GOVERNMENT
FINANCE
STATISTICS
YEARBOOK

Cataloging-in-Publication Data
Joint Bank-Fund Library

Names: International Monetary Fund | International Monetary Fund. Statistics Department.
Title: Government Finance Statistics Yearbook 2016.
Description: Washington, DC : International Monetary Fund, 2017. | Prepared by the IMF Statistics Department. | Includes bibliographical references.
Identifiers: ISBN 978-1-47558-533-9 (paper) | ISBN 978-1-47558-542-1 (PDF)
Subjects: LCSH: Finance, Public | Fiscal policy.
Classification: LCC HJ101.G68 2017

For information related to this publication, please:
fax the Statistics Department at (202) 623-6460,
or write to:

Statistics Department
International Monetary Fund
Washington, D.C. 20431

or refer to the IMF Data Help page at http://datahelp.imf.org for further assistance.
For copyright inquiries, please fax the Editorial Division at (202) 623-6579.
For purchases only, please contact Publication Services (see information below).

Address orders to:
International Monetary Fund
Attention: Publication Services
P.O. Box 92780
Washington, D.C. 20090
U.S.A.
Telephone: (202) 623-7430
Telefax: (202) 623-7201
E-mail: publications@imf.org
Internet: http://www.imf.org

YEARBOOK 2016

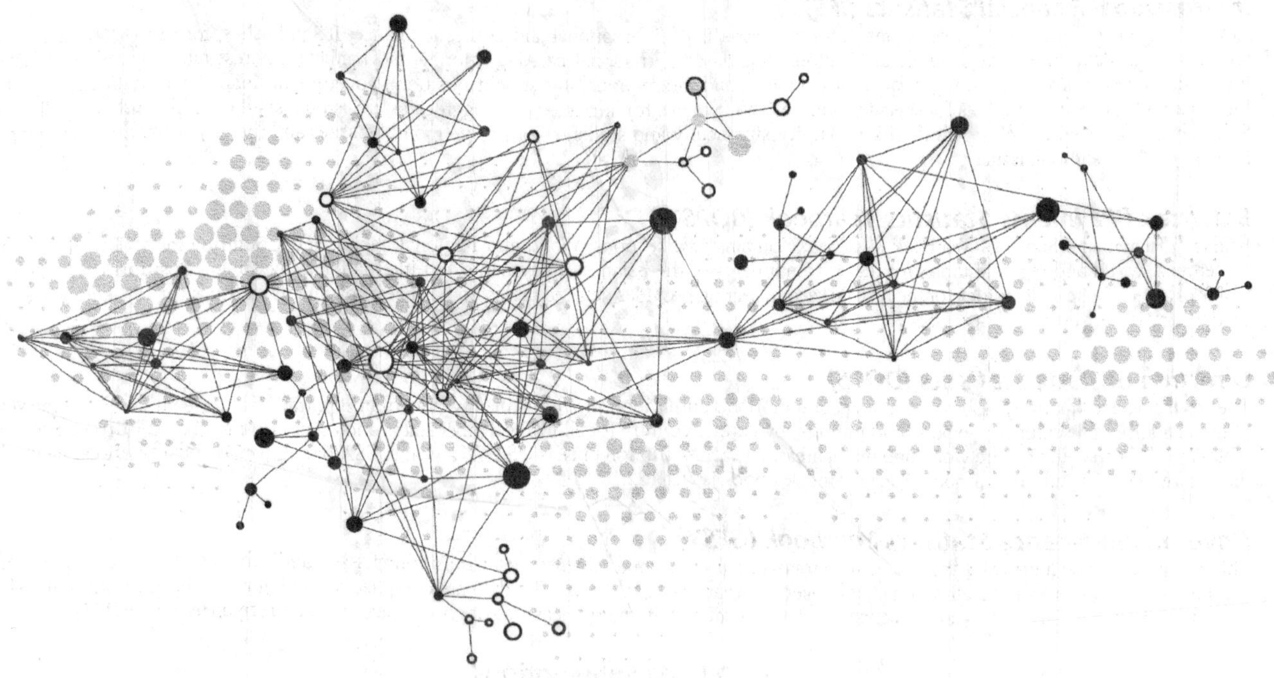

GOVERNMENT FINANCE STATISTICS

INTERNATIONAL MONETARY FUND

Selection of Statistical Publications

International Financial Statistics (IFS)

Acknowledged as a standard source of statistics on all aspects of international and domestic finance, IFS publishes, for most countries of the world, current data on exchange rates, international liquidity, international banking, money and banking, interest rates, prices, production, international transactions (including balance of payments and international investment position), government finance, and national accounts. Information is presented in tables for specific countries and in tables for area and world aggregates. IFS is published monthly and annually. Price: Subscription price is US$945 a year (US$614 to university faculty and students) for twelve monthly issues and the yearbook. Single copy price is US$191 for a yearbook issue.

Balance of Payments Statistics Yearbook (BOPSY)

Balance of Payments Statistics Yearbook (BOPSY): Contains two sections; World and Regional Tables, and Country Tables. The first section presents 21 world and regional tables for major components of the balance of payments, net International Investment Position (IIP), and total financial assets and total liabilities for the IIP. The second section provides detailed tables on balance of payments statistics for 192 economies and IIP data for 152 economies. Price: US$171.

Direction of Trade Statistics (DOTS)

The yearbook and quarterly issues of the Direction of Trade publication provide tables with current reported data (or estimates) on the value of merchandise trade statistics (exports and imports) by partner country for all IMF member states and other non-member countries. Summary tables are also presented for the world and major areas. Price: Subscription price is US$276 a year (US$236 to university faculty and students) for the quarterly issues and the yearbook. Price for the yearbook is US$122.

Government Finance Statistics Yearbook (GFSY)

This annual publication provides detailed data on transactions in revenue, expense, net acquisition of assets and liabilities, other economic flows, and balances of assets and liabilities of general government and its subsectors. The data are compiled according to the framework of the 2001 Government Finance Statistics Manual, which provides for several summary measures of government fiscal performance. Price: US$119.

DVD-ROM Subscriptions

International Financial Statistics (IFS), Balance of Payments Statistics (BOPS), Direction of Trade Statistics (DOTS), and Government Finance Statistics (GFS) are available on DVD-ROM by annual subscription. The DVD-ROMs incorporate a Windows-based browser facility, as well as a flat file of the database in scientific notation. Price of each subscription: US$250 a year for single-user PC license (US$125 for university faculty and students). Network and redistribution licenses are negotiated on a case-by-case basis. Please visit www.bookstore.imf.org/pricing for information.

Subscription Packages

Combined Subscription Package

The combined subscription package includes all issues of IFS, DOTS, GFS, and BOPSY. Combined subscription price: US$1,505 a year (US$1,204 for university faculty and students). Expedited delivery available at additional cost; please inquire.

Combined Statistical Yearbook Subscription

This subscription comprises BOPSY, IFSY, GFSY, and DOTSY at a combined rate of US$597. Because of different publication dates of the four yearbooks, it may take up to one year to service an order. Expedited delivery available at additional cost; please inquire.

IFS, BOPS, DOTS, GFS on the Internet

The Statistics Department of the Fund is pleased to make available to users the International Financial Statistics (IFS), Balance of Payments Statistics (BOPS), Direction of Trade Statistics (DOTS), and Government Finance Statistics (GFS) databases through the new, easy-to-use data.IMF.org online service. New features include Data Portals, which provide quick access to predefined tables, maps, graphs, and charts aimed at visualizing many common data searches. Data.IMF.org lets you create a basic custom-built data query using the Query tool which offers great flexibility to create larger and more complex queries. Once you have defined your query, you can structure the table the way you want it, and then convert your data into a chart or download it. A number of personalization options are available in the "My data" section such as accessing your favorites and saved queries. Free registration for My data can be obtained by clicking on the Sign In or Register link on the data.IMF.org home page.

Address orders to

Publication Services, International Monetary Fund, PO Box 92780, Washington, DC 20090, USA Telephone: (202) 623-7430 Fax: (202) 623-7201 E-mail: publications@imf.org
Internet: http://www.bookstore.imf.org

Note: Prices include the cost of delivery by surface mail. Expedited delivery is available for an additional charge.

Contents

"Country" in this publication does not always refer to a territorial entity that is a state as understood by international law and practice; the term also covers the euro area and some nonsovereign territorial entities, for which statistical data are provided internationally on a separate basis.

"Country" in this publication does not always refer to a territorial entity that is a state as understood by international law and practice; the term also covers the euro area and some nonsovereign territorial entities, for which statistical data are provided internationally on a separate basis.

"Country" in this publication does not always refer to a territorial entity that is a state as understood by international law and practice; the term also covers the euro area and some nonsovereign territorial entities, for which statistical data are provided internationally on a separate basis.

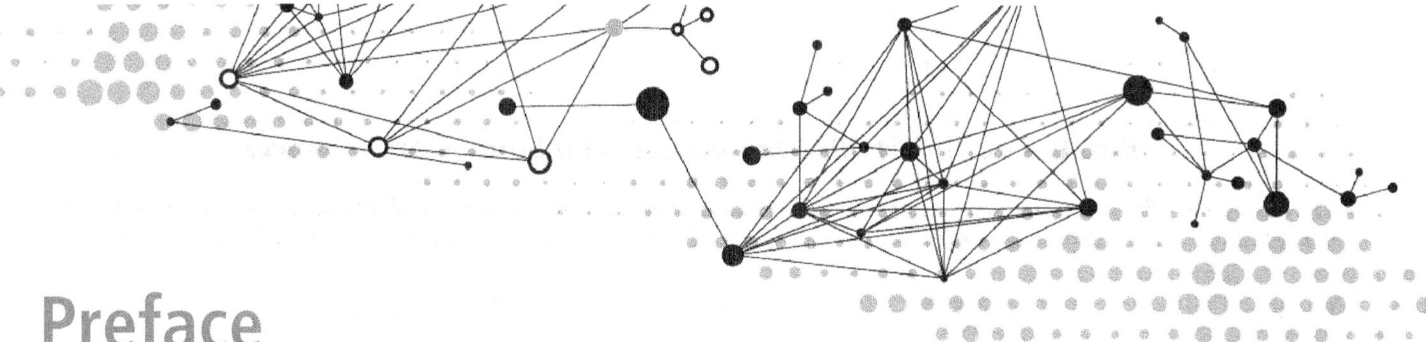

Preface

The *Government Finance Statistics Yearbook (GFS Yearbook)* contains detailed data on revenue, expense, transactions in assets and liabilities, and stock positions in assets and liabilities of the general government sector and its subsectors, as reported by countries. Data are presented in world and country tables for all reporting countries in the framework of the *Government Finance Statistics Manual, 2014* (*GFSM 2014*).[1] The *GFSM 2014* classifications remain largely the same as in the *GFSM 2001* presentation. However, some tables now include an expanded list of GFS items, where others have dropped some GFS items. Nonetheless, there are no changes in the major aggregates and balancing items of the converted data when compared with the *GFSM 2001* data. Many countries already report data in the *GFSM 2014* format for this edition of the *GFS Yearbook*. All new data reported in the *GFSM 2001* format, as well as historical data in the GFS database, have been converted to the *GFSM 2014* format. Corresponding metadata are provided in country-specific metadata tables, which are available through the IMF eLibrary Government Finance Statistics portal under the metadata table tab on the "By Country" pages at (http://data.imf.org).

The *GFS Yearbook* is supplemented by the presentation of subannual GFS according to the GFS framework in *International Financial Statistics (IFS)*. The *IFS* presents the Statement of Government Operations and Balance Sheet information, where available, and/or a Statement of Sources and Uses of Cash. These quarterly or monthly data provide timely indicators of the fiscal stance of the sector(s) reported. The presentation of these data in both publications represents a significant step forward in the worldwide effort to improve the comprehensiveness and transparency of the government finance statistics (GFS).

The *GFSM 2014* analytic framework, though conceived from an accrual perspective, can be used to present data generated by a variety of accounting practices, including cash basis. Starting with the 2014 *GFS Yearbook*, data for all countries are summarized in the Statement of Government Operations, regardless of the basis of recording used in each country, for some or all subsectors of general government. In addition, the Statement of Sources and Uses of Cash is presented for countries reporting data on a basis of recording other than cash basis, as well as cash data for some or all subsectors of general government, as relevant.

1 The text of the *GFSM 2014* is on the IMF website: http://www.imf.org/external/Pubs/FT/GFS/Manual/2014/gfsfinal.pdf

The GFS framework integrates flows (transactions and other economic flows) and stock positions (balance sheets), thereby providing the detailed information needed to fully reconcile opening and closing stock positions for government assets and liabilities. The *GFS Yearbook* presents balance sheet information which is particularly useful for fiscal policy analysis (see Box 1). Annex I to this preface further illustrates the salient features of the *GFSM 2014* framework. The concepts and principles set out in the *GFSM 2014* are also harmonized with the other macroeconomic statistical standards[2] to facilitate consistency of statistical analysis, including the "Balance Sheet Approach."

The remainder of this preface elaborates on the composition of the world, country, and metadata tables, the symbols and conventions used, and the enhanced *GFS Database and Browser* on the new offline tool (1972–present, in *GFSM 2014* format).

World and Country Tables

World tables

The *GFS Yearbook* world tables provide cross-country comparisons of data for the broadest level of government available for each country, showing the main *GFSM 2014* aggregates, balances, and other select indictors, as a percentage of gross domestic product (GDP). The level of government and basis of recording to which the data refer are shown as metadata in each world table. The world tables are supported by a set of detailed country tables that incorporate an integrated classification coding system of flows and stock positions.[3]

Country tables

To facilitate international comparisons, the *GFSM 2014* emphasizes the presentation of fiscal data for the general government sector, which should be uniformly defined across countries, consistent with the *System of National Accounts, 2008* definition of the general government sector.

2 System of National Accounts 2008; Balance of Payments and International Investment Position Manual, Sixth Edition, 2009; and Monetary and Financial Statistics Manual, 2000.

3 The GDP data are sourced from the *International Financial Statistics (IFS)* or, if not available in *IFS*, from the *World Economic Outlook (WEO)* database. As relevant, these numbers were adjusted to correspond with the fiscal years in countries.

Box 1. The *GFSM 2014* Statements and Some Core Balances

The **Statement of Operations** summarizes government transactions in an analytically useful manner by grouping transactions that affect net worth and those only changing its composition. The statement distinguishes between the following transactions:

Revenue	An increase in net worth resulting from a transaction.
Expense	A decrease in net worth resulting from a transaction.
Net investment in nonfinancial assets	Transactions that affect the stock of nonfinancial assets, i.e., acquisitions minus disposals minus consumption of fixed capital.
Financing	Transactions that affect the stock of financial assets and liabilities, i.e., net acquisition of financial assets minus net incurrence of liabilities.

The analysis of government operations is supported by two key fiscal indicators:

Operating balance	A summary measure of the effects of revenue and expense transactions on net worth. The net operating balance (NOB) equals revenue minus expense. The gross operating balance (GOB) equals revenue minus expense other than consumption of fixed capital. 1/
Net lending/net borrowing	The net financial resources that government absorbs from, or releases to, other sectors of the economy. It is calculated as the NOB minus the net acquisition of nonfinancial assets. Net lending/net borrowing is also equal to the net acquisition of financial assets minus net incurrence of liabilities.

The **Balance Sheet** focuses on an assessment of the sustainability of government operations from a fiscal perspective. It shows government's net worth on the balance sheet date. The sustainability of fiscal policy depends in part on how the government's net worth changes over time. Changes in net worth can be explained not only by government transactions but also by other economic flows attributable to gains or losses resulting from changes in the prices of assets and liabilities, as well as other changes in their volume. Key balance sheet measures published in the *GFS Yearbook*, in addition to the stock positions of assets and liabilities, comprise:

Net worth	The total stock of assets minus liabilities. The net worth in period (t) can also be calculated as the net worth of the previous period (t-1), plus changes in net worth in period (t) due to transactions (the NOB), plus changes in net worth in period (t) due to other economic flows.
Net financial worth	The total stock of financial assets minus liabilities.
Debt	At market, face, and nominal value(s), as relevant.

The **Statement of Sources and Uses of Cash** shows cash flows associated with revenue and expense transactions as well as the net cash flow from investment in nonfinancial assets, which yields the cash surplus/deficit. The assessment of government's level of cash holdings (liquidity) and its determinants is a key element in analyzing interrelationships with monetary policy.

Cash surplus/deficit	Net cash inflow from operating activities minus the net cash outflow from investment in nonfinancial assets.

1/ The NOB/GOB excludes the net acquisition of nonfinancial assets. The latter does not affect net worth because it represents only an accumulation of assets in exchange for an accumulation of liabilities or use of existing assets.

Starting with the 2014 *GFS Yearbook*, the central government excludes the social security funds subsector, which is presented as a separate subsector of the general government, along with central government, state governments, and local governments, as applicable. However, for comparability and consistency purposes, a memorandum column is included, where the former *GFS Yearbook* definition of the central government (i.e., budgetary central government, extrabudgetary funds, and social security funds, as applicable) is presented.

The hard copy edition of the 2014 *GFS Yearbook* shows, for each country, four main levels of government: the budgetary central government, the central government (budgetary central government and extrabudgetary funds), the central government including social security funds (i.e., the former *GFS Yearbook* presentation of central government), and the general government, as applicable. Data reported for the latest three years are presented in the hard copy of the *GFS Yearbook*. Data for all reported subsectors, as relevant, are shown in the *GFS Database and Browser* on the new offline tool (1972–present in *GFSM 2014* format) as well as through the IMF eLibrary Government Finance Statistics portal at (http://data.imf.org).[4]

If no data are available for the published subsectors for a specific detailed classification table or summary statement, only the statement or table headings are presented in the hard copy of the *GFS Yearbook*.

Table A of the Guide to Country Tables indicates the sectors and years for which data are available—hard copy and GFS offline tool—for each country. Table B of the Guide to Country Tables indicates the current accounting basis for compiling the data in the individual country tables for each reported subsector of general government. The basis of recording of the data in the individual country tables is identified as cash or noncash, where the latter encompasses any recording basis other than cash (including accrual).

In the hard copy of the GFS Yearbook, data are summarized in the Statement of Government Operations for all countries, regardless of the basis of recording. No Statement of Sources and Uses of Cash is presented in the hard copy of the GFS Yearbook for any country. In the online database and offline tool, data on the Statement of Sources and Uses of Cash are included if reported. If a country does not report data on consumption of fixed capital, the net operating balance and the total change in net worth resulting from transactions are not published.

Users should exercise caution when making country comparisons using the Classification of the Functions of Government (Table 7), insofar as the definition of expenditure may be different between countries or over time. The *GFSM 2014* (and its predecessor, *GFSM 2001*) framework defines expenditure by function of government (COFOG) as the sum of expense and the net investment in nonfinancial assets. This is a change from the definition of the outlays concept under the *GFSM 1986*, which was defined as the sum of expense and gross acquisition of nonfinancial assets. Expenditure in Table 7 may be defined in either way, depending on the reporting country.

4 In the GFS database, data from 1972 onward that were reported in the *GFSM 1986* framework were reclassified to the *GFSM 2001* framework. Subsequently, all data in the *GFSM 2001* framework were reclassified to the *GFSM 2014* framework.

Metadata tables

For each country, a standardized metadata overview describes the composition and structure of its general government sector. The overview also provides data coverage details and information on accounting practices. Furthermore, the overview describes a country's *GFSM 2001/2014* implementation plans, where applicable and reported. Breaks in the comparability of time series from 1990 onward are also explained. In addition to the hard copy edition,metadata tables are available through the IMF eLibrary Government Finance Statistics portal under the metadata table tab on the "By Country" pages at (http://data.imf.org).

Symbols, Conventions, and Statistical Adjustment

The following symbols and conventions are used throughout the *GFS Yearbook*:

- Captions or sub-headers identify the units in which data are expressed.
- Billion means one thousand million.
- A dash (—) indicates that a figure is zero.
- A zero (0) indicates that a figure is less than half of a significant digit.
- An ellipsis (....) indicates the absence of data.
- The letter **E** denotes forecasted or projected data.
- The letter **P** denotes data that are preliminary or provisional.
- The letter **B** marks a break in the comparability of data; that is, data appearing in the year where the symbol appears do not form a consistent time series with those for earlier years. Typically, break symbols will appear in the summary statements or detailed tables when, for example, changes have occurred in the coverage and classification of data, when the basis of recording has changed from cash to noncash, or when valuation of stock positions have changed. Break symbols in the time series of individual countries are explained in the coverage note included in the metadata table for that country. In addition, **FB** denotes final data with a break symbol, while **PB** denotes preliminary data with a break symbol.
- For data relating to a fiscal year that does not correspond to the calendar year, the country and world tables present the data with reference to the calendar year for which the greatest number of monthly observations exist. Unless otherwise

indicated, for fiscal years ending June 30 or later, the tables present the data in the calendar year when the fiscal year ends. For example, the fiscal year July 1, 2008–June 30, 2009 is shown as calendar year 2009 in the country tables. Conversely, for fiscal years ending June 29 or earlier, the tables present the data in the calendar year when the fiscal year begins. Changes in fiscal years are indicated by the break symbol B. Minor differences between published totals and the sum of the corresponding components are attributable to rounding.

- The GFS offline tool (1972–present in *GFSM 2014* format) contains statistical adjustment lines for most aggregates. However, only three statistical adjustment lines are used in the data presented in the *GFS Yearbook*: (1) the Statement of Government Operations includes a statistical discrepancy between net lending/net borrowing and financing; (2) the Statement of Sources and Uses of Cash includes a statistical discrepancy between the cash surplus/deficit and financing; and, (3) the Classification of the Functions of Government (Table 7) includes a line for the statistical discrepancy between the reported components and total outlays.

GFS offline tool

The *GFS Database and Browser* on the new offline tool (1972–present in *GFSM 2014* format), which contains annual time series for all reported subsectors of general government, is issued quarterly and is updated as new data are received. Most of the data prior to 2000 reflect reclassified data previously reported by member countries using the *GFSM 1986* format. Users should exercise caution when comparing data over time because shortcomings have been identified in the data for the years prior to 2000 that have been reclassified according to the *GFSM 2001* framework.

The data browser enables users to view and extract data for analytical purposes. The browser software is an easy-to-use interface for accessing the database, selecting specific data series, displaying the selected series in a spread- sheet format, and saving the selected series for export to other software systems, such as Microsoft Excel.

Seven databases are provided for browsing GFS data contained within the new offline tool:

- Main aggregates and balances;
- Revenue;
- Expense;
- Expenditure by function of government (COFOG)[5];
- Integrated balance sheet (stock positions and flows in assets and liabilities); and
- Financial assets and liabilities by counterpart sector[6].

The offline tool allows viewing the data by country, by indicator, or by level of government. Each of the databases also provides different supplementary dimensions to present and analyze the data, such as by type of stock position/flow or by instrument. The offline tool also provides access to metadata attributes, for example, the basis of recording.

The documents module of the GFS offline tool contains the metadata tables (previously called "institutional tables") for each country.

The incorporated "help" module provides information on how to use the GFS offline tool.

For users seeking access to historical data, two options exist:

- The *Historical Government Finance Statistics Database and Browser* on CD-ROM contains time series for reporting countries from 1972 to 1989, presented in the framework of the *GFSM 1986*. Users interested in converting the historical series may refer to the document "Classification of *GFSM 1986* Data to the *GFSM 2001* Framework," available on the IMF's website: (http://www.imf.org/external/pubs/ft/gfs/manual/comp.htm).
- The historical *GFSM 2001* data, covering time series from 1990 through 2012, is available on the Archive tab of the GFS online data portal at: http://data.imf.org/GFS01.

5 Classification of the Functions of Government (COFOG).

6 Classifications of the counterpart of transactions and stock positions in financial assets and liabilities by institutional sector.

Annex I. HIGHLIGHTS OF THE *GFSM 2014* FRAMEWORK

This annex provides a synopsis of the GFS framework as it relates to the treatment of flows and stock positions, the four financial statements that comprise the analytical framework of the GFS, and salient features of coverage, classification, basis of recording, and valuation under the *GFSM 2014* (and its predecessor *GFSM 2001*).

The Treatment of Flow and Balance Sheet Data

The GFS framework fully integrates flows (used to report the results of events that occur during the reporting period) and stock positions (used to compile the Balance Sheet at the beginning and end of the reporting period). The comprehensive treatment of flows in the GFS framework enables the opening and closing stock positions to be fully reconciled. In other words, the following relationship is valid for each item on the Balance Sheet:

$$\mathbf{S_1 = S_0 + F}$$

where $\mathbf{S_0}$ and $\mathbf{S_1}$ represent the values of an item on the Balance Sheet at two points in time (0,1) and F represents the cumulative value of all flows between times 0 and 1 that affect that particular item. More generally, any stock, including net worth, is the cumulative value of all flows that have occurred over the lifetime of the item.

The GFS framework provides a range of possibilities for fiscal analysis, especially concerning fiscal liquidity and policy sustainability issues. The liquidity constraint, measured as the net change in the stock of cash, should prove useful for fiscal policy decision makers. This measure is shown in the Statement of Sources and Uses of Cash, which also contains information on the types of aggregate receipts and payments that contribute to the change in the stock of cash.

The GFS framework includes the Statement of Operations that allows a nuanced view of fiscal sustainability through the measurement of transactions affecting net worth, as well as the net/gross operating balance and net lending/net borrowing. When compiled using comprehensive accrual information, these measures reflect more accurately the impact of resource flows. The analysis of net worth (the stock of assets minus liabilities) should focus policy attention on the structure of the government's balance sheet and the portfolio choice among assets (and liabilities). The net/gross operating balance is a summary measure of the change in net worth owing to transactions that occurred in the period; revenue and expense are the only transactions that affect net worth. Net lending/net borrowing shows the extent to which the government absorbs or provides financial resources to the rest of the economy and the rest of the world.

The Four Main Financial Statements of the GFS

The core of the analytic framework is presented in four financial statements. Three of the statements can be combined to demonstrate that all changes in stock positions result from flows (see Figure 1). These are (1) the Statement of Operations, (2) the Statement of Other Economic Flows, and (3) the Balance Sheet. The fourth statement—the Statement of Sources and Uses of Cash—provides key information on liquidity.

The Statement of Operations summarizes all transactions and derives important analytic balances from this information. Revenue minus expense equals the net/gross operating balance, which is a summary measure of the effect of the government's transactions on net worth. The subsequent deduction of the net/gross investment in nonfinancial assets from the net/gross operating balance produces a balance called net lending/net borrowing, which measures the extent to which government either provides financial resources to the other sectors of the economy and the rest of the world (net lending) or uses financial resources generated by the other sectors (net borrowing). Net lending/net borrowing is also equal to the government financing requirement derived as the net of transactions in financial assets and liabilities. It is a measure of the financial impact of government activity on the rest of the economy.

Statement of Operations	
1	Revenue
2	Expense
NOB/ GOB	***Net/gross operating balance (1–2=31+32–33)***
31	Net/gross investment in nonfinancial assets
2M	Expenditure (2+ 31)
NLB	***Net lending (+)/net borrowing (–) (1–2–31=1–2M=32–33)***
32	Net acquisition of financial assets
33	Net incurrence of liabilities

The Statement of Other Economic Flows presents information on changes in net worth that arise from flows other than transactions. These flows are classified as either changes in the value (revaluations, or holding gains and losses) or the volume of assets and liabilities. The balancing item in this statement is the change in net worth due to other economic flows.

Statement of Other Economic Flows	
9	***Change in net worth due to other economic flows (9=4+5)***
4	Change in net worth due to holding gains and losses (4=41+42–43)
41	Nonfinancial assets
42	Financial assets
43	Liabilities
5	Change in net worth due to other changes in the volume of assets and liabilities (5=51+52–53)
51	Nonfinancial assets
52	Financial assets
53	Liabilities

Figure 1: Structure of the GFS Analytical Framework

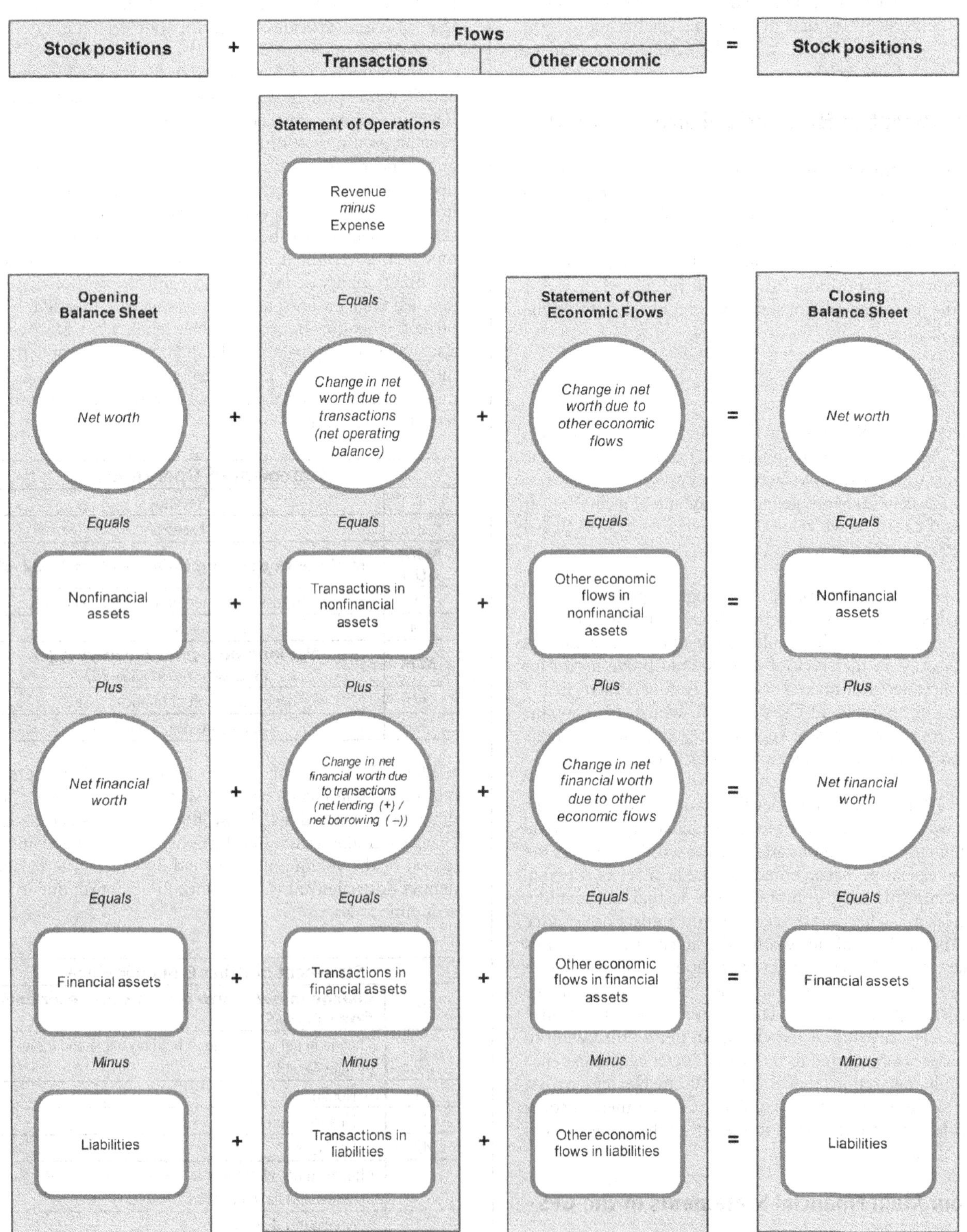

Annex I. HIGHLIGHTS OF THE *GFSM 2014* FRAMEWORK

The Balance Sheet presents the stock positions of assets, liabilities (including debt), and net worth at the end of the reporting period. The government's net worth is defined as the difference between total assets and total liabilities. Another balancing item that can be derived from the Balance Sheet is net financial worth, which is defined as total financial assets minus total liabilities. The change in net financial worth is linked to the net lending/net borrowing balance.

Balance Sheet	
6	***Net worth (61+62–63)***
61	Nonfinancial assets
62	Financial assets
63	Liabilities

The Statement of Sources and Uses of Cash shows the amounts of cash generated and used in operations, cash flows resulting from transactions in nonfinancial assets, and cash flows involving financial assets and liabilities, excluding cash itself. The balancing item, net change in the stock of cash, is the sum of the net cash received from these three sources of cash flows.

Statement of Sources and Uses of Cash	
C1	Revenue cash flows
C2	Expense cash flows
CIO	***Net cash inflow from operating activities (1–2=31+32–33)***
C31	Net cash outflow from investment in nonfinancial assets
C2M	Expenditure cash flows (2+31)
CSD	***Cash surplus (+)/deficit (–) (1–2–31=1–2M=32–33)***
C32x	Net acquisition of financial assets other than cash
C33	Net incurrence of liabilities
NFB	***Net cash inflow from financing activities (33–32x)***
NCB	***Net change in the stock of cash (CSD+NFB=3202=3212+3222)***[1]

Coverage of the GFS Framework

The main focus of the coverage of the GFS framework is the general government and public sectors, defined consistent with the *System of National Accounts, 2008* (*2008 SNA*). These sectors are defined on the basis of institutional units.[2] The comprehensive conceptual and reporting framework of the GFS applies to both the general government and the broader public sector; however, the coverage of the *GFS Yearbook* database has not yet been extended to include the public sector.[3]

Government units are unique kinds of legal entities established by political processes that have legislative, judicial, or executive authority over other institutional units within a given area and that fulfill the functions of government as their primary activity. That is, they:

- assume responsibility for the provision of goods and services to the community as a whole or to individual households on a nonmarket basis;
- redistribute income and wealth by means of transfers;
- engage primarily in nonmarket production; and
- finance their activities, primarily out of taxation or other compulsory transfers.

All government units are members of the general government sector, which also consists of all nonmarket nonprofit institutions (NPIs) that are controlled by government units. These are legally nongovernment entities, but they are considered to be carrying out government policies and, effectively, are part of government. The general government sector does not include public corporations or quasi-corporations.

Frequently, units of the broader public sector (public nonfinancial corporations and public financial corporations) carry out some functions of government. To capture the fiscal transactions and activities taking place outside the general government sector, the GFS framework separately identifies transactions between units of the general government sector and public corporations and encourages the compilation of statistics on the public sector.

In the GFS system, provision is made for subsectors of general government: central; state, provincial, or regional, and local; plus social security funds, as relevant. Not all countries have all levels of government or report on all those levels; some may have only a central government or a central government and one lower level. Other countries may have more levels. In such cases, the various units should all be classified as one of the levels suggested in the GFS framework.

The central government subsector is large and complex in most countries. It is generally composed of a central group of departments or ministries that make up a single institutional unit plus, in many countries, other units operating under the authority of the central government with a separate legal identity and enough autonomy to form additional government

1 Domestic currency and deposits (3212) and external currency and deposits (3222).

2 This type of unit can, in its own right, own assets, incur liabilities, and engage in economic activities and transactions with other entities.

3 The general government sector consists of entities that implement public policy through the provision of primarily nonmarket services and the redistribution of income and wealth, with both activities supported mainly by compulsory levies on other sectors. The public sector consists of the general government sector plus government-controlled entities, known as public corporations, whose primary activity is to engage in commercial activities.

Figure 2: The Classification Coding System for GFS

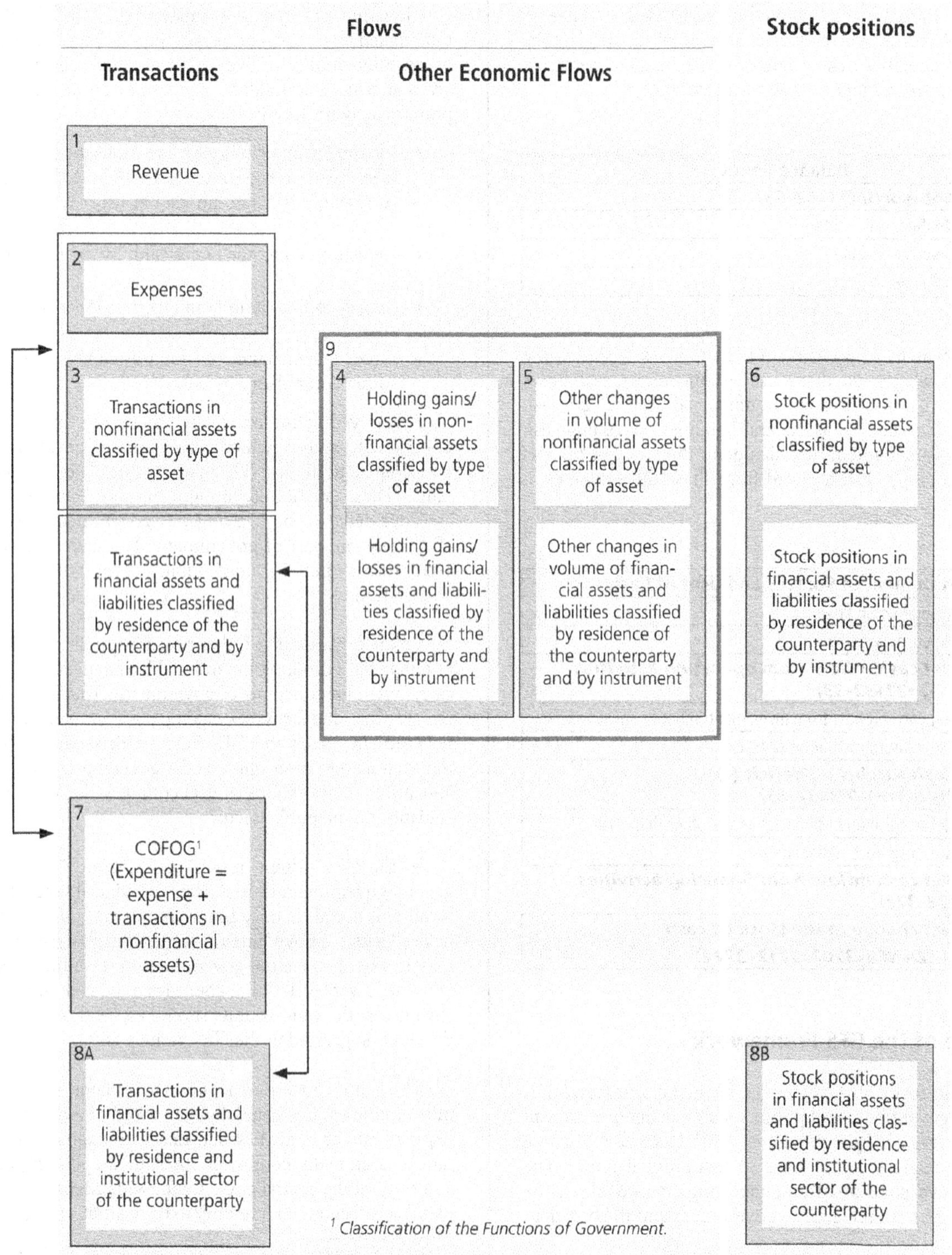

[1] *Classification of the Functions of Government.*

units (extrabudgetary accounts/funds). These units may also exist at the state or local government levels. The GFS encourages the creation of subsectors at each level of government based on whether the units are financed by the legislative budgets of that level of government or by extrabudgetary sources.[4]

The GFS Classifications

Classification codes are used in the GFS framework to identify types of transactions, other economic flows, and stock positions of assets and liabilities. The overall organization of the codes is outlined in Figure 2.

Codes beginning with 1 refer to revenue; codes beginning with 2 refer to expense; and codes beginning with 3 refer to transactions in nonfinancial assets, financial assets, and liabilities. For financial assets and liabilities, code 3 also signifies that they have been classified by financial instrument.

The first digit of the classification code for an other economic flows is always 4 or 5. Codes beginning with 4 refer to holding gains or losses and codes beginning with 5 refer to other changes in the volume of assets and liabilities.[5] The first digit of the classification code for the stock position of a type of asset or liability is always 6 for the classification by type of nonfinancial assets and type of financial instrument. Codes beginning with 68 refer to the classification of the stock positions in financial assets and liabilities by institutional sector of the counterparty.

Transactions in assets and liabilities, other economic flows, and stocks of assets and liabilities all refer to types of assets and liabilities. Hence, the second and subsequent dig- its of each code are identical for each type of asset or liability. That is, 311 refers to transactions in fixed assets, 411 to holding gains in fixed assets, 511 to other changes in the volume of fixed assets, and 611 to the stock of fixed assets. Each asset and liability also has a unique code.

4 Separately classifying these units is analytically useful in distinguishing their differing sources of financing and differing types of public oversight of their operations.

5 Where it is not possible to separately compile statistics on holding gains or losses and other changes in the volume of assets and liabilities, codes beginning with 9 refer to total other economic flows.

Expense transactions and transactions in nonfinancial assets can also be classified using the Classification of Functions of Government (COFOG).[6] All COFOG classification codes begin with 7. Transactions in financial assets and liabilities can be classified according to the sector of the other party to the financial instrument as well as according to the type of financial instrument. When classified by sector, the classification codes for these transactions begin with 8.

The GFS framework also encourages the recording of memorandum items to provide supplemental information about items related to, but not included on, the Balance Sheet (e.g., measures of debt). Where reported, these data have been included in the *GFS Yearbook* and on the GFS offline tool.

Basis and Time of Recording

In the integrated GFS framework, flows are recorded on an accrual basis, which means that flows are recorded at the time economic value is created, transformed, exchanged, transferred, or extinguished. Using the accrual basis also means that non-monetary transactions are fully integrated into the GFS framework. The GFS framework also records flows on a cash basis. These data are reported in the Statement of Sources and Uses of Cash in the Country Tables of the *GFS Yearbook* and on the GFS offline tool.

Valuation of Flows and Stock Positions

Flows as well as stock positions of assets, liabilities, and net worth (a balancing item) are valued at current market prices in the GFS framework. Specifically, flows are to be valued at prices current on the dates for which they are recorded, while stock positions are to be valued at current prices on the Balance Sheet date. The face and market values of gross and net debt are shown as memorandum items to the Balance Sheet.

6 Data are collected and published for a selected subset of functions.

Guide to Country Tables

Table A: Sector and Data Availability

Government Sector
- BA Budgetary Central Government
- EA Extra-Budgetary Units/Entities
- SSF Social Security Funds
- CG Central Government (excl. social security funds)
- SG State Governments
- LG Local Governments
- GG General Government (consolidated)
- GL2 Central Government (incl. social security funds)

X Indicates that gaps exist in the time series

For each country listed:
- Existing Sectors correspond to those described in the Metadata Tables published in this edition of the GFS Yearbook.
- Reported Sectors GFS Offline Tool refers to those sectors for which the country has actually reported (all reported sectors may not be available for each year of the series included on the GFS Offline Tool).
- Reported Sectors GFS Yearbook refers to the most recent three-year period for which data on the indicated sector(s) are published in the GFS Yearbook.
- The GFS Yearbook only includes countries that have reported data for 2008 or subsequent years.

For EU countries listed:

In line with the presentation adopted within the European Union, data on BA operations may include the operations of EA.

			GFS Offline Tool		GFS Yearbook	
	Country	**Existing Sectors**	**Reported Sectors**	**Years**	**Reported Sectors**	**Years**
512	Afghanistan, Islamic Republic of	BA,CG,GL2,EA,GG,LG	BA,CG,GL2,EA,GG,LG	2003-2013	BA,CG,GL2,GG	2011-2013
914	Albania	BA,CG,GL2,EA,GG,LG,SSF	BA,CG,GL2,GG,LG,SSF	1995-2015 X	BA,CG,GL2,GG	2013-2015
612	Algeria	BA,CG,GL2,EA,GG,LG,SSF,SG	BA,CG,GL2,EA,GG,LG,SSF,SG	1994-2011	BA,CG,GL2,GG	2009-2011
614	Angola	BA,CG,GL2,EA,GG,LG,SSF	BA	1999-2015	BA	2013-2015
312	Anguilla	BA,CG,GL2,GG,SSF	BA	2000-2014	BA	2012-2014
311	Antigua and Barbuda	BA,CG,GL2,EA,GG,LG,SSF	BA	2000-2014	BA	2012-2014
213	Argentina	BA,CG,GL2,EA,GG,LG,SSF,SG	BA,CG,GL2,EA,SSF	1990-2015 X	BA,CG,GL2	2013-2015
911	Armenia, Republic of	BA,CG,GL2,EA,GG,LG,SSF	BA,GL2,EA,GG,LG	2003-2015 X	BA,GL2,GG	2013-2015
193	Australia	BA,CG,GL2,GG,LG,SG	BA,CG,GL2,GG,LG,SG	1972-2015 X	BA,CG,GL2,GG	2013-2015
122	Austria	BA,CG,GL2,EA,GG,LG,SSF,SG	CG,GL2,GG,LG,SSF,SG	1972-2015	CG,GL2,GG	2013-2015
912	Azerbaijan, Republic of	BA,CG,GL2,EA,GG,LG,SSF,SG	BA,CG,GL2,EA,GG,LG,SSF,SG	1994-2015 X	BA,CG,GL2,GG	2013-2015
313	Bahamas, The	BA,CG,GL2,GG,SSF	BA,CG	1973-2015 X	BA,CG	2013-2015
419	Bahrain, Kingdom of	BA,CG,GL2,EA,GG,SSF	BA	1974-2013 X	BA	2011-2013
513	Bangladesh	BA,CG,GL2,EA,GG,LG	BA	2001-2015	BA	2013-2015
316	Barbados	BA,CG,GL2,EA,GG,SSF	BA	1972-2013 X	BA	2011-2013
913	Belarus	BA,CG,GL2,GG,LG,SSF	BA,CG,GL2,GG,LG,SSF	1992-2015	BA,CG,GL2,GG	2013-2015
124	Belgium	BA,CG,GL2,EA,GG,LG,SSF,SG	CG,GL2,GG,LG,SSF,SG	1978-2015	CG,GL2,GG	2013-2015
339	Belize	BA,CG,GL2,EA,GG,LG,SSF	BA	1990-2014	BA	2012-2014
638	Benin	BA,CG,GL2,EA,GG,LG,SSF	BA	1977-2013 X	BA	2011-2013
514	Bhutan	BA,CG,GL2,GG	BA,CG,GL2,GG	1982-2014 X	BA,CG,GL2,GG	2012-2014
963	Bosnia and Herzegovina	BA,CG,GL2,EA,GG,LG,SSF	BA,CG,GL2,EA,GG,LG,SSF	2003-2015	BA,CG,GL2,GG	2013-2015
616	Botswana	BA,CG,GL2,EA,GG,LG,SSF,SG	BA	1990-2014 X	BA	2012-2014
223	Brazil	BA,CG,GL2,EA,GG,LG,SG	CG,GL2,GG,LG,SG	1980-2015 X	CG,GL2,GG	2013-2015
918	Bulgaria	BA,CG,GL2,EA,GG,LG,SSF	CG,GL2,GG,LG,SSF	1990-2015	CG,GL2,GG	2013-2015
748	Burkina Faso	BA,CG,GL2,EA,GG,LG,SSF	BA	1973-2015 X	BA	2013-2015
618	Burundi	BA,CG,GL2,EA,GG,LG,SSF	BA	1973-2013 X	BA	2011-2013
624	Cabo Verde	BA,CG,GL2,EA,GG,LG,SSF	BA,CG,EA,LG	2005-2012	BA,CG	2010-2012
522	Cambodia	BA,CG,GL2,EA,GG,LG	BA	2002-2015	BA	2013-2015
156	Canada	BA,CG,GL2,GG,LG,SSF,SG	CG,GL2,GG,LG,SSF,SG	1978-2015	CG,GL2,GG	2013-2015
626	Central African Republic	BA,CG,GL2,EA,GG,LG,SSF	BA	2004-2012 X	BA	2010-2012
228	Chile	BA,CG,GL2,EA,GG,LG	GL2,GG,LG	1972-2015	GL2,GG	2013-2015
924	China, P.R.: Mainland	BA,CG,GL2,EA,GG,LG,SSF,SG	BA,CG,GL2,EA,GG,LG,SSF,SG	1990-2014	BA,CG,GL2,GG	2012-2014
532	China, P.R.: Hong Kong	GG	GG	2002-2014	GG	2012-2014
546	China, P.R.: Macao	BA,CG,GL2,EA,GG,SSF	BA,CG,GL2,EA,GG,SSF	1996-2015	BA,CG,GL2,GG	2013-2015
233	Colombia	BA,CG,GL2,EA,GG,LG,SSF,SG	BA,CG,GL2,EA,GG,LG,SSF,SG	1990-2015	BA,CG,GL2,GG	2013-2015
636	Congo, Democratic Republic of	BA,CG,GL2,EA,GG,LG,SSF,SG	BA	1972-2010 X	BA	2008-2010

Country		Existing Sectors	GFS Offline Tool Reported Sectors	Years	GFS Yearbook Reported Sectors	Years
634	Congo, Republic of	BA,CG,GL2,EA,GG,LG,SSF	BA,CG,GL2,EA,GG,LG,SSF	1972-2012 X	BA,CG,GL2,GG	2010-2012
238	Costa Rica	BA,CG,GL2,EA,GG,LG,SSF	BA,CG,GL2,EA,GG,LG,SSF	1972-2015	BA,CG,GL2,GG	2013-2015
662	Cote d'Ivoire	BA,CG,GL2,EA,GG,LG,SSF	BA	1994-2014	BA	2012-2014
960	Croatia	BA,CG,GL2,EA,GG,LG,SSF	BA,GL2,EA,GG,LG	1991-2014	BA,GL2,GG	2012-2014
423	Cyprus	BA,CG,GL2,EA,GG,LG,SSF	CG,GL2,GG,LG,SSF	1972-2015	CG,GL2,GG	2013-2015
935	Czech Republic	BA,CG,GL2,EA,GG,LG,SSF	BA,CG,GL2,EA,GG,LG,SSF	1993-2015	BA,CG,GL2,GG	2013-2015
128	Denmark	BA,CG,GL2,EA,GG,LG,SSF	CG,GL2,GG,LG,SSF	1972-2015	CG,GL2,GG	2013-2015
321	Dominica	BA,CG,GL2,EA,GG,LG,SSF	BA	2000-2014	BA	2012-2014
243	Dominican Republic	BA,CG,GL2,EA,GG,LG,SSF	BA,CG,GL2,EA,SSF	1972-2015	BA,CG,GL2	2013-2015
469	Egypt	BA,CG,GL2,EA,GG,SSF	BA,GL2,GG	1975-2015 X	BA,GL2,GG	2013-2015
253	El Salvador	BA,CG,GL2,EA,GG,LG,SSF	BA,CG,GL2,EA,GG,LG,SSF	1990-2015	BA,CG,GL2,GG	2013-2015
642	Equatorial Guinea	BA,CG,GL2,GG,LG,SSF	BA	2007-2009	BA	2007-2009
939	Estonia	BA,CG,GL2,EA,GG,LG,SSF	CG,GL2,GG,LG,SSF	1991-2015	CG,GL2,GG	2013-2015
644	Ethiopia	BA,CG,GL2,EA,GG,LG,SSF,SG	BA	1990-2011 X	BA	2009-2011
819	Fiji	BA,CG,GL2,EA,GG,LG	BA	1990-2013 X	BA	2011-2013
172	Finland	BA,CG,GL2,EA,GG,LG,SSF	CG,GL2,GG,LG,SSF	1972-2015	CG,GL2,GG	2013-2015
132	France	BA,CG,GL2,EA,GG,LG,SSF	CG,GL2,GG,LG,SSF	1972-2015	CG,GL2,GG	2013-2015
648	Gambia, The	BA,CG,GL2,EA,GG,LG	CG,GL2	1990-2009 X	CG,GL2	2007-2009
915	Georgia	BA,CG,GL2,GG,LG	BA,CG,GL2,GG,LG	1995-2015	BA,CG,GL2,GG	2013-2015
134	Germany	BA,CG,GL2,EA,GG,LG,SSF,SG	BA,CG,GL2,EA,GG,LG,SSF,SG	1972-2015	BA,CG,GL2,GG	2013-2015
652	Ghana	BA,CG,GL2,EA,GG,LG,SG	BA,EA	1990-2011 X	BA	2009-2011
174	Greece	BA,CG,GL2,EA,GG,LG,SSF	CG,GL2,GG,LG,SSF	1972-2015	CG,GL2,GG	2013-2015
328	Grenada	BA,CG,GL2,EA,GG,LG,SSF	BA	1999-2014	BA	2012-2014
258	Guatemala	BA,CG,GL2,EA,GG,LG,SSF	BA	1990-2013	BA	2011-2013
268	Honduras	BA,CG,GL2,EA,GG,LG,SSF	BA,CG,GL2,EA,GG,LG,SSF	1972-2015 X	BA,CG,GL2,GG	2013-2015
944	Hungary	BA,CG,GL2,EA,GG,LG,SSF	CG,GL2,GG,LG,SSF	1981-2015	CG,GL2,GG	2013-2015
176	Iceland	BA,CG,GL2,GG,LG,SSF	BA,CG,GL2,GG,LG,SSF	1972-2015	BA,CG,GL2,GG	2013-2015
534	India	BA,CG,GL2,GG,LG,SG	BA,CG,GL2	1974-2013	BA,CG,GL2	2011-2013
536	Indonesia	BA,CG,GL2,EA,GG,LG	CG,GL2,GG,LG	1972-2015 X	CG,GL2,GG	2013-2015
429	Iran, Islamic Republic of	BA,CG,GL2,EA,GG,LG,SSF	BA,CG,GL2,EA,GG,LG,SSF	1972-2009	BA,CG,GL2,GG	2007-2009
433	Iraq	BA,CG,GL2,EA,GG,LG,SSF	BA	2014-2014	BA	2012-2014
178	Ireland	BA,CG,GL2,EA,GG,LG	CG,GL2,GG,LG	1972-2015	CG,GL2,GG	2013-2015
436	Israel	BA,CG,GL2,EA,GG,LG,SSF	BA,CG,GL2,EA,GG,LG,SSF	1972-2015	BA,CG,GL2,GG	2013-2015
136	Italy	BA,CG,GL2,EA,GG,LG,SSF	CG,GL2,GG,LG,SSF	1973-2015	CG,GL2,GG	2013-2015
343	Jamaica	BA,CG,GL2,EA,GG,LG,SSF	BA,CG,GL2,EA,GG,SSF	1975-2015 X	BA,CG,GL2,GG	2013-2015
158	Japan	BA,CG,GL2,EA,GG,LG,SSF	CG,GG,LG	1972-2014 X	CG,GG	2012-2014
439	Jordan	BA,CG,GL2,EA,GG,LG,SSF	BA	1990-2015	BA	2013-2015
916	Kazakhstan	BA,CG,GL2,GG,LG,SSF	BA,CG,GL2,GG,LG,SSF	1997-2015	BA,CG,GL2,GG	2013-2015
664	Kenya	BA,CG,GL2,EA,GG,LG,SSF	BA,CG,GL2,EA,GG,LG,SSF	1991-2015	BA,CG,GL2,GG	2013-2015
826	Kiribati	BA,CG,GL2,EA,GG,LG	BA,CG,GL2,EA,GG,LG	2010-2015	BA,CG,GL2,GG	2013-2015
542	Korea, Republic of	BA,CG,GL2,EA,GG,LG,SSF	BA,GL2,EA,GG,LG	1972-2015	BA,GL2,GG	2013-2015
443	Kuwait	BA,CG,GL2,EA,GG,SSF	BA,CG,EA	1972-2015 X	BA,CG	2013-2015
917	Kyrgyz Republic	BA,CG,GL2,GG,LG,SSF	BA,CG,GL2,GG,LG,SSF	1993-2015 X	BA,CG,GL2,GG	2013-2015
544	Lao People's Democratic Republic	BA,CG,GL2,EA,GG,SSF	BA	2006-2015	BA	2013-2015
941	Latvia	BA,CG,GL2,EA,GG,LG,SSF	CG,GL2,GG,LG,SSF	1994-2015	CG,GL2,GG	2013-2015
446	Lebanon	BA,CG,GL2,EA,GG,LG,SSF	BA	1993-2015	BA	2013-2015
666	Lesotho	BA,CG,GL2,EA,GG,LG,SSF,SG	BA,CG,EA,GG,LG,SSF,SG	1972-2013 X	BA,CG,GG	2011-2013
668	Liberia	BA,CG,GL2,GG,LG,SSF	BA,CG	1974-2013 X	BA,CG	2011-2013
946	Lithuania	BA,CG,GL2,EA,GG,LG,SSF,SG	BA,CG,GL2,EA,GG,LG,SSF,SG	1991-2015 X	BA,CG,GL2,GG	2013-2015
137	Luxembourg	BA,CG,GL2,EA,GG,LG,SSF	CG,GL2,GG,LG,SSF	1972-2015 X	CG,GL2,GG	2013-2015
962	Macedonia, FYR	BA,CG,GL2,EA,GG,LG,SSF	GL2	2005-2012	GL2	2010-2012
674	Madagascar	BA,CG,GL2,EA,GG,LG,SSF	CG,GL2	1972-2014 X	CG,GL2	2012-2014
676	Malawi	BA,CG,GL2,EA,GG,LG	BA,LG	2009-2016	BA	2014-2016
548	Malaysia	BA,CG,GL2,EA,GG,LG,SSF,SG	BA	1972-2015	BA	2013-2015
556	Maldives	BA,CG,GL2,GG	BA,CG,GL2,GG	1979-2014 X	BA,CG,GL2,GG	2012-2014

Country		Existing Sectors	GFS Offline Tool		GFS Yearbook	
			Reported Sectors	Years	Reported Sectors	Years
678	Mali	BA,CG,GL2,EA,GG,LG,SSF	BA	1975-2015 X	BA	2013-2015
181	Malta	BA,CG,GL2,EA,GG,LG,SSF,SG	CG,GL2,GG,LG,SSF,SG	1972-2015 X	CG,GL2,GG	2013-2015
867	Marshall Islands, Republic of	BA,CG,GL2,EA,GG,LG,SSF	BA	2008-2015	BA	2013-2015
684	Mauritius	BA,CG,GL2,EA,GG,LG,SSF,SG	BA,CG,GL2,EA,GG,LG,SSF,SG	1973-2014	BA,CG,GL2,GG	2012-2014
868	Micronesia, Federated States of	BA,CG,GL2,EA,GG,LG,SSF,SG	BA,SG	2008-2015	BA	2013-2015
921	Moldova	BA,CG,GL2,GG,LG,SSF	BA,CG,GL2,GG,LG,SSF	1994-2015	BA,CG,GL2,GG	2013-2015
948	Mongolia	BA,CG,GL2,EA,GG,LG,SSF	BA,CG,GL2,EA,GG,LG,SSF	1992-2013 X	BA,CG,GL2,GG	2011-2013
351	Montserrat	BA,CG,GL2,EA,GG,SSF	BA	2000-2014	BA	2012-2014
686	Morocco	BA,CG,GL2,EA,GG,LG,SSF	BA	1972-2015 X	BA	2013-2015
688	Mozambique	BA,CG,GL2,EA,GG,LG,SSF	BA	2010-2013	BA	2011-2013
728	Namibia	BA,CG,GL2,EA,GG,LG,SSF	BA	1990-2015	BA	2013-2015
558	Nepal	BA,CG,GL2,EA,GG,LG	BA	1972-2016	BA	2014-2016
138	Netherlands	BA,CG,GL2,EA,GG,LG,SSF	BA,CG,GL2,EA,GG,LG,SSF	1973-2015	BA,CG,GL2,GG	2013-2015
196	New Zealand	BA,CG,GL2,EA,GG,LG,SSF	GL2,LG	1972-2015 X	GL2	2013-2015
278	Nicaragua	BA,CG,GL2,EA,GG,LG,SSF,SG	BA,SSF	1972-2015 X	BA	2013-2015
694	Nigeria	BA,CG,GL2,EA,GG,LG,SG	BA	2003-2013	BA	2011-2013
142	Norway	BA,CG,GL2,EA,GG,LG,SSF	CG,GL2,GG,LG	1972-2015	CG,GL2,GG	2013-2015
449	Oman	BA,CG,GL2,EA,GG,SSF	BA	1990-2013	BA	2011-2013
564	Pakistan	BA,CG,GL2,EA,GG,LG,SG	BA	1973-2014 X	BA	2012-2014
565	Palau	BA,CG,GL2,EA,GG,SSF,SG	BA	2008-2015	BA	2013-2015
288	Paraguay	BA,CG,GL2,EA,GG,LG,SSF,SG	BA,CG,GL2,EA,GG,LG,SSF,SG	1990-2015	BA,CG,GL2,GG	2013-2015
293	Peru	BA,CG,GL2,EA,GG,LG,SSF,SG	BA,CG,GL2,EA,GG,LG,SSF,SG	1972-2015	BA,CG,GL2,GG	2013-2015
566	Philippines	BA,CG,GL2,EA,GG,LG,SSF	BA	1990-2015	BA	2013-2015
964	Poland	BA,CG,GL2,EA,GG,LG,SSF	CG,GL2,GG,LG,SSF	1984-2015 X	CG,GL2,GG	2013-2015
182	Portugal	BA,CG,GL2,EA,GG,LG,SSF	BA,CG,GL2,EA,GG,LG,SSF	1975-2015	BA,CG,GL2,GG	2013-2015
453	Qatar	BA,CG,GL2,EA,GG	BA	2004-2010	BA	2008-2010
968	Romania	BA,CG,GL2,EA,GG,LG,SSF	CG,GL2,GG,LG,SSF	1972-2015	CG,GL2,GG	2013-2015
922	Russian Federation	BA,CG,GL2,EA,GG,LG,SSF,SG	BA,CG,GL2,EA,GG,LG,SSF,SG	1994-2015 X	BA,CG,GL2,GG	2013-2015
714	Rwanda	BA,CG,GL2,EA,GG,LG,SSF	BA,CG,GL2,EA,GG,LG,SSF	1973-2015 X	BA,CG,GL2,GG	2013-2015
862	Samoa	BA,CG,GL2,EA,GG,SSF	BA	2010-2016	BA	2014-2016
135	San Marino	BA,CG,GL2,EA,GG,SSF	BA,CG,GL2,EA,GG,SSF	1995-2015 X	BA,CG,GL2,GG	2013-2015
716	Sao Tome and Principe	BA,CG,GL2,EA,GG,LG,SSF	BA	2002-2012	BA	2010-2012
722	Senegal	BA,CG,GL2,EA,GG,LG,SSF	BA	1996-2015 X	BA	2013-2015
942	Serbia, Republic of	BA,CG,GL2,EA,GG,LG,SSF	BA,CG,GL2,EA,GG,LG,SSF	2007-2012	BA,CG,GL2,GG	2010-2012
718	Seychelles	BA,CG,GL2,GG	BA,CG,GL2,GG	1985-2015 X	BA,CG,GL2,GG	2013-2015
724	Sierra Leone	BA,CG,GL2,EA,GG,LG,SSF,SG	BA,CG,GL2,EA,GG,LG,SSF,SG	1990-2014	BA,CG,GL2,GG	2012-2014
576	Singapore	BA,CG,GL2,EA,GG	BA,CG,GL2,EA,GG	1972-2015	BA,CG,GL2,GG	2013-2015
936	Slovak Republic	BA,CG,GL2,EA,GG,LG,SSF	CG,GL2,GG,LG,SSF	1995-2015	CG,GL2,GG	2013-2015
961	Slovenia	BA,CG,GL2,EA,GG,LG,SSF	CG,GL2,GG,LG,SSF	1992-2015	CG,GL2,GG	2013-2015
813	Solomon Islands	BA,CG,GL2,EA,GG,LG,SG	BA	2011-2015	BA	2013-2015
199	South Africa	BA,CG,GL2,EA,GG,LG,SSF,SG	BA,CG,GL2,EA,GG,LG,SSF,SG	1972-2015	BA,CG,GL2,GG	2013-2015
184	Spain	BA,CG,GL2,EA,GG,LG,SSF,SG	BA,CG,GL2,EA,GG,LG,SSF,SG	1972-2015	BA,CG,GL2,GG	2013-2015
524	Sri Lanka	BA,CG,GL2,EA,GG,LG,SG	BA	1990-2015	BA	2013-2015
361	St. Kitts and Nevis	BA,CG,GL2,EA,GG,SSF	BA	1985-2014 X	BA	2012-2014
362	St. Lucia	BA,CG,GL2,EA,GG,LG,SSF	BA	2000-2014	BA	2012-2014
364	St. Vincent and the Grenadines	BA,CG,GL2,GG,LG,SSF	BA	1978-2014	BA	2012-2014
366	Suriname	BA,CG,GL2,EA,GG,LG,SSF	BA	2001-2012	BA	2010-2012
734	Swaziland	BA,CG,GL2,EA,GG,LG	BA	1999-2012	BA	2010-2012
144	Sweden	BA,CG,GL2,EA,GG,LG,SSF	CG,GL2,GG,LG,SSF	1972-2015	CG,GL2,GG	2013-2015
146	Switzerland	BA,CG,GL2,EA,GG,LG,SSF,SG	CG,GL2,SSF	1972-2015 X	CG,GL2	2013-2015
463	Syrian Arab Republic	BA,CG,GL2,EA,GG,LG	BA	1972-2009 X	BA	2007-2009
738	Tanzania	BA,CG,GL2,EA,GG,LG,SSF	BA,LG	2009-2016	BA	2014-2016
578	Thailand	BA,CG,GL2,EA,GG,LG,SSF	BA,CG,GL2,EA,GG,LG,SSF	1972-2015	BA,CG,GL2,GG	2013-2015
537	Timor-Leste, Dem. Rep. of	BA,CG,GL2,EA,GG	BA,CG,GL2,EA,GG	2010-2015	BA,CG,GL2,GG	2013-2015
742	Togo	BA,CG,GL2,EA,GG,LG,SSF	BA	1977-2015 X	BA	2013-2015

	Country	Existing Sectors	GFS Offline Tool Reported Sectors	Years	GFS Yearbook Reported Sectors	Years
369	Trinidad and Tobago	BA,CG,GL2,EA,GG,LG,SSF	GL2	1976-2012 X	GL2	2010-2012
744	Tunisia	BA,CG,GL2,EA,GG,LG,SSF	BA,GL2,GG,LG,SSF	1972-2012	BA,GL2,GG	2010-2012
186	Turkey	BA,CG,GL2,EA,GG,LG,SSF	BA,CG,GL2,EA,GG,LG,SSF	1972-2015 X	BA,CG,GL2,GG	2013-2015
746	Uganda	BA,CG,GL2,EA,GG,LG,SSF,SG	BA,CG,GL2,EA,GG,LG,SSF,SG	1998-2015	BA,CG,GL2,GG	2013-2015
926	Ukraine	BA,CG,GL2,GG,LG,SSF	BA,CG,GL2,GG,LG,SSF	1999-2015	BA,CG,GL2,GG	2013-2015
466	United Arab Emirates	BA,CG,GL2,EA,GG,SSF,SG	BA,CG,GL2,EA,GG,SSF,SG	1997-2015 X	BA,CG,GL2,GG	2013-2015
112	United Kingdom	BA,CG,GL2,GG,LG	BA,CG,GL2,GG,LG	1972-2015	BA,CG,GL2,GG	2013-2015
111	United States	BA,CG,GL2,GG,SSF,SG	BA,CG,GL2,GG,SSF,SG	1972-2015	BA,CG,GL2,GG	2013-2015
298	Uruguay	BA,CG,GL2,EA,GG,LG,SSF	CG,GL2,GG,LG,SSF	1972-2015	CG,GL2,GG	2013-2015
927	Uzbekistan	BA,CG,GL2,EA,GG,SSF,SG	BA,CG,GL2,EA,GG,SSF,SG	2011-2015	BA,CG,GL2,GG	2013-2015
846	Vanuatu	BA,CG,GL2,EA,GG,LG	BA	1981-2011 X	BA	2009-2011
487	West Bank and Gaza	BA,CG,GL2,GG,LG,SSF	BA,CG,LG	2005-2015	BA,CG	2013-2015
474	Yemen, Republic of	BA,CG,GL2,EA,GG,LG,SSF	GG	1990-2012 X	GG	2010-2012
754	Zambia	BA,CG,GL2,EA,GG,LG,SSF	BA	1990-2011 X	BA	2009-2011
698	Zimbabwe	BA,CG,GL2,EA,GG,LG,SSF	BA	1976-2012 X	BA	2010-2012

Guide to Country Tables

Table B: Basis of Recording for Latest Year Reported GFS Offline Tool and Yearbook

Government Sector
- BA Budgetary Central Government
- EA Extra-Budgetary Units/Entities
- SSF Social Security Funds
- CG Central Government (excl. social security funds)
- SG State Governments
- LG Local Governments
- GG General Government (consolidated)
- GL2 Central Government (incl. social security funds)

- CA Cash basis of recording
- AC Noncash basis of recording (including accrual basis)
- NP Sector does not exist
- NA Information Not Available

For EU countries listed:
In line with the presentation adopted within the European Union, data on BA operations may include the operations of EA.

	Country	**BA**	**EA**	**CG**	**SSF**	**SG**	**LG**	**GG**	**GL2**	**Reference Year**
512	Afghanistan, Islamic Republic of	CA	CA	CA	NP	NP	CA	CA	CA	2013
914	Albania	AC	NA	AC	AC	NP	AC	AC	AC	2015
612	Algeria	AC	NA	NA	NA	NP	NA	NA	NA	2011
614	Angola	AC	NA	NA	NA	NP	NA	NA	NA	2015
312	Anguilla	CA	NP	NA	NA	NP	NP	NA	NA	2014
311	Antigua and Barbuda	CA	NA	NA	NA	NP	NA	NA	NA	2014
213	Argentina	AC	AC	AC	AC	NA	NA	NA	AC	2015
911	Armenia, Republic of	CA	CA	NA	NA	NP	CA	CA	CA	2015
193	Australia	AC	NP	AC	NP	AC	AC	AC	AC	2015
122	Austria	NA	NA	AC	AC	AC	AC	AC	AC	2015
912	Azerbaijan, Republic of	CA	CA	CA	CA	CA	CA	CA	CA	2015
313	Bahamas, The	CA	NP	CA	NA	NP	NP	NA	NA	2015
419	Bahrain, Kingdom of	AC	NA	NA	NA	NP	NP	NA	NA	2013
513	Bangladesh	CA	NA	NA	NP	NP	NA	NA	NA	2015
316	Barbados	AC	NA	NA	NA	NP	NP	NA	NA	2013
913	Belarus	AC	NP	AC	AC	NP	CA	AC	AC	2015
124	Belgium	NA	NA	AC	AC	AC	AC	AC	AC	2015
339	Belize	CA	NA	NA	NA	NP	NA	NA	NA	2014
638	Benin	AC	NA	NA	NA	NP	NA	NA	NA	2013
514	Bhutan	CA	NP	CA	NP	NP	NP	CA	CA	2014
963	Bosnia and Herzegovina	AC	AC	AC	AC	NP	AC	AC	AC	2015
616	Botswana	CA	NA	NA	NA	NA	NA	NA	NA	2014
223	Brazil	NA	NA	AC	NP	AC	AC	AC	AC	2015
918	Bulgaria	NA	NA	AC	AC	NP	AC	AC	AC	2015
748	Burkina Faso	AC	NA	NA	NA	NP	NA	NA	NA	2015
618	Burundi	AC	NA	NA	NA	NP	NA	NA	NA	2013
624	Cabo Verde	CA	CA	CA	NA	NP	CA	NA	NA	2012
522	Cambodia	AC	NA	NA	NP	NP	NA	NA	NA	2015
156	Canada	NA	NP	AC	AC	AC	AC	AC	AC	2015
626	Central African Republic	AC	NA	NA	NA	NP	NA	NA	NA	2012
228	Chile	NA	NA	NA	NP	NP	AC	AC	AC	2015

Country		BA	EA	CG	SSF	SG	LG	GG	GL2	Reference Year
924	China, P.R.: Mainland	CA	CA	CA	CA	CA	CA	CA	CA	2014
532	China, P.R.: Hong Kong	NP	NP	NP	NP	NP	NP	AC	NP	2014
546	China, P.R.: Macao	CA	CA	CA	CA	NP	NP	CA	CA	2015
233	Colombia	AC	AC	AC	AC	AC	AC	AC	AC	2015
636	Congo, Democratic Republic of	CA	NA	NA	NA	NP	NA	NA	NA	2010
634	Congo, Republic of	AC	AC	AC	AC	NP	AC	AC	AC	2012
238	Costa Rica	AC	CA	AC	AC	NP	CA	AC	AC	2015
662	Cote d'Ivoire	AC	NA	NA	NA	NP	NA	NA	NA	2014
960	Croatia	CA	CA	NA	NA	NP	CA	CA	CA	2014
423	Cyprus	NA	NA	AC	AC	NP	AC	AC	AC	2015
935	Czech Republic	CA	CA	CA	CA	NP	CA	CA	CA	2015
128	Denmark	NA	NA	AC	AC	NP	AC	AC	AC	2015
321	Dominica	CA	NA	NA	NA	NP	NA	NA	NA	2014
243	Dominican Republic	AC	AC	AC	AC	NP	NA	NA	AC	2015
469	Egypt	CA	NA	NA	NA	NP	NP	CA	CA	2015
253	El Salvador	AC	AC	AC	AC	NP	AC	AC	AC	2015
642	Equatorial Guinea	CA	NP	NA	NA	NP	NA	NA	NA	2009
939	Estonia	NA	NA	AC	AC	NP	AC	AC	AC	2015
644	Ethiopia	CA	NA	NA	NA	NA	NA	NA	NA	2011
819	Fiji	CA	NA	NA	NP	NP	NA	NA	NA	2013
172	Finland	NA	NA	AC	AC	NP	AC	AC	AC	2015
132	France	NA	NA	AC	AC	NP	AC	AC	AC	2015
648	Gambia, The	NA	NA	CA	NP	NP	NA	NA	NP	2009
915	Georgia	CA	NP	CA	NP	NP	CA	CA	CA	2015
134	Germany	AC	AC	AC	AC	AC	AC	AC	AC	2015
652	Ghana	CA	CA	NA	NP	NA	NA	NA	NA	2011
174	Greece	NA	NA	AC	AC	NP	AC	AC	AC	2015
328	Grenada	CA	NA	NA	NA	NP	NA	NA	NA	2014
258	Guatemala	CA	NA	NA	NA	NP	NA	NA	NA	2013
268	Honduras	AC	AC	AC	AC	NP	AC	AC	AC	2015
944	Hungary	NA	NA	AC	AC	NP	AC	AC	AC	2015
176	Iceland	AC	NP	AC	AC	NP	AC	AC	AC	2015
534	India	CA	NP	CA	NP	NA	NA	NA	CA	2013
536	Indonesia	NA	NA	AC	NP	NP	AC	AC	AC	2015
429	Iran, Islamic Republic of	CA	CA	CA	CA	NP	CA	CA	CA	2009
433	Iraq	AC	NA	NA	NA	NP	NA	NA	NA	2014
178	Ireland	NA	NA	AC	NP	NP	AC	AC	AC	2015
436	Israel	AC	AC	AC	AC	NP	AC	AC	AC	2015
136	Italy	NA	NA	AC	AC	NP	AC	AC	AC	2015
343	Jamaica	CA	AC	AC	AC	NP	NA	AC	AC	2015
158	Japan	NA	NA	AC	NA	NP	AC	AC	NA	2014
439	Jordan	CA	NA	NA	NA	NP	NA	NA	NA	2015
916	Kazakhstan	CA	NP	CA	CA	NP	CA	CA	CA	2015
664	Kenya	AC	AC	AC	AC	NP	AC	AC	AC	2015
826	Kiribati	CA	CA	CA	NP	NP	CA	CA	CA	2015
542	Korea, Republic of	AC	AC	NA	NA	NP	AC	AC	AC	2015
443	Kuwait	CA	CA	CA	NA	NP	NP	NA	NA	2015
917	Kyrgyz Republic	CA	NP	CA	CA	NP	CA	CA	CA	2015
544	Lao People's Democratic Republic	CA	NA	NA	NA	NP	NP	NA	NA	2015

Country		BA	EA	CG	SSF	SG	LG	GG	GL2	Reference Year
941	Latvia	NA	NA	AC	AC	NP	AC	AC	AC	2015
446	Lebanon	CA	NA	NA	NA	NP	NA	NA	NA	2015
666	Lesotho	CA	NA	NA	NP	NP	NA	NA	NA	2013
668	Liberia	CA	NP	CA	NA	NP	NA	NA	NA	2013
946	Lithuania	AC	AC	AC	AC	AC	AC	AC	AC	2015
137	Luxembourg	NA	NA	AC	AC	NP	AC	AC	AC	2015
962	Macedonia, FYR	NA	NA	NA	NA	NP	NA	NA	CA	2012
674	Madagascar	NA	NA	AC	NA	NP	NA	NA	AC	2014
676	Malawi	CA	NA	NA	NP	NP	CA	NA	NA	2016
548	Malaysia	CA	NA	NA	NA	NA	NA	NA	NA	2015
556	Maldives	CA	NP	CA	NP	NP	NP	CA	CA	2014
678	Mali	AC	NA	NA	NA	NP	NA	NA	NA	2015
181	Malta	NA	NA	AC	AC	AC	AC	AC	AC	2015
867	Marshall Islands, Republic of	AC	NA	NA	NA	NP	NA	NA	NA	2015
684	Mauritius	AC	AC	AC	AC	AC	AC	AC	AC	2014
868	Micronesia, Federated States of	AC	NA	NA	NA	AC	NA	NA	NA	2015
921	Moldova	CA	NP	CA	CA	NP	CA	CA	CA	2015
948	Mongolia	CA	CA	CA	CA	NP	CA	CA	CA	2013
351	Montserrat	CA	NA	NA	NA	NP	NP	NA	NA	2014
686	Morocco	AC	NA	NA	NA	NP	NA	NA	NA	2015
688	Mozambique	CA	NA	NA	NA	NP	NA	NA	NA	2013
728	Namibia	CA	NA	NA	NA	NP	NA	NA	NA	2015
558	Nepal	CA	NA	NA	NP	NP	NA	NA	NA	2016
138	Netherlands	AC	AC	AC	AC	NP	AC	AC	AC	2015
196	New Zealand	NA	NA	NA	NA	NP	AC	NA	AC	2015
278	Nicaragua	CA	NA	NA	CA	NA	NA	NA	NA	2015
694	Nigeria	CA	NA	NA	NP	NA	NA	NA	NA	2013
142	Norway	NA	NA	AC	NA	NP	AC	AC	AC	2015
449	Oman	CA	NA	NA	NA	NP	NP	NA	NA	2013
564	Pakistan	CA	NA	NA	NP	NA	NA	NA	NP	2014
565	Palau	AC	NA	NA	NA	NA	NP	NA	NA	2015
288	Paraguay	AC	AC	AC	AC	AC	AC	AC	AC	2015
293	Peru	CA	CA	CA	CA	CA	CA	CA	CA	2015
566	Philippines	CA	NA	NA	NA	NP	NA	NA	NA	2015
964	Poland	NA	NA	AC	AC	NP	AC	AC	AC	2015
182	Portugal	AC	AC	AC	AC	NP	AC	AC	AC	2015
453	Qatar	CA	NA	NA	NP	NP	NP	NA	NA	2010
968	Romania	NA	NA	AC	AC	NP	AC	AC	AC	2015
922	Russian Federation	AC	AC	AC	AC	AC	AC	AC	AC	2015
714	Rwanda	AC	AC	AC	AC	NP	AC	AC	AC	2015
862	Samoa	CA	NA	NA	NA	NP	NP	NA	NA	2016
135	San Marino	AC	AC	AC	AC	CA	CA	AC	AC	2015
716	Sao Tome and Principe	AC	NA	NA	NA	NP	NA	NA	NA	2012
722	Senegal	AC	NA	NA	NA	NP	NA	NA	NA	2015
942	Serbia, Republic of	CA	CA	CA	CA	NP	CA	CA	CA	2012
718	Seychelles	CA	NP	CA	NP	NP	NP	CA	CA	2015
724	Sierra Leone	CA	NA	NA	NA	NP	NA	NA	NA	2014
576	Singapore	CA	CA	CA	NP	NP	NP	CA	CA	2015
936	Slovak Republic	NA	NA	AC	AC	NP	AC	AC	AC	2015

Country		BA	EA	CG	SSF	SG	LG	GG	GL2	Reference Year
961	Slovenia	NA	NA	AC	AC	NP	AC	AC	AC	2015
813	Solomon Islands	CA	NA	NA	NP	NA	NA	NA	NA	2015
199	South Africa	CA	CA	CA	AC	CA	AC	CA	CA	2015
184	Spain	AC	AC	AC	AC	AC	AC	AC	AC	2015
524	Sri Lanka	CA	NA	NA	NP	NA	NA	NA	NA	2015
361	St. Kitts and Nevis	CA	NA	NA	NA	NP	NP	NA	NA	2014
362	St. Lucia	CA	NA	NA	NA	NP	NA	NA	NA	2014
364	St. Vincent and the Grenadines	CA	NP	NA	NA	NP	NA	NA	NA	2014
366	Suriname	CA	NA	NA	NA	NP	NA	NA	NA	2012
734	Swaziland	CA	NA	NA	NP	NP	NA	NA	NP	2012
144	Sweden	NA	NA	AC	AC	AC	AC	AC	AC	2015
146	Switzerland	NA	NA	AC	AC	NA	NA	NA	AC	2015
463	Syrian Arab Republic	CA	NA	NA	NP	NP	NA	NA	NP	2009
738	Tanzania	CA	NA	NA	NA	NP	CA	NA	NA	2016
578	Thailand	AC	AC	AC	AC	NP	CA	AC	AC	2015
537	Timor-Leste, Dem. Rep. of	CA	CA	CA	NP	NP	NP	CA	CA	2015
742	Togo	AC	NA	NA	NA	NP	NA	NA	NA	2015
369	Trinidad and Tobago	NA	NA	NA	NA	NP	NA	NA	CA	2012
744	Tunisia	CA	NA	NA	CA	NP	CA	CA	CA	2012
186	Turkey	AC	AC	AC	AC	NP	AC	AC	AC	2015
746	Uganda	AC	AC	AC	CA	CA	AC	AC	CA	2015
926	Ukraine	CA	NP	CA	CA	NP	CA	CA	CA	2015
466	United Arab Emirates	AC	AC	AC	AC	AC	NP	AC	AC	2015
112	United Kingdom	AC	NP	AC	NP	NP	AC	AC	AC	2015
111	United States	AC	NP	AC	AC	AC	NP	AC	AC	2015
298	Uruguay	NA	NA	CA	CA	NP	CA	CA	CA	2015
927	Uzbekistan	CA	CA	CA	CA	CA	NP	CA	CA	2015
846	Vanuatu	AC	NA	NA	NP	NP	NA	NA	NP	2011
487	West Bank and Gaza	AC	NP	AC	NA	NP	AC	NA	NA	2015
474	Yemen, Republic of	NA	NA	NA	NA	NP	NA	CA	NA	2012
754	Zambia	CA	NA	NA	NA	NP	NA	NA	NA	2011
698	Zimbabwe	CA	NA	NA	NA	NP	NA	NA	NA	2012

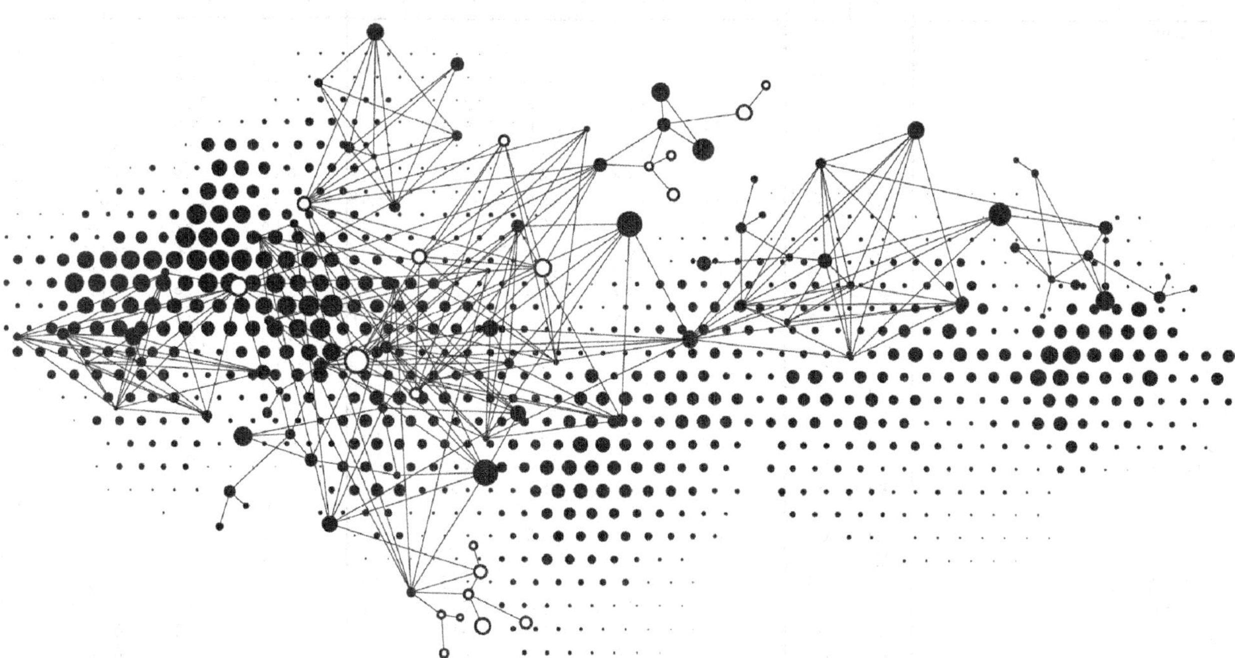

World Tables

Table W1. Main Balances

(Percent of GDP)

BR: Basis of recording (Cash/Non Cash); GL: Government sector

		BR	GL	Net lending / borrowing					Primary net lending / borrowing				
				2011	2012	2013	2014	2015	2011	2012	2013	2014	2015
	Advanced Economies												
	Euro Area												
122	Austria	AC	GG	-2.6	-2.2	-1.4	-2.7	-1.1	0.4	0.7	1.4	-0.1	1.5
124	Belgium	AC	GG	-4.1 P	-4.2 P	-3.0 P	-3.1 P	-2.5 P	-0.4 P	-0.4 P	0.6 P	0.5 P	0.7 P
423	Cyprus	AC	GG	-5.7 P	-5.8 P	-4.9 P	-8.9 P	-1.1 P	-3.5 P	-2.9 P	-1.8 P	-6.0 P	1.7 P
939	Estonia	AC	GG	1.2 P	-0.3 P	-0.2 P	0.7 P	0.1 P	1.3 P	-0.1 P	0.0 P	0.9 P	0.3 P
172	Finland	AC	GG	-1.0 P	-2.2 P	-2.6 P	-3.2 P	-2.8 P	0.4 P	-0.7 P	-1.3 P	-1.9 P	-1.5 P
132	France	AC	GG	-5.1 P	-4.8 P	-4.0 P	-4.0 P	-3.5 P	-2.5 P	-2.2 P	-1.8 P	-1.8 P	-1.5 P
134	Germany	AC	GG	-1.0	-0.1	-0.2	0.3	0.7	1.6	2.2	1.8	2.1	2.3
174	Greece	AC	GG	-10.3 P	-8.8 P	-13.2 P	-3.6 P	-7.5 P	-3.0 P	-3.7 P	-9.1 P	0.4 P	-3.9 P
178	Ireland	AC	GG	-12.6 P	-8.0 P	-5.7 P	-3.7 P	-1.9 P	-9.3 P	-3.9 P	-1.4 P	0.1 P	0.7 P
136	Italy	AC	GG	-3.7 P	-2.9 P	-2.7 P	-3.0 P	-2.6 P	1.0 P	2.3 P	2.1 P	1.6 P	1.5 P
941	Latvia	AC	GG	-3.4 P	-0.8 P	-0.9 P	-1.6 P	-1.3 P	-1.5 P	0.9 P	0.7 P	0.0 P	0.2 P
946	Lithuania	AC	GG	-8.9 P	-3.1 P	-2.6 P	-0.7 P	-0.2 P	-7.1 P	-1.2 P	-0.9 P	0.9 P	1.3 P
137	Luxembourg	AC	GG	0.5	0.3	1.0	1.5	1.5 P	1.0	0.9	1.5	1.9	1.9 P
181	Malta	AC	GG	-2.5 P	-3.6 P	-2.6 P	-2.1 P	-1.4 P	0.7 P	-0.6 P	0.3 P	0.9 P	1.3 P
138	Netherlands	AC	GG	-4.3 P	-3.9 P	-2.4 P	-2.3 P	-1.9 P	-2.5 P	-2.2 P	-0.9 P	-0.8 P	-0.6 P
182	Portugal	AC	GG	-7.4 P	-5.7 P	-4.8 P	-7.2 P	-4.4 P	-3.1 P	-0.8 P	0.0 P	-2.3 P	0.2 P
936	Slovak Republic	AC	GG	-4.3 P	-4.4 P	-2.7 P	-2.7 P	-2.7 P	-2.8 P	-2.6 P	-0.9 P	-0.8 P	-1.0 P
961	Slovenia	AC	GG	-6.7	-4.1	-15.0	-5.0	-2.7	-4.8	-2.1	-12.5	-1.9	0.3
184	Spain	AC	GG	-9.5	-10.4	...	-6.0	-5.1 P	-7.0	-7.5	...	-2.5	-2.0 P
193	Australia	AC	GG	-4.6	-4.2	-2.6	-2.9	-2.9	-3.5	-2.9	-1.3	-1.5	-1.4
156	Canada	AC	GG	-3.3	-2.5	-1.4	0.0	-1.1	0.4	1.0	1.9	3.2	2.1
532	China, P.R.: Hong Kong SAR	AC	GG	3.8	3.5	0.7	4.2	...	3.9	3.6	0.8	4.4	...
546	China, P.R.: Macao SAR	CA	GG	24.8	24.1	27.0	23.9	13.5	24.8	24.1	27.0	23.9	13.5
935	Czech Republic	CA	GG	-4.2	-2.3	-1.2 P	-1.7	-0.7	-3.1	-1.2	0.1 P	-0.6	0.3
128	Denmark	AC	GG	-2.1 P	-3.5 P	-1.0 P	1.5 P	-1.4 P	-0.1 P	-1.7 P	0.7 P	3.0 P	0.2 P
176	Iceland	AC	GG	-5.3	-3.7	-1.4	-0.1	-0.8	-0.4	1.7	3.4	4.7	3.8
436	Israel	AC	GG	-2.7	-4.7	-4.0	-3.2	-2.1	1.5	-0.5	-0.2	0.4	1.3
158	Japan	AC	GG	-8.8	-8.6	-7.6	-5.2	...	-6.4	-6.3	-5.3	-2.9	...
542	Korea, Republic of	AC	GG	1.9	1.2	1.5	1.4	1.3	3.0	2.8	3.0	2.9	2.7
196	New Zealand	AC	GL2	-7.8	-0.4	-0.6 NA	-1.1	0.1	-6.0	1.2	1.3 NA	0.4	1.6
142	Norway	AC	GG	13.4 P	13.8 P	10.8 P	8.7 P	6.4 P	14.3 P	14.6 P	11.5 P	9.4 P	7.1 P
135	San Marino	AC	GG	...	...	...	...	...	...	...	...	...	...
576	Singapore	CA	GG	9.2	8.6	8.3	7.3	4.4	9.2	8.6	8.3	7.3	4.4
144	Sweden	AC	GG	-0.2 P	-1.0 P	-1.4 P	-1.6 P	0.2 P	1.0 P	0.0 P	-0.5 P	-0.8 P	0.8 P
146	Switzerland	AC	GL2	0.7 P	0.6 P	0.3 P	0.3 P	0.5 P	1.1 P	1.0 P	0.6 P	0.7 P	0.8 P
112	United Kingdom	AC	GG	-7.6 P	-8.3 P	-5.7 P	-5.7 P	-4.3 P	-4.4 P	-5.4 P	-2.8 P	-3.0 P	-2.0 P
111	United States	AC	GG	-10.7	-9.0	-5.5	-4.9	-4.3	-6.8	-5.1	-1.8	-1.3	-0.9
	Emerging and Developing Economies												
	Emerging and Developing Asia												
513	Bangladesh	CA	BA	-0.8	-0.1	0.1	-0.7	-1.2	0.8	1.7	2.0	1.2	0.7
514	Bhutan	CA	GG	-1.7	-1.8	-5.3	4.6	...	0.6	0.2	-2.7	6.5	...
522	Cambodia	AC	BA	-4.6	-0.7	-2.7	-1.3	-0.8 P	-4.3	-0.4	-2.4	-1.0	-0.5 P
924	China, P.R.: Mainland	CA	BA	...	...	...	...	...	...	...	...	...	...
819	Fiji	CA	BA	-2.1	-1.8	-0.9	...	...	2.8	2.8	2.6	...	...
534	India	CA	GL2	-3.2	-3.8	-4.1 P	...	...	-0.6	-0.6	-0.8 P	...	...
536	Indonesia	AC	GG	-0.6	-1.3	-1.8	-1.7 P	-2.7 P	0.6	-0.2	-0.6	-0.5 P	-1.3 P
826	Kiribati	CA	GG	-7.1	3.5	20.1	50.8	69.7 P	-4.8	7.1	21.1	50.8	69.8 P
544	Lao People's Democratic Republic	CA	BA	-1.0	-0.7	-5.3	-2.4	-4.3	-0.3	0.0	-4.1	-1.5	-3.2
548	Malaysia	CA	BA	-4.6	-4.4	-3.8	-3.3	-3.2	-2.7	-2.4	-1.7	-1.3	-1.1
556	Maldives	CA	GG	-7.7	...	...	...	...	-5.7	...	...	...	...
867	Marshall Islands, Republic of	AC	BA	2.1	-0.7	0.7	3.2	2.7 P	2.9	0.0	1.4	3.6	2.9 P
868	Micronesia, Federated States of	AC	BA	0.4	2.4	3.5	13.5	11.1	0.6	2.6	3.8	13.7	11.4
948	Mongolia	CA	GG	-2.6	-7.3	-0.5	...	...	-2.3	-6.5	0.9	...	...
558	Nepal	CA	BA	-1.0	-0.6	1.7	1.8	1.1	-0.1	0.4	2.5	2.4	1.5
565	Palau	AC	BA	1.3	1.0	0.7	3.5	5.0	1.6	1.3	1.0	3.7	5.3
566	Philippines	CA	BA	-1.8	-1.9	-1.2	-0.5	-1.3 P	1.2	1.0	1.6	2.1	1.0 P
862	Samoa	CA	BA	-5.3	-7.2	-3.8	-5.3	-3.9	-4.6	-6.4	-3.0	-4.5	-3.0
813	Solomon Islands	CA	BA	7.4	5.4	4.1	2.5	0.9	7.7	5.6	4.3	2.6	1.1
524	Sri Lanka	CA	BA	-6.4	-6.1	-5.8	-5.9 P	-7.4 P	-1.0	-0.7	-0.7	-1.4 P	-2.9 P
578	Thailand	AC	GG	-0.6	-0.8	0.4	-0.1	0.1 E	0.6	0.3	1.5	1.1	1.1 E
537	Timor-Leste	CA	GG	41.6	39.9	42.7	22.5	4.5	41.6	39.9	42.7	22.5	4.5
846	Vanuatu	AC	BA	-2.3	...	...	...	...	-1.7	...	...	...	...
582	Vietnam	CA	BA	0.6	-5.5	-5.7	...	...	1.6	-4.3 P	-4.2 P	...	...
	Europe												
	Central and Eastern Europe												
914	Albania	AC	GG	-4.0	-4.1	-5.5	-3.0	-3.2	-0.8	-1.0	-2.3	-0.2	-0.5
963	Bosnia and Herzegovina	AC	GG	-1.2	-2.0	-2.2	-2.0	0.7	-0.6	-1.2	-1.4	-1.2	1.6
918	Bulgaria	AC	GG	-2.0 P	-0.3 P	-0.4 P	-5.5 P	-1.7 P	-1.3 P	0.5 P	0.3 P	-4.6 P	-0.8 P
960	Croatia	CA	GG	-4.5	-3.3	-5.3	-3.8	...	-2.2	-0.6	-2.4	-0.6	...
944	Hungary	AC	GG	-5.5 P	-2.3 P	-2.6 P	-2.1 P	-1.6 P	-1.3 P	2.3 P	2.0 P	1.9 P	2.0 P

Table W1. Main Balances

(Percent of GDP)

BR: Basis of recording (Cash/Non Cash); GL: Government sector

		BR	GL	Net lending / borrowing					Primary net lending / borrowing				
				2011	2012	2013	2014	2015	2011	2012	2013	2014	2015
967	Kosovo, Republic of	CA	GG	...	-2.3	-3.2	-2.6	-1.8	...	-2.1	-3.0	-2.3	-1.5
962	Macedonia, F.Y.R. of	CA	GL2	-2.7	-4.0	...	...	...	-1.9	-3.1	...	...	...
964	Poland	AC	GG	-4.8 P	-3.7 P	-4.1 P	-3.4 P	-2.6 P	-2.3 P	-1.0 P	-1.5 P	-1.5 P	-0.8 P
968	Romania	AC	GG	-5.4 P	-3.7 P	-2.1 P	-0.8 P	-0.8 P	-3.8 P	-1.9 P	-0.3 P	0.8 P	0.9 P
942	Serbia, Republic of	CA	GG	-4.6	-6.1 P	...	...	...	-3.3	-4.2 P	...	...	...
186	Turkey	AC	GG	-0.8	-0.2	0.2	0.4	1.7	2.5	3.1	3.1	3.1	4.1
	CIS												
911	Armenia	AC	GL2	-2.8	-1.3	...	-1.8	-4.7	-1.8	-0.4	...	-0.5	-3.2
912	Azerbaijan	CA	GG	13.1	5.8	4.5	4.5	-2.8	13.4	5.9	4.7	4.6	-2.4
913	Belarus	AC	GG	3.1	0.8	-0.2	0.9	2.3	4.2	2.2	0.8	1.9	4.1
915	Georgia	CA	GG	-0.9	-0.6	-1.1	-2.0	-1.1	0.3	0.4	-0.2	-1.1	-0.0
916	Kazakhstan	CA	GG	8.0	5.8	4.9	3.4	-2.2	8.3	6.1	5.3	3.9	-1.6
917	Kyrgyz Republic	CA	GG	...	...	...	...	-1.0	...	...	...	...	-0.1
921	Moldova	CA	GG	-2.4	-2.2	-1.8	-1.8	-2.3	-1.6	-1.4	-1.3	-1.3	-1.4
922	Russian Federation	AC	GG	3.1	2.7	0.7	-0.9 P	-0.7 P	3.7	3.3	1.4	-0.2 P	0.3 P
926	Ukraine	CA	GG	-2.3	-3.9	-4.3	-4.5	-0.8 P	-0.3	-2.0	-1.8	-1.1	3.7 P
927	Uzbekistan	CA	GG	9.6	11.2	6.0	5.3	4.0	9.6	11.2	6.0	5.3	4.0
	Middle East, North Africa and Pakistan												
512	Afghanistan, Islamic Republic of	CA	GG	-0.4	-0.5	2.3	...	...	-0.4	-0.5	2.3	...	...
612	Algeria	AC	BA	-0.3	...	...	...	...	-0.0	...	...	...	...
419	Bahrain, Kingdom of	AC	BA	-0.5	...	-3.5	...	...	0.5	...	-1.9	...	...
469	Egypt	CA	GG	-9.6	-10.1	-12.8	-11.2	-10.8 P	-4.3	-4.5	-5.4	-3.6	-3.4 P
433	Iraq	AC	BA	...	...	...	-2.8 P	...	...	...	...	-2.6 P	...
439	Jordan	CA	BA	-6.8	-8.3	-5.5	-2.3	-3.5	-4.7	-5.6	-2.4	1.3	-0.0
443	Kuwait	CA	CG	26.4 NA	26.1 NA	26.1	7.6	-21.0	26.4 NA	26.1 NA	26.1	7.6	-21.0
446	Lebanon	CA	BA	-6.4	-8.6	-9.9	-7.9	-6.8	2.9	-0.4	-1.9	0.5	1.9
686	Morocco	AC	BA	-6.6	-7.2	-5.1	-4.9	...	-4.4	-4.8	-2.6	-2.2	...
449	Oman	CA	BA	8.7	6.2	4.7	...	...	8.9	6.3	4.9	...	...
564	Pakistan	CA	BA	-6.4	-8.0	-5.2	-6.5 P	...	-1.7	-3.1	-0.1	-0.8 P	...
744	Tunisia	CA	GG	-3.5	-4.5	...	...	...	-1.6	-2.7	...	...	...
466	United Arab Emirates	AC	GG	2.8	3.8	2.7	-2.3	-6.6	3.0	4.2	3.1	-2.0	-6.3
487	West Bank and Gaza	AC	CG	-0.6	-0.7	0.3	0.4	-0.3	-0.4	-0.6	0.5	0.5	-0.1
474	Yemen, Republic of	CA	GG	-9.3	-6.9	...	...	...	-5.8	-2.0	...	...	...
	Sub-Saharan Africa												
	CEMAC												
626	Central African Republic	AC	BA	-6.6 P	0.7 P	...	...	...	-5.9 P	1.2 P	...	...	...
634	Congo, Republic of	AC	GG	17.4	6.6	...	...	...	17.5	6.8	...	...	...
	WAEMU												
638	Benin	AC	BA	2.6	1.6	2.7	...	...	3.0	2.1	3.2	...	...
748	Burkina Faso	AC	BA	-2.3	-3.1	-3.9	-1.9	-2.3	-1.7	-2.4	-3.3	-1.2	-1.6
662	Côte d'Ivoire	AC	BA	-3.4	-2.8	-2.3	-1.9	...	-1.6	-1.1	-0.9	-1.1	...
678	Mali	AC	BA	-2.9	0.0	-1.2	-1.2	-2.6	-2.4	0.4	-0.6	-0.6	-1.9
722	Senegal	AC	BA	-6.2 P	-5.2 P	-5.5 P	-4.4 P	-4.8 P	-4.7 P	-3.8 P	-4.0 P	-2.6 P	-2.8 P
742	Togo	AC	BA	-1.1	-6.1	-4.6	...	-11.5	-0.4	-5.2	-3.4	...	-9.7
614	Angola	AC	BA	11.4	6.7	-4.5	-11.9 P	-6.9 P	12.3	7.6	-3.7	-10.8 P	-4.9 P
616	Botswana	CA	BA	-0.4	1.1	5.6	3.7	...	0.1	1.7	6.2	4.2	...
618	Burundi	AC	BA	-2.9	-2.6	-2.0	...	...	-1.7	-1.7	-1.2	...	...
624	Cabo Verde	CA	CG	...	-12.3	...	...	...	...	-10.4	...	...	...
644	Ethiopia	CA	BA	-1.4	...	...	...	...	-1.0	...	...	...	...
652	Ghana	CA	BA	-3.9	...	...	...	...	-1.2	...	...	...	...
664	Kenya	AC	GG	...	...	...	-4.1 P	-8.8 P	...	...	...	-1.5 P	-6.0 P
666	Lesotho	CA	BA	-12.0	3.3	3.9	...	...	-11.2	4.2	5.0	...	...
668	Liberia	CA	CG	-1.6	-1.7	-0.7	...	...	-0.5	-1.5	...	...	...
674	Madagascar	AC	GL2	-1.7	-1.1	-1.7	-2.1	...	-1.0	-0.5	-1.1	-1.6	...
676	Malawi	CA	BA	-1.8	-5.3	-0.9	-4.8	-4.4	-0.0	-3.8	0.7	-1.3	-1.5
684	Mauritius	AC	GG	-1.2	-0.5	-3.2	-2.2 FB	...	0.8	1.4	-1.5	-0.4 FB	...
688	Mozambique	AC	BA	-3.5	-2.7	...	...	...	-2.6	-1.7	...	...	...
728	Namibia	CA	BA	-5.5	1.0	-3.2	-6.0 P	-8.0 P	-4.2	2.6	-1.8	-4.5 P	-6.2 P
694	Nigeria	CA	BA	-1.8	-1.3	-1.4	...	...	-1.0	-0.4	-0.4	...	...
714	Rwanda	AC	GG	...	...	...	-1.9 P	-2.4 P	...	...	...	-1.0 P	-1.6 P
716	São Tomé and Príncipe	AC	BA	-12.4	-12.4	...	...	...	-11.8	-11.8	...	...	...
718	Seychelles	CA	GG	5.8	5.1	2.4 P	1.5 P	1.1 P	8.7	9.0	5.1 P	4.3 P	4.5 P
724	Sierra Leone	CA	BA	-5.1	-5.7	-2.5	-3.1 P	...	-3.1	-4.0	-1.1	-2.1 P	...
199	South Africa	CA	GG	-5.1	-5.3	-6.2	-5.6 P	-4.9 P	-2.3	-2.3	-3.1	-2.3 P	-1.4 P
734	Swaziland	CA	BA	-7.7	2.9	...	...	...	-7.0	3.6	...	...	...
738	Tanzania	CA	BA	-1.5	-2.5	-1.3	-2.9	-1.1 P	-0.9	-1.8	-0.2	-1.6	0.3 P
746	Uganda	AC	GG	...	...	...	...	-3.4	...	...	...	...	-2.2
754	Zambia	CA	BA	4.7 P	...	...	...	...	5.7 P	...	...	...	...
698	Zimbabwe	CA	BA	1.1	-0.6	...	...	...	1.4	-0.4	...	...	...
	Western Hemisphere												
	ECCU												
312	Anguilla	CA	BA	2.7	1.5	0.6	2.6	...	3.9	2.6	1.8	3.7	...

Table W1. Main Balances

(Percent of GDP)

BR: Basis of recording (Cash/Non Cash); GL: Government sector

		BR	GL	Net lending / borrowing					Primary net lending / borrowing				
				2011	2012	2013	2014	2015	2011	2012	2013	2014	2015
311	Antigua and Barbuda	CA	BA	-4.3	-1.3	-4.5	-2.7	...	-1.8	1.1	-2.4	-0.1	...
321	Dominica	CA	BA	-8.3	-8.7	-9.3	-3.7	...	-6.5	-7.3	-7.2	-2.0	...
328	Grenada	CA	BA	-3.2	-5.5	-6.6	-4.8	...	-0.7	-2.1	-3.4	-1.2	...
351	Montserrat	CA	BA	7.7	-6.9	-16.8	-5.8	...	7.7	-6.9	-16.8	-5.7	...
361	St. Kitts and Nevis	CA	BA	-2.5	-1.9	-5.7	-3.4	...	-0.2	0.3	-3.5	-1.4	...
362	St. Lucia	CA	BA	-4.6	-6.5	-6.7	-3.1	...	-1.8	-3.0	-2.9	0.8	...
364	St. Vincent and the Grenadines	CA	BA	-2.7	-2.1	-6.2	-3.9	...	-0.2	0.3	-3.7	-1.6	...
213	Argentina	AC	GL2	...	...	...	...	-3.5	...	...	...	...	-1.6
313	Bahamas, The	CA	CG	-3.7	-4.0	-5.2 P	-4.6 P	-3.3 P	-1.0	-1.8	-2.9 P	-2.2 P	-0.6 P
316	Barbados	AC	BA	-4.6	-9.9	-12.2	...	...	1.5	-3.4	-5.3	...	...
339	Belize	CA	BA	-1.6	-1.2	-1.7	-3.7	...	1.8	0.7	1.0	-1.1	...
223	Brazil	AC	GG	-2.4	-1.9	-2.9	-5.9	-9.0	5.7	5.4	4.4	2.1	3.6
228	Chile	AC	GG	1.4	0.7	-0.5 P	-1.4 P	-2.1 P	2.0	1.3	0.1 P	-0.9 P	-1.4 P
233	Colombia	AC	GG	-1.3	6.1	-4.6 P	-5.9 P	-4.8 P	1.4	8.6	-2.1 P	-3.3 P	-2.1 P
238	Costa Rica	AC	BA	-4.0	-4.5	-5.4	-6.8	-6.6	-1.9	-2.4	-2.8	-4.2	-3.8
243	Dominican Republic	AC	GL2	-2.5	-6.2	-3.2	-2.7 P	0.3 P	-0.5	-3.8	-0.9	-0.2 P	2.9 P
253	El Salvador	AC	GG	-2.3	-0.9	-1.6	-2.5	-1.2	-0.0	1.3	0.8	0.0	1.1
258	Guatemala	CA	BA	-2.7	-2.3	-0.4	...	...	-1.3	-0.8	1.1	...	...
268	Honduras	AC	GG	-2.9	-3.5	-5.7	-2.7	-0.8 P	-1.7	-2.0	-4.2	-1.0	1.1 P
343	Jamaica	AC	GG	-5.9	-3.3	0.8 P	-0.3 P	-0.6 P	3.9	6.5	8.6 P	8.3 P	7.4 P
278	Nicaragua	CA	BA	0.5	0.5	0.1	-0.3	-0.6 P	1.5	1.5	1.0	0.6	0.3 P
288	Paraguay	AC	GG	1.5	-1.2	-1.3	-0.2	-0.7	1.8	-0.9	-1.0	0.2	-0.0
293	Peru	CA	GG	2.0	2.1	0.9	-0.3	-2.2	3.2	3.1	2.0	0.8	-1.2
366	Suriname	CA	BA	-0.8	-1.2 P	...	...	...	0.2	-0.3 P	...	...	...
369	Trinidad and Tobago	CA	GL2	-3.1	-1.5	...	...	...	-1.1	0.5	...	...	...
298	Uruguay	CA	GL2	-0.6	-2.0	-1.5	-6.2	...	1.9	0.3	0.9	-3.9	...

Table W2. Other Balances

(Percent of GDP) *BR: Basis of recording (Cash/Non Cash); GL: Government sector*

				Gross operating balance						Net financial worth				
		BR	GL	2011	2012	2013	2014	2015	GL	2011	2012	2013	2014	2015
	Advanced Economies													
	Euro Area													
122	Austria	AC	GG	0.5	0.7	1.0	0.2	1.9	GG	-52.9	-58.4	-57.5	-60.5	-58.5
124	Belgium	AC	GG	-1.6 P	-1.6 P	-0.7 P	-0.7 P	-0.3 P	GG	-83.1 P	-91.9 P	-90.0 P	-100.2 P	-98.0 P
423	Cyprus	AC	GG	-2.0 P	-3.2 P	-3.9 P	-7.1 P	0.8 P	GG	-38.8 P	-45.2 P	-60.0 P	-66.2 P	-68.5 P
939	Estonia	AC	GG	4.6 P	5.9 P	4.9 P	5.6 P	5.2 P	GG	33.4 P	31.3 P	31.2 P	30.4 P	41.6 P
172	Finland	AC	GG	2.5 P	1.6 P	1.3 P	0.8 P	0.9 P	GG	48.8 P	49.4 P	53.0 P	53.8 P	54.0 P
132	France	AC	GG	-1.1 P	-0.7 P	0.1 P	-0.1 P	0.1 P	GG	-59.5 P	-67.4 P	-66.4 P	-74.7 P	-76.1 P
134	Germany	AC	GG	1.3	2.1	1.9	2.3	2.8	GG	-50.3	-49.7	-46.2	-46.1	-42.7
174	Greece	AC	GG	-7.8 P	-6.3 P	-8.4 P	0.4 P	-2.8 P	...	...	...	...	...	...
178	Ireland	AC	GG	-10.1 P	-6.0 P	-4.1 P	-1.5 P	-0.1 P	GG	-60.5 P	-77.8 P	-80.6 P	-79.4 P	-58.8 P
136	Italy	AC	GG	-0.9 P	-0.4 P	-0.5 P	-0.7 P	-0.3 P	GG	-95.9 P	-111.7 P	-118.1 P	-131.0 P	-132.8 P
941	Latvia	AC	GG	1.4 P	3.9 P	3.5 P	2.9 P	3.4 P	GG	-14.9 P	-12.2 P	-14.0 P	-15.8 P	-17.5 P
946	Lithuania	AC	GG	-4.5 P	0.6 P	0.8 P	2.7 P	3.4 P	GG	-21.2 P	-26.3 P	-25.8 P	-25.4 P	-24.4 P
137	Luxembourg	AC	GG	4.7	4.4	4.6	5.2	5.3 P	GG	41.7	50.2	50.8	51.3	49.7 P
181	Malta	AC	GG	0.2 P	-0.3 P	0.3 P	1.6 P	3.0 P	GG	-52.3 P	-49.0 P	-48.9 P	-55.2 P	-53.0 P
138	Netherlands	AC	GG	-0.5 P	-0.3 P	0.5 P	1.0 P	1.3 P	GG	-37.2 P	-39.7 P	-40.2 P	-43.9 P	-42.8 P
182	Portugal	AC	GG	-3.9 P	-3.4 P	-2.6 P	-5.1 P	-2.0 P	GG	-66.6 P	-89.3 P	-97.5 P	-107.7 P	-108.6 P
936	Slovak Republic	AC	GG	-0.6 P	-0.9 P	0.7 P	1.0 P	3.7 P	GG	-32.9 P	-31.3 P	-32.8 P	-35.6 P	-35.5 P
961	Slovenia	AC	GG	-2.5	-0.0	-10.4	-0.1	2.1	GG	-2.4	-8.7	-13.9	-20.6	-24.5
184	Spain	AC	GG	-5.9	-8.0	...	-3.8	-2.7 P	GG	-47.1	-58.7	-69.3	-81.9	-81.4 P
193	Australia	AC	GG	-1.1	-1.0	0.1	0.1	0.0	GG	-3.8	-18.9	-13.9	-16.2	-19.7
156	Canada	AC	GG	1.1	1.8	2.5	3.4	2.7	GG	-200.4	-211.4	-198.4	-187.2	-190.2
532	China, P.R.: Hong Kong SAR	AC	GG	5.2	4.9	2.1	5.8	...	GG	15.9	16.3	15.6	16.6	...
546	China, P.R.: Macao SAR	CA	GG	28.0	28.1	27.8	25.6	16.0	...	...	...	...	...	...
935	Czech Republic	CA	GG	-2.2	-0.5	0.5 P	0.2	1.5	...	...	...	...	...	...
128	Denmark	AC	GG	1.2 P	0.2 P	2.6 P	5.3 P	2.1 P	GG	-1.1 P	-6.6 P	-4.0 P	-4.9 P	-5.7 P
176	Iceland	AC	GG	-3.6	-1.7	1.4	3.0	2.1	GG	-51.0	-56.5	-51.4	-49.9	-48.8
436	Israel	AC	GG	-1.4	-3.0	-2.1	-1.4	-0.6	...	...	...	...	...	...
158	Japan	AC	GG	-5.4	-5.2	-3.8	-1.4	...	GG	-126.5	-129.4	-123.3	-125.3	...
542	Korea, Republic of	AC	GG	6.0	6.0	6.1	5.8	5.8	GG	...	31.1	30.8	32.3	33.8
196	New Zealand	AC	GL2	-5.2	1.2	1.3 NA	1.2	2.2	GL2	0.8	-8.5	-6.4 NA	-3.5	-0.4
142	Norway	AC	GG	17.4 P	17.6 P	15.0 P	13.3 P	11.2 P	GG	160.1 P	169.1 P	207.4 P	248.3 P	283.5 P
135	San Marino	AC	GG	-0.1	1.1	-2.4	...	-0.4	GG	34.8	31.3	32.6	...	33.8
576	Singapore	CA	GG	4.3	5.2	5.0	5.0	2.2	...	...	...	...	...	...
144	Sweden	AC	GG	4.2 P	3.5 P	3.0 P	2.8 P	4.5 P	GG	19.2 P	21.1 P	20.8 P	20.1 P	19.3 P
146	Switzerland	AC	GL2	1.7 P	1.4 P	1.3 P	1.2 P	1.5 P	GL2	-6.1 P	-4.5 P	-3.6 P	-1.6 P	-3.0 P
112	United Kingdom	AC	GG	-4.7 P	-5.6 P	-3.1 P	-3.1 P	-1.8 P	GG	-71.2 P	-73.2 P	-71.3 P	-82.3 P	-82.1 P
111	United States	AC	GG	-7.0	-5.5	-2.3	-1.8	-1.4	GG	-99.4	-102.4	-100.8	-100.0	-100.7
	Emerging and Developing Economies													
	Emerging and Developing Asia													
513	Bangladesh	CA	BA	0.8	1.7	2.1	1.7	0.9	...	...	...	...	...	...
514	Bhutan	CA	GG	11.8	14.1	9.3	14.0	...	GG	38.2	24.7	7.3	5.9	...
522	Cambodia	AC	BA	4.1	7.8	6.0	6.7	6.4 P	...	...	...	...	...	...
924	China, P.R.: Mainland	CA	BA	...	...	...	...	...	...	...	...	...	...	...
819	Fiji	CA	BA	2.3	2.4	1.8	...	...	...	...	...	...	...	...
534	India	CA	GL2	-3.0	-3.5	-4.0 P	...	...	...	...	...	...	...	...
536	Indonesia	AC	GG	2.3	1.9	1.4	1.4 P	1.3 P	GG	-6.3	-6.2	-6.8	-7.1 P	-2.9 P
826	Kiribati	CA	GG	-1.2	8.5	24.4	56.1	74.0 P	...	...	...	...	...	...
544	Lao People's Democratic Republic	CA	BA	9.6	10.7	4.6	7.3	6.2	...	...	...	...	...	...
548	Malaysia	CA	BA	0.6	0.4	0.3	0.3	0.3	...	...	...	...	...	...
556	Maldives	CA	GG	0.8	...	...	1.1	...	...	...	...	...	...	...
867	Marshall Islands, Republic of	AC	BA	9.7	3.2	4.5	6.1	6.8 P	BA	-23.0	-22.3	-15.7	-19.2	-22.9 P
868	Micronesia, Federated States of	AC	BA	19.0	21.3	16.3	20.7	17.2	BA	9.8	13.1	14.9	30.2	39.9
948	Mongolia	CA	GG	8.8	3.1	7.2	...	...	GG	41.8	80.2	-1.3	...	...
558	Nepal	CA	BA	2.6	2.7	4.9	5.2	5.2	BA	...	...	...	...	...
565	Palau	AC	BA	8.5	9.2	5.0	7.9	9.7	BA	-11.4	-10.5	-10.0	-8.5	-43.6
566	Philippines	CA	BA	-0.1	0.3	1.1	1.7	1.3 P	...	...	...	...	...	...
862	Samoa	CA	BA	2.7	0.5	0.6	1.4	0.4	...	...	...	...	...	...
813	Solomon Islands	CA	BA	9.4	10.1	17.2	13.6	13.4	GG	...	...	...	...	7.6 NA
524	Sri Lanka	CA	BA	-3.3	-3.8	-2.9	-3.5 P	-4.6 P	...	...	...	...	...	...
578	Thailand	AC	GG	2.3	2.2	3.4	2.8	3.7 E	GG	...	17.4	25.9	...	...
537	Timor-Leste	CA	GG	52.2	47.9	49.0	32.8	15.8	...	...	...	...	...	...
846	Vanuatu	AC	BA	2.6	...	...	...	...	...	...	...	...	...	...
582	Vietnam	CA	BA	5.6	0.9 P	0.3 P	...	...	...	...	...	...	...	...
	Europe													
	Central and Eastern Europe													
914	Albania	AC	GG	2.2	1.2	-0.6	2.2	2.0	GG	-60.9	-56.4	-56.5	-55.3	-60.1
963	Bosnia and Herzegovina	AC	GG	1.7	1.1	1.8	2.2	2.7	GG	-16.1	-20.6	-19.5	-23.6	...
918	Bulgaria	AC	GG	1.4 P	3.0 P	3.4 P	-0.5 P	4.6 P	GG	1.4 P	2.9 P	1.6 P	-3.2 P	-5.0 P
960	Croatia	CA	GG	-3.0	-1.9	-3.7	-2.3	...	...	...	...	...	...	...
944	Hungary	AC	GG	-2.1 P	1.3 P	1.7 P	2.9 P	5.1 P	GG	-62.5 P	-69.8 P	-70.5 P	-71.4 P	-67.5 P

Table W2. Other Balances

(Percent of GDP)

BR: Basis of recording (Cash/Non Cash); GL: Government sector

				Gross operating balance						Net financial worth				
		BR	GL	2011	2012	2013	2014	2015	GL	2011	2012	2013	2014	2015
967	Kosovo, Republic of	CA	GG	...	8.3	6.6	4.5	4.8	...	...	...	...	...	...
962	Macedonia, F.Y.R. of	CA	GL2	-0.4	-0.9	...	...	...	...	...	...	...	...	...
964	Poland	AC	GG	0.9 P	0.8 P	-0.3 P	0.7 P	1.7 P	GG	-30.3 P	-31.4 P	-35.0 P	-38.0 P	-38.9 P
968	Romania	AC	GG	0.0 P	1.2 P	2.5 P	3.0 P	4.4 P	GG	-15.4 P	-18.2 P	-20.8 P	-20.6 P	-19.9 P
942	Serbia, Republic of	CA	GG	-1.4	-2.8 P	...	...	...	BA	-6.5 P	-4.1 P	...	...	...
186	Turkey	AC	GG	2.2	3.0	3.3	3.2	4.8	GG	-21.7	-21.6	-17.0	-16.8	-13.7
	CIS													
911	Armenia	CA	GG	2.0	2.0	...	1.2	-1.2 E	...	...	...	...	...	...
912	Azerbaijan	CA	GG	27.6	19.4	19.7	17.8	9.5	...	...	...	...	...	...
913	Belarus	AC	GG	6.0	5.0	4.8	4.4	5.1	GG	...	...	...	9.3	...
915	Georgia	CA	GG	4.5	4.1	2.6	1.3	2.5	...	...	...	...	...	...
916	Kazakhstan	CA	GG	12.2	9.9	8.6	7.4	1.0	GL2	...	-8.7	32.7	37.2	11.0
917	Kyrgyz Republic	CA	GG	...	...	...	...	6.1	GG	...	...	...	...	-38.3
921	Moldova	CA	GG	1.1	1.4	1.8	2.5	0.4	GG	25.1	23.7	19.4	16.4	10.8
922	Russian Federation	AC	GG	10.8	8.2	5.2	2.6 P	5.1 P	GG	21.8	21.6	22.1	23.7 P	23.8 P
926	Ukraine	CA	GG	-0.8	-2.5	-3.2	-3.7	0.5 P	GG	-17.2	-16.6	-18.8	-36.5	-41.6 P
927	Uzbekistan	CA	GG	12.6	14.6	9.7	8.8	7.3	...	...	...	...	...	...
	Middle East, North Africa and Pakistan													
512	Afghanistan, Islamic Republic of	CA	GG	31.1	22.8	25.7	...	...	BA	...	...	...	...	...
612	Algeria	AC	BA	10.9	...	...	...	...	...	...	...	...	...	...
419	Bahrain, Kingdom of	AC	BA	3.8	...	0.8	...	...	...	...	...	...	...	...
469	Egypt	CA	GG	-6.8	-7.9	-10.6	-8.7	-8.2 P	...	...	...	...	...	...
433	Iraq	AC	BA	...	...	...	13.8 P	...	...	...	...	...	...	...
439	Jordan	CA	BA	-3.1	-6.5	-2.8	0.3	-0.9	BA	-57.9	-63.3	-69.9	-72.5	...
443	Kuwait	CA	CG	31.1 NA	30.3 NA	30.3	12.7	-13.4	...	...	...	...	...	...
446	Lebanon	CA	BA	-4.5	-6.8	-8.1	-5.8	-5.1	...	...	...	...	...	...
686	Morocco	AC	BA	-2.2	-1.7	0.0	0.5	...	...	...	...	...	...	...
449	Oman	CA	BA	20.0	16.1	15.1	...	...	BA	65.9	65.4	67.8	...	...
564	Pakistan	CA	BA	-5.2	-5.9	-2.9	-3.5 P	...	...	...	...	...	...	...
744	Tunisia	CA	GG	-0.2	-1.9	...	...	...	...	...	...	...	...	...
466	United Arab Emirates	AC	GG	6.7	7.3	5.3	0.7	-3.6	GG	...	...	3.7	...	...
487	West Bank and Gaza	AC	CG	-0.1	-0.4	0.5	0.7	-0.1	...	...	...	...	...	...
474	Yemen, Republic of	CA	GG	-7.4	-0.7	...	...	...	...	...	...	...	...	...
	Sub-Saharan Africa													
	CEMAC													
626	Central African Republic	AC	BA	-2.8 P	8.7 P	...	...	...	...	...	...	...	...	...
634	Congo, Republic of	AC	GG	32.1	28.8	...	...	...	BA	...	...	...	...	...
	WAEMU													
638	Benin	AC	BA	5.9	4.0	5.0	...	...	...	...	...	...	...	...
748	Burkina Faso	AC	BA	8.3	7.9	10.3	7.1	5.4	...	...	...	...	...	...
662	Côte d'Ivoire	AC	BA	-1.1	1.6	3.7	3.9	...	...	...	...	...	...	...
678	Mali	AC	BA	4.3	2.1	4.8	1.6	4.2	...	...	...	...	...	...
722	Senegal	AC	BA	4.9 P	6.0 P	5.4 P	2.1 P	1.7 P	...	...	...	...	...	...
742	Togo	AC	BA	7.1	2.6	3.0	...	-0.3	...	...	...	...	...	...
614	Angola	AC	BA	19.2	14.2	8.2	3.4 P	-2.3 P	...	...	...	...	...	...
616	Botswana	CA	BA	7.1	7.2	11.2	10.8	...	...	...	...	...	...	...
618	Burundi	AC	BA	18.1	9.3	8.8	...	...	...	...	...	...	...	...
624	Cabo Verde	CA	CG	...	1.6	...	...	...	...	...	...	...	...	...
644	Ethiopia	CA	BA	4.5	...	...	...	...	...	...	...	...	...	...
652	Ghana	CA	BA	0.5	...	...	...	...	...	...	...	...	...	...
664	Kenya	AC	GG	...	...	...	1.7 P	0.3 P	...	...	...	...	...	...
666	Lesotho	CA	BA	3.5	20.5	16.3	...	...	...	...	...	...	...	...
668	Liberia	CA	CG	2.4	1.3	0.6	...	...	...	...	...	...	...	...
674	Madagascar	AC	GL2	2.5	1.6	1.5	1.8	...	...	...	...	...	...	...
676	Malawi	CA	BA	3.5	-0.1	4.5	-0.4	0.5	BA	-24.2	-39.1	-33.0	8.8	-7.9
684	Mauritius	AC	GG	2.5	3.3	1.0	1.1 FB	...	...	...	...	...	...	...
688	Mozambique	AC	BA	4.3	4.5	...	...	...	...	...	...	...	...	...
728	Namibia	CA	BA	-0.9	4.3	0.9	0.2 P	-1.8 P	...	...	...	...	...	...
694	Nigeria	CA	BA	-0.4	-0.1	-0.1	...	...	...	...	...	...	...	...
714	Rwanda	AC	GG	...	...	...	11.2 P	10.8 P	...	...	...	...	...	...
716	São Tomé and Príncipe	AC	BA	20.4	14.9	...	...	...	...	...	...	...	...	...
718	Seychelles	CA	GG	10.7	9.7	6.6 P	5.5 P	5.5 P	GG	-74.0	-61.7	-29.4 P	-52.3 P	-45.8 P
724	Sierra Leone	CA	BA	3.9	1.9	2.9	2.3 P	...	...	...	...	...	...	...
199	South Africa	CA	GG	-2.1	-2.1	-3.0	-2.2 P	-1.5 P	BA	-32.5	-35.5	-38.8	-41.5 P	-45.0 P
734	Swaziland	CA	BA	-4.9	6.5	...	...	...	...	...	...	...	...	...
738	Tanzania	CA	BA	0.3	0.6	0.8	-2.1	-0.7 P	...	...	...	...	...	...
746	Uganda	AC	GG	...	...	...	...	0.8	GG	...	...	...	...	-16.8
754	Zambia	CA	BA	6.3 P	...	...	...	...	...	...	...	...	...	...
698	Zimbabwe	CA	BA	2.1	0.3	...	...	...	...	...	...	...	...	...

Table W2. Other Balances

(Percent of GDP)

BR: Basis of recording (Cash/Non Cash); GL: Government sector

		BR	GL	Gross operating balance					GL	Net financial worth				
				2011	2012	2013	2014	2015		2011	2012	2013	2014	2015
	Western Hemisphere													
	ECCU													
312	Anguilla	CA	BA	3.9	2.7	1.7	3.0	...	...	...	...	...	...	...
311	Antigua and Barbuda	CA	BA	-3.1	-0.8	-3.2	-1.2	...	...	...	...	...	...	...
321	Dominica	CA	BA	4.4	3.2	2.2	4.6	...	...	...	...	...	...	...
328	Grenada	CA	BA	3.1	-0.5	0.3	4.7	...	...	...	...	...	...	...
351	Montserrat	CA	BA	23.8	16.3	28.4	19.0	...	...	...	...	...	...	...
361	St. Kitts and Nevis	CA	BA	0.2	0.5	-0.1	1.6	...	...	...	...	...	...	...
362	St. Lucia	CA	BA	3.0	0.2	1.0	2.8	...	...	...	...	...	...	...
364	St. Vincent and the Grenadines	CA	BA	0.2	0.5	-0.1	1.9	...	...	...	...	...	...	...
213	Argentina	AC	GL2	...	...	...	...	-2.9	...	...	...	...	...	...
313	Bahamas, The	CA	CG	-1.2	-1.5	-2.5 P	-1.7 P	-0.2 P	...	...	...	...	...	...
316	Barbados	AC	BA	-4.1	-9.2	-11.2	...	...	BA	-77.0	-87.0	-94.1	...	...
339	Belize	CA	BA	3.2	3.2	5.0	3.5	...	...	...	...	...	...	...
223	Brazil	AC	GG	-0.3	0.2	-0.8	-3.6	-7.4	GG	-35.1	-32.9	-31.2	-33.7	-38.5
228	Chile	AC	GG	3.8	3.0	1.7 P	0.8 P	0.5 P	...	...	...	...	...	...
233	Colombia	AC	GG	1.4	5.0	-2.1 P	-3.4 P	-1.1 P	GG	-28.7	-27.2	-26.7 P	-31.1 P	-26.8 P
238	Costa Rica	AC	GG	-1.9	-2.3	-2.8	-2.8	-4.3	BA	-36.7	-37.9	-43.0	-29.2	-11.5
243	Dominican Republic	AC	GL2	0.4	-1.0	-0.2	-0.5 P	2.7 P	BA	...	...	...	...	...
253	El Salvador	AC	GG	0.5	1.1	1.4	1.1	1.3	GG	...	...	-39.1	-40.3	-41.1
258	Guatemala	CA	BA	-1.0	-1.4	-1.2	...	...	...	...	...	...	...	...
268	Honduras	AC	GG	0.8	-0.1	-1.0	1.0	2.4 P	...	...	...	...	...	...
343	Jamaica	AC	GG	-4.0	-1.4	2.3 P	2.6 P	3.0 P	...	...	...	...	...	...
278	Nicaragua	CA	BA	2.2	2.4	2.1	2.0	1.8 P	...	...	...	...	...	...
288	Paraguay	AC	GG	4.2	2.2	2.1	3.1	3.0	...	...	...	...	...	...
293	Peru	CA	GG	6.9	7.4	6.4	5.2	2.5	GG	-8.7	-5.2	-3.9	-4.3	-7.0
366	Suriname	CA	BA	3.6	3.3 P	...	...	...	...	...	...	...	...	...
369	Trinidad and Tobago	CA	GL2	1.7	1.6	...	...	...	...	...	...	...	...	...
298	Uruguay	CA	CG	0.9	-0.5	-0.1	-0.9	-1.6	GG	-35.1	-33.7	-34.1	-35.7	-41.9

Table W3. Major Categories

(Percent of GDP)

BR: Basis of recording (Cash/Non Cash); GL: Government sector

		Year	GL	Revenue			Expenditure: Expense, excl. consumption of fixed capital			Expenditure: Gross investment in nonfinancial assets			Expenditure: Total			Net acquisition of financial assets			Net incurrence of liabilities		
	Advanced Economies																				
	Euro Area																				
122	Austria	2015	GG	AC	50.9	...	AC	49.0	...	AC	2.9	...	AC	51.9	...	AC	-0.2	...	AC	1.1	...
124	Belgium	2015	GG	AC	50.9	P	AC	51.1	P	AC	2.3	P	AC	53.4	P	AC	-0.2	P	AC	2.5	P
423	Cyprus	2015	GG	AC	39.5	P	AC	38.7	P	AC	1.9	P	AC	40.6	P	AC	-1.4	P	AC	-0.3	P
939	Estonia	2015	GG	AC	39.2	P	AC	34.1	P	AC	5.0	P	AC	39.1	P	AC	-0.7	P	AC	-0.8	P
172	Finland	2015	GG	AC	53.9	P	AC	53.0	P	AC	3.6	P	AC	56.7	P	AC	1.3	P	AC	4.0	P
132	France	2015	GG	AC	53.5	P	AC	53.4	P	AC	3.6	P	AC	57.0	P	AC	0.7	P	AC	4.1	P
134	Germany	2015	GG	AC	44.7	...	AC	41.9	...	AC	2.1	...	AC	43.9	...	AC	-0.0	...	AC	-0.8	...
174	Greece	2015	GG	AC	47.8	P	AC	50.6	P	AC	4.8	P	AC	55.3	P	AC	...	P	AC	...	P
178	Ireland	2015	GG	AC	27.6	P	AC	27.7	P	AC	1.7	P	AC	29.4	P	AC	-2.8	P	AC	-1.0	P
136	Italy	2015	GG	AC	48.0	P	AC	48.3	P	AC	2.3	P	AC	50.6	P	AC	-0.7	P	AC	1.9	P
941	Latvia	2015	GG	AC	35.8	P	AC	32.4	P	AC	4.7	P	AC	37.1	P	AC	-5.2	P	AC	-3.9	P
946	Lithuania	2015	GG	AC	35.1	P	AC	31.6	P	AC	3.6	P	AC	35.3	P	AC	0.9	P	AC	1.2	P
137	Luxembourg	2015	GG	AC	42.9	P	AC	37.6	P	AC	3.8	P	AC	41.4	P	AC	2.2	P	AC	0.7	P
181	Malta	2015	GG	AC	41.8	P	AC	38.7	P	AC	4.4	P	AC	43.1	P	AC	0.9	P	AC	2.2	P
138	Netherlands	2015	GG	AC	43.2	P	AC	41.9	P	AC	3.2	P	AC	45.1	P	AC	-2.9	P	AC	-1.0	P
182	Portugal	2015	GG	AC	44.0	P	AC	46.0	P	AC	2.4	P	AC	48.4	P	AC	-2.4	P	AC	2.0	P
936	Slovak Republic	2015	GG	AC	43.2	P	AC	39.4	P	AC	6.5	P	AC	45.9	P	AC	-1.0	P	AC	1.7	P
961	Slovenia	2015	GG	AC	45.1	...	AC	43.0	...	AC	4.8	...	AC	47.8	...	AC	2.0	...	AC	4.7	...
184	Spain	2015	GG	AC	37.8	P	AC	40.5	P	AC	2.4	P	AC	42.9	P	AC	-1.4	P	AC	3.7	P
193	Australia	2015	GG	AC	34.1	...	AC	34.1	...	AC	2.9	...	AC	37.0	...	AC	1.3	...	AC	4.2	...
156	Canada	2015	GG	AC	39.2	...	AC	36.6	...	AC	3.7	...	AC	40.3	...	AC	5.7	...	AC	6.8	...
532	China, P.R.: Hong Kong SAR	2014	GG	AC	23.6	...	AC	17.8	...	AC	1.5	...	AC	19.3	...	AC	5.2	...	AC	1.0	...
546	China, P.R.: Macao SAR	2015	GG	CA	31.0	...	CA	15.0	...	CA	2.5	...	CA	17.5	...	CA	13.5	...	CA	–	...
935	Czech Republic	2015	GG	AC	38.1	...	CA	36.6	...	CA	2.2	...	CA	38.8	...	CA	-0.3	...	CA	0.4	...
128	Denmark	2015	GG	AC	54.6	P	AC	52.5	P	AC	3.5	P	AC	56.0	P	AC	-5.3	P	AC	-3.6	P
176	Iceland	2015	GG	AC	42.2	...	AC	40.1	...	AC	2.9	...	AC	43.0	...	AC	-8.0	...	AC	-7.2	...
436	Israel	2015	GG	AC	37.0	...	AC	37.5	...	AC	1.5	...	AC	39.0	...	NA	...	...	NA	...	...
158	Japan	2014	GG	AC	50.8	...	AC	52.2	...	AC	3.8	...	AC	56.0	...	AC	2.3	...	AC	6.9	...
542	Korea, Republic of	2015	GG	AC	34.3	...	AC	28.5	...	AC	4.6	...	AC	33.0	...	AC	4.6	...	AC	3.3	...
196	New Zealand	2015	GL2	AC	33.9	...	AC	31.7	...	AC	2.1	...	AC	33.7	...	NA	...	...	NA	...	...
142	Norway	2015	GG	AC	55.0	P	AC	43.8	P	AC	4.8	P	AC	48.6	P	AC	11.9	P	AC	5.8	P
135	San Marino	2015	GG	AC	39.2	...	AC	39.6	...	NA	...	...	AC	...	...	NA	...	...	NA	...	...
576	Singapore	2015	GG	CA	18.9	...	CA	16.8	...	CA	-2.2	...	CA	14.5	...	CA	14.4	...	CA	10.0	...
144	Sweden	2015	GG	AC	49.8	P	AC	45.3	P	AC	4.2	P	AC	49.5	P	AC	-0.7	P	AC	-1.0	P
146	Switzerland	2015	GL2	AC	18.2	P	AC	16.8	P	AC	0.9	P	AC	17.7	P	NA	...	P	NA	...	P
112	United Kingdom	2015	GG	AC	38.5	P	AC	40.3	P	AC	2.6	P	AC	42.9	P	AC	-0.1	P	AC	4.2	P
111	United States	2015	GG	AC	31.8		AC	33.2		AC	2.9		AC	36.1		AC	1.7		AC	5.7	
	Emerging and Developing Economies																				
	Emerging and Developing Asia																				
513	Bangladesh	2015	BA	CA	9.3	...	CA	8.4	...	CA	2.2	...	CA	10.6	...	CA	2.3	...	CA	3.5	...
514	Bhutan	2014	GG	CA	33.3	...	CA	19.3	...	CA	9.3	...	CA	28.6	...	CA	4.0	...	CA	-0.6	...
522	Cambodia	2015	BA	AC	18.0	P	AC	11.6	P	AC	7.2	P	AC	18.8	P	AC	2.7	P	AC	3.5	P
924	China, P.R.: Mainland	2014	GG	CA	28.6	...	CA	...	...	CA	0.3	...	CA	...	...	CA	...	...	CA	1.4	...
819	Fiji	2013	BA	CA	27.1	...	CA	25.3	...	CA	2.6	...	CA	28.0	...	CA	0.4	...	CA	1.3	...
534	India	2013	GL2	CA	12.6	P	CA	16.6	P	CA	0.0	P	CA	16.6	P	CA	1.1	P	CA	4.7	P
536	Indonesia	2015	GG	CA	15.1	P	AC	13.8	P	AC	4.0	P	AC	17.8	P	AC	0.6	P	AC	3.3	P
826	Kiribati	2015	GG	CA	147.9	P	CA	73.9	P	CA	4.3	P	CA	78.2	P	CA	80.5	P	CA	10.8	P
544	Lao People's Democratic Republic	2015	BA	CA	23.3	...	CA	17.0	...	CA	10.5	...	CA	27.5	...	CA	0.1	...	CA	4.9	...
548	Malaysia	2015	BA	CA	18.9	...	CA	18.6	...	CA	3.5	...	CA	22.1	...	CA	0.3	...	CA	3.4	...
556	Maldives	2014	GG	CA	31.3	...	CA	30.2	...	CA	...	...	CA	...	...	NA	...	...	NA	...	...
867	Marshall Islands, Republic of	2015	BA	AC	57.0	P	AC	50.2	P	AC	4.0	P	AC	54.2	P	AC	0.6	P	AC	-2.1	P
868	Micronesia, Federated States of	2015	BA	AC	34.7	...	AC	17.6	...	AC	6.0	...	AC	23.6	...	AC	13.8	...	AC	2.7	...
948	Mongolia	2013	GG	CA	31.5	...	CA	24.3	...	CA	7.7	...	CA	32.0	...	CA	5.6	...	CA	6.1	...
558	Nepal	2016	BA	CA	22.9	P	CA	16.5	P	CA	5.1	P	CA	21.6	P	CA	5.6	P	CA	3.2	P
565	Palau	2015	BA	AC	40.6	...	AC	30.9	...	AC	4.7	...	AC	35.6	...	AC	3.3	...	AC	-1.7	...
566	Philippines	2015	BA	CA	15.4	P	CA	14.1	P	CA	2.6	P	CA	16.7	P	CA	-0.4	P	CA	0.9	P
862	Samoa	2016	BA	CA	29.5	...	CA	25.0	...	CA	4.9	...	CA	29.9	...	CA	-0.4	...	CA	-0.0	...
813	Solomon Islands	2015	BA	CA	49.0	...	CA	35.5	...	CA	12.5	...	CA	48.0	...	CA	-1.9	...	CA	-2.0	...
524	Sri Lanka	2015	BA	CA	13.1	P	CA	17.7	P	CA	2.8	P	CA	20.5	P	CA	0.0	P	CA	7.5	P
578	Thailand	2015	GG	AC	22.4	E	AC	18.7	E	AC	3.6	E	AC	22.3	E	AC	0.8	E	AC	0.7	E
537	Timor-Leste	2015	GG	CA	56.3	...	CA	40.6	...	CA	11.3	...	CA	51.8	...	CA	0.4	...	CA	–	...
846	Vanuatu	2011	BA	AC	24.6	...	AC	22.0	...	AC	4.9	...	AC	26.9	...	AC	-0.8	...	AC	1.6	...
582	Vietnam	2013	BA	CA	21.8	...	CA	21.6	P	CA	5.9	P	CA	27.5	P	CA	...	P	CA	...	P
	Europe																				
	Central and Eastern Europe																				
914	Albania	2015	GG	CA	26.4	...	AC	24.4	...	AC	5.2	...	AC	29.6	...	AC	0.7	...	AC	3.8	...
963	Bosnia and Herzegovina	2015	GG	AC	43.7	...	AC	41.1	...	AC	2.0	...	AC	43.0	...	AC	0.2	...	AC	0.4	...

Table W3. Major Categories

(Percent of GDP)

BR: Basis of recording (Cash/Non Cash); GL: Government sector

		Year	GL	Revenue			Expenditure: Expense, excl. consumption of fixed capital			Expenditure: Gross investment in nonfinancial assets			Expenditure: Total			Net acquisition of financial assets			Net incurrence of liabilities		
918	Bulgaria	2015	GG	AC	40.0	P	AC	35.4	P	AC	6.3	P	AC	41.7	P	AC	-2.3	P	AC	-0.5	P
960	Croatia	2014	GG	CA	40.2	...	CA	42.5	...	CA	1.5	...	CA	44.0	...	CA	-0.7	...	CA	3.1	...
944	Hungary	2015	GG	AC	48.9	P	AC	43.8	P	AC	6.7	P	AC	50.5	P	AC	0.2	P	AC	1.8	P
967	Kosovo, Republic of	2015	GG	CA	25.6	...	CA	20.8	...	CA	6.6	...	CA	27.4	...	CA	0.6	...	CA	2.4	...
962	Macedonia, F.Y.R. of	2012	GL2	CA	29.0	...	CA	29.9	...	CA	3.1	...	CA	33.0	...	CA	2.5	...	CA	6.5	...
964	Poland	2015	GG	AC	39.1	P	AC	37.5	P	AC	4.2	P	AC	41.7	P	AC	0.1	P	AC	2.6	P
968	Romania	2015	GG	AC	34.9	P	AC	30.5	P	AC	5.2	P	AC	35.7	P	AC	0.5	P	AC	1.3	P
942	Serbia, Republic of	2012	GG	CA	40.8	P	CA	43.6	P	CA	3.3	P	CA	46.9	P	CA	1.2	P	CA	7.3	P
186	Turkey	2015	GG	AC	40.5	...	AC	35.8	...	AC	3.1	...	AC	38.9	...	AC	3.3	...	AC	1.6	...
	CIS																				
911	Armenia	2015	GG	CA	25.1	E	CA	26.3	E	NA	...	E	AC	...	E	NA	...	E	NA	...	E
912	Azerbaijan	2015	GG	CA	34.4	...	CA	24.9	...	CA	12.3	...	CA	37.2	...	CA	-3.9	...	CA	-1.0	...
913	Belarus	2015	GG	AC	43.3	...	AC	38.2	...	AC	2.7	...	AC	41.0	...	AC	1.8	...	AC	-0.5	...
915	Georgia	2015	GG	CA	28.3	...	CA	25.8	...	CA	3.5	...	CA	29.4	...	CA	1.9	...	CA	2.9	...
916	Kazakhstan	2015	GG	CA	17.6	...	CA	16.6	...	CA	3.2	...	CA	19.8	...	CA	0.4	...	CA	2.6	...
917	Kyrgyz Republic	2015	GG	CA	36.1	...	CA	30.1	...	CA	7.0	...	CA	37.1	...	CA	3.0	...	CA	4.0	...
921	Moldova	2015	GG	CA	35.8	...	CA	35.3	...	CA	2.8	...	CA	38.1	...	CA	-0.3	...	CA	2.0	...
922	Russian Federation	2015	GG	AC	41.1	P	AC	36.0	P	AC	5.8	P	AC	41.8	P	AC	0.2	P	AC	0.9	P
926	Ukraine	2015	GG	CA	42.0	P	CA	41.5	P	CA	1.3	P	CA	42.8	P	CA	4.6	P	CA	5.4	P
927	Uzbekistan	2015	GG	CA	33.8	...	CA	26.5	...	CA	3.3	...	CA	29.8	...	CA	4.1	...	CA	0.1	...
	Middle East, North Africa and Pakistan																				
512	Afghanistan, Islamic Republic of	2013	GG	CA	68.8	...	CA	43.1	...	CA	23.4	...	CA	66.5	...	CA	0.0	...	CA	-2.3	...
612	Algeria	2011	BA	AC	40.4	...	AC	29.5	...	AC	11.2	...	AC	40.7	...	AC	3.1	...	AC	3.4	...
419	Bahrain, Kingdom of	2013	BA	AC	23.8	...	AC	23.0	...	AC	4.3	...	AC	27.2	...	AC	6.9	...	AC	10.5	...
469	Egypt	2015	GG	CA	22.2	P	CA	30.4	P	CA	2.5	P	CA	32.9	P	CA	...	P	CA	...	P
433	Iraq	2014	BA	CA	40.0	P	AC	26.3	P	AC	16.6	P	AC	42.9	P	CA	0.9	P	CA	3.3	P
439	Jordan	2015	BA	CA	25.5	...	CA	26.4	...	CA	2.5	...	CA	29.0	...	CA	...	...	CA	4.7	...
443	Kuwait	2015	CG	CA	38.8	...	CA	52.2	...	CA	7.6	...	CA	59.8	...	NA	...	...	NA	...	...
446	Lebanon	2015	BA	CA	17.3	...	CA	22.3	...	CA	1.7	...	CA	24.1	...	CA	1.2	...	CA	7.9	...
686	Morocco	2015	BA	AC	...	...	AC	...	...	AC	...	...	AC	...	...	AC	...	...	AC	...	...
449	Oman	2013	BA	CA	49.9	...	CA	34.8	...	CA	10.3	...	CA	45.2	...	CA	5.1	...	CA	0.4	...
564	Pakistan	2014	BA	CA	14.3	P	CA	17.8	P	CA	3.0	P	CA	20.8	P	CA	...	P	CA	...	P
744	Tunisia	2012	GG	CA	32.7	...	CA	34.5	...	CA	2.7	...	CA	37.2	...	CA	-1.9	...	CA	2.6	...
466	United Arab Emirates	2015	GG	AC	20.7	...	AC	24.3	...	AC	2.9	...	AC	27.2	...	AC	-3.4	...	AC	3.2	...
487	West Bank and Gaza	2015	CG	AC	7.6	...	AC	7.7	...	AC	0.3	...	AC	7.9	...	AC	0.9	...	AC	0.7	...
474	Yemen, Republic of	2012	GG	CA	30.0	...	CA	30.7	...	CA	6.3	...	CA	36.9	...	CA	0.1	...	CA	7.0	...
	Sub-Saharan Africa																				
	CEMAC																				
626	Central African Republic	2012	BA	AC	18.2	P	AC	9.5	P	AC	8.1	P	AC	17.5	P	AC	...	P	AC	...	P
634	Congo, Republic of	2012	GG	CA	44.3	...	AC	15.5	...	AC	22.2	...	AC	37.8	...	AC	...	...	AC	7.1	...
	WAEMU			...	...	...	...	...	...	...	...	...	...	...	...	...	...	...	...	...	...
638	Benin	2013	BA	AC	17.8	...	AC	12.8	...	AC	2.3	...	AC	15.1	...	AC	-0.1	...	AC	3.6	...
748	Burkina Faso	2015	BA	CA	19.6	...	AC	14.2	...	AC	7.7	...	AC	21.9	...	AC	-1.1	...	AC	1.1	...
662	Côte d'Ivoire	2014	BA	CA	16.9	...	AC	13.1	...	AC	5.8	...	AC	18.8	...	AC	0.9	...	AC	4.0	...
678	Mali	2015	BA	AC	16.5	...	AC	12.3	...	AC	6.8	...	AC	19.0	...	AC	1.2	...	AC	3.8	...
722	Senegal	2015	BA	AC	25.1	P	AC	23.4	P	AC	6.5	P	AC	29.9	P	AC	...	P	AC	...	P
742	Togo	2015	BA	CA	25.2	...	AC	25.5	...	AC	11.3	...	AC	36.7	...	NA	...	...	NA	...	...
614	Angola	2015	BA	CA	21.3	P	AC	23.6	P	AC	4.6	P	AC	28.2	P	AC	0.6	P	AC	7.5	P
616	Botswana	2014	BA	CA	39.3	...	CA	28.5	...	CA	7.1	...	CA	35.6	...	CA	4.4	...	CA	0.7	...
618	Burundi	2013	BA	AC	24.7	...	AC	15.9	...	AC	10.7	...	AC	26.7	...	AC	4.0	...	AC	5.9	...
624	Cabo Verde	2012	CG	CA	23.8	...	CA	22.2	...	CA	13.9	...	CA	36.1	...	CA	1.7	...	CA	10.9	...
644	Ethiopia	2011	BA	CA	15.2	...	CA	10.7	...	CA	5.8	...	CA	16.5	...	CA	9.7	...	CA	12.2	...
652	Ghana	2011	BA	CA	21.6	...	CA	21.1	...	CA	4.4	...	CA	25.5	...	CA	-0.1	...	CA	3.8	...
664	Kenya	2015	GG	AC	22.4	P	AC	22.1	P	AC	9.1	P	AC	31.2	P	AC	1.4	P	AC	9.6	P
666	Lesotho	2013	BA	CA	60.9	...	CA	44.6	...	CA	12.3	...	CA	57.0	...	CA	10.9	...	CA	7.0	...
668	Liberia	2013	CG	CA	26.4	...	CA	25.8	...	CA	1.3	...	CA	27.0	...	NA	...	...	NA	...	...
674	Madagascar	2014	GL2	AC	12.5	...	AC	10.7	...	AC	3.9	...	AC	14.6	...	AC	1.2	...	AC	3.3	...
676	Malawi	2016	BA	CA	19.7	...	CA	18.1	...	CA	5.0	...	CA	23.1	...	CA	5.2	...	CA	8.4	...
684	Mauritius	2014	GG	AC	23.7	FB	AC	22.6	FB	AC	3.3	FB	AC	25.9	FB	AC	2.7	FB	AC	4.9	FB
688	Mozambique	2013	BA	CA	33.2	...	CA	...	...	CA	10.9	...	CA	...	...	CA	...	...	CA	7.5	...
728	Namibia	2015	BA	CA	35.7	P	CA	37.5	P	CA	6.2	P	CA	43.7	P	CA	...	P	CA	...	P
694	Nigeria	2013	BA	CA	5.0	...	CA	5.0	...	CA	1.4	...	CA	6.4	...	CA	0.0	...	CA	1.4	...
714	Rwanda	2015	GG	AC	28.6	P	AC	17.8	P	AC	13.2	P	AC	31.0	P	AC	2.0	P	AC	4.7	P
716	São Tomé and Príncipe	2012	BA	AC	32.6	...	AC	17.7	...	AC	27.3	...	AC	44.9	...	AC	-0.7	...	AC	13.0	...
718	Seychelles	2015	GG	CA	35.1	P	CA	29.5	P	CA	4.5	P	CA	34.0	P	CA	3.0	P	CA	1.9	P
724	Sierra Leone	2014	BA	CA	14.2	P	CA	11.9	P	CA	5.4	P	CA	17.3	P	CA	...	P	CA	3.9	P
199	South Africa	2015	GG	CA	38.0	P	CA	39.5	P	CA	3.4	P	CA	42.9	P	CA	0.6	P	CA	5.6	P
734	Swaziland	2012	BA	CA	28.7	...	CA	22.2	...	CA	3.6	...	CA	25.8	...	CA	4.9	...	CA	2.0	...

Table W3. Major Categories

(Percent of GDP)

BR: Basis of recording (Cash/Non Cash); GL: Government sector

							Expenditure														
							Expense, excl. consumption of fixed capital			Gross investment in nonfinancial assets			Total			Net acquisition of financial assets			Net incurrence of liabilities		
		Year	GL		Revenue																
738	Tanzania	2016	BA	CA	13.5	P	CA	14.1	P	CA	0.2	P	CA	14.3	P	CA	0.3	P	CA	3.5	P
746	Uganda	2015	GG	CA	11.8	...	AC	11.1	...	AC	4.2	...	AC	15.2	...	CA	-5.6	...	CA	-2.2	...
754	Zambia	2011	BA	CA	23.8	P	CA	17.4	P	CA	1.7	P	CA	19.1	P	CA	5.9	P	CA	1.3	P
698	Zimbabwe	2012	BA	CA	28.0	...	CA	27.7	...	CA	0.9	...	CA	28.6	...	NA	...	...	NA	...	...
	Western Hemisphere																				
	ECCU																				
312	Anguilla	2014	BA	CA	24.5	...	CA	21.6	...	CA	0.4	...	CA	22.0	...	CA	1.4	...	CA	-1.2	...
311	Antigua and Barbuda	2014	BA	CA	19.8	...	CA	21.0	...	CA	1.6	...	CA	22.5	...	CA	-4.0	...	CA	-1.3	...
321	Dominica	2014	BA	CA	28.6	...	CA	23.9	...	CA	8.4	...	CA	32.3	...	CA	-1.7	...	CA	2.0	...
328	Grenada	2014	BA	CA	25.3	...	CA	20.6	...	CA	9.5	...	CA	30.1	...	CA	-0.4	...	CA	4.5	...
351	Montserrat	2014	BA	CA	88.2	...	CA	69.2	...	CA	24.8	...	CA	94.0	...	CA	-3.6	...	CA	2.2	...
361	St. Kitts and Nevis	2014	BA	CA	24.5	...	CA	22.8	...	CA	5.0	...	CA	27.9	...	CA	2.1	...	CA	5.5	...
362	St. Lucia	2014	BA	CA	26.1	...	CA	23.2	...	CA	5.9	...	CA	29.1	...	CA	-2.7	...	CA	0.3	...
364	St. Vincent and the Grenadines	2014	BA	CA	28.0	...	CA	26.1	...	CA	5.8	...	CA	31.9	...	CA	2.4	...	CA	6.3	...
213	Argentina	2015	GL2	CA	22.6	...	AC	25.5	...	AC	0.5	...	AC	26.0	...	AC	0.4	...	AC	3.9	...
313	Bahamas, The	2015	CG	CA	19.2	P	CA	19.4	P	CA	3.1	P	CA	22.5	P	CA	1.9	P	CA	7.7	P
316	Barbados	2013	BA	AC	27.0	...	AC	38.2	...	AC	1.1	...	AC	39.2	...	AC	6.3	...	AC	10.2	...
339	Belize	2014	BA	CA	27.8	...	CA	24.4	...	CA	7.1	...	CA	31.5	...	CA	0.2	...	CA	3.8	...
223	Brazil	2015	GG	CA	41.5	...	AC	48.9	...	AC	1.6	...	AC	50.5	...	CA	-1.0	...	CA	9.7	...
228	Chile	2015	GG	AC	23.2	P	AC	22.6	P	AC	2.6	P	AC	25.3	P	AC	-0.2	P	AC	1.9	P
233	Colombia	2015	GG	AC	29.0	P	AC	30.1	P	AC	3.7	P	AC	33.8	P	AC	-1.3	P	AC	-0.3	P
238	Costa Rica	2015	GG	CA	26.2	...	AC	30.6	...	NA	...	...	AC	...	...	NA	...	...	NA	...	...
243	Dominican Republic	2015	GL2	CA	18.7	P	AC	16.0	P	AC	2.4	P	AC	18.5	P	AC	0.0	P	AC	-0.1	P
253	El Salvador	2015	GG	AC	20.3	...	AC	19.0	...	AC	2.5	...	AC	21.5	...	AC	-2.1	...	AC	-0.9	...
258	Guatemala	2013	BA	CA	11.6	...	CA	12.8	...	CA	-0.8	...	CA	12.0	...	CA	1.6	...	CA	2.1	...
268	Honduras	2015	GG	AC	25.7	P	AC	23.3	P	AC	3.2	P	AC	26.5	P	AC	1.4	P	AC	2.4	P
343	Jamaica	2015	GG	AC	33.0	P	AC	30.0	P	AC	3.6	P	AC	33.6	P	AC	...	P	AC	...	P
278	Nicaragua	2015	BA	CA	17.8	P	CA	16.0	P	CA	2.4	P	CA	18.4	P	CA	...	P	CA	...	P
288	Paraguay	2015	GG	CA	24.4	...	AC	21.4	...	AC	3.6	...	AC	25.1	...	CA	1.6	...	CA	1.3	...
293	Peru	2015	GG	CA	20.4	...	CA	17.9	...	CA	4.7	...	CA	22.5	...	CA	-1.0	...	CA	1.2	...
366	Suriname	2012	BA	CA	25.7	P	CA	22.4	P	CA	4.4	P	CA	26.8	P	CA	1.5	P	CA	2.7	P
369	Trinidad and Tobago	2012	GL2	CA	34.9	...	CA	33.3	...	CA	3.1	...	CA	36.3	...	CA	-0.0	...	CA	1.9	...
298	Uruguay	2015	GL2	CA	35.3	...	CA	...	...	CA	...	...	CA	...	...	CA	2.1	...	CA	5.1	...

Table W4. Revenue Categories

(Percent of GDP)

BR: Basis of recording (Cash/Non Cash); GL: Government sector

		Year	GL	BR	Taxes									
					Taxes on income, profits, and capital gains	Taxes on payroll and workforce	Taxes on property	Taxes on goods and services	Taxes on international trade and transactions	Other taxes	Total	Social contributions	Grants	Other revenue
	Advanced Economies													
	Euro Area													
122	Austria	2015	GG	AC	13.6	2.7	0.3	12.4	–	0.1	29.1	15.5	0.1	6.2
124	Belgium	2015	GG	AC	16.1 P	–	2.3 P	11.9 P	–	0.0 P	30.4 P	16.6 P	0.1 P	3.8 P
423	Cyprus	2015	GG	AC	8.9 P	0.9 P	1.2 P	13.6 P	0.0 P	0.2 P	24.8 P	8.5 P	...	...
939	Estonia	2015	GG	AC	7.9 P	–	0.3 P	14.0 P	–	–	22.2 P	11.4 P	1.9 P	3.7 P
172	Finland	2015	GG	AC	15.5 P	–	1.1 P	14.6 P	–	–	31.2 P	12.9 P	0.2 P	9.7 P
132	France	2015	GG	AC	11.5 P	1.6 P	4.2 P	11.7 P	0.0 P	0.1 P	29.1 P	18.9 P	...	...
134	Germany	2015	GG	AC	11.8	–	0.6	10.5	–	0.4	23.3	16.5	0.2	4.7
174	Greece	2015	GG	AC	8.2 P	–	2.7 P	14.4 P	–	0.2 P	25.5 P	13.9 P	...	...
178	Ireland	2015	GG	AC	10.4 P	0.1 P	0.9 P	8.3 P	–	0.0 P	19.8 P	4.5 P	...	...
136	Italy	2015	GG	AC	14.4 P	–	1.6 P	12.5 P	–	1.7 P	30.2 P	13.4 P	...	...
941	Latvia	2015	GG	AC	7.5 P	0.0 P	0.8 P	12.3 P	0.0 P	–	20.7 P	8.7 P	...	...
946	Lithuania	2015	GG	AC	5.4 P	0.0 P	0.3 P	11.4 P	–	0.2 P	17.3 P	12.0 P	2.0 P	3.7 P
137	Luxembourg	2015	GG	AC	13.5 P	–	1.0 P	12.0 P	–	–	26.4 P	12.0 P	0.3 P	4.2 P
181	Malta	2015	GG	AC	13.5 P	–	0.2 P	14.1 P	–	0.0 P	27.8 P	6.8 P	0.4 P	6.8 P
138	Netherlands	2015	GG	AC	10.5 P	0.0 P	1.1 P	10.4 P	0.0 P	1.1 P	23.1 P	14.7 P	0.0 P	5.4 P
182	Portugal	2015	GG	AC	10.4 P	–	0.9 P	13.1 P	0.0 P	1.0 P	25.4 P	11.6 P	...	...
936	Slovak Republic	2015	GG	AC	7.1 P	–	0.4 P	10.8 P	0.0 P	–	18.4 P	14.1 P	...	...
961	Slovenia	2015	GG	AC	6.6	0.1	0.5	14.9	–	0.0	22.2	14.8	...	...
184	Spain	2015	GG	AC	9.7 P	–	2.0 P	10.8 P	0.0 P	–	22.5 P	12.2 P	0.5 P	2.6 P
193	Australia	2015	GG	AC	15.9	1.4	1.5	7.9	0.7	–	27.4	–	0.0	6.7
156	Canada	2015	GG	AC	15.5	0.7	...	...	0.3	0.0	27.5	4.8	0.1	6.9
532	China, P.R.: Hong Kong SAR	2014	GG	AC	8.8	–	1.1	5.4	0.0	0.1	15.5	0.0	–	8.1
546	China, P.R.: Macao SAR	2015	GG	CA	2.2	–	0.2	25.9	–	0.2	28.4	0.1	–	2.5
935	Czech Republic	2015	GG	CA	6.8	–	0.1	11.2	0.0	0.0	18.1	13.1	4.2	2.7
128	Denmark	2015	GG	AC	29.4 P	0.7 P	2.4 P	14.7 P	–	0.3 P	47.4 P	1.0 P	...	...
176	Iceland	2015	GG	AC	17.3	0.3	2.0	11.7	0.2	1.7	33.2	3.6	0.1	5.3
436	Israel	2015	GG	AC	10.1	1.2	2.1	12.3	0.2	–	25.9	5.9	1.1	4.1
158	Japan	2014	GG	AC	9.0	–	2.4	7.8	0.2	0.2	19.6	13.2	14.2	3.8
542	Korea, Republic of	2015	GG	AC	7.8	–	1.6	7.9	0.5	0.9	18.7	7.0	–	8.6
196	New Zealand	2015	GL2	AC	17.6	–	–	9.6	1.0	–	28.1	1.0	0.1	4.6
142	Norway	2015	GG	AC	15.5 P	0.0 P	0.8 P	11.7 P	0.1 P	0.0 P	28.2 P	10.4 P	...	...
135	San Marino	2015	GG	AC	6.6	–	0.7	8.6	0.2	0.3	16.3	12.2	0.0	10.7
576	Singapore	2015	GG	CA	6.2	–	1.1	4.4	–	2.1	13.8	–	–	5.1
144	Sweden	2015	GG	AC	18.2 P	9.0 P	0.8 P	12.5 P	–	–	40.6 P	3.7 P	0.1 P	5.4 P
146	Switzerland	2015	GL2	AC	4.1 P	–	–	5.7 P	0.2 P	–	10.0 P	6.9 P	0.1 P	1.3 P
112	United Kingdom	2015	GG	AC	11.6 P	–	3.3 P	11.8 P	–	0.2 P	27.0 P	7.8 P	0.0 P	3.8 P
111	United States	2015	GG	AC	12.9	–	2.7	4.3	0.2	–	20.1	6.7	0.0	5.0
	Emerging and Developing Economies													
	Emerging and Developing Asia													
513	Bangladesh	2015	BA	CA	2.5	–	–	2.9	2.2	0.3	7.9	–	0.1	1.3
514	Bhutan	2014	GG	CA	8.3	–	–	5.6	0.3	–	14.2	0.0	12.7	6.4
522	Cambodia	2015	BA	AC	3.4 P	–	–	8.2 P	2.6 P	0.0 P	14.2 P	–	2.1 P	1.8 P
924	China, P.R.: Mainland	2014	GG	CA	4.9	–	1.6	12.5	0.4	0.2	19.7	4.6	–	4.2
819	Fiji	2013	BA	CA	6.0	–	–	13.1	5.5	–	24.6	–	0.4	2.1
534	India	2013	GL2	CA	5.9 P	–	0.0 P	3.4 P	1.7 P	–	11.0 P	0.0 P	0.0 P	1.6 P
536	Indonesia	2015	GG	AC	5.2 P	–	0.3 P	6.2 P	0.3 P	0.0 P	12.0 P	–	0.1 P	3.0 P
826	Kiribati	2015	GG	CA	7.7 P	–	–	15.0 P	1.5 P	–	24.2 P	–	6.4 P	117.2 P
544	Lao People's Democratic Republic	2015	BA	CA	2.2	–	0.1	10.6	1.5	–	15.4	–	5.2	2.6
548	Malaysia	2015	BA	CA	8.8	–	–	4.3	0.3	0.9	14.3	–	–	4.6
556	Maldives	2014	GG	CA	6.4	–	–	12.8	4.2	0.1	23.5	–	0.3	7.5
867	Marshall Islands, Republic of	2015	BA	AC	6.4 P	–	0.0 P	2.8 P	4.0 P	0.1 P	13.3 P	–	30.6 P	13.1 P
868	Micronesia, Federated States of	2015	BA	AC	2.6	–	–	1.4	1.4	0.1	5.4	–	6.5	22.9
948	Mongolia	2013	GG	CA	5.7	–	0.2	10.6	2.0	0.2	18.8	5.3	–	7.4
558	Nepal	2016	BA	CA	5.1 P	0.1 P	0.0 P	9.7 P	3.7 P	0.1 P	18.7 P	–	1.4 P	2.8 P
565	Palau	2015	BA	AC	3.2	0.5	–	7.8	5.0	3.2	19.7	–	15.3	5.7
566	Philippines	2015	BA	CA	6.4 P	–	–	4.0 P	2.8 P	0.6 P	13.6 P	–	0.0 P	1.7 P
862	Samoa	2016	BA	CA	5.7	–	0.1	16.2	2.7	–	24.7	–	2.3	2.6
813	Solomon Islands	2015	BA	CA	10.7	–	0.3	6.5	12.2	–	29.8	–	13.2	6.0
524	Sri Lanka	2015	BA	CA	2.3 P	–	–	6.5 P	2.2 P	1.1 P	12.1 P	0.1 P	0.1 P	0.8 P
578	Thailand	2015	GG	AC	6.6 E	–	0.2 E	10.0 E	0.7 E	0.1 E	17.8 E	1.2 E	0.0 E	3.4 E
537	Timor-Leste	2015	GG	CA	16.3	–	–	3.3	0.4	0.0	20.0	–	4.8	31.5
846	Vanuatu	2011	BA	AC	–	–	–	12.3	3.7	–	16.0	–	6.1	2.5
582	Vietnam	2013	BA	CA	7.7	–	0.0	8.8	2.2	0.3	19.1	–	0.3	2.4

Table W4. Revenue Categories

(Percent of GDP)

BR: Basis of recording (Cash/Non Cash); GL: Government sector

Code	Country	Year	GL	BR	Taxes: Taxes on income, profits, and capital gains	Taxes: Taxes on payroll and workforce	Taxes: Taxes on property	Taxes: Taxes on goods and services	Taxes: Taxes on international trade and transactions	Taxes: Other taxes	Taxes: Total	Social contributions	Grants	Other revenue
	Europe													
	Central and Eastern Europe													
914	Albania	2015	GG	CA	3.9	–	0.2	14.2	0.7	0.0	19.1	4.8	0.8	1.7
963	Bosnia and Herzegovina	2015	GG	AC	3.1	–	0.4	19.3	0.0	0.1	22.8	15.3	0.2	5.4
918	Bulgaria	2015	GG	AC	5.4 P	0.0 P	0.6 P	15.4 P	0.0 P	0.2 P	21.6 P	8.1 P	...	...
960	Croatia	2014	GG	CA	4.9	–	0.5	17.2	0.1	0.1	22.8	12.7	0.7	4.0
944	Hungary	2015	GG	AC	6.9 P	0.6 P	0.6 P	18.0 P	–	–	26.1 P	13.3 P	4.5 P	5.0 P
967	Kosovo, Republic of	2015	GG	CA	1.8	1.2	0.3	17.8	2.3	0.0	23.5	–	0.3	1.9
962	Macedonia, F.Y.R. of	2012	GL2	CA	3.1	–	–	12.0	0.9	0.7	16.7	8.9	0.7	2.8
964	Poland	2015	GG	AC	6.5 P	0.2 P	1.3 P	11.8 P	–	0.1 P	19.9 P	13.4 P	...	...
968	Romania	2015	GG	AC	6.2 P	–	0.8 P	12.8 P	0.0 P	0.1 P	19.9 P	8.1 P	...	...
942	Serbia, Republic of	2012	GG	CA	6.1 P	–	0.4 P	16.5 P	1.0 P	0.1 P	24.2 P	12.4 P	0.1 P	4.1 P
186	Turkey	2015	GG	AC	6.2	–	0.4	14.8	0.4	0.7	22.4	11.3	0.0	6.9
	CIS													
911	Armenia	2015	GG	CA	8.5 E	–	0.5 E	9.4 E	1.2 E	2.1 E	21.6 E	–	0.6 E	2.9 E
912	Azerbaijan	2015	GG	CA	6.0	–	0.4	8.2	1.1	0.2	15.8	3.3	0.0	15.3
913	Belarus	2015	GG	AC	7.0	–	1.4	12.5	4.6	0.1	25.6	11.2	0.1	6.4
915	Georgia	2015	GG	CA	10.3	–	0.9	13.8	0.2	0.1	25.3	–	1.0	2.0
916	Kazakhstan	2015	GG	CA	6.0	1.1	0.5	3.0	2.7	0.2	13.6	0.6	0.0	3.5
917	Kyrgyz Republic	2015	GG	CA	5.1	–	0.5	12.0	2.3	0.0	20.0	5.7	2.2	8.2
921	Moldova	2015	GG	CA	4.5	–	0.3	15.9	1.1	–	21.8	9.9	1.6	2.5
922	Russian Federation	2015	GG	AC	7.1 P	–	1.2 P	6.9 P	4.2 P	0.0 P	19.4 P	6.8 P	0.0 P	14.9 P
926	Ukraine	2015	GG	CA	7.0 P	0.3 P	0.3 P	15.3 P	2.1 P	–	25.0 P	9.6 P	0.1 P	7.3 P
927	Uzbekistan	2015	GG	CA	7.8	–	1.3	12.0	3.9	–	24.9	6.2	–	2.8
	Middle East, North Africa and Pakistan													
512	Afghanistan, Islamic Republic of	2013	GG	CA	2.5	–	0.1	1.7	2.5	0.4	7.3	0.3	58.9	2.4
612	Algeria	2011	BA	AC	24.3	–	0.0	10.6	1.5	0.7	37.2	–	–	3.2
419	Bahrain, Kingdom of	2013	BA	AC	0.1	–	–	–	0.9	–	1.1	–	–	22.7
469	Egypt	2015	GG	CA	5.3 P	–	0.1 P	5.8 P	0.9 P	0.4 P	12.6 P	–	1.0 P	8.5 P
433	Iraq	2014	BA	CA	0.5 P	–	0.0 P	0.1 P	0.2 P	0.1 P	0.9 P	0.0 P	–	39.1 P
439	Jordan	2015	BA	CA	3.2	–	0.5	10.4	1.2	–	15.4	0.1	3.3	6.7
443	Kuwait	2015	CG	CA	–	–	–	0.5	0.9	–	1.4	–	–	37.4
446	Lebanon	2015	BA	CA	3.7	–	1.5	6.3	0.9	0.6	13.1	0.2	0.0	3.9
686	Morocco	2015	BA	AC	...	...	...	...	...	...	...	...	...	...
449	Oman	2013	BA	CA	1.3	0.5	–	–	0.7	–	2.5	–	0.0	47.3
564	Pakistan	2014	BA	CA	3.5 P	–	–	4.5 P	0.9 P	0.9 P	9.9 P	–	0.2 P	4.3 P
744	Tunisia	2012	GG	CA	8.6	0.3	0.1	10.1	1.9	0.5	21.5	8.2	0.9	2.1
466	United Arab Emirates	2015	GG	AC	0.8	–	–	10.2	0.8	0.0	11.8	0.3	–	8.6
487	West Bank and Gaza	2015	CG	AC	0.2	0.1	0.0	3.4	1.8	–	5.6	–	1.6	0.4
474	Yemen, Republic of	2012	GG	CA	3.2	0.0	–	3.1	1.2	0.2	7.7	–	2.8	19.5
	Sub-Saharan Africa													
	CEMAC													
626	Central African Republic	2012	BA	AC	1.3 P	0.7 P	0.1 P	2.7 P	4.6 P	0.1 P	9.5 P	0.2 P	7.1 P	1.4 P
634	Congo, Republic of	2012	GG	CA	3.6	–	0.1	4.4	1.6	0.0	9.6	0.8	0.2	33.7
	WAEMU													
638	Benin	2013	BA	AC	3.0	0.1	0.0	7.8	4.3	0.2	15.5	0.5	1.0	0.9
748	Burkina Faso	2015	BA	CA	3.6	0.1	0.1	8.1	2.2	0.1	14.3	–	3.5	1.8
662	Côte d'Ivoire	2014	BA	CA	3.7	–	0.1	3.6	7.0	–	14.3	–	1.8	0.7
678	Mali	2015	BA	AC	3.9	0.1	0.0	7.3	1.8	0.9	14.1	–	1.6	0.8
722	Senegal	2015	BA	AC	5.4 P	0.3 P	0.0 P	11.0 P	2.8 P	0.3 P	19.8 P	–	2.9 P	2.4 P
742	Togo	2015	BA	CA	4.0	0.1	0.1	12.2	4.9	0.1	21.4	–	2.3	1.5
614	Angola	2015	BA	CA	8.6 P	–	0.2 P	1.4 P	1.1 P	1.2 P	12.5 P	1.2 P	–	7.6 P
616	Botswana	2014	BA	CA	11.2	–	0.0	4.2	11.1	–	26.5	–	0.3	12.6
618	Burundi	2013	BA	AC	3.6	–	–	7.8	1.2	–	12.6	–	11.1	1.0
624	Cabo Verde	2012	CG	CA	5.7	–	–	8.5	3.7	–	17.9	0.0	2.8	3.1
644	Ethiopia	2011	BA	CA	2.4	–	–	2.4	4.5	–	9.3	–	4.2	1.7
652	Ghana	2011	BA	CA	5.3	–	–	5.9	3.6	–	14.9	0.1	2.3	4.4
664	Kenya	2015	GG	AC	8.2 P	–	–	6.4 P	1.6 P	0.2 P	16.4 P	0.4 P	0.5 P	5.2 P
666	Lesotho	2013	BA	CA	14.3	–	0.9	9.8	28.9	0.0	53.9	–	2.1	4.9
668	Liberia	2013	CG	CA	8.2	0.0	0.2	3.3	7.9	0.6	20.2	–	1.9	4.3
674	Madagascar	2014	GL2	AC	2.4	–	0.1	2.6	4.9	0.0	9.9	–	2.3	0.3
676	Malawi	2016	BA	CA	7.6	–	–	6.7	1.4	0.0	15.6	–	3.4	0.8
684	Mauritius	2014	GG	AC	4.4 FB	0.1 FB	0.2 FB	13.3 FB	0.3 FB	0.4 FB	18.8 FB	1.9 FB	0.2 FB	2.8 FB
688	Mozambique	2013	BA	CA	10.6	–	–	10.9	1.9	0.6	24.0	0.5	6.5	2.2
728	Namibia	2015	BA	CA	12.7 P	–	0.2 P	8.5 P	11.8 P	0.2 P	33.4 P	0.2 P	0.1 P	1.9 P
694	Nigeria	2013	BA	CA	1.3	–	–	0.1	–	–	1.5	–	–	3.5
714	Rwanda	2015	GG	AC	5.9 P	–	0.0 P	7.2 P	1.1 P	–	14.2 P	1.7 P	7.8 P	4.9 P
716	São Tomé and Príncipe	2012	BA	AC	4.2	–	0.3	1.1	6.7	1.9	14.2	–	17.0	1.4

Table W4. Revenue Categories

(Percent of GDP)

BR: Basis of recording (Cash/Non Cash); GL: Government sector

		Year	GL	BR	Taxes									
					Taxes on income, profits, and capital gains	Taxes on payroll and workforce	Taxes on property	Taxes on goods and services	Taxes on international trade and transactions	Other taxes	Total	Social contributions	Grants	Other revenue
718	Seychelles	2015	GG	CA	4.9 P	5.2 P	–	15.4 P	1.8 P	–	30.0 P	0.0 P	0.7 P	4.4 P
724	Sierra Leone	2014	BA	CA	4.0 P	–	–	3.4 P	1.3 P	–	8.7 P	–	4.3 P	1.2 P
199	South Africa	2015	GG	CA	15.1 P	0.4 P	1.7 P	10.8 P	1.1 P	0.0 P	29.1 P	0.6 P	0.1 P	8.3 P
734	Swaziland	2012	BA	CA	5.4	0.0	0.0	5.2	17.5	0.0	28.1	–	0.0	0.6
738	Tanzania	2016	BA	CA	4.4 P	0.3 P	0.1 P	6.0 P	1.2 P	0.1 P	12.0 P	–	0.5 P	1.1 P
746	Uganda	2015	GG	CA	3.3	...	0.0	5.7	1.1	0.1	10.2	...	0.7	0.9
754	Zambia	2011	BA	CA	11.4 P	–	–	3.9 P	2.9 P	–	18.2 P	–	4.0 P	1.5 P
698	Zimbabwe	2012	BA	CA	9.0	–	–	10.0	5.5	–	24.5	0.0	–	3.5
	Western Hemisphere													
	ECCU													
312	Anguilla	2014	BA	CA	1.6	–	0.5	7.0	9.7	–	18.9	–	1.8	3.8
311	Antigua and Barbuda	2014	BA	CA	2.1	–	0.7	7.8	6.1	–	16.7	–	0.4	2.7
321	Dominica	2014	BA	CA	3.9	–	0.5	12.8	4.3	–	21.5	–	3.0	4.1
328	Grenada	2014	BA	CA	3.8	–	0.9	9.1	6.0	0.2	20.1	–	4.2	1.0
351	Montserrat	2014	BA	CA	9.8	–	0.5	2.9	10.6	–	23.8	–	61.6	2.8
361	St. Kitts and Nevis	2014	BA	CA	6.1	–	0.2	10.7	3.8	–	20.8	–	1.3	2.4
362	St. Lucia	2014	BA	CA	5.9	–	0.2	10.4	6.7	–	23.2	–	1.6	1.2
364	St. Vincent and the Grenadines	2014	BA	CA	7.0	–	0.2	12.2	4.3	–	23.7	–	1.5	2.8
213	Argentina	2015	GL2	CA	3.4	0.1	0.1	6.3	1.8	0.8	12.6	7.0	0.0	3.0
313	Bahamas, The	2015	CG	CA	–	–	3.4 P	5.4 P	8.2 P	–	16.9 P	–	0.0 P	2.2 P
316	Barbados	2013	BA	AC	7.5	–	1.6	13.5	2.3	0.4	25.2	0.0	0.0	1.8
339	Belize	2014	BA	CA	8.1	...	0.2	9.7	5.6	–	23.5	–	1.2	3.2
223	Brazil	2015	GG	CA	6.8	0.4	1.5	13.8	0.7	0.0	23.1	10.9	0.0	7.4
228	Chile	2015	GG	AC	6.4 P	–	0.7 P	11.2 P	0.2 P	0.8 P	19.3 P	1.4 P	0.0 P	2.5 P
233	Colombia	2015	GG	AC	5.6 P	1.0 P	1.0 P	9.0 P	0.7 P	1.3 P	18.6 P	2.5 P	0.1 P	7.8 P
238	Costa Rica	2015	GG	CA	4.0	–	1.0	8.4	1.3	0.2	14.9	8.9	0.0	2.4
243	Dominican Republic	2015	GL2	CA	3.9 P	–	0.6 P	8.0 P	1.0 P	0.0 P	13.6 P	0.4 P	0.1 P	4.7 P
253	El Salvador	2015	GG	AC	5.4	–	0.4	9.0	0.8	0.0	15.5	2.4	0.1	2.2
258	Guatemala	2013	BA	CA	3.8	–	0.0	6.5	0.5	0.1	10.9	0.3	0.1	0.2
268	Honduras	2015	GG	AC	5.5 P	–	0.6 P	11.3 P	0.8 P	–	18.2 P	3.0 P	0.9 P	3.5 P
343	Jamaica	2015	GG	AC	10.5 P	–	–	6.5 P	9.1 P	0.7 P	26.8 P	1.0 P	1.2 P	4.1 P
278	Nicaragua	2015	BA	CA	6.0 P	–	0.1 P	8.8 P	0.7 P	0.0 P	15.7 P	–	1.0 P	1.1 P
288	Paraguay	2015	GG	CA	2.7	–	0.3	9.0	1.2	0.2	13.4	4.9	0.2	5.8
293	Peru	2015	GG	CA	5.7	–	0.3	7.5	0.3	1.5	15.2	2.2	0.0	3.0
366	Suriname	2012	BA	CA	8.2 P	–	0.0 P	8.1 P	2.3 P	0.9 P	19.5 P	–	–	6.1 P
369	Trinidad and Tobago	2012	GL2	CA	18.5	3.6	0.0	5.3	1.5	0.1	29.1	2.0	0.0	3.8
298	Uruguay	2015	GL2	CA	5.7	...	1.2	10.0	1.1	0.5	18.5	10.3	4.9	1.6

Table W5. Expense Categories

(Percent of GDP) *BR: Basis of recording (Cash/Non Cash); GL: Government sector*

		Year	GL	BR	Compensation of employees	Use of goods and services	Consumption of fixed capital	Interest	Subsidies	Grants	Social benefits	Other expense
	Advanced Economies											
	Euro Area											
122	Austria	2015	GG	AC	10.9	6.3	2.6	2.5	1.4	1.5	23.4	3.0
124	Belgium	2015	GG	AC	12.1 P	3.8 P	2.2 P	3.2 P	3.4 P	1.2 P	25.3 P	2.1 P
423	Cyprus	2015	GG	AC	12.8 P	4.0 P	1.5 P	2.8 P	0.4 P	...	14.2 P	...
939	Estonia	2015	GG	AC	11.0 P	6.4 P	3.0 P	0.2 P	0.4 P	1.1 P	13.3 P	1.7 P
172	Finland	2015	GG	AC	13.5 P	11.0 P	3.3 P	1.2 P	1.4 P	1.3 P	22.7 P	2.0 P
132	France	2015	GG	AC	12.9 P	5.1 P	3.4 P	2.0 P	2.5 P	...	26.0 P	...
134	Germany	2015	GG	AC	7.5	4.5	2.2	1.6	0.9	1.3	23.9	2.2
174	Greece	2015	GG	AC	12.3 P	4.8 P	3.7 P	3.6 P	0.9 P	...	22.1 P	...
178	Ireland	2015	GG	AC	7.4 P	3.6 P	1.4 P	2.6 P	0.7 P	...	11.0 P	...
136	Italy	2015	GG	AC	9.9 P	5.5 P	2.7 P	4.2 P	1.7 P	...	23.0 P	...
941	Latvia	2015	GG	AC	9.9 P	6.0 P	4.0 P	1.5 P	0.2 P	...	11.3 P	...
946	Lithuania	2015	GG	AC	9.7 P	5.2 P	3.0 P	1.5 P	0.4 P	0.9 P	12.6 P	1.3 P
137	Luxembourg	2015	GG	AC	8.7 P	3.5 P	2.1 P	0.4 P	1.4 P	1.9 P	19.7 P	2.0 P
181	Malta	2015	GG	AC	12.7 P	6.8 P	2.0 P	2.7 P	1.3 P	0.9 P	11.7 P	2.7 P
138	Netherlands	2015	GG	AC	8.8 P	6.0 P	3.3 P	1.3 P	1.2 P	1.3 P	22.1 P	1.3 P
182	Portugal	2015	GG	AC	11.3 P	5.8 P	2.9 P	4.6 P	0.6 P	...	19.3 P	...
936	Slovak Republic	2015	GG	AC	9.0 P	6.0 P	3.9 P	1.8 P	0.6 P	...	19.2 P	...
961	Slovenia	2015	GG	AC	11.2	6.7	2.8	2.9	0.8	...	18.2	...
184	Spain	2015	GG	AC	10.6 P	5.1 P	2.5 P	3.1 P	1.2 P	1.0 P	18.4 P	1.2 P
193	Australia	2015	GG	AC	9.6	6.6	1.7	1.5	1.4	0.3	11.0	3.7
156	Canada	2015	GG	AC	12.2	8.5	3.3	3.1	0.9	0.2	9.7	1.8
532	China, P.R.: Hong Kong SAR	2014	GG	AC	4.1	6.4	0.5	0.1	0.1	-0.0	2.7	4.3
546	China, P.R.: Macao SAR	2015	GG	CA	4.6	2.6	...	–	0.6	0.0	4.0	3.2
935	Czech Republic	2015	GG	CA	3.4	2.7	...	1.0	7.8	0.9	16.5	4.3
128	Denmark	2015	GG	AC	16.4 P	9.2 P	3.0 P	1.6 P	2.1 P	...	19.0 P	...
176	Iceland	2015	GG	AC	13.9	11.0	1.8	4.6	1.4	0.2	6.4	2.6
436	Israel	2015	GG	AC	9.8	8.8	1.8	3.4	0.7	0.1	11.7	3.1
158	Japan	2014	GG	AC	6.0	4.0	3.0	2.3	0.6	14.4	22.6	2.4
542	Korea, Republic of	2015	GG	AC	6.1	6.4	1.7	1.4	4.9	0.0	6.4	3.2
196	New Zealand	2015	GL2	AC	8.4	3.9	1.2	1.5	0.2	0.8	14.2	2.7
142	Norway	2015	GG	AC	14.7 P	6.6 P	3.2 P	0.7 P	2.0 P	...	16.9 P	...
135	San Marino	2015	GG	AC	12.0	8.7	1.6	0.4	2.2	–	15.2	1.0
576	Singapore	2015	GG	CA	4.0	4.8	...	0.0	–	0.0	...	...
144	Sweden	2015	GG	AC	12.6 P	7.2 P	3.2 P	0.5 P	1.6 P	1.6 P	17.2 P	4.7 P
146	Switzerland	2015	GL2	AC	1.2 P	1.2 P	0.8 P	0.3 P	0.5 P	3.6 P	9.2 P	0.8 P
112	United Kingdom	2015	GG	AC	9.3 P	8.7 P	1.6 P	2.3 P	0.6 P	0.4 P	16.3 P	2.5 P
111	United States	2015	GG	AC	9.2	5.2	2.5	3.5	0.3	0.3	14.7	0.0
	Emerging and Developing Economies											
	Emerging and Developing Asia											
513	Bangladesh	2015	BA	CA	1.8	1.2	...	1.9	0.7	1.3	0.7	0.8
514	Bhutan	2014	GG	CA	7.4	6.1	...	1.9	0.2	0.1	0.6	3.0
522	Cambodia	2015	BA	AC	5.1 P	2.8 P	...	0.3 P	0.0 P	1.3 P	1.3 P	0.8 P
924	China, P.R.: Mainland	2006	BA	CA	...	...	...	0.5	...	...	...	...
819	Fiji	2013	BA	CA	8.2	3.5	...	3.5	1.1	6.3	1.4	1.3
534	India	2013	GL2	CA	1.3 P	1.4 P	...	3.2 P	3.7 P	6.7 P	–	0.1 P
536	Indonesia	2015	GG	AC	5.3 P	3.4 P	1.0 P	1.4 P	1.6 P	1.2 P	0.9 P	0.1 P
826	Kiribati	2015	GG	CA	29.2 P	33.3 P	...	0.1 P	6.2 P	–	2.7 P	2.4 P
544	Lao People's Democratic Republic	2015	BA	CA	8.5	4.9	...	1.1	1.2	0.0	–	1.2
548	Malaysia	2015	BA	CA	6.1	3.1	...	2.1	2.4	3.2	1.6	0.1
556	Maldives	2014	GG	CA	12.4	6.1	...	2.1	3.6	0.0	5.0	1.2
867	Marshall Islands, Republic of	2015	BA	AC	22.1 P	13.7 P	2.7 P	0.2 P	6.2 P	4.0 P	–	4.1 P
868	Micronesia, Federated States of	2015	BA	AC	5.7	9.9	3.0	0.2	–	0.3	–	1.4
948	Mongolia	2013	GG	CA	7.9	5.1	...	1.4	0.5	0.0	8.7	0.6
558	Nepal	2016	BA	CA	4.0 P	2.0 P	...	0.4 P	0.0 P	7.6 P	2.5 P	0.0 P
565	Palau	2015	BA	AC	13.6	8.8	8.8	0.3	1.2	4.0	–	3.1
566	Philippines	2015	BA	CA	5.0 P	3.0 P	...	2.4 P	0.6 P	2.9 P	–	0.2 P
862	Samoa	2016	BA	CA	8.1	6.0	...	0.9	0.7	8.1	0.9	0.3
813	Solomon Islands	2015	BA	CA	11.9	16.9	...	0.1	0.2	1.8	1.2	3.4
524	Sri Lanka	2015	BA	CA	5.0 P	1.9 P	...	4.6 P	0.7 P	2.5 P	3.1 P	–
578	Thailand	2015	GG	AC	6.6 E	6.1 E	...	1.0 E	1.1 E	0.0 E	2.3 E	0.7 E
537	Timor-Leste	2015	GG	CA	6.8	16.5	...	0.0	–	–	6.0	11.2
846	Vanuatu	2011	BA	AC	11.4	6.1	...	0.7	0.2	2.5	0.5	0.7
582	Vietnam	2013	BA	CA	...	...	...	1.5	...	...	...	...
	Europe											
	Central and Eastern Europe											
914	Albania	2015	GG	AC	6.8	2.7	...	2.7	0.1	0.1	9.7	2.3
963	Bosnia and Herzegovina	2015	GG	AC	11.7	7.6	...	0.9	1.4	0.0	16.8	2.7
918	Bulgaria	2015	GG	AC	9.7 P	5.4 P	2.7 P	1.0 P	1.9 P	...	14.3 P	...
960	Croatia	2014	GG	CA	10.4	4.6	...	3.2	1.9	1.6	18.4	2.4
944	Hungary	2015	GG	AC	10.6 P	7.4 P	3.6 P	3.6 P	1.4 P	1.4 P	15.3 P	4.1 P

Table W5. Expense Categories

(Percent of GDP)

BR: Basis of recording (Cash/Non Cash); GL: Government sector

		Year	GL	BR	Compensation of employees	Use of goods and services	Consumption of fixed capital	Interest	Subsidies	Grants	Social benefits	Other expense
967	Kosovo, Republic of	2015	GG	CA	9.1	3.2	...	0.3	1.9	0.1	5.8	0.4
962	Macedonia, F.Y.R. of	2012	GL2	CA	5.0	3.2	...	0.9	5.4	...	15.2	0.3
964	Poland	2015	GG	AC	10.3 P	5.9 P	2.2 P	1.8 P	0.5 P	...	16.2 P	...
968	Romania	2015	GG	AC	7.7 P	5.6 P	1.7 P	1.6 P	0.5 P	...	11.5 P	...
942	Serbia, Republic of	2012	GG	CA	12.3 P	6.6 P	...	1.9 P	3.5 P	0.0 P	18.2 P	1.0 P
186	Turkey	2015	GG	AC	9.3	6.0	1.0	2.4	1.3	0.1	15.0	1.6
	CIS											
911	Armenia	2015	GG	CA	5.7 E	4.8 E	–	1.5 E	0.8 E	0.2 E	7.9 E	5.5 E
912	Azerbaijan	2015	GG	CA	...	...	...	0.4	3.3	0.0	...	7.7
913	Belarus	2015	GG	AC	9.7	7.0	...	1.7	4.3	0.1	14.7	0.7
915	Georgia	2015	GG	CA	5.1	3.8	...	1.0	2.3	0.1	9.6	4.0
916	Kazakhstan	2015	GG	CA	2.9	7.0	...	0.6	0.8	0.0	5.0	0.3
917	Kyrgyz Republic	2015	GG	CA	12.2	5.4	...	0.8	0.8	0.1	10.2	0.5
921	Moldova	2015	GG	CA	8.4	8.3	...	0.9	0.8	–	12.5	4.3
922	Russian Federation	2015	GG	AC	9.6 P	5.6 P	1.8 P	1.0 P	4.1 P	0.2 P	14.2 P	1.2 P
926	Ukraine	2015	GG	CA	9.6 P	7.3 P	...	4.5 P	1.3 P	0.1 P	18.0 P	0.8 P
927	Uzbekistan	2015	GG	CA	...	...	...	0.0	...	...	...	...
	Middle East, North Africa and Pakistan											
512	Afghanistan, Islamic Republic of	2013	GG	CA	12.5	28.9	...	0.0	0.1	–	1.1	0.5
612	Algeria	2011	BA	AC	11.9	2.7	...	0.3	2.4	4.9	6.0	1.4
419	Bahrain, Kingdom of	2013	BA	AC	10.5	3.3	0.1	1.6	0.4	5.6	1.6	-0.0
469	Egypt	2015	GG	CA	8.3 P	1.3 P	...	7.4 P	6.2 P	0.0 P	5.1 P	2.1 P
433	Iraq	2014	BA	AC	11.6 P	3.4 P	–	0.3 P	1.6 P	0.6 P	6.6 P	2.1 P
439	Jordan	2015	BA	CA	12.7	2.0	...	3.4	1.1	1.4	5.4	0.4
443	Kuwait	2015	CG	CA	17.0	8.9	...	–	6.8	1.9	–	10.1
446	Lebanon	2015	BA	CA	5.6	1.0	...	8.7	2.7	-0.6	4.4	0.6
686	Morocco	2015	BA	AC	...	...	...	...	...	...	...	...
449	Oman	2013	BA	CA	8.2	19.1	...	0.2	7.2	0.2	–	–
564	Pakistan	2014	BA	CA	1.8 P	1.7 P	...	5.7 P	1.3 P	1.3 P	0.7 P	5.3 P
744	Tunisia	2012	GG	CA	12.8	1.8	...	1.8	7.0	–	7.8	3.3
466	United Arab Emirates	2015	GG	AC	4.6	4.4	0.3	0.2	0.9	0.6	3.1	10.4
487	West Bank and Gaza	2015	CG	AC	4.2	1.4	...	0.2	0.0	0.1	1.6	0.1
474	Yemen, Republic of	2012	GG	CA	12.9	4.0	...	4.9	–	–	4.6	4.3
	Sub-Saharan Africa											
	CEMAC											
626	Central African Republic	2012	BA	AC	4.6 P	2.3 P	...	0.5 P	2.1 P	–	–	–
634	Congo, Republic of	2012	GG	AC	4.1	6.8	...	0.2	0.1	2.7	0.7	0.9
	WAEMU											
638	Benin	2013	BA	AC	6.6	2.4	...	0.4	1.1	2.0	0.0	0.3
748	Burkina Faso	2015	BA	AC	7.2	1.7	...	0.7	0.2	1.4	–	3.1
662	Côte d'Ivoire	2014	BA	AC	7.0	2.8	...	0.8	0.8	0.6	–	1.2
678	Mali	2015	BA	AC	4.7	2.9	...	0.7	1.0	1.8	0.1	1.2
722	Senegal	2015	BA	AC	6.5 P	4.8 P	...	2.0 P	0.6 P	7.4 P	0.7 P	1.3 P
742	Togo	2015	BA	AC	7.0	6.8	...	1.8	5.2	1.2	–	3.5
614	Angola	2015	BA	AC	11.3 P	5.2 P	...	2.0 P	2.3 P	0.0 P	2.3 P	0.5 P
616	Botswana	2014	BA	CA	11.7	9.2	...	0.5	...	...	...	...
618	Burundi	2013	BA	AC	7.2	3.0	...	0.7	–	4.9	0.1	0.0
624	Cabo Verde	2012	CG	CA	10.4	3.3	...	1.9	0.2	2.7	2.6	1.2
644	Ethiopia	2011	BA	CA	1.4	2.1	...	0.4	5.4	1.4	–	–
652	Ghana	2011	BA	CA	8.1	3.3	...	2.7	–	5.2	1.8	–
664	Kenya	2015	GG	AC	9.0 P	6.3 P	...	2.8 P	0.5 P	2.4 P	0.6 P	0.2 P
666	Lesotho	2013	BA	CA	19.6	12.4	...	1.1	1.1	3.8	3.4	3.4
668	Liberia	2013	CG	CA	10.5	...	...	...	...	5.6	0.1	–
674	Madagascar	2015	BA	AC	5.5 P	0.5 P	–	0.8 P	3.0 P	0.0 P	0.2 P	1.4 P
676	Malawi	2016	BA	CA	5.8	3.7	...	3.2	1.8	2.3	1.1	0.1
684	Mauritius	2014	GG	AC	9.2 FB	2.8 FB	–	1.8 FB	0.5 FB	0.1 FB	6.1 FB	2.2 FB
688	Mozambique	2012	BA	CA	10.5	7.2	–	1.0	1.2	0.6	2.6	1.8
728	Namibia	2015	BA	CA	16.3 P	6.0 P	...	1.8 P	5.7 P	6.7 P	0.7 P	0.3 P
694	Nigeria	2013	BA	CA	2.1	0.6	...	1.0	0.2	0.3	0.8	–
714	Rwanda	2015	GG	AC	6.5 P	5.9 P	...	0.8 P	1.2 P	0.0 P	1.3 P	2.0 P
716	São Tomé and Príncipe	2012	BA	AC	8.5	4.0	...	0.6	0.0	3.3	–	1.3
718	Seychelles	2015	GG	CA	6.7 P	6.0 P	...	3.4 P	7.9 P	–	3.0 P	2.5 P
724	Sierra Leone	2014	BA	CA	6.4 P	2.8 P	...	1.0 P	–	1.3 P	0.3 P	0.1 P
199	South Africa	2015	GG	CA	14.3 P	10.9 P	0.9 P	3.5 P	1.1 P	1.3 P	5.6 P	2.9 P
734	Swaziland	2012	BA	CA	11.1	4.6	...	0.7	0.3	5.2	0.3	0.1
738	Tanzania	2016	BA	CA	3.5 P	1.9 P	...	1.4 P	0.4 P	6.3 P	0.4 P	0.2 P
746	Uganda	2015	GG	AC	3.8	4.0	0.1	1.2	0.0	1.1	0.3	0.6
754	Zambia	2011	BA	CA	7.0 P	8.2 P	...	1.1 P	0.0 P	0.6 P	0.1 P	0.4 P
698	Zimbabwe	2012	BA	CA	17.4	3.5	...	0.2	...	...	0.2	–

Table W5. Expense Categories

(Percent of GDP)

BR: Basis of recording (Cash/Non Cash); GL: Government sector

		Year	GL	BR	Compensation of employees	Use of goods and services	Consumption of fixed capital	Interest	Subsidies	Grants	Social benefits	Other expense
	Western Hemisphere											
	ECCU											
312	Anguilla	2014	BA	CA	9.8	5.1	...	1.1	4.5	–	1.0	–
311	Antigua and Barbuda	2014	BA	CA	9.0	3.6	...	2.6	4.0	–	1.8	–
321	Dominica	2014	BA	CA	9.9	7.4	...	1.8	3.6	–	1.2	–
328	Grenada	2014	BA	CA	10.2	3.0	...	3.6	2.4	–	1.4	–
351	Montserrat	2014	BA	CA	25.1	17.2	...	0.0	18.0	–	8.9	–
361	St. Kitts and Nevis	2014	BA	CA	11.0	3.3	...	2.0	3.9	–	2.6	–
362	St. Lucia	2014	BA	CA	10.2	4.3	...	3.9	2.9	–	1.9	–
364	St. Vincent and the Grenadines	2014	BA	CA	12.6	3.7	...	2.3	4.5	–	3.0	–
213	Argentina	2015	GL2	AC	3.4	1.2	0.0	1.9	4.4	1.7	10.6	2.4
313	Bahamas, The	2015	CG	CA	7.2 P	3.7 P	...	2.6 P	3.7 P	–	1.4 P	0.7 P
316	Barbados	2013	BA	AC	10.5	5.1	0.6	7.0	10.8	0.3	4.5	–
339	Belize	2014	BA	CA	9.9	5.5	...	2.6	4.4	–	1.9	–
223	Brazil	2015	GG	AC	13.1	5.5	1.5	12.6	0.4	0.0	15.8	1.5
228	Chile	2015	GG	AC	6.4 P	3.0 P	1.0 P	0.7 P	3.4 P	0.0 P	4.9 P	4.2 P
233	Colombia	2015	GG	AC	4.8 P	9.4 P	0.5 P	2.7 P	0.4 P	–	8.0 P	4.8 P
238	Costa Rica	2015	GG	AC	13.8	3.3	...	2.9	–	0.0	6.2	3.7
243	Dominican Republic	2015	GL2	AC	6.2 P	2.8 P	0.1 P	2.7 P	1.1 P	0.6 P	1.0 P	1.7 P
253	El Salvador	2015	GG	AC	9.7	3.7	0.3	2.4	0.4	0.0	2.4	0.3
258	Guatemala	2013	BA	CA	4.0	2.0	...	1.5	0.1	3.2	0.9	1.2
268	Honduras	2015	GG	AC	10.7 P	4.2 P	...	1.9 P	0.0 P	0.0 P	0.4 P	6.1 P
343	Jamaica	2015	GG	AC	11.5 P	3.7 P	...	8.0 P	–	3.1 P	3.3 P	0.3 P
278	Nicaragua	2015	BA	CA	5.9 P	2.5 P	...	0.9 P	0.1 P	5.1 P	0.4 P	1.1 P
288	Paraguay	2015	GG	AC	12.0	2.7	...	0.6	–	0.0	4.6	1.4
293	Peru	2015	GG	CA	6.1	6.6	...	1.0	–	–	1.9	2.3
366	Suriname	2012	BA	CA	8.0 P	7.6 P	...	0.9 P	6.0 P	–	–	–
369	Trinidad and Tobago	2012	GL2	CA	8.1	7.3	...	2.0	0.1	7.3	6.1	2.3
298	Uruguay	2015	CG	CA	7.0	3.6	...	2.3	0.3	4.9	2.5	1.0

Table W6. Expenditure by Function

(Percent of Total Expenditure)

BR: Basis of recording (Cash/Non Cash); GL: Government sector

		Year	GL	BR	General public services	Defense	Public order and safety	Economic affairs	Environ-mental protection	Housing and community amenities	Health	Recreation, culture and religion	Education	Social protection
	Advanced Economies													
	Euro Area													
122	Austria	2015	GG	AC	13.2	1.1	2.7	11.9	0.9	0.7	15.5	2.4	9.6	42.0
124	Belgium	2014	GG	AC	15.4 P	1.6 P	3.4 P	12.8 P	1.7 P	0.7 P	14.6 P	2.3 P	11.4 P	36.1 P
423	Cyprus	2014	GG	AC	38.5 P	3.0 P	3.6 P	5.7 P	0.5 P	4.6 P	5.5 P	1.8 P	11.8 P	25.0 P
939	Estonia	2014	GG	AC	10.3 P	4.7 P	5.1 P	12.6 P	1.6 P	1.2 P	13.6 P	5.2 P	14.7 P	31.1 P
172	Finland	2014	GG	AC	14.3 P	2.4 P	2.3 P	8.3 P	0.4 P	0.7 P	14.3 P	2.5 P	11.0 P	43.8 P
132	France	2014	GG	AC	11.6 P	3.0 P	2.8 P	8.8 P	1.7 P	2.5 P	14.3 P	2.5 P	9.6 P	43.1 P
134	Germany	2015	GG	AC	13.4	2.3	3.6	7.1	1.4	0.9	16.3	2.3	9.6	43.2
174	Greece	2015	GG	AC	17.8 P	4.9 P	3.8 P	16.0 P	2.7 P	0.4 P	8.2 P	1.3 P	7.8 P	37.0 P
178	Ireland	2014	GG	AC	15.9 P	0.9 P	3.7 P	8.4 P	1.5 P	1.9 P	19.9 P	2.0 P	11.1 P	34.6 P
136	Italy	2015	GG	AC	16.6 P	2.4 P	3.7 P	8.1 P	1.9 P	1.2 P	14.1 P	1.5 P	7.9 P	42.6 P
941	Latvia	2014	GG	AC	13.0 P	2.4 P	5.4 P	13.1 P	1.8 P	3.0 P	10.2 P	4.5 P	15.8 P	30.7 P
946	Lithuania	2014	GG	AC	13.3 P	3.0 P	4.8 P	9.3 P	1.6 P	1.0 P	15.9 P	2.6 P	15.5 P	33.0 P
137	Luxembourg	2015	GG	AC	10.7 P	0.7 P	2.4 P	11.7 P	2.6 P	1.2 P	10.9 P	2.8 P	12.3 P	44.8 P
181	Malta	2014	GG	AC	16.5 P	1.8 P	3.2 P	12.5 P	3.7 P	0.8 P	13.9 P	2.5 P	13.4 P	31.7 P
138	Netherlands	2015	GG	AC	11.1 P	2.5 P	4.0 P	8.8 P	3.2 P	0.7 P	17.7 P	3.1 P	12.0 P	36.8 P
182	Portugal	2014	GG	AC	16.9 P	1.9 P	4.3 P	13.3 P	0.9 P	1.2 P	12.1 P	1.7 P	12.0 P	35.7 P
936	Slovak Republic	2014	GG	AC	13.6 P	2.2 P	5.4 P	10.8 P	1.7 P	1.5 P	4.5 P	2.2 P	9.9 P	48.1 P
961	Slovenia	2014	GG	AC	15.1	1.7	3.3	11.5	2.0	1.8	13.2	3.4	11.9	36.2
184	Spain	2015	GG	AC	14.5 P	2.2 P	4.7 P	9.7 P	1.9 P	1.1 P	14.1 P	2.6 P	9.4 P	39.7 P
193	Australia	2015	GG	AC	13.0	4.5	4.6	11.8	1.9	2.1	18.5	2.1	14.2	27.3
156	Canada	2015	GG	AC	...	...	...	...	...	...	...	...	...	...
532	China, P.R.: Hong Kong SAR	2014	GG	AC	15.6	–	9.4	14.4	3.6	7.1	14.6	3.1	17.5	14.6
546	China, P.R.: Macao SAR	2015	GG	CA	15.7	–	14.5	12.5	1.3	2.9	10.2	3.8	14.7	24.3
935	Czech Republic	2015	GG	CA	10.5	2.1	4.7	18.5	3.6	2.3	15.1	2.7	9.3	31.0
128	Denmark	2015	GG	AC	13.5 P	2.0 P	1.8 P	6.7 P	0.8 P	0.4 P	15.6 P	3.2 P	12.8 P	43.0 P
176	Iceland	2015	GG	AC	18.0	0.0	3.6	11.6	1.3	1.1	17.4	7.5	17.4	22.1
436	Israel	2015	GG	AC	12.3	15.2	3.9	6.0	1.3	0.1	12.8	3.6	17.4	27.5
158	Japan	2014	GG	AC	7.7	1.7	2.4	7.3	2.2	1.4	13.2	0.7	6.3	31.6
542	Korea, Republic of	2015	GG	AC	...	...	...	...	...	...	...	...	...	...
196	New Zealand	2015	GL2	AC	9.4	2.9	5.4	7.4	0.8	0.5	20.3	1.1	18.3	34.0
142	Norway	2015	GG	AC	9.6 P	3.1 P	2.2 P	10.5 P	1.8 P	1.5 P	17.2 P	3.0 P	11.2 P	39.8 P
135	San Marino	2007	GG	AC	...	...	...	...	...	...	...	...	...	...
576	Singapore	2015	GG	CA	6.0	18.4	5.5	21.5	1.3	4.6	12.1	3.7	16.4	10.6
144	Sweden	2015	GG	AC	14.1 P	2.3 P	2.6 P	8.4 P	0.6 P	1.5 P	13.8 P	2.2 P	13.0 P	41.6 P
146	Switzerland	2015	GL2	AC	18.6 P	4.1 P	1.0 P	13.2 P	0.6 P	0.0 P	0.3 P	0.4 P	3.3 P	58.4 P
112	United Kingdom	2015	GG	AC	10.6 P	5.0 P	4.7 P	7.1 P	1.8 P	1.1 P	17.8 P	1.5 P	12.0 P	38.4 P
111	United States	2015	GG	AC	13.8	8.8	5.4	8.7	–	1.4	24.2	0.7	16.2	20.8
	Emerging and Developing Economies													
	Emerging and Developing Asia													
513	Bangladesh	2015	BA	CA	24.3	10.3	8.1	26.2	0.1	2.0	5.8	0.8	16.0	6.5
514	Bhutan	2014	GG	CA	21.0	0.1	6.4	31.9	0.2	5.0	9.2	6.0	20.2	0.1
522	Cambodia	2015	BA	AC	...	...	...	...	...	...	...	...	...	...
924	China, P.R.: Mainland	2014	GG	CA	9.2	4.4	4.4	27.7	2.0	7.8	3.1	1.5	12.8	27.1
819	Fiji	2013	BA	CA	...	...	...	...	...	...	...	...	...	...
534	India	2013	GL2	CA	56.1 P	10.9 P	–	20.8 P	–	7.0 P	1.9 P	–	3.3 P	–
536	Indonesia	2015	GG	AC	47.7 P	5.2 P	3.3 P	12.0 P	1.2 P	7.0 P	4.8 P	0.7 P	16.7 P	1.5 P
826	Kiribati	2015	GG	CA	35.8 P	–	5.9 P	27.4 P	2.1 P	–	13.5 P	...	13.5 P	1.8 P
544	Lao People's Democratic Republic	2015	BA	CA	...	...	...	...	...	...	...	...	...	...
548	Malaysia	2015	BA	CA	...	6.8	5.7	15.5	...	5.7	9.1	...	22.2	...
556	Maldives	2011	GG	CA	32.7	7.2	10.8	8.9	1.5	10.2	2.9	2.6	14.2	9.0
867	Marshall Islands, Republic of	2015	BA	AC	27.3 P	–	6.3 P	14.5 P	4.9 P	1.5 P	14.2 P	0.3 P	31.1 P	–
868	Micronesia, Federated States of	2015	BA	AC	50.7	–	9.6	19.1	2.6	–	7.1	–	9.0	1.8
948	Mongolia	2013	GG	CA	...	...	...	...	...	...	...	...	...	...
558	Nepal	2016	BA	CA	18.4 P	7.4 P	7.4 P	28.1 P	2.5 P	4.8 P	7.2 P	0.8 P	19.2 P	4.1 P
565	Palau	2015	BA	AC	30.0	–	5.1	24.4	6.7	0.2	17.5	1.3	14.5	0.3
566	Philippines	2015	BA	CA	45.3 P	3.5 P	7.8 P	20.0 P	0.2 P	0.6 P	4.9 P	0.3 P	17.4 P	8.3 P
862	Samoa	2016	BA	CA	23.1	–	6.9	28.6	3.0	3.5	14.4	0.8	14.4	5.3
813	Solomon Islands	2015	GG	AC	18.5 NA	...	9.2 NA	25.0 NA	1.2 NA	1.6 NA	12.1 NA	0.4 NA	30.1 NA	1.8 NA
524	Sri Lanka	2015	BA	CA	28.8 P	10.2 P	3.4 P	26.3 P	...	12.5 P	7.8 P	...	9.8 P	24.0 P
578	Thailand	2015	GG	AC	...	...	...	...	...	...	...	...	...	...
537	Timor-Leste	2013	GG	CA	...	...	...	...	...	...	...	...	...	...
846	Vanuatu	2011	BA	AC	...	...	...	...	...	...	...	...	...	...
582	Vietnam	2002	BA	CA	...	...	...	...	...	...	...	...	...	9.8
	Europe													
	Central and Eastern Europe													
914	Albania	2015	GG	AC	18.9	2.4	5.9	13.9	0.3	6.5	9.2	1.5	10.4	30.8
963	Bosnia and Herzegovina	2015	GG	AC	...	...	...	...	...	...	...	...	...	...
918	Bulgaria	2014	GG	AC	14.9 P	3.3 P	6.5 P	11.7 P	1.6 P	3.9 P	13.0 P	3.5 P	9.7 P	31.9 P
960	Croatia	2014	GG	CA	15.3	2.9	5.2	10.1	0.5	3.1	15.5	2.6	10.2	34.5

Table W6. Expenditure by Function

(Percent of Total Expenditure)

BR: Basis of recording (Cash/Non Cash); GL: Government sector

		Year	GL	BR	General public services	Defense	Public order and safety	Economic affairs	Environ-mental protection	Housing and community amenities	Health	Recreation, culture and religion	Education	Social protection
944	Hungary	2014	GG	AC	20.4 P	1.2 P	3.9 P	14.8 P	2.4 P	1.8 P	10.0 P	4.0 P	10.3 P	31.2 P
967	Kosovo, Republic of	2015	GG	CA	...	...	...	...	...	...	...	...	...	...
962	Macedonia, F.Y.R. of	2012	GL2	CA	...	...	...	...	...	...	...	...	...	...
964	Poland	2014	GG	AC	11.9 P	3.5 P	5.3 P	11.0 P	2.1 P	1.7 P	11.0 P	2.8 P	12.5 P	38.2 P
968	Romania	2014	GG	AC	13.4 P	2.4 P	6.0 P	17.1 P	2.2 P	3.3 P	11.5 P	2.7 P	8.6 P	32.7 P
942	Serbia, Republic of	2012	GG	CA	11.0 P	3.2 P	6.4 P	13.6 P	0.9 P	3.4 P	12.8 P	2.4 P	8.7 P	37.5 P
186	Turkey	2015	GG	AC	14.4	4.0	6.0	8.9	1.1	2.3	16.1	2.5	11.5	33.4
	CIS													
911	Armenia	2015	BA	AC	20.4	14.4	8.8	8.0	0.4	2.8	6.2	2.2	8.9	27.8
912	Azerbaijan	2015	GG	CA	16.6	8.4	5.7	35.5	0.1	2.1	3.6	1.4	8.3	18.3
913	Belarus	2015	GG	AC	13.5	2.7	4.7	11.4	0.2	4.5	10.9	2.6	13.1	36.5
915	Georgia	2015	GG	CA	8.4	7.1	10.9	13.8	1.4	4.4	9.7	6.2	11.5	26.5
916	Kazakhstan	2015	GG	CA	13.4	5.6	6.9	14.7	0.2	5.5	10.6	3.6	16.8	22.7
917	Kyrgyz Republic	2015	GG	CA	...	...	...	...	...	...	...	...	...	...
921	Moldova	2015	GG	CA	9.8	1.0	6.5	11.3	1.0	2.2	13.9	2.4	18.2	33.8
922	Russian Federation	2015	GG	AC	40.2 P	5.2 P	5.8 P	6.5 P	0.1 P	2.0 P	6.7 P	0.9 P	2.1 P	30.5 P
926	Ukraine	2015	GG	CA	13.0 P	6.1 P	6.5 P	4.5 P	0.7 P	1.9 P	8.4 P	1.9 P	13.5 P	43.5 P
927	Uzbekistan	2015	GG	CA	4.6	...	...	13.5	...	...	10.2	...	24.5	...
	Middle East, North Africa and													
512	Afghanistan, Islamic Republic of	2013	GG	CA	4.6	46.6	21.8	14.2	0.5	0.5	2.7	0.5	7.1	1.5
612	Algeria	2011	BA	AC	...	...	...	...	...	...	...	...	...	...
419	Bahrain, Kingdom of	2013	BA	AC	10.3	12.5	13.9	21.0	0.2	6.3	11.0	3.4	12.0	9.5
469	Egypt	2015	GG	CA	29.0 P	6.0 P	6.0 P	6.0 P	0.3 P	3.0 P	5.0 P	4.0 P	12.0 P	29.0 P
433	Iraq	2014	BA	AC	...	...	...	...	...	...	...	...	...	...
439	Jordan	2015	BA	CA	17.8	12.1	13.5	6.6	0.6	3.1	11.3	2.0	13.5	19.5
443	Kuwait	2015	CG	CA	13.1	8.5	7.2	11.6	0.1	6.4	7.8	2.7	13.8	16.3
446	Lebanon	2015	BA	CA	50.1	9.6	5.8	16.7	0.1	0.6	3.4	0.4	8.0	5.2
686	Morocco	2015	BA	AC	...	...	...	...	...	...	...	...	...	...
449	Oman	2013	BA	CA	5.3	33.1	1.5	7.2	0.2	6.3	4.3	1.6	11.1	4.2
564	Pakistan	2014	BA	CA	80.4 P	11.9 P	1.5 P	3.1 P	0.0 P	0.5 P	0.7 P	0.1 P	1.7 P	0.1 P
744	Tunisia	2012	GG	CA	10.9	...	...	...	...	...	...	...	...	...
466	United Arab Emirates	2015	GG	AC	40.8	2.9	11.3	12.9	1.8	4.5	8.6	1.5	6.1	9.7
487	West Bank and Gaza	2014	CG	AC	12.7	–	29.2	3.7	0.1	1.1	13.2	2.6	18.7	20.0
474	Yemen, Republic of	2012	GG	CA	23.3	11.7	6.3	14.8	16.3	1.2	4.6	1.4	–	20.3
	Sub-Saharan Africa													
	CEMAC													
626	Central African Republic	2012	BA	AC	...	...	...	...	...	...	...	...	...	...
634	Congo, Republic of	2012	BA	AC	26.5	7.5	3.4	22.3	0.0	24.7	5.6	1.8	7.6	0.5
	WAEMU													
638	Benin	2013	BA	AC	...	...	...	...	...	...	...	...	...	...
748	Burkina Faso	2015	BA	AC	...	...	...	...	...	...	...	...	...	...
662	Côte d'Ivoire	2014	BA	AC	36.4	8.0	5.0	8.6	1.7	18.6	7.1	1.5	26.5	1.0
678	Mali	2015	BA	AC	...	...	...	...	...	...	...	...	...	...
722	Senegal	2015	BA	AC	...	...	...	...	...	...	...	...	...	...
742	Togo	2015	BA	AC	...	...	...	...	...	...	...	...	...	...
614	Angola	2015	BA	AC	20.4 P	22.7 P	4.6 P	12.4 P	0.6 P	5.0 P	5.6 P	1.0 P	12.1 P	15.7 P
616	Botswana	2014	BA	CA	...	...	...	...	...	...	...	...	...	...
618	Burundi	2013	BA	AC	16.0	8.9	6.8	8.1	0.5	0.4	8.4	0.2	18.5	0.9
624	Cabo Verde	2012	CG	CA	22.0	1.5	5.8	30.7	2.1	4.8	6.4	3.2	16.4	8.4
644	Ethiopia	2011	BA	CA	...	...	...	...	...	...	...	...	...	...
652	Ghana	2011	BA	CA	...	...	...	...	...	...	...	...	...	...
664	Kenya	2015	GG	AC	...	...	...	...	...	...	...	...	...	...
666	Lesotho	2013	BA	CA	...	...	...	...	...	...	...	...	...	...
668	Liberia	2013	CG	CA	31.4	2.8	11.7	...	1.1	2.6	10.2	...	13.2	1.6
674	Madagascar	2015	BA	AC	55.3 P	9.4 P	5.1 P	2.9 P	0.3 P	0.5 P	5.1 P	0.5 P	20.5 P	0.2 P
676	Malawi	2016	BA	CA	...	...	...	...	...	...	...	...	...	...
684	Mauritius	2014	GG	AC	16.9 FB	–	9.4 FB	10.7 FB	2.1 FB	6.4 FB	9.8 FB	1.2 FB	15.5 FB	28.0 FB
688	Mozambique	2012	BA	AC	...	...	...	...	...	...	...	...	...	...
728	Namibia	2015	BA	CA	19.4 P	10.5 P	9.5 P	14.3 P	0.9 P	4.6 P	8.4 P	2.0 P	23.4 P	6.9 P
694	Nigeria	2013	BA	CA	15.1	5.9	5.9	15.2	...	0.2	4.1	...	8.2	7.0
714	Rwanda	2011	BA	CA	...	...	...	...	...	...	...	...	...	...
716	São Tomé and Príncipe	2012	BA	AC	...	...	...	...	...	...	...	...	...	...
718	Seychelles	2015	GG	CA	31.0 P	4.1 P	9.8 P	8.5 P	4.3 P	3.8 P	10.7 P	3.9 P	12.6 P	11.5 P
724	Sierra Leone	2014	BA	CA	...	...	...	...	...	...	...	...	...	...
199	South Africa	2015	GG	CA	45.1 P	2.1 P	6.4 P	9.3 P	0.5 P	5.0 P	7.7 P	2.1 P	12.6 P	9.2 P
734	Swaziland	2012	BA	CA	38.4	...	17.2	18.1	...	...	12.3	...	20.6	4.7
738	Tanzania	2015	BA	CA	...	...	...	...	...	...	...	...	...	...
746	Uganda	2015	GG	AC	23.2	8.9	6.0	24.9	0.7	3.8	8.4	0.1	20.2	3.8
754	Zambia	2011	BA	CA	19.8 P	8.7 P	5.2 P	31.2 P	0.2 P	1.6 P	9.7 P	0.9 P	17.7 P	4.9 P
698	Zimbabwe	2012	BA	CA	...	...	...	...	...	...	...	...	...	...

Table W6. Expenditure by Function

(Percent of Total Expenditure)

BR: Basis of recording (Cash/Non Cash); GL: Government sector

		Year	GL	BR	General public services	Defense	Public order and safety	Economic affairs	Environ-mental protection	Housing and community amenities	Health	Recreation, culture and religion	Education	Social protection
	Western Hemisphere													
	ECCU													
312	Anguilla	...	...	...	...	...	...	...	...	...	...	...	...	...
311	Antigua and Barbuda	...	...	...	...	...	...	...	...	...	...	...	...	...
321	Dominica	2001	BA	AC	...	...	...	...	...	...	...	...	...	...
328	Grenada	1995	BA	AC	21.4	–	10.0	28.4	...	2.1	10.4	2.1	16.8	8.6
351	Montserrat	...	...	...	...	...	...	...	...	...	...	...	...	...
361	St. Kitts and Nevis	2001	BA	AC	...	...	...	...	...	...	...	...	...	...
362	St. Lucia	...	...	...	...	...	...	...	...	...	...	...	...	...
364	St. Vincent and the Grenadines	1999	CG	AC	24.8	–	7.3	11.1	...	1.7	10.7	–	15.0	7.7
213	Argentina	2015	GL2	AC	13.1	1.8	4.9	21.3	0.1	2.4	7.1	0.3	6.5	42.4
313	Bahamas, The	2015	CG	CA	30.7 P	7.4 P	10.3 P	14.8 P	0.1 P	0.2 P	14.2 P	1.4 P	13.3 P	7.6 P
316	Barbados	2013	BA	AC	...	...	...	...	...	...	...	...	...	...
339	Belize	2014	BA	CA	...	...	...	...	...	...	...	...	...	...
223	Brazil	2015	GG	AC	...	...	...	...	...	...	...	...	...	...
228	Chile	2015	GG	AC	...	...	...	...	...	...	...	...	...	...
233	Colombia	2015	GG	AC	...	...	...	...	...	...	...	...	...	...
238	Costa Rica	2015	GG	AC	14.2	–	8.3	6.4	0.4	4.2	20.5	0.6	23.7	21.7
243	Dominican Republic	2015	BA	AC	26.3 P	2.7 P	4.3 P	16.1 P	0.4 P	1.8 P	10.5 P	0.9 P	22.9 P	10.4 P
253	El Salvador	2015	GG	AC	23.2	2.9	12.3	15.0	0.6	2.5	16.3	0.4	17.2	9.5
258	Guatemala	2013	BA	CA	18.4	2.6	11.1	12.8	1.0	12.1	8.5	1.5	21.4	11.2
268	Honduras	2015	GG	AC	...	...	...	...	...	...	...	...	...	...
343	Jamaica	2015	GG	AC	...	...	...	...	...	...	...	...	...	...
278	Nicaragua	2015	BA	CA	...	...	...	...	...	...	...	...	...	...
288	Paraguay	2014	GG	CA	...	...	...	...	...	...	...	...	...	...
293	Peru	2015	GG	CA	...	...	...	...	...	...	...	...	...	...
366	Suriname	2012	BA	CA	...	...	...	...	...	...	...	...	...	...
369	Trinidad and Tobago	2012	GL2	CA	23.2	1.7	7.6	17.4	1.8	7.7	7.2	1.9	15.2	18.1
298	Uruguay	2014	GL2	CA	...	...	...	...	...	...	...	...	...	...

GDP used for calculations

Domestic Currency

Code	Country	Scale	2011	2012	2013	2014	2015
	Advanced Economies						
	Euro Area						
122	Austria	Millions	308,630	317,056	322,878	329,296	337,286
124	Belgium	Millions	379,106	387,447	392,675	400,408	409,407
423	Cyprus	Millions	19,547	19,469	18,065	17,394	17,421
939	Estonia	Millions	16,668	18,006	19,015	19,963	20,461
172	Finland	Millions	196,869	199,793	203,338	205,364	209,149
132	France	Billions	2,059	2,087	2,115	2,140	2,181
134	Germany	Billions	2,703	2,758	2,826	2,924	3,033
174	Greece	Millions	207,029	191,204	180,389	177,559	176,023
178	Ireland	Millions	173,070	175,754	180,209	193,160	255,815
136	Italy	Billions	1,637	1,613	1,604	1,612	1,636
941	Latvia	Millions	20,244	21,819	22,741	23,556	24,294
946	Lithuania	Millions	31,263	33,335	34,962	36,444	37,124
137	Luxembourg	Millions	42,227	43,574	46,541	48,898	52,112
181	Malta	Millions	6,875	7,209	7,671	8,093	8,788
138	Netherlands	Millions	642,929	645,164	652,748	663,008	676,531
182	Portugal	Millions	176,167	168,398	170,269	173,446	179,369
936	Slovak Republic	Millions	70,444	72,420	73,835	75,560	78,071
961	Slovenia	Millions	36,896	36,003	35,917	37,332	38,570
184	Spain	Billions	1,070	1,043	1,031	1,041	1,081
193	Australia	Billions	1,457	1,505	1,555	1,600	1,628
156	Canada	Billions	1,770	1,823	1,892	1,973	1,983
532	China, P.R.: Hong Kong SAR	Billions	1,934	2,037	2,138	2,258	2,403
546	China, P.R.: Macao SAR	Millions	294,347	343,795	411,839	443,468	368,728
935	Czech Republic	Billions	4,034	4,060	4,098	4,314	4,555
128	Denmark	Billions	1,833	1,883	1,904	1,943	1,985
176	Iceland	Billions	1,701	1,777	1,889	2,004	2,205
436	Israel	Millions	935,225	993,441	1,059,101	1,104,746	1,163,769
158	Japan	Billions	474,244	474,726	482,734	490,471	...
542	Korea, Republic of	Trillions	1,333	1,377	1,429	1,486	1,559
196	New Zealand	Millions	211,219	216,604	226,658	238,277	246,086
142	Norway	Billions	2,792	2,965	3,071	3,154	3,131
135	San Marino	Millions	1,478	1,401	1,405	1,391	1,404
576	Singapore	Millions	346,173	361,499	375,751	388,169	402,458
144	Sweden	Billions	3,657	3,685	3,770	3,918	4,159
146	Switzerland	Millions	618,628	623,939	635,136	642,426	639,026
112	United Kingdom	Billions	1,628	1,675	1,740	1,822	1,870
111	United States	Billions	15,518	16,155	16,692	17,393	18,037
	Emerging and Developing Economies						
	Emerging and Developing Asia						
513	Bangladesh	Billions	9,855	11,271	12,713	14,297	16,227
514	Bhutan	Millions	78,723	91,201	101,416	112,462	125,185
522	Cambodia	Billions	52,069	56,682	61,390	67,740	73,423
924	China, P.R.: Mainland	Billions	48,604	54,099	59,696	64,849	69,630
819	Fiji	Millions	5,385	5,613	7,428	8,095	...
534	India	Billions	87,360	99,513	112,728	124,882	135,761
536	Indonesia	Trillions	7,832	8,616	9,546	10,566	11,541
826	Kiribati	Thousands	171,739	181,614	193,854	206,423	213,138
544	Lao People's Democratic Republic	Billions	64,727	75,251	84,572	95,406	102,543
548	Malaysia	Millions	911,733	971,251	1,018,614	1,106,465	1,157,138
556	Maldives	Millions	35,768	38,693	42,952	47,122	48,044
867	Marshall Islands, Republic of	Thousands	172,957	184,359	190,180	186,717	184,598
868	Micronesia, Federated States of	Thousands	310,439	325,835	315,726	318,072	317,842
948	Mongolia	Billions	11,168	14,621	19,326	21,937	...
558	Nepal	Millions	1,366,954	1,527,344	1,695,011	1,964,540	2,120,470
565	Palau	Thousands	199,850	214,160	228,721	250,879	287,413
566	Philippines	Billions	9,708	10,561	11,538	12,645	13,307
862	Samoa	Thousands	1,765,126	1,843,384	1,838,907	1,866,419	1,948,940
813	Solomon Islands	Millions	6,776	7,541	8,109	8,530	8,937
524	Sri Lanka	Billions	6,543	7,579	8,674	9,785	11,183
578	Thailand	Billions	11,300	12,349	12,901	13,132	13,537
537	Timor-Leste	Millions	5,973	6,809	5,641	4,175	2,874
846	Vanuatu	Millions	70,873	72,415	75,803	79,819	...
582	Vietnam	Billions	2,779,880	3,245,419	3,584,300	3,937,856	...
	Europe						
	Central and Eastern Europe						
914	Albania	Millions	1,300,624	1,332,811	1,350,053	1,394,419	1,435,751
963	Bosnia and Herzegovina	Millions	26,210	26,193	26,743	27,304	28,208
918	Bulgaria	Millions	80,100	81,544	81,971	83,612	86,373
960	Croatia	Millions	332,587	330,456	329,571	328,431	...
944	Hungary	Billions	28,134	28,628	30,065	32,180	33,712
967	Kosovo, Republic of	Millions	4,815	5,059	5,327	5,568	5,772
962	Macedonia, F.Y.R. of	Millions	459,789	458,621	474,196	525,843	...

GDP used for calculations

Domestic Currency

	Country	Scale	2011	2012	2013	2014	2015
964	Poland	Millions	1,566,557	1,628,992	1,656,341	1,719,146	1,789,696
968	Romania	Millions	565,097	595,367	637,456	667,577	712,832
942	Serbia, Republic of	Billions	3,408	3,584	3,876	3,878	...
186	Turkey	Billions	1,298	1,417	1,567	1,748	1,954
	CIS						
911	Armenia	Billions	3,778	4,266	4,556	4,829	5,032
912	Azerbaijan	Millions	51,158	53,968	57,708	58,978	54,352
913	Belarus	Billions	297,158	530,356	649,111	778,095	869,702
915	Georgia	Millions	24,344	26,167	26,847	29,150	31,692
916	Kazakhstan	Billions	29,380	32,194	37,085	40,755	40,878
917	Kyrgyz Republic	Millions	285,989	310,471	355,295	400,694	423,636
921	Moldova	Millions	82,349	88,228	100,510	112,050	122,170
922	Russian Federation	Billions	59,698	66,927	71,017	77,945	80,804
926	Ukraine	Millions	1,299,991	1,404,669	1,465,198	1,586,915	1,979,458
927	Uzbekistan	Billions	77,866	96,723	119,750	145,999	171,369
	Middle East, North Africa and Pakistan						
512	Afghanistan, Islamic Republic of	Millions	943,671	1,113,941	1,116,827	1,173,182	...
612	Algeria	Billions	14,589	16,209	16,644	17,205	...
419	Bahrain, Kingdom of	Millions	10,921	11,416	12,370	12,735	...
469	Egypt	Billions	1,442	1,657	1,844	2,102	2,430
433	Iraq	Billions	211,310	214,768	235,550	260,610	...
439	Jordan	Millions	20,477	21,965	23,852	25,437	26,637
443	Kuwait	Millions	42,512	48,722	49,392	46,285	34,315
446	Lebanon	Billions	60,414	66,481	71,755	75,291	77,136
686	Morocco	Millions	820,077	847,881	901,366	924,769	...
449	Oman	Millions	26,033	29,004	30,061	31,451	24,655
564	Pakistan	Billions	18,276	20,047	22,489	25,402	...
744	Tunisia	Millions	64,690	70,658	76,351	82,562	...
466	United Arab Emirates	Millions	1,279,969	1,371,429	1,427,128	1,476,191	1,359,913
487	West Bank and Gaza	Millions	37,337	43,322	44,843	45,429	49,290
474	Yemen, Republic of	Billions	6,645	6,875	7,460	9,289	...
	Sub-Saharan Africa						
	CEMAC						
626	Central African Republic	Millions	1,036,029	1,107,694	759,705	851,644	...
634	Congo, Republic of	Billions	6,804	6,979	6,657	6,690	5,228
	WAEMU						
638	Benin	Billions	3,687	4,144	4,501	4,734	5,010
748	Burkina Faso	Billions	5,060	5,701	6,026	6,162	6,509
662	Côte d'Ivoire	Billions	11,977	13,805	15,460	17,021	...
678	Mali	Billions	6,124	6,352	6,544	7,114	7,748
722	Senegal	Billions	6,783	7,263	7,338	7,583	8,078
742	Togo	Billions	1,772	1,999	2,149	2,277	2,464
614	Angola	Billions	9,780	11,011	12,056	12,462	12,321
616	Botswana	Millions	107,057	112,732	120,858	141,942	...
618	Burundi	Billions	2,820	3,524	4,074	4,669	...
624	Cabo Verde	Millions	147,924	150,351	152,640	154,156	...
644	Ethiopia	Millions	511,157	747,326	864,673	1,047,393	...
652	Ghana	Millions	59,816	73,109	93,462	113,344	...
664	Kenya	Billions	3,726	4,261	4,745	5,398	6,224
666	Lesotho	Millions	18,324	19,783	21,975	24,071	...
668	Liberia	Thousands	1,540,276	1,745,871	1,961,991	2,013,381	...
674	Madagascar	Billions	20,034	21,774	23,397	25,775	28,585
676	Malawi	Billions	1,253	1,502	2,011	2,570	3,201
684	Mauritius	Millions	322,958	343,973	366,228	387,068	...
688	Mozambique	Millions	383,608	423,734	465,326	525,871	...
728	Namibia	Millions	90,108	106,864	122,749	139,500	146,619
694	Nigeria	Billions	63,713	72,600	81,010	90,137	...
714	Rwanda	Billions	3,846	4,437	4,864	5,394	5,837
716	São Tomé and Príncipe	Billions	4,469	4,952	5,582	6,237	...
718	Seychelles	Millions	12,609	14,519	15,864	17,199	18,102
724	Sierra Leone	Billions	12,753	16,461	21,287	22,415	...
199	South Africa	Billions	3,024	3,254	3,549	3,813	4,014
734	Swaziland	Millions	36,037	40,334	44,051	47,892	...
738	Tanzania	Billions	52,763	61,434	70,953	79,718	90,864
746	Uganda	Billions	53,249	61,662	66,214	71,544	78,783
754	Zambia	Millions	101,184	116,348	144,775	163,733	...
698	Zimbabwe		10,956	12,472	13,490	13,833	...
	Western Hemisphere						
	ECCU						
312	Anguilla	Thousands	797,230	768,740	782,250	826,690	...
311	Antigua and Barbuda	Millions	3,051	3,253	3,242	3,427	...
321	Dominica	Millions	1,373	1,390	1,395	1,452	...
328	Grenada	Millions	2,102	2,160	2,256	2,382	...
351	Montserrat	Thousands	171,990	170,760	162,620	170,330	...

GDP used for calculations

Domestic Currency

	Country	Scale	2011	2012	2013	2014	2015
361	St. Kitts and Nevis	Millions	1,966	1,976	2,090	2,251	...
362	St. Lucia	Millions	3,482	3,517	3,607	3,687	...
364	St. Vincent and the Grenadines	Millions	1,828	1,875	1,941	1,967	...
213	Argentina	Millions	2,179,024	2,637,914	3,348,308	4,579,086	5,843,142
313	Bahamas, The	Millions	7,890	8,399	8,522	8,618	8,854
316	Barbados	Millions	8,666	8,626	8,562	8,709	...
339	Belize	Millions	3,017	3,173	3,223	3,398	...
223	Brazil	Billions	4,374	4,806	5,316	5,687	5,904
228	Chile	Billions	121,232	128,997	137,235	147,562	157,130
233	Colombia	Billions	619,894	664,240	710,497	757,506	800,849
238	Costa Rica	Billions	21,392	23,371	24,781	26,703	28,279
243	Dominican Republic	Billions	2,218	2,378	2,559	2,786	3,023
253	El Salvador	Millions	23,139	23,814	24,351	25,054	25,850
258	Guatemala	Millions	371,278	394,634	423,115	454,098	...
268	Honduras	Millions	335,028	361,349	376,539	409,612	451,279
343	Jamaica	Billions	1,240	1,314	1,431	1,542	1,667
278	Nicaragua	Millions	218,763	245,800	268,854	306,061	345,959
288	Paraguay	Billions	105,203	108,832	125,152	137,798	144,249
293	Peru	Millions	469,883	507,697	545,822	575,814	611,903
366	Suriname	Millions	14,452	16,434	16,932	17,194	...
369	Trinidad and Tobago	Millions	145,964	149,717	155,395	185,057	...
298	Uruguay	Millions	926,356	1,041,211	1,178,332	1,330,508	1,460,439

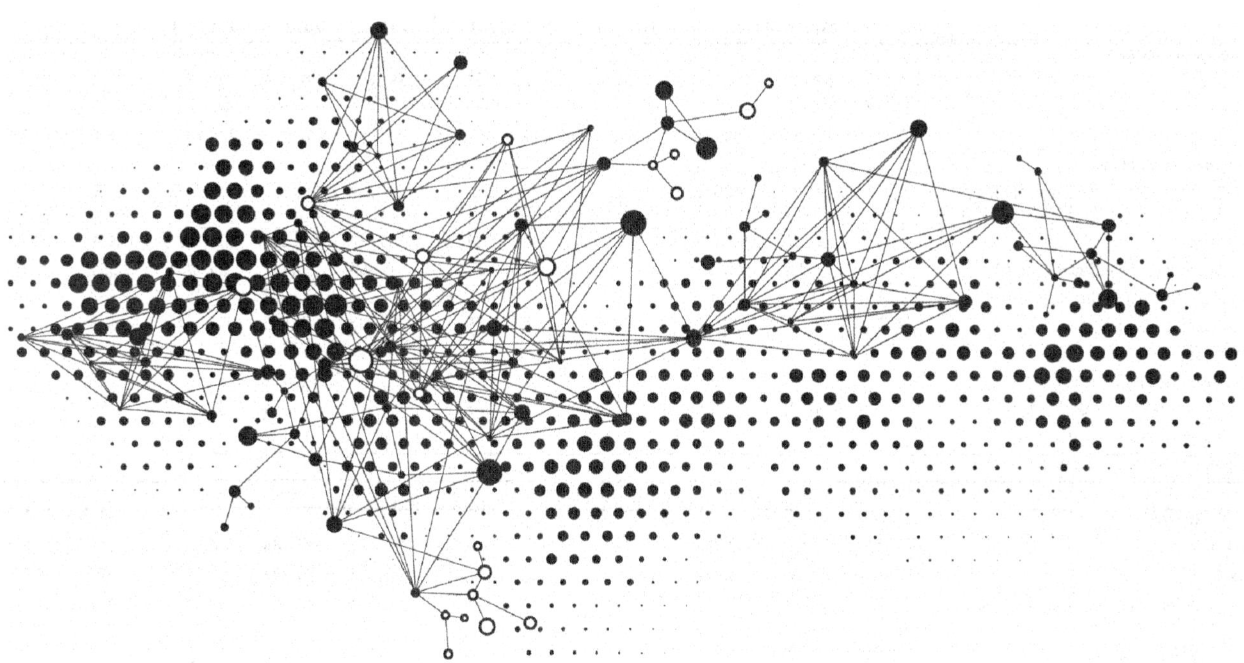

Country Tables

Afghanistan, Islamic Republic of (512)

In Millions of Afghanis (AFN) / Fiscal Year Ends March 20th

		Budgetary Central Government			Central Government (excl. Social Security)			Central Government (incl. Social Security)			General Government		
		2011	2012	2013	2011	2012	2013	2011	2012	2013	2011	2012	2013
	Statement of operations												
1	Revenue	190,816	228,522	302,720	...	...	764,535	797,697	687,744	764,535	801,049	691,315	768,300
2	Expense	168,339	196,232	230,373	...	...	479,367	505,827	435,481	479,367	507,118	437,320	481,469
GOB	**Gross operating balance**	**22,477**	**32,290**	**72,347**	**291,870**	**252,263**	**285,168**	**291,870**	**252,263**	**285,168**	**293,930**	**253,995**	**286,831**
NOB	**Net operating balance**	...	...	...	...	...	...	...	...	...	...	...	...
31	Net/Gross investment in nonfinancial assets	27,766	39,118	46,346	...	...	259,175	297,234	258,855	259,175	297,490	259,442	261,541
2M	Expenditure	196,105	235,350	276,719	...	...	738,542	803,061	694,336	738,542	804,608	696,762	743,010
NLB	**Net lending (+) / Net borrowing (-)**	**-5,289**	**-6,828**	**26,001**	...	...	**25,993**	**-5,364**	**-6,592**	**25,993**	**-3,559**	**-5,447**	**25,290**
32	Net acquisition of financial assets	9,185	21,913	963	...	...	859	9,951	22,073	859	11,756	23,219	157
33	Net incurrence of liabilities	14,474	28,741	-25,038	...	...	-25,134	15,315	28,665	-25,134	15,315	28,665	-25,134
NLBz	Statistical discrepancy	0	0	-0	...	...	0	0	-0	0	0	0	1
	Memorandum items												
PB	Primary net lending / net borrowing	-5,197	-6,715	26,269	...	...	26,261	-5,272	-6,474	26,261	-3,457	-5,279	25,578
GB	Government balance per national definition	...	...	...	...	...	...	...	...	...	...	...	...
	Statement of other economic flows												
	Balance sheet												
	Table 1 Revenue												
1	**Revenue**	**190,816**	**228,522**	**302,720**	...	...	**764,535**	**797,697**	**687,744**	**764,535**	**801,049**	**691,315**	**768,300**
11	**Taxes**	**75,530**	**79,057**	**80,822**	...	...	**81,115**	**75,824**	**79,297**	**81,115**	**76,776**	**80,011**	**81,149**
111	Taxes on income, profits, and capital gains	21,517	25,610	27,674	...	...	27,653	21,517	25,610	27,653	22,466	26,320	27,685
1111	Payable by individuals	7,668	9,809	9,963	...	...	9,963	7,668	9,809	9,963	8,617	10,519	9,994
1112	Payable by corporations and other enterprises	11,434	13,831	16,258	...	...	16,258	11,434	13,831	16,258	11,434	13,831	16,258
1113	Other taxes on income, profits, and capital gains	2,414	1,970	1,453	...	...	1,432	2,414	1,970	1,432	2,414	1,970	1,432
112	Taxes on payroll and workforce	—	—	—	—	—	—	—	—	—	—	—	—
113	Taxes on property	1,411	2,143	1,233	...	...	1,233	1,411	2,143	1,233	1,412	2,146	1,236
114	Taxes on goods and services	20,942	21,529	19,386	...	...	19,386	20,919	21,452	19,386	20,922	21,453	19,387
1141	General taxes on goods and services	19,084	19,932	18,145	...	...	18,145	19,060	19,856	18,145	19,063	19,856	18,145
1142	Excises	—	—	—	—	—	—	—	—	—	—	—	—
115	Taxes on international trade and transactions	30,557	29,055	28,316	...	...	28,316	30,557	29,055	28,316	30,557	29,055	28,316
116	Other taxes	1,103	720	4,213	...	...	4,526	1,420	1,037	4,526	1,420	1,037	4,526
12	**Social contributions**	**2,735**	**3,119**	**3,478**	...	...	**3,478**	**2,735**	**3,119**	**3,478**	**2,735**	**3,119**	**3,478**
121	Social security contributions	2,735	3,119	3,478	...	...	3,478	2,735	3,119	3,478	2,735	3,119	3,478
122	Other social contributions	—	—	—	—	—	—	—	—	—	—	—	—
13	**Grants**	**93,541**	**124,148**	**196,297**	...	...	**657,423**	**699,820**	**582,801**	**657,423**	**699,820**	**582,801**	**657,423**
131	From foreign governments	67,572	88,627	140,082	...	...	601,208	673,851	547,280	601,208	673,851	547,280	601,208
132	From international organizations	25,970	35,521	56,215	...	...	56,215	25,970	35,521	56,215	25,970	35,521	56,215
133	From other general government units	—	—	—	—	—	—	—	—	—	—	—	—
1331	Current	—	—	—	—	—	—	—	—	—	—	—	—
1332	Capital	—	—	—	—	—	—	—	—	—	—	—	—
14	**Other revenue**	**19,009**	**22,199**	**22,122**	...	...	**22,519**	**19,317**	**22,527**	**22,519**	**21,717**	**25,385**	**26,250**
	Table 2 Expense by economic type												
2	**Expense**	**168,339**	**196,232**	**230,373**	...	...	**479,367**	**505,827**	**435,481**	**479,367**	**507,118**	**437,320**	**481,469**
21	**Compensation of employees**	**110,897**	**125,314**	**137,772**	...	...	**138,204**	**111,122**	**125,459**	**138,204**	**112,008**	**126,362**	**139,207**
211	Wages and salaries	110,897	125,314	137,772	...	...	138,204	111,122	125,459	138,204	112,008	126,362	139,207
212	Employers' social contributions	—	—	—	—	—	—	—	—	—	—	—	—
22	**Use of goods and services**	**45,734**	**57,611**	**72,864**	...	...	**321,312**	**383,081**	**296,595**	**321,312**	**384,182**	**297,822**	**323,012**
23	**Consumption of fixed capital**	—	...	...	—	—	...	—	—	...	—	—	...
24	**Interest**	**92**	**113**	**268**	...	...	**268**	**92**	**118**	**268**	**103**	**167**	**288**
25	**Subsidies**	**1,100**	**1,275**	**900**	...	...	**900**	**1,100**	**1,275**	**900**	**1,100**	**1,275**	**900**
26	**Grants**	**963**	**381**	**880**	—	—	**880**	**716**	**381**	**880**	—	—	—
261	To foreign governments	—	—	—	—	—	—	—	—	—	—	—	—
262	To international organizations	—	—	—	—	—	—	—	—	—	—	—	—
263	To other general government units	963	381	880	—	—	880	716	381	880	—	—	—
2631	Current	1	—	74	—	—	74	1	—	74	—	—	—
2632	Capital	961	381	806	—	—	806	715	381	806	—	—	—

Afghanistan, Islamic Republic of (512)

In Millions of Afghanis (AFN) / Fiscal Year Ends March 20th

		Budgetary Central Government			Central Government (excl. Social Security)			Central Government (incl. Social Security)			General Government		
		2011	2012	2013	2011	2012	2013	2011	2012	2013	2011	2012	2013
27	**Social benefits**	**8,605**	**10,070**	**12,028**	**...**	**...**	**12,048**	**8,613**	**10,070**	**12,048**	**8,620**	**10,090**	**12,296**
271	Social security benefits	4,198	5,147	6,544	...	...	6,544	4,198	5,147	6,544	4,198	5,147	6,544
272	Social assistance benefits	3,587	3,925	3,757	...	...	3,757	3,587	3,925	3,757	3,587	3,925	3,757
273	Employment-related social benefits	820	998	1,727	...	...	1,748	828	998	1,748	835	1,018	1,995
28	**Other expense**	**949**	**1,469**	**5,662**	**...**	**...**	**5,755**	**1,104**	**1,583**	**5,755**	**1,106**	**1,604**	**5,767**
281	Property expense other than interest	246	218	178	...	...	178	246	218	178	246	220	178
282	Transfers not elsewhere classified	703	1,251	5,484	...	...	5,576	858	1,365	5,576	860	1,384	5,589
2821	Current	703	1,251	5,484	...	...	5,484	703	1,251	5,484	705	1,270	5,496
2822	Capital	—	—	—	...	...	93	155	114	93	155	114	93
	Table 3 Transactions in assets and liabilities												
3	**Change in net worth from transactions**	**...**	**...**	**...**	**...**	**...**	**...**	**...**	**...**	**...**	**...**	**...**	**...**
31	**Net/Gross investment in nonfinancial assets**	**27,766**	**39,118**	**46,346**	**...**	**...**	**259,175**	**297,234**	**258,855**	**259,175**	**297,490**	**259,442**	**261,541**
311	Fixed assets	30,031	42,406	46,753	...	...	259,581	299,495	262,143	259,581	301,422	264,028	262,945
3111	Buildings and structures	20,697	29,558	36,189	...	...	94,326	73,196	94,762	94,326	74,871	96,643	97,627
3112	Machinery and equipment	9,334	12,848	10,563	...	...	165,255	226,300	167,381	165,255	226,551	167,385	165,318
3113	Other fixed assets	—	—	—	—	—	—	—	—	—	—	—	—
3114	Weapons systems	—	—	—	—	—	—	—	—	—	—	—	—
312	Inventories	—	—	—	—	—	—	—	—	—	—	—	—
313	Valuables	4	14	1	—	...	1	4	14	1	4	14	1
314	Nonproduced assets	-2,270	-3,302	-408	...	...	-408	-2,266	-3,302	-408	-3,937	-4,600	-1,406
3141	Land	601	291	570	...	...	570	605	291	570	-1,066	-1,007	-428
3142	Mineral and energy resources	-2,871	-3,593	-978	...	...	-978	-2,871	-3,593	-978	-2,871	-3,593	-978
3143	Other naturally occurring assets	—	—	—	—	—	—	—	—	—	—	—	—
3144	Intangible nonproduced assets	—	—	—	—	—	—	—	—	—	—	—	—
32	**Net acquisition of financial assets**	**9,185**	**21,913**	**963**	**...**	**...**	**859**	**9,951**	**22,073**	**859**	**11,756**	**23,219**	**157**
	By instrument												
3201	Monetary gold and SDRs	—	—	—	—	—	—	—	—	—	—	—	—
3202	Currency and deposits	7,802	24,084	2,935	...	...	1,542	8,520	24,188	1,542	10,239	25,272	768
3203	Debt securities	—	—	—	—	—	—	—	—	—	—	—	—
3204	Loans	-24	-25	-18	...	...	718	-24	-20	718	-24	-20	718
3205	Equity and investment fund shares	—	—	—	—	—	—	1	—	—	1	—	—
3206	Insurance, pension, and standardized guarantee schemes	—	—	—	—	—	—	—	—	—	—	—	—
3207	Financial derivatives and employee stock options	—	—	—	—	—	—	—	—	—	—	—	—
3208	Other accounts receivable	1,406	-2,145	-1,954	...	...	-1,401	1,454	-2,095	-1,401	1,539	-2,033	-1,329
	By debtor												
321	Domestic debtors	9,185	21,913	963	...	...	859	9,951	22,073	859	11,756	23,219	157
322	External debtors	—	—	—	—	—	—	—	—	—	—	—	—
33	**Net incurrence of liabilities**	**14,474**	**28,741**	**-25,038**	**...**	**...**	**-25,134**	**15,315**	**28,665**	**-25,134**	**15,315**	**28,665**	**-25,134**
	By instrument												
3301	Special Drawing Rights (SDRs)	—	—	—	—	—	—	—	—	—	—	—	—
3302	Currency and deposits	—	—	—	—	—	—	—	—	—	—	—	—
3303	Debt securities	—	—	—	—	—	—	—	—	—	—	—	—
3304	Loans	2,257	3,681	1,335	...	...	1,335	2,527	3,681	1,335	2,527	3,681	1,335
3305	Equity and investment fund shares	—	—	—	—	—	—	—	—	—	—	—	—
3306	Insurance, pension, and standardized guarantee schemes	—	—	—	—	—	—	—	—	—	—	—	—
3307	Financial derivatives and employee stock options	—	—	—	—	—	—	—	—	—	—	—	—
3308	Other accounts payable	12,216	25,060	-26,373	...	...	-26,469	12,788	24,984	-26,469	12,788	24,984	-26,469
	By creditor												
331	Domestic creditors	2,910	3,192	2,925	...	...	2,829	3,482	3,116	2,829	3,482	3,116	2,829
332	External creditors	11,564	25,549	-27,963	...	...	-27,963	11,833	25,549	-27,963	11,833	25,549	-27,963
	Table 4 Holding gains and losses in assets and liabilities												
	Table 5 Holding gains and losses in assets and liabilities												
	Table 6 Balance sheet												

Afghanistan, Islamic Republic of (512)

In Millions of Afghanis (AFN) / Fiscal Year Ends March 20th

		Budgetary Central Government			Central Government (excl. Social Security)			Central Government (incl. Social Security)			General Government		
		2011	2012	2013	2011	2012	2013	2011	2012	2013	2011	2012	2013
	Table 7 Expenditure by functions of government												
7	**Expenditure**	**196,105**	**235,350**	**276,719**	**...**	**...**	**738,542**	**803,061**	**694,336**	**738,542**	**804,608**	**696,762**	**743,010**
701	**General public services**	**16,973**	**19,680**	**22,658**	**...**	**...**	**34,278**	**51,185**	**54,395**	**34,278**	**51,494**	**55,075**	**34,480**
7017	Public debt transactions	92	113	268	...	...	268	92	118	268	103	167	288
7018	Transfers of general character between levels of government	...	...	880	...	...	880	...	...	880	...	...	—
702	**Defense**	**45,806**	**54,957**	**77,385**	**...**	**...**	**345,906**	**310,778**	**281,471**	**345,906**	**310,778**	**281,471**	**345,906**
703	**Public order and safety**	**42,159**	**49,954**	**54,990**	**...**	**...**	**161,765**	**208,836**	**147,435**	**161,765**	**208,836**	**147,435**	**161,765**
704	**Economic affairs**	**42,123**	**55,439**	**60,067**	**...**	**...**	**103,536**	**130,942**	**116,003**	**103,536**	**131,329**	**116,812**	**105,868**
7042	Agriculture, forestry, fishing, and hunting	8,346	10,125	13,460	...	...	13,460	...	...	13,460	...	...	13,460
7043	Fuel and energy	3,343	3,774	2,783	...	...	2,783	...	...	2,783	...	...	2,783
7044	Mining, manufacturing, and construction	471	1,205	605	...	...	605	...	...	605	...	...	605
7045	Transport	15,869	19,932	17,614	...	...	17,614	...	...	17,614	...	...	19,811
7046	Communication	1,570	1,618	1,771	...	...	1,771	...	...	1,771	...	...	1,771
705	**Environmental protection**	**178**	**207**	**179**	**...**	**...**	**2,915**	**2,812**	**2,577**	**2,915**	**3,059**	**2,847**	**3,345**
706	**Housing and community amenities**	**877**	**1,115**	**1,763**	**...**	**...**	**2,640**	**5,266**	**4,977**	**2,640**	**5,807**	**5,576**	**4,036**
707	**Health**	**7,137**	**8,196**	**10,281**	**...**	**...**	**20,322**	**31,199**	**22,601**	**20,322**	**31,199**	**22,601**	**20,322**
7072	Outpatient services	...	...	—	...	...	—	...	...	—	...	...	—
7073	Hospital services	...	...	—	...	...	2,490	...	...	2,490	...	...	2,490
7074	Public health services	...	...	—	...	...	1,807	...	...	1,807	...	...	1,807
708	**Recreation, culture and religion**	**1,996**	**2,170**	**2,542**	**...**	**...**	**3,239**	**3,465**	**3,419**	**3,239**	**3,527**	**3,487**	**3,346**
709	**Education**	**30,636**	**34,359**	**39,753**	**...**	**...**	**52,992**	**41,413**	**45,216**	**52,992**	**41,413**	**45,216**	**52,992**
7091	Pre-primary and primary education	...	...	8,639	...	...	8,639	...	...	8,639	...	...	8,639
7092	Secondary education	...	...	24,512	...	...	24,512	...	...	24,512	...	...	24,512
7094	Tertiary education	...	...	4,215	...	...	4,215	...	...	4,215	...	...	4,215
710	**Social protection**	**8,221**	**9,274**	**7,101**	**...**	**...**	**10,950**	**17,167**	**16,242**	**10,950**	**17,167**	**16,242**	**10,950**
7z	Statistical discrepancy: Expenditure	—	—	...	—	—	...	0	0	...	0	0	...
	Table 8 Financial transactions by counterpart sector												
	Table 9 Total other economic flows in assets and liabilities												

Albania (914)

In Millions of Albanian Leks (ALL) / Fiscal Year Ends December 31st

		Budgetary Central Government			Central Government (excl. Social Security)			Central Government (incl. Social Security)			General Government		
		2013	2014	2015	2013	2014	2015	2013	2014	2015	2013	2014	2015
	Statement of operations												
1	Revenue	248,839	283,134	296,513	248,839	283,134	296,513	307,109	352,632	366,138	318,982	366,612	379,381
2	Expense	268,375	277,593	278,855	268,375	277,593	278,855	326,183	340,213	350,633	326,416	336,445	350,062
GOB	**Gross operating balance**	**-19,536**	**5,541**	**17,657**	**-19,536**	**5,541**	**17,657**	**-19,075**	**12,420**	**15,505**	**-7,434**	**30,167**	**29,319**
NOB	**Net operating balance**	...	...	...	...	...	...	...	...	...	...	...	...
31	Net/Gross investment in nonfinancial assets	52,618	56,153	58,671	52,618	56,153	58,671	52,827	56,289	58,941	66,167	72,042	75,021
2M	Expenditure	320,993	333,746	337,526	320,993	333,746	337,526	379,010	396,501	409,574	392,583	408,488	425,082
NLB	**Net lending (+) / Net borrowing (-)**	**-72,154**	**-50,612**	**-41,014**	**-72,154**	**-50,612**	**-41,014**	**-71,901**	**-43,869**	**-43,436**	**-73,601**	**-41,875**	**-45,701**
32	Net acquisition of financial assets	7,960	-3,854	7,031	7,960	-3,854	7,031	8,045	1,476	4,848	6,859	1,545	9,346
33	Net incurrence of liabilities	80,114	46,758	48,045	80,114	46,758	48,045	79,946	45,344	48,282	80,460	43,419	55,046
NLBz	Statistical discrepancy	0	1	0	0	1	0	1	1	2	0	2	1
	Memorandum items												
PB	Primary net lending / net borrowing	-28,818	-10,676	-2,371	-28,818	-10,676	-2,371	-28,768	-4,127	-4,910	-30,436	-2,107	-7,120
GB	Government balance per national definition	...	...	...	...	...	...	...	...	...	...	...	...
	Statement of other economic flows												
	Balance sheet												
6	**Net worth**	**-281,621**	**-245,596**	**-200,945**	**-281,621**	**-245,596**	**-200,945**	**-273,259**	**-224,392**	**-182,980**	**-93,706**	**-20,922**	**53,060**
61	Nonfinancial assets	496,608	554,562	663,946	496,608	554,562	663,946	498,680	556,650	666,257	669,384	750,168	915,883
62	Financial assets	165,533	218,544	273,812	165,533	218,544	273,812	180,939	241,998	296,263	206,791	265,060	297,636
63	Liabilities	943,762	1,018,701	1,138,703	943,762	1,018,701	1,138,703	952,878	1,023,041	1,145,501	969,881	1,036,151	1,160,459
	Table 1 Revenue												
1	**Revenue**	**248,839**	**283,134**	**296,513**	**248,839**	**283,134**	**296,513**	**307,109**	**352,632**	**366,138**	**318,982**	**366,612**	**379,381**
11	**Taxes**	**222,803**	**255,368**	**265,573**	**222,803**	**255,368**	**265,573**	**222,803**	**255,368**	**265,573**	**231,055**	**265,291**	**274,792**
111	Taxes on income, profits, and capital gains	44,012	48,712	54,624	44,012	48,712	54,624	44,012	48,712	54,624	46,087	50,392	56,666
1111	Payable by individuals	21,278	19,462	21,183	21,278	19,462	21,183	21,278	19,462	21,183	21,278	19,463	21,183
1112	Payable by corporations and other enterprises	15,300	21,686	24,976	15,300	21,686	24,976	15,300	21,686	24,976	17,244	23,366	27,018
1113	Other taxes on income, profits, and capital gains	7,434	7,563	8,465	7,434	7,563	8,465	7,434	7,563	8,465	7,564	7,563	8,465
112	Taxes on payroll and workforce	—	—	—	—	—	—	—	—	—	—	—	—
113	Taxes on property	1,016	0	—	1,016	0	—	1,016	0	—	2,855	3,101	3,315
114	Taxes on goods and services	166,375	195,998	200,013	166,375	195,998	200,013	166,375	195,998	200,013	170,169	200,532	203,500
1141	General taxes on goods and services	104,742	125,393	125,783	104,742	125,393	125,783	104,742	125,393	125,783	105,355	125,974	126,389
1142	Excises	42,250	44,813	42,321	42,250	44,813	42,321	42,250	44,813	42,321	42,250	44,813	42,321
115	Taxes on international trade and transactions	10,948	10,234	10,656	10,948	10,234	10,656	10,948	10,234	10,656	10,948	10,234	10,656
116	Other taxes	452	425	280	452	425	280	452	425	280	995	1,032	656
12	**Social contributions**	—	—	—	—	—	—	**57,792**	**68,655**	**69,235**	**57,792**	**68,655**	**69,235**
121	Social security contributions	—	—	—	—	—	—	57,792	68,655	69,235	57,792	68,655	69,235
122	Other social contributions	—	—	—	—	—	—	—	—	—	—	—	—
13	**Grants**	**5,980**	**10,432**	**11,317**	**5,980**	**10,432**	**11,317**	**5,980**	**10,432**	**11,317**	**6,073**	**10,631**	**11,420**
131	From foreign governments	1,973	1,299	164	1,973	1,299	164	1,973	1,299	164	1,964	1,380	213
132	From international organizations	4,007	9,124	11,137	4,007	9,124	11,137	4,007	9,124	11,137	4,108	9,251	11,207
133	From other general government units	0	9	16	0	9	16	—	9	16	-0	—	-0
1331	Current	0	9	16	0	9	16	—	9	16	-0	—	-0
1332	Capital	—	—	—	—	—	—	—	—	—	—	—	—
14	**Other revenue**	**20,056**	**17,334**	**19,622**	**20,056**	**17,334**	**19,622**	**20,534**	**18,177**	**20,012**	**24,063**	**22,034**	**23,933**
	Table 2 Expense by economic type												
2	**Expense**	**268,375**	**277,593**	**278,855**	**268,375**	**277,593**	**278,855**	**326,183**	**340,213**	**350,633**	**326,416**	**336,445**	**350,062**
21	**Compensation of employees**	**81,930**	**82,984**	**84,175**	**81,930**	**82,984**	**84,175**	**83,480**	**84,615**	**85,803**	**95,844**	**97,186**	**97,905**
211	Wages and salaries	70,548	71,265	72,341	70,548	71,265	72,341	71,883	72,674	73,741	82,608	83,554	84,213
212	Employers' social contributions	11,383	11,719	11,834	11,383	11,719	11,834	11,597	11,941	12,062	13,236	13,632	13,692
22	**Use of goods and services**	**32,023**	**24,250**	**28,227**	**32,023**	**24,250**	**28,227**	**32,878**	**25,116**	**29,190**	**41,065**	**34,021**	**38,147**
23	**Consumption of fixed capital**	...	...	...	...	...	...	...	...	...	...	...	...
24	**Interest**	**43,336**	**39,936**	**38,642**	**43,336**	**39,936**	**38,642**	**43,133**	**39,742**	**38,526**	**43,165**	**39,769**	**38,582**
25	**Subsidies**	**975**	**1,151**	**1,305**	**975**	**1,151**	**1,305**	**975**	**1,151**	**1,305**	**1,875**	**1,761**	**1,862**

Albania (914)

In Millions of Albanian Leks (ALL) / Fiscal Year Ends December 31st

		Budgetary Central Government			Central Government (excl. Social Security)			Central Government (incl. Social Security)			General Government		
		2013	2014	2015	2013	2014	2015	2013	2014	2015	2013	2014	2015
26	**Grants**	**97,333**	**105,417**	**97,217**	**97,333**	**105,417**	**97,217**	**43,642**	**49,053**	**44,827**	**1,485**	**1,655**	**1,687**
261	To foreign governments	—	—	—	—	—	—	—	—	—	—	—	—
262	To international organizations	1,470	1,651	1,679	1,470	1,651	1,679	1,472	1,652	1,683	1,485	1,655	1,687
263	To other general government units	95,863	103,766	95,538	95,863	103,766	95,538	42,170	47,401	43,143	-0	0	—
2631	Current	88,928	94,944	87,161	88,928	94,944	87,161	35,235	38,578	34,766	-0	-0	—
2632	Capital	6,935	8,822	8,378	6,935	8,822	8,378	6,935	8,822	8,378	—	0	—
27	**Social benefits**	**5,108**	**4,566**	**3,977**	**5,108**	**4,566**	**3,977**	**107,152**	**113,804**	**118,615**	**127,242**	**134,415**	**138,891**
271	Social security benefits	—	—	—	—	—	—	102,033	109,228	114,627	102,033	109,228	114,627
272	Social assistance benefits	5,106	4,560	3,975	5,106	4,560	3,975	5,106	4,560	3,975	25,196	25,171	24,250
273	Employment-related social benefits	2	6	2	2	6	2	13	16	14	14	16	14
28	**Other expense**	**7,670**	**19,290**	**25,312**	**7,670**	**19,290**	**25,312**	**14,922**	**26,731**	**32,367**	**15,741**	**27,638**	**32,988**
281	Property expense other than interest	—	—	—	—	—	—	—	—	—	—	—	—
282	Transfers not elsewhere classified	7,670	19,290	25,312	7,670	19,290	25,312	14,922	26,731	32,367	15,741	27,638	32,988
2821	Current	7,670	14,693	18,969	7,670	14,693	18,969	14,922	22,135	26,024	15,711	23,037	26,645
2822	Capital	—	4,596	6,343	—	4,596	6,343	—	4,596	6,343	30	4,602	6,343
	Table 3 Transactions in assets and liabilities												
3	**Change in net worth from transactions**	...	...	...	...	...	...	...	...	...	...	...	...
31	**Net/Gross investment in nonfinancial assets**	**52,618**	**56,153**	**58,671**	**52,618**	**56,153**	**58,671**	**52,827**	**56,289**	**58,941**	**66,167**	**72,042**	**75,021**
311	Fixed assets	25,755	29,243	33,317	25,755	29,243	33,317	25,948	29,277	33,442	38,753	44,217	47,863
3111	Buildings and structures	17,541	20,412	23,481	17,541	20,412	23,481	17,635	20,434	23,587	29,705	34,698	37,500
3112	Machinery and equipment	4,896	6,284	5,103	4,896	6,284	5,103	4,995	6,296	5,121	5,301	6,552	5,320
3113	Other fixed assets	3,317	2,548	4,734	3,317	2,548	4,734	3,317	2,548	4,735	3,747	2,967	5,043
3114	Weapons systems	...	...	...	...	...	...	...	...	...	...	...	...
312	Inventories	848	1,263	1,310	848	1,263	1,310	864	1,275	1,340	1,010	1,378	1,465
313	Valuables	33	—	84	33	—	84	33	—	84	49	—	234
314	Nonproduced assets	25,982	25,647	23,960	25,982	25,647	23,960	25,982	25,736	24,075	26,355	26,447	25,459
3141	Land	25,583	25,562	23,518	25,583	25,562	23,518	25,583	25,562	23,518	25,947	26,225	24,866
3142	Mineral and energy resources	—	—	—	—	—	—	—	—	—	—	—	—
3143	Other naturally occurring assets	6	10	248	6	10	248	6	10	248	8	10	248
3144	Intangible nonproduced assets	393	75	195	393	75	195	393	164	310	400	212	346
32	**Net acquisition of financial assets**	**7,960**	**-3,854**	**7,031**	**7,960**	**-3,854**	**7,031**	**8,045**	**1,476**	**4,848**	**6,859**	**1,545**	**9,346**
	By instrument												
3201	Monetary gold and SDRs	—	—	—	—	—	—	—	—	—	—	—	—
3202	Currency and deposits	9,019	-2,273	4,197	9,019	-2,465	4,197	8,882	2,479	2,396	7,647	3,256	3,530
3203	Debt securities	—	—	—	—	—	—	—	—	—	—	—	—
3204	Loans	-1,059	-1,581	2,835	-1,059	-1,389	2,835	-1,059	-1,389	2,835	-1,010	-1,581	6,199
3205	Equity and investment fund shares	—	—	...	—	—	—	—	—	—	—	—	—
3206	Insurance, pension, and standardized guarantee schemes	—	—	—	—	—	—	—	—	—	—	—	—
3207	Financial derivatives and employee stock options	—	—	—	—	—	—	—	—	—	—	—	—
3208	Other accounts receivable	...	...	...	...	...	...	222	386	-383	222	-130	-383
	By debtor												
321	Domestic debtors	7,343	-4,213	1,091	7,343	-4,213	1,091	7,428	1,117	-1,093	6,242	1,186	3,405
322	External debtors	617	359	5,941	617	359	5,941	617	359	5,941	617	359	5,941
33	**Net incurrence of liabilities**	**80,114**	**46,758**	**48,045**	**80,114**	**46,758**	**48,045**	**79,946**	**45,344**	**48,282**	**80,460**	**43,419**	**55,046**
	By instrument												
3301	Special Drawing Rights (SDRs)	—	—	—	—	—	—	—	—	—	—	—	—
3302	Currency and deposits	—	—	—	—	—	—	—	—	—	—	—	—
3303	Debt securities	46,196	37,750	2,383	46,196	37,750	2,383	46,199	36,069	2,111	46,199	36,069	2,111
3304	Loans	9,214	35,979	54,204	9,214	35,979	54,204	9,214	35,979	54,203	9,682	36,441	61,016
3305	Equity and investment fund shares	—	—	—	—	—	—	—	—	—	—	—	—
3306	Insurance, pension, and standardized guarantee schemes	—	—	—	—	—	—	—	—	—	—	—	—
3307	Financial derivatives and employee stock options	—	—	—	—	—	—	—	—	—	—	—	—
3308	Other accounts payable	24,704	-26,971	-8,542	24,704	-26,971	-8,542	24,533	-26,705	-8,032	24,579	-29,092	-8,080

Albania (914)

In Millions of Albanian Leks (ALL) / Fiscal Year Ends December 31st

		Budgetary Central Government			Central Government (excl. Social Security)			Central Government (incl. Social Security)			General Government		
		2013	2014	2015	2013	2014	2015	2013	2014	2015	2013	2014	2015
	By creditor												
331	Domestic creditors	70,900	10,778	-25,894	70,900	10,778	-25,894	70,732	9,365	-25,656	70,880	7,439	-18,893
332	External creditors	9,214	35,979	73,939	9,214	35,979	73,939	9,214	35,979	73,939	9,580	35,979	73,939
	Table 4 Holding gains and losses in assets and liabilities												
	Table 5 Holding gains and losses in assets and liabilities												
	Table 6 Balance sheet												
6	**Net worth**	**-281,621**	**-245,596**	**-200,945**	**-281,621**	**-245,596**	**-200,945**	**-273,259**	**-224,392**	**-182,980**	**-93,706**	**-20,922**	**53,060**
61	**Nonfinancial assets**	**496,608**	**554,562**	**663,946**	**496,608**	**554,562**	**663,946**	**498,680**	**556,650**	**666,257**	**669,384**	**750,168**	**915,883**
611	Fixed assets	375,917	398,081	447,396	375,917	398,081	447,396	377,787	399,863	449,365	539,956	578,974	685,831
6111	Buildings and structures	295,406	321,823	350,837	295,406	321,823	350,837	296,418	322,708	352,065	442,869	489,802	571,670
6112	Machinery and equipment	62,125	55,402	70,837	62,125	55,402	70,837	62,983	56,299	71,576	70,770	60,006	79,479
6113	Other fixed assets	18,386	20,856	25,723	18,386	20,856	25,723	18,386	20,856	25,723	26,317	29,165	34,681
6114	Weapons systems	...	...	...	...	...	...	...	...	...	...	...	...
612	Inventories	18,963	26,167	28,158	18,963	26,167	28,158	19,049	26,263	28,219	22,117	32,686	31,792
613	Valuables	...	—	-679	...	—	-679	...	...	-679	...	—	43
614	Nonproduced assets	101,728	130,313	189,071	101,728	130,313	189,071	101,843	130,524	189,353	107,311	138,509	198,217
6141	Land	99,674	128,081	185,668	99,674	128,081	185,668	99,707	128,114	185,702	104,681	135,515	193,842
6142	Mineral and energy resources	—	—	—	—	—	—	—	—	—	—	—	—
6143	Other naturally occurring assets	601	881	1,215	601	881	1,215	601	881	1,215	1,089	1,413	1,850
6144	Intangible nonproduced assets	1,453	1,351	2,188	1,453	1,351	2,188	1,535	1,529	2,436	1,541	1,581	2,525
62	**Financial assets**	**165,533**	**218,544**	**273,812**	**165,533**	**218,544**	**273,812**	**180,939**	**241,998**	**296,263**	**206,791**	**265,060**	**297,636**
	By instrument												
6201	Monetary gold and SDRs	—	—	—	—	—	—	—	—	—	—	—	—
6202	Currency and deposits	22,325	18,634	24,364	22,325	18,634	24,364	28,955	30,703	34,636	28,955	30,703	34,636
6203	Debt securities	—	—	—	—	—	—	—	0	—	0	0	—
6204	Loans	...	59,936	60,216	...	59,936	60,216	—	59,936	60,216	—	59,378	35,856
6205	Equity and investment fund shares	...	...	...	...	...	...	—	—	—	8,372	8,661	8,661
6206	Insurance, pension, and standardized guarantee schemes	—	—	—	—	—	—	—	—	—	—	—	—
6207	Financial derivatives and employee stock options	—	—	—	—	—	—	—	—	—	—	—	—
6208	Other accounts receivable	143,208	139,974	189,231	143,208	139,974	189,231	151,984	151,359	201,412	169,463	166,318	218,483
	By debtor												
621	Domestic debtors	163,739	216,374	265,717	163,739	216,374	265,717	179,145	239,828	288,169	204,996	262,890	289,541
622	External debtors	1,794	2,170	8,095	1,794	2,170	8,095	1,794	2,170	8,095	1,794	2,170	8,095
63	**Liabilities**	**943,762**	**1,018,701**	**1,138,703**	**943,762**	**1,018,701**	**1,138,703**	**952,878**	**1,023,041**	**1,145,501**	**969,881**	**1,036,151**	**1,160,459**
	By instrument												
6301	Special Drawing Rights (SDRs)	—	—	—	—	—	—	—	—	—	—	—	—
6302	Currency and deposits	—	—	—	—	—	—	—	—	—	—	—	—
6303	Debt securities	542,928	580,682	582,712	542,928	580,682	582,712	550,364	575,119	576,827	539,045	575,119	576,827
6304	Loans	290,440	341,881	403,530	290,440	341,881	403,530	291,842	341,881	403,419	290,831	342,730	404,464
6305	Equity and investment fund shares	—	—	—	—	—	—	—	—	—	—	—	—
6306	Insurance, pension, and standardized guarantee schemes	—	—	—	—	—	—	—	—	—	—	—	—
6307	Financial derivatives and employee stock options	—	—	—	—	—	—	—	—	—	—	—	—
6308	Other accounts payable	110,394	96,138	152,461	110,394	96,138	152,461	110,672	106,041	165,255	140,005	118,302	179,168
	By creditor												
631	Domestic creditors	611,262	634,779	673,397	611,262	634,779	673,397	620,378	639,119	680,306	637,381	652,229	695,153
632	External creditors	332,500	383,922	465,306	332,500	383,922	465,306	332,500	383,922	465,195	332,500	383,922	465,306
	Memorandum items												
6M2	Net financial worth	-778,229	-800,158	-864,892	-778,229	-800,158	-864,892	-771,938	-781,042	-849,238	-763,090	-771,091	-862,823
6M3	Gross debt (D4) at market value	...	...	...	...	...	...	...	...	...	...	...	...
6M3D3	D3 debt liabilities at market value	...	...	...	...	...	...	...	...	...	...	...	...
6M3D2	D2 debt liabilities at market value	...	...	...	...	...	...	...	...	...	...	...	...
6M3D1	D1 debt liabilities at market value	...	...	...	...	...	...	...	...	...	...	...	...
6M4	Gross debt (D4) at nominal value	943,762	1,018,701	1,138,703	943,762	1,018,701	1,138,703	952,878	1,023,041	1,145,501	969,881	1,036,151	1,160,459
6M4D3	D3 debt liabilities at nominal value	943,762	1,018,701	1,138,703	943,762	1,018,701	1,138,703	952,878	1,023,041	1,145,501	969,881	1,036,151	1,160,459
6M4D2	D2 debt liabilities at nominal value	833,368	922,563	986,242	833,368	922,563	986,242	842,206	917,000	980,246	829,876	917,849	981,291
6M4D1	D1 debt liabilities at nominal value	833,368	922,563	986,242	833,368	922,563	986,242	842,206	917,000	980,246	829,876	917,849	981,291

Albania (914)

In Millions of Albanian Leks (ALL) / Fiscal Year Ends December 31st

		Budgetary Central Government			Central Government (excl. Social Security)			Central Government (incl. Social Security)			General Government		
		2013	2014	2015	2013	2014	2015	2013	2014	2015	2013	2014	2015
6M35	Gross debt (D4) at face value	...	...	...	...	...	...	...	...	...	...	...	...
6M35D3	D3 debt liabilities at face value	...	...	...	...	...	...	...	...	...	...	...	...
6M35D2	D2 debt liabilities at face value	...	...	...	...	...	...	...	...	...	...	...	...
6M35D1	D1 debt liabilities at face value	...	...	...	...	...	...	...	...	...	...	...	...
6M93	Government gross debt per national definition	...	...	...	...	...	...	...	...	...	...	...	...
6M5	Arrears	...	...	...	...	...	...	...	...	...	...	...	...
6M6	Explicit contingent liabilities	...	...	...	...	...	...	...	...	...	...	...	...
6M61	of which: Publicly guaranteed debt	...	...	...	...	...	...	...	...	...	...	...	...
6M7	Net implicit obligations for social security benefits	...	...	...	...	...	...	...	...	...	...	...	...
	Table 7 Expenditure by functions of government												
7	**Expenditure**	**320,993**	**333,746**	**337,526**	**320,993**	**333,746**	**337,526**	**379,009**	**396,501**	**409,574**	**392,584**	**408,488**	**425,082**
701	**General public services**	**71,991**	**67,029**	**70,809**	**71,991**	**67,029**	**70,809**	**71,789**	**66,835**	**70,692**	**81,686**	**77,372**	**80,321**
7017	Public debt transactions	43,336	39,936	38,642	43,336	39,936	38,642	43,133	39,742	38,526	43,165	39,769	38,582
7018	Transfers of general character between levels of government	—	—	—	—	—	—	—	—	—	—	—	—
702	**Defense**	**13,465**	**11,400**	**10,287**	**13,465**	**11,400**	**10,287**	**13,465**	**11,400**	**10,287**	**13,465**	**11,400**	**10,287**
703	**Public order and safety**	**20,389**	**23,429**	**24,915**	**20,389**	**23,429**	**24,915**	**20,389**	**23,429**	**24,915**	**20,578**	**23,641**	**25,105**
704	**Economic affairs**	**47,690**	**55,537**	**65,247**	**47,690**	**55,537**	**65,247**	**47,690**	**55,537**	**65,247**	**40,798**	**47,242**	**59,066**
7042	Agriculture, forestry, fishing, and hunting	6,828	7,082	8,288	6,828	7,082	8,288	6,828	7,082	8,288	6,845	7,113	8,306
7043	Fuel and energy	-16,387	5,936	7,440	-16,387	5,936	7,440	-16,387	5,936	7,440	-16,387	5,936	7,440
7044	Mining, manufacturing, and construction	253	530	774	253	530	774	253	530	774	253	530	774
7045	Transport	43,811	25,627	29,954	43,811	25,627	29,954	43,811	25,627	29,954	48,670	30,418	35,939
7046	Communication	—	—	—	—	—	—	—	—	—	—	—	—
705	**Environmental protection**	**624**	**916**	**1,383**	**624**	**916**	**1,383**	**624**	**916**	**1,383**	**624**	**917**	**1,383**
706	**Housing and community amenities**	**18,190**	**22,515**	**19,937**	**18,190**	**22,515**	**19,937**	**18,190**	**22,515**	**19,937**	**24,568**	**30,016**	**27,650**
707	**Health**	**30,834**	**30,419**	**31,956**	**30,834**	**30,419**	**31,956**	**37,776**	**38,289**	**39,260**	**37,787**	**38,300**	**39,306**
7072	Outpatient services	9,641	8,743	9,322	9,641	8,743	9,322	16,584	16,689	17,681	16,593	16,698	17,726
7073	Hospital services	18,773	19,611	20,054	18,773	19,611	20,054	18,773	19,535	18,999	18,773	19,536	18,999
7074	Public health services	2,420	2,066	2,581	2,420	2,066	2,581	2,420	2,065	2,581	2,420	2,066	2,581
708	**Recreation, culture and religion**	**2,622**	**4,482**	**5,028**	**2,622**	**4,482**	**5,028**	**2,622**	**4,482**	**5,028**	**4,070**	**5,932**	**6,457**
709	**Education**	**43,403**	**42,503**	**42,073**	**43,403**	**42,503**	**42,073**	**43,403**	**42,503**	**42,073**	**45,461**	**44,886**	**44,383**
7091	Pre-primary and primary education	24,298	24,454	23,917	24,298	24,454	23,917	24,298	24,454	23,917	25,973	26,458	25,817
7092	Secondary education	8,134	8,089	8,272	8,134	8,089	8,272	8,134	8,089	8,272	8,517	8,468	8,682
7094	Tertiary education	10,502	9,645	9,525	10,502	9,645	9,525	10,502	9,645	9,525	10,502	9,645	9,525
710	**Social protection**	**71,785**	**75,515**	**65,892**	**71,785**	**75,515**	**65,892**	**123,061**	**130,594**	**130,754**	**123,546**	**128,781**	**131,126**
7z	Statistical discrepancy: Expenditure	...	...	...	...	...	...	...	...	...	...	...	...
	Table 8 Financial transactions by counterpart sector												
32	**Net acquisition of financial assets**	**7,960**	**-3,854**	**7,031**	**7,960**	**-3,854**	**7,031**	**8,045**	**1,476**	**4,848**	**6,859**	**1,545**	**9,346**
321	Domestic debtors	7,343	-4,213	1,091	7,343	-4,213	1,091	7,428	1,117	-1,093	6,242	1,186	3,405
8211	General government	...	...	...	...	...	...	...	...	...	...	...	...
8212	Central bank	...	...	...	...	...	...	...	...	...	...	...	...
8213	Deposit-taking corporations except the central bank	...	...	...	...	...	...	...	...	...	...	...	...
8214	Other financial corporations	...	...	...	...	...	...	...	...	...	...	...	...
8215	Nonfinancial corporations	...	...	...	...	...	...	...	...	...	...	...	...
8216	Households & nonprofit institutions serving households	...	...	...	...	...	...	...	...	...	...	...	...
322	External debtors	617	359	5,941	617	359	5,941	617	359	5,941	617	359	5,941
8221	General government	...	...	...	...	...	...	...	...	...	...	...	...
8227	International organizations	...	...	...	...	...	...	...	...	...	...	...	...
8228	Financial corporations other than international organizations	...	...	...	...	...	...	...	...	...	...	...	...
8229	Other nonresidents	...	...	...	...	...	...	...	...	...	...	...	...

Albania (914)

In Millions of Albanian Leks (ALL) / Fiscal Year Ends December 31st

		Budgetary Central Government			Central Government (excl. Social Security)			Central Government (incl. Social Security)			General Government		
		2013	2014	2015	2013	2014	2015	2013	2014	2015	2013	2014	2015
33	**Net incurrence of liabilities**	**80,114**	**46,758**	**48,045**	**80,114**	**46,758**	**48,045**	**79,946**	**45,344**	**48,282**	**80,460**	**43,419**	**55,046**
331	Domestic creditors	70,900	10,778	-25,894	70,900	10,778	-25,894	70,732	9,365	-25,656	70,880	7,439	-18,893
8311	General government	...	...	...	...	...	...	...	...	...	...	...	...
8312	Central bank	...	...	...	...	...	...	...	...	...	...	...	...
8313	Deposit-taking corporations except the central bank	...	...	...	...	...	...	...	...	...	...	...	...
8314	Other financial corporations	...	...	...	...	...	...	...	...	...	...	...	...
8315	Nonfinancial corporations	...	...	...	...	...	...	...	...	...	...	...	...
8316	Households & nonprofit institutions serving households	...	...	...	...	...	...	...	...	...	...	...	...
332	External creditors	9,214	35,979	73,939	9,214	35,979	73,939	9,214	35,979	73,939	9,580	35,979	73,939
8321	General government	...	...	...	...	...	...	...	...	...	...	...	...
8327	International organizations	...	...	...	...	...	...	...	...	...	...	...	...
8328	Financial corporations other than international organizations	...	...	...	...	...	...	...	...	...	...	...	...
8329	Other nonresidents	...	...	...	...	...	...	...	...	...	...	...	...
	Table 9 Total other economic flows in assets and liabilities												

Algeria (612)

In Billions of Algerian Dinars (DZD) / Fiscal Year Ends December 31st

		Budgetary Central Government			Central Government (excl. Social Security)			Central Government (incl. Social Security)			General Government		
		2009	2010	2011	2009	2010	2011	2009	2010	2011	2009	2010	2011
	Statement of operations												
1	Revenue	3,741	4,443	5,897	...	...	...	...	...	...	...	...	...
2	Expense	2,557	2,934	4,308	...	...	...	...	...	...	...	...	...
GOB	**Gross operating balance**	**1,184**	**1,509**	**1,589**	...	...	...	...	...	...	...	...	...
NOB	**Net operating balance**	...	...	...	...	...	...	...	...	...	...	...	...
31	Net/Gross investment in nonfinancial assets	1,631	1,460	1,631	...	...	...	...	...	...	...	...	...
2M	Expenditure	4,188	4,395	5,939	...	...	...	...	...	...	...	...	...
NLB	**Net lending (+) / Net borrowing (-)**	**-448**	**49**	**-41**	...	...	...	...	...	...	...	...	...
32	Net acquisition of financial assets	83	651	453	...	...	...	...	...	...	...	...	...
33	Net incurrence of liabilities	602	603	494	...	...	...	...	...	...	...	...	...
NLBz	Statistical discrepancy	-71	-0	0	...	...	...	...	...	...	...	...	...
	Memorandum items												
PB	Primary net lending / net borrowing	-412	79	-4	...	...	...	...	...	...	...	...	...
GB	Government balance per national definition	...	...	...	...	...	...	...	...	...	...	...	...
	Statement of other economic flows												
	Balance sheet												
	Table 1 Revenue												
1	**Revenue**	**3,741**	**4,443**	**5,897**	...	...	...	...	...	...	...	...	...
11	**Taxes**	**3,503**	**4,125**	**5,425**	...	...	...	...	...	...	...	...	...
111	Taxes on income, profits, and capital gains	2,232	2,622	3,550	...	...	...	...	...	...	...	...	...
1111	Payable by individuals	184	245	383	...	...	...	...	...	...	...	...	...
1112	Payable by corporations and other enterprises	2,003	2,322	3,118	...	...	...	...	...	...	...	...	...
1113	Other taxes on income, profits, and capital gains	45	56	49	...	...	...	...	...	...	...	...	...
112	Taxes on payroll and workforce	—	—	—	...	...	...	...	...	...	...	...	...
113	Taxes on property	0	0	0	...	...	...	...	...	...	...	...	...
114	Taxes on goods and services	1,049	1,270	1,548	...	...	...	...	...	...	...	...	...
1141	General taxes on goods and services	450	470	533	...	...	...	...	...	...	...	...	...
1142	Excises	592	791	1,004	...	...	...	...	...	...	...	...	...
115	Taxes on international trade and transactions	166	174	223	...	...	...	...	...	...	...	...	...
116	Other taxes	56	59	103	...	...	...	...	...	...	...	...	...
12	**Social contributions**	—	—	—	...	...	...	...	...	...	...	...	...
121	Social security contributions	—	—	—	...	...	...	...	...	...	...	...	...
122	Other social contributions	—	—	—	...	...	...	...	...	...	...	...	...
13	**Grants**	—	—	—	...	...	...	...	...	...	...	...	...
131	From foreign governments	—	—	—	...	...	...	...	...	...	...	...	...
132	From international organizations	—	—	—	...	...	...	...	...	...	...	...	...
133	From other general government units	—	—	—	...	...	...	...	...	...	...	...	...
1331	Current	—	—	—	...	...	...	...	...	...	...	...	...
1332	Capital	—	—	—	...	...	...	...	...	...	...	...	...
14	**Other revenue**	**237**	**318**	**473**	...	...	...	...	...	...	...	...	...
	Table 2 Expense by economic type												
2	**Expense**	**2,557**	**2,934**	**4,308**	...	...	...	...	...	...	...	...	...
21	**Compensation of employees**	**861**	**1,113**	**1,733**	...	...	...	...	...	...	...	...	...
211	Wages and salaries	860	1,113	1,733	...	...	...	...	...	...	...	...	...
212	Employers' social contributions	1	—	—	...	...	...	...	...	...	...	...	...
22	**Use of goods and services**	**288**	**356**	**397**	...	...	...	...	...	...	...	...	...
23	**Consumption of fixed capital**	...	...	...	...	...	...	...	...	...	...	...	...
24	**Interest**	**36**	**30**	**38**	...	...	...	...	...	...	...	...	...
25	**Subsidies**	**155**	**179**	**346**	...	...	...	...	...	...	...	...	...
26	**Grants**	**449**	**450**	**719**	...	...	...	...	...	...	...	...	...
261	To foreign governments	—	—	—	...	...	...	...	...	...	...	...	...
262	To international organizations	21	—	20	...	...	...	...	...	...	...	...	...
263	To other general government units	428	450	699	...	...	...	...	...	...	...	...	...
2631	Current	334	374	635	...	...	...	...	...	...	...	...	...
2632	Capital	94	76	64	...	...	...	...	...	...	...	...	...

Algeria (612)

In Billions of Algerian Dinars (DZD) / Fiscal Year Ends December 31st

		Budgetary Central Government			Central Government (excl. Social Security)			Central Government (incl. Social Security)			General Government		
		2009	2010	2011	2009	2010	2011	2009	2010	2011	2009	2010	2011
27	**Social benefits**	**556**	**677**	**870**	...	...	...	...	...	...	...	...	...
271	Social security benefits	9	52	51	...	...	...	...	...	...	...	...	...
272	Social assistance benefits	296	308	320	...	...	...	...	...	...	...	...	...
273	Employment-related social benefits	251	317	499	...	...	...	...	...	...	...	...	...
28	**Other expense**	**212**	**129**	**206**	...	...	...	...	...	...	...	...	...
281	Property expense other than interest	1	2	1	...	...	...	...	...	...	...	...	...
282	Transfers not elsewhere classified	211	127	204	...	...	...	...	...	...	...	...	...
2821	Current	125	26	91	...	...	...	...	...	...	...	...	...
2822	Capital	86	102	113	...	...	...	...	...	...	...	...	...
	Table 3 Transactions in assets and liabilities												
3	**Change in net worth from transactions**	...	...	...	...	...	...	...	...	...	...	...	...
31	**Net/Gross investment in nonfinancial assets**	**1,631**	**1,460**	**1,631**	...	...	...	...	...	...	...	...	...
311	Fixed assets	1,625	1,442	1,624	...	...	...	...	...	...	...	...	...
3111	Buildings and structures	—	...	...	...	...	...	...	...	...	...	...	...
3112	Machinery and equipment	—	...	...	...	...	...	...	...	...	...	...	...
3113	Other fixed assets	1,625	...	...	...	...	...	...	...	...	...	...	...
3114	Weapons systems	...	...	...	...	...	...	...	...	...	...	...	...
312	Inventories	—	—	—	...	...	...	...	...	...	...	...	...
313	Valuables	—	—	—	...	...	...	...	...	...	...	...	...
314	Nonproduced assets	6	18	7	...	...	...	...	...	...	...	...	...
3141	Land	—	...	...	...	...	...	...	...	...	...	...	...
3142	Mineral and energy resources	—	...	...	...	...	...	...	...	...	...	...	...
3143	Other naturally occurring assets	—	...	...	...	...	...	...	...	...	...	...	...
3144	Intangible nonproduced assets	6	...	...	...	...	...	...	...	...	...	...	...
32	**Net acquisition of financial assets**	**83**	**651**	**453**	...	...	...	...	...	...	...	...	...
	By instrument												
3201	Monetary gold and SDRs	—	—	—	...	...	...	...	...	...	...	...	...
3202	Currency and deposits	-73	424	277	...	...	...	...	...	...	...	...	...
3203	Debt securities	2	...	...	...	...	...	...	...	...	...	...	...
3204	Loans	141	...	...	...	...	...	...	...	...	...	...	...
3205	Equity and investment fund shares	14	...	...	...	...	...	...	...	...	...	...	...
3206	Insurance, pension, and standardized guarantee schemes	—	...	...	...	...	...	...	...	...	...	...	...
3207	Financial derivatives and employee stock options	—	...	...	...	...	...	...	...	...	...	...	...
3208	Other accounts receivable	—	...	...	...	...	...	...	...	...	...	...	...
	By debtor												
321	Domestic debtors	83	651	453	...	...	...	...	...	...	...	...	...
322	External debtors	—	—	—	...	...	...	...	...	...	...	...	...
33	**Net incurrence of liabilities**	**602**	**603**	**494**	...	...	...	...	...	...	...	...	...
	By instrument												
3301	Special Drawing Rights (SDRs)	—	...	...	...	...	...	...	...	...	...	...	...
3302	Currency and deposits	549	...	...	...	...	...	...	...	...	...	...	...
3303	Debt securities	84	...	...	...	...	...	...	...	...	...	...	...
3304	Loans	-1	...	...	...	...	...	...	...	...	...	...	...
3305	Equity and investment fund shares	—	...	...	...	...	...	...	...	...	...	...	...
3306	Insurance, pension, and standardized guarantee schemes	—	...	...	...	...	...	...	...	...	...	...	...
3307	Financial derivatives and employee stock options	—	...	...	...	...	...	...	...	...	...	...	...
3308	Other accounts payable	-30	...	...	...	...	...	...	...	...	...	...	...
	By creditor												
331	Domestic creditors	603	603	495	...	...	...	...	...	...	...	...	...
332	External creditors	-1	—	-1	...	...	...	...	...	...	...	...	...
	Table 4 Holding gains and losses in assets and liabilities												
	Table 5 Holding gains and losses in assets and liabilities												
	Table 6 Balance sheet												

Algeria (612)

In Billions of Algerian Dinars (DZD) / Fiscal Year Ends December 31st

		Budgetary Central Government			Central Government (excl. Social Security)			Central Government (incl. Social Security)			General Government		
		2009	2010	2011	2009	2010	2011	2009	2010	2011	2009	2010	2011
	Table 7 Expenditure by functions of government												
7	**Expenditure**	**4,188**	**4,395**	**5,939**	...	...	...	...	...	...	...	...	...
701	**General public services**	**804**	...	...	...	...	...	...	...	...	...	...	...
7017	Public debt transactions	36	30	38	...	...	...	...	...	...	...	...	...
7018	Transfers of general character between levels of government	253	...	...	...	...	...	...	...	...	...	...	...
702	**Defense**	**407**	...	...	...	...	...	...	...	...	...	...	...
703	**Public order and safety**	**183**	...	...	...	...	...	...	...	...	...	...	...
704	**Economic affairs**	**814**	...	...	...	...	...	...	...	...	...	...	...
7042	Agriculture, forestry, fishing, and hunting	153	...	...	...	...	...	...	...	...	...	...	...
7043	Fuel and energy	1	...	...	...	...	...	...	...	...	...	...	...
7044	Mining, manufacturing, and construction	17	...	...	...	...	...	...	...	...	...	...	...
7045	Transport	392	...	...	...	...	...	...	...	...	...	...	...
7046	Communication	15	...	...	...	...	...	...	...	...	...	...	...
705	**Environmental protection**	**12**	...	...	...	...	...	...	...	...	...	...	...
706	**Housing and community amenities**	**439**	...	...	...	...	...	...	...	...	...	...	...
707	**Health**	**230**	...	...	...	...	...	...	...	...	...	...	...
7072	Outpatient services	23	...	...	...	...	...	...	...	...	...	...	...
7073	Hospital services	204	...	...	...	...	...	...	...	...	...	...	...
7074	Public health services	0	...	...	...	...	...	...	...	...	...	...	...
708	**Recreation, culture and religion**	**86**	...	...	...	...	...	...	...	...	...	...	...
709	**Education**	**601**	...	...	...	...	...	...	...	...	...	...	...
7091	Pre-primary and primary education	235	...	...	...	...	...	...	...	...	...	...	...
7092	Secondary education	86	...	...	...	...	...	...	...	...	...	...	...
7094	Tertiary education	158	...	...	...	...	...	...	...	...	...	...	...
710	**Social protection**	**613**	...	...	...	...	...	...	...	...	...	...	...
7z	Statistical discrepancy: Expenditure	-0	...	...	...	...	...	...	...	...	...	...	...
	Table 8 Financial transactions by counterpart sector												
	Table 9 Total other economic flows in assets and liabilities												

Angola (614)

In Billions of Angolan Kwanzas (AOA) / Fiscal Year Ends December 31st

		Budgetary Central Government			Central Government (excl. Social Security)			Central Government (incl. Social Security)			General Government		
		2013	2014P	2015P	2013	2014	2015	2013	2014	2015	2013	2014	2015
	Statement of operations												
1	Revenue	4,711	4,424	2,619	...	...	...	...	...	...	...	...	...
2	Expense	3,722	4,006	2,904	...	...	...	...	...	...	...	...	...
GOB	**Gross operating balance**	**989**	**418**	**-285**	...	...	...	...	...	...	...	...	...
NOB	**Net operating balance**	...	...	...	...	...	...	...	...	...	...	...	...
31	Net/Gross investment in nonfinancial assets	1,533	1,906	568	...	...	...	...	...	...	...	...	...
2M	Expenditure	5,255	5,912	3,473	...	...	...	...	...	...	...	...	...
NLB	**Net lending (+) / Net borrowing (-)**	**-544**	**-1,488**	**-853**	...	...	...	...	...	...	...	...	...
32	Net acquisition of financial assets	-179	-447	75	...	...	...	...	...	...	...	...	...
33	Net incurrence of liabilities	364	762	928	...	...	...	...	...	...	...	...	...
NLBz	Statistical discrepancy	-0	279	0	...	...	...	...	...	...	...	...	...
	Memorandum items												
PB	Primary net lending / net borrowing	-444	-1,341	-605	...	...	...	...	...	...	...	...	...
GB	Government balance per national definition	...	...	...	...	...	...	...	...	...	...	...	...
	Statement of other economic flows												
	Balance sheet												
	Table 1 Revenue												
1	**Revenue**	**4,711**	**4,424**	**2,619**	...	...	...	...	...	...	...	...	...
11	**Taxes**	**1,872**	**1,940**	**1,535**	...	...	...	...	...	...	...	...	...
111	Taxes on income, profits, and capital gains	1,401	1,356	1,054	...	...	...	...	...	...	...	...	...
1111	Payable by individuals	153	184	204	...	...	...	...	...	...	...	...	...
1112	Payable by corporations and other enterprises	1,248	1,173	850	...	...	...	...	...	...	...	...	...
1113	Other taxes on income, profits, and capital gains	—	—	—	...	...	...	...	...	...	...	...	...
112	Taxes on payroll and workforce	—	—	—	...	...	...	...	...	...	...	...	...
113	Taxes on property	20	28	30	...	...	...	...	...	...	...	...	...
114	Taxes on goods and services	202	229	177	...	...	...	...	...	...	...	...	...
1141	General taxes on goods and services	153	184	134	...	...	...	...	...	...	...	...	...
1142	Excises	25	16	15	...	...	...	...	...	...	...	...	...
115	Taxes on international trade and transactions	124	182	130	...	...	...	...	...	...	...	...	...
116	Other taxes	124	144	143	...	...	...	...	...	...	...	...	...
12	**Social contributions**	**121**	**87**	**151**	...	...	...	...	...	...	...	...	...
121	Social security contributions	121	87	151	...	...	...	...	...	...	...	...	...
122	Other social contributions	—	—	—	...	...	...	...	...	...	...	...	...
13	**Grants**	—	—	—	...	...	...	...	...	...	...	...	...
131	From foreign governments	—	—	—	...	...	...	...	...	...	...	...	...
132	From international organizations	—	—	—	...	...	...	...	...	...	...	...	...
133	From other general government units	—	—	—	...	...	...	...	...	...	...	...	...
1331	Current	—	—	—	...	...	...	...	...	...	...	...	...
1332	Capital	—	—	—	...	...	...	...	...	...	...	...	...
14	**Other revenue**	**2,719**	**2,397**	**934**	...	...	...	...	...	...	...	...	...
	Table 2 Expense by economic type												
2	**Expense**	**3,722**	**4,006**	**2,904**	...	...	...	...	...	...	...	...	...
21	**Compensation of employees**	**1,155**	**1,319**	**1,390**	...	...	...	...	...	...	...	...	...
211	Wages and salaries	1,084	1,247	1,313	...	...	...	...	...	...	...	...	...
212	Employers' social contributions	71	72	77	...	...	...	...	...	...	...	...	...
22	**Use of goods and services**	**1,510**	**1,371**	**637**	...	...	...	...	...	...	...	...	...
23	**Consumption of fixed capital**	...	...	...	...	...	...	...	...	...	...	...	...
24	**Interest**	**99**	**147**	**248**	...	...	...	...	...	...	...	...	...
25	**Subsidies**	**710**	**735**	**278**	...	...	...	...	...	...	...	...	...
26	**Grants**	**3**	**100**	**4**	...	...	...	...	...	...	...	...	...
261	To foreign governments	3	4	4	...	...	...	...	...	...	...	...	...
262	To international organizations	—	—	—	...	...	...	...	...	...	...	...	...
263	To other general government units	0	96	—	...	...	...	...	...	...	...	...	...
2631	Current	0	96	—	...	...	...	...	...	...	...	...	...
2632	Capital	—	—	—	...	...	...	...	...	...	...	...	...

Angola (614)

In Billions of Angolan Kwanzas (AOA) / Fiscal Year Ends December 31st

		Budgetary Central Government			Central Government (excl. Social Security)			Central Government (incl. Social Security)			General Government		
		2013	2014P	2015P	2013	2014	2015	2013	2014	2015	2013	2014	2015
27	**Social benefits**	**210**	**233**	**283**	...	...	...	...	...	...	...	...	...
271	Social security benefits	—	—	—	...	...	...	...	...	...	...	...	...
272	Social assistance benefits	—	—	—	...	...	...	...	...	...	...	...	...
273	Employment-related social benefits	210	233	283	...	...	...	...	...	...	...	...	...
28	**Other expense**	**34**	**100**	**63**	...	...	...	...	...	...	...	...	...
281	Property expense other than interest	—	—	—	...	...	...	...	...	...	...	...	...
282	Transfers not elsewhere classified	34	100	63	...	...	...	...	...	...	...	...	...
2821	Current	32	43	46	...	...	...	...	...	...	...	...	...
2822	Capital	3	57	17	...	...	...	...	...	...	...	...	...
	Table 3 Transactions in assets and liabilities												
3	**Change in net worth from transactions**	...	...	...	...	...	...	...	...	...	...	...	...
31	**Net/Gross investment in nonfinancial assets**	**1,533**	**1,906**	**568**	...	...	...	...	...	...	...	...	...
311	Fixed assets	1,533	1,906	568	...	...	...	...	...	...	...	...	...
3111	Buildings and structures	1,378	1,636	502	...	...	...	...	...	...	...	...	...
3112	Machinery and equipment	155	269	66	...	...	...	...	...	...	...	...	...
3113	Other fixed assets	0	1	1	...	...	...	...	...	...	...	...	...
3114	Weapons systems	—	—	—	...	...	...	...	...	...	...	...	...
312	Inventories	—	—	—	...	...	...	...	...	...	...	...	...
313	Valuables	—	—	—	...	...	...	...	...	...	...	...	...
314	Nonproduced assets	—	0	—	...	...	...	...	...	...	...	...	...
3141	Land	—	0	—	...	...	...	...	...	...	...	...	...
3142	Mineral and energy resources	—	—	—	...	...	...	...	...	...	...	...	...
3143	Other naturally occurring assets	—	—	—	...	...	...	...	...	...	...	...	...
3144	Intangible nonproduced assets	—	—	—	...	...	...	...	...	...	...	...	...
32	**Net acquisition of financial assets**	**-179**	**-447**	**75**	...	...	...	...	...	...	...	...	...
	By instrument												
3201	Monetary gold and SDRs	—	—	—	...	...	...	...	...	...	...	...	...
3202	Currency and deposits	-475	-691	39	...	...	...	...	...	...	...	...	...
3203	Debt securities	9	—	—	...	...	...	...	...	...	...	...	...
3204	Loans	1	—	—	...	...	...	...	...	...	...	...	...
3205	Equity and investment fund shares	286	243	36	...	...	...	...	...	...	...	...	...
3206	Insurance, pension, and standardized guarantee schemes	—	—	—	...	...	...	...	...	...	...	...	...
3207	Financial derivatives and employee stock options	—	—	—	...	...	...	...	...	...	...	...	...
3208	Other accounts receivable	...	...	...	...	...	...	...	...	...	...	...	...
	By debtor												
321	Domestic debtors	-179	-447	75	...	...	...	...	...	...	...	...	...
322	External debtors	—	—	—	...	...	...	...	...	...	...	...	...
33	**Net incurrence of liabilities**	**364**	**762**	**928**	...	...	...	...	...	...	...	...	...
	By instrument												
3301	Special Drawing Rights (SDRs)	—	—	—	...	...	...	...	...	...	...	...	...
3302	Currency and deposits	—	—	—	...	...	...	...	...	...	...	...	...
3303	Debt securities	339	—	—	...	...	...	...	...	...	...	...	...
3304	Loans	25	762	433	...	...	...	...	...	...	...	...	...
3305	Equity and investment fund shares	—	—	—	...	...	...	...	...	...	...	...	...
3306	Insurance, pension, and standardized guarantee schemes	—	—	—	...	...	...	...	...	...	...	...	...
3307	Financial derivatives and employee stock options	—	—	—	...	...	...	...	...	...	...	...	...
3308	Other accounts payable	...	...	496	...	...	...	...	...	...	...	...	...
	By creditor												
331	Domestic creditors	25	279	720	...	...	...	...	...	...	...	...	...
332	External creditors	339	483	208	...	...	...	...	...	...	...	...	...
	Table 4 Holding gains and losses in assets and liabilities												
	Table 5 Holding gains and losses in assets and liabilities												
	Table 6 Balance sheet												

Angola (614)

In Billions of Angolan Kwanzas (AOA) / Fiscal Year Ends December 31st

		Budgetary Central Government			Central Government (excl. Social Security)			Central Government (incl. Social Security)			General Government		
		2013	2014P	2015P	2013	2014	2015	2013	2014	2015	2013	2014	2015
	Table 7 Expenditure by functions of government												
7	**Expenditure**	**5,255**	**5,912**	**3,474**	...	...	...	...	...	...	...	...	...
701	**General public services**	**1,913**	**1,397**	**707**	...	...	...	...	...	...	...	...	...
7017	Public debt transactions	99	147	248	...	...	...	...	...	...	...	...	...
7018	Transfers of general character between levels of government	—	—	—	...	...	...	...	...	...	...	...	...
702	**Defense**	**613**	**672**	**789**	...	...	...	...	...	...	...	...	...
703	**Public order and safety**	**374**	**511**	**159**	...	...	...	...	...	...	...	...	...
704	**Economic affairs**	**1,240**	**1,137**	**431**	...	...	...	...	...	...	...	...	...
7042	Agriculture, forestry, fishing, and hunting	68	51	31	...	...	...	...	...	...	...	...	...
7043	Fuel and energy	278	287	182	...	...	...	...	...	...	...	...	...
7044	Mining, manufacturing, and construction	194	53	14	...	...	...	...	...	...	...	...	...
7045	Transport	475	378	134	...	...	...	...	...	...	...	...	...
7046	Communication	17	31	23	...	...	...	...	...	...	...	...	...
705	**Environmental protection**	**49**	**37**	**21**	...	...	...	...	...	...	...	...	...
706	**Housing and community amenities**	**192**	**552**	**175**	...	...	...	...	...	...	...	...	...
707	**Health**	**318**	**276**	**193**	...	...	...	...	...	...	...	...	...
7072	Outpatient services	27	5	3	...	...	...	...	...	...	...	...	...
7073	Hospital services	201	202	129	...	...	...	...	...	...	...	...	...
7074	Public health services	66	64	59	...	...	...	...	...	...	...	...	...
708	**Recreation, culture and religion**	**89**	**72**	**34**	...	...	...	...	...	...	...	...	...
709	**Education**	**496**	**405**	**420**	...	...	...	...	...	...	...	...	...
7091	Pre-primary and primary education	286	222	292	...	...	...	...	...	...	...	...	...
7092	Secondary education	69	76	49	...	...	...	...	...	...	...	...	...
7094	Tertiary education	69	80	66	...	...	...	...	...	...	...	...	...
710	**Social protection**	**837**	**853**	**544**	...	...	...	...	...	...	...	...	...
7z	Statistical discrepancy: Expenditure	—	—	—	...	...	...	...	...	...	...	...	...
	Table 8 Financial transactions by counterpart sector												
	Table 9 Total other economic flows in assets and liabilities												

Anguilla (312)

In Thousands of Eastern Caribbean Dollars (XCD) / Fiscal Year Ends December 31st

		Budgetary Central Government			Central Government (excl. Social Security)			Central Government (incl. Social Security)			General Government		
		2012	2013	2014	2012	2013	2014	2012	2013	2014	2012	2013	2014
	Statement of operations												
1	Revenue	191,525	189,134	202,857	...	...	...	...	...	...	...	...	...
2	Expense	170,427	175,784	178,168	...	...	...	...	...	...	...	...	...
GOB	**Gross operating balance**	**21,098**	**13,350**	**24,689**	...	...	...	...	...	...	...	...	...
NOB	**Net operating balance**	...	...	...	...	...	...	...	...	...	...	...	...
31	Net/Gross investment in nonfinancial assets	9,513	8,265	3,430	...	...	...	...	...	...	...	...	...
2M	Expenditure	179,940	184,049	181,598	...	...	...	...	...	...	...	...	...
NLB	**Net lending (+) / Net borrowing (-)**	**11,585**	**5,085**	**21,259**	...	...	...	...	...	...	...	...	...
32	Net acquisition of financial assets	3,992	-4,103	11,688	...	...	...	...	...	...	...	...	...
33	Net incurrence of liabilities	-7,593	-9,188	-9,571	...	...	...	...	...	...	...	...	...
NLBz	Statistical discrepancy	—	0	-0	...	...	...	...	...	...	...	...	...
	Memorandum items												
PB	Primary net lending / net borrowing	19,931	14,190	30,650	...	...	...	...	...	...	...	...	...
GB	Government balance per national definition	...	...	...	...	...	...	...	...	...	...	...	...
	Statement of other economic flows												
	Balance sheet												
	Table 1 Revenue												
1	**Revenue**	**191,525**	**189,134**	**202,857**	...	...	...	...	...	...	...	...	...
11	**Taxes**	**155,131**	**147,466**	**156,314**	...	...	...	...	...	...	...	...	...
111	Taxes on income, profits, and capital gains	13,858	12,772	13,215	...	...	...	...	...	...	...	...	...
1111	Payable by individuals	...	...	...	...	...	...	...	...	...	...	...	...
1112	Payable by corporations and other enterprises	...	...	...	...	...	...	...	...	...	...	...	...
1113	Other taxes on income, profits, and capital gains	...	...	...	...	...	...	...	...	...	...	...	...
112	Taxes on payroll and workforce	—	—	—	...	...	...	...	...	...	...	...	...
113	Taxes on property	3,911	3,624	4,463	...	...	...	...	...	...	...	...	...
114	Taxes on goods and services	66,034	52,446	58,209	...	...	...	...	...	...	...	...	...
1141	General taxes on goods and services	18,579	13,622	16,107	...	...	...	...	...	...	...	...	...
1142	Excises	—	—	—	...	...	...	...	...	...	...	...	...
115	Taxes on international trade and transactions	71,328	78,624	80,427	...	...	...	...	...	...	...	...	...
116	Other taxes	—	—	—	...	...	...	...	...	...	...	...	...
12	**Social contributions**	—	—	—	...	...	...	...	...	...	...	...	...
121	Social security contributions	—	—	—	...	...	...	...	...	...	...	...	...
122	Other social contributions	—	—	—	...	...	...	...	...	...	...	...	...
13	**Grants**	**11,640**	**15,723**	**14,819**	...	...	...	...	...	...	...	...	...
131	From foreign governments	11,640	15,723	14,819	...	...	...	...	...	...	...	...	...
132	From international organizations	—	—	—	...	...	...	...	...	...	...	...	...
133	From other general government units	—	—	—	...	...	...	...	...	...	...	...	...
1331	Current	—	—	—	...	...	...	...	...	...	...	...	...
1332	Capital	—	—	—	...	...	...	...	...	...	...	...	...
14	**Other revenue**	**24,755**	**25,944**	**31,724**	...	...	...	...	...	...	...	...	...
	Table 2 Expense by economic type												
2	**Expense**	**170,427**	**175,784**	**178,168**	...	...	...	...	...	...	...	...	...
21	**Compensation of employees**	**79,911**	**80,319**	**81,152**	...	...	...	...	...	...	...	...	...
211	Wages and salaries	79,911	80,319	81,152	...	...	...	...	...	...	...	...	...
212	Employers' social contributions	—	—	—	...	...	...	...	...	...	...	...	...
22	**Use of goods and services**	**38,334**	**40,451**	**42,198**	...	...	...	...	...	...	...	...	...
23	**Consumption of fixed capital**	...	...	...	...	...	...	...	...	...	...	...	...
24	**Interest**	**8,346**	**9,105**	**9,391**	...	...	...	...	...	...	...	...	...
25	**Subsidies**	**36,072**	**37,697**	**37,474**	...	...	...	...	...	...	...	...	...
26	**Grants**	—	—	—	...	...	...	...	...	...	...	...	...
261	To foreign governments	—	—	—	...	...	...	...	...	...	...	...	...
262	To international organizations	—	—	—	...	...	...	...	...	...	...	...	...
263	To other general government units	—	—	—	...	...	...	...	...	...	...	...	...
2631	Current	—	—	—	...	...	...	...	...	...	...	...	...
2632	Capital	—	—	—	...	...	...	...	...	...	...	...	...

Anguilla (312)

In Thousands of Eastern Caribbean Dollars (XCD) / Fiscal Year Ends December 31st

		Budgetary Central Government			Central Government (excl. Social Security)			Central Government (incl. Social Security)			General Government		
		2012	2013	2014	2012	2013	2014	2012	2013	2014	2012	2013	2014
27	**Social benefits**	**7,765**	**8,211**	**7,952**	...	...	...	...	...	...	...	...	...
271	Social security benefits	7,765	8,211	7,952	...	...	...	...	...	...	...	...	...
272	Social assistance benefits	—	—	—	...	...	...	...	...	...	...	...	...
273	Employment-related social benefits	—	—	—	...	...	...	...	...	...	...	...	...
28	**Other expense**	—	—	—	...	...	...	...	...	...	...	...	...
281	Property expense other than interest	—	—	—	...	...	...	...	...	...	...	...	...
282	Transfers not elsewhere classified	—	—	—	...	...	...	...	...	...	...	...	...
2821	Current	—	—	—	...	...	...	...	...	...	...	...	...
2822	Capital	—	—	—	...	...	...	...	...	...	...	...	...
	Table 3 Transactions in assets and liabilities												
3	**Change in net worth from transactions**	...	...	...	...	...	...	...	...	...	...	...	...
31	**Net/Gross investment in nonfinancial assets**	**9,513**	**8,265**	**3,430**	...	...	...	...	...	...	...	...	...
311	Fixed assets	9,513	8,265	3,430	...	...	...	...	...	...	...	...	...
3111	Buildings and structures	...	...	...	...	...	...	...	...	...	...	...	...
3112	Machinery and equipment	...	...	...	...	...	...	...	...	...	...	...	...
3113	Other fixed assets	...	...	...	...	...	...	...	...	...	...	...	...
3114	Weapons systems	...	...	...	...	...	...	...	...	...	...	...	...
312	Inventories	—	—	—	...	...	...	...	...	...	...	...	...
313	Valuables	—	—	—	...	...	...	...	...	...	...	...	...
314	Nonproduced assets	—	—	—	...	...	...	...	...	...	...	...	...
3141	Land	—	—	—	...	...	...	...	...	...	...	...	...
3142	Mineral and energy resources	—	—	—	...	...	...	...	...	...	...	...	...
3143	Other naturally occurring assets	—	—	—	...	...	...	...	...	...	...	...	...
3144	Intangible nonproduced assets	—	—	—	...	...	...	...	...	...	...	...	...
32	**Net acquisition of financial assets**	**3,992**	**-4,103**	**11,688**	...	...	...	...	...	...	...	...	...
	By instrument												
3201	Monetary gold and SDRs	—	—	—	—	—	—	—	—	—	—	—	—
3202	Currency and deposits	3,992	-4,103	11,688	...	...	...	...	...	...	...	...	...
3203	Debt securities	—	—	—	...	...	...	...	...	...	...	...	...
3204	Loans	—	—	—	...	...	...	...	...	...	...	...	...
3205	Equity and investment fund shares	—	—	—	...	...	...	...	...	...	...	...	...
3206	Insurance, pension, and standardized guarantee schemes	—	—	—	...	...	...	...	...	...	...	...	...
3207	Financial derivatives and employee stock options	—	—	—	...	...	...	...	...	...	...	...	...
3208	Other accounts receivable	...	...	...	...	...	...	...	...	...	...	...	...
	By debtor												
321	Domestic debtors	3,992	-4,103	11,688	...	...	...	...	...	...	...	...	...
322	External debtors	—	—	—	...	...	...	...	...	...	...	...	...
33	**Net incurrence of liabilities**	**-7,593**	**-9,188**	**-9,571**	...	...	...	...	...	...	...	...	...
	By instrument												
3301	Special Drawing Rights (SDRs)	—	—	—	—	—	—	—	—	—	—	—	—
3302	Currency and deposits	—	—	—	...	...	...	...	...	...	...	...	...
3303	Debt securities	—	—	—	...	...	...	...	...	...	...	...	...
3304	Loans	-4,573	-9,176	-9,688	...	...	...	...	...	...	...	...	...
3305	Equity and investment fund shares	—	—	—	...	...	...	...	...	...	...	...	...
3306	Insurance, pension, and standardized guarantee schemes	—	—	—	...	...	...	...	...	...	...	...	...
3307	Financial derivatives and employee stock options	—	—	—	...	...	...	...	...	...	...	...	...
3308	Other accounts payable	-3,020	-11	117	...	...	...	...	...	...	...	...	...
	By creditor												
331	Domestic creditors	-6,516	-8,143	-8,452	...	...	...	...	...	...	...	...	...
332	External creditors	-1,077	-1,044	-1,119	...	...	...	...	...	...	...	...	...
	Table 4 Holding gains and losses in assets and liabilities												
	Table 5 Holding gains and losses in assets and liabilities												
	Table 6 Balance sheet												

Anguilla (312)

In Thousands of Eastern Caribbean Dollars (XCD) / Fiscal Year Ends December 31st

	Budgetary Central Government			Central Government (excl. Social Security)			Central Government (incl. Social Security)			General Government		
	2012	2013	2014	2012	2013	2014	2012	2013	2014	2012	2013	2014
Table 7 Expenditure by functions of government												
Table 8 Financial transactions by counterpart sector												
Table 9 Total other economic flows in assets and liabilities												

Antigua and Barbuda (311)

In Millions of Eastern Caribbean Dollars (XCD) / Fiscal Year Ends December 31st

		Budgetary Central Government			Central Government (excl. Social Security)			Central Government (incl. Social Security)			General Government		
		2012	2013	2014	2012	2013	2014	2012	2013	2014	2012	2013	2014
	Statement of operations												
1	Revenue	647	598	679	...	...	...	...	...	...	...	...	...
2	Expense	671	700	718	...	...	...	...	...	...	...	...	...
GOB	**Gross operating balance**	**-25**	**-103**	**-39**	...	...	...	...	...	...	...	...	...
NOB	**Net operating balance**	...	...	...	...	...	...	...	...	...	...	...	...
31	Net/Gross investment in nonfinancial assets	19	42	54	...	...	...	...	...	...	...	...	...
2M	Expenditure	690	742	772	...	...	...	...	...	...	...	...	...
NLB	**Net lending (+) / Net borrowing (-)**	**-44**	**-144**	**-93**	...	...	...	...	...	...	...	...	...
32	Net acquisition of financial assets	-117	-109	-137	...	...	...	...	...	...	...	...	...
33	Net incurrence of liabilities	-73	35	-44	...	...	...	...	...	...	...	...	...
NLBz	Statistical discrepancy	—	-0	-1	...	...	...	...	...	...	...	...	...
	Memorandum items												
PB	Primary net lending / net borrowing	36	-78	-4	...	...	...	...	...	...	...	...	...
GB	Government balance per national definition	...	...	...	...	...	...	...	...	...	...	...	...
	Statement of other economic flows												
	Balance sheet												
	Table 1 Revenue												
1	**Revenue**	**647**	**598**	**679**	...	...	...	...	...	...	...	...	...
11	**Taxes**	**604**	**555**	**572**	...	...	...	...	...	...	...	...	...
111	Taxes on income, profits, and capital gains	77	85	73	...	...	...	...	...	...	...	...	...
1111	Payable by individuals	42	40	37	...	...	...	...	...	...	...	...	...
1112	Payable by corporations and other enterprises	35	44	36	...	...	...	...	...	...	...	...	...
1113	Other taxes on income, profits, and capital gains	0	0	—	...	...	...	...	...	...	...	...	...
112	Taxes on payroll and workforce	—	—	—	...	...	...	...	...	...	...	...	...
113	Taxes on property	20	18	22	...	...	...	...	...	...	...	...	...
114	Taxes on goods and services	275	245	268	...	...	...	...	...	...	...	...	...
1141	General taxes on goods and services	40	28	32	...	...	...	...	...	...	...	...	...
1142	Excises	—	—	—	...	...	...	...	...	...	...	...	...
115	Taxes on international trade and transactions	231	208	209	...	...	...	...	...	...	...	...	...
116	Other taxes	—	—	—	...	...	...	...	...	...	...	...	...
12	**Social contributions**	—	—	—	...	...	...	...	...	...	...	...	...
121	Social security contributions	—	—	—	...	...	...	...	...	...	...	...	...
122	Other social contributions	—	—	—	...	...	...	...	...	...	...	...	...
13	**Grants**	—	—	**14**	...	...	...	...	...	...	...	...	...
131	From foreign governments	—	—	14	...	...	...	...	...	...	...	...	...
132	From international organizations	—	—	—	...	...	...	...	...	...	...	...	...
133	From other general government units	—	—	—	...	...	...	...	...	...	...	...	...
1331	Current	—	—	—	...	...	...	...	...	...	...	...	...
1332	Capital	—	—	—	...	...	...	...	...	...	...	...	...
14	**Other revenue**	**42**	**43**	**93**	...	...	...	...	...	...	...	...	...
	Table 2 Expense by economic type												
2	**Expense**	**671**	**700**	**718**	...	...	...	...	...	...	...	...	...
21	**Compensation of employees**	**274**	**277**	**308**	...	...	...	...	...	...	...	...	...
211	Wages and salaries	274	277	308	...	...	...	...	...	...	...	...	...
212	Employers' social contributions	—	—	—	...	...	...	...	...	...	...	...	...
22	**Use of goods and services**	**114**	**148**	**125**	...	...	...	...	...	...	...	...	...
23	**Consumption of fixed capital**	...	...	...	...	...	...	...	...	...	...	...	...
24	**Interest**	**80**	**66**	**89**	...	...	...	...	...	...	...	...	...
25	**Subsidies**	**133**	**134**	**137**	...	...	...	...	...	...	...	...	...
26	**Grants**	—	—	—	...	...	...	...	...	...	...	...	...
261	To foreign governments	—	—	—	...	...	...	...	...	...	...	...	...
262	To international organizations	—	—	—	...	...	...	...	...	...	...	...	...
263	To other general government units	—	—	—	...	...	...	...	...	...	...	...	...
2631	Current	—	—	—	...	...	...	...	...	...	...	...	...
2632	Capital	—	—	—	...	...	...	...	...	...	...	...	...

Antigua and Barbuda (311)

In Millions of Eastern Caribbean Dollars (XCD) / Fiscal Year Ends December 31st

		Budgetary Central Government			Central Government (excl. Social Security)			Central Government (incl. Social Security)			General Government		
		2012	2013	2014	2012	2013	2014	2012	2013	2014	2012	2013	2014
27	**Social benefits**	**71**	**76**	**61**	...	...	...	...	...	...	...	...	...
271	Social security benefits	71	76	61	...	...	...	...	...	...	...	...	...
272	Social assistance benefits	—	—	—	...	...	...	...	...	...	...	...	...
273	Employment-related social benefits	—	—	—	...	...	...	...	...	...	...	...	...
28	**Other expense**	—	—	—	...	...	...	...	...	...	...	...	...
281	Property expense other than interest	—	—	—	...	...	...	...	...	...	...	...	...
282	Transfers not elsewhere classified	—	—	—	...	...	...	...	...	...	...	...	...
2821	Current	—	—	—	...	...	...	...	...	...	...	...	...
2822	Capital	—	—	—	...	...	...	...	...	...	...	...	...
	Table 3 Transactions in assets and liabilities												
3	**Change in net worth from transactions**	...	...	...	...	...	...	...	...	...	...	...	...
31	**Net/Gross investment in nonfinancial assets**	**19**	**42**	**54**	...	...	...	...	...	...	...	...	...
311	Fixed assets	21	43	55	...	...	...	...	...	...	...	...	...
3111	Buildings and structures	—	—	—	...	...	...	...	...	...	...	...	...
3112	Machinery and equipment	—	—	—	...	...	...	...	...	...	...	...	...
3113	Other fixed assets	—	—	—	...	...	...	...	...	...	...	...	...
3114	Weapons systems	...	...	...	...	...	...	...	...	...	...	...	...
312	Inventories	—	—	—	...	...	...	...	...	...	...	...	...
313	Valuables	—	—	—	...	...	...	...	...	...	...	...	...
314	Nonproduced assets	-2	-1	-1	...	...	...	...	...	...	...	...	...
3141	Land	-2	-1	-1	...	...	...	...	...	...	...	...	...
3142	Mineral and energy resources	—	—	—	...	...	...	...	...	...	...	...	...
3143	Other naturally occurring assets	—	—	—	...	...	...	...	...	...	...	...	...
3144	Intangible nonproduced assets	—	—	—	...	...	...	...	...	...	...	...	...
32	**Net acquisition of financial assets**	**-117**	**-109**	**-137**	...	...	...	...	...	...	...	...	...
	By instrument												
3201	Monetary gold and SDRs	—	—	—	...	...	...	...	...	...	...	...	...
3202	Currency and deposits	-117	-109	-137	...	...	...	...	...	...	...	...	...
3203	Debt securities	—	—	—	...	...	...	...	...	...	...	...	...
3204	Loans	—	—	—	...	...	...	...	...	...	...	...	...
3205	Equity and investment fund shares	—	—	—	...	...	...	...	...	...	...	...	...
3206	Insurance, pension, and standardized guarantee schemes	—	—	—	...	...	...	...	...	...	...	...	...
3207	Financial derivatives and employee stock options	—	—	—	...	...	...	...	...	...	...	...	...
3208	Other accounts receivable	...	...	...	...	...	...	...	...	...	...	...	...
	By debtor												
321	Domestic debtors	-108	-112	-137	...	...	...	...	...	...	...	...	...
322	External debtors	-9	3	-0	...	...	...	...	...	...	...	...	...
33	**Net incurrence of liabilities**	**-73**	**35**	**-44**	...	...	...	...	...	...	...	...	...
	By instrument												
3301	Special Drawing Rights (SDRs)	...	...	...	...	...	...	...	...	...	...	...	...
3302	Currency and deposits	—	—	—	...	...	...	...	...	...	...	...	...
3303	Debt securities	—	—	—	...	...	...	...	...	...	...	...	...
3304	Loans	35	55	-89	...	...	...	...	...	...	...	...	...
3305	Equity and investment fund shares	—	—	—	...	...	...	...	...	...	...	...	...
3306	Insurance, pension, and standardized guarantee schemes	—	—	—	...	...	...	...	...	...	...	...	...
3307	Financial derivatives and employee stock options	—	—	—	...	...	...	...	...	...	...	...	...
3308	Other accounts payable	-108	-19	45	...	...	...	...	...	...	...	...	...
	By creditor												
331	Domestic creditors	-7	-56	-2	...	...	...	...	...	...	...	...	...
332	External creditors	-66	91	-42	...	...	...	...	...	...	...	...	...
	Table 4 Holding gains and losses in assets and liabilities												
	Table 5 Holding gains and losses in assets and liabilities												
	Table 6 Balance sheet												

Antigua and Barbuda (311)

In Millions of Eastern Caribbean Dollars (XCD) / Fiscal Year Ends December 31st

	Budgetary Central Government			Central Government (excl. Social Security)			Central Government (incl. Social Security)			General Government		
	2012	2013	2014	2012	2013	2014	2012	2013	2014	2012	2013	2014
Table 7 Expenditure by functions of government												
Table 8 Financial transactions by counterpart sector												
Table 9 Total other economic flows in assets and liabilities												

Armenia, Republic of (911)

In Billions of Armenian Drams (AMD) / Fiscal Year Ends December 31st

		Budgetary Central Government			Central Government (excl. Social Security)			Central Government (incl. Social Security)			General Government		
		2013	2014	2015	2013	2014	2015	2013	2014	2015	2013	2014	2015E
	Statement of operations												
1	Revenue	...	1,145	1,168	...	...	1,198	...	1,207	1,198	...	1,252	1,264
2	Expense	...	1,101	1,239	...	...	1,265	...	1,158	1,265	...	1,192	1,323
GOB	**Gross operating balance**	**...**	**43**	**-71**	**...**	**...**	**-67**	**...**	**48**	**-67**	**...**	**60**	**-59**
NOB	**Net operating balance**	**...**	**...**	**...**	**...**	**...**	**...**	**...**	**...**	**...**	**...**	**...**	**...**
31	Net/Gross investment in nonfinancial assets	...	134	170	...	...	...	...	134	170	...	146	170
2M	Expenditure	...	1,235	1,409	...	...	1,435	...	1,292	1,435	...	1,338	...
NLB	**Net lending (+) / Net borrowing (-)**	**...**	**-90**	**-241**	**...**	**...**	**-237**	**...**	**-85**	**-237**	**...**	**-86**	**...**
32	Net acquisition of financial assets	...	-7	28	...	...	...	...	-2	29	...	-50	...
33	Net incurrence of liabilities	...	84	317	...	...	...	...	84	317	...	84	...
NLBz	Statistical discrepancy	...	0	-48	...	...	-51	...	0	-51	...	-48	...
	Memorandum items												
PB	Primary net lending / net borrowing	...	-29	-167	...	...	-163	...	-24	-163	...	-24	...
GB	Government balance per national definition	...	...	...	...	...	...	...	...	...	...	...	...
	Statement of other economic flows												
	Balance sheet												
	Table 1 Revenue												
1	**Revenue**	**...**	**1,145**	**1,168**	**...**	**...**	**1,198**	**...**	**1,207**	**1,198**	**...**	**1,252**	**1,264**
11	**Taxes**	**...**	**1,047**	**1,059**	**...**	**...**	**1,056**	**...**	**1,043**	**1,056**	**...**	**1,066**	**1,088**
111	Taxes on income, profits, and capital gains	...	409	427	...	...	427	...	409	427	...	409	427
1111	Payable by individuals	...	289	312	...	...	312	...	289	312	...	289	312
1112	Payable by corporations and other enterprises	...	104	104	...	...	104	...	104	104	...	104	104
1113	Other taxes on income, profits, and capital gains	...	16	12	...	...	12	...	16	12	...	16	12
112	Taxes on payroll and workforce	...	—	—	...	...	—	...	—	—	...	—	—
113	Taxes on property	...	0	0	...	...	0	...	0	0	...	19	23
114	Taxes on goods and services	...	533	473	...	...	473	...	533	473	...	537	473
1141	General taxes on goods and services	...	440	424	...	...	424	...	440	424	...	440	424
1142	Excises	...	51	49	...	...	49	...	51	49	...	51	49
115	Taxes on international trade and transactions	...	48	61	...	...	61	...	48	61	...	48	61
116	Other taxes	...	57	98	...	...	94	...	53	94	...	53	103
12	**Social contributions**	**...**	**17**	**9**	**...**	**...**	**9**	**...**	**17**	**9**	**...**	**17**	**—**
121	Social security contributions	...	17	9	...	...	9	...	17	9	...	17	—
122	Other social contributions	...	—	—	...	...	—	...	—	—	...	—	—
13	**Grants**	**...**	**17**	**30**	**...**	**...**	**33**	**...**	**23**	**33**	**...**	**23**	**31**
131	From foreign governments	...	3	17	...	...	17	...	3	17	...	3	17
132	From international organizations	...	15	13	...	...	16	...	15	16	...	15	16
133	From other general government units	...	—	—	...	...	0	...	6	0	...	5	-3
1331	Current	...	—	—	...	...	0	...	6	0	...	5	-3
1332	Capital	...	—	—	...	...	—	...	—	—	...	—	1
14	**Other revenue**	**...**	**63**	**70**	**...**	**...**	**100**	**...**	**124**	**100**	**...**	**146**	**145**
	Table 2 Expense by economic type												
2	**Expense**	**...**	**1,101**	**1,239**	**...**	**...**	**1,265**	**...**	**1,158**	**1,265**	**...**	**1,192**	**1,323**
21	**Compensation of employees**	**...**	**119**	**141**	**...**	**...**	**266**	**...**	**250**	**266**	**...**	**270**	**288**
211	Wages and salaries	...	...	...	...	...	...	...	250	...	...	...	...
212	Employers' social contributions	...	...	...	...	...	...	...	...	...	...	...	...
22	**Use of goods and services**	**...**	**237**	**259**	**...**	**...**	**201**	**...**	**198**	**201**	**...**	**223**	**242**
23	**Consumption of fixed capital**	**...**	**...**	**—**	**...**	**...**	**...**	**...**	**...**	**...**	**...**	**...**	**—**
24	**Interest**	**...**	**62**	**74**	**...**	**...**	**74**	**...**	**62**	**74**	**...**	**62**	**74**
25	**Subsidies**	**...**	**28**	**33**	**...**	**...**	**14**	**...**	**12**	**14**	**...**	**35**	**40**
26	**Grants**	**...**	**139**	**93**	**...**	**...**	**64**	**...**	**113**	**64**	**...**	**62**	**8**
261	To foreign governments	...	0	0	...	...	0	...	0	0	...	0	0
262	To international organizations	...	2	2	...	...	2	...	2	2	...	2	2
263	To other general government units	...	137	90	...	...	62	...	111	62	...	60	6
2631	Current	...	129	87	...	...	59	...	102	59	...	52	2
2632	Capital	...	8	3	...	...	...	...	8	3	...	8	4

Armenia, Republic of (911)

In Billions of Armenian Drams (AMD) / Fiscal Year Ends December 31st

		Budgetary Central Government			Central Government (excl. Social Security)			Central Government (incl. Social Security)			General Government		
		2013	2014	2015	2013	2014	2015	2013	2014	2015	2013	2014	2015E
27	**Social benefits**	**...**	**348**	**391**	**...**	**...**	**393**	**...**	**350**	**393**	**...**	**353**	**396**
271	Social security benefits	...	294	268	...	...	268	...	296	0	...	296	0
272	Social assistance benefits	...	54	123	...	...	125	...	54	393	...	57	396
273	Employment-related social benefits	...	—	—	...	...	—	...	—	—	...	—	—
28	**Other expense**	**...**	**168**	**249**	**...**	**...**	**252**	**...**	**174**	**252**	**...**	**187**	**274**
281	Property expense other than interest	...	—	—	...	...	—	...	—	—	...	—	—
282	Transfers not elsewhere classified	...	168	249	...	...	252	...	174	252	...	187	274
2821	Current	...	168	249	...	...	252	...	174	252	...	187	274
2822	Capital	...	—	—	...	...	—	...	—	—	...	—	...
	Table 3 Transactions in assets and liabilities												
3	**Change in net worth from transactions**	**...**	**...**	**-119**	**...**	**...**	**...**	**...**	**...**	**-118**	**...**	**...**	**...**
31	**Net/Gross investment in nonfinancial assets**	**...**	**134**	**170**	**...**	**...**	**...**	**...**	**134**	**170**	**...**	**146**	**170**
311	Fixed assets	...	134	170	...	...	...	...	134	...	...	160	...
3111	Buildings and structures	...	...	126	...	...	...	...	...	...	...	...	...
3112	Machinery and equipment	...	...	37	...	...	...	...	...	...	...	...	...
3113	Other fixed assets	...	...	7	...	...	...	...	...	...	...	...	...
3114	Weapons systems	...	...	—	...	...	...	...	...	...	...	...	...
312	Inventories	...	—	0	...	...	...	...	—	...	...	0	...
313	Valuables	...	—	—	...	...	...	...	—	...	...	—	...
314	Nonproduced assets	...	0	0	...	...	...	...	0	...	...	-14	...
3141	Land	...	0	0	...	...	...	...	...	...	...	...	...
3142	Mineral and energy resources	...	0	0	...	...	...	...	...	...	...	...	...
3143	Other naturally occurring assets	...	0	—	...	...	...	...	...	...	...	...	...
3144	Intangible nonproduced assets	...	0	—	...	...	...	...	...	...	...	...	...
32	**Net acquisition of financial assets**	**...**	**-7**	**28**	**...**	**...**	**...**	**...**	**-2**	**29**	**...**	**-50**	**...**
	By instrument												
3201	Monetary gold and SDRs	...	—	—	...	...	...	...	—	—	...	—	...
3202	Currency and deposits	...	-74	-33	...	...	...	...	-70	-32	...	-70	...
3203	Debt securities	...	—	—	...	...	...	...	—	—	...	—	...
3204	Loans	...	68	59	...	...	...	...	68	59	...	68	...
3205	Equity and investment fund shares	...	—	2	...	...	...	...	—	2	...	—	...
3206	Insurance, pension, and standardized guarantee schemes	...	—	—	...	...	...	...	—	—	...	—	...
3207	Financial derivatives and employee stock options	...	—	—	...	...	...	...	—	—	...	—	...
3208	Other accounts receivable	...	...	—	...	...	...	...	...	—	...	...	...
	By debtor												
321	Domestic debtors	...	-55	-45	...	...	...	...	-50	-44	...	-50	...
322	External debtors	...	48	73	...	...	...	...	48	73	...	48	...
33	**Net incurrence of liabilities**	**...**	**84**	**317**	**...**	**...**	**...**	**...**	**84**	**317**	**...**	**84**	**...**
	By instrument												
3301	Special Drawing Rights (SDRs)	...	—	—	...	...	...	...	—	—	...	—	...
3302	Currency and deposits	...	—	—	...	...	...	...	—	—	...	—	...
3303	Debt securities	...	15	151	...	...	...	...	15	151	...	15	...
3304	Loans	...	69	166	...	...	...	...	69	166	...	69	...
3305	Equity and investment fund shares	...	—	—	...	...	...	...	—	—	...	—	...
3306	Insurance, pension, and standardized guarantee schemes	...	—	—	...	...	...	...	—	—	...	—	...
3307	Financial derivatives and employee stock options	...	—	—	...	...	...	...	—	—	...	—	...
3308	Other accounts payable	...	...	—	...	...	...	...	...	—	...	...	...
	By creditor												
331	Domestic creditors	...	15	14	...	...	...	...	15	14	...	15	...
332	External creditors	...	69	303	...	...	...	...	69	303	...	69	...
	Table 4 Holding gains and losses in assets and liabilities												
	Table 5 Holding gains and losses in assets and liabilities												
	Table 6 Balance sheet												

Armenia, Republic of (911)

In Billions of Armenian Drams (AMD) / Fiscal Year Ends December 31st

		Budgetary Central Government			Central Government (excl. Social Security)			Central Government (incl. Social Security)			General Government		
		2013	2014	2015	2013	2014	2015	2013	2014	2015	2013	2014	2015E
	Table 7 Expenditure by functions of government												
7	**Expenditure**	...	**1,235**	**1,379**	...	...	...	...	**1,292**	...	...	**1,338**	...
701	**General public services**	...	**217**	**281**	...	...	...	...	...	...	...	...	...
7017	Public debt transactions	...	62	74	...	...	...	...	62	...	...	62	...
7018	Transfers of general character between levels of government	...	41	47	...	...	...	...	...	...	...	...	...
702	**Defense**	...	**190**	**199**	...	...	...	...	...	...	...	...	...
703	**Public order and safety**	...	**105**	**122**	...	...	...	...	...	...	...	...	...
704	**Economic affairs**	...	**83**	**110**	...	...	...	...	...	...	...	...	...
7042	Agriculture, forestry, fishing, and hunting	...	20	34	...	...	...	...	...	...	...	...	...
7043	Fuel and energy	...	1	7	...	...	...	...	...	...	...	...	...
7044	Mining, manufacturing, and construction	...	0	0	...	...	...	...	...	...	...	...	...
7045	Transport	...	55	64	...	...	...	...	...	...	...	...	...
7046	Communication	...	0	0	...	...	...	...	...	...	...	...	...
705	**Environmental protection**	...	**5**	**6**	...	...	...	...	...	...	...	...	...
706	**Housing and community amenities**	...	**31**	**39**	...	...	...	...	...	...	...	...	...
707	**Health**	...	**77**	**86**	...	...	...	...	...	...	...	...	...
7072	Outpatient services	...	26	28	...	...	...	...	...	...	...	...	...
7073	Hospital services	...	36	40	...	...	...	...	...	...	...	...	...
7074	Public health services	...	5	5	...	...	...	...	...	...	...	...	...
708	**Recreation, culture and religion**	...	**21**	**30**	...	...	...	...	...	...	...	...	...
709	**Education**	...	**116**	**122**	...	...	...	...	...	...	...	...	...
7091	Pre-primary and primary education	...	24	28	...	...	...	...	...	...	...	...	...
7092	Secondary education	...	53	53	...	...	...	...	...	...	...	...	...
7094	Tertiary education	...	9	11	...	...	...	...	...	...	...	...	...
710	**Social protection**	...	**342**	**384**	...	...	...	...	...	...	...	...	...
7z	Statistical discrepancy: Expenditure	...	...	...	...	...	...	...	...	...	...	...	...
	Table 8 Financial transactions by counterpart sector												
	Table 9 Total other economic flows in assets and liabilities												

Argentina (213)

In Millions of Argentine Pesos (ARS) / Fiscal Year Ends December 31st

		Budgetary Central Government			Central Government (excl. Social Security)			Central Government (incl. Social Security)			General Government		
		2013	2014	2015	2013	2014	2015	2013	2014	2015	2013	2014	2015
	Statement of operations												
1	Revenue	...	...	739,301	...	...	864,363	...	...	1,319,349	...	...	...
2	Expense	...	...	981,110	...	...	1,099,293	...	...	1,489,128	...	...	...
GOB	**Gross operating balance**	...	...	**-241,809**	...	...	**-234,929**	...	...	**-169,778**	...	...	...
NOB	**Net operating balance**	...	...	**-241,809**	...	...	**-234,929**	...	...	**-169,779**	...	...	...
31	Net/Gross investment in nonfinancial assets	...	...	29,230	...	...	29,898	...	...	32,086	...	...	...
2M	Expenditure	...	...	1,010,340	...	...	1,129,191	...	...	1,521,213	...	...	...
NLB	**Net lending (+) / Net borrowing (-)**	...	...	**-271,039**	...	...	**-264,828**	...	...	**-201,864**	...	...	...
32	Net acquisition of financial assets	...	...	-27,561	...	...	-31,958	...	...	23,949	...	...	...
33	Net incurrence of liabilities	...	...	243,478	...	...	232,870	...	...	225,814	...	...	...
NLBz	Statistical discrepancy	...	...	0	...	...	-0	...	...	-0	...	...	...
	Memorandum items												
PB	Primary net lending / net borrowing	...	...	-163,738	...	...	-155,016	...	...	-92,053	...	...	...
GB	Government balance per national definition	...	...	...	...	...	...	...	...	...	...	...	...
	Statement of other economic flows												
	Balance sheet												
	Table 1 Revenue												
1	**Revenue**	...	...	**739,301**	...	...	**864,363**	...	...	**1,319,349**	...	...	...
11	**Taxes**	...	...	**542,721**	...	...	**594,423**	...	...	**734,579**	...	...	...
111	Taxes on income, profits, and capital gains	...	...	124,189	...	...	124,189	...	...	199,987	...	...	...
1111	Payable by individuals	...	...	37,434	...	...	37,434	...	...	60,173	...	...	...
1112	Payable by corporations and other enterprises	...	...	86,755	...	...	86,755	...	...	139,813	...	...	...
1113	Other taxes on income, profits, and capital gains	...	...	—	...	...	—	...	...	—	...	...	...
112	Taxes on payroll and workforce	...	...	—	...	...	—	...	...	3,969	...	...	...
113	Taxes on property	...	...	7,686	...	...	7,686	...	...	7,686	...	...	...
114	Taxes on goods and services	...	...	286,311	...	...	309,030	...	...	369,418	...	...	...
1141	General taxes on goods and services	...	...	250,442	...	...	250,442	...	...	293,715	...	...	...
1142	Excises	...	...	23,309	...	...	23,309	...	...	40,425	...	...	...
115	Taxes on international trade and transactions	...	...	106,146	...	...	106,146	...	...	106,146	...	...	...
116	Other taxes	...	...	18,390	...	...	47,373	...	...	47,373	...	...	...
12	**Social contributions**	...	...	**10,226**	...	...	**64,359**	...	...	**410,854**	...	...	...
121	Social security contributions	...	...	4,568	...	...	...	...	...	...	...	...	...
122	Other social contributions	...	...	5,657	...	...	...	...	...	...	...	...	...
13	**Grants**	...	...	**73,560**	...	...	**86,292**	...	...	**479**	...	...	...
131	From foreign governments	...	...	36	...	...	36	...	...	36	...	...	...
132	From international organizations	...	...	191	...	...	191	...	...	191	...	...	...
133	From other general government units	...	...	73,333	...	...	86,065	...	...	252	...	...	...
1331	Current	...	...	71,324	...	...	84,056	...	...	252	...	...	...
1332	Capital	...	...	2,009	...	...	2,009	...	...	—	...	...	...
14	**Other revenue**	...	...	**112,795**	...	...	**119,289**	...	...	**173,436**	...	...	...
	Table 2 Expense by economic type												
2	**Expense**	...	...	**981,110**	...	...	**1,099,293**	...	...	**1,489,128**	...	...	...
21	**Compensation of employees**	...	...	**153,134**	...	...	**187,407**	...	...	**196,094**	...	...	...
211	Wages and salaries	...	...	127,372	...	...	161,645	...	...	168,587	...	...	...
212	Employers' social contributions	...	...	25,762	...	...	25,762	...	...	27,507	...	...	...
22	**Use of goods and services**	...	...	**56,088**	...	...	**64,895**	...	...	**69,224**	...	...	...
23	**Consumption of fixed capital**	...	...	—	...	...	**0**	...	...	**0**	...	...	...
24	**Interest**	...	...	**107,301**	...	...	**109,811**	...	...	**109,811**	...	...	...
25	**Subsidies**	...	...	**216,864**	...	...	**255,863**	...	...	**255,866**	...	...	...
26	**Grants**	...	...	**289,423**	...	...	**256,316**	...	...	**98,594**	...	...	...
261	To foreign governments	...	...	0	...	...	0	...	...	0	...	...	...
262	To international organizations	...	...	1,583	...	...	1,585	...	...	1,587	...	...	...
263	To other general government units	...	...	287,839	...	...	254,731	...	...	97,007	...	...	...
2631	Current	...	...	215,910	...	...	182,024	...	...	28,634	...	...	...
2632	Capital	...	...	71,929	...	...	72,707	...	...	68,373	...	...	...

Argentina (213)

In Millions of Argentine Pesos (ARS) / Fiscal Year Ends December 31st

		Budgetary Central Government			Central Government (excl. Social Security)			Central Government (incl. Social Security)			General Government		
		2013	2014	2015	2013	2014	2015	2013	2014	2015	2013	2014	2015
27	**Social benefits**	...	...	**86,176**	...	...	**86,176**	...	...	**620,674**	...	...	...
271	Social security benefits	...	...	68,643	...	...	68,643	...	...	527,917	...	...	...
272	Social assistance benefits	...	...	17,469	...	...	17,469	...	...	92,693	...	...	...
273	Employment-related social benefits	...	...	64	...	...	64	...	...	64	...	...	...
28	**Other expense**	...	...	**72,124**	...	...	**138,824**	...	...	**138,864**	...	...	...
281	Property expense other than interest	...	...	10	...	...	16	...	...	31	...	...	...
282	Transfers not elsewhere classified	...	...	72,114	...	...	138,807	...	...	138,833	...	...	...
2821	Current	...	...	68,917	...	...	132,454	...	...	132,473	...	...	...
2822	Capital	...	...	3,197	...	...	6,353	...	...	6,361	...	...	...
	Table 3 Transactions in assets and liabilities												
3	**Change in net worth from transactions**	...	...	**-241,809**	...	...	**-234,930**	...	...	**-169,779**	...	...	...
31	**Net/Gross investment in nonfinancial assets**	...	...	**29,230**	...	...	**29,898**	...	...	**32,086**	...	...	...
311	Fixed assets	...	...	28,365	...	...	29,033	...	...	31,220	...	...	...
3111	Buildings and structures	...	...	21,427	...	...	21,448	...	...	21,661	...	...	...
3112	Machinery and equipment	...	...	6,475	...	...	7,123	...	...	9,015	...	...	...
3113	Other fixed assets	...	...	463	...	...	463	...	...	545	...	...	...
3114	Weapons systems	...	...	—	...	...	—	...	...	—	...	...	...
312	Inventories	...	...	—	...	...	—	...	...	—	...	...	...
313	Valuables	...	...	673	...	...	673	...	...	673	...	...	...
314	Nonproduced assets	...	...	193	...	...	193	...	...	193	...	...	...
3141	Land	...	...	192	...	...	192	...	...	192	...	...	...
3142	Mineral and energy resources	...	...	—	...	...	—	...	...	—	...	...	...
3143	Other naturally occurring assets	...	...	0	...	...	0	...	...	0	...	...	...
3144	Intangible nonproduced assets	...	...	—	...	...	—	...	...	—	...	...	...
32	**Net acquisition of financial assets**	...	...	**-27,561**	...	...	**-31,958**	...	...	**23,949**	...	...	...
	By instrument												
3201	Monetary gold and SDRs	...	...	—	...	...	—	...	...	—	...	...	...
3202	Currency and deposits	...	...	-68,343	...	...	-62,931	...	...	-57,655	...	...	...
3203	Debt securities	...	...	-891	...	...	-9,280	...	...	13,789	...	...	...
3204	Loans	...	...	198	...	...	341	...	...	341	...	...	...
3205	Equity and investment fund shares	...	...	11,081	...	...	11,081	...	...	11,081	...	...	...
3206	Insurance, pension, and standardized guarantee schemes	...	...	—	...	...	—	...	...	—	...	...	...
3207	Financial derivatives and employee stock options	...	...	—	...	...	—	...	...	—	...	...	...
3208	Other accounts receivable	...	...	30,394	...	...	28,831	...	...	56,394	...	...	...
	By debtor												
321	Domestic debtors	...	...	-28,737	...	...	-33,134	...	...	22,773	...	...	...
322	External debtors	...	...	1,176	...	...	1,176	...	...	1,176	...	...	...
33	**Net incurrence of liabilities**	...	...	**243,478**	...	...	**232,870**	...	...	**225,814**	...	...	...
	By instrument												
3301	Special Drawing Rights (SDRs)	...	...	—	...	...	—	...	...	—	...	...	...
3302	Currency and deposits	...	...	—	...	...	—	...	...	—	...	...	...
3303	Debt securities	...	...	220,268	...	...	220,267	...	...	208,630	...	...	...
3304	Loans	...	...	19,985	...	...	10,610	...	...	10,610	...	...	...
3305	Equity and investment fund shares	...	...	—	...	...	—	...	...	—	...	...	...
3306	Insurance, pension, and standardized guarantee schemes	...	...	—	...	...	—	...	...	—	...	...	...
3307	Financial derivatives and employee stock options	...	...	—	...	...	—	...	...	—	...	...	...
3308	Other accounts payable	...	...	3,225	...	...	1,993	...	...	6,573	...	...	...
	By creditor												
331	Domestic creditors	...	...	106,889	...	...	96,281	...	...	89,224	...	...	...
332	External creditors	...	...	136,589	...	...	136,589	...	...	136,589	...	...	...
	Table 4 Holding gains and losses in assets and liabilities												
	Table 5 Holding gains and losses in assets and liabilities												
	Table 6 Balance sheet												

Argentina (213)

In Millions of Argentine Pesos (ARS) / Fiscal Year Ends December 31st

		Budgetary Central Government			Central Government (excl. Social Security)			Central Government (incl. Social Security)			General Government		
		2013	2014	2015	2013	2014	2015	2013	2014	2015	2013	2014	2015
	Table 7 Expenditure by functions of government												
7	**Expenditure**	...	...	**1,010,339**	...	...	**1,129,191**	...	...	**1,521,213**	...	...	...
701	**General public services**	...	...	**332,373**	...	...	**360,925**	...	...	**198,809**	...	...	...
7017	Public debt transactions	...	...	107,301	...	...	109,811	...	...	109,811	...	...	...
7018	Transfers of general character between levels of government	...	...	187,280	...	...	189,508	...	...	27,392	...	...	...
702	**Defense**	...	...	**27,349**	...	...	**27,349**	...	...	**27,349**	...	...	...
703	**Public order and safety**	...	...	**74,361**	...	...	**74,361**	...	...	**74,361**	...	...	...
704	**Economic affairs**	...	...	**307,409**	...	...	**324,620**	...	...	**324,681**	...	...	...
7042	Agriculture, forestry, fishing, and hunting	...	...	7,260	...	...	7,263	...	...	7,263	...	...	...
7043	Fuel and energy	...	...	175,305	...	...	179,575	...	...	179,575	...	...	...
7044	Mining, manufacturing, and construction	...	...	6,393	...	...	4,763	...	...	4,763	...	...	...
7045	Transport	...	...	89,036	...	...	103,178	...	...	103,178	...	...	...
7046	Communication	...	...	11,854	...	...	11,868	...	...	11,868	...	...	...
705	**Environmental protection**	...	...	**3,298**	...	...	**2,128**	...	...	**2,128**	...	...	...
706	**Housing and community amenities**	...	...	**36,623**	...	...	**36,759**	...	...	**36,759**	...	...	...
707	**Health**	...	...	**40,997**	...	...	**103,889**	...	...	**107,938**	...	...	...
7072	Outpatient services	...	...	...	...	...	...	...	...	...	...	...	...
7073	Hospital services	...	...	...	...	...	...	...	...	...	...	...	...
7074	Public health services	...	...	...	...	...	...	...	...	...	...	...	...
708	**Recreation, culture and religion**	...	...	**3,464**	...	...	**4,471**	...	...	**4,471**	...	...	...
709	**Education**	...	...	**90,058**	...	...	**90,043**	...	...	**99,316**	...	...	...
7091	Pre-primary and primary education	...	...	...	...	...	...	...	...	...	...	...	...
7092	Secondary education	...	...	...	...	...	...	...	...	...	...	...	...
7094	Tertiary education	...	...	...	...	...	...	...	...	...	...	...	...
710	**Social protection**	...	...	**94,406**	...	...	**104,645**	...	...	**645,400**	...	...	...
7z	Statistical discrepancy: Expenditure	...	...	...	...	...	...	...	...	...	...	...	...
	Table 8 Financial transactions by counterpart sector												
	Table 9 Total other economic flows in assets and liabilities												

Australia (193)

In Billions of Australian Dollars (AUD) / Fiscal Year Ends June 30th

		Budgetary Central Government			Central Government (excl. Social Security)			Central Government (incl. Social Security)			General Government		
		2013	2014	2015	2013	2014	2015	2013	2014	2015	2013	2014	2015
	Statement of operations												
1	Revenue	376	389	398	376	389	398	376	391	398	518	539	556
2	Expense	398	420	434	398	420	434	397	420	434	541	564	583
GOB	**Gross operating balance**	**-15**	**-23**	**-28**	**-15**	**-23**	**-28**	**-13**	**-21**	**-28**	**2**	**2**	**1**
NOB	**Net operating balance**	**-22**	**-30**	**-37**	**-22**	**-30**	**-37**	**-21**	**-29**	**-37**	**-23**	**-25**	**-27**
31	Net/Gross investment in nonfinancial assets	2	6	6	2	6	6	1	5	6	18	22	20
2M	Expenditure	400	425	441	400	425	441	398	425	441	559	585	603
NLB	**Net lending (+) / Net borrowing (-)**	**-23**	**-36**	**-43**	**-23**	**-36**	**-43**	**-22**	**-35**	**-43**	**-41**	**-46**	**-47**
32	Net acquisition of financial assets	14	24	18	14	24	18	14	24	18	14	30	21
33	Net incurrence of liabilities	37	60	61	37	60	61	37	60	61	55	76	68
NLBz	Statistical discrepancy	0	—	0	0	—	—	-1	-1	-0	—	—	—
	Memorandum items												
PB	Primary net lending / net borrowing	-10	-22	-19	-10	-22	-28	-9	-21	-28	-20	-24	-23
GB	Government balance per national definition	...	...	...	...	...	...	...	...	...	...	...	...
	Statement of other economic flows												
9	**Change in net worth due to other economic flows**	**75**	**-1**	**...**	**75**	**-1**	**...**	**75**	**-1**	**...**	**133**	**26**	**...**
4	Change in net worth due to holding gains and losses	...	...	...	...	...	...	...	...	...	...	...	...
41	Nonfinancial assets	...	...	...	...	...	...	...	...	...	...	...	...
42	Financial assets	...	...	...	...	...	...	...	...	...	...	...	...
43	Liabilities	...	...	...	...	...	...	...	...	...	...	...	...
5	Change in net worth due to volume changes	...	...	...	...	...	...	...	...	...	...	...	...
51	Nonfinancial assets	...	...	...	...	...	...	...	...	...	...	...	...
52	Financial assets	...	...	...	...	...	...	...	...	...	...	...	...
53	Liabilities	...	...	...	...	...	...	...	...	...	...	...	...
	Balance sheet												
6	**Net worth**	**-157**	**-190**	**-245**	**-157**	**-190**	**-245**	**-162**	**-197**	**-245**	**839**	**833**	**837**
61	Nonfinancial assets	143	154	169	143	154	169	138	146	169	1,060	1,097	1,163
62	Financial assets	285	331	349	285	331	349	285	331	349	694	764	802
63	Liabilities	584	675	763	584	675	763	584	675	763	916	1,028	1,129
	Table 1 Revenue												
1	**Revenue**	**376**	**389**	**398**	**376**	**389**	**398**	**376**	**391**	**398**	**518**	**539**	**556**
11	**Taxes**	**340**	**353**	**357**	**340**	**353**	**357**	**338**	**352**	**357**	**416**	**436**	**446**
111	Taxes on income, profits, and capital gains	242	248	259	242	248	259	242	248	259	242	248	259
1111	Payable by individuals	163	170	183	163	170	183	163	170	183	163	170	183
1112	Payable by corporations and other enterprises	78	77	74	78	77	74	78	77	74	78	77	74
1113	Other taxes on income, profits, and capital gains	1	2	2	1	2	2	1	1	2	1	2	2
112	Taxes on payroll and workforce	1	1	1	1	1	1	1	1	1	21	22	22
113	Taxes on property	—	—	—	—	—	—	—	—	—	22	24	25
114	Taxes on goods and services	89	95	87	89	95	87	88	93	87	124	133	129
1141	General taxes on goods and services	52	57	58	52	57	58	51	57	58	66	74	78
1142	Excises	26	26	24	26	26	24	26	26	24	26	27	25
115	Taxes on international trade and transactions	8	9	11	8	9	11	8	9	11	8	9	11
116	Other taxes	—	—	—	—	—	—	—	—	—	—	—	—
12	**Social contributions**	—	—	—	—	—	—	—	—	—	—	—	—
121	Social security contributions	—	—	—	—	—	—	—	—	—	—	—	—
122	Other social contributions	—	—	—	—	—	—	—	—	—	—	—	—
13	**Grants**	**1**	**1**	**0**	**1**	**1**	**1**	**1**	**1**	**0**	**0**	**0**	**0**
131	From foreign governments	—	—	—	—	—	—	—	—	—	0	0	0
132	From international organizations	—	—	—	—	—	—	—	—	—	—	—	—
133	From other general government units	1	1	0	1	1	1	1	1	0	—	—	—
1331	Current	1	1	0	1	1	0	1	0	0	—	—	—
1332	Capital	0	0	0	0	0	0	0	0	0	—	—	—
14	**Other revenue**	**36**	**36**	**40**	**36**	**36**	**40**	**37**	**39**	**40**	**101**	**103**	**110**

Australia (193)

In Billions of Australian Dollars (AUD) / Fiscal Year Ends June 30th

		Budgetary Central Government			Central Government (excl. Social Security)			Central Government (incl. Social Security)			General Government		
		2013	2014	2015	2013	2014	2015	2013	2014	2015	2013	2014	2015
	Table 2 Expense by economic type												
2	**Expense**	**398**	**420**	**434**	**398**	**420**	**434**	**397**	**420**	**434**	**541**	**564**	**583**
21	**Compensation of employees**	**46**	**44**	**45**	**46**	**44**	**45**	**46**	**44**	**45**	**151**	**152**	**157**
211	Wages and salaries	36	37	37	36	37	37	35	37	37	131	134	137
212	Employers' social contributions	10	8	9	10	8	9	10	8	9	20	18	20
22	**Use of goods and services**	**40**	**42**	**44**	**40**	**42**	**44**	**40**	**42**	**44**	**99**	**103**	**107**
23	**Consumption of fixed capital**	**7**	**8**	**8**	**7**	**8**	**8**	**7**	**8**	**8**	**25**	**26**	**28**
24	**Interest**	**13**	**14**	**24**	**13**	**14**	**15**	**13**	**14**	**15**	**21**	**22**	**24**
25	**Subsidies**	**14**	**16**	**13**	**14**	**16**	**13**	**14**	**16**	**13**	**23**	**25**	**22**
26	**Grants**	**96**	**102**	**108**	**96**	**102**	**108**	**96**	**102**	**108**	**4**	**4**	**4**
261	To foreign governments	4	4	4	4	4	4	4	4	4	4	4	4
262	To international organizations	—	—	—	—	—	—	—	—	—	—	—	—
263	To other general government units	92	98	103	92	98	104	92	98	103	—	—	—
2631	Current	85	89	96	85	89	96	85	89	96	—	—	—
2632	Capital	7	10	7	7	10	7	7	9	7	—	—	—
27	**Social benefits**	**157**	**166**	**173**	**157**	**166**	**173**	**157**	**166**	**173**	**163**	**173**	**180**
271	Social security benefits	117	125	131	117	125	131	...	125	131	119	127	133
272	Social assistance benefits	40	41	43	40	41	43	...	41	43	43	46	46
273	Employment-related social benefits	—	—	—	—	—	—	—	—	—	—	—	—
28	**Other expense**	**25**	**27**	**18**	**25**	**27**	**27**	**24**	**27**	**27**	**55**	**59**	**61**
281	Property expense other than interest	7	8	—	7	8	9	7	8	9	11	13	14
282	Transfers not elsewhere classified	18	19	18	18	19	18	17	19	18	44	46	47
2821	Current	14	14	15	14	14	15	14	14	15	34	36	39
2822	Capital	4	5	3	4	5	3	3	4	3	9	9	8
	Table 3 Transactions in assets and liabilities												
3	**Change in net worth from transactions**	**-22**	**-30**	**-37**	**-22**	**-30**	**-37**	**-21**	**-29**	**-37**	**-23**	**-25**	**-27**
31	**Net/Gross investment in nonfinancial assets**	**2**	**6**	**6**	**2**	**6**	**6**	**1**	**5**	**6**	**18**	**22**	**20**
311	Fixed assets	4	5	6	4	5	6	3	4	6	21	20	19
3111	Buildings and structures	...	...	...	...	...	...	...	...	...	...	...	...
3112	Machinery and equipment	...	...	...	...	...	...	...	...	...	...	...	...
3113	Other fixed assets	...	...	...	...	...	...	...	...	...	...	...	...
3114	Weapons systems	...	...	...	...	...	...	...	...	...	...	...	...
312	Inventories	1	1	1	1	1	1	1	1	1	1	1	1
313	Valuables	—	—	—	—	—	—	—	—	—	—	—	—
314	Nonproduced assets	-3	0	0	-3	0	—	-3	0	0	-4	1	1
3141	Land	...	...	...	...	...	—	0	-0	...	...	...	...
3142	Mineral and energy resources	...	...	...	...	...	—	—	—	...	...	...	...
3143	Other naturally occurring assets	...	...	...	...	...	—	—	—	...	...	...	...
3144	Intangible nonproduced assets	...	...	...	...	...	—	-3	0	...	...	...	...
32	**Net acquisition of financial assets**	**14**	**24**	**18**	**14**	**24**	**18**	**14**	**24**	**18**	**14**	**30**	**21**
	By instrument												
3201	Monetary gold and SDRs	—	—	—	—	—	—	—	—	—	—	—	—
3202	Currency and deposits	-0	2	-0	-0	2	-1	-0	2	-0	1	2	4
3203	Debt securities	6	8	12	6	8	12	6	8	12	9	14	15
3204	Loans	5	3	6	5	3	6	5	3	6	5	4	5
3205	Equity and investment fund shares	3	12	-1	3	12	-1	3	12	-1	-1	11	-3
3206	Insurance, pension, and standardized guarantee schemes	—	—	—	—	—	—	—	—	—	—	—	—
3207	Financial derivatives and employee stock options	—	—	—	—	—	—	—	—	—	—	—	—
3208	Other accounts receivable	1	-1	1	1	-1	1	1	-1	1	0	-1	0
	By debtor												
321	Domestic debtors	...	...	...	...	...	...	...	...	...	...	...	...
322	External debtors	...	...	...	...	...	...	...	...	...	...	...	...
33	**Net incurrence of liabilities**	**37**	**60**	**61**	**37**	**60**	**61**	**37**	**60**	**61**	**55**	**76**	**68**
	By instrument												
3301	Special Drawing Rights (SDRs)	—	—	—	—	—	—	—	—	—	—	—	—
3302	Currency and deposits	0	0	0	0	0	0	0	0	0	—	-1	-0
3303	Debt securities	28	64	53	28	64	53	28	64	53	29	64	53
3304	Loans	...	...	...	...	...	...	...	...	...	18	10	2

Australia (193)

In Billions of Australian Dollars (AUD) / Fiscal Year Ends June 30th

		Budgetary Central Government			Central Government (excl. Social Security)			Central Government (incl. Social Security)			General Government		
		2013	2014	2015	2013	2014	2015	2013	2014	2015	2013	2014	2015
3305	Equity and investment fund shares	—	—	—	—	—	—	—	—	—	—	—	—
3306	Insurance, pension, and standardized guarantee schemes	9	6	7	9	6	7	9	6	7	12	10	10
3307	Financial derivatives and employee stock options	—	—	—	—	—	—	—	—	—	—	—	—
3308	Other accounts payable	1	-10	1	1	-10	1	1	-10	1	-4	-7	4
	By creditor												
331	Domestic creditors	...	...	...	...	...	...	...	...	...	...	...	...
332	External creditors	...	...	...	...	...	...	...	...	...	...	...	...
	Table 4 Holding gains and losses in assets and liabilities												
	Table 5 Holding gains and losses in assets and liabilities												
	Table 6 Balance sheet												
6	**Net worth**	**-157**	**-190**	**-245**	**-157**	**-190**	**-245**	**-162**	**-197**	**-245**	**839**	**833**	**837**
61	**Nonfinancial assets**	**143**	**154**	**169**	**143**	**154**	**169**	**138**	**146**	**169**	**1,060**	**1,097**	**1,163**
611	Fixed assets	106	116	129	106	116	129	101	108	129	718	755	801
6111	Buildings and structures	52	54	57	52	54	57	51	54	57	635	667	702
6112	Machinery and equipment	16	17	18	16	17	18	45	49	18	39	38	39
6113	Other fixed assets	4	5	5	4	5	5	4	5	5	9	9	10
6114	Weapons systems	34	40	50	34	40	50	—	—	50	34	40	50
612	Inventories	8	8	9	8	8	9	8	8	9	9	10	10
613	Valuables	11	12	12	11	12	12	11	12	12	25	25	27
614	Nonproduced assets	18	18	20	18	18	20	18	18	20	309	307	325
6141	Land	15	16	16	15	16	16	15	15	16	302	300	317
6142	Mineral and energy resources	...	...	...	...	...	...	—	—	...	...	...	...
6143	Other naturally occurring assets	—	—	—	—	—	—	0	0	—	0	—	—
6144	Intangible nonproduced assets	3	3	3	3	3	3	2	3	3	7	7	9
62	**Financial assets**	**285**	**331**	**349**	**285**	**331**	**349**	**285**	**331**	**349**	**694**	**764**	**802**
	By instrument												
6201	Monetary gold and SDRs	—	—	—	—	—	—	—	—	—	—	—	—
6202	Currency and deposits	6	7	7	6	7	7	6	7	7	32	36	40
6203	Debt securities	116	126	145	116	126	145	116	126	145	180	191	214
6204	Loans	37	43	46	37	43	46	37	43	46	49	60	60
6205	Equity and investment fund shares	60	85	85	60	85	85	60	85	85	340	382	392
6206	Insurance, pension, and standardized guarantee schemes	—	—	—	—	—	—	—	—	—	—	—	—
6207	Financial derivatives and employee stock options	—	—	—	—	—	—	—	—	—	—	—	—
6208	Other accounts receivable	66	70	66	66	70	66	66	70	66	92	96	96
	By debtor												
621	Domestic debtors	...	...	...	...	...	...	...	...	...	...	...	...
622	External debtors	...	...	...	...	...	...	...	...	...	...	...	...
63	**Liabilities**	**584**	**675**	**763**	**584**	**675**	**763**	**584**	**675**	**763**	**916**	**1,028**	**1,129**
	By instrument												
6301	Special Drawing Rights (SDRs)	5	5	6	5	5	6	5	5	6	5	5	6
6302	Currency and deposits	4	4	4	4	4	4	4	4	4	8	8	8
6303	Debt securities	296	357	417	296	357	417	296	357	417	298	360	419
6304	Loans	6	9	11	6	9	11	6	9	11	136	150	155
6305	Equity and investment fund shares	—	—	—	—	—	—	—	—	—	—	—	—
6306	Insurance, pension, and standardized guarantee schemes	201	228	257	201	228	257	201	228	257	328	364	399
6307	Financial derivatives and employee stock options	—	—	—	—	—	—	—	—	—	—	—	—
6308	Other accounts payable	74	72	69	74	72	69	74	72	69	141	142	142
	By creditor												
631	Domestic creditors	...	...	...	...	...	...	...	...	...	...	...	...
632	External creditors	...	...	...	...	...	...	...	...	...	...	...	...
	Memorandum items												
6M2	Net financial worth	-295	-338	-408	-295	-338	-408	-300	-343	-414	-216	-259	-321

Australia (193)

In Billions of Australian Dollars (AUD) / Fiscal Year Ends June 30th

		Budgetary Central Government			Central Government (excl. Social Security)			Central Government (incl. Social Security)			General Government		
		2013	2014	2015	2013	2014	2015	2013	2014	2015	2013	2014	2015
6M3	Gross debt (D4) at market value	584	675	763	584	675	763	584	675	763	916	1,028	1,129
6M3D3	D3 debt liabilities at market value	384	447	506	384	447	506	383	446	506	588	664	729
6M3D2	D2 debt liabilities at market value	310	375	437	310	375	437	310	375	437	447	522	587
6M3D1	D1 debt liabilities at market value	301	366	427	301	366	427	301	366	427	433	509	574
6M4	Gross debt (D4) at nominal value	...	...	...	...	...	...	...	...	...	...	...	...
6M4D3	D3 debt liabilities at nominal value	...	...	...	...	...	...	...	...	...	...	...	...
6M4D2	D2 debt liabilities at nominal value	...	...	...	...	...	...	...	...	...	...	...	...
6M4D1	D1 debt liabilities at nominal value	...	...	...	...	...	...	...	...	...	...	...	...
6M35	Gross debt (D4) at face value	...	...	...	...	...	...	...	...	...	...	...	...
6M35D3	D3 debt liabilities at face value	...	...	...	...	...	...	...	...	...	...	...	...
6M35D2	D2 debt liabilities at face value	...	...	...	...	...	...	...	...	...	...	...	...
6M35D1	D1 debt liabilities at face value	...	...	...	...	...	...	...	...	...	...	...	...
6M93	Government gross debt per national definition	...	...	...	...	...	...	...	...	...	...	...	...
6M5	Arrears	...	...	...	...	...	...	...	...	...	...	...	...
6M6	Explicit contingent liabilities	...	...	...	...	...	...	...	...	...	...	...	...
6M61	of which: Publicly guaranteed debt	...	...	...	...	...	...	...	...	...	...	...	...
6M7	Net implicit obligations for social security benefits	...	...	...	...	...	...	...	...	...	...	...	...
	Table 7 Expenditure by functions of government												
7	**Expenditure**	**400**	**425**	**434**	**400**	**425**	**441**	**398**	**425**	**441**	**559**	**585**	**603**
701	**General public services**	**97**	**101**	**107**	**97**	**101**	**108**	**97**	**101**	**108**	**71**	**75**	**78**
7017	Public debt transactions	13	14	24	13	14	15	13	14	15	21	22	24
7018	Transfers of general character between levels of government	52	54	60	52	54	60	52	54	60	1	1	1
702	**Defense**	**22**	**25**	**24**	**22**	**25**	**27**	**22**	**25**	**27**	**22**	**25**	**27**
703	**Public order and safety**	**4**	**4**	**4**	**4**	**4**	**4**	**4**	**4**	**4**	**26**	**26**	**28**
704	**Economic affairs**	**24**	**31**	**29**	**24**	**31**	**29**	**24**	**31**	**29**	**67**	**72**	**71**
7042	Agriculture, forestry, fishing, and hunting	2	2	2	2	2	2	2	2	2	4	4	4
7043	Fuel and energy	6	6	7	6	6	7	6	6	7	8	8	8
7044	Mining, manufacturing, and construction	3	4	4	3	4	4	3	4	4	5	5	5
7045	Transport	5	8	6	5	8	6	5	8	6	38	38	39
7046	Communication	-3	0	1	-3	0	1	-3	0	1	-3	0	1
705	**Environmental protection**	**7**	**7**	**3**	**7**	**7**	**3**	**7**	**7**	**3**	**15**	**15**	**11**
706	**Housing and community amenities**	**3**	**4**	**4**	**3**	**4**	**4**	**3**	**4**	**4**	**12**	**12**	**13**
707	**Health**	**61**	**64**	**66**	**61**	**64**	**66**	**61**	**64**	**66**	**105**	**108**	**112**
7072	Outpatient services	24	25	27	24	25	27	24	25	27	36	36	38
7073	Hospital services	16	17	18	16	17	18	16	17	18	44	46	49
7074	Public health services	21	22	21	21	22	21	21	22	21	26	27	25
708	**Recreation, culture and religion**	**3**	**3**	**3**	**3**	**3**	**3**	**3**	**3**	**3**	**12**	**13**	**13**
709	**Education**	**45**	**46**	**47**	**45**	**46**	**48**	**45**	**46**	**48**	**82**	**84**	**86**
7091	Pre-primary and primary education	—	—	—	—	—	—	—	—	—	22	23	24
7092	Secondary education	—	—	0	—	—	—	—	—	—	18	19	19
7094	Tertiary education	27	27	28	27	27	29	27	27	29	31	31	32
710	**Social protection**	**134**	**141**	**148**	**134**	**141**	**148**	**134**	**141**	**148**	**147**	**156**	**165**
7z	Statistical discrepancy: Expenditure	...	...	...	—	—	—	—	—	—	—	—	—

Australia (193)

In Billions of Australian Dollars (AUD) / Fiscal Year Ends June 30th

		Budgetary Central Government			Central Government (excl. Social Security)			Central Government (incl. Social Security)			General Government		
		2013	2014	2015	2013	2014	2015	2013	2014	2015	2013	2014	2015
	Table 8 Financial transactions by counterpart sector												
32	**Net acquisition of financial assets**	**14**	**24**	**18**	**14**	**24**	**18**	**14**	**24**	**18**	**14**	**30**	**21**
321	Domestic debtors	...	...	...	...	...	...	...	...	...	...	...	...
8211	General government	...	...	...	...	...	...	...	...	...	...	...	...
8212	Central bank	...	...	...	...	...	...	...	...	...	...	...	...
8213	Deposit-taking corporations except the central bank	...	...	...	...	...	...	...	...	...	...	...	...
8214	Other financial corporations	...	...	...	...	...	...	...	...	...	...	...	...
8215	Nonfinancial corporations	...	...	...	...	...	...	...	...	...	...	...	...
8216	Households & nonprofit institutions serving households	...	...	...	...	...	...	...	...	...	...	...	...
322	External debtors	...	...	...	...	...	...	...	...	...	...	...	...
8221	General government	...	...	...	...	...	...	...	...	...	...	...	...
8227	International organizations	...	...	...	...	...	...	...	...	...	...	...	...
8228	Financial corporations other than international organizations	...	...	...	...	...	...	...	...	...	...	...	...
8229	Other nonresidents	...	...	...	...	...	...	...	...	...	...	...	...
33	**Net incurrence of liabilities**	**37**	**60**	**61**	**37**	**60**	**61**	**37**	**60**	**61**	**55**	**76**	**68**
331	Domestic creditors	...	...	...	...	...	...	...	...	...	...	...	...
8311	General government	...	...	...	...	...	...	...	...	...	...	...	...
8312	Central bank	...	...	...	...	...	...	...	...	...	...	...	...
8313	Deposit-taking corporations except the central bank	...	...	...	...	...	...	...	...	...	...	...	...
8314	Other financial corporations	...	...	...	...	...	...	...	...	...	...	...	...
8315	Nonfinancial corporations	...	...	...	...	...	...	...	...	...	...	...	...
8316	Households & nonprofit institutions serving households	...	...	...	...	...	...	...	...	...	...	...	...
332	External creditors	...	...	...	...	...	...	...	...	...	...	...	...
8321	General government	...	...	...	...	...	...	...	...	...	...	...	...
8327	International organizations	...	...	...	...	...	...	...	...	...	...	...	...
8328	Financial corporations other than international organizations	...	...	...	...	...	...	...	...	...	...	...	...
8329	Other nonresidents	...	...	...	...	...	...	...	...	...	...	...	...
	Table 9 Total other economic flows in assets and liabilities												
9	**Change in net worth due to other economic flows**	**75**	**-1**	**...**	**75**	**-1**	**...**	**75**	**-1**	**...**	**133**	**26**	**...**
91	**Other economic flows in nonfinancial assets**	**3**	**3**	**...**	**3**	**3**	**...**	**3**	**3**	**...**	**25**	**13**	**...**
911	Fixed assets	-0	2	...	-0	2	...	-0	2	...	21	16	...
912	Inventories	-0	-0	...	-0	-0	...	-0	-0	...	-1	-0	...
913	Valuables	0	0	...	0	0	...	0	0	...	-1	0	...
914	Nonproduced assets	3	0	...	3	0	...	3	0	...	4	-2	...
92	**Other economic flows in financial assets**	**17**	**22**	**...**	**17**	**22**	**...**	**17**	**22**	**...**	**42**	**44**	**...**
	By instrument												
9201	Monetary gold and SDRs	—	—	...	—	—	...	—	—	...	—	—	...
9202	Currency and deposits	-0	-0	...	-0	-0	...	-0	-0	...	1	2	...
9203	Debt securities	7	2	...	7	2	...	7	2	...	7	-3	...
9204	Loans	-2	3	...	-2	3	...	-2	3	...	1	7	...
9205	Equity and investment fund shares	6	13	...	6	13	...	6	13	...	22	34	...
9206	Insurance, pension, and standardized guarantee schemes	—	—	...	—	—	...	—	—	...	—	—	...
9207	Financial derivatives and employee stock options	—	—	...	—	—	...	—	—	...	—	—	...
9208	Other accounts receivable	6	5	...	6	5	...	6	5	...	10	5	...
	By debtor												
921	Domestic debtors	...	...	...	...	...	...	...	...	...	...	...	...
922	External debtors	...	...	...	...	...	...	...	...	...	...	...	...
93	**Other economic flows in liabilities**	**-55**	**26**	**...**	**-55**	**26**	**...**	**-55**	**26**	**...**	**-66**	**32**	**...**

Australia (193)

In Billions of Australian Dollars (AUD) / Fiscal Year Ends June 30th

		Budgetary Central Government			Central Government (excl. Social Security)			Central Government (incl. Social Security)			General Government		
		2013	2014	2015	2013	2014	2015	2013	2014	2015	2013	2014	2015
	By instrument												
9301	Special Drawing Rights (SDRs)	0	-5	...	0	-5	...	0	-5	...	0	-5	...
9302	Currency and deposits	-0	0	...	-0	0	...	-0	0	...	-0	0	...
9303	Debt securities	20	62	...	20	62	...	20	62	...	20	62	...
9304	Loans	-27	-60	...	-27	-60	...	-27	-60	...	-19	-60	...
9305	Equity and investment fund shares	—	—	...	—	—	...	—	—	...	—	—	...
9306	Insurance, pension, and standardized guarantee schemes	-50	21	...	-50	21	...	-50	21	...	-78	27	...
9307	Financial derivatives and employee stock options	—	—	...	—	—	...	—	—	...	—	—	...
9308	Other accounts payable	1	9	...	1	9	...	1	9	...	10	8	...
	By creditor												
931	Domestic creditors	...	...	...	...	...	...	...	...	...	...	...	...
932	External creditors	...	...	...	...	...	...	...	...	...	...	...	...
	Memorandum items												
9M2	Change in net financial worth due to other economic flows	72	-4	...	72	-4	...	72	-4	...	108	12	...
9M3	Gross debt (D4) at market value: other economic flows	-55	26	...	-55	26	...	-55	26	...	-66	32	...
9M3D3	D3 debt liabilities at market value: other economic flows	-5	5	...	-5	5	...	-5	5	...	11	5	...
9M3D2	D2 debt liabilities at market value: other economic flows	-6	-4	...	-6	-4	...	-6	-4	...	1	-3	...
9M3D1	D1 debt liabilities at market value: other economic flows	-6	1	...	-6	1	...	-6	1	...	1	2	...

Austria (122)

In Millions of Euros (EUR) / Fiscal Year Ends December 31st

		Budgetary Central Government			Central Government (excl. Social Security)			Central Government (incl. Social Security)			General Government		
		2013	2014	2015	2013	2014	2015	2013	2014	2015	2013	2014	2015
	Statement of operations												
1	Revenue	...	...	...	106,003	108,679	113,424	145,906	149,833	156,280	160,699	165,036	171,630
2	Expense	...	...	...	111,520	117,327	116,640	150,992	158,183	159,230	165,917	173,110	174,134
GOB	**Gross operating balance**	...	...	...	**-1,023**	**-4,091**	**1,400**	**-424**	**-3,624**	**1,837**	**3,387**	**664**	**6,335**
NOB	**Net operating balance**	...	...	...	**-5,517**	**-8,648**	**-3,216**	**-5,086**	**-8,350**	**-2,949**	**-5,218**	**-8,074**	**-2,504**
31	Net/Gross investment in nonfinancial assets	...	...	...	-936	678	772	-923	673	773	-808	981	1,038
2M	Expenditure	...	...	...	110,584	118,004	117,412	150,069	158,856	160,003	165,108	174,090	175,173
NLB	**Net lending (+) / Net borrowing (-)**	...	...	...	**-4,581**	**-9,326**	**-3,988**	**-4,163**	**-9,024**	**-3,722**	**-4,409**	**-9,055**	**-3,543**
32	Net acquisition of financial assets	...	...	...	-2,002	-1,657	-1,437	...	...	...	-1,776	-2,168	-528
33	Net incurrence of liabilities	...	...	...	2,204	8,326	3,260	...	...	...	2,201	7,367	3,609
NLBz	Statistical discrepancy	...	...	...	375	-657	-708	...	...	...	433	-481	-594
	Memorandum items												
PB	Primary net lending / net borrowing	...	...	...	3,620	-1,423	3,899	4,041	-1,118	4,168	4,471	-492	4,940
GB	Government balance per national definition	...	...	...	...	...	...	...	...	...	...	...	...
	Statement of other economic flows												
	Balance sheet												
6	**Net worth**	...	...	...	...	...	...	...	...	...	...	...	...
61	Nonfinancial assets	...	...	...	...	...	...	...	...	...	...	...	...
62	Financial assets	...	...	...	78,579	98,814	109,004	...	...	...	144,702	165,525	175,413
63	Liabilities	...	...	...	282,125	317,258	325,302	...	...	...	330,230	364,770	372,879
	Table 1 Revenue												
1	**Revenue**	...	...	...	**106,003**	**108,679**	**113,424**	**145,906**	**149,833**	**156,280**	**160,699**	**165,036**	**171,630**
11	**Taxes**	...	...	...	**85,561**	**88,010**	**92,272**	**85,561**	**88,010**	**92,272**	**91,237**	**93,859**	**98,142**
111	Taxes on income, profits, and capital gains	...	...	...	39,960	41,841	44,941	39,960	41,841	44,941	40,976	42,882	45,994
1111	Payable by individuals	...	...	...	31,940	33,770	36,174	31,940	33,770	36,174	32,820	34,673	37,089
1112	Payable by corporations and other enterprises	...	...	...	7,105	7,135	7,801	7,105	7,135	7,801	7,240	7,273	7,939
1113	Other taxes on income, profits, and capital gains	...	...	...	915	936	965	915	936	965	915	936	965
112	Taxes on payroll and workforce	...	...	...	5,574	5,755	5,895	5,574	5,755	5,895	8,574	8,844	9,068
113	Taxes on property	...	...	...	789	341	131	789	341	131	1,483	1,044	849
114	Taxes on goods and services	...	...	...	39,041	39,843	41,097	39,041	39,843	41,097	39,966	40,817	41,989
1141	General taxes on goods and services	...	...	...	25,752	26,331	27,362	25,752	26,331	27,362	25,752	26,331	27,362
1142	Excises	...	...	...	7,520	7,500	7,666	7,520	7,500	7,666	7,519	7,500	7,666
115	Taxes on international trade and transactions	...	...	...	—	—	—	—	—	—	—	—	—
116	Other taxes	...	...	...	197	230	210	197	230	210	238	272	242
12	**Social contributions**	...	...	...	**7,959**	**8,154**	**8,421**	**47,287**	**48,776**	**50,519**	**49,116**	**50,532**	**52,286**
121	Social security contributions	...	...	...	285	287	286	39,560	40,859	42,336	39,590	40,896	42,374
122	Other social contributions	...	...	...	7,675	7,867	8,135	7,728	7,918	8,183	9,527	9,637	9,912
13	**Grants**	...	...	...	**1,029**	**1,040**	**1,040**	**730**	**754**	**911**	**163**	**188**	**241**
131	From foreign governments	...	...	...	—	—	—	—	—	—	—	—	—
132	From international organizations	...	...	...	125	154	204	142	158	211	163	188	241
133	From other general government units	...	...	...	904	886	835	587	596	699	—	—	—
1331	Current	...	...	...	833	839	795	516	550	645	—	—	—
1332	Capital	...	...	...	71	46	40	71	47	54	—	—	—
14	**Other revenue**	...	...	...	**11,453**	**11,475**	**11,691**	**12,328**	**12,292**	**12,579**	**20,183**	**20,457**	**20,962**
	Table 2 Expense by economic type												
2	**Expense**	...	...	...	**111,520**	**117,327**	**116,640**	**150,992**	**158,183**	**159,230**	**165,917**	**173,110**	**174,134**
21	**Compensation of employees**	...	...	...	**13,981**	**14,273**	**14,802**	**15,801**	**16,124**	**16,677**	**34,632**	**35,342**	**36,640**
211	Wages and salaries	...	...	...	11,429	11,682	12,053	12,945	13,225	13,619	28,112	28,715	29,709
212	Employers' social contributions	...	...	...	2,553	2,591	2,750	2,856	2,899	3,059	6,519	6,627	6,931
22	**Use of goods and services**	...	...	...	**8,648**	**8,597**	**8,742**	**9,488**	**9,483**	**9,661**	**20,461**	**20,679**	**21,163**
23	**Consumption of fixed capital**	...	...	...	**4,495**	**4,558**	**4,616**	**4,661**	**4,727**	**4,786**	**8,604**	**8,738**	**8,839**
24	**Interest**	...	...	...	**8,201**	**7,903**	**7,887**	**8,204**	**7,906**	**7,890**	**8,880**	**8,562**	**8,483**
25	**Subsidies**	...	...	...	**2,865**	**3,101**	**3,179**	**3,005**	**3,225**	**3,306**	**4,379**	**4,654**	**4,680**

Austria (122)

In Millions of Euros (EUR) / Fiscal Year Ends December 31st

		Budgetary Central Government			Central Government (excl. Social Security)			Central Government (incl. Social Security)			General Government		
		2013	2014	2015	2013	2014	2015	2013	2014	2015	2013	2014	2015
26	**Grants**	...	...	...	**50,787**	**52,017**	**55,160**	**40,029**	**40,841**	**44,324**	**3,855**	**3,378**	**5,216**
261	To foreign governments	...	...	...	713	720	2,381	734	741	2,402	742	749	2,410
262	To international organizations	...	...	...	3,114	2,629	2,806	3,114	2,629	2,806	3,114	2,629	2,806
263	To other general government units	...	...	...	46,961	48,669	49,973	36,181	37,471	39,116	—	—	—
2631	Current	...	...	...	46,114	48,014	49,135	35,528	36,827	38,280	—	—	—
2632	Capital	...	...	...	847	655	838	654	645	836	—	—	—
27	**Social benefits**	...	...	...	**18,202**	**18,562**	**19,294**	**65,361**	**67,459**	**69,522**	**74,029**	**76,594**	**79,049**
271	Social security benefits	...	...	...	...	...	...	...	...	...	...	...	...
272	Social assistance benefits	...	...	...	...	...	...	...	...	...	...	...	...
273	Employment-related social benefits	...	...	...	...	...	...	...	...	...	...	...	...
28	**Other expense**	...	...	...	**4,342**	**8,316**	**2,960**	**4,443**	**8,418**	**3,063**	**11,076**	**15,162**	**10,064**
281	Property expense other than interest	...	...	...	—	—	6	—	—	6	7	7	16
282	Transfers not elsewhere classified	...	...	...	4,336	8,311	2,949	4,437	8,413	3,052	10,986	15,069	9,960
2821	Current	...	...	...	2,042	2,187	2,316	2,136	2,282	2,413	6,708	7,136	7,560
2822	Capital	...	...	...	2,294	6,125	633	2,301	6,132	640	4,278	7,933	2,401
	Table 3 Transactions in assets and liabilities												
3	**Change in net worth from transactions**	...	...	...	**-5,142**	**-9,305**	**-3,925**	...	...	...	**-4,784**	**-8,555**	**-3,099**
31	**Net/Gross investment in nonfinancial assets**	...	...	...	**-936**	**678**	**772**	**-923**	**673**	**773**	**-808**	**981**	**1,038**
311	Fixed assets	...	...	...	1,038	709	812	1,053	705	813	1,247	1,101	1,099
3111	Buildings and structures	...	...	...	859	786	748	...	...	...	931	1,035	963
3112	Machinery and equipment	...	...	...	...	...	...	...	...	...	...	...	...
3113	Other fixed assets	...	...	...	259	189	201	...	...	...	313	233	235
3114	Weapons systems	...	...	...	...	...	...	...	...	...	...	...	...
312	Inventories	...	...	...	21	-1	-18	...	...	...	4	5	-5
313	Valuables	...	...	...	1	1	1	...	...	...	1	1	1
314	Nonproduced assets	...	...	...	-1,996	-30	-23	-1,997	-32	-23	-2,060	-126	-56
3141	Land	...	...	...	...	...	...	...	...	...	...	...	...
3142	Mineral and energy resources	...	...	...	...	...	...	...	...	...	...	...	...
3143	Other naturally occurring assets	...	...	...	...	...	...	...	...	...	...	...	...
3144	Intangible nonproduced assets	...	...	...	...	...	...	...	...	...	...	...	...
32	**Net acquisition of financial assets**	...	...	...	**-2,002**	**-1,657**	**-1,437**	...	...	...	**-1,776**	**-2,168**	**-528**
	By instrument												
3201	Monetary gold and SDRs	...	...	...	—	—	—	...	...	...	—	—	—
3202	Currency and deposits	...	...	...	-609	-407	2,381	...	...	...	694	-982	3,266
3203	Debt securities	...	...	...	-932	-2,335	-2,429	...	...	...	-2,247	-2,616	-2,236
3204	Loans	...	...	...	257	1,251	-21	...	...	...	960	730	-284
3205	Equity and investment fund shares	...	...	...	-464	-877	-863	...	...	...	-904	-426	-1,093
3206	Insurance, pension, and standardized guarantee schemes	...	...	...	—	—	—	...	...	...	0	0	-1
3207	Financial derivatives and employee stock options	...	...	...	-130	-247	-105	...	...	...	-234	-239	-106
3208	Other accounts receivable	...	...	...	-123	958	-400	...	...	...	-46	1,365	-73
	By debtor												
321	Domestic debtors	...	...	...	...	...	...	...	...	...	...	...	...
322	External debtors	...	...	...	...	...	...	...	...	...	...	...	...
33	**Net incurrence of liabilities**	...	...	...	**2,204**	**8,326**	**3,260**	...	...	...	**2,201**	**7,367**	**3,609**
	By instrument												
3301	Special Drawing Rights (SDRs)	...	...	...	—	—	—	...	...	...	—	—	—
3302	Currency and deposits	...	...	...	-1,328	1,010	-1,567	...	...	...	-1,333	1,010	-1,563
3303	Debt securities	...	...	...	3,433	1,816	5,596	...	...	...	3,531	1,056	5,612
3304	Loans	...	...	...	750	1,325	-1,272	...	...	...	419	1,090	-962
3305	Equity and investment fund shares	...	...	...	-16	-1	42	...	...	...	-3	2	108
3306	Insurance, pension, and standardized guarantee schemes	...	...	...	-7	-2	-10	...	...	...	-7	-2	-10
3307	Financial derivatives and employee stock options	...	...	...	-733	-461	-403	...	...	...	-829	-569	-508
3308	Other accounts payable	...	...	...	104	4,639	874	...	...	...	422	4,781	933

Austria (122)

In Millions of Euros (EUR) / Fiscal Year Ends December 31st

		Budgetary Central Government			Central Government (excl. Social Security)			Central Government (incl. Social Security)			General Government		
		2013	2014	2015	2013	2014	2015	2013	2014	2015	2013	2014	2015
	By creditor												
331	Domestic creditors	...	...	...	...	...	...	...	...	...	...	...	...
332	External creditors	...	...	...	...	...	...	...	...	...	...	...	...
	Table 4 Holding gains and losses in assets and liabilities												
	Table 5 Holding gains and losses in assets and liabilities												
	Table 6 Balance sheet												
6	**Net worth**	...	...	...	...	...	...	...	...	...	...	...	...
61	**Nonfinancial assets**	...	...	...	...	...	...	...	...	...	...	...	...
611	Fixed assets	...	...	...	...	...	...	...	...	...	196,016	199,959	203,997
6111	Buildings and structures	...	...	...	...	...	...	...	...	...	162,993	166,506	170,031
6112	Machinery and equipment	...	...	...	...	...	...	...	...	...	...	...	...
6113	Other fixed assets	...	...	...	...	...	...	...	...	...	15,537	16,071	16,578
6114	Weapons systems	...	...	...	...	...	...	...	...	...	...	...	...
612	Inventories	...	...	...	...	...	...	...	...	...	...	...	...
613	Valuables	...	...	...	...	...	...	...	...	...	...	...	...
614	Nonproduced assets	...	...	...	...	...	...	...	...	...	...	...	...
6141	Land	...	...	...	...	...	...	...	...	...	...	...	...
6142	Mineral and energy resources	...	...	...	...	...	...	...	...	...	...	...	...
6143	Other naturally occurring assets	...	...	...	...	...	...	...	...	...	...	...	...
6144	Intangible nonproduced assets	...	...	...	...	...	...	...	...	...	...	...	...
62	**Financial assets**	...	...	...	**78,579**	**98,814**	**109,004**	...	...	...	**144,702**	**165,525**	**175,413**
	By instrument												
6201	Monetary gold and SDRs	...	...	...	—	—	—	...	...	...	—	—	—
6202	Currency and deposits	...	...	...	7,979	14,661	20,042	...	...	...	20,017	26,067	32,407
6203	Debt securities	...	...	...	6,211	5,845	5,984	...	...	...	9,507	8,772	8,698
6204	Loans	...	...	...	22,064	32,600	36,050	...	...	...	36,639	46,524	48,786
6205	Equity and investment fund shares	...	...	...	30,010	31,788	32,509	...	...	...	51,929	55,467	56,101
6206	Insurance, pension, and standardized guarantee schemes	...	...	...	—	—	—	...	...	...	4	4	4
6207	Financial derivatives and employee stock options	...	...	...	668	1,094	1,535	...	...	...	668	1,104	1,545
6208	Other accounts receivable	...	...	...	11,647	12,827	12,883	...	...	...	25,938	27,588	27,871
	By debtor												
621	Domestic debtors	...	...	...	...	...	...	...	...	...	...	...	...
622	External debtors	...	...	...	...	...	...	...	...	...	...	...	...
63	**Liabilities**	...	...	...	**282,125**	**317,258**	**325,302**	...	...	...	**330,230**	**364,770**	**372,879**
	By instrument												
6301	Special Drawing Rights (SDRs)	...	...	...	—	—	—	...	...	...	—	—	—
6302	Currency and deposits	...	...	...	3,324	4,398	5,430	...	...	...	3,314	4,388	5,415
6303	Debt securities	...	...	...	234,868	262,656	266,551	...	...	...	242,696	269,827	273,771
6304	Loans	...	...	...	25,449	31,387	32,950	...	...	...	42,455	48,183	49,544
6305	Equity and investment fund shares	...	...	...	7,923	7,921	8,281	...	...	...	15,175	15,285	15,811
6306	Insurance, pension, and standardized guarantee schemes	...	...	...	153	151	141	...	...	...	153	151	141
6307	Financial derivatives and employee stock options	...	...	...	1,199	1,047	1,302	...	...	...	1,215	1,053	1,306
6308	Other accounts payable	...	...	...	9,208	9,698	10,647	...	...	...	25,223	25,884	26,891
	By creditor												
631	Domestic creditors	...	...	...	...	...	...	...	...	...	...	...	...
632	External creditors	...	...	...	...	...	...	...	...	...	...	...	...
	Memorandum items												
6M2	Net financial worth	...	...	...	-203,546	-218,444	-216,298	...	...	...	-185,528	-199,245	-197,467
6M3	Gross debt (D4) at market value	...	...	...	273,003	308,290	315,719	...	...	...	313,841	348,433	355,762
6M3D3	D3 debt liabilities at market value	...	...	...	272,850	308,139	315,578	...	...	...	313,688	348,282	355,621
6M3D2	D2 debt liabilities at market value	...	...	...	263,642	298,441	304,931	...	...	...	288,465	322,398	328,730
6M3D1	D1 debt liabilities at market value	...	...	...	260,318	294,043	299,501	...	...	...	285,151	318,010	323,315
6M4	Gross debt (D4) at nominal value	...	...	...	...	...	...	...	...	...	...	...	...
6M4D3	D3 debt liabilities at nominal value	...	...	...	...	...	...	...	...	...	...	...	...
6M4D2	D2 debt liabilities at nominal value	...	...	...	...	...	...	...	...	...	...	...	...
6M4D1	D1 debt liabilities at nominal value	...	...	...	...	...	...	...	...	...	...	...	...

Austria (122)

In Millions of Euros (EUR) / Fiscal Year Ends December 31st

		Budgetary Central Government			Central Government (excl. Social Security)			Central Government (incl. Social Security)			General Government		
		2013	2014	2015	2013	2014	2015	2013	2014	2015	2013	2014	2015
6M35	Gross debt (D4) at face value	...	...	...	...	...	...	...	...	...	...	...	...
6M35D3	D3 debt liabilities at face value	...	...	...	246,735	264,799	277,998	...	...	...	287,523	304,803	317,653
6M35D2	D2 debt liabilities at face value	...	...	...	237,527	255,101	267,352	...	...	...	262,300	278,919	290,762
6M35D1	D1 debt liabilities at face value	...	...	...	234,203	250,703	261,922	...	...	...	258,986	274,531	285,347
6M93	Government gross debt per national definition	...	...	...	237,527	255,101	267,352	...	...	...	262,300	278,919	290,762
6M5	Arrears	...	...	...	...	...	...	...	...	...	...	...	...
6M6	Explicit contingent liabilities	...	...	...	...	...	...	...	...	...	...	...	...
6M61	of which: Publicly guaranteed debt	...	...	...	...	...	...	...	...	...	...	...	...
6M7	Net implicit obligations for social security benefits	...	...	...	...	...	...	...	...	...	...	...	...
	Table 7 Expenditure by functions of government												
7	**Expenditure**	...	...	...	**110,584**	**118,004**	**117,412**	...	...	...	**165,108**	**174,090**	**175,173**
701	**General public services**	...	...	...	**39,917**	**39,889**	**41,307**	...	...	...	**23,190**	**22,502**	**23,044**
7017	Public debt transactions	...	...	...	...	...	...	...	...	...	8,898	8,582	8,499
7018	Transfers of general character between levels of government	...	...	...	...	...	...	...	...	...	136	110	70
702	**Defense**	...	...	...	**2,010**	**1,924**	**1,948**	...	...	...	**2,013**	**1,928**	**1,952**
703	**Public order and safety**	...	...	...	**3,712**	**3,841**	**4,065**	...	...	...	**4,280**	**4,460**	**4,700**
704	**Economic affairs**	...	...	...	**11,589**	**17,547**	**13,981**	...	...	...	**18,326**	**24,559**	**20,928**
7042	Agriculture, forestry, fishing, and hunting	...	...	...	...	...	...	...	...	...	1,353	1,356	1,272
7043	Fuel and energy	...	...	...	...	...	...	...	...	...	35	29	37
7044	Mining, manufacturing, and construction	...	...	...	...	...	...	...	...	...	86	32	31
7045	Transport	...	...	...	...	...	...	...	...	...	9,653	9,747	9,695
7046	Communication	...	...	...	...	...	...	...	...	...	-1,888	135	158
705	**Environmental protection**	...	...	...	**830**	**811**	**748**	...	...	...	**1,636**	**1,567**	**1,527**
706	**Housing and community amenities**	...	...	...	**145**	**128**	**158**	...	...	...	**1,184**	**1,206**	**1,194**
707	**Health**	...	...	...	**4,211**	**4,130**	**4,461**	...	...	...	**25,195**	**26,067**	**27,172**
7072	Outpatient services	...	...	...	...	...	...	...	...	...	4,706	4,807	4,978
7073	Hospital services	...	...	...	...	...	...	...	...	...	14,045	14,536	15,135
7074	Public health services	...	...	...	...	...	...	...	...	...	524	557	600
708	**Recreation, culture and religion**	...	...	...	**2,006**	**1,968**	**2,060**	...	...	...	**4,062**	**4,018**	**4,203**
709	**Education**	...	...	...	**11,046**	**11,049**	**11,364**	...	...	...	**16,270**	**16,406**	**16,855**
7091	Pre-primary and primary education	...	...	...	...	...	...	...	...	...	4,444	4,651	4,847
7092	Secondary education	...	...	...	...	...	...	...	...	...	7,264	7,313	7,415
7094	Tertiary education	...	...	...	...	...	...	...	...	...	2,667	2,526	2,604
710	**Social protection**	...	...	...	**35,119**	**36,716**	**37,320**	...	...	...	**68,953**	**71,378**	**73,599**
7z	Statistical discrepancy: Expenditure	...	...	...	-0	-0	-0	...	...	...	0	—	—
	Table 8 Financial transactions by counterpart sector												
32	**Net acquisition of financial assets**	...	...	...	**-2,002**	**-1,657**	**-1,437**	...	...	...	**-1,776**	**-2,168**	**-528**
321	Domestic debtors	...	...	...	...	...	...	...	...	...	...	...	...
8211	General government	...	...	...	...	...	...	...	...	...	—	—	—
8212	Central bank	...	...	...	...	...	...	...	...	...	...	...	...
8213	Deposit-taking corporations except the central bank	...	...	...	...	...	...	...	...	...	...	...	...
8214	Other financial corporations	...	...	...	...	...	...	...	...	...	...	...	...
8215	Nonfinancial corporations	...	...	...	...	...	...	...	...	...	...	...	...
8216	Households & nonprofit institutions serving households	...	...	...	...	...	...	...	...	...	...	...	...
322	External debtors	...	...	...	...	...	...	...	...	...	...	...	...
8221	General government	...	...	...	...	...	...	...	...	...	...	...	...
8227	International organizations	...	...	...	...	...	...	...	...	...	...	...	...
8228	Financial corporations other than international organizations	...	...	...	...	...	...	...	...	...	...	...	...
8229	Other nonresidents	...	...	...	...	...	...	...	...	...	...	...	...

Austria (122)

In Millions of Euros (EUR) / Fiscal Year Ends December 31st

		Budgetary Central Government			Central Government (excl. Social Security)			Central Government (incl. Social Security)			General Government		
		2013	2014	2015	2013	2014	2015	2013	2014	2015	2013	2014	2015
33	**Net incurrence of liabilities**	**...**	**...**	**...**	**2,204**	**8,326**	**3,260**	**...**	**...**	**...**	**2,201**	**7,367**	**3,609**
331	Domestic creditors	...	...	...	...	...	...	...	...	...	...	...	...
8311	General government	...	...	...	...	...	...	...	...	...	—	—	—
8312	Central bank	...	...	...	...	...	...	...	...	...	...	...	...
8313	Deposit-taking corporations except the central bank	...	...	...	...	...	...	...	...	...	...	...	...
8314	Other financial corporations	...	...	...	...	...	...	...	...	...	...	...	...
8315	Nonfinancial corporations	...	...	...	...	...	...	...	...	...	...	...	...
8316	Households & nonprofit institutions serving households	...	...	...	...	...	...	...	...	...	...	...	...
332	External creditors	...	...	...	...	...	...	...	...	...	...	...	...
8321	General government	...	...	...	...	...	...	...	...	...	...	...	...
8327	International organizations	...	...	...	...	...	...	...	...	...	...	...	...
8328	Financial corporations other than international organizations	...	...	...	...	...	...	...	...	...	...	...	...
8329	Other nonresidents	...	...	...	...	...	...	...	...	...	...	...	...
	Table 9 Total other economic flows in assets and liabilities												
9	**Change in net worth due to other economic flows**	**...**	**...**	**...**	**...**	**...**	**...**	**...**	**...**	**...**	**...**	**...**	**...**
91	**Other economic flows in nonfinancial assets**	**...**	**...**	**...**	**...**	**...**	**...**	**...**	**...**	**...**	**...**	**...**	**...**
911	Fixed assets	...	...	...	...	...	...	...	...	...	...	...	...
912	Inventories	...	...	...	...	...	...	...	...	...	...	...	...
913	Valuables	...	...	...	...	...	...	...	...	...	...	...	...
914	Nonproduced assets	...	...	...	...	...	...	...	...	...	...	...	...
92	**Other economic flows in financial assets**	**...**	**...**	**...**	**-3,632**	**21,892**	**11,626**	**...**	**...**	**...**	**-4,663**	**22,991**	**10,416**
	By instrument												
9201	Monetary gold and SDRs	...	...	...	—	—	—	...	...	...	—	—	—
9202	Currency and deposits	...	...	...	145	7,089	3,000	...	...	...	125	7,031	3,074
9203	Debt securities	...	...	...	-142	1,968	2,568	...	...	...	-200	1,881	2,162
9204	Loans	...	...	...	-11	9,285	3,471	...	...	...	-145	9,155	2,547
9205	Equity and investment fund shares	...	...	...	-3,180	2,655	1,584	...	...	...	-3,623	3,964	1,728
9206	Insurance, pension, and standardized guarantee schemes	...	...	...	—	—	—	...	...	...	0	0	1
9207	Financial derivatives and employee stock options	...	...	...	-289	673	547	...	...	...	-637	675	547
9208	Other accounts receivable	...	...	...	-155	222	456	...	...	...	-183	285	356
	By debtor												
921	Domestic debtors	...	...	...	...	...	...	...	...	...	...	...	...
922	External debtors	...	...	...	...	...	...	...	...	...	...	...	...
93	**Other economic flows in liabilities**	**...**	**...**	**...**	**-8,650**	**26,807**	**4,784**	**...**	**...**	**...**	**-8,373**	**27,173**	**4,500**
	By instrument												
9301	Special Drawing Rights (SDRs)	...	...	...	—	—	—	...	...	...	—	—	—
9302	Currency and deposits	...	...	...	66	64	2,599	...	...	...	66	64	2,590
9303	Debt securities	...	...	...	-8,983	25,972	-1,702	...	...	...	-8,930	26,074	-1,668
9304	Loans	...	...	...	0	4,612	2,836	...	...	...	-24	4,639	2,322
9305	Equity and investment fund shares	...	...	...	42	-1	317	...	...	...	173	108	419
9306	Insurance, pension, and standardized guarantee schemes	...	...	...	-0	0	0	...	...	...	-0	0	0
9307	Financial derivatives and employee stock options	...	...	...	310	309	658	...	...	...	411	407	762
9308	Other accounts payable	...	...	...	-85	-4,149	75	...	...	...	-69	-4,120	75
	By creditor												
931	Domestic creditors	...	...	...	...	...	...	...	...	...	...	...	...
932	External creditors	...	...	...	...	...	...	...	...	...	...	...	...
	Memorandum items												
9M2	Change in net financial worth due to other economic flows	...	...	...	5,018	-4,915	6,842	...	...	...	3,710	-4,182	5,916

Austria (122)

In Millions of Euros (EUR) / Fiscal Year Ends December 31st

		Budgetary Central Government			Central Government (excl. Social Security)			Central Government (incl. Social Security)			General Government		
		2013	2014	2015	2013	2014	2015	2013	2014	2015	2013	2014	2015
9M3	Gross debt (D4) at market value: other economic flows	...	...	...	-9,002	26,499	3,808	...	...	...	-8,957	26,658	3,319
9M3D3	D3 debt liabilities at market value: other economic flows	...	...	...	-9,002	26,499	3,808	...	...	...	-8,957	26,657	3,319
9M3D2	D2 debt liabilities at market value: other economic flows	...	...	...	-8,917	30,648	3,734	...	...	...	-8,888	30,777	3,244
9M3D1	D1 debt liabilities at market value: other economic flows	...	...	...	-8,983	30,584	1,135	...	...	...	-8,954	30,713	654

Azerbaijan, Republic of (912)

In Millions of Azerbaijan Manat (AZN) / Fiscal Year Ends December 31st

		Budgetary Central Government			Central Government (excl. Social Security)			Central Government (incl. Social Security)			General Government		
		2013	2014	2015	2013	2014	2015	2013	2014	2015	2013	2014	2015
	Statement of operations												
1	Revenue	19,664	18,396	17,143	21,915	21,790	16,789	23,509	23,545	18,604	23,591	23,642	18,696
2	Expense	9,751	10,536	10,582	10,667	11,316	11,645	12,175	13,043	13,480	12,243	13,149	13,535
GOB	**Gross operating balance**	**9,913**	**7,860**	**6,561**	**11,248**	**10,474**	**5,144**	**11,334**	**10,502**	**5,124**	**11,348**	**10,493**	**5,161**
NOB	**Net operating balance**	...	...	...	...	...	...	...	...	...	...	...	...
31	Net/Gross investment in nonfinancial assets	8,455	7,773	6,603	8,492	7,773	6,603	8,496	7,774	6,605	8,773	7,852	6,679
2M	Expenditure	18,206	18,309	17,185	19,158	19,089	18,248	20,671	20,816	20,085	21,017	21,001	20,214
NLB	**Net lending (+) / Net borrowing (-)**	**1,458**	**87**	**-42**	**2,756**	**2,701**	**-1,459**	**2,838**	**2,728**	**-1,481**	**2,575**	**2,641**	**-1,518**
32	Net acquisition of financial assets	518	792	-573	1,815	3,406	-2,039	1,897	3,434	-2,061	1,634	3,347	-2,098
33	Net incurrence of liabilities	-941	706	-531	-941	706	-531	-941	706	-531	-941	706	-531
NLBz	Statistical discrepancy	—	—	—	—	—	-50	—	—	-50	—	—	-50
	Memorandum items												
PB	Primary net lending / net borrowing	1,613	171	169	2,911	2,785	-1,248	2,992	2,812	-1,270	2,732	2,725	-1,306
GB	Government balance per national definition	...	...	...	...	...	...	...	...	...	...	...	...
	Statement of other economic flows												
	Balance sheet												
	Table 1 Revenue												
1	**Revenue**	**19,664**	**18,396**	**17,143**	**21,915**	**21,790**	**16,789**	**23,509**	**23,545**	**18,604**	**23,591**	**23,642**	**18,696**
11	**Taxes**	**7,790**	**8,387**	**8,485**	**7,790**	**8,387**	**8,485**	**7,790**	**8,387**	**8,485**	**7,860**	**8,468**	**8,564**
111	Taxes on income, profits, and capital gains	3,247	3,292	3,217	3,247	3,292	3,217	3,247	3,292	3,217	3,262	3,309	3,237
1111	Payable by individuals	864	984	992	864	984	992	864	984	992	877	999	1,011
1112	Payable by corporations and other enterprises	2,383	2,308	2,225	2,383	2,308	2,225	2,383	2,308	2,225	2,385	2,310	2,227
1113	Other taxes on income, profits, and capital gains	—	—	—	—	—	—	—	—	—	—	—	—
112	Taxes on payroll and workforce	—	—	—	—	—	—	—	—	—	—	—	—
113	Taxes on property	160	179	200	160	179	200	160	179	200	172	191	212
114	Taxes on goods and services	3,494	4,146	4,404	3,494	4,146	4,404	3,494	4,146	4,404	3,536	4,196	4,450
1141	General taxes on goods and services	2,859	3,309	3,676	2,859	3,309	3,676	2,859	3,309	3,676	2,895	3,354	3,717
1142	Excises	593	797	649	593	797	649	593	797	649	598	802	652
115	Taxes on international trade and transactions	669	679	571	669	679	571	669	679	571	670	681	572
116	Other taxes	219	91	93	219	91	93	219	91	93	220	92	93
12	**Social contributions**	—	—	—	—	—	—	**1,584**	**1,744**	**1,805**	**1,584**	**1,744**	**1,805**
121	Social security contributions	—	—	—	—	—	—	1,584	1,744	1,805	1,584	1,744	1,805
122	Other social contributions	—	—	—	—	—	—	—	—	—	—	—	—
13	**Grants**	**11,350**	**9,337**	**8,145**	—	—	**15**	—	—	**15**	—	—	**15**
131	From foreign governments	—	—	—	—	—	—	—	—	—	—	—	—
132	From international organizations	—	—	15	—	—	15	—	—	15	—	—	15
133	From other general government units	11,350	9,337	8,130	—	—	—	—	—	—	—	—	—
1331	Current	11,350	9,337	8,130	—	—	—	—	—	—	—	—	—
1332	Capital	—	—	—	—	—	—	—	—	—	—	—	—
14	**Other revenue**	**525**	**671**	**513**	**14,125**	**13,402**	**8,289**	**14,135**	**13,413**	**8,299**	**14,147**	**13,431**	**8,313**
	Table 2 Expense by economic type												
2	**Expense**	**9,751**	**10,536**	**10,582**	**10,667**	**11,316**	**11,645**	**12,175**	**13,043**	**13,480**	**12,243**	**13,149**	**13,535**
21	**Compensation of employees**	**1,708**	**1,926**	**1,938**	**1,710**	**1,926**	**1,944**	**1,724**	**1,946**	...	**1,831**	**2,069**	...
211	Wages and salaries	1,400	1,578	1,589	1,403	1,578	...	1,414	1,595	...	1,501	1,695	...
212	Employers' social contributions	308	348	350	308	348	...	310	351	...	330	374	...
22	**Use of goods and services**	**1,450**	**1,632**	**1,627**	**1,451**	**1,632**	...	**1,473**	**1,652**	...	**1,529**	**1,718**	...
23	**Consumption of fixed capital**	...	...	...	...	...	...	...	...	...	...	...	...
24	**Interest**	**155**	**84**	**211**	**155**	**84**	**211**	**155**	**84**	**211**	**158**	**84**	**211**
25	**Subsidies**	**334**	**683**	**805**	**1,206**	**1,384**	**1,799**	**1,206**	**1,384**	**1,799**	**1,216**	**1,391**	**1,807**
26	**Grants**	**1,373**	**1,444**	**1,418**	**1,373**	**1,444**	**1,418**	**296**	**302**	**318**	**13**	**13**	**15**
261	To foreign governments	—	—	—	—	—	—	—	—	—	—	—	—
262	To international organizations	13	13	15	13	13	15	13	13	15	13	13	15
263	To other general government units	1,360	1,431	1,403	1,360	1,431	1,403	283	289	303	—	—	—
2631	Current	1,360	289	1,403	1,360	289	1,403	283	289	303	—	—	—
2632	Capital	—	1,142	—	—	1,142	—	—	—	—	—	—	—

Azerbaijan, Republic of (912)

In Millions of Azerbaijan Manat (AZN) / Fiscal Year Ends December 31st

		Budgetary Central Government			Central Government (excl. Social Security)			Central Government (incl. Social Security)			General Government		
		2013	2014	2015	2013	2014	2015	2013	2014	2015	2013	2014	2015
27	**Social benefits**	**566**	**635**	**647**	**566**	**635**	**...**	**3,096**	**3,462**	**...**	**3,109**	**3,477**	**...**
271	Social security benefits	266	288	293	266	288	...	2,796	3,115	...	2,801	3,121	...
272	Social assistance benefits	299	347	353	299	347	...	299	347	...	307	355	...
273	Employment-related social benefits	1	1	1	1	1	...	1	1	...	1	1	...
28	**Other expense**	**4,167**	**4,132**	**3,936**	**4,207**	**4,212**	**3,999**	**4,225**	**4,212**	**4,024**	**4,388**	**4,398**	**4,181**
281	Property expense other than interest	—	—	30	—	—	30	—	—	30	—	—	30
282	Transfers not elsewhere classified	4,167	4,132	3,905	4,207	4,212	3,969	4,225	4,212	3,994	4,388	4,398	4,151
2821	Current	4,167	3,821	3,745	4,207	3,901	3,809	4,225	3,901	3,834	4,388	4,087	3,991
2822	Capital	—	311	160	—	311	160	—	311	160	—	311	160
	Table 3 Transactions in assets and liabilities												
3	**Change in net worth from transactions**	**...**	**...**	**...**	**...**	**...**	**...**	**...**	**...**	**...**	**...**	**...**	**...**
31	**Net/Gross investment in nonfinancial assets**	**8,455**	**7,773**	**6,603**	**8,492**	**7,773**	**6,603**	**8,496**	**7,774**	**6,605**	**8,773**	**7,852**	**6,679**
311	Fixed assets	8,449	7,764	6,597	8,486	7,764	6,597	8,490	7,765	6,598	8,790	7,863	6,678
3111	Buildings and structures	7,064	6,342	5,177	7,064	6,342	5,177	7,067	6,342	5,178	7,359	6,434	5,252
3112	Machinery and equipment	1,308	1,348	1,367	1,308	1,348	1,367	1,310	1,348	1,368	1,314	1,351	1,371
3113	Other fixed assets	77	74	52	114	74	52	114	74	52	117	79	55
3114	Weapons systems	...	...	—	...	...	—	...	...	—	...	...	—
312	Inventories	—	—	...	—	—	...	—	—	...	—	—	...
313	Valuables	—	—	...	—	—	...	—	—	...	—	—	...
314	Nonproduced assets	5	9	6	5	9	6	6	9	7	-17	-11	0
3141	Land	—	—	—	—	—	—	—	—	—	-23	-21	-7
3142	Mineral and energy resources	—	—	—	—	—	—	—	—	—	—	—	—
3143	Other naturally occurring assets	—	—	—	—	—	—	—	—	—	—	—	—
3144	Intangible nonproduced assets	5	9	6	5	9	6	6	9	7	6	9	7
32	**Net acquisition of financial assets**	**518**	**792**	**-573**	**1,815**	**3,406**	**-2,039**	**1,897**	**3,434**	**-2,061**	**1,634**	**3,347**	**-2,098**
	By instrument												
3201	Monetary gold and SDRs	—	—	—	—	—	—	...	...	...	—	—	—
3202	Currency and deposits	518	732	-644	1,815	3,346	-2,111	...	...	...	1,634	3,286	-2,169
3203	Debt securities	—	—	—	—	—	—	...	...	...	—	—	—
3204	Loans	0	61	72	0	61	72	...	...	...	0	61	72
3205	Equity and investment fund shares	—	—	—	...	...	...	...	...	...	...	...	...
3206	Insurance, pension, and standardized guarantee schemes	—	—	—	...	...	...	...	...	...	...	...	...
3207	Financial derivatives and employee stock options	—	—	—	...	...	...	...	...	...	...	...	...
3208	Other accounts receivable	...	...	...	...	...	...	...	...	...	...	...	...
	By debtor												
321	Domestic debtors	518	732	-644	1,815	3,346	...	1,897	3,373	...	1,634	3,286	...
322	External debtors	—	61	72	—	61	...	—	61	...	—	61	...
33	**Net incurrence of liabilities**	**-941**	**706**	**-531**	**-941**	**706**	**-531**	**-941**	**706**	**-531**	**-941**	**706**	**-531**
	By instrument												
3301	Special Drawing Rights (SDRs)	—	—	—	—	—	—	—	—	—	—	—	—
3302	Currency and deposits	-324	—	—	-324	—	—	-324	—	—	-324	—	—
3303	Debt securities	-146	987	-91	-146	987	-91	-146	987	-91	-146	987	-91
3304	Loans	-471	-282	-440	-471	-282	-440	-471	-282	-440	-471	-282	-440
3305	Equity and investment fund shares	—	—	—	—	—	—	—	—	—	—	—	—
3306	Insurance, pension, and standardized guarantee schemes	—	—	—	—	—	—	—	—	—	—	—	—
3307	Financial derivatives and employee stock options	—	—	—	—	—	—	—	—	—	—	—	—
3308	Other accounts payable	...	...	...	...	...	...	...	...	...	...	...	...
	By creditor												
331	Domestic creditors	-470	987	-91	-470	987	-91	-470	987	-91	-470	987	-91
332	External creditors	-471	-282	-440	-471	-282	-440	-471	-282	-440	-471	-282	-440
	Table 4 Holding gains and losses in assets and liabilities												
	Table 5 Holding gains and losses in assets and liabilities												
	Table 6 Balance sheet												

Azerbaijan, Republic of (912)

In Millions of Azerbaijan Manat (AZN) / Fiscal Year Ends December 31st

		Budgetary Central Government			Central Government (excl. Social Security)			Central Government (incl. Social Security)			General Government		
		2013	2014	2015	2013	2014	2015	2013	2014	2015	2013	2014	2015
	Table 7 Expenditure by functions of government												
7	**Expenditure**	**18,206**	**18,309**	**17,194**	**19,158**	**19,089**	**18,257**	**20,671**	**20,816**	**20,094**	**21,017**	**21,001**	**20,224**
701	**General public services**	**3,382**	**3,606**	**3,527**	**3,382**	**3,606**	**3,527**	**3,382**	**3,606**	**3,527**	**2,152**	**3,474**	**3,364**
7017	Public debt transactions	155	84	211	155	84	211	155	84	211	158	84	211
7018	Transfers of general character between levels of government	1,360	289	1,403	1,360	289	1,403	12,710	289	1,403	—	—	1,100
702	**Defense**	**1,485**	**1,516**	**1,701**	**1,485**	**1,516**	**1,701**	**1,485**	**1,516**	**1,701**	**1,490**	**1,522**	**1,707**
703	**Public order and safety**	**1,049**	**1,104**	**1,106**	**1,049**	**1,104**	**1,106**	**1,049**	**1,104**	**1,106**	**1,086**	**1,145**	**1,149**
704	**Economic affairs**	**7,796**	**7,168**	**6,009**	**8,749**	**7,948**	**7,072**	**8,749**	**7,948**	**7,072**	**9,077**	**8,074**	**7,182**
7042	Agriculture, forestry, fishing, and hunting	475	491	537	475	491	537	475	491	537	498	515	564
7043	Fuel and energy	2	2	4	2	2	4	2	2	4	2	2	4
7044	Mining, manufacturing, and construction	6,933	17	—	7,885	797	1,063	7,885	797	1,063	8,169	879	1,063
7045	Transport	73	80	77	73	80	77	73	80	77	85	94	91
7046	Communication	38	8	42	38	8	42	38	8	42	38	8	42
705	**Environmental protection**	**13**	**14**	**13**	**13**	**14**	**13**	**13**	**14**	**13**	**14**	**15**	**14**
706	**Housing and community amenities**	**398**	**417**	**396**	**398**	**417**	**396**	**398**	**417**	**396**	**432**	**451**	**418**
707	**Health**	**619**	**665**	**708**	**619**	**665**	**708**	**619**	**665**	**708**	**633**	**685**	**728**
7072	Outpatient services	95	104	98	95	104	98	95	104	98	97	107	100
7073	Hospital services	319	349	282	319	349	282	319	349	282	329	364	297
7074	Public health services	5	6	5	5	6	5	5	6	5	5	7	5
708	**Recreation, culture and religion**	**275**	**294**	**272**	**275**	**294**	**272**	**275**	**294**	**272**	**283**	**303**	**281**
709	**Education**	**1,438**	**1,554**	**1,605**	**1,438**	**1,554**	**1,605**	**1,438**	**1,554**	**1,605**	**1,496**	**1,617**	**1,671**
7091	Pre-primary and primary education	144	159	152	144	159	152	144	159	152	146	161	155
7092	Secondary education	776	822	867	776	822	867	776	822	867	815	865	915
7094	Tertiary education	139	161	170	139	161	170	139	161	170	140	162	170
710	**Social protection**	**1,750**	**1,971**	**1,857**	**1,750**	**1,971**	**1,857**	**3,263**	**3,699**	**3,694**	**4,354**	**3,714**	**3,710**
7z	Statistical discrepancy: Expenditure	—	—	—	—	—	0	—	—	0	—	—	—
	Table 8 Financial transactions by counterpart sector												
32	**Net acquisition of financial assets**	**518**	**792**	**-573**	**1,815**	**3,406**	**-2,039**	**1,897**	**3,434**	**-2,061**	**1,634**	**3,347**	**-2,098**
321	Domestic debtors	518	732	-644	1,815	3,346	...	1,897	3,373	...	1,634	3,286	...
8211	General government	—	—	...	—	—	...	—	—	...	—	—	...
8212	Central bank	519	724	...	519	724	...	519	724	...	519	724	...
8213	Deposit-taking corporations except the central bank	-2	8	...	1,296	2,622	...	1,378	2,649	...	1,115	2,562	...
8214	Other financial corporations	—	—	...	—	—	...	—	—	...	—	—	...
8215	Nonfinancial corporations	—	—	...	—	—	...	—	—	...	—	—	...
8216	Households & nonprofit institutions serving households	—	—	...	—	—	...	—	—	...	—	—	...
322	External debtors	—	61	72	—	61	...	—	61	...	—	61	...
8221	General government	—	—	...	—	—	...	—	—	...	—	—	...
8227	International organizations	—	61	...	—	61	...	—	61	...	—	61	...
8228	Financial corporations other than international organizations	—	—	...	—	—	...	—	—	...	—	—	...
8229	Other nonresidents	—	—	...	—	—	...	—	—	...	—	—	...

Azerbaijan, Republic of (912)

In Millions of Azerbaijan Manat (AZN) / Fiscal Year Ends December 31st

		Budgetary Central Government			Central Government (excl. Social Security)			Central Government (incl. Social Security)			General Government		
		2013	2014	2015	2013	2014	2015	2013	2014	2015	2013	2014	2015
33	**Net incurrence of liabilities**	**-941**	**706**	**-531**	**-941**	**706**	**-531**	**-941**	**706**	**-531**	**-941**	**706**	**-531**
331	Domestic creditors	-470	987	-91	-470	987	-91	-470	987	-91	-470	987	-91
8311	General government	-324	—	...	-324	—	...	-324	—	...	-324	—	...
8312	Central bank	—	—	...	—	—	...	—	—	...	—	—	...
8313	Deposit-taking corporations except the central bank	-146	987	...	-146	987	...	-146	987	...	-146	987	...
8314	Other financial corporations	—	—	...	—	—	...	—	—	...	—	—	...
8315	Nonfinancial corporations	—	—	...	—	—	...	—	—	...	—	—	...
8316	Households & nonprofit institutions serving households	—	—	...	—	—	...	—	—	...	—	—	...
332	External creditors	-471	-282	-440	-471	-282	-440	-471	-282	-440	-471	-282	-440
8321	General government	—	—	...	—	—	...	—	—	...	—	—	...
8327	International organizations	-471	-282	...	-471	-282	...	-471	-282	...	-471	-282	...
8328	Financial corporations other than international organizations	—	—	...	—	—	...	—	—	...	—	—	...
8329	Other nonresidents	—	—	...	—	—	...	—	—	...	—	—	...
	Table 9 Total other economic flows in assets and liabilities												

Bahamas, The (313)

In Millions of Bahamian Dollars (BSD) / Fiscal Year Ends June 30th

		Budgetary Central Government			Central Government (excl. Social Security)			Central Government (incl. Social Security)			General Government		
		2013P	2014P	2015P	2013P	2014P	2015P	2013	2014	2015	2013	2014	2015
	Statement of operations												
1	Revenue	1,353	1,449	1,698	1,353	1,449	1,698	...	...	...	...	...	...
2	Expense	1,565	1,599	1,714	1,565	1,599	1,714	...	...	...	...	...	...
GOB	**Gross operating balance**	**-212**	**-150**	**-17**	**-212**	**-150**	**-17**	...	...	...	...	...	...
NOB	**Net operating balance**	...	...	...	...	...	...	...	...	...	...	...	...
31	Net/Gross investment in nonfinancial assets	231	247	273	231	247	273	...	...	...	...	...	...
2M	Expenditure	1,796	1,847	1,988	1,796	1,847	1,988	...	...	...	...	...	...
NLB	**Net lending (+) / Net borrowing (-)**	**-443**	**-397**	**-290**	**-443**	**-397**	**-290**	...	...	...	...	...	...
32	Net acquisition of financial assets	131	134	169	131	134	169	...	...	...	...	...	...
33	Net incurrence of liabilities	824	1,036	680	824	1,036	680	...	...	...	...	...	...
NLBz	Statistical discrepancy	-251	-506	-221	-251	-506	-221	...	...	...	...	...	...
	Memorandum items												
PB	Primary net lending / net borrowing	-245	-185	-57	-245	-185	-57	...	...	...	...	...	...
GB	Government balance per national definition	...	...	...	...	...	...	...	...	...	...	...	...
	Statement of other economic flows												
	Balance sheet												
	Table 1 Revenue												
1	**Revenue**	**1,353**	**1,449**	**1,698**	**1,353**	**1,449**	**1,698**	...	...	...	...	...	...
11	**Taxes**	**1,216**	**1,246**	**1,500**	**1,216**	**1,246**	**1,500**	...	...	...	...	...	...
111	Taxes on income, profits, and capital gains	—	—	—	—	—	—	...	...	...	...	...	...
1111	Payable by individuals	—	—	—	—	—	—	...	...	...	...	...	...
1112	Payable by corporations and other enterprises	—	—	—	—	—	—	...	...	...	...	...	...
1113	Other taxes on income, profits, and capital gains	—	—	—	—	—	—	...	...	...	...	...	...
112	Taxes on payroll and workforce	—	—	—	—	—	—	...	...	...	...	...	...
113	Taxes on property	275	268	298	275	268	298	...	...	...	...	...	...
114	Taxes on goods and services	186	259	478	186	259	478	...	...	...	...	...	...
1141	General taxes on goods and services	—	—	219	—	—	219	...	...	...	...	...	...
1142	Excises	—	—	—	—	—	—	...	...	...	...	...	...
115	Taxes on international trade and transactions	754	719	724	754	719	724	...	...	...	...	...	...
116	Other taxes	—	—	—	—	—	—	...	...	...	...	...	...
12	**Social contributions**	—	—	—	—	—	—	...	...	...	...	...	...
121	Social security contributions	—	—	—	—	—	—	...	...	...	...	...	...
122	Other social contributions	—	—	—	—	—	—	...	...	...	...	...	...
13	**Grants**	**0**	**0**	**0**	**0**	**0**	**0**	...	...	...	...	...	...
131	From foreign governments	0	0	0	0	0	0	...	...	...	...	...	...
132	From international organizations	—	—	—	—	—	—	...	...	...	...	...	...
133	From other general government units	—	—	—	—	—	—	...	...	...	...	...	...
1331	Current	—	—	—	—	—	—	...	...	...	...	...	...
1332	Capital	—	—	—	—	—	—	...	...	...	...	...	...
14	**Other revenue**	**137**	**203**	**197**	**137**	**203**	**197**	...	...	...	...	...	...
	Table 2 Expense by economic type												
2	**Expense**	**1,565**	**1,599**	**1,714**	**1,565**	**1,599**	**1,714**	...	...	...	...	...	...
21	**Compensation of employees**	**594**	**624**	**640**	**594**	**624**	**640**	...	...	...	...	...	...
211	Wages and salaries	594	624	640	594	624	640	...	...	...	...	...	...
212	Employers' social contributions	—	—	—	—	—	—	...	...	...	...	...	...
22	**Use of goods and services**	**354**	**308**	**331**	**354**	**308**	**331**	...	...	...	...	...	...
23	**Consumption of fixed capital**	...	...	...	...	...	...	...	...	...	...	...	...
24	**Interest**	**198**	**212**	**233**	**198**	**212**	**233**	...	...	...	...	...	...
25	**Subsidies**	**261**	**276**	**331**	**261**	**276**	**331**	...	...	...	...	...	...
26	**Grants**	—	—	—	—	—	—	...	...	...	...	...	...
261	To foreign governments	—	—	—	—	—	—	...	...	...	...	...	...
262	To international organizations	—	—	—	—	—	—	...	...	...	...	...	...
263	To other general government units	—	—	—	—	—	—	...	...	...	...	...	...
2631	Current	—	—	—	—	—	—	...	...	...	...	...	...
2632	Capital	—	—	—	—	—	—	...	...	...	...	...	...

Bahamas, The (313)

In Millions of Bahamian Dollars (BSD) / Fiscal Year Ends June 30th

		Budgetary Central Government			Central Government (excl. Social Security)			Central Government (incl. Social Security)			General Government		
		2013P	2014P	2015P	2013P	2014P	2015P	2013	2014	2015	2013	2014	2015
27	**Social benefits**	**105**	**115**	**121**	**105**	**115**	**121**	**...**	**...**	**...**	**...**	**...**	**...**
271	Social security benefits	105	115	121	105	115	121	...	...	...	...	...	...
272	Social assistance benefits	—	—	—	—	—	—	...	...	...	...	...	...
273	Employment-related social benefits	—	—	—	—	—	—	...	...	...	...	...	...
28	**Other expense**	**53**	**64**	**58**	**53**	**64**	**58**	**...**	**...**	**...**	**...**	**...**	**...**
281	Property expense other than interest	—	—	—	—	—	—	...	...	...	...	...	...
282	Transfers not elsewhere classified	53	64	58	53	64	58	...	...	...	...	...	...
2821	Current	53	64	58	53	64	58	...	...	...	...	...	...
2822	Capital	—	—	—	—	—	—	...	...	...	...	...	...
	Table 3 Transactions in assets and liabilities												
3	**Change in net worth from transactions**	**...**	**...**	**...**	**...**	**...**	**...**	**...**	**...**	**...**	**...**	**...**	**...**
31	**Net/Gross investment in nonfinancial assets**	**231**	**247**	**273**	**231**	**247**	**273**	**...**	**...**	**...**	**...**	**...**	**...**
311	Fixed assets	228	237	259	228	237	259	...	...	...	...	...	...
3111	Buildings and structures	209	156	161	209	156	161	...	...	...	...	...	...
3112	Machinery and equipment	—	—	—	—	—	—	...	...	...	...	...	...
3113	Other fixed assets	19	81	98	19	81	98	...	...	...	...	...	...
3114	Weapons systems	—	—	—	—	—	—	...	...	...	...	...	...
312	Inventories	—	—	—	—	—	—	...	...	...	...	...	...
313	Valuables	—	—	—	—	—	—	...	...	...	...	...	...
314	Nonproduced assets	3	11	14	3	11	14	...	...	...	...	...	...
3141	Land	3	11	14	3	11	14	...	...	...	...	...	...
3142	Mineral and energy resources	—	—	—	—	—	—	...	...	...	...	...	...
3143	Other naturally occurring assets	—	—	—	—	—	—	...	...	...	...	...	...
3144	Intangible nonproduced assets	—	—	—	—	—	—	...	...	...	...	...	...
32	**Net acquisition of financial assets**	**131**	**134**	**169**	**131**	**134**	**169**	**...**	**...**	**...**	**...**	**...**	**...**
	By instrument												
3201	Monetary gold and SDRs	—	—	—	—	—	—	...	...	...	...	...	...
3202	Currency and deposits	28	51	77	28	51	77	...	...	...	...	...	...
3203	Debt securities	—	—	—	—	—	—	...	...	...	...	...	...
3204	Loans	96	82	92	96	82	92	...	...	...	...	...	...
3205	Equity and investment fund shares	7	1	0	7	1	0	...	...	...	...	...	...
3206	Insurance, pension, and standardized guarantee schemes	—	—	—	—	—	—	...	...	...	...	...	...
3207	Financial derivatives and employee stock options	—	—	—	—	—	—	...	...	...	...	...	...
3208	Other accounts receivable	...	...	...	...	...	...	...	...	...	...	...	...
	By debtor												
321	Domestic debtors	131	134	169	131	134	169	...	...	...	...	...	...
322	External debtors	—	—	—	—	—	—	...	...	...	...	...	...
33	**Net incurrence of liabilities**	**824**	**1,036**	**680**	**824**	**1,036**	**680**	**...**	**...**	**...**	**...**	**...**	**...**
	By instrument												
3301	Special Drawing Rights (SDRs)	—	—	—	—	—	—	...	...	...	...	...	...
3302	Currency and deposits	—	—	—	—	—	—	...	...	...	...	...	...
3303	Debt securities	669	496	305	669	496	305	...	...	...	...	...	...
3304	Loans	272	485	441	272	485	441	...	...	...	...	...	...
3305	Equity and investment fund shares	—	—	—	—	—	—	...	...	...	...	...	...
3306	Insurance, pension, and standardized guarantee schemes	—	—	—	—	—	—	...	...	...	...	...	...
3307	Financial derivatives and employee stock options	—	—	—	—	—	—	...	...	...	...	...	...
3308	Other accounts payable	-117	56	-66	-117	56	-66	...	...	...	...	...	...
	By creditor												
331	Domestic creditors	584	594	532	584	594	532	...	...	...	...	...	...
332	External creditors	240	442	148	240	442	148	...	...	...	...	...	...
	Table 4 Holding gains and losses in assets and liabilities												
	Table 5 Holding gains and losses in assets and liabilities												
	Table 6 Balance sheet												

Bahamas, The (313)

In Millions of Bahamian Dollars (BSD) / Fiscal Year Ends June 30th

		Budgetary Central Government			Central Government (excl. Social Security)			Central Government (incl. Social Security)			General Government		
		2013P	2014P	2015P	2013P	2014P	2015P	2013	2014	2015	2013	2014	2015
	Table 7 Expenditure by functions of government												
7	**Expenditure**	**1,804**	**1,849**	**1,992**	**1,804**	**1,849**	**1,992**	...	...	...	...	...	...
701	**General public services**	**500**	**523**	**611**	**500**	**523**	**611**	...	...	...	...	...	...
7017	Public debt transactions	198	212	233	198	212	233	...	...	...	...	...	...
7018	Transfers of general character between levels of government	—	—	—	—	—	—	...	...	...	...	...	...
702	**Defense**	**54**	**119**	**147**	**54**	**119**	**147**	...	...	...	...	...	...
703	**Public order and safety**	**213**	**205**	**206**	**213**	**205**	**206**	...	...	...	...	...	...
704	**Economic affairs**	**322**	**290**	**295**	**322**	**290**	**295**	...	...	...	...	...	...
7042	Agriculture, forestry, fishing, and hunting	14	15	12	14	15	12	...	...	...	...	...	...
7043	Fuel and energy	—	—	—	—	—	—	...	...	...	...	...	...
7044	Mining, manufacturing, and construction	—	—	—	—	—	—	...	...	...	...	...	...
7045	Transport	46	29	29	46	29	29	...	...	...	...	...	...
7046	Communication	4	3	3	4	3	3	...	...	...	...	...	...
705	**Environmental protection**	**1**	**1**	**2**	**1**	**1**	**2**	...	...	...	...	...	...
706	**Housing and community amenities**	**4**	**4**	**4**	**4**	**4**	**4**	...	...	...	...	...	...
707	**Health**	**272**	**271**	**282**	**272**	**271**	**282**	...	...	...	...	...	...
7072	Outpatient services	—	—	—	—	—	—	...	...	...	...	...	...
7073	Hospital services	—	—	—	—	—	—	...	...	...	...	...	...
7074	Public health services	—	—	—	—	—	—	...	...	...	...	...	...
708	**Recreation, culture and religion**	**19**	**22**	**28**	**19**	**22**	**28**	...	...	...	...	...	...
709	**Education**	**288**	**276**	**265**	**288**	**276**	**265**	...	...	...	...	...	...
7091	Pre-primary and primary education	—	—	—	—	—	—	...	...	...	...	...	...
7092	Secondary education	—	—	—	—	—	—	...	...	...	...	...	...
7094	Tertiary education	36	30	24	36	30	24	...	...	...	...	...	...
710	**Social protection**	**131**	**139**	**151**	**131**	**139**	**151**	...	...	...	...	...	...
7z	Statistical discrepancy: Expenditure	—	—	—	—	—	—	...	...	...	...	...	...
	Table 8 Financial transactions by counterpart sector												
	Table 9 Total other economic flows in assets and liabilities												

Bahrain, Kingdom of (419)

In Millions of Bahrain Dinars (BHD) / Fiscal Year Ends December 31st

		Budgetary Central Government			Central Government (excl. Social Security)			Central Government (incl. Social Security)			General Government		
		2011	2012	2013	2011	2012	2013	2011	2012	2013	2011	2012	2013
	Statement of operations												
1	Revenue	2,819	...	2,942	...	...	...	...	...	...	...	...	...
2	Expense	2,435	...	2,857	...	...	...	...	...	...	...	...	...
GOB	**Gross operating balance**	**415**	**...**	**101**	**...**	**...**	**...**	**...**	**...**	**...**	**...**	**...**	**...**
NOB	**Net operating balance**	**384**	**...**	**84**	**...**	**...**	**...**	**...**	**...**	**...**	**...**	**...**	**...**
31	Net/Gross investment in nonfinancial assets	443	...	511	...	...	...	...	...	...	...	...	...
2M	Expenditure	2,878	...	3,369	...	...	...	...	...	...	...	...	...
NLB	**Net lending (+) / Net borrowing (-)**	**-58**	**...**	**-427**	**...**	**...**	**...**	**...**	**...**	**...**	**...**	**...**	**...**
32	Net acquisition of financial assets	781	...	856	...	...	...	...	...	...	...	...	...
33	Net incurrence of liabilities	821	...	1,293	...	...	...	...	...	...	...	...	...
NLBz	Statistical discrepancy	19	...	-10	...	...	...	...	...	...	...	...	...
	Memorandum items												
PB	Primary net lending / net borrowing	56	...	-235	...	...	...	...	...	...	...	...	...
GB	Government balance per national definition	...	...	...	...	...	...	...	...	...	...	...	...
	Statement of other economic flows												
	Balance sheet												
	Table 1 Revenue												
1	**Revenue**	**2,819**	**...**	**2,942**	**...**	**...**	**...**	**...**	**...**	**...**	**...**	**...**	**...**
11	**Taxes**	**121**	**...**	**131**	**...**	**...**	**...**	**...**	**...**	**...**	**...**	**...**	**...**
111	Taxes on income, profits, and capital gains	19	...	16	...	...	...	...	...	...	...	...	...
1111	Payable by individuals	—	...	—	...	...	...	...	...	...	...	...	...
1112	Payable by corporations and other enterprises	19	...	16	...	...	...	...	...	...	...	...	...
1113	Other taxes on income, profits, and capital gains	—	...	—	...	...	...	...	...	...	...	...	...
112	Taxes on payroll and workforce	—	...	—	...	...	...	...	...	...	...	...	...
113	Taxes on property	—	...	—	...	...	...	...	...	...	...	...	...
114	Taxes on goods and services	—	...	—	...	...	...	...	...	...	...	...	...
1141	General taxes on goods and services	—	...	—	...	...	...	...	...	...	...	...	...
1142	Excises	—	...	—	...	...	...	...	...	...	...	...	...
115	Taxes on international trade and transactions	102	...	115	...	...	...	...	...	...	...	...	...
116	Other taxes	—	...	—	...	...	...	...	...	...	...	...	...
12	**Social contributions**	**—**	**...**	**—**	**...**	**...**	**...**	**...**	**...**	**...**	**...**	**...**	**...**
121	Social security contributions	—	...	—	...	...	...	...	...	...	...	...	...
122	Other social contributions	—	...	—	...	...	...	...	...	...	...	...	...
13	**Grants**	**100**	**...**	**—**	**...**	**...**	**...**	**...**	**...**	**...**	**...**	**...**	**...**
131	From foreign governments	100	...	—	...	...	...	...	...	...	...	...	...
132	From international organizations	—	...	—	...	...	...	...	...	...	...	...	...
133	From other general government units	—	...	—	...	...	...	...	...	...	...	...	...
1331	Current	—	...	—	...	...	...	...	...	...	...	...	...
1332	Capital	—	...	—	...	...	...	...	...	...	...	...	...
14	**Other revenue**	**2,599**	**...**	**2,811**	**...**	**...**	**...**	**...**	**...**	**...**	**...**	**...**	**...**
	Table 2 Expense by economic type												
2	**Expense**	**2,435**	**...**	**2,857**	**...**	**...**	**...**	**...**	**...**	**...**	**...**	**...**	**...**
21	**Compensation of employees**	**1,005**	**...**	**1,300**	**...**	**...**	**...**	**...**	**...**	**...**	**...**	**...**	**...**
211	Wages and salaries	...	...	...	...	...	...	...	...	...	...	...	...
212	Employers' social contributions	...	...	...	...	...	...	...	...	...	...	...	...
22	**Use of goods and services**	**318**	**...**	**406**	**...**	**...**	**...**	**...**	**...**	**...**	**...**	**...**	**...**
23	**Consumption of fixed capital**	**31**	**...**	**17**	**...**	**...**	**...**	**...**	**...**	**...**	**...**	**...**	**...**
24	**Interest**	**115**	**...**	**192**	**...**	**...**	**...**	**...**	**...**	**...**	**...**	**...**	**...**
25	**Subsidies**	**86**	**...**	**52**	**...**	**...**	**...**	**...**	**...**	**...**	**...**	**...**	**...**
26	**Grants**	**635**	**...**	**695**	**...**	**...**	**...**	**...**	**...**	**...**	**...**	**...**	**...**
261	To foreign governments	0	...	0	...	...	...	...	...	...	...	...	...
262	To international organizations	—	...	—	...	...	...	...	...	...	...	...	...
263	To other general government units	635	...	695	...	...	...	...	...	...	...	...	...
2631	Current	635	...	695	...	...	...	...	...	...	...	...	...
2632	Capital	—	...	—	...	...	...	...	...	...	...	...	...

Bahrain, Kingdom of (419)

In Millions of Bahrain Dinars (BHD) / Fiscal Year Ends December 31st

		Budgetary Central Government			Central Government (excl. Social Security)			Central Government (incl. Social Security)			General Government		
		2011	2012	2013	2011	2012	2013	2011	2012	2013	2011	2012	2013
27	**Social benefits**	**218**	**...**	**197**	**...**	**...**	**...**	**...**	**...**	**...**	**...**	**...**	**...**
271	Social security benefits	...	...	...	...	...	...	...	...	...	...	...	...
272	Social assistance benefits	...	...	...	...	...	...	...	...	...	...	...	...
273	Employment-related social benefits	...	...	...	...	...	...	...	...	...	...	...	...
28	**Other expense**	**28**	**...**	**-3**	**...**	**...**	**...**	**...**	**...**	**...**	**...**	**...**	**...**
281	Property expense other than interest	—	...	—	...	...	...	...	...	...	...	...	...
282	Transfers not elsewhere classified	28	...	-3	...	...	...	...	...	...	...	...	...
2821	Current	28	...	-3	...	...	...	...	...	...	...	...	...
2822	Capital	—	...	—	...	...	...	...	...	...	...	...	...
	Table 3 Transactions in assets and liabilities												
3	**Change in net worth from transactions**	**403**	**...**	**-782**	**...**	**...**	**...**	**...**	**...**	**...**	**...**	**...**	**...**
31	**Net/Gross investment in nonfinancial assets**	**443**	**...**	**511**	**...**	**...**	**...**	**...**	**...**	**...**	**...**	**...**	**...**
311	Fixed assets	440	...	506	...	...	...	...	...	...	...	...	...
3111	Buildings and structures	...	...	...	...	...	...	...	...	...	...	...	...
3112	Machinery and equipment	...	...	...	...	...	...	...	...	...	...	...	...
3113	Other fixed assets	...	...	...	...	...	...	...	...	...	...	...	...
3114	Weapons systems	...	...	...	...	...	...	...	...	...	...	...	...
312	Inventories	2	...	5	...	...	...	...	...	...	...	...	...
313	Valuables	—	...	—	...	...	...	...	...	...	...	...	...
314	Nonproduced assets	—	...	—	...	...	...	...	...	...	...	...	...
3141	Land	—	...	—	...	...	...	...	...	...	...	...	...
3142	Mineral and energy resources	—	...	—	...	...	...	...	...	...	...	...	...
3143	Other naturally occurring assets	—	...	—	...	...	...	...	...	...	...	...	...
3144	Intangible nonproduced assets	—	...	—	...	...	...	...	...	...	...	...	...
32	**Net acquisition of financial assets**	**781**	**...**	**856**	**...**	**...**	**...**	**...**	**...**	**...**	**...**	**...**	**...**
	By instrument												
3201	Monetary gold and SDRs	—	...	—	...	...	...	...	...	...	...	...	...
3202	Currency and deposits	795	...	856	...	...	...	...	...	...	...	...	...
3203	Debt securities	—	...	—	...	...	...	...	...	...	...	...	...
3204	Loans	—	...	—	...	...	...	...	...	...	...	...	...
3205	Equity and investment fund shares	—	...	—	...	...	...	...	...	...	...	...	...
3206	Insurance, pension, and standardized guarantee schemes	—	...	—	...	...	...	...	...	...	...	...	...
3207	Financial derivatives and employee stock options	—	...	—	...	...	...	...	...	...	...	...	...
3208	Other accounts receivable	-13	...	—	...	...	...	...	...	...	...	...	...
	By debtor												
321	Domestic debtors	781	...	—	...	...	...	...	...	...	...	...	...
322	External debtors	—	...	—	...	...	...	...	...	...	...	...	...
33	**Net incurrence of liabilities**	**821**	**...**	**1,293**	**...**	**...**	**...**	**...**	**...**	**...**	**...**	**...**	**...**
	By instrument												
3301	Special Drawing Rights (SDRs)	—	...	—	...	...	...	...	...	...	...	...	...
3302	Currency and deposits	—	...	—	...	...	...	...	...	...	...	...	...
3303	Debt securities	—	...	—	...	...	...	...	...	...	...	...	...
3304	Loans	677	...	1,190	...	...	...	...	...	...	...	...	...
3305	Equity and investment fund shares	—	...	—	...	...	...	...	...	...	...	...	...
3306	Insurance, pension, and standardized guarantee schemes	—	...	—	...	...	...	...	...	...	...	...	...
3307	Financial derivatives and employee stock options	—	...	—	...	...	...	...	...	...	...	...	...
3308	Other accounts payable	144	...	104	...	...	...	...	...	...	...	...	...
	By creditor												
331	Domestic creditors	549	...	770	...	...	...	...	...	...	...	...	...
332	External creditors	272	...	524	...	...	...	...	...	...	...	...	...
	Table 4 Holding gains and losses in assets and liabilities												
	Table 5 Holding gains and losses in assets and liabilities												
	Table 6 Balance sheet												

Bahrain, Kingdom of (419)

In Millions of Bahrain Dinars (BHD) / Fiscal Year Ends December 31st

		Budgetary Central Government			Central Government (excl. Social Security)			Central Government (incl. Social Security)			General Government		
		2011	2012	2013	2011	2012	2013	2011	2012	2013	2011	2012	2013
	Table 7 Expenditure by functions of government												
7	**Expenditure**	**2,878**	**...**	**3,349**	**...**	**...**	**...**	**...**	**...**	**...**	**...**	**...**	**...**
701	**General public services**	**264**	**...**	**344**	**...**	**...**	**...**	**...**	**...**	**...**	**...**	**...**	**...**
7017	Public debt transactions	115	...	139	...	...	...	...	...	...	...	...	...
7018	Transfers of general character between levels of government	...	...	206	...	...	...	...	...	...	...	...	...
702	**Defense**	**360**	**...**	**418**	**...**	**...**	**...**	**...**	**...**	**...**	**...**	**...**	**...**
703	**Public order and safety**	**424**	**...**	**464**	**...**	**...**	**...**	**...**	**...**	**...**	**...**	**...**	**...**
704	**Economic affairs**	**529**	**...**	**703**	**...**	**...**	**...**	**...**	**...**	**...**	**...**	**...**	**...**
7042	Agriculture, forestry, fishing, and hunting	...	...	...	...	...	...	...	...	...	...	...	...
7043	Fuel and energy	300	...	355	...	...	...	...	...	...	...	...	...
7044	Mining, manufacturing, and construction	...	...	...	...	...	...	...	...	...	...	...	...
7045	Transport	181	...	281	...	...	...	...	...	...	...	...	...
7046	Communication	...	...	3	...	...	...	...	...	...	...	...	...
705	**Environmental protection**	**9**	**...**	**7**	**...**	**...**	**...**	**...**	**...**	**...**	**...**	**...**	**...**
706	**Housing and community amenities**	**214**	**...**	**210**	**...**	**...**	**...**	**...**	**...**	**...**	**...**	**...**	**...**
707	**Health**	**263**	**...**	**369**	**...**	**...**	**...**	**...**	**...**	**...**	**...**	**...**	**...**
7072	Outpatient services	...	...	...	...	...	...	...	...	...	...	...	...
7073	Hospital services	51	...	113	...	...	...	...	...	...	...	...	...
7074	Public health services	...	...	...	...	...	...	...	...	...	...	...	...
708	**Recreation, culture and religion**	**105**	**...**	**112**	**...**	**...**	**...**	**...**	**...**	**...**	**...**	**...**	**...**
709	**Education**	**328**	**...**	**402**	**...**	**...**	**...**	**...**	**...**	**...**	**...**	**...**	**...**
7091	Pre-primary and primary education	...	...	...	...	...	...	...	...	...	...	...	...
7092	Secondary education	...	...	...	...	...	...	...	...	...	...	...	...
7094	Tertiary education	63	...	63	...	...	...	...	...	...	...	...	...
710	**Social protection**	**352**	**...**	**319**	**...**	**...**	**...**	**...**	**...**	**...**	**...**	**...**	**...**
7z	Statistical discrepancy: Expenditure	...	...	—	...	...	...	...	...	...	...	...	...
	Table 8 Financial transactions by counterpart sector												
	Table 9 Total other economic flows in assets and liabilities												

Bangladesh (513)

In Billions of Bangladesh Taka (BDT) / Fiscal Year Ends June 30th

		Budgetary Central Government			Central Government (excl. Social Security)			Central Government (incl. Social Security)			General Government		
		2013	2014	2015	2013	2014	2015	2013	2014	2015	2013	2014	2015
	Statement of operations												
1	Revenue	1,407	1,519	1,516	...	...	...	...	...	...	...	...	...
2	Expense	1,140	1,277	1,365	...	...	...	...	...	...	...	...	...
GOB	**Gross operating balance**	**267**	**242**	**151**	...	...	...	...	...	...	...	...	...
NOB	**Net operating balance**	...	...	...	...	...	...	...	...	...	...	...	...
31	Net/Gross investment in nonfinancial assets	259	345	354	...	...	...	...	...	...	...	...	...
2M	Expenditure	1,399	1,622	1,719	...	...	...	...	...	...	...	...	...
NLB	**Net lending (+) / Net borrowing (-)**	**8**	**-103**	**-203**	...	...	...	...	...	...	...	...	...
32	Net acquisition of financial assets	391	358	365	...	...	...	...	...	...	...	...	...
33	Net incurrence of liabilities	399	422	562	...	...	...	...	...	...	...	...	...
NLBz	Statistical discrepancy	-16	40	6	...	...	...	...	...	...	...	...	...
	Memorandum items												
PB	Primary net lending / net borrowing	250	177	107	...	...	...	...	...	...	...	...	...
GB	Government balance per national definition	...	...	...	...	...	...	...	...	...	...	...	...
	Statement of other economic flows												
	Balance sheet												
	Table 1 Revenue												
1	**Revenue**	**1,407**	**1,519**	**1,516**	...	...	...	...	...	...	...	...	...
11	**Taxes**	**1,075**	**1,160**	**1,288**	...	...	...	...	...	...	...	...	...
111	Taxes on income, profits, and capital gains	344	378	407	...	...	...	...	...	...	...	...	...
1111	Payable by individuals	104	108	130	...	...	...	...	...	...	...	...	...
1112	Payable by corporations and other enterprises	240	270	277	...	...	...	...	...	...	...	...	...
1113	Other taxes on income, profits, and capital gains	—	—	—	...	...	...	...	...	...	...	...	...
112	Taxes on payroll and workforce	—	—	—	...	...	...	...	...	...	...	...	...
113	Taxes on property	—	—	—	...	...	...	...	...	...	...	...	...
114	Taxes on goods and services	402	429	474	...	...	...	...	...	...	...	...	...
1141	General taxes on goods and services	387	411	454	...	...	...	...	...	...	...	...	...
1142	Excises	8	8	10	...	...	...	...	...	...	...	...	...
115	Taxes on international trade and transactions	289	311	360	...	...	...	...	...	...	...	...	...
116	Other taxes	39	43	47	...	...	...	...	...	...	...	...	...
12	**Social contributions**	—	—	—	...	...	...	...	...	...	...	...	...
121	Social security contributions	—	—	—	...	...	...	...	...	...	...	...	...
122	Other social contributions	—	—	—	...	...	...	...	...	...	...	...	...
13	**Grants**	**69**	**59**	**24**	...	...	...	...	...	...	...	...	...
131	From foreign governments	39	49	15	...	...	...	...	...	...	...	...	...
132	From international organizations	30	9	9	...	...	...	...	...	...	...	...	...
133	From other general government units	—	—	—	...	...	...	...	...	...	...	...	...
1331	Current	—	—	—	...	...	...	...	...	...	...	...	...
1332	Capital	—	—	—	...	...	...	...	...	...	...	...	...
14	**Other revenue**	**264**	**300**	**204**	...	...	...	...	...	...	...	...	...
	Table 2 Expense by economic type												
2	**Expense**	**1,140**	**1,277**	**1,365**	...	...	...	...	...	...	...	...	...
21	**Compensation of employees**	**220**	**268**	**295**	...	...	...	...	...	...	...	...	...
211	Wages and salaries	220	268	295	...	...	...	...	...	...	...	...	...
212	Employers' social contributions	—	—	—	...	...	...	...	...	...	...	...	...
22	**Use of goods and services**	**163**	**190**	**200**	...	...	...	...	...	...	...	...	...
23	**Consumption of fixed capital**	...	...	...	...	...	...	...	...	...	...	...	...
24	**Interest**	**242**	**280**	**310**	...	...	...	...	...	...	...	...	...
25	**Subsidies**	**144**	**124**	**113**	...	...	...	...	...	...	...	...	...
26	**Grants**	**173**	**190**	**205**	...	...	...	...	...	...	...	...	...
261	To foreign governments	—	—	—	...	...	...	...	...	...	...	...	...
262	To international organizations	—	—	—	...	...	...	...	...	...	...	...	...
263	To other general government units	173	190	205	...	...	...	...	...	...	...	...	...
2631	Current	91	105	114	...	...	...	...	...	...	...	...	...
2632	Capital	82	85	91	...	...	...	...	...	...	...	...	...

Bangladesh (513)

In Billions of Bangladesh Taka (BDT) / Fiscal Year Ends June 30th

		Budgetary Central Government			Central Government (excl. Social Security)			Central Government (incl. Social Security)			General Government		
		2013	2014	2015	2013	2014	2015	2013	2014	2015	2013	2014	2015
27	**Social benefits**	**100**	**103**	**116**	...	...	...	...	...	...	...	...	...
271	Social security benefits	—	—	—	...	...	...	...	...	...	...	...	...
272	Social assistance benefits	41	50	63	...	...	...	...	...	...	...	...	...
273	Employment-related social benefits	59	53	53	...	...	...	...	...	...	...	...	...
28	**Other expense**	**98**	**123**	**127**	...	...	...	...	...	...	...	...	...
281	Property expense other than interest	—	—	—	...	...	...	...	...	...	...	...	...
282	Transfers not elsewhere classified	98	123	127	...	...	...	...	...	...	...	...	...
2821	Current	35	40	43	...	...	...	...	...	...	...	...	...
2822	Capital	62	82	84	...	...	...	...	...	...	...	...	...
	Table 3 Transactions in assets and liabilities												
3	**Change in net worth from transactions**	...	...	...	...	...	...	...	...	...	...	...	...
31	**Net/Gross investment in nonfinancial assets**	**259**	**345**	**354**	...	...	...	...	...	...	...	...	...
311	Fixed assets	247	327	340	...	...	...	...	...	...	...	...	...
3111	Buildings and structures	...	...	...	...	...	...	...	...	...	...	...	...
3112	Machinery and equipment	...	...	...	...	...	...	...	...	...	...	...	...
3113	Other fixed assets	...	...	...	...	...	...	...	...	...	...	...	...
3114	Weapons systems	...	...	...	...	...	...	...	...	...	...	...	...
312	Inventories	—	—	—	...	...	...	...	...	...	...	...	...
313	Valuables	—	—	—	...	...	...	...	...	...	...	...	...
314	Nonproduced assets	11	18	14	...	...	...	...	...	...	...	...	...
3141	Land	11	18	14	...	...	...	...	...	...	...	...	...
3142	Mineral and energy resources	—	—	—	...	...	...	...	...	...	...	...	...
3143	Other naturally occurring assets	—	—	—	...	...	...	...	...	...	...	...	...
3144	Intangible nonproduced assets	—	—	—	...	...	...	...	...	...	...	...	...
32	**Net acquisition of financial assets**	**391**	**358**	**365**	...	...	...	...	...	...	...	...	...
	By instrument												
3201	Monetary gold and SDRs	—	—	—	...	...	...	...	...	...	...	...	...
3202	Currency and deposits	67	80	119	...	...	...	...	...	...	...	...	...
3203	Debt securities	—	—	—	...	...	...	...	...	...	...	...	...
3204	Loans	270	181	158	...	...	...	...	...	...	...	...	...
3205	Equity and investment fund shares	54	98	87	...	...	...	...	...	...	...	...	...
3206	Insurance, pension, and standardized guarantee schemes	—	—	—	...	...	...	...	...	...	...	...	...
3207	Financial derivatives and employee stock options	—	—	—	...	...	...	...	...	...	...	...	...
3208	Other accounts receivable	...	...	...	...	...	...	...	...	...	...	...	...
	By debtor												
321	Domestic debtors	391	358	365	...	...	...	...	...	...	...	...	...
322	External debtors	—	—	—	...	...	...	...	...	...	...	...	...
33	**Net incurrence of liabilities**	**399**	**422**	**562**	...	...	...	...	...	...	...	...	...
	By instrument												
3301	Special Drawing Rights (SDRs)	—	—	—	...	...	...	...	...	...	...	...	...
3302	Currency and deposits	—	—	—	...	...	...	...	...	...	...	...	...
3303	Debt securities	8	118	287	...	...	...	...	...	...	...	...	...
3304	Loans	391	304	275	...	...	...	...	...	...	...	...	...
3305	Equity and investment fund shares	—	—	—	...	...	...	...	...	...	...	...	...
3306	Insurance, pension, and standardized guarantee schemes	—	—	—	...	...	...	...	...	...	...	...	...
3307	Financial derivatives and employee stock options	—	—	—	...	...	...	...	...	...	...	...	...
3308	Other accounts payable	...	...	...	...	...	...	...	...	...	...	...	...
	By creditor												
331	Domestic creditors	341	385	513	...	...	...	...	...	...	...	...	...
332	External creditors	58	36	49	...	...	...	...	...	...	...	...	...
	Table 4 Holding gains and losses in assets and liabilities												
	Table 5 Holding gains and losses in assets and liabilities												
	Table 6 Balance sheet												

Bangladesh (513)

In Billions of Bangladesh Taka (BDT) / Fiscal Year Ends June 30th

		Budgetary Central Government			Central Government (excl. Social Security)			Central Government (incl. Social Security)			General Government		
		2013	2014	2015	2013	2014	2015	2013	2014	2015	2013	2014	2015
	Table 7 Expenditure by functions of government												
7	**Expenditure**	**1,399**	**1,622**	**1,719**	...	...	...	...	...	...	...	...	...
701	**General public services**	**337**	**401**	**418**	...	...	...	...	...	...	...	...	...
7017	Public debt transactions	242	280	310	...	...	...	...	...	...	...	...	...
7018	Transfers of general character between levels of government	18	17	12	...	...	...	...	...	...	...	...	...
702	**Defense**	**131**	**165**	**176**	...	...	...	...	...	...	...	...	...
703	**Public order and safety**	**102**	**130**	**139**	...	...	...	...	...	...	...	...	...
704	**Economic affairs**	**415**	**423**	**450**	...	...	...	...	...	...	...	...	...
7042	Agriculture, forestry, fishing, and hunting	169	140	134	...	...	...	...	...	...	...	...	...
7043	Fuel and energy	4	14	17	...	...	...	...	...	...	...	...	...
7044	Mining, manufacturing, and construction	0	0	0	...	...	...	...	...	...	...	...	...
7045	Transport	101	111	121	...	...	...	...	...	...	...	...	...
7046	Communication	10	9	12	...	...	...	...	...	...	...	...	...
705	**Environmental protection**	**4**	**2**	**2**	...	...	...	...	...	...	...	...	...
706	**Housing and community amenities**	**25**	**32**	**34**	...	...	...	...	...	...	...	...	...
707	**Health**	**82**	**93**	**100**	...	...	...	...	...	...	...	...	...
7072	Outpatient services	4	5	5	...	...	...	...	...	...	...	...	...
7073	Hospital services	14	17	18	...	...	...	...	...	...	...	...	...
7074	Public health services	10	12	12	...	...	...	...	...	...	...	...	...
708	**Recreation, culture and religion**	**10**	**13**	**14**	...	...	...	...	...	...	...	...	...
709	**Education**	**202**	**259**	**275**	...	...	...	...	...	...	...	...	...
7091	Pre-primary and primary education	82	104	105	...	...	...	...	...	...	...	...	...
7092	Secondary education	62	82	81	...	...	...	...	...	...	...	...	...
7094	Tertiary education	22	27	30	...	...	...	...	...	...	...	...	...
710	**Social protection**	**89**	**105**	**111**	...	...	...	...	...	...	...	...	...
7z	Statistical discrepancy: Expenditure	—	-0	-0	...	...	...	...	...	...	...	...	...
	Table 8 Financial transactions by counterpart sector												
	Table 9 Total other economic flows in assets and liabilities												

Barbados (316)

In Millions of Barbados Dollars (BBD) / Fiscal Year Ends March 31st

		Budgetary Central Government			Central Government (excl. Social Security)			Central Government (incl. Social Security)			General Government		
		2011	2012	2013	2011	2012	2013	2011	2012	2013	2011	2012	2013
	Statement of operations												
1	Revenue	2,597	2,426	2,312	...	...	...	...	...	...	...	...	...
2	Expense	3,006	3,275	3,322	...	...	...	...	...	...	...	...	...
GOB	**Gross operating balance**	**-357**	**-797**	**-957**	...	...	...	...	...	...	...	...	...
NOB	**Net operating balance**	**-409**	**-849**	**-1,010**	...	...	...	...	...	...	...	...	...
31	Net/Gross investment in nonfinancial assets	-9	6	38	...	...	...	...	...	...	...	...	...
2M	Expenditure	2,997	3,280	3,360	...	...	...	...	...	...	...	...	...
NLB	**Net lending (+) / Net borrowing (-)**	**-400**	**-855**	**-1,048**	...	...	...	...	...	...	...	...	...
32	Net acquisition of financial assets	398	319	540	...	...	...	...	...	...	...	...	...
33	Net incurrence of liabilities	672	1,065	876	...	...	...	...	...	...	...	...	...
NLBz	Statistical discrepancy	126	109	713	...	...	...	...	...	...	...	...	...
	Memorandum items												
PB	Primary net lending / net borrowing	127	-290	-450	...	...	...	...	...	...	...	...	...
GB	Government balance per national definition	...	...	...	...	...	...	...	...	...	...	...	...
	Statement of other economic flows												
9	**Change in net worth due to other economic flows**	...	...	...	...	...	...	...	...	...	...	...	...
4	Change in net worth due to holding gains and losses	1	-0	0	...	...	...	...	...	...	...	...	...
41	Nonfinancial assets	—	—	—	...	...	...	...	...	...	...	...	...
42	Financial assets	1	-0	0	...	...	...	...	...	...	...	...	...
43	Liabilities	—	—	—	...	...	...	...	...	...	...	...	...
5	Change in net worth due to volume changes	...	...	...	...	...	...	...	...	...	...	...	...
51	Nonfinancial assets	...	...	...	...	...	...	...	...	...	...	...	...
52	Financial assets	...	...	...	...	...	...	...	...	...	...	...	...
53	Liabilities	...	...	...	...	...	...	...	...	...	...	...	...
	Balance sheet												
6	**Net worth**	**-3,732**	**-4,553**	**-5,062**	...	...	...	...	...	...	...	...	...
61	Nonfinancial assets	2,943	2,953	2,997	...	...	...	...	...	...	...	...	...
62	Financial assets	2,663	2,891	3,212	...	...	...	...	...	...	...	...	...
63	Liabilities	9,338	10,398	11,270	...	...	...	...	...	...	...	...	...
	Table 1 Revenue												
1	**Revenue**	**2,597**	**2,426**	**2,312**	...	...	...	...	...	...	...	...	...
11	**Taxes**	**2,416**	**2,255**	**2,157**	...	...	...	...	...	...	...	...	...
111	Taxes on income, profits, and capital gains	772	746	639	...	...	...	...	...	...	...	...	...
1111	Payable by individuals	420	397	379	...	...	...	...	...	...	...	...	...
1112	Payable by corporations and other enterprises	286	269	180	...	...	...	...	...	...	...	...	...
1113	Other taxes on income, profits, and capital gains	66	80	81	...	...	...	...	...	...	...	...	...
112	Taxes on payroll and workforce	—	—	—	...	...	...	...	...	...	...	...	...
113	Taxes on property	131	132	138	...	...	...	...	...	...	...	...	...
114	Taxes on goods and services	1,284	1,145	1,152	...	...	...	...	...	...	...	...	...
1141	General taxes on goods and services	1,015	893	924	...	...	...	...	...	...	...	...	...
1142	Excises	161	141	115	...	...	...	...	...	...	...	...	...
115	Taxes on international trade and transactions	200	202	194	...	...	...	...	...	...	...	...	...
116	Other taxes	29	30	35	...	...	...	...	...	...	...	...	...
12	**Social contributions**	**1**	**0**	**0**	...	...	...	...	...	...	...	...	...
121	Social security contributions	—	—	—	...	...	...	...	...	...	...	...	...
122	Other social contributions	1	0	0	...	...	...	...	...	...	...	...	...
13	**Grants**	**16**	**34**	**0**	...	...	...	...	...	...	...	...	...
131	From foreign governments	—	—	—	...	...	...	...	...	...	...	...	...
132	From international organizations	16	34	0	...	...	...	...	...	...	...	...	...
133	From other general government units	—	—	—	...	...	...	...	...	...	...	...	...
1331	Current	—	—	—	...	...	...	...	...	...	...	...	...
1332	Capital	—	—	—	...	...	...	...	...	...	...	...	...
14	**Other revenue**	**164**	**137**	**155**	...	...	...	...	...	...	...	...	...

Barbados (316)

In Millions of Barbados Dollars (BBD) / Fiscal Year Ends March 31st

		Budgetary Central Government			Central Government (excl. Social Security)			Central Government (incl. Social Security)			General Government		
		2011	2012	2013	2011	2012	2013	2011	2012	2013	2011	2012	2013
	Table 2 Expense by economic type												
2	**Expense**	**3,006**	**3,275**	**3,322**	...	...	...	...	...	...	...	...	...
21	**Compensation of employees**	**893**	**906**	**896**	...	...	...	...	...	...	...	...	...
211	Wages and salaries	828	840	830	...	...	...	...	...	...	...	...	...
212	Employers' social contributions	65	66	66	...	...	...	...	...	...	...	...	...
22	**Use of goods and services**	**459**	**469**	**439**	...	...	...	...	...	...	...	...	...
23	**Consumption of fixed capital**	**53**	**52**	**53**	...	...	...	...	...	...	...	...	...
24	**Interest**	**527**	**565**	**598**	...	...	...	...	...	...	...	...	...
25	**Subsidies**	**709**	**882**	**927**	...	...	...	...	...	...	...	...	...
26	**Grants**	**26**	**23**	**23**	...	...	...	...	...	...	...	...	...
261	To foreign governments	—	—	—	...	...	...	...	...	...	...	...	...
262	To international organizations	26	23	23	...	...	...	...	...	...	...	...	...
263	To other general government units	—	—	—	...	...	...	...	...	...	...	...	...
2631	Current	—	—	—	...	...	...	...	...	...	...	...	...
2632	Capital	—	—	—	...	...	...	...	...	...	...	...	...
27	**Social benefits**	**339**	**378**	**387**	...	...	...	...	...	...	...	...	...
271	Social security benefits	189	199	209	...	...	...	...	...	...	...	...	...
272	Social assistance benefits	150	179	178	...	...	...	...	...	...	...	...	...
273	Employment-related social benefits	—	—	—	...	...	...	...	...	...	...	...	...
28	**Other expense**	**—**	**—**	**—**	...	...	...	...	...	...	...	...	...
281	Property expense other than interest	—	—	—	...	...	...	...	...	...	...	...	...
282	Transfers not elsewhere classified	—	—	—	...	...	...	...	...	...	...	...	...
2821	Current	—	—	—	...	...	...	...	...	...	...	...	...
2822	Capital	—	—	—	...	...	...	...	...	...	...	...	...
	Table 3 Transactions in assets and liabilities												
3	**Change in net worth from transactions**	**-283**	**-740**	**-298**	...	...	...	...	...	...	...	...	...
31	**Net/Gross investment in nonfinancial assets**	**-9**	**6**	**38**	...	...	...	...	...	...	...	...	...
311	Fixed assets	-17	-0	31	...	...	...	...	...	...	...	...	...
3111	Buildings and structures	-46	-29	-51	...	...	...	...	...	...	...	...	...
3112	Machinery and equipment	8	4	7	...	...	...	...	...	...	...	...	...
3113	Other fixed assets	22	25	75	...	...	...	...	...	...	...	...	...
3114	Weapons systems	—	—	—	...	...	...	...	...	...	...	...	...
312	Inventories	—	—	—	...	...	...	...	...	...	...	...	...
313	Valuables	—	—	—	...	...	...	...	...	...	...	...	...
314	Nonproduced assets	7	6	7	...	...	...	...	...	...	...	...	...
3141	Land	6	4	6	...	...	...	...	...	...	...	...	...
3142	Mineral and energy resources	—	—	—	...	...	...	...	...	...	...	...	...
3143	Other naturally occurring assets	—	—	—	...	...	...	...	...	...	...	...	...
3144	Intangible nonproduced assets	2	2	1	...	...	...	...	...	...	...	...	...
32	**Net acquisition of financial assets**	**398**	**319**	**540**	...	...	...	...	...	...	...	...	...
	By instrument												
3201	Monetary gold and SDRs	—	—	—	...	...	...	...	...	...	...	...	...
3202	Currency and deposits	327	-27	185	...	...	...	...	...	...	...	...	...
3203	Debt securities	—	—	—	...	...	...	...	...	...	...	...	...
3204	Loans	1	109	-6	...	...	...	...	...	...	...	...	...
3205	Equity and investment fund shares	5	61	21	...	...	...	...	...	...	...	...	...
3206	Insurance, pension, and standardized guarantee schemes	—	—	—	...	...	...	...	...	...	...	...	...
3207	Financial derivatives and employee stock options	—	—	—	...	...	...	...	...	...	...	...	...
3208	Other accounts receivable	65	176	341	...	...	...	...	...	...	...	...	...
	By debtor												
321	Domestic debtors	398	319	540	...	...	...	...	...	...	...	...	...
322	External debtors	—	—	—	...	...	...	...	...	...	...	...	...
33	**Net incurrence of liabilities**	**672**	**1,065**	**876**	...	...	...	...	...	...	...	...	...
	By instrument												
3301	Special Drawing Rights (SDRs)	—	—	—	...	...	...	...	...	...	...	...	...
3302	Currency and deposits	25	64	123	...	...	...	...	...	...	...	...	...
3303	Debt securities	461	1,063	756	...	...	...	...	...	...	...	...	...
3304	Loans	224	-119	-1	...	...	...	...	...	...	...	...	...

Barbados (316)

In Millions of Barbados Dollars (BBD) / Fiscal Year Ends March 31st

		Budgetary Central Government			Central Government (excl. Social Security)			Central Government (incl. Social Security)			General Government		
		2011	2012	2013	2011	2012	2013	2011	2012	2013	2011	2012	2013
3305	Equity and investment fund shares	—	—	—	...	...	...	...	...	...	...	...	...
3306	Insurance, pension, and standardized guarantee schemes	—	—	—	...	...	...	...	...	...	...	...	...
3307	Financial derivatives and employee stock options	—	—	—	...	...	...	...	...	...	...	...	...
3308	Other accounts payable	-38	57	-2	...	...	...	...	...	...	...	...	...
	By creditor												
331	Domestic creditors	480	1,183	879	...	...	...	...	...	...	...	...	...
332	External creditors	192	-119	-3	...	...	...	...	...	...	...	...	...
	Table 4 Holding gains and losses in assets and liabilities												
4	**Change in net worth due to holding gains and losses**	1	-0	0	...	...	...	...	...	...	...	...	...
41	**Holding gains and losses in nonfinancial assets**	—	—	—	...	...	...	...	...	...	...	...	...
411	Fixed assets	—	—	—	...	...	...	...	...	...	...	...	...
412	Inventories	—	—	—	...	...	...	...	...	...	...	...	...
413	Valuables	—	—	—	...	...	...	...	...	...	...	...	...
414	Nonproduced assets	—	—	—	...	...	...	...	...	...	...	...	...
42	**Holding gains and losses in financial assets**	1	-0	0	...	...	...	...	...	...	...	...	...
	By instrument												
4201	Monetary gold and SDRs	—	—	—	...	...	...	...	...	...	...	...	...
4202	Currency and deposits	—	—	—	...	...	...	...	...	...	...	...	...
4203	Debt securities	—	—	—	...	...	...	...	...	...	...	...	...
4204	Loans	—	—	—	...	...	...	...	...	...	...	...	...
4205	Equity and investment fund shares	—	—	—	...	...	...	...	...	...	...	...	...
4206	Insurance, pension, and standardized guarantee schemes	—	—	—	...	...	...	...	...	...	...	...	...
4207	Financial derivatives and employee stock options	—	—	—	...	...	...	...	...	...	...	...	...
4208	Other accounts receivable	—	—	—	...	...	...	...	...	...	...	...	...
	By debtor												
421	Domestic debtors	1	-0	0	...	...	...	...	...	...	...	...	...
422	External debtors	—	—	—	...	...	...	...	...	...	...	...	...
43	**Holding gains and losses in liabilities**	—	—	—	...	...	...	...	...	...	...	...	...
	By instrument												
4301	Special Drawing Rights (SDRs)	—	—	—	...	...	...	...	...	...	...	...	...
4302	Currency and deposits	—	—	—	...	...	...	...	...	...	...	...	...
4303	Debt securities	—	—	—	...	...	...	...	...	...	...	...	...
4304	Loans	—	—	—	...	...	...	...	...	...	...	...	...
4305	Equity and investment fund shares	—	—	—	...	...	...	...	...	...	...	...	...
4306	Insurance, pension, and standardized guarantee schemes	—	—	—	...	...	...	...	...	...	...	...	...
4307	Financial derivatives and employee stock options	—	—	—	...	...	...	...	...	...	...	...	...
4308	Other accounts payable	—	—	—	...	...	...	...	...	...	...	...	...
	By creditor												
431	Domestic creditors	—	—	—	...	...	...	...	...	...	...	...	...
432	External creditors	—	—	—	...	...	...	...	...	...	...	...	...
	Table 5 Holding gains and losses in assets and liabilities												
	Table 6 Balance sheet												
6	**Net worth**	**-3,732**	**-4,553**	**-5,062**	...	...	...	...	...	...	...	...	...
61	**Nonfinancial assets**	**2,943**	**2,953**	**2,997**	...	...	...	...	...	...	...	...	...
611	Fixed assets	1,530	1,537	1,574	...	...	...	...	...	...	...	...	...
6111	Buildings and structures	1,137	1,127	1,094	...	...	...	...	...	...	...	...	...
6112	Machinery and equipment	141	138	138	...	...	...	...	...	...	...	...	...
6113	Other fixed assets	252	271	341	...	...	...	...	...	...	...	...	...
6114	Weapons systems	—	—	—	...	...	...	...	...	...	...	...	...
612	Inventories	1	1	0	...	...	...	...	...	...	...	...	...
613	Valuables	—	—	—	...	...	...	...	...	...	...	...	...
614	Nonproduced assets	1,411	1,416	1,423	...	...	...	...	...	...	...	...	...
6141	Land	1,402	1,406	1,413	...	...	...	...	...	...	...	...	...

Barbados (316)

In Millions of Barbados Dollars (BBD) / Fiscal Year Ends March 31st

		Budgetary Central Government			Central Government (excl. Social Security)			Central Government (incl. Social Security)			General Government		
		2011	2012	2013	2011	2012	2013	2011	2012	2013	2011	2012	2013
6142	Mineral and energy resources	—	—	—	...	...	...	...	...	...	...	...	...
6143	Other naturally occurring assets	—	—	—	...	...	...	...	...	...	...	...	...
6144	Intangible nonproduced assets	10	10	10	...	...	...	...	...	...	...	...	...
62	**Financial assets**	**2,663**	**2,891**	**3,212**	...	...	...	...	...	...	...	...	...
	By instrument												
6201	Monetary gold and SDRs	—	—	—	...	...	...	...	...	...	...	...	...
6202	Currency and deposits	1,229	1,110	1,251	...	...	...	...	...	...	...	...	...
6203	Debt securities	—	—	—	...	...	...	...	...	...	...	...	...
6204	Loans	300	410	403	...	...	...	...	...	...	...	...	...
6205	Equity and investment fund shares	230	291	312	...	...	...	...	...	...	...	...	...
6206	Insurance, pension, and standardized guarantee schemes	—	—	—	...	...	...	...	...	...	...	...	...
6207	Financial derivatives and employee stock options	—	—	—	...	...	...	...	...	...	...	...	...
6208	Other accounts receivable	904	1,080	1,245	...	...	...	...	...	...	...	...	...
	By debtor												
621	Domestic debtors	2,663	2,891	3,212	...	...	...	...	...	...	...	...	...
622	External debtors	—	—	—	...	...	...	...	...	...	...	...	...
63	**Liabilities**	**9,338**	**10,398**	**11,270**	...	...	...	...	...	...	...	...	...
	By instrument												
6301	Special Drawing Rights (SDRs)	—	—	—	...	...	...	...	...	...	...	...	...
6302	Currency and deposits	143	206	329	...	...	...	...	...	...	...	...	...
6303	Debt securities	5,782	6,846	7,603	...	...	...	...	...	...	...	...	...
6304	Loans	3,351	3,227	3,222	...	...	...	...	...	...	...	...	...
6305	Equity and investment fund shares	—	—	—	...	...	...	...	...	...	...	...	...
6306	Insurance, pension, and standardized guarantee schemes	—	—	—	...	...	...	...	...	...	...	...	...
6307	Financial derivatives and employee stock options	—	—	—	...	...	...	...	...	...	...	...	...
6308	Other accounts payable	62	119	116	...	...	...	...	...	...	...	...	...
	By creditor												
631	Domestic creditors	6,520	7,698	8,574	...	...	...	...	...	...	...	...	...
632	External creditors	2,818	2,700	2,697	...	...	...	...	...	...	...	...	...
	Memorandum items												
6M2	Net financial worth	-6,675	-7,507	-8,058	...	...	...	...	...	...	...	...	...
6M3	Gross debt (D4) at market value	...	...	...	...	...	...	...	...	...	...	...	...
6M3D3	D3 debt liabilities at market value	...	...	...	...	...	...	...	...	...	...	...	...
6M3D2	D2 debt liabilities at market value	...	...	...	...	...	...	...	...	...	...	...	...
6M3D1	D1 debt liabilities at market value	...	...	...	...	...	...	...	...	...	...	...	...
6M4	Gross debt (D4) at nominal value	...	...	...	...	...	...	...	...	...	...	...	...
6M4D3	D3 debt liabilities at nominal value	...	...	...	...	...	...	...	...	...	...	...	...
6M4D2	D2 debt liabilities at nominal value	...	...	...	...	...	...	...	...	...	...	...	...
6M4D1	D1 debt liabilities at nominal value	...	...	...	...	...	...	...	...	...	...	...	...
6M35	Gross debt (D4) at face value	9,338	10,398	11,270	...	...	...	...	...	...	...	...	...
6M35D3	D3 debt liabilities at face value	9,338	10,398	11,270	...	...	...	...	...	...	...	...	...
6M35D2	D2 debt liabilities at face value	9,276	10,279	11,154	...	...	...	...	...	...	...	...	...
6M35D1	D1 debt liabilities at face value	9,134	10,073	10,825	...	...	...	...	...	...	...	...	...
6M93	Government gross debt per national definition	...	...	...	...	...	...	...	...	...	...	...	...
6M5	Arrears	...	...	...	...	...	...	...	...	...	...	...	...
6M6	Explicit contingent liabilities	...	...	...	...	...	...	...	...	...	...	...	...
6M61	of which: Publicly guaranteed debt	...	...	...	...	...	...	...	...	...	...	...	...
6M7	Net implicit obligations for social security benefits	...	...	...	...	...	...	...	...	...	...	...	...
	Table 7 Expenditure by functions of government												
7	**Expenditure**	**2,997**	**3,280**	**3,360**	...	...	...	...	...	...	...	...	...
701	**General public services**	...	...	...	...	...	...	...	...	...	...	...	...
7017	Public debt transactions	527	565	598	...	...	...	...	...	...	...	...	...
7018	Transfers of general character between levels of government	...	...	...	...	...	...	...	...	...	...	...	...
702	**Defense**	...	...	...	...	...	...	...	...	...	...	...	...

Barbados (316)

In Millions of Barbados Dollars (BBD) / Fiscal Year Ends March 31st

		Budgetary Central Government			Central Government (excl. Social Security)			Central Government (incl. Social Security)			General Government		
		2011	2012	2013	2011	2012	2013	2011	2012	2013	2011	2012	2013
703	**Public order and safety**	...	...	...	...	...	...	...	...	...	...	...	...
704	**Economic affairs**	...	...	...	...	...	...	...	...	...	...	...	...
7042	Agriculture, forestry, fishing, and hunting	...	...	...	...	...	...	...	...	...	...	...	...
7043	Fuel and energy	...	...	...	...	...	...	...	...	...	...	...	...
7044	Mining, manufacturing, and construction	...	...	...	...	...	...	...	...	...	...	...	...
7045	Transport	...	...	...	...	...	...	...	...	...	...	...	...
7046	Communication	...	...	...	...	...	...	...	...	...	...	...	...
705	**Environmental protection**	...	...	...	...	...	...	...	...	...	...	...	...
706	**Housing and community amenities**	...	...	...	...	...	...	...	...	...	...	...	...
707	**Health**	...	...	...	...	...	...	...	...	...	...	...	...
7072	Outpatient services	...	...	...	...	...	...	...	...	...	...	...	...
7073	Hospital services	...	...	...	...	...	...	...	...	...	...	...	...
7074	Public health services	...	...	...	...	...	...	...	...	...	...	...	...
708	**Recreation, culture and religion**	...	...	...	...	...	...	...	...	...	...	...	...
709	**Education**	...	...	...	...	...	...	...	...	...	...	...	...
7091	Pre-primary and primary education	...	...	...	...	...	...	...	...	...	...	...	...
7092	Secondary education	...	...	...	...	...	...	...	...	...	...	...	...
7094	Tertiary education	...	...	...	...	...	...	...	...	...	...	...	...
710	**Social protection**	...	...	...	...	...	...	...	...	...	...	...	...
7z	Statistical discrepancy: Expenditure	...	...	...	...	...	...	...	...	...	...	...	...
	Table 8 Financial transactions by counterpart sector												
32	**Net acquisition of financial assets**	**398**	**319**	**540**	...	...	...	...	...	...	...	...	...
321	Domestic debtors	398	319	540	...	...	...	...	...	...	...	...	...
8211	General government	...	...	...	...	...	...	...	...	...	...	...	...
8212	Central bank	...	...	...	...	...	...	...	...	...	...	...	...
8213	Deposit-taking corporations except the central bank	...	...	...	...	...	...	...	...	...	...	...	...
8214	Other financial corporations	...	...	...	...	...	...	...	...	...	...	...	...
8215	Nonfinancial corporations	...	...	...	...	...	...	...	...	...	...	...	...
8216	Households & nonprofit institutions serving households	...	...	...	...	...	...	...	...	...	...	...	...
322	External debtors	—	—	—	...	...	...	...	...	...	...	...	...
8221	General government	—	—	—	...	...	...	...	...	...	...	...	...
8227	International organizations	—	—	—	...	...	...	...	...	...	...	...	...
8228	Financial corporations other than international organizations	—	—	—	...	...	...	...	...	...	...	...	...
8229	Other nonresidents	—	—	—	...	...	...	...	...	...	...	...	...
33	**Net incurrence of liabilities**	**672**	**1,065**	**876**	...	...	...	...	...	...	...	...	...
331	Domestic creditors	480	1,183	879	...	...	...	...	...	...	...	...	...
8311	General government	...	...	...	...	...	...	...	...	...	...	...	...
8312	Central bank	...	...	...	...	...	...	...	...	...	...	...	...
8313	Deposit-taking corporations except the central bank	...	...	...	...	...	...	...	...	...	...	...	...
8314	Other financial corporations	...	...	...	...	...	...	...	...	...	...	...	...
8315	Nonfinancial corporations	...	...	...	...	...	...	...	...	...	...	...	...
8316	Households & nonprofit institutions serving households	...	...	...	...	...	...	...	...	...	...	...	...
332	External creditors	192	-119	-3	...	...	...	...	...	...	...	...	...
8321	General government	...	...	...	...	...	...	...	...	...	...	...	...
8327	International organizations	...	...	...	...	...	...	...	...	...	...	...	...
8328	Financial corporations other than international organizations	...	...	...	...	...	...	...	...	...	...	...	...
8329	Other nonresidents	...	...	...	...	...	...	...	...	...	...	...	...
	Table 9 Total other economic flows in assets and liabilities												

Belarus (913)

In Billions of Belarusian Rubels (BYR) / Fiscal Year Ends December 31st

		Budgetary Central Government			Central Government (excl. Social Security)			Central Government (incl. Social Security)			General Government		
		2013	2014	2015	2013	2014	2015	2013	2014	2015	2013	2014	2015
	Statement of operations												
1	Revenue	114,740	...	175,682	114,863	138,670	175,682	192,636	232,734	280,467	277,593	323,842	376,665
2	Expense	111,124	...	144,552	111,242	127,110	144,552	189,501	220,871	252,741	246,669	289,300	332,509
GOB	**Gross operating balance**	**3,616**	**...**	**31,130**	**3,621**	**11,560**	**31,130**	**3,135**	**11,863**	**27,726**	**30,924**	**34,542**	**44,157**
NOB	**Net operating balance**	...	...	...	...	...	...	...	...	...	...	...	...
31	Net/Gross investment in nonfinancial assets	8,656	...	7,460	8,660	8,379	7,460	8,697	8,455	7,464	32,300	27,925	23,790
2M	Expenditure	119,780	...	152,012	119,902	135,489	152,012	198,198	229,326	260,205	278,969	317,225	356,299
NLB	**Net lending (+) / Net borrowing (-)**	**-5,040**	**...**	**23,670**	**-5,039**	**3,181**	**23,670**	**-5,562**	**3,408**	**20,263**	**-1,376**	**6,617**	**20,366**
32	Net acquisition of financial assets	-3,200	...	19,294	-3,200	5,032	19,294	-3,723	5,258	15,886	601	10,291	15,599
33	Net incurrence of liabilities	1,840	...	-4,376	1,840	1,851	-4,376	1,840	1,851	-4,376	1,976	3,674	-4,768
NLBz	Statistical discrepancy	0	...	-0	-0	-0	-0	-1	-0	-0	1	-0	-0
	Memorandum items												
PB	Primary net lending / net borrowing	400	...	37,155	400	10,433	37,155	-122	10,660	33,748	5,238	14,959	35,415
GB	Government balance per national definition	...	...	...	...	...	...	...	...	...	...	...	...
	Statement of other economic flows												
	Balance sheet												
6	**Net worth**	...	...	...	...	...	...	...	...	...	...	...	...
61	Nonfinancial assets	...	...	...	...	...	...	...	...	...	...	...	...
62	Financial assets	...	...	...	...	...	...	...	...	...	...	...	...
63	Liabilities	159,874	...	338,045	159,874	197,812	338,045	159,874	197,812	338,045	...	215,284	348,063
	Table 1 Revenue												
1	**Revenue**	**114,740**	**...**	**175,682**	**114,863**	**138,670**	**175,682**	**192,636**	**232,734**	**280,467**	**277,593**	**323,842**	**376,665**
11	**Taxes**	**89,570**	**...**	**127,430**	**89,570**	**102,317**	**127,430**	**89,570**	**102,317**	**127,430**	**164,922**	**189,017**	**222,767**
111	Taxes on income, profits, and capital gains	5,247	...	8,192	5,247	6,584	8,192	5,247	6,584	8,192	50,058	53,751	60,859
1111	Payable by individuals	—	...	—	—	—	—	—	—	—	26,992	32,092	37,009
1112	Payable by corporations and other enterprises	5,247	...	8,192	5,247	6,584	8,192	5,247	6,584	8,192	23,066	21,659	23,850
1113	Other taxes on income, profits, and capital gains	—	...	—	—	—	—	—	—	—	—	—	—
112	Taxes on payroll and workforce	—	...	—	—	—	—	—	—	—	—	—	—
113	Taxes on property	—	...	—	—	—	—	—	—	—	7,591	9,618	12,336
114	Taxes on goods and services	59,947	...	78,650	59,947	75,291	78,650	59,947	75,291	78,650	82,686	105,168	108,947
1141	General taxes on goods and services	39,356	...	50,143	39,356	48,182	50,143	39,356	48,182	50,143	60,505	75,040	78,350
1142	Excises	17,519	...	19,442	17,519	21,231	19,442	17,519	21,231	19,442	17,519	21,231	19,442
115	Taxes on international trade and transactions	23,328	...	39,586	23,328	19,411	39,586	23,328	19,411	39,586	23,328	19,411	39,586
116	Other taxes	1,049	...	1,002	1,049	1,031	1,002	1,049	1,031	1,002	1,260	1,067	1,039
12	**Social contributions**	—	...	—	—	—	—	**76,298**	**90,909**	**97,152**	**76,298**	**90,909**	**97,152**
121	Social security contributions	—	...	—	—	—	—	76,298	90,909	97,152	76,298	90,909	97,152
122	Other social contributions	—	...	—	—	—	—	—	—	—	—	—	—
13	**Grants**	**1**	**...**	**8,369**	**1**	**6,413**	**8,369**	**1**	**7,741**	**13,643**	—	**937**	**755**
131	From foreign governments	—	...	755	—	937	755	—	937	755	—	937	755
132	From international organizations	—	...	—	—	—	—	—	—	—	—	—	—
133	From other general government units	1	...	7,613	1	5,477	7,613	1	6,805	12,888	0	0	—
1331	Current	1	...	7,613	1	5,411	7,613	1	6,739	12,888	0	0	—
1332	Capital	—	...	—	—	65	—	—	65	—	0	0	—
14	**Other revenue**	**25,169**	**...**	**39,883**	**25,292**	**29,939**	**39,883**	**26,767**	**31,766**	**42,242**	**36,373**	**42,979**	**55,991**
	Table 2 Expense by economic type												
2	**Expense**	**111,124**	**...**	**144,552**	**111,242**	**127,110**	**144,552**	**189,501**	**220,871**	**252,741**	**246,669**	**289,300**	**332,509**
21	**Compensation of employees**	**22,668**	**...**	**30,929**	**22,752**	**26,269**	**30,929**	**22,895**	**26,446**	**31,124**	**60,002**	**70,598**	**84,206**
211	Wages and salaries	19,072	...	26,056	19,135	22,016	26,056	19,242	22,148	26,201	47,091	55,084	65,850
212	Employers' social contributions	3,596	...	4,873	3,617	4,252	4,873	3,653	4,298	4,923	12,911	15,514	18,356
22	**Use of goods and services**	**21,162**	**...**	**27,267**	**21,196**	**26,861**	**27,267**	**21,896**	**27,654**	**28,150**	**48,600**	**58,742**	**61,062**
23	**Consumption of fixed capital**	...	...	...	...	...	...	...	...	...	...	...	...
24	**Interest**	**5,439**	**...**	**13,485**	**5,439**	**7,252**	**13,485**	**5,439**	**7,252**	**13,485**	**6,614**	**8,342**	**15,049**
25	**Subsidies**	**10,646**	**...**	**16,794**	**10,646**	**12,501**	**16,794**	**10,828**	**12,698**	**17,021**	**31,710**	**35,249**	**37,572**

Belarus (913)

In Billions of Belarusian Rubels (BYR) / Fiscal Year Ends December 31st

		Budgetary Central Government			Central Government (excl. Social Security)			Central Government (incl. Social Security)			General Government		
		2013	2014	2015	2013	2014	2015	2013	2014	2015	2013	2014	2015
26	**Grants**	**36,758**	**...**	**37,467**	**36,758**	**39,041**	**37,467**	**37,049**	**39,291**	**37,745**	**658**	**658**	**716**
261	To foreign governments	62	...	118	62	82	118	62	82	118	62	82	118
262	To international organizations	595	...	597	595	577	597	595	577	597	595	577	597
263	To other general government units	36,100	...	36,751	36,100	38,383	36,751	36,392	38,633	37,030	0	—	0
2631	Current	32,401	...	33,572	32,401	35,072	33,572	32,580	35,255	33,757	0	—	0
2632	Capital	3,699	...	3,179	3,699	3,311	3,179	3,811	3,378	3,273	0	—	—
27	**Social benefits**	**10,461**	**...**	**15,425**	**10,461**	**11,644**	**15,425**	**87,404**	**103,987**	**122,030**	**91,358**	**108,722**	**127,688**
271	Social security benefits	4,838	...	6,846	4,838	6,100	6,846	81,375	97,894	112,804	81,500	97,999	112,925
272	Social assistance benefits	5,623	...	8,579	5,623	5,544	8,579	6,028	6,093	9,225	9,859	10,723	14,764
273	Employment-related social benefits	—	...	—	—	—	—	—	—	—	—	—	—
28	**Other expense**	**3,991**	**...**	**3,185**	**3,991**	**3,543**	**3,185**	**3,991**	**3,543**	**3,185**	**7,726**	**6,989**	**6,215**
281	Property expense other than interest	—	...	—	—	—	—	—	—	—	—	—	—
282	Transfers not elsewhere classified	3,991	...	3,185	3,991	3,543	3,185	3,991	3,543	3,185	7,726	6,989	6,215
2821	Current	964	...	1,087	964	1,042	1,087	964	1,042	1,087	1,173	1,268	1,326
2822	Capital	3,027	...	2,098	3,027	2,501	2,098	3,027	2,501	2,098	6,553	5,721	4,889
	Table 3 Transactions in assets and liabilities												
3	**Change in net worth from transactions**	**...**	**...**	**...**	**...**	**...**	**...**	**...**	**...**	**...**	**...**	**...**	**...**
31	**Net/Gross investment in nonfinancial assets**	**8,656**	**...**	**7,460**	**8,660**	**8,379**	**7,460**	**8,697**	**8,455**	**7,464**	**32,300**	**27,925**	**23,790**
311	Fixed assets	8,970	...	7,924	8,974	8,711	7,924	9,011	8,788	7,927	32,824	28,554	24,657
3111	Buildings and structures	5,809	...	5,271	5,809	6,172	5,271	5,839	6,204	5,271	27,920	24,888	21,166
3112	Machinery and equipment	3,136	...	2,568	3,140	2,498	2,568	3,146	2,543	2,571	4,879	3,622	3,404
3113	Other fixed assets	25	...	85	25	41	85	25	41	85	25	43	87
3114	Weapons systems	...	...	...	...	...	...	...	...	...	...	...	...
312	Inventories	-347	...	-495	-347	-275	-495	-347	-275	-495	-356	-281	-504
313	Valuables	33	...	31	33	-58	31	33	-58	31	33	-58	31
314	Nonproduced assets	—	...	—	—	—	—	—	—	—	-201	-290	-394
3141	Land	—	...	—	—	—	—	—	—	—	-201	-290	-394
3142	Mineral and energy resources	—	...	—	—	—	—	—	—	—	—	—	—
3143	Other naturally occurring assets	—	...	—	—	—	—	—	—	—	—	—	—
3144	Intangible nonproduced assets	—	...	—	—	—	—	—	—	—	—	—	—
32	**Net acquisition of financial assets**	**-3,200**	**...**	**19,294**	**-3,200**	**5,032**	**19,294**	**-3,723**	**5,258**	**15,886**	**601**	**10,291**	**15,599**
	By instrument												
3201	Monetary gold and SDRs	—	...	—	—	—	—	—	—	—	—	—	—
3202	Currency and deposits	-8,777	...	-7,810	-8,777	185	-7,810	-9,300	411	-11,217	-5,591	2,039	-12,291
3203	Debt securities	-0	...	-0	-0	-0	-0	-0	-0	-0	-0	-0	-0
3204	Loans	-244	...	13,275	-244	170	13,275	-244	170	13,275	-1,232	2,142	11,750
3205	Equity and investment fund shares	5,821	...	13,828	5,821	4,676	13,828	5,821	4,676	13,828	7,425	6,110	16,139
3206	Insurance, pension, and standardized guarantee schemes	—	...	—	—	—	—	—	—	—	—	—	—
3207	Financial derivatives and employee stock options	—	...	—	—	—	—	—	—	—	—	—	—
3208	Other accounts receivable	...	...	...	...	...	...	...	...	—	...	...	...
	By debtor												
321	Domestic debtors	-3,200	...	19,294	-3,200	5,032	19,294	-3,723	5,258	15,886	601	10,291	15,599
322	External debtors	—	...	—	—	—	—	—	—	—	—	—	—
33	**Net incurrence of liabilities**	**1,840**	**...**	**-4,376**	**1,840**	**1,851**	**-4,376**	**1,840**	**1,851**	**-4,376**	**1,976**	**3,674**	**-4,768**
	By instrument												
3301	Special Drawing Rights (SDRs)	—	...	—	—	—	—	—	—	—	—	—	—
3302	Currency and deposits	—	...	—	—	—	—	—	—	—	—	—	—
3303	Debt securities	7,835	...	13,611	7,835	7,426	13,611	7,835	7,426	13,611	8,199	9,660	14,525
3304	Loans	-5,995	...	-3,381	-5,995	-5,576	-3,381	-5,995	-5,576	-3,381	-5,995	-5,986	-3,381
3305	Equity and investment fund shares	—	...	—	—	—	—	—	—	—	—	—	—
3306	Insurance, pension, and standardized guarantee schemes	—	...	—	—	—	—	—	—	—	—	—	—
3307	Financial derivatives and employee stock options	—	...	—	—	—	—	—	—	—	—	—	—
3308	Other accounts payable	...	...	-14,607	...	...	-14,607	...	...	-14,607	-227	...	-15,912

Belarus (913)

In Billions of Belarusian Rubels (BYR) / Fiscal Year Ends December 31st

		Budgetary Central Government			Central Government (excl. Social Security)			Central Government (incl. Social Security)			General Government		
		2013	2014	2015	2013	2014	2015	2013	2014	2015	2013	2014	2015
	By creditor												
331	Domestic creditors	7,836	...	14,130	7,836	7,647	14,130	7,836	7,647	14,130	7,972	9,470	13,739
332	External creditors	-5,996	...	-18,507	-5,996	-5,796	-18,507	-5,996	-5,796	-18,507	-5,996	-5,796	-18,507
	Table 4 Holding gains and losses in assets and liabilities												
	Table 5 Holding gains and losses in assets and liabilities												
	Table 6 Balance sheet												
6	**Net worth**	...	...	...	...	...	...	...	...	...	...	...	...
61	**Nonfinancial assets**	...	...	...	...	...	...	...	...	...	...	...	...
611	Fixed assets	63,629	...	95,399	...	72,303	95,399	...	73,193	96,296	...	207,254	239,819
6111	Buildings and structures	46,258	...	68,127	...	51,439	68,127	...	52,081	68,774	...	163,690	186,544
6112	Machinery and equipment	16,487	...	24,732	...	18,979	24,732	...	19,226	24,980	...	40,905	49,827
6113	Other fixed assets	884	...	2,540	...	1,884	2,540	...	1,886	2,542	...	2,659	3,448
6114	Weapons systems	...	...	...	...	...	...	...	...	...	...	...	...
612	Inventories	2,626	...	4,308	...	3,220	4,308	...	3,224	4,312	...	5,997	7,781
613	Valuables	—	...	...	...	—	...	...	—	...	...	—	...
614	Nonproduced assets	...	...	...	...	...	...	...	...	...	...	435,923	614,833
6141	Land	...	...	...	...	...	...	...	...	...	...	326,019	388,610
6142	Mineral and energy resources	...	...	...	...	...	...	...	...	...	...	...	...
6143	Other naturally occurring assets	...	...	...	...	...	...	...	...	...	...	109,904	226,223
6144	Intangible nonproduced assets	...	...	...	...	...	...	...	...	...	...	...	...
62	**Financial assets**	...	...	...	...	...	...	...	...	...	...	...	...
	By instrument												
6201	Monetary gold and SDRs	5,436	...	9,567	5,436	6,634	9,567	5,436	6,634	9,567	5,436	6,634	9,567
6202	Currency and deposits	...	...	...	...	...	...	...	...	...	...	...	...
6203	Debt securities	1,038	...	412	...	715	412	...	715	412	...	715	412
6204	Loans	6,570	...	41,800	...	9,094	41,800	...	9,094	48,425	...	16,532	46,094
6205	Equity and investment fund shares	151,167	...	61,561	...	196,544	61,561	...	196,544	65,796	...	270,485	65,796
6206	Insurance, pension, and standardized guarantee schemes	—	...	—	...	—	—	...	—	—	...	—	—
6207	Financial derivatives and employee stock options	—	...	—	...	—	—	...	—	—	...	—	—
6208	Other accounts receivable	...	...	...	...	...	...	...	...	...	...	...	...
	By debtor												
621	Domestic debtors	...	...	...	...	206,353	...	...	206,353	...	...	...	...
622	External debtors	...	...	...	...	...	...	...	...	...	...	...	...
63	**Liabilities**	**159,874**	**...**	**338,045**	**159,874**	**197,812**	**338,045**	**159,874**	**197,812**	**338,045**	**...**	**215,284**	**348,063**
	By instrument												
6301	Special Drawing Rights (SDRs)	5,399	...	9,486	5,399	6,369	9,486	5,399	6,369	9,486	5,399	6,369	9,486
6302	Currency and deposits	—	...	—	—	—	—	—	—	—	...	—	—
6303	Debt securities	52,814	...	112,299	52,814	69,710	112,299	52,814	69,710	112,299	...	77,804	121,835
6304	Loans	101,194	...	216,260	101,194	127,745	216,260	101,194	127,745	216,260	...	130,145	216,260
6305	Equity and investment fund shares	—	...	—	—	—	—	—	—	—	...	—	—
6306	Insurance, pension, and standardized guarantee schemes	—	...	—	—	—	—	—	—	—	...	—	—
6307	Financial derivatives and employee stock options	—	...	—	—	—	—	—	—	—	...	—	—
6308	Other accounts payable	467	...	...	467	357	...	467	357	—	...	965	482
	By creditor												
631	Domestic creditors	36,163	...	97,443	36,163	48,737	97,443	36,163	48,737	97,443	...	59,840	107,462
632	External creditors	123,711	...	240,601	123,711	155,444	240,601	123,711	155,444	240,601	...	149,075	240,601
	Memorandum items												
6M2	Net financial worth	4,338	...	...	...	8,541	...	...	8,541	...	...	72,448	...
6M3	Gross debt (D4) at market value	...	...	...	...	...	...	...	...	...	...	...	...
6M3D3	D3 debt liabilities at market value	...	...	...	...	...	...	...	...	...	...	...	...
6M3D2	D2 debt liabilities at market value	...	...	...	...	...	...	...	...	...	...	...	...
6M3D1	D1 debt liabilities at market value	...	...	...	...	...	...	...	...	...	...	...	...
6M4	Gross debt (D4) at nominal value	...	...	...	...	...	...	...	...	...	...	...	...
6M4D3	D3 debt liabilities at nominal value	...	...	...	...	...	...	...	...	...	...	...	...
6M4D2	D2 debt liabilities at nominal value	...	...	...	...	...	...	...	...	...	...	...	...
6M4D1	D1 debt liabilities at nominal value	...	...	...	...	...	...	...	...	...	...	...	...

Belarus (913)

In Billions of Belarusian Rubels (BYR) / Fiscal Year Ends December 31st

		Budgetary Central Government			Central Government (excl. Social Security)			Central Government (incl. Social Security)			General Government		
		2013	2014	2015	2013	2014	2015	2013	2014	2015	2013	2014	2015
6M35	Gross debt (D4) at face value	159,874	...	...	...	204,181	...	...	204,181	338,045	...	215,284	348,063
6M35D3	D3 debt liabilities at face value	159,874	...	...	159,874	204,181	...	159,874	204,181	338,045	...	215,284	348,063
6M35D2	D2 debt liabilities at face value	159,407	...	338,045	159,407	203,824	338,045	159,407	203,824	338,045	...	214,319	347,581
6M35D1	D1 debt liabilities at face value	154,008	...	328,559	154,008	197,455	328,559	154,008	197,455	328,559	...	207,950	338,096
6M93	Government gross debt per national definition	...	...	328,559	...	...	328,559	...	...	328,559	...	...	328,559
6M5	Arrears	...	...	...	...	...	...	...	...	...	...	...	...
6M6	Explicit contingent liabilities	...	...	...	...	...	...	...	...	...	...	...	...
6M61	of which: Publicly guaranteed debt	52,805	...	...	...	67,949	...	...	67,949	...	...	97,490	...
6M7	Net implicit obligations for social security benefits	...	...	...	...	...	...	...	...	...	...	...	...
	Table 7 Expenditure by functions of government												
7	**Expenditure**	**119,780**	**...**	**152,012**	**119,902**	**135,489**	**152,012**	**198,198**	**229,326**	**260,205**	**278,968**	**317,225**	**356,299**
701	**General public services**	**54,497**	**...**	**62,763**	**54,497**	**55,439**	**62,763**	**54,497**	**55,689**	**63,042**	**45,448**	**22,975**	**48,133**
7017	Public debt transactions	5,439	...	13,485	5,439	7,252	13,485	5,439	7,252	13,485	6,614	8,342	15,049
7018	Transfers of general character between levels of government	36,100	...	36,751	36,100	38,383	36,751	36,100	38,633	37,030	-0	0	—
702	**Defense**	**6,300**	**...**	**9,422**	**6,300**	**7,472**	**9,422**	**6,300**	**7,472**	**9,422**	**6,329**	**7,509**	**9,458**
703	**Public order and safety**	**14,469**	**...**	**16,039**	**14,469**	**18,492**	**16,039**	**14,469**	**18,492**	**16,039**	**15,061**	**19,199**	**16,768**
704	**Economic affairs**	**17,233**	**...**	**25,826**	**17,356**	**20,099**	**25,826**	**17,356**	**20,099**	**25,826**	**31,739**	**37,575**	**40,579**
7042	Agriculture, forestry, fishing, and hunting	7,760	...	11,184	7,796	9,059	11,184	7,796	9,059	11,184	7,796	19,165	20,330
7043	Fuel and energy	2,293	...	1,951	2,354	2,544	1,951	2,354	2,544	1,951	2,354	2,918	2,271
7044	Mining, manufacturing, and construction	2,699	...	6,784	2,725	4,409	6,784	2,725	4,409	6,784	2,725	4,606	6,851
7045	Transport	2,731	...	455	2,731	437	455	2,731	437	455	2,731	4,787	3,743
7046	Communication	82	...	83	82	79	83	82	79	83	82	79	83
705	**Environmental protection**	**538**	**...**	**668**	**538**	**686**	**668**	**538**	**686**	**668**	**734**	**936**	**796**
706	**Housing and community amenities**	**125**	**...**	**157**	**125**	**1,177**	**157**	**125**	**1,177**	**157**	**15,938**	**29,226**	**16,177**
707	**Health**	**5,619**	**...**	**7,569**	**5,619**	**6,829**	**7,569**	**5,619**	**6,829**	**7,569**	**27,736**	**34,588**	**38,723**
7072	Outpatient services	—	...	—	—	—	—	—	—	—	—	—	—
7073	Hospital services	—	...	—	—	—	—	—	—	—	—	—	—
7074	Public health services	42	...	—	42	—	—	42	—	—	42	—	—
708	**Recreation, culture and religion**	**2,266**	**...**	**3,471**	**2,266**	**3,790**	**3,471**	**2,266**	**3,790**	**3,471**	**6,943**	**11,265**	**9,253**
709	**Education**	**8,419**	**...**	**10,640**	**8,419**	**9,862**	**10,640**	**8,419**	**9,862**	**10,640**	**35,635**	**42,891**	**46,499**
7091	Pre-primary and primary education	33	...	35	33	87	35	33	87	35	33	8,868	9,775
7092	Secondary education	1,322	...	301	1,322	371	301	1,322	371	301	1,322	17,924	19,181
7094	Tertiary education	6,331	...	7,937	6,331	7,174	7,937	6,331	7,174	7,937	6,331	7,176	7,937
710	**Social protection**	**10,313**	**...**	**15,457**	**10,313**	**11,643**	**15,457**	**88,609**	**105,231**	**123,371**	**93,407**	**111,062**	**129,914**
7z	Statistical discrepancy: Expenditure	1	...	...	-0	-0	...	0	—	...	-0	—	—
	Table 8 Financial transactions by counterpart sector												
32	**Net acquisition of financial assets**	**-3,200**	**...**	**19,294**	**-3,200**	**5,032**	**19,294**	**-3,723**	**5,258**	**15,886**	**601**	**10,291**	**15,599**
321	Domestic debtors	-3,200	...	19,294	-3,200	5,032	19,294	-3,723	5,258	15,886	601	10,291	15,599
8211	General government	-154	...	225	-154	111	225	-154	111	225	-154	—	0
8212	Central bank	-8,777	...	-7,962	-8,777	185	-7,962	-8,777	185	-11,369	-8,777	185	-11,369
8213	Deposit-taking corporations except the central bank	1,651	...	—	1,651	70	—	1,651	70	—	4,837	3,403	-1,074
8214	Other financial corporations	—	...	—	—	—	—	—	—	—	—	—	—
8215	Nonfinancial corporations	4,080	...	27,031	4,080	4,665	27,031	4,080	4,665	27,031	4,696	6,703	28,042
8216	Households & nonprofit institutions serving households	—	...	—	—	—	—	—	—	—	—	—	—
322	External debtors	—	...	—	—	—	—	—	—	—	—	—	—
8221	General government	—	...	—	—	—	—	—	—	—	—	—	—
8227	International organizations	—	...	—	—	—	—	—	—	—	—	—	—
8228	Financial corporations other than international organizations	—	...	—	—	—	—	—	—	—	—	—	—
8229	Other nonresidents	—	...	—	—	—	—	—	—	—	—	—	—

Belarus (913)

In Billions of Belarusian Rubels (BYR) / Fiscal Year Ends December 31st

		Budgetary Central Government			Central Government (excl. Social Security)			Central Government (incl. Social Security)			General Government		
		2013	2014	2015	2013	2014	2015	2013	2014	2015	2013	2014	2015
33	**Net incurrence of liabilities**	**1,840**	**...**	**-4,376**	**1,840**	**1,851**	**-4,376**	**1,840**	**1,851**	**-4,376**	**1,976**	**3,674**	**-4,768**
331	Domestic creditors	7,836	...	14,130	7,836	7,647	14,130	7,836	7,647	14,130	7,972	9,470	13,739
3311	General government	—	...	—	—	—	—	—	—	—	0	—	—
3312	Central bank	—	...	—	—	—	—	—	—	—	—	—	—
3313	Deposit-taking corporations except the central bank	6,299	...	14,130	6,299	8,001	14,130	6,299	8,001	14,130	6,436	9,824	13,739
3314	Other financial corporations	—	...	—	—	-162	—	—	-162	—	—	-162	—
3315	Nonfinancial corporations	-701	...	—	-701	—	—	-701	—	—	-701	—	—
3316	Households & nonprofit institutions serving households	2,237	...	—	2,237	-192	—	2,237	-192	—	2,237	-192	—
332	External creditors	-5,996	...	-18,507	-5,996	-5,796	-18,507	-5,996	-5,796	-18,507	-5,996	-5,796	-18,507
3321	General government	1,139	...	3,896	1,139	—	3,896	1,139	—	3,896	1,139	—	3,896
3327	International organizations	-7,135	...	-7,276	-7,135	10,112	-7,276	-7,135	10,112	-7,276	-7,135	10,112	-7,276
3328	Financial corporations other than international organizations	—	...	-15,126	—	-15,908	-15,126	—	-15,908	-15,126	—	-15,908	-15,126
3329	Other nonresidents	—	...	—	—	—	—	—	—	—	—	—	—
	Table 9 Total other economic flows in assets and liabilities												

Belgium (124)

In Millions of Euros (EUR) / Fiscal Year Ends December 31st

		Budgetary Central Government			Central Government (excl. Social Security)			Central Government (incl. Social Security)			General Government		
		2013	2014	2015	2013P	2014P	2015P	2013P	2014P	2015P	2013P	2014P	2015P
	Statement of operations												
1	Revenue	...	...	...	110,809	112,214	107,265	168,462	170,621	167,124	204,194	206,369	208,267
2	Expense	...	...	...	120,741	122,505	112,917	178,576	180,836	172,296	215,713	218,146	218,230
GOB	**Gross operating balance**	**...**	**...**	**...**	**-8,915**	**-9,267**	**-4,617**	**-9,040**	**-9,135**	**-4,083**	**-2,718**	**-2,890**	**-1,031**
NOB	**Net operating balance**	**...**	**...**	**...**	**-9,932**	**-10,292**	**-5,652**	**-10,114**	**-10,215**	**-5,172**	**-11,519**	**-11,777**	**-9,962**
31	Net/Gross investment in nonfinancial assets	...	...	...	-127	-123	-371	-122	-74	-374	302	477	383
2M	Expenditure	...	...	...	120,614	122,382	112,546	178,454	180,762	171,922	216,015	218,623	218,612
NLB	**Net lending (+) / Net borrowing (-)**	**...**	**...**	**...**	**-9,805**	**-10,169**	**-5,281**	**-9,992**	**-10,141**	**-4,798**	**-11,821**	**-12,255**	**-10,345**
32	Net acquisition of financial assets	...	...	...	-1,686	631	4,662	...	...	...	-2,431	2,441	-660
33	Net incurrence of liabilities	...	...	...	8,681	10,130	9,617	...	...	...	9,546	15,067	10,251
NLBz	Statistical discrepancy	...	...	...	-562	669	325	...	...	...	-156	-372	-566
	Memorandum items												
PB	Primary net lending / net borrowing	...	...	...	2,088	1,658	5,653	1,731	1,547	5,992	2,381	1,901	2,784
GB	Government balance per national definition	...	...	...	...	...	...	...	...	...	...	...	...
	Statement of other economic flows												
9	**Change in net worth due to other economic flows**	**...**	**...**	**...**	**...**	**...**	**...**	**...**	**...**	**...**	**...**	**...**	**...**
4	Change in net worth due to holding gains and losses	...	...	...	...	...	...	...	...	...	...	...	...
41	Nonfinancial assets	...	...	...	...	...	...	...	...	...	...	...	...
42	Financial assets	...	...	...	1,571	4,611	464	...	...	...	1,940	4,769	1,489
43	Liabilities	...	...	...	-11,892	29,363	-9,401	...	...	...	-11,583	27,983	-9,064
5	Change in net worth due to volume changes	...	...	...	...	...	...	...	...	...	...	...	...
51	Nonfinancial assets	...	...	...	...	...	...	...	...	...	...	...	...
52	Financial assets	...	...	...	47	576	-61	...	...	...	1,214	764	62
53	Liabilities	...	...	...	144	11,811	-0	...	...	...	33	12,402	17
	Balance sheet												
6	**Net worth**	**...**	**...**	**...**	**...**	**...**	**...**	**...**	**...**	**...**	**...**	**...**	**...**
61	Nonfinancial assets	...	...	...	...	...	...	...	...	...	...	...	...
62	Financial assets	...	...	...	58,962	64,780	69,845	...	...	...	109,986	117,960	118,850
63	Liabilities	...	...	...	397,923	449,227	449,443	...	...	...	463,370	519,075	519,934
	Table 1 Revenue												
1	**Revenue**	**...**	**...**	**...**	**110,809**	**112,214**	**107,265**	**168,462**	**170,621**	**167,124**	**204,194**	**206,369**	**208,267**
11	**Taxes**	**...**	**...**	**...**	**99,786**	**102,120**	**98,173**	**102,675**	**105,006**	**101,060**	**120,799**	**123,065**	**124,261**
111	Taxes on income, profits, and capital gains	...	...	...	59,818	61,609	57,512	60,935	62,725	58,619	63,806	65,301	66,057
1111	Payable by individuals	...	...	...	46,713	47,699	42,733	47,830	48,815	43,840	50,701	51,391	51,278
1112	Payable by corporations and other enterprises	...	...	...	12,209	12,890	13,817	12,209	12,890	13,817	12,209	12,890	13,817
1113	Other taxes on income, profits, and capital gains	...	...	...	896	1,020	962	896	1,020	962	896	1,020	962
112	Taxes on payroll and workforce	...	...	...	—	—	—	—	—	—	—	—	—
113	Taxes on property	...	...	...	676	844	604	985	1,152	922	9,469	9,551	9,381
114	Taxes on goods and services	...	...	...	39,292	39,667	40,056	40,756	41,128	41,520	47,467	48,156	48,763
1141	General taxes on goods and services	...	...	...	27,698	28,001	28,142	27,698	28,001	28,142	31,136	31,599	31,905
1142	Excises	...	...	...	8,050	8,223	8,655	8,050	8,223	8,655	8,053	8,226	8,658
115	Taxes on international trade and transactions	...	...	...	—	—	—	—	—	—	—	—	—
116	Other taxes	...	...	...	—	—	—	—	—	—	57	56	61
12	**Social contributions**	**...**	**...**	**...**	**4,805**	**4,834**	**4,684**	**58,872**	**59,652**	**60,849**	**65,996**	**66,785**	**67,789**
121	Social security contributions	...	...	...	226	226	249	54,285	55,037	56,414	54,285	55,037	56,414
122	Other social contributions	...	...	...	4,579	4,608	4,435	4,586	4,615	4,435	11,711	11,749	11,375
13	**Grants**	**...**	**...**	**...**	**429**	**320**	**358**	**509**	**404**	**307**	**599**	**424**	**461**
131	From foreign governments	...	...	...	111	62	56	111	62	56	129	80	86
132	From international organizations	...	...	...	149	56	33	149	56	33	470	344	375
133	From other general government units	...	...	...	169	203	269	248	286	218	—	—	—
1331	Current	...	...	...	169	203	269	248	286	218	—	—	—
1332	Capital	...	...	...	—	—	—	—	—	—	—	—	—
14	**Other revenue**	**...**	**...**	**...**	**5,789**	**4,939**	**4,051**	**6,407**	**5,560**	**4,908**	**16,800**	**16,095**	**15,756**

Belgium (124)

In Millions of Euros (EUR) / Fiscal Year Ends December 31st

		Budgetary Central Government			Central Government (excl. Social Security)			Central Government (incl. Social Security)			General Government		
		2013	2014	2015	2013P	2014P	2015P	2013P	2014P	2015P	2013P	2014P	2015P
	Table 2 Expense by economic type												
2	**Expense**	...	...	...	120,741	122,505	112,917	178,576	180,836	172,296	215,713	218,146	218,230
21	**Compensation of employees**	...	...	...	9,079	9,081	8,794	10,662	10,712	10,360	48,264	49,127	49,363
211	Wages and salaries	...	...	...	6,078	6,046	5,721	7,203	7,217	6,835	31,896	32,613	32,417
212	Employers' social contributions	...	...	...	3,001	3,035	3,073	3,459	3,495	3,525	16,368	16,514	16,946
22	**Use of goods and services**	...	...	...	2,994	2,947	2,909	3,991	3,988	3,880	15,330	15,388	15,636
23	**Consumption of fixed capital**	...	...	...	1,017	1,025	1,036	1,073	1,079	1,089	8,801	8,887	8,931
24	**Interest**	...	...	...	11,893	11,826	10,934	11,723	11,687	10,790	14,202	14,155	13,129
25	**Subsidies**	...	...	...	4,811	4,890	4,929	9,737	9,924	6,628	13,672	13,766	13,815
26	**Grants**	...	...	...	77,330	79,147	72,115	48,723	49,156	54,801	5,354	4,972	4,998
261	To foreign governments	...	...	...	1,177	1,260	907	1,177	1,260	907	1,244	1,326	992
262	To international organizations	...	...	...	4,083	3,623	3,981	4,110	3,645	4,006	4,110	3,645	4,006
263	To other general government units	...	...	...	72,070	74,264	67,227	43,437	44,251	49,888	—	—	—
2631	Current	...	...	...	71,901	74,188	67,159	43,268	44,174	49,820	—	—	—
2632	Capital	...	...	...	169	76	68	169	76	68	—	—	—
27	**Social benefits**	...	...	...	9,354	9,587	9,088	86,799	88,525	80,229	99,373	101,266	103,586
271	Social security benefits	...	...	...	...	...	...	...	...	...	...	...	...
272	Social assistance benefits	...	...	...	...	...	...	...	...	...	...	...	...
273	Employment-related social benefits	...	...	...	...	...	...	...	...	...	...	...	...
28	**Other expense**	...	...	...	4,263	4,002	3,113	5,870	5,765	4,520	10,718	10,585	8,773
281	Property expense other than interest	...	...	...	—	—	—	—	—	—	6	3	3
282	Transfers not elsewhere classified	...	...	...	4,263	4,002	3,112	5,870	5,765	4,519	10,451	10,314	8,501
2821	Current	...	...	...	1,116	1,087	998	1,511	1,539	1,428	3,408	3,659	3,513
2822	Capital	...	...	...	3,147	2,915	2,115	4,359	4,226	3,091	7,042	6,655	4,988
	Table 3 Transactions in assets and liabilities												
3	**Change in net worth from transactions**	...	...	...	-10,494	-9,623	-5,327	...	...	...	-11,675	-12,149	-10,528
31	**Net/Gross investment in nonfinancial assets**	...	...	...	-127	-123	-371	-122	-74	-374	302	477	383
311	Fixed assets	...	...	...	-51	-45	-121	-46	4	-124	297	510	592
3111	Buildings and structures	...	...	...	...	...	...	...	...	...	...	...	...
3112	Machinery and equipment	...	...	...	...	...	...	...	...	...	...	...	...
3113	Other fixed assets	...	...	...	...	...	...	...	...	...	...	...	...
3114	Weapons systems	...	...	...	...	...	...	...	...	...	...	...	...
312	Inventories	...	...	...	...	...	...	...	...	...	...	...	...
313	Valuables	...	...	...	...	...	...	...	...	...	...	...	...
314	Nonproduced assets	...	...	...	-369	-0	-200	-369	-0	-200	-235	104	-99
3141	Land	...	...	...	...	...	...	...	...	...	...	...	...
3142	Mineral and energy resources	...	...	...	...	...	...	...	...	...	...	...	...
3143	Other naturally occurring assets	...	...	...	...	...	...	...	...	...	...	...	...
3144	Intangible nonproduced assets	...	...	...	...	...	...	...	...	...	...	...	...
32	**Net acquisition of financial assets**	...	...	...	-1,686	631	4,662	...	...	...	-2,431	2,441	-660
	By instrument												
3201	Monetary gold and SDRs	...	...	...	—	—	—	...	...	...	—	—	—
3202	Currency and deposits	...	...	...	-288	-595	-230	...	...	...	-329	-587	196
3203	Debt securities	...	...	...	57	-1,084	-50	...	...	...	-219	-403	-84
3204	Loans	...	...	...	1,850	-262	-493	...	...	...	2,712	1,728	489
3205	Equity and investment fund shares	...	...	...	-2,646	694	91	...	...	...	-4,259	844	-3,242
3206	Insurance, pension, and standardized guarantee schemes	...	...	...	—	—	—	...	...	...	—	—	—
3207	Financial derivatives and employee stock options	...	...	...	-769	10	841	...	...	...	-627	185	1,019
3208	Other accounts receivable	...	...	...	110	1,867	4,502	...	...	...	290	673	962
	By debtor												
321	Domestic debtors	...	...	...	-4,572	-551	5,136	...	...	...	-5,310	1,241	-147
322	External debtors	...	...	...	2,886	1,182	-474	...	...	...	...	...	...
33	**Net incurrence of liabilities**	...	...	...	8,681	10,130	9,617	...	...	...	9,546	15,067	10,251
	By instrument												
3301	Special Drawing Rights (SDRs)	...	...	...	—	—	—	...	...	...	—	—	—
3302	Currency and deposits	...	...	...	-52	-47	32	...	...	...	-54	-47	32
3303	Debt securities	...	...	...	7,270	10,500	9,462	...	...	...	6,150	11,351	10,828
3304	Loans	...	...	...	2,023	-71	-30	...	...	...	4,396	4,782	-1,321

Belgium (124)

In Millions of Euros (EUR) / Fiscal Year Ends December 31st

		Budgetary Central Government			Central Government (excl. Social Security)			Central Government (incl. Social Security)			General Government		
		2013	2014	2015	2013P	2014P	2015P	2013P	2014P	2015P	2013P	2014P	2015P
3305	Equity and investment fund shares	...	...	...	—	—	—	...	...	...	—	—	—
3306	Insurance, pension, and standardized guarantee schemes	...	...	...	—	—	—	...	...	...	51	23	11
3307	Financial derivatives and employee stock options	...	...	...	-144	—	—	...	...	...	-144	—	—
3308	Other accounts payable	...	...	...	-415	-252	154	...	...	...	-855	-1,045	701
	By creditor												
331	Domestic creditors	...	...	...	-11,879	-8,299	14,174	...	...	...	-9,605	-4,047	13,589
332	External creditors	...	...	...	20,560	18,429	-4,557	...	...	...	...	...	...
	Table 4 Holding gains and losses in assets and liabilities												
4	**Change in net worth due to holding gains and losses**	...	...	...	...	...	...	...	...	...	...	...	...
41	**Holding gains and losses in nonfinancial assets**	...	...	...	...	...	...	...	...	...	...	...	...
411	Fixed assets	...	...	...	...	...	...	...	...	...	...	...	...
412	Inventories	...	...	...	...	...	...	...	...	...	...	...	...
413	Valuables	...	...	...	...	...	...	...	...	...	...	...	...
414	Nonproduced assets	...	...	...	...	...	...	...	...	...	...	...	...
42	**Holding gains and losses in financial assets**	...	...	...	**1,571**	**4,611**	**464**	...	...	...	**1,940**	**4,769**	**1,489**
	By instrument												
4201	Monetary gold and SDRs	...	...	...	—	—	—	...	...	...	—	—	—
4202	Currency and deposits	...	...	...	-0	0	0	...	...	...	-0	0	-1
4203	Debt securities	...	...	...	0	5	-2	...	...	...	0	84	1
4204	Loans	...	...	...	130	1	-0	...	...	...	131	1	0
4205	Equity and investment fund shares	...	...	...	672	4,616	1,307	...	...	...	1,182	4,870	2,508
4206	Insurance, pension, and standardized guarantee schemes	...	...	...	—	—	—	...	...	...	—	—	—
4207	Financial derivatives and employee stock options	...	...	...	769	-10	-841	...	...	...	627	-186	-1,019
4208	Other accounts receivable	...	...	...	-0	0	-0	...	...	...	0	-0	-0
	By debtor												
421	Domestic debtors	...	...	...	-386	5,521	12	...	...	...	-17	5,506	1,038
422	External debtors	...	...	...	1,957	-910	452	...	...	...	1,957	-737	451
43	**Holding gains and losses in liabilities**	...	...	...	**-11,892**	**29,363**	**-9,401**	...	...	...	**-11,583**	**27,983**	**-9,064**
	By instrument												
4301	Special Drawing Rights (SDRs)	...	...	...	—	—	—	...	...	...	—	—	—
4302	Currency and deposits	...	...	...	—	—	—	...	...	...	—	—	—
4303	Debt securities	...	...	...	-11,895	29,547	-9,852	...	...	...	-11,585	28,415	-9,861
4304	Loans	...	...	...	2	62	105	...	...	...	2	62	105
4305	Equity and investment fund shares	...	...	...	—	-247	346	...	...	...	—	-247	346
4306	Insurance, pension, and standardized guarantee schemes	...	...	...	—	—	—	...	...	...	—	-247	346
4307	Financial derivatives and employee stock options	...	...	...	—	—	—	...	...	...	—	—	—
4308	Other accounts payable	...	...	...	0	-0	0	...	...	...	0	-0	-0
	By creditor												
431	Domestic creditors	...	...	...	-6,195	12,342	-8,829	...	...	...	-5,885	11,158	-8,594
432	External creditors	...	...	...	-5,698	17,020	-572	...	...	...	-5,698	16,826	-471
	Table 5 Holding gains and losses in assets and liabilities												
5	**Change in net worth due to other volume changes**	...	...	...	...	...	...	...	...	...	...	...	...
51	**Other volume changes in nonfinancial assets**	...	...	...	...	...	...	...	...	...	...	...	...
511	Fixed assets	...	...	...	...	...	...	...	...	...	...	...	...
512	Inventories	...	...	...	...	...	...	...	...	...	...	...	...
513	Valuables	...	...	...	...	...	...	...	...	...	...	...	...
514	Nonproduced assets	...	...	...	...	...	...	...	...	...	...	...	...
52	**Other volume changes in financial assets**	...	...	...	**47**	**576**	**-61**	...	...	...	**1,214**	**764**	**62**

Belgium (124)

In Millions of Euros (EUR) / Fiscal Year Ends December 31st

		Budgetary Central Government			Central Government (excl. Social Security)			Central Government (incl. Social Security)			General Government		
		2013	2014	2015	2013P	2014P	2015P	2013P	2014P	2015P	2013P	2014P	2015P
	By instrument												
5201	Monetary gold and SDRs	...	...	...	—	—	—	...	...	...	—	—	—
5202	Currency and deposits	...	...	...	—	784	—	...	...	...	—	894	—
5203	Debt securities	...	...	...	—	-0	-0	...	...	...	—	-40	-5
5204	Loans	...	...	...	-589	308	-0	...	...	...	-745	327	-145
5205	Equity and investment fund shares	...	...	...	—	-623	-41	...	...	...	1,323	-554	230
5206	Insurance, pension, and standardized guarantee schemes	...	...	...	—	—	—	...	...	...	—	—	—
5207	Financial derivatives and employee stock options	...	...	...	—	—	—	...	...	...	—	—	—
5208	Other accounts receivable	...	...	...	636	106	-20	...	...	...	636	137	-19
	By debtor												
521	Domestic debtors	...	...	...	47	576	-48	...	...	...	1,214	846	73
522	External debtors	...	...	...	—	—	-13	...	...	...	—	-82	-12
53	**Other volume changes in liabilities**	...	...	...	**144**	**11,811**	**-0**	...	...	...	**33**	**12,402**	**17**
	By instrument												
5301	Special Drawing Rights (SDRs)	...	...	...	—	—	—	...	...	...	—	—	—
5302	Currency and deposits	...	...	...	—	—	—	...	...	...	—	—	—
5303	Debt securities	...	...	...	0	9,407	-0	...	...	...	-111	5,688	-20
5304	Loans	...	...	...	—	1,611	—	...	...	...	-0	5,336	—
5305	Equity and investment fund shares	...	...	...	—	659	—	...	...	...	—	659	—
5306	Insurance, pension, and standardized guarantee schemes	...	...	...	—	—	—	...	...	...	—	—	—
5307	Financial derivatives and employee stock options	...	...	...	144	—	—	...	...	...	144	—	—
5308	Other accounts payable	...	...	...	—	134	-0	...	...	...	—	719	37
	By creditor												
531	Domestic creditors	...	...	...	144	-4,977	89	...	...	...	144	-9,249	519
532	External creditors	...	...	...	0	16,788	-89	...	...	...	-111	21,651	-502
	Table 6 Balance sheet												
6	**Net worth**	...	...	...	...	...	...	...	...	...	...	...	...
61	**Nonfinancial assets**	...	...	...	...	...	...	...	...	...	...	...	...
611	Fixed assets	...	...	...	...	...	...	...	...	...	151,216	150,965	...
6111	Buildings and structures	...	...	...	...	...	...	...	...	...	131,407	131,277	...
6112	Machinery and equipment	...	...	...	...	...	...	...	...	...	...	...	...
6113	Other fixed assets	...	...	...	...	...	...	...	...	...	11,471	11,643	...
6114	Weapons systems	...	...	...	...	...	...	...	...	...	...	...	...
612	Inventories	...	...	...	...	...	...	...	...	...	2,503	...	...
613	Valuables	...	...	...	...	...	...	...	...	...	...	...	...
614	Nonproduced assets	...	...	...	...	...	...	...	...	...	...	...	...
6141	Land	...	...	...	...	...	...	...	...	...	...	...	...
6142	Mineral and energy resources	...	...	...	...	...	...	...	...	...	...	...	...
6143	Other naturally occurring assets	...	...	...	...	...	...	...	...	...	...	...	...
6144	Intangible nonproduced assets	...	...	...	...	...	...	...	...	...	...	...	...
62	**Financial assets**	...	...	...	**58,962**	**64,780**	**69,845**	...	...	...	**109,986**	**117,960**	**118,850**
	By instrument												
6201	Monetary gold and SDRs	...	...	...	—	—	—	...	...	...	—	—	—
6202	Currency and deposits	...	...	...	1,856	2,046	1,816	...	...	...	17,180	17,488	17,683
6203	Debt securities	...	...	...	1,246	167	115	...	...	...	1,546	1,186	1,099
6204	Loans	...	...	...	12,355	12,402	11,909	...	...	...	31,816	33,872	34,216
6205	Equity and investment fund shares	...	...	...	34,506	39,193	40,550	...	...	...	39,201	44,360	43,857
6206	Insurance, pension, and standardized guarantee schemes	...	...	...	—	—	—	...	...	...	—	—	—
6207	Financial derivatives and employee stock options	...	...	...	—	—	—	...	...	...	—	—	—
6208	Other accounts receivable	...	...	...	9,000	10,973	15,455	...	...	...	20,243	21,053	21,996
	By debtor												
621	Domestic debtors	...	...	...	39,008	44,554	49,654	...	...	...	89,987	97,581	98,545
622	External debtors	...	...	...	19,954	20,226	20,191	...	...	...	19,999	20,379	20,306
63	**Liabilities**	...	...	...	**397,923**	**449,227**	**449,443**	...	...	...	**463,370**	**519,075**	**519,934**

Belgium (124)

In Millions of Euros (EUR) / Fiscal Year Ends December 31st

		Budgetary Central Government			Central Government (excl. Social Security)			Central Government (incl. Social Security)			General Government		
		2013	2014	2015	2013P	2014P	2015P	2013P	2014P	2015P	2013P	2014P	2015P
	By instrument												
6301	Special Drawing Rights (SDRs)	...	...	...	—	—	—	...	...	...	—	—	—
6302	Currency and deposits	...	...	...	1,395	1,348	1,380	...	...	...	1,395	1,348	1,380
6303	Debt securities	...	...	...	367,386	416,840	416,451	...	...	...	376,798	422,252	423,199
6304	Loans	...	...	...	20,010	21,614	21,688	...	...	...	70,659	80,840	79,624
6305	Equity and investment fund shares	...	...	...	—	412	758	...	...	...	—	412	758
6306	Insurance, pension, and standardized guarantee schemes	...	...	...	—	—	—	...	...	...	789	820	833
6307	Financial derivatives and employee stock options	...	...	...	—	—	—	...	...	...	—	—	—
6308	Other accounts payable	...	...	...	9,132	9,013	9,166	...	...	...	13,729	13,404	14,141
	By creditor												
631	Domestic creditors	...	...	...	181,849	180,916	186,349	...	...	...	239,501	237,615	242,786
632	External creditors	...	...	...	216,074	268,311	263,094	...	...	...	223,869	281,460	277,148
	Memorandum items												
6M2	Net financial worth	...	...	...	-338,961	-384,447	-379,598	...	...	...	-353,384	-401,115	-401,084
6M3	Gross debt (D4) at market value	...	...	...	397,923	448,815	448,685	...	...	...	463,370	518,663	519,177
6M3D3	D3 debt liabilities at market value	...	...	...	397,923	448,815	448,685	...	...	...	462,581	517,844	518,344
6M3D2	D2 debt liabilities at market value	...	...	...	388,791	439,802	439,519	...	...	...	448,852	504,440	504,203
6M3D1	D1 debt liabilities at market value	...	...	...	387,396	438,454	438,139	...	...	...	447,457	503,092	502,823
6M4	Gross debt (D4) at nominal value	...	...	...	...	...	...	...	...	...	...	...	...
6M4D3	D3 debt liabilities at nominal value	...	...	...	...	...	...	...	...	...	...	...	...
6M4D2	D2 debt liabilities at nominal value	...	...	...	...	...	...	...	...	...	...	...	...
6M4D1	D1 debt liabilities at nominal value	...	...	...	...	...	...	...	...	...	...	...	...
6M35	Gross debt (D4) at face value	...	...	...	...	...	...	...	...	...	...	...	...
6M35D3	D3 debt liabilities at face value	...	...	...	361,172	374,587	387,200	...	...	...	426,703	444,545	459,872
6M35D2	D2 debt liabilities at face value	...	...	...	352,040	365,574	378,034	...	...	...	412,974	431,141	445,730
6M35D1	D1 debt liabilities at face value	...	...	...	350,645	364,211	376,692	...	...	...	411,579	429,778	444,388
6M93	Government gross debt per national definition	...	...	...	352,040	360,580	367,875	...	...	...	412,974	426,663	433,992
6M5	Arrears	...	...	...	...	...	...	...	...	...	...	...	...
6M6	Explicit contingent liabilities	...	...	...	...	...	...	...	...	...	...	...	...
6M61	of which: Publicly guaranteed debt	...	...	...	...	...	...	...	...	...	...	...	...
6M7	Net implicit obligations for social security benefits	...	...	...	...	...	...	...	...	...	...	...	...
	Table 7 Expenditure by functions of government												
7	**Expenditure**	...	...	...	**121,000**	**122,714**	...	...	...	...	**218,657**	**221,108**	...
701	**General public services**	...	...	...	**81,274**	**82,935**	...	...	...	...	**34,232**	**33,983**	...
7017	Public debt transactions	...	...	...	11,852	11,793	...	...	...	...	13,982	13,838	...
7018	Transfers of general character between levels of government	...	...	...	59,765	61,906	...	...	...	...	5	-3	...
702	**Defense**	...	...	...	**3,667**	**3,547**	...	...	...	...	**3,667**	**3,547**	...
703	**Public order and safety**	...	...	...	**4,541**	**4,693**	...	...	...	...	**7,337**	**7,538**	...
704	**Economic affairs**	...	...	...	**9,076**	**9,358**	...	...	...	...	**27,022**	**28,218**	...
7042	Agriculture, forestry, fishing, and hunting	...	...	...	13	11	...	...	...	...	241	179	...
7043	Fuel and energy	...	...	...	644	302	...	...	...	...	729	392	...
7044	Mining, manufacturing, and construction	...	...	...	0	0	...	...	...	...	18	13	...
7045	Transport	...	...	...	3,340	3,397	...	...	...	...	10,619	10,908	...
7046	Communication	...	...	...	4	342	...	...	...	...	-53	355	...
705	**Environmental protection**	...	...	...	**1,290**	**660**	...	...	...	...	**4,550**	**3,793**	...
706	**Housing and community amenities**	...	...	...	—	**1**	...	...	...	...	**1,607**	**1,524**	...
707	**Health**	...	...	...	**3,361**	**3,434**	...	...	...	...	**31,375**	**32,352**	...
7072	Outpatient services	...	...	...	16	17	...	...	...	...	11,304	11,618	...
7073	Hospital services	...	...	...	46	31	...	...	...	...	15,451	15,939	...
7074	Public health services	...	...	...	265	296	...	...	...	...	587	599	...
708	**Recreation, culture and religion**	...	...	...	**277**	**304**	...	...	...	...	**5,050**	**5,066**	...
709	**Education**	...	...	...	**5,778**	**5,966**	...	...	...	...	**25,043**	**25,193**	...
7091	Pre-primary and primary education	...	...	...	2,078	2,145	...	...	...	...	8,191	8,271	...
7092	Secondary education	...	...	...	2,790	2,885	...	...	...	...	9,781	9,816	...
7094	Tertiary education	...	...	...	771	793	...	...	...	...	3,875	3,728	...

Belgium (124)

In Millions of Euros (EUR) / Fiscal Year Ends December 31st

		Budgetary Central Government			Central Government (excl. Social Security)			Central Government (incl. Social Security)			General Government		
		2013	2014	2015	2013P	2014P	2015P	2013P	2014P	2015P	2013P	2014P	2015P
710	**Social protection**	...	...	...	11,736	11,817	...	...	...	...	78,774	79,894	...
7z	Statistical discrepancy: Expenditure	...	...	...	0	-0	...	...	...	...	-0	0	...
	Table 8 Financial transactions by counterpart sector												
32	**Net acquisition of financial assets**	...	...	...	-1,686	631	4,662	...	...	...	-2,431	2,441	-660
321	Domestic debtors	...	...	...	-4,572	-551	5,136	...	...	...	-5,310	1,241	-147
8211	General government	...	...	...	609	-780	4,552	...	...	...	—	—	—
8212	Central bank	...	...	...	-165	-122	0	...	...	...	-165	-122	0
8213	Deposit-taking corporations except the central bank	...	...	...	-4,172	-474	576	...	...	...	-4,112	-314	1,139
8214	Other financial corporations	...	...	...	-855	-517	-0	...	...	...	-2,417	-1,227	-3,093
8215	Nonfinancial corporations	...	...	...	-179	1,580	138	...	...	...	197	2,982	1,294
8216	Households & nonprofit institutions serving households	...	...	...	190	-239	-130	...	...	...	1,187	-78	513
322	External debtors	...	...	...	2,886	1,182	-474	...	...	...	...	...	...
8221	General government	...	...	...	...	...	...	...	...	...	...	...	...
8227	International organizations	...	...	...	...	...	...	...	...	...	...	...	...
8228	Financial corporations other than international organizations	...	...	...	...	...	...	...	...	...	...	...	...
8229	Other nonresidents	...	...	...	...	...	...	...	...	...	...	...	...
33	**Net incurrence of liabilities**	...	...	...	8,681	10,130	9,617	...	...	...	9,546	15,067	10,251
331	Domestic creditors	...	...	...	-11,879	-8,299	14,174	...	...	...	-9,605	-4,047	13,589
8311	General government	...	...	...	863	945	944	...	...	...	—	—	—
8312	Central bank	...	...	...	-28	-438	14,065	...	...	...	-28	-438	14,065
8313	Deposit-taking corporations except the central bank	...	...	...	-5,879	-5,951	-4,509	...	...	...	-4,952	-2,980	-5,092
8314	Other financial corporations	...	...	...	-4,097	285	3,588	...	...	...	-3,634	1,183	3,991
8315	Nonfinancial corporations	...	...	...	-587	-1,329	-196	...	...	...	1,036	-599	260
8316	Households & nonprofit institutions serving households	...	...	...	-2,151	-1,811	283	...	...	...	-2,026	-1,212	365
332	External creditors	...	...	...	20,560	18,429	-4,557	...	...	...	...	...	...
8321	General government	...	...	...	...	...	...	...	...	...	...	...	...
8327	International organizations	...	...	...	...	...	...	...	...	...	...	...	...
8328	Financial corporations other than international organizations	...	...	...	...	...	...	...	...	...	...	...	...
8329	Other nonresidents	...	...	...	...	...	...	...	...	...	...	...	...
	Table 9 Total other economic flows in assets and liabilities												
9	**Change in net worth due to other economic flows**	...	...	...	...	...	...	...	...	...	...	...	...
91	**Other economic flows in nonfinancial assets**	...	...	...	...	...	...	...	...	...	...	...	...
911	Fixed assets	...	...	...	...	...	...	...	...	...	...	...	...
912	Inventories	...	...	...	...	...	...	...	...	...	...	...	...
913	Valuables	...	...	...	...	...	...	...	...	...	...	...	...
914	Nonproduced assets	...	...	...	...	...	...	...	...	...	...	...	...
92	**Other economic flows in financial assets**	...	...	...	1,618	5,187	403	...	...	...	3,153	5,533	1,551
	By instrument												
9201	Monetary gold and SDRs	...	...	...	—	—	—	...	...	...	—	—	—
9202	Currency and deposits	...	...	...	-0	784	-0	...	...	...	0	895	-1
9203	Debt securities	...	...	...	0	5	-2	...	...	...	-0	44	-3
9204	Loans	...	...	...	-459	309	-0	...	...	...	-613	328	-146
9205	Equity and investment fund shares	...	...	...	672	3,993	1,266	...	...	...	2,505	4,315	2,739
9206	Insurance, pension, and standardized guarantee schemes	...	...	...	—	—	—	...	...	...	—	—	—
9207	Financial derivatives and employee stock options	...	...	...	769	-10	-841	...	...	...	627	-185	-1,019
9208	Other accounts receivable	...	...	...	636	106	-20	...	...	...	636	137	-19
	By debtor												
921	Domestic debtors	...	...	...	...	...	...	...	...	...	...	...	...
922	External debtors	...	...	...	...	...	...	...	...	...	...	...	...
93	**Other economic flows in liabilities**	...	...	...	-11,748	41,174	-9,401	...	...	...	-11,550	40,638	-9,392

Belgium (124)

In Millions of Euros (EUR) / Fiscal Year Ends December 31st

		Budgetary Central Government			Central Government (excl. Social Security)			Central Government (incl. Social Security)			General Government		
		2013	2014	2015	2013P	2014P	2015P	2013P	2014P	2015P	2013P	2014P	2015P
	By instrument												
9301	Special Drawing Rights (SDRs)	...	...	...	—	—	—	...	...	...	—	—	—
9302	Currency and deposits	...	...	...	—	—	—	...	...	...	2	0	-0
9303	Debt securities	...	...	...	-11,895	38,954	-9,852	...	...	...	-11,695	34,103	-9,882
9304	Loans	...	...	...	2	1,674	105	...	...	...	2	5,399	105
9305	Equity and investment fund shares	...	...	...	—	412	346	...	...	...	—	412	346
9306	Insurance, pension, and standardized guarantee schemes	...	...	...	—	—	—	...	...	...	-1	7	2
9307	Financial derivatives and employee stock options	...	...	...	144	—	—	...	...	...	144	—	—
9308	Other accounts payable	...	...	...	-0	134	-0	...	...	...	0	719	37
	By creditor												
931	Domestic creditors	...	...	...	...	...	...	...	...	...	...	...	...
932	External creditors	...	...	...	...	...	...	...	...	...	...	...	...
	Memorandum items												
9M2	Change in net financial worth due to other economic flows	...	...	...	13,367	-35,987	9,804	...	...	...	14,703	-35,105	10,943
9M3	Gross debt (D4) at market value: other economic flows	...	...	...	-11,892	40,762	-9,747	...	...	...	-11,692	40,229	-9,738
9M3D3	D3 debt liabilities at market value: other economic flows	...	...	...	-11,892	40,762	-9,747	...	...	...	-11,691	40,222	-9,740
9M3D2	D2 debt liabilities at market value: other economic flows	...	...	...	-11,892	40,628	-9,747	...	...	...	-11,691	39,503	-9,777
9M3D1	D1 debt liabilities at market value: other economic flows	...	...	...	-11,892	40,628	-9,747	...	...	...	-11,693	39,502	-9,776

Belize (339)

In Millions of Belize Dollars (BZD) / Fiscal Year Ends March 31st

		Budgetary Central Government			Central Government (excl. Social Security)			Central Government (incl. Social Security)			General Government		
		2012	2013	2014	2012	2013	2014	2012	2013	2014	2012	2013	2014
	Statement of operations												
1	Revenue	808	938	946	...	...	...	...	...	...	...	...	...
2	Expense	708	777	828	...	...	...	...	...	...	...	...	...
GOB	**Gross operating balance**	**100**	**160**	**118**	...	...	...	...	...	...	...	...	...
NOB	**Net operating balance**	...	...	...	...	...	...	...	...	...	...	...	...
31	Net/Gross investment in nonfinancial assets	137	214	242	...	...	...	...	...	...	...	...	...
2M	Expenditure	844	991	1,070	...	...	...	...	...	...	...	...	...
NLB	**Net lending (+) / Net borrowing (-)**	**-37**	**-53**	**-124**	...	...	...	...	...	...	...	...	...
32	Net acquisition of financial assets	16	118	6	...	...	...	...	...	...	...	...	...
33	Net incurrence of liabilities	53	172	130	...	...	...	...	...	...	...	...	...
NLBz	Statistical discrepancy	—	—	0	...	...	...	...	...	...	...	...	...
	Memorandum items												
PB	Primary net lending / net borrowing	22	31	-37	...	...	...	...	...	...	...	...	...
GB	Government balance per national definition	...	...	...	...	...	...	...	...	...	...	...	...
	Statement of other economic flows												
	Balance sheet												
	Table 1 Revenue												
1	**Revenue**	**808**	**938**	**946**	...	...	...	...	...	...	...	...	...
11	**Taxes**	**707**	**752**	**798**	...	...	...	...	...	...	...	...	...
111	Taxes on income, profits, and capital gains	236	247	274	...	...	...	...	...	...	...	...	...
1111	Payable by individuals	...	...	...	...	...	...	...	...	...	...	...	...
1112	Payable by corporations and other enterprises	...	...	...	...	...	...	...	...	...	...	...	...
1113	Other taxes on income, profits, and capital gains	...	...	...	...	...	...	...	...	...	...	...	...
112	Taxes on payroll and workforce	...	...	...	...	...	...	...	...	...	...	...	...
113	Taxes on property	5	6	6	...	...	...	...	...	...	...	...	...
114	Taxes on goods and services	277	305	330	...	...	...	...	...	...	...	...	...
1141	General taxes on goods and services	277	305	330	...	...	...	...	...	...	...	...	...
1142	Excises	...	...	...	...	...	...	...	...	...	...	...	...
115	Taxes on international trade and transactions	189	194	189	...	...	...	...	...	...	...	...	...
116	Other taxes	—	—	—	...	...	...	...	...	...	...	...	...
12	**Social contributions**	—	—	—	...	...	...	...	...	...	...	...	...
121	Social security contributions	—	—	—	...	...	...	...	...	...	...	...	...
122	Other social contributions	—	—	—	...	...	...	...	...	...	...	...	...
13	**Grants**	**21**	**72**	**39**	...	...	...	...	...	...	...	...	...
131	From foreign governments	21	72	39	...	...	...	...	...	...	...	...	...
132	From international organizations	—	—	—	...	...	...	...	...	...	...	...	...
133	From other general government units	—	—	—	...	...	...	...	...	...	...	...	...
1331	Current	—	—	—	...	...	...	...	...	...	...	...	...
1332	Capital	—	—	—	...	...	...	...	...	...	...	...	...
14	**Other revenue**	**80**	**113**	**108**	...	...	...	...	...	...	...	...	...
	Table 2 Expense by economic type												
2	**Expense**	**708**	**777**	**828**	...	...	...	...	...	...	...	...	...
21	**Compensation of employees**	**297**	**303**	**338**	...	...	...	...	...	...	...	...	...
211	Wages and salaries	297	303	338	...	...	...	...	...	...	...	...	...
212	Employers' social contributions	—	—	—	...	...	...	...	...	...	...	...	...
22	**Use of goods and services**	**179**	**200**	**187**	...	...	...	...	...	...	...	...	...
23	**Consumption of fixed capital**	...	...	...	...	...	...	...	...	...	...	...	...
24	**Interest**	**59**	**84**	**87**	...	...	...	...	...	...	...	...	...
25	**Subsidies**	**119**	**137**	**151**	...	...	...	...	...	...	...	...	...
26	**Grants**	—	—	—	...	...	...	...	...	...	...	...	...
261	To foreign governments	—	—	—	...	...	...	...	...	...	...	...	...
262	To international organizations	—	—	—	...	...	...	...	...	...	...	...	...
263	To other general government units	—	—	—	...	...	...	...	...	...	...	...	...
2631	Current	—	—	—	...	...	...	...	...	...	...	...	...
2632	Capital	—	—	—	...	...	...	...	...	...	...	...	...

Belize (339)

In Millions of Belize Dollars (BZD) / Fiscal Year Ends March 31st

		Budgetary Central Government			Central Government (excl. Social Security)			Central Government (incl. Social Security)			General Government		
		2012	2013	2014	2012	2013	2014	2012	2013	2014	2012	2013	2014
27	**Social benefits**	**54**	**54**	**64**	**...**	**...**	**...**	**...**	**...**	**...**	**...**	**...**	**...**
271	Social security benefits	54	54	64	...	...	...	...	...	...	...	...	...
272	Social assistance benefits	...	...	...	...	...	...	...	...	...	...	...	...
273	Employment-related social benefits	...	...	...	...	...	...	...	...	...	...	...	...
28	**Other expense**	**—**	**—**	**—**	**...**	**...**	**...**	**...**	**...**	**...**	**...**	**...**	**...**
281	Property expense other than interest	—	—	—	...	...	...	...	...	...	...	...	...
282	Transfers not elsewhere classified	—	—	—	...	...	...	...	...	...	...	...	...
2821	Current	—	—	—	...	...	...	...	...	...	...	...	...
2822	Capital	—	—	—	...	...	...	...	...	...	...	...	...
	Table 3 Transactions in assets and liabilities												
3	**Change in net worth from transactions**	**...**	**...**	**...**	**...**	**...**	**...**	**...**	**...**	**...**	**...**	**...**	**...**
31	**Net/Gross investment in nonfinancial assets**	**137**	**214**	**242**	**...**	**...**	**...**	**...**	**...**	**...**	**...**	**...**	**...**
311	Fixed assets	137	214	242	...	...	...	...	...	...	...	...	...
3111	Buildings and structures	...	...	...	...	...	...	...	...	...	...	...	...
3112	Machinery and equipment	...	...	...	...	...	...	...	...	...	...	...	...
3113	Other fixed assets	...	...	...	...	...	...	...	...	...	...	...	...
3114	Weapons systems	...	...	...	...	...	...	...	...	...	...	...	...
312	Inventories	...	...	...	...	...	...	...	...	...	...	...	...
313	Valuables	...	...	...	...	...	...	...	...	...	...	...	...
314	Nonproduced assets	...	...	...	...	...	...	...	...	...	...	...	...
3141	Land	...	...	...	...	...	...	...	...	...	...	...	...
3142	Mineral and energy resources	...	...	...	...	...	...	...	...	...	...	...	...
3143	Other naturally occurring assets	...	...	...	...	...	...	...	...	...	...	...	...
3144	Intangible nonproduced assets	...	...	...	...	...	...	...	...	...	...	...	...
32	**Net acquisition of financial assets**	**16**	**118**	**6**	**...**	**...**	**...**	**...**	**...**	**...**	**...**	**...**	**...**
	By instrument												
3201	Monetary gold and SDRs	—	—	—	...	...	...	...	...	...	...	...	...
3202	Currency and deposits	41	116	4	...	...	...	...	...	...	...	...	...
3203	Debt securities	—	—	—	...	...	...	...	...	...	...	...	...
3204	Loans	-25	2	2	...	...	...	...	...	...	...	...	...
3205	Equity and investment fund shares	—	—	—	...	...	...	...	...	...	...	...	...
3206	Insurance, pension, and standardized guarantee schemes	—	—	—	...	...	...	...	...	...	...	...	...
3207	Financial derivatives and employee stock options	—	—	—	...	...	...	...	...	...	...	...	...
3208	Other accounts receivable	...	...	...	...	...	...	...	...	...	...	...	...
	By debtor												
321	Domestic debtors	16	118	6	...	...	...	...	...	...	...	...	...
322	External debtors	—	—	—	...	...	...	...	...	...	...	...	...
33	**Net incurrence of liabilities**	**53**	**172**	**130**	**...**	**...**	**...**	**...**	**...**	**...**	**...**	**...**	**...**
	By instrument												
3301	Special Drawing Rights (SDRs)	—	—	—	...	...	...	...	...	...	...	...	...
3302	Currency and deposits	—	—	—	...	...	...	...	...	...	...	...	...
3303	Debt securities	5	-14	15	...	...	...	...	...	...	...	...	...
3304	Loans	48	186	115	...	...	...	...	...	...	...	...	...
3305	Equity and investment fund shares	—	—	—	...	...	...	...	...	...	...	...	...
3306	Insurance, pension, and standardized guarantee schemes	—	—	—	...	...	...	...	...	...	...	...	...
3307	Financial derivatives and employee stock options	—	—	—	...	...	...	...	...	...	...	...	...
3308	Other accounts payable	...	...	...	...	...	...	...	...	...	...	...	...
	By creditor												
331	Domestic creditors	6	-4	33	...	...	...	...	...	...	...	...	...
332	External creditors	47	176	97	...	...	...	...	...	...	...	...	...
	Table 4 Holding gains and losses in assets and liabilities												
	Table 5 Holding gains and losses in assets and liabilities												
	Table 6 Balance sheet												

Belize (339)

In Millions of Belize Dollars (BZD) / Fiscal Year Ends March 31st

	Budgetary Central Government			Central Government (excl. Social Security)			Central Government (incl. Social Security)			General Government		
	2012	2013	2014	2012	2013	2014	2012	2013	2014	2012	2013	2014
Table 7 Expenditure by functions of government												
Table 8 Financial transactions by counterpart sector												
Table 9 Total other economic flows in assets and liabilities												

Benin (638)

In Billions of CFA (BEAC) Francs (XAF) / Fiscal Year Ends December 31st

		Budgetary Central Government			Central Government (excl. Social Security)			Central Government (incl. Social Security)			General Government		
		2011	2012	2013	2011	2012	2013	2011	2012	2013	2011	2012	2013
	Statement of operations												
1	Revenue	677	701	803	...	...	...	...	...	...	...	...	...
2	Expense	458	535	578	...	...	...	...	...	...	...	...	...
GOB	**Gross operating balance**	**219**	**167**	**226**	...	...	...	...	...	...	...	...	...
NOB	**Net operating balance**	...	...	...	...	...	...	...	...	...	...	...	...
31	Net/Gross investment in nonfinancial assets	125	101	102	...	...	...	...	...	...	...	...	...
2M	Expenditure	583	636	680	...	...	...	...	...	...	...	...	...
NLB	**Net lending (+) / Net borrowing (-)**	**94**	**66**	**123**	...	...	...	...	...	...	...	...	...
32	Net acquisition of financial assets	-1	-17	-6	...	...	...	...	...	...	...	...	...
33	Net incurrence of liabilities	134	81	161	...	...	...	...	...	...	...	...	...
NLBz	Statistical discrepancy	-229	-163	-290	...	...	...	...	...	...	...	...	...
	Memorandum items												
PB	Primary net lending / net borrowing	109	89	143	...	...	...	...	...	...	...	...	...
GB	Government balance per national definition	...	...	...	...	...	...	...	...	...	...	...	...
	Statement of other economic flows												
	Balance sheet												
	Table 1 Revenue												
1	**Revenue**	**677**	**701**	**803**	...	...	...	...	...	...	...	...	...
11	**Taxes**	**547**	**600**	**696**	...	...	...	...	...	...	...	...	...
111	Taxes on income, profits, and capital gains	114	118	134	...	...	...	...	...	...	...	...	...
1111	Payable by individuals	52	56	60	...	...	...	...	...	...	...	...	...
1112	Payable by corporations and other enterprises	53	53	64	...	...	...	...	...	...	...	...	...
1113	Other taxes on income, profits, and capital gains	10	9	11	...	...	...	...	...	...	...	...	...
112	Taxes on payroll and workforce	5	6	6	...	...	...	...	...	...	...	...	...
113	Taxes on property	2	1	2	...	...	...	...	...	...	...	...	...
114	Taxes on goods and services	283	302	350	...	...	...	...	...	...	...	...	...
1141	General taxes on goods and services	240	270	309	...	...	...	...	...	...	...	...	...
1142	Excises	21	9	23	...	...	...	...	...	...	...	...	...
115	Taxes on international trade and transactions	133	164	194	...	...	...	...	...	...	...	...	...
116	Other taxes	9	9	10	...	...	...	...	...	...	...	...	...
12	**Social contributions**	**19**	**21**	**23**	...	...	...	...	...	...	...	...	...
121	Social security contributions	19	21	23	...	...	...	...	...	...	...	...	...
122	Other social contributions	—	—	—	...	...	...	...	...	...	...	...	...
13	**Grants**	**81**	**47**	**46**	...	...	...	...	...	...	...	...	...
131	From foreign governments	77	43	41	...	...	...	...	...	...	...	...	...
132	From international organizations	—	—	—	...	...	...	...	...	...	...	...	...
133	From other general government units	4	3	5	...	...	...	...	...	...	...	...	...
1331	Current	4	3	5	...	...	...	...	...	...	...	...	...
1332	Capital	—	—	—	...	...	...	...	...	...	...	...	...
14	**Other revenue**	**31**	**34**	**38**	...	...	...	...	...	...	...	...	...
	Table 2 Expense by economic type												
2	**Expense**	**458**	**535**	**578**	...	...	...	...	...	...	...	...	...
21	**Compensation of employees**	**242**	**268**	**296**	...	...	...	...	...	...	...	...	...
211	Wages and salaries	242	268	296	...	...	...	...	...	...	...	...	...
212	Employers' social contributions	—	—	—	...	...	...	...	...	...	...	...	...
22	**Use of goods and services**	**69**	**94**	**106**	...	...	...	...	...	...	...	...	...
23	**Consumption of fixed capital**	...	...	...	...	...	...	...	...	...	...	...	...
24	**Interest**	**15**	**23**	**20**	...	...	...	...	...	...	...	...	...
25	**Subsidies**	**34**	**55**	**50**	...	...	...	...	...	...	...	...	...
26	**Grants**	**87**	**81**	**91**	...	...	...	...	...	...	...	...	...
261	To foreign governments	—	—	—	...	...	...	...	...	...	...	...	...
262	To international organizations	6	7	8	...	...	...	...	...	...	...	...	...
263	To other general government units	81	74	83	...	...	...	...	...	...	...	...	...
2631	Current	81	74	83	...	...	...	...	...	...	...	...	...
2632	Capital	—	—	—	...	...	...	...	...	...	...	...	...

Benin (638)

In Billions of CFA (BEAC) Francs (XAF) / Fiscal Year Ends December 31st

		Budgetary Central Government			Central Government (excl. Social Security)			Central Government (incl. Social Security)			General Government		
		2011	2012	2013	2011	2012	2013	2011	2012	2013	2011	2012	2013
27	**Social benefits**	**1**	**1**	**1**	**...**	**...**	**...**	**...**	**...**	**...**	**...**	**...**	**...**
271	Social security benefits	—	—	—	...	...	...	...	...	...	...	...	...
272	Social assistance benefits	—	—	—	...	...	...	...	...	...	...	...	...
273	Employment-related social benefits	1	1	1	...	...	...	...	...	...	...	...	...
28	**Other expense**	**10**	**13**	**14**	**...**	**...**	**...**	**...**	**...**	**...**	**...**	**...**	**...**
281	Property expense other than interest	—	—	—	...	...	...	...	...	...	...	...	...
282	Transfers not elsewhere classified	10	13	14	...	...	...	...	...	...	...	...	...
2821	Current	10	13	14	...	...	...	...	...	...	...	...	...
2822	Capital	—	—	—	...	...	...	...	...	...	...	...	...
	Table 3 Transactions in assets and liabilities												
3	**Change in net worth from transactions**	**...**	**...**	**...**	**...**	**...**	**...**	**...**	**...**	**...**	**...**	**...**	**...**
31	**Net/Gross investment in nonfinancial assets**	**125**	**101**	**102**	**...**	**...**	**...**	**...**	**...**	**...**	**...**	**...**	**...**
311	Fixed assets	130	153	155	...	...	...	...	...	...	...	...	...
3111	Buildings and structures	...	...	...	...	...	...	...	...	...	...	...	...
3112	Machinery and equipment	...	...	...	...	...	...	...	...	...	...	...	...
3113	Other fixed assets	...	...	...	...	...	...	...	...	...	...	...	...
3114	Weapons systems	...	...	...	...	...	...	...	...	...	...	...	...
312	Inventories	—	—	—	...	...	...	...	...	...	...	...	...
313	Valuables	—	—	—	...	...	...	...	...	...	...	...	...
314	Nonproduced assets	-5	-52	-52	...	...	...	...	...	...	...	...	...
3141	Land	...	...	...	...	...	...	...	...	...	...	...	...
3142	Mineral and energy resources	...	...	...	...	...	...	...	...	...	...	...	...
3143	Other naturally occurring assets	...	...	...	...	...	...	...	...	...	...	...	...
3144	Intangible nonproduced assets	...	...	...	...	...	...	...	...	...	...	...	...
32	**Net acquisition of financial assets**	**-1**	**-17**	**-6**	**...**	**...**	**...**	**...**	**...**	**...**	**...**	**...**	**...**
	By instrument												
3201	Monetary gold and SDRs	—	—	—	...	...	...	...	...	...	...	...	...
3202	Currency and deposits	-11	-20	-34	...	...	...	...	...	...	...	...	...
3203	Debt securities	—	—	—	...	...	...	...	...	...	...	...	...
3204	Loans	11	3	28	...	...	...	...	...	...	...	...	...
3205	Equity and investment fund shares	—	—	—	...	...	...	...	...	...	...	...	...
3206	Insurance, pension, and standardized guarantee schemes	—	—	—	...	...	...	...	...	...	...	...	...
3207	Financial derivatives and employee stock options	—	—	—	...	...	...	...	...	...	...	...	...
3208	Other accounts receivable	—	—	—	...	...	...	...	...	...	...	...	...
	By debtor												
321	Domestic debtors	-1	-17	-6	...	...	...	...	...	...	...	...	...
322	External debtors	—	—	—	...	...	...	...	...	...	...	...	...
33	**Net incurrence of liabilities**	**134**	**81**	**161**	**...**	**...**	**...**	**...**	**...**	**...**	**...**	**...**	**...**
	By instrument												
3301	Special Drawing Rights (SDRs)	—	—	—	...	...	...	...	...	...	...	...	...
3302	Currency and deposits	—	—	—	...	...	...	...	...	...	...	...	...
3303	Debt securities	113	39	2	...	...	...	...	...	...	...	...	...
3304	Loans	68	58	188	...	...	...	...	...	...	...	...	...
3305	Equity and investment fund shares	—	—	—	...	...	...	...	...	...	...	...	...
3306	Insurance, pension, and standardized guarantee schemes	—	—	—	...	...	...	...	...	...	...	...	...
3307	Financial derivatives and employee stock options	—	—	—	...	...	...	...	...	...	...	...	...
3308	Other accounts payable	-47	-16	-28	...	...	...	...	...	...	...	...	...
	By creditor												
331	Domestic creditors	91	37	-2	...	...	...	...	...	...	...	...	...
332	External creditors	42	44	163	...	...	...	...	...	...	...	...	...
	Table 4 Holding gains and losses in assets and liabilities												
	Table 5 Holding gains and losses in assets and liabilities												
	Table 6 Balance sheet												

Benin (638)

In Billions of CFA (BEAC) Francs (XAF) / Fiscal Year Ends December 31st

	Budgetary Central Government			Central Government (excl. Social Security)			Central Government (incl. Social Security)			General Government		
	2011	2012	2013	2011	2012	2013	2011	2012	2013	2011	2012	2013
Table 7 Expenditure by functions of government												
Table 8 Financial transactions by counterpart sector												
Table 9 Total other economic flows in assets and liabilities												

Bhutan (514)

In Millions of Bhutanese Ngultrum (BTN) / Fiscal Year Ends June 30th

		Budgetary Central Government			Central Government (excl. Social Security)			Central Government (incl. Social Security)			General Government		
		2012	2013	2014	2012	2013	2014	2012	2013	2014	2012	2013	2014
	Statement of operations												
1	Revenue	32,796	30,613	37,425	32,796	30,613	37,425	32,796	30,613	37,425	32,796	30,613	37,425
2	Expense	19,915	21,226	21,715	19,915	21,226	21,715	19,915	21,226	21,715	19,915	21,226	21,715
GOB	**Gross operating balance**	**12,880**	**9,388**	**15,710**	**12,880**	**9,388**	**15,710**	**12,880**	**9,388**	**15,710**	**12,880**	**9,388**	**15,710**
NOB	**Net operating balance**	...	...	...	...	...	...	...	...	...	...	...	...
31	Net/Gross investment in nonfinancial assets	14,550	14,741	10,499	14,550	14,741	10,499	14,550	14,741	10,499	14,550	14,741	10,499
2M	Expenditure	34,466	35,966	32,215	34,466	35,966	32,215	34,466	35,966	32,215	34,466	35,966	32,215
NLB	**Net lending (+) / Net borrowing (-)**	**-1,670**	**-5,353**	**5,211**	**-1,670**	**-5,353**	**5,211**	**-1,670**	**-5,353**	**5,211**	**-1,670**	**-5,353**	**5,211**
32	Net acquisition of financial assets	-2,887	-4,869	4,507	-2,887	-4,869	4,507	-2,887	-4,869	4,507	-2,887	-4,869	4,507
33	Net incurrence of liabilities	-1,217	484	-704	-1,217	484	-704	-1,217	484	-704	-1,217	484	-704
NLBz	Statistical discrepancy	0	0	0	0	0	0	0	0	0	0	0	0
	Memorandum items												
PB	Primary net lending / net borrowing	216	-2,711	7,301	216	-2,711	7,301	216	-2,711	7,301	216	-2,711	7,301
GB	Government balance per national definition	...	...	...	...	...	...	...	...	...	...	...	...
	Statement of other economic flows												
	Balance sheet												
6	**Net worth**	...	...	...	...	...	...	...	...	...	...	...	...
61	Nonfinancial assets	...	...	...	...	...	...	...	...	...	...	...	...
62	Financial assets	93,218	108,687	115,000	93,218	108,687	115,000	93,218	108,687	115,000	93,218	108,687	115,000
63	Liabilities	70,669	101,310	108,370	70,669	101,310	108,370	70,669	101,310	108,370	70,669	101,310	108,370
	Table 1 Revenue												
1	**Revenue**	**32,796**	**30,613**	**37,425**	**32,796**	**30,613**	**37,425**	**32,796**	**30,613**	**37,425**	**32,796**	**30,613**	**37,425**
11	**Taxes**	**14,330**	**15,151**	**15,944**	**14,330**	**15,151**	**15,944**	**14,330**	**15,151**	**15,944**	**14,330**	**15,151**	**15,944**
111	Taxes on income, profits, and capital gains	7,542	7,813	9,350	7,542	7,813	9,350	7,542	7,813	9,350	7,542	7,813	9,350
1111	Payable by individuals	1,057	1,258	1,438	1,057	1,258	1,438	1,057	1,258	1,438	1,057	1,258	1,438
1112	Payable by corporations and other enterprises	6,485	6,555	7,911	6,485	6,555	7,911	6,485	6,555	7,911	6,485	6,555	7,911
1113	Other taxes on income, profits, and capital gains	—	—	—	—	—	—	—	—	—	—	—	—
112	Taxes on payroll and workforce	—	—	—	—	—	—	—	—	—	—	—	—
113	Taxes on property	—	—	—	—	—	—	—	—	—	—	—	—
114	Taxes on goods and services	6,405	7,052	6,286	6,405	7,052	6,286	6,405	7,052	6,286	6,405	7,052	6,286
1141	General taxes on goods and services	2,392	2,171	2,163	2,392	2,171	2,163	2,392	2,171	2,163	2,392	2,171	2,163
1142	Excises	2,837	3,482	2,556	2,837	3,482	2,556	2,837	3,482	2,556	2,837	3,482	2,556
115	Taxes on international trade and transactions	382	287	308	382	287	308	382	287	308	382	287	308
116	Other taxes	—	—	—	—	—	—	—	—	—	—	—	—
12	**Social contributions**	**23**	**23**	**24**	**23**	**23**	**24**	**23**	**23**	**24**	**23**	**23**	**24**
121	Social security contributions	23	23	24	23	23	24	23	23	24	23	23	24
122	Other social contributions	—	—	—	—	—	—	—	—	—	—	—	—
13	**Grants**	**12,502**	**9,563**	**14,236**	**12,502**	**9,563**	**14,236**	**12,502**	**9,563**	**14,236**	**12,502**	**9,563**	**14,236**
131	From foreign governments	10,473	6,346	12,271	10,473	6,346	12,271	10,473	6,346	12,271	10,473	6,346	12,271
132	From international organizations	2,029	3,217	1,965	2,029	3,217	1,965	2,029	3,217	1,965	2,029	3,217	1,965
133	From other general government units	—	—	—	—	—	—	—	—	—	—	—	—
1331	Current	—	—	—	—	—	—	—	—	—	—	—	—
1332	Capital	—	—	—	—	—	—	—	—	—	—	—	—
14	**Other revenue**	**5,941**	**5,877**	**7,221**	**5,941**	**5,877**	**7,221**	**5,941**	**5,877**	**7,221**	**5,941**	**5,877**	**7,221**
	Table 2 Expense by economic type												
2	**Expense**	**19,915**	**21,226**	**21,715**	**19,915**	**21,226**	**21,715**	**19,915**	**21,226**	**21,715**	**19,915**	**21,226**	**21,715**
21	**Compensation of employees**	**7,577**	**7,954**	**8,271**	**7,577**	**7,954**	**8,271**	**7,577**	**7,954**	**8,271**	**7,577**	**7,954**	**8,271**
211	Wages and salaries	7,074	7,427	7,722	7,074	7,427	7,722	7,074	7,427	7,722	7,074	7,427	7,722
212	Employers' social contributions	503	527	549	503	527	549	503	527	549	503	527	549
22	**Use of goods and services**	**7,103**	**6,999**	**6,905**	**7,103**	**6,999**	**6,905**	**7,103**	**6,999**	**6,905**	**7,103**	**6,999**	**6,905**
23	**Consumption of fixed capital**	...	...	...	...	...	...	...	...	...	...	...	...
24	**Interest**	**1,886**	**2,642**	**2,090**	**1,886**	**2,642**	**2,090**	**1,886**	**2,642**	**2,090**	**1,886**	**2,642**	**2,090**
25	**Subsidies**	**283**	**323**	**200**	**283**	**323**	**200**	**283**	**323**	**200**	**283**	**323**	**200**

Bhutan (514)

In Millions of Bhutanese Ngultrum (BTN) / Fiscal Year Ends June 30th

		Budgetary Central Government			Central Government (excl. Social Security)			Central Government (incl. Social Security)			General Government		
		2012	2013	2014	2012	2013	2014	2012	2013	2014	2012	2013	2014
26	**Grants**	**66**	**95**	**119**	**66**	**95**	**119**	**66**	**95**	**119**	**66**	**95**	**119**
261	To foreign governments	—	—	—	—	—	—	—	—	—	—	—	—
262	To international organizations	65	95	119	65	95	119	65	95	119	65	95	119
263	To other general government units	1	—	—	1	—	—	1	—	—	1	—	—
2631	Current	1	—	—	1	—	—	1	—	—	1	—	—
2632	Capital	—	—	—	—	—	—	—	—	—	—	—	—
27	**Social benefits**	**632**	**750**	**720**	**632**	**750**	**720**	**632**	**750**	**720**	**632**	**750**	**720**
271	Social security benefits	526	638	597	526	638	597	526	638	597	526	638	597
272	Social assistance benefits	106	113	123	106	113	123	106	113	123	106	113	123
273	Employment-related social benefits	—	—	—	—	—	—	—	—	—	—	—	—
28	**Other expense**	**2,368**	**2,462**	**3,410**	**2,368**	**2,462**	**3,410**	**2,368**	**2,462**	**3,410**	**2,368**	**2,462**	**3,410**
281	Property expense other than interest	—	—	—	—	—	—	—	—	—	—	—	—
282	Transfers not elsewhere classified	2,368	2,462	3,410	2,368	2,462	3,410	2,368	2,462	3,410	2,368	2,462	3,410
2821	Current	1,477	1,508	1,750	1,477	1,508	1,750	1,477	1,508	1,750	1,477	1,508	1,750
2822	Capital	892	954	1,660	892	954	1,660	892	954	1,660	892	954	1,660
	Table 3 Transactions in assets and liabilities												
3	**Change in net worth from transactions**	...	...	...	...	...	...	...	...	...	...	...	...
31	**Net/Gross investment in nonfinancial assets**	**14,550**	**14,741**	**10,499**	**14,550**	**14,741**	**10,499**	**14,550**	**14,741**	**10,499**	**14,550**	**14,741**	**10,499**
311	Fixed assets	14,548	14,744	10,524	14,548	14,744	10,524	14,548	14,744	10,524	14,548	14,744	10,524
3111	Buildings and structures	12,188	12,703	8,862	12,188	12,703	8,862	12,188	12,703	8,862	12,188	12,703	8,862
3112	Machinery and equipment	2,246	1,940	1,505	2,246	1,940	1,505	2,246	1,940	1,505	2,246	1,940	1,505
3113	Other fixed assets	114	102	157	114	102	157	114	102	157	114	102	157
3114	Weapons systems	—	—	—	—	—	—	—	—	—	—	—	—
312	Inventories	—	—	—	—	—	—	—	—	—	—	—	—
313	Valuables	—	—	—	—	—	—	—	—	—	—	—	—
314	Nonproduced assets	3	-3	-24	3	-3	-24	3	-3	-24	3	-3	-24
3141	Land	52	46	25	52	46	25	52	46	25	52	46	25
3142	Mineral and energy resources	-50	-50	-50	-50	-50	-50	-50	-50	-50	-50	-50	-50
3143	Other naturally occurring assets	—	—	—	—	—	—	—	—	—	—	—	—
3144	Intangible nonproduced assets	—	—	—	—	—	—	—	—	—	—	—	—
32	**Net acquisition of financial assets**	**-2,887**	**-4,869**	**4,507**	**-2,887**	**-4,869**	**4,507**	**-2,887**	**-4,869**	**4,507**	**-2,887**	**-4,869**	**4,507**
	By instrument												
3201	Monetary gold and SDRs	—	—	—	—	—	—	—	—	—	—	—	—
3202	Currency and deposits	-2,049	-3,752	3,254	-2,049	-3,752	3,254	-2,049	-3,752	3,254	-2,049	-3,752	3,254
3203	Debt securities	—	—	—	—	—	—	—	—	—	—	—	—
3204	Loans	-1,037	-740	768	-1,037	-740	768	-1,037	-740	768	-1,037	-740	768
3205	Equity and investment fund shares	317	510	240	317	510	240	317	510	240	317	510	240
3206	Insurance, pension, and standardized guarantee schemes	—	—	—	—	—	—	—	—	—	—	—	—
3207	Financial derivatives and employee stock options	—	—	—	—	—	—	—	—	—	—	—	—
3208	Other accounts receivable	-118	-887	245	-118	-887	245	-118	-887	245	-118	-887	245
	By debtor												
321	Domestic debtors	-3,204	-5,379	4,267	-3,204	-5,379	4,267	-3,204	-5,379	4,267	-3,204	-5,379	4,267
322	External debtors	317	510	240	317	510	240	317	510	240	317	510	240
33	**Net incurrence of liabilities**	**-1,217**	**484**	**-704**	**-1,217**	**484**	**-704**	**-1,217**	**484**	**-704**	**-1,217**	**484**	**-704**
	By instrument												
3301	Special Drawing Rights (SDRs)	—	—	—	—	—	—	—	—	—	—	—	—
3302	Currency and deposits	—	—	—	—	—	—	—	—	—	—	—	—
3303	Debt securities	216	-175	-175	216	-175	-175	216	-175	-175	216	-175	-175
3304	Loans	-1,223	668	-867	-1,223	668	-867	-1,223	668	-867	-1,223	668	-867
3305	Equity and investment fund shares	—	—	—	—	—	—	—	—	—	—	—	—
3306	Insurance, pension, and standardized guarantee schemes	—	—	—	—	—	—	—	—	—	—	—	—
3307	Financial derivatives and employee stock options	—	—	—	—	—	—	—	—	—	—	—	—
3308	Other accounts payable	-210	-8	338	-210	-8	338	-210	-8	338	-210	-8	338

Bhutan (514)

In Millions of Bhutanese Ngultrum (BTN) / Fiscal Year Ends June 30th

		Budgetary Central Government			Central Government (excl. Social Security)			Central Government (incl. Social Security)			General Government		
		2012	2013	2014	2012	2013	2014	2012	2013	2014	2012	2013	2014
	By creditor												
331	Domestic creditors	6	-184	163	6	-184	163	6	-184	163	6	-184	163
332	External creditors	-1,223	668	-867	-1,223	668	-867	-1,223	668	-867	-1,223	668	-867
	Table 4 Holding gains and losses in assets and liabilities												
	Table 5 Holding gains and losses in assets and liabilities												
	Table 6 Balance sheet												
6	**Net worth**	...	...	...	...	...	...	...	...	...	...	...	...
61	**Nonfinancial assets**	...	...	...	...	...	...	...	...	...	...	...	...
611	Fixed assets	...	...	...	...	...	...	...	...	...	...	...	...
6111	Buildings and structures	...	...	...	...	...	...	...	...	...	...	...	...
6112	Machinery and equipment	...	...	...	...	...	...	...	...	...	...	...	...
6113	Other fixed assets	...	...	...	...	...	...	...	...	...	...	...	...
6114	Weapons systems	...	...	...	...	...	...	...	...	...	...	...	...
612	Inventories	...	...	...	...	...	...	...	...	...	...	...	...
613	Valuables	...	...	...	...	...	...	...	...	...	...	...	...
614	Nonproduced assets	...	...	...	...	...	...	...	...	...	...	...	...
6141	Land	...	...	...	...	...	...	...	...	...	...	...	...
6142	Mineral and energy resources	...	...	...	...	...	...	...	...	...	...	...	...
6143	Other naturally occurring assets	...	...	...	...	...	...	...	...	...	...	...	...
6144	Intangible nonproduced assets	...	...	...	...	...	...	...	...	...	...	...	...
62	**Financial assets**	**93,218**	**108,687**	**115,000**	**93,218**	**108,687**	**115,000**	**93,218**	**108,687**	**115,000**	**93,218**	**108,687**	**115,000**
	By instrument												
6201	Monetary gold and SDRs	—	—	—	—	—	—	—	—	—	—	—	—
6202	Currency and deposits	...	...	...	...	...	...	...	...	...	...	...	...
6203	Debt securities	—	—	—	—	—	—	—	—	—	—	—	—
6204	Loans	46,133	59,347	61,447	46,133	59,347	61,447	46,133	59,347	61,447	46,133	59,347	61,447
6205	Equity and investment fund shares	49,149	55,156	56,115	49,149	55,156	56,115	49,149	55,156	56,115	49,149	55,156	56,115
6206	Insurance, pension, and standardized guarantee schemes	—	—	—	—	—	—	—	—	—	—	—	—
6207	Financial derivatives and employee stock options	—	—	—	—	—	—	—	—	—	—	—	—
6208	Other accounts receivable	...	...	...	...	...	...	...	...	...	...	...	...
	By debtor												
621	Domestic debtors	93,218	108,687	115,000	93,218	108,687	115,000	93,218	108,687	115,000	93,218	108,687	115,000
622	External debtors	—	—	—	—	—	—	—	—	—	—	—	—
63	**Liabilities**	**70,669**	**101,310**	**108,370**	**70,669**	**101,310**	**108,370**	**70,669**	**101,310**	**108,370**	**70,669**	**101,310**	**108,370**
	By instrument												
6301	Special Drawing Rights (SDRs)	—	—	—	—	—	—	—	—	—	—	—	—
6302	Currency and deposits	—	—	—	—	—	—	—	—	—	—	—	—
6303	Debt securities	1,093	6,343	2,913	1,093	6,343	2,913	1,093	6,343	2,913	1,093	6,343	2,913
6304	Loans	69,576	94,968	105,457	69,576	94,968	105,457	69,576	94,968	105,457	69,576	94,968	105,457
6305	Equity and investment fund shares	—	—	—	—	—	—	—	—	—	—	—	—
6306	Insurance, pension, and standardized guarantee schemes	—	—	—	—	—	—	—	—	—	—	—	—
6307	Financial derivatives and employee stock options	—	—	—	—	—	—	—	—	—	—	—	—
6308	Other accounts payable	...	...	...	...	...	...	...	...	...	...	...	...
	By creditor												
631	Domestic creditors	1,093	6,343	2,913	1,093	6,343	2,913	1,093	6,343	2,913	1,093	6,343	2,913
632	External creditors	69,576	94,968	105,457	69,576	94,968	105,457	69,576	94,968	105,457	69,576	94,968	105,457
	Memorandum items												
6M2	Net financial worth	22,549	7,377	6,630	22,549	7,377	6,630	22,549	7,377	6,630	22,549	7,377	6,630
6M3	Gross debt (D4) at market value	...	...	...	...	...	...	...	...	...	...	...	...
6M3D3	D3 debt liabilities at market value	...	...	...	...	...	...	...	...	...	...	...	...
6M3D2	D2 debt liabilities at market value	...	...	...	...	...	...	...	...	...	...	...	...
6M3D1	D1 debt liabilities at market value	...	...	...	...	...	...	...	...	...	...	...	...
6M4	Gross debt (D4) at nominal value	...	...	...	...	...	...	...	...	...	...	...	...
6M4D3	D3 debt liabilities at nominal value	...	...	...	...	...	...	...	...	...	...	...	...
6M4D2	D2 debt liabilities at nominal value	...	...	...	...	...	...	...	...	...	...	...	...
6M4D1	D1 debt liabilities at nominal value	...	...	...	...	...	...	...	...	...	...	...	...

Bhutan (514)

In Millions of Bhutanese Ngultrum (BTN) / Fiscal Year Ends June 30th

		Budgetary Central Government			Central Government (excl. Social Security)			Central Government (incl. Social Security)			General Government		
		2012	2013	2014	2012	2013	2014	2012	2013	2014	2012	2013	2014
6M35	Gross debt (D4) at face value	...	...	...	...	...	...	...	...	108,370	...	...	...
6M35D3	D3 debt liabilities at face value	...	...	...	...	...	...	...	...	...	...	...	...
6M35D2	D2 debt liabilities at face value	70,669	101,310	108,370	70,669	101,310	108,370	70,669	101,310	108,370	70,669	101,310	108,370
6M35D1	D1 debt liabilities at face value	70,669	101,310	108,370	70,669	101,310	108,370	70,669	101,310	108,370	70,669	101,310	108,370
6M93	Government gross debt per national definition	...	...	...	...	...	...	...	...	...	...	...	...
6M5	Arrears	...	...	...	...	...	...	...	...	...	...	...	...
6M6	Explicit contingent liabilities	...	...	...	...	...	...	...	...	...	...	...	...
6M61	of which: Publicly guaranteed debt	...	...	...	...	...	...	...	...	...	...	...	...
6M7	Net implicit obligations for social security benefits	...	...	...	...	...	...	...	...	...	...	...	...
	Table 7 Expenditure by functions of government												
7	**Expenditure**	**34,466**	**35,966**	**32,215**	**34,466**	**35,966**	**32,215**	**34,466**	**35,966**	**32,215**	**34,466**	**35,966**	**32,215**
701	**General public services**	**6,389**	**7,077**	**6,767**	**6,389**	**7,077**	**6,767**	**6,389**	**7,077**	**6,767**	**6,389**	**7,077**	**6,767**
7017	Public debt transactions	1,886	2,642	2,090	1,886	2,642	2,090	1,886	2,642	2,090	1,886	2,642	2,090
7018	Transfers of general character between levels of government	—	—	—	—	—	—	—	—	—	—	—	—
702	**Defense**	**67**	**29**	**23**	**67**	**29**	**23**	**67**	**29**	**23**	**67**	**29**	**23**
703	**Public order and safety**	**2,122**	**2,120**	**2,054**	**2,122**	**2,120**	**2,054**	**2,122**	**2,120**	**2,054**	**2,122**	**2,120**	**2,054**
704	**Economic affairs**	**12,219**	**12,261**	**10,275**	**12,219**	**12,261**	**10,275**	**12,219**	**12,261**	**10,275**	**12,219**	**12,261**	**10,275**
7042	Agriculture, forestry, fishing, and hunting	4,869	4,897	4,245	4,869	4,897	4,245	4,869	4,897	4,245	4,869	4,897	4,245
7043	Fuel and energy	601	427	375	601	427	375	601	427	375	601	427	375
7044	Mining, manufacturing, and construction	150	200	183	150	200	183	150	200	183	150	200	183
7045	Transport	4,372	4,647	3,915	4,372	4,647	3,915	4,372	4,647	3,915	4,372	4,647	3,915
7046	Communication	1,044	911	378	1,044	911	378	1,044	911	378	1,044	911	378
705	**Environmental protection**	**84**	**62**	**67**	**84**	**62**	**67**	**84**	**62**	**67**	**84**	**62**	**67**
706	**Housing and community amenities**	**1,485**	**1,637**	**1,604**	**1,485**	**1,637**	**1,604**	**1,485**	**1,637**	**1,604**	**1,485**	**1,637**	**1,604**
707	**Health**	**2,955**	**2,952**	**2,974**	**2,955**	**2,952**	**2,974**	**2,955**	**2,952**	**2,974**	**2,955**	**2,952**	**2,974**
7072	Outpatient services	2,760	391	361	2,760	391	361	2,760	391	361	2,760	391	361
7073	Hospital services	—	2,344	2,412	—	2,344	2,412	—	2,344	2,412	—	2,344	2,412
7074	Public health services	—	—	—	—	—	—	—	—	—	—	—	—
708	**Recreation, culture and religion**	**1,847**	**2,047**	**1,926**	**1,847**	**2,047**	**1,926**	**1,847**	**2,047**	**1,926**	**1,847**	**2,047**	**1,926**
709	**Education**	**7,269**	**7,749**	**6,500**	**7,269**	**7,749**	**6,500**	**7,269**	**7,749**	**6,500**	**7,269**	**7,749**	**6,500**
7091	Pre-primary and primary education	5,344	5,477	4,858	5,344	5,477	4,858	5,344	5,477	4,858	5,344	5,477	4,858
7092	Secondary education	68	68	78	68	68	78	68	68	78	68	68	78
7094	Tertiary education	1,217	1,490	760	1,217	1,490	760	1,217	1,490	760	1,217	1,490	760
710	**Social protection**	**30**	**34**	**23**	**30**	**34**	**23**	**30**	**34**	**23**	**30**	**34**	**23**
7z	Statistical discrepancy: Expenditure	...	...	...	...	...	...	...	...	...	...	...	...
	Table 8 Financial transactions by counterpart sector												
32	**Net acquisition of financial assets**	**-2,887**	**-4,869**	**4,507**	**-2,887**	**-4,869**	**4,507**	**-2,887**	**-4,869**	**4,507**	**-2,887**	**-4,869**	**4,507**
321	Domestic debtors	-3,204	-5,379	4,267	-3,204	-5,379	4,267	-3,204	-5,379	4,267	-3,204	-5,379	4,267
8211	General government	—	—	—	—	—	—	—	—	—	—	—	—
8212	Central bank	-2,049	-3,752	3,254	-2,049	-3,752	3,254	-2,049	-3,752	3,254	-2,049	-3,752	3,254
8213	Deposit-taking corporations except the central bank	—	—	—	—	—	—	—	—	—	—	—	—
8214	Other financial corporations	—	—	—	—	—	—	—	—	—	—	—	—
8215	Nonfinancial corporations	-1,037	-740	768	-1,037	-740	768	-1,037	-740	768	-1,037	-740	768
8216	Households & nonprofit institutions serving households	-118	-887	245	-118	-887	245	118	-887	245	-118	-887	245
322	External debtors	317	510	240	317	510	240	317	510	240	317	510	240
8221	General government	—	—	—	—	—	—	—	—	—	—	—	—
8227	International organizations	317	510	240	317	510	240	317	510	240	317	510	240
8228	Financial corporations other than international organizations	—	—	—	—	—	—	—	—	—	—	—	—
8229	Other nonresidents	—	—	—	—	—	—	—	—	—	—	—	—

Bhutan (514)

In Millions of Bhutanese Ngultrum (BTN) / Fiscal Year Ends June 30th

		Budgetary Central Government			Central Government (excl. Social Security)			Central Government (incl. Social Security)			General Government		
		2012	2013	2014	2012	2013	2014	2012	2013	2014	2012	2013	2014
33	**Net incurrence of liabilities**	**-1,217**	**484**	**-704**	**-1,217**	**484**	**-704**	**-1,217**	**484**	**-704**	**-1,217**	**484**	**-704**
331	Domestic creditors	6	-184	163	6	-184	163	6	-184	163	6	-184	163
8311	General government	—	—	—	—	—	—	—	—	—	—	—	—
8312	Central bank	—	—	—	—	—	—	—	—	—	—	—	—
8313	Deposit-taking corporations except the central bank	216	—	—	216	—	—	216	—	—	216	—	—
8314	Other financial corporations	—	—	—	—	—	—	—	—	—	—	—	—
8315	Nonfinancial corporations	—	-175	-175	—	-175	-175	—	-175	-175	—	-175	-175
8316	Households & nonprofit institutions serving households	-210	-8	338	-210	-8	338	-210	-8	338	-210	-8	338
332	External creditors	-1,223	668	-867	-1,223	668	-867	-1,223	668	-867	-1,223	668	-867
8321	General government	-2,385	-2,326	-3,160	-2,385	-2,326	-3,160	-2,385	-2,326	-3,160	-2,385	-2,326	-3,160
8327	International organizations	1,162	2,994	2,293	1,162	2,994	2,293	1,162	2,994	2,293	1,162	2,994	2,293
8328	Financial corporations other than international organizations	—	—	—	—	—	—	—	—	—	—	—	—
8329	Other nonresidents	—	—	—	—	—	—	—	—	—	—	—	—
	Table 9 Total other economic flows in assets and liabilities												

Bosnia and Herzegovina (963)

In Millions of Convertible Marka (BAM) / Fiscal Year Ends December 31st

		Budgetary Central Government			Central Government (excl. Social Security)			Central Government (incl. Social Security)			General Government		
		2013	2014	2015	2013	2014	2015	2013	2014	2015	2013	2014	2015
	Statement of operations												
1	Revenue	5,929	6,469	6,359	6,178	6,554	6,691	10,359	10,854	11,079	11,408	11,962	12,335
2	Expense	5,696	6,082	5,889	5,759	6,025	6,076	10,006	10,929	10,553	10,939	11,350	11,584
GOB	**Gross operating balance**	**233**	**386**	**469**	**419**	**529**	**615**	**353**	**-74**	**526**	**469**	**612**	**751**
NOB	**Net operating balance**	...	...	...	...	...	...	...	...	...	...	...	...
31	Net/Gross investment in nonfinancial assets	169	333	212	881	998	395	909	1,028	422	1,047	1,167	559
2M	Expenditure	5,865	6,416	6,101	6,640	7,023	6,470	10,915	11,956	10,975	11,986	12,517	12,143
NLB	**Net lending (+) / Net borrowing (-)**	**63**	**53**	**258**	**-462**	**-469**	**220**	**-556**	**-1,102**	**104**	**-578**	**-555**	**192**
32	Net acquisition of financial assets	532	953	48	292	160	62	235	44	62	276	90	50
33	Net incurrence of liabilities	467	920	75	753	599	114	789	629	186	848	648	102
NLBz	Statistical discrepancy	1	-20	-286	1	29	-273	2	517	-228	6	-3	-245
	Memorandum items												
PB	Primary net lending / net borrowing	222	346	466	-295	-267	444	-377	-888	344	-377	-316	456
GB	Government balance per national definition	...	...	...	...	...	...	...	...	...	...	...	...
	Statement of other economic flows												
9	**Change in net worth due to other economic flows**	...	...	...	...	...	...	...	...	...	...	...	...
4	Change in net worth due to holding gains and losses	...	...	...	...	...	...	...	...	...	...	...	...
41	Nonfinancial assets	...	...	...	...	...	...	...	...	...	...	...	...
42	Financial assets	149	...	...	...	...	...	...	...	...	...	...	...
43	Liabilities	20	...	...	...	...	...	...	...	...	...	...	...
5	Change in net worth due to volume changes	...	...	...	...	...	...	...	...	...	...	...	...
51	Nonfinancial assets	...	...	...	...	...	...	...	...	...	...	...	...
52	Financial assets	...	...	...	...	...	...	...	...	...	...	...	...
53	Liabilities	...	...	...	...	...	...	...	...	...	...	...	...
	Balance sheet												
6	**Net worth**	...	...	...	...	...	...	...	...	...	...	...	...
61	Nonfinancial assets	...	...	...	...	...	...	...	...	...	...	...	...
62	Financial assets	8,438	9,028	...	7,474	7,790	...	...	...	...	9,207	9,366	...
63	Liabilities	11,909	13,077	...	12,303	13,672	...	...	...	...	14,432	15,807	...
	Table 1 Revenue												
1	**Revenue**	**5,929**	**6,469**	**6,359**	**6,178**	**6,554**	**6,691**	**10,359**	**10,854**	**11,079**	**11,408**	**11,962**	**12,335**
11	**Taxes**	**5,127**	**5,255**	**5,462**	**5,289**	**5,411**	**5,699**	**5,289**	**5,411**	**5,699**	**5,919**	**6,079**	**6,440**
111	Taxes on income, profits, and capital gains	711	704	753	711	704	753	711	704	753	829	817	876
1111	Payable by individuals	412	396	407	412	396	407	412	396	407	530	509	530
1112	Payable by corporations and other enterprises	299	308	346	299	308	346	299	308	346	299	308	347
1113	Other taxes on income, profits, and capital gains	—	—	—	—	—	—	—	—	—	—	—	—
112	Taxes on payroll and workforce	6	5	—	6	5	—	6	5	—	9	7	—
113	Taxes on property	12	12	7	12	12	7	12	12	7	98	99	100
114	Taxes on goods and services	4,382	4,509	4,675	4,544	4,665	4,911	4,544	4,665	4,911	4,963	5,128	5,435
1141	General taxes on goods and services	4,221	4,382	4,509	4,383	4,538	4,692	4,383	4,538	4,692	4,802	5,001	5,213
1142	Excises	48	41	27	48	41	81	48	41	81	48	41	83
115	Taxes on international trade and transactions	—	—	0	—	—	0	—	—	0	—	—	0
116	Other taxes	17	25	27	17	25	27	17	25	27	20	28	28
12	**Social contributions**	—	—	—	—	—	—	**4,117**	**4,235**	**4,330**	**4,117**	**4,235**	**4,330**
121	Social security contributions	—	—	—	—	—	—	4,105	4,235	4,330	4,105	4,235	4,330
122	Other social contributions	—	—	—	—	—	—	11	—	—	11	—	—
13	**Grants**	**61**	**138**	**45**	**61**	**68**	**45**	**63**	**70**	**47**	**66**	**77**	**55**
131	From foreign governments	3	2	42	3	2	42	5	4	42	7	8	49
132	From international organizations	57	66	2	57	66	2	57	66	2	59	69	4
133	From other general government units	2	70	2	2	-0	2	2	-0	3	-0	-0	2
1331	Current	2	69	2	2	-0	2	2	-0	3	-0	-0	2
1332	Capital	—	0	—	0	-0	—	0	-0	—	0	-0	0
14	**Other revenue**	**740**	**1,076**	**851**	**828**	**1,075**	**946**	**890**	**1,138**	**1,004**	**1,306**	**1,571**	**1,511**

Bosnia and Herzegovina (963)

In Millions of Convertible Marka (BAM) / Fiscal Year Ends December 31st

		Budgetary Central Government			Central Government (excl. Social Security)			Central Government (incl. Social Security)			General Government		
		2013	2014	2015	2013	2014	2015	2013	2014	2015	2013	2014	2015
	Table 2 Expense by economic type												
2	**Expense**	**5,696**	**6,082**	**5,889**	**5,759**	**6,025**	**6,076**	**10,006**	**10,929**	**10,553**	**10,939**	**11,350**	**11,584**
21	**Compensation of employees**	**2,761**	**2,745**	**2,760**	**2,777**	**2,762**	**2,781**	**2,879**	**2,870**	**2,891**	**3,278**	**3,266**	**3,294**
211	Wages and salaries	2,629	2,615	2,631	2,642	2,629	2,648	2,739	2,731	2,752	3,121	3,109	3,138
212	Employers' social contributions	132	130	129	135	133	133	140	139	139	158	157	157
22	**Use of goods and services**	**597**	**554**	**546**	**706**	**675**	**680**	**1,869**	**1,853**	**1,878**	**2,123**	**2,127**	**2,138**
23	**Consumption of fixed capital**	...	...	...	...	...	...	...	...	...	...	...	...
24	**Interest**	**159**	**293**	**208**	**167**	**201**	**223**	**179**	**214**	**240**	**201**	**239**	**264**
25	**Subsidies**	**326**	**302**	**313**	**326**	**302**	**313**	**349**	**328**	**346**	**384**	**365**	**385**
26	**Grants**	**596**	**734**	**567**	**521**	**620**	**567**	**61**	**620**	**31**	**1**	**3**	**5**
261	To foreign governments	—	—	—	—	—	—	—	—	—	0	—	—
262	To international organizations	1	3	2	1	3	2	1	3	2	1	3	3
263	To other general government units	595	731	565	520	616	565	60	80	29	0	-0	2
2631	Current	508	677	564	508	606	564	48	69	28	0	—	1
2632	Capital	87	54	1	12	11	1	12	11	1	0	-0	1
27	**Social benefits**	**947**	**986**	**961**	**948**	**986**	**961**	**4,318**	**4,530**	**4,598**	**4,424**	**4,658**	**4,729**
271	Social security benefits	3	1	3	3	1	3	3,309	3,475	3,568	3,309	3,475	3,568
272	Social assistance benefits	922	962	926	922	962	926	985	1,031	997	1,091	1,159	1,129
273	Employment-related social benefits	23	24	32	23	24	32	24	24	33	24	24	33
28	**Other expense**	**309**	**467**	**534**	**315**	**477**	**550**	**351**	**513**	**569**	**528**	**692**	**768**
281	Property expense other than interest	—	—	0	—	—	0	—	—	0	—	—	0
282	Transfers not elsewhere classified	309	467	534	315	477	550	351	513	569	528	692	768
2821	Current	266	378	454	272	388	467	285	401	482	407	519	606
2822	Capital	43	90	80	43	90	82	66	112	87	121	173	162
	Table 3 Transactions in assets and liabilities												
3	**Change in net worth from transactions**	...	...	...	...	...	...	...	...	...	...	...	...
31	**Net/Gross investment in nonfinancial assets**	**169**	**333**	**212**	**881**	**998**	**395**	**909**	**1,028**	**422**	**1,047**	**1,167**	**559**
311	Fixed assets	150	306	195	793	944	368	820	968	374	955	1,105	499
3111	Buildings and structures	67	183	99	554	706	162	555	707	164	676	831	284
3112	Machinery and equipment	74	112	88	82	113	197	106	137	200	118	148	213
3113	Other fixed assets	9	10	9	157	124	9	158	124	10	160	126	2
3114	Weapons systems	...	...	...	...	...	...	...	...	...	...	...	...
312	Inventories	8	12	4	8	12	4	8	12	24	5	12	24
313	Valuables	—	0	0	—	0	0	—	0	0	—	0	0
314	Nonproduced assets	11	16	12	81	42	23	82	47	24	87	50	35
3141	Land	0	1	1	63	24	9	63	24	9	63	19	16
3142	Mineral and energy resources	—	—	—	—	—	—	—	—	—	—	—	0
3143	Other naturally occurring assets	0	0	—	0	0	—	0	0	0	0	0	1
3144	Intangible nonproduced assets	11	14	11	18	18	13	20	23	14	24	31	19
32	**Net acquisition of financial assets**	**532**	**953**	**48**	**292**	**160**	**62**	**235**	**44**	**62**	**276**	**90**	**50**
	By instrument												
3201	Monetary gold and SDRs	—	—	—	—	—	—	—	—	—	—	—	—
3202	Currency and deposits	57	187	137	118	228	102	98	218	73	116	232	106
3203	Debt securities	7	-60	1	7	2	1	7	3	1	7	1	1
3204	Loans	412	909	-151	72	61	-86	88	36	-98	81	39	-113
3205	Equity and investment fund shares	-10	1	7	-10	1	7	-9	1	7	-3	1	5
3206	Insurance, pension, and standardized guarantee schemes	—	—	—	—	—	—	—	—	—	—	—	—
3207	Financial derivatives and employee stock options	—	—	—	—	—	—	—	—	—	—	—	—
3208	Other accounts receivable	65	-83	53	105	-133	37	51	-214	79	75	-183	52
	By debtor												
321	Domestic debtors	512	1,008	69	273	214	83	215	98	84	256	144	71
322	External debtors	20	-54	-22	20	-54	-22	20	-54	-22	20	-54	-22
33	**Net incurrence of liabilities**	**467**	**920**	**75**	**753**	**599**	**114**	**789**	**629**	**186**	**848**	**648**	**102**
	By instrument												
3301	Special Drawing Rights (SDRs)	—	—	—	—	—	—	—	—	—	—	—	—
3302	Currency and deposits	—	—	—	—	—	—	—	—	—	—	—	—
3303	Debt securities	-58	81	170	-58	144	170	-58	144	170	-64	137	164
3304	Loans	353	930	-114	542	526	-49	574	593	-25	632	597	-67

Bosnia and Herzegovina (963)

In Millions of Convertible Marka (BAM) / Fiscal Year Ends December 31st

		Budgetary Central Government			Central Government (excl. Social Security)			Central Government (incl. Social Security)			General Government		
		2013	2014	2015	2013	2014	2015	2013	2014	2015	2013	2014	2015
3305	Equity and investment fund shares	—	—	—	—	—	—	—	—	—	—	—	—
3306	Insurance, pension, and standardized guarantee schemes	—	—	—	—	—	—	—	—	—	—	—	—
3307	Financial derivatives and employee stock options	—	—	—	—	—	—	—	—	—	—	—	—
3308	Other accounts payable	172	-90	19	270	-70	-7	274	-107	41	281	-86	5
	By creditor												
331	Domestic creditors	42	609	281	290	244	283	326	277	354	384	296	270
332	External creditors	425	312	-206	463	355	-169	463	352	-168	463	352	-168
	Table 4 Holding gains and losses in assets and liabilities												
4	**Change in net worth due to holding gains and losses**	...	...	...	...	...	...	...	...	...	...	...	...
41	**Holding gains and losses in nonfinancial assets**	...	...	...	...	...	...	...	...	...	...	...	...
411	Fixed assets	...	...	...	...	...	...	...	...	...	...	...	...
412	Inventories	...	...	...	...	...	...	...	...	...	...	...	...
413	Valuables	...	...	...	...	...	...	...	...	...	...	...	...
414	Nonproduced assets	...	...	...	...	...	...	...	...	...	...	...	...
42	**Holding gains and losses in financial assets**	**149**	...	...	...	...	...	...	...	...	...	...	...
	By instrument												
4201	Monetary gold and SDRs	—	...	...	...	...	...	...	...	...	...	...	...
4202	Currency and deposits	15	...	...	...	...	...	...	...	...	...	...	...
4203	Debt securities	—	...	...	...	...	...	...	...	...	...	...	...
4204	Loans	—	...	...	...	...	...	...	...	...	...	...	...
4205	Equity and investment fund shares	134	...	...	...	...	...	...	...	...	...	...	...
4206	Insurance, pension, and standardized guarantee schemes	—	...	...	...	...	...	...	...	...	...	...	...
4207	Financial derivatives and employee stock options	—	...	...	...	...	...	...	...	...	...	...	...
4208	Other accounts receivable	—	...	...	...	...	...	...	...	...	...	...	...
	By debtor												
421	Domestic debtors	...	...	...	...	...	...	...	...	...	...	...	...
422	External debtors	...	...	...	...	...	...	...	...	...	...	...	...
43	**Holding gains and losses in liabilities**	**20**	...	...	...	...	...	...	...	...	...	...	...
	By instrument												
4301	Special Drawing Rights (SDRs)	—	...	...	...	...	...	...	...	...	...	...	...
4302	Currency and deposits	—	...	...	...	...	...	...	...	...	...	...	...
4303	Debt securities	107	...	...	...	...	...	...	...	...	...	...	...
4304	Loans	-87	...	...	...	...	...	...	...	...	...	...	...
4305	Equity and investment fund shares	—	...	...	...	...	...	...	...	...	...	...	...
4306	Insurance, pension, and standardized guarantee schemes	—	...	...	...	...	...	...	...	...	...	...	...
4307	Financial derivatives and employee stock options	—	...	...	...	...	...	...	...	...	...	...	...
4308	Other accounts payable	—	...	...	...	...	...	...	...	...	...	...	...
	By creditor												
431	Domestic creditors	...	...	...	...	...	...	...	...	...	...	...	...
432	External creditors	...	...	...	...	...	...	...	...	...	...	...	...
	Table 5 Holding gains and losses in assets and liabilities												
	Table 6 Balance sheet												
6	**Net worth**	...	...	...	...	...	...	...	...	...	...	...	...
61	**Nonfinancial assets**	...	...	...	...	...	...	...	...	...	...	...	...
611	Fixed assets	...	...	...	...	...	...	...	...	...	...	...	...
6111	Buildings and structures	...	...	...	...	...	...	...	...	...	...	...	...
6112	Machinery and equipment	...	...	...	...	...	...	...	...	...	...	...	...
6113	Other fixed assets	...	...	...	...	...	...	...	...	...	...	...	...
6114	Weapons systems	...	...	...	...	...	...	...	...	...	...	...	...
612	Inventories	...	...	...	...	...	...	...	...	...	...	...	...
613	Valuables	...	...	...	...	...	...	...	...	...	...	...	...
614	Nonproduced assets	...	...	...	...	...	...	...	...	...	...	...	...
6141	Land	...	...	...	...	...	...	...	...	...	...	...	...

Bosnia and Herzegovina (963)

In Millions of Convertible Marka (BAM) / Fiscal Year Ends December 31st

		Budgetary Central Government			Central Government (excl. Social Security)			Central Government (incl. Social Security)			General Government		
		2013	2014	2015	2013	2014	2015	2013	2014	2015	2013	2014	2015
6142	Mineral and energy resources	...	...	...	...	...	...	...	...	...	...	...	...
6143	Other naturally occurring assets	...	...	...	...	...	...	...	...	...	...	...	...
6144	Intangible nonproduced assets	...	...	...	...	...	...	...	...	...	...	...	...
62	**Financial assets**	**8,438**	**9,028**	**...**	**7,474**	**7,790**	**...**	**...**	**...**	**...**	**9,207**	**9,366**	**...**
	By instrument												
6201	Monetary gold and SDRs	3	5	...	3	5	...	3	5	...	3	5	...
6202	Currency and deposits	1,092	1,279	...	1,171	1,399	...	...	1,656	...	1,637	1,869	...
6203	Debt securities	2	4	...	2	4	...	...	4	...	3	4	...
6204	Loans	3,456	3,990	...	2,295	2,565	...	...	...	...	2,058	2,215	...
6205	Equity and investment fund shares	3,149	3,095	...	3,149	3,095	...	...	3,383	...	3,591	3,541	...
6206	Insurance, pension, and standardized guarantee schemes	—	—	...	—	—	...	...	—	...	—	—	...
6207	Financial derivatives and employee stock options	—	—	...	—	—	...	...	—	...	—	—	...
6208	Other accounts receivable	737	654	...	855	722	...	...	1,377	...	1,916	1,733	...
	By debtor												
621	Domestic debtors	8,244	8,885	...	7,279	7,647	...	...	...	...	9,012	9,223	...
622	External debtors	195	143	...	195	143	...	...	478	...	195	143	...
63	**Liabilities**	**11,909**	**13,077**	**...**	**12,303**	**13,672**	**...**	**...**	**...**	**...**	**14,432**	**15,807**	**...**
	By instrument												
6301	Special Drawing Rights (SDRs)	352	376	...	352	376	...	352	376	...	352	376	...
6302	Currency and deposits	—	—	...	—	—	...	...	—	...	—	—	...
6303	Debt securities	1,770	1,990	...	1,770	1,990	...	...	1,990	...	1,822	2,040	...
6304	Loans	7,425	8,440	...	7,511	8,705	...	...	...	...	7,963	9,183	...
6305	Equity and investment fund shares	—	—	...	—	—	...	...	—	...	—	—	...
6306	Insurance, pension, and standardized guarantee schemes	—	—	...	—	—	...	...	—	...	—	—	...
6307	Financial derivatives and employee stock options	—	—	...	—	—	...	...	—	...	—	—	...
6308	Other accounts payable	2,362	2,272	...	2,671	2,601	...	...	3,555	...	4,295	4,209	...
	By creditor												
631	Domestic creditors	4,147	4,477	...	4,337	4,822	...	...	...	...	6,454	6,948	...
632	External creditors	7,761	8,601	...	7,966	8,850	...	...	8,858	...	7,979	8,859	...
	Memorandum items												
6M2	Net financial worth	-3,470	-4,050	...	-4,829	-5,881	...	-4,886	...	...	-5,225	-6,441	...
6M3	Gross debt (D4) at market value	...	...	...	...	...	...	...	...	...	...	...	...
6M3D3	D3 debt liabilities at market value	...	...	...	...	...	...	...	...	...	...	...	...
6M3D2	D2 debt liabilities at market value	...	...	...	...	...	...	...	...	...	...	...	...
6M3D1	D1 debt liabilities at market value	...	...	...	...	...	...	...	...	...	...	...	...
6M4	Gross debt (D4) at nominal value	...	...	...	...	...	...	...	...	...	...	...	...
6M4D3	D3 debt liabilities at nominal value	...	...	...	...	...	...	...	...	...	...	...	...
6M4D2	D2 debt liabilities at nominal value	...	...	...	...	...	...	...	...	...	...	...	...
6M4D1	D1 debt liabilities at nominal value	...	...	...	...	...	...	...	...	...	...	...	...
6M35	Gross debt (D4) at face value	11,909	13,077	...	12,303	13,672	...	...	...	...	14,432	15,807	...
6M35D3	D3 debt liabilities at face value	11,909	13,077	...	12,303	13,672	...	...	...	...	14,432	15,807	...
6M35D2	D2 debt liabilities at face value	9,547	10,806	...	9,632	11,071	...	...	...	...	10,137	11,598	...
6M35D1	D1 debt liabilities at face value	9,195	10,430	...	9,280	10,695	...	...	...	...	9,785	11,222	...
6M93	Government gross debt per national definition	...	...	...	...	...	...	...	...	...	...	...	...
6M5	Arrears	...	...	...	...	...	...	...	...	...	...	...	...
6M6	Explicit contingent liabilities	...	...	...	...	...	...	...	...	...	...	...	...
6M61	of which: Publicly guaranteed debt	...	...	...	...	...	...	...	...	...	...	...	...
6M7	Net implicit obligations for social security benefits	...	...	...	...	...	...	...	...	...	...	...	...
	Table 7 Expenditure by functions of government												
7	**Expenditure**	**5,865**	**6,416**	**6,101**	**6,640**	**7,023**	**6,470**	**10,915**	**11,956**	**10,975**	**11,986**	**12,517**	**12,143**
701	**General public services**	**...**	**...**	**...**	**...**	**...**	**...**	**...**	**...**	**...**	**...**	**...**	**...**
7017	Public debt transactions	159	293	208	167	201	223	179	214	240	201	239	264
7018	Transfers of general character between levels of government	...	...	...	...	...	...	...	...	...	...	...	...
702	**Defense**	**...**	**...**	**...**	**...**	**...**	**...**	**...**	**...**	**...**	**...**	**...**	**...**

Bosnia and Herzegovina (963)

In Millions of Convertible Marka (BAM) / Fiscal Year Ends December 31st

		Budgetary Central Government			Central Government (excl. Social Security)			Central Government (incl. Social Security)			General Government		
		2013	2014	2015	2013	2014	2015	2013	2014	2015	2013	2014	2015
703	**Public order and safety**	...	...	...	...	...	...	...	...	...	...	...	...
704	**Economic affairs**	...	...	...	...	...	...	...	...	...	...	...	...
7042	Agriculture, forestry, fishing, and hunting	...	...	...	...	...	...	...	...	...	...	...	...
7043	Fuel and energy	...	...	...	...	...	...	...	...	...	...	...	...
7044	Mining, manufacturing, and construction	...	...	...	...	...	...	...	...	...	...	...	...
7045	Transport	...	...	...	...	...	...	...	...	...	...	...	...
7046	Communication	...	...	...	...	...	...	...	...	...	...	...	...
705	**Environmental protection**	...	...	...	...	...	...	...	...	...	...	...	...
706	**Housing and community amenities**	...	...	...	...	...	...	...	...	...	...	...	...
707	**Health**	...	...	...	...	...	...	...	...	...	...	...	...
7072	Outpatient services	...	...	...	...	...	...	...	...	...	...	...	...
7073	Hospital services	...	...	...	...	...	...	...	...	...	...	...	...
7074	Public health services	...	...	...	...	...	...	...	...	...	...	...	...
708	**Recreation, culture and religion**	...	...	...	...	...	...	...	...	...	...	...	...
709	**Education**	...	...	...	...	...	...	...	...	...	...	...	...
7091	Pre-primary and primary education	...	...	...	...	...	...	...	...	...	...	...	...
7092	Secondary education	...	...	...	...	...	...	...	...	...	...	...	...
7094	Tertiary education	...	...	...	...	...	...	...	...	...	...	...	...
710	**Social protection**	...	...	...	...	...	...	...	...	...	...	...	...
7z	Statistical discrepancy: Expenditure	...	...	...	...	...	...	...	...	...	...	...	...
	Table 8 Financial transactions by counterpart sector												
32	**Net acquisition of financial assets**	**532**	**953**	**48**	**292**	**160**	**62**	**235**	**44**	**62**	**276**	**90**	**50**
321	Domestic debtors	512	1,008	69	273	214	83	215	98	84	256	144	71
8211	General government	...	...	...	...	...	...	...	...	...	...	...	...
8212	Central bank	...	...	...	...	...	...	...	...	...	...	...	...
8213	Deposit-taking corporations except the central bank	...	...	...	...	...	...	...	...	...	...	...	...
8214	Other financial corporations	...	...	...	...	...	...	...	...	...	...	...	...
8215	Nonfinancial corporations	...	...	...	...	...	...	...	...	...	...	...	...
8216	Households & nonprofit institutions serving households	...	...	...	...	...	...	...	...	...	...	...	...
322	External debtors	20	-54	-22	20	-54	-22	20	-54	-22	20	-54	-22
8221	General government	...	...	...	...	...	...	...	...	...	...	...	...
8227	International organizations	...	...	...	...	...	...	...	...	...	...	...	...
8228	Financial corporations other than international organizations	...	...	...	...	...	...	...	...	...	...	...	...
8229	Other nonresidents	...	...	...	...	...	...	...	...	...	...	...	...
33	**Net incurrence of liabilities**	**467**	**920**	**75**	**753**	**599**	**114**	**789**	**629**	**186**	**848**	**648**	**102**
331	Domestic creditors	42	609	281	290	244	283	326	277	354	384	296	270
8311	General government	...	...	...	...	...	...	...	...	...	...	...	...
8312	Central bank	...	...	...	...	...	...	...	...	...	...	...	...
8313	Deposit-taking corporations except the central bank	...	...	...	...	...	...	...	...	...	...	...	...
8314	Other financial corporations	...	...	...	...	...	...	...	...	...	...	...	...
8315	Nonfinancial corporations	...	...	...	...	...	...	...	...	...	...	...	...
8316	Households & nonprofit institutions serving households	...	...	...	...	...	...	...	...	...	...	...	...
332	External creditors	425	312	-206	463	355	-169	463	352	-168	463	352	-168
8321	General government	...	...	...	...	...	...	...	...	...	...	...	...
8327	International organizations	...	...	...	...	...	...	...	...	...	...	...	...
8328	Financial corporations other than international organizations	...	...	...	...	...	...	...	...	...	...	...	...
8329	Other nonresidents	...	...	...	...	...	...	...	...	...	...	...	...
	Table 9 Total other economic flows in assets and liabilities												

Botswana (616)

In Millions of Botswana Pula (BWP) / Fiscal Year Ends March 31st

		Budgetary Central Government			Central Government (excl. Social Security)			Central Government (incl. Social Security)			General Government		
		2012	2013	2014	2012	2013	2014	2012	2013	2014	2012	2013	2014
	Statement of operations												
1	Revenue	41,591	48,882	55,843	...	...	...	...	...	...	...	...	...
2	Expense	33,493	35,344	40,453	...	...	...	...	...	...	...	...	...
GOB	**Gross operating balance**	**8,098**	**13,538**	**15,390**	...	...	...	...	...	...	...	...	...
NOB	**Net operating balance**	...	...	...	...	...	...	...	...	...	...	...	...
31	Net/Gross investment in nonfinancial assets	6,828	6,737	10,140	...	...	...	...	...	...	...	...	...
2M	Expenditure	40,321	42,080	50,594	...	...	...	...	...	...	...	...	...
NLB	**Net lending (+) / Net borrowing (-)**	**1,270**	**6,802**	**5,249**	...	...	...	...	...	...	...	...	...
32	Net acquisition of financial assets	-1,181	8,323	6,255	...	...	...	...	...	...	...	...	...
33	Net incurrence of liabilities	-2,451	1,521	1,005	...	...	...	...	...	...	...	...	...
NLBz	Statistical discrepancy	0	0	0	...	...	...	...	...	...	...	...	...
	Memorandum items												
PB	Primary net lending / net borrowing	1,942	7,489	5,951	...	...	...	...	...	...	...	...	...
GB	Government balance per national definition	...	...	...	...	...	...	...	...	...	...	...	...
	Statement of other economic flows												
	Balance sheet												
	Table 1 Revenue												
1	**Revenue**	**41,591**	**48,882**	**55,843**	...	...	...	...	...	...	...	...	...
11	**Taxes**	**29,792**	**32,053**	**37,621**	...	...	...	...	...	...	...	...	...
111	Taxes on income, profits, and capital gains	9,987	13,661	15,882	...	...	...	...	...	...	...	...	...
1111	Payable by individuals	—	—	—	...	...	...	...	...	...	...	...	...
1112	Payable by corporations and other enterprises	3,262	6,190	7,498	...	...	...	...	...	...	...	...	...
1113	Other taxes on income, profits, and capital gains	6,725	7,471	8,384	...	...	...	...	...	...	...	...	...
112	Taxes on payroll and workforce	—	—	—	...	...	...	...	...	...	...	...	...
113	Taxes on property	51	55	54	...	...	...	...	...	...	...	...	...
114	Taxes on goods and services	5,536	5,166	5,993	...	...	...	...	...	...	...	...	...
1141	General taxes on goods and services	5,283	4,885	5,710	...	...	...	...	...	...	...	...	...
1142	Excises	—	—	—	...	...	...	...	...	...	...	...	...
115	Taxes on international trade and transactions	14,218	13,172	15,692	...	...	...	...	...	...	...	...	...
116	Other taxes	—	—	—	...	...	...	...	...	...	...	...	...
12	**Social contributions**	—	—	—	...	...	...	...	...	...	...	...	...
121	Social security contributions	—	—	—	...	...	...	...	...	...	...	...	...
122	Other social contributions	—	—	—	...	...	...	...	...	...	...	...	...
13	**Grants**	**507**	**326**	**380**	...	...	...	...	...	...	...	...	...
131	From foreign governments	...	...	...	...	...	...	...	...	...	...	...	...
132	From international organizations	...	...	...	...	...	...	...	...	...	...	...	...
133	From other general government units	...	...	...	...	...	...	...	...	...	...	...	...
1331	Current	...	...	...	...	...	...	...	...	...	...	...	...
1332	Capital	...	...	...	...	...	...	...	...	...	...	...	...
14	**Other revenue**	**11,293**	**16,503**	**17,842**	...	...	...	...	...	...	...	...	...
	Table 2 Expense by economic type												
2	**Expense**	**33,493**	**35,344**	**40,453**	...	...	...	...	...	...	...	...	...
21	**Compensation of employees**	**14,548**	**15,338**	**16,589**	...	...	...	...	...	...	...	...	...
211	Wages and salaries	...	...	...	...	...	...	...	...	...	...	...	...
212	Employers' social contributions	...	...	...	...	...	...	...	...	...	...	...	...
22	**Use of goods and services**	**10,183**	**10,856**	**13,019**	...	...	...	...	...	...	...	...	...
23	**Consumption of fixed capital**	...	...	...	...	...	...	...	...	...	...	...	...
24	**Interest**	**672**	**687**	**702**	...	...	...	...	...	...	...	...	...
25	**Subsidies**	...	...	...	...	...	...	...	...	...	...	...	...
26	**Grants**	...	...	...	...	...	...	...	...	...	...	...	...
261	To foreign governments	...	...	...	...	...	...	...	...	...	...	...	...
262	To international organizations	...	...	...	...	...	...	...	...	...	...	...	...
263	To other general government units	...	...	...	...	...	...	...	...	...	...	...	...
2631	Current	...	...	...	...	...	...	...	...	...	...	...	...
2632	Capital	...	...	...	...	...	...	...	...	...	...	...	...

Botswana (616)

In Millions of Botswana Pula (BWP) / Fiscal Year Ends March 31st

		Budgetary Central Government			Central Government (excl. Social Security)			Central Government (incl. Social Security)			General Government		
		2012	2013	2014	2012	2013	2014	2012	2013	2014	2012	2013	2014
27	**Social benefits**	...	...	...	...	...	...	...	...	...	...	...	...
271	Social security benefits	...	...	...	...	...	...	...	...	...	...	...	...
272	Social assistance benefits	...	...	...	...	...	...	...	...	...	...	...	...
273	Employment-related social benefits	...	...	...	...	...	...	...	...	...	...	...	...
28	**Other expense**	...	...	...	...	...	...	...	...	...	...	...	...
281	Property expense other than interest	...	...	...	...	...	...	...	...	...	...	...	...
282	Transfers not elsewhere classified	...	...	...	...	...	...	...	...	...	...	...	...
2821	Current	...	...	...	...	...	...	...	...	...	...	...	...
2822	Capital	...	...	...	...	...	...	...	...	...	...	...	...
	Table 3 Transactions in assets and liabilities												
3	**Change in net worth from transactions**	...	...	...	...	...	...	...	...	...	...	...	...
31	**Net/Gross investment in nonfinancial assets**	**6,828**	**6,737**	**10,140**	...	...	...	...	...	...	...	...	...
311	Fixed assets	...	...	...	...	...	...	...	...	...	...	...	...
3111	Buildings and structures	...	...	...	...	...	...	...	...	...	...	...	...
3112	Machinery and equipment	...	...	...	...	...	...	...	...	...	...	...	...
3113	Other fixed assets	...	...	...	...	...	...	...	...	...	...	...	...
3114	Weapons systems	...	...	...	...	...	...	...	...	...	...	...	...
312	Inventories	...	...	...	...	...	...	...	...	...	...	...	...
313	Valuables	...	...	...	...	...	...	...	...	...	...	...	...
314	Nonproduced assets	...	...	...	...	...	...	...	...	...	...	...	...
3141	Land	...	...	...	...	...	...	...	...	...	...	...	...
3142	Mineral and energy resources	...	...	...	...	...	...	...	...	...	...	...	...
3143	Other naturally occurring assets	...	...	...	...	...	...	...	...	...	...	...	...
3144	Intangible nonproduced assets	...	...	...	...	...	...	...	...	...	...	...	...
32	**Net acquisition of financial assets**	**-1,181**	**8,323**	**6,255**	...	...	...	...	...	...	...	...	...
	By instrument												
3201	Monetary gold and SDRs	—	—	—	...	...	...	...	...	...	...	...	...
3202	Currency and deposits	2,435	-8,722	-6,346	...	...	...	...	...	...	...	...	...
3203	Debt securities	...	...	...	...	...	...	...	...	...	...	...	...
3204	Loans	...	...	...	...	...	...	...	...	...	...	...	...
3205	Equity and investment fund shares	...	...	...	...	...	...	...	...	...	...	...	...
3206	Insurance, pension, and standardized guarantee schemes	...	...	...	...	...	...	...	...	...	...	...	...
3207	Financial derivatives and employee stock options	...	...	...	...	...	...	...	...	...	...	...	...
3208	Other accounts receivable	...	...	...	...	...	...	...	...	...	...	...	...
	By debtor												
321	Domestic debtors	-1,181	8,323	6,255	...	...	...	...	...	...	...	...	...
322	External debtors	—	—	—	...	...	...	...	...	...	...	...	...
33	**Net incurrence of liabilities**	**-2,451**	**1,521**	**1,005**	...	...	...	...	...	...	...	...	...
	By instrument												
3301	Special Drawing Rights (SDRs)	...	...	...	...	...	...	...	...	...	...	...	...
3302	Currency and deposits	...	...	...	...	...	...	...	...	...	...	...	...
3303	Debt securities	...	...	...	...	...	...	...	...	...	...	...	...
3304	Loans	...	...	...	...	...	...	...	...	...	...	...	...
3305	Equity and investment fund shares	...	...	...	...	...	...	...	...	...	...	...	...
3306	Insurance, pension, and standardized guarantee schemes	...	...	...	...	...	...	...	...	...	...	...	...
3307	Financial derivatives and employee stock options	...	...	...	...	...	...	...	...	...	...	...	...
3308	Other accounts payable	...	...	...	...	...	...	...	...	...	...	...	...
	By creditor												
331	Domestic creditors	-1,437	1,588	1,638	...	...	...	...	...	...	...	...	...
332	External creditors	-1,014	-66	-633	...	...	...	...	...	...	...	...	...
	Table 4 Holding gains and losses in assets and liabilities												
	Table 5 Holding gains and losses in assets and liabilities												
	Table 6 Balance sheet												

Botswana (616)

In Millions of Botswana Pula (BWP) / Fiscal Year Ends March 31st

	Budgetary Central Government			Central Government (excl. Social Security)			Central Government (incl. Social Security)			General Government		
	2012	2013	2014	2012	2013	2014	2012	2013	2014	2012	2013	2014
Table 7 Expenditure by functions of government												
Table 8 Financial transactions by counterpart sector												
Table 9 Total other economic flows in assets and liabilities												

Brazil (223)

In Billions of Brazilian Reais (BRL) / Fiscal Year Ends December 31st

		Budgetary Central Government			Central Government (excl. Social Security)			Central Government (incl. Social Security)			General Government		
		2013	2014	2015	2013	2014	2015	2013	2014	2015	2013	2014	2015
	Statement of operations												
1	Revenue	...	...	...	1,503	1,553	1,729	1,503	1,553	1,729	2,134	2,246	2,450
2	Expense	...	...	...	1,628	1,834	2,196	1,628	1,834	2,196	2,246	2,529	2,974
GOB	**Gross operating balance**	...	...	...	**-103**	**-257**	**-438**	**-103**	**-257**	**-438**	**-42**	**-204**	**-437**
NOB	**Net operating balance**	...	...	...	**-125**	**-281**	**-466**	**-125**	**-281**	**-466**	**-112**	**-282**	**-524**
31	Net/Gross investment in nonfinancial assets	...	...	...	7	8	-6	7	8	-6	42	53	8
2M	Expenditure	...	...	...	1,635	1,842	2,190	1,635	1,842	2,190	2,288	2,581	2,983
NLB	**Net lending (+) / Net borrowing (-)**	...	...	...	**-132**	**-289**	**-460**	**-132**	**-289**	**-460**	**-154**	**-335**	**-533**
32	Net acquisition of financial assets	...	...	...	13	19	-1	13	19	-1	4	2	-61
33	Net incurrence of liabilities	...	...	...	154	314	543	154	314	543	189	361	573
NLBz	Statistical discrepancy	...	...	...	-9	-5	-84	-9	-5	-84	-31	-24	-101
	Memorandum items												
PB	Primary net lending / net borrowing	...	...	...	252	158	268	252	158	268	235	120	210
GB	Government balance per national definition	...	...	...	...	...	...	...	...	...	...	...	...
	Statement of other economic flows												
9	**Change in net worth due to other economic flows**	...	...	...	...	...	...	...	...	...	...	...	...
4	Change in net worth due to holding gains and losses	...	...	...	...	...	...	...	...	...	...	...	...
41	Nonfinancial assets	...	...	...	...	...	...	...	...	...	...	...	...
42	Financial assets	...	...	...	95	107	460	95	107	460	95	107	460
43	Liabilities	...	...	...	14	13	47	14	13	47	20	23	86
5	Change in net worth due to volume changes	...	...	...	...	...	...	...	...	...	...	...	...
51	Nonfinancial assets	...	...	...	...	...	...	...	...	...	...	...	...
52	Financial assets	...	...	...	33	18	-16	33	18	-16	33	19	-16
53	Liabilities	...	...	...	2	-0	81	2	-0	81	2	0	81
	Balance sheet												
6	**Net worth**	...	...	...	...	...	...	...	...	...	...	...	...
61	Nonfinancial assets	...	...	...	...	...	...	...	...	...	...	...	...
62	Financial assets	...	...	...	1,961	2,106	2,549	1,961	2,106	2,549	1,517	1,645	2,029
63	Liabilities	...	...	...	3,051	3,378	4,049	3,051	3,378	4,049	3,177	3,561	4,301
	Table 1 Revenue												
1	**Revenue**	...	...	...	**1,503**	**1,553**	**1,729**	**1,503**	**1,553**	**1,729**	**2,134**	**2,246**	**2,450**
11	**Taxes**	...	...	...	**717**	**737**	**769**	**717**	**737**	**769**	**1,243**	**1,305**	**1,366**
111	Taxes on income, profits, and capital gains	...	...	...	326	342	355	326	342	355	361	382	401
1111	Payable by individuals	...	...	...	92	100	103	92	100	103	127	141	149
1112	Payable by corporations and other enterprises	...	...	...	171	172	164	171	172	164	171	172	164
1113	Other taxes on income, profits, and capital gains	...	...	...	63	70	88	63	70	88	63	70	88
112	Taxes on payroll and workforce	...	...	...	19	21	21	19	21	21	19	21	21
113	Taxes on property	...	...	...	1	1	1	1	1	1	69	76	86
114	Taxes on goods and services	...	...	...	333	337	353	333	337	353	756	789	818
1141	General taxes on goods and services	...	...	...	314	317	328	314	317	328	726	757	779
1142	Excises	...	...	...	1	0	4	1	0	4	1	0	4
115	Taxes on international trade and transactions	...	...	...	37	37	40	37	37	40	37	37	40
116	Other taxes	...	...	...	1	0	-0	1	0	-0	1	0	1
12	**Social contributions**	...	...	...	**485**	**526**	**548**	**485**	**526**	**548**	**564**	**613**	**645**
121	Social security contributions	...	...	...	393	424	439	393	424	439	393	504	439
122	Other social contributions	...	...	...	92	102	109	92	102	109	171	109	206
13	**Grants**	...	...	...	**0**	**1**	**1**	**0**	**1**	**1**	**0**	**0**	**0**
131	From foreign governments	...	...	...	—	—	—	—	—	—	—	—	—
132	From international organizations	...	...	...	0	0	0	0	0	0	0	0	0
133	From other general government units	...	...	...	0	0	1	0	0	1	—	—	0
1331	Current	...	...	...	0	0	0	0	0	0	—	—	0
1332	Capital	...	...	...	0	0	0	0	0	0	-0	0	—
14	**Other revenue**	...	...	...	**301**	**289**	**412**	**301**	**289**	**412**	**327**	**328**	**438**

Brazil (223)

In Billions of Brazilian Reais (BRL) / Fiscal Year Ends December 31st

		Budgetary Central Government			Central Government (excl. Social Security)			Central Government (incl. Social Security)			General Government		
		2013	2014	2015	2013	2014	2015	2013	2014	2015	2013	2014	2015
	Table 2 Expense by economic type												
2	**Expense**	...	...	...	**1,628**	**1,834**	**2,196**	**1,628**	**1,834**	**2,196**	**2,246**	**2,529**	**2,974**
21	**Compensation of employees**	...	...	...	**201**	**220**	**242**	**201**	**220**	**242**	**647**	**710**	**776**
211	Wages and salaries	...	...	...	121	132	148	121	132	148	493	541	592
212	Employers' social contributions	...	...	...	79	88	94	79	88	94	155	169	183
22	**Use of goods and services**	...	...	...	**59**	**64**	**70**	**59**	**64**	**70**	**287**	**319**	**322**
23	**Consumption of fixed capital**	...	...	...	**22**	**25**	**28**	**22**	**25**	**28**	**70**	**78**	**88**
24	**Interest**	...	...	...	**384**	**447**	**729**	**384**	**447**	**729**	**389**	**455**	**743**
25	**Subsidies**	...	...	...	**25**	**30**	**21**	**25**	**30**	**21**	**26**	**30**	**21**
26	**Grants**	...	...	...	**284**	**314**	**315**	**284**	**314**	**315**	**2**	**3**	**3**
261	To foreign governments	...	...	...	—	—	—	—	—	—	—	—	—
262	To international organizations	...	...	...	2	3	3	2	3	3	2	3	3
263	To other general government units	...	...	...	283	310	313	283	310	313	-0	—	-0
2631	Current	...	...	...	268	294	299	268	294	299	-0	—	—
2632	Capital	...	...	...	14	17	13	14	17	13	-0	—	—
27	**Social benefits**	...	...	...	**629**	**707**	**767**	**629**	**707**	**767**	**758**	**856**	**934**
271	Social security benefits	...	...	...	402	455	492	402	455	492	402	455	492
272	Social assistance benefits	...	...	...	62	69	72	62	69	72	66	74	77
273	Employment-related social benefits	...	...	...	164	183	204	164	183	204	289	327	365
28	**Other expense**	...	...	...	**23**	**28**	**23**	**23**	**28**	**23**	**67**	**76**	**88**
281	Property expense other than interest	...	...	...	—	—	—	—	—	—	0	0	0
282	Transfers not elsewhere classified	...	...	...	23	28	23	23	28	23	67	76	88
2821	Current	...	...	...	7	7	8	7	7	8	50	54	71
2822	Capital	...	...	...	16	21	16	16	21	16	18	22	17
	Table 3 Transactions in assets and liabilities												
3	**Change in net worth from transactions**	...	...	...	**-134**	**-287**	**-550**	**-134**	**-287**	**-550**	**-144**	**-306**	**-625**
31	**Net/Gross investment in nonfinancial assets**	...	...	...	**7**	**8**	**-6**	**7**	**8**	**-6**	**42**	**53**	**8**
311	Fixed assets	...	...	...	11	14	-3	11	14	-3	45	60	12
3111	Buildings and structures	...	...	...	7	9	-2	7	9	-2	35	47	11
3112	Machinery and equipment	...	...	...	3	4	-1	3	4	-1	9	11	1
3113	Other fixed assets	...	...	...	1	1	-0	1	1	-0	1	1	-0
3114	Weapons systems	...	...	...	0	0	-0	0	0	-0	0	0	-0
312	Inventories	...	...	...	-1	0	1	-1	0	1	-0	0	2
313	Valuables	...	...	...	0	0	0	0	0	0	0	0	0
314	Nonproduced assets	...	...	...	-3	-7	-5	-3	-7	-5	-3	-7	-5
3141	Land	...	...	...	0	0	0	0	0	0	0	0	0
3142	Mineral and energy resources	...	...	...	—	—	—	—	—	—	—	—	—
3143	Other naturally occurring assets	...	...	...	—	—	—	—	—	—	—	—	—
3144	Intangible nonproduced assets	...	...	...	-3	-7	-5	-3	-7	-5	-3	-7	-5
32	**Net acquisition of financial assets**	...	...	...	**13**	**19**	**-1**	**13**	**19**	**-1**	**4**	**2**	**-61**
	By instrument												
3201	Monetary gold and SDRs	...	...	...	—	—	—	—	—	—	—	—	—
3202	Currency and deposits	...	...	...	-59	-71	-61	-59	-71	-61	-49	-73	-69
3203	Debt securities	...	...	...	—	—	—	—	—	—	—	—	—
3204	Loans	...	...	...	72	90	60	72	90	60	53	75	8
3205	Equity and investment fund shares	...	...	...	—	—	—	—	—	—	—	—	—
3206	Insurance, pension, and standardized guarantee schemes	...	...	...	—	—	—	—	—	—	—	—	—
3207	Financial derivatives and employee stock options	...	...	...	—	—	—	—	—	—	—	—	—
3208	Other accounts receivable	...	...	...	...	...	...	...	...	...	...	...	...
	By debtor												
321	Domestic debtors	...	...	...	14	20	-0	14	20	-0	4	2	-60
322	External debtors	...	...	...	-1	-0	-0	-1	-0	-0	-1	-0	-0
33	**Net incurrence of liabilities**	...	...	...	**154**	**314**	**543**	**154**	**314**	**543**	**189**	**361**	**573**
	By instrument												
3301	Special Drawing Rights (SDRs)	...	...	...	—	—	—	—	—	—	—	—	—
3302	Currency and deposits	...	...	...	—	—	—	—	—	—	—	—	—
3303	Debt securities	...	...	...	162	315	540	162	315	540	163	315	540
3304	Loans	...	...	...	-8	-1	4	-8	-1	4	26	46	33

Brazil (223)

In Billions of Brazilian Reais (BRL) / Fiscal Year Ends December 31st

		Budgetary Central Government			Central Government (excl. Social Security)			Central Government (incl. Social Security)			General Government		
		2013	2014	2015	2013	2014	2015	2013	2014	2015	2013	2014	2015
3305	Equity and investment fund shares	...	...	...	—	—	—	—	—	—	—	—	—
3306	Insurance, pension, and standardized guarantee schemes	...	...	...	—	—	—	—	—	—	—	—	—
3307	Financial derivatives and employee stock options	...	...	...	—	—	—	—	—	—	—	—	—
3308	Other accounts payable	...	...	...	...	...	...	...	...	...	...	...	...
	By creditor												
331	Domestic creditors	...	...	...	145	281	482	145	281	482	168	315	507
332	External creditors	...	...	...	9	32	62	9	32	62	21	46	66
	Table 4 Holding gains and losses in assets and liabilities												
4	**Change in net worth due to holding gains and losses**	...	...	...	...	...	...	...	...	...	...	...	...
41	**Holding gains and losses in nonfinancial assets**	...	...	...	...	...	...	...	...	...	...	...	...
411	Fixed assets	...	...	...	...	...	...	...	...	...	...	...	...
412	Inventories	...	...	...	...	...	...	...	...	...	...	...	...
413	Valuables	...	...	...	...	...	...	...	...	...	...	...	...
414	Nonproduced assets	...	...	...	...	...	...	...	...	...	...	...	...
42	**Holding gains and losses in financial assets**	...	...	...	**95**	**107**	**460**	**95**	**107**	**460**	**95**	**107**	**460**
	By instrument												
4201	Monetary gold and SDRs	...	...	...	—	—	—	—	—	—	—	—	—
4202	Currency and deposits	...	...	...	90	104	446	90	104	446	90	104	446
4203	Debt securities	...	...	...	—	—	—	—	—	—	—	—	—
4204	Loans	...	...	...	5	2	14	5	2	14	5	2	14
4205	Equity and investment fund shares	...	...	...	—	—	—	—	—	...	—	—	—
4206	Insurance, pension, and standardized guarantee schemes	...	...	...	—	—	—	—	—	...	—	—	—
4207	Financial derivatives and employee stock options	...	...	...	—	—	—	—	—	...	—	—	—
4208	Other accounts receivable	...	...	...	...	...	...	...	...	...	...	...	...
	By debtor												
421	Domestic debtors	...	...	...	95	107	460	95	107	460	95	107	460
422	External debtors	...	...	...	0	0	0	0	0	0	0	0	0
43	**Holding gains and losses in liabilities**	...	...	...	**14**	**13**	**47**	**14**	**13**	**47**	**20**	**23**	**86**
	By instrument												
4301	Special Drawing Rights (SDRs)	...	...	...	—	—	—	—	—	—	—	—	—
4302	Currency and deposits	...	...	...	—	—	—	—	—	—	—	—	—
4303	Debt securities	...	...	...	13	13	44	13	13	44	13	13	44
4304	Loans	...	...	...	1	1	3	1	1	3	7	10	42
4305	Equity and investment fund shares	...	...	...	—	—	—	—	—	—	—	—	—
4306	Insurance, pension, and standardized guarantee schemes	...	...	...	—	—	—	—	—	—	—	—	—
4307	Financial derivatives and employee stock options	...	...	...	—	—	—	—	—	—	—	—	—
4308	Other accounts payable	...	...	...	...	...	...	...	...	...	...	...	...
	By creditor												
431	Domestic creditors	...	...	...	-58	-54	0	-58	-54	0	-58	-54	0
432	External creditors	...	...	...	72	68	47	72	68	47	78	77	86
	Table 5 Holding gains and losses in assets and liabilities												
5	**Change in net worth due to other volume changes**	...	...	...	...	...	...	...	...	...	...	...	...
51	**Other volume changes in nonfinancial assets**	...	...	...	...	...	...	...	...	...	...	...	...
511	Fixed assets	...	...	...	...	...	...	...	...	...	...	...	...
512	Inventories	...	...	...	...	...	...	...	...	...	...	...	...
513	Valuables	...	...	...	...	...	...	...	...	...	...	...	...
514	Nonproduced assets	...	...	...	...	...	...	...	...	...	...	...	...
52	**Other volume changes in financial assets**	...	...	...	**33**	**18**	**-16**	**33**	**18**	**-16**	**33**	**19**	**-16**

Brazil (223)

In Billions of Brazilian Reais (BRL) / Fiscal Year Ends December 31st

		Budgetary Central Government			Central Government (excl. Social Security)			Central Government (incl. Social Security)			General Government		
		2013	2014	2015	2013	2014	2015	2013	2014	2015	2013	2014	2015
	By instrument												
5201	Monetary gold and SDRs	...	...	...	—	—	—	—	—	—	—	—	—
5202	Currency and deposits	...	...	...	33	19	-16	33	19	-16	33	19	-16
5203	Debt securities	...	...	...	—	—	—	—	—	—	—	—	—
5204	Loans	...	...	...	0	-1	-0	0	-1	-0	—	—	0
5205	Equity and investment fund shares	...	...	...	—	—	...	—	—	...	—	—	...
5206	Insurance, pension, and standardized guarantee schemes	...	...	...	—	—	...	—	—	...	—	—	...
5207	Financial derivatives and employee stock options	...	...	...	—	—	...	—	—	...	—	—	...
5208	Other accounts receivable	...	...	...	...	...	...	...	...	...	...	...	...
	By debtor												
521	Domestic debtors	...	...	...	33	18	-16	33	18	-16	33	19	-16
522	External debtors	...	...	...	—	—	—	—	—	—	—	—	—
53	**Other volume changes in liabilities**	**...**	**...**	**...**	**2**	**-0**	**81**	**2**	**-0**	**81**	**2**	**0**	**81**
	By instrument												
5301	Special Drawing Rights (SDRs)	...	...	...	—	—	—	—	—	—	—	—	—
5302	Currency and deposits	...	...	...	—	—	—	—	—	—	—	—	—
5303	Debt securities	...	...	...	2	-0	81	2	-0	81	2	-0	81
5304	Loans	...	...	...	—	—	—	—	—	—	0	0	0
5305	Equity and investment fund shares	...	...	...	—	—	—	—	—	—	—	—	—
5306	Insurance, pension, and standardized guarantee schemes	...	...	...	—	—	—	—	—	—	—	—	—
5307	Financial derivatives and employee stock options	...	...	...	—	—	—	—	—	—	—	—	—
5308	Other accounts payable	...	...	...	...	...	...	...	...	...	...	...	—
	By creditor												
531	Domestic creditors	...	...	...	1	0	81	1	0	81	1	0	81
532	External creditors	...	...	...	1	-0	-0	1	-0	-0	1	0	0
	Table 6 Balance sheet												
6	**Net worth**	**...**	**...**	**...**	**...**	**...**	**...**	**...**	**...**	**...**	**...**	**...**	**...**
61	**Nonfinancial assets**	**...**	**...**	**...**	**...**	**...**	**...**	**...**	**...**	**...**	**...**	**...**	**...**
611	Fixed assets	...	...	...	...	...	...	...	...	...	...	...	...
6111	Buildings and structures	...	...	...	...	...	...	...	...	...	...	...	...
6112	Machinery and equipment	...	...	...	...	...	...	...	...	...	...	...	...
6113	Other fixed assets	...	...	...	...	...	...	...	...	...	...	...	...
6114	Weapons systems	...	...	...	...	...	...	...	...	...	...	...	...
612	Inventories	...	...	...	...	...	...	...	...	...	...	...	...
613	Valuables	...	...	...	...	...	...	...	...	...	...	...	...
614	Nonproduced assets	...	...	...	...	...	...	...	...	...	...	...	...
6141	Land	...	...	...	...	...	...	...	...	...	...	...	...
6142	Mineral and energy resources	...	...	...	...	...	...	...	...	...	...	...	...
6143	Other naturally occurring assets	...	...	...	...	...	...	...	...	...	...	...	...
6144	Intangible nonproduced assets	...	...	...	...	...	...	...	...	...	...	...	...
62	**Financial assets**	**...**	**...**	**...**	**1,961**	**2,106**	**2,549**	**1,961**	**2,106**	**2,549**	**1,517**	**1,645**	**2,029**
	By instrument												
6201	Monetary gold and SDRs	...	...	...	—	—	—	—	—	—	—	—	—
6202	Currency and deposits	...	...	...	973	1,025	1,395	973	1,025	1,395	1,042	1,092	1,453
6203	Debt securities	...	...	...	—	—	—	—	—	—	—	—	—
6204	Loans	...	...	...	988	1,080	1,154	988	1,080	1,154	475	553	576
6205	Equity and investment fund shares	...	...	...	—	—	—	—	—	—	—	—	—
6206	Insurance, pension, and standardized guarantee schemes	...	...	...	—	—	—	—	—	—	—	—	—
6207	Financial derivatives and employee stock options	...	...	...	—	—	—	—	—	—	—	—	—
6208	Other accounts receivable	...	...	...	...	...	...	...	...	...	...	...	...
	By debtor												
621	Domestic debtors	...	...	...	1,960	2,105	2,549	1,960	2,105	2,549	1,517	1,645	2,028
622	External debtors	...	...	...	1	0	0	1	0	0	1	0	0
63	**Liabilities**	**...**	**...**	**...**	**3,051**	**3,378**	**4,049**	**3,051**	**3,378**	**4,049**	**3,177**	**3,561**	**4,301**

Brazil (223)

In Billions of Brazilian Reais (BRL) / Fiscal Year Ends December 31st

		Budgetary Central Government			Central Government (excl. Social Security)			Central Government (incl. Social Security)			General Government		
		2013	2014	2015	2013	2014	2015	2013	2014	2015	2013	2014	2015
	By instrument												
6301	Special Drawing Rights (SDRs)	...	...	...	—	—	—	—	—	—	—	—	—
6302	Currency and deposits	...	...	...	—	—	—	—	—	—	—	—	—
6303	Debt securities	...	...	...	3,032	3,359	4,024	3,032	3,359	4,024	3,032	3,359	4,024
6304	Loans	...	...	...	19	19	26	19	19	26	146	202	277
6305	Equity and investment fund shares	...	...	...	—	—	—	—	—	—	—	—	—
6306	Insurance, pension, and standardized guarantee schemes	...	...	...	—	—	—	—	—	—	—	—	—
6307	Financial derivatives and employee stock options	...	...	...	—	—	—	—	—	—	—	—	—
6308	Other accounts payable	...	...	...	...	...	...	...	...	...	...	...	...
	By creditor												
631	Domestic creditors	...	...	...	2,653	2,880	3,443	2,653	2,880	3,443	2,719	2,980	3,568
632	External creditors	...	...	...	399	499	607	399	499	607	458	581	733
	Memorandum items												
6M2	Net financial worth	...	...	...	-1,090	-1,273	-1,501	-1,090	-1,273	-1,501	-1,660	-1,916	-2,272
6M3	Gross debt (D4) at market value	...	...	...	...	...	...	...	...	...	...	...	...
6M3D3	D3 debt liabilities at market value	...	...	...	...	...	...	...	...	...	...	...	...
6M3D2	D2 debt liabilities at market value	...	...	...	...	...	...	...	...	...	...	...	...
6M3D1	D1 debt liabilities at market value	...	...	...	...	...	...	...	...	...	...	...	...
6M4	Gross debt (D4) at nominal value	...	...	...	...	...	...	...	...	...	...	...	...
6M4D3	D3 debt liabilities at nominal value	...	...	...	...	...	...	...	...	...	...	...	...
6M4D2	D2 debt liabilities at nominal value	...	...	...	3,051	3,378	4,049	3,051	3,378	4,049	3,177	3,561	4,301
6M4D1	D1 debt liabilities at nominal value	...	...	...	3,051	3,378	4,049	3,051	3,378	4,049	3,177	3,561	4,301
6M35	Gross debt (D4) at face value	...	...	...	...	...	...	...	...	...	...	...	...
6M35D3	D3 debt liabilities at face value	...	...	...	...	...	...	...	...	...	...	...	...
6M35D2	D2 debt liabilities at face value	...	...	...	...	...	...	...	...	...	...	...	...
6M35D1	D1 debt liabilities at face value	...	...	...	...	...	...	...	...	...	...	...	...
6M93	Government gross debt per national definition	...	...	...	2,622	3,070	3,676	2,622	3,070	3,676	2,748	3,252	3,928
6M5	Arrears	...	...	...	...	...	...	...	...	...	...	...	...
6M6	Explicit contingent liabilities	...	...	...	...	...	...	...	...	...	...	...	...
6M61	of which: Publicly guaranteed debt	...	...	...	...	...	...	...	...	...	...	...	...
6M7	Net implicit obligations for social security benefits	...	...	...	...	...	...	...	...	...	...	...	...
	Table 7 Expenditure by functions of government												
7	**Expenditure**	...	...	...	**1,635**	**1,842**	**2,190**	**1,635**	**1,842**	**2,190**	**2,288**	**2,581**	**2,983**
701	**General public services**	...	...	...	...	...	...	...	...	...	...	...	...
7017	Public debt transactions	...	...	...	384	447	729	384	447	729	389	455	743
7018	Transfers of general character between levels of government	...	...	...	...	...	...	...	...	...	...	...	...
702	**Defense**	...	...	...	...	...	...	...	...	...	...	...	...
703	**Public order and safety**	...	...	...	...	...	...	...	...	...	...	...	...
704	**Economic affairs**	...	...	...	...	...	...	...	...	...	...	...	...
7042	Agriculture, forestry, fishing, and hunting	...	...	...	...	...	...	...	...	...	...	...	...
7043	Fuel and energy	...	...	...	...	...	...	...	...	...	...	...	...
7044	Mining, manufacturing, and construction	...	...	...	...	...	...	...	...	...	...	...	...
7045	Transport	...	...	...	...	...	...	...	...	...	...	...	...
7046	Communication	...	...	...	...	...	...	...	...	...	...	...	...
705	**Environmental protection**	...	...	...	...	...	...	...	...	...	...	...	...
706	**Housing and community amenities**	...	...	...	...	...	...	...	...	...	...	...	...
707	**Health**	...	...	...	...	...	...	...	...	...	...	...	...
7072	Outpatient services	...	...	...	...	...	...	...	...	...	...	...	...
7073	Hospital services	...	...	...	...	...	...	...	...	...	...	...	...
7074	Public health services	...	...	...	...	...	...	...	...	...	...	...	...
708	**Recreation, culture and religion**	...	...	...	...	...	...	...	...	...	...	...	...
709	**Education**	...	...	...	...	...	...	...	...	...	...	...	...
7091	Pre-primary and primary education	...	...	...	...	...	...	...	...	...	...	...	...
7092	Secondary education	...	...	...	...	...	...	...	...	...	...	...	...
7094	Tertiary education	...	...	...	...	...	...	...	...	...	...	...	...

Brazil (223)

In Billions of Brazilian Reais (BRL) / Fiscal Year Ends December 31st

		Budgetary Central Government			Central Government (excl. Social Security)			Central Government (incl. Social Security)			General Government		
		2013	2014	2015	2013	2014	2015	2013	2014	2015	2013	2014	2015
710	**Social protection**	...	...	...	...	...	...	...	...	...	...	...	...
7z	Statistical discrepancy: Expenditure	...	...	...	...	...	...	...	...	...	...	...	...
	Table 8 Financial transactions by counterpart sector												
32	**Net acquisition of financial assets**	...	...	...	**13**	**19**	**-1**	**13**	**19**	**-1**	**4**	**2**	**-61**
321	Domestic debtors	...	...	...	14	20	-0	14	20	-0	4	2	-60
8211	General government	...	...	...	19	15	52	19	15	52	—	—	—
8212	Central bank	...	...	...	-71	-111	-100	-71	-111	-100	-71	-111	-100
8213	Deposit-taking corporations except the central bank	...	...	...	-1	8	3	-1	8	3	8	5	-5
8214	Other financial corporations	...	...	...	69	110	44	69	110	44	69	110	44
8215	Nonfinancial corporations	...	...	...	-2	-1	0	-2	-1	0	-2	-1	0
8216	Households & nonprofit institutions serving households	...	...	...	—	—	—	—	—	—	—	—	—
322	External debtors	...	...	...	-1	-0	-0	-1	-0	-0	-1	-0	-0
8221	General government	...	...	...	—	—	—	—	—	—	—	—	—
8227	International organizations	...	...	...	—	—	—	—	—	—	—	—	—
8228	Financial corporations other than international organizations	...	...	...	-1	-0	-0	-1	-0	-0	-1	-0	-0
8229	Other nonresidents	...	...	...	—	—	—	—	—	—	—	—	—
33	**Net incurrence of liabilities**	...	...	...	**154**	**314**	**543**	**154**	**314**	**543**	**189**	**361**	**573**
331	Domestic creditors	...	...	...	145	281	482	145	281	482	168	315	507
8311	General government	...	...	...	-0	-0	-0	-0	-0	-0	—	—	—
8312	Central bank	...	...	...	51	159	94	51	159	94	51	159	94
8313	Deposit-taking corporations except the central bank	...	...	...	44	44	125	44	44	125	57	65	140
8314	Other financial corporations	...	...	...	44	70	239	44	70	239	53	82	249
8315	Nonfinancial corporations	...	...	...	5	7	20	5	7	20	5	7	20
8316	Households & nonprofit institutions serving households	...	...	...	1	2	5	1	2	5	1	2	5
332	External creditors	...	...	...	9	32	62	9	32	62	21	46	66
8321	General government	...	...	...	—	—	—	—	—	—	—	—	—
8327	International organizations	...	...	...	-2	0	—	-2	0	—	7	10	3
8328	Financial corporations other than international organizations	...	...	...	7	27	48	7	27	48	10	31	50
8329	Other nonresidents	...	...	...	4	5	13	4	5	13	4	5	13
	Table 9 Total other economic flows in assets and liabilities												
9	**Change in net worth due to other economic flows**	...	...	...	...	...	...	...	...	...	...	...	...
91	**Other economic flows in nonfinancial assets**	...	...	...	...	...	...	...	...	...	...	...	...
911	Fixed assets	...	...	...	...	...	...	...	...	...	...	...	...
912	Inventories	...	...	...	...	...	...	...	...	...	...	...	...
913	Valuables	...	...	...	...	...	...	...	...	...	...	...	...
914	Nonproduced assets	...	...	...	...	...	...	...	...	...	...	...	...
92	**Other economic flows in financial assets**	...	...	...	**128**	**125**	**444**	**128**	**125**	**444**	**128**	**126**	**444**
	By instrument												
9201	Monetary gold and SDRs	...	...	...	—	—	—	—	—	—	—	—	—
9202	Currency and deposits	...	...	...	123	123	430	123	123	430	123	123	430
9203	Debt securities	...	...	...	—	—	—	—	—	—	—	—	—
9204	Loans	...	...	...	5	2	14	5	2	14	5	2	14
9205	Equity and investment fund shares	...	...	...	—	—	—	—	—	—	—	—	—
9206	Insurance, pension, and standardized guarantee schemes	...	...	...	—	—	—	—	—	—	—	—	—
9207	Financial derivatives and employee stock options	...	...	...	—	—	—	—	—	—	—	—	—
9208	Other accounts receivable	...	...	...	...	...	...	...	...	...	...	...	...
	By debtor												
921	Domestic debtors	...	...	...	128	125	444	128	125	444	128	126	444
922	External debtors	...	...	...	0	0	0	0	0	0	0	0	0
93	**Other economic flows in liabilities**	...	...	...	**15**	**13**	**128**	**15**	**13**	**128**	**22**	**23**	**167**

Brazil (223)

In Billions of Brazilian Reais (BRL) / Fiscal Year Ends December 31st

		Budgetary Central Government			Central Government (excl. Social Security)			Central Government (incl. Social Security)			General Government		
		2013	2014	2015	2013	2014	2015	2013	2014	2015	2013	2014	2015
	By instrument												
9301	Special Drawing Rights (SDRs)	...	...	...	—	—	—	—	—	—	—	—	—
9302	Currency and deposits	...	...	...	—	—	—	—	—	—	—	—	—
9303	Debt securities	...	...	...	14	13	125	14	13	125	14	13	125
9304	Loans	...	...	...	1	1	3	1	1	3	8	10	43
9305	Equity and investment fund shares	...	...	...	—	—	—	—	—	—	—	—	—
9306	Insurance, pension, and standardized guarantee schemes	...	...	...	—	—	—	—	—	—	—	—	—
9307	Financial derivatives and employee stock options	...	...	...	—	—	—	—	—	—	—	—	—
9308	Other accounts payable	...	...	...	...	...	...	...	...	...	...	...	...
	By creditor												
931	Domestic creditors	...	...	...	-57	-54	81	-57	-54	81	-57	-54	81
932	External creditors	...	...	...	72	68	47	72	68	47	79	77	86
	Memorandum items												
9M2	Change in net financial worth due to other economic flows	...	...	...	113	112	316	113	112	316	106	103	277
9M3	Gross debt (D4) at market value: other economic flows	...	...	...	...	...	...	...	...	...	...	...	...
9M3D3	D3 debt liabilities at market value: other economic flows	...	...	...	...	...	...	...	...	...	...	...	...
9M3D2	D2 debt liabilities at market value: other economic flows	...	...	...	15	13	128	15	13	128	22	23	167
9M3D1	D1 debt liabilities at market value: other economic flows	...	...	...	15	13	128	15	13	128	22	23	167

Bulgaria (918)

In Millions of Bulgarian Leva (BGN) / Fiscal Year Ends December 31st

		Budgetary Central Government			Central Government (excl. Social Security)			Central Government (incl. Social Security)			General Government		
		2013	2014	2015	2013P	2014P	2015P	2013P	2014P	2015P	2013P	2014P	2015P
	Statement of operations												
1	Revenue	...	...	...	21,389	21,119	24,099	...	...	...	30,518	30,618	34,548
2	Expense	...	...	...	21,418	25,165	24,669	...	...	...	29,812	33,164	32,900
GOB	**Gross operating balance**	...	...	...	**870**	**-3,082**	**957**	...	...	...	**2,824**	**-419**	**3,991**
NOB	**Net operating balance**	...	...	...	**-29**	**-4,046**	**-570**	...	...	...	**706**	**-2,546**	**1,648**
31	Net/Gross investment in nonfinancial assets	...	...	...	618	675	49	560	605	37	1,045	2,013	3,138
2M	Expenditure	...	...	...	22,036	25,839	24,718	...	...	...	30,858	35,177	36,038
NLB	**Net lending (+) / Net borrowing (-)**	...	...	...	**-647**	**-4,720**	**-619**	...	...	...	**-340**	**-4,559**	**-1,490**
32	Net acquisition of financial assets	...	...	...	-328	4,093	-705	...	...	...	224	4,137	-1,976
33	Net incurrence of liabilities	...	...	...	296	8,599	-45	...	...	...	603	8,455	-441
NLBz	Statistical discrepancy	...	...	...	23	215	-41	...	...	...	-39	240	-44
	Memorandum items												
PB	Primary net lending / net borrowing	...	...	...	-45	-4,026	176	...	...	...	263	-3,836	-667
GB	Government balance per national definition	...	...	...	...	...	...	...	...	...	...	...	...
	Statement of other economic flows												
	Balance sheet												
6	**Net worth**	...	...	...	...	...	...	...	...	...	...	...	...
61	Nonfinancial assets	...	...	...	...	...	...	...	...	...	...	...	...
62	Financial assets	...	...	...	18,319	22,942	22,102	...	...	...	21,574	26,232	24,121
63	Liabilities	...	...	...	18,069	26,839	26,808	...	...	...	20,282	28,891	28,480
	Table 1 Revenue												
1	**Revenue**	...	...	...	**21,389**	**21,119**	**24,099**	...	...	...	**30,518**	**30,618**	**34,548**
11	**Taxes**	...	...	...	**16,286**	**16,354**	**17,856**	**16,286**	**16,354**	**17,856**	**16,974**	**17,072**	**18,614**
111	Taxes on income, profits, and capital gains	...	...	...	4,055	4,387	4,617	4,055	4,387	4,617	4,069	4,400	4,629
1111	Payable by individuals	...	...	...	2,358	2,674	2,711	2,358	2,674	2,711	2,372	2,687	2,723
1112	Payable by corporations and other enterprises	...	...	...	1,696	1,696	1,888	1,696	1,696	1,888	1,696	1,696	1,888
1113	Other taxes on income, profits, and capital gains	...	...	...	2	17	18	2	17	18	2	17	18
112	Taxes on payroll and workforce	...	...	...	6	14	16	6	14	16	6	14	16
113	Taxes on property	...	...	...	—	—	—	—	—	—	459	478	502
114	Taxes on goods and services	...	...	...	12,209	11,931	13,203	12,209	11,931	13,203	12,311	12,039	13,317
1141	General taxes on goods and services	...	...	...	7,624	7,451	7,939	7,624	7,451	7,939	7,624	7,451	7,939
1142	Excises	...	...	...	4,121	4,040	4,742	4,121	4,040	4,742	4,121	4,040	4,742
115	Taxes on international trade and transactions	...	...	...	11	15	15	11	15	15	11	15	15
116	Other taxes	...	...	...	5	6	5	5	6	5	117	126	133
12	**Social contributions**	...	...	...	—	—	—	**6,116**	**6,575**	**6,966**	**6,116**	**6,575**	**6,966**
121	Social security contributions	...	...	...	—	—	—	6,116	6,575	6,966	6,116	6,575	6,966
122	Other social contributions	...	...	...	—	—	—	—	—	—	—	—	—
13	**Grants**	...	...	...	...	...	...	...	...	...	...	...	...
131	From foreign governments	...	...	...	...	...	...	...	...	...	...	...	...
132	From international organizations	...	...	...	...	...	...	...	...	...	...	...	...
133	From other general government units	...	...	...	834	950	961	...	...	...	—	—	—
1331	Current	...	...	...	834	950	961	—	—	—	—	—	—
1332	Capital	...	...	...	—	—	—	...	...	...	—	—	—
14	**Other revenue**	...	...	...	...	...	...	...	...	...	...	...	...
	Table 2 Expense by economic type												
2	**Expense**	...	...	...	**21,418**	**25,165**	**24,669**	...	...	...	**29,812**	**33,164**	**32,900**
21	**Compensation of employees**	...	...	...	**5,149**	**5,394**	**5,622**	**5,229**	**5,476**	**5,703**	**7,776**	**7,956**	**8,344**
211	Wages and salaries	...	...	...	...	...	...	...	...	...	...	...	...
212	Employers' social contributions	...	...	...	...	...	...	...	...	...	...	...	...
22	**Use of goods and services**	...	...	...	**2,727**	**2,693**	**3,061**	**2,786**	**2,751**	**3,117**	**4,668**	**4,584**	**4,648**
23	**Consumption of fixed capital**	...	...	...	**899**	**963**	**1,527**	**961**	**1,037**	**1,548**	**2,118**	**2,128**	**2,343**
24	**Interest**	...	...	...	**602**	**695**	**796**	**578**	**695**	**796**	**603**	**723**	**823**
25	**Subsidies**	...	...	...	**1,023**	**1,066**	**1,571**	**1,023**	**1,066**	**1,572**	**1,066**	**1,119**	**1,624**

Bulgaria (918)

In Millions of Bulgarian Leva (BGN) / Fiscal Year Ends December 31st

		Budgetary Central Government			Central Government (excl. Social Security)			Central Government (incl. Social Security)			General Government		
		2013	2014	2015	2013P	2014P	2015P	2013P	2014P	2015P	2013P	2014P	2015P
26	**Grants**	...	...	...	...	...	...	...	...	...	...	...	...
261	To foreign governments	...	...	...	...	...	...	...	...	...	...	...	...
262	To international organizations	...	...	...	...	...	...	...	...	...	...	...	...
263	To other general government units	...	...	...	8,596	9,476	9,626	...	...	...	—	—	—
2631	Current	...	...	...	8,596	9,476	9,626	3,292	3,772	4,013	—	—	—
2632	Capital	...	...	...	—	—	—	...	...	...	—	—	—
27	**Social benefits**	...	...	...	835	917	909	11,278	12,043	12,297	11,358	12,117	12,320
271	Social security benefits	...	...	...	...	...	...	...	...	...	...	...	...
272	Social assistance benefits	...	...	...	...	...	...	...	...	...	...	...	...
273	Employment-related social benefits	...	...	...	...	...	...	...	...	...	...	...	...
28	**Other expense**	...	...	...	...	...	...	...	...	...	...	...	...
281	Property expense other than interest	...	...	...	—	—	—	—	—	—	...	...	...
282	Transfers not elsewhere classified	...	...	...	...	...	...	...	...	...	...	...	...
2821	Current	...	...	...	...	...	...	...	...	...	...	...	...
2822	Capital	...	...	...	...	...	...	...	...	...	...	...	...
	Table 3 Transactions in assets and liabilities												
3	**Change in net worth from transactions**	...	...	...	-6	-3,831	-611	...	...	...	667	-2,306	1,604
31	**Net/Gross investment in nonfinancial assets**	...	...	...	618	675	49	560	605	37	1,045	2,013	3,138
311	Fixed assets	...	...	...	700	792	290	643	723	278	1,206	2,230	3,472
3111	Buildings and structures	...	...	...	...	...	...	...	...	...	...	...	...
3112	Machinery and equipment	...	...	...	...	...	...	...	...	...	...	...	...
3113	Other fixed assets	...	...	...	...	...	...	...	...	...	...	...	...
3114	Weapons systems	...	...	...	...	...	...	...	...	...	...	...	...
312	Inventories	...	...	...	...	...	...	...	...	...	...	...	...
313	Valuables	...	...	...	...	...	...	...	...	...	...	...	...
314	Nonproduced assets	...	...	...	-110	-99	-259	-110	-99	-259	-188	-199	-353
3141	Land	...	...	...	...	...	...	...	...	...	...	...	...
3142	Mineral and energy resources	...	...	...	...	...	...	...	...	...	...	...	...
3143	Other naturally occurring assets	...	...	...	...	...	...	...	...	...	...	...	...
3144	Intangible nonproduced assets	...	...	...	...	...	...	...	...	...	...	...	...
32	**Net acquisition of financial assets**	...	...	...	-328	4,093	-705	...	...	...	224	4,137	-1,976
	By instrument												
3201	Monetary gold and SDRs	...	...	...	—	—	—	...	...	...	—	—	—
3202	Currency and deposits	...	...	...	-1,323	1,511	-1,011	...	...	...	-1,095	1,383	-1,776
3203	Debt securities	...	...	...	1	—	—	...	...	...	1	—	—
3204	Loans	...	...	...	-34	844	-367	...	...	...	-50	816	-467
3205	Equity and investment fund shares	...	...	...	-237	893	-30	...	...	...	-228	872	-30
3206	Insurance, pension, and standardized guarantee schemes	...	...	...	-2	3	5	...	...	...	-2	4	8
3207	Financial derivatives and employee stock options	...	...	...	—	—	—	...	...	...	—	—	—
3208	Other accounts receivable	...	...	...	1,266	843	698	...	...	...	1,598	1,061	289
	By debtor												
321	Domestic debtors	...	...	...	...	...	...	...	...	...	...	...	...
322	External debtors	...	...	...	...	...	...	...	...	...	...	...	...
33	**Net incurrence of liabilities**	...	...	...	296	8,599	-45	...	...	...	603	8,455	-441
	By instrument												
3301	Special Drawing Rights (SDRs)	...	...	...	—	—	—	...	...	...	—	—	—
3302	Currency and deposits	...	...	...	...	...	...	...	...	...	...	...	...
3303	Debt securities	...	...	...	-354	5,076	3,434	...	...	...	-426	5,020	3,400
3304	Loans	...	...	...	888	3,232	-3,065	...	...	...	869	3,289	-2,991
3305	Equity and investment fund shares	...	...	...	—	—	—	...	...	...	—	—	—
3306	Insurance, pension, and standardized guarantee schemes	...	...	...	—	—	—	...	...	...	—	—	—
3307	Financial derivatives and employee stock options	...	...	...	-23	0	10	...	...	...	-23	0	10
3308	Other accounts payable	...	...	...	-216	291	-424	...	...	...	183	146	-860

Bulgaria (918)

In Millions of Bulgarian Leva (BGN) / Fiscal Year Ends December 31st

		Budgetary Central Government			Central Government (excl. Social Security)			Central Government (incl. Social Security)			General Government		
		2013	2014	2015	2013P	2014P	2015P	2013P	2014P	2015P	2013P	2014P	2015P
	By creditor												
331	Domestic creditors	...	...	...	...	...	...	...	...	...	...	...	...
332	External creditors	...	...	...	...	...	...	...	...	...	...	...	...
	Table 4 Holding gains and losses in assets and liabilities												
	Table 5 Holding gains and losses in assets and liabilities												
	Table 6 Balance sheet												
6	**Net worth**	...	...	...	...	...	...	...	...	...	...	...	...
61	**Nonfinancial assets**	...	...	...	...	...	...	...	...	...	...	...	...
611	Fixed assets	...	...	...	...	...	...	...	...	...	...	...	...
6111	Buildings and structures	...	...	...	...	...	...	...	...	...	...	...	...
6112	Machinery and equipment	...	...	...	...	...	...	...	...	...	...	...	...
6113	Other fixed assets	...	...	...	...	...	...	...	...	...	...	...	...
6114	Weapons systems	...	...	...	...	...	...	...	...	...	...	...	...
612	Inventories	...	...	...	...	...	...	...	...	...	...	...	...
613	Valuables	...	...	...	...	...	...	...	...	...	...	...	...
614	Nonproduced assets	...	...	...	...	...	...	...	...	...	...	...	...
6141	Land	...	...	...	...	...	...	...	...	...	...	...	...
6142	Mineral and energy resources	...	...	...	...	...	...	...	...	...	...	...	...
6143	Other naturally occurring assets	...	...	...	...	...	...	...	...	...	...	...	...
6144	Intangible nonproduced assets	...	...	...	...	...	...	...	...	...	...	...	...
62	**Financial assets**	...	...	...	**18,319**	**22,942**	**22,102**	...	...	...	**21,574**	**26,232**	**24,121**
	By instrument												
6201	Monetary gold and SDRs	...	...	...	—	—	—	...	...	...	—	—	—
6202	Currency and deposits	...	...	...	6,108	7,651	6,637	...	...	...	7,877	9,293	7,514
6203	Debt securities	...	...	...	1	1	1	...	...	...	1	1	1
6204	Loans	...	...	...	985	1,854	1,511	...	...	...	888	1,728	1,285
6205	Equity and investment fund shares	...	...	...	6,855	8,222	8,035	...	...	...	7,148	8,486	8,299
6206	Insurance, pension, and standardized guarantee schemes	...	...	...	20	23	27	...	...	...	28	32	41
6207	Financial derivatives and employee stock options	...	...	...	—	—	—	...	...	...	—	—	—
6208	Other accounts receivable	...	...	...	4,349	5,191	5,890	...	...	...	5,632	6,691	6,981
	By debtor												
621	Domestic debtors	...	...	...	...	...	...	...	...	...	...	...	...
622	External debtors	...	...	...	...	...	...	...	...	...	...	...	...
63	**Liabilities**	...	...	...	**18,069**	**26,839**	**26,808**	...	...	...	**20,282**	**28,891**	**28,480**
	By instrument												
6301	Special Drawing Rights (SDRs)	...	...	...	—	—	—	...	...	...	—	—	—
6302	Currency and deposits	...	...	...	...	...	...	...	...	...	...	...	...
6303	Debt securities	...	...	...	9,170	14,394	17,817	...	...	...	8,688	13,855	17,244
6304	Loans	...	...	...	4,819	8,057	5,010	...	...	...	5,526	8,827	5,870
6305	Equity and investment fund shares	...	...	...	—	—	—	...	...	...	—	—	—
6306	Insurance, pension, and standardized guarantee schemes	...	...	...	—	—	—	...	...	...	—	—	—
6307	Financial derivatives and employee stock options	...	...	...	191	209	226	...	...	...	190	208	225
6308	Other accounts payable	...	...	...	3,889	4,179	3,755	...	...	...	5,878	6,001	5,141
	By creditor												
631	Domestic creditors	...	...	...	...	...	...	...	...	...	...	...	...
632	External creditors	...	...	...	...	...	...	...	...	...	...	...	...
	Memorandum items												
6M2	Net financial worth	...	...	...	249	-3,897	-4,707	...	...	...	1,292	-2,659	-4,359
6M3	Gross debt (D4) at market value	...	...	...	17,878	26,630	26,582	...	...	...	20,092	28,683	28,255
6M3D3	D3 debt liabilities at market value	...	...	...	17,878	26,630	26,582	...	...	...	20,092	28,683	28,255
6M3D2	D2 debt liabilities at market value	...	...	...	13,990	22,451	22,827	...	...	...	14,214	22,683	23,114
6M3D1	D1 debt liabilities at market value	...	...	...	13,990	22,451	22,827	...	...	...	14,214	22,683	23,114
6M4	Gross debt (D4) at nominal value	...	...	...	...	...	...	...	...	...	...	...	...
6M4D3	D3 debt liabilities at nominal value	...	...	...	...	...	...	...	...	...	...	...	...
6M4D2	D2 debt liabilities at nominal value	...	...	...	...	...	...	...	...	...	...	...	...
6M4D1	D1 debt liabilities at nominal value	...	...	...	...	...	...	...	...	...	...	...	...

Bulgaria (918)

In Millions of Bulgarian Leva (BGN) / Fiscal Year Ends December 31st

		Budgetary Central Government			Central Government (excl. Social Security)			Central Government (incl. Social Security)			General Government		
		2013	2014	2015	2013P	2014P	2015P	2013P	2014P	2015P	2013P	2014P	2015P
6M35	Gross debt (D4) at face value	...	...	...	...	...	...	...	...	...	...	...	...
6M35D3	D3 debt liabilities at face value	...	...	...	17,642	26,498	26,518	...	...	...	19,856	28,554	28,191
6M35D2	D2 debt liabilities at face value	...	...	...	13,753	22,319	22,762	...	...	...	13,978	22,554	23,049
6M35D1	D1 debt liabilities at face value	...	...	...	13,753	22,319	22,762	...	...	...	13,978	22,554	23,049
6M93	Government gross debt per national definition	...	...	...	13,753	22,319	22,762	...	...	...	13,978	22,554	23,049
6M5	Arrears	...	...	...	...	...	...	...	...	...	...	...	...
6M6	Explicit contingent liabilities	...	...	...	...	...	...	...	...	...	...	...	...
6M61	of which: Publicly guaranteed debt	...	...	...	...	...	...	...	...	...	...	...	...
6M7	Net implicit obligations for social security benefits	...	...	...	...	...	...	...	...	...	...	...	...
	Table 7 Expenditure by functions of government												
7	**Expenditure**	...	...	...	**22,036**	**25,839**	...	...	...	...	**30,857**	**35,177**	...
701	**General public services**	...	...	...	**10,950**	**12,469**	...	...	...	...	**2,975**	**5,242**	...
7017	Public debt transactions	...	...	...	613	695	...	...	...	...	614	724	...
7018	Transfers of general character between levels of government	...	...	...	...	...	...	...	...	...	...	...	...
702	**Defense**	...	...	...	**978**	**1,034**	...	...	...	...	**978**	**1,150**	...
703	**Public order and safety**	...	...	...	**2,046**	**2,227**	...	...	...	...	**2,148**	**2,300**	...
704	**Economic affairs**	...	...	...	**3,701**	**4,287**	...	...	...	...	**4,476**	**4,106**	...
7042	Agriculture, forestry, fishing, and hunting	...	...	...	627	711	...	...	...	...	728	742	...
7043	Fuel and energy	...	...	...	83	6	...	...	...	...	89	6	...
7044	Mining, manufacturing, and construction	...	...	...	41	11	...	...	...	...	41	11	...
7045	Transport	...	...	...	2,376	2,785	...	...	...	...	2,645	2,685	...
7046	Communication	...	...	...	41	40	...	...	...	...	41	40	...
705	**Environmental protection**	...	...	...	**190**	**89**	...	...	...	...	**752**	**577**	...
706	**Housing and community amenities**	...	...	...	**59**	**94**	...	...	...	...	**1,076**	**1,367**	...
707	**Health**	...	...	...	**1,590**	**1,928**	...	...	...	...	**3,711**	**4,579**	...
7072	Outpatient services	...	...	...	106	129	...	...	...	...	669	497	...
7073	Hospital services	...	...	...	1,322	1,592	...	...	...	...	2,142	3,285	...
7074	Public health services	...	...	...	36	41	...	...	...	...	69	80	...
708	**Recreation, culture and religion**	...	...	...	**322**	**980**	...	...	...	...	**621**	**1,232**	...
709	**Education**	...	...	...	**1,149**	**1,339**	...	...	...	...	**3,021**	**3,415**	...
7091	Pre-primary and primary education	...	...	...	2	2	...	...	...	...	618	771	...
7092	Secondary education	...	...	...	311	413	...	...	...	...	1,471	1,626	...
7094	Tertiary education	...	...	...	639	743	...	...	...	...	644	744	...
710	**Social protection**	...	...	...	**1,051**	**1,391**	...	...	...	...	**11,099**	**11,208**	...
7z	Statistical discrepancy: Expenditure	...	...	...	0	0	...	...	...	...	-0	0	...
	Table 8 Financial transactions by counterpart sector												
32	**Net acquisition of financial assets**	...	...	...	**-328**	**4,093**	**-705**	...	...	...	**224**	**4,137**	**-1,976**
321	Domestic debtors	...	...	...	...	...	...	...	...	...	...	...	...
8211	General government	...	...	...	...	...	...	...	...	...	—	—	—
8212	Central bank	...	...	...	...	...	...	...	...	...	...	...	...
8213	Deposit-taking corporations except the central bank	...	...	...	...	...	...	...	...	...	...	...	...
8214	Other financial corporations	...	...	...	...	...	...	...	...	...	...	...	...
8215	Nonfinancial corporations	...	...	...	...	...	...	...	...	...	...	...	...
8216	Households & nonprofit institutions serving households	...	...	...	...	...	...	...	...	...	...	...	...
322	External debtors	...	...	...	...	...	...	...	...	...	...	...	...
8221	General government	...	...	...	...	...	...	...	...	...	...	...	...
8227	International organizations	...	...	...	...	...	...	...	...	...	...	...	...
8228	Financial corporations other than international organizations	...	...	...	...	...	...	...	...	...	...	...	...
8229	Other nonresidents	...	...	...	...	...	...	...	...	...	...	...	...

Bulgaria (918)

In Millions of Bulgarian Leva (BGN) / Fiscal Year Ends December 31st

		Budgetary Central Government			Central Government (excl. Social Security)			Central Government (incl. Social Security)			General Government		
		2013	2014	2015	2013P	2014P	2015P	2013P	2014P	2015P	2013P	2014P	2015P
33	**Net incurrence of liabilities**	...	...	...	296	8,599	-45	...	...	...	603	8,455	-441
331	Domestic creditors	...	...	...	...	...	...	...	...	...	...	...	...
8311	General government	...	...	...	...	...	...	...	...	...	—	—	—
8312	Central bank	...	...	...	...	...	...	...	...	...	...	...	...
8313	Deposit-taking corporations except the central bank	...	...	...	...	...	...	...	...	...	...	...	...
8314	Other financial corporations	...	...	...	...	...	...	...	...	...	...	...	...
8315	Nonfinancial corporations	...	...	...	...	...	...	...	...	...	...	...	...
8316	Households & nonprofit institutions serving households	...	...	...	...	...	...	...	...	...	...	...	...
332	External creditors	...	...	...	...	...	...	...	...	...	...	...	...
8321	General government	...	...	...	...	...	...	...	...	...	...	...	...
8327	International organizations	...	...	...	...	...	...	...	...	...	...	...	...
8328	Financial corporations other than international organizations	...	...	...	...	...	...	...	...	...	...	...	...
8329	Other nonresidents	...	...	...	...	...	...	...	...	...	...	...	...
	Table 9 Total other economic flows in assets and liabilities												
9	**Change in net worth due to other economic flows**	...	...	...	...	...	...	...	...	...	...	...	...
91	**Other economic flows in nonfinancial assets**	...	...	...	...	...	...	...	...	...	...	...	...
911	Fixed assets	...	...	...	...	...	...	...	...	...	...	...	...
912	Inventories	...	...	...	...	...	...	...	...	...	...	...	...
913	Valuables	...	...	...	...	...	...	...	...	...	...	...	...
914	Nonproduced assets	...	...	...	...	...	...	...	...	...	...	...	...
92	**Other economic flows in financial assets**	...	...	...	**-970**	**530**	**-136**	...	...	...	**-963**	**521**	**-135**
	By instrument												
9201	Monetary gold and SDRs	...	...	...	—	—	—	...	...	...	—	—	—
9202	Currency and deposits	...	...	...	1	33	-3	...	...	...	1	33	-3
9203	Debt securities	...	...	...	—	0	-0	...	...	...	—	0	-0
9204	Loans	...	...	...	-27	24	24	...	...	...	-27	24	24
9205	Equity and investment fund shares	...	...	...	-943	474	-157	...	...	...	-936	467	-157
9206	Insurance, pension, and standardized guarantee schemes	...	...	...	—	—	—	...	...	...	0	—	-0
9207	Financial derivatives and employee stock options	...	...	...	—	—	—	...	...	...	—	—	—
9208	Other accounts receivable	...	...	...	0	—	0	...	...	...	—	-2	0
	By debtor												
921	Domestic debtors	...	...	...	...	...	...	...	...	...	...	...	...
922	External debtors	...	...	...	...	...	...	...	...	...	...	...	...
93	**Other economic flows in liabilities**	...	...	...	**-235**	**171**	**14**	...	...	...	**-279**	**154**	**30**
	By instrument												
9301	Special Drawing Rights (SDRs)	...	...	...	—	—	—	...	...	...	—	—	—
9302	Currency and deposits	...	...	...	—	—	—	...	...	...	—	—	—
9303	Debt securities	...	...	...	-196	148	-12	...	...	...	-196	148	-12
9304	Loans	...	...	...	-48	6	18	...	...	...	-92	12	34
9305	Equity and investment fund shares	...	...	...	—	—	—	...	...	...	—	—	—
9306	Insurance, pension, and standardized guarantee schemes	...	...	...	—	—	—	...	...	...	—	—	—
9307	Financial derivatives and employee stock options	...	...	...	9	18	7	...	...	...	9	18	7
9308	Other accounts payable	...	...	...	—	-0	1	...	...	...	—	-23	1
	By creditor												
931	Domestic creditors	...	...	...	...	...	...	...	...	...	...	...	...
932	External creditors	...	...	...	...	...	...	...	...	...	...	...	...
	Memorandum items												
9M2	Change in net financial worth due to other economic flows	...	...	...	-735	359	-150	...	...	...	-683	368	-165

Bulgaria (918)

In Millions of Bulgarian Leva (BGN) / Fiscal Year Ends December 31st

		Budgetary Central Government			Central Government (excl. Social Security)			Central Government (incl. Social Security)			General Government		
		2013	2014	2015	2013P	2014P	2015P	2013P	2014P	2015P	2013P	2014P	2015P
9M3	Gross debt (D4) at market value: other economic flows	...	...	...	-244	153	7	...	...	...	-289	136	23
9M3D3	D3 debt liabilities at market value: other economic flows	...	...	...	-244	153	7	...	...	...	-289	136	23
9M3D2	D2 debt liabilities at market value: other economic flows	...	...	...	-244	153	7	...	...	...	-289	160	22
9M3D1	D1 debt liabilities at market value: other economic flows	...	...	...	-244	153	7	...	...	...	-289	160	22

Burkina Faso (748)

In Billions of CFA (BCEAO) Francs (XOF) / Fiscal Year Ends December 31st

		Budgetary Central Government			Central Government (excl. Social Security)			Central Government (incl. Social Security)			General Government		
		2013	2014	2015	2013	2014	2015	2013	2014	2015	2013	2014	2015
	Statement of operations												
1	Revenue	1,442	1,321	1,278	...	...	...	...	...	...	...	...	...
2	Expense	819	887	923	...	...	...	...	...	...	...	...	...
GOB	**Gross operating balance**	**623**	**435**	**354**	...	...	...	...	...	...	...	...	...
NOB	**Net operating balance**	...	...	...	...	...	...	...	...	...	...	...	...
31	Net/Gross investment in nonfinancial assets	858	554	501	...	...	...	...	...	...	...	...	...
2M	Expenditure	1,677	1,441	1,424	...	...	...	...	...	...	...	...	...
NLB	**Net lending (+) / Net borrowing (-)**	**-236**	**-120**	**-146**	...	...	...	...	...	...	...	...	...
32	Net acquisition of financial assets	-68	68	-73	...	...	...	...	...	...	...	...	...
33	Net incurrence of liabilities	168	188	73	...	...	...	...	...	...	...	...	...
NLBz	Statistical discrepancy	0	0	0	...	...	...	...	...	...	...	...	...
	Memorandum items												
PB	Primary net lending / net borrowing	-201	-76	-103	...	...	...	...	...	...	...	...	...
GB	Government balance per national definition	...	...	...	...	...	...	...	...	...	...	...	...
	Statement of other economic flows												
	Balance sheet												
	Table 1 Revenue												
1	**Revenue**	**1,442**	**1,321**	**1,278**	...	...	...	...	...	...	...	...	...
11	**Taxes**	**993**	**941**	**929**	...	...	...	...	...	...	...	...	...
111	Taxes on income, profits, and capital gains	277	263	234	...	...	...	...	...	...	...	...	...
1111	Payable by individuals	...	...	...	...	...	...	...	...	...	...	...	...
1112	Payable by corporations and other enterprises	...	...	...	...	...	...	...	...	...	...	...	...
1113	Other taxes on income, profits, and capital gains	...	...	...	...	...	...	...	...	...	...	...	...
112	Taxes on payroll and workforce	7	7	8	...	...	...	...	...	...	...	...	...
113	Taxes on property	7	9	7	...	...	...	...	...	...	...	...	...
114	Taxes on goods and services	523	510	529	...	...	...	...	...	...	...	...	...
1141	General taxes on goods and services	423	387	388	...	...	...	...	...	...	...	...	...
1142	Excises	100	123	140	...	...	...	...	...	...	...	...	...
115	Taxes on international trade and transactions	169	144	143	...	...	...	...	...	...	...	...	...
116	Other taxes	9	8	7	...	...	...	...	...	...	...	...	...
12	**Social contributions**	—	—	—	...	...	...	...	...	...	...	...	...
121	Social security contributions	—	—	—	...	...	...	...	...	...	...	...	...
122	Other social contributions	—	—	—	...	...	...	...	...	...	...	...	...
13	**Grants**	**324**	**256**	**230**	...	...	...	...	...	...	...	...	...
131	From foreign governments	119	99	125	...	...	...	...	...	...	...	...	...
132	From international organizations	205	158	105	...	...	...	...	...	...	...	...	...
133	From other general government units	—	—	—	...	...	...	...	...	...	...	...	...
1331	Current	—	—	—	...	...	...	...	...	...	...	...	...
1332	Capital	—	—	—	...	...	...	...	...	...	...	...	...
14	**Other revenue**	**125**	**124**	**119**	...	...	...	...	...	...	...	...	...
	Table 2 Expense by economic type												
2	**Expense**	**819**	**887**	**923**	...	...	...	...	...	...	...	...	...
21	**Compensation of employees**	**356**	**437**	**469**	...	...	...	...	...	...	...	...	...
211	Wages and salaries	...	...	...	...	...	...	...	...	...	...	...	...
212	Employers' social contributions	...	...	...	...	...	...	...	...	...	...	...	...
22	**Use of goods and services**	**119**	**102**	**109**	...	...	...	...	...	...	...	...	...
23	**Consumption of fixed capital**	...	...	...	...	...	...	...	...	...	...	...	...
24	**Interest**	**35**	**44**	**44**	...	...	...	...	...	...	...	...	...
25	**Subsidies**	**11**	**24**	**12**	...	...	...	...	...	...	...	...	...
26	**Grants**	**57**	**89**	**88**	...	...	...	...	...	...	...	...	...
261	To foreign governments	—	—	—	...	...	...	...	...	...	...	...	...
262	To international organizations	—	—	—	...	...	...	...	...	...	...	...	...
263	To other general government units	57	89	88	...	...	...	...	...	...	...	...	...
2631	Current	57	89	88	...	...	...	...	...	...	...	...	...
2632	Capital	—	—	—	...	...	...	...	...	...	...	...	...

Burkina Faso (748)

In Billions of CFA (BCEAO) Francs (XOF) / Fiscal Year Ends December 31st

		Budgetary Central Government			Central Government (excl. Social Security)			Central Government (incl. Social Security)			General Government		
		2013	2014	2015	2013	2014	2015	2013	2014	2015	2013	2014	2015
27	**Social benefits**	—	—	—	...	...	...	...	...	...	...	...	...
271	Social security benefits	—	—	—	...	...	...	...	...	...	...	...	...
272	Social assistance benefits	—	—	—	...	...	...	...	...	...	...	...	...
273	Employment-related social benefits	—	—	—	...	...	...	...	...	...	...	...	...
28	**Other expense**	**242**	**190**	**202**	...	...	...	...	...	...	...	...	...
281	Property expense other than interest	—	—	—	...	...	...	...	...	...	...	...	...
282	Transfers not elsewhere classified	242	190	202	...	...	...	...	...	...	...	...	...
2821	Current	242	190	202	...	...	...	...	...	...	...	...	...
2822	Capital	—	—	—	...	...	...	...	...	...	...	...	...
	Table 3 Transactions in assets and liabilities												
3	**Change in net worth from transactions**	...	...	...	...	...	...	...	...	...	...	...	...
31	**Net/Gross investment in nonfinancial assets**	**858**	**554**	**501**	...	...	...	...	...	...	...	...	...
311	Fixed assets	858	554	501	...	...	...	...	...	...	...	...	...
3111	Buildings and structures	...	...	...	...	...	...	...	...	...	...	...	...
3112	Machinery and equipment	...	...	...	...	...	...	...	...	...	...	...	...
3113	Other fixed assets	...	...	...	...	...	...	...	...	...	...	...	...
3114	Weapons systems	...	...	...	...	...	...	...	...	...	...	...	...
312	Inventories	—	—	—	...	...	...	...	...	...	...	...	...
313	Valuables	—	—	—	...	...	...	...	...	...	...	...	...
314	Nonproduced assets	—	—	—	...	...	...	...	...	...	...	...	...
3141	Land	—	—	—	...	...	...	...	...	...	...	...	...
3142	Mineral and energy resources	—	—	—	...	...	...	...	...	...	...	...	...
3143	Other naturally occurring assets	—	—	—	...	...	...	...	...	...	...	...	...
3144	Intangible nonproduced assets	—	—	—	...	...	...	...	...	...	...	...	...
32	**Net acquisition of financial assets**	**-68**	**68**	**-73**	...	...	...	...	...	...	...	...	...
	By instrument												
3201	Monetary gold and SDRs	—	—	—	...	...	...	...	...	...	...	...	...
3202	Currency and deposits	-43	74	-61	...	...	...	...	...	...	...	...	...
3203	Debt securities	—	—	—	...	...	...	...	...	...	...	...	...
3204	Loans	-25	-6	-13	...	...	...	...	...	...	...	...	...
3205	Equity and investment fund shares	—	—	—	...	...	...	...	...	...	...	...	...
3206	Insurance, pension, and standardized guarantee schemes	—	—	—	...	...	...	...	...	...	...	...	...
3207	Financial derivatives and employee stock options	—	—	—	...	...	...	...	...	...	...	...	...
3208	Other accounts receivable	...	...	...	...	...	...	...	...	...	...	...	...
	By debtor												
321	Domestic debtors	-68	68	-73	...	...	...	...	...	...	...	...	...
322	External debtors	—	—	—	...	...	...	...	...	...	...	...	...
33	**Net incurrence of liabilities**	**168**	**188**	**73**	...	...	...	...	...	...	...	...	...
	By instrument												
3301	Special Drawing Rights (SDRs)	—	—	—	...	...	...	...	...	...	...	...	...
3302	Currency and deposits	0	0	-7	...	...	...	...	...	...	...	...	...
3303	Debt securities	92	75	84	...	...	...	...	...	...	...	...	...
3304	Loans	97	99	99	...	...	...	...	...	...	...	...	...
3305	Equity and investment fund shares	—	—	—	...	...	...	...	...	...	...	...	...
3306	Insurance, pension, and standardized guarantee schemes	—	—	—	...	...	...	...	...	...	...	...	...
3307	Financial derivatives and employee stock options	—	—	—	...	...	...	...	...	...	...	...	...
3308	Other accounts payable	-21	14	-102	...	...	...	...	...	...	...	...	...
	By creditor												
331	Domestic creditors	134	137	-16	...	...	...	...	...	...	...	...	...
332	External creditors	34	51	89	...	...	...	...	...	...	...	...	...
	Table 4 Holding gains and losses in assets and liabilities												
	Table 5 Holding gains and losses in assets and liabilities												
	Table 6 Balance sheet												

Burkina Faso (748)

In Billions of CFA (BCEAO) Francs (XOF) / Fiscal Year Ends December 31st

	Budgetary Central Government			Central Government (excl. Social Security)			Central Government (incl. Social Security)			General Government		
	2013	2014	2015	2013	2014	2015	2013	2014	2015	2013	2014	2015
Table 7 Expenditure by functions of government												
Table 8 Financial transactions by counterpart sector												
Table 9 Total other economic flows in assets and liabilities												

Burundi (618)

In Billions of Burundi Francs (BIF) / Fiscal Year Ends December 31st

		Budgetary Central Government			Central Government (excl. Social Security)			Central Government (incl. Social Security)			General Government		
		2011	2012	2013	2011	2012	2013	2011	2012	2013	2011	2012	2013
	Statement of operations												
1	Revenue	1,075	933	1,006	...	...	...	...	...	...	...	...	...
2	Expense	564	604	649	...	...	...	...	...	...	...	...	...
GOB	**Gross operating balance**	**511**	**329**	**358**	...	...	...	...	...	...	...	...	...
NOB	**Net operating balance**	...	...	...	...	...	...	...	...	...	...	...	...
31	Net/Gross investment in nonfinancial assets	593	421	437	...	...	...	...	...	...	...	...	...
2M	Expenditure	1,156	1,025	1,086	...	...	...	...	...	...	...	...	...
NLB	**Net lending (+) / Net borrowing (-)**	**-82**	**-92**	**-80**	...	...	...	...	...	...	...	...	...
32	Net acquisition of financial assets	-60	-90	164	...	...	...	...	...	...	...	...	...
33	Net incurrence of liabilities	20	5	242	...	...	...	...	...	...	...	...	...
NLBz	Statistical discrepancy	1	-3	2	...	...	...	...	...	...	...	...	...
	Memorandum items												
PB	Primary net lending / net borrowing	-49	-58	-50	...	...	...	...	...	...	...	...	...
GB	Government balance per national definition	...	...	...	...	...	...	...	...	...	...	...	...
	Statement of other economic flows												
	Balance sheet												
	Table 1 Revenue												
1	**Revenue**	**1,075**	**933**	**1,006**	...	...	...	...	...	...	...	...	...
11	**Taxes**	**438**	**488**	**514**	...	...	...	...	...	...	...	...	...
111	Taxes on income, profits, and capital gains	125	162	146	...	...	...	...	...	...	...	...	...
1111	Payable by individuals	53	78	50	...	...	...	...	...	...	...	...	...
1112	Payable by corporations and other enterprises	71	84	96	...	...	...	...	...	...	...	...	...
1113	Other taxes on income, profits, and capital gains	1	1	0	...	...	...	...	...	...	...	...	...
112	Taxes on payroll and workforce	—	—	—	...	...	...	...	...	...	...	...	...
113	Taxes on property	—	—	—	...	...	...	...	...	...	...	...	...
114	Taxes on goods and services	245	272	317	...	...	...	...	...	...	...	...	...
1141	General taxes on goods and services	174	188	201	...	...	...	...	...	...	...	...	...
1142	Excises	69	80	110	...	...	...	...	...	...	...	...	...
115	Taxes on international trade and transactions	69	54	51	...	...	...	...	...	...	...	...	...
116	Other taxes	0	0	—	...	...	...	...	...	...	...	...	...
12	**Social contributions**	—	—	—	...	...	...	...	...	...	...	...	...
121	Social security contributions	—	—	—	...	...	...	...	...	...	...	...	...
122	Other social contributions	—	—	—	...	...	...	...	...	...	...	...	...
13	**Grants**	**603**	**395**	**452**	...	...	...	...	...	...	...	...	...
131	From foreign governments	256	96	74	...	...	...	...	...	...	...	...	...
132	From international organizations	347	299	377	...	...	...	...	...	...	...	...	...
133	From other general government units	—	—	—	...	...	...	...	...	...	...	...	...
1331	Current	—	—	—	...	...	...	...	...	...	...	...	...
1332	Capital	—	—	—	...	...	...	...	...	...	...	...	...
14	**Other revenue**	**34**	**50**	**40**	...	...	...	...	...	...	...	...	...
	Table 2 Expense by economic type												
2	**Expense**	**564**	**604**	**649**	...	...	...	...	...	...	...	...	...
21	**Compensation of employees**	**259**	**281**	**295**	...	...	...	...	...	...	...	...	...
211	Wages and salaries	236	258	270	...	...	...	...	...	...	...	...	...
212	Employers' social contributions	23	23	25	...	...	...	...	...	...	...	...	...
22	**Use of goods and services**	**105**	**105**	**120**	...	...	...	...	...	...	...	...	...
23	**Consumption of fixed capital**	...	...	...	...	...	...	...	...	...	...	...	...
24	**Interest**	**33**	**33**	**30**	...	...	...	...	...	...	...	...	...
25	**Subsidies**	—	—	—	...	...	...	...	...	...	...	...	...
26	**Grants**	**149**	**171**	**198**	...	...	...	...	...	...	...	...	...
261	To foreign governments	—	—	—	...	...	...	...	...	...	...	...	...
262	To international organizations	18	5	15	...	...	...	...	...	...	...	...	...
263	To other general government units	131	166	183	...	...	...	...	...	...	...	...	...
2631	Current	120	156	167	...	...	...	...	...	...	...	...	...
2632	Capital	11	10	16	...	...	...	...	...	...	...	...	...

Burundi (618)

In Billions of Burundi Francs (BIF) / Fiscal Year Ends December 31st

		Budgetary Central Government			Central Government (excl. Social Security)			Central Government (incl. Social Security)			General Government		
		2011	2012	2013	2011	2012	2013	2011	2012	2013	2011	2012	2013
27	**Social benefits**	**15**	**4**	**4**	...	...	...	...	...	...	...	...	...
271	Social security benefits	—	—	—	...	...	...	...	...	...	...	...	...
272	Social assistance benefits	1	1	1	...	...	...	...	...	...	...	...	...
273	Employment-related social benefits	15	3	3	...	...	...	...	...	...	...	...	...
28	**Other expense**	**2**	**9**	**2**	...	...	...	...	...	...	...	...	...
281	Property expense other than interest	—	—	—	...	...	...	...	...	...	...	...	...
282	Transfers not elsewhere classified	2	9	2	...	...	...	...	...	...	...	...	...
2821	Current	2	9	2	...	...	...	...	...	...	...	...	...
2822	Capital	—	—	—	...	...	...	...	...	...	...	...	...
	Table 3 Transactions in assets and liabilities												
3	**Change in net worth from transactions**	**512**	**326**	**359**	...	...	...	...	...	...	...	...	...
31	**Net/Gross investment in nonfinancial assets**	**593**	**421**	**437**	...	...	...	...	...	...	...	...	...
311	Fixed assets	584	413	434	...	...	...	...	...	...	...	...	...
3111	Buildings and structures	...	...	...	...	...	...	...	...	...	...	...	...
3112	Machinery and equipment	...	...	...	...	...	...	...	...	...	...	...	...
3113	Other fixed assets	...	...	...	...	...	...	...	...	...	...	...	...
3114	Weapons systems	...	...	...	...	...	...	...	...	...	...	...	...
312	Inventories	—	—	—	...	...	...	...	...	...	...	...	...
313	Valuables	—	—	—	...	...	...	...	...	...	...	...	...
314	Nonproduced assets	9	8	3	...	...	...	...	...	...	...	...	...
3141	Land	9	8	3	...	...	...	...	...	...	...	...	...
3142	Mineral and energy resources	—	—	0	...	...	...	...	...	...	...	...	...
3143	Other naturally occurring assets	—	—	—	...	...	...	...	...	...	...	...	...
3144	Intangible nonproduced assets	—	—	—	...	...	...	...	...	...	...	...	...
32	**Net acquisition of financial assets**	**-60**	**-90**	**164**	...	...	...	...	...	...	...	...	...
	By instrument												
3201	Monetary gold and SDRs	—	—	0	...	...	...	...	...	...	...	...	...
3202	Currency and deposits	-61	-78	164	...	...	...	...	...	...	...	...	...
3203	Debt securities	—	—	—	...	...	...	...	...	...	...	...	...
3204	Loans	—	-2	—	...	...	...	...	...	...	...	...	...
3205	Equity and investment fund shares	4	-6	0	...	...	...	...	...	...	...	...	...
3206	Insurance, pension, and standardized guarantee schemes	—	—	—	...	...	...	...	...	...	...	...	...
3207	Financial derivatives and employee stock options	—	—	—	...	...	...	...	...	...	...	...	...
3208	Other accounts receivable	-3	-4	—	...	...	...	...	...	...	...	...	...
	By debtor												
321	Domestic debtors	-60	-90	164	...	...	...	...	...	...	...	...	...
322	External debtors	—	—	—	...	...	...	...	...	...	...	...	...
33	**Net incurrence of liabilities**	**20**	**5**	**242**	...	...	...	...	...	...	...	...	...
	By instrument												
3301	Special Drawing Rights (SDRs)	—	—	—	...	...	...	...	...	...	...	...	...
3302	Currency and deposits	—	—	—	...	...	...	...	...	...	...	...	...
3303	Debt securities	-0	-18	58	...	...	...	...	...	...	...	...	...
3304	Loans	11	46	148	...	...	...	...	...	...	...	...	...
3305	Equity and investment fund shares	—	—	—	...	...	...	...	...	...	...	...	...
3306	Insurance, pension, and standardized guarantee schemes	—	—	—	...	...	...	...	...	...	...	...	...
3307	Financial derivatives and employee stock options	—	—	—	...	...	...	...	...	...	...	...	...
3308	Other accounts payable	10	-23	37	...	...	...	...	...	...	...	...	...
	By creditor												
331	Domestic creditors	26	-22	236	...	...	...	...	...	...	...	...	...
332	External creditors	-6	27	6	...	...	...	...	...	...	...	...	...
	Table 4 Holding gains and losses in assets and liabilities												
	Table 5 Holding gains and losses in assets and liabilities												
	Table 6 Balance sheet												

Burundi (618)

In Billions of Burundi Francs (BIF) / Fiscal Year Ends December 31st

		Budgetary Central Government			Central Government (excl. Social Security)			Central Government (incl. Social Security)			General Government		
		2011	2012	2013	2011	2012	2013	2011	2012	2013	2011	2012	2013
	Table 7 Expenditure by functions of government												
7	**Expenditure**	**1,156**	**1,025**	**1,086**	...	...	...	...	...	...	...	...	...
701	**General public services**	**199**	**220**	**173**	...	...	...	...	...	...	...	...	...
7017	Public debt transactions	33	33	30	...	...	...	...	...	...	...	...	...
7018	Transfers of general character between levels of government	...	...	...	...	...	...	...	...	...	...	...	...
702	**Defense**	**76**	**88**	**97**	...	...	...	...	...	...	...	...	...
703	**Public order and safety**	**51**	**51**	**74**	...	...	...	...	...	...	...	...	...
704	**Economic affairs**	**79**	**76**	**88**	...	...	...	...	...	...	...	...	...
7042	Agriculture, forestry, fishing, and hunting	33	31	30	...	...	...	...	...	...	...	...	...
7043	Fuel and energy	14	19	22	...	...	...	...	...	...	...	...	...
7044	Mining, manufacturing, and construction	10	5	3	...	...	...	...	...	...	...	...	...
7045	Transport	15	14	17	...	...	...	...	...	...	...	...	...
7046	Communication	4	4	6	...	...	...	...	...	...	...	...	...
705	**Environmental protection**	**5**	**4**	**5**	...	...	...	...	...	...	...	...	...
706	**Housing and community amenities**	**4**	**3**	**5**	...	...	...	...	...	...	...	...	...
707	**Health**	**68**	**89**	**91**	...	...	...	...	...	...	...	...	...
7072	Outpatient services	0	0	0	...	...	...	...	...	...	...	...	...
7073	Hospital services	15	30	33	...	...	...	...	...	...	...	...	...
7074	Public health services	2	3	3	...	...	...	...	...	...	...	...	...
708	**Recreation, culture and religion**	**2**	**2**	**3**	...	...	...	...	...	...	...	...	...
709	**Education**	**173**	**186**	**201**	...	...	...	...	...	...	...	...	...
7091	Pre-primary and primary education	86	85	101	...	...	...	...	...	...	...	...	...
7092	Secondary education	62	63	67	...	...	...	...	...	...	...	...	...
7094	Tertiary education	25	38	31	...	...	...	...	...	...	...	...	...
710	**Social protection**	**8**	**8**	**10**	...	...	...	...	...	...	...	...	...
7z	Statistical discrepancy: Expenditure	-0	—	...	...	...	...	...	...	...	...	...	...
	Table 8 Financial transactions by counterpart sector												
	Table 9 Total other economic flows in assets and liabilities												

Cabo Verde (624)

In Millions of Cape Verde Escudos (CVE) / Fiscal Year Ends December 31st

		Budgetary Central Government			Central Government (excl. Social Security)			Central Government (incl. Social Security)			General Government		
		2010	2011B	2012	2010	2011	2012	2010	2011	2012	2010	2011	2012
	Statement of operations												
1	Revenue	37,213	37,300	33,962	...	...	35,763	...	...	...	...	...	...
2	Expense	27,326	33,929	27,799	...	...	33,413	...	...	...	...	...	...
GOB	**Gross operating balance**	**9,887**	**3,371**	**6,162**	...	...	**2,350**	...	...	...	...	...	...
NOB	**Net operating balance**	...	...	...	...	...	...	...	...	...	...	...	...
31	Net/Gross investment in nonfinancial assets	21,192	14,652	20,859	...	...	20,879	...	...	...	...	...	...
2M	Expenditure	48,518	48,581	48,658	...	...	54,293	...	...	...	...	...	...
NLB	**Net lending (+) / Net borrowing (-)**	**-11,304**	**-11,281**	**-14,696**	...	...	**-18,529**	...	...	...	...	...	...
32	Net acquisition of financial assets	3,641	4,758	2,552	...	...	2,552	...	...	...	...	...	...
33	Net incurrence of liabilities	17,921	16,711	16,451	...	...	16,451	...	...	...	...	...	...
NLBz	Statistical discrepancy	-2,975	-671	797	...	...	4,630	...	...	...	...	...	...
	Memorandum items												
PB	Primary net lending / net borrowing	-9,145	-9,005	-11,839	...	...	-15,671	...	...	...	...	...	...
GB	Government balance per national definition	...	...	...	...	...	...	...	...	...	...	...	...
	Statement of other economic flows												
	Balance sheet												
	Table 1 Revenue												
1	**Revenue**	**37,213**	**37,300**	**33,962**	...	...	**35,763**	...	...	...	...	...	...
11	**Taxes**	**25,564**	**29,187**	**26,886**	...	...	**26,886**	...	...	...	...	...	...
111	Taxes on income, profits, and capital gains	7,701	8,285	8,603	...	...	8,603	...	...	...	...	...	...
1111	Payable by individuals	4,454	4,484	4,981	...	...	4,981	...	...	...	...	...	...
1112	Payable by corporations and other enterprises	3,247	3,801	3,622	...	...	3,622	...	...	...	...	...	...
1113	Other taxes on income, profits, and capital gains	—	—	—	...	...	—	...	...	...	...	...	...
112	Taxes on payroll and workforce	—	—	—	...	...	—	...	...	...	...	...	...
113	Taxes on property	—	—	—	...	...	—	...	...	...	...	...	...
114	Taxes on goods and services	12,475	14,965	12,767	...	...	12,767	...	...	...	...	...	...
1141	General taxes on goods and services	11,774	14,130	12,047	...	...	12,047	...	...	...	...	...	...
1142	Excises	—	—	—	...	...	—	...	...	...	...	...	...
115	Taxes on international trade and transactions	5,388	5,938	5,516	...	...	5,516	...	...	...	...	...	...
116	Other taxes	—	—	—	...	...	—	...	...	...	...	...	...
12	**Social contributions**	**42**	**37**	**41**	...	...	**41**	...	...	...	...	...	...
121	Social security contributions	42	37	41	...	...	41	...	...	...	...	...	...
122	Other social contributions	—	—	—	...	...	—	...	...	...	...	...	...
13	**Grants**	**9,440**	**4,343**	**4,203**	...	...	**4,203**	...	...	...	...	...	...
131	From foreign governments	9,440	4,342	—	...	...	—	...	...	...	...	...	...
132	From international organizations	—	—	4,203	...	...	4,203	...	...	...	...	...	...
133	From other general government units	—	1	—	...	...	—	...	...	...	...	...	...
1331	Current	—	—	—	...	...	—	...	...	...	...	...	...
1332	Capital	—	1	—	...	...	—	...	...	...	...	...	...
14	**Other revenue**	**2,167**	**3,733**	**2,832**	...	...	**4,634**	...	...	...	...	...	...
	Table 2 Expense by economic type												
2	**Expense**	**27,326**	**33,929**	**27,799**	...	...	**33,413**	...	...	...	...	...	...
21	**Compensation of employees**	**11,298**	**15,993**	**11,734**	...	...	**15,641**	...	...	...	...	...	...
211	Wages and salaries	10,937	15,260	11,206	...	...	14,899	...	...	...	...	...	...
212	Employers' social contributions	361	733	529	...	...	742	...	...	...	...	...	...
22	**Use of goods and services**	**4,214**	**5,312**	**3,869**	...	...	**4,934**	...	...	...	...	...	...
23	**Consumption of fixed capital**	—	—	...	...	...	...	...	...	...	...	...	...
24	**Interest**	**2,159**	**2,276**	**2,858**	...	...	**2,858**	...	...	...	...	...	...
25	**Subsidies**	**699**	**509**	**274**	...	...	**274**	...	...	...	...	...	...
26	**Grants**	**4,671**	**4,033**	**4,029**	...	...	**4,057**	...	...	...	...	...	...
261	To foreign governments	206	2	—	...	...	—	...	...	...	...	...	...
262	To international organizations	200	198	276	...	...	277	...	...	...	...	...	...
263	To other general government units	4,264	3,833	3,753	...	...	3,780	...	...	...	...	...	...
2631	Current	4,264	3,779	3,605	...	...	3,632	...	...	...	...	...	...
2632	Capital	—	55	147	...	...	147	...	...	...	...	...	...

Cabo Verde (624)

In Millions of Cape Verde Escudos (CVE) / Fiscal Year Ends December 31st

		Budgetary Central Government			Central Government (excl. Social Security)			Central Government (incl. Social Security)			General Government		
		2010	2011B	2012	2010	2011	2012	2010	2011	2012	2010	2011	2012
27	**Social benefits**	**2,830**	**4,005**	**3,845**	...	...	**3,918**	...	...	...	...	...	...
271	Social security benefits	—	—	—	...	...	—	...	...	...	...	...	...
272	Social assistance benefits	2,830	4,005	3,845	...	...	3,918	...	...	...	...	...	...
273	Employment-related social benefits	—	—	—	...	...	—	...	...	...	...	...	...
28	**Other expense**	**1,456**	**1,800**	**1,191**	...	...	**1,731**	...	...	...	...	...	...
281	Property expense other than interest	—	—	—	...	...	—	...	...	...	...	...	...
282	Transfers not elsewhere classified	1,456	1,800	1,191	...	...	1,731	...	...	...	...	...	...
2821	Current	1,456	1,800	1,191	...	...	1,731	...	...	...	...	...	...
2822	Capital	—	—	—	...	...	—	...	...	...	...	...	...
	Table 3 Transactions in assets and liabilities												
3	**Change in net worth from transactions**	...	...	...	...	...	...	...	...	...	...	...	...
31	**Net/Gross investment in nonfinancial assets**	**21,192**	**14,652**	**20,859**	...	...	**20,879**	...	...	...	...	...	...
311	Fixed assets	21,184	14,652	20,800	...	...	20,821	...	...	...	...	...	...
3111	Buildings and structures	19,335	13,629	20,044	...	...	20,048	...	...	...	...	...	...
3112	Machinery and equipment	1,437	916	730	...	...	747	...	...	...	...	...	...
3113	Other fixed assets	412	107	26	...	...	26	...	...	...	...	...	...
3114	Weapons systems	—	—	—	...	...	—	...	...	...	...	...	...
312	Inventories	—	—	1	...	...	1	...	...	...	...	...	...
313	Valuables	—	—	—	...	...	—	...	...	...	...	...	...
314	Nonproduced assets	8	1	58	...	...	58	...	...	...	...	...	...
3141	Land	8	1	30	...	...	30	...	...	...	...	...	...
3142	Mineral and energy resources	—	—	—	...	...	—	...	...	...	...	...	...
3143	Other naturally occurring assets	—	—	28	...	...	28	...	...	...	...	...	...
3144	Intangible nonproduced assets	—	—	—	...	...	—	...	...	...	...	...	...
32	**Net acquisition of financial assets**	**3,641**	**4,758**	**2,552**	...	...	**2,552**	...	...	...	...	...	...
	By instrument												
3201	Monetary gold and SDRs	—	—	—	...	...	—	...	...	...	...	...	...
3202	Currency and deposits	2,196	-597	—	...	...	—	...	...	...	...	...	...
3203	Debt securities	—	—	—	...	...	—	...	...	...	...	...	...
3204	Loans	1,430	5,310	2,465	...	...	2,465	...	...	...	...	...	...
3205	Equity and investment fund shares	15	46	1,044	...	...	1,044	...	...	...	...	...	...
3206	Insurance, pension, and standardized guarantee schemes	—	—	—	...	...	—	...	...	...	...	...	...
3207	Financial derivatives and employee stock options	—	—	—	...	...	—	...	...	...	...	...	...
3208	Other accounts receivable	—	—	-957	...	...	-957	...	...	...	...	...	...
	By debtor												
321	Domestic debtors	3,641	4,758	2,552	...	...	2,552	...	...	...	...	...	...
322	External debtors	—	—	—	...	...	—	...	...	...	...	...	...
33	**Net incurrence of liabilities**	**17,921**	**16,711**	**16,451**	...	...	**16,451**	...	...	...	...	...	...
	By instrument												
3301	Special Drawing Rights (SDRs)	—	—	—	...	...	—	...	...	...	...	...	...
3302	Currency and deposits	—	—	-3,746	...	...	-3,746	...	...	...	...	...	...
3303	Debt securities	2,545	2,539	2,648	...	...	2,648	...	...	...	...	...	...
3304	Loans	14,524	14,172	17,751	...	...	17,751	...	...	...	...	...	...
3305	Equity and investment fund shares	—	—	—	...	...	—	...	...	...	...	...	...
3306	Insurance, pension, and standardized guarantee schemes	—	—	—	...	...	—	...	...	...	...	...	...
3307	Financial derivatives and employee stock options	—	—	—	...	...	—	...	...	...	...	...	...
3308	Other accounts payable	852	—	-201	...	...	-201	...	...	...	...	...	...
	By creditor												
331	Domestic creditors	3,397	2,539	-1,299	...	...	-1,299	...	...	...	...	...	...
332	External creditors	14,524	14,172	17,751	...	...	17,751	...	...	...	...	...	...
	Table 4 Holding gains and losses in assets and liabilities												
	Table 5 Holding gains and losses in assets and liabilities												
	Table 6 Balance sheet												

Cabo Verde (624)

In Millions of Cape Verde Escudos (CVE) / Fiscal Year Ends December 31st

		Budgetary Central Government			Central Government (excl. Social Security)			Central Government (incl. Social Security)			General Government		
		2010	2011B	2012	2010	2011	2012	2010	2011	2012	2010	2011	2012
	Table 7 Expenditure by functions of government												
7	**Expenditure**	**48,518**	**48,581**	**48,658**	...	...	**54,293**	...	...	...	...	...	...
701	**General public services**	**12,428**	**13,595**	**11,579**	...	...	**11,943**	...	...	...	...	...	...
7017	Public debt transactions	2,159	2,276	2,858	...	...	2,858	...	...	...	...	...	...
7018	Transfers of general character between levels of government	—	—	740	...	...	740	...	...	...	...	...	...
702	**Defense**	**32**	**1,131**	**152**	...	...	**836**	...	...	...	...	...	...
703	**Public order and safety**	**6,955**	**3,589**	**907**	...	...	**3,146**	...	...	...	...	...	...
704	**Economic affairs**	**15,630**	**12,780**	**16,468**	...	...	**16,670**	...	...	...	...	...	...
7042	Agriculture, forestry, fishing, and hunting	1,729	966	2,675	...	...	2,675	...	...	...	...	...	...
7043	Fuel and energy	2,218	1,630	780	...	...	780	...	...	...	...	...	...
7044	Mining, manufacturing, and construction	3,353	6,136	7,053	...	...	7,053	...	...	...	...	...	...
7045	Transport	8,329	3,074	4,801	...	...	4,962	...	...	...	...	...	...
7046	Communication	0	5	1	...	...	1	...	...	...	...	...	...
705	**Environmental protection**	**544**	**800**	**1,124**	...	...	**1,124**	...	...	...	...	...	...
706	**Housing and community amenities**	**1,054**	**484**	**2,582**	...	...	**2,582**	...	...	...	...	...	...
707	**Health**	**2,637**	**3,470**	**2,749**	...	...	**3,461**	...	...	...	...	...	...
7072	Outpatient services	—	—	—	...	...	—	...	...	...	...	...	...
7073	Hospital services	576	1,557	1,211	...	...	1,922	...	...	...	...	...	...
7074	Public health services	2,061	1,913	1,539	...	...	1,539	...	...	...	...	...	...
708	**Recreation, culture and religion**	**215**	**619**	**1,661**	...	...	**1,755**	...	...	...	...	...	...
709	**Education**	**6,089**	**8,097**	**7,620**	...	...	**8,913**	...	...	...	...	...	...
7091	Pre-primary and primary education	—	—	2,856	...	...	2,856	...	...	...	...	...	...
7092	Secondary education	5,910	7,336	2,936	...	...	3,485	...	...	...	...	...	...
7094	Tertiary education	179	761	1,828	...	...	2,572	...	...	...	...	...	...
710	**Social protection**	**3,612**	**4,473**	**4,503**	...	...	**4,550**	...	...	...	...	...	...
7z	Statistical discrepancy: Expenditure	-677	-456	...	...	...	...	...	...	...	...	...	...
	Table 8 Financial transactions by counterpart sector												
	Table 9 Total other economic flows in assets and liabilities												

Cambodia (522)

In Billions of Cambodian Riels (KHR) / Fiscal Year Ends March 31st

		Budgetary Central Government			Central Government (excl. Social Security)			Central Government (incl. Social Security)			General Government		
		2013	2014	2015P	2013	2014	2015	2013	2014	2015	2013	2014	2015
	Statement of operations												
1	Revenue	10,971	12,909	13,208	...	...	...	...	...	...	...	...	...
2	Expense	7,274	8,398	8,515	...	...	...	...	...	...	...	...	...
GOB	**Gross operating balance**	**3,697**	**4,511**	**4,693**	...	...	...	...	...	...	...	...	...
NOB	**Net operating balance**	...	...	...	...	...	...	...	...	...	...	...	...
31	Net/Gross investment in nonfinancial assets	5,374	5,405	5,260	...	...	...	...	...	...	...	...	...
2M	Expenditure	12,648	13,802	13,775	...	...	...	...	...	...	...	...	...
NLB	**Net lending (+) / Net borrowing (-)**	**-1,676**	**-894**	**-567**	...	...	...	...	...	...	...	...	...
32	Net acquisition of financial assets	85	1,568	1,969	...	...	...	...	...	...	...	...	...
33	Net incurrence of liabilities	1,764	2,462	2,535	...	...	...	...	...	...	...	...	...
NLBz	Statistical discrepancy	-2	0	-0	...	...	...	...	...	...	...	...	...
	Memorandum items												
PB	Primary net lending / net borrowing	-1,472	-665	-349	...	...	...	...	...	...	...	...	...
GB	Government balance per national definition	...	...	...	...	...	...	...	...	...	...	...	...
	Statement of other economic flows												
	Balance sheet												
	Table 1 Revenue												
1	**Revenue**	**10,971**	**12,909**	**13,208**	...	...	...	...	...	...	...	...	...
11	**Taxes**	**7,408**	**9,864**	**10,403**	...	...	...	...	...	...	...	...	...
111	Taxes on income, profits, and capital gains	1,561	1,965	2,467	...	...	...	...	...	...	...	...	...
1111	Payable by individuals	377	485	...	...	...	...	...	...	...	...	...	...
1112	Payable by corporations and other enterprises	1,184	1,480	...	...	...	...	...	...	...	...	...	...
1113	Other taxes on income, profits, and capital gains	—	—	...	...	...	...	...	...	...	...	...	...
112	Taxes on payroll and workforce	—	—	—	...	...	...	...	...	...	...	...	...
113	Taxes on property	—	—	—	...	...	...	...	...	...	...	...	...
114	Taxes on goods and services	4,174	5,426	6,018	...	...	...	...	...	...	...	...	...
1141	General taxes on goods and services	2,670	3,391	3,524	...	...	...	...	...	...	...	...	...
1142	Excises	1,339	1,857	2,334	...	...	...	...	...	...	...	...	...
115	Taxes on international trade and transactions	1,667	2,466	1,911	...	...	...	...	...	...	...	...	...
116	Other taxes	5	6	7	...	...	...	...	...	...	...	...	...
12	**Social contributions**	—	—	—	...	...	...	...	...	...	...	...	...
121	Social security contributions	—	—	—	...	...	...	...	...	...	...	...	...
122	Other social contributions	—	—	—	...	...	...	...	...	...	...	...	...
13	**Grants**	**2,542**	**1,728**	**1,508**	...	...	...	...	...	...	...	...	...
131	From foreign governments	2,419	1,595	1,479	...	...	...	...	...	...	...	...	...
132	From international organizations	2	38	29	...	...	...	...	...	...	...	...	...
133	From other general government units	121	95	—	...	...	...	...	...	...	...	...	...
1331	Current	121	95	—	...	...	...	...	...	...	...	...	...
1332	Capital	—	—	—	...	...	...	...	...	...	...	...	...
14	**Other revenue**	**1,022**	**1,317**	**1,298**	...	...	...	...	...	...	...	...	...
	Table 2 Expense by economic type												
2	**Expense**	**7,274**	**8,398**	**8,515**	...	...	...	...	...	...	...	...	...
21	**Compensation of employees**	**2,746**	**3,313**	**3,721**	...	...	...	...	...	...	...	...	...
211	Wages and salaries	...	...	...	...	...	...	...	...	...	...	...	...
212	Employers' social contributions	...	...	...	...	...	...	...	...	...	...	...	...
22	**Use of goods and services**	**1,965**	**2,119**	**2,025**	...	...	...	...	...	...	...	...	...
23	**Consumption of fixed capital**	...	...	...	...	...	...	...	...	...	...	...	...
24	**Interest**	**204**	**228**	**217**	...	...	...	...	...	...	...	...	...
25	**Subsidies**	**130**	**324**	**21**	...	...	...	...	...	...	...	...	...
26	**Grants**	**710**	**727**	**977**	...	...	...	...	...	...	...	...	...
261	To foreign governments	28	—	118	...	...	...	...	...	...	...	...	...
262	To international organizations	14	21	18	...	...	...	...	...	...	...	...	...
263	To other general government units	668	707	841	...	...	...	...	...	...	...	...	...
2631	Current	...	...	...	...	...	...	...	...	...	...	...	...
2632	Capital	...	...	...	...	...	...	...	...	...	...	...	...

Cambodia (522)

In Billions of Cambodian Riels (KHR) / Fiscal Year Ends March 31st

		Budgetary Central Government			Central Government (excl. Social Security)			Central Government (incl. Social Security)			General Government		
		2013	2014	2015P	2013	2014	2015	2013	2014	2015	2013	2014	2015
27	**Social benefits**	**879**	**917**	**986**	**...**	**...**	**...**	**...**	**...**	**...**	**...**	**...**	**...**
271	Social security benefits	—	—	—	...	...	...	...	...	...	...	...	...
272	Social assistance benefits	458	369	435	...	...	...	...	...	...	...	...	...
273	Employment-related social benefits	420	548	551	...	...	...	...	...	...	...	...	...
28	**Other expense**	**640**	**769**	**567**	**...**	**...**	**...**	**...**	**...**	**...**	**...**	**...**	**...**
281	Property expense other than interest	—	—	—	...	...	...	...	...	...	...	...	...
282	Transfers not elsewhere classified	640	769	567	...	...	...	...	...	...	...	...	...
2821	Current	640	769	567	...	...	...	...	...	...	...	...	...
2822	Capital	—	—	—	...	...	...	...	...	...	...	...	...
	Table 3 Transactions in assets and liabilities												
3	**Change in net worth from transactions**	**...**	**...**	**...**	**...**	**...**	**...**	**...**	**...**	**...**	**...**	**...**	**...**
31	**Net/Gross investment in nonfinancial assets**	**5,374**	**5,405**	**5,260**	**...**	**...**	**...**	**...**	**...**	**...**	**...**	**...**	**...**
311	Fixed assets	5,374	5,392	5,106	...	...	...	...	...	...	...	...	...
3111	Buildings and structures	...	5,366	5,065	...	...	...	...	...	...	...	...	...
3112	Machinery and equipment	...	25	41	...	...	...	...	...	...	...	...	...
3113	Other fixed assets	...	2	—	...	...	...	...	...	...	...	...	...
3114	Weapons systems	...	...	...	...	...	...	...	...	...	...	...	...
312	Inventories	...	—	—	...	...	...	...	...	...	...	...	...
313	Valuables	...	—	—	...	...	...	...	...	...	...	...	...
314	Nonproduced assets	—	12	154	...	...	...	...	...	...	...	...	...
3141	Land	—	12	154	...	...	...	...	...	...	...	...	...
3142	Mineral and energy resources	—	—	—	...	...	...	...	...	...	...	...	...
3143	Other naturally occurring assets	—	—	—	...	...	...	...	...	...	...	...	...
3144	Intangible nonproduced assets	—	—	—	...	...	...	...	...	...	...	...	...
32	**Net acquisition of financial assets**	**85**	**1,568**	**1,969**	**...**	**...**	**...**	**...**	**...**	**...**	**...**	**...**	**...**
	By instrument												
3201	Monetary gold and SDRs	—	—	—	...	...	...	...	...	...	...	...	...
3202	Currency and deposits	62	1,679	2,059	...	...	...	...	...	...	...	...	...
3203	Debt securities	—	—	—	...	...	...	...	...	...	...	...	...
3204	Loans	23	-111	-91	...	...	...	...	...	...	...	...	...
3205	Equity and investment fund shares	-0	—	—	...	...	...	...	...	...	...	...	...
3206	Insurance, pension, and standardized guarantee schemes	—	—	—	...	...	...	...	...	...	...	...	...
3207	Financial derivatives and employee stock options	—	—	—	...	...	...	...	...	...	...	...	...
3208	Other accounts receivable	...	...	...	...	...	...	...	...	...	...	...	...
	By debtor												
321	Domestic debtors	85	1,568	1,969	...	...	...	...	...	...	...	...	...
322	External debtors	—	—	—	...	...	...	...	...	...	...	...	...
33	**Net incurrence of liabilities**	**1,764**	**2,462**	**2,535**	**...**	**...**	**...**	**...**	**...**	**...**	**...**	**...**	**...**
	By instrument												
3301	Special Drawing Rights (SDRs)	—	—	—	...	...	...	...	...	...	...	...	...
3302	Currency and deposits	—	—	—	...	...	...	...	...	...	...	...	...
3303	Debt securities	—	—	—	...	...	...	...	...	...	...	...	...
3304	Loans	1,923	2,306	2,250	...	...	...	...	...	...	...	...	...
3305	Equity and investment fund shares	—	—	—	...	...	...	...	...	...	...	...	...
3306	Insurance, pension, and standardized guarantee schemes	—	—	—	...	...	...	...	...	...	...	...	...
3307	Financial derivatives and employee stock options	—	—	—	...	...	...	...	...	...	...	...	...
3308	Other accounts payable	-160	156	285	...	...	...	...	...	...	...	...	...
	By creditor												
331	Domestic creditors	-160	156	285	...	...	...	...	...	...	...	...	...
332	External creditors	1,923	2,306	2,250	...	...	...	...	...	...	...	...	...
	Table 4 Holding gains and losses in assets and liabilities												
	Table 5 Holding gains and losses in assets and liabilities												
	Table 6 Balance sheet												

Cambodia (522)

In Billions of Cambodian Riels (KHR) / Fiscal Year Ends March 31st

	Budgetary Central Government			Central Government (excl. Social Security)			Central Government (incl. Social Security)			General Government		
	2013	2014	2015P	2013	2014	2015	2013	2014	2015	2013	2014	2015
Table 7 Expenditure by functions of government												
Table 8 Financial transactions by counterpart sector												
Table 9 Total other economic flows in assets and liabilities												

Canada (156)

In Billions of Canadian Dollars (CAD) / Fiscal Year Ends December 31st

		Budgetary Central Government			Central Government (excl. Social Security)			Central Government (incl. Social Security)			General Government		
		2013	2014	2015	2013	2014	2015	2013	2014	2015	2013	2014	2015
	Statement of operations												
1	Revenue	...	...	...	262	274	279	323	338	347	733	766	778
2	Expense	...	...	...	274	274	284	325	327	341	748	763	791
GOB	**Gross operating balance**	...	...	...	**-3**	**9**	**5**	**8**	**20**	**16**	**46**	**67**	**53**
NOB	**Net operating balance**	...	...	...	**-12**	**0**	**-5**	**-2**	**11**	**6**	**-15**	**3**	**-13**
31	Net/Gross investment in nonfinancial assets	...	...	...	-0	-8	-4	-0	-8	-4	12	2	8
2M	Expenditure	...	...	...	273	266	280	325	320	337	760	765	799
NLB	**Net lending (+) / Net borrowing (-)**	...	...	...	**-12**	**8**	**-1**	**-1**	**19**	**10**	**-27**	**0**	**-21**
32	Net acquisition of financial assets	...	...	...	-4	-16	42	...	...	...	35	65	113
33	Net incurrence of liabilities	...	...	...	8	-24	43	...	...	...	64	65	136
NLBz	Statistical discrepancy	...	...	...	-0	-0	0	...	...	...	-1	-1	-1
	Memorandum items												
PB	Primary net lending / net borrowing	...	...	...	16	33	23	26	44	34	37	63	41
GB	Government balance per national definition	...	...	...	...	...	...	...	...	...	...	...	...
	Statement of other economic flows												
	Balance sheet												
6	**Net worth**	...	...	...	**-578**	**-591**	**-605**	...	...	...	**18**	**-15**	**-122**
61	Nonfinancial assets	...	...	...	64	64	60	...	...	...	936	925	820
62	Financial assets	...	...	...	301	292	337	...	...	...	1,122	1,219	1,360
63	Liabilities	...	...	...	943	947	1,002	...	...	...	2,040	2,159	2,301
	Table 1 Revenue												
1	**Revenue**	...	...	...	**262**	**274**	**279**	**323**	**338**	**347**	**733**	**766**	**778**
11	**Taxes**	...	...	...	**221**	**234**	**239**	**221**	**234**	**239**	**505**	**530**	**545**
111	Taxes on income, profits, and capital gains	...	...	...	172	183	186	172	183	186	284	301	307
1111	Payable by individuals	...	...	...	...	...	...	...	...	...	...	...	...
1112	Payable by corporations and other enterprises	...	...	...	...	...	...	...	...	...	...	...	...
1113	Other taxes on income, profits, and capital gains	...	...	...	...	...	...	...	...	...	...	...	...
112	Taxes on payroll and workforce	...	...	...	—	—	—	—	—	—	12	13	13
113	Taxes on property	...	...	...	...	...	...	...	...	...	...	...	...
114	Taxes on goods and services	...	...	...	...	...	...	...	...	...	...	...	...
1141	General taxes on goods and services	...	...	...	...	...	...	...	...	...	...	...	...
1142	Excises	...	...	...	...	...	...	...	...	...	...	...	...
115	Taxes on international trade and transactions	...	...	...	4	5	5	4	5	5	4	5	5
116	Other taxes	...	...	...	—	—	—	—	—	—	0	0	0
12	**Social contributions**	...	...	...	**22**	**23**	**24**	**77**	**80**	**82**	**89**	**92**	**95**
121	Social security contributions	...	...	...	...	...	...	...	...	...	...	...	...
122	Other social contributions	...	...	...	...	...	...	...	...	...	...	...	...
13	**Grants**	...	...	...	**1**	**1**	**1**	**1**	**1**	**1**	**1**	**1**	**1**
131	From foreign governments	...	...	...	...	...	...	...	...	...	...	...	...
132	From international organizations	...	...	...	...	...	...	...	...	...	...	...	...
133	From other general government units	...	...	...	...	...	...	...	...	...	...	...	...
1331	Current	...	...	...	...	...	...	...	...	...	...	...	...
1332	Capital	...	...	...	...	...	...	...	...	...	...	...	...
14	**Other revenue**	...	...	...	**18**	**16**	**16**	**25**	**23**	**25**	**137**	**142**	**137**
	Table 2 Expense by economic type												
2	**Expense**	...	...	...	**274**	**274**	**284**	**325**	**327**	**341**	**748**	**763**	**791**
21	**Compensation of employees**	...	...	...	**39**	**38**	**37**	**39**	**38**	**37**	**230**	**236**	**243**
211	Wages and salaries	...	...	...	...	...	...	...	...	...	...	...	...
212	Employers' social contributions	...	...	...	...	...	...	...	...	...	...	...	...
22	**Use of goods and services**	...	...	...	**20**	**20**	**21**	**22**	**23**	**24**	**159**	**164**	**169**
23	**Consumption of fixed capital**	...	...	...	**9**	**9**	**9**	**9**	**9**	**9**	**61**	**64**	**66**
24	**Interest**	...	...	...	**27**	**25**	**24**	**27**	**25**	**24**	**64**	**63**	**62**
25	**Subsidies**	...	...	...	**3**	**3**	**3**	**3**	**3**	**3**	**18**	**17**	**18**

Canada (156)

In Billions of Canadian Dollars (CAD) / Fiscal Year Ends December 31st

		Budgetary Central Government			Central Government (excl. Social Security)			Central Government (incl. Social Security)			General Government		
		2013	2014	2015	2013	2014	2015	2013	2014	2015	2013	2014	2015
26	**Grants**	...	...	...	86	87	90	86	87	90	5	5	5
261	To foreign governments	...	...	...	...	...	...	...	...	...	...	...	...
262	To international organizations	...	...	...	...	...	...	...	...	...	...	...	...
263	To other general government units	...	...	...	...	...	...	...	...	...	...	...	...
2631	Current	...	...	...	...	...	...	...	...	...	...	...	...
2632	Capital	...	...	...	...	...	...	...	...	...	...	...	...
27	**Social benefits**	...	...	...	83	85	94	132	136	147	176	180	193
271	Social security benefits	...	...	...	...	...	...	...	...	...	...	...	...
272	Social assistance benefits	...	...	...	...	...	...	...	...	...	...	...	...
273	Employment-related social benefits	...	...	...	...	...	...	...	...	...	...	...	...
28	**Other expense**	...	...	...	7	6	6	7	6	6	34	34	35
281	Property expense other than interest	...	...	...	...	...	...	...	...	...	...	...	...
282	Transfers not elsewhere classified	...	...	...	...	...	...	...	...	...	...	...	...
2821	Current	...	...	...	...	...	...	...	...	...	...	...	...
2822	Capital	...	...	...	...	...	...	...	...	...	...	...	...
	Table 3 Transactions in assets and liabilities												
3	**Change in net worth from transactions**	...	...	...	-12	0	-4	...	...	...	-16	2	-14
31	**Net/Gross investment in nonfinancial assets**	...	...	...	-0	-8	-4	-0	-8	-4	12	2	8
311	Fixed assets	...	...	...	...	...	...	...	...	...	...	...	...
3111	Buildings and structures	...	...	...	...	...	...	...	...	...	...	...	...
3112	Machinery and equipment	...	...	...	...	...	...	...	...	...	...	...	...
3113	Other fixed assets	...	...	...	...	...	...	...	...	...	...	...	...
3114	Weapons systems	...	...	...	...	...	...	...	...	...	...	...	...
312	Inventories	...	...	...	...	...	...	...	...	...	...	...	...
313	Valuables	...	...	...	...	...	...	...	...	...	...	...	...
314	Nonproduced assets	...	...	...	...	...	...	...	...	...	...	...	...
3141	Land	...	...	...	...	...	...	...	...	...	...	...	...
3142	Mineral and energy resources	...	...	...	...	...	...	...	...	...	...	...	...
3143	Other naturally occurring assets	...	...	...	...	...	...	...	...	...	...	...	...
3144	Intangible nonproduced assets	...	...	...	...	...	...	...	...	...	...	...	...
32	**Net acquisition of financial assets**	...	...	...	-4	-16	42	...	...	...	35	65	113
	By instrument												
3201	Monetary gold and SDRs	...	...	...	—	—	—	...	...	...	—	—	—
3202	Currency and deposits	...	...	...	9	2	11	...	...	...	15	7	15
3203	Debt securities	...	...	...	0	-0	-0	...	...	...	6	6	40
3204	Loans	...	...	...	-21	-23	3	...	...	...	-5	-6	20
3205	Equity and investment fund shares	...	...	...	11	6	13	...	...	...	4	33	29
3206	Insurance, pension, and standardized guarantee schemes	...	...	...	—	—	—	...	...	...	—	—	—
3207	Financial derivatives and employee stock options	...	...	...	—	—	—	...	...	...	—	—	—
3208	Other accounts receivable	...	...	...	-2	-1	15	...	...	...	14	25	9
	By debtor												
321	Domestic debtors	...	...	...	...	...	...	...	...	...	...	...	...
322	External debtors	...	...	...	...	...	...	...	...	...	...	...	...
33	**Net incurrence of liabilities**	...	...	...	8	-24	43	...	...	...	64	65	136
	By instrument												
3301	Special Drawing Rights (SDRs)	...	...	...	—	—	—	...	...	...	—	—	—
3302	Currency and deposits	...	...	...	0	0	0	...	...	...	0	0	0
3303	Debt securities	...	...	...	12	-21	24	...	...	...	45	20	46
3304	Loans	...	...	...	-0	-0	1	...	...	...	9	3	1
3305	Equity and investment fund shares	...	...	...	—	—	—	...	...	...	—	—	—
3306	Insurance, pension, and standardized guarantee schemes	...	...	...	0	-0	-1	...	...	...	10	14	15
3307	Financial derivatives and employee stock options	...	...	...	—	—	—	...	...	...	—	—	—
3308	Other accounts payable	...	...	...	-4	-3	18	...	...	...	-0	28	74

Canada (156)

In Billions of Canadian Dollars (CAD) / Fiscal Year Ends December 31st

		Budgetary Central Government			Central Government (excl. Social Security)			Central Government (incl. Social Security)			General Government		
		2013	2014	2015	2013	2014	2015	2013	2014	2015	2013	2014	2015
	By creditor												
331	Domestic creditors	...	...	...	...	...	...	...	...	...	...	...	...
332	External creditors	...	...	...	...	...	...	...	...	...	...	...	...
	Table 4 Holding gains and losses in assets and liabilities												
	Table 5 Holding gains and losses in assets and liabilities												
	Table 6 Balance sheet												
6	**Net worth**	...	...	...	-578	-591	-605	...	...	...	18	-15	-122
61	**Nonfinancial assets**	...	...	...	64	64	60	...	...	...	936	925	820
611	Fixed assets	...	...	...	...	...	...	...	...	...	...	...	...
6111	Buildings and structures	...	...	...	...	...	...	...	...	...	...	...	...
6112	Machinery and equipment	...	...	...	...	...	...	...	...	...	...	...	...
6113	Other fixed assets	...	...	...	...	...	...	...	...	...	...	...	...
6114	Weapons systems	...	...	...	...	...	...	...	...	...	...	...	...
612	Inventories	...	...	...	...	...	...	...	...	...	...	...	...
613	Valuables	...	...	...	...	...	...	...	...	...	...	...	...
614	Nonproduced assets	...	...	...	...	...	...	...	...	...	...	...	...
6141	Land	...	...	...	...	...	...	...	...	...	...	...	...
6142	Mineral and energy resources	...	...	...	...	...	...	...	...	...	...	...	...
6143	Other naturally occurring assets	...	...	...	...	...	...	...	...	...	...	...	...
6144	Intangible nonproduced assets	...	...	...	...	...	...	...	...	...	...	...	...
62	**Financial assets**	...	...	...	301	292	337	...	...	...	1,122	1,219	1,360
	By instrument												
6201	Monetary gold and SDRs	...	...	...	—	—	—	...	...	...	—	—	—
6202	Currency and deposits	...	...	...	35	38	49	...	...	...	86	93	108
6203	Debt securities	...	...	...	3	3	3	...	...	...	126	136	173
6204	Loans	...	...	...	98	74	77	...	...	...	219	212	233
6205	Equity and investment fund shares	...	...	...	118	128	154	...	...	...	456	517	598
6206	Insurance, pension, and standardized guarantee schemes	...	...	...	—	—	—	...	...	...	—	—	—
6207	Financial derivatives and employee stock options	...	...	...	—	—	—	...	...	...	—	—	—
6208	Other accounts receivable	...	...	...	47	49	54	...	...	...	236	261	248
	By debtor												
621	Domestic debtors	...	...	...	...	...	...	...	...	...	...	...	...
622	External debtors	...	...	...	...	...	...	...	...	...	...	...	...
63	**Liabilities**	...	...	...	943	947	1,002	...	...	...	2,040	2,159	2,301
	By instrument												
6301	Special Drawing Rights (SDRs)	...	...	...	—	—	—	...	...	...	—	—	—
6302	Currency and deposits	...	...	...	6	6	6	...	...	...	6	6	6
6303	Debt securities	...	...	...	695	702	735	...	...	...	1,320	1,401	1,479
6304	Loans	...	...	...	4	4	5	...	...	...	60	63	67
6305	Equity and investment fund shares	...	...	...	—	—	—	...	...	...	—	—	—
6306	Insurance, pension, and standardized guarantee schemes	...	...	...	158	161	160	...	...	...	341	339	357
6307	Financial derivatives and employee stock options	...	...	...	—	—	—	...	...	...	—	—	—
6308	Other accounts payable	...	...	...	81	74	96	...	...	...	313	349	393
	By creditor												
631	Domestic creditors	...	...	...	...	...	...	...	...	...	...	...	...
632	External creditors	...	...	...	...	...	...	...	...	...	...	...	...
	Memorandum items												
6M2	Net financial worth	...	...	...	-2,596	-2,594	-2,662	...	...	...	-3,754	-3,693	-3,771
6M3	Gross debt (D4) at market value	...	...	...	...	...	...	...	...	...	...	...	...
6M3D3	D3 debt liabilities at market value	...	...	...	...	...	...	...	...	...	...	...	...
6M3D2	D2 debt liabilities at market value	...	...	...	...	...	...	...	...	...	...	...	...
6M3D1	D1 debt liabilities at market value	...	...	...	...	...	...	...	...	...	...	...	...
6M4	Gross debt (D4) at nominal value	...	...	...	...	...	...	...	...	...	...	...	...
6M4D3	D3 debt liabilities at nominal value	...	...	...	...	...	...	...	...	...	...	...	...
6M4D2	D2 debt liabilities at nominal value	...	...	...	...	...	...	...	...	...	...	...	...
6M4D1	D1 debt liabilities at nominal value	...	...	...	...	...	...	...	...	...	...	...	...

Canada (156)

In Billions of Canadian Dollars (CAD) / Fiscal Year Ends December 31st

		Budgetary Central Government			Central Government (excl. Social Security)			Central Government (incl. Social Security)			General Government		
		2013	2014	2015	2013	2014	2015	2013	2014	2015	2013	2014	2015
6M35	Gross debt (D4) at face value	...	...	...	943	947	1,002	...	...	...	2,040	2,159	2,301
6M35D3	D3 debt liabilities at face value	...	...	...	785	786	842	...	...	...	1,699	1,819	1,944
6M35D2	D2 debt liabilities at face value	...	...	...	704	712	746	...	...	...	1,386	1,470	1,551
6M35D1	D1 debt liabilities at face value	...	...	...	699	706	740	...	...	...	1,380	1,465	1,546
6M93	Government gross debt per national definition	...	...	...	...	...	...	...	...	...	...	...	...
6M5	Arrears	...	...	...	...	...	...	...	...	...	...	...	...
6M6	Explicit contingent liabilities	...	...	...	...	...	...	...	...	...	...	...	...
6M61	of which: Publicly guaranteed debt	...	...	...	...	...	...	...	...	...	...	...	...
6M7	Net implicit obligations for social security benefits	...	...	...	...	...	...	...	...	...	...	...	...
	Table 7 Expenditure by functions of government												
7	**Expenditure**	...	...	...	**273**	**266**	**280**	...	...	...	**760**	**765**	**799**
701	**General public services**	...	...	...	...	...	...	...	...	...	...	...	...
7017	Public debt transactions	...	...	...	27	25	24	...	...	...	64	63	62
7018	Transfers of general character between levels of government	...	...	...	...	...	...	...	...	...	...	...	...
702	**Defense**	...	...	...	...	...	...	...	...	...	...	...	...
703	**Public order and safety**	...	...	...	...	...	...	...	...	...	...	...	...
704	**Economic affairs**	...	...	...	...	...	...	...	...	...	...	...	...
7042	Agriculture, forestry, fishing, and hunting	...	...	...	...	...	...	...	...	...	...	...	...
7043	Fuel and energy	...	...	...	...	...	...	...	...	...	...	...	...
7044	Mining, manufacturing, and construction	...	...	...	...	...	...	...	...	...	...	...	...
7045	Transport	...	...	...	...	...	...	...	...	...	...	...	...
7046	Communication	...	...	...	...	...	...	...	...	...	...	...	...
705	**Environmental protection**	...	...	...	...	...	...	...	...	...	...	...	...
706	**Housing and community amenities**	...	...	...	...	...	...	...	...	...	...	...	...
707	**Health**	...	...	...	...	...	...	...	...	...	...	...	...
7072	Outpatient services	...	...	...	...	...	...	...	...	...	...	...	...
7073	Hospital services	...	...	...	...	...	...	...	...	...	...	...	...
7074	Public health services	...	...	...	...	...	...	...	...	...	...	...	...
708	**Recreation, culture and religion**	...	...	...	...	...	...	...	...	...	...	...	...
709	**Education**	...	...	...	...	...	...	...	...	...	...	...	...
7091	Pre-primary and primary education	...	...	...	...	...	...	...	...	...	...	...	...
7092	Secondary education	...	...	...	...	...	...	...	...	...	...	...	...
7094	Tertiary education	...	...	...	...	...	...	...	...	...	...	...	...
710	**Social protection**	...	...	...	...	...	...	...	...	...	...	...	...
7z	Statistical discrepancy: Expenditure	...	...	...	...	...	...	...	...	...	...	...	...
	Table 8 Financial transactions by counterpart sector												
32	**Net acquisition of financial assets**	...	...	...	**-4**	**-16**	**42**	...	...	...	**35**	**65**	**113**
321	Domestic debtors	...	...	...	...	...	...	...	...	...	...	...	...
8211	General government	...	...	...	...	...	...	...	...	...	...	...	...
8212	Central bank	...	...	...	...	...	...	...	...	...	...	...	...
8213	Deposit-taking corporations except the central bank	...	...	...	...	...	...	...	...	...	...	...	...
8214	Other financial corporations	...	...	...	...	...	...	...	...	...	...	...	...
8215	Nonfinancial corporations	...	...	...	...	...	...	...	...	...	...	...	...
8216	Households & nonprofit institutions serving households	...	...	...	...	...	...	...	...	...	...	...	...
322	External debtors	...	...	...	...	...	...	...	...	...	...	...	...
8221	General government	...	...	...	...	...	...	...	...	...	...	...	...
8227	International organizations	...	...	...	...	...	...	...	...	...	...	...	...
8228	Financial corporations other than international organizations	...	...	...	...	...	...	...	...	...	...	...	...
8229	Other nonresidents	...	...	...	...	...	...	...	...	...	...	...	...

Canada (156)

In Billions of Canadian Dollars (CAD) / Fiscal Year Ends December 31st

		Budgetary Central Government			Central Government (excl. Social Security)			Central Government (incl. Social Security)			General Government		
		2013	2014	2015	2013	2014	2015	2013	2014	2015	2013	2014	2015
33	**Net incurrence of liabilities**	...	...	...	8	-24	43	...	...	...	64	65	136
331	Domestic creditors	...	...	...	...	...	...	...	...	...	...	...	...
8311	General government	...	...	...	...	...	...	...	...	...	...	...	...
8312	Central bank	...	...	...	...	...	...	...	...	...	...	...	...
8313	Deposit-taking corporations except the central bank	...	...	...	...	...	...	...	...	...	...	...	...
8314	Other financial corporations	...	...	...	...	...	...	...	...	...	...	...	...
8315	Nonfinancial corporations	...	...	...	...	...	...	...	...	...	...	...	...
8316	Households & nonprofit institutions serving households	...	...	...	...	...	...	...	...	...	...	...	...
332	External creditors	...	...	...	...	...	...	...	...	...	...	...	...
8321	General government	...	...	...	...	...	...	...	...	...	...	...	...
8327	International organizations	...	...	...	...	...	...	...	...	...	...	...	...
8328	Financial corporations other than international organizations	...	...	...	...	...	...	...	...	...	...	...	...
8329	Other nonresidents	...	...	...	...	...	...	...	...	...	...	...	...
	Table 9 Total other economic flows in assets and liabilities												

Central African Republic (626)

In Millions of CFA (BEAC) Francs (XAF) / Fiscal Year Ends December 31st

		Budgetary Central Government			Central Government (excl. Social Security)			Central Government (incl. Social Security)			General Government		
		2010P	2011P	2012P	2010	2011	2012	2010	2011	2012	2010	2011	2012
	Statement of operations												
1	Revenue	159,856	125,400	201,430	176,513	138,087	...	...	...	...	...	...	...
2	Expense	173,192	154,688	104,889	189,861	167,375	...	...	...	...	...	...	...
GOB	**Gross operating balance**	**-13,335**	**-29,288**	**96,541**	**-13,347**	**-29,288**	...	...	...	...	...	...	...
NOB	**Net operating balance**	...	...	...	...	...	...	...	...	...	...	...	...
31	Net/Gross investment in nonfinancial assets	75,406	39,304	89,208	77,299	41,064	...	...	...	...	...	...	...
2M	Expenditure	248,598	193,993	194,097	267,160	208,438	...	...	...	...	...	...	...
NLB	**Net lending (+) / Net borrowing (-)**	**-88,742**	**-68,592**	**7,333**	**-90,646**	**-70,351**	...	...	...	...	...	...	...
32	Net acquisition of financial assets	...	...	...	...	...	...	...	...	...	...	...	...
33	Net incurrence of liabilities	...	...	...	...	...	...	...	...	...	...	...	...
NLBz	Statistical discrepancy	...	...	...	...	...	...	...	...	...	...	...	...
	Memorandum items												
PB	Primary net lending / net borrowing	-79,230	-61,609	13,256	-81,135	-63,368	...	...	...	...	...	...	...
GB	Government balance per national definition	...	...	...	...	...	...	...	...	...	...	...	...
	Statement of other economic flows												
	Balance sheet												
	Table 1 Revenue												
1	**Revenue**	**159,856**	**125,400**	**201,430**	**176,513**	**138,087**	...	...	...	...	...	...	...
11	**Taxes**	**89,136**	**86,631**	**104,734**	**99,072**	**96,241**	...	...	...	...	...	...	...
111	Taxes on income, profits, and capital gains	13,806	17,679	13,903	13,806	...	...	...	...	...	...	...	...
1111	Payable by individuals	7,440	7,044	322	7,440	...	...	...	...	...	...	...	...
1112	Payable by corporations and other enterprises	6,313	10,635	13,582	6,313	...	...	...	...	...	...	...	...
1113	Other taxes on income, profits, and capital gains	53	—	—	53	...	...	...	...	...	...	...	...
112	Taxes on payroll and workforce	3,263	—	8,289	3,263	...	...	...	...	...	...	...	...
113	Taxes on property	693	1,132	1,067	2,070	...	...	...	...	...	...	...	...
114	Taxes on goods and services	50,031	44,867	29,462	51,492	...	...	...	...	...	...	...	...
1141	General taxes on goods and services	33,224	32,481	16,200	33,224	...	...	...	...	...	...	...	...
1142	Excises	1,296	2,548	2,771	1,296	...	...	...	...	...	...	...	...
115	Taxes on international trade and transactions	21,343	21,076	50,627	28,441	...	...	...	...	...	...	...	...
116	Other taxes	—	1,877	1,387	—	...	...	...	...	...	...	...	...
12	**Social contributions**	**1,825**	**1,987**	**2,197**	**1,825**	**1,987**	...	...	...	...	...	...	...
121	Social security contributions	1,825	1,987	2,197	1,825	1,987	...	...	...	...	...	...	...
122	Other social contributions	—	—	—	—	—	...	...	...	...	...	...	...
13	**Grants**	**62,245**	**26,305**	**78,989**	**62,245**	**26,305**	...	...	...	...	...	...	...
131	From foreign governments	—	—	—	—	—	...	...	...	...	...	...	...
132	From international organizations	62,245	26,305	78,989	62,245	26,305	...	...	...	...	...	...	...
133	From other general government units	—	—	—	—	—	...	...	...	...	...	...	...
1331	Current	—	—	—	—	—	...	...	...	...	...	...	...
1332	Capital	—	—	—	—	—	...	...	...	...	...	...	...
14	**Other revenue**	**6,651**	**10,477**	**15,510**	**13,372**	**13,554**	...	...	...	...	...	...	...
	Table 2 Expense by economic type												
2	**Expense**	**173,192**	**154,688**	**104,889**	**189,861**	**167,375**	...	...	...	...	...	...	...
21	**Compensation of employees**	**42,810**	**45,991**	**51,213**	**42,810**	**45,991**	...	...	...	...	...	...	...
211	Wages and salaries	40,985	44,003	49,016	40,985	44,003	...	...	...	...	...	...	...
212	Employers' social contributions	1,825	1,987	2,197	1,825	1,987	...	...	...	...	...	...	...
22	**Use of goods and services**	**100,288**	**75,433**	**24,993**	**104,807**	**77,192**	...	...	...	...	...	...	...
23	**Consumption of fixed capital**	...	...	...	...	...	...	...	...	...	...	...	...
24	**Interest**	**9,512**	**6,983**	**5,924**	**9,512**	**6,983**	...	...	...	...	...	...	...
25	**Subsidies**	**20,182**	**23,281**	**22,759**	**32,332**	**34,208**	...	...	...	...	...	...	...
26	**Grants**	—	—	—	—	—	...	...	...	...	...	...	...
261	To foreign governments	—	—	—	—	—	...	...	...	...	...	...	...
262	To international organizations	—	—	—	—	—	...	...	...	...	...	...	...
263	To other general government units	—	—	—	—	—	...	...	...	...	...	...	...
2631	Current	—	—	—	—	—	...	...	...	...	...	...	...
2632	Capital	—	—	—	—	—	...	...	...	...	...	...	...

Central African Republic (626)

In Millions of CFA (BEAC) Francs (XAF) / Fiscal Year Ends December 31st

		Budgetary Central Government			Central Government (excl. Social Security)			Central Government (incl. Social Security)			General Government		
		2010P	2011P	2012P	2010	2011	2012	2010	2011	2012	2010	2011	2012
27	**Social benefits**	—	—	—	—	—	...	...	...	...	...	...	...
271	Social security benefits	—	—	—	—	—	...	...	...	...	...	...	...
272	Social assistance benefits	—	—	—	—	—	...	...	...	...	...	...	...
273	Employment-related social benefits	—	—	—	—	—	...	...	...	...	...	...	...
28	**Other expense**	**400**	**3,000**	**—**	**400**	**3,000**	...	...	...	...	...	...	...
281	Property expense other than interest	—	—	—	—	—	...	...	...	...	...	...	...
282	Transfers not elsewhere classified	400	3,000	—	400	3,000	...	...	...	...	...	...	...
2821	Current	400	3,000	—	400	3,000	...	...	...	...	...	...	...
2822	Capital	—	—	—	—	—	...	...	...	...	...	...	...
	Table 3 Transactions in assets and liabilities												
3	**Change in net worth from transactions**	...	...	...	...	...	...	...	...	...	...	...	...
31	**Net/Gross investment in nonfinancial assets**	**75,406**	**39,304**	**89,208**	**77,299**	**41,064**	...	...	...	...	...	...	...
311	Fixed assets	75,406	39,304	89,208	77,299	41,064	...	...	...	...	...	...	...
3111	Buildings and structures	10,090	30,324	73,239	10,090	30,324	...	...	...	...	...	...	...
3112	Machinery and equipment	65,317	8,980	15,970	67,210	10,739	...	...	...	...	...	...	...
3113	Other fixed assets	—	—	—	—	—	...	...	...	...	...	...	...
3114	Weapons systems	...	...	...	...	...	...	...	...	...	...	...	...
312	Inventories	—	—	—	—	—	...	...	...	...	...	...	...
313	Valuables	—	—	—	—	—	...	...	...	...	...	...	...
314	Nonproduced assets	—	—	—	—	—	...	...	...	...	...	...	...
3141	Land	—	—	—	—	—	...	...	...	...	...	...	...
3142	Mineral and energy resources	—	—	—	—	—	...	...	...	...	...	...	...
3143	Other naturally occurring assets	—	—	—	—	—	...	...	...	...	...	...	...
3144	Intangible nonproduced assets	—	—	—	—	—	...	...	...	...	...	...	...
32	**Net acquisition of financial assets**	...	...	...	...	...	...	...	...	...	...	...	...
	By instrument												
3201	Monetary gold and SDRs	...	...	...	...	...	...	...	...	...	...	...	...
3202	Currency and deposits	...	...	...	...	...	...	...	...	...	...	...	...
3203	Debt securities	...	...	...	...	...	...	...	...	...	...	...	...
3204	Loans	...	...	...	...	...	...	...	...	...	...	...	...
3205	Equity and investment fund shares	...	...	...	...	...	...	...	...	...	...	...	...
3206	Insurance, pension, and standardized guarantee schemes	...	...	...	...	...	...	...	...	...	...	...	...
3207	Financial derivatives and employee stock options	...	...	...	...	...	...	...	...	...	...	...	...
3208	Other accounts receivable	...	...	...	...	...	...	...	...	...	...	...	...
	By debtor												
321	Domestic debtors	...	...	...	...	...	...	...	...	...	...	...	...
322	External debtors	...	...	...	...	...	...	...	...	...	...	...	...
33	**Net incurrence of liabilities**	...	...	...	...	...	...	...	...	...	...	...	...
	By instrument												
3301	Special Drawing Rights (SDRs)	...	...	...	...	...	...	...	...	...	...	...	...
3302	Currency and deposits	...	...	...	...	...	...	...	...	...	...	...	...
3303	Debt securities	...	...	...	...	...	...	...	...	...	...	...	...
3304	Loans	...	...	...	...	...	...	...	...	...	...	...	...
3305	Equity and investment fund shares	...	...	...	...	...	...	...	...	...	...	...	...
3306	Insurance, pension, and standardized guarantee schemes	...	...	...	...	...	...	...	...	...	...	...	...
3307	Financial derivatives and employee stock options	...	...	...	...	...	...	...	...	...	...	...	...
3308	Other accounts payable	...	...	...	...	...	...	...	...	...	...	...	...
	By creditor												
331	Domestic creditors	...	...	...	...	...	...	...	...	...	...	...	...
332	External creditors	...	...	...	...	...	...	...	...	...	...	...	...
	Table 4 Holding gains and losses in assets and liabilities												
	Table 5 Holding gains and losses in assets and liabilities												
	Table 6 Balance sheet												

Central African Republic (626)

In Millions of CFA (BEAC) Francs (XAF) / Fiscal Year Ends December 31st

		Budgetary Central Government			Central Government (excl. Social Security)			Central Government (incl. Social Security)			General Government		
		2010P	2011P	2012P	2010	2011	2012	2010	2011	2012	2010	2011	2012
	Table 7 Expenditure by functions of government												
7	**Expenditure**	**248,598**	**193,993**	**194,097**	**267,160**	**208,438**	...	...	...	...	...	...	...
701	**General public services**	**67,306**	...	...	...	...	...	...	...	...	...	...	...
7017	Public debt transactions	9,512	6,983	5,924	9,512	6,983	...	...	...	...	...	...	...
7018	Transfers of general character between levels of government	...	...	...	...	...	...	...	...	...	...	...	...
702	**Defense**	**24,103**	...	...	...	...	...	...	...	...	...	...	...
703	**Public order and safety**	**3,181**	...	...	...	...	...	...	...	...	...	...	...
704	**Economic affairs**	**14,433**	...	...	...	...	...	...	...	...	...	...	...
7042	Agriculture, forestry, fishing, and hunting	4,384	...	...	...	...	...	...	...	...	...	...	...
7043	Fuel and energy	6,642	...	...	...	...	...	...	...	...	...	...	...
7044	Mining, manufacturing, and construction	...	...	...	...	...	...	...	...	...	...	...	...
7045	Transport	291	...	...	...	...	...	...	...	...	...	...	...
7046	Communication	3,116	...	...	...	...	...	...	...	...	...	...	...
705	**Environmental protection**	**—**	...	...	...	...	...	...	...	...	...	...	...
706	**Housing and community amenities**	**5,377**	...	...	...	...	...	...	...	...	...	...	...
707	**Health**	**6,502**	...	...	...	...	...	...	...	...	...	...	...
7072	Outpatient services	...	...	...	...	...	...	...	...	...	...	...	...
7073	Hospital services	...	...	...	...	...	...	...	...	...	...	...	...
7074	Public health services	...	...	...	...	...	...	...	...	...	...	...	...
708	**Recreation, culture and religion**	**1,833**	...	...	...	...	...	...	...	...	...	...	...
709	**Education**	**11,508**	...	...	...	...	...	...	...	...	...	...	...
7091	Pre-primary and primary education	...	...	...	...	...	...	...	...	...	...	...	...
7092	Secondary education	...	...	...	...	...	...	...	...	...	...	...	...
7094	Tertiary education	...	...	...	...	...	...	...	...	...	...	...	...
710	**Social protection**	**651**	...	...	...	...	...	...	...	...	...	...	...
7z	Statistical discrepancy: Expenditure	113,705	...	...	...	...	...	...	...	...	...	...	...
	Table 8 Financial transactions by counterpart sector												
	Table 9 Total other economic flows in assets and liabilities												

Chile (228)

In Billions of Chilean Pesos (CLP) / Fiscal Year Ends December 31st

		Budgetary Central Government			Central Government (excl. Social Security)			Central Government (incl. Social Security)			General Government		
		2013	2014	2015	2013	2014	2015	2013	2014	2015	2013P	2014P	2015P
	Statement of operations												
1	Revenue	...	...	...	...	...	...	28,835	30,571	33,548	31,081	33,076	36,391
2	Expense	...	...	...	...	...	...	28,067	31,063	34,545	30,011	33,271	37,118
GOB	**Gross operating balance**	...	...	...	...	...	...	**1,848**	**637**	**213**	**2,391**	**1,223**	**806**
NOB	**Net operating balance**	...	...	...	...	...	...	**768**	**-491**	**-996**	**1,070**	**-195**	**-727**
31	Net/Gross investment in nonfinancial assets	...	...	...	...	...	...	1,600	1,818	2,407	1,722	1,918	2,577
2M	Expenditure	...	...	...	...	...	...	29,666	32,881	36,952	31,733	35,188	39,694
NLB	**Net lending (+) / Net borrowing (-)**	...	...	...	...	...	...	**-831**	**-2,309**	**-3,404**	**-652**	**-2,112**	**-3,303**
32	Net acquisition of financial assets	...	...	...	...	...	...	-640	247	-369	-539	343	-374
33	Net incurrence of liabilities	...	...	...	...	...	...	191	2,556	3,034	114	2,456	2,929
NLBz	Statistical discrepancy	...	...	...	...	...	...	-0	-0	0	-0	-0	0
	Memorandum items												
PB	Primary net lending / net borrowing	...	...	...	...	...	...	-24	-1,503	-2,358	157	-1,304	-2,256
GB	Government balance per national definition	...	...	...	...	...	...	...	...	...	...	...	...
	Statement of other economic flows												
	Balance sheet												
	Table 1 Revenue												
1	**Revenue**	...	...	...	...	...	...	**28,835**	**30,571**	**33,548**	**31,081**	**33,076**	**36,391**
11	**Taxes**	...	...	...	...	...	...	**23,973**	**25,218**	**27,832**	**25,931**	**27,419**	**30,254**
111	Taxes on income, profits, and capital gains	...	...	...	...	...	...	8,270	8,832	10,008	8,270	8,832	10,008
1111	Payable by individuals	...	...	...	...	...	...	—	—	—	—	—	—
1112	Payable by corporations and other enterprises	...	...	...	...	...	...	446	348	146	446	348	146
1113	Other taxes on income, profits, and capital gains	...	...	...	...	...	...	7,823	8,484	9,862	7,823	8,484	9,862
112	Taxes on payroll and workforce	...	...	...	...	...	...	—	—	—	...	—	—
113	Taxes on property	...	...	...	...	...	...	—	—	—	809	910	1,039
114	Taxes on goods and services	...	...	...	...	...	...	14,090	15,048	16,281	15,239	16,339	17,664
1141	General taxes on goods and services	...	...	...	...	...	...	11,282	14,390	13,304	11,282	14,390	13,304
1142	Excises	...	...	...	...	...	...	2,561	385	2,643	2,561	385	2,643
115	Taxes on international trade and transactions	...	...	...	...	...	...	303	337	323	303	337	323
116	Other taxes	...	...	...	...	...	...	1,310	1,000	1,220	1,310	1,000	1,220
12	**Social contributions**	...	...	...	...	...	...	**1,969**	**2,110**	**2,252**	**1,969**	**2,110**	**2,252**
121	Social security contributions	...	...	...	...	...	...	1,969	2,110	2,252	1,969	2,110	2,252
122	Other social contributions	...	...	...	...	...	...	—	—	—	—	—	—
13	**Grants**	...	...	...	...	...	...	**10**	**10**	**12**	**0**	**1**	**0**
131	From foreign governments	...	...	...	...	...	...	—	—	0	0	0	0
132	From international organizations	...	...	...	...	...	...	0	1	0	0	1	0
133	From other general government units	...	...	...	...	...	...	10	9	12	0	0	-0
1331	Current	...	...	...	...	...	...	1	1	1	0	0	0
1332	Capital	...	...	...	...	...	...	9	8	11	-0	0	-0
14	**Other revenue**	...	...	...	...	...	...	**2,884**	**3,234**	**3,452**	**3,181**	**3,546**	**3,884**
	Table 2 Expense by economic type												
2	**Expense**	...	...	...	...	...	...	**28,067**	**31,063**	**34,545**	**30,011**	**33,271**	**37,118**
21	**Compensation of employees**	...	...	...	...	...	...	**5,894**	**6,511**	**7,209**	**8,116**	**9,074**	**10,103**
211	Wages and salaries	...	...	...	...	...	...	5,894	6,511	7,209	8,116	9,074	10,103
212	Employers' social contributions	...	...	...	...	...	...	—	—	—	—	—	—
22	**Use of goods and services**	...	...	...	...	...	...	**2,755**	**3,209**	**3,300**	**3,875**	**4,499**	**4,744**
23	**Consumption of fixed capital**	...	...	...	...	...	...	**1,080**	**1,129**	**1,209**	**1,322**	**1,418**	**1,532**
24	**Interest**	...	...	...	...	...	...	**807**	**806**	**1,045**	**809**	**808**	**1,047**
25	**Subsidies**	...	...	...	...	...	...	**3,979**	**4,343**	**4,754**	**4,317**	**4,877**	**5,368**
26	**Grants**	...	...	...	...	...	...	**2,118**	**2,611**	**2,844**	**32**	**36**	**41**
261	To foreign governments	...	...	...	...	...	...	0	0	0	0	0	0
262	To international organizations	...	...	...	...	...	...	32	36	41	32	36	41
263	To other general government units	...	...	...	...	...	...	2,086	2,575	2,803	0	0	0
2631	Current	...	...	...	...	...	...	1,888	2,323	2,559	0	0	0
2632	Capital	...	...	...	...	...	...	198	252	245	-0	0	—

Chile (228)

In Billions of Chilean Pesos (CLP) / Fiscal Year Ends December 31st

		Budgetary Central Government			Central Government (excl. Social Security)			Central Government (incl. Social Security)			General Government		
		2013	2014	2015	2013	2014	2015	2013	2014	2015	2013P	2014P	2015P
27	**Social benefits**	...	...	...	...	...	...	**6,521**	**7,005**	**7,618**	**6,576**	**7,061**	**7,659**
271	Social security benefits	...	...	...	...	...	...	4,538	4,814	5,141	4,588	4,858	5,172
272	Social assistance benefits	...	...	...	...	...	...	1,894	2,085	2,294	1,894	2,085	2,294
273	Employment-related social benefits	...	...	...	...	...	...	88	106	183	94	119	193
28	**Other expense**	...	...	...	...	...	...	**4,914**	**5,449**	**6,566**	**4,965**	**5,498**	**6,624**
281	Property expense other than interest	...	...	...	...	...	...	—	—	—	—	—	—
282	Transfers not elsewhere classified	...	...	...	...	...	...	4,914	5,449	6,566	4,965	5,498	6,624
2821	Current	...	...	...	...	...	...	2,809	3,044	3,768	2,854	3,084	3,817
2822	Capital	...	...	...	...	...	...	2,105	2,405	2,798	2,111	2,414	2,807
	Table 3 Transactions in assets and liabilities												
3	**Change in net worth from transactions**	...	...	...	...	...	...	**768**	**-491**	**-996**	**1,069**	**-195**	**-727**
31	**Net/Gross investment in nonfinancial assets**	...	...	...	...	...	...	**1,600**	**1,818**	**2,407**	**1,722**	**1,918**	**2,577**
311	Fixed assets	...	...	...	...	...	...	1,600	1,818	2,260	1,722	1,918	2,404
3111	Buildings and structures	...	...	...	...	...	...	...	...	1,452	...	...	1,472
3112	Machinery and equipment	...	...	...	...	...	...	...	...	248	...	...	285
3113	Other fixed assets	...	...	...	...	...	...	...	...	559	...	...	647
3114	Weapons systems	...	...	...	...	...	...	...	...	—	...	...	—
312	Inventories	...	...	...	...	...	...	—	—	—	—	—	—
313	Valuables	...	...	...	...	...	...	—	—	—	—	—	—
314	Nonproduced assets	...	...	...	...	...	...	—	—	147	—	—	172
3141	Land	...	...	...	...	...	...	—	—	147	—	—	172
3142	Mineral and energy resources	...	...	...	...	...	...	—	—	—	—	—	—
3143	Other naturally occurring assets	...	...	...	...	...	...	—	—	—	—	—	—
3144	Intangible nonproduced assets	...	...	...	...	...	...	—	—	—	—	—	—
32	**Net acquisition of financial assets**	...	...	...	...	...	...	**-640**	**247**	**-369**	**-539**	**343**	**-374**
	By instrument												
3201	Monetary gold and SDRs	...	...	...	...	...	...	—	—	—	—	—	—
3202	Currency and deposits	...	...	...	...	...	...	-641	-1,280	171	-227	-837	532
3203	Debt securities	...	...	...	...	...	...	190	1,611	-587	191	1,610	-587
3204	Loans	...	...	...	...	...	...	-189	-84	46	-503	-430	-320
3205	Equity and investment fund shares	...	...	...	...	...	...	—	—	—	—	—	—
3206	Insurance, pension, and standardized guarantee schemes	...	...	...	...	...	...	—	—	—	—	—	—
3207	Financial derivatives and employee stock options	...	...	...	...	...	...	—	—	—	—	—	—
3208	Other accounts receivable	...	...	...	...	...	...	—	—	—	—	—	—
	By debtor												
321	Domestic debtors	...	...	...	...	...	...	-819	31	-605	-717	128	-610
322	External debtors	...	...	...	...	...	...	179	216	236	179	216	236
33	**Net incurrence of liabilities**	...	...	...	...	...	...	**191**	**2,556**	**3,034**	**114**	**2,456**	**2,929**
	By instrument												
3301	Special Drawing Rights (SDRs)	...	...	...	...	...	...	—	—	—	—	—	—
3302	Currency and deposits	...	...	...	...	...	...	—	—	—	—	—	—
3303	Debt securities	...	...	...	...	...	...	-1,010	-791	-743	-1,010	-791	-743
3304	Loans	...	...	...	...	...	...	1,031	3,347	3,777	954	3,246	3,672
3305	Equity and investment fund shares	...	...	...	...	...	...	—	—	—	—	—	—
3306	Insurance, pension, and standardized guarantee schemes	...	...	...	...	...	...	170	—	—	170	—	—
3307	Financial derivatives and employee stock options	...	...	...	...	...	...	—	—	—	—	—	—
3308	Other accounts payable	...	...	...	...	...	...	—	—	—	—	—	—
	By creditor												
331	Domestic creditors	...	...	...	...	...	...	646	1,689	2,197	568	1,588	2,091
332	External creditors	...	...	...	...	...	...	-455	867	837	-455	867	837
	Table 4 Holding gains and losses in assets and liabilities												
	Table 5 Holding gains and losses in assets and liabilities												
	Table 6 Balance sheet												

Chile (228)

In Billions of Chilean Pesos (CLP) / Fiscal Year Ends December 31st

		Budgetary Central Government			Central Government (excl. Social Security)			Central Government (incl. Social Security)			General Government		
		2013	2014	2015	2013	2014	2015	2013	2014	2015	2013P	2014P	2015P
	Table 7 Expenditure by functions of government												
7	**Expenditure**	...	...	...	...	...	...	**29,712**	**32,914**	**36,994**	**31,733**	**35,188**	**39,694**
701	**General public services**	...	...	...	...	...	...	**2,363**	**2,477**	**2,867**	...	...	...
7017	Public debt transactions	...	...	...	...	...	...	807	806	1,045	809	806	1,047
7018	Transfers of general character between levels of government	...	...	...	...	...	...	—	—	—	...	...	...
702	**Defense**	...	...	...	...	...	...	**1,402**	**1,613**	**1,446**	...	...	...
703	**Public order and safety**	...	...	...	...	...	...	**2,120**	**2,403**	**2,686**	...	...	...
704	**Economic affairs**	...	...	...	...	...	...	**3,780**	**4,226**	**4,872**	...	...	...
7042	Agriculture, forestry, fishing, and hunting	...	...	...	...	...	...	494	544	608	...	...	...
7043	Fuel and energy	...	...	...	...	...	...	99	128	159	...	...	...
7044	Mining, manufacturing, and construction	...	...	...	...	...	...	34	29	42	...	...	...
7045	Transport	...	...	...	...	...	...	2,489	2,765	3,196	...	...	...
7046	Communication	...	...	...	...	...	...	14	17	23	...	...	...
705	**Environmental protection**	...	...	...	...	...	...	**114**	**132**	**136**	...	...	...
706	**Housing and community amenities**	...	...	...	...	...	...	**453**	**581**	**606**	...	...	...
707	**Health**	...	...	...	...	...	...	**5,225**	**5,975**	**6,944**	...	...	...
7072	Outpatient services	...	...	...	...	...	...	115	138	181	...	...	...
7073	Hospital services	...	...	...	...	...	...	4,054	4,663	5,426	...	...	...
7074	Public health services	...	...	...	...	...	...	100	108	133	...	...	...
708	**Recreation, culture and religion**	...	...	...	...	...	...	**249**	**260**	**293**	...	...	...
709	**Education**	...	...	...	...	...	...	**5,850**	**6,398**	**7,392**	...	...	...
7091	Pre-primary and primary education	...	...	...	...	...	...	4,409	4,830	5,025	...	...	...
7092	Secondary education	...	...	...	...	...	...	—	—	—	...	...	...
7094	Tertiary education	...	...	...	...	...	...	610	816	961	...	...	...
710	**Social protection**	...	...	...	...	...	...	**8,156**	**8,849**	**9,753**	...	...	...
7z	Statistical discrepancy: Expenditure	...	...	...	...	...	...	—	—	...	...	...	...
	Table 8 Financial transactions by counterpart sector												
	Table 9 Total other economic flows in assets and liabilities												

China, P.R.: Mainland (924)

In Billions of Chinese Yuan (CNY) / Fiscal Year Ends December 31st

		Budgetary Central Government			Central Government (excl. Social Security)			Central Government (incl. Social Security)			General Government		
		2012	2013	2014	2012	2013	2014	2012	2013	2014	2012	2013	2014
	Statement of operations												
1	Revenue	...	6,497	6,938	5,999	6,497	6,939	...	6,497	10,180	15,235	16,995	18,521
2	Expense	...	...	...	...	...	...	...	...	...	...	...	...
GOB	**Gross operating balance**	...	...	...	...	...	...	...	...	...	...	...	...
NOB	**Net operating balance**	...	...	...	...	...	...	...	...	...	...	...	...
31	Net/Gross investment in nonfinancial assets	...	37	33	...	37	33	...	37	34	...	75	171
2M	Expenditure	...	...	...	...	...	...	...	...	...	...	...	...
NLB	**Net lending (+) / Net borrowing (-)**	...	...	...	...	...	...	...	...	...	...	...	...
32	Net acquisition of financial assets	...	...	...	...	...	...	...	...	...	...	...	...
33	Net incurrence of liabilities	...	918	891	552	918	891	...	918	...	...	918	891
NLBz	Statistical discrepancy	...	...	...	...	...	...	...	...	...	...	...	...
	Memorandum items												
PB	Primary net lending / net borrowing	...	...	...	...	...	...	...	...	...	...	...	...
GB	Government balance per national definition	...	...	...	...	...	...	...	...	...	...	...	...
	Statement of other economic flows												
	Balance sheet												
	Table 1 Revenue												
1	**Revenue**	...	**6,497**	**6,938**	**5,999**	**6,497**	**6,939**	...	**6,497**	**10,180**	**15,235**	**16,995**	**18,521**
11	**Taxes**	...	**5,875**	**6,229**	**5,524**	**5,875**	**6,229**	...	**5,875**	**6,229**	**10,754**	**11,849**	**12,766**
111	Taxes on income, profits, and capital gains	...	1,836	2,024	1,558	1,836	2,024	...	1,836	2,024	2,547	2,896	3,202
1111	Payable by individuals	...	392	443	349	392	443	...	392	443	582	653	738
1112	Payable by corporations and other enterprises	...	1,444	1,581	1,208	1,444	1,581	...	1,444	1,581	1,965	2,243	2,464
1113	Other taxes on income, profits, and capital gains	...	—	—	—	—	—	...	—	—	—	—	—
112	Taxes on payroll and workforce	...	—	—	—	—	—	...	—	—	—	—	—
113	Taxes on property	...	—	—	—	—	—	...	—	—	765	888	1,036
114	Taxes on goods and services	...	3,767	3,912	3,679	3,767	3,912	...	3,767	3,912	7,047	7,672	8,102
1141	General taxes on goods and services	...	2,404	2,432	2,388	2,404	2,432	...	2,404	2,432	5,514	6,011	6,306
1142	Excises	...	1,228	1,350	1,161	1,228	1,350	...	1,228	1,350	1,193	1,263	1,388
115	Taxes on international trade and transactions	...	267	289	282	267	289	...	267	289	282	267	289
116	Other taxes	...	5	4	5	5	4	...	5	4	111	126	137
12	**Social contributions**	...	—	...	—	—	...	...	—	**3,004**	**2,370**	**2,702**	**3,004**
121	Social security contributions	...	—	...	—	—	...	...	—	3,004	2,370	2,702	3,004
122	Other social contributions	...	—	...	—	—	...	...	—	...	—	—	...
13	**Grants**	...	—	...	—	—	...	...	—	—	—	—	—
131	From foreign governments	...	—	...	—	—	...	...	—	—	—	—	...
132	From international organizations	...	—	...	—	—	...	...	—	—	—	—	...
133	From other general government units	...	—	...	—	—	...	...	—	—	—	—	—
1331	Current	...	—	...	—	—	...	...	—	—	—	—	—
1332	Capital	...	—	...	—	...	...	...	...	—	—	—	...
14	**Other revenue**	...	**622**	**710**	**475**	**622**	**710**	...	**622**	**947**	**2,112**	**2,444**	**2,751**
	Table 2 Expense by economic type												
2	**Expense**	...	...	...	...	...	...	...	...	...	...	...	...
21	**Compensation of employees**	...	...	...	...	...	...	...	...	...	...	...	...
211	Wages and salaries	...	...	...	...	...	...	...	...	...	...	...	...
212	Employers' social contributions	...	...	...	...	...	...	...	...	...	...	...	...
22	**Use of goods and services**	...	...	...	...	...	...	...	...	...	...	...	...
23	**Consumption of fixed capital**	...	...	...	...	...	...	...	...	...	...	...	...
24	**Interest**	...	**232**	...	**206**	**232**	...	...	**232**	...	**264**	**306**	...
25	**Subsidies**	...	...	...	...	...	...	...	...	...	...	...	...
26	**Grants**	...	...	...	...	...	...	...	...	...	...	...	...
261	To foreign governments	...	...	...	...	...	...	...	...	...	...	...	...
262	To international organizations	...	...	...	...	...	...	...	...	...	...	...	...
263	To other general government units	...	...	...	...	...	...	...	...	...	...	...	...
2631	Current	...	...	...	...	...	...	...	...	...	...	...	...
2632	Capital	...	...	...	...	...	...	...	...	...	...	...	...

China, P.R.: Mainland (924)

In Billions of Chinese Yuan (CNY) / Fiscal Year Ends December 31st

		Budgetary Central Government			Central Government (excl. Social Security)			Central Government (incl. Social Security)			General Government		
		2012	2013	2014	2012	2013	2014	2012	2013	2014	2012	2013	2014
27	**Social benefits**	...	...	...	...	...	...	...	...	...	...	...	...
271	Social security benefits	...	...	...	...	...	...	...	...	...	...	...	...
272	Social assistance benefits	...	...	...	...	...	...	...	...	...	...	...	...
273	Employment-related social benefits	...	...	...	...	...	...	...	...	...	...	...	...
28	**Other expense**	...	...	...	...	...	...	...	...	...	...	...	...
281	Property expense other than interest	...	...	...	...	...	...	...	...	...	...	...	...
282	Transfers not elsewhere classified	...	...	...	...	...	...	...	...	...	...	...	...
2821	Current	...	...	...	...	...	...	...	...	...	...	...	...
2822	Capital	...	...	...	...	...	...	...	...	...	...	...	...
	Table 3 Transactions in assets and liabilities												
3	**Change in net worth from transactions**	...	...	-857	...	...	...	...	...	...	...	...	...
31	**Net/Gross investment in nonfinancial assets**	...	37	33	...	37	33	...	37	34	...	75	171
311	Fixed assets	...	—	...	...	—	...	...	—	...	...	—	...
3111	Buildings and structures	...	—	...	...	—	...	...	—	...	...	—	...
3112	Machinery and equipment	...	—	...	...	—	...	...	—	...	...	—	...
3113	Other fixed assets	...	—	...	...	—	...	...	—	...	...	—	...
3114	Weapons systems	...	...	...	...	...	...	...	...	...	...	—	...
312	Inventories	...	—	...	...	—	...	...	—	...	...	...	...
313	Valuables	...	—	...	...	...	...	...	...	...	...	...	...
314	Nonproduced assets	...	37	33	...	37	33	...	37	34	...	75	171
3141	Land	...	37	33	...	37	33	...	37	34	...	75	171
3142	Mineral and energy resources	...	—	...	...	...	...	...	...	...	...	...	...
3143	Other naturally occurring assets	...	—	...	...	—	...	...	—	...	...	...	...
3144	Intangible nonproduced assets	...	—	...	...	—	...	...	—	...	...	—	...
32	**Net acquisition of financial assets**	...	...	...	...	...	...	...	...	...	...	...	...
	By instrument												
3201	Monetary gold and SDRs	...	...	...	...	...	...	...	...	...	...	...	...
3202	Currency and deposits	...	...	...	...	...	...	...	...	...	...	...	...
3203	Debt securities	...	...	...	...	...	...	...	...	...	...	...	...
3204	Loans	...	...	...	...	...	...	...	...	...	...	...	...
3205	Equity and investment fund shares	...	...	...	...	...	...	...	...	...	...	...	...
3206	Insurance, pension, and standardized guarantee schemes	...	...	...	...	...	...	...	...	...	...	...	...
3207	Financial derivatives and employee stock options	...	...	...	...	...	...	...	...	...	...	...	...
3208	Other accounts receivable	...	...	...	...	...	...	...	...	...	...	...	...
	By debtor												
321	Domestic debtors	...	...	...	...	...	...	...	...	...	...	...	...
322	External debtors	...	...	...	...	...	...	...	...	...	...	...	...
33	**Net incurrence of liabilities**	...	918	891	552	918	891	...	918	...	...	918	891
	By instrument												
3301	Special Drawing Rights (SDRs)	...	...	...	...	...	...	...	...	...	...	—	...
3302	Currency and deposits	...	...	...	...	...	...	...	...	...	...	—	...
3303	Debt securities	...	...	...	...	...	...	...	...	...	...	—	...
3304	Loans	...	...	...	...	...	...	...	...	...	...	—	...
3305	Equity and investment fund shares	...	...	...	...	...	...	...	...	...	...	...	...
3306	Insurance, pension, and standardized guarantee schemes	...	...	...	...	...	...	...	...	...	...	...	...
3307	Financial derivatives and employee stock options	...	...	...	...	...	...	...	...	...	...	...	...
3308	Other accounts payable	...	...	...	...	...	...	...	...	...	...	...	...
	By creditor												
331	Domestic creditors	...	909	884	534	909	884	...	909	...	...	909	884
332	External creditors	...	9	7	18	9	7	...	9	...	...	9	7
	Table 4 Holding gains and losses in assets and liabilities												
	Table 5 Holding gains and losses in assets and liabilities												
	Table 6 Balance sheet												

China, P.R.: Mainland (924)

In Billions of Chinese Yuan (CNY) / Fiscal Year Ends December 31st

		Budgetary Central Government			Central Government (excl. Social Security)			Central Government (incl. Social Security)			General Government		
		2012	2013	2014	2012	2013	2014	2012	2013	2014	2012	2013	2014
	Table 7 Expenditure by functions of government												
7	**Expenditure**	...	**7,198**	**7,961**	**6,705**	**7,198**	**7,961**	...	**7,198**	**10,484**	**15,256**	**17,254**	**18,894**
701	**General public services**	...	**5,195**	**5,727**	**4,899**	**5,195**	**5,727**	...	**5,195**	**5,727**	**1,488**	**1,634**	**1,737**
7017	Public debt transactions	...	232	260	206	232	260	...	232	260	264	306	359
7018	Transfers of general character between levels of government	...	4,802	5,295	—	4,802	5,295	...	4,802	5,295	—	—	—
702	**Defense**	...	**720**	**810**	**650**	**720**	**810**	...	**720**	**810**	**671**	**744**	**833**
703	**Public order and safety**	...	**130**	**148**	**118**	**130**	**148**	...	**130**	**148**	**711**	**779**	**836**
704	**Economic affairs**	...	**867**	**937**	**766**	**867**	**937**	...	**867**	**937**	**4,319**	**4,903**	**5,229**
7042	Agriculture, forestry, fishing, and hunting	...	83	83	80	83	83	...	83	83	1,365	1,515	1,599
7043	Fuel and energy	...	32	55	55	32	55	...	32	55	96	78	77
7044	Mining, manufacturing, and construction	...	16	20	53	16	20	...	16	20	149	102	100
7045	Transport	...	204	178	174	204	178	...	204	178	1,058	1,241	1,334
7046	Communication	...	7	7	8	7	7	...	7	7	33	34	36
705	**Environmental protection**	...	**10**	**30**	**6**	**10**	**30**	...	**10**	**30**	**297**	**345**	**378**
706	**Housing and community amenities**	...	**2**	**2**	**2**	**2**	**2**	...	**2**	**2**	**1,029**	**1,282**	**1,481**
707	**Health**	...	**8**	**9**	**7**	**8**	**9**	...	**8**	**9**	**472**	**526**	**586**
7072	Outpatient services	...	—	—	—	—	—	...	—	—	—	—	—
7073	Hospital services	...	5	6	5	5	6	...	5	6	212	236	269
7074	Public health services	...	1	1	1	1	1	...	1	1	200	219	237
708	**Recreation, culture and religion**	...	**23**	**25**	**22**	**23**	**25**	...	**23**	**25**	**240**	**270**	**286**
709	**Education**	...	**115**	**131**	**114**	**115**	**131**	...	**115**	**131**	**2,198**	**2,297**	**2,409**
7091	Pre-primary and primary education	...	1	1	1	1	1	...	1	1	589	625	677
7092	Secondary education	...	2	2	2	2	2	...	2	2	523	548	590
7094	Tertiary education	...	96	110	94	96	110	...	96	110	346	325	355
710	**Social protection**	...	**128**	**143**	**120**	**128**	**143**	...	**128**	**2,667**	**3,831**	**4,475**	**5,119**
7z	Statistical discrepancy: Expenditure	...	—	...	—	—	...	...	—	...	-0	-0	...
	Table 8 Financial transactions by counterpart sector												
	Table 9 Total other economic flows in assets and liabilities												

China, P.R.: Hong Kong (532)

In Billions of Hong Kong Dollars (HKD) / Fiscal Year Ends March 31st

		Budgetary Central Government			Central Government (excl. Social Security)			Central Government (incl. Social Security)			General Government		
		2012	2013	2014	2012	2013	2014	2012	2013	2014	2012	2013	2014
	Statement of operations												
1	Revenue	...	...	...	...	...	...	...	...	...	480	459	532
2	Expense	...	...	...	...	...	...	...	...	...	390	426	414
GOB	**Gross operating balance**	...	...	...	...	...	...	...	...	...	**101**	**45**	**130**
NOB	**Net operating balance**	...	...	...	...	...	...	...	...	...	**90**	**33**	**118**
31	Net/Gross investment in nonfinancial assets	...	...	...	...	...	...	...	...	...	18	18	22
2M	Expenditure	...	...	...	...	...	...	...	...	...	408	444	436
NLB	**Net lending (+) / Net borrowing (-)**	...	...	...	...	...	...	...	...	...	**72**	**14**	**96**
32	Net acquisition of financial assets	...	...	...	...	...	...	...	...	...	113	58	118
33	Net incurrence of liabilities	...	...	...	...	...	...	...	...	...	41	44	22
NLBz	Statistical discrepancy	...	...	...	...	...	...	...	...	...	—	—	—
	Memorandum items												
PB	Primary net lending / net borrowing	...	...	...	...	...	...	...	...	...	74	17	99
GB	Government balance per national definition	...	...	...	...	...	...	...	...	...	...	...	...
	Statement of other economic flows												
9	**Change in net worth due to other economic flows**	...	...	...	...	...	...	...	...	...	**-48**	**-13**	**-52**
4	Change in net worth due to holding gains and losses	...	...	...	...	...	...	...	...	...	**0**	**1**	**-0**
41	Nonfinancial assets	...	...	...	...	...	...	...	...	...	0	1	0
42	Financial assets	...	...	...	...	...	...	...	...	...	-0	-0	-1
43	Liabilities	...	...	...	...	...	...	...	...	...	—	—	—
5	Change in net worth due to volume changes	...	...	...	...	...	...	...	...	...	**-48**	**-14**	**-52**
51	Nonfinancial assets	...	...	...	...	...	...	...	...	...	—	—	—
52	Financial assets	...	...	...	...	...	...	...	...	...	6	0	—
53	Liabilities	...	...	...	...	...	...	...	...	...	54	14	52
	Balance sheet												
6	**Net worth**	...	...	...	...	...	...	...	...	...	**686**	**706**	**772**
61	Nonfinancial assets	...	...	...	...	...	...	...	...	...	354	373	396
62	Financial assets	...	...	...	...	...	...	...	...	...	1,186	1,244	1,361
63	Liabilities	...	...	...	...	...	...	...	...	...	853	911	985
	Table 1 Revenue												
1	**Revenue**	...	...	...	...	...	...	...	...	...	**480**	**459**	**532**
11	**Taxes**	...	...	...	...	...	...	...	...	...	**279**	**286**	**349**
111	Taxes on income, profits, and capital gains	...	...	...	...	...	...	...	...	...	181	182	200
1111	Payable by individuals	...	...	...	...	...	...	...	...	...	55	60	65
1112	Payable by corporations and other enterprises	...	...	...	...	...	...	...	...	...	126	122	135
1113	Other taxes on income, profits, and capital gains	...	...	...	...	...	...	...	...	...	—	—	—
112	Taxes on payroll and workforce	...	...	...	...	...	...	...	...	...	—	—	—
113	Taxes on property	...	...	...	...	...	...	...	...	...	14	18	25
114	Taxes on goods and services	...	...	...	...	...	...	...	...	...	81	83	122
1141	General taxes on goods and services	...	...	...	...	...	...	...	...	...	43	42	75
1142	Excises	...	...	...	...	...	...	...	...	...	9	10	10
115	Taxes on international trade and transactions	...	...	...	...	...	...	...	...	...	1	1	1
116	Other taxes	...	...	...	...	...	...	...	...	...	2	2	2
12	**Social contributions**	...	...	...	...	...	...	...	...	...	**0**	**0**	**0**
121	Social security contributions	...	...	...	...	...	...	...	...	...	0	0	0
122	Other social contributions	...	...	...	...	...	...	...	...	...	—	—	—
13	**Grants**	...	...	...	...	...	...	...	...	...	**—**	**—**	**—**
131	From foreign governments	...	...	...	...	...	...	...	...	...	—	—	—
132	From international organizations	...	...	...	...	...	...	...	...	...	—	—	—
133	From other general government units	...	...	...	...	...	...	...	...	...	—	—	—
1331	Current	...	...	...	...	...	...	...	...	...	—	—	—
1332	Capital	...	...	...	...	...	...	...	...	...	—	—	—
14	**Other revenue**	...	...	...	...	...	...	...	...	...	**201**	**173**	**183**

China, P.R.: Hong Kong (532)

In Billions of Hong Kong Dollars (HKD) / Fiscal Year Ends March 31st

		Budgetary Central Government			Central Government (excl. Social Security)			Central Government (incl. Social Security)			General Government		
		2012	2013	2014	2012	2013	2014	2012	2013	2014	2012	2013	2014
	Table 2 Expense by economic type												
2	**Expense**	...	...	...	...	...	...	...	...	...	**390**	**426**	**414**
21	**Compensation of employees**	...	...	...	...	...	...	...	...	...	**85**	**89**	**94**
211	Wages and salaries	...	...	...	...	...	...	...	...	...	68	70	74
212	Employers' social contributions	...	...	...	...	...	...	...	...	...	17	19	19
22	**Use of goods and services**	...	...	...	...	...	...	...	...	...	**124**	**121**	**144**
23	**Consumption of fixed capital**	...	...	...	...	...	...	...	...	...	**11**	**12**	**12**
24	**Interest**	...	...	...	...	...	...	...	...	...	**2**	**3**	**3**
25	**Subsidies**	...	...	...	...	...	...	...	...	...	**0**	**0**	**3**
26	**Grants**	...	...	...	...	...	...	...	...	...	**0**	**1**	**-0**
261	To foreign governments	...	...	...	...	...	...	...	...	...	0	0	-0
262	To international organizations	...	...	...	...	...	...	...	...	...	0	0	0
263	To other general government units	...	...	...	...	...	...	...	...	...	—	—	—
2631	Current	...	...	...	...	...	...	...	...	...	—	—	—
2632	Capital	...	...	...	...	...	...	...	...	...	—	—	—
27	**Social benefits**	...	...	...	...	...	...	...	...	...	**60**	**75**	**61**
271	Social security benefits	...	...	...	...	...	...	...	...	...	—	—	—
272	Social assistance benefits	...	...	...	...	...	...	...	...	...	59	75	61
273	Employment-related social benefits	...	...	...	...	...	...	...	...	...	0	0	1
28	**Other expense**	...	...	...	...	...	...	...	...	...	**107**	**126**	**98**
281	Property expense other than interest	...	...	...	...	...	...	...	...	...	25	24	25
282	Transfers not elsewhere classified	...	...	...	...	...	...	...	...	...	82	101	72
2821	Current	...	...	...	...	...	...	...	...	...	72	78	64
2822	Capital	...	...	...	...	...	...	...	...	...	11	23	8
	Table 3 Transactions in assets and liabilities												
3	**Change in net worth from transactions**	...	...	...	...	...	...	...	...	...	**90**	**33**	**118**
31	**Net/Gross investment in nonfinancial assets**	...	...	...	...	...	...	...	...	...	**18**	**18**	**22**
311	Fixed assets	...	...	...	...	...	...	...	...	...	18	19	21
3111	Buildings and structures	...	...	...	...	...	...	...	...	...	7	13	2
3112	Machinery and equipment	...	...	...	...	...	...	...	...	...	1	1	-0
3113	Other fixed assets	...	...	...	...	...	...	...	...	...	9	5	19
3114	Weapons systems	...	...	...	...	...	...	...	...	...	—	—	—
312	Inventories	...	...	...	...	...	...	...	...	...	0	-0	1
313	Valuables	...	...	...	...	...	...	...	...	...	—	—	—
314	Nonproduced assets	...	...	...	...	...	...	...	...	...	—	—	—
3141	Land	...	...	...	...	...	...	...	...	...	—	—	—
3142	Mineral and energy resources	...	...	...	...	...	...	...	...	...	—	—	—
3143	Other naturally occurring assets	...	...	...	...	...	...	...	...	...	—	—	—
3144	Intangible nonproduced assets	...	...	...	...	...	...	...	...	...	—	—	—
32	**Net acquisition of financial assets**	...	...	...	...	...	...	...	...	...	**113**	**58**	**118**
	By instrument												
3201	Monetary gold and SDRs	—	—	—	—	—	—	—	—	—	—	—	—
3202	Currency and deposits	...	...	...	...	...	...	...	...	...	1	0	-4
3203	Debt securities	...	...	...	...	...	...	...	...	...	—	—	—
3204	Loans	...	...	...	...	...	...	...	...	...	1	2	2
3205	Equity and investment fund shares	...	...	...	...	...	...	...	...	...	94	73	91
3206	Insurance, pension, and standardized guarantee schemes	...	...	...	...	...	...	...	...	...	—	—	—
3207	Financial derivatives and employee stock options	...	...	...	...	...	...	...	...	...	—	—	0
3208	Other accounts receivable	...	...	...	...	...	...	...	...	...	17	-17	29
	By debtor												
321	Domestic debtors	...	...	...	...	...	...	...	...	...	113	58	118
322	External debtors	...	...	...	...	...	...	...	...	...	—	—	—
33	**Net incurrence of liabilities**	...	...	...	...	...	...	...	...	...	**41**	**44**	**22**
	By instrument												
3301	Special Drawing Rights (SDRs)	—	—	—	—	—	—	—	—	—	—	—	—
3302	Currency and deposits	...	...	...	...	...	...	...	...	...	—	—	—
3303	Debt securities	...	...	...	...	...	...	...	...	...	21	23	8
3304	Loans	...	...	...	...	...	...	...	...	...	—	—	—

China, P.R.: Hong Kong (532)

In Billions of Hong Kong Dollars (HKD) / Fiscal Year Ends March 31st

		Budgetary Central Government			Central Government (excl. Social Security)			Central Government (incl. Social Security)			General Government		
		2012	2013	2014	2012	2013	2014	2012	2013	2014	2012	2013	2014
3305	Equity and investment fund shares	...	...	...	...	...	...	...	...	...	—	—	—
3306	Insurance, pension, and standardized guarantee schemes	...	...	...	...	...	...	...	...	...	20	18	17
3307	Financial derivatives and employee stock options	...	...	...	...	...	...	...	...	...	—	—	—
3308	Other accounts payable	...	...	...	...	...	...	...	...	...	0	2	-3
	By creditor												
331	Domestic creditors	...	...	...	...	...	...	...	...	...	41	43	22
332	External creditors	...	...	...	...	...	...	...	...	...	-0	0	0
	Table 4 Holding gains and losses in assets and liabilities												
4	**Change in net worth due to holding gains and losses**	...	...	...	...	...	...	...	...	...	0	1	-0
41	**Holding gains and losses in nonfinancial assets**	...	...	...	...	...	...	...	...	...	0	1	0
411	Fixed assets	...	...	...	...	...	...	...	...	...	0	1	0
412	Inventories	...	...	...	...	...	...	...	...	...	—	—	—
413	Valuables	...	...	...	...	...	...	...	...	...	—	—	—
414	Nonproduced assets	...	...	...	...	...	...	...	...	...	—	—	—
42	**Holding gains and losses in financial assets**	...	...	...	...	...	...	...	...	...	-0	-0	-1
	By instrument												
4201	Monetary gold and SDRs	...	...	...	...	...	...	...	...	...	—	—	—
4202	Currency and deposits	...	...	...	...	...	...	...	...	...	—	—	—
4203	Debt securities	...	...	...	...	...	...	...	...	...	—	—	—
4204	Loans	...	...	...	...	...	...	...	...	...	—	—	—
4205	Equity and investment fund shares	...	...	...	...	...	...	...	...	...	-0	-0	-1
4206	Insurance, pension, and standardized guarantee schemes	...	...	...	...	...	...	...	...	...	—	—	—
4207	Financial derivatives and employee stock options	...	...	...	...	...	...	...	...	...	—	—	—
4208	Other accounts receivable	...	...	...	...	...	...	...	...	...	—	—	—
	By debtor												
421	Domestic debtors	...	...	...	...	...	...	...	...	...	-0	-0	-1
422	External debtors	...	...	...	...	...	...	...	...	...	—	—	—
43	**Holding gains and losses in liabilities**	...	...	...	...	...	...	...	...	...	—	—	—
	By instrument												
4301	Special Drawing Rights (SDRs)	...	...	...	...	...	...	...	...	...	—	—	—
4302	Currency and deposits	...	...	...	...	...	...	...	...	...	—	—	—
4303	Debt securities	...	...	...	...	...	...	...	...	...	—	—	—
4304	Loans	...	...	...	...	...	...	...	...	...	—	—	—
4305	Equity and investment fund shares	...	...	...	...	...	...	...	...	...	—	—	—
4306	Insurance, pension, and standardized guarantee schemes	...	...	...	...	...	...	...	...	...	—	—	—
4307	Financial derivatives and employee stock options	...	...	...	...	...	...	...	...	...	—	—	—
4308	Other accounts payable	...	...	...	...	...	...	...	...	...	—	—	—
	By creditor												
431	Domestic creditors	...	...	...	...	...	...	...	...	...	—	—	—
432	External creditors	...	...	...	...	...	...	...	...	...	—	—	—
	Table 5 Holding gains and losses in assets and liabilities												
5	**Change in net worth due to other volume changes**	...	...	...	...	...	...	...	...	...	**-48**	**-14**	**-52**
51	**Other volume changes in nonfinancial assets**	...	...	...	...	...	...	...	...	...	—	—	—
511	Fixed assets	...	...	...	...	...	...	...	...	...	—	—	—
512	Inventories	...	...	...	...	...	...	...	...	...	—	—	—
513	Valuables	...	...	...	...	...	...	...	...	...	—	—	—
514	Nonproduced assets	...	...	...	...	...	...	...	...	...	—	—	—
52	**Other volume changes in financial assets**	...	...	...	...	...	...	...	...	...	**6**	**0**	—

China, P.R.: Hong Kong (532)

In Billions of Hong Kong Dollars (HKD) / Fiscal Year Ends March 31st

		Budgetary Central Government			Central Government (excl. Social Security)			Central Government (incl. Social Security)			General Government		
		2012	2013	2014	2012	2013	2014	2012	2013	2014	2012	2013	2014
	By instrument												
5201	Monetary gold and SDRs	...	...	...	...	...	...	...	...	...	—	—	—
5202	Currency and deposits	...	...	...	...	...	...	...	...	...	0	—	—
5203	Debt securities	...	...	...	...	...	...	...	...	...	—	—	—
5204	Loans	...	...	...	...	...	...	...	...	...	-0	—	—
5205	Equity and investment fund shares	...	...	...	...	...	...	...	...	...	6	0	—
5206	Insurance, pension, and standardized guarantee schemes	...	...	...	...	...	...	...	...	...	—	—	—
5207	Financial derivatives and employee stock options	...	...	...	...	...	...	...	...	...	—	—	—
5208	Other accounts receivable	...	...	...	...	...	...	...	...	...	—	—	—
	By debtor												
521	Domestic debtors	...	...	...	...	...	...	...	...	...	6	0	—
522	External debtors	...	...	...	...	...	...	...	...	...	—	—	—
53	**Other volume changes in liabilities**	**...**	**...**	**...**	**...**	**...**	**...**	**...**	**...**	**...**	**54**	**14**	**52**
	By instrument												
5301	Special Drawing Rights (SDRs)	...	...	...	...	...	...	...	...	...	—	—	—
5302	Currency and deposits	...	...	...	...	...	...	...	...	...	—	—	—
5303	Debt securities	...	...	...	...	...	...	...	...	...	—	—	—
5304	Loans	...	...	...	...	...	...	...	...	...	—	—	—
5305	Equity and investment fund shares	...	...	...	...	...	...	...	...	...	—	—	—
5306	Insurance, pension, and standardized guarantee schemes	...	...	...	...	...	...	...	...	...	54	14	52
5307	Financial derivatives and employee stock options	...	...	...	...	...	...	...	...	...	—	—	—
5308	Other accounts payable	...	...	...	...	...	...	...	...	...	—	—	—
	By creditor												
531	Domestic creditors	...	...	...	...	...	...	...	...	...	54	14	52
532	External creditors	...	...	...	...	...	...	...	...	...	—	—	—
	Table 6 Balance sheet												
6	**Net worth**	**...**	**...**	**...**	**...**	**...**	**...**	**...**	**...**	**...**	**686**	**706**	**772**
61	**Nonfinancial assets**	**...**	**...**	**...**	**...**	**...**	**...**	**...**	**...**	**...**	**354**	**373**	**396**
611	Fixed assets	...	...	...	...	...	...	...	...	...	351	371	392
6111	Buildings and structures	...	...	...	...	...	...	...	...	...	279	293	295
6112	Machinery and equipment	...	...	...	...	...	...	...	...	...	15	16	15
6113	Other fixed assets	...	...	...	...	...	...	...	...	...	58	63	82
6114	Weapons systems	...	...	...	...	...	...	...	...	...	—	—	—
612	Inventories	...	...	...	...	...	...	...	...	...	3	3	4
613	Valuables	...	...	...	...	...	...	...	...	...	—	—	—
614	Nonproduced assets	...	...	...	...	...	...	...	...	...	—	—	—
6141	Land	...	...	...	...	...	...	...	...	...	—	—	—
6142	Mineral and energy resources	...	...	...	...	...	...	...	...	...	—	—	—
6143	Other naturally occurring assets	...	...	...	...	...	...	...	...	...	—	—	—
6144	Intangible nonproduced assets	...	...	...	...	...	...	...	...	...	—	—	—
62	**Financial assets**	**...**	**...**	**...**	**...**	**...**	**...**	**...**	**...**	**...**	**1,186**	**1,244**	**1,361**
	By instrument												
6201	Monetary gold and SDRs	—	—	—	—	—	—	—	—	—	—	—	—
6202	Currency and deposits	...	...	...	...	...	...	...	...	...	19	19	15
6203	Debt securities	...	...	...	...	...	...	...	...	...	—	—	—
6204	Loans	...	...	...	...	...	...	...	...	...	22	24	25
6205	Equity and investment fund shares	...	...	...	...	...	...	...	...	...	1,079	1,151	1,242
6206	Insurance, pension, and standardized guarantee schemes	...	...	...	...	...	...	...	...	...	—	—	—
6207	Financial derivatives and employee stock options	...	...	...	...	...	...	...	...	...	—	—	0
6208	Other accounts receivable	...	...	...	...	...	...	...	...	...	66	49	79
	By debtor												
621	Domestic debtors	...	...	...	...	...	...	...	...	...	1,184	1,242	1,360
622	External debtors	...	...	...	...	...	...	...	...	...	1	1	1
63	**Liabilities**	**...**	**...**	**...**	**...**	**...**	**...**	**...**	**...**	**...**	**853**	**911**	**985**

China, P.R.: Hong Kong (532)

In Billions of Hong Kong Dollars (HKD) / Fiscal Year Ends March 31st

		Budgetary Central Government			Central Government (excl. Social Security)			Central Government (incl. Social Security)			General Government		
		2012	2013	2014	2012	2013	2014	2012	2013	2014	2012	2013	2014
	By instrument												
6301	Special Drawing Rights (SDRs)	—	—	—	—	—	—	—	—	—	—	—	—
6302	Currency and deposits	...	...	...	...	...	...	...	...	...	—	—	—
6303	Debt securities	...	...	...	...	...	...	...	...	...	82	105	114
6304	Loans	...	...	...	...	...	...	...	...	...	—	—	—
6305	Equity and investment fund shares	...	...	...	...	...	...	...	...	...	—	—	—
6306	Insurance, pension, and standardized guarantee schemes	...	...	...	...	...	...	...	...	...	715	747	816
6307	Financial derivatives and employee stock options	...	...	...	...	...	...	...	...	...	—	—	—
6308	Other accounts payable	...	...	...	...	...	...	...	...	...	57	59	56
	By creditor												
631	Domestic creditors	...	...	...	...	...	...	...	...	...	843	900	974
632	External creditors	...	...	...	...	...	...	...	...	...	11	11	11
	Memorandum items												
6M2	Net financial worth	...	...	...	...	...	...	...	...	...	332	333	376
6M3	Gross debt (D4) at market value	...	...	...	...	...	...	...	...	...	...	...	...
6M3D3	D3 debt liabilities at market value	...	...	...	...	...	...	...	...	...	...	...	...
6M3D2	D2 debt liabilities at market value	...	...	...	...	...	...	...	...	...	...	...	...
6M3D1	D1 debt liabilities at market value	...	...	...	...	...	...	...	...	...	...	...	...
6M4	Gross debt (D4) at nominal value	...	...	...	...	...	...	...	...	...	...	...	...
6M4D3	D3 debt liabilities at nominal value	...	...	...	...	...	...	...	...	...	...	...	...
6M4D2	D2 debt liabilities at nominal value	...	...	...	...	...	...	...	...	...	...	...	...
6M4D1	D1 debt liabilities at nominal value	...	...	...	...	...	...	...	...	...	...	...	...
6M35	Gross debt (D4) at face value	...	...	...	...	...	...	...	...	...	853	911	985
6M35D3	D3 debt liabilities at face value	...	...	...	...	...	...	...	...	...	138	164	169
6M35D2	D2 debt liabilities at face value	...	...	...	...	...	...	...	...	...	82	105	114
6M35D1	D1 debt liabilities at face value	...	...	...	...	...	...	...	...	...	82	105	114
6M93	Government gross debt per national definition	...	...	...	...	...	...	...	...	...	...	...	...
6M5	Arrears	...	...	...	...	...	...	...	...	...	29	30	...
6M6	Explicit contingent liabilities	...	...	...	...	...	...	...	...	...	124	122	108
6M61	of which: Publicly guaranteed debt	...	...	...	...	...	...	...	...	...	—	—	—
6M7	Net implicit obligations for social security benefits	...	...	...	...	...	...	...	...	...	—	—	...
	Table 7 Expenditure by functions of government												
7	**Expenditure**	**...**	**...**	**...**	**...**	**...**	**...**	**...**	**...**	**...**	**408**	**444**	**436**
701	**General public services**	**...**	**...**	**...**	**...**	**...**	**...**	**...**	**...**	**...**	**68**	**70**	**68**
7017	Public debt transactions	...	...	...	...	...	...	...	...	...	2	3	3
7018	Transfers of general character between levels of government	...	...	...	...	...	...	...	...	...	—	—	—
702	**Defense**	**...**	**...**	**...**	**...**	**...**	**...**	**...**	**...**	**...**	**—**	**—**	**—**
703	**Public order and safety**	**...**	**...**	**...**	**...**	**...**	**...**	**...**	**...**	**...**	**36**	**37**	**41**
704	**Economic affairs**	**...**	**...**	**...**	**...**	**...**	**...**	**...**	**...**	**...**	**52**	**75**	**63**
7042	Agriculture, forestry, fishing, and hunting	...	...	...	...	...	...	...	...	...	2	1	1
7043	Fuel and energy	...	...	...	...	...	...	...	...	...	0	0	0
7044	Mining, manufacturing, and construction	...	...	...	...	...	...	...	...	...	4	5	7
7045	Transport	...	...	...	...	...	...	...	...	...	35	44	45
7046	Communication	...	...	...	...	...	...	...	...	...	1	1	1
705	**Environmental protection**	**...**	**...**	**...**	**...**	**...**	**...**	**...**	**...**	**...**	**13**	**13**	**16**
706	**Housing and community amenities**	**...**	**...**	**...**	**...**	**...**	**...**	**...**	**...**	**...**	**26**	**27**	**31**
707	**Health**	**...**	**...**	**...**	**...**	**...**	**...**	**...**	**...**	**...**	**63**	**71**	**64**
7072	Outpatient services	...	...	...	...	...	...	...	...	...	1	1	1
7073	Hospital services	...	...	...	...	...	...	...	...	...	58	65	55
7074	Public health services	...	...	...	...	...	...	...	...	...	4	5	7
708	**Recreation, culture and religion**	**...**	**...**	**...**	**...**	**...**	**...**	**...**	**...**	**...**	**15**	**15**	**13**
709	**Education**	**...**	**...**	**...**	**...**	**...**	**...**	**...**	**...**	**...**	**72**	**72**	**76**
7091	Pre-primary and primary education	...	...	...	...	...	...	...	...	...	14	14	16
7092	Secondary education	...	...	...	...	...	...	...	...	...	22	24	25
7094	Tertiary education	...	...	...	...	...	...	...	...	...	24	23	18

China, P.R.: Hong Kong (532)

In Billions of Hong Kong Dollars (HKD) / Fiscal Year Ends March 31st

		Budgetary Central Government			Central Government (excl. Social Security)			Central Government (incl. Social Security)			General Government		
		2012	2013	2014	2012	2013	2014	2012	2013	2014	2012	2013	2014
710	**Social protection**	...	...	...	...	...	...	...	...	...	**63**	**64**	**64**
7z	Statistical discrepancy: Expenditure	...	...	...	...	...	...	...	...	...	—	—	—
	Table 8 Financial transactions by counterpart sector												
32	**Net acquisition of financial assets**	...	...	...	...	...	...	...	...	...	**113**	**58**	**118**
321	Domestic debtors	...	...	...	...	...	...	...	...	...	113	58	118
8211	General government	...	...	...	...	...	...	...	...	...	...	...	118
8212	Central bank	...	...	...	...	...	...	...	...	...	...	...	...
8213	Deposit-taking corporations except the central bank	...	...	...	...	...	...	...	...	...	...	...	...
8214	Other financial corporations	...	...	...	...	...	...	...	...	...	...	...	...
8215	Nonfinancial corporations	...	...	...	...	...	...	...	...	...	...	...	...
8216	Households & nonprofit institutions serving households	...	...	...	...	...	...	...	...	...	...	...	...
322	External debtors	...	...	...	...	...	...	...	...	...	—	—	—
8221	General government	...	...	...	...	...	...	...	...	...	—	—	—
8227	International organizations	...	...	...	...	...	...	...	...	...	—	—	—
8228	Financial corporations other than international organizations	...	...	...	...	...	...	...	...	...	—	—	—
8229	Other nonresidents	...	...	...	...	...	...	...	...	...	—	—	—
33	**Net incurrence of liabilities**	...	...	...	...	...	...	...	...	...	**41**	**44**	**22**
331	Domestic creditors	...	...	...	...	...	...	...	...	...	41	43	22
8311	General government	...	...	...	...	...	...	...	...	...	...	...	22
8312	Central bank	...	...	...	...	...	...	...	...	...	...	...	...
8313	Deposit-taking corporations except the central bank	...	...	...	...	...	...	...	...	...	...	...	...
8314	Other financial corporations	...	...	...	...	...	...	...	...	...	...	...	...
8315	Nonfinancial corporations	...	...	...	...	...	...	...	...	...	...	...	...
8316	Households & nonprofit institutions serving households	...	...	...	...	...	...	...	...	...	...	...	...
332	External creditors	...	...	...	...	...	...	...	...	...	-0	0	0
8321	General government	...	...	...	...	...	...	...	...	...	...	...	0
8327	International organizations	...	...	...	...	...	...	...	...	...	...	...	—
8328	Financial corporations other than international organizations	...	...	...	...	...	...	...	...	...	...	...	—
8329	Other nonresidents	...	...	...	...	...	...	...	...	...	...	...	—
	Table 9 Total other economic flows in assets and liabilities												
9	**Change in net worth due to other economic flows**	...	...	...	...	...	...	...	...	...	**-48**	**-13**	**-52**
91	**Other economic flows in nonfinancial assets**	...	...	...	...	...	...	...	...	...	**0**	**1**	**0**
911	Fixed assets	...	...	...	...	...	...	...	...	...	0	1	0
912	Inventories	...	...	...	...	...	...	...	...	...	—	—	—
913	Valuables	...	...	...	...	...	...	...	...	...	—	—	—
914	Nonproduced assets	...	...	...	...	...	...	...	...	...	—	—	—
92	**Other economic flows in financial assets**	...	...	...	...	...	...	...	...	...	**6**	**0**	**-1**
	By instrument												
9201	Monetary gold and SDRs	...	...	...	...	...	...	...	...	...	—	—	—
9202	Currency and deposits	...	...	...	...	...	...	...	...	...	0	—	—
9203	Debt securities	...	...	...	...	...	...	...	...	...	—	—	—
9204	Loans	...	...	...	...	...	...	...	...	...	-0	—	—
9205	Equity and investment fund shares	...	...	...	...	...	...	...	...	...	6	0	-1
9206	Insurance, pension, and standardized guarantee schemes	...	...	...	...	...	...	...	...	...	—	—	—
9207	Financial derivatives and employee stock options	...	...	...	...	...	...	...	...	...	—	—	—
9208	Other accounts receivable	...	...	...	...	...	...	...	...	...	—	—	—
	By debtor												
921	Domestic debtors	...	...	...	...	...	...	...	...	...	6	0	-1
922	External debtors	...	...	...	...	...	...	...	...	...	—	—	—
93	**Other economic flows in liabilities**	...	...	...	...	...	...	...	...	...	**54**	**14**	**52**

China, P.R.: Hong Kong (532)

In Billions of Hong Kong Dollars (HKD) / Fiscal Year Ends March 31st

		Budgetary Central Government			Central Government (excl. Social Security)			Central Government (incl. Social Security)			General Government		
		2012	2013	2014	2012	2013	2014	2012	2013	2014	2012	2013	2014
	By instrument												
9301	Special Drawing Rights (SDRs)	...	...	...	...	...	...	...	...	...	—	—	—
9302	Currency and deposits	...	...	...	...	...	...	...	...	...	—	—	—
9303	Debt securities	...	...	...	...	...	...	...	...	...	—	—	—
9304	Loans	...	...	...	...	...	...	...	...	...	—	—	—
9305	Equity and investment fund shares	...	...	...	...	...	...	...	...	...	—	—	—
9306	Insurance, pension, and standardized guarantee schemes	...	...	...	...	...	...	...	...	...	54	14	52
9307	Financial derivatives and employee stock options	...	...	...	...	...	...	...	...	...	—	—	—
9308	Other accounts payable	...	...	...	...	...	...	...	...	...	—	—	—
	By creditor												
931	Domestic creditors	...	...	...	...	...	...	...	...	...	54	14	52
932	External creditors	...	...	...	...	...	...	...	...	...	—	—	—
	Memorandum items												
9M2	Change in net financial worth due to other economic flows	...	...	...	...	...	...	...	...	...	-48	-14	-53
9M3	Gross debt (D4) at market value: other economic flows	...	...	...	...	...	...	...	...	...	54	14	52
9M3D3	D3 debt liabilities at market value: other economic flows	...	...	...	...	...	...	...	...	...	—	—	—
9M3D2	D2 debt liabilities at market value: other economic flows	...	...	...	...	...	...	...	...	...	—	—	—
9M3D1	D1 debt liabilities at market value: other economic flows	...	...	...	...	...	...	...	...	...	—	—	—

China, P.R.: Macao (546)

In Millions of Macao Patacas (MOP) / Fiscal Year Ends December 31st

		Budgetary Central Government			Central Government (excl. Social Security)			Central Government (incl. Social Security)			General Government		
		2013	2014	2015	2013	2014	2015	2013	2014	2015	2013	2014	2015
	Statement of operations												
1	Revenue	150,749	155,489	108,857	156,876	161,957	113,103	157,531	163,392	114,218	157,531	163,392	114,218
2	Expense	51,141	57,662	68,895	52,808	59,584	70,405	43,113	49,858	55,308	43,113	49,858	55,308
GOB	**Gross operating balance**	**99,608**	**97,826**	**39,962**	**104,068**	**102,373**	**42,699**	**114,418**	**113,534**	**58,910**	**114,418**	**113,534**	**58,910**
NOB	**Net operating balance**	...	...	...	...	...	...	...	...	...	...	...	...
31	Net/Gross investment in nonfinancial assets	2,812	6,983	8,521	3,302	7,587	9,209	3,306	7,587	9,209	3,306	7,587	9,209
2M	Expenditure	53,953	64,646	77,416	56,111	67,171	79,614	46,419	57,445	64,517	46,419	57,445	64,517
NLB	**Net lending (+) / Net borrowing (-)**	**96,796**	**90,843**	**31,441**	**100,765**	**94,786**	**33,490**	**111,112**	**105,947**	**49,701**	**111,112**	**105,947**	**49,701**
32	Net acquisition of financial assets	96,797	90,843	31,441	100,765	94,786	33,490	111,112	105,947	49,701	111,112	105,947	49,701
33	Net incurrence of liabilities	—	—	—	—	—	—	—	—	—	—	—	—
NLBz	Statistical discrepancy	0	—	-0	-0	—	0	-0	-0	—	-0	-0	—
	Memorandum items												
PB	Primary net lending / net borrowing	96,796	90,843	31,441	100,765	94,786	33,490	111,112	105,947	49,701	111,112	105,947	49,701
GB	Government balance per national definition	...	...	...	...	...	...	...	...	...	...	...	...
	Statement of other economic flows												
	Balance sheet												
	Table 1 Revenue												
1	**Revenue**	**150,749**	**155,489**	**108,857**	**156,876**	**161,957**	**113,103**	**157,531**	**163,392**	**114,218**	**157,531**	**163,392**	**114,218**
11	**Taxes**	**145,557**	**149,523**	**102,781**	**149,824**	**153,864**	**104,856**	**149,824**	**153,864**	**104,856**	**149,824**	**153,864**	**104,856**
111	Taxes on income, profits, and capital gains	4,955	6,312	7,956	4,955	6,312	7,956	4,955	6,312	7,956	4,955	6,312	7,956
1111	Payable by individuals	1,310	1,737	2,058	1,310	1,737	2,058	1,310	1,737	2,058	1,310	1,737	2,058
1112	Payable by corporations and other enterprises	3,645	4,575	5,898	3,645	4,575	5,898	3,645	4,575	5,898	3,645	4,575	5,898
1113	Other taxes on income, profits, and capital gains	—	—	—	—	—	—	—	—	—	—	—	—
112	Taxes on payroll and workforce	—	—	—	—	—	—	—	—	—	—	—	—
113	Taxes on property	462	581	765	462	581	765	462	581	765	462	581	765
114	Taxes on goods and services	139,536	141,861	93,489	143,803	146,201	95,564	143,803	146,201	95,564	143,803	146,201	95,564
1141	General taxes on goods and services	2,518	2,356	1,479	2,518	2,356	1,479	2,518	2,356	1,479	2,518	2,356	1,479
1142	Excises	1,751	1,738	1,506	1,751	1,738	1,506	1,751	1,738	1,506	1,751	1,738	1,506
115	Taxes on international trade and transactions	—	—	—	—	—	—	—	—	—	—	—	—
116	Other taxes	603	770	572	603	770	572	603	770	572	603	770	572
12	**Social contributions**	—	—	—	—	—	—	**181**	**185**	**190**	**181**	**185**	**190**
121	Social security contributions	—	—	—	—	—	—	181	185	190	181	185	190
122	Other social contributions	—	—	—	—	—	—	—	—	—	—	—	—
13	**Grants**	**2**	—	—	—	—	—	—	—	—	—	—	—
131	From foreign governments	—	—	—	—	—	—	—	—	—	—	—	—
132	From international organizations	—	—	—	—	—	—	—	—	—	—	—	—
133	From other general government units	2	—	—	0	—	—	—	—	—	0	—	—
1331	Current	2	—	—	0	—	—	—	—	—	0	—	—
1332	Capital	—	—	—	0	—	—	—	—	—	0	—	—
14	**Other revenue**	**5,190**	**5,966**	**6,076**	**7,053**	**8,094**	**8,247**	**7,527**	**9,343**	**9,172**	**7,527**	**9,343**	**9,172**
	Table 2 Expense by economic type												
2	**Expense**	**51,141**	**57,662**	**68,895**	**52,808**	**59,584**	**70,405**	**43,113**	**49,858**	**55,308**	**43,113**	**49,858**	**55,308**
21	**Compensation of employees**	**7,794**	**8,762**	**9,826**	**13,128**	**14,832**	**16,820**	**13,204**	**14,922**	**16,920**	**13,204**	**14,922**	**16,920**
211	Wages and salaries	7,794	8,762	9,826	13,128	14,832	16,820	13,204	14,922	16,920	13,204	14,922	16,920
212	Employers' social contributions	—	—	—	—	—	—	—	—	—	—	—	—
22	**Use of goods and services**	**3,156**	**3,396**	**3,544**	**7,532**	**8,724**	**9,533**	**7,556**	**8,769**	**9,599**	**7,556**	**8,769**	**9,599**
23	**Consumption of fixed capital**	...	...	...	...	...	...	...	...	...	...	...	...
24	**Interest**	—	—	—	—	—	—	—	—	—	—	—	—
25	**Subsidies**	**1,598**	**1,725**	**1,491**	**2,288**	**2,407**	**2,079**	**2,288**	**2,407**	**2,079**	**2,288**	**2,407**	**2,079**
26	**Grants**	**26,335**	**29,112**	**38,454**	**12,160**	**12,738**	**18,585**	**157**	**167**	**78**	**157**	**167**	**78**
261	To foreign governments	—	—	—	—	—	—	—	—	—	—	—	—
262	To international organizations	120	115	36	157	167	78	157	167	78	157	167	78
263	To other general government units	26,215	28,997	38,418	12,003	12,571	18,507	—	—	—	0	—	—
2631	Current	26,215	28,997	38,418	12,003	12,571	18,507	—	—	—	0	—	—
2632	Capital	—	—	—	—	—	—	—	—	—	—	—	—

China, P.R.: Macao (546)

In Millions of Macao Patacas (MOP) / Fiscal Year Ends December 31st

		Budgetary Central Government			Central Government (excl. Social Security)			Central Government (incl. Social Security)			General Government		
		2013	2014	2015	2013	2014	2015	2013	2014	2015	2013	2014	2015
27	**Social benefits**	**8,717**	**10,002**	**10,545**	**9,817**	**11,186**	**11,871**	**12,015**	**13,797**	**14,850**	**12,015**	**13,797**	**14,850**
271	Social security benefits	—	—	—	—	—	—	—	—	—	—	—	—
272	Social assistance benefits	8,594	9,773	10,266	9,624	10,829	11,437	11,820	13,440	14,416	11,820	13,440	14,416
273	Employment-related social benefits	123	228	279	194	357	434	194	357	434	194	357	434
28	**Other expense**	**3,542**	**4,665**	**5,035**	**7,883**	**9,697**	**11,517**	**7,893**	**9,795**	**11,782**	**7,893**	**9,795**	**11,782**
281	Property expense other than interest	969	1,041	1,236	1,438	1,566	1,834	1,448	1,581	1,853	1,448	1,581	1,853
282	Transfers not elsewhere classified	2,573	3,625	3,799	6,445	8,132	9,682	6,445	8,214	9,929	6,445	8,214	9,929
2821	Current	2,573	3,561	3,720	6,423	8,040	9,574	6,423	8,123	9,821	6,423	8,123	9,821
2822	Capital	0	64	79	22	91	108	22	91	108	22	91	108
	Table 3 Transactions in assets and liabilities												
3	**Change in net worth from transactions**	...	...	...	...	...	**42,699**	...	...	...	...	...	...
31	**Net/Gross investment in nonfinancial assets**	**2,812**	**6,983**	**8,521**	**3,302**	**7,587**	**9,209**	**3,306**	**7,587**	**9,209**	**3,306**	**7,587**	**9,209**
311	Fixed assets	2,812	6,983	8,521	3,302	7,587	9,209	3,306	7,587	9,209	3,306	7,587	9,209
3111	Buildings and structures	319	4,500	6,914	542	4,750	7,201	542	4,750	7,201	542	4,750	7,201
3112	Machinery and equipment	2,493	2,484	1,607	2,760	2,837	2,008	2,763	2,837	2,008	2,763	2,837	2,008
3113	Other fixed assets	0	—	—	0	—	—	0	—	—	0	—	—
3114	Weapons systems	—	—	—	—	—	—	—	—	—	—	—	—
312	Inventories	—	—	—	—	—	—	—	—	—	—	—	—
313	Valuables	—	—	—	—	—	—	—	—	—	—	—	—
314	Nonproduced assets	—	—	—	—	—	—	—	—	—	—	—	—
3141	Land	—	—	—	—	—	—	—	—	—	—	—	—
3142	Mineral and energy resources	—	—	—	—	—	—	—	—	—	—	—	—
3143	Other naturally occurring assets	—	—	—	—	—	—	—	—	—	—	—	—
3144	Intangible nonproduced assets	—	—	—	—	—	—	—	—	—	—	—	—
32	**Net acquisition of financial assets**	**96,797**	**90,843**	**31,441**	**100,765**	**94,786**	**33,490**	**111,112**	**105,947**	**49,701**	**111,112**	**105,947**	**49,701**
	By instrument												
3201	Monetary gold and SDRs	—	—	—	—	—	—	—	—	—	—	—	—
3202	Currency and deposits	96,285	90,296	29,299	99,608	94,015	31,188	109,955	105,176	47,400	109,955	105,176	47,400
3203	Debt securities	—	—	—	—	—	—	—	—	—	—	—	—
3204	Loans	-35	-35	78	210	189	193	210	189	193	210	189	193
3205	Equity and investment fund shares	547	582	2,064	948	582	2,108	948	582	2,108	948	582	2,108
3206	Insurance, pension, and standardized guarantee schemes	—	—	—	—	—	—	—	—	—	—	—	—
3207	Financial derivatives and employee stock options	—	—	—	—	—	—	—	—	—	—	—	—
3208	Other accounts receivable	...	...	...	...	...	...	...	...	...	...	...	...
	By debtor												
321	Domestic debtors	96,797	90,843	31,441	100,765	94,786	33,490	111,112	105,947	49,701	111,112	105,947	49,701
322	External debtors	—	—	—	—	—	—	—	—	—	—	—	—
33	**Net incurrence of liabilities**	—	—	—	—	—	—	—	—	—	—	—	—
	By instrument												
3301	Special Drawing Rights (SDRs)	—	—	—	—	—	—	—	—	—	—	—	—
3302	Currency and deposits	—	—	—	—	—	—	—	—	—	—	—	—
3303	Debt securities	—	—	—	—	—	—	—	—	—	—	—	—
3304	Loans	—	—	—	—	—	—	—	—	—	—	—	—
3305	Equity and investment fund shares	—	—	—	—	—	—	—	—	—	—	—	—
3306	Insurance, pension, and standardized guarantee schemes	—	—	—	—	—	—	—	—	—	—	—	—
3307	Financial derivatives and employee stock options	—	—	—	—	—	—	—	—	—	—	—	—
3308	Other accounts payable	...	...	...	...	...	...	...	...	...	...	...	...
	By creditor												
331	Domestic creditors	—	—	—	—	—	—	—	—	—	—	—	—
332	External creditors	—	—	—	—	—	—	—	—	—	—	—	—
	Table 4 Holding gains and losses in assets and liabilities												
	Table 5 Holding gains and losses in assets and liabilities												

China, P.R.: Macao (546)

In Millions of Macao Patacas (MOP) / Fiscal Year Ends December 31st

		Budgetary Central Government			Central Government (excl. Social Security)			Central Government (incl. Social Security)			General Government		
		2013	2014	2015	2013	2014	2015	2013	2014	2015	2013	2014	2015
	Table 6 Balance sheet												
6	**Net worth**	...	...	...	...	...	...	...	...	...	...	...	...
61	**Nonfinancial assets**	...	...	...	...	...	...	...	...	...	...	...	...
611	Fixed assets	...	...	...	...	...	...	...	...	...	...	...	...
6111	Buildings and structures	...	...	...	...	...	...	...	...	...	...	...	...
6112	Machinery and equipment	...	...	...	...	...	...	...	...	...	...	...	...
6113	Other fixed assets	...	...	...	...	...	...	...	...	...	...	...	...
6114	Weapons systems	...	...	...	...	...	...	...	...	...	...	...	...
612	Inventories	...	...	...	...	...	...	...	...	...	...	...	...
613	Valuables	...	...	...	...	...	...	...	...	...	...	...	...
614	Nonproduced assets	...	...	...	...	...	...	...	...	...	...	...	...
6141	Land	...	...	...	...	...	...	...	...	...	...	...	...
6142	Mineral and energy resources	...	...	...	...	...	...	...	...	...	...	...	...
6143	Other naturally occurring assets	...	...	...	...	...	...	...	...	...	...	...	...
6144	Intangible nonproduced assets	...	...	...	...	...	...	...	...	...	...	...	...
62	**Financial assets**	...	...	...	...	...	...	...	...	...	...	...	...
	By instrument												
6201	Monetary gold and SDRs	—	—	—	—	—	—	—	—	—	—	—	—
6202	Currency and deposits	...	...	...	...	...	...	...	...	...	...	...	...
6203	Debt securities	...	...	...	...	...	...	...	...	...	...	...	...
6204	Loans	...	...	...	...	...	...	...	...	...	...	...	...
6205	Equity and investment fund shares	...	...	...	...	...	...	...	...	...	...	...	...
6206	Insurance, pension, and standardized guarantee schemes	...	...	...	...	...	...	...	...	...	...	...	...
6207	Financial derivatives and employee stock options	...	...	...	...	...	...	...	...	...	...	...	...
6208	Other accounts receivable	...	...	...	...	...	...	...	...	...	...	...	...
	By debtor												
621	Domestic debtors	...	...	...	...	...	...	...	...	...	...	...	...
622	External debtors	...	...	...	...	...	...	...	...	...	...	...	...
63	**Liabilities**	...	...	...	...	...	...	...	...	...	...	...	...
	By instrument												
6301	Special Drawing Rights (SDRs)	—	—	—	—	—	—	—	—	—	—	—	—
6302	Currency and deposits	...	...	...	...	...	...	...	...	...	...	...	...
6303	Debt securities	...	...	...	...	...	...	...	...	...	...	...	...
6304	Loans	...	...	...	...	...	...	...	...	...	...	...	...
6305	Equity and investment fund shares	...	...	...	...	...	...	...	...	...	...	...	...
6306	Insurance, pension, and standardized guarantee schemes	...	...	...	...	...	...	...	...	...	...	...	...
6307	Financial derivatives and employee stock options	...	...	...	...	...	...	...	...	...	...	...	...
6308	Other accounts payable	...	...	...	...	...	...	...	...	...	...	...	...
	By creditor												
631	Domestic creditors	...	...	...	...	...	...	...	...	...	...	...	...
632	External creditors	...	...	...	...	...	...	...	...	...	...	...	...
	Memorandum items												
6M2	Net financial worth	...	...	...	...	...	...	...	...	...	...	...	...
6M3	Gross debt (D4) at market value	...	...	...	...	...	...	...	...	...	...	...	...
6M3D3	D3 debt liabilities at market value	...	...	...	...	...	...	...	...	...	...	...	...
6M3D2	D2 debt liabilities at market value	...	...	...	...	...	...	...	...	...	...	...	...
6M3D1	D1 debt liabilities at market value	...	...	...	...	...	...	...	...	...	...	...	...
6M4	Gross debt (D4) at nominal value	...	...	...	...	...	...	...	...	...	...	...	...
6M4D3	D3 debt liabilities at nominal value	...	...	...	...	...	...	...	...	...	...	...	...
6M4D2	D2 debt liabilities at nominal value	...	...	...	...	...	...	...	...	...	...	...	...
6M4D1	D1 debt liabilities at nominal value	...	...	...	...	...	...	...	...	...	...	...	...
6M35	Gross debt (D4) at face value	...	...	...	...	...	...	...	...	...	...	...	...
6M35D3	D3 debt liabilities at face value	...	...	...	...	...	...	...	...	...	...	...	...
6M35D2	D2 debt liabilities at face value	...	...	...	...	...	...	...	...	...	...	...	...
6M35D1	D1 debt liabilities at face value	...	...	...	...	...	...	...	...	...	...	...	...
6M93	Government gross debt per national definition	...	...	...	...	...	...	...	...	...	...	...	...
6M5	Arrears	...	...	...	...	...	...	...	...	...	...	...	...

China, P.R.: Macao (546)

In Millions of Macao Patacas (MOP) / Fiscal Year Ends December 31st

		Budgetary Central Government			Central Government (excl. Social Security)			Central Government (incl. Social Security)			General Government		
		2013	2014	2015	2013	2014	2015	2013	2014	2015	2013	2014	2015
6M6	Explicit contingent liabilities	...	...	...	...	...	...	...	...	...	...	...	...
6M61	of which: Publicly guaranteed debt	...	...	...	...	...	...	...	...	...	...	...	...
6M7	Net implicit obligations for social security benefits	...	...	...	...	...	...	...	...	...	...	...	...
	Table 7 Expenditure by functions of government												
7	**Expenditure**	53,953	64,646	77,416	56,111	67,171	79,614	46,419	57,445	...	46,419	57,445	64,517
701	**General public services**	29,877	32,391	43,227	19,368	20,343	28,627	7,365	7,772	...	7,365	7,772	10,120
7017	Public debt transactions	—	...	...	—	...	...	—	...	...	—	...	...
7018	Transfers of general character between levels of government	...	...	...	...	...	...	...	...	...	...	...	...
702	**Defense**	—	—	—	—	—	—	—	—	...	—	—	—
703	**Public order and safety**	5,239	5,692	8,349	6,054	6,597	9,347	6,054	6,597	...	6,054	6,597	9,347
704	**Economic affairs**	7,077	9,022	7,070	7,753	9,872	8,075	7,753	9,872	...	7,753	9,872	8,075
7042	Agriculture, forestry, fishing, and hunting	...	...	...	...	...	...	...	...	...	...	...	...
7043	Fuel and energy	...	...	...	...	...	...	...	...	...	...	...	...
7044	Mining, manufacturing, and construction	...	...	...	...	...	...	...	...	...	...	...	...
7045	Transport	...	...	...	...	...	...	...	...	...	...	...	...
7046	Communication	...	...	...	...	...	...	...	...	...	...	...	...
705	**Environmental protection**	649	950	842	761	1,074	865	761	1,074	...	761	1,074	865
706	**Housing and community amenities**	1,255	1,004	1,518	1,594	1,306	1,890	1,594	1,306	...	1,594	1,306	1,890
707	**Health**	204	387	688	4,448	5,299	6,572	4,448	5,299	...	4,448	5,299	6,572
7072	Outpatient services	...	...	...	...	...	...	...	...	...	...	...	...
7073	Hospital services	...	...	...	...	...	...	...	...	...	...	...	...
7074	Public health services	...	...	...	...	...	...	...	...	...	...	...	...
708	**Recreation, culture and religion**	557	662	539	2,127	2,501	2,452	2,127	2,501	...	2,127	2,501	2,452
709	**Education**	4,975	5,057	5,409	8,024	8,580	9,515	8,024	8,580	...	8,024	8,580	9,515
7091	Pre-primary and primary education	...	...	...	...	...	...	...	...	...	...	...	...
7092	Secondary education	...	...	...	...	...	...	...	...	...	...	...	...
7094	Tertiary education	...	...	...	...	...	...	...	...	...	...	...	...
710	**Social protection**	4,120	9,481	9,774	5,982	11,599	12,271	8,293	14,443	...	8,293	14,443	15,681
7z	Statistical discrepancy: Expenditure	—	...	...	—	...	...	—	...	...	—	...	...
	Table 8 Financial transactions by counterpart sector												
32	**Net acquisition of financial assets**	96,797	90,843	31,441	100,765	94,786	33,490	111,112	105,947	49,701	111,112	105,947	49,701
321	Domestic debtors	96,797	90,843	31,441	100,765	94,786	33,490	111,112	105,947	49,701	111,112	105,947	49,701
8211	General government	—	90,296	...	—	94,015	...	—	105,176	...	—	105,176	...
8212	Central bank	96,285	...	...	99,608	...	...	109,955	...	...	109,955	...	...
8213	Deposit-taking corporations except the central bank	-35	-35	...	210	189	...	210	189	...	210	189	...
8214	Other financial corporations	—	...	...	—	...	...	—	...	...	—	...	...
8215	Nonfinancial corporations	547	582	...	948	582	...	948	582	...	948	582	...
8216	Households & nonprofit institutions serving households	—	...	...	—	...	...	—	...	...	—	...	...
322	External debtors	—	—	—	—	—	—	—	—	—	—	—	—
8221	General government	—	—	—	—	—	—	—	—	—	—	—	—
8227	International organizations	—	—	—	—	—	—	—	—	—	—	—	—
8228	Financial corporations other than international organizations	—	—	—	—	—	—	—	—	—	—	—	—
8229	Other nonresidents	—	—	—	—	—	—	—	—	—	—	—	—

China, P.R.: Macao (546)

In Millions of Macao Patacas (MOP) / Fiscal Year Ends December 31st

		Budgetary Central Government			Central Government (excl. Social Security)			Central Government (incl. Social Security)			General Government		
		2013	2014	2015	2013	2014	2015	2013	2014	2015	2013	2014	2015
33	**Net incurrence of liabilities**	—	—	—	—	—	—	—	—	—	—	—	—
331	Domestic creditors	—	—	—	—	—	—	—	—	—	—	—	—
3311	General government	—	—	—	—	—	—	—	—	—	—	—	—
3312	Central bank	—	—	—	—	—	—	—	—	—	—	—	—
3313	Deposit-taking corporations except the central bank	—	—	—	—	—	—	—	—	—	—	—	—
3314	Other financial corporations	—	—	—	—	—	—	—	—	—	—	—	—
3315	Nonfinancial corporations	—	—	—	—	—	—	—	—	—	—	—	—
3316	Households & nonprofit institutions serving households	—	—	—	—	—	—	—	—	—	—	—	—
332	External creditors	—	—	—	—	—	—	—	—	—	—	—	—
3321	General government	—	—	—	—	—	—	—	—	—	—	—	—
3327	International organizations	—	—	—	—	—	—	—	—	—	—	—	—
3328	Financial corporations other than international organizations	—	—	—	—	—	—	—	—	—	—	—	—
3329	Other nonresidents	—	—	—	—	—	—	—	—	—	—	—	—
	Table 9 Total other economic flows in assets and liabilities												

Colombia (233)

In Billions of Colombian Pesos (COP) / Fiscal Year Ends December 31st

		Budgetary Central Government			Central Government (excl. Social Security)			Central Government (incl. Social Security)			General Government		
		2013P	2014P	2015P	2013P	2014P	2015P	2013P	2014P	2015P	2013P	2014P	2015P
	Statement of operations												
1	Revenue	153,630	158,059	148,880	176,363	162,463	158,538	209,702	195,847	199,031	209,977	226,917	232,332
2	Expense	183,269	198,593	176,048	201,740	202,661	180,325	237,687	236,759	221,500	229,099	257,400	245,330
GOB	**Gross operating balance**	**-28,344**	**-39,102**	**-25,715**	**-23,165**	**-38,018**	**-19,847**	**-25,696**	**-38,717**	**-20,507**	**-14,860**	**-26,119**	**-8,852**
NOB	**Net operating balance**	**-29,639**	**-40,534**	**-27,168**	**-25,377**	**-40,198**	**-21,786**	**-27,986**	**-40,912**	**-22,469**	**-19,122**	**-30,483**	**-12,998**
31	Net/Gross investment in nonfinancial assets	9,053	9,006	5,262	11,387	11,094	9,425	11,537	11,026	9,476	13,606	14,297	25,666
2M	Expenditure	192,322	207,599	181,310	213,126	213,755	189,750	249,225	247,785	230,977	242,706	271,698	270,997
NLB	**Net lending (+) / Net borrowing (-)**	**-38,692**	**-49,540**	**-32,430**	**-36,763**	**-51,292**	**-31,212**	**-39,523**	**-51,938**	**-31,946**	**-32,728**	**-44,780**	**-38,664**
32	Net acquisition of financial assets	9,734	2,954	-12,376	9,732	637	-12,941	6,563	3,602	-10,299	24,447	15,502	-10,162
33	Net incurrence of liabilities	42,632	62,303	52,555	42,118	62,382	47,951	41,037	61,996	-8,218	45,957	65,391	-2,707
NLBz	Statistical discrepancy	5,794	-9,810	-32,500	4,377	-10,452	-29,681	5,049	-6,456	29,865	11,219	-5,108	31,208
	Memorandum items												
PB	Primary net lending / net borrowing	-21,213	-30,239	-11,756	-19,271	-31,978	-10,424	-22,030	-32,616	-11,144	-14,634	-24,856	-17,138
GB	Government balance per national definition	...	...	...	...	...	...	...	...	...	...	...	...
	Statement of other economic flows												
9	**Change in net worth due to other economic flows**	**7,088**	**-24,203**	**-36,418**	**9,000**	**-22,246**	**-31,271**	**8,913**	**-22,045**	**-30,743**	**10,386**	**-18,647**	**-30,483**
4	Change in net worth due to holding gains and losses	**-4,032**	**-13,661**	**-31,384**	**-2,117**	**-11,703**	**-26,241**	**-2,204**	**-11,502**	**-25,713**	**-822**	**-8,028**	**-25,460**
41	Nonfinancial assets	2,155	4,379	4,031	3,777	6,108	8,840	3,685	6,392	8,929	6,130	8,718	10,798
42	Financial assets	-727	-1,148	-3,535	-421	-904	-2,818	-415	-985	-2,378	-1,398	493	-3,423
43	Liabilities	5,459	16,891	31,880	5,473	16,906	32,263	5,474	16,909	32,264	5,554	17,240	32,835
5	Change in net worth due to volume changes	**11,119**	**-10,542**	**-5,034**	**11,117**	**-10,543**	**-5,030**	**11,117**	**-10,543**	**-5,030**	**11,208**	**-10,618**	**-5,023**
51	Nonfinancial assets	11,118	-10,544	-5,034	11,116	-10,545	-5,030	11,116	-10,545	-5,030	11,207	-10,620	-5,023
52	Financial assets	—	—	—	—	—	—	—	—	—	—	—	—
53	Liabilities	-1	-2	0	-1	-2	0	-1	-2	0	-1	-2	0
	Balance sheet												
6	**Net worth**	**-79,213**	**-130,782**	**-180,769**	**-33,759**	**-93,507**	**-130,092**	**-88,637**	**-238,851**	**-122,107**	**81,301**	**-11,527**	**48,931**
61	Nonfinancial assets	139,573	142,409	146,675	173,141	170,330	183,748	173,503	126,292	184,808	270,821	224,019	263,206
62	Financial assets	188,777	196,675	194,976	205,624	214,061	212,534	217,038	242,761	229,556	333,662	352,842	373,448
63	Liabilities	407,563	469,866	522,420	412,524	477,898	526,374	479,177	607,904	536,471	523,182	588,388	587,724
	Table 1 Revenue												
1	**Revenue**	**153,630**	**158,059**	**148,880**	**176,363**	**162,463**	**158,538**	**209,702**	**195,847**	**199,031**	**209,977**	**226,917**	**232,332**
11	**Taxes**	**94,173**	**109,436**	**110,073**	**98,904**	**113,419**	**114,897**	**100,131**	**113,419**	**120,657**	**123,163**	**137,403**	**149,168**
111	Taxes on income, profits, and capital gains	33,979	39,745	45,009	33,979	39,745	45,009	33,979	39,745	45,009	34,015	39,781	45,052
1111	Payable by individuals	—	—	—	—	—	—	—	—	—	—	—	—
1112	Payable by corporations and other enterprises	—	9,235	14,275	—	9,235	14,275	—	9,235	14,275	—	9,235	14,275
1113	Other taxes on income, profits, and capital gains	33,979	30,510	30,734	33,979	30,510	30,734	33,979	30,510	30,734	34,015	30,546	30,778
112	Taxes on payroll and workforce	3,701	5,891	828	7,252	8,547	3,644	7,252	8,547	8,178	7,252	8,547	8,178
113	Taxes on property	8	30	21	447	822	928	447	822	928	6,131	7,495	8,364
114	Taxes on goods and services	44,451	50,836	53,248	44,850	51,192	53,899	46,076	51,192	55,126	60,938	66,545	71,847
1141	General taxes on goods and services	38,419	44,169	47,513	38,419	44,169	47,513	38,419	44,169	47,513	45,930	51,999	56,041
1142	Excises	2,833	2,916	3,344	3,173	3,205	3,643	3,173	3,205	3,643	7,998	8,200	9,051
115	Taxes on international trade and transactions	4,337	4,657	5,356	4,337	4,657	5,356	4,337	4,657	5,356	4,337	4,657	5,356
116	Other taxes	7,698	8,277	5,611	8,041	8,455	6,061	8,041	8,455	6,061	10,490	10,377	10,371
12	**Social contributions**	**8,108**	**12,291**	**616**	**8,108**	**12,291**	**616**	**27,224**	**24,870**	**19,732**	**27,236**	**24,872**	**19,735**
121	Social security contributions	8,108	12,291	616	8,108	12,291	616	27,224	24,870	19,732	27,236	24,872	19,735
122	Other social contributions	—	—	—	—	—	—	—	—	—	—	—	—
13	**Grants**	**11,490**	**2,390**	**2,805**	**22,884**	**-2,070**	**3,084**	**34,759**	**17,655**	**14,359**	**815**	**786**	**894**
131	From foreign governments	815	786	894	815	786	894	815	786	894	815	786	894
132	From international organizations	—	—	—	—	—	—	—	—	—	—	—	—
133	From other general government units	10,675	1,604	1,911	22,069	-2,856	2,189	33,944	16,869	13,465	—	—	—
1331	Current	9,582	1,548	1,901	20,874	-3,088	1,988	32,749	16,636	13,262	—	—	—
1332	Capital	1,094	57	10	1,196	232	202	1,196	232	202	—	—	—
14	**Other revenue**	**39,858**	**33,942**	**35,385**	**46,466**	**38,823**	**39,941**	**47,587**	**39,902**	**44,283**	**58,763**	**63,856**	**62,535**

Colombia (233)

In Billions of Colombian Pesos (COP) / Fiscal Year Ends December 31st

		Budgetary Central Government			Central Government (excl. Social Security)			Central Government (incl. Social Security)			General Government		
		2013P	2014P	2015P	2013P	2014P	2015P	2013P	2014P	2015P	2013P	2014P	2015P
	Table 2 Expense by economic type												
2	**Expense**	**183,269**	**198,593**	**176,048**	**201,740**	**202,661**	**180,325**	**237,687**	**236,759**	**221,500**	**229,099**	**257,400**	**245,330**
21	**Compensation of employees**	**15,974**	**17,620**	**19,066**	**17,989**	**19,837**	**21,535**	**18,609**	**20,191**	**21,864**	**33,607**	**36,274**	**38,788**
211	Wages and salaries	13,808	15,215	16,329	15,530	17,109	18,458	15,641	17,228	18,601	28,225	30,750	33,084
212	Employers' social contributions	2,166	2,404	2,736	2,459	2,728	3,077	2,967	2,963	3,263	5,382	5,524	5,704
22	**Use of goods and services**	**22,018**	**24,368**	**25,700**	**35,653**	**37,796**	**35,784**	**36,192**	**45,590**	**38,832**	**61,100**	**74,816**	**75,141**
23	**Consumption of fixed capital**	**1,295**	**1,433**	**1,454**	**2,211**	**2,180**	**1,940**	**2,289**	**2,195**	**1,962**	**4,262**	**4,364**	**4,146**
24	**Interest**	**17,479**	**19,301**	**20,674**	**17,493**	**19,314**	**20,787**	**17,493**	**19,321**	**20,802**	**18,095**	**19,924**	**21,526**
25	**Subsidies**	**3,606**	**3,494**	**2,732**	**3,625**	**3,508**	**2,767**	**3,625**	**3,508**	**2,767**	**4,071**	**4,054**	**3,542**
26	**Grants**	**67,802**	**73,504**	**61,554**	**66,362**	**53,656**	**46,797**	**81,246**	**53,779**	**61,682**	**—**	**—**	**—**
261	To foreign governments	—	—	—	—	—	—	—	—	—	—	—	—
262	To international organizations	—	—	—	—	—	—	—	—	—	—	—	—
263	To other general government units	67,802	73,504	61,554	66,362	53,656	46,797	81,246	53,779	61,682	—	—	—
2631	Current	57,949	65,573	54,599	56,631	46,005	40,025	71,515	46,127	54,909	—	—	—
2632	Capital	9,852	7,931	6,955	9,731	7,652	6,773	9,731	7,652	6,773	—	—	—
27	**Social benefits**	**24,517**	**29,024**	**17,549**	**26,033**	**31,929**	**20,487**	**45,173**	**56,625**	**41,545**	**64,992**	**77,251**	**63,803**
271	Social security benefits	15,822	17,711	11,017	15,845	17,725	11,062	34,972	42,346	27,978	35,820	43,217	28,353
272	Social assistance benefits	4,124	6,225	3,358	5,023	8,445	4,884	5,024	8,447	8,576	20,607	25,169	26,517
273	Employment-related social benefits	4,571	5,087	3,174	5,165	5,758	4,540	5,177	5,832	4,991	8,565	8,865	8,933
28	**Other expense**	**30,579**	**29,851**	**27,321**	**32,375**	**34,440**	**30,227**	**33,061**	**35,550**	**32,046**	**42,973**	**40,717**	**38,384**
281	Property expense other than interest	15	24	26	17	26	28	17	26	28	72	148	144
282	Transfers not elsewhere classified	30,563	29,826	27,294	32,358	34,414	30,200	33,044	35,524	32,018	42,901	40,569	38,241
2821	Current	30,563	29,826	26,996	32,356	34,414	29,901	33,042	35,524	31,719	42,891	40,563	37,933
2822	Capital	0	0	299	2	0	299	2	0	299	10	6	308
	Table 3 Transactions in assets and liabilities												
3	**Change in net worth from transactions**	**-23,846**	**-50,344**	**-59,668**	**-21,000**	**-50,650**	**-51,467**	**-22,937**	**-47,368**	**7,395**	**-7,904**	**-35,591**	**18,210**
31	**Net/Gross investment in nonfinancial assets**	**9,053**	**9,006**	**5,262**	**11,387**	**11,094**	**9,425**	**11,537**	**11,026**	**9,476**	**13,606**	**14,297**	**25,666**
311	Fixed assets	8,635	8,256	5,104	10,743	10,273	8,884	10,816	10,219	8,907	12,366	12,942	24,508
3111	Buildings and structures	6,614	6,737	4,994	8,433	8,457	8,612	8,495	8,417	8,642	9,673	10,690	23,414
3112	Machinery and equipment	1,978	1,319	137	2,185	1,544	243	2,187	1,540	241	2,511	1,946	1,046
3113	Other fixed assets	43	200	-26	126	272	30	134	262	24	182	305	48
3114	Weapons systems	—	—	—	—	—	—	—	—	—	—	—	—
312	Inventories	255	459	159	339	497	761	338	497	791	466	475	840
313	Valuables	10	21	6	16	23	9	15	23	11	28	31	28
314	Nonproduced assets	153	270	-7	289	302	-229	368	287	-233	746	849	290
3141	Land	153	270	-7	289	302	-229	368	287	-233	746	849	290
3142	Mineral and energy resources	—	—	—	—	—	—	—	—	—	—	—	—
3143	Other naturally occurring assets	—	—	—	—	—	—	—	—	—	—	—	—
3144	Intangible nonproduced assets	—	—	—	—	—	—	—	—	—	—	—	—
32	**Net acquisition of financial assets**	**9,734**	**2,954**	**-12,376**	**9,732**	**637**	**-12,941**	**6,563**	**3,602**	**-10,299**	**24,447**	**15,502**	**-10,162**
	By instrument												
3201	Monetary gold and SDRs	—	—	—	—	—	—	—	—	—	—	—	—
3202	Currency and deposits	7,812	7,199	-9,207	8,044	6,945	-9,151	9,565	6,957	-8,931	17,051	8,132	-14,037
3203	Debt securities	-1,437	-2,362	2,710	-868	-4,770	255	-1,434	-4,536	984	-319	-4,346	473
3204	Loans	904	-4,116	4,212	877	-4,118	4,268	871	-4,117	4,270	949	-4,134	4,516
3205	Equity and investment fund shares	3,854	-3,029	-21,020	3,688	-2,971	-20,930	3,629	-2,388	-20,739	4,951	-1,711	-20,360
3206	Insurance, pension, and standardized guarantee schemes	—	—	—	—	—	—	—	—	—	—	—	—
3207	Financial derivatives and employee stock options	-336	—	—	-336	—	1	-336	—	1	-336	—	1
3208	Other accounts receivable	-1,063	5,261	10,930	-1,674	5,551	12,615	-5,732	7,685	14,116	2,150	17,562	19,245
	By debtor												
321	Domestic debtors	7,360	1,988	-16,970	7,351	-354	-17,607	4,183	2,611	-14,966	22,064	14,512	-14,823
322	External debtors	2,374	965	4,594	2,380	992	4,666	2,380	992	4,666	2,383	990	4,660
33	**Net incurrence of liabilities**	**42,632**	**62,303**	**52,555**	**42,118**	**62,382**	**47,951**	**41,037**	**61,996**	**-8,218**	**45,957**	**65,391**	**-2,707**
	By instrument												
3301	Special Drawing Rights (SDRs)	—	—	—	—	—	—	—	—	—	—	—	—
3302	Currency and deposits	—	—	—	—	—	—	—	—	—	—	—	—
3303	Debt securities	26,600	34,582	29,882	26,480	33,078	29,643	26,480	33,078	29,643	26,308	33,153	29,350
3304	Loans	5,618	4,745	19,525	5,577	4,796	20,422	5,505	4,868	21,188	6,068	5,795	22,736

Colombia (233)

In Billions of Colombian Pesos (COP) / Fiscal Year Ends December 31st

		Budgetary Central Government			Central Government (excl. Social Security)			Central Government (incl. Social Security)			General Government		
		2013P	2014P	2015P	2013P	2014P	2015P	2013P	2014P	2015P	2013P	2014P	2015P
3305	Equity and investment fund shares	—	—	—	—	—	—	—	—	—	—	—	—
3306	Insurance, pension, and standardized guarantee schemes	—	—	—	—	—	—	—	—	—	—	—	—
3307	Financial derivatives and employee stock options	363	-441	-413	361	-442	-419	361	-442	-419	361	-442	-419
3308	Other accounts payable	10,050	23,417	3,560	9,701	24,950	-1,694	8,692	24,492	-58,630	13,220	26,886	-54,374
	By creditor												
331	Domestic creditors	33,634	40,437	12,010	33,124	40,486	6,524	32,114	40,028	-49,574	36,864	42,952	-44,499
332	External creditors	8,998	21,866	40,544	8,994	21,896	41,427	8,923	21,967	41,356	9,093	22,439	41,793
	Table 4 Holding gains and losses in assets and liabilities												
4	**Change in net worth due to holding gains and losses**	**-4,032**	**-13,661**	**-31,384**	**-2,117**	**-11,703**	**-26,241**	**-2,204**	**-11,502**	**-25,713**	**-822**	**-8,028**	**-25,460**
41	**Holding gains and losses in nonfinancial assets**	**2,155**	**4,379**	**4,031**	**3,777**	**6,108**	**8,840**	**3,685**	**6,392**	**8,929**	**6,130**	**8,718**	**10,798**
411	Fixed assets	1,150	1,421	2,509	1,423	2,204	3,169	1,387	2,367	3,177	1,671	3,585	3,918
412	Inventories	—	—	—	—	—	—	—	—	—	—	—	—
413	Valuables	—	—	—	—	—	—	—	—	—	—	—	—
414	Nonproduced assets	1,005	2,958	1,522	2,354	3,903	5,671	2,298	4,025	5,752	4,459	5,134	6,880
42	**Holding gains and losses in financial assets**	**-727**	**-1,148**	**-3,535**	**-421**	**-904**	**-2,818**	**-415**	**-985**	**-2,378**	**-1,398**	**493**	**-3,423**
	By instrument												
4201	Monetary gold and SDRs	—	—	—	—	—	—	—	—	—	—	—	—
4202	Currency and deposits	45	84	505	52	110	570	55	114	570	57	150	575
4203	Debt securities	1,824	2,322	2,900	2,045	2,574	3,228	2,048	2,593	3,541	2,241	2,885	3,845
4204	Loans	—	—	—	—	—	—	—	—	—	—	—	—
4205	Equity and investment fund shares	-2,774	-4,939	-10,677	-2,725	-4,986	-10,675	-2,725	-5,090	-10,548	-3,929	-3,997	-11,972
4206	Insurance, pension, and standardized guarantee schemes	—	—	—	—	—	—	—	—	—	—	—	—
4207	Financial derivatives and employee stock options	171	253	379	200	267	639	200	267	640	200	267	640
4208	Other accounts receivable	7	1,132	3,358	7	1,132	3,419	7	1,132	3,419	32	1,189	3,489
	By debtor												
421	Domestic debtors	-643	-2,051	-6,883	-344	-1,832	-6,293	-341	-1,917	-5,853	-1,352	-532	-6,973
422	External debtors	-84	902	3,348	-77	928	3,475	-74	932	3,475	-47	1,025	3,550
43	**Holding gains and losses in liabilities**	**5,459**	**16,891**	**31,880**	**5,473**	**16,906**	**32,263**	**5,474**	**16,909**	**32,264**	**5,554**	**17,240**	**32,835**
	By instrument												
4301	Special Drawing Rights (SDRs)	—	—	—	—	—	—	—	—	—	—	—	—
4302	Currency and deposits	12	182	134	12	183	146	14	185	146	15	188	147
4303	Debt securities	—	—	—	0	—	3	0	—	3	0	—	3
4304	Loans	5,000	16,709	30,584	4,999	16,707	30,783	4,999	16,707	30,783	5,078	17,031	31,357
4305	Equity and investment fund shares	—	—	—	—	—	—	—	—	—	—	—	—
4306	Insurance, pension, and standardized guarantee schemes	—	—	—	—	—	—	—	—	—	—	—	—
4307	Financial derivatives and employee stock options	531	9	—	541	18	119	541	18	120	541	18	120
4308	Other accounts payable	-83	-8	1,162	-80	-2	1,212	-80	-2	1,212	-81	3	1,208
	By creditor												
431	Domestic creditors	1,300	1,785	4,378	1,315	1,803	4,968	1,316	1,806	4,968	1,318	1,820	4,971
432	External creditors	4,160	15,107	27,501	4,158	15,103	27,295	4,158	15,103	27,295	4,236	15,420	27,864
	Table 5 Holding gains and losses in assets and liabilities												
5	**Change in net worth due to other volume changes**	**11,119**	**-10,542**	**-5,034**	**11,117**	**-10,543**	**-5,030**	**11,117**	**-10,543**	**-5,030**	**11,208**	**-10,618**	**-5,023**
51	**Other volume changes in nonfinancial assets**	**11,118**	**-10,544**	**-5,034**	**11,116**	**-10,545**	**-5,030**	**11,116**	**-10,545**	**-5,030**	**11,207**	**-10,620**	**-5,023**
511	Fixed assets	—	—	—	—	—	—	—	—	—	—	—	—
512	Inventories	7	3	15	4	2	18	4	2	18	97	-72	12
513	Valuables	—	—	—	—	—	—	—	—	—	—	—	—
514	Nonproduced assets	11,112	-10,547	-5,048	11,112	-10,547	-5,048	11,112	-10,547	-5,048	11,110	-10,548	-5,034
52	**Other volume changes in financial assets**	—	—	—	—	—	—	—	—	—	—	—	—

Colombia (233)

In Billions of Colombian Pesos (COP) / Fiscal Year Ends December 31st

		Budgetary Central Government			Central Government (excl. Social Security)			Central Government (incl. Social Security)			General Government		
		2013P	2014P	2015P	2013P	2014P	2015P	2013P	2014P	2015P	2013P	2014P	2015P
	By instrument												
5201	Monetary gold and SDRs	—	—	—	—	—	—	—	—	—	—	—	—
5202	Currency and deposits	—	—	—	—	—	—	—	—	—	—	—	—
5203	Debt securities	—	—	—	—	—	—	—	—	—	—	—	—
5204	Loans	—	—	—	—	—	—	—	—	—	—	—	—
5205	Equity and investment fund shares	—	—	—	—	—	—	—	—	—	—	—	—
5206	Insurance, pension, and standardized guarantee schemes	—	—	—	—	—	—	—	—	—	—	—	—
5207	Financial derivatives and employee stock options	—	—	—	—	—	—	—	—	—	—	—	—
5208	Other accounts receivable	—	—	—	—	—	—	—	—	—	—	—	—
	By debtor												
521	Domestic debtors	—	—	—	—	—	—	—	—	—	—	—	—
522	External debtors	—	—	—	—	—	—	—	—	—	—	—	—
53	**Other volume changes in liabilities**	**-1**	**-2**	**0**	**-1**	**-2**	**0**	**-1**	**-2**	**0**	**-1**	**-2**	**0**
	By instrument												
5301	Special Drawing Rights (SDRs)	—	—	—	—	—	—	—	—	—	—	—	—
5302	Currency and deposits	—	—	—	—	—	—	—	—	—	—	—	—
5303	Debt securities	-1	-1	0	-1	-1	0	-1	-1	0	-1	-1	0
5304	Loans	—	—	—	—	—	—	—	—	—	—	—	—
5305	Equity and investment fund shares	—	—	—	—	—	—	—	—	—	—	—	—
5306	Insurance, pension, and standardized guarantee schemes	—	—	—	—	—	—	—	—	—	—	—	—
5307	Financial derivatives and employee stock options	—	—	—	—	—	—	—	—	—	—	—	—
5308	Other accounts payable	—	-1	—	—	-1	—	—	-1	—	—	-1	—
	By creditor												
531	Domestic creditors	-1	-1	—	-1	-1	—	-1	-1	—	-1	-1	—
532	External creditors	—	-1	0	—	-1	0	—	-1	0	—	-1	0
	Table 6 Balance sheet												
6	**Net worth**	**-79,213**	**-130,782**	**-180,769**	**-33,759**	**-93,507**	**-130,092**	**-88,637**	**-238,851**	**-122,107**	**81,301**	**-11,527**	**48,931**
61	**Nonfinancial assets**	**139,573**	**142,409**	**146,675**	**173,141**	**170,330**	**183,748**	**173,503**	**126,292**	**184,808**	**270,821**	**224,019**	**263,206**
611	Fixed assets	63,274	72,931	80,548	89,321	92,314	104,531	89,577	93,325	105,332	171,689	129,046	163,271
6111	Buildings and structures	48,740	56,802	63,557	72,062	73,006	83,865	72,203	73,814	84,547	149,667	104,482	135,831
6112	Machinery and equipment	13,959	15,322	15,636	15,508	17,108	17,777	15,521	17,136	17,887	19,226	21,244	23,336
6113	Other fixed assets	574	807	1,356	1,751	2,200	2,890	1,853	2,375	2,898	2,796	3,320	4,104
6114	Weapons systems	—	—	—	—	—	—	—	—	—	—	—	—
612	Inventories	4,276	4,735	4,895	5,672	6,169	6,930	5,674	6,172	6,962	6,294	6,770	7,610
613	Valuables	294	315	320	389	412	421	389	412	423	631	663	1,330
614	Nonproduced assets	71,729	64,428	60,912	77,759	71,436	71,866	77,863	26,383	72,092	92,206	87,541	90,996
6141	Land	10,643	13,888	15,421	16,673	20,896	26,375	16,776	21,330	26,600	31,080	36,963	45,452
6142	Mineral and energy resources	61,086	50,539	45,491	61,086	50,539	45,491	61,086	5,054	45,491	61,126	50,578	45,543
6143	Other naturally occurring assets	—	—	—	—	—	—	—	—	—	-0	-0	-0
6144	Intangible nonproduced assets	—	—	—	—	—	—	—	—	—	—	—	—
62	**Financial assets**	**188,777**	**196,675**	**194,976**	**205,624**	**214,061**	**212,534**	**217,038**	**242,761**	**229,556**	**333,662**	**352,842**	**373,448**
	By instrument												
6201	Monetary gold and SDRs	—	—	—	—	—	—	—	—	—	—	—	—
6202	Currency and deposits	18,688	25,887	16,679	21,567	28,513	19,361	24,289	33,981	22,315	51,732	59,900	54,702
6203	Debt securities	14,303	11,941	14,651	19,993	18,230	18,964	20,038	18,283	19,972	25,101	24,080	25,450
6204	Loans	12,747	8,631	12,843	12,915	8,612	13,096	12,917	8,817	13,100	13,470	9,299	14,250
6205	Equity and investment fund shares	76,537	78,452	68,109	78,005	80,042	69,803	78,087	81,589	70,659	95,006	97,319	89,085
6206	Insurance, pension, and standardized guarantee schemes	—	—	—	—	—	—	—	—	—	—	—	—
6207	Financial derivatives and employee stock options	—	—	—	—	—	1	—	—	1	0	0	1
6208	Other accounts receivable	66,502	71,763	82,693	73,143	78,664	91,310	81,708	100,092	103,509	148,353	162,244	189,960
	By debtor												
621	Domestic debtors	183,098	189,717	182,910	199,848	206,980	200,273	211,263	236,187	217,294	327,878	345,752	361,184
622	External debtors	5,679	6,958	12,066	5,775	7,081	12,261	5,775	6,574	12,261	5,784	7,090	12,265
63	**Liabilities**	**407,563**	**469,866**	**522,420**	**412,524**	**477,898**	**526,374**	**479,177**	**607,904**	**536,471**	**523,182**	**588,388**	**587,724**

Colombia (233)

In Billions of Colombian Pesos (COP) / Fiscal Year Ends December 31st

		Budgetary Central Government			Central Government (excl. Social Security)			Central Government (incl. Social Security)			General Government		
		2013P	2014P	2015P	2013P	2014P	2015P	2013P	2014P	2015P	2013P	2014P	2015P
	By instrument												
6301	Special Drawing Rights (SDRs)	—	—	—	—	—	—	—	—	—	—	—	—
6302	Currency and deposits	—	—	—	—	—	—	—	—	—	—	—	—
6303	Debt securities	211,804	246,387	276,269	209,507	245,593	275,715	209,507	245,593	275,715	210,118	246,594	276,790
6304	Loans	35,892	40,637	60,161	36,062	40,873	61,311	36,064	38,492	62,149	43,756	49,714	74,492
6305	Equity and investment fund shares	—	—	—	—	—	—	—	—	—	—	—	—
6306	Insurance, pension, and standardized guarantee schemes	—	—	—	—	—	—	—	—	—	—	—	—
6307	Financial derivatives and employee stock options	363	-78	-490	365	-78	-497	365	-78	-497	365	-78	-497
6308	Other accounts payable	159,503	182,920	186,480	166,590	191,510	189,845	233,242	323,898	199,103	268,942	292,157	236,939
	By creditor												
631	Domestic creditors	337,214	377,651	389,661	342,150	385,628	392,677	408,802	515,491	402,773	450,893	493,661	451,204
632	External creditors	70,349	92,215	132,759	70,374	92,270	133,697	70,375	92,414	133,698	72,289	94,727	136,520
	Memorandum items												
6M2	Net financial worth	-218,786	-273,190	-327,444	-206,900	-263,837	-313,840	-262,139	-365,144	-306,915	-189,520	-235,546	-214,275
6M3	Gross debt (D4) at market value	...	...	...	...	...	...	...	...	...	...	...	...
6M3D3	D3 debt liabilities at market value	...	...	...	...	...	...	...	...	...	...	...	...
6M3D2	D2 debt liabilities at market value	...	...	...	...	...	...	...	...	...	...	...	...
6M3D1	D1 debt liabilities at market value	...	...	...	...	...	...	...	...	...	...	...	...
6M4	Gross debt (D4) at nominal value	407,199	469,943	522,911	412,159	477,975	526,871	478,812	607,982	536,967	522,817	588,465	588,221
6M4D3	D3 debt liabilities at nominal value	407,199	469,943	522,911	412,159	477,975	526,871	478,812	607,982	536,967	522,817	588,465	588,221
6M4D2	D2 debt liabilities at nominal value	247,696	287,024	336,430	245,569	286,466	337,025	245,570	284,084	337,864	253,874	296,308	351,281
6M4D1	D1 debt liabilities at nominal value	247,696	287,024	336,430	245,569	286,466	337,025	245,570	284,084	337,864	253,874	296,308	351,281
6M35	Gross debt (D4) at face value	...	...	...	...	...	...	...	...	...	...	...	...
6M35D3	D3 debt liabilities at face value	...	...	...	...	...	...	...	...	...	...	...	...
6M35D2	D2 debt liabilities at face value	...	...	...	...	...	...	...	...	...	...	...	...
6M35D1	D1 debt liabilities at face value	...	...	...	...	...	...	...	...	...	...	...	...
6M93	Government gross debt per national definition	...	...	...	...	...	...	...	...	...	...	...	...
6M5	Arrears	...	...	...	...	...	...	...	...	...	...	...	...
6M6	Explicit contingent liabilities	...	...	...	...	...	...	...	...	...	...	...	...
6M61	of which: Publicly guaranteed debt	...	...	...	...	...	...	...	...	...	...	...	...
6M7	Net implicit obligations for social security benefits	...	...	...	...	...	...	...	...	...	...	...	...
	Table 7 Expenditure by functions of government												
7	**Expenditure**	**192,322**	**207,599**	**181,310**	**213,126**	**213,755**	**189,750**	**249,225**	**247,785**	**230,977**	**242,706**	**271,698**	**270,997**
701	**General public services**	...	...	...	...	...	...	...	...	...	...	...	...
7017	Public debt transactions	17,479	19,301	20,674	17,493	19,314	20,787	17,493	19,321	20,802	18,095	19,924	21,526
7018	Transfers of general character between levels of government	...	...	...	...	...	...	...	...	...	...	...	...
702	**Defense**	...	...	...	...	...	...	...	...	...	...	...	...
703	**Public order and safety**	...	...	...	...	...	...	...	...	...	...	...	...
704	**Economic affairs**	...	...	...	...	...	...	...	...	...	...	...	...
7042	Agriculture, forestry, fishing, and hunting	...	...	...	...	...	...	...	...	...	...	...	...
7043	Fuel and energy	...	...	...	...	...	...	...	...	...	...	...	...
7044	Mining, manufacturing, and construction	...	...	...	...	...	...	...	...	...	...	...	...
7045	Transport	...	...	...	...	...	...	...	...	...	...	...	...
7046	Communication	...	...	...	...	...	...	...	...	...	...	...	...
705	**Environmental protection**	...	...	...	...	...	...	...	...	...	...	...	...
706	**Housing and community amenities**	...	...	...	...	...	...	...	...	...	...	...	...
707	**Health**	...	...	...	...	...	...	...	...	...	...	...	...
7072	Outpatient services	...	...	...	...	...	...	...	...	...	...	...	...
7073	Hospital services	...	...	...	...	...	...	...	...	...	...	...	...
7074	Public health services	...	...	...	...	...	...	...	...	...	...	...	...
708	**Recreation, culture and religion**	...	...	...	...	...	...	...	...	...	...	...	...
709	**Education**	...	...	...	...	...	...	...	...	...	...	...	...
7091	Pre-primary and primary education	...	...	...	...	...	...	...	...	...	...	...	...
7092	Secondary education	...	...	...	...	...	...	...	...	...	...	...	...
7094	Tertiary education	...	...	...	...	...	...	...	...	...	...	...	...

Colombia (233)

In Billions of Colombian Pesos (COP) / Fiscal Year Ends December 31st

		Budgetary Central Government			Central Government (excl. Social Security)			Central Government (incl. Social Security)			General Government		
		2013P	2014P	2015P	2013P	2014P	2015P	2013P	2014P	2015P	2013P	2014P	2015P
710	**Social protection**	...	...	...	...	...	...	...	...	...	...	...	...
7z	Statistical discrepancy: Expenditure	...	...	...	...	...	...	...	...	...	...	...	...
	Table 8 Financial transactions by counterpart sector												
32	**Net acquisition of financial assets**	**9,734**	**2,954**	**-12,376**	**9,732**	**637**	**-12,941**	**6,563**	**3,602**	**-10,299**	**24,447**	**15,502**	**-10,162**
321	Domestic debtors	7,360	1,988	-16,970	7,351	-354	-17,607	4,183	2,611	-14,966	22,064	14,512	-14,823
8211	General government	...	818	...	...	...	...	...	...	...	...	...	...
8212	Central bank	...	—	...	...	...	...	...	...	...	...	...	...
8213	Deposit-taking corporations except the central bank	...	7,202	...	...	...	...	...	...	...	...	...	...
8214	Other financial corporations	...	-2,686	...	...	...	...	...	...	...	...	...	...
8215	Nonfinancial corporations	...	-4,631	...	...	...	...	...	...	...	...	...	...
8216	Households & nonprofit institutions serving households	...	1,285	...	...	...	...	...	...	...	...	...	...
322	External debtors	2,374	965	4,594	2,380	992	4,666	2,380	992	4,666	2,383	990	4,660
8221	General government	...	790	...	...	790	...	...	...	...	...	...	...
8227	International organizations	...	—	...	...	—	...	...	...	...	...	...	...
8228	Financial corporations other than international organizations	...	215	...	...	241	...	...	...	...	...	...	...
8229	Other nonresidents	...	-39	...	...	-39	...	...	...	...	...	...	...
33	**Net incurrence of liabilities**	**42,632**	**62,303**	**52,555**	**42,118**	**62,382**	**47,951**	**41,037**	**61,996**	**-8,218**	**45,957**	**65,391**	**-2,707**
331	Domestic creditors	33,634	40,437	12,010	33,124	40,486	6,524	32,114	40,028	-49,574	36,864	42,952	-44,499
8311	General government	...	29,650	...	...	...	...	...	...	...	...	...	...
8312	Central bank	...	—	...	...	...	...	...	...	...	...	...	...
8313	Deposit-taking corporations except the central bank	...	-451	...	...	...	...	...	...	...	...	...	...
8314	Other financial corporations	...	2,250	...	...	...	...	...	...	...	...	...	...
8315	Nonfinancial corporations	...	5,039	...	...	...	...	...	...	...	...	...	...
8316	Households & nonprofit institutions serving households	...	3,947	...	...	...	...	...	...	...	...	...	...
332	External creditors	8,998	21,866	40,544	8,994	21,896	41,427	8,923	21,967	41,356	9,093	22,439	41,793
8321	General government	...	—	...	...	—	...	...	...	...	...	...	...
8327	International organizations	...	—	...	...	—	...	...	...	...	...	...	...
8328	Financial corporations other than international organizations	...	21,867	...	...	21,898	...	...	...	...	...	...	...
8329	Other nonresidents	...	—	...	...	0	...	...	...	...	...	...	...
	Table 9 Total other economic flows in assets and liabilities												
9	**Change in net worth due to other economic flows**	**7,088**	**-24,203**	**-36,418**	**9,000**	**-22,246**	**-31,271**	**8,913**	**-22,045**	**-30,743**	**10,386**	**-18,647**	**-30,483**
91	**Other economic flows in nonfinancial assets**	**13,274**	**-6,165**	**-1,003**	**14,893**	**-4,437**	**3,811**	**14,801**	**-4,153**	**3,899**	**17,337**	**-1,902**	**5,775**
911	Fixed assets	1,150	1,421	2,509	1,423	2,204	3,169	1,387	2,367	3,177	1,671	3,585	3,918
912	Inventories	7	3	15	4	2	18	4	2	18	97	-72	12
913	Valuables	—	—	—	—	—	—	—	—	—	—	—	—
914	Nonproduced assets	12,117	-7,589	-3,526	13,466	-6,643	623	13,410	-6,522	704	15,569	-5,414	1,846
92	**Other economic flows in financial assets**	**-727**	**-1,148**	**-3,535**	**-421**	**-904**	**-2,818**	**-415**	**-985**	**-2,378**	**-1,398**	**493**	**-3,423**
	By instrument												
9201	Monetary gold and SDRs	—	—	—	—	—	—	—	—	—	—	—	—
9202	Currency and deposits	45	84	505	52	110	570	55	114	570	57	150	575
9203	Debt securities	1,824	2,322	2,900	2,045	2,574	3,228	2,048	2,593	3,541	2,241	2,885	3,845
9204	Loans	—	—	—	—	—	—	—	—	—	—	—	—
9205	Equity and investment fund shares	-2,774	-4,939	-10,677	-2,725	-4,986	-10,675	-2,725	-5,090	-10,548	-3,929	-3,997	-11,972
9206	Insurance, pension, and standardized guarantee schemes	—	—	—	—	—	—	—	—	—	—	—	—
9207	Financial derivatives and employee stock options	171	253	379	200	267	639	200	267	640	200	267	640
9208	Other accounts receivable	7	1,132	3,358	7	1,132	3,419	7	1,132	3,419	32	1,189	3,489
	By debtor												
921	Domestic debtors	-643	-2,051	-6,883	-344	-1,832	-6,293	-341	-1,917	-5,853	-1,352	-532	-6,973
922	External debtors	-84	902	3,348	-77	928	3,475	-74	932	3,475	-47	1,025	3,550
93	**Other economic flows in liabilities**	**5,459**	**16,890**	**31,880**	**5,472**	**16,905**	**32,263**	**5,473**	**16,907**	**32,264**	**5,553**	**17,238**	**32,835**

Colombia (233)

In Billions of Colombian Pesos (COP) / Fiscal Year Ends December 31st

		Budgetary Central Government			Central Government (excl. Social Security)			Central Government (incl. Social Security)			General Government		
		2013P	2014P	2015P	2013P	2014P	2015P	2013P	2014P	2015P	2013P	2014P	2015P
	By instrument												
9301	Special Drawing Rights (SDRs)	—	—	—	—	—	—	—	—	—	—	—	—
9302	Currency and deposits	12	182	134	12	183	146	14	185	146	15	188	147
9303	Debt securities	-1	-1	0	-1	-1	3	-1	-1	3	-1	-1	3
9304	Loans	5,000	16,709	30,584	4,999	16,707	30,783	4,999	16,707	30,783	5,078	17,031	31,357
9305	Equity and investment fund shares	—	—	—	—	—	—	—	—	—	—	—	—
9306	Insurance, pension, and standardized guarantee schemes	—	—	—	—	—	—	—	—	—	—	—	—
9307	Financial derivatives and employee stock options	531	9	—	541	18	119	541	18	120	541	18	120
9308	Other accounts payable	-83	-9	1,162	-80	-3	1,212	-80	-3	1,212	-81	2	1,208
	By creditor												
931	Domestic creditors	1,299	1,784	4,378	1,314	1,802	4,968	1,315	1,805	4,968	1,317	1,819	4,971
932	External creditors	4,160	15,106	27,502	4,158	15,102	27,295	4,158	15,102	27,295	4,236	15,419	27,864
	Memorandum items												
9M2	Change in net financial worth due to other economic flows	-6,186	-18,038	-35,415	-5,893	-17,808	-35,082	-5,888	-17,892	-34,642	-6,951	-16,745	-36,258
9M3	Gross debt (D4) at market value: other economic flows	4,928	16,881	31,880	4,930	16,886	32,144	4,932	16,889	32,144	5,011	17,220	32,715
9M3D3	D3 debt liabilities at market value: other economic flows	4,928	16,881	31,880	4,930	16,886	32,144	4,932	16,889	32,144	5,011	17,220	32,715
9M3D2	D2 debt liabilities at market value: other economic flows	5,011	16,890	30,718	5,010	16,889	30,932	5,012	16,892	30,932	5,092	17,218	31,507
9M3D1	D1 debt liabilities at market value: other economic flows	4,999	16,708	30,585	4,998	16,706	30,786	4,998	16,706	30,786	5,077	17,030	31,360

Congo, Republic of (634)

In Billions of CFA (BEAC) Francs (XAF) / Fiscal Year Ends December 31st

		Budgetary Central Government			Central Government (excl. Social Security)			Central Government (incl. Social Security)			General Government		
		2010	2011	2012	2010	2011	2012	2010	2011	2012P	2010	2011	2012
	Statement of operations												
1	Revenue	3,610	2,887	2,979	3,644	2,954	2,997	3,789	3,021	3,074	3,808	3,040	3,095
2	Expense	700	751	1,053	711	802	1,028	796	861	1,086	794	855	1,085
GOB	**Gross operating balance**	**2,910**	**2,136**	**1,927**	**2,933**	**2,152**	**1,969**	**2,993**	**2,160**	**1,988**	**3,013**	**2,186**	**2,010**
NOB	**Net operating balance**	**2,910**	**2,136**	...	**2,933**	...	...	**2,993**	...	...	**3,013**	...	...
31	Net/Gross investment in nonfinancial assets	541	952	1,481	560	974	1,525	561	979	1,529	575	1,005	1,551
2M	Expenditure	1,241	1,703	2,533	1,270	1,777	2,553	1,357	1,840	2,615	1,369	1,859	2,636
NLB	**Net lending (+) / Net borrowing (-)**	**2,369**	**1,184**	**446**	**2,373**	**1,177**	**444**	**2,432**	**1,181**	**459**	**2,439**	**1,181**	**459**
32	Net acquisition of financial assets	293	1,178	973	...	1,200	992	...	1,202	999	...	...	...
33	Net incurrence of liabilities	-1,430	-6	513	...	-33	503	...	-35	495	...	...	495
NLBz	Statistical discrepancy	-646	0	14	...	56	45	...	56	45	...	...	...
	Memorandum items												
PB	Primary net lending / net borrowing	2,425	1,195	459	2,429	1,189	457	2,489	1,192	472	2,495	1,192	473
GB	Government balance per national definition	...	...	...	...	...	...	...	...	...	...	...	...
	Statement of other economic flows												
	Balance sheet												
	Table 1 Revenue												
1	**Revenue**	**3,610**	**2,887**	**2,979**	**3,644**	**2,954**	**2,997**	**3,789**	**3,021**	**3,074**	**3,808**	**3,040**	**3,095**
11	**Taxes**	**449**	**599**	**657**	**452**	**603**	**658**	**452**	**603**	**658**	**465**	**617**	**673**
111	Taxes on income, profits, and capital gains	175	219	250	175	219	250	175	219	250	175	219	250
1111	Payable by individuals	55	75	101	55	75	101	55	75	101	55	75	101
1112	Payable by corporations and other enterprises	120	144	148	120	144	148	120	144	148	120	144	148
1113	Other taxes on income, profits, and capital gains	—	—	—	—	—	—	—	—	—	—	—	—
112	Taxes on payroll and workforce	—	—	—	—	—	—	—	—	—	—	—	—
113	Taxes on property	2	3	3	2	3	3	2	3	3	5	6	6
114	Taxes on goods and services	198	280	293	200	283	294	200	283	294	210	294	305
1141	General taxes on goods and services	166	180	216	167	182	216	167	182	216	176	191	226
1142	Excises	21	15	16	21	15	16	21	15	16	21	15	16
115	Taxes on international trade and transactions	72	92	109	73	93	109	73	93	109	73	93	109
116	Other taxes	2	4	3	2	5	3	2	5	3	3	5	3
12	**Social contributions**	—	—	—	—	—	—	**104**	**52**	**59**	**104**	**52**	**59**
121	Social security contributions	—	—	—	—	—	—	104	52	59	104	52	59
122	Other social contributions	—	—	—	—	—	—	—	—	—	—	—	—
13	**Grants**	**1,359**	**29**	**14**	**1,359**	**29**	**14**	**1,359**	**29**	**14**	**1,359**	**29**	**14**
131	From foreign governments	1,359	29	8	1,359	29	8	1,359	29	8	1,359	29	8
132	From international organizations	—	—	6	—	1	6	0	1	6	0	1	6
133	From other general government units	—	—	—	—	-0	—	0	-0	—	0	-0	—
1331	Current	—	—	—	—	—	—	0	—	—	0	—	—
1332	Capital	—	—	—	—	-0	—	—	-0	—	—	-0	—
14	**Other revenue**	**1,802**	**2,260**	**2,308**	**1,833**	**2,322**	**2,325**	**1,874**	**2,337**	**2,343**	**1,879**	**2,342**	**2,349**
	Table 2 Expense by economic type												
2	**Expense**	**700**	**751**	**1,053**	**711**	**802**	**1,028**	**796**	**861**	**1,086**	**794**	**855**	**1,085**
21	**Compensation of employees**	**172**	**198**	**237**	**198**	**225**	**271**	**204**	**230**	**276**	**215**	**243**	**289**
211	Wages and salaries	158	166	218	182	191	250	187	195	254	198	206	267
212	Employers' social contributions	14	32	19	16	35	21	17	35	22	17	37	22
22	**Use of goods and services**	**284**	**310**	**421**	**306**	**332**	**446**	**313**	**346**	**459**	**326**	**359**	**474**
23	**Consumption of fixed capital**	—	—	...	—	**2**	...	—	...	...	—	...	...
24	**Interest**	**56**	**11**	**13**	**56**	**11**	**13**	**56**	**11**	**13**	**56**	**11**	**13**
25	**Subsidies**	**4**	**5**	**5**	**4**	**5**	**5**	**4**	**5**	**5**	**4**	**5**	**5**
26	**Grants**	**88**	**203**	**309**	**45**	**169**	**219**	**45**	**169**	**219**	**17**	**135**	**187**
261	To foreign governments	1	1	1	1	1	1	1	1	1	1	1	1
262	To international organizations	15	6	5	15	6	5	15	6	5	15	6	5
263	To other general government units	71	196	303	28	162	213	28	162	213	-0	128	181
2631	Current	52	196	238	11	164	196	11	164	196	0	149	184
2632	Capital	19	—	65	17	-2	17	17	-2	17	-0	-21	-3

Congo, Republic of (634)

In Billions of CFA (BEAC) Francs (XAF) / Fiscal Year Ends December 31st

		Budgetary Central Government			Central Government (excl. Social Security)			Central Government (incl. Social Security)			General Government		
		2010	2011	2012	2010	2011	2012	2010	2011	2012P	2010	2011	2012
27	**Social benefits**	**7**	**8**	**10**	**8**	**39**	**11**	**80**	**74**	**49**	**80**	**74**	**50**
271	Social security benefits	—	—	—	—	31	—	71	65	37	71	65	37
272	Social assistance benefits	—	—	—	0	0	0	0	0	0	0	0	0
273	Employment-related social benefits	7	8	10	8	9	11	8	9	11	9	9	12
28	**Other expense**	**89**	**17**	**58**	**93**	**19**	**61**	**93**	**21**	**62**	**94**	**23**	**65**
281	Property expense other than interest	—	—	—	—	—	—	—	—	—	—	—	—
282	Transfers not elsewhere classified	89	17	58	93	19	61	93	21	62	94	23	65
2821	Current	89	17	58	92	19	61	93	21	62	94	22	65
2822	Capital	—	—	—	1	0	—	1	0	—	1	0	—
	Table 3 Transactions in assets and liabilities												
3	**Change in net worth from transactions**	...	...	...	...	...	...	...	...	...	...	...	...
31	**Net/Gross investment in nonfinancial assets**	**541**	**952**	**1,481**	**560**	**974**	**1,525**	**561**	**979**	**1,529**	**575**	**1,005**	**1,551**
311	Fixed assets	526	936	1,478	544	957	1,522	545	962	1,526	559	987	1,547
3111	Buildings and structures	409	722	714	424	736	757	424	739	760	434	761	777
3112	Machinery and equipment	117	214	757	120	221	758	121	223	760	125	226	764
3113	Other fixed assets	0	—	6	0	0	6	0	0	6	0	0	6
3114	Weapons systems	—	...	...	—	...	...	—	...	...	—	...	...
312	Inventories	—	—	—	—	—	—	—	0	0	—	0	0
313	Valuables	—	—	—	—	—	—	—	—	—	—	—	—
314	Nonproduced assets	15	17	3	15	17	3	15	17	3	16	17	3
3141	Land	15	9	3	15	9	3	15	9	3	15	9	3
3142	Mineral and energy resources	—	—	—	—	—	—	—	—	—	—	—	—
3143	Other naturally occurring assets	—	—	—	—	—	—	—	—	—	—	—	—
3144	Intangible nonproduced assets	—	8	—	—	8	—	—	8	—	0	8	—
32	**Net acquisition of financial assets**	**293**	**1,178**	**973**	**...**	**1,200**	**992**	**...**	**1,202**	**999**	**...**	**...**	**...**
	By instrument												
3201	Monetary gold and SDRs	—	—	—	...	—	—	...	—	—	...	...	...
3202	Currency and deposits	293	984	883	...	1,002	902	...	1,002	909	...	...	...
3203	Debt securities	—	—	—	...	—	—	...	—	—	...	...	...
3204	Loans	—	175	—	...	178	2	...	178	2	...	...	...
3205	Equity and investment fund shares	0	4	89	...	4	89	...	4	89	...	...	...
3206	Insurance, pension, and standardized guarantee schemes	—	—	—	...	—	—	...	—	—	...	...	...
3207	Financial derivatives and employee stock options	—	—	—	...	—	—	...	—	—	...	...	...
3208	Other accounts receivable	—	15	1	...	16	0	...	17	-1	...	...	...
	By debtor												
321	Domestic debtors	293	412	91	...	435	110	...	436	117	...	...	...
322	External debtors	—	765	882	...	765	882	...	765	882	...	...	...
33	**Net incurrence of liabilities**	**-1,430**	**-6**	**513**	**...**	**-33**	**503**	**...**	**-35**	**495**	**...**	**...**	**495**
	By instrument												
3301	Special Drawing Rights (SDRs)	—	—	—	...	—	—	...	—	—	...	...	—
3302	Currency and deposits	—	—	—	...	—	—	...	0	-0	...	...	-0
3303	Debt securities	—	—	—	...	—	—	...	—	—	...	...	—
3304	Loans	-1,266	85	577	...	86	577	...	83	578	...	...	578
3305	Equity and investment fund shares	—	—	—	...	—	—	...	—	—	...	...	—
3306	Insurance, pension, and standardized guarantee schemes	—	—	—	...	-29	-8	...	-29	-8	...	...	-8
3307	Financial derivatives and employee stock options	—	—	—	...	—	—	...	—	—	...	...	—
3308	Other accounts payable	-164	-92	-64	...	-90	-67	...	...	-75	...	...	-76
	By creditor												
331	Domestic creditors	-164	-89	305	...	-116	295	...	-118	287	...	...	287
332	External creditors	-1,266	83	208	...	83	208	...	83	208	...	...	208
	Table 4 Holding gains and losses in assets and liabilities												
	Table 5 Holding gains and losses in assets and liabilities												
	Table 6 Balance sheet												

Congo, Republic of (634)

In Billions of CFA (BEAC) Francs (XAF) / Fiscal Year Ends December 31st

		Budgetary Central Government			Central Government (excl. Social Security)			Central Government (incl. Social Security)			General Government		
		2010	2011	2012	2010	2011	2012	2010	2011	2012P	2010	2011	2012
	Table 7 Expenditure by functions of government												
7	**Expenditure**	**1,185**	**1,717**	**2,522**	...	...	...	...	...	...	...	...	...
701	**General public services**	**304**	**429**	**668**	...	...	...	...	...	...	...	...	...
7017	Public debt transactions	56	11	13	...	...	...	...	...	...	...	...	...
7018	Transfers of general character between levels of government	...	...	...	...	...	...	...	...	...	...	...	...
702	**Defense**	**83**	**148**	**190**	...	...	...	...	...	...	...	...	...
703	**Public order and safety**	**51**	**66**	**86**	...	...	...	...	...	...	...	...	...
704	**Economic affairs**	**308**	**738**	**563**	...	...	...	...	...	...	...	...	...
7042	Agriculture, forestry, fishing, and hunting	28	53	55	...	...	...	...	...	...	...	...	...
7043	Fuel and energy	139	129	217	...	...	...	...	...	...	...	...	...
7044	Mining, manufacturing, and construction	3	403	84	...	...	...	...	...	...	...	...	...
7045	Transport	80	91	126	...	...	...	...	...	...	...	...	...
7046	Communication	13	40	45	...	...	...	...	...	...	...	...	...
705	**Environmental protection**	**2**	**3**	**1**	...	...	...	...	...	...	...	...	...
706	**Housing and community amenities**	**195**	**33**	**623**	...	...	...	...	...	...	...	...	...
707	**Health**	**74**	**102**	**142**	...	...	...	...	...	...	...	...	...
7072	Outpatient services	...	...	...	...	...	...	...	...	...	...	...	...
7073	Hospital services	...	...	...	...	...	...	...	...	...	...	...	...
7074	Public health services	...	...	...	...	...	...	...	...	...	...	...	...
708	**Recreation, culture and religion**	**32**	**35**	**45**	...	...	...	...	...	...	...	...	...
709	**Education**	**125**	**150**	**191**	...	...	...	...	...	...	...	...	...
7091	Pre-primary and primary education	49	57	74	...	...	...	...	...	...	...	...	...
7092	Secondary education	50	55	76	...	...	...	...	...	...	...	...	...
7094	Tertiary education	26	38	41	...	...	...	...	...	...	...	...	...
710	**Social protection**	**11**	**14**	**13**	...	...	...	...	...	...	...	...	...
7z	Statistical discrepancy: Expenditure	—	...	...	...	...	...	...	...	...	...	...	...
	Table 8 Financial transactions by counterpart sector												
	Table 9 Total other economic flows in assets and liabilities												

Costa Rica (238)

In Billions of Costa Rican Colones (CRC) / Fiscal Year Ends December 31st

		Budgetary Central Government			Central Government (excl. Social Security)			Central Government (incl. Social Security)			General Government		
		2013	2014	2015	2013	2014	2015	2013	2014	2015	2013	2014	2015
	Statement of operations												
1	Revenue	3,536	3,799	4,181	4,067	4,352	4,778	6,012	6,470	7,323	6,269	6,763	7,413
2	Expense	4,810	5,281	6,176	5,036	5,431	6,353	6,752	7,486	8,616	6,956	7,513	8,641
GOB	**Gross operating balance**	**-1,255**	**-1,441**	**-1,787**	**-969**	**-1,079**	**-1,575**	**-741**	**-1,017**	**-1,293**	**-686**	**-751**	**-1,228**
NOB	**Net operating balance**	**-1,274**	**-1,482**	**-1,995**	...	...	...	...	...	...	...	...	...
31	Net/Gross investment in nonfinancial assets	62	323	-119	321	633	...	367	571	...	415	633	...
2M	Expenditure	4,872	5,605	6,056	5,357	6,064	...	7,119	8,058	...	7,371	8,147	...
NLB	**Net lending (+) / Net borrowing (-)**	**-1,336**	**-1,805**	**-1,876**	**-1,290**	**-1,712**	...	**-1,107**	**-1,588**	...	**-1,101**	**-1,384**	...
32	Net acquisition of financial assets	-317	-153	-20	...	...	...	...	...	...	...	...	...
33	Net incurrence of liabilities	1,212	1,600	1,652	...	...	...	...	...	...	...	...	...
NLBz	Statistical discrepancy	-192	52	203	...	...	...	...	...	...	...	...	...
	Memorandum items												
PB	Primary net lending / net borrowing	-705	-1,109	-1,076	-657	-1,014	...	-472	-888	...	-463	-680	...
GB	Government balance per national definition	...	...	...	...	...	...	...	...	...	...	...	...
	Statement of other economic flows												
	Balance sheet												
6	**Net worth**	**2,773**	**5,853**	**13,210**	...	...	...	...	...	...	...	...	...
61	Nonfinancial assets	13,336	13,659	16,472	...	...	...	...	...	...	...	...	...
62	Financial assets	347	4,703	10,900	...	...	...	...	...	...	...	...	...
63	Liabilities	10,995	12,510	14,162	...	...	...	...	...	...	...	...	...
	Table 1 Revenue												
1	**Revenue**	**3,536**	**3,799**	**4,181**	**4,067**	**4,352**	**4,778**	**6,012**	**6,470**	**7,323**	**6,269**	**6,763**	**7,413**
11	**Taxes**	**3,292**	**3,522**	**3,862**	**3,416**	**3,653**	**3,999**	**3,416**	**3,653**	**3,999**	**3,583**	**3,843**	**4,210**
111	Taxes on income, profits, and capital gains	939	1,007	1,133	939	1,011	1,136	939	1,011	1,136	939	1,011	1,136
1111	Payable by individuals	317	349	386	317	349	386	317	349	386	317	349	386
1112	Payable by corporations and other enterprises	622	658	747	622	662	750	622	662	750	622	662	750
1113	Other taxes on income, profits, and capital gains	—	—	—	—	—	—	—	—	—	—	—	—
112	Taxes on payroll and workforce	—	—	—	—	—	—	—	—	—	—	—	—
113	Taxes on property	154	174	183	154	174	184	154	174	184	221	252	270
114	Taxes on goods and services	1,918	2,031	2,195	1,963	2,079	2,246	1,963	2,079	2,246	2,054	2,189	2,369
1141	General taxes on goods and services	1,228	1,324	1,395	1,228	1,324	1,395	1,228	1,324	1,395	1,228	1,324	1,395
1142	Excises	690	706	798	690	706	798	690	706	798	690	706	798
115	Taxes on international trade and transactions	281	311	351	305	337	378	305	337	378	307	340	381
116	Other taxes	0	0	0	55	51	55	55	51	55	61	51	55
12	**Social contributions**	**56**	**60**	**63**	**409**	**449**	**487**	**2,137**	**2,332**	**2,528**	**2,137**	**2,332**	**2,528**
121	Social security contributions	56	60	63	409	449	63	2,137	2,332	2,104	2,137	2,332	2,104
122	Other social contributions	—	—	—	—	—	424	—	—	424	—	—	424
13	**Grants**	**166**	**189**	**204**	**5**	**9**	**3**	**5**	**9**	**245**	**1**	**5**	**3**
131	From foreign governments	—	—	2	—	—	2	—	—	2	—	—	2
132	From international organizations	0	4	0	1	5	0	1	5	0	1	5	1
133	From other general government units	165	185	201	4	5	0	4	5	243	-0	0	0
1331	Current	165	184	200	4	5	0	4	5	243	-0	0	0
1332	Capital	—	1	1	0	0	0	0	0	0	0	0	-0
14	**Other revenue**	**22**	**28**	**52**	**236**	**241**	**289**	**453**	**475**	**551**	**548**	**582**	**672**
	Table 2 Expense by economic type												
2	**Expense**	**4,810**	**5,281**	**6,176**	**5,036**	**5,431**	**6,353**	**6,752**	**7,486**	**8,616**	**6,956**	**7,513**	**8,641**
21	**Compensation of employees**	**1,817**	**1,969**	**2,113**	**2,306**	**2,498**	**2,689**	**3,209**	**3,461**	**3,740**	**3,335**	**3,600**	**3,894**
211	Wages and salaries	1,523	1,650	1,757	1,945	2,108	2,254	2,809	3,025	3,233	2,921	3,148	3,369
212	Employers' social contributions	294	319	356	361	390	435	400	436	507	415	452	525
22	**Use of goods and services**	**141**	**180**	**194**	**336**	**394**	**426**	**682**	**758**	**821**	**763**	**850**	**921**
23	**Consumption of fixed capital**	**20**	**41**	**208**	...	...	...	...	...	...	...	...	...
24	**Interest**	**631**	**696**	**800**	**634**	**699**	**807**	**635**	**700**	**808**	**638**	**703**	**812**
25	**Subsidies**	—	—	—	—	—	—	—	—	—	0	0	—

Costa Rica (238)

In Billions of Costa Rican Colones (CRC) / Fiscal Year Ends December 31st

		Budgetary Central Government			Central Government (excl. Social Security)			Central Government (incl. Social Security)			General Government		
		2013	2014	2015	2013	2014	2015	2013	2014	2015	2013	2014	2015
26	**Grants**	**1,193**	**1,411**	**1,479**	**244**	**252**	**276**	**40**	**48**	**276**	**14**	**12**	**7**
261	To foreign governments	—	—	—	—	—	—	—	—	—	—	—	—
262	To international organizations	6	6	6	14	12	7	14	12	7	14	12	7
263	To other general government units	1,188	1,405	1,473	230	240	269	26	36	269	-0	0	-0
2631	Current	978	1,088	1,186	188	204	233	-14	0	233	-0	0	-0
2632	Capital	210	317	287	42	36	36	41	36	36	-0	0	-0
27	**Social benefits**	**615**	**667**	**745**	**822**	**887**	**980**	**1,453**	**1,579**	**1,752**	**1,453**	**1,579**	**1,752**
271	Social security benefits	607	653	699	607	653	699	1,154	1,264	1,378	1,154	1,264	1,378
272	Social assistance benefits	0	0	1	207	220	236	207	220	236	207	220	236
273	Employment-related social benefits	8	14	45	8	14	45	92	95	138	92	95	138
28	**Other expense**	**392**	**318**	**636**	**676**	**660**	**967**	**714**	**695**	**1,009**	**733**	**728**	**1,046**
281	Property expense other than interest	—	—	—	—	—	—	—	—	—	—	—	—
282	Transfers not elsewhere classified	392	318	636	676	660	967	714	695	1,009	733	728	1,046
2821	Current	283	257	500	560	586	817	597	621	860	612	650	891
2822	Capital	109	61	136	117	74	150	117	74	150	121	79	155
	Table 3 Transactions in assets and liabilities												
3	**Change in net worth from transactions**	**-1,467**	**-1,430**	**-1,791**	...	...	...	...	...	...	...	...	...
31	**Net/Gross investment in nonfinancial assets**	**62**	**323**	**-119**	**321**	**633**	...	**367**	**571**	...	**415**	**633**	...
311	Fixed assets	58	419	-499	297	713	...	342	655	...	389	715	...
3111	Buildings and structures	35	407	-495	38	410	...	38	410	...	39	471	...
3112	Machinery and equipment	23	12	-5	70	68	...	90	10	...	99	23	...
3113	Other fixed assets	0	-1	1	189	235	...	214	235	...	251	282	...
3114	Weapons systems	—	—	—	—	—	...	—	—	...	—	—	...
312	Inventories	—	-0	0	—	-0	...	—	-3	...	—	-3	...
313	Valuables	0	—	—	0	—	...	0	—	...	0	—	...
314	Nonproduced assets	3	-96	380	24	-80	...	25	-80	...	26	-78	...
3141	Land	1	-97	377	21	-81	...	22	-81	...	24	-79	...
3142	Mineral and energy resources	—	—	—	—	—	...	—	—	...	—	—	...
3143	Other naturally occurring assets	—	—	—	—	—	...	—	—	...	—	—	...
3144	Intangible nonproduced assets	3	1	2	3	1	...	3	1	...	3	1	...
32	**Net acquisition of financial assets**	**-317**	**-153**	**-20**	...	...	...	...	...	...	...	...	...
	By instrument												
3201	Monetary gold and SDRs	—	—	—	...	...	...	...	...	...	...	...	...
3202	Currency and deposits	-377	-153	35	...	...	...	...	...	...	...	...	...
3203	Debt securities	—	—	—	...	...	...	...	...	...	...	...	...
3204	Loans	1	—	—	...	...	...	...	...	...	...	...	...
3205	Equity and investment fund shares	—	—	-69	...	...	...	...	...	...	...	...	...
3206	Insurance, pension, and standardized guarantee schemes	—	—	—	...	...	...	...	...	...	...	...	...
3207	Financial derivatives and employee stock options	—	—	—	...	...	...	...	...	...	...	...	...
3208	Other accounts receivable	59	0	14	...	...	...	...	...	...	...	...	...
	By debtor												
321	Domestic debtors	-317	-153	-20	...	...	...	...	...	...	...	...	...
322	External debtors	—	—	—	...	...	...	...	...	...	...	...	...
33	**Net incurrence of liabilities**	**1,212**	**1,600**	**1,652**	...	...	...	...	...	...	...	...	...
	By instrument												
3301	Special Drawing Rights (SDRs)	—	—	—	...	...	...	...	...	...	...	...	...
3302	Currency and deposits	—	—	—	...	...	...	...	...	...	...	...	...
3303	Debt securities	773	1,567	1,463	...	...	...	...	...	...	...	...	...
3304	Loans	142	-21	60	...	...	...	...	...	...	...	...	...
3305	Equity and investment fund shares	—	—	—	...	...	...	...	...	...	...	...	...
3306	Insurance, pension, and standardized guarantee schemes	—	—	—	...	...	...	...	...	...	...	...	...
3307	Financial derivatives and employee stock options	—	—	—	...	...	...	...	...	...	...	...	...
3308	Other accounts payable	297	54	129	...	...	...	...	...	...	...	...	...

Costa Rica (238)

In Billions of Costa Rican Colones (CRC) / Fiscal Year Ends December 31st

		Budgetary Central Government			Central Government (excl. Social Security)			Central Government (incl. Social Security)			General Government		
		2013	2014	2015	2013	2014	2015	2013	2014	2015	2013	2014	2015
	By creditor												
331	Domestic creditors	832	956	1,056	...	...	...	...	...	...	...	...	...
332	External creditors	379	644	596	...	...	...	...	...	...	...	...	...
	Table 4 Holding gains and losses in assets and liabilities												
	Table 5 Holding gains and losses in assets and liabilities												
	Table 6 Balance sheet												
6	**Net worth**	**2,773**	**5,853**	**13,210**	...	...	...	...	...	...	...	...	...
61	**Nonfinancial assets**	**13,336**	**13,659**	**16,472**	...	...	...	...	...	...	...	...	...
611	Fixed assets	354	775	3,208	...	...	...	...	...	...	...	...	...
6111	Buildings and structures	205	612	3,050	...	...	...	...	...	...	...	...	...
6112	Machinery and equipment	149	162	156	...	...	...	...	...	...	...	...	...
6113	Other fixed assets	0	1	2	...	...	...	...	...	...	...	...	...
6114	Weapons systems	—	—	—	...	...	...	...	...	...	...	...	...
612	Inventories	2	2	2	...	...	...	...	...	...	...	...	...
613	Valuables	1	...	—	...	...	...	...	...	...	...	...	...
614	Nonproduced assets	12,979	12,883	13,263	...	...	...	...	...	...	...	...	...
6141	Land	12,964	12,867	13,245	...	...	...	...	...	...	...	...	...
6142	Mineral and energy resources	—	...	—	...	...	...	...	...	...	...	...	...
6143	Other naturally occurring assets	—	...	—	...	...	...	...	...	...	...	...	...
6144	Intangible nonproduced assets	15	16	18	...	...	...	...	...	...	...	...	...
62	**Financial assets**	**347**	**4,703**	**10,900**	...	...	...	...	...	...	...	...	...
	By instrument												
6201	Monetary gold and SDRs	—	—	—	...	...	...	...	...	...	...	...	...
6202	Currency and deposits	242	89	124	...	...	...	...	...	...	...	...	...
6203	Debt securities	—	—	—	...	...	...	...	...	...	...	...	...
6204	Loans	—	—	—	...	...	...	...	...	...	...	...	...
6205	Equity and investment fund shares	—	4,424	10,572	...	...	...	...	...	...	...	...	...
6206	Insurance, pension, and standardized guarantee schemes	—	—	—	...	...	...	...	...	...	...	...	...
6207	Financial derivatives and employee stock options	—	—	—	...	...	...	...	...	...	...	...	...
6208	Other accounts receivable	105	190	204	...	...	...	...	...	...	...	...	...
	By debtor												
621	Domestic debtors	347	4,703	10,900	...	...	...	...	...	...	...	...	...
622	External debtors	—	—	—	...	...	...	...	...	...	...	...	...
63	**Liabilities**	**10,995**	**12,510**	**14,162**	...	...	...	...	...	...	...	...	...
	By instrument												
6301	Special Drawing Rights (SDRs)	—	—	—	...	...	...	...	...	...	...	...	...
6302	Currency and deposits	—	—	—	...	...	...	...	...	...	...	...	...
6303	Debt securities	8,160	9,727	11,190	...	...	...	...	...	...	...	...	...
6304	Loans	636	615	675	...	...	...	...	...	...	...	...	...
6305	Equity and investment fund shares	—	—	—	...	...	...	...	...	...	...	...	...
6306	Insurance, pension, and standardized guarantee schemes	—	—	—	...	...	...	...	...	...	...	...	...
6307	Financial derivatives and employee stock options	—	—	—	...	...	...	...	...	...	...	...	...
6308	Other accounts payable	2,114	2,168	2,296	...	...	...	...	...	...	...	...	...
	By creditor												
631	Domestic creditors	9,145	10,101	11,157	...	...	...	...	...	...	...	...	...
632	External creditors	1,765	2,409	3,005	...	...	...	...	...	...	...	...	...
	Memorandum items												
6M2	Net financial worth	-10,648	-7,806	-3,262	...	...	...	...	...	...	...	...	...
6M3	Gross debt (D4) at market value	...	...	...	...	...	...	...	...	...	...	...	...
6M3D3	D3 debt liabilities at market value	...	...	...	...	...	...	...	...	...	...	...	...
6M3D2	D2 debt liabilities at market value	...	...	...	...	...	...	...	...	...	...	...	...
6M3D1	D1 debt liabilities at market value	...	...	...	...	...	...	...	...	...	...	...	...
6M4	Gross debt (D4) at nominal value	10,910	12,510	14,162	...	...	...	...	...	...	...	...	...
6M4D3	D3 debt liabilities at nominal value	10,910	12,510	14,162	...	...	...	...	...	...	...	...	...
6M4D2	D2 debt liabilities at nominal value	8,796	10,342	11,866	...	...	...	...	...	...	...	...	...
6M4D1	D1 debt liabilities at nominal value	8,796	10,342	11,866	...	...	...	...	...	...	...	...	...

Costa Rica (238)

In Billions of Costa Rican Colones (CRC) / Fiscal Year Ends December 31st

		Budgetary Central Government			Central Government (excl. Social Security)			Central Government (incl. Social Security)			General Government		
		2013	2014	2015	2013	2014	2015	2013	2014	2015	2013	2014	2015
6M35	Gross debt (D4) at face value	...	...	...	...	...	...	...	...	...	...	...	...
6M35D3	D3 debt liabilities at face value	...	...	...	...	...	...	...	...	...	...	...	...
6M35D2	D2 debt liabilities at face value	...	...	...	...	...	...	...	...	...	...	...	...
6M35D1	D1 debt liabilities at face value	...	...	...	...	...	...	...	...	...	...	...	...
6M93	Government gross debt per national definition	...	...	...	...	...	...	...	...	...	...	...	...
6M5	Arrears	...	...	...	...	...	...	...	...	...	...	...	...
6M6	Explicit contingent liabilities	...	...	...	...	...	...	...	...	...	...	...	...
6M61	of which: Publicly guaranteed debt	...	...	...	...	...	...	...	...	...	...	...	...
6M7	Net implicit obligations for social security benefits	...	...	...	...	...	...	...	...	...	...	...	...
	Table 7 Expenditure by functions of government												
7	**Expenditure**	**4,872**	**5,604**	**6,056**	**5,357**	**6,086**	**6,535**	**7,119**	**8,080**	**8,829**	**7,371**	**...**	**9,144**
701	**General public services**	**876**	**1,236**	**1,262**	**894**	**1,262**	**1,292**	**894**	**1,263**	**1,294**	**...**	**...**	**1,298**
7017	Public debt transactions	631	696	800	634	699	807	635	700	808	...	...	812
7018	Transfers of general character between levels of government	...	-14	30	256	31	30	256	31	30	...	...	30
702	**Defense**	—	—	—	—	—	—	—	—	—	...	...	—
703	**Public order and safety**	**616**	**671**	**745**	**638**	**705**	**762**	**638**	**705**	**762**	**...**	**...**	**756**
704	**Economic affairs**	**711**	**781**	**827**	**550**	**597**	**624**	**550**	**597**	**624**	**...**	**...**	**589**
7042	Agriculture, forestry, fishing, and hunting	396	55	61	213	116	127	213	116	127	...	...	125
7043	Fuel and energy	—	—	—	0	0	0	0	0	0	...	...	0
7044	Mining, manufacturing, and construction	—	—	—	0	0	—	0	0	—	...	...	—
7045	Transport	314	373	377	321	381	387	321	381	387	...	...	357
7046	Communication	—	—	—	16	17	19	15	17	19	...	...	19
705	**Environmental protection**	**42**	**44**	**47**	**31**	**39**	**40**	**31**	**39**	**40**	**...**	**...**	**40**
706	**Housing and community amenities**	**14**	**10**	**9**	**20**	**16**	**15**	**20**	**16**	**15**	**...**	**...**	**385**
707	**Health**	**220**	**245**	**276**	**222**	**257**	**290**	**1,627**	**1,623**	**1,885**	**...**	**...**	**1,872**
7072	Outpatient services	...	—	—	—	—	—	—	—	—	...	...	—
7073	Hospital services	...	—	—	—	—	—	—	—	—	...	...	—
7074	Public health services	...	245	276	222	253	286	1,627	1,620	286	...	...	285
708	**Recreation, culture and religion**	**35**	**40**	**41**	**54**	**57**	**58**	**54**	**57**	**58**	**...**	**...**	**55**
709	**Education**	**1,703**	**1,870**	**2,074**	**1,803**	**1,967**	**2,166**	**1,803**	**1,967**	**2,166**	**...**	**...**	**2,166**
7091	Pre-primary and primary education	...	...	—	—	...	—	—	...	—	...	...	—
7092	Secondary education	...	...	—	6	...	—	6	...	—	...	...	—
7094	Tertiary education	...	...	—	1,798	...	497	1,798	...	497	...	...	497
710	**Social protection**	**655**	**705**	**776**	**1,149**	**1,187**	**1,287**	**1,501**	**1,812**	**1,984**	**...**	**...**	**1,983**
7z	Statistical discrepancy: Expenditure	—	...	...	-0	...	...	-0	...	...	-0	...	...
	Table 8 Financial transactions by counterpart sector												
32	**Net acquisition of financial assets**	**-317**	**-153**	**-20**	**...**	**...**	**...**	**...**	**...**	**...**	**...**	**...**	**...**
321	Domestic debtors	-317	-153	-20	...	...	...	...	...	...	...	...	...
8211	General government	...	...	...	...	...	...	...	...	...	...	...	...
8212	Central bank	...	...	...	...	...	...	...	...	...	...	...	...
8213	Deposit-taking corporations except the central bank	...	...	...	...	...	...	...	...	...	...	...	...
8214	Other financial corporations	...	...	...	...	...	...	...	...	...	...	...	...
8215	Nonfinancial corporations	...	...	...	...	...	...	...	...	...	...	...	...
8216	Households & nonprofit institutions serving households	...	...	...	...	...	...	...	...	...	...	...	...
322	External debtors	—	—	—	...	...	...	...	...	...	...	...	...
8221	General government	—	—	—	...	...	...	...	...	...	...	...	...
8227	International organizations	—	—	—	...	...	...	...	...	...	...	...	...
8228	Financial corporations other than international organizations	—	—	—	...	...	...	...	...	...	...	...	...
8229	Other nonresidents	—	—	—	...	...	...	...	...	...	...	...	...

Costa Rica (238)

In Billions of Costa Rican Colones (CRC) / Fiscal Year Ends December 31st

		Budgetary Central Government			Central Government (excl. Social Security)			Central Government (incl. Social Security)			General Government		
		2013	2014	2015	2013	2014	2015	2013	2014	2015	2013	2014	2015
33	**Net incurrence of liabilities**	**1,212**	**1,600**	**1,652**	**...**	**...**	**...**	**...**	**...**	**...**	**...**	**...**	**...**
331	Domestic creditors	832	956	1,056	...	...	...	...	...	...	...	...	...
3311	General government	...	...	...	...	...	...	...	...	...	...	...	...
3312	Central bank	...	...	...	...	...	...	...	...	...	...	...	...
3313	Deposit-taking corporations except the central bank	...	...	...	...	...	...	...	...	...	...	...	...
3314	Other financial corporations	...	...	...	...	...	...	...	...	...	...	...	...
3315	Nonfinancial corporations	...	...	...	...	...	...	...	...	...	...	...	...
3316	Households & nonprofit institutions serving households	...	...	...	...	...	...	...	...	...	...	...	...
332	External creditors	379	644	596	...	...	...	...	...	...	...	...	...
3321	General government	...	...	...	...	...	...	...	...	...	...	...	...
3327	International organizations	...	...	...	...	...	...	...	...	...	...	...	...
3328	Financial corporations other than international organizations	...	...	...	...	...	...	...	...	...	...	...	...
3329	Other nonresidents	...	...	...	...	...	...	...	...	...	...	...	...
	Table 9 Total other economic flows in assets and liabilities												

Côte d'Ivoire (662)

In Billions of CFA (BCEAO) Francs (XOF) / Fiscal Year Ends December 31st

		Budgetary Central Government			Central Government (excl. Social Security)			Central Government (incl. Social Security)			General Government		
		2012	2013	2014	2012	2013	2014	2012	2013	2014	2012	2013	2014
	Statement of operations												
1	Revenue	2,326	2,675	2,881	...	...	...	...	...	...	...	...	...
2	Expense	2,098	2,097	2,223	...	...	...	...	...	...	...	...	...
GOB	**Gross operating balance**	**228**	**578**	**659**	...	...	...	...	...	...	...	...	...
NOB	**Net operating balance**	...	...	...	...	...	...	...	...	...	...	...	...
31	Net/Gross investment in nonfinancial assets	612	927	984	...	...	...	...	...	...	...	...	...
2M	Expenditure	2,711	3,024	3,206	...	...	...	...	...	...	...	...	...
NLB	**Net lending (+) / Net borrowing (-)**	**-385**	**-349**	**-325**	...	...	...	...	...	...	...	...	...
32	Net acquisition of financial assets	-48	195	160	...	...	...	...	...	...	...	...	...
33	Net incurrence of liabilities	245	550	686	...	...	...	...	...	...	...	...	...
NLBz	Statistical discrepancy	92	-6	-201	...	...	...	...	...	...	...	...	...
	Memorandum items												
PB	Primary net lending / net borrowing	-152	-135	-187	...	...	...	...	...	...	...	...	...
GB	Government balance per national definition	...	...	...	...	...	...	...	...	...	...	...	...
	Statement of other economic flows												
	Balance sheet												
	Table 1 Revenue												
1	**Revenue**	**2,326**	**2,675**	**2,881**	...	...	...	...	...	...	...	...	...
11	**Taxes**	**1,968**	**2,246**	**2,440**	...	...	...	...	...	...	...	...	...
111	Taxes on income, profits, and capital gains	498	611	636	...	...	...	...	...	...	...	...	...
1111	Payable by individuals	214	258	340	...	...	...	...	...	...	...	...	...
1112	Payable by corporations and other enterprises	228	284	227	...	...	...	...	...	...	...	...	...
1113	Other taxes on income, profits, and capital gains	56	69	69	...	...	...	...	...	...	...	...	...
112	Taxes on payroll and workforce	—	—	—	...	...	...	...	...	...	...	...	...
113	Taxes on property	9	12	13	...	...	...	...	...	...	...	...	...
114	Taxes on goods and services	550	557	605	...	...	...	...	...	...	...	...	...
1141	General taxes on goods and services	204	248	258	...	...	...	...	...	...	...	...	...
1142	Excises	74	27	38	...	...	...	...	...	...	...	...	...
115	Taxes on international trade and transactions	911	1,066	1,186	...	...	...	...	...	...	...	...	...
116	Other taxes	—	—	—	...	...	...	...	...	...	...	...	...
12	**Social contributions**	—	—	—	...	...	...	...	...	...	...	...	...
121	Social security contributions	—	—	—	...	...	...	...	...	...	...	...	...
122	Other social contributions	—	—	—	...	...	...	...	...	...	...	...	...
13	**Grants**	**81**	**201**	**314**	...	...	...	...	...	...	...	...	...
131	From foreign governments	...	...	...	...	...	...	...	...	...	...	...	...
132	From international organizations	...	...	...	...	...	...	...	...	...	...	...	...
133	From other general government units	...	...	...	...	...	...	...	...	...	...	...	...
1331	Current	...	...	...	...	...	...	...	...	...	...	...	...
1332	Capital	...	...	...	...	...	...	...	...	...	...	...	...
14	**Other revenue**	**276**	**227**	**127**	...	...	...	...	...	...	...	...	...
	Table 2 Expense by economic type												
2	**Expense**	**2,098**	**2,097**	**2,223**	...	...	...	...	...	...	...	...	...
21	**Compensation of employees**	**935**	**1,039**	**1,183**	...	...	...	...	...	...	...	...	...
211	Wages and salaries	...	...	...	...	...	...	...	...	...	...	...	...
212	Employers' social contributions	...	...	...	...	...	...	...	...	...	...	...	...
22	**Use of goods and services**	**389**	**377**	**475**	...	...	...	...	...	...	...	...	...
23	**Consumption of fixed capital**	...	...	...	...	...	...	...	...	...	...	...	...
24	**Interest**	**233**	**215**	**139**	...	...	...	...	...	...	...	...	...
25	**Subsidies**	**232**	**164**	**128**	...	...	...	...	...	...	...	...	...
26	**Grants**	**84**	**84**	**94**	...	...	...	...	...	...	...	...	...
261	To foreign governments	—	—	—	...	...	...	...	...	...	...	...	...
262	To international organizations	—	—	—	...	...	...	...	...	...	...	...	...
263	To other general government units	84	84	94	...	...	...	...	...	...	...	...	...
2631	Current	84	84	94	...	...	...	...	...	...	...	...	...
2632	Capital	—	—	—	...	...	...	...	...	...	...	...	...

Côte d'Ivoire (662)

In Billions of CFA (BCEAO) Francs (XOF) / Fiscal Year Ends December 31st

		Budgetary Central Government			Central Government (excl. Social Security)			Central Government (incl. Social Security)			General Government		
		2012	2013	2014	2012	2013	2014	2012	2013	2014	2012	2013	2014
27	**Social benefits**	**—**	**—**	**—**	**...**	**...**	**...**	**...**	**...**	**...**	**...**	**...**	**...**
271	Social security benefits	—	—	—	...	...	...	...	...	...	...	...	...
272	Social assistance benefits	—	—	—	...	...	...	...	...	...	...	...	...
273	Employment-related social benefits	—	—	—	...	...	...	...	...	...	...	...	...
28	**Other expense**	**226**	**219**	**204**	**...**	**...**	**...**	**...**	**...**	**...**	**...**	**...**	**...**
281	Property expense other than interest	—	—	—	...	...	...	...	...	...	...	...	...
282	Transfers not elsewhere classified	226	219	204	...	...	...	...	...	...	...	...	...
2821	Current	186	217	203	...	...	...	...	...	...	...	...	...
2822	Capital	40	2	1	...	...	...	...	...	...	...	...	...
	Table 3 Transactions in assets and liabilities												
3	**Change in net worth from transactions**	**...**	**...**	**...**	**...**	**...**	**...**	**...**	**...**	**...**	**...**	**...**	**...**
31	**Net/Gross investment in nonfinancial assets**	**612**	**927**	**984**	**...**	**...**	**...**	**...**	**...**	**...**	**...**	**...**	**...**
311	Fixed assets	612	927	984	...	...	...	...	...	...	...	...	...
3111	Buildings and structures	...	...	...	...	...	...	...	...	...	...	...	...
3112	Machinery and equipment	...	...	...	...	...	...	...	...	...	...	...	...
3113	Other fixed assets	...	...	...	...	...	...	...	...	...	...	...	...
3114	Weapons systems	...	...	...	...	...	...	...	...	...	...	...	...
312	Inventories	—	—	—	...	...	...	...	...	...	...	...	...
313	Valuables	—	—	—	...	...	...	...	...	...	...	...	...
314	Nonproduced assets	—	—	—	...	...	...	...	...	...	...	...	...
3141	Land	—	—	—	...	...	...	...	...	...	...	...	...
3142	Mineral and energy resources	—	—	—	...	...	...	...	...	...	...	...	...
3143	Other naturally occurring assets	—	—	—	...	...	...	...	...	...	...	...	...
3144	Intangible nonproduced assets	—	—	—	...	...	...	...	...	...	...	...	...
32	**Net acquisition of financial assets**	**-48**	**195**	**160**	**...**	**...**	**...**	**...**	**...**	**...**	**...**	**...**	**...**
	By instrument												
3201	Monetary gold and SDRs	—	—	—	...	...	...	...	...	...	...	...	...
3202	Currency and deposits	-36	213	209	...	...	...	...	...	...	...	...	...
3203	Debt securities	—	—	—	...	...	...	...	...	...	...	...	...
3204	Loans	2	-0	-2	...	...	...	...	...	...	...	...	...
3205	Equity and investment fund shares	-15	-18	-47	...	...	...	...	...	...	...	...	...
3206	Insurance, pension, and standardized guarantee schemes	—	—	—	...	...	...	...	...	...	...	...	...
3207	Financial derivatives and employee stock options	—	—	—	...	...	...	...	...	...	...	...	...
3208	Other accounts receivable	—	—	—	...	...	...	...	...	...	...	...	...
	By debtor												
321	Domestic debtors	-48	195	160	...	...	...	...	...	...	...	...	...
322	External debtors	—	—	—	...	...	...	...	...	...	...	...	...
33	**Net incurrence of liabilities**	**245**	**550**	**686**	**...**	**...**	**...**	**...**	**...**	**...**	**...**	**...**	**...**
	By instrument												
3301	Special Drawing Rights (SDRs)	—	—	—	...	...	...	...	...	...	...	...	...
3302	Currency and deposits	—	—	—	...	...	...	...	...	...	...	...	...
3303	Debt securities	237	343	858	...	...	...	...	...	...	...	...	...
3304	Loans	-75	184	8	...	...	...	...	...	...	...	...	...
3305	Equity and investment fund shares	—	—	—	...	...	...	...	...	...	...	...	...
3306	Insurance, pension, and standardized guarantee schemes	—	—	—	...	...	...	...	...	...	...	...	...
3307	Financial derivatives and employee stock options	—	—	—	...	...	...	...	...	...	...	...	...
3308	Other accounts payable	82	23	-180	...	...	...	...	...	...	...	...	...
	By creditor												
331	Domestic creditors	222	276	157	...	...	...	...	...	...	...	...	...
332	External creditors	22	274	529	...	...	...	...	...	...	...	...	...
	Table 4 Holding gains and losses in assets and liabilities												
	Table 5 Holding gains and losses in assets and liabilities												
	Table 6 Balance sheet												

Côte d'Ivoire (662)

In Billions of CFA (BCEAO) Francs (XOF) / Fiscal Year Ends December 31st

	Budgetary Central Government			Central Government (excl. Social Security)			Central Government (incl. Social Security)			General Government		
	2012	2013	2014	2012	2013	2014	2012	2013	2014	2012	2013	2014
Table 7 Expenditure by functions of government												
Table 8 Financial transactions by counterpart sector												
Table 9 Total other economic flows in assets and liabilities												

Croatia (960)

In Millions of Croatian Kunas (HRK) / Fiscal Year Ends December 31st

		Budgetary Central Government			Central Government (excl. Social Security)			Central Government (incl. Social Security)			General Government		
		2012	2013	2014	2012	2013	2014	2012	2013	2014	2012	2013	2014
	Statement of operations												
1	Revenue	109,559	108,585	114,044	...	...	118,067	112,883	112,051	118,067	126,132	125,879	131,917
2	Expense	118,730	123,506	125,689	...	...	127,920	120,930	126,410	127,920	132,413	138,217	139,532
GOB	**Gross operating balance**	**-9,171**	**-14,921**	**-11,645**	...	...	**-9,854**	**-8,047**	**-14,359**	**-9,854**	**-6,282**	**-12,338**	**-7,615**
NOB	**Net operating balance**	...	...	...	...	...	...	...	...	...	...	...	...
31	Net/Gross investment in nonfinancial assets	830	1,305	1,167	...	...	3,215	3,133	3,654	3,215	4,574	5,264	4,855
2M	Expenditure	119,560	124,811	126,857	...	...	131,136	124,064	130,064	131,136	136,987	143,481	144,387
NLB	**Net lending (+) / Net borrowing (-)**	**-10,001**	**-16,226**	**-12,812**	...	...	**-13,069**	**-11,180**	**-18,013**	**-13,069**	**-10,855**	**-17,602**	**-12,470**
32	Net acquisition of financial assets	-462	14,214	-3,466	...	...	-2,725	-166	14,146	-2,725	58	14,306	-2,325
33	Net incurrence of liabilities	9,539	30,440	9,346	...	...	10,344	11,014	32,159	10,344	10,914	31,908	10,145
NLBz	Statistical discrepancy	—	0	—	...	...	—	—	-0	—	—	-1	—
	Memorandum items												
PB	Primary net lending / net borrowing	-1,665	-6,966	-2,901	...	...	-2,643	-2,466	-8,327	-2,643	-2,007	-7,804	-1,922
GB	Government balance per national definition	...	...	...	...	...	...	...	...	...	...	...	...
	Statement of other economic flows												
	Balance sheet												
	Table 1 Revenue												
1	**Revenue**	**109,559**	**108,585**	**114,044**	...	...	**118,067**	**112,883**	**112,051**	**118,067**	**126,132**	**125,879**	**131,917**
11	**Taxes**	**64,694**	**63,045**	**63,350**	...	...	**63,350**	**64,694**	**63,045**	**63,350**	**74,118**	**74,492**	**74,888**
111	Taxes on income, profits, and capital gains	8,967	7,738	7,060	...	...	7,060	8,967	7,738	7,060	17,574	16,691	16,138
1111	Payable by individuals	1,270	1,373	1,402	...	...	1,402	1,270	1,373	1,402	9,876	10,326	10,480
1112	Payable by corporations and other enterprises	7,697	6,365	5,658	...	...	5,658	7,697	6,365	5,658	7,697	6,365	5,658
1113	Other taxes on income, profits, and capital gains	—	—	—	...	...	—	—	—	—	—	—	—
112	Taxes on payroll and workforce	—	—	—	...	...	—	—	—	—	—	—	—
113	Taxes on property	—	—	—	...	...	—	—	—	—	54	1,473	1,529
114	Taxes on goods and services	53,603	53,812	55,578	...	...	55,578	53,603	53,812	55,578	54,356	54,822	56,501
1141	General taxes on goods and services	41,177	40,851	41,463	...	...	41,463	41,177	40,851	41,463	41,583	41,347	41,878
1142	Excises	11,206	11,683	12,846	...	...	12,846	11,206	11,683	12,846	11,206	11,683	12,846
115	Taxes on international trade and transactions	1,754	1,159	425	...	...	425	1,754	1,159	425	1,754	1,159	425
116	Other taxes	370	336	288	...	...	288	370	336	288	380	345	296
12	**Social contributions**	**37,846**	**37,149**	**41,702**	...	...	**41,702**	**37,846**	**37,149**	**41,702**	**37,846**	**37,149**	**41,702**
121	Social security contributions	37,846	37,149	41,702	...	...	41,702	37,846	37,149	41,702	37,846	37,149	41,702
122	Other social contributions	—	—	—	...	...	—	—	—	—	—	—	—
13	**Grants**	**968**	**1,738**	**2,268**	...	...	**2,296**	**984**	**1,746**	**2,296**	**995**	**1,773**	**2,342**
131	From foreign governments	20	6	83	...	...	83	20	6	83	20	9	83
132	From international organizations	948	1,730	2,167	...	...	2,171	949	1,733	2,171	973	1,764	2,258
133	From other general government units	0	1	18	...	...	42	15	7	42	2	0	0
1331	Current	—	1	4	...	...	1	2	1	1	0	—	—
1332	Capital	0	0	14	...	...	41	13	5	41	2	0	0
14	**Other revenue**	**6,051**	**6,653**	**6,725**	...	...	**10,720**	**9,360**	**10,111**	**10,720**	**13,173**	**12,465**	**12,985**
	Table 2 Expense by economic type												
2	**Expense**	**118,730**	**123,506**	**125,689**	...	...	**127,920**	**120,930**	**126,410**	**127,920**	**132,413**	**138,217**	**139,532**
21	**Compensation of employees**	**31,383**	**30,462**	**30,032**	...	...	**30,311**	**31,664**	**30,764**	**30,311**	**35,381**	**34,443**	**34,130**
211	Wages and salaries	26,910	26,286	25,633	...	...	25,874	27,154	26,553	25,874	30,365	29,744	29,161
212	Employers' social contributions	4,473	4,176	4,399	...	...	4,437	4,510	4,212	4,437	5,016	4,699	4,969
22	**Use of goods and services**	**7,406**	**7,537**	**7,186**	...	...	**9,545**	**9,767**	**10,079**	**9,545**	**14,996**	**15,461**	**15,100**
23	**Consumption of fixed capital**	...	...	...	...	...	...	...	...	...	...	...	...
24	**Interest**	**8,336**	**9,259**	**9,911**	...	...	**10,426**	**8,714**	**9,685**	**10,426**	**8,849**	**9,798**	**10,548**
25	**Subsidies**	**5,762**	**5,538**	**5,174**	...	...	**5,185**	**5,763**	**5,551**	**5,185**	**6,801**	**6,730**	**6,244**
26	**Grants**	**4,844**	**6,512**	**8,535**	...	...	**6,993**	**3,306**	**5,164**	**6,993**	**1,832**	**3,523**	**5,169**
261	To foreign governments	26	9	14	...	...	14	26	9	14	26	16	17
262	To international organizations	247	2,057	3,658	...	...	3,658	247	2,057	3,658	252	2,063	3,684
263	To other general government units	4,571	4,446	4,863	...	...	3,320	3,033	3,098	3,320	1,554	1,444	1,468
2631	Current	2,441	2,362	2,445	...	...	2,413	2,435	2,365	2,413	1,131	900	935
2632	Capital	2,130	2,084	2,418	...	...	907	598	733	907	422	545	533

Croatia (960)

In Millions of Croatian Kunas (HRK) / Fiscal Year Ends December 31st

		Budgetary Central Government			Central Government (excl. Social Security)			Central Government (incl. Social Security)			General Government		
		2012	2013	2014	2012	2013	2014	2012	2013	2014	2012	2013	2014
27	**Social benefits**	**56,170**	**58,943**	**59,393**	**...**	**...**	**59,393**	**56,170**	**58,943**	**59,393**	**56,881**	**59,859**	**60,365**
271	Social security benefits	42,798	45,412	45,732	...	...	45,732	42,798	45,412	45,732	42,798	45,412	45,732
272	Social assistance benefits	13,241	13,393	13,489	...	...	13,489	13,241	13,393	13,489	13,931	14,289	14,425
273	Employment-related social benefits	131	139	173	...	...	173	131	139	173	152	159	209
28	**Other expense**	**4,829**	**5,255**	**5,457**	**...**	**...**	**6,068**	**5,546**	**6,224**	**6,068**	**7,674**	**8,403**	**7,976**
281	Property expense other than interest	0	0	0	...	...	0	0	0	0	0	0	0
282	Transfers not elsewhere classified	4,829	5,254	5,457	...	...	6,067	5,546	6,223	6,067	7,674	8,403	7,975
2821	Current	2,068	2,316	2,761	...	...	2,939	2,173	2,866	2,939	3,596	4,298	4,383
2822	Capital	2,760	2,938	2,697	...	...	3,129	3,374	3,358	3,129	4,078	4,105	3,593
	Table 3 Transactions in assets and liabilities												
3	**Change in net worth from transactions**	**...**	**...**	**-11,645**	**...**	**...**	**...**	**...**	**...**	**...**	**...**	**...**	**...**
31	**Net/Gross investment in nonfinancial assets**	**830**	**1,305**	**1,167**	**...**	**...**	**3,215**	**3,133**	**3,654**	**3,215**	**4,574**	**5,264**	**4,855**
311	Fixed assets	772	1,037	1,069	...	...	2,994	2,949	3,224	2,994	4,377	5,016	4,607
3111	Buildings and structures	266	381	332	...	...	2,195	2,421	2,546	2,195	3,562	3,976	3,444
3112	Machinery and equipment	434	610	685	...	...	738	449	625	738	683	938	1,054
3113	Other fixed assets	73	45	52	...	...	61	79	53	61	132	101	110
3114	Weapons systems	—	—	—	...	...	...	—	—	—	—	—	—
312	Inventories	29	225	-0	...	...	-0	29	225	-0	29	225	-0
313	Valuables	3	1	1	...	...	1	3	1	1	4	2	1
314	Nonproduced assets	25	41	97	...	...	221	151	203	221	164	21	247
3141	Land	-17	-16	-28	...	...	92	107	143	92	80	-77	79
3142	Mineral and energy resources	—	—	—	...	...	—	—	—	—	—	—	—
3143	Other naturally occurring assets	—	—	—	...	...	—	—	—	—	0	1	0
3144	Intangible nonproduced assets	42	57	125	...	...	129	44	60	129	84	97	168
32	**Net acquisition of financial assets**	**-462**	**14,214**	**-3,466**	**...**	**...**	**-2,725**	**-166**	**14,146**	**-2,725**	**58**	**14,306**	**-2,325**
	By instrument												
3201	Monetary gold and SDRs	—	—	—	...	...	—	—	—	—	—	—	—
3202	Currency and deposits	-1,209	4,826	-4,881	...	...	-3,918	-674	4,599	-3,918	-488	4,704	-3,548
3203	Debt securities	—	—	—	...	...	-150	—	150	-150	0	150	-150
3204	Loans	92	8,559	1,588	...	...	1,252	-58	8,430	1,252	-74	8,450	1,218
3205	Equity and investment fund shares	655	830	-379	...	...	-115	566	967	-115	620	1,002	-51
3206	Insurance, pension, and standardized guarantee schemes	—	—	206	...	...	206	—	—	206	—	—	206
3207	Financial derivatives and employee stock options	—	—	—	...	...	—	—	—	—	—	—	—
3208	Other accounts receivable	—	...	...	...	...	...	—	...	...	—	...	...
	By debtor												
321	Domestic debtors	-468	14,009	-3,672	...	...	-2,931	-172	13,941	-2,931	52	14,100	-2,531
322	External debtors	7	205	206	...	...	206	7	205	206	7	205	206
33	**Net incurrence of liabilities**	**9,539**	**30,440**	**9,346**	**...**	**...**	**10,344**	**11,014**	**32,159**	**10,344**	**10,914**	**31,908**	**10,145**
	By instrument												
3301	Special Drawing Rights (SDRs)	—	—	—	...	...	...	—	—	—	—	—	—
3302	Currency and deposits	—	—	—	...	...	—	—	—	—	—	—	—
3303	Debt securities	14,584	26,141	14,196	...	...	14,196	14,584	26,141	14,196	14,532	26,083	14,116
3304	Loans	-5,045	4,299	-4,850	...	...	-3,853	-3,570	6,018	-3,853	-3,618	5,826	-3,971
3305	Equity and investment fund shares	—	—	—	...	...	—	—	—	—	—	—	—
3306	Insurance, pension, and standardized guarantee schemes	—	—	—	...	...	—	—	—	—	—	—	—
3307	Financial derivatives and employee stock options	—	—	—	...	...	—	—	—	—	—	—	—
3308	Other accounts payable	—	...	...	...	...	...	—	...	...	—	...	...
	By creditor												
331	Domestic creditors	1,414	8,905	4,822	...	...	5,868	2,958	10,586	5,868	2,864	10,341	5,672
332	External creditors	8,125	21,535	4,524	...	...	4,476	8,056	21,573	4,476	8,050	21,568	4,473
	Table 4 Holding gains and losses in assets and liabilities												
	Table 5 Holding gains and losses in assets and liabilities												
	Table 6 Balance sheet												

Croatia (960)

In Millions of Croatian Kunas (HRK) / Fiscal Year Ends December 31st

		Budgetary Central Government			Central Government (excl. Social Security)			Central Government (incl. Social Security)			General Government		
		2012	2013	2014	2012	2013	2014	2012	2013	2014	2012	2013	2014
	Table 7 Expenditure by functions of government												
7	**Expenditure**	**119,838**	**125,070**	**127,546**	**...**	**...**	**...**	**...**	**125,070**	**127,546**	**...**	**141,029**	**143,316**
701	**General public services**	**14,767**	**17,495**	**19,676**	**...**	**...**	**...**	**...**	**17,495**	**19,676**	**...**	**19,926**	**21,989**
7017	Public debt transactions	8,393	9,424	10,086	...	...	...	...	9,424	10,086	...	9,490	10,151
7018	Transfers of general character between levels of government	1,689	1,581	1,669	...	...	...	...	1,581	1,669	...	1,595	1,680
702	**Defense**	**4,793**	**4,413**	**4,164**	**...**	**...**	**...**	**...**	**4,413**	**4,164**	**...**	**4,413**	**4,164**
703	**Public order and safety**	**7,530**	**7,164**	**7,117**	**...**	**...**	**...**	**...**	**7,164**	**7,117**	**...**	**7,558**	**7,495**
704	**Economic affairs**	**12,013**	**12,281**	**12,248**	**...**	**...**	**...**	**...**	**12,281**	**12,248**	**...**	**14,942**	**14,474**
7042	Agriculture, forestry, fishing, and hunting	3,808	3,524	3,713	...	...	...	...	3,524	3,713	...	3,742	3,906
7043	Fuel and energy	1	426	539	...	...	...	...	426	539	...	443	563
7044	Mining, manufacturing, and construction	791	955	852	...	...	...	...	955	852	...	1,018	905
7045	Transport	5,616	5,438	5,350	...	...	...	...	5,438	5,350	...	7,422	6,897
7046	Communication	13	11	98	...	...	...	...	11	98	...	12	99
705	**Environmental protection**	**462**	**462**	**402**	**...**	**...**	**...**	**...**	**462**	**402**	**...**	**1,053**	**742**
706	**Housing and community amenities**	**1,107**	**1,050**	**1,366**	**...**	**...**	**...**	**...**	**1,050**	**1,366**	**...**	**3,333**	**4,485**
707	**Health**	**19,697**	**21,484**	**21,610**	**...**	**...**	**...**	**...**	**21,484**	**21,610**	**...**	**22,184**	**22,285**
7072	Outpatient services	6,083	8,180	15,377	...	...	...	...	8,180	15,377	...	8,348	15,509
7073	Hospital services	8,435	6,889	303	...	...	...	...	6,889	303	...	6,927	332
7074	Public health services	53	53	41	...	...	...	...	53	41	...	179	165
708	**Recreation, culture and religion**	**1,592**	**1,712**	**1,757**	**...**	**...**	**...**	**...**	**1,712**	**1,757**	**...**	**3,725**	**3,690**
709	**Education**	**10,521**	**10,612**	**10,791**	**...**	**...**	**...**	**...**	**10,612**	**10,791**	**...**	**14,383**	**14,562**
7091	Pre-primary and primary education	4,700	4,597	4,639	...	...	...	...	4,597	4,639	...	7,173	7,175
7092	Secondary education	2,554	2,696	2,853	...	...	...	...	2,696	2,853	...	3,361	3,503
7094	Tertiary education	2,637	2,670	2,697	...	...	...	...	2,670	2,697	...	2,708	2,735
710	**Social protection**	**47,356**	**48,398**	**48,415**	**...**	**...**	**...**	**...**	**48,398**	**48,415**	**...**	**49,512**	**49,429**
7z	Statistical discrepancy: Expenditure	—	—	—	...	...	...	...	...	...	...	...	...
	Table 8 Financial transactions by counterpart sector												
	Table 9 Total other economic flows in assets and liabilities												

Cyprus (423)

In Millions of Euros (EUR) / Fiscal Year Ends December 31st

		Budgetary Central Government			Central Government (excl. Social Security)			Central Government (incl. Social Security)			General Government		
		2013	2014	2015	2013P	2014P	2015P	2013P	2014P	2015P	2013P	2014P	2015P
	Statement of operations												
1	Revenue	...	...	...	5,040	5,306	5,200	6,411	6,754	6,691	6,596	6,924	6,883
2	Expense	...	...	...	5,989	6,783	5,352	7,443	8,271	6,831	7,566	8,411	6,999
GOB	**Gross operating balance**	...	...	...	**-709**	**-1,249**	**80**	**-792**	**-1,289**	**93**	**-706**	**-1,235**	**141**
NOB	**Net operating balance**	...	...	...	**-949**	**-1,477**	**-152**	**-1,032**	**-1,517**	**-140**	**-971**	**-1,486**	**-116**
31	Net/Gross investment in nonfinancial assets	...	...	...	-117	32	60	-117	32	60	-80	57	81
2M	Expenditure	...	...	...	5,872	6,814	5,412	7,326	8,303	6,891	7,486	8,467	7,080
NLB	**Net lending (+) / Net borrowing (-)**	...	...	...	**-832**	**-1,508**	**-212**	**-915**	**-1,549**	**-200**	**-891**	**-1,543**	**-196**
32	Net acquisition of financial assets	...	...	...	2,313	-1,092	-227	...	...	...	2,229	-1,085	-238
33	Net incurrence of liabilities	...	...	...	3,154	413	-36	...	...	...	3,127	454	-57
NLBz	Statistical discrepancy	...	...	...	-9	4	21	...	...	...	-7	4	15
	Memorandum items												
PB	Primary net lending / net borrowing	...	...	...	-194	-974	298	-357	-1,056	289	-328	-1,046	299
GB	Government balance per national definition	...	...	...	...	...	...	...	...	...	...	...	...
	Statement of other economic flows												
	Balance sheet												
6	**Net worth**	...	...	...	...	...	...	...	...	...	...	...	...
61	Nonfinancial assets	...	...	...	...	...	...	...	...	...	...	...	...
62	Financial assets	...	...	...	7,290	7,276	7,080	...	...	...	7,610	7,603	7,396
63	Liabilities	...	...	...	26,065	26,678	26,925	...	...	...	18,455	19,110	19,336
	Table 1 Revenue												
1	**Revenue**	...	...	...	**5,040**	**5,306**	**5,200**	**6,411**	**6,754**	**6,691**	**6,596**	**6,924**	**6,883**
11	**Taxes**	...	...	...	**4,226**	**4,282**	**4,233**	**4,226**	**4,282**	**4,233**	**4,328**	**4,368**	**4,321**
111	Taxes on income, profits, and capital gains	...	...	...	1,691	1,599	1,548	1,691	1,599	1,548	1,691	1,599	1,548
1111	Payable by individuals	...	...	...	505	469	485	505	469	485	505	469	485
1112	Payable by corporations and other enterprises	...	...	...	1,171	1,112	1,046	1,171	1,112	1,046	1,171	1,112	1,046
1113	Other taxes on income, profits, and capital gains	...	...	...	14	17	17	14	17	17	14	17	17
112	Taxes on payroll and workforce	...	...	...	137	133	134	137	133	134	160	153	155
113	Taxes on property	...	...	...	150	158	167	150	158	167	206	204	213
114	Taxes on goods and services	...	...	...	2,215	2,363	2,350	2,215	2,363	2,350	2,238	2,383	2,371
1141	General taxes on goods and services	...	...	...	1,406	1,515	1,520	1,406	1,515	1,520	1,406	1,515	1,520
1142	Excises	...	...	...	600	629	613	600	629	613	600	629	613
115	Taxes on international trade and transactions	...	...	...	2	0	4	2	0	4	2	0	4
116	Other taxes	...	...	...	31	29	30	31	29	30	31	29	30
12	**Social contributions**	...	...	...	—	—	—	**1,362**	**1,445**	**1,483**	**1,362**	**1,445**	**1,483**
121	Social security contributions	...	...	...	—	—	—	1,362	1,445	1,483	1,362	1,445	1,483
122	Other social contributions	...	...	...	—	—	—	—	—	—	—	—	—
13	**Grants**	...	...	...	...	...	...	...	...	...	...	...	...
131	From foreign governments	...	...	...	...	...	...	...	...	...	...	...	...
132	From international organizations	...	...	...	...	...	...	...	...	...	...	...	...
133	From other general government units	...	...	...	—	—	—	—	—	—	—	—	—
1331	Current	...	...	...	—	—	—	—	—	—	—	—	—
1332	Capital	...	...	...	—	—	—	—	—	—	—	—	—
14	**Other revenue**	...	...	...	...	...	...	...	...	...	...	...	...
	Table 2 Expense by economic type												
2	**Expense**	...	...	...	**5,989**	**6,783**	**5,352**	**7,443**	**8,271**	**6,831**	**7,566**	**8,411**	**6,999**
21	**Compensation of employees**	...	...	...	**2,441**	**2,163**	**2,105**	**2,441**	**2,163**	**2,105**	**2,573**	**2,299**	**2,225**
211	Wages and salaries	...	...	...	...	...	...	...	...	...	...	...	...
212	Employers' social contributions	...	...	...	...	...	...	...	...	...	...	...	...
22	**Use of goods and services**	...	...	...	**652**	**561**	**569**	**666**	**574**	**581**	**744**	**655**	**692**
23	**Consumption of fixed capital**	...	...	...	**241**	**228**	**232**	**241**	**228**	**232**	**265**	**252**	**257**
24	**Interest**	...	...	...	**638**	**534**	**511**	**558**	**493**	**489**	**563**	**497**	**495**
25	**Subsidies**	...	...	...	**95**	**80**	**72**	**95**	**80**	**72**	**95**	**80**	**72**

Cyprus (423)

In Millions of Euros (EUR) / Fiscal Year Ends December 31st

		Budgetary Central Government			Central Government (excl. Social Security)			Central Government (incl. Social Security)			General Government		
		2013	2014	2015	2013P	2014P	2015P	2013P	2014P	2015P	2013P	2014P	2015P
26	**Grants**	...	...	...	...	...	...	...	...	...	...	...	...
261	To foreign governments	...	...	...	...	...	...	...	...	...	...	...	...
262	To international organizations	...	...	...	...	...	...	...	...	...	...	...	...
263	To other general government units	...	...	...	152	147	127	118	110	98	—	—	—
2631	Current	...	...	...	152	146	127	118	109	98	—	—	—
2632	Capital	...	...	...	—	1	—	—	1	—	—	—	—
27	**Social benefits**	...	...	...	**949**	**931**	**969**	**2,484**	**2,469**	**2,468**	**2,484**	**2,469**	**2,468**
271	Social security benefits	...	...	...	...	...	...	...	...	...	...	...	...
272	Social assistance benefits	...	...	...	...	...	...	...	...	...	...	...	...
273	Employment-related social benefits	...	...	...	...	...	...	...	...	...	...	...	...
28	**Other expense**	...	...	...	...	...	...	...	...	...	...	...	...
281	Property expense other than interest	...	...	...	—	—	—	—	—	—	—	—	—
282	Transfers not elsewhere classified	...	...	...	...	...	...	...	...	...	...	...	...
2821	Current	...	...	...	...	...	...	...	...	...	...	...	...
2822	Capital	...	...	...	...	...	...	...	...	...	...	...	...
	Table 3 Transactions in assets and liabilities												
3	**Change in net worth from transactions**	...	...	...	**-958**	**-1,473**	**-131**	...	...	...	**-978**	**-1,482**	**-101**
31	**Net/Gross investment in nonfinancial assets**	...	...	...	**-117**	**32**	**60**	**-117**	**32**	**60**	**-80**	**57**	**81**
311	Fixed assets	...	...	...	58	32	60	58	32	60	95	57	81
3111	Buildings and structures	...	...	...	...	...	...	...	...	...	...	...	...
3112	Machinery and equipment	...	...	...	...	...	...	...	...	...	...	...	...
3113	Other fixed assets	...	...	...	...	...	...	...	...	...	...	...	...
3114	Weapons systems	...	...	...	...	...	...	...	...	...	...	...	...
312	Inventories	...	...	...	...	...	...	...	...	...	...	...	...
313	Valuables	...	...	...	...	...	...	...	...	...	...	...	...
314	Nonproduced assets	...	...	...	-175	—	—	-175	—	—	-175	—	—
3141	Land	...	...	...	...	—	—	...	—	—	...	—	—
3142	Mineral and energy resources	...	...	...	...	—	—	...	—	—	...	—	—
3143	Other naturally occurring assets	...	...	...	...	—	—	...	—	—	...	—	—
3144	Intangible nonproduced assets	...	...	...	...	—	—	...	—	—	...	—	—
32	**Net acquisition of financial assets**	...	...	...	**2,313**	**-1,092**	**-227**	...	...	...	**2,229**	**-1,085**	**-238**
	By instrument												
3201	Monetary gold and SDRs	...	...	...	—	—	—	...	...	...	—	—	—
3202	Currency and deposits	...	...	...	726	321	-256	...	...	...	652	408	-316
3203	Debt securities	...	...	...	1,500	-1,500	—	...	...	...	1,500	-1,500	—
3204	Loans	...	...	...	1	10	-40	...	...	...	1	-70	10
3205	Equity and investment fund shares	...	...	...	68	35	6	...	...	...	68	35	6
3206	Insurance, pension, and standardized guarantee schemes	...	...	...	—	—	—	...	...	...	—	—	—
3207	Financial derivatives and employee stock options	...	...	...	—	—	—	...	...	...	—	—	—
3208	Other accounts receivable	...	...	...	18	42	64	...	...	...	8	43	63
	By debtor												
321	Domestic debtors	...	...	...	...	...	...	...	...	...	...	...	...
322	External debtors	...	...	...	...	...	...	...	...	...	...	...	...
33	**Net incurrence of liabilities**	...	...	...	**3,154**	**413**	**-36**	...	...	...	**3,127**	**454**	**-57**
	By instrument												
3301	Special Drawing Rights (SDRs)	...	...	...	—	—	—	...	...	...	—	—	—
3302	Currency and deposits	...	...	...	-6	-131	214	...	...	...	—	—	—
3303	Debt securities	...	...	...	-1,533	-812	-996	...	...	...	-1,533	-812	-839
3304	Loans	...	...	...	4,731	1,264	858	...	...	...	4,699	1,175	894
3305	Equity and investment fund shares	...	...	...	—	—	—	...	...	...	—	—	—
3306	Insurance, pension, and standardized guarantee schemes	...	...	...	—	—	—	...	...	...	-2	-1	—
3307	Financial derivatives and employee stock options	...	...	...	—	—	—	...	...	...	—	—	—
3308	Other accounts payable	...	...	...	-38	93	-112	...	...	...	-38	93	-112

Cyprus (423)

In Millions of Euros (EUR) / Fiscal Year Ends December 31st

		Budgetary Central Government			Central Government (excl. Social Security)			Central Government (incl. Social Security)			General Government		
		2013	2014	2015	2013P	2014P	2015P	2013P	2014P	2015P	2013P	2014P	2015P
	By creditor												
331	Domestic creditors	...	...	...	...	...	...	...	...	...	...	...	...
332	External creditors	...	...	...	...	...	...	...	...	...	...	...	...
	Table 4 Holding gains and losses in assets and liabilities												
	Table 5 Holding gains and losses in assets and liabilities												
	Table 6 Balance sheet												
6	**Net worth**	...	...	...	...	...	...	...	...	...	...	...	...
61	**Nonfinancial assets**	...	...	...	...	...	...	...	...	...	...	...	...
611	Fixed assets	...	...	...	...	...	...	...	...	...	...	...	...
6111	Buildings and structures	...	...	...	...	...	...	...	...	...	...	...	...
6112	Machinery and equipment	...	...	...	...	...	...	...	...	...	...	...	...
6113	Other fixed assets	...	...	...	...	...	...	...	...	...	...	...	...
6114	Weapons systems	...	...	...	...	...	...	...	...	...	...	...	...
612	Inventories	...	...	...	...	...	...	...	...	...	...	...	...
613	Valuables	...	...	...	...	...	...	...	...	...	...	...	...
614	Nonproduced assets	...	...	...	...	...	...	...	...	...	...	...	...
6141	Land	...	...	...	...	...	...	...	...	...	...	...	...
6142	Mineral and energy resources	...	...	...	...	...	...	...	...	...	...	...	...
6143	Other naturally occurring assets	...	...	...	...	...	...	...	...	...	...	...	...
6144	Intangible nonproduced assets	...	...	...	...	...	...	...	...	...	...	...	...
62	**Financial assets**	...	...	...	**7,290**	**7,276**	**7,080**	...	...	...	**7,610**	**7,603**	**7,396**
	By instrument												
6201	Monetary gold and SDRs	...	...	...	—	—	—	...	...	...	—	—	—
6202	Currency and deposits	...	...	...	1,433	1,755	1,498	...	...	...	1,746	2,154	1,837
6203	Debt securities	...	...	...	1,500	—	—	...	...	...	1,500	—	—
6204	Loans	...	...	...	1,088	1,098	1,058	...	...	...	1,088	1,018	1,028
6205	Equity and investment fund shares	...	...	...	2,914	4,026	4,063	...	...	...	2,914	4,026	4,063
6206	Insurance, pension, and standardized guarantee schemes	...	...	...	—	—	—	...	...	...	—	—	—
6207	Financial derivatives and employee stock options	...	...	...	—	—	—	...	...	...	—	—	—
6208	Other accounts receivable	...	...	...	355	397	461	...	...	...	363	405	468
	By debtor												
621	Domestic debtors	...	...	...	...	...	...	...	...	...	...	...	...
622	External debtors	...	...	...	...	...	...	...	...	...	...	...	...
63	**Liabilities**	...	...	...	**26,065**	**26,678**	**26,925**	...	...	...	**18,455**	**19,110**	**19,336**
	By instrument												
6301	Special Drawing Rights (SDRs)	...	...	...	—	—	—	...	...	...	—	—	—
6302	Currency and deposits	...	...	...	7,586	7,455	7,669	...	...	...	—	—	—
6303	Debt securities	...	...	...	7,738	7,101	6,351	...	...	...	7,318	6,680	6,088
6304	Loans	...	...	...	10,649	11,938	12,831	...	...	...	10,938	12,139	13,068
6305	Equity and investment fund shares	...	...	...	—	—	—	...	...	...	—	—	—
6306	Insurance, pension, and standardized guarantee schemes	...	...	...	—	—	—	...	...	...	107	106	106
6307	Financial derivatives and employee stock options	...	...	...	—	—	—	...	...	...	—	—	—
6308	Other accounts payable	...	...	...	92	185	74	...	...	...	92	185	74
	By creditor												
631	Domestic creditors	...	...	...	...	...	...	...	...	...	...	...	...
632	External creditors	...	...	...	...	...	...	...	...	...	...	...	...
	Memorandum items												
6M2	Net financial worth	...	...	...	-18,774	-19,403	-19,845	...	...	...	-10,845	-11,508	-11,940
6M3	Gross debt (D4) at market value	...	...	...	26,065	26,678	26,925	...	...	...	18,455	19,110	19,336
6M3D3	D3 debt liabilities at market value	...	...	...	26,065	26,678	26,925	...	...	...	18,348	19,004	19,230
6M3D2	D2 debt liabilities at market value	...	...	...	25,972	26,493	26,851	...	...	...	18,256	18,819	19,156
6M3D1	D1 debt liabilities at market value	...	...	...	18,387	19,039	19,182	...	...	...	18,256	18,819	19,156
6M4	Gross debt (D4) at nominal value	...	...	...	...	...	...	...	...	...	...	...	...
6M4D3	D3 debt liabilities at nominal value	...	...	...	...	...	...	...	...	...	...	...	...
6M4D2	D2 debt liabilities at nominal value	...	...	...	...	...	...	...	...	...	...	...	...
6M4D1	D1 debt liabilities at nominal value	...	...	...	...	...	...	...	...	...	...	...	...

Cyprus (423)

In Millions of Euros (EUR) / Fiscal Year Ends December 31st

		Budgetary Central Government			Central Government (excl. Social Security)			Central Government (incl. Social Security)			General Government		
		2013	2014	2015	2013P	2014P	2015P	2013P	2014P	2015P	2013P	2014P	2015P
6M35	Gross debt (D4) at face value	...	...	...	...	...	...	...	...	...	...	...	...
6M35D3	D3 debt liabilities at face value	...	...	...	26,328	26,678	26,734	...	...	...	18,611	19,004	19,039
6M35D2	D2 debt liabilities at face value	...	...	...	26,235	26,493	26,661	...	...	...	18,519	18,819	18,966
6M35D1	D1 debt liabilities at face value	...	...	...	18,650	19,039	18,992	...	...	...	18,519	18,819	18,966
6M93	Government gross debt per national definition	...	...	...	26,235	26,493	26,661	...	...	...	18,519	18,819	18,966
6M5	Arrears	...	...	...	...	...	...	...	...	...	...	...	...
6M6	Explicit contingent liabilities	...	...	...	...	...	...	...	...	...	...	...	...
6M61	of which: Publicly guaranteed debt	...	...	...	...	...	...	...	...	...	...	...	...
6M7	Net implicit obligations for social security benefits	...	...	...	...	...	...	...	...	...	...	...	...
	Table 7 Expenditure by functions of government												
7	**Expenditure**	...	...	...	**5,872**	**6,814**	...	...	...	...	**7,486**	**8,467**	...
701	**General public services**	...	...	...	**1,793**	**3,193**	...	...	...	...	**1,818**	**3,263**	...
7017	Public debt transactions	...	...	...	660	540	...	...	...	...	584	503	...
7018	Transfers of general character between levels of government	...	...	...	—	—	...	...	...	...	—	—	...
702	**Defense**	...	...	...	**288**	**251**	...	...	...	...	**288**	**251**	...
703	**Public order and safety**	...	...	...	**387**	**304**	...	...	...	...	**387**	**304**	...
704	**Economic affairs**	...	...	...	**526**	**480**	...	...	...	...	**526**	**480**	...
7042	Agriculture, forestry, fishing, and hunting	...	...	...	136	127	...	...	...	...	136	127	...
7043	Fuel and energy	...	...	...	36	55	...	...	...	...	36	55	...
7044	Mining, manufacturing, and construction	...	...	...	4	3	...	...	...	...	4	3	...
7045	Transport	...	...	...	138	113	...	...	...	...	138	113	...
7046	Communication	...	...	...	25	22	...	...	...	...	25	22	...
705	**Environmental protection**	...	...	...	**40**	**6**	...	...	...	...	**81**	**46**	...
706	**Housing and community amenities**	...	...	...	**389**	**420**	...	...	...	...	**348**	**388**	...
707	**Health**	...	...	...	**554**	**462**	...	...	...	...	**554**	**462**	...
7072	Outpatient services	...	...	...	21	17	...	...	...	...	21	17	...
7073	Hospital services	...	...	...	393	329	...	...	...	...	393	329	...
7074	Public health services	...	...	...	0	0	...	...	...	...	0	0	...
708	**Recreation, culture and religion**	...	...	...	**118**	**106**	...	...	...	...	**164**	**151**	...
709	**Education**	...	...	...	**1,178**	**1,003**	...	...	...	...	**1,178**	**1,003**	...
7091	Pre-primary and primary education	...	...	...	375	316	...	...	...	...	375	316	...
7092	Secondary education	...	...	...	435	365	...	...	...	...	435	365	...
7094	Tertiary education	...	...	...	182	176	...	...	...	...	182	176	...
710	**Social protection**	...	...	...	**599**	**591**	...	...	...	...	**2,143**	**2,121**	...
7z	Statistical discrepancy: Expenditure	...	...	...	—	0	...	...	...	...	—	-0	...
	Table 8 Financial transactions by counterpart sector												
32	**Net acquisition of financial assets**	...	...	...	**2,313**	**-1,092**	**-227**	...	...	...	**2,229**	**-1,085**	**-238**
321	Domestic debtors	...	...	...	...	...	...	...	...	...	...	...	...
8211	General government	...	...	...	...	...	...	...	...	...	—	—	—
8212	Central bank	...	...	...	...	...	...	...	...	...	...	...	...
8213	Deposit-taking corporations except the central bank	...	...	...	...	...	...	...	...	...	...	...	...
8214	Other financial corporations	...	...	...	...	...	...	...	...	...	...	...	...
8215	Nonfinancial corporations	...	...	...	...	...	...	...	...	...	...	...	...
8216	Households & nonprofit institutions serving households	...	...	...	...	...	...	...	...	...	...	...	...
322	External debtors	...	...	...	...	...	...	...	...	...	...	...	...
8221	General government	...	...	...	...	...	...	...	...	...	...	...	...
8227	International organizations	...	...	...	...	...	...	...	...	...	...	...	...
8228	Financial corporations other than international organizations	...	...	...	...	...	...	...	...	...	...	...	...
8229	Other nonresidents	...	...	...	...	...	...	...	...	...	...	...	...

Cyprus (423)

In Millions of Euros (EUR) / Fiscal Year Ends December 31st

		Budgetary Central Government			Central Government (excl. Social Security)			Central Government (incl. Social Security)			General Government		
		2013	2014	2015	2013P	2014P	2015P	2013P	2014P	2015P	2013P	2014P	2015P
33	**Net incurrence of liabilities**	...	...	...	**3,154**	**413**	**-36**	...	...	...	**3,127**	**454**	**-57**
331	Domestic creditors	...	...	...	...	...	...	...	...	...	...	...	...
8311	General government	...	...	...	...	...	...	...	...	...	—	—	—
8312	Central bank	...	...	...	...	...	...	...	...	...	...	...	...
8313	Deposit-taking corporations except the central bank	...	...	...	...	...	...	...	...	...	...	...	...
8314	Other financial corporations	...	...	...	...	...	...	...	...	...	...	...	...
8315	Nonfinancial corporations	...	...	...	...	...	...	...	...	...	...	...	...
8316	Households & nonprofit institutions serving households	...	...	...	...	...	...	...	...	...	...	...	...
332	External creditors	...	...	...	...	...	...	...	...	...	...	...	...
8321	General government	...	...	...	...	...	...	...	...	...	...	...	...
8327	International organizations	...	...	...	...	...	...	...	...	...	...	...	...
8328	Financial corporations other than international organizations	...	...	...	...	...	...	...	...	...	...	...	...
8329	Other nonresidents	...	...	...	...	...	...	...	...	...	...	...	...
	Table 9 Total other economic flows in assets and liabilities												
9	**Change in net worth due to other economic flows**	...	...	...	...	...	...	...	...	...	...	...	...
91	**Other economic flows in nonfinancial assets**	...	...	...	...	...	...	...	...	...	...	...	...
911	Fixed assets	...	...	...	...	...	...	...	...	...	...	...	...
912	Inventories	...	...	...	...	...	...	...	...	...	...	...	...
913	Valuables	...	...	...	...	...	...	...	...	...	...	...	...
914	Nonproduced assets	...	...	...	...	...	...	...	...	...	...	...	...
92	**Other economic flows in financial assets**	...	...	...	**-639**	**1,077**	**31**	...	...	...	**-639**	**1,077**	**31**
	By instrument												
9201	Monetary gold and SDRs	...	...	...	—	—	—	...	...	...	—	—	—
9202	Currency and deposits	...	...	...	0	-0	0	...	...	...	—	—	—
9203	Debt securities	...	...	...	—	—	—	...	...	...	—	—	—
9204	Loans	...	...	...	—	-0	—	...	...	...	—	-0	—
9205	Equity and investment fund shares	...	...	...	-639	1,077	31	...	...	...	-639	1,077	31
9206	Insurance, pension, and standardized guarantee schemes	...	...	...	—	—	—	...	...	...	—	—	—
9207	Financial derivatives and employee stock options	...	...	...	—	—	—	...	...	...	—	—	—
9208	Other accounts receivable	...	...	...	—	—	—	...	...	...	—	—	0
	By debtor												
921	Domestic debtors	...	...	...	...	...	...	...	...	...	...	...	...
922	External debtors	...	...	...	...	...	...	...	...	...	...	...	...
93	**Other economic flows in liabilities**	...	...	...	**507**	**201**	**282**	...	...	...	**507**	**201**	**282**
	By instrument												
9301	Special Drawing Rights (SDRs)	...	...	...	—	—	—	...	...	...	—	—	—
9302	Currency and deposits	...	...	...	0	—	-0	...	...	...	—	—	—
9303	Debt securities	...	...	...	513	175	247	...	...	...	513	175	247
9304	Loans	...	...	...	-6	26	35	...	...	...	-6	26	35
9305	Equity and investment fund shares	...	...	...	—	—	—	...	...	...	—	—	—
9306	Insurance, pension, and standardized guarantee schemes	...	...	...	—	—	—	...	...	...	—	—	—
9307	Financial derivatives and employee stock options	...	...	...	—	—	—	...	...	...	—	—	—
9308	Other accounts payable	...	...	...	—	—	-0	...	...	...	—	—	-0
	By creditor												
931	Domestic creditors	...	...	...	...	...	...	...	...	...	...	...	...
932	External creditors	...	...	...	...	...	...	...	...	...	...	...	...
	Memorandum items												
9M2	Change in net financial worth due to other economic flows	...	...	...	-1,146	876	-251	...	...	...	-1,146	876	-251

Cyprus (423)

In Millions of Euros (EUR) / Fiscal Year Ends December 31st

		Budgetary Central Government			Central Government (excl. Social Security)			Central Government (incl. Social Security)			General Government		
		2013	2014	2015	2013P	2014P	2015P	2013P	2014P	2015P	2013P	2014P	2015P
9M3	Gross debt (D4) at market value: other economic flows	...	...	...	507	201	282	...	...	...	507	201	282
9M3D3	D3 debt liabilities at market value: other economic flows	...	...	...	507	201	282	...	...	...	507	201	282
9M3D2	D2 debt liabilities at market value: other economic flows	...	...	...	507	201	282	...	...	...	507	201	282
9M3D1	D1 debt liabilities at market value: other economic flows	...	...	...	507	201	282	...	...	...	507	201	282

Czech Republic (935)

In Billions of Czech Koruny (CZK) / Fiscal Year Ends December 31st

		Budgetary Central Government			Central Government (excl. Social Security)			Central Government (incl. Social Security)			General Government		
		2013	2014	2015	2013P	2014	2015	2013P	2014	2015	2013P	2014	2015
	Statement of operations												
1	Revenue	1,089	1,100	1,238	1,119	1,129	1,273	1,294	1,311	1,465	1,544	1,572	1,733
2	Expense	1,150	1,192	1,278	1,178	1,219	1,317	1,353	1,458	1,508	1,523	1,564	1,665
GOB	**Gross operating balance**	**-61**	**-92**	**-40**	**-58**	**-90**	**-44**	**-59**	**-147**	**-43**	**21**	**8**	**68**
NOB	**Net operating balance**	...	...	...	...	...	...	...	...	...	...	...	...
31	Net/Gross investment in nonfinancial assets	8	-0	10	9	-0	11	9	0	11	71	83	100
2M	Expenditure	1,159	1,192	1,288	1,187	1,219	1,327	1,363	1,458	1,518	1,594	1,647	1,766
NLB	**Net lending (+) / Net borrowing (-)**	**-69**	**-92**	**-50**	**-67**	**-90**	**-54**	**-68**	**-147**	**-54**	**-50**	**-75**	**-32**
32	Net acquisition of financial assets	-67	-110	-30	-66	-108	-34	-67	-106	-34	-45	-97	-15
33	Net incurrence of liabilities	2	-18	20	1	-18	20	1	-18	20	5	-22	18
NLBz	Statistical discrepancy	-0	—	—	0	-0	—	0	60	-0	-0	-0	—
	Memorandum items												
PB	Primary net lending / net borrowing	-19	-44	-5	-17	-42	-9	-18	-99	-9	4	-25	15
GB	Government balance per national definition	...	...	...	...	...	...	...	...	...	...	...	...
	Statement of other economic flows												
	Balance sheet												
6	**Net worth**	...	...	...	...	...	...	...	...	...	...	...	...
61	Nonfinancial assets	...	...	...	...	...	...	...	...	...	...	...	...
62	Financial assets	...	...	...	...	...	...	...	...	...	...	...	...
63	Liabilities	1,665	1,648	1,673	1,665	1,648	1,673	1,664	1,648	1,673	1,779	1,761	1,776
	Table 1 Revenue												
1	**Revenue**	**1,089**	**1,100**	**1,238**	**1,119**	**1,129**	**1,273**	**1,294**	**1,311**	**1,465**	**1,544**	**1,572**	**1,733**
11	**Taxes**	**540**	**559**	**593**	**554**	**573**	**608**	**554**	**573**	**608**	**754**	**785**	**826**
111	Taxes on income, profits, and capital gains	176	188	203	176	188	203	176	188	203	271	289	309
1111	Payable by individuals	94	98	103	94	98	103	94	98	103	142	148	155
1112	Payable by corporations and other enterprises	81	89	100	81	89	100	81	89	100	129	141	154
1113	Other taxes on income, profits, and capital gains	—	—	—	—	—	—	—	—	—	—	—	—
112	Taxes on payroll and workforce	—	—	—	—	—	—	—	—	—	—	—	—
113	Taxes on property	0	0	-4	0	0	-4	0	0	-4	10	10	6
114	Taxes on goods and services	364	371	394	377	386	409	377	386	409	473	486	511
1141	General taxes on goods and services	224	234	248	224	234	248	224	234	248	311	326	342
1142	Excises	136	134	143	143	141	151	143	141	151	143	141	151
115	Taxes on international trade and transactions	0	0	0	0	0	0	0	0	0	0	0	0
116	Other taxes	0	0	0	0	0	0	0	0	0	0	0	0
12	**Social contributions**	**372**	**383**	**405**	**372**	**383**	**405**	**545**	**563**	**595**	**545**	**563**	**595**
121	Social security contributions	358	368	389	358	368	389	531	548	579	531	548	579
122	Other social contributions	14	15	16	14	15	16	14	15	16	14	15	16
13	**Grants**	**125**	**117**	**193**	**124**	**116**	**192**	**124**	**116**	**192**	**125**	**117**	**191**
131	From foreign governments	0	0	0	0	0	0	0	0	0	0	0	0
132	From international organizations	124	116	190	124	116	190	124	116	190	125	116	191
133	From other general government units	0	1	2	0	0	1	0	0	1	0	—	—
1331	Current	0	0	0	0	0	1	0	0	1	0	—	—
1332	Capital	0	1	2	0	0	0	—	0	0	0	—	—
14	**Other revenue**	**53**	**41**	**48**	**70**	**57**	**69**	**71**	**58**	**71**	**120**	**108**	**122**
	Table 2 Expense by economic type												
2	**Expense**	**1,150**	**1,192**	**1,278**	**1,178**	**1,219**	**1,317**	**1,353**	**1,458**	**1,508**	**1,523**	**1,564**	**1,665**
21	**Compensation of employees**	**95**	**99**	**107**	**96**	**100**	**108**	**99**	**104**	**112**	**139**	**146**	**155**
211	Wages and salaries	71	74	80	72	75	81	74	78	84	105	110	117
212	Employers' social contributions	24	25	27	24	25	27	25	26	28	34	36	39
22	**Use of goods and services**	**52**	**51**	**53**	**53**	**52**	**55**	**56**	**54**	**57**	**122**	**121**	**122**
23	**Consumption of fixed capital**	...	...	...	...	...	...	...	...	...	...	...	...
24	**Interest**	**50**	**48**	**45**	**50**	**48**	**45**	**50**	**48**	**45**	**54**	**50**	**47**
25	**Subsidies**	**100**	**106**	**105**	**150**	**165**	**170**	**150**	**165**	**170**	**319**	**341**	**353**

Czech Republic (935)

In Billions of Czech Koruny (CZK) / Fiscal Year Ends December 31st

		Budgetary Central Government			Central Government (excl. Social Security)			Central Government (incl. Social Security)			General Government		
		2013	2014	2015	2013P	2014	2015	2013P	2014	2015	2013P	2014	2015
26	**Grants**	**288**	**310**	**353**	**228**	**246**	**268**	**174**	**186**	**207**	**36**	**37**	**39**
261	To foreign governments	—	—	—	—	—	—	—	—	—	0	0	0
262	To international organizations	36	37	39	36	37	39	36	37	39	36	37	39
263	To other general government units	252	272	314	192	208	229	139	148	168	0	—	—
2631	Current	201	215	223	161	170	179	107	111	119	0	—	—
2632	Capital	51	57	91	31	38	49	31	38	49	0	—	—
27	**Social benefits**	**490**	**496**	**507**	**490**	**496**	**507**	**713**	**728**	**751**	**713**	**728**	**752**
271	Social security benefits	413	417	428	413	417	428	636	649	673	636	649	673
272	Social assistance benefits	77	79	79	77	79	79	77	79	79	77	79	79
273	Employment-related social benefits	0	0	0	0	0	0	0	0	0	0	0	0
28	**Other expense**	**76**	**83**	**107**	**110**	**112**	**164**	**111**	**112**	**164**	**141**	**141**	**197**
281	Property expense other than interest	0	0	0	0	0	0	0	0	0	0	0	0
282	Transfers not elsewhere classified	76	83	107	110	112	164	111	112	164	141	141	197
2821	Current	20	21	22	21	22	23	21	23	24	35	37	41
2822	Capital	56	63	85	89	90	141	89	90	141	105	104	156
	Table 3 Transactions in assets and liabilities												
3	**Change in net worth from transactions**	...	...	...	...	...	...	...	...	...	...	...	...
31	**Net/Gross investment in nonfinancial assets**	**8**	**-0**	**10**	**9**	**-0**	**11**	**9**	**0**	**11**	**71**	**83**	**100**
311	Fixed assets	12	12	15	13	12	16	13	12	16	76	96	107
3111	Buildings and structures	3	4	3	3	4	3	3	4	3	60	81	86
3112	Machinery and equipment	6	3	7	6	3	7	6	3	7	11	9	14
3113	Other fixed assets	2	4	4	2	4	4	2	4	4	4	5	6
3114	Weapons systems	2	1	1	2	1	1	2	1	1	2	1	1
312	Inventories	—	—	—	—	—	—	—	—	—	—	—	—
313	Valuables	0	0	0	0	0	0	0	0	0	0	0	0
314	Nonproduced assets	-4	-12	-5	-4	-12	-5	-4	-12	-5	-5	-13	-6
3141	Land	-2	-2	-2	-2	-2	-2	-2	-2	-2	-3	-3	-3
3142	Mineral and energy resources	—	-10	—	—	-10	—	—	-10	—	—	-10	—
3143	Other naturally occurring assets	—	—	—	—	—	—	—	—	—	—	—	—
3144	Intangible nonproduced assets	-2	—	-3	-2	—	-3	-2	—	-3	-2	—	-3
32	**Net acquisition of financial assets**	**-67**	**-110**	**-30**	**-66**	**-108**	**-34**	**-67**	**-106**	**-34**	**-45**	**-97**	**-15**
	By instrument												
3201	Monetary gold and SDRs	—	—	—	—	—	—	—	—	—	—	—	—
3202	Currency and deposits	-69	-105	-27	-67	-103	-31	-67	-102	-31	-53	-92	-24
3203	Debt securities	—	—	—	—	0	0	—	0	0	8	-2	11
3204	Loans	-0	-2	-1	-1	-2	-1	-2	-1	-1	-2	-1	-1
3205	Equity and investment fund shares	2	-3	-2	2	-3	-2	2	-3	-2	2	-2	-1
3206	Insurance, pension, and standardized guarantee schemes	—	—	—	—	—	—	—	—	—	—	—	—
3207	Financial derivatives and employee stock options	—	—	...	—	—	...	—	—	...	—	—	...
3208	Other accounts receivable	...	...	...	...	...	...	...	...	...	...	...	...
	By debtor												
321	Domestic debtors	-67	-111	-31	-66	-108	-34	-67	-106	-34	-45	-97	-15
322	External debtors	-0	0	0	-0	0	0	-0	0	0	-0	0	0
33	**Net incurrence of liabilities**	**2**	**-18**	**20**	**1**	**-18**	**20**	**1**	**-18**	**20**	**5**	**-22**	**18**
	By instrument												
3301	Special Drawing Rights (SDRs)	—	—	—	—	—	—	—	—	—	—	—	—
3302	Currency and deposits	—	—	—	—	—	—	—	—	—	—	—	—
3303	Debt securities	0	-10	22	0	-10	22	0	-10	22	0	-12	22
3304	Loans	2	-9	-2	1	-9	-2	1	-9	-2	4	-10	-4
3305	Equity and investment fund shares	—	—	—	—	—	—	—	—	—	—	—	—
3306	Insurance, pension, and standardized guarantee schemes	—	—	—	—	—	—	—	—	—	—	—	—
3307	Financial derivatives and employee stock options	—	—	...	—	—	...	—	—	...	—	—	...
3308	Other accounts payable	...	...	...	...	...	...	...	...	...	...	...	...

Czech Republic (935)

In Billions of Czech Koruny (CZK) / Fiscal Year Ends December 31st

		Budgetary Central Government			Central Government (excl. Social Security)			Central Government (incl. Social Security)			General Government		
		2013	2014	2015	2013P	2014	2015	2013P	2014	2015	2013P	2014	2015
	By creditor												
331	Domestic creditors	-44	55	-75	-44	55	-74	-44	55	-74	-46	54	-75
332	External creditors	45	-73	95	45	-73	95	45	-73	95	51	-76	93
	Table 4 Holding gains and losses in assets and liabilities												
	Table 5 Holding gains and losses in assets and liabilities												
	Table 6 Balance sheet												
6	**Net worth**	...	...	...	...	...	...	...	...	...	...	...	...
61	**Nonfinancial assets**	...	...	...	...	...	...	...	...	...	...	...	...
611	Fixed assets	...	...	...	...	...	...	...	...	...	...	...	...
6111	Buildings and structures	...	...	...	...	...	...	...	...	...	...	...	...
6112	Machinery and equipment	...	...	...	...	...	...	...	...	...	...	...	...
6113	Other fixed assets	...	...	...	...	...	...	...	...	...	...	...	...
6114	Weapons systems	...	...	...	...	...	...	...	...	...	...	...	...
612	Inventories	...	...	...	...	...	...	...	...	...	...	...	...
613	Valuables	...	...	...	...	...	...	...	...	...	...	...	...
614	Nonproduced assets	...	...	...	...	...	...	...	...	...	...	...	...
6141	Land	...	...	...	...	...	...	...	...	...	...	...	...
6142	Mineral and energy resources	...	...	...	...	...	...	...	...	...	...	...	...
6143	Other naturally occurring assets	...	...	...	...	...	...	...	...	...	...	...	...
6144	Intangible nonproduced assets	...	...	...	...	...	...	...	...	...	...	...	...
62	**Financial assets**	...	...	...	...	...	...	...	...	...	...	...	...
	By instrument												
6201	Monetary gold and SDRs	...	...	—	—	—	—	...	...	—	...	...	—
6202	Currency and deposits	...	...	...	...	...	...	...	...	...	...	...	...
6203	Debt securities	...	...	...	...	...	...	...	...	...	...	...	...
6204	Loans	...	...	...	...	...	...	...	...	...	...	...	...
6205	Equity and investment fund shares	...	...	...	...	...	...	...	...	...	...	...	...
6206	Insurance, pension, and standardized guarantee schemes	...	...	...	...	...	...	...	...	...	...	...	...
6207	Financial derivatives and employee stock options	...	...	...	—	...	...	...	...	...	...	...	...
6208	Other accounts receivable	...	...	...	...	...	...	...	...	...	...	...	...
	By debtor												
621	Domestic debtors	...	...	...	...	...	...	...	...	...	...	...	...
622	External debtors	...	...	...	...	...	...	...	...	...	...	...	...
63	**Liabilities**	**1,665**	**1,648**	**1,673**	**1,665**	**1,648**	**1,673**	**1,664**	**1,648**	**1,673**	**1,779**	**1,761**	**1,776**
	By instrument												
6301	Special Drawing Rights (SDRs)	—	—	—	—	—	—	—	—	—	—	—	—
6302	Currency and deposits	—	—	—	—	—	—	—	—	—	—	—	—
6303	Debt securities	1,593	1,586	1,612	1,593	1,586	1,612	1,593	1,585	1,612	1,606	1,596	1,623
6304	Loans	72	63	61	72	63	61	72	63	61	174	164	153
6305	Equity and investment fund shares	—	—	—	—	—	—	—	—	—	—	—	—
6306	Insurance, pension, and standardized guarantee schemes	—	—	—	—	—	—	—	—	—	—	—	—
6307	Financial derivatives and employee stock options	—	—	...	—	—	...	—	—	...	—	—	...
6308	Other accounts payable	...	...	...	...	...	...	...	...	...	...	...	...
	By creditor												
631	Domestic creditors	1,123	1,178	1,111	1,123	1,178	1,111	1,123	1,178	1,111	1,176	1,234	1,160
632	External creditors	541	470	562	541	470	562	541	470	562	603	527	616
	Memorandum items												
6M2	Net financial worth	...	...	...	...	...	...	...	...	...	...	...	...
6M3	Gross debt (D4) at market value	...	...	...	...	...	...	...	...	...	...	...	...
6M3D3	D3 debt liabilities at market value	...	...	...	...	...	...	...	...	...	...	...	...
6M3D2	D2 debt liabilities at market value	...	...	...	...	...	...	...	...	...	...	...	...
6M3D1	D1 debt liabilities at market value	...	...	...	...	...	...	...	...	...	...	...	...
6M4	Gross debt (D4) at nominal value	...	...	...	...	...	...	...	...	...	...	...	...
6M4D3	D3 debt liabilities at nominal value	...	...	...	...	...	...	...	...	...	...	...	...
6M4D2	D2 debt liabilities at nominal value	...	...	...	...	...	...	...	...	...	...	...	...
6M4D1	D1 debt liabilities at nominal value	...	...	...	...	...	...	...	...	...	...	...	...

Czech Republic (935)

In Billions of Czech Koruny (CZK) / Fiscal Year Ends December 31st

		Budgetary Central Government			Central Government (excl. Social Security)			Central Government (incl. Social Security)			General Government		
		2013	2014	2015	2013P	2014	2015	2013P	2014	2015	2013P	2014	2015
6M35	Gross debt (D4) at face value	...	...	...	...	...	...	...	...	...	...	...	...
6M35D3	D3 debt liabilities at face value	...	...	...	...	...	...	...	...	...	...	...	...
6M35D2	D2 debt liabilities at face value	1,665	1,648	1,673	1,665	1,648	1,673	1,664	1,648	1,673	1,779	1,761	1,776
6M35D1	D1 debt liabilities at face value	1,665	1,648	1,673	1,665	1,648	1,673	1,664	1,648	1,673	1,779	1,761	1,776
6M93	Government gross debt per national definition	...	...	...	...	...	...	...	...	...	...	...	...
6M5	Arrears	...	...	...	...	...	...	...	...	...	...	...	...
6M6	Explicit contingent liabilities	...	...	...	...	...	...	...	...	...	...	...	...
6M61	of which: Publicly guaranteed debt	...	...	...	...	...	...	...	...	...	...	...	...
6M7	Net implicit obligations for social security benefits	...	...	...	...	...	...	...	...	...	...	...	...
	Table 7 Expenditure by functions of government												
7	**Expenditure**	**1,159**	**1,204**	**1,295**	**1,187**	**1,231**	**1,334**	**1,363**	**1,410**	**1,525**	**1,594**	**1,665**	**1,778**
701	**General public services**	**134**	**135**	**138**	**139**	**135**	**138**	**139**	**135**	**138**	**182**	**182**	**187**
7017	Public debt transactions	50	48	45	50	48	45	50	48	45	54	50	47
7018	Transfers of general character between levels of government	11	10	10	11	10	10	11	10	10	—	—	—
702	**Defense**	**28**	**32**	**38**	**28**	**32**	**38**	**28**	**32**	**38**	**29**	**32**	**38**
703	**Public order and safety**	**60**	**65**	**75**	**60**	**65**	**75**	**60**	**65**	**75**	**66**	**73**	**84**
704	**Economic affairs**	**155**	**171**	**216**	**173**	**193**	**251**	**173**	**193**	**251**	**229**	**273**	**329**
7042	Agriculture, forestry, fishing, and hunting	48	48	47	39	48	44	39	48	44	41	50	46
7043	Fuel and energy	3	6	8	4	6	8	4	6	8	1	3	4
7044	Mining, manufacturing, and construction	2	2	1	3	3	2	3	3	2	3	3	2
7045	Transport	37	44	76	62	64	113	62	64	113	133	145	191
7046	Communication	1	1	1	1	1	1	1	1	1	1	1	1
705	**Environmental protection**	**22**	**32**	**35**	**24**	**34**	**37**	**24**	**34**	**37**	**33**	**57**	**64**
706	**Housing and community amenities**	**27**	**27**	**35**	**30**	**30**	**37**	**30**	**30**	**37**	**27**	**45**	**42**
707	**Health**	**59**	**66**	**68**	**59**	**66**	**68**	**235**	**245**	**259**	**243**	**255**	**269**
7072	Outpatient services	1	1	1	1	1	1	...	1	1	...	5	5
7073	Hospital services	1	2	2	1	2	2	...	2	2	...	7	7
7074	Public health services	54	60	0	54	60	0	...	239	0	...	240	1
708	**Recreation, culture and religion**	**16**	**16**	**16**	**16**	**16**	**16**	**16**	**16**	**16**	**38**	**46**	**48**
709	**Education**	**127**	**128**	**131**	**127**	**128**	**131**	**127**	**128**	**131**	**146**	**161**	**166**
7091	Pre-primary and primary education	0	0	0	0	0	0	...	0	0	19	24	24
7092	Secondary education	3	2	4	3	2	4	...	2	4	75	84	88
7094	Tertiary education	23	23	24	23	23	24	...	23	24	24	23	25
710	**Social protection**	**522**	**532**	**543**	**522**	**532**	**543**	**522**	**532**	**543**	**529**	**540**	**552**
7z	Statistical discrepancy: Expenditure	...	...	...	...	...	...	...	...	...	...	...	...
	Table 8 Financial transactions by counterpart sector												
32	**Net acquisition of financial assets**	**-67**	**-110**	**-30**	**-66**	**-108**	**-34**	**-67**	**-106**	**-34**	**-45**	**-97**	**-15**
321	Domestic debtors	-67	-111	-31	-66	-108	-34	-67	-106	-34	-45	-97	-15
8211	General government	...	-1	-1	...	-1	-0	...	0	0	...	—	—
8212	Central bank	...	-186	-131	...	-184	-134	...	-184	-134	...	-184	-134
8213	Deposit-taking corporations except the central bank	...	81	102	...	81	102	...	82	102	...	92	109
8214	Other financial corporations	...	-0	—	...	-0	—	...	-0	—	...	-0	0
8215	Nonfinancial corporations	...	-5	-2	...	-4	-2	...	-4	-2	...	-5	11
8216	Households & nonprofit institutions serving households	...	—	-0	...	-0	-0	...	-0	-0	...	-0	-0
322	External debtors	-0	0	0	-0	0	0	-0	0	0	-0	0	0
8221	General government	...	—	—	...	—	—	...	—	—	...	—	—
8227	International organizations	...	...	...	...	...	...	...	—	...	...	...	...
8228	Financial corporations other than international organizations	...	...	...	...	...	...	...	—	...	...	...	...
8229	Other nonresidents	...	...	...	...	...	...	...	0	...	...	...	...

Czech Republic (935)

In Billions of Czech Koruny (CZK) / Fiscal Year Ends December 31st

		Budgetary Central Government			Central Government (excl. Social Security)			Central Government (incl. Social Security)			General Government		
		2013	2014	2015	2013P	2014	2015	2013P	2014	2015	2013P	2014	2015
33	**Net incurrence of liabilities**	**2**	**-18**	**20**	**1**	**-18**	**20**	**1**	**-18**	**20**	**5**	**-22**	**18**
331	Domestic creditors	-44	55	-75	-44	55	-74	-44	55	-74	-46	54	-75
8311	General government	...	-1	-1	...	-1	-1	...	-1	-1	...	—	—
8312	Central bank	...	—	—	...	—	—	...	—	—	...	—	—
8313	Deposit-taking corporations except the central bank	...	90	-61	...	90	-61	...	90	-61	...	88	-61
8314	Other financial corporations	...	24	-25	...	24	-25	...	24	-25	...	24	-25
8315	Nonfinancial corporations	...	-49	23	...	-49	23	...	-49	23	...	-49	23
8316	Households & nonprofit institutions serving households	...	-9	-11	...	-9	-11	...	-9	-11	...	-9	-11
332	External creditors	45	-73	95	45	-73	95	45	-73	95	51	-76	93
8321	General government	...	—	—	...	—	—	...	—	—	...	—	—
8327	International organizations	...	-11	-2	...	-11	-2	...	-11	-2	...	-11	-2
8328	Financial corporations other than international organizations	...	—	...	...	—	...	...	—	...	...	—	...
8329	Other nonresidents	...	...	...	...	...	...	...	...	...	...	...	...
	Table 9 Total other economic flows in assets and liabilities												

Denmark (128)

In Billions of Danish Kroner (DKK) / Fiscal Year Ends December 31st

		Budgetary Central Government			Central Government (excl. Social Security)			Central Government (incl. Social Security)			General Government		
		2013	2014	2015	2013P	2014P	2015P	2013P	2014P	2015P	2013P	2014P	2015P
	Statement of operations												
1	Revenue	...	...	...	784	847	802	788	851	805	1,058	1,122	1,084
2	Expense	...	...	...	795	808	822	799	811	825	1,065	1,077	1,101
GOB	**Gross operating balance**	...	...	...	**15**	**68**	**9**	**15**	**68**	**9**	**49**	**103**	**42**
NOB	**Net operating balance**	...	...	...	**-12**	**40**	**-21**	**-12**	**40**	**-20**	**-7**	**45**	**-16**
31	Net/Gross investment in nonfinancial assets	...	...	...	12	15	12	12	15	12	12	17	11
2M	Expenditure	...	...	...	807	823	834	811	827	837	1,077	1,094	1,111
NLB	**Net lending (+) / Net borrowing (-)**	...	...	...	**-24**	**24**	**-32**	**-24**	**25**	**-32**	**-19**	**28**	**-27**
32	Net acquisition of financial assets	...	...	...	-18	40	-115	...	...	...	-14	50	-105
33	Net incurrence of liabilities	...	...	...	7	15	-77	...	...	...	7	22	-71
NLBz	Statistical discrepancy	...	...	...	-1	0	-6	...	...	...	-1	0	-7
	Memorandum items												
PB	Primary net lending / net borrowing	...	...	...	7	51	-2	7	52	-1	13	57	5
GB	Government balance per national definition	...	...	...	...	...	...	...	...	...	...	...	...
	Statement of other economic flows												
	Balance sheet												
6	**Net worth**	...	...	...	...	...	...	...	...	...	...	...	...
61	Nonfinancial assets	...	...	...	...	...	...	...	...	...	...	...	...
62	Financial assets	...	...	...	699	742	631	...	...	...	1,018	1,072	963
63	Liabilities	...	...	...	893	959	863	...	...	...	1,094	1,166	1,076
	Table 1 Revenue												
1	**Revenue**	...	...	...	**784**	**847**	**802**	**788**	**851**	**805**	**1,058**	**1,122**	**1,084**
11	**Taxes**	...	...	...	**657**	**729**	**692**	**657**	**729**	**692**	**893**	**971**	**941**
111	Taxes on income, profits, and capital gains	...	...	...	342	410	363	342	410	363	551	624	584
1111	Payable by individuals	...	...	...	288	354	310	288	354	310	497	568	531
1112	Payable by corporations and other enterprises	...	...	...	54	56	53	54	56	53	54	56	53
1113	Other taxes on income, profits, and capital gains	...	...	...	—	—	—	—	—	—	—	—	—
112	Taxes on payroll and workforce	...	...	...	13	13	13	13	13	13	13	13	13
113	Taxes on property	...	...	...	17	17	19	17	17	19	43	44	47
114	Taxes on goods and services	...	...	...	281	284	291	281	284	291	281	284	291
1141	General taxes on goods and services	...	...	...	177	182	186	177	182	186	177	182	186
1142	Excises	...	...	...	67	64	64	67	64	64	67	64	64
115	Taxes on international trade and transactions	...	...	...	—	—	—	—	—	—	—	—	—
116	Other taxes	...	...	...	5	5	6	5	5	6	5	5	6
12	**Social contributions**	...	...	...	**4**	**4**	**4**	**19**	**19**	**19**	**21**	**20**	**20**
121	Social security contributions	...	...	...	—	—	—	15	15	15	15	15	15
122	Other social contributions	...	...	...	4	4	4	4	4	4	6	6	6
13	**Grants**	...	...	...	...	...	...	...	...	...	...	...	...
131	From foreign governments	...	...	...	...	...	...	...	...	...	...	...	...
132	From international organizations	...	...	...	...	...	...	...	...	...	...	...	...
133	From other general government units	...	...	...	30	30	28	19	19	17	—	—	—
1331	Current	...	...	...	30	30	28	19	19	17	—	—	—
1332	Capital	...	...	...	0	0	—	0	0	—	—	—	—
14	**Other revenue**	...	...	...	...	...	...	...	...	...	...	...	...
	Table 2 Expense by economic type												
2	**Expense**	...	...	...	**795**	**808**	**822**	**799**	**811**	**825**	**1,065**	**1,077**	**1,101**
21	**Compensation of employees**	...	...	...	**85**	**86**	**87**	**87**	**88**	**90**	**317**	**322**	**326**
211	Wages and salaries	...	...	...	...	...	...	...	...	...	...	...	...
212	Employers' social contributions	...	...	...	...	...	...	...	...	...	...	...	...
22	**Use of goods and services**	...	...	...	**63**	**63**	**63**	**63**	**64**	**64**	**178**	**181**	**184**
23	**Consumption of fixed capital**	...	...	...	**27**	**28**	**30**	**27**	**28**	**30**	**56**	**58**	**59**
24	**Interest**	...	...	...	**30**	**27**	**30**	**30**	**27**	**30**	**32**	**29**	**32**
25	**Subsidies**	...	...	...	**23**	**23**	**25**	**23**	**23**	**25**	**41**	**41**	**41**

Denmark (128)

In Billions of Danish Kroner (DKK) / Fiscal Year Ends December 31st

		Budgetary Central Government			Central Government (excl. Social Security)			Central Government (incl. Social Security)			General Government		
		2013	2014	2015	2013P	2014P	2015P	2013P	2014P	2015P	2013P	2014P	2015P
26	**Grants**	...	...	...	...	...	...	...	...	...	...	...	...
261	To foreign governments	...	...	...	...	...	...	...	...	...	...	...	...
262	To international organizations	...	...	...	...	...	...	...	...	...	...	...	...
263	To other general government units	...	...	...	441	451	453	401	413	417	—	—	—
2631	Current	...	...	...	439	449	449	399	411	413	—	—	—
2632	Capital	...	...	...	1	2	4	1	2	4	—	—	—
27	**Social benefits**	...	...	...	**64**	**67**	**67**	**103**	**103**	**101**	**365**	**371**	**376**
271	Social security benefits	...	...	...	...	...	...	...	...	...	...	...	...
272	Social assistance benefits	...	...	...	...	...	...	...	...	...	...	...	...
273	Employment-related social benefits	...	...	...	...	...	...	...	...	...	...	...	...
28	**Other expense**	...	...	...	...	...	...	...	...	...	...	...	...
281	Property expense other than interest	...	...	...	—	—	—	—	—	—	—	—	—
282	Transfers not elsewhere classified	...	...	...	...	...	...	...	...	...	...	...	...
2821	Current	...	...	...	...	...	...	...	...	...	...	...	...
2822	Capital	...	...	...	...	...	...	...	...	...	...	...	...
	Table 3 Transactions in assets and liabilities												
3	**Change in net worth from transactions**	...	...	...	**-13**	**40**	**-26**	...	...	...	**-8**	**45**	**-23**
31	**Net/Gross investment in nonfinancial assets**	...	...	...	**12**	**15**	**12**	**12**	**15**	**12**	**12**	**17**	**11**
311	Fixed assets	...	...	...	12	15	11	12	15	11	14	19	15
3111	Buildings and structures	...	...	...	...	...	...	...	...	...	...	...	...
3112	Machinery and equipment	...	...	...	...	...	...	...	...	...	...	...	...
3113	Other fixed assets	...	...	...	...	...	...	...	...	...	...	...	...
3114	Weapons systems	...	...	...	...	...	...	...	...	...	...	...	...
312	Inventories	...	...	...	...	...	...	...	...	...	...	...	...
313	Valuables	...	...	...	...	...	...	...	...	...	...	...	...
314	Nonproduced assets	...	...	...	-0	1	0	-0	1	0	-2	-2	-4
3141	Land	...	...	...	...	...	...	...	...	...	...	...	...
3142	Mineral and energy resources	...	...	...	...	...	...	...	...	...	...	...	...
3143	Other naturally occurring assets	...	...	...	...	...	...	...	...	...	...	...	...
3144	Intangible nonproduced assets	...	...	...	...	...	...	...	...	...	...	...	...
32	**Net acquisition of financial assets**	...	...	...	**-18**	**40**	**-115**	...	...	...	**-14**	**50**	**-105**
	By instrument												
3201	Monetary gold and SDRs	...	...	...	—	—	—	...	...	...	—	—	—
3202	Currency and deposits	...	...	...	-1	51	-52	...	...	...	-1	52	-52
3203	Debt securities	...	...	...	-11	-37	-5	...	...	...	-12	-35	1
3204	Loans	...	...	...	10	3	7	...	...	...	12	5	1
3205	Equity and investment fund shares	...	...	...	3	2	3	...	...	...	4	2	7
3206	Insurance, pension, and standardized guarantee schemes	...	...	...	0	0	0	...	...	...	0	0	0
3207	Financial derivatives and employee stock options	...	...	...	-4	-3	-3	...	...	...	-4	-3	-3
3208	Other accounts receivable	...	...	...	-15	25	-65	...	...	...	-12	30	-59
	By debtor												
321	Domestic debtors	...	...	...	...	...	...	...	...	...	...	...	...
322	External debtors	...	...	...	...	...	...	...	...	...	...	...	...
33	**Net incurrence of liabilities**	...	...	...	**7**	**15**	**-77**	...	...	...	**7**	**22**	**-71**
	By instrument												
3301	Special Drawing Rights (SDRs)	...	...	...	—	—	—	...	...	...	—	—	—
3302	Currency and deposits	...	...	...	—	—	—	...	...	...	-0	1	1
3303	Debt securities	...	...	...	-13	15	-77	...	...	...	-12	15	-77
3304	Loans	...	...	...	3	-0	-0	...	...	...	10	2	5
3305	Equity and investment fund shares	...	...	...	—	—	—	...	...	...	—	—	—
3306	Insurance, pension, and standardized guarantee schemes	...	...	...	—	—	—	...	...	...	—	—	—
3307	Financial derivatives and employee stock options	...	...	...	—	—	—	...	...	...	—	—	—
3308	Other accounts payable	...	...	...	16	-0	0	...	...	...	8	4	1

Denmark (128)

In Billions of Danish Kroner (DKK) / Fiscal Year Ends December 31st

		Budgetary Central Government			Central Government (excl. Social Security)			Central Government (incl. Social Security)			General Government		
		2013	2014	2015	2013P	2014P	2015P	2013P	2014P	2015P	2013P	2014P	2015P
	By creditor												
331	Domestic creditors	...	...	...	...	...	...	...	...	...	...	...	...
332	External creditors	...	...	...	...	...	...	...	...	...	...	...	...
	Table 4 Holding gains and losses in assets and liabilities												
	Table 5 Holding gains and losses in assets and liabilities												
	Table 6 Balance sheet												
6	**Net worth**	**...**	**...**	**...**	**...**	**...**	**...**	**...**	**...**	**...**	**...**	**...**	**...**
61	**Nonfinancial assets**	**...**	**...**	**...**	**...**	**...**	**...**	**...**	**...**	**...**	**...**	**...**	**...**
611	Fixed assets	...	...	...	...	...	...	...	...	...	945	958	...
6111	Buildings and structures	...	...	...	...	...	...	...	...	...	664	671	...
6112	Machinery and equipment	...	...	...	...	...	...	...	...	...	...	...	...
6113	Other fixed assets	...	...	...	...	...	...	...	...	...	173	176	...
6114	Weapons systems	...	...	...	...	...	...	...	...	...	...	...	...
612	Inventories	...	...	...	...	...	...	...	...	...	...	...	...
613	Valuables	...	...	...	...	...	...	...	...	...	...	...	...
614	Nonproduced assets	...	...	...	...	...	...	...	...	...	...	...	...
6141	Land	...	...	...	...	...	...	...	...	...	...	...	...
6142	Mineral and energy resources	...	...	...	...	...	...	...	...	...	...	...	...
6143	Other naturally occurring assets	...	...	...	...	...	...	...	...	...	...	...	...
6144	Intangible nonproduced assets	...	...	...	...	...	...	...	...	...	...	...	...
62	**Financial assets**	**...**	**...**	**...**	**699**	**742**	**631**	**...**	**...**	**...**	**1,018**	**1,072**	**963**
	By instrument												
6201	Monetary gold and SDRs	...	...	...	—	—	—	...	...	...	—	—	—
6202	Currency and deposits	...	...	...	202	253	209	...	...	...	218	270	226
6203	Debt securities	...	...	...	77	39	33	...	...	...	102	67	67
6204	Loans	...	...	...	145	148	158	...	...	...	176	180	185
6205	Equity and investment fund shares	...	...	...	200	204	198	...	...	...	416	425	422
6206	Insurance, pension, and standardized guarantee schemes	...	...	...	1	1	1	...	...	...	2	2	2
6207	Financial derivatives and employee stock options	...	...	...	6	5	5	...	...	...	6	5	5
6208	Other accounts receivable	...	...	...	69	92	27	...	...	...	98	123	57
	By debtor												
621	Domestic debtors	...	...	...	...	...	...	...	...	...	...	...	...
622	External debtors	...	...	...	...	...	...	...	...	...	...	...	...
63	**Liabilities**	**...**	**...**	**...**	**893**	**959**	**863**	**...**	**...**	**...**	**1,094**	**1,166**	**1,076**
	By instrument												
6301	Special Drawing Rights (SDRs)	...	...	...	—	—	—	...	...	...	—	—	—
6302	Currency and deposits	...	...	...	—	—	—	...	...	...	15	16	16
6303	Debt securities	...	...	...	767	833	739	...	...	...	764	831	737
6304	Loans	...	...	...	41	41	40	...	...	...	163	165	170
6305	Equity and investment fund shares	...	...	...	—	—	—	...	...	...	—	—	—
6306	Insurance, pension, and standardized guarantee schemes	...	...	...	—	—	—	...	...	...	—	—	—
6307	Financial derivatives and employee stock options	...	...	...	—	—	—	...	...	...	—	—	—
6308	Other accounts payable	...	...	...	85	85	83	...	...	...	151	155	153
	By creditor												
631	Domestic creditors	...	...	...	...	...	...	...	...	...	...	...	...
632	External creditors	...	...	...	...	...	...	...	...	...	...	...	...
	Memorandum items												
6M2	Net financial worth	...	...	...	-194	-217	-232	...	...	...	-76	-94	-113
6M3	Gross debt (D4) at market value	...	...	...	893	959	863	...	...	...	1,094	1,166	1,076
6M3D3	D3 debt liabilities at market value	...	...	...	893	959	863	...	...	...	1,094	1,166	1,076
6M3D2	D2 debt liabilities at market value	...	...	...	808	874	780	...	...	...	943	1,011	923
6M3D1	D1 debt liabilities at market value	...	...	...	808	874	780	...	...	...	928	996	907
6M4	Gross debt (D4) at nominal value	...	...	...	...	...	...	...	...	...	...	...	...
6M4D3	D3 debt liabilities at nominal value	...	...	...	...	...	...	...	...	...	...	...	...
6M4D2	D2 debt liabilities at nominal value	...	...	...	...	...	...	...	...	...	...	...	...
6M4D1	D1 debt liabilities at nominal value	...	...	...	...	...	...	...	...	...	...	...	...

Denmark (128)

In Billions of Danish Kroner (DKK) / Fiscal Year Ends December 31st

		Budgetary Central Government			Central Government (excl. Social Security)			Central Government (incl. Social Security)			General Government		
		2013	2014	2015	2013P	2014P	2015P	2013P	2014P	2015P	2013P	2014P	2015P
6M35	Gross debt (D4) at face value	...	...	...	...	...	...	...	...	...	...	...	...
6M35D3	D3 debt liabilities at face value	...	...	...	801	818	742	...	...	...	1,001	1,025	955
6M35D2	D2 debt liabilities at face value	...	...	...	716	733	659	...	...	...	850	870	802
6M35D1	D1 debt liabilities at face value	...	...	...	716	733	659	...	...	...	835	854	786
6M93	Government gross debt per national definition	...	...	...	716	733	659	...	...	...	850	870	802
6M5	Arrears	...	...	...	...	...	...	...	...	...	...	...	...
6M6	Explicit contingent liabilities	...	...	...	...	...	...	...	...	...	...	...	...
6M61	of which: Publicly guaranteed debt	...	...	...	...	...	...	...	...	...	...	...	...
6M7	Net implicit obligations for social security benefits	...	...	...	...	...	...	...	...	...	...	...	...
	Table 7 Expenditure by functions of government												
7	**Expenditure**	...	...	...	**807**	**823**	**834**	...	...	...	**1,077**	**1,094**	**1,111**
701	**General public services**	...	...	...	**236**	**235**	**234**	...	...	...	**145**	**145**	**150**
7017	Public debt transactions	...	...	...	32	29	32	...	...	...	34	31	33
7018	Transfers of general character between levels of government	...	...	...	108	113	107	...	...	...	—	—	—
702	**Defense**	...	...	...	**25**	**22**	**23**	...	...	...	**25**	**23**	**23**
703	**Public order and safety**	...	...	...	**18**	**18**	**18**	...	...	...	**20**	**20**	**20**
704	**Economic affairs**	...	...	...	**47**	**51**	**52**	...	...	...	**67**	**72**	**74**
7042	Agriculture, forestry, fishing, and hunting	...	...	...	3	3	4	...	...	...	3	3	4
7043	Fuel and energy	...	...	...	6	8	9	...	...	...	6	8	9
7044	Mining, manufacturing, and construction	...	...	...	0	0	0	...	...	...	0	0	0
7045	Transport	...	...	...	21	23	24	...	...	...	40	43	45
7046	Communication	...	...	...	0	0	0	...	...	...	0	0	0
705	**Environmental protection**	...	...	...	**5**	**5**	**4**	...	...	...	**9**	**9**	**9**
706	**Housing and community amenities**	...	...	...	**3**	**3**	**5**	...	...	...	**5**	**4**	**5**
707	**Health**	...	...	...	**92**	**93**	**98**	...	...	...	**164**	**170**	**174**
7072	Outpatient services	...	...	...	0	0	0	...	...	...	23	23	24
7073	Hospital services	...	...	...	1	3	4	...	...	...	117	121	123
7074	Public health services	...	...	...	3	1	1	...	...	...	3	3	3
708	**Recreation, culture and religion**	...	...	...	**20**	**19**	**20**	...	...	...	**35**	**35**	**36**
709	**Education**	...	...	...	**78**	**84**	**85**	...	...	...	**133**	**141**	**143**
7091	Pre-primary and primary education	...	...	...	10	10	10	...	...	...	61	63	64
7092	Secondary education	...	...	...	34	37	36	...	...	...	35	38	37
7094	Tertiary education	...	...	...	31	33	35	...	...	...	31	33	35
710	**Social protection**	...	...	...	**283**	**293**	**295**	...	...	...	**473**	**475**	**478**
7z	Statistical discrepancy: Expenditure	...	...	...	—	—	-0	...	...	...	—	0	—
	Table 8 Financial transactions by counterpart sector												
32	**Net acquisition of financial assets**	...	...	...	**-18**	**40**	**-115**	...	...	...	**-14**	**50**	**-105**
321	Domestic debtors	...	...	...	...	...	...	...	...	...	...	...	...
8211	General government	...	...	...	...	...	...	...	...	...	—	—	—
8212	Central bank	...	...	...	...	...	...	...	...	...	...	...	...
8213	Deposit-taking corporations except the central bank	...	...	...	...	...	...	...	...	...	...	...	...
8214	Other financial corporations	...	...	...	...	...	...	...	...	...	...	...	...
8215	Nonfinancial corporations	...	...	...	...	...	...	...	...	...	...	...	...
8216	Households & nonprofit institutions serving households	...	...	...	...	...	...	...	...	...	...	...	...
322	External debtors	...	...	...	...	...	...	...	...	...	...	...	...
8221	General government	...	...	...	...	...	...	...	...	...	...	...	...
8227	International organizations	...	...	...	...	...	...	...	...	...	...	...	...
8228	Financial corporations other than international organizations	...	...	...	...	...	...	...	...	...	...	...	...
8229	Other nonresidents	...	...	...	...	...	...	...	...	...	...	...	...

Denmark (128)

In Billions of Danish Kroner (DKK) / Fiscal Year Ends December 31st

		Budgetary Central Government			Central Government (excl. Social Security)			Central Government (incl. Social Security)			General Government		
		2013	2014	2015	2013P	2014P	2015P	2013P	2014P	2015P	2013P	2014P	2015P
33	**Net incurrence of liabilities**	**...**	**...**	**...**	**7**	**15**	**-77**	**...**	**...**	**...**	**7**	**22**	**-71**
331	Domestic creditors	...	...	...	...	...	...	...	...	...	...	...	...
8311	General government	...	...	...	...	...	...	...	...	...	—	—	—
8312	Central bank	...	...	...	...	...	...	...	...	...	...	...	...
8313	Deposit-taking corporations except the central bank	...	...	...	...	...	...	...	...	...	...	...	...
8314	Other financial corporations	...	...	...	...	...	...	...	...	...	...	...	...
8315	Nonfinancial corporations	...	...	...	...	...	...	...	...	...	...	...	...
8316	Households & nonprofit institutions serving households	...	...	...	...	...	...	...	...	...	...	...	...
332	External creditors	...	...	...	...	...	...	...	...	...	...	...	...
8321	General government	...	...	...	...	...	...	...	...	...	...	...	...
8327	International organizations	...	...	...	...	...	...	...	...	...	...	...	...
8328	Financial corporations other than international organizations	...	...	...	...	...	...	...	...	...	...	...	...
8329	Other nonresidents	...	...	...	...	...	...	...	...	...	...	...	...
	Table 9 Total other economic flows in assets and liabilities												
9	**Change in net worth due to other economic flows**	**...**	**...**	**...**	**...**	**...**	**...**	**...**	**...**	**...**	**...**	**...**	**...**
91	**Other economic flows in nonfinancial assets**	**...**	**...**	**...**	**...**	**...**	**...**	**...**	**...**	**...**	**...**	**...**	**...**
911	Fixed assets	...	...	...	...	...	...	...	...	...	...	...	...
912	Inventories	...	...	...	...	...	...	...	...	...	...	...	...
913	Valuables	...	...	...	...	...	...	...	...	...	...	...	...
914	Nonproduced assets	...	...	...	...	...	...	...	...	...	...	...	...
92	**Other economic flows in financial assets**	**...**	**...**	**...**	**4**	**4**	**3**	**...**	**...**	**...**	**7**	**4**	**-4**
	By instrument												
9201	Monetary gold and SDRs	...	...	...	—	—	—	...	...	...	—	—	—
9202	Currency and deposits	...	...	...	—	0	7	...	...	...	0	-0	7
9203	Debt securities	...	...	...	-1	-0	-0	...	...	...	-1	-0	-1
9204	Loans	...	...	...	-0	—	3	...	...	...	-0	-0	3
9205	Equity and investment fund shares	...	...	...	-8	2	-9	...	...	...	-3	7	-10
9206	Insurance, pension, and standardized guarantee schemes	...	...	...	0	0	0	...	...	...	0	0	0
9207	Financial derivatives and employee stock options	...	...	...	-2	3	3	...	...	...	-2	3	3
9208	Other accounts receivable	...	...	...	15	-1	0	...	...	...	13	-5	-7
	By debtor												
921	Domestic debtors	...	...	...	...	...	...	...	...	...	...	...	...
922	External debtors	...	...	...	...	...	...	...	...	...	...	...	...
93	**Other economic flows in liabilities**	**...**	**...**	**...**	**-61**	**51**	**-19**	**...**	**...**	**...**	**-61**	**51**	**-19**
	By instrument												
9301	Special Drawing Rights (SDRs)	...	...	...	—	—	—	...	...	...	—	—	—
9302	Currency and deposits	...	...	...	—	—	—	...	...	...	—	0	-0
9303	Debt securities	...	...	...	-61	51	-17	...	...	...	-61	51	-17
9304	Loans	...	...	...	0	—	-0	...	...	...	-0	-0	0
9305	Equity and investment fund shares	...	...	...	—	—	—	...	...	...	—	—	—
9306	Insurance, pension, and standardized guarantee schemes	...	...	...	—	—	—	...	...	...	—	—	—
9307	Financial derivatives and employee stock options	...	...	...	—	—	—	...	...	...	—	—	—
9308	Other accounts payable	...	...	...	0	—	-3	...	...	...	0	0	-3
	By creditor												
931	Domestic creditors	...	...	...	...	...	...	...	...	...	...	...	...
932	External creditors	...	...	...	...	...	...	...	...	...	...	...	...
	Memorandum items												
9M2	Change in net financial worth due to other economic flows	...	...	...	65	-47	23	...	...	...	69	-46	15

Denmark (128)

In Billions of Danish Kroner (DKK) / Fiscal Year Ends December 31st

		Budgetary Central Government			Central Government (excl. Social Security)			Central Government (incl. Social Security)			General Government		
		2013	2014	2015	2013P	2014P	2015P	2013P	2014P	2015P	2013P	2014P	2015P
9M3	Gross debt (D4) at market value: other economic flows	...	...	...	-61	51	-19	...	...	...	-61	51	-19
9M3D3	D3 debt liabilities at market value: other economic flows	...	...	...	-61	51	-19	...	...	...	-61	51	-19
9M3D2	D2 debt liabilities at market value: other economic flows	...	...	...	-61	51	-17	...	...	...	-62	51	-17
9M3D1	D1 debt liabilities at market value: other economic flows	...	...	...	-61	51	-17	...	...	...	-62	51	-17

Dominica (321)

In Millions of Eastern Caribbean Dollars (XCD) / Fiscal Year Ends December 31st

		Budgetary Central Government			Central Government (excl. Social Security)			Central Government (incl. Social Security)			General Government		
		2012	2013	2014	2012	2013	2014	2012	2013	2014	2012	2013	2014
	Statement of operations												
1	Revenue	361	383	415	...	...	...	...	...	...	...	...	...
2	Expense	316	352	348	...	...	...	...	...	...	...	...	...
GOB	**Gross operating balance**	**44**	**31**	**67**	...	...	...	...	...	...	...	...	...
NOB	**Net operating balance**	...	...	...	...	...	...	...	...	...	...	...	...
31	Net/Gross investment in nonfinancial assets	166	160	121	...	...	...	...	...	...	...	...	...
2M	Expenditure	482	512	469	...	...	...	...	...	...	...	...	...
NLB	**Net lending (+) / Net borrowing (-)**	**-121**	**-129**	**-54**	...	...	...	...	...	...	...	...	...
32	Net acquisition of financial assets	-25	-27	-25	...	...	...	...	...	...	...	...	...
33	Net incurrence of liabilities	97	102	29	...	...	...	...	...	...	...	...	...
NLBz	Statistical discrepancy	-0	-0	0	...	...	...	...	...	...	...	...	...
	Memorandum items												
PB	Primary net lending / net borrowing	-101	-101	-29	...	...	...	...	...	...	...	...	...
GB	Government balance per national definition	...	...	...	...	...	...	...	...	...	...	...	...
	Statement of other economic flows												
	Balance sheet												
	Table 1 Revenue												
1	**Revenue**	**361**	**383**	**415**	...	...	...	...	...	...	...	...	...
11	**Taxes**	**302**	**303**	**312**	...	...	...	...	...	...	...	...	...
111	Taxes on income, profits, and capital gains	57	59	57	...	...	...	...	...	...	...	...	...
1111	Payable by individuals	32	34	33	...	...	...	...	...	...	...	...	...
1112	Payable by corporations and other enterprises	25	24	24	...	...	...	...	...	...	...	...	...
1113	Other taxes on income, profits, and capital gains	—	—	—	...	...	...	...	...	...	...	...	...
112	Taxes on payroll and workforce	—	—	—	...	...	...	...	...	...	...	...	...
113	Taxes on property	6	8	7	...	...	...	...	...	...	...	...	...
114	Taxes on goods and services	178	180	187	...	...	...	...	...	...	...	...	...
1141	General taxes on goods and services	126	124	130	...	...	...	...	...	...	...	...	...
1142	Excises	33	37	38	...	...	...	...	...	...	...	...	...
115	Taxes on international trade and transactions	61	57	62	...	...	...	...	...	...	...	...	...
116	Other taxes	—	—	—	...	...	...	...	...	...	...	...	...
12	**Social contributions**	—	—	—	...	...	...	...	...	...	...	...	...
121	Social security contributions	—	—	—	...	...	...	...	...	...	...	...	...
122	Other social contributions	—	—	—	...	...	...	...	...	...	...	...	...
13	**Grants**	**12**	**0**	**43**	...	...	...	...	...	...	...	...	...
131	From foreign governments	12	0	43	...	...	...	...	...	...	...	...	...
132	From international organizations	—	—	—	...	...	...	...	...	...	...	...	...
133	From other general government units	—	—	—	...	...	...	...	...	...	...	...	...
1331	Current	—	—	—	...	...	...	...	...	...	...	...	...
1332	Capital	—	—	—	...	...	...	...	...	...	...	...	...
14	**Other revenue**	**47**	**80**	**59**	...	...	...	...	...	...	...	...	...
	Table 2 Expense by economic type												
2	**Expense**	**316**	**352**	**348**	...	...	...	...	...	...	...	...	...
21	**Compensation of employees**	**135**	**150**	**144**	...	...	...	...	...	...	...	...	...
211	Wages and salaries	135	150	144	...	...	...	...	...	...	...	...	...
212	Employers' social contributions	—	—	—	...	...	...	...	...	...	...	...	...
22	**Use of goods and services**	**94**	**107**	**108**	...	...	...	...	...	...	...	...	...
23	**Consumption of fixed capital**	...	...	...	...	...	...	...	...	...	...	...	...
24	**Interest**	**20**	**28**	**26**	...	...	...	...	...	...	...	...	...
25	**Subsidies**	**52**	**50**	**52**	...	...	...	...	...	...	...	...	...
26	**Grants**	—	—	—	...	...	...	...	...	...	...	...	...
261	To foreign governments	—	—	—	...	...	...	...	...	...	...	...	...
262	To international organizations	—	—	—	...	...	...	...	...	...	...	...	...
263	To other general government units	—	—	—	...	...	...	...	...	...	...	...	...
2631	Current	—	—	—	...	...	...	...	...	...	...	...	...
2632	Capital	—	—	—	...	...	...	...	...	...	...	...	...

Dominica (321)

In Millions of Eastern Caribbean Dollars (XCD) / Fiscal Year Ends December 31st

		Budgetary Central Government			Central Government (excl. Social Security)			Central Government (incl. Social Security)			General Government		
		2012	2013	2014	2012	2013	2014	2012	2013	2014	2012	2013	2014
27	**Social benefits**	**15**	**17**	**18**	...	...	...	...	...	...	...	...	...
271	Social security benefits	15	17	18	...	...	...	...	...	...	...	...	...
272	Social assistance benefits	—	—	—	...	...	...	...	...	...	...	...	...
273	Employment-related social benefits	—	—	—	...	...	...	...	...	...	...	...	...
28	**Other expense**	**—**	**—**	**—**	...	...	...	...	...	...	...	...	...
281	Property expense other than interest	—	—	—	...	...	...	...	...	...	...	...	...
282	Transfers not elsewhere classified	—	—	—	...	...	...	...	...	...	...	...	...
2821	Current	—	—	—	...	...	...	...	...	...	...	...	...
2822	Capital	—	—	—	...	...	...	...	...	...	...	...	...
	Table 3 Transactions in assets and liabilities												
3	**Change in net worth from transactions**	...	...	...	...	...	...	...	...	...	...	...	...
31	**Net/Gross investment in nonfinancial assets**	**166**	**160**	**121**	...	...	...	...	...	...	...	...	...
311	Fixed assets	168	160	122	...	...	...	...	...	...	...	...	...
3111	Buildings and structures	—	—	—	...	...	...	...	...	...	...	...	...
3112	Machinery and equipment	—	—	—	...	...	...	...	...	...	...	...	...
3113	Other fixed assets	—	—	—	...	...	...	...	...	...	...	...	...
3114	Weapons systems	...	...	...	...	...	...	...	...	...	...	...	...
312	Inventories	—	—	—	...	...	...	...	...	...	...	...	...
313	Valuables	—	—	—	...	...	...	...	...	...	...	...	...
314	Nonproduced assets	-3	-0	-0	...	...	...	...	...	...	...	...	...
3141	Land	-3	-0	-0	...	...	...	...	...	...	...	...	...
3142	Mineral and energy resources	—	—	—	...	...	...	...	...	...	...	...	...
3143	Other naturally occurring assets	—	—	—	...	...	...	...	...	...	...	...	...
3144	Intangible nonproduced assets	—	—	—	...	...	...	...	...	...	...	...	...
32	**Net acquisition of financial assets**	**-25**	**-27**	**-25**	...	...	...	...	...	...	...	...	...
	By instrument												
3201	Monetary gold and SDRs	—	—	—	...	...	...	...	...	...	...	...	...
3202	Currency and deposits	-24	-27	-25	...	...	...	...	...	...	...	...	...
3203	Debt securities	—	—	—	...	...	...	...	...	...	...	...	...
3204	Loans	-1	0	0	...	...	...	...	...	...	...	...	...
3205	Equity and investment fund shares	—	—	—	...	...	...	...	...	...	...	...	...
3206	Insurance, pension, and standardized guarantee schemes	—	—	—	...	...	...	...	...	...	...	...	...
3207	Financial derivatives and employee stock options	—	—	—	...	...	...	...	...	...	...	...	...
3208	Other accounts receivable	...	...	...	...	...	...	...	...	...	...	...	...
	By debtor												
321	Domestic debtors	4	-27	-34	...	...	...	...	...	...	...	...	...
322	External debtors	-29	-0	9	...	...	...	...	...	...	...	...	...
33	**Net incurrence of liabilities**	**97**	**102**	**29**	...	...	...	...	...	...	...	...	...
	By instrument												
3301	Special Drawing Rights (SDRs)	...	...	...	...	...	...	...	...	...	...	...	...
3302	Currency and deposits	—	—	—	...	...	...	...	...	...	...	...	...
3303	Debt securities	—	—	—	...	...	...	...	...	...	...	...	...
3304	Loans	105	96	35	...	...	...	...	...	...	...	...	...
3305	Equity and investment fund shares	—	—	—	...	...	...	...	...	...	...	...	...
3306	Insurance, pension, and standardized guarantee schemes	—	—	—	...	...	...	...	...	...	...	...	...
3307	Financial derivatives and employee stock options	—	—	—	...	...	...	...	...	...	...	...	...
3308	Other accounts payable	-8	6	-6	...	...	...	...	...	...	...	...	...
	By creditor												
331	Domestic creditors	19	66	-1	...	...	...	...	...	...	...	...	...
332	External creditors	78	36	30	...	...	...	...	...	...	...	...	...
	Table 4 Holding gains and losses in assets and liabilities												
	Table 5 Holding gains and losses in assets and liabilities												
	Table 6 Balance sheet												

Dominica (321)

In Millions of Eastern Caribbean Dollars (XCD) / Fiscal Year Ends December 31st

	Budgetary Central Government			Central Government (excl. Social Security)			Central Government (incl. Social Security)			General Government		
	2012	2013	2014	2012	2013	2014	2012	2013	2014	2012	2013	2014
Table 7 Expenditure by functions of government												
Table 8 Financial transactions by counterpart sector												
Table 9 Total other economic flows in assets and liabilities												

Dominican Republic (243)

In Billions of Dominican Pesos (DOP) / Fiscal Year Ends December 31st

		Budgetary Central Government			Central Government (excl. Social Security)			Central Government (incl. Social Security)			General Government		
		2013	2014P	2015P	2013	2014P	2015P	2013	2014P	2015P	2013	2014	2015
	Statement of operations												
1	Revenue	372	419	538	391	431	553	399	443	566	...	...	...
2	Expense	382	440	468	398	451	479	405	458	487	...	...	...
GOB	**Gross operating balance**	**-8**	**-20**	**72**	**-7**	**-19**	**76**	**-6**	**-14**	**81**	...	...	...
NOB	**Net operating balance**	**-9**	**-20**	**70**	...	**-20**	**74**	...	**-14**	**79**	...	...	...
31	Net/Gross investment in nonfinancial assets	69	58	66	75	61	70	75	62	71	...	...	...
2M	Expenditure	450	498	535	473	512	550	480	519	558	...	...	...
NLB	**Net lending (+) / Net borrowing (-)**	**-78**	**-79**	**3**	**-82**	**-81**	**4**	**-82**	**-76**	**8**	...	...	...
32	Net acquisition of financial assets	13	-7	-2	14	-7	-2	14	-1	1	...	...	...
33	Net incurrence of liabilities	93	70	-3	98	73	-3	99	73	-3	...	...	...
NLBz	Statistical discrepancy	-2	1	-2	-2	1	-2	-3	1	-4	...	...	...
	Memorandum items												
PB	Primary net lending / net borrowing	-19	-9	83	-23	-11	84	-22	-6	88	...	...	...
GB	Government balance per national definition	...	...	...	...	...	...	...	...	...	...	...	...
	Statement of other economic flows												
	Balance sheet												
	Table 1 Revenue												
1	**Revenue**	**372**	**419**	**538**	**391**	**431**	**553**	**399**	**443**	**566**	...	...	...
11	**Taxes**	**354**	**392**	**410**	**354**	**392**	**411**	**354**	**392**	**411**	...	...	...
111	Taxes on income, profits, and capital gains	108	125	119	108	125	119	108	125	119	...	...	...
1111	Payable by individuals	23	27	36	23	27	36	23	27	36	...	...	...
1112	Payable by corporations and other enterprises	51	73	62	51	73	62	51	73	62	...	...	...
1113	Other taxes on income, profits, and capital gains	35	25	22	35	25	22	35	25	22	...	...	...
112	Taxes on payroll and workforce	—	—	—	—	—	—	—	—	—	...	...	...
113	Taxes on property	3	6	18	3	6	18	3	6	18	...	...	...
114	Taxes on goods and services	219	234	241	219	234	242	219	234	242	...	...	...
1141	General taxes on goods and services	133	143	147	133	143	147	133	143	147	...	...	...
1142	Excises	67	82	73	67	82	73	67	82	73	...	...	...
115	Taxes on international trade and transactions	24	27	31	24	27	31	24	27	31	...	...	...
116	Other taxes	0	0	1	0	0	1	0	0	1	...	...	...
12	**Social contributions**	**2**	**2**	**1**	**2**	**2**	**1**	**6**	**9**	**12**	...	...	...
121	Social security contributions	2	2	1	2	2	1	2	2	12	...	...	...
122	Other social contributions	—	—	—	—	—	—	4	7	—	...	...	...
13	**Grants**	**3**	**5**	**3**	**10**	**3**	**3**	**5**	**3**	**3**	...	...	...
131	From foreign governments	0	—	0	0	—	0	0	—	0	...	...	...
132	From international organizations	3	2	2	3	2	3	3	2	3	...	...	...
133	From other general government units	—	3	—	7	1	0	2	1	0	...	...	...
1331	Current	—	—	—	5	-3	0	-0	-3	0	...	...	...
1332	Capital	—	3	—	2	4	0	2	4	0	...	...	...
14	**Other revenue**	**14**	**21**	**124**	**26**	**35**	**138**	**34**	**40**	**141**	...	...	...
	Table 2 Expense by economic type												
2	**Expense**	**382**	**440**	**468**	**398**	**451**	**479**	**405**	**458**	**487**	...	...	...
21	**Compensation of employees**	**105**	**127**	**153**	**149**	**163**	**183**	**154**	**168**	**188**	...	...	...
211	Wages and salaries	96	115	138	135	149	166	139	154	171	...	...	...
212	Employers' social contributions	10	12	15	15	14	17	15	14	17	...	...	...
22	**Use of goods and services**	**39**	**44**	**49**	**55**	**66**	**72**	**66**	**78**	**86**	...	...	...
23	**Consumption of fixed capital**	**2**	**1**	**2**	...	**1**	**2**	...	**1**	**2**	...	...	...
24	**Interest**	**59**	**70**	**80**	**59**	**70**	**80**	**59**	**70**	**80**	...	...	...
25	**Subsidies**	**47**	**53**	**33**	**47**	**53**	**33**	**47**	**54**	**33**	...	...	...
26	**Grants**	**81**	**84**	**74**	**34**	**35**	**31**	**24**	**23**	**19**	...	...	...
261	To foreign governments	—	—	0	0	0	0	0	0	0	...	...	...
262	To international organizations	0	0	—	0	0	0	0	0	0	...	...	...
263	To other general government units	81	83	74	34	34	31	24	23	19	...	...	...
2631	Current	68	73	64	21	26	23	11	15	11	...	...	...
2632	Capital	13	11	10	13	8	7	13	8	7	...	...	...

Dominican Republic (243)

In Billions of Dominican Pesos (DOP) / Fiscal Year Ends December 31st

		Budgetary Central Government			Central Government (excl. Social Security)			Central Government (incl. Social Security)			General Government		
		2013	2014P	2015P	2013	2014P	2015P	2013	2014P	2015P	2013	2014	2015
27	**Social benefits**	**33**	**40**	**27**	**35**	**42**	**28**	**36**	**42**	**29**	**...**	**...**	**...**
271	Social security benefits	22	25	27	22	27	28	22	27	28	...	...	...
272	Social assistance benefits	11	15	—	13	15	1	13	15	1	...	...	...
273	Employment-related social benefits	0	0	—	0	0	—	0	0	—	...	0	...
28	**Other expense**	**15**	**21**	**50**	**16**	**22**	**51**	**16**	**22**	**51**	**...**	**...**	**...**
281	Property expense other than interest	—	—	—	—	—	—	—	—	—	...	...	...
282	Transfers not elsewhere classified	15	21	50	16	22	51	16	22	51	...	...	...
2821	Current	6	5	23	7	6	24	7	6	24	...	...	...
2822	Capital	9	16	26	9	16	26	9	16	26	...	...	...
	Table 3 Transactions in assets and liabilities												
3	**Change in net worth from transactions**	**-11**	**-20**	**68**	**...**	**-19**	**72**	**...**	**-13**	**75**	**...**	**...**	**...**
31	**Net/Gross investment in nonfinancial assets**	**69**	**58**	**66**	**75**	**61**	**70**	**75**	**62**	**71**	**...**	**...**	**...**
311	Fixed assets	66	56	64	73	59	69	73	59	69	...	...	...
3111	Buildings and structures	56	30	57	60	33	59	60	33	59	...	...	...
3112	Machinery and equipment	9	26	7	11	26	8	11	26	8	...	...	...
3113	Other fixed assets	1	0	1	1	0	1	1	0	1	...	...	...
3114	Weapons systems	...	—	—	...	—	—	...	—	—	...	...	...
312	Inventories	—	—	—	—	—	—	—	—	—	...	...	...
313	Valuables	0	0	0	0	0	0	0	0	0	...	...	...
314	Nonproduced assets	3	2	2	3	2	2	3	2	2	...	...	...
3141	Land	3	2	2	3	2	2	3	2	2	...	...	...
3142	Mineral and energy resources	—	—	—	—	—	—	—	—	—	...	...	...
3143	Other naturally occurring assets	—	—	—	—	—	—	—	—	—	...	...	...
3144	Intangible nonproduced assets	—	—	0	—	—	0	—	—	0	...	...	...
32	**Net acquisition of financial assets**	**13**	**-7**	**-2**	**14**	**-7**	**-2**	**14**	**-1**	**1**	**...**	**...**	**...**
	By instrument												
3201	Monetary gold and SDRs	—	—	—	—	—	—	—	—	—	...	...	...
3202	Currency and deposits	9	-6	-4	9	-6	-4	9	-4	-5	...	...	...
3203	Debt securities	—	—	—	—	—	—	0	4	3	...	...	...
3204	Loans	0	0	—	1	0	-0	1	0	0	...	...	...
3205	Equity and investment fund shares	2	2	2	2	2	2	2	2	2	...	...	...
3206	Insurance, pension, and standardized guarantee schemes	—	—	—	—	—	—	—	—	—	...	...	...
3207	Financial derivatives and employee stock options	—	—	—	0	0	—	0	0	—	...	...	...
3208	Other accounts receivable	2	-4	-0	...	-4	-0	...	-4	-0	...	...	...
	By debtor												
321	Domestic debtors	13	-8	-2	14	-7	-2	14	-1	1	...	...	...
322	External debtors	0	0	0	0	0	0	0	0	0	...	...	...
33	**Net incurrence of liabilities**	**93**	**70**	**-3**	**98**	**73**	**-3**	**99**	**73**	**-3**	**...**	**...**	**...**
	By instrument												
3301	Special Drawing Rights (SDRs)	—	—	—	—	—	—	—	—	—	...	...	...
3302	Currency and deposits	—	0	3	—	0	3	—	0	3	...	...	...
3303	Debt securities	84	93	189	84	93	189	84	93	189	...	...	...
3304	Loans	56	-45	-147	56	-45	-147	57	-45	-147	...	...	...
3305	Equity and investment fund shares	—	—	—	—	—	—	—	—	—	...	...	...
3306	Insurance, pension, and standardized guarantee schemes	—	—	—	—	—	—	—	—	—	...	...	...
3307	Financial derivatives and employee stock options	—	—	—	—	—	—	—	—	—	...	...	...
3308	Other accounts payable	-47	22	-48	-42	25	-48	-42	25	-48	...	...	...
	By creditor												
331	Domestic creditors	8	16	-5	13	18	-5	13	19	-5	...	...	...
332	External creditors	85	55	2	85	55	2	85	55	2	...	...	...
	Table 4 Holding gains and losses in assets and liabilities												
	Table 5 Holding gains and losses in assets and liabilities												
	Table 6 Balance sheet												

Dominican Republic (243)

In Billions of Dominican Pesos (DOP) / Fiscal Year Ends December 31st

	Budgetary Central Government			Central Government (excl. Social Security)			Central Government (incl. Social Security)			General Government		
	2013	2014P	2015P	2013	2014P	2015P	2013	2014P	2015P	2013	2014	2015
Table 7 Expenditure by functions of government												
Table 8 Financial transactions by counterpart sector												
Table 9 Total other economic flows in assets and liabilities												

Egypt (469)

In Billions of Egyptian Pounds (EGP) / Fiscal Year Ends June 30th

		Budgetary Central Government			Central Government (excl. Social Security)			Central Government (incl. Social Security)			General Government		
		2013	2014	2015P	2013	2014	2015	2013	2014	2015P	2013	2014	2015P
	Statement of operations												
1	Revenue	350	457	465	...	...	...	404	519	538	404	519	538
2	Expense	548	649	672	...	...	...	599	...	...	600	702	739
GOB	**Gross operating balance**	**-198**	**-192**	**-206**	**...**	**...**	**...**	**-195**	**...**	**...**	**-196**	**-182**	**-200**
NOB	**Net operating balance**	**...**	**...**	**...**	**...**	**...**	**...**	**...**	**...**	**...**	**...**	**...**	**...**
31	Net/Gross investment in nonfinancial assets	40	53	62	...	...	...	...	...	...	40	53	62
2M	Expenditure	588	702	733	...	...	...	...	...	...	639	755	801
NLB	**Net lending (+) / Net borrowing (-)**	**-237**	**-245**	**-268**	**...**	**...**	**...**	**...**	**...**	**...**	**-235**	**-235**	**-262**
32	Net acquisition of financial assets	...	...	...	...	...	...	...	...	...	...	...	...
33	Net incurrence of liabilities	...	...	...	...	...	...	...	...	...	...	...	...
NLBz	Statistical discrepancy	...	...	...	...	...	...	...	...	...	...	...	...
	Memorandum items												
PB	Primary net lending / net borrowing	-91	-72	-75	...	...	...	...	...	...	-100	-76	-83
GB	Government balance per national definition	...	...	...	...	...	...	...	...	...	...	...	...
	Statement of other economic flows												
	Balance sheet												
	Table 1 Revenue												
1	**Revenue**	**350**	**457**	**465**	**...**	**...**	**...**	**404**	**519**	**538**	**404**	**519**	**538**
11	**Taxes**	**251**	**260**	**306**	**...**	**...**	**...**	**251**	**260**	**306**	**251**	**260**	**306**
111	Taxes on income, profits, and capital gains	118	121	130	...	...	...	118	121	130	118	121	130
1111	Payable by individuals	26	31	38	...	...	...	26	31	38	26	31	38
1112	Payable by corporations and other enterprises	92	90	92	...	...	...	92	90	92	92	90	92
1113	Other taxes on income, profits, and capital gains	—	—	—	...	...	...	—	—	—	—	—	—
112	Taxes on payroll and workforce	—	—	—	...	...	...	—	—	—	—	—	—
113	Taxes on property	1	4	3	...	...	...	1	4	3	1	4	3
114	Taxes on goods and services	107	107	141	...	...	...	107	107	141	107	107	141
1141	General taxes on goods and services	63	68	83	...	...	...	63	68	83	63	68	83
1142	Excises	31	25	40	...	...	...	31	25	40	31	25	40
115	Taxes on international trade and transactions	17	18	22	...	...	...	17	18	22	17	18	22
116	Other taxes	9	11	10	...	...	...	9	11	10	9	11	10
12	**Social contributions**	—	—	—	**...**	**...**	**...**	—	—	—	—	—	—
121	Social security contributions	—	—	—	...	...	...	—	—	—	—	—	—
122	Other social contributions	—	—	—	...	...	...	—	—	—	—	—	—
13	**Grants**	**5**	**96**	**25**	**...**	**...**	**...**	**5**	**96**	**25**	**5**	**96**	**25**
131	From foreign governments	5	95	25	...	...	...	5	95	25	5	95	25
132	From international organizations	0	0	1	...	...	...	0	0	0	0	0	0
133	From other general government units	—	—	—	...	...	...	0	0	0	0	0	0
1331	Current	—	—	—	...	...	...	—	—	—	—	—	—
1332	Capital	—	—	—	...	...	...	—	—	—	—	—	—
14	**Other revenue**	**94**	**101**	**134**	**...**	**...**	**...**	**147**	**163**	**207**	**147**	**163**	**207**
	Table 2 Expense by economic type												
2	**Expense**	**548**	**649**	**672**	**...**	**...**	**...**	**599**	**...**	**...**	**600**	**702**	**739**
21	**Compensation of employees**	**143**	**164**	**181**	**...**	**...**	**...**	**145**	**181**	**...**	**145**	**181**	**201**
211	Wages and salaries	129	147	162	...	...	...	131	164	...	131	164	182
212	Employers' social contributions	14	17	19	...	...	...	14	17	...	14	17	19
22	**Use of goods and services**	**27**	**27**	**31**	**...**	**...**	**...**	**27**	**28**	**...**	**27**	**28**	**32**
23	**Consumption of fixed capital**	**...**	**...**	**...**	**...**	**...**	**...**	**...**	**...**	**...**	**...**	**...**	**...**
24	**Interest**	**147**	**173**	**193**	**...**	**...**	**...**	**135**	**159**	**...**	**135**	**159**	**179**
25	**Subsidies**	**171**	**188**	**150**	**...**	**...**	**...**	**171**	**188**	**...**	**171**	**188**	**150**
26	**Grants**	**5**	**5**	**6**	**...**	**...**	**...**	**0**	**0**	**...**	**0**	**0**	**0**
261	To foreign governments	0	0	0	...	...	...	0	0	...	0	0	0
262	To international organizations	0	—	—	...	...	...	0	0	...	0	0	0
263	To other general government units	5	5	6	...	...	...	—	—	...	—	—	—
2631	Current	5	5	6	...	...	...	—	—	...	—	—	—
2632	Capital	—	—	—	...	...	...	—	—	...	—	—	—

Egypt (469)

In Billions of Egyptian Pounds (EGP) / Fiscal Year Ends June 30th

		Budgetary Central Government			Central Government (excl. Social Security)			Central Government (incl. Social Security)			General Government		
		2013	2014	2015P	2013	2014	2015	2013	2014	2015P	2013	2014	2015P
27	**Social benefits**	**21**	**35**	**41**	**...**	**...**	**...**	**85**	**105**	**...**	**85**	**105**	**125**
271	Social security benefits	4	5	7	...	...	...	...	...	...	...	...	...
272	Social assistance benefits	16	29	33	...	...	...	...	...	...	...	...	...
273	Employment-related social benefits	1	1	1	...	...	...	...	...	...	...	...	...
28	**Other expense**	**35**	**41**	**50**	**...**	**...**	**...**	**35**	**41**	**...**	**36**	**42**	**52**
281	Property expense other than interest	—	—	—	...	...	...	—	—	...	—	—	—
282	Transfers not elsewhere classified	35	41	50	...	...	...	35	41	...	36	42	52
2821	Current	4	6	5	...	...	...	35	41	...	35	41	50
2822	Capital	31	35	45	...	...	...	...	...	...	1	1	1
	Table 3 Transactions in assets and liabilities												
3	**Change in net worth from transactions**	**...**	**...**	**...**	**...**	**...**	**...**	**...**	**...**	**...**	**...**	**...**	**...**
31	**Net/Gross investment in nonfinancial assets**	**40**	**53**	**62**	**...**	**...**	**...**	**...**	**...**	**...**	**40**	**53**	**62**
311	Fixed assets	32	38	46	...	...	...	...	...	...	32	38	46
3111	Buildings and structures	...	...	...	...	...	...	...	...	...	...	...	...
3112	Machinery and equipment	...	...	...	...	...	...	...	...	...	...	...	...
3113	Other fixed assets	...	...	...	...	...	...	...	...	...	...	...	...
3114	Weapons systems	...	...	...	...	...	...	...	...	...	...	...	...
312	Inventories	—	—	—	...	...	...	...	...	...	—	—	—
313	Valuables	—	—	—	...	...	...	...	...	...	—	—	—
314	Nonproduced assets	7	14	13	...	...	...	...	...	...	8	14	16
3141	Land	...	...	...	...	...	...	...	...	...	8	14	16
3142	Mineral and energy resources	...	...	...	...	...	...	...	...	...	—	—	—
3143	Other naturally occurring assets	...	...	...	...	...	...	...	...	...	—	—	—
3144	Intangible nonproduced assets	...	...	...	...	...	...	...	...	...	—	—	—
32	**Net acquisition of financial assets**	**...**	**...**	**...**	**...**	**...**	**...**	**...**	**...**	**...**	**...**	**...**	**...**
	By instrument												
3201	Monetary gold and SDRs	...	...	...	...	...	...	...	...	...	...	...	...
3202	Currency and deposits	...	...	...	...	...	...	...	...	...	...	...	...
3203	Debt securities	...	...	...	...	...	...	...	...	...	...	...	...
3204	Loans	...	...	...	...	...	...	...	...	...	...	...	...
3205	Equity and investment fund shares	...	...	...	...	...	...	...	...	...	...	...	...
3206	Insurance, pension, and standardized guarantee schemes	...	...	...	...	...	...	...	...	...	...	...	...
3207	Financial derivatives and employee stock options	...	...	...	...	...	...	...	...	...	...	...	...
3208	Other accounts receivable	...	...	...	...	...	...	...	...	...	...	...	...
	By debtor												
321	Domestic debtors	...	...	...	...	...	...	...	...	...	...	...	...
322	External debtors	...	...	...	...	...	...	...	...	...	...	...	...
33	**Net incurrence of liabilities**	**...**	**...**	**...**	**...**	**...**	**...**	**...**	**...**	**...**	**...**	**...**	**...**
	By instrument												
3301	Special Drawing Rights (SDRs)	...	...	...	...	...	...	...	...	...	...	...	...
3302	Currency and deposits	...	...	...	...	...	...	...	...	...	...	...	...
3303	Debt securities	...	...	...	...	...	...	...	...	...	...	...	...
3304	Loans	...	...	...	...	...	...	...	...	...	...	...	...
3305	Equity and investment fund shares	...	...	...	...	...	...	...	...	...	...	...	...
3306	Insurance, pension, and standardized guarantee schemes	...	...	...	...	...	...	...	...	...	...	...	...
3307	Financial derivatives and employee stock options	...	...	...	...	...	...	...	...	...	...	...	...
3308	Other accounts payable	...	...	...	...	...	...	...	...	...	...	...	...
	By creditor												
331	Domestic creditors	...	...	...	...	...	...	...	...	...	...	...	...
332	External creditors	...	...	...	...	...	...	...	...	...	...	...	...
	Table 4 Holding gains and losses in assets and liabilities												
	Table 5 Holding gains and losses in assets and liabilities												
	Table 6 Balance sheet												

Egypt (469)

In Billions of Egyptian Pounds (EGP) / Fiscal Year Ends June 30th

		Budgetary Central Government			Central Government (excl. Social Security)			Central Government (incl. Social Security)			General Government		
		2013	2014	2015P	2013	2014	2015	2013	2014	2015P	2013	2014	2015P
	Table 7 Expenditure by functions of government												
7	**Expenditure**	**588**	**686**	**715**	...	...	...	...	...	...	**639**	**755**	**801**
701	**General public services**	**170**	**199**	**207**	...	...	...	...	...	...	**185**	**219**	**232**
7017	Public debt transactions	147	173	193	...	...	...	...	...	...	135	159	179
7018	Transfers of general character between levels of government	...	...	...	...	...	...	...	...	...	—	—	—
702	**Defense**	**29**	**34**	**36**	...	...	...	...	...	...	**38**	**45**	**48**
703	**Public order and safety**	**35**	**41**	**43**	...	...	...	...	...	...	**38**	**45**	**48**
704	**Economic affairs**	**41**	**48**	**50**	...	...	...	...	...	...	**38**	**45**	**48**
7042	Agriculture, forestry, fishing, and hunting	...	...	...	...	...	...	...	...	...	...	...	...
7043	Fuel and energy	...	...	...	...	...	...	...	...	...	...	...	...
7044	Mining, manufacturing, and construction	...	...	...	...	...	...	...	...	...	...	...	...
7045	Transport	...	...	...	...	...	...	...	...	...	...	...	...
7046	Communication	...	...	...	...	...	...	...	...	...	...	...	...
705	**Environmental protection**	**2**	**2**	**2**	...	...	...	...	...	...	**2**	**2**	**2**
706	**Housing and community amenities**	**18**	**21**	**21**	...	...	...	...	...	...	**19**	**23**	**24**
707	**Health**	**41**	**48**	**50**	...	...	...	...	...	...	**32**	**38**	**40**
7072	Outpatient services	...	...	...	...	...	...	...	...	...	...	...	...
7073	Hospital services	...	...	...	...	...	...	...	...	...	...	...	...
7074	Public health services	...	...	...	...	...	...	...	...	...	...	...	...
708	**Recreation, culture and religion**	**23**	**27**	**29**	...	...	...	...	...	...	**26**	**30**	**32**
709	**Education**	**70**	**82**	**86**	...	...	...	...	...	...	**77**	**91**	**96**
7091	Pre-primary and primary education	...	...	...	...	...	...	...	...	...	...	...	...
7092	Secondary education	...	...	...	...	...	...	...	...	...	...	...	...
7094	Tertiary education	...	...	...	...	...	...	...	...	...	...	...	...
710	**Social protection**	**156**	**183**	**191**	...	...	...	...	...	...	**185**	**219**	**232**
7z	Statistical discrepancy: Expenditure	...	...	...	...	...	...	...	...	...	...	...	...
	Table 8 Financial transactions by counterpart sector												
	Table 9 Total other economic flows in assets and liabilities												

El Salvador (253)

In Millions of U.S. Dollars (USD) / Fiscal Year Ends December 31st

		Budgetary Central Government			Central Government (excl. Social Security)			Central Government (incl. Social Security)			General Government		
		2013	2014	2015	2013	2014	2015	2013	2014	2015	2013	2014	2015
	Statement of operations												
1	Revenue	3,938	3,958	4,096	4,522	4,090	4,269	5,095	5,165	5,403	5,673	5,108	5,245
2	Expense	3,978	4,054	4,162	4,479	4,078	4,271	5,057	5,144	5,335	5,462	4,836	4,978
GOB	**Gross operating balance**	**55**	**-96**	**-27**	**159**	**12**	**50**	**166**	**20**	**120**	**345**	**272**	**334**
NOB	**Net operating balance**	**-40**	**-96**	**-67**	**43**	**12**	**-2**	**38**	**20**	**68**	**212**	**272**	**267**
31	Net/Gross investment in nonfinancial assets	206	284	183	381	422	294	372	538	374	594	906	583
2M	Expenditure	4,184	4,337	4,345	4,860	4,500	4,565	5,429	5,682	5,709	6,056	5,742	5,561
NLB	**Net lending (+) / Net borrowing (-)**	**-246**	**-380**	**-249**	**-338**	**-410**	**-296**	**-334**	**-517**	**-306**	**-382**	**-634**	**-316**
32	Net acquisition of financial assets	-908	102	-317	-873	161	-491	-919	143	-554	-918	198	-543
33	Net incurrence of liabilities	-665	5	-68	-592	52	-195	-642	37	-248	-621	129	-227
NLBz	Statistical discrepancy	2	476	-0	56	518	0	57	622	0	85	703	0
	Memorandum items												
PB	Primary net lending / net borrowing	277	205	305	199	188	272	204	80	262	183	3	292
GB	Government balance per national definition	...	...	...	...	...	...	...	...	...	...	...	...
	Statement of other economic flows												
9	**Change in net worth due to other economic flows**	**21**	**-428**	**-164**	**-118**	**-469**	**-198**	**-119**	**-591**	**-317**	**-245**	**-838**	**-509**
4	Change in net worth due to holding gains and losses	**-5**	**-652**	**12**	**7**	**-346**	**12**	**7**	**-348**	**-23**	**29**	**-342**	**-15**
41	Nonfinancial assets	1	3	12	13	5	12	13	3	-23	35	9	-15
42	Financial assets	—	—	—	—	—	—	—	—	—	—	—	—
43	Liabilities	6	655	—	6	351	—	6	351	—	6	351	—
5	Change in net worth due to volume changes	**26**	**224**	**-176**	**-125**	**-123**	**-210**	**-126**	**-244**	**-294**	**-274**	**-496**	**-493**
51	Nonfinancial assets	-521	-339	-258	-617	-459	-431	-620	-574	-518	-810	-839	-715
52	Financial assets	-540	-469	-274	-749	-1,037	-839	-696	-1,032	-768	-638	-1,016	-759
53	Liabilities	-1,086	-1,031	-356	-1,241	-1,373	-1,060	-1,191	-1,362	-992	-1,174	-1,359	-981
	Balance sheet												
6	**Net worth**	**-9,204**	**-9,573**	**-9,864**	**-5,736**	**-8,017**	**-9,064**	**-5,165**	**-7,433**	**-8,482**	**-4,097**	**-6,329**	**-7,419**
61	Nonfinancial assets	1,235	1,163	1,209	4,106	2,378	1,829	4,457	2,729	2,186	5,424	3,771	3,215
62	Financial assets	1,216	1,212	1,242	3,760	974	993	4,100	1,324	1,351	4,601	1,918	1,923
63	Liabilities	11,655	11,948	12,315	13,602	11,369	11,886	13,722	11,486	12,019	14,123	12,018	12,557
	Table 1 Revenue												
1	**Revenue**	**3,938**	**3,958**	**4,096**	**4,522**	**4,090**	**4,269**	**5,095**	**5,165**	**5,403**	**5,673**	**5,108**	**5,245**
11	**Taxes**	**3,751**	**3,775**	**3,927**	**3,751**	**3,775**	**3,927**	**3,751**	**3,775**	**3,927**	**3,832**	**3,871**	**4,007**
111	Taxes on income, profits, and capital gains	1,317	1,339	1,384	1,317	1,339	1,384	1,317	1,339	1,384	1,317	1,339	1,384
1111	Payable by individuals	388	442	199	388	442	199	388	442	199	388	442	199
1112	Payable by corporations and other enterprises	793	693	704	793	693	704	793	693	704	793	693	704
1113	Other taxes on income, profits, and capital gains	135	204	481	135	204	481	135	204	481	135	204	481
112	Taxes on payroll and workforce	—	—	—	—	—	—	—	—	—	—	—	—
113	Taxes on property	21	24	20	21	24	20	21	24	20	98	115	96
114	Taxes on goods and services	2,180	2,210	2,327	2,180	2,210	2,327	2,180	2,210	2,327	2,184	2,215	2,332
1141	General taxes on goods and services	1,897	1,907	1,933	1,897	1,907	1,933	1,897	1,907	1,933	1,897	1,907	1,933
1142	Excises	271	271	295	271	271	295	271	271	295	276	276	300
115	Taxes on international trade and transactions	232	202	194	232	202	194	232	202	194	232	202	194
116	Other taxes	1	—	1	1	—	1	1	—	1	1	—	1
12	**Social contributions**	—	—	—	**13**	**11**	**17**	**561**	**582**	**625**	**561**	**582**	**625**
121	Social security contributions	—	—	—	13	11	17	561	582	625	561	582	625
122	Other social contributions	—	—	—	—	—	—	—	—	—	—	—	—
13	**Grants**	**47**	**47**	**33**	**453**	**42**	**35**	**453**	**512**	**525**	**757**	**44**	**35**
131	From foreign governments	24	25	13	28	27	16	28	27	16	29	29	16
132	From international organizations	22	15	18	23	15	19	23	15	19	25	16	19
133	From other general government units	1	8	2	403	—	—	403	470	490	702	-0	-0
1331	Current	1	3	2	395	—	—	395	133	490	465	-0	-0
1332	Capital	0	5	—	8	—	—	8	337	—	237	0	0
14	**Other revenue**	**141**	**135**	**136**	**306**	**262**	**291**	**331**	**295**	**327**	**524**	**611**	**578**

El Salvador (253)

In Millions of U.S. Dollars (USD) / Fiscal Year Ends December 31st

		Budgetary Central Government			Central Government (excl. Social Security)			Central Government (incl. Social Security)			General Government		
		2013	2014	2015	2013	2014	2015	2013	2014	2015	2013	2014	2015
	Table 2 Expense by economic type												
2	**Expense**	**3,978**	**4,054**	**4,162**	**4,479**	**4,078**	**4,271**	**5,057**	**5,144**	**5,335**	**5,462**	**4,836**	**4,978**
21	**Compensation of employees**	**1,507**	**1,580**	**1,680**	**1,896**	**1,959**	**2,081**	**2,122**	**2,200**	**2,335**	**2,289**	**2,394**	**2,511**
211	Wages and salaries	1,352	1,416	1,509	1,705	1,774	1,884	1,908	1,990	2,111	2,059	2,167	2,271
212	Employers' social contributions	155	164	170	191	185	197	215	210	223	231	228	240
22	**Use of goods and services**	**459**	**513**	**481**	**643**	**695**	**681**	**850**	**912**	**854**	**999**	**1,046**	**968**
23	**Consumption of fixed capital**	**94**	—	**40**	**116**	—	**52**	**128**	—	**52**	**133**	—	**67**
24	**Interest**	**523**	**585**	**555**	**537**	**598**	**568**	**537**	**598**	**568**	**565**	**637**	**608**
25	**Subsidies**	**184**	**77**	**102**	**184**	**77**	**102**	**184**	**77**	**102**	**184**	**77**	**102**
26	**Grants**	**850**	**1,299**	**1,306**	**426**	**750**	**788**	**-17**	**750**	**788**	**-1**	**8**	**6**
261	To foreign governments	—	—	—	—	—	—	—	—	—	—	—	—
262	To international organizations	7	7	5	7	8	6	7	8	6	7	8	6
263	To other general government units	843	1,292	1,300	419	743	782	-24	743	782	-8	0	-0
2631	Current	674	745	742	385	201	566	-59	201	566	-43	-0	0
2632	Capital	169	548	558	35	541	216	35	541	216	35	0	-0
27	**Social benefits**	**0**	—	—	**0**	—	—	**574**	**599**	**629**	**574**	**599**	**629**
271	Social security benefits	0	—	—	0	—	—	574	—	—	574	—	—
272	Social assistance benefits	—	—	—	—	—	—	—	599	629	—	599	629
273	Employment-related social benefits	—	—	—	—	—	—	—	—	—	—	—	—
28	**Other expense**	**361**	—	—	**676**	—	—	**678**	**10**	**8**	**718**	**77**	**87**
281	Property expense other than interest	—	—	—	—	—	—	—	—	—	—	—	—
282	Transfers not elsewhere classified	361	—	—	676	—	—	678	10	8	718	77	87
2821	Current	-7	—	—	242	—	—	244	10	8	277	72	82
2822	Capital	368	—	—	434	—	—	434	—	—	441	5	4
	Table 3 Transactions in assets and liabilities												
3	**Change in net worth from transactions**	**-38**	**380**	**-67**	**100**	**531**	**-2**	**94**	**643**	**68**	**297**	**975**	**267**
31	**Net/Gross investment in nonfinancial assets**	**206**	**284**	**183**	**381**	**422**	**294**	**372**	**538**	**374**	**594**	**906**	**583**
311	Fixed assets	147	204	164	260	288	274	249	300	300	465	607	503
3111	Buildings and structures	94	49	13	80	65	12	73	66	19	70	98	29
3112	Machinery and equipment	-3	53	37	-2	67	39	-1	77	57	3	90	63
3113	Other fixed assets	56	102	114	181	156	223	176	157	224	393	419	411
3114	Weapons systems	...	...	...	...	...	...	...	...	...	...	...	...
312	Inventories	58	80	24	120	134	24	120	238	78	124	295	78
313	Valuables	0	0	0	0	0	0	0	0	0	0	0	0
314	Nonproduced assets	1	0	-5	1	0	-5	2	0	-5	4	4	2
3141	Land	1	0	-5	1	0	-5	2	0	-5	4	4	2
3142	Mineral and energy resources	—	—	—	—	—	—	—	—	—	—	—	—
3143	Other naturally occurring assets	—	—	—	—	—	—	—	—	—	—	—	—
3144	Intangible nonproduced assets	—	—	—	—	—	—	—	—	—	—	—	—
32	**Net acquisition of financial assets**	**-908**	**102**	**-317**	**-873**	**161**	**-491**	**-919**	**143**	**-554**	**-918**	**198**	**-543**
	By instrument												
3201	Monetary gold and SDRs	—	—	—	—	—	—	—	—	—	—	—	—
3202	Currency and deposits	-759	-38	-95	-605	-51	-97	-558	-51	-103	-544	-53	-107
3203	Debt securities	—	—	—	5	127	43	-3	177	114	-3	176	110
3204	Loans	-7	-3	-1	-9	-5	3	-6	-8	-16	-6	-8	-16
3205	Equity and investment fund shares	4	4	2	4	4	2	4	4	2	4	4	2
3206	Insurance, pension, and standardized guarantee schemes	—	—	—	—	—	—	—	—	—	—	—	—
3207	Financial derivatives and employee stock options	—	—	—	—	—	—	—	—	—	—	—	—
3208	Other accounts receivable	-146	139	-223	-267	86	-442	-357	20	-551	-368	79	-533
	By debtor												
321	Domestic debtors	-909	139	-303	-873	152	-540	-909	142	-595	-910	195	-587
322	External debtors	0	-37	-14	-0	9	49	-10	1	41	-8	3	44
33	**Net incurrence of liabilities**	**-665**	**5**	**-68**	**-592**	**52**	**-195**	**-642**	**37**	**-248**	**-621**	**129**	**-227**
	By instrument												
3301	Special Drawing Rights (SDRs)	—	—	—	—	—	—	—	—	—	—	—	—
3302	Currency and deposits	—	—	—	—	—	—	—	—	—	—	—	—
3303	Debt securities	-62	567	463	-62	567	463	-62	567	463	-62	567	463
3304	Loans	-29	-106	-27	63	-102	-7	63	-102	-7	104	-21	21

El Salvador (253)

In Millions of U.S. Dollars (USD) / Fiscal Year Ends December 31st

		Budgetary Central Government			Central Government (excl. Social Security)			Central Government (incl. Social Security)			General Government		
		2013	2014	2015	2013	2014	2015	2013	2014	2015	2013	2014	2015
3305	Equity and investment fund shares	—	—	—	—	—	—	—	—	—	—	—	—
3306	Insurance, pension, and standardized guarantee schemes	—	—	—	—	—	—	—	—	—	—	—	—
3307	Financial derivatives and employee stock options	—	—	—	—	—	—	—	—	—	—	—	—
3308	Other accounts payable	-574	-455	-504	-593	-412	-651	-644	-427	-704	-662	-416	-711
	By creditor												
331	Domestic creditors	-846	-20	412	-706	27	279	-757	30	244	-734	121	262
332	External creditors	181	25	-480	115	25	-475	115	7	-492	113	8	-490
	Table 4 Holding gains and losses in assets and liabilities												
4	**Change in net worth due to holding gains and losses**	**-5**	**-652**	**12**	**7**	**-346**	**12**	**7**	**-348**	**-23**	**29**	**-342**	**-15**
41	**Holding gains and losses in nonfinancial assets**	**1**	**3**	**12**	**13**	**5**	**12**	**13**	**3**	**-23**	**35**	**9**	**-15**
411	Fixed assets	0	3	12	10	5	12	10	3	-23	15	9	-15
412	Inventories	—	—	—	—	—	—	—	—	—	—	—	—
413	Valuables	—	—	—	—	—	—	—	—	—	—	—	—
414	Nonproduced assets	1	—	—	3	—	—	3	—	—	20	—	—
42	**Holding gains and losses in financial assets**	**—**	**—**	**—**	**—**	**—**	**—**	**—**	**—**	**—**	**—**	**—**	**—**
	By instrument												
4201	Monetary gold and SDRs	—	—	—	—	—	—	—	—	—	—	—	—
4202	Currency and deposits	—	—	—	—	—	—	—	—	—	—	—	—
4203	Debt securities	—	—	—	—	—	—	—	—	—	—	—	—
4204	Loans	—	—	—	—	—	—	—	—	—	—	—	—
4205	Equity and investment fund shares	—	—	—	—	—	—	—	—	—	—	—	—
4206	Insurance, pension, and standardized guarantee schemes	—	—	—	—	—	—	—	—	—	—	—	—
4207	Financial derivatives and employee stock options	—	—	—	—	—	—	—	—	—	—	—	—
4208	Other accounts receivable	—	—	—	—	—	—	—	—	—	—	—	—
	By debtor												
421	Domestic debtors	—	—	—	—	—	—	—	—	—	—	—	—
422	External debtors	—	—	—	—	—	—	—	—	—	—	—	—
43	**Holding gains and losses in liabilities**	**6**	**655**	**—**	**6**	**351**	**—**	**6**	**351**	**—**	**6**	**351**	**—**
	By instrument												
4301	Special Drawing Rights (SDRs)	—	...	—	—	...	—	—	...	—	—	...	—
4302	Currency and deposits	—	...	—	—	...	—	—	...	—	—	...	—
4303	Debt securities	4	...	—	4	...	—	4	...	—	4	...	—
4304	Loans	2	...	—	2	...	—	2	...	—	2	...	—
4305	Equity and investment fund shares	—	...	—	—	...	—	—	...	—	—	...	—
4306	Insurance, pension, and standardized guarantee schemes	—	...	—	—	...	—	—	...	—	—	...	—
4307	Financial derivatives and employee stock options	—	...	—	—	...	—	—	...	—	—	...	—
4308	Other accounts payable	—	...	—	—	...	—	—	...	—	—	...	—
	By creditor												
431	Domestic creditors	5	655	—	5	351	—	5	351	—	5	351	—
432	External creditors	1	—	—	1	—	—	1	—	—	1	—	—
	Table 5 Holding gains and losses in assets and liabilities												
5	**Change in net worth due to other volume changes**	**26**	**224**	**-176**	**-125**	**-123**	**-210**	**-126**	**-244**	**-294**	**-274**	**-496**	**-493**
51	**Other volume changes in nonfinancial assets**	**-521**	**-339**	**-258**	**-617**	**-459**	**-431**	**-620**	**-574**	**-518**	**-810**	**-839**	**-715**
511	Fixed assets	-525	-188	-188	-624	-252	-300	-628	-267	-339	-817	-530	-534
512	Inventories	—	-151	-70	—	-207	-131	—	-307	-178	—	-310	-180
513	Valuables	-0	0	-0	-0	0	-0	-0	0	-0	-0	2	-0
514	Nonproduced assets	4	—	—	8	—	—	8	—	—	7	—	—
52	**Other volume changes in financial assets**	**-540**	**-469**	**-274**	**-749**	**-1,037**	**-839**	**-696**	**-1,032**	**-768**	**-638**	**-1,016**	**-759**

El Salvador (253)

In Millions of U.S. Dollars (USD) / Fiscal Year Ends December 31st

		Budgetary Central Government			Central Government (excl. Social Security)			Central Government (incl. Social Security)			General Government		
		2013	2014	2015	2013	2014	2015	2013	2014	2015	2013	2014	2015
	By instrument												
5201	Monetary gold and SDRs	—	...	...	—	...	...	—	...	...	—	...	...
5202	Currency and deposits	—	...	...	—	...	...	—	...	...	—	...	...
5203	Debt securities	—	...	...	-143	...	...	-179	...	...	-173	...	...
5204	Loans	-107	...	...	-144	...	...	-144	...	...	-144	...	...
5205	Equity and investment fund shares	—	...	...	—	...	...	-0	...	...	—	...	...
5206	Insurance, pension, and standardized guarantee schemes	—	...	...	—	...	...	—	...	...	—	...	...
5207	Financial derivatives and employee stock options	—	...	...	—	...	...	—	...	...	—	...	...
5208	Other accounts receivable	-433	...	...	-462	...	...	-373	...	...	-321	...	...
	By debtor												
521	Domestic debtors	-591	-455	-279	-800	-1,024	-844	-747	-1,018	-773	-689	-1,003	-764
522	External debtors	51	-13	5	51	-13	5	51	-13	5	51	-13	5
53	**Other volume changes in liabilities**	**-1,086**	**-1,031**	**-356**	**-1,241**	**-1,373**	**-1,060**	**-1,191**	**-1,362**	**-992**	**-1,174**	**-1,359**	**-981**
	By instrument												
5301	Special Drawing Rights (SDRs)	—	...	—	—	...	—	—	...	—	—	...	—
5302	Currency and deposits	—	...	—	—	...	—	—	...	—	—	...	—
5303	Debt securities	-200	...	—	-223	...	—	-223	...	—	-223	...	—
5304	Loans	7	...	—	-30	...	—	-30	...	—	-30	...	—
5305	Equity and investment fund shares	—	...	...	—	...	...	—	...	...	—	...	...
5306	Insurance, pension, and standardized guarantee schemes	—	...	—	—	...	—	—	...	—	—	...	—
5307	Financial derivatives and employee stock options	—	...	...	—	...	...	—	...	...	—	...	...
5308	Other accounts payable	-893	...	—	-987	...	—	-937	...	—	-920	...	—
	By creditor												
531	Domestic creditors	-893	-1,135	-783	-1,030	-1,446	-1,341	-980	-1,434	-1,273	-964	-1,431	-1,262
532	External creditors	-194	104	427	-211	72	281	-211	72	281	-211	72	281
	Table 6 Balance sheet												
6	**Net worth**	**-9,204**	**-9,573**	**-9,864**	**-5,736**	**-8,017**	**-9,064**	**-5,165**	**-7,433**	**-8,482**	**-4,097**	**-6,329**	**-7,419**
61	**Nonfinancial assets**	**1,235**	**1,163**	**1,209**	**4,106**	**2,378**	**1,829**	**4,457**	**2,729**	**2,186**	**5,424**	**3,771**	**3,215**
611	Fixed assets	842	804	827	2,942	1,550	1,207	3,124	1,726	1,389	3,444	2,070	1,744
6111	Buildings and structures	335	460	448	1,522	938	689	1,625	1,049	802	1,782	1,303	1,067
6112	Machinery and equipment	272	336	371	780	601	508	844	666	577	910	750	663
6113	Other fixed assets	235	8	9	640	11	10	655	11	10	751	18	15
6114	Weapons systems	...	...	...	...	...	...	...	...	...	...	...	...
612	Inventories	128	56	80	336	173	138	384	225	244	388	229	248
613	Valuables	1	2	2	1	2	2	1	2	2	2	4	4
614	Nonproduced assets	265	301	301	827	653	482	948	776	551	1,591	1,468	1,219
6141	Land	265	301	301	827	653	482	948	776	551	1,591	1,468	1,219
6142	Mineral and energy resources	—	—	—	—	—	—	—	—	—	—	—	—
6143	Other naturally occurring assets	—	—	—	—	—	—	—	—	—	—	—	—
6144	Intangible nonproduced assets	—	—	—	—	—	—	—	—	—	—	—	—
62	**Financial assets**	**1,216**	**1,212**	**1,242**	**3,760**	**974**	**993**	**4,100**	**1,324**	**1,351**	**4,601**	**1,918**	**1,923**
	By instrument												
6201	Monetary gold and SDRs	—	—	—	—	—	—	—	—	—	—	—	—
6202	Currency and deposits	199	193	134	865	237	219	1,056	280	256	1,184	399	366
6203	Debt securities	34	32	32	234	182	88	252	348	276	252	361	279
6204	Loans	443	457	484	1,341	245	54	1,407	307	99	1,408	308	100
6205	Equity and investment fund shares	17	32	36	526	32	21	526	32	21	529	35	24
6206	Insurance, pension, and standardized guarantee schemes	—	—	—	—	—	—	—	—	—	—	—	—
6207	Financial derivatives and employee stock options	—	—	—	—	—	—	—	—	—	—	—	—
6208	Other accounts receivable	525	499	556	794	278	610	859	357	699	1,228	815	1,153
	By debtor												
621	Domestic debtors	1,204	1,197	1,153	3,727	868	918	4,066	1,219	1,276	4,213	1,812	1,847
622	External debtors	12	16	89	34	106	75	34	106	75	388	106	75
63	**Liabilities**	**11,655**	**11,948**	**12,315**	**13,602**	**11,369**	**11,886**	**13,722**	**11,486**	**12,019**	**14,123**	**12,018**	**12,557**

El Salvador (253)

In Millions of U.S. Dollars (USD) / Fiscal Year Ends December 31st

		Budgetary Central Government			Central Government (excl. Social Security)			Central Government (incl. Social Security)			General Government		
		2013	2014	2015	2013	2014	2015	2013	2014	2015	2013	2014	2015
	By instrument												
6301	Special Drawing Rights (SDRs)	—	—	—	—	—	—	—	—	—	—	—	—
6302	Currency and deposits	—	—	—	—	—	—	—	—	—	—	—	—
6303	Debt securities	6,853	7,370	7,832	7,151	7,121	7,296	7,151	7,121	7,296	7,151	7,121	7,296
6304	Loans	3,763	3,650	3,584	4,471	3,622	3,675	4,471	3,622	3,675	4,821	4,084	4,151
6305	Equity and investment fund shares	—	—	—	—	—	—	—	—	—	—	—	—
6306	Insurance, pension, and standardized guarantee schemes	—	—	—	—	—	—	—	—	—	—	—	—
6307	Financial derivatives and employee stock options	—	—	—	—	—	—	—	—	—	—	—	—
6308	Other accounts payable	1,040	928	899	1,979	626	916	2,100	743	1,048	2,150	814	1,110
	By creditor												
631	Domestic creditors	3,086	2,537	2,986	4,543	2,015	2,605	4,664	2,131	2,736	5,058	2,652	3,260
632	External creditors	8,570	9,411	9,329	9,059	9,354	9,282	9,059	9,355	9,283	9,064	9,366	9,297
	Memorandum items												
6M2	Net financial worth	-10,439	-10,736	-11,073	-9,842	-10,395	-10,893	-9,622	-10,162	-10,668	-9,521	-10,100	-10,634
6M3	Gross debt (D4) at market value	...	...	...	...	...	...	...	...	...	...	...	...
6M3D3	D3 debt liabilities at market value	...	...	...	...	...	...	...	...	...	...	...	...
6M3D2	D2 debt liabilities at market value	...	...	...	...	...	...	...	...	...	...	...	...
6M3D1	D1 debt liabilities at market value	...	...	...	...	...	...	...	...	...	...	...	...
6M4	Gross debt (D4) at nominal value	11,655	11,948	12,315	13,602	11,369	11,886	13,722	11,486	12,019	14,123	12,018	12,557
6M4D3	D3 debt liabilities at nominal value	11,655	11,948	12,315	13,602	11,369	11,886	13,722	11,486	12,019	14,123	12,018	12,557
6M4D2	D2 debt liabilities at nominal value	10,616	11,020	11,416	11,623	10,743	10,970	11,623	10,743	10,970	11,973	11,204	11,447
6M4D1	D1 debt liabilities at nominal value	10,616	11,020	11,416	11,623	10,743	10,970	11,623	10,743	10,970	11,973	11,204	11,447
6M35	Gross debt (D4) at face value	...	...	...	...	...	...	...	...	...	...	...	...
6M35D3	D3 debt liabilities at face value	...	...	...	...	...	...	...	...	...	...	...	...
6M35D2	D2 debt liabilities at face value	...	...	...	...	...	...	...	...	...	...	...	...
6M35D1	D1 debt liabilities at face value	...	...	...	...	...	...	...	...	...	...	...	...
6M93	Government gross debt per national definition	...	...	...	...	...	...	...	...	...	...	...	...
6M5	Arrears	...	...	...	...	...	...	...	...	...	...	...	...
6M6	Explicit contingent liabilities	...	...	...	...	...	...	...	...	...	...	...	...
6M61	of which: Publicly guaranteed debt	...	...	...	...	...	...	...	...	...	...	...	...
6M7	Net implicit obligations for social security benefits	...	...	...	...	...	...	...	...	...	...	...	...
	Table 7 Expenditure by functions of government												
7	**Expenditure**	**4,184**	**4,337**	**4,345**	**4,860**	**4,500**	**4,565**	**5,429**	**5,682**	**5,709**	**6,056**	**5,742**	**5,561**
701	**General public services**	**1,594**	**1,657**	**1,269**	**2,030**	**1,541**	**1,158**	**2,030**	**1,541**	**1,163**	**2,633**	**2,046**	**1,289**
7017	Public debt transactions	523	585	555	537	598	568	537	598	568	565	637	608
7018	Transfers of general character between levels of government	381	403	—	688	741	351	688	741	351	688	768	379
702	**Defense**	**152**	**152**	**155**	**163**	**164**	**164**	**163**	**164**	**164**	**163**	**164**	**164**
703	**Public order and safety**	**554**	**640**	**677**	**554**	**630**	**682**	**554**	**630**	**682**	**554**	**630**	**682**
704	**Economic affairs**	**420**	**311**	**463**	**643**	**497**	**652**	**643**	**497**	**659**	**646**	**500**	**837**
7042	Agriculture, forestry, fishing, and hunting	59	82	71	46	72	61	46	72	61	46	72	65
7043	Fuel and energy	141	106	35	320	285	167	320	285	167	320	285	176
7044	Mining, manufacturing, and construction	—	—	69	—	—	69	—	—	75	—	—	80
7045	Transport	153	59	154	72	25	164	72	25	164	74	27	166
7046	Communication	6	6	15	6	6	15	6	6	15	6	6	15
705	**Environmental protection**	**9**	**13**	**14**	**11**	**14**	**16**	**11**	**14**	**16**	**30**	**34**	**34**
706	**Housing and community amenities**	**11**	**50**	**116**	**...**	**72**	**139**	**...**	**72**	**139**	**...**	**73**	**140**
707	**Health**	**458**	**500**	**572**	**428**	**531**	**618**	**714**	**531**	**908**	**714**	**531**	**908**
7072	Outpatient services	—	—	2	41	54	57	41	54	202	41	54	202
7073	Hospital services	245	246	270	152	142	207	438	142	345	438	142	345
7074	Public health services	209	234	298	204	306	328	204	306	328	204	306	328
708	**Recreation, culture and religion**	**30**	**31**	**31**	**30**	**16**	**22**	**30**	**16**	**22**	**30**	**17**	**23**
709	**Education**	**823**	**861**	**917**	**849**	**894**	**957**	**849**	**894**	**957**	**850**	**895**	**957**
7091	Pre-primary and primary education	598	615	627	598	615	627	598	615	627	598	615	627
7092	Secondary education	78	82	105	78	82	105	78	82	105	78	82	105
7094	Tertiary education	68	69	74	79	133	74	79	133	74	79	133	74

El Salvador (253)

In Millions of U.S. Dollars (USD) / Fiscal Year Ends December 31st

		Budgetary Central Government			Central Government (excl. Social Security)			Central Government (incl. Social Security)			General Government		
		2013	2014	2015	2013	2014	2015	2013	2014	2015	2013	2014	2015
710	**Social protection**	**134**	**122**	**131**	**...**	**141**	**157**	**...**	**1,323**	**1,000**	**...**	**852**	**527**
7z	Statistical discrepancy: Expenditure	...	...	...	...	...	...	...	...	...	...	...	...
	Table 8 Financial transactions by counterpart sector												
32	**Net acquisition of financial assets**	**-908**	**102**	**-317**	**-873**	**161**	**-491**	**-919**	**143**	**-554**	**-918**	**198**	**-543**
321	Domestic debtors	-909	139	-303	-873	152	-540	-909	142	-595	-910	195	-587
8211	General government	-367	-6	-150	-434	66	-286	-436	75	-279	-467	67	-281
8212	Central bank	-799	43	-25	-799	43	-25	-799	43	-25	-799	43	-25
8213	Deposit-taking corporations except the central bank	—	-81	-0	—	-81	-0	—	-89	-0	—	-89	-28
8214	Other financial corporations	69	9	-309	161	-56	-383	121	-70	-428	117	-46	-429
8215	Nonfinancial corporations	-773	-794	-815	-763	-788	-842	-758	-790	-841	-736	-772	-813
8216	Households & nonprofit institutions serving households	962	968	996	963	969	996	963	972	978	975	990	988
322	External debtors	0	-37	-14	-0	9	49	-10	1	41	-8	3	44
8221	General government	—	—	—	-1	45	64	-1	45	64	-1	45	64
8227	International organizations	-4	-41	-17	-4	-41	-17	-4	-41	-17	-1	-39	-14
8228	Financial corporations other than international organizations	4	4	2	4	4	2	-6	4	-6	-6	4	-6
8229	Other nonresidents	—	—	—	—	—	—	—	-7	—	—	-7	—
33	**Net incurrence of liabilities**	**-665**	**5**	**-68**	**-592**	**52**	**-195**	**-642**	**37**	**-248**	**-621**	**129**	**-227**
331	Domestic creditors	-846	-20	412	-706	27	279	-757	30	244	-734	121	262
8311	General government	-288	-10	423	-278	137	312	-338	115	251	-303	181	277
8312	Central bank	—	—	—	—	—	—	—	—	—	—	—	—
8313	Deposit-taking corporations except the central bank	—	—	—	—	—	—	—	—	—	—	0	-5
8314	Other financial corporations	-5	-3	-5	-38	1	-5	-38	1	-5	-47	5	-5
8315	Nonfinancial corporations	-539	6	3	-384	-105	-28	-389	-95	-20	-398	-80	-29
8316	Households & nonprofit institutions serving households	-14	-14	-9	-6	-6	0	8	9	18	15	16	24
332	External creditors	181	25	-480	115	25	-475	115	7	-492	113	8	-490
8321	General government	—	—	—	—	—	—	—	—	—	—	—	—
8327	International organizations	-19	-690	-480	-85	-690	-475	-85	-709	-492	-87	-718	-490
8328	Financial corporations other than international organizations	200	716	—	200	716	—	200	716	—	200	726	—
8329	Other nonresidents	—	—	—	—	—	—	—	—	—	—	—	—
	Table 9 Total other economic flows in assets and liabilities												
9	**Change in net worth due to other economic flows**	**21**	**-428**	**-164**	**-118**	**-469**	**-198**	**-119**	**-591**	**-317**	**-245**	**-838**	**-509**
91	**Other economic flows in nonfinancial assets**	**-520**	**-336**	**-246**	**-604**	**-454**	**-418**	**-608**	**-570**	**-540**	**-775**	**-829**	**-730**
911	Fixed assets	-525	-185	-175	-614	-248	-288	-618	-264	-362	-802	-521	-550
912	Inventories	—	-151	-70	—	-207	-131	—	-307	-178	—	-310	-180
913	Valuables	-0	0	-0	-0	0	-0	-0	0	-0	-0	2	-0
914	Nonproduced assets	5	—	—	11	—	—	11	—	—	27	—	—
92	**Other economic flows in financial assets**	**-540**	**-469**	**-274**	**-749**	**-1,037**	**-839**	**-696**	**-1,032**	**-768**	**-638**	**-1,016**	**-759**
	By instrument												
9201	Monetary gold and SDRs	—	...	...	—	...	...	—	...	...	—	...	...
9202	Currency and deposits	—	...	...	—	...	...	—	...	...	—	...	...
9203	Debt securities	—	...	...	-143	...	...	-179	...	...	-173	...	...
9204	Loans	-107	...	...	-144	...	...	-144	...	...	-144	...	...
9205	Equity and investment fund shares	—	...	...	—	...	...	-0	...	...	—	...	...
9206	Insurance, pension, and standardized guarantee schemes	—	...	...	—	...	...	—	...	...	—	...	...
9207	Financial derivatives and employee stock options	—	...	...	—	...	...	—	...	...	—	...	...
9208	Other accounts receivable	-433	...	...	-462	...	...	-373	...	...	-321	...	...
	By debtor												
921	Domestic debtors	-591	-455	-279	-800	-1,024	-844	-747	-1,018	-773	-689	-1,003	-764
922	External debtors	51	-13	5	51	-13	5	51	-13	5	51	-13	5
93	**Other economic flows in liabilities**	**-1,080**	**-376**	**-356**	**-1,235**	**-1,022**	**-1,060**	**-1,185**	**-1,011**	**-992**	**-1,168**	**-1,008**	**-981**

El Salvador (253)

In Millions of U.S. Dollars (USD) / Fiscal Year Ends December 31st

		Budgetary Central Government			Central Government (excl. Social Security)			Central Government (incl. Social Security)			General Government		
		2013	2014	2015	2013	2014	2015	2013	2014	2015	2013	2014	2015
	By instrument												
9301	Special Drawing Rights (SDRs)	—	...	...	—	...	...	—	...	...	—	...	...
9302	Currency and deposits	—	...	...	—	...	...	—	...	...	—	...	...
9303	Debt securities	-196	...	...	-219	...	...	-219	...	...	-219	...	...
9304	Loans	8	...	...	-28	...	...	-28	...	...	-29	...	...
9305	Equity and investment fund shares	—	...	...	—	...	...	—	...	...	—	...	...
9306	Insurance, pension, and standardized guarantee schemes	—	...	...	—	...	...	—	...	...	—	...	...
9307	Financial derivatives and employee stock options	—	...	...	—	...	...	—	...	...	—	...	...
9308	Other accounts payable	-893	...	...	-987	...	...	-937	...	...	-920	...	...
	By creditor												
931	Domestic creditors	-888	-480	-783	-1,026	-1,095	-1,341	-976	-1,083	-1,273	-959	-1,080	-1,262
932	External creditors	-192	104	427	-209	72	281	-209	72	281	-209	72	281
	Memorandum items												
9M2	Change in net financial worth due to other economic flows	541	-92	82	486	-15	221	489	-21	224	530	-8	222
9M3	Gross debt (D4) at market value: other economic flows	-1,080	...	...	-1,235	...	...	-1,185	...	...	-1,168	...	...
9M3D3	D3 debt liabilities at market value: other economic flows	-1,080	...	...	-1,235	...	...	-1,185	...	...	-1,168	...	...
9M3D2	D2 debt liabilities at market value: other economic flows	-188	...	...	-247	...	...	-247	...	...	-248	...	...
9M3D1	D1 debt liabilities at market value: other economic flows	-188	...	...	-247	...	...	-247	...	...	-248	...	...

Estonia (939)

In Millions of Euros (EUR) / Fiscal Year Ends December 31st

		Budgetary Central Government			Central Government (excl. Social Security)			Central Government (incl. Social Security)			General Government		
		2013	2014	2015	2013P	2014P	2015P	2013P	2014P	2015P	2013P	2014P	2015P
	Statement of operations												
1	Revenue	...	...	...	5,963	6,430	6,890	6,712	7,218	7,695	7,093	7,566	8,028
2	Expense	...	...	...	5,757	6,058	6,643	6,442	6,783	7,423	6,672	7,005	7,578
GOB	**Gross operating balance**	...	...	...	**601**	**812**	**718**	**667**	**878**	**746**	**935**	**1,127**	**1,059**
NOB	**Net operating balance**	...	...	...	**206**	**372**	**247**	**271**	**436**	**272**	**421**	**561**	**450**
31	Net/Gross investment in nonfinancial assets	...	...	...	213	299	299	214	299	301	454	427	423
2M	Expenditure	...	...	...	5,970	6,356	6,942	6,656	7,082	7,724	7,125	7,432	8,001
NLB	**Net lending (+) / Net borrowing (-)**	...	...	...	**-8**	**73**	**-52**	**56**	**136**	**-29**	**-32**	**134**	**27**
32	Net acquisition of financial assets	...	...	...	181	177	-149	...	...	...	154	254	-134
33	Net incurrence of liabilities	...	...	...	182	107	-105	...	...	...	193	120	-160
NLBz	Statistical discrepancy	...	...	...	7	-3	8	...	...	...	-7	0	-1
	Memorandum items												
PB	Primary net lending / net borrowing	...	...	...	9	89	-43	70	149	-21	-2	171	64
GB	Government balance per national definition	...	...	...	...	...	...	...	...	...	...	...	...
	Statement of other economic flows												
9	**Change in net worth due to other economic flows**	...	...	...	...	...	...	...	...	...	...	...	...
4	Change in net worth due to holding gains and losses	...	...	...	...	...	...	...	...	...	...	...	...
41	Nonfinancial assets	...	...	...	...	...	...	...	...	...	...	...	...
42	Financial assets	...	...	...	...	...	...	...	...	...	...	...	...
43	Liabilities	...	...	...	—	...	...	...	...	...	...	...	...
5	Change in net worth due to volume changes	...	...	...	...	...	...	...	...	...	...	...	...
51	Nonfinancial assets	...	...	...	...	...	...	...	...	...	...	...	...
52	Financial assets	...	...	...	...	...	...	...	...	...	...	...	...
53	Liabilities	...	...	...	—	...	...	...	...	...	...	...	...
	Balance sheet												
6	**Net worth**	...	...	...	...	...	...	...	...	...	...	...	...
61	Nonfinancial assets	...	...	...	...	...	...	...	...	...	...	...	...
62	Financial assets	...	...	...	8,224	8,486	10,726	...	...	...	8,506	8,858	11,123
63	Liabilities	...	...	...	2,651	2,839	2,734	...	...	...	2,581	2,782	2,621
	Table 1 Revenue												
1	**Revenue**	...	...	...	**5,963**	**6,430**	**6,890**	**6,712**	**7,218**	**7,695**	**7,093**	**7,566**	**8,028**
11	**Taxes**	...	...	...	**3,814**	**4,159**	**4,465**	**3,814**	**4,159**	**4,465**	**3,882**	**4,229**	**4,535**
111	Taxes on income, profits, and capital gains	...	...	...	1,357	1,479	1,607	1,357	1,479	1,607	1,357	1,479	1,607
1111	Payable by individuals	...	...	...	1,031	1,134	1,182	1,031	1,134	1,182	1,031	1,134	1,182
1112	Payable by corporations and other enterprises	...	...	...	327	345	424	327	345	424	327	345	424
1113	Other taxes on income, profits, and capital gains	...	...	...	—	—	—	—	—	—	—	—	—
112	Taxes on payroll and workforce	...	...	...	—	—	—	—	—	—	—	—	—
113	Taxes on property	...	...	...	—	—	—	—	—	—	57	59	58
114	Taxes on goods and services	...	...	...	2,457	2,681	2,859	2,457	2,681	2,859	2,468	2,691	2,870
1141	General taxes on goods and services	...	...	...	1,558	1,711	1,872	1,558	1,711	1,872	1,558	1,711	1,872
1142	Excises	...	...	...	802	850	875	802	850	875	802	850	875
115	Taxes on international trade and transactions	...	...	...	—	—	—	—	—	—	—	—	—
116	Other taxes	...	...	...	—	—	—	—	—	—	—	—	—
12	**Social contributions**	...	...	...	**1,113**	**1,150**	**1,225**	**2,112**	**2,217**	**2,335**	**2,116**	**2,222**	**2,339**
121	Social security contributions	...	...	...	11	12	12	1,010	1,079	1,122	1,010	1,079	1,122
122	Other social contributions	...	...	...	1,102	1,138	1,213	1,102	1,138	1,213	1,106	1,143	1,217
13	**Grants**	...	...	...	**556**	**560**	**663**	**307**	**281**	**358**	**416**	**344**	**389**
131	From foreign governments	...	...	...	63	69	78	63	69	78	70	78	82
132	From international organizations	...	...	...	231	205	255	231	205	256	346	267	308
133	From other general government units	...	...	...	262	285	330	13	6	24	—	—	—
1331	Current	...	...	...	248	279	305	4	5	5	—	—	—
1332	Capital	...	...	...	14	7	26	9	1	19	—	—	—
14	**Other revenue**	...	...	...	**479**	**560**	**537**	**480**	**561**	**537**	**680**	**771**	**765**

Estonia (939)

In Millions of Euros (EUR) / Fiscal Year Ends December 31st

		Budgetary Central Government			Central Government (excl. Social Security)			Central Government (incl. Social Security)			General Government		
		2013	2014	2015	2013P	2014P	2015P	2013P	2014P	2015P	2013P	2014P	2015P
	Table 2 Expense by economic type												
2	**Expense**	...	...	...	**5,757**	**6,058**	**6,643**	**6,442**	**6,783**	**7,423**	**6,672**	**7,005**	**7,578**
21	**Compensation of employees**	...	...	...	**1,109**	**1,208**	**1,304**	**1,144**	**1,241**	**1,340**	**1,936**	**2,085**	**2,249**
211	Wages and salaries	...	...	...	741	803	863	752	814	876	1,337	1,438	1,550
212	Employers' social contributions	...	...	...	368	405	440	393	427	464	599	647	699
22	**Use of goods and services**	...	...	...	**650**	**713**	**757**	**659**	**721**	**767**	**1,183**	**1,248**	**1,302**
23	**Consumption of fixed capital**	...	...	...	**395**	**440**	**471**	**397**	**442**	**474**	**513**	**566**	**609**
24	**Interest**	...	...	...	**16**	**15**	**9**	**14**	**13**	**8**	**30**	**37**	**37**
25	**Subsidies**	...	...	...	**102**	**70**	**64**	**107**	**74**	**69**	**124**	**94**	**91**
26	**Grants**	...	...	...	**1,422**	**1,456**	**1,614**	**1,618**	**1,674**	**1,837**	**231**	**211**	**228**
261	To foreign governments	...	...	...	33	39	31	33	39	32	35	42	32
262	To international organizations	...	...	...	197	169	196	197	169	196	197	169	196
263	To other general government units	...	...	...	1,193	1,249	1,387	1,389	1,467	1,609	—	—	—
2631	Current	...	...	...	1,126	1,218	1,310	1,318	1,431	1,527	—	—	—
2632	Capital	...	...	...	66	31	77	71	36	82	—	—	—
27	**Social benefits**	...	...	...	**1,837**	**1,943**	**2,151**	**2,271**	**2,398**	**2,648**	**2,345**	**2,473**	**2,724**
271	Social security benefits	...	...	...	...	...	...	...	...	...	...	...	...
272	Social assistance benefits	...	...	...	...	...	...	...	...	...	...	...	...
273	Employment-related social benefits	...	...	...	...	...	...	...	...	...	...	...	...
28	**Other expense**	...	...	...	**225**	**213**	**274**	**232**	**220**	**281**	**309**	**291**	**338**
281	Property expense other than interest	...	...	...	—	—	—	—	—	—	—	—	—
282	Transfers not elsewhere classified	...	...	...	223	210	271	229	217	278	305	286	333
2821	Current	...	...	...	102	104	133	106	108	136	142	142	173
2822	Capital	...	...	...	121	106	138	123	109	141	164	144	160
	Table 3 Transactions in assets and liabilities												
3	**Change in net worth from transactions**	...	...	...	**213**	**369**	**255**	...	...	...	**415**	**562**	**450**
31	**Net/Gross investment in nonfinancial assets**	...	...	...	**213**	**299**	**299**	**214**	**299**	**301**	**454**	**427**	**423**
311	Fixed assets	...	...	...	273	293	323	274	294	325	515	420	450
3111	Buildings and structures	...	...	...	...	...	...	...	...	...	...	...	...
3112	Machinery and equipment	...	...	...	...	...	...	...	...	...	...	...	...
3113	Other fixed assets	...	...	...	...	...	...	...	...	...	...	...	...
3114	Weapons systems	...	...	...	...	...	...	...	...	...	...	...	...
312	Inventories	...	...	...	...	...	...	...	...	...	...	...	...
313	Valuables	...	...	...	...	...	...	...	...	...	...	...	...
314	Nonproduced assets	...	...	...	-35	-28	-21	-35	-28	-21	-37	-27	-26
3141	Land	...	...	...	...	...	...	...	...	...	...	...	...
3142	Mineral and energy resources	...	...	...	...	...	...	...	...	...	...	...	...
3143	Other naturally occurring assets	...	...	...	...	...	...	...	...	...	...	...	...
3144	Intangible nonproduced assets	...	...	...	...	...	...	...	...	...	...	...	...
32	**Net acquisition of financial assets**	...	...	...	**181**	**177**	**-149**	...	...	...	**154**	**254**	**-134**
	By instrument												
3201	Monetary gold and SDRs	...	...	...	—	—	—	...	...	...	—	—	—
3202	Currency and deposits	...	...	...	189	-61	-298	...	...	...	180	10	-298
3203	Debt securities	...	...	...	-171	141	-47	...	...	...	-171	141	-47
3204	Loans	...	...	...	149	-20	-51	...	...	...	131	-21	-44
3205	Equity and investment fund shares	...	...	...	77	32	11	...	...	...	79	39	13
3206	Insurance, pension, and standardized guarantee schemes	...	...	...	—	—	—	...	...	...	—	—	—
3207	Financial derivatives and employee stock options	...	...	...	—	—	—	...	...	...	-3	1	0
3208	Other accounts receivable	...	...	...	-63	85	238	...	...	...	-61	84	242
	By debtor												
321	Domestic debtors	...	...	...	...	...	...	...	...	...	...	...	...
322	External debtors	...	...	...	...	...	...	...	...	...	...	...	...
33	**Net incurrence of liabilities**	...	...	...	**182**	**107**	**-105**	...	...	...	**193**	**120**	**-160**
	By instrument												
3301	Special Drawing Rights (SDRs)	...	...	...	—	—	—	...	...	...	—	—	—
3302	Currency and deposits	...	...	...	63	57	30	...	...	...	4	3	4
3303	Debt securities	...	...	...	-4	-24	-4	...	...	...	16	-8	-43
3304	Loans	...	...	...	85	70	-53	...	...	...	138	127	-34

Estonia (939)

In Millions of Euros (EUR) / Fiscal Year Ends December 31st

		Budgetary Central Government			Central Government (excl. Social Security)			Central Government (incl. Social Security)			General Government		
		2013	2014	2015	2013P	2014P	2015P	2013P	2014P	2015P	2013P	2014P	2015P
3305	Equity and investment fund shares	...	...	...	—	—	—	...	...	...	—	—	—
3306	Insurance, pension, and standardized guarantee schemes	...	...	...	—	-1	-0	...	...	...	—	-1	-0
3307	Financial derivatives and employee stock options	...	...	...	—	—	-2	...	...	...	-1	-1	-2
3308	Other accounts payable	...	...	...	37	5	-76	...	...	...	35	0	-84
	By creditor												
331	Domestic creditors	...	...	...	...	...	...	...	...	...	...	...	...
332	External creditors	...	...	...	...	...	...	...	...	...	...	...	...
	Table 4 Holding gains and losses in assets and liabilities												
4	**Change in net worth due to holding gains and losses**	...	...	...	...	...	...	...	...	...	...	...	...
41	**Holding gains and losses in nonfinancial assets**	...	...	...	...	...	...	...	...	...	...	...	...
411	Fixed assets	...	...	...	...	...	...	...	...	...	...	...	...
412	Inventories	...	...	...	...	...	...	...	...	...	...	...	...
413	Valuables	...	...	...	...	...	...	...	...	...	...	...	...
414	Nonproduced assets	...	...	...	...	...	...	...	...	...	...	...	...
42	**Holding gains and losses in financial assets**	...	...	...	...	...	...	...	...	...	...	...	...
	By instrument												
4201	Monetary gold and SDRs	...	...	...	...	...	...	...	...	...	...	...	...
4202	Currency and deposits	...	...	...	...	...	...	...	...	...	...	...	...
4203	Debt securities	...	...	...	...	...	...	...	...	...	...	...	...
4204	Loans	...	...	...	...	...	...	...	...	...	...	...	...
4205	Equity and investment fund shares	...	...	...	...	...	...	...	...	...	...	...	...
4206	Insurance, pension, and standardized guarantee schemes	...	...	...	...	...	...	...	...	...	...	...	...
4207	Financial derivatives and employee stock options	...	...	...	...	...	...	...	...	...	...	...	...
4208	Other accounts receivable	...	...	...	...	...	...	...	...	...	...	...	...
	By debtor												
421	Domestic debtors	...	...	...	...	...	...	...	...	...	...	...	...
422	External debtors	...	...	...	...	...	...	...	...	...	...	...	...
43	**Holding gains and losses in liabilities**	...	...	...	—	...	...	...	...	...	...	...	...
	By instrument												
4301	Special Drawing Rights (SDRs)	...	...	...	—	...	...	...	...	...	...	...	...
4302	Currency and deposits	...	...	...	—	...	...	...	...	...	...	...	...
4303	Debt securities	...	...	...	—	...	...	...	...	...	...	...	...
4304	Loans	...	...	...	—	...	...	...	...	...	...	...	...
4305	Equity and investment fund shares	...	...	...	—	...	...	...	...	...	...	...	...
4306	Insurance, pension, and standardized guarantee schemes	...	...	...	—	...	...	...	...	...	...	...	...
4307	Financial derivatives and employee stock options	...	...	...	—	...	...	...	...	...	...	...	...
4308	Other accounts payable	...	...	...	—	...	...	...	...	...	...	...	...
	By creditor												
431	Domestic creditors	...	...	...	—	...	...	...	...	...	...	...	...
432	External creditors	...	...	...	—	...	...	...	...	...	...	...	...
	Table 5 Holding gains and losses in assets and liabilities												
5	**Change in net worth due to other volume changes**	...	...	...	...	...	...	...	...	...	...	...	...
51	**Other volume changes in nonfinancial assets**	...	...	...	...	...	...	...	...	...	...	...	...
511	Fixed assets	...	...	...	...	...	...	...	...	...	...	...	...
512	Inventories	...	...	...	...	...	...	...	...	...	...	...	...
513	Valuables	...	...	...	...	...	...	...	...	...	...	...	...
514	Nonproduced assets	...	...	...	...	...	...	...	...	...	...	...	...
52	**Other volume changes in financial assets**	...	...	...	...	...	...	...	...	...	...	...	...

Estonia (939)

In Millions of Euros (EUR) / Fiscal Year Ends December 31st

		Budgetary Central Government			Central Government (excl. Social Security)			Central Government (incl. Social Security)			General Government		
		2013	2014	2015	2013P	2014P	2015P	2013P	2014P	2015P	2013P	2014P	2015P
	By instrument												
5201	Monetary gold and SDRs	...	...	...	...	...	...	...	...	...	...	...	...
5202	Currency and deposits	...	...	...	...	...	...	...	...	...	...	...	...
5203	Debt securities	...	...	...	...	...	...	...	...	...	...	...	...
5204	Loans	...	...	...	...	...	...	...	...	...	...	...	...
5205	Equity and investment fund shares	...	...	...	...	...	...	...	...	...	...	...	...
5206	Insurance, pension, and standardized guarantee schemes	...	...	...	...	...	...	...	...	...	...	...	...
5207	Financial derivatives and employee stock options	...	...	...	...	...	...	...	...	...	...	...	...
5208	Other accounts receivable	...	...	...	...	...	...	...	...	...	...	...	...
	By debtor												
521	Domestic debtors	...	...	...	...	...	...	...	...	...	...	...	...
522	External debtors	...	...	...	...	...	...	...	...	...	...	...	...
53	**Other volume changes in liabilities**	...	...	...	—	...	...	...	...	...	...	...	...
	By instrument												
5301	Special Drawing Rights (SDRs)	...	...	...	—	...	...	...	...	...	...	...	...
5302	Currency and deposits	...	...	...	—	...	...	...	...	...	...	...	...
5303	Debt securities	...	...	...	—	...	...	...	...	...	...	...	...
5304	Loans	...	...	...	—	...	...	...	...	...	...	...	...
5305	Equity and investment fund shares	...	...	...	—	...	...	...	...	...	...	...	...
5306	Insurance, pension, and standardized guarantee schemes	...	...	...	—	...	...	...	...	...	...	...	...
5307	Financial derivatives and employee stock options	...	...	...	—	...	...	...	...	...	...	...	...
5308	Other accounts payable	...	...	...	—	...	...	...	...	...	...	...	...
	By creditor												
531	Domestic creditors	...	...	...	—	...	...	...	...	...	...	...	...
532	External creditors	...	...	...	—	...	...	...	...	...	...	...	...
	Table 6 Balance sheet												
6	**Net worth**	...	...	...	...	...	...	...	...	...	...	...	...
61	**Nonfinancial assets**	...	...	...	...	...	...	...	...	...	...	...	...
611	Fixed assets	...	...	...	...	...	...	...	...	...	8,927	...	...
6111	Buildings and structures	...	...	...	...	...	...	...	...	...	7,448	...	...
6112	Machinery and equipment	...	...	...	...	...	...	...	...	...	...	...	...
6113	Other fixed assets	...	...	...	...	...	...	...	...	...	571	...	...
6114	Weapons systems	...	...	...	...	...	...	...	...	...	...	...	...
612	Inventories	...	...	...	...	...	...	...	...	...	204	...	...
613	Valuables	...	...	...	...	...	...	...	...	...	...	...	...
614	Nonproduced assets	...	...	...	...	...	...	...	...	...	...	...	...
6141	Land	...	...	...	...	...	...	...	...	...	...	...	...
6142	Mineral and energy resources	...	...	...	...	...	...	...	...	...	...	...	...
6143	Other naturally occurring assets	...	...	...	...	...	...	...	...	...	...	...	...
6144	Intangible nonproduced assets	...	...	...	...	...	...	...	...	...	...	...	...
62	**Financial assets**	...	...	...	**8,224**	**8,486**	**10,726**	...	...	...	**8,506**	**8,858**	**11,123**
	By instrument												
6201	Monetary gold and SDRs	...	...	...	—	—	—	...	...	...	—	—	—
6202	Currency and deposits	...	...	...	1,160	1,101	803	...	...	...	1,289	1,300	1,002
6203	Debt securities	...	...	...	738	879	825	...	...	...	738	879	825
6204	Loans	...	...	...	828	808	757	...	...	...	728	707	663
6205	Equity and investment fund shares	...	...	...	4,632	4,745	7,152	...	...	...	4,875	5,010	7,430
6206	Insurance, pension, and standardized guarantee schemes	...	...	...	1	1	—	...	...	...	1	1	1
6207	Financial derivatives and employee stock options	...	...	...	—	—	—	...	...	...	—	—	—
6208	Other accounts receivable	...	...	...	866	952	1,189	...	...	...	875	960	1,202
	By debtor												
621	Domestic debtors	...	...	...	...	...	...	...	...	...	...	...	...
622	External debtors	...	...	...	...	...	...	...	...	...	...	...	...
63	**Liabilities**	...	...	...	**2,651**	**2,839**	**2,734**	...	...	...	**2,581**	**2,782**	**2,621**

Estonia (939)

In Millions of Euros (EUR) / Fiscal Year Ends December 31st

		Budgetary Central Government			Central Government (excl. Social Security)			Central Government (incl. Social Security)			General Government		
		2013	2014	2015	2013P	2014P	2015P	2013P	2014P	2015P	2013P	2014P	2015P
	By instrument												
6301	Special Drawing Rights (SDRs)	...	...	...	—	—	—	...	...	...	—	—	—
6302	Currency and deposits	...	...	...	770	827	858	...	...	...	35	38	41
6303	Debt securities	...	...	...	86	62	58	...	...	...	279	271	228
6304	Loans	...	...	...	1,229	1,361	1,308	...	...	...	1,613	1,802	1,768
6305	Equity and investment fund shares	...	...	...	—	—	—	...	...	...	—	—	—
6306	Insurance, pension, and standardized guarantee schemes	...	...	...	8	7	6	...	...	...	8	7	6
6307	Financial derivatives and employee stock options	...	...	...	0	2	0	...	...	...	1	3	1
6308	Other accounts payable	...	...	...	559	581	505	...	...	...	645	662	577
	By creditor												
631	Domestic creditors	...	...	...	...	...	...	...	...	...	...	...	...
632	External creditors	...	...	...	...	...	...	...	...	...	...	...	...
	Memorandum items												
6M2	Net financial worth	...	...	...	5,573	5,647	7,992	...	...	...	5,925	6,076	8,502
6M3	Gross debt (D4) at market value	...	...	...	2,651	2,837	2,734	...	...	...	2,579	2,779	2,621
6M3D3	D3 debt liabilities at market value	...	...	...	2,644	2,830	2,728	...	...	...	2,572	2,772	2,615
6M3D2	D2 debt liabilities at market value	...	...	...	2,084	2,250	2,223	...	...	...	1,927	2,111	2,037
6M3D1	D1 debt liabilities at market value	...	...	...	1,314	1,422	1,366	...	...	...	1,892	2,073	1,996
6M4	Gross debt (D4) at nominal value	...	...	...	...	...	...	...	...	...	...	...	...
6M4D3	D3 debt liabilities at nominal value	...	...	...	...	...	...	...	...	...	...	...	...
6M4D2	D2 debt liabilities at nominal value	...	...	...	...	...	...	...	...	...	...	...	...
6M4D1	D1 debt liabilities at nominal value	...	...	...	...	...	...	...	...	...	...	...	...
6M35	Gross debt (D4) at face value	...	...	...	...	...	...	...	...	...	...	...	...
6M35D3	D3 debt liabilities at face value	...	...	...	2,642	2,828	2,726	...	...	...	2,568	2,770	2,613
6M35D2	D2 debt liabilities at face value	...	...	...	2,082	2,248	2,222	...	...	...	1,924	2,108	2,036
6M35D1	D1 debt liabilities at face value	...	...	...	1,312	1,421	1,364	...	...	...	1,889	2,071	1,994
6M93	Government gross debt per national definition	...	...	...	2,082	2,248	2,222	...	...	...	1,924	2,108	2,036
6M5	Arrears	...	...	...	...	...	...	...	...	...	...	...	...
6M6	Explicit contingent liabilities	...	...	...	...	...	...	...	...	...	...	...	...
6M61	of which: Publicly guaranteed debt	...	...	...	...	...	...	...	...	...	...	...	...
6M7	Net implicit obligations for social security benefits	...	...	...	...	...	...	...	...	...	...	...	...
	Table 7 Expenditure by functions of government												
7	**Expenditure**	...	...	...	**6,105**	**6,494**	...	...	...	...	**7,262**	**7,573**	...
701	**General public services**	...	...	...	**1,669**	**1,735**	...	...	...	...	**752**	**784**	...
7017	Public debt transactions	...	...	...	24	31	...	...	...	...	30	37	...
7018	Transfers of general character between levels of government	...	...	...	1,032	1,095	...	...	...	...	—	—	...
702	**Defense**	...	...	...	**343**	**357**	...	...	...	...	**343**	**355**	...
703	**Public order and safety**	...	...	...	**348**	**380**	...	...	...	...	**352**	**385**	...
704	**Economic affairs**	...	...	...	**628**	**731**	...	...	...	...	**885**	**953**	...
7042	Agriculture, forestry, fishing, and hunting	...	...	...	130	99	...	...	...	...	129	97	...
7043	Fuel and energy	...	...	...	-25	30	...	...	...	...	-21	33	...
7044	Mining, manufacturing, and construction	...	...	...	5	10	...	...	...	...	7	12	...
7045	Transport	...	...	...	371	424	...	...	...	...	570	601	...
7046	Communication	...	...	...	6	8	...	...	...	...	7	8	...
705	**Environmental protection**	...	...	...	**76**	**76**	...	...	...	...	**117**	**120**	...
706	**Housing and community amenities**	...	...	...	**1**	**1**	...	...	...	...	**101**	**90**	...
707	**Health**	...	...	...	**401**	**464**	...	...	...	...	**953**	**1,027**	...
7072	Outpatient services	...	...	...	8	13	...	...	...	...	76	88	...
7073	Hospital services	...	...	...	346	398	...	...	...	...	711	761	...
7074	Public health services	...	...	...	2	3	...	...	...	...	4	4	...
708	**Recreation, culture and religion**	...	...	...	**218**	**224**	...	...	...	...	**391**	**395**	...
709	**Education**	...	...	...	**481**	**483**	...	...	...	...	**1,121**	**1,113**	...
7091	Pre-primary and primary education	...	...	...	22	16	...	...	...	...	430	410	...
7092	Secondary education	...	...	...	81	85	...	...	...	...	269	299	...
7094	Tertiary education	...	...	...	260	250	...	...	...	...	260	250	...

Estonia (939)

In Millions of Euros (EUR) / Fiscal Year Ends December 31st

		Budgetary Central Government			Central Government (excl. Social Security)			Central Government (incl. Social Security)			General Government		
		2013	2014	2015	2013P	2014P	2015P	2013P	2014P	2015P	2013P	2014P	2015P
710	**Social protection**	...	...	...	1,940	2,042	...	...	...	...	2,248	2,353	...
7z	Statistical discrepancy: Expenditure	...	...	...	0	-0	...	...	...	...	-0	-0	...
	Table 8 Financial transactions by counterpart sector												
32	**Net acquisition of financial assets**	...	...	...	181	177	-149	...	...	...	154	254	-134
321	Domestic debtors	...	...	...	...	...	...	...	...	...	...	...	...
8211	General government	...	...	...	...	...	...	...	...	...	—	—	—
8212	Central bank	...	...	...	...	...	...	...	...	...	...	...	...
8213	Deposit-taking corporations except the central bank	...	...	...	...	...	...	...	...	...	...	...	...
8214	Other financial corporations	...	...	...	...	...	...	...	...	...	...	...	...
8215	Nonfinancial corporations	...	...	...	...	...	...	...	...	...	...	...	...
8216	Households & nonprofit institutions serving households	...	...	...	...	...	...	...	...	...	...	...	...
322	External debtors	...	...	...	...	...	...	...	...	...	...	...	...
8221	General government	...	...	...	...	...	...	...	...	...	...	...	...
8227	International organizations	...	...	...	...	...	...	...	...	...	...	...	...
8228	Financial corporations other than international organizations	...	...	...	...	...	...	...	...	...	...	...	...
8229	Other nonresidents	...	...	...	...	...	...	...	...	...	...	...	...
33	**Net incurrence of liabilities**	...	...	...	182	107	-105	...	...	...	193	120	-160
331	Domestic creditors	...	...	...	...	...	...	...	...	...	...	...	...
8311	General government	...	...	...	...	...	...	...	...	...	—	—	—
8312	Central bank	...	...	...	...	...	...	...	...	...	...	...	...
8313	Deposit-taking corporations except the central bank	...	...	...	...	...	...	...	...	...	...	...	...
8314	Other financial corporations	...	...	...	...	...	...	...	...	...	...	...	...
8315	Nonfinancial corporations	...	...	...	...	...	...	...	...	...	...	...	...
8316	Households & nonprofit institutions serving households	...	...	...	...	...	...	...	...	...	...	...	...
332	External creditors	...	...	...	...	...	...	...	...	...	...	...	...
8321	General government	...	...	...	...	...	...	...	...	...	...	...	...
8327	International organizations	...	...	...	...	...	...	...	...	...	...	...	...
8328	Financial corporations other than international organizations	...	...	...	...	...	...	...	...	...	...	...	...
8329	Other nonresidents	...	...	...	...	...	...	...	...	...	...	...	...
	Table 9 Total other economic flows in assets and liabilities												
9	**Change in net worth due to other economic flows**	...	...	...	...	...	...	...	...	...	...	...	...
91	**Other economic flows in nonfinancial assets**	...	...	...	...	...	...	...	...	...	...	...	...
911	Fixed assets	...	...	...	...	...	...	...	...	...	...	...	...
912	Inventories	...	...	...	...	...	...	...	...	...	...	...	...
913	Valuables	...	...	...	...	...	...	...	...	...	...	...	...
914	Nonproduced assets	...	...	...	...	...	...	...	...	...	...	...	...
92	**Other economic flows in financial assets**	...	...	...	350	84	2,389	...	...	...	364	98	2,399
	By instrument												
9201	Monetary gold and SDRs	...	...	...	—	—	—	...	...	...	—	—	—
9202	Currency and deposits	...	...	...	—	2	—	...	...	...	2	2	—
9203	Debt securities	...	...	...	-3	0	-7	...	...	...	-3	0	-7
9204	Loans	...	...	...	0	—	0	...	...	...	—	-0	-0
9205	Equity and investment fund shares	...	...	...	353	81	2,396	...	...	...	362	96	2,407
9206	Insurance, pension, and standardized guarantee schemes	...	...	...	—	—	-1	...	...	...	—	—	-1
9207	Financial derivatives and employee stock options	...	...	...	—	—	—	...	...	...	3	-1	-0
9208	Other accounts receivable	...	...	...	—	1	-0	...	...	...	0	1	0
	By debtor												
921	Domestic debtors	...	...	...	...	...	...	...	...	...	...	...	...
922	External debtors	...	...	...	...	...	...	...	...	...	...	...	...
93	**Other economic flows in liabilities**	...	...	...	—	81	-0	...	...	...	27	81	-0

Estonia (939)

In Millions of Euros (EUR) / Fiscal Year Ends December 31st

		Budgetary Central Government			Central Government (excl. Social Security)			Central Government (incl. Social Security)			General Government		
		2013	2014	2015	2013P	2014P	2015P	2013P	2014P	2015P	2013P	2014P	2015P
	By instrument												
9301	Special Drawing Rights (SDRs)	...	...	...	—	—	—	...	...	...	—	—	—
9302	Currency and deposits	...	...	...	0	-0	-0	...	...	...	—	—	—
9303	Debt securities	...	...	...	—	0	-0	...	...	...	16	—	0
9304	Loans	...	...	...	—	62	—	...	...	...	4	62	-0
9305	Equity and investment fund shares	...	...	...	—	—	—	...	...	...	—	—	—
9306	Insurance, pension, and standardized guarantee schemes	...	...	...	—	0	-0	...	...	...	—	0	-0
9307	Financial derivatives and employee stock options	...	...	...	—	2	-0	...	...	...	-0	2	-0
9308	Other accounts payable	...	...	...	—	17	—	...	...	...	7	17	0
	By creditor												
931	Domestic creditors	...	...	...	—	...	...	...	...	...	...	...	...
932	External creditors	...	...	...	—	...	...	...	...	...	...	...	...
	Memorandum items												
9M2	Change in net financial worth due to other economic flows	...	...	...	350	3	2,389	...	...	...	337	17	2,399
9M3	Gross debt (D4) at market value: other economic flows	...	...	...	0	79	-0	...	...	...	27	79	-0
9M3D3	D3 debt liabilities at market value: other economic flows	...	...	...	0	79	-0	...	...	...	27	79	0
9M3D2	D2 debt liabilities at market value: other economic flows	...	...	...	0	62	-0	...	...	...	20	62	0
9M3D1	D1 debt liabilities at market value: other economic flows	...	...	...	—	62	-0	...	...	...	20	62	0

Ethiopia (644)

In Millions of Ethiopian Birr (ETB) / Fiscal Year Ends July 6th

		Budgetary Central Government			Central Government (excl. Social Security)			Central Government (incl. Social Security)			General Government		
		2009	2010	2011	2009	2010	2011	2009	2010	2011	2009	2010	2011
	Statement of operations												
1	Revenue	47,749	60,382	77,455	...	...	...	...	...	...	...	...	...
2	Expense	41,073	48,247	54,516	...	...	...	...	...	...	...	...	...
GOB	**Gross operating balance**	**6,676**	**12,135**	**22,940**	...	...	...	...	...	...	...	...	...
NOB	**Net operating balance**	...	...	...	...	...	...	...	...	...	...	...	...
31	Net/Gross investment in nonfinancial assets	14,187	22,685	29,893	...	...	...	...	...	...	...	...	...
2M	Expenditure	55,261	70,932	84,408	...	...	...	...	...	...	...	...	...
NLB	**Net lending (+) / Net borrowing (-)**	**-7,512**	**-10,550**	**-6,953**	...	...	...	...	...	...	...	...	...
32	Net acquisition of financial assets	36,227	69,804	49,508	...	...	...	...	...	...	...	...	...
33	Net incurrence of liabilities	49,379	51,200	62,383	...	...	...	...	...	...	...	...	...
NLBz	Statistical discrepancy	-5,640	29,154	-5,922	...	...	...	...	...	...	...	...	...
	Memorandum items												
PB	Primary net lending / net borrowing	-6,128	-8,972	-4,949	...	...	...	...	...	...	...	...	...
GB	Government balance per national definition	...	...	...	...	...	...	...	...	...	...	...	...
	Statement of other economic flows												
	Balance sheet												
	Table 1 Revenue												
1	**Revenue**	**47,749**	**60,382**	**77,455**	...	...	...	...	...	...	...	...	...
11	**Taxes**	**22,242**	**31,501**	**47,435**	...	...	...	...	...	...	...	...	...
111	Taxes on income, profits, and capital gains	5,194	8,354	12,414	...	...	...	...	...	...	...	...	...
1111	Payable by individuals	1,558	2,129	1,703	...	...	...	...	...	...	...	...	...
1112	Payable by corporations and other enterprises	3,635	6,225	8,011	...	...	...	...	...	...	...	...	...
1113	Other taxes on income, profits, and capital gains	—	0	2,700	...	...	...	...	...	...	...	...	...
112	Taxes on payroll and workforce	—	—	—	...	...	...	...	...	...	...	...	...
113	Taxes on property	—	—	—	...	...	...	...	...	...	...	...	...
114	Taxes on goods and services	5,200	5,582	12,049	...	...	...	...	...	...	...	...	...
1141	General taxes on goods and services	4,175	2,973	9,747	...	...	...	...	...	...	...	...	...
1142	Excises	1,024	1,517	1,965	...	...	...	...	...	...	...	...	...
115	Taxes on international trade and transactions	11,849	17,565	22,973	...	...	...	...	...	...	...	...	...
116	Other taxes	—	—	—	...	...	...	...	...	...	...	...	...
12	**Social contributions**	—	—	—	...	...	...	...	...	...	...	...	...
121	Social security contributions	—	—	—	...	...	...	...	...	...	...	...	...
122	Other social contributions	—	—	—	...	...	...	...	...	...	...	...	...
13	**Grants**	**15,974**	**18,855**	**21,433**	...	...	...	...	...	...	...	...	...
131	From foreign governments	3,242	4,919	5,169	...	...	...	...	...	...	...	...	...
132	From international organizations	12,732	13,936	16,264	...	...	...	...	...	...	...	...	...
133	From other general government units	—	—	—	...	...	...	...	...	...	...	...	...
1331	Current	—	—	—	...	...	...	...	...	...	...	...	...
1332	Capital	—	—	—	...	...	...	...	...	...	...	...	...
14	**Other revenue**	**9,533**	**10,027**	**8,587**	...	...	...	...	...	...	...	...	...
	Table 2 Expense by economic type												
2	**Expense**	**41,073**	**48,247**	**54,516**	...	...	...	...	...	...	...	...	...
21	**Compensation of employees**	**6,149**	**6,979**	**6,979**	...	...	...	...	...	...	...	...	...
211	Wages and salaries	5,795	6,627	6,627	...	...	...	...	...	...	...	...	...
212	Employers' social contributions	354	352	352	...	...	...	...	...	...	...	...	...
22	**Use of goods and services**	**8,588**	**10,364**	**10,820**	...	...	...	...	...	...	...	...	...
23	**Consumption of fixed capital**	...	...	...	...	...	...	...	...	...	...	...	...
24	**Interest**	**1,384**	**1,578**	**2,004**	...	...	...	...	...	...	...	...	...
25	**Subsidies**	**18,152**	**23,662**	**27,732**	...	...	...	...	...	...	...	...	...
26	**Grants**	**5,570**	**5,526**	**6,981**	...	...	...	...	...	...	...	...	...
261	To foreign governments	—	—	—	...	...	...	...	...	...	...	...	...
262	To international organizations	48	89	117	...	...	...	...	...	...	...	...	...
263	To other general government units	5,522	5,437	6,864	...	...	...	...	...	...	...	...	...
2631	Current	—	—	—	...	...	...	...	...	...	...	...	...
2632	Capital	5,522	5,437	6,864	...	...	...	...	...	...	...	...	...

Ethiopia (644)

In Millions of Ethiopian Birr (ETB) / Fiscal Year Ends July 6th

		Budgetary Central Government			Central Government (excl. Social Security)			Central Government (incl. Social Security)			General Government		
		2009	2010	2011	2009	2010	2011	2009	2010	2011	2009	2010	2011
27	**Social benefits**	—	—	—	...	...	...	...	...	...	...	...	...
271	Social security benefits	—	—	—	...	...	...	...	...	...	...	...	...
272	Social assistance benefits	—	—	—	...	...	...	...	...	...	...	...	...
273	Employment-related social benefits	—	—	—	...	...	...	...	...	...	...	...	...
28	**Other expense**	**1,230**	**139**	**—**	...	...	...	...	...	...	...	...	...
281	Property expense other than interest	—	—	—	...	...	...	...	...	...	...	...	...
282	Transfers not elsewhere classified	1,230	139	—	...	...	...	...	...	...	...	...	...
2821	Current	1,113	—	—	...	...	...	...	...	...	...	...	...
2822	Capital	116	139	—	...	...	...	...	...	...	...	...	...
	Table 3 Transactions in assets and liabilities												
3	**Change in net worth from transactions**	...	...	...	...	...	...	...	...	...	...	...	...
31	**Net/Gross investment in nonfinancial assets**	**14,187**	**22,685**	**29,893**	...	...	...	...	...	...	...	...	...
311	Fixed assets	14,187	22,685	29,893	...	...	...	...	...	...	...	...	...
3111	Buildings and structures	12,316	19,165	24,981	...	...	...	...	...	...	...	...	...
3112	Machinery and equipment	1,871	3,520	4,912	...	...	...	...	...	...	...	...	...
3113	Other fixed assets	—	—	—	...	...	...	...	...	...	...	...	...
3114	Weapons systems	...	...	...	...	...	...	...	...	...	...	...	...
312	Inventories	—	—	—	...	...	...	...	...	...	...	...	...
313	Valuables	—	—	—	...	...	...	...	...	...	...	...	...
314	Nonproduced assets	—	—	—	...	...	...	...	...	...	...	...	...
3141	Land	—	—	—	...	...	...	...	...	...	...	...	...
3142	Mineral and energy resources	—	—	—	...	...	...	...	...	...	...	...	...
3143	Other naturally occurring assets	—	—	—	...	...	...	...	...	...	...	...	...
3144	Intangible nonproduced assets	—	—	—	...	...	...	...	...	...	...	...	...
32	**Net acquisition of financial assets**	**36,227**	**69,804**	**49,508**	...	...	...	...	...	...	...	...	...
	By instrument												
3201	Monetary gold and SDRs	—	—	—	...	...	...	...	...	...	...	...	...
3202	Currency and deposits	22,772	5,735	24,908	...	...	...	...	...	...	...	...	...
3203	Debt securities	—	44,581	—	...	...	...	...	...	...	...	...	...
3204	Loans	5,782	9,050	16,448	...	...	...	...	...	...	...	...	...
3205	Equity and investment fund shares	—	—	—	...	...	...	...	...	...	...	...	...
3206	Insurance, pension, and standardized guarantee schemes	—	—	—	...	...	...	...	...	...	...	...	...
3207	Financial derivatives and employee stock options	—	—	—	...	...	...	...	...	...	...	...	...
3208	Other accounts receivable	7,673	10,438	8,152	...	...	...	...	...	...	...	...	...
	By debtor												
321	Domestic debtors	14,451	58,976	38,057	...	...	...	...	...	...	...	...	...
322	External debtors	21,776	10,829	11,451	...	...	...	...	...	...	...	...	...
33	**Net incurrence of liabilities**	**49,379**	**51,200**	**62,383**	...	...	...	...	...	...	...	...	...
	By instrument												
3301	Special Drawing Rights (SDRs)	—	—	—	...	...	...	...	...	...	...	...	...
3302	Currency and deposits	44,297	5,688	2,172	...	...	...	...	...	...	...	...	...
3303	Debt securities	—	44,581	59,882	...	...	...	...	...	...	...	...	...
3304	Loans	4,799	170	166	...	...	...	...	...	...	...	...	...
3305	Equity and investment fund shares	—	589	—	...	...	...	...	...	...	...	...	...
3306	Insurance, pension, and standardized guarantee schemes	—	—	—	...	...	...	...	...	...	...	...	...
3307	Financial derivatives and employee stock options	—	—	—	...	...	...	...	...	...	...	...	...
3308	Other accounts payable	283	172	163	...	...	...	...	...	...	...	...	...
	By creditor												
331	Domestic creditors	44,792	51,030	60,808	...	...	...	...	...	...	...	...	...
332	External creditors	4,587	170	1,575	...	...	...	...	...	...	...	...	...
	Table 4 Holding gains and losses in assets and liabilities												
	Table 5 Holding gains and losses in assets and liabilities												
	Table 6 Balance sheet												

Ethiopia (644)

In Millions of Ethiopian Birr (ETB) / Fiscal Year Ends July 6th

	Budgetary Central Government			Central Government (excl. Social Security)			Central Government (incl. Social Security)			General Government		
	2009	2010	2011	2009	2010	2011	2009	2010	2011	2009	2010	2011
Table 7 Expenditure by functions of government												
Table 8 Financial transactions by counterpart sector												
Table 9 Total other economic flows in assets and liabilities												

Fiji (819)

In Millions of Fiji Dollars (FJD) / Fiscal Year Ends December 31st

		Budgetary Central Government			Central Government (excl. Social Security)			Central Government (incl. Social Security)			General Government		
		2011	2012	2013	2011	2012	2013	2011	2012	2013	2011	2012	2013
	Statement of operations												
1	Revenue	1,732	1,819	2,013	...	...	...	...	...	...	...	...	...
2	Expense	1,608	1,687	1,883	...	...	...	...	...	...	...	...	...
GOB	**Gross operating balance**	**124**	**132**	**130**	...	...	...	...	...	...	...	...	...
NOB	**Net operating balance**	...	...	...	...	...	...	...	...	...	...	...	...
31	Net/Gross investment in nonfinancial assets	238	235	196	...	...	...	...	...	...	...	...	...
2M	Expenditure	1,847	1,922	2,079	...	...	...	...	...	...	...	...	...
NLB	**Net lending (+) / Net borrowing (-)**	**-114**	**-102**	**-66**	...	...	...	...	...	...	...	...	...
32	Net acquisition of financial assets	28	25	27	...	...	...	...	...	...	...	...	...
33	Net incurrence of liabilities	142	127	93	...	...	...	...	...	...	...	...	...
NLBz	Statistical discrepancy	0	-0	0	...	...	...	...	...	...	...	...	...
	Memorandum items												
PB	Primary net lending / net borrowing	149	155	194	...	...	...	...	...	...	...	...	...
GB	Government balance per national definition	...	...	...	...	...	...	...	...	...	...	...	...
	Statement of other economic flows												
	Balance sheet												
	Table 1 Revenue												
1	**Revenue**	**1,732**	**1,819**	**2,013**	...	...	...	...	...	...	...	...	...
11	**Taxes**	**1,558**	**1,652**	**1,824**	...	...	...	...	...	...	...	...	...
111	Taxes on income, profits, and capital gains	478	493	443	...	...	...	...	...	...	...	...	...
1111	Payable by individuals	205	131	135	...	...	...	...	...	...	...	...	...
1112	Payable by corporations and other enterprises	177	246	203	...	...	...	...	...	...	...	...	...
1113	Other taxes on income, profits, and capital gains	96	116	104	...	...	...	...	...	...	...	...	...
112	Taxes on payroll and workforce	—	—	—	...	...	...	...	...	...	...	...	...
113	Taxes on property	—	—	—	...	...	...	...	...	...	...	...	...
114	Taxes on goods and services	775	812	974	...	...	...	...	...	...	...	...	...
1141	General taxes on goods and services	619	661	801	...	...	...	...	...	...	...	...	...
1142	Excises	99	110	130	...	...	...	...	...	...	...	...	...
115	Taxes on international trade and transactions	305	347	407	...	...	...	...	...	...	...	...	...
116	Other taxes	—	—	—	...	...	...	...	...	...	...	...	...
12	**Social contributions**	—	—	—	...	...	...	...	...	...	...	...	...
121	Social security contributions	—	—	—	...	...	...	...	...	...	...	...	...
122	Other social contributions	—	—	—	...	...	...	...	...	...	...	...	...
13	**Grants**	**21**	**20**	**29**	...	...	...	...	...	...	...	...	...
131	From foreign governments	7	13	16	...	...	...	...	...	...	...	...	...
132	From international organizations	15	7	13	...	...	...	...	...	...	...	...	...
133	From other general government units	—	—	—	...	...	...	...	...	...	...	...	...
1331	Current	—	—	—	...	...	...	...	...	...	...	...	...
1332	Capital	—	—	—	...	...	...	...	...	...	...	...	...
14	**Other revenue**	**153**	**148**	**159**	...	...	...	...	...	...	...	...	...
	Table 2 Expense by economic type												
2	**Expense**	**1,608**	**1,687**	**1,883**	...	...	...	...	...	...	...	...	...
21	**Compensation of employees**	**553**	**586**	**606**	...	...	...	...	...	...	...	...	...
211	Wages and salaries	515	544	566	...	...	...	...	...	...	...	...	...
212	Employers' social contributions	38	42	41	...	...	...	...	...	...	...	...	...
22	**Use of goods and services**	**207**	**237**	**260**	...	...	...	...	...	...	...	...	...
23	**Consumption of fixed capital**	...	...	...	...	...	...	...	...	...	...	...	...
24	**Interest**	**263**	**258**	**260**	...	...	...	...	...	...	...	...	...
25	**Subsidies**	**188**	**120**	**84**	...	...	...	...	...	...	...	...	...
26	**Grants**	**198**	**282**	**467**	...	...	...	...	...	...	...	...	...
261	To foreign governments	—	—	—	...	...	...	...	...	...	...	...	...
262	To international organizations	—	—	—	...	...	...	...	...	...	...	...	...
263	To other general government units	198	282	467	...	...	...	...	...	...	...	...	...
2631	Current	109	130	171	...	...	...	...	...	...	...	...	...
2632	Capital	89	151	296	...	...	...	...	...	...	...	...	...

Fiji (819)

In Millions of Fiji Dollars (FJD) / Fiscal Year Ends December 31st

		Budgetary Central Government			Central Government (excl. Social Security)			Central Government (incl. Social Security)			General Government		
		2011	2012	2013	2011	2012	2013	2011	2012	2013	2011	2012	2013
27	**Social benefits**	**112**	**111**	**107**	**...**	**...**	**...**	**...**	**...**	**...**	**...**	**...**	**...**
271	Social security benefits	—	—	—	...	...	...	...	...	...	...	...	...
272	Social assistance benefits	78	74	71	...	...	...	...	...	...	...	...	...
273	Employment-related social benefits	34	37	36	...	...	...	...	...	...	...	...	...
28	**Other expense**	**87**	**95**	**98**	**...**	**...**	**...**	**...**	**...**	**...**	**...**	**...**	**...**
281	Property expense other than interest	2	3	6	...	...	...	...	...	...	...	...	...
282	Transfers not elsewhere classified	85	92	91	...	...	...	...	...	...	...	...	...
2821	Current	79	86	82	...	...	...	...	...	...	...	...	...
2822	Capital	5	6	9	...	...	...	...	...	...	...	...	...
	Table 3 Transactions in assets and liabilities												
3	**Change in net worth from transactions**	**...**	**...**	**...**	**...**	**...**	**...**	**...**	**...**	**...**	**...**	**...**	**...**
31	**Net/Gross investment in nonfinancial assets**	**238**	**235**	**196**	**...**	**...**	**...**	**...**	**...**	**...**	**...**	**...**	**...**
311	Fixed assets	205	198	160	...	...	...	...	...	...	...	...	...
3111	Buildings and structures	...	...	...	...	...	...	...	...	...	...	...	...
3112	Machinery and equipment	...	...	...	...	...	...	...	...	...	...	...	...
3113	Other fixed assets	...	...	...	...	...	...	...	...	...	...	...	...
3114	Weapons systems	...	...	...	...	...	...	...	...	...	...	...	...
312	Inventories	27	29	26	...	...	...	...	...	...	...	...	...
313	Valuables	—	—	—	...	...	...	...	...	...	...	...	...
314	Nonproduced assets	6	8	10	...	...	...	...	...	...	...	...	...
3141	Land	...	...	...	...	...	...	...	...	...	...	...	...
3142	Mineral and energy resources	...	...	...	...	...	...	...	...	...	...	...	...
3143	Other naturally occurring assets	...	...	...	...	...	...	...	...	...	...	...	...
3144	Intangible nonproduced assets	...	...	...	...	...	...	...	...	...	...	...	...
32	**Net acquisition of financial assets**	**28**	**25**	**27**	**...**	**...**	**...**	**...**	**...**	**...**	**...**	**...**	**...**
	By instrument												
3201	Monetary gold and SDRs	...	...	...	...	...	...	...	...	...	—	—	...
3202	Currency and deposits	44	47	43	...	...	...	...	...	...	...	...	...
3203	Debt securities	...	...	...	...	...	...	...	...	...	...	...	...
3204	Loans	...	...	...	...	...	...	...	...	...	...	...	...
3205	Equity and investment fund shares	...	...	...	...	...	...	...	...	...	...	...	...
3206	Insurance, pension, and standardized guarantee schemes	...	...	...	...	...	...	...	...	...	...	...	...
3207	Financial derivatives and employee stock options	...	...	...	...	...	...	...	...	...	...	...	...
3208	Other accounts receivable	...	...	...	...	...	...	...	...	...	...	...	...
	By debtor												
321	Domestic debtors	28	25	27	...	...	...	...	...	...	...	...	...
322	External debtors	—	—	—	...	...	...	...	...	...	...	...	...
33	**Net incurrence of liabilities**	**142**	**127**	**93**	**...**	**...**	**...**	**...**	**...**	**...**	**...**	**...**	**...**
	By instrument												
3301	Special Drawing Rights (SDRs)	...	...	...	...	...	...	...	...	...	—	—	...
3302	Currency and deposits	...	...	...	...	...	...	...	...	...	...	...	...
3303	Debt securities	...	...	...	...	...	...	...	...	...	...	...	...
3304	Loans	...	...	...	...	...	...	...	...	...	...	...	...
3305	Equity and investment fund shares	...	...	...	...	...	...	...	...	...	...	...	...
3306	Insurance, pension, and standardized guarantee schemes	...	...	...	...	...	...	...	...	...	...	...	...
3307	Financial derivatives and employee stock options	...	...	...	...	...	...	...	...	...	...	...	...
3308	Other accounts payable	...	...	...	...	...	...	...	...	...	...	...	...
	By creditor												
331	Domestic creditors	-136	9	13	...	...	...	...	...	...	...	...	...
332	External creditors	278	118	80	...	...	...	...	...	...	...	...	...
	Table 4 Holding gains and losses in assets and liabilities												
	Table 5 Holding gains and losses in assets and liabilities												
	Table 6 Balance sheet												

Fiji (819)

In Millions of Fiji Dollars (FJD) / Fiscal Year Ends December 31st

	Budgetary Central Government			Central Government (excl. Social Security)			Central Government (incl. Social Security)			General Government		
	2011	2012	2013	2011	2012	2013	2011	2012	2013	2011	2012	2013
Table 7 Expenditure by functions of government												
Table 8 Financial transactions by counterpart sector												
Table 9 Total other economic flows in assets and liabilities												

Finland (172)

In Millions of Euros (EUR) / Fiscal Year Ends December 31st

		Budgetary Central Government			Central Government (excl. Social Security)			Central Government (incl. Social Security)			General Government		
		2013	2014	2015	2013P	2014P	2015P	2013P	2014P	2015P	2013P	2014P	2015P
	Statement of operations												
1	Revenue	...	...	...	48,718	49,164	50,407	77,916	78,547	79,985	109,462	110,640	112,748
2	Expense	...	...	...	56,370	56,936	57,056	81,915	83,784	85,019	113,541	115,857	117,771
GOB	**Gross operating balance**	**...**	**...**	**...**	**-4,009**	**-4,138**	**-2,987**	**-240**	**-1,486**	**-1,257**	**2,647**	**1,592**	**1,872**
NOB	**Net operating balance**	**...**	**...**	**...**	**-7,652**	**-7,772**	**-6,649**	**-3,999**	**-5,237**	**-5,034**	**-4,079**	**-5,217**	**-5,023**
31	Net/Gross investment in nonfinancial assets	...	...	...	-73	-113	-339	-151	-315	-608	1,236	1,278	729
2M	Expenditure	...	...	...	56,297	56,823	56,717	81,764	83,469	84,411	114,777	117,135	118,500
NLB	**Net lending (+) / Net borrowing (-)**	**...**	**...**	**...**	**-7,579**	**-7,659**	**-6,310**	**-3,848**	**-4,922**	**-4,426**	**-5,315**	**-6,495**	**-5,752**
32	Net acquisition of financial assets	...	...	...	-1,935	-1,068	-101	...	...	...	4,293	638	2,707
33	Net incurrence of liabilities	...	...	...	5,673	6,883	6,207	...	...	...	9,047	7,638	8,389
NLBz	Statistical discrepancy	...	...	...	-29	-292	2	...	...	...	561	-505	70
	Memorandum items												
PB	Primary net lending / net borrowing	...	...	...	-5,094	-5,198	-3,976	-1,387	-2,485	-2,068	-2,644	-3,818	-3,166
GB	Government balance per national definition	...	...	...	...	...	...	...	...	...	...	...	...
	Statement of other economic flows												
	Balance sheet												
6	**Net worth**	**...**	**...**	**...**	**...**	**...**	**...**	**...**	**...**	**...**	**227,520**	**232,811**	**235,874**
61	Nonfinancial assets	...	...	...	...	...	...	...	...	...	119,720	122,234	122,844
62	Financial assets	...	...	...	59,475	60,668	61,328	...	...	...	238,975	257,361	268,236
63	Liabilities	...	...	...	108,778	119,226	124,484	...	...	...	131,175	146,784	155,206
	Table 1 Revenue												
1	**Revenue**	**...**	**...**	**...**	**48,718**	**49,164**	**50,407**	**77,916**	**78,547**	**79,985**	**109,462**	**110,640**	**112,748**
11	**Taxes**	**...**	**...**	**...**	**42,179**	**42,686**	**43,346**	**42,179**	**42,686**	**43,346**	**62,889**	**63,845**	**65,195**
111	Taxes on income, profits, and capital gains	...	...	...	11,506	11,901	12,200	11,506	11,901	12,200	30,850	31,546	32,444
1111	Payable by individuals	...	...	...	8,110	9,290	9,248	8,110	9,290	9,248	25,998	27,523	27,824
1112	Payable by corporations and other enterprises	...	...	...	3,343	2,544	2,879	3,343	2,544	2,879	4,799	3,956	4,547
1113	Other taxes on income, profits, and capital gains	...	...	...	53	67	73	53	67	73	53	67	73
112	Taxes on payroll and workforce	...	...	...	1	1	—	1	1	—	1	1	—
113	Taxes on property	...	...	...	646	499	631	646	499	631	2,009	2,011	2,234
114	Taxes on goods and services	...	...	...	30,025	30,285	30,515	30,025	30,285	30,515	30,028	30,287	30,517
1141	General taxes on goods and services	...	...	...	19,478	19,656	19,757	19,478	19,656	19,757	19,478	19,656	19,757
1142	Excises	...	...	...	7,512	7,432	7,678	7,512	7,432	7,678	7,513	7,433	7,679
115	Taxes on international trade and transactions	...	...	...	1	—	—	1	—	—	1	—	—
116	Other taxes	...	...	...	—	—	—	—	—	—	—	—	—
12	**Social contributions**	**...**	**...**	**...**	**—**	**—**	**—**	**25,886**	**26,273**	**26,927**	**25,902**	**26,288**	**26,942**
121	Social security contributions	...	...	...	—	—	—	25,886	26,273	26,927	25,886	26,273	26,927
122	Other social contributions	...	...	...	—	—	—	—	—	—	16	15	15
13	**Grants**	**...**	**...**	**...**	**2,592**	**2,595**	**3,024**	**1,397**	**1,355**	**1,385**	**568**	**525**	**414**
131	From foreign governments	...	...	...	18	17	18	24	21	24	24	21	24
132	From international organizations	...	...	...	488	452	354	489	452	354	544	504	390
133	From other general government units	...	...	...	2,086	2,126	2,652	884	882	1,007	—	—	—
1331	Current	...	...	...	2,051	2,126	2,652	849	882	1,007	—	—	—
1332	Capital	...	...	...	35	—	—	35	—	—	—	—	—
14	**Other revenue**	**...**	**...**	**...**	**3,947**	**3,883**	**4,037**	**8,454**	**8,233**	**8,327**	**20,103**	**19,982**	**20,197**
	Table 2 Expense by economic type												
2	**Expense**	**...**	**...**	**...**	**56,370**	**56,936**	**57,056**	**81,915**	**83,784**	**85,019**	**113,541**	**115,857**	**117,771**
21	**Compensation of employees**	**...**	**...**	**...**	**6,206**	**6,193**	**6,059**	**6,757**	**6,760**	**6,621**	**28,247**	**28,279**	**28,166**
211	Wages and salaries	...	...	...	4,961	4,896	4,822	5,408	5,354	5,274	21,915	21,899	21,845
212	Employers' social contributions	...	...	...	1,245	1,297	1,237	1,349	1,406	1,347	6,332	6,380	6,321
22	**Use of goods and services**	**...**	**...**	**...**	**5,295**	**5,264**	**5,481**	**6,470**	**6,392**	**6,584**	**22,504**	**22,629**	**22,973**
23	**Consumption of fixed capital**	**...**	**...**	**...**	**3,643**	**3,634**	**3,662**	**3,759**	**3,751**	**3,777**	**6,726**	**6,809**	**6,895**
24	**Interest**	**...**	**...**	**...**	**2,485**	**2,461**	**2,334**	**2,461**	**2,437**	**2,358**	**2,671**	**2,677**	**2,586**
25	**Subsidies**	**...**	**...**	**...**	**2,303**	**2,282**	**2,430**	**2,303**	**2,282**	**2,430**	**2,697**	**2,689**	**2,839**

Finland (172)

In Millions of Euros (EUR) / Fiscal Year Ends December 31st

		Budgetary Central Government			Central Government (excl. Social Security)			Central Government (incl. Social Security)			General Government		
		2013	2014	2015	2013P	2014P	2015P	2013P	2014P	2015P	2013P	2014P	2015P
26	**Grants**	...	...	...	**28,907**	**29,305**	**29,127**	**17,106**	**17,013**	**16,706**	**2,983**	**2,909**	**2,733**
261	To foreign governments	...	...	...	897	1,011	927	922	1,028	949	922	1,028	949
262	To international organizations	...	...	...	2,060	1,880	1,784	2,061	1,881	1,784	2,061	1,881	1,784
263	To other general government units	...	...	...	25,950	26,414	26,416	14,123	14,104	13,973	—	—	—
2631	Current	...	...	...	25,792	26,239	26,203	13,967	13,930	13,761	—	—	—
2632	Capital	...	...	...	158	175	213	156	174	212	—	—	—
27	**Social benefits**	...	...	...	**4,491**	**4,589**	**4,652**	**39,731**	**41,626**	**42,923**	**43,928**	**45,885**	**47,429**
271	Social security benefits	...	...	...	...	...	...	...	...	...	...	...	...
272	Social assistance benefits	...	...	...	...	...	...	...	...	...	...	...	...
273	Employment-related social benefits	...	...	...	...	...	...	...	...	...	...	...	...
28	**Other expense**	...	...	...	**3,040**	**3,208**	**3,311**	**3,328**	**3,523**	**3,620**	**3,785**	**3,980**	**4,150**
281	Property expense other than interest	...	...	...	8	8	10	8	8	10	14	13	15
282	Transfers not elsewhere classified	...	...	...	...	...	...	...	...	...	...	...	...
2821	Current	...	...	...	...	...	...	...	...	...	...	...	...
2822	Capital	...	...	...	560	596	778	560	596	778	627	638	924
	Table 3 Transactions in assets and liabilities												
3	**Change in net worth from transactions**	...	...	...	**-7,681**	**-8,064**	**-6,647**	...	...	...	**-3,518**	**-5,722**	**-4,953**
31	**Net/Gross investment in nonfinancial assets**	...	...	...	**-73**	**-113**	**-339**	**-151**	**-315**	**-608**	**1,236**	**1,278**	**729**
311	Fixed assets	...	...	...	-85	-36	-351	-163	-238	-620	1,273	1,326	816
3111	Buildings and structures	...	...	...	...	...	...	...	...	...	...	...	...
3112	Machinery and equipment	...	...	...	...	...	...	...	...	...	...	...	...
3113	Other fixed assets	...	...	...	...	...	...	...	...	...	...	...	...
3114	Weapons systems	...	...	...	...	...	...	...	...	...	...	...	...
312	Inventories	...	...	...	...	...	...	...	...	...	...	...	...
313	Valuables	...	...	...	...	...	...	...	...	...	...	...	...
314	Nonproduced assets	...	...	...	9	-79	11	9	-79	11	-54	-62	-108
3141	Land	...	...	...	...	...	...	...	...	...	...	...	...
3142	Mineral and energy resources	...	...	...	...	...	...	...	...	...	...	...	...
3143	Other naturally occurring assets	...	...	...	...	...	...	...	...	...	...	...	...
3144	Intangible nonproduced assets	...	...	...	...	...	...	...	...	...	...	...	...
32	**Net acquisition of financial assets**	...	...	...	**-1,935**	**-1,068**	**-101**	...	...	...	**4,293**	**638**	**2,707**
	By instrument												
3201	Monetary gold and SDRs	...	...	...	—	—	—	...	...	...	—	—	—
3202	Currency and deposits	...	...	...	-2,274	-1,171	1,630	...	...	...	-1,578	-1,648	5,522
3203	Debt securities	...	...	...	-945	245	-414	...	...	...	2,615	-1,170	93
3204	Loans	...	...	...	1,972	-168	-538	...	...	...	934	-1,018	-510
3205	Equity and investment fund shares	...	...	...	98	-191	-596	...	...	...	4,931	1,810	-2,383
3206	Insurance, pension, and standardized guarantee schemes	...	...	...	—	—	—	...	...	...	—	18	6
3207	Financial derivatives and employee stock options	...	...	...	—	—	—	...	...	...	—	—	—
3208	Other accounts receivable	...	...	...	-786	217	-183	...	...	...	-2,609	2,646	-21
	By debtor												
321	Domestic debtors	...	...	...	574	1,239	-401	...	...	...	436	-3,412	2,338
322	External debtors	...	...	...	-2,509	-2,307	300	...	...	...	3,857	4,050	369
33	**Net incurrence of liabilities**	...	...	...	**5,673**	**6,883**	**6,207**	...	...	...	**9,047**	**7,638**	**8,389**
	By instrument												
3301	Special Drawing Rights (SDRs)	...	...	...	—	—	—	...	...	...	—	—	—
3302	Currency and deposits	...	...	...	59	138	79	...	...	...	59	138	79
3303	Debt securities	...	...	...	6,068	5,829	2,968	...	...	...	5,758	7,316	5,187
3304	Loans	...	...	...	-725	530	1,786	...	...	...	1,353	1,980	2,809
3305	Equity and investment fund shares	...	...	...	—	—	—	...	...	...	—	—	—
3306	Insurance, pension, and standardized guarantee schemes	...	...	...	5	11	7	...	...	...	5	11	7
3307	Financial derivatives and employee stock options	...	...	...	449	663	1,027	...	...	...	1,593	-1,442	-840
3308	Other accounts payable	...	...	...	-183	-288	340	...	...	...	279	-365	1,147

Finland (172)

In Millions of Euros (EUR) / Fiscal Year Ends December 31st

		Budgetary Central Government			Central Government (excl. Social Security)			Central Government (incl. Social Security)			General Government		
		2013	2014	2015	2013P	2014P	2015P	2013P	2014P	2015P	2013P	2014P	2015P
	By creditor												
331	Domestic creditors	...	...	...	-92	676	5,770	...	...	...	1,912	2,425	9,361
332	External creditors	...	...	...	5,765	6,207	437	...	...	...	7,135	5,213	-972
	Table 4 Holding gains and losses in assets and liabilities												
	Table 5 Holding gains and losses in assets and liabilities												
	Table 6 Balance sheet												
6	**Net worth**	...	...	...	...	...	...	...	...	...	**227,520**	**232,811**	**235,874**
61	**Nonfinancial assets**	...	...	...	...	...	...	...	...	...	**119,720**	**122,234**	**122,844**
611	Fixed assets	...	...	...	...	...	...	...	...	...	117,684	120,192	120,788
6111	Buildings and structures	...	...	...	...	...	...	...	...	...	96,275	98,567	98,801
6112	Machinery and equipment	...	...	...	...	...	...	...	...	...	...	...	...
6113	Other fixed assets	...	...	...	...	...	...	...	...	...	9,322	9,476	...
6114	Weapons systems	...	...	...	...	...	...	...	...	...	...	...	...
612	Inventories	...	...	...	...	...	...	...	...	...	1,943	1,953	1,963
613	Valuables	...	...	...	...	...	...	...	...	...	93	89	93
614	Nonproduced assets	...	...	...	...	...	...	...	...	...	...	...	...
6141	Land	...	...	...	...	...	...	...	...	...	34,715	35,464	36,383
6142	Mineral and energy resources	...	...	...	...	...	...	...	...	...	...	...	...
6143	Other naturally occurring assets	...	...	...	...	...	...	...	...	...	...	...	...
6144	Intangible nonproduced assets	...	...	...	...	...	...	...	...	...	...	...	...
62	**Financial assets**	...	...	...	**59,475**	**60,668**	**61,328**	...	...	...	**238,975**	**257,361**	**268,236**
	By instrument												
6201	Monetary gold and SDRs	...	...	...	—	—	—	...	...	...	—	—	—
6202	Currency and deposits	...	...	...	5,211	4,042	5,672	...	...	...	14,743	13,097	18,619
6203	Debt securities	...	...	...	305	579	1,070	...	...	...	42,507	43,598	44,184
6204	Loans	...	...	...	18,727	18,559	18,021	...	...	...	31,222	31,347	30,854
6205	Equity and investment fund shares	...	...	...	32,719	34,650	34,016	...	...	...	141,533	157,518	162,901
6206	Insurance, pension, and standardized guarantee schemes	...	...	...	—	—	—	...	...	...	84	176	176
6207	Financial derivatives and employee stock options	...	...	...	—	—	—	...	...	...	2,188	2,173	2,177
6208	Other accounts receivable	...	...	...	2,513	2,838	2,549	...	...	...	6,698	9,452	9,325
	By debtor												
621	Domestic debtors	...	...	...	44,757	48,925	48,359	...	...	...	114,923	119,837	124,870
622	External debtors	...	...	...	14,718	11,743	12,969	...	...	...	124,052	137,524	143,366
63	**Liabilities**	...	...	...	**108,778**	**119,226**	**124,484**	...	...	...	**131,175**	**146,784**	**155,206**
	By instrument												
6301	Special Drawing Rights (SDRs)	...	...	...	—	—	—	...	...	...	—	—	—
6302	Currency and deposits	...	...	...	614	752	831	...	...	...	614	752	831
6303	Debt securities	...	...	...	95,330	107,900	110,665	...	...	...	94,004	107,848	113,226
6304	Loans	...	...	...	10,866	11,396	13,182	...	...	...	25,550	27,530	30,279
6305	Equity and investment fund shares	...	...	...	—	—	—	...	...	...	521	521	521
6306	Insurance, pension, and standardized guarantee schemes	...	...	...	84	95	102	...	...	...	84	95	102
6307	Financial derivatives and employee stock options	...	...	...	-1,339	-3,852	-3,571	...	...	...	-1,039	-1,003	-1,941
6308	Other accounts payable	...	...	...	3,223	2,935	3,275	...	...	...	11,441	11,041	12,188
	By creditor												
631	Domestic creditors	...	...	...	16,152	16,256	21,500	...	...	...	33,771	36,126	44,942
632	External creditors	...	...	...	92,626	102,970	102,984	...	...	...	97,404	110,658	110,264
	Memorandum items												
6M2	Net financial worth	...	...	...	-49,303	-58,558	-63,156	...	...	...	107,800	110,577	113,030
6M3	Gross debt (D4) at market value	...	...	...	110,117	123,078	128,055	...	...	...	131,693	147,266	156,626
6M3D3	D3 debt liabilities at market value	...	...	...	110,033	122,983	127,953	...	...	...	131,609	147,171	156,524
6M3D2	D2 debt liabilities at market value	...	...	...	106,810	120,048	124,678	...	...	...	120,168	136,130	144,336
6M3D1	D1 debt liabilities at market value	...	...	...	106,196	119,296	123,847	...	...	...	119,554	135,378	143,505
6M4	Gross debt (D4) at nominal value	...	...	...	...	...	...	...	...	...	...	...	...
6M4D3	D3 debt liabilities at nominal value	...	...	...	...	...	...	...	...	...	...	...	...
6M4D2	D2 debt liabilities at nominal value	...	...	...	...	...	...	...	...	...	...	...	...
6M4D1	D1 debt liabilities at nominal value	...	...	...	...	...	...	...	...	...	...	...	...

Finland (172)

In Millions of Euros (EUR) / Fiscal Year Ends December 31st

		Budgetary Central Government			Central Government (excl. Social Security)			Central Government (incl. Social Security)			General Government		
		2013	2014	2015	2013P	2014P	2015P	2013P	2014P	2015P	2013P	2014P	2015P
6M35	Gross debt (D4) at face value	...	...	...	...	...	...	...	...	...	...	...	...
6M35D3	D3 debt liabilities at face value	...	...	...	104,454	110,344	116,674	...	...	...	126,242	134,737	145,299
6M35D2	D2 debt liabilities at face value	...	...	...	101,231	107,409	113,399	...	...	...	114,801	123,696	133,111
6M35D1	D1 debt liabilities at face value	...	...	...	100,617	106,657	112,568	...	...	...	114,187	122,944	132,280
6M93	Government gross debt per national definition	...	...	...	101,231	107,409	113,399	...	...	...	114,801	123,696	133,111
6M5	Arrears	...	...	...	...	...	...	...	...	...	...	...	...
6M6	Explicit contingent liabilities	...	...	...	...	...	...	...	...	...	...	...	...
6M61	of which: Publicly guaranteed debt	...	...	...	...	...	...	...	...	...	...	...	...
6M7	Net implicit obligations for social security benefits	...	...	...	...	...	...	...	...	...	...	...	...
	Table 7 Expenditure by functions of government												
7	**Expenditure**	...	...	...	**58,037**	**58,599**	...	...	...	...	**116,854**	**119,190**	...
701	**General public services**	...	...	...	**13,158**	**13,259**	...	...	...	...	**16,794**	**17,008**	...
7017	Public debt transactions	...	...	...	2,504	2,530	...	...	...	...	2,690	2,746	...
7018	Transfers of general character between levels of government	...	...	...	3,558	3,519	...	...	...	...	—	—	...
702	**Defense**	...	...	...	**2,981**	**2,889**	...	...	...	...	**2,981**	**2,889**	...
703	**Public order and safety**	...	...	...	**2,256**	**2,170**	...	...	...	...	**2,811**	**2,729**	...
704	**Economic affairs**	...	...	...	**6,918**	**6,915**	...	...	...	...	**9,745**	**9,946**	...
7042	Agriculture, forestry, fishing, and hunting	...	...	...	1,692	1,659	...	...	...	...	1,800	1,763	...
7043	Fuel and energy	...	...	...	102	145	...	...	...	...	158	140	...
7044	Mining, manufacturing, and construction	...	...	...	132	129	...	...	...	...	216	212	...
7045	Transport	...	...	...	2,479	2,535	...	...	...	...	4,864	5,201	...
7046	Communication	...	...	...	44	-65	...	...	...	...	44	-65	...
705	**Environmental protection**	...	...	...	**389**	**397**	...	...	...	...	**522**	**529**	...
706	**Housing and community amenities**	...	...	...	**398**	**375**	...	...	...	...	**810**	**814**	...
707	**Health**	...	...	...	**6,550**	**6,536**	...	...	...	...	**16,869**	**17,064**	...
7072	Outpatient services	...	...	...	26	31	...	...	...	...	7,529	7,741	...
7073	Hospital services	...	...	...	54	56	...	...	...	...	7,266	7,238	...
7074	Public health services	...	...	...	50	70	...	...	...	...	48	48	...
708	**Recreation, culture and religion**	...	...	...	**1,482**	**1,534**	...	...	...	...	**2,981**	**2,970**	...
709	**Education**	...	...	...	**7,208**	**7,263**	...	...	...	...	**13,011**	**13,063**	...
7091	Pre-primary and primary education	...	...	...	104	109	...	...	...	...	2,582	2,615	...
7092	Secondary education	...	...	...	3,278	3,297	...	...	...	...	5,565	5,580	...
7094	Tertiary education	...	...	...	3,488	3,523	...	...	...	...	4,009	3,990	...
710	**Social protection**	...	...	...	**16,697**	**17,261**	...	...	...	...	**50,330**	**52,178**	...
7z	Statistical discrepancy: Expenditure	...	...	...	—	—	...	...	...	...	—	—	...
	Table 8 Financial transactions by counterpart sector												
32	**Net acquisition of financial assets**	...	...	...	**-1,935**	**-1,068**	**-101**	...	...	...	**4,293**	**638**	**2,707**
321	Domestic debtors	...	...	...	574	1,239	-401	...	...	...	436	-3,412	2,338
8211	General government	...	...	...	...	...	...	...	...	...	—	—	—
8212	Central bank	...	...	...	...	...	...	...	...	...	...	...	...
8213	Deposit-taking corporations except the central bank	...	...	...	...	...	...	...	...	...	...	...	...
8214	Other financial corporations	...	...	...	...	...	...	...	...	...	...	...	...
8215	Nonfinancial corporations	...	...	...	...	...	...	...	...	...	...	...	...
8216	Households & nonprofit institutions serving households	...	...	...	...	...	...	...	...	...	...	...	...
322	External debtors	...	...	...	-2,509	-2,307	300	...	...	...	3,857	4,050	369
8221	General government	...	...	...	...	...	...	...	...	...	...	...	...
8227	International organizations	...	...	...	...	...	...	...	...	...	...	...	...
8228	Financial corporations other than international organizations	...	...	...	...	...	...	...	...	...	...	...	...
8229	Other nonresidents	...	...	...	...	...	...	...	...	...	...	...	...

Finland (172)

In Millions of Euros (EUR) / Fiscal Year Ends December 31st

		Budgetary Central Government			Central Government (excl. Social Security)			Central Government (incl. Social Security)			General Government		
		2013	2014	2015	2013P	2014P	2015P	2013P	2014P	2015P	2013P	2014P	2015P
33	**Net incurrence of liabilities**	...	...	...	**5,673**	**6,883**	**6,207**	...	...	...	**9,047**	**7,638**	**8,389**
331	Domestic creditors	...	...	...	-92	676	5,770	...	...	...	1,912	2,425	9,361
8311	General government	...	...	...	...	...	...	...	...	...	—	—	—
8312	Central bank	...	...	...	...	...	...	...	...	...	...	...	...
8313	Deposit-taking corporations except the central bank	...	...	...	...	...	...	...	...	...	...	...	...
8314	Other financial corporations	...	...	...	...	...	...	...	...	...	...	...	...
8315	Nonfinancial corporations	...	...	...	...	...	...	...	...	...	...	...	...
8316	Households & nonprofit institutions serving households	...	...	...	...	...	...	...	...	...	...	...	...
332	External creditors	...	...	...	5,765	6,207	437	...	...	...	7,135	5,213	-972
8321	General government	...	...	...	...	...	...	...	...	...	...	...	...
8327	International organizations	...	...	...	...	...	...	...	...	...	...	...	...
8328	Financial corporations other than international organizations	...	...	...	...	...	...	...	...	...	...	...	...
8329	Other nonresidents	...	...	...	...	...	...	...	...	...	...	...	...
	Table 9 Total other economic flows in assets and liabilities												
9	**Change in net worth due to other economic flows**	...	...	...	...	...	...	...	...	...	...	...	...
91	**Other economic flows in nonfinancial assets**	...	...	...	...	...	...	...	...	...	...	...	...
911	Fixed assets	...	...	...	...	...	...	...	...	...	...	...	...
912	Inventories	...	...	...	...	...	...	...	...	...	...	...	...
913	Valuables	...	...	...	...	...	...	...	...	...	...	...	...
914	Nonproduced assets	...	...	...	...	...	...	...	...	...	...	...	...
92	**Other economic flows in financial assets**	...	...	...	**2,915**	**2,261**	**761**	...	...	...	**8,376**	**17,748**	**8,168**
	By instrument												
9201	Monetary gold and SDRs	...	...	...	—	—	—	...	...	...	—	—	—
9202	Currency and deposits	...	...	...	—	2	—	...	...	...	-20	2	—
9203	Debt securities	...	...	...	1	29	905	...	...	...	-2,225	2,261	493
9204	Loans	...	...	...	—	—	—	...	...	...	-25	1,143	17
9205	Equity and investment fund shares	...	...	...	2,914	2,122	-38	...	...	...	10,813	14,175	7,766
9206	Insurance, pension, and standardized guarantee schemes	...	...	...	—	—	—	...	...	...	—	74	-6
9207	Financial derivatives and employee stock options	...	...	...	—	—	—	...	...	...	-167	-15	4
9208	Other accounts receivable	...	...	...	—	108	-106	...	...	...	—	108	-106
	By debtor												
921	Domestic debtors	...	...	...	...	...	...	...	...	...	...	...	...
922	External debtors	...	...	...	...	...	...	...	...	...	...	...	...
93	**Other economic flows in liabilities**	...	...	...	**-3,317**	**3,565**	**-949**	...	...	...	**-5,420**	**7,971**	**33**
	By instrument												
9301	Special Drawing Rights (SDRs)	...	...	...	—	—	—	...	...	...	—	—	—
9302	Currency and deposits	...	...	...	—	—	—	...	...	...	—	—	—
9303	Debt securities	...	...	...	-4,425	6,741	-203	...	...	...	-4,299	6,528	191
9304	Loans	...	...	...	0	—	—	...	...	...	-0	—	-60
9305	Equity and investment fund shares	...	...	...	—	—	—	...	...	...	—	—	—
9306	Insurance, pension, and standardized guarantee schemes	...	...	...	—	—	—	...	...	...	—	—	—
9307	Financial derivatives and employee stock options	...	...	...	1,114	-3,176	-746	...	...	...	-1,115	1,478	-98
9308	Other accounts payable	...	...	...	-6	—	—	...	...	...	-6	-35	—
	By creditor												
931	Domestic creditors	...	...	...	...	...	...	...	...	...	...	...	...
932	External creditors	...	...	...	...	...	...	...	...	...	...	...	...
	Memorandum items												
9M2	Change in net financial worth due to other economic flows	...	...	...	6,232	-1,304	1,710	...	...	...	13,796	9,777	8,135

Finland (172)

In Millions of Euros (EUR) / Fiscal Year Ends December 31st

		Budgetary Central Government			Central Government (excl. Social Security)			Central Government (incl. Social Security)			General Government		
		2013	2014	2015	2013P	2014P	2015P	2013P	2014P	2015P	2013P	2014P	2015P
9M3	Gross debt (D4) at market value: other economic flows	...	...	...	-4,431	6,741	-203	...	...	...	-4,305	6,493	131
9M3D3	D3 debt liabilities at market value: other economic flows	...	...	...	-4,431	6,741	-203	...	...	...	-4,305	6,493	131
9M3D2	D2 debt liabilities at market value: other economic flows	...	...	...	-4,425	6,741	-203	...	...	...	-4,299	6,528	131
9M3D1	D1 debt liabilities at market value: other economic flows	...	...	...	-4,425	6,741	-203	...	...	...	-4,299	6,528	131

France (132)

In Billions of Euros (EUR) / Fiscal Year Ends December 31st

		Budgetary Central Government			Central Government (excl. Social Security)			Central Government (incl. Social Security)			General Government		
		2013	2014	2015	2013P	2014P	2015P	2013P	2014P	2015P	2013P	2014P	2015P
	Statement of operations												
1	Revenue	...	...	...	419	423	429	950	968	985	1,120	1,142	1,166
2	Expense	...	...	...	488	498	502	1,027	1,049	1,063	1,192	1,219	1,238
GOB	**Gross operating balance**	...	...	...	-42	-48	-46	-42	-47	-43	2	-3	1
NOB	**Net operating balance**	...	...	...	-69	-75	-73	-77	-81	-78	-72	-77	-72
31	Net/Gross investment in nonfinancial assets	...	...	...	-1	-2	-1	0	-1	-0	14	7	4
2M	Expenditure	...	...	...	487	495	501	1,027	1,048	1,062	1,205	1,227	1,243
NLB	**Net lending (+) / Net borrowing (-)**	...	...	...	-68	-72	-72	-77	-80	-77	-85	-85	-77
32	Net acquisition of financial assets	...	...	...	7	8	10	...	...	...	3	13	16
33	Net incurrence of liabilities	...	...	...	74	82	82	...	...	...	87	101	90
NLBz	Statistical discrepancy	...	...	...	1	-2	1	...	...	...	2	-3	3
	Memorandum items												
PB	Primary net lending / net borrowing	...	...	...	-27	-33	-35	-32	-36	-35	-37	-38	-33
GB	Government balance per national definition	...	...	...	...	...	...	...	...	...	...	...	...
	Statement of other economic flows												
	Balance sheet												
6	**Net worth**	...	...	...	...	...	...	...	...	...	-202	-399	...
61	Nonfinancial assets	...	...	...	...	...	...	...	...	...	1,202	1,201	...
62	Financial assets	...	...	...	564	584	575	...	...	...	945	979	981
63	Liabilities	...	...	...	1,899	2,097	2,151	...	...	...	2,348	2,578	2,642
	Table 1 Revenue												
1	**Revenue**	...	...	...	419	423	429	950	968	985	1,120	1,142	1,166
11	**Taxes**	...	...	...	329	330	339	492	498	510	609	618	635
111	Taxes on income, profits, and capital gains	...	...	...	140	138	137	246	246	250	246	246	250
1111	Payable by individuals	...	...	...	82	82	80	187	189	192	187	189	192
1112	Payable by corporations and other enterprises	...	...	...	58	56	56	59	57	58	59	57	58
1113	Other taxes on income, profits, and capital gains	...	...	...	0	0	0	0	0	0	0	0	0
112	Taxes on payroll and workforce	...	...	...	5	5	5	25	26	26	34	35	35
113	Taxes on property	...	...	...	16	16	18	16	16	18	86	88	92
114	Taxes on goods and services	...	...	...	168	169	178	203	208	214	240	246	255
1141	General taxes on goods and services	...	...	...	136	137	141	146	149	153	155	160	164
1142	Excises	...	...	...	20	20	23	36	36	39	48	48	53
115	Taxes on international trade and transactions	...	...	...	-0	-0	-0	-0	-0	-0	1	1	1
116	Other taxes	...	...	...	2	2	1	2	2	1	2	2	1
12	**Social contributions**	...	...	...	48	48	49	398	408	412	399	409	413
121	Social security contributions	...	...	...	—	—	—	349	359	362	349	359	362
122	Other social contributions	...	...	...	48	48	49	49	49	50	50	50	51
13	**Grants**	...	...	...	...	...	...	...	...	...	...	...	...
131	From foreign governments	...	...	...	...	...	...	...	...	...	...	...	...
132	From international organizations	...	...	...	...	...	...	...	...	...	...	...	...
133	From other general government units	...	...	...	10	11	6	4	5	4	—	—	—
1331	Current	...	...	...	10	10	5	4	4	4	—	—	—
1332	Capital	...	...	...	1	1	1	1	1	1	—	—	—
14	**Other revenue**	...	...	...	...	...	...	...	...	...	...	...	...
	Table 2 Expense by economic type												
2	**Expense**	...	...	...	488	498	502	1,027	1,049	1,063	1,192	1,219	1,238
21	**Compensation of employees**	...	...	...	136	137	137	198	201	202	273	279	282
211	Wages and salaries	...	...	...	...	...	...	...	...	...	...	...	...
212	Employers' social contributions	...	...	...	...	...	...	...	...	...	...	...	...
22	**Use of goods and services**	...	...	...	32	31	32	59	58	60	110	110	112
23	**Consumption of fixed capital**	...	...	...	27	27	27	34	35	34	74	75	73
24	**Interest**	...	...	...	41	40	38	45	44	42	48	46	44
25	**Subsidies**	...	...	...	22	34	41	22	34	41	36	48	55

France (132)

In Billions of Euros (EUR) / Fiscal Year Ends December 31st

		Budgetary Central Government			Central Government (excl. Social Security)			Central Government (incl. Social Security)			General Government		
		2013	2014	2015	2013P	2014P	2015P	2013P	2014P	2015P	2013P	2014P	2015P
26	**Grants**	...	...	...	...	...	...	...	...	...	...	...	...
261	To foreign governments	...	...	...	...	...	...	...	...	...	...	...	...
262	To international organizations	...	...	...	...	...	...	...	...	...	...	...	...
263	To other general government units	...	...	...	79	78	73	69	69	64	—	—	—
2631	Current	...	...	...	69	68	64	60	59	55	—	—	—
2632	Capital	...	...	...	10	10	9	10	10	9	—	—	—
27	**Social benefits**	...	...	...	93	95	96	521	532	542	545	557	567
271	Social security benefits	...	...	...	...	...	...	...	...	...	...	...	...
272	Social assistance benefits	...	...	...	...	...	...	...	...	...	...	...	...
273	Employment-related social benefits	...	...	...	...	...	...	...	...	...	...	...	...
28	**Other expense**	...	...	...	...	...	...	...	...	...	...	...	...
281	Property expense other than interest	...	...	...	—	—	—	—	—	—	0	0	0
282	Transfers not elsewhere classified	...	...	...	...	...	...	...	...	...	...	...	...
2821	Current	...	...	...	...	...	...	...	...	...	...	...	...
2822	Capital	...	...	...	...	...	...	...	...	...	...	...	...
	Table 3 Transactions in assets and liabilities												
3	**Change in net worth from transactions**	...	...	...	-67	-77	-72	...	...	...	-70	-80	-69
31	**Net/Gross investment in nonfinancial assets**	...	...	...	-1	-2	-1	0	-1	-0	14	7	4
311	Fixed assets	...	...	...	-1	-3	-1	-0	-1	-0	10	5	2
3111	Buildings and structures	...	...	...	...	...	...	...	...	...	...	...	...
3112	Machinery and equipment	...	...	...	...	...	...	...	...	...	...	...	...
3113	Other fixed assets	...	...	...	...	...	...	...	...	...	...	...	...
3114	Weapons systems	...	...	...	...	...	...	...	...	...	...	...	...
312	Inventories	...	...	...	...	...	...	...	...	...	...	...	...
313	Valuables	...	...	...	...	...	...	...	...	...	...	...	...
314	Nonproduced assets	...	...	...	0	0	0	0	0	0	3	3	2
3141	Land	...	...	...	...	...	...	...	...	...	...	...	...
3142	Mineral and energy resources	...	...	...	...	...	...	...	...	...	...	...	...
3143	Other naturally occurring assets	...	...	...	...	...	...	...	...	...	...	...	...
3144	Intangible nonproduced assets	...	...	...	...	...	...	...	...	...	...	...	...
32	**Net acquisition of financial assets**	...	...	...	7	8	10	...	...	...	3	13	16
	By instrument												
3201	Monetary gold and SDRs	...	...	...	—	—	—	...	...	...	—	—	—
3202	Currency and deposits	...	...	...	-7	-2	6	...	...	...	-9	-3	11
3203	Debt securities	...	...	...	0	3	1	...	...	...	2	7	-5
3204	Loans	...	...	...	7	0	-3	...	...	...	7	0	-3
3205	Equity and investment fund shares	...	...	...	1	-0	2	...	...	...	-7	-4	2
3206	Insurance, pension, and standardized guarantee schemes	...	...	...	...	...	...	...	...	...	-0	0	0
3207	Financial derivatives and employee stock options	...	...	...	0	0	0	...	...	...	-0	1	1
3208	Other accounts receivable	...	...	...	6	7	5	...	...	...	9	11	10
	By debtor												
321	Domestic debtors	...	...	...	...	...	...	...	...	...	...	...	...
322	External debtors	...	...	...	...	...	...	...	...	...	...	...	...
33	**Net incurrence of liabilities**	...	...	...	74	82	82	...	...	...	87	101	90
	By instrument												
3301	Special Drawing Rights (SDRs)	...	...	...	—	—	—	...	...	...	—	—	—
3302	Currency and deposits	...	...	...	-4	-2	7	...	...	...	-2	-1	1
3303	Debt securities	...	...	...	71	73	66	...	...	...	73	78	73
3304	Loans	...	...	...	3	3	-2	...	...	...	10	12	2
3305	Equity and investment fund shares	...	...	...	...	...	...	...	...	...	...	...	...
3306	Insurance, pension, and standardized guarantee schemes	...	...	...	0	0	0	...	...	...	0	0	0
3307	Financial derivatives and employee stock options	...	...	...	0	0	0	...	...	...	1	1	0
3308	Other accounts payable	...	...	...	4	8	11	...	...	...	3	11	14

France (132)

In Billions of Euros (EUR) / Fiscal Year Ends December 31st

		Budgetary Central Government			Central Government (excl. Social Security)			Central Government (incl. Social Security)			General Government		
		2013	2014	2015	2013P	2014P	2015P	2013P	2014P	2015P	2013P	2014P	2015P
	By creditor												
331	Domestic creditors	...	...	...	...	...	...	...	...	...	...	...	...
332	External creditors	...	...	...	...	...	...	...	...	...	...	...	...
	Table 4 Holding gains and losses in assets and liabilities												
	Table 5 Holding gains and losses in assets and liabilities												
	Table 6 Balance sheet												
6	**Net worth**	**...**	**...**	**...**	**...**	**...**	**...**	**...**	**...**	**...**	**-202**	**-399**	**...**
61	**Nonfinancial assets**	**...**	**...**	**...**	**...**	**...**	**...**	**...**	**...**	**...**	**1,202**	**1,201**	**...**
611	Fixed assets	...	...	...	...	...	...	...	...	...	1,180	1,178	...
6111	Buildings and structures	...	...	...	...	...	...	...	...	...	1,028	1,027	...
6112	Machinery and equipment	...	...	...	...	...	...	...	...	...	...	...	...
6113	Other fixed assets	...	...	...	...	...	...	...	...	...	86	87	...
6114	Weapons systems	...	...	...	...	...	...	...	...	...	...	...	...
612	Inventories	...	...	...	...	...	...	...	...	...	22	22	...
613	Valuables	...	...	...	...	...	...	...	...	...	—	—	...
614	Nonproduced assets	...	...	...	...	...	...	...	...	...	...	...	...
6141	Land	...	...	...	...	...	...	...	...	...	745	714	...
6142	Mineral and energy resources	...	...	...	...	...	...	...	...	...	2	1	...
6143	Other naturally occurring assets	...	...	...	...	...	...	...	...	...	...	...	...
6144	Intangible nonproduced assets	...	...	...	...	...	...	...	...	...	0	0	...
62	**Financial assets**	**...**	**...**	**...**	**564**	**584**	**575**	**...**	**...**	**...**	**945**	**979**	**981**
	By instrument												
6201	Monetary gold and SDRs	...	...	...	—	—	—	...	...	...	—	—	—
6202	Currency and deposits	...	...	...	30	23	29	...	...	...	47	40	51
6203	Debt securities	...	...	...	8	12	13	...	...	...	37	48	41
6204	Loans	...	...	...	92	91	88	...	...	...	103	103	100
6205	Equity and investment fund shares	...	...	...	324	344	326	...	...	...	485	507	497
6206	Insurance, pension, and standardized guarantee schemes	...	...	...	...	...	...	...	...	...	6	6	6
6207	Financial derivatives and employee stock options	...	...	...	—	—	—	...	...	...	1	1	1
6208	Other accounts receivable	...	...	...	111	114	119	...	...	...	266	274	286
	By debtor												
621	Domestic debtors	...	...	...	...	...	...	...	...	...	...	...	...
622	External debtors	...	...	...	...	...	...	...	...	...	...	...	...
63	**Liabilities**	**...**	**...**	**...**	**1,899**	**2,097**	**2,151**	**...**	**...**	**...**	**2,348**	**2,578**	**2,642**
	By instrument												
6301	Special Drawing Rights (SDRs)	...	...	...	—	—	—	...	...	...	—	—	—
6302	Currency and deposits	...	...	...	89	87	94	...	...	...	40	38	39
6303	Debt securities	...	...	...	1,609	1,798	1,835	...	...	...	1,784	1,991	2,038
6304	Loans	...	...	...	67	70	68	...	...	...	286	298	300
6305	Equity and investment fund shares	...	...	...	...	...	...	...	...	...	...	...	...
6306	Insurance, pension, and standardized guarantee schemes	...	...	...	2	2	2	...	...	...	2	2	2
6307	Financial derivatives and employee stock options	...	...	...	—	—	—	...	...	...	—	—	—
6308	Other accounts payable	...	...	...	133	141	152	...	...	...	237	248	263
	By creditor												
631	Domestic creditors	...	...	...	...	...	...	...	...	...	...	...	...
632	External creditors	...	...	...	...	...	...	...	...	...	...	...	...
	Memorandum items												
6M2	Net financial worth	...	...	...	-1,335	-1,513	-1,577	...	...	...	-1,404	-1,599	-1,661
6M3	Gross debt (D4) at market value	...	...	...	1,899	2,097	2,151	...	...	...	2,348	2,578	2,642
6M3D3	D3 debt liabilities at market value	...	...	...	1,897	2,095	2,149	...	...	...	2,347	2,576	2,640
6M3D2	D2 debt liabilities at market value	...	...	...	1,765	1,955	1,997	...	...	...	2,109	2,327	2,377
6M3D1	D1 debt liabilities at market value	...	...	...	1,676	1,868	1,903	...	...	...	2,070	2,289	2,338
6M4	Gross debt (D4) at nominal value	...	...	...	...	...	...	...	...	...	...	...	...
6M4D3	D3 debt liabilities at nominal value	...	...	...	...	...	...	...	...	...	...	...	...
6M4D2	D2 debt liabilities at nominal value	...	...	...	...	...	...	...	...	...	...	...	...
6M4D1	D1 debt liabilities at nominal value	...	...	...	...	...	...	...	...	...	...	...	...

France (132)

In Billions of Euros (EUR) / Fiscal Year Ends December 31st

		Budgetary Central Government			Central Government (excl. Social Security)			Central Government (incl. Social Security)			General Government		
		2013	2014	2015	2013P	2014P	2015P	2013P	2014P	2015P	2013P	2014P	2015P
6M35	Gross debt (D4) at face value	...	...	...	...	...	...	...	...	...	...	...	...
6M35D3	D3 debt liabilities at face value	...	...	...	1,755	1,834	1,898	...	...	...	2,190	2,287	2,360
6M35D2	D2 debt liabilities at face value	...	...	...	1,622	1,693	1,746	...	...	...	1,953	2,038	2,098
6M35D1	D1 debt liabilities at face value	...	...	...	1,534	1,606	1,652	...	...	...	1,914	2,000	2,058
6M93	Government gross debt per national definition	...	...	...	1,622	1,693	1,746	...	...	...	1,953	2,038	2,098
6M5	Arrears	...	...	...	...	...	...	...	...	...	...	...	...
6M6	Explicit contingent liabilities	...	...	...	...	...	...	...	...	...	...	...	...
6M61	of which: Publicly guaranteed debt	...	...	...	...	...	...	...	...	...	...	...	...
6M7	Net implicit obligations for social security benefits	...	...	...	...	...	...	...	...	...	...	...	...
	Table 7 Expenditure by functions of government												
7	**Expenditure**	...	...	...	**488**	**495**	...	...	...	...	**1,207**	**1,227**	...
701	**General public services**	...	...	...	**152**	**148**	...	...	...	...	**146**	**142**	...
7017	Public debt transactions	...	...	...	41	40	...	...	...	...	51	49	...
7018	Transfers of general character between levels of government	...	...	...	59	58	...	...	...	...	0	0	...
702	**Defense**	...	...	...	**37**	**36**	...	...	...	...	**37**	**36**	...
703	**Public order and safety**	...	...	...	**27**	**27**	...	...	...	...	**35**	**34**	...
704	**Economic affairs**	...	...	...	**63**	**68**	...	...	...	...	**104**	**108**	...
7042	Agriculture, forestry, fishing, and hunting	...	...	...	3	3	...	...	...	...	4	4	...
7043	Fuel and energy	...	...	...	8	9	...	...	...	...	9	10	...
7044	Mining, manufacturing, and construction	...	...	...	0	1	...	...	...	...	0	1	...
7045	Transport	...	...	...	9	10	...	...	...	...	41	41	...
7046	Communication	...	...	...	1	1	...	...	...	...	1	1	...
705	**Environmental protection**	...	...	...	**3**	**3**	...	...	...	...	**21**	**21**	...
706	**Housing and community amenities**	...	...	...	**8**	**10**	...	...	...	...	**29**	**31**	...
707	**Health**	...	...	...	**6**	**6**	...	...	...	...	**172**	**175**	...
7072	Outpatient services	...	...	...	—	—	...	...	...	...	60	61	...
7073	Hospital services	...	...	...	—	—	...	...	...	...	74	75	...
7074	Public health services	...	...	...	2	2	...	...	...	...	3	3	...
708	**Recreation, culture and religion**	...	...	...	**6**	**7**	...	...	...	...	**31**	**31**	...
709	**Education**	...	...	...	**82**	**84**	...	...	...	...	**116**	**118**	...
7091	Pre-primary and primary education	...	...	...	20	20	...	...	...	...	29	29	...
7092	Secondary education	...	...	...	35	36	...	...	...	...	51	51	...
7094	Tertiary education	...	...	...	14	14	...	...	...	...	14	14	...
710	**Social protection**	...	...	...	**104**	**106**	...	...	...	...	**516**	**529**	...
7z	Statistical discrepancy: Expenditure	...	...	...	—	0	...	...	...	...	-0	0	...
	Table 8 Financial transactions by counterpart sector												
32	**Net acquisition of financial assets**	...	...	...	**7**	**8**	**10**	...	...	...	**3**	**13**	**16**
321	Domestic debtors	...	...	...	...	...	...	...	...	...	...	...	...
8211	General government	...	...	...	...	...	...	...	...	...	—	—	—
8212	Central bank	...	...	...	...	...	...	...	...	...	...	...	...
8213	Deposit-taking corporations except the central bank	...	...	...	...	...	...	...	...	...	...	...	...
8214	Other financial corporations	...	...	...	...	...	...	...	...	...	...	...	...
8215	Nonfinancial corporations	...	...	...	...	...	...	...	...	...	...	...	...
8216	Households & nonprofit institutions serving households	...	...	...	...	...	...	...	...	...	...	...	...
322	External debtors	...	...	...	...	...	...	...	...	...	...	...	...
8221	General government	...	...	...	...	...	...	...	...	...	...	...	...
8227	International organizations	...	...	...	...	...	...	...	...	...	...	...	...
8228	Financial corporations other than international organizations	...	...	...	...	...	...	...	...	...	...	...	...
8229	Other nonresidents	...	...	...	...	...	...	...	...	...	...	...	...

France (132)

In Billions of Euros (EUR) / Fiscal Year Ends December 31st

		Budgetary Central Government			Central Government (excl. Social Security)			Central Government (incl. Social Security)			General Government		
		2013	2014	2015	2013P	2014P	2015P	2013P	2014P	2015P	2013P	2014P	2015P
33	**Net incurrence of liabilities**	...	...	...	74	82	82	...	...	...	87	101	90
331	Domestic creditors	...	...	...	...	...	...	...	...	...	...	...	...
8311	General government	...	...	...	...	...	...	...	...	...	—	—	—
8312	Central bank	...	...	...	...	...	...	...	...	...	...	...	...
8313	Deposit-taking corporations except the central bank	...	...	...	...	...	...	...	...	...	...	...	...
8314	Other financial corporations	...	...	...	...	...	...	...	...	...	...	...	...
8315	Nonfinancial corporations	...	...	...	...	...	...	...	...	...	...	...	...
8316	Households & nonprofit institutions serving households	...	...	...	...	...	...	...	...	...	...	...	...
332	External creditors	...	...	...	...	...	...	...	...	...	...	...	...
8321	General government	...	...	...	...	...	...	...	...	...	...	...	...
8327	International organizations	...	...	...	...	...	...	...	...	...	...	...	...
8328	Financial corporations other than international organizations	...	...	...	...	...	...	...	...	...	...	...	...
8329	Other nonresidents	...	...	...	...	...	...	...	...	...	...	...	...
	Table 9 Total other economic flows in assets and liabilities												
9	**Change in net worth due to other economic flows**	...	...	...	...	...	...	...	...	...	...	...	...
91	**Other economic flows in nonfinancial assets**	...	...	...	...	...	...	...	...	...	...	...	...
911	Fixed assets	...	...	...	...	...	...	...	...	...	...	...	...
912	Inventories	...	...	...	...	...	...	...	...	...	...	...	...
913	Valuables	...	...	...	...	...	...	...	...	...	...	...	...
914	Nonproduced assets	...	...	...	...	...	...	...	...	...	...	...	...
92	**Other economic flows in financial assets**	...	...	...	39	12	-20	...	...	...	44	21	-14
	By instrument												
9201	Monetary gold and SDRs	...	...	...	—	—	—	...	...	...	—	—	—
9202	Currency and deposits	...	...	...	0	-4	0	...	...	...	0	-4	0
9203	Debt securities	...	...	...	-0	0	-0	...	...	...	-1	3	-1
9204	Loans	...	...	...	0	-1	0	...	...	...	0	-1	0
9205	Equity and investment fund shares	...	...	...	34	21	-20	...	...	...	41	26	-13
9206	Insurance, pension, and standardized guarantee schemes	...	...	...	—	—	—	...	...	...	—	-0	—
9207	Financial derivatives and employee stock options	...	...	...	-0	-0	-0	...	...	...	0	-1	-1
9208	Other accounts receivable	...	...	...	5	-4	-0	...	...	...	4	-3	1
	By debtor												
921	Domestic debtors	...	...	...	...	...	...	...	...	...	...	...	...
922	External debtors	...	...	...	...	...	...	...	...	...	...	...	...
93	**Other economic flows in liabilities**	...	...	...	-32	116	-28	...	...	...	-44	129	-26
	By instrument												
9301	Special Drawing Rights (SDRs)	...	...	...	—	—	—	...	...	...	—	—	—
9302	Currency and deposits	...	...	...	-0	-0	—	...	...	...	-0	-0	-0
9303	Debt securities	...	...	...	-52	116	-28	...	...	...	-59	129	-26
9304	Loans	...	...	...	4	—	-0	...	...	...	4	0	-0
9305	Equity and investment fund shares	...	...	...	—	—	—	...	...	...	—	—	—
9306	Insurance, pension, and standardized guarantee schemes	...	...	...	-0	-0	—	...	...	...	-0	-0	—
9307	Financial derivatives and employee stock options	...	...	...	-0	-0	-0	...	...	...	-1	-1	-0
9308	Other accounts payable	...	...	...	16	0	0	...	...	...	13	0	0
	By creditor												
931	Domestic creditors	...	...	...	...	...	...	...	...	...	...	...	...
932	External creditors	...	...	...	...	...	...	...	...	...	...	...	...
	Memorandum items												
9M2	Change in net financial worth due to other economic flows	...	...	...	72	-104	8	...	...	...	88	-108	12

France (132)

In Billions of Euros (EUR) / Fiscal Year Ends December 31st

		Budgetary Central Government			Central Government (excl. Social Security)			Central Government (incl. Social Security)			General Government		
		2013	2014	2015	2013P	2014P	2015P	2013P	2014P	2015P	2013P	2014P	2015P
9M3	Gross debt (D4) at market value: other economic flows	...	...	...	-32	116	-28	...	...	...	-42	130	-26
9M3D3	D3 debt liabilities at market value: other economic flows	...	...	...	-32	116	-28	...	...	...	-42	130	-26
9M3D2	D2 debt liabilities at market value: other economic flows	...	...	...	-48	116	-28	...	...	...	-55	129	-26
9M3D1	D1 debt liabilities at market value: other economic flows	...	...	...	-48	116	-28	...	...	...	-55	129	-26

Georgia (915)

In Millions of Georgian Lari (GEL) / Fiscal Year Ends December 31st

		Budgetary Central Government			Central Government (excl. Social Security)			Central Government (incl. Social Security)			General Government		
		2013	2014	2015	2013	2014	2015	2013	2014	2015	2013	2014	2015
	Statement of operations												
1	Revenue	6,840	7,435	8,171	6,840	7,435	8,171	6,840	7,435	8,171	7,434	8,119	8,963
2	Expense	6,546	7,480	8,158	6,546	7,480	8,158	6,546	7,480	8,158	6,723	7,731	8,180
GOB	**Gross operating balance**	**294**	**-45**	**13**	**294**	**-45**	**13**	**294**	**-45**	**13**	**711**	**388**	**783**
NOB	**Net operating balance**	...	...	...	...	...	...	...	...	...	...	...	...
31	Net/Gross investment in nonfinancial assets	690	618	393	690	618	393	690	618	393	1,015	968	1,124
2M	Expenditure	7,236	8,097	8,551	7,236	8,097	8,551	7,236	8,097	8,551	7,738	8,698	9,304
NLB	**Net lending (+) / Net borrowing (-)**	**-396**	**-663**	**-380**	**-396**	**-663**	**-380**	**-396**	**-663**	**-380**	**-304**	**-580**	**-341**
32	Net acquisition of financial assets	-172	347	561	-172	347	561	-172	347	561	-92	422	592
33	Net incurrence of liabilities	224	1,010	941	224	1,010	941	224	1,010	941	212	1,001	933
NLBz	Statistical discrepancy	—	—	—	—	—	—	—	—	—	—	—	—
	Memorandum items												
PB	Primary net lending / net borrowing	-163	-418	-54	-163	-418	-54	-163	-418	-54	-66	-331	-11
GB	Government balance per national definition	...	...	...	...	...	...	...	...	...	...	...	...
	Statement of other economic flows												
	Balance sheet												
6	**Net worth**	...	...	...	...	...	...	...	...	...	...	...	...
61	Nonfinancial assets	...	...	...	...	...	...	...	...	...	...	...	...
62	Financial assets	...	...	...	...	...	...	...	...	...	...	...	...
63	Liabilities	9,107	10,313	13,109	9,107	10,313	13,109	9,107	10,313	13,109	...	...	...
	Table 1 Revenue												
1	**Revenue**	**6,840**	**7,435**	**8,171**	**6,840**	**7,435**	**8,171**	**6,840**	**7,435**	**8,171**	**7,434**	**8,119**	**8,963**
11	**Taxes**	**6,288**	**6,847**	**7,550**	**6,288**	**6,847**	**7,550**	**6,288**	**6,847**	**7,550**	**6,659**	**7,242**	**8,011**
111	Taxes on income, profits, and capital gains	2,602	2,619	3,078	2,602	2,619	3,078	2,602	2,619	3,078	2,741	2,768	3,248
1111	Payable by individuals	1,795	1,790	2,052	1,795	1,790	2,052	1,795	1,790	2,052	1,934	1,939	2,223
1112	Payable by corporations and other enterprises	807	829	1,025	807	829	1,025	807	829	1,025	807	829	1,025
1113	Other taxes on income, profits, and capital gains	—	—	—	—	—	—	—	—	—	—	—	—
112	Taxes on payroll and workforce	—	—	—	—	—	—	—	—	—	—	—	—
113	Taxes on property	—	—	—	—	—	—	—	—	—	231	246	290
114	Taxes on goods and services	3,570	4,109	4,376	3,570	4,109	4,376	3,570	4,109	4,376	3,570	4,109	4,376
1141	General taxes on goods and services	2,848	3,299	3,506	2,848	3,299	3,506	2,848	3,299	3,506	2,848	3,299	3,506
1142	Excises	722	810	871	722	810	871	722	810	871	722	810	871
115	Taxes on international trade and transactions	89	95	69	89	95	69	89	95	69	89	95	69
116	Other taxes	27	24	27	27	24	27	27	24	27	28	25	27
12	**Social contributions**	—	—	—	—	—	—	—	—	—	—	—	—
121	Social security contributions	—	—	—	—	—	—	—	—	—	—	—	—
122	Other social contributions	—	—	—	—	—	—	—	—	—	—	—	—
13	**Grants**	**239**	**279**	**316**	**239**	**279**	**316**	**239**	**279**	**316**	**239**	**280**	**319**
131	From foreign governments	122	190	109	122	190	109	122	190	109	122	191	111
132	From international organizations	117	89	207	117	89	207	117	89	207	117	89	208
133	From other general government units	—	—	—	—	—	—	—	—	—	0	—	—
1331	Current	—	—	—	—	—	—	—	—	—	0	—	—
1332	Capital	—	—	—	—	—	—	—	—	—	0	—	—
14	**Other revenue**	**313**	**309**	**305**	**313**	**309**	**305**	**313**	**309**	**305**	**536**	**598**	**634**
	Table 2 Expense by economic type												
2	**Expense**	**6,546**	**7,480**	**8,158**	**6,546**	**7,480**	**8,158**	**6,546**	**7,480**	**8,158**	**6,723**	**7,731**	**8,180**
21	**Compensation of employees**	**1,188**	**1,296**	**1,377**	**1,188**	**1,296**	**1,377**	**1,188**	**1,296**	**1,377**	**1,395**	**1,522**	**1,602**
211	Wages and salaries	1,188	1,296	1,377	1,188	1,296	1,377	1,188	1,296	1,377	1,395	1,522	1,602
212	Employers' social contributions	—	—	—	—	—	—	—	—	—	—	—	—
22	**Use of goods and services**	**766**	**875**	**946**	**766**	**875**	**946**	**766**	**875**	**946**	**1,011**	**1,144**	**1,203**
23	**Consumption of fixed capital**	...	...	...	...	...	...	...	...	...	...	...	...
24	**Interest**	**233**	**245**	**327**	**233**	**245**	**327**	**233**	**245**	**327**	**238**	**249**	**330**
25	**Subsidies**	**243**	**275**	**246**	**243**	**275**	**246**	**243**	**275**	**246**	**548**	**626**	**726**

Georgia (915)

In Millions of Georgian Lari (GEL) / Fiscal Year Ends December 31st

		Budgetary Central Government			Central Government (excl. Social Security)			Central Government (incl. Social Security)			General Government		
		2013	2014	2015	2013	2014	2015	2013	2014	2015	2013	2014	2015
26	**Grants**	**1,083**	**1,068**	**1,271**	**1,083**	**1,068**	**1,271**	**1,083**	**1,068**	**1,271**	**15**	**12**	**29**
261	To foreign governments	0	—	9	0	—	9	0	—	9	0	—	9
262	To international organizations	15	12	20	15	12	20	15	12	20	15	12	20
263	To other general government units	1,069	1,056	1,242	1,069	1,056	1,242	1,069	1,056	1,242	0	—	—
2631	Current	793	803	896	793	803	896	793	803	896	0	—	—
2632	Capital	276	253	347	276	253	347	276	253	347	0	—	—
27	**Social benefits**	**2,083**	**2,548**	**2,802**	**2,083**	**2,548**	**2,802**	**2,083**	**2,548**	**2,802**	**2,295**	**2,791**	**3,037**
271	Social security benefits	2,083	2,548	—	2,083	2,548	—	2,083	2,548	—	—	—	—
272	Social assistance benefits	—	—	2,802	—	—	2,802	—	—	2,802	2,083	2,548	3,037
273	Employment-related social benefits	—	—	—	—	—	—	—	—	—	—	—	—
28	**Other expense**	**950**	**1,173**	**1,189**	**950**	**1,173**	**1,189**	**950**	**1,173**	**1,189**	**1,222**	**1,388**	**1,254**
281	Property expense other than interest	—	—	1,189	—	—	1,189	—	—	1,189	—	—	—
282	Transfers not elsewhere classified	950	1,173	—	950	1,173	—	950	1,173	—	1,222	1,388	1,254
2821	Current	727	812	—	727	812	—	727	812	—	999	1,026	957
2822	Capital	223	362	—	223	362	—	223	362	—	223	362	297
	Table 3 Transactions in assets and liabilities												
3	**Change in net worth from transactions**	...	...	...	...	...	...	...	...	...	...	...	...
31	**Net/Gross investment in nonfinancial assets**	**690**	**618**	**393**	**690**	**618**	**393**	**690**	**618**	**393**	**1,015**	**968**	**1,124**
311	Fixed assets	731	620	560	731	620	560	731	620	560	1,089	998	1,342
3111	Buildings and structures	574	528	437	574	528	437	574	528	437	560	522	420
3112	Machinery and equipment	145	87	85	145	87	85	145	87	85	145	87	85
3113	Other fixed assets	12	5	38	12	5	38	12	5	38	385	389	837
3114	Weapons systems	—	—	—	—	—	—	—	—	—	—	—	—
312	Inventories	1	10	10	1	10	10	1	10	10	0	9	9
313	Valuables	—	—	—	—	—	—	—	—	—	—	—	—
314	Nonproduced assets	-42	-12	-177	-42	-12	-177	-42	-12	-177	-75	-39	-227
3141	Land	8	5	5	8	5	5	8	5	5	-25	-22	-45
3142	Mineral and energy resources	—	—	—	—	—	—	—	—	—	—	—	—
3143	Other naturally occurring assets	-50	-17	-182	-50	-17	-182	-50	-17	-182	-50	-17	-182
3144	Intangible nonproduced assets	—	—	—	—	—	—	—	—	—	—	—	—
32	**Net acquisition of financial assets**	**-172**	**347**	**561**	**-172**	**347**	**561**	**-172**	**347**	**561**	**-92**	**422**	**592**
	By instrument												
3201	Monetary gold and SDRs	—	—	—	—	—	—	—	—	—	—	—	—
3202	Currency and deposits	-387	147	188	-387	147	188	-387	147	188	-303	205	145
3203	Debt securities	—	—	—	—	—	—	—	—	—	—	—	—
3204	Loans	79	34	109	79	34	109	79	34	109	75	50	184
3205	Equity and investment fund shares	159	166	264	159	166	264	159	166	264	159	166	264
3206	Insurance, pension, and standardized guarantee schemes	—	—	—	—	—	—	—	—	—	—	—	—
3207	Financial derivatives and employee stock options	—	—	—	—	—	—	—	—	—	—	—	—
3208	Other accounts receivable	-23	...	...	-23	...	...	-23	...	...	-23	...	...
	By debtor												
321	Domestic debtors	-172	347	561	-172	347	561	-172	347	561	-92	422	592
322	External debtors	—	—	—	—	—	—	—	—	—	—	—	—
33	**Net incurrence of liabilities**	**224**	**1,010**	**941**	**224**	**1,010**	**941**	**224**	**1,010**	**941**	**212**	**1,001**	**933**
	By instrument												
3301	Special Drawing Rights (SDRs)	—	—	—	—	—	—	—	—	—	—	—	—
3302	Currency and deposits	—	—	—	—	—	—	—	—	—	—	—	—
3303	Debt securities	98	538	280	98	538	280	98	538	280	98	538	280
3304	Loans	126	492	675	126	492	675	126	492	675	114	483	667
3305	Equity and investment fund shares	—	—	—	—	—	—	—	—	—	—	—	—
3306	Insurance, pension, and standardized guarantee schemes	—	—	—	—	—	—	—	—	—	—	—	—
3307	Financial derivatives and employee stock options	—	—	—	—	—	—	—	—	—	—	—	—
3308	Other accounts payable	...	-20	-14	...	-20	-14	...	-20	-14	...	-20	-14

Georgia (915)

In Millions of Georgian Lari (GEL) / Fiscal Year Ends December 31st

		Budgetary Central Government			Central Government (excl. Social Security)			Central Government (incl. Social Security)			General Government		
		2013	2014	2015	2013	2014	2015	2013	2014	2015	2013	2014	2015
	By creditor												
331	Domestic creditors	90	517	265	90	517	265	90	517	265	78	508	257
332	External creditors	134	494	676	134	494	676	134	494	676	134	494	676
	Table 4 Holding gains and losses in assets and liabilities												
	Table 5 Holding gains and losses in assets and liabilities												
	Table 6 Balance sheet												
6	**Net worth**	...	...	...	...	...	...	...	...	...	...	...	...
61	**Nonfinancial assets**	...	...	...	...	...	...	...	...	...	...	...	...
611	Fixed assets	...	...	...	...	...	...	...	...	...	...	...	...
6111	Buildings and structures	...	...	...	...	...	...	...	...	...	...	...	...
6112	Machinery and equipment	...	...	...	...	...	...	...	...	...	...	...	...
6113	Other fixed assets	...	...	...	...	...	...	...	...	...	...	...	...
6114	Weapons systems	...	...	...	...	...	...	...	...	...	...	...	...
612	Inventories	...	...	...	...	...	...	...	...	...	...	...	...
613	Valuables	...	...	...	...	...	...	...	...	...	...	...	...
614	Nonproduced assets	...	...	...	...	...	...	...	...	...	...	...	...
6141	Land	...	...	...	...	...	...	...	...	...	...	...	...
6142	Mineral and energy resources	...	...	...	...	...	...	...	...	...	...	...	...
6143	Other naturally occurring assets	...	...	...	...	...	...	...	...	...	...	...	...
6144	Intangible nonproduced assets	...	...	...	...	...	...	...	...	...	...	...	...
62	**Financial assets**	...	...	...	...	...	...	...	...	...	...	...	...
	By instrument												
6201	Monetary gold and SDRs	...	...	...	...	...	...	...	...	...	...	...	...
6202	Currency and deposits	...	...	...	...	...	...	...	...	...	...	...	...
6203	Debt securities	...	...	...	...	...	...	...	...	...	...	...	...
6204	Loans	...	...	...	...	...	...	...	...	...	...	...	...
6205	Equity and investment fund shares	...	...	...	...	...	...	...	...	...	...	...	...
6206	Insurance, pension, and standardized guarantee schemes	...	...	...	...	...	...	...	...	...	...	...	...
6207	Financial derivatives and employee stock options	...	...	...	...	...	...	...	...	...	...	...	...
6208	Other accounts receivable	...	...	...	...	...	...	...	...	...	...	...	...
	By debtor												
621	Domestic debtors	...	...	...	...	...	...	...	...	...	...	...	...
622	External debtors	...	...	...	...	...	...	...	...	...	...	...	...
63	**Liabilities**	**9,107**	**10,313**	**13,109**	**9,107**	**10,313**	**13,109**	**9,107**	**10,313**	**13,109**	...	...	...
	By instrument												
6301	Special Drawing Rights (SDRs)	—	—	—	—	—	—	—	—	—	...	...	...
6302	Currency and deposits	—	—	—	—	—	—	—	—	—	...	...	...
6303	Debt securities	1,349	1,373	1,598	1,349	1,373	1,598	1,349	1,373	1,598	...	...	...
6304	Loans	7,086	8,268	10,839	7,086	8,268	10,839	7,086	8,268	10,839	...	...	...
6305	Equity and investment fund shares	—	—	—	—	—	—	—	—	—	...	...	...
6306	Insurance, pension, and standardized guarantee schemes	—	—	—	—	—	—	—	—	—	...	...	...
6307	Financial derivatives and employee stock options	—	—	—	—	—	—	—	—	—	...	...	...
6308	Other accounts payable	672	672	672	672	672	672	672	672	672	...	...	...
	By creditor												
631	Domestic creditors	2,017	2,570	2,827	2,017	2,570	2,827	2,017	2,570	2,827	...	...	...
632	External creditors	7,090	7,743	10,282	7,090	7,743	10,282	7,090	7,743	10,282	...	...	...
	Memorandum items												
6M2	Net financial worth	...	...	...	...	...	...	...	...	...	...	...	...
6M3	Gross debt (D4) at market value	...	...	...	...	...	...	...	...	...	...	...	...
6M3D3	D3 debt liabilities at market value	...	...	...	...	...	...	...	...	...	...	...	...
6M3D2	D2 debt liabilities at market value	...	...	...	...	...	...	...	...	...	...	...	...
6M3D1	D1 debt liabilities at market value	...	...	...	...	...	...	...	...	...	...	...	...
6M4	Gross debt (D4) at nominal value	...	...	13,109	...	...	13,109	...	...	...	...	...	...
6M4D3	D3 debt liabilities at nominal value	...	...	13,109	...	...	13,109	...	...	...	...	...	...
6M4D2	D2 debt liabilities at nominal value	...	...	12,437	...	...	12,437	...	...	...	...	...	...
6M4D1	D1 debt liabilities at nominal value	...	...	12,437	...	...	12,437	...	...	...	...	...	...

Georgia (915)

In Millions of Georgian Lari (GEL) / Fiscal Year Ends December 31st

		Budgetary Central Government			Central Government (excl. Social Security)			Central Government (incl. Social Security)			General Government		
		2013	2014	2015	2013	2014	2015	2013	2014	2015	2013	2014	2015
6M35	Gross debt (D4) at face value	9,107	10,313	13,109	9,107	10,313	13,109	9,107	10,313	13,109	...	...	...
6M35D3	D3 debt liabilities at face value	9,107	10,313	13,109	9,107	10,313	13,109	9,107	10,313	13,109	...	...	...
6M35D2	D2 debt liabilities at face value	8,435	9,641	12,437	8,435	9,641	12,437	8,435	9,641	12,437	...	...	...
6M35D1	D1 debt liabilities at face value	8,435	9,641	12,437	8,435	9,641	12,437	8,435	9,641	12,437	...	...	...
6M93	Government gross debt per national definition	...	...	...	...	...	...	...	...	...	...	...	...
6M5	Arrears	...	...	...	...	...	...	...	...	...	...	...	...
6M6	Explicit contingent liabilities	...	...	...	...	...	...	...	...	...	...	...	...
6M61	of which: Publicly guaranteed debt	...	...	...	...	...	...	...	...	...	...	...	...
6M7	Net implicit obligations for social security benefits	...	...	...	...	...	...	...	...	...	...	...	...
	Table 7 Expenditure by functions of government												
7	**Expenditure**	**7,236**	**8,097**	**8,551**	**7,236**	**8,097**	**8,551**	**7,236**	**8,097**	**8,551**	**7,738**	**8,698**	**9,304**
701	**General public services**	**1,649**	**1,696**	**1,763**	**1,649**	**1,696**	**1,763**	**1,649**	**1,696**	**1,763**	**833**	**903**	**781**
7017	Public debt transactions	233	245	327	233	245	327	233	245	327	238	249	330
7018	Transfers of general character between levels of government	...	1,056	1,242	...	1,056	1,242	...	1,056	1,242	...	—	—
702	**Defense**	**630**	**640**	**654**	**630**	**640**	**654**	**630**	**640**	**654**	**637**	**646**	**661**
703	**Public order and safety**	**860**	**906**	**961**	**860**	**906**	**961**	**860**	**906**	**961**	**907**	**955**	**1,010**
704	**Economic affairs**	**907**	**1,007**	**950**	**907**	**1,007**	**950**	**907**	**1,007**	**950**	**1,229**	**1,304**	**1,288**
7042	Agriculture, forestry, fishing, and hunting	176	218	201	176	218	201	176	218	201	166	217	171
7043	Fuel and energy	57	85	24	57	85	24	57	85	24	57	85	24
7044	Mining, manufacturing, and construction	1	1	1	1	1	1	1	1	1	1	2	1
7045	Transport	516	581	569	516	581	569	516	581	569	795	825	857
7046	Communication	—	—	—	—	—	—	—	—	—	—	—	—
705	**Environmental protection**	**26**	**38**	**45**	**26**	**38**	**45**	**26**	**38**	**45**	**134**	**163**	**133**
706	**Housing and community amenities**	**38**	**54**	**48**	**38**	**54**	**48**	**38**	**54**	**48**	**320**	**323**	**411**
707	**Health**	**481**	**653**	**855**	**481**	**653**	**855**	**481**	**653**	**855**	**525**	**694**	**906**
7072	Outpatient services	...	370	612	...	370	612	...	370	612	...	374	615
7073	Hospital services	...	94	151	...	94	151	...	94	151	...	97	155
7074	Public health services	...	43	15	...	43	15	...	43	15	...	49	22
708	**Recreation, culture and religion**	**145**	**190**	**223**	**145**	**190**	**223**	**145**	**190**	**223**	**329**	**393**	**574**
709	**Education**	**683**	**740**	**834**	**683**	**740**	**834**	**683**	**740**	**834**	**825**	**933**	**1,074**
7091	Pre-primary and primary education	...	521	460	...	521	460	...	521	460	...	687	665
7092	Secondary education	...	15	16	...	15	16	...	15	16	...	17	25
7094	Tertiary education	...	88	133	...	88	133	...	88	133	...	91	135
710	**Social protection**	**1,817**	**2,175**	**2,218**	**1,817**	**2,175**	**2,218**	**1,817**	**2,175**	**2,218**	**1,999**	**2,385**	**2,467**
7z	Statistical discrepancy: Expenditure	—	...	...	—	...	...	—	...	...	—	...	...
	Table 8 Financial transactions by counterpart sector												
32	**Net acquisition of financial assets**	**-172**	**347**	**561**	**-172**	**347**	**561**	**-172**	**347**	**561**	**-92**	**422**	**592**
321	Domestic debtors	-172	347	561	-172	347	561	-172	347	561	-92	422	592
8211	General government	3	-15	-3	3	-15	-3	3	-15	-3	0	—	—
8212	Central bank	-387	-26	88	-387	-26	88	-387	-26	88	-387	-26	147
8213	Deposit-taking corporations except the central bank	-23	173	100	-23	173	100	-23	173	100	61	231	-2
8214	Other financial corporations	—	...	...	—	...	...	—	...	...	—	—	—
8215	Nonfinancial corporations	235	215	376	235	215	376	235	215	376	234	216	447
8216	Households & nonprofit institutions serving households	—	...	...	—	...	...	—	...	...	—	—	—
322	External debtors	—	—	—	—	—	—	—	—	—	—	—	—
8221	General government	—	—	—	—	—	—	—	—	—	—	—	—
8227	International organizations	—	—	—	—	—	—	—	—	—	—	—	—
8228	Financial corporations other than international organizations	—	—	—	—	—	—	—	—	—	—	—	—
8229	Other nonresidents	—	—	—	—	—	—	—	—	—	—	—	—

Georgia (915)

In Millions of Georgian Lari (GEL) / Fiscal Year Ends December 31st

		Budgetary Central Government			Central Government (excl. Social Security)			Central Government (incl. Social Security)			General Government		
		2013	2014	2015	2013	2014	2015	2013	2014	2015	2013	2014	2015
33	**Net incurrence of liabilities**	**224**	**1,010**	**941**	**224**	**1,010**	**941**	**224**	**1,010**	**941**	**212**	**1,001**	**933**
331	Domestic creditors	90	517	265	90	517	265	90	517	265	78	508	257
8311	General government	—	—	—	—	—	—	—	—	—	0	—	—
8312	Central bank	-35	-35	-35	-35	-35	-35	-35	-35	-35	-35	-35	-35
8313	Deposit-taking corporations except the central bank	150	572	315	150	572	315	150	572	315	142	563	307
8314	Other financial corporations	—	—	—	—	—	—	—	—	—	—	—	—
8315	Nonfinancial corporations	-25	-20	-15	-25	-20	-15	-25	-20	-15	-30	-20	-15
8316	Households & nonprofit institutions serving households	—	—	—	—	—	—	—	—	—	—	—	—
332	External creditors	134	494	676	134	494	676	134	494	676	134	494	676
8321	General government	—	22	46	—	22	46	—	22	46	—	22	46
8327	International organizations	134	471	631	134	471	631	134	471	631	134	471	631
8328	Financial corporations other than international organizations	—	—	—	—	—	—	—	—	—	—	—	—
8329	Other nonresidents	—	—	—	—	—	—	—	—	—	—	—	—
	Table 9 Total other economic flows in assets and liabilities												

Germany (134)

In Billions of Euros (EUR) / Fiscal Year Ends December 31st

		Budgetary Central Government			Central Government (excl. Social Security)			Central Government (incl. Social Security)			General Government		
		2013	2014	2015	2013	2014	2015	2013	2014	2015	2013	2014	2015
	Statement of operations												
1	Revenue	349	362	372	369	385	393	809	842	870	1,257	1,305	1,354
2	Expense	367	360	370	375	377	383	810	830	856	1,266	1,302	1,336
GOB	**Gross operating balance**	**-4**	**16**	**16**	**11**	**26**	**29**	**17**	**30**	**32**	**54**	**68**	**85**
NOB	**Net operating balance**	**-18**	**2**	**2**	**-6**	**8**	**11**	**-1**	**11**	**13**	**-9**	**3**	**18**
31	Net/Gross investment in nonfinancial assets	2	0	1	2	-0	1	2	-0	1	-4	-5	-4
2M	Expenditure	369	360	371	378	376	383	812	830	857	1,262	1,297	1,332
NLB	**Net lending (+) / Net borrowing (-)**	**-20**	**2**	**2**	**-8**	**9**	**10**	**-3**	**12**	**13**	**-5**	**9**	**22**
32	Net acquisition of financial assets	...	...	...	-4	15	-9	...	...	...	-17	12	-1
33	Net incurrence of liabilities	...	...	...	4	6	-20	...	...	...	-12	4	-24
NLBz	Statistical discrepancy	...	...	...	—	—	1	...	...	...	-0	-0	0
	Memorandum items												
PB	Primary net lending / net borrowing	10	30	27	25	40	39	31	43	41	52	62	71
GB	Government balance per national definition	...	...	...	...	...	...	...	...	...	...	...	...
	Statement of other economic flows												
	Balance sheet												
6	**Net worth**	**...**	**...**	**...**	**-716**	**-741**	**-704**	**...**	**...**	**...**	**-3**	**-28**	**...**
61	Nonfinancial assets	315	320	...	315	320	326	337	342	348	1,301	1,320	...
62	Financial assets	...	...	...	457	504	501	...	...	...	1,031	1,080	1,091
63	Liabilities	...	...	...	1,489	1,565	1,531	...	...	...	2,336	2,428	2,386
	Table 1 Revenue												
1	**Revenue**	**349**	**362**	**372**	**369**	**385**	**393**	**809**	**842**	**870**	**1,257**	**1,305**	**1,354**
11	**Taxes**	**325**	**336**	**346**	**326**	**337**	**348**	**326**	**337**	**348**	**651**	**674**	**706**
111	Taxes on income, profits, and capital gains	133	139	146	133	139	146	133	139	146	326	339	357
1111	Payable by individuals	113	118	124	113	118	124	113	118	124	251	261	276
1112	Payable by corporations and other enterprises	17	17	17	17	17	17	17	17	17	68	69	72
1113	Other taxes on income, profits, and capital gains	3	4	5	3	4	5	3	4	5	7	8	10
112	Taxes on payroll and workforce	—	—	—	—	—	—	—	—	—	—	—	—
113	Taxes on property	—	—	—	—	—	—	—	—	—	17	18	20
114	Taxes on goods and services	192	197	200	193	198	202	193	198	202	299	308	318
1141	General taxes on goods and services	105	108	111	106	109	111	106	109	111	197	203	212
1142	Excises	64	64	65	64	64	65	64	64	65	65	65	65
115	Taxes on international trade and transactions	—	—	—	—	—	—	—	—	—	—	—	—
116	Other taxes	—	—	—	—	—	—	—	—	—	8	9	11
12	**Social contributions**	**5**	**5**	**5**	**7**	**7**	**7**	**440**	**457**	**475**	**465**	**482**	**501**
121	Social security contributions	—	—	—	—	—	—	432	448	466	432	448	466
122	Other social contributions	5	5	5	7	7	7	9	9	9	33	34	35
13	**Grants**	**5**	**4**	**4**	**5**	**5**	**5**	**7**	**6**	**6**	**5**	**5**	**5**
131	From foreign governments	—	—	—	—	—	—	—	—	—	—	—	—
132	From international organizations	1	0	1	1	1	1	1	1	1	5	5	5
133	From other general government units	4	4	4	4	4	4	5	6	6	—	—	—
1331	Current	4	4	4	4	4	4	...	...	...	—	—	—
1332	Capital	0	0	0	0	0	0	...	...	...	—	—	—
14	**Other revenue**	**15**	**17**	**17**	**31**	**37**	**34**	**36**	**42**	**40**	**136**	**144**	**142**
	Table 2 Expense by economic type												
2	**Expense**	**367**	**360**	**370**	**375**	**377**	**383**	**810**	**830**	**856**	**1,266**	**1,302**	**1,336**
21	**Compensation of employees**	**25**	**25**	**25**	**28**	**29**	**29**	**48**	**49**	**51**	**218**	**224**	**229**
211	Wages and salaries	...	...	...	...	...	...	...	...	...	164	169	172
212	Employers' social contributions	...	...	...	...	...	...	...	...	...	54	55	57
22	**Use of goods and services**	**25**	**25**	**25**	**32**	**32**	**31**	**40**	**40**	**40**	**131**	**132**	**137**
23	**Consumption of fixed capital**	**14**	**14**	**14**	**17**	**17**	**18**	**18**	**19**	**19**	**63**	**65**	**67**
24	**Interest**	**30**	**28**	**25**	**33**	**31**	**29**	**33**	**32**	**29**	**57**	**53**	**48**
25	**Subsidies**	**5**	**5**	**6**	**8**	**8**	**8**	**8**	**9**	**9**	**25**	**26**	**28**

Germany (134)

In Billions of Euros (EUR) / Fiscal Year Ends December 31st

		Budgetary Central Government			Central Government (excl. Social Security)			Central Government (incl. Social Security)			General Government		
		2013	2014	2015	2013	2014	2015	2013	2014	2015	2013	2014	2015
26	**Grants**	**208**	**200**	**213**	**184**	**184**	**191**	**86**	**85**	**90**	**37**	**36**	**39**
261	To foreign governments	34	33	33	34	33	33	34	33	33	34	33	34
262	To international organizations	3	3	3	3	3	5	3	3	5	3	3	5
263	To other general government units	171	165	176	147	149	153	49	50	52	—	—	—
2631	Current	165	159	166	141	143	147	...	...	...	—	—	—
2632	Capital	6	6	10	6	6	7	...	...	...	—	—	—
27	**Social benefits**	**46**	**47**	**48**	**58**	**60**	**61**	**559**	**579**	**603**	**667**	**693**	**723**
271	Social security benefits	—	—	—	—	—	—	499	518	540	499	518	540
272	Social assistance benefits	36	37	38	49	50	51	49	50	51	120	124	130
273	Employment-related social benefits	9	10	10	10	10	10	11	12	12	48	51	53
28	**Other expense**	**14**	**15**	**14**	**15**	**16**	**15**	**17**	**18**	**16**	**68**	**74**	**66**
281	Property expense other than interest	—	—	—	—	—	—	—	—	—	—	—	—
282	Transfers not elsewhere classified	14	15	14	15	16	15	17	18	16	68	74	66
2821	Current	6	6	7	6	7	7	9	9	8	41	42	43
2822	Capital	8	9	7	8	9	8	8	9	8	27	31	23
	Table 3 Transactions in assets and liabilities												
3	**Change in net worth from transactions**	...	...	...	**-6**	**8**	**12**	...	...	...	**-10**	**3**	**18**
31	**Net/Gross investment in nonfinancial assets**	**2**	**0**	**1**	**2**	**-0**	**1**	**2**	**-0**	**1**	**-4**	**-5**	**-4**
311	Fixed assets	3	0	2	3	0	2	2	0	1	-2	-4	-2
3111	Buildings and structures	—	-0	-1	-0	-0	-1	-0	-1	-1	-8	-7	-8
3112	Machinery and equipment	2	-0	1	2	-0	1	2	-0	2	3	1	3
3113	Other fixed assets	1	1	1	1	1	1	1	1	1	3	3	2
3114	Weapons systems	—	—	—	—	—	—	—	—	—	—	—	—
312	Inventories	-0	-0	-0	-0	-0	-0	-0	-0	-0	-0	-0	-0
313	Valuables	—	—	—	—	—	—	—	—	—	0	0	0
314	Nonproduced assets	0	0	-0	-0	-0	-1	-0	-0	-1	-2	-1	-2
3141	Land	0	0	0	-0	-0	-0	-0	-0	-0	-2	-1	-1
3142	Mineral and energy resources	—	—	—	—	—	—	—	—	—	—	—	—
3143	Other naturally occurring assets	—	—	—	—	—	—	—	—	—	—	—	—
3144	Intangible nonproduced assets	—	—	-1	—	—	-1	—	—	-1	—	—	-1
32	**Net acquisition of financial assets**	...	...	...	**-4**	**15**	**-9**	...	...	...	**-17**	**12**	**-1**
	By instrument												
3201	Monetary gold and SDRs	...	...	...	—	—	—	...	...	...	—	—	—
3202	Currency and deposits	...	...	...	-14	10	5	...	...	...	-19	19	11
3203	Debt securities	...	...	...	-4	-7	-6	...	...	...	-7	-11	-3
3204	Loans	...	...	...	6	-2	-8	...	...	...	-2	-7	-13
3205	Equity and investment fund shares	...	...	...	6	4	-2	...	...	...	10	6	1
3206	Insurance, pension, and standardized guarantee schemes	...	...	...	0	0	0	...	...	...	0	0	0
3207	Financial derivatives and employee stock options	...	...	...	1	1	0	...	...	...	1	2	1
3208	Other accounts receivable	...	...	...	1	9	2	...	...	...	-1	4	2
	By debtor												
321	Domestic debtors	...	...	...	-16	-10	6	...	...	...	-29	-14	14
322	External debtors	...	...	...	11	25	-16	...	...	...	12	26	-15
33	**Net incurrence of liabilities**	...	...	...	**4**	**6**	**-20**	...	...	...	**-12**	**4**	**-24**
	By instrument												
3301	Special Drawing Rights (SDRs)	...	...	...	—	—	—	...	...	...	—	—	—
3302	Currency and deposits	...	...	...	1	2	2	...	...	...	1	2	2
3303	Debt securities	...	...	...	15	14	-18	...	...	...	8	18	-9
3304	Loans	...	...	...	-11	-12	-10	...	...	...	-23	-22	-23
3305	Equity and investment fund shares	...	...	...	—	—	—	...	...	...	—	—	—
3306	Insurance, pension, and standardized guarantee schemes	...	...	...	—	—	—	...	...	...	—	—	—
3307	Financial derivatives and employee stock options	...	...	...	—	—	—	...	...	...	—	—	—
3308	Other accounts payable	...	...	...	-1	2	5	...	...	...	2	7	6

Germany (134)

In Billions of Euros (EUR) / Fiscal Year Ends December 31st

		Budgetary Central Government			Central Government (excl. Social Security)			Central Government (incl. Social Security)			General Government		
		2013	2014	2015	2013	2014	2015	2013	2014	2015	2013	2014	2015
	By creditor												
331	Domestic creditors	...	...	...	...	...	...	...	...	...	...	...	...
332	External creditors	...	...	...	...	...	...	...	...	...	...	...	...
	Table 4 Holding gains and losses in assets and liabilities												
	Table 5 Holding gains and losses in assets and liabilities												
	Table 6 Balance sheet												
6	**Net worth**	**...**	**...**	**...**	**-716**	**-741**	**-704**	**...**	**...**	**...**	**-3**	**-28**	**...**
61	**Nonfinancial assets**	**315**	**320**	**...**	**315**	**320**	**326**	**337**	**342**	**348**	**1,301**	**1,320**	**...**
611	Fixed assets	315	320	...	315	320	326	337	342	348	1,301	1,320	...
6111	Buildings and structures	230	234	...	230	234	236	250	254	256	1,142	1,156	1,167
6112	Machinery and equipment	57	58	...	57	58	60	59	59	62	88	89	93
6113	Other fixed assets	28	29	...	28	29	30	28	29	30	71	75	78
6114	Weapons systems	...	...	...	...	...	...	—	—	...	...	...	...
612	Inventories	...	...	...	...	...	...	...	...	...	...	...	...
613	Valuables	...	...	...	...	...	...	...	...	...	...	...	...
614	Nonproduced assets	...	...	...	...	...	...	...	...	...	...	...	...
6141	Land	...	...	...	...	...	...	...	...	...	...	...	...
6142	Mineral and energy resources	...	...	...	...	...	...	...	...	...	...	...	...
6143	Other naturally occurring assets	...	...	...	...	...	...	...	...	...	...	...	...
6144	Intangible nonproduced assets	...	...	...	...	...	...	...	...	...	...	...	...
62	**Financial assets**	**...**	**...**	**...**	**457**	**504**	**501**	**...**	**...**	**...**	**1,031**	**1,080**	**1,091**
	By instrument												
6201	Monetary gold and SDRs	...	...	...	—	—	—	...	...	...	—	—	—
6202	Currency and deposits	...	...	...	64	92	99	...	...	...	260	302	314
6203	Debt securities	...	...	...	89	97	95	...	...	...	129	135	138
6204	Loans	...	...	...	131	130	121	...	...	...	190	183	169
6205	Equity and investment fund shares	...	...	...	136	141	145	...	...	...	362	370	381
6206	Insurance, pension, and standardized guarantee schemes	...	...	...	0	0	0	...	...	...	1	1	1
6207	Financial derivatives and employee stock options	...	...	...	-18	-17	-17	...	...	...	-17	-15	-14
6208	Other accounts receivable	...	...	...	55	62	58	...	...	...	105	105	102
	By debtor												
621	Domestic debtors	...	...	...	303	310	322	...	...	...	874	881	907
622	External debtors	...	...	...	154	194	180	...	...	...	157	199	184
63	**Liabilities**	**...**	**...**	**...**	**1,489**	**1,565**	**1,531**	**...**	**...**	**...**	**2,336**	**2,428**	**2,386**
	By instrument												
6301	Special Drawing Rights (SDRs)	...	...	...	—	—	—	...	...	...	—	—	—
6302	Currency and deposits	...	...	...	11	12	14	...	...	...	11	12	14
6303	Debt securities	...	...	...	1,287	1,372	1,343	...	...	...	1,686	1,796	1,773
6304	Loans	...	...	...	188	178	170	...	...	...	636	617	595
6305	Equity and investment fund shares	...	...	...	—	—	—	...	...	...	—	—	—
6306	Insurance, pension, and standardized guarantee schemes	...	...	...	—	—	—	...	...	...	—	—	—
6307	Financial derivatives and employee stock options	...	...	...	—	—	—	...	...	...	—	—	—
6308	Other accounts payable	...	...	...	3	3	3	...	...	...	3	3	3
	By creditor												
631	Domestic creditors	...	...	...	...	...	...	...	...	...	...	...	...
632	External creditors	...	...	...	...	...	...	...	...	...	...	...	...
	Memorandum items												
6M2	Net financial worth	...	...	...	-1,031	-1,061	-1,029	...	...	...	-1,305	-1,348	-1,295
6M3	Gross debt (D4) at market value	...	...	...	1,489	1,565	1,531	...	...	...	2,336	2,428	2,386
6M3D3	D3 debt liabilities at market value	...	...	...	1,489	1,565	1,531	...	...	...	2,336	2,428	2,386
6M3D2	D2 debt liabilities at market value	...	...	...	1,485	1,562	1,527	...	...	...	2,332	2,425	2,383
6M3D1	D1 debt liabilities at market value	...	...	...	1,475	1,550	1,513	...	...	...	2,322	2,413	2,369
6M4	Gross debt (D4) at nominal value	...	...	...	...	...	...	...	...	...	...	...	...
6M4D3	D3 debt liabilities at nominal value	...	...	...	...	...	...	...	...	...	...	...	...
6M4D2	D2 debt liabilities at nominal value	...	...	...	...	...	...	...	...	...	...	...	...
6M4D1	D1 debt liabilities at nominal value	...	...	...	...	...	...	...	...	...	...	...	...

Germany (134)

In Billions of Euros (EUR) / Fiscal Year Ends December 31st

		Budgetary Central Government			Central Government (excl. Social Security)			Central Government (incl. Social Security)			General Government		
		2013	2014	2015	2013	2014	2015	2013	2014	2015	2013	2014	2015
6M35	Gross debt (D4) at face value	...	...	...	...	...	...	...	...	...	...	...	...
6M35D3	D3 debt liabilities at face value	...	...	...	...	...	...	...	...	...	...	...	...
6M35D2	D2 debt liabilities at face value	...	...	...	...	...	...	...	...	...	...	...	...
6M35D1	D1 debt liabilities at face value	...	...	...	...	...	...	...	...	...	...	...	...
6M93	Government gross debt per national definition	...	...	...	...	...	...	...	...	...	...	...	...
6M5	Arrears	...	...	...	...	...	...	...	...	...	...	...	...
6M6	Explicit contingent liabilities	...	...	...	...	...	...	...	...	...	...	...	...
6M61	of which: Publicly guaranteed debt	...	...	...	...	...	...	...	...	...	...	...	...
6M7	Net implicit obligations for social security benefits	...	...	...	...	...	...	...	...	...	...	...	...
	Table 7 Expenditure by functions of government												
7	**Expenditure**	...	...	...	...	...	...	...	...	...	**1,262**	**1,297**	**1,332**
701	**General public services**	...	...	...	...	...	...	...	...	...	**181**	**187**	**178**
7017	Public debt transactions	...	...	...	...	...	...	...	...	...	57	53	48
7018	Transfers of general character between levels of government	...	...	...	...	...	...	...	...	...	—	—	—
702	**Defense**	...	...	...	...	...	...	...	...	...	**31**	**29**	**30**
703	**Public order and safety**	...	...	...	...	...	...	...	...	...	**44**	**46**	**47**
704	**Economic affairs**	...	...	...	...	...	...	...	...	...	**94**	**91**	**95**
7042	Agriculture, forestry, fishing, and hunting	...	...	...	...	...	...	...	...	...	6	6	6
7043	Fuel and energy	...	...	...	...	...	...	...	...	...	3	3	3
7044	Mining, manufacturing, and construction	...	...	...	...	...	...	...	...	...	5	5	6
7045	Transport	...	...	...	...	...	...	...	...	...	46	45	47
7046	Communication	...	...	...	...	...	...	...	...	...	0	0	0
705	**Environmental protection**	...	...	...	...	...	...	...	...	...	**17**	**18**	**18**
706	**Housing and community amenities**	...	...	...	...	...	...	...	...	...	**12**	**13**	**12**
707	**Health**	...	...	...	...	...	...	...	...	...	**199**	**209**	**217**
7072	Outpatient services	...	...	...	...	...	...	...	...	...	59	61	64
7073	Hospital services	...	...	...	...	...	...	...	...	...	78	81	84
7074	Public health services	...	...	...	...	...	...	...	...	...	2	2	2
708	**Recreation, culture and religion**	...	...	...	...	...	...	...	...	...	**29**	**30**	**31**
709	**Education**	...	...	...	...	...	...	...	...	...	**121**	**124**	**127**
7091	Pre-primary and primary education	...	...	...	...	...	...	...	...	...	34	35	36
7092	Secondary education	...	...	...	...	...	...	...	...	...	45	47	48
7094	Tertiary education	...	...	...	...	...	...	...	...	...	25	25	25
710	**Social protection**	...	...	...	...	...	...	...	...	...	**534**	**549**	**575**
7z	Statistical discrepancy: Expenditure	...	...	...	...	...	...	...	...	...	...	...	...
	Table 8 Financial transactions by counterpart sector												
32	**Net acquisition of financial assets**	...	...	...	**-4**	**15**	**-9**	...	...	...	**-17**	**12**	**-1**
321	Domestic debtors	...	...	...	-16	-10	6	...	...	...	-29	-14	14
8211	General government	...	...	...	...	...	...	...	...	...	...	...	...
8212	Central bank	...	...	...	...	...	...	...	...	...	...	...	...
8213	Deposit-taking corporations except the central bank	...	...	...	...	...	...	...	...	...	...	...	...
8214	Other financial corporations	...	...	...	...	...	...	...	...	...	...	...	...
8215	Nonfinancial corporations	...	...	...	...	...	...	...	...	...	...	...	...
8216	Households & nonprofit institutions serving households	...	...	...	...	...	...	...	...	...	...	...	...
322	External debtors	...	...	...	11	25	-16	...	...	...	12	26	-15
8221	General government	...	...	...	...	...	...	...	...	...	...	...	...
8227	International organizations	...	...	...	...	...	...	...	...	...	...	...	...
8228	Financial corporations other than international organizations	...	...	...	...	...	...	...	...	...	...	...	...
8229	Other nonresidents	...	...	...	...	...	...	...	...	...	...	...	...

Germany (134)

In Billions of Euros (EUR) / Fiscal Year Ends December 31st

		Budgetary Central Government			Central Government (excl. Social Security)			Central Government (incl. Social Security)			General Government		
		2013	2014	2015	2013	2014	2015	2013	2014	2015	2013	2014	2015
33	**Net incurrence of liabilities**	...	...	...	4	6	-20	...	...	...	-12	4	-24
331	Domestic creditors	...	...	...	...	...	...	...	...	...	...	...	...
3311	General government	...	...	...	...	...	...	...	...	...	...	...	...
3312	Central bank	...	...	...	...	...	...	...	...	...	...	...	...
3313	Deposit-taking corporations except the central bank	...	...	...	...	...	...	...	...	...	...	...	...
3314	Other financial corporations	...	...	...	...	...	...	...	...	...	...	...	...
3315	Nonfinancial corporations	...	...	...	...	...	...	...	...	...	...	...	...
3316	Households & nonprofit institutions serving households	...	...	...	...	...	...	...	...	...	...	...	...
332	External creditors	...	...	...	...	...	...	...	...	...	...	...	...
3321	General government	...	...	...	...	...	...	...	...	...	...	...	...
3327	International organizations	...	...	...	...	...	...	...	...	...	...	...	...
3328	Financial corporations other than international organizations	...	...	...	...	...	...	...	...	...	...	...	...
3329	Other nonresidents	...	...	...	...	...	...	...	...	...	...	...	...
	Table 9 Total other economic flows in assets and liabilities												

Ghana (652)

In Millions of Ghanaian Cedis (GHS) / Fiscal Year Ends December 31st

		Budgetary Central Government			Central Government (excl. Social Security)			Central Government (incl. Social Security)			General Government		
		2009	2010	2011	2009	2010P	2011	2009	2010P	2011	2009	2010	2011
	Statement of operations												
1	Revenue	6,803	8,859	12,935	...	9,210	...	...	9,210	...	...	...	...
2	Expense	6,598	9,281	12,646	...	9,443	...	...	9,443	...	...	...	...
GOB	**Gross operating balance**	**205**	**-422**	**289**	...	**-233**	...	...	**-233**	...	...	...	...
NOB	**Net operating balance**	...	...	...	...	...	...	...	...	...	...	...	...
31	Net/Gross investment in nonfinancial assets	2,271	2,893	2,633	...	3,048	...	...	3,048	...	...	...	...
2M	Expenditure	8,869	12,174	15,278	...	12,491	...	...	12,491	...	...	...	...
NLB	**Net lending (+) / Net borrowing (-)**	**-2,067**	**-3,315**	**-2,344**	...	**-3,281**	...	...	**-3,281**	...	...	...	...
32	Net acquisition of financial assets	-69	-409	-71	...	-301	...	...	-301	...	...	...	...
33	Net incurrence of liabilities	1,998	2,906	2,272	...	3,031	...	...	3,031	...	...	...	...
NLBz	Statistical discrepancy	0	-0	—	...	-51	...	...	-51	...	...	...	...
	Memorandum items												
PB	Primary net lending / net borrowing	-1,034	-1,876	-732	...	-1,822	...	...	-1,822	...	...	...	...
GB	Government balance per national definition	...	...	...	...	...	...	...	...	...	...	...	...
	Statement of other economic flows												
	Balance sheet												
	Table 1 Revenue												
1	**Revenue**	**6,803**	**8,859**	**12,935**	...	**9,210**	...	...	**9,210**	...	...	...	...
11	**Taxes**	**4,616**	**6,164**	**8,892**	...	**6,297**	...	...	**6,297**	...	...	...	...
111	Taxes on income, profits, and capital gains	1,538	2,195	3,193	...	2,195	...	...	2,195	...	...	...	...
1111	Payable by individuals	846	1,115	1,493	...	1,115	...	...	1,115	...	...	...	...
1112	Payable by corporations and other enterprises	692	1,080	1,699	...	1,080	...	...	1,080	...	...	...	...
1113	Other taxes on income, profits, and capital gains	—	—	—	...	—	...	...	—	...	...	...	...
112	Taxes on payroll and workforce	—	—	—	...	—	...	...	—	...	...	...	...
113	Taxes on property	—	—	—	...	—	...	...	—	...	...	...	...
114	Taxes on goods and services	1,996	2,437	3,549	...	2,570	...	...	2,570	...	...	...	...
1141	General taxes on goods and services	1,556	1,888	2,759	...	1,888	...	...	1,888	...	...	...	...
1142	Excises	330	374	606	...	374	...	...	374	...	...	...	...
115	Taxes on international trade and transactions	1,081	1,533	2,151	...	1,533	...	...	1,533	...	...	...	...
116	Other taxes	—	—	—	...	—	...	...	—	...	...	...	...
12	**Social contributions**	—	—	**79**	...	**87**	...	...	**87**	...	...	...	...
121	Social security contributions	—	—	—	...	—	...	...	—	...	...	...	...
122	Other social contributions	—	—	79	...	87	...	...	87	...	...	...	...
13	**Grants**	**1,160**	**1,174**	**1,347**	...	**1,174**	...	...	**1,174**	...	...	...	...
131	From foreign governments	1,001	973	1,105	...	973	...	...	973	...	...	...	...
132	From international organizations	158	201	242	...	201	...	...	201	...	...	...	...
133	From other general government units	—	—	—	...	—	...	...	—	...	...	...	...
1331	Current	—	—	—	...	—	...	...	—	...	...	...	...
1332	Capital	—	—	—	...	—	...	...	—	...	...	...	...
14	**Other revenue**	**1,027**	**1,521**	**2,617**	...	**1,652**	...	...	**1,652**	...	...	...	...
	Table 2 Expense by economic type												
2	**Expense**	**6,598**	**9,281**	**12,646**	...	**9,443**	...	...	**9,443**	...	...	...	...
21	**Compensation of employees**	**2,636**	**3,316**	**4,855**	...	**3,409**	...	...	**3,409**	...	...	...	...
211	Wages and salaries	2,479	3,183	4,535	...	3,189	...	...	3,189	...	...	...	...
212	Employers' social contributions	157	133	320	...	220	...	...	220	...	...	...	...
22	**Use of goods and services**	**1,087**	**1,372**	**2,002**	...	**1,375**	...	...	**1,375**	...	...	...	...
23	**Consumption of fixed capital**	...	...	...	...	...	...	...	...	...	...	...	...
24	**Interest**	**1,032**	**1,439**	**1,611**	...	**1,459**	...	...	**1,459**	...	...	...	...
25	**Subsidies**	—	**131**	—	...	**131**	...	...	**131**	...	...	...	...
26	**Grants**	**1,230**	**2,332**	**3,092**	...	**2,378**	...	...	**2,378**	...	...	...	...
261	To foreign governments	—	—	—	...	—	...	...	—	...	...	...	...
262	To international organizations	—	—	—	...	—	...	...	—	...	...	...	...
263	To other general government units	1,230	2,332	3,092	...	2,378	...	...	2,378	...	...	...	...
2631	Current	923	1,945	2,177	...	1,601	...	...	1,601	...	...	...	...
2632	Capital	307	387	915	...	777	...	...	777	...	...	...	...

Ghana (652)

In Millions of Ghanaian Cedis (GHS) / Fiscal Year Ends December 31st

		Budgetary Central Government			Central Government (excl. Social Security)			Central Government (incl. Social Security)			General Government		
		2009	2010	2011	2009	2010P	2011	2009	2010P	2011	2009	2010	2011
27	**Social benefits**	**612**	**691**	**1,085**	**...**	**691**	**...**	**...**	**691**	**...**	**...**	**...**	**...**
271	Social security benefits	252	304	450	...	304	...	...	304	...	...	...	...
272	Social assistance benefits	360	386	635	...	386	...	...	386	...	...	...	...
273	Employment-related social benefits	—	—	—	...	—	...	...	—	...	...	...	...
28	**Other expense**	**—**	**—**	**—**	**...**	**—**	**...**	**...**	**—**	**...**	**...**	**...**	**...**
281	Property expense other than interest	—	—	—	...	—	...	...	—	...	...	...	...
282	Transfers not elsewhere classified	—	—	—	...	—	...	...	—	...	...	...	...
2821	Current	—	—	—	...	—	...	...	—	...	...	...	...
2822	Capital	—	—	—	...	—	...	...	—	...	...	...	...
	Table 3 Transactions in assets and liabilities												
3	**Change in net worth from transactions**	**...**	**...**	**...**	**...**	**...**	**...**	**...**	**...**	**...**	**...**	**...**	**...**
31	**Net/Gross investment in nonfinancial assets**	**2,271**	**2,893**	**2,633**	**...**	**3,048**	**...**	**...**	**3,048**	**...**	**...**	**...**	**...**
311	Fixed assets	2,271	2,893	2,633	...	3,048	...	...	3,048	...	...	...	...
3111	Buildings and structures	...	...	...	...	...	...	...	...	...	...	...	...
3112	Machinery and equipment	...	...	...	...	...	...	...	...	...	...	...	...
3113	Other fixed assets	...	...	...	...	...	...	...	...	...	...	...	...
3114	Weapons systems	...	...	...	...	...	...	...	...	...	...	...	...
312	Inventories	—	—	—	...	—	...	...	—	...	...	...	...
313	Valuables	—	—	—	...	—	...	...	—	...	...	...	...
314	Nonproduced assets	—	—	—	...	—	...	...	—	...	...	...	...
3141	Land	—	—	—	...	—	...	...	—	...	...	...	...
3142	Mineral and energy resources	—	—	—	...	—	...	...	—	...	...	...	...
3143	Other naturally occurring assets	—	—	—	...	—	...	...	—	...	...	...	...
3144	Intangible nonproduced assets	—	—	—	...	—	...	...	—	...	...	...	...
32	**Net acquisition of financial assets**	**-69**	**-409**	**-71**	**...**	**-301**	**...**	**...**	**-301**	**...**	**...**	**...**	**...**
	By instrument												
3201	Monetary gold and SDRs	—	—	—	...	—	...	...	—	...	...	...	...
3202	Currency and deposits	-69	-409	-71	...	-554	...	...	-554	...	...	...	...
3203	Debt securities	—	—	—	...	—	...	...	—	...	...	...	...
3204	Loans	—	—	—	...	153	...	...	153	...	...	...	...
3205	Equity and investment fund shares	—	—	—	...	8	...	...	8	...	...	...	...
3206	Insurance, pension, and standardized guarantee schemes	—	—	—	...	—	...	...	—	...	...	...	...
3207	Financial derivatives and employee stock options	—	—	—	...	—	...	...	—	...	...	...	...
3208	Other accounts receivable	—	—	...	...	91	268	...	91	...	...	...	...
	By debtor												
321	Domestic debtors	-69	-409	-71	...	-301	...	...	-301	...	...	...	...
322	External debtors	—	—	—	...	—	...	...	—	...	...	...	...
33	**Net incurrence of liabilities**	**1,998**	**2,906**	**2,272**	**...**	**3,031**	**...**	**...**	**3,031**	**...**	**...**	**...**	**...**
	By instrument												
3301	Special Drawing Rights (SDRs)	—	—	—	...	—	...	...	—	...	...	...	...
3302	Currency and deposits	—	—	—	...	—	...	...	—	...	...	...	...
3303	Debt securities	1,042	1,698	1,416	...	1,698	...	...	1,698	...	...	...	...
3304	Loans	956	1,209	856	...	1,247	...	...	1,247	...	...	...	...
3305	Equity and investment fund shares	—	—	—	...	—	...	...	—	...	...	...	...
3306	Insurance, pension, and standardized guarantee schemes	—	—	—	...	—	...	...	—	...	...	...	...
3307	Financial derivatives and employee stock options	—	—	—	...	—	...	...	—	...	...	...	...
3308	Other accounts payable	—	—	...	...	86	793	...	86	...	...	...	...
	By creditor												
331	Domestic creditors	1,042	1,698	1,416	...	1,822	...	...	1,822	...	...	...	...
332	External creditors	956	1,209	856	...	1,209	...	...	1,209	...	...	...	...
	Table 4 Holding gains and losses in assets and liabilities												
	Table 5 Holding gains and losses in assets and liabilities												
	Table 6 Balance sheet												

Ghana (652)

In Millions of Ghanaian Cedis (GHS) / Fiscal Year Ends December 31st

	Budgetary Central Government			Central Government (excl. Social Security)			Central Government (incl. Social Security)			General Government		
	2009	2010	2011	2009	2010P	2011	2009	2010P	2011	2009	2010	2011
Table 7 Expenditure by functions of government												
Table 8 Financial transactions by counterpart sector												
Table 9 Total other economic flows in assets and liabilities												

Greece (174)

In Millions of Euros (EUR) / Fiscal Year Ends December 31st

		Budgetary Central Government			Central Government (excl. Social Security)			Central Government (incl. Social Security)			General Government		
		2013	2014	2015	2013P	2014P	2015P	2013P	2014P	2015P	2013P	2014P	2015P
	Statement of operations												
1	Revenue	...	...	...	66,216	61,704	62,281	86,078	81,166	81,693	88,779	83,602	84,110
2	Expense	...	...	...	92,585	69,074	73,899	109,081	87,789	93,837	110,898	89,602	95,421
GOB	**Gross operating balance**	...	...	...	**-20,518**	**-1,859**	**-6,252**	**-17,131**	**-1,079**	**-6,744**	**-15,152**	**687**	**-4,871**
NOB	**Net operating balance**	...	...	...	**-26,369**	**-7,370**	**-11,618**	**-23,003**	**-6,623**	**-12,144**	**-22,119**	**-6,000**	**-11,311**
31	Net/Gross investment in nonfinancial assets	...	...	...	1,490	361	1,516	1,494	364	1,550	1,640	412	1,926
2M	Expenditure	...	...	...	94,075	69,435	75,415	110,575	88,153	95,387	112,538	90,014	97,347
NLB	**Net lending (+) / Net borrowing (-)**	...	...	...	**-27,859**	**-7,731**	**-13,134**	**-24,497**	**-6,987**	**-13,694**	**-23,759**	**-6,412**	**-13,237**
32	Net acquisition of financial assets	...	...	...	...	...	...	...	...	...	...	...	...
33	Net incurrence of liabilities	...	...	...	...	...	...	...	...	...	...	...	...
NLBz	Statistical discrepancy	...	...	...	...	...	...	...	...	...	...	...	...
	Memorandum items												
PB	Primary net lending / net borrowing	...	...	...	-20,443	-512	-6,630	-17,299	104	-7,373	-16,483	685	-6,912
GB	Government balance per national definition	...	...	...	...	...	...	...	...	...	...	...	...
	Statement of other economic flows												
	Balance sheet												
	Table 1 Revenue												
1	**Revenue**	...	...	...	**66,216**	**61,704**	**62,281**	**86,078**	**81,166**	**81,693**	**88,779**	**83,602**	**84,110**
11	**Taxes**	...	...	...	**42,454**	**43,101**	**43,139**	**42,887**	**43,543**	**43,426**	**44,549**	**45,107**	**44,967**
111	Taxes on income, profits, and capital gains	...	...	...	14,005	15,138	14,352	14,015	15,148	14,361	14,015	15,148	14,361
1111	Payable by individuals	...	...	...	10,770	10,540	9,603	10,780	10,550	9,612	10,780	10,550	9,612
1112	Payable by corporations and other enterprises	...	...	...	2,071	3,349	3,800	2,071	3,349	3,800	2,071	3,349	3,800
1113	Other taxes on income, profits, and capital gains	...	...	...	1,164	1,249	949	1,164	1,249	949	1,164	1,249	949
112	Taxes on payroll and workforce	...	...	...	—	—	—	—	—	—	—	—	—
113	Taxes on property	...	...	...	2,285	2,996	3,362	2,285	2,996	3,362	3,819	4,445	4,807
114	Taxes on goods and services	...	...	...	24,594	24,489	25,025	25,017	24,921	25,303	25,145	25,036	25,399
1141	General taxes on goods and services	...	...	...	13,246	13,183	13,391	13,569	13,533	13,599	13,589	13,548	13,602
1142	Excises	...	...	...	6,820	6,756	6,722	6,820	6,756	6,722	6,820	6,756	6,722
115	Taxes on international trade and transactions	...	...	...	5	5	—	5	5	—	5	5	—
116	Other taxes	...	...	...	1,565	473	400	1,565	473	400	1,565	473	400
12	**Social contributions**	...	...	...	**5,854**	**6,253**	**6,359**	**24,455**	**24,088**	**24,422**	**24,455**	**24,088**	**24,422**
121	Social security contributions	...	...	...	—	—	—	18,598	17,833	18,062	18,598	17,833	18,062
122	Other social contributions	...	...	...	5,854	6,253	6,359	5,857	6,255	6,360	5,857	6,255	6,360
13	**Grants**	...	...	...	...	...	...	...	...	...	...	...	...
131	From foreign governments	...	...	...	...	...	...	...	...	...	...	...	...
132	From international organizations	...	...	...	...	...	...	...	...	...	...	...	...
133	From other general government units	...	...	...	16	13	6	—	—	—	—	—	—
1331	Current	...	...	...	16	13	6	—	—	—	—	—	—
1332	Capital	...	...	...	—	—	—	—	—	—	—	—	—
14	**Other revenue**	...	...	...	...	...	...	...	...	...	...	...	...
	Table 2 Expense by economic type												
2	**Expense**	...	...	...	**92,585**	**69,074**	**73,899**	**109,081**	**87,789**	**93,837**	**110,898**	**89,602**	**95,421**
21	**Compensation of employees**	...	...	...	**19,052**	**19,350**	**19,181**	**19,740**	**19,776**	**19,546**	**22,059**	**21,948**	**21,649**
211	Wages and salaries	...	...	...	...	...	...	...	...	...	...	...	...
212	Employers' social contributions	...	...	...	...	...	...	...	...	...	...	...	...
22	**Use of goods and services**	...	...	...	**6,356**	**6,643**	**6,571**	**6,948**	**7,211**	**6,941**	**8,554**	**8,708**	**8,371**
23	**Consumption of fixed capital**	...	...	...	**5,851**	**5,511**	**5,366**	**5,872**	**5,544**	**5,400**	**6,967**	**6,687**	**6,440**
24	**Interest**	...	...	...	**7,416**	**7,219**	**6,504**	**7,198**	**7,091**	**6,321**	**7,276**	**7,097**	**6,325**
25	**Subsidies**	...	...	...	**1,635**	**1,296**	**1,330**	**1,937**	**1,644**	**1,654**	**1,937**	**1,644**	**1,654**
26	**Grants**	...	...	...	...	...	...	...	...	...	...	...	...
261	To foreign governments	...	...	...	...	...	...	...	...	...	...	...	...
262	To international organizations	...	...	...	...	...	...	...	...	...	...	...	...
263	To other general government units	...	...	...	20,330	16,838	16,198	4,422	4,035	3,973	—	—	—
2631	Current	...	...	...	19,230	15,768	14,949	3,549	3,153	2,992	—	—	—
2632	Capital	...	...	...	1,100	1,070	1,249	873	882	981	—	—	—

Greece (174)

In Millions of Euros (EUR) / Fiscal Year Ends December 31st

		Budgetary Central Government			Central Government (excl. Social Security)			Central Government (incl. Social Security)			General Government		
		2013	2014	2015	2013P	2014P	2015P	2013P	2014P	2015P	2013P	2014P	2015P
27	**Social benefits**	...	...	...	6,845	7,371	7,502	37,749	37,419	38,088	38,660	38,365	38,983
271	Social security benefits	...	...	...	...	...	...	...	...	...	...	...	...
272	Social assistance benefits	...	...	...	...	...	...	...	...	...	...	...	...
273	Employment-related social benefits	...	...	...	...	...	...	...	...	...	...	...	...
28	**Other expense**	...	...	...	...	...	...	...	...	...	...	...	...
281	Property expense other than interest	...	...	...	4	—	—	4	—	—	7	3	3
282	Transfers not elsewhere classified	...	...	...	...	...	...	...	...	...	...	...	...
2821	Current	...	...	...	...	...	...	...	...	...	...	...	...
2822	Capital	...	...	...	...	...	...	...	...	...	...	...	...
	Table 3 Transactions in assets and liabilities												
3	**Change in net worth from transactions**	...	...	...	...	...	...	...	...	...	...	...	...
31	**Net/Gross investment in nonfinancial assets**	...	...	...	1,490	361	1,516	1,494	364	1,550	1,640	412	1,926
311	Fixed assets	...	...	...	-901	-196	84	-897	-193	118	-777	-161	476
3111	Buildings and structures	...	...	...	...	...	...	...	...	...	...	...	...
3112	Machinery and equipment	...	...	...	...	...	...	...	...	...	...	...	...
3113	Other fixed assets	...	...	...	...	...	...	...	...	...	...	...	...
3114	Weapons systems	...	...	...	...	...	...	...	...	...	...	...	...
312	Inventories	...	...	...	...	...	...	...	...	...	...	...	...
313	Valuables	...	...	...	...	...	...	...	...	...	...	...	...
314	Nonproduced assets	...	...	...	53	36	50	53	36	50	79	52	68
3141	Land	...	...	...	...	...	...	...	...	...	...	...	...
3142	Mineral and energy resources	...	...	...	...	...	...	...	...	...	...	...	...
3143	Other naturally occurring assets	...	...	...	...	...	...	...	...	...	...	...	...
3144	Intangible nonproduced assets	...	...	...	...	...	...	...	...	...	...	...	...
32	**Net acquisition of financial assets**	...	...	...	...	...	...	...	...	...	...	...	...
	By instrument												
3201	Monetary gold and SDRs	...	...	...	...	...	...	...	...	...	...	...	...
3202	Currency and deposits	...	...	...	...	...	...	...	...	...	...	...	...
3203	Debt securities	...	...	...	...	...	...	...	...	...	...	...	...
3204	Loans	...	...	...	...	...	...	...	...	...	...	...	...
3205	Equity and investment fund shares	...	...	...	...	...	...	...	...	...	...	...	...
3206	Insurance, pension, and standardized guarantee schemes	...	...	...	...	...	...	...	...	...	...	...	...
3207	Financial derivatives and employee stock options	...	...	...	...	...	...	...	...	...	...	...	...
3208	Other accounts receivable	...	...	...	...	...	...	...	...	...	...	...	...
	By debtor												
321	Domestic debtors	...	...	...	...	...	...	...	...	...	...	...	...
322	External debtors	...	...	...	...	...	...	...	...	...	...	...	...
33	**Net incurrence of liabilities**	...	...	...	...	...	...	...	...	...	...	...	...
	By instrument												
3301	Special Drawing Rights (SDRs)	...	...	...	...	...	...	...	...	...	...	...	...
3302	Currency and deposits	...	...	...	...	...	...	...	...	...	...	...	...
3303	Debt securities	...	...	...	...	...	...	...	...	...	...	...	...
3304	Loans	...	...	...	...	...	...	...	...	...	...	...	...
3305	Equity and investment fund shares	...	...	...	...	...	...	...	...	...	...	...	...
3306	Insurance, pension, and standardized guarantee schemes	...	...	...	...	...	...	...	...	...	...	...	...
3307	Financial derivatives and employee stock options	...	...	...	...	...	...	...	...	...	...	...	...
3308	Other accounts payable	...	...	...	...	...	...	...	...	...	...	...	...
	By creditor												
331	Domestic creditors	...	...	...	...	...	...	...	...	...	...	...	...
332	External creditors	...	...	...	...	...	...	...	...	...	...	...	...
	Table 4 Holding gains and losses in assets and liabilities												
	Table 5 Holding gains and losses in assets and liabilities												
	Table 6 Balance sheet												

Greece (174)

In Millions of Euros (EUR) / Fiscal Year Ends December 31st

		Budgetary Central Government			Central Government (excl. Social Security)			Central Government (incl. Social Security)			General Government		
		2013	2014	2015	2013P	2014P	2015P	2013P	2014P	2015P	2013P	2014P	2015P
	Table 7 Expenditure by functions of government												
7	**Expenditure**	...	...	...	**94,075**	**69,435**	**75,415**	...	...	...	**112,538**	**90,014**	**97,347**
701	**General public services**	...	...	...	**36,484**	**33,263**	**32,117**	...	...	...	**17,854**	**17,925**	**17,365**
7017	Public debt transactions	...	...	...	7,774	7,562	6,860	...	...	...	7,632	7,440	6,681
7018	Transfers of general character between levels of government	...	...	...	20,282	16,828	16,147	...	...	...	—	—	—
702	**Defense**	...	...	...	**3,879**	**4,757**	**4,792**	...	...	...	**3,879**	**4,757**	**4,792**
703	**Public order and safety**	...	...	...	**3,328**	**3,752**	**3,686**	...	...	...	**3,372**	**3,763**	**3,694**
704	**Economic affairs**	...	...	...	**28,540**	**6,144**	**13,791**	...	...	...	**29,718**	**7,350**	**15,619**
7042	Agriculture, forestry, fishing, and hunting	...	...	...	267	292	414	...	...	...	267	292	414
7043	Fuel and energy	...	...	...	5	4	2	...	...	...	5	4	2
7044	Mining, manufacturing, and construction	...	...	...	150	189	132	...	...	...	174	217	163
7045	Transport	...	...	...	5,701	3,560	4,397	...	...	...	6,734	4,512	5,524
7046	Communication	...	...	...	2	7	7	...	...	...	2	7	7
705	**Environmental protection**	...	...	...	**2,031**	**1,728**	**1,727**	...	...	...	**3,082**	**2,628**	**2,603**
706	**Housing and community amenities**	...	...	...	**124**	**117**	**113**	...	...	...	**530**	**494**	**430**
707	**Health**	...	...	...	**4,572**	**4,427**	**4,018**	...	...	...	**9,313**	**8,364**	**7,973**
7072	Outpatient services	...	...	...	—	—	—	...	...	...	874	970	825
7073	Hospital services	...	...	...	4,347	4,140	3,896	...	...	...	5,600	4,892	4,595
7074	Public health services	...	...	...	—	—	—	...	...	...	—	—	—
708	**Recreation, culture and religion**	...	...	...	**671**	**583**	**587**	...	...	...	**1,179**	**1,221**	**1,223**
709	**Education**	...	...	...	**7,626**	**7,254**	**7,072**	...	...	...	**8,257**	**7,800**	**7,593**
7091	Pre-primary and primary education	...	...	...	2,290	2,310	2,203	...	...	...	2,485	2,478	2,371
7092	Secondary education	...	...	...	2,610	2,366	2,244	...	...	...	2,610	2,366	2,244
7094	Tertiary education	...	...	...	1,633	1,601	1,656	...	...	...	1,633	1,601	1,656
710	**Social protection**	...	...	...	**6,820**	**7,410**	**7,512**	...	...	...	**35,354**	**35,712**	**36,055**
7z	Statistical discrepancy: Expenditure	...	...	...	—	—	—	...	...	...	—	—	—
	Table 8 Financial transactions by counterpart sector												
32	**Net acquisition of financial assets**	...	...	...	...	...	...	...	...	...	...	...	...
321	Domestic debtors	...	...	...	...	...	...	...	...	...	...	...	...
8211	General government	...	...	...	...	...	...	...	...	...	—	—	—
8212	Central bank	...	...	...	...	...	...	...	...	...	...	...	...
8213	Deposit-taking corporations except the central bank	...	...	...	...	...	...	...	...	...	...	...	...
8214	Other financial corporations	...	...	...	...	...	...	...	...	...	...	...	...
8215	Nonfinancial corporations	...	...	...	...	...	...	...	...	...	...	...	...
8216	Households & nonprofit institutions serving households	...	...	...	...	...	...	...	...	...	...	...	...
322	External debtors	...	...	...	...	...	...	...	...	...	...	...	...
8221	General government	...	...	...	...	...	...	...	...	...	...	...	...
8227	International organizations	...	...	...	...	...	...	...	...	...	...	...	...
8228	Financial corporations other than international organizations	...	...	...	...	...	...	...	...	...	...	...	...
8229	Other nonresidents	...	...	...	...	...	...	...	...	...	...	...	...

Greece (174)

In Millions of Euros (EUR) / Fiscal Year Ends December 31st

		Budgetary Central Government			Central Government (excl. Social Security)			Central Government (incl. Social Security)			General Government		
		2013	2014	2015	2013P	2014P	2015P	2013P	2014P	2015P	2013P	2014P	2015P
33	**Net incurrence of liabilities**	...	...	...	...	...	...	...	...	...	...	...	...
331	Domestic creditors	...	...	...	...	...	...	...	...	...	...	...	...
3311	General government	...	...	...	...	...	...	...	...	...	—	—	—
3312	Central bank	...	...	...	...	...	...	...	...	...	...	...	...
3313	Deposit-taking corporations except the central bank	...	...	...	...	...	...	...	...	...	...	...	...
3314	Other financial corporations	...	...	...	...	...	...	...	...	...	...	...	...
3315	Nonfinancial corporations	...	...	...	...	...	...	...	...	...	...	...	...
3316	Households & nonprofit institutions serving households	...	...	...	...	...	...	...	...	...	...	...	...
332	External creditors	...	...	...	...	...	...	...	...	...	...	...	...
3321	General government	...	...	...	...	...	...	...	...	...	...	...	...
3327	International organizations	...	...	...	...	...	...	...	...	...	...	...	...
3328	Financial corporations other than international organizations	...	...	...	...	...	...	...	...	...	...	...	...
3329	Other nonresidents	...	...	...	...	...	...	...	...	...	...	...	...
	Table 9 Total other economic flows in assets and liabilities												

Grenada (328)

In Millions of Eastern Caribbean Dollars (XCD) / Fiscal Year Ends December 31st

		Budgetary Central Government			Central Government (excl. Social Security)			Central Government (incl. Social Security)			General Government		
		2012	2013	2014	2012	2013	2014	2012	2013	2014	2012	2013	2014
	Statement of operations												
1	Revenue	447	468	603	...	...	...	...	...	...	...	...	...
2	Expense	458	462	491	...	...	...	...	...	...	...	...	...
GOB	**Gross operating balance**	**-11**	**6**	**111**	...	...	...	...	...	...	...	...	...
NOB	**Net operating balance**	...	...	...	...	...	...	...	...	...	...	...	...
31	Net/Gross investment in nonfinancial assets	108	154	227	...	...	...	...	...	...	...	...	...
2M	Expenditure	566	616	718	...	...	...	...	...	...	...	...	...
NLB	**Net lending (+) / Net borrowing (-)**	**-120**	**-148**	**-115**	...	...	...	...	...	...	...	...	...
32	Net acquisition of financial assets	-148	-93	-9	...	...	...	...	...	...	...	...	...
33	Net incurrence of liabilities	-28	55	106	...	...	...	...	...	...	...	...	...
NLBz	Statistical discrepancy	-0	—	—	...	...	...	...	...	...	...	...	...
	Memorandum items												
PB	Primary net lending / net borrowing	-46	-77	-28	...	...	...	...	...	...	...	...	...
GB	Government balance per national definition	...	...	...	...	...	...	...	...	...	...	...	...
	Statement of other economic flows												
	Balance sheet												
	Table 1 Revenue												
1	**Revenue**	**447**	**468**	**603**	...	...	...	...	...	...	...	...	...
11	**Taxes**	**403**	**419**	**478**	...	...	...	...	...	...	...	...	...
111	Taxes on income, profits, and capital gains	75	66	90	...	...	...	...	...	...	...	...	...
1111	Payable by individuals	28	30	46	...	...	...	...	...	...	...	...	...
1112	Payable by corporations and other enterprises	48	36	44	...	...	...	...	...	...	...	...	...
1113	Other taxes on income, profits, and capital gains	—	0	0	...	...	...	...	...	...	...	...	...
112	Taxes on payroll and workforce	—	—	—	...	...	...	...	...	...	...	...	...
113	Taxes on property	16	15	21	...	...	...	...	...	...	...	...	...
114	Taxes on goods and services	177	209	218	...	...	...	...	...	...	...	...	...
1141	General taxes on goods and services	153	158	177	...	...	...	...	...	...	...	...	...
1142	Excises	—	—	—	...	...	...	...	...	...	...	...	...
115	Taxes on international trade and transactions	122	125	143	...	...	...	...	...	...	...	...	...
116	Other taxes	13	4	6	...	...	...	...	...	...	...	...	...
12	**Social contributions**	—	—	—	...	...	...	...	...	...	...	...	...
121	Social security contributions	—	—	—	...	...	...	...	...	...	...	...	...
122	Other social contributions	—	—	—	...	...	...	...	...	...	...	...	...
13	**Grants**	**22**	**31**	**100**	...	...	...	...	...	...	...	...	...
131	From foreign governments	22	31	100	...	...	...	...	...	...	...	...	...
132	From international organizations	—	—	—	...	...	...	...	...	...	...	...	...
133	From other general government units	—	—	—	...	...	...	...	...	...	...	...	...
1331	Current	—	—	—	...	...	...	...	...	...	...	...	...
1332	Capital	—	—	—	...	...	...	...	...	...	...	...	...
14	**Other revenue**	**22**	**18**	**24**	...	...	...	...	...	...	...	...	...
	Table 2 Expense by economic type												
2	**Expense**	**458**	**462**	**491**	...	...	...	...	...	...	...	...	...
21	**Compensation of employees**	**227**	**243**	**242**	...	...	...	...	...	...	...	...	...
211	Wages and salaries	227	243	242	...	...	...	...	...	...	...	...	...
212	Employers' social contributions	—	—	—	...	...	...	...	...	...	...	...	...
22	**Use of goods and services**	**86**	**76**	**72**	...	...	...	...	...	...	...	...	...
23	**Consumption of fixed capital**	...	...	...	...	...	...	...	...	...	...	...	...
24	**Interest**	**74**	**71**	**87**	...	...	...	...	...	...	...	...	...
25	**Subsidies**	**44**	**43**	**57**	...	...	...	...	...	...	...	...	...
26	**Grants**	—	—	—	...	...	...	...	...	...	...	...	...
261	To foreign governments	—	—	—	...	...	...	...	...	...	...	...	...
262	To international organizations	—	—	—	...	...	...	...	...	...	...	...	...
263	To other general government units	—	—	—	...	...	...	...	...	...	...	...	...
2631	Current	—	—	—	...	...	...	...	...	...	...	...	...
2632	Capital	—	—	—	...	...	...	...	...	...	...	...	...

Grenada (328)

In Millions of Eastern Caribbean Dollars (XCD) / Fiscal Year Ends December 31st

		Budgetary Central Government			Central Government (excl. Social Security)			Central Government (incl. Social Security)			General Government		
		2012	2013	2014	2012	2013	2014	2012	2013	2014	2012	2013	2014
27	**Social benefits**	**27**	**29**	**33**	...	...	...	...	...	...	...	...	...
271	Social security benefits	27	29	33	...	...	...	...	...	...	...	...	...
272	Social assistance benefits	—	—	—	...	...	...	...	...	...	...	...	...
273	Employment-related social benefits	—	—	—	...	...	...	...	...	...	...	...	...
28	**Other expense**	**—**	**—**	**—**	...	...	...	...	...	...	...	...	...
281	Property expense other than interest	—	—	—	...	...	...	...	...	...	...	...	...
282	Transfers not elsewhere classified	—	—	—	...	...	...	...	...	...	...	...	...
2821	Current	—	—	—	...	...	...	...	...	...	...	...	...
2822	Capital	—	—	—	...	...	...	...	...	...	...	...	...
	Table 3 Transactions in assets and liabilities												
3	**Change in net worth from transactions**	...	...	...	...	...	...	...	...	...	...	...	...
31	**Net/Gross investment in nonfinancial assets**	**108**	**154**	**227**	...	...	...	...	...	...	...	...	...
311	Fixed assets	108	154	227	...	...	...	...	...	...	...	...	...
3111	Buildings and structures	—	—	—	...	...	...	...	...	...	...	...	...
3112	Machinery and equipment	—	—	—	...	...	...	...	...	...	...	...	...
3113	Other fixed assets	—	—	—	...	...	...	...	...	...	...	...	...
3114	Weapons systems	...	...	...	...	...	...	...	...	...	...	...	...
312	Inventories	—	—	—	...	...	...	...	...	...	...	...	...
313	Valuables	—	—	—	...	...	...	...	...	...	...	...	...
314	Nonproduced assets	-0	-0	-0	...	...	...	...	...	...	...	...	...
3141	Land	-0	-0	-0	...	...	...	...	...	...	...	...	...
3142	Mineral and energy resources	—	—	—	...	...	...	...	...	...	...	...	...
3143	Other naturally occurring assets	—	—	—	...	...	...	...	...	...	...	...	...
3144	Intangible nonproduced assets	—	—	—	...	...	...	...	...	...	...	...	...
32	**Net acquisition of financial assets**	**-148**	**-93**	**-9**	...	...	...	...	...	...	...	...	...
	By instrument												
3201	Monetary gold and SDRs	—	—	—	...	...	...	...	...	...	...	...	...
3202	Currency and deposits	-148	-93	-9	...	...	...	...	...	...	...	...	...
3203	Debt securities	—	—	—	...	...	...	...	...	...	...	...	...
3204	Loans	—	—	—	...	...	...	...	...	...	...	...	...
3205	Equity and investment fund shares	—	—	—	...	...	...	...	...	...	...	...	...
3206	Insurance, pension, and standardized guarantee schemes	—	—	—	...	...	...	...	...	...	...	...	...
3207	Financial derivatives and employee stock options	—	—	—	...	...	...	...	...	...	...	...	...
3208	Other accounts receivable	...	...	...	...	...	...	...	...	...	...	...	...
	By debtor												
321	Domestic debtors	-148	-93	-9	...	...	...	...	...	...	...	...	...
322	External debtors	—	—	—	...	...	...	...	...	...	...	...	...
33	**Net incurrence of liabilities**	**-28**	**55**	**106**	...	...	...	...	...	...	...	...	...
	By instrument												
3301	Special Drawing Rights (SDRs)	...	...	...	...	...	...	...	...	...	...	...	...
3302	Currency and deposits	—	—	—	...	...	...	...	...	...	...	...	...
3303	Debt securities	—	—	—	...	...	...	...	...	...	...	...	...
3304	Loans	-63	-4	42	...	...	...	...	...	...	...	...	...
3305	Equity and investment fund shares	—	—	—	...	...	...	...	...	...	...	...	...
3306	Insurance, pension, and standardized guarantee schemes	—	—	—	...	...	...	...	...	...	...	...	...
3307	Financial derivatives and employee stock options	—	—	—	...	...	...	...	...	...	...	...	...
3308	Other accounts payable	34	59	64	...	...	...	...	...	...	...	...	...
	By creditor												
331	Domestic creditors	-53	-55	-20	...	...	...	...	...	...	...	...	...
332	External creditors	25	110	126	...	...	...	...	...	...	...	...	...
	Table 4 Holding gains and losses in assets and liabilities												
	Table 5 Holding gains and losses in assets and liabilities												
	Table 6 Balance sheet												

Grenada (328)

In Millions of Eastern Caribbean Dollars (XCD) / Fiscal Year Ends December 31st

	Budgetary Central Government			Central Government (excl. Social Security)			Central Government (incl. Social Security)			General Government		
	2012	2013	2014	2012	2013	2014	2012	2013	2014	2012	2013	2014
Table 7 Expenditure by functions of government												
Table 8 Financial transactions by counterpart sector												
Table 9 Total other economic flows in assets and liabilities												

Guatemala (258)

In Millions of Guatemalan Quetzales (GTQ) / Fiscal Year Ends December 31st

		Budgetary Central Government			Central Government (excl. Social Security)			Central Government (incl. Social Security)			General Government		
		2011	2012	2013	2011	2012	2013	2011	2012	2013	2011	2012	2013
	Statement of operations												
1	Revenue	42,865	45,681	48,997	...	...	...	...	...	...	...	...	...
2	Expense	46,514	51,171	54,268	...	...	...	...	...	...	...	...	...
GOB	**Gross operating balance**	**-3,649**	**-5,490**	**-5,270**	...	...	...	...	...	...	...	...	...
NOB	**Net operating balance**	...	...	...	...	...	...	...	...	...	...	...	...
31	Net/Gross investment in nonfinancial assets	6,535	3,712	-3,499	...	...	...	...	...	...	...	...	...
2M	Expenditure	53,049	54,883	50,769	...	...	...	...	...	...	...	...	...
NLB	**Net lending (+) / Net borrowing (-)**	**-10,185**	**-9,201**	**-1,772**	...	...	...	...	...	...	...	...	...
32	Net acquisition of financial assets	-1,571	-1,775	6,962	...	...	...	...	...	...	...	...	...
33	Net incurrence of liabilities	8,613	7,426	8,734	...	...	...	...	...	...	...	...	...
NLBz	Statistical discrepancy	0	0	0	...	...	...	...	...	...	...	...	...
	Memorandum items												
PB	Primary net lending / net borrowing	-4,835	-3,307	4,671	...	...	...	...	...	...	...	...	...
GB	Government balance per national definition	...	...	...	...	...	...	...	...	...	...	...	...
	Statement of other economic flows												
	Balance sheet												
	Table 1 Revenue												
1	**Revenue**	**42,865**	**45,681**	**48,997**	...	...	...	...	...	...	...	...	...
11	**Taxes**	**40,210**	**42,772**	**46,228**	...	...	...	...	...	...	...	...	...
111	Taxes on income, profits, and capital gains	12,696	13,444	16,041	...	...	...	...	...	...	...	...	...
1111	Payable by individuals	1,462	1,477	1,246	...	...	...	...	...	...	...	...	...
1112	Payable by corporations and other enterprises	11,234	11,967	14,795	...	...	...	...	...	...	...	...	...
1113	Other taxes on income, profits, and capital gains	0	0	0	...	...	...	...	...	...	...	...	...
112	Taxes on payroll and workforce	—	—	—	...	...	...	...	...	...	...	...	...
113	Taxes on property	14	9	12	...	...	...	...	...	...	...	...	...
114	Taxes on goods and services	24,109	25,901	27,541	...	...	...	...	...	...	...	...	...
1141	General taxes on goods and services	22,301	20,767	21,645	...	...	...	...	...	...	...	...	...
1142	Excises	3,013	3,073	3,373	...	...	...	...	...	...	...	...	...
115	Taxes on international trade and transactions	2,752	2,542	2,205	...	...	...	...	...	...	...	...	...
116	Other taxes	638	876	430	...	...	...	...	...	...	...	...	...
12	**Social contributions**	**1,214**	**1,274**	**1,427**	...	...	...	...	...	...	...	...	...
121	Social security contributions	—	—	—	...	...	...	...	...	...	...	...	...
122	Other social contributions	1,214	1,274	1,427	...	...	...	...	...	...	...	...	...
13	**Grants**	**572**	**407**	**385**	...	...	...	...	...	...	...	...	...
131	From foreign governments	452	336	316	...	...	...	...	...	...	...	...	...
132	From international organizations	119	71	70	...	...	...	...	...	...	...	...	...
133	From other general government units	1	—	—	...	...	...	...	...	...	...	...	...
1331	Current	1	—	—	...	...	...	...	...	...	...	...	...
1332	Capital	—	—	—	...	...	...	...	...	...	...	...	...
14	**Other revenue**	**869**	**1,229**	**956**	...	...	...	...	...	...	...	...	...
	Table 2 Expense by economic type												
2	**Expense**	**46,514**	**51,171**	**54,268**	...	...	...	...	...	...	...	...	...
21	**Compensation of employees**	**14,100**	**14,974**	**16,875**	...	...	...	...	...	...	...	...	...
211	Wages and salaries	13,653	14,321	16,281	...	...	...	...	...	...	...	...	...
212	Employers' social contributions	448	653	594	...	...	...	...	...	...	...	...	...
22	**Use of goods and services**	**7,161**	**8,716**	**8,596**	...	...	...	...	...	...	...	...	...
23	**Consumption of fixed capital**	—	—	...	...	...	...	...	...	...	...	...	...
24	**Interest**	**5,350**	**5,895**	**6,443**	...	...	...	...	...	...	...	...	...
25	**Subsidies**	**30**	**591**	**245**	...	...	...	...	...	...	...	...	...
26	**Grants**	**11,558**	**12,665**	**13,394**	...	...	...	...	...	...	...	...	...
261	To foreign governments	1	1	1	...	...	...	...	...	...	...	...	...
262	To international organizations	55	75	72	...	...	...	...	...	...	...	...	...
263	To other general government units	11,502	12,589	13,321	...	...	...	...	...	...	...	...	...
2631	Current	6,178	6,284	6,582	...	...	...	...	...	...	...	...	...
2632	Capital	5,325	6,305	6,739	...	...	...	...	...	...	...	...	...

Guatemala (258)

In Millions of Guatemalan Quetzales (GTQ) / Fiscal Year Ends December 31st

		Budgetary Central Government			Central Government (excl. Social Security)			Central Government (incl. Social Security)			General Government		
		2011	2012	2013	2011	2012	2013	2011	2012	2013	2011	2012	2013
27	**Social benefits**	**3,211**	**3,423**	**3,682**	...	...	...	...	...	...	...	...	...
271	Social security benefits	—	—	3,581	...	...	...	...	...	...	...	...	...
272	Social assistance benefits	3,147	3,306	—	...	...	...	...	...	...	...	...	...
273	Employment-related social benefits	64	117	101	...	...	...	...	...	...	...	...	...
28	**Other expense**	**5,103**	**4,907**	**5,033**	...	...	...	...	...	...	...	...	...
281	Property expense other than interest	—	—	—	...	...	...	...	...	...	...	...	...
282	Transfers not elsewhere classified	5,103	4,907	5,033	...	...	...	...	...	...	...	...	...
2821	Current	2,517	2,427	2,934	...	...	...	...	...	...	...	...	...
2822	Capital	2,586	2,480	2,099	...	...	...	...	...	...	...	...	...
	Table 3 Transactions in assets and liabilities												
3	**Change in net worth from transactions**	...	...	...	...	...	...	...	...	...	...	...	...
31	**Net/Gross investment in nonfinancial assets**	**6,535**	**3,712**	**-3,499**	...	...	...	...	...	...	...	...	...
311	Fixed assets	6,505	3,703	-3,513	...	...	...	...	...	...	...	...	...
3111	Buildings and structures	6,477	3,663	-3,310	...	...	...	...	...	...	...	...	...
3112	Machinery and equipment	50	44	-203	...	...	...	...	...	...	...	...	...
3113	Other fixed assets	-23	-4	-1	...	...	...	...	...	...	...	...	...
3114	Weapons systems	—	—	—	...	...	...	...	...	...	...	...	...
312	Inventories	—	—	—	...	...	...	...	...	...	...	...	...
313	Valuables	0	0	0	...	...	...	...	...	...	...	...	...
314	Nonproduced assets	31	9	15	...	...	...	...	...	...	...	...	...
3141	Land	31	9	15	...	...	...	...	...	...	...	...	...
3142	Mineral and energy resources	—	—	—	...	...	...	...	...	...	...	...	...
3143	Other naturally occurring assets	—	—	—	...	...	...	...	...	...	...	...	...
3144	Intangible nonproduced assets	—	—	—	...	...	...	...	...	...	...	...	...
32	**Net acquisition of financial assets**	**-1,571**	**-1,775**	**6,962**	...	...	...	...	...	...	...	...	...
	By instrument												
3201	Monetary gold and SDRs	—	—	—	...	...	...	...	...	...	...	...	...
3202	Currency and deposits	-1,565	-1,765	6,967	...	...	...	...	...	...	...	...	...
3203	Debt securities	—	—	—	...	...	...	...	...	...	...	...	...
3204	Loans	-7	-11	-5	...	...	...	...	...	...	...	...	...
3205	Equity and investment fund shares	—	—	—	...	...	...	...	...	...	...	...	...
3206	Insurance, pension, and standardized guarantee schemes	—	—	—	...	...	...	...	...	...	...	...	...
3207	Financial derivatives and employee stock options	—	—	—	...	...	...	...	...	...	...	...	...
3208	Other accounts receivable	—	—	...	...	...	...	...	...	...	...	...	...
	By debtor												
321	Domestic debtors	-1,571	-1,775	6,962	...	...	...	...	...	...	...	...	...
322	External debtors	—	—	—	...	...	...	...	...	...	...	...	...
33	**Net incurrence of liabilities**	**8,613**	**7,426**	**8,734**	...	...	...	...	...	...	...	...	...
	By instrument												
3301	Special Drawing Rights (SDRs)	—	—	—	...	...	...	...	...	...	...	...	...
3302	Currency and deposits	—	—	—	...	...	...	...	...	...	...	...	...
3303	Debt securities	5,690	7,164	5,473	...	...	...	...	...	...	...	...	...
3304	Loans	2,923	262	3,261	...	...	...	...	...	...	...	...	...
3305	Equity and investment fund shares	—	—	—	...	...	...	...	...	...	...	...	...
3306	Insurance, pension, and standardized guarantee schemes	—	—	—	...	...	...	...	...	...	...	...	...
3307	Financial derivatives and employee stock options	—	—	—	...	...	...	...	...	...	...	...	...
3308	Other accounts payable	—	—	...	...	...	...	...	...	...	...	...	...
	By creditor												
331	Domestic creditors	5,690	3,629	2,205	...	...	...	...	...	...	...	...	...
332	External creditors	2,923	3,797	6,528	...	...	...	...	...	...	...	...	...
	Table 4 Holding gains and losses in assets and liabilities												
	Table 5 Holding gains and losses in assets and liabilities												
	Table 6 Balance sheet												

Guatemala (258)

In Millions of Guatemalan Quetzales (GTQ) / Fiscal Year Ends December 31st

		Budgetary Central Government			Central Government (excl. Social Security)			Central Government (incl. Social Security)			General Government		
		2011	2012	2013	2011	2012	2013	2011	2012	2013	2011	2012	2013
	Table 7 Expenditure by functions of government												
7	**Expenditure**	**53,049**	**54,883**	**57,796**	...	...	...	...	...	...	...	...	...
701	**General public services**	**12,301**	**12,720**	**10,654**	...	...	...	...	...	...	...	...	...
7017	Public debt transactions	5,350	5,895	6,443	...	...	...	...	...	...	...	...	...
7018	Transfers of general character between levels of government	...	...	...	...	...	...	...	...	...	...	...	...
702	**Defense**	**1,204**	**1,310**	**1,525**	...	...	...	...	...	...	...	...	...
703	**Public order and safety**	**5,208**	**5,750**	**6,392**	...	...	...	...	...	...	...	...	...
704	**Economic affairs**	**9,093**	**8,107**	**7,412**	...	...	...	...	...	...	...	...	...
7042	Agriculture, forestry, fishing, and hunting	1,123	1,527	1,393	...	...	...	...	...	...	...	...	...
7043	Fuel and energy	107	308	205	...	...	...	...	...	...	...	...	...
7044	Mining, manufacturing, and construction	9	9	13	...	...	...	...	...	...	...	...	...
7045	Transport	7,366	5,697	5,224	...	...	...	...	...	...	...	...	...
7046	Communication	67	107	41	...	...	...	...	...	...	...	...	...
705	**Environmental protection**	**560**	**571**	**568**	...	...	...	...	...	...	...	...	...
706	**Housing and community amenities**	**5,590**	**6,258**	**6,971**	...	...	...	...	...	...	...	...	...
707	**Health**	**4,085**	**4,193**	**4,924**	...	...	...	...	...	...	...	...	...
7072	Outpatient services	201	664	487	...	...	...	...	...	...	...	...	...
7073	Hospital services	775	1,145	2,109	...	...	...	...	...	...	...	...	...
7074	Public health services	1,218	1,353	1,723	...	...	...	...	...	...	...	...	...
708	**Recreation, culture and religion**	**930**	**975**	**884**	...	...	...	...	...	...	...	...	...
709	**Education**	**10,811**	**11,668**	**12,360**	...	...	...	...	...	...	...	...	...
7091	Pre-primary and primary education	5,908	6,643	6,838	...	...	...	...	...	...	...	...	...
7092	Secondary education	1,263	1,431	1,467	...	...	...	...	...	...	...	...	...
7094	Tertiary education	1,349	1,498	1,479	...	...	...	...	...	...	...	...	...
710	**Social protection**	**5,836**	**6,170**	**6,454**	...	...	...	...	...	...	...	...	...
7z	Statistical discrepancy: Expenditure	-2,568	-2,839	...	...	...	...	...	...	...	...	...	...
	Table 8 Financial transactions by counterpart sector												
	Table 9 Total other economic flows in assets and liabilities												

Honduras (268)

In Millions of Honduran Lempiras (HNL) / Fiscal Year Ends December 31st

		Budgetary Central Government			Central Government (excl. Social Security)			Central Government (incl. Social Security)			General Government		
		2013	2014	2015	2013	2014	2015	2013	2014	2015	2013	2014	2015P
	Statement of operations												
1	Revenue	64,119	76,768	88,226	77,617	91,802	104,203	86,984	99,168	106,954	88,721	102,925	115,896
2	Expense	84,733	86,298	93,238	89,106	95,238	101,287	89,970	100,515	101,179	92,580	99,030	105,178
GOB	**Gross operating balance**	**-20,613**	**-9,530**	**-5,013**	**-11,489**	**-3,436**	**2,916**	**-2,986**	**-1,347**	**5,775**	**-3,859**	**3,895**	**10,718**
NOB	**Net operating balance**	...	...	...	...	...	...	...	...	...	...	...	...
31	Net/Gross investment in nonfinancial assets	9,463	8,470	8,729	11,502	9,275	9,593	11,074	9,499	9,731	17,624	15,095	14,307
2M	Expenditure	94,196	94,769	101,967	100,608	104,513	110,879	101,043	110,014	110,910	110,204	114,125	119,486
NLB	**Net lending (+) / Net borrowing (-)**	**-30,076**	**-18,000**	**-13,742**	**-22,991**	**-12,711**	**-6,676**	**-14,059**	**-10,846**	**-3,956**	**-21,483**	**-11,200**	**-3,589**
32	Net acquisition of financial assets	5,692	-1,103	2,613	12,883	-108	4,148	15,912	3,354	6,209	15,532	3,459	6,491
33	Net incurrence of liabilities	35,768	16,897	16,355	35,873	12,603	11,368	36,449	14,200	10,709	37,015	14,659	10,623
NLBz	Statistical discrepancy	0	-0	0	0	-0	-544	-6,478	-0	-543	0	1	-543
	Memorandum items												
PB	Primary net lending / net borrowing	-22,313	-8,609	-2,528	-17,018	-5,142	2,057	-6,282	-3,277	4,312	-15,996	-4,137	4,834
GB	Government balance per national definition	...	...	...	...	...	...	...	...	...	...	...	...
	Statement of other economic flows												
	Balance sheet												
	Table 1 Revenue												
1	**Revenue**	**64,119**	**76,768**	**88,226**	**77,617**	**91,802**	**104,203**	**86,984**	**99,168**	**106,954**	**88,721**	**102,925**	**115,896**
11	**Taxes**	**56,719**	**68,591**	**79,855**	**56,719**	**68,591**	**79,855**	**56,719**	**68,591**	**79,855**	**59,116**	**71,228**	**82,350**
111	Taxes on income, profits, and capital gains	19,352	21,333	24,990	19,352	21,333	24,990	19,352	21,333	24,990	19,352	21,333	24,990
1111	Payable by individuals	6,478	7,312	8,791	6,478	7,312	8,791	6,478	7,312	8,791	6,478	7,312	8,791
1112	Payable by corporations and other enterprises	12,875	14,021	16,198	12,875	14,021	16,198	12,875	14,021	16,198	12,875	14,021	16,198
1113	Other taxes on income, profits, and capital gains	—	—	—	—	—	—	—	—	—	—	—	—
112	Taxes on payroll and workforce	—	—	—	—	—	—	—	—	—	—	—	—
113	Taxes on property	245	389	334	245	389	334	245	389	334	2,641	3,025	2,829
114	Taxes on goods and services	34,471	43,895	50,990	34,471	43,895	50,990	34,471	43,895	50,990	34,471	43,895	50,990
1141	General taxes on goods and services	20,935	28,009	32,571	20,935	28,009	32,571	20,935	28,009	32,571	20,935	28,009	32,571
1142	Excises	10,476	11,986	15,848	10,476	11,986	15,848	10,476	11,986	15,848	10,476	11,986	15,848
115	Taxes on international trade and transactions	2,651	2,974	3,541	2,651	2,974	3,541	2,651	2,974	3,541	2,651	2,974	3,541
116	Other taxes	—	—	—	—	—	—	—	—	—	—	—	—
12	**Social contributions**	—	—	—	**6,405**	**6,676**	**6,945**	**12,529**	**12,467**	**13,524**	**12,529**	**12,467**	**13,524**
121	Social security contributions	—	—	—	—	—	—	6,125	5,792	6,579	6,125	5,792	6,579
122	Other social contributions	—	—	—	6,405	6,676	6,945	6,405	6,676	6,945	6,405	6,676	6,945
13	**Grants**	**2,949**	**3,295**	**4,111**	**2,873**	**3,213**	**4,140**	**2,873**	**3,332**	**-612**	**2,954**	**3,307**	**4,107**
131	From foreign governments	311	311	—	311	311	—	311	311	—	311	311	—
132	From international organizations	2,562	2,902	4,107	2,562	2,902	4,107	2,562	2,902	4,107	2,643	2,996	4,107
133	From other general government units	76	82	4	0	—	33	—	119	-4,718	0	—	0
1331	Current	76	82	4	0	—	33	—	119	-523	0	—	0
1332	Capital	—	—	—	—	—	-0	—	—	-4,195	0	—	-0
14	**Other revenue**	**4,452**	**4,882**	**4,260**	**11,620**	**13,322**	**13,263**	**14,863**	**14,777**	**14,186**	**14,122**	**15,923**	**15,915**
	Table 2 Expense by economic type												
2	**Expense**	**84,733**	**86,298**	**93,238**	**89,106**	**95,238**	**101,287**	**89,970**	**100,515**	**101,179**	**92,580**	**99,030**	**105,178**
21	**Compensation of employees**	**36,033**	**36,404**	**38,187**	**42,275**	**41,975**	**43,789**	**44,969**	**44,413**	**46,259**	**47,014**	**46,272**	**48,166**
211	Wages and salaries	32,494	32,659	33,999	38,707	37,760	39,042	41,205	40,016	41,311	43,244	41,870	43,176
212	Employers' social contributions	3,539	3,745	4,188	3,568	4,215	4,747	3,764	4,397	4,948	3,770	4,402	4,990
22	**Use of goods and services**	**11,919**	**10,970**	**14,673**	**13,446**	**12,750**	**16,550**	**14,952**	**14,258**	**18,002**	**17,256**	**15,814**	**18,939**
23	**Consumption of fixed capital**	...	...	...	...	...	...	...	...	...	...	...	...
24	**Interest**	**7,764**	**9,391**	**11,214**	**5,973**	**7,569**	**8,733**	**7,777**	**7,569**	**8,269**	**5,487**	**7,063**	**8,423**
25	**Subsidies**	**351**	**181**	**189**	**351**	**181**	**189**	**351**	**181**	**189**	**351**	**181**	**189**
26	**Grants**	**14,297**	**11,728**	**10,540**	**6,863**	**5,092**	**4,914**	**404**	**5,092**	**121**	**404**	**143**	**121**
261	To foreign governments	11	11	11	11	11	11	11	11	11	11	11	11
262	To international organizations	388	129	108	393	132	110	393	132	110	393	132	110
263	To other general government units	13,899	11,588	10,421	6,459	4,949	4,794	—	4,949	-0	0	—	-0
2631	Current	7,237	6,869	5,985	511	719	598	—	719	-0	0	—	-0
2632	Capital	6,662	4,718	4,436	5,948	4,230	4,195	—	4,230	-0	0	—	-0

Honduras (268)

In Millions of Honduran Lempiras (HNL) / Fiscal Year Ends December 31st

		Budgetary Central Government			Central Government (excl. Social Security)			Central Government (incl. Social Security)			General Government		
		2013	2014	2015	2013	2014	2015	2013	2014	2015	2013	2014	2015P
27	**Social benefits**	**499**	**734**	**254**	**526**	**1,176**	**511**	**1,734**	**2,341**	**1,726**	**1,736**	**2,344**	**1,726**
271	Social security benefits	—	—	—	—	—	—	961	1,090	1,183	961	1,090	1,183
272	Social assistance benefits	—	—	—	—	—	—	—	—	—	—	—	—
273	Employment-related social benefits	499	734	254	526	1,176	511	772	1,251	544	775	1,254	544
28	**Other expense**	**13,869**	**16,891**	**18,181**	**19,672**	**26,497**	**26,600**	**19,783**	**26,662**	**26,614**	**20,332**	**27,214**	**27,614**
281	Property expense other than interest	—	—	—	—	—	—	—	—	—	—	—	—
282	Transfers not elsewhere classified	13,869	16,891	18,181	19,672	26,497	26,600	19,783	26,662	26,614	20,332	27,214	27,614
2821	Current	10,292	8,815	10,392	16,095	18,420	18,811	16,205	18,586	18,825	16,473	18,862	18,918
2822	Capital	3,577	8,076	7,789	3,577	8,076	7,789	3,577	8,076	7,789	3,859	8,352	8,696
	Table 3 Transactions in assets and liabilities												
3	**Change in net worth from transactions**	...	...	...	...	...	...	...	...	...	...	...	...
31	**Net/Gross investment in nonfinancial assets**	**9,463**	**8,470**	**8,729**	**11,502**	**9,275**	**9,593**	**11,074**	**9,499**	**9,731**	**17,624**	**15,095**	**14,307**
311	Fixed assets	9,463	8,470	8,729	11,495	9,261	9,595	11,485	9,485	9,668	18,035	15,082	14,245
3111	Buildings and structures	8,708	8,248	...	...	...	...	...	...	...	...	...	...
3112	Machinery and equipment	755	222	...	...	...	...	...	...	...	...	...	...
3113	Other fixed assets	—	—	...	...	...	...	...	...	...	...	...	...
3114	Weapons systems	—	—	...	...	...	...	...	...	...	...	...	...
312	Inventories	—	—	—	7	14	-2	-411	14	63	-411	14	63
313	Valuables	—	—	—	—	—	—	—	—	—	—	—	—
314	Nonproduced assets	—	—	—	—	—	—	—	—	—	—	—	—
3141	Land	—	—	—	—	—	—	—	—	—	—	—	—
3142	Mineral and energy resources	—	—	—	—	—	—	—	—	—	—	—	—
3143	Other naturally occurring assets	—	—	—	—	—	—	—	—	—	—	—	—
3144	Intangible nonproduced assets	—	—	—	—	—	—	—	—	—	—	—	—
32	**Net acquisition of financial assets**	**5,692**	**-1,103**	**2,613**	**12,883**	**-108**	**4,148**	**15,912**	**3,354**	**6,209**	**15,532**	**3,459**	**6,491**
	By instrument												
3201	Monetary gold and SDRs	—	—	—	—	—	—	—	—	—	—	—	—
3202	Currency and deposits	6,341	-1,127	2,418	8,942	-407	1,997	10,236	-227	3,290	10,457	29	3,607
3203	Debt securities	-227	-32	15	3,881	1,184	879	4,039	1,773	1,010	4,039	1,773	1,010
3204	Loans	-444	-17	—	-1,829	-423	544	-1,841	-423	493	-1,841	-423	493
3205	Equity and investment fund shares	—	—	—	—	—	—	—	—	—	—	—	—
3206	Insurance, pension, and standardized guarantee schemes	—	—	—	—	—	—	—	—	—	—	—	—
3207	Financial derivatives and employee stock options	—	—	—	—	—	546	—	—	1,236	—	—	1,201
3208	Other accounts receivable	23	73	180	1,888	-462	180	3,478	2,231	180	2,877	2,080	180
	By debtor												
321	Domestic debtors	5,543	-1,266	2,432	12,833	-246	3,967	15,862	3,216	6,029	15,482	3,320	6,310
322	External debtors	149	163	180	50	139	180	50	139	180	50	139	180
33	**Net incurrence of liabilities**	**35,768**	**16,897**	**16,355**	**35,873**	**12,603**	**11,368**	**36,449**	**14,200**	**10,709**	**37,015**	**14,659**	**10,623**
	By instrument												
3301	Special Drawing Rights (SDRs)	—	—	—	—	—	—	—	—	—	—	—	—
3302	Currency and deposits	—	—	—	—	—	—	—	—	—	—	—	—
3303	Debt securities	3,855	6,347	4,865	3,855	1,438	2,319	3,855	1,242	1,716	3,855	1,242	1,716
3304	Loans	31,384	12,108	11,361	31,384	12,108	11,361	31,277	11,548	12,506	30,943	11,559	12,462
3305	Equity and investment fund shares	—	—	—	—	—	—	—	—	—	—	—	—
3306	Insurance, pension, and standardized guarantee schemes	—	—	—	—	—	—	—	—	—	—	—	—
3307	Financial derivatives and employee stock options	—	—	—	—	—	—	—	—	—	—	—	—
3308	Other accounts payable	529	-1,559	128	634	-943	-2,312	1,317	1,410	-3,514	2,217	1,859	-3,555
	By creditor												
331	Domestic creditors	4,202	6,339	7,593	4,307	2,045	2,607	4,883	3,642	1,948	5,448	4,101	1,862
332	External creditors	31,567	10,558	8,761	31,567	10,558	8,761	31,567	10,558	8,761	31,566	10,558	8,761
	Table 4 Holding gains and losses in assets and liabilities												
	Table 5 Holding gains and losses in assets and liabilities												
	Table 6 Balance sheet												

Honduras (268)

In Millions of Honduran Lempiras (HNL) / Fiscal Year Ends December 31st

		Budgetary Central Government			Central Government (excl. Social Security)			Central Government (incl. Social Security)			General Government		
		2013	2014	2015	2013	2014	2015	2013	2014	2015	2013	2014	2015P
	Table 7 Expenditure by functions of government												
7	**Expenditure**	**94,196**	**94,769**	**101,967**	**100,608**	**104,513**	**110,879**	**101,043**	**110,014**	**110,910**	**110,204**	**114,125**	**119,486**
701	**General public services**	...	...	...	...	...	...	...	...	...	...	...	...
7017	Public debt transactions	7,764	9,391	11,214	5,973	7,569	8,733	7,777	7,569	8,269	5,487	7,063	8,423
7018	Transfers of general character between levels of government	...	...	...	...	...	...	...	...	...	...	...	...
702	**Defense**	...	...	...	...	...	...	...	...	...	...	...	...
703	**Public order and safety**	...	...	...	...	...	...	...	...	...	...	...	...
704	**Economic affairs**	...	...	...	...	...	...	...	...	...	...	...	...
7042	Agriculture, forestry, fishing, and hunting	...	...	...	...	...	...	...	...	...	...	...	...
7043	Fuel and energy	...	...	...	...	...	...	...	...	...	...	...	...
7044	Mining, manufacturing, and construction	...	...	...	...	...	...	...	...	...	...	...	...
7045	Transport	...	...	...	...	...	...	...	...	...	...	...	...
7046	Communication	...	...	...	...	...	...	...	...	...	...	...	...
705	**Environmental protection**	...	...	...	...	...	...	...	...	...	...	...	...
706	**Housing and community amenities**	...	...	...	...	...	...	...	...	...	...	...	...
707	**Health**	...	...	...	...	...	...	...	...	...	...	...	...
7072	Outpatient services	...	...	...	...	...	...	...	...	...	...	...	...
7073	Hospital services	...	...	...	...	...	...	...	...	...	...	...	...
7074	Public health services	...	...	...	...	...	...	...	...	...	...	...	...
708	**Recreation, culture and religion**	...	...	...	...	...	...	...	...	...	...	...	...
709	**Education**	...	...	...	...	...	...	...	...	...	...	...	...
7091	Pre-primary and primary education	...	...	...	...	...	...	...	...	...	...	...	...
7092	Secondary education	...	...	...	...	...	...	...	...	...	...	...	...
7094	Tertiary education	...	...	...	...	...	...	...	...	...	...	...	...
710	**Social protection**	...	...	...	...	...	...	...	...	...	...	...	...
7z	Statistical discrepancy: Expenditure	...	...	...	...	...	...	...	...	...	...	...	...
	Table 8 Financial transactions by counterpart sector												
32	**Net acquisition of financial assets**	**5,692**	**-1,103**	**2,613**	**12,883**	**-108**	**4,148**	**15,912**	**3,354**	**6,209**	**15,532**	**3,459**	**6,491**
321	Domestic debtors	5,543	-1,266	2,432	12,833	-246	3,967	15,862	3,216	6,029	15,482	3,320	6,310
8211	General government	...	-12	—	...	506	—	...	506	17	...	506	0
8212	Central bank	...	-1,423	1,985	...	-820	3,035	...	93	3,005	...	93	3,005
8213	Deposit-taking corporations except the central bank	...	132	487	...	1,065	99	...	916	1,602	...	1,176	1,935
8214	Other financial corporations	...	-34	-39	...	-127	-258	...	-121	-306	...	-127	-306
8215	Nonfinancial corporations	...	70	—	...	-465	1,091	...	2,228	1,712	...	2,077	1,677
8216	Households & nonprofit institutions serving households	...	—	—	...	-405	—	...	-405	—	...	-405	—
322	External debtors	149	163	180	50	139	180	50	139	180	50	139	180
8221	General government	...	163	—	...	163	—	...	163	—	...	163	—
8227	International organizations	...	—	180	...	—	180	...	—	180	...	—	180
8228	Financial corporations other than international organizations	...	—	—	...	-24	—	...	-24	—	...	-24	—
8229	Other nonresidents	...	—	—	...	—	—	...	—	—	...	—	—

Honduras (268)

In Millions of Honduran Lempiras (HNL) / Fiscal Year Ends December 31st

		Budgetary Central Government			Central Government (excl. Social Security)			Central Government (incl. Social Security)			General Government		
		2013	2014	2015	2013	2014	2015	2013	2014	2015	2013	2014	2015P
33	**Net incurrence of liabilities**	**35,768**	**16,897**	**16,355**	**35,873**	**12,603**	**11,368**	**36,449**	**14,200**	**10,709**	**37,015**	**14,659**	**10,623**
331	Domestic creditors	4,202	6,339	7,593	4,307	2,045	2,607	4,883	3,642	1,948	5,448	4,101	1,862
3311	General government	...	5,204	3,149	...	294	603	...	104	17	...	99	-0
3312	Central bank	...	-575	-576	...	-575	-576	...	-575	-576	...	-575	-576
3313	Deposit-taking corporations except the central bank	...	2,848	925	...	2,848	925	...	2,282	2,053	...	2,297	2,026
3314	Other financial corporations	...	-119	—	...	-119	—	...	-119	—	...	-119	—
3315	Nonfinancial corporations	...	-1,018	5,918	...	-403	3,477	...	1,950	2,276	...	2,399	2,235
3316	Households & nonprofit institutions serving households	...	—	-1,815	...	—	-1,815	...	—	-1,815	...	—	-1,815
332	External creditors	31,567	10,558	8,761	31,567	10,558	8,761	31,567	10,558	8,761	31,566	10,558	8,761
3321	General government	...	—	—	...	—	—	...	—	—	...	—	—
3327	International organizations	...	8,056	8,761	...	8,056	8,761	...	8,056	8,761	...	8,056	8,761
3328	Financial corporations other than international organizations	...	2,502	—	...	2,502	—	...	2,502	—	...	2,502	—
3329	Other nonresidents	...	—	—	...	—	—	...	—	—	...	—	—
	Table 9 Total other economic flows in assets and liabilities												

Hungary (944)

In Billions of Hungarian Forint (HUF) / Fiscal Year Ends December 31st

		Budgetary Central Government			Central Government (excl. Social Security)			Central Government (incl. Social Security)			General Government		
		2013	2014	2015	2013P	2014P	2015P	2013P	2014P	2015P	2013P	2014P	2015P
	Statement of operations												
1	Revenue	...	...	...	9,542	10,422	11,130	12,729	13,780	14,908	14,094	15,209	16,476
2	Expense	...	...	...	10,986	11,235	10,946	14,037	14,551	14,717	14,651	15,405	15,949
GOB	**Gross operating balance**	...	...	...	**-871**	**-196**	**851**	**-731**	**-149**	**862**	**517**	**933**	**1,724**
NOB	**Net operating balance**	...	...	...	**-1,444**	**-813**	**184**	**-1,308**	**-770**	**191**	**-558**	**-196**	**526**
31	Net/Gross investment in nonfinancial assets	...	...	...	216	347	785	213	344	782	213	476	1,060
2M	Expenditure	...	...	...	11,201	11,582	11,731	14,250	14,895	15,499	14,864	15,881	17,010
NLB	**Net lending (+) / Net borrowing (-)**	...	...	...	**-1,660**	**-1,160**	**-601**	**-1,522**	**-1,114**	**-591**	**-770**	**-673**	**-534**
32	Net acquisition of financial assets	...	...	...	-537	246	57	-396	269	56	-272	271	69
33	Net incurrence of liabilities	...	...	...	1,099	1,351	633	1,104	1,336	628	468	919	593
NLBz	Statistical discrepancy	...	...	...	23	55	24	22	47	19	30	25	10
	Memorandum items												
PB	Primary net lending / net borrowing	...	...	...	-401	50	510	-178	181	604	593	627	666
GB	Government balance per national definition	...	...	...	...	...	...	...	...	...	...	...	...
	Statement of other economic flows												
9	**Change in net worth due to other economic flows**	...	...	...	...	...	...	...	...	...	...	...	...
4	Change in net worth due to holding gains and losses	...	...	...	...	...	...	...	...	...	...	...	...
41	Nonfinancial assets	...	...	...	...	...	...	...	...	...	...	...	...
42	Financial assets	...	...	...	18	796	1,088	18	796	1,088	10	848	1,161
43	Liabilities	...	...	...	464	1,918	408	464	1,918	408	471	1,930	408
5	Change in net worth due to volume changes	...	...	...	...	...	...	...	...	...	...	...	...
51	Nonfinancial assets	...	...	...	...	...	...	...	...	...	...	...	...
52	Financial assets	...	...	...	-0	-2	3	-0	-2	3	-0	-1	3
53	Liabilities	...	...	...	-10	52	-0	-10	52	-0	-10	52	8
	Balance sheet												
6	**Net worth**	...	...	...	...	...	...	...	...	...	**12,575**	...	...
61	Nonfinancial assets	...	...	...	...	...	...	...	...	...	33,757	...	...
62	Financial assets	...	...	...	6,066	7,106	8,254	6,445	7,508	8,656	7,902	9,021	10,253
63	Liabilities	...	...	...	28,435	31,755	32,796	28,473	31,779	32,815	29,084	31,984	32,994
	Table 1 Revenue												
1	**Revenue**	...	...	...	**9,542**	**10,422**	**11,130**	**12,729**	**13,780**	**14,908**	**14,094**	**15,209**	**16,476**
11	**Taxes**	...	...	...	**6,779**	**7,376**	**7,901**	**6,871**	**7,472**	**8,014**	**7,546**	**8,170**	**8,784**
111	Taxes on income, profits, and capital gains	...	...	...	1,917	2,133	2,312	1,917	2,133	2,312	1,917	2,133	2,312
1111	Payable by individuals	...	...	...	1,501	1,598	1,698	1,501	1,598	1,698	1,501	1,598	1,698
1112	Payable by corporations and other enterprises	...	...	...	416	535	614	416	535	614	416	535	614
1113	Other taxes on income, profits, and capital gains	...	...	...	—	—	—	—	—	—	—	—	—
112	Taxes on payroll and workforce	...	...	...	159	171	189	169	180	199	169	180	199
113	Taxes on property	...	...	...	62	65	67	62	65	67	197	201	212
114	Taxes on goods and services	...	...	...	4,640	5,008	5,333	4,723	5,095	5,436	5,262	5,657	6,061
1141	General taxes on goods and services	...	...	...	2,970	3,288	3,580	3,011	3,330	3,626	3,511	3,853	4,210
1142	Excises	...	...	...	963	996	1,085	983	1,016	1,115	983	1,016	1,115
115	Taxes on international trade and transactions	...	...	...	—	—	—	—	—	—	—	—	—
116	Other taxes	...	...	...	—	—	—	—	—	—	—	—	—
12	**Social contributions**	...	...	...	**146**	**178**	**174**	**3,906**	**4,202**	**4,487**	**3,907**	**4,204**	**4,489**
121	Social security contributions	...	...	...	126	156	148	3,886	4,180	4,461	3,886	4,180	4,461
122	Other social contributions	...	...	...	20	23	26	20	23	26	22	24	28
13	**Grants**	...	...	...	**1,489**	**1,654**	**1,850**	**714**	**781**	**1,085**	**1,053**	**1,228**	**1,516**
131	From foreign governments	...	...	...	277	173	464	277	174	464	279	215	466
132	From international organizations	...	...	...	406	575	592	406	575	592	774	1,013	1,050
133	From other general government units	...	...	...	806	906	794	31	32	29	—	—	—
1331	Current	...	...	...	802	904	788	29	30	23	—	—	—
1332	Capital	...	...	...	4	2	6	2	2	6	—	—	—
14	**Other revenue**	...	...	...	**1,128**	**1,213**	**1,206**	**1,238**	**1,325**	**1,322**	**1,587**	**1,606**	**1,686**

Hungary (944)

In Billions of Hungarian Forint (HUF) / Fiscal Year Ends December 31st

		Budgetary Central Government			Central Government (excl. Social Security)			Central Government (incl. Social Security)			General Government		
		2013	2014	2015	2013P	2014P	2015P	2013P	2014P	2015P	2013P	2014P	2015P
	Table 2 Expense by economic type												
2	**Expense**	...	...	...	**10,986**	**11,235**	**10,946**	**14,037**	**14,551**	**14,717**	**14,651**	**15,405**	**15,949**
21	**Compensation of employees**	...	...	...	**2,308**	**2,537**	**2,733**	**2,322**	**2,550**	**2,746**	**3,028**	**3,339**	**3,589**
211	Wages and salaries	...	...	...	1,809	2,012	2,166	1,820	2,022	2,176	2,393	2,664	2,858
212	Employers' social contributions	...	...	...	499	525	567	502	528	570	635	674	731
22	**Use of goods and services**	...	...	...	**1,558**	**1,755**	**1,806**	**1,583**	**1,781**	**1,830**	**2,197**	**2,434**	**2,491**
23	**Consumption of fixed capital**	...	...	...	**572**	**617**	**667**	**577**	**622**	**671**	**1,074**	**1,129**	**1,197**
24	**Interest**	...	...	...	**1,258**	**1,210**	**1,110**	**1,344**	**1,296**	**1,196**	**1,363**	**1,299**	**1,200**
25	**Subsidies**	...	...	...	**321**	**350**	**375**	**321**	**350**	**375**	**398**	**438**	**465**
26	**Grants**	...	...	...	**3,017**	**2,707**	**2,117**	**1,992**	**1,870**	**1,613**	**383**	**361**	**469**
261	To foreign governments	...	...	...	29	59	72	34	65	78	35	66	80
262	To international organizations	...	...	...	347	295	388	347	295	388	348	295	389
263	To other general government units	...	...	...	2,641	2,354	1,657	1,610	1,511	1,147	—	—	—
2631	Current	...	...	...	1,831	1,781	1,402	917	939	893	—	—	—
2632	Capital	...	...	...	810	572	254	693	572	254	—	—	—
27	**Social benefits**	...	...	...	**1,058**	**997**	**972**	**4,994**	**5,004**	**5,103**	**5,126**	**5,142**	**5,169**
271	Social security benefits	...	...	...	...	...	...	...	...	...	...	...	...
272	Social assistance benefits	...	...	...	...	...	...	...	...	...	...	...	...
273	Employment-related social benefits	...	...	...	...	...	...	...	...	...	...	...	...
28	**Other expense**	...	...	...	**893**	**1,062**	**1,166**	**905**	**1,079**	**1,183**	**1,082**	**1,264**	**1,368**
281	Property expense other than interest	...	...	...	—	—	—	—	—	—	—	—	—
282	Transfers not elsewhere classified	...	...	...	893	1,062	1,166	905	1,078	1,182	1,062	1,244	1,350
2821	Current	...	...	...	558	588	492	570	604	509	656	677	604
2822	Capital	...	...	...	335	474	674	335	474	674	407	567	747
	Table 3 Transactions in assets and liabilities												
3	**Change in net worth from transactions**	...	...	...	**-1,421**	**-758**	**208**	**-1,287**	**-723**	**210**	**-527**	**-171**	**536**
31	**Net/Gross investment in nonfinancial assets**	...	...	...	**216**	**347**	**785**	**213**	**344**	**782**	**213**	**476**	**1,060**
311	Fixed assets	...	...	...	250	499	776	248	495	774	246	617	1,050
3111	Buildings and structures	...	...	...	...	...	...	...	...	...	...	...	...
3112	Machinery and equipment	...	...	...	...	...	...	...	...	...	...	...	...
3113	Other fixed assets	...	...	...	...	...	...	...	...	...	...	...	...
3114	Weapons systems	...	...	...	...	...	...	...	...	...	...	...	...
312	Inventories	...	...	...	...	...	...	...	...	...	...	...	...
313	Valuables	...	...	...	...	...	...	...	...	...	...	...	...
314	Nonproduced assets	...	...	...	-34	-154	7	-34	-154	7	-33	-144	8
3141	Land	...	...	...	...	...	...	...	...	...	...	...	...
3142	Mineral and energy resources	...	...	...	...	...	...	...	...	...	...	...	...
3143	Other naturally occurring assets	...	...	...	...	...	...	...	...	...	...	...	...
3144	Intangible nonproduced assets	...	...	...	...	...	...	...	...	...	...	...	...
32	**Net acquisition of financial assets**	...	...	...	**-537**	**246**	**57**	**-396**	**269**	**56**	**-272**	**271**	**69**
	By instrument												
3201	Monetary gold and SDRs	...	...	...	—	—	—	—	—	—	—	—	—
3202	Currency and deposits	...	...	...	-524	180	-339	-524	180	-339	-433	242	-315
3203	Debt securities	...	...	...	79	-114	0	79	-114	0	79	-114	-1
3204	Loans	...	...	...	-120	7	33	-8	2	7	-8	-9	3
3205	Equity and investment fund shares	...	...	...	-115	165	131	-115	165	131	-105	123	130
3206	Insurance, pension, and standardized guarantee schemes	...	...	...	-0	-0	-0	-0	-0	-0	-0	-0	-0
3207	Financial derivatives and employee stock options	...	...	...	-114	-97	-268	-114	-97	-268	-114	-97	-268
3208	Other accounts receivable	...	...	...	258	105	500	287	133	526	309	127	519
	By debtor												
321	Domestic debtors	...	...	...	-449	487	-347	-307	510	-347	-184	512	-335
322	External debtors	...	...	...	-88	-242	403	-88	-242	403	-88	-241	404
33	**Net incurrence of liabilities**	...	...	...	**1,099**	**1,351**	**633**	**1,104**	**1,336**	**628**	**468**	**919**	**593**
	By instrument												
3301	Special Drawing Rights (SDRs)	...	...	...	—	—	—	—	—	—	—	—	—
3302	Currency and deposits	...	...	...	-12	3	4	-11	-3	-1	0	1	6
3303	Debt securities	...	...	...	1,888	1,974	630	1,888	1,974	630	1,563	1,813	617
3304	Loans	...	...	...	-816	-583	194	-816	-583	194	-1,110	-850	200

Hungary (944)

In Billions of Hungarian Forint (HUF) / Fiscal Year Ends December 31st

		Budgetary Central Government			Central Government (excl. Social Security)			Central Government (incl. Social Security)			General Government		
		2013	2014	2015	2013P	2014P	2015P	2013P	2014P	2015P	2013P	2014P	2015P
3305	Equity and investment fund shares	...	...	...	—	—	—	—	—	—	—	—	—
3306	Insurance, pension, and standardized guarantee schemes	...	...	...	-7	-2	-1	-7	-2	-1	-7	-2	-1
3307	Financial derivatives and employee stock options	...	...	...	-32	-69	-20	-32	-69	-20	-32	-69	-20
3308	Other accounts payable	...	...	...	79	28	-174	82	18	-174	54	24	-210
	By creditor												
331	Domestic creditors	...	...	...	1,910	1,819	2,094	1,915	1,804	2,089	1,375	1,515	2,054
332	External creditors	...	...	...	-811	-468	-1,461	-811	-468	-1,461	-907	-596	-1,461
	Table 4 Holding gains and losses in assets and liabilities												
4	**Change in net worth due to holding gains and losses**	...	...	...	...	...	...	...	...	...	...	...	...
41	**Holding gains and losses in nonfinancial assets**	...	...	...	...	...	...	...	...	...	...	...	...
411	Fixed assets	...	...	...	...	...	...	...	...	...	...	...	...
412	Inventories	...	...	...	...	...	...	...	...	...	...	...	...
413	Valuables	...	...	...	...	...	...	...	...	...	...	...	...
414	Nonproduced assets	...	...	...	...	...	...	...	...	...	...	...	...
42	**Holding gains and losses in financial assets**	...	...	...	**18**	**796**	**1,088**	**18**	**796**	**1,088**	**10**	**848**	**1,161**
	By instrument												
4201	Monetary gold and SDRs	...	...	...	...	...	...	...	...	...	...	...	...
4202	Currency and deposits	...	...	...	29	42	-1	29	42	-1	30	42	-1
4203	Debt securities	...	...	...	8	2	3	8	2	3	8	3	4
4204	Loans	...	...	...	-0	-1	1	-0	-1	1	-0	-1	1
4205	Equity and investment fund shares	...	...	...	92	221	387	92	221	387	83	272	460
4206	Insurance, pension, and standardized guarantee schemes	...	...	...	—	—	—	—	—	—	—	—	—
4207	Financial derivatives and employee stock options	...	...	...	-129	523	703	-129	523	703	-129	523	703
4208	Other accounts receivable	...	...	...	18	10	-5	18	10	-5	18	10	-5
	By debtor												
421	Domestic debtors	...	...	...	144	373	533	144	373	533	135	425	606
422	External debtors	...	...	...	-126	423	555	-126	423	555	-126	423	555
43	**Holding gains and losses in liabilities**	...	...	...	**464**	**1,918**	**408**	**464**	**1,918**	**408**	**471**	**1,930**	**408**
	By instrument												
4301	Special Drawing Rights (SDRs)	...	...	...	...	...	...	...	...	...	...	...	...
4302	Currency and deposits	...	...	...	—	—	—	—	—	—	—	—	—
4303	Debt securities	...	...	...	262	1,839	434	262	1,839	434	266	1,844	434
4304	Loans	...	...	...	48	166	-7	48	166	-7	51	172	-7
4305	Equity and investment fund shares	...	...	...	—	—	—	—	—	—	—	—	—
4306	Insurance, pension, and standardized guarantee schemes	...	...	...	—	—	—	—	—	—	—	—	—
4307	Financial derivatives and employee stock options	...	...	...	153	-89	-20	153	-89	-20	153	-89	-20
4308	Other accounts payable	...	...	...	1	2	1	1	2	1	1	2	1
	By creditor												
431	Domestic creditors	...	...	...	167	370	-8	167	370	-8	171	376	-8
432	External creditors	...	...	...	297	1,548	416	297	1,548	416	300	1,553	416
	Table 5 Holding gains and losses in assets and liabilities												
5	**Change in net worth due to other volume changes**	...	...	...	...	...	...	...	...	...	...	...	...
51	**Other volume changes in nonfinancial assets**	...	...	...	...	...	...	...	...	...	...	...	...
511	Fixed assets	...	...	...	...	...	...	...	...	...	...	...	...
512	Inventories	...	...	...	...	...	...	...	...	...	...	...	...
513	Valuables	...	...	...	...	...	...	...	...	...	...	...	...
514	Nonproduced assets	...	...	...	...	...	...	...	...	...	...	...	...
52	**Other volume changes in financial assets**	...	...	...	**-0**	**-2**	**3**	**-0**	**-2**	**3**	**-0**	**-1**	**3**

Hungary (944)

In Billions of Hungarian Forint (HUF) / Fiscal Year Ends December 31st

		Budgetary Central Government			Central Government (excl. Social Security)			Central Government (incl. Social Security)			General Government		
		2013	2014	2015	2013P	2014P	2015P	2013P	2014P	2015P	2013P	2014P	2015P
	By instrument												
5201	Monetary gold and SDRs	...	...	...	...	...	...	...	...	...	...	...	...
5202	Currency and deposits	...	...	...	0	-2	1	0	-2	1	0	-1	1
5203	Debt securities	...	...	...	-0	-0	2	-0	-0	2	-0	-0	2
5204	Loans	...	...	...	-0	-33	0	-0	-33	0	-0	-33	0
5205	Equity and investment fund shares	...	...	...	—	0	—	—	0	—	-0	0	-0
5206	Insurance, pension, and standardized guarantee schemes	...	...	...	—	—	—	—	—	—	—	—	—
5207	Financial derivatives and employee stock options	...	...	...	-0	—	0	-0	—	0	-0	—	0
5208	Other accounts receivable	...	...	...	—	33	—	—	33	—	—	33	—
	By debtor												
521	Domestic debtors	...	...	...	0	-35	1	0	-35	1	0	-34	1
522	External debtors	...	...	...	-0	33	2	-0	33	2	-0	33	2
53	**Other volume changes in liabilities**	...	...	...	**-10**	**52**	**-0**	**-10**	**52**	**-0**	**-10**	**52**	**8**
	By instrument												
5301	Special Drawing Rights (SDRs)	...	...	...	...	...	...	...	...	...	...	...	...
5302	Currency and deposits	...	...	...	—	—	—	—	—	—	—	—	—
5303	Debt securities	...	...	...	-10	0	-0	-10	0	-0	-10	—	-0
5304	Loans	...	...	...	0	51	-0	0	51	-0	0	51	8
5305	Equity and investment fund shares	...	...	...	—	—	—	—	—	—	—	—	—
5306	Insurance, pension, and standardized guarantee schemes	...	...	...	—	—	—	—	—	—	—	—	—
5307	Financial derivatives and employee stock options	...	...	...	—	-0	0	—	-0	0	—	-0	0
5308	Other accounts payable	...	...	...	-0	1	-0	-0	1	-0	-0	1	-0
	By creditor												
531	Domestic creditors	...	...	...	-10	-0	53	-10	-0	53	-10	-0	62
532	External creditors	...	...	...	0	52	-53	0	52	-53	-0	52	-53
	Table 6 Balance sheet												
6	**Net worth**	...	...	...	...	...	...	...	...	...	**12,575**	...	...
61	**Nonfinancial assets**	...	...	...	...	...	...	...	...	...	**33,757**	...	...
611	Fixed assets	...	...	...	...	...	...	...	...	...	33,747	...	...
6111	Buildings and structures	...	...	...	...	...	...	...	...	...	31,602	...	...
6112	Machinery and equipment	...	...	...	...	...	...	...	...	...	...	...	...
6113	Other fixed assets	...	...	...	...	...	...	...	...	...	523	...	...
6114	Weapons systems	...	...	...	...	...	...	...	...	...	...	...	...
612	Inventories	...	...	...	...	...	...	...	...	...	10	...	...
613	Valuables	...	...	...	...	...	...	...	...	...	...	...	...
614	Nonproduced assets	...	...	...	...	...	...	...	...	...	...	...	...
6141	Land	...	...	...	...	...	...	...	...	...	...	...	...
6142	Mineral and energy resources	...	...	...	...	...	...	...	...	...	...	...	...
6143	Other naturally occurring assets	...	...	...	...	...	...	...	...	...	...	...	...
6144	Intangible nonproduced assets	...	...	...	...	...	...	...	...	...	...	...	...
62	**Financial assets**	...	...	...	**6,066**	**7,106**	**8,254**	**6,445**	**7,508**	**8,656**	**7,902**	**9,021**	**10,253**
	By instrument												
6201	Monetary gold and SDRs	...	...	...	—	—	—	—	—	—	—	—	—
6202	Currency and deposits	...	...	...	1,068	1,287	948	1,068	1,287	948	1,556	1,839	1,523
6203	Debt securities	...	...	...	177	66	71	177	66	71	180	69	74
6204	Loans	...	...	...	116	89	123	103	72	79	152	109	113
6205	Equity and investment fund shares	...	...	...	3,243	3,628	4,146	3,243	3,628	4,146	4,103	4,497	5,086
6206	Insurance, pension, and standardized guarantee schemes	...	...	...	1	1	1	1	1	1	2	2	2
6207	Financial derivatives and employee stock options	...	...	...	154	579	1,015	154	579	1,015	154	579	1,015
6208	Other accounts receivable	...	...	...	1,306	1,455	1,950	1,699	1,875	2,396	1,755	1,926	2,440
	By debtor												
621	Domestic debtors	...	...	...	5,362	6,187	6,375	5,741	6,589	6,776	7,198	8,100	8,372
622	External debtors	...	...	...	704	919	1,880	704	919	1,880	704	920	1,881
63	**Liabilities**	...	...	...	**28,435**	**31,755**	**32,796**	**28,473**	**31,779**	**32,815**	**29,084**	**31,984**	**32,994**

Hungary (944)

In Billions of Hungarian Forint (HUF) / Fiscal Year Ends December 31st

		Budgetary Central Government			Central Government (excl. Social Security)			Central Government (incl. Social Security)			General Government		
		2013	2014	2015	2013P	2014P	2015P	2013P	2014P	2015P	2013P	2014P	2015P
	By instrument												
6301	Special Drawing Rights (SDRs)	...	...	...	—	—	—	—	—	—	—	—	—
6302	Currency and deposits	...	...	...	52	55	59	48	45	44	33	35	41
6303	Debt securities	...	...	...	19,817	23,630	24,694	19,817	23,630	24,694	19,968	23,625	24,677
6304	Loans	...	...	...	3,827	3,461	3,648	3,827	3,461	3,648	4,128	3,501	3,703
6305	Equity and investment fund shares	...	...	...	—	—	—	—	—	—	—	—	—
6306	Insurance, pension, and standardized guarantee schemes	...	...	...	23	21	20	23	21	20	23	21	20
6307	Financial derivatives and employee stock options	...	...	...	245	88	47	245	88	47	245	88	47
6308	Other accounts payable	...	...	...	4,470	4,501	4,328	4,513	4,534	4,362	4,687	4,714	4,506
	By creditor												
631	Domestic creditors	...	...	...	14,057	16,245	18,384	14,095	16,269	18,404	14,584	16,475	18,582
632	External creditors	...	...	...	14,378	15,510	14,412	14,378	15,510	14,412	14,500	15,510	14,412
	Memorandum items												
6M2	Net financial worth	...	...	...	-22,369	-24,649	-24,542	-22,028	-24,271	-24,159	-21,182	-22,964	-22,741
6M3	Gross debt (D4) at market value	...	...	...	28,189	31,667	32,749	28,228	31,691	32,768	28,839	31,897	32,947
6M3D3	D3 debt liabilities at market value	...	...	...	28,167	31,646	32,728	28,206	31,671	32,748	28,816	31,876	32,927
6M3D2	D2 debt liabilities at market value	...	...	...	23,696	27,146	28,400	23,692	27,136	28,386	24,129	27,161	28,420
6M3D1	D1 debt liabilities at market value	...	...	...	23,644	27,091	28,342	23,644	27,091	28,342	24,096	27,127	28,380
6M4	Gross debt (D4) at nominal value	...	...	...	...	...	...	...	...	...	...	...	...
6M4D3	D3 debt liabilities at nominal value	...	...	...	...	...	...	...	...	...	...	...	...
6M4D2	D2 debt liabilities at nominal value	...	...	...	...	...	...	...	...	...	...	...	...
6M4D1	D1 debt liabilities at nominal value	...	...	...	...	...	...	...	...	...	...	...	...
6M35	Gross debt (D4) at face value	...	...	...	27,138	29,021	29,732	27,177	29,045	29,751	27,786	29,249	29,929
6M35D3	D3 debt liabilities at face value	...	...	...	27,115	29,000	29,711	27,154	29,024	29,731	27,763	29,229	29,908
6M35D2	D2 debt liabilities at face value	...	...	...	22,645	24,499	25,383	22,641	24,490	25,369	23,076	24,514	25,402
6M35D1	D1 debt liabilities at face value	...	...	...	22,593	24,444	25,325	22,593	24,444	25,325	23,043	24,479	25,361
6M93	Government gross debt per national definition	...	...	...	22,645	24,499	25,383	22,641	24,490	25,369	23,076	24,514	25,402
6M5	Arrears	...	...	...	...	...	...	...	...	...	...	...	...
6M6	Explicit contingent liabilities	...	...	...	...	...	...	...	...	...	...	...	...
6M61	of which: Publicly guaranteed debt	...	...	...	...	...	...	...	...	...	...	...	...
6M7	Net implicit obligations for social security benefits	...	...	...	...	...	...	...	...	...	...	...	...
	Table 7 Expenditure by functions of government												
7	**Expenditure**	...	...	...	**11,229**	**11,743**	...	...	...	...	**14,891**	**16,055**	...
701	**General public services**	...	...	...	**3,542**	**3,422**	...	...	...	...	**3,108**	**3,271**	...
7017	Public debt transactions	...	...	...	1,261	1,219	...	...	...	...	1,377	1,315	...
7018	Transfers of general character between levels of government	...	...	...	974	786	...	...	...	...	—	—	...
702	**Defense**	...	...	...	**200**	**189**	...	...	...	...	**200**	**189**	...
703	**Public order and safety**	...	...	...	**600**	**613**	...	...	...	...	**612**	**623**	...
704	**Economic affairs**	...	...	...	**1,823**	**2,137**	...	...	...	...	**2,036**	**2,381**	...
7042	Agriculture, forestry, fishing, and hunting	...	...	...	139	196	...	...	...	...	139	197	...
7043	Fuel and energy	...	...	...	38	63	...	...	...	...	38	56	...
7044	Mining, manufacturing, and construction	...	...	...	5	10	...	...	...	...	10	11	...
7045	Transport	...	...	...	901	1,183	...	...	...	...	1,113	1,460	...
7046	Communication	...	...	...	-56	-131	...	...	...	...	-56	-129	...
705	**Environmental protection**	...	...	...	**99**	**156**	...	...	...	...	**276**	**387**	...
706	**Housing and community amenities**	...	...	...	**70**	**80**	...	...	...	...	**238**	**285**	...
707	**Health**	...	...	...	**1,797**	**1,833**	...	...	...	...	**1,518**	**1,605**	...
7072	Outpatient services	...	...	...	201	187	...	...	...	...	474	482	...
7073	Hospital services	...	...	...	555	642	...	...	...	...	581	645	...
7074	Public health services	...	...	...	25	20	...	...	...	...	43	40	...
708	**Recreation, culture and religion**	...	...	...	**402**	**468**	...	...	...	...	**543**	**643**	...
709	**Education**	...	...	...	**1,224**	**1,463**	...	...	...	...	**1,386**	**1,661**	...
7091	Pre-primary and primary education	...	...	...	207	291	...	...	...	...	272	367	...
7092	Secondary education	...	...	...	409	553	...	...	...	...	429	577	...
7094	Tertiary education	...	...	...	272	328	...	...	...	...	271	328	...

Iceland (176)

In Billions of Icelandic Kronur (ISK) / Fiscal Year Ends December 31st

		Budgetary Central Government			Central Government (excl. Social Security)			Central Government (incl. Social Security)			General Government		
		2013	2014	2015	2013	2014	2015	2013	2014	2015	2013	2014	2015
	Statement of operations												
1	Revenue	588	686	692	588	686	692	584	682	688	800	907	931
2	Expense	616	662	686	616	662	686	606	659	681	812	886	926
GOB	**Gross operating balance**	**0**	**53**	**36**	**0**	**53**	**36**	**6**	**52**	**37**	**26**	**61**	**46**
NOB	**Net operating balance**	**-28**	**24**	**6**	**-28**	**24**	**6**	**-22**	**23**	**7**	**-12**	**21**	**5**
31	Net/Gross investment in nonfinancial assets	2	8	12	2	8	12	2	8	12	14	22	24
2M	Expenditure	618	670	698	618	670	698	608	667	693	826	908	949
NLB	**Net lending (+) / Net borrowing (-)**	**-30**	**16**	**-6**	**-30**	**16**	**-6**	**-24**	**15**	**-5**	**-27**	**-1**	**-18**
32	Net acquisition of financial assets	-44	62	-183	-44	62	-183	-38	...	...	-38	52	-177
33	Net incurrence of liabilities	-11	46	-177	-11	46	-177	-11	...	...	-6	54	-158
NLBz	Statistical discrepancy	-4	-0	-0	-4	-0	-0	-4	...	...	-5	0	-0
	Memorandum items												
PB	Primary net lending / net borrowing	53	104	87	53	104	87	59	102	88	64	94	84
GB	Government balance per national definition	...	...	...	...	...	...	...	...	...	...	...	...
	Statement of other economic flows												
	Balance sheet												
6	**Net worth**	...	...	...	...	...	...	...	...	...	...	...	...
61	Nonfinancial assets	...	...	...	...	...	...	...	...	...	...	...	...
62	Financial assets	1,064	1,168	1,010	1,064	1,168	1,010	...	...	...	1,199	1,291	1,138
63	Liabilities	1,939	2,034	1,929	1,939	2,034	1,929	...	...	...	2,169	2,291	2,214
	Table 1 Revenue												
1	**Revenue**	**588**	**686**	**692**	**588**	**686**	**692**	**584**	**682**	**688**	**800**	**907**	**931**
11	**Taxes**	**430**	**511**	**524**	**430**	**511**	**524**	**430**	**511**	**524**	**610**	**701**	**732**
111	Taxes on income, profits, and capital gains	168	204	211	168	204	211	168	204	211	316	360	381
1111	Payable by individuals	111	114	128	111	114	128	111	114	128	259	271	298
1112	Payable by corporations and other enterprises	40	67	53	40	67	53	40	67	53	40	67	53
1113	Other taxes on income, profits, and capital gains	16	23	30	16	23	30	16	23	30	16	23	30
112	Taxes on payroll and workforce	7	7	7	7	7	7	7	7	7	7	7	7
113	Taxes on property	16	17	9	16	17	9	16	17	9	46	50	43
114	Taxes on goods and services	223	232	255	223	232	255	223	232	255	225	234	258
1141	General taxes on goods and services	154	161	184	154	161	184	154	161	184	154	161	184
1142	Excises	55	58	57	55	58	57	55	58	57	55	58	57
115	Taxes on international trade and transactions	6	6	5	6	6	5	6	6	5	6	6	5
116	Other taxes	11	44	38	11	44	38	11	44	38	11	44	38
12	**Social contributions**	**70**	**73**	**80**	**70**	**73**	**80**	**70**	**73**	**80**	**70**	**73**	**80**
121	Social security contributions	70	73	80	70	73	80	70	73	80	70	73	80
122	Other social contributions	—	—	—	—	—	—	—	—	—	—	—	—
13	**Grants**	**10**	**10**	**11**	**10**	**10**	**11**	**4**	**4**	**4**	**3**	**3**	**3**
131	From foreign governments	0	0	0	0	0	0	0	0	0	0	0	0
132	From international organizations	3	2	3	3	2	3	3	2	3	3	2	3
133	From other general government units	8	8	8	8	8	8	1	1	1	—	—	-0
1331	Current	8	8	8	8	8	8	1	1	1	—	—	-3
1332	Capital	0	0	0	0	0	0	0	0	0	-0	—	3
14	**Other revenue**	**77**	**91**	**78**	**77**	**91**	**78**	**80**	**94**	**80**	**117**	**130**	**116**
	Table 2 Expense by economic type												
2	**Expense**	**616**	**662**	**686**	**616**	**662**	**686**	**606**	**659**	**681**	**812**	**886**	**926**
21	**Compensation of employees**	**129**	**135**	**151**	**129**	**135**	**151**	**148**	**155**	**173**	**257**	**276**	**307**
211	Wages and salaries	102	107	119	102	107	119	117	123	136	203	217	242
212	Employers' social contributions	27	29	32	27	29	32	31	33	36	54	58	65
22	**Use of goods and services**	**102**	**104**	**110**	**102**	**104**	**110**	**135**	**140**	**149**	**218**	**230**	**242**
23	**Consumption of fixed capital**	**28**	**29**	**30**	**28**	**29**	**30**	**28**	**29**	**30**	**38**	**40**	**40**
24	**Interest**	**83**	**87**	**93**	**83**	**87**	**93**	**83**	**87**	**93**	**91**	**95**	**102**
25	**Subsidies**	**26**	**25**	**25**	**26**	**25**	**25**	**26**	**25**	**25**	**31**	**29**	**30**

Iceland (176)

In Billions of Icelandic Kronur (ISK) / Fiscal Year Ends December 31st

		Budgetary Central Government			Central Government (excl. Social Security)			Central Government (incl. Social Security)			General Government		
		2013	2014	2015	2013	2014	2015	2013	2014	2015	2013	2014	2015
26	**Grants**	**195**	**200**	**211**	**195**	**200**	**211**	**33**	**34**	**35**	**4**	**5**	**5**
261	To foreign governments	—	—	—	—	—	—	—	—	—	—	—	—
262	To international organizations	4	5	5	4	5	5	4	5	5	4	5	5
263	To other general government units	191	195	206	191	195	206	28	29	30	0	—	0
2631	Current	188	191	202	188	191	202	26	25	26	0	—	0
2632	Capital	3	4	3	3	4	3	2	4	3	—	—	—
27	**Social benefits**	**20**	**19**	**18**	**20**	**19**	**18**	**120**	**126**	**128**	**132**	**139**	**142**
271	Social security benefits	—	—	—	—	—	—	100	107	110	100	107	110
272	Social assistance benefits	20	19	18	20	19	18	20	19	18	33	33	32
273	Employment-related social benefits	—	—	—	—	—	—	—	—	—	—	—	—
28	**Other expense**	**33**	**63**	**49**	**33**	**63**	**49**	**33**	**63**	**49**	**40**	**72**	**58**
281	Property expense other than interest	—	—	—	—	—	—	—	—	—	—	—	—
282	Transfers not elsewhere classified	33	63	49	33	63	49	33	63	49	40	72	58
2821	Current	19	18	21	19	18	21	19	18	21	24	25	27
2822	Capital	14	44	28	14	44	28	14	45	29	17	47	31
	Table 3 Transactions in assets and liabilities												
3	**Change in net worth from transactions**	**-32**	**24**	**6**	**-32**	**24**	**6**	**-25**	**...**	**...**	**-18**	**21**	**5**
31	**Net/Gross investment in nonfinancial assets**	**2**	**8**	**12**	**2**	**8**	**12**	**2**	**8**	**12**	**14**	**22**	**24**
311	Fixed assets	2	8	12	2	8	12	2	8	12	14	22	24
3111	Buildings and structures	...	...	...	...	...	...	...	...	...	...	...	...
3112	Machinery and equipment	...	...	...	...	...	...	...	...	...	...	...	...
3113	Other fixed assets	...	...	...	...	...	...	...	...	...	...	...	...
3114	Weapons systems	...	...	...	...	...	...	...	...	...	...	...	...
312	Inventories	—	—	—	—	—	—	—	—	—	—	—	—
313	Valuables	—	—	—	—	—	—	—	—	—	—	—	—
314	Nonproduced assets	—	—	—	—	—	—	—	—	—	—	—	—
3141	Land	—	—	—	—	—	—	—	—	—	—	—	—
3142	Mineral and energy resources	—	—	—	—	—	—	—	—	—	—	—	—
3143	Other naturally occurring assets	—	—	—	—	—	—	—	—	—	—	—	—
3144	Intangible nonproduced assets	—	—	—	—	—	—	—	—	—	—	—	—
32	**Net acquisition of financial assets**	**-44**	**62**	**-183**	**-44**	**62**	**-183**	**-38**	**...**	**...**	**-38**	**52**	**-177**
	By instrument												
3201	Monetary gold and SDRs	—	—	—	—	—	—	—	...	...	—	—	—
3202	Currency and deposits	-47	90	-113	-47	90	-113	-48	...	...	-53	88	-115
3203	Debt securities	—	—	—	—	—	—	0	...	...	0	0	0
3204	Loans	4	5	-43	4	5	-43	4	...	...	6	1	-44
3205	Equity and investment fund shares	39	0	1	39	0	1	39	...	...	40	1	0
3206	Insurance, pension, and standardized guarantee schemes	—	—	—	—	—	—	—	...	...	—	—	—
3207	Financial derivatives and employee stock options	—	—	—	—	—	—	—	...	...	—	—	—
3208	Other accounts receivable	-40	-33	-27	-40	-33	-27	-33	...	...	-31	-35	-18
	By debtor												
321	Domestic debtors	-44	62	-183	-44	62	-183	-38	...	...	-38	52	-177
322	External debtors	—	—	—	—	—	—	—	...	...	—	—	—
33	**Net incurrence of liabilities**	**-11**	**46**	**-177**	**-11**	**46**	**-177**	**-11**	**...**	**...**	**-6**	**54**	**-158**
	By instrument												
3301	Special Drawing Rights (SDRs)	—	—	—	—	—	—	—	...	...	—	—	—
3302	Currency and deposits	—	—	—	—	—	—	—	...	...	—	—	—
3303	Debt securities	-4	33	10	-4	33	10	-4	...	...	-4	33	10
3304	Loans	-13	-23	-165	-13	-23	-165	-13	...	...	-18	-27	-156
3305	Equity and investment fund shares	—	—	—	—	—	—	—	...	...	—	—	—
3306	Insurance, pension, and standardized guarantee schemes	2	2	2	2	2	2	2	...	...	4	4	4
3307	Financial derivatives and employee stock options	—	—	—	—	—	—	—	...	...	—	—	—
3308	Other accounts payable	4	33	-24	4	33	-24	4	...	...	11	43	-16

Iceland (176)

In Billions of Icelandic Kronur (ISK) / Fiscal Year Ends December 31st

		Budgetary Central Government			Central Government (excl. Social Security)			Central Government (incl. Social Security)			General Government		
		2013	2014	2015	2013	2014	2015	2013	2014	2015	2013	2014	2015
	By creditor												
331	Domestic creditors	-6	40	-70	-6	40	-70	-6	...	...	7	56	-50
332	External creditors	-4	6	-107	-4	6	-107	-4	...	...	-13	-3	-108
	Table 4 Holding gains and losses in assets and liabilities												
	Table 5 Holding gains and losses in assets and liabilities												
	Table 6 Balance sheet												
6	**Net worth**	...	...	...	...	...	...	...	...	...	...	...	...
61	**Nonfinancial assets**	...	...	...	...	...	...	...	...	...	...	...	...
611	Fixed assets	...	...	...	...	...	...	...	...	...	...	...	...
6111	Buildings and structures	...	...	...	...	...	...	...	...	...	...	...	...
6112	Machinery and equipment	...	...	...	...	...	...	...	...	...	...	...	...
6113	Other fixed assets	...	...	...	...	...	...	...	...	...	...	...	...
6114	Weapons systems	...	...	...	...	...	...	...	...	...	...	...	...
612	Inventories	...	...	...	...	...	...	...	...	...	...	...	...
613	Valuables	...	...	...	...	...	...	...	...	...	...	...	...
614	Nonproduced assets	...	...	...	...	...	...	...	...	...	...	...	...
6141	Land	...	...	...	...	...	...	...	...	...	...	...	...
6142	Mineral and energy resources	...	...	...	...	...	...	...	...	...	...	...	...
6143	Other naturally occurring assets	...	...	...	...	...	...	...	...	...	...	...	...
6144	Intangible nonproduced assets	...	...	...	...	...	...	...	...	...	...	...	...
62	**Financial assets**	**1,064**	**1,168**	**1,010**	**1,064**	**1,168**	**1,010**	...	...	...	**1,199**	**1,291**	**1,138**
	By instrument												
6201	Monetary gold and SDRs	—	—	—	—	—	—	...	...	...	—	—	—
6202	Currency and deposits	404	513	397	404	513	397	...	...	...	427	533	416
6203	Debt securities	—	—	—	—	—	—	...	...	...	0	0	0
6204	Loans	163	168	124	163	168	124	...	...	...	197	197	152
6205	Equity and investment fund shares	365	351	351	365	351	351	...	...	...	401	385	385
6206	Insurance, pension, and standardized guarantee schemes	—	—	—	—	—	—	...	...	...	—	—	—
6207	Financial derivatives and employee stock options	—	—	—	—	—	—	...	...	...	—	—	—
6208	Other accounts receivable	132	136	138	132	136	138	...	...	...	174	175	185
	By debtor												
621	Domestic debtors	1,064	1,168	1,010	1,064	1,168	1,010	...	...	...	1,199	1,291	1,138
622	External debtors	—	—	—	—	—	—	...	...	...	—	—	—
63	**Liabilities**	**1,939**	**2,034**	**1,929**	**1,939**	**2,034**	**1,929**	...	...	...	**2,169**	**2,291**	**2,214**
	By instrument												
6301	Special Drawing Rights (SDRs)	—	—	—	—	—	—	...	...	...	—	—	—
6302	Currency and deposits	—	—	—	—	—	—	...	...	...	—	—	—
6303	Debt securities	843	878	890	843	878	890	...	...	...	843	878	890
6304	Loans	621	619	453	621	619	453	...	...	...	760	775	618
6305	Equity and investment fund shares	—	—	—	—	—	—	...	...	...	—	—	—
6306	Insurance, pension, and standardized guarantee schemes	408	436	508	408	436	508	...	...	...	457	490	580
6307	Financial derivatives and employee stock options	—	—	—	—	—	—	...	...	...	—	—	—
6308	Other accounts payable	68	101	77	68	101	77	...	...	...	110	148	126
	By creditor												
631	Domestic creditors	1,550	1,620	1,624	1,550	1,620	1,624	...	...	...	1,767	1,873	1,904
632	External creditors	389	414	305	389	414	305	...	...	...	402	419	309
	Memorandum items												
6M2	Net financial worth	-874	-866	-919	-874	-866	-919	...	...	...	-971	-1,000	-1,075
6M3	Gross debt (D4) at market value	1,939	2,034	1,929	1,939	2,034	1,929	...	...	...	2,169	2,291	2,214
6M3D3	D3 debt liabilities at market value	1,531	1,598	1,420	1,531	1,598	1,420	...	...	...	1,712	1,801	1,633
6M3D2	D2 debt liabilities at market value	1,463	1,497	1,343	1,463	1,497	1,343	...	...	...	1,602	1,653	1,508
6M3D1	D1 debt liabilities at market value	1,463	1,497	1,343	1,463	1,497	1,343	...	...	...	1,602	1,653	1,508
6M4	Gross debt (D4) at nominal value	...	...	...	...	...	...	...	...	...	...	...	...
6M4D3	D3 debt liabilities at nominal value	...	...	...	...	...	...	...	...	...	...	...	...
6M4D2	D2 debt liabilities at nominal value	...	...	...	...	...	...	...	...	...	...	...	...
6M4D1	D1 debt liabilities at nominal value	...	...	...	...	...	...	...	...	...	...	...	...

Iceland (176)

In Billions of Icelandic Kronur (ISK) / Fiscal Year Ends December 31st

		Budgetary Central Government			Central Government (excl. Social Security)			Central Government (incl. Social Security)			General Government		
		2013	2014	2015	2013	2014	2015	2013	2014	2015	2013	2014	2015
6M35	Gross debt (D4) at face value	...	...	...	...	...	...	...	...	...	...	...	...
6M35D3	D3 debt liabilities at face value	...	...	...	...	...	...	...	...	...	...	...	...
6M35D2	D2 debt liabilities at face value	...	...	...	...	...	...	...	...	...	...	...	...
6M35D1	D1 debt liabilities at face value	...	...	...	...	...	...	...	...	...	...	...	...
6M93	Government gross debt per national definition	...	...	...	...	...	...	...	...	...	...	—	...
6M5	Arrears	...	...	...	...	...	...	...	...	...	...	...	...
6M6	Explicit contingent liabilities	...	...	...	...	...	...	...	...	...	...	...	...
6M61	of which: Publicly guaranteed debt	...	...	...	...	...	...	...	...	...	...	...	...
6M7	Net implicit obligations for social security benefits	...	...	...	...	...	...	...	...	...	...	...	...
	Table 7 Expenditure by functions of government												
7	**Expenditure**	**618**	**670**	**698**	**618**	**670**	**698**	...	...	...	**826**	**908**	**949**
701	**General public services**	**147**	**154**	**160**	**147**	**154**	**160**	...	...	...	**154**	**164**	**170**
7017	Public debt transactions	83	87	93	83	87	93	...	...	...	91	97	104
7018	Transfers of general character between levels of government	19	21	22	19	21	22	...	...	...	—	—	—
702	**Defense**	**1**	**0**	**0**	**1**	**0**	**0**	...	...	...	**1**	**0**	**0**
703	**Public order and safety**	**25**	**29**	**32**	**25**	**29**	**32**	...	...	...	**27**	**30**	**34**
704	**Economic affairs**	**71**	**108**	**94**	**71**	**108**	**94**	...	...	...	**89**	**118**	**110**
7042	Agriculture, forestry, fishing, and hunting	18	18	18	18	18	18	...	...	...	18	18	18
7043	Fuel and energy	3	3	4	3	3	4	...	...	...	2	2	2
7044	Mining, manufacturing, and construction	0	—	—	0	—	—	...	...	...	-0	-0	-0
7045	Transport	26	28	30	26	28	30	...	...	...	44	37	46
7046	Communication	1	1	1	1	1	1	...	...	...	1	1	1
705	**Environmental protection**	**6**	**7**	**8**	**6**	**7**	**8**	...	...	...	**11**	**13**	**13**
706	**Housing and community amenities**	**5**	**1**	**2**	**5**	**1**	**2**	...	...	...	**11**	**9**	**10**
707	**Health**	**143**	**153**	**166**	**143**	**153**	**166**	...	...	...	**140**	**151**	**165**
7072	Outpatient services	28	30	34	28	30	34	...	...	...	30	33	36
7073	Hospital services	93	100	109	93	100	109	...	...	...	94	102	112
7074	Public health services	0	0	0	0	0	0	...	...	...	0	1	1
708	**Recreation, culture and religion**	**22**	**21**	**25**	**22**	**21**	**25**	...	...	...	**61**	**63**	**71**
709	**Education**	**59**	**60**	**67**	**59**	**60**	**67**	...	...	...	**144**	**155**	**165**
7091	Pre-primary and primary education	1	1	1	1	1	1	...	...	...	60	67	70
7092	Secondary education	0	0	0	0	0	0	...	...	...	21	24	24
7094	Tertiary education	32	33	36	32	33	36	...	...	...	32	33	36
710	**Social protection**	**139**	**137**	**144**	**139**	**137**	**144**	...	...	...	**189**	**205**	**210**
7z	Statistical discrepancy: Expenditure	—	—	—	0	0	—	...	...	...	—	—	—
	Table 8 Financial transactions by counterpart sector												
32	**Net acquisition of financial assets**	**-44**	**62**	**-183**	**-44**	**62**	**-183**	**-38**	...	...	**-38**	**52**	**-177**
321	Domestic debtors	-44	62	-183	-44	62	-183	-38	...	...	-38	52	-177
8211	General government	...	...	...	...	...	...	...	...	...	...	...	...
8212	Central bank	...	...	...	...	...	...	...	...	...	...	...	...
8213	Deposit-taking corporations except the central bank	...	...	...	...	...	...	...	...	...	...	...	...
8214	Other financial corporations	...	...	...	...	...	...	...	...	...	...	...	...
8215	Nonfinancial corporations	...	...	...	...	...	...	...	...	...	...	...	...
8216	Households & nonprofit institutions serving households	...	...	...	...	...	...	...	...	...	...	...	...
322	External debtors	—	—	—	—	—	—	—	...	...	—	—	—
8221	General government	—	—	—	—	—	—	—	...	...	—	—	—
8227	International organizations	—	—	—	—	—	—	—	...	...	—	—	—
8228	Financial corporations other than international organizations	—	—	—	—	—	—	—	...	...	—	—	—
8229	Other nonresidents	—	—	—	—	—	—	—	...	...	—	—	—

Iceland (176)

In Billions of Icelandic Kronur (ISK) / Fiscal Year Ends December 31st

		Budgetary Central Government			Central Government (excl. Social Security)			Central Government (incl. Social Security)			General Government		
		2013	2014	2015	2013	2014	2015	2013	2014	2015	2013	2014	2015
33	**Net incurrence of liabilities**	**-11**	**46**	**-177**	**-11**	**46**	**-177**	**-11**	**...**	**...**	**-6**	**54**	**-158**
331	Domestic creditors	-6	40	-70	-6	40	-70	-6	...	...	7	56	-50
8311	General government	...	...	...	...	...	...	...	...	...	...	...	...
8312	Central bank	...	...	...	...	...	...	...	...	...	...	...	...
8313	Deposit-taking corporations except the central bank	...	...	...	...	...	...	...	...	...	...	...	...
8314	Other financial corporations	...	...	...	...	...	...	...	...	...	...	...	...
8315	Nonfinancial corporations	...	...	...	...	...	...	...	...	...	...	...	...
8316	Households & nonprofit institutions serving households	...	...	...	...	...	...	...	...	...	...	...	...
332	External creditors	-4	6	-107	-4	6	-107	-4	...	...	-13	-3	-108
8321	General government	...	...	...	...	...	...	...	...	...	...	...	...
8327	International organizations	...	...	...	...	...	...	...	...	...	...	...	...
8328	Financial corporations other than international organizations	...	...	...	...	...	...	...	...	...	...	...	...
8329	Other nonresidents	...	...	...	...	...	...	...	...	...	...	...	...
	Table 9 Total other economic flows in assets and liabilities												

India (534)

In Billions of Indian Rupees (INR) / Fiscal Year Ends March 31st

		Budgetary Central Government			Central Government (excl. Social Security)			Central Government (incl. Social Security)			General Government		
		2011	2012	2013P	2011	2012	2013P	2011	2012	2013P	2011	2012	2013
	Statement of operations												
1	Revenue	10,073	12,558	14,179	10,073	12,558	14,179	10,073	12,558	14,179	...	...	...
2	Expense	12,659	16,076	18,691	12,659	16,076	18,691	12,659	16,076	18,691	...	...	...
GOB	**Gross operating balance**	**-2,586**	**-3,518**	**-4,512**	**-2,586**	**-3,518**	**-4,512**	**-2,586**	**-3,518**	**-4,512**	...	...	...
NOB	**Net operating balance**	...	...	...	...	...	...	...	...	...	...	...	...
31	Net/Gross investment in nonfinancial assets	215	225	55	215	225	55	215	225	55	...	...	...
2M	Expenditure	12,874	16,302	18,746	12,874	16,302	18,746	12,874	16,302	18,746	...	...	...
NLB	**Net lending (+) / Net borrowing (-)**	**-2,801**	**-3,743**	**-4,567**	**-2,801**	**-3,743**	**-4,567**	**-2,801**	**-3,743**	**-4,567**	...	...	...
32	Net acquisition of financial assets	674	710	1,279	674	710	1,279	674	710	1,279	...	...	...
33	Net incurrence of liabilities	4,950	4,856	5,255	4,950	4,856	5,255	4,950	4,856	5,255	...	...	...
NLBz	Statistical discrepancy	-1,475	-403	591	-1,475	-403	591	-1,475	-403	591	...	...	...
	Memorandum items												
PB	Primary net lending / net borrowing	-498	-615	-925	-498	-615	-925	-498	-615	-925	...	...	...
GB	Government balance per national definition	...	...	...	...	...	...	...	...	...	...	...	...
	Statement of other economic flows												
	Balance sheet												
6	**Net worth**	...	...	...	...	...	...	...	...	...	...	...	...
61	Nonfinancial assets	...	...	...	...	...	...	...	...	...	...	...	...
62	Financial assets	...	...	...	...	...	...	...	...	...	...	...	...
63	Liabilities	45,042	50,394	56,518	45,042	50,394	56,518	45,042	50,394	56,518	...	...	...
	Table 1 Revenue												
1	**Revenue**	**10,073**	**12,558**	**14,179**	**10,073**	**12,558**	**14,179**	**10,073**	**12,558**	**14,179**	...	...	...
11	**Taxes**	**8,891**	**10,776**	**12,359**	**8,891**	**10,776**	**12,359**	**8,891**	**10,776**	**12,359**	...	...	...
111	Taxes on income, profits, and capital gains	4,874	5,631	6,604	4,874	5,631	6,604	4,874	5,631	6,604	...	...	...
1111	Payable by individuals	1,645	1,899	2,409	1,645	1,899	2,409	1,645	1,899	2,409	...	...	...
1112	Payable by corporations and other enterprises	3,228	3,732	4,195	3,228	3,732	4,195	3,228	3,732	4,195	...	...	...
1113	Other taxes on income, profits, and capital gains	0	—	—	0	—	—	0	—	—	...	...	...
112	Taxes on payroll and workforce	—	—	—	—	—	—	—	—	—	...	...	...
113	Taxes on property	8	12	10	8	12	10	8	12	10	...	...	...
114	Taxes on goods and services	2,516	3,266	3,871	2,516	3,266	3,871	2,516	3,266	3,871	...	...	...
1141	General taxes on goods and services	19	18	22	19	18	22	19	18	22	...	...	...
1142	Excises	1,453	1,941	1,972	1,453	1,941	1,972	1,453	1,941	1,972	...	...	...
115	Taxes on international trade and transactions	1,493	1,867	1,873	1,493	1,867	1,873	1,493	1,867	1,873	...	...	...
116	Other taxes	—	—	—	—	—	—	—	—	—	...	...	...
12	**Social contributions**	**15**	**30**	**27**	**15**	**30**	**27**	**15**	**30**	**27**	...	...	...
121	Social security contributions	—	—	—	—	—	—	—	—	—	...	...	...
122	Other social contributions	15	30	27	15	30	27	15	30	27	...	...	...
13	**Grants**	**30**	**29**	**15**	**30**	**29**	**15**	**30**	**29**	**15**	...	...	...
131	From foreign governments	30	29	15	30	29	15	30	29	15	...	...	...
132	From international organizations	—	—	—	—	—	—	—	—	—	...	...	...
133	From other general government units	—	—	—	—	—	—	—	—	—	...	...	...
1331	Current	—	—	—	—	—	—	—	—	—	...	...	...
1332	Capital	—	—	—	—	—	—	—	—	—	...	...	...
14	**Other revenue**	**1,137**	**1,723**	**1,779**	**1,137**	**1,723**	**1,779**	**1,137**	**1,723**	**1,779**	...	...	...
	Table 2 Expense by economic type												
2	**Expense**	**12,659**	**16,076**	**18,691**	**12,659**	**16,076**	**18,691**	**12,659**	**16,076**	**18,691**	...	...	...
21	**Compensation of employees**	**1,119**	**1,387**	**1,519**	**1,119**	**1,387**	**1,519**	**1,119**	**1,387**	**1,519**	...	...	...
211	Wages and salaries	...	...	...	...	...	...	...	...	...	...	...	...
212	Employers' social contributions	...	...	...	...	...	...	...	...	...	...	...	...
22	**Use of goods and services**	**1,184**	**1,514**	**1,634**	**1,184**	**1,514**	**1,634**	**1,184**	**1,514**	**1,634**	...	...	...
23	**Consumption of fixed capital**	...	...	...	...	...	...	...	...	...	...	...	...
24	**Interest**	**2,304**	**3,128**	**3,642**	**2,304**	**3,128**	**3,642**	**2,304**	**3,128**	**3,642**	...	...	...
25	**Subsidies**	**3,244**	**3,697**	**4,222**	**3,244**	**3,697**	**4,222**	**3,244**	**3,697**	**4,222**	...	...	...

		Budgetary Central Government			Central Government (excl. Social Security)			Central Government (incl. Social Security)			General Government		
		2011	2012	2013P	2011	2012	2013P	2011	2012	2013P	2011	2012	2013
26	**Grants**	**4,719**	**6,242**	**7,574**	**4,719**	**6,242**	**7,574**	**4,719**	**6,242**	**7,574**	**...**	**...**	**...**
261	To foreign governments	—	—	—	—	—	—	—	—	—	...	...	...
262	To international organizations	58	—	591	58	—	591	58	—	591	...	...	...
263	To other general government units	4,661	6,242	6,983	4,661	6,242	6,983	4,661	6,242	6,983	...	...	...
2631	Current	3,247	4,272	5,183	3,247	4,272	5,183	3,247	4,272	5,183	...	...	...
2632	Capital	1,413	1,970	1,800	1,413	1,970	1,800	1,413	1,970	1,800	...	...	...
27	**Social benefits**	**—**	**—**	**—**	**—**	**—**	**—**	**—**	**—**	**—**	**...**	**...**	**...**
271	Social security benefits	—	—	—	—	—	—	—	—	—	...	...	...
272	Social assistance benefits	—	—	—	—	—	—	—	—	—	...	...	...
273	Employment-related social benefits	—	—	—	—	—	—	—	—	—	...	...	...
28	**Other expense**	**90**	**108**	**100**	**90**	**108**	**100**	**90**	**108**	**100**	**...**	**...**	**...**
281	Property expense other than interest	...	...	—	...	...	—	...	...	—	...	...	...
282	Transfers not elsewhere classified	...	...	100	...	...	100	...	...	100	...	...	...
2821	Current	...	...	—	...	...	—	...	...	—	...	...	...
2822	Capital	...	...	100	...	...	100	...	...	100	...	...	...
	Table 3 Transactions in assets and liabilities												
3	**Change in net worth from transactions**	**...**	**...**	**...**	**...**	**...**	**...**	**...**	**...**	**...**	**...**	**...**	**...**
31	**Net/Gross investment in nonfinancial assets**	**215**	**225**	**55**	**215**	**225**	**55**	**215**	**225**	**55**	**...**	**...**	**...**
311	Fixed assets	396	465	613	396	465	613	396	465	613	...	...	...
3111	Buildings and structures	...	...	...	...	...	...	...	...	...	...	...	...
3112	Machinery and equipment	...	...	...	...	...	...	...	...	...	...	...	...
3113	Other fixed assets	...	...	...	...	...	...	...	...	...	...	...	...
3114	Weapons systems	...	...	...	...	...	...	...	...	...	...	...	...
312	Inventories	—	—	—	—	—	—	—	—	—	...	...	...
313	Valuables	—	—	—	—	—	—	—	—	—	...	...	...
314	Nonproduced assets	-181	-240	-558	-181	-240	-558	-181	-240	-558	...	...	...
3141	Land	...	...	...	...	...	...	...	...	...	...	...	...
3142	Mineral and energy resources	...	...	...	...	...	...	...	...	...	...	...	...
3143	Other naturally occurring assets	...	...	...	...	...	...	...	...	...	...	...	...
3144	Intangible nonproduced assets	...	...	...	...	...	...	...	...	...	...	...	...
32	**Net acquisition of financial assets**	**674**	**710**	**1,279**	**674**	**710**	**1,279**	**674**	**710**	**1,279**	**...**	**...**	**...**
	By instrument												
3201	Monetary gold and SDRs	—	—	—	—	—	—	—	—	—	...	...	...
3202	Currency and deposits	157	52	—	157	52	—	157	52	—	...	...	...
3203	Debt securities	—	—	—	—	—	—	—	—	—	...	...	...
3204	Loans	250	390	456	250	390	456	250	390	456	...	...	...
3205	Equity and investment fund shares	267	269	823	267	269	823	267	269	823	...	...	...
3206	Insurance, pension, and standardized guarantee schemes	—	—	—	—	—	—	—	—	—	...	...	...
3207	Financial derivatives and employee stock options	—	—	—	—	—	—	—	—	—	...	...	...
3208	Other accounts receivable	...	...	...	...	...	...	...	...	...	...	...	...
	By debtor												
321	Domestic debtors	674	710	1,279	674	710	1,279	674	710	1,279	...	...	...
322	External debtors	—	—	—	—	—	—	—	—	—	...	...	...
33	**Net incurrence of liabilities**	**4,950**	**4,856**	**5,255**	**4,950**	**4,856**	**5,255**	**4,950**	**4,856**	**5,255**	**...**	**...**	**...**
	By instrument												
3301	Special Drawing Rights (SDRs)	—	—	—	—	—	—	—	—	—	...	...	...
3302	Currency and deposits	—	—	—	—	—	—	—	—	—	...	...	...
3303	Debt securities	4,362	4,674	4,840	4,362	4,674	4,840	4,362	4,674	4,840	...	...	...
3304	Loans	588	182	415	588	182	415	588	182	415	...	...	...
3305	Equity and investment fund shares	—	—	—	—	—	—	—	—	—	...	...	...
3306	Insurance, pension, and standardized guarantee schemes	—	—	—	—	—	—	—	—	—	...	...	...
3307	Financial derivatives and employee stock options	—	—	—	—	—	—	—	—	—	...	...	...
3308	Other accounts payable	...	...	...	...	...	...	...	...	...	...	...	...

India (534)

In Billions of Indian Rupees (INR) / Fiscal Year Ends March 31st

		Budgetary Central Government			Central Government (excl. Social Security)			Central Government (incl. Social Security)			General Government		
		2011	2012	2013P	2011	2012	2013P	2011	2012	2013P	2011	2012	2013
	By creditor												
331	Domestic creditors	4,826	4,834	5,149	4,826	4,834	5,149	4,826	4,834	5,149	...	...	...
332	External creditors	124	22	106	124	22	106	124	22	106	...	...	...
	Table 4 Holding gains and losses in assets and liabilities												
	Table 5 Holding gains and losses in assets and liabilities												
	Table 6 Balance sheet												
6	**Net worth**	...	...	...	...	...	...	...	...	...	...	...	...
61	**Nonfinancial assets**	...	...	...	...	...	...	...	...	...	...	...	...
611	Fixed assets	...	...	...	...	...	...	...	...	...	...	...	...
6111	Buildings and structures	...	...	...	...	...	...	...	...	...	...	...	...
6112	Machinery and equipment	...	...	...	...	...	...	...	...	...	...	...	...
6113	Other fixed assets	...	...	...	...	...	...	...	...	...	...	...	...
6114	Weapons systems	...	...	...	...	...	...	...	...	...	...	...	...
612	Inventories	...	...	...	...	...	...	...	...	...	...	...	...
613	Valuables	...	...	...	...	...	...	...	...	...	...	...	...
614	Nonproduced assets	...	...	...	...	...	...	...	...	...	...	...	...
6141	Land	...	...	...	...	...	...	...	...	...	...	...	...
6142	Mineral and energy resources	...	...	...	...	...	...	...	...	...	...	...	...
6143	Other naturally occurring assets	...	...	...	...	...	...	...	...	...	...	...	...
6144	Intangible nonproduced assets	...	...	...	...	...	...	...	...	...	...	...	...
62	**Financial assets**	...	...	...	...	...	...	...	...	...	...	...	...
	By instrument												
6201	Monetary gold and SDRs	...	...	...	...	...	...	...	...	...	...	...	...
6202	Currency and deposits	...	...	...	...	...	...	...	...	...	...	...	...
6203	Debt securities	...	...	...	...	...	...	...	...	...	...	...	...
6204	Loans	...	...	...	...	...	...	...	...	...	...	...	...
6205	Equity and investment fund shares	...	...	...	...	...	...	...	...	...	...	...	...
6206	Insurance, pension, and standardized guarantee schemes	...	...	...	...	...	...	...	...	...	...	...	...
6207	Financial derivatives and employee stock options	...	...	...	...	...	...	...	...	...	...	...	...
6208	Other accounts receivable	...	...	...	...	...	...	...	...	...	...	...	...
	By debtor												
621	Domestic debtors	...	...	...	...	...	...	...	...	...	...	...	...
622	External debtors	...	...	...	...	...	...	...	...	...	...	...	...
63	**Liabilities**	**45,042**	**50,394**	**56,518**	**45,042**	**50,394**	**56,518**	**45,042**	**50,394**	**56,518**	...	...	...
	By instrument												
6301	Special Drawing Rights (SDRs)	—	—	—	—	—	—	—	—	—	...	...	...
6302	Currency and deposits	—	—	—	—	—	—	—	—	—	...	...	...
6303	Debt securities	31,864	37,019	42,110	31,864	37,019	42,110	31,864	37,019	42,110	...	...	...
6304	Loans	13,178	13,375	14,408	13,178	13,375	14,408	13,178	13,375	14,408	...	...	...
6305	Equity and investment fund shares	—	—	—	—	—	—	—	—	—	...	...	...
6306	Insurance, pension, and standardized guarantee schemes	—	—	—	—	—	—	—	—	—	...	...	...
6307	Financial derivatives and employee stock options	—	—	—	—	—	—	—	—	—	...	...	...
6308	Other accounts payable	...	...	...	...	...	...	...	...	...	...	...	...
	By creditor												
631	Domestic creditors	43,341	48,671	54,689	43,341	48,671	54,689	43,341	48,671	54,689	...	...	...
632	External creditors	1,701	1,723	1,829	1,701	1,723	1,829	1,701	1,723	1,829	...	...	...
	Memorandum items												
6M2	Net financial worth	...	...	...	...	...	...	...	...	...	...	...	...
6M3	Gross debt (D4) at market value	...	...	...	...	...	...	...	...	...	...	...	...
6M3D3	D3 debt liabilities at market value	...	...	...	...	...	...	...	...	...	...	...	...
6M3D2	D2 debt liabilities at market value	...	...	...	...	...	...	...	...	...	...	...	...
6M3D1	D1 debt liabilities at market value	...	...	...	...	...	...	...	...	...	...	...	...
6M4	Gross debt (D4) at nominal value	...	...	...	...	...	...	...	...	...	...	...	...
6M4D3	D3 debt liabilities at nominal value	...	...	...	...	...	...	...	...	...	...	...	...
6M4D2	D2 debt liabilities at nominal value	...	...	...	...	...	...	...	...	...	...	...	...
6M4D1	D1 debt liabilities at nominal value	...	...	...	...	...	...	...	...	...	...	...	...

India (534)

In Billions of Indian Rupees (INR) / Fiscal Year Ends March 31st

		Budgetary Central Government			Central Government (excl. Social Security)			Central Government (incl. Social Security)			General Government		
		2011	2012	2013P	2011	2012	2013P	2011	2012	2013P	2011	2012	2013
6M35	Gross debt (D4) at face value	...	...	...	...	...	...	...	...	...	...	...	...
6M35D3	D3 debt liabilities at face value	...	...	...	...	...	...	...	...	...	...	...	...
6M35D2	D2 debt liabilities at face value	45,042	50,394	56,518	45,042	50,394	56,518	45,042	50,394	56,518	...	...	...
6M35D1	D1 debt liabilities at face value	45,042	50,394	56,518	45,042	50,394	56,518	45,042	50,394	56,518	...	...	...
6M93	Government gross debt per national definition	...	...	...	...	...	...	...	...	...	...	...	...
6M5	Arrears	...	...	...	...	...	...	...	...	...	...	...	...
6M6	Explicit contingent liabilities	...	...	...	...	...	...	...	...	...	...	...	...
6M61	of which: Publicly guaranteed debt	...	...	...	...	...	...	...	...	...	...	...	...
6M7	Net implicit obligations for social security benefits	...	...	...	...	...	...	...	...	...	...	...	...
	Table 7 Expenditure by functions of government												
7	**Expenditure**	**12,874**	**16,302**	**18,715**	**12,874**	**16,302**	**18,715**	**12,874**	**16,302**	**18,715**	...	...	...
701	**General public services**	**6,905**	**8,084**	**10,496**	**6,905**	**8,084**	**10,496**	**6,905**	**8,084**	**10,496**	...	...	...
7017	Public debt transactions	2,304	3,128	3,642	2,304	3,128	3,642	2,304	3,128	3,642	...	...	...
7018	Transfers of general character between levels of government	2,506	3,431	...	2,506	3,431	...	2,506	3,431	...	...	...	...
702	**Defense**	**1,539**	**1,931**	**2,034**	**1,539**	**1,931**	**2,034**	**1,539**	**1,931**	**2,034**	...	...	...
703	**Public order and safety**	—	**1,025**	—	—	**1,025**	—	—	**1,025**	—	...	...	...
704	**Economic affairs**	**2,870**	**3,513**	**3,899**	**2,870**	**3,513**	**3,899**	**2,870**	**3,513**	**3,899**	...	...	...
7042	Agriculture, forestry, fishing, and hunting	955	1,030	1,118	955	1,030	1,118	955	1,030	1,118	...	...	...
7043	Fuel and energy	679	...	...	679	...	...	679	...	...	...	...	...
7044	Mining, manufacturing, and construction	—	—	1,018	—	—	1,018	—	—	1,018	...	...	...
7045	Transport	466	...	493	466	...	493	466	...	493	...	...	...
7046	Communication	—	...	...	—	...	...	—	...	...	...	...	...
705	**Environmental protection**	—	—	—	—	—	—	—	—	—	...	...	...
706	**Housing and community amenities**	**1,014**	**1,207**	**1,315**	**1,014**	**1,207**	**1,315**	**1,014**	**1,207**	**1,315**	...	...	...
707	**Health**	**244**	**317**	**351**	**244**	**317**	**351**	**244**	**317**	**351**	...	...	...
7072	Outpatient services	...	...	...	...	...	...	...	...	...	...	...	...
7073	Hospital services	...	...	...	...	...	...	...	...	...	...	...	...
7074	Public health services	...	...	...	...	...	...	...	...	...	...	...	...
708	**Recreation, culture and religion**	—	—	—	—	—	—	—	—	—	...	...	...
709	**Education**	**405**	**584**	**620**	**405**	**584**	**620**	**405**	**584**	**620**	...	...	...
7091	Pre-primary and primary education	...	...	...	...	...	...	...	...	...	...	...	...
7092	Secondary education	...	...	...	...	...	...	...	...	...	...	...	...
7094	Tertiary education	...	...	...	...	...	...	...	...	...	...	...	...
710	**Social protection**	—	—	—	—	—	—	—	—	—	...	...	...
7z	Statistical discrepancy: Expenditure	...	...	...	...	...	...	...	...	...	...	...	...
	Table 8 Financial transactions by counterpart sector												
32	**Net acquisition of financial assets**	**674**	**710**	**1,279**	**674**	**710**	**1,279**	**674**	**710**	**1,279**	...	...	...
321	Domestic debtors	674	710	1,279	674	710	1,279	674	710	1,279	...	...	...
8211	General government	...	...	...	...	...	...	...	...	...	...	...	...
8212	Central bank	...	...	...	...	...	...	...	...	...	...	...	...
8213	Deposit-taking corporations except the central bank	...	...	...	...	...	...	...	...	...	...	...	...
8214	Other financial corporations	...	...	...	...	...	...	...	...	...	...	...	...
8215	Nonfinancial corporations	...	...	...	...	...	...	...	...	...	...	...	...
8216	Households & nonprofit institutions serving households	...	...	...	...	...	...	...	...	...	...	...	...
322	External debtors	—	—	—	—	—	—	—	—	—	...	...	...
8221	General government	—	—	—	—	—	—	—	—	—	...	...	...
8227	International organizations	—	—	—	—	—	—	—	—	—	...	...	...
8228	Financial corporations other than international organizations	—	—	—	—	—	—	—	—	—	...	...	...
8229	Other nonresidents	—	—	—	—	—	—	—	—	—	...	...	...

India (534)

In Billions of Indian Rupees (INR) / Fiscal Year Ends March 31st

		Budgetary Central Government			Central Government (excl. Social Security)			Central Government (incl. Social Security)			General Government		
		2011	2012	2013P	2011	2012	2013P	2011	2012	2013P	2011	2012	2013
33	**Net incurrence of liabilities**	**4,950**	**4,856**	**5,255**	**4,950**	**4,856**	**5,255**	**4,950**	**4,856**	**5,255**	**...**	**...**	**...**
331	Domestic creditors	4,826	4,834	5,149	4,826	4,834	5,149	4,826	4,834	5,149	...	...	...
3311	General government	...	...	...	...	...	...	...	...	...	...	...	...
3312	Central bank	...	...	...	...	...	...	...	...	...	...	...	...
3313	Deposit-taking corporations except the central bank	...	...	...	...	...	...	...	...	...	...	...	...
3314	Other financial corporations	...	...	...	...	...	...	...	...	...	...	...	...
3315	Nonfinancial corporations	...	...	...	...	...	...	...	...	...	...	...	...
3316	Households & nonprofit institutions serving households	...	...	...	...	...	...	...	...	...	...	...	...
332	External creditors	124	22	106	124	22	106	124	22	106	...	...	...
3321	General government	...	...	108	...	...	108	...	...	...	...	...	...
3327	International organizations	...	...	-2	...	...	-2	...	...	...	...	...	...
3328	Financial corporations other than international organizations	...	...	—	...	...	—	...	...	...	...	...	...
3329	Other nonresidents	...	...	—	...	...	—	...	...	...	...	...	...
	Table 9 Total other economic flows in assets and liabilities												

Indonesia (536)

In Trillions of Indonesian Rupiah (IDR) / Fiscal Year Ends December 31st

		Budgetary Central Government			Central Government (excl. Social Security)			Central Government (incl. Social Security)			General Government		
		2013	2014	2015	2013	2014P	2015P	2013	2014P	2015P	2013	2014P	2015P
	Statement of operations												
1	Revenue	...	...	...	1,439	1,549	1,506	1,439	1,549	1,506	1,609	1,772	1,742
2	Expense	...	...	...	1,468	1,681	1,671	1,468	1,681	1,671	1,476	1,683	1,712
GOB	**Gross operating balance**	...	...	...	**-29**	**-132**	**-51**	**-29**	**-132**	**-51**	**132**	**151**	**144**
NOB	**Net operating balance**	...	...	...	...	...	**-165**	...	...	**-165**	...	**89**	**31**
31	Net/Gross investment in nonfinancial assets	...	...	...	180	92	134	180	92	134	304	273	342
2M	Expenditure	...	...	...	1,648	1,774	1,805	1,648	1,774	1,805	1,781	1,956	2,054
NLB	**Net lending (+) / Net borrowing (-)**	...	...	...	**-209**	**-224**	**-299**	**-209**	**-224**	**-299**	**-172**	**-184**	**-312**
32	Net acquisition of financial assets	...	...	...	13	31	82	13	31	82	49	69	68
33	Net incurrence of liabilities	...	...	...	223	256	381	223	256	381	221	253	379
NLBz	Statistical discrepancy	...	...	...	0	-0	0	0	-0	0	0	-0	0
	Memorandum items												
PB	Primary net lending / net borrowing	...	...	...	-96	-91	-143	-96	-91	-143	-58	-50	-156
GB	Government balance per national definition	...	...	...	...	...	...	...	...	...	...	...	...
	Statement of other economic flows												
	Balance sheet												
6	**Net worth**	...	...	...	**1,099**	**1,188**	**1,853**	**1,099**	**1,188**	**1,853**	**3,337**	**3,644**	**3,267**
61	Nonfinancial assets	...	...	...	1,993	2,228	2,430	1,993	2,228	2,430	3,985	4,398	3,606
62	Financial assets	...	...	...	1,758	1,859	2,916	1,758	1,859	2,916	2,001	2,141	3,157
63	Liabilities	...	...	...	2,652	2,898	3,494	2,652	2,898	3,494	2,648	2,895	3,496
	Table 1 Revenue												
1	**Revenue**	...	...	...	**1,439**	**1,549**	**1,506**	**1,439**	**1,549**	**1,506**	**1,609**	**1,772**	**1,742**
11	**Taxes**	...	...	...	**1,077**	**1,145**	**1,239**	**1,077**	**1,145**	**1,239**	**1,193**	**1,284**	**1,387**
111	Taxes on income, profits, and capital gains	...	...	...	506	546	602	506	546	602	506	546	602
1111	Payable by individuals	...	...	...	95	110	123	95	110	123	95	110	123
1112	Payable by corporations and other enterprises	...	...	...	412	436	480	412	436	480	412	436	480
1113	Other taxes on income, profits, and capital gains	...	...	...	—	—	—	—	—	—	—	—	—
112	Taxes on payroll and workforce	...	...	...	—	—	—	—	—	—	—	—	—
113	Taxes on property	...	...	...	25	23	29	25	23	29	25	23	29
114	Taxes on goods and services	...	...	...	493	528	569	493	528	569	609	666	717
1141	General taxes on goods and services	...	...	...	366	409	424	366	409	424	366	437	453
1142	Excises	...	...	...	127	118	145	127	118	145	127	118	145
115	Taxes on international trade and transactions	...	...	...	47	43	34	47	43	34	47	43	34
116	Other taxes	...	...	...	5	5	5	5	5	5	5	5	5
12	**Social contributions**	...	...	...	—	—	—	—	—	—	—	—	—
121	Social security contributions	...	...	...	—	—	—	—	—	—	—	—	—
122	Other social contributions	...	...	...	—	—	—	—	—	—	—	—	—
13	**Grants**	...	...	...	**6**	**4**	**12**	**6**	**4**	**12**	**5**	**11**	**14**
131	From foreign governments	...	...	...	5	4	3	5	4	3	5	4	3
132	From international organizations	...	...	...	—	—	—	—	—	—	—	—	—
133	From other general government units	...	...	...	1	1	9	1	1	9	—	7	11
1331	Current	...	...	...	1	1	9	1	1	9	—	7	11
1332	Capital	...	...	...	—	—	—	—	—	—	—	—	—
14	**Other revenue**	...	...	...	**355**	**400**	**255**	**355**	**400**	**255**	**411**	**477**	**341**
	Table 2 Expense by economic type												
2	**Expense**	...	...	...	**1,468**	**1,681**	**1,671**	**1,468**	**1,681**	**1,671**	**1,476**	**1,683**	**1,712**
21	**Compensation of employees**	...	...	...	**222**	**241**	**278**	**222**	**241**	**278**	**508**	**553**	**607**
211	Wages and salaries	...	...	...	222	155	186	222	155	186	508	468	515
212	Employers' social contributions	...	...	...	—	86	92	—	86	92	—	86	92
22	**Use of goods and services**	...	...	...	**155**	**167**	**201**	**155**	**167**	**201**	**299**	**333**	**396**
23	**Consumption of fixed capital**	...	...	...	...	...	**114**	...	...	**114**	...	**62**	**114**
24	**Interest**	...	...	...	**113**	**133**	**156**	**113**	**133**	**156**	**114**	**134**	**156**
25	**Subsidies**	...	...	...	**355**	**392**	**186**	**355**	**392**	**186**	**356**	**393**	**188**

Indonesia (536)

In Trillions of Indonesian Rupiah (IDR) / Fiscal Year Ends December 31st

		Budgetary Central Government			Central Government (excl. Social Security)			Central Government (incl. Social Security)			General Government		
		2013	2014	2015	2013	2014P	2015P	2013	2014P	2015P	2013	2014P	2015P
26	**Grants**	...	...	...	**515**	**575**	**627**	**515**	**575**	**627**	**0**	**89**	**134**
261	To foreign governments	...	...	...	0	0	0	0	0	0	0	0	0
262	To international organizations	...	...	...	—	0	0	—	0	0	—	0	0
263	To other general government units	...	...	...	515	575	627	515	575	627	—	89	134
2631	Current	...	...	...	515	575	627	515	575	627	—	89	134
2632	Capital	...	...	...	—	—	—	—	—	—	—	—	—
27	**Social benefits**	...	...	...	**92**	**101**	**100**	**92**	**101**	**100**	**100**	**108**	**108**
271	Social security benefits	...	...	...	—	—	—	—	—	—	8	—	—
272	Social assistance benefits	...	...	...	92	98	97	92	98	97	92	105	105
273	Employment-related social benefits	...	...	...	—	3	3	—	3	3	—	3	3
28	**Other expense**	...	...	...	**16**	**11**	**9**	**16**	**11**	**9**	**98**	**11**	**9**
281	Property expense other than interest	...	...	...	—	—	—	—	—	—	—	—	—
282	Transfers not elsewhere classified	...	...	...	16	11	9	16	11	9	98	11	9
2821	Current	...	...	...	3	9	8	3	9	8	86	10	9
2822	Capital	...	...	...	13	2	1	13	2	1	13	2	1
	Table 3 Transactions in assets and liabilities												
3	**Change in net worth from transactions**	...	...	...	...	...	**-165**	...	...	**-165**	...	...	...
31	**Net/Gross investment in nonfinancial assets**	...	...	...	**180**	**92**	**134**	**180**	**92**	**134**	**304**	**273**	**342**
311	Fixed assets	...	...	...	176	58	92	176	58	92	295	151	199
3111	Buildings and structures	...	...	...	102	45	48	102	45	48	196	124	139
3112	Machinery and equipment	...	...	...	69	7	30	69	7	30	93	19	44
3113	Other fixed assets	...	...	...	4	6	14	4	6	14	7	8	15
3114	Weapons systems	...	...	...	—	—	—	—	—	—	—	—	—
312	Inventories	...	...	...	—	8	32	—	8	32	—	8	32
313	Valuables	...	...	...	—	—	—	—	—	—	—	—	—
314	Nonproduced assets	...	...	...	5	26	9	5	26	9	9	113	111
3141	Land	...	...	...	5	26	9	5	26	9	9	113	111
3142	Mineral and energy resources	...	...	...	—	—	—	—	—	—	—	—	—
3143	Other naturally occurring assets	...	...	...	—	—	—	—	—	—	—	—	—
3144	Intangible nonproduced assets	...	...	...	—	—	—	—	—	—	—	—	—
32	**Net acquisition of financial assets**	...	...	...	**13**	**31**	**82**	**13**	**31**	**82**	**49**	**69**	**68**
	By instrument												
3201	Monetary gold and SDRs	...	...	...	—	—	—	—	—	—	—	—	—
3202	Currency and deposits	...	...	...	3	25	25	3	25	25	32	54	-0
3203	Debt securities	...	...	...	—	—	—	—	—	—	—	—	—
3204	Loans	...	...	...	-0	1	5	-0	1	5	-1	0	5
3205	Equity and investment fund shares	...	...	...	10	5	52	10	5	52	17	14	64
3206	Insurance, pension, and standardized guarantee schemes	...	...	...	—	—	—	—	—	—	—	—	—
3207	Financial derivatives and employee stock options	...	...	...	—	—	—	—	—	—	—	—	—
3208	Other accounts receivable	...	...	...	...	...	...	...	...	...	...	...	...
	By debtor												
321	Domestic debtors	...	...	...	12	27	80	12	27	80	48	65	65
322	External debtors	...	...	...	1	4	3	1	4	3	1	4	3
33	**Net incurrence of liabilities**	...	...	...	**223**	**256**	**381**	**223**	**256**	**381**	**221**	**253**	**379**
	By instrument												
3301	Special Drawing Rights (SDRs)	...	...	...	—	—	—	—	—	—	—	—	—
3302	Currency and deposits	...	...	...	—	—	—	—	—	—	—	—	—
3303	Debt securities	...	...	...	225	265	362	225	265	362	225	265	362
3304	Loans	...	...	...	-2	-9	19	-2	-9	19	-4	-11	17
3305	Equity and investment fund shares	...	...	...	—	—	—	—	—	—	—	—	—
3306	Insurance, pension, and standardized guarantee schemes	...	...	...	—	—	—	—	—	—	—	—	—
3307	Financial derivatives and employee stock options	...	...	...	—	—	—	—	—	—	—	—	—
3308	Other accounts payable	...	...	...	...	...	...	...	...	...	...	...	...

Indonesia (536)

In Trillions of Indonesian Rupiah (IDR) / Fiscal Year Ends December 31st

		Budgetary Central Government			Central Government (excl. Social Security)			Central Government (incl. Social Security)			General Government		
		2013	2014	2015	2013	2014P	2015P	2013	2014P	2015P	2013	2014P	2015P
	By creditor												
331	Domestic creditors	...	...	...	165	214	263	165	214	263	163	211	261
332	External creditors	...	...	...	58	42	118	58	42	118	58	42	118
	Table 4 Holding gains and losses in assets and liabilities												
	Table 5 Holding gains and losses in assets and liabilities												
	Table 6 Balance sheet												
6	**Net worth**	...	...	...	**1,099**	**1,188**	**1,853**	**1,099**	**1,188**	**1,853**	**3,337**	**3,644**	**3,267**
61	**Nonfinancial assets**	...	...	...	**1,993**	**2,228**	**2,430**	**1,993**	**2,228**	**2,430**	**3,985**	**4,398**	**3,606**
611	Fixed assets	...	...	...	852	1,041	1,204	852	1,041	1,204	2,241	2,522	1,990
6111	Buildings and structures	...	...	...	327	808	936	327	808	936	1,242	1,803	1,531
6112	Machinery and equipment	...	...	...	469	188	219	469	188	219	913	645	385
6113	Other fixed assets	...	...	...	56	44	49	56	44	49	86	74	74
6114	Weapons systems	...	...	...	—	—	—	—	—	—	—	—	—
612	Inventories	...	...	...	85	93	124	85	93	124	97	105	138
613	Valuables	...	...	...	—	—	—	—	—	—	—	—	—
614	Nonproduced assets	...	...	...	1,056	1,093	1,103	1,056	1,093	1,103	1,646	1,771	1,478
6141	Land	...	...	...	1,056	1,093	1,103	1,056	1,093	1,103	1,646	1,771	1,478
6142	Mineral and energy resources	...	...	...	—	—	—	—	—	—	—	—	—
6143	Other naturally occurring assets	...	...	...	—	—	—	—	—	—	—	—	—
6144	Intangible nonproduced assets	...	...	...	—	—	—	—	—	—	—	—	—
62	**Financial assets**	...	...	...	**1,758**	**1,859**	**2,916**	**1,758**	**1,859**	**2,916**	**2,001**	**2,141**	**3,157**
	By instrument												
6201	Monetary gold and SDRs	...	...	...	—	—	—	—	—	—	—	—	—
6202	Currency and deposits	...	...	...	199	224	339	199	224	339	298	352	465
6203	Debt securities	...	...	...	0	0	0	0	0	0	0	0	2
6204	Loans	...	...	...	106	102	105	106	102	105	107	103	106
6205	Equity and investment fund shares	...	...	...	1,166	1,289	2,206	1,166	1,289	2,206	1,230	1,362	2,269
6206	Insurance, pension, and standardized guarantee schemes	...	...	...	—	—	—	—	—	—	—	—	—
6207	Financial derivatives and employee stock options	...	...	...	—	—	—	—	—	—	—	—	—
6208	Other accounts receivable	...	...	...	288	244	265	288	244	265	366	323	316
	By debtor												
621	Domestic debtors	...	...	...	1,683	1,801	2,899	1,683	1,801	2,899	1,926	2,083	3,140
622	External debtors	...	...	...	75	58	17	75	58	17	75	58	17
63	**Liabilities**	...	...	...	**2,652**	**2,898**	**3,494**	**2,652**	**2,898**	**3,494**	**2,648**	**2,895**	**3,496**
	By instrument												
6301	Special Drawing Rights (SDRs)	...	...	...	—	—	—	—	—	—	—	—	—
6302	Currency and deposits	...	...	...	—	—	—	—	—	—	—	—	—
6303	Debt securities	...	...	...	1,713	1,994	2,458	1,713	1,994	2,458	1,713	1,994	2,458
6304	Loans	...	...	...	719	680	688	719	680	688	721	679	690
6305	Equity and investment fund shares	...	...	...	—	—	—	—	—	—	—	—	—
6306	Insurance, pension, and standardized guarantee schemes	...	...	...	63	—	109	63	—	109	63	—	109
6307	Financial derivatives and employee stock options	...	...	...	—	—	—	—	—	—	—	—	—
6308	Other accounts payable	...	...	...	157	224	240	157	224	240	150	221	240
	By creditor												
631	Domestic creditors	...	...	...	1,499	1,725	2,128	1,499	1,725	2,128	1,495	1,722	2,130
632	External creditors	...	...	...	1,153	1,173	1,366	1,153	1,173	1,366	1,153	1,173	1,366
	Memorandum items												
6M2	Net financial worth	...	...	...	-894	-1,039	-578	-894	-1,039	-578	-647	-754	-338
6M3	Gross debt (D4) at market value	...	...	...	...	...	...	...	...	...	...	...	...
6M3D3	D3 debt liabilities at market value	...	...	...	...	...	...	...	...	...	...	...	...
6M3D2	D2 debt liabilities at market value	...	...	...	...	...	...	...	...	...	...	...	...
6M3D1	D1 debt liabilities at market value	...	...	...	...	...	...	...	...	...	...	...	...
6M4	Gross debt (D4) at nominal value	...	...	...	2,652	2,898	3,494	2,652	2,898	3,494	2,648	2,895	3,496
6M4D3	D3 debt liabilities at nominal value	...	...	...	2,589	2,898	3,385	2,589	2,898	3,385	2,585	2,895	3,387
6M4D2	D2 debt liabilities at nominal value	...	...	...	2,432	2,674	3,145	2,432	2,674	3,145	2,435	2,674	3,147
6M4D1	D1 debt liabilities at nominal value	...	...	...	2,432	2,674	3,145	2,432	2,674	3,145	2,435	2,674	3,147

Indonesia (536)

In Trillions of Indonesian Rupiah (IDR) / Fiscal Year Ends December 31st

		Budgetary Central Government			Central Government (excl. Social Security)			Central Government (incl. Social Security)			General Government		
		2013	2014	2015	2013	2014P	2015P	2013	2014P	2015P	2013	2014P	2015P
6M35	Gross debt (D4) at face value	...	...	...	2,652	2,898	3,494	2,652	2,898	3,494	2,648	2,895	3,496
6M35D3	D3 debt liabilities at face value	...	...	...	2,589	2,898	3,385	2,589	2,898	3,385	2,585	2,895	3,387
6M35D2	D2 debt liabilities at face value	...	...	...	2,432	2,674	3,145	2,432	2,674	3,145	2,435	2,674	3,147
6M35D1	D1 debt liabilities at face value	...	...	...	2,432	2,674	3,145	2,432	2,674	3,145	2,435	2,674	3,147
6M93	Government gross debt per national definition	...	...	...	...	...	...	...	...	...	...	...	...
6M5	Arrears	...	...	...	...	...	...	...	...	...	...	...	...
6M6	Explicit contingent liabilities	...	...	...	...	...	...	...	...	...	...	...	...
6M61	of which: Publicly guaranteed debt	...	...	...	...	...	...	...	...	...	...	...	...
6M7	Net implicit obligations for social security benefits	...	...	...	...	...	...	...	...	...	...	...	...
	Table 7 Expenditure by functions of government												
7	**Expenditure**	...	...	...	**1,648**	**1,774**	**1,805**	**1,648**	**1,774**	**1,805**	**1,781**	**1,956**	**2,054**
701	**General public services**	...	...	...	**1,023**	**1,369**	**1,247**	**1,023**	**1,369**	**1,247**	**911**	**1,036**	**980**
7017	Public debt transactions	...	...	...	113	133	156	113	133	156	114	134	156
7018	Transfers of general character between levels of government	...	...	...	515	575	627	515	575	627	—	89	134
702	**Defense**	...	...	...	**127**	**86**	**106**	**127**	**86**	**106**	**87**	**86**	**106**
703	**Public order and safety**	...	...	...	**52**	**35**	**53**	**52**	**35**	**53**	**43**	**49**	**67**
704	**Economic affairs**	...	...	...	**157**	**97**	**177**	**157**	**97**	**177**	**168**	**166**	**246**
7042	Agriculture, forestry, fishing, and hunting	...	...	...	...	...	56	...	...	56	...	...	...
7043	Fuel and energy	...	...	...	...	...	5	...	...	5	...	...	...
7044	Mining, manufacturing, and construction	...	...	...	...	...	5	...	...	5	...	...	...
7045	Transport	...	...	...	...	...	90	...	...	90	...	...	...
7046	Communication	...	...	...	...	...	0	...	...	0	...	...	...
705	**Environmental protection**	...	...	...	**15**	**9**	**10**	**15**	**9**	**10**	**26**	**24**	**24**
706	**Housing and community amenities**	...	...	...	**49**	**26**	**17**	**49**	**26**	**17**	**140**	**153**	**144**
707	**Health**	...	...	...	**25**	**11**	**23**	**25**	**11**	**23**	**79**	**86**	**99**
7072	Outpatient services	...	...	...	...	...	15	...	...	15	...	...	...
7073	Hospital services	...	...	...	...	...	2	...	...	2	...	...	...
7074	Public health services	...	...	...	...	...	3	...	...	3	...	...	...
708	**Recreation, culture and religion**	...	...	...	**8**	**5**	**8**	**8**	**5**	**8**	**10**	**11**	**13**
709	**Education**	...	...	...	**167**	**122**	**143**	**167**	**122**	**143**	**290**	**322**	**343**
7091	Pre-primary and primary education	...	...	...	...	...	31	...	...	31	...	...	...
7092	Secondary education	...	...	...	...	...	8	...	...	8	...	...	...
7094	Tertiary education	...	...	...	...	...	17	...	...	17	...	...	...
710	**Social protection**	...	...	...	**25**	**13**	**21**	**25**	**13**	**21**	**27**	**24**	**32**
7z	Statistical discrepancy: Expenditure	-0	...	...	-0	0	—	-0	0	—	0	0	0
	Table 8 Financial transactions by counterpart sector												
32	**Net acquisition of financial assets**	...	...	...	**13**	**31**	**82**	**13**	**31**	**82**	**49**	**69**	**68**
321	Domestic debtors	...	...	...	12	27	80	12	27	80	48	65	65
8211	General government	...	...	...	...	...	...	...	...	...	...	...	...
8212	Central bank	...	...	...	...	...	...	...	...	...	...	...	...
8213	Deposit-taking corporations except the central bank	...	...	...	...	...	...	...	...	...	...	...	...
8214	Other financial corporations	...	...	...	...	...	...	...	...	...	...	...	...
8215	Nonfinancial corporations	...	...	...	...	...	...	...	...	...	...	...	...
8216	Households & nonprofit institutions serving households	...	...	...	...	...	...	...	...	...	...	...	...
322	External debtors	...	...	...	1	4	3	1	4	3	1	4	3
8221	General government	...	...	...	...	...	...	...	...	...	...	...	...
8227	International organizations	...	...	...	...	...	...	...	...	...	...	...	...
8228	Financial corporations other than international organizations	...	...	...	...	...	...	...	...	...	...	...	...
8229	Other nonresidents	...	...	...	...	...	...	...	...	...	...	...	...

Indonesia (536)

In Trillions of Indonesian Rupiah (IDR) / Fiscal Year Ends December 31st

		Budgetary Central Government			Central Government (excl. Social Security)			Central Government (incl. Social Security)			General Government		
		2013	2014	2015	2013	2014P	2015P	2013	2014P	2015P	2013	2014P	2015P
33	**Net incurrence of liabilities**	...	...	...	**223**	**256**	**381**	**223**	**256**	**381**	**221**	**253**	**379**
331	Domestic creditors	...	...	...	165	214	263	165	214	263	163	211	261
8311	General government	...	...	...	...	...	...	...	...	...	...	...	...
8312	Central bank	...	...	...	...	...	...	...	...	...	...	...	...
8313	Deposit-taking corporations except the central bank	...	...	...	...	...	...	...	...	...	...	...	...
8314	Other financial corporations	...	...	...	...	...	...	...	...	...	...	...	...
8315	Nonfinancial corporations	...	...	...	...	...	...	...	...	...	...	...	...
8316	Households & nonprofit institutions serving households	...	...	...	...	...	...	...	...	...	...	...	...
332	External creditors	...	...	...	58	42	118	58	42	118	58	42	118
8321	General government	...	...	...	...	...	...	...	...	...	...	...	...
8327	International organizations	...	...	...	...	...	...	...	...	...	...	...	...
8328	Financial corporations other than international organizations	...	...	...	...	...	...	...	...	...	...	...	...
8329	Other nonresidents	...	...	...	...	...	...	...	...	...	...	...	...
	Table 9 Total other economic flows in assets and liabilities												

Iraq (433)

In Billions of Iraqi Dinars (IQD) / Fiscal Year Ends December 31st

		Budgetary Central Government			Central Government (excl. Social Security)			Central Government (incl. Social Security)			General Government		
		2012	2013	2014P	2012	2013	2014	2012	2013	2014	2012	2013	2014
	Statement of operations												
1	Revenue	...	...	104,321	...	...	...	...	...	...	...	...	...
2	Expense	...	...	68,472	...	...	...	...	...	...	...	...	...
GOB	**Gross operating balance**	...	...	**35,850**	...	...	...	...	...	...	...	...	...
NOB	**Net operating balance**	...	...	**35,850**	...	...	...	...	...	...	...	...	...
31	Net/Gross investment in nonfinancial assets	...	...	43,213	...	...	...	...	...	...	...	...	...
2M	Expenditure	...	...	111,684	...	...	...	...	...	...	...	...	...
NLB	**Net lending (+) / Net borrowing (-)**	...	...	**-7,363**	...	...	...	...	...	...	...	...	...
32	Net acquisition of financial assets	...	...	2,405	...	...	...	...	...	...	...	...	...
33	Net incurrence of liabilities	...	...	8,721	...	...	...	...	...	...	...	...	...
NLBz	Statistical discrepancy	...	...	1,047	...	...	...	...	...	...	...	...	...
	Memorandum items												
PB	Primary net lending / net borrowing	...	...	-6,651	...	...	...	...	...	...	...	...	...
GB	Government balance per national definition	...	...	...	...	...	...	...	...	...	...	...	...
	Statement of other economic flows												
	Balance sheet												
	Table 1 Revenue												
1	**Revenue**	...	...	**104,321**	...	...	...	...	...	...	...	...	...
11	**Taxes**	...	...	**2,436**	...	...	...	...	...	...	...	...	...
111	Taxes on income, profits, and capital gains	...	...	1,322	...	...	...	...	...	...	...	...	...
1111	Payable by individuals	...	...	719	...	...	...	...	...	...	...	...	...
1112	Payable by corporations and other enterprises	...	...	604	...	...	...	...	...	...	...	...	...
1113	Other taxes on income, profits, and capital gains	...	...	—	...	...	...	...	...	...	...	...	...
112	Taxes on payroll and workforce	...	...	—	...	...	...	...	...	...	...	...	...
113	Taxes on property	...	...	71	...	...	...	...	...	...	...	...	...
114	Taxes on goods and services	...	...	264	...	...	...	...	...	...	...	...	...
1141	General taxes on goods and services	...	...	1	...	...	...	...	...	...	...	...	...
1142	Excises	...	...	59	...	...	...	...	...	...	...	...	...
115	Taxes on international trade and transactions	...	...	564	...	...	...	...	...	...	...	...	...
116	Other taxes	...	...	214	...	...	...	...	...	...	...	...	...
12	**Social contributions**	...	...	**58**	...	...	...	...	...	...	...	...	...
121	Social security contributions	...	...	58	...	...	...	...	...	...	...	...	...
122	Other social contributions	...	...	0	...	...	...	...	...	...	...	...	...
13	**Grants**	...	...	—	...	...	...	...	...	...	...	...	...
131	From foreign governments	...	...	—	...	...	...	...	...	...	...	...	...
132	From international organizations	...	...	—	...	...	...	...	...	...	...	...	...
133	From other general government units	...	...	—	...	...	...	...	...	...	...	...	...
1331	Current	...	...	—	...	...	...	...	...	...	...	...	...
1332	Capital	...	...	—	...	...	...	...	...	...	...	...	...
14	**Other revenue**	...	...	**101,827**	...	...	...	...	...	...	...	...	...
	Table 2 Expense by economic type												
2	**Expense**	...	...	**68,472**	...	...	...	...	...	...	...	...	...
21	**Compensation of employees**	...	...	**30,349**	...	...	...	...	...	...	...	...	...
211	Wages and salaries	...	...	29,241	...	...	...	...	...	...	...	...	...
212	Employers' social contributions	...	...	1,108	...	...	...	...	...	...	...	...	...
22	**Use of goods and services**	...	...	**8,891**	...	...	...	...	...	...	...	...	...
23	**Consumption of fixed capital**	...	...	—	...	...	...	...	...	...	...	...	...
24	**Interest**	...	...	**712**	...	...	...	...	...	...	...	...	...
25	**Subsidies**	...	...	**4,203**	...	...	...	...	...	...	...	...	...
26	**Grants**	...	...	**1,569**	...	...	...	...	...	...	...	...	...
261	To foreign governments	...	...	58	...	...	...	...	...	...	...	...	...
262	To international organizations	...	...	37	...	...	...	...	...	...	...	...	...
263	To other general government units	...	...	1,474	...	...	...	...	...	...	...	...	...
2631	Current	...	...	1,385	...	...	...	...	...	...	...	...	...
2632	Capital	...	...	89	...	...	...	...	...	...	...	...	...

Iraq (433)

In Billions of Iraqi Dinars (IQD) / Fiscal Year Ends December 31st

		Budgetary Central Government			Central Government (excl. Social Security)			Central Government (incl. Social Security)			General Government		
		2012	2013	2014P	2012	2013	2014	2012	2013	2014	2012	2013	2014
27	**Social benefits**	...	...	**17,284**	...	...	...	...	...	...	...	...	...
271	Social security benefits	...	...	2	...	...	...	...	...	...	...	...	...
272	Social assistance benefits	...	...	7,357	...	...	...	...	...	...	...	...	...
273	Employment-related social benefits	...	...	9,924	...	...	...	...	...	...	...	...	...
28	**Other expense**	...	...	**5,464**	...	...	...	...	...	...	...	...	...
281	Property expense other than interest	...	...	—	...	...	...	...	...	...	...	...	...
282	Transfers not elsewhere classified	...	...	5,454	...	...	...	...	...	...	...	...	...
2821	Current	...	...	5,454	...	...	...	...	...	...	...	...	...
2822	Capital	...	...	—	...	...	...	...	...	...	...	...	...
	Table 3 Transactions in assets and liabilities												
3	**Change in net worth from transactions**	...	...	...	...	...	...	...	...	...	...	...	...
31	**Net/Gross investment in nonfinancial assets**	...	...	**43,213**	...	...	...	...	...	...	...	...	...
311	Fixed assets	...	...	43,213	...	...	...	...	...	...	...	...	...
3111	Buildings and structures	...	...	...	...	...	...	...	...	...	...	...	...
3112	Machinery and equipment	...	...	...	...	...	...	...	...	...	...	...	...
3113	Other fixed assets	...	...	...	...	...	...	...	...	...	...	...	...
3114	Weapons systems	...	...	...	...	...	...	...	...	...	...	...	...
312	Inventories	...	...	—	...	...	...	...	...	...	...	...	...
313	Valuables	...	...	—	...	...	...	...	...	...	...	...	...
314	Nonproduced assets	...	...	-1	...	...	...	...	...	...	...	...	...
3141	Land	...	...	...	...	...	...	...	...	...	...	...	...
3142	Mineral and energy resources	...	...	...	...	...	...	...	...	...	...	...	...
3143	Other naturally occurring assets	...	...	...	...	...	...	...	...	...	...	...	...
3144	Intangible nonproduced assets	...	...	...	...	...	...	...	...	...	...	...	...
32	**Net acquisition of financial assets**	...	...	**2,405**	...	...	...	...	...	...	...	...	...
	By instrument												
3201	Monetary gold and SDRs	...	...	—	...	...	...	...	...	...	...	...	...
3202	Currency and deposits	...	...	2,405	...	...	...	...	...	...	...	...	...
3203	Debt securities	...	...	—	...	...	...	...	...	...	...	...	...
3204	Loans	...	...	—	...	...	...	...	...	...	...	...	...
3205	Equity and investment fund shares	...	...	—	...	...	...	...	...	...	...	...	...
3206	Insurance, pension, and standardized guarantee schemes	...	...	—	...	...	...	...	...	...	...	...	...
3207	Financial derivatives and employee stock options	...	...	—	...	...	...	...	...	...	...	...	...
3208	Other accounts receivable	...	...	...	...	...	...	...	...	...	...	...	...
	By debtor												
321	Domestic debtors	...	...	2,405	...	...	...	...	...	...	...	...	...
322	External debtors	...	...	—	...	...	...	...	...	...	...	...	...
33	**Net incurrence of liabilities**	...	...	**8,721**	...	...	...	...	...	...	...	...	...
	By instrument												
3301	Special Drawing Rights (SDRs)	...	...	—	...	...	...	...	...	...	...	...	...
3302	Currency and deposits	...	...	—	...	...	...	...	...	...	...	...	...
3303	Debt securities	...	...	4,574	...	...	...	...	...	...	...	...	...
3304	Loans	...	...	66	...	...	...	...	...	...	...	...	...
3305	Equity and investment fund shares	...	...	—	...	...	...	...	...	...	...	...	...
3306	Insurance, pension, and standardized guarantee schemes	...	...	—	...	...	...	...	...	...	...	...	...
3307	Financial derivatives and employee stock options	...	...	—	...	...	...	...	...	...	...	...	...
3308	Other accounts payable	...	...	4,081	...	...	...	...	...	...	...	...	...
	By creditor												
331	Domestic creditors	...	...	6,765	...	...	...	...	...	...	...	...	...
332	External creditors	...	...	1,956	...	...	...	...	...	...	...	...	...
	Table 4 Holding gains and losses in assets and liabilities												
	Table 5 Holding gains and losses in assets and liabilities												
	Table 6 Balance sheet												

Iraq (433)

In Billions of Iraqi Dinars (IQD) / Fiscal Year Ends December 31st

	Budgetary Central Government			Central Government (excl. Social Security)			Central Government (incl. Social Security)			General Government		
	2012	2013	2014P	2012	2013	2014	2012	2013	2014	2012	2013	2014
Table 7 Expenditure by functions of government												
Table 8 Financial transactions by counterpart sector												
Table 9 Total other economic flows in assets and liabilities												

Ireland (178)

In Millions of Euros (EUR) / Fiscal Year Ends December 31st

		Budgetary Central Government			Central Government (excl. Social Security)			Central Government (incl. Social Security)			General Government		
		2013	2014	2015	2013P	2014P	2015P	2013P	2014P	2015P	2013P	2014P	2015P
	Statement of operations												
1	Revenue	...	...	...	58,004	62,388	67,001	58,004	62,388	67,001	61,522	65,803	70,534
2	Expense	...	...	...	67,898	67,995	70,915	67,898	67,995	70,915	72,092	72,201	74,540
GOB	**Gross operating balance**	...	...	...	**-8,498**	**-3,674**	**-1,787**	**-8,498**	**-3,674**	**-1,787**	**-7,303**	**-2,965**	**-380**
NOB	**Net operating balance**	...	...	...	**-9,894**	**-5,608**	**-3,915**	**-9,894**	**-5,608**	**-3,915**	**-10,570**	**-6,398**	**-4,007**
31	Net/Gross investment in nonfinancial assets	...	...	...	298	1,562	1,568	298	1,562	1,568	-377	798	779
2M	Expenditure	...	...	...	68,196	69,557	72,484	68,196	69,557	72,484	71,715	73,000	75,320
NLB	**Net lending (+) / Net borrowing (-)**	...	...	...	**-10,192**	**-7,169**	**-5,483**	**-10,192**	**-7,169**	**-5,483**	**-10,193**	**-7,197**	**-4,786**
32	Net acquisition of financial assets	...	...	...	-5,370	-18,181	-7,620	-5,370	-18,181	-7,620	-5,547	-18,849	-7,261
33	Net incurrence of liabilities	...	...	...	4,725	-10,748	-2,223	4,725	-10,748	-2,223	4,549	-11,389	-2,562
NLBz	Statistical discrepancy	...	...	...	97	-264	86	97	-264	86	97	-263	87
	Memorandum items												
PB	Primary net lending / net borrowing	...	...	...	-2,600	267	1,196	-2,600	267	1,196	-2,579	253	1,908
GB	Government balance per national definition	...	...	...	...	...	...	...	...	...	...	...	...
	Statement of other economic flows												
	Balance sheet												
6	**Net worth**	...	...	...	...	...	...	...	...	...	...	...	...
61	Nonfinancial assets	...	...	...	...	...	...	...	...	...	...	...	...
62	Financial assets	...	...	...	94,655	84,867	85,000	94,655	84,867	85,000	94,778	84,320	84,810
63	Liabilities	...	...	...	238,531	236,925	234,768	238,531	236,925	234,768	239,985	237,735	235,240
	Table 1 Revenue												
1	**Revenue**	...	...	...	**58,004**	**62,388**	**67,001**	**58,004**	**62,388**	**67,001**	**61,522**	**65,803**	**70,534**
11	**Taxes**	...	...	...	**41,092**	**45,044**	**49,410**	**41,092**	**45,044**	**49,410**	**42,499**	**46,447**	**50,735**
111	Taxes on income, profits, and capital gains	...	...	...	21,298	23,016	26,605	21,298	23,016	26,605	21,298	23,016	26,605
1111	Payable by individuals	...	...	...	16,983	18,340	19,660	16,983	18,340	19,660	16,983	18,340	19,660
1112	Payable by corporations and other enterprises	...	...	...	4,309	4,671	6,939	4,309	4,671	6,939	4,309	4,671	6,939
1113	Other taxes on income, profits, and capital gains	...	...	...	6	6	6	6	6	6	6	6	6
112	Taxes on payroll and workforce	...	...	...	314	334	354	314	334	354	314	334	354
113	Taxes on property	...	...	...	1,132	1,594	1,045	1,132	1,594	1,045	2,538	2,997	2,370
114	Taxes on goods and services	...	...	...	18,066	19,980	21,295	18,066	19,980	21,295	18,066	19,980	21,295
1141	General taxes on goods and services	...	...	...	10,775	12,073	12,703	10,775	12,073	12,703	10,775	12,073	12,703
1142	Excises	...	...	...	4,104	4,179	4,325	4,104	4,179	4,325	4,104	4,179	4,325
115	Taxes on international trade and transactions	...	...	...	—	—	—	—	—	—	—	—	—
116	Other taxes	...	...	...	282	119	110	282	119	110	282	119	110
12	**Social contributions**	...	...	...	**10,078**	**10,685**	**11,090**	**10,078**	**10,685**	**11,090**	**10,409**	**10,983**	**11,388**
121	Social security contributions	...	...	...	...	...	...	...	...	...	...	...	...
122	Other social contributions	...	...	...	...	...	...	...	...	...	...	...	...
13	**Grants**	...	...	...	...	...	...	...	...	...	...	...	...
131	From foreign governments	...	...	...	...	...	...	...	...	...	...	...	...
132	From international organizations	...	...	...	...	...	...	...	...	...	...	...	...
133	From other general government units	...	...	...	3	3	3	3	3	3	—	—	—
1331	Current	...	...	...	3	3	3	3	3	3	—	—	—
1332	Capital	...	...	...	—	—	—	—	—	—	—	—	—
14	**Other revenue**	...	...	...	...	...	...	...	...	...	...	...	...
	Table 2 Expense by economic type												
2	**Expense**	...	...	...	**67,898**	**67,995**	**70,915**	**67,898**	**67,995**	**70,915**	**72,092**	**72,201**	**74,540**
21	**Compensation of employees**	...	...	...	**16,568**	**16,791**	**17,321**	**16,568**	**16,791**	**17,321**	**18,594**	**18,344**	**18,874**
211	Wages and salaries	...	...	...	...	...	...	...	...	...	...	...	...
212	Employers' social contributions	...	...	...	...	...	...	...	...	...	...	...	...
22	**Use of goods and services**	...	...	...	**6,796**	**7,215**	**7,502**	**6,796**	**7,215**	**7,502**	**8,196**	**8,906**	**9,193**
23	**Consumption of fixed capital**	...	...	...	**1,396**	**1,933**	**2,127**	**1,396**	**1,933**	**2,127**	**3,267**	**3,433**	**3,627**
24	**Interest**	...	...	...	**7,592**	**7,436**	**6,679**	**7,592**	**7,436**	**6,679**	**7,614**	**7,449**	**6,694**
25	**Subsidies**	...	...	...	**1,913**	**1,853**	**1,785**	**1,913**	**1,853**	**1,785**	**1,913**	**1,853**	**1,785**

Ireland (178)

In Millions of Euros (EUR) / Fiscal Year Ends December 31st

		Budgetary Central Government			Central Government (excl. Social Security)			Central Government (incl. Social Security)			General Government		
		2013	2014	2015	2013P	2014P	2015P	2013P	2014P	2015P	2013P	2014P	2015P
26	**Grants**	...	...	...	...	...	...	...	...	...	...	...	...
261	To foreign governments	...	...	...	...	...	...	...	...	...	...	...	...
262	To international organizations	...	...	...	...	...	...	...	...	...	...	...	...
263	To other general government units	...	...	...	2,930	2,159	2,784	2,930	2,159	2,784	—	—	—
2631	Current	...	...	...	1,798	1,526	1,626	1,798	1,526	1,626	—	—	—
2632	Capital	...	...	...	1,132	633	1,158	1,132	633	1,158	—	—	—
27	**Social benefits**	...	...	...	**27,057**	**26,870**	**26,781**	**27,057**	**26,870**	**26,781**	**28,583**	**28,209**	**28,249**
271	Social security benefits	...	...	...	...	...	...	...	...	...	...	...	...
272	Social assistance benefits	...	...	...	...	...	...	...	...	...	...	...	...
273	Employment-related social benefits	...	...	...	...	...	...	...	...	...	...	...	...
28	**Other expense**	...	...	...	...	...	...	...	...	...	...	...	...
281	Property expense other than interest	...	...	...	—	—	—	—	—	—	—	—	—
282	Transfers not elsewhere classified	...	...	...	...	...	...	...	...	...	...	...	...
2821	Current	...	...	...	...	...	...	...	...	...	...	...	...
2822	Capital	...	...	...	...	...	...	...	...	...	...	...	...
	Table 3 Transactions in assets and liabilities												
3	**Change in net worth from transactions**	...	...	...	**-9,797**	**-5,871**	**-3,829**	**-9,797**	**-5,871**	**-3,829**	**-10,473**	**-6,662**	**-3,920**
31	**Net/Gross investment in nonfinancial assets**	...	...	...	**298**	**1,562**	**1,568**	**298**	**1,562**	**1,568**	**-377**	**798**	**779**
311	Fixed assets	...	...	...	939	1,502	1,508	939	1,502	1,508	263	738	719
3111	Buildings and structures	...	...	...	...	...	...	...	...	...	...	...	...
3112	Machinery and equipment	...	...	...	...	...	...	...	...	...	...	...	...
3113	Other fixed assets	...	...	...	...	...	...	...	...	...	...	...	...
3114	Weapons systems	...	...	...	...	...	...	...	...	...	...	...	...
312	Inventories	...	...	...	...	...	...	...	...	...	...	...	...
313	Valuables	...	...	...	...	...	...	...	...	...	...	...	...
314	Nonproduced assets	...	...	...	-723	—	—	-723	—	—	-723	—	—
3141	Land	...	...	...	...	—	—	...	—	—	...	—	—
3142	Mineral and energy resources	...	...	...	...	—	—	...	—	—	...	—	—
3143	Other naturally occurring assets	...	...	...	...	—	—	...	—	—	...	—	—
3144	Intangible nonproduced assets	...	...	...	...	—	—	...	—	—	...	—	—
32	**Net acquisition of financial assets**	...	...	...	**-5,370**	**-18,181**	**-7,620**	**-5,370**	**-18,181**	**-7,620**	**-5,547**	**-18,849**	**-7,261**
	By instrument												
3201	Monetary gold and SDRs	...	...	...	—	—	—	—	—	—	—	—	—
3202	Currency and deposits	...	...	...	-1,199	-5,780	-232	-1,199	-5,780	-232	-1,280	-6,225	-483
3203	Debt securities	...	...	...	-758	-1,429	-5,834	-758	-1,429	-5,834	-758	-1,429	-5,834
3204	Loans	...	...	...	-2,387	-11,826	-1,581	-2,387	-11,826	-1,581	-2,364	-11,847	-974
3205	Equity and investment fund shares	...	...	...	-1,307	-91	240	-1,307	-91	240	-1,307	-91	240
3206	Insurance, pension, and standardized guarantee schemes	...	...	...	—	1	-1	—	1	-1	—	1	-1
3207	Financial derivatives and employee stock options	...	...	...	196	97	-367	196	97	-367	196	97	-367
3208	Other accounts receivable	...	...	...	85	847	155	85	847	155	-34	645	158
	By debtor												
321	Domestic debtors	...	...	...	...	...	...	...	...	...	...	...	...
322	External debtors	...	...	...	...	...	...	...	...	...	...	...	...
33	**Net incurrence of liabilities**	...	...	...	**4,725**	**-10,748**	**-2,223**	**4,725**	**-10,748**	**-2,223**	**4,549**	**-11,389**	**-2,562**
	By instrument												
3301	Special Drawing Rights (SDRs)	...	...	...	—	—	—	—	—	—	—	—	—
3302	Currency and deposits	...	...	...	-30,707	-10,474	-247	-30,707	-10,474	-247	-30,707	-10,474	-247
3303	Debt securities	...	...	...	25,548	6,899	6,034	25,548	6,899	6,034	25,492	6,440	5,735
3304	Loans	...	...	...	10,711	-8,265	-8,244	10,711	-8,265	-8,244	10,635	-8,225	-8,358
3305	Equity and investment fund shares	...	...	...	...	...	...	...	...	...	...	...	...
3306	Insurance, pension, and standardized guarantee schemes	...	...	...	-1	—	—	-1	—	—	-1	—	—
3307	Financial derivatives and employee stock options	...	...	...	-1	-1	—	-1	-1	—	-1	-1	—
3308	Other accounts payable	...	...	...	-825	1,093	234	-825	1,093	234	-869	871	308

Ireland (178)

In Millions of Euros (EUR) / Fiscal Year Ends December 31st

		Budgetary Central Government			Central Government (excl. Social Security)			Central Government (incl. Social Security)			General Government		
		2013	2014	2015	2013P	2014P	2015P	2013P	2014P	2015P	2013P	2014P	2015P
	By creditor												
331	Domestic creditors	...	...	...	...	...	...	...	...	...	...	...	...
332	External creditors	...	...	...	...	...	...	...	...	...	...	...	...
	Table 4 Holding gains and losses in assets and liabilities												
	Table 5 Holding gains and losses in assets and liabilities												
	Table 6 Balance sheet												
6	**Net worth**	...	...	...	...	...	...	...	...	...	...	...	...
61	**Nonfinancial assets**	...	...	...	...	...	...	...	...	...	...	...	...
611	Fixed assets	...	...	...	...	...	...	...	...	...	...	...	...
6111	Buildings and structures	...	...	...	...	...	...	...	...	...	...	...	...
6112	Machinery and equipment	...	...	...	...	...	...	...	...	...	...	...	...
6113	Other fixed assets	...	...	...	...	...	...	...	...	...	...	...	...
6114	Weapons systems	...	...	...	...	...	...	...	...	...	...	...	...
612	Inventories	...	...	...	...	...	...	...	...	...	...	...	...
613	Valuables	...	...	...	...	...	...	...	...	...	...	...	...
614	Nonproduced assets	...	...	...	...	...	...	...	...	...	...	...	...
6141	Land	...	...	...	...	...	...	...	...	...	...	...	...
6142	Mineral and energy resources	...	...	...	...	...	...	...	...	...	...	...	...
6143	Other naturally occurring assets	...	...	...	...	...	...	...	...	...	...	...	...
6144	Intangible nonproduced assets	...	...	...	...	...	...	...	...	...	...	...	...
62	**Financial assets**	...	...	...	**94,655**	**84,867**	**85,000**	**94,655**	**84,867**	**85,000**	**94,778**	**84,320**	**84,810**
	By instrument												
6201	Monetary gold and SDRs	...	...	...	—	—	—	—	—	—	—	—	—
6202	Currency and deposits	...	...	...	22,687	16,979	16,968	22,687	16,979	16,968	23,994	17,841	17,579
6203	Debt securities	...	...	...	10,249	9,646	3,289	10,249	9,646	3,289	10,249	9,646	3,289
6204	Loans	...	...	...	22,214	11,217	10,045	22,214	11,217	10,045	20,319	9,299	8,734
6205	Equity and investment fund shares	...	...	...	30,795	38,202	45,259	30,795	38,202	45,259	30,795	38,202	45,259
6206	Insurance, pension, and standardized guarantee schemes	...	...	...	—	1	—	—	1	—	—	1	—
6207	Financial derivatives and employee stock options	...	...	...	1,135	352	812	1,135	352	812	1,135	352	812
6208	Other accounts receivable	...	...	...	7,575	8,470	8,627	7,575	8,470	8,627	8,286	8,979	9,137
	By debtor												
621	Domestic debtors	...	...	...	...	...	...	...	...	...	...	...	...
622	External debtors	...	...	...	...	...	...	...	...	...	...	...	...
63	**Liabilities**	...	...	...	**238,531**	**236,925**	**234,768**	**238,531**	**236,925**	**234,768**	**239,985**	**237,735**	**235,240**
	By instrument												
6301	Special Drawing Rights (SDRs)	...	...	...	—	—	—	—	—	—	—	—	—
6302	Currency and deposits	...	...	...	31,356	20,918	20,713	31,356	20,918	20,713	31,356	20,918	20,713
6303	Debt securities	...	...	...	126,471	143,038	147,705	126,471	143,038	147,705	126,265	142,372	146,741
6304	Loans	...	...	...	73,344	64,990	57,527	73,344	64,990	57,527	73,854	65,538	57,961
6305	Equity and investment fund shares	...	...	...	...	...	...	...	...	...	...	...	...
6306	Insurance, pension, and standardized guarantee schemes	...	...	...	—	—	—	—	—	—	—	—	—
6307	Financial derivatives and employee stock options	...	...	...	932	457	1,068	932	457	1,068	932	457	1,068
6308	Other accounts payable	...	...	...	6,428	7,522	7,755	6,428	7,522	7,755	7,578	8,450	8,757
	By creditor												
631	Domestic creditors	...	...	...	...	...	...	...	...	...	...	...	...
632	External creditors	...	...	...	...	...	...	...	...	...	...	...	...
	Memorandum items												
6M2	Net financial worth	...	...	...	-143,876	-152,058	-149,768	-143,876	-152,058	-149,768	-145,207	-153,415	-150,430
6M3	Gross debt (D4) at market value	...	...	...	237,599	236,468	233,700	237,599	236,468	233,700	239,053	237,278	234,172
6M3D3	D3 debt liabilities at market value	...	...	...	237,599	236,468	233,700	237,599	236,468	233,700	239,053	237,278	234,172
6M3D2	D2 debt liabilities at market value	...	...	...	231,171	228,946	225,945	231,171	228,946	225,945	231,475	228,828	225,415
6M3D1	D1 debt liabilities at market value	...	...	...	199,815	208,028	205,232	199,815	208,028	205,232	200,119	207,910	204,702
6M4	Gross debt (D4) at nominal value	...	...	...	...	...	...	...	...	...	...	...	...
6M4D3	D3 debt liabilities at nominal value	...	...	...	...	...	...	...	...	...	...	...	...
6M4D2	D2 debt liabilities at nominal value	...	...	...	...	...	...	...	...	...	...	...	...
6M4D1	D1 debt liabilities at nominal value	...	...	...	...	...	...	...	...	...	...	...	...

Ireland (178)

In Millions of Euros (EUR) / Fiscal Year Ends December 31st

		Budgetary Central Government			Central Government (excl. Social Security)			Central Government (incl. Social Security)			General Government		
		2013	2014	2015	2013P	2014P	2015P	2013P	2014P	2015P	2013P	2014P	2015P
6M35	Gross debt (D4) at face value	...	...	...	...	...	...	...	...	...	...	...	...
6M35D3	D3 debt liabilities at face value	...	...	...	221,395	210,927	209,430	221,395	210,927	209,430	222,876	211,749	209,891
6M35D2	D2 debt liabilities at face value	...	...	...	214,967	203,405	201,675	214,967	203,405	201,675	215,298	203,299	201,134
6M35D1	D1 debt liabilities at face value	...	...	...	183,611	182,487	180,962	183,611	182,487	180,962	183,942	182,381	180,421
6M93	Government gross debt per national definition	...	...	...	214,967	203,405	201,675	...	...	...	215,298	203,299	201,134
6M5	Arrears	...	...	...	...	...	...	...	...	...	...	...	...
6M6	Explicit contingent liabilities	...	...	...	...	...	...	...	...	...	...	...	...
6M61	of which: Publicly guaranteed debt	...	...	...	...	...	...	...	...	...	...	...	...
6M7	Net implicit obligations for social security benefits	...	...	...	...	...	...	...	...	...	...	...	...
	Table 7 Expenditure by functions of government												
7	**Expenditure**	...	...	...	**67,622**	**68,758**	...	...	...	...	**71,192**	**72,320**	...
701	**General public services**	...	...	...	**12,253**	**11,944**	...	...	...	...	**11,847**	**11,526**	...
7017	Public debt transactions	...	...	...	7,676	7,520	...	...	...	...	7,698	7,542	...
7018	Transfers of general character between levels of government	...	...	...	664	642	...	...	...	...	—	-23	...
702	**Defense**	...	...	...	**671**	**686**	...	...	...	...	**666**	**681**	...
703	**Public order and safety**	...	...	...	**2,389**	**2,470**	...	...	...	...	**2,617**	**2,685**	...
704	**Economic affairs**	...	...	...	**4,109**	**5,119**	...	...	...	...	**4,873**	**6,086**	...
7042	Agriculture, forestry, fishing, and hunting	...	...	...	724	738	...	...	...	...	737	750	...
7043	Fuel and energy	...	...	...	325	443	...	...	...	...	335	453	...
7044	Mining, manufacturing, and construction	...	...	...	148	150	...	...	...	...	148	150	...
7045	Transport	...	...	...	1,761	1,784	...	...	...	...	2,288	2,531	...
7046	Communication	...	...	...	-697	28	...	...	...	...	-697	28	...
705	**Environmental protection**	...	...	...	**550**	**536**	...	...	...	...	**1,092**	**1,052**	...
706	**Housing and community amenities**	...	...	...	**466**	**739**	...	...	...	...	**1,216**	**1,361**	...
707	**Health**	...	...	...	**14,213**	**14,396**	...	...	...	...	**14,213**	**14,396**	...
7072	Outpatient services	...	...	...	6,075	6,244	...	...	...	...	6,075	6,244	...
7073	Hospital services	...	...	...	3,934	4,006	...	...	...	...	3,934	4,006	...
7074	Public health services	...	...	...	491	420	...	...	...	...	491	420	...
708	**Recreation, culture and religion**	...	...	...	**946**	**1,025**	...	...	...	...	**1,366**	**1,425**	...
709	**Education**	...	...	...	**8,150**	**8,279**	...	...	...	...	**8,040**	**8,061**	...
7091	Pre-primary and primary education	...	...	...	2,774	2,821	...	...	...	...	2,774	2,821	...
7092	Secondary education	...	...	...	3,053	3,027	...	...	...	...	2,940	2,797	...
7094	Tertiary education	...	...	...	1,594	1,694	...	...	...	...	1,595	1,702	...
710	**Social protection**	...	...	...	**23,877**	**23,563**	...	...	...	...	**25,262**	**25,048**	...
7z	Statistical discrepancy: Expenditure	...	...	...	0	-0	...	...	...	...	—	-0	...
	Table 8 Financial transactions by counterpart sector												
32	**Net acquisition of financial assets**	...	...	...	**-5,370**	**-18,181**	**-7,620**	**-5,370**	**-18,181**	**-7,620**	**-5,547**	**-18,849**	**-7,261**
321	Domestic debtors	...	...	...	...	...	...	...	...	...	...	...	...
8211	General government	...	...	...	...	...	...	...	...	...	—	—	—
8212	Central bank	...	...	...	...	...	...	...	...	...	...	...	...
8213	Deposit-taking corporations except the central bank	...	...	...	...	...	...	...	...	...	...	...	...
8214	Other financial corporations	...	...	...	...	...	...	...	...	...	...	...	...
8215	Nonfinancial corporations	...	...	...	...	...	...	...	...	...	...	...	...
8216	Households & nonprofit institutions serving households	...	...	...	...	...	...	...	...	...	...	...	...
322	External debtors	...	...	...	...	...	...	...	...	...	...	...	...
8221	General government	...	...	...	...	...	...	...	...	...	...	...	...
8227	International organizations	...	...	...	...	...	...	...	...	...	...	...	...
8228	Financial corporations other than international organizations	...	...	...	...	...	...	...	...	...	...	...	...
8229	Other nonresidents	...	...	...	...	...	...	...	...	...	...	...	...

Ireland (178)

In Millions of Euros (EUR) / Fiscal Year Ends December 31st

		Budgetary Central Government			Central Government (excl. Social Security)			Central Government (incl. Social Security)			General Government		
		2013	2014	2015	2013P	2014P	2015P	2013P	2014P	2015P	2013P	2014P	2015P
33	**Net incurrence of liabilities**	...	...	...	4,725	-10,748	-2,223	4,725	-10,748	-2,223	4,549	-11,389	-2,562
331	Domestic creditors	...	...	...	...	...	...	...	...	...	...	...	...
8311	General government	...	...	...	...	...	...	...	...	...	—	—	—
8312	Central bank	...	...	...	...	...	...	...	...	...	...	...	...
8313	Deposit-taking corporations except the central bank	...	...	...	...	...	...	...	...	...	...	...	...
8314	Other financial corporations	...	...	...	...	...	...	...	...	...	...	...	...
8315	Nonfinancial corporations	...	...	...	...	...	...	...	...	...	...	...	...
8316	Households & nonprofit institutions serving households	...	...	...	...	...	...	...	...	...	...	...	...
332	External creditors	...	...	...	...	...	...	...	...	...	...	...	...
8321	General government	...	...	...	...	...	...	...	...	...	...	...	...
8327	International organizations	...	...	...	...	...	...	...	...	...	...	...	...
8328	Financial corporations other than international organizations	...	...	...	...	...	...	...	...	...	...	...	...
8329	Other nonresidents	...	...	...	...	...	...	...	...	...	...	...	...
	Table 9 Total other economic flows in assets and liabilities												
9	**Change in net worth due to other economic flows**	...	...	...	...	...	...	...	...	...	...	...	...
91	**Other economic flows in nonfinancial assets**	...	...	...	...	...	...	...	...	...	...	...	...
911	Fixed assets	...	...	...	...	...	...	...	...	...	...	...	...
912	Inventories	...	...	...	...	...	...	...	...	...	...	...	...
913	Valuables	...	...	...	...	...	...	...	...	...	...	...	...
914	Nonproduced assets	...	...	...	...	...	...	...	...	...	...	...	...
92	**Other economic flows in financial assets**	...	...	...	7,268	8,393	7,753	...	...	...	7,266	8,391	7,751
	By instrument												
9201	Monetary gold and SDRs	...	...	...	—	—	—	...	...	...	—	—	—
9202	Currency and deposits	...	...	...	—	72	221	...	...	...	—	72	221
9203	Debt securities	...	...	...	1,537	826	-523	...	...	...	1,537	826	-523
9204	Loans	...	...	...	-1,281	829	409	...	...	...	-1,282	827	409
9205	Equity and investment fund shares	...	...	...	7,004	7,498	6,817	...	...	...	7,004	7,498	6,817
9206	Insurance, pension, and standardized guarantee schemes	...	...	...	—	—	—	...	...	...	—	—	—
9207	Financial derivatives and employee stock options	...	...	...	42	-880	827	...	...	...	42	-880	827
9208	Other accounts receivable	...	...	...	-34	48	2	...	...	...	-35	48	—
	By debtor												
921	Domestic debtors	...	...	...	...	...	...	...	...	...	...	...	...
922	External debtors	...	...	...	...	...	...	...	...	...	...	...	...
93	**Other economic flows in liabilities**	...	...	...	5,600	9,142	66	...	...	...	5,598	9,139	67
	By instrument												
9301	Special Drawing Rights (SDRs)	...	...	...	—	—	—	...	...	...	—	—	—
9302	Currency and deposits	...	...	...	-36	36	42	...	...	...	-36	36	42
9303	Debt securities	...	...	...	6,487	9,668	-1,367	...	...	...	6,486	9,667	-1,366
9304	Loans	...	...	...	1,018	-89	781	...	...	...	1,017	-91	781
9305	Equity and investment fund shares	...	...	...	—	—	—	...	...	...	—	—	—
9306	Insurance, pension, and standardized guarantee schemes	...	...	...	—	—	—	...	...	...	—	—	—
9307	Financial derivatives and employee stock options	...	...	...	-1,869	-474	611	...	...	...	-1,869	-474	611
9308	Other accounts payable	...	...	...	—	1	-1	...	...	...	—	1	-1
	By creditor												
931	Domestic creditors	...	...	...	...	...	...	...	...	...	...	...	...
932	External creditors	...	...	...	...	...	...	...	...	...	...	...	...
	Memorandum items												
9M2	Change in net financial worth due to other economic flows	...	...	...	1,668	-749	7,687	...	...	...	1,668	-748	7,684

Ireland (178)

In Millions of Euros (EUR) / Fiscal Year Ends December 31st

		Budgetary Central Government			Central Government (excl. Social Security)			Central Government (incl. Social Security)			General Government		
		2013	2014	2015	2013P	2014P	2015P	2013P	2014P	2015P	2013P	2014P	2015P
9M3	Gross debt (D4) at market value: other economic flows	...	...	...	7,469	9,616	-545	...	...	...	7,467	9,613	-544
9M3D3	D3 debt liabilities at market value: other economic flows	...	...	...	7,469	9,616	-545	...	...	...	7,467	9,613	-544
9M3D2	D2 debt liabilities at market value: other economic flows	...	...	...	7,469	9,615	-544	...	...	...	7,467	9,612	-543
9M3D1	D1 debt liabilities at market value: other economic flows	...	...	...	7,505	9,579	-586	...	...	...	7,503	9,576	-585

Israel (436)

In Millions of Israeli New Sheqalim (ILS) / Fiscal Year Ends December 31st

		Budgetary Central Government			Central Government (excl. Social Security)			Central Government (incl. Social Security)			General Government		
		2013	2014	2015	2013	2014	2015	2013	2014	2015	2013	2014	2015
	Statement of operations												
1	Revenue	283,105	299,951	317,691	319,948	338,811	357,615	353,810	374,442	395,861	385,053	406,471	430,027
2	Expense	333,587	342,450	357,892	371,535	381,417	395,653	401,093	413,498	428,383	427,110	441,555	457,557
GOB	**Gross operating balance**	**-47,511**	**-39,525**	**-37,221**	**-41,730**	**-32,476**	**-27,793**	**-37,342**	**-28,844**	**-22,192**	**-22,743**	**-15,011**	**-6,922**
NOB	**Net operating balance**	**-50,482**	**-42,499**	**-40,201**	**-51,587**	**-42,606**	**-38,038**	**-47,283**	**-39,057**	**-32,521**	**-42,058**	**-35,083**	**-27,530**
31	Net/Gross investment in nonfinancial assets	-6,351	-4,674	-8,440	-4,564	-2,750	-6,523	-4,618	-2,804	-6,555	-130	497	-3,516
2M	Expenditure	327,236	337,776	349,452	366,971	378,666	389,129	396,475	410,694	421,828	426,980	442,051	454,041
NLB	**Net lending (+) / Net borrowing (-)**	**-44,131**	**-37,825**	**-31,761**	**-47,023**	**-39,855**	**-31,514**	**-42,664**	**-36,252**	**-25,966**	**-41,928**	**-35,580**	**-24,014**
32	Net acquisition of financial assets	...	...	...	...	...	...	...	...	...	...	...	...
33	Net incurrence of liabilities	...	...	...	...	...	...	...	...	...	...	...	...
NLBz	Statistical discrepancy	...	...	...	...	...	...	...	...	...	...	...	...
	Memorandum items												
PB	Primary net lending / net borrowing	1,567	7,413	13,173	-100	6,656	14,734	-3,457	2,479	12,624	-1,662	4,026	15,413
GB	Government balance per national definition	...	...	...	...	...	...	...	...	...	...	...	...
	Statement of other economic flows												
	Balance sheet												
	Table 1 Revenue												
1	**Revenue**	**283,105**	**299,951**	**317,691**	**319,948**	**338,811**	**357,615**	**353,810**	**374,442**	**395,861**	**385,053**	**406,471**	**430,027**
11	**Taxes**	**242,385**	**257,017**	**271,797**	**242,385**	**257,017**	**271,797**	**242,385**	**257,017**	**271,797**	**269,108**	**284,938**	**301,330**
111	Taxes on income, profits, and capital gains	104,436	107,759	117,565	104,436	107,759	117,565	104,436	107,759	117,565	104,436	107,759	117,565
1111	Payable by individuals	57,709	62,810	70,698	57,709	62,810	70,698	57,709	62,810	70,698	57,709	62,810	70,698
1112	Payable by corporations and other enterprises	36,639	34,967	34,668	36,639	34,967	34,668	36,639	34,967	34,668	36,639	34,967	34,668
1113	Other taxes on income, profits, and capital gains	10,088	9,982	12,199	10,088	9,982	12,199	10,088	9,982	12,199	10,088	9,982	12,199
112	Taxes on payroll and workforce	12,274	13,556	13,745	12,274	13,556	13,745	12,274	13,556	13,745	12,274	13,556	13,745
113	Taxes on property	59	95	44	59	95	44	59	95	44	21,542	22,511	24,149
114	Taxes on goods and services	123,325	132,831	137,572	123,325	132,831	137,572	123,325	132,831	137,572	128,566	138,336	143,000
1141	General taxes on goods and services	101,888	110,676	114,520	101,888	110,676	114,520	101,888	110,676	114,520	105,938	114,939	118,613
1142	Excises	16,687	17,101	17,642	16,687	17,101	17,642	16,687	17,101	17,642	16,687	17,101	17,642
115	Taxes on international trade and transactions	2,298	2,776	2,871	2,298	2,776	2,871	2,298	2,776	2,871	2,298	2,776	2,871
116	Other taxes	-7	—	—	-7	—	—	-7	—	—	-7	—	—
12	**Social contributions**	**7,275**	**7,335**	**7,421**	**7,275**	**7,335**	**7,421**	**60,640**	**63,465**	**66,983**	**62,074**	**64,907**	**68,353**
121	Social security contributions	—	—	—	—	—	—	53,364	56,130	59,561	53,364	56,130	59,561
122	Other social contributions	7,275	7,335	7,421	7,275	7,335	7,421	7,275	7,335	7,421	8,709	8,777	8,792
13	**Grants**	**16,562**	**17,552**	**19,196**	**36,163**	**38,043**	**40,598**	**16,026**	**16,944**	**18,562**	**10,944**	**11,094**	**12,910**
131	From foreign governments	10,944	11,094	12,910	10,944	11,094	12,910	10,944	11,094	12,910	10,944	11,094	12,910
132	From international organizations	—	—	—	—	—	—	—	—	—	—	—	—
133	From other general government units	5,618	6,458	6,286	25,219	26,949	27,689	5,082	5,850	5,652	—	—	—
1331	Current	5,605	6,445	6,273	25,199	26,927	27,664	5,077	5,845	5,646	—	—	—
1332	Capital	13	13	13	20	22	24	5	5	6	—	—	—
14	**Other revenue**	**16,882**	**18,046**	**19,277**	**34,125**	**36,416**	**37,798**	**34,760**	**37,016**	**38,520**	**42,927**	**45,532**	**47,434**
	Table 2 Expense by economic type												
2	**Expense**	**333,587**	**342,450**	**357,892**	**371,535**	**381,417**	**395,653**	**401,093**	**413,498**	**428,383**	**427,110**	**441,555**	**457,557**
21	**Compensation of employees**	**63,623**	**65,863**	**68,650**	**88,979**	**92,311**	**96,541**	**89,720**	**93,067**	**97,336**	**105,297**	**109,265**	**114,277**
211	Wages and salaries	49,999	51,956	54,377	72,186	75,098	78,781	72,852	75,778	79,496	85,282	88,753	93,204
212	Employers' social contributions	13,624	13,907	14,274	16,794	17,213	17,760	16,868	17,289	17,840	20,015	20,513	21,073
22	**Use of goods and services**	**51,186**	**55,245**	**57,698**	**76,191**	**81,279**	**83,852**	**76,966**	**82,094**	**84,710**	**92,515**	**98,636**	**102,385**
23	**Consumption of fixed capital**	**2,972**	**2,973**	**2,979**	**9,856**	**10,130**	**10,245**	**9,941**	**10,213**	**10,330**	**19,315**	**20,072**	**20,608**
24	**Interest**	**45,698**	**45,238**	**44,934**	**46,923**	**46,511**	**46,249**	**39,207**	**38,732**	**38,590**	**40,266**	**39,607**	**39,427**
25	**Subsidies**	**7,927**	**8,238**	**8,162**	**7,927**	**8,238**	**8,162**	**7,927**	**8,238**	**8,162**	**7,927**	**8,238**	**8,162**
26	**Grants**	**95,325**	**96,902**	**104,814**	**54,549**	**54,100**	**58,186**	**24,477**	**24,776**	**26,534**	**1,294**	**1,175**	**1,206**
261	To foreign governments	1,066	882	913	1,066	882	913	1,066	882	913	1,066	882	913
262	To international organizations	227	293	293	227	293	293	227	293	293	227	293	293
263	To other general government units	94,031	95,727	103,608	53,255	52,925	56,980	23,183	23,601	25,328	—	—	—
2631	Current	86,815	89,161	95,794	48,237	48,713	52,119	18,165	19,390	20,466	—	—	—
2632	Capital	7,216	6,565	7,813	5,018	4,212	4,862	5,018	4,212	4,862	—	—	—

Israel (436)

In Millions of Israeli New Sheqalim (ILS) / Fiscal Year Ends December 31st

		Budgetary Central Government			Central Government (excl. Social Security)			Central Government (incl. Social Security)			General Government		
		2013	2014	2015	2013	2014	2015	2013	2014	2015	2013	2014	2015
27	**Social benefits**	**35,487**	**38,057**	**39,609**	**53,862**	**56,946**	**59,284**	**119,468**	**124,336**	**129,439**	**125,004**	**130,277**	**135,828**
271	Social security benefits	—	—	—	—	—	—	65,606	67,390	70,155	65,606	67,390	70,155
272	Social assistance benefits	16,847	17,725	18,509	35,221	36,614	38,184	35,221	36,614	38,184	40,757	42,555	44,573
273	Employment-related social benefits	18,641	20,332	21,100	18,641	20,332	21,100	18,641	20,332	21,100	18,641	20,332	21,100
28	**Other expense**	**31,369**	**29,933**	**31,045**	**33,248**	**31,902**	**33,133**	**33,387**	**32,042**	**33,282**	**35,492**	**34,284**	**35,665**
281	Property expense other than interest	—	—	—	—	—	—	—	—	—	—	—	—
282	Transfers not elsewhere classified	31,369	29,933	31,045	33,248	31,902	33,133	33,387	32,042	33,282	35,492	34,284	35,665
2821	Current	10,519	10,386	11,603	12,316	12,262	13,584	12,440	12,386	13,715	14,142	14,156	15,595
2822	Capital	20,850	19,547	19,442	20,932	19,640	19,549	20,948	19,656	19,567	21,350	20,128	20,069
	Table 3 Transactions in assets and liabilities												
3	**Change in net worth from transactions**	**-6,351**	**-4,674**	**-8,440**	**-4,564**	**-2,750**	**-6,523**	**-4,618**	**-2,804**	**-6,555**	**-130**	**497**	**-3,516**
31	**Net/Gross investment in nonfinancial assets**	**-6,351**	**-4,674**	**-8,440**	**-4,564**	**-2,750**	**-6,523**	**-4,618**	**-2,804**	**-6,555**	**-130**	**497**	**-3,516**
311	Fixed assets	-1,982	-1,298	-1,091	-195	625	826	-249	571	794	3,907	3,554	3,549
3111	Buildings and structures	-1,725	-1,171	-977	-342	338	606	-388	292	579	3,127	2,810	2,900
3112	Machinery and equipment	-304	-207	-172	-60	60	107	-69	51	102	552	496	512
3113	Other fixed assets	47	80	59	208	228	113	208	228	113	228	249	138
3114	Weapons systems	—	—	—	—	—	—	—	—	—	—	—	—
312	Inventories	—	—	—	—	—	—	—	—	—	—	—	—
313	Valuables	—	—	—	—	—	—	—	—	—	—	—	—
314	Nonproduced assets	-4,369	-3,376	-7,349	-4,369	-3,376	-7,349	-4,369	-3,376	-7,349	-4,037	-3,058	-7,065
3141	Land	-4,369	-3,376	-7,349	-4,369	-3,376	-7,349	-4,369	-3,376	-7,349	-4,037	-3,058	-7,065
3142	Mineral and energy resources	—	—	—	—	—	—	—	—	—	—	—	—
3143	Other naturally occurring assets	—	—	—	—	—	—	—	—	—	—	—	—
3144	Intangible nonproduced assets	—	—	—	—	—	—	—	—	—	—	—	—
32	**Net acquisition of financial assets**	**...**	**...**	**...**	**...**	**...**	**...**	**...**	**...**	**...**	**...**	**...**	**...**
	By instrument												
3201	Monetary gold and SDRs	...	...	...	...	...	...	...	...	...	...	...	...
3202	Currency and deposits	...	...	...	...	...	...	...	...	...	...	...	...
3203	Debt securities	...	...	...	...	...	...	...	...	...	...	...	...
3204	Loans	...	...	...	...	...	...	...	...	...	...	...	...
3205	Equity and investment fund shares	...	...	...	...	...	...	...	...	...	...	...	...
3206	Insurance, pension, and standardized guarantee schemes	...	...	...	...	...	...	...	...	...	...	...	...
3207	Financial derivatives and employee stock options	...	...	...	...	...	...	...	...	...	...	...	...
3208	Other accounts receivable	...	...	...	...	...	...	...	...	...	...	...	...
	By debtor												
321	Domestic debtors	...	...	...	...	...	...	...	...	...	...	...	...
322	External debtors	...	...	...	...	...	...	...	...	...	...	...	...
33	**Net incurrence of liabilities**	**...**	**...**	**...**	**...**	**...**	**...**	**...**	**...**	**...**	**...**	**...**	**...**
	By instrument												
3301	Special Drawing Rights (SDRs)	...	...	...	...	...	...	...	...	...	...	...	...
3302	Currency and deposits	...	...	...	...	...	...	...	...	...	...	...	...
3303	Debt securities	...	...	...	...	...	...	...	...	...	...	...	...
3304	Loans	...	...	...	...	...	...	...	...	...	...	...	...
3305	Equity and investment fund shares	...	...	...	...	...	...	...	...	...	...	...	...
3306	Insurance, pension, and standardized guarantee schemes	...	...	...	...	...	...	...	...	...	...	...	...
3307	Financial derivatives and employee stock options	...	...	...	...	...	...	...	...	...	...	...	...
3308	Other accounts payable	...	...	...	...	...	...	...	...	...	...	...	...
	By creditor												
331	Domestic creditors	...	...	...	...	...	...	...	...	...	...	...	...
332	External creditors	...	...	...	...	...	...	...	...	...	...	...	...
	Table 4 Holding gains and losses in assets and liabilities												
	Table 5 Holding gains and losses in assets and liabilities												
	Table 6 Balance sheet												

Israel (436)

In Millions of Israeli New Sheqalim (ILS) / Fiscal Year Ends December 31st

		Budgetary Central Government			Central Government (excl. Social Security)			Central Government (incl. Social Security)			General Government		
		2013	2014	2015	2013	2014	2015	2013	2014	2015	2013	2014	2015
	Table 7 Expenditure by functions of government												
7	**Expenditure**	**327,235**	**337,776**	**349,452**	**366,971**	**378,666**	**389,129**	**396,474**	**410,694**	**421,828**	**426,980**	**442,051**	**454,041**
701	**General public services**	**59,852**	**59,575**	**59,981**	**60,453**	**60,298**	**60,603**	**52,737**	**52,519**	**52,944**	**55,770**	**55,044**	**55,955**
7017	Public debt transactions	45,698	45,238	44,934	46,923	46,511	46,249	39,207	38,732	38,590	40,266	39,607	39,427
7018	Transfers of general character between levels of government	3,876	4,305	4,431	3,876	4,305	4,431	3,876	4,305	4,431	—	—	—
702	**Defense**	**62,464**	**66,052**	**68,682**	**62,456**	**66,031**	**68,668**	**62,456**	**66,031**	**68,668**	**62,695**	**66,291**	**68,943**
703	**Public order and safety**	**16,019**	**16,903**	**17,555**	**16,008**	**16,886**	**17,539**	**16,008**	**16,886**	**17,539**	**16,294**	**17,138**	**17,804**
704	**Economic affairs**	**27,135**	**27,017**	**25,948**	**26,404**	**26,465**	**24,958**	**26,404**	**26,465**	**24,958**	**28,490**	**29,101**	**27,029**
7042	Agriculture, forestry, fishing, and hunting	2,005	2,410	2,618	1,448	2,034	1,818	1,448	2,034	1,818	1,481	2,071	1,858
7043	Fuel and energy	1,054	346	285	1,054	346	285	1,054	346	285	1,056	352	291
7044	Mining, manufacturing, and construction	2,022	2,328	1,866	2,022	2,328	1,866	2,022	2,328	1,866	2,042	2,338	1,876
7045	Transport	17,221	15,691	15,444	17,237	15,710	15,466	17,237	15,710	15,466	18,329	17,218	16,466
7046	Communication	211	121	201	211	118	200	211	118	200	211	118	200
705	**Environmental protection**	**1,294**	**1,081**	**1,027**	**1,292**	**1,079**	**1,025**	**1,292**	**1,079**	**1,025**	**6,011**	**6,069**	**5,767**
706	**Housing and community amenities**	**-1,123**	**-1,048**	**-2,724**	**-1,011**	**-928**	**-2,581**	**-1,011**	**-928**	**-2,581**	**1,973**	**1,887**	**301**
707	**Health**	**27,829**	**30,824**	**31,950**	**51,063**	**54,341**	**54,950**	**53,818**	**57,314**	**58,027**	**53,958**	**57,445**	**58,170**
7072	Outpatient services	1,201	1,288	1,083	15,495	16,945	17,242	15,495	16,945	17,242	15,567	17,012	17,312
7073	Hospital services	24,763	27,520	28,805	26,663	28,536	28,835	29,364	31,453	31,853	29,364	31,449	31,853
7074	Public health services	1,171	1,202	1,224	1,171	1,202	1,224	1,171	1,202	1,224	1,217	1,249	1,274
708	**Recreation, culture and religion**	**3,255**	**3,733**	**4,189**	**9,161**	**9,894**	**10,663**	**9,161**	**9,894**	**10,663**	**14,874**	**15,327**	**16,364**
709	**Education**	**56,446**	**58,867**	**62,465**	**65,064**	**67,726**	**70,746**	**65,255**	**67,927**	**70,943**	**72,296**	**75,554**	**79,016**
7091	Pre-primary and primary education	28,454	29,249	31,191	26,637	27,508	29,301	26,828	27,708	29,498	27,988	29,204	31,055
7092	Secondary education	16,209	17,635	18,516	15,888	17,153	17,707	15,888	17,153	17,707	16,535	17,552	18,121
7094	Tertiary education	6,858	6,850	7,409	17,938	18,413	18,879	17,938	18,413	18,879	17,938	18,413	18,879
710	**Social protection**	**74,066**	**74,771**	**80,378**	**76,080**	**76,873**	**82,558**	**110,354**	**113,507**	**119,641**	**114,618**	**118,195**	**124,694**
7z	Statistical discrepancy: Expenditure	1	10	—	1	10	—	0	8	—	0	8	—
	Table 8 Financial transactions by counterpart sector												
	Table 9 Total other economic flows in assets and liabilities												

Italy (136)

In Billions of Euros (EUR) / Fiscal Year Ends December 31st

		Budgetary Central Government			Central Government (excl. Social Security)			Central Government (incl. Social Security)			General Government		
		2013	2014	2015	2013P	2014P	2015P	2013P	2014P	2015P	2013P	2014P	2015P
	Statement of operations												
1	Revenue	...	...	...	423	427	434	632	635	648	772	777	785
2	Expense	...	...	...	477	483	491	684	690	703	824	832	835
GOB	**Gross operating balance**	**...**	**...**	**...**	**-32**	**-35**	**-35**	**-30**	**-34**	**-33**	**-8**	**-11**	**-6**
NOB	**Net operating balance**	**...**	**...**	**...**	**-54**	**-56**	**-57**	**-52**	**-55**	**-55**	**-52**	**-55**	**-50**
31	Net/Gross investment in nonfinancial assets	...	...	...	-9	-4	-7	-9	-5	-7	-9	-7	-7
2M	Expenditure	...	...	...	468	479	485	675	686	696	816	825	828
NLB	**Net lending (+) / Net borrowing (-)**	**...**	**...**	**...**	**-45**	**-52**	**-50**	**-43**	**-51**	**-48**	**-43**	**-48**	**-43**
32	Net acquisition of financial assets	...	...	...	41	29	-13	...	...	...	26	21	-12
33	Net incurrence of liabilities	...	...	...	85	81	38	...	...	...	72	67	32
NLBz	Statistical discrepancy	...	...	...	0	-0	-0	...	...	...	-2	2	-1
	Memorandum items												
PB	Primary net lending / net borrowing	...	...	...	30	20	16	32	21	19	34	26	25
GB	Government balance per national definition	...	...	...	...	...	...	...	...	...	...	...	...
	Statement of other economic flows												
9	**Change in net worth due to other economic flows**	**...**	**...**	**...**	**...**	**...**	**...**	**...**	**...**	**...**	**...**	**...**	**...**
4	Change in net worth due to holding gains and losses	...	...	...	...	...	...	...	...	...	...	...	...
41	Nonfinancial assets	...	...	...	...	...	...	...	...	...	...	...	...
42	Financial assets	...	...	...	...	...	...	...	...	...	...	...	...
43	Liabilities	...	...	...	...	...	...	...	...	...	...	...	...
5	Change in net worth due to volume changes	...	...	...	...	...	...	...	...	...	...	...	...
51	Nonfinancial assets	...	...	...	...	...	...	...	...	...	...	...	...
52	Financial assets	...	...	...	—	—	—	...	...	...	0	—	0
53	Liabilities	...	...	...	—	0	-0	...	...	...	0	0	-0
	Balance sheet												
6	**Net worth**	**...**	**...**	**...**	**...**	**...**	**...**	**...**	**...**	**...**	**...**	**...**	**...**
61	Nonfinancial assets	...	...	...	...	...	...	...	...	...	...	...	...
62	Financial assets	...	...	...	317	342	335	...	...	...	439	456	447
63	Liabilities	...	...	...	2,169	2,416	2,475	...	...	...	2,334	2,568	2,621
	Table 1 Revenue												
1	**Revenue**	**...**	**...**	**...**	**423**	**427**	**434**	**632**	**635**	**648**	**772**	**777**	**785**
11	**Taxes**	**...**	**...**	**...**	**381**	**382**	**389**	**381**	**382**	**389**	**485**	**488**	**494**
111	Taxes on income, profits, and capital gains	...	...	...	205	201	206	205	201	206	234	230	235
1111	Payable by individuals	...	...	...	166	168	174	166	168	174	192	195	201
1112	Payable by corporations and other enterprises	...	...	...	38	33	32	38	33	32	40	35	33
1113	Other taxes on income, profits, and capital gains	...	...	...	1	0	0	1	0	0	1	0	0
112	Taxes on payroll and workforce	...	...	...	—	—	—	—	—	—	—	—	—
113	Taxes on property	...	...	...	8	5	5	8	5	5	25	27	27
114	Taxes on goods and services	...	...	...	143	150	154	143	150	154	200	204	205
1141	General taxes on goods and services	...	...	...	88	91	95	88	91	95	94	97	102
1142	Excises	...	...	...	43	46	43	43	46	43	45	48	45
115	Taxes on international trade and transactions	...	...	...	—	—	—	—	—	—	—	—	—
116	Other taxes	...	...	...	25	25	25	25	25	25	27	28	27
12	**Social contributions**	**...**	**...**	**...**	**2**	**2**	**2**	**214**	**213**	**217**	**215**	**214**	**219**
121	Social security contributions	...	...	...	—	—	—	211	210	215	211	210	215
122	Other social contributions	...	...	...	2	2	2	3	3	3	4	4	4
13	**Grants**	**...**	**...**	**...**	**...**	**...**	**...**	**...**	**...**	**...**	**...**	**...**	**...**
131	From foreign governments	...	...	...	...	...	...	...	...	...	...	...	...
132	From international organizations	...	...	...	...	...	...	...	...	...	...	...	...
133	From other general government units	...	...	...	11	11	13	5	6	8	—	—	—
1331	Current	...	...	...	7	7	9	1	2	4	—	—	—
1332	Capital	...	...	...	4	4	4	4	4	4	—	—	—
14	**Other revenue**	**...**	**...**	**...**	**...**	**...**	**...**	**...**	**...**	**...**	**...**	**...**	**...**

Italy (136)

In Billions of Euros (EUR) / Fiscal Year Ends December 31st

		Budgetary Central Government			Central Government (excl. Social Security)			Central Government (incl. Social Security)			General Government		
		2013	2014	2015	2013P	2014P	2015P	2013P	2014P	2015P	2013P	2014P	2015P
	Table 2 Expense by economic type												
2	**Expense**	...	...	...	477	483	491	684	690	703	824	832	835
21	**Compensation of employees**	...	...	...	93	94	93	97	97	96	165	164	161
211	Wages and salaries	...	...	...	...	...	...	...	...	...	...	...	...
212	Employers' social contributions	...	...	...	...	...	...	...	...	...	...	...	...
22	**Use of goods and services**	...	...	...	20	19	21	23	21	23	90	88	89
23	**Consumption of fixed capital**	...	...	...	21	21	22	22	22	22	44	44	45
24	**Interest**	...	...	...	75	72	67	75	72	67	78	74	68
25	**Subsidies**	...	...	...	16	18	17	17	19	17	28	30	28
26	**Grants**	...	...	...	...	...	...	...	...	...	...	...	...
261	To foreign governments	...	...	...	...	...	...	...	...	...	...	...	...
262	To international organizations	...	...	...	...	...	...	...	...	...	...	...	...
263	To other general government units	...	...	...	208	206	211	94	92	97	—	—	—
2631	Current	...	...	...	197	201	206	84	87	92	—	—	—
2632	Capital	...	...	...	10	5	5	10	5	5	—	—	—
27	**Social benefits**	...	...	...	5	12	15	318	325	332	363	371	377
271	Social security benefits	...	...	...	...	...	...	...	...	...	...	...	...
272	Social assistance benefits	...	...	...	...	...	...	...	...	...	...	...	...
273	Employment-related social benefits	...	...	...	...	...	...	...	...	...	...	...	...
28	**Other expense**	...	...	...	...	...	...	...	...	...	...	...	...
281	Property expense other than interest	...	...	...	0	0	0	0	0	0	0	0	0
282	Transfers not elsewhere classified	...	...	...	...	...	...	...	...	...	...	...	...
2821	Current	...	...	...	...	...	...	...	...	...	...	...	...
2822	Capital	...	...	...	...	...	...	...	...	...	...	...	...
	Table 3 Transactions in assets and liabilities												
3	**Change in net worth from transactions**	...	...	...	-53	-57	-57	...	...	...	-54	-53	-51
31	**Net/Gross investment in nonfinancial assets**	...	...	...	-9	-4	-7	-9	-5	-7	-9	-7	-7
311	Fixed assets	...	...	...	-5	-4	-7	-6	-5	-7	-6	-7	-8
3111	Buildings and structures	...	...	...	...	...	...	...	...	...	...	...	...
3112	Machinery and equipment	...	...	...	...	...	...	...	...	...	...	...	...
3113	Other fixed assets	...	...	...	...	...	...	...	...	...	...	...	...
3114	Weapons systems	...	...	...	...	...	...	...	...	...	...	...	...
312	Inventories	...	...	...	...	...	...	...	...	...	...	...	...
313	Valuables	...	...	...	...	...	...	...	...	...	...	...	...
314	Nonproduced assets	...	...	...	-3	0	0	-3	0	0	-3	1	0
3141	Land	...	...	...	...	...	...	...	...	...	...	...	...
3142	Mineral and energy resources	...	...	...	...	...	...	...	...	...	...	...	...
3143	Other naturally occurring assets	...	...	...	...	...	...	...	...	...	...	...	...
3144	Intangible nonproduced assets	...	...	...	...	...	...	...	...	...	...	...	...
32	**Net acquisition of financial assets**	...	...	...	41	29	-13	...	...	...	26	21	-12
	By instrument												
3201	Monetary gold and SDRs	...	...	...	—	—	—	...	...	...	—	—	—
3202	Currency and deposits	...	...	...	3	8	-10	...	...	...	1	9	-10
3203	Debt securities	...	...	...	0	0	0	...	...	...	1	1	3
3204	Loans	...	...	...	20	13	-1	...	...	...	7	2	-3
3205	Equity and investment fund shares	...	...	...	8	0	-6	...	...	...	8	1	-5
3206	Insurance, pension, and standardized guarantee schemes	...	...	...	-0	—	-0	...	...	...	-0	-0	-0
3207	Financial derivatives and employee stock options	...	...	...	3	3	3	...	...	...	3	4	3
3208	Other accounts receivable	...	...	...	7	4	1	...	...	...	7	5	-1
	By debtor												
321	Domestic debtors	...	...	...	...	...	...	...	...	...	...	...	...
322	External debtors	...	...	...	...	...	...	...	...	...	...	...	...
33	**Net incurrence of liabilities**	...	...	...	85	81	38	...	...	...	72	67	32
	By instrument												
3301	Special Drawing Rights (SDRs)	...	...	...	—	—	—	...	...	...	—	—	—
3302	Currency and deposits	...	...	...	-2	15	5	...	...	...	-2	15	5
3303	Debt securities	...	...	...	86	66	36	...	...	...	83	65	33
3304	Loans	...	...	...	4	1	3	...	...	...	-1	-7	0

Italy (136)

In Billions of Euros (EUR) / Fiscal Year Ends December 31st

		Budgetary Central Government			Central Government (excl. Social Security)			Central Government (incl. Social Security)			General Government		
		2013	2014	2015	2013P	2014P	2015P	2013P	2014P	2015P	2013P	2014P	2015P
3305	Equity and investment fund shares	...	...	...	—	—	—	...	...	...	—	—	—
3306	Insurance, pension, and standardized guarantee schemes	...	...	...	1	1	1	...	...	...	1	1	1
3307	Financial derivatives and employee stock options	...	...	...	-1	-2	-4	...	...	...	-1	-2	-4
3308	Other accounts payable	...	...	...	-3	1	-3	...	...	...	-9	-4	-4
	By creditor												
331	Domestic creditors	...	...	...	...	...	...	...	...	...	...	...	...
332	External creditors	...	...	...	...	...	...	...	...	...	...	...	...
	Table 4 Holding gains and losses in assets and liabilities												
	Table 5 Holding gains and losses in assets and liabilities												
5	**Change in net worth due to other volume changes**	...	...	...	...	...	...	...	...	...	...	...	...
51	**Other volume changes in nonfinancial assets**	...	...	...	...	...	...	...	...	...	...	...	...
511	Fixed assets	...	...	...	...	...	...	...	...	...	...	...	...
512	Inventories	...	...	...	...	...	...	...	...	...	...	...	...
513	Valuables	...	...	...	...	...	...	...	...	...	...	...	...
514	Nonproduced assets	...	...	...	...	...	...	...	...	...	...	...	...
52	**Other volume changes in financial assets**	...	...	...	—	—	—	...	...	...	0	—	0
	By instrument												
5201	Monetary gold and SDRs	...	...	...	—	—	—	...	...	...	—	—	—
5202	Currency and deposits	...	...	...	—	—	—	...	...	...	—	—	—
5203	Debt securities	...	...	...	—	—	—	...	...	...	—	—	—
5204	Loans	...	...	...	—	—	—	...	...	...	—	—	—
5205	Equity and investment fund shares	...	...	...	—	—	—	...	...	...	—	—	—
5206	Insurance, pension, and standardized guarantee schemes	...	...	...	—	—	—	...	...	...	—	—	—
5207	Financial derivatives and employee stock options	...	...	...	—	—	—	...	...	...	—	—	—
5208	Other accounts receivable	...	...	...	—	—	—	...	...	...	0	—	0
	By debtor												
521	Domestic debtors	...	...	...	—	—	—	...	...	...	...	—	...
522	External debtors	...	...	...	—	—	—	...	...	...	...	—	...
53	**Other volume changes in liabilities**	...	...	...	—	0	-0	...	...	...	0	0	-0
	By instrument												
5301	Special Drawing Rights (SDRs)	...	...	...	—	—	—	...	...	...	—	—	—
5302	Currency and deposits	...	...	...	—	—	—	...	...	...	—	—	—
5303	Debt securities	...	...	...	—	0	-0	...	...	...	—	0	-0
5304	Loans	...	...	...	—	—	—	...	...	...	—	—	—
5305	Equity and investment fund shares	...	...	...	—	—	—	...	...	...	—	—	—
5306	Insurance, pension, and standardized guarantee schemes	...	...	...	—	—	—	...	...	...	—	—	—
5307	Financial derivatives and employee stock options	...	...	...	—	—	—	...	...	...	—	—	—
5308	Other accounts payable	...	...	...	—	—	0	...	...	...	0	—	0
	By creditor												
531	Domestic creditors	...	...	...	—	...	...	...	...	...	...	...	...
532	External creditors	...	...	...	—	...	...	...	...	...	...	...	...
	Table 6 Balance sheet												
6	**Net worth**	...	...	...	...	...	...	...	...	...	...	...	...
61	**Nonfinancial assets**	...	...	...	...	...	...	...	...	...	...	...	...
611	Fixed assets	...	...	...	...	...	...	...	...	...	890	885	878
6111	Buildings and structures	...	...	...	...	...	...	...	...	...	770	765	758
6112	Machinery and equipment	...	...	...	...	...	...	...	...	...	...	...	...
6113	Other fixed assets	...	...	...	...	...	...	...	...	...	46	45	46
6114	Weapons systems	...	...	...	...	...	...	...	...	...	...	...	...
612	Inventories	...	...	...	...	...	...	...	...	...	...	...	...
613	Valuables	...	...	...	...	...	...	...	...	...	...	...	...
614	Nonproduced assets	...	...	...	...	...	...	...	...	...	...	...	...
6141	Land	...	...	...	...	...	...	...	...	...	...	...	...

Italy (136)

In Billions of Euros (EUR) / Fiscal Year Ends December 31st

		Budgetary Central Government			Central Government (excl. Social Security)			Central Government (incl. Social Security)			General Government		
		2013	2014	2015	2013P	2014P	2015P	2013P	2014P	2015P	2013P	2014P	2015P
6142	Mineral and energy resources	...	...	...	...	...	...	...	...	...	...	...	...
6143	Other naturally occurring assets	...	...	...	...	...	...	...	...	...	...	...	...
6144	Intangible nonproduced assets	...	...	...	...	...	...	...	...	...	...	...	...
62	**Financial assets**	...	...	...	**317**	**342**	**335**	...	...	...	**439**	**456**	**447**
	By instrument												
6201	Monetary gold and SDRs	...	...	...	—	—	—	...	...	...	—	—	—
6202	Currency and deposits	...	...	...	49	58	48	...	...	...	76	86	76
6203	Debt securities	...	...	...	1	1	2	...	...	...	27	28	31
6204	Loans	...	...	...	109	122	122	...	...	...	95	96	94
6205	Equity and investment fund shares	...	...	...	105	105	106	...	...	...	125	124	126
6206	Insurance, pension, and standardized guarantee schemes	...	...	...	0	0	0	...	...	...	1	1	1
6207	Financial derivatives and employee stock options	...	...	...	—	—	—	...	...	...	—	—	—
6208	Other accounts receivable	...	...	...	52	56	57	...	...	...	115	120	119
	By debtor												
621	Domestic debtors	...	...	...	...	...	...	...	...	...	...	...	...
622	External debtors	...	...	...	...	...	...	...	...	...	...	...	...
63	**Liabilities**	...	...	...	**2,169**	**2,416**	**2,475**	...	...	...	**2,334**	**2,568**	**2,621**
	By instrument												
6301	Special Drawing Rights (SDRs)	...	...	...	—	—	—	...	...	...	—	—	—
6302	Currency and deposits	...	...	...	220	235	240	...	...	...	220	235	240
6303	Debt securities	...	...	...	1,809	2,028	2,090	...	...	...	1,820	2,038	2,097
6304	Loans	...	...	...	97	97	100	...	...	...	184	177	177
6305	Equity and investment fund shares	...	...	...	—	—	—	...	...	...	—	—	—
6306	Insurance, pension, and standardized guarantee schemes	...	...	...	2	3	4	...	...	...	2	3	4
6307	Financial derivatives and employee stock options	...	...	...	28	39	31	...	...	...	29	41	32
6308	Other accounts payable	...	...	...	12	13	10	...	...	...	79	75	71
	By creditor												
631	Domestic creditors	...	...	...	...	...	...	...	...	...	...	...	...
632	External creditors	...	...	...	...	...	...	...	...	...	...	...	...
	Memorandum items												
6M2	Net financial worth	...	...	...	-1,852	-2,074	-2,140	...	...	...	-1,895	-2,112	-2,174
6M3	Gross debt (D4) at market value	...	...	...	2,141	2,377	2,444	...	...	...	2,305	2,527	2,589
6M3D3	D3 debt liabilities at market value	...	...	...	2,139	2,374	2,440	...	...	...	2,303	2,524	2,585
6M3D2	D2 debt liabilities at market value	...	...	...	2,126	2,361	2,430	...	...	...	2,224	2,449	2,514
6M3D1	D1 debt liabilities at market value	...	...	...	1,906	2,126	2,190	...	...	...	2,004	2,215	2,274
6M4	Gross debt (D4) at nominal value	...	...	...	...	...	...	...	...	...	...	...	...
6M4D3	D3 debt liabilities at nominal value	...	...	...	...	...	...	...	...	...	...	...	...
6M4D2	D2 debt liabilities at nominal value	...	...	...	...	...	...	...	...	...	...	...	...
6M4D1	D1 debt liabilities at nominal value	...	...	...	...	...	...	...	...	...	...	...	...
6M35	Gross debt (D4) at face value	...	...	...	...	...	...	...	...	...	...	...	...
6M35D3	D3 debt liabilities at face value	...	...	...	1,986	2,063	2,099	...	...	...	2,149	2,212	2,244
6M35D2	D2 debt liabilities at face value	...	...	...	1,973	2,049	2,089	...	...	...	2,070	2,137	2,173
6M35D1	D1 debt liabilities at face value	...	...	...	1,815	1,876	1,911	...	...	...	1,912	1,964	1,994
6M93	Government gross debt per national definition	...	...	...	1,973	2,049	2,089	...	...	...	2,070	2,137	2,173
6M5	Arrears	...	...	...	...	...	...	...	...	...	...	...	...
6M6	Explicit contingent liabilities	...	...	...	...	...	...	...	...	...	...	...	...
6M61	of which: Publicly guaranteed debt	...	...	...	...	...	...	...	...	...	...	...	...
6M7	Net implicit obligations for social security benefits	...	...	...	...	...	...	...	...	...	...	...	...
	Table 7 Expenditure by functions of government												
7	**Expenditure**	...	...	...	**468**	**479**	**485**	...	...	...	**816**	**825**	**828**
701	**General public services**	...	...	...	**144**	**129**	**134**	...	...	...	**146**	**145**	**138**
7017	Public debt transactions	...	...	...	76	74	68	...	...	...	80	77	71
7018	Transfers of general character between levels of government	...	...	...	25	14	24	...	...	...	—	—	—
702	**Defense**	...	...	...	**19**	**20**	**20**	...	...	...	**19**	**20**	**20**

Italy (136)

In Billions of Euros (EUR) / Fiscal Year Ends December 31st

		Budgetary Central Government			Central Government (excl. Social Security)			Central Government (incl. Social Security)			General Government		
		2013	2014	2015	2013P	2014P	2015P	2013P	2014P	2015P	2013P	2014P	2015P
703	**Public order and safety**	...	...	...	27	27	27	...	...	...	31	31	31
704	**Economic affairs**	...	...	...	53	58	62	...	...	...	62	67	67
7042	Agriculture, forestry, fishing, and hunting	...	...	...	2	3	2	...	...	...	5	5	4
7043	Fuel and energy	...	...	...	12	14	13	...	...	...	12	14	14
7044	Mining, manufacturing, and construction	...	...	...	4	4	4	...	...	...	7	7	7
7045	Transport	...	...	...	17	16	16	...	...	...	29	27	27
7046	Communication	...	...	...	-2	1	1	...	...	...	-2	1	1
705	**Environmental protection**	...	...	...	2	2	2	...	...	...	15	15	16
706	**Housing and community amenities**	...	...	...	5	3	4	...	...	...	11	10	10
707	**Health**	...	...	...	53	63	57	...	...	...	115	116	117
7072	Outpatient services	...	...	...	0	1	1	...	...	...	43	44	44
7073	Hospital services	...	...	...	0	0	0	...	...	...	52	51	51
7074	Public health services	...	...	...	0	0	0	...	...	...	4	5	5
708	**Recreation, culture and religion**	...	...	...	7	7	8	...	...	...	12	12	12
709	**Education**	...	...	...	53	58	58	...	...	...	66	66	65
7091	Pre-primary and primary education	...	...	...	21	21	22	...	...	...	24	25	25
7092	Secondary education	...	...	...	27	27	27	...	...	...	29	29	29
7094	Tertiary education	...	...	...	4	8	8	...	...	...	6	6	6
710	**Social protection**	...	...	...	105	114	113	...	...	...	338	345	353
7z	Statistical discrepancy: Expenditure	...	...	...	—	—	—	...	...	...	—	—	—
	Table 8 Financial transactions by counterpart sector												
32	**Net acquisition of financial assets**	...	...	...	41	29	-13	...	...	...	26	21	-12
321	Domestic debtors	...	...	...	...	...	...	...	...	...	...	...	...
8211	General government	...	...	...	...	...	...	...	...	...	—	—	—
8212	Central bank	...	...	...	...	...	...	...	...	...	...	...	...
8213	Deposit-taking corporations except the central bank	...	...	...	...	...	...	...	...	...	...	...	...
8214	Other financial corporations	...	...	...	...	...	...	...	...	...	...	...	...
8215	Nonfinancial corporations	...	...	...	...	...	...	...	...	...	...	...	...
8216	Households & nonprofit institutions serving households	...	...	...	...	...	...	...	...	...	...	...	...
322	External debtors	...	...	...	...	...	...	...	...	...	...	...	...
8221	General government	...	...	...	...	...	...	...	...	...	...	...	...
8227	International organizations	...	...	...	...	...	...	...	...	...	...	...	...
8228	Financial corporations other than international organizations	...	...	...	...	...	...	...	...	...	...	...	...
8229	Other nonresidents	...	...	...	...	...	...	...	...	...	...	...	...
33	**Net incurrence of liabilities**	...	...	...	85	81	38	...	...	...	72	67	32
331	Domestic creditors	...	...	...	...	...	...	...	...	...	...	...	...
8311	General government	...	...	...	...	...	...	...	...	...	—	—	—
8312	Central bank	...	...	...	...	...	...	...	...	...	...	...	...
8313	Deposit-taking corporations except the central bank	...	...	...	...	...	...	...	...	...	...	...	...
8314	Other financial corporations	...	...	...	...	...	...	...	...	...	...	...	...
8315	Nonfinancial corporations	...	...	...	...	...	...	...	...	...	...	...	...
8316	Households & nonprofit institutions serving households	...	...	...	...	...	...	...	...	...	...	...	...
332	External creditors	...	...	...	...	...	...	...	...	...	...	...	...
8321	General government	...	...	...	...	...	...	...	...	...	...	...	...
8327	International organizations	...	...	...	...	...	...	...	...	...	...	...	...
8328	Financial corporations other than international organizations	...	...	...	...	...	...	...	...	...	...	...	...
8329	Other nonresidents	...	...	...	...	...	...	...	...	...	...	...	...
	Table 9 Total other economic flows in assets and liabilities												
9	**Change in net worth due to other economic flows**	...	...	...	...	...	...	...	...	...	...	...	...

Italy (136)

In Billions of Euros (EUR) / Fiscal Year Ends December 31st

		Budgetary Central Government			Central Government (excl. Social Security)			Central Government (incl. Social Security)			General Government		
		2013	2014	2015	2013P	2014P	2015P	2013P	2014P	2015P	2013P	2014P	2015P
91	**Other economic flows in nonfinancial assets**	...	...	...	...	...	...	...	...	...	...	...	...
911	Fixed assets	...	...	...	...	...	...	...	...	...	...	...	...
912	Inventories	...	...	...	...	...	...	...	...	...	...	...	...
913	Valuables	...	...	...	...	...	...	...	...	...	...	...	...
914	Nonproduced assets	...	...	...	...	...	...	...	...	...	...	...	...
92	**Other economic flows in financial assets**	...	...	...	**-16**	**-4**	**5**	...	...	...	**-17**	**-5**	**4**
	By instrument												
9201	Monetary gold and SDRs	...	...	...	—	—	—	...	...	...	—	—	—
9202	Currency and deposits	...	...	...	0	0	0	...	...	...	-1	0	0
9203	Debt securities	...	...	...	0	-0	0	...	...	...	0	-0	0
9204	Loans	...	...	...	0	0	0	...	...	...	0	0	0
9205	Equity and investment fund shares	...	...	...	-13	-1	7	...	...	...	-13	-1	6
9206	Insurance, pension, and standardized guarantee schemes	...	...	...	—	-0	0	...	...	...	-0	0	-0
9207	Financial derivatives and employee stock options	...	...	...	-3	-3	-3	...	...	...	-3	-4	-3
9208	Other accounts receivable	...	...	...	—	—	—	...	...	...	—	-0	0
	By debtor												
921	Domestic debtors	...	...	...	...	...	...	...	...	...	...	...	...
922	External debtors	...	...	...	...	...	...	...	...	...	...	...	...
93	**Other economic flows in liabilities**	...	...	...	**31**	**166**	**20**	...	...	...	**31**	**166**	**22**
	By instrument												
9301	Special Drawing Rights (SDRs)	...	...	...	—	—	—	...	...	...	—	—	—
9302	Currency and deposits	...	...	...	0	—	—	...	...	...	0	—	—
9303	Debt securities	...	...	...	35	153	25	...	...	...	35	153	27
9304	Loans	...	...	...	0	—	0	...	...	...	0	-0	—
9305	Equity and investment fund shares	...	...	...	—	—	—	...	...	...	—	—	—
9306	Insurance, pension, and standardized guarantee schemes	...	...	...	—	0	-0	...	...	...	—	0	-0
9307	Financial derivatives and employee stock options	...	...	...	-4	13	-5	...	...	...	-5	14	-5
9308	Other accounts payable	...	...	...	—	—	0	...	...	...	0	—	0
	By creditor												
931	Domestic creditors	...	...	...	...	...	...	...	...	...	...	...	...
932	External creditors	...	...	...	...	...	...	...	...	...	...	...	...
	Memorandum items												
9M2	Change in net financial worth due to other economic flows	...	...	...	-46	-170	-15	...	...	...	-47	-171	-18
9M3	Gross debt (D4) at market value: other economic flows	...	...	...	35	153	25	...	...	...	35	153	27
9M3D3	D3 debt liabilities at market value: other economic flows	...	...	...	35	153	25	...	...	...	35	153	27
9M3D2	D2 debt liabilities at market value: other economic flows	...	...	...	35	153	25	...	...	...	35	153	27
9M3D1	D1 debt liabilities at market value: other economic flows	...	...	...	35	153	25	...	...	...	35	153	27

Jamaica (343)

In Billions of Jamaican Dollars (JMD) / Fiscal Year Ends March 31st

		Budgetary Central Government			Central Government (excl. Social Security)			Central Government (incl. Social Security)			General Government		
		2013P	2014P	2015P	2013P	2014P	2015P	2013P	2014P	2015P	2013P	2014P	2015P
	Statement of operations												
1	Revenue	396	412	456	456	483	529	475	504	551	475	504	551
2	Expense	391	396	427	423	444	481	441	463	500	441	463	500
GOB	**Gross operating balance**	**5**	**16**	**29**	**33**	**40**	**49**	**33**	**41**	**50**	**33**	**41**	**50**
NOB	**Net operating balance**	...	...	...	...	...	...	...	...	...	...	...	...
31	Net/Gross investment in nonfinancial assets	22	23	35	22	45	60	22	45	60	22	45	60
2M	Expenditure	413	419	461	445	489	541	463	508	561	463	508	561
NLB	**Net lending (+) / Net borrowing (-)**	**-17**	**-7**	**-6**	**11**	**-6**	**-12**	**12**	**-5**	**-10**	**12**	**-5**	**-10**
32	Net acquisition of financial assets	-8	72	-45	15	82	-25	14	...	...	14	...	...
33	Net incurrence of liabilities	-13	...	...	...	...	...	...	...	...	...	...	...
NLBz	Statistical discrepancy	22	...	...	...	...	...	...	...	...	...	...	...
	Memorandum items												
PB	Primary net lending / net borrowing	93	117	120	123	126	122	123	127	123	123	127	123
GB	Government balance per national definition	...	...	...	...	...	...	...	...	...	...	...	...
	Statement of other economic flows												
	Balance sheet												
	Table 1 Revenue												
1	**Revenue**	**396**	**412**	**456**	**456**	**483**	**529**	**475**	**504**	**551**	**475**	**504**	**551**
11	**Taxes**	**344**	**371**	**412**	**381**	**406**	**446**	**381**	**406**	**446**	**381**	**406**	**446**
111	Taxes on income, profits, and capital gains	131	141	153	131	164	175	131	164	175	131	164	175
1111	Payable by individuals	96	91	96	96	...	...	96	...	...	96	...	...
1112	Payable by corporations and other enterprises	35	50	57	35	...	...	35	...	...	35	...	...
1113	Other taxes on income, profits, and capital gains	—	—	—	—	...	...	—	...	...	—	...	...
112	Taxes on payroll and workforce	—	—	—	27	—	—	27	—	—	27	—	—
113	Taxes on property	—	—	—	5	—	—	5	—	—	5	—	—
114	Taxes on goods and services	168	92	102	172	98	108	172	98	108	172	98	108
1141	General taxes on goods and services	122	64	73	122	64	73	122	64	73	122	64	73
1142	Excises	38	10	14	40	13	17	40	13	17	40	13	17
115	Taxes on international trade and transactions	35	127	147	35	132	152	35	132	152	35	132	152
116	Other taxes	11	11	10	11	11	11	11	11	11	11	11	11
12	**Social contributions**	—	—	—	—	—	—	**14**	**16**	**16**	**14**	**16**	**16**
121	Social security contributions	—	—	—	—	—	—	14	16	16	14	16	16
122	Other social contributions	—	—	—	—	—	—	—	—	—	—	—	—
13	**Grants**	**10**	**5**	**5**	**12**	**17**	**21**	**12**	**17**	**21**	**12**	**17**	**21**
131	From foreign governments	...	5	5	...	5	5	...	5	5	...	5	5
132	From international organizations	—	—	—	—	—	—	—	—	—	—	—	—
133	From other general government units	...	—	—	...	12	15	...	12	15	...	12	15
1331	Current	...	—	—	...	...	...	...	...	...	...	...	...
1332	Capital	...	—	—	...	...	...	...	...	...	...	...	...
14	**Other revenue**	**42**	**36**	**39**	**63**	**61**	**63**	**68**	**65**	**68**	**68**	**65**	**68**
	Table 2 Expense by economic type												
2	**Expense**	**391**	**396**	**427**	**423**	**444**	**481**	**441**	**463**	**500**	**441**	**463**	**500**
21	**Compensation of employees**	**170**	**170**	**182**	**181**	**178**	**192**	**181**	**178**	**192**	**181**	**178**	**192**
211	Wages and salaries	...	...	...	...	...	...	...	...	...	...	...	...
212	Employers' social contributions	...	...	...	...	...	...	...	...	...	...	...	...
22	**Use of goods and services**	**38**	**37**	**52**	**53**	**45**	**62**	**53**	**45**	**62**	**53**	**45**	**62**
23	**Consumption of fixed capital**	...	...	...	...	...	...	...	...	...	...	...	...
24	**Interest**	**110**	**125**	**126**	**111**	**132**	**133**	**111**	**132**	**133**	**111**	**132**	**133**
25	**Subsidies**	1	—	—	1	—	—	1	—	—	1	—	—
26	**Grants**	**—**	**31**	**31**	**—**	**47**	**49**	**3**	**51**	**52**	**3**	**51**	**52**
261	To foreign governments	—	...	...	—	...	...	—	...	...	—	...	...
262	To international organizations	—	...	...	—	...	...	—	...	...	—	...	...
263	To other general government units	—	...	...	—	...	...	3	...	...	3	...	...
2631	Current	—	...	...	—	...	...	3	...	...	3	...	...
2632	Capital	—	...	...	—	...	...	—	...	...	—	...	...

Jamaica (343)

In Billions of Jamaican Dollars (JMD) / Fiscal Year Ends March 31st

		Budgetary Central Government			Central Government (excl. Social Security)			Central Government (incl. Social Security)			General Government		
		2013P	2014P	2015P	2013P	2014P	2015P	2013P	2014P	2015P	2013P	2014P	2015P
27	**Social benefits**	**25**	**33**	**35**	**25**	**37**	**40**	**40**	**52**	**55**	**40**	**52**	**55**
271	Social security benefits	—	—	—	—	...	...	15	...	...	15	...	...
272	Social assistance benefits	—	7	7	—	...	...	—	...	...	—	...	...
273	Employment-related social benefits	25	26	28	25	...	...	25	...	...	25	...	...
28	**Other expense**	**48**	**—**	**0**	**51**	**3**	**4**	**52**	**4**	**5**	**52**	**4**	**5**
281	Property expense other than interest	—	—	—	—	—	—	—	—	—	—	—	—
282	Transfers not elsewhere classified	48	—	0	51	3	4	52	4	5	52	4	5
2821	Current	29	—	0	32	...	...	33	...	...	33	...	...
2822	Capital	19	—	—	20	...	...	20	...	...	20	...	...
	Table 3 Transactions in assets and liabilities												
3	**Change in net worth from transactions**	...	...	...	...	...	...	...	...	...	...	...	...
31	**Net/Gross investment in nonfinancial assets**	**22**	**23**	**35**	**22**	**45**	**60**	**22**	**45**	**60**	**22**	**45**	**60**
311	Fixed assets	22	23	35	22	45	61	22	45	61	22	45	61
3111	Buildings and structures	...	...	...	...	...	...	...	...	...	...	...	...
3112	Machinery and equipment	...	...	...	...	...	...	...	...	...	...	...	...
3113	Other fixed assets	...	...	...	...	...	...	...	...	...	...	...	...
3114	Weapons systems	...	...	...	...	...	...	...	...	...	...	...	...
312	Inventories	—	—	—	-0	-0	-0	-0	-0	-0	-0	-0	-0
313	Valuables	—	—	—	—	—	—	—	—	—	—	—	—
314	Nonproduced assets	—	—	—	—	—	—	—	—	—	—	—	—
3141	Land	—	—	—	—	—	—	—	—	—	—	—	—
3142	Mineral and energy resources	—	—	—	—	—	—	—	—	—	—	—	—
3143	Other naturally occurring assets	—	—	—	—	—	—	—	—	—	—	—	—
3144	Intangible nonproduced assets	—	—	—	—	—	—	—	—	—	—	—	—
32	**Net acquisition of financial assets**	**-8**	**72**	**-45**	**15**	**82**	**-25**	**14**	**...**	**...**	**14**	**...**	**...**
	By instrument												
3201	Monetary gold and SDRs	—	—	—	—	—	—	—	...	...	—	...	...
3202	Currency and deposits	-8	72	-45	-1	73	-42	-1	...	...	-1	...	...
3203	Debt securities	—	—	—	8	—	—	8	...	...	8	...	...
3204	Loans	—	—	—	23	9	9	23	...	...	23	...	...
3205	Equity and investment fund shares	—	—	—	—	—	—	—	...	...	—	...	...
3206	Insurance, pension, and standardized guarantee schemes	—	—	—	—	—	—	—	...	...	—	...	...
3207	Financial derivatives and employee stock options	—	—	—	—	—	—	—	...	...	—	...	...
3208	Other accounts receivable	...	...	...	...	...	...	...	...	...	...	...	...
	By debtor												
321	Domestic debtors	-8	...	...	15	...	...	14	...	...	14	...	...
322	External debtors	—	...	...	—	...	...	—	...	...	—	...	...
33	**Net incurrence of liabilities**	**-13**	**...**	**...**	**...**	**...**	**...**	**...**	**...**	**...**	**...**	**...**	**...**
	By instrument												
3301	Special Drawing Rights (SDRs)	—	...	...	...	...	...	...	...	...	...	...	...
3302	Currency and deposits	—	...	...	...	...	...	...	...	...	...	...	...
3303	Debt securities	—	...	...	...	...	...	...	...	...	...	...	...
3304	Loans	-13	...	...	...	...	...	...	...	...	...	...	...
3305	Equity and investment fund shares	—	...	...	...	...	...	...	...	...	...	...	...
3306	Insurance, pension, and standardized guarantee schemes	—	...	...	...	...	...	...	...	...	...	...	...
3307	Financial derivatives and employee stock options	—	...	...	...	...	...	...	...	...	...	...	...
3308	Other accounts payable	...	...	...	...	...	...	...	...	...	...	...	...
	By creditor												
331	Domestic creditors	-53	...	...	...	...	...	...	...	...	...	...	...
332	External creditors	40	...	...	...	...	...	...	...	...	...	...	...
	Table 4 Holding gains and losses in assets and liabilities												
	Table 5 Holding gains and losses in assets and liabilities												
	Table 6 Balance sheet												

Jamaica (343)

In Billions of Jamaican Dollars (JMD) / Fiscal Year Ends March 31st

		Budgetary Central Government			Central Government (excl. Social Security)			Central Government (incl. Social Security)			General Government		
		2013P	2014P	2015P	2013P	2014P	2015P	2013P	2014P	2015P	2013P	2014P	2015P
	Table 7 Expenditure by functions of government												
7	**Expenditure**	**413**	**449**	**481**	**445**	**489**	**541**	**463**	**508**	**561**	**463**	**508**	**561**
701	**General public services**	**169**	**190**	**219**	**...**	**...**	**...**	**...**	**...**	**...**	**...**	**...**	**...**
7017	Public debt transactions	110	125	126	111	132	133	111	132	133	111	132	133
7018	Transfers of general character between levels of government	...	...	...	...	...	...	...	...	...	...	...	...
702	**Defense**	**13**	**14**	**14**	**...**	**...**	**...**	**...**	**...**	**...**	**...**	**...**	**...**
703	**Public order and safety**	**44**	**47**	**48**	**...**	**...**	**...**	**...**	**...**	**...**	**...**	**...**	**...**
704	**Economic affairs**	**36**	**40**	**36**	**...**	**...**	**...**	**...**	**...**	**...**	**...**	**...**	**...**
7042	Agriculture, forestry, fishing, and hunting	—	10	11	...	...	...	...	...	...	...	...	...
7043	Fuel and energy	1	1	1	...	...	...	...	...	...	...	...	...
7044	Mining, manufacturing, and construction	0	0	0	...	...	...	...	...	...	...	...	...
7045	Transport	15	17	12	...	...	...	...	...	...	...	...	...
7046	Communication	2	4	3	...	...	...	...	...	...	...	...	...
705	**Environmental protection**	**2**	**2**	**2**	**...**	**...**	**...**	**...**	**...**	**...**	**...**	**...**	**...**
706	**Housing and community amenities**	**9**	**10**	**9**	**...**	**...**	**...**	**...**	**...**	**...**	**...**	**...**	**...**
707	**Health**	**41**	**45**	**53**	**...**	**...**	**...**	**...**	**...**	**...**	**...**	**...**	**...**
7072	Outpatient services	...	...	...	...	...	...	...	...	...	...	...	...
7073	Hospital services	...	...	...	...	...	...	...	...	...	...	...	...
7074	Public health services	...	...	...	...	...	...	...	...	...	...	...	...
708	**Recreation, culture and religion**	**3**	**4**	**4**	**...**	**...**	**...**	**...**	**...**	**...**	**...**	**...**	**...**
709	**Education**	**87**	**86**	**85**	**...**	**...**	**...**	**...**	**...**	**...**	**...**	**...**	**...**
7091	Pre-primary and primary education	...	...	...	...	...	...	...	...	...	...	...	...
7092	Secondary education	...	...	...	...	...	...	...	...	...	...	...	...
7094	Tertiary education	...	...	...	...	...	...	...	...	...	...	...	...
710	**Social protection**	**9**	**11**	**11**	**...**	**...**	**...**	**...**	**...**	**...**	**...**	**...**	**...**
7z	Statistical discrepancy: Expenditure	...	...	...	...	...	...	...	...	...	...	...	...
	Table 8 Financial transactions by counterpart sector												
	Table 9 Total other economic flows in assets and liabilities												

Japan (158)

In Billions of Japanese Yen (JPY) / Fiscal Year Ends March 31st

		Budgetary Central Government			Central Government (excl. Social Security)			Central Government (incl. Social Security)			General Government		
		2012	2013	2014	2012	2013	2014	2012	2013	2014	2012	2013	2014
	Statement of operations												
1	Revenue	...	...	...	54,419	59,118	65,478	...	...	...	227,345	236,666	249,151
2	Expense	...	...	...	90,907	92,737	91,661	...	...	...	266,463	269,288	270,956
GOB	**Gross operating balance**	...	...	...	**-33,130**	**-29,945**	**-22,838**	...	...	...	**-24,823**	**-18,123**	**-7,019**
NOB	**Net operating balance**	...	...	...	**-36,488**	**-33,618**	**-26,184**	...	...	...	**-39,118**	**-32,622**	**-21,805**
31	Net/Gross investment in nonfinancial assets	...	...	...	433	1,159	773	...	...	...	1,871	4,189	3,620
2M	Expenditure	...	...	...	91,340	93,895	92,435	...	...	...	268,334	273,477	274,576
NLB	**Net lending (+) / Net borrowing (-)**	...	...	...	**-36,921**	**-34,777**	**-26,957**	...	...	...	**-40,989**	**-36,811**	**-25,425**
32	Net acquisition of financial assets	...	...	...	-173	7,342	6,744	...	...	...	-3,610	3,944	11,042
33	Net incurrence of liabilities	...	...	...	33,504	38,350	33,149	...	...	...	33,734	38,109	33,974
NLBz	Statistical discrepancy	...	...	...	3,244	3,770	552	...	...	...	3,645	2,646	2,493
	Memorandum items												
PB	Primary net lending / net borrowing	...	...	...	-28,454	-26,232	-18,334	...	...	...	-29,693	-25,595	-14,317
GB	Government balance per national definition	...	...	...	...	...	...	...	...	...	...	...	...
	Statement of other economic flows												
	Balance sheet												
6	**Net worth**	...	...	...	...	...	...	...	...	...	**-41,923**	**-5,908**	**-13,502**
61	Nonfinancial assets	...	...	...	...	...	...	...	...	...	572,244	589,256	601,171
62	Financial assets	...	...	...	235,067	273,133	280,632	...	...	...	515,119	576,088	598,191
63	Liabilities	...	...	...	929,198	969,643	1,010,154	...	...	...	1,129,286	1,171,251	1,212,863
	Table 1 Revenue												
1	**Revenue**	...	...	...	**54,419**	**59,118**	**65,478**	...	...	...	**227,345**	**236,666**	**249,151**
11	**Taxes**	...	...	...	**47,924**	**52,132**	**58,938**	...	...	...	**82,610**	**87,774**	**95,995**
111	Taxes on income, profits, and capital gains	...	...	...	25,010	28,157	29,375	...	...	...	38,782	42,350	44,138
1111	Payable by individuals	...	...	...	12,867	14,283	15,384	...	...	...	24,140	25,944	27,209
1112	Payable by corporations and other enterprises	...	...	...	12,144	13,874	13,991	...	...	...	14,528	16,292	16,817
1113	Other taxes on income, profits, and capital gains	...	...	...	—	—	—	...	...	...	114	114	111
112	Taxes on payroll and workforce	...	...	...	—	—	—	...	...	...	—	—	—
113	Taxes on property	...	...	...	1,504	1,574	1,883	...	...	...	11,257	11,415	11,863
114	Taxes on goods and services	...	...	...	20,513	21,366	26,606	...	...	...	30,859	32,151	38,035
1141	General taxes on goods and services	...	...	...	11,428	11,955	17,064	...	...	...	14,310	14,958	20,539
1142	Excises	...	...	...	6,407	6,434	6,179	...	...	...	8,698	8,711	8,295
115	Taxes on international trade and transactions	...	...	...	897	1,034	1,073	...	...	...	897	1,034	1,073
116	Other taxes	...	...	...	—	—	—	...	...	...	815	824	887
12	**Social contributions**	...	...	...	**546**	**531**	**508**	...	...	...	**61,167**	**62,663**	**64,879**
121	Social security contributions	...	...	...	—	—	—	...	...	...	58,068	59,800	62,232
122	Other social contributions	...	...	...	546	531	508	...	...	...	3,098	2,864	2,647
13	**Grants**	...	...	...	**1,238**	**1,107**	**982**	...	...	...	**69,065**	**70,038**	**69,808**
131	From foreign governments	...	...	...	0	1	1	...	...	...	0	1	1
132	From international organizations	...	...	...	—	—	0	...	...	...	—	—	0
133	From other general government units	...	...	...	1,237	1,106	981	...	...	...	69,064	70,037	69,807
1331	Current	...	...	...	343	369	285	...	...	...	60,928	61,436	62,770
1332	Capital	...	...	...	894	737	697	...	...	...	8,137	8,601	7,037
14	**Other revenue**	...	...	...	**4,712**	**5,349**	**5,050**	...	...	...	**14,503**	**16,191**	**18,468**
	Table 2 Expense by economic type												
2	**Expense**	...	...	...	**90,907**	**92,737**	**91,661**	...	...	...	**266,463**	**269,288**	**270,956**
21	**Compensation of employees**	...	...	...	**5,771**	**5,722**	**6,199**	...	...	...	**29,089**	**28,366**	**29,347**
211	Wages and salaries	...	...	...	...	...	...	...	...	...	...	...	...
212	Employers' social contributions	...	...	...	...	...	...	...	...	...	...	...	...
22	**Use of goods and services**	...	...	...	**6,069**	**6,658**	**6,882**	...	...	...	**18,201**	**19,194**	**19,574**
23	**Consumption of fixed capital**	...	...	...	**3,358**	**3,673**	**3,346**	...	...	...	**14,296**	**14,499**	**14,786**
24	**Interest**	...	...	...	**8,467**	**8,545**	**8,623**	...	...	...	**11,296**	**11,216**	**11,108**
25	**Subsidies**	...	...	...	**901**	**825**	**777**	...	...	...	**3,030**	**2,967**	**2,854**

Japan (158)

In Billions of Japanese Yen (JPY) / Fiscal Year Ends March 31st

		Budgetary Central Government			Central Government (excl. Social Security)			Central Government (incl. Social Security)			General Government		
		2012	2013	2014	2012	2013	2014	2012	2013	2014	2012	2013	2014
26	**Grants**	...	...	...	**59,782**	**61,076**	**60,581**	...	...	...	**69,762**	**70,887**	**70,435**
261	To foreign governments	...	...	...	360	456	214	...	...	...	360	456	214
262	To international organizations	...	...	...	337	394	414	...	...	...	337	394	414
263	To other general government units	...	...	...	59,084	60,226	59,953	...	...	...	69,064	70,037	69,807
2631	Current	...	...	...	51,847	52,365	53,616	...	...	...	60,928	61,436	62,770
2632	Capital	...	...	...	7,237	7,861	6,337	...	...	...	8,137	8,601	7,037
27	**Social benefits**	...	...	...	**1,298**	**1,216**	**1,108**	...	...	...	**108,436**	**109,652**	**110,874**
271	Social security benefits	...	...	...	—	—	—	...	...	...	95,771	97,170	98,013
272	Social assistance benefits	...	...	...	753	685	600	...	...	...	9,567	9,618	10,214
273	Employment-related social benefits	...	...	...	546	531	508	...	...	...	3,098	2,864	2,647
28	**Other expense**	...	...	...	**5,261**	**5,022**	**4,146**	...	...	...	**12,353**	**12,508**	**11,978**
281	Property expense other than interest	...	...	...	113	112	115	...	...	...	353	348	353
282	Transfers not elsewhere classified	...	...	...	5,148	4,910	4,031	...	...	...	12,000	12,160	11,625
2821	Current	...	...	...	2,111	2,132	2,232	...	...	...	6,739	6,848	7,039
2822	Capital	...	...	...	3,037	2,778	1,799	...	...	...	5,260	5,312	4,586
	Table 3 Transactions in assets and liabilities												
3	**Change in net worth from transactions**	...	...	...	**-33,244**	**-29,849**	**-25,632**	...	...	...	**-35,473**	**-29,976**	**-19,312**
31	**Net/Gross investment in nonfinancial assets**	...	...	...	**433**	**1,159**	**773**	...	...	...	**1,871**	**4,189**	**3,620**
311	Fixed assets	...	...	...	142	776	403	...	...	...	533	2,712	2,276
3111	Buildings and structures	...	...	...	—	...	...	...	...	...	...	...	...
3112	Machinery and equipment	...	...	...	—	...	...	...	...	...	...	...	...
3113	Other fixed assets	...	...	...	—	...	...	...	...	...	...	...	...
3114	Weapons systems	...	...	...	...	...	...	...	...	...	...	...	...
312	Inventories	...	...	...	-18	24	83	...	...	...	-18	24	83
313	Valuables	...	...	...	—	—	—	...	...	...	—	—	—
314	Nonproduced assets	...	...	...	309	359	287	...	...	...	1,356	1,454	1,261
3141	Land	...	...	...	309	359	287	...	...	...	1,356	1,454	1,261
3142	Mineral and energy resources	...	...	...	—	—	—	...	...	...	—	—	—
3143	Other naturally occurring assets	...	...	...	—	—	—	...	...	...	—	—	—
3144	Intangible nonproduced assets	...	...	...	—	—	—	...	...	...	—	—	—
32	**Net acquisition of financial assets**	...	...	...	**-173**	**7,342**	**6,744**	...	...	...	**-3,610**	**3,944**	**11,042**
	By instrument												
3201	Monetary gold and SDRs	...	...	...	—	—	—	...	...	...	—	—	—
3202	Currency and deposits	...	...	...	-2,260	-3,200	2,624	...	...	...	1,271	-1,844	9,552
3203	Debt securities	...	...	...	789	4,400	-165	...	...	...	-111	1,378	-13,611
3204	Loans	...	...	...	1,674	947	7,314	...	...	...	-67	-375	6,811
3205	Equity and investment fund shares	...	...	...	-171	253	282	...	...	...	-1,092	-57	3,445
3206	Insurance, pension, and standardized guarantee schemes	...	...	...	—	—	—	...	...	...	—	—	—
3207	Financial derivatives and employee stock options	...	...	...	—	—	—	...	...	...	—	—	—
3208	Other accounts receivable	...	...	...	-205	4,943	-3,310	...	...	...	-3,611	4,842	4,845
	By debtor												
321	Domestic debtors	...	...	...	...	...	...	...	...	...	...	...	...
322	External debtors	...	...	...	...	...	...	...	...	...	...	...	...
33	**Net incurrence of liabilities**	...	...	...	**33,504**	**38,350**	**33,149**	...	...	...	**33,734**	**38,109**	**33,974**
	By instrument												
3301	Special Drawing Rights (SDRs)	...	...	...	—	—	—	...	...	...	—	—	—
3302	Currency and deposits	...	...	...	—	—	—	...	...	...	—	—	—
3303	Debt securities	...	...	...	33,543	38,865	30,975	...	...	...	35,164	39,490	31,321
3304	Loans	...	...	...	1,093	643	-640	...	...	...	-282	56	-570
3305	Equity and investment fund shares	...	...	...	235	-104	-94	...	...	...	397	-66	24
3306	Insurance, pension, and standardized guarantee schemes	...	...	...	—	—	—	...	...	...	—	—	—
3307	Financial derivatives and employee stock options	...	...	...	—	—	—	...	...	...	—	—	—
3308	Other accounts payable	...	...	...	-1,367	-1,054	2,909	...	...	...	-1,546	-1,371	3,198

Japan (158)

In Billions of Japanese Yen (JPY) / Fiscal Year Ends March 31st

		Budgetary Central Government			Central Government (excl. Social Security)			Central Government (incl. Social Security)			General Government		
		2012	2013	2014	2012	2013	2014	2012	2013	2014	2012	2013	2014
	By creditor												
331	Domestic creditors	...	...	...	...	...	...	...	...	...	...	...	...
332	External creditors	...	...	...	...	...	...	...	...	...	...	...	...
	Table 4 Holding gains and losses in assets and liabilities												
	Table 5 Holding gains and losses in assets and liabilities												
	Table 6 Balance sheet												
6	**Net worth**	...	...	...	...	...	...	...	...	...	**-41,923**	**-5,908**	**-13,502**
61	**Nonfinancial assets**	...	...	...	...	...	...	...	...	...	**572,244**	**589,256**	**601,171**
611	Fixed assets	...	...	...	...	...	...	...	...	...	451,190	469,287	482,509
6111	Buildings and structures	...	...	...	...	...	...	...	...	...	440,343	458,542	471,713
6112	Machinery and equipment	...	...	...	...	...	...	...	...	...	9,202	9,078	9,039
6113	Other fixed assets	...	...	...	...	...	...	...	...	...	1,644	1,667	1,758
6114	Weapons systems	...	...	...	...	...	...	...	...	...	—	—	—
612	Inventories	...	...	...	...	...	...	...	...	...	2,288	2,636	1,982
613	Valuables	...	...	...	...	...	...	...	...	...	—	—	—
614	Nonproduced assets	...	...	...	23,860	23,594	23,568	...	...	...	118,767	117,333	116,679
6141	Land	...	...	...	23,860	23,594	23,568	...	...	...	118,767	117,333	116,679
6142	Mineral and energy resources	...	...	...	—	—	—	...	...	...	—	—	—
6143	Other naturally occurring assets	...	...	...	—	—	—	...	...	...	—	—	—
6144	Intangible nonproduced assets	...	...	...	—	—	—	...	...	...	—	—	—
62	**Financial assets**	...	...	...	**235,067**	**273,133**	**280,632**	...	...	...	**515,119**	**576,088**	**598,191**
	By instrument												
6201	Monetary gold and SDRs	...	...	...	3,062	3,759	3,862	...	...	...	3,062	3,759	3,862
6202	Currency and deposits	...	...	...	21,647	20,811	24,849	...	...	...	76,103	78,668	93,950
6203	Debt securities	...	...	...	23,704	13,292	855	...	...	...	122,683	114,831	89,796
6204	Loans	...	...	...	19,417	22,522	18,739	...	...	...	33,859	35,574	30,944
6205	Equity and investment fund shares	...	...	...	55,658	76,956	78,248	...	...	...	120,630	153,652	160,329
6206	Insurance, pension, and standardized guarantee schemes	...	...	...	—	—	—	...	...	...	—	—	—
6207	Financial derivatives and employee stock options	...	...	...	—	461	47	...	...	...	—	461	47
6208	Other accounts receivable	...	...	...	111,580	135,331	154,033	...	...	...	158,782	189,142	219,264
	By debtor												
621	Domestic debtors	...	...	...	...	...	...	...	...	...	...	...	...
622	External debtors	...	...	...	...	...	...	...	...	...	...	...	...
63	**Liabilities**	...	...	...	**929,198**	**969,643**	**1,010,154**	...	...	...	**1,129,286**	**1,171,251**	**1,212,863**
	By instrument												
6301	Special Drawing Rights (SDRs)	...	...	...	1,630	1,994	2,133	...	...	...	1,630	1,994	2,133
6302	Currency and deposits	...	...	...	—	—	—	...	...	...	—	—	—
6303	Debt securities	...	...	...	843,707	880,419	920,280	...	...	...	915,584	953,256	994,365
6304	Loans	...	...	...	54,295	54,869	54,805	...	...	...	163,249	164,238	163,836
6305	Equity and investment fund shares	...	...	...	13,229	13,141	13,068	...	...	...	24,365	24,316	24,361
6306	Insurance, pension, and standardized guarantee schemes	...	...	...	—	—	—	...	...	...	—	—	—
6307	Financial derivatives and employee stock options	...	...	...	58	54	43	...	...	...	58	54	43
6308	Other accounts payable	...	...	...	16,280	19,167	19,825	...	...	...	24,401	27,395	28,125
	By creditor												
631	Domestic creditors	...	...	...	...	...	...	...	...	...	...	...	...
632	External creditors	...	...	...	...	...	...	...	...	...	...	...	...
	Memorandum items												
6M2	Net financial worth	...	...	...	-694,131	-696,510	-729,523	...	...	...	-614,167	-595,164	-614,672
6M3	Gross debt (D4) at market value	...	...	...	915,912	956,448	997,043	...	...	...	1,104,864	1,146,882	1,188,459
6M3D3	D3 debt liabilities at market value	...	...	...	915,912	956,448	997,043	...	...	...	1,104,864	1,146,882	1,188,459
6M3D2	D2 debt liabilities at market value	...	...	...	899,632	937,282	977,219	...	...	...	1,080,462	1,119,487	1,160,335
6M3D1	D1 debt liabilities at market value	...	...	...	898,002	935,288	975,086	...	...	...	1,078,833	1,117,493	1,158,202
6M4	Gross debt (D4) at nominal value	...	...	...	...	...	...	...	...	...	...	...	...
6M4D3	D3 debt liabilities at nominal value	...	...	...	...	...	...	...	...	...	...	...	...
6M4D2	D2 debt liabilities at nominal value	...	...	...	...	...	...	...	...	...	...	...	...
6M4D1	D1 debt liabilities at nominal value	...	...	...	...	...	...	...	...	...	...	...	...

Japan (158)

In Billions of Japanese Yen (JPY) / Fiscal Year Ends March 31st

		Budgetary Central Government			Central Government (excl. Social Security)			Central Government (incl. Social Security)			General Government		
		2012	2013	2014	2012	2013	2014	2012	2013	2014	2012	2013	2014
6M35	Gross debt (D4) at face value	...	...	...	...	...	...	...	...	...	...	...	...
6M35D3	D3 debt liabilities at face value	...	...	...	...	...	...	...	...	...	...	...	...
6M35D2	D2 debt liabilities at face value	...	...	...	...	...	...	...	...	...	...	...	...
6M35D1	D1 debt liabilities at face value	...	...	...	...	...	...	...	...	...	...	...	...
6M93	Government gross debt per national definition	...	...	...	...	...	...	...	...	...	...	...	...
6M5	Arrears	...	...	...	...	...	...	...	...	...	...	...	...
6M6	Explicit contingent liabilities	...	...	...	...	...	...	...	...	...	...	...	...
6M61	of which: Publicly guaranteed debt	...	...	...	...	...	...	...	...	...	...	...	...
6M7	Net implicit obligations for social security benefits	...	...	...	...	...	...	...	...	...	...	...	...
	Table 7 Expenditure by functions of government												
7	**Expenditure**	...	...	...	91,340	93,895	92,435	...	...	...	268,333	273,477	274,576
701	**General public services**	...	...	...	...	...	...	...	...	...	21,037	21,518	21,221
7017	Public debt transactions	...	...	...	8,467	8,545	8,623	...	...	...	11,329	11,264	11,154
7018	Transfers of general character between levels of government	...	...	...	...	...	...	...	...	...	...	...	...
702	**Defense**	...	...	...	...	...	...	...	...	...	4,347	4,368	4,591
703	**Public order and safety**	...	...	...	...	...	...	...	...	...	6,267	6,359	6,672
704	**Economic affairs**	...	...	...	...	...	...	...	...	...	19,985	21,132	20,013
7042	Agriculture, forestry, fishing, and hunting	...	...	...	...	...	...	...	...	...	6,382	6,747	6,250
7043	Fuel and energy	...	...	...	...	...	...	...	...	...	2,199	2,152	1,781
7044	Mining, manufacturing, and construction	...	...	...	...	...	...	...	...	...	1,373	1,413	1,416
7045	Transport	...	...	...	...	...	...	...	...	...	11,508	12,423	12,351
7046	Communication	...	...	...	...	...	...	...	...	...	246	302	201
705	**Environmental protection**	...	...	...	...	...	...	...	...	...	5,383	5,599	6,000
706	**Housing and community amenities**	...	...	...	...	...	...	...	...	...	3,198	3,711	3,861
707	**Health**	...	...	...	...	...	...	...	...	...	35,162	35,627	36,357
7072	Outpatient services	...	...	...	...	...	...	...	...	...	13,560	13,753	14,026
7073	Hospital services	...	...	...	...	...	...	...	...	...	12,736	12,813	13,062
7074	Public health services	...	...	...	...	...	...	...	...	...	1,637	1,615	1,688
708	**Recreation, culture and religion**	...	...	...	...	...	...	...	...	...	1,684	1,749	1,901
709	**Education**	...	...	...	...	...	...	...	...	...	16,909	17,168	17,275
7091	Pre-primary and primary education	...	...	...	...	...	...	...	...	...	4,976	4,937	4,909
7092	Secondary education	...	...	...	...	...	...	...	...	...	4,996	4,969	5,149
7094	Tertiary education	...	...	...	...	...	...	...	...	...	2,555	2,780	2,594
710	**Social protection**	...	...	...	...	...	...	...	...	...	85,297	86,210	86,878
7z	Statistical discrepancy: Expenditure	...	...	...	...	...	...	...	...	...	69,064	70,037	69,807
	Table 8 Financial transactions by counterpart sector												
32	**Net acquisition of financial assets**	...	...	...	-173	7,342	6,744	...	...	...	-3,610	3,944	11,042
321	Domestic debtors	...	...	...	...	...	...	...	...	...	...	...	...
8211	General government	...	...	...	...	...	...	...	...	...	...	...	...
8212	Central bank	...	...	...	...	...	...	...	...	...	...	...	...
8213	Deposit-taking corporations except the central bank	...	...	...	...	...	...	...	...	...	...	...	...
8214	Other financial corporations	...	...	...	...	...	...	...	...	...	...	...	...
8215	Nonfinancial corporations	...	...	...	...	...	...	...	...	...	...	...	...
8216	Households & nonprofit institutions serving households	...	...	...	...	...	...	...	...	...	...	...	...
322	External debtors	...	...	...	...	...	...	...	...	...	...	...	...
8221	General government	...	...	...	...	...	...	...	...	...	...	...	...
8227	International organizations	...	...	...	...	...	...	...	...	...	...	...	...
8228	Financial corporations other than international organizations	...	...	...	...	...	...	...	...	...	...	...	...
8229	Other nonresidents	...	...	...	...	...	...	...	...	...	...	...	...

Japan (158)

In Billions of Japanese Yen (JPY) / Fiscal Year Ends March 31st

		Budgetary Central Government			Central Government (excl. Social Security)			Central Government (incl. Social Security)			General Government		
		2012	2013	2014	2012	2013	2014	2012	2013	2014	2012	2013	2014
33	**Net incurrence of liabilities**	...	...	...	33,504	38,350	33,149	...	...	...	33,734	38,109	33,974
331	Domestic creditors	...	...	...	...	...	...	...	...	...	...	...	...
8311	General government	...	...	...	...	...	...	...	...	...	...	...	...
8312	Central bank	...	...	...	...	...	...	...	...	...	...	...	...
8313	Deposit-taking corporations except the central bank	...	...	...	...	...	...	...	...	...	...	...	...
8314	Other financial corporations	...	...	...	...	...	...	...	...	...	...	...	...
8315	Nonfinancial corporations	...	...	...	...	...	...	...	...	...	...	...	...
8316	Households & nonprofit institutions serving households	...	...	...	...	...	...	...	...	...	...	...	...
332	External creditors	...	...	...	...	...	...	...	...	...	...	...	...
8321	General government	...	...	...	...	...	...	...	...	...	...	...	...
8327	International organizations	...	...	...	...	...	...	...	...	...	...	...	...
8328	Financial corporations other than international organizations	...	...	...	...	...	...	...	...	...	...	...	...
8329	Other nonresidents	...	...	...	...	...	...	...	...	...	...	...	...
	Table 9 Total other economic flows in assets and liabilities												

Jordan (439)

In Millions of Jordanian Dinars (JOD) / Fiscal Year Ends December 31st

		Budgetary Central Government			Central Government (excl. Social Security)			Central Government (incl. Social Security)			General Government		
		2013	2014	2015	2013	2014	2015	2013	2014	2015	2013	2014	2015
	Statement of operations												
1	Revenue	5,759	7,268	6,796	6,310	...	...	...	...	...	8,064	...	...
2	Expense	6,419	7,191	7,045	6,795	...	...	7,440	...	...	7,771	...	...
GOB	**Gross operating balance**	**-660**	**76**	**-249**	**-485**	...	...	...	...	...	**293**	...	...
NOB	**Net operating balance**	**-660**	...	...	...	...	...	...	...	...	...	...	...
31	Net/Gross investment in nonfinancial assets	658	660	678	743	...	...	743	...	...	906	...	...
2M	Expenditure	7,077	7,851	7,723	7,537	...	...	8,183	...	...	8,677	...	...
NLB	**Net lending (+) / Net borrowing (-)**	**-1,318**	**-584**	**-927**	**-1,227**	...	...	...	...	...	**-613**	...	...
32	Net acquisition of financial assets	1,853	1,773	...	...	...	...	...	...	...	...	...	...
33	Net incurrence of liabilities	3,171	2,357	1,258	...	...	...	...	...	...	...	...	...
NLBz	Statistical discrepancy	—	—	...	...	...	...	...	...	...	...	...	...
	Memorandum items												
PB	Primary net lending / net borrowing	-582	343	-12	-491	...	...	...	...	...	149	...	...
GB	Government balance per national definition	...	...	...	...	...	...	...	...	...	...	...	...
	Statement of other economic flows												
	Balance sheet												
	Table 1 Revenue												
1	**Revenue**	**5,759**	**7,268**	**6,796**	**6,310**	...	...	...	...	...	**8,064**	...	...
11	**Taxes**	**3,652**	**4,037**	**4,096**	**3,656**	...	...	...	...	...	**3,847**	...	...
111	Taxes on income, profits, and capital gains	682	766	859	682	...	...	...	...	...	682	...	...
1111	Payable by individuals	132	154	207	132	...	...	...	...	...	132	...	...
1112	Payable by corporations and other enterprises	550	612	652	550	...	...	...	...	...	550	...	...
1113	Other taxes on income, profits, and capital gains	—	—	—	—	...	...	...	...	...	—	...	...
112	Taxes on payroll and workforce	—	—	—	—	...	...	...	...	...	—	...	...
113	Taxes on property	—	—	125	—	...	...	...	...	...	100	...	...
114	Taxes on goods and services	2,646	2,944	2,780	2,646	...	...	...	...	...	2,736	...	...
1141	General taxes on goods and services	2,646	2,944	2,780	2,646	...	...	...	...	...	2,646	...	...
1142	Excises	—	—	—	—	...	...	...	...	...	91	...	...
115	Taxes on international trade and transactions	325	327	333	325	...	...	...	...	...	325	...	...
116	Other taxes	—	—	—	4	...	...	...	...	...	4	...	...
12	**Social contributions**	**22**	**21**	**19**	**22**	...	...	...	...	...	**978**	...	...
121	Social security contributions	22	21	19	22	...	...	...	...	...	978	...	...
122	Other social contributions	—	—	—	—	...	...	...	...	...	—	...	...
13	**Grants**	**639**	**1,237**	**886**	**639**	...	...	...	...	...	**639**	...	...
131	From foreign governments	639	1,237	886	639	...	...	...	...	...	639	...	...
132	From international organizations	—	—	—	—	...	...	...	...	...	—	...	...
133	From other general government units	—	—	—	—	...	...	...	...	...	—	...	...
1331	Current	—	—	—	...	...	...	...	...	...	—	...	...
1332	Capital	—	—	—	...	...	...	...	...	...	—	...	...
14	**Other revenue**	**1,445**	**1,973**	**1,795**	**1,993**	...	...	...	...	...	**2,600**	...	...
	Table 2 Expense by economic type												
2	**Expense**	**6,419**	**7,191**	**7,045**	**6,795**	...	...	**7,440**	...	...	**7,771**	...	...
21	**Compensation of employees**	**3,099**	**3,288**	**3,387**	**3,187**	...	...	**3,203**	...	...	**3,461**	...	...
211	Wages and salaries	3,015	3,201	3,287	3,096	...	...	3,111	...	...	3,341	...	...
212	Employers' social contributions	84	87	100	91	...	...	93	...	...	120	...	...
22	**Use of goods and services**	**419**	**680**	**541**	**642**	...	...	**663**	...	...	**701**	...	...
23	**Consumption of fixed capital**	...	...	...	...	...	...	...	...	...	...	...	...
24	**Interest**	**737**	**926**	**915**	**737**	...	...	**737**	...	...	**762**	...	...
25	**Subsidies**	**340**	**298**	**291**	**341**	...	...	**341**	...	...	**341**	...	...
26	**Grants**	**371**	**456**	**369**	**340**	...	...	**340**	...	...	**330**	...	...
261	To foreign governments	—	—	—	—	...	...	—	...	...	—	...	...
262	To international organizations	—	—	—	—	...	...	—	...	...	—	...	...
263	To other general government units	371	456	369	340	...	...	340	...	...	330	...	...
2631	Current	193	206	117	...	...	...	...	...	...	—	...	...
2632	Capital	178	250	252	...	...	...	...	...	...	—	...	...

Jordan (439)

In Millions of Jordanian Dinars (JOD) / Fiscal Year Ends December 31st

		Budgetary Central Government			Central Government (excl. Social Security)			Central Government (incl. Social Security)			General Government		
		2013	2014	2015	2013	2014	2015	2013	2014	2015	2013	2014	2015
27	**Social benefits**	**1,358**	**1,473**	**1,442**	**1,358**	**...**	**...**	**1,967**	**...**	**...**	**1,967**	**...**	**...**
271	Social security benefits	1,047	1,116	1,163	1,047	...	...	1,655	...	...	1,655	...	...
272	Social assistance benefits	312	357	279	312	...	...	312	...	...	312	...	...
273	Employment-related social benefits	—	—	—	—	...	...	—	...	...	—	...	...
28	**Other expense**	**96**	**71**	**100**	**191**	**...**	**...**	**191**	**...**	**...**	**209**	**...**	**...**
281	Property expense other than interest	—	—	—	—	...	...	—	...	...	—	...	...
282	Transfers not elsewhere classified	96	71	100	191	...	...	191	...	...	209	...	...
2821	Current	96	71	79	191	...	...	191	...	...	209	...	...
2822	Capital	—	—	21	—	...	...	—	...	...	—	...	...
	Table 3 Transactions in assets and liabilities												
3	**Change in net worth from transactions**	...	...	...	...	...	...	...	...	...	...	...	...
31	**Net/Gross investment in nonfinancial assets**	**658**	**660**	**678**	**743**	**...**	**...**	**743**	**...**	**...**	**906**	**...**	**...**
311	Fixed assets	539	615	626	624	...	...	624	...	...	787	...	...
3111	Buildings and structures	457	460	498	...	...	...	...	...	...	...	...	...
3112	Machinery and equipment	76	147	119	...	...	...	...	...	...	...	...	...
3113	Other fixed assets	7	8	9	...	...	...	...	...	...	...	...	...
3114	Weapons systems	...	—	—	...	...	...	...	...	...	...	...	...
312	Inventories	-34	32	20	-34	...	...	-34	...	...	-34	...	...
313	Valuables	—	—	—	—	...	...	—	...	...	—	...	...
314	Nonproduced assets	85	13	32	85	...	...	85	...	...	85	...	...
3141	Land	...	13	32	...	...	...	...	...	...	...	...	...
3142	Mineral and energy resources	...	—	—	...	...	...	...	...	...	...	...	...
3143	Other naturally occurring assets	...	—	—	...	...	...	...	...	...	...	...	...
3144	Intangible nonproduced assets	...	—	—	...	...	...	...	...	...	...	...	...
32	**Net acquisition of financial assets**	**1,853**	**1,773**	**...**	**...**	**...**	**...**	**...**	**...**	**...**	**...**	**...**	**...**
	By instrument												
3201	Monetary gold and SDRs	—	—	...	...	...	...	...	...	...	...	...	...
3202	Currency and deposits	1,853	1,773	...	...	...	...	...	...	...	...	...	...
3203	Debt securities	—	—	...	...	...	...	...	...	...	...	...	...
3204	Loans	—	—	...	...	...	...	...	...	...	...	...	...
3205	Equity and investment fund shares	—	—	...	...	...	...	...	...	...	...	...	...
3206	Insurance, pension, and standardized guarantee schemes	—	—	...	...	...	...	...	...	...	...	...	...
3207	Financial derivatives and employee stock options	—	—	...	...	...	...	...	...	...	...	...	...
3208	Other accounts receivable	...	...	...	...	...	...	...	...	...	...	...	...
	By debtor												
321	Domestic debtors	1,853	1,773	...	...	...	...	...	...	...	...	...	...
322	External debtors	—	—	...	...	...	...	...	...	...	...	...	...
33	**Net incurrence of liabilities**	**3,171**	**2,357**	**1,258**	**...**	**...**	**...**	**...**	**...**	**...**	**...**	**...**	**...**
	By instrument												
3301	Special Drawing Rights (SDRs)	—	—	—	...	...	...	...	...	...	...	...	...
3302	Currency and deposits	—	—	—	...	...	...	...	...	...	...	...	...
3303	Debt securities	3,171	2,357	—	...	...	...	...	...	...	...	...	...
3304	Loans	—	—	1,258	...	...	...	...	...	...	...	...	...
3305	Equity and investment fund shares	—	—	—	...	...	...	...	...	...	...	...	...
3306	Insurance, pension, and standardized guarantee schemes	—	—	—	...	...	...	...	...	...	...	...	...
3307	Financial derivatives and employee stock options	—	—	—	...	...	...	...	...	...	...	...	...
3308	Other accounts payable	...	...	...	...	...	...	...	...	...	...	...	...
	By creditor												
331	Domestic creditors	1,146	1,523	-167	...	...	...	...	...	...	...	...	...
332	External creditors	2,025	834	1,425	...	...	...	...	...	...	...	...	...
	Table 4 Holding gains and losses in assets and liabilities												
	Table 5 Holding gains and losses in assets and liabilities												
	Table 6 Balance sheet												

Jordan (439)

In Millions of Jordanian Dinars (JOD) / Fiscal Year Ends December 31st

		Budgetary Central Government			Central Government (excl. Social Security)			Central Government (incl. Social Security)			General Government		
		2013	2014	2015	2013	2014	2015	2013	2014	2015	2013	2014	2015
	Table 7 Expenditure by functions of government												
7	**Expenditure**	**7,077**	**7,851**	**7,722**	**7,537**	**...**	**...**	**8,183**	**...**	**...**	**8,677**	**...**	**...**
701	**General public services**	**1,135**	**1,445**	**1,371**	**...**	**...**	**...**	**...**	**...**	**...**	**...**	**...**	**...**
7017	Public debt transactions	737	926	915	737	...	...	737	...	...	762	...	...
7018	Transfers of general character between levels of government	...	...	—	...	...	...	...	...	...	...	...	...
702	**Defense**	**849**	**899**	**936**	**...**	**...**	**...**	**...**	**...**	**...**	**...**	**...**	**...**
703	**Public order and safety**	**919**	**1,006**	**1,044**	**...**	**...**	**...**	**...**	**...**	**...**	**...**	**...**	**...**
704	**Economic affairs**	**408**	**578**	**512**	**...**	**...**	**...**	**...**	**...**	**...**	**...**	**...**	**...**
7042	Agriculture, forestry, fishing, and hunting	50	55	57	...	...	...	...	...	...	...	...	...
7043	Fuel and energy	21	137	154	...	...	...	...	...	...	...	...	...
7044	Mining, manufacturing, and construction	6	5	1	...	...	...	...	...	...	...	...	...
7045	Transport	230	213	164	...	...	...	...	...	...	...	...	...
7046	Communication	11	10	17	...	...	...	...	...	...	...	...	...
705	**Environmental protection**	**64**	**41**	**44**	**...**	**...**	**...**	**...**	**...**	**...**	**...**	**...**	**...**
706	**Housing and community amenities**	**279**	**220**	**239**	**...**	**...**	**...**	**...**	**...**	**...**	**...**	**...**	**...**
707	**Health**	**715**	**871**	**876**	**...**	**...**	**...**	**...**	**...**	**...**	**...**	**...**	**...**
7072	Outpatient services	2	1	2	...	...	...	...	...	...	...	...	...
7073	Hospital services	443	438	465	...	...	...	...	...	...	...	...	...
7074	Public health services	70	135	110	...	...	...	...	...	...	...	...	...
708	**Recreation, culture and religion**	**135**	**140**	**155**	**...**	**...**	**...**	**...**	**...**	**...**	**...**	**...**	**...**
709	**Education**	**943**	**1,006**	**1,042**	**...**	**...**	**...**	**...**	**...**	**...**	**...**	**...**	**...**
7091	Pre-primary and primary education	658	695	708	...	...	...	...	...	...	...	...	...
7092	Secondary education	121	131	126	...	...	...	...	...	...	...	...	...
7094	Tertiary education	85	96	122	...	...	...	...	...	...	...	...	...
710	**Social protection**	**1,630**	**1,646**	**1,504**	**...**	**...**	**...**	**...**	**...**	**...**	**...**	**...**	**...**
7z	Statistical discrepancy: Expenditure	—	—	...	...	...	...	...	...	...	...	...	...
	Table 8 Financial transactions by counterpart sector												
	Table 9 Total other economic flows in assets and liabilities												

Kazakhstan (916)

In Billions of Kazakhstani Tenge (KZT) / Fiscal Year Ends December 31st

		Budgetary Central Government			Central Government (excl. Social Security)			Central Government (incl. Social Security)			General Government		
		2013	2014	2015	2013	2014	2015	2013	2014	2015	2013	2014	2015
	Statement of operations												
1	Revenue	7,327	7,632	5,512	7,327	7,632	5,512	7,531	7,858	5,757	8,707	9,224	7,205
2	Expense	5,174	5,960	6,244	5,174	5,960	6,244	5,259	6,074	6,332	5,500	6,193	6,791
GOB	**Gross operating balance**	**2,153**	**1,671**	**-732**	**2,153**	**1,671**	**-732**	**2,272**	**1,784**	**-574**	**3,207**	**3,031**	**414**
NOB	**Net operating balance**	...	...	...	...	...	...	...	...	...	...	...	...
31	Net/Gross investment in nonfinancial assets	505	491	414	505	491	414	505	491	414	1,390	1,643	1,323
2M	Expenditure	5,679	6,452	6,659	5,679	6,452	6,659	5,764	6,565	6,746	6,890	7,836	8,114
NLB	**Net lending (+) / Net borrowing (-)**	**1,648**	**1,180**	**-1,146**	**1,648**	**1,180**	**-1,146**	**1,767**	**1,293**	**-989**	**1,818**	**1,387**	**-909**
32	Net acquisition of financial assets	2,425	2,185	27	2,425	2,185	27	2,419	2,198	102	2,470	2,293	168
33	Net incurrence of liabilities	777	1,005	1,174	777	1,005	1,174	652	905	1,090	652	905	1,077
NLBz	Statistical discrepancy	0	0	0	0	0	0	0	0	0	0	0	0
	Memorandum items												
PB	Primary net lending / net borrowing	1,825	1,412	-848	1,825	1,412	-848	1,922	1,495	-731	1,973	1,590	-650
GB	Government balance per national definition	...	...	...	...	...	...	...	...	...	...	...	...
	Statement of other economic flows												
	Balance sheet												
6	**Net worth**	...	...	...	...	...	...	...	...	...	...	...	...
61	Nonfinancial assets	...	...	...	...	...	...	...	...	...	...	...	...
62	Financial assets	16,012	20,156	17,864	16,012	20,156	17,864	16,038	20,195	18,012	16,038	...	...
63	Liabilities	4,398	5,613	8,666	4,398	5,613	8,666	3,903	5,018	7,894	3,918	5,033	7,896
	Table 1 Revenue												
1	**Revenue**	**7,327**	**7,632**	**5,512**	**7,327**	**7,632**	**5,512**	**7,531**	**7,858**	**5,757**	**8,707**	**9,224**	**7,205**
11	**Taxes**	**5,771**	**5,631**	**4,021**	**5,771**	**5,631**	**4,021**	**5,771**	**5,631**	**4,021**	**7,024**	**7,065**	**5,551**
111	Taxes on income, profits, and capital gains	2,435	2,562	1,869	2,435	2,562	1,869	2,435	2,562	1,869	2,928	3,114	2,468
1111	Payable by individuals	—	—	—	—	—	—	—	—	—	493	552	599
1112	Payable by corporations and other enterprises	2,435	2,562	1,869	2,435	2,562	1,869	2,435	2,562	1,869	2,435	2,562	1,869
1113	Other taxes on income, profits, and capital gains	—	—	—	—	—	—	—	—	—	—	—	—
112	Taxes on payroll and workforce	—	—	—	—	—	—	—	—	—	380	428	465
113	Taxes on property	—	—	—	—	—	—	—	—	—	157	188	225
114	Taxes on goods and services	1,391	1,277	1,042	1,391	1,277	1,042	1,391	1,277	1,042	1,521	1,444	1,221
1141	General taxes on goods and services	1,328	1,198	944	1,328	1,198	944	1,328	1,198	944	1,328	1,198	944
1142	Excises	34	46	61	34	46	61	34	46	61	104	147	161
115	Taxes on international trade and transactions	1,764	1,793	1,110	1,764	1,793	1,110	1,764	1,793	1,110	1,764	1,793	1,110
116	Other taxes	180	0	0	180	0	0	180	0	0	273	98	64
12	**Social contributions**	—	—	—	—	—	—	**203**	**225**	**241**	**203**	**225**	**241**
121	Social security contributions	—	—	—	—	—	—	203	225	241	203	225	241
122	Other social contributions	—	—	—	—	—	—	—	—	—	—	—	—
13	**Grants**	**139**	**139**	**170**	**139**	**139**	**170**	**139**	**139**	**170**	**0**	**1**	**1**
131	From foreign governments	—	—	—	—	—	—	—	—	—	—	—	—
132	From international organizations	0	1	1	0	1	1	0	1	1	0	1	1
133	From other general government units	139	139	170	139	139	170	139	139	170	0	0	—
1331	Current	137	138	170	137	138	170	137	138	170	0	0	—
1332	Capital	2	1	—	2	1	—	2	1	—	—	—	—
14	**Other revenue**	**1,417**	**1,861**	**1,321**	**1,417**	**1,861**	**1,321**	**1,417**	**1,862**	**1,326**	**1,479**	**1,933**	**1,413**
	Table 2 Expense by economic type												
2	**Expense**	**5,174**	**5,960**	**6,244**	**5,174**	**5,960**	**6,244**	**5,259**	**6,074**	**6,332**	**5,500**	**6,193**	**6,791**
21	**Compensation of employees**	**410**	**427**	**435**	**410**	**427**	**435**	**411**	**427**	**435**	**1,078**	**1,148**	**1,187**
211	Wages and salaries	398	414	422	398	414	422	399	415	423	1,042	1,110	1,148
212	Employers' social contributions	12	12	12	12	12	12	12	12	12	36	38	39
22	**Use of goods and services**	**1,001**	**1,179**	**1,479**	**1,001**	**1,179**	**1,479**	**1,001**	**1,180**	**1,479**	**2,262**	**2,465**	**2,846**
23	**Consumption of fixed capital**	...	...	...	...	...	...	...	...	...	...	...	...
24	**Interest**	**177**	**232**	**298**	**177**	**232**	**298**	**155**	**202**	**258**	**156**	**202**	**259**
25	**Subsidies**	**69**	**88**	**97**	**69**	**88**	**97**	**69**	**88**	**97**	**223**	**311**	**338**

Kazakhstan (916)

In Billions of Kazakhstani Tenge (KZT) / Fiscal Year Ends December 31st

		Budgetary Central Government			Central Government (excl. Social Security)			Central Government (incl. Social Security)			General Government		
		2013	2014	2015	2013	2014	2015	2013	2014	2015	2013	2014	2015
26	**Grants**	**1,949**	**2,220**	**1,994**	**1,949**	**2,220**	**1,994**	**1,949**	**2,220**	**1,994**	**36**	**38**	**8**
261	To foreign governments	—	—	—	—	—	—	—	—	—	—	—	—
262	To international organizations	36	38	8	36	38	8	36	38	8	36	38	8
263	To other general government units	1,913	2,182	1,986	1,913	2,182	1,986	1,913	2,182	1,986	—	—	—
2631	Current	1,376	1,555	1,506	1,376	1,555	1,506	1,376	1,555	1,506	—	—	—
2632	Capital	537	627	480	537	627	480	537	627	480	—	—	—
27	**Social benefits**	**1,450**	**1,670**	**1,856**	**1,450**	**1,670**	**1,856**	**1,556**	**1,813**	**1,982**	**1,594**	**1,852**	**2,032**
271	Social security benefits	917	1,067	1,199	917	1,067	1,199	1,024	1,210	1,326	1,024	1,210	1,326
272	Social assistance benefits	526	595	645	526	595	645	526	595	645	565	634	695
273	Employment-related social benefits	6	9	11	6	9	11	6	9	11	6	9	11
28	**Other expense**	**118**	**144**	**86**	**118**	**144**	**86**	**119**	**145**	**87**	**150**	**176**	**122**
281	Property expense other than interest	—	—	—	—	—	—	—	—	—	—	—	—
282	Transfers not elsewhere classified	118	144	86	118	144	86	119	144	87	150	176	122
2821	Current	118	99	86	118	99	86	119	99	87	150	130	122
2822	Capital	—	46	—	—	46	—	—	46	—	—	46	—
	Table 3 Transactions in assets and liabilities												
3	**Change in net worth from transactions**	...	...	...	...	...	...	...	...	...	...	...	...
31	**Net/Gross investment in nonfinancial assets**	**505**	**491**	**414**	**505**	**491**	**414**	**505**	**491**	**414**	**1,390**	**1,643**	**1,323**
311	Fixed assets	482	460	381	482	460	381	482	460	382	1,355	1,605	1,283
3111	Buildings and structures	465	462	385	465	462	385	465	462	385	1,305	1,581	1,290
3112	Machinery and equipment	3	0	—	3	0	—	3	0	—	64	71	41
3113	Other fixed assets	15	-3	-3	15	-3	-3	15	-3	-3	-14	-46	-47
3114	Weapons systems	—	—	—	—	—	—	—	—	0	—	—	0
312	Inventories	2	5	15	2	5	15	2	5	15	2	5	15
313	Valuables	—	—	—	—	—	—	—	—	—	—	—	—
314	Nonproduced assets	20	27	18	20	27	18	20	27	18	33	34	24
3141	Land	-1	-1	-1	-1	-1	-1	-1	-1	-1	12	5	6
3142	Mineral and energy resources	—	—	—	—	—	—	—	—	—	—	—	—
3143	Other naturally occurring assets	—	—	—	—	—	—	—	—	—	0	—	0
3144	Intangible nonproduced assets	21	28	19	21	28	19	21	28	19	21	28	19
32	**Net acquisition of financial assets**	**2,425**	**2,185**	**27**	**2,425**	**2,185**	**27**	**2,419**	**2,198**	**102**	**2,470**	**2,293**	**168**
	By instrument												
3201	Monetary gold and SDRs	—	—	—	—	—	—	—	—	—	—	—	—
3202	Currency and deposits	773	-845	113	773	-845	113	767	-831	191	784	-834	175
3203	Debt securities	1,120	1,934	-376	1,120	1,934	-376	1,120	1,934	-379	1,120	1,934	-379
3204	Loans	38	39	78	38	39	78	38	39	78	26	43	85
3205	Equity and investment fund shares	494	1,056	211	494	1,056	211	494	1,056	211	540	1,150	288
3206	Insurance, pension, and standardized guarantee schemes	—	—	—	—	—	—	—	—	—	—	—	—
3207	Financial derivatives and employee stock options	—	—	—	—	—	—	—	—	—	—	—	—
3208	Other accounts receivable	...	...	...	...	...	...	...	...	...	...	...	...
	By debtor												
321	Domestic debtors	968	-327	490	968	-327	490	962	-314	564	1,012	-219	631
322	External debtors	1,457	2,512	-463	1,457	2,512	-463	1,457	2,512	-463	1,457	2,512	-463
33	**Net incurrence of liabilities**	**777**	**1,005**	**1,174**	**777**	**1,005**	**1,174**	**652**	**905**	**1,090**	**652**	**905**	**1,077**
	By instrument												
3301	Special Drawing Rights (SDRs)	—	—	—	—	—	—	—	—	—	—	—	—
3302	Currency and deposits	—	—	—	—	—	—	—	—	—	—	—	—
3303	Debt securities	714	537	180	714	537	180	571	401	97	571	401	97
3304	Loans	63	468	994	63	468	994	63	468	994	63	468	994
3305	Equity and investment fund shares	—	—	—	—	—	—	—	—	—	—	—	-13
3306	Insurance, pension, and standardized guarantee schemes	—	—	—	—	—	—	—	—	—	—	—	—
3307	Financial derivatives and employee stock options	—	—	—	—	—	—	—	—	—	—	—	—
3308	Other accounts payable	...	...	...	...	...	...	...	...	...	...	...	...

Kazakhstan (916)

In Billions of Kazakhstani Tenge (KZT) / Fiscal Year Ends December 31st

		Budgetary Central Government			Central Government (excl. Social Security)			Central Government (incl. Social Security)			General Government		
		2013	2014	2015	2013	2014	2015	2013	2014	2015	2013	2014	2015
	By creditor												
331	Domestic creditors	714	537	180	714	537	180	589	437	97	589	437	84
332	External creditors	63	468	994	63	468	994	63	468	994	63	468	994
	Table 4 Holding gains and losses in assets and liabilities												
	Table 5 Holding gains and losses in assets and liabilities												
	Table 6 Balance sheet												
6	**Net worth**	...	...	...	...	...	...	...	...	...	...	...	...
61	**Nonfinancial assets**	...	...	...	...	...	...	...	...	...	...	...	...
611	Fixed assets	...	...	...	...	...	...	...	...	...	...	...	...
6111	Buildings and structures	...	...	...	...	...	...	...	...	...	...	...	...
6112	Machinery and equipment	...	...	...	...	...	...	...	...	...	...	...	...
6113	Other fixed assets	...	...	...	...	...	...	...	...	...	...	...	...
6114	Weapons systems	...	...	...	...	...	...	...	...	...	...	...	...
612	Inventories	...	...	...	...	...	...	...	...	...	...	...	...
613	Valuables	...	...	...	...	...	...	...	...	...	...	...	...
614	Nonproduced assets	...	...	...	...	...	...	...	...	...	...	...	...
6141	Land	...	...	...	...	...	...	...	...	...	...	...	...
6142	Mineral and energy resources	...	...	...	...	...	...	...	...	...	...	...	...
6143	Other naturally occurring assets	...	...	...	...	...	...	...	...	...	...	...	...
6144	Intangible nonproduced assets	...	...	...	...	...	...	...	...	...	...	...	...
62	**Financial assets**	**16,012**	**20,156**	**17,864**	**16,012**	**20,156**	**17,864**	**16,038**	**20,195**	**18,012**	**16,038**	**...**	**...**
	By instrument												
6201	Monetary gold and SDRs	—	—	—	—	—	—	—	—	—	—	...	...
6202	Currency and deposits	6,071	6,497	3,363	6,071	6,497	3,363	6,093	6,533	3,476	6,093	...	...
6203	Debt securities	7,654	11,043	7,896	7,654	11,043	7,896	7,659	11,046	7,931	7,659	...	...
6204	Loans	482	521	443	482	521	443	482	521	443	482	...	...
6205	Equity and investment fund shares	1,804	2,095	6,162	1,804	2,095	6,162	1,804	2,095	6,162	1,804	...	...
6206	Insurance, pension, and standardized guarantee schemes	—	—	—	—	—	—	—	—	—	—	...	...
6207	Financial derivatives and employee stock options	—	—	—	—	—	—	—	—	—	—	...	...
6208	Other accounts receivable	...	...	...	...	...	...	0	0	...	...	...	...
	By debtor												
621	Domestic debtors	8,157	11,013	8,131	8,157	11,013	8,131	8,183	11,052	8,280	8,183	...	...
622	External debtors	7,855	9,143	9,733	7,855	9,143	9,733	7,855	9,143	9,733	7,855	...	...
63	**Liabilities**	**4,398**	**5,613**	**8,666**	**4,398**	**5,613**	**8,666**	**3,903**	**5,018**	**7,894**	**3,918**	**5,033**	**7,896**
	By instrument												
6301	Special Drawing Rights (SDRs)	—	—	—	—	—	—	—	—	—	—	—	—
6302	Currency and deposits	—	—	—	—	—	—	—	—	—	—	—	—
6303	Debt securities	3,615	4,634	6,556	3,615	4,634	6,556	3,027	3,910	5,784	3,040	3,923	5,784
6304	Loans	784	979	2,110	784	979	2,110	784	979	2,110	784	982	2,112
6305	Equity and investment fund shares	—	—	—	—	—	—	—	—	—	—	—	—
6306	Insurance, pension, and standardized guarantee schemes	—	—	—	—	—	—	—	—	—	—	—	—
6307	Financial derivatives and employee stock options	—	—	—	—	—	—	—	—	—	—	—	—
6308	Other accounts payable	...	...	...	...	...	...	...	...	...	...	...	...
	By creditor												
631	Domestic creditors	3,615	4,178	4,349	3,615	4,178	4,349	3,119	3,583	3,578	3,134	3,583	3,580
632	External creditors	784	1,435	4,316	784	1,435	4,316	784	1,435	4,316	784	1,435	4,316
	Memorandum items												
6M2	Net financial worth	11,614	14,543	12,251	11,614	14,543	12,251	12,135	15,178	4,500	12,136	...	...
6M3	Gross debt (D4) at market value	...	...	...	...	...	...	...	...	...	...	...	...
6M3D3	D3 debt liabilities at market value	...	...	...	...	...	...	...	...	...	...	...	...
6M3D2	D2 debt liabilities at market value	...	...	...	...	...	...	...	...	...	...	...	...
6M3D1	D1 debt liabilities at market value	...	...	...	...	...	...	...	...	...	...	...	...
6M4	Gross debt (D4) at nominal value	...	...	...	...	...	...	...	...	...	...	...	...
6M4D3	D3 debt liabilities at nominal value	...	...	...	...	...	...	...	...	...	...	...	...
6M4D2	D2 debt liabilities at nominal value	...	...	...	...	...	...	...	...	...	...	...	...
6M4D1	D1 debt liabilities at nominal value	...	...	...	...	...	...	...	...	...	...	...	...

Kazakhstan (916)

In Billions of Kazakhstani Tenge (KZT) / Fiscal Year Ends December 31st

		Budgetary Central Government			Central Government (excl. Social Security)			Central Government (incl. Social Security)			General Government		
		2013	2014	2015	2013	2014	2015	2013	2014	2015	2013	2014	2015
6M35	Gross debt (D4) at face value	...	...	...	...	...	...	...	...	...	...	...	...
6M35D3	D3 debt liabilities at face value	...	...	...	...	...	...	...	...	...	...	...	...
6M35D2	D2 debt liabilities at face value	4,398	5,613	8,666	4,398	5,613	8,666	3,811	4,890	7,894	3,824	4,905	7,896
6M35D1	D1 debt liabilities at face value	4,398	5,613	8,666	4,398	5,613	8,666	3,811	4,890	7,894	3,824	4,905	7,896
6M93	Government gross debt per national definition	...	...	...	...	...	...	...	...	...	...	...	...
6M5	Arrears	...	...	...	...	...	...	...	...	...	...	...	...
6M6	Explicit contingent liabilities	...	...	...	...	...	...	...	...	...	...	...	...
6M61	of which: Publicly guaranteed debt	...	...	...	...	...	...	...	...	...	...	...	...
6M7	Net implicit obligations for social security benefits	...	...	...	...	...	...	...	...	...	...	...	...
	Table 7 Expenditure by functions of government												
7	**Expenditure**	**5,679**	**6,452**	**6,659**	**5,679**	**6,452**	**6,659**	**5,764**	**6,528**	**6,746**	**6,890**	**7,836**	**8,114**
701	**General public services**	**1,544**	**1,871**	**2,063**	**1,544**	**1,871**	**2,063**	**1,522**	**1,840**	**2,022**	**756**	**909**	**1,084**
7017	Public debt transactions	177	232	298	177	232	298	155	201	258	156	202	259
7018	Transfers of general character between levels of government	851	978	904	851	978	904	851	978	904	—	—	—
702	**Defense**	**388**	**413**	**441**	**388**	**413**	**441**	**388**	**413**	**441**	**397**	**432**	**454**
703	**Public order and safety**	**509**	**478**	**434**	**509**	**478**	**434**	**509**	**478**	**434**	**608**	**601**	**557**
704	**Economic affairs**	**676**	**748**	**755**	**676**	**748**	**755**	**676**	**748**	**755**	**899**	**1,114**	**1,194**
7042	Agriculture, forestry, fishing, and hunting	114	114	161	114	114	161	114	114	161	172	269	349
7043	Fuel and energy	1	22	80	1	22	80	1	22	80	1	22	112
7044	Mining, manufacturing, and construction	9	8	14	9	8	14	9	8	14	26	29	62
7045	Transport	361	380	482	361	380	482	361	380	482	481	543	651
7046	Communication	6	14	11	6	14	11	6	14	11	6	14	11
705	**Environmental protection**	**10**	**5**	**5**	**10**	**5**	**5**	**10**	**5**	**5**	**23**	**20**	**18**
706	**Housing and community amenities**	**244**	**283**	**153**	**244**	**283**	**153**	**244**	**283**	**153**	**472**	**555**	**443**
707	**Health**	**499**	**642**	**658**	**499**	**642**	**658**	**499**	**642**	**658**	**795**	**856**	**864**
7072	Outpatient services	15	—	—	15	—	—	15	—	—	265	150	163
7073	Hospital services	7	5	5	7	5	5	7	5	5	9	8	8
7074	Public health services	375	548	590	375	548	590	375	548	590	338	528	561
708	**Recreation, culture and religion**	**94**	**106**	**105**	**94**	**106**	**105**	**94**	**106**	**105**	**258**	**298**	**294**
709	**Education**	**453**	**465**	**444**	**453**	**465**	**444**	**453**	**465**	**444**	**1,237**	**1,358**	**1,365**
7091	Pre-primary and primary education	53	56	68	53	56	68	53	56	68	100	119	135
7092	Secondary education	23	40	44	23	40	44	23	40	44	593	654	687
7094	Tertiary education	141	144	140	141	144	140	141	144	140	141	144	140
710	**Social protection**	**1,261**	**1,442**	**1,602**	**1,261**	**1,442**	**1,602**	**1,368**	**1,585**	**1,730**	**1,425**	**1,694**	**1,841**
7z	Statistical discrepancy: Expenditure	—	—	—	—	—	—	0	-0	-0	0	—	—
	Table 8 Financial transactions by counterpart sector												
32	**Net acquisition of financial assets**	**2,425**	**2,185**	**27**	**2,425**	**2,185**	**27**	**2,419**	**2,198**	**102**	**2,470**	**2,293**	**168**
321	Domestic debtors	968	-327	490	968	-327	490	962	-314	564	1,012	-219	631
8211	General government	42	26	73	42	26	73	42	26	73	-0	0	-0
8212	Central bank	773	-845	113	773	-845	113	767	-831	191	784	-834	175
8213	Deposit-taking corporations except the central bank	-60	—	—	-60	—	—	-60	—	—	-62	-2	—
8214	Other financial corporations	179	452	271	179	452	271	178	451	268	179	451	271
8215	Nonfinancial corporations	36	42	34	36	42	34	36	42	34	82	135	108
8216	Households & nonprofit institutions serving households	-1	-1	-1	-1	-1	-1	-1	-1	-1	31	30	77
322	External debtors	1,457	2,512	-463	1,457	2,512	-463	1,457	2,512	-463	1,457	2,512	-463
8221	General government	-0	—	-0	-0	—	-0	-0	—	-0	-0	—	-0
8227	International organizations	2	1	1	2	1	1	2	1	1	2	1	1
8228	Financial corporations other than international organizations	—	—	—	—	—	—	—	—	—	—	—	—
8229	Other nonresidents	1,455	2,511	-463	1,455	2,511	-463	1,455	2,511	-463	1,455	2,511	-463

Kazakhstan (916)

In Billions of Kazakhstani Tenge (KZT) / Fiscal Year Ends December 31st

		Budgetary Central Government			Central Government (excl. Social Security)			Central Government (incl. Social Security)			General Government		
		2013	2014	2015	2013	2014	2015	2013	2014	2015	2013	2014	2015
33	**Net incurrence of liabilities**	**777**	**1,005**	**1,174**	**777**	**1,005**	**1,174**	**652**	**905**	**1,090**	**652**	**905**	**1,077**
331	Domestic creditors	714	537	180	714	537	180	589	437	97	589	437	84
8311	General government	143	136	...	143	136	...	0	—	-83	0	—	—
8312	Central bank	—	—	—	—	—	—	—	—	—	—	—	—
8313	Deposit-taking corporations except the central bank	61	2	-126	61	2	-126	61	2	-126	61	2	-126
8314	Other financial corporations	510	399	306	510	399	306	510	399	306	510	399	306
8315	Nonfinancial corporations	—	—	—	—	—	—	0	—	—	0	—	—
8316	Households & nonprofit institutions serving households	—	—	-0	—	—	-0	18	37	-0	18	37	-0
332	External creditors	63	468	994	63	468	994	63	468	994	63	468	994
8321	General government	-1	436	973	-1	436	973	-1	436	973	-1	436	973
8327	International organizations	64	32	21	64	32	21	64	32	21	64	32	21
8328	Financial corporations other than international organizations	—	—	—	—	—	—	—	—	—	—	—	—
8329	Other nonresidents	—	—	—	—	—	—	—	—	—	—	—	—
	Table 9 Total other economic flows in assets and liabilities												

Kenya (664)

In Billions of Kenya Shillings (KES) / Fiscal Year Ends June 30th

		Budgetary Central Government			Central Government (excl. Social Security)			Central Government (incl. Social Security)			General Government		
		2013	2014	2015	2013	2014P	2015P	2013	2014	2015	2013	2014P	2015P
	Statement of operations												
1	Revenue	806	1,000	1,133	...	1,171	1,325	...	1,201	1,360	...	1,228	1,394
2	Expense	919	1,174	1,364	...	1,219	1,407	...	1,233	1,426	...	1,136	1,373
GOB	**Gross operating balance**	**-114**	**-174**	**-230**	**...**	**-48**	**-82**	**...**	**-32**	**-66**	**...**	**91**	**21**
NOB	**Net operating balance**	**...**	**...**	**...**	**...**	**...**	**...**	**...**	**...**	**...**	**...**	**...**	**...**
31	Net/Gross investment in nonfinancial assets	140	138	336	...	265	483	...	268	481	...	311	569
2M	Expenditure	1,059	1,312	1,699	...	1,485	1,889	...	1,501	1,908	...	1,447	1,942
NLB	**Net lending (+) / Net borrowing (-)**	**-253**	**-312**	**-566**	**...**	**-313**	**-564**	**...**	**-300**	**-547**	**...**	**-219**	**-548**
32	Net acquisition of financial assets	—	-31	49	...	0	74	...	13	88	...	44	84
33	Net incurrence of liabilities	—	333	607	...	334	599	...	332	599	...	335	599
NLBz	Statistical discrepancy	...	-52	8	...	-21	39	...	-18	36	...	-73	33
	Memorandum items												
PB	Primary net lending / net borrowing	-160	-180	-399	...	-181	-396	...	-167	-379	...	-82	-375
GB	Government balance per national definition	...	...	...	...	...	...	...	...	...	...	...	...
	Statement of other economic flows												
	Balance sheet												
	Table 1 Revenue												
1	**Revenue**	**806**	**1,000**	**1,133**	**...**	**1,171**	**1,325**	**...**	**1,201**	**1,360**	**...**	**1,228**	**1,394**
11	**Taxes**	**735**	**912**	**1,022**	**...**	**912**	**1,022**	**...**	**912**	**1,022**	**...**	**912**	**1,022**
111	Taxes on income, profits, and capital gains	373	450	509	...	450	509	...	450	509	...	450	509
1111	Payable by individuals	200	250	280	...	250	280	...	250	280	...	250	280
1112	Payable by corporations and other enterprises	173	200	229	...	200	229	...	200	229	...	200	229
1113	Other taxes on income, profits, and capital gains	—	—	1	...	—	1	...	—	1	...	—	1
112	Taxes on payroll and workforce	—	—	—	...	—	—	...	—	—	...	—	—
113	Taxes on property	0	—	—	...	—	—	...	—	—	...	—	—
114	Taxes on goods and services	271	358	400	...	358	400	...	358	400	...	358	400
1141	General taxes on goods and services	185	233	260	...	233	260	...	233	260	...	233	260
1142	Excises	86	102	116	...	102	116	...	102	116	...	102	116
115	Taxes on international trade and transactions	82	94	101	...	94	101	...	94	101	...	94	101
116	Other taxes	9	10	11	...	10	11	...	10	11	...	10	11
12	**Social contributions**	**1**	**0**	**0**	**...**	**0**	**0**	**...**	**19**	**22**	**...**	**19**	**22**
121	Social security contributions	1	0	0	...	0	0	...	19	22	...	19	22
122	Other social contributions	—	—	—	...	—	—	...	—	—	...	—	—
13	**Grants**	**21**	**27**	**28**	**...**	**27**	**28**	**...**	**27**	**28**	**...**	**27**	**28**
131	From foreign governments	5	27	—	...	27	—	...	27	—	...	27	—
132	From international organizations	15	—	28	...	—	28	...	—	28	...	—	28
133	From other general government units	0	—	—	...	—	—	...	—	—	...	—	—
1331	Current	—	—	—	...	—	—	...	—	—	...	—	—
1332	Capital	0	—	—	...	—	—	...	—	—	...	—	—
14	**Other revenue**	**50**	**61**	**83**	**...**	**232**	**275**	**...**	**244**	**288**	**...**	**270**	**322**
	Table 2 Expense by economic type												
2	**Expense**	**919**	**1,174**	**1,364**	**...**	**1,219**	**1,407**	**...**	**1,233**	**1,426**	**...**	**1,136**	**1,373**
21	**Compensation of employees**	**279**	**338**	**363**	**...**	**433**	**461**	**...**	**438**	**467**	**...**	**503**	**563**
211	Wages and salaries	279	...	...	...	...	...	...	...	...	...	...	...
212	Employers' social contributions	—	...	...	...	...	...	...	...	...	...	...	...
22	**Use of goods and services**	**112**	**132**	**174**	**...**	**271**	**325**	**...**	**278**	**337**	**...**	**313**	**393**
23	**Consumption of fixed capital**	**...**	**...**	**...**	**...**	**...**	**...**	**...**	**...**	**...**	**...**	**...**	**...**
24	**Interest**	**93**	**132**	**167**	**...**	**132**	**168**	**...**	**132**	**168**	**...**	**137**	**173**
25	**Subsidies**	**0**	**22**	**31**	**...**	**22**	**31**	**...**	**22**	**31**	**...**	**23**	**31**
26	**Grants**	**401**	**516**	**591**	**...**	**316**	**372**	**...**	**316**	**372**	**...**	**113**	**148**
261	To foreign governments	—	—	—	...	—	—	...	—	—	...	—	—
262	To international organizations	2	3	3	...	3	3	...	3	3	...	3	3
263	To other general government units	399	513	588	...	313	369	...	313	369	...	110	145
2631	Current	272	343	403	...	209	295	...	209	295	...	5	72
2632	Capital	127	170	185	...	105	74	...	105	74	...	105	74

Kenya (664)

In Billions of Kenya Shillings (KES) / Fiscal Year Ends June 30th

		Budgetary Central Government			Central Government (excl. Social Security)			Central Government (incl. Social Security)			General Government		
		2013	2014	2015	2013	2014P	2015P	2013	2014	2015	2013	2014P	2015P
27	**Social benefits**	**29**	**29**	**34**	**...**	**30**	**34**	**...**	**30**	**34**	**...**	**30**	**40**
271	Social security benefits	29	29	34	...	30	34	...	30	34	...	30	34
272	Social assistance benefits	—	—	—	...	—	—	...	—	0	...	—	6
273	Employment-related social benefits	—	—	—	...	—	—	...	—	—	...	—	—
28	**Other expense**	**5**	**5**	**4**	**...**	**5**	**4**	**...**	**5**	**4**	**...**	**7**	**11**
281	Property expense other than interest	3	—	—	...	—	—	...	0	—	...	0	—
282	Transfers not elsewhere classified	2	5	4	...	5	4	...	5	4	...	7	11
2821	Current	2	5	4	...	5	4	...	5	4	...	7	11
2822	Capital	—	—	—	...	—	—	...	—	—	...	—	—
	Table 3 Transactions in assets and liabilities												
3	**Change in net worth from transactions**	**...**	**...**	**...**	**...**	**...**	**...**	**...**	**...**	**...**	**...**	**...**	**...**
31	**Net/Gross investment in nonfinancial assets**	**140**	**138**	**336**	**...**	**265**	**483**	**...**	**268**	**481**	**...**	**311**	**569**
311	Fixed assets	136	133	328	...	239	456	...	242	455	...	278	541
3111	Buildings and structures	109	108	296	...	215	410	...	216	409	...	243	478
3112	Machinery and equipment	27	25	33	...	24	46	...	25	46	...	35	63
3113	Other fixed assets	—	—	—	...	—	—	...	—	—	...	—	—
3114	Weapons systems	—	—	—	...	—	—	...	—	—	...	—	—
312	Inventories	3	4	6	...	5	9	...	5	9	...	5	10
313	Valuables	—	—	—	...	—	—	...	—	—	...	—	—
314	Nonproduced assets	1	1	2	...	21	17	...	22	17	...	28	18
3141	Land	1	1	2	...	21	17	...	22	17	...	28	18
3142	Mineral and energy resources	—	—	—	...	—	—	...	—	—	...	—	—
3143	Other naturally occurring assets	—	—	—	...	—	—	...	—	—	...	—	—
3144	Intangible nonproduced assets	—	—	—	...	—	—	...	—	—	...	—	—
32	**Net acquisition of financial assets**	**—**	**-31**	**49**	**...**	**0**	**74**	**...**	**13**	**88**	**...**	**44**	**84**
	By instrument												
3201	Monetary gold and SDRs	...	—	—	...	—	—	...	—	—	...	—	—
3202	Currency and deposits	...	-38	31	...	-22	38	...	-17	45	...	11	37
3203	Debt securities	...	—	—	...	8	2	...	17	9	...	17	9
3204	Loans	...	7	18	...	49	27	...	48	27	...	49	31
3205	Equity and investment fund shares	...	—	—	...	2	2	...	2	1	...	2	1
3206	Insurance, pension, and standardized guarantee schemes	...	—	—	...	—	—	...	—	—	...	—	—
3207	Financial derivatives and employee stock options	...	—	—	...	—	—	...	—	—	...	—	—
3208	Other accounts receivable	...	...	...	...	...	...	...	...	...	...	...	...
	By debtor												
321	Domestic debtors	—	-31	49	...	0	74	...	13	88	...	44	84
322	External debtors	—	—	—	...	—	—	...	—	—	...	—	—
33	**Net incurrence of liabilities**	**—**	**333**	**607**	**...**	**334**	**599**	**...**	**332**	**599**	**...**	**335**	**599**
	By instrument												
3301	Special Drawing Rights (SDRs)	...	—	—	...	—	—	...	—	—	...	—	—
3302	Currency and deposits	...	—	—	...	—	—	...	—	—	...	—	—
3303	Debt securities	...	201	311	...	201	311	...	201	311	...	201	311
3304	Loans	...	132	297	...	144	305	...	144	305	...	144	305
3305	Equity and investment fund shares	...	—	—	...	—	—	...	—	—	...	—	—
3306	Insurance, pension, and standardized guarantee schemes	...	—	—	...	—	—	...	—	—	...	—	—
3307	Financial derivatives and employee stock options	...	—	—	...	—	—	...	—	—	...	—	—
3308	Other accounts payable	...	...	...	...	...	...	...	...	...	...	...	...
	By creditor												
331	Domestic creditors	—	165	128	...	167	119	...	164	120	...	168	120
332	External creditors	—	168	479	...	168	479	...	168	479	...	168	479
	Table 4 Holding gains and losses in assets and liabilities												
	Table 5 Holding gains and losses in assets and liabilities												
	Table 6 Balance sheet												

Kenya (664)

In Billions of Kenya Shillings (KES) / Fiscal Year Ends June 30th

		Budgetary Central Government			Central Government (excl. Social Security)			Central Government (incl. Social Security)			General Government		
		2013	2014	2015	2013	2014P	2015P	2013	2014	2015	2013	2014P	2015P
	Table 7 Expenditure by functions of government												
7	**Expenditure**	**1,059**	**1,312**	**1,699**	**...**	**1,485**	**1,889**	**...**	**1,501**	**1,908**	**...**	**1,447**	**1,942**
701	**General public services**	**330**	**...**	**...**	**...**	**...**	**...**	**...**	**...**	**...**	**...**	**...**	**...**
7017	Public debt transactions	93	132	167	...	132	168	...	132	168	...	137	173
7018	Transfers of general character between levels of government	21	...	...	...	...	...	...	...	...	...	...	...
702	**Defense**	**76**	**...**	**...**	**...**	**...**	**...**	**...**	**...**	**...**	**...**	**...**	**...**
703	**Public order and safety**	**105**	**...**	**...**	**...**	**...**	**...**	**...**	**...**	**...**	**...**	**...**	**...**
704	**Economic affairs**	**258**	**...**	**...**	**...**	**...**	**...**	**...**	**...**	**...**	**...**	**...**	**...**
7042	Agriculture, forestry, fishing, and hunting	44	...	...	...	...	...	...	...	...	...	...	...
7043	Fuel and energy	60	...	...	...	...	...	...	...	...	...	...	...
7044	Mining, manufacturing, and construction	1	...	...	...	...	...	...	...	...	...	...	...
7045	Transport	116	...	...	...	...	...	...	...	...	...	...	...
7046	Communication	6	...	...	...	...	...	...	...	...	...	...	...
705	**Environmental protection**	**24**	**...**	**...**	**...**	**...**	**...**	**...**	**...**	**...**	**...**	**...**	**...**
706	**Housing and community amenities**	**13**	**...**	**...**	**...**	**...**	**...**	**...**	**...**	**...**	**...**	**...**	**...**
707	**Health**	**72**	**...**	**...**	**...**	**...**	**...**	**...**	**...**	**...**	**...**	**...**	**...**
7072	Outpatient services	15	...	...	...	...	...	...	...	...	...	...	...
7073	Hospital services	37	...	...	...	...	...	...	...	...	...	...	...
7074	Public health services	18	...	...	...	...	...	...	...	...	...	...	...
708	**Recreation, culture and religion**	**1**	**...**	**...**	**...**	**...**	**...**	**...**	**...**	**...**	**...**	**...**	**...**
709	**Education**	**220**	**...**	**...**	**...**	**...**	**...**	**...**	**...**	**...**	**...**	**...**	**...**
7091	Pre-primary and primary education	86	...	...	...	...	...	...	...	...	...	...	...
7092	Secondary education	72	...	...	...	...	...	...	...	...	...	...	...
7094	Tertiary education	46	...	...	...	...	...	...	...	...	...	...	...
710	**Social protection**	**33**	**...**	**...**	**...**	**...**	**...**	**...**	**...**	**...**	**...**	**...**	**...**
7z	Statistical discrepancy: Expenditure	...	...	...	...	...	...	...	...	...	...	...	...
	Table 8 Financial transactions by counterpart sector												
	Table 9 Total other economic flows in assets and liabilities												

Kiribati (826)

In Thousands of Australian Dollars (AUD) / Fiscal Year Ends June 30th

		Budgetary Central Government			Central Government (excl. Social Security)			Central Government (incl. Social Security)			General Government		
		2013	2014	2015P	2013	2014	2015P	2013	2014	2015P	2013	2014	2015P
	Statement of operations												
1	Revenue	130,166	191,728	257,514	173,459	242,670	312,240	173,459	242,670	312,240	176,875	245,925	315,239
2	Expense	102,538	112,054	133,884	125,800	126,820	155,454	125,800	126,820	155,454	129,480	130,124	157,514
GOB	**Gross operating balance**	**27,628**	**79,674**	**123,630**	**47,659**	**115,850**	**156,786**	**47,659**	**115,850**	**156,786**	**47,395**	**115,802**	**157,726**
NOB	**Net operating balance**	...	...	...	...	...	...	...	...	...	...	...	...
31	Net/Gross investment in nonfinancial assets	3,694	4,206	546	8,414	10,839	9,206	8,414	10,839	9,206	8,414	10,839	9,206
2M	Expenditure	106,232	116,260	134,431	134,214	137,659	164,659	134,214	137,659	164,659	137,895	140,963	166,719
NLB	**Net lending (+) / Net borrowing (-)**	**23,933**	**75,468**	**123,083**	**39,245**	**105,011**	**147,581**	**39,245**	**105,011**	**147,581**	**38,980**	**104,963**	**148,520**
32	Net acquisition of financial assets	18,266	81,015	146,135	19,578	90,558	170,632	19,578	90,558	170,632	19,229	90,422	171,610
33	Net incurrence of liabilities	-5,667	5,547	23,051	-19,667	-14,453	23,051	-19,667	-14,453	23,051	-19,751	-14,541	23,090
NLBz	Statistical discrepancy	-0	-0	—	0	-0	-0	0	-0	-0	0	—	0
	Memorandum items												
PB	Primary net lending / net borrowing	25,771	75,468	123,248	41,082	105,011	147,745	41,082	105,011	147,745	40,818	104,963	148,684
GB	Government balance per national definition	...	...	...	...	...	...	...	...	...	...	...	...
	Statement of other economic flows												
	Balance sheet												
	Table 1 Revenue												
1	**Revenue**	**130,166**	**191,728**	**257,514**	**173,459**	**242,670**	**312,240**	**173,459**	**242,670**	**312,240**	**176,875**	**245,925**	**315,239**
11	**Taxes**	**30,896**	**30,249**	**45,053**	**34,589**	**33,204**	**50,310**	**34,589**	**33,204**	**50,310**	**35,733**	**34,421**	**51,627**
111	Taxes on income, profits, and capital gains	12,196	11,442	14,256	12,690	11,442	16,273	12,690	11,442	16,273	12,767	11,557	16,415
1111	Payable by individuals	7,310	6,963	6,794	7,310	6,963	6,794	7,310	6,963	6,794	7,379	7,067	6,926
1112	Payable by corporations and other enterprises	4,886	4,478	7,461	5,380	4,478	9,479	5,380	4,478	9,479	5,388	4,491	9,489
1113	Other taxes on income, profits, and capital gains	—	—	—	—	—	—	—	—	—	—	—	—
112	Taxes on payroll and workforce	—	—	—	—	—	—	—	—	—	—	—	—
113	Taxes on property	—	—	—	—	—	—	—	—	—	—	—	—
114	Taxes on goods and services	1,345	14,769	30,797	1,345	14,769	30,797	1,345	14,769	30,797	2,411	15,871	31,972
1141	General taxes on goods and services	—	8,427	14,548	—	8,427	14,548	—	8,427	14,548	—	8,427	14,548
1142	Excises	—	4,466	6,173	—	4,466	6,173	—	4,466	6,173	—	4,466	6,173
115	Taxes on international trade and transactions	17,356	4,006	—	20,554	6,961	3,240	20,554	6,961	3,240	20,554	6,961	3,240
116	Other taxes	—	33	—	—	33	—	—	33	—	—	33	—
12	**Social contributions**	—	—	—	—	—	—	—	—	—	—	—	—
121	Social security contributions	—	—	—	—	—	—	—	—	—	—	—	—
122	Other social contributions	—	—	—	—	—	—	—	—	—	—	—	—
13	**Grants**	—	**10,401**	**4,781**	**25,867**	**27,722**	**13,718**	**25,867**	**27,722**	**13,718**	**25,867**	**27,722**	**13,718**
131	From foreign governments	—	1,000	1,000	22,315	10,565	4,836	22,315	10,565	4,836	22,315	10,565	4,836
132	From international organizations	—	9,401	3,781	3,552	17,157	8,882	3,552	17,157	8,882	3,552	17,157	8,882
133	From other general government units	—	—	—	—	—	—	—	—	—	—	—	0
1331	Current	—	—	—	—	—	—	—	—	—	—	—	0
1332	Capital	—	—	—	—	—	—	—	—	—	—	—	—
14	**Other revenue**	**99,269**	**151,078**	**207,680**	**113,002**	**181,744**	**248,212**	**113,002**	**181,744**	**248,212**	**115,275**	**183,782**	**249,894**
	Table 2 Expense by economic type												
2	**Expense**	**102,538**	**112,054**	**133,884**	**125,800**	**126,820**	**155,454**	**125,800**	**126,820**	**155,454**	**129,480**	**130,124**	**157,514**
21	**Compensation of employees**	**48,551**	**54,301**	**56,869**	**49,458**	**54,431**	**59,717**	**49,458**	**54,431**	**59,717**	**52,305**	**57,206**	**62,273**
211	Wages and salaries	45,658	51,357	53,926	46,561	51,484	56,743	46,561	51,484	56,743	49,002	54,052	59,107
212	Employers' social contributions	2,894	2,943	2,943	2,897	2,947	2,974	2,897	2,947	2,974	3,303	3,154	3,166
22	**Use of goods and services**	**24,453**	**27,148**	**30,947**	**48,974**	**44,903**	**69,611**	**48,974**	**44,903**	**69,611**	**51,001**	**46,668**	**71,070**
23	**Consumption of fixed capital**	...	...	...	...	...	...	...	...	...	...	...	...
24	**Interest**	**1,838**	—	**164**	**1,838**	—	**164**	**1,838**	—	**164**	**1,838**	—	**164**
25	**Subsidies**	**9,628**	**10,954**	**10,312**	**11,759**	**13,222**	**13,149**	**11,759**	**13,222**	**13,149**	**11,759**	**13,222**	**13,149**
26	**Grants**	**9,458**	**10,440**	**25,105**	**2,236**	**1,655**	**1,955**	**2,236**	**1,655**	**1,955**	**1,044**	**418**	—
261	To foreign governments	—	—	—	—	—	—	—	—	—	—	—	—
262	To international organizations	368	—	—	1,044	418	—	1,044	418	—	1,044	418	—
263	To other general government units	9,091	10,440	25,105	1,193	1,237	1,955	1,193	1,237	1,955	—	—	—
2631	Current	9,091	10,373	23,739	1,193	1,237	1,955	1,193	1,237	1,955	—	—	—
2632	Capital	—	68	1,367	—	—	—	—	—	—	—	—	—

Kiribati (826)

In Thousands of Australian Dollars (AUD) / Fiscal Year Ends June 30th

		Budgetary Central Government			Central Government (excl. Social Security)			Central Government (incl. Social Security)			General Government		
		2013	2014	2015P	2013	2014	2015P	2013	2014	2015P	2013	2014	2015P
27	**Social benefits**	**5,060**	**5,000**	**5,695**	**5,923**	**5,111**	**5,695**	**5,923**	**5,111**	**5,695**	**5,923**	**5,111**	**5,695**
271	Social security benefits	—	—	—	—	—	—	—	—	—	—	—	—
272	Social assistance benefits	5,060	5,000	5,695	5,923	5,111	5,695	5,923	5,111	5,695	5,923	5,111	5,695
273	Employment-related social benefits	—	—	—	—	—	—	—	—	—	—	—	—
28	**Other expense**	**3,550**	**4,212**	**4,792**	**5,611**	**7,498**	**5,162**	**5,611**	**7,498**	**5,162**	**5,611**	**7,498**	**5,162**
281	Property expense other than interest	2,967	2,907	2,816	2,967	2,907	2,816	2,967	2,907	2,816	2,967	2,907	2,816
282	Transfers not elsewhere classified	583	1,305	1,976	2,644	4,591	2,345	2,644	4,591	2,345	2,644	4,591	2,345
2821	Current	583	1,305	1,775	2,644	4,591	2,144	2,644	4,591	2,144	2,644	4,591	2,144
2822	Capital	—	—	201	—	—	201	—	—	201	—	—	201
	Table 3 Transactions in assets and liabilities												
3	**Change in net worth from transactions**	**27,628**	**79,674**	**123,630**	**47,659**	**115,850**	**156,786**	**47,659**	**115,850**	**156,786**	**47,395**	**115,802**	**157,726**
31	**Net/Gross investment in nonfinancial assets**	**3,694**	**4,206**	**546**	**8,414**	**10,839**	**9,206**	**8,414**	**10,839**	**9,206**	**8,414**	**10,839**	**9,206**
311	Fixed assets	3,694	4,207	548	8,414	10,840	9,207	8,414	10,840	9,207	8,414	10,840	9,207
3111	Buildings and structures	705	712	226	4,932	5,000	8,884	4,932	5,000	8,884	4,932	5,000	8,884
3112	Machinery and equipment	2,990	3,495	321	3,482	5,840	323	3,482	5,840	323	3,482	5,840	323
3113	Other fixed assets	—	—	—	—	—	—	—	—	—	—	—	—
3114	Weapons systems	—	—	—	—	—	—	—	—	—	—	—	—
312	Inventories	—	—	—	—	—	—	—	—	—	—	—	—
313	Valuables	—	—	—	—	—	—	—	—	—	—	—	—
314	Nonproduced assets	—	-1	-1	—	-1	-1	—	-1	-1	—	-1	-1
3141	Land	—	-1	-1	—	-1	-1	—	-1	-1	—	-1	-1
3142	Mineral and energy resources	—	—	—	—	—	—	—	—	—	—	—	—
3143	Other naturally occurring assets	—	—	—	—	—	—	—	—	—	—	—	—
3144	Intangible nonproduced assets	—	—	—	—	—	—	—	—	—	—	—	—
32	**Net acquisition of financial assets**	**18,266**	**81,015**	**146,135**	**19,578**	**90,558**	**170,632**	**19,578**	**90,558**	**170,632**	**19,229**	**90,422**	**171,610**
	By instrument												
3201	Monetary gold and SDRs	—	—	—	—	—	—	—	—	—	—	—	—
3202	Currency and deposits	24,339	79,590	-29,592	59,359	334,718	-222,359	59,359	334,718	-222,359	59,010	334,582	-221,381
3203	Debt securities	—	—	—	27,248	-237,133	211,693	27,248	-237,133	211,693	27,248	-237,133	211,693
3204	Loans	928	1,425	726	928	1,425	726	928	1,425	726	928	1,425	726
3205	Equity and investment fund shares	-7,000	—	175,000	-67,957	-8,452	180,572	-67,957	-8,452	180,572	-67,957	-8,452	180,572
3206	Insurance, pension, and standardized guarantee schemes	—	—	—	—	—	—	—	—	—	—	—	—
3207	Financial derivatives and employee stock options	—	—	—	—	—	—	—	—	—	—	—	—
3208	Other accounts receivable	...	...	...	...	...	...	...	...	...	...	...	...
	By debtor												
321	Domestic debtors	18,893	81,641	146,754	46,914	316,770	-221,014	46,914	316,770	-221,014	46,565	316,634	-220,036
322	External debtors	-627	-627	-619	-27,336	-226,212	391,646	-27,336	-226,212	391,646	-27,336	-226,212	391,646
33	**Net incurrence of liabilities**	**-5,667**	**5,547**	**23,051**	**-19,667**	**-14,453**	**23,051**	**-19,667**	**-14,453**	**23,051**	**-19,751**	**-14,541**	**23,090**
	By instrument												
3301	Special Drawing Rights (SDRs)	—	—	—	—	—	—	—	—	—	—	—	—
3302	Currency and deposits	-4,786	15,612	23,906	-4,786	15,612	23,906	-4,786	15,612	23,906	-4,786	15,612	23,906
3303	Debt securities	—	—	—	—	—	—	—	—	—	—	—	—
3304	Loans	-881	-10,065	-855	-881	-10,065	-855	-881	-10,065	-855	-965	-10,153	-816
3305	Equity and investment fund shares	—	—	—	-14,000	-20,000	—	-14,000	-20,000	—	-14,000	-20,000	—
3306	Insurance, pension, and standardized guarantee schemes	—	—	—	—	—	—	—	—	—	—	—	—
3307	Financial derivatives and employee stock options	—	—	—	—	—	—	—	—	—	—	—	—
3308	Other accounts payable	...	...	...	...	...	...	...	...	...	...	...	...
	By creditor												
331	Domestic creditors	-4,764	6,509	24,136	-18,764	-13,491	24,136	-18,764	-13,491	24,136	-18,848	-13,579	24,175
332	External creditors	-903	-962	-1,085	-903	-962	-1,085	-903	-962	-1,085	-903	-962	-1,085
	Table 4 Holding gains and losses in assets and liabilities												
	Table 5 Holding gains and losses in assets and liabilities												
	Table 6 Balance sheet												

Kiribati (826)

In Thousands of Australian Dollars (AUD) / Fiscal Year Ends June 30th

		Budgetary Central Government			Central Government (excl. Social Security)			Central Government (incl. Social Security)			General Government		
		2013	2014	2015P	2013	2014	2015P	2013	2014	2015P	2013	2014	2015P
	Table 7 Expenditure by functions of government												
7	**Expenditure**	106,233	116,260	134,431	134,215	137,659	164,659	134,215	137,659	164,659	137,896	140,963	166,719
701	**General public services**	39,587	45,101	61,316	45,518	44,576	57,646	45,518	44,576	57,646	49,199	47,879	59,706
7017	Public debt transactions	...	...	...	...	...	...	...	...	...	...	...	...
7018	Transfers of general character between levels of government	...	...	...	...	...	...	...	...	...	...	...	...
702	**Defense**	...	—	—	—	—	—	—	—	—	—	—	—
703	**Public order and safety**	9,029	9,545	9,519	9,917	9,784	9,859	9,917	9,784	9,859	9,917	9,784	9,859
704	**Economic affairs**	20,885	22,248	22,070	34,581	35,017	45,602	34,581	35,017	45,602	34,581	35,017	45,602
7042	Agriculture, forestry, fishing, and hunting	...	...	...	...	...	...	...	...	...	...	...	...
7043	Fuel and energy	...	...	...	...	...	...	...	...	...	...	...	...
7044	Mining, manufacturing, and construction	...	...	...	...	...	...	...	...	...	...	...	...
7045	Transport	...	...	...	...	...	...	...	...	...	...	...	...
7046	Communication	...	...	...	...	...	...	...	...	...	...	...	...
705	**Environmental protection**	2,288	2,277	2,439	2,870	3,067	3,582	2,870	3,067	3,582	2,870	3,067	3,582
706	**Housing and community amenities**	...	...	—	—	—	—	—	—	—	—	—	—
707	**Health**	14,780	16,128	17,687	17,573	20,201	22,456	17,573	20,201	22,456	17,573	20,201	22,456
7072	Outpatient services	...	...	...	...	...	...	...	...	...	...	...	...
7073	Hospital services	...	...	...	...	...	...	...	...	...	...	...	...
7074	Public health services	...	...	...	...	...	...	...	...	...	...	...	...
708	**Recreation, culture and religion**	163	...	—	201	...	—	201	...	...	201	...	...
709	**Education**	19,080	19,645	19,834	23,060	22,393	22,465	23,060	22,393	22,465	23,060	22,393	22,465
7091	Pre-primary and primary education	...	...	...	...	...	...	...	...	...	...	...	...
7092	Secondary education	...	...	...	...	...	...	...	...	...	...	...	...
7094	Tertiary education	...	...	...	...	...	...	...	...	...	...	...	...
710	**Social protection**	422	1,317	1,565	495	2,621	3,050	495	2,621	3,050	495	2,621	3,050
7z	Statistical discrepancy: Expenditure	...	...	...	...	...	...	...	...	...	...	...	...
	Table 8 Financial transactions by counterpart sector												
	Table 9 Total other economic flows in assets and liabilities												

Korea, Republic of (542)

In Trillions of Korean Won (KRW) / Fiscal Year Ends December 31st

		Budgetary Central Government			Central Government (excl. Social Security)			Central Government (incl. Social Security)			General Government		
		2013	2014	2015	2013	2014	2015	2013	2014	2015	2013	2014	2015
	Statement of operations												
1	Revenue	333	339	354	...	...	...	392	398	416	484	505	535
2	Expense	310	318	337	...	...	...	361	369	389	421	443	470
GOB	**Gross operating balance**	**35**	**33**	**29**	**...**	**...**	**...**	**45**	**42**	**40**	**87**	**87**	**91**
NOB	**Net operating balance**	**23**	**21**	**16**	**...**	**...**	**...**	**32**	**29**	**26**	**63**	**62**	**64**
31	Net/Gross investment in nonfinancial assets	11	11	11	...	...	...	12	13	14	42	41	45
2M	Expenditure	320	329	349	...	...	...	373	382	403	463	484	515
NLB	**Net lending (+) / Net borrowing (-)**	**13**	**10**	**5**	**...**	**...**	**...**	**19**	**16**	**13**	**21**	**21**	**20**
32	Net acquisition of financial assets	64	53	55	...	...	...	74	60	60	75	72	72
33	Net incurrence of liabilities	52	43	50	...	...	...	55	44	48	54	51	52
NLBz	Statistical discrepancy	-0	—	—	...	...	...	0	—	—	-0	—	0
	Memorandum items												
PB	Primary net lending / net borrowing	32	29	25	...	...	...	40	37	33	43	43	42
GB	Government balance per national definition	...	...	...	...	...	...	...	...	...	...	...	...
	Statement of other economic flows												
	Balance sheet												
6	**Net worth**	**1,194**	**1,234**	**1,282**	**...**	**...**	**...**	**1,234**	**1,286**	**1,345**	**2,310**	**2,393**	**2,491**
61	Nonfinancial assets	810	822	837	...	...	...	840	854	874	1,870	1,913	1,965
62	Financial assets	865	939	1,025	...	...	...	918	1,002	1,092	1,007	1,102	1,203
63	Liabilities	481	527	580	...	...	...	524	570	622	567	622	677
	Table 1 Revenue												
1	**Revenue**	**333**	**339**	**354**	**...**	**...**	**...**	**392**	**398**	**416**	**484**	**505**	**535**
11	**Taxes**	**205**	**207**	**218**	**...**	**...**	**...**	**205**	**207**	**218**	**260**	**271**	**291**
111	Taxes on income, profits, and capital gains	94	99	109	...	...	...	94	99	109	105	110	122
1111	Payable by individuals	50	56	63	...	...	...	50	56	63	61	66	76
1112	Payable by corporations and other enterprises	44	43	46	...	...	...	44	43	46	44	43	46
1113	Other taxes on income, profits, and capital gains	—	—	—	...	...	...	—	—	—	—	—	—
112	Taxes on payroll and workforce	—	—	—	...	...	...	—	—	—	—	—	—
113	Taxes on property	6	7	6	...	...	...	6	7	6	23	25	24
114	Taxes on goods and services	85	87	88	...	...	...	85	87	88	108	116	122
1141	General taxes on goods and services	63	65	63	...	...	...	63	65	63	79	87	90
1142	Excises	22	22	25	...	...	...	22	22	25	25	25	28
115	Taxes on international trade and transactions	11	9	9	...	...	...	11	9	9	11	9	9
116	Other taxes	8	6	6	...	...	...	8	6	6	14	11	14
12	**Social contributions**	**54**	**58**	**62**	**...**	**...**	**...**	**96**	**103**	**109**	**96**	**103**	**109**
121	Social security contributions	45	48	51	...	...	...	86	92	99	86	92	99
122	Other social contributions	9	10	11	...	...	...	9	10	11	9	10	11
13	**Grants**	**—**	**—**	**1**	**...**	**...**	**...**	**0**	**7**	**4**	**—**	**0**	**—**
131	From foreign governments	—	—	—	...	...	...	—	—	—	—	—	—
132	From international organizations	—	—	—	...	...	...	—	0	0	—	0	—
133	From other general government units	—	—	1	...	...	...	0	7	4	—	—	—
1331	Current	—	—	...	...	...	...	...	...	...	—	—	—
1332	Capital	—	—	...	...	...	...	...	...	...	—	—	—
14	**Other revenue**	**74**	**74**	**73**	**...**	**...**	**...**	**92**	**81**	**84**	**129**	**132**	**134**
	Table 2 Expense by economic type												
2	**Expense**	**310**	**318**	**337**	**...**	**...**	**...**	**361**	**369**	**389**	**421**	**443**	**470**
21	**Compensation of employees**	**31**	**33**	**34**	**...**	**...**	**...**	**37**	**38**	**40**	**86**	**90**	**95**
211	Wages and salaries	30	31	33	...	...	...	35	37	38	79	82	85
212	Employers' social contributions	1	1	1	...	...	...	2	1	2	8	9	10
22	**Use of goods and services**	**26**	**25**	**28**	**...**	**...**	**...**	**47**	**49**	**57**	**86**	**92**	**99**
23	**Consumption of fixed capital**	**12**	**12**	**13**	**...**	**...**	**...**	**13**	**13**	**14**	**24**	**25**	**27**
24	**Interest**	**19**	**20**	**20**	**...**	**...**	**...**	**20**	**21**	**21**	**22**	**23**	**22**
25	**Subsidies**	**21**	**16**	**17**	**...**	**...**	**...**	**25**	**20**	**22**	**71**	**70**	**77**

Korea, Republic of (542)

In Trillions of Korean Won (KRW) / Fiscal Year Ends December 31st

		Budgetary Central Government			Central Government (excl. Social Security)			Central Government (incl. Social Security)			General Government		
		2013	2014	2015	2013	2014	2015	2013	2014	2015	2013	2014	2015
26	**Grants**	**140**	**150**	**160**	**...**	**...**	**...**	**115**	**117**	**118**	**1**	**1**	**1**
261	To foreign governments	—	—	—	...	...	...	0	1	1	0	1	1
262	To international organizations	0	0	0	...	...	...	0	0	0	0	0	0
263	To other general government units	140	150	160	...	...	...	114	117	118	—	—	—
2631	Current	...	...	...	...	...	...	...	...	...	—	—	—
2632	Capital	...	...	...	...	...	...	...	...	...	—	—	—
27	**Social benefits**	**43**	**46**	**50**	**...**	**...**	**...**	**86**	**93**	**100**	**86**	**93**	**100**
271	Social security benefits	43	46	50	...	...	...	86	93	100	86	93	100
272	Social assistance benefits	0	0	0	...	...	...	0	0	0	0	0	0
273	Employment-related social benefits	—	—	—	...	...	...	—	—	—	—	—	—
28	**Other expense**	**17**	**15**	**15**	**...**	**...**	**...**	**18**	**18**	**16**	**46**	**50**	**50**
281	Property expense other than interest	0	0	0	...	...	...	0	0	0	0	0	0
282	Transfers not elsewhere classified	17	15	15	...	...	...	18	17	16	46	50	50
2821	Current	16	15	15	...	...	...	17	17	16	45	49	50
2822	Capital	1	0	0	...	...	...	1	0	0	1	0	0
	Table 3 Transactions in assets and liabilities												
3	**Change in net worth from transactions**	**23**	**21**	**16**	**...**	**...**	**...**	**32**	**29**	**26**	**63**	**62**	**64**
31	**Net/Gross investment in nonfinancial assets**	**11**	**11**	**11**	**...**	**...**	**...**	**12**	**13**	**14**	**42**	**41**	**45**
311	Fixed assets	10	10	10	...	...	...	11	11	11	30	27	27
3111	Buildings and structures	...	...	8	...	...	...	...	...	9	...	...	22
3112	Machinery and equipment	...	...	3	...	...	...	...	...	3	...	...	3
3113	Other fixed assets	...	...	-0	...	...	...	...	...	-0	...	...	1
3114	Weapons systems	...	...	...	...	...	...	...	...	...	...	...	...
312	Inventories	-1	0	1	...	...	...	-1	1	1	1	0	1
313	Valuables	—	—	—	...	...	...	—	—	—	—	—	—
314	Nonproduced assets	2	1	0	...	...	...	2	1	1	12	14	17
3141	Land	...	...	...	...	...	...	...	...	...	...	...	...
3142	Mineral and energy resources	...	...	...	...	...	...	...	...	...	...	...	...
3143	Other naturally occurring assets	...	...	...	...	...	...	...	...	...	...	...	...
3144	Intangible nonproduced assets	...	...	...	...	...	...	...	...	...	...	...	...
32	**Net acquisition of financial assets**	**64**	**53**	**55**	**...**	**...**	**...**	**74**	**60**	**60**	**75**	**72**	**72**
	By instrument												
3201	Monetary gold and SDRs	—	—	—	...	...	...	—	—	—	—	—	—
3202	Currency and deposits	-3	-18	-11	...	...	...	2	-11	-4	4	-5	10
3203	Debt securities	9	11	-4	...	...	...	8	12	-4	12	17	-4
3204	Loans	-2	6	1	...	...	...	0	4	0	-7	1	-2
3205	Equity and investment fund shares	39	32	59	...	...	...	39	32	59	42	33	59
3206	Insurance, pension, and standardized guarantee schemes	—	—	—	...	...	...	—	—	—	—	—	—
3207	Financial derivatives and employee stock options	-3	-2	-5	...	...	...	-3	-2	-5	-3	-2	-5
3208	Other accounts receivable	24	23	14	...	...	...	28	25	14	27	28	13
	By debtor												
321	Domestic debtors	50	...	54	...	...	...	61	...	59	61	...	71
322	External debtors	14	...	1	...	...	...	14	...	1	14	...	1
33	**Net incurrence of liabilities**	**52**	**43**	**50**	**...**	**...**	**...**	**55**	**44**	**48**	**54**	**51**	**52**
	By instrument												
3301	Special Drawing Rights (SDRs)	—	—	—	...	...	...	—	—	—	—	—	—
3302	Currency and deposits	—	—	—	...	...	...	—	—	—	—	—	—
3303	Debt securities	42	33	40	...	...	...	46	34	38	48	35	39
3304	Loans	13	9	12	...	...	...	12	9	12	8	12	16
3305	Equity and investment fund shares	—	—	—	...	...	...	-0	—	-0	-0	—	-0
3306	Insurance, pension, and standardized guarantee schemes	...	...	...	...	...	...	...	...	...	...	...	...
3307	Financial derivatives and employee stock options	-2	-2	-3	...	...	...	-2	-2	-3	-2	-2	-3
3308	Other accounts payable	-2	3	0	...	...	...	-1	4	1	0	7	0

Korea, Republic of (542)

In Trillions of Korean Won (KRW) / Fiscal Year Ends December 31st

		Budgetary Central Government			Central Government (excl. Social Security)			Central Government (incl. Social Security)			General Government		
		2013	2014	2015	2013	2014	2015	2013	2014	2015	2013	2014	2015
	By creditor												
331	Domestic creditors	-7	...	48	...	...	...	-4	...	46	-5	...	51
332	External creditors	59	...	1	...	...	...	59	...	1	59	...	...
	Table 4 Holding gains and losses in assets and liabilities												
	Table 5 Holding gains and losses in assets and liabilities												
	Table 6 Balance sheet												
6	**Net worth**	**1,194**	**1,234**	**1,282**	**...**	**...**	**...**	**1,234**	**1,286**	**1,345**	**2,310**	**2,393**	**2,491**
61	**Nonfinancial assets**	**810**	**822**	**837**	**...**	**...**	**...**	**840**	**854**	**874**	**1,870**	**1,913**	**1,965**
611	Fixed assets	369	378	384	...	...	...	389	400	406	1,044	1,070	1,093
6111	Buildings and structures	...	...	271	...	...	...	...	...	289	...	...	957
6112	Machinery and equipment	...	...	91	...	...	...	...	...	96	...	...	109
6113	Other fixed assets	...	...	21	...	...	...	...	...	21	...	...	27
6114	Weapons systems	...	...	...	...	...	...	...	...	...	...	...	...
612	Inventories	6	6	6	...	...	...	8	9	10	14	15	15
613	Valuables	—	—	—	...	...	...	—	—	—	—	—	—
614	Nonproduced assets	436	438	447	...	...	...	443	445	458	811	828	857
6141	Land	...	...	447	...	...	...	...	...	...	...	...	...
6142	Mineral and energy resources	...	...	—	...	...	...	...	...	...	...	...	...
6143	Other naturally occurring assets	...	...	—	...	...	...	...	...	...	...	...	...
6144	Intangible nonproduced assets	...	...	0	...	...	...	...	...	...	...	...	...
62	**Financial assets**	**865**	**939**	**1,025**	**...**	**...**	**...**	**918**	**1,002**	**1,092**	**1,007**	**1,102**	**1,203**
	By instrument												
6201	Monetary gold and SDRs	—	—	—	...	...	...	—	—	—	—	—	—
6202	Currency and deposits	126	111	108	...	...	...	148	144	148	197	198	216
6203	Debt securities	129	144	140	...	...	...	130	144	141	123	143	140
6204	Loans	139	145	150	...	...	...	154	159	162	159	162	163
6205	Equity and investment fund shares	371	408	478	...	...	...	369	406	476	398	436	506
6206	Insurance, pension, and standardized guarantee schemes	—	—	—	...	...	...	—	—	—	—	—	—
6207	Financial derivatives and employee stock options	1	3	1	...	...	...	1	3	2	1	3	2
6208	Other accounts receivable	101	128	147	...	...	...	117	146	163	129	160	177
	By debtor												
621	Domestic debtors	...	...	1,009	...	...	...	...	...	1,077	...	...	1,188
622	External debtors	...	...	16	...	...	...	...	...	16	...	...	16
63	**Liabilities**	**481**	**527**	**580**	**...**	**...**	**...**	**524**	**570**	**622**	**567**	**622**	**677**
	By instrument												
6301	Special Drawing Rights (SDRs)	—	—	—	...	...	...	—	—	—	—	—	—
6302	Currency and deposits	—	—	—	...	...	...	—	—	—	—	—	—
6303	Debt securities	402	435	476	...	...	...	434	469	507	449	485	525
6304	Loans	45	54	66	...	...	...	46	55	67	57	70	93
6305	Equity and investment fund shares	—	—	—	...	...	...	0	0	0	0	0	0
6306	Insurance, pension, and standardized guarantee schemes	...	...	...	...	...	...	—	—	—	...	...	...
6307	Financial derivatives and employee stock options	1	1	1	...	...	...	1	1	1	1	1	1
6308	Other accounts payable	33	37	37	...	...	...	42	46	46	60	66	58
	By creditor												
631	Domestic creditors	...	...	512	...	...	...	...	...	554	...	...	609
632	External creditors	...	...	68	...	...	...	...	...	68	...	...	68
	Memorandum items												
6M2	Net financial worth	385	413	445	...	...	...	394	432	471	440	481	526
6M3	Gross debt (D4) at market value	...	...	...	...	...	...	...	...	...	...	...	...
6M3D3	D3 debt liabilities at market value	...	...	...	...	...	...	...	...	...	...	...	...
6M3D2	D2 debt liabilities at market value	...	...	...	...	...	...	...	...	...	...	...	...
6M3D1	D1 debt liabilities at market value	...	...	...	...	...	...	...	...	...	...	...	...
6M4	Gross debt (D4) at nominal value	...	...	...	...	...	...	...	...	...	...	...	...
6M4D3	D3 debt liabilities at nominal value	...	...	...	...	...	...	...	...	...	...	...	...
6M4D2	D2 debt liabilities at nominal value	...	...	...	...	...	...	...	...	...	...	...	...
6M4D1	D1 debt liabilities at nominal value	...	...	...	...	...	...	...	...	...	...	...	...

Korea, Republic of (542)

In Trillions of Korean Won (KRW) / Fiscal Year Ends December 31st

		Budgetary Central Government			Central Government (excl. Social Security)			Central Government (incl. Social Security)			General Government		
		2013	2014	2015	2013	2014	2015	2013	2014	2015	2013	2014	2015
6M35	Gross debt (D4) at face value	...	...	...	...	...	...	...	...	...	...	...	...
6M35D3	D3 debt liabilities at face value	480	526	579	...	...	...	522	569	620	566	621	676
6M35D2	D2 debt liabilities at face value	446	489	542	...	...	...	480	524	574	506	555	618
6M35D1	D1 debt liabilities at face value	446	489	542	...	...	...	480	524	574	506	555	618
6M93	Government gross debt per national definition	...	...	...	...	...	...	...	...	...	...	...	...
6M5	Arrears	...	...	...	...	...	...	...	...	...	...	...	...
6M6	Explicit contingent liabilities	...	...	...	...	...	...	...	...	...	...	...	...
6M61	of which: Publicly guaranteed debt	...	...	...	...	...	...	...	...	...	...	...	...
6M7	Net implicit obligations for social security benefits	...	...	...	...	...	...	...	...	...	...	...	...
	Table 7 Expenditure by functions of government												
7	**Expenditure**	**320**	**329**	**349**	**...**	**...**	**...**	**373**	**382**	**403**	**463**	**484**	**515**
701	**General public services**	...	...	...	...	...	...	...	...	...	...	...	...
7017	Public debt transactions	19	20	20	...	...	...	20	21	21	22	23	22
7018	Transfers of general character between levels of government	...	...	...	...	...	...	...	...	...	...	...	...
702	**Defense**	...	...	...	...	...	...	...	...	...	...	...	...
703	**Public order and safety**	...	...	...	...	...	...	...	...	...	...	...	...
704	**Economic affairs**	...	...	...	...	...	...	...	...	...	...	...	...
7042	Agriculture, forestry, fishing, and hunting	...	...	...	...	...	...	...	...	...	...	...	...
7043	Fuel and energy	...	...	...	...	...	...	...	...	...	...	...	...
7044	Mining, manufacturing, and construction	...	...	...	...	...	...	...	...	...	...	...	...
7045	Transport	...	...	...	...	...	...	...	...	...	...	...	...
7046	Communication	...	...	...	...	...	...	...	...	...	...	...	...
705	**Environmental protection**	...	...	...	...	...	...	...	...	...	...	...	...
706	**Housing and community amenities**	...	...	...	...	...	...	...	...	...	...	...	...
707	**Health**	...	...	...	...	...	...	...	...	...	...	...	...
7072	Outpatient services	...	...	...	...	...	...	...	...	...	...	...	...
7073	Hospital services	...	...	...	...	...	...	...	...	...	...	...	...
7074	Public health services	...	...	...	...	...	...	...	...	...	...	...	...
708	**Recreation, culture and religion**	...	...	...	...	...	...	...	...	...	...	...	...
709	**Education**	...	...	...	...	...	...	...	...	...	...	...	...
7091	Pre-primary and primary education	...	...	...	...	...	...	...	...	...	...	...	...
7092	Secondary education	...	...	...	...	...	...	...	...	...	...	...	...
7094	Tertiary education	...	...	...	...	...	...	...	...	...	...	...	...
710	**Social protection**	...	...	...	...	...	...	...	...	...	...	...	...
7z	Statistical discrepancy: Expenditure	...	...	...	...	...	...	...	...	...	...	...	...
	Table 8 Financial transactions by counterpart sector												
32	**Net acquisition of financial assets**	**64**	**53**	**55**	**...**	**...**	**...**	**74**	**60**	**60**	**75**	**72**	**72**
321	Domestic debtors	50	...	54	...	...	...	61	...	59	61	...	71
8211	General government	...	...	...	...	...	...	...	...	...	...	...	...
8212	Central bank	...	...	...	...	...	...	...	...	...	...	...	...
8213	Deposit-taking corporations except the central bank	...	...	...	...	...	...	...	...	...	...	...	...
8214	Other financial corporations	...	...	...	...	...	...	...	...	...	...	...	...
8215	Nonfinancial corporations	...	...	...	...	...	...	...	...	...	...	...	...
8216	Households & nonprofit institutions serving households	...	...	...	...	...	...	...	...	...	...	...	...
322	External debtors	14	...	1	...	...	...	14	...	1	14	...	1
8221	General government	...	...	...	...	...	...	...	...	...	...	...	...
8227	International organizations	...	...	...	...	...	...	...	...	...	...	...	...
8228	Financial corporations other than international organizations	...	...	...	...	...	...	...	...	...	...	...	...
8229	Other nonresidents	...	...	...	...	...	...	...	...	...	...	...	...

Korea, Republic of (542)

In Trillions of Korean Won (KRW) / Fiscal Year Ends December 31st

		Budgetary Central Government			Central Government (excl. Social Security)			Central Government (incl. Social Security)			General Government		
		2013	2014	2015	2013	2014	2015	2013	2014	2015	2013	2014	2015
33	**Net incurrence of liabilities**	52	43	50	...	...	...	55	44	48	54	51	52
331	Domestic creditors	-7	...	48	...	...	...	-4	...	46	-5	...	51
3311	General government	...	...	...	...	...	...	...	...	...	...	...	...
3312	Central bank	...	...	...	...	...	...	...	...	...	...	...	...
3313	Deposit-taking corporations except the central bank	...	...	...	...	...	...	...	...	...	...	...	...
3314	Other financial corporations	...	...	...	...	...	...	...	...	...	...	...	...
3315	Nonfinancial corporations	...	...	...	...	...	...	...	...	...	...	...	...
3316	Households & nonprofit institutions serving households	...	...	...	...	...	...	...	...	...	...	...	...
332	External creditors	59	...	1	...	...	...	59	...	1	59	...	...
3321	General government	...	...	...	...	...	...	...	...	...	...	...	...
3327	International organizations	...	...	...	...	...	...	...	...	...	...	...	...
3328	Financial corporations other than international organizations	...	...	...	...	...	...	...	...	...	...	...	...
3329	Other nonresidents	...	...	...	...	...	...	...	...	...	...	...	...
	Table 9 Total other economic flows in assets and liabilities												

Kosovo, Republic of (967)

In Millions of Euros (EUR) / Fiscal Year Ends December 31st

		Budgetary Central Government			Central Government (excl. Social Security)			Central Government (incl. Social Security)			General Government		
		2013	2014	2015	2013	2014	2015	2013	2014	2015	2013	2014	2015
	Statement of operations												
1	Revenue	...	...	...	...	...	...	...	...	...	1,325	1,345	1,479
2	Expense	...	...	...	...	...	...	...	...	...	976	1,092	1,201
GOB	**Gross operating balance**	...	...	...	...	...	...	...	...	...	**349**	**253**	**278**
NOB	**Net operating balance**	...	...	...	...	...	...	...	...	...	...	...	...
31	Net/Gross investment in nonfinancial assets	...	...	...	...	...	...	...	...	...	521	396	383
2M	Expenditure	...	...	...	...	...	...	...	...	...	1,497	1,488	1,584
NLB	**Net lending (+) / Net borrowing (-)**	...	...	...	...	...	...	...	...	...	**-172**	**-143**	**-104**
32	Net acquisition of financial assets	...	...	...	...	...	...	...	...	...	-99	-51	33
33	Net incurrence of liabilities	...	...	...	...	...	...	...	...	...	70	92	137
NLBz	Statistical discrepancy	...	...	...	...	...	...	...	...	...	4	1	0
	Memorandum items												
PB	Primary net lending / net borrowing	...	...	...	...	...	...	...	...	...	-161	-130	-88
GB	Government balance per national definition	...	...	...	...	...	...	...	...	...	...	...	...
	Statement of other economic flows												
	Balance sheet												
	Table 1 Revenue												
1	**Revenue**	...	...	...	...	...	...	...	...	...	**1,325**	**1,345**	**1,479**
11	**Taxes**	...	...	...	...	...	...	...	...	...	**1,171**	**1,213**	**1,355**
111	Taxes on income, profits, and capital gains	...	...	...	...	...	...	...	...	...	154	165	103
1111	Payable by individuals	...	...	...	...	...	...	...	...	...	91	111	8
1112	Payable by corporations and other enterprises	...	...	...	...	...	...	...	...	...	63	55	95
1113	Other taxes on income, profits, and capital gains	...	...	...	...	...	...	...	...	...	—	—	—
112	Taxes on payroll and workforce	...	...	...	...	...	...	...	...	...	—	—	72
113	Taxes on property	...	...	...	...	...	...	...	...	...	16	20	20
114	Taxes on goods and services	...	...	...	...	...	...	...	...	...	880	899	1,029
1141	General taxes on goods and services	...	...	...	...	...	...	...	...	...	525	528	584
1142	Excises	...	...	...	...	...	...	...	...	...	301	315	356
115	Taxes on international trade and transactions	...	...	...	...	...	...	...	...	...	121	128	131
116	Other taxes	...	...	...	...	...	...	...	...	...	0	1	1
12	**Social contributions**	...	...	...	...	...	...	...	...	...	—	—	—
121	Social security contributions	...	...	...	...	...	...	...	...	...	—	—	—
122	Other social contributions	...	...	...	...	...	...	...	...	...	—	—	—
13	**Grants**	...	...	...	...	...	...	...	...	...	**13**	**12**	**15**
131	From foreign governments	...	...	...	...	...	...	...	...	...	—	—	13
132	From international organizations	...	...	...	...	...	...	...	...	...	13	12	1
133	From other general government units	...	...	...	...	...	...	...	...	...	—	—	—
1331	Current	...	...	...	...	...	...	...	...	...	—	—	—
1332	Capital	...	...	...	...	...	...	...	...	...	—	—	—
14	**Other revenue**	...	...	...	...	...	...	...	...	...	**141**	**120**	**109**
	Table 2 Expense by economic type												
2	**Expense**	...	...	...	...	...	...	...	...	...	**976**	**1,092**	**1,201**
21	**Compensation of employees**	...	...	...	...	...	...	...	...	...	**419**	**487**	**526**
211	Wages and salaries	...	...	...	...	...	...	...	...	...	...	...	476
212	Employers' social contributions	...	...	...	...	...	...	...	...	...	...	...	50
22	**Use of goods and services**	...	...	...	...	...	...	...	...	...	**217**	**211**	**184**
23	**Consumption of fixed capital**	...	...	...	...	...	...	...	...	...	...	...	...
24	**Interest**	...	...	...	...	...	...	...	...	...	**11**	**13**	**16**
25	**Subsidies**	...	...	...	...	...	...	...	...	...	**93**	**90**	**110**
26	**Grants**	...	...	...	...	...	...	...	...	...	**7**	**5**	**3**
261	To foreign governments	...	...	...	...	...	...	...	...	...	—	—	—
262	To international organizations	...	...	...	...	...	...	...	...	...	—	—	0
263	To other general government units	...	...	...	...	...	...	...	...	...	7	5	3
2631	Current	...	...	...	...	...	...	...	...	...	...	...	3
2632	Capital	...	...	...	...	...	...	...	...	...	...	...	—

Kosovo, Republic of (967)

In Millions of Euros (EUR) / Fiscal Year Ends December 31st

		Budgetary Central Government			Central Government (excl. Social Security)			Central Government (incl. Social Security)			General Government		
		2013	2014	2015	2013	2014	2015	2013	2014	2015	2013	2014	2015
27	**Social benefits**	...	...	...	...	...	...	...	...	...	**215**	**267**	**336**
271	Social security benefits	...	...	...	...	...	...	...	...	...	187	241	304
272	Social assistance benefits	...	...	...	...	...	...	...	...	...	27	27	32
273	Employment-related social benefits	...	...	...	...	...	...	...	...	...	—	—	—
28	**Other expense**	...	...	...	...	...	...	...	...	...	**14**	**19**	**25**
281	Property expense other than interest	...	...	...	...	...	...	...	...	...	—	—	—
282	Transfers not elsewhere classified	...	...	...	...	...	...	...	...	...	14	19	25
2821	Current	...	...	...	...	...	...	...	...	...	1	2	5
2822	Capital	...	...	...	...	...	...	...	...	...	13	17	20
	Table 3 Transactions in assets and liabilities												
3	**Change in net worth from transactions**	...	...	...	...	...	...	...	...	...	...	...	...
31	**Net/Gross investment in nonfinancial assets**	...	...	...	...	...	...	...	...	...	**521**	**396**	**383**
311	Fixed assets	...	...	...	...	...	...	...	...	...	481	362	344
3111	Buildings and structures	...	...	...	...	...	...	...	...	...	398	276	299
3112	Machinery and equipment	...	...	...	...	...	...	...	...	...	83	85	36
3113	Other fixed assets	...	...	...	...	...	...	...	...	...	0	0	9
3114	Weapons systems	...	...	...	...	...	...	...	...	...	—	—	—
312	Inventories	...	...	...	...	...	...	...	...	...	—	—	4
313	Valuables	...	...	...	...	...	...	...	...	...	—	—	—
314	Nonproduced assets	...	...	...	...	...	...	...	...	...	40	34	35
3141	Land	...	...	...	...	...	...	...	...	...	40	34	34
3142	Mineral and energy resources	...	...	...	...	...	...	...	...	...	—	—	—
3143	Other naturally occurring assets	...	...	...	...	...	...	...	...	...	—	—	0
3144	Intangible nonproduced assets	...	...	...	...	...	...	...	...	...	—	—	0
32	**Net acquisition of financial assets**	...	...	...	...	...	...	...	...	...	**-99**	**-51**	**33**
	By instrument												
3201	Monetary gold and SDRs	...	...	...	...	...	...	...	...	...	—	—	—
3202	Currency and deposits	...	...	...	...	...	...	...	...	...	-66	-48	93
3203	Debt securities	...	...	...	...	...	...	...	...	...	—	—	—
3204	Loans	...	...	...	...	...	...	...	...	...	-6	—	1
3205	Equity and investment fund shares	...	...	...	...	...	...	...	...	...	-26	-2	-61
3206	Insurance, pension, and standardized guarantee schemes	...	...	...	...	...	...	...	...	...	—	—	—
3207	Financial derivatives and employee stock options	...	...	...	...	...	...	...	...	...	—	—	—
3208	Other accounts receivable	...	...	...	...	...	...	...	...	...	...	...	...
	By debtor												
321	Domestic debtors	...	...	...	...	...	...	...	...	...	-99	-51	33
322	External debtors	...	...	...	...	...	...	...	...	...	—	—	—
33	**Net incurrence of liabilities**	...	...	...	...	...	...	...	...	...	**70**	**92**	**137**
	By instrument												
3301	Special Drawing Rights (SDRs)	...	...	...	...	...	...	...	...	...	—	—	—
3302	Currency and deposits	...	...	...	...	...	...	...	...	...	—	—	-1
3303	Debt securities	...	...	...	...	...	...	...	...	...	79	104	121
3304	Loans	...	...	...	...	...	...	...	...	...	-9	-12	17
3305	Equity and investment fund shares	...	...	...	...	...	...	...	...	...	—	—	—
3306	Insurance, pension, and standardized guarantee schemes	...	...	...	...	...	...	...	...	...	—	—	—
3307	Financial derivatives and employee stock options	...	...	...	...	...	...	...	...	...	—	—	—
3308	Other accounts payable	...	...	...	...	...	...	...	...	...	...	...	...
	By creditor												
331	Domestic creditors	...	...	...	...	...	...	...	...	...	79	104	120
332	External creditors	...	...	...	...	...	...	...	...	...	-9	-12	17
	Table 4 Holding gains and losses in assets and liabilities												
	Table 5 Holding gains and losses in assets and liabilities												
	Table 6 Balance sheet												

Kosovo, Republic of (967)

In Millions of Euros (EUR) / Fiscal Year Ends December 31st

	Budgetary Central Government			Central Government (excl. Social Security)			Central Government (incl. Social Security)			General Government		
	2013	2014	2015	2013	2014	2015	2013	2014	2015	2013	2014	2015
Table 7 Expenditure by functions of government												
Table 8 Financial transactions by counterpart sector												
Table 9 Total other economic flows in assets and liabilities												

Kuwait (443)

In Millions of Kuwaiti Dinars (KWD) / Fiscal Year Ends March 31st

		Budgetary Central Government			Central Government (excl. Social Security)			Central Government (incl. Social Security)			General Government		
		2013	2014	2015	2013	2014	2015	2013	2014	2015	2013	2014	2015
	Statement of operations												
1	Revenue	31,445	24,526	13,236	31,508	24,615	13,314	...	...	...	...	...	...
2	Expense	14,860	17,363	15,974	16,561	18,743	17,926	...	...	...	...	...	...
GOB	**Gross operating balance**	**16,585**	**7,163**	**-2,738**	**14,947**	**5,872**	**-4,612**	**...**	**...**	**...**	**...**	**...**	**...**
NOB	**Net operating balance**	**...**	**...**	**...**	**...**	**...**	**...**	**...**	**...**	**...**	**...**	**...**	**...**
31	Net/Gross investment in nonfinancial assets	1,725	1,994	2,239	2,039	2,361	2,610	...	...	...	...	...	...
2M	Expenditure	16,585	19,357	18,213	18,600	21,104	20,536	...	...	...	...	...	...
NLB	**Net lending (+) / Net borrowing (-)**	**14,860**	**5,169**	**-4,977**	**12,908**	**3,511**	**-7,222**	**...**	**...**	**...**	**...**	**...**	**...**
32	Net acquisition of financial assets	...	...	...	...	...	...	...	...	...	...	...	...
33	Net incurrence of liabilities	...	...	...	...	...	...	...	...	...	...	...	...
NLBz	Statistical discrepancy	...	...	...	...	...	...	...	...	...	...	...	...
	Memorandum items												
PB	Primary net lending / net borrowing	14,860	5,169	-4,977	12,908	3,511	-7,222	...	...	...	...	...	...
GB	Government balance per national definition	...	...	...	...	...	...	...	...	...	...	...	...
	Statement of other economic flows												
	Balance sheet												
	Table 1 Revenue												
1	**Revenue**	**31,445**	**24,526**	**13,236**	**31,508**	**24,615**	**13,314**	**...**	**...**	**...**	**...**	**...**	**...**
11	**Taxes**	**384**	**412**	**476**	**384**	**412**	**476**	**...**	**...**	**...**	**...**	**...**	**...**
111	Taxes on income, profits, and capital gains	—	—	—	—	—	—	...	...	...	...	...	...
1111	Payable by individuals	—	—	—	—	—	—	...	...	...	...	...	...
1112	Payable by corporations and other enterprises	—	—	—	—	—	—	...	...	...	...	...	...
1113	Other taxes on income, profits, and capital gains	—	—	—	—	—	—	...	...	...	...	...	...
112	Taxes on payroll and workforce	—	—	—	—	—	—	...	...	...	...	...	...
113	Taxes on property	—	—	—	—	—	—	...	...	...	...	...	...
114	Taxes on goods and services	108	121	158	108	121	158	...	...	...	...	...	...
1141	General taxes on goods and services	21	21	16	21	21	16	...	...	...	...	...	...
1142	Excises	—	—	—	—	—	—	...	...	...	...	...	...
115	Taxes on international trade and transactions	276	291	318	276	291	318	...	...	...	...	...	...
116	Other taxes	—	—	—	—	—	—	...	...	...	...	...	...
12	**Social contributions**	**—**	**—**	**—**	**—**	**—**	**—**	**...**	**...**	**...**	**...**	**...**	**...**
121	Social security contributions	—	—	—	—	—	—	...	...	...	...	...	...
122	Other social contributions	—	—	—	—	—	—	...	...	...	...	...	...
13	**Grants**	**—**	**—**	**—**	**—**	**—**	**—**	**...**	**...**	**...**	**...**	**...**	**...**
131	From foreign governments	—	—	—	—	—	—	...	...	...	...	...	...
132	From international organizations	—	—	—	—	—	—	...	...	...	...	...	...
133	From other general government units	—	—	—	—	—	—	...	...	...	...	...	...
1331	Current	—	—	—	—	—	—	...	...	...	...	...	...
1332	Capital	—	—	—	—	—	—	...	...	...	...	...	...
14	**Other revenue**	**31,061**	**24,114**	**12,760**	**31,124**	**24,203**	**12,838**	**...**	**...**	**...**	**...**	**...**	**...**
	Table 2 Expense by economic type												
2	**Expense**	**14,860**	**17,363**	**15,974**	**16,561**	**18,743**	**17,926**	**...**	**...**	**...**	**...**	**...**	**...**
21	**Compensation of employees**	**4,643**	**5,221**	**5,027**	**5,433**	**6,017**	**5,840**	**...**	**...**	**...**	**...**	**...**	**...**
211	Wages and salaries	4,338	4,897	4,674	5,080	5,641	5,434	...	...	...	...	...	...
212	Employers' social contributions	305	324	353	353	376	406	...	...	...	...	...	...
22	**Use of goods and services**	**2,477**	**2,687**	**2,846**	**2,694**	**2,900**	**3,054**	**...**	**...**	**...**	**...**	**...**	**...**
23	**Consumption of fixed capital**	**...**	**...**	**...**	**...**	**...**	**...**	**...**	**...**	**...**	**...**	**...**	**...**
24	**Interest**	**—**	**—**	**—**	**—**	**—**	**—**	**...**	**...**	**...**	**...**	**...**	**...**
25	**Subsidies**	**3,580**	**3,975**	**2,323**	**3,580**	**3,975**	**2,323**	**...**	**...**	**...**	**...**	**...**	**...**
26	**Grants**	**436**	**1,032**	**639**	**436**	**1,032**	**639**	**...**	**...**	**...**	**...**	**...**	**...**
261	To foreign governments	413	990	614	413	990	614	...	...	...	...	...	...
262	To international organizations	23	42	25	23	42	25	...	...	...	...	...	...
263	To other general government units	—	—	—	—	—	—	...	...	...	...	...	...
2631	Current	—	—	—	—	—	—	...	...	...	...	...	...
2632	Capital	—	—	—	—	—	—	...	...	...	...	...	...

Kuwait (443)

In Millions of Kuwaiti Dinars (KWD) / Fiscal Year Ends March 31st

		Budgetary Central Government			Central Government (excl. Social Security)			Central Government (incl. Social Security)			General Government		
		2013	2014	2015	2013	2014	2015	2013	2014	2015	2013	2014	2015
27	**Social benefits**	**—**	**—**	**—**	**—**	**—**	**—**	**...**	**...**	**...**	**...**	**...**	**...**
271	Social security benefits	—	—	—	—	—	—	...	...	...	...	...	...
272	Social assistance benefits	—	—	—	—	—	—	...	...	...	...	...	...
273	Employment-related social benefits	—	—	—	—	—	—	...	...	...	...	...	...
28	**Other expense**	**3,724**	**4,448**	**2,900**	**4,418**	**4,819**	**3,460**	**...**	**...**	**...**	**...**	**...**	**...**
281	Property expense other than interest	3,724	4,448	2,900	4,418	4,819	3,460	...	...	...	...	...	...
282	Transfers not elsewhere classified	—	—	—	—	—	—	...	...	...	...	...	...
2821	Current	—	—	—	—	—	—	...	...	...	...	...	...
2822	Capital	—	—	—	—	—	—	...	...	...	...	...	...
	Table 3 Transactions in assets and liabilities												
3	**Change in net worth from transactions**	**...**	**...**	**...**	**...**	**...**	**...**	**...**	**...**	**...**	**...**	**...**	**...**
31	**Net/Gross investment in nonfinancial assets**	**1,725**	**1,994**	**2,239**	**2,039**	**2,361**	**2,610**	**...**	**...**	**...**	**...**	**...**	**...**
311	Fixed assets	1,712	1,943	2,235	2,026	2,310	2,606	...	...	...	...	...	...
3111	Buildings and structures	1,504	1,746	2,010	1,793	2,078	2,353	...	...	...	...	...	...
3112	Machinery and equipment	208	226	226	233	261	254	...	...	...	...	...	...
3113	Other fixed assets	—	—	—	—	—	—	...	...	...	...	...	...
3114	Weapons systems	—	...	...	—	...	...	...	...	...	...	...	...
312	Inventories	—	—	—	—	—	—	...	...	...	...	...	...
313	Valuables	—	—	—	—	—	—	...	...	...	...	...	...
314	Nonproduced assets	13	51	4	13	51	4	...	...	...	...	...	...
3141	Land	13	51	4	13	51	4	...	...	...	...	...	...
3142	Mineral and energy resources	—	—	—	—	—	—	...	...	...	...	...	...
3143	Other naturally occurring assets	—	—	—	—	—	—	...	...	...	...	...	...
3144	Intangible nonproduced assets	—	—	—	—	—	—	...	...	...	...	...	...
32	**Net acquisition of financial assets**	**...**	**...**	**...**	**...**	**...**	**...**	**...**	**...**	**...**	**...**	**...**	**...**
	By instrument												
3201	Monetary gold and SDRs	...	...	...	...	...	...	...	...	...	...	...	...
3202	Currency and deposits	...	...	...	...	...	...	...	...	...	...	...	...
3203	Debt securities	...	...	...	...	...	...	...	...	...	...	...	...
3204	Loans	...	...	...	...	...	...	...	...	...	...	...	...
3205	Equity and investment fund shares	...	...	...	...	...	...	...	...	...	...	...	...
3206	Insurance, pension, and standardized guarantee schemes	...	...	...	...	...	...	...	...	...	...	...	...
3207	Financial derivatives and employee stock options	...	...	...	...	...	...	...	...	...	...	...	...
3208	Other accounts receivable	...	...	...	...	...	...	...	...	...	...	...	...
	By debtor												
321	Domestic debtors	...	...	...	...	...	...	...	...	...	...	...	...
322	External debtors	...	...	...	...	...	...	...	...	...	...	...	...
33	**Net incurrence of liabilities**	**...**	**...**	**...**	**...**	**...**	**...**	**...**	**...**	**...**	**...**	**...**	**...**
	By instrument												
3301	Special Drawing Rights (SDRs)	...	...	...	...	...	...	...	...	...	...	...	...
3302	Currency and deposits	...	...	...	...	...	...	...	...	...	...	...	...
3303	Debt securities	...	...	...	...	...	...	...	...	...	...	...	...
3304	Loans	...	...	...	...	...	...	...	...	...	...	...	...
3305	Equity and investment fund shares	...	...	...	...	...	...	...	...	...	...	...	...
3306	Insurance, pension, and standardized guarantee schemes	...	...	...	...	...	...	...	...	...	...	...	...
3307	Financial derivatives and employee stock options	...	...	...	...	...	...	...	...	...	...	...	...
3308	Other accounts payable	...	...	...	...	...	...	...	...	...	...	...	...
	By creditor												
331	Domestic creditors	...	...	...	...	...	...	...	...	...	...	...	...
332	External creditors	...	...	...	...	...	...	...	...	...	...	...	...
	Table 4 Holding gains and losses in assets and liabilities												
	Table 5 Holding gains and losses in assets and liabilities												
	Table 6 Balance sheet												

Kuwait (443)

In Millions of Kuwaiti Dinars (KWD) / Fiscal Year Ends March 31st

		Budgetary Central Government			Central Government (excl. Social Security)			Central Government (incl. Social Security)			General Government		
		2013	2014	2015	2013	2014	2015	2013	2014	2015	2013	2014	2015
	Table 7 Expenditure by functions of government												
7	**Expenditure**	**16,585**	**19,357**	**18,213**	**18,600**	**21,104**	**20,536**	**...**	**...**	**...**	**...**	**...**	**...**
701	**General public services**	**2,039**	**2,699**	**2,396**	**2,216**	**2,923**	**2,680**	**...**	**...**	**...**	**...**	**...**	**...**
7017	Public debt transactions	—	—	—	—	—	—	...	...	...	...	...	...
7018	Transfers of general character between levels of government	...	...	...	—	...	...	...	...	...	...	...	...
702	**Defense**	**1,590**	**1,683**	**1,741**	**1,590**	**1,683**	**1,741**	**...**	**...**	**...**	**...**	**...**	**...**
703	**Public order and safety**	**1,222**	**1,332**	**1,347**	**1,342**	**1,454**	**1,475**	**...**	**...**	**...**	**...**	**...**	**...**
704	**Economic affairs**	**3,358**	**3,287**	**2,278**	**3,472**	**3,394**	**2,382**	**...**	**...**	**...**	**...**	**...**	**...**
7042	Agriculture, forestry, fishing, and hunting	—	—	—	114	107	104	...	...	...	...	...	...
7043	Fuel and energy	3,187	3,109	2,107	3,187	3,109	2,107	...	...	...	...	...	...
7044	Mining, manufacturing, and construction	47	54	54	47	54	54	...	...	...	...	...	...
7045	Transport	124	124	117	124	124	117	...	...	...	...	...	...
7046	Communication	—	—	—	—	—	—	...	...	...	...	...	...
705	**Environmental protection**	**—**	**—**	**—**	**14**	**16**	**14**	**...**	**...**	**...**	**...**	**...**	**...**
706	**Housing and community amenities**	**559**	**901**	**912**	**1,082**	**1,107**	**1,308**	**...**	**...**	**...**	**...**	**...**	**...**
707	**Health**	**1,355**	**1,694**	**1,596**	**1,355**	**1,694**	**1,596**	**...**	**...**	**...**	**...**	**...**	**...**
7072	Outpatient services	...	...	...	—	...	...	...	...	...	...	...	...
7073	Hospital services	...	...	...	—	...	...	...	...	...	...	...	...
7074	Public health services	...	...	...	—	...	...	...	...	...	...	...	...
708	**Recreation, culture and religion**	**423**	**453**	**463**	**523**	**565**	**564**	**...**	**...**	**...**	**...**	**...**	**...**
709	**Education**	**1,916**	**2,036**	**2,061**	**2,712**	**2,853**	**2,825**	**...**	**...**	**...**	**...**	**...**	**...**
7091	Pre-primary and primary education	...	...	...	—	...	...	...	...	...	...	...	...
7092	Secondary education	...	...	...	—	...	...	...	...	...	...	...	...
7094	Tertiary education	...	...	...	—	...	...	...	...	...	...	...	...
710	**Social protection**	**4,123**	**5,272**	**3,180**	**4,294**	**5,415**	**3,341**	**...**	**...**	**...**	**...**	**...**	**...**
7z	Statistical discrepancy: Expenditure	...	...	...	...	...	...	...	...	...	...	...	...
	Table 8 Financial transactions by counterpart sector												
	Table 9 Total other economic flows in assets and liabilities												

Kyrgyz Republic (917)

In Millions of Kyrgyz Soms (KGS) / Fiscal Year Ends December 31st

		Budgetary Central Government			Central Government (excl. Social Security)			Central Government (incl. Social Security)			General Government		
		2013	2014	2015	2013	2014	2015	2013	2014	2015	2013	2014	2015
	Statement of operations												
1	Revenue	89,268	105,261	113,890	89,268	105,261	113,890	...	...	139,312	...	...	153,112
2	Expense	75,947	84,152	94,472	75,947	84,152	94,472	...	...	117,274	...	...	127,442
GOB	**Gross operating balance**	**13,321**	**21,109**	**19,419**	**13,321**	**21,109**	**19,419**	...	...	**22,038**	...	...	**25,669**
NOB	**Net operating balance**	...	...	...	...	...	...	...	...	...	...	...	...
31	Net/Gross investment in nonfinancial assets	16,155	23,245	25,947	16,155	23,245	25,947	...	...	26,545	...	...	29,787
2M	Expenditure	92,102	107,397	120,418	92,102	107,397	120,418	...	...	143,818	...	...	157,229
NLB	**Net lending (+) / Net borrowing (-)**	**-2,834**	**-2,136**	**-6,528**	**-2,834**	**-2,136**	**-6,528**	...	...	**-4,507**	...	...	**-4,118**
32	Net acquisition of financial assets	13,618	20,226	12,382	13,618	20,226	12,382	...	...	12,612	...	...	12,702
33	Net incurrence of liabilities	16,453	22,520	18,910	16,453	22,520	18,910	...	...	17,118	...	...	16,830
NLBz	Statistical discrepancy	—	-158	—	—	-158	—	...	...	—	...	...	-10
	Memorandum items												
PB	Primary net lending / net borrowing	128	1,317	-2,431	128	1,317	-2,431	...	...	-410	...	...	-590
GB	Government balance per national definition	...	...	...	...	...	...	...	...	...	...	...	...
	Statement of other economic flows												
	Balance sheet												
6	**Net worth**	**29,697**	**89,500**	**-34,634**	**29,697**	**89,500**	**-34,634**	...	...	**-24,822**	...	...	**11,027**
61	Nonfinancial assets	112,814	137,813	130,905	112,814	137,813	130,905	...	...	137,891	...	...	173,335
62	Financial assets	68,978	103,432	134,467	68,978	103,432	134,467	...	...	149,205	...	...	151,363
63	Liabilities	152,096	151,745	300,006	152,096	151,745	300,006	...	...	311,918	...	...	313,671
	Table 1 Revenue												
1	**Revenue**	**89,268**	**105,261**	**113,890**	**89,268**	**105,261**	**113,890**	...	...	**139,312**	...	...	**153,112**
11	**Taxes**	**62,414**	**70,945**	**72,329**	**62,414**	**70,945**	**72,329**	...	...	**72,329**	...	...	**84,655**
111	Taxes on income, profits, and capital gains	12,213	13,900	15,598	12,213	13,900	15,598	...	...	15,598	...	...	21,773
1111	Payable by individuals	...	...	5,613	...	...	5,613	...	...	5,613	...	...	9,514
1112	Payable by corporations and other enterprises	...	...	9,985	...	...	9,985	...	...	9,985	...	...	12,259
1113	Other taxes on income, profits, and capital gains	...	...	—	...	...	—	...	...	—	...	...	—
112	Taxes on payroll and workforce	—	—	—	—	—	—	...	...	—	...	...	...
113	Taxes on property	—	—	—	—	—	—	...	...	—	...	...	2,286
114	Taxes on goods and services	38,235	43,267	47,045	38,235	43,267	47,045	...	...	47,045	...	...	50,909
1141	General taxes on goods and services	33,330	36,295	36,975	33,330	36,295	36,975	...	...	36,975	...	...	40,729
1142	Excises	4,090	6,334	7,757	4,090	6,334	7,757	...	...	7,757	...	...	7,757
115	Taxes on international trade and transactions	11,886	13,771	9,684	11,886	13,771	9,684	...	...	9,684	...	...	9,684
116	Other taxes	80	7	2	80	7	2	...	...	2	...	...	3
12	**Social contributions**	—	—	—	—	—	—	...	...	**24,267**	...	...	**24,267**
121	Social security contributions	—	—	—	—	—	—	...	...	24,267	...	...	24,267
122	Other social contributions	—	—	—	—	—	—	...	...	—	...	...	—
13	**Grants**	**9,189**	**9,959**	**9,881**	**9,189**	**9,959**	**9,881**	...	...	**9,881**	...	...	**9,309**
131	From foreign governments	3,715	4,926	3,883	3,715	4,926	3,883	...	...	3,883	...	...	3,883
132	From international organizations	5,474	5,033	5,426	5,474	5,033	5,426	...	...	5,426	...	...	5,426
133	From other general government units	—	—	572	—	—	572	...	...	572	...	...	—
1331	Current	—	—	572	—	—	572	...	...	572	...	...	—
1332	Capital	—	—	—	—	—	—	...	...	—	...	...	—
14	**Other revenue**	**17,664**	**24,357**	**31,680**	**17,664**	**24,357**	**31,680**	...	...	**32,834**	...	...	**34,881**
	Table 2 Expense by economic type												
2	**Expense**	**75,947**	**84,152**	**94,472**	**75,947**	**84,152**	**94,472**	...	...	**117,274**	...	...	**127,442**
21	**Compensation of employees**	**24,223**	**34,292**	**39,054**	**24,223**	**34,292**	**39,054**	...	...	**46,938**	...	...	**51,838**
211	Wages and salaries	21,644	30,473	34,719	21,644	30,473	34,719	...	...	41,456	...	...	45,668
212	Employers' social contributions	2,579	3,819	4,336	2,579	3,819	4,336	...	...	5,482	...	...	6,169
22	**Use of goods and services**	**18,208**	**19,549**	**13,450**	**18,208**	**19,549**	**13,450**	...	...	**17,021**	...	...	**22,883**
23	**Consumption of fixed capital**	...	...	...	...	...	...	...	...	...	...	...	...
24	**Interest**	**2,962**	**3,452**	**4,097**	**2,962**	**3,452**	**4,097**	...	...	**4,097**	...	...	**3,528**
25	**Subsidies**	**1,627**	**1,993**	**2,159**	**1,627**	**1,993**	**2,159**	...	...	**2,159**	...	...	**3,521**

Kyrgyz Republic (917)

In Millions of Kyrgyz Soms (KGS) / Fiscal Year Ends December 31st

		Budgetary Central Government			Central Government (excl. Social Security)			Central Government (incl. Social Security)			General Government		
		2013	2014	2015	2013	2014	2015	2013	2014	2015	2013	2014	2015
26	**Grants**	**8,736**	**2,155**	**27,856**	**8,736**	**2,155**	**27,856**	**...**	**...**	**2,200**	**...**	**...**	**279**
261	To foreign governments	—	—	—	—	—	—	...	...	—	...	...	—
262	To international organizations	158	210	275	158	210	275	...	...	279	...	...	279
263	To other general government units	8,578	1,945	27,581	8,578	1,945	27,581	...	...	1,921	...	...	—
2631	Current	8,578	1,945	27,581	8,578	1,945	27,581	...	...	1,921	...	...	—
2632	Capital	—	—	—	—	—	—	...	...	—	...	...	—
27	**Social benefits**	**19,681**	**22,236**	**7,410**	**19,681**	**22,236**	**7,410**	**...**	**...**	**42,919**	**...**	**...**	**43,388**
271	Social security benefits	13,399	15,860	—	13,399	15,860	—	...	...	35,509	...	...	35,509
272	Social assistance benefits	6,282	6,376	7,410	6,282	6,376	7,410	...	...	7,410	...	...	7,879
273	Employment-related social benefits	—	—	—	—	—	—	...	...	—	...	...	—
28	**Other expense**	**509**	**477**	**446**	**509**	**477**	**446**	**...**	**...**	**1,940**	**...**	**...**	**2,006**
281	Property expense other than interest	—	—	—	—	—	—	...	...	—	...	...	—
282	Transfers not elsewhere classified	509	477	446	509	477	446	...	...	1,940	...	...	2,006
2821	Current	509	477	446	509	477	446	...	...	1,940	...	...	1,955
2822	Capital	—	—	—	—	—	—	...	...	—	...	...	51
	Table 3 Transactions in assets and liabilities												
3	**Change in net worth from transactions**	**...**	**...**	**...**	**...**	**...**	**...**	**...**	**...**	**...**	**...**	**...**	**...**
31	**Net/Gross investment in nonfinancial assets**	**16,155**	**23,245**	**25,947**	**16,155**	**23,245**	**25,947**	**...**	**...**	**26,545**	**...**	**...**	**29,787**
311	Fixed assets	16,155	23,243	25,451	16,155	23,243	25,451	...	...	26,049	...	...	29,323
3111	Buildings and structures	14,589	21,490	22,875	14,589	21,490	22,875	...	...	22,996	...	...	25,683
3112	Machinery and equipment	1,562	1,719	2,489	1,562	1,719	2,489	...	...	2,966	...	...	3,544
3113	Other fixed assets	5	33	87	5	33	87	...	...	87	...	...	96
3114	Weapons systems	...	...	...	...	...	...	...	...	...	...	...	...
312	Inventories	-1	1	496	-1	1	496	...	...	496	...	...	509
313	Valuables	1	1	1	1	1	1	...	...	1	...	...	1
314	Nonproduced assets	—	—	—	—	—	—	...	...	—	...	...	-45
3141	Land	—	—	—	—	—	—	...	...	—	...	...	-45
3142	Mineral and energy resources	—	—	—	—	—	—	...	...	—	...	...	—
3143	Other naturally occurring assets	—	—	—	—	—	—	...	...	—	...	...	—
3144	Intangible nonproduced assets	—	—	—	—	—	—	...	...	—	...	...	—
32	**Net acquisition of financial assets**	**13,618**	**20,226**	**12,382**	**13,618**	**20,226**	**12,382**	**...**	**...**	**12,612**	**...**	**...**	**12,702**
	By instrument												
3201	Monetary gold and SDRs	—	—	—	—	—	—	...	...	—	...	...	—
3202	Currency and deposits	2,917	4,377	2,945	2,917	4,377	2,945	...	...	3,075	...	...	3,159
3203	Debt securities	—	—	—	—	—	—	...	...	—	...	...	—
3204	Loans	10,698	15,796	8,624	10,698	15,796	8,624	...	...	8,624	...	...	8,731
3205	Equity and investment fund shares	4	53	813	4	53	813	...	...	813	...	...	813
3206	Insurance, pension, and standardized guarantee schemes	—	—	—	—	—	—	...	...	—	...	...	—
3207	Financial derivatives and employee stock options	—	—	—	—	—	—	...	...	—	...	...	—
3208	Other accounts receivable	...	...	...	...	...	...	...	...	...	...	...	...
	By debtor												
321	Domestic debtors	13,618	20,226	12,382	13,618	20,226	12,382	...	...	12,612	...	...	12,702
322	External debtors	—	—	—	—	—	—	...	...	—	...	...	—
33	**Net incurrence of liabilities**	**16,453**	**22,520**	**18,910**	**16,453**	**22,520**	**18,910**	**...**	**...**	**17,118**	**...**	**...**	**16,830**
	By instrument												
3301	Special Drawing Rights (SDRs)	—	—	—	—	—	—	...	...	—	...	...	—
3302	Currency and deposits	—	—	—	—	—	—	...	...	—	...	...	—
3303	Debt securities	-1,257	382	2,611	-1,257	382	2,611	...	...	720	...	...	665
3304	Loans	17,710	22,138	16,298	17,710	22,138	16,298	...	...	16,298	...	...	16,165
3305	Equity and investment fund shares	—	—	—	—	—	—	...	...	—	...	...	—
3306	Insurance, pension, and standardized guarantee schemes	—	—	—	—	—	—	...	...	—	...	...	—
3307	Financial derivatives and employee stock options	—	—	—	—	—	—	...	...	—	...	...	—
3308	Other accounts payable	...	...	...	...	...	...	...	...	...	...	...	...

Kyrgyz Republic (917)

In Millions of Kyrgyz Soms (KGS) / Fiscal Year Ends December 31st

		Budgetary Central Government			Central Government (excl. Social Security)			Central Government (incl. Social Security)			General Government		
		2013	2014	2015	2013	2014	2015	2013	2014	2015	2013	2014	2015
	By creditor												
331	Domestic creditors	-1,257	382	2,611	-1,257	382	2,611	...	...	820	...	...	532
332	External creditors	17,710	22,138	16,298	17,710	22,138	16,298	...	...	16,298	...	...	16,298
	Table 4 Holding gains and losses in assets and liabilities												
	Table 5 Holding gains and losses in assets and liabilities												
	Table 6 Balance sheet												
6	**Net worth**	**29,697**	**89,500**	**-34,634**	**29,697**	**89,500**	**-34,634**	**...**	**...**	**-24,822**	**...**	**...**	**11,027**
61	**Nonfinancial assets**	**112,814**	**137,813**	**130,905**	**112,814**	**137,813**	**130,905**	**...**	**...**	**137,891**	**...**	**...**	**173,335**
611	Fixed assets	103,923	127,546	121,593	103,923	127,546	121,593	...	...	126,640	...	...	153,486
6111	Buildings and structures	...	29,218	44,540	...	29,218	44,540	...	...	45,950	...	...	65,921
6112	Machinery and equipment	...	17,307	18,165	...	17,307	18,165	...	...	21,768	...	...	25,161
6113	Other fixed assets	...	81,021	58,887	...	81,021	58,887	...	...	58,923	...	...	62,403
6114	Weapons systems	...	...	...	...	...	...	...	...	...	...	...	...
612	Inventories	8,873	10,249	9,268	8,873	10,249	9,268	...	...	11,207	...	...	12,679
613	Valuables	11	12	37	11	12	37	...	...	37	...	...	37
614	Nonproduced assets	6	6	6	6	6	6	...	...	6	...	...	7,132
6141	Land	...	6	6	...	6	6	...	...	6	...	...	7,132
6142	Mineral and energy resources	...	—	—	...	—	—	...	...	—	...	...	—
6143	Other naturally occurring assets	...	—	—	...	—	—	...	...	—	...	...	—
6144	Intangible nonproduced assets	...	—	—	...	—	—	...	...	—	...	...	—
62	**Financial assets**	**68,978**	**103,432**	**134,467**	**68,978**	**103,432**	**134,467**	**...**	**...**	**149,205**	**...**	**...**	**151,363**
	By instrument												
6201	Monetary gold and SDRs	—	—	—	—	—	—	...	...	—	...	...	—
6202	Currency and deposits	7,288	11,665	14,247	7,288	11,665	14,247	...	...	18,873	...	...	20,295
6203	Debt securities	1	1	2	1	1	2	...	...	5,896	...	...	5,896
6204	Loans	52,466	79,659	106,883	52,466	79,659	106,883	...	...	106,894	...	...	106,910
6205	Equity and investment fund shares	734	734	734	734	734	734	...	...	737	...	...	737
6206	Insurance, pension, and standardized guarantee schemes	—	—	—	—	—	—	...	...	—	...	...	—
6207	Financial derivatives and employee stock options	—	—	—	—	—	—	...	...	—	...	...	—
6208	Other accounts receivable	8,488	11,372	12,601	8,488	11,372	12,601	...	...	16,805	...	...	17,525
	By debtor												
621	Domestic debtors	68,515	102,493	132,947	68,515	102,493	132,947	...	...	147,685	...	...	149,843
622	External debtors	464	939	1,520	464	939	1,520	...	...	1,520	...	...	1,520
63	**Liabilities**	**152,096**	**151,745**	**300,006**	**152,096**	**151,745**	**300,006**	**...**	**...**	**311,918**	**...**	**...**	**313,671**
	By instrument												
6301	Special Drawing Rights (SDRs)	—	—	—	—	—	—	...	...	—	...	...	—
6302	Currency and deposits	—	—	—	—	—	—	...	...	—	...	...	—
6303	Debt securities	10,864	11,246	15,484	10,864	11,246	15,484	...	...	14,357	...	...	14,357
6304	Loans	136,287	136,123	273,538	136,287	136,123	273,538	...	...	273,538	...	...	274,600
6305	Equity and investment fund shares	—	—	—	—	—	—	...	...	—	...	...	—
6306	Insurance, pension, and standardized guarantee schemes	—	—	—	—	—	—	...	...	—	...	...	—
6307	Financial derivatives and employee stock options	—	—	—	—	—	—	...	...	—	...	...	—
6308	Other accounts payable	4,944	4,376	10,985	4,944	4,376	10,985	...	...	24,024	...	...	24,714
	By creditor												
631	Domestic creditors	15,849	15,786	20,041	15,849	15,786	20,041	...	...	31,953	...	...	33,706
632	External creditors	136,246	135,959	279,965	136,246	135,959	279,965	...	...	279,965	...	...	279,965
	Memorandum items												
6M2	Net financial worth	-83,117	-48,313	-165,539	-83,117	-48,313	-165,539	...	...	-162,712	...	...	-162,308
6M3	Gross debt (D4) at market value	...	...	...	...	...	...	...	...	...	...	...	...
6M3D3	D3 debt liabilities at market value	...	...	...	...	...	...	...	...	...	...	...	...
6M3D2	D2 debt liabilities at market value	...	...	...	...	...	...	...	...	...	...	...	...
6M3D1	D1 debt liabilities at market value	...	...	...	...	...	...	...	...	...	...	...	...
6M4	Gross debt (D4) at nominal value	...	...	...	...	...	...	...	...	...	...	...	...
6M4D3	D3 debt liabilities at nominal value	...	...	...	...	...	...	...	...	...	...	...	...
6M4D2	D2 debt liabilities at nominal value	...	...	...	...	...	...	...	...	...	...	...	...
6M4D1	D1 debt liabilities at nominal value	...	...	...	...	...	...	...	...	...	...	...	...

Kyrgyz Republic (917)

In Millions of Kyrgyz Soms (KGS) / Fiscal Year Ends December 31st

		Budgetary Central Government			Central Government (excl. Social Security)			Central Government (incl. Social Security)			General Government		
		2013	2014	2015	2013	2014	2015	2013	2014	2015	2013	2014	2015
6M35	Gross debt (D4) at face value	152,096	151,745	300,006	152,096	151,745	300,006	...	...	311,918	...	...	313,671
6M35D3	D3 debt liabilities at face value	152,096	151,745	300,006	152,096	151,745	300,006	...	...	311,918	...	...	313,671
6M35D2	D2 debt liabilities at face value	147,151	147,369	289,021	147,151	147,369	289,021	...	...	287,894	...	...	288,957
6M35D1	D1 debt liabilities at face value	147,151	147,369	289,021	147,151	147,369	289,021	...	...	287,894	...	...	288,957
6M93	Government gross debt per national definition	...	...	...	...	...	...	...	...	...	...	...	...
6M5	Arrears	...	...	...	...	...	...	...	...	...	...	...	...
6M6	Explicit contingent liabilities	...	...	...	...	...	...	...	...	...	...	...	...
6M61	of which: Publicly guaranteed debt	...	...	...	...	...	...	...	...	...	...	...	...
6M7	Net implicit obligations for social security benefits	...	...	...	...	...	...	...	...	...	...	...	...
	Table 7 Expenditure by functions of government												
7	**Expenditure**	**92,102**	**107,397**	**120,418**	**92,102**	**107,397**	**120,418**	...	...	**143,818**	...	...	**157,239**
701	**General public services**	**17,737**	**12,228**	**40,101**	**17,737**	**12,228**	...	...	...	...	...	...	...
7017	Public debt transactions	2,962	...	4,097	2,962	...	...	...	...	...	...	...	...
7018	Transfers of general character between levels of government	...	...	27,581	...	...	...	...	...	...	...	...	...
702	**Defense**	...	...	...	...	...	...	...	...	...	...	...	...
703	**Public order and safety**	...	...	...	...	...	...	...	...	...	...	...	...
704	**Economic affairs**	**14,787**	**19,890**	**20,345**	**14,787**	**19,890**	...	...	...	...	...	...	...
7042	Agriculture, forestry, fishing, and hunting	...	...	2,158	...	...	...	...	...	...	...	...	...
7043	Fuel and energy	...	...	63	...	...	...	...	...	...	...	...	...
7044	Mining, manufacturing, and construction	...	...	125	...	...	...	...	...	...	...	...	...
7045	Transport	...	...	10,807	...	...	...	...	...	...	...	...	...
7046	Communication	...	...	129	...	...	...	...	...	...	...	...	...
705	**Environmental protection**	**561**	**665**	**810**	**561**	**665**	...	...	...	...	...	...	...
706	**Housing and community amenities**	**1,416**	**2,290**	**3,593**	**1,416**	**2,290**	...	...	...	...	...	...	...
707	**Health**	**10,758**	**11,324**	**3,615**	**10,758**	**11,324**	...	...	...	...	...	...	...
7072	Outpatient services	...	...	33	...	...	...	...	...	...	...	...	...
7073	Hospital services	...	...	1,240	...	...	...	...	...	...	...	...	...
7074	Public health services	...	...	905	...	...	...	...	...	...	...	...	...
708	**Recreation, culture and religion**	**2,179**	**2,482**	**2,808**	**2,179**	**2,482**	...	...	...	...	...	...	...
709	**Education**	**12,604**	**21,006**	**24,258**	**12,604**	**21,006**	...	...	...	...	...	...	...
7091	Pre-primary and primary education	...	...	1,705	...	...	...	...	...	...	...	...	...
7092	Secondary education	...	...	13,149	...	...	...	...	...	...	...	...	...
7094	Tertiary education	...	...	3,854	...	...	...	...	...	...	...	...	...
710	**Social protection**	**19,864**	**22,648**	**7,811**	**19,864**	**22,648**	...	...	...	...	...	...	...
7z	Statistical discrepancy: Expenditure	...	...	...	...	...	...	...	...	...	...	...	...
	Table 8 Financial transactions by counterpart sector												
32	**Net acquisition of financial assets**	**13,618**	**20,226**	**12,382**	**13,618**	**20,226**	**12,382**	...	...	**12,612**	...	...	**12,702**
321	Domestic debtors	13,618	20,226	12,382	13,618	20,226	12,382	...	...	12,612	...	...	12,702
8211	General government	...	...	...	...	...	...	...	...	...	...	...	...
8212	Central bank	...	...	...	...	...	...	...	...	...	...	...	...
8213	Deposit-taking corporations except the central bank	...	...	...	...	...	...	...	...	...	...	...	...
8214	Other financial corporations	...	...	...	...	...	...	...	...	...	...	...	...
8215	Nonfinancial corporations	...	...	...	...	...	...	...	...	...	...	...	...
8216	Households & nonprofit institutions serving households	...	...	...	...	...	...	...	...	...	...	...	...
322	External debtors	—	—	—	—	—	—	...	...	—	...	...	—
8221	General government	—	—	—	—	—	—	...	...	—	...	...	—
8227	International organizations	—	—	—	—	—	—	...	...	—	...	...	—
8228	Financial corporations other than international organizations	—	—	—	—	—	—	...	...	—	...	...	—
8229	Other nonresidents	—	—	—	—	—	—	...	...	—	...	...	—

Kyrgyz Republic (917)

In Millions of Kyrgyz Soms (KGS) / Fiscal Year Ends December 31st

		Budgetary Central Government			Central Government (excl. Social Security)			Central Government (incl. Social Security)			General Government		
		2013	2014	2015	2013	2014	2015	2013	2014	2015	2013	2014	2015
33	**Net incurrence of liabilities**	**16,453**	**22,520**	**18,910**	**16,453**	**22,520**	**18,910**	**...**	**...**	**17,118**	**...**	**...**	**16,830**
331	Domestic creditors	-1,257	382	2,611	-1,257	382	2,611	...	...	820	...	...	532
8311	General government	...	...	...	...	...	...	...	...	...	...	...	...
8312	Central bank	...	...	...	...	...	...	...	...	...	...	...	...
8313	Deposit-taking corporations except the central bank	...	...	...	...	...	...	...	...	...	...	...	...
8314	Other financial corporations	...	...	...	...	...	...	...	...	...	...	...	...
8315	Nonfinancial corporations	...	...	...	...	...	...	...	...	...	...	...	...
8316	Households & nonprofit institutions serving households	...	...	...	...	...	...	...	...	...	...	...	...
332	External creditors	17,710	22,138	16,298	17,710	22,138	16,298	...	...	16,298	...	...	16,298
8321	General government	...	...	...	...	...	...	...	...	...	...	...	...
8327	International organizations	...	...	...	...	...	...	...	...	...	...	...	...
8328	Financial corporations other than international organizations	...	...	...	...	...	...	...	...	...	...	...	...
8329	Other nonresidents	...	...	...	...	...	...	...	...	...	...	...	...
	Table 9 Total other economic flows in assets and liabilities												

Lao People's Democratic Republic (544)

In Billions of Lao Kip (LAK) / Fiscal Year Ends September 30th

		Budgetary Central Government			Central Government (excl. Social Security)			Central Government (incl. Social Security)			General Government		
		2013	2014	2015	2013	2014	2015	2013	2014	2015	2013	2014	2015
	Statement of operations												
1	Revenue	19,711	22,733	23,868	...	...	...	...	...	...	...	...	...
2	Expense	15,782	15,785	17,462	...	...	...	...	...	...	...	...	...
GOB	**Gross operating balance**	**3,929**	**6,949**	**6,406**	...	...	...	...	...	...	...	...	...
NOB	**Net operating balance**	...	...	...	...	...	...	...	...	...	...	...	...
31	Net/Gross investment in nonfinancial assets	8,379	9,280	10,782	...	...	...	...	...	...	...	...	...
2M	Expenditure	24,162	25,065	28,244	...	...	...	...	...	...	...	...	...
NLB	**Net lending (+) / Net borrowing (-)**	**-4,450**	**-2,331**	**-4,376**	...	...	...	...	...	...	...	...	...
32	Net acquisition of financial assets	-2,751	963	73	...	...	...	...	...	...	...	...	...
33	Net incurrence of liabilities	381	3,826	4,998	...	...	...	...	...	...	...	...	...
NLBz	Statistical discrepancy	1,318	-532	-550	...	...	...	...	...	...	...	...	...
	Memorandum items												
PB	Primary net lending / net borrowing	-3,445	-1,451	-3,249	...	...	...	...	...	...	...	...	...
GB	Government balance per national definition	...	...	...	...	...	...	...	...	...	...	...	...
	Statement of other economic flows												
	Balance sheet												
	Table 1 Revenue												
1	**Revenue**	**19,711**	**22,733**	**23,868**	...	...	...	...	...	...	...	...	...
11	**Taxes**	**12,928**	**15,175**	**15,836**	...	...	...	...	...	...	...	...	...
111	Taxes on income, profits, and capital gains	3,228	2,848	2,232	...	...	...	...	...	...	...	...	...
1111	Payable by individuals	...	...	...	...	...	...	...	...	...	...	...	...
1112	Payable by corporations and other enterprises	...	...	...	...	...	...	...	...	...	...	...	...
1113	Other taxes on income, profits, and capital gains	...	...	...	...	...	...	...	...	...	...	...	...
112	Taxes on payroll and workforce	—	—	—	...	...	...	...	...	...	...	...	...
113	Taxes on property	176	110	131	...	...	...	...	...	...	...	...	...
114	Taxes on goods and services	8,228	10,392	10,887	...	...	...	...	...	...	...	...	...
1141	General taxes on goods and services	3,410	3,886	4,728	...	...	...	...	...	...	...	...	...
1142	Excises	2,720	3,357	3,363	...	...	...	...	...	...	...	...	...
115	Taxes on international trade and transactions	1,297	1,825	1,586	...	...	...	...	...	...	...	...	...
116	Other taxes	—	—	—	...	...	...	...	...	...	...	...	...
12	**Social contributions**	—	—	—	...	...	...	...	...	...	...	...	...
121	Social security contributions	—	—	—	...	...	...	...	...	...	...	...	...
122	Other social contributions	—	—	—	...	...	...	...	...	...	...	...	...
13	**Grants**	**4,913**	**4,870**	**5,324**	...	...	...	...	...	...	...	...	...
131	From foreign governments	4,913	4,870	5,324	...	...	...	...	...	...	...	...	...
132	From international organizations	—	—	—	...	...	...	...	...	...	...	...	...
133	From other general government units	—	—	—	...	...	...	...	...	...	...	...	...
1331	Current	—	—	—	...	...	...	...	...	...	...	...	...
1332	Capital	—	—	—	...	...	...	...	...	...	...	...	...
14	**Other revenue**	**1,871**	**2,688**	**2,698**	...	...	...	...	...	...	...	...	...
	Table 2 Expense by economic type												
2	**Expense**	**15,782**	**15,785**	**17,462**	...	...	...	...	...	...	...	...	...
21	**Compensation of employees**	**8,884**	**8,562**	**8,765**	...	...	...	...	...	...	...	...	...
211	Wages and salaries	...	...	...	...	...	...	...	...	...	...	...	...
212	Employers' social contributions	...	...	...	...	...	...	...	...	...	...	...	...
22	**Use of goods and services**	**3,709**	**3,962**	**5,014**	...	...	...	...	...	...	...	...	...
23	**Consumption of fixed capital**	...	...	...	...	...	...	...	...	...	...	...	...
24	**Interest**	**1,005**	**881**	**1,127**	...	...	...	...	...	...	...	...	...
25	**Subsidies**	**1,096**	**1,100**	**1,258**	...	...	...	...	...	...	...	...	...
26	**Grants**	**23**	**25**	**30**	...	...	...	...	...	...	...	...	...
261	To foreign governments	—	—	—	...	...	...	...	...	...	...	...	...
262	To international organizations	23	25	30	...	...	...	...	...	...	...	...	...
263	To other general government units	—	—	—	...	...	...	...	...	...	...	...	...
2631	Current	—	—	—	...	...	...	...	...	...	...	...	...
2632	Capital	—	—	—	...	...	...	...	...	...	...	...	...

Lao People's Democratic Republic (544)

In Billions of Lao Kip (LAK) / Fiscal Year Ends September 30th

		Budgetary Central Government			Central Government (excl. Social Security)			Central Government (incl. Social Security)			General Government		
		2013	2014	2015	2013	2014	2015	2013	2014	2015	2013	2014	2015
27	**Social benefits**	—	—	—	...	...	...	...	...	...	...	...	...
271	Social security benefits	—	—	—	...	...	...	...	...	...	...	...	...
272	Social assistance benefits	—	—	—	...	...	...	...	...	...	...	...	...
273	Employment-related social benefits	—	—	—	...	...	...	...	...	...	...	...	...
28	**Other expense**	**1,065**	**1,255**	**1,269**	...	...	...	...	...	...	...	...	...
281	Property expense other than interest	—	—	—	...	...	...	...	...	...	...	...	...
282	Transfers not elsewhere classified	1,065	1,255	1,269	...	...	...	...	...	...	...	...	...
2821	Current	1,065	1,255	1,269	...	...	...	...	...	...	...	...	...
2822	Capital	—	—	—	...	...	...	...	...	...	...	...	...
	Table 3 Transactions in assets and liabilities												
3	**Change in net worth from transactions**	...	...	...	...	...	...	...	...	...	...	...	...
31	**Net/Gross investment in nonfinancial assets**	**8,379**	**9,280**	**10,782**	...	...	...	...	...	...	...	...	...
311	Fixed assets	8,379	9,280	10,782	...	...	...	...	...	...	...	...	...
3111	Buildings and structures	...	...	...	...	...	...	...	...	...	...	...	...
3112	Machinery and equipment	...	...	...	...	...	...	...	...	...	...	...	...
3113	Other fixed assets	...	...	...	...	...	...	...	...	...	...	...	...
3114	Weapons systems	...	...	...	...	...	...	...	...	...	...	...	...
312	Inventories	—	—	—	...	...	...	...	...	...	...	...	...
313	Valuables	—	—	—	...	...	...	...	...	...	...	...	...
314	Nonproduced assets	—	—	—	...	...	...	...	...	...	...	...	...
3141	Land	—	—	—	...	...	...	...	...	...	...	...	...
3142	Mineral and energy resources	—	—	—	...	...	...	...	...	...	...	...	...
3143	Other naturally occurring assets	—	—	—	...	...	...	...	...	...	...	...	...
3144	Intangible nonproduced assets	—	—	—	...	...	...	...	...	...	...	...	...
32	**Net acquisition of financial assets**	**-2,751**	**963**	**73**	...	...	...	...	...	...	...	...	...
	By instrument												
3201	Monetary gold and SDRs	—	—	—	...	...	...	...	...	...	...	...	...
3202	Currency and deposits	-2,559	1,059	-781	...	...	...	...	...	...	...	...	...
3203	Debt securities	—	—	—	...	...	...	...	...	...	...	...	...
3204	Loans	-192	-96	853	...	...	...	...	...	...	...	...	...
3205	Equity and investment fund shares	—	—	—	...	...	...	...	...	...	...	...	...
3206	Insurance, pension, and standardized guarantee schemes	—	—	—	...	...	...	...	...	...	...	...	...
3207	Financial derivatives and employee stock options	—	—	—	...	...	...	...	...	...	...	...	...
3208	Other accounts receivable	...	...	...	...	...	...	...	...	...	...	...	...
	By debtor												
321	Domestic debtors	-2,751	963	73	...	...	...	...	...	...	...	...	...
322	External debtors	—	—	—	...	...	...	...	...	...	...	...	...
33	**Net incurrence of liabilities**	**381**	**3,826**	**4,998**	...	...	...	...	...	...	...	...	...
	By instrument												
3301	Special Drawing Rights (SDRs)	—	—	—	...	...	...	...	...	...	...	...	...
3302	Currency and deposits	—	—	—	...	...	...	...	...	...	...	...	...
3303	Debt securities	-542	2,800	3,461	...	...	...	...	...	...	...	...	...
3304	Loans	923	1,027	1,537	...	...	...	...	...	...	...	...	...
3305	Equity and investment fund shares	—	—	—	...	...	...	...	...	...	...	...	...
3306	Insurance, pension, and standardized guarantee schemes	—	—	—	...	...	...	...	...	...	...	...	...
3307	Financial derivatives and employee stock options	—	—	—	...	...	...	...	...	...	...	...	...
3308	Other accounts payable	...	...	...	...	...	...	...	...	...	...	...	...
	By creditor												
331	Domestic creditors	-542	2,800	887	...	...	...	...	...	...	...	...	...
332	External creditors	923	1,027	4,111	...	...	...	...	...	...	...	...	...
	Table 4 Holding gains and losses in assets and liabilities												
	Table 5 Holding gains and losses in assets and liabilities												
	Table 6 Balance sheet												

Lao People's Democratic Republic (544)

In Billions of Lao Kip (LAK) / Fiscal Year Ends September 30th

	Budgetary Central Government			Central Government (excl. Social Security)			Central Government (incl. Social Security)			General Government		
	2013	2014	2015	2013	2014	2015	2013	2014	2015	2013	2014	2015
Table 7 Expenditure by functions of government												
Table 8 Financial transactions by counterpart sector												
Table 9 Total other economic flows in assets and liabilities												

Latvia (941)

In Millions of Euros (EUR) / Fiscal Year Ends December 31st

		Budgetary Central Government			Central Government (excl. Social Security)			Central Government (incl. Social Security)			General Government		
		2013	2014	2015	2013P	2014P	2015P	2013P	2014P	2015P	2013P	2014P	2015P
	Statement of operations												
1	Revenue	...	...	...	4,763	4,936	5,071	6,757	6,952	7,132	8,129	8,388	8,702
2	Expense	...	...	...	4,823	5,339	5,240	6,899	7,272	7,269	8,291	8,663	8,845
GOB	**Gross operating balance**	**...**	**...**	**...**	**489**	**168**	**400**	**409**	**253**	**433**	**803**	**691**	**824**
NOB	**Net operating balance**	**...**	**...**	**...**	**-60**	**-403**	**-168**	**-142**	**-320**	**-137**	**-162**	**-275**	**-143**
31	Net/Gross investment in nonfinancial assets	...	...	...	-35	-0	253	-36	-1	252	45	95	166
2M	Expenditure	...	...	...	4,789	5,339	5,493	6,863	7,271	7,520	8,335	8,758	9,011
NLB	**Net lending (+) / Net borrowing (-)**	**...**	**...**	**...**	**-26**	**-403**	**-421**	**-106**	**-318**	**-389**	**-207**	**-369**	**-309**
32	Net acquisition of financial assets	...	...	...	-186	350	-1,231	...	...	...	-336	279	-1,257
33	Net incurrence of liabilities	...	...	...	-152	751	-815	...	...	...	-118	641	-951
NLBz	Statistical discrepancy	...	...	...	-8	2	5	...	...	...	-11	7	3
	Memorandum items												
PB	Primary net lending / net borrowing	...	...	...	284	-91	-121	203	-8	-90	156	-2	43
GB	Government balance per national definition	...	...	...	...	...	...	...	...	...	...	...	...
	Statement of other economic flows												
	Balance sheet												
6	**Net worth**	**...**	**...**	**...**	**...**	**...**	**...**	**...**	**...**	**...**	**31,947**	**...**	**...**
61	Nonfinancial assets	...	...	...	...	...	...	...	...	...	35,121	...	...
62	Financial assets	...	...	...	6,176	6,799	5,364	...	...	...	6,870	7,413	5,943
63	Liabilities	...	...	...	9,471	10,509	9,738	...	...	...	10,043	11,126	10,191
	Table 1 Revenue												
1	**Revenue**	**...**	**...**	**...**	**4,763**	**4,936**	**5,071**	**6,757**	**6,952**	**7,132**	**8,129**	**8,388**	**8,702**
11	**Taxes**	**...**	**...**	**...**	**3,310**	**3,497**	**3,658**	**3,310**	**3,497**	**3,658**	**4,553**	**4,825**	**5,029**
111	Taxes on income, profits, and capital gains	...	...	...	636	641	677	636	641	677	1,690	1,761	1,833
1111	Payable by individuals	...	...	...	266	277	289	266	277	289	1,320	1,397	1,445
1112	Payable by corporations and other enterprises	...	...	...	370	364	389	370	364	389	370	364	389
1113	Other taxes on income, profits, and capital gains	...	...	...	—	—	—	—	—	—	—	—	—
112	Taxes on payroll and workforce	...	...	...	3	3	3	3	3	3	3	3	3
113	Taxes on property	...	...	...	2	2	3	2	2	3	175	194	200
114	Taxes on goods and services	...	...	...	2,667	2,848	2,973	2,667	2,848	2,973	2,684	2,866	2,991
1141	General taxes on goods and services	...	...	...	1,733	1,867	1,949	1,733	1,867	1,949	1,733	1,867	1,949
1142	Excises	...	...	...	733	751	796	733	751	796	733	751	796
115	Taxes on international trade and transactions	...	...	...	2	2	2	2	2	2	2	2	2
116	Other taxes	...	...	...	—	—	—	—	—	—	—	—	—
12	**Social contributions**	**...**	**...**	**...**	**43**	**53**	**59**	**1,981**	**2,040**	**2,094**	**1,992**	**2,054**	**2,111**
121	Social security contributions	...	...	...	—	—	—	1,933	1,982	2,030	1,933	1,982	2,030
122	Other social contributions	...	...	...	43	53	59	47	58	64	59	71	80
13	**Grants**	**...**	**...**	**...**	**...**	**...**	**...**	**...**	**...**	**...**	**...**	**...**	**...**
131	From foreign governments	...	...	...	...	...	...	...	...	...	...	...	...
132	From international organizations	...	...	...	...	...	...	...	...	...	...	...	...
133	From other general government units	...	...	...	4	3	4	5	5	5	—	—	—
1331	Current	...	...	...	4	3	4	4	3	4	—	—	—
1332	Capital	...	...	...	—	—	—	1	2	1	—	—	—
14	**Other revenue**	**...**	**...**	**...**	**...**	**...**	**...**	**...**	**...**	**...**	**...**	**...**	**...**
	Table 2 Expense by economic type												
2	**Expense**	**...**	**...**	**...**	**4,823**	**5,339**	**5,240**	**6,899**	**7,272**	**7,269**	**8,291**	**8,663**	**8,845**
21	**Compensation of employees**	**...**	**...**	**...**	**1,141**	**1,231**	**1,296**	**1,151**	**1,242**	**1,307**	**2,140**	**2,268**	**2,414**
211	Wages and salaries	...	...	...	...	...	...	...	...	...	1,682	1,776	1,884
212	Employers' social contributions	...	...	...	...	...	...	...	...	...	459	492	530
22	**Use of goods and services**	**...**	**...**	**...**	**834**	**894**	**932**	**837**	**897**	**936**	**1,390**	**1,405**	**1,469**
23	**Consumption of fixed capital**	**...**	**...**	**...**	**549**	**572**	**568**	**551**	**573**	**570**	**964**	**966**	**967**
24	**Interest**	**...**	**...**	**...**	**309**	**311**	**300**	**309**	**310**	**298**	**363**	**368**	**352**
25	**Subsidies**	**...**	**...**	**...**	**85**	**94**	**46**	**85**	**94**	**46**	**134**	**160**	**53**

Latvia (941)

In Millions of Euros (EUR) / Fiscal Year Ends December 31st

		Budgetary Central Government			Central Government (excl. Social Security)			Central Government (incl. Social Security)			General Government		
		2013	2014	2015	2013P	2014P	2015P	2013P	2014P	2015P	2013P	2014P	2015P
26	**Grants**	...	...	...	...	...	...	...	...	...	...	...	...
261	To foreign governments	...	...	...	...	...	...	...	...	...	...	...	...
262	To international organizations	...	...	...	...	...	...	...	...	...	...	...	...
263	To other general government units	...	...	...	761	978	949	733	765	747	—	—	—
2631	Current	...	...	...	600	858	870	572	644	669	—	—	—
2632	Capital	...	...	...	161	121	79	161	121	79	—	—	—
27	**Social benefits**	...	...	...	**403**	**437**	**376**	**2,478**	**2,539**	**2,560**	**2,608**	**2,664**	**2,733**
271	Social security benefits	...	...	...	...	...	...	...	...	...	...	...	...
272	Social assistance benefits	...	...	...	...	...	...	...	...	...	...	...	...
273	Employment-related social benefits	...	...	...	...	...	...	...	...	...	...	...	...
28	**Other expense**	...	...	...	...	...	...	...	...	...	...	...	...
281	Property expense other than interest	...	...	...	—	—	—	—	—	—	—	—	—
282	Transfers not elsewhere classified	...	...	...	...	...	...	...	...	...	...	...	...
2821	Current	...	...	...	...	...	...	...	...	...	...	...	...
2822	Capital	...	...	...	...	...	...	...	...	...	...	...	...
	Table 3 Transactions in assets and liabilities												
3	**Change in net worth from transactions**	...	...	...	**-69**	**-402**	**-164**	...	...	...	**-173**	**-268**	**-140**
31	**Net/Gross investment in nonfinancial assets**	...	...	...	**-35**	**-0**	**253**	**-36**	**-1**	**252**	**45**	**95**	**166**
311	Fixed assets	...	...	...	-68	-3	223	-69	-4	222	42	91	148
3111	Buildings and structures	...	...	...	...	...	...	...	...	...	...	...	...
3112	Machinery and equipment	...	...	...	...	...	...	...	...	...	...	...	...
3113	Other fixed assets	...	...	...	...	...	...	...	...	...	...	...	...
3114	Weapons systems	...	...	...	...	...	...	...	...	...	...	...	...
312	Inventories	...	...	...	...	...	...	...	...	...	...	...	...
313	Valuables	...	...	...	...	...	...	...	...	...	...	...	...
314	Nonproduced assets	...	...	...	-2	0	9	-2	0	9	-8	-9	0
3141	Land	...	...	...	...	...	...	...	...	...	...	...	...
3142	Mineral and energy resources	...	...	...	...	...	...	...	...	...	...	...	...
3143	Other naturally occurring assets	...	...	...	...	...	...	...	...	...	...	...	...
3144	Intangible nonproduced assets	...	...	...	...	...	...	...	...	...	...	...	...
32	**Net acquisition of financial assets**	...	...	...	**-186**	**350**	**-1,231**	...	...	...	**-336**	**279**	**-1,257**
	By instrument												
3201	Monetary gold and SDRs	...	...	...	—	—	—	...	...	...	—	—	—
3202	Currency and deposits	...	...	...	-326	205	-1,209	...	...	...	-352	199	-1,192
3203	Debt securities	...	...	...	60	-49	-11	...	...	...	60	-49	-11
3204	Loans	...	...	...	44	18	-25	...	...	...	-67	-83	-89
3205	Equity and investment fund shares	...	...	...	9	17	-10	...	...	...	18	29	-4
3206	Insurance, pension, and standardized guarantee schemes	...	...	...	0	1	0	...	...	...	1	1	0
3207	Financial derivatives and employee stock options	...	...	...	-2	-2	-18	...	...	...	-2	-2	-18
3208	Other accounts receivable	...	...	...	29	161	42	...	...	...	8	184	57
	By debtor												
321	Domestic debtors	...	...	...	...	...	...	...	...	...	...	...	...
322	External debtors	...	...	...	...	...	...	...	...	...	...	...	...
33	**Net incurrence of liabilities**	...	...	...	**-152**	**751**	**-815**	...	...	...	**-118**	**641**	**-951**
	By instrument												
3301	Special Drawing Rights (SDRs)	...	...	...	21	—	—	...	...	...	21	—	—
3302	Currency and deposits	...	...	...	-172	109	-25	...	...	...	-101	23	-107
3303	Debt securities	...	...	...	12	1,691	619	...	...	...	12	1,691	619
3304	Loans	...	...	...	-24	-1,127	-1,258	...	...	...	-55	-1,169	-1,297
3305	Equity and investment fund shares	...	...	...	—	—	—	...	...	...	2	1	0
3306	Insurance, pension, and standardized guarantee schemes	...	...	...	...	...	...	...	...	...	...	...	...
3307	Financial derivatives and employee stock options	...	...	...	-11	-14	-46	...	...	...	-10	-21	-59
3308	Other accounts payable	...	...	...	21	93	-105	...	...	...	13	116	-107

Latvia (941)

In Millions of Euros (EUR) / Fiscal Year Ends December 31st

		Budgetary Central Government			Central Government (excl. Social Security)			Central Government (incl. Social Security)			General Government		
		2013	2014	2015	2013P	2014P	2015P	2013P	2014P	2015P	2013P	2014P	2015P
	By creditor												
331	Domestic creditors	...	...	...	...	...	...	...	...	...	...	...	...
332	External creditors	...	...	...	...	...	...	...	...	...	...	...	...
	Table 4 Holding gains and losses in assets and liabilities												
	Table 5 Holding gains and losses in assets and liabilities												
	Table 6 Balance sheet												
6	**Net worth**	...	...	...	...	...	...	...	...	...	**31,947**	...	...
61	**Nonfinancial assets**	...	...	...	...	...	...	...	...	...	**35,121**	...	...
611	Fixed assets	...	...	...	...	...	...	...	...	...	34,647	...	...
6111	Buildings and structures	...	...	...	...	...	...	...	...	...	32,854	...	...
6112	Machinery and equipment	...	...	...	...	...	...	...	...	...	...	...	...
6113	Other fixed assets	...	...	...	...	...	...	...	...	...	562	...	...
6114	Weapons systems	...	...	...	...	...	...	...	...	...	...	...	...
612	Inventories	...	...	...	...	...	...	...	...	...	464	...	...
613	Valuables	...	...	...	...	...	...	...	...	...	10	...	...
614	Nonproduced assets	...	...	...	...	...	...	...	...	...	...	...	...
6141	Land	...	...	...	...	...	...	...	...	...	...	...	...
6142	Mineral and energy resources	...	...	...	...	...	...	...	...	...	...	...	...
6143	Other naturally occurring assets	...	...	...	...	...	...	...	...	...	...	...	...
6144	Intangible nonproduced assets	...	...	...	...	...	...	...	...	...	...	...	...
62	**Financial assets**	...	...	...	**6,176**	**6,799**	**5,364**	...	...	...	**6,870**	**7,413**	**5,943**
	By instrument												
6201	Monetary gold and SDRs	...	...	...	—	—	—	...	...	...	—	—	—
6202	Currency and deposits	...	...	...	1,445	1,707	512	...	...	...	1,645	1,901	723
6203	Debt securities	...	...	...	60	16	1	...	...	...	60	16	1
6204	Loans	...	...	...	1,286	1,471	1,440	...	...	...	530	617	522
6205	Equity and investment fund shares	...	...	...	2,568	2,614	2,321	...	...	...	3,557	3,598	3,299
6206	Insurance, pension, and standardized guarantee schemes	...	...	...	2	3	3	...	...	...	3	4	5
6207	Financial derivatives and employee stock options	...	...	...	1	1	53	...	...	...	1	1	53
6208	Other accounts receivable	...	...	...	815	988	1,034	...	...	...	1,075	1,277	1,340
	By debtor												
621	Domestic debtors	...	...	...	...	...	...	...	...	...	...	...	...
622	External debtors	...	...	...	...	...	...	...	...	...	...	...	...
63	**Liabilities**	...	...	...	**9,471**	**10,509**	**9,738**	...	...	...	**10,043**	**11,126**	**10,191**
	By instrument												
6301	Special Drawing Rights (SDRs)	...	...	...	136	144	154	...	...	...	136	144	154
6302	Currency and deposits	...	...	...	594	774	749	...	...	...	233	327	220
6303	Debt securities	...	...	...	3,924	5,570	6,163	...	...	...	3,924	5,570	6,163
6304	Loans	...	...	...	4,271	3,275	2,022	...	...	...	4,951	3,945	2,623
6305	Equity and investment fund shares	...	...	...	20	10	18	...	...	...	38	28	37
6306	Insurance, pension, and standardized guarantee schemes	...	...	...	...	...	...	...	...	...	...	...	...
6307	Financial derivatives and employee stock options	...	...	...	95	158	174	...	...	...	95	256	260
6308	Other accounts payable	...	...	...	432	578	458	...	...	...	666	855	734
	By creditor												
631	Domestic creditors	...	...	...	...	...	...	...	...	...	...	...	...
632	External creditors	...	...	...	...	...	...	...	...	...	...	...	...
	Memorandum items												
6M2	Net financial worth	...	...	...	-3,296	-3,710	-4,374	...	...	...	-3,173	-3,713	-4,249
6M3	Gross debt (D4) at market value	...	...	...	...	...	...	...	...	...	...	...	...
6M3D3	D3 debt liabilities at market value	...	...	...	9,357	10,341	9,546	...	...	...	9,910	10,842	9,894
6M3D2	D2 debt liabilities at market value	...	...	...	8,925	9,763	9,088	...	...	...	9,244	9,986	9,161
6M3D1	D1 debt liabilities at market value	...	...	...	8,195	8,845	8,185	...	...	...	8,875	9,515	8,787
6M4	Gross debt (D4) at nominal value	...	...	...	...	...	...	...	...	...	...	...	...
6M4D3	D3 debt liabilities at nominal value	...	...	...	...	...	...	...	...	...	...	...	...
6M4D2	D2 debt liabilities at nominal value	...	...	...	...	...	...	...	...	...	...	...	...
6M4D1	D1 debt liabilities at nominal value	...	...	...	...	...	...	...	...	...	...	...	...

Latvia (941)

In Millions of Euros (EUR) / Fiscal Year Ends December 31st

		Budgetary Central Government			Central Government (excl. Social Security)			Central Government (incl. Social Security)			General Government		
		2013	2014	2015	2013P	2014P	2015P	2013P	2014P	2015P	2013P	2014P	2015P
6M35	Gross debt (D4) at face value	...	...	...	...	...	...	...	...	...	...	...	...
6M35D3	D3 debt liabilities at face value	...	...	...	9,352	10,357	9,602	...	...	...	9,831	10,760	9,888
6M35D2	D2 debt liabilities at face value	...	...	...	8,785	9,635	8,990	...	...	...	9,029	9,761	9,000
6M35D1	D1 debt liabilities at face value	...	...	...	8,055	8,718	8,090	...	...	...	8,660	9,289	8,626
6M93	Government gross debt per national definition	...	...	...	8,649	9,491	8,836	...	...	...	8,893	9,616	8,846
6M5	Arrears	...	...	...	...	...	...	...	...	...	...	...	...
6M6	Explicit contingent liabilities	...	...	...	...	...	...	...	...	...	...	...	...
6M61	of which: Publicly guaranteed debt	...	...	...	...	...	...	...	...	...	...	...	...
6M7	Net implicit obligations for social security benefits	...	...	...	...	...	...	...	...	...	...	...	...
	Table 7 Expenditure by functions of government												
7	**Expenditure**	...	...	...	**4,755**	**5,291**	...	...	...	...	**8,379**	**8,789**	...
701	**General public services**	...	...	...	**976**	**1,037**	...	...	...	...	**1,085**	**1,147**	...
7017	Public debt transactions	...	...	...	350	357	...	...	...	...	371	376	...
7018	Transfers of general character between levels of government	...	...	...	31	31	...	...	...	...	0	0	...
702	**Defense**	...	...	...	**202**	**210**	...	...	...	...	**202**	**210**	...
703	**Public order and safety**	...	...	...	**400**	**434**	...	...	...	...	**438**	**476**	...
704	**Economic affairs**	...	...	...	**922**	**1,003**	...	...	...	...	**1,097**	**1,150**	...
7042	Agriculture, forestry, fishing, and hunting	...	...	...	113	120	...	...	...	...	98	113	...
7043	Fuel and energy	...	...	...	29	60	...	...	...	...	31	63	...
7044	Mining, manufacturing, and construction	...	...	...	74	1	...	...	...	...	86	11	...
7045	Transport	...	...	...	489	497	...	...	...	...	656	637	...
7046	Communication	...	...	...	0	4	...	...	...	...	2	6	...
705	**Environmental protection**	...	...	...	**137**	**137**	...	...	...	...	**151**	**160**	...
706	**Housing and community amenities**	...	...	...	**86**	**72**	...	...	...	...	**277**	**261**	...
707	**Health**	...	...	...	**754**	**820**	...	...	...	...	**835**	**898**	...
7072	Outpatient services	...	...	...	206	215	...	...	...	...	219	231	...
7073	Hospital services	...	...	...	386	446	...	...	...	...	451	506	...
7074	Public health services	...	...	...	10	11	...	...	...	...	11	11	...
708	**Recreation, culture and religion**	...	...	...	**179**	**193**	...	...	...	...	**359**	**399**	...
709	**Education**	...	...	...	**781**	**843**	...	...	...	...	**1,308**	**1,387**	...
7091	Pre-primary and primary education	...	...	...	24	37	...	...	...	...	456	510	...
7092	Secondary education	...	...	...	312	362	...	...	...	...	345	397	...
7094	Tertiary education	...	...	...	226	215	...	...	...	...	226	215	...
710	**Social protection**	...	...	...	**318**	**542**	...	...	...	...	**2,628**	**2,701**	...
7z	Statistical discrepancy: Expenditure	...	...	...	-0	0	...	...	...	...	0	-0	...
	Table 8 Financial transactions by counterpart sector												
32	**Net acquisition of financial assets**	...	...	...	**-186**	**350**	**-1,231**	...	...	...	**-336**	**279**	**-1,257**
321	Domestic debtors	...	...	...	...	...	...	...	...	...	...	...	...
8211	General government	...	...	...	...	...	...	...	...	...	—	—	—
8212	Central bank	...	...	...	...	...	...	...	...	...	...	...	...
8213	Deposit-taking corporations except the central bank	...	...	...	...	...	...	...	...	...	...	...	...
8214	Other financial corporations	...	...	...	...	...	...	...	...	...	...	...	...
8215	Nonfinancial corporations	...	...	...	...	...	...	...	...	...	...	...	...
8216	Households & nonprofit institutions serving households	...	...	...	...	...	...	...	...	...	...	...	...
322	External debtors	...	...	...	...	...	...	...	...	...	...	...	...
8221	General government	...	...	...	...	...	...	...	...	...	...	...	...
8227	International organizations	...	...	...	...	...	...	...	...	...	...	...	...
8228	Financial corporations other than international organizations	...	...	...	...	...	...	...	...	...	...	...	...
8229	Other nonresidents	...	...	...	...	...	...	...	...	...	...	...	...

Latvia (941)

In Millions of Euros (EUR) / Fiscal Year Ends December 31st

		Budgetary Central Government			Central Government (excl. Social Security)			Central Government (incl. Social Security)			General Government		
		2013	2014	2015	2013P	2014P	2015P	2013P	2014P	2015P	2013P	2014P	2015P
33	**Net incurrence of liabilities**	...	...	...	-152	751	-815	...	...	...	-118	641	-951
331	Domestic creditors	...	...	...	...	...	...	...	...	...	...	...	...
3311	General government	...	...	...	...	...	...	...	...	...	—	—	—
3312	Central bank	...	...	...	...	...	...	...	...	...	...	...	...
3313	Deposit-taking corporations except the central bank	...	...	...	...	...	...	...	...	...	...	...	...
3314	Other financial corporations	...	...	...	...	...	...	...	...	...	...	...	...
3315	Nonfinancial corporations	...	...	...	...	...	...	...	...	...	...	...	...
3316	Households & nonprofit institutions serving households	...	...	...	...	...	...	...	...	...	...	...	...
332	External creditors	...	...	...	...	...	...	...	...	...	...	...	...
3321	General government	...	...	...	...	...	...	...	...	...	...	...	...
3327	International organizations	...	...	...	...	...	...	...	...	...	...	...	...
3328	Financial corporations other than international organizations	...	...	...	...	...	...	...	...	...	...	...	...
3329	Other nonresidents	...	...	...	...	...	...	...	...	...	...	...	...
	Table 9 Total other economic flows in assets and liabilities												
9	**Change in net worth due to other economic flows**	...	...	...	...	...	...	...	...	...	...	...	...
91	**Other economic flows in nonfinancial assets**	...	...	...	...	...	...	...	...	...	...	...	...
911	Fixed assets	...	...	...	...	...	...	...	...	...	...	...	...
912	Inventories	...	...	...	...	...	...	...	...	...	...	...	...
913	Valuables	...	...	...	...	...	...	...	...	...	...	...	...
914	Nonproduced assets	...	...	...	...	...	...	...	...	...	...	...	...
92	**Other economic flows in financial assets**	...	...	...	-297	274	-204	...	...	...	-263	265	-214
	By instrument												
9201	Monetary gold and SDRs	...	...	...	—	—	—	...	...	...	—	—	—
9202	Currency and deposits	...	...	...	1	57	14	...	...	...	1	58	14
9203	Debt securities	...	...	...	-0	6	-4	...	...	...	-0	6	-4
9204	Loans	...	...	...	-143	168	-6	...	...	...	-143	170	-6
9205	Equity and investment fund shares	...	...	...	-69	29	-283	...	...	...	-34	12	-294
9206	Insurance, pension, and standardized guarantee schemes	...	...	...	-0	—	—	...	...	...	—	—	0
9207	Financial derivatives and employee stock options	...	...	...	2	2	70	...	...	...	2	2	70
9208	Other accounts receivable	...	...	...	-87	12	4	...	...	...	-88	18	6
	By debtor												
921	Domestic debtors	...	...	...	...	...	...	...	...	...	...	...	...
922	External debtors	...	...	...	...	...	...	...	...	...	...	...	...
93	**Other economic flows in liabilities**	...	...	...	20	287	43	...	...	...	24	443	16
	By instrument												
9301	Special Drawing Rights (SDRs)	...	...	...	-4	8	10	...	...	...	-4	8	10
9302	Currency and deposits	...	...	...	-0	71	-0	...	...	...	-0	71	-0
9303	Debt securities	...	...	...	15	-45	-25	...	...	...	15	-45	-25
9304	Loans	...	...	...	2	132	4	...	...	...	8	163	-25
9305	Equity and investment fund shares	...	...	...	-8	-9	7	...	...	...	-8	-11	9
9306	Insurance, pension, and standardized guarantee schemes	...	...	...	—	—	—	...	...	...	—	—	—
9307	Financial derivatives and employee stock options	...	...	...	29	77	62	...	...	...	28	183	62
9308	Other accounts payable	...	...	...	-15	53	-15	...	...	...	-16	73	-14
	By creditor												
931	Domestic creditors	...	...	...	...	...	...	...	...	...	...	...	...
932	External creditors	...	...	...	...	...	...	...	...	...	...	...	...
	Memorandum items												
9M2	Change in net financial worth due to other economic flows	...	...	...	-316	-13	-248	...	...	...	-287	-178	-230

Latvia (941)

In Millions of Euros (EUR) / Fiscal Year Ends December 31st

		Budgetary Central Government			Central Government (excl. Social Security)			Central Government (incl. Social Security)			General Government		
		2013	2014	2015	2013P	2014P	2015P	2013P	2014P	2015P	2013P	2014P	2015P
9M3	Gross debt (D4) at market value: other economic flows	...	...	...	-2	219	-26	...	...	...	3	271	-55
9M3D3	D3 debt liabilities at market value: other economic flows	...	...	...	-2	219	-26	...	...	...	3	271	-55
9M3D2	D2 debt liabilities at market value: other economic flows	...	...	...	13	166	-11	...	...	...	19	198	-40
9M3D1	D1 debt liabilities at market value: other economic flows	...	...	...	17	87	-21	...	...	...	24	118	-49

Lebanon (446)

In Billions of Lebanese Pounds (LBP) / Fiscal Year Ends December 31st

		Budgetary Central Government			Central Government (excl. Social Security)			Central Government (incl. Social Security)			General Government		
		2013	2014	2015	2013	2014	2015	2013	2014	2015	2013	2014	2015
	Statement of operations												
1	Revenue	13,086	14,467	13,330	...	...	...	...	...	...	...	...	...
2	Expense	18,864	18,812	17,235	...	...	...	...	...	...	...	...	...
GOB	**Gross operating balance**	**-5,778**	**-4,345**	**-3,905**	...	...	...	...	...	...	...	...	...
NOB	**Net operating balance**	...	...	**-3,905**	...	...	...	...	...	...	...	...	...
31	Net/Gross investment in nonfinancial assets	1,325	1,621	1,324	...	...	...	...	...	...	...	...	...
2M	Expenditure	20,189	20,433	18,559	...	...	...	...	...	...	...	...	...
NLB	**Net lending (+) / Net borrowing (-)**	**-7,103**	**-5,966**	**-5,229**	...	...	...	...	...	...	...	...	...
32	Net acquisition of financial assets	1,735	-615	889	...	...	...	...	...	...	...	...	...
33	Net incurrence of liabilities	8,838	5,351	6,118	...	...	...	...	...	...	...	...	...
NLBz	Statistical discrepancy	0	-0	-0	...	...	...	...	...	...	...	...	...
	Memorandum items												
PB	Primary net lending / net borrowing	-1,389	348	1,493	...	...	...	...	...	...	...	...	...
GB	Government balance per national definition	...	...	...	...	...	...	...	...	...	...	...	...
	Statement of other economic flows												
	Balance sheet												
	Table 1 Revenue												
1	**Revenue**	**13,086**	**14,467**	**13,330**	...	...	...	...	...	...	...	...	...
11	**Taxes**	**9,941**	**10,230**	**10,135**	...	...	...	...	...	...	...	...	...
111	Taxes on income, profits, and capital gains	2,502	2,795	2,887	...	...	...	...	...	...	...	...	...
1111	Payable by individuals	...	...	—	...	...	...	...	...	...	...	...	...
1112	Payable by corporations and other enterprises	...	...	—	...	...	...	...	...	...	...	...	...
1113	Other taxes on income, profits, and capital gains	...	...	2,887	...	...	...	...	...	...	...	...	...
112	Taxes on payroll and workforce	—	—	—	...	...	...	...	...	...	...	...	...
113	Taxes on property	1,201	1,245	1,179	...	...	...	...	...	...	...	...	...
114	Taxes on goods and services	4,948	4,929	4,872	...	...	...	...	...	...	...	...	...
1141	General taxes on goods and services	2,996	3,027	2,854	...	...	...	...	...	...	...	...	...
1142	Excises	1,346	1,281	1,355	...	...	...	...	...	...	...	...	...
115	Taxes on international trade and transactions	817	766	713	...	...	...	...	...	...	...	...	...
116	Other taxes	473	495	483	...	...	...	...	...	...	...	...	...
12	**Social contributions**	**128**	**136**	**139**	...	...	...	...	...	...	...	...	...
121	Social security contributions	—	—	—	...	...	...	...	...	...	...	...	...
122	Other social contributions	128	136	139	...	...	...	...	...	...	...	...	...
13	**Grants**	**8**	**26**	**27**	...	...	...	...	...	...	...	...	...
131	From foreign governments	4	20	1	...	...	...	...	...	...	...	...	...
132	From international organizations	4	6	26	...	...	...	...	...	...	...	...	...
133	From other general government units	—	—	—	...	...	...	...	...	...	...	...	...
1331	Current	—	—	—	...	...	...	...	...	...	...	...	...
1332	Capital	—	—	—	...	...	...	...	...	...	...	...	...
14	**Other revenue**	**3,009**	**4,075**	**3,029**	...	...	...	...	...	...	...	...	...
	Table 2 Expense by economic type												
2	**Expense**	**18,864**	**18,812**	**17,235**	...	...	...	...	...	...	...	...	...
21	**Compensation of employees**	**4,002**	**4,144**	**4,307**	...	...	...	...	...	...	...	...	...
211	Wages and salaries	3,684	3,766	3,983	...	...	...	...	...	...	...	...	...
212	Employers' social contributions	318	378	325	...	...	...	...	...	...	...	...	...
22	**Use of goods and services**	**792**	**767**	**747**	...	...	...	...	...	...	...	...	...
23	**Consumption of fixed capital**	...	...	...	...	...	...	...	...	...	...	...	...
24	**Interest**	**5,714**	**6,314**	**6,722**	...	...	...	...	...	...	...	...	...
25	**Subsidies**	**3,282**	**3,342**	**2,064**	...	...	...	...	...	...	...	...	...
26	**Grants**	**804**	**517**	**-466**	...	...	...	...	...	...	...	...	...
261	To foreign governments	—	—	—	...	...	...	...	...	...	...	...	...
262	To international organizations	141	10	28	...	...	...	...	...	...	...	...	...
263	To other general government units	663	507	-495	...	...	...	...	...	...	...	...	...
2631	Current	663	507	-495	...	...	...	...	...	...	...	...	...
2632	Capital	—	—	—	...	...	...	...	...	...	...	...	...

Lebanon (446)

In Billions of Lebanese Pounds (LBP) / Fiscal Year Ends December 31st

		Budgetary Central Government			Central Government (excl. Social Security)			Central Government (incl. Social Security)			General Government		
		2013	2014	2015	2013	2014	2015	2013	2014	2015	2013	2014	2015
27	**Social benefits**	**3,731**	**3,249**	**3,406**	...	...	...	...	...	...	...	...	...
271	Social security benefits	—	—	—	...	...	...	...	...	...	...	...	...
272	Social assistance benefits	996	596	683	...	...	...	...	...	...	...	...	...
273	Employment-related social benefits	2,735	2,653	2,724	...	...	...	...	...	...	...	...	...
28	**Other expense**	**538**	**480**	**454**	...	...	...	...	...	...	...	...	...
281	Property expense other than interest	19	22	—	...	...	...	...	...	...	...	...	...
282	Transfers not elsewhere classified	519	458	454	...	...	...	...	...	...	...	...	...
2821	Current	519	458	454	...	...	...	...	...	...	...	...	...
2822	Capital	—	—	—	...	...	...	...	...	...	...	...	...
	Table 3 Transactions in assets and liabilities												
3	**Change in net worth from transactions**	...	...	...	...	...	...	...	...	...	...	...	...
31	**Net/Gross investment in nonfinancial assets**	**1,325**	**1,621**	**1,324**	...	...	...	...	...	...	...	...	...
311	Fixed assets	1,311	1,548	1,309	...	...	...	...	...	...	...	...	...
3111	Buildings and structures	1,181	1,392	1,130	...	...	...	...	...	...	...	...	...
3112	Machinery and equipment	89	76	98	...	...	...	...	...	...	...	...	...
3113	Other fixed assets	41	79	81	...	...	...	...	...	...	...	...	...
3114	Weapons systems	...	...	...	...	...	...	...	...	...	...	...	...
312	Inventories	—	—	—	...	...	...	...	...	...	...	...	...
313	Valuables	—	—	—	...	...	...	...	...	...	...	...	...
314	Nonproduced assets	14	73	15	...	...	...	...	...	...	...	...	...
3141	Land	14	73	15	...	...	...	...	...	...	...	...	...
3142	Mineral and energy resources	—	—	—	...	...	...	...	...	...	...	...	...
3143	Other naturally occurring assets	—	—	—	...	...	...	...	...	...	...	...	...
3144	Intangible nonproduced assets	—	—	—	...	...	...	...	...	...	...	...	...
32	**Net acquisition of financial assets**	**1,735**	**-615**	**889**	...	...	...	...	...	...	...	...	...
	By instrument												
3201	Monetary gold and SDRs	—	—	—	...	...	...	...	...	...	...	...	...
3202	Currency and deposits	1,735	-615	889	...	...	...	...	...	...	...	...	...
3203	Debt securities	—	—	—	...	...	...	...	...	...	...	...	...
3204	Loans	—	—	—	...	...	...	...	...	...	...	...	...
3205	Equity and investment fund shares	—	—	—	...	...	...	...	...	...	...	...	...
3206	Insurance, pension, and standardized guarantee schemes	—	—	—	...	...	...	...	...	...	...	...	...
3207	Financial derivatives and employee stock options	—	—	—	...	...	...	...	...	...	...	...	...
3208	Other accounts receivable	...	...	...	...	...	...	...	...	...	...	...	...
	By debtor												
321	Domestic debtors	4,862	4,243	2,026	...	...	...	...	...	...	...	...	...
322	External debtors	-3,127	-4,858	-1,137	...	...	...	...	...	...	...	...	...
33	**Net incurrence of liabilities**	**8,838**	**5,351**	**6,118**	...	...	...	...	...	...	...	...	...
	By instrument												
3301	Special Drawing Rights (SDRs)	—	—	—	...	...	...	...	...	...	...	...	...
3302	Currency and deposits	-655	-13	73	...	...	...	...	...	...	...	...	...
3303	Debt securities	8,771	4,581	6,139	...	...	...	...	...	...	...	...	...
3304	Loans	-170	-43	-486	...	...	...	...	...	...	...	...	...
3305	Equity and investment fund shares	—	—	—	...	...	...	...	...	...	...	...	...
3306	Insurance, pension, and standardized guarantee schemes	—	—	—	...	...	...	...	...	...	...	...	...
3307	Financial derivatives and employee stock options	—	—	—	...	...	...	...	...	...	...	...	...
3308	Other accounts payable	892	826	392	...	...	...	...	...	...	...	...	...
	By creditor												
331	Domestic creditors	6,263	6,101	3,940	...	...	...	...	...	...	...	...	...
332	External creditors	2,575	-750	2,178	...	...	...	...	...	...	...	...	...
	Table 4 Holding gains and losses in assets and liabilities												
	Table 5 Holding gains and losses in assets and liabilities												
	Table 6 Balance sheet												

Lebanon (446)

In Billions of Lebanese Pounds (LBP) / Fiscal Year Ends December 31st

		Budgetary Central Government			Central Government (excl. Social Security)			Central Government (incl. Social Security)			General Government		
		2013	2014	2015	2013	2014	2015	2013	2014	2015	2013	2014	2015
	Table 7 Expenditure by functions of government												
7	**Expenditure**	**20,189**	**20,433**	**18,559**	...	...	...	...	...	...	...	...	...
701	**General public services**	**9,906**	**10,373**	**9,304**	...	...	...	...	...	...	...	...	...
7017	Public debt transactions	5,714	6,314	6,722	...	...	...	...	...	...	...	...	...
7018	Transfers of general character between levels of government	4,193	4,059	2,582	...	...	...	...	...	...	...	...	...
702	**Defense**	**1,838**	**1,750**	**1,790**	...	...	...	...	...	...	...	...	...
703	**Public order and safety**	**871**	**1,082**	**1,067**	...	...	...	...	...	...	...	...	...
704	**Economic affairs**	**5,356**	**5,045**	**3,101**	...	...	...	...	...	...	...	...	...
7042	Agriculture, forestry, fishing, and hunting	...	...	86	...	...	...	...	...	...	...	...	...
7043	Fuel and energy	3,027	3,614	1,874	...	...	...	...	...	...	...	...	...
7044	Mining, manufacturing, and construction	...	...	—	...	...	...	...	...	...	...	...	...
7045	Transport	...	...	196	...	...	...	...	...	...	...	...	...
7046	Communication	...	...	—	...	...	...	...	...	...	...	...	...
705	**Environmental protection**	**5**	**25**	**24**	...	...	...	...	...	...	...	...	...
706	**Housing and community amenities**	**42**	**37**	**118**	...	...	...	...	...	...	...	...	...
707	**Health**	**465**	**545**	**632**	...	...	...	...	...	...	...	...	...
7072	Outpatient services	...	...	—	...	...	...	...	...	...	...	...	...
7073	Hospital services	...	...	—	...	...	...	...	...	...	...	...	...
7074	Public health services	...	...	—	...	...	...	...	...	...	...	...	...
708	**Recreation, culture and religion**	**74**	**85**	**77**	...	...	...	...	...	...	...	...	...
709	**Education**	**1,416**	**1,433**	**1,484**	...	...	...	...	...	...	...	...	...
7091	Pre-primary and primary education	...	...	—	...	...	...	...	...	...	...	...	...
7092	Secondary education	...	...	—	...	...	...	...	...	...	...	...	...
7094	Tertiary education	...	...	—	...	...	...	...	...	...	...	...	...
710	**Social protection**	**216**	**57**	**960**	...	...	...	...	...	...	...	...	...
7z	Statistical discrepancy: Expenditure	-0	0	0	...	...	...	...	...	...	...	...	...
	Table 8 Financial transactions by counterpart sector												
	Table 9 Total other economic flows in assets and liabilities												

Lesotho (666)

In Millions of Lesotho Maloti (LSL) / Fiscal Year Ends March 31st

		Budgetary Central Government			Central Government (excl. Social Security)			Central Government (incl. Social Security)			General Government		
		2011	2012	2013	2011	2012	2013	2011	2012	2013	2011	2012	2013
	Statement of operations												
1	Revenue	9,337	13,160	13,386	...	...	...	...	...	...	...	...	...
2	Expense	8,699	9,104	9,810	...	...	...	...	...	...	...	...	...
GOB	**Gross operating balance**	**639**	**4,055**	**3,575**	...	...	...	...	...	...	...	...	...
NOB	**Net operating balance**	...	...	...	...	...	...	...	...	...	...	...	...
31	Net/Gross investment in nonfinancial assets	2,832	3,395	2,709	...	...	...	...	...	...	...	...	...
2M	Expenditure	11,530	12,500	12,519	...	...	...	...	...	...	...	...	...
NLB	**Net lending (+) / Net borrowing (-)**	**-2,193**	**660**	**866**	...	...	...	...	...	...	...	...	...
32	Net acquisition of financial assets	-1,663	1,723	2,404	...	...	...	...	...	...	...	...	...
33	Net incurrence of liabilities	530	1,063	1,538	...	...	...	...	...	...	...	...	...
NLBz	Statistical discrepancy	-0	-0	0	...	...	...	...	...	...	...	...	...
	Memorandum items												
PB	Primary net lending / net borrowing	-2,056	826	1,098	...	...	...	...	...	...	...	...	...
GB	Government balance per national definition	...	...	...	...	...	...	...	...	...	...	...	...
	Statement of other economic flows												
	Balance sheet												
	Table 1 Revenue												
1	**Revenue**	**9,337**	**13,160**	**13,386**	...	...	...	...	...	...	...	...	...
11	**Taxes**	**7,035**	**10,759**	**11,855**	...	...	...	...	...	...	...	...	...
111	Taxes on income, profits, and capital gains	2,395	2,401	3,148	...	...	...	...	...	...	...	...	...
1111	Payable by individuals	1,469	1,498	1,914	...	...	...	...	...	...	...	...	...
1112	Payable by corporations and other enterprises	556	453	717	...	...	...	...	...	...	...	...	...
1113	Other taxes on income, profits, and capital gains	370	450	517	...	...	...	...	...	...	...	...	...
112	Taxes on payroll and workforce	—	—	—	...	...	...	...	...	...	...	...	...
113	Taxes on property	125	150	191	...	...	...	...	...	...	...	...	...
114	Taxes on goods and services	1,590	1,965	2,162	...	...	...	...	...	...	...	...	...
1141	General taxes on goods and services	1,370	1,640	1,919	...	...	...	...	...	...	...	...	...
1142	Excises	201	309	223	...	...	...	...	...	...	...	...	...
115	Taxes on international trade and transactions	2,904	6,244	6,348	...	...	...	...	...	...	...	...	...
116	Other taxes	21	1	7	...	...	...	...	...	...	...	...	...
12	**Social contributions**	—	—	—	...	...	...	...	...	...	...	...	...
121	Social security contributions	—	—	—	...	...	...	...	...	...	...	...	...
122	Other social contributions	—	—	—	...	...	...	...	...	...	...	...	...
13	**Grants**	**1,147**	**1,507**	**455**	...	...	...	...	...	...	...	...	...
131	From foreign governments	1,147	1,507	455	...	...	...	...	...	...	...	...	...
132	From international organizations	—	—	—	...	...	...	...	...	...	...	...	...
133	From other general government units	—	—	—	...	...	...	...	...	...	...	...	...
1331	Current	—	—	—	...	...	...	...	...	...	...	...	...
1332	Capital	—	—	—	...	...	...	...	...	...	...	...	...
14	**Other revenue**	**1,155**	**893**	**1,075**	...	...	...	...	...	...	...	...	...
	Table 2 Expense by economic type												
2	**Expense**	**8,699**	**9,104**	**9,810**	...	...	...	...	...	...	...	...	...
21	**Compensation of employees**	**3,638**	**3,769**	**4,307**	...	...	...	...	...	...	...	...	...
211	Wages and salaries	3,126	3,317	3,800	...	...	...	...	...	...	...	...	...
212	Employers' social contributions	512	452	507	...	...	...	...	...	...	...	...	...
22	**Use of goods and services**	**2,199**	**2,784**	**2,729**	...	...	...	...	...	...	...	...	...
23	**Consumption of fixed capital**	...	...	...	...	...	...	...	...	...	...	...	...
24	**Interest**	**137**	**166**	**232**	...	...	...	...	...	...	...	...	...
25	**Subsidies**	**210**	**230**	**235**	...	...	...	...	...	...	...	...	...
26	**Grants**	**958**	**874**	**828**	...	...	...	...	...	...	...	...	...
261	To foreign governments	—	—	—	...	...	...	...	...	...	...	...	...
262	To international organizations	0	13	—	...	...	...	...	...	...	...	...	...
263	To other general government units	958	860	828	...	...	...	...	...	...	...	...	...
2631	Current	753	705	683	...	...	...	...	...	...	...	...	...
2632	Capital	205	156	145	...	...	...	...	...	...	...	...	...

Lesotho (666)

In Millions of Lesotho Maloti (LSL) / Fiscal Year Ends March 31st

		Budgetary Central Government			Central Government (excl. Social Security)			Central Government (incl. Social Security)			General Government		
		2011	2012	2013	2011	2012	2013	2011	2012	2013	2011	2012	2013
27	**Social benefits**	**613**	**630**	**742**	**...**	**...**	**...**	**...**	**...**	**...**	**...**	**...**	**...**
271	Social security benefits	—	—	—	...	...	...	...	...	...	...	...	...
272	Social assistance benefits	595	621	731	...	...	...	...	...	...	...	...	...
273	Employment-related social benefits	18	9	11	...	...	...	...	...	...	...	...	...
28	**Other expense**	**943**	**652**	**737**	**...**	**...**	**...**	**...**	**...**	**...**	**...**	**...**	**...**
281	Property expense other than interest	9	9	6	...	...	...	...	...	...	...	...	...
282	Transfers not elsewhere classified	934	643	732	...	...	...	...	...	...	...	...	...
2821	Current	934	643	732	...	...	...	...	...	...	...	...	...
2822	Capital	—	—	—	...	...	...	...	...	...	...	...	...
	Table 3 Transactions in assets and liabilities												
3	**Change in net worth from transactions**	**...**	**...**	**...**	**...**	**...**	**...**	**...**	**...**	**...**	**...**	**...**	**...**
31	**Net/Gross investment in nonfinancial assets**	**2,832**	**3,395**	**2,709**	**...**	**...**	**...**	**...**	**...**	**...**	**...**	**...**	**...**
311	Fixed assets	2,832	3,395	2,709	...	...	...	...	...	...	...	...	...
3111	Buildings and structures	1,758	1,205	1,573	...	...	...	...	...	...	...	...	...
3112	Machinery and equipment	217	267	208	...	...	...	...	...	...	...	...	...
3113	Other fixed assets	857	1,923	928	...	...	...	...	...	...	...	...	...
3114	Weapons systems	...	...	...	...	...	...	...	...	...	...	...	...
312	Inventories	—	—	—	...	...	...	...	...	...	...	...	...
313	Valuables	—	—	—	...	...	...	...	...	...	...	...	...
314	Nonproduced assets	—	—	—	...	...	...	...	...	...	...	...	...
3141	Land	—	—	—	...	...	...	...	...	...	...	...	...
3142	Mineral and energy resources	—	—	—	...	...	...	...	...	...	...	...	...
3143	Other naturally occurring assets	—	—	—	...	...	...	...	...	...	...	...	...
3144	Intangible nonproduced assets	—	—	—	...	...	...	...	...	...	...	...	...
32	**Net acquisition of financial assets**	**-1,663**	**1,723**	**2,404**	**...**	**...**	**...**	**...**	**...**	**...**	**...**	**...**	**...**
	By instrument												
3201	Monetary gold and SDRs	0	—	—	...	...	...	...	...	...	...	...	...
3202	Currency and deposits	-1,663	1,723	2,404	...	...	...	...	...	...	...	...	...
3203	Debt securities	—	—	—	...	...	...	...	...	...	...	...	...
3204	Loans	—	—	—	...	...	...	...	...	...	...	...	...
3205	Equity and investment fund shares	—	—	—	...	...	...	...	...	...	...	...	...
3206	Insurance, pension, and standardized guarantee schemes	—	—	—	...	...	...	...	...	...	...	...	...
3207	Financial derivatives and employee stock options	—	—	—	...	...	...	...	...	...	...	...	...
3208	Other accounts receivable	—	...	...	...	...	...	...	...	...	...	...	...
	By debtor												
321	Domestic debtors	-1,663	1,723	2,404	...	...	...	...	...	...	...	...	...
322	External debtors	0	—	—	...	...	...	...	...	...	...	...	...
33	**Net incurrence of liabilities**	**530**	**1,063**	**1,538**	**...**	**...**	**...**	**...**	**...**	**...**	**...**	**...**	**...**
	By instrument												
3301	Special Drawing Rights (SDRs)	—	—	—	...	...	...	...	...	...	...	...	...
3302	Currency and deposits	—	—	—	...	...	...	...	...	...	...	...	...
3303	Debt securities	324	-10	-5	...	...	...	...	...	...	...	...	...
3304	Loans	205	1,115	1,652	...	...	...	...	...	...	...	...	...
3305	Equity and investment fund shares	—	—	—	...	...	...	...	...	...	...	...	...
3306	Insurance, pension, and standardized guarantee schemes	—	-42	-110	...	...	...	...	...	...	...	...	...
3307	Financial derivatives and employee stock options	—	—	—	...	...	...	...	...	...	...	...	...
3308	Other accounts payable	—	...	...	...	...	...	...	...	...	...	...	...
	By creditor												
331	Domestic creditors	364	247	14	...	...	...	...	...	...	...	...	...
332	External creditors	166	816	1,524	...	...	...	...	...	...	...	...	...
	Table 4 Holding gains and losses in assets and liabilities												
	Table 5 Holding gains and losses in assets and liabilities												
	Table 6 Balance sheet												

Lesotho (666)

In Millions of Lesotho Maloti (LSL) / Fiscal Year Ends March 31st

		Budgetary Central Government			Central Government (excl. Social Security)			Central Government (incl. Social Security)			General Government		
		2011	2012	2013	2011	2012	2013	2011	2012	2013	2011	2012	2013
	Table 7 Expenditure by functions of government												
7	**Expenditure**	11,530	12,500	12,519	...	...	...	...	...	...	...	...	...
701	**General public services**	...	...	...	...	...	...	...	...	...	...	...	...
7017	Public debt transactions	137	166	232	...	...	...	...	...	...	...	...	...
7018	Transfers of general character between levels of government	...	...	...	...	...	...	...	...	...	...	...	...
702	**Defense**	...	...	...	...	...	...	...	...	...	...	...	...
703	**Public order and safety**	...	...	...	...	...	...	...	...	...	...	...	...
704	**Economic affairs**	...	...	...	...	...	...	...	...	...	...	...	...
7042	Agriculture, forestry, fishing, and hunting	...	...	...	...	...	...	...	...	...	...	...	...
7043	Fuel and energy	...	...	...	...	...	...	...	...	...	...	...	...
7044	Mining, manufacturing, and construction	...	...	...	...	...	...	...	...	...	...	...	...
7045	Transport	...	...	...	...	...	...	...	...	...	...	...	...
7046	Communication	...	...	...	...	...	...	...	...	...	...	...	...
705	**Environmental protection**	...	...	...	...	...	...	...	...	...	...	...	...
706	**Housing and community amenities**	...	...	...	...	...	...	...	...	...	...	...	...
707	**Health**	...	...	...	...	...	...	...	...	...	...	...	...
7072	Outpatient services	...	...	...	...	...	...	...	...	...	...	...	...
7073	Hospital services	...	...	...	...	...	...	...	...	...	...	...	...
7074	Public health services	...	...	...	...	...	...	...	...	...	...	...	...
708	**Recreation, culture and religion**	...	...	...	...	...	...	...	...	...	...	...	...
709	**Education**	...	...	...	...	...	...	...	...	...	...	...	...
7091	Pre-primary and primary education	...	...	...	...	...	...	...	...	...	...	...	...
7092	Secondary education	...	...	...	...	...	...	...	...	...	...	...	...
7094	Tertiary education	...	...	...	...	...	...	...	...	...	...	...	...
710	**Social protection**	...	...	...	...	...	...	...	...	...	...	...	...
7z	Statistical discrepancy: Expenditure	...	...	...	...	...	...	...	...	...	...	...	...
	Table 8 Financial transactions by counterpart sector												
	Table 9 Total other economic flows in assets and liabilities												

Liberia (668)

In Thousands of U.S. Dollars (USD) / Fiscal Year Ends June 30th

		Budgetary Central Government			Central Government (excl. Social Security)			Central Government (incl. Social Security)			General Government		
		2011	2012	2013	2011	2012	2013	2011	2012	2013	2011	2012	2013
	Statement of operations												
1	Revenue	359,948	458,932	517,197	359,948	458,932	517,197	...	...	...	...	...	...
2	Expense	322,408	436,207	505,591	322,408	436,207	505,591	...	...	...	...	...	...
GOB	**Gross operating balance**	**37,540**	**22,725**	**11,606**	**37,540**	**22,725**	**11,606**	...	...	...	...	...	...
NOB	**Net operating balance**	...	...	...	...	...	...	...	...	...	...	...	...
31	Net/Gross investment in nonfinancial assets	62,311	52,012	24,891	62,311	52,012	24,891	...	...	...	...	...	...
2M	Expenditure	384,718	488,219	530,482	384,718	488,219	530,482	...	...	...	...	...	...
NLB	**Net lending (+) / Net borrowing (-)**	**-24,771**	**-29,287**	**-13,285**	**-24,771**	**-29,287**	**-13,285**	...	...	...	...	...	...
32	Net acquisition of financial assets	...	...	...	...	...	...	...	...	...	...	...	...
33	Net incurrence of liabilities	...	...	...	...	...	...	...	...	...	...	...	...
NLBz	Statistical discrepancy	...	...	...	...	...	...	...	...	...	...	...	...
	Memorandum items												
PB	Primary net lending / net borrowing	-7,120	-25,882	...	-7,120	-25,882	...	...	...	...	...	...	...
GB	Government balance per national definition	...	...	...	...	...	...	...	...	...	...	...	...
	Statement of other economic flows												
	Balance sheet												
	Table 1 Revenue												
1	**Revenue**	**359,948**	**458,932**	**517,197**	**359,948**	**458,932**	**517,197**	...	...	...	...	...	...
11	**Taxes**	**267,348**	**362,116**	**395,924**	**267,348**	**362,116**	**395,924**	...	...	...	...	...	...
111	Taxes on income, profits, and capital gains	95,563	127,250	161,458	95,563	127,250	161,458	...	...	...	...	...	...
1111	Payable by individuals	42,025	34,277	141,846	42,025	34,277	141,846	...	...	...	...	...	...
1112	Payable by corporations and other enterprises	52,283	72,623	18,436	52,283	72,623	18,436	...	...	...	...	...	...
1113	Other taxes on income, profits, and capital gains	1,255	20,350	1,175	1,255	20,350	1,175	...	...	...	...	...	...
112	Taxes on payroll and workforce	—	—	0	—	—	0	...	...	...	...	...	...
113	Taxes on property	2,206	2,540	4,123	2,206	2,540	4,123	...	...	...	...	...	...
114	Taxes on goods and services	52,941	61,115	63,903	52,941	61,115	63,903	...	...	...	...	...	...
1141	General taxes on goods and services	12,263	17,731	32,765	12,263	17,731	32,765	...	...	...	...	...	...
1142	Excises	9,705	11,495	—	9,705	11,495	—	...	...	...	...	...	...
115	Taxes on international trade and transactions	106,673	151,887	155,200	106,673	151,887	155,200	...	...	...	...	...	...
116	Other taxes	9,965	19,325	11,240	9,965	19,325	11,240	...	...	...	...	...	...
12	**Social contributions**	—	**2,350**	—	—	**2,350**	—	...	...	...	...	...	...
121	Social security contributions	—	2,350	—	—	2,350	—	...	...	...	...	...	...
122	Other social contributions	—	—	—	—	—	—	...	...	...	...	...	...
13	**Grants**	**40,300**	**28,250**	**36,373**	**40,300**	**28,250**	**36,373**	...	...	...	...	...	...
131	From foreign governments	—	—	—	—	—	—	...	...	...	...	...	...
132	From international organizations	40,300	28,250	2,638	40,300	28,250	2,638	...	...	...	...	...	...
133	From other general government units	—	—	33,735	—	—	33,735	...	...	...	...	...	...
1331	Current	—	—	28,444	—	—	28,444	...	...	...	...	...	...
1332	Capital	—	—	5,291	—	—	5,291	...	...	...	...	...	...
14	**Other revenue**	**52,300**	**66,215**	**84,900**	**52,300**	**66,215**	**84,900**	...	...	...	...	...	...
	Table 2 Expense by economic type												
2	**Expense**	**322,408**	**436,207**	**505,591**	**322,408**	**436,207**	**505,591**	...	...	...	...	...	...
21	**Compensation of employees**	**137,443**	**181,500**	**206,856**	**137,443**	**181,500**	**206,856**	...	...	...	...	...	...
211	Wages and salaries	131,826	...	...	131,826	...	...	...	...	...	...	...	...
212	Employers' social contributions	5,617	...	...	5,617	...	...	...	...	...	...	...	...
22	**Use of goods and services**	**85,600**	**121,000**	...	**85,600**	**121,000**	...	...	...	...	...	...	...
23	**Consumption of fixed capital**	...	...	...	...	...	...	...	...	...	...	...	...
24	**Interest**	**17,650**	**3,406**	...	**17,650**	**3,406**	...	...	...	...	...	...	...
25	**Subsidies**	**14,501**	**37,311**	...	**14,501**	**37,311**	...	...	...	...	...	...	...
26	**Grants**	**66,701**	**87,205**	**110,274**	**66,701**	**87,205**	**110,274**	...	...	...	...	...	...
261	To foreign governments	...	...	...	...	...	...	...	...	...	...	...	...
262	To international organizations	...	...	...	...	...	...	...	...	...	...	...	...
263	To other general government units	...	...	...	...	...	...	...	...	...	...	...	...
2631	Current	...	...	...	...	...	...	...	...	...	...	...	...
2632	Capital	...	...	...	...	...	...	...	...	...	...	...	...

Liberia (668)

In Thousands of U.S. Dollars (USD) / Fiscal Year Ends June 30th

		Budgetary Central Government			Central Government (excl. Social Security)			Central Government (incl. Social Security)			General Government		
		2011	2012	2013	2011	2012	2013	2011	2012	2013	2011	2012	2013
27	**Social benefits**	**512**	**450**	**1,067**	**512**	**450**	**1,067**	**...**	**...**	**...**	**...**	**...**	**...**
271	Social security benefits	...	...	...	...	...	...	...	...	...	...	...	...
272	Social assistance benefits	...	...	...	...	...	...	...	...	...	...	...	...
273	Employment-related social benefits	...	...	...	...	...	...	...	...	...	...	...	...
28	**Other expense**	**—**	**—**	**—**	**—**	**—**	**—**	**...**	**...**	**...**	**...**	**...**	**...**
281	Property expense other than interest	—	—	—	—	—	—	...	...	...	...	...	...
282	Transfers not elsewhere classified	—	—	—	—	—	—	...	...	...	...	...	...
2821	Current	—	—	—	—	—	—	...	...	...	...	...	...
2822	Capital	—	—	—	—	—	—	...	...	...	...	...	...
	Table 3 Transactions in assets and liabilities												
3	**Change in net worth from transactions**	**...**	**...**	**...**	**...**	**...**	**...**	**...**	**...**	**...**	**...**	**...**	**...**
31	**Net/Gross investment in nonfinancial assets**	**62,311**	**52,012**	**24,891**	**62,311**	**52,012**	**24,891**	**...**	**...**	**...**	**...**	**...**	**...**
311	Fixed assets	62,311	52,012	24,891	62,311	52,012	24,891	...	...	...	...	...	...
3111	Buildings and structures	...	...	...	...	...	...	...	...	...	...	...	...
3112	Machinery and equipment	...	...	...	...	...	...	...	...	...	...	...	...
3113	Other fixed assets	...	...	...	...	...	...	...	...	...	...	...	...
3114	Weapons systems	...	...	...	...	...	...	...	...	...	...	...	...
312	Inventories	—	—	—	—	—	—	...	...	...	...	...	...
313	Valuables	—	—	—	—	—	—	...	...	...	...	...	...
314	Nonproduced assets	—	—	—	—	—	—	...	...	...	...	...	...
3141	Land	—	—	—	—	—	—	...	...	...	...	...	...
3142	Mineral and energy resources	—	—	—	—	—	—	...	...	...	...	...	...
3143	Other naturally occurring assets	—	—	—	—	—	—	...	...	...	...	...	...
3144	Intangible nonproduced assets	—	—	—	—	—	—	...	...	...	...	...	...
32	**Net acquisition of financial assets**	**...**	**...**	**...**	**...**	**...**	**...**	**...**	**...**	**...**	**...**	**...**	**...**
	By instrument												
3201	Monetary gold and SDRs	...	...	...	...	...	...	...	...	...	...	...	...
3202	Currency and deposits	...	...	...	...	...	...	...	...	...	...	...	...
3203	Debt securities	...	...	...	...	...	...	...	...	...	...	...	...
3204	Loans	...	...	...	...	...	...	...	...	...	...	...	...
3205	Equity and investment fund shares	...	...	...	...	...	...	...	...	...	...	...	...
3206	Insurance, pension, and standardized guarantee schemes	...	...	...	...	...	...	...	...	...	...	...	...
3207	Financial derivatives and employee stock options	...	...	...	...	...	...	...	...	...	...	...	...
3208	Other accounts receivable	...	...	...	...	...	...	...	...	...	...	...	...
	By debtor												
321	Domestic debtors	—	—	—	—	—	—	...	...	...	...	...	...
322	External debtors	—	—	—	—	—	—	...	...	...	...	...	...
33	**Net incurrence of liabilities**	**...**	**...**	**...**	**...**	**...**	**...**	**...**	**...**	**...**	**...**	**...**	**...**
	By instrument												
3301	Special Drawing Rights (SDRs)	...	...	...	...	...	...	...	...	...	...	...	...
3302	Currency and deposits	...	...	...	...	...	...	...	...	...	...	...	...
3303	Debt securities	...	...	...	...	...	...	...	...	...	...	...	...
3304	Loans	...	...	...	...	...	...	...	...	...	...	...	...
3305	Equity and investment fund shares	...	...	...	...	...	...	...	...	...	...	...	...
3306	Insurance, pension, and standardized guarantee schemes	...	...	...	...	...	...	...	...	...	...	...	...
3307	Financial derivatives and employee stock options	...	...	...	...	...	...	...	...	...	...	...	...
3308	Other accounts payable	...	...	...	...	...	...	...	...	...	...	...	...
	By creditor												
331	Domestic creditors	—	—	—	—	—	—	...	...	...	...	...	...
332	External creditors	—	—	—	—	—	—	...	...	...	...	...	...
	Table 4 Holding gains and losses in assets and liabilities												
	Table 5 Holding gains and losses in assets and liabilities												
	Table 6 Balance sheet												

Liberia (668)

In Thousands of U.S. Dollars (USD) / Fiscal Year Ends June 30th

		Budgetary Central Government			Central Government (excl. Social Security)			Central Government (incl. Social Security)			General Government		
		2011	2012	2013	2011	2012	2013	2011	2012	2013	2011	2012	2013
	Table 7 Expenditure by functions of government												
7	**Expenditure**	**384,718**	**488,219**	**530,482**	**384,718**	**488,219**	**530,482**	**...**	**...**	**...**	**...**	**...**	**...**
701	**General public services**	**160,200**	**176,300**	**166,674**	**160,200**	**176,300**	**166,674**	**...**	**...**	**...**	**...**	**...**	**...**
7017	Public debt transactions	17,650	3,406	...	17,650	3,406	...	...	...	...	...	...	...
7018	Transfers of general character between levels of government	...	...	...	...	...	...	...	...	...	...	...	...
702	**Defense**	**...**	**...**	**14,658**	**...**	**...**	**14,658**	**...**	**...**	**...**	**...**	**...**	**...**
703	**Public order and safety**	**...**	**...**	**62,054**	**...**	**...**	**62,054**	**...**	**...**	**...**	**...**	**...**	**...**
704	**Economic affairs**	**53,000**	**69,400**	**...**	**53,000**	**69,400**	**...**	**...**	**...**	**...**	**...**	**...**	**...**
7042	Agriculture, forestry, fishing, and hunting	11,600	9,600	...	11,600	9,600	...	...	...	...	...	...	...
7043	Fuel and energy	...	...	...	...	...	...	...	...	...	...	...	...
7044	Mining, manufacturing, and construction	...	...	...	...	...	...	...	...	...	...	...	...
7045	Transport	...	...	...	...	...	...	...	...	...	...	...	...
7046	Communication	...	...	...	...	...	...	...	...	...	...	...	...
705	**Environmental protection**	**...**	**...**	**5,596**	**...**	**...**	**5,596**	**...**	**...**	**...**	**...**	**...**	**...**
706	**Housing and community amenities**	**...**	**...**	**13,834**	**...**	**...**	**13,834**	**...**	**...**	**...**	**...**	**...**	**...**
707	**Health**	**33,900**	**49,400**	**54,162**	**33,900**	**49,400**	**54,162**	**...**	**...**	**...**	**...**	**...**	**...**
7072	Outpatient services	...	...	—	...	...	—	...	...	...	...	...	...
7073	Hospital services	...	...	—	...	...	—	...	...	...	...	...	...
7074	Public health services	...	...	54,162	...	...	54,162	...	...	...	...	...	...
708	**Recreation, culture and religion**	**...**	**...**	**...**	**...**	**...**	**...**	**...**	**...**	**...**	**...**	**...**	**...**
709	**Education**	**34,500**	**70,600**	**70,253**	**34,500**	**70,600**	**70,253**	**...**	**...**	**...**	**...**	**...**	**...**
7091	Pre-primary and primary education	...	...	—	...	...	—	...	...	...	...	...	...
7092	Secondary education	...	...	—	...	...	—	...	...	...	...	...	...
7094	Tertiary education	...	...	70,253	...	...	70,253	...	...	...	...	...	...
710	**Social protection**	**...**	**...**	**8,328**	**...**	**...**	**8,328**	**...**	**...**	**...**	**...**	**...**	**...**
7z	Statistical discrepancy: Expenditure	...	...	...	...	...	...	...	...	...	...	...	...
	Table 8 Financial transactions by counterpart sector												
	Table 9 Total other economic flows in assets and liabilities												

Lithuania (946)

In Millions of Euros (EUR) / Fiscal Year Ends December 31st

		Budgetary Central Government			Central Government (excl. Social Security)			Central Government (incl. Social Security)			General Government		
		2013P	2014P	2015P	2013P	2014P	2015P	2013P	2014P	2015P	2013P	2014P	2015P
	Statement of operations												
1	Revenue	7,094	7,355	7,834	7,885	8,539	8,783	11,180	12,083	12,594	11,512	12,452	13,014
2	Expense	...	...	...	8,048	8,073	8,570	11,695	12,070	12,380	12,252	12,533	12,838
GOB	**Gross operating balance**	**...**	**...**	**...**	**292**	**960**	**745**	**-57**	**512**	**750**	**285**	**988**	**1,274**
NOB	**Net operating balance**	**...**	**...**	**...**	**-162**	**465**	**213**	**-515**	**14**	**214**	**-740**	**-81**	**176**
31	Net/Gross investment in nonfinancial assets	...	...	...	304	305	411	307	308	412	177	171	252
2M	Expenditure	...	...	...	8,352	8,378	8,981	12,002	12,378	12,792	12,429	12,703	13,090
NLB	**Net lending (+) / Net borrowing (-)**	**...**	**...**	**...**	**-466**	**160**	**-198**	**-821**	**-295**	**-198**	**-917**	**-251**	**-76**
32	Net acquisition of financial assets	...	...	...	27	1,492	376	...	...	...	-375	1,236	343
33	Net incurrence of liabilities	...	...	...	469	1,326	591	...	...	...	525	1,483	448
NLBz	Statistical discrepancy	...	...	...	24	6	-18	...	...	...	17	4	-29
	Memorandum items												
PB	Primary net lending / net borrowing	...	...	...	134	734	368	-217	282	368	-302	336	493
GB	Government balance per national definition	...	...	...	...	...	...	...	...	...	...	...	...
	Statement of other economic flows												
	Balance sheet												
6	**Net worth**	**...**	**...**	**...**	**...**	**...**	**...**	**...**	**...**	**...**	**...**	**...**	**...**
61	Nonfinancial assets	...	...	...	...	...	...	...	...	...	...	...	...
62	Financial assets	...	...	...	9,223	11,501	12,730	...	...	...	7,791	9,977	11,118
63	Liabilities	...	...	...	15,391	17,659	18,741	...	...	...	16,798	19,223	20,163
	Table 1 Revenue												
1	**Revenue**	**7,094**	**7,355**	**7,834**	**7,885**	**8,539**	**8,783**	**11,180**	**12,083**	**12,594**	**11,512**	**12,452**	**13,014**
11	**Taxes**	**5,405**	**5,727**	**6,164**	**5,470**	**5,797**	**6,247**	**5,470**	**5,797**	**6,247**	**5,621**	**5,965**	**6,436**
111	Taxes on income, profits, and capital gains	1,726	1,825	2,013	1,726	1,825	2,013	1,726	1,825	2,013	1,726	1,825	2,013
1111	Payable by individuals	1,250	1,325	1,440	1,250	1,325	1,440	1,250	1,325	1,440	1,250	1,325	1,440
1112	Payable by corporations and other enterprises	477	500	574	477	500	574	477	500	574	477	500	574
1113	Other taxes on income, profits, and capital gains	—	—	—	—	—	—	—	—	—	—	—	—
112	Taxes on payroll and workforce	—	—	—	12	14	16	12	14	16	12	14	16
113	Taxes on property	1	2	1	1	2	1	1	2	1	97	108	126
114	Taxes on goods and services	3,651	3,874	4,125	3,704	3,930	4,192	3,704	3,930	4,192	3,726	3,953	4,215
1141	General taxes on goods and services	2,611	2,764	2,912	2,611	2,764	2,912	2,611	2,764	2,912	2,611	2,764	2,912
1142	Excises	989	1,054	1,164	989	1,054	1,164	989	1,054	1,164	989	1,054	1,164
115	Taxes on international trade and transactions	—	—	—	—	—	—	—	—	—	—	—	—
116	Other taxes	26	26	25	26	26	25	26	26	25	60	64	64
12	**Social contributions**	**98**	**108**	**113**	**98**	**108**	**113**	**3,892**	**4,173**	**4,453**	**3,893**	**4,174**	**4,456**
121	Social security contributions	—	—	—	—	—	—	3,794	4,065	4,340	3,794	4,065	4,340
122	Other social contributions	98	108	113	98	108	113	98	109	113	99	109	116
13	**Grants**	**787**	**725**	**701**	**1,230**	**1,174**	**1,147**	**879**	**796**	**738**	**879**	**796**	**738**
131	From foreign governments	11	13	26	11	13	26	11	13	26	11	13	26
132	From international organizations	776	712	675	868	783	711	868	783	711	868	783	711
133	From other general government units	—	—	—	351	378	410	—	—	—	—	—	—
1331	Current	—	—	—	351	378	410	—	—	—	—	—	—
1332	Capital	—	—	—	—	—	—	—	—	—	—	—	—
14	**Other revenue**	**805**	**794**	**856**	**1,088**	**1,460**	**1,276**	**939**	**1,317**	**1,157**	**1,120**	**1,518**	**1,384**
	Table 2 Expense by economic type												
2	**Expense**	**...**	**...**	**...**	**8,048**	**8,073**	**8,570**	**11,695**	**12,070**	**12,380**	**12,252**	**12,533**	**12,838**
21	**Compensation of employees**	**1,461**	**1,540**	**1,580**	**1,795**	**1,886**	**1,942**	**1,857**	**1,953**	**2,011**	**3,328**	**3,451**	**3,594**
211	Wages and salaries	1,052	1,103	1,132	1,305	1,365	1,407	1,352	1,416	1,459	2,475	2,559	2,665
212	Employers' social contributions	409	437	448	490	521	536	505	537	552	853	892	929
22	**Use of goods and services**	**764**	**806**	**893**	**1,033**	**1,097**	**1,200**	**1,065**	**1,122**	**1,232**	**1,652**	**1,734**	**1,923**
23	**Consumption of fixed capital**	**407**	**427**	**468**	**455**	**495**	**532**	**458**	**499**	**536**	**1,025**	**1,069**	**1,098**
24	**Interest**	**...**	**...**	**...**	**601**	**574**	**565**	**605**	**577**	**566**	**615**	**587**	**569**
25	**Subsidies**	**...**	**...**	**...**	**78**	**89**	**114**	**105**	**110**	**139**	**116**	**119**	**148**

Lithuania (946)

In Millions of Euros (EUR) / Fiscal Year Ends December 31st

		Budgetary Central Government			Central Government (excl. Social Security)			Central Government (incl. Social Security)			General Government		
		2013P	2014P	2015P	2013P	2014P	2015P	2013P	2014P	2015P	2013P	2014P	2015P
26	**Grants**	**2,510**	**2,664**	**2,830**	**2,561**	**2,572**	**2,718**	**2,833**	**2,873**	**2,983**	**361**	**308**	**346**
261	To foreign governments	1	1	2	1	1	2	1	1	2	1	1	2
262	To international organizations	360	307	334	360	307	344	360	307	344	360	307	344
263	To other general government units	2,150	2,356	2,495	2,200	2,264	2,372	2,472	2,566	2,638	—	—	—
2631	Current	1,777	1,907	2,024	1,865	1,833	1,948	2,137	2,262	2,363	—	—	—
2632	Capital	372	449	471	335	432	424	335	303	275	—	—	—
27	**Social benefits**	**962**	**1,038**	**1,073**	**962**	**1,038**	**1,073**	**4,207**	**4,308**	**4,483**	**4,508**	**4,545**	**4,672**
271	Social security benefits	—	—	—	—	—	—	3,245	3,269	3,410	3,245	3,269	3,410
272	Social assistance benefits	864	930	960	864	930	960	864	930	960	1,164	1,167	1,146
273	Employment-related social benefits	98	108	113	98	108	113	98	109	113	99	109	116
28	**Other expense**	**233**	**239**	**386**	**564**	**323**	**427**	**566**	**628**	**429**	**649**	**720**	**489**
281	Property expense other than interest	0	0	0	0	0	0	0	0	0	0	0	0
282	Transfers not elsewhere classified	233	239	386	564	323	427	565	628	429	649	720	489
2821	Current	117	127	167	122	133	173	123	137	175	200	216	224
2822	Capital	116	112	219	442	190	254	442	492	254	449	504	265
	Table 3 Transactions in assets and liabilities												
3	**Change in net worth from transactions**	**...**	**...**	**...**	**-138**	**471**	**196**	**...**	**...**	**...**	**-722**	**-76**	**147**
31	**Net/Gross investment in nonfinancial assets**	**...**	**...**	**...**	**304**	**305**	**411**	**307**	**308**	**412**	**177**	**171**	**252**
311	Fixed assets	...	...	...	399	356	414	402	359	415	286	229	258
3111	Buildings and structures	...	...	...	...	...	...	...	...	...	...	...	...
3112	Machinery and equipment	...	...	...	...	...	...	...	...	...	...	...	...
3113	Other fixed assets	...	...	...	...	...	...	...	...	...	...	...	...
3114	Weapons systems	...	...	...	...	...	...	...	...	...	...	...	...
312	Inventories	2	9	40	3	10	39	...	...	...	3	10	39
313	Valuables	—	—	-0	5	7	5	...	...	...	6	11	6
314	Nonproduced assets	-103	-68	-47	-102	-68	-46	-102	-68	-46	-118	-78	-52
3141	Land	...	...	...	...	...	...	...	...	...	...	...	...
3142	Mineral and energy resources	...	...	...	...	...	...	...	...	...	...	...	...
3143	Other naturally occurring assets	...	...	...	...	...	...	...	...	...	...	...	...
3144	Intangible nonproduced assets	...	...	...	...	...	...	...	...	...	...	...	...
32	**Net acquisition of financial assets**	**...**	**...**	**...**	**27**	**1,492**	**376**	**...**	**...**	**...**	**-375**	**1,236**	**343**
	By instrument												
3201	Monetary gold and SDRs	...	...	...	—	—	—	...	...	...	—	—	—
3202	Currency and deposits	...	...	...	-499	1,092	-39	...	...	...	-487	1,211	45
3203	Debt securities	...	...	...	—	50	-49	...	...	...	—	50	-49
3204	Loans	...	...	...	440	386	173	...	...	...	5	6	0
3205	Equity and investment fund shares	...	...	...	-1	1	70	...	...	...	-3	-1	70
3206	Insurance, pension, and standardized guarantee schemes	...	...	...	-0	0	0	...	...	...	-0	0	0
3207	Financial derivatives and employee stock options	...	...	...	-19	-11	-335	...	...	...	-19	-11	-335
3208	Other accounts receivable	...	...	...	105	-27	556	...	...	...	129	-21	612
	By debtor												
321	Domestic debtors	...	...	...	-158	1,438	-20	...	...	...	-560	1,182	-52
322	External debtors	...	...	...	185	54	396	...	...	...	185	54	396
33	**Net incurrence of liabilities**	**...**	**...**	**...**	**469**	**1,326**	**591**	**...**	**...**	**...**	**525**	**1,483**	**448**
	By instrument												
3301	Special Drawing Rights (SDRs)	...	...	...	—	—	—	...	...	...	—	—	—
3302	Currency and deposits	...	...	...	53	59	168	...	...	...	53	59	167
3303	Debt securities	...	...	...	-43	1,196	786	...	...	...	-43	1,196	786
3304	Loans	...	...	...	295	-30	102	...	...	...	303	27	80
3305	Equity and investment fund shares	...	...	...	—	—	—	...	...	...	—	—	—
3306	Insurance, pension, and standardized guarantee schemes	...	...	...	1	-1	-1	...	...	...	1	-1	-1
3307	Financial derivatives and employee stock options	...	...	...	—	—	—	...	...	...	—	—	—
3308	Other accounts payable	...	...	...	164	102	-464	...	...	...	211	202	-585

Lithuania (946)

In Millions of Euros (EUR) / Fiscal Year Ends December 31st

		Budgetary Central Government			Central Government (excl. Social Security)			Central Government (incl. Social Security)			General Government		
		2013P	2014P	2015P	2013P	2014P	2015P	2013P	2014P	2015P	2013P	2014P	2015P
	By creditor												
331	Domestic creditors	...	...	...	962	81	41	...	...	...	1,004	235	-97
332	External creditors	...	...	...	-493	1,245	550	...	...	...	-480	1,249	545
	Table 4 Holding gains and losses in assets and liabilities												
	Table 5 Holding gains and losses in assets and liabilities												
	Table 6 Balance sheet												
6	**Net worth**	...	...	...	...	...	...	...	...	...	...	...	...
61	**Nonfinancial assets**	...	...	...	...	...	...	...	...	...	...	...	...
611	Fixed assets	...	...	...	...	...	...	...	...	...	...	...	...
6111	Buildings and structures	...	...	...	...	...	...	...	...	...	...	...	...
6112	Machinery and equipment	...	...	...	...	...	...	...	...	...	...	...	...
6113	Other fixed assets	...	...	...	...	...	...	...	...	...	...	...	...
6114	Weapons systems	...	...	...	...	...	...	...	...	...	...	...	...
612	Inventories	...	...	...	...	...	...	...	...	...	...	...	...
613	Valuables	...	...	...	...	...	...	...	...	...	...	...	...
614	Nonproduced assets	...	...	...	...	...	...	...	...	...	...	...	...
6141	Land	...	...	...	...	...	...	...	...	...	...	...	...
6142	Mineral and energy resources	...	...	...	...	...	...	...	...	...	...	...	...
6143	Other naturally occurring assets	...	...	...	...	...	...	...	...	...	...	...	...
6144	Intangible nonproduced assets	...	...	...	...	...	...	...	...	...	...	...	...
62	**Financial assets**	...	...	...	**9,223**	**11,501**	**12,730**	...	...	...	**7,791**	**9,977**	**11,118**
	By instrument												
6201	Monetary gold and SDRs	...	...	...	—	—	—	...	...	...	—	—	—
6202	Currency and deposits	...	...	...	1,221	2,308	2,264	...	...	...	1,504	2,710	2,749
6203	Debt securities	...	...	...	1	51	2	...	...	...	1	51	2
6204	Loans	...	...	...	2,998	3,385	3,557	...	...	...	90	96	97
6205	Equity and investment fund shares	...	...	...	3,459	4,109	4,829	...	...	...	4,413	5,226	5,892
6206	Insurance, pension, and standardized guarantee schemes	...	...	...	1	1	1	...	...	...	1	1	1
6207	Financial derivatives and employee stock options	...	...	...	68	201	76	...	...	...	68	201	76
6208	Other accounts receivable	...	...	...	1,475	1,447	2,001	...	...	...	1,714	1,693	2,302
	By debtor												
621	Domestic debtors	...	...	...	...	...	...	...	...	...	...	...	...
622	External debtors	...	...	...	...	...	...	...	...	...	...	...	...
63	**Liabilities**	...	...	...	**15,391**	**17,659**	**18,741**	...	...	...	**16,798**	**19,223**	**20,163**
	By instrument												
6301	Special Drawing Rights (SDRs)	...	...	...	—	—	—	...	...	...	—	—	—
6302	Currency and deposits	...	...	...	248	307	536	...	...	...	248	307	535
6303	Debt securities	...	...	...	11,845	14,001	15,218	...	...	...	11,845	14,001	15,218
6304	Loans	...	...	...	1,781	1,751	1,853	...	...	...	2,821	2,848	2,928
6305	Equity and investment fund shares	...	...	...	—	—	—	...	...	...	—	—	—
6306	Insurance, pension, and standardized guarantee schemes	...	...	...	21	20	19	...	...	...	21	20	19
6307	Financial derivatives and employee stock options	...	...	...	19	—	—	...	...	...	19	—	—
6308	Other accounts payable	...	...	...	1,477	1,579	1,115	...	...	...	1,845	2,047	1,463
	By creditor												
631	Domestic creditors	...	...	...	...	...	...	...	...	...	...	...	...
632	External creditors	...	...	...	...	...	...	...	...	...	...	...	...
	Memorandum items												
6M2	Net financial worth	...	...	...	-6,169	-6,158	-6,012	...	...	...	-9,007	-9,246	-9,045
6M3	Gross debt (D4) at market value	...	...	...	15,372	17,659	18,741	...	...	...	16,779	19,223	20,163
6M3D3	D3 debt liabilities at market value	...	...	...	15,351	17,639	18,722	...	...	...	16,758	19,203	20,144
6M3D2	D2 debt liabilities at market value	...	...	...	13,874	16,060	17,607	...	...	...	14,913	17,156	18,681
6M3D1	D1 debt liabilities at market value	...	...	...	13,626	15,753	17,071	...	...	...	14,665	16,849	18,146
6M4	Gross debt (D4) at nominal value	...	...	...	...	...	...	...	...	...	...	...	...
6M4D3	D3 debt liabilities at nominal value	...	...	...	...	...	...	...	...	...	...	...	...
6M4D2	D2 debt liabilities at nominal value	...	...	...	...	...	...	...	...	...	...	...	...
6M4D1	D1 debt liabilities at nominal value	...	...	...	...	...	...	...	...	...	...	...	...

Lithuania (946)

In Millions of Euros (EUR) / Fiscal Year Ends December 31st

		Budgetary Central Government			Central Government (excl. Social Security)			Central Government (incl. Social Security)			General Government		
		2013P	2014P	2015P	2013P	2014P	2015P	2013P	2014P	2015P	2013P	2014P	2015P
6M35	Gross debt (D4) at face value	...	...	...	...	...	...	...	...	...	...	...	...
6M35D3	D3 debt liabilities at face value	...	...	...	14,018	15,340	16,010	...	...	...	15,395	16,872	17,402
6M35D2	D2 debt liabilities at face value	...	...	...	12,540	13,761	14,895	...	...	...	13,550	14,825	15,940
6M35D1	D1 debt liabilities at face value	...	...	...	12,294	13,456	14,360	...	...	...	13,304	14,520	15,406
6M93	Government gross debt per national definition	...	...	...	12,540	13,761	14,895	...	...	...	13,550	14,825	15,940
6M5	Arrears	...	...	...	...	...	...	...	...	...	...	...	...
6M6	Explicit contingent liabilities	...	...	...	...	...	...	...	...	...	...	...	...
6M61	of which: Publicly guaranteed debt	...	...	...	...	...	...	...	...	...	...	...	...
6M7	Net implicit obligations for social security benefits	...	...	...	...	...	...	...	...	...	...	...	...
	Table 7 Expenditure by functions of government												
7	**Expenditure**	...	...	...	8,352	8,355	...	...	...	...	12,429	12,683	...
701	**General public services**	...	...	...	3,833	3,585	...	...	...	...	1,848	1,692	...
7017	Public debt transactions	...	...	...	645	638	...	...	...	...	669	659	...
7018	Transfers of general character between levels of government	...	...	...	2,194	2,124	...	...	...	...	—	—	...
702	**Defense**	...	...	...	340	383	...	...	...	...	342	385	...
703	**Public order and safety**	...	...	...	474	518	...	...	...	...	578	613	...
704	**Economic affairs**	...	...	...	935	920	...	...	...	...	1,217	1,174	...
7042	Agriculture, forestry, fishing, and hunting	...	...	...	245	246	...	...	...	...	317	325	...
7043	Fuel and energy	...	...	...	189	158	...	...	...	...	230	171	...
7044	Mining, manufacturing, and construction	...	...	...	6	6	...	...	...	...	8	10	...
7045	Transport	...	...	...	349	335	...	...	...	...	461	424	...
7046	Communication	...	...	...	46	60	...	...	...	...	47	61	...
705	**Environmental protection**	...	...	...	57	99	...	...	...	...	164	206	...
706	**Housing and community amenities**	...	...	...	3	22	...	...	...	...	88	123	...
707	**Health**	...	...	...	995	1,007	...	...	...	...	1,971	2,017	...
7072	Outpatient services	...	...	...	223	217	...	...	...	...	503	507	...
7073	Hospital services	...	...	...	311	304	...	...	...	...	733	738	...
7074	Public health services	...	...	...	16	16	...	...	...	...	21	26	...
708	**Recreation, culture and religion**	...	...	...	162	182	...	...	...	...	287	325	...
709	**Education**	...	...	...	901	900	...	...	...	...	1,964	1,965	...
7091	Pre-primary and primary education	...	...	...	1	1	...	...	...	...	277	288	...
7092	Secondary education	...	...	...	27	29	...	...	...	...	658	666	...
7094	Tertiary education	...	...	...	484	449	...	...	...	...	484	449	...
710	**Social protection**	...	...	...	651	740	...	...	...	...	3,971	4,184	...
7z	Statistical discrepancy: Expenditure	...	...	...	-0	—	...	...	...	...	0	—	...
	Table 8 Financial transactions by counterpart sector												
32	**Net acquisition of financial assets**	...	...	...	27	1,492	376	...	...	...	-375	1,236	343
321	Domestic debtors	...	...	...	-158	1,438	-20	...	...	...	-560	1,182	-52
8211	General government	...	...	...	...	...	...	...	...	...	—	—	—
8212	Central bank	...	...	...	...	...	...	...	...	...	...	...	...
8213	Deposit-taking corporations except the central bank	...	...	...	...	...	...	...	...	...	...	...	...
8214	Other financial corporations	...	...	...	...	...	...	...	...	...	...	...	...
8215	Nonfinancial corporations	...	...	...	...	...	...	...	...	...	...	...	...
8216	Households & nonprofit institutions serving households	...	...	...	...	...	...	...	...	...	...	...	...
322	External debtors	...	...	...	185	54	396	...	...	...	185	54	396
8221	General government	...	...	...	...	...	...	...	...	...	...	...	...
8227	International organizations	...	...	...	...	...	...	...	...	...	...	...	...
8228	Financial corporations other than international organizations	...	...	...	...	...	...	...	...	...	...	...	...
8229	Other nonresidents	...	...	...	...	...	...	...	...	...	...	...	...

Lithuania (946)

In Millions of Euros (EUR) / Fiscal Year Ends December 31st

		Budgetary Central Government			Central Government (excl. Social Security)			Central Government (incl. Social Security)			General Government		
		2013P	2014P	2015P	2013P	2014P	2015P	2013P	2014P	2015P	2013P	2014P	2015P
33	**Net incurrence of liabilities**	...	...	...	**469**	**1,326**	**591**	...	...	...	**525**	**1,483**	**448**
331	Domestic creditors	...	...	...	962	81	41	...	...	...	1,004	235	-97
8311	General government	...	...	...	...	...	...	...	...	...	—	—	—
8312	Central bank	...	...	...	...	...	...	...	...	...	...	...	...
8313	Deposit-taking corporations except the central bank	...	...	...	...	...	...	...	...	...	...	...	...
8314	Other financial corporations	...	...	...	...	...	...	...	...	...	...	...	...
8315	Nonfinancial corporations	...	...	...	...	...	...	...	...	...	...	...	...
8316	Households & nonprofit institutions serving households	...	...	...	...	...	...	...	...	...	...	...	...
332	External creditors	...	...	...	-493	1,245	550	...	...	...	-480	1,249	545
8321	General government	...	...	...	...	...	...	...	...	...	...	...	...
8327	International organizations	...	...	...	...	...	...	...	...	...	...	...	...
8328	Financial corporations other than international organizations	...	...	...	...	...	...	...	...	...	...	...	...
8329	Other nonresidents	...	...	...	...	...	...	...	...	...	...	...	...
	Table 9 Total other economic flows in assets and liabilities												
9	**Change in net worth due to other economic flows**	...	...	...	...	...	...	...	...	...	...	...	...
91	**Other economic flows in nonfinancial assets**	...	...	...	...	...	...	...	...	...	...	...	...
911	Fixed assets	...	...	...	...	...	...	...	...	...	...	...	...
912	Inventories	...	...	...	...	...	...	...	...	...	...	...	...
913	Valuables	...	...	...	...	...	...	...	...	...	...	...	...
914	Nonproduced assets	...	...	...	...	...	...	...	...	...	...	...	...
92	**Other economic flows in financial assets**	...	...	...	**-21**	**787**	**852**	...	...	...	**-146**	**950**	**798**
	By instrument												
9201	Monetary gold and SDRs	...	...	...	—	—	—	...	...	...	—	—	—
9202	Currency and deposits	...	...	...	-24	-5	-5	...	...	...	-36	-5	-6
9203	Debt securities	...	...	...	0	-1	0	...	...	...	0	-1	0
9204	Loans	...	...	...	-2	-0	0	...	...	...	-2	-0	0
9205	Equity and investment fund shares	...	...	...	41	649	650	...	...	...	-69	813	597
9206	Insurance, pension, and standardized guarantee schemes	...	...	...	-0	0	0	...	...	...	-0	0	0
9207	Financial derivatives and employee stock options	...	...	...	-23	143	210	...	...	...	-23	143	210
9208	Other accounts receivable	...	...	...	-12	0	-3	...	...	...	-16	—	-3
	By debtor												
921	Domestic debtors	...	...	...	...	...	...	...	...	...	...	...	...
922	External debtors	...	...	...	...	...	...	...	...	...	...	...	...
93	**Other economic flows in liabilities**	...	...	...	**-817**	**942**	**491**	...	...	...	**-820**	**942**	**491**
	By instrument												
9301	Special Drawing Rights (SDRs)	...	...	...	—	—	—	...	...	...	—	—	—
9302	Currency and deposits	...	...	...	-0	—	60	...	...	...	-0	—	60
9303	Debt securities	...	...	...	-816	961	431	...	...	...	-816	961	431
9304	Loans	...	...	...	-3	0	0	...	...	...	-3	0	0
9305	Equity and investment fund shares	...	...	...	—	—	—	...	...	...	—	—	—
9306	Insurance, pension, and standardized guarantee schemes	...	...	...	—	-0	—	...	...	...	—	-0	—
9307	Financial derivatives and employee stock options	...	...	...	19	-19	—	...	...	...	19	-19	—
9308	Other accounts payable	...	...	...	-18	—	0	...	...	...	-21	—	—
	By creditor												
931	Domestic creditors	...	...	...	...	...	...	...	...	...	...	...	...
932	External creditors	...	...	...	...	...	...	...	...	...	...	...	...
	Memorandum items												
9M2	Change in net financial worth due to other economic flows	...	...	...	796	-155	361	...	...	...	674	8	307

Lithuania (946)

In Millions of Euros (EUR) / Fiscal Year Ends December 31st

		Budgetary Central Government			Central Government (excl. Social Security)			Central Government (incl. Social Security)			General Government		
		2013P	2014P	2015P	2013P	2014P	2015P	2013P	2014P	2015P	2013P	2014P	2015P
9M3	Gross debt (D4) at market value: other economic flows	...	...	...	-837	961	491	...	...	...	-839	961	491
9M3D3	D3 debt liabilities at market value: other economic flows	...	...	...	-837	961	491	...	...	...	-839	961	491
9M3D2	D2 debt liabilities at market value: other economic flows	...	...	...	-818	961	491	...	...	...	-818	961	491
9M3D1	D1 debt liabilities at market value: other economic flows	...	...	...	-818	961	431	...	...	...	-818	961	431

Luxembourg (137)

In Millions of Euros (EUR) / Fiscal Year Ends December 31st

		Budgetary Central Government			Central Government (excl. Social Security)			Central Government (incl. Social Security)			General Government		
		2013	2014	2015	2013	2014	2015P	2013	2014	2015P	2013	2014	2015P
	Statement of operations												
1	Revenue	...	...	...	14,213	15,000	15,495	19,613	20,573	21,317	20,581	21,570	22,369
2	Expense	...	...	...	14,308	14,663	15,070	18,966	19,534	20,028	19,485	20,086	20,696
GOB	**Gross operating balance**	**...**	**...**	**...**	**549**	**1,006**	**1,118**	**1,312**	**1,728**	**2,003**	**2,122**	**2,553**	**2,781**
NOB	**Net operating balance**	**...**	**...**	**...**	**-95**	**338**	**425**	**647**	**1,039**	**1,289**	**1,096**	**1,484**	**1,674**
31	Net/Gross investment in nonfinancial assets	...	...	...	371	479	600	363	467	702	651	766	878
2M	Expenditure	...	...	...	14,680	15,142	15,670	19,329	20,001	20,730	20,136	20,852	21,573
NLB	**Net lending (+) / Net borrowing (-)**	**...**	**...**	**...**	**-467**	**-141**	**-176**	**284**	**572**	**587**	**445**	**718**	**796**
32	Net acquisition of financial assets	...	...	...	637	248	-17	1,277	1,575	817	1,400	1,740	1,160
33	Net incurrence of liabilities	...	...	...	1,104	389	159	1,001	1,008	236	955	1,022	363
NLBz	Statistical discrepancy	...	...	...	0	-0	0	-7	-5	-6	-0	-0	0
	Memorandum items												
PB	Primary net lending / net borrowing	...	...	...	-211	65	35	540	779	798	701	924	1,005
GB	Government balance per national definition	...	...	...	-467	-141	-176	...	...	...	445	718	796
	Statement of other economic flows												
9	**Change in net worth due to other economic flows**	**...**	**...**	**...**	**...**	**...**	**...**	**...**	**...**	**...**	**...**	**...**	**...**
4	Change in net worth due to holding gains and losses	...	...	...	...	...	...	...	...	...	...	...	...
41	Nonfinancial assets	...	...	...	...	...	...	...	...	...	...	...	...
42	Financial assets	...	...	...	667	288	-174	...	...	...	1,080	1,438	15
43	Liabilities	...	...	...	-260	702	-0	...	...	...	-260	702	-0
5	Change in net worth due to volume changes	...	...	...	...	...	...	...	...	...	...	...	...
51	Nonfinancial assets	...	...	...	...	...	...	...	...	...	...	...	...
52	Financial assets	...	...	...	...	...	...	...	...	...	...	...	...
53	Liabilities	...	...	...	...	...	...	...	...	...	...	...	...
	Balance sheet												
6	**Net worth**	**...**	**...**	**...**	**...**	**...**	**...**	**...**	**...**	**...**	**...**	**...**	**...**
61	Nonfinancial assets	...	...	...	...	...	...	...	...	...	...	...	...
62	Financial assets	...	...	...	19,493	20,029	19,838	35,714	38,707	39,520	37,639	40,817	41,992
63	Liabilities	...	...	...	12,270	13,362	13,520	13,969	15,679	15,915	13,993	15,717	16,081
	Table 1 Revenue												
1	**Revenue**	**...**	**...**	**...**	**14,213**	**15,000**	**15,495**	**19,613**	**20,573**	**21,317**	**20,581**	**21,570**	**22,369**
11	**Taxes**	**...**	**...**	**...**	**12,026**	**12,797**	**13,097**	**12,026**	**12,797**	**13,097**	**12,651**	**13,409**	**13,768**
111	Taxes on income, profits, and capital gains	...	...	...	5,706	5,922	6,406	5,706	5,922	6,406	6,275	6,468	7,012
1111	Payable by individuals	...	...	...	4,062	4,329	4,717	4,062	4,329	4,717	4,062	4,329	4,717
1112	Payable by corporations and other enterprises	...	...	...	1,644	1,594	1,689	1,644	1,594	1,689	2,213	2,140	2,295
1113	Other taxes on income, profits, and capital gains	...	...	...	—	—	—	—	—	—	—	—	—
112	Taxes on payroll and workforce	...	...	...	—	—	—	—	—	—	—	—	—
113	Taxes on property	...	...	...	341	348	459	341	348	459	374	382	496
114	Taxes on goods and services	...	...	...	5,979	6,527	6,232	5,979	6,527	6,232	6,002	6,559	6,260
1141	General taxes on goods and services	...	...	...	3,696	4,078	3,832	3,696	4,078	3,832	3,707	4,097	3,848
1142	Excises	...	...	...	1,406	1,484	1,294	1,406	1,484	1,294	1,406	1,484	1,294
115	Taxes on international trade and transactions	...	...	...	—	—	—	—	—	—	—	—	—
116	Other taxes	...	...	...	—	—	—	—	—	—	—	—	—
12	**Social contributions**	**...**	**...**	**...**	**719**	**751**	**781**	**5,779**	**5,960**	**6,232**	**5,783**	**5,964**	**6,236**
121	Social security contributions	...	...	...	—	—	—	5,046	5,193	5,434	5,046	5,193	5,434
122	Other social contributions	...	...	...	719	751	781	733	766	798	737	770	802
13	**Grants**	**...**	**...**	**...**	**309**	**285**	**387**	**266**	**224**	**321**	**106**	**73**	**161**
131	From foreign governments	...	...	...	97	63	152	97	63	152	101	67	156
132	From international organizations	...	...	...	5	5	5	5	5	5	5	6	5
133	From other general government units	...	...	...	208	217	229	165	157	164	—	—	—
1331	Current	...	...	...	188	187	199	165	157	164	—	—	—
1332	Capital	...	...	...	20	30	31	—	—	—	—	—	—
14	**Other revenue**	**...**	**...**	**...**	**1,159**	**1,168**	**1,230**	**1,542**	**1,592**	**1,667**	**2,041**	**2,124**	**2,203**

Luxembourg (137)

In Millions of Euros (EUR) / Fiscal Year Ends December 31st

		Budgetary Central Government			Central Government (excl. Social Security)			Central Government (incl. Social Security)			General Government		
		2013	2014	2015	2013	2014	2015P	2013	2014	2015P	2013	2014	2015P
	Table 2 Expense by economic type												
2	**Expense**	...	...	...	**14,308**	**14,663**	**15,070**	**18,966**	**19,534**	**20,028**	**19,485**	**20,086**	**20,696**
21	**Compensation of employees**	...	...	...	**3,265**	**3,405**	**3,528**	**3,369**	**3,513**	**3,640**	**4,176**	**4,357**	**4,525**
211	Wages and salaries	...	...	...	2,524	2,630	2,724	2,608	2,717	2,814	3,288	3,427	3,563
212	Employers' social contributions	...	...	...	741	775	803	761	796	827	889	930	962
22	**Use of goods and services**	...	...	...	**1,105**	**1,124**	**1,189**	**1,207**	**1,226**	**1,282**	**1,726**	**1,767**	**1,840**
23	**Consumption of fixed capital**	...	...	...	**644**	**669**	**694**	**665**	**689**	**714**	**1,026**	**1,069**	**1,107**
24	**Interest**	...	...	...	**256**	**207**	**211**	**256**	**207**	**211**	**256**	**206**	**208**
25	**Subsidies**	...	...	...	**593**	**627**	**636**	**593**	**627**	**636**	**661**	**704**	**712**
26	**Grants**	...	...	...	**6,060**	**6,173**	**6,298**	**2,315**	**2,278**	**2,338**	**969**	**880**	**984**
261	To foreign governments	...	...	...	651	596	623	651	596	623	659	602	630
262	To international organizations	...	...	...	311	278	354	311	278	354	311	278	354
263	To other general government units	...	...	...	5,099	5,299	5,321	1,353	1,404	1,361	—	—	—
2631	Current	...	...	...	4,903	5,087	5,128	...	...	...	—	—	—
2632	Capital	...	...	...	195	212	194	...	...	...	—	—	—
27	**Social benefits**	...	...	...	**1,529**	**1,558**	**1,571**	**9,691**	**10,078**	**10,249**	**9,723**	**10,110**	**10,283**
271	Social security benefits	...	...	...	1,529	1,558	1,571	9,691	10,078	10,249	9,723	10,110	10,283
272	Social assistance benefits	...	...	...	—	—	—	—	—	—	—	—	—
273	Employment-related social benefits	...	...	...	—	—	—	—	—	—	—	—	—
28	**Other expense**	...	...	...	**856**	**901**	**944**	**869**	**916**	**959**	**947**	**994**	**1,036**
281	Property expense other than interest	...	...	...	0	0	0	0	0	0	0	0	0
282	Transfers not elsewhere classified	...	...	...	853	896	939	866	912	953	938	984	1,026
2821	Current	...	...	...	853	896	939	853	897	940	920	962	1,001
2822	Capital	...	...	...	—	—	—	12	15	14	19	22	25
	Table 3 Transactions in assets and liabilities												
3	**Change in net worth from transactions**	...	...	...	**-95**	**338**	**425**	**640**	**1,034**	**1,283**	**1,096**	**1,484**	**1,674**
31	**Net/Gross investment in nonfinancial assets**	...	...	...	**371**	**479**	**600**	**363**	**467**	**702**	**651**	**766**	**878**
311	Fixed assets	...	...	...	361	469	694	347	456	676	601	723	922
3111	Buildings and structures	...	...	...	...	...	...	...	...	...	...	...	...
3112	Machinery and equipment	...	...	...	...	...	...	...	...	...	...	...	...
3113	Other fixed assets	...	...	...	...	...	...	...	...	...	...	...	...
3114	Weapons systems	...	...	...	...	...	...	...	...	...	...	...	...
312	Inventories	...	...	...	-4	-1	-3	-4	-1	-3	-4	-1	-3
313	Valuables	...	...	...	1	1	0	1	1	0	1	1	1
314	Nonproduced assets	...	...	...	14	10	-91	19	11	28	53	43	-43
3141	Land	...	...	...	...	...	...	...	...	...	...	...	...
3142	Mineral and energy resources	...	...	...	...	...	...	...	...	...	...	...	...
3143	Other naturally occurring assets	...	...	...	...	...	...	...	...	...	...	...	...
3144	Intangible nonproduced assets	...	...	...	...	...	...	...	...	...	...	...	...
32	**Net acquisition of financial assets**	...	...	...	**637**	**248**	**-17**	**1,277**	**1,575**	**817**	**1,400**	**1,740**	**1,160**
	By instrument												
3201	Monetary gold and SDRs	...	...	...	—	—	—	—	—	—	—	—	—
3202	Currency and deposits	...	...	...	322	-308	-352	196	313	-42	402	557	323
3203	Debt securities	...	...	...	-61	-135	-22	677	90	707	677	90	707
3204	Loans	...	...	...	153	374	-19	134	322	-58	149	339	-40
3205	Equity and investment fund shares	...	...	...	90	17	89	443	227	-257	443	227	-255
3206	Insurance, pension, and standardized guarantee schemes	...	...		—	—	—	—	—	—	—	—	—
3207	Financial derivatives and employee stock options	...	...	...	-3	-0	—	-199	91	268	-199	91	268
3208	Other accounts receivable	...	...	...	136	300	287	26	533	198	-73	436	156
	By debtor												
321	Domestic debtors	...	...	...	509	298	12	100	1,199	457	224	1,364	800
322	External debtors	...	...	...	128	-51	-29	1,177	376	360	1,177	376	360
33	**Net incurrence of liabilities**	...	...	...	**1,104**	**389**	**159**	**1,001**	**1,008**	**236**	**955**	**1,022**	**363**
	By instrument												
3301	Special Drawing Rights (SDRs)	...	...	...	—	—	—	—	—	—	—	—	—
3302	Currency and deposits	...	...	...	12	11	11	12	11	11	12	11	11
3303	Debt securities	...	...	...	1,050	200	—	1,050	200	—	1,050	200	—
3304	Loans	...	...	...	232	49	20	232	49	21	245	108	94

Luxembourg (137)

In Millions of Euros (EUR) / Fiscal Year Ends December 31st

		Budgetary Central Government			Central Government (excl. Social Security)			Central Government (incl. Social Security)			General Government		
		2013	2014	2015	2013	2014	2015P	2013	2014	2015P	2013	2014	2015P
3305	Equity and investment fund shares	...	...	...	—	—	—	—	—	—	—	—	—
3306	Insurance, pension, and standardized guarantee schemes	...	...	...	-0	0	0	-0	0	0	-0	0	0
3307	Financial derivatives and employee stock options	...	...	...	—	—	—	—	—	—	—	—	—
3308	Other accounts payable	...	...	...	-190	128	127	-293	747	203	-352	703	258
	By creditor												
331	Domestic creditors	...	...	...	-167	252	961	-281	945	1,038	-327	960	1,166
332	External creditors	...	...	...	1,271	137	-802	1,282	62	-802	1,282	62	-802
	Table 4 Holding gains and losses in assets and liabilities												
4	**Change in net worth due to holding gains and losses**	...	...	...	...	...	...	...	...	...	...	...	...
41	**Holding gains and losses in nonfinancial assets**	...	...	...	...	...	...	...	...	...	...	...	...
411	Fixed assets	...	...	...	...	...	...	...	...	...	...	...	...
412	Inventories	...	...	...	...	...	...	...	...	...	...	...	...
413	Valuables	...	...	...	...	...	...	...	...	...	...	...	...
414	Nonproduced assets	...	...	...	...	...	...	...	...	...	...	...	...
42	**Holding gains and losses in financial assets**	...	...	...	**667**	**288**	**-174**	...	...	...	**1,080**	**1,438**	**15**
	By instrument												
4201	Monetary gold and SDRs	...	...	...	—	—	—	...	...	...	—	—	—
4202	Currency and deposits	...	...	...	—	—	—	...	...	...	—	—	—
4203	Debt securities	...	...	...	-6	0	1	...	...	...	-314	577	48
4204	Loans	...	...	...	—	—	—	...	...	...	—	—	—
4205	Equity and investment fund shares	...	...	...	669	288	-176	...	...	...	1,216	1,043	176
4206	Insurance, pension, and standardized guarantee schemes	...	...	...	—	—	—	...	...	...	—	—	—
4207	Financial derivatives and employee stock options	...	...	...	4	0	—	...	...	...	179	-182	-208
4208	Other accounts receivable	...	...	...	—	—	—	...	...	...	—	—	—
	By debtor												
421	Domestic debtors	...	...	...	492	385	-222	...	...	...	690	202	-333
422	External debtors	...	...	...	174	-96	47	...	...	...	390	1,236	348
43	**Holding gains and losses in liabilities**	...	...	...	**-260**	**702**	**-0**	...	...	...	**-260**	**702**	**-0**
	By instrument												
4301	Special Drawing Rights (SDRs)	...	...	...	—	—	—	...	...	...	—	—	—
4302	Currency and deposits	...	...	...	—	—	—	...	...	...	—	—	—
4303	Debt securities	...	...	...	-260	702	-0	...	...	...	-260	702	-0
4304	Loans	...	...	...	—	—	—	...	...	...	—	—	—
4305	Equity and investment fund shares	...	...	...	—	—	—	...	...	...	—	—	—
4306	Insurance, pension, and standardized guarantee schemes	...	...	...	—	—	—	...	...	...	—	—	—
4307	Financial derivatives and employee stock options	...	...	...	—	—	—	...	...	...	—	—	—
4308	Other accounts payable	...	...	...	—	—	—	...	...	...	—	—	—
	By creditor												
431	Domestic creditors	...	...	...	-85	189	109	...	...	...	-85	189	109
432	External creditors	...	...	...	-174	513	-109	...	...	...	-174	513	-109
	Table 5 Holding gains and losses in assets and liabilities												
	Table 6 Balance sheet												
6	**Net worth**	...	...	...	...	...	...	...	...	...	...	...	...
61	**Nonfinancial assets**	...	...	...	...	...	...	...	...	...	...	...	...
611	Fixed assets	...	...	...	...	...	...	...	...	...	...	...	...
6111	Buildings and structures	...	...	...	...	...	...	...	...	...	...	...	...
6112	Machinery and equipment	...	...	...	...	...	...	...	...	...	...	...	...
6113	Other fixed assets	...	...	...	...	...	...	...	...	...	...	...	...
6114	Weapons systems	...	...	...	...	...	...	...	...	...	...	...	...
612	Inventories	...	...	...	...	...	...	...	...	...	...	...	...
613	Valuables	...	...	...	...	...	...	...	...	...	...	...	...
614	Nonproduced assets	...	...	...	...	...	...	...	...	...	...	...	...
6141	Land	...	...	...	...	...	...	...	...	...	...	...	...

Luxembourg (137)

In Millions of Euros (EUR) / Fiscal Year Ends December 31st

		Budgetary Central Government			Central Government (excl. Social Security)			Central Government (incl. Social Security)			General Government		
		2013	2014	2015	2013	2014	2015P	2013	2014	2015P	2013	2014	2015P
6142	Mineral and energy resources	...	...	...	...	...	...	...	...	...	...	...	...
6143	Other naturally occurring assets	...	...	...	...	...	...	...	...	...	...	...	...
6144	Intangible nonproduced assets	...	...	...	...	...	...	...	...	...	...	...	...
62	**Financial assets**	...	...	...	**19,493**	**20,029**	**19,838**	**35,714**	**38,707**	**39,520**	**37,639**	**40,817**	**41,992**
	By instrument												
6201	Monetary gold and SDRs	...	...	...	—	—	—	—	—	—	—	—	—
6202	Currency and deposits	...	...	...	3,068	2,760	2,408	4,781	5,093	5,051	6,219	6,776	7,099
6203	Debt securities	...	...	...	176	41	20	7,280	7,947	8,702	7,280	7,947	8,702
6204	Loans	...	...	...	1,483	1,857	1,838	1,836	2,158	2,100	1,641	1,980	1,940
6205	Equity and investment fund shares	...	...	...	11,893	12,197	12,111	16,380	17,630	17,529	16,959	18,229	18,149
6206	Insurance, pension, and standardized guarantee schemes	...	...	...	—	—	—	—	—	—	—	—	—
6207	Financial derivatives and employee stock options	...	...	...	-0	—	—	47	-44	16	47	-44	16
6208	Other accounts receivable	...	...	...	2,873	3,174	3,461	5,390	5,923	6,121	5,493	5,929	6,086
	By debtor												
621	Domestic debtors	...	...	...	17,507	18,190	17,980	22,250	23,630	23,736	24,174	25,741	26,208
622	External debtors	...	...	...	1,986	1,839	1,857	13,465	15,077	15,784	13,465	15,077	15,784
63	**Liabilities**	...	...	...	**12,270**	**13,362**	**13,520**	**13,969**	**15,679**	**15,915**	**13,993**	**15,717**	**16,081**
	By instrument												
6301	Special Drawing Rights (SDRs)	...	...	...	—	—	—	—	—	—	—	—	—
6302	Currency and deposits	...	...	...	249	260	272	249	260	272	249	260	272
6303	Debt securities	...	...	...	6,247	7,149	7,149	6,247	7,149	7,149	6,247	7,149	7,149
6304	Loans	...	...	...	3,848	3,898	3,917	3,848	3,898	3,919	4,590	4,698	4,792
6305	Equity and investment fund shares	...	...	...	—	—	—	—	—	—	—	—	—
6306	Insurance, pension, and standardized guarantee schemes	...	...	...	0	0	0	0	0	0	0	0	0
6307	Financial derivatives and employee stock options	...	...	...	—	—	—	—	—	—	—	—	—
6308	Other accounts payable	...	...	...	1,926	2,054	2,182	3,625	4,372	4,575	2,907	3,610	3,867
	By creditor												
631	Domestic creditors	...	...	...	7,335	7,776	8,845	8,691	9,825	10,972	8,714	9,863	11,138
632	External creditors	...	...	...	4,936	5,586	4,674	5,279	5,854	4,943	5,279	5,854	4,943
	Memorandum items												
6M2	Net financial worth	...	...	...	7,223	6,668	6,318	21,745	23,028	23,605	23,646	25,100	25,912
6M3	Gross debt (D4) at market value	...	...	...	12,270	13,362	13,520	13,969	15,679	15,915	13,993	15,717	16,081
6M3D3	D3 debt liabilities at market value	...	...	...	12,270	13,361	13,520	13,969	15,679	15,915	13,992	15,717	16,080
6M3D2	D2 debt liabilities at market value	...	...	...	10,344	11,307	11,338	10,344	11,307	11,339	11,086	12,107	12,213
6M3D1	D1 debt liabilities at market value	...	...	...	10,095	11,047	11,066	10,095	11,047	11,068	10,837	11,847	11,941
6M4	Gross debt (D4) at nominal value	...	...	...	12,074	12,463	12,621	...	...	...	13,796	14,818	15,182
6M4D3	D3 debt liabilities at nominal value	...	...	...	12,073	12,462	12,621	...	...	...	13,796	14,818	15,181
6M4D2	D2 debt liabilities at nominal value	...	...	...	10,147	10,408	10,439	...	...	...	10,889	11,208	11,314
6M4D1	D1 debt liabilities at nominal value	...	...	...	9,898	10,148	10,167	...	...	...	10,640	10,948	11,042
6M35	Gross debt (D4) at face value	...	...	...	12,074	12,463	12,621	...	...	...	13,796	14,818	15,182
6M35D3	D3 debt liabilities at face value	...	...	...	12,073	12,462	12,621	...	...	...	13,796	14,818	15,181
6M35D2	D2 debt liabilities at face value	...	...	...	10,147	10,408	10,439	...	...	...	10,889	11,208	11,314
6M35D1	D1 debt liabilities at face value	...	...	...	9,898	10,148	10,167	...	...	...	10,640	10,948	11,042
6M93	Government gross debt per national definition	...	...	...	10,147	10,408	10,439	...	...	...	10,889	11,208	11,314
6M5	Arrears	...	...	...	...	...	...	...	...	...	...	...	...
6M6	Explicit contingent liabilities	...	...	...	...	...	...	...	...	...	...	...	...
6M61	of which: Publicly guaranteed debt	...	...	...	...	...	...	...	...	...	...	...	...
6M7	Net implicit obligations for social security benefits	...	...	...	...	...	...	...	...	...	...	...	...
	Table 7 Expenditure by functions of government												
7	**Expenditure**	...	...	...	**14,680**	**15,142**	**15,670**	**23,125**	**23,962**	**24,762**	**20,136**	**20,852**	**21,573**
701	**General public services**	...	...	...	**3,471**	**3,315**	**3,568**	...	...	...	**2,250**	**2,213**	**2,307**
7017	Public debt transactions	...	...	...	256	207	211	283	232	219	283	231	217
7018	Transfers of general character between levels of government	...	...	...	0	0	—	...	...	...	0	0	—
702	**Defense**	...	...	...	**299**	**275**	**257**	...	...	...	**162**	**151**	**143**

Luxembourg (137)

In Millions of Euros (EUR) / Fiscal Year Ends December 31st

		Budgetary Central Government			Central Government (excl. Social Security)			Central Government (incl. Social Security)			General Government		
		2013	2014	2015	2013	2014	2015P	2013	2014	2015P	2013	2014	2015P
703	**Public order and safety**	...	...	...	**464**	**437**	**459**	...	...	...	**480**	**489**	**512**
704	**Economic affairs**	...	...	...	**2,117**	**2,286**	**2,447**	...	...	...	**2,185**	**2,363**	**2,527**
7042	Agriculture, forestry, fishing, and hunting	...	...	...	177	184	196	...	...	...	170	173	187
7043	Fuel and energy	...	...	...	66	59	72	...	...	...	75	67	76
7044	Mining, manufacturing, and construction	...	...	...	46	43	36	...	...	...	36	34	28
7045	Transport	...	...	...	1,209	1,372	1,502	...	...	...	1,426	1,597	1,729
7046	Communication	...	...	...	52	54	51	...	...	...	30	31	29
705	**Environmental protection**	...	...	...	**219**	**238**	**242**	...	...	...	**497**	**538**	**551**
706	**Housing and community amenities**	...	...	...	**188**	**202**	**184**	...	...	...	**283**	**298**	**256**
707	**Health**	...	...	...	**597**	**568**	**583**	...	...	...	**2,344**	**2,370**	**2,342**
7072	Outpatient services	...	...	...	380	393	383	...	...	...	1,984	2,056	2,004
7073	Hospital services	...	...	...	64	51	55	...	...	...	207	189	199
7074	Public health services	...	...	...	48	21	18	...	...	...	50	23	20
708	**Recreation, culture and religion**	...	...	...	**424**	**426**	**433**	...	...	...	**604**	**607**	**611**
709	**Education**	...	...	...	**3,044**	**3,201**	**3,145**	...	...	...	**2,464**	**2,595**	**2,657**
7091	Pre-primary and primary education	...	...	...	619	637	663	...	...	...	793	812	831
7092	Secondary education	...	...	...	839	907	914	...	...	...	780	848	852
7094	Tertiary education	...	...	...	237	246	780	...	...	...	236	245	401
710	**Social protection**	...	...	...	**3,858**	**4,193**	**4,352**	...	...	...	**8,868**	**9,228**	**9,667**
7z	Statistical discrepancy: Expenditure	...	...	...	...	...	...	...	...	...	...	...	...
	Table 8 Financial transactions by counterpart sector												
32	**Net acquisition of financial assets**	...	...	...	**637**	**248**	**-17**	**1,277**	**1,575**	**817**	**1,400**	**1,740**	**1,160**
321	Domestic debtors	...	...	...	509	298	12	100	1,199	457	224	1,364	800
8211	General government	...	...	...	40	-4	13	...	...	...	—	—	—
8212	Central bank	...	...	...	...	...	...	...	...	...	...	...	...
8213	Deposit-taking corporations except the central bank	...	...	...	...	...	...	...	...	...	...	...	...
8214	Other financial corporations	...	...	...	...	...	...	...	...	...	...	...	...
8215	Nonfinancial corporations	...	...	...	...	...	...	...	...	...	...	...	...
8216	Households & nonprofit institutions serving households	...	...	...	...	...	...	...	...	...	...	...	...
322	External debtors	...	...	...	128	-51	-29	1,177	376	360	1,177	376	360
8221	General government	...	...	...	...	...	...	...	...	...	...	...	...
8227	International organizations	...	...	...	...	...	...	...	...	...	...	...	...
8228	Financial corporations other than international organizations	...	...	...	...	...	...	...	...	...	...	...	...
8229	Other nonresidents	...	...	...	...	...	...	...	...	...	...	...	...
33	**Net incurrence of liabilities**	...	...	...	**1,104**	**389**	**159**	**1,001**	**1,008**	**236**	**955**	**1,022**	**363**
331	Domestic creditors	...	...	...	-167	252	961	-281	945	1,038	-327	960	1,166
8311	General government	...	...	...	-23	-16	-135	...	...	...	—	—	—
8312	Central bank	...	...	...	...	...	...	...	...	...	...	...	...
8313	Deposit-taking corporations except the central bank	...	...	...	...	...	...	...	...	...	...	...	...
8314	Other financial corporations	...	...	...	...	...	...	...	...	...	...	...	...
8315	Nonfinancial corporations	...	...	...	...	...	...	...	...	...	...	...	...
8316	Households & nonprofit institutions serving households	...	...	...	...	...	...	...	...	...	...	...	...
332	External creditors	...	...	...	1,271	137	-802	1,282	62	-802	1,282	62	-802
8321	General government	...	...	...	...	...	...	...	...	...	...	...	...
8327	International organizations	...	...	...	...	...	...	...	...	...	...	...	...
8328	Financial corporations other than international organizations	...	...	...	...	...	...	...	...	...	...	...	...
8329	Other nonresidents	...	...	...	...	...	...	...	...	...	...	...	...
	Table 9 Total other economic flows in assets and liabilities												
9	**Change in net worth due to other economic flows**	...	...	...	...	...	...	...	...	...	...	...	...

Luxembourg (137)

In Millions of Euros (EUR) / Fiscal Year Ends December 31st

		Budgetary Central Government			Central Government (excl. Social Security)			Central Government (incl. Social Security)			General Government		
		2013	2014	2015	2013	2014	2015P	2013	2014	2015P	2013	2014	2015P
91	**Other economic flows in nonfinancial assets**	...	...	...	...	...	...	...	...	...	...	...	...
911	Fixed assets	...	...	...	...	...	...	...	...	...	...	...	...
912	Inventories	...	...	...	...	...	...	...	...	...	...	...	...
913	Valuables	...	...	...	...	...	...	...	...	...	...	...	...
914	Nonproduced assets	...	...	...	...	...	...	...	...	...	...	...	...
92	**Other economic flows in financial assets**	...	...	...	**667**	**288**	**-174**	...	...	...	**1,080**	**1,438**	**15**
	By instrument												
9201	Monetary gold and SDRs	...	...	...	—	—	—	...	...	...	—	—	—
9202	Currency and deposits	...	...	...	—	—	—	...	...	...	—	—	—
9203	Debt securities	...	...	...	-6	0	1	...	...	...	-314	577	48
9204	Loans	...	...	...	—	—	—	...	...	...	—	—	—
9205	Equity and investment fund shares	...	...	...	669	288	-176	...	...	...	1,216	1,043	176
9206	Insurance, pension, and standardized guarantee schemes	...	...	...	—	—	—	...	...	...	—	—	—
9207	Financial derivatives and employee stock options	...	...	...	4	0	—	...	...	...	179	-182	-208
9208	Other accounts receivable	...	...	...	—	—	—	...	...	...	—	—	—
	By debtor												
921	Domestic debtors	...	...	...	492	385	-222	...	...	...	690	202	-333
922	External debtors	...	...	...	174	-96	47	...	...	...	390	1,236	348
93	**Other economic flows in liabilities**	...	...	...	**-260**	**702**	**-0**	...	...	...	**-260**	**702**	**-0**
	By instrument												
9301	Special Drawing Rights (SDRs)	...	...	...	—	—	—	...	...	...	—	—	—
9302	Currency and deposits	...	...	...	—	—	—	...	...	...	—	—	—
9303	Debt securities	...	...	...	-260	702	-0	...	...	...	-260	702	-0
9304	Loans	...	...	...	—	—	—	...	...	...	—	—	—
9305	Equity and investment fund shares	...	...	...	—	—	—	...	...	...	—	—	—
9306	Insurance, pension, and standardized guarantee schemes	...	...	...	—	—	—	...	...	...	—	—	—
9307	Financial derivatives and employee stock options	...	...	...	—	—	—	...	...	...	—	—	—
9308	Other accounts payable	...	...	...	—	—	—	...	...	...	—	—	—
	By creditor												
931	Domestic creditors	...	...	...	-85	189	109	...	...	...	-85	189	109
932	External creditors	...	...	...	-174	513	-109	...	...	...	-174	513	-109
	Memorandum items												
9M2	Change in net financial worth due to other economic flows	...	...	...	926	-414	-174	...	...	...	1,340	736	16
9M3	Gross debt (D4) at market value: other economic flows	...	...	...	-260	702	-0	...	...	...	-260	702	-0
9M3D3	D3 debt liabilities at market value: other economic flows	...	...	...	-260	702	-0	...	...	...	-260	702	-0
9M3D2	D2 debt liabilities at market value: other economic flows	...	...	...	-260	702	-0	...	...	...	-260	702	-0
9M3D1	D1 debt liabilities at market value: other economic flows	...	...	...	-260	702	-0	...	...	...	-260	702	-0

Macedonia, FYR (962)

In Millions of Macedonian Denars (MKD) / Fiscal Year Ends December 31st

		Budgetary Central Government			Central Government (excl. Social Security)			Central Government (incl. Social Security)			General Government		
		2010	2011	2012	2010	2011	2012	2010	2011	2012	2010	2011	2012
	Statement of operations												
1	Revenue	...	...	...	...	...	...	127,964	132,600	133,053	...	...	...
2	Expense	...	...	...	...	...	...	131,565	134,529	137,083	...	...	...
GOB	**Gross operating balance**	**...**	**...**	**...**	**...**	**...**	**...**	**-3,601**	**-1,929**	**-4,030**	**...**	**...**	**...**
NOB	**Net operating balance**	**...**	**...**	**...**	**...**	**...**	**...**	**...**	**...**	**...**	**...**	**...**	**...**
31	Net/Gross investment in nonfinancial assets	...	...	...	...	...	...	7,467	10,333	14,324	...	...	...
2M	Expenditure	...	...	...	...	...	...	139,032	144,862	151,407	...	...	...
NLB	**Net lending (+) / Net borrowing (-)**	**...**	**...**	**...**	**...**	**...**	**...**	**-11,068**	**-12,262**	**-18,354**	**...**	**...**	**...**
32	Net acquisition of financial assets	...	...	...	...	...	...	-3,954	6,261	11,523	...	...	...
33	Net incurrence of liabilities	...	...	...	...	...	...	7,114	18,523	29,877	...	...	...
NLBz	Statistical discrepancy	...	...	...	...	...	...	—	—	—	...	...	...
	Memorandum items												
PB	Primary net lending / net borrowing	...	...	...	...	...	...	-7,894	-8,791	-14,138	...	...	...
GB	Government balance per national definition	...	...	...	...	...	...	...	...	...	...	...	...
	Statement of other economic flows												
	Balance sheet												
	Table 1 Revenue												
1	**Revenue**	**...**	**...**	**...**	**...**	**...**	**...**	**127,964**	**132,600**	**133,053**	**...**	**...**	**...**
11	**Taxes**	**...**	**...**	**...**	**...**	**...**	**...**	**73,753**	**78,910**	**76,617**	**...**	**...**	**...**
111	Taxes on income, profits, and capital gains	...	...	...	...	...	...	96,277	14,105	14,203	...	...	...
1111	Payable by individuals	...	...	...	...	...	...	8,872	9,513	9,553	...	...	...
1112	Payable by corporations and other enterprises	...	...	...	...	...	...	3,690	3,888	3,652	...	...	...
1113	Other taxes on income, profits, and capital gains	...	...	...	...	...	...	815	704	998	...	...	...
112	Taxes on payroll and workforce	...	...	...	...	...	...	—	—	—	...	...	...
113	Taxes on property	...	...	...	...	...	...	—	—	—	...	...	...
114	Taxes on goods and services	...	...	...	...	...	...	52,619	57,737	55,065	...	...	...
1141	General taxes on goods and services	...	...	...	...	...	...	37,694	42,224	38,469	...	...	...
1142	Excises	...	...	...	...	...	...	14,925	15,513	16,596	...	...	...
115	Taxes on international trade and transactions	...	...	...	...	...	...	4,712	3,779	4,067	...	...	...
116	Other taxes	...	...	...	...	...	...	3,045	3,289	3,282	...	...	...
12	**Social contributions**	**...**	**...**	**...**	**...**	**...**	**...**	**38,687**	**39,759**	**40,765**	**...**	**...**	**...**
121	Social security contributions	...	...	...	...	...	...	38,687	39,759	40,765	...	...	...
122	Other social contributions	...	...	...	...	...	...	...	...	...	...	...	...
13	**Grants**	**...**	**...**	**...**	**...**	**...**	**...**	**1,458**	**1,087**	**3,045**	**...**	**...**	**...**
131	From foreign governments	...	...	...	...	...	...	1,458	1,087	3,045	...	...	...
132	From international organizations	...	...	...	...	...	...	...	...	...	...	...	...
133	From other general government units	...	...	...	...	...	...	...	...	...	...	...	...
1331	Current	...	...	...	...	...	...	...	...	...	...	...	...
1332	Capital	...	...	...	...	...	...	...	...	...	...	...	...
14	**Other revenue**	**...**	**...**	**...**	**...**	**...**	**...**	**14,066**	**12,844**	**12,626**	**...**	**...**	**...**
	Table 2 Expense by economic type												
2	**Expense**	**...**	**...**	**...**	**...**	**...**	**...**	**131,565**	**134,529**	**137,083**	**...**	**...**	**...**
21	**Compensation of employees**	**...**	**...**	**...**	**...**	**...**	**...**	**22,638**	**23,147**	**22,714**	**...**	**...**	**...**
211	Wages and salaries	...	...	...	...	...	...	22,638	23,147	22,714	...	...	...
212	Employers' social contributions	...	...	...	...	...	...	...	...	...	...	...	...
22	**Use of goods and services**	**...**	**...**	**...**	**...**	**...**	**...**	**14,681**	**13,958**	**14,652**	**...**	**...**	**...**
23	**Consumption of fixed capital**	**...**	**...**	**...**	**...**	**...**	**...**	**...**	**...**	**...**	**...**	**...**	**...**
24	**Interest**	**...**	**...**	**...**	**...**	**...**	**...**	**3,174**	**3,471**	**4,216**	**...**	**...**	**...**
25	**Subsidies**	**...**	**...**	**...**	**...**	**...**	**...**	**21,893**	**22,378**	**24,629**	**...**	**...**	**...**
26	**Grants**	**...**	**...**	**...**	**...**	**...**	**...**	**...**	**...**	**...**	**...**	**...**	**...**
261	To foreign governments	...	...	...	...	...	...	...	...	...	...	...	...
262	To international organizations	...	...	...	...	...	...	...	...	...	...	...	...
263	To other general government units	...	...	...	...	...	...	...	...	...	...	...	...
2631	Current	...	...	...	...	...	...	...	...	...	...	...	...
2632	Capital	...	...	...	...	...	...	...	...	...	...	...	...

Macedonia, FYR (962)

In Millions of Macedonian Denars (MKD) / Fiscal Year Ends December 31st

		Budgetary Central Government			Central Government (excl. Social Security)			Central Government (incl. Social Security)			General Government		
		2010	2011	2012	2010	2011	2012	2010	2011	2012	2010	2011	2012
27	**Social benefits**	...	...	...	...	...	...	**63,786**	**67,188**	**69,676**	...	...	...
271	Social security benefits	...	...	...	...	...	...	37,614	39,234	40,893	...	...	...
272	Social assistance benefits	...	...	...	...	...	...	26,172	27,954	28,783	...	...	...
273	Employment-related social benefits	...	...	...	...	...	...	...	—	...	...	...	...
28	**Other expense**	...	...	...	...	...	...	**5,393**	**4,387**	**1,196**	...	...	...
281	Property expense other than interest	...	...	...	...	...	...	...	...	...	...	...	...
282	Transfers not elsewhere classified	...	...	...	...	...	...	5,393	4,387	1,196	...	...	...
2821	Current	...	...	...	...	...	...	1,185	797	1,196	...	...	...
2822	Capital	...	...	...	...	...	...	4,208	3,590	...	...	...	...
	Table 3 Transactions in assets and liabilities												
3	**Change in net worth from transactions**	...	...	...	...	...	...	...	...	...	...	...	...
31	**Net/Gross investment in nonfinancial assets**	...	...	...	...	...	...	**7,467**	**10,333**	**14,324**	...	...	...
311	Fixed assets	...	...	...	...	...	...	7,467	10,333	14,324	...	...	...
3111	Buildings and structures	...	...	...	...	...	...	...	...	...	...	...	...
3112	Machinery and equipment	...	...	...	...	...	...	...	...	...	...	...	...
3113	Other fixed assets	...	...	...	...	...	...	...	...	...	...	...	...
3114	Weapons systems	...	...	...	...	...	...	...	...	...	...	...	...
312	Inventories	...	...	...	...	...	...	...	...	...	...	...	...
313	Valuables	...	...	...	...	...	...	...	...	...	...	...	...
314	Nonproduced assets	...	...	...	...	...	...	...	...	...	...	...	...
3141	Land	...	...	...	...	...	...	...	...	...	...	...	...
3142	Mineral and energy resources	...	...	...	...	...	...	...	...	...	...	...	...
3143	Other naturally occurring assets	...	...	...	...	...	...	...	...	...	...	...	...
3144	Intangible nonproduced assets	...	...	...	...	...	...	...	...	...	...	...	...
32	**Net acquisition of financial assets**	...	...	...	...	...	...	**-3,954**	**6,261**	**11,523**	...	...	...
	By instrument												
3201	Monetary gold and SDRs	...	...	...	...	...	...	—	—	—	...	...	...
3202	Currency and deposits	...	...	...	...	...	...	-3,390	7,316	12,272	...	...	...
3203	Debt securities	...	...	...	...	...	...	—	—	—	...	...	...
3204	Loans	...	...	...	...	...	...	-524	-779	-629	...	...	...
3205	Equity and investment fund shares	...	...	...	...	...	...	-40	-276	-120	...	...	...
3206	Insurance, pension, and standardized guarantee schemes	...	...	...	...	...	...	—	—	—	...	...	...
3207	Financial derivatives and employee stock options	...	...	...	...	...	...	—	—	—	...	...	...
3208	Other accounts receivable	...	...	...	...	...	...	...	...	...	...	...	...
	By debtor												
321	Domestic debtors	...	...	...	...	...	...	-3,954	6,261	11,523	...	...	...
322	External debtors	...	...	...	...	...	...	...	...	...	...	...	...
33	**Net incurrence of liabilities**	...	...	...	...	...	...	**7,114**	**18,523**	**29,877**	...	...	...
	By instrument												
3301	Special Drawing Rights (SDRs)	...	...	...	...	...	...	—	—	—	...	...	...
3302	Currency and deposits	...	...	...	...	...	...	—	—	—	...	...	...
3303	Debt securities	...	...	...	...	...	...	1,904	-2,097	25,552	...	...	...
3304	Loans	...	...	...	...	...	...	5,210	20,620	4,325	...	...	...
3305	Equity and investment fund shares	...	...	...	...	...	...	—	—	—	...	...	...
3306	Insurance, pension, and standardized guarantee schemes	...	...	...	...	...	...	...	...	...	...	...	...
3307	Financial derivatives and employee stock options	...	...	...	...	...	...	—	—	—	...	...	...
3308	Other accounts payable	...	...	...	...	...	...	...	...	...	...	...	...
	By creditor												
331	Domestic creditors	...	...	...	...	...	...	1,904	-2,097	25,552	...	...	...
332	External creditors	...	...	...	...	...	...	5,210	20,620	4,325	...	...	...
	Table 4 Holding gains and losses in assets and liabilities												
	Table 5 Holding gains and losses in assets and liabilities												
	Table 6 Balance sheet												

Macedonia, FYR (962)

In Millions of Macedonian Denars (MKD) / Fiscal Year Ends December 31st

	Budgetary Central Government			Central Government (excl. Social Security)			Central Government (incl. Social Security)			General Government		
	2010	2011	2012	2010	2011	2012	2010	2011	2012	2010	2011	2012
Table 7 Expenditure by functions of government												
Table 8 Financial transactions by counterpart sector												
Table 9 Total other economic flows in assets and liabilities												

Madagascar (674)

In Billions of Malagasy Ariary (MGA) / Fiscal Year Ends December 31st

		Budgetary Central Government			Central Government (excl. Social Security)			Central Government (incl. Social Security)			General Government		
		2012	2013	2014	2012	2013	2014	2012	2013	2014	2012	2013	2014
	Statement of operations												
1	Revenue	...	...	...	2,511	2,776	3,210	2,511	2,776	3,210	...	...	...
2	Expense	...	...	...	2,158	2,434	2,757	2,158	2,434	2,757	...	...	...
GOB	**Gross operating balance**	...	...	...	**353**	**343**	**453**	**353**	**343**	**453**	...	...	...
NOB	**Net operating balance**	...	...	...	...	...	...	...	...	...	...	...	...
31	Net/Gross investment in nonfinancial assets	...	...	...	595	730	999	595	730	999	...	...	...
2M	Expenditure	...	...	...	2,753	3,164	3,757	2,753	3,164	3,757	...	...	...
NLB	**Net lending (+) / Net borrowing (-)**	...	...	...	**-242**	**-388**	**-547**	**-242**	**-388**	**-547**	...	...	...
32	Net acquisition of financial assets	...	...	...	61	-337	315	61	-337	315	...	...	...
33	Net incurrence of liabilities	...	...	...	297	50	855	297	50	855	...	...	...
NLBz	Statistical discrepancy	...	...	...	7	0	7	7	0	7	...	...	...
	Memorandum items												
PB	Primary net lending / net borrowing	...	...	...	-98	-264	-404	-98	-264	-404	...	...	...
GB	Government balance per national definition	...	...	...	...	...	...	...	...	...	...	...	...
	Statement of other economic flows												
	Balance sheet												
	Table 1 Revenue												
1	**Revenue**	...	...	...	**2,511**	**2,776**	**3,210**	**2,511**	**2,776**	**3,210**	...	...	...
11	**Taxes**	...	...	...	**2,127**	**2,409**	**2,553**	**2,127**	**2,409**	**2,553**	...	...	...
111	Taxes on income, profits, and capital gains	...	...	...	513	568	611	513	568	611	...	...	...
1111	Payable by individuals	...	...	...	—	—	—	—	—	—	...	...	...
1112	Payable by corporations and other enterprises	...	...	...	—	—	—	—	—	—	...	...	...
1113	Other taxes on income, profits, and capital gains	...	...	...	513	568	611	513	568	611	...	...	...
112	Taxes on payroll and workforce	...	...	...	—	—	—	—	—	—	...	...	...
113	Taxes on property	...	...	...	14	15	19	14	15	19	...	...	...
114	Taxes on goods and services	...	...	...	549	647	665	549	647	665	...	...	...
1141	General taxes on goods and services	...	...	...	308	392	421	308	392	421	...	...	...
1142	Excises	...	...	...	234	248	237	234	248	237	...	...	...
115	Taxes on international trade and transactions	...	...	...	1,049	1,172	1,255	1,049	1,172	1,255	...	...	...
116	Other taxes	...	...	...	3	6	3	3	6	3	...	...	...
12	**Social contributions**	...	...	...	—	—	—	—	—	—	...	...	...
121	Social security contributions	...	...	...	—	—	—	—	—	—	...	...	...
122	Other social contributions	...	...	...	—	—	—	—	—	—	...	...	...
13	**Grants**	...	...	...	**263**	**296**	**593**	**263**	**296**	**593**	...	...	...
131	From foreign governments	...	...	...	13	40	23	13	40	23	...	...	...
132	From international organizations	...	...	...	250	256	570	250	256	570	...	...	...
133	From other general government units	...	...	...	—	—	—	—	—	—	...	...	...
1331	Current	...	...	...	—	—	—	—	—	—	...	...	...
1332	Capital	...	...	...	—	—	—	—	—	—	...	...	...
14	**Other revenue**	...	...	...	**121**	**71**	**65**	**121**	**71**	**65**	...	...	...
	Table 2 Expense by economic type												
2	**Expense**	...	...	...	**2,158**	**2,434**	**2,757**	**2,158**	**2,434**	**2,757**	...	...	...
21	**Compensation of employees**	...	...	...	**1,167**	**1,342**	**1,446**	**1,167**	**1,342**	**1,446**	...	...	...
211	Wages and salaries	...	...	...	1,167	1,342	1,446	1,167	1,342	1,446	...	...	...
212	Employers' social contributions	...	...	...	—	—	—	—	—	—	...	...	...
22	**Use of goods and services**	...	...	...	**169**	**150**	**220**	**169**	**150**	**220**	...	...	...
23	**Consumption of fixed capital**	...	...	...	...	...	...	...	...	...	...	...	...
24	**Interest**	...	...	...	**144**	**124**	**142**	**144**	**124**	**142**	...	...	...
25	**Subsidies**	...	...	...	**62**	**176**	**177**	**62**	**176**	**177**	...	...	...
26	**Grants**	...	...	...	**65**	**52**	**40**	**65**	**52**	**40**	...	...	...
261	To foreign governments	...	...	...	—	—	—	—	—	—	...	...	...
262	To international organizations	...	...	...	—	—	—	—	—	—	...	...	...
263	To other general government units	...	...	...	65	52	40	65	52	40	...	...	...
2631	Current	...	...	...	65	52	40	65	52	40	...	...	...
2632	Capital	...	...	...	—	—	—	—	—	—	...	...	...

Madagascar (674)

In Billions of Malagasy Ariary (MGA) / Fiscal Year Ends December 31st

		Budgetary Central Government			Central Government (excl. Social Security)			Central Government (incl. Social Security)			General Government		
		2012	2013	2014	2012	2013	2014	2012	2013	2014	2012	2013	2014
27	**Social benefits**	...	...	...	—	—	—	—	—	—	...	...	...
271	Social security benefits	...	...	...	—	—	—	—	—	—	...	...	...
272	Social assistance benefits	...	...	...	—	—	—	—	—	—	...	...	...
273	Employment-related social benefits	...	...	...	—	—	—	—	—	—	...	...	...
28	**Other expense**	...	...	...	**551**	**590**	**733**	**551**	**590**	**733**	...	...	...
281	Property expense other than interest	...	...	...	—	—	—	—	—	—	...	...	...
282	Transfers not elsewhere classified	...	...	...	551	590	733	551	590	733	...	...	...
2821	Current	...	...	...	551	590	733	551	590	733	...	...	...
2822	Capital	...	...	...	—	—	—	—	—	—	...	...	...
	Table 3 Transactions in assets and liabilities												
3	**Change in net worth from transactions**	...	...	...	**360**	**343**	**459**	**360**	**343**	**459**	...	...	...
31	**Net/Gross investment in nonfinancial assets**	...	...	...	**595**	**730**	**999**	**595**	**730**	**999**	...	...	...
311	Fixed assets	...	...	...	595	730	999	595	730	999	...	...	...
3111	Buildings and structures	...	...	...	—	—	—	—	—	—	...	...	...
3112	Machinery and equipment	...	...	...	—	—	—	—	—	—	...	...	...
3113	Other fixed assets	...	...	...	595	730	999	595	730	999	...	...	...
3114	Weapons systems	...	...	...	...	...	...	...	...	...	...	...	...
312	Inventories	...	...	...	—	—	—	—	—	—	...	...	...
313	Valuables	...	...	...	—	—	—	—	—	—	...	...	...
314	Nonproduced assets	...	...	...	—	—	—	—	—	—	...	...	...
3141	Land	...	...	...	—	—	—	—	—	—	...	...	...
3142	Mineral and energy resources	...	...	...	—	—	—	—	—	—	...	...	...
3143	Other naturally occurring assets	...	...	...	—	—	—	—	—	—	...	...	...
3144	Intangible nonproduced assets	...	...	...	—	—	—	—	—	—	...	...	...
32	**Net acquisition of financial assets**	...	...	...	**61**	**-337**	**315**	**61**	**-337**	**315**	...	...	...
	By instrument												
3201	Monetary gold and SDRs	...	...	...	—	—	—	—	—	—	...	...	...
3202	Currency and deposits	...	...	...	22	-367	278	22	-367	278	...	...	...
3203	Debt securities	...	...	...	—	—	—	—	—	—	...	...	...
3204	Loans	...	...	...	—	—	—	—	—	—	...	...	...
3205	Equity and investment fund shares	...	...	...	33	30	31	33	30	31	...	...	...
3206	Insurance, pension, and standardized guarantee schemes	...	...	...	—	—	—	—	—	—	...	...	...
3207	Financial derivatives and employee stock options	...	...	...	7	—	7	7	—	7	...	...	...
3208	Other accounts receivable	...	...	...	—	—	—	—	—	—	...	...	...
	By debtor												
321	Domestic debtors	...	...	...	-8	-401	183	-8	-401	183	...	...	...
322	External debtors	...	...	...	69	63	133	69	63	133	...	...	...
33	**Net incurrence of liabilities**	...	...	...	**297**	**50**	**855**	**297**	**50**	**855**	...	...	...
	By instrument												
3301	Special Drawing Rights (SDRs)	...	...	...	—	—	—	—	—	—	...	...	...
3302	Currency and deposits	...	...	...	39	-268	183	39	-268	183	...	...	...
3303	Debt securities	...	...	...	118	18	-99	118	18	-99	...	...	...
3304	Loans	...	...	...	160	340	820	160	340	820	...	...	...
3305	Equity and investment fund shares	...	...	...	—	—	—	—	—	—	...	...	...
3306	Insurance, pension, and standardized guarantee schemes	...	...	...	—	—	—	—	—	—	...	...	...
3307	Financial derivatives and employee stock options	...	...	...	—	—	—	—	—	—	...	...	...
3308	Other accounts payable	...	...	...	-20	-40	-49	-20	-40	-49	...	...	...
	By creditor												
331	Domestic creditors	...	...	...	129	-247	413	129	-247	413	...	...	...
332	External creditors	...	...	...	168	297	443	168	297	443	...	...	...
	Table 4 Holding gains and losses in assets and liabilities												
	Table 5 Holding gains and losses in assets and liabilities												
	Table 6 Balance sheet												

Madagascar (674)

In Billions of Malagasy Ariary (MGA) / Fiscal Year Ends December 31st

		Budgetary Central Government			Central Government (excl. Social Security)			Central Government (incl. Social Security)			General Government		
		2012	2013	2014	2012	2013	2014	2012	2013	2014	2012	2013	2014
	Table 7 Expenditure by functions of government												
7	**Expenditure**	...	...	...	**2,158**	**2,434**	**2,757**	**2,158**	**2,434**	**2,757**	...	...	...
701	**General public services**	...	...	...	**863**	**1,075**	**1,298**	**863**	**1,075**	**1,298**	...	...	...
7017	Public debt transactions	...	...	...	144	124	142	144	124	142	...	...	...
7018	Transfers of general character between levels of government	...	...	...	65	52	40	65	52	40	...	...	...
702	**Defense**	...	...	...	**245**	**273**	**298**	**245**	**273**	**298**	...	...	...
703	**Public order and safety**	...	...	...	**142**	**153**	**161**	**142**	**153**	**161**	...	...	...
704	**Economic affairs**	...	...	...	**88**	**82**	**106**	**88**	**82**	**106**	...	...	...
7042	Agriculture, forestry, fishing, and hunting	...	...	...	33	28	38	33	28	38	...	...	...
7043	Fuel and energy	...	...	...	6	2	7	6	2	7	...	...	...
7044	Mining, manufacturing, and construction	...	...	...	11	10	10	11	10	10	...	...	...
7045	Transport	...	...	...	13	17	16	13	17	16	...	...	...
7046	Communication	...	...	...	7	7	9	7	7	9	...	...	...
705	**Environmental protection**	...	...	...	**7**	**7**	**8**	**7**	**7**	**8**	...	...	...
706	**Housing and community amenities**	...	...	...	**110**	**100**	**24**	**110**	**100**	**24**	...	...	...
707	**Health**	...	...	...	**131**	**151**	**176**	**131**	**151**	**176**	...	...	...
7072	Outpatient services	...	...	...	—	—	—	—	—	—	...	...	...
7073	Hospital services	...	...	...	—	—	—	—	—	—	...	...	...
7074	Public health services	...	...	...	—	—	—	—	—	—	...	...	...
708	**Recreation, culture and religion**	...	...	...	**15**	**16**	**17**	**15**	**16**	**17**	...	...	...
709	**Education**	...	...	...	**539**	**572**	**654**	**539**	**572**	**654**	...	...	...
7091	Pre-primary and primary education	...	...	...	430	456	491	430	456	491	...	...	...
7092	Secondary education	...	...	...	1	2	3	1	2	3	...	...	...
7094	Tertiary education	...	...	...	104	109	155	104	109	155	...	...	...
710	**Social protection**	...	...	...	**17**	**6**	**16**	**17**	**6**	**16**	...	...	...
7z	Statistical discrepancy: Expenditure	...	...	...	—	—	—	—	—	—	...	...	...
	Table 8 Financial transactions by counterpart sector												
	Table 9 Total other economic flows in assets and liabilities												

Malawi (676)

In Billions of Malawi Kwacha (MWK) / Fiscal Year Ends June 30th

		Budgetary Central Government			Central Government (excl. Social Security)			Central Government (incl. Social Security)			General Government		
		2014	2015	2016	2014	2015	2016	2014	2015	2016	2014	2015	2016
	Statement of operations												
1	Revenue	515	610	765	...	...	...	...	...	...	...	...	...
2	Expense	526	595	700	...	...	...	...	...	...	...	...	...
GOB	**Gross operating balance**	**-11**	**15**	**65**	...	...	...	...	...	...	...	...	...
NOB	**Net operating balance**	...	...	...	...	...	...	...	...	...	...	...	...
31	Net/Gross investment in nonfinancial assets	113	157	195	...	...	...	...	...	...	...	...	...
2M	Expenditure	639	751	895	...	...	...	...	...	...	...	...	...
NLB	**Net lending (+) / Net borrowing (-)**	**-125**	**-142**	**-130**	...	...	...	...	...	...	...	...	...
32	Net acquisition of financial assets	13	23	200	...	...	...	...	...	...	...	...	...
33	Net incurrence of liabilities	138	164	325	...	...	...	...	...	...	...	...	...
NLBz	Statistical discrepancy	-0	-0	5	...	...	...	...	...	...	...	...	...
	Memorandum items												
PB	Primary net lending / net borrowing	-34	-47	-4	...	...	...	...	...	...	...	...	...
GB	Government balance per national definition	...	...	...	...	...	...	...	...	...	...	...	...
	Statement of other economic flows												
	Balance sheet												
	Table 1 Revenue												
1	**Revenue**	**515**	**610**	**765**	...	...	...	...	...	...	...	...	...
11	**Taxes**	**409**	**485**	**604**	...	...	...	...	...	...	...	...	...
111	Taxes on income, profits, and capital gains	183	236	293	...	...	...	...	...	...	...	...	...
1111	Payable by individuals	102	139	187	...	...	...	...	...	...	...	...	...
1112	Payable by corporations and other enterprises	81	97	106	...	...	...	...	...	...	...	...	...
1113	Other taxes on income, profits, and capital gains	—	—	—	...	...	...	...	...	...	...	...	...
112	Taxes on payroll and workforce	—	—	—	...	...	...	...	...	...	...	...	...
113	Taxes on property	—	—	—	...	...	...	...	...	...	...	...	...
114	Taxes on goods and services	185	202	258	...	...	...	...	...	...	...	...	...
1141	General taxes on goods and services	121	138	167	...	...	...	...	...	...	...	...	...
1142	Excises	60	61	87	...	...	...	...	...	...	...	...	...
115	Taxes on international trade and transactions	41	46	53	...	...	...	...	...	...	...	...	...
116	Other taxes	0	1	1	...	...	...	...	...	...	...	...	...
12	**Social contributions**	—	—	—	...	...	...	...	...	...	...	...	...
121	Social security contributions	—	—	—	...	...	...	...	...	...	...	...	...
122	Other social contributions	—	—	—	...	...	...	...	...	...	...	...	...
13	**Grants**	**74**	**79**	**131**	...	...	...	...	...	...	...	...	...
131	From foreign governments	57	68	54	...	...	...	...	...	...	...	...	...
132	From international organizations	17	11	77	...	...	...	...	...	...	...	...	...
133	From other general government units	—	—	—	...	...	...	...	...	...	...	...	...
1331	Current	—	—	—	...	...	...	...	...	...	...	...	...
1332	Capital	—	—	—	...	...	...	...	...	...	...	...	...
14	**Other revenue**	**32**	**45**	**30**	...	...	...	...	...	...	...	...	...
	Table 2 Expense by economic type												
2	**Expense**	**526**	**595**	**700**	...	...	...	...	...	...	...	...	...
21	**Compensation of employees**	**140**	**197**	**226**	...	...	...	...	...	...	...	...	...
211	Wages and salaries	...	...	226	...	...	...	...	...	...	...	...	...
212	Employers' social contributions	...	...	—	...	...	...	...	...	...	...	...	...
22	**Use of goods and services**	**125**	**136**	**145**	...	...	...	...	...	...	...	...	...
23	**Consumption of fixed capital**	...	...	...	...	...	...	...	...	...	...	...	...
24	**Interest**	**91**	**94**	**126**	...	...	...	...	...	...	...	...	...
25	**Subsidies**	**60**	**58**	**68**	...	...	...	...	...	...	...	...	...
26	**Grants**	**84**	**70**	**88**	...	...	...	...	...	...	...	...	...
261	To foreign governments	—	—	—	...	...	...	...	...	...	...	...	...
262	To international organizations	—	—	—	...	...	...	...	...	...	...	...	...
263	To other general government units	84	70	88	...	...	...	...	...	...	...	...	...
2631	Current	74	64	85	...	...	...	...	...	...	...	...	...
2632	Capital	10	6	3	...	...	...	...	...	...	...	...	...

Malawi (676)

In Billions of Malawi Kwacha (MWK) / Fiscal Year Ends June 30th

		Budgetary Central Government			Central Government (excl. Social Security)			Central Government (incl. Social Security)			General Government		
		2014	2015	2016	2014	2015	2016	2014	2015	2016	2014	2015	2016
27	**Social benefits**	**20**	**31**	**42**	...	...	...	...	...	...	...	...	...
271	Social security benefits	—	—	—	...	...	...	...	...	...	...	...	...
272	Social assistance benefits	—	—	—	...	...	...	...	...	...	...	...	...
273	Employment-related social benefits	20	31	42	...	...	...	...	...	...	...	...	...
28	**Other expense**	**7**	**8**	**5**	...	...	...	...	...	...	...	...	...
281	Property expense other than interest	—	—	—	...	...	...	...	...	...	...	...	...
282	Transfers not elsewhere classified	7	8	5	...	...	...	...	...	...	...	...	...
2821	Current	7	8	5	...	...	...	...	...	...	...	...	...
2822	Capital	—	—	—	...	...	...	...	...	...	...	...	...
	Table 3 Transactions in assets and liabilities												
3	**Change in net worth from transactions**	...	...	...	...	...	...	...	...	...	...	...	...
31	**Net/Gross investment in nonfinancial assets**	**113**	**157**	**195**	...	...	...	...	...	...	...	...	...
311	Fixed assets	100	152	157	...	...	...	...	...	...	...	...	...
3111	Buildings and structures	...	...	...	...	...	...	...	...	...	...	...	...
3112	Machinery and equipment	...	...	...	...	...	...	...	...	...	...	...	...
3113	Other fixed assets	...	...	...	...	...	...	...	...	...	...	...	...
3114	Weapons systems	...	...	...	...	...	...	...	...	...	...	...	...
312	Inventories	14	5	26	...	...	...	...	...	...	...	...	...
313	Valuables	—	—	—	...	...	...	...	...	...	...	...	...
314	Nonproduced assets	—	—	12	...	...	...	...	...	...	...	...	...
3141	Land	—	—	...	...	...	...	...	...	...	...	...	...
3142	Mineral and energy resources	—	—	...	...	...	...	...	...	...	...	...	...
3143	Other naturally occurring assets	—	—	...	...	...	...	...	...	...	...	...	...
3144	Intangible nonproduced assets	—	—	...	...	...	...	...	...	...	...	...	...
32	**Net acquisition of financial assets**	**13**	**23**	**200**	...	...	...	...	...	...	...	...	...
	By instrument												
3201	Monetary gold and SDRs	—	—	—	...	...	...	...	...	...	...	...	...
3202	Currency and deposits	13	22	199	...	...	...	...	...	...	...	...	...
3203	Debt securities	—	—	—	...	...	...	...	...	...	...	...	...
3204	Loans	—	1	1	...	...	...	...	...	...	...	...	...
3205	Equity and investment fund shares	—	—	—	...	...	...	...	...	...	...	...	...
3206	Insurance, pension, and standardized guarantee schemes	—	—	—	...	...	...	...	...	...	...	...	...
3207	Financial derivatives and employee stock options	—	—	—	...	...	...	...	...	...	...	...	...
3208	Other accounts receivable	...	...	...	...	...	...	...	...	...	...	...	...
	By debtor												
321	Domestic debtors	13	23	200	...	...	...	...	...	...	...	...	...
322	External debtors	—	—	—	...	...	...	...	...	...	...	...	...
33	**Net incurrence of liabilities**	**138**	**164**	**325**	...	...	...	...	...	...	...	...	...
	By instrument												
3301	Special Drawing Rights (SDRs)	—	—	—	...	...	...	...	...	...	...	...	...
3302	Currency and deposits	—	—	—	...	...	...	...	...	...	...	...	...
3303	Debt securities	93	94	259	...	...	...	...	...	...	...	...	...
3304	Loans	45	70	66	...	...	...	...	...	...	...	...	...
3305	Equity and investment fund shares	—	—	—	...	...	...	...	...	...	...	...	...
3306	Insurance, pension, and standardized guarantee schemes	—	—	—	...	...	...	...	...	...	...	...	...
3307	Financial derivatives and employee stock options	—	—	—	...	...	...	...	...	...	...	...	...
3308	Other accounts payable	...	...	...	...	...	...	...	...	...	...	...	...
	By creditor												
331	Domestic creditors	93	94	259	...	...	...	...	...	...	...	...	...
332	External creditors	45	70	66	...	...	...	...	...	...	...	...	...
	Table 4 Holding gains and losses in assets and liabilities												
	Table 5 Holding gains and losses in assets and liabilities												
	Table 6 Balance sheet												

Malawi (676)

In Billions of Malawi Kwacha (MWK) / Fiscal Year Ends June 30th

	Budgetary Central Government			Central Government (excl. Social Security)			Central Government (incl. Social Security)			General Government		
	2014	2015	2016	2014	2015	2016	2014	2015	2016	2014	2015	2016
Table 7 Expenditure by functions of government												
Table 8 Financial transactions by counterpart sector												
Table 9 Total other economic flows in assets and liabilities												

Malaysia (548)

In Millions of Malaysian Ringgit (MYR) / Fiscal Year Ends December 31st

		Budgetary Central Government			Central Government (excl. Social Security)			Central Government (incl. Social Security)			General Government		
		2013	2014	2015	2013	2014	2015	2013	2014	2015	2013	2014	2015
	Statement of operations												
1	Revenue	213,370	220,625	219,089	...	...	...	...	...	...	...	...	...
2	Expense	209,856	217,787	215,274	...	...	...	...	...	...	...	...	...
GOB	**Gross operating balance**	**3,514**	**2,839**	**3,815**	...	...	...	...	...	...	...	...	...
NOB	**Net operating balance**	...	...	...	...	...	...	...	...	...	...	...	...
31	Net/Gross investment in nonfinancial assets	41,888	39,426	40,319	...	...	...	...	...	...	...	...	...
2M	Expenditure	251,744	257,213	255,593	...	...	...	...	...	...	...	...	...
NLB	**Net lending (+) / Net borrowing (-)**	**-38,374**	**-36,588**	**-36,504**	...	...	...	...	...	...	...	...	...
32	Net acquisition of financial assets	931	614	3,403	...	...	...	...	...	...	...	...	...
33	Net incurrence of liabilities	39,305	37,201	39,658	...	...	...	...	...	...	...	...	...
NLBz	Statistical discrepancy	1	1	249	...	...	...	...	...	...	...	...	...
	Memorandum items												
PB	Primary net lending / net borrowing	-17,598	-13,999	-12,221	...	...	...	...	...	...	...	...	...
GB	Government balance per national definition	...	...	...	...	...	...	...	...	...	...	...	...
	Statement of other economic flows												
	Balance sheet												
	Table 1 Revenue												
1	**Revenue**	**213,370**	**220,625**	**219,089**	...	...	...	...	...	...	...	...	...
11	**Taxes**	**155,952**	**164,205**	**165,441**	...	...	...	...	...	...	...	...	...
111	Taxes on income, profits, and capital gains	110,983	116,618	101,559	...	...	...	...	...	...	...	...	...
1111	Payable by individuals	23,055	24,423	26,321	...	...	...	...	...	...	...	...	...
1112	Payable by corporations and other enterprises	87,928	92,196	75,238	...	...	...	...	...	...	...	...	...
1113	Other taxes on income, profits, and capital gains	—	—	—	...	...	...	...	...	...	...	...	...
112	Taxes on payroll and workforce	—	—	—	...	...	...	...	...	...	...	...	...
113	Taxes on property	—	—	—	...	...	...	...	...	...	...	...	...
114	Taxes on goods and services	30,975	32,900	49,899	...	...	...	...	...	...	...	...	...
1141	General taxes on goods and services	10,068	10,939	32,235	...	...	...	...	...	...	...	...	...
1142	Excises	12,193	12,924	11,890	...	...	...	...	...	...	...	...	...
115	Taxes on international trade and transactions	4,454	4,563	3,771	...	...	...	...	...	...	...	...	...
116	Other taxes	9,541	10,124	10,212	...	...	...	...	...	...	...	...	...
12	**Social contributions**	—	—	—	...	...	...	...	...	...	...	...	...
121	Social security contributions	—	—	—	...	...	...	...	...	...	...	...	...
122	Other social contributions	—	—	—	...	...	...	...	...	...	...	...	...
13	**Grants**	—	—	—	...	...	...	...	...	...	...	...	...
131	From foreign governments	—	—	—	...	...	...	...	...	...	...	...	...
132	From international organizations	—	—	—	...	...	...	...	...	...	...	...	...
133	From other general government units	—	—	—	...	...	...	...	...	...	...	...	...
1331	Current	—	—	—	...	...	...	...	...	...	...	...	...
1332	Capital	—	—	—	...	...	...	...	...	...	...	...	...
14	**Other revenue**	**57,418**	**56,421**	**53,648**	...	...	...	...	...	...	...	...	...
	Table 2 Expense by economic type												
2	**Expense**	**209,856**	**217,787**	**215,274**	...	...	...	...	...	...	...	...	...
21	**Compensation of employees**	**61,002**	**66,947**	**70,050**	...	...	...	...	...	...	...	...	...
211	Wages and salaries	61,002	66,947	70,050	...	...	...	...	...	...	...	...	...
212	Employers' social contributions	—	—	—	...	...	...	...	...	...	...	...	...
22	**Use of goods and services**	**33,860**	**34,259**	**36,373**	...	...	...	...	...	...	...	...	...
23	**Consumption of fixed capital**	...	...	...	...	...	...	...	...	...	...	...	...
24	**Interest**	**20,776**	**22,588**	**24,283**	...	...	...	...	...	...	...	...	...
25	**Subsidies**	**43,349**	**39,703**	**27,269**	...	...	...	...	...	...	...	...	...
26	**Grants**	**34,796**	**34,587**	**37,319**	...	...	...	...	...	...	...	...	...
261	To foreign governments	...	...	...	...	...	...	...	...	...	...	...	...
262	To international organizations	...	...	...	...	...	...	...	...	...	...	...	...
263	To other general government units	...	...	...	...	...	...	...	...	...	...	...	...
2631	Current	...	...	...	...	...	...	...	...	...	...	...	...
2632	Capital	...	...	...	...	...	...	...	...	...	...	...	...

Malaysia (548)

In Millions of Malaysian Ringgit (MYR) / Fiscal Year Ends December 31st

		Budgetary Central Government			Central Government (excl. Social Security)			Central Government (incl. Social Security)			General Government		
		2013	2014	2015	2013	2014	2015	2013	2014	2015	2013	2014	2015
27	**Social benefits**	**14,842**	**18,218**	**18,872**	...	...	...	...	...	...	...	...	...
271	Social security benefits	...	...	...	...	...	...	...	...	...	...	...	...
272	Social assistance benefits	...	...	...	...	...	...	...	...	...	...	...	...
273	Employment-related social benefits	...	...	...	...	...	...	...	...	...	...	...	...
28	**Other expense**	**1,232**	**1,484**	**1,108**	...	...	...	...	...	...	...	...	...
281	Property expense other than interest	—	—	—	...	...	...	...	...	...	...	...	...
282	Transfers not elsewhere classified	1,232	1,484	1,108	...	...	...	...	...	...	...	...	...
2821	Current	1,232	1,484	1,108	...	...	...	...	...	...	...	...	...
2822	Capital	—	—	—	...	...	...	...	...	...	...	...	...
	Table 3 Transactions in assets and liabilities												
3	**Change in net worth from transactions**	...	...	...	...	...	...	...	...	...	...	...	...
31	**Net/Gross investment in nonfinancial assets**	**41,888**	**39,426**	**40,319**	...	...	...	...	...	...	...	...	...
311	Fixed assets	...	...	...	...	...	...	...	...	...	...	...	...
3111	Buildings and structures	...	...	...	...	...	...	...	...	...	...	...	...
3112	Machinery and equipment	...	...	...	...	...	...	...	...	...	...	...	...
3113	Other fixed assets	...	...	...	...	...	...	...	...	...	...	...	...
3114	Weapons systems	...	...	...	...	...	...	...	...	...	...	...	...
312	Inventories	...	...	...	...	...	...	...	...	...	...	...	...
313	Valuables	—	—	—	...	...	...	...	...	...	...	...	...
314	Nonproduced assets	...	...	...	...	...	...	...	...	...	...	...	...
3141	Land	...	...	...	...	...	...	...	...	...	...	...	...
3142	Mineral and energy resources	...	...	...	...	...	...	...	...	...	...	...	...
3143	Other naturally occurring assets	...	...	...	...	...	...	...	...	...	...	...	...
3144	Intangible nonproduced assets	...	...	...	...	...	...	...	...	...	...	...	...
32	**Net acquisition of financial assets**	**931**	**614**	**3,403**	...	...	...	...	...	...	...	...	...
	By instrument												
3201	Monetary gold and SDRs	—	—	—	...	...	...	...	...	...	...	...	...
3202	Currency and deposits	721	-213	2,464	...	...	...	...	...	...	...	...	...
3203	Debt securities	—	—	—	...	...	...	...	...	...	...	...	...
3204	Loans	210	827	939	...	...	...	...	...	...	...	...	...
3205	Equity and investment fund shares	—	—	—	...	...	...	...	...	...	...	...	...
3206	Insurance, pension, and standardized guarantee schemes	—	—	—	...	...	...	...	...	...	...	...	...
3207	Financial derivatives and employee stock options	—	—	—	...	...	...	...	...	...	...	...	...
3208	Other accounts receivable	...	...	...	...	...	...	...	...	...	...	...	...
	By debtor												
321	Domestic debtors	931	614	3,403	...	...	...	...	...	...	...	...	...
322	External debtors	—	—	—	...	...	...	...	...	...	...	...	...
33	**Net incurrence of liabilities**	**39,305**	**37,201**	**39,658**	...	...	...	...	...	...	...	...	...
	By instrument												
3301	Special Drawing Rights (SDRs)	—	—	—	...	...	...	...	...	...	...	...	...
3302	Currency and deposits	—	—	—	...	...	...	...	...	...	...	...	...
3303	Debt securities	39,526	37,557	38,931	...	...	...	...	...	...	...	...	...
3304	Loans	-222	-356	727	...	...	...	...	...	...	...	...	...
3305	Equity and investment fund shares	—	—	—	...	...	...	...	...	...	...	...	...
3306	Insurance, pension, and standardized guarantee schemes	—	—	—	...	...	...	...	...	...	...	...	...
3307	Financial derivatives and employee stock options	—	—	—	...	...	...	...	...	...	...	...	...
3308	Other accounts payable	...	...	...	...	...	...	...	...	...	...	...	...
	By creditor												
331	Domestic creditors	30,268	28,459	38,931	...	...	...	...	...	...	...	...	...
332	External creditors	9,037	8,742	727	...	...	...	...	...	...	...	...	...
	Table 4 Holding gains and losses in assets and liabilities												
	Table 5 Holding gains and losses in assets and liabilities												
	Table 6 Balance sheet												

Malaysia (548)

In Millions of Malaysian Ringgit (MYR) / Fiscal Year Ends December 31st

		Budgetary Central Government			Central Government (excl. Social Security)			Central Government (incl. Social Security)			General Government		
		2013	2014	2015	2013	2014	2015	2013	2014	2015	2013	2014	2015
	Table 7 Expenditure by functions of government												
7	**Expenditure**	**251,744**	**257,213**	**255,593**	...	...	...	...	...	...	...	...	...
701	**General public services**	...	...	...	...	...	...	...	...	...	...	...	...
7017	Public debt transactions	20,776	22,588	24,283	...	...	...	...	...	...	...	...	...
7018	Transfers of general character between levels of government	...	...	...	...	...	...	...	...	...	...	...	...
702	**Defense**	**16,247**	**16,830**	**17,476**	...	...	...	...	...	...	...	...	...
703	**Public order and safety**	**12,423**	**13,455**	**14,461**	...	...	...	...	...	...	...	...	...
704	**Economic affairs**	**40,027**	**39,038**	**39,559**	...	...	...	...	...	...	...	...	...
7042	Agriculture, forestry, fishing, and hunting	7,617	8,290	7,882	...	...	...	...	...	...	...	...	...
7043	Fuel and energy	...	...	...	...	...	...	...	...	...	...	...	...
7044	Mining, manufacturing, and construction	...	...	...	...	...	...	...	...	...	...	...	...
7045	Transport	13,172	12,625	12,211	...	...	...	...	...	...	...	...	...
7046	Communication	272	253	140	...	...	...	...	...	...	...	...	...
705	**Environmental protection**	...	...	...	...	...	...	...	...	...	...	...	...
706	**Housing and community amenities**	**11,542**	**13,307**	**14,444**	...	...	...	...	...	...	...	...	...
707	**Health**	**19,421**	**22,120**	**23,366**	...	...	...	...	...	...	...	...	...
7072	Outpatient services	...	...	...	...	...	...	...	...	...	...	...	...
7073	Hospital services	...	...	...	...	...	...	...	...	...	...	...	...
7074	Public health services	...	...	...	...	...	...	...	...	...	...	...	...
708	**Recreation, culture and religion**	...	...	...	...	...	...	...	...	...	...	...	...
709	**Education**	**54,411**	**56,627**	**56,817**	...	...	...	...	...	...	...	...	...
7091	Pre-primary and primary education	...	...	...	...	...	...	...	...	...	...	...	...
7092	Secondary education	...	...	...	...	...	...	...	...	...	...	...	...
7094	Tertiary education	...	...	...	...	...	...	...	...	...	...	...	...
710	**Social protection**	...	...	...	...	...	...	...	...	...	...	...	...
7z	Statistical discrepancy: Expenditure	—	—	—	...	...	...	...	...	...	...	...	...
	Table 8 Financial transactions by counterpart sector												
	Table 9 Total other economic flows in assets and liabilities												

Maldives (556)

In Millions of Maldivian Rufiyaa (MVR) / Fiscal Year Ends December 31st

		Budgetary Central Government			Central Government (excl. Social Security)			Central Government (incl. Social Security)			General Government		
		2012	2013	2014	2012	2013	2014	2012	2013	2014	2012	2013	2014
	Statement of operations												
1	Revenue	...	...	14,751	...	...	14,751	...	...	14,751	...	...	14,751
2	Expense	...	...	14,252	...	...	14,252	...	...	14,252	...	...	14,252
GOB	**Gross operating balance**	**...**	**...**	**499**	**...**	**...**	**499**	**...**	**...**	**499**	**...**	**...**	**499**
NOB	**Net operating balance**	**...**	**...**	**...**	**...**	**...**	**...**	**...**	**...**	**...**	**...**	**...**	**...**
31	Net/Gross investment in nonfinancial assets	...	...	...	...	...	...	...	...	...	...	...	...
2M	Expenditure	...	...	...	...	...	...	...	...	...	...	...	...
NLB	**Net lending (+) / Net borrowing (-)**	**...**	**...**	**...**	**...**	**...**	**...**	**...**	**...**	**...**	**...**	**...**	**...**
32	Net acquisition of financial assets	...	...	...	...	...	...	...	...	...	...	...	...
33	Net incurrence of liabilities	...	...	...	...	...	...	...	...	...	...	...	...
NLBz	Statistical discrepancy	...	...	...	...	...	...	...	...	...	...	...	...
	Memorandum items												
PB	Primary net lending / net borrowing	...	...	...	...	...	...	...	...	...	...	...	...
GB	Government balance per national definition	...	...	...	...	...	...	...	...	...	...	...	...
	Statement of other economic flows												
	Balance sheet												
	Table 1 Revenue												
1	**Revenue**	**...**	**...**	**14,751**	**...**	**...**	**14,751**	**...**	**...**	**14,751**	**...**	**...**	**14,751**
11	**Taxes**	**...**	**...**	**11,068**	**...**	**...**	**11,068**	**...**	**...**	**11,068**	**...**	**...**	**11,068**
111	Taxes on income, profits, and capital gains	...	...	3,009	...	...	3,009	...	...	3,009	...	...	3,009
1111	Payable by individuals	...	...	55	...	...	55	...	...	55	...	...	55
1112	Payable by corporations and other enterprises	...	...	2,954	...	...	2,954	...	...	2,954	...	...	2,954
1113	Other taxes on income, profits, and capital gains	...	...	—	...	...	—	...	...	—	...	...	—
112	Taxes on payroll and workforce	...	...	—	...	...	—	...	...	—	...	...	—
113	Taxes on property	...	...	—	...	...	—	...	...	—	...	...	—
114	Taxes on goods and services	...	...	6,074	...	...	6,044	...	...	6,044	...	...	6,044
1141	General taxes on goods and services	...	...	4,515	...	...	4,515	...	...	4,515	...	...	4,515
1142	Excises	...	...	—	...	...	—	...	...	—	...	...	—
115	Taxes on international trade and transactions	...	...	1,985	...	...	1,985	...	...	1,985	...	...	1,985
116	Other taxes	...	...	—	...	...	31	...	...	31	...	...	31
12	**Social contributions**	**...**	**...**	**—**	**...**	**...**	**—**	**...**	**...**	**—**	**...**	**...**	**—**
121	Social security contributions	...	...	—	...	...	—	...	...	—	...	...	—
122	Other social contributions	...	...	—	...	...	—	...	...	—	...	...	—
13	**Grants**	**...**	**...**	**164**	**...**	**...**	**164**	**...**	**...**	**164**	**...**	**...**	**164**
131	From foreign governments	...	...	46	...	...	46	...	...	46	...	...	46
132	From international organizations	...	...	118	...	...	118	...	...	118	...	...	118
133	From other general government units	...	...	—	...	...	—	...	...	—	...	...	—
1331	Current	...	...	—	...	...	—	...	...	—	...	...	—
1332	Capital	...	...	—	...	...	—	...	...	—	...	...	—
14	**Other revenue**	**...**	**...**	**3,519**	**...**	**...**	**3,519**	**...**	**...**	**3,519**	**...**	**...**	**3,519**
	Table 2 Expense by economic type												
2	**Expense**	**...**	**...**	**14,252**	**...**	**...**	**14,252**	**...**	**...**	**14,252**	**...**	**...**	**14,252**
21	**Compensation of employees**	**...**	**...**	**5,842**	**...**	**...**	**5,842**	**...**	**...**	**5,842**	**...**	**...**	**5,842**
211	Wages and salaries	...	...	5,842	...	...	5,842	...	...	5,842	...	...	5,842
212	Employers' social contributions	...	...	—	...	...	—	...	...	—	...	...	—
22	**Use of goods and services**	**...**	**...**	**2,851**	**...**	**...**	**2,851**	**...**	**...**	**2,851**	**...**	**...**	**2,851**
23	**Consumption of fixed capital**	**...**	**...**	**...**	**...**	**...**	**...**	**...**	**...**	**...**	**...**	**...**	**...**
24	**Interest**	**...**	**...**	**978**	**...**	**...**	**978**	**...**	**...**	**978**	**...**	**...**	**978**
25	**Subsidies**	**...**	**...**	**1,678**	**...**	**...**	**1,678**	**...**	**...**	**1,678**	**...**	**...**	**1,678**
26	**Grants**	**...**	**...**	**0**	**...**	**...**	**0**	**...**	**...**	**0**	**...**	**...**	**0**
261	To foreign governments	...	...	0	...	...	0	...	...	0	...	...	0
262	To international organizations	...	...	—	...	...	—	...	...	—	...	...	—
263	To other general government units	...	...	—	...	...	—	...	...	—	...	...	—
2631	Current	...	...	—	...	...	—	...	...	—	...	...	—
2632	Capital	...	...	—	...	...	—	...	...	—	...	...	—

Maldives (556)

In Millions of Maldivian Rufiyaa (MVR) / Fiscal Year Ends December 31st

		Budgetary Central Government			Central Government (excl. Social Security)			Central Government (incl. Social Security)			General Government		
		2012	2013	2014	2012	2013	2014	2012	2013	2014	2012	2013	2014
27	**Social benefits**	...	...	**2,358**	...	...	**2,358**	...	...	**2,358**	...	...	**2,358**
271	Social security benefits	...	...	143	...	...	143	...	...	143	...	...	143
272	Social assistance benefits	...	...	2,215	...	...	2,215	...	...	2,215	...	...	2,215
273	Employment-related social benefits	...	...	—	...	...	—	...	...	—	...	...	—
28	**Other expense**	...	...	**544**	...	...	**544**	...	...	**544**	...	...	**544**
281	Property expense other than interest	...	...	22	...	...	22	...	...	22	...	...	22
282	Transfers not elsewhere classified	...	...	523	...	...	523	...	...	523	...	...	523
2821	Current	...	...	206	...	...	206	...	...	206	...	...	206
2822	Capital	...	...	317	...	...	317	...	...	317	...	...	317
	Table 3 Transactions in assets and liabilities												
	Table 4 Holding gains and losses in assets and liabilities												
	Table 5 Holding gains and losses in assets and liabilities												
	Table 6 Balance sheet												
	Table 7 Expenditure by functions of government												
	Table 8 Financial transactions by counterpart sector												
	Table 9 Total other economic flows in assets and liabilities												

Mali (678)

In Billions of CFA (BCEAO) Francs (XOF) / Fiscal Year Ends December 31st

		Budgetary Central Government			Central Government (excl. Social Security)			Central Government (incl. Social Security)			General Government		
		2013	2014	2015	2013	2014	2015	2013	2014	2015	2013	2014	2015
	Statement of operations												
1	Revenue	1,179	1,032	1,275	...	...	...	...	...	...	...	...	...
2	Expense	867	919	951	...	...	...	...	...	...	...	...	...
GOB	**Gross operating balance**	**312**	**112**	**324**	...	...	...	...	...	...	...	...	...
NOB	**Net operating balance**	...	...	...	...	...	...	...	...	...	...	...	...
31	Net/Gross investment in nonfinancial assets	389	198	525	...	...	...	...	...	...	...	...	...
2M	Expenditure	1,256	1,118	1,476	...	...	...	...	...	...	...	...	...
NLB	**Net lending (+) / Net borrowing (-)**	**-77**	**-86**	**-201**	...	...	...	...	...	...	...	...	...
32	Net acquisition of financial assets	77	131	92	...	...	...	...	...	...	...	...	...
33	Net incurrence of liabilities	154	216	293	...	...	...	...	...	...	...	...	...
NLBz	Statistical discrepancy	-0	0	0	...	...	...	...	...	...	...	...	...
	Memorandum items												
PB	Primary net lending / net borrowing	-39	-44	-149	...	...	...	...	...	...	...	...	...
GB	Government balance per national definition	...	...	...	...	...	...	...	...	...	...	...	...
	Statement of other economic flows												
	Balance sheet												
	Table 1 Revenue												
1	**Revenue**	**1,179**	**1,032**	**1,275**	...	...	...	...	...	...	...	...	...
11	**Taxes**	**852**	**897**	**1,092**	...	...	...	...	...	...	...	...	...
111	Taxes on income, profits, and capital gains	258	299	301	...	...	...	...	...	...	...	...	...
1111	Payable by individuals	...	34	86	...	...	...	...	...	...	...	...	...
1112	Payable by corporations and other enterprises	...	196	181	...	...	...	...	...	...	...	...	...
1113	Other taxes on income, profits, and capital gains	...	69	34	...	...	...	...	...	...	...	...	...
112	Taxes on payroll and workforce	—	—	12	...	...	...	...	...	...	...	...	...
113	Taxes on property	—	0	0	...	...	...	...	...	...	...	...	...
114	Taxes on goods and services	353	386	566	...	...	...	...	...	...	...	...	...
1141	General taxes on goods and services	331	280	371	...	...	...	...	...	...	...	...	...
1142	Excises	22	101	167	...	...	...	...	...	...	...	...	...
115	Taxes on international trade and transactions	112	134	143	...	...	...	...	...	...	...	...	...
116	Other taxes	129	78	71	...	...	...	...	...	...	...	...	...
12	**Social contributions**	—	—	—	...	...	...	...	...	...	...	...	...
121	Social security contributions	—	—	—	...	...	...	...	...	...	...	...	...
122	Other social contributions	—	—	—	...	...	...	...	...	...	...	...	...
13	**Grants**	**215**	**95**	**123**	...	...	...	...	...	...	...	...	...
131	From foreign governments	71	23	40	...	...	...	...	...	...	...	...	...
132	From international organizations	145	7	36	...	...	...	...	...	...	...	...	...
133	From other general government units	—	65	47	...	...	...	...	...	...	...	...	...
1331	Current	—	65	47	...	...	...	...	...	...	...	...	...
1332	Capital	—	—	—	...	...	...	...	...	...	...	...	...
14	**Other revenue**	**111**	**39**	**60**	...	...	...	...	...	...	...	...	...
	Table 2 Expense by economic type												
2	**Expense**	**867**	**919**	**951**	...	...	...	...	...	...	...	...	...
21	**Compensation of employees**	**307**	**315**	**362**	...	...	...	...	...	...	...	...	...
211	Wages and salaries	291	299	345	...	...	...	...	...	...	...	...	...
212	Employers' social contributions	16	16	17	...	...	...	...	...	...	...	...	...
22	**Use of goods and services**	**240**	**279**	**222**	...	...	...	...	...	...	...	...	...
23	**Consumption of fixed capital**	...	...	...	...	...	...	...	...	...	...	...	...
24	**Interest**	**39**	**42**	**52**	...	...	...	...	...	...	...	...	...
25	**Subsidies**	**87**	**26**	**77**	...	...	...	...	...	...	...	...	...
26	**Grants**	**111**	**104**	**139**	...	...	...	...	...	...	...	...	...
261	To foreign governments	—	—	—	...	...	...	...	...	...	...	...	...
262	To international organizations	—	—	—	...	...	...	...	...	...	...	...	...
263	To other general government units	111	104	139	...	...	...	...	...	...	...	...	...
2631	Current	111	104	139	...	...	...	...	...	...	...	...	...
2632	Capital	—	...	—	...	...	...	...	...	...	...	...	...

Mali (678)

In Billions of CFA (BCEAO) Francs (XOF) / Fiscal Year Ends December 31st

		Budgetary Central Government			Central Government (excl. Social Security)			Central Government (incl. Social Security)			General Government		
		2013	2014	2015	2013	2014	2015	2013	2014	2015	2013	2014	2015
27	**Social benefits**	**—**	**4**	**5**	**...**	**...**	**...**	**...**	**...**	**...**	**...**	**...**	**...**
271	Social security benefits	—	3	—	...	...	...	...	...	...	...	...	...
272	Social assistance benefits	—	1	5	...	...	...	...	...	...	...	...	...
273	Employment-related social benefits	—	—	—	...	...	...	...	...	...	...	...	...
28	**Other expense**	**84**	**150**	**95**	**...**	**...**	**...**	**...**	**...**	**...**	**...**	**...**	**...**
281	Property expense other than interest	—	—	—	...	...	...	...	...	...	...	...	...
282	Transfers not elsewhere classified	84	150	95	...	...	...	...	...	...	...	...	...
2821	Current	84	150	95	...	...	...	...	...	...	...	...	...
2822	Capital	—	—	0	...	...	...	...	...	...	...	...	...
	Table 3 Transactions in assets and liabilities												
3	**Change in net worth from transactions**	**...**	**...**	**...**	**...**	**...**	**...**	**...**	**...**	**...**	**...**	**...**	**...**
31	**Net/Gross investment in nonfinancial assets**	**389**	**198**	**525**	**...**	**...**	**...**	**...**	**...**	**...**	**...**	**...**	**...**
311	Fixed assets	389	198	525	...	...	...	...	...	...	...	...	...
3111	Buildings and structures	...	168	515	...	...	...	...	...	...	...	...	...
3112	Machinery and equipment	...	27	6	...	...	...	...	...	...	...	...	...
3113	Other fixed assets	...	3	4	...	...	...	...	...	...	...	...	...
3114	Weapons systems	...	—	—	...	...	...	...	...	...	...	...	...
312	Inventories	—	—	—	...	...	...	...	...	...	...	...	...
313	Valuables	—	—	—	...	...	...	...	...	...	...	...	...
314	Nonproduced assets	—	—	—	...	...	...	...	...	...	...	...	...
3141	Land	—	—	—	...	...	...	...	...	...	...	...	...
3142	Mineral and energy resources	—	—	—	...	...	...	...	...	...	...	...	...
3143	Other naturally occurring assets	—	—	—	...	...	...	...	...	...	...	...	...
3144	Intangible nonproduced assets	—	—	—	...	...	...	...	...	...	...	...	...
32	**Net acquisition of financial assets**	**77**	**131**	**92**	**...**	**...**	**...**	**...**	**...**	**...**	**...**	**...**	**...**
	By instrument												
3201	Monetary gold and SDRs	—	—	—	...	...	...	...	...	...	...	...	...
3202	Currency and deposits	118	108	87	...	...	...	...	...	...	...	...	...
3203	Debt securities	—	—	—	...	...	...	...	...	...	...	...	...
3204	Loans	-6	-5	-7	...	...	...	...	...	...	...	...	...
3205	Equity and investment fund shares	—	7	11	...	...	...	...	...	...	...	...	...
3206	Insurance, pension, and standardized guarantee schemes	—	—	—	...	...	...	...	...	...	...	...	...
3207	Financial derivatives and employee stock options	—	—	—	...	...	...	...	...	...	...	...	...
3208	Other accounts receivable	-35	21	...	...	...	...	...	...	...	...	...	...
	By debtor												
321	Domestic debtors	77	131	92	...	...	...	...	...	...	...	...	...
322	External debtors	—	—	—	...	...	...	...	...	...	...	...	...
33	**Net incurrence of liabilities**	**154**	**216**	**293**	**...**	**...**	**...**	**...**	**...**	**...**	**...**	**...**	**...**
	By instrument												
3301	Special Drawing Rights (SDRs)	—	—	—	...	...	...	...	...	...	...	...	...
3302	Currency and deposits	42	55	167	...	...	...	...	...	...	...	...	...
3303	Debt securities	—	67	56	...	...	...	...	...	...	...	...	...
3304	Loans	152	91	176	...	...	...	...	...	...	...	...	...
3305	Equity and investment fund shares	—	—	—	...	...	...	...	...	...	...	...	...
3306	Insurance, pension, and standardized guarantee schemes	—	—	—	...	...	...	...	...	...	...	...	...
3307	Financial derivatives and employee stock options	—	—	—	...	...	...	...	...	...	...	...	...
3308	Other accounts payable	-40	3	-107	...	...	...	...	...	...	...	...	...
	By creditor												
331	Domestic creditors	84	185	134	...	...	...	...	...	...	...	...	...
332	External creditors	70	31	158	...	...	...	...	...	...	...	...	...
	Table 4 Holding gains and losses in assets and liabilities												
	Table 5 Holding gains and losses in assets and liabilities												
	Table 6 Balance sheet												

Mali (678)

In Billions of CFA (BCEAO) Francs (XOF) / Fiscal Year Ends December 31st

	Budgetary Central Government			Central Government (excl. Social Security)			Central Government (incl. Social Security)			General Government		
	2013	2014	2015	2013	2014	2015	2013	2014	2015	2013	2014	2015
Table 7 Expenditure by functions of government												
Table 8 Financial transactions by counterpart sector												
Table 9 Total other economic flows in assets and liabilities												

Malta (181)

In Millions of Euros (EUR) / Fiscal Year Ends December 31st

		Budgetary Central Government			Central Government (excl. Social Security)			Central Government (incl. Social Security)			General Government		
		2013	2014	2015	2013P	2014P	2015P	2013P	2014P	2015P	2013P	2014P	2015P
	Statement of operations												
1	Revenue	...	...	...	2,961	3,284	3,648	2,961	3,284	3,648	2,977	3,303	3,669
2	Expense	...	...	...	3,117	3,335	3,569	3,117	3,335	3,569	3,128	3,348	3,582
GOB	**Gross operating balance**	...	...	...	**6**	**114**	**249**	**6**	**114**	**249**	**19**	**127**	**266**
NOB	**Net operating balance**	...	...	...	**-157**	**-51**	**79**	**-157**	**-51**	**79**	**-150**	**-44**	**88**
31	Net/Gross investment in nonfinancial assets	...	...	...	40	117	205	40	117	205	49	121	208
2M	Expenditure	...	...	...	3,158	3,452	3,774	3,158	3,452	3,774	3,177	3,469	3,789
NLB	**Net lending (+) / Net borrowing (-)**	...	...	...	**-197**	**-168**	**-126**	**-197**	**-168**	**-126**	**-199**	**-166**	**-120**
32	Net acquisition of financial assets	...	...	...	164	105	74	...	...	...	161	110	80
33	Net incurrence of liabilities	...	...	...	359	262	196	...	...	...	357	264	196
NLBz	Statistical discrepancy	...	...	...	2	11	5	...	...	...	4	12	5
	Memorandum items												
PB	Primary net lending / net borrowing	...	...	...	28	68	108	28	68	108	26	70	113
GB	Government balance per national definition	...	...	...	...	...	...	...	...	...	...	...	...
	Statement of other economic flows												
	Balance sheet												
6	**Net worth**	...	...	...	...	...	...	...	...	...	...	...	...
61	Nonfinancial assets	...	...	...	...	...	...	...	...	...	...	...	...
62	Financial assets	...	...	...	2,674	2,656	2,826	...	...	...	2,708	2,694	2,870
63	Liabilities	...	...	...	6,429	7,133	7,498	...	...	...	6,457	7,162	7,527
	Table 1 Revenue												
1	**Revenue**	...	...	...	**2,961**	**3,284**	**3,648**	**2,961**	**3,284**	**3,648**	**2,977**	**3,303**	**3,669**
11	**Taxes**	...	...	...	**2,037**	**2,265**	**2,441**	**2,037**	**2,265**	**2,441**	**2,037**	**2,265**	**2,441**
111	Taxes on income, profits, and capital gains	...	...	...	1,003	1,077	1,187	1,003	1,077	1,187	1,003	1,077	1,187
1111	Payable by individuals	...	...	...	523	560	596	523	560	596	523	560	596
1112	Payable by corporations and other enterprises	...	...	...	476	513	586	476	513	586	476	513	586
1113	Other taxes on income, profits, and capital gains	...	...	...	4	4	5	4	4	5	4	4	5
112	Taxes on payroll and workforce	...	...	...	—	—	—	—	—	—	—	—	—
113	Taxes on property	...	...	...	13	12	15	13	12	15	13	12	15
114	Taxes on goods and services	...	...	...	1,021	1,144	1,239	1,021	1,144	1,239	1,021	1,144	1,239
1141	General taxes on goods and services	...	...	...	637	705	764	637	705	764	637	705	764
1142	Excises	...	...	...	207	243	258	207	243	258	207	243	258
115	Taxes on international trade and transactions	...	...	...	—	32	—	—	32	—	—	32	—
116	Other taxes	...	...	...	0	0	0	0	0	0	0	0	0
12	**Social contributions**	...	...	...	**525**	**560**	**596**	**525**	**560**	**596**	**525**	**560**	**596**
121	Social security contributions	...	...	...	37	38	41	37	38	41	37	38	41
122	Other social contributions	...	...	...	488	522	555	488	522	555	488	522	555
13	**Grants**	...	...	...	**31**	**35**	**24**	**31**	**35**	**24**	**40**	**46**	**36**
131	From foreign governments	...	...	...	-122	-172	6	-122	-172	6	-121	-171	-250
132	From international organizations	...	...	...	153	206	18	153	206	18	161	217	286
133	From other general government units	...	...	...	—	—	—	—	—	—	—	—	—
1331	Current	...	...	...	—	—	—	—	—	—	—	—	—
1332	Capital	...	...	...	—	—	—	—	—	—	—	—	—
14	**Other revenue**	...	...	...	**368**	**424**	**586**	**368**	**424**	**586**	**376**	**432**	**596**
	Table 2 Expense by economic type												
2	**Expense**	...	...	...	**3,117**	**3,335**	**3,569**	**3,117**	**3,335**	**3,569**	**3,128**	**3,348**	**3,582**
21	**Compensation of employees**	...	...	...	**970**	**1,043**	**1,110**	**970**	**1,043**	**1,110**	**977**	**1,050**	**1,117**
211	Wages and salaries	...	...	...	...	...	...	...	...	...	...	...	...
212	Employers' social contributions	...	...	...	147	156	160	147	156	160	148	157	161
22	**Use of goods and services**	...	...	...	**437**	**490**	**564**	**437**	**490**	**564**	**468**	**521**	**594**
23	**Consumption of fixed capital**	...	...	...	**163**	**165**	**170**	**163**	**165**	**170**	**169**	**172**	**178**
24	**Interest**	...	...	...	**225**	**236**	**234**	**225**	**236**	**234**	**225**	**236**	**234**
25	**Subsidies**	...	...	...	**80**	**105**	**111**	**80**	**105**	**111**	**80**	**105**	**111**

Malta (181)

In Millions of Euros (EUR) / Fiscal Year Ends December 31st

		Budgetary Central Government			Central Government (excl. Social Security)			Central Government (incl. Social Security)			General Government		
		2013	2014	2015	2013P	2014P	2015P	2013P	2014P	2015P	2013P	2014P	2015P
26	**Grants**	...	...	...	**116**	**119**	**115**	**116**	**119**	**115**	**81**	**85**	**81**
261	To foreign governments	...	...	...	3	3	3	3	3	3	3	3	3
262	To international organizations	...	...	...	78	82	78	78	82	78	78	82	78
263	To other general government units	...	...	...	35	34	34	35	34	34	—	—	—
2631	Current	...	...	...	35	34	34	35	34	34	—	—	—
2632	Capital	...	...	...	—	—	—	—	—	—	—	—	—
27	**Social benefits**	...	...	...	**964**	**1,005**	**1,031**	**964**	**1,005**	**1,031**	**964**	**1,005**	**1,031**
271	Social security benefits	...	...	...	...	...	...	...	...	...	...	...	...
272	Social assistance benefits	...	...	...	...	...	...	...	...	...	...	...	...
273	Employment-related social benefits	...	...	...	...	...	...	...	...	...	...	...	...
28	**Other expense**	...	...	...	**163**	**173**	**235**	**163**	**173**	**235**	**163**	**174**	**235**
281	Property expense other than interest	...	...	...	1	1	2	1	1	2	1	1	2
282	Transfers not elsewhere classified	...	...	...	464	495	582	464	495	582	464	496	583
2821	Current	...	...	...	368	404	448	368	404	448	368	404	448
2822	Capital	...	...	...	95	91	134	95	91	134	95	92	135
	Table 3 Transactions in assets and liabilities												
3	**Change in net worth from transactions**	...	...	...	**-155**	**-40**	**83**	...	...	...	**-146**	**-33**	**93**
31	**Net/Gross investment in nonfinancial assets**	...	...	...	**40**	**117**	**205**	**40**	**117**	**205**	**49**	**121**	**208**
311	Fixed assets	...	...	...	41	125	216	41	125	216	50	129	219
3111	Buildings and structures	...	...	...	...	...	...	...	...	...	...	...	...
3112	Machinery and equipment	...	...	...	...	...	...	...	...	...	...	...	...
3113	Other fixed assets	...	...	...	...	...	...	...	...	...	...	...	...
3114	Weapons systems	...	...	...	...	...	...	...	...	...	...	...	...
312	Inventories	...	...	...	...	...	...	...	...	...	...	...	...
313	Valuables	...	...	...	...	...	...	...	...	...	...	...	...
314	Nonproduced assets	...	...	...	2	-3	-1	2	-3	-1	2	-3	-1
3141	Land	...	...	...	...	...	...	...	...	...	...	...	...
3142	Mineral and energy resources	...	...	...	...	...	...	...	...	...	...	...	...
3143	Other naturally occurring assets	...	...	...	...	...	...	...	...	...	...	...	...
3144	Intangible nonproduced assets	...	...	...	...	...	...	...	...	...	...	...	...
32	**Net acquisition of financial assets**	...	...	...	**164**	**105**	**74**	...	...	...	**161**	**110**	**80**
	By instrument												
3201	Monetary gold and SDRs	...	...	...	—	—	—	...	...	...	—	—	—
3202	Currency and deposits	...	...	...	-17	75	40	...	...	...	-19	77	44
3203	Debt securities	...	...	...	—	—	—	...	...	...	—	—	-0
3204	Loans	...	...	...	36	11	-52	...	...	...	36	11	-52
3205	Equity and investment fund shares	...	...	...	26	15	-9	...	...	...	26	15	-9
3206	Insurance, pension, and standardized guarantee schemes	...	...	...	—	—	—	...	...	...	—	—	—
3207	Financial derivatives and employee stock options	...	...	...	—	—	—	...	...	...	—	—	—
3208	Other accounts receivable	...	...	...	118	4	96	...	...	...	118	6	98
	By debtor												
321	Domestic debtors	...	...	...	...	...	...	...	...	...	...	...	...
322	External debtors	...	...	...	...	...	...	...	...	...	...	...	...
33	**Net incurrence of liabilities**	...	...	...	**359**	**262**	**196**	...	...	...	**357**	**264**	**196**
	By instrument												
3301	Special Drawing Rights (SDRs)	...	...	...	—	—	—	...	...	...	—	—	—
3302	Currency and deposits	...	...	...	5	5	8	...	...	...	5	5	8
3303	Debt securities	...	...	...	334	159	210	...	...	...	334	159	210
3304	Loans	...	...	...	32	15	-15	...	...	...	32	15	-15
3305	Equity and investment fund shares	...	...	...	—	—	—	...	...	...	—	—	—
3306	Insurance, pension, and standardized guarantee schemes	...	...	...	—	—	—	...	...	...	—	—	—
3307	Financial derivatives and employee stock options	...	...	...	—	—	—	...	...	...	—	—	—
3308	Other accounts payable	...	...	...	-12	83	-8	...	...	...	-14	85	-8

Malta (181)

In Millions of Euros (EUR) / Fiscal Year Ends December 31st

		Budgetary Central Government			Central Government (excl. Social Security)			Central Government (incl. Social Security)			General Government		
		2013	2014	2015	2013P	2014P	2015P	2013P	2014P	2015P	2013P	2014P	2015P
	By creditor												
331	Domestic creditors	...	...	...	...	...	...	...	...	...	...	...	...
332	External creditors	...	...	...	...	...	...	...	...	...	...	...	...
	Table 4 Holding gains and losses in assets and liabilities												
	Table 5 Holding gains and losses in assets and liabilities												
	Table 6 Balance sheet												
6	**Net worth**	...	...	...	...	...	...	...	...	...	...	...	...
61	**Nonfinancial assets**	...	...	...	...	...	...	...	...	...	...	...	...
611	Fixed assets	...	...	...	...	...	...	...	...	...	...	...	...
6111	Buildings and structures	...	...	...	...	...	...	...	...	...	...	...	...
6112	Machinery and equipment	...	...	...	...	...	...	...	...	...	...	...	...
6113	Other fixed assets	...	...	...	...	...	...	...	...	...	...	...	...
6114	Weapons systems	...	...	...	...	...	...	...	...	...	...	...	...
612	Inventories	...	...	...	...	...	...	...	...	...	...	...	...
613	Valuables	...	...	...	...	...	...	...	...	...	...	...	...
614	Nonproduced assets	...	...	...	...	...	...	...	...	...	...	...	...
6141	Land	...	...	...	...	...	...	...	...	...	...	...	...
6142	Mineral and energy resources	...	...	...	...	...	...	...	...	...	...	...	...
6143	Other naturally occurring assets	...	...	...	...	...	...	...	...	...	...	...	...
6144	Intangible nonproduced assets	...	...	...	...	...	...	...	...	...	...	...	...
62	**Financial assets**	...	...	...	**2,674**	**2,656**	**2,826**	...	...	...	**2,708**	**2,694**	**2,870**
	By instrument												
6201	Monetary gold and SDRs	...	...	...	—	—	—	...	...	...	—	—	—
6202	Currency and deposits	...	...	...	394	472	516	...	...	...	409	489	537
6203	Debt securities	...	...	...	—	—	—	...	...	...	0	0	—
6204	Loans	...	...	...	293	304	254	...	...	...	293	304	254
6205	Equity and investment fund shares	...	...	...	1,186	1,074	1,154	...	...	...	1,186	1,075	1,154
6206	Insurance, pension, and standardized guarantee schemes	...	...	...	—	—	—	...	...	...	—	—	—
6207	Financial derivatives and employee stock options	...	...	...	—	—	—	...	...	...	—	—	—
6208	Other accounts receivable	...	...	...	801	805	901	...	...	...	820	826	924
	By debtor												
621	Domestic debtors	...	...	...	...	...	...	...	...	...	...	...	...
622	External debtors	...	...	...	...	...	...	...	...	...	...	...	...
63	**Liabilities**	...	...	...	**6,429**	**7,133**	**7,498**	...	...	...	**6,457**	**7,162**	**7,527**
	By instrument												
6301	Special Drawing Rights (SDRs)	...	...	...	—	—	—	...	...	...	—	—	—
6302	Currency and deposits	...	...	...	55	60	69	...	...	...	55	60	69
6303	Debt securities	...	...	...	5,292	5,889	6,264	...	...	...	5,292	5,889	6,264
6304	Loans	...	...	...	375	390	375	...	...	...	379	394	379
6305	Equity and investment fund shares	...	...	...	0	0	0	...	...	...	0	0	0
6306	Insurance, pension, and standardized guarantee schemes	...	...	...	—	—	—	...	...	...	—	—	—
6307	Financial derivatives and employee stock options	...	...	...	—	—	—	...	...	...	—	—	—
6308	Other accounts payable	...	...	...	708	793	790	...	...	...	731	818	815
	By creditor												
631	Domestic creditors	...	...	...	...	...	...	...	...	...	...	...	...
632	External creditors	...	...	...	...	...	...	...	...	...	...	...	...
	Memorandum items												
6M2	Net financial worth	...	...	...	-3,755	-4,477	-4,672	...	...	...	-3,748	-4,468	-4,657
6M3	Gross debt (D4) at market value	...	...	...	6,429	7,133	7,498	...	...	...	6,457	7,162	7,527
6M3D3	D3 debt liabilities at market value	...	...	...	6,429	7,133	7,498	...	...	...	6,457	7,162	7,527
6M3D2	D2 debt liabilities at market value	...	...	...	5,722	6,339	6,707	...	...	...	5,726	6,344	6,711
6M3D1	D1 debt liabilities at market value	...	...	...	5,667	6,279	6,639	...	...	...	5,671	6,283	6,643
6M4	Gross debt (D4) at nominal value	...	...	...	...	...	...	...	...	...	...	...	...
6M4D3	D3 debt liabilities at nominal value	...	...	...	...	...	...	...	...	...	...	...	...
6M4D2	D2 debt liabilities at nominal value	...	...	...	...	...	...	...	...	...	...	...	...
6M4D1	D1 debt liabilities at nominal value	...	...	...	...	...	...	...	...	...	...	...	...

Malta (181)

In Millions of Euros (EUR) / Fiscal Year Ends December 31st

		Budgetary Central Government			Central Government (excl. Social Security)			Central Government (incl. Social Security)			General Government		
		2013	2014	2015	2013P	2014P	2015P	2013P	2014P	2015P	2013P	2014P	2015P
6M35	Gross debt (D4) at face value	...	...	...	...	...	...	...	...	...	...	...	...
6M35D3	D3 debt liabilities at face value	...	...	...	5,950	6,210	6,409	...	...	...	5,977	6,239	6,437
6M35D2	D2 debt liabilities at face value	...	...	...	5,242	5,417	5,618	...	...	...	5,246	5,421	5,622
6M35D1	D1 debt liabilities at face value	...	...	...	5,187	5,357	5,550	...	...	...	5,191	5,361	5,553
6M93	Government gross debt per national definition	...	...	...	5,242	5,417	5,618	...	...	...	5,246	5,421	5,622
6M5	Arrears	...	...	...	...	...	...	...	...	...	...	...	...
6M6	Explicit contingent liabilities	...	...	...	...	...	...	...	...	...	...	...	...
6M61	of which: Publicly guaranteed debt	...	...	...	...	...	...	...	...	...	...	...	...
6M7	Net implicit obligations for social security benefits	...	...	...	...	...	...	...	...	...	...	...	...
	Table 7 Expenditure by functions of government												
7	**Expenditure**	...	...	...	**3,193**	**3,480**	...	...	...	...	**3,212**	**3,498**	...
701	**General public services**	...	...	...	**544**	**586**	...	...	...	...	**537**	**576**	...
7017	Public debt transactions	...	...	...	225	236	...	...	...	...	225	236	...
7018	Transfers of general character between levels of government	...	...	...	35	34	...	...	...	...	—	—	...
702	**Defense**	...	...	...	**49**	**63**	...	...	...	...	**49**	**63**	...
703	**Public order and safety**	...	...	...	**104**	**109**	...	...	...	...	**107**	**111**	...
704	**Economic affairs**	...	...	...	**382**	**428**	...	...	...	...	**391**	**437**	...
7042	Agriculture, forestry, fishing, and hunting	...	...	...	40	33	...	...	...	...	40	33	...
7043	Fuel and energy	...	...	...	33	46	...	...	...	...	33	46	...
7044	Mining, manufacturing, and construction	...	...	...	37	37	...	...	...	...	37	37	...
7045	Transport	...	...	...	64	119	...	...	...	...	73	127	...
7046	Communication	...	...	...	7	8	...	...	...	...	7	8	...
705	**Environmental protection**	...	...	...	**92**	**113**	...	...	...	...	**104**	**128**	...
706	**Housing and community amenities**	...	...	...	**26**	**28**	...	...	...	...	**26**	**28**	...
707	**Health**	...	...	...	**434**	**486**	...	...	...	...	**434**	**486**	...
7072	Outpatient services	...	...	...	75	84	...	...	...	...	75	84	...
7073	Hospital services	...	...	...	283	325	...	...	...	...	283	325	...
7074	Public health services	...	...	...	3	2	...	...	...	...	3	2	...
708	**Recreation, culture and religion**	...	...	...	**66**	**86**	...	...	...	...	**68**	**88**	...
709	**Education**	...	...	...	**442**	**470**	...	...	...	...	**442**	**470**	...
7091	Pre-primary and primary education	...	...	...	105	122	...	...	...	...	105	122	...
7092	Secondary education	...	...	...	160	166	...	...	...	...	160	166	...
7094	Tertiary education	...	...	...	86	85	...	...	...	...	86	85	...
710	**Social protection**	...	...	...	**1,054**	**1,110**	...	...	...	...	**1,054**	**1,110**	...
7z	Statistical discrepancy: Expenditure	...	...	...	-0	-0	...	...	...	...	-0	0	...
	Table 8 Financial transactions by counterpart sector												
32	**Net acquisition of financial assets**	...	...	...	**164**	**105**	**74**	...	...	...	**161**	**110**	**80**
321	Domestic debtors	...	...	...	...	...	...	...	...	...	...	...	...
8211	General government	...	...	...	...	...	...	...	...	...	—	—	—
8212	Central bank	...	...	...	...	...	...	...	...	...	...	...	...
8213	Deposit-taking corporations except the central bank	...	...	...	...	...	...	...	...	...	...	...	...
8214	Other financial corporations	...	...	...	...	...	...	...	...	...	...	...	...
8215	Nonfinancial corporations	...	...	...	...	...	...	...	...	...	...	...	...
8216	Households & nonprofit institutions serving households	...	...	...	...	...	...	...	...	...	...	...	...
322	External debtors	...	...	...	...	...	...	...	...	...	...	...	...
8221	General government	...	...	...	...	...	...	...	...	...	...	...	...
8227	International organizations	...	...	...	...	...	...	...	...	...	...	...	...
8228	Financial corporations other than international organizations	...	...	...	...	...	...	...	...	...	...	...	...
8229	Other nonresidents	...	...	...	...	...	...	...	...	...	...	...	...

Malta (181)

In Millions of Euros (EUR) / Fiscal Year Ends December 31st

		Budgetary Central Government			Central Government (excl. Social Security)			Central Government (incl. Social Security)			General Government		
		2013	2014	2015	2013P	2014P	2015P	2013P	2014P	2015P	2013P	2014P	2015P
33	**Net incurrence of liabilities**	...	...	...	**359**	**262**	**196**	...	...	...	**357**	**264**	**196**
331	Domestic creditors	...	...	...	...	...	...	...	...	...	...	...	...
8311	General government	...	...	...	...	...	...	...	...	...	—	—	—
8312	Central bank	...	...	...	...	...	...	...	...	...	...	...	...
8313	Deposit-taking corporations except the central bank	...	...	...	...	...	...	...	...	...	...	...	...
8314	Other financial corporations	...	...	...	...	...	...	...	...	...	...	...	...
8315	Nonfinancial corporations	...	...	...	...	...	...	...	...	...	...	...	...
8316	Households & nonprofit institutions serving households	...	...	...	...	...	...	...	...	...	...	...	...
332	External creditors	...	...	...	...	...	...	...	...	...	...	...	...
8321	General government	...	...	...	...	...	...	...	...	...	...	...	...
8327	International organizations	...	...	...	...	...	...	...	...	...	...	...	...
8328	Financial corporations other than international organizations	...	...	...	...	...	...	...	...	...	...	...	...
8329	Other nonresidents	...	...	...	...	...	...	...	...	...	...	...	...
	Table 9 Total other economic flows in assets and liabilities												
9	**Change in net worth due to other economic flows**	...	...	...	...	...	...	...	...	...	...	...	...
91	**Other economic flows in nonfinancial assets**	...	...	...	...	...	...	...	...	...	...	...	...
911	Fixed assets	...	...	...	...	...	...	...	...	...	...	...	...
912	Inventories	...	...	...	...	...	...	...	...	...	...	...	...
913	Valuables	...	...	...	...	...	...	...	...	...	...	...	...
914	Nonproduced assets	...	...	...	...	...	...	...	...	...	...	...	...
92	**Other economic flows in financial assets**	...	...	...	**43**	**-124**	**95**	...	...	...	**43**	**-124**	**95**
	By instrument												
9201	Monetary gold and SDRs	...	...	...	—	—	—	...	...	...	—	—	—
9202	Currency and deposits	...	...	...	-3	3	4	...	...	...	-3	3	4
9203	Debt securities	...	...	...	—	—	—	...	...	...	-0	0	—
9204	Loans	...	...	...	—	—	2	...	...	...	—	—	2
9205	Equity and investment fund shares	...	...	...	46	-127	89	...	...	...	46	-127	89
9206	Insurance, pension, and standardized guarantee schemes	...	...	...	—	—	—	...	...	...	—	—	—
9207	Financial derivatives and employee stock options	...	...	...	—	—	—	...	...	...	—	—	—
9208	Other accounts receivable	...	...	...	—	0	0	...	...	...	-0	0	0
	By debtor												
921	Domestic debtors	...	...	...	...	...	...	...	...	...	...	...	...
922	External debtors	...	...	...	...	...	...	...	...	...	...	...	...
93	**Other economic flows in liabilities**	...	...	...	**66**	**441**	**169**	...	...	...	**66**	**441**	**169**
	By instrument												
9301	Special Drawing Rights (SDRs)	...	...	...	—	—	—	...	...	...	—	—	—
9302	Currency and deposits	...	...	...	0	-0	0	...	...	...	0	-0	0
9303	Debt securities	...	...	...	70	439	164	...	...	...	70	439	164
9304	Loans	...	...	...	-0	0	0	...	...	...	-0	0	0
9305	Equity and investment fund shares	...	...	...	—	—	—	...	...	...	—	—	—
9306	Insurance, pension, and standardized guarantee schemes	...	...	...	—	—	—	...	...	...	—	—	—
9307	Financial derivatives and employee stock options	...	...	...	—	—	—	...	...	...	—	—	—
9308	Other accounts payable	...	...	...	-4	3	5	...	...	...	-4	3	5
	By creditor												
931	Domestic creditors	...	...	...	...	...	...	...	...	...	...	...	...
932	External creditors	...	...	...	...	...	...	...	...	...	...	...	...
	Memorandum items												
9M2	Change in net financial worth due to other economic flows	...	...	...	-23	-565	-74	...	...	...	-23	-565	-74

Malta (181)

In Millions of Euros (EUR) / Fiscal Year Ends December 31st

		Budgetary Central Government			Central Government (excl. Social Security)			Central Government (incl. Social Security)			General Government		
		2013	2014	2015	2013P	2014P	2015P	2013P	2014P	2015P	2013P	2014P	2015P
9M3	Gross debt (D4) at market value: other economic flows	...	...	...	66	441	169	...	...	...	66	441	169
9M3D3	D3 debt liabilities at market value: other economic flows	...	...	...	66	441	169	...	...	...	66	441	169
9M3D2	D2 debt liabilities at market value: other economic flows	...	...	...	70	439	164	...	...	...	70	439	164
9M3D1	D1 debt liabilities at market value: other economic flows	...	...	...	70	439	164	...	...	...	70	439	164

Marshall Islands, Republic of (867)

In Thousands of U.S. Dollars (USD) / Fiscal Year Ends September 30th

		Budgetary Central Government			Central Government (excl. Social Security)			Central Government (incl. Social Security)			General Government		
		2013	2014	2015P	2013	2014	2015	2013	2014	2015	2013	2014	2015
	Statement of operations												
1	Revenue	102,919	97,476	105,147	...	...	...	...	...	...	...	...	...
2	Expense	98,926	91,076	97,615	...	...	...	...	...	...	...	...	...
GOB	**Gross operating balance**	**8,576**	**11,373**	**12,505**	...	...	...	...	...	...	...	...	...
NOB	**Net operating balance**	**3,993**	**6,400**	**7,532**	...	...	...	...	...	...	...	...	...
31	Net/Gross investment in nonfinancial assets	2,587	455	2,463	...	...	...	...	...	...	...	...	...
2M	Expenditure	101,513	91,531	100,078	...	...	...	...	...	...	...	...	...
NLB	**Net lending (+) / Net borrowing (-)**	**1,406**	**5,944**	**5,069**	...	...	...	...	...	...	...	...	...
32	Net acquisition of financial assets	1,250	1,791	1,152	...	...	...	...	...	...	...	...	...
33	Net incurrence of liabilities	-156	-4,153	-3,896	...	...	...	...	...	...	...	...	...
NLBz	Statistical discrepancy	0	-0	-20	...	...	...	...	...	...	...	...	...
	Memorandum items												
PB	Primary net lending / net borrowing	2,579	6,694	5,380	...	...	...	...	...	...	...	...	...
GB	Government balance per national definition	...	...	...	...	...	...	...	...	...	...	...	...
	Statement of other economic flows												
	Balance sheet												
6	**Net worth**	**61,625**	**62,656**	**53,803**	...	...	...	...	...	...	...	...	...
61	Nonfinancial assets	91,466	98,493	96,030	...	...	...	...	...	...	...	...	...
62	Financial assets	49,112	56,276	45,990	...	...	...	...	...	...	...	...	...
63	Liabilities	78,952	92,113	88,217	...	...	...	...	...	...	...	...	...
	Table 1 Revenue												
1	**Revenue**	**102,919**	**97,476**	**105,147**	...	...	...	...	...	...	...	...	...
11	**Taxes**	**26,385**	**24,380**	**24,529**	...	...	...	...	...	...	...	...	...
111	Taxes on income, profits, and capital gains	11,865	11,509	11,763	...	...	...	...	...	...	...	...	...
1111	Payable by individuals	11,865	11,509	11,763	...	...	...	...	...	...	...	...	...
1112	Payable by corporations and other enterprises	—	—	—	...	...	...	...	...	...	...	...	...
1113	Other taxes on income, profits, and capital gains	—	—	—	...	...	...	...	...	...	...	...	...
112	Taxes on payroll and workforce	—	—	—	...	...	...	...	...	...	...	...	...
113	Taxes on property	393	—	43	...	...	...	...	...	...	...	...	...
114	Taxes on goods and services	6,530	5,850	5,126	...	...	...	...	...	...	...	...	...
1141	General taxes on goods and services	6,466	5,782	4,977	...	...	...	...	...	...	...	...	...
1142	Excises	—	—	—	...	...	...	...	...	...	...	...	...
115	Taxes on international trade and transactions	7,455	6,889	7,444	...	...	...	...	...	...	...	...	...
116	Other taxes	141	132	153	...	...	...	...	...	...	...	...	...
12	**Social contributions**	—	—	—	...	...	...	...	...	...	...	...	...
121	Social security contributions	—	—	—	...	...	...	...	...	...	...	...	...
122	Other social contributions	—	—	—	...	...	...	...	...	...	...	...	...
13	**Grants**	**62,138**	**53,853**	**56,487**	...	...	...	...	...	...	...	...	...
131	From foreign governments	61,791	53,562	56,487	...	...	...	...	...	...	...	...	...
132	From international organizations	—	—	—	...	...	...	...	...	...	...	...	...
133	From other general government units	347	291	—	...	...	...	...	...	...	...	...	...
1331	Current	347	291	—	...	...	...	...	...	...	...	...	...
1332	Capital	—	—	—	...	...	...	...	...	...	...	...	...
14	**Other revenue**	**14,396**	**19,242**	**24,131**	...	...	...	...	...	...	...	...	...
	Table 2 Expense by economic type												
2	**Expense**	**98,926**	**91,076**	**97,615**	...	...	...	...	...	...	...	...	...
21	**Compensation of employees**	**40,466**	**40,258**	**40,837**	...	...	...	...	...	...	...	...	...
211	Wages and salaries	36,692	36,500	37,021	...	...	...	...	...	...	...	...	...
212	Employers' social contributions	3,774	3,758	3,816	...	...	...	...	...	...	...	...	...
22	**Use of goods and services**	**28,490**	**25,397**	**25,201**	...	...	...	...	...	...	...	...	...
23	**Consumption of fixed capital**	**4,583**	**4,973**	**4,973**	...	...	...	...	...	...	...	...	...
24	**Interest**	**1,173**	**750**	**311**	...	...	...	...	...	...	...	...	...
25	**Subsidies**	**9,734**	**5,750**	**11,493**	...	...	...	...	...	...	...	...	...

Marshall Islands, Republic of (867)

In Thousands of U.S. Dollars (USD) / Fiscal Year Ends September 30th

		Budgetary Central Government			Central Government (excl. Social Security)			Central Government (incl. Social Security)			General Government		
		2013	2014	2015P	2013	2014	2015	2013	2014	2015	2013	2014	2015
26	**Grants**	**4,653**	**5,757**	**7,294**	...	...	...	...	...	...	...	...	...
261	To foreign governments	—	75	75	...	...	...	...	...	...	...	...	...
262	To international organizations	—	—	445	...	...	...	...	...	...	...	...	...
263	To other general government units	4,653	5,682	6,774	...	...	...	...	...	...	...	...	...
2631	Current	4,653	5,682	6,774	...	...	...	...	...	...	...	...	...
2632	Capital	—	—	—	...	...	...	...	...	...	...	...	...
27	**Social benefits**	**—**	**—**	**—**	...	...	...	...	...	...	...	...	...
271	Social security benefits	—	—	—	...	...	...	...	...	...	...	...	...
272	Social assistance benefits	—	—	—	...	...	...	...	...	...	...	...	...
273	Employment-related social benefits	—	—	—	...	...	...	...	...	...	...	...	...
28	**Other expense**	**9,827**	**8,191**	**7,506**	...	...	...	...	...	...	...	...	...
281	Property expense other than interest	1,042	976	1,353	...	...	...	...	...	...	...	...	...
282	Transfers not elsewhere classified	8,785	7,216	6,153	...	...	...	...	...	...	...	...	...
2821	Current	8,785	7,216	6,153	...	...	...	...	...	...	...	...	...
2822	Capital	—	—	—	...	...	...	...	...	...	...	...	...
	Table 3 Transactions in assets and liabilities												
3	**Change in net worth from transactions**	**3,993**	**6,400**	**7,511**	...	...	...	...	...	...	...	...	...
31	**Net/Gross investment in nonfinancial assets**	**2,587**	**455**	**2,463**	...	...	...	...	...	...	...	...	...
311	Fixed assets	2,693	561	2,569	...	...	...	...	...	...	...	...	...
3111	Buildings and structures	2,428	-949	-620	...	...	...	...	...	...	...	...	...
3112	Machinery and equipment	265	1,510	3,189	...	...	...	...	...	...	...	...	...
3113	Other fixed assets	—	—	—	...	...	...	...	...	...	...	...	...
3114	Weapons systems	—	—	—	...	...	...	...	...	...	...	...	...
312	Inventories	—	—	—	...	...	...	...	...	...	...	...	...
313	Valuables	—	—	—	...	...	...	...	...	...	...	...	...
314	Nonproduced assets	-106	-106	-106	...	...	...	...	...	...	...	...	...
3141	Land	—	—	—	...	...	...	...	...	...	...	...	...
3142	Mineral and energy resources	—	—	—	...	...	...	...	...	...	...	...	...
3143	Other naturally occurring assets	—	—	—	...	...	...	...	...	...	...	...	...
3144	Intangible nonproduced assets	-106	-106	-106	...	...	...	...	...	...	...	...	...
32	**Net acquisition of financial assets**	**1,250**	**1,791**	**1,152**	...	...	...	...	...	...	...	...	...
	By instrument												
3201	Monetary gold and SDRs	—	—	—	...	...	...	...	...	...	...	...	...
3202	Currency and deposits	-1,058	3,315	4,195	...	...	...	...	...	...	...	...	...
3203	Debt securities	—	—	—	...	...	...	...	...	...	...	...	...
3204	Loans	—	—	—	...	...	...	...	...	...	...	...	...
3205	Equity and investment fund shares	-69	250	250	...	...	...	...	...	...	...	...	...
3206	Insurance, pension, and standardized guarantee schemes	—	—	—	...	...	...	...	...	...	...	...	...
3207	Financial derivatives and employee stock options	—	—	—	...	...	...	...	...	...	...	...	...
3208	Other accounts receivable	2,377	-1,774	-3,293	...	...	...	...	...	...	...	...	...
	By debtor												
321	Domestic debtors	1,051	-1,680	-3,293	...	...	...	...	...	...	...	...	...
322	External debtors	199	3,471	4,445	...	...	...	...	...	...	...	...	...
33	**Net incurrence of liabilities**	**-156**	**-4,153**	**-3,896**	...	...	...	...	...	...	...	...	...
	By instrument												
3301	Special Drawing Rights (SDRs)	—	—	—	...	...	...	...	...	...	...	...	...
3302	Currency and deposits	—	—	—	...	...	...	...	...	...	...	...	...
3303	Debt securities	—	—	—	...	...	...	...	...	...	...	...	...
3304	Loans	2,545	-2,488	-3,200	...	...	...	...	...	...	...	...	...
3305	Equity and investment fund shares	—	—	—	...	...	...	...	...	...	...	...	...
3306	Insurance, pension, and standardized guarantee schemes	—	—	—	...	...	...	...	...	...	...	...	...
3307	Financial derivatives and employee stock options	—	—	—	...	...	...	...	...	...	...	...	...
3308	Other accounts payable	-2,701	-1,666	-696	...	...	...	...	...	...	...	...	...

Marshall Islands, Republic of (867)

In Thousands of U.S. Dollars (USD) / Fiscal Year Ends September 30th

		Budgetary Central Government			Central Government (excl. Social Security)			Central Government (incl. Social Security)			General Government		
		2013	2014	2015P	2013	2014	2015	2013	2014	2015	2013	2014	2015
	By creditor												
331	Domestic creditors	-2,058	-663	-696	...	...	...	...	...	...	...	...	...
332	External creditors	1,902	-3,490	-3,200	...	...	...	...	...	...	...	...	...
	Table 4 Holding gains and losses in assets and liabilities												
	Table 5 Holding gains and losses in assets and liabilities												
	Table 6 Balance sheet												
6	**Net worth**	**61,625**	**62,656**	**53,803**	...	...	...	...	...	...	...	...	...
61	**Nonfinancial assets**	**91,466**	**98,493**	**96,030**	...	...	...	...	...	...	...	...	...
611	Fixed assets	90,830	97,963	95,394	...	...	...	...	...	...	...	...	...
6111	Buildings and structures	82,280	78,949	79,570	...	...	...	...	...	...	...	...	...
6112	Machinery and equipment	8,550	19,014	15,825	...	...	...	...	...	...	...	...	...
6113	Other fixed assets	—	—	—	...	...	...	...	...	...	...	...	...
6114	Weapons systems	—	—	—	...	...	...	...	...	...	...	...	...
612	Inventories	—	—	—	...	...	...	...	...	...	...	...	...
613	Valuables	—	—	—	...	...	...	...	...	...	...	...	...
614	Nonproduced assets	636	530	636	...	...	...	...	...	...	...	...	...
6141	Land	—	—	—	...	...	...	...	...	...	...	...	...
6142	Mineral and energy resources	—	—	—	...	...	...	...	...	...	...	...	...
6143	Other naturally occurring assets	—	—	—	...	...	...	...	...	...	...	...	...
6144	Intangible nonproduced assets	636	530	636	...	...	...	...	...	...	...	...	...
62	**Financial assets**	**49,112**	**56,276**	**45,990**	...	...	...	...	...	...	...	...	...
	By instrument												
6201	Monetary gold and SDRs	—	—	—	...	...	...	...	...	...	...	...	...
6202	Currency and deposits	6,332	9,647	5,452	...	...	...	...	...	...	...	...	...
6203	Debt securities	—	—	—	...	...	...	...	...	...	...	...	...
6204	Loans	—	—	—	...	...	...	...	...	...	...	...	...
6205	Equity and investment fund shares	748	998	748	...	...	...	...	...	...	...	...	...
6206	Insurance, pension, and standardized guarantee schemes	—	—	—	...	...	...	...	...	...	...	...	...
6207	Financial derivatives and employee stock options	—	—	—	...	...	...	...	...	...	...	...	...
6208	Other accounts receivable	42,032	45,631	39,790	...	...	...	...	...	...	...	...	...
	By debtor												
621	Domestic debtors	32,803	36,497	39,790	...	...	...	...	...	...	...	...	...
622	External debtors	16,308	19,779	6,200	...	...	...	...	...	...	...	...	...
63	**Liabilities**	**78,952**	**92,113**	**88,217**	...	...	...	...	...	...	...	...	...
	By instrument												
6301	Special Drawing Rights (SDRs)	—	—	—	...	...	...	...	...	...	...	...	...
6302	Currency and deposits	—	—	—	...	...	...	...	...	...	...	...	...
6303	Debt securities	—	—	—	...	...	...	...	...	...	...	...	...
6304	Loans	64,714	62,217	59,017	...	...	...	...	...	...	...	...	...
6305	Equity and investment fund shares	—	—	—	...	...	...	...	...	...	...	...	...
6306	Insurance, pension, and standardized guarantee schemes	—	—	—	...	...	...	...	...	...	...	...	...
6307	Financial derivatives and employee stock options	—	—	—	...	...	...	...	...	...	...	...	...
6308	Other accounts payable	14,238	29,896	29,199	...	...	...	...	...	...	...	...	...
	By creditor												
631	Domestic creditors	14,072	29,896	29,199	...	...	...	...	...	...	...	...	...
632	External creditors	64,880	62,217	59,017	...	...	...	...	...	...	...	...	...
	Memorandum items												
6M2	Net financial worth	-29,841	-35,837	-42,227	...	...	...	...	...	...	...	...	...
6M3	Gross debt (D4) at market value	78,952	92,113	88,217	...	...	...	...	...	...	...	...	...
6M3D3	D3 debt liabilities at market value	78,952	92,113	88,217	...	...	...	...	...	...	...	...	...
6M3D2	D2 debt liabilities at market value	64,714	62,217	59,017	...	...	...	...	...	...	...	...	...
6M3D1	D1 debt liabilities at market value	64,714	62,217	59,017	...	...	...	...	...	...	...	...	...
6M4	Gross debt (D4) at nominal value	...	...	...	...	...	...	...	...	...	...	...	...
6M4D3	D3 debt liabilities at nominal value	...	...	...	...	...	...	...	...	...	...	...	...
6M4D2	D2 debt liabilities at nominal value	...	...	...	...	...	...	...	...	...	...	...	...
6M4D1	D1 debt liabilities at nominal value	...	...	...	...	...	...	...	...	...	...	...	...

Marshall Islands, Republic of (867)

In Thousands of U.S. Dollars (USD) / Fiscal Year Ends September 30th

		Budgetary Central Government			Central Government (excl. Social Security)			Central Government (incl. Social Security)			General Government		
		2013	2014	2015P	2013	2014	2015	2013	2014	2015	2013	2014	2015
6M35	Gross debt (D4) at face value	...	...	...	...	...	...	...	...	...	...	...	...
6M35D3	D3 debt liabilities at face value	...	...	...	...	...	...	...	...	...	...	...	...
6M35D2	D2 debt liabilities at face value	...	...	...	...	...	...	...	...	...	...	...	...
6M35D1	D1 debt liabilities at face value	...	...	...	...	...	...	...	...	...	...	...	...
6M93	Government gross debt per national definition	...	...	...	...	...	...	...	...	...	...	...	...
6M5	Arrears	...	...	...	...	...	...	...	...	...	...	...	...
6M6	Explicit contingent liabilities	...	...	...	...	...	...	...	...	...	...	...	...
6M61	of which: Publicly guaranteed debt	...	...	...	...	...	...	...	...	...	...	...	...
6M7	Net implicit obligations for social security benefits	...	...	...	...	...	...	...	...	...	...	...	...
	Table 7 Expenditure by functions of government												
7	**Expenditure**	**98,926**	**91,076**	**97,615**	...	...	...	...	...	...	...	...	...
701	**General public services**	**32,278**	**24,250**	**26,658**	...	...	...	...	...	...	...	...	...
7017	Public debt transactions	1,164	750	311	...	...	...	...	...	...	...	...	...
7018	Transfers of general character between levels of government	—	—	—	...	...	...	...	...	...	...	...	...
702	**Defense**	—	—	—	...	...	...	...	...	...	...	...	...
703	**Public order and safety**	**6,411**	**5,802**	**6,167**	...	...	...	...	...	...	...	...	...
704	**Economic affairs**	**12,751**	**13,443**	**14,174**	...	...	...	...	...	...	...	...	...
7042	Agriculture, forestry, fishing, and hunting	2,408	2,504	2,665	...	...	...	...	...	...	...	...	...
7043	Fuel and energy	3,126	3,440	3,669	...	...	...	...	...	...	...	...	...
7044	Mining, manufacturing, and construction	4,603	4,559	4,748	...	...	...	...	...	...	...	...	...
7045	Transport	1,747	1,960	2,064	...	...	...	...	...	...	...	...	...
7046	Communication	868	980	1,028	...	...	...	...	...	...	...	...	...
705	**Environmental protection**	**4,210**	**4,468**	**4,760**	...	...	...	...	...	...	...	...	...
706	**Housing and community amenities**	**1,211**	**1,332**	**1,421**	...	...	...	...	...	...	...	...	...
707	**Health**	**12,284**	**13,000**	**13,836**	...	...	...	...	...	...	...	...	...
7072	Outpatient services	2,168	2,294	2,442	...	...	...	...	...	...	...	...	...
7073	Hospital services	3,613	3,824	4,069	...	...	...	...	...	...	...	...	...
7074	Public health services	6,503	6,882	7,325	...	...	...	...	...	...	...	...	...
708	**Recreation, culture and religion**	**222**	**244**	**260**	...	...	...	...	...	...	...	...	...
709	**Education**	**29,560**	**28,536**	**30,338**	...	...	...	...	...	...	...	...	...
7091	Pre-primary and primary education	13,318	12,858	13,666	...	...	...	...	...	...	...	...	...
7092	Secondary education	11,780	11,366	12,084	...	...	...	...	...	...	...	...	...
7094	Tertiary education	4,462	4,311	4,588	...	...	...	...	...	...	...	...	...
710	**Social protection**	—	—	—	...	...	...	...	...	...	...	...	...
7z	Statistical discrepancy: Expenditure	...	...	...	...	...	...	...	...	...	...	...	...
	Table 8 Financial transactions by counterpart sector												
32	**Net acquisition of financial assets**	**1,250**	**1,791**	**1,152**	...	...	...	...	...	...	...	...	...
321	Domestic debtors	1,051	-1,680	-3,293	...	...	...	...	...	...	...	...	...
8211	General government	—	—	—	...	...	...	...	...	...	...	...	...
8212	Central bank	—	—	—	...	...	...	...	...	...	...	...	...
8213	Deposit-taking corporations except the central bank	—	—	—	...	...	...	...	...	...	...	...	...
8214	Other financial corporations	—	—	—	...	...	...	...	...	...	...	...	...
8215	Nonfinancial corporations	1,051	-1,680	-3,293	...	...	...	...	...	...	...	...	...
8216	Households & nonprofit institutions serving households	—	—	—	...	...	...	...	...	...	...	...	...
322	External debtors	199	3,471	4,445	...	...	...	...	...	...	...	...	...
8221	General government	—	—	—	...	...	...	...	...	...	...	...	...
8227	International organizations	1,326	156	250	...	...	...	...	...	...	...	...	...
8228	Financial corporations other than international organizations	-1,127	3,315	4,195	...	...	...	...	...	...	...	...	...
8229	Other nonresidents	—	—	—	...	...	...	...	...	...	...	...	...

Marshall Islands, Republic of (867)

In Thousands of U.S. Dollars (USD) / Fiscal Year Ends September 30th

		Budgetary Central Government			Central Government (excl. Social Security)			Central Government (incl. Social Security)			General Government		
		2013	2014	2015P	2013	2014	2015	2013	2014	2015	2013	2014	2015
33	**Net incurrence of liabilities**	**-156**	**-4,153**	**-3,896**	...	...	...	...	...	...	...	...	...
331	Domestic creditors	-2,058	-663	-696	...	...	...	...	...	...	...	...	...
8311	General government	—	—	—	...	...	...	...	...	...	...	...	...
8312	Central bank	—	—	—	...	...	...	...	...	...	...	...	...
8313	Deposit-taking corporations except the central bank	—	—	—	...	...	...	...	...	...	...	...	...
8314	Other financial corporations	—	—	—	...	...	...	...	...	...	...	...	...
8315	Nonfinancial corporations	-2,058	-663	-696	...	...	...	...	...	...	...	...	...
8316	Households & nonprofit institutions serving households	—	—	—	...	...	...	...	...	...	...	...	...
332	External creditors	1,902	-3,490	-3,200	...	...	...	...	...	...	...	...	...
8321	General government	—	—	—	...	...	...	...	...	...	...	...	...
8327	International organizations	-643	-1,002	—	...	...	...	...	...	...	...	...	...
8328	Financial corporations other than international organizations	2,545	-2,488	-3,200	...	...	...	...	...	...	...	...	...
8329	Other nonresidents	—	—	—	...	...	...	...	...	...	...	...	...
	Table 9 Total other economic flows in assets and liabilities												

Mauritius (684)

In Millions of Mauritian Rupees (MUR) / Fiscal Year Ends December 31st

		Budgetary Central Government			Central Government (excl. Social Security)			Central Government (incl. Social Security)			General Government		
		2012	2013	2014FB	2012	2013	2014FB	2012	2013	2014FB	2012	2013	2014FB
	Statement of operations												
1	Revenue	75,047	79,753	81,226	77,701	81,262	86,019	81,539	84,803	...	82,411	85,675	91,762
2	Expense	71,509	81,415	84,249	72,924	82,381	88,095	71,378	81,466	...	71,210	81,971	87,478
GOB	**Gross operating balance**	**3,538**	**-1,662**	**-3,023**	**4,777**	**-1,118**	**-2,076**	**10,161**	**3,337**	**...**	**11,202**	**3,703**	**4,284**
NOB	**Net operating balance**	**3,538**	**...**	**-3,023**	**4,777**	**-1,118**	**-2,076**	**10,161**	**3,337**	**...**	**11,202**	**3,703**	**4,284**
31	Net/Gross investment in nonfinancial assets	9,616	11,161	9,528	12,150	14,060	11,820	12,196	14,149	...	13,037	15,442	12,828
2M	Expenditure	81,125	92,576	93,777	85,074	96,440	99,915	83,574	95,616	...	84,247	97,413	100,306
NLB	**Net lending (+) / Net borrowing (-)**	**-6,078**	**-12,823**	**-12,551**	**-7,374**	**-15,178**	**-13,896**	**-2,035**	**-10,813**	**...**	**-1,835**	**-11,739**	**-8,544**
32	Net acquisition of financial assets	2,401	9,937	5,966	1,105	4,322	4,919	6,143	8,687	...	6,343	7,759	10,537
33	Net incurrence of liabilities	8,479	22,760	18,517	...	19,500	18,814	8,178	19,500	...	8,178	19,498	19,081
NLBz	Statistical discrepancy	0	-0	0	...	-0	0	—	-0	...	0	-0	0
	Memorandum items												
PB	Primary net lending / net borrowing	4,052	-3,194	-2,434	2,759	-5,547	-3,774	4,575	-4,462	...	4,775	-5,387	-1,727
GB	Government balance per national definition	...	...	...	...	...	...	...	...	...	...	...	...
	Statement of other economic flows												
	Balance sheet												
6	**Net worth**	...	...	...	...	...	...	...	...	...	...	...	...
61	Nonfinancial assets	...	...	...	...	...	...	...	...	...	...	...	...
62	Financial assets	...	...	...	...	...	...	...	...	...	...	...	...
63	Liabilities	172,183	...	...	172,363	...	...	128,016	...	...	...	...	...
	Table 1 Revenue												
1	**Revenue**	**75,047**	**79,753**	**81,226**	**77,701**	**81,262**	**86,019**	**81,539**	**84,803**	**...**	**82,411**	**85,675**	**91,762**
11	**Taxes**	**64,919**	**67,991**	**71,727**	**65,296**	**68,397**	**72,399**	**65,296**	**68,397**	**...**	**65,906**	**68,660**	**72,677**
111	Taxes on income, profits, and capital gains	14,634	15,920	17,089	14,634	15,920	17,089	14,634	15,920	...	14,634	15,920	17,089
1111	Payable by individuals	5,331	6,215	7,049	5,331	6,215	7,049	5,331	6,215	...	5,331	6,215	7,049
1112	Payable by corporations and other enterprises	8,372	8,727	8,972	8,372	8,727	8,972	8,372	8,727	...	8,372	8,727	8,972
1113	Other taxes on income, profits, and capital gains	931	979	1,068	931	979	1,068	931	979	...	931	979	1,068
112	Taxes on payroll and workforce	—	—	—	201	235	507	201	235	...	201	235	507
113	Taxes on property	53	102	521	53	102	521	53	102	...	288	364	796
114	Taxes on goods and services	47,511	49,344	51,297	47,687	49,515	51,462	47,687	49,515	...	48,044	49,517	51,465
1141	General taxes on goods and services	29,461	30,380	31,385	29,609	30,538	31,550	29,609	30,538	...	29,707	30,538	31,550
1142	Excises	13,039	13,557	14,423	13,052	13,570	14,423	13,052	13,570	...	13,052	13,570	14,423
115	Taxes on international trade and transactions	1,506	1,389	1,239	1,506	1,389	1,239	1,506	1,389	...	1,506	1,389	1,239
116	Other taxes	1,215	1,235	1,582	1,215	1,235	1,582	1,215	1,235	...	1,233	1,235	1,582
12	**Social contributions**	**2,304**	**2,797**	**2,836**	**3,252**	**3,844**	**3,959**	**5,743**	**6,394**	**...**	**5,743**	**6,394**	**7,488**
121	Social security contributions	768	932	945	782	947	945	3,273	3,496	...	3,273	3,496	4,474
122	Other social contributions	1,536	1,865	1,891	2,470	2,898	3,014	2,470	2,898	...	2,470	2,898	3,015
13	**Grants**	**2,398**	**2,603**	**406**	**2,398**	**1,416**	**940**	**2,398**	**1,416**	**...**	**2,398**	**1,416**	**940**
131	From foreign governments	122	118	58	122	121	569	122	121	...	122	121	569
132	From international organizations	2,276	1,285	348	2,276	1,295	371	2,276	1,295	...	2,276	1,295	371
133	From other general government units	—	1,200	—	—	—	—	—	—	...	—	0	—
1331	Current	—	—	—	—	—	—	—	—	...	—	0	—
1332	Capital	—	1,200	—	—	—	—	—	—	...	—	0	—
14	**Other revenue**	**5,426**	**6,363**	**6,256**	**6,755**	**7,606**	**8,720**	**8,102**	**8,597**	**...**	**8,364**	**9,205**	**10,657**
	Table 2 Expense by economic type												
2	**Expense**	**71,509**	**81,415**	**84,249**	**72,924**	**82,381**	**88,095**	**71,378**	**81,466**	**...**	**71,210**	**81,971**	**87,478**
21	**Compensation of employees**	**20,871**	**25,259**	**26,700**	**25,655**	**30,784**	**32,630**	**25,662**	**30,794**	**...**	**28,067**	**33,676**	**35,688**
211	Wages and salaries	18,478	22,458	23,716	23,005	27,736	29,285	23,013	27,746	...	25,202	30,422	32,096
212	Employers' social contributions	2,393	2,802	2,984	2,650	3,048	3,345	2,650	3,048	...	2,866	3,254	3,592
22	**Use of goods and services**	**6,516**	**7,087**	**7,546**	**8,465**	**9,037**	**9,703**	**8,573**	**9,292**	**...**	**9,533**	**10,352**	**11,023**
23	**Consumption of fixed capital**	—	...	—	—	—	—	—	—	...	—	—	—
24	**Interest**	**10,129**	**9,630**	**10,118**	**10,133**	**9,631**	**10,122**	**6,611**	**6,351**	**...**	**6,611**	**6,352**	**6,817**
25	**Subsidies**	**1,147**	**1,426**	**1,578**	**1,374**	**1,630**	**1,862**	**1,374**	**1,630**	**...**	**1,378**	**1,634**	**1,868**

Mauritius (684)

In Millions of Mauritian Rupees (MUR) / Fiscal Year Ends December 31st

		Budgetary Central Government			Central Government (excl. Social Security)			Central Government (incl. Social Security)			General Government		
		2012	2013	2014FB	2012	2013	2014FB	2012	2013	2014FB	2012	2013	2014FB
26	**Grants**	**25,228**	**28,692**	**16,957**	**14,709**	**15,622**	**5,222**	**4,554**	**4,604**	**...**	**238**	**259**	**241**
261	To foreign governments	3	5	—	3	5	—	3	5	...	3	5	—
262	To international organizations	236	254	241	236	254	241	236	254	...	236	254	241
263	To other general government units	24,990	28,434	16,716	14,470	15,363	4,982	4,316	4,345	...	—	0	—
2631	Current	22,166	25,334	15,404	13,781	14,938	4,494	3,626	3,920	...	—	0	—
2632	Capital	2,824	3,100	1,311	690	425	487	690	425	...	—	0	—
27	**Social benefits**	**5,245**	**6,487**	**19,250**	**6,158**	**7,524**	**20,329**	**18,174**	**20,643**	**...**	**18,828**	**21,378**	**23,428**
271	Social security benefits	—	—	—	—	9	—	12,016	13,128	...	12,298	13,415	2,792
272	Social assistance benefits	1,029	1,125	13,650	1,029	1,126	14,724	1,029	1,126	...	1,139	1,264	14,749
273	Employment-related social benefits	4,216	5,361	5,600	5,129	6,388	5,605	5,129	6,388	...	5,391	6,698	5,887
28	**Other expense**	**2,373**	**2,835**	**2,102**	**6,430**	**8,153**	**8,227**	**6,430**	**8,153**	**...**	**6,554**	**8,321**	**8,414**
281	Property expense other than interest	—	—	—	—	—	11	—	—	...	—	—	11
282	Transfers not elsewhere classified	2,373	2,835	2,102	6,430	8,153	8,215	6,430	8,153	...	6,554	8,321	8,403
2821	Current	1,505	1,857	1,441	5,386	6,641	6,834	5,386	6,641	...	5,511	6,808	7,022
2822	Capital	867	978	660	1,043	1,513	1,381	1,043	1,513	...	1,043	1,513	1,381
	Table 3 Transactions in assets and liabilities												
3	**Change in net worth from transactions**	...	...	...	...	...	...	...	...	...	...	...	...
31	**Net/Gross investment in nonfinancial assets**	**9,616**	**11,161**	**9,528**	**12,150**	**14,060**	**11,820**	**12,196**	**14,149**	**...**	**13,037**	**15,442**	**12,828**
311	Fixed assets	9,187	10,518	8,272	11,721	13,417	10,328	11,767	13,506	...	12,605	14,798	11,312
3111	Buildings and structures	7,807	7,723	5,623	10,103	10,318	7,599	10,103	10,318	...	10,827	11,434	8,336
3112	Machinery and equipment	964	1,817	1,690	1,148	2,015	1,766	1,193	2,105	...	1,277	2,243	1,946
3113	Other fixed assets	416	978	959	471	1,083	963	471	1,083	...	501	1,121	1,030
3114	Weapons systems	—	—	—	—	—	—	—	—	...	—	—	—
312	Inventories	—	—	—	—	—	196	—	—	...	—	—	196
313	Valuables	—	—	—	—	—	—	—	—	...	—	—	—
314	Nonproduced assets	429	643	1,256	429	643	1,297	429	643	...	432	644	1,321
3141	Land	429	643	1,256	429	643	1,273	429	643	...	432	644	1,297
3142	Mineral and energy resources	—	—	—	—	—	—	—	—	...	—	—	—
3143	Other naturally occurring assets	—	—	—	—	—	—	—	—	...	—	—	—
3144	Intangible nonproduced assets	—	—	—	—	—	23	—	—	...	—	—	23
32	**Net acquisition of financial assets**	**2,401**	**9,937**	**5,966**	**1,105**	**4,322**	**4,919**	**6,143**	**8,687**	**...**	**6,343**	**7,759**	**10,537**
	By instrument												
3201	Monetary gold and SDRs	96	191	34	96	191	34	96	191	...	96	191	34
3202	Currency and deposits	978	3,959	4,970	982	5,904	2,130	4,331	1,929	...	4,531	1,001	1,727
3203	Debt securities	—	—	—	—	-3,260	—	463	3,551	...	463	3,551	3,986
3204	Loans	137	5,113	851	-1,163	813	2,443	-1,231	752	...	-1,231	752	2,447
3205	Equity and investment fund shares	1,191	674	111	1,191	674	311	2,485	2,265	...	2,485	2,265	2,428
3206	Insurance, pension, and standardized guarantee schemes	—	—	—	—	—	—	—	—	...	—	—	—
3207	Financial derivatives and employee stock options	—	—	—	—	—	—	—	—	...	—	—	—
3208	Other accounts receivable	—	—	—	—	—	—	—	—	...	—	—	-84
	By debtor												
321	Domestic debtors	2,015	9,627	5,825	719	4,013	4,777	5,114	6,893	...	5,314	5,965	9,570
322	External debtors	386	309	141	386	309	141	1,029	1,794	...	1,029	1,794	967
33	**Net incurrence of liabilities**	**8,479**	**22,760**	**18,517**	**...**	**19,500**	**18,814**	**8,178**	**19,500**	**...**	**8,178**	**19,498**	**19,081**
	By instrument												
3301	Special Drawing Rights (SDRs)	—	—	—	—	—	—	—	—	...	—	—	—
3302	Currency and deposits	-1,551	2,182	-2,422	...	2,182	-2,422	-251	2,182	...	-251	2,182	-2,382
3303	Debt securities	6,727	9,638	16,904	...	6,378	16,904	5,127	6,378	...	5,127	6,378	15,266
3304	Loans	3,022	10,621	4,426	...	10,621	4,724	3,022	10,621	...	3,022	10,619	4,666
3305	Equity and investment fund shares	—	—	—	—	—	—	—	—	...	—	—	—
3306	Insurance, pension, and standardized guarantee schemes	—	—	—	—	—	—	—	—	...	—	—	140
3307	Financial derivatives and employee stock options	—	—	—	—	—	—	—	—	...	—	—	—
3308	Other accounts payable	280	320	-392	...	320	-392	280	320	...	280	320	1,391

Mauritius (684)

In Millions of Mauritian Rupees (MUR) / Fiscal Year Ends December 31st

		Budgetary Central Government			Central Government (excl. Social Security)			Central Government (incl. Social Security)			General Government		
		2012	2013	2014FB	2012	2013	2014FB	2012	2013	2014FB	2012	2013	2014FB
	By creditor												
331	Domestic creditors	5,496	12,078	14,281	...	8,819	14,578	5,196	8,819	...	5,196	8,816	14,844
332	External creditors	2,982	10,682	4,237	...	10,682	4,237	2,982	10,682	...	2,982	10,682	4,237
	Table 4 Holding gains and losses in assets and liabilities												
	Table 5 Holding gains and losses in assets and liabilities												
	Table 6 Balance sheet												
6	**Net worth**	...	...	...	...	...	...	...	...	...	...	...	...
61	**Nonfinancial assets**	...	...	...	...	...	...	...	...	...	...	...	...
611	Fixed assets	...	...	...	...	...	...	...	...	...	...	...	...
6111	Buildings and structures	...	...	...	...	...	...	...	...	...	...	...	...
6112	Machinery and equipment	...	...	...	...	...	...	...	...	...	...	...	...
6113	Other fixed assets	...	...	...	...	...	...	...	...	...	...	...	...
6114	Weapons systems	...	...	...	...	...	...	...	...	...	...	...	...
612	Inventories	...	...	...	...	...	...	...	...	...	...	...	...
613	Valuables	...	...	...	...	...	...	...	...	...	...	...	...
614	Nonproduced assets	...	...	...	...	...	...	...	...	...	...	...	...
6141	Land	...	...	...	...	...	...	...	...	...	...	...	...
6142	Mineral and energy resources	...	...	...	...	...	...	...	...	...	...	...	...
6143	Other naturally occurring assets	...	...	...	...	...	...	...	...	...	...	...	...
6144	Intangible nonproduced assets	...	...	...	...	...	...	...	...	...	...	...	...
62	**Financial assets**	...	...	...	...	...	...	...	...	...	...	...	...
	By instrument												
6201	Monetary gold and SDRs	...	...	...	...	...	...	...	...	...	...	...	...
6202	Currency and deposits	...	...	...	...	...	...	...	...	...	...	...	...
6203	Debt securities	...	...	...	...	...	...	...	...	...	...	...	...
6204	Loans	...	...	...	...	...	...	...	...	...	...	...	...
6205	Equity and investment fund shares	...	...	...	...	...	...	...	...	...	...	...	...
6206	Insurance, pension, and standardized guarantee schemes	...	...	...	...	...	...	...	...	...	...	...	...
6207	Financial derivatives and employee stock options	...	...	...	...	...	...	...	...	...	...	...	...
6208	Other accounts receivable	...	...	...	...	...	...	...	...	...	...	...	...
	By debtor												
621	Domestic debtors	...	...	...	...	...	...	...	...	...	...	...	...
622	External debtors	...	...	...	...	...	...	...	...	...	...	...	...
63	**Liabilities**	**172,183**	...	...	**172,363**	...	...	**128,016**	...	...	...	...	...
	By instrument												
6301	Special Drawing Rights (SDRs)	—	...	...	—	...	...	—	...	...	...	...	...
6302	Currency and deposits	—	...	...	—	...	...	—	...	...	...	...	...
6303	Debt securities	141,030	...	...	141,030	...	...	96,683	...	...	...	...	...
6304	Loans	31,153	...	...	31,334	...	...	31,334	...	...	...	...	...
6305	Equity and investment fund shares	—	...	...	—	...	...	—	...	...	...	...	...
6306	Insurance, pension, and standardized guarantee schemes	—	...	...	—	...	...	—	...	...	...	...	...
6307	Financial derivatives and employee stock options	—	...	...	—	...	...	—	...	...	...	...	...
6308	Other accounts payable	—	...	...	—	...	...	—	...	...	...	...	...
	By creditor												
631	Domestic creditors	141,030	...	...	141,030	...	...	96,683	...	...	...	...	...
632	External creditors	31,153	...	...	31,334	...	...	31,334	...	...	...	...	...
	Memorandum items												
6M2	Net financial worth	...	...	...	...	...	...	...	...	...	...	...	...
6M3	Gross debt (D4) at market value	...	...	...	...	...	...	...	...	...	...	...	...
6M3D3	D3 debt liabilities at market value	...	...	...	...	...	...	...	...	...	...	...	...
6M3D2	D2 debt liabilities at market value	...	...	...	...	...	...	...	...	...	...	...	...
6M3D1	D1 debt liabilities at market value	...	...	...	...	...	...	...	...	...	...	...	...
6M4	Gross debt (D4) at nominal value	...	...	...	...	...	...	...	...	...	...	...	...
6M4D3	D3 debt liabilities at nominal value	...	...	...	...	...	...	...	...	...	...	...	...
6M4D2	D2 debt liabilities at nominal value	...	...	...	...	...	...	...	...	...	...	...	...
6M4D1	D1 debt liabilities at nominal value	0	...	...	180	...	...	0	...	...	...	...	...

Mauritius (684)

In Millions of Mauritian Rupees (MUR) / Fiscal Year Ends December 31st

		Budgetary Central Government			Central Government (excl. Social Security)			Central Government (incl. Social Security)			General Government		
		2012	2013	2014FB	2012	2013	2014FB	2012	2013	2014FB	2012	2013	2014FB
6M35	Gross debt (D4) at face value	...	...	...	...	...	...	...	...	...	...	...	...
6M35D3	D3 debt liabilities at face value	...	...	...	...	...	...	...	...	...	...	...	...
6M35D2	D2 debt liabilities at face value	...	...	...	...	...	...	...	...	...	...	...	...
6M35D1	D1 debt liabilities at face value	...	...	...	...	...	...	...	...	...	...	...	...
6M93	Government gross debt per national definition	...	...	...	...	...	...	...	...	...	...	...	...
6M5	Arrears	...	...	...	...	...	...	...	...	...	...	...	...
6M6	Explicit contingent liabilities	...	...	...	...	...	...	...	...	...	...	...	...
6M61	of which: Publicly guaranteed debt	...	...	...	...	...	...	...	...	...	...	...	...
6M7	Net implicit obligations for social security benefits	...	...	...	...	...	...	...	...	...	...	...	...
	Table 7 Expenditure by functions of government												
7	**Expenditure**	**81,125**	**92,576**	**93,777**	**85,074**	**96,441**	**99,915**	**83,574**	**95,616**	...	**84,247**	**97,413**	**100,306**
701	**General public services**	**20,747**	**22,681**	**23,757**	**21,349**	**23,277**	**23,771**	**17,826**	**19,996**	...	**14,563**	**17,211**	**17,000**
7017	Public debt transactions	10,129	9,630	10,118	10,133	9,631	10,122	6,611	6,351	...	6,611	6,352	6,817
7018	Transfers of general character between levels of government	4,316	4,345	4,982	4,316	4,345	4,982	4,316	4,345	...	—	0	—
702	**Defense**	—	—	—	—	—	—	—	—	...	—	—	—
703	**Public order and safety**	**7,368**	**9,950**	**9,404**	**7,354**	**9,955**	**9,407**	**7,354**	**9,955**	...	**7,388**	**9,996**	**9,453**
704	**Economic affairs**	**9,129**	**9,746**	**7,157**	**10,228**	**11,489**	**9,402**	**10,228**	**11,489**	...	**11,350**	**12,702**	**10,777**
7042	Agriculture, forestry, fishing, and hunting	2,070	2,444	2,310	2,272	2,422	2,301	2,272	2,422	...	2,441	2,606	2,490
7043	Fuel and energy	99	101	46	96	...	130	96	323	...	96	323	130
7044	Mining, manufacturing, and construction	331	389	411	353	400	419	353	400	...	849	883	1,313
7045	Transport	5,548	5,594	3,119	5,902	6,394	4,266	5,902	6,394	...	6,332	6,911	4,532
7046	Communication	—	—	—	200	169	152	200	169	...	203	172	152
705	**Environmental protection**	**2,594**	**1,293**	**1,329**	**2,605**	**1,300**	**1,337**	**2,605**	**1,300**	...	**3,146**	**2,052**	**2,123**
706	**Housing and community amenities**	**2,703**	**4,547**	**4,413**	**2,762**	**4,135**	**5,733**	**2,762**	**4,135**	...	**3,418**	**4,990**	**6,378**
707	**Health**	**7,753**	**8,716**	**9,416**	**7,775**	**8,712**	**9,470**	**7,775**	**8,712**	...	**8,100**	**9,055**	**9,832**
7072	Outpatient services	...	...	...	...	...	...	...	...	...	...	...	...
7073	Hospital services	...	...	...	...	...	...	...	...	...	...	...	...
7074	Public health services	...	...	...	...	...	...	...	...	...	...	...	...
708	**Recreation, culture and religion**	**742**	**834**	**856**	**726**	**817**	**875**	**726**	**817**	...	**978**	**1,169**	**1,168**
709	**Education**	**11,111**	**13,015**	**13,932**	**12,370**	**13,956**	**15,227**	**12,370**	**13,956**	...	**12,612**	**14,210**	**15,515**
7091	Pre-primary and primary education	...	...	...	...	...	...	...	...	...	...	...	...
7092	Secondary education	...	...	...	...	...	...	...	...	...	...	...	...
7094	Tertiary education	...	...	...	...	...	...	...	...	...	...	...	...
710	**Social protection**	**18,977**	**21,795**	**23,514**	**19,905**	**22,800**	**24,694**	**21,928**	**25,255**	...	**22,691**	**26,028**	**28,060**
7z	Statistical discrepancy: Expenditure	—	—	—	—	—	—	—	—	...	—	—	—
	Table 8 Financial transactions by counterpart sector												
32	**Net acquisition of financial assets**	**2,401**	**9,937**	**5,966**	**1,105**	**4,322**	**4,919**	**6,143**	**8,687**	...	**6,343**	**7,759**	**10,537**
321	Domestic debtors	2,015	9,627	5,825	719	4,013	4,777	5,114	6,893	...	5,314	5,965	9,570
8211	General government	—	4,298	-369	-1,300	-3,262	-70	1	—	...	1	0	...
8212	Central bank	—	...	...	—	—	...	-331	1,359	...	-331	1,359	1,286
8213	Deposit-taking corporations except the central bank	1,002	3,443	4,860	1,006	5,388	2,030	3,761	1,634	...	3,961	706	3,070
8214	Other financial corporations	-2	-2	-2	-2	-2	-2	96	1,285	...	96	1,285	55
8215	Nonfinancial corporations	1,055	1,189	873	1,055	1,189	873	1,627	1,915	...	1,627	1,915	3,421
8216	Households & nonprofit institutions serving households	-40	700	464	-40	700	1,947	-40	700	...	-40	700	1,738
322	External debtors	386	309	141	386	309	141	1,029	1,794	...	1,029	1,794	967
8221	General government	—	—	—	—	—	—	—	—	...	—	—	—
8227	International organizations	295	298	145	295	298	145	295	298	...	295	298	145
8228	Financial corporations other than international organizations	92	12	-4	92	12	-4	734	1,497	...	734	1,497	822
8229	Other nonresidents	—	—	—	—	—	—	—	—	...	—	—	—

Mauritius (684)

In Millions of Mauritian Rupees (MUR) / Fiscal Year Ends December 31st

		Budgetary Central Government			Central Government (excl. Social Security)			Central Government (incl. Social Security)			General Government		
		2012	2013	2014FB	2012	2013	2014FB	2012	2013	2014FB	2012	2013	2014FB
33	**Net incurrence of liabilities**	**8,479**	**22,760**	**18,517**	**...**	**19,500**	**18,814**	**8,178**	**19,500**	**...**	**8,178**	**19,498**	**19,081**
331	Domestic creditors	5,496	12,078	14,281	...	8,819	14,578	5,196	8,819	...	5,196	8,816	14,844
3311	General government	300	3,262	1,341	...	2	1,638	—	2	...	—	0	0
3312	Central bank	-3,959	776	-1,776	...	776	-1,776	-3,959	776	...	-3,959	776	-1,776
3313	Deposit-taking corporations except the central bank	5,550	5,121	12,458	...	5,121	12,458	5,550	5,121	...	5,550	5,121	12,440
3314	Other financial corporations	3,633	3,105	1,041	...	3,105	1,041	3,633	3,105	...	3,633	3,105	1,041
3315	Nonfinancial corporations	66	-71	-38	...	-71	-38	66	-71	...	66	-71	88
3316	Households & nonprofit institutions serving households	-93	-114	1,256	...	-114	1,256	-93	-114	...	-93	-114	3,053
332	External creditors	2,982	10,682	4,237	...	10,682	4,237	2,982	10,682	...	2,982	10,682	4,237
3321	General government	—	2,250	...	—	2,250	...	—	2,250	...	—	2,250	—
3327	International organizations	2,666	7,372	4,151	...	7,372	4,151	2,666	7,372	...	2,666	7,372	4,151
3328	Financial corporations other than international organizations	—	1,058	276	—	1,058	276	—	1,058	...	—	1,058	276
3329	Other nonresidents	316	1	-190	...	1	-190	316	1	...	316	1	-190
	Table 9 Total other economic flows in assets and liabilities												

Micronesia, Federated States of (868)

In Thousands of U.S. Dollars (USD) / Fiscal Year Ends September 30th

		Budgetary Central Government			Central Government (excl. Social Security)			Central Government (incl. Social Security)			General Government		
		2013	2014	2015	2013	2014	2015	2013	2014	2015	2013	2014	2015
	Statement of operations												
1	Revenue	100,255	114,061	110,404	...	...	...	...	...	...	...	...	...
2	Expense	57,721	57,789	65,364	...	...	...	...	...	...	...	...	...
GOB	**Gross operating balance**	**51,578**	**65,692**	**54,553**	...	...	...	...	...	...	...	...	...
NOB	**Net operating balance**	**42,535**	**56,272**	**45,040**	...	...	...	...	...	...	...	...	...
31	Net/Gross investment in nonfinancial assets	31,341	13,348	9,662	...	...	...	...	...	...	...	...	...
2M	Expenditure	89,062	71,137	75,025	...	...	...	...	...	...	...	...	...
NLB	**Net lending (+) / Net borrowing (-)**	**11,194**	**42,924**	**35,379**	...	...	...	...	...	...	...	...	...
32	Net acquisition of financial assets	5,952	34,110	44,015	...	...	...	...	...	...	...	...	...
33	Net incurrence of liabilities	-5,241	-8,813	8,637	...	...	...	...	...	...	...	...	...
NLBz	Statistical discrepancy	0	-0	-0	...	...	...	...	...	...	...	...	...
	Memorandum items												
PB	Primary net lending / net borrowing	11,927	43,712	36,167	...	...	...	...	...	...	...	...	...
GB	Government balance per national definition	...	...	...	...	...	...	...	...	...	...	...	...
	Statement of other economic flows												
	Balance sheet												
6	**Net worth**	**274,016**	**298,811**	**339,914**	...	...	...	...	...	...	...	...	...
61	Nonfinancial assets	227,100	202,866	212,999	...	...	...	...	...	...	...	...	...
62	Financial assets	130,417	170,622	221,682	...	...	...	...	...	...	...	...	...
63	Liabilities	83,500	74,677	94,767	...	...	...	...	...	...	...	...	...
	Table 1 Revenue												
1	**Revenue**	**100,255**	**114,061**	**110,404**	...	...	...	...	...	...	...	...	...
11	**Taxes**	**17,341**	**40,050**	**17,148**	...	...	...	...	...	...	...	...	...
111	Taxes on income, profits, and capital gains	8,258	31,700	8,334	...	...	...	...	...	...	...	...	...
1111	Payable by individuals	3,880	4,070	4,196	...	...	...	...	...	...	...	...	...
1112	Payable by corporations and other enterprises	4,378	27,630	4,138	...	...	...	...	...	...	...	...	...
1113	Other taxes on income, profits, and capital gains	—	—	—	...	...	...	...	...	...	...	...	...
112	Taxes on payroll and workforce	—	—	—	...	...	...	...	...	...	...	...	...
113	Taxes on property	—	—	—	...	...	...	...	...	...	...	...	...
114	Taxes on goods and services	4,853	4,450	4,322	...	...	...	...	...	...	...	...	...
1141	General taxes on goods and services	4,543	4,380	4,170	...	...	...	...	...	...	...	...	...
1142	Excises	—	—	—	...	...	...	...	...	...	...	...	...
115	Taxes on international trade and transactions	4,041	3,796	4,302	...	...	...	...	...	...	...	...	...
116	Other taxes	188	103	190	...	...	...	...	...	...	...	...	...
12	**Social contributions**	—	—	—	...	...	...	...	...	...	...	...	...
121	Social security contributions	—	—	—	...	...	...	...	...	...	...	...	...
122	Other social contributions	—	—	—	...	...	...	...	...	...	...	...	...
13	**Grants**	**43,828**	**22,465**	**20,604**	...	...	...	...	...	...	...	...	...
131	From foreign governments	43,828	22,465	20,604	...	...	...	...	...	...	...	...	...
132	From international organizations	—	—	—	...	...	...	...	...	...	...	...	...
133	From other general government units	—	—	—	...	...	...	...	...	...	...	...	...
1331	Current	—	—	—	...	...	...	...	...	...	...	...	...
1332	Capital	—	—	—	...	...	...	...	...	...	...	...	...
14	**Other revenue**	**39,087**	**51,546**	**72,652**	...	...	...	...	...	...	...	...	...
	Table 2 Expense by economic type												
2	**Expense**	**57,721**	**57,789**	**65,364**	...	...	...	...	...	...	...	...	...
21	**Compensation of employees**	**17,908**	**16,972**	**18,206**	...	...	...	...	...	...	...	...	...
211	Wages and salaries	17,908	16,972	18,206	...	...	...	...	...	...	...	...	...
212	Employers' social contributions	—	—	—	...	...	...	...	...	...	...	...	...
22	**Use of goods and services**	**20,688**	**24,513**	**31,327**	...	...	...	...	...	...	...	...	...
23	**Consumption of fixed capital**	**9,043**	**9,420**	**9,513**	...	...	...	...	...	...	...	...	...
24	**Interest**	**733**	**788**	**788**	...	...	...	...	...	...	...	...	...
25	**Subsidies**	**305**	**347**	—	...	...	...	...	...	...	...	...	...

Micronesia, Federated States of (868)

In Thousands of U.S. Dollars (USD) / Fiscal Year Ends September 30th

		Budgetary Central Government			Central Government (excl. Social Security)			Central Government (incl. Social Security)			General Government		
		2013	2014	2015	2013	2014	2015	2013	2014	2015	2013	2014	2015
26	**Grants**	**1,039**	**1,746**	**1,101**	**...**	**...**	**...**	**...**	**...**	**...**	**...**	**...**	**...**
261	To foreign governments	—	—	—	...	...	...	...	...	...	...	...	...
262	To international organizations	—	—	—	...	...	...	...	...	...	...	...	...
263	To other general government units	1,039	1,746	1,101	...	...	...	...	...	...	...	...	...
2631	Current	1,039	1,746	1,101	...	...	...	...	...	...	...	...	...
2632	Capital	—	—	—	...	...	...	...	...	...	...	...	...
27	**Social benefits**	**—**	**—**	**—**	**...**	**...**	**...**	**...**	**...**	**...**	**...**	**...**	**...**
271	Social security benefits	—	—	—	...	...	...	...	...	...	...	...	...
272	Social assistance benefits	—	—	—	...	...	...	...	...	...	...	...	...
273	Employment-related social benefits	—	—	—	...	...	...	...	...	...	...	...	...
28	**Other expense**	**8,004**	**4,004**	**4,429**	**...**	**...**	**...**	**...**	**...**	**...**	**...**	**...**	**...**
281	Property expense other than interest	—	—	—	...	...	...	...	...	...	...	...	...
282	Transfers not elsewhere classified	8,004	4,004	4,429	...	...	...	...	...	...	...	...	...
2821	Current	8,004	4,004	4,429	...	...	...	...	...	...	...	...	...
2822	Capital	—	—	—	...	...	...	...	...	...	...	...	...
	Table 3 Transactions in assets and liabilities												
3	**Change in net worth from transactions**	**42,535**	**56,272**	**45,040**	**...**	**...**	**...**	**...**	**...**	**...**	**...**	**...**	**...**
31	**Net/Gross investment in nonfinancial assets**	**31,341**	**13,348**	**9,662**	**...**	**...**	**...**	**...**	**...**	**...**	**...**	**...**	**...**
311	Fixed assets	31,341	13,348	9,662	...	...	...	...	...	...	...	...	...
3111	Buildings and structures	32,040	13,104	9,425	...	...	...	...	...	...	...	...	...
3112	Machinery and equipment	-699	244	236	...	...	...	...	...	...	...	...	...
3113	Other fixed assets	—	—	—	...	...	...	...	...	...	...	...	...
3114	Weapons systems	—	—	—	...	...	...	...	...	...	...	...	...
312	Inventories	—	—	—	...	...	...	...	...	...	...	...	...
313	Valuables	—	—	—	...	...	...	...	...	...	...	...	...
314	Nonproduced assets	—	—	—	...	...	...	...	...	...	...	...	...
3141	Land	—	—	—	...	...	...	...	...	...	...	...	...
3142	Mineral and energy resources	—	—	—	...	...	...	...	...	...	...	...	...
3143	Other naturally occurring assets	—	—	—	...	...	...	...	...	...	...	...	...
3144	Intangible nonproduced assets	—	—	—	...	...	...	...	...	...	...	...	...
32	**Net acquisition of financial assets**	**5,952**	**34,110**	**44,015**	**...**	**...**	**...**	**...**	**...**	**...**	**...**	**...**	**...**
	By instrument												
3201	Monetary gold and SDRs	—	—	—	...	...	...	...	...	...	...	...	...
3202	Currency and deposits	5,153	32,605	8,247	...	...	...	...	...	...	...	...	...
3203	Debt securities	-1,532	-6,094	1,090	...	...	...	...	...	...	...	...	...
3204	Loans	-2,703	1,822	-975	...	...	...	...	...	...	...	...	...
3205	Equity and investment fund shares	2,243	12,519	34,818	...	...	...	...	...	...	...	...	...
3206	Insurance, pension, and standardized guarantee schemes	—	—	—	...	...	...	...	...	...	...	...	...
3207	Financial derivatives and employee stock options	—	—	—	...	...	...	...	...	...	...	...	...
3208	Other accounts receivable	2,791	-6,742	836	...	...	...	...	...	...	...	...	...
	By debtor												
321	Domestic debtors	6,787	34,383	13,574	...	...	...	...	...	...	...	...	...
322	External debtors	-835	-273	30,441	...	...	...	...	...	...	...	...	...
33	**Net incurrence of liabilities**	**-5,241**	**-8,813**	**8,637**	**...**	**...**	**...**	**...**	**...**	**...**	**...**	**...**	**...**
	By instrument												
3301	Special Drawing Rights (SDRs)	—	—	—	...	...	...	...	...	...	...	...	...
3302	Currency and deposits	—	—	—	...	...	...	...	...	...	...	...	...
3303	Debt securities	—	—	—	...	...	...	...	...	...	...	...	...
3304	Loans	927	-383	-395	...	...	...	...	...	...	...	...	...
3305	Equity and investment fund shares	—	—	—	...	...	...	...	...	...	...	...	...
3306	Insurance, pension, and standardized guarantee schemes	—	—	—	...	...	...	...	...	...	...	...	...
3307	Financial derivatives and employee stock options	—	—	—	...	...	...	...	...	...	...	...	...
3308	Other accounts payable	-6,168	-8,431	9,032	...	...	...	...	...	...	...	...	...

Micronesia, Federated States of (868)

In Thousands of U.S. Dollars (USD) / Fiscal Year Ends September 30th

		Budgetary Central Government			Central Government (excl. Social Security)			Central Government (incl. Social Security)			General Government		
		2013	2014	2015	2013	2014	2015	2013	2014	2015	2013	2014	2015
	By creditor												
331	Domestic creditors	-6,168	-8,431	9,032	...	...	...	...	...	...	...	...	...
332	External creditors	927	-383	-395	...	...	...	...	...	...	...	...	...
	Table 4 Holding gains and losses in assets and liabilities												
	Table 5 Holding gains and losses in assets and liabilities												
	Table 6 Balance sheet												
6	**Net worth**	**274,016**	**298,811**	**339,914**	...	...	...	...	...	...	...	...	...
61	**Nonfinancial assets**	**227,100**	**202,866**	**212,999**	...	...	...	...	...	...	...	...	...
611	Fixed assets	227,100	202,866	212,989	...	...	...	...	...	...	...	...	...
6111	Buildings and structures	216,788	193,357	203,361	...	...	...	...	...	...	...	...	...
6112	Machinery and equipment	10,312	9,509	9,628	...	...	...	...	...	...	...	...	...
6113	Other fixed assets	—	—	—	...	...	...	...	...	...	...	...	...
6114	Weapons systems	—	—	—	...	...	...	...	...	...	...	...	...
612	Inventories	—	—	—	...	...	...	...	...	...	...	...	...
613	Valuables	—	—	—	...	...	...	...	...	...	...	...	...
614	Nonproduced assets	—	—	10	...	...	...	...	...	...	...	...	...
6141	Land	—	—	10	...	...	...	...	...	...	...	...	...
6142	Mineral and energy resources	—	—	—	...	...	...	...	...	...	...	...	...
6143	Other naturally occurring assets	—	—	—	...	...	...	...	...	...	...	...	...
6144	Intangible nonproduced assets	—	—	—	...	...	...	...	...	...	...	...	...
62	**Financial assets**	**130,417**	**170,622**	**221,682**	...	...	...	...	...	...	...	...	...
	By instrument												
6201	Monetary gold and SDRs	—	—	—	...	...	...	...	...	...	...	...	...
6202	Currency and deposits	31,374	63,979	69,888	...	...	...	...	...	...	...	...	...
6203	Debt securities	—	—	—	...	...	...	...	...	...	...	...	...
6204	Loans	39,468	41,290	40,314	...	...	...	...	...	...	...	...	...
6205	Equity and investment fund shares	34,030	46,549	81,367	...	...	...	...	...	...	...	...	...
6206	Insurance, pension, and standardized guarantee schemes	—	—	—	...	...	...	...	...	...	...	...	...
6207	Financial derivatives and employee stock options	—	—	—	...	...	...	...	...	...	...	...	...
6208	Other accounts receivable	25,545	18,803	30,112	...	...	...	...	...	...	...	...	...
	By debtor												
621	Domestic debtors	65,876	100,259	124,307	...	...	...	...	...	...	...	...	...
622	External debtors	64,541	70,362	97,375	...	...	...	...	...	...	...	...	...
63	**Liabilities**	**83,500**	**74,677**	**94,767**	...	...	...	...	...	...	...	...	...
	By instrument												
6301	Special Drawing Rights (SDRs)	—	—	—	...	...	...	...	...	...	...	...	...
6302	Currency and deposits	—	—	—	...	...	...	...	...	...	...	...	...
6303	Debt securities	—	—	—	...	...	...	...	...	...	...	...	...
6304	Loans	57,257	56,993	50,656	...	...	...	...	...	...	...	...	...
6305	Equity and investment fund shares	—	—	—	...	...	...	...	...	...	...	...	...
6306	Insurance, pension, and standardized guarantee schemes	—	—	—	...	...	...	...	...	...	...	...	...
6307	Financial derivatives and employee stock options	—	—	—	...	...	...	...	...	...	...	...	...
6308	Other accounts payable	26,243	17,684	44,111	...	...	...	...	...	...	...	...	...
	By creditor												
631	Domestic creditors	25,117	16,557	42,984	...	...	...	...	...	...	...	...	...
632	External creditors	58,384	58,119	51,783	...	...	...	...	...	...	...	...	...
	Memorandum items												
6M2	Net financial worth	46,917	95,945	126,915	...	...	...	...	...	...	...	...	...
6M3	Gross debt (D4) at market value	...	...	...	...	...	...	...	...	...	...	...	...
6M3D3	D3 debt liabilities at market value	...	...	...	...	...	...	...	...	...	...	...	...
6M3D2	D2 debt liabilities at market value	...	...	...	...	...	...	...	...	...	...	...	...
6M3D1	D1 debt liabilities at market value	...	...	...	...	...	...	...	...	...	...	...	...
6M4	Gross debt (D4) at nominal value	...	...	...	...	...	...	...	...	...	...	...	...
6M4D3	D3 debt liabilities at nominal value	...	...	...	...	...	...	...	...	...	...	...	...
6M4D2	D2 debt liabilities at nominal value	...	...	...	...	...	...	...	...	...	...	...	...
6M4D1	D1 debt liabilities at nominal value	...	...	...	...	...	...	...	...	...	...	...	...

Micronesia, Federated States of (868)

In Thousands of U.S. Dollars (USD) / Fiscal Year Ends September 30th

		Budgetary Central Government			Central Government (excl. Social Security)			Central Government (incl. Social Security)			General Government		
		2013	2014	2015	2013	2014	2015	2013	2014	2015	2013	2014	2015
6M35	Gross debt (D4) at face value	83,500	74,677	94,767	...	...	...	...	...	...	...	...	...
6M35D3	D3 debt liabilities at face value	83,500	74,677	94,767	...	...	...	...	...	...	...	...	...
6M35D2	D2 debt liabilities at face value	57,257	56,993	50,656	...	...	...	...	...	...	...	...	...
6M35D1	D1 debt liabilities at face value	57,257	56,993	50,656	...	...	...	...	...	...	...	...	...
6M93	Government gross debt per national definition	...	...	...	...	...	...	...	...	...	...	...	...
6M5	Arrears	...	...	...	...	...	...	...	...	...	...	...	...
6M6	Explicit contingent liabilities	...	...	...	...	...	...	...	...	...	...	...	...
6M61	of which: Publicly guaranteed debt	...	...	...	...	...	...	...	...	...	...	...	...
6M7	Net implicit obligations for social security benefits	...	...	...	...	...	...	...	...	...	...	...	...
	Table 7 Expenditure by functions of government												
7	**Expenditure**	**57,721**	**57,789**	**65,364**	...	...	...	...	...	...	...	...	...
701	**General public services**	**19,773**	**21,067**	**33,126**	...	...	...	...	...	...	...	...	...
7017	Public debt transactions	733	788	788	...	...	...	...	...	...	...	...	...
7018	Transfers of general character between levels of government	1,085	1,806	7,282	...	...	...	...	...	...	...	...	...
702	**Defense**	—	—	—	...	...	...	...	...	...	...	...	...
703	**Public order and safety**	**4,921**	**4,453**	**6,289**	...	...	...	...	...	...	...	...	...
704	**Economic affairs**	**21,751**	**22,329**	**12,492**	...	...	...	...	...	...	...	...	...
7042	Agriculture, forestry, fishing, and hunting	1,540	3,806	1,168	...	...	...	...	...	...	...	...	...
7043	Fuel and energy	—	—	—	...	...	...	...	...	...	...	...	...
7044	Mining, manufacturing, and construction	9,095	8,335	5,096	...	...	...	...	...	...	...	...	...
7045	Transport	7,074	6,483	3,963	...	...	...	...	...	...	...	...	...
7046	Communication	4,042	3,705	2,265	...	...	...	...	...	...	...	...	...
705	**Environmental protection**	**494**	**664**	**1,732**	...	...	...	...	...	...	...	...	...
706	**Housing and community amenities**	—	—	—	...	...	...	...	...	...	...	...	...
707	**Health**	**5,241**	**4,735**	**4,651**	...	...	...	...	...	...	...	...	...
7072	Outpatient services	655	592	581	...	...	...	...	...	...	...	...	...
7073	Hospital services	1,638	1,480	1,453	...	...	...	...	...	...	...	...	...
7074	Public health services	2,948	2,664	2,616	...	...	...	...	...	...	...	...	...
708	**Recreation, culture and religion**	—	—	—	...	...	...	...	...	...	...	...	...
709	**Education**	**4,230**	**3,357**	**5,912**	...	...	...	...	...	...	...	...	...
7091	Pre-primary and primary education	—	—	—	...	...	...	...	...	...	...	...	...
7092	Secondary education	—	—	—	...	...	...	...	...	...	...	...	...
7094	Tertiary education	—	—	—	...	...	...	...	...	...	...	...	...
710	**Social protection**	**1,310**	**1,184**	**1,163**	...	...	...	...	...	...	...	...	...
7z	Statistical discrepancy: Expenditure	...	...	...	...	...	...	...	...	...	...	...	...
	Table 8 Financial transactions by counterpart sector												
32	**Net acquisition of financial assets**	**5,952**	**34,110**	**44,015**	...	...	...	...	...	...	...	...	...
321	Domestic debtors	6,787	34,383	13,574	...	...	...	...	...	...	...	...	...
8211	General government	...	...	...	...	...	...	...	...	...	...	...	...
8212	Central bank	...	...	...	...	...	...	...	...	...	...	...	...
8213	Deposit-taking corporations except the central bank	...	...	...	...	...	...	...	...	...	...	...	...
8214	Other financial corporations	...	...	...	...	...	...	...	...	...	...	...	...
8215	Nonfinancial corporations	...	...	...	...	...	...	...	...	...	...	...	...
8216	Households & nonprofit institutions serving households	...	...	...	...	...	...	...	...	...	...	...	...
322	External debtors	-835	-273	30,441	...	...	...	...	...	...	...	...	...
8221	General government	...	...	...	...	...	...	...	...	...	...	...	...
8227	International organizations	...	...	...	...	...	...	...	...	...	...	...	...
8228	Financial corporations other than international organizations	...	...	...	...	...	...	...	...	...	...	...	...
8229	Other nonresidents	...	...	...	...	...	...	...	...	...	...	...	...

Micronesia, Federated States of (868)

In Thousands of U.S. Dollars (USD) / Fiscal Year Ends September 30th

		Budgetary Central Government			Central Government (excl. Social Security)			Central Government (incl. Social Security)			General Government		
		2013	2014	2015	2013	2014	2015	2013	2014	2015	2013	2014	2015
33	**Net incurrence of liabilities**	**-5,241**	**-8,813**	**8,637**	...	...	...	...	...	...	...	...	...
331	Domestic creditors	-6,168	-8,431	9,032	...	...	...	...	...	...	...	...	...
8311	General government	...	...	...	...	...	...	...	...	...	...	...	...
8312	Central bank	...	...	...	...	...	...	...	...	...	...	...	...
8313	Deposit-taking corporations except the central bank	...	...	...	...	...	...	...	...	...	...	...	...
8314	Other financial corporations	...	...	...	...	...	...	...	...	...	...	...	...
8315	Nonfinancial corporations	...	...	...	...	...	...	...	...	...	...	...	...
8316	Households & nonprofit institutions serving households	...	...	...	...	...	...	...	...	...	...	...	...
332	External creditors	927	-383	-395	...	...	...	...	...	...	...	...	...
8321	General government	...	...	...	...	...	...	...	...	...	...	...	...
8327	International organizations	...	...	...	...	...	...	...	...	...	...	...	...
8328	Financial corporations other than international organizations	...	...	...	...	...	...	...	...	...	...	...	...
8329	Other nonresidents	...	...	...	...	...	...	...	...	...	...	...	...
	Table 9 Total other economic flows in assets and liabilities												

Moldova (921)

In Millions of Moldovan Lei (MDL) / Fiscal Year Ends December 31st

		Budgetary Central Government			Central Government (excl. Social Security)			Central Government (incl. Social Security)			General Government		
		2013	2014	2015	2013	2014	2015	2013	2014	2015	2013	2014	2015
	Statement of operations												
1	Revenue	22,437	27,718	28,055	22,437	27,718	28,055	32,197	38,495	40,179	36,900	42,447	43,681
2	Expense	22,475	27,945	29,300	22,475	27,945	29,300	32,427	38,755	41,572	35,125	39,661	43,154
GOB	**Gross operating balance**	**-39**	**-227**	**-1,246**	**-39**	**-227**	**-1,246**	**-230**	**-259**	**-1,393**	**1,774**	**2,786**	**527**
NOB	**Net operating balance**	...	...	...	...	...	...	...	...	...	...	...	...
31	Net/Gross investment in nonfinancial assets	1,518	1,545	985	1,518	1,545	985	1,518	1,545	985	3,604	4,819	3,386
2M	Expenditure	23,994	29,490	30,285	23,994	29,490	30,285	33,945	40,300	42,557	38,729	44,480	46,540
NLB	**Net lending (+) / Net borrowing (-)**	**-1,557**	**-1,772**	**-2,231**	**-1,557**	**-1,772**	**-2,231**	**-1,748**	**-1,805**	**-2,378**	**-1,830**	**-2,033**	**-2,859**
32	Net acquisition of financial assets	-315	153	40	-315	153	40	-506	121	-108	-584	-81	-367
33	Net incurrence of liabilities	1,242	1,925	2,271	1,242	1,925	2,271	1,242	1,925	2,271	1,246	1,953	2,492
NLBz	Statistical discrepancy	—	—	—	—	—	—	—	—	—	—	—	—
	Memorandum items												
PB	Primary net lending / net borrowing	-1,064	-1,180	-1,188	-1,064	-1,180	-1,188	-1,256	-1,213	-1,335	-1,303	-1,409	-1,760
GB	Government balance per national definition	...	...	...	...	...	...	...	...	...	...	...	...
	Statement of other economic flows												
9	**Change in net worth due to other economic flows**	...	...	...	—	...	...	...	...	...	—	...	...
4	Change in net worth due to holding gains and losses	...	...	**-4,084**	...	...	**-4,084**	...	...	**-4,084**	...	...	**-4,129**
41	Nonfinancial assets	...	...	—	...	...	—	...	...	—	...	...	—
42	Financial assets	...	...	—	—	...	—	...	...	—	—	...	—
43	Liabilities	...	...	4,084	—	...	4,084	...	...	4,084	—	...	4,129
5	Change in net worth due to volume changes	...	...	...	...	...	...	...	...	...	...	...	...
51	Nonfinancial assets	...	...	...	...	...	...	...	...	...	...	...	...
52	Financial assets	...	...	...	—	...	...	...	...	...	—	...	...
53	Liabilities	...	2,078	...	—	2,078	...	...	2,078	...	—	2,101	...
	Balance sheet												
6	**Net worth**	**22,578**	**23,200**	**20,454**	**22,578**	**23,200**	**20,454**	**23,210**	**23,821**	**20,934**	**59,784**	**63,544**	**63,736**
61	Nonfinancial assets	12,805	14,499	16,525	12,805	14,499	16,525	13,074	14,790	16,821	40,264	45,161	50,560
62	Financial assets	33,582	36,500	34,930	33,582	36,500	34,930	33,945	36,831	35,114	43,741	46,616	44,901
63	Liabilities	23,809	27,800	31,001	23,809	27,800	31,001	23,809	27,800	31,001	24,221	28,234	31,724
	Table 1 Revenue												
1	**Revenue**	**22,437**	**27,718**	**28,055**	**22,437**	**27,718**	**28,055**	**32,197**	**38,495**	**40,179**	**36,900**	**42,447**	**43,681**
11	**Taxes**	**18,491**	**22,208**	**23,905**	**18,491**	**22,208**	**23,905**	**18,491**	**22,208**	**23,905**	**22,934**	**25,498**	**26,624**
111	Taxes on income, profits, and capital gains	801	2,626	3,983	801	2,626	3,983	801	2,626	3,983	4,258	4,878	5,554
1111	Payable by individuals	—	789	1,211	—	789	1,211	—	789	1,211	2,206	2,447	2,745
1112	Payable by corporations and other enterprises	801	1,837	2,772	801	1,837	2,772	801	1,837	2,772	2,053	2,431	2,808
1113	Other taxes on income, profits, and capital gains	—	—	—	—	—	—	—	—	—	—	—	—
112	Taxes on payroll and workforce	—	—	—	—	—	—	—	—	—	—	—	—
113	Taxes on property	1	2	0	1	2	0	1	2	0	317	346	361
114	Taxes on goods and services	16,272	18,122	18,594	16,272	18,122	18,594	16,272	18,122	18,594	16,942	18,817	19,381
1141	General taxes on goods and services	12,130	12,815	13,672	12,130	12,815	13,672	12,130	12,815	13,672	12,174	12,852	13,714
1142	Excises	3,501	3,427	3,844	3,501	3,427	3,844	3,501	3,427	3,844	3,508	3,428	3,844
115	Taxes on international trade and transactions	1,417	1,458	1,328	1,417	1,458	1,328	1,417	1,458	1,328	1,417	1,458	1,328
116	Other taxes	—	—	—	—	—	—	—	—	—	—	—	—
12	**Social contributions**	—	—	—	—	—	—	**9,723**	**10,777**	**12,128**	**9,723**	**10,777**	**12,128**
121	Social security contributions	—	—	—	—	—	—	9,723	10,777	12,128	9,723	10,777	12,128
122	Other social contributions	—	—	—	—	—	—	—	—	—	—	—	—
13	**Grants**	**2,198**	**3,883**	**1,763**	**2,198**	**3,883**	**1,763**	**2,197**	**3,855**	**1,743**	**1,947**	**3,914**	**1,906**
131	From foreign governments	1,893	3,826	1,710	1,893	3,826	1,710	1,893	3,826	1,710	1,947	3,914	1,906
132	From international organizations	—	—	—	—	—	—	—	—	—	—	—	—
133	From other general government units	305	57	53	305	57	53	304	29	33	0	—	—
1331	Current	278	2	1	278	2	1	279	2	1	0	—	—
1332	Capital	28	56	52	28	56	52	25	27	32	0	—	—
14	**Other revenue**	**1,747**	**1,627**	**2,386**	**1,747**	**1,627**	**2,386**	**1,785**	**1,656**	**2,403**	**2,295**	**2,258**	**3,024**

Moldova (921)

In Millions of Moldovan Lei (MDL) / Fiscal Year Ends December 31st

		Budgetary Central Government			Central Government (excl. Social Security)			Central Government (incl. Social Security)			General Government		
		2013	2014	2015	2013	2014	2015	2013	2014	2015	2013	2014	2015
	Table 2 Expense by economic type												
2	**Expense**	**22,475**	**27,945**	**29,300**	**22,475**	**27,945**	**29,300**	**32,427**	**38,755**	**41,572**	**35,125**	**39,661**	**43,154**
21	**Compensation of employees**	**3,875**	**4,253**	**4,738**	**3,875**	**4,253**	**4,738**	**3,875**	**4,253**	**4,738**	**8,297**	**9,089**	**10,300**
211	Wages and salaries	3,339	3,671	4,101	3,339	3,671	4,101	3,339	3,671	4,101	6,871	7,519	8,514
212	Employers' social contributions	537	582	637	537	582	637	537	582	637	1,426	1,570	1,785
22	**Use of goods and services**	**3,235**	**3,345**	**3,025**	**3,235**	**3,345**	**3,025**	**7,460**	**7,996**	**8,157**	**9,260**	**9,960**	**10,200**
23	**Consumption of fixed capital**	...	...	...	...	...	...	...	...	...	...	...	...
24	**Interest**	**493**	**592**	**1,043**	**493**	**592**	**1,043**	**493**	**592**	**1,043**	**527**	**624**	**1,099**
25	**Subsidies**	**786**	**1,015**	**637**	**786**	**1,015**	**637**	**786**	**1,015**	**637**	**1,119**	**1,358**	**1,022**
26	**Grants**	**9,429**	**12,967**	**13,855**	**9,429**	**12,967**	**13,855**	**4,439**	**7,107**	**7,504**	**—**	**—**	**—**
261	To foreign governments	—	—	—	—	—	—	—	—	—	—	—	—
262	To international organizations	—	—	—	—	—	—	—	—	—	—	—	—
263	To other general government units	9,429	12,967	13,855	9,429	12,967	13,855	4,439	7,107	7,504	0	—	—
2631	Current	9,136	11,776	13,399	9,136	11,776	13,399	4,147	5,915	7,048	0	—	—
2632	Capital	293	1,191	456	293	1,191	456	293	1,191	456	0	—	—
27	**Social benefits**	**1,115**	**1,171**	**1,254**	**1,115**	**1,171**	**1,254**	**11,831**	**13,190**	**14,744**	**12,173**	**13,562**	**15,226**
271	Social security benefits	798	844	904	798	844	904	11,515	10,371	11,159	11,515	10,371	11,159
272	Social assistance benefits	168	175	152	168	175	152	168	2,667	3,387	486	3,018	3,789
273	Employment-related social benefits	149	152	199	149	152	199	149	152	199	173	173	278
28	**Other expense**	**3,544**	**4,603**	**4,748**	**3,544**	**4,603**	**4,748**	**3,544**	**4,603**	**4,748**	**3,749**	**5,067**	**5,308**
281	Property expense other than interest	—	—	—	—	—	—	—	—	—	—	—	—
282	Transfers not elsewhere classified	3,544	4,603	4,748	3,544	4,603	4,748	3,544	4,603	4,748	3,749	5,067	5,308
2821	Current	2,827	284	4,392	2,827	284	4,392	2,827	284	4,392	2,908	391	4,707
2822	Capital	717	4,319	357	717	4,319	357	717	4,319	357	841	4,677	601
	Table 3 Transactions in assets and liabilities												
3	**Change in net worth from transactions**	...	...	...	...	...	...	...	...	...	...	...	...
31	**Net/Gross investment in nonfinancial assets**	**1,518**	**1,545**	**985**	**1,518**	**1,545**	**985**	**1,518**	**1,545**	**985**	**3,604**	**4,819**	**3,386**
311	Fixed assets	892	890	384	892	890	384	892	890	384	2,145	3,243	1,923
3111	Buildings and structures	892	890	...	892	890	...	892	890	...	2,145	3,243	...
3112	Machinery and equipment	—	—	...	—	—	...	—	—	...	—	—	...
3113	Other fixed assets	—	—	...	—	—	...	—	—	...	—	—	...
3114	Weapons systems	—	—	...	—	—	...	—	—	...	—	—	...
312	Inventories	626	655	602	626	655	602	626	655	602	1,459	1,575	1,463
313	Valuables	—	—	—	—	—	—	—	—	—	—	—	—
314	Nonproduced assets	—	—	—	—	—	—	—	—	—	0	1	0
3141	Land	—	—	—	—	—	—	—	—	—	0	1	0
3142	Mineral and energy resources	—	—	—	—	—	—	—	—	—	—	—	—
3143	Other naturally occurring assets	—	—	—	—	—	—	—	—	—	—	—	—
3144	Intangible nonproduced assets	—	—	—	—	—	—	—	—	—	—	—	—
32	**Net acquisition of financial assets**	**-315**	**153**	**40**	**-315**	**153**	**40**	**-506**	**121**	**-108**	**-584**	**-81**	**-367**
	By instrument												
3201	Monetary gold and SDRs	—	—	—	—	—	—	—	—	—	—	—	—
3202	Currency and deposits	-130	486	259	-130	486	259	-321	454	112	-186	434	-4
3203	Debt securities	—	—	—	—	—	—	—	—	—	—	—	—
3204	Loans	-87	-161	-202	-87	-161	-202	-87	-161	-202	-82	-147	-171
3205	Equity and investment fund shares	-98	-173	-17	-98	-173	-17	-98	-173	-17	-316	-367	-193
3206	Insurance, pension, and standardized guarantee schemes	—	—	—	—	—	—	—	—	—	—	—	—
3207	Financial derivatives and employee stock options	—	—	—	—	—	—	—	—	—	—	—	—
3208	Other accounts receivable	...	...	...	...	...	...	...	...	...	...	...	...
	By debtor												
321	Domestic debtors	-315	153	40	-315	153	40	-506	121	-108	-584	-81	-367
322	External debtors	—	—	—	—	—	—	—	—	—	—	—	—
33	**Net incurrence of liabilities**	**1,242**	**1,925**	**2,271**	**1,242**	**1,925**	**2,271**	**1,242**	**1,925**	**2,271**	**1,246**	**1,953**	**2,492**
	By instrument												
3301	Special Drawing Rights (SDRs)	—	—	—	—	—	—	—	—	—	—	—	—
3302	Currency and deposits	—	—	—	—	—	—	—	—	—	—	—	—
3303	Debt securities	517	400	150	517	400	150	517	400	150	517	400	150
3304	Loans	588	1,427	1,914	588	1,427	1,914	588	1,427	1,914	585	1,449	2,132

Moldova (921)

In Millions of Moldovan Lei (MDL) / Fiscal Year Ends December 31st

		Budgetary Central Government			Central Government (excl. Social Security)			Central Government (incl. Social Security)			General Government		
		2013	2014	2015	2013	2014	2015	2013	2014	2015	2013	2014	2015
3305	Equity and investment fund shares	—	—	—	—	—	—	—	—	—	—	—	—
3306	Insurance, pension, and standardized guarantee schemes	—	—	—	—	—	—	—	—	—	—	—	—
3307	Financial derivatives and employee stock options	—	—	—	—	—	—	—	—	—	—	—	—
3308	Other accounts payable	137	98	207	137	98	207	137	98	207	144	104	211
	By creditor												
331	Domestic creditors	654	498	465	654	498	465	654	498	465	729	522	625
332	External creditors	588	1,427	1,806	588	1,427	1,806	588	1,427	1,806	516	1,431	1,867
	Table 4 Holding gains and losses in assets and liabilities												
4	**Change in net worth due to holding gains and losses**	...	...	**-4,084**	...	...	**-4,084**	...	...	**-4,084**	...	...	**-4,129**
41	**Holding gains and losses in nonfinancial assets**	...	...	—	...	...	—	...	...	—	...	...	—
411	Fixed assets	...	...	—	...	...	—	...	...	—	...	...	—
412	Inventories	...	...	—	...	...	—	...	...	—	...	...	—
413	Valuables	...	...	—	...	...	—	...	...	—	...	...	—
414	Nonproduced assets	...	...	—	...	...	—	...	...	—	...	...	—
42	**Holding gains and losses in financial assets**	...	...	—	—	...	—	...	...	—	—	...	—
	By instrument												
4201	Monetary gold and SDRs	...	...	—	—	...	—	...	...	—	—	...	—
4202	Currency and deposits	...	...	—	—	...	—	...	...	—	—	...	—
4203	Debt securities	...	...	—	—	...	—	...	...	—	—	...	—
4204	Loans	...	...	—	—	...	—	...	...	—	—	...	—
4205	Equity and investment fund shares	...	...	—	—	...	—	...	...	—	—	...	—
4206	Insurance, pension, and standardized guarantee schemes	...	...	—	—	...	—	...	...	—	—	...	—
4207	Financial derivatives and employee stock options	...	...	—	—	...	—	...	...	—	—	...	—
4208	Other accounts receivable	...	...	—	—	...	—	...	...	—	—	...	—
	By debtor												
421	Domestic debtors	...	...	—	—	...	—	...	...	—	—	...	—
422	External debtors	...	...	—	—	...	—	...	...	—	—	...	—
43	**Holding gains and losses in liabilities**	...	...	**4,084**	—	...	**4,084**	...	...	**4,084**	—	...	**4,129**
	By instrument												
4301	Special Drawing Rights (SDRs)	...	...	547	—	...	547	...	...	547	—	...	547
4302	Currency and deposits	...	...	—	—	...	—	...	...	—	—	...	—
4303	Debt securities	...	...	—	—	...	—	...	...	—	—	...	—
4304	Loans	...	...	3,537	—	...	3,537	...	...	3,537	—	...	3,582
4305	Equity and investment fund shares	...	...	—	—	...	—	...	...	—	—	...	—
4306	Insurance, pension, and standardized guarantee schemes	...	...	—	—	...	—	...	...	—	—	...	—
4307	Financial derivatives and employee stock options	...	...	—	—	...	—	...	...	—	—	...	—
4308	Other accounts payable	...	...	—	—	...	—	...	...	—	—	...	—
	By creditor												
431	Domestic creditors	...	...	—	—	...	—	...	...	—	—	...	—
432	External creditors	...	...	4,084	—	...	4,084	...	...	4,084	—	...	4,129
	Table 5 Holding gains and losses in assets and liabilities												
5	**Change in net worth due to other volume changes**	...	...	...	...	...	...	...	...	...	...	...	...
51	**Other volume changes in nonfinancial assets**	...	...	...	...	...	...	...	...	...	...	...	...
511	Fixed assets	...	...	...	...	...	...	...	...	...	...	...	...
512	Inventories	...	...	...	...	...	...	...	...	...	...	...	...
513	Valuables	...	...	...	...	...	...	...	...	...	...	...	...
514	Nonproduced assets	...	...	...	...	...	...	...	...	...	...	...	...
52	**Other volume changes in financial assets**	...	...	...	—	...	...	...	...	...	—	...	...

		Budgetary Central Government			Central Government (excl. Social Security)			Central Government (incl. Social Security)			General Government		
		2013	2014	2015	2013	2014	2015	2013	2014	2015	2013	2014	2015
	By instrument												
5201	Monetary gold and SDRs	...	...	...	—	...	...	...	...	...	—	...	...
5202	Currency and deposits	...	...	...	—	...	...	...	...	...	—	...	...
5203	Debt securities	...	...	...	—	...	...	...	...	...	—	...	...
5204	Loans	...	...	...	—	...	...	...	...	...	—	...	...
5205	Equity and investment fund shares	...	...	...	—	...	...	...	...	...	—	...	...
5206	Insurance, pension, and standardized guarantee schemes	...	...	...	—	...	...	...	...	...	—	...	...
5207	Financial derivatives and employee stock options	...	...	...	—	...	...	...	...	...	—	...	...
5208	Other accounts receivable	...	...	...	—	...	...	...	...	...	—	...	...
	By debtor												
521	Domestic debtors	...	...	...	—	...	...	...	...	...	—	...	...
522	External debtors	...	...	...	—	...	...	...	...	...	—	...	...
53	**Other volume changes in liabilities**	**...**	**2,078**	**...**	**—**	**2,078**	**...**	**...**	**2,078**	**...**	**—**	**2,101**	**...**
	By instrument												
5301	Special Drawing Rights (SDRs)	...	295	...	—	295	...	...	295	...	—	295	...
5302	Currency and deposits	...	—	...	—	...	...	...	—	...	—	—	...
5303	Debt securities	...	—	...	—	...	...	...	—	...	—	—	...
5304	Loans	...	1,782	...	—	1,782	...	...	1,782	...	—	1,806	...
5305	Equity and investment fund shares	...	—	...	—	...	...	...	—	...	—	—	...
5306	Insurance, pension, and standardized guarantee schemes	...	—	...	—	...	...	...	—	...	—	—	...
5307	Financial derivatives and employee stock options	...	—	...	—	...	...	...	—	...	—	—	...
5308	Other accounts payable	...	—	...	—	...	...	...	—	...	—	—	...
	By creditor												
531	Domestic creditors	...	...	...	—	...	...	...	—	...	—	—	...
532	External creditors	...	...	...	—	...	...	...	2,078	...	—	2,101	...
	Table 6 Balance sheet												
6	**Net worth**	**22,578**	**23,200**	**20,454**	**22,578**	**23,200**	**20,454**	**23,210**	**23,821**	**20,934**	**59,784**	**63,544**	**63,736**
61	**Nonfinancial assets**	**12,805**	**14,499**	**16,525**	**12,805**	**14,499**	**16,525**	**13,074**	**14,790**	**16,821**	**40,264**	**45,161**	**50,560**
611	Fixed assets	10,559	12,005	13,455	10,559	12,005	13,455	10,822	12,278	13,734	34,455	38,513	43,067
6111	Buildings and structures	5,857	6,253	6,405	5,857	6,253	6,405	5,978	6,382	6,539	26,657	29,283	30,926
6112	Machinery and equipment	2,555	3,065	3,832	2,555	3,065	3,832	2,569	3,132	3,898	3,181	3,821	5,054
6113	Other fixed assets	2,147	2,687	3,219	2,147	2,687	3,219	2,275	2,763	3,298	4,618	5,409	7,087
6114	Weapons systems	—	—	—	—	—	—	—	—	—	—	—	—
612	Inventories	944	1,006	1,528	944	1,006	1,528	949	1,011	1,534	1,138	1,213	1,992
613	Valuables	—	—	—	—	—	—	—	—	—	—	—	—
614	Nonproduced assets	1,302	1,489	1,542	1,302	1,489	1,542	1,302	1,501	1,553	4,671	5,435	5,502
6141	Land	1,302	1,489	1,542	1,302	1,489	1,542	1,302	1,501	1,553	4,671	5,435	5,502
6142	Mineral and energy resources	—	—	—	—	—	—	—	—	—	—	—	—
6143	Other naturally occurring assets	—	—	—	—	—	—	—	—	—	—	—	—
6144	Intangible nonproduced assets	—	—	—	—	—	—	—	—	—	—	—	—
62	**Financial assets**	**33,582**	**36,500**	**34,930**	**33,582**	**36,500**	**34,930**	**33,945**	**36,831**	**35,114**	**43,741**	**46,616**	**44,901**
	By instrument												
6201	Monetary gold and SDRs	—	—	—	—	—	—	—	—	—	—	—	—
6202	Currency and deposits	1,620	2,106	2,328	1,620	2,106	2,328	1,983	2,437	2,511	2,816	3,250	3,208
6203	Debt securities	—	—	—	—	—	—	—	—	—	—	—	—
6204	Loans	4,259	4,828	5,821	4,259	4,828	5,821	4,259	4,828	5,821	3,932	4,368	5,101
6205	Equity and investment fund shares	25,868	27,614	24,957	25,868	27,614	24,957	25,868	27,614	24,957	35,159	37,046	34,763
6206	Insurance, pension, and standardized guarantee schemes	—	—	—	—	—	—	—	—	—	—	—	—
6207	Financial derivatives and employee stock options	—	—	—	—	—	—	—	—	—	—	—	—
6208	Other accounts receivable	1,835	1,952	1,824	1,835	1,952	1,824	1,835	1,952	1,824	1,835	1,953	1,828
	By debtor												
621	Domestic debtors	33,582	36,500	34,930	33,582	36,500	34,930	33,945	36,831	35,114	43,741	46,616	44,901
622	External debtors	—	—	—	—	—	—	—	—	—	—	—	—
63	**Liabilities**	**23,809**	**27,800**	**31,001**	**23,809**	**27,800**	**31,001**	**23,809**	**27,800**	**31,001**	**24,221**	**28,234**	**31,724**

Moldova (921)

In Millions of Moldovan Lei (MDL) / Fiscal Year Ends December 31st

		Budgetary Central Government			Central Government (excl. Social Security)			Central Government (incl. Social Security)			General Government		
		2013	2014	2015	2013	2014	2015	2013	2014	2015	2013	2014	2015
	By instrument												
6301	Special Drawing Rights (SDRs)	—	—	—	—	—	—	—	—	—	—	—	—
6302	Currency and deposits	—	—	—	—	—	—	—	—	—	—	—	—
6303	Debt securities	6,676	7,075	7,225	6,676	7,075	7,225	6,676	7,075	7,225	6,676	7,075	7,225
6304	Loans	16,846	20,395	23,075	16,846	20,395	23,075	14,479	17,733	23,075	17,258	20,856	23,795
6305	Equity and investment fund shares	—	—	—	—	—	—	—	—	—	—	—	—
6306	Insurance, pension, and standardized guarantee schemes	—	—	—	—	—	—	—	—	—	—	—	—
6307	Financial derivatives and employee stock options	—	—	—	—	—	—	—	—	—	—	—	—
6308	Other accounts payable	287	329	701	287	329	701	287	329	701	287	302	704
	By creditor												
631	Domestic creditors	6,963	7,404	7,927	6,963	7,404	7,927	6,963	7,404	7,927	7,179	7,616	8,322
632	External creditors	16,846	20,395	26,284	16,846	20,395	26,284	16,846	20,395	26,284	17,042	20,618	26,612
	Memorandum items												
6M2	Net financial worth	9,773	8,700	3,929	9,773	8,700	3,929	10,137	9,031	4,113	19,520	18,383	13,176
6M3	Gross debt (D4) at market value	...	...	...	...	...	...	...	...	...	...	...	...
6M3D3	D3 debt liabilities at market value	...	...	...	...	...	...	...	...	...	...	...	...
6M3D2	D2 debt liabilities at market value	...	...	...	...	...	...	...	...	...	...	...	...
6M3D1	D1 debt liabilities at market value	...	...	...	...	...	...	...	...	...	...	...	...
6M4	Gross debt (D4) at nominal value	23,809	27,800	31,001	23,809	27,800	31,001	21,442	25,137	31,001	24,221	28,234	31,724
6M4D3	D3 debt liabilities at nominal value	23,809	27,800	31,001	23,809	27,800	31,001	21,442	25,137	31,001	24,221	28,234	31,724
6M4D2	D2 debt liabilities at nominal value	23,522	27,471	30,300	23,522	27,471	30,300	21,155	24,808	30,300	23,934	27,932	31,020
6M4D1	D1 debt liabilities at nominal value	23,522	27,471	30,300	23,522	27,471	30,300	21,155	24,808	30,300	23,934	27,932	31,020
6M35	Gross debt (D4) at face value	...	...	...	...	...	...	...	...	...	...	...	...
6M35D3	D3 debt liabilities at face value	...	...	...	...	...	...	...	...	...	...	...	...
6M35D2	D2 debt liabilities at face value	...	...	...	...	...	...	...	...	...	...	...	...
6M35D1	D1 debt liabilities at face value	...	...	...	...	...	...	...	...	...	...	...	...
6M93	Government gross debt per national definition	...	...	...	...	...	...	...	...	...	...	...	...
6M5	Arrears	...	...	...	...	...	...	...	...	...	...	...	...
6M6	Explicit contingent liabilities	...	...	...	...	...	...	...	...	...	...	...	...
6M61	of which: Publicly guaranteed debt	...	...	...	...	...	...	...	...	...	...	...	...
6M7	Net implicit obligations for social security benefits	...	...	...	...	...	...	...	...	...	...	...	...
	Table 7 Expenditure by functions of government												
7	**Expenditure**	**23,994**	**29,490**	**30,285**	**23,994**	**29,490**	**30,285**	**33,945**	**40,300**	**42,557**	**38,729**	**44,480**	**46,540**
701	**General public services**	**6,859**	**7,588**	**4,474**	**6,859**	**7,588**	**4,474**	**6,859**	**7,588**	**4,474**	**3,753**	**3,977**	**4,574**
7017	Public debt transactions	493	592	1,043	493	592	1,043	493	592	1,043	527	624	1,099
7018	Transfers of general character between levels of government	4,114	4,702	1,079	4,114	4,702	1,079	4,114	4,702	1,079	—	—	—
702	**Defense**	**328**	**401**	**450**	**328**	**401**	**450**	**328**	**401**	**450**	**336**	**409**	**460**
703	**Public order and safety**	**2,439**	**2,800**	**2,985**	**2,439**	**2,800**	**2,985**	**2,439**	**2,800**	**2,985**	**2,442**	**2,806**	**3,003**
704	**Economic affairs**	**4,115**	**5,415**	**4,387**	**4,115**	**5,415**	**4,387**	**4,115**	**5,415**	**4,387**	**4,626**	**6,168**	**5,267**
7042	Agriculture, forestry, fishing, and hunting	1,364	1,462	1,110	1,364	1,462	1,110	1,364	1,462	1,110	1,390	1,480	1,126
7043	Fuel and energy	243	130	39	243	130	39	243	130	39	253	143	42
7044	Mining, manufacturing, and construction	37	3	3	37	3	3	37	3	3	58	3	3
7045	Transport	2,241	2,875	1,714	2,241	2,875	1,714	2,241	2,875	1,714	2,680	3,464	2,430
7046	Communication	—	—	—	—	—	—	—	—	—	—	—	—
705	**Environmental protection**	**401**	**566**	**176**	**401**	**566**	**176**	**401**	**566**	**176**	**391**	**579**	**450**
706	**Housing and community amenities**	**351**	**427**	**382**	**351**	**427**	**382**	**351**	**427**	**382**	**1,172**	**1,497**	**1,036**
707	**Health**	**3,067**	**3,302**	**3,390**	**3,067**	**3,302**	**3,390**	**5,130**	**5,753**	**6,324**	**5,227**	**5,890**	**6,456**
7072	Outpatient services	2	2	3	2	2	3	2	2,033	2,316	5	2,046	2,320
7073	Hospital services	—	—	—	—	—	—	—	2,196	2,401	1	2,202	2,407
7074	Public health services	3,056	3,205	3,285	3,056	3,205	3,285	5,119	1,180	1,279	5,208	1,188	1,288
708	**Recreation, culture and religion**	**377**	**373**	**540**	**377**	**373**	**540**	**377**	**373**	**540**	**1,020**	**1,185**	**1,116**
709	**Education**	**1,816**	**3,427**	**7,721**	**1,816**	**3,427**	**7,721**	**1,816**	**3,427**	**7,721**	**7,064**	**7,824**	**8,462**
7091	Pre-primary and primary education	12	1,615	5,833	12	1,615	5,833	12	1,615	5,833	1,787	2,118	2,474
7092	Secondary education	1,037	607	621	1,037	607	621	1,037	607	621	4,045	3,993	4,171
7094	Tertiary education	707	703	739	707	703	739	707	703	739	707	703	739

Moldova (921)

In Millions of Moldovan Lei (MDL) / Fiscal Year Ends December 31st

		Budgetary Central Government			Central Government (excl. Social Security)			Central Government (incl. Social Security)			General Government		
		2013	2014	2015	2013	2014	2015	2013	2014	2015	2013	2014	2015
710	**Social protection**	4,243	5,190	5,781	4,243	5,190	5,781	12,131	13,550	15,118	12,696	14,145	15,717
7z	Statistical discrepancy: Expenditure	...	...	...	...	...	...	...	...	...	...	...	...
	Table 8 Financial transactions by counterpart sector												
32	**Net acquisition of financial assets**	-315	153	40	-315	153	40	-506	121	-108	-584	-81	-367
321	Domestic debtors	-315	153	40	-315	153	40	-506	121	-108	-584	-81	-367
8211	General government	...	...	...	...	...	...	...	...	...	...	...	...
8212	Central bank	...	...	...	...	...	...	...	...	...	...	...	...
8213	Deposit-taking corporations except the central bank	...	...	...	...	...	...	...	...	...	...	...	...
8214	Other financial corporations	...	...	...	...	...	...	...	...	...	...	...	...
8215	Nonfinancial corporations	...	...	-220	...	...	-220	...	...	-220	...	...	-406
8216	Households & nonprofit institutions serving households	...	...	...	...	...	...	...	...	...	...	...	...
322	External debtors	—	—	—	—	—	—	—	—	—	—	—	—
8221	General government	—	—	—	—	—	—	—	—	—	—	—	—
8227	International organizations	—	—	—	—	—	—	—	—	—	—	—	—
8228	Financial corporations other than international organizations	—	—	—	—	—	—	—	—	—	—	—	—
8229	Other nonresidents	—	—	—	—	—	—	—	—	—	—	—	—
33	**Net incurrence of liabilities**	1,242	1,925	2,271	1,242	1,925	2,271	1,242	1,925	2,271	1,246	1,953	2,492
331	Domestic creditors	654	498	465	654	498	465	654	498	465	729	522	625
8311	General government	...	...	—	...	...	—	...	...	—	...	...	—
8312	Central bank	...	...	—	...	...	—	...	...	—	...	...	—
8313	Deposit-taking corporations except the central bank	...	...	150	...	...	150	...	...	150	...	...	176
8314	Other financial corporations	...	...	—	...	...	—	...	...	—	...	...	—
8315	Nonfinancial corporations	...	...	315	...	...	315	...	...	315	...	...	450
8316	Households & nonprofit institutions serving households	...	...	—	...	...	—	...	...	—	...	...	—
332	External creditors	588	1,427	1,806	588	1,427	1,806	588	1,427	1,806	516	1,431	1,867
8321	General government	...	...	466	...	...	466	...	...	466	...	...	466
8327	International organizations	...	...	1,357	...	...	1,357	...	...	1,357	...	...	1,418
8328	Financial corporations other than international organizations	...	...	-18	...	...	-18	...	...	-18	...	...	-18
8329	Other nonresidents	...	...	—	...	...	—	...	...	—	...	...	—
	Table 9 Total other economic flows in assets and liabilities												
9	**Change in net worth due to other economic flows**	...	...	...	—	...	...	...	...	...	—	...	...
91	**Other economic flows in nonfinancial assets**	...	...	...	—	...	...	...	...	...	—	...	...
911	Fixed assets	...	...	...	—	...	...	...	...	...	—	...	...
912	Inventories	...	...	...	—	...	...	...	...	...	—	...	...
913	Valuables	...	...	...	—	...	...	...	...	...	—	...	...
914	Nonproduced assets	...	...	...	—	...	...	...	...	...	—	...	...
92	**Other economic flows in financial assets**	...	...	...	—	...	...	...	...	...	—	...	...
	By instrument												
9201	Monetary gold and SDRs	...	...	...	—	...	...	...	...	...	—	...	...
9202	Currency and deposits	...	...	...	—	...	...	...	...	...	—	...	...
9203	Debt securities	...	...	...	—	...	...	...	...	...	—	...	...
9204	Loans	...	...	...	—	...	...	...	...	...	—	...	...
9205	Equity and investment fund shares	...	...	...	—	...	...	...	...	...	—	...	...
9206	Insurance, pension, and standardized guarantee schemes	...	...	...	—	...	...	...	...	...	—	...	...
9207	Financial derivatives and employee stock options	...	...	...	—	...	...	...	...	...	—	...	...
9208	Other accounts receivable	...	...	...	—	...	...	...	...	...	—	...	...
	By debtor												
921	Domestic debtors	...	...	...	—	...	...	...	...	...	—	...	...
922	External debtors	...	...	...	—	...	...	...	...	...	—	...	...
93	**Other economic flows in liabilities**	...	2,078	...	—	2,078	...	...	2,078	...	—	2,101	...

Moldova (921)

In Millions of Moldovan Lei (MDL) / Fiscal Year Ends December 31st

		Budgetary Central Government			Central Government (excl. Social Security)			Central Government (incl. Social Security)			General Government		
		2013	2014	2015	2013	2014	2015	2013	2014	2015	2013	2014	2015
	By instrument												
9301	Special Drawing Rights (SDRs)	...	295	...	—	295	...	...	295	...	—	295	...
9302	Currency and deposits	...	...	...	—	...	...	...	—	...	—	...	...
9303	Debt securities	...	...	...	—	...	...	...	—	...	—	...	...
9304	Loans	...	1,782	...	—	1,782	...	...	1,782	...	—	1,806	...
9305	Equity and investment fund shares	...	...	...	—	...	...	...	—	...	—	...	...
9306	Insurance, pension, and standardized guarantee schemes	...	...	...	—	...	...	...	—	...	—	...	...
9307	Financial derivatives and employee stock options	...	...	...	—	...	...	...	—	...	—	...	...
9308	Other accounts payable	...	...	...	—	...	...	...	—	...	—	...	...
	By creditor												
931	Domestic creditors	...	...	...	—	...	...	...	—	...	—	...	...
932	External creditors	...	2,078	...	—	2,078	...	...	2,078	...	—	2,101	...
	Memorandum items												
9M2	Change in net financial worth due to other economic flows	...	-2,078	...	—	-2,078	...	...	-2,078	...	...	-2,101	...
9M3	Gross debt (D4) at market value: other economic flows	...	2,078	...	—	2,078	...	...	2,078	...	...	2,101	...
9M3D3	D3 debt liabilities at market value: other economic flows	...	2,078	...	—	2,078	...	...	2,078	...	...	2,101	...
9M3D2	D2 debt liabilities at market value: other economic flows	...	2,078	...	—	2,078	...	...	2,078	...	...	2,101	...
9M3D1	D1 debt liabilities at market value: other economic flows	...	1,782	...	—	1,782	...	...	1,782	...	...	1,806	...

Mongolia (948)

In Billions of Mongolian Togrogs (MNT) / Fiscal Year Ends December 31st

		Budgetary Central Government			Central Government (excl. Social Security)			Central Government (incl. Social Security)			General Government		
		2011	2012	2013	2011	2012	2013	2011	2012	2013	2011	2012	2013
	Statement of operations												
1	Revenue	3,110	3,387	4,010	3,409	3,815	4,392	3,921	4,537	5,321	4,291	5,006	6,085
2	Expense	2,040	3,038	3,484	2,811	3,874	3,750	3,166	4,440	4,449	3,312	4,553	4,697
GOB	**Gross operating balance**	**1,070**	**349**	**527**	**598**	**-59**	**642**	**755**	**96**	**872**	**979**	**453**	**1,387**
NOB	**Net operating balance**	...	...	...	...	...	...	...	...	...	...	...	...
31	Net/Gross investment in nonfinancial assets	1,102	1,277	1,078	1,102	1,277	1,078	1,104	1,279	1,083	1,269	1,525	1,491
2M	Expenditure	3,142	4,315	4,562	3,913	5,152	4,828	4,270	5,720	5,532	4,581	6,078	6,188
NLB	**Net lending (+) / Net borrowing (-)**	**-32**	**-929**	**-551**	**-504**	**-1,336**	**-436**	**-349**	**-1,183**	**-211**	**-290**	**-1,072**	**-103**
32	Net acquisition of financial assets	481	1,529	763	470	1,497	750	626	1,650	975	684	1,761	1,082
33	Net incurrence of liabilities	513	2,457	1,315	974	2,834	1,186	974	2,834	1,186	974	2,834	1,186
NLBz	Statistical discrepancy	0	-0	-0	-0	-0	0	-0	0	0	—	-0	0
	Memorandum items												
PB	Primary net lending / net borrowing	6	-822	-290	-467	-1,210	-166	-311	-1,057	59	-253	-946	167
GB	Government balance per national definition	...	...	...	...	...	...	...	...	...	...	...	...
	Statement of other economic flows												
	Balance sheet												
6	**Net worth**	**7,495**	**8,118**	**2,133**	...	...	**4,459**	...	...	**5,399**	**11,527**	**11,731**	**9,015**
61	Nonfinancial assets	4,287	5,086	4,777	...	...	6,798	...	...	6,817	6,858	7,937	9,270
62	Financial assets	6,785	10,074	6,024	...	...	6,443	...	...	7,380	11,961	15,659	8,893
63	Liabilities	3,576	7,042	8,668	—	—	8,782	...	...	8,798	7,292	11,864	9,148
	Table 1 Revenue												
1	**Revenue**	**3,110**	**3,387**	**4,010**	**3,409**	**3,815**	**4,392**	**3,921**	**4,537**	**5,321**	**4,291**	**5,006**	**6,085**
11	**Taxes**	**2,433**	**2,555**	**3,016**	**2,433**	**2,555**	**3,016**	**2,433**	**2,555**	**3,016**	**2,735**	**2,998**	**3,626**
111	Taxes on income, profits, and capital gains	601	524	660	601	524	660	601	524	660	834	871	1,109
1111	Payable by individuals	—	—	—	—	—	—	—	—	—	232	347	449
1112	Payable by corporations and other enterprises	601	524	660	601	524	660	601	524	660	601	524	660
1113	Other taxes on income, profits, and capital gains	—	0	—	—	0	—	—	0	—	—	0	—
112	Taxes on payroll and workforce	—	—	—	—	—	—	—	—	—	—	—	—
113	Taxes on property	—	—	—	—	—	—	—	—	—	17	22	44
114	Taxes on goods and services	1,440	1,646	1,959	1,440	1,646	1,959	1,440	1,646	1,959	1,470	1,692	2,045
1141	General taxes on goods and services	1,114	1,296	1,435	1,114	1,296	1,435	1,114	1,296	1,435	1,114	1,296	1,435
1142	Excises	294	312	449	294	312	449	294	312	449	294	312	449
115	Taxes on international trade and transactions	337	327	381	337	327	381	337	327	381	337	327	381
116	Other taxes	54	57	16	54	57	16	54	57	16	77	86	47
12	**Social contributions**	—	—	—	—	—	—	**565**	**799**	**1,019**	**565**	**799**	**1,019**
121	Social security contributions	—	—	—	—	—	—	565	799	1,019	565	799	1,019
122	Other social contributions	—	—	—	—	—	—	—	—	—	—	—	—
13	**Grants**	**223**	**352**	**114**	**207**	**339**	**102**	**154**	**261**	**12**	**2**	**25**	—
131	From foreign governments	2	25	—	2	25	—	2	25	—	2	25	—
132	From international organizations	—	—	—	—	—	—	—	—	—	—	—	—
133	From other general government units	221	327	114	206	315	102	153	237	12	—	—	0
1331	Current	221	327	114	206	315	102	153	237	12	—	—	0
1332	Capital	—	—	—	—	—	—	—	—	—	—	—	0
14	**Other revenue**	**455**	**480**	**880**	**769**	**921**	**1,274**	**769**	**921**	**1,274**	**990**	**1,184**	**1,439**
	Table 2 Expense by economic type												
2	**Expense**	**2,040**	**3,038**	**3,484**	**2,811**	**3,874**	**3,750**	**3,166**	**4,440**	**4,449**	**3,312**	**4,553**	**4,697**
21	**Compensation of employees**	**792**	**1,184**	**817**	**792**	**1,184**	**817**	**802**	**1,197**	**831**	**878**	**1,310**	**1,534**
211	Wages and salaries	725	1,084	756	725	1,084	756	733	1,095	768	802	1,197	1,402
212	Employers' social contributions	67	100	61	67	100	61	68	102	63	76	113	132
22	**Use of goods and services**	**611**	**711**	**582**	**611**	**711**	**582**	**612**	**714**	**585**	**702**	**855**	**990**
23	**Consumption of fixed capital**	...	...	...	...	...	...	...	...	...	...	...	...
24	**Interest**	**37**	**107**	**261**	**37**	**126**	**270**	**37**	**126**	**270**	**37**	**126**	**270**
25	**Subsidies**	**87**	**77**	**86**	**87**	**77**	**86**	**90**	**82**	**96**	**96**	**83**	**97**

Mongolia (948)

In Billions of Mongolian Togrogs (MNT) / Fiscal Year Ends December 31st

		Budgetary Central Government			Central Government (excl. Social Security)			Central Government (incl. Social Security)			General Government		
		2011	2012	2013	2011	2012	2013	2011	2012	2013	2011	2012	2013
26	**Grants**	**223**	**480**	**1,394**	**223**	**480**	**1,394**	**48**	**219**	**1,129**	**3**	**3**	**4**
261	To foreign governments	—	—	—	—	—	—	—	—	—	—	—	—
262	To international organizations	2	2	4	2	2	4	2	2	4	3	3	4
263	To other general government units	220	478	1,390	220	478	1,390	45	217	1,126	—	—	0
2631	Current	220	478	1,390	220	478	1,390	45	217	1,126	—	—	0
2632	Capital	—	—	—	—	—	—	—	—	—	—	—	0
27	**Social benefits**	**180**	**289**	**278**	**884**	**1,035**	**535**	**1,385**	**1,822**	**1,450**	**1,388**	**1,831**	**1,678**
271	Social security benefits	0	0	0	0	0	0	499	785	913	499	785	922
272	Social assistance benefits	180	289	278	884	1,035	535	886	1,037	537	889	1,046	756
273	Employment-related social benefits	—	—	—	—	—	—	—	—	—	—	—	—
28	**Other expense**	**110**	**190**	**66**	**177**	**261**	**66**	**192**	**280**	**88**	**208**	**346**	**124**
281	Property expense other than interest	—	—	—	—	—	—	—	—	—	—	—	—
282	Transfers not elsewhere classified	110	190	66	177	261	66	192	280	88	208	346	124
2821	Current	110	190	—	177	261	—	177	261	0	181	326	34
2822	Capital	—	—	66	—	—	66	15	19	88	26	20	90
	Table 3 Transactions in assets and liabilities												
3	**Change in net worth from transactions**	...	...	...	...	...	...	...	...	...	...	...	...
31	**Net/Gross investment in nonfinancial assets**	**1,102**	**1,277**	**1,078**	**1,102**	**1,277**	**1,078**	**1,104**	**1,279**	**1,083**	**1,269**	**1,525**	**1,491**
311	Fixed assets	1,068	1,220	1,034	1,068	1,220	1,034	1,071	1,222	1,039	1,230	1,459	1,445
3111	Buildings and structures	1,068	1,220	1,034	1,068	1,220	1,034	1,071	1,222	1,039	1,230	1,459	1,445
3112	Machinery and equipment	—	—	—	—	—	—	—	—	—	—	—	—
3113	Other fixed assets	—	—	—	—	—	—	—	—	—	—	—	—
3114	Weapons systems	—	—	—	—	—	—	—	—	—	—	—	—
312	Inventories	25	50	32	25	50	32	25	50	32	31	59	33
313	Valuables	—	—	—	—	—	—	—	—	—	—	—	—
314	Nonproduced assets	9	7	12	9	7	12	9	7	12	9	7	13
3141	Land	4	4	7	4	4	7	4	4	7	4	4	7
3142	Mineral and energy resources	—	—	5	—	—	5	—	—	5	—	—	6
3143	Other naturally occurring assets	5	3	—	5	3	—	5	3	—	5	3	—
3144	Intangible nonproduced assets	—	—	—	—	—	—	—	—	—	—	—	—
32	**Net acquisition of financial assets**	**481**	**1,529**	**763**	**470**	**1,497**	**750**	**626**	**1,650**	**975**	**684**	**1,761**	**1,082**
	By instrument												
3201	Monetary gold and SDRs	—	—	—	—	—	—	—	—	—	—	—	—
3202	Currency and deposits	10	1,466	642	-1	1,434	628	155	1,587	853	218	1,703	964
3203	Debt securities	—	—	—	—	—	—	—	—	—	—	—	—
3204	Loans	480	64	121	480	64	121	480	64	121	480	64	121
3205	Equity and investment fund shares	-9	-1	—	-9	-1	—	-9	-1	—	-14	-6	-3
3206	Insurance, pension, and standardized guarantee schemes	—	—	—	—	—	—	—	—	—	—	—	—
3207	Financial derivatives and employee stock options	—	—	—	—	—	—	—	—	—	—	—	—
3208	Other accounts receivable	...	...	...	...	...	...	...	...	...	...	...	...
	By debtor												
321	Domestic debtors	481	1,529	763	470	1,497	750	626	1,650	975	684	1,761	1,082
322	External debtors	—	—	—	—	—	—	—	—	—	—	—	—
33	**Net incurrence of liabilities**	**513**	**2,457**	**1,315**	**974**	**2,834**	**1,186**	**974**	**2,834**	**1,186**	**974**	**2,834**	**1,186**
	By instrument												
3301	Special Drawing Rights (SDRs)	—	—	—	—	—	—	—	—	—	—	—	—
3302	Currency and deposits	—	—	—	—	—	—	—	—	—	—	—	—
3303	Debt securities	318	2,275	1,092	318	2,588	1,039	318	2,588	1,039	318	2,588	1,039
3304	Loans	195	183	223	195	183	223	195	183	223	195	183	223
3305	Equity and investment fund shares	—	—	—	—	—	—	—	—	—	—	—	—
3306	Insurance, pension, and standardized guarantee schemes	—	—	—	—	—	—	—	—	—	—	—	—
3307	Financial derivatives and employee stock options	—	—	—	—	—	—	—	—	—	—	—	—
3308	Other accounts payable	...	...	...	461	63	-77	461	63	-77	461	63	-77

Mongolia (948)

In Billions of Mongolian Togrogs (MNT) / Fiscal Year Ends December 31st

		Budgetary Central Government			Central Government (excl. Social Security)			Central Government (incl. Social Security)			General Government		
		2011	2012	2013	2011	2012	2013	2011	2012	2013	2011	2012	2013
	By creditor												
331	Domestic creditors	313	183	1,088	775	559	959	775	559	959	775	559	959
332	External creditors	199	2,274	226	199	2,274	226	199	2,274	226	199	2,274	226
	Table 4 Holding gains and losses in assets and liabilities												
	Table 5 Holding gains and losses in assets and liabilities												
	Table 6 Balance sheet												
6	**Net worth**	**7,495**	**8,118**	**2,133**	**...**	**...**	**4,459**	**...**	**...**	**5,399**	**11,527**	**11,731**	**9,015**
61	**Nonfinancial assets**	**4,287**	**5,086**	**4,777**	**...**	**...**	**6,798**	**...**	**...**	**6,817**	**6,858**	**7,937**	**9,270**
611	Fixed assets	3,821	4,343	4,207	...	...	6,148	...	...	6,165	5,818	6,729	8,506
6111	Buildings and structures	...	...	3,345	...	...	4,895	...	...	4,909	...	...	6,690
6112	Machinery and equipment	...	...	797	...	...	1,012	...	...	1,015	...	...	1,366
6113	Other fixed assets	...	...	65	...	...	242	...	...	242	...	...	450
6114	Weapons systems	...	...	—	...	...	—	...	...	—	...	...	—
612	Inventories	447	722	569	...	...	650	...	...	652	798	1,141	763
613	Valuables	—	—	—	—	—	—	...	...	—	—	—	—
614	Nonproduced assets	19	22	0	...	...	0	...	...	0	243	67	1
6141	Land	0	0	0	—	—	0	...	...	0	1	1	1
6142	Mineral and energy resources	—	—	—	—	—	—	...	...	—	—	—	—
6143	Other naturally occurring assets	—	—	—	—	—	—	...	...	—	—	—	—
6144	Intangible nonproduced assets	19	22	—	...	...	—	...	...	—	242	66	—
62	**Financial assets**	**6,785**	**10,074**	**6,024**	**...**	**...**	**6,443**	**...**	**...**	**7,380**	**11,961**	**15,659**	**8,893**
	By instrument												
6201	Monetary gold and SDRs	—	—	—	—	—	—	...	...	—	—	—	—
6202	Currency and deposits	834	2,679	710	...	...	1,102	...	...	1,922	1,662	3,665	3,276
6203	Debt securities	...	—	2,051	...	—	2,051	...	...	2,051	...	—	2,051
6204	Loans	1,481	393	2,595	...	...	2,603	...	...	2,603	1,481	1,433	2,603
6205	Equity and investment fund shares	3,496	4,059	—	...	...	—	...	...	—	5,764	5,865	—
6206	Insurance, pension, and standardized guarantee schemes	...	—	—	...	—	—	...	...	—	...	—	—
6207	Financial derivatives and employee stock options	...	—	—	...	—	—	...	...	—	...	—	—
6208	Other accounts receivable	915	2,942	668	...	...	687	...	...	804	2,896	4,695	964
	By debtor												
621	Domestic debtors	...	...	6,001	—	—	6,410	...	...	7,348	...	...	7,982
622	External debtors	...	...	22	...	...	32	...	...	32	...	...	911
63	**Liabilities**	**3,576**	**7,042**	**8,668**	**—**	**—**	**8,782**	**...**	**...**	**8,798**	**7,292**	**11,864**	**9,148**
	By instrument												
6301	Special Drawing Rights (SDRs)	—	—	—	—	—	—	...	...	—	—	—	—
6302	Currency and deposits	—	—	—	—	—	—	...	...	—	—	—	—
6303	Debt securities	611	1,510	2,209	—	—	2,209	...	...	2,209	1,410	2,936	2,325
6304	Loans	2,704	5,021	6,125	—	—	6,130	...	...	6,130	3,830	6,401	6,302
6305	Equity and investment fund shares	—	—	—	—	—	—	...	...	—	—	—	—
6306	Insurance, pension, and standardized guarantee schemes	—	—	—	—	—	—	...	...	—	—	—	—
6307	Financial derivatives and employee stock options	—	—	—	—	—	—	...	...	—	—	—	—
6308	Other accounts payable	262	511	334	...	...	443	...	...	459	2,052	2,527	522
	By creditor												
631	Domestic creditors	...	...	4,839	—	—	4,953	...	...	4,970	...	...	5,318
632	External creditors	...	...	3,829	—	—	3,829	...	...	3,829	...	...	3,830
	Memorandum items												
6M2	Net financial worth	3,208	8,118	-2,644	...	...	-2,339	...	...	-1,418	4,669	11,731	-255
6M3	Gross debt (D4) at market value	...	...	...	...	...	...	...	...	...	...	...	...
6M3D3	D3 debt liabilities at market value	...	...	...	...	...	...	...	...	...	...	...	...
6M3D2	D2 debt liabilities at market value	...	...	...	...	...	...	...	...	...	...	...	...
6M3D1	D1 debt liabilities at market value	...	...	...	...	...	...	...	...	...	...	...	...
6M4	Gross debt (D4) at nominal value	...	...	...	...	...	...	...	...	...	...	...	...
6M4D3	D3 debt liabilities at nominal value	...	...	...	...	...	...	...	...	...	...	...	...
6M4D2	D2 debt liabilities at nominal value	...	...	...	...	...	...	...	...	...	...	...	...
6M4D1	D1 debt liabilities at nominal value	...	...	...	...	...	...	...	...	...	...	...	...

Mongolia (948)

In Billions of Mongolian Togrogs (MNT) / Fiscal Year Ends December 31st

		Budgetary Central Government			Central Government (excl. Social Security)			Central Government (incl. Social Security)			General Government		
		2011	2012	2013	2011	2012	2013	2011	2012	2013	2011	2012	2013
6M35	Gross debt (D4) at face value	...	...	...	...	...	...	...	...	...	...	...	...
6M35D3	D3 debt liabilities at face value	...	...	...	...	...	...	...	...	...	...	...	...
6M35D2	D2 debt liabilities at face value	...	...	...	...	...	...	...	...	...	...	...	...
6M35D1	D1 debt liabilities at face value	3,576	7,042	...	...	...	...	...	...	...	7,292	11,864	...
6M93	Government gross debt per national definition	...	...	...	...	...	...	...	...	...	...	...	...
6M5	Arrears	...	...	...	...	...	...	...	...	...	...	...	...
6M6	Explicit contingent liabilities	...	...	...	...	...	...	...	...	...	...	...	...
6M61	of which: Publicly guaranteed debt	...	...	...	...	...	...	...	...	...	...	...	...
6M7	Net implicit obligations for social security benefits	...	...	...	...	...	...	...	...	...	...	...	...
	Table 7 Expenditure by functions of government												
7	**Expenditure**	**3,142**	**4,315**	**4,562**	**3,913**	**5,152**	**4,828**	**4,270**	**5,720**	**5,532**	**4,581**	**6,078**	**6,188**
701	**General public services**	**328**	**1,039**	**...**	**328**	**1,027**	**...**	**—**	**1,039**	**...**	**581**	**661**	**...**
7017	Public debt transactions	37	107	261	37	126	270	37	126	270	37	126	270
7018	Transfers of general character between levels of government	...	...	...	—	—	...	—	...	...	—	—	...
702	**Defense**	**151**	**226**	**...**	**151**	**226**	**...**	**—**	**226**	**...**	**151**	**226**	**...**
703	**Public order and safety**	**199**	**280**	**...**	**199**	**280**	**...**	**—**	**280**	**...**	**199**	**280**	**...**
704	**Economic affairs**	**1,289**	**633**	**...**	**1,289**	**633**	**...**	**1,289**	**633**	**...**	**1,306**	**649**	**...**
7042	Agriculture, forestry, fishing, and hunting	281	104	...	281	104	...	281	104	...	284	107	...
7043	Fuel and energy	154	167	...	154	167	...	154	167	...	154	167	...
7044	Mining, manufacturing, and construction	326	80	...	326	80	...	326	80	...	326	80	...
7045	Transport	...	...	...	...	...	...	...	...	...	...	...	...
7046	Communication	...	...	...	...	...	...	...	...	...	...	...	...
705	**Environmental protection**	**...**	**—**	**...**	**...**	**—**	**...**	**...**	**—**	**...**	**...**	**—**	**...**
706	**Housing and community amenities**	**12**	**45**	**...**	**12**	**45**	**...**	**12**	**45**	**...**	**26**	**71**	**...**
707	**Health**	**329**	**436**	**...**	**329**	**436**	**...**	**329**	**436**	**...**	**329**	**436**	**...**
7072	Outpatient services	...	...	...	...	...	...	...	...	...	...	...	...
7073	Hospital services	...	...	...	...	...	...	...	...	...	...	...	...
7074	Public health services	...	...	...	...	...	...	...	...	...	...	...	...
708	**Recreation, culture and religion**	**81**	**84**	**...**	**81**	**84**	**...**	**81**	**84**	**...**	**82**	**85**	**...**
709	**Education**	**621**	**951**	**...**	**621**	**951**	**...**	**621**	**951**	**...**	**637**	**966**	**...**
7091	Pre-primary and primary education	...	...	...	...	...	...	...	...	...	...	...	...
7092	Secondary education	...	...	...	...	...	...	...	...	...	...	...	...
7094	Tertiary education	...	...	...	...	...	...	...	...	...	...	...	...
710	**Social protection**	**331**	**466**	**...**	**1,135**	**1,307**	**...**	**1,734**	**2,225**	**...**	**1,734**	**2,250**	**...**
7z	Statistical discrepancy: Expenditure	...	155	...	...	...	...	...	-199	...	...	-445	...
	Table 8 Financial transactions by counterpart sector												
32	**Net acquisition of financial assets**	**481**	**1,529**	**763**	**470**	**1,497**	**750**	**626**	**1,650**	**975**	**684**	**1,761**	**1,082**
321	Domestic debtors	481	1,529	763	470	1,497	750	626	1,650	975	684	1,761	1,082
8211	General government	...	...	...	...	...	...	...	...	...	...	...	...
8212	Central bank	...	...	...	...	...	...	...	...	...	...	...	...
8213	Deposit-taking corporations except the central bank	...	...	...	...	...	...	...	...	...	...	...	...
8214	Other financial corporations	...	...	...	...	...	...	...	...	...	...	...	...
8215	Nonfinancial corporations	...	...	...	...	...	...	...	...	...	...	...	...
8216	Households & nonprofit institutions serving households	...	...	...	...	...	...	...	...	...	...	...	...
322	External debtors	—	—	—	—	—	—	—	—	—	—	—	—
8221	General government	—	—	—	—	—	—	—	—	—	—	—	—
8227	International organizations	—	—	—	—	—	—	—	—	—	—	—	—
8228	Financial corporations other than international organizations	—	—	—	—	—	—	—	—	—	—	—	—
8229	Other nonresidents		—	—	—	—	—	—	—	—	—	—	—

Mongolia (948)

In Billions of Mongolian Togrogs (MNT) / Fiscal Year Ends December 31st

		Budgetary Central Government			Central Government (excl. Social Security)			Central Government (incl. Social Security)			General Government		
		2011	2012	2013	2011	2012	2013	2011	2012	2013	2011	2012	2013
33	**Net incurrence of liabilities**	**513**	**2,457**	**1,315**	**974**	**2,834**	**1,186**	**974**	**2,834**	**1,186**	**974**	**2,834**	**1,186**
331	Domestic creditors	313	183	1,088	775	559	959	775	559	959	775	559	959
3311	General government	...	...	...	...	...	...	...	...	...	...	...	...
3312	Central bank	...	...	...	...	...	...	...	...	...	...	...	...
3313	Deposit-taking corporations except the central bank	...	...	...	...	...	...	...	...	...	...	...	...
3314	Other financial corporations	...	...	...	...	...	...	...	...	...	...	...	...
3315	Nonfinancial corporations	...	...	...	...	...	...	...	...	...	...	...	...
3316	Households & nonprofit institutions serving households	...	...	...	...	...	...	...	...	...	...	...	...
332	External creditors	199	2,274	226	199	2,274	226	199	2,274	226	199	2,274	226
3321	General government	...	...	...	...	...	...	...	...	...	...	...	...
3327	International organizations	...	...	...	...	...	...	...	...	...	...	...	...
3328	Financial corporations other than international organizations	...	...	...	...	...	...	...	...	...	...	...	...
3329	Other nonresidents	...	...	...	...	...	...	...	...	...	...	...	...
	Table 9 Total other economic flows in assets and liabilities												

Montserrat (351)

In Thousands of Eastern Caribbean Dollars (XCD) / Fiscal Year Ends December 31st

		Budgetary Central Government			Central Government (excl. Social Security)			Central Government (incl. Social Security)			General Government		
		2012	2013	2014	2012	2013	2014	2012	2013	2014	2012	2013	2014
	Statement of operations												
1	Revenue	139,518	153,919	150,258	...	...	...	...	...	...	...	...	...
2	Expense	111,757	107,740	117,859	...	...	...	...	...	...	...	...	...
GOB	**Gross operating balance**	**27,761**	**46,179**	**32,399**	...	...	...	...	...	...	...	...	...
NOB	**Net operating balance**	...	...	...	...	...	...	...	...	...	...	...	...
31	Net/Gross investment in nonfinancial assets	39,601	73,513	42,200	...	...	...	...	...	...	...	...	...
2M	Expenditure	151,358	181,253	160,059	...	...	...	...	...	...	...	...	...
NLB	**Net lending (+) / Net borrowing (-)**	**-11,840**	**-27,334**	**-9,801**	...	...	...	...	...	...	...	...	...
32	Net acquisition of financial assets	-21,651	-19,769	-6,048	...	...	...	...	...	...	...	...	...
33	Net incurrence of liabilities	-9,811	7,565	3,753	...	...	...	...	...	...	...	...	...
NLBz	Statistical discrepancy	-0	—	-0	...	...	...	...	...	...	...	...	...
	Memorandum items												
PB	Primary net lending / net borrowing	-11,814	-27,301	-9,771	...	...	...	...	...	...	...	...	...
GB	Government balance per national definition	...	...	...	...	...	...	...	...	...	...	...	...
	Statement of other economic flows												
	Balance sheet												
	Table 1 Revenue												
1	**Revenue**	**139,518**	**153,919**	**150,258**	...	...	...	...	...	...	...	...	...
11	**Taxes**	**37,178**	**35,703**	**40,460**	...	...	...	...	...	...	...	...	...
111	Taxes on income, profits, and capital gains	15,550	14,975	16,697	...	...	...	...	...	...	...	...	...
1111	Payable by individuals	12,161	11,896	12,347	...	...	...	...	...	...	...	...	...
1112	Payable by corporations and other enterprises	2,782	2,431	3,595	...	...	...	...	...	...	...	...	...
1113	Other taxes on income, profits, and capital gains	607	648	755	...	...	...	...	...	...	...	...	...
112	Taxes on payroll and workforce	—	—	—	...	...	...	...	...	...	...	...	...
113	Taxes on property	854	1,018	807	...	...	...	...	...	...	...	...	...
114	Taxes on goods and services	3,495	3,691	4,915	...	...	...	...	...	...	...	...	...
1141	General taxes on goods and services	2,188	2,355	3,436	...	...	...	...	...	...	...	...	...
1142	Excises	—	—	—	...	...	...	...	...	...	...	...	...
115	Taxes on international trade and transactions	17,279	16,019	18,042	...	...	...	...	...	...	...	...	...
116	Other taxes	—	—	—	...	...	...	...	...	...	...	...	...
12	**Social contributions**	—	—	—	...	...	...	...	...	...	...	...	...
121	Social security contributions	—	—	—	...	...	...	...	...	...	...	...	...
122	Other social contributions	—	—	—	...	...	...	...	...	...	...	...	...
13	**Grants**	**97,031**	**112,187**	**104,948**	...	...	...	...	...	...	...	...	...
131	From foreign governments	97,031	112,187	104,948	...	...	...	...	...	...	...	...	...
132	From international organizations	—	—	—	...	...	...	...	...	...	...	...	...
133	From other general government units	—	—	—	...	...	...	...	...	...	...	...	...
1331	Current	—	—	—	...	...	...	...	...	...	...	...	...
1332	Capital	—	—	—	...	...	...	...	...	...	...	...	...
14	**Other revenue**	**5,310**	**6,028**	**4,850**	...	...	...	...	...	...	...	...	...
	Table 2 Expense by economic type												
2	**Expense**	**111,757**	**107,740**	**117,859**	...	...	...	...	...	...	...	...	...
21	**Compensation of employees**	**42,323**	**41,770**	**42,723**	...	...	...	...	...	...	...	...	...
211	Wages and salaries	42,323	41,770	42,723	...	...	...	...	...	...	...	...	...
212	Employers' social contributions	—	—	—	...	...	...	...	...	...	...	...	...
22	**Use of goods and services**	**22,142**	**26,233**	**29,366**	...	...	...	...	...	...	...	...	...
23	**Consumption of fixed capital**	...	...	...	...	...	...	...	...	...	...	...	...
24	**Interest**	**26**	**33**	**30**	...	...	...	...	...	...	...	...	...
25	**Subsidies**	**17,500**	**28,191**	**30,633**	...	...	...	...	...	...	...	...	...
26	**Grants**	—	—	—	...	...	...	...	...	...	...	...	...
261	To foreign governments	—	—	—	...	...	...	...	...	...	...	...	...
262	To international organizations	—	—	—	...	...	...	...	...	...	...	...	...
263	To other general government units	—	—	—	...	...	...	...	...	...	...	...	...
2631	Current	—	—	—	...	...	...	...	...	...	...	...	...
2632	Capital	—	—	—	...	...	...	...	...	...	...	...	...

Montserrat (351)

In Thousands of Eastern Caribbean Dollars (XCD) / Fiscal Year Ends December 31st

		Budgetary Central Government			Central Government (excl. Social Security)			Central Government (incl. Social Security)			General Government		
		2012	2013	2014	2012	2013	2014	2012	2013	2014	2012	2013	2014
27	**Social benefits**	**29,766**	**11,513**	**15,107**	...	...	...	...	...	...	...	...	...
271	Social security benefits	29,766	11,513	15,107	...	...	...	...	...	...	...	...	...
272	Social assistance benefits	—	—	—	...	...	...	...	...	...	...	...	...
273	Employment-related social benefits	—	—	—	...	...	...	...	...	...	...	...	...
28	**Other expense**	—	—	—	...	...	...	...	...	...	...	...	...
281	Property expense other than interest	—	—	—	...	...	...	...	...	...	...	...	...
282	Transfers not elsewhere classified	—	—	—	...	...	...	...	...	...	...	...	...
2821	Current	—	—	—	...	...	...	...	...	...	...	...	...
2822	Capital	—	—	—	...	...	...	...	...	...	...	...	...
	Table 3 Transactions in assets and liabilities												
3	**Change in net worth from transactions**	...	...	...	...	...	...	...	...	...	...	...	...
31	**Net/Gross investment in nonfinancial assets**	**39,601**	**73,513**	**42,200**	...	...	...	...	...	...	...	...	...
311	Fixed assets	39,601	73,513	42,200	...	...	...	...	...	...	...	...	...
3111	Buildings and structures	...	...	...	...	...	...	...	...	...	...	...	...
3112	Machinery and equipment	...	...	...	...	...	...	...	...	...	...	...	...
3113	Other fixed assets	...	...	...	...	...	...	...	...	...	...	...	...
3114	Weapons systems	...	...	...	...	...	...	...	...	...	...	...	...
312	Inventories	—	—	—	...	...	...	...	...	...	...	...	...
313	Valuables	—	—	—	...	...	...	...	...	...	...	...	...
314	Nonproduced assets	—	—	—	...	...	...	...	...	...	...	...	...
3141	Land	—	—	—	...	...	...	...	...	...	...	...	...
3142	Mineral and energy resources	—	—	—	...	...	...	...	...	...	...	...	...
3143	Other naturally occurring assets	—	—	—	...	...	...	...	...	...	...	...	...
3144	Intangible nonproduced assets	—	—	—	...	...	...	...	...	...	...	...	...
32	**Net acquisition of financial assets**	**-21,651**	**-19,769**	**-6,048**	...	...	...	...	...	...	...	...	...
	By instrument												
3201	Monetary gold and SDRs	—	—	—	—	—	—	—	—	—	—	—	—
3202	Currency and deposits	-21,651	-19,769	-6,048	...	...	...	...	...	...	...	...	...
3203	Debt securities	—	—	—	...	...	...	...	...	...	...	...	...
3204	Loans	—	—	—	...	...	...	...	...	...	...	...	...
3205	Equity and investment fund shares	—	—	—	...	...	...	...	...	...	...	...	...
3206	Insurance, pension, and standardized guarantee schemes	—	—	—	...	...	...	...	...	...	...	...	...
3207	Financial derivatives and employee stock options	—	—	—	...	...	...	...	...	...	...	...	...
3208	Other accounts receivable	...	...	...	...	...	...	...	...	...	...	...	...
	By debtor												
321	Domestic debtors	-21,651	-19,769	-6,048	...	...	...	...	...	...	...	...	...
322	External debtors	—	—	—	...	...	...	...	...	...	...	...	...
33	**Net incurrence of liabilities**	**-9,811**	**7,565**	**3,753**	...	...	...	...	...	...	...	...	...
	By instrument												
3301	Special Drawing Rights (SDRs)	—	—	—	—	—	—	—	—	—	—	—	—
3302	Currency and deposits	—	—	—	...	...	...	...	...	...	...	...	...
3303	Debt securities	—	—	—	...	...	...	...	...	...	...	...	...
3304	Loans	-9,811	7,565	3,753	...	...	...	...	...	...	...	...	...
3305	Equity and investment fund shares	—	—	—	...	...	...	...	...	...	...	...	...
3306	Insurance, pension, and standardized guarantee schemes	—	—	—	...	...	...	...	...	...	...	...	...
3307	Financial derivatives and employee stock options	—	—	—	...	...	...	...	...	...	...	...	...
3308	Other accounts payable	...	...	...	...	...	...	...	...	...	...	...	...
	By creditor												
331	Domestic creditors	-9,693	7,682	3,870	...	...	...	...	...	...	...	...	...
332	External creditors	-118	-118	-118	...	...	...	...	...	...	...	...	...
	Table 4 Holding gains and losses in assets and liabilities												
	Table 5 Holding gains and losses in assets and liabilities												
	Table 6 Balance sheet												

Montserrat (351)

In Thousands of Eastern Caribbean Dollars (XCD) / Fiscal Year Ends December 31st

	Budgetary Central Government			Central Government (excl. Social Security)			Central Government (incl. Social Security)			General Government		
	2012	2013	2014	2012	2013	2014	2012	2013	2014	2012	2013	2014
Table 7 Expenditure by functions of government												
Table 8 Financial transactions by counterpart sector												
Table 9 Total other economic flows in assets and liabilities												

Morocco (686)

In Millions of Moroccan Dirhams (MAD) / Fiscal Year Ends December 31st

		Budgetary Central Government			Central Government (excl. Social Security)			Central Government (incl. Social Security)			General Government		
		2013	2014	2015	2013	2014	2015	2013	2014	2015	2013	2014	2015
	Statement of operations												
1	Revenue	250,022	259,347	260,389	...	...	...	...	...	...	...	...	...
2	Expense	250,009	254,540	248,621	...	...	...	...	...	...	...	...	...
GOB	**Gross operating balance**	**13**	**4,807**	**11,768**	...	...	...	...	...	...	...	...	...
NOB	**Net operating balance**	...	...	...	...	...	...	...	...	...	...	...	...
31	Net/Gross investment in nonfinancial assets	45,702	49,673	2,239	...	...	...	...	...	...	...	...	...
2M	Expenditure	295,711	304,213	250,860	...	...	...	...	...	...	...	...	...
NLB	**Net lending (+) / Net borrowing (-)**	**-45,689**	**-44,866**	**9,529**	...	...	...	...	...	...	...	...	...
32	Net acquisition of financial assets	...	...	...	...	...	...	...	...	...	...	...	...
33	Net incurrence of liabilities	...	...	...	...	...	...	...	...	...	...	...	...
NLBz	Statistical discrepancy	...	...	...	...	...	...	...	...	...	...	...	...
	Memorandum items												
PB	Primary net lending / net borrowing	-23,187	-20,083	36,818	...	...	...	...	...	...	...	...	...
GB	Government balance per national definition	...	...	...	...	...	...	...	...	...	...	...	...
	Statement of other economic flows												
	Balance sheet												
	Table 1 Revenue												
1	**Revenue**	**250,022**	**259,347**	**260,389**	...	...	...	...	...	...	...	...	...
11	**Taxes**	**200,678**	**203,832**	**209,559**	...	...	...	...	...	...	...	...	...
111	Taxes on income, profits, and capital gains	75,704	76,348	78,957	...	...	...	...	...	...	...	...	...
1111	Payable by individuals	34,425	34,672	37,220	...	...	...	...	...	...	...	...	...
1112	Payable by corporations and other enterprises	40,825	41,677	41,736	...	...	...	...	...	...	...	...	...
1113	Other taxes on income, profits, and capital gains	—	—	—	...	...	...	...	...	...	...	...	...
112	Taxes on payroll and workforce	—	—	—	...	...	...	...	...	...	...	...	...
113	Taxes on property	—	—	—	...	...	...	...	...	...	...	...	...
114	Taxes on goods and services	111,694	114,610	117,313	...	...	...	...	...	...	...	...	...
1141	General taxes on goods and services	86,998	88,901	89,933	...	...	...	...	...	...	...	...	...
1142	Excises	22,875	23,849	25,366	...	...	...	...	...	...	...	...	...
115	Taxes on international trade and transactions	8,092	8,136	8,102	...	...	...	...	...	...	...	...	...
116	Other taxes	5,188	4,738	5,187	...	...	...	...	...	...	...	...	...
12	**Social contributions**	—	—	—	...	...	...	...	...	...	...	...	...
121	Social security contributions	—	—	—	...	...	...	...	...	...	...	...	...
122	Other social contributions	—	—	—	...	...	...	...	...	...	...	...	...
13	**Grants**	**6,111**	**13,838**	**4,971**	...	...	...	...	...	...	...	...	...
131	From foreign governments	6,111	13,838	4,971	...	...	...	...	...	...	...	...	...
132	From international organizations	—	—	—	...	...	...	...	...	...	...	...	...
133	From other general government units	—	—	—	...	...	...	...	...	...	...	...	...
1331	Current	—	—	—	...	...	...	...	...	...	...	...	...
1332	Capital	—	—	—	...	...	...	...	...	...	...	...	...
14	**Other revenue**	**43,234**	**41,676**	**45,859**	...	...	...	...	...	...	...	...	...
	Table 2 Expense by economic type												
2	**Expense**	**250,009**	**254,540**	**248,621**	...	...	...	...	...	...	...	...	...
21	**Compensation of employees**	**112,762**	**117,309**	**118,202**	...	...	...	...	...	...	...	...	...
211	Wages and salaries	99,044	101,645	102,669	...	...	...	...	...	...	...	...	...
212	Employers' social contributions	13,718	15,664	15,533	...	...	...	...	...	...	...	...	...
22	**Use of goods and services**	**21,529**	**23,646**	**25,136**	...	...	...	...	...	...	...	...	...
23	**Consumption of fixed capital**	...	...	...	...	...	...	...	...	...	...	...	...
24	**Interest**	**22,502**	**24,784**	**27,289**	...	...	...	...	...	...	...	...	...
25	**Subsidies**	**41,600**	**32,648**	**13,977**	...	...	...	...	...	...	...	...	...
26	**Grants**	**37,765**	**41,383**	**47,262**	...	...	...	...	...	...	...	...	...
261	To foreign governments	—	—	—	...	...	...	...	...	...	...	...	...
262	To international organizations	—	—	—	...	...	...	...	...	...	...	...	...
263	To other general government units	37,765	41,383	47,262	...	...	...	...	...	...	...	...	...
2631	Current	...	...	47,262	...	...	...	...	...	...	...	...	...
2632	Capital	...	...	—	...	...	...	...	...	...	...	...	...

Morocco (686)

In Millions of Moroccan Dirhams (MAD) / Fiscal Year Ends December 31st

		Budgetary Central Government			Central Government (excl. Social Security)			Central Government (incl. Social Security)			General Government		
		2013	2014	2015	2013	2014	2015	2013	2014	2015	2013	2014	2015
27	**Social benefits**	—	—	—	...	...	...	...	...	...	...	...	...
271	Social security benefits	—	—	—	...	...	...	...	...	...	...	...	...
272	Social assistance benefits	—	—	—	...	...	...	...	...	...	...	...	...
273	Employment-related social benefits	—	—	—	...	...	...	...	...	...	...	...	...
28	**Other expense**	**13,851**	**14,770**	**16,754**	...	...	...	...	...	...	...	...	...
281	Property expense other than interest	—	—	—	...	...	...	...	...	...	...	...	...
282	Transfers not elsewhere classified	13,851	14,770	16,754	...	...	...	...	...	...	...	...	...
2821	Current	...	...	...	...	...	...	...	...	...	...	...	...
2822	Capital	...	...	...	...	...	...	...	...	...	...	...	...
	Table 3 Transactions in assets and liabilities												
3	**Change in net worth from transactions**	...	...	...	...	...	...	...	...	...	...	...	...
31	**Net/Gross investment in nonfinancial assets**	**45,702**	**49,673**	**2,239**	...	...	...	...	...	...	...	...	...
311	Fixed assets	...	...	...	...	...	...	...	...	...	...	...	...
3111	Buildings and structures	...	...	...	...	...	...	...	...	...	...	...	...
3112	Machinery and equipment	...	...	...	...	...	...	...	...	...	...	...	...
3113	Other fixed assets	...	...	...	...	...	...	...	...	...	...	...	...
3114	Weapons systems	...	...	...	...	...	...	...	...	...	...	...	...
312	Inventories	...	...	...	...	...	...	...	...	...	...	...	...
313	Valuables	...	...	...	...	...	...	...	...	...	...	...	...
314	Nonproduced assets	...	...	...	...	...	...	...	...	...	...	...	...
3141	Land	...	...	...	...	...	...	...	...	...	...	...	...
3142	Mineral and energy resources	...	...	...	...	...	...	...	...	...	...	...	...
3143	Other naturally occurring assets	...	...	...	...	...	...	...	...	...	...	...	...
3144	Intangible nonproduced assets	...	...	...	...	...	...	...	...	...	...	...	...
32	**Net acquisition of financial assets**	...	...	...	...	...	...	...	...	...	...	...	...
	By instrument												
3201	Monetary gold and SDRs	...	...	...	...	...	...	...	...	...	...	...	...
3202	Currency and deposits	...	...	...	...	...	...	...	...	...	...	...	...
3203	Debt securities	...	...	...	...	...	...	...	...	...	...	...	...
3204	Loans	...	...	...	...	...	...	...	...	...	...	...	...
3205	Equity and investment fund shares	...	...	...	...	...	...	...	...	...	...	...	...
3206	Insurance, pension, and standardized guarantee schemes	...	...	...	...	...	...	...	...	...	...	...	...
3207	Financial derivatives and employee stock options	...	...	...	...	...	...	...	...	...	...	...	...
3208	Other accounts receivable	...	...	...	...	...	...	...	...	...	...	...	...
	By debtor												
321	Domestic debtors	...	...	...	...	...	...	...	...	...	...	...	...
322	External debtors	...	...	...	...	...	...	...	...	...	...	...	...
33	**Net incurrence of liabilities**	...	...	...	...	...	...	...	...	...	...	...	...
	By instrument												
3301	Special Drawing Rights (SDRs)	...	...	...	...	...	...	...	...	...	...	...	...
3302	Currency and deposits	...	...	...	...	...	...	...	...	...	...	...	...
3303	Debt securities	...	...	...	...	...	...	...	...	...	...	...	...
3304	Loans	...	...	...	...	...	...	...	...	...	...	...	...
3305	Equity and investment fund shares	...	...	...	...	...	...	...	...	...	...	...	...
3306	Insurance, pension, and standardized guarantee schemes	...	...	...	...	...	...	...	...	...	...	...	...
3307	Financial derivatives and employee stock options	...	...	...	...	...	...	...	...	...	...	...	...
3308	Other accounts payable	...	...	...	...	...	...	...	...	...	...	...	...
	By creditor												
331	Domestic creditors	...	...	...	...	...	...	...	...	...	...	...	...
332	External creditors	...	...	...	...	...	...	...	...	...	...	...	...
	Table 4 Holding gains and losses in assets and liabilities												
	Table 5 Holding gains and losses in assets and liabilities												
	Table 6 Balance sheet												

Morocco (686)

In Millions of Moroccan Dirhams (MAD) / Fiscal Year Ends December 31st

	Budgetary Central Government			Central Government (excl. Social Security)			Central Government (incl. Social Security)			General Government		
	2013	2014	2015	2013	2014	2015	2013	2014	2015	2013	2014	2015
Table 7 Expenditure by functions of government												
Table 8 Financial transactions by counterpart sector												
Table 9 Total other economic flows in assets and liabilities												

Mozambique (688)

In Millions of Mozambican Meticais (MZN) / Fiscal Year Ends December 31st

		Budgetary Central Government			Central Government (excl. Social Security)			Central Government (incl. Social Security)			General Government		
		2011	2012	2013	2011	2012	2013	2011	2012	2013	2011	2012	2013
	Statement of operations												
1	Revenue	106,839	124,454	154,285	...	...	...	...	...	...	...	...	...
2	Expense	90,492	105,321	...	...	...	...	...	...	...	...	...	...
GOB	**Gross operating balance**	**16,347**	**19,133**	**...**	**...**	**...**	**...**	**...**	**...**	**...**	**...**	**...**	**...**
NOB	**Net operating balance**	**...**	**...**	**...**	**...**	**...**	**...**	**...**	**...**	**...**	**...**	**...**	**...**
31	Net/Gross investment in nonfinancial assets	29,850	30,586	50,888	...	...	...	...	...	...	...	...	...
2M	Expenditure	120,342	135,907	...	...	...	...	...	...	...	...	...	...
NLB	**Net lending (+) / Net borrowing (-)**	**-13,502**	**-11,453**	**...**	**...**	**...**	**...**	**...**	**...**	**...**	**...**	**...**	**...**
32	Net acquisition of financial assets	3,671	4,092	...	...	...	...	...	...	...	...	...	...
33	Net incurrence of liabilities	17,174	15,425	34,689	...	...	...	...	...	...	...	...	...
NLBz	Statistical discrepancy	-1	119	...	...	...	...	...	...	...	...	...	...
	Memorandum items												
PB	Primary net lending / net borrowing	-10,001	-7,327	...	...	...	...	...	...	...	...	...	...
GB	Government balance per national definition	...	...	...	...	...	...	...	...	...	...	...	...
	Statement of other economic flows												
	Balance sheet												
	Table 1 Revenue												
1	**Revenue**	**106,839**	**124,454**	**154,285**	**...**	**...**	**...**	**...**	**...**	**...**	**...**	**...**	**...**
11	**Taxes**	**71,389**	**88,206**	**111,523**	**...**	**...**	**...**	**...**	**...**	**...**	**...**	**...**	**...**
111	Taxes on income, profits, and capital gains	25,032	36,772	49,322	...	...	...	...	...	...	...	...	...
1111	Payable by individuals	10,819	12,015	14,836	...	...	...	...	...	...	...	...	...
1112	Payable by corporations and other enterprises	14,213	24,757	34,486	...	...	...	...	...	...	...	...	...
1113	Other taxes on income, profits, and capital gains	—	—	—	...	...	...	...	...	...	...	...	...
112	Taxes on payroll and workforce	—	—	—	...	...	...	...	...	...	...	...	...
113	Taxes on property	—	—	—	...	...	...	...	...	...	...	...	...
114	Taxes on goods and services	38,880	42,665	50,753	...	...	...	...	...	...	...	...	...
1141	General taxes on goods and services	29,229	31,981	38,116	...	...	...	...	...	...	...	...	...
1142	Excises	9,180	9,923	11,807	...	...	...	...	...	...	...	...	...
115	Taxes on international trade and transactions	5,609	6,816	8,700	...	...	...	...	...	...	...	...	...
116	Other taxes	1,868	1,953	2,747	...	...	...	...	...	...	...	...	...
12	**Social contributions**	**1,421**	**1,687**	**2,108**	**...**	**...**	**...**	**...**	**...**	**...**	**...**	**...**	**...**
121	Social security contributions	1,421	1,687	2,108	...	...	...	...	...	...	...	...	...
122	Other social contributions	—	—	—	...	...	...	...	...	...	...	...	...
13	**Grants**	**27,399**	**27,332**	**30,299**	**...**	**...**	**...**	**...**	**...**	**...**	**...**	**...**	**...**
131	From foreign governments	27,399	27,332	30,299	...	...	...	...	...	...	...	...	...
132	From international organizations	—	—	—	...	...	...	...	...	...	...	...	...
133	From other general government units	—	—	—	...	...	...	...	...	...	...	...	...
1331	Current	—	—	—	...	...	...	...	...	...	...	...	...
1332	Capital	—	—	—	...	...	...	...	...	...	...	...	...
14	**Other revenue**	**6,631**	**7,229**	**10,355**	**...**	**...**	**...**	**...**	**...**	**...**	**...**	**...**	**...**
	Table 2 Expense by economic type												
2	**Expense**	**90,492**	**105,321**	**...**	**...**	**...**	**...**	**...**	**...**	**...**	**...**	**...**	**...**
21	**Compensation of employees**	**39,033**	**44,373**	**...**	**...**	**...**	**...**	**...**	**...**	**...**	**...**	**...**	**...**
211	Wages and salaries	39,033	44,373	...	...	...	...	...	...	...	...	...	...
212	Employers' social contributions	—	—	...	...	...	...	...	...	...	...	...	...
22	**Use of goods and services**	**25,205**	**30,521**	**...**	**...**	**...**	**...**	**...**	**...**	**...**	**...**	**...**	**...**
23	**Consumption of fixed capital**	**—**	**—**	**...**	**...**	**...**	**...**	**...**	**...**	**...**	**...**	**...**	**...**
24	**Interest**	**3,501**	**4,125**	**...**	**...**	**...**	**...**	**...**	**...**	**...**	**...**	**...**	**...**
25	**Subsidies**	**5,238**	**5,240**	**...**	**...**	**...**	**...**	**...**	**...**	**...**	**...**	**...**	**...**
26	**Grants**	**2,040**	**2,489**	**...**	**...**	**...**	**...**	**...**	**...**	**...**	**...**	**...**	**...**
261	To foreign governments	—	—	...	...	...	...	...	...	...	...	...	...
262	To international organizations	252	232	...	...	...	...	...	...	...	...	...	...
263	To other general government units	1,787	2,257	...	...	...	...	...	...	...	...	...	...
2631	Current	1,158	1,452	...	...	...	...	...	...	...	...	...	...
2632	Capital	629	806	...	...	...	...	...	...	...	...	...	...

Mozambique (688)

In Millions of Mozambican Meticais (MZN) / Fiscal Year Ends December 31st

		Budgetary Central Government			Central Government (excl. Social Security)			Central Government (incl. Social Security)			General Government		
		2011	2012	2013	2011	2012	2013	2011	2012	2013	2011	2012	2013
27	**Social benefits**	**8,396**	**11,051**	**...**	**...**	**...**	**...**	**...**	**...**	**...**	**...**	**...**	**...**
271	Social security benefits	—	—	...	...	...	...	...	...	...	...	...	...
272	Social assistance benefits	764	1,295	...	...	...	...	...	...	...	...	...	...
273	Employment-related social benefits	7,632	9,757	...	...	...	...	...	...	...	...	...	...
28	**Other expense**	**7,079**	**7,521**	**...**	**...**	**...**	**...**	**...**	**...**	**...**	**...**	**...**	**...**
281	Property expense other than interest	—	—	...	...	...	...	...	...	...	...	...	...
282	Transfers not elsewhere classified	7,079	7,521	...	...	...	...	...	...	...	...	...	...
2821	Current	5,830	6,086	...	...	...	...	...	...	...	...	...	...
2822	Capital	1,249	1,435	...	...	...	...	...	...	...	...	...	...
	Table 3 Transactions in assets and liabilities												
3	**Change in net worth from transactions**	**...**	**...**	**...**	**...**	**...**	**...**	**...**	**...**	**...**	**...**	**...**	**...**
31	**Net/Gross investment in nonfinancial assets**	**29,850**	**30,586**	**50,888**	**...**	**...**	**...**	**...**	**...**	**...**	**...**	**...**	**...**
311	Fixed assets	29,850	30,586	50,888	...	...	...	...	...	...	...	...	...
3111	Buildings and structures	...	...	29,143	...	...	...	...	...	...	...	...	...
3112	Machinery and equipment	...	...	21,927	...	...	...	...	...	...	...	...	...
3113	Other fixed assets	...	...	—	...	...	...	...	...	...	...	...	...
3114	Weapons systems	...	...	...	...	...	...	...	...	...	...	...	...
312	Inventories	—	—	—	...	...	...	...	...	...	...	...	...
313	Valuables	—	—	—	...	...	...	...	...	...	...	...	...
314	Nonproduced assets	—	—	—	...	...	...	...	...	...	...	...	...
3141	Land	—	—	—	...	...	...	...	...	...	...	...	...
3142	Mineral and energy resources	—	—	—	...	...	...	...	...	...	...	...	...
3143	Other naturally occurring assets	—	—	—	...	...	...	...	...	...	...	...	...
3144	Intangible nonproduced assets	—	—	—	...	...	...	...	...	...	...	...	...
32	**Net acquisition of financial assets**	**3,671**	**4,092**	**...**	**...**	**...**	**...**	**...**	**...**	**...**	**...**	**...**	**...**
	By instrument												
3201	Monetary gold and SDRs	—	—	—	...	...	...	...	...	...	...	...	...
3202	Currency and deposits	-201	-736	...	...	...	...	...	...	...	...	...	...
3203	Debt securities	—	—	—	...	...	...	...	...	...	...	...	...
3204	Loans	3,871	4,820	9,994	...	...	...	...	...	...	...	...	...
3205	Equity and investment fund shares	—	7	—	...	...	...	...	...	...	...	...	...
3206	Insurance, pension, and standardized guarantee schemes	—	—	—	...	...	...	...	...	...	...	...	...
3207	Financial derivatives and employee stock options	—	—	—	...	...	...	...	...	...	...	...	...
3208	Other accounts receivable	—	—	...	...	...	...	...	...	...	...	...	...
	By debtor												
321	Domestic debtors	3,671	4,092	...	...	...	...	...	...	...	...	...	...
322	External debtors	—	—	—	...	...	...	...	...	...	...	...	...
33	**Net incurrence of liabilities**	**17,174**	**15,425**	**34,689**	**...**	**...**	**...**	**...**	**...**	**...**	**...**	**...**	**...**
	By instrument												
3301	Special Drawing Rights (SDRs)	—	—	—	...	...	...	...	...	...	...	...	...
3302	Currency and deposits	—	—	—	...	...	...	...	...	...	...	...	...
3303	Debt securities	2,385	2,650	6,208	...	...	...	...	...	...	...	...	...
3304	Loans	14,789	12,775	28,481	...	...	...	...	...	...	...	...	...
3305	Equity and investment fund shares	—	—	—	...	...	...	...	...	...	...	...	...
3306	Insurance, pension, and standardized guarantee schemes	—	—	—	...	...	...	...	...	...	...	...	...
3307	Financial derivatives and employee stock options	—	—	—	...	...	...	...	...	...	...	...	...
3308	Other accounts payable	—	—	...	...	...	...	...	...	...	...	...	...
	By creditor												
331	Domestic creditors	3,583	1,408	5,990	...	...	...	...	...	...	...	...	...
332	External creditors	13,591	14,017	28,699	...	...	...	...	...	...	...	...	...
	Table 4 Holding gains and losses in assets and liabilities												
	Table 5 Holding gains and losses in assets and liabilities												
	Table 6 Balance sheet												

Mozambique (688)

In Millions of Mozambican Meticais (MZN) / Fiscal Year Ends December 31st

		Budgetary Central Government			Central Government (excl. Social Security)			Central Government (incl. Social Security)			General Government		
		2011	2012	2013	2011	2012	2013	2011	2012	2013	2011	2012	2013
	Table 7 Expenditure by functions of government												
7	**Expenditure**	**120,342**	**135,907**	...	...	...	...	...	...	...	...	...	...
701	**General public services**	**33,952**	...	...	...	...	...	...	...	...	...	...	...
7017	Public debt transactions	3,501	4,125	...	...	...	...	...	...	...	...	...	...
7018	Transfers of general character between levels of government	...	...	...	...	...	...	...	...	...	...	...	...
702	**Defense**	**3,627**	...	...	...	...	...	...	...	...	...	...	...
703	**Public order and safety**	**7,777**	...	...	...	...	...	...	...	...	...	...	...
704	**Economic affairs**	**22,379**	...	...	...	...	...	...	...	...	...	...	...
7042	Agriculture, forestry, fishing, and hunting	3,980	...	...	...	...	...	...	...	...	...	...	...
7043	Fuel and energy	...	...	...	...	...	...	...	...	...	...	...	...
7044	Mining, manufacturing, and construction	...	...	...	...	...	...	...	...	...	...	...	...
7045	Transport	...	...	...	...	...	...	...	...	...	...	...	...
7046	Communication	...	...	...	...	...	...	...	...	...	...	...	...
705	**Environmental protection**	**1,241**	...	...	...	...	...	...	...	...	...	...	...
706	**Housing and community amenities**	**6,631**	...	...	...	...	...	...	...	...	...	...	...
707	**Health**	**9,407**	...	...	...	...	...	...	...	...	...	...	...
7072	Outpatient services	...	...	...	...	...	...	...	...	...	...	...	...
7073	Hospital services	...	...	...	...	...	...	...	...	...	...	...	...
7074	Public health services	...	...	...	...	...	...	...	...	...	...	...	...
708	**Recreation, culture and religion**	**4,547**	...	...	...	...	...	...	...	...	...	...	...
709	**Education**	**23,896**	...	...	...	...	...	...	...	...	...	...	...
7091	Pre-primary and primary education	...	...	...	...	...	...	...	...	...	...	...	...
7092	Secondary education	...	...	...	...	...	...	...	...	...	...	...	...
7094	Tertiary education	...	...	...	...	...	...	...	...	...	...	...	...
710	**Social protection**	**8,545**	...	...	...	...	...	...	...	...	...	...	...
7z	Statistical discrepancy: Expenditure	-1,659	...	...	...	...	...	...	...	...	...	...	...
	Table 8 Financial transactions by counterpart sector												
	Table 9 Total other economic flows in assets and liabilities												

Namibia (728)

In Millions of Namibia Dollars (NAD) / Fiscal Year Ends December 31st

		Budgetary Central Government			Central Government (excl. Social Security)			Central Government (incl. Social Security)			General Government		
		2013	2014P	2015P	2013	2014	2015	2013	2014	2015	2013	2014	2015
	Statement of operations												
1	Revenue	42,527	50,142	52,282	...	...	...	...	...	...	...	...	...
2	Expense	41,376	49,834	54,990	...	...	...	...	...	...	...	...	...
GOB	**Gross operating balance**	**1,151**	**308**	**-2,708**	...	...	...	...	...	...	...	...	...
NOB	**Net operating balance**	...	...	...	...	...	...	...	...	...	...	...	...
31	Net/Gross investment in nonfinancial assets	5,098	8,646	9,055	...	...	...	...	...	...	...	...	...
2M	Expenditure	46,474	58,480	64,045	...	...	...	...	...	...	...	...	...
NLB	**Net lending (+) / Net borrowing (-)**	**-3,947**	**-8,338**	**-11,763**	...	...	...	...	...	...	...	...	...
32	Net acquisition of financial assets	-2,048	-3,227	...	...	...	...	...	...	...	...	...	...
33	Net incurrence of liabilities	1,899	5,111	...	...	...	...	...	...	...	...	...	...
NLBz	Statistical discrepancy	-0	0	...	...	...	...	...	...	...	...	...	...
	Memorandum items												
PB	Primary net lending / net borrowing	-2,158	-6,278	-9,136	...	...	...	...	...	...	...	...	...
GB	Government balance per national definition	...	...	...	...	...	...	...	...	...	...	...	...
	Statement of other economic flows												
	Balance sheet												
	Table 1 Revenue												
1	**Revenue**	**42,527**	**50,142**	**52,282**	...	...	...	...	...	...	...	...	...
11	**Taxes**	**38,917**	**46,847**	**49,004**	...	...	...	...	...	...	...	...	...
111	Taxes on income, profits, and capital gains	13,685	17,438	18,658	...	...	...	...	...	...	...	...	...
1111	Payable by individuals	9,537	10,197	10,556	...	...	...	...	...	...	...	...	...
1112	Payable by corporations and other enterprises	3,434	7,019	8,041	...	...	...	...	...	...	...	...	...
1113	Other taxes on income, profits, and capital gains	713	223	61	...	...	...	...	...	...	...	...	...
112	Taxes on payroll and workforce	—	—	—	...	...	...	...	...	...	...	...	...
113	Taxes on property	261	286	313	...	...	...	...	...	...	...	...	...
114	Taxes on goods and services	9,993	10,744	12,442	...	...	...	...	...	...	...	...	...
1141	General taxes on goods and services	9,671	10,549	12,104	...	...	...	...	...	...	...	...	...
1142	Excises	131	42	219	...	...	...	...	...	...	...	...	...
115	Taxes on international trade and transactions	14,737	18,128	17,357	...	...	...	...	...	...	...	...	...
116	Other taxes	241	251	234	...	...	...	...	...	...	...	...	...
12	**Social contributions**	**269**	**309**	**352**	...	...	...	...	...	...	...	...	...
121	Social security contributions	...	...	...	...	...	...	...	...	...	...	...	...
122	Other social contributions	...	...	...	...	...	...	...	...	...	...	...	...
13	**Grants**	**278**	**110**	**152**	...	...	...	...	...	...	...	...	...
131	From foreign governments	278	110	152	...	...	...	...	...	...	...	...	...
132	From international organizations	—	—	—	...	...	...	...	...	...	...	...	...
133	From other general government units	—	—	—	...	...	...	...	...	...	...	...	...
1331	Current	—	—	—	...	...	...	...	...	...	...	...	...
1332	Capital	—	—	—	...	...	...	...	...	...	...	...	...
14	**Other revenue**	**3,063**	**2,875**	**2,775**	...	...	...	...	...	...	...	...	...
	Table 2 Expense by economic type												
2	**Expense**	**41,376**	**49,834**	**54,990**	...	...	...	...	...	...	...	...	...
21	**Compensation of employees**	**17,932**	**21,655**	**23,947**	...	...	...	...	...	...	...	...	...
211	Wages and salaries	16,169	19,490	21,588	...	...	...	...	...	...	...	...	...
212	Employers' social contributions	1,763	2,164	2,359	...	...	...	...	...	...	...	...	...
22	**Use of goods and services**	**6,755**	**8,585**	**8,831**	...	...	...	...	...	...	...	...	...
23	**Consumption of fixed capital**	...	...	...	...	...	...	...	...	...	...	...	...
24	**Interest**	**1,788**	**2,060**	**2,626**	...	...	...	...	...	...	...	...	...
25	**Subsidies**	**5,025**	**6,048**	**8,301**	...	...	...	...	...	...	...	...	...
26	**Grants**	**9,349**	**10,264**	**9,781**	...	...	...	...	...	...	...	...	...
261	To foreign governments	196	214	173	...	...	...	...	...	...	...	...	...
262	To international organizations	6,822	8,273	8,262	...	...	...	...	...	...	...	...	...
263	To other general government units	2,331	1,777	1,346	...	...	...	...	...	...	...	...	...
2631	Current	...	...	...	...	...	...	...	...	...	...	...	...
2632	Capital	...	...	...	...	...	...	...	...	...	...	...	...

Namibia (728)

In Millions of Namibia Dollars (NAD) / Fiscal Year Ends December 31st

		Budgetary Central Government			Central Government (excl. Social Security)			Central Government (incl. Social Security)			General Government		
		2013	2014P	2015P	2013	2014	2015	2013	2014	2015	2013	2014	2015
27	**Social benefits**	**343**	**663**	**1,098**	**...**	**...**	**...**	**...**	**...**	**...**	**...**	**...**	**...**
271	Social security benefits	...	...	...	...	...	...	...	...	...	...	...	...
272	Social assistance benefits	...	...	...	...	...	...	...	...	...	...	...	...
273	Employment-related social benefits	...	...	...	...	...	...	...	...	...	...	...	...
28	**Other expense**	**184**	**559**	**406**	**...**	**...**	**...**	**...**	**...**	**...**	**...**	**...**	**...**
281	Property expense other than interest	—	—	—	...	...	...	...	...	...	...	...	...
282	Transfers not elsewhere classified	184	559	406	...	...	...	...	...	...	...	...	...
2821	Current	—	—	—	...	...	...	...	...	...	...	...	...
2822	Capital	184	559	406	...	...	...	...	...	...	...	...	...
	Table 3 Transactions in assets and liabilities												
3	**Change in net worth from transactions**	**...**	**...**	**...**	**...**	**...**	**...**	**...**	**...**	**...**	**...**	**...**	**...**
31	**Net/Gross investment in nonfinancial assets**	**5,098**	**8,646**	**9,055**	**...**	**...**	**...**	**...**	**...**	**...**	**...**	**...**	**...**
311	Fixed assets	5,075	8,616	9,051	...	...	...	...	...	...	...	...	...
3111	Buildings and structures	3,413	4,785	5,992	...	...	...	...	...	...	...	...	...
3112	Machinery and equipment	1,259	3,204	2,274	...	...	...	...	...	...	...	...	...
3113	Other fixed assets	402	627	785	...	...	...	...	...	...	...	...	...
3114	Weapons systems	...	...	...	...	...	...	...	...	...	...	...	...
312	Inventories	—	—	—	...	...	...	...	...	...	...	...	...
313	Valuables	—	—	—	...	...	...	...	...	...	...	...	...
314	Nonproduced assets	22	30	4	...	...	...	...	...	...	...	...	...
3141	Land	22	30	4	...	...	...	...	...	...	...	...	...
3142	Mineral and energy resources	—	—	—	...	...	...	...	...	...	...	...	...
3143	Other naturally occurring assets	—	—	—	...	...	...	...	...	...	...	...	...
3144	Intangible nonproduced assets	—	—	—	...	...	...	...	...	...	...	...	...
32	**Net acquisition of financial assets**	**-2,048**	**-3,227**	**...**	**...**	**...**	**...**	**...**	**...**	**...**	**...**	**...**	**...**
	By instrument												
3201	Monetary gold and SDRs	...	...	...	...	...	...	...	...	...	...	...	...
3202	Currency and deposits	-2,042	-3,228	...	...	...	...	...	...	...	...	...	...
3203	Debt securities	—	—	...	...	...	...	...	...	...	...	...	...
3204	Loans	-6	0	...	...	...	...	...	...	...	...	...	...
3205	Equity and investment fund shares	—	—	...	...	...	...	...	...	...	...	...	...
3206	Insurance, pension, and standardized guarantee schemes	—	—	...	...	...	...	...	...	...	...	...	...
3207	Financial derivatives and employee stock options	—	—	...	...	...	...	...	...	...	...	...	...
3208	Other accounts receivable	...	...	...	...	...	...	...	...	...	...	...	...
	By debtor												
321	Domestic debtors	-2,048	-3,227	...	...	...	...	...	...	...	...	...	...
322	External debtors	—	—	...	...	...	...	...	...	...	...	...	...
33	**Net incurrence of liabilities**	**1,899**	**5,111**	**...**	**...**	**...**	**...**	**...**	**...**	**...**	**...**	**...**	**...**
	By instrument												
3301	Special Drawing Rights (SDRs)	—	—	...	...	...	...	...	...	...	...	...	...
3302	Currency and deposits	—	—	...	...	...	...	...	...	...	...	...	...
3303	Debt securities	1,925	4,858	...	...	...	...	...	...	...	...	...	...
3304	Loans	-26	252	...	...	...	...	...	...	...	...	...	...
3305	Equity and investment fund shares	—	—	...	...	...	...	...	...	...	...	...	...
3306	Insurance, pension, and standardized guarantee schemes	—	—	...	...	...	...	...	...	...	...	...	...
3307	Financial derivatives and employee stock options	—	—	...	...	...	...	...	...	...	...	...	...
3308	Other accounts payable	...	...	...	...	...	...	...	...	...	...	...	...
	By creditor												
331	Domestic creditors	1,925	4,858	...	...	...	...	...	...	...	...	...	...
332	External creditors	-26	252	...	...	...	...	...	...	...	...	...	...
	Table 4 Holding gains and losses in assets and liabilities												
	Table 5 Holding gains and losses in assets and liabilities												
	Table 6 Balance sheet												

Namibia (728)

In Millions of Namibia Dollars (NAD) / Fiscal Year Ends December 31st

		Budgetary Central Government			Central Government (excl. Social Security)			Central Government (incl. Social Security)			General Government		
		2013	2014P	2015P	2013	2014	2015	2013	2014	2015	2013	2014	2015
	Table 7 Expenditure by functions of government												
7	**Expenditure**	**46,474**	**58,480**	**64,045**	...	...	...	...	...	...	...	...	...
701	**General public services**	**7,375**	**11,943**	**12,423**	...	...	...	...	...	...	...	...	...
7017	Public debt transactions	1,788	2,060	2,626	...	...	...	...	...	...	...	...	...
7018	Transfers of general character between levels of government	2,331	1,777	1,346	...	...	...	...	...	...	...	...	...
702	**Defense**	**3,771**	**5,731**	**6,750**	...	...	...	...	...	...	...	...	...
703	**Public order and safety**	**4,402**	**5,744**	**6,091**	...	...	...	...	...	...	...	...	...
704	**Economic affairs**	**6,812**	**8,296**	**9,162**	...	...	...	...	...	...	...	...	...
7042	Agriculture, forestry, fishing, and hunting	1,301	1,306	1,307	...	...	...	...	...	...	...	...	...
7043	Fuel and energy	—	—	—	...	...	...	...	...	...	...	...	...
7044	Mining, manufacturing, and construction	881	923	968	...	...	...	...	...	...	...	...	...
7045	Transport	3,499	4,298	4,567	...	...	...	...	...	...	...	...	...
7046	Communication	0	376	337	...	...	...	...	...	...	...	...	...
705	**Environmental protection**	**638**	**590**	**545**	...	...	...	...	...	...	...	...	...
706	**Housing and community amenities**	**2,042**	**2,457**	**2,975**	...	...	...	...	...	...	...	...	...
707	**Health**	**7,007**	**6,500**	**5,408**	...	...	...	...	...	...	...	...	...
7072	Outpatient services	—	—	—	...	...	...	...	...	...	...	...	...
7073	Hospital services	3,544	2,690	1,265	...	...	...	...	...	...	...	...	...
7074	Public health services	3,270	3,684	4,040	...	...	...	...	...	...	...	...	...
708	**Recreation, culture and religion**	**784**	**942**	**1,293**	...	...	...	...	...	...	...	...	...
709	**Education**	**10,889**	**12,802**	**14,995**	...	...	...	...	...	...	...	...	...
7091	Pre-primary and primary education	4,776	5,590	6,753	...	...	...	...	...	...	...	...	...
7092	Secondary education	1,921	2,199	2,495	...	...	...	...	...	...	...	...	...
7094	Tertiary education	2,345	2,900	3,386	...	...	...	...	...	...	...	...	...
710	**Social protection**	**2,755**	**3,474**	**4,404**	...	...	...	...	...	...	...	...	...
7z	Statistical discrepancy: Expenditure	...	...	...	...	...	...	...	...	...	...	...	...
	Table 8 Financial transactions by counterpart sector												
	Table 9 Total other economic flows in assets and liabilities												

Nepal (558)

In Millions of Nepalese Rupees (NPR) / Fiscal Year Ends July 15th

		Budgetary Central Government			Central Government (excl. Social Security)			Central Government (incl. Social Security)			General Government		
		2014	2015	2016P	2014	2015	2016	2014	2015	2016	2014	2015	2016
	Statement of operations												
1	Revenue	404,631	450,014	515,391	...	...	...	...	...	...	...	...	...
2	Expense	303,244	339,062	370,097	...	...	...	...	...	...	...	...	...
GOB	**Gross operating balance**	**101,388**	**110,952**	**145,295**	...	...	...	...	...	...	...	...	...
NOB	**Net operating balance**	...	...	...	...	...	...	...	...	...	...	...	...
31	Net/Gross investment in nonfinancial assets	66,485	88,424	114,715	...	...	...	...	...	...	...	...	...
2M	Expenditure	369,728	427,486	484,811	...	...	...	...	...	...	...	...	...
NLB	**Net lending (+) / Net borrowing (-)**	**34,903**	**22,528**	**30,580**	...	...	...	...	...	...	...	...	...
32	Net acquisition of financial assets	31,008	49,162	126,175	...	...	...	...	...	...	...	...	...
33	Net incurrence of liabilities	-3,895	3,497	72,485	...	...	...	...	...	...	...	...	...
NLBz	Statistical discrepancy	—	23,137	23,110	...	...	...	...	...	...	...	...	...
	Memorandum items												
PB	Primary net lending / net borrowing	46,941	31,791	39,253	...	...	...	...	...	...	...	...	...
GB	Government balance per national definition	...	...	...	...	...	...	...	...	...	...	...	...
	Statement of other economic flows												
	Balance sheet												
	Table 1 Revenue												
1	**Revenue**	**404,631**	**450,014**	**515,391**	...	...	...	...	...	...	...	...	...
11	**Taxes**	**312,440**	**355,943**	**419,481**	...	...	...	...	...	...	...	...	...
111	Taxes on income, profits, and capital gains	75,608	86,168	114,169	...	...	...	...	...	...	...	...	...
1111	Payable by individuals	19,432	8,536	9,747	...	...	...	...	...	...	...	...	...
1112	Payable by corporations and other enterprises	45,420	63,422	84,534	...	...	...	...	...	...	...	...	...
1113	Other taxes on income, profits, and capital gains	10,756	14,209	19,888	...	...	...	...	...	...	...	...	...
112	Taxes on payroll and workforce	2,449	2,928	3,274	...	...	...	...	...	...	...	...	...
113	Taxes on property	28	9	6	...	...	...	...	...	...	...	...	...
114	Taxes on goods and services	164,365	189,422	218,703	...	...	...	...	...	...	...	...	...
1141	General taxes on goods and services	107,753	121,904	135,457	...	...	...	...	...	...	...	...	...
1142	Excises	45,411	53,540	65,768	...	...	...	...	...	...	...	...	...
115	Taxes on international trade and transactions	67,981	74,844	82,185	...	...	...	...	...	...	...	...	...
116	Other taxes	2,008	2,572	1,144	...	...	...	...	...	...	...	...	...
12	**Social contributions**	—	—	—	...	...	...	...	...	...	...	...	...
121	Social security contributions	—	—	—	...	...	...	...	...	...	...	...	...
122	Other social contributions	—	—	—	...	...	...	...	...	...	...	...	...
13	**Grants**	**42,206**	**38,174**	**32,478**	...	...	...	...	...	...	...	...	...
131	From foreign governments	20,718	13,339	12,966	...	...	...	...	...	...	...	...	...
132	From international organizations	21,487	24,836	19,511	...	...	...	...	...	...	...	...	...
133	From other general government units	—	—	—	...	...	...	...	...	...	...	...	...
1331	Current	—	—	—	...	...	...	...	...	...	...	...	...
1332	Capital	—	—	—	...	...	...	...	...	...	...	...	...
14	**Other revenue**	**49,986**	**55,896**	**63,432**	...	...	...	...	...	...	...	...	...
	Table 2 Expense by economic type												
2	**Expense**	**303,244**	**339,062**	**370,097**	...	...	...	...	...	...	...	...	...
21	**Compensation of employees**	**84,357**	**88,543**	**89,268**	...	...	...	...	...	...	...	...	...
211	Wages and salaries	84,357	88,543	89,268	...	...	...	...	...	...	...	...	...
212	Employers' social contributions	—	—	—	...	...	...	...	...	...	...	...	...
22	**Use of goods and services**	**29,950**	**31,824**	**44,378**	...	...	...	...	...	...	...	...	...
23	**Consumption of fixed capital**	...	...	...	...	...	...	...	...	...	...	...	...
24	**Interest**	**12,038**	**9,263**	**8,673**	...	...	...	...	...	...	...	...	...
25	**Subsidies**	**1,146**	**1,019**	**942**	...	...	...	...	...	...	...	...	...
26	**Grants**	**133,392**	**157,691**	**170,069**	...	...	...	...	...	...	...	...	...
261	To foreign governments	—	—	—	...	...	...	...	...	...	...	...	...
262	To international organizations	—	365	185	...	...	...	...	...	...	...	...	...
263	To other general government units	133,392	157,325	169,884	...	...	...	...	...	...	...	...	...
2631	Current	83,013	113,374	101,339	...	...	...	...	...	...	...	...	...
2632	Capital	50,379	43,952	68,545	...	...	...	...	...	...	...	...	...

Nepal (558)

In Millions of Nepalese Rupees (NPR) / Fiscal Year Ends July 15th

		Budgetary Central Government			Central Government (excl. Social Security)			Central Government (incl. Social Security)			General Government		
		2014	2015	2016P	2014	2015	2016	2014	2015	2016	2014	2015	2016
27	**Social benefits**	**39,028**	**50,758**	**56,760**	...	...	...	...	...	...	...	...	...
271	Social security benefits	—	—	—	...	...	...	...	...	...	...	...	...
272	Social assistance benefits	12,084	16,357	20,997	...	...	...	...	...	...	...	...	...
273	Employment-related social benefits	26,944	34,401	35,763	...	...	...	...	...	...	...	...	...
28	**Other expense**	**3,333**	**9**	**6**	...	...	...	...	...	...	...	...	...
281	Property expense other than interest	10	9	6	...	...	...	...	...	...	...	...	...
282	Transfers not elsewhere classified	3,323	—	—	...	...	...	...	...	...	...	...	...
2821	Current	3,323	—	—	...	...	...	...	...	...	...	...	...
2822	Capital	—	—	—	...	...	...	...	...	...	...	...	...
	Table 3 Transactions in assets and liabilities												
3	**Change in net worth from transactions**	...	...	...	...	...	...	...	...	...	...	...	...
31	**Net/Gross investment in nonfinancial assets**	**66,485**	**88,424**	**114,715**	...	...	...	...	...	...	...	...	...
311	Fixed assets	65,069	86,007	120,179	...	...	...	...	...	...	...	...	...
3111	Buildings and structures	7,372	74,236	107,199	...	...	...	...	...	...	...	...	...
3112	Machinery and equipment	10,012	7,876	7,317	...	...	...	...	...	...	...	...	...
3113	Other fixed assets	47,685	3,895	5,663	...	...	...	...	...	...	...	...	...
3114	Weapons systems	—	—	—	...	...	...	...	...	...	...	...	...
312	Inventories	-205	-390	-969	...	...	...	...	...	...	...	...	...
313	Valuables	—	—	—	...	...	...	...	...	...	...	...	...
314	Nonproduced assets	1,621	2,807	2,822	...	...	...	...	...	...	...	...	...
3141	Land	1,621	2,807	2,822	...	...	...	...	...	...	...	...	...
3142	Mineral and energy resources	—	—	—	...	...	...	...	...	...	...	...	...
3143	Other naturally occurring assets	—	—	—	...	...	...	...	...	...	...	...	...
3144	Intangible nonproduced assets	—	—	—	...	...	...	...	...	...	...	...	...
32	**Net acquisition of financial assets**	**31,008**	**49,162**	**126,175**	...	...	...	...	...	...	...	...	...
	By instrument												
3201	Monetary gold and SDRs	—	—	—	...	...	...	...	...	...	...	...	...
3202	Currency and deposits	8,059	10,312	93,567	...	...	...	...	...	...	...	...	...
3203	Debt securities	—	—	—	...	...	...	...	...	...	...	...	...
3204	Loans	13,498	28,339	20,518	...	...	...	...	...	...	...	...	...
3205	Equity and investment fund shares	9,451	10,510	12,090	...	...	...	...	...	...	...	...	...
3206	Insurance, pension, and standardized guarantee schemes	—	—	—	...	...	...	...	...	...	...	...	...
3207	Financial derivatives and employee stock options	—	—	—	...	...	...	...	...	...	...	...	...
3208	Other accounts receivable	...	...	...	...	...	...	...	...	...	...	...	...
	By debtor												
321	Domestic debtors	30,969	47,175	125,999	...	...	...	...	...	...	...	...	...
322	External debtors	39	1,986	176	...	...	...	...	...	...	...	...	...
33	**Net incurrence of liabilities**	**-3,895**	**3,497**	**72,485**	...	...	...	...	...	...	...	...	...
	By instrument												
3301	Special Drawing Rights (SDRs)	—	—	—	...	...	...	...	...	...	...	...	...
3302	Currency and deposits	—	—	—	...	...	...	...	...	...	...	...	...
3303	Debt securities	—	—	—	...	...	...	...	...	...	...	...	...
3304	Loans	-3,895	3,497	72,485	...	...	...	...	...	...	...	...	...
3305	Equity and investment fund shares	—	—	—	...	...	...	...	...	...	...	...	...
3306	Insurance, pension, and standardized guarantee schemes	—	—	—	...	...	...	...	...	...	...	...	...
3307	Financial derivatives and employee stock options	—	—	—	...	...	...	...	...	...	...	...	...
3308	Other accounts payable	...	...	...	...	...	...	...	...	...	...	...	...
	By creditor												
331	Domestic creditors	-5,170	-5,007	37,440	...	...	...	...	...	...	...	...	...
332	External creditors	1,274	8,503	35,045	...	...	...	...	...	...	...	...	...
	Table 4 Holding gains and losses in assets and liabilities												
	Table 5 Holding gains and losses in assets and liabilities												
	Table 6 Balance sheet												

Nepal (558)

In Millions of Nepalese Rupees (NPR) / Fiscal Year Ends July 15th

		Budgetary Central Government			Central Government (excl. Social Security)			Central Government (incl. Social Security)			General Government		
		2014	2015	2016P	2014	2015	2016	2014	2015	2016	2014	2015	2016
	Table 7 Expenditure by functions of government												
7	**Expenditure**	**363,839**	**439,155**	**471,683**	...	...	...	...	...	...	...	...	...
701	**General public services**	**57,816**	**96,304**	**86,699**	...	...	...	...	...	...	...	...	...
7017	Public debt transactions	12,038	9,263	8,673	...	...	...	...	...	...	...	...	...
7018	Transfers of general character between levels of government	14,513	21,213	25,291	...	...	...	...	...	...	...	...	...
702	**Defense**	**31,042**	**33,156**	**35,099**	...	...	...	...	...	...	...	...	...
703	**Public order and safety**	**44,968**	**33,969**	**34,719**	...	...	...	...	...	...	...	...	...
704	**Economic affairs**	**94,120**	**123,604**	**132,607**	...	...	...	...	...	...	...	...	...
7042	Agriculture, forestry, fishing, and hunting	39,963	47,158	57,153	...	...	...	...	...	...	...	...	...
7043	Fuel and energy	4,001	26,902	17,151	...	...	...	...	...	...	...	...	...
7044	Mining, manufacturing, and construction	1,428	1,868	2,395	...	...	...	...	...	...	...	...	...
7045	Transport	33,230	43,578	51,863	...	...	...	...	...	...	...	...	...
7046	Communication	3,425	4,098	4,046	...	...	...	...	...	...	...	...	...
705	**Environmental protection**	**2,002**	**7,542**	**11,743**	...	...	...	...	...	...	...	...	...
706	**Housing and community amenities**	**13,099**	**16,935**	**22,791**	...	...	...	...	...	...	...	...	...
707	**Health**	**26,518**	**29,468**	**34,020**	...	...	...	...	...	...	...	...	...
7072	Outpatient services	2,036	1,843	4,308	...	...	...	...	...	...	...	...	...
7073	Hospital services	8,993	12,408	12,219	...	...	...	...	...	...	...	...	...
7074	Public health services	12,152	15,218	17,493	...	...	...	...	...	...	...	...	...
708	**Recreation, culture and religion**	**3,912**	**3,351**	**3,967**	...	...	...	...	...	...	...	...	...
709	**Education**	**77,826**	**79,841**	**90,690**	...	...	...	...	...	...	...	...	...
7091	Pre-primary and primary education	25,402	28,364	28,457	...	...	...	...	...	...	...	...	...
7092	Secondary education	12,968	14,249	14,375	...	...	...	...	...	...	...	...	...
7094	Tertiary education	39,456	37,228	47,857	...	...	...	...	...	...	...	...	...
710	**Social protection**	**12,534**	**14,985**	**19,348**	...	...	...	...	...	...	...	...	...
7z	Statistical discrepancy: Expenditure	—	...	...	...	...	...	...	...	...	...	...	...
	Table 8 Financial transactions by counterpart sector												
	Table 9 Total other economic flows in assets and liabilities												

Netherlands (138)

In Millions of Euros (EUR) / Fiscal Year Ends December 31st

		Budgetary Central Government			Central Government (excl. Social Security)			Central Government (incl. Social Security)			General Government		
		2013P	2014P	2015P	2013P	2014P	2015P	2013P	2014P	2015P	2013P	2014P	2015P
	Statement of operations												
1	Revenue	...	...	...	164,282	168,722	171,677	260,457	265,161	266,874	286,539	291,176	292,596
2	Expense	...	...	...	172,627	175,975	183,016	277,284	278,891	277,206	304,895	306,398	305,788
GOB	**Gross operating balance**	...	...	...	**1,982**	**3,194**	**-768**	**-6,376**	**-3,163**	**350**	**3,486**	**6,895**	**9,025**
NOB	**Net operating balance**	...	...	...	**-8,345**	**-7,253**	**-11,339**	**-16,827**	**-13,730**	**-10,332**	**-18,356**	**-15,222**	**-13,192**
31	Net/Gross investment in nonfinancial assets	-4,392	-678	-67	-3,555	-177	130	-3,616	-276	108	-2,859	-194	-433
2M	Expenditure	...	...	...	169,072	175,798	183,146	273,668	278,615	277,314	302,036	306,204	305,355
NLB	**Net lending (+) / Net borrowing (-)**	...	...	...	**-4,790**	**-7,076**	**-11,469**	**-13,211**	**-13,454**	**-10,440**	**-15,497**	**-15,028**	**-12,759**
32	Net acquisition of financial assets	10,611	1,277	-10,731	10,987	879	-13,837	3,369	-2,461	-15,323	-5,333	-5,965	-19,503
33	Net incurrence of liabilities	15,901	8,239	260	15,609	8,058	-2,461	16,411	11,096	-5,016	10,070	8,910	-6,836
NLBz	Statistical discrepancy	...	...	...	168	-103	93	169	-103	133	94	153	92
	Memorandum items												
PB	Primary net lending / net borrowing	...	...	...	4,417	1,933	-3,168	-4,054	-4,498	-2,184	-5,584	-5,600	-4,280
GB	Government balance per national definition	...	...	...	...	...	...	...	...	...	...	...	...
	Statement of other economic flows												
9	**Change in net worth due to other economic flows**	...	...	...	...	...	...	...	...	...	...	...	...
4	Change in net worth due to holding gains and losses	...	...	...	...	...	...	—	—	—	...	...	...
41	Nonfinancial assets	...	...	...	...	...	...	—	—	—	...	...	...
42	Financial assets	...	...	...	-9,553	15,344	8,178	—	—	—	-9,547	15,634	9,380
43	Liabilities	...	...	...	-19,181	29,784	-5,608	-17,330	29,803	-4,488	-16,973	29,796	-4,462
5	Change in net worth due to volume changes	...	...	...	...	...	...	...	...	...	...	...	...
51	Nonfinancial assets	...	...	...	...	...	...	...	...	...	...	...	...
52	Financial assets	...	...	...	5,898	219	1,740	5,898	219	640	6,832	-233	641
53	Liabilities	...	...	...	6,758	42	1,243	4,925	42	143	5,015	-291	143
	Balance sheet												
6	**Net worth**	...	...	...	...	...	...	...	...	...	...	...	...
61	Nonfinancial assets	...	...	...	...	...	...	...	...	...	...	...	...
62	Financial assets	201,556	218,488	215,107	209,862	226,304	222,385	187,660	200,762	195,357	237,597	247,033	237,551
63	Liabilities	439,301	477,332	473,084	445,677	483,561	476,735	445,914	486,836	477,455	499,749	538,164	527,009
	Table 1 Revenue												
1	**Revenue**	...	...	...	**164,282**	**168,722**	**171,677**	**260,457**	**265,161**	**266,874**	**286,539**	**291,176**	**292,596**
11	**Taxes**	...	...	...	**130,069**	**138,383**	**146,623**	**130,069**	**138,383**	**146,623**	**139,107**	**147,758**	**156,213**
111	Taxes on income, profits, and capital gains	...	...	...	59,085	63,671	70,849	59,085	63,671	70,849	59,085	63,671	70,849
1111	Payable by individuals	...	...	...	44,830	46,581	52,419	44,830	46,581	52,419	44,830	46,581	52,419
1112	Payable by corporations and other enterprises	...	...	...	14,255	17,090	18,430	14,255	17,090	18,430	14,255	17,090	18,430
1113	Other taxes on income, profits, and capital gains	...	...	...	—	—	—	—	—	—	—	—	—
112	Taxes on payroll and workforce	...	...	...	804	951	218	804	951	218	804	951	218
113	Taxes on property	...	...	...	2,287	3,204	2,959	2,287	3,204	2,959	6,488	7,524	7,432
114	Taxes on goods and services	...	...	...	64,750	67,050	69,075	64,750	67,050	69,075	65,774	68,123	70,143
1141	General taxes on goods and services	...	...	...	43,528	44,274	46,651	43,528	44,274	46,651	43,528	44,274	46,651
1142	Excises	...	...	...	13,769	14,542	14,828	13,769	14,542	14,828	13,769	14,542	14,828
115	Taxes on international trade and transactions	...	...	...	96	108	108	96	108	108	96	108	108
116	Other taxes	...	...	...	3,047	3,399	3,414	3,047	3,399	3,414	6,860	7,381	7,463
12	**Social contributions**	...	...	...	**1,745**	**1,713**	**1,485**	**99,173**	**100,387**	**97,929**	**100,786**	**101,931**	**99,621**
121	Social security contributions	...	...	...	—	—	—	97,372	98,616	96,386	97,372	98,616	96,386
122	Other social contributions	...	...	...	1,745	1,713	1,485	1,801	1,771	1,543	3,414	3,315	3,235
13	**Grants**	...	...	...	**2,175**	**3,289**	**2,903**	**852**	**952**	**1,537**	**106**	**88**	**135**
131	From foreign governments	...	...	...	...	...	...	...	...	...	...	...	...
132	From international organizations	...	...	...	27	43	92	27	43	92	106	88	135
133	From other general government units	...	...	...	2,148	3,246	2,811	825	909	1,445	—	—	—
1331	Current	...	...	...	1,560	1,589	1,629	237	269	263	—	—	—
1332	Capital	...	...	...	588	1,657	1,182	588	640	1,182	—	—	—
14	**Other revenue**	...	...	...	**30,293**	**25,337**	**20,666**	**30,363**	**25,439**	**20,785**	**46,540**	**41,399**	**36,627**

Netherlands (138)

In Millions of Euros (EUR) / Fiscal Year Ends December 31st

		Budgetary Central Government			Central Government (excl. Social Security)			Central Government (incl. Social Security)			General Government		
		2013P	2014P	2015P	2013P	2014P	2015P	2013P	2014P	2015P	2013P	2014P	2015P
	Table 2 Expense by economic type												
2	**Expense**	...	...	...	**172,627**	**175,975**	**183,016**	**277,284**	**278,891**	**277,206**	**304,895**	**306,398**	**305,788**
21	**Compensation of employees**	...	...	...	**21,148**	**21,516**	**21,686**	**22,613**	**23,081**	**23,149**	**60,193**	**60,423**	**59,796**
211	Wages and salaries	...	...	...	15,270	15,586	16,174	16,374	16,774	17,285	44,559	44,614	44,885
212	Employers' social contributions	...	...	...	5,878	5,930	5,512	6,239	6,307	5,864	15,634	15,809	14,911
22	**Use of goods and services**	...	...	...	**13,449**	**13,415**	**13,339**	**16,864**	**17,291**	**14,936**	**41,845**	**42,906**	**40,718**
23	**Consumption of fixed capital**	...	...	...	**10,327**	**10,447**	**10,571**	**10,451**	**10,567**	**10,682**	**21,842**	**22,117**	**22,217**
24	**Interest**	...	...	...	**9,207**	**9,009**	**8,301**	**9,157**	**8,956**	**8,256**	**9,913**	**9,428**	**8,479**
25	**Subsidies**	...	...	...	**3,789**	**3,904**	**3,865**	**5,667**	**5,559**	**5,645**	**8,211**	**8,021**	**8,039**
26	**Grants**	...	...	...	**85,184**	**90,376**	**98,269**	**70,628**	**72,030**	**76,987**	**7,494**	**8,784**	**8,728**
261	To foreign governments	...	...	...	...	...	...	...	...	...	...	...	...
262	To international organizations	...	...	...	7,481	8,772	8,713	7,481	8,772	8,713	7,494	8,784	8,728
263	To other general government units	...	...	...	77,703	81,604	89,556	63,147	63,258	68,274	—	—	—
2631	Current	...	...	...	74,977	78,826	86,760	60,421	60,480	65,478	—	—	—
2632	Capital	...	...	...	2,726	2,778	2,796	2,726	2,778	2,796	—	—	—
27	**Social benefits**	...	...	...	**22,748**	**21,679**	**21,117**	**135,124**	**135,773**	**131,678**	**145,287**	**146,204**	**149,315**
271	Social security benefits	...	...	...	—	—	—	52,261	53,518	54,826	52,261	53,518	54,826
272	Social assistance benefits	...	...	...	21,003	19,966	19,632	81,062	80,484	75,309	89,612	89,371	91,254
273	Employment-related social benefits	...	...	...	1,745	1,713	1,485	1,801	1,771	1,543	3,414	3,315	3,235
28	**Other expense**	...	...	...	**6,775**	**5,629**	**5,868**	**6,780**	**5,634**	**5,873**	**10,110**	**8,515**	**8,496**
281	Property expense other than interest	...	...	...	—	—	—	—	—	—	27	24	20
282	Transfers not elsewhere classified	...	...	...	6,775	5,629	5,868	6,780	5,634	5,873	10,083	8,491	8,476
2821	Current	...	...	...	2,365	2,578	2,616	2,370	2,583	2,621	5,001	4,675	4,530
2822	Capital	...	...	...	4,410	3,051	3,252	4,410	3,051	3,252	5,082	3,816	3,946
	Table 3 Transactions in assets and liabilities												
3	**Change in net worth from transactions**	**-9,682**	**-7,640**	**-11,058**	**-8,177**	**-7,356**	**-11,246**	**-16,658**	**-13,833**	**-10,199**	**-18,262**	**-15,069**	**-13,100**
31	**Net/Gross investment in nonfinancial assets**	**-4,392**	**-678**	**-67**	**-3,555**	**-177**	**130**	**-3,616**	**-276**	**108**	**-2,859**	**-194**	**-433**
311	Fixed assets	-628	-646	-39	266	356	808	205	257	786	1,915	1,181	1,693
3111	Buildings and structures	...	...	...	...	...	...	...	...	...	...	...	...
3112	Machinery and equipment	...	...	...	...	...	...	...	...	...	...	...	...
3113	Other fixed assets	...	...	...	...	...	...	...	...	...	...	...	...
3114	Weapons systems	...	...	...	...	...	...	...	...	...	...	...	...
312	Inventories	...	...	...	...	...	...	...	...	...	...	...	...
313	Valuables	...	...	...	...	...	...	...	...	...	...	...	...
314	Nonproduced assets	-3,764	-32	-28	-3,821	-533	-678	-3,821	-533	-678	-4,803	-1,400	-2,151
3141	Land	...	...	...	...	...	...	...	...	...	...	...	...
3142	Mineral and energy resources	...	...	...	...	...	...	...	...	...	...	...	...
3143	Other naturally occurring assets	...	...	...	...	...	...	...	...	...	...	...	...
3144	Intangible nonproduced assets	...	...	...	...	...	...	...	...	...	...	...	...
32	**Net acquisition of financial assets**	**10,611**	**1,277**	**-10,731**	**10,987**	**879**	**-13,837**	**3,369**	**-2,461**	**-15,323**	**-5,333**	**-5,965**	**-19,503**
	By instrument												
3201	Monetary gold and SDRs	—	—	—	—	—	—	—	—	—	—	—	—
3202	Currency and deposits	270	1,009	-684	435	966	-608	423	988	-611	-3,546	-859	-1,379
3203	Debt securities	-4,467	-3,919	148	-4,482	-3,916	148	-4,482	-3,916	148	-6,434	-4,772	-977
3204	Loans	11,335	6,396	-866	11,609	5,975	-991	5,143	1,180	-2,452	3,052	325	-4,176
3205	Equity and investment fund shares	1,662	-1,239	-1,419	1,678	-1,238	-4,500	1,678	-1,238	-4,500	1,280	-1,451	-4,665
3206	Insurance, pension, and standardized guarantee schemes	—	—	—	—	—	—	—	—	—	—	—	—
3207	Financial derivatives and employee stock options	1,536	-1,037	-5,753	1,536	-1,037	-5,753	1,536	-1,037	-5,753	1,536	-1,035	-5,753
3208	Other accounts receivable	275	67	-2,157	211	129	-2,133	-929	1,562	-2,155	-1,221	1,827	-2,553
	By debtor												
321	Domestic debtors	...	...	...	...	...	...	...	...	...	...	...	...
322	External debtors	...	...	...	...	...	...	...	...	...	...	...	...
33	**Net incurrence of liabilities**	**15,901**	**8,239**	**260**	**15,609**	**8,058**	**-2,461**	**16,411**	**11,096**	**-5,016**	**10,070**	**8,910**	**-6,836**
	By instrument												
3301	Special Drawing Rights (SDRs)	—	—	—	—	—	—	—	—	—	—	—	—
3302	Currency and deposits	5,674	34	7,414	5,848	-8	7,402	5,836	420	2,352	94	-136	967
3303	Debt securities	17,351	5,788	-8,741	17,357	9,295	-9,655	17,357	9,295	-9,655	16,511	9,523	-9,367
3304	Loans	-7,568	3,548	499	-7,683	-30	-1,440	-7,685	-30	-1,439	-6,671	-1,237	-1,636

Netherlands (138)

In Millions of Euros (EUR) / Fiscal Year Ends December 31st

		Budgetary Central Government			Central Government (excl. Social Security)			Central Government (incl. Social Security)			General Government		
		2013P	2014P	2015P	2013P	2014P	2015P	2013P	2014P	2015P	2013P	2014P	2015P
3305	Equity and investment fund shares	...	...	...	—	—	—	—	—	—	—	—	—
3306	Insurance, pension, and standardized guarantee schemes	—	—	—	—	—	—	—	—	—	—	—	—
3307	Financial derivatives and employee stock options	...	...	...	—	—	—	—	—	—	—	—	—
3308	Other accounts payable	444	-1,131	1,088	87	-1,199	1,232	903	1,411	3,726	136	760	3,200
	By creditor												
331	Domestic creditors	...	...	...	...	...	...	...	...	...	...	...	...
332	External creditors	...	...	...	...	...	...	...	...	...	...	...	...
	Table 4 Holding gains and losses in assets and liabilities												
4	**Change in net worth due to holding gains and losses**	...	...	...	...	...	...	—	—	—	...	...	...
41	**Holding gains and losses in nonfinancial assets**	...	...	...	...	...	...	—	—	—	...	...	...
411	Fixed assets	...	...	...	...	...	...	—	—	—	...	...	...
412	Inventories	...	...	...	...	...	...	—	—	—	...	...	...
413	Valuables	...	...	...	...	...	...	—	—	—	...	...	...
414	Nonproduced assets	...	...	...	...	...	...	—	—	—	...	...	...
42	**Holding gains and losses in financial assets**	...	...	...	**-9,553**	**15,344**	**8,178**	—	—	—	**-9,547**	**15,634**	**9,380**
	By instrument												
4201	Monetary gold and SDRs	...	...	...	—	—	—	—	—	—	—	—	—
4202	Currency and deposits	...	...	...	—	—	—	—	—	—	-68	22	59
4203	Debt securities	...	...	...	-521	317	140	-521	317	140	-346	378	196
4204	Loans	...	...	...	—	-124	-1,100	—	-124	—	60	-124	—
4205	Equity and investment fund shares	...	...	...	-4,362	73	9,174	-4,362	73	9,174	-4,854	367	9,162
4206	Insurance, pension, and standardized guarantee schemes	...	...	...	—	—	—	18	19	20	—	—	-1
4207	Financial derivatives and employee stock options	...	...	...	-4,670	15,024	-36	-4,702	15,124	-36	-4,548	14,940	-36
4208	Other accounts receivable	...	...	...	—	54	—	—	54	—	209	51	—
	By debtor												
421	Domestic debtors	...	...	...	...	...	...	—	—	—	...	...	...
422	External debtors	...	...	...	...	...	...	—	—	—	...	...	...
43	**Holding gains and losses in liabilities**	...	...	...	**-19,181**	**29,784**	**-5,608**	**-17,330**	**29,803**	**-4,488**	**-16,973**	**29,796**	**-4,462**
	By instrument												
4301	Special Drawing Rights (SDRs)	...	...	...	—	—	—	—	—	—	—	—	—
4302	Currency and deposits	...	...	...	-632	—	—	—	—	—	—	—	—
4303	Debt securities	...	...	...	-17,139	29,349	-4,532	-17,132	29,349	-4,532	-17,162	29,339	-4,545
4304	Loans	...	...	...	-1,023	79	-1,076	-216	79	24	59	101	83
4305	Equity and investment fund shares	...	...	...	—	—	—	—	—	—	—	—	—
4306	Insurance, pension, and standardized guarantee schemes	...	...	...	—	—	—	18	19	20	—	—	—
4307	Financial derivatives and employee stock options	...	...	...	—	—	—	—	—	—	—	—	—
4308	Other accounts payable	...	...	...	-387	356	—	—	356	—	130	356	—
	By creditor												
431	Domestic creditors	...	...	...	...	...	...	...	...	...	...	...	...
432	External creditors	...	...	...	...	...	...	...	...	...	...	...	...
	Table 5 Holding gains and losses in assets and liabilities												
5	**Change in net worth due to other volume changes**	...	...	...	...	...	...	...	...	...	...	...	...
51	**Other volume changes in nonfinancial assets**	...	...	...	...	...	...	...	...	...	...	...	...
511	Fixed assets	...	...	...	...	...	...	...	...	...	...	...	...
512	Inventories	...	...	...	...	...	...	...	...	...	...	...	...
513	Valuables	...	...	...	...	...	...	...	...	...	...	...	...
514	Nonproduced assets	...	...	...	...	...	...	...	...	...	...	...	...
52	**Other volume changes in financial assets**	...	...	...	**5,898**	**219**	**1,740**	**5,898**	**219**	**640**	**6,832**	**-233**	**641**

Netherlands (138)

In Millions of Euros (EUR) / Fiscal Year Ends December 31st

		Budgetary Central Government			Central Government (excl. Social Security)			Central Government (incl. Social Security)			General Government		
		2013P	2014P	2015P	2013P	2014P	2015P	2013P	2014P	2015P	2013P	2014P	2015P
	By instrument												
5201	Monetary gold and SDRs	...	...	...	—	—	—	—	—	—	—	—	—
5202	Currency and deposits	...	...	...	170	114	71	170	114	71	15	-168	71
5203	Debt securities	...	...	...	—	—	—	—	—	—	—	12	—
5204	Loans	...	...	...	5,925	88	472	5,925	88	-628	6,701	3	-628
5205	Equity and investment fund shares	...	...	...	-3	-1	1,182	-3	-1	1,182	-8	-18	1,182
5206	Insurance, pension, and standardized guarantee schemes	...	...	...	—	—	—	—	—	—	—	—	1
5207	Financial derivatives and employee stock options	...	...	...	—	—	—	—	—	—	—	—	—
5208	Other accounts receivable	...	...	...	-194	18	15	-194	18	15	124	-62	15
	By debtor												
521	Domestic debtors	...	...	...	4,740	131	1,635	4,740	131	535	5,674	-388	536
522	External debtors	...	...	...	1,158	88	105	1,158	88	105	1,158	155	105
53	**Other volume changes in liabilities**	**...**	**...**	**...**	**6,758**	**42**	**1,243**	**4,925**	**42**	**143**	**5,015**	**-291**	**143**
	By instrument												
5301	Special Drawing Rights (SDRs)	...	...	...	—	—	—	—	—	—	—	—	—
5302	Currency and deposits	...	...	...	—	—	—	-632	—	—	—	—	—
5303	Debt securities	...	...	...	—	—	55	-7	—	55	-7	—	55
5304	Loans	...	...	...	5,627	—	1,100	4,820	—	—	4,867	-103	—
5305	Equity and investment fund shares	...	...	...	—	—	—	—	—	—	—	—	—
5306	Insurance, pension, and standardized guarantee schemes	...	...	...	—	—	—	—	—	—	—	—	—
5307	Financial derivatives and employee stock options	...	...	...	—	—	—	—	—	—	—	—	—
5308	Other accounts payable	...	...	...	1,131	42	88	744	42	88	155	-188	88
	By creditor												
531	Domestic creditors	...	...	...	6,410	1,022	1,188	4,577	1,022	88	4,667	685	88
532	External creditors	...	...	...	348	-980	55	348	-980	55	348	-976	55
	Table 6 Balance sheet												
6	**Net worth**	...	...	...	...	...	...	...	...	...	...	...	...
61	**Nonfinancial assets**	...	...	...	...	...	...	...	...	...	...	...	...
611	Fixed assets	...	...	...	...	...	...	...	...	...	740,560	746,104	738,278
6111	Buildings and structures	...	...	...	...	...	...	...	...	...	357,061	359,546	355,223
6112	Machinery and equipment	...	...	...	...	...	...	...	...	...	...	...	...
6113	Other fixed assets	...	...	...	...	...	...	...	...	...	26,438	27,012	27,832
6114	Weapons systems	...	...	...	...	...	...	...	...	...	...	...	...
612	Inventories	...	...	...	...	...	...	...	...	...	—	—	—
613	Valuables	...	...	...	...	...	...	...	...	...	...	...	...
614	Nonproduced assets	...	...	...	...	...	...	...	...	...	...	...	...
6141	Land	...	...	...	...	...	...	...	...	...	39,462	36,296	36,820
6142	Mineral and energy resources	...	...	...	...	...	...	...	...	...	154,721	124,185	105,324
6143	Other naturally occurring assets	...	...	...	...	...	...	...	...	...	...	...	...
6144	Intangible nonproduced assets	...	...	...	...	...	...	...	...	...	...	...	...
62	**Financial assets**	**201,556**	**218,488**	**215,107**	**209,862**	**226,304**	**222,385**	**187,660**	**200,762**	**195,357**	**237,597**	**247,033**	**237,551**
	By instrument												
6201	Monetary gold and SDRs	—	—	—	—	—	—	—	—	—	—	—	—
6202	Currency and deposits	508	1,517	833	2,518	3,598	3,061	2,597	3,699	3,159	11,928	10,923	9,674
6203	Debt securities	4,724	1,122	1,410	4,857	1,258	1,546	4,857	1,258	1,546	13,287	8,905	8,124
6204	Loans	79,903	86,386	85,625	85,961	91,900	90,281	56,044	57,188	54,108	67,618	67,822	63,018
6205	Equity and investment fund shares	66,979	65,813	71,535	67,117	65,951	71,807	67,117	65,951	71,807	89,883	88,781	94,460
6206	Insurance, pension, and standardized guarantee schemes	—	—	—	—	—	—	—	—	—	—	—	—
6207	Financial derivatives and employee stock options	10,064	24,151	18,362	9,859	23,846	18,057	9,859	23,846	18,057	9,714	23,619	17,830
6208	Other accounts receivable	39,378	39,499	37,342	39,550	39,751	37,633	47,186	48,820	46,680	45,167	46,983	44,445
	By debtor												
621	Domestic debtors	...	...	...	...	...	...	...	...	...	...	...	...
622	External debtors	...	...	...	...	...	...	...	...	...	...	...	...
63	**Liabilities**	**439,301**	**477,332**	**473,084**	**445,677**	**483,561**	**476,735**	**445,914**	**486,836**	**477,455**	**499,749**	**538,164**	**527,009**

Netherlands (138)

In Millions of Euros (EUR) / Fiscal Year Ends December 31st

		Budgetary Central Government			Central Government (excl. Social Security)			Central Government (incl. Social Security)			General Government		
		2013P	2014P	2015P	2013P	2014P	2015P	2013P	2014P	2015P	2013P	2014P	2015P
	By instrument												
6301	Special Drawing Rights (SDRs)	—	—	—	—	—	—	—	—	—	—	—	—
6302	Currency and deposits	19,914	19,948	27,362	17,212	17,204	24,606	9,069	9,489	11,841	1,262	1,126	2,093
6303	Debt securities	378,375	413,520	400,247	378,332	416,976	402,844	378,332	416,976	402,844	376,994	415,856	401,999
6304	Loans	32,887	36,514	37,037	38,676	38,725	37,309	38,676	38,725	37,310	93,861	92,622	91,069
6305	Equity and investment fund shares	—	—	—	—	—	—	—	—	—	—	—	—
6306	Insurance, pension, and standardized guarantee schemes	—	—	—	—	—	—	—	—	—	—	—	—
6307	Financial derivatives and employee stock options	—	—	—	—	—	—	—	—	—	—	—	—
6308	Other accounts payable	8,125	7,350	8,438	11,457	10,656	11,976	19,837	21,646	25,460	27,632	28,560	31,848
	By creditor												
631	Domestic creditors	...	...	...	...	...	...	...	...	...	...	...	...
632	External creditors	...	...	...	...	...	...	...	...	...	...	...	...
	Memorandum items												
6M2	Net financial worth	-237,745	-258,844	-257,977	-235,815	-257,257	-254,350	-258,254	-286,074	-282,098	-262,152	-291,131	-289,458
6M3	Gross debt (D4) at market value	439,301	477,332	473,084	445,677	483,561	476,735	445,914	486,836	477,455	499,749	538,164	527,009
6M3D3	D3 debt liabilities at market value	439,301	477,332	473,084	445,677	483,561	476,735	445,914	486,836	477,455	499,749	538,164	527,009
6M3D2	D2 debt liabilities at market value	431,176	469,982	464,646	434,220	472,905	464,759	426,077	465,190	451,995	472,117	509,604	495,161
6M3D1	D1 debt liabilities at market value	411,262	450,034	437,284	417,008	455,701	440,153	417,008	455,701	440,154	470,855	508,478	493,068
6M4	Gross debt (D4) at nominal value	...	...	...	...	...	...	...	...	...	...	...	...
6M4D3	D3 debt liabilities at nominal value	...	...	...	...	...	...	...	...	...	...	...	...
6M4D2	D2 debt liabilities at nominal value	...	...	...	...	...	...	...	...	...	...	...	...
6M4D1	D1 debt liabilities at nominal value	...	...	...	...	...	...	...	...	...	...	...	...
6M35	Gross debt (D4) at face value	...	...	...	415,554	424,116	421,859	415,791	427,391	422,579	27,632	28,560	31,848
6M35D3	D3 debt liabilities at face value	...	...	...	415,554	424,116	421,859	415,791	427,391	422,579	27,632	28,560	31,848
6M35D2	D2 debt liabilities at face value	...	...	...	404,097	413,460	409,883	395,954	405,745	397,119	442,174	450,487	440,552
6M35D1	D1 debt liabilities at face value	...	...	...	386,885	396,256	385,277	386,885	396,256	385,278	440,912	449,361	438,459
6M93	Government gross debt per national definition	...	...	...	404,097	413,460	409,883	...	...	...	442,174	450,487	440,552
6M5	Arrears	...	...	...	...	...	...	...	...	...	...	...	...
6M6	Explicit contingent liabilities	...	...	...	...	...	...	...	...	...	...	...	...
6M61	of which: Publicly guaranteed debt	...	...	...	33,754	15,310	17,494	33,754	15,310	17,494	41,233	22,053	24,240
6M7	Net implicit obligations for social security benefits	...	...	...	...	...	...	...	...	...	...	...	...
	Table 7 Expenditure by functions of government												
7	**Expenditure**	...	...	...	**169,072**	**175,798**	**183,146**	...	...	...	**302,036**	**306,204**	**305,355**
701	**General public services**	...	...	...	**47,914**	**49,871**	**58,298**	...	...	...	**33,472**	**34,764**	**33,961**
7017	Public debt transactions	...	...	...	9,634	9,392	8,663	...	...	...	11,562	11,115	10,229
7018	Transfers of general character between levels of government	...	...	...	21,283	21,804	30,786	...	...	...	—	—	—
702	**Defense**	...	...	...	**7,541**	**7,325**	**7,722**	...	...	...	**7,541**	**7,325**	**7,719**
703	**Public order and safety**	...	...	...	**11,491**	**11,080**	**11,029**	...	...	...	**12,880**	**12,353**	**12,264**
704	**Economic affairs**	...	...	...	**16,061**	**18,698**	**17,555**	...	...	...	**25,062**	**27,639**	**26,873**
7042	Agriculture, forestry, fishing, and hunting	...	...	...	1,188	1,014	977	...	...	...	1,011	559	410
7043	Fuel and energy	...	...	...	808	801	844	...	...	...	864	871	906
7044	Mining, manufacturing, and construction	...	...	...	27	27	6	...	...	...	605	525	457
7045	Transport	...	...	...	10,412	9,998	9,802	...	...	...	15,659	15,825	15,407
7046	Communication	...	...	...	-3,734	61	53	...	...	...	-3,720	77	69
705	**Environmental protection**	...	...	...	**1,056**	**679**	**644**	...	...	...	**10,076**	**9,770**	**9,675**
706	**Housing and community amenities**	...	...	...	**891**	**941**	**399**	...	...	...	**3,437**	**3,051**	**2,174**
707	**Health**	...	...	...	**10,170**	**10,697**	**11,479**	...	...	...	**53,561**	**54,044**	**54,078**
7072	Outpatient services	...	...	...	3,680	4,142	5,063	...	...	...	14,004	13,952	14,730
7073	Hospital services	...	...	...	68	52	321	...	...	...	28,342	28,667	27,869
7074	Public health services	...	...	...	594	612	174	...	...	...	1,354	1,354	1,424
708	**Recreation, culture and religion**	...	...	...	**1,860**	**1,986**	**2,024**	...	...	...	**10,024**	**9,644**	**9,502**
709	**Education**	...	...	...	**30,806**	**30,644**	**32,298**	...	...	...	**35,268**	**35,727**	**36,786**
7091	Pre-primary and primary education	...	...	...	9,961	9,566	10,065	...	...	...	11,181	11,333	11,583
7092	Secondary education	...	...	...	12,118	12,361	13,116	...	...	...	13,450	13,991	14,526
7094	Tertiary education	...	...	...	7,810	7,899	8,420	...	...	...	8,905	8,969	9,356

Netherlands (138)

In Millions of Euros (EUR) / Fiscal Year Ends December 31st

		Budgetary Central Government			Central Government (excl. Social Security)			Central Government (incl. Social Security)			General Government		
		2013P	2014P	2015P	2013P	2014P	2015P	2013P	2014P	2015P	2013P	2014P	2015P
710	**Social protection**	...	...	...	41,282	43,877	41,698	...	...	...	110,715	111,887	112,323
7z	Statistical discrepancy: Expenditure	...	...	...	—	—	—	...	...	...	—	—	—
	Table 8 Financial transactions by counterpart sector												
32	**Net acquisition of financial assets**	10,611	1,277	-10,731	10,987	879	-13,837	3,369	-2,461	-15,323	-5,333	-5,965	-19,503
321	Domestic debtors	...	...	...	...	...	...	...	...	...	...	...	...
8211	General government	...	...	...	...	...	...	...	...	...	—	—	—
8212	Central bank	...	...	...	...	...	...	...	...	...	...	...	...
8213	Deposit-taking corporations except the central bank	...	...	...	...	...	...	...	...	...	...	...	...
8214	Other financial corporations	...	...	...	...	...	...	...	...	...	...	...	...
8215	Nonfinancial corporations	...	...	...	...	...	...	...	...	...	...	...	...
8216	Households & nonprofit institutions serving households	...	...	...	...	...	...	...	...	...	...	...	...
322	External debtors	...	...	...	...	...	...	...	...	...	...	...	...
8221	General government	...	...	...	...	...	...	...	...	...	...	...	...
8227	International organizations	...	...	...	...	...	...	...	...	...	...	...	...
8228	Financial corporations other than international organizations	...	...	...	...	...	...	...	...	...	...	...	...
8229	Other nonresidents	...	...	...	...	...	...	...	...	...	...	...	...
33	**Net incurrence of liabilities**	15,901	8,239	260	15,609	8,058	-2,461	16,411	11,096	-5,016	10,070	8,910	-6,836
331	Domestic creditors	...	...	...	...	...	...	...	...	...	...	...	...
8311	General government	...	...	...	...	...	...	...	...	...	—	—	—
8312	Central bank	...	...	...	...	...	...	...	...	...	...	...	...
8313	Deposit-taking corporations except the central bank	...	...	...	...	...	...	...	...	...	...	...	...
8314	Other financial corporations	...	...	...	...	...	...	...	...	...	...	...	...
8315	Nonfinancial corporations	...	...	...	...	...	...	...	...	...	...	...	...
8316	Households & nonprofit institutions serving households	...	...	...	...	...	...	...	...	...	...	...	...
332	External creditors	...	...	...	...	...	...	...	...	...	...	...	...
8321	General government	...	...	...	...	...	...	...	...	...	...	...	...
8327	International organizations	...	...	...	...	...	...	...	...	...	...	...	...
8328	Financial corporations other than international organizations	...	...	...	...	...	...	...	...	...	...	...	...
8329	Other nonresidents	...	...	...	...	...	...	...	...	...	...	...	...
	Table 9 Total other economic flows in assets and liabilities												
9	**Change in net worth due to other economic flows**	...	...	...	...	...	...	...	...	...	...	...	...
91	**Other economic flows in nonfinancial assets**	...	...	...	...	...	...	...	...	...	...	...	...
911	Fixed assets	...	...	...	...	...	...	...	...	...	...	...	...
912	Inventories	...	...	...	...	...	...	...	...	...	...	...	...
913	Valuables	...	...	...	...	...	...	...	...	...	...	...	...
914	Nonproduced assets	...	...	...	...	...	...	...	...	...	...	...	...
92	**Other economic flows in financial assets**	-9,571	15,655	7,350	-3,655	15,563	9,918	-3,669	15,682	9,938	-2,715	15,401	10,021
	By instrument												
9201	Monetary gold and SDRs	—	—	—	—	—	—	—	—	—	—	—	—
9202	Currency and deposits	—	—	—	170	114	71	170	114	71	-53	-146	130
9203	Debt securities	-521	317	140	-521	317	140	-521	317	140	-346	390	196
9204	Loans	14	87	105	5,925	-36	-628	5,925	-36	-628	6,761	-121	-628
9205	Equity and investment fund shares	-4,362	73	7,141	-4,365	72	10,356	-4,365	72	10,356	-4,862	349	10,344
9206	Insurance, pension, and standardized guarantee schemes	—	—	—	—	—	—	18	19	20	—	—	—
9207	Financial derivatives and employee stock options	-4,702	15,124	-36	-4,670	15,024	-36	-4,702	15,124	-36	-4,548	14,940	-36
9208	Other accounts receivable	—	54	—	-194	72	15	-194	72	15	333	-11	15
	By debtor												
921	Domestic debtors	...	...	...	...	...	...	...	...	...	...	...	...
922	External debtors	...	...	...	...	...	...	...	...	...	...	...	...
93	**Other economic flows in liabilities**	-17,350	29,792	-4,508	-12,423	29,826	-4,365	-12,405	29,845	-4,345	-11,958	29,505	-4,319

Netherlands (138)

In Millions of Euros (EUR) / Fiscal Year Ends December 31st

		Budgetary Central Government			Central Government (excl. Social Security)			Central Government (incl. Social Security)			General Government		
		2013P	2014P	2015P	2013P	2014P	2015P	2013P	2014P	2015P	2013P	2014P	2015P
	By instrument												
9301	Special Drawing Rights (SDRs)	—	—	—	—	—	—	—	—	—	—	—	—
9302	Currency and deposits	—	—	—	-632	—	—	-632	—	—	—	—	—
9303	Debt securities	-17,134	29,357	-4,532	-17,139	29,349	-4,477	-17,139	29,349	-4,477	-17,169	29,339	-4,490
9304	Loans	-216	79	24	4,604	79	24	4,604	79	24	4,926	-2	83
9305	Equity and investment fund shares	—	—	—	—	—	—	—	—	—	—	—	—
9306	Insurance, pension, and standardized guarantee schemes	—	—	—	—	—	—	18	19	20	—	—	—
9307	Financial derivatives and employee stock options	—	—	—	—	—	—	—	—	—	—	—	—
9308	Other accounts payable	—	356	—	744	398	88	744	398	88	285	168	88
	By creditor												
931	Domestic creditors	...	...	...	...	...	...	...	...	...	...	...	...
932	External creditors	...	...	...	...	...	...	...	...	...	...	...	...
	Memorandum items												
9M2	Change in net financial worth due to other economic flows	7,779	-14,137	11,858	8,768	-14,263	14,283	8,736	-14,163	14,283	9,243	-14,104	14,340
9M3	Gross debt (D4) at market value: other economic flows	-17,350	29,792	-4,508	-12,423	29,826	-4,365	-12,405	29,845	-4,345	-11,958	29,505	-4,319
9M3D3	D3 debt liabilities at market value: other economic flows	-17,350	29,792	-4,508	-12,423	29,826	-4,365	-12,423	29,826	-4,365	-11,958	29,505	-4,319
9M3D2	D2 debt liabilities at market value: other economic flows	-17,350	29,436	-4,508	-13,167	29,428	-4,453	-13,167	29,428	-4,453	-12,243	29,337	-4,407
9M3D1	D1 debt liabilities at market value: other economic flows	-17,350	29,436	-4,508	-12,535	29,428	-4,453	-12,535	29,428	-4,453	-12,243	29,337	-4,407

New Zealand (196)

In Millions of New Zealand Dollars (NZD) / Fiscal Year Ends June 30th

		Budgetary Central Government			Central Government (excl. Social Security)			Central Government (incl. Social Security)			General Government		
		2013	2014	2015	2013	2014	2015	2013	2014	2015	2013	2014	2015
	Statement of operations												
1	Revenue	...	...	...	...	...	...	75,839	78,688	83,340	...	...	...
2	Expense	...	...	...	...	...	...	75,427	78,598	80,821	...	...	...
GOB	**Gross operating balance**	**...**	**...**	**...**	**...**	**...**	**...**	**3,034**	**2,833**	**5,388**	**...**	**...**	**...**
NOB	**Net operating balance**	**...**	**...**	**...**	**...**	**...**	**...**	**412**	**90**	**2,519**	**...**	**...**	**...**
31	Net/Gross investment in nonfinancial assets	...	...	...	...	...	...	1,685	2,784	2,232	...	...	...
2M	Expenditure	...	...	...	...	...	...	77,112	81,382	83,053	...	...	...
NLB	**Net lending (+) / Net borrowing (-)**	**...**	**...**	**...**	**...**	**...**	**...**	**-1,273**	**-2,694**	**287**	**...**	**...**	**...**
32	Net acquisition of financial assets	...	...	...	...	...	...	...	...	...	...	...	...
33	Net incurrence of liabilities	...	...	...	...	...	...	...	...	...	...	...	...
NLBz	Statistical discrepancy	...	...	...	...	...	...	...	...	...	...	...	...
	Memorandum items												
PB	Primary net lending / net borrowing	...	...	...	...	...	...	3,047	851	3,955	...	...	...
GB	Government balance per national definition	...	...	...	...	...	...	...	...	...	...	...	...
	Statement of other economic flows												
	Balance sheet												
6	**Net worth**	**...**	**...**	**...**	**...**	**...**	**...**	**60,601**	**73,454**	**80,639**	**...**	**...**	**...**
61	Nonfinancial assets	...	...	...	...	...	...	75,168	81,876	81,626	...	...	...
62	Financial assets	...	...	...	...	...	...	123,373	128,951	141,834	...	...	...
63	Liabilities	...	...	...	...	...	...	137,940	137,373	142,821	...	...	...
	Table 1 Revenue												
1	**Revenue**	**...**	**...**	**...**	**...**	**...**	**...**	**75,839**	**78,688**	**83,340**	**...**	**...**	**...**
11	**Taxes**	**...**	**...**	**...**	**...**	**...**	**...**	**62,233**	**64,312**	**69,267**	**...**	**...**	**...**
111	Taxes on income, profits, and capital gains	...	...	...	...	...	...	38,157	40,012	43,224	...	...	...
1111	Payable by individuals	...	...	...	...	...	...	27,058	28,412	30,549	...	...	...
1112	Payable by corporations and other enterprises	...	...	...	...	...	...	11,099	11,600	12,675	...	...	...
1113	Other taxes on income, profits, and capital gains	...	...	...	...	...	...	...	...	—	...	...	...
112	Taxes on payroll and workforce	...	...	...	...	...	...	...	...	—	...	...	...
113	Taxes on property	...	...	...	...	...	...	—	—	—	...	...	...
114	Taxes on goods and services	...	...	...	...	...	...	21,905	22,015	23,594	...	...	...
1141	General taxes on goods and services	...	...	...	...	...	...	16,713	16,582	17,605	...	...	...
1142	Excises	...	...	...	...	...	...	2,080	2,098	2,271	...	...	...
115	Taxes on international trade and transactions	...	...	...	...	...	...	2,124	2,237	2,449	...	...	...
116	Other taxes	...	...	...	...	...	...	47	48	—	...	...	...
12	**Social contributions**	**...**	**...**	**...**	**...**	**...**	**...**	**2,586**	**2,618**	**2,453**	**...**	**...**	**...**
121	Social security contributions	...	...	...	...	...	...	2,586	2,618	2,453	...	...	...
122	Other social contributions	...	...	...	...	...	...	—	—	...	...	...	...
13	**Grants**	**...**	**...**	**...**	**...**	**...**	**...**	**185**	**214**	**238**	**...**	**...**	**...**
131	From foreign governments	...	...	...	...	...	...	...	...	238	...	...	...
132	From international organizations	...	...	...	...	...	...	...	...	—	...	...	...
133	From other general government units	...	...	...	...	...	...	185	214	—	...	...	...
1331	Current	...	...	...	...	...	...	185	214	—	...	...	...
1332	Capital	...	...	...	...	...	...	...	...	—	...	...	...
14	**Other revenue**	**...**	**...**	**...**	**...**	**...**	**...**	**10,835**	**11,544**	**11,382**	**...**	**...**	**...**
	Table 2 Expense by economic type												
2	**Expense**	**...**	**...**	**...**	**...**	**...**	**...**	**75,427**	**78,598**	**80,821**	**...**	**...**	**...**
21	**Compensation of employees**	**...**	**...**	**...**	**...**	**...**	**...**	**19,119**	**20,027**	**20,628**	**...**	**...**	**...**
211	Wages and salaries	...	...	...	...	...	...	...	...	...	...	...	...
212	Employers' social contributions	...	...	...	...	...	...	...	...	...	...	...	...
22	**Use of goods and services**	**...**	**...**	**...**	**...**	**...**	**...**	**9,117**	**9,753**	**9,542**	**...**	**...**	**...**
23	**Consumption of fixed capital**	**...**	**...**	**...**	**...**	**...**	**...**	**2,622**	**2,743**	**2,869**	**...**	**...**	**...**
24	**Interest**	**...**	**...**	**...**	**...**	**...**	**...**	**4,320**	**3,545**	**3,668**	**...**	**...**	**...**
25	**Subsidies**	**...**	**...**	**...**	**...**	**...**	**...**	**685**	**540**	**499**	**...**	**...**	**...**

New Zealand (196)

In Millions of New Zealand Dollars (NZD) / Fiscal Year Ends June 30th

		Budgetary Central Government			Central Government (excl. Social Security)			Central Government (incl. Social Security)			General Government		
		2013	2014	2015	2013	2014	2015	2013	2014	2015	2013	2014	2015
26	**Grants**	...	...	...	...	...	...	**1,439**	**1,948**	**1,983**	...	...	...
261	To foreign governments	...	...	...	...	...	...	—	—	—	...	...	...
262	To international organizations	...	...	...	...	...	...	—	—	—	...	...	...
263	To other general government units	...	...	...	...	...	...	1,439	1,948	1,983	...	...	...
2631	Current	...	...	...	...	...	...	801	1,339	1,438	...	...	...
2632	Capital	...	...	...	...	...	...	638	608	545	...	...	...
27	**Social benefits**	...	...	...	...	...	...	**32,493**	**33,377**	**35,067**	...	...	...
271	Social security benefits	...	...	...	...	...	...	...	...	...	...	...	...
272	Social assistance benefits	...	...	...	...	...	...	...	...	...	...	...	...
273	Employment-related social benefits	...	...	...	...	...	...	...	...	...	...	...	...
28	**Other expense**	...	...	...	...	...	...	**5,632**	**6,666**	**6,565**	...	...	...
281	Property expense other than interest	...	...	...	...	...	...	—	—	—	...	...	...
282	Transfers not elsewhere classified	...	...	...	...	...	...	5,632	6,666	6,565	...	...	...
2821	Current	...	...	...	...	...	...	5,216	5,465	6,128	...	...	...
2822	Capital	...	...	...	...	...	...	416	1,201	437	...	...	...
	Table 3 Transactions in assets and liabilities												
3	**Change in net worth from transactions**	...	...	...	...	...	...	...	...	**2,232**	...	...	...
31	**Net/Gross investment in nonfinancial assets**	...	...	...	...	...	...	**1,685**	**2,784**	**2,232**	...	...	...
311	Fixed assets	...	...	...	...	...	...	1,497	1,968	2,041	...	...	...
3111	Buildings and structures	...	...	...	...	...	...	1,481	2,096	2,240	...	...	...
3112	Machinery and equipment	...	...	...	...	...	...	-42	-258	-284	...	...	...
3113	Other fixed assets	...	...	...	...	...	...	58	130	85	...	...	...
3114	Weapons systems	...	...	...	...	...	...	—	—	—	...	...	...
312	Inventories	...	...	...	...	...	...	-74	-30	22	...	...	...
313	Valuables	...	...	...	...	...	...	10	2	2	...	...	...
314	Nonproduced assets	...	...	...	...	...	...	252	845	167	...	...	...
3141	Land	...	...	...	...	...	...	223	758	95	...	...	...
3142	Mineral and energy resources	...	...	...	...	...	...	—	—	—	...	...	...
3143	Other naturally occurring assets	...	...	...	...	...	...	—	—	—	...	...	...
3144	Intangible nonproduced assets	...	...	...	...	...	...	29	88	72	...	...	...
32	**Net acquisition of financial assets**	...	...	...	...	...	...	...	...	...	...	...	...
	By instrument												
3201	Monetary gold and SDRs	...	...	...	...	...	...	...	...	...	...	...	...
3202	Currency and deposits	...	...	...	...	...	...	...	...	...	...	...	...
3203	Debt securities	...	...	...	...	...	...	...	...	...	...	...	...
3204	Loans	...	...	...	...	...	...	...	...	...	...	...	...
3205	Equity and investment fund shares	...	...	...	...	...	...	...	...	...	...	...	...
3206	Insurance, pension, and standardized guarantee schemes	...	...	...	...	...	...	...	...	...	...	...	...
3207	Financial derivatives and employee stock options	...	...	...	...	...	...	...	...	...	...	...	...
3208	Other accounts receivable	...	...	...	...	...	...	...	...	...	...	...	...
	By debtor												
321	Domestic debtors	...	...	...	...	...	...	...	...	...	...	...	...
322	External debtors	...	...	...	...	...	...	...	...	...	...	...	...
33	**Net incurrence of liabilities**	...	...	...	...	...	...	...	...	...	...	...	...
	By instrument												
3301	Special Drawing Rights (SDRs)	...	...	...	...	...	...	...	...	...	...	...	...
3302	Currency and deposits	...	...	...	...	...	...	...	...	...	...	...	...
3303	Debt securities	...	...	...	...	...	...	...	...	...	...	...	...
3304	Loans	...	...	...	...	...	...	...	...	...	...	...	...
3305	Equity and investment fund shares	...	...	...	...	...	...	...	...	...	...	...	...
3306	Insurance, pension, and standardized guarantee schemes	...	...	...	...	...	...	...	...	...	...	...	...
3307	Financial derivatives and employee stock options	...	...	...	...	...	...	...	...	...	...	...	...
3308	Other accounts payable	...	...	...	...	...	...	...	...	...	...	...	...

New Zealand (196)

In Millions of New Zealand Dollars (NZD) / Fiscal Year Ends June 30th

		Budgetary Central Government			Central Government (excl. Social Security)			Central Government (incl. Social Security)			General Government		
		2013	2014	2015	2013	2014	2015	2013	2014	2015	2013	2014	2015
	By creditor												
331	Domestic creditors	...	...	...	...	...	...	...	...	...	...	...	...
332	External creditors	...	...	...	...	...	...	...	...	...	...	...	...
	Table 4 Holding gains and losses in assets and liabilities												
	Table 5 Holding gains and losses in assets and liabilities												
	Table 6 Balance sheet												
6	**Net worth**	...	...	...	...	...	...	**60,601**	**73,454**	**80,639**	...	...	...
61	**Nonfinancial assets**	...	...	...	...	...	...	**75,168**	**81,876**	**81,626**	...	...	...
611	Fixed assets	...	...	...	...	...	...	52,827	57,708	56,337	...	...	...
6111	Buildings and structures	...	...	...	...	...	...	44,093	48,892	52,002	...	...	...
6112	Machinery and equipment	...	...	...	...	...	...	3,541	2,941	2,927	...	...	...
6113	Other fixed assets	...	...	...	...	...	...	5,193	5,875	1,408	...	...	...
6114	Weapons systems	...	...	...	...	...	...	—	—	—	...	...	...
612	Inventories	...	...	...	...	...	...	539	515	535	...	...	...
613	Valuables	...	...	...	...	...	...	80	0	—	...	...	...
614	Nonproduced assets	...	...	...	...	...	...	21,722	23,652	24,754	...	...	...
6141	Land	...	...	...	...	...	...	21,312	23,386	24,495	...	...	...
6142	Mineral and energy resources	...	...	...	...	...	...	—	—	—	...	...	...
6143	Other naturally occurring assets	...	...	...	...	...	...	—	—	—	...	...	...
6144	Intangible nonproduced assets	...	...	...	...	...	...	410	266	259	...	...	...
62	**Financial assets**	...	...	...	...	...	...	**123,373**	**128,951**	**141,834**	...	...	...
	By instrument												
6201	Monetary gold and SDRs	...	...	...	...	...	...	—	—	—	...	...	...
6202	Currency and deposits	...	...	...	...	...	...	10,183	14,792	14,669	...	...	...
6203	Debt securities	...	...	...	...	...	...	11,645	22,602	25,684	...	...	...
6204	Loans	...	...	...	...	...	...	17,324	16,057	17,255	...	...	...
6205	Equity and investment fund shares	...	...	...	...	...	...	60,973	55,965	65,065	...	...	...
6206	Insurance, pension, and standardized guarantee schemes	...	...	...	...	...	...	—	—	—	...	...	...
6207	Financial derivatives and employee stock options	...	...	...	...	...	...	—	—	—	...	...	...
6208	Other accounts receivable	...	...	...	...	...	...	23,248	19,535	19,161	...	...	...
	By debtor												
621	Domestic debtors	...	...	...	...	...	...	...	...	...	...	...	...
622	External debtors	...	...	...	...	...	...	...	...	...	...	...	...
63	**Liabilities**	...	...	...	...	...	...	**137,940**	**137,373**	**142,821**	...	...	...
	By instrument												
6301	Special Drawing Rights (SDRs)	...	...	...	...	...	...	—	—	—	...	...	...
6302	Currency and deposits	...	...	...	...	...	...	—	...	—	...	...	...
6303	Debt securities	...	...	...	...	...	...	65,286	67,127	68,885	...	...	...
6304	Loans	...	...	...	...	...	...	5,548	4,258	4,229	...	...	...
6305	Equity and investment fund shares	...	...	...	...	...	...	—	—	—	...	...	...
6306	Insurance, pension, and standardized guarantee schemes	...	...	...	...	...	...	49,719	46,514	47,300	...	...	...
6307	Financial derivatives and employee stock options	...	...	...	...	...	...	—	—	—	...	...	...
6308	Other accounts payable	...	...	...	...	...	...	17,387	19,473	22,407	...	...	...
	By creditor												
631	Domestic creditors	...	...	...	...	...	...	...	...	...	...	...	...
632	External creditors	...	...	...	...	...	...	...	...	...	...	...	...
	Memorandum items												
6M2	Net financial worth	...	...	...	...	...	...	-14,567	-8,422	-987	...	...	...
6M3	Gross debt (D4) at market value	...	...	...	...	...	...	...	...	...	...	...	...
6M3D3	D3 debt liabilities at market value	...	...	...	...	...	...	...	...	...	...	...	...
6M3D2	D2 debt liabilities at market value	...	...	...	...	...	...	...	...	...	...	...	...
6M3D1	D1 debt liabilities at market value	...	...	...	...	...	...	...	...	...	...	...	...
6M4	Gross debt (D4) at nominal value	...	...	...	...	...	...	...	...	...	...	...	...
6M4D3	D3 debt liabilities at nominal value	...	...	...	...	...	...	...	...	...	...	...	...
6M4D2	D2 debt liabilities at nominal value	...	...	...	...	...	...	...	...	...	...	...	...
6M4D1	D1 debt liabilities at nominal value	...	...	...	...	...	...	...	...	...	...	...	...

New Zealand (196)

In Millions of New Zealand Dollars (NZD) / Fiscal Year Ends June 30th

		Budgetary Central Government			Central Government (excl. Social Security)			Central Government (incl. Social Security)			General Government		
		2013	2014	2015	2013	2014	2015	2013	2014	2015	2013	2014	2015
6M35	Gross debt (D4) at face value	...	...	...	...	...	...	...	...	142,821	...	...	...
6M35D3	D3 debt liabilities at face value	...	...	...	...	...	...	...	...	95,521	...	...	...
6M35D2	D2 debt liabilities at face value	...	...	...	...	...	...	...	...	73,114	...	...	...
6M35D1	D1 debt liabilities at face value	...	...	...	...	...	...	...	71,385	73,114	...	...	...
6M93	Government gross debt per national definition	...	...	...	...	...	...	...	...	...	...	...	...
6M5	Arrears	...	...	...	...	...	...	...	...	...	...	...	...
6M6	Explicit contingent liabilities	...	...	...	...	...	...	...	...	...	...	...	...
6M61	of which: Publicly guaranteed debt	...	...	...	...	...	...	...	...	...	...	...	...
6M7	Net implicit obligations for social security benefits	...	...	...	...	...	...	...	...	...	...	...	...
	Table 7 Expenditure by functions of government												
7	**Expenditure**	...	...	...	...	...	...	77,112	78,598	83,053	...	...	...
701	**General public services**	...	...	...	...	...	...	20,240	20,655	7,835	...	...	...
7017	Public debt transactions	...	...	...	...	...	...	4,320	3,545	...	...	...	...
7018	Transfers of general character between levels of government	...	...	...	...	...	...	...	...	...	...	...	...
702	**Defense**	...	...	...	...	...	...	1,662	1,879	2,423	...	...	...
703	**Public order and safety**	...	...	...	...	...	...	5,137	4,769	4,508	...	...	...
704	**Economic affairs**	...	...	...	...	...	...	6,612	5,733	6,107	...	...	...
7042	Agriculture, forestry, fishing, and hunting	...	...	...	...	...	...	...	...	...	...	...	...
7043	Fuel and energy	...	...	...	...	...	...	...	...	...	...	...	...
7044	Mining, manufacturing, and construction	...	...	...	...	...	...	...	...	...	...	...	...
7045	Transport	...	...	...	...	...	...	...	...	...	...	...	...
7046	Communication	...	...	...	...	...	...	...	...	...	...	...	...
705	**Environmental protection**	...	...	...	...	...	...	667	700	629	...	...	...
706	**Housing and community amenities**	...	...	...	...	...	...	294	351	419	...	...	...
707	**Health**	...	...	...	...	...	...	15,293	15,916	16,836	...	...	...
7072	Outpatient services	...	...	...	...	...	...	...	...	...	...	...	...
7073	Hospital services	...	...	...	...	...	...	...	...	...	...	...	...
7074	Public health services	...	...	...	...	...	...	...	...	...	...	...	...
708	**Recreation, culture and religion**	...	...	...	...	...	...	882	902	912	...	...	...
709	**Education**	...	...	...	...	...	...	14,428	14,718	15,173	...	...	...
7091	Pre-primary and primary education	...	...	...	...	...	...	...	...	...	...	...	...
7092	Secondary education	...	...	...	...	...	...	...	...	...	...	...	...
7094	Tertiary education	...	...	...	...	...	...	...	...	...	...	...	...
710	**Social protection**	...	...	...	...	...	...	11,897	12,975	28,211	...	...	...
7z	Statistical discrepancy: Expenditure	...	...	...	...	...	...	...	...	...	...	...	...
	Table 8 Financial transactions by counterpart sector												
32	**Net acquisition of financial assets**	...	...	...	...	...	...	...	...	...	...	...	...
321	Domestic debtors	...	...	...	...	...	...	...	...	...	...	...	...
322	External debtors	...	...	...	...	...	...	...	...	...	...	...	...
33	**Net incurrence of liabilities**	...	...	...	...	...	...	...	...	...	...	...	...
331	Domestic creditors	...	...	...	...	...	...	...	...	...	...	...	...
332	External creditors	...	...	...	...	...	...	...	...	...	...	...	...
	Table 9 Total other economic flows in assets and liabilities												

Nicaragua (278)

In Millions of Nicaraguan Cordobas (NIO) / Fiscal Year Ends December 31st

		Budgetary Central Government			Central Government (excl. Social Security)			Central Government (incl. Social Security)			General Government		
		2013	2014	2015P	2013	2014	2015	2013	2014	2015	2013	2014	2015
	Statement of operations												
1	Revenue	46,701	53,731	61,470	...	...	...	...	...	...	...	...	...
2	Expense	40,976	47,580	55,371	...	...	...	...	...	...	...	...	...
GOB	**Gross operating balance**	**5,725**	**6,151**	**6,099**	...	...	...	...	...	...	...	...	...
NOB	**Net operating balance**	...	...	...	...	...	...	...	...	...	...	...	...
31	Net/Gross investment in nonfinancial assets	5,549	7,104	8,270	...	...	...	...	...	...	...	...	...
2M	Expenditure	46,524	54,684	63,641	...	...	...	...	...	...	...	...	...
NLB	**Net lending (+) / Net borrowing (-)**	**177**	**-953**	**-2,171**	...	...	...	...	...	...	...	...	...
32	Net acquisition of financial assets	...	...	...	...	...	...	...	...	...	...	...	...
33	Net incurrence of liabilities	...	...	...	...	...	...	...	...	...	...	...	...
NLBz	Statistical discrepancy	...	...	...	...	...	...	...	...	...	...	...	...
	Memorandum items												
PB	Primary net lending / net borrowing	2,696	1,686	879	...	...	...	...	...	...	...	...	...
GB	Government balance per national definition	...	...	...	...	...	...	...	...	...	...	...	...
	Statement of other economic flows												
	Balance sheet												
	Table 1 Revenue												
1	**Revenue**	**46,701**	**53,731**	**61,470**	...	...	...	...	...	...	...	...	...
11	**Taxes**	**40,785**	**47,236**	**54,206**	...	...	...	...	...	...	...	...	...
111	Taxes on income, profits, and capital gains	14,521	17,658	20,800	...	...	...	...	...	...	...	...	...
1111	Payable by individuals	...	...	...	...	...	...	...	...	...	...	...	...
1112	Payable by corporations and other enterprises	...	...	...	...	...	...	...	...	...	...	...	...
1113	Other taxes on income, profits, and capital gains	...	...	...	...	...	...	...	...	...	...	...	...
112	Taxes on payroll and workforce	—	—	—	...	...	...	...	...	...	...	...	...
113	Taxes on property	311	374	513	...	...	...	...	...	...	...	...	...
114	Taxes on goods and services	23,990	27,139	30,486	...	...	...	...	...	...	...	...	...
1141	General taxes on goods and services	16,736	19,385	20,714	...	...	...	...	...	...	...	...	...
1142	Excises	7,254	7,755	9,773	...	...	...	...	...	...	...	...	...
115	Taxes on international trade and transactions	1,886	1,977	2,317	...	...	...	...	...	...	...	...	...
116	Other taxes	77	87	90	...	...	...	...	...	...	...	...	...
12	**Social contributions**	—	—	—	...	...	...	...	...	...	...	...	...
121	Social security contributions	—	—	—	...	...	...	...	...	...	...	...	...
122	Other social contributions	—	—	—	...	...	...	...	...	...	...	...	...
13	**Grants**	**2,667**	**3,046**	**3,306**	...	...	...	...	...	...	...	...	...
131	From foreign governments	...	...	...	...	...	...	...	...	...	...	...	...
132	From international organizations	...	...	...	...	...	...	...	...	...	...	...	...
133	From other general government units	...	...	...	...	...	...	...	...	...	...	...	...
1331	Current	...	...	...	...	...	...	...	...	...	...	...	...
1332	Capital	...	...	...	...	...	...	...	...	...	...	...	...
14	**Other revenue**	**3,249**	**3,449**	**3,959**	...	...	...	...	...	...	...	...	...
	Table 2 Expense by economic type												
2	**Expense**	**40,976**	**47,580**	**55,371**	...	...	...	...	...	...	...	...	...
21	**Compensation of employees**	**15,204**	**18,305**	**20,547**	...	...	...	...	...	...	...	...	...
211	Wages and salaries	13,450	16,236	18,124	...	...	...	...	...	...	...	...	...
212	Employers' social contributions	1,754	2,070	2,423	...	...	...	...	...	...	...	...	...
22	**Use of goods and services**	**6,350**	**7,433**	**8,589**	...	...	...	...	...	...	...	...	...
23	**Consumption of fixed capital**	...	...	...	...	...	...	...	...	...	...	...	...
24	**Interest**	**2,520**	**2,639**	**3,050**	...	...	...	...	...	...	...	...	...
25	**Subsidies**	**144**	**231**	**195**	...	...	...	...	...	...	...	...	...
26	**Grants**	**12,848**	**14,288**	**17,811**	...	...	...	...	...	...	...	...	...
261	To foreign governments	—	—	—	...	...	...	...	...	...	...	...	...
262	To international organizations	142	151	164	...	...	...	...	...	...	...	...	...
263	To other general government units	12,705	14,137	17,647	...	...	...	...	...	...	...	...	...
2631	Current	7,938	8,884	10,307	...	...	...	...	...	...	...	...	...
2632	Capital	4,768	5,253	7,340	...	...	...	...	...	...	...	...	...

Nicaragua (278)

In Millions of Nicaraguan Cordobas (NIO) / Fiscal Year Ends December 31st

		Budgetary Central Government			Central Government (excl. Social Security)			Central Government (incl. Social Security)			General Government		
		2013	2014	2015P	2013	2014	2015	2013	2014	2015	2013	2014	2015
27	**Social benefits**	**964**	**1,104**	**1,224**	**...**	**...**	**...**	**...**	**...**	**...**	**...**	**...**	**...**
271	Social security benefits	...	...	...	...	...	...	...	...	...	...	...	...
272	Social assistance benefits	...	...	...	...	...	...	...	...	...	...	...	...
273	Employment-related social benefits	...	...	...	...	...	...	...	...	...	...	...	...
28	**Other expense**	**2,947**	**3,581**	**3,955**	**...**	**...**	**...**	**...**	**...**	**...**	**...**	**...**	**...**
281	Property expense other than interest	—	—	—	...	...	...	...	...	...	...	...	...
282	Transfers not elsewhere classified	2,947	3,581	3,955	...	...	...	...	...	...	...	...	...
2821	Current	1,609	1,993	2,002	...	...	...	...	...	...	...	...	...
2822	Capital	1,338	1,587	1,954	...	...	...	...	...	...	...	...	...
	Table 3 Transactions in assets and liabilities												
3	**Change in net worth from transactions**	**...**	**...**	**...**	**...**	**...**	**...**	**...**	**...**	**...**	**...**	**...**	**...**
31	**Net/Gross investment in nonfinancial assets**	**5,549**	**7,104**	**8,270**	**...**	**...**	**...**	**...**	**...**	**...**	**...**	**...**	**...**
311	Fixed assets	5,549	7,104	8,270	...	...	...	...	...	...	...	...	...
3111	Buildings and structures	...	...	...	...	...	...	...	...	...	...	...	...
3112	Machinery and equipment	...	...	...	...	...	...	...	...	...	...	...	...
3113	Other fixed assets	...	...	...	...	...	...	...	...	...	...	...	...
3114	Weapons systems	...	...	...	...	...	...	...	...	...	...	...	...
312	Inventories	—	—	—	...	...	...	...	...	...	...	...	...
313	Valuables	—	—	—	...	...	...	...	...	...	...	...	...
314	Nonproduced assets	—	—	—	...	...	...	...	...	...	...	...	...
3141	Land	—	—	—	...	...	...	...	...	...	...	...	...
3142	Mineral and energy resources	—	—	—	...	...	...	...	...	...	...	...	...
3143	Other naturally occurring assets	—	—	—	...	...	...	...	...	...	...	...	...
3144	Intangible nonproduced assets	—	—	—	...	...	...	...	...	...	...	...	...
32	**Net acquisition of financial assets**	**...**	**...**	**...**	**...**	**...**	**...**	**...**	**...**	**...**	**...**	**...**	**...**
	By instrument												
3201	Monetary gold and SDRs	...	...	...	...	...	...	...	...	...	...	...	...
3202	Currency and deposits	...	...	...	...	...	...	...	...	...	...	...	...
3203	Debt securities	...	...	...	...	...	...	...	...	...	...	...	...
3204	Loans	...	...	...	...	...	...	...	...	...	...	...	...
3205	Equity and investment fund shares	...	...	...	...	...	...	...	...	...	...	...	...
3206	Insurance, pension, and standardized guarantee schemes	...	...	...	...	...	...	...	...	...	...	...	...
3207	Financial derivatives and employee stock options	...	...	...	...	...	...	...	...	...	...	...	...
3208	Other accounts receivable	...	...	...	...	...	...	...	...	...	...	...	...
	By debtor												
321	Domestic debtors	...	...	...	...	...	...	...	...	...	...	...	...
322	External debtors	...	...	...	...	...	...	...	...	...	...	...	...
33	**Net incurrence of liabilities**	**...**	**...**	**...**	**...**	**...**	**...**	**...**	**...**	**...**	**...**	**...**	**...**
	By instrument												
3301	Special Drawing Rights (SDRs)	...	...	...	...	...	...	...	...	...	...	...	...
3302	Currency and deposits	...	...	...	...	...	...	...	...	...	...	...	...
3303	Debt securities	...	...	...	...	...	...	...	...	...	...	...	...
3304	Loans	...	...	...	...	...	...	...	...	...	...	...	...
3305	Equity and investment fund shares	...	...	...	...	...	...	...	...	...	...	...	...
3306	Insurance, pension, and standardized guarantee schemes	...	...	...	...	...	...	...	...	...	...	...	...
3307	Financial derivatives and employee stock options	...	...	...	...	...	...	...	...	...	...	...	...
3308	Other accounts payable	...	...	...	...	...	...	...	...	...	...	...	...
	By creditor												
331	Domestic creditors	...	...	...	...	...	...	...	...	...	...	...	...
332	External creditors	...	...	...	...	...	...	...	...	...	...	...	...
	Table 4 Holding gains and losses in assets and liabilities												
	Table 5 Holding gains and losses in assets and liabilities												
	Table 6 Balance sheet												

Nicaragua (278)

In Millions of Nicaraguan Cordobas (NIO) / Fiscal Year Ends December 31st

	Budgetary Central Government			Central Government (excl. Social Security)			Central Government (incl. Social Security)			General Government		
	2013	2014	2015P	2013	2014	2015	2013	2014	2015	2013	2014	2015
Table 7 Expenditure by functions of government												
Table 8 Financial transactions by counterpart sector												
Table 9 Total other economic flows in assets and liabilities												

Nigeria (694)

In Billions of Nigerian Naira (NGN) / Fiscal Year Ends December 31st

		Budgetary Central Government			Central Government (excl. Social Security)			Central Government (incl. Social Security)			General Government		
		2011	2012	2013	2011	2012	2013	2011	2012	2013	2011	2012	2013
	Statement of operations												
1	Revenue	3,554	3,630	4,032	...	...	...	...	...	...	...	...	...
2	Expense	3,794	3,731	4,077	...	...	...	...	...	...	...	...	...
GOB	**Gross operating balance**	**-240**	**-101**	**-45**	...	...	...	...	...	...	...	...	...
NOB	**Net operating balance**	...	...	...	...	...	...	...	...	...	...	...	...
31	Net/Gross investment in nonfinancial assets	919	875	1,108	...	...	...	...	...	...	...	...	...
2M	Expenditure	4,712	4,605	5,185	...	...	...	...	...	...	...	...	...
NLB	**Net lending (+) / Net borrowing (-)**	**-1,159**	**-976**	**-1,153**	...	...	...	...	...	...	...	...	...
32	Net acquisition of financial assets	-230	0	0	...	...	...	...	...	...	...	...	...
33	Net incurrence of liabilities	929	976	1,154	...	...	...	...	...	...	...	...	...
NLBz	Statistical discrepancy	—	—	—	...	...	...	...	...	...	...	...	...
	Memorandum items												
PB	Primary net lending / net borrowing	-632	-296	-325	...	...	...	...	...	...	...	...	...
GB	Government balance per national definition	...	...	...	...	...	...	...	...	...	...	...	...
	Statement of other economic flows												
	Balance sheet												
	Table 1 Revenue												
1	**Revenue**	**3,554**	**3,630**	**4,032**	...	...	...	...	...	...	...	...	...
11	**Taxes**	**1,150**	**1,130**	**1,201**	...	...	...	...	...	...	...	...	...
111	Taxes on income, profits, and capital gains	1,056	1,028	1,086	...	...	...	...	...	...	...	...	...
1111	Payable by individuals	...	...	...	...	...	...	...	...	...	...	...	...
1112	Payable by corporations and other enterprises	...	...	...	...	...	...	...	...	...	...	...	...
1113	Other taxes on income, profits, and capital gains	...	...	...	...	...	...	...	...	...	...	...	...
112	Taxes on payroll and workforce	—	—	—	...	...	...	...	...	...	...	...	...
113	Taxes on property	—	—	—	...	...	...	...	...	...	...	...	...
114	Taxes on goods and services	94	102	115	...	...	...	...	...	...	...	...	...
1141	General taxes on goods and services	94	102	115	...	...	...	...	...	...	...	...	...
1142	Excises	—	—	—	...	...	...	...	...	...	...	...	...
115	Taxes on international trade and transactions	—	—	—	...	...	...	...	...	...	...	...	...
116	Other taxes	—	—	—	...	...	...	...	...	...	...	...	...
12	**Social contributions**	—	—	—	...	...	...	...	...	...	...	...	...
121	Social security contributions	—	—	—	...	...	...	...	...	...	...	...	...
122	Other social contributions	—	—	—	...	...	...	...	...	...	...	...	...
13	**Grants**	—	—	—	...	...	...	...	...	...	...	...	...
131	From foreign governments	—	—	—	...	...	...	...	...	...	...	...	...
132	From international organizations	—	—	—	...	...	...	...	...	...	...	...	...
133	From other general government units	—	—	—	...	...	...	...	...	...	...	...	...
1331	Current	—	—	—	...	...	...	...	...	...	...	...	...
1332	Capital	—	—	—	...	...	...	...	...	...	...	...	...
14	**Other revenue**	**2,404**	**2,500**	**2,831**	...	...	...	...	...	...	...	...	...
	Table 2 Expense by economic type												
2	**Expense**	**3,794**	**3,731**	**4,077**	...	...	...	...	...	...	...	...	...
21	**Compensation of employees**	**1,722**	**1,664**	**1,721**	...	...	...	...	...	...	...	...	...
211	Wages and salaries	1,722	1,664	1,721	...	...	...	...	...	...	...	...	...
212	Employers' social contributions	—	—	—	...	...	...	...	...	...	...	...	...
22	**Use of goods and services**	**673**	**590**	**526**	...	...	...	...	...	...	...	...	...
23	**Consumption of fixed capital**	...	...	...	...	...	...	...	...	...	...	...	...
24	**Interest**	**527**	**679**	**828**	...	...	...	...	...	...	...	...	...
25	**Subsidies**	**263**	**247**	**183**	...	...	...	...	...	...	...	...	...
26	**Grants**	**216**	**159**	**204**	...	...	...	...	...	...	...	...	...
261	To foreign governments	—	—	—	...	...	...	...	...	...	...	...	...
262	To international organizations	—	—	—	...	...	...	...	...	...	...	...	...
263	To other general government units	216	159	204	...	...	...	...	...	...	...	...	...
2631	Current	...	...	...	...	...	...	...	...	...	...	...	...
2632	Capital	...	...	...	...	...	...	...	...	...	...	...	...

Nigeria (694)

In Billions of Nigerian Naira (NGN) / Fiscal Year Ends December 31st

		Budgetary Central Government			Central Government (excl. Social Security)			Central Government (incl. Social Security)			General Government		
		2011	2012	2013	2011	2012	2013	2011	2012	2013	2011	2012	2013
27	**Social benefits**	**392**	**393**	**614**	...	...	...	...	...	...	...	...	...
271	Social security benefits	—	—	—	...	...	...	...	...	...	...	...	...
272	Social assistance benefits	260	246	474	...	...	...	...	...	...	...	...	...
273	Employment-related social benefits	132	147	140	...	...	...	...	...	...	...	...	...
28	**Other expense**	**—**	**—**	**—**	...	...	...	...	...	...	...	...	...
281	Property expense other than interest	—	—	—	...	...	...	...	...	...	...	...	...
282	Transfers not elsewhere classified	—	—	—	...	...	...	...	...	...	...	...	...
2821	Current	—	—	—	...	...	...	...	...	...	...	...	...
2822	Capital	—	—	—	...	...	...	...	...	...	...	...	...
	Table 3 Transactions in assets and liabilities												
3	**Change in net worth from transactions**	...	...	...	...	...	...	...	...	...	...	...	...
31	**Net/Gross investment in nonfinancial assets**	**919**	**875**	**1,108**	...	...	...	...	...	...	...	...	...
311	Fixed assets	919	875	1,108	...	...	...	...	...	...	...	...	...
3111	Buildings and structures	...	...	...	...	...	...	...	...	...	...	...	...
3112	Machinery and equipment	...	...	...	...	...	...	...	...	...	...	...	...
3113	Other fixed assets	...	...	...	...	...	...	...	...	...	...	...	...
3114	Weapons systems	...	...	...	...	...	...	...	...	...	...	...	...
312	Inventories	—	—	—	...	...	...	...	...	...	...	...	...
313	Valuables	—	—	—	...	...	...	...	...	...	...	...	...
314	Nonproduced assets	—	—	—	...	...	...	...	...	...	...	...	...
3141	Land	—	—	—	...	...	...	...	...	...	...	...	...
3142	Mineral and energy resources	—	—	—	...	...	...	...	...	...	...	...	...
3143	Other naturally occurring assets	—	—	—	...	...	...	...	...	...	...	...	...
3144	Intangible nonproduced assets	—	—	—	...	...	...	...	...	...	...	...	...
32	**Net acquisition of financial assets**	**-230**	**0**	**0**	...	...	...	...	...	...	...	...	...
	By instrument												
3201	Monetary gold and SDRs	—	—	—	...	...	...	...	...	...	...	...	...
3202	Currency and deposits	-227	8	0	...	...	...	...	...	...	...	...	...
3203	Debt securities	—	—	—	...	...	...	...	...	...	...	...	...
3204	Loans	—	—	—	...	...	...	...	...	...	...	...	...
3205	Equity and investment fund shares	-3	-8	—	...	...	...	...	...	...	...	...	...
3206	Insurance, pension, and standardized guarantee schemes	—	—	—	...	...	...	...	...	...	...	...	...
3207	Financial derivatives and employee stock options	—	—	—	...	...	...	...	...	...	...	...	...
3208	Other accounts receivable	—	...	...	...	...	...	...	...	...	...	...	...
	By debtor												
321	Domestic debtors	-230	0	0	...	...	...	...	...	...	...	...	...
322	External debtors	—	—	—	...	...	...	...	...	...	...	...	...
33	**Net incurrence of liabilities**	**929**	**976**	**1,154**	...	...	...	...	...	...	...	...	...
	By instrument												
3301	Special Drawing Rights (SDRs)	...	...	...	...	...	...	...	...	...	...	...	...
3302	Currency and deposits	...	...	...	...	...	...	...	...	...	...	...	...
3303	Debt securities	...	...	...	...	...	...	...	...	...	...	...	...
3304	Loans	...	...	...	...	...	...	...	...	...	...	...	...
3305	Equity and investment fund shares	...	...	...	...	...	...	...	...	...	...	...	...
3306	Insurance, pension, and standardized guarantee schemes	...	...	...	...	...	...	...	...	...	...	...	...
3307	Financial derivatives and employee stock options	...	...	...	...	...	...	...	...	...	...	...	...
3308	Other accounts payable	...	...	...	...	...	...	...	...	...	...	...	...
	By creditor												
331	Domestic creditors	855	976	1,154	...	...	...	...	...	...	...	...	...
332	External creditors	73	—	—	...	...	...	...	...	...	...	...	...
	Table 4 Holding gains and losses in assets and liabilities												
	Table 5 Holding gains and losses in assets and liabilities												
	Table 6 Balance sheet												

Nigeria (694)

In Billions of Nigerian Naira (NGN) / Fiscal Year Ends December 31st

		Budgetary Central Government			Central Government (excl. Social Security)			Central Government (incl. Social Security)			General Government		
		2011	2012	2013	2011	2012	2013	2011	2012	2013	2011	2012	2013
	Table 7 Expenditure by functions of government												
7	**Expenditure**	**4,712**	**4,605**	**5,185**	...	...	...	...	...	...	...	...	...
701	**General public services**	**1,003**	**745**	**785**	...	...	...	...	...	...	...	...	...
7017	Public debt transactions	527	679	828	...	...	...	...	...	...	...	...	...
7018	Transfers of general character between levels of government	—	—	—	...	...	...	...	...	...	...	...	...
702	**Defense**	**311**	**334**	**306**	...	...	...	...	...	...	...	...	...
703	**Public order and safety**	**346**	**421**	**305**	...	...	...	...	...	...	...	...	...
704	**Economic affairs**	**675**	**524**	**786**	...	...	...	...	...	...	...	...	...
7042	Agriculture, forestry, fishing, and hunting	104	97	96	...	...	...	...	...	...	...	...	...
7043	Fuel and energy	—	—	—	...	...	...	...	...	...	...	...	...
7044	Mining, manufacturing, and construction	—	—	—	...	...	...	...	...	...	...	...	...
7045	Transport	—	—	—	...	...	...	...	...	...	...	...	...
7046	Communication	—	—	—	...	...	...	...	...	...	...	...	...
705	**Environmental protection**	...	...	...	...	...	...	...	...	...	...	...	...
706	**Housing and community amenities**	**22**	**27**	**11**	...	...	...	...	...	...	...	...	...
707	**Health**	**271**	**243**	**212**	...	...	...	...	...	...	...	...	...
7072	Outpatient services	—	—	—	...	...	...	...	...	...	...	...	...
7073	Hospital services	—	—	—	...	...	...	...	...	...	...	...	...
7074	Public health services	—	—	—	...	...	...	...	...	...	...	...	...
708	**Recreation, culture and religion**	...	...	...	...	...	...	...	...	...	...	...	...
709	**Education**	**371**	**396**	**426**	...	...	...	...	...	...	...	...	...
7091	Pre-primary and primary education	—	—	—	...	...	...	...	...	...	...	...	...
7092	Secondary education	—	—	—	...	...	...	...	...	...	...	...	...
7094	Tertiary education	—	—	—	...	...	...	...	...	...	...	...	...
710	**Social protection**	**70**	**99**	**361**	...	...	...	...	...	...	...	...	...
7z	Statistical discrepancy: Expenditure	...	...	...	...	...	...	...	...	...	...	...	...
	Table 8 Financial transactions by counterpart sector												
	Table 9 Total other economic flows in assets and liabilities												

Norway (142)

In Billions of Norwegian Kroner (NOK) / Fiscal Year Ends December 31st

		Budgetary Central Government			Central Government (excl. Social Security)			Central Government (incl. Social Security)			General Government		
		2013	2014	2015	2013P	2014P	2015P	2013P	2014P	2015P	2013P	2014P	2015P
	Statement of operations												
1	Revenue	...	...	...	1,447	1,470	1,453	1,447	1,470	1,453	1,684	1,716	1,722
2	Expense	...	...	...	1,071	1,142	1,209	1,071	1,142	1,209	1,313	1,393	1,472
GOB	**Gross operating balance**	...	...	...	**429**	**384**	**303**	**429**	**384**	**303**	**460**	**419**	**352**
NOB	**Net operating balance**	...	...	...	**377**	**328**	**244**	**377**	**328**	**244**	**370**	**323**	**250**
31	Net/Gross investment in nonfinancial assets	...	...	...	22	30	30	22	30	30	39	47	49
2M	Expenditure	...	...	...	1,093	1,171	1,239	1,093	1,171	1,239	1,352	1,441	1,521
NLB	**Net lending (+) / Net borrowing (-)**	...	...	...	**355**	**298**	**214**	**355**	**298**	**214**	**331**	**275**	**201**
32	Net acquisition of financial assets	...	...	...	387	211	348	...	...	...	401	227	372
33	Net incurrence of liabilities	...	...	...	28	-96	142	...	...	...	58	-62	182
NLBz	Statistical discrepancy	...	...	...	4	9	-8	...	...	...	11	14	-11
	Memorandum items												
PB	Primary net lending / net borrowing	...	...	...	365	309	224	365	309	224	352	296	221
GB	Government balance per national definition	...	...	...	...	...	...	...	...	...	...	...	...
	Statement of other economic flows												
	Balance sheet												
6	**Net worth**	...	...	...	...	...	...	...	...	...	...	...	...
61	Nonfinancial assets	...	...	...	...	...	...	...	...	...	...	...	...
62	Financial assets	...	...	...	7,146	8,537	9,726	...	...	...	7,461	8,875	10,096
63	Liabilities	...	...	...	659	577	713	...	...	...	1,091	1,044	1,219
	Table 1 Revenue												
1	**Revenue**	...	...	...	**1,447**	**1,470**	**1,453**	**1,447**	**1,470**	**1,453**	**1,684**	**1,716**	**1,722**
11	**Taxes**	...	...	...	**771**	**738**	**700**	**771**	**738**	**700**	**934**	**908**	**883**
111	Taxes on income, profits, and capital gains	...	...	...	418	373	326	418	373	326	561	522	486
1111	Payable by individuals	...	...	...	161	161	174	161	161	174	304	310	334
1112	Payable by corporations and other enterprises	...	...	...	254	209	151	254	209	151	254	209	151
1113	Other taxes on income, profits, and capital gains	...	...	...	3	4	1	3	4	1	3	4	1
112	Taxes on payroll and workforce	...	...	...	0	0	0	0	0	0	0	0	0
113	Taxes on property	...	...	...	9	8	4	9	8	4	27	27	26
114	Taxes on goods and services	...	...	...	340	353	365	340	353	365	342	355	367
1141	General taxes on goods and services	...	...	...	242	251	264	242	251	264	242	251	264
1142	Excises	...	...	...	56	59	60	56	59	60	56	59	60
115	Taxes on international trade and transactions	...	...	...	3	3	3	3	3	3	3	3	3
116	Other taxes	...	...	...	0	0	0	0	0	0	0	0	0
12	**Social contributions**	...	...	...	**293**	**313**	**326**	**293**	**313**	**326**	**293**	**313**	**326**
121	Social security contributions	...	...	...	17	19	22	17	19	22	17	19	22
122	Other social contributions	...	...	...	276	295	305	276	295	305	276	295	305
13	**Grants**	...	...	...	...	...	...	...	...	...	...	...	...
131	From foreign governments	...	...	...	...	...	...	...	...	...	...	...	...
132	From international organizations	...	...	...	...	...	...	...	...	...	...	...	...
133	From other general government units	...	...	...	7	8	3	7	8	3	—	—	—
1331	Current	...	...	...	7	8	3	7	8	3	—	—	—
1332	Capital	...	...	...	—	—	—	—	—	—	—	—	—
14	**Other revenue**	...	...	...	...	...	...	...	...	...	...	...	...
	Table 2 Expense by economic type												
2	**Expense**	...	...	...	**1,071**	**1,142**	**1,209**	**1,071**	**1,142**	**1,209**	**1,313**	**1,393**	**1,472**
21	**Compensation of employees**	...	...	...	**180**	**193**	**204**	**180**	**193**	**204**	**418**	**441**	**462**
211	Wages and salaries	...	...	...	...	...	...	...	...	...	...	...	...
212	Employers' social contributions	...	...	...	...	...	...	...	...	...	...	...	...
22	**Use of goods and services**	...	...	...	**97**	**104**	**110**	**97**	**104**	**110**	**184**	**195**	**206**
23	**Consumption of fixed capital**	...	...	...	**52**	**56**	**59**	**52**	**56**	**59**	**90**	**96**	**102**
24	**Interest**	...	...	...	**10**	**10**	**10**	**10**	**10**	**10**	**21**	**21**	**20**
25	**Subsidies**	...	...	...	**43**	**45**	**47**	**43**	**45**	**47**	**57**	**60**	**63**

Norway (142)

In Billions of Norwegian Kroner (NOK) / Fiscal Year Ends December 31st

		Budgetary Central Government			Central Government (excl. Social Security)			Central Government (incl. Social Security)			General Government		
		2013	2014	2015	2013P	2014P	2015P	2013P	2014P	2015P	2013P	2014P	2015P
26	**Grants**	...	...	...	...	...	...	...	...	...	...	...	...
261	To foreign governments	...	...	...	...	...	...	...	...	...	...	...	...
262	To international organizations	...	...	...	...	...	...	...	...	...	...	...	...
263	To other general government units	...	...	...	194	208	217	194	208	217	—	—	—
2631	Current	...	...	...	194	208	217	194	208	217	—	—	—
2632	Capital	...	...	...	—	—	—	—	—	—	—	—	—
27	**Social benefits**	...	...	...	**432**	**459**	**490**	**432**	**459**	**490**	**468**	**497**	**530**
271	Social security benefits	...	...	...	...	...	...	...	...	...	...	...	...
272	Social assistance benefits	...	...	...	...	...	...	...	...	...	...	...	...
273	Employment-related social benefits	...	...	...	...	...	...	...	...	...	...	...	...
28	**Other expense**	...	...	...	...	...	...	...	...	...	...	...	...
281	Property expense other than interest	...	...	...	0	0	0	0	0	0	0	0	0
282	Transfers not elsewhere classified	...	...	...	...	...	...	...	...	...	...	...	...
2821	Current	...	...	...	...	...	...	...	...	...	...	...	...
2822	Capital	...	...	...	...	...	...	...	...	...	...	...	...
	Table 3 Transactions in assets and liabilities												
3	**Change in net worth from transactions**	...	...	...	**381**	**337**	**236**	...	...	...	**381**	**336**	**239**
31	**Net/Gross investment in nonfinancial assets**	...	...	...	**22**	**30**	**30**	**22**	**30**	**30**	**39**	**47**	**49**
311	Fixed assets	...	...	...	23	29	29	23	29	29	42	48	52
3111	Buildings and structures	...	...	...	...	...	...	...	...	...	...	...	...
3112	Machinery and equipment	...	...	...	...	...	...	...	...	...	...	...	...
3113	Other fixed assets	...	...	...	...	...	...	...	...	...	...	...	...
3114	Weapons systems	...	...	...	...	...	...	...	...	...	...	...	...
312	Inventories	...	...	...	...	...	...	...	...	...	...	...	...
313	Valuables	...	...	...	...	...	...	...	...	...	...	...	...
314	Nonproduced assets	...	...	...	-1	0	0	-1	0	0	-3	-1	-3
3141	Land	...	...	...	...	...	...	...	...	...	...	...	...
3142	Mineral and energy resources	...	...	...	...	...	...	...	...	...	...	...	...
3143	Other naturally occurring assets	...	...	...	...	...	...	...	...	...	...	...	...
3144	Intangible nonproduced assets	...	...	...	...	...	...	...	...	...	...	...	...
32	**Net acquisition of financial assets**	...	...	...	**387**	**211**	**348**	...	...	...	**401**	**227**	**372**
	By instrument												
3201	Monetary gold and SDRs	...	...	...	—	—	—	...	...	...	—	—	—
3202	Currency and deposits	...	...	...	-48	36	-26	...	...	...	-45	36	-14
3203	Debt securities	...	...	...	347	77	145	...	...	...	345	79	144
3204	Loans	...	...	...	60	-64	87	...	...	...	66	-58	91
3205	Equity and investment fund shares	...	...	...	47	168	135	...	...	...	54	167	135
3206	Insurance, pension, and standardized guarantee schemes	...	...	...	—	0	0	...	...	...	3	4	4
3207	Financial derivatives and employee stock options	...	...	...	-0	9	1	...	...	...	-0	9	1
3208	Other accounts receivable	...	...	...	-19	-14	6	...	...	...	-21	-9	12
	By debtor												
321	Domestic debtors	...	...	...	...	...	...	...	...	...	...	...	...
322	External debtors	...	...	...	...	...	...	...	...	...	...	...	...
33	**Net incurrence of liabilities**	...	...	...	**28**	**-96**	**142**	...	...	...	**58**	**-62**	**182**
	By instrument												
3301	Special Drawing Rights (SDRs)	...	...	...	—	—	—	...	...	...	—	—	—
3302	Currency and deposits	...	...	...	...	...	...	...	...	...	...	...	...
3303	Debt securities	...	...	...	-33	-38	12	...	...	...	-22	-17	32
3304	Loans	...	...	...	50	-66	108	...	...	...	72	-51	123
3305	Equity and investment fund shares	...	...	...	...	...	...	...	...	...	...	...	...
3306	Insurance, pension, and standardized guarantee schemes	...	...	...	...	...	...	...	...	...	...	...	...
3307	Financial derivatives and employee stock options	...	...	...	1	8	-1	...	...	...	1	8	-1
3308	Other accounts payable	...	...	...	11	1	23	...	...	...	7	-1	29

Norway (142)

In Billions of Norwegian Kroner (NOK) / Fiscal Year Ends December 31st

		Budgetary Central Government			Central Government (excl. Social Security)			Central Government (incl. Social Security)			General Government		
		2013	2014	2015	2013P	2014P	2015P	2013P	2014P	2015P	2013P	2014P	2015P
	By creditor												
331	Domestic creditors	...	...	...	...	...	...	...	...	...	...	...	...
332	External creditors	...	...	...	...	...	...	...	...	...	...	...	...
	Table 4 Holding gains and losses in assets and liabilities												
	Table 5 Holding gains and losses in assets and liabilities												
	Table 6 Balance sheet												
6	**Net worth**	...	...	...	...	...	...	...	...	...	...	...	...
61	**Nonfinancial assets**	...	...	...	...	...	...	...	...	...	...	...	...
611	Fixed assets	...	...	...	...	...	...	...	...	...	...	...	...
6111	Buildings and structures	...	...	...	...	...	...	...	...	...	...	...	...
6112	Machinery and equipment	...	...	...	...	...	...	...	...	...	...	...	...
6113	Other fixed assets	...	...	...	...	...	...	...	...	...	...	...	...
6114	Weapons systems	...	...	...	...	...	...	...	...	...	...	...	...
612	Inventories	...	...	...	...	...	...	...	...	...	...	...	...
613	Valuables	...	...	...	...	...	...	...	...	...	...	...	...
614	Nonproduced assets	...	...	...	...	...	...	...	...	...	...	...	...
6141	Land	...	...	...	...	...	...	...	...	...	...	...	...
6142	Mineral and energy resources	...	...	...	...	...	...	...	...	...	...	...	...
6143	Other naturally occurring assets	...	...	...	...	...	...	...	...	...	...	...	...
6144	Intangible nonproduced assets	...	...	...	...	...	...	...	...	...	...	...	...
62	**Financial assets**	...	...	...	**7,146**	**8,537**	**9,726**	...	...	...	**7,461**	**8,875**	**10,096**
	By instrument												
6201	Monetary gold and SDRs	...	...	...	—	—	—	...	...	...	—	—	—
6202	Currency and deposits	...	...	...	117	154	129	...	...	...	191	228	215
6203	Debt securities	...	...	...	1,935	2,404	2,775	...	...	...	1,944	2,415	2,785
6204	Loans	...	...	...	613	562	658	...	...	...	683	638	738
6205	Equity and investment fund shares	...	...	...	4,214	5,159	5,897	...	...	...	4,288	5,233	5,977
6206	Insurance, pension, and standardized guarantee schemes	...	...	...	—	2	3	...	...	...	52	64	72
6207	Financial derivatives and employee stock options	...	...	...	3	9	11	...	...	...	3	9	12
6208	Other accounts receivable	...	...	...	263	247	252	...	...	...	299	287	298
	By debtor												
621	Domestic debtors	...	...	...	...	...	...	...	...	...	...	...	...
622	External debtors	...	...	...	...	...	...	...	...	...	...	...	...
63	**Liabilities**	...	...	...	**659**	**577**	**713**	...	...	...	**1,091**	**1,044**	**1,219**
	By instrument												
6301	Special Drawing Rights (SDRs)	...	...	...	—	—	—	...	...	...	—	—	—
6302	Currency and deposits	...	...	...	...	...	...	...	...	...	...	...	...
6303	Debt securities	...	...	...	404	376	383	...	...	...	497	491	517
6304	Loans	...	...	...	142	80	189	...	...	...	442	394	518
6305	Equity and investment fund shares	...	...	...	...	...	...	...	...	...	...	...	...
6306	Insurance, pension, and standardized guarantee schemes	...	...	...	...	...	...	...	...	...	...	...	...
6307	Financial derivatives and employee stock options	...	...	...	5	11	9	...	...	...	5	12	9
6308	Other accounts payable	...	...	...	109	110	133	...	...	...	147	146	175
	By creditor												
631	Domestic creditors	...	...	...	...	...	...	...	...	...	...	...	...
632	External creditors	...	...	...	...	...	...	...	...	...	...	...	...
	Memorandum items												
6M2	Net financial worth	...	...	...	6,487	7,960	9,013	...	...	...	6,370	7,831	8,876
6M3	Gross debt (D4) at market value	...	...	...	...	...	...	...	...	...	...	...	...
6M3D3	D3 debt liabilities at market value	...	...	...	655	566	704	...	...	...	1,086	1,032	1,210
6M3D2	D2 debt liabilities at market value	...	...	...	546	456	571	...	...	...	939	886	1,035
6M3D1	D1 debt liabilities at market value	...	...	...	546	456	571	...	...	...	939	886	1,035
6M4	Gross debt (D4) at nominal value	...	...	...	...	...	...	...	...	...	...	...	...
6M4D3	D3 debt liabilities at nominal value	...	...	...	...	...	...	...	...	...	...	...	...
6M4D2	D2 debt liabilities at nominal value	...	...	...	...	...	...	...	...	...	...	...	...
6M4D1	D1 debt liabilities at nominal value	...	...	...	...	...	...	...	...	...	...	...	...

Norway (142)

In Billions of Norwegian Kroner (NOK) / Fiscal Year Ends December 31st

		Budgetary Central Government			Central Government (excl. Social Security)			Central Government (incl. Social Security)			General Government		
		2013	2014	2015	2013P	2014P	2015P	2013P	2014P	2015P	2013P	2014P	2015P
6M35	Gross debt (D4) at face value	...	...	...	...	...	...	...	...	...	...	...	...
6M35D3	D3 debt liabilities at face value	...	...	...	631	544	668	...	...	...	1,061	1,008	1,172
6M35D2	D2 debt liabilities at face value	...	...	...	522	435	535	...	...	...	914	862	997
6M35D1	D1 debt liabilities at face value	...	...	...	522	435	535	...	...	...	914	862	997
6M93	Government gross debt per national definition	...	...	...	522	435	535	...	...	...	914	862	997
6M5	Arrears	...	...	...	...	...	...	...	...	...	...	...	...
6M6	Explicit contingent liabilities	...	...	...	...	...	...	...	...	...	...	...	...
6M61	of which: Publicly guaranteed debt	...	...	...	...	...	...	...	...	...	...	...	...
6M7	Net implicit obligations for social security benefits	...	...	...	...	...	...	...	...	...	...	...	...
	Table 7 Expenditure by functions of government												
7	**Expenditure**	...	...	...	**1,093**	**1,171**	**1,239**	...	...	...	**1,352**	**1,441**	**1,521**
701	**General public services**	...	...	...	**251**	**266**	**278**	...	...	...	**132**	**139**	**146**
7017	Public debt transactions	...	...	...	13	12	12	...	...	...	26	25	25
7018	Transfers of general character between levels of government	...	...	...	161	170	174	...	...	...	—	—	—
702	**Defense**	...	...	...	**42**	**45**	**48**	...	...	...	**42**	**45**	**48**
703	**Public order and safety**	...	...	...	**26**	**27**	**28**	...	...	...	**31**	**32**	**34**
704	**Economic affairs**	...	...	...	**100**	**113**	**115**	...	...	...	**140**	**154**	**160**
7042	Agriculture, forestry, fishing, and hunting	...	...	...	18	18	18	...	...	...	18	18	18
7043	Fuel and energy	...	...	...	3	3	3	...	...	...	3	3	3
7044	Mining, manufacturing, and construction	...	...	...	0	0	0	...	...	...	0	0	0
7045	Transport	...	...	...	53	62	65	...	...	...	88	97	104
7046	Communication	...	...	...	-0	1	1	...	...	...	-0	1	1
705	**Environmental protection**	...	...	...	**8**	**7**	**7**	...	...	...	**25**	**26**	**27**
706	**Housing and community amenities**	...	...	...	**1**	**2**	**2**	...	...	...	**19**	**22**	**24**
707	**Health**	...	...	...	**170**	**183**	**195**	...	...	...	**230**	**247**	**261**
7072	Outpatient services	...	...	...	42	45	48	...	...	...	53	57	60
7073	Hospital services	...	...	...	93	101	106	...	...	...	138	150	156
7074	Public health services	...	...	...	4	3	4	...	...	...	8	7	8
708	**Recreation, culture and religion**	...	...	...	**19**	**21**	**23**	...	...	...	**43**	**44**	**46**
709	**Education**	...	...	...	**43**	**50**	**53**	...	...	...	**151**	**161**	**170**
7091	Pre-primary and primary education	...	...	...	2	2	3	...	...	...	67	70	75
7092	Secondary education	...	...	...	5	6	5	...	...	...	37	38	39
7094	Tertiary education	...	...	...	28	34	36	...	...	...	28	34	36
710	**Social protection**	...	...	...	**433**	**457**	**491**	...	...	...	**541**	**570**	**606**
7z	Statistical discrepancy: Expenditure	...	...	...	—	—	—	...	...	...	—	—	—
	Table 8 Financial transactions by counterpart sector												
32	**Net acquisition of financial assets**	...	...	...	**387**	**211**	**348**	...	...	...	**401**	**227**	**372**
321	Domestic debtors	...	...	...	...	...	...	...	...	...	...	...	...
8211	General government	...	...	...	...	...	...	...	...	...	—	—	—
8212	Central bank	...	...	...	...	...	...	...	...	...	...	...	...
8213	Deposit-taking corporations except the central bank	...	...	...	...	...	...	...	...	...	...	...	...
8214	Other financial corporations	...	...	...	...	...	...	...	...	...	...	...	...
8215	Nonfinancial corporations	...	...	...	...	...	...	...	...	...	...	...	...
8216	Households & nonprofit institutions serving households	...	...	...	...	...	...	...	...	...	...	...	...
322	External debtors	...	...	...	...	...	...	...	...	...	...	...	...
8221	General government	...	...	...	...	...	...	...	...	...	...	...	...
8227	International organizations	...	...	...	...	...	...	...	...	...	...	...	...
8228	Financial corporations other than international organizations	...	...	...	...	...	...	...	...	...	...	...	...
8229	Other nonresidents	...	...	...	...	...	...	...	...	...	...	...	...

Norway (142)

In Billions of Norwegian Kroner (NOK) / Fiscal Year Ends December 31st

		Budgetary Central Government			Central Government (excl. Social Security)			Central Government (incl. Social Security)			General Government		
		2013	2014	2015	2013P	2014P	2015P	2013P	2014P	2015P	2013P	2014P	2015P
33	**Net incurrence of liabilities**	...	...	...	28	-96	142	...	...	...	58	-62	182
331	Domestic creditors	...	...	...	...	...	...	...	...	...	...	...	...
3311	General government	...	...	...	...	...	...	...	...	...	—	—	—
3312	Central bank	...	...	...	...	...	...	...	...	...	...	...	...
3313	Deposit-taking corporations except the central bank	...	...	...	...	...	...	...	...	...	...	...	...
3314	Other financial corporations	...	...	...	...	...	...	...	...	...	...	...	...
3315	Nonfinancial corporations	...	...	...	...	...	...	...	...	...	...	...	...
3316	Households & nonprofit institutions serving households	...	...	...	...	...	...	...	...	...	...	...	...
332	External creditors	...	...	...	...	...	...	...	...	...	...	...	...
3321	General government	...	...	...	...	...	...	...	...	...	...	...	...
3327	International organizations	...	...	...	...	...	...	...	...	...	...	...	...
3328	Financial corporations other than international organizations	...	...	...	...	...	...	...	...	...	...	...	...
3329	Other nonresidents	...	...	...	...	...	...	...	...	...	...	...	...
	Table 9 Total other economic flows in assets and liabilities												
9	**Change in net worth due to other economic flows**	...	...	...	...	...	...	...	...	...	...	...	...
91	**Other economic flows in nonfinancial assets**	...	...	...	...	...	...	...	...	...	...	...	...
911	Fixed assets	...	...	...	...	...	...	...	...	...	...	...	...
912	Inventories	...	...	...	...	...	...	...	...	...	...	...	...
913	Valuables	...	...	...	...	...	...	...	...	...	...	...	...
914	Nonproduced assets	...	...	...	...	...	...	...	...	...	...	...	...
92	**Other economic flows in financial assets**	...	...	...	996	1,179	841	...	...	...	1,010	1,187	849
	By instrument												
9201	Monetary gold and SDRs	...	...	...	—	—	—	...	...	...	—	—	—
9202	Currency and deposits	...	...	...	0	1	1	...	...	...	0	1	1
9203	Debt securities	...	...	...	66	392	226	...	...	...	66	393	226
9204	Loans	...	...	...	12	13	9	...	...	...	12	13	9
9205	Equity and investment fund shares	...	...	...	919	776	604	...	...	...	920	778	609
9206	Insurance, pension, and standardized guarantee schemes	...	...	...	—	2	0	...	...	...	13	8	3
9207	Financial derivatives and employee stock options	...	...	...	0	-3	2	...	...	...	0	-3	2
9208	Other accounts receivable	...	...	...	-1	-2	-1	...	...	...	-1	-2	-2
	By debtor												
921	Domestic debtors	...	...	...	...	...	...	...	...	...	...	...	...
922	External debtors	...	...	...	...	...	...	...	...	...	...	...	...
93	**Other economic flows in liabilities**	...	...	...	-4	14	-6	...	...	...	-4	15	-6
	By instrument												
9301	Special Drawing Rights (SDRs)	...	...	...	—	—	—	...	...	...	—	—	—
9302	Currency and deposits	...	...	...	—	—	—	...	...	...	—	—	—
9303	Debt securities	...	...	...	-8	11	-5	...	...	...	-8	12	-6
9304	Loans	...	...	...	5	4	1	...	...	...	5	4	1
9305	Equity and investment fund shares	...	...	...	—	—	—	...	...	...	—	—	—
9306	Insurance, pension, and standardized guarantee schemes	...	...	...	—	—	—	...	...	...	—	—	—
9307	Financial derivatives and employee stock options	...	...	...	-1	-1	-1	...	...	...	-1	-1	-1
9308	Other accounts payable	...	...	...	0	0	—	...	...	...	0	0	—
	By creditor												
931	Domestic creditors	...	...	...	...	...	...	...	...	...	...	...	...
932	External creditors	...	...	...	...	...	...	...	...	...	...	...	...
	Memorandum items												
9M2	Change in net financial worth due to other economic flows	...	...	...	1,000	1,166	847	...	...	...	1,014	1,172	855

Norway (142)

In Billions of Norwegian Kroner (NOK) / Fiscal Year Ends December 31st

		Budgetary Central Government			Central Government (excl. Social Security)			Central Government (incl. Social Security)			General Government		
		2013	2014	2015	2013P	2014P	2015P	2013P	2014P	2015P	2013P	2014P	2015P
9M3	Gross debt (D4) at market value: other economic flows	...	...	...	-3	15	-4	...	...	...	-3	16	-5
9M3D3	D3 debt liabilities at market value: other economic flows	...	...	...	-3	15	-4	...	...	...	-3	16	-5
9M3D2	D2 debt liabilities at market value: other economic flows	...	...	...	-3	15	-4	...	...	...	-3	16	-5
9M3D1	D1 debt liabilities at market value: other economic flows	...	...	...	-3	15	-4	...	...	...	-3	16	-5

Oman (449)

In Millions of Rials Omani (OMR) / Fiscal Year Ends December 31st

		Budgetary Central Government			Central Government (excl. Social Security)			Central Government (incl. Social Security)			General Government		
		2011	2012	2013	2011	2012	2013	2011	2012	2013	2011	2012	2013
	Statement of operations												
1	Revenue	12,536	14,766	14,995	...	...	...	...	...	...	...	...	...
2	Expense	7,319	10,096	10,468	...	...	...	...	...	...	...	...	...
GOB	**Gross operating balance**	**5,217**	**4,670**	**4,527**	...	...	...	...	...	...	...	...	...
NOB	**Net operating balance**	...	...	...	...	...	...	...	...	...	...	...	...
31	Net/Gross investment in nonfinancial assets	2,943	2,875	3,110	...	...	...	...	...	...	...	...	...
2M	Expenditure	10,262	12,971	13,578	...	...	...	...	...	...	...	...	...
NLB	**Net lending (+) / Net borrowing (-)**	**2,274**	**1,796**	**1,417**	...	...	...	...	...	...	...	...	...
32	Net acquisition of financial assets	2,385	1,911	1,544	...	...	...	...	...	...	...	...	...
33	Net incurrence of liabilities	111	113	126	...	...	...	...	...	...	...	...	...
NLBz	Statistical discrepancy	—	2	1	...	...	...	...	...	...	...	...	...
	Memorandum items												
PB	Primary net lending / net borrowing	2,312	1,841	1,471	...	...	...	...	...	...	...	...	...
GB	Government balance per national definition	...	...	...	...	...	...	...	...	...	...	...	...
	Statement of other economic flows												
	Balance sheet												
6	**Net worth**	...	...	...	...	...	...	...	...	...	...	...	...
61	Nonfinancial assets	...	...	...	...	...	...	...	...	...	...	...	...
62	Financial assets	18,407	20,317	21,861	...	...	...	...	...	...	...	...	...
63	Liabilities	1,247	1,361	1,487	...	...	...	...	...	...	...	...	...
	Table 1 Revenue												
1	**Revenue**	**12,536**	**14,766**	**14,995**	...	...	...	...	...	...	...	...	...
11	**Taxes**	**594**	**767**	**766**	...	...	...	...	...	...	...	...	...
111	Taxes on income, profits, and capital gains	282	353	394	...	...	...	...	...	...	...	...	...
1111	Payable by individuals	—	—	—	...	...	...	...	...	...	...	...	...
1112	Payable by corporations and other enterprises	282	353	394	...	...	...	...	...	...	...	...	...
1113	Other taxes on income, profits, and capital gains	—	—	—	...	...	...	...	...	...	...	...	...
112	Taxes on payroll and workforce	151	164	155	...	...	...	...	...	...	...	...	...
113	Taxes on property	—	—	—	...	...	...	...	...	...	...	...	...
114	Taxes on goods and services	—	—	—	...	...	...	...	...	...	...	...	...
1141	General taxes on goods and services	—	—	—	...	...	...	...	...	...	...	...	...
1142	Excises	—	—	—	...	...	...	...	...	...	...	...	...
115	Taxes on international trade and transactions	161	250	217	...	...	...	...	...	...	...	...	...
116	Other taxes	—	—	—	...	...	...	...	...	...	...	...	...
12	**Social contributions**	—	—	—	...	...	...	...	...	...	...	...	...
121	Social security contributions	—	—	—	...	...	...	...	...	...	...	...	...
122	Other social contributions	—	—	—	...	...	...	...	...	...	...	...	...
13	**Grants**	**14**	**6**	**6**	...	...	...	...	...	...	...	...	...
131	From foreign governments	...	6	6	...	...	...	...	...	...	...	...	...
132	From international organizations	...	—	—	...	...	...	...	...	...	...	...	...
133	From other general government units	...	—	—	...	...	...	...	...	...	...	...	...
1331	Current	...	—	—	...	...	...	...	...	...	...	...	...
1332	Capital	...	—	—	...	...	...	...	...	...	...	...	...
14	**Other revenue**	**11,929**	**13,993**	**14,223**	...	...	...	...	...	...	...	...	...
	Table 2 Expense by economic type												
2	**Expense**	**7,319**	**10,096**	**10,468**	...	...	...	...	...	...	...	...	...
21	**Compensation of employees**	**1,935**	**2,308**	**2,472**	...	...	...	...	...	...	...	...	...
211	Wages and salaries	1,777	2,107	2,260	...	...	...	...	...	...	...	...	...
212	Employers' social contributions	158	201	212	...	...	...	...	...	...	...	...	...
22	**Use of goods and services**	**3,464**	**5,885**	**5,734**	...	...	...	...	...	...	...	...	...
23	**Consumption of fixed capital**	...	...	...	...	...	...	...	...	...	...	...	...
24	**Interest**	**38**	**45**	**54**	...	...	...	...	...	...	...	...	...
25	**Subsidies**	**1,813**	**1,819**	**2,159**	...	...	...	...	...	...	...	...	...

Oman (449)

In Millions of Rials Omani (OMR) / Fiscal Year Ends December 31st

		Budgetary Central Government			Central Government (excl. Social Security)			Central Government (incl. Social Security)			General Government		
		2011	2012	2013	2011	2012	2013	2011	2012	2013	2011	2012	2013
26	**Grants**	**69**	**39**	**49**	**...**	**...**	**...**	**...**	**...**	**...**	**...**	**...**	**...**
261	To foreign governments	...	...	49	...	...	...	...	...	...	...	...	...
262	To international organizations	...	...	—	...	...	...	...	...	...	...	...	...
263	To other general government units	...	...	—	...	...	...	...	...	...	...	...	...
2631	Current	...	...	—	...	...	...	...	...	...	...	...	...
2632	Capital	...	...	—	...	...	...	...	...	...	...	...	...
27	**Social benefits**	**—**	**—**	**—**	**...**	**...**	**...**	**...**	**...**	**...**	**...**	**...**	**...**
271	Social security benefits	—	—	—	...	...	...	...	...	...	...	...	...
272	Social assistance benefits	—	—	—	...	...	...	...	...	...	...	...	...
273	Employment-related social benefits	—	—	—	...	...	...	...	...	...	...	...	...
28	**Other expense**	**—**	**—**	**—**	**...**	**...**	**...**	**...**	**...**	**...**	**...**	**...**	**...**
281	Property expense other than interest	—	—	—	...	...	...	...	...	...	...	...	...
282	Transfers not elsewhere classified	—	—	—	...	...	...	...	...	...	...	...	...
2821	Current	—	—	—	...	...	...	...	...	...	...	...	...
2822	Capital	—	—	—	...	...	...	...	...	...	...	...	...
	Table 3 Transactions in assets and liabilities												
3	**Change in net worth from transactions**	**...**	**...**	**...**	**...**	**...**	**...**	**...**	**...**	**...**	**...**	**...**	**...**
31	**Net/Gross investment in nonfinancial assets**	**2,943**	**2,875**	**3,110**	**...**	**...**	**...**	**...**	**...**	**...**	**...**	**...**	**...**
311	Fixed assets	2,958	2,886	3,119	...	...	...	...	...	...	...	...	...
3111	Buildings and structures	...	...	...	...	...	...	...	...	...	...	...	...
3112	Machinery and equipment	...	...	...	...	...	...	...	...	...	...	...	...
3113	Other fixed assets	...	...	...	...	...	...	...	...	...	...	...	...
3114	Weapons systems	...	...	...	...	...	...	...	...	...	...	...	...
312	Inventories	—	—	—	...	...	...	...	...	...	...	...	...
313	Valuables	—	—	—	...	...	...	...	...	...	...	...	...
314	Nonproduced assets	-15	-11	-9	...	...	...	...	...	...	...	...	...
3141	Land	-15	-11	-9	...	...	...	...	...	...	...	...	...
3142	Mineral and energy resources	—	—	—	...	...	...	...	...	...	...	...	...
3143	Other naturally occurring assets	—	—	—	...	...	...	...	...	...	...	...	...
3144	Intangible nonproduced assets	—	—	—	...	...	...	...	...	...	...	...	...
32	**Net acquisition of financial assets**	**2,385**	**1,911**	**1,544**	**...**	**...**	**...**	**...**	**...**	**...**	**...**	**...**	**...**
	By instrument												
3201	Monetary gold and SDRs	—	—	—	...	...	...	...	...	...	...	...	...
3202	Currency and deposits	1,896	1,255	1,113	...	...	...	...	...	...	...	...	...
3203	Debt securities	—	—	—	...	...	...	...	...	...	...	...	...
3204	Loans	28	5	368	...	...	...	...	...	...	...	...	...
3205	Equity and investment fund shares	461	651	63	...	...	...	...	...	...	...	...	...
3206	Insurance, pension, and standardized guarantee schemes	—	—	—	...	...	...	...	...	...	...	...	...
3207	Financial derivatives and employee stock options	—	—	—	...	...	...	...	...	...	...	...	...
3208	Other accounts receivable	...	...	...	...	...	...	...	...	...	...	...	...
	By debtor												
321	Domestic debtors	2,417	1,908	1,543	...	...	...	...	...	...	...	...	...
322	External debtors	-32	3	1	...	...	...	...	...	...	...	...	...
33	**Net incurrence of liabilities**	**111**	**113**	**126**	**...**	**...**	**...**	**...**	**...**	**...**	**...**	**...**	**...**
	By instrument												
3301	Special Drawing Rights (SDRs)	—	—	—	...	...	...	...	...	...	...	...	...
3302	Currency and deposits	—	—	—	...	...	...	...	...	...	...	...	...
3303	Debt securities	150	150	200	...	...	...	...	...	...	...	...	...
3304	Loans	-39	-37	-74	...	...	...	...	...	...	...	...	...
3305	Equity and investment fund shares	—	—	—	...	...	...	...	...	...	...	...	...
3306	Insurance, pension, and standardized guarantee schemes	—	—	—	...	...	...	...	...	...	...	...	...
3307	Financial derivatives and employee stock options	—	—	—	...	...	...	...	...	...	...	...	...
3308	Other accounts payable	...	...	...	...	...	...	...	...	...	...	...	...

Oman (449)

In Millions of Rials Omani (OMR) / Fiscal Year Ends December 31st

		Budgetary Central Government			Central Government (excl. Social Security)			Central Government (incl. Social Security)			General Government		
		2011	2012	2013	2011	2012	2013	2011	2012	2013	2011	2012	2013
	By creditor												
331	Domestic creditors	150	150	200	...	...	...	...	...	...	...	...	...
332	External creditors	-39	-37	-74	...	...	...	...	...	...	...	...	...
	Table 4 Holding gains and losses in assets and liabilities												
	Table 5 Holding gains and losses in assets and liabilities												
	Table 6 Balance sheet												
6	**Net worth**	...	...	...	...	...	...	...	...	...	...	...	...
61	**Nonfinancial assets**	...	...	...	...	...	...	...	...	...	...	...	...
611	Fixed assets	...	...	...	...	...	...	...	...	...	...	...	...
6111	Buildings and structures	...	...	...	...	...	...	...	...	...	...	...	...
6112	Machinery and equipment	...	...	...	...	...	...	...	...	...	...	...	...
6113	Other fixed assets	...	...	...	...	...	...	...	...	...	...	...	...
6114	Weapons systems	...	...	...	...	...	...	...	...	...	...	...	...
612	Inventories	...	...	...	...	...	...	...	...	...	...	...	...
613	Valuables	...	...	...	...	...	...	...	...	...	...	...	...
614	Nonproduced assets	...	...	...	...	...	...	...	...	...	...	...	...
6141	Land	...	...	...	...	...	...	...	...	...	...	...	...
6142	Mineral and energy resources	...	...	...	...	...	...	...	...	...	...	...	...
6143	Other naturally occurring assets	...	...	...	...	...	...	...	...	...	...	...	...
6144	Intangible nonproduced assets	...	...	...	...	...	...	...	...	...	...	...	...
62	**Financial assets**	**18,407**	**20,317**	**21,861**	...	...	...	...	...	...	...	...	...
	By instrument												
6201	Monetary gold and SDRs	—	—	—	...	...	...	...	...	...	...	...	...
6202	Currency and deposits	13,756	15,011	16,124	...	...	...	...	...	...	...	...	...
6203	Debt securities	—	—	—	...	...	...	...	...	...	...	...	...
6204	Loans	362	366	734	...	...	...	...	...	...	...	...	...
6205	Equity and investment fund shares	4,289	4,941	5,003	...	...	...	...	...	...	...	...	...
6206	Insurance, pension, and standardized guarantee schemes	—	—	—	...	...	...	...	...	...	...	...	...
6207	Financial derivatives and employee stock options	—	—	—	...	...	...	...	...	...	...	...	...
6208	Other accounts receivable	...	...	...	...	...	...	...	...	...	...	...	...
	By debtor												
621	Domestic debtors	5,497	5,809	6,902	...	...	...	...	...	...	...	...	...
622	External debtors	12,910	14,508	14,960	...	...	...	...	...	...	...	...	...
63	**Liabilities**	**1,247**	**1,361**	**1,487**	...	...	...	...	...	...	...	...	...
	By instrument												
6301	Special Drawing Rights (SDRs)	—	—	—	...	...	...	...	...	...	...	...	...
6302	Currency and deposits	—	—	—	...	...	...	...	...	...	...	...	...
6303	Debt securities	480	630	830	...	...	...	...	...	...	...	...	...
6304	Loans	767	731	657	...	...	...	...	...	...	...	...	...
6305	Equity and investment fund shares	—	—	—	...	...	...	...	...	...	...	...	...
6306	Insurance, pension, and standardized guarantee schemes	—	—	—	...	...	...	...	...	...	...	...	...
6307	Financial derivatives and employee stock options	—	—	—	...	...	...	...	...	...	...	...	...
6308	Other accounts payable	...	...	...	...	...	...	...	...	...	...	...	...
	By creditor												
631	Domestic creditors	480	630	830	...	...	...	...	...	...	...	...	...
632	External creditors	767	731	657	...	...	...	...	...	...	...	...	...
	Memorandum items												
6M2	Net financial worth	17,160	18,957	20,375	...	...	...	...	...	...	...	...	...
6M3	Gross debt (D4) at market value	...	...	...	...	...	...	...	...	...	...	...	...
6M3D3	D3 debt liabilities at market value	...	...	...	...	...	...	...	...	...	...	...	...
6M3D2	D2 debt liabilities at market value	...	...	...	...	...	...	...	...	...	...	...	...
6M3D1	D1 debt liabilities at market value	...	...	...	...	...	...	...	...	...	...	...	...
6M4	Gross debt (D4) at nominal value	...	...	...	...	...	...	...	...	...	...	...	...
6M4D3	D3 debt liabilities at nominal value	...	...	...	...	...	...	...	...	...	...	...	...
6M4D2	D2 debt liabilities at nominal value	1,247	1,361	1,487	...	...	...	...	...	...	...	...	...
6M4D1	D1 debt liabilities at nominal value	1,247	1,361	1,487	...	...	...	...	...	...	...	...	...

Oman (449)

In Millions of Rials Omani (OMR) / Fiscal Year Ends December 31st

		Budgetary Central Government			Central Government (excl. Social Security)			Central Government (incl. Social Security)			General Government		
		2011	2012	2013	2011	2012	2013	2011	2012	2013	2011	2012	2013
6M35	Gross debt (D4) at face value	...	...	...	...	...	...	...	...	...	...	...	...
6M35D3	D3 debt liabilities at face value	...	...	...	...	...	...	...	...	...	...	...	...
6M35D2	D2 debt liabilities at face value	...	...	...	...	...	...	...	...	...	...	...	...
6M35D1	D1 debt liabilities at face value	...	...	...	...	...	...	...	...	...	...	...	...
6M93	Government gross debt per national definition	...	...	...	...	...	...	...	...	...	...	...	...
6M5	Arrears	...	...	...	...	...	...	...	...	...	...	...	...
6M6	Explicit contingent liabilities	...	...	...	...	...	...	...	...	...	...	...	...
6M61	of which: Publicly guaranteed debt	...	...	...	...	...	...	...	...	...	...	...	...
6M7	Net implicit obligations for social security benefits	...	...	...	...	...	...	...	...	...	...	...	...
	Table 7 Expenditure by functions of government												
7	**Expenditure**	**10,262**	**12,971**	**13,578**	...	...	...	...	...	...	...	...	...
701	**General public services**	**666**	**711**	**721**	...	...	...	...	...	...	...	...	...
7017	Public debt transactions	38	45	54	...	...	...	...	...	...	...	...	...
7018	Transfers of general character between levels of government	...	...	...	...	...	...	...	...	...	...	...	...
702	**Defense**	**2,564**	**4,743**	**4,494**	...	...	...	...	...	...	...	...	...
703	**Public order and safety**	**101**	**104**	**203**	...	...	...	...	...	...	...	...	...
704	**Economic affairs**	**1,114**	**832**	**982**	...	...	...	...	...	...	...	...	...
7042	Agriculture, forestry, fishing, and hunting	67	69	77	...	...	...	...	...	...	...	...	...
7043	Fuel and energy	4	5	5	...	...	...	...	...	...	...	...	...
7044	Mining, manufacturing, and construction	1	1	1	...	...	...	...	...	...	...	...	...
7045	Transport	843	716	840	...	...	...	...	...	...	...	...	...
7046	Communication	200	41	60	...	...	...	...	...	...	...	...	...
705	**Environmental protection**	**12**	**16**	**29**	...	...	...	...	...	...	...	...	...
706	**Housing and community amenities**	**960**	**870**	**849**	...	...	...	...	...	...	...	...	...
707	**Health**	**420**	**475**	**580**	...	...	...	...	...	...	...	...	...
7072	Outpatient services	...	...	...	...	...	...	...	...	...	...	...	...
7073	Hospital services	...	...	...	...	...	...	...	...	...	...	...	...
7074	Public health services	...	...	...	...	...	...	...	...	...	...	...	...
708	**Recreation, culture and religion**	**150**	**184**	**215**	...	...	...	...	...	...	...	...	...
709	**Education**	**1,161**	**1,392**	**1,503**	...	...	...	...	...	...	...	...	...
7091	Pre-primary and primary education	...	...	...	...	...	...	...	...	...	...	...	...
7092	Secondary education	...	...	...	...	...	...	...	...	...	...	...	...
7094	Tertiary education	...	...	...	...	...	...	...	...	...	...	...	...
710	**Social protection**	**640**	**554**	**572**	...	...	...	...	...	...	...	...	...
7z	Statistical discrepancy: Expenditure	...	...	...	...	...	...	...	...	...	...	...	...
	Table 8 Financial transactions by counterpart sector												
32	**Net acquisition of financial assets**	**2,385**	**1,911**	**1,544**	...	...	...	...	...	...	...	...	...
321	Domestic debtors	2,417	1,908	1,543	...	...	...	...	...	...	...	...	...
8211	General government	...	...	...	...	...	...	...	...	...	...	...	...
8212	Central bank	...	...	...	...	...	...	...	...	...	...	...	...
8213	Deposit-taking corporations except the central bank	...	...	...	...	...	...	...	...	...	...	...	...
8214	Other financial corporations	...	...	...	...	...	...	...	...	...	...	...	...
8215	Nonfinancial corporations	...	...	...	...	...	...	...	...	...	...	...	...
8216	Households & nonprofit institutions serving households	...	...	...	...	...	...	...	...	...	...	...	...
322	External debtors	-32	3	1	...	...	...	...	...	...	...	...	...
8221	General government	...	...	...	...	...	...	...	...	...	...	...	...
8227	International organizations	...	...	...	...	...	...	...	...	...	...	...	...
8228	Financial corporations other than international organizations	...	...	...	...	...	...	...	...	...	...	...	...
8229	Other nonresidents	...	...	...	...	...	...	...	...	...	...	...	...

Oman (449)

In Millions of Rials Omani (OMR) / Fiscal Year Ends December 31st

		Budgetary Central Government			Central Government (excl. Social Security)			Central Government (incl. Social Security)			General Government		
		2011	2012	2013	2011	2012	2013	2011	2012	2013	2011	2012	2013
33	**Net incurrence of liabilities**	**111**	**113**	**126**	**...**	**...**	**...**	**...**	**...**	**...**	**...**	**...**	**...**
331	Domestic creditors	150	150	200	...	...	...	...	...	...	...	...	...
3311	General government	...	...	...	...	...	...	...	...	...	...	...	...
3312	Central bank	...	...	...	...	...	...	...	...	...	...	...	...
3313	Deposit-taking corporations except the central bank	...	...	...	...	...	...	...	...	...	...	...	...
3314	Other financial corporations	...	...	...	...	...	...	...	...	...	...	...	...
3315	Nonfinancial corporations	...	...	...	...	...	...	...	...	...	...	...	...
3316	Households & nonprofit institutions serving households	...	...	...	...	...	...	...	...	...	...	...	...
332	External creditors	-39	-37	-74	...	...	...	...	...	...	...	...	...
3321	General government	...	...	...	...	...	...	...	...	...	...	...	...
3327	International organizations	...	...	...	...	...	...	...	...	...	...	...	...
3328	Financial corporations other than international organizations	...	...	...	...	...	...	...	...	...	...	...	...
3329	Other nonresidents	...	...	...	...	...	...	...	...	...	...	...	...
	Table 9 Total other economic flows in assets and liabilities												

Pakistan (564)

In Billions of Pakistani Rupees (PKR) / Fiscal Year Ends June 30th

		Budgetary Central Government			Central Government (excl. Social Security)			Central Government (incl. Social Security)			General Government		
		2012	2013	2014P	2012	2013	2014	2012	2013	2014	2012	2013	2014
	Statement of operations												
1	Revenue	2,582	3,346	3,636	...	...	...	...	...	...	...	...	...
2	Expense	3,769	3,991	4,533	...	...	...	...	...	...	...	...	...
GOB	**Gross operating balance**	**-1,186**	**-645**	**-897**	...	...	...	...	...	...	...	...	...
NOB	**Net operating balance**	...	...	...	...	...	...	...	...	...	...	...	...
31	Net/Gross investment in nonfinancial assets	419	527	755	...	...	...	...	...	...	...	...	...
2M	Expenditure	4,187	4,517	5,289	...	...	...	...	...	...	...	...	...
NLB	**Net lending (+) / Net borrowing (-)**	**-1,605**	**-1,171**	**-1,653**	...	...	...	...	...	...	...	...	...
32	Net acquisition of financial assets	...	...	...	...	...	...	...	...	...	...	...	...
33	Net incurrence of liabilities	...	...	...	...	...	...	...	...	...	...	...	...
NLBz	Statistical discrepancy	...	...	...	...	...	...	...	...	...	...	...	...
	Memorandum items												
PB	Primary net lending / net borrowing	-624	-30	-202	...	...	...	...	...	...	...	...	...
GB	Government balance per national definition	...	...	...	...	...	...	...	...	...	...	...	...
	Statement of other economic flows												
	Balance sheet												
	Table 1 Revenue												
1	**Revenue**	**2,582**	**3,346**	**3,636**	...	...	...	...	...	...	...	...	...
11	**Taxes**	**2,025**	**2,504**	**2,514**	...	...	...	...	...	...	...	...	...
111	Taxes on income, profits, and capital gains	745	932	891	...	...	...	...	...	...	...	...	...
1111	Payable by individuals	730	914	877	...	...	...	...	...	...	...	...	...
1112	Payable by corporations and other enterprises	—	—	14	...	...	...	...	...	...	...	...	...
1113	Other taxes on income, profits, and capital gains	15	18	—	...	...	...	...	...	...	...	...	...
112	Taxes on payroll and workforce	—	—	—	...	...	...	...	...	...	...	...	...
113	Taxes on property	—	—	—	...	...	...	...	...	...	...	...	...
114	Taxes on goods and services	992	1,202	1,143	...	...	...	...	...	...	...	...	...
1141	General taxes on goods and services	852	1,077	1,005	...	...	...	...	...	...	...	...	...
1142	Excises	140	125	138	...	...	...	...	...	...	...	...	...
115	Taxes on international trade and transactions	215	248	241	...	...	...	...	...	...	...	...	...
116	Other taxes	73	123	239	...	...	...	...	...	...	...	...	...
12	**Social contributions**	—	—	—	...	...	...	...	...	...	...	...	...
121	Social security contributions	—	—	—	...	...	...	...	...	...	...	...	...
122	Other social contributions	—	—	—	...	...	...	...	...	...	...	...	...
13	**Grants**	**46**	**112**	**39**	...	...	...	...	...	...	...	...	...
131	From foreign governments	46	112	39	...	...	...	...	...	...	...	...	...
132	From international organizations	—	—	—	...	...	...	...	...	...	...	...	...
133	From other general government units	—	—	—	...	...	...	...	...	...	...	...	...
1331	Current	—	—	—	...	...	...	...	...	...	...	...	...
1332	Capital	—	—	—	...	...	...	...	...	...	...	...	...
14	**Other revenue**	**512**	**730**	**1,083**	...	...	...	...	...	...	...	...	...
	Table 2 Expense by economic type												
2	**Expense**	**3,769**	**3,991**	**4,533**	...	...	...	...	...	...	...	...	...
21	**Compensation of employees**	**134**	**155**	**452**	...	...	...	...	...	...	...	...	...
211	Wages and salaries	134	155	452	...	...	...	...	...	...	...	...	...
212	Employers' social contributions	—	—	—	...	...	...	...	...	...	...	...	...
22	**Use of goods and services**	**755**	**884**	**435**	...	...	...	...	...	...	...	...	...
23	**Consumption of fixed capital**	...	...	...	...	...	...	...	...	...	...	...	...
24	**Interest**	**981**	**1,142**	**1,451**	...	...	...	...	...	...	...	...	...
25	**Subsidies**	**512**	**209**	**323**	...	...	...	...	...	...	...	...	...
26	**Grants**	**251**	**312**	**336**	...	...	...	...	...	...	...	...	...
261	To foreign governments	...	...	...	...	...	...	...	...	...	...	...	...
262	To international organizations	...	...	...	...	...	...	...	...	...	...	...	...
263	To other general government units	...	...	...	...	...	...	...	...	...	...	...	...
2631	Current	...	...	...	...	...	...	...	...	...	...	...	...
2632	Capital	...	...	...	...	...	...	...	...	...	...	...	...

Pakistan (564)

In Billions of Pakistani Rupees (PKR) / Fiscal Year Ends June 30th

		Budgetary Central Government			Central Government (excl. Social Security)			Central Government (incl. Social Security)			General Government		
		2012	2013	2014P	2012	2013	2014	2012	2013	2014	2012	2013	2014
27	**Social benefits**	149	144	188	...	...	...	...	...	...	...	...	...
271	Social security benefits	...	...	...	...	...	...	...	...	...	...	...	...
272	Social assistance benefits	...	...	...	...	...	...	...	...	...	...	...	...
273	Employment-related social benefits	...	...	...	...	...	...	...	...	...	...	...	...
28	**Other expense**	986	1,145	1,350	...	...	...	...	...	...	...	...	...
281	Property expense other than interest	...	...	...	...	...	...	...	...	...	...	...	...
282	Transfers not elsewhere classified	...	...	—	...	...	...	...	...	...	...	...	...
2821	Current	...	...	—	...	...	...	...	...	...	...	...	...
2822	Capital	...	...	—	...	...	...	...	...	...	...	...	...
	Table 3 Transactions in assets and liabilities												
3	**Change in net worth from transactions**	...	...	...	...	...	...	...	...	...	...	...	...
31	**Net/Gross investment in nonfinancial assets**	419	527	755	...	...	...	...	...	...	...	...	...
311	Fixed assets	419	527	755	...	...	...	...	...	...	...	...	...
3111	Buildings and structures	...	...	...	...	...	...	...	...	...	...	...	...
3112	Machinery and equipment	...	...	...	...	...	...	...	...	...	...	...	...
3113	Other fixed assets	...	...	...	...	...	...	...	...	...	...	...	...
3114	Weapons systems	...	...	...	...	...	...	...	...	...	...	...	...
312	Inventories	—	—	—	...	...	...	...	...	...	...	...	...
313	Valuables	—	—	—	...	...	...	...	...	...	...	...	...
314	Nonproduced assets	—	—	—	...	...	...	...	...	...	...	...	...
3141	Land	—	—	—	...	...	...	...	...	...	...	...	...
3142	Mineral and energy resources	—	—	—	...	...	...	...	...	...	...	...	...
3143	Other naturally occurring assets	—	—	—	...	...	...	...	...	...	...	...	...
3144	Intangible nonproduced assets	—	—	—	...	...	...	...	...	...	...	...	...
32	**Net acquisition of financial assets**	...	...	...	...	...	...	...	...	...	...	...	...
	By instrument												
3201	Monetary gold and SDRs	...	...	...	...	...	...	...	...	...	...	...	...
3202	Currency and deposits	...	...	...	...	...	...	...	...	...	...	...	...
3203	Debt securities	...	...	...	...	...	...	...	...	...	...	...	...
3204	Loans	...	...	...	...	...	...	...	...	...	...	...	...
3205	Equity and investment fund shares	...	...	...	...	...	...	...	...	...	...	...	...
3206	Insurance, pension, and standardized guarantee schemes	...	...	...	...	...	...	...	...	...	...	...	...
3207	Financial derivatives and employee stock options	...	...	...	...	...	...	...	...	...	...	...	...
3208	Other accounts receivable	...	...	...	...	...	...	...	...	...	...	...	...
	By debtor												
321	Domestic debtors	—	—	—	...	...	...	...	...	...	...	...	...
322	External debtors	—	—	—	...	...	...	...	...	...	...	...	...
33	**Net incurrence of liabilities**	...	...	...	...	...	...	...	...	...	...	...	...
	By instrument												
3301	Special Drawing Rights (SDRs)	...	...	...	...	...	...	...	...	...	...	...	...
3302	Currency and deposits	...	...	...	...	...	...	...	...	...	...	...	...
3303	Debt securities	...	...	...	...	...	...	...	...	...	...	...	...
3304	Loans	...	...	...	...	...	...	...	...	...	...	...	...
3305	Equity and investment fund shares	...	...	...	...	...	...	...	...	...	...	...	...
3306	Insurance, pension, and standardized guarantee schemes	...	...	...	...	...	...	...	...	...	...	...	...
3307	Financial derivatives and employee stock options	...	...	...	...	...	...	...	...	...	...	...	...
3308	Other accounts payable	...	...	...	...	...	...	...	...	...	...	...	...
	By creditor												
331	Domestic creditors	—	—	—	...	...	...	...	...	...	...	...	...
332	External creditors	—	—	—	...	...	...	...	...	...	...	...	...
	Table 4 Holding gains and losses in assets and liabilities												
	Table 5 Holding gains and losses in assets and liabilities												
	Table 6 Balance sheet												

Pakistan (564)

In Billions of Pakistani Rupees (PKR) / Fiscal Year Ends June 30th

		Budgetary Central Government			Central Government (excl. Social Security)			Central Government (incl. Social Security)			General Government		
		2012	2013	2014P	2012	2013	2014	2012	2013	2014	2012	2013	2014
	Table 7 Expenditure by functions of government												
7	**Expenditure**	**4,187**	**4,517**	**5,289**	...	...	...	...	...	...	...	...	...
701	**General public services**	**3,315**	**3,641**	**4,251**	...	...	...	...	...	...	...	...	...
7017	Public debt transactions	981	1,142	1,451	...	...	...	...	...	...	...	...	...
7018	Transfers of general character between levels of government	...	...	...	...	...	...	...	...	...	...	...	...
702	**Defense**	**510**	**545**	**630**	...	...	...	...	...	...	...	...	...
703	**Public order and safety**	**66**	**76**	**80**	...	...	...	...	...	...	...	...	...
704	**Economic affairs**	**182**	**156**	**162**	...	...	...	...	...	...	...	...	...
7042	Agriculture, forestry, fishing, and hunting	122	87	100	...	...	...	...	...	...	...	...	...
7043	Fuel and energy	1	1	1	...	...	...	...	...	...	...	...	...
7044	Mining, manufacturing, and construction	4	3	3	...	...	...	...	...	...	...	...	...
7045	Transport	15	13	17	...	...	...	...	...	...	...	...	...
7046	Communication	13	17	19	...	...	...	...	...	...	...	...	...
705	**Environmental protection**	**1**	**1**	**1**	...	...	...	...	...	...	...	...	...
706	**Housing and community amenities**	**5**	**4**	**27**	...	...	...	...	...	...	...	...	...
707	**Health**	**7**	**9**	**37**	...	...	...	...	...	...	...	...	...
7072	Outpatient services	—	—	...	...	...	...	...	...	...	...	...	...
7073	Hospital services	6	7	9	...	...	...	...	...	...	...	...	...
7074	Public health services	1	1	5	...	...	...	...	...	...	...	...	...
708	**Recreation, culture and religion**	**5**	**6**	**7**	...	...	...	...	...	...	...	...	...
709	**Education**	**61**	**65**	**88**	...	...	...	...	...	...	...	...	...
7091	Pre-primary and primary education	4	5	6	...	...	...	...	...	...	...	...	...
7092	Secondary education	6	6	7	...	...	...	...	...	...	...	...	...
7094	Tertiary education	0	0	0	...	...	...	...	...	...	...	...	...
710	**Social protection**	**35**	**12**	**5**	...	...	...	...	...	...	...	...	...
7z	Statistical discrepancy: Expenditure	...	—	...	...	...	...	...	...	...	...	...	...
	Table 8 Financial transactions by counterpart sector												
	Table 9 Total other economic flows in assets and liabilities												

Palau (565)

In Thousands of U.S. Dollars (USD) / Fiscal Year Ends September 30th

		Budgetary Central Government			Central Government (excl. Social Security)			Central Government (incl. Social Security)			General Government		
		2013	2014	2015	2013	2014	2015	2013	2014	2015	2013	2014	2015
	Statement of operations												
1	Revenue	93,868	108,561	116,822	...	...	...	...	...	...	...	...	...
2	Expense	111,693	114,915	114,175	...	...	...	...	...	...	...	...	...
GOB	**Gross operating balance**	**11,407**	**19,767**	**27,910**	...	...	...	...	...	...	...	...	...
NOB	**Net operating balance**	**-17,825**	**-6,354**	**2,646**	...	...	...	...	...	...	...	...	...
31	Net/Gross investment in nonfinancial assets	-19,499	-15,125	-11,784	...	...	...	...	...	...	...	...	...
2M	Expenditure	92,194	99,790	102,392	...	...	...	...	...	...	...	...	...
NLB	**Net lending (+) / Net borrowing (-)**	**1,674**	**8,771**	**14,430**	...	...	...	...	...	...	...	...	...
32	Net acquisition of financial assets	-6,114	9,665	9,405	...	...	...	...	...	...	...	...	...
33	Net incurrence of liabilities	-7,788	894	-5,025	...	...	...	...	...	...	...	...	...
NLBz	Statistical discrepancy	0	-0	—	...	...	...	...	...	...	...	...	...
	Memorandum items												
PB	Primary net lending / net borrowing	2,263	9,313	15,178	...	...	...	...	...	...	...	...	...
GB	Government balance per national definition	...	...	...	...	...	...	...	...	...	...	...	...
	Statement of other economic flows												
	Balance sheet												
6	**Net worth**	**160,793**	**147,893**	**29,832**	...	...	...	...	...	...	...	...	...
61	Nonfinancial assets	183,638	169,184	155,067	...	...	...	...	...	...	...	...	...
62	Financial assets	28,501	31,580	52,757	...	...	...	...	...	...	...	...	...
63	Liabilities	51,346	52,871	177,992	...	...	...	...	...	...	...	...	...
	Table 1 Revenue												
1	**Revenue**	**93,868**	**108,561**	**116,822**	...	...	...	...	...	...	...	...	...
11	**Taxes**	**41,365**	**47,172**	**56,607**	...	...	...	...	...	...	...	...	...
111	Taxes on income, profits, and capital gains	7,357	8,151	9,143	...	...	...	...	...	...	...	...	...
1111	Payable by individuals	7,357	8,151	9,143	...	...	...	...	...	...	...	...	...
1112	Payable by corporations and other enterprises	—	—	—	...	...	...	...	...	...	...	...	...
1113	Other taxes on income, profits, and capital gains	—	—	—	...	...	...	...	...	...	...	...	...
112	Taxes on payroll and workforce	967	1,147	1,387	...	...	...	...	...	...	...	...	...
113	Taxes on property	—	—	—	...	...	...	...	...	...	...	...	...
114	Taxes on goods and services	17,617	19,581	22,459	...	...	...	...	...	...	...	...	...
1141	General taxes on goods and services	12,196	13,020	14,525	...	...	...	...	...	...	...	...	...
1142	Excises	—	—	—	...	...	...	...	...	...	...	...	...
115	Taxes on international trade and transactions	9,642	11,555	14,426	...	...	...	...	...	...	...	...	...
116	Other taxes	5,783	6,739	9,193	...	...	...	...	...	...	...	...	...
12	**Social contributions**	—	—	—	...	...	...	...	...	...	...	...	...
121	Social security contributions	—	—	—	...	...	...	...	...	...	...	...	...
122	Other social contributions	—	—	—	...	...	...	...	...	...	...	...	...
13	**Grants**	**42,049**	**47,302**	**43,835**	...	...	...	...	...	...	...	...	...
131	From foreign governments	42,049	47,302	43,835	...	...	...	...	...	...	...	...	...
132	From international organizations	—	—	—	...	...	...	...	...	...	...	...	...
133	From other general government units	—	—	—	...	...	...	...	...	...	...	...	...
1331	Current	—	—	—	...	...	...	...	...	...	...	...	...
1332	Capital	—	—	—	...	...	...	...	...	...	...	...	...
14	**Other revenue**	**10,454**	**14,086**	**16,379**	...	...	...	...	...	...	...	...	...
	Table 2 Expense by economic type												
2	**Expense**	**111,693**	**114,915**	**114,175**	...	...	...	...	...	...	...	...	...
21	**Compensation of employees**	**37,288**	**38,098**	**38,997**	...	...	...	...	...	...	...	...	...
211	Wages and salaries	33,410	33,660	34,903	...	...	...	...	...	...	...	...	...
212	Employers' social contributions	3,878	4,438	4,094	...	...	...	...	...	...	...	...	...
22	**Use of goods and services**	**23,344**	**24,869**	**25,369**	...	...	...	...	...	...	...	...	...
23	**Consumption of fixed capital**	**29,233**	**26,121**	**25,263**	...	...	...	...	...	...	...	...	...
24	**Interest**	**589**	**542**	**748**	...	...	...	...	...	...	...	...	...
25	**Subsidies**	**1,820**	**1,742**	**3,419**	...	...	...	...	...	...	...	...	...

Palau (565)

In Thousands of U.S. Dollars (USD) / Fiscal Year Ends September 30th

		Budgetary Central Government			Central Government (excl. Social Security)			Central Government (incl. Social Security)			General Government		
		2013	2014	2015	2013	2014	2015	2013	2014	2015	2013	2014	2015
26	**Grants**	**12,112**	**12,874**	**11,456**	...	...	...	...	...	...	...	...	...
261	To foreign governments	—	—	—	...	...	...	...	...	...	...	...	...
262	To international organizations	—	—	250	...	...	...	...	...	...	...	...	...
263	To other general government units	12,112	12,874	11,206	...	...	...	...	...	...	...	...	...
2631	Current	11,845	12,517	11,206	...	...	...	...	...	...	...	...	...
2632	Capital	267	357	—	...	...	...	...	...	...	...	...	...
27	**Social benefits**	**—**	**—**	**—**	...	...	...	...	...	...	...	...	...
271	Social security benefits	—	—	—	...	...	...	...	...	...	...	...	...
272	Social assistance benefits	—	—	—	...	...	...	...	...	...	...	...	...
273	Employment-related social benefits	—	—	—	...	...	...	...	...	...	...	...	...
28	**Other expense**	**7,309**	**10,668**	**8,923**	...	...	...	...	...	...	...	...	...
281	Property expense other than interest	—	—	—	...	...	...	...	...	...	...	...	...
282	Transfers not elsewhere classified	7,309	10,668	8,923	...	...	...	...	...	...	...	...	...
2821	Current	7,309	10,668	8,923	...	...	...	...	...	...	...	...	...
2822	Capital	—	—	—	...	...	...	...	...	...	...	...	...
	Table 3 Transactions in assets and liabilities												
3	**Change in net worth from transactions**	**-17,825**	**-6,354**	**2,646**	...	...	...	...	...	...	...	...	...
31	**Net/Gross investment in nonfinancial assets**	**-19,499**	**-15,125**	**-11,784**	...	...	...	...	...	...	...	...	...
311	Fixed assets	-19,548	-15,125	-11,737	...	...	...	...	...	...	...	...	...
3111	Buildings and structures	-17,215	-16,269	-13,060	...	...	...	...	...	...	...	...	...
3112	Machinery and equipment	-2,373	50	1,282	...	...	...	...	...	...	...	...	...
3113	Other fixed assets	39	1,094	41	...	...	...	...	...	...	...	...	...
3114	Weapons systems	—	—	—	...	...	...	...	...	...	...	...	...
312	Inventories	—	—	-46	...	...	...	...	...	...	...	...	...
313	Valuables	—	—	—	...	...	...	...	...	...	...	...	...
314	Nonproduced assets	49	—	—	...	...	...	...	...	...	...	...	...
3141	Land	49	—	—	...	...	...	...	...	...	...	...	...
3142	Mineral and energy resources	—	—	—	...	...	...	...	...	...	...	...	...
3143	Other naturally occurring assets	—	—	—	...	...	...	...	...	...	...	...	...
3144	Intangible nonproduced assets	—	—	—	...	...	...	...	...	...	...	...	...
32	**Net acquisition of financial assets**	**-6,114**	**9,665**	**9,405**	...	...	...	...	...	...	...	...	...
	By instrument												
3201	Monetary gold and SDRs	—	—	—	...	...	...	...	...	...	...	...	...
3202	Currency and deposits	-4,852	3,367	8,762	...	...	...	...	...	...	...	...	...
3203	Debt securities	—	—	—	...	...	...	...	...	...	...	...	...
3204	Loans	—	—	—	...	...	...	...	...	...	...	...	...
3205	Equity and investment fund shares	444	597	-110	...	...	...	...	...	...	...	...	...
3206	Insurance, pension, and standardized guarantee schemes	—	—	—	...	...	...	...	...	...	...	...	...
3207	Financial derivatives and employee stock options	—	—	—	...	...	...	...	...	...	...	...	...
3208	Other accounts receivable	-1,707	5,701	754	...	...	...	...	...	...	...	...	...
	By debtor												
321	Domestic debtors	-7,042	8,648	7,769	...	...	...	...	...	...	...	...	...
322	External debtors	927	1,017	1,636	...	...	...	...	...	...	...	...	...
33	**Net incurrence of liabilities**	**-7,788**	**894**	**-5,025**	...	...	...	...	...	...	...	...	...
	By instrument												
3301	Special Drawing Rights (SDRs)	—	—	—	...	...	...	...	...	...	...	...	...
3302	Currency and deposits	—	—	—	...	...	...	...	...	...	...	...	...
3303	Debt securities	—	—	—	...	...	...	...	...	...	...	...	...
3304	Loans	-1,600	4,317	-2,209	...	...	...	...	...	...	...	...	...
3305	Equity and investment fund shares	—	—	—	...	...	...	...	...	...	...	...	...
3306	Insurance, pension, and standardized guarantee schemes	—	—	—	...	...	...	...	...	...	...	...	...
3307	Financial derivatives and employee stock options	—	—	—	...	...	...	...	...	...	...	...	...
3308	Other accounts payable	-6,188	-3,423	-2,815	...	...	...	...	...	...	...	...	...

Palau (565)

In Thousands of U.S. Dollars (USD) / Fiscal Year Ends September 30th

		Budgetary Central Government			Central Government (excl. Social Security)			Central Government (incl. Social Security)			General Government		
		2013	2014	2015	2013	2014	2015	2013	2014	2015	2013	2014	2015
	By creditor												
331	Domestic creditors	-4,285	-3,423	-2,815	...	...	...	...	...	...	...	...	...
332	External creditors	-3,503	4,317	-2,209	...	...	...	...	...	...	...	...	...
	Table 4 Holding gains and losses in assets and liabilities												
	Table 5 Holding gains and losses in assets and liabilities												
	Table 6 Balance sheet												
6	**Net worth**	**160,793**	**147,893**	**29,832**	...	...	...	...	...	...	...	...	...
61	**Nonfinancial assets**	**183,638**	**169,184**	**155,067**	...	...	...	...	...	...	...	...	...
611	Fixed assets	179,693	165,238	151,167	...	...	...	...	...	...	...	...	...
6111	Buildings and structures	176,618	160,893	146,672	...	...	...	...	...	...	...	...	...
6112	Machinery and equipment	3,074	4,345	4,495	...	...	...	...	...	...	...	...	...
6113	Other fixed assets	—	—	—	...	...	...	...	...	...	...	...	...
6114	Weapons systems	—	—	—	...	...	...	...	...	...	...	...	...
612	Inventories	46	46	—	...	...	...	...	...	...	...	...	...
613	Valuables	—	—	—	...	...	...	...	...	...	...	...	...
614	Nonproduced assets	3,899	3,899	3,899	...	...	...	...	...	...	...	...	...
6141	Land	3,899	3,899	3,899	...	...	...	...	...	...	...	...	...
6142	Mineral and energy resources	—	—	—	...	...	...	...	...	...	...	...	...
6143	Other naturally occurring assets	—	—	—	...	...	...	...	...	...	...	...	...
6144	Intangible nonproduced assets	—	—	—	...	...	...	...	...	...	...	...	...
62	**Financial assets**	**28,501**	**31,580**	**52,757**	...	...	...	...	...	...	...	...	...
	By instrument												
6201	Monetary gold and SDRs	—	—	—	...	...	...	...	...	...	...	...	...
6202	Currency and deposits	6,237	9,605	18,367	...	...	...	...	...	...	...	...	...
6203	Debt securities	—	—	—	...	...	...	...	...	...	...	...	...
6204	Loans	—	—	—	...	...	...	...	...	...	...	...	...
6205	Equity and investment fund shares	7,592	8,189	8,079	...	...	...	...	...	...	...	...	...
6206	Insurance, pension, and standardized guarantee schemes	—	—	—	...	...	...	...	...	...	...	...	...
6207	Financial derivatives and employee stock options	—	—	—	...	...	...	...	...	...	...	...	...
6208	Other accounts receivable	14,672	13,787	26,312	...	...	...	...	...	...	...	...	...
	By debtor												
621	Domestic debtors	16,608	18,925	38,463	...	...	...	...	...	...	...	...	...
622	External debtors	11,893	12,655	14,294	...	...	...	...	...	...	...	...	...
63	**Liabilities**	**51,346**	**52,871**	**177,992**	...	...	...	...	...	...	...	...	...
	By instrument												
6301	Special Drawing Rights (SDRs)	—	—	—	...	...	...	...	...	...	...	...	...
6302	Currency and deposits	—	—	—	...	...	...	...	...	...	...	...	...
6303	Debt securities	—	—	—	...	...	...	...	...	...	...	...	...
6304	Loans	21,584	27,645	23,179	...	...	...	...	...	...	...	...	...
6305	Equity and investment fund shares	—	—	—	...	...	...	...	...	...	...	...	...
6306	Insurance, pension, and standardized guarantee schemes	—	—	129,958	...	...	...	...	...	...	...	...	...
6307	Financial derivatives and employee stock options	—	—	—	...	...	...	...	...	...	...	...	...
6308	Other accounts payable	29,762	25,226	24,855	...	...	...	...	...	...	...	...	...
	By creditor												
631	Domestic creditors	26,762	22,226	146,324	...	...	...	...	...	...	...	...	...
632	External creditors	24,584	30,645	31,668	...	...	...	...	...	...	...	...	...
	Memorandum items												
6M2	Net financial worth	-22,846	-21,291	-125,235	...	...	...	...	...	...	...	...	...
6M3	Gross debt (D4) at market value	51,346	52,871	177,992	...	...	...	...	...	...	...	...	...
6M3D3	D3 debt liabilities at market value	51,346	52,871	48,034	...	...	...	...	...	...	...	...	...
6M3D2	D2 debt liabilities at market value	21,584	27,645	23,179	...	...	...	...	...	...	...	...	...
6M3D1	D1 debt liabilities at market value	21,584	27,645	23,179	...	...	...	...	...	...	...	...	...
6M4	Gross debt (D4) at nominal value	...	...	...	...	...	...	...	...	...	...	...	...
6M4D3	D3 debt liabilities at nominal value	...	...	...	...	...	...	...	...	...	...	...	...
6M4D2	D2 debt liabilities at nominal value	...	...	...	...	...	...	...	...	...	...	...	...
6M4D1	D1 debt liabilities at nominal value	...	...	...	...	...	...	...	...	...	...	...	...

Palau (565)

In Thousands of U.S. Dollars (USD) / Fiscal Year Ends September 30th

		Budgetary Central Government			Central Government (excl. Social Security)			Central Government (incl. Social Security)			General Government		
		2013	2014	2015	2013	2014	2015	2013	2014	2015	2013	2014	2015
6M35	Gross debt (D4) at face value	...	...	...	...	...	...	...	...	...	...	...	...
6M35D3	D3 debt liabilities at face value	...	...	...	...	...	...	...	...	...	...	...	...
6M35D2	D2 debt liabilities at face value	...	...	...	...	...	...	...	...	...	...	...	...
6M35D1	D1 debt liabilities at face value	...	...	...	...	...	...	...	...	...	...	...	...
6M93	Government gross debt per national definition	...	...	...	...	...	...	...	...	...	...	...	...
6M5	Arrears	...	...	...	...	...	...	...	...	...	...	...	...
6M6	Explicit contingent liabilities	...	...	...	...	...	...	...	...	...	...	...	...
6M61	of which: Publicly guaranteed debt	...	...	...	...	...	...	...	...	...	...	...	...
6M7	Net implicit obligations for social security benefits	...	...	...	...	...	...	...	...	...	...	...	...
	Table 7 Expenditure by functions of government												
7	**Expenditure**	**111,693**	**114,915**	**114,175**	...	...	...	...	...	...	...	...	...
701	**General public services**	**31,064**	**34,914**	**34,231**	...	...	...	...	...	...	...	...	...
7017	Public debt transactions	589	542	748	...	...	...	...	...	...	...	...	...
7018	Transfers of general character between levels of government	5,363	5,624	6,241	...	...	...	...	...	...	...	...	...
702	**Defense**	—	—	—	...	...	...	...	...	...	...	...	...
703	**Public order and safety**	**5,712**	**6,237**	**5,776**	...	...	...	...	...	...	...	...	...
704	**Economic affairs**	**29,657**	**27,331**	**27,878**	...	...	...	...	...	...	...	...	...
7042	Agriculture, forestry, fishing, and hunting	438	433	506	...	...	...	...	...	...	...	...	...
7043	Fuel and energy	10,489	9,224	9,054	...	...	...	...	...	...	...	...	...
7044	Mining, manufacturing, and construction	—	—	—	...	...	...	...	...	...	...	...	...
7045	Transport	10,214	9,662	9,597	...	...	...	...	...	...	...	...	...
7046	Communication	324	346	389	...	...	...	...	...	...	...	...	...
705	**Environmental protection**	**6,929**	**8,223**	**7,698**	...	...	...	...	...	...	...	...	...
706	**Housing and community amenities**	**196**	**175**	**275**	...	...	...	...	...	...	...	...	...
707	**Health**	**18,454**	**19,022**	**19,958**	...	...	...	...	...	...	...	...	...
7072	Outpatient services	7,305	6,883	7,274	...	...	...	...	...	...	...	...	...
7073	Hospital services	—	—	—	...	...	...	...	...	...	...	...	...
7074	Public health services	2,110	1,078	1,078	...	...	...	...	...	...	...	...	...
708	**Recreation, culture and religion**	**999**	**1,343**	**1,456**	...	...	...	...	...	...	...	...	...
709	**Education**	**15,442**	**15,901**	**16,553**	...	...	...	...	...	...	...	...	...
7091	Pre-primary and primary education	225	241	150	...	...	...	...	...	...	...	...	...
7092	Secondary education	510	527	496	...	...	...	...	...	...	...	...	...
7094	Tertiary education	3,538	2,436	2,436	...	...	...	...	...	...	...	...	...
710	**Social protection**	**3,240**	**1,768**	**351**	...	...	...	...	...	...	...	...	...
7z	Statistical discrepancy: Expenditure	-19,499	-15,125	...	...	...	...	...	...	...	...	...	...
	Table 8 Financial transactions by counterpart sector												
32	**Net acquisition of financial assets**	**-6,114**	**9,665**	**9,405**	...	...	...	...	...	...	...	...	...
321	Domestic debtors	-7,042	8,648	7,769	...	...	...	...	...	...	...	...	...
8211	General government	...	...	...	...	...	...	...	...	...	...	...	...
8212	Central bank	...	...	...	...	...	...	...	...	...	...	...	...
8213	Deposit-taking corporations except the central bank	...	...	...	...	...	...	...	...	...	...	...	...
8214	Other financial corporations	...	...	...	...	...	...	...	...	...	...	...	...
8215	Nonfinancial corporations	...	...	...	...	...	...	...	...	...	...	...	...
8216	Households & nonprofit institutions serving households	...	...	...	...	...	...	...	...	...	...	...	...
322	External debtors	927	1,017	1,636	...	...	...	...	...	...	...	...	...
8221	General government	...	...	...	...	...	...	...	...	...	...	...	...
8227	International organizations	...	...	...	...	...	...	...	...	...	...	...	...
8228	Financial corporations other than international organizations	...	...	...	...	...	...	...	...	...	...	...	...
8229	Other nonresidents	...	...	...	...	...	...	...	...	...	...	...	...

Palau (565)

In Thousands of U.S. Dollars (USD) / Fiscal Year Ends September 30th

		Budgetary Central Government			Central Government (excl. Social Security)			Central Government (incl. Social Security)			General Government		
		2013	2014	2015	2013	2014	2015	2013	2014	2015	2013	2014	2015
33	**Net incurrence of liabilities**	**-7,788**	**894**	**-5,025**	**...**	**...**	**...**	**...**	**...**	**...**	**...**	**...**	**...**
331	Domestic creditors	-4,285	-3,423	-2,815	...	...	...	...	...	...	...	...	...
3311	General government	...	...	...	...	...	...	...	...	...	...	...	...
3312	Central bank	...	...	...	...	...	...	...	...	...	...	...	...
3313	Deposit-taking corporations except the central bank	...	...	...	...	...	...	...	...	...	...	...	...
3314	Other financial corporations	...	...	...	...	...	...	...	...	...	...	...	...
3315	Nonfinancial corporations	...	...	...	...	...	...	...	...	...	...	...	...
3316	Households & nonprofit institutions serving households	...	...	...	...	...	...	...	...	...	...	...	...
332	External creditors	-3,503	4,317	-2,209	...	...	...	...	...	...	...	...	...
3321	General government	...	...	...	...	...	...	...	...	...	...	...	...
3327	International organizations	...	...	...	...	...	...	...	...	...	...	...	...
3328	Financial corporations other than international organizations	...	...	...	...	...	...	...	...	...	...	...	...
3329	Other nonresidents	...	...	...	...	...	...	...	...	...	...	...	...
	Table 9 Total other economic flows in assets and liabilities												

Paraguay (288)

In Billions of Paraguayan Guaranies (PYG) / Fiscal Year Ends December 31st

		Budgetary Central Government			Central Government (excl. Social Security)			Central Government (incl. Social Security)			General Government		
		2013	2014	2015	2013	2014	2015	2013	2014	2015	2013	2014	2015
	Statement of operations												
1	Revenue	20,942	24,147	26,565	21,678	24,958	27,494	25,866	30,364	33,624	27,269	31,658	35,181
2	Expense	20,373	21,931	25,339	20,819	22,376	26,125	24,132	26,503	30,476	24,610	27,317	30,911
GOB	**Gross operating balance**	**569**	**2,216**	**1,226**	**859**	**2,583**	**1,369**	**1,734**	**3,861**	**3,148**	**2,659**	**4,341**	**4,270**
NOB	**Net operating balance**	...	...	...	...	...	...	...	...	...	...	...	...
31	Net/Gross investment in nonfinancial assets	2,923	3,294	3,749	3,334	3,830	4,203	3,526	3,947	...	4,337	4,659	5,245
2M	Expenditure	23,296	25,224	29,088	24,153	26,206	30,328	27,659	30,450	...	28,948	31,976	36,156
NLB	**Net lending (+) / Net borrowing (-)**	**-2,354**	**-1,078**	**-2,523**	**-2,475**	**-1,248**	**-2,834**	**-1,792**	**-86**	**...**	**-1,678**	**-318**	**-975**
32	Net acquisition of financial assets	1,149	4,018	275	1,148	3,890	380	1,316	3,980	...	1,081	3,778	2,342
33	Net incurrence of liabilities	3,272	5,057	1,704	3,193	5,341	2,023	3,192	5,340	...	3,129	5,284	1,913
NLBz	Statistical discrepancy	232	38	1,094	431	-203	1,191	-83	-1,275	...	-370	-1,188	1,405
	Memorandum items												
PB	Primary net lending / net borrowing	-1,938	-551	-1,630	-2,059	-721	-1,941	-1,376	441	...	-1,251	221	-65
GB	Government balance per national definition	...	...	—	...	...	—	...	...	...	...	...	—
	Statement of other economic flows												
	Balance sheet												
	Table 1 Revenue												
1	**Revenue**	**20,942**	**24,147**	**26,565**	**21,678**	**24,958**	**27,494**	**25,866**	**30,364**	**33,624**	**27,269**	**31,658**	**35,181**
11	**Taxes**	**14,888**	**17,485**	**18,212**	**14,959**	**17,558**	**18,340**	**14,959**	**17,558**	**18,351**	**15,942**	**18,552**	**19,377**
111	Taxes on income, profits, and capital gains	3,098	3,682	3,918	3,098	3,682	3,918	3,098	3,682	3,918	3,104	4,675	3,918
1111	Payable by individuals	13	84	126	13	84	126	13	84	126	13	84	126
1112	Payable by corporations and other enterprises	3,084	3,597	3,792	3,084	3,597	3,792	3,084	3,597	3,792	3,090	4,591	3,792
1113	Other taxes on income, profits, and capital gains	—	—	—	—	—	—	—	—	—	—	—	—
112	Taxes on payroll and workforce	—	—	—	—	—	—	—	—	—	—	—	—
113	Taxes on property	—	—	—	—	—	—	—	—	—	973	—	432
114	Taxes on goods and services	10,047	11,844	12,363	10,118	11,918	12,491	10,118	11,918	12,503	10,124	11,918	13,011
1141	General taxes on goods and services	7,893	9,345	9,810	7,958	9,419	9,893	7,958	9,419	9,893	7,959	9,419	9,893
1142	Excises	2,055	2,449	2,427	2,055	2,449	2,427	2,055	2,449	2,427	2,057	2,449	2,427
115	Taxes on international trade and transactions	1,632	1,788	1,672	1,632	1,788	1,672	1,632	1,788	1,672	1,632	1,788	1,672
116	Other taxes	111	172	260	111	171	259	111	171	259	111	171	343
12	**Social contributions**	**1,607**	**2,313**	**2,029**	**1,607**	**2,313**	**2,029**	**5,544**	**6,746**	**7,085**	**5,554**	**6,746**	**7,085**
121	Social security contributions	—	41	41	—	41	41	3,937	4,474	5,097	3,942	4,474	5,097
122	Other social contributions	1,607	2,272	1,988	1,607	2,272	1,988	1,607	2,272	1,988	1,612	2,272	1,988
13	**Grants**	**551**	**530**	**716**	**219**	**242**	**312**	**219**	**242**	**346**	**313**	**242**	**312**
131	From foreign governments	82	102	159	82	103	159	82	103	159	177	103	159
132	From international organizations	136	139	152	136	139	152	136	139	152	136	139	153
133	From other general government units	332	289	405	0	—	—	—	—	34	0	—	—
1331	Current	332	289	405	0	—	—	—	—	34	0	—	—
1332	Capital	—	—	—	0	—	—	—	—	—	0	—	—
14	**Other revenue**	**3,897**	**3,818**	**5,608**	**4,894**	**4,845**	**6,813**	**5,145**	**5,818**	**7,842**	**5,460**	**6,118**	**8,408**
	Table 2 Expense by economic type												
2	**Expense**	**20,373**	**21,931**	**25,339**	**20,819**	**22,376**	**26,125**	**24,132**	**26,503**	**30,476**	**24,610**	**27,317**	**30,911**
21	**Compensation of employees**	**10,996**	**12,131**	**13,194**	**12,639**	**13,905**	**15,084**	**13,696**	**14,980**	**16,217**	**14,636**	**15,841**	**17,351**
211	Wages and salaries	10,996	12,131	13,194	12,639	13,905	15,084	13,696	14,980	16,217	14,636	15,841	17,351
212	Employers' social contributions	—	—	—	—	—	—	—	—	—	—	—	—
22	**Use of goods and services**	**1,677**	**2,042**	**2,263**	**1,963**	**2,382**	**2,602**	**2,449**	**3,428**	**3,484**	**2,871**	**3,823**	**3,938**
23	**Consumption of fixed capital**	...	...	...	...	...	...	...	...	...	...	...	...
24	**Interest**	**416**	**527**	**893**	**416**	**527**	**893**	**416**	**527**	**893**	**427**	**540**	**910**
25	**Subsidies**	**45**	**45**	—	**45**	**45**	—	**45**	**45**	—	**45**	**45**	—
26	**Grants**	**3,394**	**3,234**	**3,895**	**1,599**	**1,311**	**2,064**	**1,600**	**1,312**	**2,078**	**42**	**67**	**66**
261	To foreign governments	—	—	—	—	—	—	—	—	—	—	—	—
262	To international organizations	37	62	52	42	67	65	42	67	66	42	67	66
263	To other general government units	3,357	3,172	3,843	1,557	1,245	1,999	1,557	1,245	2,012	0	—	—
2631	Current	1,891	1,981	2,303	553	512	1,168	553	512	1,168	0	—	—
2632	Capital	1,466	1,191	1,540	1,004	733	831	1,004	733	844	0	—	—

Paraguay (288)

In Billions of Paraguayan Guaranies (PYG) / Fiscal Year Ends December 31st

		Budgetary Central Government			Central Government (excl. Social Security)			Central Government (incl. Social Security)			General Government		
		2013	2014	2015	2013	2014	2015	2013	2014	2015	2013	2014	2015
27	**Social benefits**	**2,943**	**2,999**	**3,873**	**2,986**	**3,043**	**3,918**	**4,692**	**4,987**	**6,138**	**4,727**	**5,080**	**6,636**
271	Social security benefits	280	310	2,072	280	310	2,072	1,726	1,978	3,988	1,726	1,979	3,988
272	Social assistance benefits	241	268	1,566	241	268	1,571	241	268	1,692	241	268	2,139
273	Employment-related social benefits	2,421	2,421	236	2,464	2,465	276	2,725	2,741	459	2,760	2,834	509
28	**Other expense**	**902**	**953**	**1,220**	**1,172**	**1,162**	**1,564**	**1,234**	**1,224**	**1,665**	**1,862**	**1,922**	**2,011**
281	Property expense other than interest	—	—	—	—	—	—	—	—	—	—	—	—
282	Transfers not elsewhere classified	902	953	1,220	1,172	1,162	1,564	1,234	1,224	1,665	1,862	1,922	2,011
2821	Current	637	833	974	682	893	1,019	744	955	1,121	1,167	1,503	1,282
2822	Capital	265	120	246	489	269	544	489	269	544	695	419	728
	Table 3 Transactions in assets and liabilities												
3	**Change in net worth from transactions**	...	...	...	...	...	...	...	...	...	...	...	...
31	**Net/Gross investment in nonfinancial assets**	**2,923**	**3,294**	**3,749**	**3,334**	**3,830**	**4,203**	**3,526**	**3,947**	**...**	**4,337**	**4,659**	**5,245**
311	Fixed assets	2,898	3,260	3,723	3,112	3,601	4,070	3,305	3,717	...	4,107	4,423	5,105
3111	Buildings and structures	2,464	2,777	3,162	2,587	2,980	3,398	2,692	3,043	...	3,387	3,628	4,289
3112	Machinery and equipment	405	419	502	486	542	608	570	584	...	658	693	730
3113	Other fixed assets	29	64	59	40	78	64	43	91	...	62	102	86
3114	Weapons systems	—	—	—	—	—	—	—	—	...	—	—	—
312	Inventories	18	23	23	18	24	24	18	24	...	27	30	32
313	Valuables	—	—	—	—	—	—	—	—	...	—	—	—
314	Nonproduced assets	8	11	3	203	206	109	203	206	...	203	206	109
3141	Land	8	11	3	203	206	109	203	206	...	203	206	109
3142	Mineral and energy resources	—	—	—	—	—	—	—	—	...	—	—	—
3143	Other naturally occurring assets	—	—	—	—	—	—	—	—	...	—	—	—
3144	Intangible nonproduced assets	—	—	—	—	—	—	—	—	...	—	—	—
32	**Net acquisition of financial assets**	**1,149**	**4,018**	**275**	**1,148**	**3,890**	**380**	**1,316**	**3,980**	**...**	**1,081**	**3,778**	**2,342**
	By instrument												
3201	Monetary gold and SDRs	—	—	—	—	—	—	—	—	...	—	—	—
3202	Currency and deposits	798	2,415	-1,032	798	2,300	-916	798	2,410	...	566	2,208	870
3203	Debt securities	200	300	300	200	300	300	71	122	...	70	122	188
3204	Loans	76	960	734	75	948	723	372	1,105	...	369	1,105	1,006
3205	Equity and investment fund shares	75	343	273	75	343	273	75	343	...	75	343	278
3206	Insurance, pension, and standardized guarantee schemes	—	—	—	—	—	—	—	—	...	—	—	—
3207	Financial derivatives and employee stock options	—	—	—	—	—	—	—	—	...	—	—	—
3208	Other accounts receivable	...	...	...	...	...	...	...	...	...	...	...	...
	By debtor												
321	Domestic debtors	1,149	4,018	275	1,148	3,890	380	1,316	3,980	...	1,081	3,778	2,342
322	External debtors	—	—	—	—	—	—	—	—	...	—	—	—
33	**Net incurrence of liabilities**	**3,272**	**5,057**	**1,704**	**3,193**	**5,341**	**2,023**	**3,192**	**5,340**	**...**	**3,129**	**5,284**	**1,913**
	By instrument												
3301	Special Drawing Rights (SDRs)	—	—	—	—	—	—	—	—	...	—	—	—
3302	Currency and deposits	—	—	—	—	—	—	—	—	...	—	—	—
3303	Debt securities	3,160	5,345	2,039	3,160	5,345	2,039	3,160	5,345	...	3,226	5,445	2,040
3304	Loans	-115	-509	-488	-116	-509	-488	-116	-509	...	-166	-576	-486
3305	Equity and investment fund shares	—	—	—	—	—	—	—	—	...	—	—	—
3306	Insurance, pension, and standardized guarantee schemes	—	—	—	—	—	—	—	—	...	—	—	—
3307	Financial derivatives and employee stock options	—	—	—	—	—	—	—	—	...	—	—	—
3308	Other accounts payable	227	221	153	149	505	472	148	504	...	68	415	359
	By creditor												
331	Domestic creditors	1,127	824	237	1,048	1,107	556	1,047	1,107	...	984	1,048	446
332	External creditors	2,145	4,234	1,467	2,145	4,234	1,467	2,145	4,234	...	2,144	4,236	1,467
	Table 4 Holding gains and losses in assets and liabilities												
	Table 5 Holding gains and losses in assets and liabilities												
	Table 6 Balance sheet												

Paraguay (288)

In Billions of Paraguayan Guaranies (PYG) / Fiscal Year Ends December 31st

	Budgetary Central Government			Central Government (excl. Social Security)			Central Government (incl. Social Security)			General Government		
	2013	2014	2015	2013	2014	2015	2013	2014	2015	2013	2014	2015
Table 7 Expenditure by functions of government												
Table 8 Financial transactions by counterpart sector												
Table 9 Total other economic flows in assets and liabilities												

Peru (293)

In Millions of Peruvian Nuevos Soles (PEN) / Fiscal Year Ends December 31st

		Budgetary Central Government			Central Government (excl. Social Security)			Central Government (incl. Social Security)			General Government		
		2013	2014	2015	2013	2014	2015	2013	2014	2015	2013	2014	2015
	Statement of operations												
1	Revenue	104,705	110,356	102,665	105,018	110,767	103,190	117,577	124,335	118,474	123,127	129,999	124,560
2	Expense	92,019	102,927	109,759	92,198	103,203	110,156	103,049	115,399	124,412	88,430	99,862	109,256
GOB	**Gross operating balance**	**12,686**	**7,429**	**-7,093**	**12,820**	**7,564**	**-6,966**	**14,528**	**8,936**	**-5,938**	**34,697**	**30,137**	**15,303**
NOB	**Net operating balance**	...	...	...	...	...	...	...	...	...	...	...	...
31	Net/Gross investment in nonfinancial assets	8,524	11,127	11,827	8,551	11,202	11,907	8,795	11,431	12,126	30,002	31,627	28,682
2M	Expenditure	100,543	114,054	121,585	100,749	114,405	122,063	111,844	126,830	136,538	118,432	131,489	137,938
NLB	**Net lending (+) / Net borrowing (-)**	**4,162**	**-3,698**	**-18,920**	**4,268**	**-3,638**	**-18,873**	**5,733**	**-2,496**	**-18,064**	**4,695**	**-1,490**	**-13,379**
32	Net acquisition of financial assets	-1,843	-9,070	-11,408	-1,736	-9,010	-11,361	-271	-7,867	-9,219	-1,310	-6,862	-5,867
33	Net incurrence of liabilities	-6,005	-5,372	7,512	-6,005	-5,372	7,512	-6,005	-5,372	7,512	-6,005	-5,372	7,512
NLBz	Statistical discrepancy	-0	-0	-0	0	-0	-0	-0	-0	1,333	0	-0	-0
	Memorandum items												
PB	Primary net lending / net borrowing	9,886	2,080	-13,066	9,992	2,141	-13,019	11,665	3,513	-11,913	10,653	4,559	-7,198
GB	Government balance per national definition	...	...	...	...	...	...	...	...	...	...	...	...
	Statement of other economic flows												
	Balance sheet												
6	**Net worth**	...	...	...	...	...	...	...	...	...	...	...	...
61	Nonfinancial assets	...	...	...	...	...	...	...	...	...	...	...	...
62	Financial assets	65,244	71,717	78,529	65,640	72,173	79,008	75,023	81,836	89,324	83,467	88,484	97,522
63	Liabilities	92,694	103,312	129,759	92,694	103,312	129,759	99,984	110,267	136,469	104,981	113,189	140,616
	Table 1 Revenue												
1	**Revenue**	**104,705**	**110,356**	**102,665**	**105,018**	**110,767**	**103,190**	**117,577**	**124,335**	**118,474**	**123,127**	**129,999**	**124,560**
11	**Taxes**	**89,323**	**95,310**	**90,177**	**89,323**	**95,310**	**90,177**	**89,323**	**95,310**	**90,177**	**91,617**	**97,646**	**92,788**
111	Taxes on income, profits, and capital gains	36,512	40,157	34,745	36,512	40,157	34,745	36,512	40,157	34,745	36,512	40,157	34,745
1111	Payable by individuals	10,570	11,423	11,137	10,570	11,423	11,137	10,570	11,423	11,137	10,570	11,423	11,137
1112	Payable by corporations and other enterprises	25,942	28,734	23,608	25,942	28,734	23,608	25,942	28,734	23,608	25,942	28,734	23,608
1113	Other taxes on income, profits, and capital gains	—	—	—	—	—	—	—	—	—	—	—	—
112	Taxes on payroll and workforce	—	—	—	—	—	—	—	—	—	—	—	—
113	Taxes on property	—	—	—	—	—	—	—	—	—	1,359	1,499	1,740
114	Taxes on goods and services	42,169	44,931	45,647	42,169	44,931	45,647	42,169	44,931	45,647	42,169	44,931	45,647
1141	General taxes on goods and services	36,690	39,796	40,152	36,690	39,796	40,152	36,690	39,796	40,152	36,690	39,796	40,152
1142	Excises	5,480	5,135	5,495	5,480	5,135	5,495	5,480	5,135	5,495	5,480	5,135	5,495
115	Taxes on international trade and transactions	1,706	1,790	1,775	1,706	1,790	1,775	1,706	1,790	1,775	1,706	1,790	1,775
116	Other taxes	8,935	8,433	8,010	8,935	8,433	8,010	8,935	8,433	8,010	9,870	9,269	8,881
12	**Social contributions**	—	—	—	—	—	—	**11,493**	**12,513**	**13,402**	**11,493**	**12,513**	**13,402**
121	Social security contributions	—	—	—	—	—	—	11,493	12,513	13,402	11,493	12,513	13,402
122	Other social contributions	—	—	—	—	—	—	—	—	—	—	—	—
13	**Grants**	**606**	**524**	**519**	**445**	**349**	**331**	**445**	**349**	**331**	**202**	**258**	**243**
131	From foreign governments	21	87	51	21	87	51	21	87	51	32	94	65
132	From international organizations	106	109	132	106	109	132	106	109	132	171	165	178
133	From other general government units	479	328	335	318	153	147	318	153	147	-0	—	—
1331	Current	161	175	188	-0	-0	—	—	—	—	-0	—	—
1332	Capital	318	153	147	318	153	147	318	153	147	-0	—	—
14	**Other revenue**	**14,776**	**14,522**	**11,969**	**15,250**	**15,108**	**12,682**	**16,316**	**16,162**	**14,564**	**19,814**	**19,582**	**18,126**
	Table 2 Expense by economic type												
2	**Expense**	**92,019**	**102,927**	**109,759**	**92,198**	**103,203**	**110,156**	**103,049**	**115,399**	**124,412**	**88,430**	**99,862**	**109,256**
21	**Compensation of employees**	**15,964**	**18,750**	**19,319**	**16,145**	**18,969**	**19,596**	**19,008**	**22,067**	**23,046**	**31,019**	**35,895**	**37,304**
211	Wages and salaries	14,944	17,580	18,081	...	...	...	...	...	...	...	...	...
212	Employers' social contributions	1,020	1,170	1,237	...	...	...	...	...	...	...	...	...
22	**Use of goods and services**	**17,355**	**19,680**	**24,241**	**17,474**	**19,847**	**24,484**	**20,907**	**24,081**	**28,941**	**31,424**	**35,065**	**40,642**
23	**Consumption of fixed capital**	...	...	...	...	...	...	...	...	...	...	...	...
24	**Interest**	**5,724**	**5,778**	**5,854**	**5,724**	**5,778**	**5,854**	**5,932**	**6,008**	**6,151**	**5,958**	**6,049**	**6,180**
25	**Subsidies**	—	—	—	—	—	—	—	—	—	—	—	—

Peru (293)

In Millions of Peruvian Nuevos Soles (PEN) / Fiscal Year Ends December 31st

		Budgetary Central Government			Central Government (excl. Social Security)			Central Government (incl. Social Security)			General Government		
		2013	2014	2015	2013	2014	2015	2013	2014	2015	2013	2014	2015
26	**Grants**	**42,100**	**45,512**	**44,229**	**41,932**	**45,331**	**44,035**	**40,293**	**43,563**	**44,035**	**—**	**—**	**—**
261	To foreign governments	—	—	—	—	—	—	—	—	—	—	—	—
262	To international organizations	—	—	—	—	—	—	—	—	—	—	—	—
263	To other general government units	42,100	45,512	44,229	41,932	45,331	44,035	40,293	43,563	44,035	—	—	—
2631	Current	30,681	33,024	31,870	30,514	32,843	31,677	28,874	31,075	31,677	—	—	—
2632	Capital	11,419	12,488	12,359	11,419	12,488	12,359	11,419	12,488	12,359	—	—	—
27	**Social benefits**	**3,718**	**4,355**	**4,083**	**3,721**	**4,358**	**4,086**	**9,122**	**10,162**	**9,485**	**10,935**	**12,226**	**11,345**
271	Social security benefits	—	—	—	—	—	—	5,402	5,804	5,399	5,402	5,804	5,399
272	Social assistance benefits	417	629	708	417	629	708	417	629	708	417	629	708
273	Employment-related social benefits	3,301	3,726	3,375	3,303	3,730	3,378	3,303	3,730	3,378	5,116	5,794	5,238
28	**Other expense**	**7,158**	**8,852**	**12,033**	**7,202**	**8,919**	**12,101**	**7,787**	**9,518**	**12,755**	**9,094**	**10,627**	**13,786**
281	Property expense other than interest	—	—	—	—	—	—	—	—	—	—	—	—
282	Transfers not elsewhere classified	7,158	8,852	12,033	7,202	8,919	12,101	7,787	9,518	12,755	9,094	10,627	13,786
2821	Current	4,767	6,325	7,710	4,812	6,392	7,778	5,397	6,991	8,432	6,393	7,903	9,305
2822	Capital	2,390	2,527	4,323	2,390	2,527	4,323	2,390	2,527	4,323	2,701	2,723	4,481
	Table 3 Transactions in assets and liabilities												
3	**Change in net worth from transactions**	...	...	...	...	...	...	...	...	...	...	...	...
31	**Net/Gross investment in nonfinancial assets**	**8,524**	**11,127**	**11,827**	**8,551**	**11,202**	**11,907**	**8,795**	**11,431**	**12,126**	**30,002**	**31,627**	**28,682**
311	Fixed assets	8,524	11,127	11,827	8,551	11,202	11,907	8,795	11,431	12,126	30,002	31,627	28,682
3111	Buildings and structures	...	...	...	...	...	...	...	...	...	...	...	...
3112	Machinery and equipment	...	...	...	...	...	...	...	...	...	...	...	...
3113	Other fixed assets	...	...	...	...	...	...	...	...	...	...	...	...
3114	Weapons systems	...	...	...	...	...	...	...	...	...	...	...	...
312	Inventories	—	—	—	—	—	—	—	—	—	—	—	—
313	Valuables	—	—	—	—	—	—	—	—	—	—	—	—
314	Nonproduced assets	—	—	—	—	—	—	—	—	—	—	—	—
3141	Land	—	—	—	—	—	—	—	—	—	—	—	—
3142	Mineral and energy resources	—	—	—	—	—	—	—	—	—	—	—	—
3143	Other naturally occurring assets	—	—	—	—	—	—	—	—	—	—	—	—
3144	Intangible nonproduced assets	—	—	—	—	—	—	—	—	—	—	—	—
32	**Net acquisition of financial assets**	**-1,843**	**-9,070**	**-11,408**	**-1,736**	**-9,010**	**-11,361**	**-271**	**-7,867**	**-9,219**	**-1,310**	**-6,862**	**-5,867**
	By instrument												
3201	Monetary gold and SDRs	—	—	—	—	—	—	—	—	—	—	—	—
3202	Currency and deposits	-1,830	-9,041	-11,408	-1,724	-8,980	-11,361	-164	-8,806	-9,223	-1,202	-7,800	-5,870
3203	Debt securities	-12	-29	—	-12	-29	—	-107	938	4	-107	938	4
3204	Loans	—	—	—	—	—	—	—	—	—	—	—	—
3205	Equity and investment fund shares	—	—	—	—	—	—	—	—	—	—	—	—
3206	Insurance, pension, and standardized guarantee schemes	—	—	—	—	—	—	—	—	—	—	—	—
3207	Financial derivatives and employee stock options	—	—	—	—	—	—	—	—	—	—	—	—
3208	Other accounts receivable	...	...	...	...	...	...	...	...	...	...	...	...
	By debtor												
321	Domestic debtors	-1,830	-9,041	-11,408	-1,724	-8,980	-11,361	-164	-8,806	-9,223	-1,202	-7,800	-5,870
322	External debtors	-12	-29	—	-12	-29	—	-107	938	4	-107	938	4
33	**Net incurrence of liabilities**	**-6,005**	**-5,372**	**7,512**	**-6,005**	**-5,372**	**7,512**	**-6,005**	**-5,372**	**7,512**	**-6,005**	**-5,372**	**7,512**
	By instrument												
3301	Special Drawing Rights (SDRs)	—	—	—	—	—	—	—	—	—	—	—	—
3302	Currency and deposits	—	—	—	—	—	—	—	—	—	—	—	—
3303	Debt securities	-797	-4,924	5,299	-797	-4,924	5,299	-797	-4,924	5,299	-797	-4,924	5,299
3304	Loans	-5,207	-448	2,213	-5,207	-448	2,213	-5,207	-448	2,213	-5,207	-448	2,213
3305	Equity and investment fund shares	—	—	—	—	—	—	—	—	—	—	—	—
3306	Insurance, pension, and standardized guarantee schemes	—	—	—	—	—	—	—	—	—	—	—	—
3307	Financial derivatives and employee stock options	—	—	—	—	—	—	—	—	—	—	—	—
3308	Other accounts payable	...	...	...	...	...	...	...	...	...	...	...	...

Peru (293)

In Millions of Peruvian Nuevos Soles (PEN) / Fiscal Year Ends December 31st

		Budgetary Central Government			Central Government (excl. Social Security)			Central Government (incl. Social Security)			General Government		
		2013	2014	2015	2013	2014	2015	2013	2014	2015	2013	2014	2015
	By creditor												
331	Domestic creditors	-797	-3,867	-2,731	-797	-3,867	-2,731	-797	-3,867	-2,731	-797	-3,867	-2,731
332	External creditors	-5,207	-1,505	10,243	-5,207	-1,505	10,243	-5,207	-1,505	10,243	-5,207	-1,505	10,243
	Table 4 Holding gains and losses in assets and liabilities												
	Table 5 Holding gains and losses in assets and liabilities												
	Table 6 Balance sheet												
6	**Net worth**	...	...	...	...	...	...	...	...	...	...	...	...
61	**Nonfinancial assets**	...	...	...	...	...	...	...	...	...	...	...	...
611	Fixed assets	...	...	...	...	...	...	...	...	...	...	...	...
6111	Buildings and structures	...	...	...	...	...	...	...	...	...	...	...	...
6112	Machinery and equipment	...	...	...	...	...	...	...	...	...	...	...	...
6113	Other fixed assets	...	...	...	...	...	...	...	...	...	...	...	...
6114	Weapons systems	...	...	...	...	...	...	...	...	...	...	...	...
612	Inventories	...	...	...	...	...	...	...	...	...	...	...	...
613	Valuables	...	...	...	...	...	...	...	...	...	...	...	...
614	Nonproduced assets	...	...	...	...	...	...	...	...	...	...	...	...
6141	Land	...	...	...	...	...	...	...	...	...	...	...	...
6142	Mineral and energy resources	...	...	...	...	...	...	...	...	...	...	...	...
6143	Other naturally occurring assets	...	...	...	...	...	...	...	...	...	...	...	...
6144	Intangible nonproduced assets	...	...	...	...	...	...	...	...	...	...	...	...
62	**Financial assets**	**65,244**	**71,717**	**78,529**	**65,640**	**72,173**	**79,008**	**75,023**	**81,836**	**89,324**	**83,467**	**88,484**	**97,522**
	By instrument												
6201	Monetary gold and SDRs	—	—	—	—	—	—	—	—	—	—	—	—
6202	Currency and deposits	65,244	71,717	78,529	65,640	72,173	79,008	75,023	81,836	89,324	83,467	88,484	97,522
6203	Debt securities	—	—	—	—	—	—	—	—	—	—	—	—
6204	Loans	—	—	—	—	—	—	—	—	—	—	—	—
6205	Equity and investment fund shares	—	—	—	—	—	—	—	—	—	—	—	—
6206	Insurance, pension, and standardized guarantee schemes	—	—	—	—	—	—	—	—	—	—	—	—
6207	Financial derivatives and employee stock options	—	—	—	—	—	—	—	—	—	—	—	—
6208	Other accounts receivable	...	...	...	...	...	...	...	...	...	...	...	...
	By debtor												
621	Domestic debtors	65,244	71,717	78,529	65,640	72,173	79,008	73,355	79,059	86,135	81,800	85,707	94,332
622	External debtors	—	—	—	—	—	—	1,667	2,777	3,189	1,667	2,777	3,189
63	**Liabilities**	**92,694**	**103,312**	**129,759**	**92,694**	**103,312**	**129,759**	**99,984**	**110,267**	**136,469**	**104,981**	**113,189**	**140,616**
	By instrument												
6301	Special Drawing Rights (SDRs)	—	—	—	—	—	—	—	—	—	—	—	—
6302	Currency and deposits	—	—	—	—	—	—	—	—	—	—	—	—
6303	Debt securities	64,655	73,356	90,921	64,655	73,356	90,921	71,945	80,310	97,631	71,945	80,310	97,631
6304	Loans	23,594	25,667	33,878	23,594	25,667	33,878	23,594	25,667	33,878	23,986	26,059	34,184
6305	Equity and investment fund shares	—	—	—	—	—	—	—	—	—	—	—	—
6306	Insurance, pension, and standardized guarantee schemes	—	—	—	—	—	—	—	—	—	—	—	—
6307	Financial derivatives and employee stock options	—	—	—	—	—	—	—	—	—	—	—	—
6308	Other accounts payable	4,445	4,289	4,960	...	...	4,960	...	...	4,960	...	...	8,802
	By creditor												
631	Domestic creditors	44,611	52,939	61,753	44,611	52,939	61,753	51,900	59,894	68,463	56,897	62,817	72,610
632	External creditors	48,084	50,373	68,006	48,084	50,373	68,006	48,084	50,373	68,006	48,084	50,373	68,006
	Memorandum items												
6M2	Net financial worth	-27,450	-31,595	-51,230	-27,055	-31,139	-50,751	-24,961	-28,431	-47,145	-21,514	-24,705	-43,095
6M3	Gross debt (D4) at market value	...	...	...	...	...	...	...	...	...	...	...	...
6M3D3	D3 debt liabilities at market value	...	...	...	...	...	...	...	...	...	...	...	...
6M3D2	D2 debt liabilities at market value	...	...	...	...	...	...	...	...	...	...	...	...
6M3D1	D1 debt liabilities at market value	...	...	...	...	...	...	...	...	...	...	...	...
6M4	Gross debt (D4) at nominal value	...	...	...	...	...	...	...	...	...	...	...	...
6M4D3	D3 debt liabilities at nominal value	...	...	...	...	...	...	...	...	...	...	...	...
6M4D2	D2 debt liabilities at nominal value	...	...	...	...	...	...	...	...	...	...	...	...
6M4D1	D1 debt liabilities at nominal value	...	...	...	...	...	...	...	...	...	...	...	...

Peru (293)

In Millions of Peruvian Nuevos Soles (PEN) / Fiscal Year Ends December 31st

		Budgetary Central Government			Central Government (excl. Social Security)			Central Government (incl. Social Security)			General Government		
		2013	2014	2015	2013	2014	2015	2013	2014	2015	2013	2014	2015
6M35	Gross debt (D4) at face value	92,694	103,312	129,759	...	...	129,759	...	...	136,469	...	...	140,616
6M35D3	D3 debt liabilities at face value	92,694	103,312	129,759	...	...	129,759	...	...	136,469	...	...	140,616
6M35D2	D2 debt liabilities at face value	88,249	99,023	124,800	88,249	99,023	124,800	95,539	105,978	131,509	95,931	106,370	131,815
6M35D1	D1 debt liabilities at face value	88,249	99,023	124,800	88,249	99,023	124,800	95,539	105,978	131,509	95,931	106,370	131,815
6M93	Government gross debt per national definition	...	...	...	...	...	...	...	...	...	...	...	...
6M5	Arrears	...	...	...	...	...	...	...	...	...	...	...	...
6M6	Explicit contingent liabilities	...	...	...	...	...	...	...	...	...	...	...	...
6M61	of which: Publicly guaranteed debt	...	...	...	...	...	...	...	...	...	...	...	...
6M7	Net implicit obligations for social security benefits	...	...	...	...	...	...	...	...	...	...	...	...
	Table 7 Expenditure by functions of government												
7	**Expenditure**	**100,543**	**114,054**	**121,585**	**97,470**	**110,869**	**122,063**	**111,844**	**126,830**	**136,538**	**118,432**	**131,489**	**137,938**
701	**General public services**	**...**	**...**	**...**	**...**	**...**	**...**	**...**	**...**	**...**	**...**	**...**	**...**
7017	Public debt transactions	5,724	5,778	5,854	5,724	5,778	5,854	5,932	6,008	6,151	5,958	6,049	6,180
7018	Transfers of general character between levels of government	...	...	...	...	...	...	...	...	...	...	...	...
702	**Defense**	**...**	**...**	**...**	**...**	**...**	**...**	**...**	**...**	**...**	**...**	**...**	**...**
703	**Public order and safety**	**...**	**...**	**...**	**...**	**...**	**...**	**...**	**...**	**...**	**...**	**...**	**...**
704	**Economic affairs**	**...**	**...**	**...**	**...**	**...**	**...**	**...**	**...**	**...**	**...**	**...**	**...**
7042	Agriculture, forestry, fishing, and hunting	...	...	...	...	...	...	...	...	...	...	...	...
7043	Fuel and energy	...	...	...	...	...	...	...	...	...	...	...	...
7044	Mining, manufacturing, and construction	...	...	...	...	...	...	...	...	...	...	...	...
7045	Transport	...	...	...	...	...	...	...	...	...	...	...	...
7046	Communication	...	...	...	...	...	...	...	...	...	...	...	...
705	**Environmental protection**	**...**	**...**	**...**	**...**	**...**	**...**	**...**	**...**	**...**	**...**	**...**	**...**
706	**Housing and community amenities**	**...**	**...**	**...**	**...**	**...**	**...**	**...**	**...**	**...**	**...**	**...**	**...**
707	**Health**	**...**	**...**	**...**	**...**	**...**	**...**	**...**	**...**	**...**	**...**	**...**	**...**
7072	Outpatient services	...	...	...	...	...	...	...	...	...	...	...	...
7073	Hospital services	...	...	...	...	...	...	...	...	...	...	...	...
7074	Public health services	...	...	...	...	...	...	...	...	...	...	...	...
708	**Recreation, culture and religion**	**...**	**...**	**...**	**...**	**...**	**...**	**...**	**...**	**...**	**...**	**...**	**...**
709	**Education**	**...**	**...**	**...**	**...**	**...**	**...**	**...**	**...**	**...**	**...**	**...**	**...**
7091	Pre-primary and primary education	...	...	...	...	...	...	...	...	...	...	...	...
7092	Secondary education	...	...	...	...	...	...	...	...	...	...	...	...
7094	Tertiary education	...	...	...	...	...	...	...	...	...	...	...	...
710	**Social protection**	**...**	**...**	**...**	**...**	**...**	**...**	**...**	**...**	**...**	**...**	**...**	**...**
7z	Statistical discrepancy: Expenditure	...	...	...	...	...	...	...	...	...	...	...	...
	Table 8 Financial transactions by counterpart sector												
32	**Net acquisition of financial assets**	**-1,843**	**-9,070**	**-11,408**	**-1,736**	**-9,010**	**-11,361**	**-271**	**-7,867**	**-9,219**	**-1,310**	**-6,862**	**-5,867**
321	Domestic debtors	-1,830	-9,041	-11,408	-1,724	-8,980	-11,361	-164	-8,806	-9,223	-1,202	-7,800	-5,870
8211	General government	—	—	...	—	—	...	—	—	...	—	—	...
8212	Central bank	—	—	...	—	—	...	—	—	...	—	—	...
8213	Deposit-taking corporations except the central bank	-1,830	-9,041	...	-1,724	-8,980	...	-164	-8,806	...	-1,202	-7,800	...
8214	Other financial corporations	—	—	...	—	—	...	—	—	...	—	—	...
8215	Nonfinancial corporations	—	—	...	—	—	...	—	—	...	—	—	...
8216	Households & nonprofit institutions serving households	—	—	...	—	—	...	—	—	...	—	—	...
322	External debtors	-12	-29	—	-12	-29	—	-107	938	4	-107	938	4
8221	General government	—	—	—	—	—	—	—	—	...	—	—	...
8227	International organizations	—	—	—	—	—	—	—	—	...	—	—	...
8228	Financial corporations other than international organizations	-12	-29	—	-12	-29	—	-107	938	...	-107	938	...
8229	Other nonresidents	—	—	—	—	—	—	—	—	...	—	—	...

Peru (293)

In Millions of Peruvian Nuevos Soles (PEN) / Fiscal Year Ends December 31st

		Budgetary Central Government			Central Government (excl. Social Security)			Central Government (incl. Social Security)			General Government		
		2013	2014	2015	2013	2014	2015	2013	2014	2015	2013	2014	2015
33	**Net incurrence of liabilities**	**-6,005**	**-5,372**	**7,512**	**-6,005**	**-5,372**	**7,512**	**-6,005**	**-5,372**	**7,512**	**-6,005**	**-5,372**	**7,512**
331	Domestic creditors	-797	-3,867	-2,731	-797	-3,867	-2,731	-797	-3,867	-2,731	-797	-3,867	-2,731
8311	General government	—	—	...	—	—	...	—	—	...	—	—	...
8312	Central bank	—	—	...	—	—	...	—	—	...	—	—	...
8313	Deposit-taking corporations except the central bank	—	—	...	—	—	...	—	—	...	—	—	...
8314	Other financial corporations	-797	-3,867	...	-797	-3,867	...	-797	-3,867	...	-797	-3,867	...
8315	Nonfinancial corporations	—	—	...	—	—	...	—	—	...	—	—	...
8316	Households & nonprofit institutions serving households	—	—	...	—	—	...	—	—	...	—	—	...
332	External creditors	-5,207	-1,505	10,243	-5,207	-1,505	10,243	-5,207	-1,505	10,243	-5,207	-1,505	10,243
8321	General government	—	—	...	—	—	...	—	—	...	—	—	...
8327	International organizations	-5,207	-448	...	-5,207	-448	...	-5,207	-448	...	-5,207	-448	...
8328	Financial corporations other than international organizations	—	-1,057	...	—	-1,057	...	—	-1,057	...	—	-1,057	...
8329	Other nonresidents	—	—	...	—	—	...	—	—	...	—	—	...
	Table 9 Total other economic flows in assets and liabilities												

Philippines (566)

In Billions of Philippine Pesos (PHP) / Fiscal Year Ends December 31st

		Budgetary Central Government			Central Government (excl. Social Security)			Central Government (incl. Social Security)			General Government		
		2013	2014	2015P	2013	2014	2015	2013	2014	2015	2013	2014	2015
	Statement of operations												
1	Revenue	1,713	1,907	2,047	...	...	...	...	...	...	...	...	...
2	Expense	1,592	1,693	1,879	...	...	...	...	...	...	...	...	...
GOB	**Gross operating balance**	**122**	**213**	**168**	...	...	...	...	...	...	...	...	...
NOB	**Net operating balance**	...	...	...	...	...	...	...	...	...	...	...	...
31	Net/Gross investment in nonfinancial assets	262	276	345	...	...	...	...	...	...	...	...	...
2M	Expenditure	1,853	1,969	2,225	...	...	...	...	...	...	...	...	...
NLB	**Net lending (+) / Net borrowing (-)**	**-140**	**-63**	**-178**	...	...	...	...	...	...	...	...	...
32	Net acquisition of financial assets	91	51	-54	...	...	...	...	...	...	...	...	...
33	Net incurrence of liabilities	231	114	124	...	...	...	...	...	...	...	...	...
NLBz	Statistical discrepancy	-0	0	—	...	...	...	...	...	...	...	...	...
	Memorandum items												
PB	Primary net lending / net borrowing	185	261	136	...	...	...	...	...	...	...	...	...
GB	Government balance per national definition	...	...	...	...	...	...	...	...	...	...	...	...
	Statement of other economic flows												
	Balance sheet												
6	**Net worth**	...	...	...	...	...	...	...	...	...	...	...	...
61	Nonfinancial assets	...	...	...	...	...	...	...	...	...	...	...	...
62	Financial assets	...	...	...	...	...	...	...	...	...	...	...	...
63	Liabilities	5,681	5,735	...	...	...	...	...	...	...	...	...	...
	Table 1 Revenue												
1	**Revenue**	**1,713**	**1,907**	**2,047**	...	...	...	...	...	...	...	...	...
11	**Taxes**	**1,536**	**1,719**	**1,815**	...	...	...	...	...	...	...	...	...
111	Taxes on income, profits, and capital gains	718	785	846	...	...	...	...	...	...	...	...	...
1111	Payable by individuals	247	284	309	...	...	...	...	...	...	...	...	...
1112	Payable by corporations and other enterprises	424	455	490	...	...	...	...	...	...	...	...	...
1113	Other taxes on income, profits, and capital gains	47	46	47	...	...	...	...	...	...	...	...	...
112	Taxes on payroll and workforce	—	—	—	...	...	...	...	...	...	...	...	...
113	Taxes on property	3	5	—	...	...	...	...	...	...	...	...	...
114	Taxes on goods and services	441	482	527	...	...	...	...	...	...	...	...	...
1141	General taxes on goods and services	250	279	296	...	...	...	...	...	...	...	...	...
1142	Excises	119	135	158	...	...	...	...	...	...	...	...	...
115	Taxes on international trade and transactions	305	369	368	...	...	...	...	...	...	...	...	...
116	Other taxes	68	77	83	...	...	...	...	...	...	...	...	...
12	**Social contributions**	—	—	—	...	...	...	...	...	...	...	...	...
121	Social security contributions	—	—	—	...	...	...	...	...	...	...	...	...
122	Other social contributions	—	—	—	...	...	...	...	...	...	...	...	...
13	**Grants**	**0**	**0**	**0**	...	...	...	...	...	...	...	...	...
131	From foreign governments	0	0	0	...	...	...	...	...	...	...	...	...
132	From international organizations	0	0	—	...	...	...	...	...	...	...	...	...
133	From other general government units	—	—	—	...	...	...	...	...	...	...	...	...
1331	Current	—	—	—	...	...	...	...	...	...	...	...	...
1332	Capital	—	—	—	...	...	...	...	...	...	...	...	...
14	**Other revenue**	**177**	**188**	**231**	...	...	...	...	...	...	...	...	...
	Table 2 Expense by economic type												
2	**Expense**	**1,592**	**1,693**	**1,879**	...	...	...	...	...	...	...	...	...
21	**Compensation of employees**	**582**	**604**	**664**	...	...	...	...	...	...	...	...	...
211	Wages and salaries	...	...	...	...	...	...	...	...	...	...	...	...
212	Employers' social contributions	...	...	...	...	...	...	...	...	...	...	...	...
22	**Use of goods and services**	**283**	**309**	**403**	...	...	...	...	...	...	...	...	...
23	**Consumption of fixed capital**	...	...	...	...	...	...	...	...	...	...	...	...
24	**Interest**	**325**	**324**	**314**	...	...	...	...	...	...	...	...	...
25	**Subsidies**	**66**	**80**	**78**	...	...	...	...	...	...	...	...	...

Philippines (566)

In Billions of Philippine Pesos (PHP) / Fiscal Year Ends December 31st

		Budgetary Central Government			Central Government (excl. Social Security)			Central Government (incl. Social Security)			General Government		
		2013	2014	2015P	2013	2014	2015	2013	2014	2015	2013	2014	2015
26	**Grants**	**317**	**344**	**388**	...	...	...	...	...	...	...	...	...
261	To foreign governments	—	—	—	...	...	...	...	...	...	...	...	...
262	To international organizations	—	—	—	...	...	...	...	...	...	...	...	...
263	To other general government units	317	344	388	...	...	...	...	...	...	...	...	...
2631	Current	317	344	388	...	...	...	...	...	...	...	...	...
2632	Capital	—	—	—	...	...	...	...	...	...	...	...	...
27	**Social benefits**	**—**	**—**	**—**	...	...	...	...	...	...	...	...	...
271	Social security benefits	—	—	—	...	...	...	...	...	...	...	...	...
272	Social assistance benefits	—	—	—	...	...	...	...	...	...	...	...	...
273	Employment-related social benefits	—	—	—	...	...	...	...	...	...	...	...	...
28	**Other expense**	**19**	**32**	**32**	...	...	...	...	...	...	...	...	...
281	Property expense other than interest	—	—	—	...	...	...	...	...	...	...	...	...
282	Transfers not elsewhere classified	19	32	32	...	...	...	...	...	...	...	...	...
2821	Current	19	32	32	...	...	...	...	...	...	...	...	...
2822	Capital	—	—	—	...	...	...	...	...	...	...	...	...
	Table 3 Transactions in assets and liabilities												
3	**Change in net worth from transactions**	...	...	...	...	...	...	...	...	...	...	...	...
31	**Net/Gross investment in nonfinancial assets**	**262**	**276**	**345**	...	...	...	...	...	...	...	...	...
311	Fixed assets	...	...	...	...	...	...	...	...	...	...	...	...
3111	Buildings and structures	...	...	...	...	...	...	...	...	...	...	...	...
3112	Machinery and equipment	...	...	...	...	...	...	...	...	...	...	...	...
3113	Other fixed assets	...	...	...	...	...	...	...	...	...	...	...	...
3114	Weapons systems	...	...	...	...	...	...	...	...	...	...	...	...
312	Inventories	...	...	...	...	...	...	...	...	...	...	...	...
313	Valuables	...	...	...	...	...	...	...	...	...	...	...	...
314	Nonproduced assets	...	...	...	...	...	...	...	...	...	...	...	...
3141	Land	...	...	...	...	...	...	...	...	...	...	...	...
3142	Mineral and energy resources	...	...	...	...	...	...	...	...	...	...	...	...
3143	Other naturally occurring assets	...	...	...	...	...	...	...	...	...	...	...	...
3144	Intangible nonproduced assets	...	...	...	...	...	...	...	...	...	...	...	...
32	**Net acquisition of financial assets**	**91**	**51**	**-54**	...	...	...	...	...	...	...	...	...
	By instrument												
3201	Monetary gold and SDRs	—	—	—	...	...	...	...	...	...	...	...	...
3202	Currency and deposits	66	38	-2	...	...	...	...	...	...	...	...	...
3203	Debt securities	—	—	—	...	...	...	...	...	...	...	...	...
3204	Loans	17	13	10	...	...	...	...	...	...	...	...	...
3205	Equity and investment fund shares	9	-0	-62	...	...	...	...	...	...	...	...	...
3206	Insurance, pension, and standardized guarantee schemes	—	—	—	...	...	...	...	...	...	...	...	...
3207	Financial derivatives and employee stock options	—	—	—	...	...	...	...	...	...	...	...	...
3208	Other accounts receivable	...	...	...	...	...	...	...	...	...	...	...	...
	By debtor												
321	Domestic debtors	91	51	-54	...	...	...	...	...	...	...	...	...
322	External debtors	—	—	—	...	...	...	...	...	...	...	...	...
33	**Net incurrence of liabilities**	**231**	**114**	**124**	...	...	...	...	...	...	...	...	...
	By instrument												
3301	Special Drawing Rights (SDRs)	—	—	—	...	...	...	...	...	...	...	...	...
3302	Currency and deposits	—	—	—	...	...	...	...	...	...	...	...	...
3303	Debt securities	403	146	153	...	...	...	...	...	...	...	...	...
3304	Loans	-172	-33	-29	...	...	...	...	...	...	...	...	...
3305	Equity and investment fund shares	—	—	—	...	...	...	...	...	...	...	...	...
3306	Insurance, pension, and standardized guarantee schemes	—	—	—	...	...	...	...	...	...	...	...	...
3307	Financial derivatives and employee stock options	—	—	—	...	...	...	...	...	...	...	...	...
3308	Other accounts payable	...	...	...	...	...	...	...	...	...	...	...	...

Philippines (566)

In Billions of Philippine Pesos (PHP) / Fiscal Year Ends December 31st

		Budgetary Central Government			Central Government (excl. Social Security)			Central Government (incl. Social Security)			General Government		
		2013	2014	2015P	2013	2014	2015	2013	2014	2015	2013	2014	2015
	By creditor												
331	Domestic creditors	313	99	58	...	...	...	...	...	...	...	...	...
332	External creditors	-82	15	66	...	...	...	...	...	...	...	...	...
	Table 4 Holding gains and losses in assets and liabilities												
	Table 5 Holding gains and losses in assets and liabilities												
	Table 6 Balance sheet												
6	**Net worth**	...	...	...	...	...	...	...	...	...	...	...	...
61	**Nonfinancial assets**	...	...	...	...	...	...	...	...	...	...	...	...
611	Fixed assets	...	...	...	...	...	...	...	...	...	...	...	...
6111	Buildings and structures	...	...	...	...	...	...	...	...	...	...	...	...
6112	Machinery and equipment	...	...	...	...	...	...	...	...	...	...	...	...
6113	Other fixed assets	...	...	...	...	...	...	...	...	...	...	...	...
6114	Weapons systems	...	...	...	...	...	...	...	...	...	...	...	...
612	Inventories	...	...	...	...	...	...	...	...	...	...	...	...
613	Valuables	...	...	...	...	...	...	...	...	...	...	...	...
614	Nonproduced assets	...	...	...	...	...	...	...	...	...	...	...	...
6141	Land	...	...	...	...	...	...	...	...	...	...	...	...
6142	Mineral and energy resources	...	...	...	...	...	...	...	...	...	...	...	...
6143	Other naturally occurring assets	...	...	...	...	...	...	...	...	...	...	...	...
6144	Intangible nonproduced assets	...	...	...	...	...	...	...	...	...	...	...	...
62	**Financial assets**	...	...	...	...	...	...	...	...	...	...	...	...
	By instrument												
6201	Monetary gold and SDRs	...	...	...	...	...	...	...	...	...	...	...	...
6202	Currency and deposits	...	...	...	...	...	...	...	...	...	...	...	...
6203	Debt securities	...	...	...	...	...	...	...	...	...	...	...	...
6204	Loans	...	...	...	...	...	...	...	...	...	...	...	...
6205	Equity and investment fund shares	...	...	...	...	...	...	...	...	...	...	...	...
6206	Insurance, pension, and standardized guarantee schemes	...	...	...	...	...	...	...	...	...	...	...	...
6207	Financial derivatives and employee stock options	...	...	...	...	...	...	...	...	...	...	...	...
6208	Other accounts receivable	...	...	...	...	...	...	...	...	...	...	...	...
	By debtor												
621	Domestic debtors	...	...	...	...	...	...	...	...	...	...	...	...
622	External debtors	...	...	...	...	...	...	...	...	...	...	...	...
63	**Liabilities**	**5,681**	**5,735**	...	...	...	...	...	...	...	...	...	...
	By instrument												
6301	Special Drawing Rights (SDRs)	—	—	...	...	...	...	...	...	...	...	...	...
6302	Currency and deposits	—	—	...	...	...	...	...	...	...	...	...	...
6303	Debt securities	4,981	5,051	...	...	...	...	...	...	...	...	...	...
6304	Loans	700	684	...	...	...	...	...	...	...	...	...	...
6305	Equity and investment fund shares	—	—	...	...	...	...	...	...	...	...	...	...
6306	Insurance, pension, and standardized guarantee schemes	—	—	...	...	...	...	...	...	...	...	...	...
6307	Financial derivatives and employee stock options	—	—	...	...	...	...	...	...	...	...	...	...
6308	Other accounts payable	...	...	...	...	...	...	...	...	...	...	...	...
	By creditor												
631	Domestic creditors	3,733	3,821	...	...	...	...	...	...	...	...	...	...
632	External creditors	1,948	1,915	...	...	...	...	...	...	...	...	...	...
	Memorandum items												
6M2	Net financial worth	...	...	...	...	...	...	...	...	...	...	...	...
6M3	Gross debt (D4) at market value	...	...	...	...	...	...	...	...	...	...	...	...
6M3D3	D3 debt liabilities at market value	...	...	...	...	...	...	...	...	...	...	...	...
6M3D2	D2 debt liabilities at market value	...	...	...	...	...	...	...	...	...	...	...	...
6M3D1	D1 debt liabilities at market value	...	...	...	...	...	...	...	...	...	...	...	...
6M4	Gross debt (D4) at nominal value	...	...	...	...	...	...	...	...	...	...	...	...
6M4D3	D3 debt liabilities at nominal value	...	...	...	...	...	...	...	...	...	...	...	...
6M4D2	D2 debt liabilities at nominal value	...	...	...	...	...	...	...	...	...	...	...	...
6M4D1	D1 debt liabilities at nominal value	...	...	...	...	...	...	...	...	...	...	...	...

Philippines (566)

In Billions of Philippine Pesos (PHP) / Fiscal Year Ends December 31st

		Budgetary Central Government			Central Government (excl. Social Security)			Central Government (incl. Social Security)			General Government		
		2013	2014	2015P	2013	2014	2015	2013	2014	2015	2013	2014	2015
6M35	Gross debt (D4) at face value	...	...	...	...	...	...	...	...	...	...	...	...
6M35D3	D3 debt liabilities at face value	...	...	...	...	...	...	...	...	...	...	...	...
6M35D2	D2 debt liabilities at face value	5,681	5,735	...	...	...	...	...	...	...	...	...	...
6M35D1	D1 debt liabilities at face value	5,681	5,735	...	...	...	...	...	...	...	...	...	...
6M93	Government gross debt per national definition	...	...	...	...	...	...	...	...	...	...	...	...
6M5	Arrears	...	...	...	...	...	...	...	...	...	...	...	...
6M6	Explicit contingent liabilities	...	...	...	...	...	...	...	...	...	...	...	...
6M61	of which: Publicly guaranteed debt	...	...	...	...	...	...	...	...	...	...	...	...
6M7	Net implicit obligations for social security benefits	...	...	...	...	...	...	...	...	...	...	...	...
	Table 7 Expenditure by functions of government												
7	**Expenditure**	**1,853**	**1,969**	**2,224**	...	...	...	...	...	...	...	...	...
701	**General public services**	**641**	**542**	**1,007**	...	...	...	...	...	...	...	...	...
7017	Public debt transactions	325	324	314	...	...	...	...	...	...	...	...	...
7018	Transfers of general character between levels of government	...	...	407	...	...	...	...	...	...	...	...	...
702	**Defense**	**90**	**90**	**79**	...	...	...	...	...	...	...	...	...
703	**Public order and safety**	**124**	**134**	**174**	...	...	...	...	...	...	...	...	...
704	**Economic affairs**	**378**	**448**	**445**	...	...	...	...	...	...	...	...	...
7042	Agriculture, forestry, fishing, and hunting	111	112	119	...	...	...	...	...	...	...	...	...
7043	Fuel and energy	11	14	8	...	...	...	...	...	...	...	...	...
7044	Mining, manufacturing, and construction	1	1	1	...	...	...	...	...	...	...	...	...
7045	Transport	204	261	292	...	...	...	...	...	...	...	...	...
7046	Communication	—	—	1	...	...	...	...	...	...	...	...	...
705	**Environmental protection**	**26**	**25**	**5**	...	...	...	...	...	...	...	...	...
706	**Housing and community amenities**	**23**	**18**	**12**	...	...	...	...	...	...	...	...	...
707	**Health**	**58**	**91**	**109**	...	...	...	...	...	...	...	...	...
7072	Outpatient services	...	...	0	...	...	...	...	...	...	...	...	...
7073	Hospital services	...	...	32	...	...	...	...	...	...	...	...	...
7074	Public health services	...	...	38	...	...	...	...	...	...	...	...	...
708	**Recreation, culture and religion**	**15**	**23**	**6**	...	...	...	...	...	...	...	...	...
709	**Education**	**329**	**382**	**387**	...	...	...	...	...	...	...	...	...
7091	Pre-primary and primary education	...	...	161	...	...	...	...	...	...	...	...	...
7092	Secondary education	...	...	84	...	...	...	...	...	...	...	...	...
7094	Tertiary education	...	...	34	...	...	...	...	...	...	...	...	...
710	**Social protection**	**170**	**218**	**184**	...	...	...	...	...	...	...	...	...
7z	Statistical discrepancy: Expenditure	192	...	—	...	...	...	...	...	...	...	...	...
	Table 8 Financial transactions by counterpart sector												
32	**Net acquisition of financial assets**	**91**	**51**	**-54**	...	...	...	...	...	...	...	...	...
321	Domestic debtors	91	51	-54	...	...	...	...	...	...	...	...	...
8211	General government	0	0	—	...	...	...	...	...	...	...	...	...
8212	Central bank	—	—	—	...	...	...	...	...	...	...	...	...
8213	Deposit-taking corporations except the central bank	66	38	-2	...	...	...	...	...	...	...	...	...
8214	Other financial corporations	—	—	—	...	...	...	...	...	...	...	...	...
8215	Nonfinancial corporations	25	13	-52	...	...	...	...	...	...	...	...	...
8216	Households & nonprofit institutions serving households	—	—	—	...	...	...	...	...	...	...	...	...
322	External debtors	—	—	—	...	...	...	...	...	...	...	...	...
8221	General government	—	—	—	...	...	...	...	...	...	...	...	...
8227	International organizations	—	—	—	...	...	...	...	...	...	...	...	...
8228	Financial corporations other than international organizations	—	—	—	...	...	...	...	...	...	...	...	...
8229	Other nonresidents	—	—	—	...	...	...	...	...	...	...	...	...

Philippines (566)

In Billions of Philippine Pesos (PHP) / Fiscal Year Ends December 31st

		Budgetary Central Government			Central Government (excl. Social Security)			Central Government (incl. Social Security)			General Government		
		2013	2014	2015P	2013	2014	2015	2013	2014	2015	2013	2014	2015
33	**Net incurrence of liabilities**	**231**	**114**	**124**	...	...	...	...	...	...	...	...	...
331	Domestic creditors	313	99	58	...	...	...	...	...	...	...	...	...
8311	General government	-48	-25	25	...	...	...	...	...	...	...	...	...
8312	Central bank	—	—	—	...	...	...	...	...	...	...	...	...
8313	Deposit-taking corporations except the central bank	—	—	—	...	...	...	...	...	...	...	...	...
8314	Other financial corporations	361	124	33	...	...	...	...	...	...	...	...	...
8315	Nonfinancial corporations	—	—	—	...	...	...	...	...	...	...	...	...
8316	Households & nonprofit institutions serving households	—	—	—	...	...	...	...	...	...	...	...	...
332	External creditors	-82	15	66	...	...	...	...	...	...	...	...	...
8321	General government	2	2	1	...	...	...	...	...	...	...	...	...
8327	International organizations	-84	-16	30	...	...	...	...	...	...	...	...	...
8328	Financial corporations other than international organizations	—	29	35	...	...	...	...	...	...	...	...	...
8329	Other nonresidents	—	—	—	...	...	...	...	...	...	...	...	...
	Table 9 Total other economic flows in assets and liabilities												

Poland (964)

In Millions of Polish Zlotys (PLN) / Fiscal Year Ends December 31st

		Budgetary Central Government			Central Government (excl. Social Security)			Central Government (incl. Social Security)			General Government		
		2013	2014	2015	2013P	2014P	2015P	2013P	2014P	2015P	2013P	2014P	2015P
	Statement of operations												
1	Revenue	...	...	...	337,235	351,589	372,543	531,102	551,946	586,207	635,909	665,167	700,326
2	Expense	...	...	...	388,334	380,925	395,401	586,646	598,254	615,583	677,458	692,352	710,360
GOB	**Gross operating balance**	...	...	...	**-29,345**	**-5,762**	**592**	**-33,460**	**-22,390**	**-5,553**	**-4,572**	**12,204**	**29,724**
NOB	**Net operating balance**	...	...	...	**-51,099**	**-29,337**	**-22,858**	**-55,544**	**-46,308**	**-29,376**	**-41,549**	**-27,185**	**-10,033**
31	Net/Gross investment in nonfinancial assets	...	...	...	8,476	9,466	16,577	8,660	9,432	16,650	25,581	31,796	35,942
2M	Expenditure	...	...	...	396,810	390,391	411,978	595,306	607,686	632,233	703,039	724,147	746,302
NLB	**Net lending (+) / Net borrowing (-)**	...	...	...	**-59,575**	**-38,803**	**-39,435**	**-64,204**	**-55,740**	**-46,025**	**-67,130**	**-58,980**	**-45,976**
32	Net acquisition of financial assets	...	...	...	-13,780	21,035	3,611	...	...	...	-19,370	14,903	1,629
33	Net incurrence of liabilities	...	...	...	45,150	59,465	42,387	...	...	...	47,050	73,321	46,842
NLBz	Statistical discrepancy	...	...	...	645	373	659	...	...	...	710	562	763
	Memorandum items												
PB	Primary net lending / net borrowing	...	...	...	-20,599	-6,818	-8,374	-25,485	-24,350	-16,226	-25,630	-25,478	-14,415
GB	Government balance per national definition	...	...	...	...	...	...	...	...	...	...	...	...
	Statement of other economic flows												
	Balance sheet												
6	**Net worth**	...	...	...	...	...	...	...	...	...	...	...	...
61	Nonfinancial assets	...	...	...	...	...	...	...	...	...	...	...	...
62	Financial assets	...	...	...	354,118	387,979	397,301	...	...	...	454,467	481,368	492,468
63	Liabilities	...	...	...	958,540	911,766	959,605	...	...	...	1,033,768	1,134,464	1,189,027
	Table 1 Revenue												
1	**Revenue**	...	...	...	**337,235**	**351,589**	**372,543**	**531,102**	**551,946**	**586,207**	**635,909**	**665,167**	**700,326**
11	**Taxes**	...	...	...	**257,852**	**266,613**	**280,865**	**257,852**	**266,613**	**280,865**	**324,479**	**337,741**	**355,985**
111	Taxes on income, profits, and capital gains	...	...	...	64,522	66,829	71,381	64,522	66,829	71,381	103,567	108,759	117,078
1111	Payable by individuals	...	...	...	41,437	43,299	45,462	41,437	43,299	45,462	74,216	78,719	83,974
1112	Payable by corporations and other enterprises	...	...	...	23,085	23,530	25,919	23,085	23,530	25,919	29,351	30,040	33,104
1113	Other taxes on income, profits, and capital gains	...	...	...	—	—	—	—	—	—	—	—	—
112	Taxes on payroll and workforce	...	...	...	3,998	4,042	4,028	3,998	4,042	4,028	3,998	4,042	4,028
113	Taxes on property	...	...	...	—	—	—	—	—	—	20,999	21,686	22,452
114	Taxes on goods and services	...	...	...	189,332	195,742	205,456	189,332	195,742	205,456	194,402	201,638	211,372
1141	General taxes on goods and services	...	...	...	116,607	122,671	125,836	116,607	122,671	125,836	118,240	124,476	127,613
1142	Excises	...	...	...	66,310	67,136	70,632	66,310	67,136	70,632	66,310	67,136	70,632
115	Taxes on international trade and transactions	...	...	...	—	—	—	—	—	—	—	—	—
116	Other taxes	...	...	...	—	—	—	—	—	—	1,513	1,616	1,055
12	**Social contributions**	...	...	...	**14,965**	**15,569**	**15,864**	**217,594**	**225,471**	**240,685**	**217,594**	**225,471**	**240,685**
121	Social security contributions	...	...	...	—	—	—	202,629	209,902	224,821	202,629	209,902	224,821
122	Other social contributions	...	...	...	14,965	15,569	15,864	14,965	15,569	15,864	14,965	15,569	15,864
13	**Grants**	...	...	...	...	...	...	...	...	...	...	...	...
131	From foreign governments	...	...	...	...	...	...	...	...	...	...	...	...
132	From international organizations	...	...	...	...	...	...	...	...	...	...	...	...
133	From other general government units	...	...	...	13,489	14,098	14,548	2,739	3,151	2,556	—	—	—
1331	Current	...	...	...	13,308	13,629	14,128	2,558	2,682	2,136	—	—	—
1332	Capital	...	...	...	181	470	420	181	470	420	—	—	—
14	**Other revenue**	...	...	...	...	...	...	...	...	...	...	...	...
	Table 2 Expense by economic type												
2	**Expense**	...	...	...	**388,334**	**380,925**	**395,401**	**586,646**	**598,254**	**615,583**	**677,458**	**692,352**	**710,360**
21	**Compensation of employees**	...	...	...	**77,266**	**81,797**	**84,256**	**80,572**	**85,106**	**87,583**	**171,795**	**178,708**	**184,200**
211	Wages and salaries	...	...	...	...	...	...	...	...	...	...	...	...
212	Employers' social contributions	...	...	...	...	...	...	...	...	...	...	...	...
22	**Use of goods and services**	...	...	...	**36,550**	**39,027**	**41,884**	**38,200**	**40,586**	**43,654**	**96,545**	**101,209**	**105,228**
23	**Consumption of fixed capital**	...	...	...	**21,754**	**23,575**	**23,450**	**22,084**	**23,918**	**23,822**	**36,977**	**39,389**	**39,757**
24	**Interest**	...	...	...	**38,976**	**31,985**	**31,060**	**38,719**	**31,390**	**29,800**	**41,500**	**33,502**	**31,560**
25	**Subsidies**	...	...	...	**9,691**	**9,878**	**6,826**	**10,759**	**10,991**	**8,230**	**11,032**	**11,278**	**8,642**

Poland (964)

In Millions of Polish Zlotys (PLN) / Fiscal Year Ends December 31st

		Budgetary Central Government			Central Government (excl. Social Security)			Central Government (incl. Social Security)			General Government		
		2013	2014	2015	2013P	2014P	2015P	2013P	2014P	2015P	2013P	2014P	2015P
26	**Grants**	...	...	...	...	...	...	...	...	...	...	...	...
261	To foreign governments	...	...	...	...	...	...	...	...	...	...	...	...
262	To international organizations	...	...	...	...	...	...	...	...	...	...	...	...
263	To other general government units	...	...	...	145,139	136,778	147,956	106,222	108,868	112,987	—	—	—
2631	Current	...	...	...	141,693	132,992	143,439	102,774	105,080	108,467	—	—	—
2632	Capital	...	...	...	3,446	3,785	4,517	3,448	3,788	4,520	—	—	—
27	**Social benefits**	...	...	...	**23,638**	**24,412**	**24,315**	**252,030**	**259,920**	**271,136**	**270,367**	**278,842**	**290,307**
271	Social security benefits	...	...	...	...	...	...	...	...	...	...	...	...
272	Social assistance benefits	...	...	...	...	...	...	...	...	...	...	...	...
273	Employment-related social benefits	...	...	...	...	...	...	...	...	...	...	...	...
28	**Other expense**	...	...	...	...	...	...	...	...	...	...	...	...
281	Property expense other than interest	...	...	...	—	—	—	—	—	—	—	—	—
282	Transfers not elsewhere classified	...	...	...	...	...	...	...	...	...	...	...	...
2821	Current	...	...	...	...	...	...	...	...	...	...	...	...
2822	Capital	...	...	...	...	...	...	...	...	...	...	...	...
	Table 3 Transactions in assets and liabilities												
3	**Change in net worth from transactions**	...	...	...	**-50,454**	**-28,964**	**-22,199**	...	...	...	**-40,839**	**-26,623**	**-9,271**
31	**Net/Gross investment in nonfinancial assets**	...	...	...	**8,476**	**9,466**	**16,577**	**8,660**	**9,432**	**16,650**	**25,581**	**31,796**	**35,942**
311	Fixed assets	...	...	...	12,229	12,992	17,703	12,413	12,958	17,779	31,465	38,128	39,406
3111	Buildings and structures	...	...	...	...	...	...	...	...	...	...	...	...
3112	Machinery and equipment	...	...	...	...	...	...	...	...	...	...	...	...
3113	Other fixed assets	...	...	...	...	...	...	...	...	...	...	...	...
3114	Weapons systems	...	...	...	...	...	...	...	...	...	...	...	...
312	Inventories	...	...	...	...	...	...	...	...	...	...	...	...
313	Valuables	...	...	...	...	...	...	...	...	...	...	...	...
314	Nonproduced assets	...	...	...	-3,958	-4,107	-2,060	-3,958	-4,107	-2,060	-6,233	-7,074	-4,391
3141	Land	...	...	...	...	...	...	...	...	...	...	...	...
3142	Mineral and energy resources	...	...	...	...	...	...	...	...	...	...	...	...
3143	Other naturally occurring assets	...	...	...	...	...	...	...	...	...	...	...	...
3144	Intangible nonproduced assets	...	...	...	...	...	...	...	...	...	...	...	...
32	**Net acquisition of financial assets**	...	...	...	**-13,780**	**21,035**	**3,611**	...	...	...	**-19,370**	**14,903**	**1,629**
	By instrument												
3201	Monetary gold and SDRs	...	...	...	—	—	—	...	...	...	—	—	—
3202	Currency and deposits	...	...	...	-17,915	10,436	-20,158	...	...	...	-18,882	10,735	-16,860
3203	Debt securities	...	...	...	3,192	-3,869	104	...	...	...	3,220	-3,877	143
3204	Loans	...	...	...	11,726	11,198	4,120	...	...	...	-19	2,943	-212
3205	Equity and investment fund shares	...	...	...	-9,190	3,821	-32	...	...	...	-9,569	3,525	-485
3206	Insurance, pension, and standardized guarantee schemes	...	...	...	35	27	-190	...	...	...	44	34	-238
3207	Financial derivatives and employee stock options	...	...	...	-16	97	35	...	...	...	-16	97	35
3208	Other accounts receivable	...	...	...	-1,612	-675	19,732	...	...	...	5,852	1,446	19,246
	By debtor												
321	Domestic debtors	...	...	...	...	...	...	...	...	...	...	...	...
322	External debtors	...	...	...	...	...	...	...	...	...	...	...	...
33	**Net incurrence of liabilities**	...	...	...	**45,150**	**59,465**	**42,387**	...	...	...	**47,050**	**73,321**	**46,842**
	By instrument												
3301	Special Drawing Rights (SDRs)	...	...	...	—	—	—	...	...	...	—	—	—
3302	Currency and deposits	...	...	...	-31	1,457	5,486	...	...	...	—	391	3,851
3303	Debt securities	...	...	...	35,036	46,345	31,651	...	...	...	34,322	-100,937	31,315
3304	Loans	...	...	...	12,037	11,103	10,073	...	...	...	12,353	15,650	11,457
3305	Equity and investment fund shares	...	...	...	...	...	...	...	...	...	...	...	...
3306	Insurance, pension, and standardized guarantee schemes	...	...	...	34	45	99	...	...	...	34	45	99
3307	Financial derivatives and employee stock options	...	...	...	-5	—	—	...	...	...	-5	—	—
3308	Other accounts payable	...	...	...	-1,921	515	-4,922	...	...	...	346	158,172	120

Poland (964)

In Millions of Polish Zlotys (PLN) / Fiscal Year Ends December 31st

		Budgetary Central Government			Central Government (excl. Social Security)			Central Government (incl. Social Security)			General Government		
		2013	2014	2015	2013P	2014P	2015P	2013P	2014P	2015P	2013P	2014P	2015P
	By creditor												
331	Domestic creditors	...	...	...	...	...	...	...	...	...	...	...	...
332	External creditors	...	...	...	...	...	...	...	...	...	...	...	...
	Table 4 Holding gains and losses in assets and liabilities												
	Table 5 Holding gains and losses in assets and liabilities												
	Table 6 Balance sheet												
6	**Net worth**	**...**	**...**	**...**	**...**	**...**	**...**	**...**	**...**	**...**	**...**	**...**	**...**
61	**Nonfinancial assets**	**...**	**...**	**...**	**...**	**...**	**...**	**...**	**...**	**...**	**...**	**...**	**...**
611	Fixed assets	...	...	...	...	...	...	...	...	...	555,668	...	...
6111	Buildings and structures	...	...	...	...	...	...	...	...	...	432,069	...	...
6112	Machinery and equipment	...	...	...	...	...	...	...	...	...	...	...	...
6113	Other fixed assets	...	...	...	...	...	...	...	...	...	21,847	...	...
6114	Weapons systems	...	...	...	...	...	...	...	...	...	...	...	...
612	Inventories	...	...	...	...	...	...	...	...	...	5,989	...	...
613	Valuables	...	...	...	...	...	...	...	...	...	...	...	...
614	Nonproduced assets	...	...	...	...	...	...	...	...	...	...	...	...
6141	Land	...	...	...	...	...	...	...	...	...	...	...	...
6142	Mineral and energy resources	...	...	...	...	...	...	...	...	...	...	...	...
6143	Other naturally occurring assets	...	...	...	...	...	...	...	...	...	...	...	...
6144	Intangible nonproduced assets	...	...	...	...	...	...	...	...	...	...	...	...
62	**Financial assets**	**...**	**...**	**...**	**354,118**	**387,979**	**397,301**	**...**	**...**	**...**	**454,467**	**481,368**	**492,468**
	By instrument												
6201	Monetary gold and SDRs	...	...	...	—	—	—	...	...	...	—	—	—
6202	Currency and deposits	...	...	...	35,766	54,700	36,820	...	...	...	57,689	77,010	63,542
6203	Debt securities	...	...	...	6,300	2,431	2,595	...	...	...	6,384	2,508	2,720
6204	Loans	...	...	...	45,019	56,864	59,858	...	...	...	15,664	19,316	18,555
6205	Equity and investment fund shares	...	...	...	191,819	196,420	197,900	...	...	...	262,345	266,660	267,851
6206	Insurance, pension, and standardized guarantee schemes	...	...	...	1,083	1,110	920	...	...	...	1,354	1,388	1,150
6207	Financial derivatives and employee stock options	...	...	...	4,088	4,185	4,220	...	...	...	4,088	4,185	4,220
6208	Other accounts receivable	...	...	...	70,043	72,269	94,988	...	...	...	106,943	110,301	134,430
	By debtor												
621	Domestic debtors	...	...	...	...	...	...	...	...	...	...	...	...
622	External debtors	...	...	...	...	...	...	...	...	...	...	...	...
63	**Liabilities**	**...**	**...**	**...**	**958,540**	**911,766**	**959,605**	**...**	**...**	**...**	**1,033,768**	**1,134,464**	**1,189,027**
	By instrument												
6301	Special Drawing Rights (SDRs)	...	...	...	—	—	—	...	...	...	—	—	—
6302	Currency and deposits	...	...	...	9,576	11,034	16,519	...	...	...	—	391	4,241
6303	Debt securities	...	...	...	772,659	702,426	738,708	...	...	...	761,691	678,238	714,182
6304	Loans	...	...	...	100,099	119,542	131,055	...	...	...	163,518	187,382	200,350
6305	Equity and investment fund shares	...	...	...	...	...	...	...	...	...	...	...	...
6306	Insurance, pension, and standardized guarantee schemes	...	...	...	44	89	189	...	...	...	44	89	189
6307	Financial derivatives and employee stock options	...	...	...	—	—	—	...	...	...	—	—	—
6308	Other accounts payable	...	...	...	76,162	78,675	73,134	...	...	...	108,515	268,364	270,065
	By creditor												
631	Domestic creditors	...	...	...	...	...	...	...	...	...	...	...	...
632	External creditors	...	...	...	...	...	...	...	...	...	...	...	...
	Memorandum items												
6M2	Net financial worth	...	...	...	-604,422	-523,787	-562,304	...	...	...	-579,301	-653,096	-696,559
6M3	Gross debt (D4) at market value	...	...	...	958,540	911,766	959,605	...	...	...	1,033,768	1,134,464	1,189,027
6M3D3	D3 debt liabilities at market value	...	...	...	958,496	911,677	959,416	...	...	...	1,033,724	1,134,375	1,188,838
6M3D2	D2 debt liabilities at market value	...	...	...	882,334	833,002	886,282	...	...	...	925,209	866,011	918,773
6M3D1	D1 debt liabilities at market value	...	...	...	872,758	821,968	869,763	...	...	...	925,209	865,620	914,532

Poland (964)

In Millions of Polish Zlotys (PLN) / Fiscal Year Ends December 31st

		Budgetary Central Government			Central Government (excl. Social Security)			Central Government (incl. Social Security)			General Government		
		2013	2014	2015	2013P	2014P	2015P	2013P	2014P	2015P	2013P	2014P	2015P
6M4	Gross debt (D4) at nominal value	...	...	...	...	...	...	...	...	...	...	...	...
6M4D3	D3 debt liabilities at nominal value	...	...	...	...	...	...	...	...	...	...	...	...
6M4D2	D2 debt liabilities at nominal value	...	...	...	...	...	...	...	...	...	...	...	...
6M4D1	D1 debt liabilities at nominal value	...	...	...	...	...	...	...	...	...	...	...	...
6M35	Gross debt (D4) at face value	...	...	...	...	...	...	...	...	...	...	...	...
6M35D3	D3 debt liabilities at face value	...	...	...	955,619	907,847	958,751	...	...	...	1,031,078	1,132,174	1,189,725
6M35D2	D2 debt liabilities at face value	...	...	...	879,457	829,172	885,617	...	...	...	922,563	863,810	919,660
6M35D1	D1 debt liabilities at face value	...	...	...	869,880	818,138	869,100	...	...	...	922,563	863,419	915,418
6M93	Government gross debt per national definition	...	...	...	879,457	829,172	885,617	...	...	...	922,563	863,810	919,660
6M5	Arrears	...	...	...	...	...	...	...	...	...	...	...	...
6M6	Explicit contingent liabilities	...	...	...	...	...	...	...	...	...	...	...	...
6M61	of which: Publicly guaranteed debt	...	...	...	...	...	...	...	...	...	...	...	...
6M7	Net implicit obligations for social security benefits	...	...	...	...	...	...	...	...	...	...	...	...
	Table 7 Expenditure by functions of government												
7	**Expenditure**	...	...	...	**394,219**	**387,066**	...	...	...	...	**702,166**	**724,465**	...
701	**General public services**	...	...	...	**86,976**	**79,040**	...	...	...	...	**94,428**	**86,200**	...
7017	Public debt transactions	...	...	...	40,099	33,036	...	...	...	...	42,760	34,769	...
7018	Transfers of general character between levels of government	...	...	...	11,417	10,490	...	...	...	...	—	—	...
702	**Defense**	...	...	...	**27,433**	**25,591**	...	...	...	...	**27,459**	**25,568**	...
703	**Public order and safety**	...	...	...	**34,551**	**35,728**	...	...	...	...	**36,995**	**38,435**	...
704	**Economic affairs**	...	...	...	**35,708**	**46,306**	...	...	...	...	**67,678**	**79,724**	...
7042	Agriculture, forestry, fishing, and hunting	...	...	...	6,056	6,469	...	...	...	...	6,987	6,691	...
7043	Fuel and energy	...	...	...	1,119	1,215	...	...	...	...	1,326	1,474	...
7044	Mining, manufacturing, and construction	...	...	...	640	895	...	...	...	...	1,428	1,395	...
7045	Transport	...	...	...	19,111	26,882	...	...	...	...	48,266	58,442	...
7046	Communication	...	...	...	-800	-886	...	...	...	...	-675	-464	...
705	**Environmental protection**	...	...	...	**3,292**	**3,852**	...	...	...	...	**12,299**	**14,872**	...
706	**Housing and community amenities**	...	...	...	**3,710**	**2,933**	...	...	...	...	**12,250**	**12,322**	...
707	**Health**	...	...	...	**20,246**	**20,707**	...	...	...	...	**76,807**	**79,734**	...
7072	Outpatient services	...	...	...	6,053	6,040	...	...	...	...	24,648	25,028	...
7073	Hospital services	...	...	...	10,197	10,616	...	...	...	...	46,604	49,074	...
7074	Public health services	...	...	...	1,110	1,110	...	...	...	...	1,312	1,276	...
708	**Recreation, culture and religion**	...	...	...	**4,349**	**4,242**	...	...	...	...	**18,308**	**20,180**	...
709	**Education**	...	...	...	**65,889**	**68,976**	...	...	...	...	**87,406**	**90,482**	...
7091	Pre-primary and primary education	...	...	...	554	1,850	...	...	...	...	29,753	30,834	...
7092	Secondary education	...	...	...	1,024	1,113	...	...	...	...	23,961	23,964	...
7094	Tertiary education	...	...	...	23,428	25,154	...	...	...	...	23,370	25,226	...
710	**Social protection**	...	...	...	**112,065**	**99,692**	...	...	...	...	**268,536**	**276,949**	...
7z	Statistical discrepancy: Expenditure	...	...	...	—	-0	...	...	...	...	—	-0	...
	Table 8 Financial transactions by counterpart sector												
32	**Net acquisition of financial assets**	...	...	...	**-13,780**	**21,035**	**3,611**	...	...	...	**-19,370**	**14,903**	**1,629**
321	Domestic debtors	...	...	...	...	...	...	...	...	...	...	...	...
8211	General government	...	...	...	...	...	...	...	...	...	—	—	—
8212	Central bank	...	...	...	...	...	...	...	...	...	...	...	...
8213	Deposit-taking corporations except the central bank	...	...	...	...	...	...	...	...	...	...	...	...
8214	Other financial corporations	...	...	...	...	...	...	...	...	...	...	...	...
8215	Nonfinancial corporations	...	...	...	...	...	...	...	...	...	...	...	...
8216	Households & nonprofit institutions serving households	...	...	...	...	...	...	...	...	...	...	...	...
322	External debtors	...	...	...	...	...	...	...	...	...	...	...	...
8221	General government	...	...	...	...	...	...	...	...	...	...	...	...
8227	International organizations	...	...	...	...	...	...	...	...	...	...	...	...
8228	Financial corporations other than international organizations	...	...	...	...	...	...	...	...	...	...	...	...
8229	Other nonresidents	...	...	...	...	...	...	...	...	...	...	...	...

Poland (964)

In Millions of Polish Zlotys (PLN) / Fiscal Year Ends December 31st

		Budgetary Central Government			Central Government (excl. Social Security)			Central Government (incl. Social Security)			General Government		
		2013	2014	2015	2013P	2014P	2015P	2013P	2014P	2015P	2013P	2014P	2015P
33	**Net incurrence of liabilities**	...	...	...	45,150	59,465	42,387	...	...	...	47,050	73,321	46,842
331	Domestic creditors	...	...	...	...	...	...	...	...	...	...	...	...
3311	General government	...	...	...	...	...	...	...	...	...	—	—	—
3312	Central bank	...	...	...	...	...	...	...	...	...	...	...	...
3313	Deposit-taking corporations except the central bank	...	...	...	...	...	...	...	...	...	...	...	...
3314	Other financial corporations	...	...	...	...	...	...	...	...	...	...	...	...
3315	Nonfinancial corporations	...	...	...	...	...	...	...	...	...	...	...	...
3316	Households & nonprofit institutions serving households	...	...	...	...	...	...	...	...	...	...	...	...
332	External creditors	...	...	...	...	...	...	...	...	...	...	...	...
3321	General government	...	...	...	...	...	...	...	...	...	...	...	...
3327	International organizations	...	...	...	...	...	...	...	...	...	...	...	...
3328	Financial corporations other than international organizations	...	...	...	...	...	...	...	...	...	...	...	...
3329	Other nonresidents	...	...	...	...	...	...	...	...	...	...	...	...
	Table 9 Total other economic flows in assets and liabilities												
9	**Change in net worth due to other economic flows**	...	...	...	...	...	...	...	...	...	...	...	...
91	**Other economic flows in nonfinancial assets**	...	...	...	...	...	...	...	...	...	...	...	...
911	Fixed assets	...	...	...	...	...	...	...	...	...	...	...	...
912	Inventories	...	...	...	...	...	...	...	...	...	...	...	...
913	Valuables	...	...	...	...	...	...	...	...	...	...	...	...
914	Nonproduced assets	...	...	...	...	...	...	...	...	...	...	...	...
92	**Other economic flows in financial assets**	...	...	...	2,508	12,826	5,711	...	...	...	-2,547	11,998	9,471
	By instrument												
9201	Monetary gold and SDRs	...	...	...	—	—	—	...	...	...	—	—	—
9202	Currency and deposits	...	...	...	-393	8,498	2,278	...	...	...	-380	8,586	3,392
9203	Debt securities	...	...	...	—	—	60	...	...	...	44	1	69
9204	Loans	...	...	...	442	647	-1,126	...	...	...	427	709	-549
9205	Equity and investment fund shares	...	...	...	140	780	1,512	...	...	...	149	790	1,676
9206	Insurance, pension, and standardized guarantee schemes	...	...	...	—	—	—	...	...	...	—	—	—
9207	Financial derivatives and employee stock options	...	...	...	8	—	—	...	...	...	8	—	—
9208	Other accounts receivable	...	...	...	2,311	2,901	2,987	...	...	...	-2,795	1,912	4,883
	By debtor												
921	Domestic debtors	...	...	...	...	...	...	...	...	...	...	...	...
922	External debtors	...	...	...	...	...	...	...	...	...	...	...	...
93	**Other economic flows in liabilities**	...	...	...	-2,118	-106,239	5,452	...	...	...	-1,841	27,375	7,721
	By instrument												
9301	Special Drawing Rights (SDRs)	...	...	...	—	—	—	...	...	...	—	—	—
9302	Currency and deposits	...	...	...	-6	1	-1	...	...	...	—	—	-1
9303	Debt securities	...	...	...	-1,411	-116,578	4,631	...	...	...	-1,938	17,484	4,629
9304	Loans	...	...	...	629	8,340	1,440	...	...	...	711	8,214	1,511
9305	Equity and investment fund shares	...	...	...	—	—	—	...	...	...	—	—	—
9306	Insurance, pension, and standardized guarantee schemes	...	...	...	—	—	1	...	...	...	—	—	1
9307	Financial derivatives and employee stock options	...	...	...	5	—	—	...	...	...	5	—	—
9308	Other accounts payable	...	...	...	-1,335	1,998	-619	...	...	...	-619	1,677	1,581
	By creditor												
931	Domestic creditors	...	...	...	...	...	...	...	...	...	...	...	...
932	External creditors	...	...	...	...	...	...	...	...	...	...	...	...
	Memorandum items												
9M2	Change in net financial worth due to other economic flows	...	...	...	4,626	119,065	259	...	...	...	-706	-15,377	1,750

Poland (964)

In Millions of Polish Zlotys (PLN) / Fiscal Year Ends December 31st

		Budgetary Central Government			Central Government (excl. Social Security)			Central Government (incl. Social Security)			General Government		
		2013	2014	2015	2013P	2014P	2015P	2013P	2014P	2015P	2013P	2014P	2015P
9M3	Gross debt (D4) at market value: other economic flows	...	...	...	-2,123	-106,239	5,452	...	...	...	-1,846	27,375	7,721
9M3D3	D3 debt liabilities at market value: other economic flows	...	...	...	-2,123	-106,239	5,451	...	...	...	-1,846	27,375	7,720
9M3D2	D2 debt liabilities at market value: other economic flows	...	...	...	-788	-108,237	6,070	...	...	...	-1,227	25,698	6,139
9M3D1	D1 debt liabilities at market value: other economic flows	...	...	...	-782	-108,238	6,071	...	...	...	-1,227	25,698	6,140

Portugal (182)

In Millions of Euros (EUR) / Fiscal Year Ends December 31st

		Budgetary Central Government			Central Government (excl. Social Security)			Central Government (incl. Social Security)			General Government		
		2013P	2014P	2015P	2013P	2014P	2015P	2013P	2014P	2015P	2013P	2014P	2015P
	Statement of operations												
1	Revenue	43,654	43,820	44,747	54,649	54,843	56,141	68,799	69,274	70,637	76,787	77,196	79,004
2	Expense	54,940	57,640	58,091	64,684	69,771	66,453	78,505	83,418	79,864	86,276	91,158	87,757
GOB	**Gross operating balance**	**-10,689**	**-13,256**	**-12,797**	**-7,021**	**-11,925**	**-7,258**	**-6,648**	**-11,100**	**-6,129**	**-4,397**	**-8,875**	**-3,505**
NOB	**Net operating balance**	**-11,286**	**-13,819**	**-13,343**	**-10,036**	**-14,928**	**-10,313**	**-9,706**	**-14,145**	**-9,226**	**-9,489**	**-13,962**	**-8,753**
31	Net/Gross investment in nonfinancial assets	...	...	...	-1,154	-1,077	-562	-1,172	-1,092	-588	-1,244	-1,560	-932
2M	Expenditure	...	...	...	63,530	68,694	65,892	77,333	82,326	79,276	85,032	89,598	86,825
NLB	**Net lending (+) / Net borrowing (-)**	...	...	...	**-8,882**	**-13,851**	**-9,751**	**-8,534**	**-13,053**	**-8,638**	**-8,245**	**-12,402**	**-7,821**
32	Net acquisition of financial assets	...	...	...	-1,283	-5,252	-4,709	...	...	...	-1,826	-6,527	-4,235
33	Net incurrence of liabilities	...	...	...	7,599	8,598	5,043	...	...	...	6,419	5,876	3,586
NLBz	Statistical discrepancy	...	...	...	-0	0	0	...	...	...	0	-0	-0
	Memorandum items												
PB	Primary net lending / net borrowing	...	...	...	-585	-5,294	-1,373	-433	-4,720	-575	13	-3,919	370
GB	Government balance per national definition	...	...	...	...	...	...	...	...	...	...	...	...
	Statement of other economic flows												
9	**Change in net worth due to other economic flows**	...	...	...	...	...	...	...	...	...	...	...	...
4	Change in net worth due to holding gains and losses	...	...	...	...	...	...	...	...	...	...	...	...
41	Nonfinancial assets	...	...	...	...	...	...	...	...	...	...	...	...
42	Financial assets	...	...	...	-4,962	7,652	1,419	...	...	...	-4,699	7,876	1,508
43	Liabilities	...	...	...	2,422	16,247	2,017	...	...	...	2,215	15,411	2,056
5	Change in net worth due to volume changes	...	...	...	...	...	...	...	...	...	...	...	...
51	Nonfinancial assets	...	...	...	...	...	...	...	...	...	...	...	...
52	Financial assets	...	...	...	239	75	556	...	...	...	233	99	553
53	Liabilities	...	...	...	834	415	-88	...	...	...	682	1,006	119
	Balance sheet												
6	**Net worth**	...	...	...	...	...	...	...	...	...	...	...	...
61	Nonfinancial assets	...	...	...	...	...	...	...	...	...	...	...	...
62	Financial assets	...	...	...	68,843	71,317	68,584	...	...	...	77,429	78,878	76,704
63	Liabilities	...	...	...	237,515	262,775	269,747	...	...	...	243,361	265,654	271,415
	Table 1 Revenue												
1	**Revenue**	**43,654**	**43,820**	**44,747**	**54,649**	**54,843**	**56,141**	**68,799**	**69,274**	**70,637**	**76,787**	**77,196**	**79,004**
11	**Taxes**	**35,764**	**36,259**	**37,730**	**37,581**	**38,170**	**39,872**	**38,737**	**39,329**	**41,065**	**42,733**	**43,564**	**45,542**
111	Taxes on income, profits, and capital gains	17,402	17,036	17,476	17,424	17,086	17,495	17,424	17,086	17,495	18,664	18,253	18,742
1111	Payable by individuals	12,312	12,519	12,283	12,325	12,569	12,296	12,325	12,569	12,296	13,120	13,356	13,128
1112	Payable by corporations and other enterprises	5,091	4,517	5,193	5,099	4,517	5,199	5,099	4,517	5,199	5,545	4,897	5,614
1113	Other taxes on income, profits, and capital gains	—	—	—	—	—	—	—	—	—	—	—	—
112	Taxes on payroll and workforce	—	—	—	—	—	—	—	—	—	—	—	—
113	Taxes on property	2	—	0	14	34	13	14	34	13	1,351	1,478	1,527
114	Taxes on goods and services	16,906	17,809	18,792	18,497	19,424	20,695	19,649	20,579	21,881	20,993	22,163	23,551
1141	General taxes on goods and services	12,171	12,994	13,692	12,248	13,075	13,751	13,218	14,051	14,745	14,066	15,165	15,943
1142	Excises	3,579	3,590	3,707	4,135	4,168	4,426	4,135	4,168	4,426	4,313	4,347	4,618
115	Taxes on international trade and transactions	—	—	—	0	0	0	0	0	0	0	0	0
116	Other taxes	1,453	1,414	1,461	1,645	1,626	1,669	1,650	1,630	1,676	1,724	1,670	1,722
12	**Social contributions**	**4,859**	**4,862**	**4,621**	**6,404**	**6,279**	**6,039**	**19,691**	**19,825**	**20,198**	**20,449**	**20,457**	**20,775**
121	Social security contributions	1,652	1,849	1,862	—	—	—	13,253	13,503	14,099	13,253	13,503	14,099
122	Other social contributions	3,206	3,013	2,758	6,404	6,279	6,039	6,438	6,323	6,099	7,196	6,955	6,676
13	**Grants**	**121**	**118**	**103**	...	...	...	...	...	...	...	...	...
131	From foreign governments	121	118	103	...	...	...	...	...	...	...	...	...
132	From international organizations	—	—	—	...	...	...	...	...	...	...	...	...
133	From other general government units	—	—	—	841	797	1,325	83	71	73	—	—	—
1331	Current	—	—	—	831	786	1,315	73	60	63	—	—	—
1332	Capital	—	—	—	10	11	9	10	11	9	—	—	—
14	**Other revenue**	**2,910**	**2,581**	**2,294**	...	...	...	...	...	...	...	...	...

Portugal (182)

In Millions of Euros (EUR) / Fiscal Year Ends December 31st

		Budgetary Central Government			Central Government (excl. Social Security)			Central Government (incl. Social Security)			General Government		
		2013P	2014P	2015P	2013P	2014P	2015P	2013P	2014P	2015P	2013P	2014P	2015P
	Table 2 Expense by economic type												
2	**Expense**	**54,940**	**57,640**	**58,091**	**64,684**	**69,771**	**66,453**	**78,505**	**83,418**	**79,864**	**86,276**	**91,158**	**87,757**
21	**Compensation of employees**	**10,148**	**9,885**	**9,659**	**17,179**	**16,631**	**16,464**	**17,457**	**16,902**	**16,733**	**21,317**	**20,515**	**20,273**
211	Wages and salaries	7,128	6,873	6,895	12,112	...	11,756	...	...	...	...	...	...
212	Employers' social contributions	3,021	3,012	2,764	5,068	...	4,708	...	...	...	...	...	...
22	**Use of goods and services**	**1,848**	**1,626**	**1,766**	**6,711**	**7,031**	**7,480**	**6,799**	**7,119**	**7,560**	**9,611**	**9,847**	**10,329**
23	**Consumption of fixed capital**	**597**	**564**	**547**	**3,015**	**3,003**	**3,055**	**3,058**	**3,045**	**3,098**	**5,092**	**5,088**	**5,248**
24	**Interest**	**7,536**	**7,941**	**7,968**	**8,296**	**8,556**	**8,378**	**8,101**	**8,332**	**8,063**	**8,258**	**8,483**	**8,191**
25	**Subsidies**	**198**	**177**	**134**	**749**	**993**	**905**	**904**	**1,117**	**981**	**1,031**	**1,230**	**1,110**
26	**Grants**	**13,845**	**12,936**	**12,640**	...	...	...	...	...	...	...	...	...
261	To foreign governments	285	272	242	...	...	...	...	...	...	...	...	...
262	To international organizations	1,634	1,429	1,495	...	...	...	...	...	...	...	...	...
263	To other general government units	11,926	11,235	10,904	12,095	11,259	10,985	3,405	2,931	2,975	—	—	—
2631	Current	10,978	10,604	10,233	11,131	10,616	10,300	2,454	2,291	2,292	—	—	—
2632	Capital	948	631	670	964	643	684	950	641	683	—	—	—
27	**Social benefits**	**8,593**	**8,721**	**9,746**	**12,825**	**12,837**	**13,876**	**33,672**	**33,133**	**33,736**	**34,785**	**34,088**	**34,637**
271	Social security benefits	...	...	...	...	...	...	...	...	...	...	...	...
272	Social assistance benefits	...	...	...	...	...	...	...	...	...	...	...	...
273	Employment-related social benefits	...	...	...	...	...	...	...	...	...	...	...	...
28	**Other expense**	**12,175**	**15,790**	**15,631**	...	...	...	...	...	...	...	...	...
281	Property expense other than interest	—	—	—	0	0	—	0	0	—	13	13	14
282	Transfers not elsewhere classified	12,175	15,790	15,631	...	...	...	...	...	...	...	...	...
2821	Current	10,276	10,237	10,252	...	...	...	...	...	...	...	...	...
2822	Capital	1,899	5,553	5,379	...	...	...	...	...	...	...	...	...
	Table 3 Transactions in assets and liabilities												
3	**Change in net worth from transactions**	...	...	...	**-10,036**	**-14,928**	**-10,313**	...	...	...	**-9,489**	**-13,962**	**-8,753**
31	**Net/Gross investment in nonfinancial assets**	...	...	...	**-1,154**	**-1,077**	**-562**	**-1,172**	**-1,092**	**-588**	**-1,244**	**-1,560**	**-932**
311	Fixed assets	...	...	...	-1,208	-1,081	-660	-1,230	-1,099	-689	-1,391	-1,641	-1,164
3111	Buildings and structures	...	...	...	...	...	...	...	...	...	...	...	...
3112	Machinery and equipment	...	...	...	...	...	...	...	...	...	...	...	...
3113	Other fixed assets	...	...	...	...	...	...	...	...	...	...	...	...
3114	Weapons systems	...	...	...	...	...	...	...	...	...	...	...	...
312	Inventories	...	...	...	...	...	...	...	...	...	...	...	...
313	Valuables	...	...	...	...	...	...	...	...	...	...	...	...
314	Nonproduced assets	...	...	...	24	18	4	28	21	6	105	81	130
3141	Land	...	...	...	...	...	...	...	...	...	...	...	...
3142	Mineral and energy resources	...	...	...	...	...	...	...	...	...	...	...	...
3143	Other naturally occurring assets	...	...	...	...	...	...	...	...	...	...	...	...
3144	Intangible nonproduced assets	...	...	...	...	...	...	...	...	...	...	...	...
32	**Net acquisition of financial assets**	...	...	...	**-1,283**	**-5,252**	**-4,709**	...	...	...	**-1,826**	**-6,527**	**-4,235**
	By instrument												
3201	Monetary gold and SDRs	...	...	...	—	—	—	...	...	...	—	—	—
3202	Currency and deposits	...	...	...	323	-428	-4,369	...	...	...	1,211	-4	-3,115
3203	Debt securities	...	...	...	189	-3,363	-636	...	...	...	-282	-4,705	-967
3204	Loans	...	...	...	1,182	38	488	...	...	...	258	-149	242
3205	Equity and investment fund shares	...	...	...	-1,274	-1,478	146	...	...	...	-1,090	-2,097	-189
3206	Insurance, pension, and standardized guarantee schemes	...	...	...	-0	1	-1	...	...	...	-0	1	-1
3207	Financial derivatives and employee stock options	...	...	...	56	26	-414	...	...	...	-23	112	-291
3208	Other accounts receivable	...	...	...	-1,759	-47	76	...	...	...	-1,900	316	85
	By debtor												
321	Domestic debtors	...	...	...	-1,878	-5,552	-3,868	...	...	...	-2,070	-5,331	-2,812
322	External debtors	...	...	...	595	300	-840	...	...	...	245	-1,196	-1,423
33	**Net incurrence of liabilities**	...	...	...	**7,599**	**8,598**	**5,043**	...	...	...	**6,419**	**5,876**	**3,586**
	By instrument												
3301	Special Drawing Rights (SDRs)	...	...	...	—	—	—	...	...	...	—	—	—
3302	Currency and deposits	...	...	...	872	4,534	4,525	...	...	...	1,223	4,919	3,969
3303	Debt securities	...	...	...	-2,041	218	10,555	...	...	...	-2,777	-1,834	11,192
3304	Loans	...	...	...	9,516	4,116	-8,550	...	...	...	8,997	3,613	-9,379

Portugal (182)

In Millions of Euros (EUR) / Fiscal Year Ends December 31st

		Budgetary Central Government			Central Government (excl. Social Security)			Central Government (incl. Social Security)			General Government		
		2013P	2014P	2015P	2013P	2014P	2015P	2013P	2014P	2015P	2013P	2014P	2015P
3305	Equity and investment fund shares	...	...	...	-340	12	-137	...	...	...	-340	12	-137
3306	Insurance, pension, and standardized guarantee schemes	...	...	...	—	—	-24	...	...	...	—	—	-24
3307	Financial derivatives and employee stock options	...	...	...	18	-6	—	...	...	...	18	-6	—
3308	Other accounts payable	...	...	...	-427	-276	-1,327	...	...	...	-701	-828	-2,036
	By creditor												
331	Domestic creditors	...	...	...	199	-4,748	12,077	...	...	...	-729	-7,398	10,660
332	External creditors	...	...	...	7,400	13,347	-7,034	...	...	...	7,148	13,274	-7,074
	Table 4 Holding gains and losses in assets and liabilities												
4	**Change in net worth due to holding gains and losses**	...	...	...	...	...	...	...	...	...	...	...	...
41	**Holding gains and losses in nonfinancial assets**	...	...	...	...	...	...	...	...	...	...	...	...
411	Fixed assets	...	...	...	...	...	...	...	...	...	...	...	...
412	Inventories	...	...	...	...	...	...	...	...	...	...	...	...
413	Valuables	...	...	...	...	...	...	...	...	...	...	...	...
414	Nonproduced assets	...	...	...	...	...	...	...	...	...	...	...	...
42	**Holding gains and losses in financial assets**	...	...	...	**-4,962**	**7,652**	**1,419**	...	...	...	**-4,699**	**7,876**	**1,508**
	By instrument												
4201	Monetary gold and SDRs	...	...	...	—	—	—	...	...	...	—	—	—
4202	Currency and deposits	...	...	...	-1	0	1	...	...	...	-4	3	7
4203	Debt securities	...	...	...	13	-12	-3	...	...	...	-135	219	21
4204	Loans	...	...	...	-86	99	92	...	...	...	-86	99	92
4205	Equity and investment fund shares	...	...	...	-4,392	6,232	-263	...	...	...	-4,073	6,346	-119
4206	Insurance, pension, and standardized guarantee schemes	...	...	...	-0	—	-0	...	...	...	-0	—	-0
4207	Financial derivatives and employee stock options	...	...	...	-495	1,332	1,619	...	...	...	-402	1,210	1,533
4208	Other accounts receivable	...	...	...	-0	—	-26	...	...	...	—	—	-26
	By debtor												
421	Domestic debtors	...	...	...	...	...	...	...	...	...	...	...	...
422	External debtors	...	...	...	...	...	...	...	...	...	...	...	...
43	**Holding gains and losses in liabilities**	...	...	...	**2,422**	**16,247**	**2,017**	...	...	...	**2,215**	**15,411**	**2,056**
	By instrument												
4301	Special Drawing Rights (SDRs)	...	...	...	—	—	—	...	...	...	—	—	—
4302	Currency and deposits	...	...	...	-0	-0	0	...	...	...	—	—	—
4303	Debt securities	...	...	...	3,636	14,244	515	...	...	...	3,410	13,239	595
4304	Loans	...	...	...	-964	1,733	1,804	...	...	...	-964	1,735	1,810
4305	Equity and investment fund shares	...	...	...	-20	-226	-7	...	...	...	-1	-59	-7
4306	Insurance, pension, and standardized guarantee schemes	...	...	...	—	—	—	...	...	...	—	—	—
4307	Financial derivatives and employee stock options	...	...	...	-230	481	-226	...	...	...	-230	481	-226
4308	Other accounts payable	...	...	...	0	14	-70	...	...	...	0	14	-116
	By creditor												
431	Domestic creditors	...	...	...	...	...	...	...	...	...	...	...	...
432	External creditors	...	...	...	...	...	...	...	...	...	...	...	...
	Table 5 Holding gains and losses in assets and liabilities												
5	**Change in net worth due to other volume changes**	...	...	...	...	...	...	...	...	...	...	...	...
51	**Other volume changes in nonfinancial assets**	...	...	...	...	...	...	...	...	...	...	...	...
511	Fixed assets	...	...	...	...	...	...	...	...	...	...	...	...
512	Inventories	...	...	...	...	...	...	...	...	...	...	...	...
513	Valuables	...	...	...	...	...	...	...	...	...	...	...	...
514	Nonproduced assets	...	...	...	...	...	...	...	...	...	...	...	...
52	**Other volume changes in financial assets**	...	...	...	**239**	**75**	**556**	...	...	...	**233**	**99**	**553**

Portugal (182)

In Millions of Euros (EUR) / Fiscal Year Ends December 31st

		Budgetary Central Government			Central Government (excl. Social Security)			Central Government (incl. Social Security)			General Government		
		2013P	2014P	2015P	2013P	2014P	2015P	2013P	2014P	2015P	2013P	2014P	2015P
	By instrument												
5201	Monetary gold and SDRs	...	...	...	—	—	—	...	...	...	—	—	—
5202	Currency and deposits	...	...	...	-0	-90	18	...	...	...	-6	-74	15
5203	Debt securities	...	...	...	—	—	-125	...	...	...	-1	—	-125
5204	Loans	...	...	...	253	75	-179	...	...	...	253	75	-179
5205	Equity and investment fund shares	...	...	...	-14	91	822	...	...	...	-14	98	822
5206	Insurance, pension, and standardized guarantee schemes	...	...	...	—	—	—	...	...	...	—	—	—
5207	Financial derivatives and employee stock options	...	...	...	—	—	—	...	...	...	—	—	—
5208	Other accounts receivable	...	...	...	0	—	19	...	...	...	0	—	19
	By debtor												
521	Domestic debtors	...	...	...	...	...	...	...	...	...	...	...	...
522	External debtors	...	...	...	...	...	...	...	...	...	...	...	...
53	**Other volume changes in liabilities**	**...**	**...**	**...**	**834**	**415**	**-88**	**...**	**...**	**...**	**682**	**1,006**	**119**
	By instrument												
5301	Special Drawing Rights (SDRs)	...	...	...	—	—	—	...	...	...	—	—	—
5302	Currency and deposits	...	...	...	-182	-359	—	...	...	...	-162	-317	—
5303	Debt securities	...	...	...	—	—	-24	...	...	...	—	—	-24
5304	Loans	...	...	...	227	-75	-18	...	...	...	355	268	-64
5305	Equity and investment fund shares	...	...	...	—	—	-7	...	...	...	—	—	-7
5306	Insurance, pension, and standardized guarantee schemes	...	...	...	—	—	24	...	...	...	—	—	24
5307	Financial derivatives and employee stock options	...	...	...	28	45	—	...	...	...	28	45	—
5308	Other accounts payable	...	...	...	761	804	-63	...	...	...	461	1,010	190
	By creditor												
531	Domestic creditors	...	...	...	...	...	...	...	...	...	...	...	...
532	External creditors	...	...	...	...	...	...	...	...	...	...	...	...
	Table 6 Balance sheet												
6	**Net worth**	**...**	**...**	**...**	**...**	**...**	**...**	**...**	**...**	**...**	**...**	**...**	**...**
61	**Nonfinancial assets**	**...**	**...**	**...**	**...**	**...**	**...**	**...**	**...**	**...**	**...**	**...**	**...**
611	Fixed assets	...	...	...	...	...	...	...	...	...	138,255	...	...
6111	Buildings and structures	...	...	...	...	...	...	...	...	...	129,193	...	...
6112	Machinery and equipment	...	...	...	...	...	...	...	...	...	...	...	...
6113	Other fixed assets	...	...	...	...	...	...	...	...	...	4,441	...	...
6114	Weapons systems	...	...	...	...	...	...	...	...	...	...	...	...
612	Inventories	...	...	...	...	...	...	...	...	...	628	...	...
613	Valuables	...	...	...	...	...	...	...	...	...	...	...	...
614	Nonproduced assets	...	...	...	...	...	...	...	...	...	...	...	...
6141	Land	...	...	...	...	...	...	...	...	...	...	...	...
6142	Mineral and energy resources	...	...	...	...	...	...	...	...	...	...	...	...
6143	Other naturally occurring assets	...	...	...	...	...	...	...	...	...	...	...	...
6144	Intangible nonproduced assets	...	...	...	...	...	...	...	...	...	...	...	...
62	**Financial assets**	**...**	**...**	**...**	**68,843**	**71,317**	**68,584**	**...**	**...**	**...**	**77,429**	**78,878**	**76,704**
	By instrument												
6201	Monetary gold and SDRs	...	...	...	—	—	—	...	...	...	—	—	—
6202	Currency and deposits	...	...	...	18,126	17,608	13,258	...	...	...	21,347	21,271	18,178
6203	Debt securities	...	...	...	6,453	3,078	2,314	...	...	...	8,967	4,481	3,410
6204	Loans	...	...	...	11,330	11,542	11,942	...	...	...	9,234	9,259	9,414
6205	Equity and investment fund shares	...	...	...	24,715	29,560	30,265	...	...	...	27,895	32,241	32,756
6206	Insurance, pension, and standardized guarantee schemes	...	...	...	19	19	18	...	...	...	19	19	18
6207	Financial derivatives and employee stock options	...	...	...	-42	1,316	2,522	...	...	...	-27	1,295	2,538
6208	Other accounts receivable	...	...	...	8,242	8,195	8,264	...	...	...	9,995	10,312	10,390
	By debtor												
621	Domestic debtors	...	...	...	59,186	59,543	55,703	...	...	...	63,381	63,905	61,140
622	External debtors	...	...	...	9,657	11,775	12,881	...	...	...	14,048	14,972	15,564
63	**Liabilities**	**...**	**...**	**...**	**237,515**	**262,775**	**269,747**	**...**	**...**	**...**	**243,361**	**265,654**	**271,415**

Portugal (182)

In Millions of Euros (EUR) / Fiscal Year Ends December 31st

		Budgetary Central Government			Central Government (excl. Social Security)			Central Government (incl. Social Security)			General Government		
		2013P	2014P	2015P	2013P	2014P	2015P	2013P	2014P	2015P	2013P	2014P	2015P
	By instrument												
6301	Special Drawing Rights (SDRs)	...	...	...	—	—	—	...	...	...	—	—	—
6302	Currency and deposits	...	...	...	15,839	20,014	24,540	...	...	...	14,748	19,350	23,319
6303	Debt securities	...	...	...	118,625	133,087	144,134	...	...	...	112,124	123,530	135,293
6304	Loans	...	...	...	87,419	93,194	86,431	...	...	...	95,698	101,314	93,682
6305	Equity and investment fund shares	...	...	...	917	703	553	...	...	...	1,623	1,576	1,426
6306	Insurance, pension, and standardized guarantee schemes	...	...	...	—	—	—	...	...	...	—	—	—
6307	Financial derivatives and employee stock options	...	...	...	1,017	1,537	1,311	...	...	...	1,017	1,537	1,311
6308	Other accounts payable	...	...	...	13,698	14,240	12,779	...	...	...	18,150	18,347	16,385
	By creditor												
631	Domestic creditors	...	...	...	92,450	93,922	106,236	...	...	...	96,804	95,335	106,478
632	External creditors	...	...	...	145,064	168,853	163,511	...	...	...	146,556	170,319	164,937
	Memorandum items												
6M2	Net financial worth	...	...	...	-168,672	-191,458	-201,163	...	...	...	-165,932	-186,776	-194,711
6M3	Gross debt (D4) at market value	...	...	...	235,581	260,535	267,883	...	...	...	240,721	262,541	268,678
6M3D3	D3 debt liabilities at market value	...	...	...	235,581	260,535	267,883	...	...	...	240,721	262,541	268,678
6M3D2	D2 debt liabilities at market value	...	...	...	221,884	246,296	255,104	...	...	...	222,571	244,194	252,293
6M3D1	D1 debt liabilities at market value	...	...	...	206,045	226,282	230,564	...	...	...	207,823	224,844	228,975
6M4	Gross debt (D4) at nominal value	...	...	...	...	...	...	...	...	...	...	...	...
6M4D3	D3 debt liabilities at nominal value	...	...	...	...	...	...	...	...	...	...	...	...
6M4D2	D2 debt liabilities at nominal value	...	...	...	...	...	...	...	...	...	...	...	...
6M4D1	D1 debt liabilities at nominal value	...	...	...	...	...	...	...	...	...	...	...	...
6M35	Gross debt (D4) at face value	...	...	...	...	...	...	...	...	...	...	...	...
6M35D3	D3 debt liabilities at face value	...	...	...	233,003	241,271	245,906	...	...	...	237,865	244,393	247,969
6M35D2	D2 debt liabilities at face value	...	...	...	219,305	227,032	233,126	...	...	...	219,715	226,046	231,584
6M35D1	D1 debt liabilities at face value	...	...	...	207,724	211,445	213,259	...	...	...	209,224	211,123	212,938
6M93	Government gross debt per national definition	...	...	...	219,305	227,032	233,126	...	...	...	219,715	226,046	231,584
6M5	Arrears	...	...	...	...	...	...	...	...	...	...	...	...
6M6	Explicit contingent liabilities	...	...	...	...	...	...	...	...	...	...	...	...
6M61	of which: Publicly guaranteed debt	...	...	...	...	...	...	...	...	...	...	...	...
6M7	Net implicit obligations for social security benefits	...	...	...	...	...	...	...	...	...	...	...	...
	Table 7 Expenditure by functions of government												
7	**Expenditure**	...	...	...	**63,530**	**68,558**	...	...	...	...	**85,032**	**89,677**	...
701	**General public services**	...	...	...	**24,474**	**23,776**	...	...	...	...	**15,167**	**15,189**	...
7017	Public debt transactions	...	...	...	8,638	8,931	...	...	...	...	8,653	8,935	...
7018	Transfers of general character between levels of government	...	...	...	12,095	11,315	...	...	...	...	...	...	...
702	**Defense**	...	...	...	**1,873**	**1,730**	...	...	...	...	**1,873**	**1,730**	...
703	**Public order and safety**	...	...	...	**3,401**	**3,381**	...	...	...	...	**3,909**	**3,881**	...
704	**Economic affairs**	...	...	...	**4,719**	**10,330**	...	...	...	...	**6,475**	**11,886**	...
7042	Agriculture, forestry, fishing, and hunting	...	...	...	457	497	...	...	...	...	626	668	...
7043	Fuel and energy	...	...	...	207	52	...	...	...	...	221	76	...
7044	Mining, manufacturing, and construction	...	...	...	33	36	...	...	...	...	298	274	...
7045	Transport	...	...	...	1,839	3,273	...	...	...	...	2,850	4,087	...
7046	Communication	...	...	...	35	77	...	...	...	...	36	78	...
705	**Environmental protection**	...	...	...	**126**	**156**	...	...	...	...	**788**	**781**	...
706	**Housing and community amenities**	...	...	...	**154**	**192**	...	...	...	...	**1,070**	**1,040**	...
707	**Health**	...	...	...	**10,149**	**10,116**	...	...	...	...	**10,883**	**10,824**	...
7072	Outpatient services	...	...	...	3,208	3,708	...	...	...	...	3,405	3,896	...
7073	Hospital services	...	...	...	5,836	5,230	...	...	...	...	6,328	5,706	...
7074	Public health services	...	...	...	36	36	...	...	...	...	57	56	...
708	**Recreation, culture and religion**	...	...	...	**501**	**567**	...	...	...	...	**1,538**	**1,557**	...
709	**Education**	...	...	...	**8,917**	**9,130**	...	...	...	...	**10,638**	**10,739**	...
7091	Pre-primary and primary education	...	...	...	2,666	2,677	...	...	...	...	3,198	3,186	...
7092	Secondary education	...	...	...	2,753	2,763	...	...	...	...	3,170	3,159	...
7094	Tertiary education	...	...	...	1,777	1,839	...	...	...	...	1,783	1,844	...

Portugal (182)

In Millions of Euros (EUR) / Fiscal Year Ends December 31st

		Budgetary Central Government			Central Government (excl. Social Security)			Central Government (incl. Social Security)			General Government		
		2013P	2014P	2015P	2013P	2014P	2015P	2013P	2014P	2015P	2013P	2014P	2015P
710	**Social protection**	...	...	...	9,216	9,179	...	...	...	...	32,690	32,050	...
7z	Statistical discrepancy: Expenditure	...	...	...	-0	-0	...	...	...	...	-0	0	...
	Table 8 Financial transactions by counterpart sector												
32	**Net acquisition of financial assets**	...	...	...	-1,283	-5,252	-4,709	...	...	...	-1,826	-6,527	-4,235
321	Domestic debtors	...	...	...	-1,878	-5,552	-3,868	...	...	...	-2,070	-5,331	-2,812
8211	General government	...	...	...	...	...	...	...	...	...	—	—	—
8212	Central bank	...	...	...	...	...	...	...	...	...	...	...	...
8213	Deposit-taking corporations except the central bank	...	...	...	...	...	...	...	...	...	...	...	...
8214	Other financial corporations	...	...	...	...	...	...	...	...	...	...	...	...
8215	Nonfinancial corporations	...	...	...	...	...	...	...	...	...	...	...	...
8216	Households & nonprofit institutions serving households	...	...	...	...	...	...	...	...	...	...	...	...
322	External debtors	...	...	...	595	300	-840	...	...	...	245	-1,196	-1,423
8221	General government	...	...	...	...	...	...	...	...	...	...	...	...
8227	International organizations	...	...	...	...	...	...	...	...	...	...	...	...
8228	Financial corporations other than international organizations	...	...	...	...	...	...	...	...	...	...	...	...
8229	Other nonresidents	...	...	...	...	...	...	...	...	...	...	...	...
33	**Net incurrence of liabilities**	...	...	...	7,599	8,598	5,043	...	...	...	6,419	5,876	3,586
331	Domestic creditors	...	...	...	199	-4,748	12,077	...	...	...	-729	-7,398	10,660
8311	General government	...	...	...	...	...	...	...	...	...	—	—	—
8312	Central bank	...	...	...	...	...	...	...	...	...	...	...	...
8313	Deposit-taking corporations except the central bank	...	...	...	...	...	...	...	...	...	...	...	...
8314	Other financial corporations	...	...	...	...	...	...	...	...	...	...	...	...
8315	Nonfinancial corporations	...	...	...	...	...	...	...	...	...	...	...	...
8316	Households & nonprofit institutions serving households	...	...	...	...	...	...	...	...	...	...	...	...
332	External creditors	...	...	...	7,400	13,347	-7,034	...	...	...	7,148	13,274	-7,074
8321	General government	...	...	...	...	...	...	...	...	...	...	...	...
8327	International organizations	...	...	...	...	...	...	...	...	...	...	...	...
8328	Financial corporations other than international organizations	...	...	...	...	...	...	...	...	...	...	...	...
8329	Other nonresidents	...	...	...	...	...	...	...	...	...	...	...	...
	Table 9 Total other economic flows in assets and liabilities												
9	**Change in net worth due to other economic flows**	...	...	...	...	...	...	...	...	...	...	...	...
91	**Other economic flows in nonfinancial assets**	...	...	...	...	...	...	...	...	...	...	...	...
911	Fixed assets	...	...	...	...	...	...	...	...	...	...	...	...
912	Inventories	...	...	...	...	...	...	...	...	...	...	...	...
913	Valuables	...	...	...	...	...	...	...	...	...	...	...	...
914	Nonproduced assets	...	...	...	...	...	...	...	...	...	...	...	...
92	**Other economic flows in financial assets**	...	...	...	-4,723	7,727	1,975	...	...	...	-4,466	7,976	2,061
	By instrument												
9201	Monetary gold and SDRs	...	...	...	—	—	—	...	...	...	—	—	—
9202	Currency and deposits	...	...	...	-1	-90	19	...	...	...	-9	-71	22
9203	Debt securities	...	...	...	13	-12	-128	...	...	...	-136	219	-103
9204	Loans	...	...	...	167	174	-87	...	...	...	167	174	-87
9205	Equity and investment fund shares	...	...	...	-4,406	6,323	560	...	...	...	-4,087	6,444	703
9206	Insurance, pension, and standardized guarantee schemes	...	...	...	-0	—	-0	...	...	...	-0	—	-0
9207	Financial derivatives and employee stock options	...	...	...	-495	1,332	1,619	...	...	...	-402	1,210	1,533
9208	Other accounts receivable	...	...	...	0	0	-7	...	...	...	0	—	-7
	By debtor												
921	Domestic debtors	...	...	...	-4,396	5,908	29	...	...	...	-4,339	5,855	47
922	External debtors	...	...	...	-327	1,819	1,946	...	...	...	-127	2,121	2,014
93	**Other economic flows in liabilities**	...	...	...	3,256	16,662	1,929	...	...	...	2,897	16,417	2,175

Portugal (182)

In Millions of Euros (EUR) / Fiscal Year Ends December 31st

		Budgetary Central Government			Central Government (excl. Social Security)			Central Government (incl. Social Security)			General Government		
		2013P	2014P	2015P	2013P	2014P	2015P	2013P	2014P	2015P	2013P	2014P	2015P
	By instrument												
9301	Special Drawing Rights (SDRs)	...	...	...	—	—	—	...	...	...	—	—	—
9302	Currency and deposits	...	...	...	-182	-359	0	...	...	...	-162	-317	—
9303	Debt securities	...	...	...	3,636	14,244	491	...	...	...	3,410	13,239	571
9304	Loans	...	...	...	-737	1,658	1,786	...	...	...	-610	2,003	1,746
9305	Equity and investment fund shares	...	...	...	-20	-226	-13	...	...	...	-1	-59	-13
9306	Insurance, pension, and standardized guarantee schemes	...	...	...	—	—	24	...	...	...	—	—	24
9307	Financial derivatives and employee stock options	...	...	...	-202	526	-226	...	...	...	-202	526	-226
9308	Other accounts payable	...	...	...	761	818	-133	...	...	...	461	1,024	74
	By creditor												
931	Domestic creditors	...	...	...	1,867	6,220	237	...	...	...	1,483	5,928	483
932	External creditors	...	...	...	1,389	10,442	1,692	...	...	...	1,414	10,489	1,692
	Memorandum items												
9M2	Change in net financial worth due to other economic flows	...	...	...	-7,978	-8,935	46	...	...	...	-7,363	-8,442	-115
9M3	Gross debt (D4) at market value: other economic flows	...	...	...	3,478	16,362	2,169	...	...	...	3,099	15,950	2,415
9M3D3	D3 debt liabilities at market value: other economic flows	...	...	...	3,478	16,362	2,145	...	...	...	3,099	15,950	2,391
9M3D2	D2 debt liabilities at market value: other economic flows	...	...	...	2,717	15,543	2,278	...	...	...	2,638	14,926	2,316
9M3D1	D1 debt liabilities at market value: other economic flows	...	...	...	2,899	15,902	2,278	...	...	...	2,801	15,243	2,316

Romania (968)

In Millions of Romanian Lei (RON) / Fiscal Year Ends December 31st

		Budgetary Central Government			Central Government (excl. Social Security)			Central Government (incl. Social Security)			General Government		
		2013	2014	2015	2013P	2014P	2015P	2013P	2014P	2015P	2013P	2014P	2015P
	Statement of operations												
1	Revenue	...	...	...	142,384	153,699	175,689	195,554	209,107	231,817	212,186	224,352	248,803
2	Expense	...	...	...	150,593	158,469	177,926	201,279	213,023	232,843	209,309	215,638	229,144
GOB	**Gross operating balance**	...	...	...	**-1,820**	**1,099**	**4,217**	**1,097**	**2,388**	**5,864**	**15,828**	**20,087**	**31,581**
NOB	**Net operating balance**	...	...	...	**-8,209**	**-4,770**	**-2,237**	**-5,725**	**-3,916**	**-1,027**	**2,877**	**8,714**	**19,660**
31	Net/Gross investment in nonfinancial assets	...	...	...	8,688	5,506	9,948	8,282	5,128	9,562	16,166	14,364	25,046
2M	Expenditure	...	...	...	159,281	163,975	187,874	209,561	218,151	242,405	225,475	230,002	254,190
NLB	**Net lending (+) / Net borrowing (-)**	...	...	...	**-16,897**	**-10,276**	**-12,184**	**-14,007**	**-9,044**	**-10,589**	**-13,290**	**-5,650**	**-5,387**
32	Net acquisition of financial assets	...	...	...	4,315	14,450	2,223	...	...	...	4,476	15,458	3,524
33	Net incurrence of liabilities	...	...	...	21,521	24,150	14,469	...	...	...	18,240	20,578	9,103
NLBz	Statistical discrepancy	...	...	...	-308	576	-62	...	...	...	-474	530	-193
	Memorandum items												
PB	Primary net lending / net borrowing	...	...	...	-6,505	117	-1,071	-3,658	1,299	479	-2,110	5,361	6,232
GB	Government balance per national definition	...	...	...	...	...	...	...	...	...	...	...	...
	Statement of other economic flows												
	Balance sheet												
6	**Net worth**	...	...	...	...	...	...	...	...	...	...	...	...
61	Nonfinancial assets	...	...	...	...	...	...	...	...	...	...	...	...
62	Financial assets	...	...	...	155,597	175,326	177,263	...	...	...	167,822	188,198	191,925
63	Liabilities	...	...	...	275,957	306,162	319,683	...	...	...	300,637	325,637	334,106
	Table 1 Revenue												
1	**Revenue**	...	...	...	**142,384**	**153,699**	**175,689**	**195,554**	**209,107**	**231,817**	**212,186**	**224,352**	**248,803**
11	**Taxes**	...	...	...	**111,201**	**118,244**	**133,151**	**112,265**	**119,765**	**134,775**	**118,632**	**126,397**	**141,658**
111	Taxes on income, profits, and capital gains	...	...	...	34,835	38,504	43,986	34,835	38,504	43,986	34,908	38,597	44,098
1111	Payable by individuals	...	...	...	22,069	24,390	27,359	22,069	24,390	27,359	22,081	24,400	27,371
1112	Payable by corporations and other enterprises	...	...	...	12,765	14,113	16,626	12,765	14,113	16,626	12,826	14,196	16,727
1113	Other taxes on income, profits, and capital gains	...	...	...	1	0	1	1	0	1	1	0	1
112	Taxes on payroll and workforce	...	...	...	—	—	—	—	—	—	—	—	—
113	Taxes on property	...	...	...	—	1,562	1,057	—	1,562	1,057	4,085	5,860	5,431
114	Taxes on goods and services	...	...	...	76,151	77,966	87,742	77,215	79,487	89,366	79,053	81,421	91,461
1141	General taxes on goods and services	...	...	...	52,083	51,445	57,912	53,147	52,966	59,536	53,373	53,212	59,848
1142	Excises	...	...	...	21,292	23,697	26,503	21,292	23,697	26,503	21,292	23,697	26,503
115	Taxes on international trade and transactions	...	...	...	165	88	251	165	88	251	165	88	251
116	Other taxes	...	...	...	51	125	116	51	125	116	422	432	417
12	**Social contributions**	...	...	...	**180**	**185**	**199**	**54,817**	**56,983**	**57,604**	**54,817**	**56,983**	**57,604**
121	Social security contributions	...	...	...	—	—	—	54,637	56,798	57,405	54,637	56,798	57,405
122	Other social contributions	...	...	...	180	185	199	180	185	199	180	185	199
13	**Grants**	...	...	...	...	...	...	...	...	...	...	...	...
131	From foreign governments	...	...	...	...	...	...	...	...	...	...	...	...
132	From international organizations	...	...	...	...	...	...	...	...	...	...	...	...
133	From other general government units	...	...	...	3,261	3,633	3,737	—	—	—	—	—	—
1331	Current	...	...	...	3,261	3,633	3,737	—	—	—	—	—	—
1332	Capital	...	...	...	—	—	—	—	—	—	—	—	—
14	**Other revenue**	...	...	...	...	...	...	...	...	...	...	...	...
	Table 2 Expense by economic type												
2	**Expense**	...	...	...	**150,593**	**158,469**	**177,926**	**201,279**	**213,023**	**232,843**	**209,309**	**215,638**	**229,144**
21	**Compensation of employees**	...	...	...	**30,475**	**30,849**	**32,598**	**30,911**	**31,251**	**33,023**	**51,681**	**51,419**	**54,618**
211	Wages and salaries	...	...	...	...	...	...	...	...	...	...	...	...
212	Employers' social contributions	...	...	...	...	...	...	...	...	...	...	...	...
22	**Use of goods and services**	...	...	...	**15,479**	**16,449**	**17,459**	**20,618**	**21,722**	**23,287**	**36,421**	**37,948**	**40,208**
23	**Consumption of fixed capital**	...	...	...	**6,389**	**5,869**	**6,454**	**6,822**	**6,304**	**6,891**	**12,952**	**11,373**	**11,921**
24	**Interest**	...	...	...	**10,392**	**10,393**	**11,114**	**10,349**	**10,343**	**11,068**	**11,179**	**11,011**	**11,619**
25	**Subsidies**	...	...	...	**1,871**	**1,233**	**1,291**	**1,873**	**1,237**	**1,304**	**3,450**	**3,187**	**3,521**

Romania (968)

In Millions of Romanian Lei (RON) / Fiscal Year Ends December 31st

		Budgetary Central Government			Central Government (excl. Social Security)			Central Government (incl. Social Security)			General Government		
		2013	2014	2015	2013P	2014P	2015P	2013P	2014P	2015P	2013P	2014P	2015P
26	**Grants**	...	...	...	...	...	...	...	...	...	...	...	...
261	To foreign governments	...	...	...	...	...	...	...	...	...	...	...	...
262	To international organizations	...	...	...	...	...	...	...	...	...	...	...	...
263	To other general government units	...	...	...	54,721	58,525	70,401	42,540	48,175	57,366	—	—	—
2631	Current	...	...	...	51,561	55,028	62,525	39,380	44,678	49,490	—	—	—
2632	Capital	...	...	...	3,160	3,497	7,876	3,160	3,497	7,876	—	—	—
27	**Social benefits**	...	...	...	**14,267**	**14,783**	**16,635**	**71,089**	**73,455**	**77,833**	**74,460**	**76,684**	**81,687**
271	Social security benefits	...	...	...	...	...	...	...	...	...	...	...	...
272	Social assistance benefits	...	...	...	...	...	...	...	...	...	...	...	...
273	Employment-related social benefits	...	...	...	...	...	...	...	...	...	...	...	...
28	**Other expense**	...	...	...	...	...	...	...	...	...	...	...	...
281	Property expense other than interest	...	...	...	—	—	—	—	—	—	—	—	—
282	Transfers not elsewhere classified	...	...	...	...	...	...	...	...	...	...	...	...
2821	Current	...	...	...	...	...	...	...	...	...	...	...	...
2822	Capital	...	...	...	...	...	...	...	...	...	...	...	...
	Table 3 Transactions in assets and liabilities												
3	**Change in net worth from transactions**	...	...	...	**-8,517**	**-4,194**	**-2,299**	...	...	...	**2,403**	**9,244**	**19,467**
31	**Net/Gross investment in nonfinancial assets**	...	...	...	**8,688**	**5,506**	**9,948**	**8,282**	**5,128**	**9,562**	**16,166**	**14,364**	**25,046**
311	Fixed assets	...	...	...	8,449	8,245	9,690	8,043	7,867	9,304	15,837	17,112	24,783
3111	Buildings and structures	...	...	...	...	...	...	...	...	...	...	...	...
3112	Machinery and equipment	...	...	...	...	...	...	...	...	...	...	...	...
3113	Other fixed assets	...	...	...	...	...	...	...	...	...	...	...	...
3114	Weapons systems	...	...	...	...	...	...	...	...	...	...	...	...
312	Inventories	...	...	...	...	...	...	...	...	...	...	...	...
313	Valuables	...	...	...	...	...	...	...	...	...	...	...	...
314	Nonproduced assets	...	...	...	97	-2,935	59	97	-2,935	59	163	-2,923	73
3141	Land	...	...	...	...	...	...	...	...	...	...	...	...
3142	Mineral and energy resources	...	...	...	...	...	...	...	...	...	...	...	...
3143	Other naturally occurring assets	...	...	...	...	...	...	...	...	...	...	...	...
3144	Intangible nonproduced assets	...	...	...	...	...	...	...	...	...	...	...	...
32	**Net acquisition of financial assets**	...	...	...	**4,315**	**14,450**	**2,223**	...	...	...	**4,476**	**15,458**	**3,524**
	By instrument												
3201	Monetary gold and SDRs	...	...	...	—	—	—	...	...	...	—	—	—
3202	Currency and deposits	...	...	...	5,920	10,585	-3,851	...	...	...	6,041	10,844	-3,833
3203	Debt securities	...	...	...	—	10	-96	...	...	...	—	10	-96
3204	Loans	...	...	...	1,020	-336	1,775	...	...	...	250	10	4
3205	Equity and investment fund shares	...	...	...	-2,014	-298	-594	...	...	...	-2,015	-298	-594
3206	Insurance, pension, and standardized guarantee schemes	...	...	...	18	-6	7	...	...	...	18	5	100
3207	Financial derivatives and employee stock options	...	...	...	—	—	—	...	...	...	—	—	—
3208	Other accounts receivable	...	...	...	-629	4,495	4,981	...	...	...	181	4,887	7,943
	By debtor												
321	Domestic debtors	...	...	...	...	...	...	...	...	...	...	...	...
322	External debtors	...	...	...	...	...	...	...	...	...	...	...	...
33	**Net incurrence of liabilities**	...	...	...	**21,521**	**24,150**	**14,469**	...	...	...	**18,240**	**20,578**	**9,103**
	By instrument												
3301	Special Drawing Rights (SDRs)	...	...	...	—	—	—	...	...	...	—	—	—
3302	Currency and deposits	...	...	...	-87	4,650	4,987	...	...	...	-765	2,533	1,999
3303	Debt securities	...	...	...	22,226	27,492	12,439	...	...	...	22,164	27,496	12,391
3304	Loans	...	...	...	-2,053	-5,756	-5,783	...	...	...	-1,978	-5,183	-6,060
3305	Equity and investment fund shares	...	...	...	—	—	—	...	...	...	—	—	—
3306	Insurance, pension, and standardized guarantee schemes	...	...	...	36	38	57	...	...	...	36	38	57
3307	Financial derivatives and employee stock options	...	...	...	—	—	—	...	...	...	—	—	—
3308	Other accounts payable	...	...	...	1,399	-2,276	2,769	...	...	...	-1,218	-4,306	717

Romania (968)

In Millions of Romanian Lei (RON) / Fiscal Year Ends December 31st

		Budgetary Central Government			Central Government (excl. Social Security)			Central Government (incl. Social Security)			General Government		
		2013	2014	2015	2013P	2014P	2015P	2013P	2014P	2015P	2013P	2014P	2015P
	By creditor												
331	Domestic creditors	...	...	...	...	...	...	...	...	...	...	...	...
332	External creditors	...	...	...	...	...	...	...	...	...	...	...	...
	Table 4 Holding gains and losses in assets and liabilities												
	Table 5 Holding gains and losses in assets and liabilities												
	Table 6 Balance sheet												
6	**Net worth**	...	...	...	...	...	...	...	...	...	...	...	...
61	**Nonfinancial assets**	...	...	...	...	...	...	...	...	...	...	...	...
611	Fixed assets	...	...	...	...	...	...	...	...	...	...	...	...
6111	Buildings and structures	...	...	...	...	...	...	...	...	...	...	...	...
6112	Machinery and equipment	...	...	...	...	...	...	...	...	...	...	...	...
6113	Other fixed assets	...	...	...	...	...	...	...	...	...	...	...	...
6114	Weapons systems	...	...	...	...	...	...	...	...	...	...	...	...
612	Inventories	...	...	...	...	...	...	...	...	...	...	...	...
613	Valuables	...	...	...	...	...	...	...	...	...	...	...	...
614	Nonproduced assets	...	...	...	...	...	...	...	...	...	...	...	...
6141	Land	...	...	...	...	...	...	...	...	...	...	...	...
6142	Mineral and energy resources	...	...	...	...	...	...	...	...	...	...	...	...
6143	Other naturally occurring assets	...	...	...	...	...	...	...	...	...	...	...	...
6144	Intangible nonproduced assets	...	...	...	...	...	...	...	...	...	...	...	...
62	**Financial assets**	...	...	...	**155,597**	**175,326**	**177,263**	...	...	...	**167,822**	**188,198**	**191,925**
	By instrument												
6201	Monetary gold and SDRs	...	...	...	—	—	—	...	...	...	—	—	—
6202	Currency and deposits	...	...	...	37,166	47,828	44,476	...	...	...	38,464	49,353	46,012
6203	Debt securities	...	...	...	187	197	100	...	...	...	187	197	100
6204	Loans	...	...	...	10,032	9,693	11,572	...	...	...	6,603	6,610	6,718
6205	Equity and investment fund shares	...	...	...	73,653	77,848	75,467	...	...	...	74,215	78,397	76,266
6206	Insurance, pension, and standardized guarantee schemes	...	...	...	18	12	20	...	...	...	18	23	123
6207	Financial derivatives and employee stock options	...	...	...	—	—	—	...	...	...	—	—	—
6208	Other accounts receivable	...	...	...	34,541	39,748	45,629	...	...	...	48,335	53,618	62,707
	By debtor												
621	Domestic debtors	...	...	...	...	...	...	...	...	...	...	...	...
622	External debtors	...	...	...	...	...	...	...	...	...	...	...	...
63	**Liabilities**	...	...	...	**275,957**	**306,162**	**319,683**	...	...	...	**300,637**	**325,637**	**334,106**
	By instrument												
6301	Special Drawing Rights (SDRs)	...	...	...	—	—	—	...	...	...	—	—	—
6302	Currency and deposits	...	...	...	12,422	17,072	22,059	...	...	...	4,222	6,755	8,754
6303	Debt securities	...	...	...	162,458	196,517	207,797	...	...	...	165,612	199,583	210,816
6304	Loans	...	...	...	69,086	63,212	57,505	...	...	...	81,662	76,209	70,321
6305	Equity and investment fund shares	...	...	...	—	—	—	...	...	...	—	—	—
6306	Insurance, pension, and standardized guarantee schemes	...	...	...	164	202	259	...	...	...	164	202	259
6307	Financial derivatives and employee stock options	...	...	...	—	—	—	...	...	...	—	—	—
6308	Other accounts payable	...	...	...	31,828	29,159	32,063	...	...	...	48,977	42,888	43,957
	By creditor												
631	Domestic creditors	...	...	...	...	...	...	...	...	...	...	...	...
632	External creditors	...	...	...	...	...	...	...	...	...	...	...	...
	Memorandum items												
6M2	Net financial worth	...	...	...	-120,360	-130,836	-142,420	...	...	...	-132,815	-137,439	-142,181
6M3	Gross debt (D4) at market value	...	...	...	275,957	306,162	319,683	...	...	...	300,637	325,637	334,106
6M3D3	D3 debt liabilities at market value	...	...	...	275,793	305,960	319,424	...	...	...	300,473	325,435	333,847
6M3D2	D2 debt liabilities at market value	...	...	...	243,965	276,801	287,361	...	...	...	251,496	282,547	289,891
6M3D1	D1 debt liabilities at market value	...	...	...	231,543	259,729	265,302	...	...	...	247,274	275,792	281,137
6M4	Gross debt (D4) at nominal value	...	...	...	...	...	...	...	...	...	...	...	...
6M4D3	D3 debt liabilities at nominal value	...	...	...	...	...	...	...	...	...	...	...	...
6M4D2	D2 debt liabilities at nominal value	...	...	...	...	...	...	...	...	...	...	...	...
6M4D1	D1 debt liabilities at nominal value	...	...	...	...	...	...	...	...	...	...	...	...

Romania (968)

In Millions of Romanian Lei (RON) / Fiscal Year Ends December 31st

		Budgetary Central Government			Central Government (excl. Social Security)			Central Government (incl. Social Security)			General Government		
		2013	2014	2015	2013P	2014P	2015P	2013P	2014P	2015P	2013P	2014P	2015P
6M35	Gross debt (D4) at face value	...	...	...	...	...	...	...	...	...	...	...	...
6M35D3	D3 debt liabilities at face value	...	...	...	265,272	286,629	299,758	...	...	...	289,754	306,042	314,034
6M35D2	D2 debt liabilities at face value	...	...	...	233,444	257,470	267,696	...	...	...	240,777	263,153	270,077
6M35D1	D1 debt liabilities at face value	...	...	...	221,022	240,399	245,638	...	...	...	236,555	256,399	261,325
6M93	Government gross debt per national definition	...	...	...	233,444	257,470	267,696	...	...	...	240,777	263,153	270,077
6M5	Arrears	...	...	...	...	...	...	...	...	...	...	...	...
6M6	Explicit contingent liabilities	...	...	...	...	...	...	...	...	...	...	...	...
6M61	of which: Publicly guaranteed debt	...	...	...	...	...	...	...	...	...	...	...	...
6M7	Net implicit obligations for social security benefits	...	...	...	...	...	...	...	...	...	...	...	...
	Table 7 Expenditure by functions of government												
7	**Expenditure**	...	...	...	**158,342**	**166,696**	...	...	...	...	**224,466**	**232,690**	...
701	**General public services**	...	...	...	**43,791**	**42,099**	...	...	...	...	**31,290**	**31,289**	...
7017	Public debt transactions	...	...	...	10,800	10,871	...	...	...	...	11,636	11,548	...
7018	Transfers of general character between levels of government	...	...	...	17,493	16,741	...	...	...	...	—	—	...
702	**Defense**	...	...	...	**4,984**	**5,540**	...	...	...	...	**5,000**	**5,554**	...
703	**Public order and safety**	...	...	...	**13,372**	**13,449**	...	...	...	...	**13,993**	**14,056**	...
704	**Economic affairs**	...	...	...	**58,638**	**62,539**	...	...	...	...	**39,316**	**39,703**	...
7042	Agriculture, forestry, fishing, and hunting	...	...	...	5,578	5,857	...	...	...	...	5,744	5,391	...
7043	Fuel and energy	...	...	...	235	168	...	...	...	...	2,318	1,710	...
7044	Mining, manufacturing, and construction	...	...	...	1,608	1,772	...	...	...	...	1,555	1,772	...
7045	Transport	...	...	...	15,908	17,456	...	...	...	...	23,435	26,432	...
7046	Communication	...	...	...	558	427	...	...	...	...	554	427	...
705	**Environmental protection**	...	...	...	**2,543**	**2,914**	...	...	...	...	**5,341**	**5,102**	...
706	**Housing and community amenities**	...	...	...	**2,073**	**4,275**	...	...	...	...	**7,396**	**7,723**	...
707	**Health**	...	...	...	**7,954**	**8,138**	...	...	...	...	**25,576**	**26,749**	...
7072	Outpatient services	...	...	...	206	210	...	...	...	...	790	506	...
7073	Hospital services	...	...	...	4,065	4,149	...	...	...	...	13,363	13,296	...
7074	Public health services	...	...	...	184	188	...	...	...	...	340	343	...
708	**Recreation, culture and religion**	...	...	...	**1,712**	**2,094**	...	...	...	...	**5,536**	**6,353**	...
709	**Education**	...	...	...	**5,789**	**7,834**	...	...	...	...	**17,869**	**20,043**	...
7091	Pre-primary and primary education	...	...	...	14	1,364	...	...	...	...	4,622	5,191	...
7092	Secondary education	...	...	...	214	801	...	...	...	...	6,511	8,065	...
7094	Tertiary education	...	...	...	4,558	4,230	...	...	...	...	4,558	4,201	...
710	**Social protection**	...	...	...	**17,486**	**17,813**	...	...	...	...	**73,147**	**76,118**	...
7z	Statistical discrepancy: Expenditure	...	...	...	0	0	...	...	...	...	—	-0	...
	Table 8 Financial transactions by counterpart sector												
32	**Net acquisition of financial assets**	...	...	...	**4,315**	**14,450**	**2,223**	...	...	...	**4,476**	**15,458**	**3,524**
321	Domestic debtors	...	...	...	...	...	...	...	...	...	...	...	...
8211	General government	...	...	...	...	...	...	...	...	...	—	—	—
8212	Central bank	...	...	...	...	...	...	...	...	...	...	...	...
8213	Deposit-taking corporations except the central bank	...	...	...	...	...	...	...	...	...	...	...	...
8214	Other financial corporations	...	...	...	...	...	...	...	...	...	...	...	...
8215	Nonfinancial corporations	...	...	...	...	...	...	...	...	...	...	...	...
8216	Households & nonprofit institutions serving households	...	...	...	...	...	...	...	...	...	...	...	...
322	External debtors	...	...	...	...	...	...	...	...	...	...	...	...
8221	General government	...	...	...	...	...	...	...	...	...	...	...	...
8227	International organizations	...	...	...	...	...	...	...	...	...	...	...	...
8228	Financial corporations other than international organizations	...	...	...	...	...	...	...	...	...	...	...	...
8229	Other nonresidents	...	...	...	...	...	...	...	...	...	...	...	...

Romania (968)

In Millions of Romanian Lei (RON) / Fiscal Year Ends December 31st

		Budgetary Central Government			Central Government (excl. Social Security)			Central Government (incl. Social Security)			General Government		
		2013	2014	2015	2013P	2014P	2015P	2013P	2014P	2015P	2013P	2014P	2015P
33	**Net incurrence of liabilities**	...	...	...	21,521	24,150	14,469	...	...	...	18,240	20,578	9,103
331	Domestic creditors	...	...	...	...	...	...	...	...	...	...	...	...
8311	General government	...	...	...	...	...	...	...	...	...	—	—	—
8312	Central bank	...	...	...	...	...	...	...	...	...	...	...	...
8313	Deposit-taking corporations except the central bank	...	...	...	...	...	...	...	...	...	...	...	...
8314	Other financial corporations	...	...	...	...	...	...	...	...	...	...	...	...
8315	Nonfinancial corporations	...	...	...	...	...	...	...	...	...	...	...	...
8316	Households & nonprofit institutions serving households	...	...	...	...	...	...	...	...	...	...	...	...
332	External creditors	...	...	...	...	...	...	...	...	...	...	...	...
8321	General government	...	...	...	...	...	...	...	...	...	...	...	...
8327	International organizations	...	...	...	...	...	...	...	...	...	...	...	...
8328	Financial corporations other than international organizations	...	...	...	...	...	...	...	...	...	...	...	...
8329	Other nonresidents	...	...	...	...	...	...	...	...	...	...	...	...
	Table 9 Total other economic flows in assets and liabilities												
9	**Change in net worth due to other economic flows**	...	...	...	...	...	...	...	...	...	...	...	...
91	**Other economic flows in nonfinancial assets**	...	...	...	...	...	...	...	...	...	...	...	...
911	Fixed assets	...	...	...	...	...	...	...	...	...	...	...	...
912	Inventories	...	...	...	...	...	...	...	...	...	...	...	...
913	Valuables	...	...	...	...	...	...	...	...	...	...	...	...
914	Nonproduced assets	...	...	...	...	...	...	...	...	...	...	...	...
92	**Other economic flows in financial assets**	...	...	...	-7,059	5,279	-285	...	...	...	-6,987	4,919	203
	By instrument												
9201	Monetary gold and SDRs	...	...	...	—	—	—	...	...	...	—	—	—
9202	Currency and deposits	...	...	...	353	77	499	...	...	...	467	45	492
9203	Debt securities	...	...	...	—	—	-0	...	...	...	—	—	-0
9204	Loans	...	...	...	-313	-3	104	...	...	...	-313	-3	104
9205	Equity and investment fund shares	...	...	...	-6,764	4,493	-1,788	...	...	...	-6,753	4,480	-1,537
9206	Insurance, pension, and standardized guarantee schemes	...	...	...	—	0	—	...	...	...	—	0	—
9207	Financial derivatives and employee stock options	...	...	...	—	—	—	...	...	...	—	—	—
9208	Other accounts receivable	...	...	...	-335	712	900	...	...	...	-388	397	1,146
	By debtor												
921	Domestic debtors	...	...	...	...	...	...	...	...	...	...	...	...
922	External debtors	...	...	...	...	...	...	...	...	...	...	...	...
93	**Other economic flows in liabilities**	...	...	...	2,349	6,055	-948	...	...	...	3,446	4,422	-634
	By instrument												
9301	Special Drawing Rights (SDRs)	...	...	...	—	—	—	...	...	...	—	—	—
9302	Currency and deposits	...	...	...	0	-1	0	...	...	...	—	-1	0
9303	Debt securities	...	...	...	-77	6,567	-1,159	...	...	...	-70	6,474	-1,157
9304	Loans	...	...	...	860	-118	76	...	...	...	1,087	-269	171
9305	Equity and investment fund shares	...	...	...	-2	—	—	...	...	...	-2	—	—
9306	Insurance, pension, and standardized guarantee schemes	...	...	...	-0	—	0	...	...	...	-0	—	0
9307	Financial derivatives and employee stock options	...	...	...	—	—	—	...	...	...	—	—	—
9308	Other accounts payable	...	...	...	1,568	-393	135	...	...	...	2,432	-1,783	352
	By creditor												
931	Domestic creditors	...	...	...	...	...	...	...	...	...	...	...	...
932	External creditors	...	...	...	...	...	...	...	...	...	...	...	...
	Memorandum items												
9M2	Change in net financial worth due to other economic flows	...	...	...	-9,408	-776	663	...	...	...	-10,433	496	838

Romania (968)

In Millions of Romanian Lei (RON) / Fiscal Year Ends December 31st

		Budgetary Central Government			Central Government (excl. Social Security)			Central Government (incl. Social Security)			General Government		
		2013	2014	2015	2013P	2014P	2015P	2013P	2014P	2015P	2013P	2014P	2015P
9M3	Gross debt (D4) at market value: other economic flows	...	...	...	2,351	6,055	-948	...	...	...	3,448	4,422	-634
9M3D3	D3 debt liabilities at market value: other economic flows	...	...	...	2,351	6,055	-948	...	...	...	3,448	4,422	-634
9M3D2	D2 debt liabilities at market value: other economic flows	...	...	...	783	6,448	-1,083	...	...	...	1,017	6,205	-986
9M3D1	D1 debt liabilities at market value: other economic flows	...	...	...	783	6,449	-1,083	...	...	...	1,017	6,206	-986

Russian Federation (922)

In Billions of Russian Rubles (RUB) / Fiscal Year Ends December 31st

		Budgetary Central Government			Central Government (excl. Social Security)			Central Government (incl. Social Security)			General Government		
		2013	2014P	2015P	2013	2014P	2015P	2013	2014P	2015P	2013	2014P	2015P
	Statement of operations												
1	Revenue	13,638	15,297	14,174	14,451	15,757	15,237	19,579	21,533	26,109	28,752	31,046	33,194
2	Expense	12,349	15,046	13,303	12,968	15,364	13,980	17,959	20,913	25,524	26,365	30,373	30,564
GOB	**Gross operating balance**	**1,923**	**835**	**1,572**	**2,246**	**1,117**	**2,102**	**2,391**	**1,355**	**1,442**	**3,722**	**1,991**	**4,088**
NOB	**Net operating balance**	**1,289**	**251**	**871**	**1,483**	**394**	**1,256**	**1,620**	**621**	**586**	**2,387**	**673**	**2,630**
31	Net/Gross investment in nonfinancial assets	508	1,222	1,870	990	1,346	2,244	998	1,350	2,245	1,872	1,352	3,195
2M	Expenditure	12,857	16,268	15,173	13,959	16,709	16,225	18,957	22,263	27,768	28,237	31,725	33,758
NLB	**Net lending (+) / Net borrowing (-)**	**781**	**-971**	**-999**	**493**	**-952**	**-988**	**623**	**-729**	**-1,659**	**515**	**-679**	**-565**
32	Net acquisition of financial assets	1,664	248	-770	1,397	291	-719	1,544	500	-1,178	1,887	812	139
33	Net incurrence of liabilities	883	1,219	229	905	1,243	269	922	1,229	481	1,372	1,491	704
NLBz	Statistical discrepancy	—	0	-0	—	-0	-0	—	-0	0	—	-0	-0
	Memorandum items												
PB	Primary net lending / net borrowing	1,151	-537	-335	873	-518	-310	1,004	-296	-982	983	-128	246
GB	Government balance per national definition	...	...	...	...	...	...	...	...	...	...	...	...
	Statement of other economic flows												
9	**Change in net worth due to other economic flows**	**848**	**18,646**	**-1,204**	**577**	**18,643**	**-1,503**	**573**	**5,507**	**-1,509**	**764**	**25,949**	**-654**
4	**Change in net worth due to holding gains and losses**	**941**	**18,510**	**-796**	**667**	**18,508**	**-1,108**	**667**	**5,379**	**-1,108**	**876**	**25,857**	**-221**
41	Nonfinancial assets	383	10,732	-2,900	109	14,856	-2,903	109	1,729	-2,903	320	22,302	-2,023
42	Financial assets	475	8,778	2,739	475	4,651	2,429	475	4,659	2,431	473	4,554	2,435
43	Liabilities	-83	1,000	634	-83	1,000	634	-83	1,009	636	-83	1,000	634
5	**Change in net worth due to volume changes**	**-93**	**135**	**-409**	**-90**	**135**	**-395**	**-94**	**128**	**-401**	**-112**	**92**	**-433**
51	Nonfinancial assets	-2	-0	-7	-3	-1	7	-3	-1	7	-11	-13	35
52	Financial assets	-90	131	-85	-86	131	85	-90	125	875	-99	95	663
53	Liabilities	2	-5	316	2	-5	488	2	-5	1,282	2	-9	1,130
	Balance sheet												
6	**Net worth**	**29,404**	**48,301**	**47,968**	**28,985**	**48,016**	**47,769**	**31,423**	**45,405**	**49,766**	**46,588**	**73,020**	**74,996**
61	Nonfinancial assets	14,938	26,892	25,854	16,693	32,888	32,236	16,755	32,970	32,318	30,872	54,521	55,728
62	Financial assets	20,877	30,033	31,917	21,295	23,958	25,754	21,287	21,287	28,698	23,932	29,210	32,447
63	Liabilities	6,410	8,624	9,803	9,004	8,831	10,221	6,618	8,852	11,251	8,216	10,711	13,179
	Table 1 Revenue												
1	**Revenue**	**13,638**	**15,297**	**14,174**	**14,451**	**15,757**	**15,237**	**19,579**	**21,533**	**26,109**	**28,752**	**31,046**	**33,194**
11	**Taxes**	**9,440**	**10,476**	**8,842**	**9,440**	**10,476**	**8,842**	**9,440**	**10,476**	**8,842**	**15,324**	**16,743**	**15,672**
111	Taxes on income, profits, and capital gains	337	408	486	337	408	486	337	408	486	4,814	5,225	5,746
1111	Payable by individuals	—	9	2	—	9	2	—	9	2	2,506	2,631	2,780
1112	Payable by corporations and other enterprises	346	406	497	346	406	497	346	406	497	2,026	2,292	2,637
1113	Other taxes on income, profits, and capital gains	-9	-7	-13	-9	-7	-13	-9	-7	-13	283	301	328
112	Taxes on payroll and workforce	—	—	—	—	—	—	—	—	—	—	—	—
113	Taxes on property	0	0	0	0	0	0	0	0	0	782	850	931
114	Taxes on goods and services	4,129	4,661	4,970	4,129	4,661	4,970	4,129	4,661	4,970	4,753	5,262	5,610
1141	General taxes on goods and services	3,582	4,055	4,387	3,582	4,055	4,387	3,582	4,055	4,387	3,582	4,055	4,388
1142	Excises	547	606	583	547	606	583	547	606	583	1,056	1,076	1,064
115	Taxes on international trade and transactions	4,974	5,406	3,386	4,974	5,406	3,386	4,974	5,406	3,386	4,974	5,406	3,386
116	Other taxes	-0	0	0	-0	0	0	-0	0	0	-0	0	0
12	**Social contributions**	**-7**	**1**	**2**	**-7**	**1**	**2**	**4,933**	**5,624**	**5,483**	**4,602**	**5,222**	**5,483**
121	Social security contributions	-7	1	2	-7	1	2	4,933	5,624	5,483	4,602	5,222	5,483
122	Other social contributions	—	—	—	—	—	—	—	—	—	—	—	—
13	**Grants**	**113**	**75**	**257**	**208**	**75**	**253**	**208**	**75**	**5,264**	**—**	**0**	**0**
131	From foreign governments	—	—	—	—	—	—	—	—	—	—	—	—
132	From international organizations	—	—	—	—	0	0	—	0	0	—	0	0
133	From other general government units	113	75	257	208	75	253	208	75	5,264	0	0	-0
1331	Current	113	75	257	208	75	253	208	75	5,264	0	0	-0
1332	Capital	—	—	—	—	—	—	—	—	—	0	—	—
14	**Other revenue**	**4,093**	**4,745**	**5,073**	**4,811**	**5,205**	**6,139**	**4,999**	**5,359**	**6,520**	**8,826**	**9,081**	**12,039**

Russian Federation (922)

In Billions of Russian Rubles (RUB) / Fiscal Year Ends December 31st

		Budgetary Central Government			Central Government (excl. Social Security)			Central Government (incl. Social Security)			General Government		
		2013	2014P	2015P	2013	2014P	2015P	2013	2014P	2015P	2013	2014P	2015P
	Table 2 Expense by economic type												
2	**Expense**	**12,349**	**15,046**	**13,303**	**12,968**	**15,364**	**13,980**	**17,959**	**20,913**	**25,524**	**26,365**	**30,373**	**30,564**
21	**Compensation of employees**	**2,445**	**2,557**	**2,518**	**3,173**	**3,363**	**3,391**	**3,264**	**3,459**	**3,498**	**6,929**	**7,513**	**7,797**
211	Wages and salaries	2,282	2,382	2,337	2,859	3,022	3,024	2,930	3,097	3,107	5,791	6,254	6,440
212	Employers' social contributions	164	176	181	314	341	367	334	362	391	1,138	1,259	1,357
22	**Use of goods and services**	**1,459**	**1,639**	**1,465**	**1,863**	**2,118**	**1,966**	**1,931**	**2,189**	**2,038**	**4,299**	**4,593**	**4,517**
23	**Consumption of fixed capital**	**634**	**584**	**701**	**763**	**723**	**845**	**771**	**734**	**856**	**1,335**	**1,319**	**1,457**
24	**Interest**	**370**	**434**	**664**	**381**	**434**	**678**	**381**	**434**	**678**	**468**	**551**	**811**
25	**Subsidies**	**956**	**1,810**	**809**	**983**	**1,830**	**862**	**983**	**1,833**	**862**	**3,075**	**4,293**	**3,313**
26	**Grants**	**5,650**	**7,075**	**6,120**	**4,827**	**5,823**	**5,020**	**1,720**	**3,236**	**6,716**	**94**	**1,733**	**184**
261	To foreign governments	28	1,461	46	28	1,461	46	28	1,461	46	28	1,462	46
262	To international organizations	65	82	137	65	85	138	65	85	138	66	85	138
263	To other general government units	5,556	5,533	5,936	4,734	4,277	4,836	1,627	1,691	6,532	0	186	—
2631	Current	5,556	5,533	5,936	4,734	4,277	4,836	1,627	1,691	6,532	0	186	—
2632	Capital	—	—	—	—	—	—	—	—	—	0	—	—
27	**Social benefits**	**728**	**836**	**894**	**728**	**837**	**895**	**8,286**	**8,789**	**10,026**	**9,344**	**9,959**	**11,492**
271	Social security benefits	—	—	—	—	—	—	6,788	7,218	8,295	6,790	7,220	8,317
272	Social assistance benefits	194	244	248	195	244	249	954	969	1,074	1,989	2,111	2,491
273	Employment-related social benefits	534	593	646	534	593	646	543	602	657	566	627	684
28	**Other expense**	**108**	**111**	**132**	**250**	**236**	**324**	**624**	**239**	**849**	**821**	**411**	**992**
281	Property expense other than interest	—	—	—	—	—	—	—	—	—	—	—	—
282	Transfers not elsewhere classified	108	111	132	250	236	324	624	239	849	821	411	992
2821	Current	108	111	132	250	236	324	624	239	849	821	411	992
2822	Capital	—	—	—	—	—	—	—	—	—	—	—	—
	Table 3 Transactions in assets and liabilities												
3	**Change in net worth from transactions**	**1,289**	**251**	**871**	**1,483**	**394**	**1,256**	**1,620**	**621**	**586**	**2,387**	**673**	**2,630**
31	**Net/Gross investment in nonfinancial assets**	**508**	**1,222**	**1,870**	**990**	**1,346**	**2,244**	**998**	**1,350**	**2,245**	**1,872**	**1,352**	**3,195**
311	Fixed assets	157	822	1,745	634	928	1,884	641	932	1,885	1,130	1,587	2,182
3111	Buildings and structures	361	193	811	502	314	1,107	504	318	1,110	712	638	1,186
3112	Machinery and equipment	213	239	385	248	271	394	251	270	392	328	264	355
3113	Other fixed assets	-417	389	549	-116	343	382	-115	344	383	90	685	641
3114	Weapons systems	...	...	...	...	...	...	...	...	...	...	...	...
312	Inventories	193	417	173	199	435	182	199	435	182	223	471	236
313	Valuables	—	—	—	—	—	—	—	—	—	—	—	—
314	Nonproduced assets	158	-17	-48	158	-17	178	158	-17	178	520	-706	777
3141	Land	158	-18	-48	158	-19	176	158	-19	176	520	-712	773
3142	Mineral and energy resources	—	1	—	—	1	0	—	1	0	—	1	0
3143	Other naturally occurring assets	—	1	0	—	1	2	—	1	2	—	5	4
3144	Intangible nonproduced assets	—	—	0	—	—	0	—	—	—	—	—	0
32	**Net acquisition of financial assets**	**1,664**	**248**	**-770**	**1,397**	**291**	**-719**	**1,544**	**500**	**-1,178**	**1,887**	**812**	**139**
	By instrument												
3201	Monetary gold and SDRs	—	...	—	—	—	—	—	—	—	—	—	—
3202	Currency and deposits	80	108	-2,784	108	106	-2,786	74	49	-3,283	-19	49	-3,115
3203	Debt securities	97	5	265	97	26	265	98	24	122	101	25	122
3204	Loans	205	-1,174	260	196	-1,172	284	196	-1,172	284	143	-1,341	120
3205	Equity and investment fund shares	459	463	577	187	467	591	187	467	591	546	703	835
3206	Insurance, pension, and standardized guarantee schemes	—	—	—	—	—	—	—	—	—	—	—	—
3207	Financial derivatives and employee stock options	—	—	—	—	—	—	—	—	—	—	—	—
3208	Other accounts receivable	822	847	912	808	865	927	989	1,132	1,108	1,115	1,376	2,177
	By debtor												
321	Domestic debtors	1,664	248	-770	1,397	291	-719	1,544	500	-1,178	1,887	812	139
322	External debtors	—	—	—	—	—	—	—	—	—	—	—	—
33	**Net incurrence of liabilities**	**883**	**1,219**	**229**	**905**	**1,243**	**269**	**922**	**1,229**	**481**	**1,372**	**1,491**	**704**
	By instrument												
3301	Special Drawing Rights (SDRs)	—	—	—	—	—	—	—	—	—	—	—	—
3302	Currency and deposits	—	—	—	—	—	—	—	—	—	—	—	—
3303	Debt securities	639	925	-22	639	925	17	639	925	17	639	935	28
3304	Loans	62	50	-51	77	62	-46	77	62	-46	449	285	31

Russian Federation (922)

In Billions of Russian Rubles (RUB) / Fiscal Year Ends December 31st

		Budgetary Central Government			Central Government (excl. Social Security)			Central Government (incl. Social Security)			General Government		
		2013	2014P	2015P	2013	2014P	2015P	2013	2014P	2015P	2013	2014P	2015P
3305	Equity and investment fund shares	—	—	—	—	—	—	—	—	—	—	—	—
3306	Insurance, pension, and standardized guarantee schemes	—	—	—	—	—	—	—	—	—	—	—	—
3307	Financial derivatives and employee stock options	—	—	—	—	—	—	—	—	—	—	—	—
3308	Other accounts payable	182	243	302	189	256	298	206	242	509	285	272	645
	By creditor												
331	Domestic creditors	626	293	462	648	317	502	665	303	714	1,114	556	935
332	External creditors	257	926	-232	257	926	-232	257	926	-232	258	936	-232
	Table 4 Holding gains and losses in assets and liabilities												
4	**Change in net worth due to holding gains and losses**	**941**	**18,510**	**-796**	**667**	**18,508**	**-1,108**	**667**	**5,379**	**-1,108**	**876**	**25,857**	**-221**
41	**Holding gains and losses in nonfinancial assets**	**383**	**10,732**	**-2,900**	**109**	**14,856**	**-2,903**	**109**	**1,729**	**-2,903**	**320**	**22,302**	**-2,023**
411	Fixed assets	...	1,512	224	...	1,729	221	...	1,729	221	...	1,916	459
412	Inventories	...	0	1	...	0	1	...	0	1	...	0	1
413	Valuables	...	—	—	...	—	—	...	—	—	...	—	—
414	Nonproduced assets	...	9,221	-3,125	...	13,127	-3,125	...	...	-3,125	...	20,386	-2,483
42	**Holding gains and losses in financial assets**	**475**	**8,778**	**2,739**	**475**	**4,651**	**2,429**	**475**	**4,659**	**2,431**	**473**	**4,554**	**2,435**
	By instrument												
4201	Monetary gold and SDRs	—	—	—	—	—	—	—	—	—	—	—	—
4202	Currency and deposits	481	3,487	1,779	481	3,490	1,781	481	3,490	1,781	479	3,490	1,788
4203	Debt securities	—	72	85	—	72	85	—	72	85	—	72	85
4204	Loans	—	1,122	550	—	1,122	550	—	1,122	550	—	1,122	550
4205	Equity and investment fund shares	—	3,935	316	—	-195	1	—	-186	3	—	-195	1
4206	Insurance, pension, and standardized guarantee schemes	—	—	—	—	—	—	—	—	—	—	—	—
4207	Financial derivatives and employee stock options	—	—	—	—	—	—	—	—	—	—	—	—
4208	Other accounts receivable	-6	162	7	-6	162	11	-6	161	11	-6	66	10
	By debtor												
421	Domestic debtors	475	3,932	2,739	475	-198	2,429	475	-189	2,431	473	-198	2,435
422	External debtors	—	4,846	—	—	4,850	—	—	4,848	—	—	4,753	—
43	**Holding gains and losses in liabilities**	**-83**	**1,000**	**634**	**-83**	**1,000**	**634**	**-83**	**1,009**	**636**	**-83**	**1,000**	**634**
	By instrument												
4301	Special Drawing Rights (SDRs)	—	—	—	—	—	—	—	—	—	—	—	—
4302	Currency and deposits	—	—	—	—	—	—	—	—	—	—	—	—
4303	Debt securities	—	—	591	—	—	591	—	—	591	—	—	591
4304	Loans	-83	999	43	-83	999	43	-83	999	43	-83	999	43
4305	Equity and investment fund shares	—	—	—	—	—	—	—	9	2	—	—	—
4306	Insurance, pension, and standardized guarantee schemes	—	—	—	—	—	—	—	—	—	—	—	—
4307	Financial derivatives and employee stock options	—	—	—	—	—	—	—	—	—	—	—	—
4308	Other accounts payable	—	0	-0	—	0	-0	—	0	-0	—	0	-0
	By creditor												
431	Domestic creditors	-83	0	-0	-83	0	-0	-83	9	2	-83	0	-0
432	External creditors	—	1,000	634	—	1,000	634	—	1,000	634	—	1,000	634
	Table 5 Holding gains and losses in assets and liabilities												
5	**Change in net worth due to other volume changes**	**-93**	**135**	**-409**	**-90**	**135**	**-395**	**-94**	**128**	**-401**	**-112**	**92**	**-433**
51	**Other volume changes in nonfinancial assets**	**-2**	**-0**	**-7**	**-3**	**-1**	**7**	**-3**	**-1**	**7**	**-11**	**-13**	**35**
511	Fixed assets	...	-0	-7	...	-1	7	...	-1	7	...	-13	2
512	Inventories	...	-0	-0	...	-0	-0	...	-0	-0	...	-0	3
513	Valuables	...	—	—	...	—	—	...	—	—	...	—	—
514	Nonproduced assets	...	—	—	...	—	—	...	—	—	...	—	30
52	**Other volume changes in financial assets**	**-90**	**131**	**-85**	**-86**	**131**	**85**	**-90**	**125**	**875**	**-99**	**95**	**663**

Russian Federation (922)

In Billions of Russian Rubles (RUB) / Fiscal Year Ends December 31st

		Budgetary Central Government			Central Government (excl. Social Security)			Central Government (incl. Social Security)			General Government		
		2013	2014P	2015P	2013	2014P	2015P	2013	2014P	2015P	2013	2014P	2015P
	By instrument												
5201	Monetary gold and SDRs	—	—	—	—	—	—	—	—	—	—	—	—
5202	Currency and deposits	—	—	-8	—	—	-3	—	—	353	—	—	352
5203	Debt securities	—	—	—	—	—	—	—	—	1,664	-5	-0	833
5204	Loans	-7	-0	-106	-7	-0	-106	-7	-0	-106	-8	-7	-106
5205	Equity and investment fund shares	—	—	-7	—	—	-7	—	—	-6	—	-5	-6
5206	Insurance, pension, and standardized guarantee schemes	—	—	—	—	—	—	—	—	—	—	—	—
5207	Financial derivatives and employee stock options	—	—	—	—	—	—	—	—	—	—	—	—
5208	Other accounts receivable	-82	131	36	-78	132	202	-82	125	-1,030	-86	108	-410
	By debtor												
521	Domestic debtors	-90	131	-85	-86	131	85	-90	125	875	-99	95	663
522	External debtors	—	—	—	—	—	—	—	—	—	—	—	—
53	**Other volume changes in liabilities**	**2**	**-5**	**316**	**2**	**-5**	**488**	**2**	**-5**	**1,282**	**2**	**-9**	**1,130**
	By instrument												
5301	Special Drawing Rights (SDRs)	—	—	—	—	—	—	—	—	—	—	—	—
5302	Currency and deposits	—	—	—	—	—	—	—	—	—	—	—	—
5303	Debt securities	—	1	-62	—	1	-62	—	1	-62	—	1	-908
5304	Loans	2	-7	0	2	-7	1	2	-7	1	2	-11	16
5305	Equity and investment fund shares	—	—	—	—	—	—	—	—	—	—	—	4
5306	Insurance, pension, and standardized guarantee schemes	—	—	—	—	—	—	—	—	—	—	—	—
5307	Financial derivatives and employee stock options	—	—	—	—	—	—	—	—	—	—	—	—
5308	Other accounts payable	—	1	378	—	1	549	—	1	1,344	—	1	2,019
	By creditor												
531	Domestic creditors	2	-5	316	2	-5	487	2	-5	1,282	2	-9	1,129
532	External creditors	—	—	1	—	—	1	—	—	1	—	—	1
	Table 6 Balance sheet												
6	**Net worth**	**29,404**	**48,301**	**47,968**	**28,985**	**48,016**	**47,769**	**31,423**	**45,405**	**49,766**	**46,588**	**73,020**	**74,996**
61	**Nonfinancial assets**	**14,938**	**26,892**	**25,854**	**16,693**	**32,888**	**32,236**	**16,755**	**32,970**	**32,318**	**30,872**	**54,521**	**55,728**
611	Fixed assets	9,643	11,976	13,938	11,304	13,955	16,067	11,365	14,024	16,137	23,033	26,536	29,180
6111	Buildings and structures	2,726	2,919	5,658	3,739	4,045	7,095	3,774	4,087	7,139	7,966	8,605	11,950
6112	Machinery and equipment	1,883	2,123	2,507	2,272	2,542	2,938	2,286	2,557	2,952	2,998	3,264	3,623
6113	Other fixed assets	5,034	6,934	5,772	5,294	7,368	6,035	5,305	7,380	6,047	12,069	14,668	13,607
6114	Weapons systems	...	...	...	...	...	...	...	...	...	...	...	...
612	Inventories	3,353	3,770	3,944	3,446	3,881	4,064	3,448	3,883	4,066	3,798	4,270	4,510
613	Valuables	—	—	—	—	—	—	—	—	—	—	—	—
614	Nonproduced assets	1,942	11,146	7,972	1,942	15,053	12,105	1,942	15,063	12,115	4,041	23,715	22,038
6141	Land	1,942	11,143	7,972	1,942	15,049	12,103	1,942	15,059	12,113	4,040	23,702	22,024
6142	Mineral and energy resources	—	1	—	—	1	0	—	1	0	1	1	1
6143	Other naturally occurring assets	—	2	0	—	3	2	—	3	2	—	12	14
6144	Intangible nonproduced assets	—	—	—	—	—	—	—	—	—	—	—	—
62	**Financial assets**	**20,877**	**30,033**	**31,917**	**21,295**	**23,958**	**25,754**	**21,287**	**21,287**	**28,698**	**23,932**	**29,210**	**32,447**
	By instrument												
6201	Monetary gold and SDRs	—	—	—	—	—	—	—	—	—	—	—	—
6202	Currency and deposits	6,581	10,178	9,165	6,892	10,490	9,483	7,914	11,456	10,309	8,855	12,397	11,428
6203	Debt securities	100	177	527	100	197	548	246	341	2,212	261	358	1,398
6204	Loans	2,843	2,790	3,495	2,865	2,815	3,543	2,865	2,815	3,543	2,477	2,250	2,815
6205	Equity and investment fund shares	8,005	12,401	13,288	8,086	5,945	6,529	5,674	5,954	6,542	7,531	7,841	8,667
6206	Insurance, pension, and standardized guarantee schemes	—	—	—	—	—	—	—	—	—	—	—	—
6207	Financial derivatives and employee stock options	—	—	—	—	—	—	—	—	—	—	—	—
6208	Other accounts receivable	3,348	4,486	5,442	3,352	4,511	5,650	4,588	6,005	6,092	4,808	6,364	8,139
	By debtor												
621	Domestic debtors	20,877	30,033	31,917	21,295	23,958	25,754	21,287	26,571	28,698	23,932	29,210	32,447
622	External debtors	—	—	—	—	—	—	—	—	—	—	—	—
63	**Liabilities**	**6,410**	**8,624**	**9,803**	**9,004**	**8,831**	**10,221**	**6,618**	**8,852**	**11,251**	**8,216**	**10,711**	**13,179**

Russian Federation (922)

In Billions of Russian Rubles (RUB) / Fiscal Year Ends December 31st

		Budgetary Central Government			Central Government (excl. Social Security)			Central Government (incl. Social Security)			General Government		
		2013	2014P	2015P	2013	2014P	2015P	2013	2014P	2015P	2013	2014P	2015P
	By instrument												
6301	Special Drawing Rights (SDRs)	—	—	—	—	—	—	—	—	—	—	—	—
6302	Currency and deposits	—	—	—	1	—	—	1	—	—	1	—	—
6303	Debt securities	5,764	7,686	8,191	5,764	7,742	8,287	5,764	7,742	8,287	6,219	8,189	7,898
6304	Loans	124	171	165	249	252	251	249	252	251	1,124	1,364	1,455
6305	Equity and investment fund shares	—	—	—	2,411	—	-0	—	9	11	0	—	—
6306	Insurance, pension, and standardized guarantee schemes	—	—	—	—	—	—	—	—	—	—	—	—
6307	Financial derivatives and employee stock options	—	—	—	—	—	—	—	—	—	—	—	—
6308	Other accounts payable	523	767	1,448	578	837	1,684	604	849	2,702	871	1,157	3,825
	By creditor												
631	Domestic creditors	4,955	6,243	7,021	7,549	6,450	7,439	5,163	6,471	8,468	6,743	8,294	10,358
632	External creditors	1,455	2,381	2,782	1,455	2,381	2,782	1,455	2,381	2,782	1,473	2,417	2,820
	Memorandum items												
6M2	Net financial worth	14,467	21,409	22,114	12,292	15,127	15,533	14,669	17,719	17,448	15,716	18,499	19,269
6M3	Gross debt (D4) at market value	...	...	...	...	...	...	...	...	...	...	...	...
6M3D3	D3 debt liabilities at market value	...	...	...	...	...	...	...	...	...	...	...	...
6M3D2	D2 debt liabilities at market value	...	...	...	...	...	...	...	...	...	...	...	...
6M3D1	D1 debt liabilities at market value	...	...	...	...	...	...	...	...	...	...	...	...
6M4	Gross debt (D4) at nominal value	...	...	...	...	...	...	...	...	...	...	...	...
6M4D3	D3 debt liabilities at nominal value	...	...	...	...	...	...	...	...	...	...	...	...
6M4D2	D2 debt liabilities at nominal value	...	...	...	...	...	...	...	...	...	...	...	...
6M4D1	D1 debt liabilities at nominal value	7,548	...	...	...	...	...	7,548	...	...	7,548	...	...
6M35	Gross debt (D4) at face value	6,410	8,624	9,803	6,592	8,831	10,221	6,618	8,843	11,239	8,216	10,711	13,179
6M35D3	D3 debt liabilities at face value	6,410	8,624	9,803	6,592	8,831	10,221	6,618	8,843	11,239	8,216	10,711	13,179
6M35D2	D2 debt liabilities at face value	5,887	7,857	8,355	6,014	7,994	8,538	6,014	7,994	8,538	7,345	9,553	9,354
6M35D1	D1 debt liabilities at face value	5,887	7,857	8,355	6,013	7,994	8,538	6,013	7,994	8,538	7,343	9,553	9,354
6M93	Government gross debt per national definition	...	...	...	...	...	...	...	...	...	...	...	...
6M5	Arrears	...	...	...	...	...	...	...	...	...	...	...	...
6M6	Explicit contingent liabilities	...	...	...	...	...	...	...	...	...	...	...	...
6M61	of which: Publicly guaranteed debt	...	...	...	...	...	...	...	...	...	...	...	...
6M7	Net implicit obligations for social security benefits	...	...	...	...	...	...	...	...	...	...	...	...
	Table 7 Expenditure by functions of government												
7	**Expenditure**	**12,857**	**16,268**	**15,173**	**13,959**	**16,709**	**16,225**	**18,957**	**26,200**	**27,768**	**28,237**	**31,870**	**33,758**
701	**General public services**	**2,381**	**4,832**	**4,328**	**3,417**	**5,104**	**6,232**	**3,422**	**5,265**	**6,397**	**6,370**	**8,034**	**13,573**
7017	Public debt transactions	370	434	664	381	434	678	381	434	678	468	551	811
7018	Transfers of general character between levels of government	677	819	682	...	819	682	723	839	702	15	25	20
702	**Defense**	**1,664**	**1,932**	**1,798**	**1,664**	**1,932**	**1,782**	**1,664**	**1,932**	**1,782**	**1,654**	**1,916**	**1,758**
703	**Public order and safety**	**1,905**	**1,949**	**1,862**	**1,905**	**1,949**	**1,853**	**1,905**	**1,949**	**1,853**	**1,994**	**2,050**	**1,941**
704	**Economic affairs**	**1,503**	**2,678**	**1,500**	**1,512**	**2,795**	**1,373**	**1,512**	**2,795**	**1,373**	**2,666**	**4,121**	**2,179**
7042	Agriculture, forestry, fishing, and hunting	238	212	223	238	212	201	238	212	201	395	359	309
7043	Fuel and energy	20	26	27	20	26	26	20	26	26	33	34	45
7044	Mining, manufacturing, and construction	—	38	32	—	38	30	—	38	30	—	39	30
7045	Transport	349	210	243	358	327	289	358	327	289	533	735	359
7046	Communication	38	40	32	38	40	32	38	40	32	84	86	77
705	**Environmental protection**	**25**	**42**	**49**	**25**	**42**	**26**	**25**	**42**	**26**	**47**	**64**	**40**
706	**Housing and community amenities**	**95**	**87**	**103**	**151**	**141**	**74**	**151**	**141**	**74**	**908**	**870**	**666**
707	**Health**	**464**	**530**	**511**	**464**	**530**	**333**	**1,642**	**3,210**	**3,535**	**2,286**	**2,485**	**2,265**
7072	Outpatient services	97	113	127	97	113	122	98	113	122	163	159	83
7073	Hospital services	157	272	220	157	272	119	157	272	119	446	533	169
7074	Public health services	—	46	48	—	46	32	—	47	32	—	67	39
708	**Recreation, culture and religion**	**364**	**204**	**189**	**364**	**204**	**120**	**364**	**204**	**120**	**822**	**709**	**304**
709	**Education**	**647**	**619**	**598**	**647**	**619**	**198**	**648**	**619**	**198**	**2,824**	**2,921**	**722**
7091	Pre-primary and primary education	50	59	37	50	59	36	50	59	36	548	595	150
7092	Secondary education	76	33	41	76	33	31	76	33	31	1,500	1,567	314
7094	Tertiary education	480	483	488	480	483	110	480	483	110	496	501	113

Russian Federation (922)

In Billions of Russian Rubles (RUB) / Fiscal Year Ends December 31st

		Budgetary Central Government			Central Government (excl. Social Security)			Central Government (incl. Social Security)			General Government		
		2013	2014P	2015P	2013	2014P	2015P	2013	2014P	2015P	2013	2014P	2015P
710	**Social protection**	3,808	3,394	4,236	3,808	3,394	4,235	7,623	10,044	12,411	8,667	8,702	10,308
7z	Statistical discrepancy: Expenditure	—	...	...	—	...	...	—	...	...	—	...	...
	Table 8 Financial transactions by counterpart sector												
32	**Net acquisition of financial assets**	**1,664**	**248**	**-770**	**1,397**	**291**	**-719**	**1,544**	**500**	**-1,178**	**1,887**	**812**	**139**
321	Domestic debtors	1,664	248	-770	1,397	291	-719	1,544	500	-1,178	1,887	812	139
8211	General government	...	...	...	...	...	...	...	...	...	...	...	...
8212	Central bank	...	...	...	...	...	...	...	...	...	...	...	...
8213	Deposit-taking corporations except the central bank	...	...	...	...	...	...	...	...	...	...	...	...
8214	Other financial corporations	...	...	...	...	...	...	...	...	...	...	...	...
8215	Nonfinancial corporations	...	...	...	...	...	...	...	...	...	...	...	...
8216	Households & nonprofit institutions serving households	...	...	...	...	...	...	...	...	...	...	...	...
322	External debtors	—	—	—	—	—	—	—	—	—	—	—	—
8221	General government	—	—	—	—	—	—	—	—	—	—	—	—
8227	International organizations	—	—	—	—	—	—	—	—	—	—	—	—
8228	Financial corporations other than international organizations	—	—	—	—	—	—	—	—	—	—	—	—
8229	Other nonresidents	—	—	—	—	—	—	—	—	—	—	—	—
33	**Net incurrence of liabilities**	**883**	**1,219**	**229**	**905**	**1,243**	**269**	**922**	**1,229**	**481**	**1,372**	**1,491**	**704**
331	Domestic creditors	626	293	462	648	317	502	665	303	714	1,114	556	935
8311	General government	...	...	...	...	...	...	...	...	...	...	...	...
8312	Central bank	...	...	...	...	...	...	...	...	...	...	...	...
8313	Deposit-taking corporations except the central bank	...	...	...	...	...	...	...	...	...	...	...	...
8314	Other financial corporations	...	...	...	...	...	...	...	...	...	...	...	...
8315	Nonfinancial corporations	...	...	...	...	...	...	...	...	...	...	...	...
8316	Households & nonprofit institutions serving households	...	...	...	...	...	...	...	...	...	...	...	...
332	External creditors	257	926	-232	257	926	-232	257	926	-232	258	936	-232
8321	General government	...	...	...	...	...	...	...	...	...	...	...	...
8327	International organizations	...	...	...	...	...	...	...	...	...	...	...	...
8328	Financial corporations other than international organizations	...	...	...	...	...	...	...	...	...	...	...	...
8329	Other nonresidents	...	...	...	...	...	...	...	...	...	...	...	...
	Table 9 Total other economic flows in assets and liabilities												
9	**Change in net worth due to other economic flows**	**848**	**18,646**	**-1,204**	**577**	**18,643**	**-1,503**	**573**	**5,507**	**-1,509**	**764**	**25,949**	**-654**
91	**Other economic flows in nonfinancial assets**	**381**	**10,732**	**-2,908**	**107**	**14,855**	**-2,896**	**107**	**1,727**	**-2,896**	**309**	**22,289**	**-1,988**
911	Fixed assets	...	1,511	217	...	1,727	229	...	1,727	228	...	1,903	461
912	Inventories	...	-0	1	...	-0	1	...	-0	1	...	-0	4
913	Valuables	...	—	—	...	—	—	...	—	—	...	—	—
914	Nonproduced assets	...	9,221	-3,125	...	13,127	-3,125	...	—	-3,125	...	20,386	-2,454
92	**Other economic flows in financial assets**	**386**	**8,909**	**2,653**	**390**	**4,783**	**2,515**	**386**	**4,784**	**3,305**	**374**	**4,650**	**3,098**
	By instrument												
9201	Monetary gold and SDRs	—	—	—	—	—	—	—	—	—	—	—	—
9202	Currency and deposits	481	3,487	1,771	481	3,490	1,778	481	3,490	2,134	479	3,490	2,141
9203	Debt securities	—	72	85	—	72	85	—	72	1,749	-5	71	918
9204	Loans	-7	1,122	445	-7	1,122	445	-7	1,122	445	-8	1,115	445
9205	Equity and investment fund shares	—	3,935	309	—	-195	-6	—	-186	-3	—	-200	-5
9206	Insurance, pension, and standardized guarantee schemes	—	—	—	—	—	—	—	—	—	—	—	—
9207	Financial derivatives and employee stock options	—	—	—	—	—	—	—	—	—	—	—	—
9208	Other accounts receivable	-88	293	44	-84	294	213	-88	286	-1,019	-92	173	-400
	By debtor												
921	Domestic debtors	386	4,063	2,653	390	-67	2,515	386	-64	3,305	374	-103	3,098
922	External debtors	—	4,846	—	—	4,850	—	—	4,848	—	—	4,753	—
93	**Other economic flows in liabilities**	**-81**	**995**	**950**	**-81**	**995**	**1,121**	**-81**	**1,004**	**1,918**	**-81**	**991**	**1,764**

Russian Federation (922)

In Billions of Russian Rubles (RUB) / Fiscal Year Ends December 31st

		Budgetary Central Government			Central Government (excl. Social Security)			Central Government (incl. Social Security)			General Government		
		2013	2014P	2015P	2013	2014P	2015P	2013	2014P	2015P	2013	2014P	2015P
	By instrument												
9301	Special Drawing Rights (SDRs)	—	—	—	—	—	—	—	—	—	—	—	—
9302	Currency and deposits	—	—	—	—	—	—	—	—	—	—	—	—
9303	Debt securities	—	1	528	—	1	528	—	1	528	—	1	-318
9304	Loans	-81	993	44	-81	993	44	-81	993	44	-81	989	59
9305	Equity and investment fund shares	—	—	—	—	—	—	—	9	2	—	—	4
9306	Insurance, pension, and standardized guarantee schemes	—	—	—	—	—	—	—	—	—	—	—	—
9307	Financial derivatives and employee stock options	—	—	—	—	—	—	—	—	—	—	—	—
9308	Other accounts payable	—	1	378	—	1	549	—	1	1,344	—	1	2,018
	By creditor												
931	Domestic creditors	-81	-5	316	-81	-5	487	-81	4	1,283	-81	-9	1,129
932	External creditors	—	1,000	634	—	1,000	634	—	1,000	634	—	1,000	635
	Memorandum items												
9M2	Change in net financial worth due to other economic flows	466	7,914	1,703	471	3,788	1,393	467	3,780	1,387	455	3,659	1,334
9M3	Gross debt (D4) at market value: other economic flows	-81	995	950	-81	995	1,121	-81	995	1,916	-81	991	1,760
9M3D3	D3 debt liabilities at market value: other economic flows	-81	995	950	-81	995	1,121	-81	995	1,916	-81	991	1,760
9M3D2	D2 debt liabilities at market value: other economic flows	-81	994	572	-81	994	572	-81	994	572	-81	990	-258
9M3D1	D1 debt liabilities at market value: other economic flows	-81	994	572	-81	994	572	-81	994	572	-81	990	-258

Rwanda (714)

In Billions of Rwanda Francs (RWF) / Fiscal Year Ends June 30th

		Budgetary Central Government			Central Government (excl. Social Security)			Central Government (incl. Social Security)			General Government		
		2013	2014P	2015P	2013	2014P	2015P	2013	2014P	2015P	2013	2014P	2015P
	Statement of operations												
1	Revenue	...	1,339	1,406	...	1,386	1,455	...	1,515	1,589	...	1,578	1,669
2	Expense	...	907	975	...	935	996	...	977	1,039	...	972	1,040
GOB	**Gross operating balance**	...	**432**	**431**	...	**451**	**459**	...	**538**	**550**	...	**606**	**630**
NOB	**Net operating balance**	...	...	...	...	...	...	...	...	...	...	...	...
31	Net/Gross investment in nonfinancial assets	...	640	677	...	651	697	...	634	694	...	707	769
2M	Expenditure	...	1,547	1,652	...	1,586	1,693	...	1,611	1,733	...	1,678	1,809
NLB	**Net lending (+) / Net borrowing (-)**	...	**-208**	**-246**	...	**-200**	**-239**	...	**-96**	**-145**	...	**-100**	**-139**
32	Net acquisition of financial assets	...	-63	18	...	-54	26	...	50	112	...	43	114
33	Net incurrence of liabilities	...	130	280	...	129	282	...	133	276	...	134	275
NLBz	Statistical discrepancy	...	15	-17	...	16	-18	...	13	-20	...	9	-21
	Memorandum items												
PB	Primary net lending / net borrowing	...	-164	-200	...	-156	-193	...	-52	-99	...	-56	-93
GB	Government balance per national definition	...	...	...	...	...	...	...	...	...	...	...	...
	Statement of other economic flows												
	Balance sheet												
	Table 1 Revenue												
1	**Revenue**	...	**1,339**	**1,406**	...	**1,386**	**1,455**	...	**1,515**	**1,589**	...	**1,578**	**1,669**
11	**Taxes**	...	**728**	**818**	...	**728**	**818**	...	**728**	**818**	...	**740**	**830**
111	Taxes on income, profits, and capital gains	...	288	335	...	288	335	...	288	335	...	297	345
1111	Payable by individuals	...	234	267	...	234	267	...	234	267	...	244	267
1112	Payable by corporations and other enterprises	...	52	65	...	52	65	...	52	65	...	52	65
1113	Other taxes on income, profits, and capital gains	...	2	3	...	2	3	...	2	3	...	2	13
112	Taxes on payroll and workforce	...	...	...	...	—	—	...	...	...	...	—	—
113	Taxes on property	...	1	1	...	1	1	...	1	1	...	4	3
114	Taxes on goods and services	...	383	418	...	383	418	...	383	418	...	383	418
1141	General taxes on goods and services	...	257	281	...	257	281	...	257	281	...	257	281
1142	Excises	...	126	137	...	126	137	...	126	137	...	126	137
115	Taxes on international trade and transactions	...	56	64	...	56	64	...	56	64	...	56	64
116	Other taxes	...	...	...	...	—	—	...	...	...	...	—	—
12	**Social contributions**	...	...	...	...	—	—	...	**92**	**98**	...	**92**	**98**
121	Social security contributions	...	...	...	...	—	—	...	92	98	...	92	98
122	Other social contributions	...	...	...	...	—	—	...	...	...	...	—	—
13	**Grants**	...	**474**	**416**	...	**486**	**429**	...	**489**	**429**	...	**517**	**457**
131	From foreign governments	...	...	...	...	—	—	...	...	416	...	0	0
132	From international organizations	...	474	416	...	486	429	...	486	13	...	517	457
133	From other general government units	...	...	...	...	—	—	...	4	...	...	—	—
1331	Current	...	...	...	...	—	—	...	4	...	...	—	—
1332	Capital	...	...	...	...	—	—	...	...	...	...	—	—
14	**Other revenue**	...	**136**	**173**	...	**172**	**208**	...	**207**	**244**	...	**229**	**283**
	Table 2 Expense by economic type												
2	**Expense**	...	**907**	**975**	...	**935**	**996**	...	**977**	**1,039**	...	**972**	**1,040**
21	**Compensation of employees**	...	**177**	**188**	...	**211**	**231**	...	**217**	**237**	...	**353**	**379**
211	Wages and salaries	...	177	188	...	211	231	...	217	237	...	353	379
212	Employers' social contributions	...	...	...	...	—	—	...	...	...	...	—	—
22	**Use of goods and services**	...	**279**	**257**	...	**315**	**300**	...	**319**	**305**	...	**363**	**347**
23	**Consumption of fixed capital**	...	...	...	...	...	...	...	...	...	...	...	...
24	**Interest**	...	**44**	**46**	...	**44**	**46**	...	**44**	**46**	...	**44**	**46**
25	**Subsidies**	...	**63**	**71**	...	**63**	**71**	...	**63**	**71**	...	**63**	**71**
26	**Grants**	...	**289**	**323**	...	**245**	**257**	...	**245**	**257**	...	**-0**	**-0**
261	To foreign governments	...	...	...	...	—	—	...	...	...	...	—	—
262	To international organizations	...	...	...	...	—	—	...	...	...	...	—	—
263	To other general government units	...	289	323	...	245	257	...	245	257	...	-0	-0
2631	Current	...	289	323	...	245	257	...	245	257	...	-0	-0
2632	Capital	...	...	...	...	—	—	...	...	...	...	—	—

Rwanda (714)

In Billions of Rwanda Francs (RWF) / Fiscal Year Ends June 30th

		Budgetary Central Government			Central Government (excl. Social Security)			Central Government (incl. Social Security)			General Government		
		2013	2014P	2015P	2013	2014P	2015P	2013	2014P	2015P	2013	2014P	2015P
27	**Social benefits**	...	**23**	**23**	...	**23**	**23**	...	**52**	**54**	...	**74**	**77**
271	Social security benefits	...	...	...	...	—	—	...	...	...	...	—	—
272	Social assistance benefits	...	23	23	...	23	23	...	52	54	...	74	77
273	Employment-related social benefits	...	...	...	...	—	—	...	...	...	...	—	—
28	**Other expense**	...	**32**	**68**	...	**34**	**69**	...	**37**	**70**	...	**74**	**119**
281	Property expense other than interest	...	...	...	...	—	—	...	...	...	...	—	—
282	Transfers not elsewhere classified	...	32	68	...	34	69	...	37	70	...	74	119
2821	Current	...	32	68	...	34	69	...	37	70	...	74	119
2822	Capital	...	...	...	...	—	—	...	...	...	...	—	—
	Table 3 Transactions in assets and liabilities												
3	**Change in net worth from transactions**	...	**447**	**415**	...	**467**	**440**	...	**551**	**529**	...	**615**	**609**
31	**Net/Gross investment in nonfinancial assets**	...	**640**	**677**	...	**651**	**697**	...	**634**	**694**	...	**707**	**769**
311	Fixed assets	...	636	671	...	647	691	...	630	688	...	703	763
3111	Buildings and structures	...	636	671	...	647	691	...	630	688	...	703	763
3112	Machinery and equipment	...	...	...	...	—	—	...	...	...	...	—	—
3113	Other fixed assets	...	...	...	...	—	—	...	...	...	...	—	—
3114	Weapons systems	...	...	...	...	—	—	...	...	...	...	—	—
312	Inventories	...	2	2	...	2	2	...	2	2	...	2	2
313	Valuables	...	...	...	...	—	—	...	...	...	...	—	—
314	Nonproduced assets	...	2	4	...	2	4	...	2	4	...	2	4
3141	Land	...	2	4	...	2	4	...	2	4	...	2	4
3142	Mineral and energy resources	...	...	...	...	—	—	...	...	...	...	—	—
3143	Other naturally occurring assets	...	...	...	...	—	—	...	...	...	...	—	—
3144	Intangible nonproduced assets	...	...	...	...	—	—	...	...	...	...	—	—
32	**Net acquisition of financial assets**	...	**-63**	**18**	...	**-54**	**26**	...	**50**	**112**	...	**43**	**114**
	By instrument												
3201	Monetary gold and SDRs	...	...	...	...	—	—	...	—	—	...	—	—
3202	Currency and deposits	...	-89	-45	...	-87	-43	...	3	-10	...	-2	-6
3203	Debt securities	...	...	...	...	—	—	...	-19	15	...	-19	15
3204	Loans	...	26	64	...	33	64	...	30	62	...	30	62
3205	Equity and investment fund shares	...	...	...	...	—	—	...	29	48	...	29	48
3206	Insurance, pension, and standardized guarantee schemes	...	...	...	...	—	—	...	...	...	...	—	—
3207	Financial derivatives and employee stock options	...	...	...	...	—	—	...	...	...	...	—	—
3208	Other accounts receivable	...	...	...	...	—	5	...	7	-3	...	5	-5
	By debtor												
321	Domestic debtors	...	-63	18	...	-54	26	...	50	112	...	43	114
322	External debtors	...	...	...	...	—	—	...	...	—	...	—	—
33	**Net incurrence of liabilities**	...	**130**	**280**	...	**129**	**282**	...	**133**	**276**	...	**134**	**275**
	By instrument												
3301	Special Drawing Rights (SDRs)	...	...	...	...	—	—	...	...	...	...	—	—
3302	Currency and deposits	...	...	...	...	—	—	...	—	...	...	—	—
3303	Debt securities	...	35	111	...	35	111	...	35	111	...	35	111
3304	Loans	...	93	159	...	95	163	...	95	163	...	94	163
3305	Equity and investment fund shares	...	...	...	...	—	—	...	...	...	...	—	—
3306	Insurance, pension, and standardized guarantee schemes	...	—	...	...	—	—	...	0	...	...	0	—
3307	Financial derivatives and employee stock options	...	...	...	...	—	—	...	...	...	...	—	—
3308	Other accounts payable	...	1	10	...	-1	9	...	3	2	...	4	1
	By creditor												
331	Domestic creditors	...	25	280	...	24	282	...	28	276	...	29	275
332	External creditors	...	105	...	...	105	—	...	105	...	...	105	—
	Table 4 Holding gains and losses in assets and liabilities												
	Table 5 Holding gains and losses in assets and liabilities												
	Table 6 Balance sheet												

Rwanda (714)

In Billions of Rwanda Francs (RWF) / Fiscal Year Ends June 30th

	Budgetary Central Government			Central Government (excl. Social Security)			Central Government (incl. Social Security)			General Government		
	2013	2014P	2015P	2013	2014P	2015P	2013	2014P	2015P	2013	2014P	2015P
Table 7 Expenditure by functions of government												
Table 8 Financial transactions by counterpart sector												
Table 9 Total other economic flows in assets and liabilities												

Samoa (862)

In Thousands of Samoa Tala (WST) / Fiscal Year Ends June 30th

		Budgetary Central Government			Central Government (excl. Social Security)			Central Government (incl. Social Security)			General Government		
		2014	2015	2016	2014	2015	2016	2014	2015	2016	2014	2015	2016
	Statement of operations												
1	Revenue	555,388	534,355	595,587	...	...	...	...	...	...	...	...	...
2	Expense	529,866	526,698	503,926	...	...	...	...	...	...	...	...	...
GOB	**Gross operating balance**	**25,522**	**7,657**	**91,661**	...	...	...	...	...	...	...	...	...
NOB	**Net operating balance**	...	...	...	...	...	...	...	...	...	...	...	...
31	Net/Gross investment in nonfinancial assets	124,244	83,316	99,300	...	...	...	...	...	...	...	...	...
2M	Expenditure	654,110	610,015	603,226	...	...	...	...	...	...	...	...	...
NLB	**Net lending (+) / Net borrowing (-)**	**-98,722**	**-75,659**	**-7,639**	...	...	...	...	...	...	...	...	...
32	Net acquisition of financial assets	-10,425	-35,247	-8,474	...	...	...	...	...	...	...	...	...
33	Net incurrence of liabilities	88,297	40,412	-835	...	...	...	...	...	...	...	...	...
NLBz	Statistical discrepancy	-0	0	0	...	...	...	...	...	...	...	...	...
	Memorandum items												
PB	Primary net lending / net borrowing	-83,838	-57,739	10,803	...	...	...	...	...	...	...	...	...
GB	Government balance per national definition	...	...	...	...	...	...	...	...	...	...	...	...
	Statement of other economic flows												
	Balance sheet												
	Table 1 Revenue												
1	**Revenue**	**555,388**	**534,355**	**595,587**	...	...	...	...	...	...	...	...	...
11	**Taxes**	**430,360**	**442,022**	**497,562**	...	...	...	...	...	...	...	...	...
111	Taxes on income, profits, and capital gains	103,319	107,385	114,323	...	...	...	...	...	...	...	...	...
1111	Payable by individuals	57,843	59,431	63,805	...	...	...	...	...	...	...	...	...
1112	Payable by corporations and other enterprises	45,476	47,954	50,518	...	...	...	...	...	...	...	...	...
1113	Other taxes on income, profits, and capital gains	—	—	—	...	...	...	...	...	...	...	...	...
112	Taxes on payroll and workforce	—	—	—	...	...	...	...	...	...	...	...	...
113	Taxes on property	3,013	2,404	2,869	...	...	...	...	...	...	...	...	...
114	Taxes on goods and services	271,297	282,157	325,957	...	...	...	...	...	...	...	...	...
1141	General taxes on goods and services	169,928	177,176	199,627	...	...	...	...	...	...	...	...	...
1142	Excises	9,623	9,934	12,049	...	...	...	...	...	...	...	...	...
115	Taxes on international trade and transactions	52,731	50,077	54,414	...	...	...	...	...	...	...	...	...
116	Other taxes	—	—	—	...	...	...	...	...	...	...	...	...
12	**Social contributions**	—	—	—	...	...	...	...	...	...	...	...	...
121	Social security contributions	—	—	—	...	...	...	...	...	...	...	...	...
122	Other social contributions	—	—	—	...	...	...	...	...	...	...	...	...
13	**Grants**	**81,834**	**41,167**	**45,426**	...	...	...	...	...	...	...	...	...
131	From foreign governments	81,834	41,167	45,426	...	...	...	...	...	...	...	...	...
132	From international organizations	—	—	—	...	...	...	...	...	...	...	...	...
133	From other general government units	—	—	—	...	...	...	...	...	...	...	...	...
1331	Current	—	—	—	...	...	...	...	...	...	...	...	...
1332	Capital	—	—	—	...	...	...	...	...	...	...	...	...
14	**Other revenue**	**43,194**	**51,166**	**52,599**	...	...	...	...	...	...	...	...	...
	Table 2 Expense by economic type												
2	**Expense**	**529,866**	**526,698**	**503,926**	...	...	...	...	...	...	...	...	...
21	**Compensation of employees**	**143,863**	**154,553**	**163,452**	...	...	...	...	...	...	...	...	...
211	Wages and salaries	135,990	146,086	153,042	...	...	...	...	...	...	...	...	...
212	Employers' social contributions	7,874	8,468	10,410	...	...	...	...	...	...	...	...	...
22	**Use of goods and services**	**142,685**	**151,689**	**120,339**	...	...	...	...	...	...	...	...	...
23	**Consumption of fixed capital**	...	...	...	...	...	...	...	...	...	...	...	...
24	**Interest**	**14,884**	**17,920**	**18,442**	...	...	...	...	...	...	...	...	...
25	**Subsidies**	**17,792**	**17,818**	**15,066**	...	...	...	...	...	...	...	...	...
26	**Grants**	**189,697**	**165,243**	**163,605**	...	...	...	...	...	...	...	...	...
261	To foreign governments	—	—	—	...	...	...	...	...	...	...	...	...
262	To international organizations	—	—	—	...	...	...	...	...	...	...	...	...
263	To other general government units	189,697	165,243	163,605	...	...	...	...	...	...	...	...	...
2631	Current	189,697	165,243	163,605	...	...	...	...	...	...	...	...	...
2632	Capital	—	—	—	...	...	...	...	...	...	...	...	...

Samoa (862)

In Thousands of Samoa Tala (WST) / Fiscal Year Ends June 30th

		Budgetary Central Government			Central Government (excl. Social Security)			Central Government (incl. Social Security)			General Government		
		2014	2015	2016	2014	2015	2016	2014	2015	2016	2014	2015	2016
27	**Social benefits**	**17,610**	**17,647**	**17,872**	**...**	**...**	**...**	**...**	**...**	**...**	**...**	**...**	**...**
271	Social security benefits	—	—	—	...	...	...	...	...	...	...	...	...
272	Social assistance benefits	17,610	17,647	17,872	...	...	...	...	...	...	...	...	...
273	Employment-related social benefits	—	—	—	...	...	...	...	...	...	...	...	...
28	**Other expense**	**3,335**	**1,828**	**5,149**	**...**	**...**	**...**	**...**	**...**	**...**	**...**	**...**	**...**
281	Property expense other than interest	—	—	—	...	...	...	...	...	...	...	...	...
282	Transfers not elsewhere classified	3,335	1,828	5,149	...	...	...	...	...	...	...	...	...
2821	Current	3,335	1,828	5,149	...	...	...	...	...	...	...	...	...
2822	Capital	—	—	—	...	...	...	...	...	...	...	...	...
	Table 3 Transactions in assets and liabilities												
3	**Change in net worth from transactions**	**...**	**...**	**...**	**...**	**...**	**...**	**...**	**...**	**...**	**...**	**...**	**...**
31	**Net/Gross investment in nonfinancial assets**	**124,244**	**83,316**	**99,300**	**...**	**...**	**...**	**...**	**...**	**...**	**...**	**...**	**...**
311	Fixed assets	124,244	83,316	99,300	...	...	...	...	...	...	...	...	...
3111	Buildings and structures	124,244	83,316	99,300	...	...	...	...	...	...	...	...	...
3112	Machinery and equipment	...	...	...	...	...	...	...	...	...	...	...	...
3113	Other fixed assets	...	...	...	...	...	...	...	...	...	...	...	...
3114	Weapons systems	...	...	...	...	...	...	...	...	...	...	...	...
312	Inventories	—	—	—	...	...	...	...	...	...	...	...	...
313	Valuables	—	—	—	...	...	...	...	...	...	...	...	...
314	Nonproduced assets	—	—	—	...	...	...	...	...	...	...	...	...
3141	Land	—	—	—	...	...	...	...	...	...	...	...	...
3142	Mineral and energy resources	—	—	—	...	...	...	...	...	...	...	...	...
3143	Other naturally occurring assets	—	—	—	...	...	...	...	...	...	...	...	...
3144	Intangible nonproduced assets	—	—	—	...	...	...	...	...	...	...	...	...
32	**Net acquisition of financial assets**	**-10,425**	**-35,247**	**-8,474**	**...**	**...**	**...**	**...**	**...**	**...**	**...**	**...**	**...**
	By instrument												
3201	Monetary gold and SDRs	—	—	—	...	...	...	...	...	...	...	...	...
3202	Currency and deposits	-10,425	-35,247	-8,474	...	...	...	...	...	...	...	...	...
3203	Debt securities	—	—	—	...	...	...	...	...	...	...	...	...
3204	Loans	—	—	—	...	...	...	...	...	...	...	...	...
3205	Equity and investment fund shares	—	—	—	...	...	...	...	...	...	...	...	...
3206	Insurance, pension, and standardized guarantee schemes	—	—	—	...	...	...	...	...	...	...	...	...
3207	Financial derivatives and employee stock options	—	—	—	...	...	...	...	...	...	...	...	...
3208	Other accounts receivable	...	...	...	...	...	...	...	...	...	...	...	...
	By debtor												
321	Domestic debtors	-10,425	-35,247	-8,474	...	...	...	...	...	...	...	...	...
322	External debtors	—	—	—	...	...	...	...	...	...	...	...	...
33	**Net incurrence of liabilities**	**88,297**	**40,412**	**-835**	**...**	**...**	**...**	**...**	**...**	**...**	**...**	**...**	**...**
	By instrument												
3301	Special Drawing Rights (SDRs)	—	—	—	...	...	...	...	...	...	...	...	...
3302	Currency and deposits	—	—	—	...	...	...	...	...	...	...	...	...
3303	Debt securities	—	—	—	...	...	...	...	...	...	...	...	...
3304	Loans	88,297	40,412	-835	...	...	...	...	...	...	...	...	...
3305	Equity and investment fund shares	—	—	—	...	...	...	...	...	...	...	...	...
3306	Insurance, pension, and standardized guarantee schemes	—	—	—	...	...	...	...	...	...	...	...	...
3307	Financial derivatives and employee stock options	—	—	—	...	...	...	...	...	...	...	...	...
3308	Other accounts payable	...	...	...	...	...	...	...	...	...	...	...	...
	By creditor												
331	Domestic creditors	35,385	-4,920	-9,936	...	...	...	...	...	...	...	...	...
332	External creditors	52,912	45,332	9,102	...	...	...	...	...	...	...	...	...
	Table 4 Holding gains and losses in assets and liabilities												
	Table 5 Holding gains and losses in assets and liabilities												
	Table 6 Balance sheet												

Samoa (862)

In Thousands of Samoa Tala (WST) / Fiscal Year Ends June 30th

		Budgetary Central Government			Central Government (excl. Social Security)			Central Government (incl. Social Security)			General Government		
		2014	2015	2016	2014	2015	2016	2014	2015	2016	2014	2015	2016
	Table 7 Expenditure by functions of government												
7	**Expenditure**	**654,110**	**610,015**	**603,226**	...	...	...	...	...	...	...	...	...
701	**General public services**	**146,384**	**153,120**	**139,327**	...	...	...	...	...	...	...	...	...
7017	Public debt transactions	13,955	11,438	17,838	...	...	...	...	...	...	...	...	...
7018	Transfers of general character between levels of government	—	—	—	...	...	...	...	...	...	...	...	...
702	**Defense**	—	—	—	...	...	...	...	...	...	...	...	...
703	**Public order and safety**	**37,585**	**40,181**	**41,487**	...	...	...	...	...	...	...	...	...
704	**Economic affairs**	**155,736**	**136,133**	**172,390**	...	...	...	...	...	...	...	...	...
7042	Agriculture, forestry, fishing, and hunting	12,027	21,951	14,215	...	...	...	...	...	...	...	...	...
7043	Fuel and energy	34,728	25,800	21,335	...	...	...	...	...	...	...	...	...
7044	Mining, manufacturing, and construction	1,689	1,593	1,559	...	...	...	...	...	...	...	...	...
7045	Transport	40,854	59,111	101,068	...	...	...	...	...	...	...	...	...
7046	Communication	42,262	3,941	5,878	...	...	...	...	...	...	...	...	...
705	**Environmental protection**	**20,060**	**19,281**	**18,085**	...	...	...	...	...	...	...	...	...
706	**Housing and community amenities**	**28,366**	**28,750**	**21,357**	...	...	...	...	...	...	...	...	...
707	**Health**	**135,021**	**103,444**	**86,786**	...	...	...	...	...	...	...	...	...
7072	Outpatient services	...	...	...	...	...	...	...	...	...	...	...	...
7073	Hospital services	...	...	...	...	...	...	...	...	...	...	...	...
7074	Public health services	...	...	...	...	...	...	...	...	...	...	...	...
708	**Recreation, culture and religion**	**4,516**	**4,426**	**4,791**	...	...	...	...	...	...	...	...	...
709	**Education**	**95,074**	**85,362**	**86,893**	...	...	...	...	...	...	...	...	...
7091	Pre-primary and primary education	...	...	...	...	...	...	...	...	...	...	...	...
7092	Secondary education	...	...	...	...	...	...	...	...	...	...	...	...
7094	Tertiary education	...	...	...	...	...	...	...	...	...	...	...	...
710	**Social protection**	**31,367**	**39,317**	**32,111**	...	...	...	...	...	...	...	...	...
7z	Statistical discrepancy: Expenditure	...	...	...	...	...	...	...	...	...	...	...	...
	Table 8 Financial transactions by counterpart sector												
	Table 9 Total other economic flows in assets and liabilities												

San Marino (135)

In Millions of Euros (EUR) / Fiscal Year Ends December 31st

		Budgetary Central Government			Central Government (excl. Social Security)			Central Government (incl. Social Security)			General Government		
		2013	2014	2015	2013	2014	2015	2013	2014	2015	2013	2014	2015
	Statement of operations												
1	Revenue	275	...	289	367	...	391	528	...	551	528	...	551
2	Expense	305	...	304	396	...	400	582	...	579	582	...	579
GOB	**Gross operating balance**	**-16**	**...**	**-1**	**-9**	**...**	**12**	**-34**	**...**	**-6**	**-34**	**...**	**-6**
NOB	**Net operating balance**	**-30**	**...**	**-16**	**-29**	**...**	**-8**	**-54**	**...**	**-28**	**-54**	**...**	**-28**
31	Net/Gross investment in nonfinancial assets	...	...	...	...	...	...	...	...	...	...	...	...
2M	Expenditure	...	...	...	...	...	...	...	...	...	...	...	...
NLB	**Net lending (+) / Net borrowing (-)**	**...**	**...**	**...**	**...**	**...**	**...**	**...**	**...**	**...**	**...**	**...**	**...**
32	Net acquisition of financial assets	...	...	...	...	...	...	...	...	...	...	...	...
33	Net incurrence of liabilities	...	...	...	...	...	...	...	...	...	...	...	...
NLBz	Statistical discrepancy	...	...	...	...	...	...	...	...	...	...	...	...
	Memorandum items												
PB	Primary net lending / net borrowing	...	...	...	...	...	...	...	...	...	...	...	...
GB	Government balance per national definition	...	...	...	...	...	...	...	...	...	...	...	...
	Statement of other economic flows												
	Balance sheet												
6	**Net worth**	**300**	**...**	**309**	**437**	**...**	**449**	**861**	**...**	**879**	**861**	**...**	**879**
61	Nonfinancial assets	335	...	335	385	...	386	402	...	405	402	...	405
62	Financial assets	576	...	638	652	...	785	1,141	...	1,202	1,141	...	1,202
63	Liabilities	610	...	664	600	...	722	683	...	728	683	...	728
	Table 1 Revenue												
1	**Revenue**	**275**	**...**	**289**	**367**	**...**	**391**	**528**	**...**	**551**	**528**	**...**	**551**
11	**Taxes**	**210**	**...**	**225**	**216**	**...**	**229**	**216**	**...**	**229**	**216**	**...**	**229**
111	Taxes on income, profits, and capital gains	82	...	92	82	...	92	82	...	92	82	...	92
1111	Payable by individuals	82	...	92	82	...	92	82	...	92	82	...	92
1112	Payable by corporations and other enterprises	—	...	—	—	...	—	—	...	—	—	...	—
1113	Other taxes on income, profits, and capital gains	—	...	—	—	...	—	—	...	—	—	...	—
112	Taxes on payroll and workforce	—	...	—	—	...	—	—	...	—	—	...	—
113	Taxes on property	2	...	9	2	...	9	2	...	9	2	...	9
114	Taxes on goods and services	121	...	118	125	...	120	125	...	120	125	...	120
1141	General taxes on goods and services	66	...	62	66	...	62	66	...	62	66	...	62
1142	Excises	34	...	33	34	...	33	34	...	33	34	...	33
115	Taxes on international trade and transactions	3	...	3	3	...	3	3	...	3	3	...	3
116	Other taxes	2	...	3	4	...	4	4	...	4	4	...	4
12	**Social contributions**	**—**	**...**	**—**	**—**	**...**	**—**	**168**	**...**	**172**	**168**	**...**	**172**
121	Social security contributions	—	...	—	—	...	—	168	...	171	168	...	171
122	Other social contributions	—	...	—	—	...	—	1	...	1	1	...	1
13	**Grants**	**1**	**...**	**1**	**1**	**...**	**25**	**0**	**...**	**0**	**—**	**...**	**0**
131	From foreign governments	—	...	—	—	...	—	—	...	—	—	...	—
132	From international organizations	—	...	—	—	...	—	—	...	—	—	...	—
133	From other general government units	1	...	1	1	...	25	0	...	0	—	...	0
1331	Current	1	...	1	1	...	25	0	...	0	—	...	0
1332	Capital	—	...	—	—	...	—	0	...	—	—	...	—
14	**Other revenue**	**64**	**...**	**63**	**150**	**...**	**138**	**144**	**...**	**150**	**144**	**...**	**150**
	Table 2 Expense by economic type												
2	**Expense**	**305**	**...**	**304**	**396**	**...**	**400**	**582**	**...**	**579**	**582**	**...**	**579**
21	**Compensation of employees**	**99**	**...**	**92**	**124**	**...**	**118**	**175**	**...**	**169**	**175**	**...**	**169**
211	Wages and salaries	81	...	75	106	...	99	148	...	141	148	...	141
212	Employers' social contributions	18	...	17	19	...	19	28	...	28	28	...	28
22	**Use of goods and services**	**50**	**...**	**45**	**121**	**...**	**97**	**132**	**...**	**123**	**132**	**...**	**123**
23	**Consumption of fixed capital**	**14**	**...**	**14**	**20**	**...**	**20**	**20**	**...**	**22**	**20**	**...**	**22**
24	**Interest**	**3**	**...**	**5**	**4**	**...**	**6**	**4**	**...**	**6**	**4**	**...**	**6**
25	**Subsidies**	**1**	**...**	**1**	**5**	**...**	**9**	**29**	**...**	**30**	**29**	**...**	**30**

San Marino (135)

In Millions of Euros (EUR) / Fiscal Year Ends December 31st

		Budgetary Central Government			Central Government (excl. Social Security)			Central Government (incl. Social Security)			General Government		
		2013	2014	2015	2013	2014	2015	2013	2014	2015	2013	2014	2015
26	**Grants**	**111**	**...**	**125**	**91**	**...**	**125**	**0**	**...**	**—**	**0**	**...**	**—**
261	To foreign governments	—	...	—	—	...	—	—	...	—	—	...	—
262	To international organizations	—	...	—	—	...	—	—	...	—	—	...	—
263	To other general government units	111	...	125	91	...	125	0	...	—	0	...	—
2631	Current	111	...	125	91	...	125	0	...	—	0	...	—
2632	Capital	—	...	—	—	...	—	—	...	—	—	...	—
27	**Social benefits**	**13**	**...**	**12**	**13**	**...**	**12**	**204**	**...**	**214**	**204**	**...**	**214**
271	Social security benefits	13	...	12	13	...	12	204	...	214	204	...	214
272	Social assistance benefits	—	...	—	—	...	—	—	...	—	—	...	—
273	Employment-related social benefits	—	...	—	—	...	—	—	...	—	—	...	—
28	**Other expense**	**14**	**...**	**10**	**17**	**...**	**13**	**18**	**...**	**14**	**18**	**...**	**14**
281	Property expense other than interest	—	...	—	—	...	—	—	...	—	—	...	—
282	Transfers not elsewhere classified	14	...	10	17	...	13	18	...	14	18	...	14
2821	Current	10	...	8	11	...	10	11	...	10	11	...	10
2822	Capital	4	...	1	6	...	3	7	...	4	7	...	4
	Table 3 Transactions in assets and liabilities												
	Table 4 Holding gains and losses in assets and liabilities												
	Table 5 Holding gains and losses in assets and liabilities												
	Table 6 Balance sheet												
6	**Net worth**	**300**	**...**	**309**	**437**	**...**	**449**	**861**	**...**	**879**	**861**	**...**	**879**
61	**Nonfinancial assets**	**335**	**...**	**335**	**385**	**...**	**386**	**402**	**...**	**405**	**402**	**...**	**405**
611	Fixed assets	272	...	274	321	...	323	336	...	339	336	...	339
6111	Buildings and structures	266	...	268	270	...	272	274	...	276	274	...	276
6112	Machinery and equipment	5	...	5	48	...	48	58	...	58	58	...	58
6113	Other fixed assets	2	...	2	3	...	3	4	...	5	4	...	5
6114	Weapons systems	—	...	—	—	...	—	—	...	—	—	...	—
612	Inventories	56	...	53	58	...	55	60	...	57	60	...	57
613	Valuables	6	...	8	6	...	8	6	...	8	6	...	8
614	Nonproduced assets	—	...	—	—	...	—	—	...	—	—	...	—
6141	Land	—	...	—	—	...	—	—	...	—	—	...	—
6142	Mineral and energy resources	—	...	—	—	...	—	—	...	—	—	...	—
6143	Other naturally occurring assets	—	...	—	—	...	—	—	...	—	—	...	—
6144	Intangible nonproduced assets	—	...	—	—	...	—	—	...	—	—	...	—
62	**Financial assets**	**576**	**...**	**638**	**652**	**...**	**785**	**1,141**	**...**	**1,202**	**1,141**	**...**	**1,202**
	By instrument												
6201	Monetary gold and SDRs	—	...	—	—	...	—	—	...	—	—	...	—
6202	Currency and deposits	56	...	33	125	...	101	510	...	505	510	...	505
6203	Debt securities	201	...	197	203	...	199	203	...	199	203	...	199
6204	Loans	—	...	—	—	...	—	—	...	—	—	...	—
6205	Equity and investment fund shares	1	...	1	1	...	1	1	...	1	1	...	1
6206	Insurance, pension, and standardized guarantee schemes	—	...	—	—	...	—	—	...	—	—	...	—
6207	Financial derivatives and employee stock options	—	...	—	—	...	—	—	...	—	—	...	—
6208	Other accounts receivable	318	...	406	323	...	484	428	...	497	428	...	497
	By debtor												
621	Domestic debtors	576	...	638	652	...	785	1,141	...	1,150	1,141	...	1,150
622	External debtors	—	...	—	—	...	—	—	...	52	—	...	52
63	**Liabilities**	**610**	**...**	**664**	**600**	**...**	**722**	**683**	**...**	**728**	**683**	**...**	**728**
	By instrument												
6301	Special Drawing Rights (SDRs)	—	...	—	—	...	—	—	...	—	—	...	—
6302	Currency and deposits	—	...	—	—	...	—	—	...	—	—	...	—
6303	Debt securities	—	...	—	—	...	—	—	...	—	—	...	—
6304	Loans	191	...	178	191	...	178	191	...	178	191	...	178
6305	Equity and investment fund shares	—	...	—	—	...	—	—	...	—	—	...	—
6306	Insurance, pension, and standardized guarantee schemes	—	...	—	—	...	—	—	...	—	—	...	—
6307	Financial derivatives and employee stock options	—	...	—	—	...	—	—	...	—	—	...	—
6308	Other accounts payable	419	...	486	409	...	544	492	...	550	492	...	550

San Marino (135)

In Millions of Euros (EUR) / Fiscal Year Ends December 31st

		Budgetary Central Government			Central Government (excl. Social Security)			Central Government (incl. Social Security)			General Government		
		2013	2014	2015	2013	2014	2015	2013	2014	2015	2013	2014	2015
	By creditor												
631	Domestic creditors	602	...	655	592	...	714	592	...	623	592	...	623
632	External creditors	9	...	9	9	...	9	91	...	105	91	...	105
	Memorandum items												
6M2	Net financial worth	-34	...	-26	51	...	63	458	...	474	458	...	474
6M3	Gross debt (D4) at market value	...	...	...	...	...	...	...	...	...	...	...	...
6M3D3	D3 debt liabilities at market value	...	...	...	...	...	...	...	...	...	...	...	...
6M3D2	D2 debt liabilities at market value	...	...	...	...	...	...	...	...	...	...	...	...
6M3D1	D1 debt liabilities at market value	...	...	...	...	...	...	683	...	...	683	...	...
6M4	Gross debt (D4) at nominal value	...	...	...	...	...	...	...	...	...	...	...	...
6M4D3	D3 debt liabilities at nominal value	...	...	...	...	...	...	...	...	...	...	...	...
6M4D2	D2 debt liabilities at nominal value	...	...	...	...	...	...	...	...	...	...	...	...
6M4D1	D1 debt liabilities at nominal value	...	...	...	...	...	...	...	...	...	...	...	...
6M35	Gross debt (D4) at face value	610	...	664	600	...	722	683	...	728	683	...	728
6M35D3	D3 debt liabilities at face value	610	...	664	600	...	722	683	...	728	683	...	728
6M35D2	D2 debt liabilities at face value	191	...	178	191	...	178	191	...	178	191	...	178
6M35D1	D1 debt liabilities at face value	191	...	178	191	...	178	191	...	178	191	...	178
6M93	Government gross debt per national definition	...	...	...	...	...	...	...	...	...	...	...	...
6M5	Arrears	...	...	...	...	...	...	...	...	...	...	...	...
6M6	Explicit contingent liabilities	...	...	...	...	...	...	...	...	...	...	...	...
6M61	of which: Publicly guaranteed debt	...	...	...	...	...	...	...	...	...	...	...	...
6M7	Net implicit obligations for social security benefits	...	...	...	...	...	...	...	...	...	...	...	...
	Table 7 Expenditure by functions of government												
7	**Expenditure**	...	...	...	...	...	...	...	...	...	...	...	...
701	**General public services**	...	...	...	...	...	...	...	...	...	...	...	...
7017	Public debt transactions	3	...	...	4	...	...	4	...	...	4	...	...
7018	Transfers of general character between levels of government	...	...	...	...	...	...	...	...	...	...	...	...
702	**Defense**	...	...	...	...	...	...	...	...	...	...	...	...
703	**Public order and safety**	...	...	...	...	...	...	...	...	...	...	...	...
704	**Economic affairs**	...	...	...	...	...	...	...	...	...	...	...	...
7042	Agriculture, forestry, fishing, and hunting	...	...	...	...	...	...	...	...	...	...	...	...
7043	Fuel and energy	...	...	...	...	...	...	...	...	...	...	...	...
7044	Mining, manufacturing, and construction	...	...	...	...	...	...	...	...	...	...	...	...
7045	Transport	...	...	...	...	...	...	...	...	...	...	...	...
7046	Communication	...	...	...	...	...	...	...	...	...	...	...	...
705	**Environmental protection**	...	...	...	...	...	...	...	...	...	...	...	...
706	**Housing and community amenities**	...	...	...	...	...	...	...	...	...	...	...	...
707	**Health**	...	...	...	...	...	...	...	...	...	...	...	...
7072	Outpatient services	...	...	...	...	...	...	...	...	...	...	...	...
7073	Hospital services	...	...	...	...	...	...	...	...	...	...	...	...
7074	Public health services	...	...	...	...	...	...	...	...	...	...	...	...
708	**Recreation, culture and religion**	...	...	...	...	...	...	...	...	...	...	...	...
709	**Education**	...	...	...	...	...	...	...	...	...	...	...	...
7091	Pre-primary and primary education	...	...	...	...	...	...	...	...	...	...	...	...
7092	Secondary education	...	...	...	...	...	...	...	...	...	...	...	...
7094	Tertiary education	...	...	...	...	...	...	...	...	...	...	...	...
710	**Social protection**	...	...	...	...	...	...	...	...	...	...	...	...
7z	Statistical discrepancy: Expenditure	...	...	...	...	...	...	...	...	...	...	...	...
	Table 8 Financial transactions by counterpart sector												
	Table 9 Total other economic flows in assets and liabilities												

São Tomé and Príncipe (716)

In Billions of Sao Tome and Principe Dobras (STD) / Fiscal Year Ends December 31st

		Budgetary Central Government			Central Government (excl. Social Security)			Central Government (incl. Social Security)			General Government		
		2010	2011	2012	2010	2011	2012	2010	2011	2012	2010	2011	2012
	Statement of operations												
1	Revenue	1,459	1,765	1,612	...	...	...	...	...	...	...	...	...
2	Expense	767	851	875	...	...	...	...	...	...	...	...	...
GOB	**Gross operating balance**	**692**	**914**	**737**	...	...	...	...	...	...	...	...	...
NOB	**Net operating balance**	...	...	...	...	...	...	...	...	...	...	...	...
31	Net/Gross investment in nonfinancial assets	1,081	1,466	1,350	...	...	...	...	...	...	...	...	...
2M	Expenditure	1,848	2,317	2,226	...	...	...	...	...	...	...	...	...
NLB	**Net lending (+) / Net borrowing (-)**	**-389**	**-552**	**-613**	...	...	...	...	...	...	...	...	...
32	Net acquisition of financial assets	...	44	-34	...	...	...	...	...	...	...	...	...
33	Net incurrence of liabilities	...	508	645	...	...	...	...	...	...	...	...	...
NLBz	Statistical discrepancy	...	89	-65	...	...	...	...	...	...	...	...	...
	Memorandum items												
PB	Primary net lending / net borrowing	-373	-528	-584	...	...	...	...	...	...	...	...	...
GB	Government balance per national definition	...	...	...	...	...	...	...	...	...	...	...	...
	Statement of other economic flows												
	Balance sheet												
	Table 1 Revenue												
1	**Revenue**	**1,459**	**1,765**	**1,612**	...	...	...	...	...	...	...	...	...
11	**Taxes**	**647**	**726**	**704**	...	...	...	...	...	...	...	...	...
111	Taxes on income, profits, and capital gains	168	226	207	...	...	...	...	...	...	...	...	...
1111	Payable by individuals	106	130	150	...	...	...	...	...	...	...	...	...
1112	Payable by corporations and other enterprises	62	95	57	...	...	...	...	...	...	...	...	...
1113	Other taxes on income, profits, and capital gains	—	—	—	...	...	...	...	...	...	...	...	...
112	Taxes on payroll and workforce	—	—	—	...	...	...	...	...	...	...	...	...
113	Taxes on property	13	9	16	...	...	...	...	...	...	...	...	...
114	Taxes on goods and services	63	56	54	...	...	...	...	...	...	...	...	...
1141	General taxes on goods and services	—	—	—	...	...	...	...	...	...	...	...	...
1142	Excises	—	—	—	...	...	...	...	...	...	...	...	...
115	Taxes on international trade and transactions	312	300	334	...	...	...	...	...	...	...	...	...
116	Other taxes	91	136	93	...	...	...	...	...	...	...	...	...
12	**Social contributions**	—	—	—	...	...	...	...	...	...	...	...	...
121	Social security contributions	—	—	—	...	...	...	...	...	...	...	...	...
122	Other social contributions	—	—	—	...	...	...	...	...	...	...	...	...
13	**Grants**	**752**	**977**	**841**	...	...	...	...	...	...	...	...	...
131	From foreign governments	520	485	178	...	...	...	...	...	...	...	...	...
132	From international organizations	232	492	663	...	...	...	...	...	...	...	...	...
133	From other general government units	—	—	—	...	...	...	...	...	...	...	...	...
1331	Current	—	—	—	...	...	...	...	...	...	...	...	...
1332	Capital	—	—	—	...	...	...	...	...	...	...	...	...
14	**Other revenue**	**60**	**61**	**67**	...	...	...	...	...	...	...	...	...
	Table 2 Expense by economic type												
2	**Expense**	**767**	**851**	**875**	...	...	...	...	...	...	...	...	...
21	**Compensation of employees**	**338**	**369**	**419**	...	...	...	...	...	...	...	...	...
211	Wages and salaries	328	360	409	...	...	...	...	...	...	...	...	...
212	Employers' social contributions	10	10	10	...	...	...	...	...	...	...	...	...
22	**Use of goods and services**	**191**	**234**	**198**	...	...	...	...	...	...	...	...	...
23	**Consumption of fixed capital**	...	...	...	...	...	...	...	...	...	...	...	...
24	**Interest**	**16**	**24**	**30**	...	...	...	...	...	...	...	...	...
25	**Subsidies**	—	—	**0**	...	...	...	...	...	...	...	...	...
26	**Grants**	**137**	**139**	**163**	...	...	...	...	...	...	...	...	...
261	To foreign governments	—	—	—	...	...	...	...	...	...	...	...	...
262	To international organizations	1	5	8	...	...	...	...	...	...	...	...	...
263	To other general government units	136	133	155	...	...	...	...	...	...	...	...	...
2631	Current	136	133	155	...	...	...	...	...	...	...	...	...
2632	Capital	—	—	—	...	...	...	...	...	...	...	...	...

São Tomé and Príncipe (716)

In Billions of Sao Tome and Principe Dobras (STD) / Fiscal Year Ends December 31st

		Budgetary Central Government			Central Government (excl. Social Security)			Central Government (incl. Social Security)			General Government		
		2010	2011	2012	2010	2011	2012	2010	2011	2012	2010	2011	2012
27	**Social benefits**	**—**	**—**	**—**	**...**	**...**	**...**	**...**	**...**	**...**	**...**	**...**	**...**
271	Social security benefits	—	—	—	...	...	...	...	...	...	...	...	...
272	Social assistance benefits	—	—	—	...	...	...	...	...	...	...	...	...
273	Employment-related social benefits	—	—	—	...	...	...	...	...	...	...	...	...
28	**Other expense**	**84**	**85**	**65**	**...**	**...**	**...**	**...**	**...**	**...**	**...**	**...**	**...**
281	Property expense other than interest	—	—	—	...	...	...	...	...	...	...	...	...
282	Transfers not elsewhere classified	84	85	65	...	...	...	...	...	...	...	...	...
2821	Current	84	85	65	...	...	...	...	...	...	...	...	...
2822	Capital	—	—	—	...	...	...	...	...	...	...	...	...
	Table 3 Transactions in assets and liabilities												
3	**Change in net worth from transactions**	**...**	**...**	**...**	**...**	**...**	**...**	**...**	**...**	**...**	**...**	**...**	**...**
31	**Net/Gross investment in nonfinancial assets**	**1,081**	**1,466**	**1,350**	**...**	**...**	**...**	**...**	**...**	**...**	**...**	**...**	**...**
311	Fixed assets	1,081	1,466	1,350	...	...	...	...	...	...	...	...	...
3111	Buildings and structures	...	...	...	...	...	...	...	...	...	...	...	...
3112	Machinery and equipment	...	...	...	...	...	...	...	...	...	...	...	...
3113	Other fixed assets	...	...	...	...	...	...	...	...	...	...	...	...
3114	Weapons systems	...	...	...	...	...	...	...	...	...	...	...	...
312	Inventories	...	...	...	...	...	...	...	...	...	...	...	...
313	Valuables	...	...	...	...	...	...	...	...	...	...	...	...
314	Nonproduced assets	...	...	...	...	...	...	...	...	...	...	...	...
3141	Land	...	...	...	...	...	...	...	...	...	...	...	...
3142	Mineral and energy resources	...	...	...	...	...	...	...	...	...	...	...	...
3143	Other naturally occurring assets	...	...	...	...	...	...	...	...	...	...	...	...
3144	Intangible nonproduced assets	...	...	...	...	...	...	...	...	...	...	...	...
32	**Net acquisition of financial assets**	**...**	**44**	**-34**	**...**	**...**	**...**	**...**	**...**	**...**	**...**	**...**	**...**
	By instrument												
3201	Monetary gold and SDRs	...	—	—	...	...	...	...	...	...	...	...	...
3202	Currency and deposits	...	44	-34	...	...	...	...	...	...	...	...	...
3203	Debt securities	...	—	—	...	...	...	...	...	...	...	...	...
3204	Loans	...	—	—	...	...	...	...	...	...	...	...	...
3205	Equity and investment fund shares	...	—	—	...	...	...	...	...	...	...	...	...
3206	Insurance, pension, and standardized guarantee schemes	...	—	—	...	...	...	...	...	...	...	...	...
3207	Financial derivatives and employee stock options	...	—	—	...	...	...	...	...	...	...	...	...
3208	Other accounts receivable	...	—	—	...	...	...	...	...	...	...	...	...
	By debtor												
321	Domestic debtors	...	44	-34	...	...	...	...	...	...	...	...	...
322	External debtors	...	—	—	...	...	...	...	...	...	...	...	...
33	**Net incurrence of liabilities**	**...**	**508**	**645**	**...**	**...**	**...**	**...**	**...**	**...**	**...**	**...**	**...**
	By instrument												
3301	Special Drawing Rights (SDRs)	...	—	—	...	...	...	...	...	...	...	...	...
3302	Currency and deposits	...	—	—	...	...	...	...	...	...	...	...	...
3303	Debt securities	...	—	—	...	...	...	...	...	...	...	...	...
3304	Loans	...	449	558	...	...	...	...	...	...	...	...	...
3305	Equity and investment fund shares	...	—	—	...	...	...	...	...	...	...	...	...
3306	Insurance, pension, and standardized guarantee schemes	...	—	—	...	...	...	...	...	...	...	...	...
3307	Financial derivatives and employee stock options	...	—	—	...	...	...	...	...	...	...	...	...
3308	Other accounts payable	...	59	87	...	...	...	...	...	...	...	...	...
	By creditor												
331	Domestic creditors	...	59	87	...	...	...	...	...	...	...	...	...
332	External creditors	...	449	558	...	...	...	...	...	...	...	...	...
	Table 4 Holding gains and losses in assets and liabilities												
	Table 5 Holding gains and losses in assets and liabilities												
	Table 6 Balance sheet												

São Tomé and Príncipe (716)

In Billions of Sao Tome and Principe Dobras (STD) / Fiscal Year Ends December 31st

	Budgetary Central Government			Central Government (excl. Social Security)			Central Government (incl. Social Security)			General Government		
	2010	2011	2012	2010	2011	2012	2010	2011	2012	2010	2011	2012
Table 7 Expenditure by functions of government												
Table 8 Financial transactions by counterpart sector												
Table 9 Total other economic flows in assets and liabilities												

Senegal (722)

In Billions of CFA (BCEAO) Francs (XOF) / Fiscal Year Ends December 31st

		Budgetary Central Government			Central Government (excl. Social Security)			Central Government (incl. Social Security)			General Government		
		2013P	2014P	2015P	2013	2014	2015	2013	2014	2015	2013	2014	2015
	Statement of operations												
1	Revenue	1,659	1,935	2,026	...	...	...	...	...	...	...	...	...
2	Expense	1,263	1,776	1,889	...	...	...	...	...	...	...	...	...
GOB	**Gross operating balance**	**396**	**160**	**137**	...	...	...	...	...	...	...	...	...
NOB	**Net operating balance**	...	...	...	...	...	...	...	...	...	...	...	...
31	Net/Gross investment in nonfinancial assets	801	492	524	...	...	...	...	...	...	...	...	...
2M	Expenditure	2,064	2,268	2,413	...	...	...	...	...	...	...	...	...
NLB	**Net lending (+) / Net borrowing (-)**	**-405**	**-332**	**-387**	...	...	...	...	...	...	...	...	...
32	Net acquisition of financial assets	...	122	...	...	...	...	...	...	...	...	...	...
33	Net incurrence of liabilities	...	455	...	...	...	...	...	...	...	...	...	...
NLBz	Statistical discrepancy	...	-0	...	...	...	...	...	...	...	...	...	...
	Memorandum items												
PB	Primary net lending / net borrowing	-292	-193	-227	...	...	...	...	...	...	...	...	...
GB	Government balance per national definition	...	...	...	...	...	...	...	...	...	...	...	...
	Statement of other economic flows												
	Balance sheet												
	Table 1 Revenue												
1	**Revenue**	**1,659**	**1,935**	**2,026**	...	...	...	...	...	...	...	...	...
11	**Taxes**	...	**1,483**	**1,597**	...	...	...	...	...	...	...	...	...
111	Taxes on income, profits, and capital gains	...	402	435	...	...	...	...	...	...	...	...	...
1111	Payable by individuals	...	188	218	...	...	...	...	...	...	...	...	...
1112	Payable by corporations and other enterprises	...	139	151	...	...	...	...	...	...	...	...	...
1113	Other taxes on income, profits, and capital gains	...	75	67	...	...	...	...	...	...	...	...	...
112	Taxes on payroll and workforce	...	21	20	...	...	...	...	...	...	...	...	...
113	Taxes on property	...	26	2	...	...	...	...	...	...	...	...	...
114	Taxes on goods and services	...	787	885	...	...	...	...	...	...	...	...	...
1141	General taxes on goods and services	...	316	651	...	...	...	...	...	...	...	...	...
1142	Excises	...	398	158	...	...	...	...	...	...	...	...	...
115	Taxes on international trade and transactions	...	219	228	...	...	...	...	...	...	...	...	...
116	Other taxes	...	28	27	...	...	...	...	...	...	...	...	...
12	**Social contributions**	—	—	—	...	...	...	...	...	...	...	...	...
121	Social security contributions	—	—	—	...	...	...	...	...	...	...	...	...
122	Other social contributions	—	—	—	...	...	...	...	...	...	...	...	...
13	**Grants**	**188**	**312**	**232**	...	...	...	...	...	...	...	...	...
131	From foreign governments	...	234	223	...	...	...	...	...	...	...	...	...
132	From international organizations	...	66	9	...	...	...	...	...	...	...	...	...
133	From other general government units	...	12	—	...	...	...	...	...	...	...	...	...
1331	Current	...	—	—	...	...	...	...	...	...	...	...	...
1332	Capital	...	12	—	...	...	...	...	...	...	...	...	...
14	**Other revenue**	...	**141**	**197**	...	...	...	...	...	...	...	...	...
	Table 2 Expense by economic type												
2	**Expense**	**1,263**	**1,776**	**1,889**	...	...	...	...	...	...	...	...	...
21	**Compensation of employees**	**465**	**490**	**526**	...	...	...	...	...	...	...	...	...
211	Wages and salaries	...	482	525	...	...	...	...	...	...	...	...	...
212	Employers' social contributions	...	8	1	...	...	...	...	...	...	...	...	...
22	**Use of goods and services**	**314**	**361**	**384**	...	...	...	...	...	...	...	...	...
23	**Consumption of fixed capital**	...	...	...	...	...	...	...	...	...	...	...	...
24	**Interest**	**113**	**139**	**160**	...	...	...	...	...	...	...	...	...
25	**Subsidies**	...	**12**	**51**	...	...	...	...	...	...	...	...	...
26	**Grants**	...	**570**	**600**	...	...	...	...	...	...	...	...	...
261	To foreign governments	...	—	0	...	...	...	...	...	...	...	...	...
262	To international organizations	...	7	9	...	...	...	...	...	...	...	...	...
263	To other general government units	...	563	591	...	...	...	...	...	...	...	...	...
2631	Current	...	208	206	...	...	...	...	...	...	...	...	...
2632	Capital	...	355	385	...	...	...	...	...	...	...	...	...

Senegal (722)

In Billions of CFA (BCEAO) Francs (XOF) / Fiscal Year Ends December 31st

		Budgetary Central Government			Central Government (excl. Social Security)			Central Government (incl. Social Security)			General Government		
		2013P	2014P	2015P	2013	2014	2015	2013	2014	2015	2013	2014	2015
27	**Social benefits**	...	**30**	**60**	...	...	...	...	...	...	...	...	...
271	Social security benefits	...	—	—	...	...	...	...	...	...	...	...	...
272	Social assistance benefits	...	29	54	...	...	...	...	...	...	...	...	...
273	Employment-related social benefits	...	1	6	...	...	...	...	...	...	...	...	...
28	**Other expense**	...	**173**	**108**	...	...	...	...	...	...	...	...	...
281	Property expense other than interest	...	—	—	...	...	...	...	...	...	...	...	...
282	Transfers not elsewhere classified	...	173	108	...	...	...	...	...	...	...	...	...
2821	Current	...	137	108	...	...	...	...	...	...	...	...	...
2822	Capital	...	36	—	...	...	...	...	...	...	...	...	...
	Table 3 Transactions in assets and liabilities												
3	**Change in net worth from transactions**	...	...	...	...	...	...	...	...	...	...	...	...
31	**Net/Gross investment in nonfinancial assets**	**801**	**492**	**524**	...	...	...	...	...	...	...	...	...
311	Fixed assets	...	490	522	...	...	...	...	...	...	...	...	...
3111	Buildings and structures	...	42	42	...	...	...	...	...	...	...	...	...
3112	Machinery and equipment	...	49	73	...	...	...	...	...	...	...	...	...
3113	Other fixed assets	...	399	407	...	...	...	...	...	...	...	...	...
3114	Weapons systems	...	—	—	...	...	...	...	...	...	...	...	...
312	Inventories	...	1	0	...	...	...	...	...	...	...	...	...
313	Valuables	...	—	—	...	...	...	...	...	...	...	...	...
314	Nonproduced assets	...	1	2	...	...	...	...	...	...	...	...	...
3141	Land	...	1	1	...	...	...	...	...	...	...	...	...
3142	Mineral and energy resources	...	—	—	...	...	...	...	...	...	...	...	...
3143	Other naturally occurring assets	...	0	0	...	...	...	...	...	...	...	...	...
3144	Intangible nonproduced assets	...	—	—	...	...	...	...	...	...	...	...	...
32	**Net acquisition of financial assets**	...	**122**	...	...	...	...	...	...	...	...	...	...
	By instrument												
3201	Monetary gold and SDRs	...	—	...	...	...	...	...	...	...	...	...	...
3202	Currency and deposits	...	112	...	...	...	...	...	...	...	...	...	...
3203	Debt securities	...	8	...	...	...	...	...	...	...	...	...	...
3204	Loans	...	-1	...	...	...	...	...	...	...	...	...	...
3205	Equity and investment fund shares	...	—	...	...	...	...	...	...	...	...	...	...
3206	Insurance, pension, and standardized guarantee schemes	...	—	...	...	...	...	...	...	...	...	...	...
3207	Financial derivatives and employee stock options	...	—	...	...	...	...	...	...	...	...	...	...
3208	Other accounts receivable	...	3	...	...	...	...	...	...	...	...	...	...
	By debtor												
321	Domestic debtors	...	106	...	...	...	...	...	...	...	...	...	...
322	External debtors	...	16	...	...	...	...	...	...	...	...	...	...
33	**Net incurrence of liabilities**	...	**455**	...	...	...	...	...	...	...	...	...	...
	By instrument												
3301	Special Drawing Rights (SDRs)	...	-21	...	...	...	...	...	...	...	...	...	...
3302	Currency and deposits	...	19	...	...	...	...	...	...	...	...	...	...
3303	Debt securities	...	285	...	...	...	...	...	...	...	...	...	...
3304	Loans	...	326	...	...	...	...	...	...	...	...	...	...
3305	Equity and investment fund shares	...	—	...	...	...	...	...	...	...	...	...	...
3306	Insurance, pension, and standardized guarantee schemes	...	—	...	...	...	...	...	...	...	...	...	...
3307	Financial derivatives and employee stock options	...	—	...	...	...	...	...	...	...	...	...	...
3308	Other accounts payable	...	-154	...	...	...	...	...	...	...	...	...	...
	By creditor												
331	Domestic creditors	...	-80	...	...	...	...	...	...	...	...	...	...
332	External creditors	...	535	...	...	...	...	...	...	...	...	...	...
	Table 4 Holding gains and losses in assets and liabilities												
	Table 5 Holding gains and losses in assets and liabilities												
	Table 6 Balance sheet												

Senegal (722)

In Billions of CFA (BCEAO) Francs (XOF) / Fiscal Year Ends December 31st

	Budgetary Central Government			Central Government (excl. Social Security)			Central Government (incl. Social Security)			General Government		
	2013P	2014P	2015P	2013	2014	2015	2013	2014	2015	2013	2014	2015
Table 7 Expenditure by functions of government												
Table 8 Financial transactions by counterpart sector												
Table 9 Total other economic flows in assets and liabilities												

Serbia, Republic of (942)

In Billions of Serbian Dinars (RSD) / Fiscal Year Ends December 31st

		Budgetary Central Government			Central Government (excl. Social Security)			Central Government (incl. Social Security)			General Government		
		2010P	2011P	2012P	2010P	2011P	2012P	2010P	2011P	2012P	2010P	2011P	2012P
	Statement of operations												
1	Revenue	710	743	781	743	780	800	1,127	1,194	1,254	1,277	1,363	1,463
2	Expense	781	849	946	807	871	957	1,188	1,281	1,406	1,310	1,413	1,563
GOB	**Gross operating balance**	**-70**	**-106**	**-165**	**-64**	**-92**	**-157**	**-62**	**-87**	**-152**	**-33**	**-49**	**-100**
NOB	**Net operating balance**	...	...	...	...	...	...	...	...	...	...	...	...
31	Net/Gross investment in nonfinancial assets	38	39	48	52	54	66	54	55	66	103	109	118
2M	Expenditure	818	887	994	859	925	1,022	1,242	1,336	1,472	1,413	1,522	1,680
NLB	**Net lending (+) / Net borrowing (-)**	**-108**	**-144**	**-213**	**-116**	**-146**	**-223**	**-115**	**-142**	**-218**	**-136**	**-158**	**-217**
32	Net acquisition of financial assets	-15	35	29	-15	36	29	-15	40	34	-24	39	43
33	Net incurrence of liabilities	93	179	242	101	182	252	101	182	252	112	198	260
NLBz	Statistical discrepancy	0	0	0	0	-0	-0	0	-0	0	0	-0	0
	Memorandum items												
PB	Primary net lending / net borrowing	-78	-104	-150	-84	-103	-159	-83	-100	-154	-102	-114	-149
GB	Government balance per national definition	...	...	...	...	...	...	...	...	...	...	...	...
	Statement of other economic flows												
	Balance sheet												
6	**Net worth**	**335**	**172**	**264**	...	...	...	...	...	...	...	...	...
61	Nonfinancial assets	378	394	413	...	...	...	...	...	...	...	...	...
62	Financial assets	1,073	1,100	1,533	...	...	...	...	...	...	...	...	...
63	Liabilities	1,115	1,323	1,682	...	...	...	...	...	...	...	...	...
	Table 1 Revenue												
1	**Revenue**	**710**	**743**	**781**	**743**	**780**	**800**	**1,127**	**1,194**	**1,254**	**1,277**	**1,363**	**1,463**
11	**Taxes**	**625**	**654**	**691**	**658**	**688**	**707**	**658**	**688**	**707**	**758**	**803**	**867**
111	Taxes on income, profits, and capital gains	105	104	95	105	104	95	105	104	95	172	189	220
1111	Payable by individuals	75	70	46	75	70	46	75	70	46	139	151	165
1112	Payable by corporations and other enterprises	30	34	49	30	34	49	30	34	49	33	38	55
1113	Other taxes on income, profits, and capital gains	—	—	—	—	—	—	—	—	—	—	—	—
112	Taxes on payroll and workforce	—	—	—	—	—	—	—	—	—	—	—	—
113	Taxes on property	—	—	—	—	—	—	—	—	—	13	14	15
114	Taxes on goods and services	476	511	559	508	545	576	508	545	576	524	557	591
1141	General taxes on goods and services	319	342	367	319	342	367	319	342	367	326	350	374
1142	Excises	136	152	181	152	171	181	152	171	181	152	171	181
115	Taxes on international trade and transactions	44	39	36	44	39	36	44	39	36	44	39	36
116	Other taxes	0	0	0	0	0	0	0	0	0	5	5	4
12	**Social contributions**	—	—	—	—	—	—	**379**	**407**	**446**	**379**	**407**	**446**
121	Social security contributions	—	—	—	—	—	—	379	407	446	379	407	446
122	Other social contributions	—	—	—	—	—	—	—	—	—	—	—	—
13	**Grants**	**7**	**2**	**2**	**7**	**2**	**2**	**7**	**2**	**2**	**7**	**3**	**3**
131	From foreign governments	0	0	0	0	0	0	0	0	0	0	0	0
132	From international organizations	6	2	2	6	2	2	6	2	2	7	2	3
133	From other general government units	—	—	—	—	—	—	—	—	—	—	—	—
1331	Current	—	—	—	—	—	—	—	—	—	—	—	—
1332	Capital	—	—	—	—	—	—	—	—	—	—	—	—
14	**Other revenue**	**78**	**87**	**88**	**79**	**89**	**91**	**83**	**97**	**99**	**133**	**151**	**148**
	Table 2 Expense by economic type												
2	**Expense**	**781**	**849**	**946**	**807**	**871**	**957**	**1,188**	**1,281**	**1,406**	**1,310**	**1,413**	**1,563**
21	**Compensation of employees**	**192**	**215**	**239**	**193**	**216**	**240**	**295**	**328**	**357**	**365**	**403**	**441**
211	Wages and salaries	163	183	203	164	184	204	251	279	303	310	342	375
212	Employers' social contributions	30	32	36	30	33	36	45	49	54	55	60	67
22	**Use of goods and services**	**60**	**65**	**69**	**80**	**84**	**85**	**158**	**166**	**175**	**203**	**216**	**236**
23	**Consumption of fixed capital**	...	...	...	...	...	...	...	...	...	...	...	...
24	**Interest**	**30**	**40**	**63**	**32**	**42**	**64**	**33**	**42**	**64**	**34**	**45**	**68**
25	**Subsidies**	**75**	**81**	**93**	**78**	**81**	**93**	**78**	**81**	**93**	**108**	**105**	**127**

Serbia, Republic of (942)

In Billions of Serbian Dinars (RSD) / Fiscal Year Ends December 31st

		Budgetary Central Government			Central Government (excl. Social Security)			Central Government (incl. Social Security)			General Government		
		2010P	2011P	2012P	2010P	2011P	2012P	2010P	2011P	2012P	2010P	2011P	2012P
26	**Grants**	**304**	**321**	**369**	**304**	**321**	**361**	**61**	**68**	**74**	**1**	**1**	**1**
261	To foreign governments	—	—	—	—	—	—	—	—	—	—	—	—
262	To international organizations	1	1	1	1	1	1	1	1	1	1	1	1
263	To other general government units	303	320	368	303	320	360	61	67	73	—	—	—
2631	Current	303	318	364	303	318	355	61	65	68	—	—	—
2632	Capital	—	2	5	—	2	5	—	2	5	—	—	—
27	**Social benefits**	**108**	**110**	**92**	**108**	**110**	**92**	**551**	**579**	**619**	**577**	**609**	**652**
271	Social security benefits	—	—	—	—	—	—	443	469	527	443	469	527
272	Social assistance benefits	108	110	92	108	110	92	108	110	92	134	140	126
273	Employment-related social benefits	—	—	—	—	—	—	—	—	—	—	—	—
28	**Other expense**	**11**	**17**	**20**	**12**	**17**	**21**	**12**	**17**	**22**	**22**	**34**	**37**
281	Property expense other than interest	—	—	—	—	—	—	—	—	—	—	—	—
282	Transfers not elsewhere classified	11	17	20	12	17	21	12	17	22	22	34	37
2821	Current	11	16	18	12	16	19	12	16	20	22	33	35
2822	Capital	—	1	2	—	1	2	—	1	2	—	1	2
	Table 3 Transactions in assets and liabilities												
3	**Change in net worth from transactions**	...	...	...	...	...	...	...	...	...	...	...	...
31	**Net/Gross investment in nonfinancial assets**	**38**	**39**	**48**	**52**	**54**	**66**	**54**	**55**	**66**	**103**	**109**	**118**
311	Fixed assets	35	37	44	48	50	59	49	51	60	97	104	111
3111	Buildings and structures	28	29	38	40	42	53	42	43	54	90	96	105
3112	Machinery and equipment	7	7	5	7	7	6	7	7	6	7	7	6
3113	Other fixed assets	—	0	0	0	0	0	0	0	0	0	0	0
3114	Weapons systems	...	...	...	...	...	...	...	...	...	...	...	...
312	Inventories	1	1	2	1	1	2	1	1	2	1	2	3
313	Valuables	—	—	—	—	—	—	—	—	—	—	—	—
314	Nonproduced assets	1	1	2	4	3	4	4	3	4	5	3	3
3141	Land	0	1	2	3	3	4	3	3	4	4	3	3
3142	Mineral and energy resources	—	—	—	—	—	—	—	—	—	—	—	—
3143	Other naturally occurring assets	—	—	—	—	—	—	—	—	—	—	—	—
3144	Intangible nonproduced assets	1	—	—	1	—	—	1	—	—	1	—	—
32	**Net acquisition of financial assets**	**-15**	**35**	**29**	**-15**	**36**	**29**	**-15**	**40**	**34**	**-24**	**39**	**43**
	By instrument												
3201	Monetary gold and SDRs	—	—	—	—	—	—	—	—	—	—	—	—
3202	Currency and deposits	-10	35	20	-11	37	20	-9	41	25	-17	42	32
3203	Debt securities	—	—	—	—	—	—	—	—	—	—	—	—
3204	Loans	-1	-1	-1	-1	-1	-1	-1	-1	-2	-1	-1	-2
3205	Equity and investment fund shares	-4	0	10	-4	0	10	-4	-0	10	-6	-2	13
3206	Insurance, pension, and standardized guarantee schemes	—	—	—	—	—	—	—	—	—	—	—	—
3207	Financial derivatives and employee stock options	—	—	—	—	—	—	—	—	—	—	—	—
3208	Other accounts receivable	—	—	...	—	—	...	—	—	...	—	—	...
	By debtor												
321	Domestic debtors	-15	35	29	-15	36	29	-15	40	34	-24	39	43
322	External debtors	—	—	—	—	—	—	—	—	—	—	—	—
33	**Net incurrence of liabilities**	**93**	**179**	**242**	**101**	**182**	**252**	**101**	**182**	**252**	**112**	**198**	**260**
	By instrument												
3301	Special Drawing Rights (SDRs)	—	—	—	—	—	—	—	—	—	—	—	—
3302	Currency and deposits	—	—	—	—	—	—	—	—	—	—	—	—
3303	Debt securities	34	176	278	34	176	278	34	176	278	34	176	282
3304	Loans	59	3	-35	67	6	-26	67	6	-26	78	22	-21
3305	Equity and investment fund shares	—	—	—	—	—	—	—	—	—	—	—	—
3306	Insurance, pension, and standardized guarantee schemes	—	—	—	—	—	—	—	—	—	—	—	—
3307	Financial derivatives and employee stock options	—	—	—	—	—	—	—	—	—	—	—	—
3308	Other accounts payable	—	—	...	—	—	...	—	—	...	—	—	..

Serbia, Republic of (942)

In Billions of Serbian Dinars (RSD) / Fiscal Year Ends December 31st

		Budgetary Central Government			Central Government (excl. Social Security)			Central Government (incl. Social Security)			General Government		
		2010P	2011P	2012P	2010P	2011P	2012P	2010P	2011P	2012P	2010P	2011P	2012P
	By creditor												
331	Domestic creditors	69	67	108	69	62	105	69	62	105	75	68	109
332	External creditors	24	112	134	32	119	147	32	119	147	37	130	152
	Table 4 Holding gains and losses in assets and liabilities												
	Table 5 Holding gains and losses in assets and liabilities												
	Table 6 Balance sheet												
6	**Net worth**	**335**	**172**	**264**	**...**	**...**	**...**	**...**	**...**	**...**	**...**	**...**	**...**
61	**Nonfinancial assets**	**378**	**394**	**413**	**...**	**...**	**...**	**...**	**...**	**...**	**...**	**...**	**...**
611	Fixed assets	378	394	413	...	...	...	...	...	...	...	...	...
6111	Buildings and structures	324	337	352	...	...	...	...	...	...	...	...	...
6112	Machinery and equipment	51	53	58	...	...	...	...	...	...	...	...	...
6113	Other fixed assets	3	3	3	...	...	...	...	...	...	...	...	...
6114	Weapons systems	...	...	...	...	...	...	...	...	...	...	...	...
612	Inventories	—	—	—	...	...	...	...	...	...	...	...	...
613	Valuables	—	—	—	...	...	...	...	...	...	...	...	...
614	Nonproduced assets	—	—	—	...	...	...	...	...	...	...	...	...
6141	Land	—	—	—	...	...	...	...	...	...	...	...	...
6142	Mineral and energy resources	—	—	—	...	...	...	...	...	...	...	...	...
6143	Other naturally occurring assets	—	—	—	...	...	...	...	...	...	...	...	...
6144	Intangible nonproduced assets	—	—	—	...	...	...	...	...	...	...	...	...
62	**Financial assets**	**1,073**	**1,100**	**1,533**	**...**	**...**	**...**	**...**	**...**	**...**	**...**	**...**	**...**
	By instrument												
6201	Monetary gold and SDRs	—	—	—	...	...	...	...	...	...	...	...	...
6202	Currency and deposits	83	123	139	...	...	...	...	...	...	...	...	...
6203	Debt securities	0	0	0	...	...	...	...	...	...	...	...	...
6204	Loans	64	70	100	...	...	...	...	...	...	...	...	...
6205	Equity and investment fund shares	189	187	507	...	...	...	...	...	...	...	...	...
6206	Insurance, pension, and standardized guarantee schemes	—	—	—	...	...	...	...	...	...	...	...	...
6207	Financial derivatives and employee stock options	—	—	—	...	...	...	...	...	...	...	...	...
6208	Other accounts receivable	736	721	787	...	...	...	...	...	...	...	...	...
	By debtor												
621	Domestic debtors	1,069	1,096	1,528	...	...	...	...	...	...	...	...	...
622	External debtors	4	4	5	...	...	...	...	...	...	...	...	...
63	**Liabilities**	**1,115**	**1,323**	**1,682**	**...**	**...**	**...**	**...**	**...**	**...**	**...**	**...**	**...**
	By instrument												
6301	Special Drawing Rights (SDRs)	—	—	—	...	...	...	...	...	...	...	...	...
6302	Currency and deposits	—	—	—	...	...	...	...	...	...	...	...	...
6303	Debt securities	165	269	671	...	...	...	...	...	...	...	...	...
6304	Loans	943	1,045	1,001	...	...	...	...	...	...	...	...	...
6305	Equity and investment fund shares	—	—	—	...	...	...	...	...	...	...	...	...
6306	Insurance, pension, and standardized guarantee schemes	—	—	—	...	...	...	...	...	...	...	...	...
6307	Financial derivatives and employee stock options	—	—	—	...	...	...	...	...	...	...	...	...
6308	Other accounts payable	8	9	9	...	...	...	...	...	...	...	...	...
	By creditor												
631	Domestic creditors	496	565	701	...	...	...	...	...	...	...	...	...
632	External creditors	620	758	980	...	...	...	...	...	...	...	...	...
	Memorandum items												
6M2	Net financial worth	-43	-222	-149	...	...	...	...	...	...	...	...	...
6M3	Gross debt (D4) at market value	...	...	...	...	...	...	...	...	...	...	...	...
6M3D3	D3 debt liabilities at market value	...	...	...	...	...	...	...	...	...	...	...	...
6M3D2	D2 debt liabilities at market value	...	...	...	...	...	...	...	...	...	...	...	...
6M3D1	D1 debt liabilities at market value	...	...	...	...	...	...	...	...	...	...	...	...
6M4	Gross debt (D4) at nominal value	...	...	...	...	...	...	...	...	...	...	...	...
6M4D3	D3 debt liabilities at nominal value	...	...	...	...	...	...	...	...	...	...	...	...
6M4D2	D2 debt liabilities at nominal value	...	...	...	...	...	...	...	...	...	...	...	...
6M4D1	D1 debt liabilities at nominal value	...	...	...	...	...	...	...	...	...	...	...	...

Serbia, Republic of (942)

In Billions of Serbian Dinars (RSD) / Fiscal Year Ends December 31st

		Budgetary Central Government			Central Government (excl. Social Security)			Central Government (incl. Social Security)			General Government		
		2010P	2011P	2012P	2010P	2011P	2012P	2010P	2011P	2012P	2010P	2011P	2012P
6M35	Gross debt (D4) at face value	...	...	1,682	...	...	...	...	...	...	...	...	...
6M35D3	D3 debt liabilities at face value	...	...	1,682	...	...	...	...	...	...	...	...	...
6M35D2	D2 debt liabilities at face value	...	...	1,672	...	...	...	...	...	...	...	...	...
6M35D1	D1 debt liabilities at face value	1,115	1,323	1,672	...	...	...	...	...	...	...	...	...
6M93	Government gross debt per national definition	...	...	...	...	...	...	...	...	...	...	...	...
6M5	Arrears	...	...	...	...	...	...	...	...	...	...	...	...
6M6	Explicit contingent liabilities	...	...	...	...	...	...	...	...	...	...	...	...
6M61	of which: Publicly guaranteed debt	...	...	...	...	...	...	...	...	...	...	...	...
6M7	Net implicit obligations for social security benefits	...	...	...	...	...	...	...	...	...	...	...	...
	Table 7 Expenditure by functions of government												
7	**Expenditure**	**818**	**887**	**994**	**859**	**925**	**1,022**	**1,242**	**1,336**	**1,472**	**1,413**	**1,522**	**1,680**
701	**General public services**	**107**	**137**	**169**	**108**	**138**	**170**	**109**	**138**	**170**	**126**	**154**	**185**
7017	Public debt transactions	30	40	63	32	42	64	33	42	64	34	45	68
7018	Transfers of general character between levels of government	...	33	38	...	33	38	...	33	38	—	—	—
702	**Defense**	**72**	**74**	**54**	**72**	**74**	**54**	**72**	**74**	**54**	**72**	**74**	**54**
703	**Public order and safety**	**76**	**90**	**106**	**76**	**90**	**106**	**76**	**90**	**106**	**76**	**91**	**107**
704	**Economic affairs**	**109**	**113**	**142**	**148**	**149**	**170**	**148**	**149**	**170**	**198**	**201**	**229**
7042	Agriculture, forestry, fishing, and hunting	24	22	32	24	22	32	24	22	32	...	28	39
7043	Fuel and energy	1	0	0	1	0	0	1	0	0	...	2	2
7044	Mining, manufacturing, and construction	2	2	2	2	2	2	2	2	2	...	2	2
7045	Transport	19	22	49	58	58	76	58	58	76	...	92	114
7046	Communication	1	2	2	1	2	2	1	2	2	...	2	2
705	**Environmental protection**	**4**	**5**	**7**	**4**	**5**	**7**	**4**	**5**	**7**	**11**	**12**	**15**
706	**Housing and community amenities**	**7**	**6**	**6**	**7**	**6**	**6**	**7**	**6**	**6**	**47**	**52**	**57**
707	**Health**	**7**	**8**	**8**	**7**	**8**	**8**	**186**	**199**	**213**	**187**	**201**	**215**
7072	Outpatient services	...	...	...	...	...	...	...	...	...	...	...	...
7073	Hospital services	...	...	...	...	...	...	...	...	...	...	...	...
7074	Public health services	...	...	...	...	...	...	...	...	...	...	...	...
708	**Recreation, culture and religion**	**9**	**11**	**10**	**9**	**11**	**10**	**9**	**11**	**10**	**33**	**38**	**40**
709	**Education**	**109**	**117**	**123**	**109**	**117**	**123**	**109**	**117**	**123**	**127**	**135**	**147**
7091	Pre-primary and primary education	53	57	60	53	57	60	53	57	60	...	69	75
7092	Secondary education	24	26	27	24	26	27	24	26	27	...	32	35
7094	Tertiary education	22	24	25	22	24	25	22	24	25	...	23	26
710	**Social protection**	**318**	**328**	**369**	**318**	**328**	**369**	**522**	**548**	**614**	**535**	**563**	**630**
7z	Statistical discrepancy: Expenditure	—	—	...	—	—	...	—	—	...	0	—	...
	Table 8 Financial transactions by counterpart sector												
32	**Net acquisition of financial assets**	**-15**	**35**	**29**	**-15**	**36**	**29**	**-15**	**40**	**34**	**-24**	**39**	**43**
321	Domestic debtors	-15	35	29	-15	36	29	-15	40	34	-24	39	43
8211	General government	—	—	—	—	—	—	—	—	—	—	—	—
8212	Central bank	-10	35	20	-12	35	20	-10	40	25	-18	41	32
8213	Deposit-taking corporations except the central bank	—	—	29	1	2	29	1	2	29	1	2	37
8214	Other financial corporations	—	—	—	—	—	—	—	—	—	—	—	-5
8215	Nonfinancial corporations	-4	0	-19	-4	0	-19	-5	-0	-19	-7	-2	-20
8216	Households & nonprofit institutions serving households	-1	-1	-1	-1	-1	-1	-1	-1	-1	-1	-1	-1
322	External debtors	—	—	—	—	—	—	—	—	—	—	—	—
8221	General government	—	—	—	—	—	—	—	—	—	—	—	—
8227	International organizations	—	—	—	—	—	—	—	—	—	—	—	—
8228	Financial corporations other than international organizations	—	—	—	—	—	—	—	—	—	—	—	—
8229	Other nonresidents	—	—	—	—	—	—	—	—	—	—	—	—

Serbia, Republic of (942)

In Billions of Serbian Dinars (RSD) / Fiscal Year Ends December 31st

		Budgetary Central Government			Central Government (excl. Social Security)			Central Government (incl. Social Security)			General Government		
		2010P	2011P	2012P	2010P	2011P	2012P	2010P	2011P	2012P	2010P	2011P	2012P
33	**Net incurrence of liabilities**	**93**	**179**	**242**	**101**	**182**	**252**	**101**	**182**	**252**	**112**	**198**	**260**
331	Domestic creditors	69	67	108	69	62	105	69	62	105	75	68	109
8311	General government	—	—	—	—	—	—	—	—	—	—	—	—
8312	Central bank	—	—	—	—	—	—	—	—	—	—	—	—
8313	Deposit-taking corporations except the central bank	105	99	140	105	94	137	104	94	137	110	100	141
8314	Other financial corporations	-0	—	—	-0	—	—	-0	—	—	-0	—	—
8315	Nonfinancial corporations	—	—	-0	—	—	-0	—	—	-0	—	—	-0
8316	Households & nonprofit institutions serving households	-35	-32	-32	-35	-32	-32	-35	-32	-32	-35	-32	-32
332	External creditors	24	112	134	32	119	147	32	119	147	37	130	152
8321	General government	—	—	—	—	—	—	—	—	—	—	—	—
8327	International organizations	24	1	-21	32	9	-8	32	9	-8	37	19	-4
8328	Financial corporations other than international organizations	—	111	155	—	111	155	—	111	155	—	111	155
8329	Other nonresidents	—	—	—	—	—	—	—	—	—	—	—	—
	Table 9 Total other economic flows in assets and liabilities												

Seychelles (718)

In Millions of Seychelles Rupees (SCR) / Fiscal Year Ends December 31st

		Budgetary Central Government			Central Government (excl. Social Security)			Central Government (incl. Social Security)			General Government		
		2013P	2014P	2015P	2013P	2014P	2015P	2013P	2014P	2015P	2013P	2014P	2015P
	Statement of operations												
1	Revenue	5,467	5,932	6,349	5,467	5,932	6,349	5,467	5,932	6,349	5,467	5,932	6,349
2	Expense	4,427	4,980	5,346	4,427	4,980	5,346	4,427	4,980	5,346	4,427	4,980	5,346
GOB	**Gross operating balance**	**1,040**	**952**	**1,003**	**1,040**	**952**	**1,003**	**1,040**	**952**	**1,003**	**1,040**	**952**	**1,003**
NOB	**Net operating balance**	...	...	...	...	...	...	...	...	...	...	...	...
31	Net/Gross investment in nonfinancial assets	662	692	807	662	692	807	662	692	807	662	692	807
2M	Expenditure	5,090	5,672	6,153	5,090	5,672	6,153	5,090	5,672	6,153	5,090	5,672	6,153
NLB	**Net lending (+) / Net borrowing (-)**	**377**	**261**	**196**	**377**	**261**	**196**	**377**	**261**	**196**	**377**	**261**	**196**
32	Net acquisition of financial assets	65	1,066	543	65	1,066	543	65	1,066	543	65	1,066	543
33	Net incurrence of liabilities	-312	806	347	-312	806	347	-312	806	347	-312	806	347
NLBz	Statistical discrepancy	-0	-0	0	-0	-0	0	-0	-0	0	-0	-0	0
	Memorandum items												
PB	Primary net lending / net borrowing	804	737	810	804	737	810	804	737	810	804	737	810
GB	Government balance per national definition	...	...	...	...	...	...	...	...	...	...	...	...
	Statement of other economic flows												
	Balance sheet												
6	**Net worth**	...	...	...	...	...	...	...	...	...	...	...	...
61	Nonfinancial assets	...	...	...	...	...	...	...	...	...	...	...	...
62	Financial assets	2,263	3,374	3,334	2,263	3,374	3,334	2,263	3,374	3,334	2,263	3,374	3,334
63	Liabilities	8,256	11,784	11,617	8,256	11,784	11,617	8,256	11,784	11,617	8,256	11,784	11,617
	Table 1 Revenue												
1	**Revenue**	**5,467**	**5,932**	**6,349**	**5,467**	**5,932**	**6,349**	**5,467**	**5,932**	**6,349**	**5,467**	**5,932**	**6,349**
11	**Taxes**	**4,495**	**5,150**	**5,428**	**4,495**	**5,150**	**5,428**	**4,495**	**5,150**	**5,428**	**4,495**	**5,150**	**5,428**
111	Taxes on income, profits, and capital gains	882	907	883	882	907	883	882	907	883	882	907	883
1111	Payable by individuals	17	23	—	17	23	—	17	23	—	17	23	—
1112	Payable by corporations and other enterprises	865	883	759	865	883	759	865	883	759	865	883	759
1113	Other taxes on income, profits, and capital gains	—	0	125	—	0	125	—	0	125	—	0	125
112	Taxes on payroll and workforce	754	878	948	754	878	948	754	878	948	754	878	948
113	Taxes on property	5	96	—	5	96	—	5	96	—	5	96	—
114	Taxes on goods and services	2,423	2,889	2,788	2,423	2,889	2,788	2,423	2,889	2,788	2,423	2,889	2,788
1141	General taxes on goods and services	1,623	1,820	1,827	1,623	1,820	1,827	1,623	1,820	1,827	1,623	1,820	1,827
1142	Excises	652	858	961	652	858	961	652	858	961	652	858	961
115	Taxes on international trade and transactions	431	381	331	431	381	331	431	381	331	431	381	331
116	Other taxes	—	—	—	—	—	—	—	—	—	—	—	—
12	**Social contributions**	—	**0**	**0**	—	**0**	**0**	—	**0**	**0**	—	**0**	**0**
121	Social security contributions	—	0	0	—	0	0	—	0	0	—	0	0
122	Other social contributions	—	—	—	—	—	—	—	—	—	—	—	—
13	**Grants**	**44**	**94**	**121**	**44**	**94**	**121**	**44**	**94**	**121**	**44**	**94**	**121**
131	From foreign governments	—	—	—	—	—	—	—	—	—	—	—	—
132	From international organizations	44	94	121	44	94	121	44	94	121	44	94	121
133	From other general government units	—	—	—	—	—	—	—	—	—	—	—	—
1331	Current	—	—	—	—	—	—	—	—	—	—	—	—
1332	Capital	—	—	—	—	—	—	—	—	—	—	—	—
14	**Other revenue**	**929**	**688**	**799**	**929**	**688**	**799**	**929**	**688**	**799**	**929**	**688**	**799**
	Table 2 Expense by economic type												
2	**Expense**	**4,427**	**4,980**	**5,346**	**4,427**	**4,980**	**5,346**	**4,427**	**4,980**	**5,346**	**4,427**	**4,980**	**5,346**
21	**Compensation of employees**	**1,367**	**1,646**	**1,209**	**1,367**	**1,646**	**1,209**	**1,367**	**1,646**	**1,209**	**1,367**	**1,646**	**1,209**
211	Wages and salaries	1,310	1,646	1,209	1,310	1,646	1,209	1,310	1,646	1,209	1,310	1,646	1,209
212	Employers' social contributions	57	—	—	57	—	—	57	—	—	57	—	—
22	**Use of goods and services**	**1,623**	**1,736**	**1,089**	**1,623**	**1,736**	**1,089**	**1,623**	**1,736**	**1,089**	**1,623**	**1,736**	**1,089**
23	**Consumption of fixed capital**	...	...	...	...	...	...	...	...	...	...	...	...
24	**Interest**	**427**	**476**	**613**	**427**	**476**	**613**	**427**	**476**	**613**	**427**	**476**	**613**
25	**Subsidies**	**91**	**90**	**1,438**	**91**	**90**	**1,438**	**91**	**90**	**1,438**	**91**	**90**	**1,438**

Seychelles (718)

In Millions of Seychelles Rupees (SCR) / Fiscal Year Ends December 31st

		Budgetary Central Government			Central Government (excl. Social Security)			Central Government (incl. Social Security)			General Government		
		2013P	2014P	2015P	2013P	2014P	2015P	2013P	2014P	2015P	2013P	2014P	2015P
26	**Grants**	—	—	—	—	—	—	—	—	—	—	—	—
261	To foreign governments	—	—	—	—	—	—	—	—	—	—	—	—
262	To international organizations	—	—	—	—	—	—	—	—	—	—	—	—
263	To other general government units	—	—	—	—	—	—	—	—	—	—	—	—
2631	Current	—	—	—	—	—	—	—	—	—	—	—	—
2632	Capital	—	—	—	—	—	—	—	—	—	—	—	—
27	**Social benefits**	**530**	**580**	**552**	**530**	**580**	**552**	**530**	**580**	**552**	**530**	**580**	**552**
271	Social security benefits	351	380	402	351	380	402	351	380	402	351	380	402
272	Social assistance benefits	179	109	150	179	109	150	179	109	150	179	109	150
273	Employment-related social benefits	—	91	—	—	91	—	—	91	—	—	91	—
28	**Other expense**	**390**	**452**	**444**	**390**	**452**	**444**	**390**	**452**	**444**	**390**	**452**	**444**
281	Property expense other than interest	—	—	—	—	—	—	—	—	—	—	—	—
282	Transfers not elsewhere classified	390	452	444	390	452	444	390	452	444	390	452	444
2821	Current	390	452	444	390	452	444	390	452	444	390	452	444
2822	Capital	1	2	3	1	2	3	1	2	3	1	2	3
	Table 3 Transactions in assets and liabilities												
3	**Change in net worth from transactions**	...	...	**1,003**	...	...	**1,003**	...	...	**1,003**	...	...	**1,003**
31	**Net/Gross investment in nonfinancial assets**	**662**	**692**	**807**	**662**	**692**	**807**	**662**	**692**	**807**	**662**	**692**	**807**
311	Fixed assets	682	715	832	682	715	832	682	715	832	682	715	832
3111	Buildings and structures	471	529	696	471	529	696	471	529	696	471	529	696
3112	Machinery and equipment	206	180	129	206	180	129	206	180	129	206	180	129
3113	Other fixed assets	5	6	7	5	6	7	5	6	7	5	6	7
3114	Weapons systems	—	—	—	—	—	—	—	—	—	—	—	—
312	Inventories	—	—	—	—	—	—	—	—	—	—	—	—
313	Valuables	0	1	0	0	1	0	0	1	0	0	1	0
314	Nonproduced assets	-20	-25	-25	-20	-25	-25	-20	-25	-25	-20	-25	-25
3141	Land	-20	-25	-43	-20	-25	-43	-20	-25	-43	-20	-25	-43
3142	Mineral and energy resources	—	—	0	—	—	0	—	—	0	—	—	0
3143	Other naturally occurring assets	—	—	18	—	—	18	—	—	18	—	—	18
3144	Intangible nonproduced assets	—	—	—	—	—	—	—	—	—	—	—	—
32	**Net acquisition of financial assets**	**65**	**1,066**	**543**	**65**	**1,066**	**543**	**65**	**1,066**	**543**	**65**	**1,066**	**543**
	By instrument												
3201	Monetary gold and SDRs	—	—	—	—	—	—	—	—	—	—	—	—
3202	Currency and deposits	72	1,048	543	72	1,048	543	72	1,048	543	72	1,048	543
3203	Debt securities	—	—	—	—	—	—	—	—	—	—	—	—
3204	Loans	-7	18	-0	-7	18	-0	-7	18	-0	-7	18	-0
3205	Equity and investment fund shares	—	0	0	—	0	0	—	0	0	—	0	0
3206	Insurance, pension, and standardized guarantee schemes	—	—	—	—	—	—	—	—	—	—	—	—
3207	Financial derivatives and employee stock options	—	—	—	—	—	—	—	—	—	—	—	—
3208	Other accounts receivable	...	...	...	...	...	...	...	...	...	...	...	...
	By debtor												
321	Domestic debtors	65	1,065	543	65	1,065	543	65	1,065	543	65	1,065	543
322	External debtors	—	—	—	—	—	—	—	—	—	—	—	—
33	**Net incurrence of liabilities**	**-312**	**806**	**347**	**-312**	**806**	**347**	**-312**	**806**	**347**	**-312**	**806**	**347**
	By instrument												
3301	Special Drawing Rights (SDRs)	—	—	—	—	—	—	—	—	—	—	—	—
3302	Currency and deposits	13	114	-27	13	114	-27	13	114	-27	13	114	-27
3303	Debt securities	-260	705	516	-260	705	516	-260	705	516	-260	705	516
3304	Loans	-65	-14	-142	-65	-14	-142	-65	-14	-142	-65	-14	-142
3305	Equity and investment fund shares	—	0	0	—	0	0	—	0	0	—	0	0
3306	Insurance, pension, and standardized guarantee schemes	—	—	—	—	—	—	—	—	—	—	—	—
3307	Financial derivatives and employee stock options	—	—	—	—	—	—	—	—	—	—	—	—
3308	Other accounts payable	...	...	...	...	...	...	...	...	...	...	...	...

Seychelles (718)

In Millions of Seychelles Rupees (SCR) / Fiscal Year Ends December 31st

		Budgetary Central Government			Central Government (excl. Social Security)			Central Government (incl. Social Security)			General Government		
		2013P	2014P	2015P	2013P	2014P	2015P	2013P	2014P	2015P	2013P	2014P	2015P
	By creditor												
331	Domestic creditors	-363	742	437	-363	742	437	-363	742	437	-363	742	437
332	External creditors	51	63	-90	51	63	-90	51	63	-90	51	63	-90
	Table 4 Holding gains and losses in assets and liabilities												
	Table 5 Holding gains and losses in assets and liabilities												
	Table 6 Balance sheet												
6	**Net worth**	...	...	...	...	...	...	...	...	...	...	...	...
61	**Nonfinancial assets**	...	...	...	...	...	...	...	...	...	...	...	...
611	Fixed assets	...	...	...	...	...	...	...	...	...	...	...	...
6111	Buildings and structures	...	...	...	...	...	...	...	...	...	...	...	...
6112	Machinery and equipment	...	...	...	...	...	...	...	...	...	...	...	...
6113	Other fixed assets	...	...	...	...	...	...	...	...	...	...	...	...
6114	Weapons systems	...	...	...	...	...	...	...	...	...	...	...	...
612	Inventories	...	...	...	...	...	...	...	...	...	...	...	...
613	Valuables	...	...	...	...	...	...	...	...	...	...	...	...
614	Nonproduced assets	...	...	...	...	...	...	...	...	...	...	...	...
6141	Land	...	...	...	...	...	...	...	...	...	...	...	...
6142	Mineral and energy resources	...	...	...	...	...	...	...	...	...	...	...	...
6143	Other naturally occurring assets	...	...	...	...	...	...	...	...	...	...	...	...
6144	Intangible nonproduced assets	...	...	...	...	...	...	...	...	...	...	...	...
62	**Financial assets**	**2,263**	**3,374**	**3,334**	**2,263**	**3,374**	**3,334**	**2,263**	**3,374**	**3,334**	**2,263**	**3,374**	**3,334**
	By instrument												
6201	Monetary gold and SDRs	—	—	—	—	—	—	—	—	—	—	—	—
6202	Currency and deposits	1,989	3,072	3,026	1,989	3,072	3,026	1,989	3,072	3,026	1,989	3,072	3,026
6203	Debt securities	—	...	—	—	...	—	—	...	—	—	...	—
6204	Loans	272	306	306	272	306	306	272	306	306	272	306	306
6205	Equity and investment fund shares	1	2	2	1	2	2	1	2	2	1	2	2
6206	Insurance, pension, and standardized guarantee schemes	—	—	—	—	—	—	—	—	—	—	—	—
6207	Financial derivatives and employee stock options	—	—	—	—	—	—	—	—	—	—	—	—
6208	Other accounts receivable	...	...	...	...	...	...	...	...	...	...	...	...
	By debtor												
621	Domestic debtors	2,263	3,374	3,334	2,263	3,374	3,334	2,263	3,374	3,334	2,263	3,374	3,334
622	External debtors	—	—	—	—	—	—	—	—	—	—	—	—
63	**Liabilities**	**8,256**	**11,784**	**11,617**	**8,256**	**11,784**	**11,617**	**8,256**	**11,784**	**11,617**	**8,256**	**11,784**	**11,617**
	By instrument												
6301	Special Drawing Rights (SDRs)	—	—	—	—	—	—	—	—	—	—	—	—
6302	Currency and deposits	36	179	154	36	179	154	36	179	154	36	179	154
6303	Debt securities	3,121	5,226	5,724	3,121	5,226	5,724	3,121	5,226	5,724	3,121	5,226	5,724
6304	Loans	5,098	6,379	5,739	5,098	6,379	5,739	5,098	6,379	5,739	5,098	6,379	5,739
6305	Equity and investment fund shares	—	—	—	—	—	—	—	—	—	—	—	—
6306	Insurance, pension, and standardized guarantee schemes	—	—	—	—	—	—	—	—	—	—	—	—
6307	Financial derivatives and employee stock options	—	—	—	—	—	—	—	—	—	—	—	—
6308	Other accounts payable	...	...	...	...	...	...	...	...	...	...	...	...
	By creditor												
631	Domestic creditors	3,157	5,406	5,877	3,157	5,406	5,877	3,157	5,406	5,877	3,157	5,406	5,877
632	External creditors	5,098	6,379	5,739	5,098	6,379	5,739	5,098	6,379	5,739	5,098	6,379	5,739
	Memorandum items												
6M2	Net financial worth	-4,670	-8,994	-8,283	-4,670	-8,994	-8,283	-4,670	-8,994	-8,283	-4,670	-8,994	-8,283
6M3	Gross debt (D4) at market value	...	...	...	...	...	...	...	...	...	...	...	...
6M3D3	D3 debt liabilities at market value	...	...	...	...	...	...	...	...	...	...	...	...
6M3D2	D2 debt liabilities at market value	...	...	...	...	...	...	...	...	...	...	...	...
6M3D1	D1 debt liabilities at market value	...	...	...	...	...	...	...	...	...	...	...	...
6M4	Gross debt (D4) at nominal value	...	...	...	...	...	...	...	...	...	...	...	...
6M4D3	D3 debt liabilities at nominal value	...	...	...	...	...	...	...	...	...	...	...	...
6M4D2	D2 debt liabilities at nominal value	...	...	...	...	...	...	...	...	...	...	...	...
6M4D1	D1 debt liabilities at nominal value	...	...	...	...	...	...	...	...	...	...	...	...

Seychelles (718)

In Millions of Seychelles Rupees (SCR) / Fiscal Year Ends December 31st

		Budgetary Central Government			Central Government (excl. Social Security)			Central Government (incl. Social Security)			General Government		
		2013P	2014P	2015P	2013P	2014P	2015P	2013P	2014P	2015P	2013P	2014P	2015P
6M35	Gross debt (D4) at face value	8,256	11,784	11,617	8,256	11,784	11,617	8,256	11,784	11,617	8,256	11,784	11,617
6M35D3	D3 debt liabilities at face value	...	...	...	...	...	...	...	...	...	...	...	...
6M35D2	D2 debt liabilities at face value	8,256	11,784	11,617	8,256	11,784	11,617	8,256	11,784	11,617	8,256	11,784	11,617
6M35D1	D1 debt liabilities at face value	8,219	11,605	11,463	8,219	11,605	11,463	8,219	11,605	11,463	8,219	11,605	11,463
6M93	Government gross debt per national definition	...	...	...	...	...	...	...	...	...	...	...	...
6M5	Arrears	...	...	...	...	...	...	...	...	...	...	...	...
6M6	Explicit contingent liabilities	...	...	...	...	...	...	...	...	...	...	...	...
6M61	of which: Publicly guaranteed debt	...	...	...	...	...	...	...	...	...	...	...	...
6M7	Net implicit obligations for social security benefits	...	...	...	...	...	...	...	...	...	...	...	...
	Table 7 Expenditure by functions of government												
7	**Expenditure**	**5,090**	**5,672**	**6,153**	**5,090**	**5,672**	**6,153**	**5,090**	**5,672**	**6,153**	**5,090**	**5,672**	**6,153**
701	**General public services**	**1,485**	**1,663**	**1,906**	**1,485**	**1,663**	**1,906**	**1,485**	**1,663**	**1,906**	**1,485**	**1,663**	**1,906**
7017	Public debt transactions	427	476	613	427	476	613	427	476	613	427	476	613
7018	Transfers of general character between levels of government	—	—	—	—	—	—	—	—	—	—	—	—
702	**Defense**	**212**	**274**	**251**	**212**	**274**	**251**	**212**	**274**	**251**	**212**	**274**	**251**
703	**Public order and safety**	**509**	**566**	**602**	**509**	**566**	**602**	**509**	**566**	**602**	**509**	**566**	**602**
704	**Economic affairs**	**445**	**392**	**521**	**445**	**392**	**521**	**445**	**392**	**521**	**445**	**392**	**521**
7042	Agriculture, forestry, fishing, and hunting	91	92	149	91	92	149	91	92	149	91	92	149
7043	Fuel and energy	...	3	3	...	3	3	...	3	3	...	3	3
7044	Mining, manufacturing, and construction	...	—	—	...	—	—	...	—	—	...	—	—
7045	Transport	108	112	135	108	112	135	108	112	135	108	112	135
7046	Communication	97	35	39	97	35	39	97	35	39	97	35	39
705	**Environmental protection**	**202**	**263**	**264**	**202**	**263**	**264**	**202**	**263**	**264**	**202**	**263**	**264**
706	**Housing and community amenities**	**222**	**289**	**231**	**222**	**289**	**231**	**222**	**289**	**231**	**222**	**289**	**231**
707	**Health**	**578**	**629**	**658**	**578**	**629**	**658**	**578**	**629**	**658**	**578**	**629**	**658**
7072	Outpatient services	1	112	120	1	112	120	1	112	120	1	112	120
7073	Hospital services	...	291	292	...	291	292	...	291	292	...	291	292
7074	Public health services	571	225	245	571	225	245	571	225	245	571	225	245
708	**Recreation, culture and religion**	**97**	**205**	**238**	**97**	**205**	**238**	**97**	**205**	**238**	**97**	**205**	**238**
709	**Education**	**713**	**729**	**774**	**713**	**729**	**774**	**713**	**729**	**774**	**713**	**729**	**774**
7091	Pre-primary and primary education	5	6	157	5	6	157	5	6	157	5	6	157
7092	Secondary education	4	4	110	4	4	110	4	4	110	4	4	110
7094	Tertiary education	39	54	69	39	54	69	39	54	69	39	54	69
710	**Social protection**	**627**	**664**	**709**	**627**	**664**	**709**	**627**	**664**	**709**	**627**	**664**	**709**
7z	Statistical discrepancy: Expenditure	—	...	...	—	...	...	—	...	...	—	...	...
	Table 8 Financial transactions by counterpart sector												
32	**Net acquisition of financial assets**	**65**	**1,066**	**543**	**65**	**1,066**	**543**	**65**	**1,066**	**543**	**65**	**1,066**	**543**
321	Domestic debtors	65	1,065	543	65	1,065	543	65	1,065	543	65	1,065	543
8211	General government	...	...	...	...	...	...	...	...	...	...	...	...
8212	Central bank	...	...	...	...	...	...	...	...	...	...	...	...
8213	Deposit-taking corporations except the central bank	...	...	...	...	...	...	...	...	...	...	...	...
8214	Other financial corporations	...	...	...	...	...	...	...	...	...	...	...	...
8215	Nonfinancial corporations	...	...	...	...	...	...	...	...	...	...	...	...
8216	Households & nonprofit institutions serving households	...	...	...	...	...	...	...	...	...	...	...	...
322	External debtors	—	—	—	—	—	—	—	—	—	—	—	—
8221	General government	—	—	—	—	—	—	—	—	—	—	—	—
8227	International organizations	—	—	—	—	—	—	—	—	—	—	—	—
8228	Financial corporations other than international organizations	—	—	—	—	—	—	—	—	—	—	—	—
8229	Other nonresidents	—	—	—	—	—	—	—	—	—	—	—	—

Seychelles (718)

In Millions of Seychelles Rupees (SCR) / Fiscal Year Ends December 31st

		Budgetary Central Government			Central Government (excl. Social Security)			Central Government (incl. Social Security)			General Government		
		2013P	2014P	2015P	2013P	2014P	2015P	2013P	2014P	2015P	2013P	2014P	2015P
33	**Net incurrence of liabilities**	**-312**	**806**	**347**	**-312**	**806**	**347**	**-312**	**806**	**347**	**-312**	**806**	**347**
331	Domestic creditors	-363	742	437	-363	742	437	-363	742	437	-363	742	437
3311	General government	...	...	...	...	...	...	...	...	...	...	...	...
3312	Central bank	...	...	...	...	...	...	...	...	...	...	...	...
3313	Deposit-taking corporations except the central bank	...	...	...	...	...	...	...	...	...	...	...	...
3314	Other financial corporations	...	...	...	...	...	...	...	...	...	...	...	...
3315	Nonfinancial corporations	...	...	...	...	...	...	...	...	...	...	...	...
3316	Households & nonprofit institutions serving households	...	...	...	...	...	...	...	...	...	...	...	...
332	External creditors	51	63	-90	51	63	-90	51	63	-90	51	63	-90
3321	General government	...	...	...	...	...	...	...	...	...	...	...	...
3327	International organizations	...	...	...	...	...	...	...	...	...	...	...	...
3328	Financial corporations other than international organizations	...	...	...	...	...	...	...	...	...	...	...	...
3329	Other nonresidents	...	...	...	...	...	...	...	...	...	...	...	...
	Table 9 Total other economic flows in assets and liabilities												

Sierra Leone (724)

In Billions of Sierra Leonean Leones (SLL) / Fiscal Year Ends December 31st

		Budgetary Central Government			Central Government (excl. Social Security)			Central Government (incl. Social Security)			General Government		
		2012	2013	2014P	2012	2013	2014	2012	2013	2014	2012	2013	2014
	Statement of operations												
1	Revenue	2,506	2,828	3,186	...	...	...	...	...	...	...	...	...
2	Expense	2,186	2,210	2,671	...	...	...	...	...	...	...	...	...
GOB	**Gross operating balance**	**320**	**618**	**515**	...	...	...	...	...	...	...	...	...
NOB	**Net operating balance**	...	...	...	...	...	...	...	...	...	...	...	...
31	Net/Gross investment in nonfinancial assets	1,263	1,147	1,205	...	...	...	...	...	...	...	...	...
2M	Expenditure	3,449	3,356	3,875	...	...	...	...	...	...	...	...	...
NLB	**Net lending (+) / Net borrowing (-)**	**-943**	**-528**	**-690**	...	...	...	...	...	...	...	...	...
32	Net acquisition of financial assets	...	...	...	...	...	...	...	...	...	...	...	...
33	Net incurrence of liabilities	871	525	867	...	...	...	...	...	...	...	...	...
NLBz	Statistical discrepancy	...	...	...	...	...	...	...	...	...	...	...	...
	Memorandum items												
PB	Primary net lending / net borrowing	-652	-227	-468	...	...	...	...	...	...	...	...	...
GB	Government balance per national definition	...	...	...	...	...	...	...	...	...	...	...	...
	Statement of other economic flows												
	Balance sheet												
	Table 1 Revenue												
1	**Revenue**	**2,506**	**2,828**	**3,186**	...	...	...	...	...	...	...	...	...
11	**Taxes**	**1,571**	**1,944**	**1,950**	...	...	...	...	...	...	...	...	...
111	Taxes on income, profits, and capital gains	778	929	896	...	...	...	...	...	...	...	...	...
1111	Payable by individuals	571	657	618	...	...	...	...	...	...	...	...	...
1112	Payable by corporations and other enterprises	203	267	270	...	...	...	...	...	...	...	...	...
1113	Other taxes on income, profits, and capital gains	5	6	7	...	...	...	...	...	...	...	...	...
112	Taxes on payroll and workforce	—	—	—	...	...	...	...	...	...	...	...	...
113	Taxes on property	—	—	—	...	...	...	...	...	...	...	...	...
114	Taxes on goods and services	556	746	769	...	...	...	...	...	...	...	...	...
1141	General taxes on goods and services	419	440	459	...	...	...	...	...	...	...	...	...
1142	Excises	99	221	222	...	...	...	...	...	...	...	...	...
115	Taxes on international trade and transactions	237	269	285	...	...	...	...	...	...	...	...	...
116	Other taxes	—	—	—	...	...	...	...	...	...	...	...	...
12	**Social contributions**	—	—	—	...	...	...	...	...	...	...	...	...
121	Social security contributions	—	—	—	...	...	...	...	...	...	...	...	...
122	Other social contributions	—	—	—	...	...	...	...	...	...	...	...	...
13	**Grants**	**633**	**548**	**959**	...	...	...	...	...	...	...	...	...
131	From foreign governments	281	170	677	...	...	...	...	...	...	...	...	...
132	From international organizations	352	378	283	...	...	...	...	...	...	...	...	...
133	From other general government units	—	—	—	...	...	...	...	...	...	...	...	...
1331	Current	—	—	—	...	...	...	...	...	...	...	...	...
1332	Capital	—	—	—	...	...	...	...	...	...	...	...	...
14	**Other revenue**	**302**	**336**	**276**	...	...	...	...	...	...	...	...	...
	Table 2 Expense by economic type												
2	**Expense**	**2,186**	**2,210**	**2,671**	...	...	...	...	...	...	...	...	...
21	**Compensation of employees**	**948**	**1,066**	**1,443**	...	...	...	...	...	...	...	...	...
211	Wages and salaries	...	...	...	...	...	...	...	...	...	...	...	...
212	Employers' social contributions	...	...	...	...	...	...	...	...	...	...	...	...
22	**Use of goods and services**	**541**	**538**	**636**	...	...	...	...	...	...	...	...	...
23	**Consumption of fixed capital**	...	...	...	...	...	...	...	...	...	...	...	...
24	**Interest**	**291**	**301**	**221**	...	...	...	...	...	...	...	...	...
25	**Subsidies**	—	—	—	...	...	...	...	...	...	...	...	...
26	**Grants**	**229**	**294**	**297**	...	...	...	...	...	...	...	...	...
261	To foreign governments	—	—	—	...	...	...	...	...	...	...	...	...
262	To international organizations	—	—	—	...	...	...	...	...	...	...	...	...
263	To other general government units	229	294	297	...	...	...	...	...	...	...	...	...
2631	Current	229	294	297	...	...	...	...	...	...	...	...	...
2632	Capital	—	—	—	...	...	...	...	...	...	...	...	...

Sierra Leone (724)

In Billions of Sierra Leonean Leones (SLL) / Fiscal Year Ends December 31st

		Budgetary Central Government			Central Government (excl. Social Security)			Central Government (incl. Social Security)			General Government		
		2012	2013	2014P	2012	2013	2014	2012	2013	2014	2012	2013	2014
27	**Social benefits**	**—**	**—**	**58**	**...**	**...**	**...**	**...**	**...**	**...**	**...**	**...**	**...**
271	Social security benefits	—	—	...	...	...	...	...	...	...	...	...	...
272	Social assistance benefits	—	—	...	...	...	...	...	...	...	...	...	...
273	Employment-related social benefits	—	—	...	...	...	...	...	...	...	...	...	...
28	**Other expense**	**178**	**10**	**16**	**...**	**...**	**...**	**...**	**...**	**...**	**...**	**...**	**...**
281	Property expense other than interest	—	—	—	...	...	...	...	...	...	...	...	...
282	Transfers not elsewhere classified	178	10	16	...	...	...	...	...	...	...	...	...
2821	Current	...	...	...	...	...	...	...	...	...	...	...	...
2822	Capital	...	...	...	...	...	...	...	...	...	...	...	...
	Table 3 Transactions in assets and liabilities												
3	**Change in net worth from transactions**	**...**	**...**	**...**	**...**	**...**	**...**	**...**	**...**	**...**	**...**	**...**	**...**
31	**Net/Gross investment in nonfinancial assets**	**1,263**	**1,147**	**1,205**	**...**	**...**	**...**	**...**	**...**	**...**	**...**	**...**	**...**
311	Fixed assets	1,263	1,147	1,205	...	...	...	...	...	...	...	...	...
3111	Buildings and structures	...	...	...	...	...	...	...	...	...	...	...	...
3112	Machinery and equipment	...	...	...	...	...	...	...	...	...	...	...	...
3113	Other fixed assets	...	...	...	...	...	...	...	...	...	...	...	...
3114	Weapons systems	...	...	...	...	...	...	...	...	...	...	...	...
312	Inventories	—	—	—	...	...	...	...	...	...	...	...	...
313	Valuables	—	—	—	...	...	...	...	...	...	...	...	...
314	Nonproduced assets	—	—	—	...	...	...	...	...	...	...	...	...
3141	Land	—	—	—	...	...	...	...	...	...	...	...	...
3142	Mineral and energy resources	—	—	—	...	...	...	...	...	...	...	...	...
3143	Other naturally occurring assets	—	—	—	...	...	...	...	...	...	...	...	...
3144	Intangible nonproduced assets	—	—	—	...	...	...	...	...	...	...	...	...
32	**Net acquisition of financial assets**	**...**	**...**	**...**	**...**	**...**	**...**	**...**	**...**	**...**	**...**	**...**	**...**
	By instrument												
3201	Monetary gold and SDRs	...	...	...	...	...	...	...	...	...	...	...	...
3202	Currency and deposits	...	...	...	...	...	...	...	...	...	...	...	...
3203	Debt securities	...	...	...	...	...	...	...	...	...	...	...	...
3204	Loans	...	...	...	...	...	...	...	...	...	...	...	...
3205	Equity and investment fund shares	...	...	...	...	...	...	...	...	...	...	...	...
3206	Insurance, pension, and standardized guarantee schemes	...	...	...	...	...	...	...	...	...	...	...	...
3207	Financial derivatives and employee stock options	...	...	...	...	...	...	...	...	...	...	...	...
3208	Other accounts receivable	...	...	...	...	...	...	...	...	...	...	...	...
	By debtor												
321	Domestic debtors	—	—	—	...	...	...	...	...	...	...	...	...
322	External debtors	—	—	—	...	...	...	...	...	...	...	...	...
33	**Net incurrence of liabilities**	**871**	**525**	**867**	**...**	**...**	**...**	**...**	**...**	**...**	**...**	**...**	**...**
	By instrument												
3301	Special Drawing Rights (SDRs)	...	...	...	...	...	...	...	...	...	...	...	...
3302	Currency and deposits	...	...	...	...	...	...	...	...	...	...	...	...
3303	Debt securities	...	...	...	...	...	...	...	...	...	...	...	...
3304	Loans	...	...	...	...	...	...	...	...	...	...	...	...
3305	Equity and investment fund shares	...	...	...	...	...	...	...	...	...	...	...	...
3306	Insurance, pension, and standardized guarantee schemes	...	...	...	...	...	...	...	...	...	...	...	...
3307	Financial derivatives and employee stock options	...	...	...	...	...	...	...	...	...	...	...	...
3308	Other accounts payable	...	...	...	...	...	...	...	...	...	...	...	...
	By creditor												
331	Domestic creditors	347	231	601	...	...	...	...	...	...	...	...	...
332	External creditors	523	294	266	...	...	...	...	...	...	...	...	...
	Table 4 Holding gains and losses in assets and liabilities												
	Table 5 Holding gains and losses in assets and liabilities												
	Table 6 Balance sheet												

Sierra Leone (724)

In Billions of Sierra Leonean Leones (SLL) / Fiscal Year Ends December 31st

	Budgetary Central Government			Central Government (excl. Social Security)			Central Government (incl. Social Security)			General Government		
	2012	2013	2014P	2012	2013	2014	2012	2013	2014	2012	2013	2014
Table 7 Expenditure by functions of government												
Table 8 Financial transactions by counterpart sector												
Table 9 Total other economic flows in assets and liabilities												

Singapore (576)

In Millions of Singapore Dollars (SGD) / Fiscal Year Ends March 31st

		Budgetary Central Government			Central Government (excl. Social Security)			Central Government (incl. Social Security)			General Government		
		2013	2014	2015	2013	2014	2015	2013	2014	2015	2013	2014	2015
	Statement of operations												
1	Revenue	64,750	69,973	74,244	66,350	71,894	76,208	66,350	71,894	76,208	66,350	71,894	76,208
2	Expense	51,773	56,519	72,244	47,629	52,466	67,436	47,629	52,466	67,436	47,629	52,466	67,436
GOB	**Gross operating balance**	**12,977**	**13,454**	**2,000**	**18,721**	**19,428**	**8,772**	**18,721**	**19,428**	**8,772**	**18,721**	**19,428**	**8,772**
NOB	**Net operating balance**	...	...	...	...	...	...	...	...	...	...	...	...
31	Net/Gross investment in nonfinancial assets	-12,285	-8,905	-9,006	-12,285	-8,905	-9,006	-12,285	-8,905	-9,006	-12,285	-8,905	-9,006
2M	Expenditure	39,488	47,615	63,238	35,344	43,561	58,430	35,344	43,561	58,430	35,344	43,561	58,430
NLB	**Net lending (+) / Net borrowing (-)**	**25,262**	**22,358**	**11,006**	**31,006**	**28,333**	**17,778**	**31,006**	**28,333**	**17,778**	**31,006**	**28,333**	**17,778**
32	Net acquisition of financial assets	10,363	37,010	51,121	16,108	42,984	57,893	16,108	42,984	57,893	16,108	42,984	57,893
33	Net incurrence of liabilities	-14,899	14,652	40,115	-14,899	14,652	40,115	-14,899	14,652	40,115	-14,899	14,652	40,115
NLBz	Statistical discrepancy	—	—	—	—	—	—	—	—	—	—	—	—
	Memorandum items												
PB	Primary net lending / net borrowing	25,262	22,358	11,006	31,009	28,334	17,780	31,009	28,334	17,780	31,009	28,334	17,780
GB	Government balance per national definition	...	...	...	...	...	...	...	...	...	...	...	...
	Statement of other economic flows												
	Balance sheet												
	Table 1 Revenue												
1	**Revenue**	**64,750**	**69,973**	**74,244**	**66,350**	**71,894**	**76,208**	**66,350**	**71,894**	**76,208**	**66,350**	**71,894**	**76,208**
11	**Taxes**	**51,146**	**54,110**	**55,647**	**51,077**	**54,084**	**55,640**	**51,077**	**54,084**	**55,640**	**51,077**	**54,084**	**55,640**
111	Taxes on income, profits, and capital gains	22,050	23,940	24,890	21,981	23,914	24,883	21,981	23,914	24,883	21,981	23,914	24,883
1111	Payable by individuals	7,688	8,927	9,235	7,688	8,927	9,235	7,688	8,927	9,235	7,688	8,927	9,235
1112	Payable by corporations and other enterprises	14,362	15,013	15,655	14,293	14,987	15,648	14,293	14,987	15,648	14,293	14,987	15,648
1113	Other taxes on income, profits, and capital gains	—	—	—	—	—	—	—	—	—	—	—	—
112	Taxes on payroll and workforce	—	—	—	—	—	—	—	—	—	—	—	—
113	Taxes on property	4,182	4,341	4,455	4,182	4,341	4,455	4,182	4,341	4,455	4,182	4,341	4,455
114	Taxes on goods and services	15,736	16,949	17,657	15,736	16,949	17,657	15,736	16,949	17,657	15,736	16,949	17,657
1141	General taxes on goods and services	9,513	10,215	10,345	9,513	10,215	10,345	9,513	10,215	10,345	9,513	10,215	10,345
1142	Excises	2,189	2,540	2,833	2,189	2,540	2,833	2,189	2,540	2,833	2,189	2,540	2,833
115	Taxes on international trade and transactions	—	—	—	—	—	—	—	—	—	—	—	—
116	Other taxes	9,178	8,881	8,645	9,178	8,881	8,645	9,178	8,881	8,645	9,178	8,881	8,645
12	**Social contributions**	—	—	—	—	—	—	—	—	—	—	—	—
121	Social security contributions	—	—	—	—	—	—	—	—	—	—	—	—
122	Other social contributions	—	—	—	—	—	—	—	—	—	—	—	—
13	**Grants**	—	—	—	—	—	—	—	—	—	—	—	—
131	From foreign governments	—	—	—	—	—	—	—	—	—	—	—	—
132	From international organizations	—	—	—	—	—	—	—	—	—	—	—	—
133	From other general government units	—	—	—	—	—	—	—	—	—	—	—	—
1331	Current	—	—	—	—	—	—	—	—	—	—	—	—
1332	Capital	—	—	—	—	—	—	—	—	—	—	—	—
14	**Other revenue**	**13,605**	**15,863**	**18,596**	**15,273**	**17,810**	**20,568**	**15,273**	**17,810**	**20,568**	**15,273**	**17,810**	**20,568**
	Table 2 Expense by economic type												
2	**Expense**	**51,773**	**56,519**	**72,244**	**47,629**	**52,466**	**67,436**	**47,629**	**52,466**	**67,436**	**47,629**	**52,466**	**67,436**
21	**Compensation of employees**	**11,351**	**12,132**	**13,045**	**14,110**	**15,034**	**16,076**	**14,110**	**15,034**	**16,076**	**14,110**	**15,034**	**16,076**
211	Wages and salaries	11,351	12,132	13,045	14,110	15,034	16,076	14,110	15,034	16,076	14,110	15,034	16,076
212	Employers' social contributions	—	—	—	—	—	—	—	—	—	—	—	—
22	**Use of goods and services**	**11,797**	**12,799**	**13,997**	**15,720**	**17,147**	**19,299**	**15,720**	**17,147**	**19,299**	**15,720**	**17,147**	**19,299**
23	**Consumption of fixed capital**	...	...	...	...	...	...	...	...	...	...	...	...
24	**Interest**	—	—	—	**3**	**1**	**2**	**3**	**1**	**2**	**3**	**1**	**2**
25	**Subsidies**	...	...	—	...	...	—	...	...	—	...	...	—
26	**Grants**	**11,001**	**11,427**	**13,318**	**171**	**123**	**175**	**171**	**123**	**175**	**171**	**123**	**175**
261	To foreign governments	—	—	—	—	—	—	—	—	—	—	—	—
262	To international organizations	171	123	175	171	123	175	171	123	175	171	123	175
263	To other general government units	10,830	11,304	13,143	—	—	—	—	—	—	—	—	—
2631	Current	4,495	5,072	5,805	—	—	—	—	—	—	—	—	—
2632	Capital	6,334	6,232	7,339	—	—	—	—	—	—	—	—	—

Singapore (576)

In Millions of Singapore Dollars (SGD) / Fiscal Year Ends March 31st

		Budgetary Central Government			Central Government (excl. Social Security)			Central Government (incl. Social Security)			General Government		
		2013	2014	2015	2013	2014	2015	2013	2014	2015	2013	2014	2015
27	**Social benefits**	...	...	...	...	...	...	...	...	...	...	...	...
271	Social security benefits	...	...	...	...	...	...	...	...	...	...	...	...
272	Social assistance benefits	...	...	...	...	...	...	...	...	...	...	...	...
273	Employment-related social benefits	...	...	...	...	...	...	...	...	...	...	...	...
28	**Other expense**	...	...	...	...	...	...	...	...	...	...	...	...
281	Property expense other than interest	...	...	...	...	...	...	...	...	...	...	...	...
282	Transfers not elsewhere classified	...	...	...	...	...	...	...	...	...	...	...	...
2821	Current	...	...	...	...	...	...	...	...	...	...	...	...
2822	Capital	...	...	...	...	...	...	...	...	...	...	...	...
	Table 3 Transactions in assets and liabilities												
3	**Change in net worth from transactions**	...	...	...	...	...	...	...	...	...	...	...	...
31	**Net/Gross investment in nonfinancial assets**	**-12,285**	**-8,905**	**-9,006**	**-12,285**	**-8,905**	**-9,006**	**-12,285**	**-8,905**	**-9,006**	**-12,285**	**-8,905**	**-9,006**
311	Fixed assets	3,828	4,619	5,123	3,828	4,619	5,123	3,828	4,619	5,123	3,828	4,619	5,123
3111	Buildings and structures	...	...	...	...	...	...	...	...	...	...	...	...
3112	Machinery and equipment	...	...	...	...	...	...	...	...	...	...	...	...
3113	Other fixed assets	...	...	...	...	...	...	...	...	...	...	...	...
3114	Weapons systems	...	...	...	...	...	...	...	...	...	...	...	...
312	Inventories	—	—	—	—	—	—	—	—	—	—	—	—
313	Valuables	—	—	—	—	—	—	—	—	—	—	—	—
314	Nonproduced assets	-16,113	-13,524	-14,128	-16,113	-13,524	-14,128	-16,113	-13,524	-14,128	-16,113	-13,524	-14,128
3141	Land	...	...	...	...	...	...	...	...	...	...	...	...
3142	Mineral and energy resources	...	...	...	...	...	...	...	...	...	...	...	...
3143	Other naturally occurring assets	...	...	...	...	...	...	...	...	...	...	...	...
3144	Intangible nonproduced assets	...	...	...	...	...	...	...	...	...	...	...	...
32	**Net acquisition of financial assets**	**10,363**	**37,010**	**51,121**	**16,108**	**42,984**	**57,893**	**16,108**	**42,984**	**57,893**	**16,108**	**42,984**	**57,893**
	By instrument												
3201	Monetary gold and SDRs	—	—	—	—	—	—	—	—	—	—	—	—
3202	Currency and deposits	9,948	37,812	48,572	15,692	43,786	55,344	15,692	43,786	55,344	15,692	43,786	55,344
3203	Debt securities	—	—	—	—	—	—	—	—	—	—	—	—
3204	Loans	415	-802	2,548	415	-802	2,548	415	-802	2,548	415	-802	2,548
3205	Equity and investment fund shares	—	—	—	—	—	—	—	—	—	—	—	—
3206	Insurance, pension, and standardized guarantee schemes	—	—	—	—	—	—	—	—	—	—	—	—
3207	Financial derivatives and employee stock options	—	—	—	—	—	—	—	—	—	—	—	—
3208	Other accounts receivable	...	...	...	...	...	...	...	...	...	...	...	...
	By debtor												
321	Domestic debtors	10,363	37,010	51,121	16,108	42,984	57,893	16,108	42,984	57,893	16,108	42,984	57,893
322	External debtors	—	—	—	—	—	—	—	—	—	—	—	—
33	**Net incurrence of liabilities**	**-14,899**	**14,652**	**40,115**	**-14,899**	**14,652**	**40,115**	**-14,899**	**14,652**	**40,115**	**-14,899**	**14,652**	**40,115**
	By instrument												
3301	Special Drawing Rights (SDRs)	—	—	—	—	—	—	—	—	—	—	—	—
3302	Currency and deposits	—	—	—	—	—	—	—	—	—	—	—	—
3303	Debt securities	-14,899	14,652	40,115	-14,899	14,652	40,115	-14,899	14,652	40,115	-14,899	14,652	40,115
3304	Loans	—	—	—	—	—	—	—	—	—	—	—	—
3305	Equity and investment fund shares	—	—	—	—	—	—	—	—	—	—	—	—
3306	Insurance, pension, and standardized guarantee schemes	—	—	—	—	—	—	—	—	—	—	—	—
3307	Financial derivatives and employee stock options	—	—	—	—	—	—	—	—	—	—	—	—
3308	Other accounts payable	...	...	...	...	...	...	...	...	...	...	...	...
	By creditor												
331	Domestic creditors	-14,899	14,652	40,115	-14,899	14,652	40,115	-14,899	14,652	40,115	-14,899	14,652	40,115
332	External creditors	—	—	—	—	—	—	—	—	—	—	—	—
	Table 4 Holding gains and losses in assets and liabilities												
	Table 5 Holding gains and losses in assets and liabilities												
	Table 6 Balance sheet												

Singapore (576)

In Millions of Singapore Dollars (SGD) / Fiscal Year Ends March 31st

		Budgetary Central Government			Central Government (excl. Social Security)			Central Government (incl. Social Security)			General Government		
		2013	2014	2015	2013	2014	2015	2013	2014	2015	2013	2014	2015
	Table 7 Expenditure by functions of government												
7	**Expenditure**	**57,038**	**62,541**	**78,780**	**52,895**	**58,445**	**73,972**	**52,895**	**58,445**	**73,972**	**52,895**	**58,445**	**73,972**
701	**General public services**	**3,897**	**4,356**	**4,425**	**3,897**	**4,356**	**4,425**	**3,897**	**4,356**	**4,425**	**3,897**	**4,356**	**4,425**
7017	Public debt transactions	—	—	—	3	—	—	3	—	—	3	—	—
7018	Transfers of general character between levels of government	...	...	...	...	...	...	...	...	...	...	...	...
702	**Defense**	**12,157**	**12,714**	**13,593**	**12,157**	**12,714**	**13,593**	**12,157**	**12,714**	**13,593**	**12,157**	**12,714**	**13,593**
703	**Public order and safety**	**3,222**	**3,754**	**4,102**	**3,222**	**3,754**	**4,102**	**3,222**	**3,754**	**4,102**	**3,222**	**3,754**	**4,102**
704	**Economic affairs**	**10,681**	**11,571**	**21,540**	**6,071**	**6,857**	**15,869**	**6,071**	**6,857**	**15,869**	**6,071**	**6,857**	**15,869**
7042	Agriculture, forestry, fishing, and hunting	107	127	140	146	159	185	146	159	185	146	159	185
7043	Fuel and energy	...	...	—	...	...	—	...	...	—	...	...	—
7044	Mining, manufacturing, and construction	50	89	82	208	260	82	208	260	82	208	260	82
7045	Transport	6,182	6,264	14,226	2,969	3,385	10,702	2,969	3,385	10,702	2,969	3,385	10,702
7046	Communication	...	...	—	...	...	—	...	...	—	...	...	—
705	**Environmental protection**	**—**	**—**	**941**	**—**	**—**	**963**	**—**	**—**	**963**	**—**	**—**	**963**
706	**Housing and community amenities**	**3,271**	**4,043**	**3,404**	**2,924**	**3,626**	**3,395**	**2,924**	**3,626**	**3,395**	**2,924**	**3,626**	**3,395**
707	**Health**	**5,816**	**7,071**	**8,929**	**5,824**	**7,075**	**8,937**	**5,824**	**7,075**	**8,937**	**5,824**	**7,075**	**8,937**
7072	Outpatient services	—	—	—	—	—	—	—	—	—	—	—	—
7073	Hospital services	3,464	4,269	5,315	3,464	4,269	5,315	3,464	4,269	5,315	3,464	4,269	5,315
7074	Public health services	2,352	2,802	3,614	2,360	2,806	3,622	2,360	2,806	3,622	2,360	2,806	3,622
708	**Recreation, culture and religion**	**800**	**1,100**	**2,121**	**1,609**	**2,041**	**2,752**	**1,609**	**2,041**	**2,752**	**1,609**	**2,041**	**2,752**
709	**Education**	**11,620**	**11,577**	**11,911**	**11,615**	**11,667**	**12,124**	**11,615**	**11,667**	**12,124**	**11,615**	**11,667**	**12,124**
7091	Pre-primary and primary education	...	...	6,791	...	...	6,791	...	...	6,791	...	...	6,791
7092	Secondary education	...	...	—	...	...	—	...	...	—	...	...	—
7094	Tertiary education	5,159	4,739	4,755	5,154	4,829	4,968	5,154	4,829	4,968	5,154	4,829	4,968
710	**Social protection**	**5,575**	**6,355**	**7,814**	**5,575**	**6,355**	**7,814**	**5,575**	**6,355**	**7,814**	**5,575**	**6,355**	**7,814**
7z	Statistical discrepancy: Expenditure	...	...	...	...	...	...	...	...	...	...	...	...
	Table 8 Financial transactions by counterpart sector												
	Table 9 Total other economic flows in assets and liabilities												

Slovak Republic (936)

In Millions of Euros (EUR) / Fiscal Year Ends December 31st

		Budgetary Central Government			Central Government (excl. Social Security)			Central Government (incl. Social Security)			General Government		
		2013	2014	2015	2013P	2014P	2015P	2013P	2014P	2015P	2013P	2014P	2015P
	Statement of operations												
1	Revenue	...	...	...	17,426	18,244	21,266	27,073	28,231	31,912	28,719	29,855	33,720
2	Expense	...	...	...	19,441	20,076	21,705	29,313	30,206	32,555	30,891	31,952	33,827
GOB	**Gross operating balance**	...	...	...	**-45**	**275**	**1,787**	**-229**	**176**	**1,626**	**535**	**785**	**2,926**
NOB	**Net operating balance**	...	...	...	**-2,015**	**-1,832**	**-439**	**-2,241**	**-1,974**	**-643**	**-2,172**	**-2,098**	**-107**
31	Net/Gross investment in nonfinancial assets	...	...	...	-28	72	1,642	-61	39	1,608	-155	-42	2,023
2M	Expenditure	...	...	...	19,412	20,148	23,347	29,253	30,245	34,163	30,737	31,911	35,850
NLB	**Net lending (+) / Net borrowing (-)**	...	...	...	**-1,986**	**-1,904**	**-2,081**	**-2,180**	**-2,013**	**-2,252**	**-2,017**	**-2,056**	**-2,130**
32	Net acquisition of financial assets	...	...	...	1,134	-1,366	-841	...	...	...	1,268	-1,434	-755
33	Net incurrence of liabilities	...	...	...	3,211	523	1,197	...	...	...	3,378	608	1,314
NLBz	Statistical discrepancy	...	...	...	-91	16	43	...	...	...	-92	14	61
	Memorandum items												
PB	Primary net lending / net borrowing	...	...	...	-630	-484	-728	-824	-593	-898	-630	-613	-751
GB	Government balance per national definition	...	...	...	...	...	...	...	...	...	...	...	...
	Statement of other economic flows												
	Balance sheet												
6	**Net worth**	...	...	...	...	...	...	...	...	...	...	...	...
61	Nonfinancial assets	...	...	...	...	...	...	...	...	...	...	...	...
62	Financial assets	...	...	...	18,456	16,451	16,267	...	...	...	21,115	19,048	18,959
63	Liabilities	...	...	...	43,535	44,051	44,526	...	...	...	45,360	45,980	46,669
	Table 1 Revenue												
1	**Revenue**	...	...	...	**17,426**	**18,244**	**21,266**	**27,073**	**28,231**	**31,912**	**28,719**	**29,855**	**33,720**
11	**Taxes**	...	...	...	**11,810**	**12,706**	**13,913**	**11,810**	**12,706**	**13,913**	**12,347**	**13,252**	**14,331**
111	Taxes on income, profits, and capital gains	...	...	...	4,471	4,955	5,572	4,471	4,955	5,572	4,471	4,955	5,572
1111	Payable by individuals	...	...	...	2,175	2,275	2,464	2,175	2,275	2,464	2,175	2,275	2,464
1112	Payable by corporations and other enterprises	...	...	...	2,118	2,504	2,945	2,118	2,504	2,945	2,118	2,504	2,945
1113	Other taxes on income, profits, and capital gains	...	...	...	178	175	162	178	175	162	178	175	162
112	Taxes on payroll and workforce	...	...	...	—	—	—	—	—	—	—	—	—
113	Taxes on property	...	...	...	0	0	-0	0	0	-0	327	331	335
114	Taxes on goods and services	...	...	...	7,339	7,752	8,342	7,339	7,752	8,342	7,549	7,967	8,424
1141	General taxes on goods and services	...	...	...	4,696	5,021	5,420	4,696	5,021	5,420	4,696	5,021	5,420
1142	Excises	...	...	...	1,985	2,015	2,108	1,985	2,015	2,108	1,985	2,015	2,108
115	Taxes on international trade and transactions	...	...	...	0	-0	0	0	-0	0	0	-0	0
116	Other taxes	...	...	...	—	—	—	—	—	—	—	—	—
12	**Social contributions**	...	...	...	**333**	**365**	**385**	**9,977**	**10,328**	**11,006**	**10,007**	**10,360**	**11,042**
121	Social security contributions	...	...	...	0	0	1	9,643	9,962	10,619	9,643	9,962	10,619
122	Other social contributions	...	...	...	332	364	385	334	366	387	364	398	424
13	**Grants**	...	...	...	...	...	...	...	...	...	...	...	...
131	From foreign governments	...	...	...	...	...	...	...	...	...	...	...	...
132	From international organizations	...	...	...	...	...	...	...	...	...	...	...	...
133	From other general government units	...	...	...	31	45	41	2	1	0	—	—	—
1331	Current	...	...	...	30	45	41	0	1	0	—	—	—
1332	Capital	...	...	...	1	—	0	1	—	0	—	—	—
14	**Other revenue**	...	...	...	...	...	...	...	...	...	...	...	...
	Table 2 Expense by economic type												
2	**Expense**	...	...	...	**19,441**	**20,076**	**21,705**	**29,313**	**30,206**	**32,555**	**30,891**	**31,952**	**33,827**
21	**Compensation of employees**	...	...	...	**3,975**	**4,132**	**4,320**	**4,097**	**4,259**	**4,454**	**6,356**	**6,694**	**7,049**
211	Wages and salaries	...	...	...	...	...	...	...	...	...	...	...	...
212	Employers' social contributions	...	...	...	...	...	...	...	...	...	...	...	...
22	**Use of goods and services**	...	...	...	**2,630**	**2,741**	**3,140**	**2,764**	**2,881**	**3,249**	**4,102**	**4,266**	**4,655**
23	**Consumption of fixed capital**	...	...	...	**1,970**	**2,107**	**2,226**	**2,012**	**2,151**	**2,269**	**2,707**	**2,883**	**3,033**
24	**Interest**	...	...	...	**1,356**	**1,421**	**1,353**	**1,356**	**1,420**	**1,353**	**1,387**	**1,444**	**1,379**
25	**Subsidies**	...	...	...	**333**	**246**	**193**	**333**	**246**	**193**	**574**	**520**	**464**

Slovak Republic (936)

In Millions of Euros (EUR) / Fiscal Year Ends December 31st

		Budgetary Central Government			Central Government (excl. Social Security)			Central Government (incl. Social Security)			General Government		
		2013	2014	2015	2013P	2014P	2015P	2013P	2014P	2015P	2013P	2014P	2015P
26	**Grants**	...	...	...	...	...	...	...	...	...	...	...	...
261	To foreign governments	...	...	...	...	...	...	...	...	...	...	...	...
262	To international organizations	...	...	...	...	...	...	...	...	...	...	...	...
263	To other general government units	...	...	...	3,964	4,290	4,644	3,260	3,389	4,184	—	—	—
2631	Current	...	...	...	3,577	3,975	4,083	2,872	3,074	3,623	—	—	—
2632	Capital	...	...	...	388	316	561	388	316	561	—	—	—
27	**Social benefits**	...	...	...	**3,847**	**3,774**	**3,907**	**14,027**	**14,428**	**14,883**	**14,098**	**14,501**	**14,960**
271	Social security benefits	...	...	...	...	...	...	...	...	...	...	...	...
272	Social assistance benefits	...	...	...	...	...	...	...	...	...	...	...	...
273	Employment-related social benefits	...	...	...	...	...	...	...	...	...	...	...	...
28	**Other expense**	...	...	...	...	...	...	...	...	...	...	...	...
281	Property expense other than interest	...	...	...	—	—	—	—	—	—	—	—	—
282	Transfers not elsewhere classified	...	...	...	...	...	...	...	...	...	...	...	...
2821	Current	...	...	...	...	...	...	...	...	...	...	...	...
2822	Capital	...	...	...	...	...	...	...	...	...	...	...	...
	Table 3 Transactions in assets and liabilities												
3	**Change in net worth from transactions**	...	...	...	**-2,106**	**-1,816**	**-396**	...	...	...	**-2,264**	**-2,084**	**-46**
31	**Net/Gross investment in nonfinancial assets**	...	...	...	**-28**	**72**	**1,642**	**-61**	**39**	**1,608**	**-155**	**-42**	**2,023**
311	Fixed assets	...	...	...	-157	203	1,511	-190	169	1,477	-241	140	1,918
3111	Buildings and structures	...	...	...	...	...	...	...	...	...	...	...	...
3112	Machinery and equipment	...	...	...	...	...	...	...	...	...	...	...	...
3113	Other fixed assets	...	...	...	...	...	...	...	...	...	...	...	...
3114	Weapons systems	...	...	...	...	...	...	...	...	...	...	...	...
312	Inventories	...	...	...	...	...	...	...	...	...	...	...	...
313	Valuables	...	...	...	...	...	...	...	...	...	...	...	...
314	Nonproduced assets	...	...	...	69	-178	126	69	-176	126	26	-229	99
3141	Land	...	...	...	...	...	...	...	...	...	...	...	...
3142	Mineral and energy resources	...	...	...	...	...	...	...	...	...	...	...	...
3143	Other naturally occurring assets	...	...	...	...	...	...	...	...	...	...	...	...
3144	Intangible nonproduced assets	...	...	...	...	...	...	...	...	...	...	...	...
32	**Net acquisition of financial assets**	...	...	...	**1,134**	**-1,366**	**-841**	...	...	...	**1,268**	**-1,434**	**-755**
	By instrument												
3201	Monetary gold and SDRs	...	...	...	—	—	—	...	...	...	—	—	—
3202	Currency and deposits	...	...	...	323	-2,125	396	...	...	...	388	-2,210	530
3203	Debt securities	...	...	...	2	-11	-36	...	...	...	1	-10	-37
3204	Loans	...	...	...	462	114	0	...	...	...	456	112	-45
3205	Equity and investment fund shares	...	...	...	-63	-203	-1,051	...	...	...	-55	-197	-1,034
3206	Insurance, pension, and standardized guarantee schemes	...	...	...	—	—	—	...	...	...	—	—	—
3207	Financial derivatives and employee stock options	...	...	...	—	—	—	...	...	...	—	—	—
3208	Other accounts receivable	...	...	...	410	859	-150	...	...	...	479	870	-169
	By debtor												
321	Domestic debtors	...	...	...	...	...	...	...	...	...	...	...	...
322	External debtors	...	...	...	...	...	...	...	...	...	...	...	...
33	**Net incurrence of liabilities**	...	...	...	**3,211**	**523**	**1,197**	...	...	...	**3,378**	**608**	**1,314**
	By instrument												
3301	Special Drawing Rights (SDRs)	...	...	...	—	—	—	...	...	...	—	—	—
3302	Currency and deposits	...	...	...	20	-56	669	...	...	...	17	-5	315
3303	Debt securities	...	...	...	1,788	884	271	...	...	...	1,788	886	274
3304	Loans	...	...	...	1,132	-529	48	...	...	...	1,081	-529	102
3305	Equity and investment fund shares	...	...	...	-0	—	-0	...	...	...	-0	—	—
3306	Insurance, pension, and standardized guarantee schemes	...	...	...	6	-2	-1	...	...	...	6	-2	-1
3307	Financial derivatives and employee stock options	...	...	...	—	—	—	...	...	...	—	—	—
3308	Other accounts payable	...	...	...	265	226	210	...	...	...	485	257	624

Slovak Republic (936)

In Millions of Euros (EUR) / Fiscal Year Ends December 31st

		Budgetary Central Government			Central Government (excl. Social Security)			Central Government (incl. Social Security)			General Government		
		2013	2014	2015	2013P	2014P	2015P	2013P	2014P	2015P	2013P	2014P	2015P
	By creditor												
331	Domestic creditors	...	...	...	...	...	...	...	...	...	...	...	...
332	External creditors	...	...	...	...	...	...	...	...	...	...	...	...
	Table 4 Holding gains and losses in assets and liabilities												
	Table 5 Holding gains and losses in assets and liabilities												
	Table 6 Balance sheet												
6	**Net worth**	...	...	...	...	...	...	...	...	...	...	...	...
61	**Nonfinancial assets**	...	...	...	...	...	...	...	...	...	...	...	...
611	Fixed assets	...	...	...	...	...	...	...	...	...	...	...	...
6111	Buildings and structures	...	...	...	...	...	...	...	...	...	...	...	...
6112	Machinery and equipment	...	...	...	...	...	...	...	...	...	...	...	...
6113	Other fixed assets	...	...	...	...	...	...	...	...	...	...	...	...
6114	Weapons systems	...	...	...	...	...	...	...	...	...	...	...	...
612	Inventories	...	...	...	...	...	...	...	...	...	...	...	...
613	Valuables	...	...	...	...	...	...	...	...	...	...	...	...
614	Nonproduced assets	...	...	...	...	...	...	...	...	...	...	...	...
6141	Land	...	...	...	...	...	...	...	...	...	...	...	...
6142	Mineral and energy resources	...	...	...	...	...	...	...	...	...	...	...	...
6143	Other naturally occurring assets	...	...	...	...	...	...	...	...	...	...	...	...
6144	Intangible nonproduced assets	...	...	...	...	...	...	...	...	...	...	...	...
62	**Financial assets**	...	...	...	**18,456**	**16,451**	**16,267**	...	...	...	**21,115**	**19,048**	**18,959**
	By instrument												
6201	Monetary gold and SDRs	...	...	...	—	—	—	...	...	...	—	—	—
6202	Currency and deposits	...	...	...	4,321	2,243	2,642	...	...	...	4,965	2,836	3,337
6203	Debt securities	...	...	...	16	47	17	...	...	...	20	50	20
6204	Loans	...	...	...	3,781	4,063	4,083	...	...	...	3,297	3,578	3,581
6205	Equity and investment fund shares	...	...	...	7,070	6,936	6,548	...	...	...	8,546	8,392	8,007
6206	Insurance, pension, and standardized guarantee schemes	...	...	...	—	—	—	...	...	...	—	—	—
6207	Financial derivatives and employee stock options	...	...	...	—	—	—	...	...	...	0	0	1
6208	Other accounts receivable	...	...	...	3,268	3,162	2,976	...	...	...	4,286	4,192	4,013
	By debtor												
621	Domestic debtors	...	...	...	...	...	...	...	...	...	...	...	...
622	External debtors	...	...	...	...	...	...	...	...	...	...	...	...
63	**Liabilities**	...	...	...	**43,535**	**44,051**	**44,526**	...	...	...	**45,360**	**45,980**	**46,669**
	By instrument												
6301	Special Drawing Rights (SDRs)	...	...	...	—	—	—	...	...	...	—	—	—
6302	Currency and deposits	...	...	...	1,017	962	1,631	...	...	...	110	105	421
6303	Debt securities	...	...	...	34,989	36,153	35,943	...	...	...	34,997	36,161	35,952
6304	Loans	...	...	...	5,155	4,407	4,521	...	...	...	6,155	5,452	5,706
6305	Equity and investment fund shares	...	...	...	—	—	—	...	...	...	—	—	—
6306	Insurance, pension, and standardized guarantee schemes	...	...	...	37	35	34	...	...	...	37	35	34
6307	Financial derivatives and employee stock options	...	...	...	—	0	0	...	...	...	—	0	0
6308	Other accounts payable	...	...	...	2,336	2,494	2,399	...	...	...	4,061	4,227	4,556
	By creditor												
631	Domestic creditors	...	...	...	...	...	...	...	...	...	...	...	...
632	External creditors	...	...	...	...	...	...	...	...	...	...	...	...
	Memorandum items												
6M2	Net financial worth	...	...	...	-25,079	-27,600	-28,259	...	...	...	-24,246	-26,932	-27,710
6M3	Gross debt (D4) at market value	...	...	...	43,535	44,051	44,526	...	...	...	45,360	45,980	46,669
6M3D3	D3 debt liabilities at market value	...	...	...	43,498	44,016	44,493	...	...	...	45,323	45,945	46,636
6M3D2	D2 debt liabilities at market value	...	...	...	41,162	41,522	42,094	...	...	...	41,262	41,718	42,080
6M3D1	D1 debt liabilities at market value	...	...	...	40,145	40,560	40,463	...	...	...	41,152	41,613	41,659
6M4	Gross debt (D4) at nominal value	...	...	...	...	...	...	...	...	...	...	...	...
6M4D3	D3 debt liabilities at nominal value	...	...	...	...	...	...	...	...	...	...	...	...
6M4D2	D2 debt liabilities at nominal value	...	...	...	...	...	...	...	...	...	...	...	...
6M4D1	D1 debt liabilities at nominal value	...	...	...	...	...	...	...	...	...	...	...	...

lovak Republic (936)

Millions of Euros (EUR) / Fiscal Year Ends December 31st

		Budgetary Central Government			Central Government (excl. Social Security)			Central Government (incl. Social Security)			General Government		
		2013	2014	2015	2013P	2014P	2015P	2013P	2014P	2015P	2013P	2014P	2015P
6M35	Gross debt (D4) at face value	...	...	...	...	...	...	...	...	...	...	...	...
6M35D3	D3 debt liabilities at face value	...	...	...	42,837	43,025	43,740	...	...	...	44,661	44,952	45,849
6M35D2	D2 debt liabilities at face value	...	...	...	40,500	40,531	41,341	...	...	...	40,600	40,725	41,293
6M35D1	D1 debt liabilities at face value	...	...	...	39,483	39,570	39,710	...	...	...	40,490	40,620	40,872
6M93	Government gross debt per national definition	...	...	...	40,500	40,531	41,341	...	...	...	40,600	40,725	41,293
6M5	Arrears	...	...	...	...	...	...	...	...	...	...	...	...
6M6	Explicit contingent liabilities	...	...	...	...	...	...	...	...	...	...	...	...
6M61	of which: Publicly guaranteed debt	...	...	...	...	...	...	...	...	...	...	...	...
6M7	Net implicit obligations for social security benefits	...	...	...	...	...	...	...	...	...	...	...	...
	Table 7 Expenditure by functions of government												
7	**Expenditure**	...	...	...	**18,960**	**19,697**	...	...	...	...	**30,284**	**31,462**	...
701	**General public services**	...	...	...	**5,272**	**5,517**	...	...	...	...	**4,064**	**4,294**	...
7017	Public debt transactions	...	...	...	1,407	1,477	...	...	...	...	1,446	1,509	...
7018	Transfers of general character between levels of government	...	...	...	—	—	...	...	...	...	—	—	...
702	**Defense**	...	...	...	**669**	**695**	...	...	...	...	**669**	**695**	...
703	**Public order and safety**	...	...	...	**1,562**	**1,646**	...	...	...	...	**1,618**	**1,706**	...
704	**Economic affairs**	...	...	...	**2,663**	**2,800**	...	...	...	...	**3,192**	**3,387**	...
7042	Agriculture, forestry, fishing, and hunting	...	...	...	259	247	...	...	...	...	259	246	...
7043	Fuel and energy	...	...	...	18	18	...	...	...	...	19	20	...
7044	Mining, manufacturing, and construction	...	...	...	12	13	...	...	...	...	45	48	...
7045	Transport	...	...	...	2,156	2,294	...	...	...	...	2,657	2,852	...
7046	Communication	...	...	...	4	4	...	...	...	...	7	8	...
705	**Environmental protection**	...	...	...	**229**	**226**	...	...	...	...	**524**	**535**	...
706	**Housing and community amenities**	...	...	...	**135**	**135**	...	...	...	...	**446**	**465**	...
707	**Health**	...	...	...	**1,229**	**1,291**	...	...	...	...	**1,342**	**1,409**	...
7072	Outpatient services	...	...	...	54	56	...	...	...	...	64	65	...
7073	Hospital services	...	...	...	1,045	1,097	...	...	...	...	1,144	1,202	...
7074	Public health services	...	...	...	32	33	...	...	...	...	32	33	...
708	**Recreation, culture and religion**	...	...	...	**393**	**416**	...	...	...	...	**667**	**705**	...
709	**Education**	...	...	...	**2,114**	**2,259**	...	...	...	...	**2,928**	**3,121**	...
7091	Pre-primary and primary education	...	...	...	93	97	...	...	...	...	1,118	1,196	...
7092	Secondary education	...	...	...	439	475	...	...	...	...	505	532	...
7094	Tertiary education	...	...	...	474	493	...	...	...	...	474	493	...
710	**Social protection**	...	...	...	**4,694**	**4,711**	...	...	...	...	**14,834**	**15,145**	...
7z	Statistical discrepancy: Expenditure	...	...	...	-0	0	...	...	...	...	-0	—	...
	Table 8 Financial transactions by counterpart sector												
32	**Net acquisition of financial assets**	...	...	...	**1,134**	**-1,366**	**-841**	...	...	...	**1,268**	**-1,434**	**-755**
321	Domestic debtors	...	...	...	...	...	...	...	...	...	...	...	...
8211	General government	...	...	...	...	...	...	...	...	...	...	...	...
8212	Central bank	...	...	...	...	...	...	...	...	...	—	—	—
8213	Deposit-taking corporations except the central bank	...	...	...	...	...	...	...	...	...	...	...	...
8214	Other financial corporations	...	...	...	...	...	...	...	...	...	...	...	...
8215	Nonfinancial corporations	...	...	...	...	...	...	...	...	...	...	...	...
8216	Households & nonprofit institutions serving households	...	...	...	...	...	...	...	...	...	...	...	...
322	External debtors	...	...	...	...	...	...	...	...	...	...	...	...
8221	General government	...	...	...	...	...	...	...	...	...	...	...	...
8227	International organizations	...	...	...	...	...	...	...	...	...	...	...	...
8228	Financial corporations other than international organizations	...	...	...	...	...	...	...	...	...	...	...	...
8229	Other nonresidents	...	...	...	...	...	...	...	...	...	...	...	...

Slovak Republic (936)

In Millions of Euros (EUR) / Fiscal Year Ends December 31st

		Budgetary Central Government			Central Government (excl. Social Security)			Central Government (incl. Social Security)			General Government		
		2013	2014	2015	2013P	2014P	2015P	2013P	2014P	2015P	2013P	2014P	2015P
33	**Net incurrence of liabilities**	**...**	**...**	**...**	**3,211**	**523**	**1,197**	**...**	**...**	**...**	**3,378**	**608**	**1,314**
331	Domestic creditors	...	...	...	...	...	...	...	...	...	...	...	...
8311	General government	...	...	...	...	...	...	...	...	...	—	—	—
8312	Central bank	...	...	...	...	...	...	...	...	...	...	...	...
8313	Deposit-taking corporations except the central bank	...	...	...	...	...	...	...	...	...	...	...	...
8314	Other financial corporations	...	...	...	...	...	...	...	...	...	...	...	...
8315	Nonfinancial corporations	...	...	...	...	...	...	...	...	...	...	...	...
8316	Households & nonprofit institutions serving households	...	...	...	...	...	...	...	...	...	...	...	...
332	External creditors	...	...	...	...	...	...	...	...	...	...	...	...
8321	General government	...	...	...	...	...	...	...	...	...	...	...	...
8327	International organizations	...	...	...	...	...	...	...	...	...	...	...	...
8328	Financial corporations other than international organizations	...	...	...	...	...	...	...	...	...	...	...	...
8329	Other nonresidents	...	...	...	...	...	...	...	...	...	...	...	...
	Table 9 Total other economic flows in assets and liabilities												
9	**Change in net worth due to other economic flows**	**...**	**...**	**...**	**...**	**...**	**...**	**...**	**...**	**...**	**...**	**...**	**...**
91	**Other economic flows in nonfinancial assets**	**...**	**...**	**...**	**...**	**...**	**...**	**...**	**...**	**...**	**...**	**...**	**...**
911	Fixed assets	...	...	...	...	...	...	...	...	...	...	...	...
912	Inventories	...	...	...	...	...	...	...	...	...	...	...	...
913	Valuables	...	...	...	...	...	...	...	...	...	...	...	...
914	Nonproduced assets	...	...	...	...	...	...	...	...	...	...	...	...
92	**Other economic flows in financial assets**	**...**	**...**	**...**	**129**	**-640**	**658**	**...**	**...**	**...**	**114**	**-632**	**665**
	By instrument												
9201	Monetary gold and SDRs	...	...	...	—	—	—	...	...	...	—	—	—
9202	Currency and deposits	...	...	...	7	46	4	...	...	...	4	80	-29
9203	Debt securities	...	...	...	-189	42	6	...	...	...	-187	40	7
9204	Loans	...	...	...	-15	168	20	...	...	...	-18	168	48
9205	Equity and investment fund shares	...	...	...	231	69	663	...	...	...	173	43	649
9206	Insurance, pension, and standardized guarantee schemes	...	...	...	—	—	—	...	...	...	—	—	—
9207	Financial derivatives and employee stock options	...	...	...	—	—	—	...	...	...	—	—	0
9208	Other accounts receivable	...	...	...	95	-966	-35	...	...	...	143	-964	-10
	By debtor												
921	Domestic debtors	...	...	...	...	...	...	...	...	...	...	...	...
922	External debtors	...	...	...	...	...	...	...	...	...	...	...	...
93	**Other economic flows in liabilities**	**...**	**...**	**...**	**-375**	**-7**	**-721**	**...**	**...**	**...**	**-405**	**12**	**-625**
	By instrument												
9301	Special Drawing Rights (SDRs)	...	...	...	—	—	—	...	...	...	—	—	—
9302	Currency and deposits	...	...	...	0	0	—	...	...	...	—	0	0
9303	Debt securities	...	...	...	-277	280	-482	...	...	...	-277	278	-483
9304	Loans	...	...	...	39	-219	65	...	...	...	32	-175	153
9305	Equity and investment fund shares	...	...	...	0	—	0	...	...	...	0	—	—
9306	Insurance, pension, and standardized guarantee schemes	...	...	...	-0	0	—	...	...	...	-0	0	—
9307	Financial derivatives and employee stock options	...	...	...	—	0	0	...	...	...	—	0	-0
9308	Other accounts payable	...	...	...	-137	-68	-304	...	...	...	-161	-91	-295
	By creditor												
931	Domestic creditors	...	...	...	...	...	...	...	...	...	...	...	...
932	External creditors	...	...	...	...	...	...	...	...	...	...	...	...
	Memorandum items												
9M2	Change in net financial worth due to other economic flows	...	...	...	503	-633	1,379	...	...	...	519	-644	1,291

Slovak Republic (936)

In Millions of Euros (EUR) / Fiscal Year Ends December 31st

		Budgetary Central Government			Central Government (excl. Social Security)			Central Government (incl. Social Security)			General Government		
		2013	2014	2015	2013P	2014P	2015P	2013P	2014P	2015P	2013P	2014P	2015P
9M3	Gross debt (D4) at market value: other economic flows	...	...	...	-375	-7	-721	...	...	...	-406	12	-625
9M3D3	D3 debt liabilities at market value: other economic flows	...	...	...	-375	-7	-721	...	...	...	-406	12	-625
9M3D2	D2 debt liabilities at market value: other economic flows	...	...	...	-238	61	-417	...	...	...	-244	103	-330
9M3D1	D1 debt liabilities at market value: other economic flows	...	...	...	-238	61	-417	...	...	...	-244	103	-330

Slovenia (961)

In Millions of Euros (EUR) / Fiscal Year Ends December 31st

		Budgetary Central Government			Central Government (excl. Social Security)			Central Government (incl. Social Security)			General Government		
		2013	2014	2015	2013	2014	2015	2013	2014	2015	2013	2014	2015
	Statement of operations												
1	Revenue	...	...	...	9,797	10,315	10,834	14,154	14,686	15,408	16,267	16,787	17,407
2	Expense	...	...	...	15,000	12,115	11,709	19,299	16,415	16,244	21,048	17,884	17,679
GOB	**Gross operating balance**	...	...	...	**-4,489**	**-1,081**	**-138**	**-4,417**	**-996**	**-83**	**-3,732**	**-34**	**817**
NOB	**Net operating balance**	...	...	...	**-5,203**	**-1,800**	**-876**	**-5,145**	**-1,729**	**-836**	**-4,781**	**-1,096**	**-272**
31	Net/Gross investment in nonfinancial assets	...	...	...	207	110	320	200	107	315	615	784	759
2M	Expenditure	...	...	...	15,207	12,225	12,030	19,499	16,522	16,559	21,663	18,667	18,438
NLB	**Net lending (+) / Net borrowing (-)**	...	...	...	**-5,409**	**-1,909**	**-1,196**	**-5,345**	**-1,836**	**-1,151**	**-5,396**	**-1,880**	**-1,031**
32	Net acquisition of financial assets	...	...	...	961	3,011	700	...	...	...	974	3,017	774
33	Net incurrence of liabilities	...	...	...	6,361	4,919	1,887	...	...	...	6,386	4,913	1,802
NLBz	Statistical discrepancy	...	...	...	9	2	8	...	...	...	-16	-16	3
	Memorandum items												
PB	Primary net lending / net borrowing	...	...	...	-4,503	-741	-71	-4,440	-671	-26	-4,476	-697	106
GB	Government balance per national definition	...	...	...	...	...	...	...	...	...	...	...	...
	Statement of other economic flows												
	Balance sheet												
6	**Net worth**	...	...	...	...	...	...	...	...	...	...	...	...
61	Nonfinancial assets	...	...	...	...	...	...	...	...	...	...	...	...
62	Financial assets	...	...	...	22,065	26,894	26,552	...	...	...	23,598	28,605	28,237
63	Liabilities	...	...	...	27,408	35,136	36,603	...	...	...	28,596	36,300	37,675
	Table 1 Revenue												
1	**Revenue**	...	...	...	**9,797**	**10,315**	**10,834**	**14,154**	**14,686**	**15,408**	**16,267**	**16,787**	**17,407**
11	**Taxes**	...	...	...	**6,524**	**6,837**	**7,192**	**6,524**	**6,837**	**7,192**	**7,968**	**8,285**	**8,546**
111	Taxes on income, profits, and capital gains	...	...	...	1,154	1,310	1,535	1,154	1,310	1,535	2,285	2,437	2,554
1111	Payable by individuals	...	...	...	718	779	965	718	779	965	1,849	1,907	1,984
1112	Payable by corporations and other enterprises	...	...	...	433	529	568	433	529	568	433	529	568
1113	Other taxes on income, profits, and capital gains	...	...	...	3	2	2	3	2	2	3	2	2
112	Taxes on payroll and workforce	...	...	...	23	20	20	23	20	20	23	20	20
113	Taxes on property	...	...	...	14	5	2	14	5	2	209	207	211
114	Taxes on goods and services	...	...	...	5,326	5,495	5,627	5,326	5,495	5,627	5,443	5,612	5,753
1141	General taxes on goods and services	...	...	...	3,044	3,153	3,217	3,044	3,153	3,217	3,067	3,179	3,246
1142	Excises	...	...	...	1,549	1,571	1,594	1,549	1,571	1,594	1,549	1,571	1,594
115	Taxes on international trade and transactions	...	...	...	—	—	—	—	—	—	—	—	—
116	Other taxes	...	...	...	8	8	8	8	8	8	8	8	8
12	**Social contributions**	...	...	...	**129**	**131**	**135**	**5,346**	**5,444**	**5,683**	**5,387**	**5,485**	**5,725**
121	Social security contributions	...	...	...	6	5	5	5,223	5,316	5,552	5,223	5,316	5,552
122	Other social contributions	...	...	...	122	127	130	124	128	131	164	169	173
13	**Grants**	...	...	...	...	...	...	...	...	...	...	...	...
131	From foreign governments	...	...	...	...	...	...	...	...	...	...	...	...
132	From international organizations	...	...	...	...	...	...	...	...	...	...	...	...
133	From other general government units	...	...	...	1,053	1,069	1,122	24	21	20	—	—	—
1331	Current	...	...	...	1,053	1,068	1,122	24	20	20	—	—	—
1332	Capital	...	...	...	0	1	—	0	1	—	—	—	—
14	**Other revenue**	...	...	...	...	...	...	...	...	...	...	...	...
	Table 2 Expense by economic type												
2	**Expense**	...	...	...	**15,000**	**12,115**	**11,709**	**19,299**	**16,415**	**16,244**	**21,048**	**17,884**	**17,679**
21	**Compensation of employees**	...	...	...	**2,801**	**2,742**	**2,780**	**2,849**	**2,788**	**2,826**	**4,328**	**4,255**	**4,313**
211	Wages and salaries	...	...	...	...	...	...	...	...	...	...	...	...
212	Employers' social contributions	...	...	...	...	...	...	...	...	...	...	...	...
22	**Use of goods and services**	...	...	...	**1,663**	**1,703**	**1,772**	**1,694**	**1,732**	**1,800**	**2,471**	**2,492**	**2,567**
23	**Consumption of fixed capital**	...	...	...	**714**	**719**	**738**	**728**	**733**	**753**	**1,049**	**1,063**	**1,089**
24	**Interest**	...	...	...	**907**	**1,169**	**1,125**	**905**	**1,165**	**1,125**	**920**	**1,183**	**1,137**
25	**Subsidies**	...	...	...	**274**	**231**	**227**	**274**	**231**	**227**	**380**	**329**	**320**

Slovenia (961)

In Millions of Euros (EUR) / Fiscal Year Ends December 31st

		Budgetary Central Government			Central Government (excl. Social Security)			Central Government (incl. Social Security)			General Government		
		2013	2014	2015	2013	2014	2015	2013	2014	2015	2013	2014	2015
26	**Grants**	...	...	...	...	...	...	...	...	...	...	...	...
261	To foreign governments	...	...	...	...	...	...	...	...	...	...	...	...
262	To international organizations	...	...	...	...	...	...	...	...	...	...	...	...
263	To other general government units	...	...	...	2,576	2,757	2,666	1,318	1,511	1,566	—	—	—
2631	Current	...	...	...	2,343	2,329	2,230	1,084	1,083	1,130	—	—	—
2632	Capital	...	...	...	233	428	436	233	428	436	—	—	—
27	**Social benefits**	...	...	...	**1,337**	**1,321**	**1,330**	**6,759**	**6,723**	**6,820**	**6,947**	**6,919**	**7,020**
271	Social security benefits	...	...	...	...	...	...	...	...	...	...	...	...
272	Social assistance benefits	...	...	...	...	...	...	...	...	...	...	...	...
273	Employment-related social benefits	...	...	...	...	...	...	...	...	...	...	...	...
28	**Other expense**	...	...	...	...	...	...	...	...	...	...	...	...
281	Property expense other than interest	...	...	...	—	—	—	—	—	—	—	—	—
282	Transfers not elsewhere classified	...	...	...	...	...	...	...	...	...	...	...	...
2821	Current	...	...	...	...	...	...	...	...	...	...	...	...
2822	Capital	...	...	...	...	...	...	...	...	...	...	...	...
	Table 3 Transactions in assets and liabilities												
3	**Change in net worth from transactions**	...	...	...	**-5,193**	**-1,798**	**-867**	...	...	...	**-4,797**	**-1,112**	**-269**
31	**Net/Gross investment in nonfinancial assets**	...	...	...	**207**	**110**	**320**	**200**	**107**	**315**	**615**	**784**	**759**
311	Fixed assets	...	...	...	127	169	292	121	167	287	527	844	737
3111	Buildings and structures	...	...	...	...	...	...	...	...	...	...	...	...
3112	Machinery and equipment	...	...	...	...	...	...	...	...	...	...	...	...
3113	Other fixed assets	...	...	...	...	...	...	...	...	...	...	...	...
3114	Weapons systems	...	...	...	...	...	...	...	...	...	...	...	...
312	Inventories	...	...	...	...	...	...	...	...	...	...	...	...
313	Valuables	...	...	...	...	...	...	...	...	...	...	...	...
314	Nonproduced assets	...	...	...	25	-65	23	25	-65	23	32	-66	16
3141	Land	...	...	...	...	...	...	...	...	...	...	...	...
3142	Mineral and energy resources	...	...	...	...	...	...	...	...	...	...	...	...
3143	Other naturally occurring assets	...	...	...	...	...	...	...	...	...	...	...	...
3144	Intangible nonproduced assets	...	...	...	...	...	...	...	...	...	...	...	...
32	**Net acquisition of financial assets**	...	...	...	**961**	**3,011**	**700**	...	...	...	**974**	**3,017**	**774**
	By instrument												
3201	Monetary gold and SDRs	...	...	...	—	—	—	...	...	...	—	—	—
3202	Currency and deposits	...	...	...	-224	2,104	1,070	...	...	...	-281	2,180	1,140
3203	Debt securities	...	...	...	24	-8	39	...	...	...	-3	-38	34
3204	Loans	...	...	...	860	821	-658	...	...	...	852	807	-665
3205	Equity and investment fund shares	...	...	...	208	0	71	...	...	...	217	-14	72
3206	Insurance, pension, and standardized guarantee schemes	...	...	...	1	1	0	...	...	...	0	2	0
3207	Financial derivatives and employee stock options	...	...	...	-1	-1	-0	...	...	...	-1	-1	-0
3208	Other accounts receivable	...	...	...	93	94	178	...	...	...	190	79	193
	By debtor												
321	Domestic debtors	...	...	...	...	...	...	...	...	...	...	...	...
322	External debtors	...	...	...	...	...	...	...	...	...	...	...	...
33	**Net incurrence of liabilities**	...	...	...	**6,361**	**4,919**	**1,887**	...	...	...	**6,386**	**4,913**	**1,802**
	By instrument												
3301	Special Drawing Rights (SDRs)	...	...	...	—	—	—	...	...	...	—	—	—
3302	Currency and deposits	...	...	...	22	-8	5	...	...	...	22	-8	5
3303	Debt securities	...	...	...	5,756	4,377	1,003	...	...	...	5,762	4,393	1,007
3304	Loans	...	...	...	374	338	888	...	...	...	332	381	872
3305	Equity and investment fund shares	...	...	...	0	-0	104	...	...	...	0	0	110
3306	Insurance, pension, and standardized guarantee schemes	...	...	...	—	—	—	...	...	...	—	—	—
3307	Financial derivatives and employee stock options	...	...	...	-1	-2	-2	...	...	...	-1	-2	-2
3308	Other accounts payable	...	...	...	209	214	-111	...	...	...	270	149	-190

Slovenia (961)

In Millions of Euros (EUR) / Fiscal Year Ends December 31st

		Budgetary Central Government			Central Government (excl. Social Security)			Central Government (incl. Social Security)			General Government		
		2013	2014	2015	2013	2014	2015	2013	2014	2015	2013	2014	2015
	By creditor												
331	Domestic creditors	...	...	...	...	...	...	...	...	...	...	...	...
332	External creditors	...	...	...	...	...	...	...	...	...	...	...	...
	Table 4 Holding gains and losses in assets and liabilities												
	Table 5 Holding gains and losses in assets and liabilities												
	Table 6 Balance sheet												
6	**Net worth**	...	...	...	...	...	...	...	...	...	...	...	...
61	**Nonfinancial assets**	...	...	...	...	...	...	...	...	...	...	...	...
611	Fixed assets	...	...	...	...	...	...	...	...	...	22,060	...	...
6111	Buildings and structures	...	...	...	...	...	...	...	...	...	19,166	...	...
6112	Machinery and equipment	...	...	...	...	...	...	...	...	...	...	...	...
6113	Other fixed assets	...	...	...	...	...	...	...	...	...	1,115	...	...
6114	Weapons systems	...	...	...	...	...	...	...	...	...	...	...	...
612	Inventories	...	...	...	...	...	...	...	...	...	836	...	...
613	Valuables	...	...	...	...	...	...	...	...	...	...	...	...
614	Nonproduced assets	...	...	...	...	...	...	...	...	...	...	...	...
6141	Land	...	...	...	...	...	...	...	...	...	...	...	...
6142	Mineral and energy resources	...	...	...	...	...	...	...	...	...	...	...	...
6143	Other naturally occurring assets	...	...	...	...	...	...	...	...	...	...	...	...
6144	Intangible nonproduced assets	...	...	...	...	...	...	...	...	...	...	...	...
62	**Financial assets**	...	...	...	**22,065**	**26,894**	**26,552**	...	...	...	**23,598**	**28,605**	**28,237**
	By instrument												
6201	Monetary gold and SDRs	...	...	...	—	—	—	...	...	...	—	—	—
6202	Currency and deposits	...	...	...	3,611	5,729	6,814	...	...	...	4,000	6,197	7,356
6203	Debt securities	...	...	...	147	144	179	...	...	...	203	172	201
6204	Loans	...	...	...	4,920	6,450	4,880	...	...	...	4,831	6,346	4,762
6205	Equity and investment fund shares	...	...	...	11,563	12,629	12,540	...	...	...	12,099	13,321	13,135
6206	Insurance, pension, and standardized guarantee schemes	...	...	...	2	11	22	...	...	...	2	12	23
6207	Financial derivatives and employee stock options	...	...	...	1	0	—	...	...	...	1	0	—
6208	Other accounts receivable	...	...	...	1,820	1,931	2,118	...	...	...	2,462	2,557	2,760
	By debtor												
621	Domestic debtors	...	...	...	...	...	...	...	...	...	...	...	...
622	External debtors	...	...	...	...	...	...	...	...	...	...	...	...
63	**Liabilities**	...	...	...	**27,408**	**35,136**	**36,603**	...	...	...	**28,596**	**36,300**	**37,675**
	By instrument												
6301	Special Drawing Rights (SDRs)	...	...	...	—	—	—	...	...	...	—	—	—
6302	Currency and deposits	...	...	...	170	163	169	...	...	...	170	163	169
6303	Debt securities	...	...	...	22,528	29,699	30,676	...	...	...	22,441	29,610	30,586
6304	Loans	...	...	...	2,696	3,036	3,921	...	...	...	3,339	3,722	4,588
6305	Equity and investment fund shares	...	...	...	52	48	147	...	...	...	45	43	149
6306	Insurance, pension, and standardized guarantee schemes	...	...	...	—	—	—	...	...	...	—	—	—
6307	Financial derivatives and employee stock options	...	...	...	4	5	3	...	...	...	4	5	3
6308	Other accounts payable	...	...	...	1,957	2,185	1,687	...	...	...	2,597	2,757	2,179
	By creditor												
631	Domestic creditors	...	...	...	...	...	...	...	...	...	...	...	...
632	External creditors	...	...	...	...	...	...	...	...	...	...	...	...
	Memorandum items												
6M2	Net financial worth	...	...	...	-5,343	-8,242	-10,051	...	...	...	-4,998	-7,696	-9,438
6M3	Gross debt (D4) at market value	...	...	...	27,352	35,082	36,453	...	...	...	28,547	36,252	37,523
6M3D3	D3 debt liabilities at market value	...	...	...	27,352	35,082	36,453	...	...	...	28,547	36,252	37,523
6M3D2	D2 debt liabilities at market value	...	...	...	25,395	32,898	34,766	...	...	...	25,950	33,495	35,344
6M3D1	D1 debt liabilities at market value	...	...	...	25,224	32,735	34,597	...	...	...	25,780	33,333	35,175
6M4	Gross debt (D4) at nominal value	...	...	...	...	...	...	...	...	...	...	...	...
6M4D3	D3 debt liabilities at nominal value	...	...	...	...	...	...	...	...	...	...	...	...
6M4D2	D2 debt liabilities at nominal value	...	...	...	...	...	...	...	...	...	...	...	...
6M4D1	D1 debt liabilities at nominal value	...	...	...	...	...	...	...	...	...	...	...	...

Slovenia (961)

In Millions of Euros (EUR) / Fiscal Year Ends December 31st

		Budgetary Central Government			Central Government (excl. Social Security)			Central Government (incl. Social Security)			General Government		
		2013	2014	2015	2013	2014	2015	2013	2014	2015	2013	2014	2015
6M35	Gross debt (D4) at face value	...	...	...	...	...	...	...	...	...	...	...	...
6M35D3	D3 debt liabilities at face value	...	...	...	26,908	31,776	33,168	...	...	...	28,102	32,956	34,250
6M35D2	D2 debt liabilities at face value	...	...	...	24,951	29,592	31,481	...	...	...	25,505	30,199	32,071
6M35D1	D1 debt liabilities at face value	...	...	...	24,781	29,429	31,312	...	...	...	25,335	30,037	31,902
6M93	Government gross debt per national definition	...	...	...	24,951	29,592	31,481	...	...	...	25,505	30,199	32,071
6M5	Arrears	...	...	...	...	...	...	...	...	...	...	...	...
6M6	Explicit contingent liabilities	...	...	...	...	...	...	...	...	...	...	...	...
6M61	of which: Publicly guaranteed debt	...	...	...	...	...	...	...	...	...	...	...	...
6M7	Net implicit obligations for social security benefits	...	...	...	...	...	...	...	...	...	...	...	...
	Table 7 Expenditure by functions of government												
7	**Expenditure**	...	...	...	**15,190**	**12,157**	...	...	...	...	**21,642**	**18,591**	...
701	**General public services**	...	...	...	**2,141**	**2,491**	...	...	...	...	**2,459**	**2,808**	...
7017	Public debt transactions	...	...	...	985	1,221	...	...	...	...	998	1,235	...
7018	Transfers of general character between levels of government	...	...	...	—	—	...	...	...	...	—	—	...
702	**Defense**	...	...	...	**347**	**320**	...	...	...	...	**347**	**320**	...
703	**Public order and safety**	...	...	...	**608**	**568**	...	...	...	...	**655**	**611**	...
704	**Economic affairs**	...	...	...	**5,121**	**1,889**	...	...	...	...	**5,397**	**2,134**	...
7042	Agriculture, forestry, fishing, and hunting	...	...	...	203	144	...	...	...	...	219	163	...
7043	Fuel and energy	...	...	...	134	122	...	...	...	...	123	91	...
7044	Mining, manufacturing, and construction	...	...	...	10	38	...	...	...	...	10	38	...
7045	Transport	...	...	...	602	708	...	...	...	...	876	977	...
7046	Communication	...	...	...	14	-83	...	...	...	...	20	-81	...
705	**Environmental protection**	...	...	...	**174**	**327**	...	...	...	...	**283**	**371**	...
706	**Housing and community amenities**	...	...	...	**98**	**69**	...	...	...	...	**267**	**332**	...
707	**Health**	...	...	...	**1,394**	**1,361**	...	...	...	...	**2,487**	**2,453**	...
7072	Outpatient services	...	...	...	240	231	...	...	...	...	828	819	...
7073	Hospital services	...	...	...	990	975	...	...	...	...	1,027	1,010	...
7074	Public health services	...	...	...	99	90	...	...	...	...	137	126	...
708	**Recreation, culture and religion**	...	...	...	**400**	**380**	...	...	...	...	**646**	**629**	...
709	**Education**	...	...	...	**1,759**	**1,605**	...	...	...	...	**2,351**	**2,210**	...
7091	Pre-primary and primary education	...	...	...	447	427	...	...	...	...	827	833	...
7092	Secondary education	...	...	...	706	614	...	...	...	...	865	763	...
7094	Tertiary education	...	...	...	465	436	...	...	...	...	471	438	...
710	**Social protection**	...	...	...	**3,150**	**3,147**	...	...	...	...	**6,750**	**6,723**	...
7z	Statistical discrepancy: Expenditure	...	...	...	0	0	...	...	...	...	0	-0	...
	Table 8 Financial transactions by counterpart sector												
32	**Net acquisition of financial assets**	...	...	...	**961**	**3,011**	**700**	...	...	...	**974**	**3,017**	**774**
321	Domestic debtors	...	...	...	...	...	...	...	...	...	...	...	...
8211	General government	...	...	...	...	...	...	...	...	...	...	...	...
8212	Central bank	...	...	...	...	...	...	...	...	...	—	—	—
8213	Deposit-taking corporations except the central bank	...	...	...	...	...	...	...	...	...	...	...	...
8214	Other financial corporations	...	...	...	...	...	...	...	...	...	...	...	...
8215	Nonfinancial corporations	...	...	...	...	...	...	...	...	...	...	...	...
8216	Households & nonprofit institutions serving households	...	...	...	...	...	...	...	...	...	...	...	...
322	External debtors	...	...	...	...	...	...	...	...	...	...	...	...
8221	General government	...	...	...	...	...	...	...	...	...	...	...	...
8227	International organizations	...	...	...	...	...	...	...	...	...	...	...	...
8228	Financial corporations other than international organizations	...	...	...	...	...	...	...	...	...	...	...	...
8229	Other nonresidents	...	...	...	...	...	...	...	...	...	...	...	...

Slovenia (961)

In Millions of Euros (EUR) / Fiscal Year Ends December 31st

		Budgetary Central Government			Central Government (excl. Social Security)			Central Government (incl. Social Security)			General Government		
		2013	2014	2015	2013	2014	2015	2013	2014	2015	2013	2014	2015
33	**Net incurrence of liabilities**	...	...	...	**6,361**	**4,919**	**1,887**	...	...	...	**6,386**	**4,913**	**1,802**
331	Domestic creditors	...	...	...	...	...	...	...	...	...	...	...	...
3311	General government	...	...	...	...	...	...	...	...	...	—	—	—
3312	Central bank	...	...	...	...	...	...	...	...	...	...	...	...
3313	Deposit-taking corporations except the central bank	...	...	...	...	...	...	...	...	...	...	...	...
3314	Other financial corporations	...	...	...	...	...	...	...	...	...	...	...	...
3315	Nonfinancial corporations	...	...	...	...	...	...	...	...	...	...	...	...
3316	Households & nonprofit institutions serving households	...	...	...	...	...	...	...	...	...	...	...	...
332	External creditors	...	...	...	...	...	...	...	...	...	...	...	...
3321	General government	...	...	...	...	...	...	...	...	...	...	...	...
3327	International organizations	...	...	...	...	...	...	...	...	...	...	...	...
3328	Financial corporations other than international organizations	...	...	...	...	...	...	...	...	...	...	...	...
3329	Other nonresidents	...	...	...	...	...	...	...	...	...	...	...	...
	Table 9 Total other economic flows in assets and liabilities												
9	**Change in net worth due to other economic flows**	...	...	...	...	...	...	...	...	...	...	...	...
91	**Other economic flows in nonfinancial assets**	...	...	...	...	...	...	...	...	...	...	...	...
911	Fixed assets	...	...	...	...	...	...	...	...	...	...	...	...
912	Inventories	...	...	...	...	...	...	...	...	...	...	...	...
913	Valuables	...	...	...	...	...	...	...	...	...	...	...	...
914	Nonproduced assets	...	...	...	...	...	...	...	...	...	...	...	...
92	**Other economic flows in financial assets**	...	...	...	**4,437**	**1,817**	**-1,041**	...	...	...	**3,920**	**1,990**	**-1,142**
	By instrument												
9201	Monetary gold and SDRs	...	...	...	—	—	—	...	...	...	—	—	—
9202	Currency and deposits	...	...	...	-4	14	15	...	...	...	-4	16	20
9203	Debt securities	...	...	...	-14	4	-4	...	...	...	-16	6	-4
9204	Loans	...	...	...	2,322	709	-912	...	...	...	2,322	708	-919
9205	Equity and investment fund shares	...	...	...	2,131	1,066	-160	...	...	...	1,606	1,236	-259
9206	Insurance, pension, and standardized guarantee schemes	...	...	...	-0	8	10	...	...	...	0	8	10
9207	Financial derivatives and employee stock options	...	...	...	-0	0	—	...	...	...	-0	0	—
9208	Other accounts receivable	...	...	...	3	17	9	...	...	...	12	16	10
	By debtor												
921	Domestic debtors	...	...	...	...	...	...	...	...	...	...	...	...
922	External debtors	...	...	...	...	...	...	...	...	...	...	...	...
93	**Other economic flows in liabilities**	...	...	...	**346**	**2,809**	**-420**	...	...	...	**359**	**2,792**	**-427**
	By instrument												
9301	Special Drawing Rights (SDRs)	...	...	...	—	—	—	...	...	...	—	—	—
9302	Currency and deposits	...	...	...	0	-0	2	...	...	...	0	-0	2
9303	Debt securities	...	...	...	366	2,794	-27	...	...	...	358	2,777	-31
9304	Loans	...	...	...	-8	2	-3	...	...	...	1	2	-6
9305	Equity and investment fund shares	...	...	...	-13	-4	-6	...	...	...	1	-2	-5
9306	Insurance, pension, and standardized guarantee schemes	...	...	...	—	—	—	...	...	...	—	—	—
9307	Financial derivatives and employee stock options	...	...	...	-2	4	-1	...	...	...	-2	4	-1
9308	Other accounts payable	...	...	...	3	13	-387	...	...	...	1	11	-387
	By creditor												
931	Domestic creditors	...	...	...	...	...	...	...	...	...	...	...	...
932	External creditors	...	...	...	...	...	...	...	...	...	...	...	...
	Memorandum items												
9M2	Change in net financial worth due to other economic flows	...	...	...	4,091	-992	-621	...	...	...	3,561	-802	-714

Slovenia (961)

In Millions of Euros (EUR) / Fiscal Year Ends December 31st

		Budgetary Central Government			Central Government (excl. Social Security)			Central Government (incl. Social Security)			General Government		
		2013	2014	2015	2013	2014	2015	2013	2014	2015	2013	2014	2015
9M3	Gross debt (D4) at market value: other economic flows	...	...	...	361	2,809	-414	...	...	...	360	2,790	-422
9M3D3	D3 debt liabilities at market value: other economic flows	...	...	...	361	2,809	-414	...	...	...	360	2,790	-422
9M3D2	D2 debt liabilities at market value: other economic flows	...	...	...	358	2,796	-27	...	...	...	359	2,779	-35
9M3D1	D1 debt liabilities at market value: other economic flows	...	...	...	358	2,796	-29	...	...	...	359	2,779	-37

Solomon Islands (813)

In Millions of Solomon Islands Dollars (SBD) / Fiscal Year Ends December 31st

		Budgetary Central Government			Central Government (excl. Social Security)			Central Government (incl. Social Security)			General Government		
		2013	2014	2015	2013	2014	2015	2013	2014	2015	2013	2014	2015
	Statement of operations												
1	Revenue	4,259	4,134	4,375	...	...	...	...	...	...	...	...	...
2	Expense	2,864	2,971	3,175	...	...	...	...	...	...	...	...	...
GOB	**Gross operating balance**	**1,395**	**1,163**	**1,200**	...	...	...	...	...	...	...	...	...
NOB	**Net operating balance**	...	...	...	...	...	...	...	...	...	...	...	...
31	Net/Gross investment in nonfinancial assets	1,060	954	1,116	...	...	...	...	...	...	...	...	...
2M	Expenditure	3,923	3,924	4,292	...	...	...	...	...	...	...	...	...
NLB	**Net lending (+) / Net borrowing (-)**	**335**	**210**	**84**	...	...	...	...	...	...	...	...	...
32	Net acquisition of financial assets	237	88	-171	...	...	...	...	...	...	...	...	...
33	Net incurrence of liabilities	-83	-78	-175	...	...	...	...	...	...	...	...	...
NLBz	Statistical discrepancy	-16	-43	-79	...	...	...	...	...	...	...	...	...
	Memorandum items												
PB	Primary net lending / net borrowing	350	223	95	...	...	...	...	...	...	...	...	...
GB	Government balance per national definition	...	...	...	...	...	...	...	...	...	...	...	...
	Statement of other economic flows												
	Balance sheet												
6	**Net worth**	...	...	...	...	...	...	...	...	...	...	...	...
61	Nonfinancial assets	...	...	...	...	...	...	...	...	...	...	...	...
62	Financial assets	1,457	1,545	1,374	...	...	1,374	...	...	...	...	...	1,374
63	Liabilities	949	859	697	...	...	697	...	...	...	...	...	697
	Table 1 Revenue												
1	**Revenue**	**4,259**	**4,134**	**4,375**	...	...	...	...	...	...	...	...	...
11	**Taxes**	**2,498**	**2,521**	**2,664**	...	...	...	...	...	...	...	...	...
111	Taxes on income, profits, and capital gains	908	834	955	...	...	...	...	...	...	...	...	...
1111	Payable by individuals	409	403	433	...	...	...	...	...	...	...	...	...
1112	Payable by corporations and other enterprises	500	431	522	...	...	...	...	...	...	...	...	...
1113	Other taxes on income, profits, and capital gains	—	—	...	...	...	...	...	...	...	...	...	...
112	Taxes on payroll and workforce	—	—	—	...	...	...	...	...	...	...	...	...
113	Taxes on property	24	24	29	...	...	...	...	...	...	...	...	...
114	Taxes on goods and services	583	642	585	...	...	...	...	...	...	...	...	...
1141	General taxes on goods and services	423	459	411	...	...	...	...	...	...	...	...	...
1142	Excises	138	158	144	...	...	...	...	...	...	...	...	...
115	Taxes on international trade and transactions	983	1,021	1,094	...	...	...	...	...	...	...	...	...
116	Other taxes	—	—	—	...	...	...	...	...	...	...	...	...
12	**Social contributions**	—	—	—	...	...	...	...	...	...	...	...	...
121	Social security contributions	—	—	—	...	...	...	...	...	...	...	...	...
122	Other social contributions	—	—	—	...	...	...	...	...	...	...	...	...
13	**Grants**	**1,440**	**1,255**	**1,175**	...	...	...	...	...	...	...	...	...
131	From foreign governments	1,020	899	774	...	...	...	...	...	...	...	...	...
132	From international organizations	420	355	402	...	...	...	...	...	...	...	...	...
133	From other general government units	—	—	—	...	...	...	...	...	...	...	...	...
1331	Current	—	—	—	...	...	...	...	...	...	...	...	...
1332	Capital	—	—	—	...	...	...	...	...	...	...	...	...
14	**Other revenue**	**321**	**358**	**535**	...	...	...	...	...	...	...	...	...
	Table 2 Expense by economic type												
2	**Expense**	**2,864**	**2,971**	**3,175**	...	...	...	...	...	...	...	...	...
21	**Compensation of employees**	**888**	**949**	**1,060**	...	...	...	...	...	...	...	...	...
211	Wages and salaries	839	897	1,002	...	...	...	...	...	...	...	...	...
212	Employers' social contributions	49	53	58	...	...	...	...	...	...	...	...	...
22	**Use of goods and services**	**1,497**	**1,575**	**1,513**	...	...	...	...	...	...	...	...	...
23	**Consumption of fixed capital**	...	...	...	...	...	...	...	...	...	...	...	...
24	**Interest**	**15**	**13**	**12**	...	...	...	...	...	...	...	...	...
25	**Subsidies**	**2**	**0**	**20**	...	...	...	...	...	...	...	...	...

Solomon Islands (813)

In Millions of Solomon Islands Dollars (SBD) / Fiscal Year Ends December 31st

		Budgetary Central Government			Central Government (excl. Social Security)			Central Government (incl. Social Security)			General Government		
		2013	2014	2015	2013	2014	2015	2013	2014	2015	2013	2014	2015
26	**Grants**	**228**	**183**	**161**	**...**	**...**	**...**	**...**	**...**	**...**	**...**	**...**	**...**
261	To foreign governments	—	—	—	...	...	...	...	...	...	...	...	...
262	To international organizations	—	—	—	...	...	...	...	...	...	...	...	...
263	To other general government units	228	183	161	...	...	...	...	...	...	...	...	...
2631	Current	228	183	161	...	...	...	...	...	...	...	...	...
2632	Capital	—	—	—	...	...	...	...	...	...	...	...	...
27	**Social benefits**	**19**	**40**	**108**	**...**	**...**	**...**	**...**	**...**	**...**	**...**	**...**	**...**
271	Social security benefits	—	—	—	...	...	...	...	...	...	...	...	...
272	Social assistance benefits	—	—	—	...	...	...	...	...	...	...	...	...
273	Employment-related social benefits	19	40	108	...	...	...	...	...	...	...	...	...
28	**Other expense**	**215**	**210**	**302**	**...**	**...**	**...**	**...**	**...**	**...**	**...**	**...**	**...**
281	Property expense other than interest	3	2	2	...	...	...	...	...	...	...	...	...
282	Transfers not elsewhere classified	212	207	299	...	...	...	...	...	...	...	...	...
2821	Current	200	195	263	...	...	...	...	...	...	...	...	...
2822	Capital	12	11	36	...	...	...	...	...	...	...	...	...
	Table 3 Transactions in assets and liabilities												
3	**Change in net worth from transactions**	**...**	**...**	**...**	**...**	**...**	**...**	**...**	**...**	**...**	**...**	**...**	**...**
31	**Net/Gross investment in nonfinancial assets**	**1,060**	**954**	**1,116**	**...**	**...**	**...**	**...**	**...**	**...**	**...**	**...**	**...**
311	Fixed assets	1,050	944	1,078	...	...	...	...	...	...	...	...	...
3111	Buildings and structures	880	809	809	...	...	...	...	...	...	...	...	...
3112	Machinery and equipment	168	133	266	...	...	...	...	...	...	...	...	...
3113	Other fixed assets	2	2	3	...	...	...	...	...	...	...	...	...
3114	Weapons systems	—	—	—	...	...	...	...	...	...	...	...	...
312	Inventories	—	—	—	...	...	...	...	...	...	...	...	...
313	Valuables	0	0	—	...	...	...	...	...	...	...	...	...
314	Nonproduced assets	9	9	39	...	...	...	...	...	...	...	...	...
3141	Land	9	9	39	...	...	...	...	...	...	...	...	...
3142	Mineral and energy resources	—	—	—	...	...	...	...	...	...	...	...	...
3143	Other naturally occurring assets	—	—	—	...	...	...	...	...	...	...	...	...
3144	Intangible nonproduced assets	—	—	—	...	...	...	...	...	...	...	...	...
32	**Net acquisition of financial assets**	**237**	**88**	**-171**	**...**	**...**	**...**	**...**	**...**	**...**	**...**	**...**	**...**
	By instrument												
3201	Monetary gold and SDRs	—	—	—	...	...	...	...	...	...	...	...	...
3202	Currency and deposits	239	90	-175	...	...	...	...	...	...	...	...	...
3203	Debt securities	—	—	—	...	...	...	...	...	...	...	...	...
3204	Loans	—	—	—	...	...	...	...	...	...	...	...	...
3205	Equity and investment fund shares	—	—	—	...	...	...	...	...	...	...	...	...
3206	Insurance, pension, and standardized guarantee schemes	—	—	—	...	...	...	...	...	...	...	...	...
3207	Financial derivatives and employee stock options	—	—	—	...	...	...	...	...	...	...	...	...
3208	Other accounts receivable	-1	-2	5	...	...	...	...	...	...	...	...	...
	By debtor												
321	Domestic debtors	239	123	-163	...	...	...	...	...	...	...	...	...
322	External debtors	-2	-35	-8	...	...	...	...	...	...	...	...	...
33	**Net incurrence of liabilities**	**-83**	**-78**	**-175**	**...**	**...**	**...**	**...**	**...**	**...**	**...**	**...**	**...**
	By instrument												
3301	Special Drawing Rights (SDRs)	—	—	—	...	...	...	...	...	...	...	...	...
3302	Currency and deposits	—	—	—	...	...	...	...	...	...	...	...	...
3303	Debt securities	-30	-27	-132	...	...	...	...	...	...	...	...	...
3304	Loans	-49	-50	-43	...	...	...	...	...	...	...	...	...
3305	Equity and investment fund shares	—	—	—	...	...	...	...	...	...	...	...	...
3306	Insurance, pension, and standardized guarantee schemes	—	—	—	...	...	...	...	...	...	...	...	...
3307	Financial derivatives and employee stock options	—	—	—	...	...	...	...	...	...	...	...	...
3308	Other accounts payable	-3	-2	-1	...	...	...	...	...	...	...	...	...

Solomon Islands (813)

In Millions of Solomon Islands Dollars (SBD) / Fiscal Year Ends December 31st

		Budgetary Central Government			Central Government (excl. Social Security)			Central Government (incl. Social Security)			General Government		
		2013	2014	2015	2013	2014	2015	2013	2014	2015	2013	2014	2015
	By creditor												
331	Domestic creditors	-36	-29	-133	...	...	...	...	...	...	...	...	...
332	External creditors	-47	-50	-43	...	...	...	...	...	...	...	...	...
	Table 4 Holding gains and losses in assets and liabilities												
	Table 5 Holding gains and losses in assets and liabilities												
	Table 6 Balance sheet												
6	**Net worth**	...	...	...	...	...	...	...	...	...	...	...	...
61	**Nonfinancial assets**	...	...	...	...	...	...	...	...	...	...	...	...
611	Fixed assets	...	...	...	...	...	...	...	...	...	...	...	...
6111	Buildings and structures	...	...	...	...	...	...	...	...	...	...	...	...
6112	Machinery and equipment	...	...	...	...	...	...	...	...	...	...	...	...
6113	Other fixed assets	...	...	...	...	...	...	...	...	...	...	...	...
6114	Weapons systems	...	...	...	...	...	...	...	...	...	...	...	...
612	Inventories	...	...	...	...	...	...	...	...	...	...	...	...
613	Valuables	...	...	...	...	...	...	...	...	...	...	...	...
614	Nonproduced assets	...	...	...	...	...	...	...	...	...	...	...	...
6141	Land	...	...	...	...	...	...	...	...	...	...	...	...
6142	Mineral and energy resources	...	...	...	...	...	...	...	...	...	...	...	...
6143	Other naturally occurring assets	...	...	...	...	...	...	...	...	...	...	...	...
6144	Intangible nonproduced assets	...	...	...	...	...	...	...	...	...	...	...	...
62	**Financial assets**	**1,457**	**1,545**	**1,374**	...	...	**1,374**	...	...	...	...	...	**1,374**
	By instrument												
6201	Monetary gold and SDRs	—	—	—	...	...	...	...	...	...	...	...	...
6202	Currency and deposits	1,450	1,540	1,365	...	...	1,365	...	...	...	...	...	1,365
6203	Debt securities	—	—	—	...	...	...	...	...	...	...	...	...
6204	Loans	—	—	—	...	...	...	...	...	...	...	...	...
6205	Equity and investment fund shares	—	—	—	...	...	...	...	...	...	...	...	...
6206	Insurance, pension, and standardized guarantee schemes	—	—	—	...	...	...	...	...	...	...	...	...
6207	Financial derivatives and employee stock options	—	—	—	...	...	...	...	...	...	...	...	...
6208	Other accounts receivable	7	5	10	...	...	10	...	...	...	...	...	10
	By debtor												
621	Domestic debtors	1,400	1,523	1,360	...	...	1,360	...	...	...	...	...	1,360
622	External debtors	57	22	14	...	...	14	...	...	...	...	...	14
63	**Liabilities**	**949**	**859**	**697**	...	...	**697**	...	...	...	...	...	**697**
	By instrument												
6301	Special Drawing Rights (SDRs)	—	—	—	...	...	...	...	...	...	...	...	...
6302	Currency and deposits	—	—	—	...	...	...	...	...	...	...	...	...
6303	Debt securities	201	173	43	...	...	43	...	...	...	...	...	43
6304	Loans	743	685	655	...	...	655	...	...	...	...	...	655
6305	Equity and investment fund shares	—	—	—	...	...	...	...	...	...	...	...	...
6306	Insurance, pension, and standardized guarantee schemes	—	—	—	...	...	...	...	...	...	...	...	...
6307	Financial derivatives and employee stock options	—	—	—	...	...	...	...	...	...	...	...	...
6308	Other accounts payable	5	1	—	...	...	—	...	...	...	...	...	—
	By creditor												
631	Domestic creditors	206	174	43	...	...	43	...	...	...	...	...	43
632	External creditors	743	685	655	...	...	655	...	...	...	...	...	655
	Memorandum items												
6M2	Net financial worth	508	686	677	...	...	677	...	...	...	...	...	677
6M3	Gross debt (D4) at market value	949	859	697	...	...	...	...	...	...	...	...	...
6M3D3	D3 debt liabilities at market value	949	859	697	...	...	...	...	...	...	...	...	...
6M3D2	D2 debt liabilities at market value	944	858	697	...	...	...	...	...	...	...	...	...
6M3D1	D1 debt liabilities at market value	944	858	697	...	...	...	...	...	...	...	...	...
6M4	Gross debt (D4) at nominal value	...	...	...	...	...	...	...	...	...	...	...	...
6M4D3	D3 debt liabilities at nominal value	...	...	...	...	...	...	...	...	...	...	...	...
6M4D2	D2 debt liabilities at nominal value	...	...	...	...	...	...	...	...	...	...	...	...
6M4D1	D1 debt liabilities at nominal value	...	...	...	...	...	...	...	...	...	...	...	...

Solomon Islands (813)

In Millions of Solomon Islands Dollars (SBD) / Fiscal Year Ends December 31st

		Budgetary Central Government			Central Government (excl. Social Security)			Central Government (incl. Social Security)			General Government		
		2013	2014	2015	2013	2014	2015	2013	2014	2015	2013	2014	2015
6M35	Gross debt (D4) at face value	...	...	...	...	...	...	...	...	...	...	...	...
6M35D3	D3 debt liabilities at face value	...	...	...	...	...	...	...	...	...	...	...	...
6M35D2	D2 debt liabilities at face value	...	...	...	...	...	...	...	...	...	...	...	...
6M35D1	D1 debt liabilities at face value	...	...	...	...	...	...	...	...	...	...	...	...
6M93	Government gross debt per national definition	...	...	...	...	...	...	...	...	...	...	...	...
6M5	Arrears	...	...	...	...	...	...	...	...	...	...	...	...
6M6	Explicit contingent liabilities	...	...	...	...	...	...	...	...	...	...	...	...
6M61	of which: Publicly guaranteed debt	...	...	...	...	...	...	...	...	...	...	...	...
6M7	Net implicit obligations for social security benefits	...	...	...	...	...	...	...	...	...	...	...	...
	Table 7 Expenditure by functions of government												
7	**Expenditure**	**3,923**	**3,924**	**4,292**	**...**	**...**	**4,292**	**...**	**...**	**...**	**...**	**...**	**4,292**
701	**General public services**	**775**	**831**	**795**	**...**	**...**	**795**	**...**	**...**	**...**	**...**	**...**	**795**
7017	Public debt transactions	15	13	12	...	...	12	...	...	...	...	...	12
7018	Transfers of general character between levels of government	6	37	6	...	...	6	...	...	...	...	...	6
702	**Defense**	**—**	**—**	**—**	**...**	**...**	**...**	**...**	**...**	**...**	**...**	**...**	**...**
703	**Public order and safety**	**266**	**317**	**395**	**...**	**...**	**395**	**...**	**...**	**...**	**...**	**...**	**395**
704	**Economic affairs**	**946**	**875**	**1,074**	**...**	**...**	**1,074**	**...**	**...**	**...**	**...**	**...**	**1,074**
7042	Agriculture, forestry, fishing, and hunting	169	135	158	...	...	158	...	...	...	...	...	158
7043	Fuel and energy	25	18	19	...	...	19	...	...	...	...	...	19
7044	Mining, manufacturing, and construction	16	14	19	...	...	19	...	...	...	...	...	19
7045	Transport	360	337	351	...	...	351	...	...	...	...	...	351
7046	Communication	0	7	13	...	...	13	...	...	...	...	...	13
705	**Environmental protection**	**37**	**37**	**52**	**...**	**...**	**52**	**...**	**...**	**...**	**...**	**...**	**52**
706	**Housing and community amenities**	**78**	**83**	**71**	**...**	**...**	**71**	**...**	**...**	**...**	**...**	**...**	**71**
707	**Health**	**501**	**528**	**518**	**...**	**...**	**518**	**...**	**...**	**...**	**...**	**...**	**518**
7072	Outpatient services	20	19	23	...	...	23	...	...	...	...	...	23
7073	Hospital services	86	96	104	...	...	104	...	...	...	...	...	104
7074	Public health services	24	26	16	...	...	16	...	...	...	...	...	16
708	**Recreation, culture and religion**	**15**	**14**	**19**	**...**	**...**	**19**	**...**	**...**	**...**	**...**	**...**	**19**
709	**Education**	**1,219**	**1,175**	**1,292**	**...**	**...**	**1,292**	**...**	**...**	**...**	**...**	**...**	**1,292**
7091	Pre-primary and primary education	336	362	396	...	...	396	...	...	...	...	...	396
7092	Secondary education	249	247	284	...	...	284	...	...	...	...	...	284
7094	Tertiary education	451	369	389	...	...	389	...	...	...	...	...	389
710	**Social protection**	**87**	**65**	**77**	**...**	**...**	**77**	**...**	**...**	**...**	**...**	**...**	**77**
7z	Statistical discrepancy: Expenditure	...	...	...	...	...	...	...	...	...	...	...	...
	Table 8 Financial transactions by counterpart sector												
32	**Net acquisition of financial assets**	**237**	**88**	**-171**	**...**	**...**	**...**	**...**	**...**	**...**	**...**	**...**	**...**
321	Domestic debtors	239	123	-163	...	...	...	...	...	...	...	...	...
8211	General government	...	...	...	...	...	...	...	...	...	...	...	...
8212	Central bank	...	...	...	...	...	...	...	...	...	...	...	...
8213	Deposit-taking corporations except the central bank	...	...	...	...	...	...	...	...	...	...	...	...
8214	Other financial corporations	...	...	...	...	...	...	...	...	...	...	...	...
8215	Nonfinancial corporations	...	...	...	...	...	...	...	...	...	...	...	...
8216	Households & nonprofit institutions serving households	...	...	...	...	...	...	...	...	...	...	...	...
322	External debtors	-2	-35	-8	...	...	...	...	...	...	...	...	...
8221	General government	...	...	...	...	...	...	...	...	...	...	...	...
8227	International organizations	...	...	...	...	...	...	...	...	...	...	...	...
8228	Financial corporations other than international organizations	...	...	...	...	...	...	...	...	...	...	...	...
8229	Other nonresidents	...	...	...	...	...	...	...	...	...	...	...	...

Solomon Islands (813)

In Millions of Solomon Islands Dollars (SBD) / Fiscal Year Ends December 31st

		Budgetary Central Government			Central Government (excl. Social Security)			Central Government (incl. Social Security)			General Government		
		2013	2014	2015	2013	2014	2015	2013	2014	2015	2013	2014	2015
33	**Net incurrence of liabilities**	**-83**	**-78**	**-175**	**...**	**...**	**...**	**...**	**...**	**...**	**...**	**...**	**...**
331	Domestic creditors	-36	-29	-133	...	...	...	...	...	...	...	...	...
8311	General government	...	...	...	...	...	...	...	...	...	...	...	...
8312	Central bank	...	...	...	...	...	...	...	...	...	...	...	...
8313	Deposit-taking corporations except the central bank	...	...	...	...	...	...	...	...	...	...	...	...
8314	Other financial corporations	...	...	...	...	...	...	...	...	...	...	...	...
8315	Nonfinancial corporations	...	...	...	...	...	...	...	...	...	...	...	...
8316	Households & nonprofit institutions serving households	...	...	...	...	...	...	...	...	...	...	...	...
332	External creditors	-47	-50	-43	...	...	...	...	...	...	...	...	...
8321	General government	...	...	...	...	...	...	...	...	...	...	...	...
8327	International organizations	...	...	...	...	...	...	...	...	...	...	...	...
8328	Financial corporations other than international organizations	...	...	...	...	...	...	...	...	...	...	...	...
8329	Other nonresidents	...	...	...	...	...	...	...	...	...	...	...	...
	Table 9 Total other economic flows in assets and liabilities												

.th Africa (199)

.ons of South African Rand (ZAR) / Fiscal Year Ends March 31st

		Budgetary Central Government			Central Government (excl. Social Security)			Central Government (incl. Social Security)			General Government		
		2013	2014P	2015P	2013	2014P	2015P	2013	2014P	2015P	2013	2014P	2015P
	Statement of operations												
1	Revenue	919	1,004	1,120	996	1,105	1,211	1,048	1,171	1,281	1,251	1,400	1,527
2	Expense	1,103	1,198	1,274	1,165	1,280	1,345	1,228	1,339	1,440	1,387	1,516	1,620
GOB	**Gross operating balance**	**-178**	**-186**	**-145**	**-156**	**-160**	**-119**	**-167**	**-154**	**-144**	**-107**	**-86**	**-59**
NOB	**Net operating balance**	**-184**	**-194**	**-154**	**-169**	**-174**	**-135**	**-180**	**-168**	**-160**	**-135**	**-116**	**-94**
31	Net/Gross investment in nonfinancial assets	14	14	16	19	24	33	19	24	33	84	97	102
2M	Expenditure	1,118	1,212	1,290	1,185	1,304	1,378	1,248	1,363	1,473	1,470	1,613	1,722
NLB	**Net lending (+) / Net borrowing (-)**	**-198**	**-208**	**-170**	**-188**	**-199**	**-167**	**-199**	**-192**	**-192**	**-219**	**-213**	**-195**
32	Net acquisition of financial assets	-17	-25	-12	1	-10	6	13	20	23	74	92	22
33	Net incurrence of liabilities	181	183	158	185	189	160	202	211	199	193	227	225
NLBz	Statistical discrepancy	0	0	-0	4	-1	14	11	0	16	100	77	-7
	Memorandum items												
PB	Primary net lending / net borrowing	-97	-93	-41	-86	-81	-36	-97	-75	-61	-109	-89	-56
GB	Government balance per national definition	...	...	...	...	...	...	...	...	...	...	...	...
	Statement of other economic flows												
	Balance sheet												
6	**Net worth**	...	...	...	...	...	...	...	...	...	...	...	...
61	Nonfinancial assets	...	...	...	...	...	...	...	...	...	...	...	...
62	Financial assets	207	218	211	...	...	...	...	...	...	...	...	...
63	Liabilities	1,585	1,799	2,019	...	...	...	...	...	...	...	...	...
	Table 1 Revenue												
1	**Revenue**	**919**	**1,004**	**1,120**	**996**	**1,105**	**1,211**	**1,048**	**1,171**	**1,281**	**1,251**	**1,400**	**1,527**
11	**Taxes**	**898**	**984**	**1,068**	**901**	**987**	**1,071**	**922**	**1,010**	**1,104**	**973**	**1,069**	**1,168**
111	Taxes on income, profits, and capital gains	508	562	607	508	562	607	508	562	607	508	562	607
1111	Payable by individuals	311	354	389	311	354	389	311	354	389	311	354	389
1112	Payable by corporations and other enterprises	197	208	218	197	208	218	197	208	218	197	208	218
1113	Other taxes on income, profits, and capital gains	—	—	—	—	—	—	—	—	—	—	—	—
112	Taxes on payroll and workforce	12	14	15	12	14	15	12	14	15	12	14	15
113	Taxes on property	10	12	15	10	12	15	10	12	15	52	60	67
114	Taxes on goods and services	324	356	385	327	359	388	347	381	421	357	392	434
1141	General taxes on goods and services	238	261	281	238	261	281	238	262	281	238	262	281
1142	Excises	75	83	93	77	86	93	77	86	93	77	86	93
115	Taxes on international trade and transactions	44	40	46	44	40	46	44	40	46	44	40	46
116	Other taxes	0	-0	-0	0	-0	-0	0	-0	-0	0	-0	-0
12	**Social contributions**	—	—	—	—	—	—	**22**	**24**	**24**	**22**	**24**	**24**
121	Social security contributions	—	—	—	—	—	—	22	24	24	22	24	24
122	Other social contributions	—	—	—	—	—	—	—	—	—	—	—	—
13	**Grants**	**4**	**4**	**2**	**5**	**6**	**4**	**5**	**6**	**4**	**4**	**5**	**2**
131	From foreign governments	2	2	2	3	3	2	3	3	2	3	3	2
132	From international organizations	2	2	—	2	2	0	2	2	0	2	2	0
133	From other general government units	—	—	—	0	1	2	0	1	2	0	0	-0
1331	Current	—	—	—	0	1	2	0	1	2	0	0	-0
1332	Capital	—	—	—	—	—	—	—	—	—	—	—	—
14	**Other revenue**	**17**	**15**	**50**	**90**	**113**	**136**	**99**	**131**	**148**	**251**	**302**	**332**
	Table 2 Expense by economic type												
2	**Expense**	**1,103**	**1,198**	**1,274**	**1,165**	**1,280**	**1,345**	**1,228**	**1,339**	**1,440**	**1,387**	**1,516**	**1,620**
21	**Compensation of employees**	**116**	**126**	**134**	**169**	**183**	**201**	**171**	**185**	**204**	**496**	**534**	**573**
211	Wages and salaries	96	105	111	145	158	176	147	160	178	424	460	532
212	Employers' social contributions	19	21	22	25	25	26	25	25	26	72	75	42
22	**Use of goods and services**	**58**	**58**	**59**	**155**	**179**	**162**	**157**	**180**	**167**	**397**	**442**	**437**
23	**Consumption of fixed capital**	**6**	**8**	**9**	**13**	**14**	**16**	**13**	**14**	**16**	**28**	**31**	**34**
24	**Interest**	**101**	**115**	**129**	**102**	**117**	**131**	**103**	**117**	**131**	**110**	**124**	**140**
25	**Subsidies**	**39**	**44**	**36**	**39**	**44**	**36**	**39**	**44**	**36**	**46**	**51**	**43**

South Africa (199)

In Billions of South African Rand (ZAR) / Fiscal Year Ends March 31st

		Budgetary Central Government			Central Government (excl. Social Security)			Central Government (incl. Social Security)			General Government		
		2013	2014P	2015P	2013	2014P	2015P	2013	2014P	2015P	2013	2014P	2015P
26	**Grants**	**642**	**694**	**734**	**543**	**586**	**623**	**543**	**586**	**623**	**44**	**53**	**51**
261	To foreign governments	42	50	49	42	50	49	42	50	49	42	50	49
262	To international organizations	2	3	2	2	3	2	2	3	2	2	3	2
263	To other general government units	598	641	683	498	533	571	498	533	571	0	0	0
2631	Current	532	569	611	433	461	500	433	461	500	0	0	0
2632	Capital	66	72	72	66	72	72	66	72	72	-0	0	-0
27	**Social benefits**	**120**	**131**	**136**	**120**	**131**	**136**	**175**	**185**	**218**	**177**	**187**	**225**
271	Social security benefits	—	—	—	—	—	—	56	54	82	56	54	82
272	Social assistance benefits	116	131	122	116	131	122	116	131	122	116	131	122
273	Employment-related social benefits	4	—	14	4	—	14	4	—	14	5	2	21
28	**Other expense**	**22**	**22**	**38**	**25**	**25**	**41**	**27**	**26**	**46**	**88**	**92**	**117**
281	Property expense other than interest	—	—	—	—	0	0	—	0	0	0	0	0
282	Transfers not elsewhere classified	22	22	38	25	25	41	27	26	46	88	92	117
2821	Current	18	18	7	21	21	11	23	22	15	67	70	68
2822	Capital	4	3	30	4	4	31	4	4	31	21	22	49
	Table 3 Transactions in assets and liabilities												
3	**Change in net worth from transactions**	**-184**	**-194**	**-154**	**-165**	**-175**	**-121**	**-169**	**-168**	**-143**	**-35**	**-39**	**-101**
31	**Net/Gross investment in nonfinancial assets**	**14**	**14**	**16**	**19**	**24**	**33**	**19**	**24**	**33**	**84**	**97**	**102**
311	Fixed assets	14	14	16	18	23	33	18	23	33	82	95	101
3111	Buildings and structures	7	8	8	9	16	8	9	16	8	70	85	74
3112	Machinery and equipment	4	3	4	5	4	22	5	4	22	7	7	24
3113	Other fixed assets	3	3	3	3	3	3	3	3	3	4	4	3
3114	Weapons systems	...	...	...	...	...	...	...	...	...	...	...	...
312	Inventories	—	—	—	0	-0	—	0	-0	0	0	-0	0
313	Valuables	—	—	—	—	0	-0	—	0	-0	0	0	-0
314	Nonproduced assets	0	—	0	1	1	0	1	1	0	2	2	1
3141	Land	0	—	0	1	1	0	1	1	0	2	2	1
3142	Mineral and energy resources	—	—	—	—	—	—	—	—	—	—	—	—
3143	Other naturally occurring assets	—	—	—	—	—	—	—	—	—	—	—	0
3144	Intangible nonproduced assets	—	—	—	—	—	—	—	—	—	—	—	—
32	**Net acquisition of financial assets**	**-17**	**-25**	**-12**	**1**	**-10**	**6**	**13**	**20**	**23**	**74**	**92**	**22**
	By instrument												
3201	Monetary gold and SDRs	...	—	—	—	—	—	—	—	—	—	—	—
3202	Currency and deposits	-18	-26	-13	-11	-20	-4	-15	-21	-1	-2	6	-25
3203	Debt securities	—	—	—	3	1	1	12	23	9	12	23	9
3204	Loans	—	—	—	1	-1	0	1	-1	1	-4	1	3
3205	Equity and investment fund shares	—	—	—	2	6	8	10	12	10	10	16	9
3206	Insurance, pension, and standardized guarantee schemes	—	—	—	0	-0	—	0	-0	—	0	-0	—
3207	Financial derivatives and employee stock options	—	—	—	—	—	—	-0	—	—	-0	—	—
3208	Other accounts receivable	1	1	1	6	4	1	4	7	4	57	46	25
	By debtor												
321	Domestic debtors	-17	-25	-12	1	-10	6	13	20	23	74	92	22
322	External debtors	—	—	—	—	—	—	—	—	—	0	—	—
33	**Net incurrence of liabilities**	**181**	**183**	**158**	**185**	**189**	**160**	**202**	**211**	**199**	**193**	**227**	**225**
	By instrument												
3301	Special Drawing Rights (SDRs)	—	—	—	—	—	—	—	—	—	—	—	—
3302	Currency and deposits	—	—	—	0	0	—	0	0	—	0	0	—
3303	Debt securities	174	169	134	174	169	134	174	169	134	176	171	134
3304	Loans	6	14	-2	3	14	-1	3	14	-1	3	17	9
3305	Equity and investment fund shares	—	—	—	—	—	—	—	—	—	—	—	—
3306	Insurance, pension, and standardized guarantee schemes	—	—	—	0	1	0	0	1	0	-1	1	1
3307	Financial derivatives and employee stock options	—	—	—	—	—	—	0	-0	—	0	-0	—
3308	Other accounts payable	2	1	27	8	5	27	25	27	66	14	38	82

South Africa (199)

In Billions of South African Rand (ZAR) / Fiscal Year Ends March 31st

		Budgetary Central Government			Central Government (excl. Social Security)			Central Government (incl. Social Security)			General Government		
		2013	2014P	2015P	2013	2014P	2015P	2013	2014P	2015P	2013	2014P	2015P
	By creditor												
331	Domestic creditors	176	170	161	179	175	162	196	198	202	187	213	227
332	External creditors	6	14	-2	6	14	-2	6	14	-2	6	14	-2
	Table 4 Holding gains and losses in assets and liabilities												
	Table 5 Holding gains and losses in assets and liabilities												
	Table 6 Balance sheet												
6	**Net worth**	...	...	...	...	...	...	...	...	...	...	...	...
61	**Nonfinancial assets**	...	...	...	...	...	...	...	...	...	...	...	...
611	Fixed assets	...	...	...	...	...	...	...	...	...	...	...	...
6111	Buildings and structures	...	...	...	...	...	...	...	...	...	...	...	...
6112	Machinery and equipment	...	...	...	...	...	...	...	...	...	...	...	...
6113	Other fixed assets	...	...	...	...	...	...	...	...	...	...	...	...
6114	Weapons systems	...	...	...	...	...	...	...	...	...	...	...	...
612	Inventories	...	...	...	...	...	...	...	...	...	...	...	...
613	Valuables	...	...	...	...	...	...	...	...	...	...	...	...
614	Nonproduced assets	...	...	...	...	...	...	...	...	...	...	...	...
6141	Land	...	...	...	...	...	...	...	...	...	...	...	...
6142	Mineral and energy resources	...	...	...	...	...	...	...	...	...	...	...	...
6143	Other naturally occurring assets	...	...	...	...	...	...	...	...	...	...	...	...
6144	Intangible nonproduced assets	...	...	...	...	...	...	...	...	...	...	...	...
62	**Financial assets**	**207**	**218**	**211**	...	...	...	...	...	...	...	...	...
	By instrument												
6201	Monetary gold and SDRs	—	—	—	...	...	...	...	...	...	...	...	...
6202	Currency and deposits	207	218	211	...	...	...	...	...	...	...	...	...
6203	Debt securities	—	—	—	...	...	...	...	...	...	...	...	...
6204	Loans	—	—	—	...	...	...	...	...	...	...	...	...
6205	Equity and investment fund shares	—	—	—	...	...	...	...	...	...	...	...	...
6206	Insurance, pension, and standardized guarantee schemes	—	—	—	...	...	...	...	...	...	...	...	...
6207	Financial derivatives and employee stock options	—	—	—	...	...	...	...	...	...	...	...	...
6208	Other accounts receivable	—	...	...	...	...	...	...	...	...	...	...	...
	By debtor												
621	Domestic debtors	207	218	211	...	...	...	...	...	...	...	...	...
622	External debtors	—	—	—	...	...	...	...	...	...	...	...	...
63	**Liabilities**	**1,585**	**1,799**	**2,019**	...	...	...	...	...	...	...	...	...
	By instrument												
6301	Special Drawing Rights (SDRs)	—	—	—	...	...	...	...	...	...	...	...	...
6302	Currency and deposits	—	—	—	...	...	...	...	...	...	...	...	...
6303	Debt securities	1,546	1,766	1,981	...	...	...	...	...	...	...	...	...
6304	Loans	38	33	38	...	...	...	...	...	...	...	...	...
6305	Equity and investment fund shares	—	—	—	...	...	...	...	...	...	...	...	...
6306	Insurance, pension, and standardized guarantee schemes	—	—	—	...	...	...	...	...	...	...	...	...
6307	Financial derivatives and employee stock options	—	—	—	...	...	...	...	...	...	...	...	...
6308	Other accounts payable	...	...	...	...	...	...	...	...	...	...	...	...
	By creditor												
631	Domestic creditors	1,441	1,632	1,819	...	...	...	...	...	...	...	...	...
632	External creditors	144	167	200	...	...	...	...	...	...	...	...	...
	Memorandum items												
6M2	Net financial worth	-1,378	-1,581	-1,808	...	...	...	...	...	...	...	...	...
6M3	Gross debt (D4) at market value	...	...	...	...	...	...	...	...	...	...	...	...
6M3D3	D3 debt liabilities at market value	...	...	...	...	...	...	...	...	...	...	...	...
6M3D2	D2 debt liabilities at market value	...	...	...	...	...	...	...	...	...	...	...	...
6M3D1	D1 debt liabilities at market value	...	...	...	...	...	...	...	...	...	...	...	...
6M4	Gross debt (D4) at nominal value	...	...	...	...	...	...	...	...	...	...	...	...
6M4D3	D3 debt liabilities at nominal value	...	...	...	...	...	...	...	...	...	...	...	...
6M4D2	D2 debt liabilities at nominal value	...	...	...	...	...	...	...	...	...	...	...	...
6M4D1	D1 debt liabilities at nominal value	...	...	...	...	...	...	...	...	...	...	...	...

South Africa (199)

In Billions of South African Rand (ZAR) / Fiscal Year Ends March 31st

		Budgetary Central Government			Central Government (excl. Social Security)			Central Government (incl. Social Security)			General Government		
		2013	2014P	2015P	2013	2014P	2015P	2013	2014P	2015P	2013	2014P	2015P
6M35	Gross debt (D4) at face value	...	...	...	...	...	...	...	...	...	...	...	...
6M35D3	D3 debt liabilities at face value	...	...	...	...	...	...	...	...	...	...	...	...
6M35D2	D2 debt liabilities at face value	1,585	1,799	2,019	...	...	...	...	...	...	...	...	...
6M35D1	D1 debt liabilities at face value	1,585	1,799	2,019	...	...	...	...	...	...	...	...	...
6M93	Government gross debt per national definition	...	...	...	...	...	...	...	...	...	...	...	...
6M5	Arrears	...	...	...	...	...	...	...	...	...	...	...	...
6M6	Explicit contingent liabilities	...	...	...	...	...	...	...	...	...	...	...	...
6M61	of which: Publicly guaranteed debt	...	...	...	...	...	...	...	...	...	...	...	...
6M7	Net implicit obligations for social security benefits	...	...	...	...	...	...	...	...	...	...	...	...
	Table 7 Expenditure by functions of government												
7	**Expenditure**	**1,118**	**1,212**	**1,290**	**1,284**	**1,412**	**1,489**	**1,347**	**1,471**	**1,584**	**2,071**	**2,258**	**2,412**
701	**General public services**	**603**	**656**	**698**	**629**	**691**	**734**	**662**	**720**	**781**	**882**	**962**	**1,089**
7017	Public debt transactions	101	115	129	102	117	131	103	117	131	110	124	140
7018	Transfers of general character between levels of government	388	415	442	388	415	442	421	444	488	506	535	594
702	**Defense**	**40**	**43**	**45**	**48**	**49**	**50**	**48**	**49**	**50**	**48**	**49**	**50**
703	**Public order and safety**	**104**	**110**	**117**	**107**	**114**	**120**	**107**	**114**	**120**	**143**	**146**	**153**
704	**Economic affairs**	**95**	**103**	**110**	**125**	**141**	**149**	**125**	**141**	**149**	**184**	**229**	**224**
7042	Agriculture, forestry, fishing, and hunting	13	13	14	16	18	19	16	18	19	25	28	29
7043	Fuel and energy	6	6	7	7	7	7	7	7	7	24	51	40
7044	Mining, manufacturing, and construction	8	9	9	12	14	13	12	14	13	12	14	13
7045	Transport	44	50	53	49	56	61	49	56	61	70	79	82
7046	Communication	3	2	3	4	4	4	4	4	4	4	4	4
705	**Environmental protection**	**3**	**3**	**3**	**8**	**9**	**8**	**8**	**9**	**8**	**13**	**14**	**13**
706	**Housing and community amenities**	**58**	**62**	**66**	**68**	**77**	**82**	**68**	**77**	**82**	**108**	**117**	**121**
707	**Health**	**35**	**39**	**42**	**41**	**46**	**49**	**41**	**46**	**49**	**174**	**188**	**185**
7072	Outpatient services	—	—	—	—	—	—	—	—	—	0	0	0
7073	Hospital services	20	21	22	20	21	22	20	21	22	100	109	106
7074	Public health services	11	13	14	11	13	14	11	13	14	61	66	65
708	**Recreation, culture and religion**	**5**	**6**	**7**	**13**	**15**	**17**	**13**	**15**	**17**	**53**	**48**	**50**
709	**Education**	**53**	**58**	**61**	**110**	**125**	**126**	**110**	**125**	**126**	**284**	**309**	**305**
7091	Pre-primary and primary education	5	6	6	5	6	6	5	6	6	83	86	85
7092	Secondary education	1	0	0	1	0	0	1	0	0	62	65	64
7094	Tertiary education	29	32	34	86	98	98	86	98	98	86	98	98
710	**Social protection**	**121**	**132**	**140**	**134**	**146**	**154**	**164**	**176**	**202**	**182**	**197**	**222**
7z	Statistical discrepancy: Expenditure	...	...	...	...	...	...	...	...	...	...	...	...
	Table 8 Financial transactions by counterpart sector												
32	**Net acquisition of financial assets**	**-17**	**-25**	**-12**	**1**	**-10**	**6**	**13**	**20**	**23**	**74**	**92**	**22**
321	Domestic debtors	-17	-25	-12	1	-10	6	13	20	23	74	92	22
8211	General government	...	...	...	...	...	...	...	...	...	...	...	...
8212	Central bank	...	...	...	...	...	...	...	...	...	...	...	...
8213	Deposit-taking corporations except the central bank	...	...	...	...	...	...	...	...	...	...	...	...
8214	Other financial corporations	...	...	...	...	...	...	...	...	...	...	...	...
8215	Nonfinancial corporations	...	...	...	...	...	...	...	...	...	...	...	...
8216	Households & nonprofit institutions serving households	...	...	...	...	...	...	...	...	...	...	...	...
322	External debtors	—	—	—	—	—	—	—	—	—	0	—	—
8221	General government	—	—	—	—	—	—	—	—	—	...	—	—
8227	International organizations	—	—	—	—	—	—	—	—	—	...	—	—
8228	Financial corporations other than international organizations	—	—	—	—	—	—	—	—	—	...	—	—
8229	Other nonresidents	—	—	—	—	—	—	—	—	—	...	—	—

South Africa (199)

In Billions of South African Rand (ZAR) / Fiscal Year Ends March 31st

		Budgetary Central Government			Central Government (excl. Social Security)			Central Government (incl. Social Security)			General Government		
		2013	2014P	2015P	2013	2014P	2015P	2013	2014P	2015P	2013	2014P	2015P
33	**Net incurrence of liabilities**	**181**	**183**	**158**	**185**	**189**	**160**	**202**	**211**	**199**	**193**	**227**	**225**
331	Domestic creditors	176	170	161	179	175	162	196	198	202	187	213	227
3311	General government	...	...	...	...	...	...	...	...	...	...	...	...
3312	Central bank	...	...	...	...	...	...	...	...	...	...	...	...
3313	Deposit-taking corporations except the central bank	...	...	...	...	...	...	...	...	...	...	...	...
3314	Other financial corporations	...	...	...	...	...	...	...	...	...	...	...	...
3315	Nonfinancial corporations	...	...	...	...	...	...	...	...	...	...	...	...
3316	Households & nonprofit institutions serving households	...	...	...	...	...	...	...	...	...	...	...	...
332	External creditors	6	14	-2	6	14	-2	6	14	-2	6	14	-2
3321	General government	...	...	...	...	...	...	...	...	...	...	...	...
3327	International organizations	...	...	...	...	...	...	...	...	...	...	...	...
3328	Financial corporations other than international organizations	...	...	...	...	...	...	...	...	...	...	...	...
3329	Other nonresidents	...	...	...	...	...	...	...	...	...	...	...	...
	Table 9 Total other economic flows in assets and liabilities												

Spain (184)

In Billions of Euros (EUR) / Fiscal Year Ends December 31st

		Budgetary Central Government			Central Government (excl. Social Security)			Central Government (incl. Social Security)			General Government		
		2013	2014	2015P	2013	2014	2015P	2013	2014	2015P	2013	2014	2015P
	Statement of operations												
1	Revenue	181	185	191	181	185	191	...	...	...	389	397	408
2	Expense	...	226	222	...	226	222	...	...	...	...	463	465
GOB	**Gross operating balance**	**...**	**-31**	**-22**	**...**	**-31**	**-22**	**...**	**...**	**...**	**...**	**-40**	**-30**
NOB	**Net operating balance**	**...**	**-41**	**-31**	**...**	**-41**	**-31**	**...**	**...**	**...**	**...**	**-67**	**-57**
31	Net/Gross investment in nonfinancial assets	-1	-3	-3	-1	-3	-3	...	...	...	-4	-5	-1
2M	Expenditure	...	224	219	...	224	219	...	...	...	...	459	463
NLB	**Net lending (+) / Net borrowing (-)**	**...**	**-38**	**-28**	**...**	**-38**	**-28**	**...**	**...**	**...**	**...**	**-62**	**-55**
32	Net acquisition of financial assets	54	42	18	54	42	18	12	23	18	-10	5	-15
33	Net incurrence of liabilities	104	80	47	104	80	47	73	72	60	62	67	40
NLBz	Statistical discrepancy	...	-0	-0	...	-0	-0	...	...	...	...	0	0
	Memorandum items												
PB	Primary net lending / net borrowing	...	-6	1	...	-6	1	...	...	...	...	-26	-22
GB	Government balance per national definition	...	...	...	...	...	...	...	...	...	...	...	...
	Statement of other economic flows												
9	**Change in net worth due to other economic flows**	...	...	...	...	...	...	...	...	...	...	...	...
4	Change in net worth due to holding gains and losses	...	...	...	...	...	...	...	...	...	...	...	...
41	Nonfinancial assets	...	...	...	...	...	...	...	...	...	...	...	...
42	Financial assets	1	7	10	1	7	10	1	6	11	2	6	12
43	Liabilities	34	77	-14	34	77	-14	31	78	-14	37	83	-14
5	Change in net worth due to volume changes	...	...	...	...	...	...	...	...	...	...	...	...
51	Nonfinancial assets	...	...	...	...	...	...	...	...	...	...	...	...
52	Financial assets	15	-18	-63	15	-18	-63	29	0	-0	29	0	-0
53	Liabilities	9	-18	-64	9	-18	-64	23	-1	-1	23	-0	-1
	Balance sheet												
6	**Net worth**	...	...	...	...	...	...	...	...	...	...	...	...
61	Nonfinancial assets	...	...	...	...	...	...	...	...	...	...	...	...
62	Financial assets	516	546	512	516	546	512	420	449	478	369	380	377
63	Liabilities	1,019	1,158	1,127	1,019	1,158	1,127	874	1,024	1,069	1,084	1,233	1,257
	Table 1 Revenue												
1	**Revenue**	**181**	**185**	**191**	**181**	**185**	**191**	**...**	**...**	**...**	**389**	**397**	**408**
11	**Taxes**	**144**	**148**	**156**	**144**	**148**	**156**	**...**	**...**	**...**	**225**	**231**	**243**
111	Taxes on income, profits, and capital gains	62	63	65	62	63	65	...	...	...	101	102	105
1111	Payable by individuals	42	43	40	42	43	40	...	...	...	79	80	79
1112	Payable by corporations and other enterprises	21	20	25	21	20	25	...	...	...	22	22	26
1113	Other taxes on income, profits, and capital gains	—	—	—	—	—	—	...	...	...	—	—	—
112	Taxes on payroll and workforce	—	—	—	—	—	—	...	...	...	—	—	—
113	Taxes on property	1	1	1	1	1	1	...	...	...	19	20	21
114	Taxes on goods and services	80	84	90	80	84	90	...	...	...	105	109	117
1141	General taxes on goods and services	55	58	63	55	58	63	...	...	...	68	71	77
1142	Excises	19	19	20	19	19	20	...	...	...	23	22	23
115	Taxes on international trade and transactions	—	—	—	—	—	—	...	...	...	0	0	0
116	Other taxes	—	—	—	—	—	—	...	...	...	0	—	—
12	**Social contributions**	**11**	**10**	**11**	**11**	**10**	**11**	**...**	**...**	**...**	**128**	**130**	**132**
121	Social security contributions	—	—	—	—	—	—	...	...	...	117	119	121
122	Other social contributions	11	10	11	11	10	11	...	...	...	11	11	11
13	**Grants**	**12**	**12**	**15**	**12**	**12**	**15**	**...**	**...**	**...**	**6**	**5**	**5**
131	From foreign governments	—	—	—	—	—	—	...	...	...	—	—	—
132	From international organizations	2	1	1	2	1	1	...	...	...	6	5	5
133	From other general government units	11	11	13	11	11	13	...	...	...	—	—	—
1331	Current	10	11	13	10	11	13	...	...	...	—	—	—
1332	Capital	0	0	0	0	0	0	...	...	...	—	—	—
14	**Other revenue**	**14**	**15**	**10**	**14**	**15**	**10**	**...**	**...**	**...**	**29**	**30**	**28**

Spain (184)

In Billions of Euros (EUR) / Fiscal Year Ends December 31st

		Budgetary Central Government			Central Government (excl. Social Security)			Central Government (incl. Social Security)			General Government		
		2013	2014	2015P	2013	2014	2015P	2013	2014	2015P	2013	2014	2015P
	Table 2 Expense by economic type												
2	**Expense**	**...**	**226**	**222**	**...**	**226**	**222**	**...**	**...**	**...**	**...**	**463**	**465**
21	**Compensation of employees**	**23**	**22**	**23**	**23**	**22**	**23**	**...**	**...**	**...**	**110**	**111**	**115**
211	Wages and salaries	17	17	17	17	17	17	...	...	...	85	85	89
212	Employers' social contributions	6	5	6	6	5	6	...	...	...	25	26	26
22	**Use of goods and services**	**8**	**8**	**8**	**8**	**8**	**8**	**...**	**...**	**...**	**53**	**53**	**55**
23	**Consumption of fixed capital**	**9**	**9**	**9**	**9**	**9**	**9**	**...**	**...**	**...**	**27**	**27**	**27**
24	**Interest**	**32**	**32**	**30**	**32**	**32**	**30**	**...**	**...**	**...**	**36**	**36**	**33**
25	**Subsidies**	**5**	**5**	**6**	**5**	**5**	**6**	**...**	**...**	**...**	**11**	**11**	**12**
26	**Grants**	**...**	**125**	**123**	**...**	**125**	**123**	**...**	**...**	**...**	**...**	**11**	**10**
261	To foreign governments	...	—	—	...	—	—	...	...	...	...	—	—
262	To international organizations	12	11	10	12	11	10	...	...	...	12	11	10
263	To other general government units	118	114	112	118	114	112	...	...	...	—	—	—
2631	Current	116	112	110	116	112	110	...	...	...	—	—	—
2632	Capital	2	2	2	2	2	2	...	...	...	—	—	—
27	**Social benefits**	**17**	**17**	**18**	**17**	**17**	**18**	**...**	**...**	**...**	**199**	**199**	**199**
271	Social security benefits	—	—	—	—	—	—	...	...	...	147	147	146
272	Social assistance benefits	3	3	3	3	3	3	...	...	...	37	37	37
273	Employment-related social benefits	14	14	15	14	14	15	...	...	...	15	15	15
28	**Other expense**	**10**	**7**	**6**	**10**	**7**	**6**	**...**	**...**	**...**	**17**	**15**	**13**
281	Property expense other than interest	0	0	0	0	0	0	...	...	...	0	0	0
282	Transfers not elsewhere classified	9	7	6	9	7	6	...	...	...	17	15	13
2821	Current	2	2	2	2	2	2	...	...	...	6	6	6
2822	Capital	7	5	3	7	5	3	...	...	...	11	9	7
	Table 3 Transactions in assets and liabilities												
3	**Change in net worth from transactions**	**-51**	**-41**	**-31**	**-51**	**-41**	**-31**	**...**	**...**	**...**	**-76**	**-67**	**-57**
31	**Net/Gross investment in nonfinancial assets**	**-1**	**-3**	**-3**	**-1**	**-3**	**-3**	**...**	**...**	**...**	**-4**	**-5**	**-1**
311	Fixed assets	-2	-3	-2	-2	-3	-2	...	...	...	-5	-5	-1
3111	Buildings and structures	...	...	...	...	...	...	...	...	...	...	...	...
3112	Machinery and equipment	...	...	...	...	...	...	...	...	...	...	...	...
3113	Other fixed assets	...	...	...	...	...	...	...	...	...	...	...	...
3114	Weapons systems	...	...	...	...	...	...	...	...	...	...	...	...
312	Inventories	-0	-0	-0	-0	-0	-0	...	...	...	0	-0	-0
313	Valuables	...	—	—	—	—	—	...	...	...	—	—	—
314	Nonproduced assets	0	0	-1	0	0	-1	...	...	...	1	1	-1
3141	Land	...	...	...	...	...	...	...	...	...	...	...	...
3142	Mineral and energy resources	...	...	...	...	...	...	...	...	...	...	...	...
3143	Other naturally occurring assets	...	...	...	...	...	...	...	...	...	...	...	...
3144	Intangible nonproduced assets	...	...	...	...	...	...	...	...	...	...	...	...
32	**Net acquisition of financial assets**	**54**	**42**	**18**	**54**	**42**	**18**	**12**	**23**	**18**	**-10**	**5**	**-15**
	By instrument												
3201	Monetary gold and SDRs	—	—	—	—	—	—	—	—	—	—	—	—
3202	Currency and deposits	-25	8	-2	-25	8	-2	-26	10	-1	-24	11	2
3203	Debt securities	-16	-8	-3	-16	-8	-3	-13	-5	-4	-13	-5	-4
3204	Loans	74	47	34	74	47	34	32	24	34	3	1	-3
3205	Equity and investment fund shares	12	-2	-3	12	-2	-3	12	-2	-4	12	-2	-4
3206	Insurance, pension, and standardized guarantee schemes	—	—	—	—	—	—	—	—	—	—	—	—
3207	Financial derivatives and employee stock options	-0	—	—	-0	—	—	-0	—	—	0	—	—
3208	Other accounts receivable	10	-3	-8	10	-3	-8	7	-4	-7	11	-0	-6
	By debtor												
321	Domestic debtors	48	40	23	48	40	23	6	23	23	-16	4	-11
322	External debtors	6	2	-4	6	2	-4	6	0	-5	6	1	-4
33	**Net incurrence of liabilities**	**104**	**80**	**47**	**104**	**80**	**47**	**73**	**72**	**60**	**62**	**67**	**40**
	By instrument												
3301	Special Drawing Rights (SDRs)	—	—	—	—	—	—	—	—	—	—	—	—
3302	Currency and deposits	0	0	0	0	0	0	0	0	0	0	0	0
3303	Debt securities	89	53	58	89	53	58	101	68	67	95	66	59
3304	Loans	18	22	-12	18	22	-12	-24	-0	-12	-28	2	-20

		Budgetary Central Government			Central Government (excl. Social Security)			Central Government (incl. Social Security)			General Government		
		2013	2014	2015P	2013	2014	2015P	2013	2014	2015P	2013	2014	2015P
3305	Equity and investment fund shares	—	—	—	—	—	—	—	—	—	—	—	—
3306	Insurance, pension, and standardized guarantee schemes	—	—	—	—	—	—	—	—	—	—	—	—
3307	Financial derivatives and employee stock options	—	—	—	—	—	—	—	—	—	—	—	—
3308	Other accounts payable	-3	5	0	-3	5	0	-3	4	5	-6	-1	1
	By creditor												
331	Domestic creditors	28	25	-17	28	25	-17	-3	17	-5	-13	14	-22
332	External creditors	76	56	64	76	56	64	76	56	64	74	53	62
	Table 4 Holding gains and losses in assets and liabilities												
4	**Change in net worth due to holding gains and losses**	...	...	...	...	...	...	...	...	...	...	...	...
41	**Holding gains and losses in nonfinancial assets**	...	...	...	...	...	...	...	...	...	...	...	...
411	Fixed assets	...	...	...	...	...	...	...	...	...	...	...	...
412	Inventories	...	...	...	...	...	...	...	...	...	...	...	...
413	Valuables	...	...	...	...	...	...	...	...	...	...	...	...
414	Nonproduced assets	...	...	...	...	...	...	...	...	...	...	...	...
42	**Holding gains and losses in financial assets**	**1**	**7**	**10**	**1**	**7**	**10**	**1**	**6**	**11**	**2**	**6**	**12**
	By instrument												
4201	Monetary gold and SDRs	—	—	—	—	—	—	—	—	—	—	—	—
4202	Currency and deposits	0	-0	-0	0	-0	-0	-0	0	-0	-0	0	-0
4203	Debt securities	0	0	-2	0	0	-2	-0	-0	-1	-0	-0	-1
4204	Loans	-2	0	0	-2	0	0	-2	0	0	-2	0	0
4205	Equity and investment fund shares	3	6	12	3	6	12	3	6	12	4	6	13
4206	Insurance, pension, and standardized guarantee schemes	—	—	—	—	—	—	—	—	—	—	—	—
4207	Financial derivatives and employee stock options	0	—	—	0	—	—	0	—	—	-0	—	—
4208	Other accounts receivable	-0	0	-0	-0	0	-0	-0	0	-0	0	0	-0
	By debtor												
421	Domestic debtors	...	...	...	...	...	...	...	...	...	...	...	...
422	External debtors	...	...	...	...	...	...	...	...	...	...	...	...
43	**Holding gains and losses in liabilities**	**34**	**77**	**-14**	**34**	**77**	**-14**	**31**	**78**	**-14**	**37**	**83**	**-14**
	By instrument												
4301	Special Drawing Rights (SDRs)	—	—	—	—	—	—	—	—	—	—	—	—
4302	Currency and deposits	—	—	—	—	—	—	—	—	—	—	—	—
4303	Debt securities	34	77	-14	34	77	-14	32	78	-14	38	83	-14
4304	Loans	-0	-0	-0	-0	-0	-0	-0	-0	-0	-0	-0	-0
4305	Equity and investment fund shares	—	—	—	—	—	—	—	—	—	—	—	—
4306	Insurance, pension, and standardized guarantee schemes	—	—	—	—	—	—	—	—	—	—	—	—
4307	Financial derivatives and employee stock options	—	—	—	—	—	—	—	—	—	—	—	—
4308	Other accounts payable	-0	0	-0	-0	0	-0	-0	0	-0	-0	0	-0
	By creditor												
431	Domestic creditors	...	...	...	...	...	...	...	...	...	...	...	...
432	External creditors	...	...	...	...	...	...	...	...	...	...	...	...
	Table 5 Holding gains and losses in assets and liabilities												
5	**Change in net worth due to other volume changes**	...	...	...	...	...	...	...	...	...	...	...	...
51	**Other volume changes in nonfinancial assets**	...	...	...	...	...	...	...	...	...	...	...	...
511	Fixed assets	...	...	...	...	...	...	...	...	...	...	...	...
512	Inventories	...	...	...	...	...	...	...	...	...	...	...	...
513	Valuables	...	...	...	...	...	...	...	...	...	...	...	...
514	Nonproduced assets	...	...	...	...	...	...	...	...	...	...	...	...
52	**Other volume changes in financial assets**	**15**	**-18**	**-63**	**15**	**-18**	**-63**	**29**	**0**	**-0**	**29**	**0**	**-0**

Spain (184)

In Billions of Euros (EUR) / Fiscal Year Ends December 31st

		Budgetary Central Government			Central Government (excl. Social Security)			Central Government (incl. Social Security)			General Government		
		2013	2014	2015P	2013	2014	2015P	2013	2014	2015P	2013	2014	2015P
	By instrument												
5201	Monetary gold and SDRs	—	—	—	—	—	—	—	—	—	—	—	—
5202	Currency and deposits	12	—	—	12	—	—	12	—	—	12	—	—
5203	Debt securities	35	—	—	35	—	—	22	—	—	22	—	—
5204	Loans	-24	-18	-63	-24	-18	-63	3	0	-0	3	0	-0
5205	Equity and investment fund shares	-9	—	—	-9	—	—	-9	—	—	-9	—	—
5206	Insurance, pension, and standardized guarantee schemes	—	—	—	—	—	—	—	—	—	—	—	—
5207	Financial derivatives and employee stock options	—	—	—	—	—	—	—	—	—	—	—	—
5208	Other accounts receivable	1	0	0	1	0	0	1	0	0	1	0	0
	By debtor												
521	Domestic debtors	...	...	...	...	...	...	...	...	...	...	...	...
522	External debtors	...	...	...	...	...	...	...	...	...	...	...	...
53	**Other volume changes in liabilities**	**9**	**-18**	**-64**	**9**	**-18**	**-64**	**23**	**-1**	**-1**	**23**	**-0**	**-1**
	By instrument												
5301	Special Drawing Rights (SDRs)	—	—	—	—	—	—	—	—	—	—	—	—
5302	Currency and deposits	—	—	—	—	—	—	—	—	—	—	—	—
5303	Debt securities	12	—	—	12	—	—	-1	—	—	-1	—	—
5304	Loans	-3	-18	-62	-3	-18	-62	24	0	0	24	0	0
5305	Equity and investment fund shares	—	—	—	—	—	—	—	—	—	—	—	—
5306	Insurance, pension, and standardized guarantee schemes	—	—	—	—	—	—	—	—	—	—	—	—
5307	Financial derivatives and employee stock options	—	—	—	—	—	—	—	—	—	—	—	—
5308	Other accounts payable	-0	-1	-1	-0	-1	-1	-0	-1	-1	-0	-0	-2
	By creditor												
531	Domestic creditors	...	...	...	...	...	...	...	...	...	...	...	...
532	External creditors	...	...	...	...	...	...	...	...	...	...	...	...
	Table 6 Balance sheet												
6	**Net worth**	...	...	...	...	...	...	...	...	...	...	...	...
61	**Nonfinancial assets**	...	...	...	...	...	...	...	...	...	...	...	...
611	Fixed assets	...	...	...	...	...	...	...	...	...	...	...	...
6111	Buildings and structures	...	...	...	...	...	...	...	...	...	...	...	...
6112	Machinery and equipment	...	...	...	...	...	...	...	...	...	...	...	...
6113	Other fixed assets	...	...	...	...	...	...	...	...	...	...	...	...
6114	Weapons systems	...	...	...	...	...	...	...	...	...	...	...	...
612	Inventories	...	...	...	...	...	...	...	...	...	...	...	...
613	Valuables	...	...	...	...	...	...	...	...	...	...	...	...
614	Nonproduced assets	...	...	...	...	...	...	...	...	...	...	...	...
6141	Land	...	...	...	...	...	...	...	...	...	...	...	...
6142	Mineral and energy resources	...	...	...	...	...	...	...	...	...	...	...	...
6143	Other naturally occurring assets	...	...	...	...	...	...	...	...	...	...	...	...
6144	Intangible nonproduced assets	...	...	...	...	...	...	...	...	...	...	...	...
62	**Financial assets**	**516**	**546**	**512**	**516**	**546**	**512**	**420**	**449**	**478**	**369**	**380**	**377**
	By instrument												
6201	Monetary gold and SDRs	—	—	—	—	—	—	—	—	—	—	—	—
6202	Currency and deposits	38	46	44	38	46	44	47	56	55	73	84	85
6203	Debt securities	28	21	16	28	21	16	14	8	4	14	9	4
6204	Loans	221	250	221	221	250	221	132	157	191	61	61	59
6205	Equity and investment fund shares	133	137	146	133	137	146	134	138	146	150	155	164
6206	Insurance, pension, and standardized guarantee schemes	—	—	—	—	—	—	—	—	—	—	—	—
6207	Financial derivatives and employee stock options	—	—	—	—	—	—	—	—	—	—	—	—
6208	Other accounts receivable	96	92	85	96	92	85	93	89	82	72	72	66
	By debtor												
621	Domestic debtors	460	488	457	460	488	457	361	389	423	309	319	321
622	External debtors	56	59	54	56	59	54	59	59	55	60	61	57
63	**Liabilities**	**1,019**	**1,158**	**1,127**	**1,019**	**1,158**	**1,127**	**874**	**1,024**	**1,069**	**1,084**	**1,233**	**1,257**

Spain (184)

In Billions of Euros (EUR) / Fiscal Year Ends December 31st

		Budgetary Central Government			Central Government (excl. Social Security)			Central Government (incl. Social Security)			General Government		
		2013	2014	2015P	2013	2014	2015P	2013	2014	2015P	2013	2014	2015P
	By instrument												
6301	Special Drawing Rights (SDRs)	—	—	—	—	—	—	—	—	—	—	—	—
6302	Currency and deposits	4	4	4	4	4	4	4	4	4	4	4	4
6303	Debt securities	818	948	993	818	948	993	745	891	944	807	956	1,001
6304	Loans	165	169	95	165	169	95	94	93	81	213	215	196
6305	Equity and investment fund shares	—	—	—	—	—	—	—	—	—	—	—	—
6306	Insurance, pension, and standardized guarantee schemes	—	—	—	—	—	—	—	—	—	—	—	—
6307	Financial derivatives and employee stock options	—	—	—	—	—	—	—	—	—	—	—	—
6308	Other accounts payable	33	37	36	33	37	36	32	36	39	59	58	57
	By creditor												
631	Domestic creditors	649	707	627	649	707	627	504	573	569	662	732	710
632	External creditors	370	451	500	370	451	500	370	451	500	421	501	547
	Memorandum items												
6M2	Net financial worth	-504	-612	-615	-504	-612	-615	-454	-575	-591	-715	-853	-880
6M3	Gross debt (D4) at market value	1,019	1,158	1,127	1,019	1,158	1,127	874	1,024	1,069	1,084	1,233	1,257
6M3D3	D3 debt liabilities at market value	1,019	1,158	1,127	1,019	1,158	1,127	874	1,024	1,069	1,084	1,233	1,257
6M3D2	D2 debt liabilities at market value	987	1,121	1,091	987	1,121	1,091	842	988	1,029	1,024	1,175	1,200
6M3D1	D1 debt liabilities at market value	983	1,118	1,087	983	1,118	1,087	838	984	1,025	1,021	1,171	1,196
6M4	Gross debt (D4) at nominal value	...	...	...	...	...	...	...	...	...	...	...	...
6M4D3	D3 debt liabilities at nominal value	...	...	...	...	...	...	...	...	...	...	...	...
6M4D2	D2 debt liabilities at nominal value	...	...	...	...	...	...	...	...	...	...	...	...
6M4D1	D1 debt liabilities at nominal value	...	...	...	...	...	...	...	...	...	...	...	...
6M35	Gross debt (D4) at face value	971	1,027	1,001	971	1,027	1,001	899	950	991	1,038	1,099	1,130
6M35D3	D3 debt liabilities at face value	971	1,027	1,001	971	1,027	1,001	899	950	991	1,038	1,099	1,130
6M35D2	D2 debt liabilities at face value	939	990	965	939	990	965	867	914	952	978	1,041	1,073
6M35D1	D1 debt liabilities at face value	935	987	961	935	987	961	863	910	948	975	1,037	1,069
6M93	Government gross debt per national definition	850	902	940	850	902	940	812	880	926	978	1,041	1,073
6M5	Arrears	...	...	...	...	...	...	...	...	...	...	...	...
6M6	Explicit contingent liabilities	...	...	...	...	...	...	...	...	...	...	...	...
6M61	of which: Publicly guaranteed debt	...	...	...	...	...	...	...	...	...	...	...	...
6M7	Net implicit obligations for social security benefits	...	...	...	...	...	...	...	...	...	...	...	...
	Table 7 Expenditure by functions of government												
7	**Expenditure**	**231**	**223**	**219**	**231**	**223**	**219**	...	...	...	**460**	**456**	**463**
701	**General public services**	**168**	**163**	**158**	**168**	**163**	**158**	...	...	...	**71**	**69**	**67**
7017	Public debt transactions	32	32	30	32	32	30	...	...	...	37	37	35
7018	Transfers of general character between levels of government	118	115	112	118	115	112	...	...	...	—	—	—
702	**Defense**	**10**	**9**	**10**	**10**	**9**	**10**	...	...	...	**10**	**9**	**10**
703	**Public order and safety**	**11**	**11**	**11**	**11**	**11**	**11**	...	...	...	**21**	**21**	**22**
704	**Economic affairs**	**19**	**17**	**16**	**19**	**17**	**16**	...	...	...	**45**	**44**	**45**
7042	Agriculture, forestry, fishing, and hunting	1	1	1	1	1	1	...	...	...	4	4	4
7043	Fuel and energy	3	6	5	3	6	5	...	...	...	4	6	5
7044	Mining, manufacturing, and construction	0	1	0	0	1	0	...	...	...	1	1	1
7045	Transport	5	5	6	5	5	6	...	...	...	16	16	19
7046	Communication	0	1	1	0	1	-1	...	...	...	1	1	-1
705	**Environmental protection**	**0**	**0**	**0**	**0**	**0**	**0**	...	...	...	**8**	**8**	**9**
706	**Housing and community amenities**	**0**	**0**	**0**	**0**	**0**	**0**	...	...	...	**5**	**5**	**5**
707	**Health**	**3**	**3**	**3**	**3**	**3**	**3**	...	...	...	**62**	**62**	**65**
7072	Outpatient services	2	2	2	2	2	2	...	...	...	48	49	52
7073	Hospital services	...	...	...	—	—	—	...	...	...	—	—	—
7074	Public health services	0	0	0	0	0	0	...	...	...	1	1	1
708	**Recreation, culture and religion**	**2**	**2**	**2**	**2**	**2**	**2**	...	...	...	**12**	**12**	**12**
709	**Education**	**2**	**2**	**2**	**2**	**2**	**2**	...	...	...	**42**	**42**	**44**
7091	Pre-primary and primary education	0	0	0	0	0	0	...	...	...	17	17	17
7092	Secondary education	0	0	0	0	0	0	...	...	...	16	16	16
7094	Tertiary education	1	1	1	1	1	1	...	...	...	6	6	6

Spain (184)

In Billions of Euros (EUR) / Fiscal Year Ends December 31st

		Budgetary Central Government			Central Government (excl. Social Security)			Central Government (incl. Social Security)			General Government		
		2013	2014	2015P	2013	2014	2015P	2013	2014	2015P	2013	2014	2015P
710	**Social protection**	**16**	**16**	**16**	**16**	**16**	**16**	**...**	**...**	**...**	**184**	**183**	**184**
7z	Statistical discrepancy: Expenditure	...	...	...	...	...	...	...	...	...	...	...	...
	Table 8 Financial transactions by counterpart sector												
32	**Net acquisition of financial assets**	**54**	**42**	**18**	**54**	**42**	**18**	**12**	**23**	**18**	**-10**	**5**	**-15**
321	Domestic debtors	48	40	23	48	40	23	6	23	23	-16	4	-11
8211	General government	...	...	...	...	...	...	...	...	...	...	...	...
8212	Central bank	...	...	...	...	...	...	...	...	...	...	...	...
8213	Deposit-taking corporations except the central bank	...	...	...	...	...	...	...	...	...	...	...	...
8214	Other financial corporations	...	...	...	...	...	...	...	...	...	...	...	...
8215	Nonfinancial corporations	...	...	...	...	...	...	...	...	...	...	...	...
8216	Households & nonprofit institutions serving households	...	...	...	...	...	...	...	...	...	...	...	...
322	External debtors	6	2	-4	6	2	-4	6	0	-5	6	1	-4
8221	General government	...	...	...	...	...	...	...	...	...	...	...	...
8227	International organizations	...	...	...	...	...	...	...	...	...	...	...	...
8228	Financial corporations other than international organizations	...	...	...	...	...	...	...	...	...	...	...	...
8229	Other nonresidents	...	...	...	...	...	...	...	...	...	...	...	...
33	**Net incurrence of liabilities**	**104**	**80**	**47**	**104**	**80**	**47**	**73**	**72**	**60**	**62**	**67**	**40**
331	Domestic creditors	28	25	-17	28	25	-17	-3	17	-5	-13	14	-22
8311	General government	...	...	...	...	...	...	...	...	...	...	...	...
8312	Central bank	...	...	...	...	...	...	...	...	...	...	...	...
8313	Deposit-taking corporations except the central bank	...	...	...	...	...	...	...	...	...	...	...	...
8314	Other financial corporations	...	...	...	...	...	...	...	...	...	...	...	...
8315	Nonfinancial corporations	...	...	...	...	...	...	...	...	...	...	...	...
8316	Households & nonprofit institutions serving households	...	...	...	...	...	...	...	...	...	...	...	...
332	External creditors	76	56	64	76	56	64	76	56	64	74	53	62
8321	General government	...	...	...	...	...	...	...	...	...	...	...	...
8327	International organizations	...	...	...	...	...	...	...	...	...	...	...	...
8328	Financial corporations other than international organizations	...	...	...	...	...	...	...	...	...	...	...	...
8329	Other nonresidents	...	...	...	...	...	...	...	...	...	...	...	...
	Table 9 Total other economic flows in assets and liabilities												
9	**Change in net worth due to other economic flows**	**...**	**...**	**...**	**...**	**...**	**...**	**...**	**...**	**...**	**...**	**...**	**...**
91	**Other economic flows in nonfinancial assets**	**...**	**...**	**...**	**...**	**...**	**...**	**...**	**...**	**...**	**...**	**...**	**...**
911	Fixed assets	...	...	...	...	...	...	...	...	...	...	...	...
912	Inventories	...	...	...	...	...	...	...	...	...	...	...	...
913	Valuables	...	...	...	...	...	...	...	...	...	...	...	...
914	Nonproduced assets	...	...	...	...	...	...	...	...	...	...	...	...
92	**Other economic flows in financial assets**	**16**	**-11**	**-53**	**16**	**-11**	**-53**	**30**	**6**	**11**	**31**	**6**	**12**
	By instrument												
9201	Monetary gold and SDRs	—	—	—	—	—	—	—	—	—	—	—	—
9202	Currency and deposits	12	-0	-0	12	-0	-0	12	0	-0	12	0	-0
9203	Debt securities	35	0	-2	35	0	-2	22	-0	-1	22	-0	-1
9204	Loans	-26	-17	-63	-26	-17	-63	2	0	0	2	0	0
9205	Equity and investment fund shares	-6	6	12	-6	6	12	-6	6	12	-5	6	13
9206	Insurance, pension, and standardized guarantee schemes	—	—	—	—	—	—	—	—	—	—	—	—
9207	Financial derivatives and employee stock options	0	—	—	0	—	—	0	—	—	-0	—	—
9208	Other accounts receivable	1	0	-0	1	0	-0	1	0	-0	1	0	-0
	By debtor												
921	Domestic debtors	...	...	...	...	...	...	...	...	...	...	...	...
922	External debtors	...	...	...	...	...	...	...	...	...	...	...	...
93	**Other economic flows in liabilities**	**43**	**59**	**-78**	**43**	**59**	**-78**	**55**	**78**	**-15**	**61**	**82**	**-16**

Spain (184)

In Billions of Euros (EUR) / Fiscal Year Ends December 31st

		Budgetary Central Government			Central Government (excl. Social Security)			Central Government (incl. Social Security)			General Government		
		2013	2014	2015P	2013	2014	2015P	2013	2014	2015P	2013	2014	2015P
	By instrument												
9301	Special Drawing Rights (SDRs)	—	—	—	—	—	—	—	—	—	—	—	—
9302	Currency and deposits	—	—	—	—	—	—	—	—	—	—	—	—
9303	Debt securities	46	77	-14	46	77	-14	31	78	-14	37	83	-14
9304	Loans	-3	-18	-63	-3	-18	-63	24	-0	0	24	-0	0
9305	Equity and investment fund shares	—	—	—	—	—	—	—	—	—	—	—	—
9306	Insurance, pension, and standardized guarantee schemes	—	—	—	—	—	—	—	—	—	—	—	—
9307	Financial derivatives and employee stock options	—	—	—	—	—	—	—	—	—	—	—	—
9308	Other accounts payable	-0	-1	-1	-0	-1	-1	-0	-1	-1	-0	-0	-2
	By creditor												
931	Domestic creditors	...	...	...	...	...	...	...	...	...	...	...	...
932	External creditors	...	...	...	...	...	...	...	...	...	...	...	...
	Memorandum items												
9M2	Change in net financial worth due to other economic flows	-27	-70	25	-27	-70	25	-25	-72	26	-29	-76	28
9M3	Gross debt (D4) at market value: other economic flows	43	59	-78	43	59	-78	55	78	-15	61	82	-16
9M3D3	D3 debt liabilities at market value: other economic flows	43	59	-78	43	59	-78	55	78	-15	61	82	-16
9M3D2	D2 debt liabilities at market value: other economic flows	43	59	-76	43	59	-76	55	78	-14	61	83	-14
9M3D1	D1 debt liabilities at market value: other economic flows	43	59	-76	43	59	-76	55	78	-14	61	83	-14

Sri Lanka (524)

In Billions of Sri Lanka Rupees (LKR) / Fiscal Year Ends December 31st

		Budgetary Central Government			Central Government (excl. Social Security)			Central Government (incl. Social Security)			General Government		
		2013	2014P	2015P	2013	2014	2015	2013	2014	2015	2013	2014	2015
	Statement of operations												
1	Revenue	1,153	1,187	1,461	...	...	...	...	...	...	...	...	...
2	Expense	1,407	1,530	1,977	...	...	...	...	...	...	...	...	...
GOB	**Gross operating balance**	**-254**	**-343**	**-516**	...	...	...	...	...	...	...	...	...
NOB	**Net operating balance**	...	...	...	...	...	...	...	...	...	...	...	...
31	Net/Gross investment in nonfinancial assets	253	235	313	...	...	...	...	...	...	...	...	...
2M	Expenditure	1,659	1,765	2,290	...	...	...	...	...	...	...	...	...
NLB	**Net lending (+) / Net borrowing (-)**	**-506**	**-578**	**-829**	...	...	...	...	...	...	...	...	...
32	Net acquisition of financial assets	10	27	5	...	...	...	...	...	...	...	...	...
33	Net incurrence of liabilities	516	605	834	...	...	...	...	...	...	...	...	...
NLBz	Statistical discrepancy	-0	-0	0	...	...	...	...	...	...	...	...	...
	Memorandum items												
PB	Primary net lending / net borrowing	-62	-142	-319	...	...	...	...	...	...	...	...	...
GB	Government balance per national definition	...	...	...	...	...	...	...	...	...	...	...	...
	Statement of other economic flows												
	Balance sheet												
	Table 1 Revenue												
1	**Revenue**	**1,153**	**1,187**	**1,461**	...	...	...	...	...	...	...	...	...
11	**Taxes**	**1,006**	**1,050**	**1,356**	...	...	...	...	...	...	...	...	...
111	Taxes on income, profits, and capital gains	206	198	263	...	...	...	...	...	...	...	...	...
1111	Payable by individuals	27	31	38	...	...	...	...	...	...	...	...	...
1112	Payable by corporations and other enterprises	101	98	162	...	...	...	...	...	...	...	...	...
1113	Other taxes on income, profits, and capital gains	78	69	62	...	...	...	...	...	...	...	...	...
112	Taxes on payroll and workforce	—	—	—	...	...	...	...	...	...	...	...	...
113	Taxes on property	—	—	—	...	...	...	...	...	...	...	...	...
114	Taxes on goods and services	507	539	724	...	...	...	...	...	...	...	...	...
1141	General taxes on goods and services	251	275	220	...	...	...	...	...	...	...	...	...
1142	Excises	251	257	498	...	...	...	...	...	...	...	...	...
115	Taxes on international trade and transactions	192	198	244	...	...	...	...	...	...	...	...	...
116	Other taxes	102	115	125	...	...	...	...	...	...	...	...	...
12	**Social contributions**	**15**	**15**	**15**	...	...	...	...	...	...	...	...	...
121	Social security contributions	15	15	15	...	...	...	...	...	...	...	...	...
122	Other social contributions	—	—	—	...	...	...	...	...	...	...	...	...
13	**Grants**	**16**	**9**	**6**	...	...	...	...	...	...	...	...	...
131	From foreign governments	16	9	6	...	...	...	...	...	...	...	...	...
132	From international organizations	—	—	—	...	...	...	...	...	...	...	...	...
133	From other general government units	—	—	—	...	...	...	...	...	...	...	...	...
1331	Current	—	—	—	...	...	...	...	...	...	...	...	...
1332	Capital	—	—	—	...	...	...	...	...	...	...	...	...
14	**Other revenue**	**116**	**112**	**84**	...	...	...	...	...	...	...	...	...
	Table 2 Expense by economic type												
2	**Expense**	**1,407**	**1,530**	**1,977**	...	...	...	...	...	...	...	...	...
21	**Compensation of employees**	**393**	**441**	**562**	...	...	...	...	...	...	...	...	...
211	Wages and salaries	393	441	562	...	...	...	...	...	...	...	...	...
212	Employers' social contributions	—	—	—	...	...	...	...	...	...	...	...	...
22	**Use of goods and services**	**119**	**163**	**211**	...	...	...	...	...	...	...	...	...
23	**Consumption of fixed capital**	...	...	...	...	...	...	...	...	...	...	...	...
24	**Interest**	**444**	**436**	**510**	...	...	...	...	...	...	...	...	...
25	**Subsidies**	**53**	**66**	**74**	...	...	...	...	...	...	...	...	...
26	**Grants**	**202**	**208**	**275**	...	...	...	...	...	...	...	...	...
261	To foreign governments	1	1	1	...	...	...	...	...	...	...	...	...
262	To international organizations	—	—	—	...	...	...	...	...	...	...	...	...
263	To other general government units	200	207	274	...	...	...	...	...	...	...	...	...
2631	Current	—	—	—	...	...	...	...	...	...	...	...	...
2632	Capital	200	207	274	...	...	...	...	...	...	...	...	...

Sri Lanka (524)

In Billions of Sri Lanka Rupees (LKR) / Fiscal Year Ends December 31st

		Budgetary Central Government			Central Government (excl. Social Security)			Central Government (incl. Social Security)			General Government		
		2013	2014P	2015P	2013	2014	2015	2013	2014	2015	2013	2014	2015
27	**Social benefits**	**195**	**217**	**345**	...	...	...	...	...	...	...	...	...
271	Social security benefits	123	126	155	...	...	...	...	...	...	...	...	...
272	Social assistance benefits	72	91	190	...	...	...	...	...	...	...	...	...
273	Employment-related social benefits	—	—	—	...	...	...	...	...	...	...	...	...
28	**Other expense**	—	—	—	...	...	...	...	...	...	...	...	...
281	Property expense other than interest	—	—	—	...	...	...	...	...	...	...	...	...
282	Transfers not elsewhere classified	—	—	—	...	...	...	...	...	...	...	...	...
2821	Current	—	—	—	...	...	...	...	...	...	...	...	...
2822	Capital	—	—	—	...	...	...	...	...	...	...	...	...
	Table 3 Transactions in assets and liabilities												
3	**Change in net worth from transactions**	...	...	...	...	...	...	...	...	...	...	...	...
31	**Net/Gross investment in nonfinancial assets**	**253**	**235**	**313**	...	...	...	...	...	...	...	...	...
311	Fixed assets	253	235	313	...	...	...	...	...	...	...	...	...
3111	Buildings and structures	...	...	...	...	...	...	...	...	...	...	...	...
3112	Machinery and equipment	...	...	...	...	...	...	...	...	...	...	...	...
3113	Other fixed assets	...	...	...	...	...	...	...	...	...	...	...	...
3114	Weapons systems	...	...	...	...	...	...	...	...	...	...	...	...
312	Inventories	—	—	—	...	...	...	...	...	...	...	...	...
313	Valuables	—	—	—	...	...	...	...	...	...	...	...	...
314	Nonproduced assets	—	—	—	...	...	...	...	...	...	...	...	...
3141	Land	—	—	—	...	...	...	...	...	...	...	...	...
3142	Mineral and energy resources	—	—	—	...	...	...	...	...	...	...	...	...
3143	Other naturally occurring assets	—	—	—	...	...	...	...	...	...	...	...	...
3144	Intangible nonproduced assets	—	—	—	...	...	...	...	...	...	...	...	...
32	**Net acquisition of financial assets**	**10**	**27**	**5**	...	...	...	...	...	...	...	...	...
	By instrument												
3201	Monetary gold and SDRs	—	—	—	...	...	...	...	...	...	...	...	...
3202	Currency and deposits	—	14	4	...	...	...	...	...	...	...	...	...
3203	Debt securities	—	—	—	...	...	...	...	...	...	...	...	...
3204	Loans	10	13	1	...	...	...	...	...	...	...	...	...
3205	Equity and investment fund shares	—	—	—	...	...	...	...	...	...	...	...	...
3206	Insurance, pension, and standardized guarantee schemes	—	—	—	...	...	...	...	...	...	...	...	...
3207	Financial derivatives and employee stock options	—	—	—	...	...	...	...	...	...	...	...	...
3208	Other accounts receivable	...	...	...	...	...	...	...	...	...	...	...	...
	By debtor												
321	Domestic debtors	10	27	5	...	...	...	...	...	...	...	...	...
322	External debtors	—	—	—	...	...	...	...	...	...	...	...	...
33	**Net incurrence of liabilities**	**516**	**605**	**834**	...	...	...	...	...	...	...	...	...
	By instrument												
3301	Special Drawing Rights (SDRs)	—	—	—	...	...	...	...	...	...	...	...	...
3302	Currency and deposits	—	14	—	...	...	...	...	...	...	...	...	...
3303	Debt securities	446	396	...	...	...	...	...	...	...	...	...	...
3304	Loans	70	195	...	...	...	...	...	...	...	...	...	...
3305	Equity and investment fund shares	—	—	—	...	...	...	...	...	...	...	...	...
3306	Insurance, pension, and standardized guarantee schemes	—	—	—	...	...	...	...	...	...	...	...	...
3307	Financial derivatives and employee stock options	—	—	—	...	...	...	...	...	...	...	...	...
3308	Other accounts payable	...	...	...	...	...	...	...	...	...	...	...	...
	By creditor												
331	Domestic creditors	392	392	597	...	...	...	...	...	...	...	...	...
332	External creditors	124	213	237	...	...	...	...	...	...	...	...	...
	Table 4 Holding gains and losses in assets and liabilities												
	Table 5 Holding gains and losses in assets and liabilities												
	Table 6 Balance sheet												

Sri Lanka (524)

In Billions of Sri Lanka Rupees (LKR) / Fiscal Year Ends December 31st

		Budgetary Central Government			Central Government (excl. Social Security)			Central Government (incl. Social Security)			General Government		
		2013	2014P	2015P	2013	2014	2015	2013	2014	2015	2013	2014	2015
	Table 7 Expenditure by functions of government												
7	**Expenditure**	**1,659**	**1,765**	**2,290**	...	...	...	...	...	...	...	...	...
701	**General public services**	**530**	**550**	**660**	...	...	...	...	...	...	...	...	...
7017	Public debt transactions	444	436	510	...	...	...	...	...	...	...	...	...
7018	Transfers of general character between levels of government	—	—	—	...	...	...	...	...	...	...	...	...
702	**Defense**	**170**	**195**	**234**	...	...	...	...	...	...	...	...	...
703	**Public order and safety**	**47**	**69**	**79**	...	...	...	...	...	...	...	...	...
704	**Economic affairs**	**452**	**435**	**602**	...	...	...	...	...	...	...	...	...
7042	Agriculture, forestry, fishing, and hunting	67	104	146	...	...	...	...	...	...	...	...	...
7043	Fuel and energy	92	52	61	...	...	...	...	...	...	...	...	...
7044	Mining, manufacturing, and construction	—	—	—	...	...	...	...	...	...	...	...	...
7045	Transport	247	219	296	...	...	...	...	...	...	...	...	...
7046	Communication	—	—	—	...	...	...	...	...	...	...	...	...
705	**Environmental protection**	...	...	...	...	...	...	...	...	...	...	...	...
706	**Housing and community amenities**	**46**	**65**	**286**	...	...	...	...	...	...	...	...	...
707	**Health**	**120**	**138**	**178**	...	...	...	...	...	...	...	...	...
7072	Outpatient services	—	—	—	...	...	...	...	...	...	...	...	...
7073	Hospital services	—	—	—	...	...	...	...	...	...	...	...	...
7074	Public health services	—	—	—	...	...	...	...	...	...	...	...	...
708	**Recreation, culture and religion**	...	...	...	...	...	...	...	...	...	...	...	...
709	**Education**	**152**	**190**	**225**	...	...	...	...	...	...	...	...	...
7091	Pre-primary and primary education	152	190	225	...	...	...	...	...	...	...	...	...
7092	Secondary education	—	—	—	...	...	...	...	...	...	...	...	...
7094	Tertiary education	—	—	—	...	...	...	...	...	...	...	...	...
710	**Social protection**	**614**	**603**	**550**	...	...	...	...	...	...	...	...	...
7z	Statistical discrepancy: Expenditure	-471	-481	-524	...	...	...	...	...	...	...	...	...
	Table 8 Financial transactions by counterpart sector												
	Table 9 Total other economic flows in assets and liabilities												

St. Kitts and Nevis (361)

In Millions of Eastern Caribbean Dollars (XCD) / Fiscal Year Ends December 31st

		Budgetary Central Government			Central Government (excl. Social Security)			Central Government (incl. Social Security)			General Government		
		2012	2013	2014	2012	2013	2014	2012	2013	2014	2012	2013	2014
	Statement of operations												
1	Revenue	499	489	551	...	...	...	...	...	...	...	...	...
2	Expense	489	491	514	...	...	...	...	...	...	...	...	...
GOB	**Gross operating balance**	**10**	**-3**	**37**	...	...	...	...	...	...	...	...	...
NOB	**Net operating balance**	...	...	...	...	...	...	...	...	...	...	...	...
31	Net/Gross investment in nonfinancial assets	49	117	114	...	...	...	...	...	...	...	...	...
2M	Expenditure	538	609	628	...	...	...	...	...	...	...	...	...
NLB	**Net lending (+) / Net borrowing (-)**	**-38**	**-120**	**-77**	...	...	...	...	...	...	...	...	...
32	Net acquisition of financial assets	4	0	48	...	...	...	...	...	...	...	...	...
33	Net incurrence of liabilities	43	120	124	...	...	...	...	...	...	...	...	...
NLBz	Statistical discrepancy	-0	-0	-0	...	...	...	...	...	...	...	...	...
	Memorandum items												
PB	Primary net lending / net borrowing	6	-72	-31	...	...	...	...	...	...	...	...	...
GB	Government balance per national definition	...	...	...	...	...	...	...	...	...	...	...	...
	Statement of other economic flows												
	Balance sheet												
	Table 1 Revenue												
1	**Revenue**	**499**	**489**	**551**	...	...	...	...	...	...	...	...	...
11	**Taxes**	**431**	**421**	**467**	...	...	...	...	...	...	...	...	...
111	Taxes on income, profits, and capital gains	122	111	137	...	...	...	...	...	...	...	...	...
1111	Payable by individuals	72	69	72	...	...	...	...	...	...	...	...	...
1112	Payable by corporations and other enterprises	41	30	40	...	...	...	...	...	...	...	...	...
1113	Other taxes on income, profits, and capital gains	10	12	25	...	...	...	...	...	...	...	...	...
112	Taxes on payroll and workforce	—	—	—	...	...	...	...	...	...	...	...	...
113	Taxes on property	3	4	4	...	...	...	...	...	...	...	...	...
114	Taxes on goods and services	224	223	240	...	...	...	...	...	...	...	...	...
1141	General taxes on goods and services	134	131	138	...	...	...	...	...	...	...	...	...
1142	Excises	—	—	—	...	...	...	...	...	...	...	...	...
115	Taxes on international trade and transactions	81	82	85	...	...	...	...	...	...	...	...	...
116	Other taxes	—	—	—	...	...	...	...	...	...	...	...	...
12	**Social contributions**	—	—	—	...	...	...	...	...	...	...	...	...
121	Social security contributions	—	—	—	...	...	...	...	...	...	...	...	...
122	Other social contributions	—	—	—	...	...	...	...	...	...	...	...	...
13	**Grants**	**27**	**26**	**29**	...	...	...	...	...	...	...	...	...
131	From foreign governments	27	26	29	...	...	...	...	...	...	...	...	...
132	From international organizations	—	—	—	...	...	...	...	...	...	...	...	...
133	From other general government units	—	—	—	...	...	...	...	...	...	...	...	...
1331	Current	—	—	—	...	...	...	...	...	...	...	...	...
1332	Capital	—	—	—	...	...	...	...	...	...	...	...	...
14	**Other revenue**	**42**	**42**	**55**	...	...	...	...	...	...	...	...	...
	Table 2 Expense by economic type												
2	**Expense**	**489**	**491**	**514**	...	...	...	...	...	...	...	...	...
21	**Compensation of employees**	**243**	**251**	**248**	...	...	...	...	...	...	...	...	...
211	Wages and salaries	243	251	248	...	...	...	...	...	...	...	...	...
212	Employers' social contributions	—	—	—	...	...	...	...	...	...	...	...	...
22	**Use of goods and services**	**70**	**66**	**74**	...	...	...	...	...	...	...	...	...
23	**Consumption of fixed capital**	...	...	...	...	...	...	...	...	...	...	...	...
24	**Interest**	**44**	**48**	**46**	...	...	...	...	...	...	...	...	...
25	**Subsidies**	**82**	**72**	**89**	...	...	...	...	...	...	...	...	...
26	**Grants**	—	—	—	...	...	...	...	...	...	...	...	...
261	To foreign governments	—	—	—	...	...	...	...	...	...	...	...	...
262	To international organizations	—	—	—	...	...	...	...	...	...	...	...	...
263	To other general government units	—	—	—	...	...	...	...	...	...	...	...	...
2631	Current	—	—	—	...	...	...	...	...	...	...	...	...
2632	Capital	—	—	—	...	...	...	...	...	...	...	...	...

St. Kitts and Nevis (361)

In Millions of Eastern Caribbean Dollars (XCD) / Fiscal Year Ends December 31st

		Budgetary Central Government			Central Government (excl. Social Security)			Central Government (incl. Social Security)			General Government		
		2012	2013	2014	2012	2013	2014	2012	2013	2014	2012	2013	2014
27	**Social benefits**	**50**	**54**	**58**	**...**	**...**	**...**	**...**	**...**	**...**	**...**	**...**	**...**
271	Social security benefits	50	54	58	...	...	...	...	...	...	...	...	...
272	Social assistance benefits	—	—	—	...	...	...	...	...	...	...	...	...
273	Employment-related social benefits	—	—	—	...	...	...	...	...	...	...	...	...
28	**Other expense**	**—**	**—**	**—**	**...**	**...**	**...**	**...**	**...**	**...**	**...**	**...**	**...**
281	Property expense other than interest	—	—	—	...	...	...	...	...	...	...	...	...
282	Transfers not elsewhere classified	—	—	—	...	...	...	...	...	...	...	...	...
2821	Current	—	—	—	...	...	...	...	...	...	...	...	...
2822	Capital	—	—	—	...	...	...	...	...	...	...	...	...
	Table 3 Transactions in assets and liabilities												
3	**Change in net worth from transactions**	**...**	**...**	**...**	**...**	**...**	**...**	**...**	**...**	**...**	**...**	**...**	**...**
31	**Net/Gross investment in nonfinancial assets**	**49**	**117**	**114**	**...**	**...**	**...**	**...**	**...**	**...**	**...**	**...**	**...**
311	Fixed assets	54	152	114	...	...	...	...	...	...	...	...	...
3111	Buildings and structures	—	—	—	...	...	...	...	...	...	...	...	...
3112	Machinery and equipment	—	—	—	...	...	...	...	...	...	...	...	...
3113	Other fixed assets	—	—	—	...	...	...	...	...	...	...	...	...
3114	Weapons systems	...	...	...	...	...	...	...	...	...	...	...	...
312	Inventories	—	—	—	...	...	...	...	...	...	...	...	...
313	Valuables	—	—	—	...	...	...	...	...	...	...	...	...
314	Nonproduced assets	-5	-34	-1	...	...	...	...	...	...	...	...	...
3141	Land	-5	-34	-1	...	...	...	...	...	...	...	...	...
3142	Mineral and energy resources	—	—	—	...	...	...	...	...	...	...	...	...
3143	Other naturally occurring assets	—	—	—	...	...	...	...	...	...	...	...	...
3144	Intangible nonproduced assets	—	—	—	...	...	...	...	...	...	...	...	...
32	**Net acquisition of financial assets**	**4**	**0**	**48**	**...**	**...**	**...**	**...**	**...**	**...**	**...**	**...**	**...**
	By instrument												
3201	Monetary gold and SDRs	—	—	—	...	...	...	...	...	...	...	...	...
3202	Currency and deposits	4	0	48	...	...	...	...	...	...	...	...	...
3203	Debt securities	—	—	—	...	...	...	...	...	...	...	...	...
3204	Loans	—	—	—	...	...	...	...	...	...	...	...	...
3205	Equity and investment fund shares	—	—	—	...	...	...	...	...	...	...	...	...
3206	Insurance, pension, and standardized guarantee schemes	—	—	—	...	...	...	...	...	...	...	...	...
3207	Financial derivatives and employee stock options	—	—	—	...	...	...	...	...	...	...	...	...
3208	Other accounts receivable	...	...	...	...	...	...	...	...	...	...	...	...
	By debtor												
321	Domestic debtors	4	0	48	...	...	...	...	...	...	...	...	...
322	External debtors	—	—	—	...	...	...	...	...	...	...	...	...
33	**Net incurrence of liabilities**	**43**	**120**	**124**	**...**	**...**	**...**	**...**	**...**	**...**	**...**	**...**	**...**
	By instrument												
3301	Special Drawing Rights (SDRs)	...	...	...	...	...	...	...	...	...	...	...	...
3302	Currency and deposits	—	—	—	...	...	...	...	...	...	...	...	...
3303	Debt securities	27	8	22	...	...	...	...	...	...	...	...	...
3304	Loans	-21	103	99	...	...	...	...	...	...	...	...	...
3305	Equity and investment fund shares	—	—	—	...	...	...	...	...	...	...	...	...
3306	Insurance, pension, and standardized guarantee schemes	—	—	—	...	...	...	...	...	...	...	...	...
3307	Financial derivatives and employee stock options	—	—	—	...	...	...	...	...	...	...	...	...
3308	Other accounts payable	37	9	3	...	...	...	...	...	...	...	...	...
	By creditor												
331	Domestic creditors	42	24	27	...	...	...	...	...	...	...	...	...
332	External creditors	1	96	97	...	...	...	...	...	...	...	...	...
	Table 4 Holding gains and losses in assets and liabilities												
	Table 5 Holding gains and losses in assets and liabilities												
	Table 6 Balance sheet												

St. Kitts and Nevis (361)

In Millions of Eastern Caribbean Dollars (XCD) / Fiscal Year Ends December 31st

	Budgetary Central Government			Central Government (excl. Social Security)			Central Government (incl. Social Security)			General Government		
	2012	2013	2014	2012	2013	2014	2012	2013	2014	2012	2013	2014
Table 7 Expenditure by functions of government												
Table 8 Financial transactions by counterpart sector												
Table 9 Total other economic flows in assets and liabilities												

St. Lucia (362)

In Millions of Eastern Caribbean Dollars (XCD) / Fiscal Year Ends December 31st

		Budgetary Central Government			Central Government (excl. Social Security)			Central Government (incl. Social Security)			General Government		
		2012	2013	2014	2012	2013	2014	2012	2013	2014	2012	2013	2014
	Statement of operations												
1	Revenue	833	883	961	...	...	...	...	...	...	...	...	...
2	Expense	826	848	856	...	...	...	...	...	...	...	...	...
GOB	**Gross operating balance**	**8**	**35**	**104**	...	...	...	...	...	...	...	...	...
NOB	**Net operating balance**	...	...	...	...	...	...	...	...	...	...	...	...
31	Net/Gross investment in nonfinancial assets	236	276	218	...	...	...	...	...	...	...	...	...
2M	Expenditure	1,062	1,124	1,074	...	...	...	...	...	...	...	...	...
NLB	**Net lending (+) / Net borrowing (-)**	**-229**	**-241**	**-114**	...	...	...	...	...	...	...	...	...
32	Net acquisition of financial assets	-23	-129	-101	...	...	...	...	...	...	...	...	...
33	Net incurrence of liabilities	206	112	12	...	...	...	...	...	...	...	...	...
NLBz	Statistical discrepancy	—	—	—	...	...	...	...	...	...	...	...	...
	Memorandum items												
PB	Primary net lending / net borrowing	-106	-106	30	...	...	...	...	...	...	...	...	...
GB	Government balance per national definition	...	...	...	...	...	...	...	...	...	...	...	...
	Statement of other economic flows												
	Balance sheet												
	Table 1 Revenue												
1	**Revenue**	**833**	**883**	**961**	...	...	...	...	...	...	...	...	...
11	**Taxes**	**740**	**814**	**856**	...	...	...	...	...	...	...	...	...
111	Taxes on income, profits, and capital gains	226	223	219	...	...	...	...	...	...	...	...	...
1111	Payable by individuals	93	94	101	...	...	...	...	...	...	...	...	...
1112	Payable by corporations and other enterprises	80	62	63	...	...	...	...	...	...	...	...	...
1113	Other taxes on income, profits, and capital gains	53	67	55	...	...	...	...	...	...	...	...	...
112	Taxes on payroll and workforce	—	—	—	...	...	...	...	...	...	...	...	...
113	Taxes on property	5	8	8	...	...	...	...	...	...	...	...	...
114	Taxes on goods and services	183	363	383	...	...	...	...	...	...	...	...	...
1141	General taxes on goods and services	93	301	325	...	...	...	...	...	...	...	...	...
1142	Excises	6	1	0	...	...	...	...	...	...	...	...	...
115	Taxes on international trade and transactions	327	220	245	...	...	...	...	...	...	...	...	...
116	Other taxes	—	—	—	...	...	...	...	...	...	...	...	...
12	**Social contributions**	**—**	**—**	**—**	...	...	...	...	...	...	...	...	...
121	Social security contributions	—	—	—	...	...	...	...	...	...	...	...	...
122	Other social contributions	—	—	—	...	...	...	...	...	...	...	...	...
13	**Grants**	**23**	**17**	**59**	...	...	...	...	...	...	...	...	...
131	From foreign governments	23	17	59	...	...	...	...	...	...	...	...	...
132	From international organizations	—	—	—	...	...	...	...	...	...	...	...	...
133	From other general government units	—	—	—	...	...	...	...	...	...	...	...	...
1331	Current	—	—	—	...	...	...	...	...	...	...	...	...
1332	Capital	—	—	—	...	...	...	...	...	...	...	...	...
14	**Other revenue**	**70**	**51**	**46**	...	...	...	...	...	...	...	...	...
	Table 2 Expense by economic type												
2	**Expense**	**826**	**848**	**856**	...	...	...	...	...	...	...	...	...
21	**Compensation of employees**	**359**	**373**	**377**	...	...	...	...	...	...	...	...	...
211	Wages and salaries	359	373	377	...	...	...	...	...	...	...	...	...
212	Employers' social contributions	—	—	—	...	...	...	...	...	...	...	...	...
22	**Use of goods and services**	**160**	**168**	**159**	...	...	...	...	...	...	...	...	...
23	**Consumption of fixed capital**	...	...	...	...	...	...	...	...	...	...	...	...
24	**Interest**	**123**	**135**	**144**	...	...	...	...	...	...	...	...	...
25	**Subsidies**	**121**	**108**	**105**	...	...	...	...	...	...	...	...	...
26	**Grants**	**—**	**—**	**—**	...	...	...	...	...	...	...	...	...
261	To foreign governments	—	—	—	...	...	...	...	...	...	...	...	...
262	To international organizations	—	—	—	...	...	...	...	...	...	...	...	...
263	To other general government units	—	—	—	...	...	...	...	...	...	...	...	...
2631	Current	—	—	—	...	...	...	...	...	...	...	...	...
2632	Capital	—	—	—	...	...	...	...	...	...	...	...	...

St. Lucia (362)

In Millions of Eastern Caribbean Dollars (XCD) / Fiscal Year Ends December 31st

		Budgetary Central Government			Central Government (excl. Social Security)			Central Government (incl. Social Security)			General Government		
		2012	2013	2014	2012	2013	2014	2012	2013	2014	2012	2013	2014
27	**Social benefits**	**62**	**64**	**71**	**...**	**...**	**...**	**...**	**...**	**...**	**...**	**...**	**...**
271	Social security benefits	62	64	71	...	...	...	...	...	...	...	...	...
272	Social assistance benefits	—	—	—	...	...	...	...	...	...	...	...	...
273	Employment-related social benefits	—	—	—	...	...	...	...	...	...	...	...	...
28	**Other expense**	**—**	**—**	**—**	**...**	**...**	**...**	**...**	**...**	**...**	**...**	**...**	**...**
281	Property expense other than interest	—	—	—	...	...	...	...	...	...	...	...	...
282	Transfers not elsewhere classified	—	—	—	...	...	...	...	...	...	...	...	...
2821	Current	—	—	—	...	...	...	...	...	...	...	...	...
2822	Capital	—	—	—	...	...	...	...	...	...	...	...	...
	Table 3 Transactions in assets and liabilities												
3	**Change in net worth from transactions**	**...**	**...**	**...**	**...**	**...**	**...**	**...**	**...**	**...**	**...**	**...**	**...**
31	**Net/Gross investment in nonfinancial assets**	**236**	**276**	**218**	**...**	**...**	**...**	**...**	**...**	**...**	**...**	**...**	**...**
311	Fixed assets	242	276	218	...	...	...	...	...	...	...	...	...
3111	Buildings and structures	...	...	...	...	...	...	...	...	...	...	...	...
3112	Machinery and equipment	...	...	...	...	...	...	...	...	...	...	...	...
3113	Other fixed assets	...	...	...	...	...	...	...	...	...	...	...	...
3114	Weapons systems	...	...	...	...	...	...	...	...	...	...	...	...
312	Inventories	—	—	—	...	...	...	...	...	...	...	...	...
313	Valuables	—	—	—	...	...	...	...	...	...	...	...	...
314	Nonproduced assets	-6	-0	-0	...	...	...	...	...	...	...	...	...
3141	Land	-6	-0	-0	...	...	...	...	...	...	...	...	...
3142	Mineral and energy resources	—	—	—	...	...	...	...	...	...	...	...	...
3143	Other naturally occurring assets	—	—	—	...	...	...	...	...	...	...	...	...
3144	Intangible nonproduced assets	—	—	—	...	...	...	...	...	...	...	...	...
32	**Net acquisition of financial assets**	**-23**	**-129**	**-101**	**...**	**...**	**...**	**...**	**...**	**...**	**...**	**...**	**...**
	By instrument												
3201	Monetary gold and SDRs	—	—	—	...	...	...	...	...	...	...	...	...
3202	Currency and deposits	-23	-129	-101	...	...	...	...	...	...	...	...	...
3203	Debt securities	—	—	—	...	...	...	...	...	...	...	...	...
3204	Loans	—	—	—	...	...	...	...	...	...	...	...	...
3205	Equity and investment fund shares	—	—	—	...	...	...	...	...	...	...	...	...
3206	Insurance, pension, and standardized guarantee schemes	—	—	—	...	...	...	...	...	...	...	...	...
3207	Financial derivatives and employee stock options	—	—	—	...	...	...	...	...	...	...	...	...
3208	Other accounts receivable	...	...	...	...	...	...	...	...	...	...	...	...
	By debtor												
321	Domestic debtors	-23	-129	-101	...	...	...	...	...	...	...	...	...
322	External debtors	—	—	—	...	...	...	...	...	...	...	...	...
33	**Net incurrence of liabilities**	**206**	**112**	**12**	**...**	**...**	**...**	**...**	**...**	**...**	**...**	**...**	**...**
	By instrument												
3301	Special Drawing Rights (SDRs)	...	...	...	...	...	...	...	...	...	...	...	...
3302	Currency and deposits	—	—	—	...	...	...	...	...	...	...	...	...
3303	Debt securities	—	—	—	...	...	...	...	...	...	...	...	...
3304	Loans	206	112	12	...	...	...	...	...	...	...	...	...
3305	Equity and investment fund shares	—	—	—	...	...	...	...	...	...	...	...	...
3306	Insurance, pension, and standardized guarantee schemes	—	—	—	...	...	...	...	...	...	...	...	...
3307	Financial derivatives and employee stock options	—	—	—	...	...	...	...	...	...	...	...	...
3308	Other accounts payable	...	...	...	...	...	...	...	...	...	...	...	...
	By creditor												
331	Domestic creditors	163	146	-51	...	...	...	...	...	...	...	...	...
332	External creditors	43	-33	63	...	...	...	...	...	...	...	...	...
	Table 4 Holding gains and losses in assets and liabilities												
	Table 5 Holding gains and losses in assets and liabilities												
	Table 6 Balance sheet												

St. Lucia (362)

In Millions of Eastern Caribbean Dollars (XCD) / Fiscal Year Ends December 31st

	Budgetary Central Government			Central Government (excl. Social Security)			Central Government (incl. Social Security)			General Government		
	2012	2013	2014	2012	2013	2014	2012	2013	2014	2012	2013	2014
Table 7 Expenditure by functions of government												
Table 8 Financial transactions by counterpart sector												
Table 9 Total other economic flows in assets and liabilities												

St. Vincent and the Grenadines (364)

In Millions of Eastern Caribbean Dollars (XCD) / Fiscal Year Ends December 31st

		Budgetary Central Government			Central Government (excl. Social Security)			Central Government (incl. Social Security)			General Government		
		2012	2013	2014	2012	2013	2014	2012	2013	2014	2012	2013	2014
	Statement of operations												
1	Revenue	499	489	551	...	...	...	...	...	...	...	...	...
2	Expense	489	491	514	...	...	...	...	...	...	...	...	...
GOB	**Gross operating balance**	**10**	**-3**	**37**	...	...	...	...	...	...	...	...	...
NOB	**Net operating balance**	...	...	...	...	...	...	...	...	...	...	...	...
31	Net/Gross investment in nonfinancial assets	49	117	114	...	...	...	...	...	...	...	...	...
2M	Expenditure	538	609	628	...	...	...	...	...	...	...	...	...
NLB	**Net lending (+) / Net borrowing (-)**	**-38**	**-120**	**-77**	...	...	...	...	...	...	...	...	...
32	Net acquisition of financial assets	4	0	48	...	...	...	...	...	...	...	...	...
33	Net incurrence of liabilities	43	120	124	...	...	...	...	...	...	...	...	...
NLBz	Statistical discrepancy	-0	-0	-0	...	...	...	...	...	...	...	...	...
	Memorandum items												
PB	Primary net lending / net borrowing	6	-72	-31	...	...	...	...	...	...	...	...	...
GB	Government balance per national definition	...	...	...	...	...	...	...	...	...	...	...	...
	Statement of other economic flows												
	Balance sheet												
	Table 1 Revenue												
1	**Revenue**	**499**	**489**	**551**	...	...	...	...	...	...	...	...	...
11	**Taxes**	**431**	**421**	**467**	...	...	...	...	...	...	...	...	...
111	Taxes on income, profits, and capital gains	122	111	137	...	...	...	...	...	...	...	...	...
1111	Payable by individuals	72	69	72	...	...	...	...	...	...	...	...	...
1112	Payable by corporations and other enterprises	41	30	40	...	...	...	...	...	...	...	...	...
1113	Other taxes on income, profits, and capital gains	10	12	25	...	...	...	...	...	...	...	...	...
112	Taxes on payroll and workforce	—	—	—	...	...	...	...	...	...	...	...	...
113	Taxes on property	3	4	4	...	...	...	...	...	...	...	...	...
114	Taxes on goods and services	224	223	240	...	...	...	...	...	...	...	...	...
1141	General taxes on goods and services	134	131	138	...	...	...	...	...	...	...	...	...
1142	Excises	28	25	—	...	...	...	...	...	...	...	...	...
115	Taxes on international trade and transactions	81	82	85	...	...	...	...	...	...	...	...	...
116	Other taxes	—	—	—	...	...	...	...	...	...	...	...	...
12	**Social contributions**	—	—	—	...	...	...	...	...	...	...	...	...
121	Social security contributions	—	—	—	...	...	...	...	...	...	...	...	...
122	Other social contributions	—	—	—	...	...	...	...	...	...	...	...	...
13	**Grants**	**27**	**26**	**29**	...	...	...	...	...	...	...	...	...
131	From foreign governments	27	26	29	...	...	...	...	...	...	...	...	...
132	From international organizations	—	—	—	...	...	...	...	...	...	...	...	...
133	From other general government units	—	—	—	...	...	...	...	...	...	...	...	...
1331	Current	—	—	—	...	...	...	...	...	...	...	...	...
1332	Capital	—	—	—	...	...	...	...	...	...	...	...	...
14	**Other revenue**	**42**	**42**	**55**	...	...	...	...	...	...	...	...	...
	Table 2 Expense by economic type												
2	**Expense**	**489**	**491**	**514**	...	...	...	...	...	...	...	...	...
21	**Compensation of employees**	**243**	**251**	**248**	...	...	...	...	...	...	...	...	...
211	Wages and salaries	243	251	248	...	...	...	...	...	...	...	...	...
212	Employers' social contributions		—	—	...	...	...	...	...	...	...	...	...
22	**Use of goods and services**	**70**	**66**	**74**	...	...	...	...	...	...	...	...	...
23	**Consumption of fixed capital**	...	...	...	...	...	...	...	...	...	...	...	...
24	**Interest**	**44**	**48**	**46**	...	...	...	...	...	...	...	...	...
25	**Subsidies**	**82**	**72**	**89**	...	...	...	...	...	...	...	...	...
26	**Grants**	—	—	—	...	...	...	...	...	...	...	...	...
261	To foreign governments	—	—	—	...	...	...	...	...	...	...	...	...
262	To international organizations	—	—	—	...	...	...	...	...	...	...	...	...
263	To other general government units	—	—	—	...	...	...	...	...	...	...	...	...
2631	Current	—	—	—	...	...	...	...	...	...	...	...	...
2632	Capital	—	—	—	...	...	...	...	...	...	...	...	...

St. Vincent and the Grenadines (364)

In Millions of Eastern Caribbean Dollars (XCD) / Fiscal Year Ends December 31st

		Budgetary Central Government			Central Government (excl. Social Security)			Central Government (incl. Social Security)			General Government		
		2012	2013	2014	2012	2013	2014	2012	2013	2014	2012	2013	2014
27	**Social benefits**	**50**	**54**	**58**	...	...	...	...	...	...	...	...	...
271	Social security benefits	50	54	58	...	...	...	...	...	...	...	...	...
272	Social assistance benefits	—	—	—	...	...	...	...	...	...	...	...	...
273	Employment-related social benefits	—	—	—	...	...	...	...	...	...	...	...	...
28	**Other expense**	—	—	—	...	...	...	...	...	...	...	...	...
281	Property expense other than interest	—	—	—	...	...	...	...	...	...	...	...	...
282	Transfers not elsewhere classified	—	—	—	...	...	...	...	...	...	...	...	...
2821	Current	—	—	—	...	...	...	...	...	...	...	...	...
2822	Capital	—	—	—	...	...	...	...	...	...	...	...	...
	Table 3 Transactions in assets and liabilities												
3	**Change in net worth from transactions**	...	...	...	...	...	...	...	...	...	...	...	...
31	**Net/Gross investment in nonfinancial assets**	**49**	**117**	**114**	...	...	...	...	...	...	...	...	...
311	Fixed assets	54	152	114	...	...	...	...	...	...	...	...	...
3111	Buildings and structures	...	...	...	...	...	...	...	...	...	...	...	...
3112	Machinery and equipment	...	...	...	...	...	...	...	...	...	...	...	...
3113	Other fixed assets	...	...	...	...	...	...	...	...	...	...	...	...
3114	Weapons systems	...	...	...	...	...	...	...	...	...	...	...	...
312	Inventories	—	—	—	...	...	...	...	...	...	...	...	...
313	Valuables	—	—	—	...	...	...	...	...	...	...	...	...
314	Nonproduced assets	-5	-34	-1	...	...	...	...	...	...	...	...	...
3141	Land	-5	-34	-1	...	...	...	...	...	...	...	...	...
3142	Mineral and energy resources	—	—	—	...	...	...	...	...	...	...	...	...
3143	Other naturally occurring assets	—	—	—	...	...	...	...	...	...	...	...	...
3144	Intangible nonproduced assets	—	—	—	...	...	...	...	...	...	...	...	...
32	**Net acquisition of financial assets**	**4**	**0**	**48**	...	...	...	...	...	...	...	...	...
	By instrument												
3201	Monetary gold and SDRs	—	—	—	...	...	...	...	...	...	...	...	...
3202	Currency and deposits	4	0	48	...	...	...	...	...	...	...	...	...
3203	Debt securities	—	—	—	...	...	...	...	...	...	...	...	...
3204	Loans	—	—	—	...	...	...	...	...	...	...	...	...
3205	Equity and investment fund shares	—	—	—	...	...	...	...	...	...	...	...	...
3206	Insurance, pension, and standardized guarantee schemes	—	—	—	...	...	...	...	...	...	...	...	...
3207	Financial derivatives and employee stock options	—	—	—	...	...	...	...	...	...	...	...	...
3208	Other accounts receivable	...	...	...	...	...	...	...	...	...	...	...	...
	By debtor												
321	Domestic debtors	4	0	48	...	...	...	...	...	...	...	...	...
322	External debtors	—	—	—	...	...	...	...	...	...	...	...	...
33	**Net incurrence of liabilities**	**43**	**120**	**124**	...	...	...	...	...	...	...	...	...
	By instrument												
3301	Special Drawing Rights (SDRs)	...	...	...	...	...	...	...	...	...	...	...	...
3302	Currency and deposits	—	—	—	...	...	...	...	...	...	...	...	...
3303	Debt securities	5	15	25	...	...	...	...	...	...	...	...	...
3304	Loans	1	96	97	...	...	...	...	...	...	...	...	...
3305	Equity and investment fund shares	—	—	—	...	...	...	...	...	...	...	...	...
3306	Insurance, pension, and standardized guarantee schemes	—	—	—	...	...	...	...	...	...	...	...	...
3307	Financial derivatives and employee stock options	—	—	—	...	...	...	...	...	...	...	...	...
3308	Other accounts payable	37	9	3	...	...	...	...	...	...	...	...	...
	By creditor												
331	Domestic creditors	42	24	27	...	...	...	...	...	...	...	...	...
332	External creditors	1	96	97	...	...	...	...	...	...	...	...	...
	Table 4 Holding gains and losses in assets and liabilities												
	Table 5 Holding gains and losses in assets and liabilities												
	Table 6 Balance sheet												

St. Vincent and the Grenadines (364)

In Millions of Eastern Caribbean Dollars (XCD) / Fiscal Year Ends December 31st

	Budgetary Central Government			Central Government (excl. Social Security)			Central Government (incl. Social Security)			General Government		
	2012	2013	2014	2012	2013	2014	2012	2013	2014	2012	2013	2014
Table 7 Expenditure by functions of government												
Table 8 Financial transactions by counterpart sector												
Table 9 Total other economic flows in assets and liabilities												

Suriname (366)

In Millions of Surinamese Dollars (SRD) / Fiscal Year Ends December 31st

		Budgetary Central Government			Central Government (excl. Social Security)			Central Government (incl. Social Security)			General Government		
		2010	2011	2012P	2010	2011	2012	2010	2011	2012	2010	2011	2012
	Statement of operations												
1	Revenue	2,606	3,537	4,217	...	...	...	...	...	...	...	...	...
2	Expense	2,502	3,020	3,681	...	...	...	...	...	...	...	...	...
GOB	**Gross operating balance**	**104**	**518**	**536**	...	...	...	...	...	...	...	...	...
NOB	**Net operating balance**	...	...	...	...	...	...	...	...	...	...	...	...
31	Net/Gross investment in nonfinancial assets	354	632	728	...	...	...	...	...	...	...	...	...
2M	Expenditure	2,855	3,651	4,410	...	...	...	...	...	...	...	...	...
NLB	**Net lending (+) / Net borrowing (-)**	**-249**	**-114**	**-192**	...	...	...	...	...	...	...	...	...
32	Net acquisition of financial assets	-46	171	251	...	...	...	...	...	...	...	...	...
33	Net incurrence of liabilities	203	285	443	...	...	...	...	...	...	...	...	...
NLBz	Statistical discrepancy	—	-0	—	...	...	...	...	...	...	...	...	...
	Memorandum items												
PB	Primary net lending / net borrowing	-146	26	-52	...	...	...	...	...	...	...	...	...
GB	Government balance per national definition	...	...	...	...	...	...	...	...	...	...	...	...
	Statement of other economic flows												
	Balance sheet												
	Table 1 Revenue												
1	**Revenue**	**2,606**	**3,537**	**4,217**	...	...	...	...	...	...	...	...	...
11	**Taxes**	**1,878**	**2,667**	**3,212**	...	...	...	...	...	...	...	...	...
111	Taxes on income, profits, and capital gains	722	1,040	1,345	...	...	...	...	...	...	...	...	...
1111	Payable by individuals	389	390	434	...	...	...	...	...	...	...	...	...
1112	Payable by corporations and other enterprises	328	642	907	...	...	...	...	...	...	...	...	...
1113	Other taxes on income, profits, and capital gains	5	9	4	...	...	...	...	...	...	...	...	...
112	Taxes on payroll and workforce	—	—	—	...	...	...	...	...	...	...	...	...
113	Taxes on property	3	4	6	...	...	...	...	...	...	...	...	...
114	Taxes on goods and services	795	1,146	1,327	...	...	...	...	...	...	...	...	...
1141	General taxes on goods and services	437	555	698	...	...	...	...	...	...	...	...	...
1142	Excises	121	148	156	...	...	...	...	...	...	...	...	...
115	Taxes on international trade and transactions	267	359	380	...	...	...	...	...	...	...	...	...
116	Other taxes	89	117	155	...	...	...	...	...	...	...	...	...
12	**Social contributions**	—	—	—	...	...	...	...	...	...	...	...	...
121	Social security contributions	—	—	—	...	...	...	...	...	...	...	...	...
122	Other social contributions	—	—	—	...	...	...	...	...	...	...	...	...
13	**Grants**	**149**	**115**	—	...	...	...	...	...	...	...	...	...
131	From foreign governments	149	115	—	...	...	...	...	...	...	...	...	...
132	From international organizations	—	—	—	...	...	...	...	...	...	...	...	...
133	From other general government units	—	—	—	...	...	...	...	...	...	...	...	...
1331	Current	—	—	—	...	...	...	...	...	...	...	...	...
1332	Capital	—	—	—	...	...	...	...	...	...	...	...	...
14	**Other revenue**	**579**	**755**	**1,005**	...	...	...	...	...	...	...	...	...
	Table 2 Expense by economic type												
2	**Expense**	**2,502**	**3,020**	**3,681**	...	...	...	...	...	...	...	...	...
21	**Compensation of employees**	**1,075**	**1,209**	**1,316**	...	...	...	...	...	...	...	...	...
211	Wages and salaries	1,075	1,209	1,316	...	...	...	...	...	...	...	...	...
212	Employers' social contributions	—	—	—	...	...	...	...	...	...	...	...	...
22	**Use of goods and services**	**639**	**772**	**1,246**	...	...	...	...	...	...	...	...	...
23	**Consumption of fixed capital**	...	...	...	...	...	...	...	...	...	...	...	...
24	**Interest**	**104**	**140**	**141**	...	...	...	...	...	...	...	...	...
25	**Subsidies**	**535**	**784**	**979**	...	...	...	...	...	...	...	...	...
26	**Grants**	—	—	—	...	...	...	...	...	...	...	...	...
261	To foreign governments	—	—	—	...	...	...	...	...	...	...	...	...
262	To international organizations	—	—	—	...	...	...	...	...	...	...	...	...
263	To other general government units	—	—	—	...	...	...	...	...	...	...	...	...
2631	Current	—	—	—	...	...	...	...	...	...	...	...	...
2632	Capital	—	—	—	...	...	...	...	...	...	...	...	...

Suriname (366)

In Millions of Surinamese Dollars (SRD) / Fiscal Year Ends December 31st

		Budgetary Central Government			Central Government (excl. Social Security)			Central Government (incl. Social Security)			General Government		
		2010	2011	2012P	2010	2011	2012	2010	2011	2012	2010	2011	2012
27	**Social benefits**	**—**	**—**	**—**	**...**	**...**	**...**	**...**	**...**	**...**	**...**	**...**	**...**
271	Social security benefits	—	—	—	...	...	...	...	...	...	...	...	...
272	Social assistance benefits	—	—	—	...	...	...	...	...	...	...	...	...
273	Employment-related social benefits	—	—	—	...	...	...	...	...	...	...	...	...
28	**Other expense**	**149**	**115**	**—**	**...**	**...**	**...**	**...**	**...**	**...**	**...**	**...**	**...**
281	Property expense other than interest	—	—	—	...	...	...	...	...	...	...	...	...
282	Transfers not elsewhere classified	149	115	—	...	...	...	...	...	...	...	...	...
2821	Current	—	—	—	...	...	...	...	...	...	...	...	...
2822	Capital	149	115	—	...	...	...	...	...	...	...	...	...
	Table 3 Transactions in assets and liabilities												
3	**Change in net worth from transactions**	**...**	**...**	**...**	**...**	**...**	**...**	**...**	**...**	**...**	**...**	**...**	**...**
31	**Net/Gross investment in nonfinancial assets**	**354**	**632**	**728**	**...**	**...**	**...**	**...**	**...**	**...**	**...**	**...**	**...**
311	Fixed assets	354	632	728	...	...	...	...	...	...	...	...	...
3111	Buildings and structures	...	...	...	...	...	...	...	...	...	...	...	...
3112	Machinery and equipment	...	...	...	...	...	...	...	...	...	...	...	...
3113	Other fixed assets	...	...	...	...	...	...	...	...	...	...	...	...
3114	Weapons systems	...	...	...	...	...	...	...	...	...	...	...	...
312	Inventories	—	—	—	...	...	...	...	...	...	...	...	...
313	Valuables	—	—	—	...	...	...	...	...	...	...	...	...
314	Nonproduced assets	—	—	—	...	...	...	...	...	...	...	...	...
3141	Land	—	—	—	...	...	...	...	...	...	...	...	...
3142	Mineral and energy resources	—	—	—	...	...	...	...	...	...	...	...	...
3143	Other naturally occurring assets	—	—	—	...	...	...	...	...	...	...	...	...
3144	Intangible nonproduced assets	—	—	—	...	...	...	...	...	...	...	...	...
32	**Net acquisition of financial assets**	**-46**	**171**	**251**	**...**	**...**	**...**	**...**	**...**	**...**	**...**	**...**	**...**
	By instrument												
3201	Monetary gold and SDRs	—	—	—	...	...	...	...	...	...	...	...	...
3202	Currency and deposits	-46	171	251	...	...	...	...	...	...	...	...	...
3203	Debt securities	—	—	—	...	...	...	...	...	...	...	...	...
3204	Loans	—	—	—	...	...	...	...	...	...	...	...	...
3205	Equity and investment fund shares	—	—	—	...	...	...	...	...	...	...	...	...
3206	Insurance, pension, and standardized guarantee schemes	—	—	—	...	...	...	...	...	...	...	...	...
3207	Financial derivatives and employee stock options	—	—	—	...	...	...	...	...	...	...	...	...
3208	Other accounts receivable	—	—	...	...	...	...	...	...	...	...	...	...
	By debtor												
321	Domestic debtors	-46	171	251	...	...	...	...	...	...	...	...	...
322	External debtors	—	—	—	...	...	...	...	...	...	...	...	...
33	**Net incurrence of liabilities**	**203**	**285**	**443**	**...**	**...**	**...**	**...**	**...**	**...**	**...**	**...**	**...**
	By instrument												
3301	Special Drawing Rights (SDRs)	—	—	—	...	...	...	...	...	...	...	...	...
3302	Currency and deposits	—	—	—	...	...	...	...	...	...	...	...	...
3303	Debt securities	105	152	-74	...	...	...	...	...	...	...	...	...
3304	Loans	98	132	518	...	...	...	...	...	...	...	...	...
3305	Equity and investment fund shares	—	—	—	...	...	...	...	...	...	...	...	...
3306	Insurance, pension, and standardized guarantee schemes	—	—	—	...	...	...	...	...	...	...	...	...
3307	Financial derivatives and employee stock options	—	—	—	...	...	...	...	...	...	...	...	...
3308	Other accounts payable	—	—	...	...	...	...	...	...	...	...	...	...
	By creditor												
331	Domestic creditors	18	-129	96	...	...	...	...	...	...	...	...	...
332	External creditors	185	414	348	...	...	...	...	...	...	...	...	...
	Table 4 Holding gains and losses in assets and liabilities												
	Table 5 Holding gains and losses in assets and liabilities												
	Table 6 Balance sheet												

Suriname (366)

In Millions of Surinamese Dollars (SRD) / Fiscal Year Ends December 31st

	Budgetary Central Government			Central Government (excl. Social Security)			Central Government (incl. Social Security)			General Government		
	2010	2011	2012P	2010	2011	2012	2010	2011	2012	2010	2011	2012
Table 7 Expenditure by functions of government												
Table 8 Financial transactions by counterpart sector												
Table 9 Total other economic flows in assets and liabilities												

Swaziland (734)

In Millions of Swaziland Emalangeni (SZL) / Fiscal Year Ends March 31st

		Budgetary Central Government			Central Government (excl. Social Security)			Central Government (incl. Social Security)			General Government		
		2010	2011	2012	2010	2011	2012	2010	2011	2012	2010	2011	2012
	Statement of operations												
1	Revenue	5,572	6,010	11,584	...	...	...	...	...	...	...	...	...
2	Expense	8,023	7,779	8,959	...	...	...	...	...	...	...	...	...
GOB	**Gross operating balance**	**-2,450**	**-1,768**	**2,626**	...	...	...	...	...	...	...	...	...
NOB	**Net operating balance**	...	...	...	...	...	...	...	...	...	...	...	...
31	Net/Gross investment in nonfinancial assets	1,913	1,010	1,459	...	...	...	...	...	...	...	...	...
2M	Expenditure	9,935	8,789	10,418	...	...	...	...	...	...	...	...	...
NLB	**Net lending (+) / Net borrowing (-)**	**-4,363**	**-2,779**	**1,166**	...	...	...	...	...	...	...	...	...
32	Net acquisition of financial assets	-3,416	-2,455	1,987	...	...	...	...	...	...	...	...	...
33	Net incurrence of liabilities	947	324	821	...	...	...	...	...	...	...	...	...
NLBz	Statistical discrepancy	0	0	—	...	...	...	...	...	...	...	...	...
	Memorandum items												
PB	Primary net lending / net borrowing	-4,135	-2,518	1,436	...	...	...	...	...	...	...	...	...
GB	Government balance per national definition	...	...	...	...	...	...	...	...	...	...	...	...
	Statement of other economic flows												
	Balance sheet												
	Table 1 Revenue												
1	**Revenue**	**5,572**	**6,010**	**11,584**	...	...	...	...	...	...	...	...	...
11	**Taxes**	**5,200**	**5,708**	**11,327**	...	...	...	...	...	...	...	...	...
111	Taxes on income, profits, and capital gains	2,311	2,471	2,160	...	...	...	...	...	...	...	...	...
1111	Payable by individuals	1,558	1,650	1,417	...	...	...	...	...	...	...	...	...
1112	Payable by corporations and other enterprises	752	821	743	...	...	...	...	...	...	...	...	...
1113	Other taxes on income, profits, and capital gains	—	—	—	...	...	...	...	...	...	...	...	...
112	Taxes on payroll and workforce	4	3	2	...	...	...	...	...	...	...	...	...
113	Taxes on property	15	22	17	...	...	...	...	...	...	...	...	...
114	Taxes on goods and services	232	318	2,080	...	...	...	...	...	...	...	...	...
1141	General taxes on goods and services	—	—	1,623	...	...	...	...	...	...	...	...	...
1142	Excises	—	—	—	...	...	...	...	...	...	...	...	...
115	Taxes on international trade and transactions	2,629	2,881	7,063	...	...	...	...	...	...	...	...	...
116	Other taxes	9	11	5	...	...	...	...	...	...	...	...	...
12	**Social contributions**	—	—	—	...	...	...	...	...	...	...	...	...
121	Social security contributions	—	—	—	...	...	...	...	...	...	...	...	...
122	Other social contributions	—	—	—	...	...	...	...	...	...	...	...	...
13	**Grants**	**10**	**18**	**15**	...	...	...	...	...	...	...	...	...
131	From foreign governments	10	18	13	...	...	...	...	...	...	...	...	...
132	From international organizations	—	—	2	...	...	...	...	...	...	...	...	...
133	From other general government units	—	—	—	...	...	...	...	...	...	...	...	...
1331	Current	—	—	—	...	...	...	...	...	...	...	...	...
1332	Capital	—	—	—	...	...	...	...	...	...	...	...	...
14	**Other revenue**	**362**	**285**	**242**	...	...	...	...	...	...	...	...	...
	Table 2 Expense by economic type												
2	**Expense**	**8,023**	**7,779**	**8,959**	...	...	...	...	...	...	...	...	...
21	**Compensation of employees**	**4,445**	**4,406**	**4,486**	...	...	...	...	...	...	...	...	...
211	Wages and salaries	3,920	3,830	3,940	...	...	...	...	...	...	...	...	...
212	Employers' social contributions	525	576	546	...	...	...	...	...	...	...	...	...
22	**Use of goods and services**	**1,658**	**1,427**	**1,850**	...	...	...	...	...	...	...	...	...
23	**Consumption of fixed capital**	...	...	...	...	...	...	...	...	...	...	...	...
24	**Interest**	**228**	**261**	**270**	...	...	...	...	...	...	...	...	...
25	**Subsidies**	**44**	**41**	**115**	...	...	...	...	...	...	...	...	...
26	**Grants**	**1,398**	**1,395**	**2,077**	...	...	...	...	...	...	...	...	...
261	To foreign governments	—	—	—	...	...	...	...	...	...	...	...	...
262	To international organizations	36	32	47	...	...	...	...	...	...	...	...	...
263	To other general government units	1,362	1,364	2,031	...	...	...	...	...	...	...	...	...
2631	Current	1,362	1,364	2,031	...	...	...	...	...	...	...	...	...
2632	Capital	—	—	—	...	...	...	...	...	...	...	...	...

Swaziland (734)

In Millions of Swaziland Emalangeni (SZL) / Fiscal Year Ends March 31st

		Budgetary Central Government			Central Government (excl. Social Security)			Central Government (incl. Social Security)			General Government		
		2010	2011	2012	2010	2011	2012	2010	2011	2012	2010	2011	2012
27	**Social benefits**	**222**	**230**	**132**	...	...	...	...	...	...	...	...	...
271	Social security benefits	—	—	—	...	...	...	...	...	...	...	...	...
272	Social assistance benefits	221	230	140	...	...	...	...	...	...	...	...	...
273	Employment-related social benefits	1	0	-7	...	...	...	...	...	...	...	...	...
28	**Other expense**	**30**	**18**	**28**	...	...	...	...	...	...	...	...	...
281	Property expense other than interest	...	...	...	...	...	...	...	...	...	...	...	...
282	Transfers not elsewhere classified	...	...	...	...	...	...	...	...	...	...	...	...
2821	Current	...	...	...	...	...	...	...	...	...	...	...	...
2822	Capital	...	...	...	...	...	...	...	...	...	...	...	...
	Table 3 Transactions in assets and liabilities												
3	**Change in net worth from transactions**	...	...	...	...	...	...	...	...	...	...	...	...
31	**Net/Gross investment in nonfinancial assets**	**1,913**	**1,010**	**1,459**	...	...	...	...	...	...	...	...	...
311	Fixed assets	1,883	993	1,415	...	...	...	...	...	...	...	...	...
3111	Buildings and structures	...	...	...	...	...	...	...	...	...	...	...	...
3112	Machinery and equipment	...	...	...	...	...	...	...	...	...	...	...	...
3113	Other fixed assets	...	...	...	...	...	...	...	...	...	...	...	...
3114	Weapons systems	...	...	...	...	...	...	...	...	...	...	...	...
312	Inventories	30	18	45	...	...	...	...	...	...	...	...	...
313	Valuables	—	—	—	...	...	...	...	...	...	...	...	...
314	Nonproduced assets	—	—	—	...	...	...	...	...	...	...	...	...
3141	Land	—	—	—	...	...	...	...	...	...	...	...	...
3142	Mineral and energy resources	—	—	—	...	...	...	...	...	...	...	...	...
3143	Other naturally occurring assets	—	—	—	...	...	...	...	...	...	...	...	...
3144	Intangible nonproduced assets	—	—	—	...	...	...	...	...	...	...	...	...
32	**Net acquisition of financial assets**	**-3,416**	**-2,455**	**1,987**	...	...	...	...	...	...	...	...	...
	By instrument												
3201	Monetary gold and SDRs	—	—	—	...	...	...	...	...	...	...	...	...
3202	Currency and deposits	-3,431	-2,455	1,977	...	...	...	...	...	...	...	...	...
3203	Debt securities	—	—	—	...	...	...	...	...	...	...	...	...
3204	Loans	15	—	10	...	...	...	...	...	...	...	...	...
3205	Equity and investment fund shares	—	—	—	...	...	...	...	...	...	...	...	...
3206	Insurance, pension, and standardized guarantee schemes	—	—	—	...	...	...	...	...	...	...	...	...
3207	Financial derivatives and employee stock options	—	—	—	...	...	...	...	...	...	...	...	...
3208	Other accounts receivable	—	—	...	...	...	...	...	...	...	...	...	...
	By debtor												
321	Domestic debtors	-3,416	-2,455	1,987	...	...	...	...	...	...	...	...	...
322	External debtors	—	—	—	...	...	...	...	...	...	...	...	...
33	**Net incurrence of liabilities**	**947**	**324**	**821**	...	...	...	...	...	...	...	...	...
	By instrument												
3301	Special Drawing Rights (SDRs)	—	—	—	...	...	...	...	...	...	...	...	...
3302	Currency and deposits	—	—	—	...	...	...	...	...	...	...	...	...
3303	Debt securities	1,066	460	968	...	...	...	...	...	...	...	...	...
3304	Loans	-119	-136	-147	...	...	...	...	...	...	...	...	...
3305	Equity and investment fund shares	—	—	—	...	...	...	...	...	...	...	...	...
3306	Insurance, pension, and standardized guarantee schemes	—	—	—	...	...	...	...	...	...	...	...	...
3307	Financial derivatives and employee stock options	—	—	—	...	...	...	...	...	...	...	...	...
3308	Other accounts payable	—	—	...	...	...	...	...	...	...	...	...	...
	By creditor												
331	Domestic creditors	1,066	460	968	...	...	...	...	...	...	...	...	...
332	External creditors	-119	-136	-147	...	...	...	...	...	...	...	...	...
	Table 4 Holding gains and losses in assets and liabilities												
	Table 5 Holding gains and losses in assets and liabilities												
	Table 6 Balance sheet												

Swaziland (734)

In Millions of Swaziland Emalangeni (SZL) / Fiscal Year Ends March 31st

		Budgetary Central Government			Central Government (excl. Social Security)			Central Government (incl. Social Security)			General Government		
		2010	2011	2012	2010	2011	2012	2010	2011	2012	2010	2011	2012
	Table 7 Expenditure by functions of government												
7	**Expenditure**	**9,935**	**8,789**	**10,418**	...	...	...	...	...	...	...	...	...
701	**General public services**	**2,548**	**2,059**	**4,004**	...	...	...	...	...	...	...	...	...
7017	Public debt transactions	228	261	270	...	...	...	...	...	...	...	...	...
7018	Transfers of general character between levels of government	...	...	...	...	...	...	...	...	...	...	...	...
702	**Defense**	...	...	...	...	...	...	...	...	...	...	...	...
703	**Public order and safety**	**1,666**	**1,660**	**1,791**	...	...	...	...	...	...	...	...	...
704	**Economic affairs**	**2,002**	**1,556**	**1,882**	...	...	...	...	...	...	...	...	...
7042	Agriculture, forestry, fishing, and hunting	536	304	440	...	...	...	...	...	...	...	...	...
7043	Fuel and energy	...	...	...	...	...	...	...	...	...	...	...	...
7044	Mining, manufacturing, and construction	323	256	326	...	...	...	...	...	...	...	...	...
7045	Transport	...	...	...	...	...	...	...	...	...	...	...	...
7046	Communication	...	...	...	...	...	...	...	...	...	...	...	...
705	**Environmental protection**	...	...	...	...	...	...	...	...	...	...	...	...
706	**Housing and community amenities**	...	...	...	...	...	...	...	...	...	...	...	...
707	**Health**	**1,183**	**1,106**	**1,277**	...	...	...	...	...	...	...	...	...
7072	Outpatient services	...	...	...	...	...	...	...	...	...	...	...	...
7073	Hospital services	...	...	...	...	...	...	...	...	...	...	...	...
7074	Public health services	...	...	...	...	...	...	...	...	...	...	...	...
708	**Recreation, culture and religion**	...	...	...	...	...	...	...	...	...	...	...	...
709	**Education**	**2,050**	**1,984**	**2,147**	...	...	...	...	...	...	...	...	...
7091	Pre-primary and primary education	...	...	...	...	...	...	...	...	...	...	...	...
7092	Secondary education	...	...	...	...	...	...	...	...	...	...	...	...
7094	Tertiary education	...	...	...	...	...	...	...	...	...	...	...	...
710	**Social protection**	**647**	**449**	**485**	...	...	...	...	...	...	...	...	...
7z	Statistical discrepancy: Expenditure	...	...	...	...	...	...	...	...	...	...	...	...
	Table 8 Financial transactions by counterpart sector												
	Table 9 Total other economic flows in assets and liabilities												

Sweden (144)

In Billions of Swedish Kronor (SEK) / Fiscal Year Ends December 31st

		Budgetary Central Government			Central Government (excl. Social Security)			Central Government (incl. Social Security)			General Government		
		2013	2014	2015	2013P	2014P	2015P	2013P	2014P	2015P	2013P	2014P	2015P
	Statement of operations												
1	Revenue	...	...	...	1,093	1,125	1,224	1,223	1,259	1,369	1,884	1,926	2,070
2	Expense	...	...	...	1,124	1,164	1,204	1,258	1,295	1,340	1,897	1,948	2,017
GOB	**Gross operating balance**	...	...	...	**45**	**38**	**98**	**40**	**41**	**107**	**114**	**109**	**186**
NOB	**Net operating balance**	...	...	...	**-30**	**-39**	**20**	**-36**	**-36**	**28**	**-13**	**-22**	**53**
31	Net/Gross investment in nonfinancial assets	...	...	...	14	11	9	14	11	9	39	41	43
2M	Expenditure	...	...	...	1,138	1,176	1,213	1,272	1,306	1,349	1,937	1,989	2,060
NLB	**Net lending (+) / Net borrowing (-)**	...	...	...	**-44**	**-51**	**11**	**-49**	**-47**	**19**	**-52**	**-63**	**10**
32	Net acquisition of financial assets	...	...	...	48	60	25	...	...	...	46	96	-29
33	Net incurrence of liabilities	...	...	...	90	108	12	...	...	...	91	153	-41
NLBz	Statistical discrepancy	...	...	...	3	3	1	...	...	...	8	5	2
	Memorandum items												
PB	Primary net lending / net borrowing	...	...	...	-18	-26	29	-25	-25	37	-19	-33	33
GB	Government balance per national definition	...	...	...	...	...	...	...	...	...	...	...	...
	Statement of other economic flows												
9	**Change in net worth due to other economic flows**	...	...	...	...	...	...	...	...	...	...	...	...
4	Change in net worth due to holding gains and losses	...	...	...	...	...	...	...	...	...	...	...	...
41	Nonfinancial assets	...	...	...	...	...	...	...	...	...	...	...	...
42	Financial assets	...	...	...	-48	61	7	...	...	...	96	272	121
43	Liabilities	...	...	...	5	130	31	...	...	...	48	217	119
5	Change in net worth due to volume changes	...	...	...	...	...	...	...	...	...	...	...	...
51	Nonfinancial assets	...	...	...	...	...	...	...	...	...	...	...	...
52	Financial assets	...	...	...	1	3	—	...	...	...	13	5	—
53	Liabilities	...	...	...	0	-0	0	...	...	...	10	-1	0
	Balance sheet												
6	**Net worth**	...	...	...	...	...	...	...	...	...	**3,570**	...	...
61	Nonfinancial assets	...	...	...	...	...	...	...	...	...	2,787	...	...
62	Financial assets	...	...	...	1,366	1,490	1,521	...	...	...	2,940	3,313	3,406
63	Liabilities	...	...	...	1,660	1,898	1,941	...	...	...	2,157	2,526	2,605
	Table 1 Revenue												
1	**Revenue**	...	...	...	**1,093**	**1,125**	**1,224**	**1,223**	**1,259**	**1,369**	**1,884**	**1,926**	**2,070**
11	**Taxes**	...	...	...	**990**	**1,035**	**1,132**	**990**	**1,035**	**1,132**	**1,506**	**1,561**	**1,688**
111	Taxes on income, profits, and capital gains	...	...	...	161	181	219	161	181	219	662	691	759
1111	Payable by individuals	...	...	...	58	75	93	58	75	93	559	584	632
1112	Payable by corporations and other enterprises	...	...	...	101	103	124	101	103	124	101	103	124
1113	Other taxes on income, profits, and capital gains	...	...	...	2	3	2	2	3	2	2	3	2
112	Taxes on payroll and workforce	...	...	...	342	353	375	342	353	375	342	353	375
113	Taxes on property	...	...	...	16	16	18	16	16	18	32	32	33
114	Taxes on goods and services	...	...	...	471	485	520	471	485	520	471	485	520
1141	General taxes on goods and services	...	...	...	347	363	390	347	363	390	347	363	390
1142	Excises	...	...	...	91	89	95	91	89	95	91	89	95
115	Taxes on international trade and transactions	...	...	...	—	—	—	—	—	—	—	—	—
116	Other taxes	...	...	...	—	—	—	—	—	—	—	—	—
12	**Social contributions**	...	...	...	**12**	**12**	**12**	**118**	**122**	**128**	**142**	**147**	**155**
121	Social security contributions	...	...	...	—	—	—	107	110	116	107	110	116
122	Other social contributions	...	...	...	12	12	12	12	12	13	36	37	39
13	**Grants**	...	...	...	**11**	**11**	**13**	**11**	**11**	**12**	**3**	**3**	**3**
131	From foreign governments	...	...	...	1	1	2	1	1	2	1	1	2
132	From international organizations	...	...	...	1	1	1	1	1	1	2	2	1
133	From other general government units	...	...	...	10	10	10	9	9	9	—	—	—
1331	Current	...	...	...	8	9	9	8	8	8	—	—	—
1332	Capital	...	...	...	1	1	2	1	1	2	—	—	—
14	**Other revenue**	...	...	...	**81**	**66**	**66**	**104**	**91**	**96**	**233**	**216**	**225**

Sweden (144)

In Billions of Swedish Kronor (SEK) / Fiscal Year Ends December 31st

		Budgetary Central Government			Central Government (excl. Social Security)			Central Government (incl. Social Security)			General Government		
		2013	2014	2015	2013P	2014P	2015P	2013P	2014P	2015P	2013P	2014P	2015P
	Table 2 Expense by economic type												
2	**Expense**	...	...	...	**1,124**	**1,164**	**1,204**	**1,258**	**1,295**	**1,340**	**1,897**	**1,948**	**2,017**
21	**Compensation of employees**	...	...	...	**115**	**118**	**122**	**116**	**119**	**123**	**481**	**500**	**523**
211	Wages and salaries	...	...	...	93	96	99	94	97	100	406	422	441
212	Employers' social contributions	...	...	...	22	22	23	22	22	23	75	78	82
22	**Use of goods and services**	...	...	...	**71**	**70**	**75**	**73**	**73**	**77**	**280**	**287**	**299**
23	**Consumption of fixed capital**	...	...	...	**75**	**77**	**78**	**75**	**77**	**78**	**127**	**131**	**133**
24	**Interest**	...	...	...	**26**	**25**	**18**	**25**	**23**	**18**	**33**	**30**	**23**
25	**Subsidies**	...	...	...	**42**	**43**	**42**	**42**	**43**	**42**	**63**	**67**	**67**
26	**Grants**	...	...	...	**457**	**485**	**513**	**335**	**359**	**381**	**63**	**63**	**65**
261	To foreign governments	...	...	...	27	27	28	27	27	28	27	27	28
262	To international organizations	...	...	...	36	37	37	36	37	37	36	37	37
263	To other general government units	...	...	...	394	422	448	272	296	317	—	—	—
2631	Current	...	...	...	392	421	448	271	295	316	—	—	—
2632	Capital	...	...	...	1	1	1	1	1	1	—	—	—
27	**Social benefits**	...	...	...	**269**	**275**	**283**	**523**	**531**	**548**	**671**	**686**	**715**
271	Social security benefits	...	...	...	174	176	181	428	431	446	546	557	582
272	Social assistance benefits	...	...	...	86	89	91	86	89	91	99	102	104
273	Employment-related social benefits	...	...	...	10	10	10	10	11	11	26	27	28
28	**Other expense**	...	...	...	**69**	**71**	**73**	**69**	**70**	**72**	**179**	**185**	**194**
281	Property expense other than interest	...	...	...	4	4	5	4	4	5	6	6	7
282	Transfers not elsewhere classified	...	...	...	65	66	68	64	66	67	172	178	185
2821	Current	...	...	...	62	63	64	61	62	63	167	172	179
2822	Capital	...	...	...	3	4	4	3	4	4	4	6	6
	Table 3 Transactions in assets and liabilities												
3	**Change in net worth from transactions**	...	...	...	**-27**	**-37**	**21**	...	...	...	**-6**	**-17**	**55**
31	**Net/Gross investment in nonfinancial assets**	...	...	...	**14**	**11**	**9**	**14**	**11**	**9**	**39**	**41**	**43**
311	Fixed assets	...	...	...	13	10	5	13	10	5	41	43	41
3111	Buildings and structures	...	...	...	...	...	...	...	...	...	...	...	...
3112	Machinery and equipment	...	...	...	...	...	...	...	...	...	...	...	...
3113	Other fixed assets	...	...	...	...	...	...	...	...	...	...	...	...
3114	Weapons systems	...	...	...	...	...	...	...	...	...	...	...	...
312	Inventories	...	...	...	0	1	3	...	...	...	0	1	3
313	Valuables	...	...	...	—	—	—	...	...	...	—	—	—
314	Nonproduced assets	...	...	...	1	0	0	1	0	0	-2	-3	-2
3141	Land	...	...	...	1	0	0	...	...	...	-2	-3	-2
3142	Mineral and energy resources	...	...	...	—	—	—	...	...	...	—	—	—
3143	Other naturally occurring assets	...	...	...	—	—	—	...	...	...	—	—	—
3144	Intangible nonproduced assets	...	...	...	—	—	—	...	...	...	—	—	—
32	**Net acquisition of financial assets**	...	...	...	**48**	**60**	**25**	...	...	...	**46**	**96**	**-29**
	By instrument												
3201	Monetary gold and SDRs	...	...	...	—	—	—	...	...	...	—	—	—
3202	Currency and deposits	...	...	...	-11	66	-24	...	...	...	-7	79	-16
3203	Debt securities	...	...	...	1	1	2	...	...	...	1	57	8
3204	Loans	...	...	...	111	6	6	...	...	...	128	32	36
3205	Equity and investment fund shares	...	...	...	-43	-0	-11	...	...	...	-21	-15	-57
3206	Insurance, pension, and standardized guarantee schemes	...	...	...	—	—	—	...	...	...	—	—	—
3207	Financial derivatives and employee stock options	...	...	...	-27	-23	-35	...	...	...	-79	-68	-97
3208	Other accounts receivable	...	...	...	18	11	88	...	...	...	23	12	98
	By debtor												
321	Domestic debtors	...	...	...	62	78	42	...	...	...	89	106	54
322	External debtors	...	...	...	-14	-18	-17	...	...	...	-43	-10	-83
33	**Net incurrence of liabilities**	...	...	...	**90**	**108**	**12**	...	...	...	**91**	**153**	**-41**
	By instrument												
3301	Special Drawing Rights (SDRs)	...	...	...	—	—	—	...	...	...	—	—	—
3302	Currency and deposits	...	...	...	-20	2	-14	...	...	...	-20	1	-15
3303	Debt securities	...	...	...	109	62	4	...	...	...	107	104	55
3304	Loans	...	...	...	11	63	-11	...	...	...	18	104	-11

Sweden (144)

In Billions of Swedish Kronor (SEK) / Fiscal Year Ends December 31st

		Budgetary Central Government			Central Government (excl. Social Security)			Central Government (incl. Social Security)			General Government		
		2013	2014	2015	2013P	2014P	2015P	2013P	2014P	2015P	2013P	2014P	2015P
3305	Equity and investment fund shares	...	...	...	—	—	—	...	...	...	—	—	—
3306	Insurance, pension, and standardized guarantee schemes	...	...	...	2	2	2	...	...	...	11	13	13
3307	Financial derivatives and employee stock options	...	...	...	-11	-10	-18	...	...	...	-38	-73	-128
3308	Other accounts payable	...	...	...	-2	-11	49	...	...	...	13	4	45
	By creditor												
331	Domestic creditors	...	...	...	8	42	134	...	...	...	37	139	138
332	External creditors	...	...	...	82	66	-122	...	...	...	54	14	-178
	Table 4 Holding gains and losses in assets and liabilities												
4	**Change in net worth due to holding gains and losses**	...	...	...	...	...	...	...	...	...	...	...	...
41	**Holding gains and losses in nonfinancial assets**	...	...	...	...	...	...	...	...	...	...	...	...
411	Fixed assets	...	...	...	...	...	...	...	...	...	...	...	...
412	Inventories	...	...	...	...	...	...	...	...	...	...	...	...
413	Valuables	...	...	...	...	...	...	...	...	...	...	...	...
414	Nonproduced assets	...	...	...	...	...	...	...	...	...	...	...	...
42	**Holding gains and losses in financial assets**	...	...	...	**-48**	**61**	**7**	...	...	...	**96**	**272**	**121**
	By instrument												
4201	Monetary gold and SDRs	...	...	...	—	—	—	...	...	...	—	—	—
4202	Currency and deposits	...	...	...	0	—	—	...	...	...	0	—	—
4203	Debt securities	...	...	...	-1	2	-1	...	...	...	-6	41	1
4204	Loans	...	...	...	3	34	14	...	...	...	2	34	15
4205	Equity and investment fund shares	...	...	...	-61	-9	-32	...	...	...	43	128	15
4206	Insurance, pension, and standardized guarantee schemes	...	...	...	—	—	—	...	...	...	—	—	—
4207	Financial derivatives and employee stock options	...	...	...	12	33	26	...	...	...	57	69	90
4208	Other accounts receivable	...	...	...	—	—	—	...	...	...	—	—	—
	By debtor												
421	Domestic debtors	...	...	...	-58	43	-5	...	...	...	-1	80	44
422	External debtors	...	...	...	10	17	12	...	...	...	97	192	78
43	**Holding gains and losses in liabilities**	...	...	...	**5**	**130**	**31**	...	...	...	**48**	**217**	**119**
	By instrument												
4301	Special Drawing Rights (SDRs)	...	...	...	—	—	—	...	...	...	—	—	—
4302	Currency and deposits	...	...	...	0	1	0	...	...	...	0	1	0
4303	Debt securities	...	...	...	-11	111	5	...	...	...	-8	108	7
4304	Loans	...	...	...	0	0	0	...	...	...	0	0	0
4305	Equity and investment fund shares	...	...	...	—	—	—	...	...	...	—	—	—
4306	Insurance, pension, and standardized guarantee schemes	...	...	...	5	5	4	...	...	...	13	3	4
4307	Financial derivatives and employee stock options	...	...	...	11	13	22	...	...	...	43	105	108
4308	Other accounts payable	...	...	...	—	—	-0	...	...	...	—	0	-0
	By creditor												
431	Domestic creditors	...	...	...	-14	56	10	...	...	...	6	83	35
432	External creditors	...	...	...	19	74	20	...	...	...	42	134	84
	Table 5 Holding gains and losses in assets and liabilities												
5	**Change in net worth due to other volume changes**	...	...	...	...	...	...	...	...	...	...	...	...
51	**Other volume changes in nonfinancial assets**	...	...	...	...	...	...	...	...	...	...	...	...
511	Fixed assets	...	...	...	...	...	...	...	...	...	...	...	...
512	Inventories	...	...	...	...	...	...	...	...	...	...	...	...
513	Valuables	...	...	...	...	...	...	...	...	...	...	...	...
514	Nonproduced assets	...	...	...	...	...	...	...	...	...	...	...	...
52	**Other volume changes in financial assets**	...	...	...	**1**	**3**	—	...	...	...	**13**	**5**	—

Sweden (144)

In Billions of Swedish Kronor (SEK) / Fiscal Year Ends December 31st

		Budgetary Central Government			Central Government (excl. Social Security)			Central Government (incl. Social Security)			General Government		
		2013	2014	2015	2013P	2014P	2015P	2013P	2014P	2015P	2013P	2014P	2015P
	By instrument												
5201	Monetary gold and SDRs	...	...	...	—	—	—	...	...	...	—	—	—
5202	Currency and deposits	...	...	...	—	4	—	...	...	...	0	4	—
5203	Debt securities	...	...	...	3	-1	—	...	...	...	3	-1	-1
5204	Loans	...	...	...	-3	-0	—	...	...	...	-6	-0	1
5205	Equity and investment fund shares	...	...	...	—	—	—	...	...	...	14	1	—
5206	Insurance, pension, and standardized guarantee schemes	...	...	...	—	—	—	...	...	...	—	—	—
5207	Financial derivatives and employee stock options	...	...	...	—	—	—	...	...	...	-0	—	—
5208	Other accounts receivable	...	...	...	-0	0	—	...	...	...	0	0	—
	By debtor												
521	Domestic debtors	...	...	...	-3	1	—	...	...	...	7	-1	-1
522	External debtors	...	...	...	3	2	—	...	...	...	6	6	1
53	**Other volume changes in liabilities**	...	...	...	**0**	**-0**	**0**	...	...	...	**10**	**-1**	**0**
	By instrument												
5301	Special Drawing Rights (SDRs)	...	...	...	—	—	—	...	...	...	—	—	—
5302	Currency and deposits	...	...	...	—	-0	-0	...	...	...	—	-0	-0
5303	Debt securities	...	...	...	—	-0	—	...	...	...	—	-0	—
5304	Loans	...	...	...	0	0	—	...	...	...	9	0	—
5305	Equity and investment fund shares	...	...	...	—	—	—	...	...	...	—	—	—
5306	Insurance, pension, and standardized guarantee schemes	...	...	...	—	—	—	...	...	...	—	-1	—
5307	Financial derivatives and employee stock options	...	...	...	—	—	—	...	...	...	—	—	—
5308	Other accounts payable	...	...	...	0	0	0	...	...	...	0	-0	0
	By creditor												
531	Domestic creditors	...	...	...	1	-74	0	...	...	...	7	-75	0
532	External creditors	...	...	...	-1	74	-0	...	...	...	3	74	-0
	Table 6 Balance sheet												
6	**Net worth**	...	...	...	...	...	...	...	...	...	**3,570**	...	...
61	**Nonfinancial assets**	...	...	...	...	...	...	...	...	...	**2,787**	...	...
611	Fixed assets	...	...	...	...	...	...	...	...	...	2,727	...	...
6111	Buildings and structures	...	...	...	...	...	...	...	...	...	2,164	...	...
6112	Machinery and equipment	...	...	...	...	...	...	...	...	...	...	...	...
6113	Other fixed assets	...	...	...	...	...	...	...	...	...	...	...	...
6114	Weapons systems	...	...	...	...	...	...	...	...	...	...	...	...
612	Inventories	...	...	...	...	...	...	...	...	...	60	...	...
613	Valuables	...	...	...	...	...	...	...	...	...	...	...	...
614	Nonproduced assets	...	...	...	...	...	...	...	...	...	...	...	...
6141	Land	...	...	...	...	...	...	...	...	...	...	...	...
6142	Mineral and energy resources	...	...	...	...	...	...	...	...	...	...	...	...
6143	Other naturally occurring assets	...	...	...	...	...	...	...	...	...	...	...	...
6144	Intangible nonproduced assets	...	...	...	...	...	...	...	...	...	...	...	...
62	**Financial assets**	...	...	...	**1,366**	**1,490**	**1,521**	...	...	...	**2,940**	**3,313**	**3,406**
	By instrument												
6201	Monetary gold and SDRs	...	...	...	—	—	—	...	...	...	—	—	—
6202	Currency and deposits	...	...	...	16	86	62	...	...	...	90	173	156
6203	Debt securities	...	...	...	40	43	44	...	...	...	342	439	448
6204	Loans	...	...	...	414	454	474	...	...	...	665	731	783
6205	Equity and investment fund shares	...	...	...	618	609	565	...	...	...	1,474	1,588	1,546
6206	Insurance, pension, and standardized guarantee schemes	...	...	...	—	—	—	...	...	...	—	—	—
6207	Financial derivatives and employee stock options	...	...	...	32	42	32	...	...	...	54	54	47
6208	Other accounts receivable	...	...	...	245	256	344	...	...	...	316	329	426
	By debtor												
621	Domestic debtors	...	...	...	1,302	1,424	1,461	...	...	...	2,217	2,402	2,499
622	External debtors	...	...	...	64	65	60	...	...	...	723	911	906
63	**Liabilities**	...	...	...	**1,660**	**1,898**	**1,941**	...	...	...	**2,157**	**2,526**	**2,605**

Sweden (144)

In Billions of Swedish Kronor (SEK) / Fiscal Year Ends December 31st

		Budgetary Central Government			Central Government (excl. Social Security)			Central Government (incl. Social Security)			General Government		
		2013	2014	2015	2013P	2014P	2015P	2013P	2014P	2015P	2013P	2014P	2015P
	By instrument												
6301	Special Drawing Rights (SDRs)	...	...	...	—	—	—	...	...	...	—	—	—
6302	Currency and deposits	...	...	...	55	58	44	...	...	...	51	53	38
6303	Debt securities	...	...	...	1,206	1,379	1,388	...	...	...	1,215	1,426	1,487
6304	Loans	...	...	...	65	128	117	...	...	...	329	434	423
6305	Equity and investment fund shares	...	...	...	—	—	—	...	...	...	—	—	—
6306	Insurance, pension, and standardized guarantee schemes	...	...	...	209	216	223	...	...	...	323	339	355
6307	Financial derivatives and employee stock options	...	...	...	2	5	9	...	...	...	12	44	25
6308	Other accounts payable	...	...	...	123	112	161	...	...	...	227	231	276
	By creditor												
631	Domestic creditors	...	...	...	1,093	1,117	1,262	...	...	...	1,542	1,689	1,862
632	External creditors	...	...	...	567	781	679	...	...	...	616	838	743
	Memorandum items												
6M2	Net financial worth	...	...	...	-294	-409	-420	...	...	...	783	787	801
6M3	Gross debt (D4) at market value	...	...	...	1,658	1,893	1,932	...	...	...	2,146	2,482	2,580
6M3D3	D3 debt liabilities at market value	...	...	...	1,449	1,677	1,710	...	...	...	1,822	2,143	2,225
6M3D2	D2 debt liabilities at market value	...	...	...	1,326	1,565	1,549	...	...	...	1,595	1,912	1,948
6M3D1	D1 debt liabilities at market value	...	...	...	1,271	1,507	1,505	...	...	...	1,544	1,859	1,910
6M4	Gross debt (D4) at nominal value	...	...	...	...	...	...	...	...	...	...	...	...
6M4D3	D3 debt liabilities at nominal value	...	...	...	...	...	...	...	...	...	...	...	...
6M4D2	D2 debt liabilities at nominal value	...	...	...	...	...	...	...	...	...	...	...	...
6M4D1	D1 debt liabilities at nominal value	...	...	...	...	...	...	...	...	...	...	...	...
6M35	Gross debt (D4) at face value	...	...	...	...	...	...	...	...	...	...	...	...
6M35D3	D3 debt liabilities at face value	...	...	...	1,372	1,538	1,595	...	...	...	1,752	2,012	2,113
6M35D2	D2 debt liabilities at face value	...	...	...	1,250	1,425	1,434	...	...	...	1,524	1,781	1,837
6M35D1	D1 debt liabilities at face value	...	...	...	1,195	1,368	1,391	...	...	...	1,473	1,728	1,799
6M93	Government gross debt per national definition	...	...	...	1,250	1,425	1,434	...	...	...	1,524	1,781	1,837
6M5	Arrears	...	...	...	...	...	...	...	...	...	...	...	...
6M6	Explicit contingent liabilities	...	...	...	...	...	...	...	...	...	...	...	...
6M61	of which: Publicly guaranteed debt	...	...	...	...	...	...	...	...	...	...	...	...
6M7	Net implicit obligations for social security benefits	...	...	...	...	...	...	...	...	...	...	...	...
	Table 7 Expenditure by functions of government												
7	**Expenditure**	...	...	...	**1,167**	**1,206**	**1,242**	...	...	...	**1,975**	**2,028**	**2,099**
701	**General public services**	...	...	...	**375**	**397**	**406**	...	...	...	**293**	**295**	**295**
7017	Public debt transactions	...	...	...	25	24	18	...	...	...	32	29	22
7018	Transfers of general character between levels of government	...	...	...	175	191	205	...	...	...	—	—	—
702	**Defense**	...	...	...	**55**	**51**	**47**	...	...	...	**55**	**51**	**47**
703	**Public order and safety**	...	...	...	**44**	**46**	**46**	...	...	...	**52**	**53**	**55**
704	**Economic affairs**	...	...	...	**114**	**118**	**120**	...	...	...	**164**	**171**	**175**
7042	Agriculture, forestry, fishing, and hunting	...	...	...	7	6	6	...	...	...	6	6	6
7043	Fuel and energy	...	...	...	2	2	2	...	...	...	3	3	3
7044	Mining, manufacturing, and construction	...	...	...	—	—	—	...	...	...	4	4	4
7045	Transport	...	...	...	64	65	67	...	...	...	102	106	110
7046	Communication	...	...	...	1	2	1	...	...	...	1	2	1
705	**Environmental protection**	...	...	...	**5**	**5**	**6**	...	...	...	**13**	**12**	**12**
706	**Housing and community amenities**	...	...	...	**3**	**3**	**3**	...	...	...	**28**	**31**	**31**
707	**Health**	...	...	...	**47**	**48**	**49**	...	...	...	**264**	**276**	**291**
7072	Outpatient services	...	...	...	12	12	12	...	...	...	116	121	125
7073	Hospital services	...	...	...	5	5	6	...	...	...	97	104	110
7074	Public health services	...	...	...	1	1	1	...	...	...	8	8	9
708	**Recreation, culture and religion**	...	...	...	**14**	**14**	**14**	...	...	...	**42**	**45**	**46**
709	**Education**	...	...	...	**66**	**68**	**71**	...	...	...	**248**	**259**	**273**
7091	Pre-primary and primary education	...	...	...	8	10	10	...	...	...	147	158	169
7092	Secondary education	...	...	...	2	2	3	...	...	...	43	43	44
7094	Tertiary education	...	...	...	47	47	48	...	...	...	46	46	47

Sweden (144)

In Billions of Swedish Kronor (SEK) / Fiscal Year Ends December 31st

		Budgetary Central Government			Central Government (excl. Social Security)			Central Government (incl. Social Security)			General Government		
		2013	2014	2015	2013P	2014P	2015P	2013P	2014P	2015P	2013P	2014P	2015P
710	**Social protection**	...	...	...	443	456	477	...	...	...	817	836	874
7z	Statistical discrepancy: Expenditure	...	...	...	—	—	—	...	...	...	—	—	—
	Table 8 Financial transactions by counterpart sector												
32	**Net acquisition of financial assets**	...	...	...	48	60	25	...	...	...	46	96	-29
321	Domestic debtors	...	...	...	62	78	42	...	...	...	89	106	54
8211	General government	...	...	...	-0	2	1	...	...	...	—	—	—
8212	Central bank	...	...	...	99	-2	-3	...	...	...	99	-2	-3
8213	Deposit-taking corporations except the central bank	...	...	...	-55	56	-42	...	...	...	-68	60	-58
8214	Other financial corporations	...	...	...	-1	1	3	...	...	...	6	14	12
8215	Nonfinancial corporations	...	...	...	24	19	71	...	...	...	57	32	92
8216	Households & nonprofit institutions serving households	...	...	...	-6	2	12	...	...	...	-6	2	12
322	External debtors	...	...	...	-14	-18	-17	...	...	...	-43	-10	-83
8221	General government	...	...	...	...	...	...	...	...	...	...	...	...
8227	International organizations	...	...	...	...	...	...	...	...	...	...	...	...
8228	Financial corporations other than international organizations	...	...	...	...	...	...	...	...	...	...	...	...
8229	Other nonresidents	...	...	...	...	...	...	...	...	...	...	...	...
33	**Net incurrence of liabilities**	...	...	...	90	108	12	...	...	...	91	153	-41
331	Domestic creditors	...	...	...	8	42	134	...	...	...	37	139	138
8311	General government	...	...	...	-4	-19	-10	...	...	...	—	—	—
8312	Central bank	...	...	...	6	1	159	...	...	...	6	1	159
8313	Deposit-taking corporations except the central bank	...	...	...	-18	72	-46	...	...	...	-21	113	-63
8314	Other financial corporations	...	...	...	8	1	-0	...	...	...	18	12	-12
8315	Nonfinancial corporations	...	...	...	16	-6	-12	...	...	...	24	9	-2
8316	Households & nonprofit institutions serving households	...	...	...	-0	-7	44	...	...	...	10	4	55
332	External creditors	...	...	...	82	66	-122	...	...	...	54	14	-178
8321	General government	...	...	...	...	...	...	...	...	...	...	...	...
8327	International organizations	...	...	...	...	...	...	...	...	...	...	...	...
8328	Financial corporations other than international organizations	...	...	...	...	...	...	...	...	...	...	...	...
8329	Other nonresidents	...	...	...	...	...	...	...	...	...	...	...	...
	Table 9 Total other economic flows in assets and liabilities												
9	**Change in net worth due to other economic flows**	...	...	...	...	...	...	...	...	...	...	...	...
91	**Other economic flows in nonfinancial assets**	...	...	...	...	...	...	...	...	...	...	...	...
911	Fixed assets	...	...	...	...	...	...	...	...	...	...	...	...
912	Inventories	...	...	...	...	...	...	...	...	...	...	...	...
913	Valuables	...	...	...	...	...	...	...	...	...	...	...	...
914	Nonproduced assets	...	...	...	...	...	...	...	...	...	...	...	...
92	**Other economic flows in financial assets**	...	...	...	-47	63	7	...	...	...	109	277	121
	By instrument												
9201	Monetary gold and SDRs	...	...	...	—	—	—	...	...	...	—	—	—
9202	Currency and deposits	...	...	...	0	4	—	...	...	...	1	4	—
9203	Debt securities	...	...	...	2	2	-1	...	...	...	-3	40	1
9204	Loans	...	...	...	-0	34	14	...	...	...	-4	34	15
9205	Equity and investment fund shares	...	...	...	-61	-9	-32	...	...	...	58	130	15
9206	Insurance, pension, and standardized guarantee schemes	...	...	...	—	—	—	...	...	...	—	—	—
9207	Financial derivatives and employee stock options	...	...	...	12	33	26	...	...	...	57	69	90
9208	Other accounts receivable	...	...	...	-0	0	—	...	...	...	0	0	—
	By debtor												
921	Domestic debtors	...	...	...	...	...	...	...	...	...	...	...	...
922	External debtors	...	...	...	...	...	...	...	...	...	...	...	...
93	**Other economic flows in liabilities**	...	...	...	6	130	31	...	...	...	57	216	119

Sweden (144)

In Billions of Swedish Kronor (SEK) / Fiscal Year Ends December 31st

		Budgetary Central Government			Central Government (excl. Social Security)			Central Government (incl. Social Security)			General Government		
		2013	2014	2015	2013P	2014P	2015P	2013P	2014P	2015P	2013P	2014P	2015P
	By instrument												
9301	Special Drawing Rights (SDRs)	...	...	...	—	—	—	...	...	...	—	—	—
9302	Currency and deposits	...	...	...	0	1	-0	...	...	...	0	1	-0
9303	Debt securities	...	...	...	-11	111	5	...	...	...	-8	107	7
9304	Loans	...	...	...	0	0	0	...	...	...	9	0	0
9305	Equity and investment fund shares	...	...	...	—	—	—	...	...	...	—	—	—
9306	Insurance, pension, and standardized guarantee schemes	...	...	...	5	5	4	...	...	...	13	2	4
9307	Financial derivatives and employee stock options	...	...	...	11	13	22	...	...	...	43	105	108
9308	Other accounts payable	...	...	...	0	0	0	...	...	...	0	0	0
	By creditor												
931	Domestic creditors	...	...	...	...	...	...	...	...	...	...	...	...
932	External creditors	...	...	...	...	...	...	...	...	...	...	...	...
	Memorandum items												
9M2	Change in net financial worth due to other economic flows	...	...	...	-53	-66	-24	...	...	...	51	61	2
9M3	Gross debt (D4) at market value: other economic flows	...	...	...	-6	117	9	...	...	...	15	110	11
9M3D3	D3 debt liabilities at market value: other economic flows	...	...	...	-10	112	5	...	...	...	2	108	7
9M3D2	D2 debt liabilities at market value: other economic flows	...	...	...	-11	112	5	...	...	...	1	108	7
9M3D1	D1 debt liabilities at market value: other economic flows	...	...	...	-11	111	5	...	...	...	1	107	7

Switzerland (146)

In Millions of Swiss Francs (CHF) / Fiscal Year Ends December 31st

		Budgetary Central Government			Central Government (excl. Social Security)			Central Government (incl. Social Security)			General Government		
		2013	2014	2015	2013P	2014P	2015P	2013P	2014P	2015P	2013P	2014P	2015
	Statement of operations												
1	Revenue	...	...	...	67,312	67,082	70,782	111,813	112,492	116,511	207,834	210,448	...
2	Expense	...	...	...	66,574	66,546	68,400	109,036	109,781	112,494	207,844	210,684	...
GOB	**Gross operating balance**	...	...	...	**5,944**	**5,838**	**7,710**	**7,990**	**8,021**	**9,352**	**18,297**	**18,498**	...
NOB	**Net operating balance**	...	...	...	**738**	**536**	**2,383**	**2,777**	**2,711**	**4,017**	**-10**	**-236**	...
31	Net/Gross investment in nonfinancial assets	...	...	...	802	529	524	797	524	518	943	922	...
2M	Expenditure	...	...	...	67,376	67,075	68,924	109,833	110,304	113,012	208,787	211,605	...
NLB	**Net lending (+) / Net borrowing (-)**	...	...	...	**-64**	**7**	**1,858**	**1,980**	**2,187**	**3,499**	**-953**	**-1,157**	...
32	Net acquisition of financial assets	...	...	...	...	...	...	...	...	...	...	...	...
33	Net incurrence of liabilities	...	...	...	...	...	...	...	...	...	...	...	...
NLBz	Statistical discrepancy	...	...	...	...	...	...	...	...	...	...	...	...
	Memorandum items												
PB	Primary net lending / net borrowing	...	...	...	2,040	1,980	3,740	4,126	4,206	5,423	3,020	2,552	...
GB	Government balance per national definition	...	...	...	2,470	194	2,706	4,617	2,351	4,379	1,270	-1,050	...
	Statement of other economic flows												
	Balance sheet												
6	**Net worth**	...	...	...	**31,901**	**41,683**	**32,336**	**64,383**	**77,708**	**69,140**	**152,027**	**200,902**	...
61	Nonfinancial assets	...	...	...	87,386	87,529	87,916	87,530	87,675	88,087	192,022	205,995	...
62	Financial assets	...	...	...	86,251	99,806	92,946	117,885	136,006	129,518	246,754	291,416	...
63	Liabilities	...	...	...	141,735	145,651	148,527	141,032	145,973	148,465	286,749	296,508	...
	Table 1 Revenue												
1	**Revenue**	...	...	...	**67,312**	**67,082**	**70,782**	**111,813**	**112,492**	**116,511**	**207,834**	**210,448**	...
11	**Taxes**	...	...	...	**60,763**	**61,127**	**63,921**	**60,763**	**61,127**	**63,921**	**128,143**	**130,435**	...
111	Taxes on income, profits, and capital gains	...	...	...	23,406	23,666	26,338	23,406	23,666	26,338	77,789	79,252	...
1111	Payable by individuals	...	...	...	9,818	9,661	10,567	9,818	9,661	10,567	53,205	53,753	...
1112	Payable by corporations and other enterprises	...	...	...	8,769	8,559	9,806	8,769	8,559	9,806	17,760	18,074	...
1113	Other taxes on income, profits, and capital gains	...	...	...	4,818	5,447	5,965	4,818	5,447	5,965	6,825	7,425	...
112	Taxes on payroll and workforce	...	...	...	—	—	—	—	—	—	—	—	...
113	Taxes on property	...	...	...	—	—	—	—	—	—	9,407	10,001	...
114	Taxes on goods and services	...	...	...	36,298	36,393	36,527	36,298	36,393	36,527	39,122	39,270	...
1141	General taxes on goods and services	...	...	...	24,008	24,023	24,163	24,008	24,023	24,163	24,079	24,090	...
1142	Excises	...	...	...	8,099	8,097	8,056	8,099	8,097	8,056	8,099	8,097	...
115	Taxes on international trade and transactions	...	...	...	1,059	1,068	1,056	1,059	1,068	1,056	1,059	1,068	...
116	Other taxes	...	...	...	—	—	—	—	—	—	766	844	...
12	**Social contributions**	...	...	...	**69**	**60**	**61**	**42,589**	**43,213**	**43,989**	**43,011**	**43,515**	...
121	Social security contributions	...	...	...	—	—	—	42,518	43,152	43,926	42,518	43,152	...
122	Other social contributions	...	...	...	69	60	61	71	61	63	493	363	...
13	**Grants**	...	...	...	**148**	**158**	**135**	**344**	**355**	**335**	**244**	**258**	...
131	From foreign governments	...	...	...	135	142	135	135	142	135	244	258	...
132	From international organizations	...	...	...	—	—	—	—	—	—	—	—	...
133	From other general government units	...	...	...	12	15	0	209	212	200	—	—	...
1331	Current	...	...	...	12	15	0	209	212	200	—	—	...
1332	Capital	...	...	...	—	—	0	—	—	0	—	—	...
14	**Other revenue**	...	...	...	**6,333**	**5,737**	**6,665**	**8,117**	**7,797**	**8,266**	**36,436**	**36,240**	...
	Table 2 Expense by economic type												
2	**Expense**	...	...	...	**66,574**	**66,546**	**68,400**	**109,036**	**109,781**	**112,494**	**207,844**	**210,684**	...
21	**Compensation of employees**	...	...	...	**7,355**	**7,333**	**7,409**	**7,753**	**7,739**	**7,824**	**48,003**	**48,558**	...
211	Wages and salaries	...	...	...	5,823	6,002	6,122	6,157	6,342	6,470	39,578	40,263	...
212	Employers' social contributions	...	...	...	1,532	1,332	1,287	1,596	1,397	1,354	8,424	8,295	...
22	**Use of goods and services**	...	...	...	**6,276**	**5,978**	**6,240**	**7,475**	**7,191**	**7,478**	**23,667**	**23,907**	...
23	**Consumption of fixed capital**	...	...	...	**5,205**	**5,301**	**5,328**	**5,214**	**5,309**	**5,336**	**18,308**	**18,734**	...
24	**Interest**	...	...	...	**2,104**	**1,972**	**1,882**	**2,146**	**2,018**	**1,925**	**3,973**	**3,710**	...
25	**Subsidies**	...	...	...	**2,639**	**2,730**	**2,985**	**2,712**	**2,814**	**3,066**	**19,206**	**19,219**	...

Switzerland (146)

In Millions of Swiss Francs (CHF) / Fiscal Year Ends December 31st

		Budgetary Central Government			Central Government (excl. Social Security)			Central Government (incl. Social Security)			General Government		
		2013	2014	2015	2013P	2014P	2015P	2013P	2014P	2015P	2013P	2014P	2015
26	**Grants**	...	...	...	**38,167**	**38,407**	**39,172**	**22,504**	**22,412**	**23,090**	**4,021**	**3,771**	...
261	To foreign governments	...	...	...	2,140	1,812	2,088	2,140	1,812	2,088	2,521	2,205	...
262	To international organizations	...	...	...	1,501	1,565	1,638	1,501	1,565	1,638	1,501	1,565	...
263	To other general government units	...	...	...	34,526	35,029	35,446	18,864	19,034	19,364	—	—	...
2631	Current	...	...	...	32,746	33,292	33,894	17,083	17,298	17,811	—	—	...
2632	Capital	...	...	...	1,780	1,736	1,552	1,780	1,736	1,552	—	—	...
27	**Social benefits**	...	...	...	**355**	**336**	**424**	**56,431**	**57,477**	**58,499**	**71,432**	**72,766**	...
271	Social security benefits	...	...	...	—	—	—	56,073	57,140	58,074	56,073	57,140	...
272	Social assistance benefits	...	...	...	286	276	362	286	276	362	14,865	15,263	...
273	Employment-related social benefits	...	...	...	69	60	61	71	61	63	493	363	...
28	**Other expense**	...	...	...	**4,472**	**4,488**	**4,961**	**4,802**	**4,820**	**5,277**	**19,234**	**20,019**	...
281	Property expense other than interest	...	...	...	—	—	—	—	—	—	—	—	...
282	Transfers not elsewhere classified	...	...	...	4,472	4,488	4,961	4,802	4,820	5,277	17,420	17,545	...
2821	Current	...	...	...	1,184	1,247	1,416	1,494	1,557	1,711	10,732	11,132	...
2822	Capital	...	...	...	3,288	3,240	3,545	3,308	3,263	3,567	6,689	6,413	...
	Table 3 Transactions in assets and liabilities												
3	**Change in net worth from transactions**	...	...	...	**802**	**529**	**524**	**797**	**524**	**518**	**943**	**922**	...
31	**Net/Gross investment in nonfinancial assets**	...	...	...	**802**	**529**	**524**	**797**	**524**	**518**	**943**	**922**	...
311	Fixed assets	...	...	...	652	413	578	646	408	572	792	805	...
3111	Buildings and structures	...	...	...	1,677	1,711	1,802	1,672	1,707	1,796	5,162	5,323	...
3112	Machinery and equipment	...	...	...	308	220	223	305	218	222	-738	-703	...
3113	Other fixed assets	...	...	...	-1,333	-1,518	-1,446	-1,331	-1,517	-1,446	-3,632	-3,815	...
3114	Weapons systems	...	...	...	...	...	...	...	...	...	...	...	...
312	Inventories	...	...	...	150	116	85	150	116	85	151	117	...
313	Valuables	...	...	...	...	...	...	...	...	...	...	...	...
314	Nonproduced assets	...	...	...	—	—	-139	—	—	-139	—	—	...
3141	Land	...	...	...	—	—	—	—	—	—	—	—	...
3142	Mineral and energy resources	...	...	...	—	—	—	—	—	—	—	—	...
3143	Other naturally occurring assets	...	...	...	—	—	-139	—	—	-139	—	—	...
3144	Intangible nonproduced assets	...	...	...	—	—	—	—	—	—	—	—	...
32	**Net acquisition of financial assets**	...	...	...	...	...	...	...	...	...	...	...	...
	By instrument												
3201	Monetary gold and SDRs	...	...	...	...	...	...	...	...	...	...	...	...
3202	Currency and deposits	...	...	...	...	...	...	...	...	...	...	...	...
3203	Debt securities	...	...	...	...	...	...	...	...	...	...	...	...
3204	Loans	...	...	...	...	...	...	...	...	...	...	...	...
3205	Equity and investment fund shares	...	...	...	...	...	...	...	...	...	...	...	...
3206	Insurance, pension, and standardized guarantee schemes	...	...	...	...	...	...	...	...	...	...	...	...
3207	Financial derivatives and employee stock options	...	...	...	...	...	...	...	...	...	...	...	...
3208	Other accounts receivable	...	...	...	...	...	...	...	...	...	...	...	...
	By debtor												
321	Domestic debtors	...	...	...	...	...	...	...	...	...	...	...	...
322	External debtors	...	...	...	...	...	...	...	...	...	...	...	...
33	**Net incurrence of liabilities**	...	...	...	...	...	...	...	...	...	...	...	...
	By instrument												
3301	Special Drawing Rights (SDRs)	...	...	...	...	...	...	...	...	...	...	...	...
3302	Currency and deposits	...	...	...	...	...	...	...	...	...	...	...	...
3303	Debt securities	...	...	...	...	...	...	...	...	...	...	...	...
3304	Loans	...	...	...	...	...	...	...	...	...	...	...	...
3305	Equity and investment fund shares	...	...	...	...	...	...	...	...	...	...	...	...
3306	Insurance, pension, and standardized guarantee schemes	...	...	...	...	...	...	...	...	...	...	...	...
3307	Financial derivatives and employee stock options	...	...	...	...	...	...	...	...	...	...	...	...
3308	Other accounts payable	...	...	...	...	...	...	...	...	...	...	...	...

Switzerland (146)

In Millions of Swiss Francs (CHF) / Fiscal Year Ends December 31st

		Budgetary Central Government			Central Government (excl. Social Security)			Central Government (incl. Social Security)			General Government		
		2013	2014	2015	2013P	2014P	2015P	2013P	2014P	2015P	2013P	2014P	2015
	By creditor												
331	Domestic creditors	...	...	...	...	...	...	...	...	...	...	...	...
332	External creditors	...	...	...	...	...	...	...	...	...	...	...	...
	Table 4 Holding gains and losses in assets and liabilities												
	Table 5 Holding gains and losses in assets and liabilities												
	Table 6 Balance sheet												
6	**Net worth**	...	...	...	**31,901**	**41,683**	**32,336**	**64,383**	**77,708**	**69,140**	**152,027**	**200,902**	...
61	**Nonfinancial assets**	...	...	...	**87,386**	**87,529**	**87,916**	**87,530**	**87,675**	**88,087**	**192,022**	**205,995**	...
611	Fixed assets	...	...	...	78,876	79,072	79,529	79,020	79,218	79,699	170,451	179,918	...
6111	Buildings and structures	...	...	...	45,878	46,382	47,599	46,010	46,517	47,764	120,017	129,439	...
6112	Machinery and equipment	...	...	...	1,304	1,726	1,463	1,315	1,734	1,468	5,983	6,257	...
6113	Other fixed assets	...	...	...	31,694	30,963	30,467	31,696	30,966	30,467	44,452	44,221	...
6114	Weapons systems	...	...	...	...	...	...	...	...	...	...	...	...
612	Inventories	...	...	...	335	292	209	335	292	209	727	655	...
613	Valuables	...	...	...	...	...	...	...	...	...	...	...	...
614	Nonproduced assets	...	...	...	8,175	8,165	8,179	8,175	8,165	8,179	20,843	25,422	...
6141	Land	...	...	...	8,173	8,164	8,177	8,173	8,164	8,177	20,842	25,420	...
6142	Mineral and energy resources	...	...	...	—	—	—	—	—	—	—	—	...
6143	Other naturally occurring assets	...	...	...	—	—	—	—	—	—	—	—	...
6144	Intangible nonproduced assets	...	...	...	1	1	1	1	1	1	1	2	...
62	**Financial assets**	...	...	...	**86,251**	**99,806**	**92,946**	**117,885**	**136,006**	**129,518**	**246,754**	**291,416**	...
	By instrument												
6201	Monetary gold and SDRs	...	...	...	—	—	—	—	—	—	—	—	...
6202	Currency and deposits	...	...	...	13,484	11,717	12,426	17,542	14,229	16,071	37,145	33,743	...
6203	Debt securities	...	...	...	253	215	216	14,913	16,734	14,353	20,989	23,410	...
6204	Loans	...	...	...	18,830	19,292	19,212	18,021	19,228	19,927	29,743	31,513	...
6205	Equity and investment fund shares	...	...	...	46,975	61,986	53,317	55,261	73,463	66,240	109,252	150,008	...
6206	Insurance, pension, and standardized guarantee schemes	...	...	...	—	—	—	—	—	—	—	—	...
6207	Financial derivatives and employee stock options	...	...	...	76	211	177	390	472	421	390	472	...
6208	Other accounts receivable	...	...	...	6,634	6,386	7,598	11,759	11,879	12,506	49,237	52,269	...
	By debtor												
621	Domestic debtors	...	...	...	84,464	97,713	91,021	98,706	112,601	106,869	227,575	268,011	...
622	External debtors	...	...	...	1,787	2,093	1,925	19,179	23,405	22,649	19,179	23,405	...
63	**Liabilities**	...	...	...	**141,735**	**145,651**	**148,527**	**141,032**	**145,973**	**148,465**	**286,749**	**296,508**	...
	By instrument												
6301	Special Drawing Rights (SDRs)	...	...	...	—	—	—	—	—	—	—	—	...
6302	Currency and deposits	...	...	...	8,401	9,168	8,980	8,601	9,568	8,980	8,601	9,568	...
6303	Debt securities	...	...	...	101,277	104,179	101,103	101,277	104,179	101,103	132,153	146,136	...
6304	Loans	...	...	...	4,950	4,506	5,030	3,463	3,108	3,781	63,019	61,722	...
6305	Equity and investment fund shares	...	...	...	—	—	—	—	—	—	—	—	...
6306	Insurance, pension, and standardized guarantee schemes	...	...	...	2,378	2,476	4,523	2,378	2,476	4,523	11,406	8,143	...
6307	Financial derivatives and employee stock options	...	...	...	225	166	203	381	913	905	393	951	...
6308	Other accounts payable	...	...	...	24,505	25,155	28,688	24,933	25,729	29,174	71,177	69,988	...
	By creditor												
631	Domestic creditors	...	...	...	120,937	124,412	127,740	120,233	124,734	127,678	244,140	251,578	...
632	External creditors	...	...	...	20,799	21,239	20,787	20,799	21,239	20,787	42,609	44,930	...
	Memorandum items												
6M2	Net financial worth	...	...	...	-55,485	-45,845	-55,581	-23,147	-9,967	-18,947	-39,995	-5,092	...
6M3	Gross debt (D4) at market value	...	...	...	141,511	145,485	148,324	140,652	145,060	147,560	286,356	295,557	...
6M3D3	D3 debt liabilities at market value	...	...	...	139,132	143,008	143,801	138,273	142,584	143,038	274,950	287,414	...
6M3D2	D2 debt liabilities at market value	...	...	...	114,627	117,853	115,113	113,341	116,854	113,864	203,773	217,425	...
6M3D1	D1 debt liabilities at market value	...	...	...	106,226	108,685	106,133	104,740	107,286	104,884	195,172	207,857	...
6M4	Gross debt (D4) at nominal value	...	...	...	...	...	...	...	...	...	...	...	...
6M4D3	D3 debt liabilities at nominal value	...	...	...	...	...	...	...	...	...	...	...	...
6M4D2	D2 debt liabilities at nominal value	...	...	...	...	...	...	...	...	...	...	...	...
6M4D1	D1 debt liabilities at nominal value	...	...	...	...	...	...	...	...	...	...	...	...

Switzerland (146)

In Millions of Swiss Francs (CHF) / Fiscal Year Ends December 31st

		Budgetary Central Government			Central Government (excl. Social Security)			Central Government (incl. Social Security)			General Government		
		2013	2014	2015	2013P	2014P	2015P	2013P	2014P	2015P	2013P	2014P	2015
6M35	Gross debt (D4) at face value	...	...	...	...	...	...	...	...	...	...	...	...
6M35D3	D3 debt liabilities at face value	...	...	...	...	...	...	...	...	...	...	...	...
6M35D2	D2 debt liabilities at face value	...	...	...	...	...	...	...	...	...	...	...	...
6M35D1	D1 debt liabilities at face value	...	...	...	...	...	...	...	...	...	...	...	...
6M93	Government gross debt per national definition	...	...	...	...	...	...	...	...	...	...	...	...
6M5	Arrears	...	...	...	...	...	...	...	...	...	...	...	...
6M6	Explicit contingent liabilities	...	...	...	...	...	...	...	...	...	...	...	...
6M61	of which: Publicly guaranteed debt	...	...	...	...	...	...	...	...	...	...	...	...
6M7	Net implicit obligations for social security benefits	...	...	...	...	...	...	...	...	...	...	...	...
	Table 7 Expenditure by functions of government												
7	**Expenditure**	...	...	...	**67,376**	**67,075**	**68,924**	**109,833**	**110,304**	**113,012**	**208,787**	**211,605**	...
701	**General public services**	...	...	...	**20,058**	**20,041**	**20,913**	**20,190**	**20,161**	**21,031**	**30,437**	**31,373**	...
7017	Public debt transactions	...	...	...	2,104	1,972	1,882	2,146	2,018	1,925	3,973	3,710	...
7018	Transfers of general character between levels of government	...	...	...	6,890	6,847	7,368	6,890	6,847	7,368	—	—	...
702	**Defense**	...	...	...	**5,057**	**4,687**	**4,639**	**5,057**	**4,687**	**4,639**	**5,456**	**5,072**	...
703	**Public order and safety**	...	...	...	**1,067**	**1,053**	**1,139**	**1,067**	**1,053**	**1,139**	**10,178**	**10,297**	...
704	**Economic affairs**	...	...	...	**14,498**	**14,467**	**14,929**	**14,498**	**14,467**	**14,929**	**25,277**	**25,090**	...
7042	Agriculture, forestry, fishing, and hunting	...	...	...	3,750	3,774	3,786	3,750	3,774	3,786	4,726	4,754	...
7043	Fuel and energy	...	...	...	476	630	1,104	476	630	1,104	1,618	1,745	...
7044	Mining, manufacturing, and construction	...	...	...	—	—	—	—	—	—	—	—	...
7045	Transport	...	...	...	9,213	9,032	9,116	9,213	9,032	9,116	17,237	16,906	...
7046	Communication	...	...	...	41	43	-93	41	43	-93	43	53	...
705	**Environmental protection**	...	...	...	**972**	**915**	**690**	**972**	**915**	**690**	**4,819**	**4,669**	...
706	**Housing and community amenities**	...	...	...	**15**	**15**	**15**	**15**	**15**	**15**	**1,225**	**1,224**	...
707	**Health**	...	...	...	**379**	**287**	**309**	**379**	**287**	**309**	**13,640**	**13,820**	...
7072	Outpatient services	...	...	...	—	—	—	—	—	—	1,043	1,049	...
7073	Hospital services	...	...	...	3	1	0	3	1	0	10,740	10,980	...
7074	Public health services	...	...	...	234	219	215	234	219	215	787	783	...
708	**Recreation, culture and religion**	...	...	...	**471**	**479**	**499**	**471**	**479**	**499**	**5,131**	**5,292**	...
709	**Education**	...	...	...	**3,784**	**3,588**	**3,715**	**3,784**	**3,588**	**3,715**	**32,317**	**32,811**	...
7091	Pre-primary and primary education	...	...	...	—	—	—	—	—	—	7,979	8,147	...
7092	Secondary education	...	...	...	760	771	782	760	771	782	10,174	10,117	...
7094	Tertiary education	...	...	...	2,407	2,433	2,457	2,407	2,433	2,457	7,740	8,009	...
710	**Social protection**	...	...	...	**21,073**	**21,543**	**22,076**	**63,398**	**64,652**	**66,045**	**80,307**	**81,957**	...
7z	Statistical discrepancy: Expenditure	...	...	...	—	—	—	—	—	—	—	—	...
	Table 8 Financial transactions by counterpart sector												
32	**Net acquisition of financial assets**	...	...	...	...	...	...	...	...	...	...	...	...
321	Domestic debtors	...	...	...	...	...	...	...	...	...	...	...	...
322	External debtors	...	...	...	...	...	...	...	...	...	...	...	...
33	**Net incurrence of liabilities**	...	...	...	...	...	...	...	...	...	...	...	...
331	Domestic creditors	...	...	...	...	...	...	...	...	...	...	...	...
332	External creditors	...	...	...	...	...	...	...	...	...	...	...	...
	Table 9 Total other economic flows in assets and liabilities												

Tanzania (738)

In Billions of Tanzania Shillings (TZS) / Fiscal Year Ends June 30th

		Budgetary Central Government			Central Government (excl. Social Security)			Central Government (incl. Social Security)			General Government		
		2014	2015P	2016P	2014	2015	2016	2014	2015	2016	2014	2015	2016
	Statement of operations												
1	Revenue	11,582	13,418	13,921	12,590	...	...	15,068	...	...	15,418	...	...
2	Expense	13,282	14,030	14,487	13,087	...	...	14,757	...	...	13,982	...	...
GOB	**Gross operating balance**	**-1,700**	**-612**	**-566**	**-497**	**...**	**...**	**312**	**...**	**...**	**1,436**	**...**	**...**
NOB	**Net operating balance**	**...**	**...**	**...**	**...**	**...**	**...**	**...**	**...**	**...**	**...**	**...**	**...**
31	Net/Gross investment in nonfinancial assets	588	391	209	1,800	...	...	2,008	...	...	2,521	...	...
2M	Expenditure	13,870	14,421	14,696	14,887	...	...	16,764	...	...	16,503	...	...
NLB	**Net lending (+) / Net borrowing (-)**	**-2,288**	**-1,003**	**-775**	**-2,297**	**...**	**...**	**-1,696**	**...**	**...**	**-1,085**	**...**	**...**
32	Net acquisition of financial assets	169	-486	277	620	...	...	1,233	...	...	...	...	...
33	Net incurrence of liabilities	3,263	5,070	3,566	3,733	...	...	3,878	...	...	...	...	...
NLBz	Statistical discrepancy	-806	-4,553	-2,514	-816	...	...	-950	...	...	...	...	...
	Memorandum items												
PB	Primary net lending / net borrowing	-1,311	261	677	-1,293	...	...	-692	...	...	-80	...	...
GB	Government balance per national definition	...	...	...	...	...	...	...	...	...	...	...	...
	Statement of other economic flows												
	Balance sheet												
	Table 1 Revenue												
1	**Revenue**	**11,582**	**13,418**	**13,921**	**12,590**	**...**	**...**	**15,068**	**...**	**...**	**15,418**	**...**	**...**
11	**Taxes**	**9,387**	**9,900**	**12,343**	**9,459**	**...**	**...**	**9,459**	**...**	**...**	**9,636**	**...**	**...**
111	Taxes on income, profits, and capital gains	3,700	3,648	4,525	...	...	...	...	...	...	...	...	...
1111	Payable by individuals	1,714	1,853	2,389	...	...	...	...	...	...	...	...	...
1112	Payable by corporations and other enterprises	1,484	1,183	2,061	...	...	...	...	...	...	...	...	...
1113	Other taxes on income, profits, and capital gains	502	612	75	...	...	...	...	...	...	...	...	...
112	Taxes on payroll and workforce	169	181	262	...	...	...	...	...	...	...	...	...
113	Taxes on property	95	64	75	...	...	...	...	...	...	...	...	...
114	Taxes on goods and services	4,601	5,083	6,133	...	...	...	...	...	...	...	...	...
1141	General taxes on goods and services	2,183	2,496	2,984	...	...	...	...	...	...	...	...	...
1142	Excises	2,260	2,401	3,149	...	...	...	...	...	...	...	...	...
115	Taxes on international trade and transactions	749	846	1,242	...	...	...	...	...	...	...	...	...
116	Other taxes	74	78	106	...	...	...	...	...	...	...	...	...
12	**Social contributions**	**—**	**—**	**—**	**—**	**...**	**...**	**1,896**	**...**	**...**	**1,901**	**...**	**...**
121	Social security contributions	—	—	—	—	...	...	...	...	...	...	...	...
122	Other social contributions	—	—	—	—	...	...	...	...	...	...	...	...
13	**Grants**	**1,473**	**2,678**	**481**	**1,473**	**...**	**...**	**1,500**	**...**	**...**	**1,530**	**...**	**...**
131	From foreign governments	437	1,870	318	437	...	...	437	...	...	494	...	...
132	From international organizations	1,036	808	163	1,036	...	...	1,036	...	...	1,036	...	...
133	From other general government units	—	—	—	—	...	...	27	...	...	—	...	...
1331	Current	—	—	—	—	...	...	27	...	...	—	...	...
1332	Capital	—	—	—	—	...	...	—	...	...	—	...	...
14	**Other revenue**	**722**	**840**	**1,097**	**1,657**	**...**	**...**	**2,213**	**...**	**...**	**2,351**	**...**	**...**
	Table 2 Expense by economic type												
2	**Expense**	**13,282**	**14,030**	**14,487**	**13,087**	**...**	**...**	**14,757**	**...**	**...**	**13,982**	**...**	**...**
21	**Compensation of employees**	**2,611**	**2,992**	**3,565**	**3,467**	**...**	**...**	**3,651**	**...**	**...**	**5,278**	**...**	**...**
211	Wages and salaries	1,912	2,198	2,603	...	...	...	...	...	...	...	...	...
212	Employers' social contributions	699	794	961	...	...	...	...	...	...	...	...	...
22	**Use of goods and services**	**2,495**	**2,369**	**1,913**	**3,950**	**...**	**...**	**4,037**	**...**	**...**	**4,589**	**...**	**...**
23	**Consumption of fixed capital**	**...**	**...**	**...**	**...**	**...**	**...**	**...**	**...**	**...**	**...**	**...**	**...**
24	**Interest**	**977**	**1,264**	**1,452**	**1,004**	**...**	**...**	**1,004**	**...**	**...**	**1,005**	**...**	**...**
25	**Subsidies**	**1**	**174**	**461**	**1**	**...**	**...**	**1**	**...**	**...**	**1**	**...**	**...**
26	**Grants**	**6,720**	**6,698**	**6,461**	**4,159**	**...**	**...**	**4,159**	**...**	**...**	**1,189**	**...**	**...**
261	To foreign governments	—	—	—	...	...	...	...	...	...	...	...	...
262	To international organizations	48	59	33	...	...	...	...	...	...	...	...	...
263	To other general government units	6,672	6,639	6,427	...	...	...	...	...	...	...	...	...
2631	Current	6,672	6,636	6,383	...	...	...	...	...	...	...	...	...
2632	Capital	—	3	45	...	...	...	...	...	...	...	...	...

Tanzania (738)

In Billions of Tanzania Shillings (TZS) / Fiscal Year Ends June 30th

		Budgetary Central Government			Central Government (excl. Social Security)			Central Government (incl. Social Security)			General Government		
		2014	2015P	2016P	2014	2015	2016	2014	2015	2016	2014	2015	2016
27	**Social benefits**	**273**	**280**	**427**	**296**	**...**	**...**	**1,673**	**...**	**...**	**1,675**	**...**	**...**
271	Social security benefits	0	0	0	...	...	...	...	...	...	...	...	...
272	Social assistance benefits	13	16	12	...	...	...	...	...	...	...	...	...
273	Employment-related social benefits	260	264	415	...	...	...	...	...	...	...	...	...
28	**Other expense**	**205**	**253**	**209**	**210**	**...**	**...**	**232**	**...**	**...**	**244**	**...**	**...**
281	Property expense other than interest	—	—	—	...	...	...	...	...	...	...	...	...
282	Transfers not elsewhere classified	205	253	209	...	...	...	...	...	...	...	...	...
2821	Current	...	...	...	...	...	...	...	...	...	...	...	...
2822	Capital	...	...	...	...	...	...	...	...	...	...	...	...
	Table 3 Transactions in assets and liabilities												
3	**Change in net worth from transactions**	**...**	**...**	**...**	**...**	**...**	**...**	**...**	**...**	**...**	**...**	**...**	**...**
31	**Net/Gross investment in nonfinancial assets**	**588**	**391**	**209**	**1,800**	**...**	**...**	**2,008**	**...**	**...**	**2,521**	**...**	**...**
311	Fixed assets	588	384	209	1,795	...	...	2,003	...	...	2,510	...	...
3111	Buildings and structures	389	128	73	...	...	...	...	...	...	...	...	...
3112	Machinery and equipment	188	252	135	...	...	...	...	...	...	...	...	...
3113	Other fixed assets	4	4	0	...	...	...	...	...	...	...	...	...
3114	Weapons systems	7	—	0	...	...	...	...	...	...	...	...	...
312	Inventories	—	—	—	—	...	...	—	...	...	1	...	...
313	Valuables	—	—	—	—	...	...	—	...	...	—	...	...
314	Nonproduced assets	—	7	—	5	...	...	5	...	...	9	...	...
3141	Land	—	5	—	5	...	...	5	...	...	5	...	...
3142	Mineral and energy resources	—	—	—	—	...	...	—	...	...	—	...	...
3143	Other naturally occurring assets	—	0	—	—	...	...	—	...	...	1	...	...
3144	Intangible nonproduced assets	—	2	—	—	...	...	—	...	...	3	...	...
32	**Net acquisition of financial assets**	**169**	**-486**	**277**	**620**	**...**	**...**	**1,233**	**...**	**...**	**...**	**...**	**...**
	By instrument												
3201	Monetary gold and SDRs	—	—	—	—	...	...	—	...	...	...	...	...
3202	Currency and deposits	149	-516	97	149	...	...	149	...	...	...	...	...
3203	Debt securities	—	—	—	—	...	...	613	...	...	...	...	...
3204	Loans	—	—	—	—	...	...	—	...	...	...	...	...
3205	Equity and investment fund shares	15	32	180	15	...	...	15	...	...	...	...	...
3206	Insurance, pension, and standardized guarantee schemes	—	—	—	—	...	...	—	...	...	...	...	...
3207	Financial derivatives and employee stock options	—	—	—	—	...	...	—	...	...	...	...	...
3208	Other accounts receivable	4	-2	...	455	...	...	455	...	...	...	...	...
	By debtor												
321	Domestic debtors	164	-486	277	615	...	...	1,228	...	...	...	...	...
322	External debtors	5	—	—	5	...	...	5	...	...	...	...	...
33	**Net incurrence of liabilities**	**3,263**	**5,070**	**3,566**	**3,733**	**...**	**...**	**3,878**	**...**	**...**	**...**	**...**	**...**
	By instrument												
3301	Special Drawing Rights (SDRs)	—	—	—	—	...	...	—	...	...	...	...	...
3302	Currency and deposits	—	—	—	—	...	...	—	...	...	...	...	...
3303	Debt securities	851	1,697	2,748	851	...	...	996	...	...	...	...	...
3304	Loans	2,412	3,373	818	2,412	...	...	2,412	...	...	...	...	...
3305	Equity and investment fund shares	—	—	—	—	...	...	—	...	...	...	...	...
3306	Insurance, pension, and standardized guarantee schemes	—	—	—	—	...	...	—	...	...	...	...	...
3307	Financial derivatives and employee stock options	—	—	—	—	...	...	—	...	...	...	...	...
3308	Other accounts payable	...	...	...	470	...	...	470	...	...	...	...	...
	By creditor												
331	Domestic creditors	848	1,694	2,763	1,317	...	...	1,463	...	...	...	...	...
332	External creditors	2,415	3,376	803	2,415	...	...	2,415	...	...	...	...	...
	Table 4 Holding gains and losses in assets and liabilities												
	Table 5 Holding gains and losses in assets and liabilities												
	Table 6 Balance sheet												

Tanzania (738)

In Billions of Tanzania Shillings (TZS) / Fiscal Year Ends June 30th

		Budgetary Central Government			Central Government (excl. Social Security)			Central Government (incl. Social Security)			General Government		
		2014	2015P	2016P	2014	2015	2016	2014	2015	2016	2014	2015	2016
	Table 7 Expenditure by functions of government												
7	**Expenditure**	**13,870**	**14,421**	...	**14,887**	...	...	**16,764**	...	...	**16,503**	...	...
701	**General public services**	...	...	...	...	...	...	...	...	...	...	...	...
7017	Public debt transactions	977	1,264	1,452	1,004	...	...	1,004	...	...	1,005	...	...
7018	Transfers of general character between levels of government	...	...	...	...	...	...	...	...	...	...	...	...
702	**Defense**	...	...	...	...	...	...	...	...	...	...	...	...
703	**Public order and safety**	...	...	...	...	...	...	...	...	...	...	...	...
704	**Economic affairs**	...	...	...	...	...	...	...	...	...	...	...	...
7042	Agriculture, forestry, fishing, and hunting	...	...	...	...	...	...	...	...	...	...	...	...
7043	Fuel and energy	...	...	...	...	...	...	...	...	...	...	...	...
7044	Mining, manufacturing, and construction	...	...	...	...	...	...	...	...	...	...	...	...
7045	Transport	...	...	...	...	...	...	...	...	...	...	...	...
7046	Communication	...	...	...	...	...	...	...	...	...	...	...	...
705	**Environmental protection**	...	...	...	...	...	...	...	...	...	...	...	...
706	**Housing and community amenities**	...	...	...	...	...	...	...	...	...	...	...	...
707	**Health**	...	...	...	...	...	...	...	...	...	...	...	...
7072	Outpatient services	...	...	...	...	...	...	...	...	...	...	...	...
7073	Hospital services	...	...	...	...	...	...	...	...	...	...	...	...
7074	Public health services	...	...	...	...	...	...	...	...	...	...	...	...
708	**Recreation, culture and religion**	...	...	...	...	...	...	...	...	...	...	...	...
709	**Education**	...	...	...	...	...	...	...	...	...	...	...	...
7091	Pre-primary and primary education	...	...	...	...	...	...	...	...	...	...	...	...
7092	Secondary education	...	...	...	...	...	...	...	...	...	...	...	...
7094	Tertiary education	...	...	...	...	...	...	...	...	...	...	...	...
710	**Social protection**	...	...	...	...	...	...	...	...	...	...	...	...
7z	Statistical discrepancy: Expenditure	...	...	...	...	...	...	...	...	...	...	...	...
	Table 8 Financial transactions by counterpart sector												
	Table 9 Total other economic flows in assets and liabilities												

Thailand (578)

In Billions of Thai Baht (THB) / Fiscal Year Ends September 30th

		Budgetary Central Government			Central Government (excl. Social Security)			Central Government (incl. Social Security)			General Government		
		2013	2014	2015	2013	2014	2015	2013	2014	2015	2013	2014	2015E
	Statement of operations												
1	Revenue	2,378	2,314	2,483	2,522	2,414	2,625	2,673	2,598	2,830	2,870	2,795	3,032
2	Expense	2,414	2,444	2,470	2,430	2,512	2,537	2,464	2,555	2,578	2,426	2,433	2,531
GOB	**Gross operating balance**	**66**	**-36**	**122**	**194**	**-3**	**198**	**312**	**138**	**362**	**444**	**362**	**501**
NOB	**Net operating balance**	**-36**	**-130**	**13**	**92**	**-98**	**88**	**209**	**43**	**252**	**...**	**...**	**...**
31	Net/Gross investment in nonfinancial assets	198	169	260	199	168	264	199	168	264	398	371	483
2M	Expenditure	2,613	2,613	2,730	2,630	2,680	2,801	2,663	2,723	2,842	2,823	2,804	3,014
NLB	**Net lending (+) / Net borrowing (-)**	**-234**	**-299**	**-247**	**-108**	**-266**	**-176**	**10**	**-125**	**-12**	**47**	**-9**	**18**
32	Net acquisition of financial assets	3	-145	-130	128	-114	-57	253	43	80	288	61	109
33	Net incurrence of liabilities	237	154	117	236	152	119	243	168	92	242	165	91
NLBz	Statistical discrepancy	0	0	0	0	0	0	0	0	0	0	-95	0
	Memorandum items												
PB	Primary net lending / net borrowing	-92	-153	-112	35	-120	-40	152	21	123	191	139	155
GB	Government balance per national definition	...	...	...	...	...	...	...	...	...	...	...	...
	Statement of other economic flows												
	Balance sheet												
6	**Net worth**	**5,351**	**...**	**...**	**6,997**	**...**	**...**	**8,377**	**...**	**...**	**8,887**	**...**	**...**
61	Nonfinancial assets	5,399	...	...	5,422	...	...	5,422	...	...	5,543	...	...
62	Financial assets	3,726	...	...	5,348	...	...	6,729	...	...	7,147	...	...
63	Liabilities	3,774	3,965	4,157	3,774	3,965	...	3,774	3,965	...	3,803	3,993	...
	Table 1 Revenue												
1	**Revenue**	**2,378**	**2,314**	**2,483**	**2,522**	**2,414**	**2,625**	**2,673**	**2,598**	**2,830**	**2,870**	**2,795**	**3,032**
11	**Taxes**	**2,138**	**2,041**	**2,115**	**2,235**	**2,105**	**2,227**	**2,235**	**2,105**	**2,227**	**2,418**	**2,285**	**2,407**
111	Taxes on income, profits, and capital gains	959	899	895	959	899	895	959	899	895	959	899	895
1111	Payable by individuals	268	237	268	268	237	268	268	237	268	268	237	268
1112	Payable by corporations and other enterprises	691	662	627	691	662	627	691	662	627	691	662	627
1113	Other taxes on income, profits, and capital gains	—	—	—	—	—	—	—	—	—	—	—	—
112	Taxes on payroll and workforce	—	—	—	—	—	—	—	—	—	—	—	—
113	Taxes on property	—	—	—	—	—	—	—	—	—	24	25	34
114	Taxes on goods and services	1,054	1,022	1,102	1,150	1,086	1,213	1,150	1,086	1,213	1,310	1,241	1,360
1141	General taxes on goods and services	476	491	481	476	491	481	476	491	481	566	579	545
1142	Excises	429	379	435	499	425	529	499	425	529	539	461	570
115	Taxes on international trade and transactions	110	105	100	110	105	100	110	105	100	110	105	100
116	Other taxes	15	15	18	15	15	18	15	15	18	15	15	18
12	**Social contributions**	**—**	**—**	**—**	**—**	**—**	**—**	**108**	**140**	**160**	**108**	**140**	**160**
121	Social security contributions	—	—	—	—	—	—	108	140	160	108	140	160
122	Other social contributions	—	—	—	—	—	—	—	—	—	—	—	—
13	**Grants**	**2**	**5**	**19**	**2**	**5**	**1**	**2**	**5**	**1**	**2**	**5**	**1**
131	From foreign governments	2	5	1	2	5	1	2	5	1	2	5	1
132	From international organizations	—	—	—	0	0	0	0	0	0	0	0	0
133	From other general government units	—	—	17	—	—	—	—	—	—	—	—	—
1331	Current	—	—	17	—	—	—	—	—	—	—	—	—
1332	Capital	—	—	—	—	—	—	—	—	—	—	—	—
14	**Other revenue**	**238**	**268**	**349**	**285**	**304**	**397**	**329**	**347**	**442**	**342**	**364**	**464**
	Table 2 Expense by economic type												
2	**Expense**	**2,414**	**2,444**	**2,470**	**2,430**	**2,512**	**2,537**	**2,464**	**2,555**	**2,578**	**2,426**	**2,433**	**2,531**
21	**Compensation of employees**	**709**	**718**	**742**	**714**	**723**	**747**	**714**	**723**	**747**	**848**	**854**	**898**
211	Wages and salaries	689	697	718	694	702	724	694	702	724	828	833	875
212	Employers' social contributions	20	21	23	20	21	23	20	21	23	20	21	23
22	**Use of goods and services**	**446**	**485**	**507**	**604**	**641**	**650**	**610**	**645**	**655**	**753**	**811**	**828**
23	**Consumption of fixed capital**	**102**	**94**	**109**	**103**	**95**	**110**	**103**	**95**	**110**	**...**	**...**	**...**
24	**Interest**	**142**	**146**	**135**	**142**	**146**	**135**	**142**	**146**	**135**	**144**	**148**	**137**
25	**Subsidies**	**108**	**124**	**115**	**170**	**198**	**151**	**170**	**198**	**151**	**170**	**198**	**151**

Thailand (578)

In Billions of Thai Baht (THB) / Fiscal Year Ends September 30th

		Budgetary Central Government			Central Government (excl. Social Security)			Central Government (incl. Social Security)			General Government		
		2013	2014	2015	2013	2014	2015	2013	2014	2015	2013	2014	2015E
26	**Grants**	**606**	**565**	**571**	**372**	**383**	**434**	**342**	**359**	**407**	**2**	**2**	**2**
261	To foreign governments	1	1	1	1	1	1	1	1	1	1	1	1
262	To international organizations	1	1	1	1	1	1	1	1	1	1	1	1
263	To other general government units	604	563	569	369	381	432	340	357	405	-0	—	—
2631	Current	584	541	514	349	360	377	320	335	350	-0	—	—
2632	Capital	20	22	55	20	22	55	20	22	55	—	—	—
27	**Social benefits**	**204**	**212**	**234**	**215**	**221**	**242**	**271**	**284**	**305**	**272**	**284**	**305**
271	Social security benefits	—	—	—	—	—	—	57	63	63	57	63	63
272	Social assistance benefits	3	1	1	14	10	9	14	10	9	14	10	9
273	Employment-related social benefits	201	211	232	201	211	232	201	211	232	201	211	233
28	**Other expense**	**97**	**99**	**57**	**111**	**104**	**66**	**111**	**104**	**66**	**134**	**134**	**99**
281	Property expense other than interest	0	0	0	0	0	0	0	0	0	0	0	0
282	Transfers not elsewhere classified	97	99	57	111	104	66	111	104	66	134	134	99
2821	Current	64	73	29	78	78	39	78	78	39	101	108	71
2822	Capital	33	26	27	33	26	27	33	26	27	33	26	27
	Table 3 Transactions in assets and liabilities												
3	**Change in net worth from transactions**	**-36**	**-130**	**13**	**92**	**-98**	**88**	**209**	**43**	**252**	**444**	**267**	**501**
31	**Net/Gross investment in nonfinancial assets**	**198**	**169**	**260**	**199**	**168**	**264**	**199**	**168**	**264**	**398**	**371**	**483**
311	Fixed assets	198	169	260	200	168	264	200	168	264	398	371	484
3111	Buildings and structures	149	154	234	149	154	237	149	154	237	256	279	372
3112	Machinery and equipment	48	14	22	50	14	22	50	14	22	140	91	106
3113	Other fixed assets	2	1	2	2	1	3	2	1	3	2	1	3
3114	Weapons systems	—	—	2	—	—	2	—	—	2	—	—	2
312	Inventories	—	—	—	-1	-0	-0	-1	-0	-0	-1	-0	-0
313	Valuables	—	—	—	—	—	—	—	—	—	—	—	—
314	Nonproduced assets	—	—	—	—	0	0	—	0	0	—	0	0
3141	Land	—	—	—	—	—	—	—	—	—	—	—	—
3142	Mineral and energy resources	—	—	—	—	—	—	—	—	—	—	—	—
3143	Other naturally occurring assets	—	—	—	—	—	—	—	—	—	—	—	—
3144	Intangible nonproduced assets	—	—	—	—	0	0	—	0	0	—	0	0
32	**Net acquisition of financial assets**	**3**	**-145**	**-130**	**128**	**-114**	**-57**	**253**	**43**	**80**	**288**	**61**	**109**
	By instrument												
3201	Monetary gold and SDRs	—	—	—	—	—	—	—	—	—	—	—	—
3202	Currency and deposits	-41	-165	-147	-6	-150	-97	16	-162	-90	51	-144	-62
3203	Debt securities	-0	-0	—	53	0	8	145	163	127	145	163	127
3204	Loans	44	20	27	82	34	44	82	34	44	82	34	44
3205	Equity and investment fund shares	3	1	1	2	1	1	2	1	1	2	1	1
3206	Insurance, pension, and standardized guarantee schemes	—	—	—	—	—	—	—	—	—	—	—	—
3207	Financial derivatives and employee stock options	—	—	—	—	—	—	—	—	—	—	—	—
3208	Other accounts receivable	-2	-1	-11	-3	1	-14	8	7	-2	8	7	-2
	By debtor												
321	Domestic debtors	3	-145	-130	128	-114	-57	253	43	80	288	61	109
322	External debtors	—	—	—	—	—	—	—	—	—	—	—	—
33	**Net incurrence of liabilities**	**237**	**154**	**117**	**236**	**152**	**119**	**243**	**168**	**92**	**242**	**165**	**91**
	By instrument												
3301	Special Drawing Rights (SDRs)	—	—	—	—	—	—	—	—	—	—	—	—
3302	Currency and deposits	—	—	—	—	—	—	—	—	—	—	—	—
3303	Debt securities	206	130	101	206	130	101	206	130	101	206	130	101
3304	Loans	32	24	16	32	22	20	32	22	20	30	19	18
3305	Equity and investment fund shares	—	—	—	-1	-2	-4	-1	9	-20	-1	9	-20
3306	Insurance, pension, and standardized guarantee schemes	—	—	—	—	-0	—	—	-0	—	—	-0	—
3307	Financial derivatives and employee stock options	—	—	—	—	—	—	—	—	—	—	—	—
3308	Other accounts payable	—	—	—	-1	2	1	6	7	-9	6	7	-9

Thailand (578)

In Billions of Thai Baht (THB) / Fiscal Year Ends September 30th

		Budgetary Central Government			Central Government (excl. Social Security)			Central Government (incl. Social Security)			General Government		
		2013	2014	2015	2013	2014	2015	2013	2014	2015	2013	2014	2015E
	By creditor												
331	Domestic creditors	95	113	149	94	111	151	101	127	124	100	124	122
332	External creditors	142	41	-32	142	41	-32	142	41	-32	142	41	-32
	Table 4 Holding gains and losses in assets and liabilities												
	Table 5 Holding gains and losses in assets and liabilities												
	Table 6 Balance sheet												
6	**Net worth**	**5,351**	**...**	**...**	**6,997**	**...**	**...**	**8,377**	**...**	**...**	**8,887**	**...**	**...**
61	**Nonfinancial assets**	**5,399**	**...**	**...**	**5,422**	**...**	**...**	**5,422**	**...**	**...**	**5,543**	**...**	**...**
611	Fixed assets	...	...	...	...	...	...	...	...	...	...	...	...
6111	Buildings and structures	...	...	...	...	...	...	...	...	...	...	...	...
6112	Machinery and equipment	...	...	...	...	...	...	...	...	...	...	...	...
6113	Other fixed assets	...	...	...	...	...	...	...	...	...	...	...	...
6114	Weapons systems	...	...	...	...	...	...	...	...	...	...	...	...
612	Inventories	...	...	...	...	...	...	...	...	...	...	...	...
613	Valuables	...	...	...	...	...	...	...	...	...	...	...	...
614	Nonproduced assets	...	...	...	...	...	...	...	...	...	...	...	...
6141	Land	...	...	...	...	...	...	...	...	...	...	...	...
6142	Mineral and energy resources	...	...	...	...	...	...	...	...	...	...	...	...
6143	Other naturally occurring assets	...	...	...	...	...	...	...	...	...	...	...	...
6144	Intangible nonproduced assets	...	...	...	...	...	...	...	...	...	...	...	...
62	**Financial assets**	**3,726**	**...**	**...**	**5,348**	**...**	**...**	**6,729**	**...**	**...**	**7,147**	**...**	**...**
	By instrument												
6201	Monetary gold and SDRs	—	—	—	—	...	...	—	...	...	—	...	...
6202	Currency and deposits	865	496	426	1,050	...	...	1,271	...	...	1,644	...	...
6203	Debt securities	156	...	...	156	...	...	1,192	...	...	1,192	...	...
6204	Loans	969	...	...	2,357	...	...	2,357	...	...	2,357	...	...
6205	Equity and investment fund shares	1,642	...	...	1,642	...	...	1,642	...	...	1,644	...	...
6206	Insurance, pension, and standardized guarantee schemes	—	...	...	—	...	...	—	...	...	—	...	...
6207	Financial derivatives and employee stock options	—	...	...	—	...	...	—	...	...	—	...	...
6208	Other accounts receivable	94	...	...	144	...	...	267	...	...	311	...	...
	By debtor												
621	Domestic debtors	...	...	...	...	...	...	...	...	...	...	...	...
622	External debtors	...	...	...	...	...	...	...	...	...	...	...	...
63	**Liabilities**	**3,774**	**3,965**	**4,157**	**3,774**	**3,965**	**...**	**3,774**	**3,965**	**...**	**3,803**	**3,993**	**...**
	By instrument												
6301	Special Drawing Rights (SDRs)	—	—	—	—	—	...	—	—	...	—	—	...
6302	Currency and deposits	—	—	—	—	—	...	—	—	...	—	—	...
6303	Debt securities	3,660	3,828	4,004	3,660	3,828	...	3,660	3,828	...	3,660	3,828	...
6304	Loans	114	137	153	114	137	...	114	137	...	142	165	...
6305	Equity and investment fund shares	—	—	—	—	—	...	—	—	...	—	—	...
6306	Insurance, pension, and standardized guarantee schemes	—	—	—	—	—	...	—	—	...	—	—	...
6307	Financial derivatives and employee stock options	—	—	—	—	—	...	—	—	...	—	—	...
6308	Other accounts payable	—	—	—	—	—	...	—	—	...	—	—	...
	By creditor												
631	Domestic creditors	3,705	3,890	3,505	3,705	3,890	...	3,705	3,890	...	3,734	3,918	...
632	External creditors	69	75	652	69	75	...	69	75	...	69	75	...
	Memorandum items												
6M2	Net financial worth	-48	...	...	1,574	...	...	2,955	...	...	3,345	...	...
6M3	Gross debt (D4) at market value	...	...	...	...	...	...	...	...	...	...	...	...
6M3D3	D3 debt liabilities at market value	...	...	...	...	...	...	...	...	...	...	...	...
6M3D2	D2 debt liabilities at market value	...	...	...	...	...	...	...	...	...	...	...	...
6M3D1	D1 debt liabilities at market value	...	...	...	...	...	...	...	...	...	...	...	...
6M4	Gross debt (D4) at nominal value	...	...	...	...	...	...	...	...	...	...	...	...
6M4D3	D3 debt liabilities at nominal value	...	...	...	...	...	...	...	...	...	...	...	...
6M4D2	D2 debt liabilities at nominal value	...	...	...	...	...	...	...	...	...	...	...	...
6M4D1	D1 debt liabilities at nominal value	...	...	...	...	...	...	...	...	...	...	...	...

Thailand (578)

In Billions of Thai Baht (THB) / Fiscal Year Ends September 30th

		Budgetary Central Government			Central Government (excl. Social Security)			Central Government (incl. Social Security)			General Government		
		2013	2014	2015	2013	2014	2015	2013	2014	2015	2013	2014	2015E
6M35	Gross debt (D4) at face value	3,774	3,965	4,157	3,774	3,965	...	3,774	3,965	...	3,803	3,993	...
6M35D3	D3 debt liabilities at face value	3,774	3,965	4,157	3,774	3,965	...	3,774	3,965	...	3,803	3,993	...
6M35D2	D2 debt liabilities at face value	3,774	3,965	4,157	3,774	3,965	...	3,774	3,965	...	3,803	3,993	...
6M35D1	D1 debt liabilities at face value	3,774	3,965	4,157	3,774	3,965	...	3,774	3,965	...	3,803	3,993	...
6M93	Government gross debt per national definition	...	...	...	...	...	...	...	...	...	...	...	...
6M5	Arrears	...	...	...	...	...	...	...	...	...	...	...	...
6M6	Explicit contingent liabilities	...	...	...	...	...	...	...	...	...	...	...	...
6M61	of which: Publicly guaranteed debt	...	...	...	...	...	...	...	...	...	...	...	...
6M7	Net implicit obligations for social security benefits	...	...	...	...	...	...	...	...	...	...	...	...
	Table 7 Expenditure by functions of government												
7	**Expenditure**	**2,613**	**2,613**	**2,730**	**2,630**	**2,680**	**2,801**	**2,663**	**2,723**	**2,842**	**2,823**	**2,899**	**3,014**
701	**General public services**	**611**	**624**	**1,004**	**381**	**445**	**873**	**352**	**421**	**846**	**...**	**...**	**...**
7017	Public debt transactions	142	146	135	142	146	135	142	146	135	144	149	137
7018	Transfers of general character between levels of government	604	563	569	369	381	432	345	357	405	—	—	—
702	**Defense**	**181**	**176**	**190**	**181**	**176**	**190**	**181**	**176**	**190**	**...**	**...**	**...**
703	**Public order and safety**	**146**	**151**	**172**	**146**	**151**	**172**	**146**	**151**	**172**	**...**	**...**	**...**
704	**Economic affairs**	**489**	**525**	**423**	**611**	**645**	**509**	**611**	**645**	**509**	**...**	**...**	**...**
7042	Agriculture, forestry, fishing, and hunting	153	186	196	168	208	213	168	208	213	...	...	...
7043	Fuel and energy	8	3	3	87	89	53	87	89	53	...	...	...
7044	Mining, manufacturing, and construction	22	12	12	22	12	12	22	12	12	...	...	...
7045	Transport	86	118	168	93	122	179	93	122	179	...	...	...
7046	Communication	2	4	4	2	4	4	2	4	4	...	...	...
705	**Environmental protection**	**2**	**3**	**4**	**3**	**3**	**4**	**3**	**3**	**4**	**...**	**...**	**...**
706	**Housing and community amenities**	**152**	**61**	**72**	**153**	**61**	**73**	**153**	**61**	**73**	**...**	**...**	**...**
707	**Health**	**267**	**267**	**149**	**272**	**273**	**156**	**272**	**273**	**156**	**...**	**...**	**...**
7072	Outpatient services	2	2	0	2	2	0	...	...	0	...	...	...
7073	Hospital services	61	61	120	61	61	120	...	...	120	...	...	...
7074	Public health services	86	85	4	90	91	9	...	...	9	...	...	...
708	**Recreation, culture and religion**	**28**	**27**	**30**	**29**	**28**	**32**	**29**	**28**	**32**	**...**	**...**	**...**
709	**Education**	**505**	**531**	**513**	**506**	**532**	**516**	**506**	**532**	**516**	**...**	**...**	**...**
7091	Pre-primary and primary education	221	237	206	222	237	206	...	...	206	...	...	...
7092	Secondary education	119	146	173	...	...	173	...	...	173	...	...	...
7094	Tertiary education	70	96	97	...	...	97	...	...	97	...	...	...
710	**Social protection**	**232**	**249**	**173**	**347**	**364**	**277**	**410**	**431**	**345**	**...**	**...**	**...**
7z	Statistical discrepancy: Expenditure	0	-0	—	—	—	—	—	—	—	—	—	—
	Table 8 Financial transactions by counterpart sector												
32	**Net acquisition of financial assets**	**3**	**-145**	**-130**	**128**	**-114**	**-57**	**253**	**43**	**80**	**288**	**61**	**109**
321	Domestic debtors	3	-145	-130	128	-114	-57	253	43	80	288	61	109
8211	General government	-87	-57	-71	-67	-44	-72	-52	-31	-56	-52	-31	-56
8212	Central bank	54	-113	-75	54	-113	-75	54	-113	-75	54	-113	-75
8213	Deposit-taking corporations except the central bank	-10	3	6	57	6	64	166	150	185	202	168	214
8214	Other financial corporations	3	1	1	3	1	1	3	1	1	3	1	1
8215	Nonfinancial corporations	44	20	9	49	22	8	49	22	8	49	22	8
8216	Households & nonprofit institutions serving households	—	—	—	32	14	16	33	14	16	33	14	16
322	External debtors	—	—	—	—	—	—	—	—	—	—	—	—
8221	General government	—	—	—	—	—	—	—	—	—	—	—	—
8227	International organizations	—	—	—	—	—	—	—	—	—	—	—	—
8228	Financial corporations other than international organizations	—	—	—	—	—	—	—	—	—	—	—	—
8229	Other nonresidents	—	—	—	—	—	—	—	—	—	—	—	—

Thailand (578)

In Billions of Thai Baht (THB) / Fiscal Year Ends September 30th

		Budgetary Central Government			Central Government (excl. Social Security)			Central Government (incl. Social Security)			General Government		
		2013	2014	2015	2013	2014	2015	2013	2014	2015	2013	2014	2015E
33	**Net incurrence of liabilities**	**237**	**154**	**117**	**236**	**152**	**119**	**243**	**168**	**92**	**242**	**165**	**91**
331	Domestic creditors	95	113	149	94	111	151	101	127	124	100	124	122
8311	General government	14	27	51	14	25	47	14	36	31	14	36	31
8312	Central bank	50	-67	32	50	-67	32	50	-67	32	50	-67	32
8313	Deposit-taking corporations except the central bank	153	154	142	153	152	146	153	152	146	152	149	144
8314	Other financial corporations	-155	82	-95	-155	82	-95	-155	82	-95	-155	82	-95
8315	Nonfinancial corporations	31	10	-5	29	12	-5	29	12	-5	29	12	-5
8316	Households & nonprofit institutions serving households	2	-92	23	2	-92	24	10	-87	14	10	-87	14
332	External creditors	142	41	-32	142	41	-32	142	41	-32	142	41	-32
8321	General government	-3	7	6	-3	7	6	-3	7	6	-3	7	6
8327	International organizations	29	-0	1	29	-0	1	29	-0	1	29	-0	1
8328	Financial corporations other than international organizations	—	34	2	—	34	2	—	34	2	—	34	2
8329	Other nonresidents	116	—	-41	116	—	-41	116	—	-41	116	—	-41
	Table 9 Total other economic flows in assets and liabilities												

Timor-Leste, Dem. Rep. of (537)

In Millions of U.S. Dollars (USD) / Fiscal Year Ends December 31st

		Budgetary Central Government			Central Government (excl. Social Security)			Central Government (incl. Social Security)			General Government		
		2013	2014	2015	2013	2014	2015	2013	2014	2015	2013	2014	2015
	Statement of operations												
1	Revenue	...	859	1,452	3,644	2,345	1,618	3,644	2,345	1,618	3,644	2,345	1,618
2	Expense	...	913	1,028	878	975	1,165	878	975	1,165	878	975	1,165
GOB	**Gross operating balance**	...	**-54**	**424**	**2,766**	**1,370**	**453**	**2,766**	**1,370**	**453**	**2,766**	**1,370**	**453**
NOB	**Net operating balance**	...	...	...	...	...	...	...	...	...	...	...	...
31	Net/Gross investment in nonfinancial assets	...	425	307	358	432	324	358	432	324	358	432	324
2M	Expenditure	...	1,337	1,335	1,236	1,407	1,490	1,236	1,407	1,490	1,236	1,407	1,490
NLB	**Net lending (+) / Net borrowing (-)**	...	**-478**	**117**	**2,408**	**939**	**129**	**2,408**	**939**	**129**	**2,408**	**939**	**129**
32	Net acquisition of financial assets	...	-43	1	2,992	1,351	12	2,992	1,351	12	2,992	1,351	12
33	Net incurrence of liabilities	...	3	—	—	3	—	—	3	—	—	3	—
NLBz	Statistical discrepancy	...	432	-116	584	409	-116	584	409	-116	584	409	-116
	Memorandum items												
PB	Primary net lending / net borrowing	...	-478	117	2,408	939	129	2,408	939	129	2,408	939	129
GB	Government balance per national definition	...	...	...	...	...	...	...	...	...	...	...	...
	Statement of other economic flows												
	Balance sheet												
	Table 1 Revenue												
1	**Revenue**	...	**859**	**1,452**	**3,644**	**2,345**	**1,618**	**3,644**	**2,345**	**1,618**	**3,644**	**2,345**	**1,618**
11	**Taxes**	...	**127**	**125**	**1,310**	**909**	**575**	**1,310**	**909**	**575**	**1,310**	**909**	**575**
111	Taxes on income, profits, and capital gains	...	53	53	1,191	805	468	1,191	805	468	1,191	805	468
1111	Payable by individuals	...	45	45	...	...	...	...	...	...	...	...	...
1112	Payable by corporations and other enterprises	...	8	8	...	...	...	...	...	...	...	...	...
1113	Other taxes on income, profits, and capital gains	...	—	—	...	...	...	...	...	...	...	...	...
112	Taxes on payroll and workforce	...	—	—	—	—	—	—	—	—	—	—	—
113	Taxes on property	...	—	—	...	—	—	...	—	—	...	—	—
114	Taxes on goods and services	...	60	59	...	90	95	...	90	95	...	90	95
1141	General taxes on goods and services	...	15	14	...	...	...	...	...	...	...	...	...
1142	Excises	...	40	40	...	...	...	...	...	...	...	...	...
115	Taxes on international trade and transactions	...	13	12	13	13	12	13	13	12	13	13	12
116	Other taxes	...	0	0	4	0	0	4	0	0	4	0	0
12	**Social contributions**	...	—	—	—	—	—	—	—	—	—	—	—
121	Social security contributions	...	—	—	—	—	—	—	—	—	—	—	—
122	Other social contributions	...	—	—	—	—	—	—	—	—	—	—	—
13	**Grants**	...	**732**	**1,279**	**133**	**53**	**139**	**133**	**53**	**139**	**133**	**53**	**139**
131	From foreign governments	...	—	—	...	53	139	...	53	139	...	53	139
132	From international organizations	...	—	—	...	—	—	...	—	—	...	—	—
133	From other general government units	...	732	1,279	...	—	—	...	—	—	...	—	—
1331	Current	...	732	1,279	...	—	—	...	—	—	...	—	—
1332	Capital	...	—	—	...	—	—	...	—	—	...	—	—
14	**Other revenue**	...	**1**	**49**	**2,201**	**1,384**	**904**	**2,201**	**1,384**	**904**	**2,201**	**1,384**	**904**
	Table 2 Expense by economic type												
2	**Expense**	...	**913**	**1,028**	**878**	**975**	**1,165**	**878**	**975**	**1,165**	**878**	**975**	**1,165**
21	**Compensation of employees**	...	**169**	**179**	**149**	**172**	**196**	**149**	**172**	**196**	**149**	**172**	**196**
211	Wages and salaries	...	169	179	...	172	196	...	172	196	...	172	196
212	Employers' social contributions	...	—	—	...	—	—	...	—	—	...	—	—
22	**Use of goods and services**	...	**445**	**410**	**445**	**477**	**474**	**445**	**477**	**474**	**445**	**477**	**474**
23	**Consumption of fixed capital**	...	...	...	...	...	...	...	...	...	...	...	...
24	**Interest**	...	—	**0**	—	—	**0**	—	—	**0**	—	—	**0**
25	**Subsidies**	...	—	—	—	—	—	—	—	—	—	—	—
26	**Grants**	...	—	—	—	—	—	—	—	—	—	—	—
261	To foreign governments	...	—	—	—	—	—	—	—	—	—	—	—
262	To international organizations	...	—	—	—	—	—	—	—	—	—	—	—
263	To other general government units	...	—	—	—	—	—	—	—	—	—	—	—
2631	Current	...	—	—	—	—	—	—	—	—	—	—	—
2632	Capital	...	—	—	—	—	—	—	—	—	—	—	—

Timor-Leste, Dem. Rep. of (537)

In Millions of U.S. Dollars (USD) / Fiscal Year Ends December 31st

		Budgetary Central Government			Central Government (excl. Social Security)			Central Government (incl. Social Security)			General Government		
		2013	2014	2015	2013	2014	2015	2013	2014	2015	2013	2014	2015
27	**Social benefits**	...	117	174	124	117	174	124	117	174	124	117	174
271	Social security benefits	...	—	—	...	—	—	...	—	—	...	—	—
272	Social assistance benefits	...	117	174	...	117	174	...	117	174	...	117	174
273	Employment-related social benefits	...	—	—	...	—	—	...	—	—	...	—	—
28	**Other expense**	...	182	265	160	209	322	160	209	322	160	209	322
281	Property expense other than interest	...	—	—	...	—	—	...	—	—	...	—	—
282	Transfers not elsewhere classified	...	182	265	...	209	322	...	209	322	...	209	322
2821	Current	...	182	265	...	209	322	...	209	322	...	209	322
2822	Capital	...	—	—	...	—	—	...	—	—	...	—	—
	Table 3 Transactions in assets and liabilities												
3	**Change in net worth from transactions**	...	379	308	...	1,779	337	...	1,779	337	...	1,779	337
31	**Net/Gross investment in nonfinancial assets**	...	425	307	358	432	324	358	432	324	358	432	324
311	Fixed assets	...	425	307	...	432	324	...	432	324	...	432	324
3111	Buildings and structures	...	371	273	...	378	289	...	378	289	...	378	289
3112	Machinery and equipment	...	53	34	...	53	35	...	53	35	...	53	35
3113	Other fixed assets	...	—	—	...	—	—	...	—	—	...	—	—
3114	Weapons systems	...	—	—	...	—	—	...	—	—	...	—	—
312	Inventories	...	...	—	...	...	—	...	...	—	...	—	—
313	Valuables	...	...	—	...	...	—	...	...	—	...	—	—
314	Nonproduced assets	...	...	—	...	...	—	...	...	—	...	—	—
3141	Land	...	...	—	...	...	—	...	...	—	...	—	—
3142	Mineral and energy resources	...	...	—	...	...	—	...	...	—	...	—	—
3143	Other naturally occurring assets	...	...	—	...	...	—	...	...	—	...	—	—
3144	Intangible nonproduced assets	...	...	—	...	...	—	...	...	—	...	—	—
32	**Net acquisition of financial assets**	...	-43	1	2,992	1,351	12	2,992	1,351	12	2,992	1,351	12
	By instrument												
3201	Monetary gold and SDRs	...	—	—	—	—	—	—	—	—	—	—	—
3202	Currency and deposits	...	-59	1	25	218	69	25	218	69	25	218	69
3203	Debt securities	...	—	—	2,023	602	-38	2,023	602	-38	2,023	602	-38
3204	Loans	...	16	—	—	16	—	—	16	—	—	16	—
3205	Equity and investment fund shares	...	—	—	883	383	-25	883	383	-25	883	383	-25
3206	Insurance, pension, and standardized guarantee schemes	...	—	—	—	—	—	—	—	—	—	—	—
3207	Financial derivatives and employee stock options	...	—	—	—	—	—	—	—	—	—	—	—
3208	Other accounts receivable	...	...	...	60	132	7	60	132	7	60	132	7
	By debtor												
321	Domestic debtors	...	-59	1	...	-59	1	—	-59	1	...	-59	1
322	External debtors	...	16	—	...	1,410	12	—	1,410	12	...	1,410	12
33	**Net incurrence of liabilities**	...	3	—	—	3	—	—	3	—	—	3	—
	By instrument												
3301	Special Drawing Rights (SDRs)	...	—	—	—	—	—	—	—	—	—	—	—
3302	Currency and deposits	...	—	—	—	—	—	—	—	—	—	—	—
3303	Debt securities	...	—	—	—	—	—	—	—	—	—	—	—
3304	Loans	...	3	—	—	3	—	—	3	—	—	3	—
3305	Equity and investment fund shares	...	—	—	—	—	—	—	—	—	—	—	—
3306	Insurance, pension, and standardized guarantee schemes	...	—	—	—	—	—	—	—	—	—	—	—
3307	Financial derivatives and employee stock options	...	—	—	—	—	—	—	—	—	—	—	—
3308	Other accounts payable	...	...	...	...	...	...	...	...	...	...	...	...
	By creditor												
331	Domestic creditors	...	—	—	—	—	—	—	—	—	—	—	—
332	External creditors	...	3	—	—	3	—	—	3	—	—	3	—
	Table 4 Holding gains and losses in assets and liabilities												
	Table 5 Holding gains and losses in assets and liabilities												
	Table 6 Balance sheet												

Timor-Leste, Dem. Rep. of (537)

In Millions of U.S. Dollars (USD) / Fiscal Year Ends December 31st

	Budgetary Central Government			Central Government (excl. Social Security)			Central Government (incl. Social Security)			General Government		
	2013	2014	2015	2013	2014	2015	2013	2014	2015	2013	2014	2015
Table 7 Expenditure by functions of government												
Table 8 Financial transactions by counterpart sector												
Table 9 Total other economic flows in assets and liabilities												

Togo (742)

In Billions of CFA (BCEAO) Francs (XOF) / Fiscal Year Ends December 31st

		Budgetary Central Government			Central Government (excl. Social Security)			Central Government (incl. Social Security)			General Government		
		2013	2014	2015	2013	2014	2015	2013	2014	2015	2013	2014	2015
	Statement of operations												
1	Revenue	523	...	621	...	...	...	...	...	...	...	...	...
2	Expense	459	...	628	...	...	...	...	...	...	...	...	...
GOB	**Gross operating balance**	**64**	...	**-7**	...	...	...	...	...	...	...	...	...
NOB	**Net operating balance**	...	...	...	...	...	...	...	...	...	...	...	...
31	Net/Gross investment in nonfinancial assets	162	...	278	...	...	...	...	...	...	...	...	...
2M	Expenditure	621	...	905	...	...	...	...	...	...	...	...	...
NLB	**Net lending (+) / Net borrowing (-)**	**-98**	...	**-285**	...	...	...	...	...	...	...	...	...
32	Net acquisition of financial assets	24	...	...	...	...	...	...	...	...	...	...	...
33	Net incurrence of liabilities	122	...	...	...	...	...	...	...	...	...	...	...
NLBz	Statistical discrepancy	-0	...	...	...	...	...	...	...	...	...	...	...
	Memorandum items												
PB	Primary net lending / net borrowing	-72	...	-239	...	...	...	...	...	...	...	...	...
GB	Government balance per national definition	...	...	...	...	...	...	...	...	...	...	...	...
	Statement of other economic flows												
	Balance sheet												
	Table 1 Revenue												
1	**Revenue**	**523**	...	**621**	...	...	...	...	...	...	...	...	...
11	**Taxes**	**404**	...	**527**	...	...	...	...	...	...	...	...	...
111	Taxes on income, profits, and capital gains	58	...	98	...	...	...	...	...	...	...	...	...
1111	Payable by individuals	22	...	24	...	...	...	...	...	...	...	...	...
1112	Payable by corporations and other enterprises	32	...	74	...	...	...	...	...	...	...	...	...
1113	Other taxes on income, profits, and capital gains	4	...	—	...	...	...	...	...	...	...	...	...
112	Taxes on payroll and workforce	3	...	3	...	...	...	...	...	...	...	...	...
113	Taxes on property	0	...	2	...	...	...	...	...	...	...	...	...
114	Taxes on goods and services	178	...	300	...	...	...	...	...	...	...	...	...
1141	General taxes on goods and services	153	...	256	...	...	...	...	...	...	...	...	...
1142	Excises	24	...	35	...	...	...	...	...	...	...	...	...
115	Taxes on international trade and transactions	96	...	121	...	...	...	...	...	...	...	...	...
116	Other taxes	68	...	3	...	...	...	...	...	...	...	...	...
12	**Social contributions**	—	...	—	...	...	...	...	...	...	...	...	...
121	Social security contributions	—	...	—	...	...	...	...	...	...	...	...	...
122	Other social contributions	—	...	—	...	...	...	...	...	...	...	...	...
13	**Grants**	**74**	...	**57**	...	...	...	...	...	...	...	...	...
131	From foreign governments	74	...	57	...	...	...	...	...	...	...	...	...
132	From international organizations	—	...	—	...	...	...	...	...	...	...	...	...
133	From other general government units	—	...	—	...	...	...	...	...	...	...	...	...
1331	Current	—	...	—	...	...	...	...	...	...	...	...	...
1332	Capital	—	...	—	...	...	...	...	...	...	...	...	...
14	**Other revenue**	**46**	...	**37**	...	...	...	...	...	...	...	...	...
	Table 2 Expense by economic type												
2	**Expense**	**459**	...	**628**	...	...	...	...	...	...	...	...	...
21	**Compensation of employees**	**131**	...	**172**	...	...	...	...	...	...	...	...	...
211	Wages and salaries	...	...	...	...	...	...	...	...	...	...	...	...
212	Employers' social contributions	...	...	...	...	...	...	...	...	...	...	...	...
22	**Use of goods and services**	**129**	...	**167**	...	...	...	...	...	...	...	...	...
23	**Consumption of fixed capital**	...	...	...	...	...	...	...	...	...	...	...	...
24	**Interest**	**26**	...	**45**	...	...	...	...	...	...	...	...	...
25	**Subsidies**	**128**	...	**128**	...	...	...	...	...	...	...	...	...
26	**Grants**	**34**	...	**30**	...	...	...	...	...	...	...	...	...
261	To foreign governments	—	...	—	...	...	...	...	...	...	...	...	...
262	To international organizations	—	...	—	...	...	...	...	...	...	...	...	...
263	To other general government units	34	...	30	...	...	...	...	...	...	...	...	...
2631	Current	34	...	30	...	...	...	...	...	...	...	...	...
2632	Capital	—	...	—	...	...	...	...	...	...	...	...	...

Togo (742)

In Billions of CFA (BCEAO) Francs (XOF) / Fiscal Year Ends December 31st

		Budgetary Central Government			Central Government (excl. Social Security)			Central Government (incl. Social Security)			General Government		
		2013	2014	2015	2013	2014	2015	2013	2014	2015	2013	2014	2015
27	**Social benefits**	—	...	—	...	...	...	...	...	...	...	...	...
271	Social security benefits	—	...	—	...	...	...	...	...	...	...	...	...
272	Social assistance benefits	—	...	—	...	...	...	...	...	...	...	...	...
273	Employment-related social benefits	—	...	—	...	...	...	...	...	...	...	...	...
28	**Other expense**	**11**	...	**86**	...	...	...	...	...	...	...	...	...
281	Property expense other than interest	—	...	—	...	...	...	...	...	...	...	...	...
282	Transfers not elsewhere classified	11	...	86	...	...	...	...	...	...	...	...	...
2821	Current	11	...	86	...	...	...	...	...	...	...	...	...
2822	Capital	—	...	—	...	...	...	...	...	...	...	...	...
	Table 3 Transactions in assets and liabilities												
3	**Change in net worth from transactions**	...	...	...	...	...	...	...	...	...	...	...	...
31	**Net/Gross investment in nonfinancial assets**	**162**	...	**278**	...	...	...	...	...	...	...	...	...
311	Fixed assets	162	...	278	...	...	...	...	...	...	...	...	...
3111	Buildings and structures	...	...	...	...	...	...	...	...	...	...	...	...
3112	Machinery and equipment	...	...	...	...	...	...	...	...	...	...	...	...
3113	Other fixed assets	...	...	...	...	...	...	...	...	...	...	...	...
3114	Weapons systems	...	...	...	...	...	...	...	...	...	...	...	...
312	Inventories	—	...	...	...	...	...	...	...	...	...	...	...
313	Valuables	—	...	...	...	...	...	...	...	...	...	...	...
314	Nonproduced assets	—	...	...	...	...	...	...	...	...	...	...	...
3141	Land	—	...	...	...	...	...	...	...	...	...	...	...
3142	Mineral and energy resources	—	...	...	...	...	...	...	...	...	...	...	...
3143	Other naturally occurring assets	—	...	...	...	...	...	...	...	...	...	...	...
3144	Intangible nonproduced assets	—	...	...	...	...	...	...	...	...	...	...	...
32	**Net acquisition of financial assets**	**24**	...	...	...	...	...	...	...	...	...	...	...
	By instrument												
3201	Monetary gold and SDRs	—	...	...	...	...	...	...	...	...	...	...	...
3202	Currency and deposits	48	...	...	...	...	...	...	...	...	...	...	...
3203	Debt securities	—	...	...	...	...	...	...	...	...	...	...	...
3204	Loans	-0	...	...	...	...	...	...	...	...	...	...	...
3205	Equity and investment fund shares	-23	...	...	...	...	...	...	...	...	...	...	...
3206	Insurance, pension, and standardized guarantee schemes	—	...	...	...	...	...	...	...	...	...	...	...
3207	Financial derivatives and employee stock options	—	...	...	...	...	...	...	...	...	...	...	...
3208	Other accounts receivable	...	...	...	...	...	...	...	...	...	...	...	...
	By debtor												
321	Domestic debtors	24	...	...	...	...	...	...	...	...	...	...	...
322	External debtors	—	...	...	...	...	...	...	...	...	...	...	...
33	**Net incurrence of liabilities**	**122**	...	...	...	...	...	...	...	...	...	...	...
	By instrument												
3301	Special Drawing Rights (SDRs)	—	...	...	...	...	...	...	...	...	...	...	...
3302	Currency and deposits	10	...	...	...	...	...	...	...	...	...	...	...
3303	Debt securities	65	...	...	...	...	...	...	...	...	...	...	...
3304	Loans	31	...	...	...	...	...	...	...	...	...	...	...
3305	Equity and investment fund shares	—	...	...	...	...	...	...	...	...	...	...	...
3306	Insurance, pension, and standardized guarantee schemes	—	...	...	...	...	...	...	...	...	...	...	...
3307	Financial derivatives and employee stock options	—	...	...	...	...	...	...	...	...	...	...	...
3308	Other accounts payable	16	...	...	...	...	...	...	...	...	...	...	...
	By creditor												
331	Domestic creditors	101	...	...	...	...	...	...	...	...	...	...	...
332	External creditors	20	...	...	...	...	...	...	...	...	...	...	...
	Table 4 Holding gains and losses in assets and liabilities												
	Table 5 Holding gains and losses in assets and liabilities												
	Table 6 Balance sheet												

Togo (742)

In Billions of CFA (BCEAO) Francs (XOF) / Fiscal Year Ends December 31st

	Budgetary Central Government			Central Government (excl. Social Security)			Central Government (incl. Social Security)			General Government		
	2013	2014	2015	2013	2014	2015	2013	2014	2015	2013	2014	2015
Table 7 Expenditure by functions of government												
Table 8 Financial transactions by counterpart sector												
Table 9 Total other economic flows in assets and liabilities												

Trinidad and Tobago (369)

In Millions of Trinidad and Tobago Dollars (TTD) / Fiscal Year Ends September 30th

		Budgetary Central Government			Central Government (excl. Social Security)			Central Government (incl. Social Security)			General Government		
		2010	2011	2012	2010	2011	2012	2010	2011	2012	2010	2011	2012
	Statement of operations												
1	Revenue	...	...	...	...	...	...	46,517	47,015	52,204	...	...	...
2	Expense	...	...	...	...	...	...	43,366	44,540	49,787	...	...	...
GOB	**Gross operating balance**	...	...	...	...	...	...	**3,151**	**2,475**	**2,418**	...	...	...
NOB	**Net operating balance**	...	...	...	...	...	...	**3,151**	...	...	...	...	...
31	Net/Gross investment in nonfinancial assets	...	...	...	...	...	...	5,242	6,943	4,624	...	...	...
2M	Expenditure	...	...	...	...	...	...	48,608	51,483	54,411	...	...	...
NLB	**Net lending (+) / Net borrowing (-)**	...	...	...	...	...	...	**-2,091**	**-4,468**	**-2,206**	...	...	...
32	Net acquisition of financial assets	...	...	...	...	...	...	-4,216	-476	-32	...	...	...
33	Net incurrence of liabilities	...	...	...	...	...	...	-2,125	3,992	2,808	...	...	...
NLBz	Statistical discrepancy	...	...	...	...	...	...	—	—	-634	...	...	...
	Memorandum items												
PB	Primary net lending / net borrowing	...	...	...	...	...	...	1,199	-1,602	731	...	...	...
GB	Government balance per national definition	...	...	...	...	...	...	...	...	...	...	...	...
	Statement of other economic flows												
	Balance sheet												
	Table 1 Revenue												
1	**Revenue**	...	...	...	...	...	...	**46,517**	**47,015**	**52,204**	...	...	...
11	**Taxes**	...	...	...	...	...	...	**37,074**	**41,801**	**43,569**	...	...	...
111	Taxes on income, profits, and capital gains	...	...	...	...	...	...	23,071	30,226	27,670	...	...	...
1111	Payable by individuals	...	...	...	...	...	...	207	4,961	214	...	...	...
1112	Payable by corporations and other enterprises	...	...	...	...	...	...	22,864	25,056	27,456	...	...	...
1113	Other taxes on income, profits, and capital gains	...	...	...	...	...	...	—	209	—	...	...	...
112	Taxes on payroll and workforce	...	...	...	...	...	...	4,467	2,438	5,435	...	...	...
113	Taxes on property	...	...	...	...	...	...	22	32	62	...	...	...
114	Taxes on goods and services	...	...	...	...	...	...	7,437	6,753	7,869	...	...	...
1141	General taxes on goods and services	...	...	...	...	...	...	6,086	4,917	6,337	...	...	...
1142	Excises	...	...	...	...	...	...	705	705	725	...	...	...
115	Taxes on international trade and transactions	...	...	...	...	...	...	1,906	2,168	2,319	...	...	...
116	Other taxes	...	...	...	...	...	...	172	185	214	...	...	...
12	**Social contributions**	...	...	...	...	...	...	**2,702**	**216**	**2,982**	...	...	...
121	Social security contributions	...	...	...	...	...	...	2,665	...	2,942	...	...	...
122	Other social contributions	...	...	...	...	...	...	37	...	39	...	...	...
13	**Grants**	...	...	...	...	...	...	—	**242**	**1**	...	...	...
131	From foreign governments	...	...	...	...	...	...	—	242	—	...	...	...
132	From international organizations	...	...	...	...	...	...	—	—	1	...	...	...
133	From other general government units	...	...	...	...	...	...	—	—	—	...	...	...
1331	Current	...	...	...	...	...	...	—	—	—	...	...	...
1332	Capital	...	...	...	...	...	...	—	—	—	...	...	...
14	**Other revenue**	...	...	...	...	...	...	**6,740**	**4,756**	**5,653**	...	...	...
	Table 2 Expense by economic type												
2	**Expense**	...	...	...	...	...	...	**43,366**	**44,540**	**49,787**	...	...	...
21	**Compensation of employees**	...	...	...	...	...	...	**10,452**	**7,180**	**12,071**	...	...	...
211	Wages and salaries	...	...	...	...	...	...	6,385	...	6,933	...	...	...
212	Employers' social contributions	...	...	...	...	...	...	4,068	...	5,138	...	...	...
22	**Use of goods and services**	...	...	...	...	...	...	**7,887**	**6,504**	**10,961**	...	...	...
23	**Consumption of fixed capital**	...	...	...	...	...	...	—	...	...	...	...	...
24	**Interest**	...	...	...	...	...	...	**3,290**	**2,866**	**2,937**	...	...	...
25	**Subsidies**	...	...	...	...	...	...	**205**	...	**214**	...	...	...
26	**Grants**	...	...	...	...	...	...	**8,746**	...	**10,889**	...	...	...
261	To foreign governments	...	...	...	...	...	...	—	...	—	...	...	...
262	To international organizations	...	...	...	...	...	...	—	...	—	...	...	...
263	To other general government units	...	...	...	...	...	...	8,746	...	10,889	...	...	...
2631	Current	...	...	...	...	...	...	8,746	...	10,889	...	...	...
2632	Capital	...	...	...	...	...	...	—	...	—	...	...	...

Trinidad and Tobago (369)

In Millions of Trinidad and Tobago Dollars (TTD) / Fiscal Year Ends September 30th

		Budgetary Central Government			Central Government (excl. Social Security)			Central Government (incl. Social Security)			General Government		
		2010	2011	2012	2010	2011	2012	2010	2011	2012	2010	2011	2012
27	**Social benefits**	...	...	...	...	...	...	**9,200**	...	**9,197**	...	...	...
271	Social security benefits	...	...	...	...	...	...	—	...	—	...	...	...
272	Social assistance benefits	...	...	...	...	...	...	9,200	...	9,197	...	...	...
273	Employment-related social benefits	...	...	...	...	...	...	—	...	—	...	...	...
28	**Other expense**	...	...	...	...	...	...	**3,586**	...	**3,517**	...	...	...
281	Property expense other than interest	...	...	...	...	...	...	—	...	—	...	...	...
282	Transfers not elsewhere classified	...	...	...	...	...	...	3,586	...	3,517	...	...	...
2821	Current	...	...	...	...	...	...	3,586	...	3,517	...	...	...
2822	Capital	...	...	...	...	...	...	—	...	—	...	...	...
	Table 3 Transactions in assets and liabilities												
3	**Change in net worth from transactions**	...	...	...	...	...	...	...	...	...	...	...	...
31	**Net/Gross investment in nonfinancial assets**	...	...	...	...	...	...	**5,242**	**6,943**	**4,624**	...	...	...
311	Fixed assets	...	...	...	...	...	...	4,910	...	3,974	...	...	...
3111	Buildings and structures	...	...	...	...	...	...	4,015	...	3,019	...	...	...
3112	Machinery and equipment	...	...	...	...	...	...	898	...	958	...	...	...
3113	Other fixed assets	...	...	...	...	...	...	-3	...	-4	...	...	...
3114	Weapons systems	...	...	...	...	...	...	—	...	—	...	...	...
312	Inventories	...	...	...	...	...	...	—	...	—	...	...	...
313	Valuables	...	...	...	...	...	...	—	...	—	...	...	...
314	Nonproduced assets	...	...	...	...	...	...	332	...	650	...	...	...
3141	Land	...	...	...	...	...	...	332	...	650	...	...	...
3142	Mineral and energy resources	...	...	...	...	...	...	—	...	—	...	...	...
3143	Other naturally occurring assets	...	...	...	...	...	...	—	...	—	...	...	...
3144	Intangible nonproduced assets	...	...	...	...	...	...	—	...	—	...	...	...
32	**Net acquisition of financial assets**	...	...	...	...	...	...	**-4,216**	**-476**	**-32**	...	...	...
	By instrument												
3201	Monetary gold and SDRs	...	...	...	...	...	...	—	—	—	...	...	...
3202	Currency and deposits	...	...	...	...	...	...	-4,186	-441	—	...	...	...
3203	Debt securities	...	...	...	...	...	...	—	—	—	...	...	...
3204	Loans	...	...	...	...	...	...	-30	-35	-32	...	...	...
3205	Equity and investment fund shares	...	...	...	...	...	...	—	—	—	...	...	...
3206	Insurance, pension, and standardized guarantee schemes	...	...	...	...	...	...	—	—	—	...	...	...
3207	Financial derivatives and employee stock options	...	...	...	...	...	...	—	—	—	...	...	...
3208	Other accounts receivable	...	...	...	...	...	...	—	...	...	...	...	...
	By debtor												
321	Domestic debtors	...	...	...	...	...	...	-4,216	-476	-32	...	...	...
322	External debtors	...	...	...	...	...	...	—	—	—	...	...	...
33	**Net incurrence of liabilities**	...	...	...	...	...	...	**-2,125**	**3,992**	**2,808**	...	...	...
	By instrument												
3301	Special Drawing Rights (SDRs)	...	...	...	...	...	...	—	—	—	...	...	...
3302	Currency and deposits	...	...	...	...	...	...	—	—	—	...	...	...
3303	Debt securities	...	...	...	...	...	...	—	3,447	2,808	...	...	...
3304	Loans	...	...	...	...	...	...	-2,125	545	—	...	...	...
3305	Equity and investment fund shares	...	...	...	...	...	...	—	—	—	...	...	...
3306	Insurance, pension, and standardized guarantee schemes	...	...	...	...	...	...	—	—	—	...	...	...
3307	Financial derivatives and employee stock options	...	...	...	...	...	...	—	—	—	...	...	...
3308	Other accounts payable	...	...	...	...	...	...	—	...	...	...	...	...
	By creditor												
331	Domestic creditors	...	...	...	...	...	...	-1,056	3,447	1,754	...	...	...
332	External creditors	...	...	...	...	...	...	-1,069	545	1,054	...	...	...
	Table 4 Holding gains and losses in assets and liabilities												
	Table 5 Holding gains and losses in assets and liabilities												
	Table 6 Balance sheet												

Trinidad and Tobago (369)

In Millions of Trinidad and Tobago Dollars (TTD) / Fiscal Year Ends September 30th

		Budgetary Central Government			Central Government (excl. Social Security)			Central Government (incl. Social Security)			General Government		
		2010	2011	2012	2010	2011	2012	2010	2011	2012	2010	2011	2012
	Table 7 Expenditure by functions of government												
7	**Expenditure**	...	...	...	...	...	...	**48,608**	**51,483**	**54,411**	...	...	...
701	**General public services**	...	...	...	...	...	...	**15,259**	**9,874**	**12,606**	...	...	...
7017	Public debt transactions	...	...	...	...	...	...	3,290	2,866	2,937	...	...	...
7018	Transfers of general character between levels of government	...	...	...	...	...	...	2,973	...	3,508	...	...	...
702	**Defense**	...	...	...	...	...	...	**973**	**923**	**947**	...	...	...
703	**Public order and safety**	...	...	...	...	...	...	**3,712**	**3,310**	**4,156**	...	...	...
704	**Economic affairs**	...	...	...	...	...	...	**5,687**	**5,582**	**9,489**	...	...	...
7042	Agriculture, forestry, fishing, and hunting	...	...	...	...	...	...	780	1,023	1,187	...	...	...
7043	Fuel and energy	...	...	...	...	...	...	1,572	3,022	2,292	...	...	...
7044	Mining, manufacturing, and construction	...	...	...	...	...	...	32	—	792	...	...	...
7045	Transport	...	...	...	...	...	...	2,323	1,537	2,234	...	...	...
7046	Communication	...	...	...	...	...	...	200	—	181	...	...	...
705	**Environmental protection**	...	...	...	...	...	...	**551**	...	**983**	...	...	...
706	**Housing and community amenities**	...	...	...	...	...	...	**3,669**	**2,427**	**4,169**	...	...	...
707	**Health**	...	...	...	...	...	...	**3,750**	**3,576**	**3,906**	...	...	...
7072	Outpatient services	...	...	...	...	...	...	—	...	—	...	...	...
7073	Hospital services	...	...	...	...	...	...	2,751	...	2,837	...	...	...
7074	Public health services	...	...	...	...	...	...	62	...	79	...	...	...
708	**Recreation, culture and religion**	...	...	...	...	...	...	**806**	**693**	**1,057**	...	...	...
709	**Education**	...	...	...	...	...	...	**7,150**	**6,277**	**8,285**	...	...	...
7091	Pre-primary and primary education	...	...	...	...	...	...	1,195	1,005	1,327	...	...	...
7092	Secondary education	...	...	...	...	...	...	1,456	1,218	1,478	...	...	...
7094	Tertiary education	...	...	...	...	...	...	2,021	2,229	3,250	...	...	...
710	**Social protection**	...	...	...	...	...	...	**7,057**	**8,472**	**9,849**	...	...	...
7z	Statistical discrepancy: Expenditure	...	...	...	...	...	...	...	...	...	...	...	...
	Table 8 Financial transactions by counterpart sector												
	Table 9 Total other economic flows in assets and liabilities												

Tunisia (744)

In Millions of Tunisian Dinars (TND) / Fiscal Year Ends December 31st

		Budgetary Central Government			Central Government (excl. Social Security)			Central Government (incl. Social Security)			General Government		
		2010	2011	2012	2010	2011	2012	2010	2011	2012	2010	2011	2012
	Statement of operations												
1	Revenue	14,401	16,051	16,940	...	...	...	18,356	21,318	22,710	18,752	21,589	23,072
2	Expense	13,223	17,182	19,345	...	...	...	17,685	22,292	24,950	17,345	21,738	24,389
GOB	**Gross operating balance**	**1,178**	**-1,131**	**-2,405**	**...**	**...**	**...**	**671**	**-974**	**-2,240**	**1,407**	**-149**	**-1,318**
NOB	**Net operating balance**	...	...	...	...	...	...	...	...	...	...	...	...
31	Net/Gross investment in nonfinancial assets	1,404	1,225	1,042	...	...	...	1,537	1,508	1,320	2,147	2,083	1,896
2M	Expenditure	14,627	18,406	20,387	...	...	...	19,222	23,799	26,271	19,491	23,821	26,285
NLB	**Net lending (+) / Net borrowing (-)**	**-225**	**-2,356**	**-3,448**	**...**	**...**	**...**	**-866**	**-2,481**	**-3,561**	**-739**	**-2,232**	**-3,213**
32	Net acquisition of financial assets	-84	-1,041	-1,535	...	...	...	-725	-1,167	-1,648	-603	-952	-1,345
33	Net incurrence of liabilities	141	1,314	1,913	...	...	...	141	1,314	1,913	137	1,281	1,869
NLBz	Statistical discrepancy	0	—	—	...	...	...	0	—	—	-0	—	—
	Memorandum items												
PB	Primary net lending / net borrowing	927	-1,166	-2,176	...	...	...	286	-1,291	-2,289	439	-1,011	-1,911
GB	Government balance per national definition	...	...	...	...	...	...	...	...	...	...	...	...
	Statement of other economic flows												
	Balance sheet												
	Table 1 Revenue												
1	**Revenue**	**14,401**	**16,051**	**16,940**	**...**	**...**	**...**	**18,356**	**21,318**	**22,710**	**18,752**	**21,589**	**23,072**
11	**Taxes**	**12,699**	**13,668**	**14,864**	**...**	**...**	**...**	**12,699**	**13,668**	**14,864**	**13,016**	**13,882**	**15,162**
111	Taxes on income, profits, and capital gains	5,033	5,936	6,062	...	...	...	5,033	5,936	6,062	5,033	5,936	6,062
1111	Payable by individuals	2,599	2,890	3,188	...	...	...	2,599	2,890	3,188	2,599	2,890	3,188
1112	Payable by corporations and other enterprises	2,433	3,046	2,873	...	...	...	2,433	3,046	2,873	2,433	3,046	2,873
1113	Other taxes on income, profits, and capital gains	—	—	—	...	...	...	—	—	—	—	—	—
112	Taxes on payroll and workforce	199	212	224	...	...	...	199	212	224	199	212	224
113	Taxes on property	10	5	8	...	...	...	10	5	8	65	37	52
114	Taxes on goods and services	6,019	6,123	6,928	...	...	...	6,019	6,123	6,928	6,254	6,289	7,161
1141	General taxes on goods and services	4,301	4,403	4,989	...	...	...	4,301	4,403	4,989	4,439	4,511	5,147
1142	Excises	1,270	1,281	1,431	...	...	...	1,270	1,281	1,431	1,302	1,303	1,461
115	Taxes on international trade and transactions	1,143	1,077	1,334	...	...	...	1,143	1,077	1,334	1,143	1,077	1,334
116	Other taxes	296	315	309	...	...	...	296	315	309	323	331	330
12	**Social contributions**	—	—	—	**...**	**...**	**...**	**3,881**	**5,210**	**5,782**	**3,881**	**5,210**	**5,782**
121	Social security contributions	—	—	—	...	...	...	3,881	5,210	5,782	3,881	5,210	5,782
122	Other social contributions	—	—	—	...	...	...	—	—	—	—	—	—
13	**Grants**	**54**	**208**	**742**	**...**	**...**	**...**	**54**	**207**	**633**	**54**	**207**	**633**
131	From foreign governments	54	207	633	...	...	...	54	207	633	54	207	633
132	From international organizations	—	—	—	...	...	...	—	—	—	—	—	—
133	From other general government units	—	1	109	...	...	...	—	—	—	—	—	—
1331	Current	—	1	109	...	...	...	—	—	—	—	—	—
1332	Capital	—	—	—	...	...	...	—	—	—	—	—	—
14	**Other revenue**	**1,649**	**2,175**	**1,334**	**...**	**...**	**...**	**1,722**	**2,233**	**1,431**	**1,801**	**2,290**	**1,494**
	Table 2 Expense by economic type												
2	**Expense**	**13,223**	**17,182**	**19,345**	**...**	**...**	**...**	**17,685**	**22,292**	**24,950**	**17,345**	**21,738**	**24,389**
21	**Compensation of employees**	**6,007**	**7,648**	**8,617**	**...**	**...**	**...**	**6,127**	**7,768**	**8,746**	**6,376**	**8,062**	**9,080**
211	Wages and salaries	6,007	6,794	7,551	...	...	...	6,127	6,913	7,680	6,356	7,184	7,987
212	Employers' social contributions	—	854	1,065	...	...	...	—	854	1,065	20	878	1,092
22	**Use of goods and services**	**1,059**	**1,081**	**1,061**	**...**	**...**	**...**	**1,095**	**1,117**	**1,088**	**1,257**	**1,269**	**1,252**
23	**Consumption of fixed capital**	...	...	...	...	...	...	...	...	...	...	...	...
24	**Interest**	**1,152**	**1,190**	**1,272**	**...**	**...**	**...**	**1,152**	**1,190**	**1,272**	**1,179**	**1,221**	**1,302**
25	**Subsidies**	**2,126**	**3,846**	**4,917**	**...**	**...**	**...**	**2,126**	**3,846**	**4,917**	**2,153**	**3,878**	**4,957**
26	**Grants**	**805**	**1,092**	**1,160**	**...**	**...**	**...**	**805**	**1,063**	**1,129**	—	—	—
261	To foreign governments	—	—	—	...	...	...	—	—	—	—	—	—
262	To international organizations	—	—	—	...	...	...	—	—	—	—	—	—
263	To other general government units	805	1,092	1,160	...	...	...	805	1,063	1,129	—	—	—
2631	Current	154	369	364	...	...	...	154	341	332	—	—	—
2632	Capital	651	722	797	...	...	...	651	722	797	—	—	—

Tunisia (744)

In Millions of Tunisian Dinars (TND) / Fiscal Year Ends December 31st

		Budgetary Central Government			Central Government (excl. Social Security)			Central Government (incl. Social Security)			General Government		
		2010	2011	2012	2010	2011	2012	2010	2011	2012	2010	2011	2012
27	**Social benefits**	—	—	—	...	...	...	**4,306**	**4,983**	**5,481**	**4,306**	**4,983**	**5,481**
271	Social security benefits	—	—	—	...	...	...	4,306	4,983	5,481	4,306	4,983	5,481
272	Social assistance benefits	—	—	—	...	...	...	—	—	—	—	—	—
273	Employment-related social benefits	—	—	—	...	...	...	—	—	—	—	—	—
28	**Other expense**	**2,074**	**2,325**	**2,318**	...	...	...	**2,074**	**2,325**	**2,318**	**2,074**	**2,325**	**2,318**
281	Property expense other than interest	—	—	—	...	...	...	—	—	—	—	—	—
282	Transfers not elsewhere classified	2,074	2,325	2,318	...	...	...	2,074	2,325	2,318	2,074	2,325	2,318
2821	Current	—	—	—	...	...	...	—	—	—	—	—	—
2822	Capital	2,074	2,325	2,318	...	...	...	2,074	2,325	2,318	2,074	2,325	2,318
	Table 3 Transactions in assets and liabilities												
3	**Change in net worth from transactions**	...	...	...	...	...	...	...	...	...	...	...	...
31	**Net/Gross investment in nonfinancial assets**	**1,404**	**1,225**	**1,042**	...	...	...	**1,537**	**1,508**	**1,320**	**2,147**	**2,083**	**1,896**
311	Fixed assets	1,404	1,225	1,042	...	...	...	1,537	1,508	1,320	2,147	2,083	1,896
3111	Buildings and structures	...	...	...	...	...	...	...	...	...	...	...	...
3112	Machinery and equipment	...	...	...	...	...	...	...	...	...	...	...	...
3113	Other fixed assets	...	...	...	...	...	...	...	...	...	...	...	...
3114	Weapons systems	...	...	...	...	...	...	...	...	...	...	...	...
312	Inventories	—	—	—	...	...	...	—	—	—	—	—	—
313	Valuables	—	—	—	...	...	...	—	—	—	—	—	—
314	Nonproduced assets	—	—	—	...	...	...	—	—	—	—	—	—
3141	Land	—	—	—	...	...	...	—	—	—	—	—	—
3142	Mineral and energy resources	—	—	—	...	...	...	—	—	—	—	—	—
3143	Other naturally occurring assets	—	—	—	...	...	...	—	—	—	—	—	—
3144	Intangible nonproduced assets	—	—	—	...	...	...	—	—	—	—	—	—
32	**Net acquisition of financial assets**	**-84**	**-1,041**	**-1,535**	...	...	...	**-725**	**-1,167**	**-1,648**	**-603**	**-952**	**-1,345**
	By instrument												
3201	Monetary gold and SDRs	—	—	—	...	...	...	—	—	—	—	—	—
3202	Currency and deposits	209	-399	10	...	...	...	-520	-586	-186	-398	-371	117
3203	Debt securities	—	—	—	...	...	...	—	—	—	—	—	—
3204	Loans	-293	-259	-439	...	...	...	-205	-198	-357	-205	-198	-357
3205	Equity and investment fund shares	—	-383	-1,105	...	...	...	—	-383	-1,105	—	-383	-1,105
3206	Insurance, pension, and standardized guarantee schemes	—	—	—	...	...	...	—	—	—	—	—	—
3207	Financial derivatives and employee stock options	—	—	—	...	...	...	—	—	—	—	—	—
3208	Other accounts receivable	...	...	...	...	...	...	...	...	...	...	...	...
	By debtor												
321	Domestic debtors	-84	-1,041	-1,535	...	...	...	-725	-1,167	-1,648	-603	-952	-1,345
322	External debtors	—	—	—	...	...	...	—	—	—	—	—	—
33	**Net incurrence of liabilities**	**141**	**1,314**	**1,913**	...	...	...	**141**	**1,314**	**1,913**	**137**	**1,281**	**1,869**
	By instrument												
3301	Special Drawing Rights (SDRs)	—	—	—	...	...	...	—	—	—	—	—	—
3302	Currency and deposits	746	—	—	...	...	...	746	—	—	746	—	—
3303	Debt securities	-18	-250	1,127	...	...	...	-18	-250	1,127	-21	-281	1,086
3304	Loans	-588	1,565	786	...	...	...	-588	1,565	786	-589	1,562	782
3305	Equity and investment fund shares	—	—	—	...	...	...	—	—	—	—	—	—
3306	Insurance, pension, and standardized guarantee schemes	—	—	—	...	...	...	—	—	—	—	—	—
3307	Financial derivatives and employee stock options	—	—	—	...	...	...	—	—	—	—	—	—
3308	Other accounts payable	...	...	...	...	...	...	...	...	...	...	...	...
	By creditor												
331	Domestic creditors	371	914	593	...	...	...	371	914	593	368	883	552
332	External creditors	-230	400	1,320	...	...	...	-230	400	1,320	-231	397	1,317
	Table 4 Holding gains and losses in assets and liabilities												
	Table 5 Holding gains and losses in assets and liabilities												
	Table 6 Balance sheet												

Tunisia (744)

In Millions of Tunisian Dinars (TND) / Fiscal Year Ends December 31st

		Budgetary Central Government			Central Government (excl. Social Security)			Central Government (incl. Social Security)			General Government		
		2010	2011	2012	2010	2011	2012	2010	2011	2012	2010	2011	2012
	Table 7 Expenditure by functions of government												
7	**Expenditure**	**14,627**	**18,406**	**20,387**	...	...	...	**19,222**	**23,799**	**26,271**	**19,491**	**23,821**	**26,285**
701	**General public services**	**2,407**	**3,009**	**2,844**	...	...	...	**2,407**	**3,009**	**2,844**	...	...	**2,858**
7017	Public debt transactions	1,152	1,190	1,272	...	...	...	1,152	1,190	1,272	1,179	1,221	1,302
7018	Transfers of general character between levels of government	...	...	...	...	...	...	...	...	...	...	...	...
702	**Defense**	**818**	**1,007**	**1,064**	...	...	...	**818**	**1,007**	**1,064**	...	...	...
703	**Public order and safety**	**1,295**	**1,620**	**2,001**	...	...	...	**1,295**	**1,620**	**2,001**	...	...	...
704	**Economic affairs**	**3,468**	**5,100**	**5,919**	...	...	...	**3,468**	**5,100**	**5,919**	...	...	...
7042	Agriculture, forestry, fishing, and hunting	802	945	1,093	...	...	...	802	945	1,093	...	...	...
7043	Fuel and energy	...	...	...	...	...	...	...	...	...	...	...	...
7044	Mining, manufacturing, and construction	907	1,923	1,622	...	...	...	907	1,923	1,622	...	...	...
7045	Transport	659	735	551	...	...	...	659	735	551	...	...	...
7046	Communication	...	32	88	...	...	...	...	32	88	...	...	...
705	**Environmental protection**	**235**	**222**	**219**	...	...	...	**235**	**222**	**219**	...	...	...
706	**Housing and community amenities**	**1,118**	**916**	**843**	...	...	...	**1,118**	**916**	**843**	...	...	...
707	**Health**	**905**	**978**	**1,172**	...	...	...	**905**	**978**	**1,172**	...	...	...
7072	Outpatient services	...	...	...	...	...	...	...	...	...	...	...	...
7073	Hospital services	...	...	...	...	...	...	...	...	...	...	...	...
7074	Public health services	...	...	...	...	...	...	...	...	...	...	...	...
708	**Recreation, culture and religion**	**487**	**511**	**633**	...	...	...	**487**	**511**	**633**	...	...	...
709	**Education**	**3,556**	**3,767**	**4,013**	...	...	...	**3,556**	**3,767**	**4,013**	...	...	...
7091	Pre-primary and primary education	—	—	—	...	...	...	—	—	—	...	...	...
7092	Secondary education	2,580	2,758	2,942	...	...	...	2,580	2,758	2,942	...	...	...
7094	Tertiary education	976	1,010	1,071	...	...	...	976	1,010	1,071	...	...	...
710	**Social protection**	**338**	**1,276**	**1,679**	...	...	...	**4,933**	**6,669**	**7,563**	...	...	...
7z	Statistical discrepancy: Expenditure	—	—	...	...	...	...	—	—	...	...	...	...
	Table 8 Financial transactions by counterpart sector												
	Table 9 Total other economic flows in assets and liabilities												

Turkey (186)

In Billions of Turkish Liras (TRY) / Fiscal Year Ends December 31st

		Budgetary Central Government			Central Government (excl. Social Security)			Central Government (incl. Social Security)			General Government		
		2013	2014	2015	2013	2014	2015	2013	2014	2015	2013	2014	2015
	Statement of operations												
1	Revenue	394	431	492	404	451	540	568	638	760	595	663	792
2	Expense	385	425	467	396	446	507	543	611	707	552	628	718
GOB	**Gross operating balance**	**14**	**21**	**39**	**14**	**21**	**47**	**31**	**42**	**68**	**51**	**55**	**93**
NOB	**Net operating balance**	**9**	**6**	**26**	**8**	**5**	**33**	**26**	**26**	**53**	**43**	**35**	**74**
31	Net/Gross investment in nonfinancial assets	22	18	21	21	18	27	21	18	27	39	28	41
2M	Expenditure	407	443	488	417	464	534	564	629	733	591	656	759
NLB	**Net lending (+) / Net borrowing (-)**	**-12**	**-12**	**5**	**-13**	**-12**	**6**	**4**	**9**	**26**	**4**	**7**	**33**
32	Net acquisition of financial assets	13	13	37	...	14	42	23	24	50	31	31	64
33	Net incurrence of liabilities	26	25	33	...	27	37	20	16	25	28	24	32
NLBz	Statistical discrepancy	-0	-0	-1	...	-1	-1	-2	-1	-1	-1	-1	-1
	Memorandum items												
PB	Primary net lending / net borrowing	36	40	57	35	39	59	47	53	71	48	54	80
GB	Government balance per national definition	...	...	...	...	...	...	...	...	...	...	...	...
	Statement of other economic flows												
9	**Change in net worth due to other economic flows**	**26**	**488**	**30**	**42**	**490**	**32**	**54**	**473**	**27**	**65**	**470**	**36**
4	Change in net worth due to holding gains and losses	**24**	**-31**	**7**	**40**	**-28**	**12**	**35**	**-25**	**6**	**34**	**-21**	**6**
41	Nonfinancial assets	—	—	—	—	—	—	-0	-0	—	0	-0	—
42	Financial assets	6	14	15	23	16	19	23	17	14	23	20	15
43	Liabilities	-17	45	8	-17	45	8	-12	41	8	-11	40	9
5	Change in net worth due to volume changes	**3**	**519**	**22**	**2**	**518**	**21**	**19**	**497**	**20**	**31**	**491**	**30**
51	Nonfinancial assets	18	541	40	19	541	40	19	541	40	28	536	51
52	Financial assets	-15	-22	-18	-17	-23	-20	-28	-44	-20	-28	-48	-22
53	Liabilities	—	—	0	-0	—	0	-28	—	0	-31	-3	-0
	Balance sheet												
6	**Net worth**	**-266**	**256**	**311**	**...**	**316**	**390**	**-84**	**445**	**534**	**117**	**654**	**773**
61	Nonfinancial assets	176	735	796	181	740	807	185	744	811	384	948	1,040
62	Financial assets	204	235	269	...	287	340	326	347	404	364	390	466
63	Liabilities	646	714	754	...	633	756	596	645	680	631	684	733
	Table 1 Revenue												
1	**Revenue**	**394**	**431**	**492**	**404**	**451**	**540**	**568**	**638**	**760**	**595**	**663**	**792**
11	**Taxes**	**334**	**368**	**423**	**335**	**369**	**427**	**335**	**369**	**426**	**344**	**380**	**438**
111	Taxes on income, profits, and capital gains	93	111	121	93	111	121	93	111	121	93	111	121
1111	Payable by individuals	65	76	88	65	76	88	65	76	87	65	76	87
1112	Payable by corporations and other enterprises	27	35	33	27	35	33	27	35	33	27	35	33
1113	Other taxes on income, profits, and capital gains	—	—	—	—	—	—	—	—	—	—	—	—
112	Taxes on payroll and workforce	—	—	...	—	—	—	—	—	—	—	—	—
113	Taxes on property	0	0	0	0	0	0	0	0	0	5	7	7
114	Taxes on goods and services	230	240	280	230	240	284	230	240	284	233	244	288
1141	General taxes on goods and services	111	105	123	111	105	123	111	105	123	111	105	123
1142	Excises	86	91	107	86	91	107	86	91	107	87	92	109
115	Taxes on international trade and transactions	7	7	9	7	7	9	7	7	9	7	7	9
116	Other taxes	4	10	12	5	11	13	5	11	13	7	11	13
12	**Social contributions**	**4**	**4**	**4**	**4**	**4**	**4**	**159**	**184**	**218**	**160**	**185**	**220**
121	Social security contributions	—	—	—	—	—	—	155	180	214	155	180	214
122	Other social contributions	4	4	4	4	4	4	4	4	5	5	6	6
13	**Grants**	**8**	**8**	**9**	**2**	**4**	**1**	**2**	**4**	**1**	**0**	**0**	**0**
131	From foreign governments	—	—	—	—	—	—	—	—	—	—	—	—
132	From international organizations	0	0	0	0	0	0	0	0	0	0	0	0
133	From other general government units	8	8	9	2	4	1	2	4	1	—	—	—
1331	Current	6	7	8	0	3	0	0	3	0	—	—	—
1332	Capital	2	1	1	2	1	1	2	1	1	—	—	—
14	**Other revenue**	**48**	**51**	**56**	**63**	**74**	**107**	**72**	**80**	**113**	**90**	**97**	**134**

Turkey (186)

In Billions of Turkish Liras (TRY) / Fiscal Year Ends December 31st

		Budgetary Central Government			Central Government (excl. Social Security)			Central Government (incl. Social Security)			General Government		
		2013	2014	2015	2013	2014	2015	2013	2014	2015	2013	2014	2015
	Table 2 Expense by economic type												
2	**Expense**	**385**	**425**	**467**	**396**	**446**	**507**	**543**	**611**	**707**	**552**	**628**	**718**
21	**Compensation of employees**	**111**	**129**	**146**	**126**	**147**	**165**	**128**	**148**	**167**	**141**	**164**	**183**
211	Wages and salaries	91	106	121	106	124	140	107	125	141	118	137	153
212	Employers' social contributions	20	23	26	20	23	26	21	23	26	24	27	30
22	**Use of goods and services**	**44**	**49**	**52**	**67**	**77**	**78**	**69**	**79**	**82**	**97**	**109**	**117**
23	**Consumption of fixed capital**	**5**	**15**	**14**	**6**	**16**	**14**	**6**	**16**	**15**	**9**	**20**	**19**
24	**Interest**	**48**	**52**	**52**	**48**	**52**	**52**	**43**	**45**	**45**	**44**	**47**	**48**
25	**Subsidies**	**18**	**23**	**26**	**18**	**23**	**26**	**18**	**23**	**26**	**18**	**23**	**26**
26	**Grants**	**75**	**77**	**81**	**41**	**45**	**68**	**46**	**47**	**56**	**2**	**2**	**3**
261	To foreign governments	1	1	1	1	1	1	1	1	1	1	1	1
262	To international organizations	1	1	1	1	1	2	1	1	2	1	1	2
263	To other general government units	73	75	79	40	43	66	44	45	53	—	—	0
2631	Current	65	71	70	31	39	61	36	40	48	—	—	—
2632	Capital	8	4	8	8	4	5	8	4	5	—	—	0
27	**Social benefits**	**68**	**63**	**76**	**70**	**63**	**77**	**213**	**228**	**291**	**216**	**231**	**293**
271	Social security benefits	—	—	0	—	—	0	143	165	214	143	165	214
272	Social assistance benefits	64	48	59	66	48	59	66	48	59	67	49	60
273	Employment-related social benefits	4	15	18	4	15	18	4	15	18	5	17	19
28	**Other expense**	**16**	**17**	**19**	**21**	**24**	**26**	**21**	**25**	**26**	**25**	**32**	**31**
281	Property expense other than interest	—	—	—	—	—	—	—	—	—	—	—	—
282	Transfers not elsewhere classified	16	17	19	21	24	26	21	25	26	25	32	31
2821	Current	10	11	13	14	17	20	15	19	21	17	24	24
2822	Capital	6	6	5	6	6	5	6	6	5	7	8	7
	Table 3 Transactions in assets and liabilities												
3	**Change in net worth from transactions**	**9**	**6**	**25**	**...**	**4**	**32**	**24**	**25**	**52**	**42**	**34**	**73**
31	**Net/Gross investment in nonfinancial assets**	**22**	**18**	**21**	**21**	**18**	**27**	**21**	**18**	**27**	**39**	**28**	**41**
311	Fixed assets	26	18	30	26	18	35	26	17	35	42	28	50
3111	Buildings and structures	26	19	26	27	19	27	26	18	27	43	29	40
3112	Machinery and equipment	-1	-1	3	-1	-1	9	-1	-1	9	-1	-1	10
3113	Other fixed assets	—	0	0	-0	-0	0	-0	-0	0	-0	-0	0
3114	Weapons systems	...	...	...	...	...	...	...	...	...	...	...	...
312	Inventories	-1	0	0	-1	0	0	-1	0	0	-1	-0	1
313	Valuables	—	0	-0	-0	0	-0	-0	0	-0	-0	-0	-0
314	Nonproduced assets	-3	-0	-9	-3	-0	-9	-3	0	-9	-2	1	-9
3141	Land	-3	-0	2	-4	-0	2	-4	0	2	-3	1	1
3142	Mineral and energy resources	—	—	—	—	—	—	—	—	—	—	—	—
3143	Other naturally occurring assets	—	—	—	—	—	—	—	—	—	—	—	—
3144	Intangible nonproduced assets	0	—	-11	0	—	-11	0	—	-11	0	-0	-11
32	**Net acquisition of financial assets**	**13**	**13**	**37**	**...**	**14**	**42**	**23**	**24**	**50**	**31**	**31**	**64**
	By instrument												
3201	Monetary gold and SDRs	—	—	—	—	—	—	—	—	—	—	—	—
3202	Currency and deposits	9	0	5	4	-2	15	8	-1	15	11	-2	22
3203	Debt securities	0	0	-0	0	-0	0	0	-0	0	0	-0	-0
3204	Loans	-3	2	6	...	2	5	-1	2	5	0	1	5
3205	Equity and investment fund shares	-3	0	12	-13	4	13	-13	4	13	-11	6	14
3206	Insurance, pension, and standardized guarantee schemes	—	—	—	—	—	—	—	—	—	—	—	—
3207	Financial derivatives and employee stock options	—	—	—	—	—	—	—	—	—	—	—	—
3208	Other accounts receivable	11	11	14	...	9	10	28	19	18	31	26	23
	By debtor												
321	Domestic debtors	10	15	41	...	20	40	20	31	48	29	37	60
322	External debtors	3	-2	-4	2	-7	2	2	-7	2	2	-7	3
33	**Net incurrence of liabilities**	**26**	**25**	**33**	**...**	**27**	**37**	**20**	**16**	**25**	**28**	**24**	**32**
	By instrument												
3301	Special Drawing Rights (SDRs)	—	—	—	—	—	—	—	—	—	—	—	—
3302	Currency and deposits	0	0	0	0	0	0	0	0	0	0	0	0
3303	Debt securities	24	25	27	25	25	27	20	13	14	20	13	14
3304	Loans	-1	-1	-2	...	-0	-2	-1	-0	-2	5	5	0

Turkey (186)

In Billions of Turkish Liras (TRY) / Fiscal Year Ends December 31st

		Budgetary Central Government			Central Government (excl. Social Security)			Central Government (incl. Social Security)			General Government		
		2013	2014	2015	2013	2014	2015	2013	2014	2015	2013	2014	2015
3305	Equity and investment fund shares	—	—	—	0	—	—	—	—	—	—	—	—
3306	Insurance, pension, and standardized guarantee schemes	—	—	0	—	—	0	—	—	0	—	—	1
3307	Financial derivatives and employee stock options	—	—	—	—	—	—	—	—	—	—	—	—
3308	Other accounts payable	3	1	8	...	2	12	0	4	12	3	6	16
	By creditor												
331	Domestic creditors	18	17	35	...	19	39	12	8	27	19	16	34
332	External creditors	8	8	-2	8	8	-2	8	8	-2	9	8	-2
	Table 4 Holding gains and losses in assets and liabilities												
4	**Change in net worth due to holding gains and losses**	**24**	**-31**	**7**	**40**	**-28**	**12**	**35**	**-25**	**6**	**34**	**-21**	**6**
41	**Holding gains and losses in nonfinancial assets**	**—**	**—**	**—**	**—**	**—**	**—**	**-0**	**-0**	**—**	**0**	**-0**	**—**
411	Fixed assets	—	—	—	—	—	—	-0	—	—	0	—	—
412	Inventories	—	—	—	—	—	—	—	—	—	0	—	—
413	Valuables	—	—	—	—	—	—	—	—	—	—	—	—
414	Nonproduced assets	—	—	—	—	—	—	—	-0	—	-0	-0	—
42	**Holding gains and losses in financial assets**	**6**	**14**	**15**	**23**	**16**	**19**	**23**	**17**	**14**	**23**	**20**	**15**
	By instrument												
4201	Monetary gold and SDRs	—	—	—	—	—	—	—	—	—	—	—	—
4202	Currency and deposits	1	0	2	4	1	2	4	1	2	3	1	2
4203	Debt securities	—	—	—	—	—	—	—	—	-5	0	—	-5
4204	Loans	3	1	4	3	1	4	3	1	4	4	4	4
4205	Equity and investment fund shares	2	12	9	16	14	10	16	14	10	16	14	10
4206	Insurance, pension, and standardized guarantee schemes	—	—	—	—	—	—	—	—	—	—	—	—
4207	Financial derivatives and employee stock options	—	—	—	—	—	—	—	—	—	—	—	—
4208	Other accounts receivable	—	-0	-0	-0	-0	3	-0	-0	3	-0	-0	4
	By debtor												
421	Domestic debtors	3	12	11	17	14	15	17	14	9	17	17	11
422	External debtors	3	1	4	5	2	5	6	3	5	5	3	4
43	**Holding gains and losses in liabilities**	**-17**	**45**	**8**	**-17**	**45**	**8**	**-12**	**41**	**8**	**-11**	**40**	**9**
	By instrument												
4301	Special Drawing Rights (SDRs)	—	—	—	—	—	—	—	—	—	—	—	—
4302	Currency and deposits	—	—	—	—	—	—	—	—	—	—	—	—
4303	Debt securities	-28	45	-3	-28	45	-3	-23	41	-3	-23	41	-3
4304	Loans	10	-1	11	10	-1	11	10	-1	11	11	-1	12
4305	Equity and investment fund shares	—	—	—	—	—	—	—	—	—	—	—	—
4306	Insurance, pension, and standardized guarantee schemes	—	—	0	—	—	0	—	—	0	—	—	0
4307	Financial derivatives and employee stock options	—	—	—	—	—	—	—	—	—	—	—	—
4308	Other accounts payable	—	0	0	-0	0	0	0	0	0	0	0	0
	By creditor												
431	Domestic creditors	-31	24	-29	-31	24	-29	-26	20	-29	-24	20	-29
432	External creditors	13	21	36	13	21	36	13	21	36	13	21	37
	Table 5 Holding gains and losses in assets and liabilities												
5	**Change in net worth due to other volume changes**	**3**	**519**	**22**	**2**	**518**	**21**	**19**	**497**	**20**	**31**	**491**	**30**
51	**Other volume changes in nonfinancial assets**	**18**	**541**	**40**	**19**	**541**	**40**	**19**	**541**	**40**	**28**	**536**	**51**
511	Fixed assets	1	113	11	2	113	11	2	113	11	6	96	20
512	Inventories	1	-0	0	1	-0	0	1	-0	0	1	0	-0
513	Valuables	-0	0	0	-0	0	0	-0	0	0	-0	0	0
514	Nonproduced assets	15	429	29	16	429	29	16	429	29	21	440	32
52	**Other volume changes in financial assets**	**-15**	**-22**	**-18**	**-17**	**-23**	**-20**	**-28**	**-44**	**-20**	**-28**	**-48**	**-22**

Turkey (186)

In Billions of Turkish Liras (TRY) / Fiscal Year Ends December 31st

		Budgetary Central Government			Central Government (excl. Social Security)			Central Government (incl. Social Security)			General Government		
		2013	2014	2015	2013	2014	2015	2013	2014	2015	2013	2014	2015
	By instrument												
5201	Monetary gold and SDRs	—	—	—	—	—	—	—	—	—	—	—	—
5202	Currency and deposits	—	—	1	—	—	1	—	—	1	—	-2	-0
5203	Debt securities	—	—	—	—	—	—	—	—	—	—	-0	-0
5204	Loans	-1	-1	-3	-1	-1	-4	-1	-1	-4	-1	-1	-4
5205	Equity and investment fund shares	2	—	—	2	—	—	2	—	—	2	-0	—
5206	Insurance, pension, and standardized guarantee schemes	—	—	—	—	—	—	—	—	—	—	—	—
5207	Financial derivatives and employee stock options	—	—	—	—	—	—	—	—	—	—	—	—
5208	Other accounts receivable	-16	-21	-16	-18	-22	-17	-28	-43	-17	-29	-44	-18
	By debtor												
521	Domestic debtors	-15	-22	-18	-17	-23	-20	-28	-44	-20	-28	-48	-22
522	External debtors	—	—	—	—	—	—	—	—	—	—	-0	—
53	**Other volume changes in liabilities**	**—**	**—**	**0**	**-0**	**—**	**0**	**-28**	**—**	**0**	**-31**	**-3**	**-0**
	By instrument												
5301	Special Drawing Rights (SDRs)	—	—	—	—	—	—	—	—	—	—	—	—
5302	Currency and deposits	—	—	—	—	—	—	—	—	—	—	—	—
5303	Debt securities	—	—	—	—	—	—	—	—	—	—	—	—
5304	Loans	—	—	—	—	—	—	—	—	—	-3	-2	-0
5305	Equity and investment fund shares	—	—	—	—	—	—	—	—	—	—	—	—
5306	Insurance, pension, and standardized guarantee schemes	—	—	0	—	—	0	—	—	0	—	—	-0
5307	Financial derivatives and employee stock options	—	—	—	—	—	—	—	—	—	—	—	—
5308	Other accounts payable	—	—	0	-0	—	0	-28	—	0	-28	-1	-0
	By creditor												
531	Domestic creditors	—	—	0	-0	—	0	-28	—	0	-31	-3	-0
532	External creditors	—	—	—	—	—	—	—	—	—	-0	-0	—
	Table 6 Balance sheet												
6	**Net worth**	**-266**	**256**	**311**	**...**	**316**	**390**	**-84**	**445**	**534**	**117**	**654**	**773**
61	**Nonfinancial assets**	**176**	**735**	**796**	**181**	**740**	**807**	**185**	**744**	**811**	**384**	**948**	**1,040**
611	Fixed assets	147	279	320	150	281	328	153	284	331	276	401	471
6111	Buildings and structures	125	255	292	126	256	293	129	258	296	246	371	430
6112	Machinery and equipment	22	24	27	23	25	34	23	26	34	30	30	41
6113	Other fixed assets	0	0	0	0	0	0	0	0	0	0	0	0
6114	Weapons systems	...	...	...	...	...	...	...	...	...	...	...	...
612	Inventories	4	4	4	5	5	6	5	5	6	8	7	8
613	Valuables	0	0	0	0	0	0	0	0	0	0	0	0
614	Nonproduced assets	25	452	473	26	453	473	27	454	474	100	539	561
6141	Land	24	452	473	24	453	473	25	454	474	99	539	561
6142	Mineral and energy resources	—	—	—	—	—	—	—	—	—	—	—	—
6143	Other naturally occurring assets	—	—	—	—	—	—	—	—	—	—	—	—
6144	Intangible nonproduced assets	1	0	0	2	0	0	2	0	0	2	0	0
62	**Financial assets**	**204**	**235**	**269**	**...**	**287**	**340**	**326**	**347**	**404**	**364**	**390**	**466**
	By instrument												
6201	Monetary gold and SDRs	—	—	—	—	—	—	—	—	—	—	—	—
6202	Currency and deposits	33	34	33	42	41	51	54	55	65	70	68	84
6203	Debt securities	0	0	0	0	0	0	0	0	0	0	0	0
6204	Loans	38	48	58	...	50	59	40	50	59	33	45	55
6205	Equity and investment fund shares	72	85	112	94	106	135	88	106	135	98	118	149
6206	Insurance, pension, and standardized guarantee schemes	—	—	—	—	—	—	—	—	—	—	—	—
6207	Financial derivatives and employee stock options	—	—	—	—	—	—	—	—	—	—	—	—
6208	Other accounts receivable	60	68	65	...	90	95	144	135	144	163	160	178
	By debtor												
621	Domestic debtors	178	210	244	...	262	308	296	322	372	334	365	433
622	External debtors	26	25	25	29	25	32	30	25	32	30	26	33
63	**Liabilities**	**646**	**714**	**754**	**...**	**633**	**756**	**596**	**645**	**680**	**631**	**684**	**733**

Turkey (186)

In Billions of Turkish Liras (TRY) / Fiscal Year Ends December 31st

		Budgetary Central Government			Central Government (excl. Social Security)			Central Government (incl. Social Security)			General Government		
		2013	2014	2015	2013	2014	2015	2013	2014	2015	2013	2014	2015
	By instrument												
6301	Special Drawing Rights (SDRs)	—	—	—	—	—	—	—	—	—	—	—	—
6302	Currency and deposits	3	2	2	3	2	2	3	2	2	3	2	2
6303	Debt securities	548	618	642	548	539	642	485	539	556	485	539	556
6304	Loans	65	63	71	...	64	71	65	64	71	85	86	99
6305	Equity and investment fund shares	—	—	—	6	—	—	—	—	—	—	—	—
6306	Insurance, pension, and standardized guarantee schemes	—	—	0	—	—	0	—	—	0	—	—	2
6307	Financial derivatives and employee stock options	—	—	—	—	—	—	—	—	—	—	—	—
6308	Other accounts payable	31	31	39	...	28	41	42	41	50	58	57	73
	By creditor												
631	Domestic creditors	456	494	500	...	413	502	405	426	426	434	458	472
632	External creditors	191	220	254	191	220	254	191	220	254	197	226	261
	Memorandum items												
6M2	Net financial worth	-442	-479	-485	...	-424	-416	-270	-299	-277	-267	-294	-267
6M3	Gross debt (D4) at market value	...	...	754	...	...	756	...	...	680	...	...	733
6M3D3	D3 debt liabilities at market value	...	...	754	...	...	756	...	...	680	...	...	731
6M3D2	D2 debt liabilities at market value	...	...	715	...	...	715	...	...	630	...	...	657
6M3D1	D1 debt liabilities at market value	...	...	713	...	...	713	...	...	628	...	...	655
6M4	Gross debt (D4) at nominal value	...	...	...	...	...	...	...	...	...	...	...	...
6M4D3	D3 debt liabilities at nominal value	...	...	...	...	...	...	...	...	...	...	...	...
6M4D2	D2 debt liabilities at nominal value	...	...	...	...	...	...	...	...	...	...	...	...
6M4D1	D1 debt liabilities at nominal value	...	...	...	...	...	...	...	...	...	...	...	...
6M35	Gross debt (D4) at face value	646	714	...	...	633	...	596	645	...	631	684	...
6M35D3	D3 debt liabilities at face value	646	714	...	...	633	...	596	645	...	631	684	...
6M35D2	D2 debt liabilities at face value	616	683	...	...	605	...	553	605	...	573	627	...
6M35D1	D1 debt liabilities at face value	613	681	...	...	603	...	551	603	...	570	625	...
6M93	Government gross debt per national definition	...	...	...	...	...	...	...	...	...	...	...	...
6M5	Arrears	...	...	...	...	...	...	...	...	...	...	...	...
6M6	Explicit contingent liabilities	23	26	33	...	...	...	...	...	...	...	...	...
6M61	of which: Publicly guaranteed debt	...	...	...	...	...	...	...	...	...	...	...	...
6M7	Net implicit obligations for social security benefits	...	...	...	...	...	...	...	...	...	...	...	...
	Table 7 Expenditure by functions of government												
7	**Expenditure**	**407**	**443**	**488**	**442**	**464**	**534**	**564**	**629**	**733**	**591**	**656**	**759**
701	**General public services**	**118**	**129**	**142**	**111**	**122**	**134**	**107**	**116**	**128**	**103**	**99**	**109**
7017	Public debt transactions	48	52	52	48	52	52	43	45	45	44	47	48
7018	Transfers of general character between levels of government	38	47	55	32	39	47	32	39	47	—	—	1
702	**Defense**	**20**	**22**	**24**	**24**	**28**	**30**	**24**	**28**	**30**	**24**	**28**	**30**
703	**Public order and safety**	**28**	**34**	**41**	**29**	**35**	**42**	**29**	**35**	**42**	**31**	**38**	**45**
704	**Economic affairs**	**52**	**55**	**52**	**56**	**59**	**53**	**56**	**60**	**53**	**65**	**70**	**67**
7042	Agriculture, forestry, fishing, and hunting	18	18	20	17	20	23	17	20	23	18	21	24
7043	Fuel and energy	1	1	3	1	1	1	1	1	1	1	1	1
7044	Mining, manufacturing, and construction	1	1	2	1	1	2	1	1	2	3	3	4
7045	Transport	25	20	23	25	20	21	25	20	21	30	26	31
7046	Communication	1	0	-10	1	0	-10	1	0	-10	1	0	-10
705	**Environmental protection**	**0**	**1**	**1**	**0**	**1**	**1**	**0**	**1**	**1**	**6**	**7**	**8**
706	**Housing and community amenities**	**7**	**6**	**6**	**7**	**6**	**6**	**7**	**6**	**6**	**15**	**22**	**17**
707	**Health**	**20**	**20**	**26**	**47**	**30**	**63**	**69**	**80**	**121**	**70**	**81**	**122**
7072	Outpatient services	4	5	5	4	5	5	4	5	5	5	5	5
7073	Hospital services	12	12	15	12	44	53	12	44	53	12	44	53
7074	Public health services	3	4	5	3	4	5	3	4	5	3	4	5
708	**Recreation, culture and religion**	**9**	**10**	**11**	**10**	**12**	**13**	**10**	**12**	**13**	**14**	**16**	**19**
709	**Education**	**63**	**74**	**85**	**64**	**75**	**87**	**64**	**75**	**87**	**64**	**77**	**87**
7091	Pre-primary and primary education	26	29	32	26	29	32	26	29	32	28	30	33
7092	Secondary education	15	18	21	15	18	21	15	18	21	16	18	21
7094	Tertiary education	13	15	17	13	15	17	13	15	17	13	15	17

Turkey (186)

In Billions of Turkish Liras (TRY) / Fiscal Year Ends December 31st

		Budgetary Central Government			Central Government (excl. Social Security)			Central Government (incl. Social Security)			General Government		
		2013	2014	2015	2013	2014	2015	2013	2014	2015	2013	2014	2015
710	**Social protection**	**89**	**92**	**100**	**93**	**96**	**105**	**197**	**216**	**253**	**199**	**217**	**254**
7z	Statistical discrepancy: Expenditure	—	-0	...	—	—	...	...	0	...	—	-0	...
	Table 8 Financial transactions by counterpart sector												
32	**Net acquisition of financial assets**	**13**	**13**	**37**	**...**	**14**	**42**	**23**	**24**	**50**	**31**	**31**	**64**
321	Domestic debtors	10	15	41	...	20	40	20	31	48	29	37	60
8211	General government	...	...	...	...	...	...	...	...	...	...	...	...
8212	Central bank	...	...	...	...	...	...	...	...	...	...	...	...
8213	Deposit-taking corporations except the central bank	...	...	...	...	...	...	...	...	...	...	...	...
8214	Other financial corporations	...	...	...	...	...	...	...	...	...	...	...	...
8215	Nonfinancial corporations	...	...	...	...	...	...	...	...	...	...	...	...
8216	Households & nonprofit institutions serving households	...	...	...	...	...	...	...	...	...	...	...	...
322	External debtors	3	-2	-4	2	-7	2	2	-7	2	2	-7	3
8221	General government	...	...	...	...	...	...	...	...	...	...	...	...
8227	International organizations	...	...	...	...	...	...	...	...	...	...	...	...
8228	Financial corporations other than international organizations	...	...	...	...	...	...	...	...	...	...	...	...
8229	Other nonresidents	...	...	...	...	...	...	...	...	...	...	...	...
33	**Net incurrence of liabilities**	**26**	**25**	**33**	**...**	**27**	**37**	**20**	**16**	**25**	**28**	**24**	**32**
331	Domestic creditors	18	17	35	...	19	39	12	8	27	19	16	34
8311	General government	...	...	...	...	...	...	...	...	...	...	...	...
8312	Central bank	...	...	...	...	...	...	...	...	...	...	...	...
8313	Deposit-taking corporations except the central bank	...	...	...	...	...	...	...	...	...	...	...	...
8314	Other financial corporations	...	...	...	...	...	...	...	...	...	...	...	...
8315	Nonfinancial corporations	...	...	...	...	...	...	...	...	...	...	...	...
8316	Households & nonprofit institutions serving households	...	...	...	...	...	...	...	...	...	...	...	...
332	External creditors	8	8	-2	8	8	-2	8	8	-2	9	8	-2
8321	General government	...	...	...	...	...	...	...	...	...	...	...	...
8327	International organizations	...	...	...	...	...	...	...	...	...	...	...	...
8328	Financial corporations other than international organizations	...	...	...	...	...	...	...	...	...	...	...	...
8329	Other nonresidents	...	...	...	...	...	...	...	...	...	...	...	...
	Table 9 Total other economic flows in assets and liabilities												
9	**Change in net worth due to other economic flows**	**26**	**488**	**30**	**42**	**490**	**32**	**54**	**473**	**27**	**65**	**470**	**36**
91	**Other economic flows in nonfinancial assets**	**18**	**541**	**40**	**19**	**541**	**40**	**19**	**541**	**40**	**29**	**536**	**51**
911	Fixed assets	1	113	11	2	113	11	2	113	11	6	96	20
912	Inventories	1	-0	0	1	-0	0	1	-0	0	1	0	-0
913	Valuables	-0	0	0	-0	0	0	-0	0	0	-0	0	0
914	Nonproduced assets	15	429	29	16	429	29	16	428	29	21	440	32
92	**Other economic flows in financial assets**	**-9**	**-8**	**-3**	**5**	**-6**	**-0**	**-5**	**-27**	**-6**	**-5**	**-28**	**-7**
	By instrument												
9201	Monetary gold and SDRs	—	—	—	—	—	—	—	—	—	—	—	—
9202	Currency and deposits	1	0	3	4	1	3	4	1	3	3	-1	1
9203	Debt securities	—	—	—	—	—	—	—	—	-5	0	-0	-5
9204	Loans	2	-0	1	2	-0	1	2	-0	1	2	3	1
9205	Equity and investment fund shares	3	12	9	18	14	10	18	14	10	18	14	10
9206	Insurance, pension, and standardized guarantee schemes	—	—	—	—	—	—	—	—	—	—	—	—
9207	Financial derivatives and employee stock options	—	—	—	—	—	—	—	—	—	—	—	—
9208	Other accounts receivable	-16	-21	-16	-18	-22	-13	-28	-43	-14	-29	-44	-14
	By debtor												
921	Domestic debtors	-12	-10	-7	0	-9	-5	-11	-30	-11	-11	-30	-11
922	External debtors	3	1	4	5	2	5	6	3	5	5	3	4
93	**Other economic flows in liabilities**	**-17**	**45**	**8**	**-17**	**45**	**8**	**-41**	**41**	**8**	**-42**	**38**	**8**

Turkey (186)

In Billions of Turkish Liras (TRY) / Fiscal Year Ends December 31st

		Budgetary Central Government			Central Government (excl. Social Security)			Central Government (incl. Social Security)			General Government		
		2013	2014	2015	2013	2014	2015	2013	2014	2015	2013	2014	2015
	By instrument												
9301	Special Drawing Rights (SDRs)	—	—	—	—	—	—	—	—	—	—	—	—
9302	Currency and deposits	—	—	—	—	—	—	—	—	—	—	—	—
9303	Debt securities	-28	45	-3	-28	45	-3	-23	41	-3	-23	41	-3
9304	Loans	10	-1	11	10	-1	11	10	-1	11	9	-2	12
9305	Equity and investment fund shares	—	—	—	—	—	—	—	—	—	—	—	—
9306	Insurance, pension, and standardized guarantee schemes	—	—	0	—	—	0	—	—	0	—	—	-0
9307	Financial derivatives and employee stock options	—	—	—	—	—	—	—	—	—	—	—	—
9308	Other accounts payable	—	0	0	-0	0	0	-28	0	0	-28	-1	-0
	By creditor												
931	Domestic creditors	-31	24	-29	-31	24	-29	-54	20	-29	-55	17	-29
932	External creditors	13	21	36	13	21	36	13	21	36	13	21	37
	Memorandum items												
9M2	Change in net financial worth due to other economic flows	9	-53	-10	23	-51	-8	35	-68	-14	36	-65	-16
9M3	Gross debt (D4) at market value: other economic flows	-17	45	8	-17	45	8	-41	41	8	-42	38	8
9M3D3	D3 debt liabilities at market value: other economic flows	-17	45	8	-17	45	8	-41	41	8	-42	38	8
9M3D2	D2 debt liabilities at market value: other economic flows	-17	45	8	-17	45	8	-12	41	8	-14	39	9
9M3D1	D1 debt liabilities at market value: other economic flows	-17	45	8	-17	45	8	-12	41	8	-14	39	9

Uganda (746)

In Billions of Uganda Shillings (UGX) / Fiscal Year Ends June 30th

		Budgetary Central Government			Central Government (excl. Social Security)			Central Government (incl. Social Security)			General Government		
		2013	2014	2015	2013	2014	2015	2013	2014	2015	2013	2014	2015
	Statement of operations												
1	Revenue	8,277	8,870	8,870	...	...	9,028	...	...	...	...	...	9,306
2	Expense	7,454	8,583	8,583	...	...	8,705	...	...	...	...	...	8,779
GOB	**Gross operating balance**	**822**	**287**	**287**	**...**	**...**	**385**	**...**	**...**	**...**	**...**	**...**	**592**
NOB	**Net operating balance**	**...**	**...**	**...**	**...**	**...**	**322**	**...**	**...**	**...**	**...**	**...**	**527**
31	Net/Gross investment in nonfinancial assets	...	3,060	3,060	...	...	3,083	...	...	...	...	...	3,233
2M	Expenditure	...	11,643	11,643	...	...	11,788	...	...	...	...	...	12,013
NLB	**Net lending (+) / Net borrowing (-)**	**...**	**-2,772**	**-2,772**	**...**	**...**	**-2,761**	**...**	**...**	**...**	**...**	**...**	**-2,707**
32	Net acquisition of financial assets	...	-4,434	-4,434	...	...	-4,455	...	...	...	...	...	-4,404
33	Net incurrence of liabilities	...	-1,936	-1,849	...	...	-1,800	...	...	...	...	...	-1,763
NLBz	Statistical discrepancy	...	275	187	...	...	106	...	...	...	...	...	65
	Memorandum items												
PB	Primary net lending / net borrowing	...	-1,802	-1,802	...	...	-1,790	...	...	...	...	...	-1,736
GB	Government balance per national definition	...	...	...	...	...	...	...	...	...	...	...	...
	Statement of other economic flows												
9	**Change in net worth due to other economic flows**	**...**	**...**	**-24**	**...**	**...**	**-24**	**...**	**...**	**...**	**...**	**...**	**-24**
4	Change in net worth due to holding gains and losses	**...**	**...**	**-281**	**...**	**...**	**-281**	**...**	**...**	**...**	**...**	**...**	**-281**
41	Nonfinancial assets	...	...	...	...	...	...	...	...	...	...	...	...
42	Financial assets	...	...	-281	...	...	-281	...	...	...	...	...	-281
43	Liabilities	...	...	...	...	...	...	...	...	...	...	...	...
5	Change in net worth due to volume changes	**...**	**...**	**257**	**...**	**...**	**257**	**...**	**...**	**...**	**...**	**...**	**257**
51	Nonfinancial assets	...	...	...	...	...	...	...	...	...	...	...	...
52	Financial assets	...	...	257	...	...	257	...	...	...	...	...	257
53	Liabilities	...	...	...	...	...	...	...	...	...	...	...	...
	Balance sheet												
6	**Net worth**	**...**	**...**	**-12,794**	**...**	**...**	**-12,794**	**...**	**...**	**...**	**...**	**...**	**-12,794**
61	Nonfinancial assets	...	...	428	...	...	428	...	...	...	...	...	428
62	Financial assets	...	7,207	6,592	...	...	6,592	...	...	...	...	...	6,592
63	Liabilities	...	20,718	19,814	...	...	19,814	...	...	...	...	...	19,814
	Table 1 Revenue												
1	**Revenue**	**8,277**	**8,870**	**8,870**	**...**	**...**	**9,028**	**...**	**...**	**...**	**...**	**...**	**9,306**
11	**Taxes**	**7,149**	**8,031**	**8,031**	**...**	**...**	**8,031**	**...**	**...**	**...**	**...**	**...**	**8,063**
111	Taxes on income, profits, and capital gains	2,426	2,613	2,613	...	...	2,613	...	...	...	...	...	2,613
1111	Payable by individuals	1,197	1,398	1,398	...	...	1,398	...	...	...	...	...	1,398
1112	Payable by corporations and other enterprises	598	487	1,162	...	...	1,162	...	...	...	...	...	1,162
1113	Other taxes on income, profits, and capital gains	632	729	54	...	...	54	...	...	...	...	...	54
112	Taxes on payroll and workforce	—	—	...	...	...	...	...	...	...	...	...	...
113	Taxes on property	—	—	...	...	...	...	...	...	...	...	...	10
114	Taxes on goods and services	3,959	4,536	4,496	...	...	4,496	...	...	...	...	...	4,496
1141	General taxes on goods and services	2,353	2,570	2,570	...	...	2,570	...	...	...	...	...	2,570
1142	Excises	1,466	1,757	1,757	...	...	1,757	...	...	...	...	...	1,757
115	Taxes on international trade and transactions	753	882	882	...	...	882	...	...	...	...	...	882
116	Other taxes	12	—	40	...	...	40	...	...	...	...	...	61
12	**Social contributions**	**—**	**—**	**...**	**...**	**...**	**...**	**...**	**...**	**...**	**...**	**...**	**...**
121	Social security contributions	—	—	...	...	...	...	...	...	...	...	...	...
122	Other social contributions	—	—	...	...	...	...	...	...	...	...	...	...
13	**Grants**	**936**	**702**	**702**	**...**	**...**	**360**	**...**	**...**	**...**	**...**	**...**	**557**
131	From foreign governments	...	511	702	...	...	740	...	...	...	...	...	873
132	From international organizations	...	191	...	...	...	...	...	...	...	...	...	...
133	From other general government units	...	—	...	...	...	-381	...	...	...	...	...	-316
1331	Current	...	—	...	...	...	-484	...	...	...	...	...	-419
1332	Capital	...	—	...	...	...	103	...	...	...	...	...	103
14	**Other revenue**	**191**	**137**	**137**	**...**	**...**	**637**	**...**	**...**	**...**	**...**	**...**	**687**

Uganda (746)

In Billions of Uganda Shillings (UGX) / Fiscal Year Ends June 30th

		Budgetary Central Government			Central Government (excl. Social Security)			Central Government (incl. Social Security)			General Government		
		2013	2014	2015	2013	2014	2015	2013	2014	2015	2013	2014	2015
	Table 2 Expense by economic type												
2	**Expense**	**7,454**	**8,583**	**8,583**	**...**	**...**	**8,705**	**...**	**...**	**...**	**...**	**...**	**8,779**
21	**Compensation of employees**	**1,403**	**1,516**	**1,516**	**...**	**...**	**1,891**	**...**	**...**	**...**	**...**	**...**	**3,020**
211	Wages and salaries	...	...	1,516	...	...	1,865	...	...	...	...	...	2,995
212	Employers' social contributions	...	...	...	...	...	25	...	...	...	...	...	25
22	**Use of goods and services**	**1,709**	**2,160**	**2,160**	**...**	**...**	**2,630**	**...**	**...**	**...**	**...**	**...**	**3,124**
23	**Consumption of fixed capital**	**...**	**...**	**...**	**...**	**...**	**63**	**...**	**...**	**...**	**...**	**...**	**66**
24	**Interest**	**890**	**970**	**970**	**...**	**...**	**970**	**...**	**...**	**...**	**...**	**...**	**970**
25	**Subsidies**	**29**	**36**	**36**	**...**	**...**	**36**	**...**	**...**	**...**	**...**	**...**	**36**
26	**Grants**	**2,879**	**3,257**	**3,257**	**...**	**...**	**2,408**	**...**	**...**	**...**	**...**	**...**	**839**
261	To foreign governments	—	—	...	...	...	...	...	...	...	...	...	...
262	To international organizations	29	—	43	...	...	43	...	...	...	...	...	43
263	To other general government units	2,850	3,257	3,214	...	...	2,365	...	...	...	...	...	796
2631	Current	2,283	3,257	3,214	...	...	2,365	...	...	...	...	...	796
2632	Capital	567	—	...	...	...	...	...	...	...	...	...	...
27	**Social benefits**	**260**	**229**	**229**	**...**	**...**	**229**	**...**	**...**	**...**	**...**	**...**	**232**
271	Social security benefits	—	—	229	...	...	229	...	...	...	...	...	232
272	Social assistance benefits	260	229	...	...	...	...	...	...	...	...	...	...
273	Employment-related social benefits	—	—	...	...	...	...	...	...	...	...	...	...
28	**Other expense**	**284**	**415**	**415**	**...**	**...**	**479**	**...**	**...**	**...**	**...**	**...**	**492**
281	Property expense other than interest	—	—	...	...	...	...	...	...	...	...	...	...
282	Transfers not elsewhere classified	284	415	415	...	...	479	...	...	...	...	...	492
2821	Current	...	...	415	...	...	479	...	...	...	...	...	492
2822	Capital	...	...	...	...	...	...	...	...	...	...	...	...
	Table 3 Transactions in assets and liabilities												
3	**Change in net worth from transactions**	**...**	**...**	**475**	**...**	**...**	**428**	**...**	**...**	**...**	**...**	**...**	**592**
31	**Net/Gross investment in nonfinancial assets**	**...**	**3,060**	**3,060**	**...**	**...**	**3,083**	**...**	**...**	**...**	**...**	**...**	**3,233**
311	Fixed assets	...	2,791	2,791	...	...	2,807	...	...	...	...	...	2,956
3111	Buildings and structures	...	2,029	970	...	...	974	...	...	...	...	...	1,122
3112	Machinery and equipment	...	304	287	...	...	300	...	...	...	...	...	300
3113	Other fixed assets	...	457	1,534	...	...	1,534	...	...	...	...	...	1,534
3114	Weapons systems	...	—	...	...	...	...	...	...	...	...	...	...
312	Inventories	...	—	...	...	...	...	...	...	...	...	...	0
313	Valuables	...	—	...	...	...	...	...	...	...	...	...	...
314	Nonproduced assets	...	269	269	...	...	276	...	...	...	...	...	278
3141	Land	...	269	269	...	...	276	...	...	...	...	...	278
3142	Mineral and energy resources	...	—	...	...	...	...	...	...	...	...	...	...
3143	Other naturally occurring assets	...	—	...	...	...	...	...	...	...	...	...	...
3144	Intangible nonproduced assets	...	—	...	...	...	...	...	...	...	...	...	...
32	**Net acquisition of financial assets**	**...**	**-4,434**	**-4,434**	**...**	**...**	**-4,455**	**...**	**...**	**...**	**...**	**...**	**-4,404**
	By instrument												
3201	Monetary gold and SDRs	...	—	...	...	...	...	...	...	...	...	...	...
3202	Currency and deposits	...	-4,453	-4,453	...	...	-4,453	...	...	...	...	...	-4,402
3203	Debt securities	...	—	...	...	...	...	...	...	...	...	...	...
3204	Loans	...	19	19	...	...	19	...	...	...	...	...	19
3205	Equity and investment fund shares	...	—	—	...	...	—	...	...	...	...	...	—
3206	Insurance, pension, and standardized guarantee schemes	...	—	...	...	...	...	...	...	...	...	...	...
3207	Financial derivatives and employee stock options	...	—	...	...	...	...	...	...	...	...	...	...
3208	Other accounts receivable	...	...	...	...	...	-21	...	...	...	...	...	-21
	By debtor												
321	Domestic debtors	...	-4,434	-4,434	...	...	-4,455	...	...	...	...	...	-4,404
322	External debtors	...	—	...	...	...	...	...	...	...	...	...	...
33	**Net incurrence of liabilities**	**...**	**-1,936**	**-1,849**	**...**	**...**	**-1,800**	**...**	**...**	**...**	**...**	**...**	**-1,763**
	By instrument												
3301	Special Drawing Rights (SDRs)	...	—	...	...	...	...	...	...	...	...	...	...
3302	Currency and deposits	...	—	...	...	...	...	...	...	...	...	...	...
3303	Debt securities	...	2,033	1,977	...	...	1,977	...	...	...	...	...	1,977
3304	Loans	...	-4,027	-3,971	...	...	-3,971	...	...	...	...	...	-3,971

Uganda (746)

In Billions of Uganda Shillings (UGX) / Fiscal Year Ends June 30th

		Budgetary Central Government			Central Government (excl. Social Security)			Central Government (incl. Social Security)			General Government		
		2013	2014	2015	2013	2014	2015	2013	2014	2015	2013	2014	2015
3305	Equity and investment fund shares	...	—	...	...	...	...	...	...	...	...	...	...
3306	Insurance, pension, and standardized guarantee schemes	...	—	...	...	...	...	...	...	...	...	...	...
3307	Financial derivatives and employee stock options	...	—	...	...	...	...	...	...	...	...	...	...
3308	Other accounts payable	...	57	145	...	...	193	...	...	...	...	...	231
	By creditor												
331	Domestic creditors	...	-2,823	-2,736	...	...	-2,687	...	...	...	...	...	-2,650
332	External creditors	...	887	887	...	...	887	...	...	...	...	...	887
	Table 4 Holding gains and losses in assets and liabilities												
4	**Change in net worth due to holding gains and losses**	...	...	**-281**	...	...	**-281**	...	...	...	...	...	**-281**
41	**Holding gains and losses in nonfinancial assets**	...	...	...	...	...	...	...	...	...	...	...	...
411	Fixed assets	...	...	...	...	...	...	...	...	...	...	...	...
412	Inventories	...	...	...	...	...	...	...	...	...	...	...	...
413	Valuables	...	...	...	...	...	...	...	...	...	...	...	...
414	Nonproduced assets	...	...	...	...	...	...	...	...	...	...	...	...
42	**Holding gains and losses in financial assets**	...	...	**-281**	...	...	**-281**	...	...	...	...	...	**-281**
	By instrument												
4201	Monetary gold and SDRs	...	...	...	...	...	...	...	...	...	...	...	...
4202	Currency and deposits	...	...	-281	...	...	-281	...	...	...	...	...	-281
4203	Debt securities	...	...	...	...	...	...	...	...	...	...	...	...
4204	Loans	...	...	...	...	...	...	...	...	...	...	...	...
4205	Equity and investment fund shares	...	...	...	...	...	...	...	...	...	...	...	...
4206	Insurance, pension, and standardized guarantee schemes	...	...	...	...	...	...	...	...	...	...	...	...
4207	Financial derivatives and employee stock options	...	...	...	...	...	...	...	...	...	...	...	...
4208	Other accounts receivable	...	...	...	...	...	...	...	...	...	...	...	...
	By debtor												
421	Domestic debtors	...	...	...	...	...	...	...	...	...	...	...	...
422	External debtors	...	...	...	...	...	...	...	...	...	...	...	...
43	**Holding gains and losses in liabilities**	...	...	...	...	...	...	...	...	...	...	...	...
	By instrument												
4301	Special Drawing Rights (SDRs)	...	...	...	...	...	...	...	...	...	...	...	...
4302	Currency and deposits	...	...	...	...	...	...	...	...	...	...	...	...
4303	Debt securities	...	...	...	...	...	...	...	...	...	...	...	...
4304	Loans	...	...	...	...	...	...	...	...	...	...	...	...
4305	Equity and investment fund shares	...	...	...	...	...	...	...	...	...	...	...	...
4306	Insurance, pension, and standardized guarantee schemes	...	...	...	...	...	...	...	...	...	...	...	...
4307	Financial derivatives and employee stock options	...	...	...	...	...	...	...	...	...	...	...	...
4308	Other accounts payable	...	...	...	...	...	...	...	...	...	...	...	...
	By creditor												
431	Domestic creditors	...	...	...	...	...	...	...	...	...	...	...	...
432	External creditors	...	...	...	...	...	...	...	...	...	...	...	...
	Table 5 Holding gains and losses in assets and liabilities												
5	**Change in net worth due to other volume changes**	...	...	**257**	...	...	**257**	...	...	...	...	...	**257**
51	**Other volume changes in nonfinancial assets**	...	...	...	...	...	...	...	...	...	...	...	...
511	Fixed assets	...	...	...	...	...	...	...	...	...	...	...	...
512	Inventories	...	...	...	...	...	...	...	...	...	...	...	...
513	Valuables	...	...	...	...	...	...	...	...	...	...	...	...
514	Nonproduced assets	...	...	...	...	...	...	...	...	...	...	...	...
52	**Other volume changes in financial assets**	...	...	**257**	...	...	**257**	...	...	...	...	...	**257**

Uganda (746)

In Billions of Uganda Shillings (UGX) / Fiscal Year Ends June 30th

		Budgetary Central Government			Central Government (excl. Social Security)			Central Government (incl. Social Security)			General Government		
		2013	2014	2015	2013	2014	2015	2013	2014	2015	2013	2014	2015
	By instrument												
5201	Monetary gold and SDRs	...	...	...	...	...	...	...	...	...	...	...	...
5202	Currency and deposits	...	...	...	...	...	...	...	...	...	...	...	...
5203	Debt securities	...	...	...	...	...	...	...	...	...	...	...	...
5204	Loans	...	...	...	...	...	...	...	...	...	...	...	...
5205	Equity and investment fund shares	...	...	257	...	...	257	...	...	...	...	...	257
5206	Insurance, pension, and standardized guarantee schemes	...	...	...	...	...	...	...	...	...	...	...	...
5207	Financial derivatives and employee stock options	...	...	...	...	...	...	...	...	...	...	...	...
5208	Other accounts receivable	...	...	...	...	...	...	...	...	...	...	...	...
	By debtor												
521	Domestic debtors	...	...	...	...	...	...	...	...	...	...	...	...
522	External debtors	...	...	...	...	...	...	...	...	...	...	...	...
53	**Other volume changes in liabilities**	**...**	**...**	**...**	**...**	**...**	**...**	**...**	**...**	**...**	**...**	**...**	**...**
	By instrument												
5301	Special Drawing Rights (SDRs)	...	...	...	...	...	...	...	...	...	...	...	...
5302	Currency and deposits	...	...	...	...	...	...	...	...	...	...	...	...
5303	Debt securities	...	...	...	...	...	...	...	...	...	...	...	...
5304	Loans	...	...	...	...	...	...	...	...	...	...	...	...
5305	Equity and investment fund shares	...	...	...	...	...	...	...	...	...	...	...	...
5306	Insurance, pension, and standardized guarantee schemes	...	...	...	...	...	...	...	...	...	...	...	...
5307	Financial derivatives and employee stock options	...	...	...	...	...	...	...	...	...	...	...	...
5308	Other accounts payable	...	...	...	...	...	...	...	...	...	...	...	...
	By creditor												
531	Domestic creditors	...	...	...	...	...	...	...	...	...	...	...	...
532	External creditors	...	...	...	...	...	...	...	...	...	...	...	...
	Table 6 Balance sheet												
6	**Net worth**	**...**	**...**	**-12,794**	**...**	**...**	**-12,794**	**...**	**...**	**...**	**...**	**...**	**-12,794**
61	**Nonfinancial assets**	**...**	**...**	**428**	**...**	**...**	**428**	**...**	**...**	**...**	**...**	**...**	**428**
611	Fixed assets	...	...	...	...	...	...	...	...	...	...	...	...
6111	Buildings and structures	...	...	...	...	...	...	...	...	...	...	...	...
6112	Machinery and equipment	...	...	...	...	...	...	...	...	...	...	...	...
6113	Other fixed assets	...	...	...	...	...	...	...	...	...	...	...	...
6114	Weapons systems	...	...	...	...	...	...	...	...	...	...	...	...
612	Inventories	...	...	22	...	...	22	...	...	...	...	...	22
613	Valuables	...	...	...	...	...	...	...	...	...	...	...	...
614	Nonproduced assets	...	430	406	...	...	406	...	...	...	...	...	406
6141	Land	...	408	406	...	...	406	...	...	...	...	...	406
6142	Mineral and energy resources	...	—	...	...	...	...	...	...	...	...	...	...
6143	Other naturally occurring assets	...	1	1	...	...	1	...	...	...	...	...	1
6144	Intangible nonproduced assets	...	22	...	...	...	...	...	...	...	...	...	...
62	**Financial assets**	**...**	**7,207**	**6,592**	**...**	**...**	**6,592**	**...**	**...**	**...**	**...**	**...**	**6,592**
	By instrument												
6201	Monetary gold and SDRs	...	—	...	...	...	...	...	...	...	...	...	...
6202	Currency and deposits	...	2,923	3,036	...	...	3,036	...	...	...	...	...	3,036
6203	Debt securities	...	—	7	...	...	7	...	...	...	...	...	7
6204	Loans	...	—	971	...	...	971	...	...	...	...	...	971
6205	Equity and investment fund shares	...	2,946	2,209	...	...	2,209	...	...	...	...	...	2,209
6206	Insurance, pension, and standardized guarantee schemes	...	—	...	...	...	...	...	...	...	...	...	...
6207	Financial derivatives and employee stock options	...	—	...	...	...	...	...	...	...	...	...	...
6208	Other accounts receivable	...	1,337	368	...	...	368	...	...	...	...	...	368
	By debtor												
621	Domestic debtors	...	7,207	6,283	...	...	6,283	...	...	...	...	...	6,283
622	External debtors	...	—	309	...	...	309	...	...	...	...	...	309
63	**Liabilities**	**...**	**20,718**	**19,814**	**...**	**...**	**19,814**	**...**	**...**	**...**	**...**	**...**	**19,814**

Uganda (746)

In Billions of Uganda Shillings (UGX) / Fiscal Year Ends June 30th

		Budgetary Central Government			Central Government (excl. Social Security)			Central Government (incl. Social Security)			General Government		
		2013	2014	2015	2013	2014	2015	2013	2014	2015	2013	2014	2015
	By instrument												
6301	Special Drawing Rights (SDRs)	...	—	...	...	...	...	...	...	...	...	...	...
6302	Currency and deposits	...	—	...	...	...	...	...	...	...	...	...	...
6303	Debt securities	...	7,728	5,985	...	...	5,985	...	...	...	...	...	5,985
6304	Loans	...	12,286	12,442	...	...	12,442	...	...	...	...	...	12,442
6305	Equity and investment fund shares	...	—	...	...	...	...	...	...	...	...	...	...
6306	Insurance, pension, and standardized guarantee schemes	...	—	...	...	...	...	...	...	...	...	...	...
6307	Financial derivatives and employee stock options	...	—	...	...	...	...	...	...	...	...	...	...
6308	Other accounts payable	...	703	1,388	...	...	1,388	...	...	...	...	...	1,388
	By creditor												
631	Domestic creditors	...	9,800	8,819	...	...	8,819	...	...	...	...	...	8,819
632	External creditors	...	10,918	10,996	...	...	10,996	...	...	...	...	...	10,996
	Memorandum items												
6M2	Net financial worth	...	-13,511	-13,223	...	...	-13,223	...	...	...	...	...	-13,223
6M3	Gross debt (D4) at market value	...	...	...	...	...	...	...	...	...	...	...	...
6M3D3	D3 debt liabilities at market value	...	...	...	...	...	...	...	...	...	...	...	...
6M3D2	D2 debt liabilities at market value	...	...	...	...	...	...	...	...	...	...	...	...
6M3D1	D1 debt liabilities at market value	...	...	...	...	...	...	...	...	...	...	...	...
6M4	Gross debt (D4) at nominal value	...	...	...	...	...	...	...	...	...	...	...	...
6M4D3	D3 debt liabilities at nominal value	...	...	...	...	...	...	...	...	...	...	...	...
6M4D2	D2 debt liabilities at nominal value	...	...	...	...	...	...	...	...	...	...	...	...
6M4D1	D1 debt liabilities at nominal value	...	...	...	...	...	...	...	...	...	...	...	...
6M35	Gross debt (D4) at face value	...	20,718	...	...	...	...	...	...	...	...	...	...
6M35D3	D3 debt liabilities at face value	...	20,718	...	...	...	...	...	...	...	...	...	...
6M35D2	D2 debt liabilities at face value	...	20,014	...	...	...	...	...	...	...	...	...	...
6M35D1	D1 debt liabilities at face value	...	20,014	...	...	...	...	...	...	...	...	...	...
6M93	Government gross debt per national definition	...	...	...	...	...	...	...	...	...	...	...	...
6M5	Arrears	...	...	...	...	...	...	...	...	...	...	...	...
6M6	Explicit contingent liabilities	...	...	...	...	...	...	...	...	...	...	...	...
6M61	of which: Publicly guaranteed debt	...	...	...	...	...	...	...	...	...	...	...	...
6M7	Net implicit obligations for social security benefits	...	...	...	...	...	...	...	...	...	...	...	...
	Table 7 Expenditure by functions of government												
7	**Expenditure**	**10,049**	**11,643**	**11,643**	**...**	**...**	**11,643**	**...**	**...**	**...**	**...**	**...**	**14,139**
701	**General public services**	**2,512**	**2,803**	**2,803**	**...**	**...**	**2,803**	**...**	**...**	**...**	**...**	**...**	**3,280**
7017	Public debt transactions	890	970	970	...	...	970	...	...	...	...	...	970
7018	Transfers of general character between levels of government	217	244	244	...	...	244	...	...	...	...	...	244
702	**Defense**	**980**	**1,259**	**1,259**	**...**	**...**	**1,259**	**...**	**...**	**...**	**...**	**...**	**1,259**
703	**Public order and safety**	**618**	**851**	**851**	**...**	**...**	**851**	**...**	**...**	**...**	**...**	**...**	**852**
704	**Economic affairs**	**2,613**	**3,248**	**3,248**	**...**	**...**	**3,248**	**...**	**...**	**...**	**...**	**...**	**3,521**
7042	Agriculture, forestry, fishing, and hunting	466	524	524	...	...	524	...	...	...	...	...	578
7043	Fuel and energy	266	315	315	...	...	315	...	...	...	...	...	315
7044	Mining, manufacturing, and construction	13	28	28	...	...	28	...	...	...	...	...	28
7045	Transport	1,696	2,108	2,108	...	...	2,108	...	...	...	...	...	2,214
7046	Communication	14	50	50	...	...	50	...	...	...	...	...	50
705	**Environmental protection**	**63**	**93**	**93**	**...**	**...**	**93**	**...**	**...**	**...**	**...**	**...**	**105**
706	**Housing and community amenities**	**257**	**418**	**418**	**...**	**...**	**418**	**...**	**...**	**...**	**...**	**...**	**531**
707	**Health**	**1,075**	**827**	**827**	**...**	**...**	**827**	**...**	**...**	**...**	**...**	**...**	**1,190**
7072	Outpatient services	8	8	8	...	...	8	...	...	...	...	...	8
7073	Hospital services	131	201	201	...	...	201	...	...	...	...	...	218
7074	Public health services	217	273	273	...	...	273	...	...	...	...	...	389
708	**Recreation, culture and religion**	**7**	**8**	**8**	**...**	**...**	**8**	**...**	**...**	**...**	**...**	**...**	**9**
709	**Education**	**1,454**	**1,632**	**1,632**	**...**	**...**	**1,632**	**...**	**...**	**...**	**...**	**...**	**2,855**
7091	Pre-primary and primary education	675	757	757	...	...	757	...	...	...	...	...	1,448
7092	Secondary education	324	501	501	...	...	501	...	...	...	...	...	740
7094	Tertiary education	276	249	249	...	...	249	...	...	...	...	...	302

Uganda (746)

In Billions of Uganda Shillings (UGX) / Fiscal Year Ends June 30th

		Budgetary Central Government			Central Government (excl. Social Security)			Central Government (incl. Social Security)			General Government		
		2013	2014	2015	2013	2014	2015	2013	2014	2015	2013	2014	2015
710	**Social protection**	**471**	**504**	**504**	**...**	**...**	**504**	**...**	**...**	**...**	**...**	**...**	**536**
7z	Statistical discrepancy: Expenditure	...	...	...	...	...	...	...	...	...	...	...	...
	Table 8 Financial transactions by counterpart sector												
32	**Net acquisition of financial assets**	**...**	**-4,434**	**-4,434**	**...**	**...**	**-4,455**	**...**	**...**	**...**	**...**	**...**	**-4,404**
321	Domestic debtors	...	-4,434	-4,434	...	...	-4,455	...	...	...	...	...	-4,404
8211	General government	...	...	...	...	...	...	...	...	...	...	...	...
8212	Central bank	...	...	...	...	...	...	...	...	...	...	...	...
8213	Deposit-taking corporations except the central bank	...	...	...	...	...	...	...	...	...	...	...	...
8214	Other financial corporations	...	...	...	...	...	...	...	...	...	...	...	...
8215	Nonfinancial corporations	...	...	...	...	...	...	...	...	...	...	...	...
8216	Households & nonprofit institutions serving households	...	...	...	...	...	...	...	...	...	...	...	...
322	External debtors	...	—	...	...	...	...	...	...	...	...	...	...
8221	General government	...	—	...	...	...	...	...	...	...	...	...	...
8227	International organizations	...	—	...	...	...	...	...	...	...	...	...	...
8228	Financial corporations other than international organizations	...	—	...	...	...	...	...	...	...	...	...	...
8229	Other nonresidents	...	—	...	...	...	...	...	...	...	...	...	...
33	**Net incurrence of liabilities**	**...**	**-1,936**	**-1,849**	**...**	**...**	**-1,800**	**...**	**...**	**...**	**...**	**...**	**-1,763**
331	Domestic creditors	...	-2,823	-2,736	...	...	-2,687	...	...	...	...	...	-2,650
8311	General government	...	...	...	...	...	...	...	...	...	...	...	...
8312	Central bank	...	...	...	...	...	...	...	...	...	...	...	...
8313	Deposit-taking corporations except the central bank	...	...	...	...	...	...	...	...	...	...	...	...
8314	Other financial corporations	...	...	...	...	...	...	...	...	...	...	...	...
8315	Nonfinancial corporations	...	...	...	...	...	...	...	...	...	...	...	...
8316	Households & nonprofit institutions serving households	...	...	...	...	...	...	...	...	...	...	...	...
332	External creditors	...	887	887	...	...	887	...	...	...	...	...	887
8321	General government	...	...	...	...	...	...	...	...	...	...	...	...
8327	International organizations	...	...	...	...	...	...	...	...	...	...	...	...
8328	Financial corporations other than international organizations	...	...	...	...	...	...	...	...	...	...	...	...
8329	Other nonresidents	...	...	...	...	...	...	...	...	...	...	...	...
	Table 9 Total other economic flows in assets and liabilities												
9	**Change in net worth due to other economic flows**	**...**	**...**	**-24**	**...**	**...**	**-24**	**...**	**...**	**...**	**...**	**...**	**-24**
91	**Other economic flows in nonfinancial assets**	**...**	**...**	**...**	**...**	**...**	**...**	**...**	**...**	**...**	**...**	**...**	**...**
911	Fixed assets	...	...	...	...	...	...	...	...	...	...	...	...
912	Inventories	...	...	...	...	...	...	...	...	...	...	...	...
913	Valuables	...	...	...	...	...	...	...	...	...	...	...	...
914	Nonproduced assets	...	...	...	...	...	...	...	...	...	...	...	...
92	**Other economic flows in financial assets**	**...**	**...**	**-24**	**...**	**...**	**-24**	**...**	**...**	**...**	**...**	**...**	**-24**
	By instrument												
9201	Monetary gold and SDRs	...	...	...	...	...	...	...	...	...	...	...	...
9202	Currency and deposits	...	...	-281	...	...	-281	...	...	...	...	...	-281
9203	Debt securities	...	...	...	...	...	...	...	...	...	...	...	...
9204	Loans	...	...	...	...	...	...	...	...	...	...	...	...
9205	Equity and investment fund shares	...	...	257	...	...	257	...	...	...	...	...	257
9206	Insurance, pension, and standardized guarantee schemes	...	...	...	...	...	...	...	...	...	...	...	...
9207	Financial derivatives and employee stock options	...	...	...	...	...	...	...	...	...	...	...	...
9208	Other accounts receivable	...	...	...	...	...	...	...	...	...	...	...	...
	By debtor												
921	Domestic debtors	...	...	...	...	...	...	...	...	...	...	...	...
922	External debtors	...	...	...	...	...	...	...	...	...	...	...	...
93	**Other economic flows in liabilities**	**...**	**...**	**...**	**...**	**...**	**...**	**...**	**...**	**...**	**...**	**...**	**...**

Uganda (746)

In Billions of Uganda Shillings (UGX) / Fiscal Year Ends June 30th

		Budgetary Central Government			Central Government (excl. Social Security)			Central Government (incl. Social Security)			General Government		
		2013	2014	2015	2013	2014	2015	2013	2014	2015	2013	2014	2015
	By instrument												
9301	Special Drawing Rights (SDRs)	...	...	...	...	...	...	...	...	...	...	...	...
9302	Currency and deposits	...	...	...	...	...	...	...	...	...	...	...	...
9303	Debt securities	...	...	...	...	...	...	...	...	...	...	...	...
9304	Loans	...	...	...	...	...	...	...	...	...	...	...	...
9305	Equity and investment fund shares	...	...	...	...	...	...	...	...	...	...	...	...
9306	Insurance, pension, and standardized guarantee schemes	...	...	...	...	...	...	...	...	...	...	...	...
9307	Financial derivatives and employee stock options	...	...	...	...	...	...	...	...	...	...	...	...
9308	Other accounts payable	...	...	...	...	...	...	...	...	...	...	...	...
	By creditor												
931	Domestic creditors	...	...	...	...	...	...	...	...	...	...	...	...
932	External creditors	...	...	...	...	...	...	...	...	...	...	...	...
	Memorandum items												
9M2	Change in net financial worth due to other economic flows	...	...	-24	...	...	-24	...	...	...	...	...	-24
9M3	Gross debt (D4) at market value: other economic flows	...	...	...	...	...	...	...	...	...	...	...	...
9M3D3	D3 debt liabilities at market value: other economic flows	...	...	...	...	...	...	...	...	...	...	...	...
9M3D2	D2 debt liabilities at market value: other economic flows	...	...	...	...	...	...	...	...	...	...	...	...
9M3D1	D1 debt liabilities at market value: other economic flows	...	...	...	...	...	...	...	...	...	...	...	...

Ukraine (926)

In Millions of Ukrainian Hryvnias (UAH) / Fiscal Year Ends December 31st

		Budgetary Central Government			Central Government (excl. Social Security)			Central Government (incl. Social Security)			General Government		
		2013	2014	2015P	2013	2014	2015P	2013	2014	2015P	2013	2014	2015P
	Statement of operations												
1	Revenue	338,971	356,196	525,753	338,971	356,196	525,753	532,569	617,954	716,098	634,749	639,957	831,806
2	Expense	396,332	425,638	550,500	396,332	425,638	550,500	588,988	690,954	743,094	681,438	697,964	821,916
GOB	**Gross operating balance**	**-57,361**	**-69,442**	**-24,747**	**-57,361**	**-69,442**	**-24,747**	**-56,419**	**-73,000**	**-26,996**	**-46,689**	**-58,006**	**9,891**
NOB	**Net operating balance**	...	...	...	...	...	...	...	...	...	...	...	...
31	Net/Gross investment in nonfinancial assets	6,869	3,691	2,678	6,869	3,691	2,678	7,039	3,705	2,700	15,595	12,624	25,211
2M	Expenditure	403,201	429,330	553,178	403,201	429,330	553,178	596,027	694,659	745,795	697,033	710,588	847,126
NLB	**Net lending (+) / Net borrowing (-)**	**-64,230**	**-73,134**	**-27,426**	**-64,230**	**-73,134**	**-27,426**	**-63,458**	**-76,706**	**-29,696**	**-62,284**	**-70,630**	**-15,320**
32	Net acquisition of financial assets	16,810	128,700	82,416	16,810	128,700	82,416	17,892	126,097	80,146	23,449	130,590	91,818
33	Net incurrence of liabilities	81,039	201,834	109,842	81,039	201,834	109,842	81,350	202,803	109,842	85,733	201,220	107,137
NLBz	Statistical discrepancy	1	—	0	1	—	0	0	-0	0	0	-0	0
	Memorandum items												
PB	Primary net lending / net borrowing	-29,821	-22,115	59,383	-29,821	-22,115	59,383	-29,049	-25,687	57,112	-26,380	-18,147	73,164
GB	Government balance per national definition	...	...	-45,168	...	...	-45,168	...	...	-16,629	...	...	-30,898
	Statement of other economic flows												
	Balance sheet												
6	**Net worth**	**207,496**	**-85,397**	**-315,503**	**207,496**	**-85,397**	**-315,503**	**183,827**	**-115,558**	**-346,962**	**402,616**	**113,244**	**-75,365**
61	Nonfinancial assets	457,462	463,167	496,713	457,462	463,167	496,713	461,902	467,309	500,786	678,203	692,528	748,516
62	Financial assets	241,690	408,146	532,401	241,690	408,146	532,401	264,469	427,447	549,380	288,055	454,889	588,075
63	Liabilities	491,656	956,710	1,344,616	491,656	956,710	1,344,616	542,544	1,010,315	1,397,128	563,642	1,034,173	1,411,956
	Table 1 Revenue												
1	**Revenue**	**338,971**	**356,196**	**525,753**	**338,971**	**356,196**	**525,753**	**532,569**	**617,954**	**716,098**	**634,749**	**639,957**	**831,806**
11	**Taxes**	**257,309**	**274,447**	**406,684**	**257,309**	**274,447**	**406,684**	**257,309**	**274,447**	**406,684**	**339,918**	**353,612**	**495,002**
111	Taxes on income, profits, and capital gains	61,883	52,588	79,838	61,883	52,588	79,838	61,883	52,588	79,838	127,145	115,404	139,036
1111	Payable by individuals	7,565	12,646	45,062	7,565	12,646	45,062	7,565	12,646	45,062	72,151	75,203	99,983
1112	Payable by corporations and other enterprises	54,318	39,942	34,776	54,318	39,942	34,776	54,318	39,942	34,776	54,994	40,202	39,053
1113	Other taxes on income, profits, and capital gains	—	—	—	—	—	—	—	—	—	—	—	—
112	Taxes on payroll and workforce	—	—	—	—	—	—	—	—	—	6,641	7,414	6,745
113	Taxes on property	—	—	—	—	—	—	—	—	—	3,366	3,161	5,240
114	Taxes on goods and services	181,864	209,004	286,484	181,864	209,004	286,484	181,864	209,004	286,484	189,074	214,655	303,073
1141	General taxes on goods and services	128,269	139,024	180,485	128,269	139,024	180,485	128,269	139,024	180,485	128,269	139,024	180,485
1142	Excises	35,309	44,941	63,111	35,309	44,941	63,111	35,309	44,941	63,111	36,668	45,100	70,795
115	Taxes on international trade and transactions	13,561	12,855	40,908	13,561	12,855	40,908	13,561	12,855	40,908	13,561	12,855	40,908
116	Other taxes	—	—	-546	—	—	-546	—	—	-546	131	122	—
12	**Social contributions**	—	—	—	—	—	—	**191,822**	**185,420**	**190,081**	**191,822**	**185,420**	**190,081**
121	Social security contributions	—	—	—	—	—	—	191,521	185,192	190,081	191,521	185,192	190,081
122	Other social contributions	—	—	—	—	—	—	301	228	—	301	228	—
13	**Grants**	**3,139**	**7,501**	**4,944**	**3,139**	**7,501**	**4,944**	**3,177**	**83,409**	**5,027**	**1,568**	**5,439**	**1,965**
131	From foreign governments	—	—	—	—	—	—	39	56	83	39	56	83
132	From international organizations	1,529	5,383	1,800	1,529	5,383	1,800	1,529	5,383	1,800	1,529	5,383	1,882
133	From other general government units	1,609	2,118	3,144	1,609	2,118	3,144	1,609	2,118	3,144	0	—	—
1331	Current	1,526	2,055	2,871	1,526	2,055	2,871	1,526	2,055	2,871	0	—	—
1332	Capital	83	63	273	83	63	273	83	63	273	0	—	—
14	**Other revenue**	**78,524**	**74,249**	**114,124**	**78,524**	**74,249**	**114,124**	**80,261**	**74,678**	**114,307**	**101,441**	**95,486**	**144,760**
	Table 2 Expense by economic type												
2	**Expense**	**396,332**	**425,638**	**550,500**	**396,332**	**425,638**	**550,500**	**588,988**	**690,954**	**743,094**	**681,438**	**697,964**	**821,916**
21	**Compensation of employees**	**64,314**	**69,284**	**79,855**	**64,314**	**69,284**	**79,855**	**68,280**	**72,988**	**83,594**	**171,642**	**166,157**	**189,305**
211	Wages and salaries	48,633	52,554	61,025	48,633	52,554	61,025	51,557	55,287	63,789	127,782	123,956	141,645
212	Employers' social contributions	15,681	16,730	18,830	15,681	16,730	18,830	16,723	17,701	19,805	43,861	42,201	47,660
22	**Use of goods and services**	**61,326**	**65,432**	**87,324**	**61,326**	**65,432**	**87,324**	**62,624**	**66,130**	**88,147**	**100,409**	**108,649**	**143,517**
23	**Consumption of fixed capital**	...	...	...	...	...	...	...	...	...	...	...	...
24	**Interest**	**34,409**	**51,018**	**86,808**	**34,409**	**51,018**	**86,808**	**34,409**	**51,018**	**86,808**	**35,904**	**52,484**	**88,484**
25	**Subsidies**	**19,269**	**17,111**	**10,139**	**19,269**	**17,111**	**10,139**	**20,010**	**17,132**	**10,139**	**30,122**	**37,078**	**25,609**

Ukraine (926)

In Millions of Ukrainian Hryvnias (UAH) / Fiscal Year Ends December 31st

		Budgetary Central Government			Central Government (excl. Social Security)			Central Government (incl. Social Security)			General Government		
		2013	2014	2015P	2013	2014	2015P	2013	2014	2015P	2013	2014	2015P
26	**Grants**	**199,543**	**206,643**	**270,420**	**199,543**	**206,643**	**270,420**	**116,179**	**206,643**	**175,587**	**332**	**192**	**1,608**
261	To foreign governments	—	—	—	—	—	—	—	—	—	—	—	—
262	To international organizations	330	191	1,607	330	191	1,607	330	191	1,607	332	192	1,608
263	To other general government units	199,213	206,453	268,812	199,213	206,453	268,812	115,848	130,601	173,980	0	—	—
2631	Current	196,592	205,367	266,180	196,592	205,367	266,180	113,228	129,515	171,348	0	—	—
2632	Capital	2,621	1,086	2,633	2,621	1,086	2,633	2,621	1,086	2,633	0	—	—
27	**Social benefits**	**4,745**	**5,366**	**9,176**	**4,745**	**5,366**	**9,176**	**274,744**	**266,246**	**292,019**	**324,771**	**317,627**	**357,119**
271	Social security benefits	—	—	—	—	—	—	218,825	209,669	227,965	218,825	209,669	227,965
272	Social assistance benefits	4,745	5,366	9,176	4,745	5,366	9,176	55,919	56,578	64,055	105,946	107,958	129,154
273	Employment-related social benefits	—	—	—	—	—	—	—	—	—	—	—	—
28	**Other expense**	**12,725**	**10,784**	**6,779**	**12,725**	**10,784**	**6,779**	**12,742**	**10,796**	**6,800**	**18,258**	**15,778**	**16,274**
281	Property expense other than interest	—	—	—	—	—	—	—	—	—	—	—	—
282	Transfers not elsewhere classified	12,725	10,784	6,779	12,725	10,784	6,779	12,742	10,796	6,800	18,258	15,778	16,274
2821	Current	4,626	9,050	3,549	4,626	9,050	3,549	4,643	9,062	3,571	5,940	10,204	5,280
2822	Capital	8,099	1,734	3,230	8,099	1,734	3,230	8,099	1,734	3,230	12,318	5,574	10,994
	Table 3 Transactions in assets and liabilities												
3	**Change in net worth from transactions**	...	...	...	...	...	...	...	...	...	...	...	...
31	**Net/Gross investment in nonfinancial assets**	**6,869**	**3,691**	**2,678**	**6,869**	**3,691**	**2,678**	**7,039**	**3,705**	**2,700**	**15,595**	**12,624**	**25,211**
311	Fixed assets	6,701	4,119	9,980	6,701	4,119	9,980	6,871	4,133	10,002	16,105	13,562	32,762
3111	Buildings and structures	1,229	807	2,879	1,229	807	2,879	1,242	812	2,896	2,546	2,137	9,202
3112	Machinery and equipment	3,681	2,720	4,602	3,681	2,720	4,602	3,718	2,722	4,603	6,452	5,811	8,792
3113	Other fixed assets	1,790	592	2,498	1,790	592	2,498	1,910	598	2,502	7,107	5,613	14,769
3114	Weapons systems	...	...	...	—	...	...	—	...	...	—	...	...
312	Inventories	-41	-832	229	-41	-832	229	-41	-832	229	-41	-832	229
313	Valuables	-7	-9	-7	-7	-9	-7	-7	-9	-7	26	-9	-7
314	Nonproduced assets	217	413	-7,523	217	413	-7,523	217	413	-7,523	-495	-97	-7,774
3141	Land	217	413	1,247	217	413	1,247	217	413	1,247	-495	-97	997
3142	Mineral and energy resources	—	—	—	—	—	—	—	—	—	—	—	—
3143	Other naturally occurring assets	—	—	—	—	—	—	—	—	—	—	—	—
3144	Intangible nonproduced assets	—	—	-8,770	—	—	-8,770	—	—	-8,770	—	—	-8,770
32	**Net acquisition of financial assets**	**16,810**	**128,700**	**82,416**	**16,810**	**128,700**	**82,416**	**17,892**	**126,097**	**80,146**	**23,449**	**130,590**	**91,818**
	By instrument												
3201	Monetary gold and SDRs	—	—	—	—	—	—	—	—	—	—	—	—
3202	Currency and deposits	3,112	922	-2,541	3,112	922	-2,541	4,194	-1,682	-4,865	9,709	2,771	6,700
3203	Debt securities	—	—	—	—	—	—	—	—	—	—	—	—
3204	Loans	478	4,919	2,951	478	4,919	2,951	478	4,919	2,951	535	4,972	3,011
3205	Equity and investment fund shares	13,220	122,859	74,886	13,220	122,859	74,886	13,220	122,859	74,886	13,204	122,847	74,932
3206	Insurance, pension, and standardized guarantee schemes	—	—	—	—	—	—	—	—	—	—	—	—
3207	Financial derivatives and employee stock options	—	—	—	—	—	—	—	—	—	—	—	—
3208	Other accounts receivable	...	...	7,121	...	...	7,121	...	...	7,174	...	...	7,174
	By debtor												
321	Domestic debtors	16,810	128,700	82,416	16,810	128,700	82,416	17,892	126,097	80,146	23,449	130,590	91,818
322	External debtors	—	—	—	—	—	—	—	—	—	—	—	—
33	**Net incurrence of liabilities**	**81,039**	**201,834**	**109,842**	**81,039**	**201,834**	**109,842**	**81,350**	**202,803**	**109,842**	**85,733**	**201,220**	**107,137**
	By instrument												
3301	Special Drawing Rights (SDRs)	—	—	848	—	—	848	—	—	848	—	—	848
3302	Currency and deposits	—	—	—	—	—	—	—	—	—	—	—	—
3303	Debt securities	—	—	8,999	—	—	8,999	—	—	8,999	—	—	6,673
3304	Loans	81,039	201,834	99,995	81,039	201,834	99,995	81,350	202,803	99,995	85,733	201,220	99,614
3305	Equity and investment fund shares	—	—	—	—	—	—	—	—	—	—	—	—
3306	Insurance, pension, and standardized guarantee schemes	—	—	—	—	—	—	—	—	—	—	—	—
3307	Financial derivatives and employee stock options	—	—	—	—	—	—	—	—	—	—	—	—
3308	Other accounts payable	...	...	...	...	...	...	...	...	...	...	...	2

Ukraine (926)

In Millions of Ukrainian Hryvnias (UAH) / Fiscal Year Ends December 31st

		Budgetary Central Government			Central Government (excl. Social Security)			Central Government (incl. Social Security)			General Government		
		2013	2014	2015P	2013	2014	2015P	2013	2014	2015P	2013	2014	2015P
	By creditor												
331	Domestic creditors	67,109	159,577	7,817	67,109	159,577	7,817	67,420	160,546	7,817	71,834	159,045	5,152
332	External creditors	13,930	42,256	102,025	13,930	42,256	102,025	13,930	42,256	102,025	13,899	42,175	101,986
	Table 4 Holding gains and losses in assets and liabilities												
	Table 5 Holding gains and losses in assets and liabilities												
	Table 6 Balance sheet												
6	**Net worth**	**207,496**	**-85,397**	**-315,503**	**207,496**	**-85,397**	**-315,503**	**183,827**	**-115,558**	**-346,962**	**402,616**	**113,244**	**-75,365**
61	**Nonfinancial assets**	**457,462**	**463,167**	**496,713**	**457,462**	**463,167**	**496,713**	**461,902**	**467,309**	**500,786**	**678,203**	**692,528**	**748,516**
611	Fixed assets	410,167	415,299	446,926	410,167	415,299	446,926	414,481	419,342	450,894	630,782	644,561	698,624
6111	Buildings and structures	...	...	...	...	...	...	...	...	...	...	...	...
6112	Machinery and equipment	...	...	...	...	...	...	...	...	...	...	...	...
6113	Other fixed assets	...	...	...	...	...	...	...	...	...	...	...	...
6114	Weapons systems	...	...	...	...	...	...	...	...	...	...	...	...
612	Inventories	47,295	47,868	49,787	47,295	47,868	49,787	47,421	47,967	49,892	47,421	47,967	49,892
613	Valuables	—	—	—	—	—	—	—	—	—	—	—	—
614	Nonproduced assets	—	—	—	—	—	—	—	—	—	—	—	—
6141	Land	—	—	—	—	—	—	—	—	—	—	—	—
6142	Mineral and energy resources	—	—	—	—	—	—	—	—	—	—	—	—
6143	Other naturally occurring assets	—	—	—	—	—	—	—	—	—	—	—	—
6144	Intangible nonproduced assets	—	—	—	—	—	—	—	—	—	—	—	—
62	**Financial assets**	**241,690**	**408,146**	**532,401**	**241,690**	**408,146**	**532,401**	**264,469**	**427,447**	**549,380**	**288,055**	**454,889**	**588,075**
	By instrument												
6201	Monetary gold and SDRs	—	—	—	—	—	—	—	—	—	—	—	—
6202	Currency and deposits	3,869	13,252	38,270	3,869	13,252	38,270	10,563	18,411	42,097	10,868	18,779	42,622
6203	Debt securities	176	347	52,146	176	347	52,146	176	347	52,146	176	347	52,146
6204	Loans	88,757	120,889	151,140	88,757	120,889	151,140	88,757	120,889	151,140	89,526	121,703	152,041
6205	Equity and investment fund shares	118,314	241,640	265,059	118,314	241,640	265,059	118,314	241,640	265,059	118,524	241,850	265,316
6206	Insurance, pension, and standardized guarantee schemes	—	—	—	—	—	—	—	—	—	—	—	—
6207	Financial derivatives and employee stock options	—	—	—	—	—	—	—	—	—	—	—	—
6208	Other accounts receivable	30,574	32,019	25,786	30,574	32,019	25,786	46,659	46,161	38,938	68,962	72,210	75,951
	By debtor												
621	Domestic debtors	241,690	408,146	532,401	241,690	408,146	532,401	264,469	427,447	549,380	288,055	454,889	588,075
622	External debtors	—	—	—	—	—	—	—	—	—	—	—	—
63	**Liabilities**	**491,656**	**956,710**	**1,344,616**	**491,656**	**956,710**	**1,344,616**	**542,544**	**1,010,315**	**1,397,128**	**563,642**	**1,034,173**	**1,411,956**
	By instrument												
6301	Special Drawing Rights (SDRs)	15,167	28,054	2,709	15,167	28,054	2,709	15,167	28,054	2,709	15,167	28,054	2,709
6302	Currency and deposits	—	—	—	—	—	—	—	—	—	—	—	—
6303	Debt securities	392,959	730,736	920,626	392,959	730,736	920,626	392,959	730,736	920,626	403,353	744,889	923,683
6304	Loans	72,093	188,240	410,526	72,093	188,240	410,526	121,525	238,641	460,926	132,120	248,237	472,698
6305	Equity and investment fund shares	—	—	—	—	—	—	—	—	—	—	—	—
6306	Insurance, pension, and standardized guarantee schemes	—	—	—	—	—	—	—	—	—	—	—	—
6307	Financial derivatives and employee stock options	—	—	—	—	—	—	—	—	—	—	—	—
6308	Other accounts payable	11,437	9,680	10,756	11,437	9,680	10,756	12,893	12,884	12,867	13,003	12,993	12,867
	By creditor												
631	Domestic creditors	268,397	470,683	518,757	268,397	470,683	518,757	319,285	524,288	571,268	335,872	539,377	583,581
632	External creditors	223,259	486,027	825,860	223,259	486,027	825,860	223,259	486,027	825,860	227,770	494,796	828,376
	Memorandum items												
6M2	Net financial worth	-249,966	-548,564	-812,215	-249,966	-548,564	-812,215	-278,075	-582,867	-847,748	-275,587	-579,284	-823,881
6M3	Gross debt (D4) at market value	...	...	...	...	...	...	...	...	...	...	...	...
6M3D3	D3 debt liabilities at market value	...	...	...	...	...	...	...	...	...	...	...	...
6M3D2	D2 debt liabilities at market value	...	...	...	...	...	...	...	...	...	...	...	...
6M3D1	D1 debt liabilities at market value	...	...	...	...	...	...	...	...	...	...	...	...
6M4	Gross debt (D4) at nominal value	491,656	956,710	1,344,616	491,656	956,710	1,344,616	542,544	1,010,315	1,397,128	563,642	1,034,173	1,411,956
6M4D3	D3 debt liabilities at nominal value	491,656	956,710	1,344,616	491,656	956,710	1,344,616	542,544	1,010,315	1,397,128	563,642	1,034,173	1,411,956
6M4D2	D2 debt liabilities at nominal value	480,219	947,030	1,333,861	480,219	947,030	1,333,861	529,651	997,431	1,384,261	550,640	1,021,180	1,399,089
6M4D1	D1 debt liabilities at nominal value	465,052	918,976	1,331,152	465,052	918,976	1,331,152	514,484	969,376	1,381,552	535,473	993,126	1,396,381

Ukraine (926)

In Millions of Ukrainian Hryvnias (UAH) / Fiscal Year Ends December 31st

		Budgetary Central Government			Central Government (excl. Social Security)			Central Government (incl. Social Security)			General Government		
		2013	2014	2015P	2013	2014	2015P	2013	2014	2015P	2013	2014	2015P
6M35	Gross debt (D4) at face value	...	...	...	...	...	...	...	...	...	...	...	...
6M35D3	D3 debt liabilities at face value	...	...	...	...	...	...	...	...	...	...	...	...
6M35D2	D2 debt liabilities at face value	...	...	...	...	...	...	...	...	...	...	...	...
6M35D1	D1 debt liabilities at face value	...	...	...	...	...	...	...	...	...	...	...	...
6M93	Government gross debt per national definition	...	...	...	...	...	...	...	...	...	...	...	...
6M5	Arrears	...	...	...	...	...	...	...	...	...	...	...	...
6M6	Explicit contingent liabilities	104,151	...	...	104,151	...	...	104,151	...	...	105,812	...	...
6M61	of which: Publicly guaranteed debt	...	153,802	237,905	...	153,802	237,905	...	153,802	237,905	...	157,463	243,162
6M7	Net implicit obligations for social security benefits	...	...	...	...	...	...	...	...	...	...	...	...
	Table 7 Expenditure by functions of government												
7	**Expenditure**	**403,201**	**429,330**	**553,179**	**403,201**	**429,330**	**553,179**	**596,027**	**770,511**	**745,795**	**697,033**	**710,588**	**847,127**
701	**General public services**	**168,729**	**198,622**	**271,219**	**168,729**	**198,622**	**271,219**	**168,729**	**198,622**	**176,387**	**64,482**	**77,913**	**110,137**
7017	Public debt transactions	34,409	51,018	86,808	34,409	51,018	86,808	34,409	51,018	86,808	35,904	52,484	88,484
7018	Transfers of general character between levels of government	115,848	130,601	173,980	115,848	130,601	173,980	115,848	130,601	79,148	0	—	—
702	**Defense**	**14,843**	**27,363**	**52,005**	**14,843**	**27,363**	**52,005**	**14,843**	**27,363**	**52,005**	**14,844**	**27,366**	**52,016**
703	**Public order and safety**	**39,191**	**44,619**	**54,643**	**39,191**	**44,619**	**54,643**	**39,191**	**44,619**	**54,643**	**39,409**	**44,865**	**54,963**
704	**Economic affairs**	**38,520**	**31,328**	**19,280**	**38,520**	**31,328**	**19,280**	**39,762**	**31,328**	**19,280**	**49,220**	**40,555**	**38,402**
7042	Agriculture, forestry, fishing, and hunting	7,561	5,759	4,733	7,561	5,759	4,733	7,561	5,759	4,733	7,705	5,868	6,063
7043	Fuel and energy	15,389	9,336	1,890	15,389	9,336	1,890	15,389	9,336	1,890	15,422	9,339	1,896
7044	Mining, manufacturing, and construction	431	249	275	431	249	275	431	249	275	505	343	438
7045	Transport	11,427	11,458	5,458	11,427	11,458	5,458	11,427	11,458	5,458	15,117	15,806	13,464
7046	Communication	127	123	124	127	123	124	127	123	124	186	190	263
705	**Environmental protection**	**4,595**	**2,597**	**4,053**	**4,595**	**2,597**	**4,053**	**4,595**	**2,597**	**4,053**	**5,594**	**3,482**	**5,530**
706	**Housing and community amenities**	**97**	**112**	**22**	**97**	**112**	**22**	**97**	**112**	**22**	**7,705**	**17,809**	**15,700**
707	**Health**	**12,879**	**10,581**	**11,450**	**12,879**	**10,581**	**11,450**	**14,881**	**11,995**	**11,851**	**63,570**	**58,565**	**71,402**
7072	Outpatient services	1,639	624	666	1,639	624	666	1,653	635	679	12,733	12,319	14,232
7073	Hospital services	6,622	5,492	4,474	6,622	5,492	4,474	8,517	6,842	4,776	42,147	38,213	46,316
7074	Public health services	4,287	1,019	1,110	4,287	1,019	1,110	4,287	1,019	1,110	8,266	1,051	1,144
708	**Recreation, culture and religion**	**5,112**	**4,872**	**6,619**	**5,112**	**4,872**	**6,619**	**5,315**	**5,051**	**6,619**	**13,864**	**14,037**	**16,228**
709	**Education**	**30,943**	**28,678**	**30,186**	**30,943**	**28,678**	**30,186**	**30,943**	**28,678**	**30,186**	**105,539**	**100,110**	**114,193**
7091	Pre-primary and primary education	72	65	95	72	65	95	72	65	95	15,662	15,186	18,142
7092	Secondary education	221	194	188	221	194	188	221	194	188	44,233	42,422	49,668
7094	Tertiary education	27,654	26,068	28,542	27,654	26,068	28,542	27,654	26,068	28,542	30,998	29,237	31,934
710	**Social protection**	**88,547**	**80,558**	**103,701**	**88,547**	**80,558**	**103,701**	**277,927**	**420,146**	**390,749**	**334,443**	**325,889**	**368,555**
7z	Statistical discrepancy: Expenditure	—	—	—	—	—	—	0	0	0	0	0	0
	Table 8 Financial transactions by counterpart sector												
32	**Net acquisition of financial assets**	**16,810**	**128,700**	**82,416**	**16,810**	**128,700**	**82,416**	**17,892**	**126,097**	**80,146**	**23,449**	**130,590**	**91,818**
321	Domestic debtors	16,810	128,700	82,416	16,810	128,700	82,416	17,892	126,097	80,146	23,449	130,590	91,818
3211	General government	-1,480	-467	...	-1,480	-467	...	-398	-3,070	...	5,117	1,382	...
3212	Central bank	3,112	922	...	3,112	922	...	3,112	922	...	3,112	922	...
3213	Deposit-taking corporations except the central bank	1,400	16,599	...	1,400	16,599	...	1,400	16,599	...	1,384	16,587	...
3214	Other financial corporations	—	10,118	...	—	10,118	...	—	10,118	...	—	10,118	...
3215	Nonfinancial corporations	13,778	101,538	...	13,778	101,538	...	13,778	101,538	...	13,835	101,546	...
3216	Households & nonprofit institutions serving households	—	-9	...	—	-9	...	—	-9	...	—	36	...
322	External debtors	—	—	—	—	—	—	—	—	—	—	—	—
3221	General government	—	—	—	—	—	—	—	—	—	—	—	—
3227	International organizations	—	—	—	—	—	—	—	—	—	—	—	—
3228	Financial corporations other than international organizations	—	—	—	—	—	—	—	—	—	—	—	—
3229	Other nonresidents	—	—	—	—	—	—	—	—	—	—	—	—

Ukraine (926)

In Millions of Ukrainian Hryvnias (UAH) / Fiscal Year Ends December 31st

		Budgetary Central Government			Central Government (excl. Social Security)			Central Government (incl. Social Security)			General Government		
		2013	2014	2015P	2013	2014	2015P	2013	2014	2015P	2013	2014	2015P
33	**Net incurrence of liabilities**	**81,039**	**201,834**	**109,842**	**81,039**	**201,834**	**109,842**	**81,350**	**202,803**	**109,842**	**85,733**	**201,220**	**107,137**
331	Domestic creditors	67,109	159,577	7,817	67,109	159,577	7,817	67,420	160,546	7,817	71,834	159,045	5,152
8311	General government	—	—	...	—	—	...	311	969	...	5,253	278	...
8312	Central bank	-132	159,577	...	-132	159,577	...	-132	159,577	...	-376	159,078	...
8313	Deposit-taking corporations except the central bank	67,241	—	...	67,241	—	...	67,241	—	...	66,957	-310	...
8314	Other financial corporations	—	—	...	—	—	...	—	—	...	—	—	...
8315	Nonfinancial corporations	—	—	...	—	—	...	—	—	...	—	—	...
8316	Households & nonprofit institutions serving households	—	—	...	—	—	...	—	—	...	—	—	...
332	External creditors	13,930	42,256	102,025	13,930	42,256	102,025	13,930	42,256	102,025	13,899	42,175	101,986
8321	General government	-1,505	2,566	...	-1,505	2,566	...	-1,505	2,566	...	-1,505	2,566	...
8327	International organizations	-18,536	39,813	...	-18,536	39,813	...	-18,536	39,813	...	-18,527	39,816	...
8328	Financial corporations other than international organizations	—	—	...	—	—	...	—	—	...	-42	-85	...
8329	Other nonresidents	33,970	-122	...	33,970	-122	...	33,970	-122	...	33,973	-122	...
	Table 9 Total other economic flows in assets and liabilities												

United Arab Emirates (466)

In Millions of U.A.E. Dirhams (AED) / Fiscal Year Ends December 31st

		Budgetary Central Government			Central Government (excl. Social Security)			Central Government (incl. Social Security)			General Government		
		2013	2014	2015	2013	2014	2015	2013	2014	2015	2013	2014	2015
	Statement of operations												
1	Revenue	45,947	45,221	46,116	58,271	57,332	60,175	62,605	61,777	64,201	412,072	380,655	281,261
2	Expense	42,282	44,224	44,654	54,043	54,644	53,647	57,465	57,670	56,405	340,265	374,725	335,334
GOB	**Gross operating balance**	**3,665**	**997**	**1,463**	**4,228**	**2,688**	**6,528**	**5,509**	**4,529**	**8,504**	**75,128**	**9,696**	**-49,481**
NOB	**Net operating balance**	...	...	...	...	...	...	**5,140**	**4,107**	**7,796**	**71,807**	**5,930**	**-54,073**
31	Net/Gross investment in nonfinancial assets	1,396	1,602	2,259	1,864	5,375	7,865	1,870	5,378	7,887	33,505	39,886	35,066
2M	Expenditure	43,678	45,826	46,913	55,907	60,019	61,512	59,335	63,049	64,291	373,770	414,611	370,399
NLB	**Net lending (+) / Net borrowing (-)**	**2,270**	**-604**	**-797**	**2,364**	**-2,688**	**-1,337**	**3,270**	**-1,271**	**-90**	**38,302**	**-33,956**	**-89,138**
32	Net acquisition of financial assets	-32,685	-4,389	-22	-31,185	-2,570	11,044	-28,131	-1,235	12,433	72,303	-16,776	-46,035
33	Net incurrence of liabilities	-34,954	-3,785	775	-33,549	118	12,380	-31,401	36	12,523	34,001	17,180	43,104
NLBz	Statistical discrepancy	-0	0	0	0	0	0	0	-0	0	-0	0	0
	Memorandum items												
PB	Primary net lending / net borrowing	2,270	-604	-797	2,364	-2,688	-1,337	3,270	-1,271	-90	44,210	-29,881	-86,348
GB	Government balance per national definition	...	...	...	...	...	...	...	...	...	...	...	...
	Statement of other economic flows												
	Balance sheet												
6	**Net worth**	...	...	...	...	...	...	...	...	...	...	...	...
61	Nonfinancial assets	...	...	...	...	...	...	...	...	...	...	...	...
62	Financial assets	39,451	...	...	46,518	...	...	46,561	...	...	289,790	...	...
63	Liabilities	22,503	...	...	27,126	...	...	27,128	...	...	237,069	...	...
	Table 1 Revenue												
1	**Revenue**	**45,947**	**45,221**	**46,116**	**58,271**	**57,332**	**60,175**	**62,605**	**61,777**	**64,201**	**412,072**	**380,655**	**281,261**
11	**Taxes**	**1,131**	**1,001**	**903**	**1,131**	**1,001**	**1,107**	**5,307**	**5,267**	**759**	**314,875**	**275,622**	**160,031**
111	Taxes on income, profits, and capital gains	—	—	—	—	—	—	—	—	—	14,350	15,479	10,478
1111	Payable by individuals	—	—	—	—	—	—	—	—	—	—	—	—
1112	Payable by corporations and other enterprises	—	—	—	—	—	—	—	—	—	14,350	15,479	10,478
1113	Other taxes on income, profits, and capital gains	—	—	—	—	—	—	—	—	—	—	—	—
112	Taxes on payroll and workforce	—	—	—	—	—	—	—	—	—	—	—	—
113	Taxes on property	—	—	—	—	—	—	—	—	—	342	—	—
114	Taxes on goods and services	996	843	774	996	843	978	5,173	5,109	631	290,342	249,442	138,278
1141	General taxes on goods and services	—	—	—	—	—	—	—	—	—	285,626	243,948	132,330
1142	Excises	—	—	—	—	—	—	—	—	—	—	—	—
115	Taxes on international trade and transactions	134	158	128	134	158	129	134	158	129	9,760	10,639	11,180
116	Other taxes	—	—	—	—	—	—	—	—	—	82	63	96
12	**Social contributions**	**1,473**	**1,643**	**712**	**1,473**	**1,643**	**712**	**5,079**	**5,271**	**4,271**	**5,104**	**5,297**	**4,297**
121	Social security contributions	1,473	1,643	—	1,473	1,643	—	5,079	5,271	3,559	5,104	5,297	3,585
122	Other social contributions	—	—	712	—	—	712	—	—	712	—	—	712
13	**Grants**	**16,116**	**16,039**	**17,320**	**17,695**	**17,223**	**17,767**	**17,695**	**17,223**	**17,767**	—	—	—
131	From foreign governments	—	—	—	—	—	—	—	—	—	—	—	—
132	From international organizations	—	—	—	—	—	—	—	—	—	—	—	—
133	From other general government units	16,116	16,039	17,320	17,695	17,223	17,767	17,695	17,223	17,767	—	—	—
1331	Current	12,053	12,053	12,053	13,629	13,235	12,053	13,629	13,235	12,053	—	—	—
1332	Capital	4,063	3,986	5,267	4,066	3,988	5,714	4,066	3,988	5,714	—	—	—
14	**Other revenue**	**27,228**	**26,539**	**27,181**	**37,973**	**37,465**	**40,589**	**34,524**	**34,016**	**41,403**	**92,093**	**99,736**	**116,932**
	Table 2 Expense by economic type												
2	**Expense**	**42,282**	**44,224**	**44,654**	**54,043**	**54,644**	**53,647**	**57,465**	**57,670**	**56,405**	**340,265**	**374,725**	**335,334**
21	**Compensation of employees**	**14,998**	**16,116**	**16,155**	**18,465**	**19,706**	**20,623**	**18,519**	**19,762**	**20,683**	**42,127**	**47,519**	**63,010**
211	Wages and salaries	14,957	16,064	16,155	18,316	19,536	20,618	18,370	19,592	20,679	41,885	47,253	62,971
212	Employers' social contributions	41	52	—	149	170	5	149	170	5	242	266	38
22	**Use of goods and services**	**11,937**	**12,153**	**12,625**	**16,770**	**16,915**	**20,712**	**16,797**	**16,950**	**20,748**	**43,183**	**49,505**	**59,800**
23	**Consumption of fixed capital**	...	...	...	...	...	...	**369**	**422**	**708**	**3,321**	**3,766**	**4,591**
24	**Interest**	—	—	—	—	—	—	—	—	—	**5,909**	**4,075**	**2,791**
25	**Subsidies**	**20**	**12**	**12**	**20**	**12**	**497**	**20**	**12**	**497**	**10,066**	**12,079**	**12,286**

United Arab Emirates (466)

In Millions of U.A.E. Dirhams (AED) / Fiscal Year Ends December 31st

		Budgetary Central Government			Central Government (excl. Social Security)			Central Government (incl. Social Security)			General Government		
		2013	2014	2015	2013	2014	2015	2013	2014	2015	2013	2014	2015
26	**Grants**	**5,562**	**5,717**	**6,218**	**768**	**857**	**671**	**768**	**857**	**671**	**21,630**	**21,944**	**8,771**
261	To foreign governments	32	6	26	474	534	384	474	534	384	21,336	21,621	8,484
262	To international organizations	294	323	286	294	323	287	294	323	287	294	323	287
263	To other general government units	5,236	5,387	5,906	—	—	0	—	—	0	—	—	0
2631	Current	5,236	5,387	5,906	—	—	0	—	—	0	—	—	0
2632	Capital	—	—	—	—	—	—	—	—	—	—	—	-0
27	**Social benefits**	**9,617**	**9,090**	**7,373**	**10,576**	**9,979**	**8,085**	**13,900**	**12,886**	**10,735**	**52,449**	**61,442**	**42,595**
271	Social security benefits	2	—	—	3	—	—	2,759	2,341	1	2,872	2,504	8
272	Social assistance benefits	4,044	4,059	2,736	4,528	4,515	3,196	5,089	5,077	3,196	41,494	51,589	31,253
273	Employment-related social benefits	5,571	5,031	4,638	6,046	5,463	4,889	6,053	5,467	7,538	8,084	7,348	11,334
28	**Other expense**	**149**	**1,137**	**2,271**	**7,076**	**6,759**	**2,363**	**7,091**	**6,782**	**2,363**	**161,581**	**174,395**	**141,490**
281	Property expense other than interest	—	—	—	—	—	—	—	—	—	—	—	—
282	Transfers not elsewhere classified	149	1,137	2,271	7,076	6,759	2,363	7,091	6,782	2,363	161,581	174,395	141,490
2821	Current	144	1,137	2,271	7,072	6,759	2,363	7,087	6,782	2,363	61,137	64,899	65,773
2822	Capital	4	—	—	4	—	—	4	—	—	100,444	109,496	75,717
	Table 3 Transactions in assets and liabilities												
3	**Change in net worth from transactions**	...	...	...	...	...	...	**5,140**	**4,107**	**7,796**	**71,807**	**5,930**	**-54,073**
31	**Net/Gross investment in nonfinancial assets**	**1,396**	**1,602**	**2,259**	**1,864**	**5,375**	**7,865**	**1,870**	**5,378**	**7,887**	**33,505**	**39,886**	**35,066**
311	Fixed assets	1,396	1,602	2,259	1,806	5,310	7,727	1,811	5,313	7,749	33,959	39,840	35,513
3111	Buildings and structures	879	1,081	1,430	-705	4,492	6,563	-706	4,490	6,562	17,863	24,521	23,931
3112	Machinery and equipment	494	390	602	2,469	630	836	2,468	629	833	15,983	14,881	10,916
3113	Other fixed assets	22	130	227	42	188	328	49	193	353	113	437	665
3114	Weapons systems	—	—	—	—	—	—	—	—	—	—	—	—
312	Inventories	—	—	—	59	65	138	59	65	138	63	66	141
313	Valuables	—	—	—	—	—	—	—	—	—	—	—	—
314	Nonproduced assets	—	—	—	—	—	—	—	—	—	-517	-20	-588
3141	Land	—	—	—	—	—	—	—	—	—	-517	-20	-588
3142	Mineral and energy resources	—	—	—	—	—	—	—	—	—	—	—	—
3143	Other naturally occurring assets	—	—	—	—	—	—	—	—	—	-0	—	—
3144	Intangible nonproduced assets	—	—	—	—	—	—	—	—	—	—	—	—
32	**Net acquisition of financial assets**	**-32,685**	**-4,389**	**-22**	**-31,185**	**-2,570**	**11,044**	**-28,131**	**-1,235**	**12,433**	**72,303**	**-16,776**	**-46,035**
	By instrument												
3201	Monetary gold and SDRs	—	—	—	—	—	—	—	—	—	—	—	—
3202	Currency and deposits	897	954	-937	2,837	2,704	2,796	-2,861	-1,517	-3,948	-31,255	-103,449	-134,701
3203	Debt securities	—	—	—	—	—	—	-134	—	260	-564	-8	260
3204	Loans	—	—	—	-252	-276	—	9,247	-276	187	107,109	33,539	29,230
3205	Equity and investment fund shares	1,000	1,750	768	1,173	1,969	1,112	1,416	8,813	8,647	36,114	52,958	23,637
3206	Insurance, pension, and standardized guarantee schemes	—	—	—	—	—	—	—	—	—	-26	—	—
3207	Financial derivatives and employee stock options	—	—	—	—	—	—	—	—	—	—	—	—
3208	Other accounts receivable	-34,582	-7,093	147	-34,944	-6,966	7,135	-35,799	-8,255	7,287	-39,076	184	35,540
	By debtor												
321	Domestic debtors	-32,685	-4,389	-22	-31,185	-2,570	11,044	-37,495	-1,862	12,355	62,948	-17,402	-46,113
322	External debtors	—	—	—	—	—	—	9,364	626	78	9,354	626	78
33	**Net incurrence of liabilities**	**-34,954**	**-3,785**	**775**	**-33,549**	**118**	**12,380**	**-31,401**	**36**	**12,523**	**34,001**	**17,180**	**43,104**
	By instrument												
3301	Special Drawing Rights (SDRs)	—	—	—	—	—	—	—	—	—	—	—	—
3302	Currency and deposits	—	—	—	—	—	—	—	—	—	-132	—	—
3303	Debt securities	—	—	—	—	—	—	—	—	—	84,191	-274	-2,005
3304	Loans	—	—	—	45	—	—	45	—	—	-26,583	3,063	5,973
3305	Equity and investment fund shares	—	—	—	—	—	—	—	—	—	—	—	—
3306	Insurance, pension, and standardized guarantee schemes	—	—	—	—	—	—	—	—	—	—	—	—
3307	Financial derivatives and employee stock options	—	—	—	—	—	—	—	—	—	—	—	—
3308	Other accounts payable	-34,954	-3,785	775	-33,594	118	12,380	-31,446	36	12,523	-23,475	14,392	39,136

United Arab Emirates (466)

In Millions of U.A.E. Dirhams (AED) / Fiscal Year Ends December 31st

		Budgetary Central Government			Central Government (excl. Social Security)			Central Government (incl. Social Security)			General Government		
		2013	2014	2015	2013	2014	2015	2013	2014	2015	2013	2014	2015
	By creditor												
331	Domestic creditors	-34,954	-3,785	775	-33,549	118	12,380	-31,401	36	12,523	34,001	17,180	43,104
332	External creditors	—	—	—	—	—	—	—	—	—	-0	—	—
	Table 4 Holding gains and losses in assets and liabilities												
	Table 5 Holding gains and losses in assets and liabilities												
	Table 6 Balance sheet												
6	**Net worth**	...	...	...	...	...	...	...	...	...	...	...	...
61	**Nonfinancial assets**	...	...	...	...	...	...	...	...	...	...	...	...
611	Fixed assets	...	...	...	...	...	...	...	...	...	...	...	...
6111	Buildings and structures	...	...	...	...	...	...	...	...	...	...	...	...
6112	Machinery and equipment	...	...	...	...	...	...	...	...	...	...	...	...
6113	Other fixed assets	...	...	...	...	...	...	...	...	...	...	...	...
6114	Weapons systems	...	...	...	...	...	...	...	...	...	...	...	...
612	Inventories	...	...	...	...	...	...	...	...	...	...	...	...
613	Valuables	...	...	...	...	...	...	...	...	...	...	...	...
614	Nonproduced assets	...	...	...	...	...	...	...	...	...	...	...	...
6141	Land	...	...	...	...	...	...	...	...	...	...	...	...
6142	Mineral and energy resources	...	...	...	...	...	...	...	...	...	...	...	...
6143	Other naturally occurring assets	...	...	...	...	...	...	...	...	...	...	...	...
6144	Intangible nonproduced assets	...	...	...	...	...	...	...	...	...	...	...	...
62	**Financial assets**	**39,451**	...	...	**46,518**	...	...	**46,561**	...	...	**289,790**	...	...
	By instrument												
6201	Monetary gold and SDRs	—	...	...	—	...	...	—	...	...	—	...	...
6202	Currency and deposits	4,612	...	...	10,861	...	...	10,884	...	...	25,141	...	...
6203	Debt securities	—	...	...	—	...	...	1	...	...	1,074	...	...
6204	Loans	—	...	...	—	...	...	—	...	...	98,404	...	...
6205	Equity and investment fund shares	12,350	...	...	12,350	...	...	12,362	...	...	72,135	...	...
6206	Insurance, pension, and standardized guarantee schemes	—	...	...	—	...	...	—	...	...	—	...	...
6207	Financial derivatives and employee stock options	—	...	...	—	...	...	—	...	...	—	...	...
6208	Other accounts receivable	22,489	...	...	23,307	...	...	23,314	...	...	93,036	...	...
	By debtor												
621	Domestic debtors	39,451	...	...	46,518	...	...	46,561	...	...	289,790	...	...
622	External debtors	—	...	...	—	...	...	—	...	...	—	...	...
63	**Liabilities**	**22,503**	...	...	**27,126**	...	...	**27,128**	...	...	**237,069**	...	...
	By instrument												
6301	Special Drawing Rights (SDRs)	—	...	...	—	...	...	—	...	...	—	...	...
6302	Currency and deposits	678	...	...	688	...	...	688	...	...	701	...	...
6303	Debt securities	—	...	...	—	...	...	—	...	...	101,592	...	...
6304	Loans	—	...	...	—	...	...	—	...	...	7,042	...	...
6305	Equity and investment fund shares	—	...	...	—	...	...	—	...	...	—	...	...
6306	Insurance, pension, and standardized guarantee schemes	—	...	...	—	...	...	—	...	...	—	...	...
6307	Financial derivatives and employee stock options	—	...	...	—	...	...	—	...	...	—	...	...
6308	Other accounts payable	21,825	...	...	26,438	...	...	26,440	...	...	127,734	...	...
	By creditor												
631	Domestic creditors	22,503	...	...	27,126	...	...	27,128	...	...	237,069	...	...
632	External creditors	—	...	...	—	...	...	—	...	...	—	...	...
	Memorandum items												
6M2	Net financial worth	16,948	...	...	19,392	...	...	19,433	...	...	52,721	...	...
6M3	Gross debt (D4) at market value	...	...	...	...	...	...	...	...	...	...	...	...
6M3D3	D3 debt liabilities at market value	...	...	...	...	...	...	...	...	...	...	...	...
6M3D2	D2 debt liabilities at market value	...	...	...	...	...	...	...	...	...	...	...	...
6M3D1	D1 debt liabilities at market value	...	...	...	...	...	...	...	...	...	...	...	...
6M4	Gross debt (D4) at nominal value	...	...	...	...	...	...	...	...	...	...	...	...
6M4D3	D3 debt liabilities at nominal value	...	...	...	...	...	...	...	...	...	...	...	...
6M4D2	D2 debt liabilities at nominal value	...	...	...	...	...	...	...	...	...	...	...	...
6M4D1	D1 debt liabilities at nominal value	...	...	...	...	...	...	...	...	...	...	...	...

United Arab Emirates (466)

In Millions of U.A.E. Dirhams (AED) / Fiscal Year Ends December 31st

		Budgetary Central Government			Central Government (excl. Social Security)			Central Government (incl. Social Security)			General Government		
		2013	2014	2015	2013	2014	2015	2013	2014	2015	2013	2014	2015
6M35	Gross debt (D4) at face value	22,503	...	...	27,126	...	...	27,128	...	...	237,069	...	...
6M35D3	D3 debt liabilities at face value	22,503	...	...	27,126	...	...	27,128	...	...	237,069	...	...
6M35D2	D2 debt liabilities at face value	678	...	...	688	...	...	688	...	...	109,335	...	...
6M35D1	D1 debt liabilities at face value	—	...	...	—	...	...	—	...	...	108,634	...	...
6M93	Government gross debt per national definition	...	...	...	...	...	...	...	...	...	...	...	...
6M5	Arrears	...	...	...	...	...	...	...	...	...	...	...	...
6M6	Explicit contingent liabilities	...	...	...	...	...	...	...	...	...	...	...	...
6M61	of which: Publicly guaranteed debt	...	...	...	...	...	...	...	...	...	...	...	...
6M7	Net implicit obligations for social security benefits	...	...	...	...	...	...	...	...	...	...	...	...
	Table 7 Expenditure by functions of government												
7	**Expenditure**	43,678	45,826	46,913	55,907	60,019	61,512	59,335	63,049	64,291	373,770	414,611	370,401
701	**General public services**	13,749	16,674	16,885	8,901	11,660	12,878	8,901	11,660	12,878	178,748	203,593	151,254
7017	Public debt transactions	—	—	—	—	—	—	—	—	—	5,909	4,075	2,791
7018	Transfers of general character between levels of government	...	...	—	...	...	—	...	...	—	...	...	—
702	**Defense**	6,143	7,473	6,144	6,143	7,473	6,144	6,143	7,473	6,144	9,348	12,319	10,704
703	**Public order and safety**	9,186	7,934	9,733	9,186	7,934	9,733	9,186	7,934	9,733	27,574	25,435	41,789
704	**Economic affairs**	821	804	833	11,334	12,279	9,433	11,334	12,279	9,433	42,563	44,696	47,702
7042	Agriculture, forestry, fishing, and hunting	...	...	—	...	...	—	...	...	—	...	...	—
7043	Fuel and energy	...	...	—	...	...	—	...	...	—	...	...	—
7044	Mining, manufacturing, and construction	...	...	—	...	...	—	...	...	—	...	...	—
7045	Transport	...	...	—	...	...	—	...	...	—	...	...	—
7046	Communication	...	...	—	...	...	—	...	...	—	...	...	—
705	**Environmental protection**	310	281	288	310	281	288	310	281	288	6,083	6,663	6,550
706	**Housing and community amenities**	556	158	160	611	226	3,410	611	226	3,410	12,554	12,352	16,614
707	**Health**	3,368	3,210	3,421	3,368	3,210	3,421	3,368	3,210	3,421	25,793	29,382	31,857
7072	Outpatient services	...	...	—	...	...	—	...	...	—	...	...	—
7073	Hospital services	...	...	—	...	...	—	...	...	—	...	...	—
7074	Public health services	...	...	—	...	...	—	...	...	—	...	...	—
708	**Recreation, culture and religion**	178	170	173	978	1,081	1,160	978	1,081	1,160	4,278	3,605	5,442
709	**Education**	6,389	6,161	6,300	9,496	9,965	9,688	9,496	9,965	9,688	20,717	22,760	22,480
7091	Pre-primary and primary education	...	...	—	...	...	—	...	...	—	...	...	—
7092	Secondary education	...	...	—	...	...	—	...	...	—	...	...	—
7094	Tertiary education	...	...	—	...	...	—	...	...	—	...	...	—
710	**Social protection**	2,978	2,961	2,976	5,580	5,911	5,358	9,008	8,941	8,138	46,113	53,806	36,009
7z	Statistical discrepancy: Expenditure	...	...	—	...	...	—	...	...	—	...	...	—
	Table 8 Financial transactions by counterpart sector												
32	**Net acquisition of financial assets**	-32,685	-4,389	-22	-31,185	-2,570	11,044	-28,131	-1,235	12,433	72,303	-16,776	-46,035
321	Domestic debtors	-32,685	-4,389	-22	-31,185	-2,570	11,044	-37,495	-1,862	12,355	62,948	-17,402	-46,113
8211	General government	...	...	...	...	...	...	...	...	...	...	...	...
8212	Central bank	...	...	...	...	...	...	...	...	...	...	...	...
8213	Deposit-taking corporations except the central bank	...	...	...	...	...	...	...	...	...	...	...	...
8214	Other financial corporations	...	...	...	...	...	...	...	...	...	...	...	...
8215	Nonfinancial corporations	...	...	...	...	...	...	...	...	...	...	...	...
8216	Households & nonprofit institutions serving households	...	...	...	...	...	...	...	...	...	...	...	...
322	External debtors	—	—	—	—	—	—	9,364	626	78	9,354	626	78
8221	General government	—	—	—	—	—	—	...	...	...	...	...	...
8227	International organizations	—	—	—	—	—	—	...	...	...	...	...	...
8228	Financial corporations other than international organizations	—	—	—	—	—	—	...	...	...	...	...	...
8229	Other nonresidents	—	—	—	—	—	—	...	...	...	...	...	...

United Arab Emirates (466)

In Millions of U.A.E. Dirhams (AED) / Fiscal Year Ends December 31st

		Budgetary Central Government			Central Government (excl. Social Security)			Central Government (incl. Social Security)			General Government		
		2013	2014	2015	2013	2014	2015	2013	2014	2015	2013	2014	2015
33	**Net incurrence of liabilities**	**-34,954**	**-3,785**	**775**	**-33,549**	**118**	**12,380**	**-31,401**	**36**	**12,523**	**34,001**	**17,180**	**43,104**
331	Domestic creditors	-34,954	-3,785	775	-33,549	118	12,380	-31,401	36	12,523	34,001	17,180	43,104
8311	General government	...	...	...	...	...	...	...	...	...	...	...	...
8312	Central bank	...	...	...	...	...	...	...	...	...	...	...	...
8313	Deposit-taking corporations except the central bank	...	...	...	...	...	...	...	...	...	...	...	...
8314	Other financial corporations	...	...	...	...	...	...	...	...	...	...	...	...
8315	Nonfinancial corporations	...	...	...	...	...	...	...	...	...	...	...	...
8316	Households & nonprofit institutions serving households	...	...	...	...	...	...	...	...	...	...	...	...
332	External creditors	—	—	—	—	—	—	—	—	—	-0	—	—
8321	General government	—	—	—	—	—	—	—	—	—	...	—	—
8327	International organizations	—	—	—	—	—	—	—	—	—	...	—	—
8328	Financial corporations other than international organizations	—	—	—	—	—	—	—	—	—	...	—	—
8329	Other nonresidents	—	—	—	—	—	—	—	—	—	...	—	—
	Table 9 Total other economic flows in assets and liabilities												

United Kingdom (112)

In Billions of Pounds Sterling (GBP) / Fiscal Year Ends December 31st

		Budgetary Central Government			Central Government (excl. Social Security)			Central Government (incl. Social Security)			General Government		
		2013P	2014P	2015P	2013P	2014P	2015P	2013P	2014P	2015P	2013P	2014P	2015P
	Statement of operations												
1	Revenue	620	631	659	620	631	659	620	631	659	679	692	720
2	Expense	703	720	723	703	720	723	703	720	723	761	776	783
GOB	**Gross operating balance**	**-65**	**-72**	**-46**	**-65**	**-72**	**-46**	**-65**	**-72**	**-46**	**-55**	**-56**	**-33**
NOB	**Net operating balance**	**-83**	**-89**	**-64**	**-83**	**-89**	**-64**	**-83**	**-89**	**-64**	**-82**	**-84**	**-62**
31	Net/Gross investment in nonfinancial assets	11	15	13	11	15	13	11	15	13	16	20	19
2M	Expenditure	714	735	736	714	735	736	714	735	736	777	796	802
NLB	**Net lending (+) / Net borrowing (-)**	**-94**	**-104**	**-77**	**-94**	**-104**	**-77**	**-94**	**-104**	**-77**	**-99**	**-104**	**-81**
32	Net acquisition of financial assets	-24	8	-1	-24	8	-1	-24	8	-1	-25	12	-1
33	Net incurrence of liabilities	72	108	75	72	108	75	72	108	75	75	111	78
NLBz	Statistical discrepancy	-1	4	1	-1	4	1	-1	4	1	-2	6	2
	Memorandum items												
PB	Primary net lending / net borrowing	-44	-55	-34	-44	-55	-34	-44	-55	-34	-49	-55	-37
GB	Government balance per national definition	...	...	...	...	...	...	...	...	...	...	...	...
	Statement of other economic flows												
	Balance sheet												
6	**Net worth**	**-732**	**-992**	**-1,017**	**-732**	**-992**	**-1,017**	**-732**	**-992**	**-1,017**	**-205**	**-433**	**-422**
61	Nonfinancial assets	511	522	541	511	522	541	511	522	541	1,035	1,067	1,112
62	Financial assets	453	465	458	453	465	458	453	465	458	551	570	564
63	Liabilities	1,696	1,979	2,016	1,696	1,979	2,016	1,696	1,979	2,016	1,791	2,070	2,098
	Table 1 Revenue												
1	**Revenue**	**620**	**631**	**659**	**620**	**631**	**659**	**620**	**631**	**659**	**679**	**692**	**720**
11	**Taxes**	**440**	**455**	**475**	**440**	**455**	**475**	**440**	**455**	**475**	**468**	**484**	**504**
111	Taxes on income, profits, and capital gains	203	207	218	203	207	218	203	207	218	203	207	218
1111	Payable by individuals	159	163	171	159	163	171	159	163	171	159	163	171
1112	Payable by corporations and other enterprises	44	44	46	44	44	46	44	44	46	44	44	46
1113	Other taxes on income, profits, and capital gains	—	—	—	—	—	—	—	—	—	—	—	—
112	Taxes on payroll and workforce	—	—	—	—	—	—	—	—	—	—	—	—
113	Taxes on property	31	31	32	31	31	32	31	31	32	59	60	62
114	Taxes on goods and services	204	215	221	204	215	221	204	215	221	204	215	221
1141	General taxes on goods and services	130	138	143	130	138	143	130	138	143	130	138	143
1142	Excises	56	58	59	56	58	59	56	58	59	56	58	59
115	Taxes on international trade and transactions	—	—	—	—	—	—	—	—	—	—	—	—
116	Other taxes	2	3	3	2	3	3	2	3	3	2	3	3
12	**Social contributions**	**130**	**133**	**140**	**130**	**133**	**140**	**130**	**133**	**140**	**135**	**139**	**146**
121	Social security contributions	106	109	114	106	109	114	106	109	114	106	109	114
122	Other social contributions	24	24	26	24	24	26	24	24	26	29	30	32
13	**Grants**	**0**	**0**	**1**	**0**	**0**	**1**	**0**	**0**	**1**	**0**	**0**	**0**
131	From foreign governments	—	—	—	—	—	—	—	—	—	—	—	—
132	From international organizations	0	0	0	0	0	0	0	0	0	0	0	0
133	From other general government units	0	0	1	0	0	1	0	0	1	—	—	—
1331	Current	—	—	—	—	—	—	—	—	—	—	—	—
1332	Capital	0	0	1	0	0	1	0	0	1	—	—	—
14	**Other revenue**	**50**	**42**	**43**	**50**	**42**	**43**	**50**	**42**	**43**	**76**	**68**	**70**
	Table 2 Expense by economic type												
2	**Expense**	**703**	**720**	**723**	**703**	**720**	**723**	**703**	**720**	**723**	**761**	**776**	**783**
21	**Compensation of employees**	**99**	**106**	**108**	**99**	**106**	**108**	**99**	**106**	**108**	**169**	**173**	**174**
211	Wages and salaries	80	86	87	80	86	87	80	86	87	129	132	131
212	Employers' social contributions	19	20	22	19	20	22	19	20	22	40	41	43
22	**Use of goods and services**	**98**	**101**	**103**	**98**	**101**	**103**	**98**	**101**	**103**	**156**	**160**	**163**
23	**Consumption of fixed capital**	**17**	**18**	**18**	**17**	**18**	**18**	**17**	**18**	**18**	**27**	**28**	**29**
24	**Interest**	**49**	**49**	**43**	**49**	**49**	**43**	**49**	**49**	**43**	**50**	**49**	**44**
25	**Subsidies**	**7**	**8**	**10**	**7**	**8**	**10**	**7**	**8**	**10**	**9**	**10**	**12**

United Kingdom (112)

In Billions of Pounds Sterling (GBP) / Fiscal Year Ends December 31st

		Budgetary Central Government			Central Government (excl. Social Security)			Central Government (incl. Social Security)			General Government		
		2013P	2014P	2015P	2013P	2014P	2015P	2013P	2014P	2015P	2013P	2014P	2015P
26	**Grants**	**155**	**157**	**154**	**155**	**157**	**154**	**155**	**157**	**154**	**9**	**9**	**8**
261	To foreign governments	—	—	—	—	—	—	—	—	—	—	—	—
262	To international organizations	22	21	20	22	21	20	22	21	20	9	9	8
263	To other general government units	133	136	134	133	136	134	133	136	134	—	—	—
2631	Current	122	124	121	122	124	121	122	124	121	—	—	—
2632	Capital	11	12	13	11	12	13	11	12	13	—	—	—
27	**Social benefits**	**245**	**253**	**257**	**245**	**253**	**257**	**245**	**253**	**257**	**291**	**301**	**305**
271	Social security benefits	119	125	127	119	125	127	119	125	127	134	140	142
272	Social assistance benefits	93	94	94	93	94	94	93	94	94	120	121	122
273	Employment-related social benefits	32	35	36	32	35	36	32	35	36	38	40	42
28	**Other expense**	**31**	**30**	**30**	**31**	**30**	**30**	**31**	**30**	**30**	**49**	**46**	**47**
281	Property expense other than interest	—	—	—	—	—	—	—	—	—	—	—	—
282	Transfers not elsewhere classified	31	30	30	31	30	30	31	30	30	49	46	47
2821	Current	22	20	19	22	20	19	22	20	19	37	34	32
2822	Capital	9	9	11	9	9	11	9	9	11	12	12	14
	Table 3 Transactions in assets and liabilities												
3	**Change in net worth from transactions**	**-84**	**-86**	**-63**	**-84**	**-86**	**-63**	**-84**	**-86**	**-63**	**-84**	**-78**	**-60**
31	**Net/Gross investment in nonfinancial assets**	**11**	**15**	**13**	**11**	**15**	**13**	**11**	**15**	**13**	**16**	**20**	**19**
311	Fixed assets	11	15	13	11	15	13	11	15	13	18	23	21
3111	Buildings and structures	...	...	...	...	...	...	...	...	...	...	...	...
3112	Machinery and equipment	...	...	...	...	...	...	...	...	...	...	...	...
3113	Other fixed assets	...	...	...	...	...	...	...	...	...	...	...	...
3114	Weapons systems	...	...	...	...	...	...	...	...	...	...	...	...
312	Inventories	-0	-0	-0	-0	-0	-0	...	...	...	-0	-0	-0
313	Valuables	0	0	0	0	0	0	...	...	...	0	0	0
314	Nonproduced assets	-0	-1	-0	-0	-1	-0	-0	-1	-0	-2	-2	-3
3141	Land	...	...	...	...	...	...	...	...	...	...	...	...
3142	Mineral and energy resources	...	...	...	...	...	...	...	...	...	...	...	...
3143	Other naturally occurring assets	...	...	...	...	...	...	...	...	...	...	...	...
3144	Intangible nonproduced assets	...	...	...	...	...	...	...	...	...	...	...	...
32	**Net acquisition of financial assets**	**-24**	**8**	**-1**	**-24**	**8**	**-1**	**-24**	**8**	**-1**	**-25**	**12**	**-1**
	By instrument												
3201	Monetary gold and SDRs	0	-0	0	0	-0	0	0	-0	0	0	-0	0
3202	Currency and deposits	7	6	-8	7	6	-8	7	6	-8	5	6	-4
3203	Debt securities	-4	5	16	-4	5	16	-4	5	16	-4	6	16
3204	Loans	-0	3	-4	-0	3	-4	-0	3	-4	1	6	-2
3205	Equity and investment fund shares	-30	-8	-12	-30	-8	-12	-30	-8	-12	-29	-8	-13
3206	Insurance, pension, and standardized guarantee schemes	—	—	—	—	—	—	—	—	—	-0	—	-0
3207	Financial derivatives and employee stock options	-0	-1	-1	-0	-1	-1	-0	-1	-1	-0	-1	-1
3208	Other accounts receivable	4	3	8	4	3	8	4	3	8	1	3	3
	By debtor												
321	Domestic debtors	...	...	...	...	...	...	...	...	...	...	...	...
322	External debtors	...	...	...	...	...	...	...	...	...	...	...	...
33	**Net incurrence of liabilities**	**72**	**108**	**75**	**72**	**108**	**75**	**72**	**108**	**75**	**75**	**111**	**78**
	By instrument												
3301	Special Drawing Rights (SDRs)	—	—	—	—	—	—	—	—	—	—	—	—
3302	Currency and deposits	-8	18	11	-8	18	11	-8	18	11	-7	18	11
3303	Debt securities	80	87	58	80	87	58	80	87	58	79	87	59
3304	Loans	1	-0	5	1	-0	5	1	-0	5	1	1	5
3305	Equity and investment fund shares	—	—	—	—	—	—	—	—	—	—	—	—
3306	Insurance, pension, and standardized guarantee schemes	—	0	0	—	0	0	—	0	0	2	2	2
3307	Financial derivatives and employee stock options	—	—	—	—	—	—	—	—	—	—	—	—
3308	Other accounts payable	-2	3	1	-2	3	1	-2	3	1	-0	3	1

United Kingdom (112)

In Billions of Pounds Sterling (GBP) / Fiscal Year Ends December 31st

		Budgetary Central Government			Central Government (excl. Social Security)			Central Government (incl. Social Security)			General Government		
		2013P	2014P	2015P	2013P	2014P	2015P	2013P	2014P	2015P	2013P	2014P	2015P
	By creditor												
331	Domestic creditors	...	...	...	...	...	...	...	...	...	...	...	...
332	External creditors	...	...	...	...	...	...	...	...	...	...	...	...
	Table 4 Holding gains and losses in assets and liabilities												
	Table 5 Holding gains and losses in assets and liabilities												
	Table 6 Balance sheet												
6	**Net worth**	**-732**	**-992**	**-1,017**	**-732**	**-992**	**-1,017**	**-732**	**-992**	**-1,017**	**-205**	**-433**	**-422**
61	**Nonfinancial assets**	**511**	**522**	**541**	**511**	**522**	**541**	**511**	**522**	**541**	**1,035**	**1,067**	**1,112**
611	Fixed assets	510	521	540	510	521	540	510	521	540	1,034	1,066	1,112
6111	Buildings and structures	359	366	379	359	366	379	359	366	379	444	465	487
6112	Machinery and equipment	...	...	...	...	...	...	...	...	...	...	...	...
6113	Other fixed assets	18	17	17	18	17	17	18	17	17	32	31	29
6114	Weapons systems	...	...	...	...	...	...	...	...	...	...	...	...
612	Inventories	1	1	1	1	1	1	1	1	1	1	1	1
613	Valuables	...	...	...	...	...	...	...	...	...	...	...	...
614	Nonproduced assets	...	...	...	...	...	...	...	...	...	...	...	...
6141	Land	...	...	...	...	...	...	...	...	...	...	...	...
6142	Mineral and energy resources	...	...	...	...	...	...	...	...	...	...	...	...
6143	Other naturally occurring assets	...	...	...	...	...	...	...	...	...	...	...	...
6144	Intangible nonproduced assets	...	...	...	...	...	...	...	...	...	...	...	...
62	**Financial assets**	**453**	**465**	**458**	**453**	**465**	**458**	**453**	**465**	**458**	**551**	**570**	**564**
	By instrument												
6201	Monetary gold and SDRs	16	17	16	16	17	16	16	17	16	16	17	16
6202	Currency and deposits	50	50	38	50	50	38	50	50	38	80	81	74
6203	Debt securities	47	52	68	47	52	68	47	52	68	49	55	71
6204	Loans	201	204	202	201	204	202	201	204	202	148	153	151
6205	Equity and investment fund shares	71	73	57	71	73	57	71	73	57	196	201	188
6206	Insurance, pension, and standardized guarantee schemes	—	—	—	—	—	—	—	—	—	1	1	1
6207	Financial derivatives and employee stock options	3	2	1	3	2	1	3	2	1	3	2	1
6208	Other accounts receivable	65	67	75	65	67	75	65	67	75	58	60	62
	By debtor												
621	Domestic debtors	...	...	...	...	...	...	...	...	...	...	...	...
622	External debtors	...	...	...	...	...	...	...	...	...	...	...	...
63	**Liabilities**	**1,696**	**1,979**	**2,016**	**1,696**	**1,979**	**2,016**	**1,696**	**1,979**	**2,016**	**1,791**	**2,070**	**2,098**
	By instrument												
6301	Special Drawing Rights (SDRs)	9	9	9	9	9	9	9	9	9	9	9	9
6302	Currency and deposits	127	145	156	127	145	156	127	145	156	126	144	155
6303	Debt securities	1,488	1,751	1,770	1,488	1,751	1,770	1,488	1,751	1,770	1,488	1,751	1,771
6304	Loans	12	12	16	12	12	16	12	12	16	30	30	35
6305	Equity and investment fund shares	—	—	—	—	—	—	—	—	—	—	—	—
6306	Insurance, pension, and standardized guarantee schemes	—	0	0	—	0	0	—	0	0	68	63	54
6307	Financial derivatives and employee stock options	1	1	1	1	1	1	1	1	1	1	1	1
6308	Other accounts payable	58	61	63	58	61	63	58	61	63	69	71	72
	By creditor												
631	Domestic creditors	...	...	...	...	...	...	...	...	...	...	...	...
632	External creditors	...	...	...	...	...	...	...	...	...	...	...	...
	Memorandum items												
6M2	Net financial worth	-1,243	-1,514	-1,558	-1,243	-1,514	-1,558	-1,243	-1,514	-1,558	-1,240	-1,500	-1,534
6M3	Gross debt (D4) at market value	1,695	1,978	2,014	1,695	1,978	2,014	1,695	1,978	2,014	1,789	2,068	2,096
6M3D3	D3 debt liabilities at market value	1,695	1,978	2,014	1,695	1,978	2,014	1,695	1,978	2,014	1,722	2,005	2,042
6M3D2	D2 debt liabilities at market value	1,637	1,917	1,952	1,637	1,917	1,952	1,637	1,917	1,952	1,653	1,934	1,970
6M3D1	D1 debt liabilities at market value	1,500	1,762	1,786	1,500	1,762	1,786	1,500	1,762	1,786	1,518	1,781	1,806
6M4	Gross debt (D4) at nominal value	...	...	...	...	...	...	...	...	...	...	...	...
6M4D3	D3 debt liabilities at nominal value	...	...	...	...	...	...	...	...	...	...	...	...
6M4D2	D2 debt liabilities at nominal value	...	...	...	...	...	...	...	...	...	...	...	...
6M4D1	D1 debt liabilities at nominal value	...	...	...	...	...	...	...	...	...	...	...	...

United Kingdom (112)

In Billions of Pounds Sterling (GBP) / Fiscal Year Ends December 31st

		Budgetary Central Government			Central Government (excl. Social Security)			Central Government (incl. Social Security)			General Government		
		2013P	2014P	2015P	2013P	2014P	2015P	2013P	2014P	2015P	2013P	2014P	2015P
6M35	Gross debt (D4) at face value	...	...	...	...	...	...	...	...	...	...	...	...
6M35D3	D3 debt liabilities at face value	1,561	1,668	1,729	1,561	1,668	1,729	1,561	1,668	1,729	1,588	1,695	1,757
6M35D2	D2 debt liabilities at face value	1,493	1,597	1,657	1,493	1,597	1,657	1,493	1,597	1,657	1,509	1,614	1,675
6M35D1	D1 debt liabilities at face value	1,357	1,443	1,492	1,357	1,443	1,492	1,357	1,443	1,492	1,374	1,461	1,511
6M93	Government gross debt per national definition	...	...	...	1,484	1,587	1,648	...	...	...	1,500	1,605	1,666
6M5	Arrears	...	...	...	...	...	...	...	...	...	...	...	...
6M6	Explicit contingent liabilities	...	...	...	...	...	...	...	...	...	...	...	...
6M61	of which: Publicly guaranteed debt	...	...	...	...	...	...	...	...	...	...	...	...
6M7	Net implicit obligations for social security benefits	...	...	...	...	...	...	...	...	...	...	...	...
	Table 7 Expenditure by functions of government												
7	**Expenditure**	**714**	**735**	**736**	**714**	**735**	**736**	**714**	**735**	**736**	**777**	**796**	**802**
701	**General public services**	**99**	**97**	**89**	**99**	**97**	**89**	**99**	**97**	**89**	**93**	**93**	**85**
7017	Public debt transactions	49	49	43	49	49	43	49	49	43	50	49	44
7018	Transfers of general character between levels of government	17	16	16	17	16	16	17	16	16	—	—	—
702	**Defense**	**39**	**39**	**40**	**39**	**39**	**40**	**39**	**39**	**40**	**39**	**39**	**40**
703	**Public order and safety**	**30**	**30**	**31**	**30**	**30**	**31**	**30**	**30**	**31**	**38**	**37**	**37**
704	**Economic affairs**	**44**	**46**	**47**	**44**	**46**	**47**	**44**	**46**	**47**	**54**	**55**	**57**
7042	Agriculture, forestry, fishing, and hunting	2	2	2	2	2	2	2	2	2	2	2	2
7043	Fuel and energy	3	3	4	3	3	4	3	3	4	3	3	4
7044	Mining, manufacturing, and construction	0	0	0	0	0	0	0	0	0	0	0	0
7045	Transport	24	25	24	24	25	24	24	25	24	30	30	32
7046	Communication	1	1	1	1	1	1	1	1	1	1	1	1
705	**Environmental protection**	**6**	**8**	**7**	**6**	**8**	**7**	**6**	**8**	**7**	**14**	**15**	**15**
706	**Housing and community amenities**	**28**	**33**	**31**	**28**	**33**	**31**	**28**	**33**	**31**	**8**	**8**	**9**
707	**Health**	**130**	**137**	**143**	**130**	**137**	**143**	**130**	**137**	**143**	**130**	**138**	**143**
7072	Outpatient services	14	15	15	14	15	15	14	15	15	14	15	15
7073	Hospital services	100	104	107	100	104	107	100	104	107	100	103	107
7074	Public health services	1	1	1	1	1	1	1	1	1	3	4	4
708	**Recreation, culture and religion**	**8**	**8**	**9**	**8**	**8**	**9**	**8**	**8**	**9**	**13**	**12**	**12**
709	**Education**	**77**	**81**	**78**	**77**	**81**	**78**	**77**	**81**	**78**	**94**	**98**	**96**
7091	Pre-primary and primary education	2	1	1	2	1	1	2	1	1	26	25	26
7092	Secondary education	16	22	21	16	22	21	16	22	21	37	42	40
7094	Tertiary education	9	9	6	9	9	6	9	9	6	9	9	6
710	**Social protection**	**253**	**256**	**261**	**253**	**256**	**261**	**253**	**256**	**261**	**295**	**301**	**308**
7z	Statistical discrepancy: Expenditure	—	—	—	—	—	—	—	—	—	—	—	—
	Table 8 Financial transactions by counterpart sector												
32	**Net acquisition of financial assets**	**-24**	**8**	**-1**	**-24**	**8**	**-1**	**-24**	**8**	**-1**	**-25**	**12**	**-1**
321	Domestic debtors	...	...	...	...	...	...	...	...	...	...	...	...
8211	General government	...	...	...	...	...	...	...	...	...	—	—	—
8212	Central bank	...	...	...	...	...	...	...	...	...	...	...	...
8213	Deposit-taking corporations except the central bank	...	...	...	...	...	...	...	...	...	...	...	...
8214	Other financial corporations	...	...	...	...	...	...	...	...	...	...	...	...
8215	Nonfinancial corporations	...	...	...	...	...	...	...	...	...	...	...	...
8216	Households & nonprofit institutions serving households	...	...	...	...	...	...	...	...	...	...	...	...
322	External debtors	...	...	...	...	...	...	...	...	...	...	...	...
8221	General government	...	...	...	...	...	...	...	...	...	...	...	...
8227	International organizations	...	...	...	...	...	...	...	...	...	...	...	...
8228	Financial corporations other than international organizations	...	...	...	...	...	...	...	...	...	...	...	...
8229	Other nonresidents	...	...	...	...	...	...	...	...	...	...	...	...

United Kingdom (112)

In Billions of Pounds Sterling (GBP) / Fiscal Year Ends December 31st

		Budgetary Central Government			Central Government (excl. Social Security)			Central Government (incl. Social Security)			General Government		
		2013P	2014P	2015P	2013P	2014P	2015P	2013P	2014P	2015P	2013P	2014P	2015P
33	**Net incurrence of liabilities**	**72**	**108**	**75**	**72**	**108**	**75**	**72**	**108**	**75**	**75**	**111**	**78**
331	Domestic creditors	...	...	...	...	...	...	...	...	...	...	...	...
8311	General government	...	...	...	...	...	...	...	...	...	—	—	—
8312	Central bank	...	...	...	...	...	...	...	...	...	...	...	...
8313	Deposit-taking corporations except the central bank	...	...	...	...	...	...	...	...	...	...	...	...
8314	Other financial corporations	...	...	...	...	...	...	...	...	...	...	...	...
8315	Nonfinancial corporations	...	...	...	...	...	...	...	...	...	...	...	...
8316	Households & nonprofit institutions serving households	...	...	...	...	...	...	...	...	...	...	...	...
332	External creditors	...	...	...	...	...	...	...	...	...	...	...	...
8321	General government	...	...	...	...	...	...	...	...	...	...	...	...
8327	International organizations	...	...	...	...	...	...	...	...	...	...	...	...
8328	Financial corporations other than international organizations	...	...	...	...	...	...	...	...	...	...	...	...
8329	Other nonresidents	...	...	...	...	...	...	...	...	...	...	...	...
	Table 9 Total other economic flows in assets and liabilities												
9	**Change in net worth due to other economic flows**	**...**	**...**	**...**	**...**	**...**	**...**	**...**	**...**	**...**	**...**	**...**	**...**
91	**Other economic flows in nonfinancial assets**	**...**	**...**	**...**	**...**	**...**	**...**	**...**	**...**	**...**	**...**	**...**	**...**
911	Fixed assets	...	...	...	...	...	...	...	...	...	...	...	...
912	Inventories	...	...	...	...	...	...	...	...	...	...	...	...
913	Valuables	...	...	...	...	...	...	...	...	...	...	...	...
914	Nonproduced assets	...	...	...	...	...	...	...	...	...	...	...	...
92	**Other economic flows in financial assets**	**2**	**4**	**-6**	**2**	**4**	**-6**	**2**	**4**	**-6**	**2**	**7**	**-5**
	By instrument												
9201	Monetary gold and SDRs	-3	0	-1	-3	0	-1	-3	0	-1	-3	0	-1
9202	Currency and deposits	-2	-6	-3	-2	-6	-3	-2	-6	-3	-3	-5	-3
9203	Debt securities	-1	-0	-0	-1	-0	-0	-1	-0	-0	-1	-0	-0
9204	Loans	0	0	2	0	0	2	0	0	2	-1	-2	-0
9205	Equity and investment fund shares	9	10	-3	9	10	-3	9	10	-3	11	13	-0
9206	Insurance, pension, and standardized guarantee schemes	—	—	—	—	—	—	—	—	—	—	—	—
9207	Financial derivatives and employee stock options	-0	0	0	-0	0	0	-0	0	0	-0	0	0
9208	Other accounts receivable	-0	-0	-1	-0	-0	-1	-0	-0	-1	-0	-0	-1
	By debtor												
921	Domestic debtors	...	...	...	...	...	...	...	...	...	...	...	...
922	External debtors	...	...	...	...	...	...	...	...	...	...	...	...
93	**Other economic flows in liabilities**	**-76**	**175**	**-39**	**-76**	**175**	**-39**	**-76**	**175**	**-39**	**-83**	**168**	**-50**
	By instrument												
9301	Special Drawing Rights (SDRs)	-0	-0	0	-0	-0	0	-0	-0	0	-0	-0	0
9302	Currency and deposits	0	-0	-0	0	-0	-0	0	-0	-0	0	-0	-0
9303	Debt securities	-73	175	-39	-73	175	-39	-73	175	-39	-73	175	-39
9304	Loans	-1	-0	-0	-1	-0	-0	-1	-0	-0	-1	-0	-0
9305	Equity and investment fund shares	—	—	—	—	—	—	—	—	—	—	—	—
9306	Insurance, pension, and standardized guarantee schemes	—	—	—	—	—	—	—	—	—	-8	-7	-11
9307	Financial derivatives and employee stock options	-1	-0	0	-1	-0	0	-1	-0	0	-1	-0	0
9308	Other accounts payable	-0	-0	-0	-0	-0	-0	-0	-0	-0	-0	-0	-0
	By creditor												
931	Domestic creditors	...	...	...	...	...	...	...	...	...	...	...	...
932	External creditors	...	...	...	...	...	...	...	...	...	...	...	...
	Memorandum items												
9M2	Change in net financial worth due to other economic flows	78	-170	32	78	-170	32	78	-170	32	86	-161	45

United Kingdom (112)

In Billions of Pounds Sterling (GBP) / Fiscal Year Ends December 31st

		Budgetary Central Government			Central Government (excl. Social Security)			Central Government (incl. Social Security)			General Government		
		2013P	2014P	2015P	2013P	2014P	2015P	2013P	2014P	2015P	2013P	2014P	2015P
9M3	Gross debt (D4) at market value: other economic flows	-75	175	-39	-75	175	-39	-75	175	-39	-82	168	-50
9M3D3	D3 debt liabilities at market value: other economic flows	-75	175	-39	-75	175	-39	-75	175	-39	-75	175	-39
9M3D2	D2 debt liabilities at market value: other economic flows	-74	175	-39	-74	175	-39	-74	175	-39	-74	175	-39
9M3D1	D1 debt liabilities at market value: other economic flows	-74	175	-39	-74	175	-39	-74	175	-39	-74	175	-39

United States (111)

In Billions of U.S. Dollars (USD) / Fiscal Year Ends December 31st

		Budgetary Central Government			Central Government (excl. Social Security)			Central Government (incl. Social Security)			General Government		
		2013	2014	2015	2013	2014	2015	2013	2014	2015	2013	2014	2015
	Statement of operations												
1	Revenue	2,077	2,177	2,294	2,077	2,177	2,294	3,168	3,318	3,483	5,277	5,486	5,733
2	Expense	2,315	2,396	2,446	2,315	2,396	2,446	3,870	3,989	4,104	6,098	6,256	6,446
GOB	**Gross operating balance**	**20**	**43**	**109**	**20**	**43**	**109**	**-443**	**-410**	**-359**	**-379**	**-320**	**-259**
NOB	**Net operating balance**	**-239**	**-219**	**-153**	**-239**	**-219**	**-153**	**-702**	**-672**	**-621**	**-821**	**-771**	**-713**
31	Net/Gross investment in nonfinancial assets	-2	-11	-41	-2	-11	-41	-2	-11	-41	93	83	69
2M	Expenditure	2,314	2,385	2,405	2,314	2,385	2,405	3,868	3,978	4,063	6,191	6,339	6,515
NLB	**Net lending (+) / Net borrowing (-)**	**-237**	**-208**	**-112**	**-237**	**-208**	**-112**	**-700**	**-660**	**-580**	**-913**	**-854**	**-782**
32	Net acquisition of financial assets	...	...	...	218	173	252	218	173	252	215	226	303
33	Net incurrence of liabilities	...	...	...	879	773	766	879	773	766	1,126	1,003	1,028
NLBz	Statistical discrepancy	...	...	...	-424	-392	-402	39	60	66	3	77	57
	Memorandum items												
PB	Primary net lending / net borrowing	179	233	327	179	233	327	-284	-220	-142	-294	-228	-156
GB	Government balance per national definition	...	...	...	...	...	...	...	...	...	...	...	...
	Statement of other economic flows												
	Balance sheet												
6	**Net worth**	**...**	**...**	**...**	**-11,191**	**-11,729**	**-12,238**	**-11,191**	**-11,729**	**-12,238**	**-3,905**	**-4,147**	**-4,765**
61	Nonfinancial assets	...	...	...	3,217	3,269	3,268	3,217	3,269	3,268	12,927	13,238	13,404
62	Financial assets	...	...	...	1,717	1,892	2,141	1,717	1,892	2,141	3,992	4,239	4,546
63	Liabilities	...	...	...	16,125	16,890	17,647	16,125	16,890	17,647	20,825	21,624	22,715
	Table 1 Revenue												
1	**Revenue**	**2,077**	**2,177**	**2,294**	**2,077**	**2,177**	**2,294**	**3,168**	**3,318**	**3,483**	**5,277**	**5,486**	**5,733**
11	**Taxes**	**1,765**	**1,917**	**2,059**	**1,765**	**1,917**	**2,059**	**1,765**	**1,917**	**2,059**	**3,252**	**3,441**	**3,629**
111	Taxes on income, profits, and capital gains	1,620	1,764	1,899	1,620	1,764	1,899	1,620	1,764	1,899	2,018	2,173	2,331
1111	Payable by individuals	1,321	1,424	1,555	1,321	1,424	1,555	1,321	1,424	1,555	1,664	1,775	1,926
1112	Payable by corporations and other enterprises	298	340	345	298	340	345	298	340	345	354	398	405
1113	Other taxes on income, profits, and capital gains	—	—	—	—	—	—	—	—	—	—	—	—
112	Taxes on payroll and workforce	—	—	—	—	—	—	—	—	—	—	—	—
113	Taxes on property	21	19	20	21	19	20	21	19	20	482	485	490
114	Taxes on goods and services	89	97	101	89	97	101	89	97	101	716	745	770
1141	General taxes on goods and services	—	—	—	—	—	—	—	—	—	337	353	367
1142	Excises	67	66	66	67	66	66	67	66	66	162	161	162
115	Taxes on international trade and transactions	35	37	38	35	37	38	35	37	38	35	37	38
116	Other taxes	—	—	—	—	—	—	—	—	—	—	—	—
12	**Social contributions**	—	—	—	—	—	—	**1,091**	**1,141**	**1,190**	**1,110**	**1,160**	**1,209**
121	Social security contributions	—	—	—	—	—	—	1,082	1,131	1,180	1,100	1,150	1,199
122	Other social contributions	—	—	—	—	—	—	9	10	10	9	10	10
13	**Grants**	**1**	**1**	**1**	**1**	**1**	**1**	**1**	**1**	**1**	**1**	**1**	**1**
131	From foreign governments	1	1	1	1	1	1	1	1	1	1	1	1
132	From international organizations	—	—	—	—	—	—	—	—	—	—	—	—
133	From other general government units	—	—	—	—	—	—	—	—	—	—	—	—
1331	Current	—	—	—	—	—	—	—	—	—	—	—	—
1332	Capital	—	—	—	—	—	—	—	—	—	—	—	—
14	**Other revenue**	**310**	**259**	**234**	**310**	**259**	**234**	**310**	**259**	**234**	**914**	**884**	**895**
	Table 2 Expense by economic type												
2	**Expense**	**2,315**	**2,396**	**2,446**	**2,315**	**2,396**	**2,446**	**3,870**	**3,989**	**4,104**	**6,098**	**6,256**	**6,446**
21	**Compensation of employees**	**314**	**316**	**319**	**314**	**316**	**319**	**391**	**395**	**400**	**1,580**	**1,619**	**1,667**
211	Wages and salaries	...	...	...	...	...	...	...	...	...	...	...	...
212	Employers' social contributions	...	...	...	...	...	...	...	...	...	...	...	...
22	**Use of goods and services**	**320**	**310**	**312**	**320**	**310**	**312**	**320**	**310**	**312**	**926**	**926**	**935**
23	**Consumption of fixed capital**	**259**	**262**	**262**	**259**	**262**	**262**	**259**	**262**	**262**	**441**	**450**	**454**
24	**Interest**	**416**	**441**	**438**	**416**	**441**	**438**	**416**	**441**	**438**	**619**	**625**	**626**
25	**Subsidies**	**59**	**56**	**56**	**59**	**56**	**56**	**59**	**56**	**56**	**59**	**57**	**57**

United States (111)

In Billions of U.S. Dollars (USD) / Fiscal Year Ends December 31st

		Budgetary Central Government			Central Government (excl. Social Security)			Central Government (incl. Social Security)			General Government		
		2013	2014	2015	2013	2014	2015	2013	2014	2015	2013	2014	2015
26	**Grants**	**571**	**613**	**648**	**571**	**613**	**648**	**571**	**613**	**648**	**55**	**53**	**52**
261	To foreign governments	55	53	52	55	53	52	55	53	52	55	53	52
262	To international organizations	—	—	—	—	—	—	—	—	—	—	—	—
263	To other general government units	516	560	595	516	560	595	516	560	595	—	—	—
2631	Current	450	495	531	450	495	531	450	495	531	—	—	—
2632	Capital	66	66	64	66	66	64	66	66	64	—	—	—
27	**Social benefits**	**365**	**387**	**404**	**365**	**387**	**404**	**1,842**	**1,902**	**1,982**	**2,406**	**2,514**	**2,648**
271	Social security benefits	—	—	—	—	—	—	1,477	1,514	1,577	1,493	1,531	1,594
272	Social assistance benefits	365	387	404	365	387	404	365	387	404	913	983	1,053
273	Employment-related social benefits	—	—	—	—	—	—	—	—	—	—	—	—
28	**Other expense**	**12**	**11**	**7**	**12**	**11**	**7**	**12**	**11**	**7**	**12**	**12**	**8**
281	Property expense other than interest	—	—	—	—	—	—	—	—	—	—	—	—
282	Transfers not elsewhere classified	12	11	7	12	11	7	12	11	7	12	11	7
2821	Current	...	...	...	...	...	...	...	...	...	...	...	...
2822	Capital	...	...	...	...	...	...	...	...	...	...	...	...
	Table 3 Transactions in assets and liabilities												
3	**Change in net worth from transactions**	**...**	**...**	**...**	**-663**	**-612**	**-555**	**-663**	**-612**	**-555**	**-818**	**-694**	**-656**
31	**Net/Gross investment in nonfinancial assets**	**-2**	**-11**	**-41**	**-2**	**-11**	**-41**	**-2**	**-11**	**-41**	**93**	**83**	**69**
311	Fixed assets	0	-8	-10	0	-8	-10	0	-8	-10	86	77	91
3111	Buildings and structures	-8	-10	-10	-8	-10	-10	-8	-10	-10	74	73	88
3112	Machinery and equipment	-0	1	3	-0	1	3	-0	1	3	-1	0	3
3113	Other fixed assets	5	-1	-1	5	-1	-1	5	-1	-1	9	3	3
3114	Weapons systems	4	1	-2	4	1	-2	4	1	-2	4	1	-2
312	Inventories	0	-0	0	0	-0	0	0	-0	0	0	-0	0
313	Valuables	—	—	—	—	—	—	—	—	—	—	—	—
314	Nonproduced assets	-2	-3	-31	-2	-3	-31	-2	-3	-31	7	6	-22
3141	Land	...	...	...	...	...	...	...	...	...	...	...	...
3142	Mineral and energy resources	...	...	...	...	...	...	...	...	...	...	...	...
3143	Other naturally occurring assets	...	...	...	...	...	...	...	...	...	...	...	...
3144	Intangible nonproduced assets	...	...	...	...	...	...	...	...	...	...	...	...
32	**Net acquisition of financial assets**	**...**	**...**	**...**	**218**	**173**	**252**	**218**	**173**	**252**	**215**	**226**	**303**
	By instrument												
3201	Monetary gold and SDRs	...	...	...	0	0	0	0	0	0	0	0	0
3202	Currency and deposits	...	...	...	66	57	104	66	57	104	91	82	108
3203	Debt securities	...	...	...	-0	-0	-0	-0	-0	-0	-44	-19	-13
3204	Loans	...	...	...	124	114	106	124	114	106	125	126	129
3205	Equity and investment fund shares	...	...	...	-4	1	2	-4	1	2	-5	10	22
3206	Insurance, pension, and standardized guarantee schemes	...	...	...	—	—	—	—	—	—	—	—	—
3207	Financial derivatives and employee stock options	...	...	...	—	—	—	—	—	—	—	—	—
3208	Other accounts receivable	...	...	...	32	1	41	32	1	41	49	26	57
	By debtor												
321	Domestic debtors	...	...	...	219	174	257	219	174	257	216	227	308
322	External debtors	...	...	...	-1	-1	-4	-1	-1	-4	-1	-1	-4
33	**Net incurrence of liabilities**	**...**	**...**	**...**	**879**	**773**	**766**	**879**	**773**	**766**	**1,126**	**1,003**	**1,028**
	By instrument												
3301	Special Drawing Rights (SDRs)	...	...	...	—	—	—	—	—	—	—	—	—
3302	Currency and deposits	...	...	...	-0	-0	-0	-0	-0	-0	-0	-0	-0
3303	Debt securities	...	...	...	857	736	725	857	736	725	821	665	690
3304	Loans	...	...	...	—	—	—	—	—	—	1	0	0
3305	Equity and investment fund shares	...	...	...	—	—	—	—	—	—	—	—	—
3306	Insurance, pension, and standardized guarantee schemes	...	...	...	3	33	26	3	33	26	248	294	282
3307	Financial derivatives and employee stock options	...	...	...	—	—	—	—	—	—	—	—	—
3308	Other accounts payable	...	...	...	19	4	16	19	4	16	57	43	56

United States (111)

In Billions of U.S. Dollars (USD) / Fiscal Year Ends December 31st

		Budgetary Central Government			Central Government (excl. Social Security)			Central Government (incl. Social Security)			General Government		
		2013	2014	2015	2013	2014	2015	2013	2014	2015	2013	2014	2015
	By creditor												
331	Domestic creditors	...	...	...	...	...	...	...	...	...	...	...	...
332	External creditors	...	...	...	...	...	...	...	...	...	...	...	...
	Table 4 Holding gains and losses in assets and liabilities												
	Table 5 Holding gains and losses in assets and liabilities												
	Table 6 Balance sheet												
6	**Net worth**	**...**	**...**	**...**	**-11,191**	**-11,729**	**-12,238**	**-11,191**	**-11,729**	**-12,238**	**-3,905**	**-4,147**	**-4,765**
61	**Nonfinancial assets**	**...**	**...**	**...**	**3,217**	**3,269**	**3,268**	**3,217**	**3,269**	**3,268**	**12,927**	**13,238**	**13,404**
611	Fixed assets	...	...	...	3,217	3,269	3,268	3,217	3,269	3,268	12,927	13,238	13,404
6111	Buildings and structures	...	...	...	1,481	1,512	1,508	1,481	1,512	1,508	10,823	11,106	11,264
6112	Machinery and equipment	...	...	...	734	746	743	734	746	743	982	995	993
6113	Other fixed assets	...	...	...	1,001	1,012	1,016	1,001	1,012	1,016	1,122	1,137	1,147
6114	Weapons systems	...	...	...	...	...	...	...	...	...	...	...	...
612	Inventories	...	...	...	...	...	...	...	...	...	...	...	...
613	Valuables	...	...	...	...	...	...	...	...	...	...	...	...
614	Nonproduced assets	...	...	...	...	...	...	...	...	...	...	...	...
6141	Land	...	...	...	...	...	...	...	...	...	...	...	...
6142	Mineral and energy resources	...	...	...	...	...	...	...	...	...	...	...	...
6143	Other naturally occurring assets	...	...	...	...	...	...	...	...	...	...	...	...
6144	Intangible nonproduced assets	...	...	...	...	...	...	...	...	...	...	...	...
62	**Financial assets**	**...**	**...**	**...**	**1,717**	**1,892**	**2,141**	**1,717**	**1,892**	**2,141**	**3,992**	**4,239**	**4,546**
	By instrument												
6201	Monetary gold and SDRs	...	...	...	55	52	50	55	52	50	55	52	50
6202	Currency and deposits	...	...	...	222	277	380	222	277	380	660	740	847
6203	Debt securities	...	...	...	1	1	0	1	1	0	705	686	673
6204	Loans	...	...	...	1,044	1,159	1,264	1,044	1,159	1,264	1,375	1,500	1,628
6205	Equity and investment fund shares	...	...	...	95	96	98	95	96	98	495	519	540
6206	Insurance, pension, and standardized guarantee schemes	...	...	...	—	—	—	—	—	—	—	—	—
6207	Financial derivatives and employee stock options	...	...	...	—	—	—	—	—	—	—	—	—
6208	Other accounts receivable	...	...	...	300	308	348	300	308	348	702	741	808
	By debtor												
621	Domestic debtors	...	...	...	1,545	1,729	1,986	1,545	1,729	1,986	3,820	4,076	4,392
622	External debtors	...	...	...	172	163	154	172	163	154	172	163	154
63	**Liabilities**	**...**	**...**	**...**	**16,125**	**16,890**	**17,647**	**16,125**	**16,890**	**17,647**	**20,825**	**21,624**	**22,715**
	By instrument												
6301	Special Drawing Rights (SDRs)	...	...	...	60	56	54	60	56	54	60	56	54
6302	Currency and deposits	...	...	...	26	25	25	26	25	25	26	25	25
6303	Debt securities	...	...	...	13,705	14,441	15,166	13,705	14,441	15,166	16,167	16,832	17,522
6304	Loans	...	...	...	—	—	—	—	—	—	16	17	17
6305	Equity and investment fund shares	...	...	...	—	—	—	—	—	—	—	—	—
6306	Insurance, pension, and standardized guarantee schemes	...	...	...	2,083	2,115	2,138	2,083	2,115	2,138	3,521	3,619	3,969
6307	Financial derivatives and employee stock options	...	...	...	—	—	—	—	—	—	—	—	—
6308	Other accounts payable	...	...	...	252	253	264	252	253	264	1,036	1,075	1,127
	By creditor												
631	Domestic creditors	...	...	...	...	...	...	...	...	...	...	...	...
632	External creditors	...	...	...	...	...	...	...	...	...	...	...	...
	Memorandum items												
6M2	Net financial worth	...	...	...	-14,408	-14,998	-15,506	-14,408	-14,998	-15,506	-16,833	-17,385	-18,169
6M3	Gross debt (D4) at market value	...	...	...	16,125	16,890	17,647	16,125	16,890	17,647	20,825	21,624	22,715
6M3D3	D3 debt liabilities at market value	...	...	...	14,042	14,775	15,509	14,042	14,775	15,509	17,304	18,005	18,745
6M3D2	D2 debt liabilities at market value	...	...	...	13,790	14,523	15,245	13,790	14,523	15,245	16,268	16,930	17,618
6M3D1	D1 debt liabilities at market value	...	...	...	13,705	14,441	15,166	13,705	14,441	15,166	16,183	16,849	17,539
6M4	Gross debt (D4) at nominal value	...	...	...	...	...	...	...	...	...	...	...	...
6M4D3	D3 debt liabilities at nominal value	...	...	...	...	...	...	...	...	...	...	...	...
6M4D2	D2 debt liabilities at nominal value	...	...	...	...	...	...	...	...	...	...	...	...
6M4D1	D1 debt liabilities at nominal value	...	...	...	...	...	...	...	...	...	...	...	...

United States (111)

In Billions of U.S. Dollars (USD) / Fiscal Year Ends December 31st

		Budgetary Central Government			Central Government (excl. Social Security)			Central Government (incl. Social Security)			General Government		
		2013	2014	2015	2013	2014	2015	2013	2014	2015	2013	2014	2015
6M35	Gross debt (D4) at face value	...	...	...	...	...	...	...	...	...	...	...	...
6M35D3	D3 debt liabilities at face value	...	...	...	...	...	...	...	...	...	...	...	...
6M35D2	D2 debt liabilities at face value	...	...	...	...	...	...	...	...	...	...	...	...
6M35D1	D1 debt liabilities at face value	...	...	...	...	...	...	...	...	...	...	...	...
6M93	Government gross debt per national definition	...	...	...	...	...	...	...	...	...	...	...	...
6M5	Arrears	...	...	...	...	...	...	...	...	...	...	...	...
6M6	Explicit contingent liabilities	...	...	...	...	...	...	...	...	...	...	...	...
6M61	of which: Publicly guaranteed debt	...	...	...	...	...	...	...	...	...	...	...	...
6M7	Net implicit obligations for social security benefits	...	...	...	...	...	...	...	...	...	...	...	...
	Table 7 Expenditure by functions of government												
7	**Expenditure**	...	...	...	...	...	...	**3,906**	**4,015**	**4,100**	**6,466**	**6,621**	**6,806**
701	**General public services**	...	...	...	...	...	...	**526**	**548**	**546**	**926**	**934**	**940**
7017	Public debt transactions	...	...	...	...	...	...	416	441	438	619	625	626
7018	Transfers of general character between levels of government	...	...	...	...	...	...	...	...	...	...	...	...
702	**Defense**	...	...	...	...	...	...	**632**	**611**	**600**	**631**	**611**	**599**
703	**Public order and safety**	...	...	...	...	...	...	**56**	**56**	**56**	**349**	**358**	**367**
704	**Economic affairs**	...	...	...	...	...	...	**222**	**219**	**193**	**586**	**599**	**595**
7042	Agriculture, forestry, fishing, and hunting	...	...	...	...	...	...	...	...	...	...	...	...
7043	Fuel and energy	...	...	...	...	...	...	...	...	...	...	...	...
7044	Mining, manufacturing, and construction	...	...	...	...	...	...	...	...	...	...	...	...
7045	Transport	...	...	...	...	...	...	...	...	...	...	...	...
7046	Communication	...	...	...	...	...	...	...	...	...	...	...	...
705	**Environmental protection**	...	...	...	...	...	...	—	—	—	—	—	—
706	**Housing and community amenities**	...	...	...	...	...	...	**67**	**68**	**66**	**93**	**93**	**96**
707	**Health**	...	...	...	...	...	...	**1,006**	**1,102**	**1,184**	**1,440**	**1,543**	**1,646**
7072	Outpatient services	...	...	...	...	...	...	...	...	...	...	...	...
7073	Hospital services	...	...	...	...	...	...	...	...	...	...	...	...
7074	Public health services	...	...	...	...	...	...	...	...	...	...	...	...
708	**Recreation, culture and religion**	...	...	...	...	...	...	**5**	**5**	**5**	**43**	**44**	**45**
709	**Education**	...	...	...	...	...	...	**109**	**108**	**107**	**1,045**	**1,071**	**1,105**
7091	Pre-primary and primary education	...	...	...	...	...	...	...	...	...	...	...	...
7092	Secondary education	...	...	...	...	...	...	...	...	...	...	...	...
7094	Tertiary education	...	...	...	...	...	...	...	...	...	...	...	...
710	**Social protection**	...	...	...	...	...	...	**1,283**	**1,297**	**1,343**	**1,352**	**1,368**	**1,415**
7z	Statistical discrepancy: Expenditure	...	...	...	...	...	...	...	...	...	...	...	...
	Table 8 Financial transactions by counterpart sector												
32	**Net acquisition of financial assets**	...	...	...	**218**	**173**	**252**	**218**	**173**	**252**	**215**	**226**	**303**
321	Domestic debtors	...	...	...	219	174	257	219	174	257	216	227	308
8211	General government	...	...	...	...	...	...	...	...	...	...	...	...
8212	Central bank	...	...	...	...	...	...	...	...	...	...	...	...
8213	Deposit-taking corporations except the central bank	...	...	...	...	...	...	...	...	...	...	...	...
8214	Other financial corporations	...	...	...	...	...	...	...	...	...	...	...	...
8215	Nonfinancial corporations	...	...	...	...	...	...	...	...	...	...	...	...
8216	Households & nonprofit institutions serving households	...	...	...	...	...	...	...	...	...	...	...	...
322	External debtors	...	...	...	-1	-1	-4	-1	-1	-4	-1	-1	-4
8221	General government	...	...	...	...	...	...	...	...	...	...	...	...
8227	International organizations	...	...	...	...	...	...	...	...	...	...	...	...
8228	Financial corporations other than international organizations	...	...	...	...	...	...	...	...	...	...	...	...
8229	Other nonresidents	...	...	...	...	...	...	...	...	...	...	...	...

United States (111)

In Billions of U.S. Dollars (USD) / Fiscal Year Ends December 31st

		Budgetary Central Government			Central Government (excl. Social Security)			Central Government (incl. Social Security)			General Government		
		2013	2014	2015	2013	2014	2015	2013	2014	2015	2013	2014	2015
33	**Net incurrence of liabilities**	...	...	...	879	773	766	879	773	766	1,126	1,003	1,028
331	Domestic creditors	...	...	...	...	...	...	...	...	...	...	...	...
3311	General government	...	...	...	...	...	...	...	...	...	...	...	...
3312	Central bank	...	...	...	...	...	...	...	...	...	...	...	...
3313	Deposit-taking corporations except the central bank	...	...	...	...	...	...	...	...	...	...	...	...
3314	Other financial corporations	...	...	...	...	...	...	...	...	...	...	...	...
3315	Nonfinancial corporations	...	...	...	...	...	...	...	...	...	...	...	...
3316	Households & nonprofit institutions serving households	...	...	...	...	...	...	...	...	...	...	...	...
332	External creditors	...	...	...	...	...	...	...	...	...	...	...	...
3321	General government	...	...	...	...	...	...	...	...	...	...	...	...
3327	International organizations	...	...	...	...	...	...	...	...	...	...	...	...
3328	Financial corporations other than international organizations	...	...	...	...	...	...	...	...	...	...	...	...
3329	Other nonresidents	...	...	...	...	...	...	...	...	...	...	...	...
	Table 9 Total other economic flows in assets and liabilities												

Uruguay (298)

In Millions of Uruguayan Pesos (UYU) / Fiscal Year Ends December 31st

		Budgetary Central Government			Central Government (excl. Social Security)			Central Government (incl. Social Security)			General Government		
		2013	2014	2015	2013	2014	2015	2013	2014	2015	2013	2014	2015
	Statement of operations												
1	Revenue	...	...	...	247,827	271,555	292,497	366,411	384,908	514,887	...	...	...
2	Expense	...	...	...	249,175	283,836	315,388	367,722	448,455	...	...	...	...
GOB	**Gross operating balance**	...	...	...	**-1,348**	**-12,281**	**-22,891**	**-1,311**	**-63,547**	...	...	...	...
NOB	**Net operating balance**	...	...	...	...	...	...	...	...	...	...	...	...
31	Net/Gross investment in nonfinancial assets	...	...	...	16,571	18,439	...	16,571	18,439	...	...	...	...
2M	Expenditure	...	...	...	265,746	302,275	...	384,293	466,894	...	...	...	...
NLB	**Net lending (+) / Net borrowing (-)**	...	...	...	**-17,919**	**-30,720**	...	**-17,882**	**-81,987**	...	...	...	...
32	Net acquisition of financial assets	...	...	...	-3,502	2,915	31,786	-3,406	3,131	31,213	-3,796	2,863	32,437
33	Net incurrence of liabilities	...	...	...	15,179	33,314	73,612	15,512	33,661	74,067	16,011	35,518	73,787
NLBz	Statistical discrepancy	...	...	...	-761	321	...	-1,035	51,456	...	...	...	...
	Memorandum items												
PB	Primary net lending / net borrowing	...	...	...	10,067	-429	...	10,104	-51,696	...	...	...	...
GB	Government balance per national definition	...	...	...	...	...	...	...	...	...	...	...	...
	Statement of other economic flows												
	Balance sheet												
6	**Net worth**	...	...	...	...	...	...	...	...	...	...	...	...
61	Nonfinancial assets	...	...	...	...	...	...	...	...	...	...	...	...
62	Financial assets	...	...	...	104,017	119,386	137,513	105,197	120,752	138,378	107,569	123,566	142,045
63	Liabilities	...	...	...	502,495	588,694	743,250	503,629	590,186	745,197	508,885	598,468	753,775
	Table 1 Revenue												
1	**Revenue**	...	...	...	**247,827**	**271,555**	**292,497**	**366,411**	**384,908**	**514,887**	...	...	...
11	**Taxes**	...	...	...	**224,371**	**247,032**	**269,470**	**224,371**	**247,032**	**269,470**	...	...	...
111	Taxes on income, profits, and capital gains	...	...	...	70,877	73,033	82,996	70,877	73,033	82,996	...	...	...
1111	Payable by individuals	...	...	...	37,006	38,898	50,319	37,006	38,898	50,319	...	...	...
1112	Payable by corporations and other enterprises	...	...	...	33,871	34,136	32,677	33,871	34,136	32,677	...	...	...
1113	Other taxes on income, profits, and capital gains	...	...	...	—	—	—	—	—	—	...	...	...
112	Taxes on payroll and workforce	...	...	...	—	—	...	—	—	...	...	...	...
113	Taxes on property	...	...	...	13,966	14,063	17,086	13,966	14,063	17,086	...	...	...
114	Taxes on goods and services	...	...	...	135,437	137,512	146,757	135,437	137,512	146,757	...	...	...
1141	General taxes on goods and services	...	...	...	112,816	114,795	118,472	112,816	114,795	118,472	...	...	...
1142	Excises	...	...	...	18,882	18,888	24,025	18,882	18,888	24,025	...	...	...
115	Taxes on international trade and transactions	...	...	...	13,020	15,169	15,440	13,020	15,169	15,440	...	...	...
116	Other taxes	...	...	...	-8,929	7,255	7,191	-8,929	7,255	7,191	...	...	...
12	**Social contributions**	...	...	...	—	—	—	**118,584**	**113,353**	**150,802**	...	...	...
121	Social security contributions	...	...	...	—	—	—	118,584	113,353	150,802	...	...	...
122	Other social contributions	...	...	...	—	—	—	—	—	—	...	...	...
13	**Grants**	...	...	...	—	**398**	—	—	**398**	**71,588**	...	...	...
131	From foreign governments	...	...	...	—	398	—	—	398	—	...	...	...
132	From international organizations	...	...	...	—	—	—	—	—	—	...	...	...
133	From other general government units	...	...	...	—	—	—	—	—	71,588	...	...	...
1331	Current	...	...	...	—	—	—	—	—	71,588	...	...	...
1332	Capital	...	...	...	—	—	—	—	—	—	...	...	...
14	**Other revenue**	...	...	...	**23,456**	**24,126**	**23,027**	**23,456**	**24,126**	**23,027**	...	...	...
	Table 2 Expense by economic type												
2	**Expense**	...	...	...	**249,175**	**283,836**	**315,388**	**367,722**	**448,455**	...	...	...	...
21	**Compensation of employees**	...	...	...	**80,821**	**94,510**	**102,441**	**84,789**	**98,506**	**107,131**	...	...	...
211	Wages and salaries	...	...	...	62,623	72,877	78,913	...	...	83,603	...	...	...
212	Employers' social contributions	...	...	...	18,199	21,633	23,527	...	...	23,527	...	...	...
22	**Use of goods and services**	...	...	...	**41,291**	**46,938**	**52,025**	**43,255**	**48,966**	**54,053**	...	...	...
23	**Consumption of fixed capital**	...	...	...	...	...	...	...	...	...	...	...	...
24	**Interest**	...	...	...	**27,987**	**30,291**	**33,558**	**27,987**	**30,291**	**33,558**	...	...	...
25	**Subsidies**	...	...	...	**2,926**	**3,308**	**4,019**	**2,926**	**3,308**	**4,019**	...	...	...

Uruguay (298)

In Millions of Uruguayan Pesos (UYU) / Fiscal Year Ends December 31st

		Budgetary Central Government			Central Government (excl. Social Security)			Central Government (incl. Social Security)			General Government		
		2013	2014	2015	2013	2014	2015	2013	2014	2015	2013	2014	2015
26	**Grants**	...	...	...	**51,758**	**56,977**	**71,588**	**—**	**12,972**	**71,588**	...	...	...
261	To foreign governments	...	...	...	—	—	—	—	—	—	...	...	...
262	To international organizations	...	...	...	—	—	—	—	—	—	...	...	...
263	To other general government units	...	...	...	51,758	56,977	71,588	—	12,972	71,588	...	...	...
2631	Current	...	...	...	51,758	56,977	71,588	—	12,972	71,588	...	...	...
2632	Capital	...	...	...	—	—	—	—	—	—	...	...	...
27	**Social benefits**	...	...	...	**28,709**	**32,799**	**36,839**	**170,624**	**176,304**	**222,354**	...	...	...
271	Social security benefits	...	...	...	17,997	20,777	24,116	105,256	108,906	136,564	...	...	...
272	Social assistance benefits	...	...	...	—	—	12,723	54,656	55,376	85,790	...	...	...
273	Employment-related social benefits	...	...	...	10,712	12,022	—	10,712	12,022	—	...	...	...
28	**Other expense**	...	...	...	**15,683**	**19,014**	**14,918**	**38,141**	**39,054**	**44,536**	...	...	...
281	Property expense other than interest	...	...	...	—	—	—	—	—	—	...	...	...
282	Transfers not elsewhere classified	...	...	...	15,683	19,014	14,918	38,141	39,054	44,536	...	...	...
2821	Current	...	...	...	15,683	19,014	14,918	38,141	39,054	44,536	...	...	...
2822	Capital	...	...	...	—	—	—	—	—	—	...	...	...
	Table 3 Transactions in assets and liabilities												
3	**Change in net worth from transactions**	...	...	...	...	...	...	...	...	...	...	...	...
31	**Net/Gross investment in nonfinancial assets**	...	...	...	**16,571**	**18,439**	...	**16,571**	**18,439**	...	...	...	...
311	Fixed assets	...	...	...	16,571	18,439	17,939	16,571	18,439	17,939	...	...	...
3111	Buildings and structures	...	...	...	...	...	17,939	...	...	17,939	...	...	...
3112	Machinery and equipment	...	...	...	...	...	...	...	...	...	...	...	...
3113	Other fixed assets	...	...	...	...	...	...	...	...	...	...	...	...
3114	Weapons systems	...	...	...	...	...	...	...	...	...	...	...	...
312	Inventories	...	...	...	—	—	...	—	—	...	...	...	...
313	Valuables	...	...	...	—	—	...	—	—	...	...	...	...
314	Nonproduced assets	...	...	...	—	—	...	—	—	...	...	...	...
3141	Land	...	...	...	—	—	...	—	—	...	...	...	...
3142	Mineral and energy resources	...	...	...	—	—	...	—	—	...	...	...	...
3143	Other naturally occurring assets	...	...	...	—	—	...	—	—	...	...	...	...
3144	Intangible nonproduced assets	...	...	...	—	—	...	—	—	...	...	...	...
32	**Net acquisition of financial assets**	...	...	...	**-3,502**	**2,915**	**31,786**	**-3,406**	**3,131**	**31,213**	**-3,796**	**2,863**	**32,437**
	By instrument												
3201	Monetary gold and SDRs	...	...	...	—	—	—	—	—	—	—	—	—
3202	Currency and deposits	...	...	...	-11,261	8,823	27,115	-11,165	9,038	26,543	-11,385	8,770	27,223
3203	Debt securities	...	...	...	-1,305	-401	-1,800	-1,305	-401	-1,800	-1,305	-401	-1,800
3204	Loans	...	...	...	9,064	-5,506	6,470	9,064	-5,506	6,470	8,894	-5,506	7,014
3205	Equity and investment fund shares	...	...	...	—	—	—	—	—	—	—	—	—
3206	Insurance, pension, and standardized guarantee schemes	...	...	...	—	—	—	—	—	—	—	—	—
3207	Financial derivatives and employee stock options	...	...	...	—	—	—	—	—	—	—	—	—
3208	Other accounts receivable	...	...	...	...	...	...	...	...	...	...	...	...
	By debtor												
321	Domestic debtors	...	...	...	-3,493	2,992	31,622	-3,397	3,207	31,050	-3,787	2,939	32,273
322	External debtors	...	...	...	-9	-76	164	-9	-76	164	-9	-76	164
33	**Net incurrence of liabilities**	...	...	...	**15,179**	**33,314**	**73,612**	**15,512**	**33,661**	**74,067**	**16,011**	**35,518**	**73,787**
	By instrument												
3301	Special Drawing Rights (SDRs)	...	...	...	—	—	—	—	—	—	—	—	—
3302	Currency and deposits	...	...	...	—	—	—	—	—	—	182	—	—
3303	Debt securities	...	...	...	24,898	30,429	71,725	24,898	30,429	71,725	24,898	30,429	71,725
3304	Loans	...	...	...	-9,720	2,886	1,887	-9,387	3,233	2,342	-9,069	5,089	2,063
3305	Equity and investment fund shares	...	...	...	—	—	—	—	—	—	—	—	—
3306	Insurance, pension, and standardized guarantee schemes	...	...	...	—	—	—	—	—	—	—	—	—
3307	Financial derivatives and employee stock options	...	...	...	—	—	—	—	—	—	—	—	—
3308	Other accounts payable	...	...	...	...	...	...	...	...	...	...	...	...

Uruguay (298)

In Millions of Uruguayan Pesos (UYU) / Fiscal Year Ends December 31st

Code	Item	Budgetary Central Government			Central Government (excl. Social Security)			Central Government (incl. Social Security)			General Government		
		2013	2014	2015	2013	2014	2015	2013	2014	2015	2013	2014	2015
	By creditor												
331	Domestic creditors	...	...	...	-16,381	692	42,815	-16,048	1,039	43,270	-15,867	2,924	43,381
332	External creditors	...	...	...	31,560	32,622	30,797	31,560	32,622	30,797	31,878	32,594	30,407
	Table 4 Holding gains and losses in assets and liabilities												
	Table 5 Holding gains and losses in assets and liabilities												
	Table 6 Balance sheet												
6	**Net worth**	...	...	...	...	...	...	...	...	...	...	...	...
61	**Nonfinancial assets**	...	...	...	...	...	...	...	...	...	...	...	...
611	Fixed assets	...	...	...	...	...	...	...	...	...	...	...	...
6111	Buildings and structures	...	...	...	...	...	...	...	...	...	...	...	...
6112	Machinery and equipment	...	...	...	...	...	...	...	...	...	...	...	...
6113	Other fixed assets	...	...	...	...	...	...	...	...	...	...	...	...
6114	Weapons systems	...	...	...	...	...	...	...	...	...	...	...	...
612	Inventories	...	...	...	...	...	...	...	...	...	...	...	...
613	Valuables	...	...	...	...	...	...	...	...	...	...	...	...
614	Nonproduced assets	...	...	...	...	...	...	...	...	...	...	...	...
6141	Land	...	...	...	...	...	...	...	...	...	...	...	...
6142	Mineral and energy resources	...	...	...	...	...	...	...	...	...	...	...	...
6143	Other naturally occurring assets	...	...	...	...	...	...	...	...	...	...	...	...
6144	Intangible nonproduced assets	...	...	...	...	...	...	...	...	...	...	...	...
62	**Financial assets**	...	...	...	**104,017**	**119,386**	**137,513**	**105,197**	**120,752**	**138,378**	**107,569**	**123,566**	**142,045**
	By instrument												
6201	Monetary gold and SDRs	...	...	...	—	—	—	—	—	...	—	—	—
6202	Currency and deposits	...	...	...	53,937	69,512	83,716	55,117	70,877	84,581	58,084	73,691	88,248
6203	Debt securities	...	...	...	25,917	29,719	31,284	25,917	29,719	31,284	25,917	29,719	31,284
6204	Loans	...	...	...	20,415	16,218	18,575	20,415	16,218	18,575	19,820	16,218	18,575
6205	Equity and investment fund shares	...	...	...	3,748	3,938	3,938	3,748	3,938	3,938	3,748	3,938	3,938
6206	Insurance, pension, and standardized guarantee schemes	...	...	...	—	—	—	—	—	—	—	—	—
6207	Financial derivatives and employee stock options	...	...	...	—	—	—	—	—	—	—	—	—
6208	Other accounts receivable	...	...	...	...	...	...	...	...	...	...	...	...
	By debtor												
621	Domestic debtors	...	...	...	103,865	119,296	137,221	105,045	120,661	138,086	107,416	123,475	141,753
622	External debtors	...	...	...	153	90	292	153	90	292	153	90	292
63	**Liabilities**	...	...	...	**502,495**	**588,694**	**743,250**	**503,629**	**590,186**	**745,197**	**508,885**	**598,468**	**753,775**
	By instrument												
6301	Special Drawing Rights (SDRs)	...	...	...	—	—	—	—	—	—	—	—	—
6302	Currency and deposits	...	...	...	—	—	—	—	—	—	—	—	—
6303	Debt securities	...	...	...	413,732	491,875	643,772	413,732	491,875	643,772	413,732	491,875	643,772
6304	Loans	...	...	...	88,763	96,819	99,478	89,897	98,311	101,426	95,153	106,593	110,003
6305	Equity and investment fund shares	...	...	...	—	—	—	—	—	—	—	—	—
6306	Insurance, pension, and standardized guarantee schemes	...	...	...	—	—	—	—	—	—	—	—	—
6307	Financial derivatives and employee stock options	...	...	...	—	—	—	—	—	—	—	—	—
6308	Other accounts payable	...	...	...	...	...	...	...	...	...	...	...	...
	By creditor												
631	Domestic creditors	...	...	...	197,595	222,864	280,695	198,729	224,357	282,642	200,286	228,467	286,514
632	External creditors	...	...	...	304,900	365,830	462,555	304,900	365,830	462,555	308,599	370,001	467,261
	Memorandum items												
6M2	Net financial worth	...	...	...	-398,477	-469,308	-605,737	-398,431	-469,435	-606,820	-401,316	-474,903	-611,730
6M3	Gross debt (D4) at market value	...	...	...	...	...	...	...	...	...	...	...	...
6M3D3	D3 debt liabilities at market value	...	...	...	...	...	...	...	...	...	...	...	...
6M3D2	D2 debt liabilities at market value	...	...	...	...	...	...	...	...	...	...	...	...
6M3D1	D1 debt liabilities at market value	...	...	...	...	...	...	...	...	...	...	...	...
6M4	Gross debt (D4) at nominal value	...	...	...	...	...	743,250	...	...	745,197	...	...	753,775
6M4D3	D3 debt liabilities at nominal value	...	...	...	...	...	743,250	...	...	745,197	...	...	753,775
6M4D2	D2 debt liabilities at nominal value	...	...	...	...	588,694	743,250	...	590,186	745,197	...	598,468	753,775
6M4D1	D1 debt liabilities at nominal value	...	...	...	...	588,694	743,250	...	590,186	745,197	...	598,468	753,775

Uruguay (298)

In Millions of Uruguayan Pesos (UYU) / Fiscal Year Ends December 31st

		Budgetary Central Government			Central Government (excl. Social Security)			Central Government (incl. Social Security)			General Government		
		2013	2014	2015	2013	2014	2015	2013	2014	2015	2013	2014	2015
6M35	Gross debt (D4) at face value	...	...	...	...	...	...	...	...	...	...	...	...
6M35D3	D3 debt liabilities at face value	...	...	...	...	...	...	...	...	...	...	...	...
6M35D2	D2 debt liabilities at face value	...	...	...	502,495	588,694	...	503,629	590,186	...	508,885	598,468	...
6M35D1	D1 debt liabilities at face value	...	...	...	502,495	588,694	...	503,629	590,186	...	508,885	598,468	...
6M93	Government gross debt per national definition	...	...	...	...	...	...	...	...	...	...	...	...
6M5	Arrears	...	...	...	...	...	...	...	...	...	...	...	...
6M6	Explicit contingent liabilities	...	...	...	...	...	...	...	...	...	...	...	...
6M61	of which: Publicly guaranteed debt	...	...	...	...	...	...	...	...	...	...	...	...
6M7	Net implicit obligations for social security benefits	...	...	...	...	...	...	...	...	...	...	...	...
	Table 7 Expenditure by functions of government												
7	**Expenditure**	...	...	...	**265,746**	**302,275**	...	**384,293**	**427,840**	...	...	...	...
701	**General public services**	...	...	...	...	...	...	...	...	...	...	...	...
7017	Public debt transactions	...	...	...	27,987	30,291	...	27,987	30,291	...	...	...	...
7018	Transfers of general character between levels of government	...	...	...	...	...	...	...	...	...	...	...	...
702	**Defense**	...	...	...	...	...	...	...	...	...	...	...	...
703	**Public order and safety**	...	...	...	...	...	...	...	...	...	...	...	...
704	**Economic affairs**	...	...	...	...	...	...	...	...	...	...	...	...
7042	Agriculture, forestry, fishing, and hunting	...	...	...	...	...	...	...	...	...	...	...	...
7043	Fuel and energy	...	...	...	...	...	...	...	...	...	...	...	...
7044	Mining, manufacturing, and construction	...	...	...	...	...	...	...	...	...	...	...	...
7045	Transport	...	...	...	...	...	...	...	...	...	...	...	...
7046	Communication	...	...	...	...	...	...	...	...	...	...	...	...
705	**Environmental protection**	...	...	...	...	...	...	...	...	...	...	...	...
706	**Housing and community amenities**	...	...	...	...	...	...	...	...	...	...	...	...
707	**Health**	...	...	...	...	...	...	...	...	...	...	...	...
7072	Outpatient services	...	...	...	...	...	...	...	...	...	...	...	...
7073	Hospital services	...	...	...	...	...	...	...	...	...	...	...	...
7074	Public health services	...	...	...	...	...	...	...	...	...	...	...	...
708	**Recreation, culture and religion**	...	...	...	...	...	...	...	...	...	...	...	...
709	**Education**	...	...	...	...	...	...	...	...	...	...	...	...
7091	Pre-primary and primary education	...	...	...	...	...	...	...	...	...	...	...	...
7092	Secondary education	...	...	...	...	...	...	...	...	...	...	...	...
7094	Tertiary education	...	...	...	...	...	...	...	...	...	...	...	...
710	**Social protection**	...	...	...	...	...	...	...	...	...	...	...	...
7z	Statistical discrepancy: Expenditure	...	...	...	...	...	...	...	...	...	...	...	...
	Table 8 Financial transactions by counterpart sector												
32	**Net acquisition of financial assets**	...	...	...	**-3,502**	**2,915**	**31,786**	**-3,406**	**3,131**	**31,213**	**-3,796**	**2,863**	**32,437**
321	Domestic debtors	...	...	...	-3,493	2,992	31,622	-3,397	3,207	31,050	-3,787	2,939	32,273
8211	General government	...	...	...	170	—	-543	170	—	-543	—	—	—
8212	Central bank	...	...	...	-12,380	10,016	25,973	-12,314	10,190	25,390	-12,337	10,192	25,384
8213	Deposit-taking corporations except the central bank	...	...	...	1,128	-1,117	979	1,158	-1,076	989	961	-1,346	1,676
8214	Other financial corporations	...	...	...	—	—	—	—	—	—	—	—	—
8215	Nonfinancial corporations	...	...	...	7,589	-5,907	5,214	7,589	-5,907	5,214	7,589	-5,907	5,214
8216	Households & nonprofit institutions serving households	...	...	...	—	—	—	—	—	—	—	—	—
322	External debtors	...	...	...	-9	-76	164	-9	-76	164	-9	-76	164
8221	General government	...	...	...	—	—	—	—	—	—	—	—	—
8227	International organizations	...	...	...	—	—	—	—	—	—	—	—	—
8228	Financial corporations other than international organizations	...	...	...	-9	-76	164	-9	-76	164	-9	-76	164
8229	Other nonresidents	...	...	...	—	—	—	—	—	—	—	—	—

Uruguay (298)

In Millions of Uruguayan Pesos (UYU) / Fiscal Year Ends December 31st

		Budgetary Central Government			Central Government (excl. Social Security)			Central Government (incl. Social Security)			General Government		
		2013	2014	2015	2013	2014	2015	2013	2014	2015	2013	2014	2015
33	**Net incurrence of liabilities**	**...**	**...**	**...**	**15,179**	**33,314**	**73,612**	**15,512**	**33,661**	**74,067**	**16,011**	**35,518**	**73,787**
331	Domestic creditors	...	...	...	-16,381	692	42,815	-16,048	1,039	43,270	-15,867	2,924	43,381
3311	General government	...	...	...	—	—	—	—	—	—	—	—	—
3312	Central bank	...	...	...	1,757	2,847	1,907	1,757	2,847	1,907	1,757	2,847	1,907
3313	Deposit-taking corporations except the central bank	...	...	...	-3,747	-3,361	-1,055	-3,414	-3,014	-600	-3,232	-2,452	-489
3314	Other financial corporations	...	...	...	-7,974	481	47,257	-7,974	481	47,257	-7,974	481	47,257
3315	Nonfinancial corporations	...	...	...	-4,542	12,819	-6,218	-4,542	12,819	-6,218	-4,542	14,142	-6,218
3316	Households & nonprofit institutions serving households	...	...	...	-1,876	-12,095	924	-1,876	-12,095	924	-1,876	-12,095	924
332	External creditors	...	...	...	31,560	32,622	30,797	31,560	32,622	30,797	31,878	32,594	30,407
3321	General government	...	...	...	—	—	—	—	—	—	—	—	—
3327	International organizations	...	...	...	-10,621	849	908	-10,621	849	908	-10,303	821	518
3328	Financial corporations other than international organizations	...	...	...	-13	-26	-26	-13	-26	-26	-13	-26	-26
3329	Other nonresidents	...	...	...	42,194	31,799	29,916	42,194	31,799	29,916	42,194	31,799	29,916
	Table 9 Total other economic flows in assets and liabilities												

Uzbekistan (927)

In Billions of Uzbek Sum (UZS) / Fiscal Year Ends December 31st

		Budgetary Central Government			Central Government (excl. Social Security)			Central Government (incl. Social Security)			General Government		
		2013	2014	2015	2013	2014	2015	2013	2014	2015	2013	2014	2015
	Statement of operations												
1	Revenue	15,597	19,252	21,976	23,497	27,225	30,932	33,265	39,037	43,501	43,826	51,452	57,945
2	Expense	14,157	17,274	20,376	14,147	17,248	20,326	23,225	27,967	33,347	32,214	38,675	45,458
GOB	**Gross operating balance**	**1,440**	**1,979**	**1,600**	**9,349**	**9,977**	**10,606**	**10,040**	**11,070**	**10,155**	**11,613**	**12,777**	**12,488**
NOB	**Net operating balance**	...	...	...	...	...	...	...	...	...	...	...	...
31	Net/Gross investment in nonfinancial assets	815	1,098	1,325	3,282	3,864	4,329	3,286	3,864	4,329	4,458	5,100	5,629
2M	Expenditure	14,972	18,371	21,701	17,429	21,111	24,655	26,511	31,831	37,676	36,671	43,775	51,086
NLB	**Net lending (+) / Net borrowing (-)**	**625**	**881**	**275**	**6,068**	**6,113**	**6,277**	**6,754**	**7,206**	**5,826**	**7,155**	**7,677**	**6,859**
32	Net acquisition of financial assets	421	583	69	5,967	6,105	6,532	6,654	7,198	6,080	7,047	7,665	7,109
33	Net incurrence of liabilities	-204	-298	-206	-100	-8	255	-100	-8	255	-108	-12	250
NLBz	Statistical discrepancy	-0	0	-0	0	0	-0	-0	-0	0	-0	0	-0
	Memorandum items												
PB	Primary net lending / net borrowing	658	923	316	6,101	6,162	6,334	6,787	7,254	5,883	7,190	7,730	6,920
GB	Government balance per national definition	...	...	...	...	...	...	...	...	...	...	...	...
	Statement of other economic flows												
	Balance sheet												
	Table 1 Revenue												
1	**Revenue**	**15,597**	**19,252**	**21,976**	**23,497**	**27,225**	**30,932**	**33,265**	**39,037**	**43,501**	**43,826**	**51,452**	**57,945**
11	**Taxes**	**15,002**	**18,485**	**21,111**	**19,175**	**23,019**	**28,005**	**21,158**	**25,167**	**30,010**	**30,511**	**36,076**	**42,662**
111	Taxes on income, profits, and capital gains	2,962	3,590	4,184	4,629	5,580	6,096	6,612	7,728	8,101	10,593	12,231	13,368
1111	Payable by individuals	1,007	1,308	1,639	1,007	1,308	1,639	1,007	1,308	1,639	3,112	3,790	4,452
1112	Payable by corporations and other enterprises	1,955	2,282	2,544	3,622	4,273	4,457	5,605	6,420	6,462	7,482	8,441	8,917
1113	Other taxes on income, profits, and capital gains	—	—	—	—	—	—	—	—	—	—	—	—
112	Taxes on payroll and workforce	—	—	—	—	—	—	—	—	—	—	—	—
113	Taxes on property	—	—	—	—	—	—	—	—	—	1,595	1,921	2,143
114	Taxes on goods and services	10,908	13,409	15,276	10,908	13,409	15,276	10,908	13,409	15,276	14,685	17,893	20,517
1141	General taxes on goods and services	5,375	7,164	8,192	5,375	7,164	8,192	5,375	7,164	8,192	8,223	10,562	12,094
1142	Excises	3,365	3,997	4,594	3,365	3,997	4,594	3,365	3,997	4,594	4,168	4,941	5,618
115	Taxes on international trade and transactions	1,132	1,486	1,651	3,638	4,031	6,633	3,638	4,031	6,633	3,638	4,031	6,633
116	Other taxes	—	—	—	—	—	—	—	—	—	—	—	—
12	**Social contributions**	—	—	—	—	—	—	**7,760**	**9,642**	**10,539**	**7,760**	**9,642**	**10,539**
121	Social security contributions	—	—	—	—	—	—	7,760	9,642	10,539	7,760	9,642	10,539
122	Other social contributions	—	—	—	—	—	—	—	—	—	—	—	—
13	**Grants**	—	—	**25**	**19**	**8**	**12**	**19**	**8**	**12**	—	—	—
131	From foreign governments	—	—	—	—	—	—	—	—	—	—	—	—
132	From international organizations	—	—	—	—	—	—	—	—	—	—	—	—
133	From other general government units	—	—	25	19	8	12	19	8	12	—	—	—
1331	Current	—	—	—	19	8	12	19	8	12	—	—	—
1332	Capital	—	—	25	—	—	—	—	—	—	—	—	—
14	**Other revenue**	**594**	**767**	**840**	**4,304**	**4,197**	**2,915**	**4,329**	**4,220**	**2,939**	**5,556**	**5,734**	**4,743**
	Table 2 Expense by economic type												
2	**Expense**	**14,157**	**17,274**	**20,376**	**14,147**	**17,248**	**20,326**	**23,225**	**27,967**	**33,347**	**32,214**	**38,675**	**45,458**
21	**Compensation of employees**	...	...	...	...	...	...	...	...	...	...	...	...
211	Wages and salaries	...	...	...	...	...	...	...	...	...	...	...	...
212	Employers' social contributions	...	...	...	...	...	...	...	...	...	...	...	...
22	**Use of goods and services**	...	...	...	...	...	...	...	...	...	...	...	...
23	**Consumption of fixed capital**	...	...	...	...	...	...	...	...	...	...	...	...
24	**Interest**	**33**	**42**	**41**	**33**	**48**	**57**	**33**	**48**	**57**	**36**	**53**	**61**
25	**Subsidies**	...	...	...	...	...	...	...	...	...	...	...	...
26	**Grants**	...	...	...	...	...	...	...	...	...	...	...	...
261	To foreign governments	...	...	...	...	...	...	...	...	...	...	...	...
262	To international organizations	...	...	...	...	...	...	...	...	...	...	...	...
263	To other general government units	...	...	...	...	...	...	...	...	...	...	...	...
2631	Current	...	...	...	...	...	...	...	...	...	...	...	...
2632	Capital	...	...	...	...	...	...	...	...	...	...	...	...

Uzbekistan (927)

In Billions of Uzbek Sum (UZS) / Fiscal Year Ends December 31st

		Budgetary Central Government			Central Government (excl. Social Security)			Central Government (incl. Social Security)			General Government		
		2013	2014	2015	2013	2014	2015	2013	2014	2015	2013	2014	2015
27	**Social benefits**	**...**	**...**	**...**	**...**	**...**	**...**	**...**	**...**	**...**	**...**	**...**	**...**
271	Social security benefits	...	...	...	...	...	...	...	...	...	...	...	...
272	Social assistance benefits	...	...	...	...	...	...	...	...	...	...	...	...
273	Employment-related social benefits	...	...	...	...	...	...	...	...	...	...	...	...
28	**Other expense**	**...**	**...**	**...**	**...**	**...**	**...**	**...**	**...**	**...**	**...**	**...**	**...**
281	Property expense other than interest	...	...	...	...	...	...	...	...	...	...	...	...
282	Transfers not elsewhere classified	...	...	...	...	...	...	...	...	...	...	...	...
2821	Current	...	...	...	...	...	...	...	...	...	...	...	...
2822	Capital	...	...	...	...	...	...	...	...	...	...	...	...
	Table 3 Transactions in assets and liabilities												
3	**Change in net worth from transactions**	**...**	**...**	**...**	**...**	**...**	**...**	**...**	**...**	**...**	**...**	**...**	**...**
31	**Net/Gross investment in nonfinancial assets**	**815**	**1,098**	**1,325**	**3,282**	**3,864**	**4,329**	**3,286**	**3,864**	**4,329**	**4,458**	**5,100**	**5,629**
311	Fixed assets	815	1,098	1,325	3,282	3,864	4,329	3,286	3,864	4,329	4,458	5,100	5,629
3111	Buildings and structures	712	931	1,158	2,980	3,423	3,957	2,980	3,423	3,957	3,948	4,398	4,966
3112	Machinery and equipment	99	164	163	298	437	368	302	437	368	495	686	649
3113	Other fixed assets	4	3	4	4	3	4	4	3	4	14	15	14
3114	Weapons systems	—	—	—	—	—	—	—	—	—	—	—	—
312	Inventories	—	—	—	—	—	—	—	—	—	—	—	—
313	Valuables	—	—	—	—	—	—	—	—	—	—	—	—
314	Nonproduced assets	—	—	—	—	—	—	—	—	—	—	—	—
3141	Land	—	—	—	—	—	—	—	—	—	—	—	—
3142	Mineral and energy resources	—	—	—	—	—	—	—	—	—	—	—	—
3143	Other naturally occurring assets	—	—	—	—	—	—	—	—	—	—	—	—
3144	Intangible nonproduced assets	—	—	—	—	—	—	—	—	—	—	—	—
32	**Net acquisition of financial assets**	**421**	**583**	**69**	**5,967**	**6,105**	**6,532**	**6,654**	**7,198**	**6,080**	**7,047**	**7,665**	**7,109**
	By instrument												
3201	Monetary gold and SDRs	—	—	—	—	—	—	—	—	—	—	—	—
3202	Currency and deposits	5	-158	-793	4,534	4,648	5,191	5,223	5,742	4,739	5,615	6,205	5,768
3203	Debt securities	—	—	—	—	—	—	—	—	—	—	—	—
3204	Loans	361	700	837	1,422	1,248	1,409	1,419	1,247	1,409	1,419	1,247	1,409
3205	Equity and investment fund shares	55	41	25	11	209	-68	11	209	-68	12	213	-68
3206	Insurance, pension, and standardized guarantee schemes	—	—	—	—	—	—	—	—	—	—	—	—
3207	Financial derivatives and employee stock options	—	—	—	—	—	—	—	—	—	—	—	—
3208	Other accounts receivable	...	...	...	...	...	...	...	...	...	...	...	...
	By debtor												
321	Domestic debtors	421	583	69	5,967	6,105	6,532	6,654	7,198	6,080	7,047	7,665	7,109
322	External debtors	—	—	—	—	—	—	—	—	—	—	—	—
33	**Net incurrence of liabilities**	**-204**	**-298**	**-206**	**-100**	**-8**	**255**	**-100**	**-8**	**255**	**-108**	**-12**	**250**
	By instrument												
3301	Special Drawing Rights (SDRs)	—	—	—	—	—	—	—	—	—	—	—	—
3302	Currency and deposits	—	—	—	—	—	—	—	—	—	—	—	—
3303	Debt securities	—	-22	—	—	-22	—	—	-22	—	—	-22	—
3304	Loans	-204	-276	-206	-100	14	255	-100	14	255	-108	9	250
3305	Equity and investment fund shares	—	—	—	—	—	—	—	—	—	—	—	—
3306	Insurance, pension, and standardized guarantee schemes	—	—	—	—	—	—	—	—	—	—	—	—
3307	Financial derivatives and employee stock options	—	—	—	—	—	—	—	—	—	—	—	—
3308	Other accounts payable	...	...	...	...	...	...	...	...	...	...	...	...
	By creditor												
331	Domestic creditors	-14	-31	-4	-14	-31	-4	-14	-31	-4	-14	-31	-4
332	External creditors	-190	-267	-202	-86	23	259	-86	23	259	-94	19	254
	Table 4 Holding gains and losses in assets and liabilities												
	Table 5 Holding gains and losses in assets and liabilities												
	Table 6 Balance sheet												

Uzbekistan (927)

In Billions of Uzbek Sum (UZS) / Fiscal Year Ends December 31st

		Budgetary Central Government			Central Government (excl. Social Security)			Central Government (incl. Social Security)			General Government		
		2013	2014	2015	2013	2014	2015	2013	2014	2015	2013	2014	2015
	Table 7 Expenditure by functions of government												
7	**Expenditure**	**14,972**	**18,371**	**14,408**	**17,429**	**21,111**	**17,362**	**26,511**	**31,831**	**30,383**	**36,671**	**43,775**	**51,086**
701	**General public services**	**5,510**	**6,592**	**7,402**	**5,540**	**6,648**	**7,493**	**5,540**	**6,648**	**7,493**	**1,685**	**2,030**	**2,365**
7017	Public debt transactions	33	42	41	33	48	57	33	48	57	36	53	61
7018	Transfers of general character between levels of government	4,536	5,328	5,947	4,536	...	5,947	4,536	5,328	5,947	0	—	—
702	**Defense**	...	...	...	...	...	...	...	...	...	...	...	...
703	**Public order and safety**	...	...	...	...	...	...	...	...	...	...	...	...
704	**Economic affairs**	**2,608**	**3,222**	**3,929**	**4,471**	**5,224**	**6,064**	**4,497**	**5,256**	**6,100**	**5,189**	**6,072**	**6,900**
7042	Agriculture, forestry, fishing, and hunting	1,611	1,897	2,249	1,599	1,882	2,239	...	...	...	1,915	2,294	...
7043	Fuel and energy	3	3	87	3	3	87	...	...	...	14	16	...
7044	Mining, manufacturing, and construction	196	231	276	196	231	276	...	...	...	200	237	...
7045	Transport	...	...	...	1,875	2,017	2,144	...	...	...	1,993	2,158	...
7046	Communication	5	5	7	5	5	7	...	...	...	5	5	...
705	**Environmental protection**	**14**	**19**	**21**	**14**	**...**	**21**	**14**	**19**	**21**	**22**	**26**	**...**
706	**Housing and community amenities**	**—**	**0**	**1**	**—**	**0**	**1**	**—**	**0**	**1**	**429**	**609**	**...**
707	**Health**	**318**	**414**	**493**	**318**	**414**	**942**	**318**	**414**	**942**	**3,435**	**4,164**	**5,236**
7072	Outpatient services	15	17	19	15	17	19	15	17	19	1,076	1,325	1,509
7073	Hospital services	190	239	277	190	239	277	190	239	277	1,975	2,351	2,709
7074	Public health services	22	29	39	22	29	39	22	29	39	239	295	343
708	**Recreation, culture and religion**	**188**	**211**	**242**	**188**	**...**	**242**	**188**	**211**	**242**	**435**	**504**	**...**
709	**Education**	**984**	**1,168**	**1,368**	**1,572**	**1,880**	**1,648**	**1,572**	**1,880**	**1,648**	**9,517**	**11,501**	**12,529**
7091	Pre-primary and primary education	3	8	1	3	8	1	3	8	1	1,011	1,234	1,454
7092	Secondary education	240	300	354	65	85	70	65	85	70	6,470	7,862	8,846
7094	Tertiary education	590	709	850	776	934	1,143	776	934	1,143	776	934	1,143
710	**Social protection**	**604**	**738**	**953**	**604**	**738**	**953**	**9,660**	**11,426**	**13,936**	**10,903**	**12,802**	**...**
7z	Statistical discrepancy: Expenditure	...	...	...	...	...	...	...	...	...	...	...	...
	Table 8 Financial transactions by counterpart sector												
32	**Net acquisition of financial assets**	**421**	**583**	**69**	**5,967**	**6,105**	**6,532**	**6,654**	**7,198**	**6,080**	**7,047**	**7,665**	**7,109**
321	Domestic debtors	421	583	69	5,967	6,105	6,532	6,654	7,198	6,080	7,047	7,665	7,109
8211	General government	...	...	...	...	...	...	...	...	...	...	...	...
8212	Central bank	...	...	...	...	...	...	...	...	...	...	...	...
8213	Deposit-taking corporations except the central bank	...	...	...	...	...	...	...	...	...	...	...	...
8214	Other financial corporations	...	...	...	...	...	...	...	...	...	...	...	...
8215	Nonfinancial corporations	...	...	...	...	...	...	...	...	...	...	...	...
8216	Households & nonprofit institutions serving households	...	...	...	...	...	...	...	...	...	...	...	...
322	External debtors	—	—	—	—	—	—	—	—	—	—	—	—
8221	General government	—	—	—	—	—	—	—	—	—	—	—	—
8227	International organizations	—	—	—	—	—	—	—	—	—	—	—	—
8228	Financial corporations other than international organizations	—	—	—	—	—	—	—	—	—	—	—	—
8229	Other nonresidents	—	—	—	—	—	—	—	—	—	—	—	—

Uzbekistan (927)

In Billions of Uzbek Sum (UZS) / Fiscal Year Ends December 31st

		Budgetary Central Government			Central Government (excl. Social Security)			Central Government (incl. Social Security)			General Government		
		2013	2014	2015	2013	2014	2015	2013	2014	2015	2013	2014	2015
33	**Net incurrence of liabilities**	**-204**	**-298**	**-206**	**-100**	**-8**	**255**	**-100**	**-8**	**255**	**-108**	**-12**	**250**
331	Domestic creditors	-14	-31	-4	-14	-31	-4	-14	-31	-4	-14	-31	-4
8311	General government	...	...	...	...	...	...	...	...	...	...	...	...
8312	Central bank	...	...	...	...	...	...	...	...	...	...	...	...
8313	Deposit-taking corporations except the central bank	...	...	...	...	...	...	...	...	...	...	...	...
8314	Other financial corporations	...	...	...	...	...	...	...	...	...	...	...	...
8315	Nonfinancial corporations	...	...	...	...	...	...	...	...	...	...	...	...
8316	Households & nonprofit institutions serving households	...	...	...	...	...	...	...	...	...	...	...	...
332	External creditors	-190	-267	-202	-86	23	259	-86	23	259	-94	19	254
8321	General government	-190	-267	-202	-190	-267	-202	-190	-267	-202	-197	-271	-206
8327	International organizations	—	—	—	103	290	461	103	290	461	103	290	461
8328	Financial corporations other than international organizations	—	—	—	—	—	—	—	—	—	—	—	—
8329	Other nonresidents	—	—	—	—	—	—	—	—	—	—	—	—
	Table 9 Total other economic flows in assets and liabilities												

Vanuatu (846)

In Millions of Vanuatu Vatu (VUV) / Fiscal Year Ends December 31st

		Budgetary Central Government			Central Government (excl. Social Security)			Central Government (incl. Social Security)			General Government		
		2009P	2010P	2011	2009	2010	2011	2009	2010	2011	2009	2010	2011
	Statement of operations												
1	Revenue	16,900	16,715	17,447	...	...	...	...	...	...	...	...	...
2	Expense	13,272	15,109	15,615	...	...	...	...	...	...	...	...	...
GOB	**Gross operating balance**	**3,628**	**1,606**	**1,832**	...	...	...	...	...	...	...	...	...
NOB	**Net operating balance**	...	...	...	...	...	...	...	...	...	...	...	...
31	Net/Gross investment in nonfinancial assets	4,163	3,307	3,482	...	...	...	...	...	...	...	...	...
2M	Expenditure	17,435	18,416	19,096	...	...	...	...	...	...	...	...	...
NLB	**Net lending (+) / Net borrowing (-)**	**-535**	**-1,701**	**-1,649**	...	...	...	...	...	...	...	...	...
32	Net acquisition of financial assets	129	-637	-549	...	...	...	...	...	...	...	...	...
33	Net incurrence of liabilities	664	1,064	1,100	...	...	...	...	...	...	...	...	...
NLBz	Statistical discrepancy	-0	—	—	...	...	...	...	...	...	...	...	...
	Memorandum items												
PB	Primary net lending / net borrowing	-217	-1,367	-1,182	...	...	...	...	...	...	...	...	...
GB	Government balance per national definition	...	...	...	...	...	...	...	...	...	...	...	...
	Statement of other economic flows												
	Balance sheet												
	Table 1 Revenue												
1	**Revenue**	**16,900**	**16,715**	**17,447**	...	...	...	...	...	...	...	...	...
11	**Taxes**	**10,435**	**10,526**	**11,330**	...	...	...	...	...	...	...	...	...
111	Taxes on income, profits, and capital gains	—	—	—	...	...	...	...	...	...	...	...	...
1111	Payable by individuals	—	—	—	...	...	...	...	...	...	...	...	...
1112	Payable by corporations and other enterprises	—	—	—	...	...	...	...	...	...	...	...	...
1113	Other taxes on income, profits, and capital gains	—	—	—	...	...	...	...	...	...	...	...	...
112	Taxes on payroll and workforce	—	—	—	...	...	...	...	...	...	...	...	...
113	Taxes on property	...	...	—	...	...	...	...	...	...	...	...	...
114	Taxes on goods and services	...	...	8,696	...	...	...	...	...	...	...	...	...
1141	General taxes on goods and services	...	...	...	...	...	...	...	...	...	...	...	...
1142	Excises	...	1,793	...	...	...	...	...	...	...	...	...	...
115	Taxes on international trade and transactions	3,897	2,646	2,633	...	...	...	...	...	...	...	...	...
116	Other taxes	—	—	—	...	...	...	...	...	...	...	...	...
12	**Social contributions**	—	—	—	...	...	...	...	...	...	...	...	...
121	Social security contributions	—	—	—	...	...	...	...	...	...	...	...	...
122	Other social contributions	—	—	—	...	...	...	...	...	...	...	...	...
13	**Grants**	**4,610**	**4,529**	**4,316**	...	...	...	...	...	...	...	...	...
131	From foreign governments	...	...	...	...	...	...	...	...	...	...	...	...
132	From international organizations	...	...	...	...	...	...	...	...	...	...	...	...
133	From other general government units	...	...	...	...	...	...	...	...	...	...	...	...
1331	Current	...	...	...	...	...	...	...	...	...	...	...	...
1332	Capital	...	...	...	...	...	...	...	...	...	...	...	...
14	**Other revenue**	**1,855**	**1,661**	**1,801**	...	...	...	...	...	...	...	...	...
	Table 2 Expense by economic type												
2	**Expense**	**13,272**	**15,109**	**15,615**	...	...	...	...	...	...	...	...	...
21	**Compensation of employees**	**7,236**	**7,831**	**8,088**	...	...	...	...	...	...	...	...	...
211	Wages and salaries	...	...	...	...	...	...	...	...	...	...	...	...
212	Employers' social contributions	...	...	...	...	...	...	...	...	...	...	...	...
22	**Use of goods and services**	**3,920**	**4,693**	**4,309**	...	...	...	...	...	...	...	...	...
23	**Consumption of fixed capital**	...	...	...	...	...	...	...	...	...	...	...	...
24	**Interest**	**318**	**334**	**468**	...	...	...	...	...	...	...	...	...
25	**Subsidies**	**108**	—	**108**	...	...	...	...	...	...	...	...	...
26	**Grants**	**1,278**	**1,510**	**1,807**	...	...	...	...	...	...	...	...	...
261	To foreign governments	...	...	...	...	...	...	...	...	...	...	...	...
262	To international organizations	...	...	...	...	...	...	...	...	...	...	...	...
263	To other general government units	...	...	...	...	...	...	...	...	...	...	...	...
2631	Current	...	...	...	...	...	...	...	...	...	...	...	...
2632	Capital	...	...	...	...	...	...	...	...	...	...	...	...

Vanuatu (846)

In Millions of Vanuatu Vatu (VUV) / Fiscal Year Ends December 31st

		Budgetary Central Government			Central Government (excl. Social Security)			Central Government (incl. Social Security)			General Government		
		2009P	2010P	2011	2009	2010	2011	2009	2010	2011	2009	2010	2011
27	**Social benefits**	**202**	**410**	**329**	**...**	**...**	**...**	**...**	**...**	**...**	**...**	**...**	**...**
271	Social security benefits	...	...	...	...	...	...	...	...	...	...	...	...
272	Social assistance benefits	...	...	...	...	...	...	...	...	...	...	...	...
273	Employment-related social benefits	...	...	...	...	...	...	...	...	...	...	...	...
28	**Other expense**	**211**	**331**	**506**	**...**	**...**	**...**	**...**	**...**	**...**	**...**	**...**	**...**
281	Property expense other than interest	...	...	...	...	...	...	...	...	...	...	...	...
282	Transfers not elsewhere classified	...	...	...	...	...	...	...	...	...	...	...	...
2821	Current	...	...	...	...	...	...	...	...	...	...	...	...
2822	Capital	...	...	...	...	...	...	...	...	...	...	...	...
	Table 3 Transactions in assets and liabilities												
3	**Change in net worth from transactions**	**...**	**...**	**...**	**...**	**...**	**...**	**...**	**...**	**...**	**...**	**...**	**...**
31	**Net/Gross investment in nonfinancial assets**	**4,163**	**3,307**	**3,482**	**...**	**...**	**...**	**...**	**...**	**...**	**...**	**...**	**...**
311	Fixed assets	4,163	3,307	3,482	...	...	...	...	...	...	...	...	...
3111	Buildings and structures	...	...	...	...	...	...	...	...	...	...	...	...
3112	Machinery and equipment	...	...	...	...	...	...	...	...	...	...	...	...
3113	Other fixed assets	...	...	...	...	...	...	...	...	...	...	...	...
3114	Weapons systems	...	...	...	...	...	...	...	...	...	...	...	...
312	Inventories	—	—	—	...	...	...	...	...	...	...	...	...
313	Valuables	—	—	—	...	...	...	...	...	...	...	...	...
314	Nonproduced assets	—	—	—	...	...	...	...	...	...	...	...	...
3141	Land	—	—	—	...	...	...	...	...	...	...	...	...
3142	Mineral and energy resources	—	—	—	...	...	...	...	...	...	...	...	...
3143	Other naturally occurring assets	—	—	—	...	...	...	...	...	...	...	...	...
3144	Intangible nonproduced assets	—	—	—	...	...	...	...	...	...	...	...	...
32	**Net acquisition of financial assets**	**129**	**-637**	**-549**	**...**	**...**	**...**	**...**	**...**	**...**	**...**	**...**	**...**
	By instrument												
3201	Monetary gold and SDRs	—	—	—	...	...	...	...	...	...	...	...	...
3202	Currency and deposits	129	-637	-549	...	...	...	...	...	...	...	...	...
3203	Debt securities	—	—	—	...	...	...	...	...	...	...	...	...
3204	Loans	—	—	—	...	...	...	...	...	...	...	...	...
3205	Equity and investment fund shares	—	—	—	...	...	...	...	...	...	...	...	...
3206	Insurance, pension, and standardized guarantee schemes	—	—	—	...	...	...	...	...	...	...	...	...
3207	Financial derivatives and employee stock options	—	—	—	...	...	...	...	...	...	...	...	...
3208	Other accounts receivable	...	...	...	...	...	...	...	...	...	...	...	...
	By debtor												
321	Domestic debtors	129	-637	-549	...	...	...	...	...	...	...	...	...
322	External debtors	—	—	—	...	...	...	...	...	...	...	...	...
33	**Net incurrence of liabilities**	**664**	**1,064**	**1,100**	**...**	**...**	**...**	**...**	**...**	**...**	**...**	**...**	**...**
	By instrument												
3301	Special Drawing Rights (SDRs)	—	—	—	...	...	...	...	...	...	...	...	...
3302	Currency and deposits	—	—	—	...	...	...	...	...	...	...	...	...
3303	Debt securities	-98	800	871	...	...	...	...	...	...	...	...	...
3304	Loans	762	264	229	...	...	...	...	...	...	...	...	...
3305	Equity and investment fund shares	—	—	—	...	...	...	...	...	...	...	...	...
3306	Insurance, pension, and standardized guarantee schemes	—	—	—	...	...	...	...	...	...	...	...	...
3307	Financial derivatives and employee stock options	—	—	—	...	...	...	...	...	...	...	...	...
3308	Other accounts payable	...	...	...	...	...	...	...	...	...	...	...	...
	By creditor												
331	Domestic creditors	-98	800	871	...	...	...	...	...	...	...	...	...
332	External creditors	762	264	229	...	...	...	...	...	...	...	...	...
	Table 4 Holding gains and losses in assets and liabilities												
	Table 5 Holding gains and losses in assets and liabilities												
	Table 6 Balance sheet												

Vanuatu (846)

In Millions of Vanuatu Vatu (VUV) / Fiscal Year Ends December 31st

		Budgetary Central Government			Central Government (excl. Social Security)			Central Government (incl. Social Security)			General Government		
		2009P	2010P	2011	2009	2010	2011	2009	2010	2011	2009	2010	2011
	Table 7 Expenditure by functions of government												
7	**Expenditure**	**17,435**	**18,416**	**19,096**	...	...	...	...	...	...	...	...	...
701	**General public services**	...	...	...	...	...	...	...	...	...	...	...	...
7017	Public debt transactions	318	334	468	...	...	...	...	...	...	...	...	...
7018	Transfers of general character between levels of government	...	...	...	...	...	...	...	...	...	...	...	...
702	**Defense**	...	...	...	...	...	...	...	...	...	...	...	...
703	**Public order and safety**	...	...	...	...	...	...	...	...	...	...	...	...
704	**Economic affairs**	...	...	...	...	...	...	...	...	...	...	...	...
7042	Agriculture, forestry, fishing, and hunting	...	...	...	...	...	...	...	...	...	...	...	...
7043	Fuel and energy	...	...	...	...	...	...	...	...	...	...	...	...
7044	Mining, manufacturing, and construction	...	...	...	...	...	...	...	...	...	...	...	...
7045	Transport	...	...	...	...	...	...	...	...	...	...	...	...
7046	Communication	...	...	...	...	...	...	...	...	...	...	...	...
705	**Environmental protection**	...	...	...	...	...	...	...	...	...	...	...	...
706	**Housing and community amenities**	...	...	...	...	...	...	...	...	...	...	...	...
707	**Health**	...	...	...	...	...	...	...	...	...	...	...	...
7072	Outpatient services	...	...	...	...	...	...	...	...	...	...	...	...
7073	Hospital services	...	...	...	...	...	...	...	...	...	...	...	...
7074	Public health services	...	...	...	...	...	...	...	...	...	...	...	...
708	**Recreation, culture and religion**	...	...	...	...	...	...	...	...	...	...	...	...
709	**Education**	...	...	...	...	...	...	...	...	...	...	...	...
7091	Pre-primary and primary education	...	...	...	...	...	...	...	...	...	...	...	...
7092	Secondary education	...	...	...	...	...	...	...	...	...	...	...	...
7094	Tertiary education	...	...	...	...	...	...	...	...	...	...	...	...
710	**Social protection**	...	...	...	...	...	...	...	...	...	...	...	...
7z	Statistical discrepancy: Expenditure	...	...	...	...	...	...	...	...	...	...	...	...
	Table 8 Financial transactions by counterpart sector												
	Table 9 Total other economic flows in assets and liabilities												

Vietnam (582)

In Billions of Vietnamese Dong (VND) / Fiscal Year Ends December 31st

		Budgetary Central Government			Central Government (excl. Social Security)			Central Government (incl. Social Security)			General Government		
		2011	2012	2013	2011	2012	2013	2011	2012	2013	2011	2012	2013
	Statement of operations												
1	Revenue	667,579	687,980	781,954	...	...	...	...	...	...	...	...	...
2	Expense	510,945	659,230	772,863	...	...	...	...	...	...	...	...	...
GOB	**Gross operating balance**	**156,634**	**28,750**	**9,091**	...	...	...	...	...	...	...	...	...
NOB	**Net operating balance**	...	...	...	...	...	...	...	...	...	...	...	...
31	Net/Gross investment in nonfinancial assets	141,258	207,513	212,314	...	...	...	...	...	...	...	...	...
2M	Expenditure	652,203	866,743	985,177	...	...	...	...	...	...	...	...	...
NLB	**Net lending (+) / Net borrowing (-)**	**15,376**	**-178,763**	**-203,223**	...	...	...	...	...	...	...	...	...
32	Net acquisition of financial assets	...	...	...	...	...	...	...	...	...	...	...	...
33	Net incurrence of liabilities	...	...	...	...	...	...	...	...	...	...	...	...
NLBz	Statistical discrepancy	...	...	...	...	...	...	...	...	...	...	...	...
	Memorandum items												
PB	Primary net lending / net borrowing	45,162	-138,879	-149,139	...	...	...	...	...	...	...	...	...
GB	Government balance per national definition	...	...	...	...	...	...	...	...	...	...	...	...
	Statement of other economic flows												
	Balance sheet												
	Table 1 Revenue												
1	**Revenue**	**667,579**	**687,980**	**781,954**	...	...	...	...	...	...	...	...	...
11	**Taxes**	**617,368**	**615,867**	**683,514**	...	...	...	...	...	...	...	...	...
111	Taxes on income, profits, and capital gains	234,527	260,757	277,694	...	...	...	...	...	...	...	...	...
1111	Payable by individuals	38,469	44,959	46,548	...	...	...	...	...	...	...	...	...
1112	Payable by corporations and other enterprises	196,058	215,798	231,146	...	...	...	...	...	...	...	...	...
1113	Other taxes on income, profits, and capital gains	—	—	—	...	...	...	...	...	...	...	...	...
112	Taxes on payroll and workforce	—	—	—	...	...	...	...	...	...	...	...	...
113	Taxes on property	1,661	1,262	1,516	...	...	...	...	...	...	...	...	...
114	Taxes on goods and services	288,573	269,896	314,202	...	...	...	...	...	...	...	...	...
1141	General taxes on goods and services	207,764	185,872	222,131	...	...	...	...	...	...	...	...	...
1142	Excises	80,809	84,024	92,071	...	...	...	...	...	...	...	...	...
115	Taxes on international trade and transactions	81,406	71,276	78,253	...	...	...	...	...	...	...	...	...
116	Other taxes	11,201	12,676	11,849	...	...	...	...	...	...	...	...	...
12	**Social contributions**	—	—	—	...	...	...	...	...	...	...	...	...
121	Social security contributions	—	—	—	...	...	...	...	...	...	...	...	...
122	Other social contributions	—	—	—	...	...	...	...	...	...	...	...	...
13	**Grants**	**12,103**	**10,267**	**11,124**	...	...	...	...	...	...	...	...	...
131	From foreign governments	...	...	...	...	...	...	...	...	...	...	...	...
132	From international organizations	...	...	...	...	...	...	...	...	...	...	...	...
133	From other general government units	...	...	...	...	...	...	...	...	...	...	...	...
1331	Current	...	...	...	...	...	...	...	...	...	...	...	...
1332	Capital	...	...	...	...	...	...	...	...	...	...	...	...
14	**Other revenue**	**38,108**	**61,846**	**87,316**	...	...	...	...	...	...	...	...	...
	Table 2 Expense by economic type												
2	**Expense**	**510,945**	**659,230**	**772,863**	...	...	...	...	...	...	...	...	...
21	**Compensation of employees**	...	...	...	...	...	...	...	...	...	...	...	...
211	Wages and salaries	...	...	...	...	...	...	...	...	...	...	...	...
212	Employers' social contributions	...	...	...	...	...	...	...	...	...	...	...	...
22	**Use of goods and services**	...	...	...	...	...	...	...	...	...	...	...	...
23	**Consumption of fixed capital**	...	...	...	...	...	...	...	...	...	...	...	...
24	**Interest**	**29,786**	**39,884**	**54,084**	...	...	...	...	...	...	...	...	...
25	**Subsidies**	...	...	...	...	...	...	...	...	...	...	...	...
26	**Grants**	...	...	...	...	...	...	...	...	...	...	...	...
261	To foreign governments	...	...	...	...	...	...	...	...	...	...	...	...
262	To international organizations	...	...	...	...	...	...	...	...	...	...	...	...
263	To other general government units	...	...	...	...	...	...	...	...	...	...	...	...
2631	Current	...	...	...	...	...	...	...	...	...	...	...	...
2632	Capital	...	...	...	...	...	...	...	...	...	...	...	...

Vietnam (582)

In Billions of Vietnamese Dong (VND) / Fiscal Year Ends December 31st

		Budgetary Central Government			Central Government (excl. Social Security)			Central Government (incl. Social Security)			General Government		
		2011	2012	2013	2011	2012	2013	2011	2012	2013	2011	2012	2013
27	**Social benefits**	...	...	...	...	...	...	...	...	...	...	...	...
271	Social security benefits	...	...	...	...	...	...	...	...	...	...	...	...
272	Social assistance benefits	...	...	...	...	...	...	...	...	...	...	...	...
273	Employment-related social benefits	...	...	...	...	...	...	...	...	...	...	...	...
28	**Other expense**	...	...	...	...	...	...	...	...	...	...	...	...
281	Property expense other than interest	...	...	...	...	...	...	...	...	...	...	...	...
282	Transfers not elsewhere classified	...	...	...	...	...	...	...	...	...	...	...	...
2821	Current	...	...	...	...	...	...	...	...	...	...	...	...
2822	Capital	...	...	...	...	...	...	...	...	...	...	...	...
	Table 3 Transactions in assets and liabilities												
3	**Change in net worth from transactions**	...	...	...	...	...	...	...	...	...	...	...	...
31	**Net/Gross investment in nonfinancial assets**	141,258	207,513	212,314	...	...	...	...	...	...	...	...	...
311	Fixed assets	...	...	...	...	...	...	...	...	...	...	...	...
3111	Buildings and structures	...	...	...	...	...	...	...	...	...	...	...	...
3112	Machinery and equipment	...	...	...	...	...	...	...	...	...	...	...	...
3113	Other fixed assets	...	...	...	...	...	...	...	...	...	...	...	...
3114	Weapons systems	...	...	...	...	...	...	...	...	...	...	...	...
312	Inventories	...	...	...	...	...	...	...	...	...	...	...	...
313	Valuables	...	...	...	...	...	...	...	...	...	...	...	...
314	Nonproduced assets	...	...	...	...	...	...	...	...	...	...	...	...
3141	Land	...	...	...	...	...	...	...	...	...	...	...	...
3142	Mineral and energy resources	...	...	...	...	...	...	...	...	...	...	...	...
3143	Other naturally occurring assets	...	...	...	...	...	...	...	...	...	...	...	...
3144	Intangible nonproduced assets	...	...	...	...	...	...	...	...	...	...	...	...
32	**Net acquisition of financial assets**	...	...	...	...	...	...	...	...	...	...	...	...
	By instrument												
3201	Monetary gold and SDRs	...	...	...	...	...	...	...	...	...	...	...	...
3202	Currency and deposits	...	...	...	...	...	...	...	...	...	...	...	...
3203	Debt securities	...	...	...	...	...	...	...	...	...	...	...	...
3204	Loans	...	...	...	...	...	...	...	...	...	...	...	...
3205	Equity and investment fund shares	...	...	...	...	...	...	...	...	...	...	...	...
3206	Insurance, pension, and standardized guarantee schemes	...	...	...	...	...	...	...	...	...	...	...	...
3207	Financial derivatives and employee stock options	...	...	...	...	...	...	...	...	...	...	...	...
3208	Other accounts receivable	...	...	...	...	...	...	...	...	...	...	...	...
	By debtor												
321	Domestic debtors	...	...	...	...	...	...	...	...	...	...	...	...
322	External debtors	...	...	...	...	...	...	...	...	...	...	...	...
33	**Net incurrence of liabilities**	...	...	...	...	...	...	...	...	...	...	...	...
	By instrument												
3301	Special Drawing Rights (SDRs)	...	...	...	...	...	...	...	...	...	...	...	...
3302	Currency and deposits	...	...	...	...	...	...	...	...	...	...	...	...
3303	Debt securities	...	...	...	...	...	...	...	...	...	...	...	...
3304	Loans	...	...	...	...	...	...	...	...	...	...	...	...
3305	Equity and investment fund shares	...	...	...	...	...	...	...	...	...	...	...	...
3306	Insurance, pension, and standardized guarantee schemes	...	...	...	...	...	...	...	...	...	...	...	...
3307	Financial derivatives and employee stock options	...	...	...	...	...	...	...	...	...	...	...	...
3308	Other accounts payable	...	...	...	...	...	...	...	...	...	...	...	...
	By creditor												
331	Domestic creditors	...	...	...	...	...	...	...	...	...	...	...	...
332	External creditors	...	...	...	...	...	...	...	...	...	...	...	...
	Table 4 Holding gains and losses in assets and liabilities												
	Table 5 Holding gains and losses in assets and liabilities												
	Table 6 Balance sheet												

Vietnam (582)

In Billions of Vietnamese Dong (VND) / Fiscal Year Ends December 31st

	Budgetary Central Government			Central Government (excl. Social Security)			Central Government (incl. Social Security)			General Government		
	2011	2012	2013	2011	2012	2013	2011	2012	2013	2011	2012	2013
Table 7 Expenditure by functions of government												
Table 8 Financial transactions by counterpart sector												
Table 9 Total other economic flows in assets and liabilities												

West Bank and Gaza (487)

In Millions of U.S. Dollars (USD) / Fiscal Year Ends December 31st

		Budgetary Central Government			Central Government (excl. Social Security)			Central Government (incl. Social Security)			General Government		
		2013	2014	2015	2013	2014	2015	2013	2014	2015	2013	2014	2015
	Statement of operations												
1	Revenue	3,641	4,033	3,744	3,641	4,033	3,744	...	...	...	...	...	...
2	Expense	3,406	3,725	3,771	3,406	3,725	3,771	...	...	...	...	...	...
GOB	**Gross operating balance**	**235**	**308**	**-27**	**235**	**308**	**-27**	...	...	...	...	...	...
NOB	**Net operating balance**	...	...	...	...	...	...	...	...	...	...	...	...
31	Net/Gross investment in nonfinancial assets	114	143	139	114	143	139	...	...	...	...	...	...
2M	Expenditure	3,520	3,868	3,909	3,520	3,868	3,909	...	...	...	...	...	...
NLB	**Net lending (+) / Net borrowing (-)**	**121**	**164**	**-165**	**121**	**164**	**-165**	...	...	...	...	...	...
32	Net acquisition of financial assets	374	583	433	374	583	433	...	...	...	...	...	...
33	Net incurrence of liabilities	253	410	335	253	410	335	...	...	...	...	...	...
NLBz	Statistical discrepancy	-0	8	263	-0	8	263	...	...	...	...	...	...
	Memorandum items												
PB	Primary net lending / net borrowing	210	234	-72	210	234	-72	...	...	...	...	...	...
GB	Government balance per national definition	...	...	...	...	...	...	...	...	...	...	...	...
	Statement of other economic flows												
	Balance sheet												
	Table 1 Revenue												
1	**Revenue**	**3,641**	**4,033**	**3,744**	**3,641**	**4,033**	**3,744**	...	...	...	...	...	...
11	**Taxes**	**2,165**	**2,599**	**2,757**	**2,165**	**2,599**	**2,757**	...	...	...	...	...	...
111	Taxes on income, profits, and capital gains	146	141	122	146	141	122	...	...	...	...	...	...
1111	Payable by individuals	11	15	6	11	15	6	...	...	...	...	...	...
1112	Payable by corporations and other enterprises	134	127	116	134	127	116	...	...	...	...	...	...
1113	Other taxes on income, profits, and capital gains	—	—	—	—	—	—	...	...	...	...	...	...
112	Taxes on payroll and workforce	62	66	64	62	66	64	...	...	...	...	...	...
113	Taxes on property	4	3	2	4	3	2	...	...	...	...	...	...
114	Taxes on goods and services	1,326	1,613	1,696	1,326	1,613	1,696	...	...	...	...	...	...
1141	General taxes on goods and services	792	893	845	792	893	845	...	...	...	...	...	...
1142	Excises	432	639	764	432	639	764	...	...	...	...	...	...
115	Taxes on international trade and transactions	628	776	873	628	776	873	...	...	...	...	...	...
116	Other taxes	—	—	—	—	—	—	...	...	...	...	...	...
12	**Social contributions**	—	—	—	—	—	—	...	...	...	...	...	...
121	Social security contributions	—	—	—	—	—	—	...	...	...	...	...	...
122	Other social contributions	—	—	—	—	—	—	...	...	...	...	...	...
13	**Grants**	**1,358**	**1,231**	**808**	**1,358**	**1,231**	**808**	...	...	...	...	...	...
131	From foreign governments	878	710	460	878	710	460	...	...	...	...	...	...
132	From international organizations	480	521	349	480	521	349	...	...	...	...	...	...
133	From other general government units	—	—	—	—	—	—	...	...	...	...	...	...
1331	Current	—	—	—	—	—	—	...	...	...	...	...	...
1332	Capital	—	—	—	—	—	—	...	...	...	...	...	...
14	**Other revenue**	**118**	**202**	**179**	**118**	**202**	**179**	...	...	...	...	...	...
	Table 2 Expense by economic type												
2	**Expense**	**3,406**	**3,725**	**3,771**	**3,406**	**3,725**	**3,771**	...	...	...	...	...	...
21	**Compensation of employees**	**2,080**	**2,248**	**2,083**	**2,080**	**2,248**	**2,083**	...	...	...	...	...	...
211	Wages and salaries	1,904	2,057	1,903	1,904	2,057	1,903	...	...	...	...	...	...
212	Employers' social contributions	176	191	181	176	191	181	...	...	...	...	...	...
22	**Use of goods and services**	**493**	**556**	**678**	**493**	**556**	**678**	...	...	...	...	...	...
23	**Consumption of fixed capital**	...	...	...	...	...	...	...	...	...	...	...	...
24	**Interest**	**89**	**70**	**93**	**89**	**70**	**93**	...	...	...	...	...	...
25	**Subsidies**	—	**8**	**11**	—	**8**	**11**	...	...	...	...	...	...
26	**Grants**	**18**	**29**	**45**	**18**	**29**	**45**	...	...	...	...	...	...
261	To foreign governments	—	—	—	—	—	—	...	...	...	...	...	...
262	To international organizations	—	—	—	—	—	—	...	...	...	...	...	...
263	To other general government units	18	29	45	18	29	45	...	...	...	...	...	...
2631	Current	17	27	41	17	27	41	...	...	...	...	...	...
2632	Capital	0	2	4	0	2	4	...	...	...	...	...	...

West Bank and Gaza (487)

In Millions of U.S. Dollars (USD) / Fiscal Year Ends December 31st

		Budgetary Central Government			Central Government (excl. Social Security)			Central Government (incl. Social Security)			General Government		
		2013	2014	2015	2013	2014	2015	2013	2014	2015	2013	2014	2015
27	**Social benefits**	**675**	**746**	**795**	**675**	**746**	**795**	**...**	**...**	**...**	**...**	**...**	**...**
271	Social security benefits	260	278	283	260	278	283	...	...	...	...	...	...
272	Social assistance benefits	414	469	512	414	469	512	...	...	...	...	...	...
273	Employment-related social benefits	—	—	—	—	—	—	...	...	...	...	...	...
28	**Other expense**	**50**	**68**	**64**	**50**	**68**	**64**	**...**	**...**	**...**	**...**	**...**	**...**
281	Property expense other than interest	—	—	—	—	—	—	...	...	...	...	...	...
282	Transfers not elsewhere classified	50	68	64	50	68	64	...	...	...	...	...	...
2821	Current	42	55	58	42	55	58	...	...	...	...	...	...
2822	Capital	9	13	6	9	13	6	...	...	...	...	...	...
	Table 3 Transactions in assets and liabilities												
3	**Change in net worth from transactions**	**...**	**...**	**...**	**...**	**...**	**...**	**...**	**...**	**...**	**...**	**...**	**...**
31	**Net/Gross investment in nonfinancial assets**	**114**	**143**	**139**	**114**	**143**	**139**	**...**	**...**	**...**	**...**	**...**	**...**
311	Fixed assets	88	118	114	88	118	114	...	...	...	...	...	...
3111	Buildings and structures	80	105	95	80	105	95	...	...	...	...	...	...
3112	Machinery and equipment	8	13	19	8	13	19	...	...	...	...	...	...
3113	Other fixed assets	—	—	—	—	—	—	...	...	...	...	...	...
3114	Weapons systems	—	—	—	—	—	—	...	...	...	...	...	...
312	Inventories	15	18	17	15	18	17	...	...	...	...	...	...
313	Valuables	—	—	—	—	—	—	...	...	...	...	...	...
314	Nonproduced assets	12	7	7	12	7	7	...	...	...	...	...	...
3141	Land	12	7	7	12	7	7	...	...	...	...	...	...
3142	Mineral and energy resources	—	—	—	—	—	—	...	...	...	...	...	...
3143	Other naturally occurring assets	—	—	—	—	—	—	...	...	...	...	...	...
3144	Intangible nonproduced assets	—	—	—	—	—	—	...	...	...	...	...	...
32	**Net acquisition of financial assets**	**374**	**583**	**433**	**374**	**583**	**433**	**...**	**...**	**...**	**...**	**...**	**...**
	By instrument												
3201	Monetary gold and SDRs	—	—	—	—	—	—	—	—	—	—	—	—
3202	Currency and deposits	94	313	—	94	313	—	...	...	...	...	...	...
3203	Debt securities	—	—	—	—	—	—	...	...	...	...	...	...
3204	Loans	208	174	419	208	174	419	...	...	...	...	...	...
3205	Equity and investment fund shares	—	—	—	—	—	—	...	...	...	...	...	...
3206	Insurance, pension, and standardized guarantee schemes	—	—	—	—	—	—	...	...	...	...	...	...
3207	Financial derivatives and employee stock options	—	—	—	—	—	—	...	...	...	...	...	...
3208	Other accounts receivable	72	96	14	72	96	14	...	...	...	...	...	...
	By debtor												
321	Domestic debtors	322	490	423	322	490	423	...	...	...	...	...	...
322	External debtors	52	93	9	52	93	9	...	...	...	...	...	...
33	**Net incurrence of liabilities**	**253**	**410**	**335**	**253**	**410**	**335**	**...**	**...**	**...**	**...**	**...**	**...**
	By instrument												
3301	Special Drawing Rights (SDRs)	—	—	—	—	—	—	—	—	—	—	—	—
3302	Currency and deposits	—	—	—	—	—	—	...	...	...	...	...	...
3303	Debt securities	—	—	—	—	—	—	...	...	...	...	...	...
3304	Loans	-226	-5	—	-226	-5	—	...	...	...	...	...	...
3305	Equity and investment fund shares	—	—	—	—	—	—	...	...	...	...	...	...
3306	Insurance, pension, and standardized guarantee schemes	—	—	—	—	—	—	...	...	...	...	...	...
3307	Financial derivatives and employee stock options	—	—	—	—	—	—	...	...	...	...	...	...
3308	Other accounts payable	479	415	335	479	415	335	...	...	...	...	...	...
	By creditor												
331	Domestic creditors	207	420	313	207	420	313	...	...	...	...	...	...
332	External creditors	46	-10	23	46	-10	23	...	...	...	...	...	...
	Table 4 Holding gains and losses in assets and liabilities												
	Table 5 Holding gains and losses in assets and liabilities												
	Table 6 Balance sheet												

West Bank and Gaza (487)

In Millions of U.S. Dollars (USD) / Fiscal Year Ends December 31st

		Budgetary Central Government			Central Government (excl. Social Security)			Central Government (incl. Social Security)			General Government		
		2013	2014	2015	2013	2014	2015	2013	2014	2015	2013	2014	2015
	Table 7 Expenditure by functions of government												
7	**Expenditure**	**3,520**	**3,868**	**...**	**3,520**	**3,868**	**...**	**...**	**...**	**...**	**...**	**...**	**...**
701	**General public services**	**508**	**491**	**637**	**508**	**491**	**637**	**...**	**...**	**...**	**...**	**...**	**...**
7017	Public debt transactions	89	70	...	89	70	...	...	...	...	...	...	...
7018	Transfers of general character between levels of government	...	...	...	...	...	...	...	...	...	...	...	...
702	**Defense**	**—**	**—**	**...**	**—**	**—**	**...**	**...**	**...**	**...**	**...**	**...**	**...**
703	**Public order and safety**	**1,051**	**1,130**	**1,051**	**1,051**	**1,130**	**1,051**	**...**	**...**	**...**	**...**	**...**	**...**
704	**Economic affairs**	**95**	**144**	**96**	**95**	**144**	**96**	**...**	**...**	**...**	**...**	**...**	**...**
7042	Agriculture, forestry, fishing, and hunting	...	...	43	...	...	43	...	...	...	...	...	...
7043	Fuel and energy	...	...	15	...	...	15	...	...	...	...	...	...
7044	Mining, manufacturing, and construction	...	...	15	...	...	15	...	...	...	...	...	...
7045	Transport	...	...	14	...	...	14	...	...	...	...	...	...
7046	Communication	...	...	9	...	...	9	...	...	...	...	...	...
705	**Environmental protection**	**3**	**4**	**3**	**3**	**4**	**3**	**...**	**...**	**...**	**...**	**...**	**...**
706	**Housing and community amenities**	**44**	**42**	**54**	**44**	**42**	**54**	**...**	**...**	**...**	**...**	**...**	**...**
707	**Health**	**340**	**512**	**487**	**340**	**512**	**487**	**...**	**...**	**...**	**...**	**...**	**...**
7072	Outpatient services	...	...	...	...	...	...	...	...	...	...	...	...
7073	Hospital services	...	...	...	...	...	...	...	...	...	...	...	...
7074	Public health services	...	...	...	...	...	...	...	...	...	...	...	...
708	**Recreation, culture and religion**	**88**	**102**	**96**	**88**	**102**	**96**	**...**	**...**	**...**	**...**	**...**	**...**
709	**Education**	**672**	**723**	**660**	**672**	**723**	**660**	**...**	**...**	**...**	**...**	**...**	**...**
7091	Pre-primary and primary education	...	...	...	...	...	...	...	...	...	...	...	...
7092	Secondary education	...	...	...	...	...	...	...	...	...	...	...	...
7094	Tertiary education	...	...	...	...	...	...	...	...	...	...	...	...
710	**Social protection**	**717**	**775**	**687**	**717**	**775**	**687**	**...**	**...**	**...**	**...**	**...**	**...**
7z	Statistical discrepancy: Expenditure	0	—	...	0	—	...	...	...	...	...	...	...
	Table 8 Financial transactions by counterpart sector												
	Table 9 Total other economic flows in assets and liabilities												

Yemen, Republic of (474)

In Billions of Yemeni Rial (YER) / Fiscal Year Ends December 31st

		Budgetary Central Government			Central Government (excl. Social Security)			Central Government (incl. Social Security)			General Government		
		2010	2011	2012	2010	2011	2012	2010	2011	2012	2010	2011	2012
	Statement of operations												
1	Revenue	...	...	...	...	...	...	...	...	...	1,809	1,383	2,063
2	Expense	...	...	...	...	...	...	...	...	...	1,750	1,876	2,108
GOB	**Gross operating balance**	...	...	...	...	...	...	...	...	...	**59**	**-493**	**-45**
NOB	**Net operating balance**	...	...	...	...	...	...	...	...	...	...	...	...
31	Net/Gross investment in nonfinancial assets	...	...	...	...	...	...	...	...	...	275	127	430
2M	Expenditure	...	...	...	...	...	...	...	...	...	2,025	2,002	2,538
NLB	**Net lending (+) / Net borrowing (-)**	...	...	...	...	...	...	...	...	...	**-216**	**-619**	**-475**
32	Net acquisition of financial assets	...	...	...	...	...	...	...	...	...	23	-23	6
33	Net incurrence of liabilities	...	...	...	...	...	...	...	...	...	239	597	481
NLBz	Statistical discrepancy	...	...	...	...	...	...	...	...	...	—	—	—
	Memorandum items												
PB	Primary net lending / net borrowing	...	...	...	...	...	...	...	...	...	-56	-386	-139
GB	Government balance per national definition	...	...	...	...	...	...	...	...	...	...	...	...
	Statement of other economic flows												
	Balance sheet												
	Table 1 Revenue												
1	**Revenue**	...	...	...	...	...	...	...	...	...	**1,809**	**1,383**	**2,063**
11	**Taxes**	...	...	...	...	...	...	...	...	...	**455**	**519**	**527**
111	Taxes on income, profits, and capital gains	...	...	...	...	...	...	...	...	...	207	219	220
1111	Payable by individuals	...	...	...	...	...	...	...	...	...	139	150	150
1112	Payable by corporations and other enterprises	...	...	...	...	...	...	...	...	...	66	68	69
1113	Other taxes on income, profits, and capital gains	...	...	...	...	...	...	...	...	...	1	1	1
112	Taxes on payroll and workforce	...	...	...	...	...	...	...	...	...	0	0	0
113	Taxes on property	...	...	...	...	...	...	...	...	...	—	—	—
114	Taxes on goods and services	...	...	...	...	...	...	...	...	...	169	207	212
1141	General taxes on goods and services	...	...	...	...	...	...	...	...	...	162	198	198
1142	Excises	...	...	...	...	...	...	...	...	...	—	—	—
115	Taxes on international trade and transactions	...	...	...	...	...	...	...	...	...	67	80	80
116	Other taxes	...	...	...	...	...	...	...	...	...	12	13	15
12	**Social contributions**	...	...	...	...	...	...	...	...	...	—	—	—
121	Social security contributions	...	...	...	...	...	...	...	...	...	—	—	—
122	Other social contributions	...	...	...	...	...	...	...	...	...	—	—	—
13	**Grants**	...	...	...	...	...	...	...	...	...	**34**	**17**	**193**
131	From foreign governments	...	...	...	...	...	...	...	...	...	18	17	157
132	From international organizations	...	...	...	...	...	...	...	...	...	16	—	37
133	From other general government units	...	...	...	...	...	...	...	...	...	—	—	—
1331	Current	...	...	...	...	...	...	...	...	...	—	—	—
1332	Capital	...	...	...	...	...	...	...	...	...	—	—	—
14	**Other revenue**	...	...	...	...	...	...	...	...	...	**1,320**	**847**	**1,343**
	Table 2 Expense by economic type												
2	**Expense**	...	...	...	...	...	...	...	...	...	**1,750**	**1,876**	**2,108**
21	**Compensation of employees**	...	...	...	...	...	...	...	...	...	**601**	**701**	**886**
211	Wages and salaries	...	...	...	...	...	...	...	...	...	569	662	837
212	Employers' social contributions	...	...	...	...	...	...	...	...	...	32	39	50
22	**Use of goods and services**	...	...	...	...	...	...	...	...	...	**222**	**193**	**277**
23	**Consumption of fixed capital**	...	...	...	...	...	...	...	...	...	...	...	...
24	**Interest**	...	...	...	...	...	...	...	...	...	**160**	**233**	**336**
25	**Subsidies**	...	...	...	...	...	...	...	...	...	—	—	—
26	**Grants**	...	...	...	...	...	...	...	...	...	—	—	—
261	To foreign governments	...	...	...	...	...	...	...	...	...	—	—	—
262	To international organizations	...	...	...	...	...	...	...	...	...	—	—	—
263	To other general government units	...	...	...	...	...	...	...	...	...	—	—	—
2631	Current	...	...	...	...	...	...	...	...	...	—	—	—
2632	Capital	...	...	...	...	...	...	...	...	...	—	—	—

Yemen, Republic of (474)

In Billions of Yemeni Rial (YER) / Fiscal Year Ends December 31st

		Budgetary Central Government			Central Government (excl. Social Security)			Central Government (incl. Social Security)			General Government		
		2010	2011	2012	2010	2011	2012	2010	2011	2012	2010	2011	2012
27	**Social benefits**	...	...	...	...	...	...	...	...	...	**564**	**535**	**314**
271	Social security benefits	...	...	...	...	...	...	...	...	...	—	—	—
272	Social assistance benefits	...	...	...	...	...	...	...	...	...	564	535	314
273	Employment-related social benefits	...	...	...	...	...	...	...	...	...	—	—	—
28	**Other expense**	...	...	...	...	...	...	...	...	...	**203**	**213**	**296**
281	Property expense other than interest	...	...	...	...	...	...	...	...	...	—	—	—
282	Transfers not elsewhere classified	...	...	...	...	...	...	...	...	...	203	213	296
2821	Current	...	...	...	...	...	...	...	...	...	203	213	296
2822	Capital	...	...	...	...	...	...	...	...	...	—	—	—
	Table 3 Transactions in assets and liabilities												
3	**Change in net worth from transactions**	...	...	...	...	...	...	...	...	...	...	...	...
31	**Net/Gross investment in nonfinancial assets**	...	...	...	...	...	...	...	...	...	**275**	**127**	**430**
311	Fixed assets	...	...	...	...	...	...	...	...	...	264	125	425
3111	Buildings and structures	...	...	...	...	...	...	...	...	...	...	...	...
3112	Machinery and equipment	...	...	...	...	...	...	...	...	...	...	...	...
3113	Other fixed assets	...	...	...	...	...	...	...	...	...	...	...	...
3114	Weapons systems	...	...	...	...	...	...	...	...	...	...	...	...
312	Inventories	...	...	...	...	...	...	...	...	...	4	—	—
313	Valuables	...	...	...	...	...	...	...	...	...	—	—	—
314	Nonproduced assets	...	...	...	...	...	...	...	...	...	7	1	5
3141	Land	...	...	...	...	...	...	...	...	...	7	1	5
3142	Mineral and energy resources	...	...	...	...	...	...	...	...	...	—	—	—
3143	Other naturally occurring assets	...	...	...	...	...	...	...	...	...	—	—	—
3144	Intangible nonproduced assets	...	...	...	...	...	...	...	...	...	—	—	—
32	**Net acquisition of financial assets**	...	...	...	...	...	...	...	...	...	**23**	**-23**	**6**
	By instrument												
3201	Monetary gold and SDRs	...	...	...	...	...	...	...	...	...	—	—	—
3202	Currency and deposits	...	...	...	...	...	...	...	...	...	-38	-42	-86
3203	Debt securities	...	...	...	...	...	...	...	...	...	—	—	—
3204	Loans	...	...	...	...	...	...	...	...	...	61	19	92
3205	Equity and investment fund shares	...	...	...	...	...	...	...	...	...	—	—	—
3206	Insurance, pension, and standardized guarantee schemes	...	...	...	...	...	...	...	...	...	—	—	—
3207	Financial derivatives and employee stock options	...	...	...	...	...	...	...	...	...	—	—	—
3208	Other accounts receivable	...	...	...	...	...	...	...	...	...	—	—	...
	By debtor												
321	Domestic debtors	...	...	...	...	...	...	...	...	...	23	-23	6
322	External debtors	...	...	...	...	...	...	...	...	...	—	—	—
33	**Net incurrence of liabilities**	...	...	...	...	...	...	...	...	...	**239**	**597**	**481**
	By instrument												
3301	Special Drawing Rights (SDRs)	...	...	...	...	...	...	...	...	...	—	—	—
3302	Currency and deposits	...	...	...	...	...	...	...	...	...	—	—	—
3303	Debt securities	...	...	...	...	...	...	...	...	...	233	619	475
3304	Loans	...	...	...	...	...	...	...	...	...	6	-22	6
3305	Equity and investment fund shares	...	...	...	...	...	...	...	...	...	—	—	—
3306	Insurance, pension, and standardized guarantee schemes	...	...	...	...	...	...	...	...	...	—	—	—
3307	Financial derivatives and employee stock options	...	...	...	...	...	...	...	...	...	—	—	—
3308	Other accounts payable	...	...	...	...	...	...	...	...	...	—	—	...
	By creditor												
331	Domestic creditors	...	...	...	...	...	...	...	...	...	236	619	475
332	External creditors	...	...	...	...	...	...	...	...	...	3	-22	6
	Table 4 Holding gains and losses in assets and liabilities												
	Table 5 Holding gains and losses in assets and liabilities												
	Table 6 Balance sheet												

Yemen, Republic of (474)

In Billions of Yemeni Rial (YER) / Fiscal Year Ends December 31st

		Budgetary Central Government			Central Government (excl. Social Security)			Central Government (incl. Social Security)			General Government		
		2010	2011	2012	2010	2011	2012	2010	2011	2012	2010	2011	2012
	Table 7 Expenditure by functions of government												
7	**Expenditure**	...	...	...	...	...	...	...	...	...	2,090	1,799	2,633
701	**General public services**	...	...	...	...	...	...	...	...	...	383	282	613
7017	Public debt transactions	...	...	...	...	...	...	...	...	...	160	233	336
7018	Transfers of general character between levels of government	...	...	...	...	...	...	...	...	...	—	—	—
702	**Defense**	...	...	...	...	...	...	...	...	...	318	251	308
703	**Public order and safety**	...	...	...	...	...	...	...	...	...	137	131	167
704	**Economic affairs**	...	...	...	...	...	...	...	...	...	666	278	389
7042	Agriculture, forestry, fishing, and hunting	...	...	...	...	...	...	...	...	...	...	...	...
7043	Fuel and energy	...	...	...	...	...	...	...	...	...	...	...	...
7044	Mining, manufacturing, and construction	...	...	...	...	...	...	...	...	...	...	...	...
7045	Transport	...	...	...	...	...	...	...	...	...	...	...	...
7046	Communication	...	...	...	...	...	...	...	...	...	...	...	...
705	**Environmental protection**	...	...	...	...	...	...	...	...	...	325	365	429
706	**Housing and community amenities**	...	...	...	...	...	...	...	...	...	109	33	33
707	**Health**	...	...	...	...	...	...	...	...	...	77	108	122
7072	Outpatient services	...	...	...	...	...	...	...	...	...	...	...	...
7073	Hospital services	...	...	...	...	...	...	...	...	...	...	...	...
7074	Public health services	...	...	...	...	...	...	...	...	...	...	...	...
708	**Recreation, culture and religion**	...	...	...	...	...	...	...	...	...	24	33	36
709	**Education**	...	...	...	...	...	...	...	...	...	—	—	—
7091	Pre-primary and primary education	...	...	...	...	...	...	...	...	...	—	—	—
7092	Secondary education	...	...	...	...	...	...	...	...	...	—	—	—
7094	Tertiary education	...	...	...	...	...	...	...	...	...	—	—	—
710	**Social protection**	...	...	...	...	...	...	...	...	...	50	318	535
7z	Statistical discrepancy: Expenditure	...	...	...	...	...	...	...	...	...	—	—	...
	Table 8 Financial transactions by counterpart sector												
	Table 9 Total other economic flows in assets and liabilities												

Zambia (754)

In Millions of Zambian Kwacha (ZMW) / Fiscal Year Ends December 31st

		Budgetary Central Government			Central Government (excl. Social Security)			Central Government (incl. Social Security)			General Government		
		2009	2010	2011P	2009	2010	2011	2009	2010	2011	2009	2010	2011
	Statement of operations												
1	Revenue	13,523	15,173	24,034	...	...	...	...	...	...	...	...	...
2	Expense	11,314	13,324	17,628	...	...	...	...	...	...	...	...	...
GOB	**Gross operating balance**	**2,209**	**1,849**	**6,406**	...	...	...	...	...	...	...	...	...
NOB	**Net operating balance**	...	...	...	...	...	...	...	...	...	...	...	...
31	Net/Gross investment in nonfinancial assets	2,072	3,011	1,693	...	...	...	...	...	...	...	...	...
2M	Expenditure	13,386	16,335	19,321	...	...	...	...	...	...	...	...	...
NLB	**Net lending (+) / Net borrowing (-)**	**137**	**-1,161**	**4,713**	...	...	...	...	...	...	...	...	...
32	Net acquisition of financial assets	503	-886	6,003	...	...	...	...	...	...	...	...	...
33	Net incurrence of liabilities	367	276	1,290	...	...	...	...	...	...	...	...	...
NLBz	Statistical discrepancy	-0	-0	—	...	...	...	...	...	...	...	...	...
	Memorandum items												
PB	Primary net lending / net borrowing	1,281	207	5,779	...	...	...	...	...	...	...	...	...
GB	Government balance per national definition	...	...	...	...	...	...	...	...	...	...	...	...
	Statement of other economic flows												
	Balance sheet												
	Table 1 Revenue												
1	**Revenue**	**13,523**	**15,173**	**24,034**	...	...	...	...	...	...	...	...	...
11	**Taxes**	**9,668**	**12,879**	**18,414**	...	...	...	...	...	...	...	...	...
111	Taxes on income, profits, and capital gains	4,798	6,683	11,528	...	...	...	...	...	...	...	...	...
1111	Payable by individuals	3,318	4,391	...	...	...	...	...	...	...	...	...	...
1112	Payable by corporations and other enterprises	1,480	2,292	...	...	...	...	...	...	...	...	...	...
1113	Other taxes on income, profits, and capital gains	—	—	...	...	...	...	...	...	...	...	...	...
112	Taxes on payroll and workforce	—	—	—	...	...	...	...	...	...	...	...	...
113	Taxes on property	24	34	—	...	...	...	...	...	...	...	...	...
114	Taxes on goods and services	3,822	4,901	3,980	...	...	...	...	...	...	...	...	...
1141	General taxes on goods and services	2,493	3,145	3,980	...	...	...	...	...	...	...	...	...
1142	Excises	835	1,107	—	...	...	...	...	...	...	...	...	...
115	Taxes on international trade and transactions	1,023	1,261	2,906	...	...	...	...	...	...	...	...	...
116	Other taxes	—	—	—	...	...	...	...	...	...	...	...	...
12	**Social contributions**	—	—	—	...	...	...	...	...	...	...	...	...
121	Social security contributions	—	—	—	...	...	...	...	...	...	...	...	...
122	Other social contributions	—	—	—	...	...	...	...	...	...	...	...	...
13	**Grants**	**3,425**	**1,641**	**4,094**	...	...	...	...	...	...	...	...	...
131	From foreign governments	2,582	707	2,839	...	...	...	...	...	...	...	...	...
132	From international organizations	670	778	1,255	...	...	...	...	...	...	...	...	...
133	From other general government units	173	156	—	...	...	...	...	...	...	...	...	...
1331	Current	173	156	—	...	...	...	...	...	...	...	...	...
1332	Capital	—	—	—	...	...	...	...	...	...	...	...	...
14	**Other revenue**	**430**	**653**	**1,526**	...	...	...	...	...	...	...	...	...
	Table 2 Expense by economic type												
2	**Expense**	**11,314**	**13,324**	**17,628**	...	...	...	...	...	...	...	...	...
21	**Compensation of employees**	**4,951**	**5,686**	**7,127**	...	...	...	...	...	...	...	...	...
211	Wages and salaries	4,934	5,665	7,127	...	...	...	...	...	...	...	...	...
212	Employers' social contributions	17	21	—	...	...	...	...	...	...	...	...	...
22	**Use of goods and services**	**2,211**	**3,181**	**8,334**	...	...	...	...	...	...	...	...	...
23	**Consumption of fixed capital**	...	...	...	...	...	...	...	...	...	...	...	...
24	**Interest**	**1,144**	**1,369**	**1,065**	...	...	...	...	...	...	...	...	...
25	**Subsidies**	**7**	**423**	**20**	...	...	...	...	...	...	...	...	...
26	**Grants**	**2,281**	**1,431**	**585**	...	...	...	...	...	...	...	...	...
261	To foreign governments	—	—	—	...	...	...	...	...	...	...	...	...
262	To international organizations	140	39	—	...	...	...	...	...	...	...	...	...
263	To other general government units	2,142	1,392	585	...	...	...	...	...	...	...	...	...
2631	Current	2,142	1,392	585	...	...	...	...	...	...	...	...	...
2632	Capital	—	—	—	...	...	...	...	...	...	...	...	...

Zambia (754)

In Millions of Zambian Kwacha (ZMW) / Fiscal Year Ends December 31st

		Budgetary Central Government			Central Government (excl. Social Security)			Central Government (incl. Social Security)			General Government		
		2009	2010	2011P	2009	2010	2011	2009	2010	2011	2009	2010	2011
27	**Social benefits**	**205**	**180**	**89**	**...**	**...**	**...**	**...**	**...**	**...**	**...**	**...**	**...**
271	Social security benefits	121	141	—	...	...	...	...	...	...	...	...	...
272	Social assistance benefits	3	10	89	...	...	...	...	...	...	...	...	...
273	Employment-related social benefits	81	29	—	...	...	...	...	...	...	...	...	...
28	**Other expense**	**515**	**1,053**	**408**	**...**	**...**	**...**	**...**	**...**	**...**	**...**	**...**	**...**
281	Property expense other than interest	—	—	—	...	...	...	...	...	...	...	...	...
282	Transfers not elsewhere classified	515	1,053	408	...	...	...	...	...	...	...	...	...
2821	Current	515	1,053	408	...	...	...	...	...	...	...	...	...
2822	Capital	—	—	—	...	...	...	...	...	...	...	...	...
	Table 3 Transactions in assets and liabilities												
3	**Change in net worth from transactions**	**...**	**...**	**...**	**...**	**...**	**...**	**...**	**...**	**...**	**...**	**...**	**...**
31	**Net/Gross investment in nonfinancial assets**	**2,072**	**3,011**	**1,693**	**...**	**...**	**...**	**...**	**...**	**...**	**...**	**...**	**...**
311	Fixed assets	2,060	3,021	1,693	...	...	...	...	...	...	...	...	...
3111	Buildings and structures	1,645	2,218	—	...	...	...	...	...	...	...	...	...
3112	Machinery and equipment	408	784	—	...	...	...	...	...	...	...	...	...
3113	Other fixed assets	7	18	—	...	...	...	...	...	...	...	...	...
3114	Weapons systems	...	...	...	...	...	...	...	...	...	...	...	...
312	Inventories	0	0	—	...	...	...	...	...	...	...	...	...
313	Valuables	-0	-17	—	...	...	...	...	...	...	...	...	...
314	Nonproduced assets	12	7	—	...	...	...	...	...	...	...	...	...
3141	Land	11	0	—	...	...	...	...	...	...	...	...	...
3142	Mineral and energy resources	—	—	—	...	...	...	...	...	...	...	...	...
3143	Other naturally occurring assets	0	7	—	...	...	...	...	...	...	...	...	...
3144	Intangible nonproduced assets	—	—	—	...	...	...	...	...	...	...	...	...
32	**Net acquisition of financial assets**	**503**	**-886**	**6,003**	**...**	**...**	**...**	**...**	**...**	**...**	**...**	**...**	**...**
	By instrument												
3201	Monetary gold and SDRs	—	—	—	...	...	...	...	...	...	...	...	...
3202	Currency and deposits	...	...	5,911	...	...	...	...	...	...	...	...	...
3203	Debt securities	...	...	—	...	...	...	...	...	...	...	...	...
3204	Loans	...	...	92	...	...	...	...	...	...	...	...	...
3205	Equity and investment fund shares	...	...	—	...	...	...	...	...	...	...	...	...
3206	Insurance, pension, and standardized guarantee schemes	...	...	—	...	...	...	...	...	...	...	...	...
3207	Financial derivatives and employee stock options	...	...	—	...	...	...	...	...	...	...	...	...
3208	Other accounts receivable	...	...	...	...	...	...	...	...	...	...	...	...
	By debtor												
321	Domestic debtors	...	...	6,003	...	...	...	...	...	...	...	...	...
322	External debtors	—	—	—	...	...	...	...	...	...	...	...	...
33	**Net incurrence of liabilities**	**367**	**276**	**1,290**	**...**	**...**	**...**	**...**	**...**	**...**	**...**	**...**	**...**
	By instrument												
3301	Special Drawing Rights (SDRs)	...	...	—	...	...	...	...	...	...	...	...	...
3302	Currency and deposits	...	...	—	...	...	...	...	...	...	...	...	...
3303	Debt securities	...	...	2,746	...	...	...	...	...	...	...	...	...
3304	Loans	...	...	1,150	...	...	...	...	...	...	...	...	...
3305	Equity and investment fund shares	...	...	—	...	...	...	...	...	...	...	...	...
3306	Insurance, pension, and standardized guarantee schemes	...	...	—	...	...	...	...	...	...	...	...	...
3307	Financial derivatives and employee stock options	...	...	—	...	...	...	...	...	...	...	...	...
3308	Other accounts payable	...	...	-2,606	...	...	...	...	...	...	...	...	...
	By creditor												
331	Domestic creditors	...	...	140	...	...	...	...	...	...	...	...	...
332	External creditors	—	—	1,150	...	...	...	...	...	...	...	...	...
	Table 4 Holding gains and losses in assets and liabilities												
	Table 5 Holding gains and losses in assets and liabilities												
	Table 6 Balance sheet												

Zambia (754)

In Millions of Zambian Kwacha (ZMW) / Fiscal Year Ends December 31st

		Budgetary Central Government			Central Government (excl. Social Security)			Central Government (incl. Social Security)			General Government		
		2009	2010	2011P	2009	2010	2011	2009	2010	2011	2009	2010	2011
	Table 7 Expenditure by functions of government												
7	**Expenditure**	**13,386**	**16,335**	**19,321**	...	...	...	...	...	...	...	...	...
701	**General public services**	**4,160**	**5,081**	**3,828**	...	...	...	...	...	...	...	...	...
7017	Public debt transactions	1,144	1,369	1,065	...	...	...	...	...	...	...	...	...
7018	Transfers of general character between levels of government	...	...	...	...	...	...	...	...	...	...	...	...
702	**Defense**	**1,105**	**1,317**	**1,673**	...	...	...	...	...	...	...	...	...
703	**Public order and safety**	**590**	**750**	**1,003**	...	...	...	...	...	...	...	...	...
704	**Economic affairs**	**2,729**	**4,012**	**6,035**	...	...	...	...	...	...	...	...	...
7042	Agriculture, forestry, fishing, and hunting	...	...	...	...	...	...	...	...	...	...	...	...
7043	Fuel and energy	...	...	...	...	...	...	...	...	...	...	...	...
7044	Mining, manufacturing, and construction	...	...	...	...	...	...	...	...	...	...	...	...
7045	Transport	...	...	...	...	...	...	...	...	...	...	...	...
7046	Communication	...	...	...	...	...	...	...	...	...	...	...	...
705	**Environmental protection**	**55**	**47**	**43**	...	...	...	...	...	...	...	...	...
706	**Housing and community amenities**	**422**	**412**	**315**	...	...	...	...	...	...	...	...	...
707	**Health**	**1,206**	**1,464**	**1,876**	...	...	...	...	...	...	...	...	...
7072	Outpatient services	...	...	...	...	...	...	...	...	...	...	...	...
7073	Hospital services	...	...	...	...	...	...	...	...	...	...	...	...
7074	Public health services	...	...	...	...	...	...	...	...	...	...	...	...
708	**Recreation, culture and religion**	**95**	**86**	**177**	...	...	...	...	...	...	...	...	...
709	**Education**	**2,617**	**2,690**	**3,419**	...	...	...	...	...	...	...	...	...
7091	Pre-primary and primary education	...	...	...	...	...	...	...	...	...	...	...	...
7092	Secondary education	...	...	...	...	...	...	...	...	...	...	...	...
7094	Tertiary education	...	...	...	...	...	...	...	...	...	...	...	...
710	**Social protection**	**407**	**475**	**952**	...	...	...	...	...	...	...	...	...
7z	Statistical discrepancy: Expenditure	-0	—	...	...	...	...	...	...	...	...	...	...
	Table 8 Financial transactions by counterpart sector												
	Table 9 Total other economic flows in assets and liabilities												

Zimbabwe (698)

In Millions of U.S. Dollars (USD) / Fiscal Year Ends June 30th

		Budgetary Central Government			Central Government (excl. Social Security)			Central Government (incl. Social Security)			General Government		
		2010	2011	2012	2010	2011	2012	2010	2011	2012	2010	2011	2012
	Statement of operations												
1	Revenue	2,337	2,915	3,491	...	...	...	...	...	...	...	...	...
2	Expense	1,941	2,690	3,459	...	...	...	...	...	...	...	...	...
GOB	**Gross operating balance**	**396**	**225**	**31**	...	...	...	...	...	...	...	...	...
NOB	**Net operating balance**	...	...	...	...	...	...	...	...	...	...	...	...
31	Net/Gross investment in nonfinancial assets	73	109	109	...	...	...	...	...	...	...	...	...
2M	Expenditure	2,015	2,799	3,568	...	...	...	...	...	...	...	...	...
NLB	**Net lending (+) / Net borrowing (-)**	**322**	**116**	**-77**	...	...	...	...	...	...	...	...	...
32	Net acquisition of financial assets	...	...	...	...	...	...	...	...	...	...	...	...
33	Net incurrence of liabilities	...	...	...	...	...	...	...	...	...	...	...	...
NLBz	Statistical discrepancy	...	...	...	...	...	...	...	...	...	...	...	...
	Memorandum items												
PB	Primary net lending / net borrowing	353	151	-56	...	...	...	...	...	...	...	...	...
GB	Government balance per national definition	...	...	...	...	...	...	...	...	...	...	...	...
	Statement of other economic flows												
	Balance sheet												
	Table 1 Revenue												
1	**Revenue**	**2,337**	**2,915**	**3,491**	...	...	...	...	...	...	...	...	...
11	**Taxes**	**2,099**	**2,528**	**3,053**	...	...	...	...	...	...	...	...	...
111	Taxes on income, profits, and capital gains	701	901	1,122	...	...	...	...	...	...	...	...	...
1111	Payable by individuals	428	588	661	...	...	...	...	...	...	...	...	...
1112	Payable by corporations and other enterprises	256	296	445	...	...	...	...	...	...	...	...	...
1113	Other taxes on income, profits, and capital gains	17	17	17	...	...	...	...	...	...	...	...	...
112	Taxes on payroll and workforce	—	—	—	...	...	...	...	...	...	...	...	...
113	Taxes on property	—	—	—	...	...	...	...	...	...	...	...	...
114	Taxes on goods and services	677	978	1,250	...	...	...	...	...	...	...	...	...
1141	General taxes on goods and services	459	610	778	...	...	...	...	...	...	...	...	...
1142	Excises	104	212	284	...	...	...	...	...	...	...	...	...
115	Taxes on international trade and transactions	722	650	680	...	...	...	...	...	...	...	...	...
116	Other taxes	—	—	—	...	...	...	...	...	...	...	...	...
12	**Social contributions**	**1**	**4**	**2**	...	...	...	...	...	...	...	...	...
121	Social security contributions	—	—	—	...	...	...	...	...	...	...	...	...
122	Other social contributions	1	4	2	...	...	...	...	...	...	...	...	...
13	**Grants**	—	—	—	...	...	...	...	...	...	...	...	...
131	From foreign governments	—	—	—	...	...	...	...	...	...	...	...	...
132	From international organizations	—	—	—	...	...	...	...	...	...	...	...	...
133	From other general government units	—	—	—	...	...	...	...	...	...	...	...	...
1331	Current	—	—	—	...	...	...	...	...	...	...	...	...
1332	Capital	—	—	—	...	...	...	...	...	...	...	...	...
14	**Other revenue**	**236**	**383**	**436**	...	...	...	...	...	...	...	...	...
	Table 2 Expense by economic type												
2	**Expense**	**1,941**	**2,690**	**3,459**	...	...	...	...	...	...	...	...	...
21	**Compensation of employees**	**947**	**1,544**	**2,173**	...	...	...	...	...	...	...	...	...
211	Wages and salaries	758	1,269	1,771	...	...	...	...	...	...	...	...	...
212	Employers' social contributions	188	275	402	...	...	...	...	...	...	...	...	...
22	**Use of goods and services**	**291**	**387**	**440**	...	...	...	...	...	...	...	...	...
23	**Consumption of fixed capital**	...	...	...	...	...	...	...	...	...	...	...	...
24	**Interest**	**31**	**34**	**22**	...	...	...	...	...	...	...	...	...
25	**Subsidies**	...	...	...	...	...	...	...	...	...	...	...	...
26	**Grants**	...	...	...	...	...	...	...	...	...	...	...	...
261	To foreign governments	...	...	...	...	...	...	...	...	...	...	...	...
262	To international organizations	...	...	...	...	...	...	...	...	...	...	...	...
263	To other general government units	...	...	...	...	...	...	...	...	...	...	...	...
2631	Current	...	...	...	...	...	...	...	...	...	...	...	...
2632	Capital	...	...	...	...	...	...	...	...	...	...	...	...

Zimbabwe (698)

In Millions of U.S. Dollars (USD) / Fiscal Year Ends June 30th

		Budgetary Central Government			Central Government (excl. Social Security)			Central Government (incl. Social Security)			General Government		
		2010	2011	2012	2010	2011	2012	2010	2011	2012	2010	2011	2012
27	**Social benefits**	**109**	**62**	**30**	**...**	**...**	**...**	**...**	**...**	**...**	**...**	**...**	**...**
271	Social security benefits	—	—	—	...	...	...	...	...	...	...	...	...
272	Social assistance benefits	109	62	30	...	...	...	...	...	...	...	...	...
273	Employment-related social benefits	—	—	—	...	...	...	...	...	...	...	...	...
28	**Other expense**	**—**	**—**	**—**	**...**	**...**	**...**	**...**	**...**	**...**	**...**	**...**	**...**
281	Property expense other than interest	—	—	—	...	...	...	...	...	...	...	...	...
282	Transfers not elsewhere classified	—	—	—	...	...	...	...	...	...	...	...	...
2821	Current	—	—	—	...	...	...	...	...	...	...	...	...
2822	Capital	—	—	—	...	...	...	...	...	...	...	...	...
	Table 3 Transactions in assets and liabilities												
3	**Change in net worth from transactions**	**...**	**...**	**...**	**...**	**...**	**...**	**...**	**...**	**...**	**...**	**...**	**...**
31	**Net/Gross investment in nonfinancial assets**	**73**	**109**	**109**	**...**	**...**	**...**	**...**	**...**	**...**	**...**	**...**	**...**
311	Fixed assets	71	108	108	...	...	...	...	...	...	...	...	...
3111	Buildings and structures	34	62	62	...	...	...	...	...	...	...	...	...
3112	Machinery and equipment	38	46	46	...	...	...	...	...	...	...	...	...
3113	Other fixed assets	0	0	0	...	...	...	...	...	...	...	...	...
3114	Weapons systems	...	...	...	...	...	...	...	...	...	...	...	...
312	Inventories	—	—	—	...	...	...	...	...	...	...	...	...
313	Valuables	—	—	—	...	...	...	...	...	...	...	...	...
314	Nonproduced assets	2	1	1	...	...	...	...	...	...	...	...	...
3141	Land	...	...	...	...	...	...	...	...	...	...	...	...
3142	Mineral and energy resources	...	...	...	...	...	...	...	...	...	...	...	...
3143	Other naturally occurring assets	...	...	...	...	...	...	...	...	...	...	...	...
3144	Intangible nonproduced assets	...	...	...	...	...	...	...	...	...	...	...	...
32	**Net acquisition of financial assets**	**...**	**...**	**...**	**...**	**...**	**...**	**...**	**...**	**...**	**...**	**...**	**...**
	By instrument												
3201	Monetary gold and SDRs	...	...	...	...	...	...	...	...	...	...	...	...
3202	Currency and deposits	...	...	...	...	...	...	...	...	...	...	...	...
3203	Debt securities	...	...	...	...	...	...	...	...	...	...	...	...
3204	Loans	...	...	...	...	...	...	...	...	...	...	...	...
3205	Equity and investment fund shares	...	...	...	...	...	...	...	...	...	...	...	...
3206	Insurance, pension, and standardized guarantee schemes	...	...	...	...	...	...	...	...	...	...	...	...
3207	Financial derivatives and employee stock options	...	...	...	...	...	...	...	...	...	...	...	...
3208	Other accounts receivable	...	...	...	...	...	...	...	...	...	...	...	...
	By debtor												
321	Domestic debtors	...	...	...	...	...	...	...	...	...	...	...	...
322	External debtors	...	...	...	...	...	...	...	...	...	...	...	...
33	**Net incurrence of liabilities**	**...**	**...**	**...**	**...**	**...**	**...**	**...**	**...**	**...**	**...**	**...**	**...**
	By instrument												
3301	Special Drawing Rights (SDRs)	...	...	...	...	...	...	...	...	...	...	...	...
3302	Currency and deposits	...	...	...	...	...	...	...	...	...	...	...	...
3303	Debt securities	...	...	...	...	...	...	...	...	...	...	...	...
3304	Loans	...	...	...	...	...	...	...	...	...	...	...	...
3305	Equity and investment fund shares	...	...	...	...	...	...	...	...	...	...	...	...
3306	Insurance, pension, and standardized guarantee schemes	...	...	...	...	...	...	...	...	...	...	...	...
3307	Financial derivatives and employee stock options	...	...	...	...	...	...	...	...	...	...	...	...
3308	Other accounts payable	...	...	...	...	...	...	...	...	...	...	...	...
	By creditor												
331	Domestic creditors	...	...	...	...	...	...	...	...	...	...	...	...
332	External creditors	...	...	...	...	...	...	...	...	...	...	...	...
	Table 4 Holding gains and losses in assets and liabilities												
	Table 5 Holding gains and losses in assets and liabilities												
	Table 6 Balance sheet												

Zimbabwe (698)

In Millions of U.S. Dollars (USD) / Fiscal Year Ends June 30th

	Budgetary Central Government			Central Government (excl. Social Security)			Central Government (incl. Social Security)			General Government		
	2010	2011	2012	2010	2011	2012	2010	2011	2012	2010	2011	2012
Table 7 Expenditure by functions of government												
Table 8 Financial transactions by counterpart sector												
Table 9 Total other economic flows in assets and liabilities												

Metadata Tables

Afghanistan, Islamic Republic of (512)

Information Last Updated	2015
Units of General Government	
1. Budgetary Central Government	Partially covered. 1.1 Legislative, Judiciary, and Executive bodies including ministries/departments. 1.2 Other agencies or funds
2. Extrabudgetary Central Government	Afghanistan Investment Support Agency (AISA), Foreign donor operations providing benefits to the government as reported to the Ministry of Finance, Micro Finance Investment Support Facility for Afghanistan (MISFA).
3. Social Security Funds	Pension Fund.
4. State Government	Not applicable.
5. Local Government	Partially covered. 5.1 Budgetary local government units/entities: Municipalities (includes Kabul, Herat, Kandahar, Jalalabad, Mazar-I-Sharif, Balkh, etc.) 5.2 Extrabudgetary local government units
Compilation Practices	
Breaks in Series	Data in budgetary central government tables cover operations of subsectors 1-3. Government operations at the provincial level are reported as part of the operations of the ministries and agencies in central government.
Compilation Notes	Data also cover transactions in kind, including foreign grants, as reported to the Ministry of Finance of the Islamic Republic of Afghanistan. Valuation of assets and liabilities: Assets are valued at historical cost, and loans and bonds at face value. Aid in kind valued at the cost to the donor.
Implementation of GFSM 2001/2014	No information available.

Albania (914)

Information Last Updated	2017
Units of General Government	
1. Budgetary Central Government	Covered. President, Parliament, Council of Ministers, ministries, non-ministerial departments and various central institutions. These units are made up to 1300 individual spending units.
2. Extrabudgetary Central Government	Not covered.
3. Social Security Funds	Covered. National Health Institute (NHI), Social Security Institute (SSI).
4. State Government	Not applicable.
5. Local Government	Covered. Local Government had 371 units (regions, municipalities and communes. After administrative reform in 2015 year there are 61 municipalities and 12 councils of regions.
Compilation Practices	
Breaks in Series	None reported.
Compilation Notes	Data cover the activities of subsectors 1, 3 and 5. The Government acknowledged the existence of a large stock of unpaid obligations (arrears) in September 2013. The Government has taken a number of measures to address the underlying problem and has developed a strategy to clear the arrears in a transparent and equitable manner over the medium term and to prevent the creation of new arrears. The payment process started in 2014 and 33,919 million and all arrears were paid within the year. In the GFS tables payments of arrears have been recorded, according to accrual basis of recording (Debit: Other Accounts Payable and Credit: Cash and deposits).
Implementation of GFSM 2001/2014	Complete the list of public sector units, classified according to sectors (A draft list has been prepared, but not yet approved and published). Acquire source data to expand coverage to general government (Identify annual and sub-annual source data for extra-budgetary units.) Automation of GFS compilation. Publish a time series (annual and quarterly data) of GFSM 2014 General Government data. From 2016, a new project on implementation of International Public Sector Accounting Standards in Albania.

Algeria (612)

Information Last Updated	2015
Units of General Government	
1. Budgetary Central Government	Partially covered. 1.1 Legislative, Judiciary, and Executive bodies including ministries/departments. 1.2 Other agencies or funds
2. Extrabudgetary Central Government	Hospitals, industrial and commercial government agencies, and research centers.
3. Social Security Funds	National Fund for Temporary Unemployment for Workers in Public Works, National Pension Fund, and National Unemployment Insurance Fund.
4. State Government	Not applicable.
5. Local Government	Partially covered. 5.1 Budgetary local government units/entities: Communes (1552) and Wilayas (48). 5.2 Extrabudgetary local government units
Compilation Practices	
Breaks in Series	Liabilities in the balance sheet of budgetary central government reflect debt assumptions that took place in 1996 (171 billion dinars) and 1999 (346 billion dinars). These assumptions were not accounted for as transactions (financing). From 2006, expense and acquisition of nonfinancial assets are recorded on a payment order basis.
Compilation Notes	Data cover activities of subsector 1. Government Finance Statistics are compiled by the Banque d'Algérie (BA).
Implementation of GFSM 2001/2014	No information available.

Angola (614)

Information Last Updated	2017
Units of General Government	
1. Budgetary Central Government	Covered. National Assembly, President's Office, Vice-President's Office, Auditor General Office, Constitutional Court, Supreme Courts, Ministries, Attorney General, and other units of the central administration.
2. Extrabudgetary Central Government	Covered. Public Institutes or Government Agencies, Autonomous funds and services.
3. Social Security Funds	Covered. National Social Security Institute (Instituto Nacional de Segurança Nacional – INSS)
4. State Government	Not applicable.
5. Local Government	Covered. 18 Provincial Governments
Compilation Practices	
Breaks in Series	None reported.
Compilation Notes	Data in Central Government tables cover operations of subsectors 1, 3 and 5. Given that there is no decentralization of the budget, the operations imputed to local (provincial) governments are included in central government operations. Also, the operations of all subsectors including INSS and the autonomous agencies and funds are incorporated on the Integrated Financial Management System of the State (SIGFE). Therefore, the data for budgetary central government cover all subsectors. Basis of recording: Data for all subsectors are reported on a cash basis. Liquidation or complementary period: The financial year coincides with the calendar year, ending December 31. It includes the collected revenue and the surplus funds from the previous calendar year; as well as the incurred expenses. Payment orders that have not been paid by December 31 are recognized in the next following year as outstanding payments "Restos a pagar" and usually paid in the first quarter of the following year. Valuation of assets and liabilities: Financial assets at market prices, and loans and bonds at face value.
Implementation of GFSM 2001/2014	This institutional table is based on information reported in 2014.

Anguilla (312)

Information Last Updated	2015
Units of General Government	
1. Budgetary Central Government	1.1 Legislative, Judiciary, and Executive bodies including ministries/departments. 1.2 Other agencies or funds: No information available.
2. Extrabudgetary Central Government	Not applicable.
3. Social Security Funds	Social Security Board.
4. State Government	Not applicable.
5. Local Government	Not applicable.
Compilation Practices	
Breaks in Series	None reported.
Compilation Notes	Data cover the operations of subsector 1. Government Finance Statistics are compiled by the Ministry of Finance.
Implementation of GFSM 2001/2014	No information available.

Antigua and Barbuda (311)

Information Last Updated	2015
Units of General Government	
1. Budgetary Central Government	1.1 Legislative, Judiciary, and Executive bodies including ministries/departments. 1.2 Other agencies or funds: Not applicable.
2. Extrabudgetary Central Government	Board of Education, Transport Board.
3. Social Security Funds	Medical Benefits Scheme, Social Security Scheme.
4. State Government	Not applicable.
5. Local Government	5.1 Budgetary local government units/entities: 6 parishes.
Compilation Practices	
Breaks in Series	None reported.
Compilation Notes	Data cover activities of subsector 1.
Implementation of GFSM 2001/2014	No information available.

Argentina (213)

Information Last Updated 2015

Units of General Government

1. Budgetary Central Government

1.1 Legislative, Judiciary, and Executive bodies including ministries/departments:
1.2 Other agencies or funds:
Partial information was provided.
Government agencies, such as the Argentine Mining and Geological Service; National Agrofood Health and Quality Service; National Drug, Food, and Medical Technology Administration; National Fisheries Research and Development Institute; National Institute of Agricultural Technology; National Institute of Industrial Technology; and National Transportation Regulation Commission.

2. Extrabudgetary Central Government

Partially covered.
Trustee funds and other entities, such as the Federal Public Resources Administration.

3. Social Security Funds

1 unit reported.
National Social Security Administration.

4. State Government

4.1 Budgetary state government units/entities:
24 units reported.
Ciudad Autónoma de Buenos Aires and 23 provinces.
4.2 Extrabudgetary state government units:
No extrabudgetary information was provided.

5. Local Government

5.1 Budgetary local government units/entities:
2221 units reported.
Municipalities.
5.2 Extrabudgetary local government units:
No extrabudgetary information was provided.

Compilation Practices

Breaks in Series

From 2002, data are on an accrual basis.
Through 2001 the subsectors of central government are presented on a net basis (i.e., after consolidation). Starting in 2002, the subsectors of central government are presented on a gross basis (i.e., before consolidation).

Compilation Notes

Data cover activities of subsectors 1-5.
Time series for revenue and expense for general government sector cover 1990 to 2004.
Data are recorded on accrual basis for subsectors 1-5.
No information was provided.

Implementation of GFSM 2001/2014

Government Finance Statistics are compiled by the Ministerio de Economía y Finanzas Publicas, Secretaría de Hacienda.
Over the medium term, the next steps were not provided.
This institutional information was reported in 2006 in the Government Finance Statistics Yearbook (GFSY).

Armenia, Republic of (911)

Information Last Updated 2015

Units of General Government

1. Budgetary Central Government

1.1 Legislative, Judiciary, and Executive bodies including ministries/departments.
1.2 Other agencies or funds:
Not applicable.

2. Extrabudgetary Central Government

Various government nonprofit institutions, including hospitals, schools, and universities.

3. Social Security Funds

Social security fund.

4. State Government

Not applicable.

5. Local Government

5.1 Budgetary local government units/entities:
More than 900 marzes or communities.
5.2 Extrabudgetary local government units:
No information available.

Compilation Practices

Breaks in Series

From 2008, data for budgetary central government includes the data of social security funds.

Compilation Notes

Data cover activities of subsectors 1-3 and 5.
The following flows are consolidated: grants, taxes, sales of goods and services, miscellaneous and unidentified revenue and expense, use of goods and services.
Government Finance Statistics are compiled by the Ministry of Finance.

Implementation of GFSM 2001/2014

Over the medium term, the next steps will include improving the depth of data in the cash flow statement and bringing budgetary central government revenues, expense, and transactions in nonfinancial assets in line with the GFSM 2001.

Australia (193)

Information Last Updated	2017
Units of General Government	
1. Budgetary Central Government	Covered. Legislative, Judiciary, and Executive bodies including ministries/departments plus national universities.
2. Extrabudgetary Central Government	Not applicable.
3. Social Security Funds	Not applicable.
4. State Government	Covered. Budgetary state government units/entities for 8 state governments.
5. Local Government	Covered. Budgetary local government units/entities totalling approximately 560 cities, district councils, municipalities, shires, and towns. Includes a general government central borrowing authority classified to the local government sector in South Australia.
Compilation Practices	
Breaks in Series	From 2005, defence weapons platforms have been capitalised in line with the 2008 SNA, and classified as stocks and flows in nonfinancial assets. For 2003 and 2004, in the Statement of Sources and Uses of Cash, compensation of employees includes purchases of goods and services; grants includes subsidies; and social benefits includes other payments. From 2005, these details are no longer available. Since the 1998/99 reference period, Australian GFS data has been compiled on an accrual accounting basis. From 1996 onward, all local government data are compiled on a year ending June 30.
Compilation Notes	Data cover activities of subsectors Central budgetary (where BA=CG), State Governments (SG), and Local Goverrnments (LG). All data other than cash specific statements are recorded on an accrual accounting basis. Government Finance Statistics are compiled by the Australian Bureau of Statistics.
Implementation of GFSM 2001/2014	The Australian Bureau of Statistics is currently revising Australian GFS standards to bring these into alignment with GFSM 2014. Resources are also being allocated to facilitate implementation, with stakeholder engagement plus reviews of business processes and statistical outputs underway. It is intended that GFS data for the 2016/17 financial year onwards will be compiled and reported under the new standards.

Austria (122)

Information Last Updated	2015
Units of General Government	
1. Budgetary Central Government	1.1 Legislative, Judiciary, and Executive bodies including ministries/departments. 1.2 Other agencies or funds: No information available.
2. Extrabudgetary Central Government	Associations of students Federal chambers of commerce, labor, and some types of self-employed (physicians, lawyers et. al.), Federal funds Universities, Universities of applied sciences.
3. Social Security Funds	Partially covered. Social insurance institutions, hospitals of social insurance.
4. State Government	4.1 Budgetary state government units/entities: 9 states. 4.2 Extrabudgetary state government units: State funds.
5. Local Government	5.1 Budgetary local government units/entities: Municipal associations (education services), municipal funds, municipalities (2,358, excluding Vienna), and Vienna, with responsibilities both as a state and a local government, classified for 1995 ESA and GFS purposes as a local government unit. 5.2 Extrabudgetary local government units: No information available.
Compilation Practices	
Breaks in Series	From 1996 the hospital managing companies were part of state government, and their data were included in data on state government. From 1995, data are compiled in accordance with the 1995 ESA. Data are reported after FISIM allocation.
Compilation Notes	Data cover activities of general government. Data in general government sector cover tables 1, 2, partially 3, partially 6, partially 7, and partially 9. Data for all subsectors are reported on a noncash basis, consistent with the national accounts of general government prepared according to the European System of Accounts, 1995 (ESA95). Liquidation or complementary period: Complementary period is 3 weeks for component 1.1 and 4 weeks for all other subsectors. Valuation of assets and liabilities: Financial assets and liabilities are valued at market prices. The following flows are consolidated: Grants, Interest, changes in Securities other than shares, Loans, Other accounts receivable/payable. The following stocks are consolidated: Securities other than shares, Loans, Other accounts receivable/payable. Government Finance Statistics are compiled by Statistik Austria.
Implementation of GFSM 2001/2014	Austria participates in the Eurostat GFS convergence project with the IMF.

Azerbaijan, Republic of (912)

Information Last Updated	2015
Units of General Government	
1. Budgetary Central Government	1.1 Legislative, Judiciary, and Executive bodies including ministries/departments. 1.2 Other agencies or funds: 20 state committees, State Environmental Protection Fund, Fund for Securing Loans Acquired Under State Guarantees(Guarantee Fund), National Entrepreneur Assistance Fund, etc.
2. Extrabudgetary Central Government	State oil fund.
3. Social Security Funds	State Social Protection Fund.
4. State Government	4.1 Budgetary state government units/entities: Nakhichevan Autonomous Republic. 4.2 Extrabudgetary state government units: No information available.
5. Local Government	5.1 Budgetary local government units/entities: 51 districts (rayons) consisting of 5 cities and 1494 municipalities; the city of Baku, which consists of 52 municipalities; 171 Nakhichevan Autonomous Republic municipalities grouped into 7 districts and the city of Nakhichevan. 5.2 Extrabudgetary local government units: No information available.
Compilation Practices	
Breaks in Series	None.
Compilation Notes	Data cover activities of subsectors 1-5. Data are recorded on cash basis for subsectors 1-5. Government Finance Statistics are compiled by the Ministry of Finance of Azerbaijan.
Implementation of GFSM 2001/2014	No information available.

Bahamas, The (313)

Information Last Updated	2015
Units of General Government	
1. Budgetary Central Government	Covered. 1.1 Legislative, Judiciary, and Executive bodies including ministries/departments.
2. Extrabudgetary Central Government	Not applicable.
3. Social Security Funds	Not covered. National Insurance Board and Social Security Scheme.
4. State Government	Not applicable.
5. Local Government	Not applicable.
Compilation Practices	
Breaks in Series	No breaks in series.
Compilation Notes	Data cover activities of subsector 1. Data are recorded on cash basis for subsector 1. Government Finance Statistics are compiled by The Central Bank of The Bahamas.
Implementation of GFSM 2001/2014	No information available.

Bahrain, Kingdom of (419)

Information Last Updated	2015
Units of General Government	
1. Budgetary Central Government	1.1 Legislative, Judiciary, and Executive bodies including ministries/departments. 1.2 Other agencies or funds:
2. Extrabudgetary Central Government	Extrabudgetary funds.
3. Social Security Funds	Social Insurance Organization.
4. State Government	Not applicable.
5. Local Government	Not applicable.
Compilation Practices	
Breaks in Series	Prior to 1996, the line general public services of Table 7 included outlays on public order and safety. Starting in 2005, data except for the statement of sources and uses of cash are on an accrual basis. Data through 2004 are on a cash basis. Starting in 2011, data for consumption of fixed capital are reported in Table 2 and Table 3.
Compilation Notes	Data cover activities of subsector 1. Data for revenues are recorded on a modified cash basis, expenses other than manpower costs are recorded on an accrual basis. Government Finance Statistics are compiled by the Ministry of Finance.
Implementation of GFSM 2001/2014	No information available.

Bangladesh (513)

Information Last Updated	2015
Units of General Government	
1. Budgetary Central Government	1.1 Legislative, Judiciary, and Executive bodies including ministries/departments. 1.2 Other agencies or funds: Not applicable.
2. Extrabudgetary Central Government	Not applicable.
3. Social Security Funds	No information available.
4. State Government	Not applicable.
5. Local Government	5.1 Budgetary local government units/entities: City corporations, district councils, and municipalities. 5.2 Extrabudgetary local government units: No information available.
Compilation Practices	
Breaks in Series	None reported.
Compilation Notes	Data cover activities of subsector 1. Data are recorded on cash basis for subsector 1. Government Finance Statistics are compiled by the Ministry of Finance.
Implementation of GFSM 2001/2014	No information available.

Barbados (316)

Information Last Updated	2015
Units of General Government	
1. Budgetary Central Government	Covered. 1.1 Legislative, Judiciary, and Executive bodies including ministries/departments. 1.2 Other agencies or funds: Not applicable.
2. Extrabudgetary Central Government	Covered. Barbados Cadet Corps, Barbados Defense Force, Barbados Defense Force - Sports Program, Barbados Investment and Development Corporation, Barbados Tourism Authority, Child Care Board, National Assistance Board, National Conservation Commission, Sanitation Service, University of the West Indies.
3. Social Security Funds	National Insurance Fund, Severance Fund, Unemployment Fund.
4. State Government	Not applicable.
5. Local Government	Not applicable.
Compilation Practices	
Breaks in Series	The 2006 balance sheet data are on a noncash basis. From 2007, data are compiled on a noncash basis.
Compilation Notes	Data cover activities of subsector 1. Data are recorded on a mixed cash, commitment, and/or accrual basis for subsector 1. Government Finance Statistics are compiled by the Ministry of Finance.
Implementation of GFSM 2001/2014	No information provided.

Belarus (913)

Information Last Updated 2017

Units of General Government

1. Budgetary Central Government

Covered.
Administration of the President, Constitutional Court, Council of Ministers, General Prosecutor's office, National Assembly, State Control Committee, State Secretariat of the Security Council, the Supreme Court, Ministries (24/24),State committees (10/10), other bodies, budget organizations, financed from the republican budget (about 2800/2800).

2. Extrabudgetary Central Government

Covered.
Concerns (4/0).

3. Social Security Funds

Covered.
Social Protection Fund (1/1).

4. State Government

Not applicable.

5. Local Government

Covered.
Total local government agencies comprise 1,495 budgets: Oblast/Provinces (6), city of Minsk(1), oblast cities(12), rayon/districts (118), rayon cities(14), settlement/townships budgets(55), rural(1,289).

Compilation Practices

Breaks in Series

Data cover subsectors 1, 2, 3, and 5.
Since 2013, Balance Sheet data have been included.
Since 2012, data coverage has been expanded to include operations of subsector 2.
In 2011, the exchange rate on the Belarusian ruble fell from Rbl 3,000 rubles per US$ on January 1, 2011 to 8350 rubles per US$ on December 31, 2011.
On January 1, 2000, the Belarusian ruble was redenominated by a factor of 100.
In 1998, a number of extrabudgetary funds were included in the budget.
On August 20, 1994, the Belarusian ruble was redenominated by a factor of 10.

Compilation Notes

The data are noncash basis, include a non-cash transactions (set-off of mutual claims and the transfer of property).

Implementation of GFSM 2001/2014

Fiscal statements are prepared using the classifications in GFSM 2001. Over the medium term, the next step will include implementing accrual accounting in the general government sector and classifying data on GFSM 2014.

Belgium (124)

Information Last Updated 2015

Units of General Government

1. Budgetary Central Government

Covered.
1.1 Legislative, Judiciary, and Executive bodies including ministries/departments.
1.2 Other agencies or funds:
There is no breakdown between the budgetary and the extrabudgetary central government subsectors. The central government subsector covers: the legislative bodies, the civil list, the federal public services, a ministerial department (defense), the planning public services, several scientific and cultural institutions, other public bodies, one social security fund, several Services with autonomous bookkeeping, Economic and social consultative bodies, one university, Special corps, and several public corporations.

2. Extrabudgetary Central Government

Covered.
There is no breakdown between the budgetary and the extrabudgetary central government subsectors.

3. Social Security Funds

Covered.
The social-security funds subsector covers the central and primary entities in the various branches of social security for employed and self-employed persons, with the exception of the "annual holiday allowances" branch and optional insurance schemes.

The management bodies of the "annual holiday allowances" branch are included in the Federal Authority, while the parts of mutual societies managing optional insurance schemes are established as quasi-corporate enterprises and form part of the financial corporations sector. Besides compulsory insurance, mutual societies also manage optional and complementary sickness-invalidity insurance. This consists of three elements:
- Optional healthcare insurance, also known as "small risks" insurance for self-employed persons;
- Complementary insurance (daily cash benefits, hospitalization service, travel in relation to illness, healthcare abroad and miscellaneous services) offering services to which members may or may not be obliged to subscribe (depending on the mutual society and the service);
- Prenuptial savings.

The subsistence protection funds, the redundancy fund and the overseas social-security office and the care insurance companies of the Flemish Community are also part of this subsector.

4. State Government

Covered.
4.1 Budgetary state government units/entities:
Brussels Capital Region, French region, Walloon Region, French community, Flemish community, German community, Community commissions.

5. Local Government

Covered.
4.1 Budgetary local government units/entities:
Provinces (10), municipalities (589), local police zones (195) and public social assistance centers (589), Metropolitan Brussels, assistant zones (fire departments).

Compilation Practices

Breaks in Series

None reported.

Compilation Notes

Data for central government tables cover the operations of subsectors 1 and 2; no breakdown between the two subsectors is available.
Data in the state government tables cover the operations of subsector 4.
Data in the local government tables cover the operations of subsector 5.
Government Finance Statistics are compiled by the National Bank of Belgium under the legal responsibility of the National Accounts Institute.

Implementation of GFSM 2001/2014

Belgium participates in the Eurostat GFS convergence project with the IMF.

Belize (339)

Information Last Updated	2015
Units of General Government	
1. Budgetary Central Government	1.1 Legislative, Judiciary, and Executive bodies including ministries/departments. 1.2 Other agencies or funds: Not applicable.
2. Extrabudgetary Central Government	Belize Tourism Board, Protected Areas Conservation Trust, Belize Agricultural Health Authority, Statistical Institute of Belize, Belize Social Investment Fund, Belize Trade and Investment Development Service.
3. Social Security Funds	Social security board.
4. State Government	Not applicable.
5. Local Government	5.1 Budgetary local government units/entities: Belize city council and 5 town boards 5.2 Extrabudgetary local government units: No information available.
Compilation Practices	
Breaks in Series	In 1988, data for General Public Services excluded data for Public Order and Safety.
Compilation Notes	Data cover activities of subsector 1. Data are recorded on cash basis for subsector 1. Government Finance Statistics are compiled by the Ministry of Finance.
Implementation of GFSM 2001/2014	No information available.

Benin (638)

Information Last Updated	2017
Units of General Government	
1. Budgetary Central Government	1.1 Legislative, Judiciary, and Executive bodies including ministries/departments. 1.2 Other agencies or funds: Economic and Social Council, High Authority for Audiovisual Affairs and Communication, High Council of Concerted Governance, High Council of National Solidarity, High Court of Justice.
2. Extrabudgetary Central Government	40 extrabudgetary units.
3. Social Security Funds	National Social Security Fund.
4. State Government	Not applicable.
5. Local Government	5.1 Budgetary local government units/entities: 77 communes, 12 departments 5.2 Extrabudgetary local government units: No information available.
Compilation Practices	
Breaks in Series	From 2010, data on outlays by functions of government do not cover expenditures financed from external sources.
Compilation Notes	Data cover activities of subsector 1. Data are recorded on mixed cash, commitment, and/or accrual basis for subsector 1. Government Finance Statistics are compiled by the National Institute of Statistics and Economic Analysis (INSAE).
Implementation of GFSM 2001/2014	Benin is a member country of the West African Economic and Monetary Union (WAEMU). In June 2009, the WAEMU Council of Ministers adopted a new public finance harmonized framework which includes six directives of which the common reporting format on Government Financial Operations (Tableau des Opérations Financières de l'Etat - TOFE) which is compatible with the international statistical methodology of the Government Finance Statistics Manual 2001 (GFSM 2001). The member countries have until 2017 for full implementation of the framework after having incorporated the guidelines in their own legislation by late 2011.

Bhutan (514)

Information Last Updated	2015
Units of General Government	
1. Budgetary Central Government	1.1 Legislative, Judiciary, and Executive bodies including ministries/departments. 1.2 Other agencies or funds: Bhutan Information-Communication & Media Authority, Bhutan Olympic Committee, Centre for Bhutan Studies, Dzongkha Development Commission, Gross National Happiness Commission, National Environment Commission, National Land Commission, Royal Institute of Management, Royal University of Bhutan, Thimphu Thromdey Schools, 20 district administrations, and 205 Sub-district administrations.
2. Extrabudgetary Central Government	Not applicable.
3. Social Security Funds	Not applicable.
4. State Government	Not applicable.
5. Local Government	Not applicable.
Compilation Practices	
Breaks in Series	No information available.
Compilation Notes	Data cover activities of subsector 1, which is equal to the general government sector. Data are recorded on cash basis for subsector 1. Government Finance Statistics are compiled by the Ministry of Finance.
Implementation of GFSM 2001/2014	Over the medium term, the next steps will include using the Classification Assistant Table developed by the IMF for the reporting in GFSM 2001 format.

Bosnia and Herzegovina (963)

Information Last Updated	2016
Units of General Government	
1. Budgetary Central Government	Covered. 1.1 Legislative, Judiciary, and Executive bodies including ministries/departments. 1.2 Other agencies or funds: 10 Cantonal governments, Brcko District, Federation of Bosnia and Herzegovina (entity-subnational level), and Republika Srpska (entity-subnational level).
2. Extrabudgetary Central Government	Covered. Public enterprise for road maintenance and reconstruction in the Federation of Bosnia and Herzegovina, Public enterprise for highways in the Federation of Bosnia and Herzegovina, Public enterprise for road maintenance and reconstruction in the Republika Srpska, and Public enterprise for highways in the Republika Srpska as well as Federal fund for Support to the Areas Affected by Natural Disaster.
3. Social Security Funds	Covered. Child Protection Fund of the Repulika Srpska, Health Fund of the Federation of Bosnia and Herzegovina, Health Fund of the Republika Srpska, Health Fund of the Briko District and 10 Health Funds at cantonal level, Pension Fund of the Federation of Bosnia and Herzegovina and Pension Fund of the Republika Srpska, Unemployment Fund of the Federation of Bosnia and Herzegovina, Unemployment Fund of the Republika Srpska, Unemployment Fund of the Briko Distrcit and 10 Unemployment Funds at cantonal level, Federation of Bosnia and Herzegovina and Republika Srpska fund for professional rehabilitation of persons with disability.
4. State Government	Not applicable.
5. Local Government	5.1 Budgetary local government units/entities: 10 cities and 140 municipalities. 5.2 Extrabudgetary local government units: No information available.
Compilation Practices	
Breaks in Series	None reported.
Compilation Notes	Data cover activities of subsectors 1-3 and 5. Data are recorded on mixed cash, commitment, and/or accrual basis for subsectors 1, 2, 3, and 5. Government Finance Statistics are compiled by the Central Bank of Bosnia and Herzegovina.
Implementation of GFSM 2001/2014	Over the medium term, the next steps will include improving the depth of the existing data set and plan how to start compilation of the cash flow statement. The statistical coverage of general government should be further strengthened in line with international standards.

Botswana (616)

Information Last Updated	2015
Units of General Government	
1. Budgetary Central Government	1.1 Legislative, Judiciary, and Executive bodies including ministries/departments. 1.2 Other agencies or funds: Departmental enterprises.
2. Extrabudgetary Central Government	Nonprofit bodies.
3. Social Security Funds	Not applicable.
4. State Government	Not applicable.
5. Local Government	5.1 Budgetary local government units/entities: 2 city councils, 10 district councils, 4 town councils, and 12 land boards. 5.2 Extrabudgetary local government units: No information available.
Compilation Practices	
Breaks in Series	From 1986, data for Public Order and Safety are shown separately from data for General Public Services.
Compilation Notes	Data cover activities of subsector 1. Data are recorded on cash basis for subsector 1. Government Finance Statistics are compiled by the Ministry of Finance and Development Planning.
Implementation of GFSM 2001/2014	Over the medium term, the next steps are to collect detailed breakdowns of transfers.

Brazil (223)

Information Last Updated	2017
Units of General Government	
1. Budgetary Central Government	Covered. Budgetary central government subsector comprises all units included in the federal budget coverage (nationally known as "Fiscal and Social Security Budget"). It includes Legislative, Judiciary, and Executive bodies including ministries, departments, funds, agencies and foundations.
2. Extrabudgetary Central Government	Partially covered. The extrabudgetary central government subsector comprises the Fundo Remanescente do PIS/PASEP (Programa de Integração Social and Programa de Formação do Patrimônio do Servidor Público) and the Fundo de Garantia por Tempo de Serviço (FGTS), a private fund managed by the public sector. Its assets are invested in housing, basic sanitation and urban infrastructure and its main revenue source is a mandatory contribution made by employers. The remaining extrabudgetary central government units will be compiled in the future, according to database availability.
3. Social Security Funds	Covered. The Regime Próprio de Previdência Social (RPPS), covering public sector employees; and the Regime Geral de Previdência Social (RGPS), covering private sector workers.
4. State Government	Covered. State Government subsector comprises budgetary units of 26 states and 1 federal district (with status of a state).
5. Local Government	Covered. Local Government subsector comprises 5570 municipalities. The data collection process has a response rate that exceeds 90%. Statistical methodology is applied to extrapolate the coverage to the whole of municipalities.
Compilation Practices	
Breaks in Series	In 2015, the National Treasury improved the general government statistics by introducing accrual basis of recording for government expenditures. The new methodology was applied for the series beginning in 2010. Since then, fiscal statistics follow cash basis of recording for revenues and accrual for expenditures. A statement of sources and uses of cash is also included as part of the GFS framework. Furthermore, fiscal statistics presented in the statements were prepared in accordance with the guidelines of the GFSM 2014 and harmonized with the System of National Accounts (SNA 2008). This was a joint initiative between the National Treasury and the Brazilian Bureau of Statistics (IBGE). Find more information at: Manual de Estatísticas Fiscais: https://www.tesouro.fazenda.gov.br/documents/10180/476865/PFI_Manual_Estatisticas_Fiscais/945c2ec4-a584-4823-9375-ffb22c070f78 Estatísticas de Finanças Públicas e Conta Intermediária de Governo: https://www.tesouro.fazenda.gov.br/documents/10180/476865/PFI_EFP_CIG/0c46426e-14fe-4574-b01c-63ab2278d338 Previously, the statistics for the Central Government were compiled on a cash basis by a simple reclassification of the data presented in the Central Government Primary Balance Bulletin (RTN) into the GFS template. The RTN bulletin broadly follows the GFSM 1986. The basis of recording of the expenditures adopted in the RTN bulletin is known as "actual payment" in which expenses are recorded at the time the payment orders are cashed from the Treasury Single Account (TSA).
Compilation Notes	The accrued expenditures in the current period are obtained by adding the verified expenditures from the current budget and the expenditures that come from previous budgets but are verified by the spending units in the current fiscal year. Similar treatment is applied for the expenditures compiled on a cash basis in the statement of sources and uses of cash.
Implementation of GFSM 2001/2014	Improvements in 2016: Publishing of the Brazilian general government fiscal statistics on a quarterly basis, from 2010 to the second quarter of 2016. The information was compiled in accordance with the concepts and methodologies established in the GFSM 2014 and will be made available with a three-month lag. Incorporation of two extrabudgetary institutional units: FGTS and PIS/PASEP. Elaboration of the Expenditure by Functions of Government (COFOG) statement for the budgetary central government sector. Improvements for the next years: Incorporation of other extrabudgetary institutional units, such as Sistema S and Conselhos Profissionais. Elaboration of the Balance Sheet for the General Government. Elaboration of the Expenditure by Functions of Government (COFOG) for the general government sector.

Bulgaria (918)

Information Last Updated	2017
Units of General Government	
1. Budgetary Central Government	Covered. 2.1.1 Legislative, Judiciary, and Executive bodies including ministries/departments: Central Budget, National Assembly, President's Administration, Council of Ministers, Constitutional Court, National Audit Office and Supreme Judicial Council, Ministries (17/17), Agencies (4/4), Commissions (12/12), National Service for Protection, National Intelligence Service, Ombudsman, National Statistical Institute, Electronic Media Council, Agricultural Fund, National Bureau for Control of Special Intelligence Means. 2.1.2 Other agencies or funds: Bulgarian Academy of Science, Bulgarian National Radio, Bulgarian National Television, Bulgarian News Agency (BTA), Government Universities.
2. Extrabudgetary Central Government	Partially covered. In accordance with the Public Finance Act, effective since 01.01.2014, all extrabudgetary accounts and funds shall be terminated and their revenues and expenditures shall be included in the corresponding budgets, except for accounts for the European Union funds. Accounts for the European Union Funds: National Fund with the Ministry of Finance, Agricultural Fund – payment agency, Account with the Minister of Finance for receipts from sales of of AAUs, Other accounts for the European Union funds. Other units included: Enterprise for Management of Environmental Protection Activities (EMEPA), National Company "Strategic Infrastructure Projects" (NCSIP), Fund "Security of the Electricity Systems".
3. Social Security Funds	Covered. National Social Security Institute, with funds included: Public Social Security, Teachers' Pension Fund, "Guaranteed Receivables of Workers and Employees" Fund, National Health Insurance Fund.
4. State Government	Not applicable.
5. Local Government	Covered. 2.5.1 Budgetary local government units/entities: Municipalities (265/265). 2.5.2 Extrabudgetary local government units: In accordance with the Public Finance Act, effective since 01.01.2014, all extrabudgetary accounts and funds shall be terminated and their revenues and expenditures shall be included in the corresponding municipal budgets, except for accounts for the European Union funds.
Compilation Practices	
Breaks in Series	Data on general government sector have been compiled and provided since 2000 without break in series.
Compilation Notes	Data cover activities of subsectors of central government, local government and social security funds. Data disseminated for general government sector cover tables 1-3, 8a, and partially 7. Time series for revenue and expense for general government sector cover the period from 1990 to 2015. Data are recorded on cash basis for all the subsectors covered. The following flows are consolidated: Grants, changes in securities other than shares.
Implementation of GFSM 2001/2014	Government Finance Statistics at this stage are compiled by the Ministry of Finance. Since 2015 The Republic of Bulgaria has been participating in the Eurostat GFS convergence project with the IMF and thus has filled data gaps in accrual data and has been implementing the GFSM 2014 format. This institutional information was reported in 2015 in the Government Finance Statistics Yearbook (GFSY).

Burkina Faso (748)

Information Last Updated	2017
Units of General Government	
1. Budgetary Central Government	1.1 Legislative, Judiciary, and Executive bodies including ministries/departments. 1.2 Other agencies or funds: Constitutional Council, Economic and Social Council, General Delegation for Information Technology, General Inspectorate, General Secretariat of the Government, Grande Chancellerie (Awards State Decorations and Honors), Higher Council for Communications, and National Electoral Commission.
2. Extrabudgetary Central Government	68 extrabudgetary units.
3. Social Security Funds	Multipurpose: National Social Security Fund (CNSS). Pension units: Pension fund for government employees.
4. State Government	Not applicable.
5. Local Government	5.1 Budgetary local government units/entities: 13 regions, 352 rural communes, and 49 urban communes. 5.2 Extrabudgetary local government units: No information available.
Compilation Practices	
Breaks in Series	None reported.
Compilation Notes	Data cover activities of subsector 1. Government Finance Statistics are compiled by the Ministry of Economy and Finance.
Implementation of GFSM 2001/2014	Burkina Faso participates in the West African Economic and Monetary Union (WAEMU) Project on harmonization of public finances. Over the medium term, the next steps will include full implementing of the GFSM 2001/2014 framework by 2017.

Burundi (618)

Information Last Updated	2015
Units of General Government	
1. Budgetary Central Government	1.1 Legislative, Judiciary, and Executive bodies including ministries/departments. 1.2 Other agencies or funds: Budgetary agencies, provinces, and specialized schools.
2. Extrabudgetary Central Government	Burundi National Commission for UNESCO, Prince Louis Rwagasose Clinic, radio station, university, and various government centers and institutions, Civil Servants Mutual Insurance Fund.
3. Social Security Funds	National Social Security Institute of Burundi.
4. State Government	Not applicable.
5. Local Government	5.1 Budgetary local government units/entities: 120 communal administrations. 5.2 Extrabudgetary local government units: No information available.
Compilation Practices	
Breaks in Series	None reported.
Compilation Notes	Data cover activities of subsectors 1. Data are recorded on cash basis for subsectors 1. Government Finance Statistics are compiled by the Ministry of Finance.
Implementation of GFSM 2001/2014	No information available.

Cabo Verde (624)

Information Last Updated	2015
Units of General Government	
1. Budgetary Central Government	1.1 Legislative, Judiciary, and Executive bodies including ministries/departments. 1.2 Other agencies or funds: No information available.
2. Extrabudgetary Central Government	9 Funds, 2 hospitals, 8 other entities, 2 police units, 11 public institutes, and 6 universities.
3. Social Security Funds	National Institute of Social Benefits.
4. State Government	Not applicable.
5. Local Government	5.1 Budgetary local government units/entities: 22 Municipalities, 3 municipalities associations, and 15 water supply and sanitation agencies. 5.2 Extrabudgetary local government units: No information available.
Compilation Practices	
Breaks in Series	Starting in 2011, data for budgetary central government also cover extrabudgetary central government units and entities.
Compilation Notes	Data cover activities of subsectors 1 and 5. Government Finance Statistics are compiled by the Ministry of Finance and Planning.
Implementation of GFSM 2001/2014	Over the medium term, the next steps will include improving the quality of GFS compilation and reforming the accounting system with the objective of recording information on both cash and accrual bases.

Cambodia (522)

Information Last Updated	2017
Units of General Government	
1. Budgetary Central Government	Covered. 34 entities reported. Anti-corruption office, constitutional council, council of minister, judiciary, monarchy, ministries (25), national assembly, national audit authority, national election committee, and senate
2. Extrabudgetary Central Government	Not covered. 26 units reported. APSARA Authority under the Council of Ministers, Calmate Hospital under the Ministry of Health, Cambodian Agricultural Research and Development Institute under the Ministry of Agriculture, Forestry and Fisheries, Cambodian Rubber Research Institute (IRCC) under the Ministry of Agriculture, Forestry and Fisheries, Health Science Institute of Royal Cambodian Armed Forces under the Ministry of Defense, Kampongcham National College of Agriculture under the Ministry of Agriculture, Forestry and Fisheries, Khmer Soviet Friendship Hospital under the Ministry of Health, National Authority for Pheah Vihear under the Council of Ministers, National Social Security Fund for Veterans under the Ministry of Social Affairs, Veterans, and Youth Rehabilitation, National Health Product Quality Control Center under the Ministry of Health, National Management University under the Ministry of Education, Youth, and Sports, National Pediatric Hospital under the Ministry of Health, National Polytechnic Institute of Cambodia under the Ministry of Labor and Vocational Training, National Social Security Fund for Civil Servants under the Ministry of Social Affairs, Veterans, and Youth Rehabilitation, National Social Security Fund under the Ministry of Labor and Vocational Training, Preah Ang Duong Hospital under the Ministry of Health, National Institute of Public Health under the Ministry of Health, Preah Kossamak Hospital under the Ministry of Health, Prek Leap National College of Agriculture under the Ministry of Agriculture, Forestry and Fisheries, Persons with Disabilities Foundation under the Ministry of Social Affairs, Veterans, and Youth Rehabilitation, Royal Academy of Cambodia under the Council of Ministers, Royal School of Administration under the Ministry of Public Function, Royal University of Agriculture under the Ministry of Agriculture, Forestry and Fisheries, Royal University of Low and Economics under Ministry of Education, Youth, and Sports, Royal University of Fine Arts under Ministry of Cults and Fine Arts, University of Health Sciences under Ministry of Education, Youth, and Sports.
3. Social Security Funds	Not applicable.
4. State Government	Not applicable.
5. Local Government	Not covered. 14369 units reported: 1 1,633 communes 197 districts (159 districts, 26 municipalities and 12 kahns) 25 provinces (Capital Phnom Penh and 24 provinces) Villages (14,147)
Compilation Practices	
Breaks in Series	None reported.
Compilation Notes	Data cover activities of subsector 1. Data disseminated for budgetary central government sector cover statement I and tables 1-3. Data are recorded on a cash basis for revenue and non-cash basis for expenditure and selected transactions in financial assets and liabilities.
Implementation of GFSM 2001/2014	Government Finance Statistics are compiled by the Ministry of Economy and Finance. Over the medium term, the next steps will include the implementation of the new Financial Management Information System (FMIS) and Chart of Accounts. It is planned to automate the compilation of GFS with FMIS, and thus provide data for the whole general government sector.

Canada (156)

Information Last Updated 2015

Units of General Government

1. Budgetary Central Government

1.1 Legislative, Judiciary, and Executive bodies including ministries/departments.
1.2 Other agencies or funds:
No information available.

2. Extrabudgetary Central Government

70 (approximately) units/entities.

3. Social Security Funds

Canada Pension Plan, Quebec Pension Plan.

4. State Government

4.1 Budgetary state government units/entities:
10 Provincial and 3 territorial governments
4.2 Extrabudgetary state government units:
Colleges and universities, Health and social services institutions, Nonautonomous superannuation and retirement funds for public service employees, Provincial and territorial agencies, boards, and commissions.

5. Local Government

5.1 Budgetary local government units/entities:
Municipal governments.
5.2 Extrabudgetary local government units:
Agency boards, commissions, and local school boards.

Compilation Practices

Breaks in Series

Starting 1991, data are derived from quarterly GFS using Canada's System of National Accounts (CSNA) data as compiled by Statistics Canada. Annual data for earlier years (since the early 1970's) were based on Statistics Canada's Financial Management System (FMS) annual release and are thus not strictly comparable.

Compilation Notes

Data cover activities of subsectors 1-5. No breakdown into budgetary central government is available.
The following flows are consolidated: Grants, changes in securities other than shares.
The following stocks are consolidated: Securities other than shares.
Government Finance Statistics are compiled by Statistics Canada.

Implementation of GFSM 2001/2014

No information available.

Central African Republic (626)

Information Last Updated 2015

Units of General Government

1. Budgetary Central Government

1.1 Legislative, Judiciary, and Executive bodies including ministries/departments.
1.2 Other agencies or funds:
No information available.

2. Extrabudgetary Central Government

Chamber of agriculture, Chamber of commerce, Hospitals, Museum Boganda, National Laboratory, Office of war veterans, and University of Bangui.

3. Social Security Funds

National Social Security Fund.

4. State Government

Not applicable.

5. Local Government

5.1 Budgetary local government units/entities:
Cities, towns, and villages, including the municipalities of Bangui, Begoua, and Bimbo
5.2 Extrabudgetary local government units:
No information available.

Compilation Practices

Breaks in Series

None reported.

Compilation Notes

Data cover activities of subsectors 1 and 2.
Government Finance Statistics are compiled by the Ministry of Finance and Budget.

Implementation of GFSM 2001/2014

No information available.

Chile (228)

Information Last Updated	2015
Units of General Government	
1. Budgetary Central Government	Covered. 1.1 Legislative, Judiciary, and Executive bodies including ministries/departments and social security funds: 100 (approximately) government institutions. 1.2 Other agencies or funds: Fund for Economic and Social Stabilization, Pension Reserve Fund, Education Fund, Regional Support Fund.
2. Extrabudgetary Central Government	Covered. Funds in Administration by Central Bank, Oil Price Stabilization Fund, Reserved Copper Law funds, Interest accrued on Recognition Bonds.
3. Social Security Funds	Covered. 3 units, included into budgetary central government: National Fund for Welfare Pensions, Social Security Standardization Institute, National Health Fund.
4. State Government	Not applicable.
5. Local Government	Covered. 5.1 Budgetary local government units/entities: 354 Municipalities and Municipal Mutual Fund. 5.2 Extrabudgetary local government units: Not applicable.
Compilation Practices	
Breaks in Series	Data prior to 2001 are reported on a modified cash basis.
Compilation Notes	Data cover activities of subsectors 1-3 and 5. Data (except for taxes) are recorded on accrual basis for subsectors 1-3 and 5; Data for taxes are recorded on cash basis for subsectors 1-3 and 5. The following flows are consolidated: Grants, sales of goods and services, miscellaneous other expense. Data for extrabudgetary central government (subsector 2) includes interest accrued on Recognition Bonds and Codelco's transfers to government of 10% of the export value of copper production and related by-products under Law No. 13.196 (Reserved Copper Law).
Implementation of GFSM 2001/2014	Over the medium term, the next steps will include compilation of balance sheet.

China, P.R.: Mainland (924)

Information Last Updated	2015
Units of General Government	
1. Budgetary Central Government	1.1 Legislative, Judiciary, and Executive bodies including ministries/departments. 1.2 Other agencies or funds: Departments and institutions under the CPC Central Committee, General Office of the National People's Congress, General Office of the National People's Political Consultative Conference, State Council (administrations and 10 bureaus under the ministries and commissions, general office, 14 institutions, 28 commissions, 20 organizations, and 4 working organs, State-Owned Assets Supervision and Administration Commission, State-owned enterprises subject to the central government; and the Supreme People's Procuratorate.
2. Extrabudgetary Central Government	Extrabudgetary operations of central government ministries, and Government units with individual budgets.
3. Social Security Funds	Insurance for Work-Related Injuries Plan, Maternity Insurance Plan, Medical Insurance Plan, National Social Security Fund, Old Age Insurance Plan, and Unemployment Insurance Plan.
4. State Government	Not applicable.
5. Local Government	5.1 Budgetary local government units/entities: 656 cities, 2,487 counties, 31 provinces (excluding Taiwan, Hong Kong, and Macao and including Beijing, Shanghai, Chongqing, and Tianjin), 333 subprovincial administrative regions, 44,067 townships, and 678,589 villages. 5.2 Extrabudgetary local government units: Extrabudgetary operations.
Compilation Practices	
Breaks in Series	From 2002, data for central government include extrabudgetary fund transactions. From 1999, data for central government include social security. From 1994, data include tax revenue.
Compilation Notes	Data cover activities of subsectors 1-3 and 5. Government Finance Statistics are compiled by the Ministry of Finance.
Implementation of GFSM 2001/2014	No information available.

China, P.R.: Hong Kong (532)

Information Last Updated 2017

Units of General Government

1. Budgetary Central Government

Not applicable.
1.1 Legislative, Judiciary, and Executive bodies including ministries/departments:
1.2 Other agencies or funds:
Funds established under the Public Finance Ordinance, and Funds established by the Government for specific purposes, receiving their funding mainly from the government, and the government responsible for the use of their resources, Hong Kong Housing Authority, Hong Kong Link 2004 Limited.

2. Extrabudgetary Central Government

Not applicable.

3. Social Security Funds

Not applicable.

4. State Government

Not applicable.

5. Local Government

Not applicable.

Compilation Practices

Breaks in Series

From 2006, insurance technical reserves liabilities are separated from other accounts payable.

From 2004, data cover all government-owned fixed assets and their depreciation. For earlier years, the data on fixed assets and depreciation pertain to the Hong Kong Housing Authority only.

The GFS approach of referring to the report year as the year in which most months of the fiscal year fall is different than the approach of Hong Kong SAR which is to refer to the report year as the year in which the last 3 months of the fiscal year fall.

Compilation Notes

Because of the special administrative arrangements that are applied to Hong Kong SAR, there are no data for central, state or local government. Data cover operations of subsector 1, which is equal to the general government sector.

Government Finance Statistics are compiled by The Treasury.

Apart from the Hong Kong Housing Authority and Hong Kong Link 2004 Limited which maintain their accounts on accrual basis, the accounts of the Hong Kong SAR general government sector are basically recorded and prepared on cash basis. In addition to the cash accounts, the Government of HKSAR prepares annually a set of consolidated accounts on accrual basis. The GFS reported in the questionnaire are prepared based on this set of accrual-based consolidated accounts, but adjusted where necessary to conform with the scope, definition, and guidelines laid down in the GFSM 2001.

Fixed assets (including buildings, equipment, etc. but excluding land, some infrastructure assets mainly roads and drains) are stated at cost less accumulated depreciation. Capital works/projects in progress are stated at cost; no depreciation is provided for capital works/projects in progress. Inventories are stated at the lower of cost and net realizable value. Investments are mainly valued at cost or fair value at the end of the financial year. Pension liabilities are assessed by an independent qualified actuary. Contract gratuities and unused leave are accrued while other employee benefits such as housing, medical and education are recognized when they are paid. For the Government, accrual is made for major accounts receivable and accounts payable.

Hong Kong SAR government finance statistics are based upon accounting principles instead of GFSM 2014 statistical principles. While GFSM 2014 draws heavily upon the statistical framework of SNA 2008, Hong Kong SAR does not compile data according to this statistical framework.

Data on public sector debt is not available in the financial statement. The accounting consolidation approach for Hong Kong SAR is fundamentally different from the GFS consolidation approach.

Implementation of GFSM 2001/2014

The data are adjusted where necessary to conform to the scope, definitions, and guidelines of the GFSM 2001.

China, P.R.: Macao (546)

Information Last Updated 2017

Units of General Government

1. Budgetary Central Government

Covered.
1.1 Legislative, Judiciary, and Executive bodies including ministries/departments:
1.2 Other agencies or funds:
General secretariats and several nonautonomous agencies.

2. Extrabudgetary Central Government

Covered.
39 autonomous services and funds: Student Welfare Fund, Housing Loans Allowance Fund, Industrial and Commercial Development Fund , Tourism Fund, Social Welfare Bureau, Judiciary Police Welfare Association, Public Security Police Force Welfare Association, Coffer of Legal Affairs, Printing Bureau, Macao Prison Fund, Housing Bureau, Civil Aviation Authority, Macao Trade and Investment Promotion Institute, Commission Against Corruption, Health Bureau, University of Macau, Macao Polytechnic Institute, Sports Development Fund, Culture Fund, Consumer Council, Institute for Tourism Studies, Macao Public Administration Welfare Fund, Fire Services Welfare Association, Commission of Audit, Public Prosecutions Office, Presidents Office, Court of Final Appeal, Legislative Assembly, Civic and Municipal Affairs Bureau, Customs Welfare Association, Science and Technology Development Fund, Maritime Administration Welfare Association, Fishery Development and Support Fund, Housing Repair and Maintenance Fund, Educational Development Fund, Giant Panda Foundation, Environmental Protection and Energy Conservation Fund, Automobile and Maritime Security Fund, Macao Foundation, Deposit Protection Fund.

3. Social Security Funds

Covered.
Social security fund.

4. State Government

Not applicable.

5. Local Government

Not applicable.

Compilation Practices

Breaks in Series

None reported.

Compilation Notes

Data cover activities of subsectors 1-3, which represent the general government sector.
Government Finance Statistics are compiled by the Financial Services Bureau.

Implementation of GFSM 2001/2014

No information available.

Colombia (233)

Information Last Updated	2015
Units of General Government	
1. Budgetary Central Government	Covered. 1.1 Legislative, Judiciary, and Executive bodies including ministries/departments. 1.2 Other agencies or funds: 3 superintendences, 9 public funds, 28 public institutes and 19 other bodies.
2. Extrabudgetary Central Government	Covered. 3 administrative units, 3 councils, 4 autonomous patrimonies, 6 public funds, 7 extrabudgetary superintendences, 7 public institutes, 10 other corporations, 20 Education Centers, and 35 regional autonomous corporations.
3. Social Security Funds	Covered. 8 autonomous pension funds, 7 autonomous pension patrimonies, 7 retirement funds, 3 other pension funds, Social Security Institute.
4. State Government	Covered. 4.1 Budgetary state government units/entities: 5 courts, 32 state governments. 4.2 Extrabudgetary state government units: 16 universities, 20 other units, 20 state government mixed funds, 45 state institutes.
5. Local Government	Covered. 5.1 Budgetary local government units/entities: 1108 Municipalities, including the municipality of Bogotá 5.2 Extrabudgetary local government units: 4 municipal foundations, 7 municipal corporations, 13 municipal bodies, 24 centers, 39 local government funds, 54 local government associations, 61 other units, 195 municipal institutes.
Compilation Practices	
Breaks in Series	From 2008, data may not be directly comparable with those of previous years as the coverage of the Public Sector Accounting Plan and stock data were revised. From 2004, data are based on a broader institutional coverage, though still excluding 52 public entities and some state and local government decentralized units. Data prior to 2001 are reported on a cash basis. From 2001, data are based on a sample of 258 entities (153 from the central government, 46 from the state governments, and 59 from the local governments). From 1998, data for subsectors of central government are presented on gross basis (i.e., before consolidation).
Compilation Notes	Data cover activities of subsectors 1-5. Government Finance Statistics are compiled by the Ministry of Finance and Public Credit.
Implementation of GFSM 2001/2014	No information available.

Congo, Republic of (634)

Information Last Updated	2015
Units of General Government	
1. Budgetary Central Government	1.1 Legislative, Judiciary, and Executive bodies including ministries/departments. 1.2 Other agencies or funds: No information available.
2. Extrabudgetary Central Government	National Civil Aviation Agency, Marien Ngouabi University, The new Republic CENAGES, Directorate General of Merchant Shipping, National Employment and Labor Office, National Blood Transfusion Center, Congolese Foreign Trade Center, Congolese government debt management agency, National Reforestation Service, Congolese Shippers' Board, Business Start-Up Center, National Public Health Laboratory, University Hospital, Congolese Office of Information Technology, Building and Public Works Inspection Office, Building and Public Works Engineering Office, Chamber of Commerce, Industry, Agriculture, and Craft Trades, Road Fund.
3. Social Security Funds	National Social Security Fund (Caisse Nationale de Sécurité Sociale – CNSS), Civil Service Retirement Fund (Caisse de Retraite des Fonctionnaires – CRF).
4. State Government	Not applicable.
5. Local Government	5.1 Budgetary local government units/entities: 16 Municipalities. 5.2 Extrabudgetary local government units: No information available.
Compilation Practices	
Breaks in Series	None reported.
Compilation Notes	Data cover activities of subsectors 1. Government Finance Statistics are compiled by the Ministry of Economy, Finance and Budget.
Implementation of GFSM 2001/2014	No information available.

Costa Rica (238)

Information Last Updated	2016
Units of General Government	
1. Budgetary Central Government	1.1 Legislative, Judiciary, and Executive bodies including ministries/departments. 1.2 Other agencies or funds: No information available.
2. Extrabudgetary Central Government	54 assigned entities and 31 public service agencies.
3. Social Security Funds	Costa Rican Social Security Agency.
4. State Government	Not applicable.
5. Local Government	5.1 Budgetary local government units/entities: 81 municipalities. 5.2 Extrabudgetary local government units: No information available.
Compilation Practices	
Breaks in Series	Data in central government tables cover operations of subsectors 1–3. Data in local government tables cover operations of subsector 5. From 1991 onward, revenue data are not adjusted for the tax payers' use of tax credit certificates. From 2008 onward, data for budgetary central government are reported on a noncash basis.
Compilation Notes	Data are reported on a noncash basis for the budgetary central government, and on a cash basis for the remaining subsectors. Before 2008 data for all subsectors were reported on a cash basis. Financial assets are reported at market value, and liabilities at nominal value. Foreign debt is converted to national currency using end-of-year exchange rates.
Implementation of GFSM 2001/2014	There is a single accounting scheme applied to all general government units. As part of the migration plan to GFSM 2001, this accounting scheme is currently being revised to align with the International Public Sector Accounting Standards.

Côte d'Ivoire (662)

Information Last Updated	2015
Units of General Government	
1. Budgetary Central Government	Covered. 1.1 Legislative, Judiciary, and Executive bodies including ministries/departments. 1.2 Other agencies or funds: Economic and social council, various agencies.
2. Extrabudgetary Central Government	Covered. Autonomous agencies, General Pension Fund for Civil Servants.
3. Social Security Funds	Covered. National Social Security Fund, General Pension Fund for Civil Servants.
4. State Government	Not applicable.
5. Local Government	Not covered. 5.1 Budgetary local government units/entities: 197 municipalities, 31 regions, and 14 districts, and 107 departments. 5.2 Extrabudgetary local government units: No information available.
Compilation Practices	
Breaks in Series	None reported.
Compilation Notes	Data cover activities of subsector 1. Government Finance Statistics are compiled by the Ministry of Economy and Finance, Directorate of Economic Forecasting and Analysis.
Implementation of GFSM 2001/2014	Côte d'Ivoire is a member country of the West Africa Economic and Monetary Union (WAEMU). Over the medium term, the next steps will include full implementing of the GFSM 2001/2014 framework by 2017.

Croatia (960)

Information Last Updated 2015

Units of General Government

1. Budgetary Central Government
1.1 Legislative, Judiciary, and Executive bodies including ministries/departments.
1.2 Other agencies or funds:
Not applicable.

2. Extrabudgetary Central Government
2.1 Croatian Motorways Ltd., 2.2 Croatian Privatization Fund (see Data Coverage), 2.3 Croatian Roads Ltd., Croatian Waters, 2.4 Development and Employment Fund (see Data Coverage), 2.5 Fund for Environmental Protection and Energy Efficiency, 2.6 Regional Development Fund (see Data Coverage), 2.7 State Agency for Deposit Insurance and Bank Rehabilitation, 2.8 Agency for Management of the Public Property (AUDIO) (see Data Coverage), 2.9 Restructuring and Sale Center (CERP) (see Data Coverage).

3. Social Security Funds
Croatian Employment Service, Croatian Institute for Health Insurance, Croatian Pension Insurance Administration.

4. State Government
Not applicable.

5. Local Government
5.1 Budgetary local government units/entities:
City of Zagreb, 20 counties, 428 municipalities, and 127 towns.
5.2 Extrabudgetary local government units:
Not applicable.

Compilation Practices

Breaks in Series
† Starting in 2002, data for subsectors of central government are presented on a gross basis (i.e., before consolidation).

† Starting in 2006, data for public sector debt transactions (7017) in Table 7 also include outlays for underwriting and floating loans.

Compilation Notes
Data in central government tables cover subsectors 1–3. Units 2.5 and 2.7 existed as extrabudgetary units only in 2002. In later years, they have been part of budgetary central government. Unit 2.6 started operating in 2004. All contributions and the majority of the outlays of the social security funds in subsector 3 were included in subsector 1 since 2001 (unit 3.3), and 2002 (units 3.1 and 3.2), respectively.
In 2007 all the transactions of the social security funds are included in subsector 1. Starting 2008, unit 2.1 has been excluded from the general government sector. Unit 2.2 operated until 31st March 2011. From 1st April 2011 until 30th September 2013, unit 2.9 operated, which had included unit 2.2 and a former budgetary central government user – Central State Administrative Office for State Property Management. Since 1st October 2013, the tasks of unit 2.9 have been taken over by a budgetary central government user, the State Office for Management of State Property (DUUDI) and the newly founded extrabudgetary user of the State Budget – the Restructuring and Sale Center (CERP).

Data in local government tables cover the operations of 20 counties, City of Zagreb, and 32 towns, representing between 70 and 80 percent of the total operations in this subsector. As a result, not all expense for grants to other levels of general government units are eliminated in consolidation of the general government sector.

Data for Table 7, Functional Classification of Outlays, are not compiled from the same sources as Tables 2 and 3. As a result, total outlays as reflected in Table 7 differ from the sum of Expense (Table 2) and the Net acquisition of nonfinancial assets (Table 3).

Data for all subsectors are reported on a cash basis.

Debt liabilities are reported at face value.

Implementation of GFSM 2001/2014
Reporting in the GFSM 2001 format started in 2004. Pilot compilations of the full coverage of local government have been made, in order to provide a time series of satisfactory length to be published in the near future.

Cyprus (423)

Information Last Updated 2015

Units of General Government

1. Budgetary Central Government
1.1 Legislative, Judiciary, and Executive bodies including ministries/departments.
1.2 Other agencies or funds:
Independent services and offices.

2. Extrabudgetary Central Government
Aids Fund, Bank of Cyprus Oncology Centre, Council for the Preservation of the Memory of the Eoka Liberation Struggle 1955-1959, Cyprus Agricultural Payments Organization, Cyprus Broadcasting Corporation, Cyprus Children's Fund Committee, Cyprus Cultural Foundation, Cyprus Handicraft Services, Cyprus Investment Promotion Agency, Cyprus News Agency, Cyprus Organization for the Promotion of Quality, Cyprus Sports Organization, Cyprus State Scholarship Authority Foundation, Cyprus Theatrical Theatre Organization, Cyprus Tourism Organization, Cyprus University of Technology, Cyprus Youth Board, Education A' Fund, Energy Conservation and the Promotion of Utilization of Renewable Energy Sources, Financial Stability Fund, Fund for Travel Allowance to the Disabled, Funds for Additional Tax on Petrol, Funds for the Construction of Cyprus Museum, Funds of Listed Buildings for Maintenance of Old Renovated Buildings, Improvement of Community Forests, Investment Fund, Open University of Cyprus, Public Loans Fund, Relief Fund for Affected Persons, Research Promotion Foundation, School Committees, Turkish-Cypriot Property Administration Fund, University of Cyprus, Welfare Lottery Fund, Welfare Fund National Guard Personnel.

3. Social Security Funds
Central Holiday Fund, Insolvency Fund, Medical Treatment Scheme Fund, Redundancy Fund, Social Insurance Fund, Regular Employees Provident Fund.

4. State Government
Not applicable.

5. Local Government
5.1 Budgetary local government units/entities:
Districts (6), Municipalities (39), Village authorities (349).
5.2 Extrabudgetary local government units:
Not applicable.

Compilation Practices

Breaks in Series
None reported.

Compilation Notes
Data in general government tables cover operations of subsectors 1–3 and 5.
Data in local government tables cover operations of subsector 5.
Data are reported after FISIM allocation.
Data for all subsectors are reported on a noncash basis, consistent with the European System of Accounts, 1995 (ESA95).
Financial assets and liabilities are reported at market value.

Implementation of GFSM 2001/2014
Cyprus participates in the Eurostat GFS convergence project with the IMF.

Information Last Updated 2017

Units of General Government

1. Budgetary Central Government

Covered.
Central budgetary organizations - legislative, judiciary, and executive bodies including ministries/departments
Other agencies or funds:
National Fund and Privatizations Accounts.

2. Extrabudgetary Central Government

Partially covered.
Balmed Praha, state enterprise*
Central semi-budgetary organizations (0/209 units)*
Council for Public Supervisory over Audit*
CPP Transgas, state enterprise*
Czech Export Bank (CEB)*
Czech-Moravian Guarantee and Development Bank (CMZRB)*
Czech Radio*
Czech TV*
Export Guarantee and Insurance Corporation (EGAP)*
Financial Market Guarantee System*
Galileo Real*
IMOB*
Institute "Vesela veda"*
Investor Compensation Fund*
MUFIS*
Prisko, joint stock company*
Public research institutions (0/70 units)*
Public universities (0/26 units)*
Railway Infrastructure Administration, state organization (SZDC)*
School legal entities – university nursery schools (0/5 units)*
State Agricultural Intervention Fund
State Cinematography Fund
State Cultural Fund of the Czech Republic
State Environmental Fund of the Czech Republic
State Fund for Transport Infrastructure
State Housing Development Fund
Support and Guarantee Agricultural and Forestry Fund (PGRLF)*
Vine-grower Fund*

3. Social Security Funds

Partially covered.
Association of health insurance companies (0/3 units)*
Health Insurance Bureau*
Health insurance companies (0/7 units)

4. State Government

Not applicable.

5. Local Government

Partially covered.
Budgetary local government units/entities:
Municipalities and town councils (approx. 6300/6300 units)
Regional councils of cohesion regions (7/7 units)
Regional offices (14/14 units)
Voluntary association of municipalities (743/743)
Extrabudgetary local government units*:
Community interest entities (0/23 units)
Institutes (0/2 units)
Interest grouping of legal entities (0/18 units)
Local semi-budgetary organizations (0/ approx. 10340)
Public corporations as limited liability companies or join stock companies (0/13 units)
Public health facilities with the legal form of a limited liability company or joint-stock company and owned by an entity in the general government sector (0/43 units)
Public research institutions (0/1 unit)
School legal entities (0/3 units)

Compilation Practices

Breaks in Series

None reported.

Compilation Notes

The data are partially consolidated, if the required information is available.

Implementation of GFSM 2001/2014

Over the medium term, the next steps will include improving the statistical coverage of general government, and compiling accrual-recorded data.
The Ministry of Finance intends to ensure data on a cash basis for all units in S.1311 (excluding budgetary organizations and state funds) by means of a new law and corresponding decree. This step aims to fulfill the commitment resulting from the Directive 2011/85/EU of 8 November 2011 on requirements for Budgetary Frameworks of the Member States, as well as to collect source data for Statement of sources and uses of cash.
The Ministry of Finance in cooperation with the Czech Statistical Office (CZSO) intends to disseminate accrual data within GFS Yearbook and for this purpose to use "Eurostat Option" and data compiled by the CZSO for national accounts.
The Ministry of Finance in cooperation with the Czech Statistical Office (CZSO) intends to disseminate accrual data within GFS Yearbook and for this purpose to use "Eurostat Option" and data compiled by the CZSO for national accounts.

Denmark (128)

Information Last Updated	2015
Units of General Government	
1. Budgetary Central Government	1.1 Legislative, Judiciary, and Executive bodies including ministries/departments. 1.2 Other agencies or funds: Agencies, Monarchy.
2. Extrabudgetary Central Government	State church, government agencies.
3. Social Security Funds	Social security fund.
4. State Government	Not applicable.
5. Local Government	5.1 Budgetary local government units/entities: 5 regions, 98 municipalities, regional and municipal agencies. 5.2 Extrabudgetary local government units: No information available.
Compilation Practices	
Breaks in Series	In 2007, there was a structural change in the sectors of general government. The number of municipalities was reduced from 278 to 98. The 14 counties were abolished and replaced by 5 regions. Moreover, there was a shift of responsibilities between the central and local governments. From 1991, data are compiled in accordance with the ESA 95.
Compilation Notes	Data cover activities of subsectors 1-3 and 5. Government Finance Statistics are compiled by the Statistics Denmark.
Implementation of GFSM 2001/2014	Denmark participates in the Eurostat GFS convergence project with the IMF.

Dominica (321)

Information Last Updated	2015
Units of General Government	
1. Budgetary Central Government	1.1 Legislative, Judiciary, and Executive bodies including ministries/departments. 1.2 Other agencies or funds: Not applicable.
2. Extrabudgetary Central Government	Statutory Bodies.
3. Social Security Funds	Dominica Social Security Scheme.
4. State Government	Not applicable.
5. Local Government	5.1 Budgetary local government units/entities: 10 parishes. 5.2 Extrabudgetary local government units: No information available.
Compilation Practices	
Breaks in Series	
Compilation Notes	Data cover activities of subsector 1. Government Finance Statistics are compiled by the Ministry of Finance.
Implementation of GFSM 2001/2014	No information available.

Dominican Republic (243)

Information Last Updated	2015
Units of General Government	
1. Budgetary Central Government	1.1 Legislative, Judiciary, and Executive bodies including ministries/departments. 1.2 Other agencies or funds: 20 Secretariats.
2. Extrabudgetary Central Government	46 extrabudgetary units/entities.
3. Social Security Funds	Dominican Social Security Institute (IDSS), Institute of Assistance and Housing (INAVI), Superindendent of Health and Labor Risks (SISARIL), National Social Security Council, National Health Insurance (SENASA)
4. State Government	Not applicable.
5. Local Government	5.1 Budgetary local government units/entities: 317 Municipalities. 5.2 Extrabudgetary local government units: No information available.
Compilation Practices	
Breaks in Series	Through 2003, the subsectors of central government are presented on a net basis (i.e., after consolidation). Starting in 2004, data for the subsectors of central government are presented on a gross basis (i.e., before consolidation). From 2004 onwards, data are on a noncash
Compilation Notes	Data in central government sector covers activities of subsectors 1-3. Government finance statistics are compiled by the Central Bank.
Implementation of GFSM 2001/2014	Over the medium term, the next steps will include improving the integrated management system with the objective of recording information on both accrual and cash basis.

Egypt (469)

Information Last Updated	2017
Units of General Government	
1. Budgetary Central Government	Covered. 1.1 Legislative, Judiciary, and Executive bodies including ministries/departments. 1.2 Other agencies or funds: 27 governorates, and 157 public service authorities.
2. Extrabudgetary Central Government	Partially covered. National Investment Bank.
3. Social Security Funds	Partially covered. National Organization for Social Insurance (NOSI, comprising two funds).
4. State Government	Not covered.
5. Local Government	Not covered.
Compilation Practices	
Breaks in Series	Prior to 2008, data for the subsectors of central government exclude any flows that have another government unit as a counterpart. From 2002 onward, data pertaining to revenue, expense, and transactions in nonfinancial assets are compiled on a cash basis following the classifications of GFSM 2001. Financing data are derived from national classifications that are not aligned with the GFSM 2001 methodology. Prior to 1996, data in the central government tables include the operations of the Public Authority for Insurance and Pensions (pensions for government employees) and the Public Authority for Social Insurance (pensions for public enterprise employees), which were incorrectly included as social security funds, and exclude the operations of GASC.
Compilation Notes	Data cover activities of subsectors 1-3.
Implementation of GFSM 2001/2014	No information available.

El Salvador (253)

Information Last Updated	2017
Units of General Government	
1. Budgetary Central Government	1.1 Legislative, Judiciary, and Executive bodies including ministries/departments. 1.2 Other agencies or funds: No information available.
2. Extrabudgetary Central Government	National Register of Natural Persons (RNPN), National Institute of Sports of El Salvador (INDES), Salvadoran Institute for the Development of Women (ISDEMU), El Salvador Social Investment Fund for Local Development (FISDL), Agency for the Promotion of Investment and Exports (PROESA), Salvadoran Pre-investment Fund (FOSEP), Salvadoran Institute of Municipal Development (ISDEM), National Academy of Public Security (ANSP), Technical Executing Unit for the Justice Sector (UTE), National Quality Council (Began operating in November 2012), University of El Salvador (UES), National Hospitals (30), Public Health Council (CSSP), Salvadoran Institute for Rehabilitation of the Disabled (ISRI), "Narcisa Castillo" Home for the Aged, Santa Ana, Salvadoran Red Cross, Health Solidarity Fund (FOSALUD), Salvadoran Institute for Cooperative Development (INSAFOCOOP), Salvadoran Institute for Professional Training (INSAFORP), Protection Fund for the Disabled and Handicapped as a Result of the Armed Conflict, International Fair and Convention Center of El Salvador (CIFCO), National Science and technology Council (CONACYT), Public Accounting and Auditing Supervisory Council (CVPCPA), Salvadoran Coffee Council (CSC), General Superintendency of Electricity and Telecommunications (SIGET), National Electricity and Telephony Investment Fund (FINET), National Registries Center (CNR), Emergency Fund for Coffee (FEC), Salvadoran Sugar Council (CONSAA), Competition Superintendency (SC), Consumer Ombudsman (DC), National Energy Board (CNE), Salvadoran Institute for Agrarian Reform (ISTA), National Center for Agricultural and Forestry Technology (CENTA), National Agriculture School (ENA), Road Maintenance Fund (FOVIAL), Civil Aviation Authority (AAC), Maritime Ports Authority (AMP), Environmental Fund of El Salvador (FONAES), Salvadoran Institute of Tourism (ISTU), Nation Children and Adolescents Council (CONNA), National Directorate of Medicines(DNM)(Began operating in July 2012), Salvadoran Corporation of Tourism (CORSATUR), Salvadoran Institute for the Integral Development of Children and Adolescents (ISNA), National Council for Administration of Goods (CONAB).
3. Social Security Funds	National Public Employee Pension Institute (INPEP), Armed Forces Social Insurance Institute (IPSFA), Salvadoran Institute for Teachers' Welfare (ISBM), Salvadoran Social Security Institute (ISSS).
4. State Government	Not applicable.
5. Local Government	5.1 Budgetary local government units/entities: 262 Municipalities (255 reported in 2015) 5.2 Extrabudgetary local government units: No information available.
Compilation Practices	
Breaks in Series	None reported.
Compilation Notes	Data in central government tables cover operations of subsectors 1–3. Data in local government tables cover operations of 255 units of subsector 5. Nonfinancial assets are reported at historical values, financial assets and liabilities at nominal value.
Implementation of GFSM 2001/2014	Continue efforts to reflect the standards of the GFSM 2001 through the following activities: implementation of the International Public Sector Accounting Standards and revision of national budget classification to conform to those standards; incorporation of the 262 municipalities; inclusion of information on goods for public use in government assets, by assigning an economic value in line with the market valuation of the assets; revision of institutional classification of public units; implementation of financial management and accounting systems with a view to generating statements and tables in accordance with the GFSM 2001; improvement of consolidation procedures; introduction of a functional classification of government expenditure in line with COFOG; and, the publication of GFS in the website of the Ministry of Finance.

Estonia (939)

Information Last Updated	2015
Units of General Government	
1. Budgetary Central Government	1.1 Legislative, Judiciary, and Executive bodies including ministries/departments. 1.2 Other agencies or funds: No information available.
2. Extrabudgetary Central Government	20 foundations, 6 hospitals, 16 public-legal institutions.
3. Social Security Funds	Estonian Health Insurance Fund and Estonian Unemployment Insurance Fund.
4. State Government	Not applicable.
5. Local Government	5.1 Budgetary local government units/entities: 39 city councils, and 202 municipalities. 5.2 Extrabudgetary local government units: 19 hospitals (established by municipalities as foundations).
Compilation Practices	
Breaks in Series	During 2006, Statistics Estonia carried out a major revision of the national accounts data since 2000. Data for the general government sector were revised in parallel. From 1997, the local governments fiscal year changed from end March to end December. In 1995 - 1996, Local governments data refer to end March 31 fiscal year.
Compilation Notes	Data cover activities of subsectors 1-3 and 5.
Implementation of GFSM 2001/2014	Estonia participates in the Eurostat GFS convergence project with the IMF.

Ethiopia (644)

Information Last Updated	2015
Units of General Government	
1. Budgetary Central Government	1.1 Legislative, Judiciary, and Executive bodies including ministries/departments. 1.2 Other agencies or funds: Office of (the President, Prime Minister, Auditors General, Palace Administration, National Election Board, Documentation, Authentication and Registration, Government Communication Affairs, Ethiopian Intellectual Property Right, National Council for the Coordination of Public Participation on the Construction of the Grand Renaissance Dam, Ethiopian National Accreditation and Insurance Fund), Other Entities (32 Universities and Others).
2. Extrabudgetary Central Government	Food Price Subsidies Fund, Fuel Administration Fund, Industrial Development Fund and Privatization, National Disaster Prevention and Preparedness Fund Administration, Road Fund Administration Office.
3. Social Security Funds	Social Security Agency.
4. State Government	4.1 Budgetary state government units/entities: 2 administrative councils, 9 regional governments. 4.2 Extrabudgetary state government units: No information available.
5. Local Government	5.1 Budgetary local government units/entities: 66 zones, 550 woredas (districts) 5.2 Extrabudgetary local government units: No information available.
Compilation Practices	
Breaks in Series	None reported.
Compilation Notes	Data cover activities of subsector 1. Government Finance Statistics are compiled by the Ministry of Finance and Economic Development (MoFED).
Implementation of GFSM 2001/2014	No information available.

Fiji (819)

Information Last Updated	2015
Units of General Government	
1. Budgetary Central Government	Covered. 1.1 Legislative, Judiciary, and Executive bodies including ministries/departments. 1.2 Other agencies or funds: Not applicable.
2. Extrabudgetary Central Government	Not covered. No information available.
3. Social Security Funds	Not applicable.
4. State Government	Not applicable.
5. Local Government	Not covered. 5.1 Budgetary local government units/entities: No information available. 5.2 Extrabudgetary local government units: No information available.
Compilation Practices	
Breaks in Series	None reported.
Compilation Notes	Data cover the operations of subsector 1. Government Finance Statistics for budgetary central government are compiled by the Ministry of Finance.
Implementation of GFSM 2001/2014	Fiji participates in the Asia Pacific Island harmonization project with the IMF and funded by the Government of Japan. Over the medium term, Fiji Bureau of Statistics will be extending the coverage of data to extrabudgetary and other general government

Finland (172)

Information Last Updated	2015
Units of General Government	
1. Budgetary Central Government	1.1 Legislative, Judiciary, and Executive bodies including ministries/departments. 1.2 Other agencies or funds: Institutions and other bodies.
2. Extrabudgetary Central Government	Fire Protection Fund, Fund for Compensation of Oil Damages, Fund for Development of Farm Economy, Fund for Security of Supply, Government Guarantee Fund, Housing Fund, Intervention Fund for Agriculture, Nuclear Waste Fund, State Guarantee Fund, Universities (16), Solidium Ltd., Leijona Catering Ltd.
3. Social Security Funds	Burial and redundancy assistance funds (62), Education Fund, Employment pension corporations (7), Obligatory employment pension foundations (15), Employment pension funds (7), Other obligatory employment pension institutions (6), Sickness funds (141139), Social Insurance Institution, Unemployment benefit funds (32), Unemployment Insurance Fund.
4. State Government	Not applicable.
5. Local Government	5.1 Budgetary local government units/entities: Joint municipal boards established by municipalities (166162), Municipalities (336), Government of Åland and Pension Fund of the Government of Åland, Association of Finnish Municipalities and Local Authority Employers Finland, Municipal Guarantee Board, Länsimetro Oy. 5.2 Extrabudgetary local government units: No information available.
Compilation Practices	
Breaks in Series	Break symbols in Table 7 for health and social protection indicate that, from 1991 onward, data for social protection include partial data for health. Break symbols in Table 3 indicate that beginning in 1991 a separation between long- and short-term bonds cannot be made for domestic financing or financing abroad.
Compilation Notes	Data for budgetary central government also cover extrabudgetary units and entities. Data in central government tables cover operations of subsectors 1–3. Data in local government tables cover operations of subsector 5. Data are reported after FISIM allocation. Data for all subsectors are reported on a noncash basis, consistent with the national accounts of general government prepared according to the European System of Accounts, 1995 (ESA95).
Implementation of GFSM 2001/2014	Finland participates in the Eurostat GFS convergence project with the IMF.

France (132)

Information Last Updated	2015
Units of General Government	
1. Budgetary Central Government	1.1 Legislative, Judiciary, and Executive bodies including ministries/departments. 1.2 Other agencies or funds: Budget agencies.
2. Extrabudgetary Central Government	150 universities and colleges, government hospitals, government agencies.
3. Social Security Funds	A main general social security scheme (Family Benefits, Illness, Old Age, Worker's Compensation), unemployment compensation schemes, numerous other schemes.
4. State Government	Not applicable.
5. Local Government	5.1 Budgetary local government units/entities: 100 departments, 26 regions, 36000 (approximately) communes. 5.2 Extrabudgetary local government units: Primary and secondary schools, local government agencies.
Compilation Practices	
Breaks in Series	None reported.
Compilation Notes	Data cover activities of subsectors 1-3 and 5. Government Finance Statistics are compiled by the Institut National de la Statistique et des Etudes Economiques (Insee).
Implementation of GFSM 2001/2014	France participates in the Eurostat GFS convergence project with the IMF.

Georgia (915)

Information Last Updated	2015
Units of General Government	
1. Budgetary Central Government	1.1 Legislative, Judiciary, and Executive bodies including ministries/departments. 1.2 Other agencies or funds: Several scientific academies, and inspectorates.
2. Extrabudgetary Central Government	Not applicable.
3. Social Security Funds	Not applicable.
4. State Government	Not applicable.
5. Local Government	5.1 Budgetary local government units/entities: 64 units reported. Adjaria Autonomous Republic, Abkhazia Autonomous Republic, and 62 administrative districts, towns, and cities. 5.2 Extrabudgetary local government units: No information available.
Compilation Practices	
Breaks in Series	From 2007, data are consolidated and classified in accordance with the GFSM 2001 framework. In 2009, liabilities: other account payable includes non-interest bearing deposits that were taken over from the privatized banks.
Compilation Notes	Data cover activities of subsectors 1 and 5. Government Finance Statistics are compiled by the Ministry of Finance.
Implementation of GFSM 2001/2014	Over the medium term, the next steps will include improving the migration plan towards the GFSM 2001/2014 framework.

Germany (134)

Information Last Updated 2017

Units of General Government

1. Budgetary Central Government

Covered.
1.1 Legislative, Judiciary, and Executive bodies including ministries/departments.
1.2 Other agencies or funds:
Not applicable.

2. Extrabudgetary Central Government

Covered.
Special asset funds and public funds, institutions and enterprises classified to central government.

3. Social Security Funds

Covered.
German Old-age Pensions Insurance (Deutsche Rentenversicherung Bund), German Old-age Pensions Insurance Knappschaft-Bahn-See (Deutsche Rentwenversicherung Knappschaft-Bahn-See), Federal Association of Agricultural Retirement (Gesamtverband der Landwirtschaftlichen Alterskassen), Statutory Health Insurance, Social Long-term Care Insurance, Federal Employment Agency and the Statutory accident insurance.
In addition non-market producers controlled by social security funds are classified in this subsector.

4. State Government

Covered.
4.1 Budgetary state government units/entities:
16 core budget units (the Länder).
4.2 Extrabudgetary state government units.
Extrabudgetary state government units.

5. Local Government

Covered.
5.1 Budgetary local government units/entities:
12,000 (approximately) municipalities and municipal associations.
5.2 Extrabudgetary local government units:
Extrabudgetary local government units.

Compilation Practices

Breaks in Series

None reported.

Compilation Notes

In Germany, general government non-financial accounts are compiled by the Federal Statistical Office (Destatis). For information on methods, procedures and sources used for the compilation of deficit and debt data and the underlying government sector accounts, please follow this link http://ec.europa.eu/eurostat/documents/1015035/7110762/DE-EDP-Inventory-201512.pdf.

Figures on general government financial accounts are provided by the Deutsche Bundesbank; detailed information on financial accounts are available on the website of Deutsche Bundesbank following the link

http://www.bundesbank.de/Navigation/EN/Statistics/Macroeconomic_accounting_systems/Financial_accounts/financial_accounts.html

Implementation of GFSM 2001/2014

Data on nonfinancial and financial transactions of general government are recorded in line with ESA 2010 and then converted to the current GFSM format.

Ghana (652)

Information Last Updated 2015

Units of General Government

1. Budgetary Central Government

1.1 Legislative, Judiciary, and Executive bodies including ministries/departments.
1.2 Other agencies or funds:
Subvented agencies and public universities.

2. Extrabudgetary Central Government

District Assemblies Common Fund, Ghana Education Trust Fund, National Health Insurance Fund, Road Fund.

3. Social Security Funds

Not applicable.

4. State Government

Not applicable.

5. Local Government

5.1 Budgetary local government units/entities:
6 metropolitan assemblies, 46 municipal assemblies, 164 district assemblies, and 10 regional coordinating councils.
5.2 Extrabudgetary local government units:
Not applicable.

Compilation Practices

Breaks in Series

None reported.

Compilation Notes

Data in the central government tables cover the operations of subsectors 1 and 2.
Government Finance Statistics are compiled by the Ministry of Finance and Economic Planning.

Implementation of GFSM 2001/2014

No information available.

Greece (174)

Information Last Updated	2015
Units of General Government	
1. Budgetary Central Government	1.1 Legislative, Judiciary, and Executive bodies including ministries/departments. 1.2 Other agencies or funds: Not applicable.
2. Extrabudgetary Central Government	167 central government units for administrative purposes, Museums and libraries (64), National stadiums/athletic centers (18), Press agencies (1), Research institutions (54), Social welfare and charity agencies (60), State universities and other educational institutions (88), Theaters (13), State owned enterprises reclassified into central government (16).
3. Social Security Funds	Public hospitals (129), Social insurance organizations (42).
4. State Government	Not applicable.
5. Local Government	5.1 Budgetary local government units/entities: 325 municipalities, 13 regions, 522 Legal entities public law, 155 Legal entities private law. 5.2 Extrabudgetary local government units: Not applicable.
Compilation Practices	
Breaks in Series	Until 2007, data for budgetary central government also covered extrabudgetary central government units and entities. Starting in 2002, legal entities public law and private law are included in subsector 5. Data prior to 2002 include only municipalities.
Compilation Notes	Data cover activities of subsectors 1-3 and 5. Data for all subsectors are reported on a noncash basis, consistent with the European System of Accounts, 2010 (ESA2010). Government Finance Statistics are compiled by the Hellenic Statistical Authority (EL.STAT.).
Implementation of GFSM 2001/2014	Greece participates in the Eurostat GFS convergence project with the IMF.

Grenada (328)

Information Last Updated	2015
Units of General Government	
1. Budgetary Central Government	1.1 Legislative, Judiciary, and Executive bodies including ministries/departments. 1.2 Other agencies or funds: Not applicable.
2. Extrabudgetary Central Government	Tourism Board.
3. Social Security Funds	National insurance scheme.
4. State Government	Not applicable.
5. Local Government	5.1 Budgetary local government units/entities: 6 parishes.
Compilation Practices	
Breaks in Series	None reported.
Compilation Notes	Data cover activities of subsector 1. Government Finance Statistics are compiled by the Ministry of Finance.
Implementation of GFSM 2001/2014	No information available.

Guatemala (258)

Information Last Updated	2015
Units of General Government	
1. Budgetary Central Government	1.1 Legislative, Judiciary, and Executive bodies including ministries/departments. 1.2 Other agencies or funds: Not applicable.
2. Extrabudgetary Central Government	23 government agencies and institutes, National Statistical Institute, University San Carlos of Guatemala.
3. Social Security Funds	Guatemalan Social Security Institute, Military Force Social Security Institute.
4. State Government	Not applicable.
5. Local Government	5.1 Budgetary local government units/entities: 333 Municipalities and other local bodies. 5.2 Extrabudgetary local government units: No information available.
Compilation Practices	
Breaks in Series	From 1996 onward, the data reflect a number of reclassifications in line with GFSM 2001 methodology.
Compilation Notes	Data cover activities of subsector 1. Government Finance Statistics are compiled by the Ministry of Public Finance.
Implementation of GFSM 2001/2014	Over the medium term, the next steps will include broadening the statistical coverage to incorporate extrabudgetary units; developing and implementation of a single Chart of Accounts for the general government.

Information Last Updated	2015
Units of General Government	
1. Budgetary Central Government	Covered. 1.1 Legislative, Judiciary, and Executive bodies including ministries/departments, agencies not engaged in a power state and other institutions with operational independence but not financial. 1.2 Other agencies or funds: Not applicable.
2. Extrabudgetary Central Government	Not covered. 4 universities, 13 public entities.
3. Social Security Funds	Covered. Honduran Institute of Social Security (IHSS), National Institute of Retirement and Pensions of Executive Branch Employees (INJUPEMP), and National Social Insurance Institute for Judiciary Employees (INPREMA) and Institute of Military Prevision (IPM).
4. State Government	Not applicable.
5. Local Government	Partially covered. 5.1 Budgetary local government units/entities: 298 municipalities 5.2 Extrabudgetary local government units: No information available.
Compilation Practices	
Breaks in Series	None reported.
Compilation Notes	Data cover activities of subsectors 1-3 and 5. For subsector 5, data are estimated based on partial information.
Implementation of GFSM 2001/2014	Over the medium term, the next steps are advancing the public financial accounting system in line with international standards.

Information Last Updated	2017
Units of General Government	
1. Budgetary Central Government	Covered. Constitutional Court, Law Courts, Office of Ombudsman, Office of Public Prosecutors, Parliament, Presidency of the Republic, State Audit Office, Ministries, Prime Minister's Office, Central Statistical Office, Economic Competition Office, National Tax and Customs Administration, Hungarian Academy of Arts and Hungarian Academy of Sciences, Transfers to local governments, Main revenues and expenditures of the Central Budget, Repayments of lending and borrowing cost of the Central Budget, Developments from European Union subsidy (technical chapters, managed by the Minister for National Economy, Revenues and expenditures related to state property (managed by the Minister for National Development), Revenues and expenditures of National Land Fund, Research and Technological Innovation Fund, Central Nuclear Financial Fund, Wesselényi Miklós Flood and Groundwater Protection Indemnity Fund, Bethlen Gabor Fund (former Homeland Fund), Labor Market Fund, National Cultural Fund, Saving Cooperatives Integration Fund.
2. Extrabudgetary Central Government	Covered. Hungarian State Holding Company Ltd. (Magyar Nemzeti Vagyonkezelo Zrt., MNV Zrt., former State Privatization and Property Management Co., APV Zrt.), Media corporations (Hungarian Television Co. – Magyar Televizio Nonprofit Zrt., Duna Television Co. – Duna Televizio Nonprofit Zrt.; Hungarian Broadcasting Co. – Magyar Radio Nonprofit Zrt., Hungarian Press Co. – Magyar Tavirati Iroda Nonprofit Zrt), State Debt Management Co. (Allamadossag Kezelo Kozpont Zrt., AKK Zrt.), National Infrastructural Development Co. (Nemzeti Infrastruktura Fejleszto Zrt., NIF Zrt.), National Toll Payment Services Private Company Limited by Shares (Nemzeti Útdíjfizetési Szolgáltató Zrt., NÚSZ Zrt., former State Motorway Management Co., AAK Zrt.), Hungarian Tourism Company (Magyar Turizmus Zrt.), Állami Vagyonnyilvántartási Kft., National Philharmony Real Estate Co.: Nemzeti Filharmonia Ingatlanfejlesztesi Kft., merged with former Duna Museum Real Estate Co. (Duna Muzeum Ingatlan¬fejleszto Kft.) and House of Traditions Real Estate Co. (Hagyomanyok Haza Ingatlanfejleszto Kft.), MAV Start Co. (MAV Start Vasuti Szemelyszallito Zrt.), National Theatre (Nemzeti Szinhaz Kiemelkedoen Kozhasznu Nonprofit Zrt.), Nitrokemia Environmental Protection Consuting and Ministering Incorporated Company (Nitrokemia Kornyezetvedelmi Tanacsado es Szolgaltato Zrt.), Regional Development Holding Co. (Regionalis Fejlesztesi Holding Zrt.), Palace of Arts Co. (Muveszetek Palotaja Kulturális Szolgáltato Kft.), National Asset Manager Company (Nemzeti Eszkozkezelo Zrt.), Savings Cooperatives Integration Unit (Szövetkezeti Hitelintézetek Integrációs Szervezete, SZHISZ), BM Heros Javító, Gyártó, Szolgáltató és Kereskedelmi Zrt., Corvinus Nemzetközi Befektetési Zrt., FŐKEFE Rehabilitációs Foglalkoztató Ipari Közhasznú Nonprofit Kft., HM Currus Gödöllői Harcjárműtechnikai Zrt., HM Armcom Kommunikációtechnikai Zrt., HM Elektronikai, Logisztikai és Vagyonkezelő Zrt., KIVING Ingatlangazdálkodó és Beruházásszervező Kft., MNKH Magyar Nemzeti Kereskedőház Zrt., MVM Paks II.Atomerőmű Fejlesztő Zrt., ND Nemzeti Dohánykereskedelmi Nonprofit Zrt., Nemzeti Eszközgazdálkodási Zrt., NISZ Nemzeti Infokommunikációs Szolgáltató Zrt., 117 nonprofit institutions, public foundations, and public nonprofit corporations reclassified as central government units by the Hungarian Statistical Office based on statistical survey (2014), Pension Reform and Debt Reduction Fund.
3. Social Security Funds	Covered. Health Care Fund, Pension Fund.
4. State Government	Not applicable.
5. Local Government	Covered. 1 capitol, 23 capitol districts, 19 county governments, and 3,200 municipalities, Local minority governments, Gotthard-Therm Thermal Bath and Tourism Co. (Gotthard-Therm Furdo es Idegenforgalmi Kft.), Nyirseg Water Supply Engineering Co. (Nyirsegi Vizgazdalkodasi Tarsulat), Csepeli Townscape Co. (Csepeli Városkép Kft.), Szolnok Television Co. (Szolnok Televizio Zrt.), SZINT Company (SZINT Szegedi Intezmenytakarito Zrt.), Zalaegerszeg Television Co. (Zalaegerszegi Varosi Televizio Kft.), 98 nonprofit institutions, public foundations, and public nonprofit corporations reclassified as local government units by the Hungarian Statistical Office based on a statistical survey (2013).
Compilation Practices	
Breaks in Series	Data in central government tables cover operations of subsectors 1–2. Data cannot be broken down into GFS budgetary and extra-budgetary subsectors. Data in local government tables cover operations of subsector 5 and are based on information from all local governments and units reclassified into Local Government sector.
Compilation Notes	Data for all subsectors are reported on a noncash basis, consistent with the European System of Accounts, 2010 (ESA10). Liquidation or complementary period: None. Valuation of assets and liabilities: Market value for financial accounts, as in the national accounts. Nonfinancial assets are recorded using acquisition cost less tax depreciation. Maastricht Debt — memorandum item in Table 6 – is calculated according to the EU Excessive Deficit Procedure. National accounts data on nonfinancial assets and consumption of fixed capital (CFC) are available within 2⊠3 years. CFC is only available for SNA/ESA sectors (central government, social security, local government) and cannot be classified according to COFOG, in Table 7, or in Tables 2 and 3 and Statement of Government Operations.
Implementation of GFSM 2001/2014	Hungary participates in the Eurostat GFS Convergence project with the IMF. This institutional table is based on information reported in 2015.

Iceland (176)

Information Last Updated	2015
Units of General Government	
1. Budgetary Central Government	Covered. 1.1 Legislative, Judiciary, and Executive bodies including ministries/departments. 1.2 Other agencies or funds: Government agencies, public colleges and universities, and public health service units.
2. Extrabudgetary Central Government	Not applicable.
3. Social Security Funds	Covered. Health Insurance Scheme, Insurance for occupational injuries, Pension and disability schemes, Unemployment Insurance Scheme.
4. State Government	Not applicable.
5. Local Government	Covered. 5.1 Budgetary local government units/entities: 78 municipalities, including public nursery and primary schools and old age residential institutions. 5,2 Extrabudgetary local government units: Municipal Equalization Fund
Compilation Practices	
Breaks in Series	In August 1996, some education functions (mainly teachers' salaries) were transferred from central government to local governments. In 1996, the additional expenses of local governments were financed by way of an increased transfer from central government to local governments, and from 1997, by way of higher individual income tax at local government level (central government individual income tax was lowered accordingly).
Compilation Notes	Data cover activities of subsectors 1-3 and 5. Government Finance Statistics are compiled by Statistics Iceland.
Implementation of GFSM 2001/2014	Over the medium term, the next steps will include obtaining data for stocks of nonfinancial assets.

India (534)

Information Last Updated	2015
Units of General Government	
1. Budgetary Central Government	1.1 Legislative, Judiciary, and Executive bodies including ministries/departments. 1.2 Other agencies or funds: No information available.
2. Extrabudgetary Central Government	Not applicable.
3. Social Security Funds	Not applicable.
4. State Government	4.1 Budgetary state government units/entities: 28 states (with separate legislatures), and 2 union territories (with separate legislatures). 4.2 Extrabudgetary state government units: No information available.
5. Local Government	5.1 Budgetary local government units/entities: Committees, development boards, municipal boards, other local units, and port trusts. 5.2 Extrabudgetary local government units: No information available.
Compilation Practices	
Breaks in Series	None reported.
Compilation Notes	Data cover activities of subsectors 1-3.
Implementation of GFSM 2001/2014	No information available.

Indonesia (536)

Information Last Updated	2015
Units of General Government	
1. Budgetary Central Government	Covered. 1.1 Legislative, Judiciary, and Executive bodies: 86 line ministries and non-ministerial agencies. 1.2 Other agencies or funds: General State Treasurer, Semi-autonomous Agencies/Public Service Agencies.
2. Extrabudgetary Central Government	Partially covered. 89 Non-structural Agencies and other extrabudgetary entities.
3. Social Security Funds	Partially covered. Social security scheme.
4. State Government	Covered. 4.1 Budgetary provincial government units/entities: 33 provinces (including the capital and 2 special districts). 4.2 Extrabudgetary provincial government units: No information available.
5. Local Government	Covered. 5.1 Budgetary local government units/entities: 505 Local governments and municipalities. 5.2 Extrabudgetary local government units: No information available.
Compilation Practices	
Breaks in Series	Starting 2005, budgetary central government data are compiled according to a revised set of bridge tables and classifications and are thus not strictly comparable with those in prior years. Prior to 2000, natural resources oil and gas revenue were classified as corporate income tax. Data through 1999 cover fiscal years ending March 31. Data for 2000 cover the period April 1 through December 31, 2000. Starting 2001, the fiscal year ends December 31. Prior to 1999, tax on income, profits, and capital gains could not be broken into its components, and almost all of the income tax was classified as taxes paid by individuals. Prior to 1994, certain revenue components of Other Revenue were not separately identified and were instead included under Miscellaneous and Unidentified Revenue. Also prior to 1994, certain expenditure items of Social Protection; Housing and Community Amenities; and Agriculture, Forestry, Fishing, and Hunting were not separately identified and were instead included under General Public Services. Through 1993 data in provincial government tables cover operations of subsector 4 and are based on information from all provinces.
Compilation Notes	Data cover activities of subsector 1, 4, 5. Data for subsector 1, 4, and 5 are reported on a modified cash basis, which records flows in cash basis and stock in accrual basis.
Implementation of GFSM 2001/2014	The government will implement accrual accounting in 2015. Government Finance Statistics are compiled by the Ministry of Finance in 2001 format and government will move to 2014 format. Government will prepare quarterly general government from 2016.

Iraq (433)

Information Last Updated	2015
Units of General Government	
1. Budgetary Central Government	Covered. 1.1 Legislative, Judiciary, and Executive bodies including presidency of republic, prime minister office, and 26 ministries and their agencies. 1.2 Other agencies and funds: 1.2 Kurdistan Regional Government.
2. Extrabudgetary Central Government	Not applicable.
3. Social Security Funds	Not covered. Social Security Fund, Retirement Fund for Government Employees, Construction Fund.
4. State Government	Not applicable.
5. Local Government	Not covered. 5.1 Budgetary local government units/entities: 400 Municipalities, Amanat Baghdad 5.2 Extrabudgetary local government units: No information available.
Compilation Practices	
Breaks in Series	None reported.
Compilation Notes	Data cover the operations of subsector 1.
Implementation of GFSM 2001/2014	No information available.

Ireland (178)

Information Last Updated	2015
Units of General Government	
1. Budgetary Central Government	1.1 Legislative, Judiciary, and Executive bodies including ministries/departments. 1.2 Other agencies or funds: No information available.
2. Extrabudgetary Central Government	34 Central government units with individual budgets.
3. Social Security Funds	Social Insurance Fund.
4. State Government	Not applicable.
5. Local Government	5.1 Budgetary local government units/entities: 5 borough councils, 5 city councils, 29 county councils, and 75 town councils, as well as 2 regional assemblies and 8 regional authorities. 5.2 Extrabudgetary local government units: 33 vocational education committees.
Compilation Practices	
Breaks in Series	Prior to January 1, 2005, health services in Ireland were administered through regional health boards, which were included in the subsector Local Government. These were replaced by a single body, the Health Service Executive (HSE), which is responsible for the delivery of health services nationwide. The HSE is classified as a unit of Central Government, and from 2005 its activities were included directly in the accounts of the Central Government subsector 1.1. From 1995, income from value-added taxes (VAT) has been accrued with figures for prior years recorded on a cash basis. Accrual adjustments for the revenue and expense of central government departments are made for years 1995 onward. Other accrual adjustments for excise duties, pay-as-you-earn (PAYE) income taxes, and social insurance contributions have only been made for the years 1997 onward.
Compilation Notes	Data cover activities of subsectors 1, 3, and 5. Government Finance Statistics are compiled by the Department of Finance.
Implementation of GFSM 2001/2014	Ireland participates in the Eurostat GFS convergence project with the IMF.

Israel (436)

Information Last Updated	2015
Units of General Government	
1. Budgetary Central Government	1.1 Legislative, Judiciary, and Executive bodies including ministries/departments. 1.2 Other agencies or funds: Not applicable.
2. Extrabudgetary Central Government	4 bi-national research funds, Compensation Fund, various nonprofit institutions controlled and mainly financed by the government (such as environmental organizations; health care funds; universities, education, research, culture, religion, and welfare institutions; etc.).
3. Social Security Funds	National insurance institute.
4. State Government	Not applicable.
5. Local Government	5.1 Budgetary local government units/entities: 260 (approximately) Local government units (local councils, municipalities, regional councils). 5.2 Extrabudgetary local government units: 180 (approximately) religious councils.
Compilation Practices	
Breaks in Series	None reported.
Compilation Notes	Data cover activities of subsectors 1-3 and 5. Government Finance Statistics are compiled by the Central Bureau of Statistics (CBS).
Implementation of GFSM 2001/2014	No information available.

Italy (136)

Information Last Updated	2017
Units of General Government	
1. Budgetary Central Government	Covered. Legislative, Judiciary, and Executive bodies including ministries/departments.
2. Extrabudgetary Central Government	Covered. Economic services producers (50), Institutions providing cultural services and assistance at the central level (57), Research bodies (38).
3. Social Security Funds	Covered. Social security funds and institutions (22).
4. State Government	Not applicable.
5. Local Government	Covered. Budgetary local government units/entities: Chambers of commerce (124), Institutions providing education, cultural services, and assistance at the local level (529), Mountain community development bodies (246), Municipalities (8,092), Municipalities' unions (430), Other economic bodies at local level (359), Producers of health services at local level (249), Provinces (107), Regions (20), and autonomous provinces (2).
Compilation Practices	
Breaks in Series	None reported.
Compilation Notes	Data for central government includes both budgetary central government and extrabudgetary central government units and entities. Data are reported after FISIM allocation. Data for all subsectors are reported on a noncash basis, consistent with the European System of Accounts, 2010 (ESA2010). Financial assets and liabilities are reported at market value.
Implementation of GFSM 2001/2014	Italy participates in the Eurostat GFS convergence project with the IMF. The list of units is based on and coherent with information published in October 2014, with the release of the complete general government ESA2010 accounts.

Jamaica (343)

Information Last Updated	2016
Units of General Government	
1. Budgetary Central Government	Covered. Auditor General, Governor General's office, Houses of Parliament, 15 ministries, Office of the Public Defender, Office of the Contractor General, Office of the Services Commission, Office of Children's Advocate, Office of the Prime Minister, Office of the Cabinet, and Independent Commission of Investigations.
2. Extrabudgetary Central Government	Covered. Human Employment and Resource Training (HEART) Trust , National Housing Trust, National Health Fund, Spectrum Management Authority, The Office of Utilities Regulations, The Sports Development Foundation, Bureau of Standards Jamaica, Betting, Gaming and Lotteries Commission, Culture, Health, Arts Sports and Education Fund (CHASE), Jamaica Racing Commission, Public Accountancy Board, Overseas Examination Commission, Transport Authority.
3. Social Security Funds	Covered. National Insurance Fund.
4. State Government	Not applicable.
5. Local Government	Kingston and St. Andrew Corp, Portmore Municipal Council, St. Thomas Parish Council, St Catherine Parish Council, Clarendon Parish Council, Manchester Parish Council, St. Elizabeth Parish Council, St. Mary Parish Council, St. Ann Parish Council, Trelawny Parish Council, St. James Parish Council, Hanover Parish Council, Westmoreland Parish Council, Portland Parish Council.
Compilation Practices	
Breaks in Series	Starting in 2003, data are not strictly comparable with those reported through 2002 owing to changes in classification and the adoption of a noncash basis of reporting.
Compilation Notes	Data cover activities of subsectors 1-5. Government Finance Statistics are compiled by Ministry of Finance and Planning.
Implementation of GFSM 2001/2014	No information available.

Japan (158)

Information Last Updated	2015
Units of General Government	
1. Budgetary Central Government	1.1 Legislative, Judiciary, and Executive bodies including ministries/departments. 1.2 Other agencies or funds: General Accounts and Special Accounts.
2. Extrabudgetary Central Government	70 (approximately) units/entities.
3. Social Security Funds	Partially covered. Social security funds.
4. State Government	Not applicable.
5. Local Government	5.1 Budgetary local government units/entities: Ordinary Accounts and Public Management Business Accounts of 1,800 (approximately) local public entities. 5.2 Extrabudgetary local government units: Local Independent Administrative Agencies.
Compilation Practices	
Breaks in Series	Data are for fiscal year ending March 31 except for data for balance sheet summary and Tables 4, 5, 6, and 9, which represent data for December 31. Financial transaction data, financial asset and liability data, and property income data are not consolidated.
Compilation Notes	Data cover activities of subsectors 1-3 and 5. Government Finance Statistics are compiled by the Economic and Social Research Institute, Cabinet Office.
Implementation of GFSM 2001/2014	No information available.

Jordan (439)

Information Last Updated	2015
Units of General Government	
1. Budgetary Central Government	1.1 Legislative, Judiciary, and Executive bodies including ministries/departments. 1.2 Other agencies or funds: Chief Justice for religious affairs, Jordan Valley Authority, and Royal Jordanian Geographic Center.
2. Extrabudgetary Central Government	Covered. 9 Government agencies.
3. Social Security Funds	Health Security Fund.
4. State Government	Not applicable.
5. Local Government	5.1 Budgetary local government units/entities: Greater Amman Municipality, 172 municipalities, 350 village councils. 5.2 Extrabudgetary local government units: No information available.
Compilation Practices	
Breaks in Series	None reported.
Compilation Notes	Data cover activities of subsectors 1-3 and 5. Government Finance Statistics are compiled by the Ministry of Finance.
Implementation of GFSM 2001/2014	No information available.

Kazakhstan (916)

Information Last Updated 2015

Units of General Government

1. Budgetary Central Government

Covered.
1781 units reported.
2.1.1 Legislative, Judiciary, and Executive bodies including ministries (12/12), agencies (1/1) and others (13/13).
2.1.2 Other agencies or funds:
National Fund of the Republic of Kazakhstan.
Budgetary central government units (1754/1754).

2. Extrabudgetary Central Government

Not applicable.

3. Social Security Funds

Covered.
1 unit reported.
State Social Insurance Fund.

4. State Government

Not applicable.
2.4.1 Budgetary state government units/entities:
Not Applicable

5. Local Government

Covered.
2.5.1 Budgetary local government units/entities:
10745 units reported.
2 cities (Almaty and Astana), 14 oblast bodies, 10729 budgetary local government units.
2.5.2 Extrabudgetary local government units:
Not Applicable.

Compilation Practices

Breaks in Series

From 2013, the data for budgetary central government and local governments include extrabudgetary resources of budgetary units.
From 2013, the general government data include the State Social Insurance Fund.
From 2009 onward, the data for budgetary central government include transactions of the National Fund of the Republic of Kazakhstan.
From 2005, a mandatory social insurance system (State Social Insurance Fund) was established outside budgetary central government.
From 1999, the budgetary central government data include social security and extrabudgetary funds, except the National Fund of the Republic of Kazakhstan.

Compilation Notes

Data cover activities of subsectors 1, 3, and 5.
Data disseminated for general government sector cover tables 1-3, 7, 8, and partially table 6.
Time series for revenue and expense for general government sector cover 1997 to 2014.
Data are recorded on a cash basis for subsectors 1 and 5, and a non-cash basis for subsector 3.
Fixed assets are valued at historical cost. Financial assets and liabilities are valued at face value.
The following flows are consolidated: grants, interest, transactions in loans and securities other than shares. The following stocks are consolidated: stocks of securities other than shares.

Implementation of GFSM 2001/2014

GFS are compiled by the Ministry of Finance of the Republic of Kazakhstan.
Over the medium term, the next steps will include compiling and reporting accrual-recorded data for the whole general government.
This institutional information was reported in 2015 in the Government Finance Statistics Yearbook (GFSY).

Kenya (664)

Information Last Updated 2015

Units of General Government

1. Budgetary Central Government

1.1 Legislative, Judiciary, and Executive bodies including ministries/departments:
1.2 Other agencies or funds:
Consolidated Fund Services, Directorate of Personnel Management, Kenya Anti Corruption Commission, and Public Service Commission.

2. Extrabudgetary Central Government

Local Authorities Transfer Fund, Petroleum Development Fund, Roads Maintenance Levy Fund, and Rural Electrification Program.

3. Social Security Funds

National Hospital Insurance Fund, National Social Security Fund.

4. State Government

Not applicable.

5. Local Government

5.1 Budgetary local government units/entities:
46 municipal councils (including Nairobi city council), 62 town councils, and 67 county councils.
5.2 Extrabudgetary local government units:
No information available.

Compilation Practices

Breaks in Series

From 1997, data include reclassifications as a result of using the GFSM 1986 as reporting basis. From 1999, data were reported using the GFSM 2001 classification and presentation format.

Compilation Notes

Data cover activities of subsectors 1 and 5.
Government Finance Statistics are compiled by the Ministry of Finance & Planning.

Implementation of GFSM 2001/2014

No information available.

Kiribati (826)

Information Last Updated	2017
Units of General Government	
1. Budgetary Central Government	Covered.
2. Extrabudgetary Central Government	Covered.
3. Social Security Funds	Not applicable.
4. State Government	Not applicable.
5. Local Government	Covered. 5.1 Budgetary local government units/entities: Town(town) Councils (3), Island(rural) Councils (23). 5.2 Extrabudgetary local government units: No information available.
Compilation Practices	
Breaks in Series	None reported.
Compilation Notes	Data cover activities of subsectors 1 and 5. Government Finance Statistics are compiled by the Ministry of Finance.
Implementation of GFSM 2001/2014	Over the medium term, the next steps include collecting additional cash information and updating the chart of accounts to facilitate expansion of coverage and adopting the International Public Sector Accounting Standards.

Korea, Republic of (542)

Information Last Updated	2015
Units of General Government	
1. Budgetary Central Government	Covered. 1.1 Legislative, Judiciary, and Executive bodies including ministries/departments. 1.2 Other agencies or funds: 65 funds (including social security funds).
2. Extrabudgetary Central Government	Covered. 172 nonmarket nonprofit institutions.
3. Social Security Funds	Covered. Included in Budgetary central government (Employment Insurance Fund, Industrial Accident Compensation Insurance and Prevention Fund, Korea Teachers Pension Fund, and National Pension Fund).
4. State Government	Not applicable.
5. Local Government	Covered. 5.1 Budgetary local government units/entities: 9 metropolitan cities, 8 provinces 228 basic local government units, 17 education special accounts. 5.2 Extrabudgetary local government units: 90 nonmarket nonprofit institutions.
Compilation Practices	
Breaks in Series	None reported.
Compilation Notes	Data cover activities of subsectors 1-3 and 5. Government Finance Statistics are compiled by the Ministry of Finance and Economy.
Implementation of GFSM 2001/2014	Over the medium term, the next steps will include improving the migration plan towards the GFSM 2001 framework, and compiling accrual-recorded data.

Kosovo, Republic of (967)

Information Last Updated 2017

Units of General Government

1. Budgetary Central Government

Covered.
1.1 Legislative, Judiciary, and Executive bodies including ministries/departments: Assembly, Office of the President, Office of the Prime Minister. Ministries: Ministry of Finance, Ministry of Public Administration, Ministry of Agriculture Forestry and Rural Development, Ministry of Trade and Industry, Ministry of Infrastructure, Ministry of Health, Ministry of Culture Youth and Sports, Ministry of Education, Science and Technology, Ministry of Labor and Social Welfare, Ministry of Environment, Ministry of Community and Return, Ministry of Local Government Administration, Ministry of Economic Development, Ministry of Internal Affairs, Ministry of Justice, Ministry of Foreign Affairs, Ministry of Kosovo Security Force, Ministry of European Integrations, Ministry of Diaspora.
1.2 Other agencies or funds: Anticorruption Agency, Privatization Agency of Kosovo, Kosovo Property Agency, Kosovo Intelligence Agency, Agency for the Management of Memorial Complexes, National Agency for the Personal Data Protection, Agency for Free Legal Aid, Agency for Air Navigation Service.
1.3 Authorities and Offices: Regulatory Authority of Electronic and Postal Communications, Railway Regulatory Authority, Civil Aviation Authority, Kosovo Competition Authority, Energy Regulatory Office, Water and Wastewater Regulatory Office, Office of the General Auditor.
1.4 Councils and Commissions: Kosovo Judicial Council, Independent Oversight Board for the Civil Service, Kosovo Council for Cultural Heritage, Independent Commission for Mines and Minerals, Independent Media Commission, Central Election Commission, Public Procurement Regulatory Commission, Kosovo Academy of Science and Arts.
1.5 Other: University of Prishtina, Procurement Review Body, Election Complaints and Appeals Panel, Ombudsperson Institution, State Prosecutor, Constitutional Court, Kosovo Judicial Institute.

2. Extrabudgetary Central Government Not applicable.

3. Social Security Funds Not applicable.

4. State Government Not applicable.

5. Local Government

Covered.
Decan, Dragash, Ferizaj, Fushe Kosovo, Gjakove, Gjilan, Gllogoc (Drenas)Hani I Elezit, Istog, Junik, Kacanik, Kamenice, Kline, Leposaviq, Lipjan, Malisheve, Mamusha, Mitrovice, Novo Berde, Obiliq, Peje, Podujeve, Prishtine, Prizren, Rahovec, Shterpce, Shtime, Skenderaj, Suhareke, Viti, Vushtrri, ZubinPotok, Zvecan, Gracanice, Kollokt, Mitrovica North, Partesh, Ranillug.

5.2 Extrabudgetary local government units:
No extrabudgetary information was provided.

Kosovo Financial Information Manag[illegible] The consolidation of the central and local governments is automatic through the local government sub-sectors as per the GFSM 20[illegible] [illegible]Ministry of Finance has not yet published dis-aggregated data on the central and

Compilation Notes Data are recorded on a cash basis, however, liabilities are recorded fo[illegible] [illegible]d deposits.

Implementation of GFSM 2001/2014 Government Finance Statistics are compiled by the Ministry of Finance.The Min[illegible] of Finance plans to present dis-aggregated data by central and local government in 2017. The Ministry of Finance also plans to start publishing high frequency preliminary GFSM 2014 compliant data in 2017.

Kuwait (443)

Information Last Updated 2015

Units of General Government

1. Budgetary Central Government

1.1 Legislative, Judiciary, and Executive bodies including ministries/departments.
1.2 Other agencies or funds:
Not applicable.

2. Extrabudgetary Central Government

Kuwait Fire Department, Kuwait Institute for Scientific Research, Kuwait University, Municipality of Kuwait, National Assembly of Kuwait, and Zakat House (religious provident endowment fund) and 8 public authorities (including the Environment Public Authority and the Public Authority for Assessment of Damages Resulting from Iraqi Invasion).

3. Social Security Funds Public Institution for Social Security.

4. State Government Not applicable.

5. Local Government Not applicable.

Compilation Practices

Breaks in Series

From 1997, data include the operations of the Environment Public Authority.
Starting 2000, the fiscal year ends March 31 instead of June 30.

Compilation Notes

Data cover activities of subsectors 1 and 2.
Government Finance Statistics are compiled by the Ministry of Finance.

Implementation of GFSM 2001/2014 No information available.

Kyrgyz Republic (917)

Information Last Updated 2016

Units of General Government

1. Budgetary Central Government

Covered.
1.1 Legislative, Judiciary, and Executive bodies including ministries/departments.
1.2 Other agencies or funds:
17 state agencies, Central Commission for Elections and Referendums, Constitutional Court, Financial Market Supervision and Regulation Service, International University, National Statistics Committee, Ombudsman, Public Unions and Organizations, Issyk-Kul Oblast Development Fund, Naryn Oblast Development Fund, Reserve Fund (Kyrgyz Republic Development Fund).

2. Extrabudgetary Central Government

Not applicable.

3. Social Security Funds

Partially covered.
Kyrgyz Republic Social Fund, Mandatory Health Insurance Fund with the Government of the Kyrgyz Republic.

4. State Government

Not applicable.

5. Local Government

Covered.
5.1 Budgetary local government units/entities:
2 cities under republican jurisdiction (Bishkek and Osh), 4 districts (rayons) under City of Bishkek, 12 cities under provincial (oblast) jurisdiction, 11 cities under district (rayon) jurisdiction, 469 rural settlements - aiyl okmotu.
5.2 Extrabudgetary local government units:
No information available.

Compilation Practices

Breaks in Series

From 2013 onward, the data for budgetary central government include extrabudgetary funds, previously excluded from the republican budget.
From 2013 onward, the general government data include the Kyrgyz Republic Social Fund and the Mandatory Health Insurance Fund.

Compilation Notes

Data cover activities of subsectors 1, 3, and 5.
Data disseminated for general government sector cover tables 1-3, 7, and table 6. Table 7 excludes the splitting between divisions 702 and 703, and detail for groups (sub-divisions); the total amount for two divisions is attributed to 703.
Time series for revenue and expense for general government sector cover 1993 to 2012.
Data are recorded on a cash basis for subsectors 1, 3 and 5.
Fixed assets are valued at historical cost. Financial assets and liabilities are valued at book value.
The following flows are consolidated: grants, interest, transactions in securities other than shares. The following stocks are consolidated: securities other than shares.

Implementation of GFSM 2001/2014

GFS are compiled by the Mi[illegible] [illegible]yrgyz Republic.
Over the medium [illegible]ps will include implementing the new GFSM 2014-based Chart of Accounts, compiling and reporting quarterly a[illegible], including the balance sheet, for the whole general government.

Lao People's Democratic Republic (544)

Information Last Updated 2015

Units of General Government

1. Budgetary Central Government

1.1 Legislative, Judiciary, and Executive bodies including ministries/departments.
1.2 Other agencies or funds:
17 provinces and 139 districts.

2. Extrabudgetary Central Government

Road Fund and other extrabudgetary funds.

3. Social Security Funds

Social security scheme.

4. State Government

Not applicable.

5. Local Government

Not applicable.

Compilation Practices

Breaks in Series

None reported.

Compilation Notes

Data cover activities of subsector 1.
Government Finance Statistics are compiled by the Ministry of Finance.

Implementation of GFSM 2001/2014

Over the medium term, the next steps will include improving the migration plan towards the GFSM 2001 framework.
A revised chart of accounts, linked to GFSM 2014 classifications, will implemented in 2016. It is expected that detailed GFSM 2014 data will be compiled by 2017.

Latvia (941)

Information Last Updated 2015

Units of General Government

1. Budgetary Central Government
1.1 Legislative, Judiciary, and Executive bodies including ministries/departments.
1.2 Other agencies or funds
2 Public foundations; 45 Capital companies controlled and financed by central government (reclassified enterprises from S.11 to S.13 following 50% criterion), 5 Organizations non-financed from the budget, 54 Derived public persons partially financed from the budget.

2. Extrabudgetary Central Government
Not applicable.

3. Social Security Funds
Government Special Social Insurance Budget, State Social Insurance Agency.

4. State Government
Not applicable.

5. Local Government
5.1 Budgetary local government units/entities:
Municipalities of 9 cities under state jurisdiction, Amalgamated municipalities of 110 counties, Indirect local government organizations, Capital companies controlled and financed by local government (reclassified enterprises from S.11 to S.13 following 50% criterion).
5.2 Extrabudgetary local government units:
Not applicable.

Compilation Practices

Breaks in Series
The information below explaining breaks in data series refers to the data reported in 1995-2013 in the Government Finance Statistics Yearbook (GFSY) and published till 2014. From 2004, all extrabudgetary funds data are included in the budgetary central government. From 2002, revenue and expense data for budgetary central government, extrabudgetary accounts, and social security funds are presented on a gross basis. Before 2002, these data are presented net of grants among these central government units. In 1997, there were shifts of education and health functions among the components of central government, and between local government and central government. From 1996, data in the local government tables cover the operations of subsector 5; prior to 1996, data cover the operations of component 5.1 only. Prior to 1996, social security operations were included in the budgetary accounts. Also, prior to 1996, data exclude the operations of extrabudgetary entities (subsector 2).

Compilation Notes
Data reported in 1995 - 2013 in the Government Finance Statistics Yearbook (GFSY) and published till 2014 cover activities of subsectors 1, 3, and 5.
Government Finance Statistics were compiled by the Treasury of the Republic of Latvia regarding the data. Technical specifications of metadata with regards to the GFS data for FY 2013 are provided by the Central Statistical Bureau of Latvia.

Implementation of GFSM 2001/2014
Latvia participates in the Eurostat GFS convergence project with the IMF since 2014.

Lebanon (446)

Information Last Updated 2017

Units of General Government

1. Budgetary Central Government
Covered.
1.1 Legislative, Judiciary, and Executive bodies including ministries/departments.
1.2 Other agencies or funds:
Not applicable.

2. Extrabudgetary Central Government
Not covered.
Agency for Lebanese Standards and Specifications, Bureau for Tobacco, Center for Civil Aviation Safety, Committee of Control on Insurance Companies, Council for Development and Reconstruction, Council of the South, Displaced Fund, Educational Center for Research and Development, Elissar Agency, Higher Relief Committee, Internal Fund for Vocational and Technical Education, International Exhibition of Rashid Karameh, Investment Development Authority of Lebanon (IDAL), Lebanese University, National Archives Agency, National Council for Scientific Research, National Institute of Administration, National Employment Agency, National Fund for the Displaced, National Higher Institute of Music, National Office of Medicine, Organization on Traffic Management, Machines and Transportation, Organization for Establishment and Management of Industrial Parks, Project for Activating Animal Products, Public Agency for Consumption Markets, Public Agency for Securing Investments, Railways and Public Transportation Agency, Solidarity Fund for the Lebanese University Teachers, Sports City Agency, Public Hospitals, and Scientific Agricultural Research Agency.

3. Social Security Funds
Not covered.
National Social Security Fund.

4. State Government
Not covered.

5. Local Government
Not covered.
5.1 Budgetary local government units/entities:
42 unions of municipalities and 943 Municipalities.
5.2 Extrabudgetary local government units:
No information available.

Compilation Practices

Breaks in Series
Prior to 1999, excise taxes levied on imported products are included with other import duties.

Compilation Notes
Data cover activities of subsector 1.
Government Finance Statistics are compiled by the Ministry of Finance.

Implementation of GFSM 2001/2014
No information available.

Lesotho (666)

Information Last Updated	2015
Units of General Government	
1. Budgetary Central Government	1.1 Legislative, Judiciary, and Executive bodies including ministries/departments. 1.2 Other agencies or funds: Monarchy, public service commission.
2. Extrabudgetary Central Government	Basotho Enterprise Development Corporation, Lesotho Communication Authority, Lesotho Electricity Authority, Lesotho Revenue Authority, National Aids Commission Petroleum Fund, and Road Fund.
3. Social Security Funds	Not applicable.
4. State Government	Not applicable.
5. Local Government	5.1 Budgetary local government units/entities: 10 District Councils (including 128 Community Councils), and Maseru City Council. 5.2 Extrabudgetary local government units: No information available.
Compilation Practices	
Breaks in Series	None reported.
Compilation Notes	Data cover activities of subsectors 1, 2, and 5. Government Finance Statistics are compiled by the Ministry of Finance and Development Planning.
Implementation of GFSM 2001/2014	No information available.

Liberia (668)

Information Last Updated	2015
Units of General Government	
1. Budgetary Central Government	1.1 Legislative, Judiciary, and Executive bodies including ministries/departments. 1.2 Other agencies or funds: Bureau of state enterprises, Mano River union, National food assistance agency, General auditing commission, National Election Commission, Public procurement and concessions commission, Centre for national records and archives, Liberia anti corruption commission, Land Commission, Liberia extractive industries initiative, Human Rights commission, John F,Kennedy medical center , Phebe hospital, Liberian institute of biomedical Research, Liberia medicines and human regulatory authority, National aids commission, Jackson F Doe hospital, National commission on disabilities, National veteran bureau, 2 universities, 12 tertiary educational Institution, West African examination council, Environmental protection Agency, cooperation Development Agency, National investment commission, Liberia industrial property system, and Liberia copyright office, National lottery. Other agencies.
2. Extrabudgetary Central Government	Forestry development authority, Liberia water and sewer corporation, Liberia produce marketing corporation, Liberia rubber Development authority, Liberia Broadcasting System, National housing authority, National transit authority, Liberia electricity corporation, Monrovia transit authority, National housing and savings bank, Liberia airport authority, Liberia industrial free zone authority, Liberian maritime authority, National Ports authority, and Bureau of concessions.
3. Social Security Funds	National Social Security and Welfare Corporation.
4. State Government	Not applicable.
5. Local Government	5.1 Budgetary local government units/entities: 15 countries and 133 districts. Monrovia City Corporation and several other local government units. 5.2 Extrabudgetary local government units: No information available.
Compilation Practices	
Breaks in Series	In 2007, revenue, expense, net cash flow from investments in nonfinancial assets rose sharply following the government's strong effort to improve tax and customs administration, and to improve the pace of expenditure approvals by the Cash Management Committee (IMF Country Report No. 06/412). Operations of all local governments (excluding Monrovia) are presently reported under the Ministry of Internal Affairs.
Compilation Notes	Data cover activities of subsectors 1 and 5. Government Finance Statistics are compiled by the Ministry of Finance.
Implementation of GFSM 2001/2014	Over the medium term, the next steps including broadening the coverage and depth of GFS, including financial balance sheet.

Information Last Updated	2015
Units of General Government	
1. Budgetary Central Government	Covered. 1.1 Legislative, Judiciary, and Executive bodies including ministries/departments. 1.2 Other agencies or funds: National museums, National Parks, Public higher education institutions, Regional Offices and Research Institutes.
2. Extrabudgetary Central Government	Covered. Fund for Decommission of Ignalina Nuclear Power Station, State Enterprise Ignalina Nuclear Power Plant, State Enterprise Lithuanian Oil Products Agency, Public enterprise Turto Bankas, Guarantee Fund, Reserve (Stabilization) Fund, State Enterprise Deposit and Investment Insurance, Privatization Fund, License Warehouse Fund, Account for plants, which direct payments are paid for, insurance contributions to agricultural entities and partial compensation of expenditure incurred by insurance undertakings. Health care institutions, National Centre of Remote Sensing and Geoinformatics "GIS-Centras", Agriculture Information and Rural Business Centre, Agricultural Loan Guarantee Fund, Lithuanian National Radio and Television (LRT).
3. Social Security Funds	Covered. State Social Security Fund, Compulsory Health Insurance Fund.
4. State Government	Not applicable.
5. Local Government	Covered. 5.1 Budgetary local government units/entities: 60 local governments and nonprofit institutions (including nursing homes, pre-primary, primary, and secondary schools, etc.), which are controlled and mainly financed by local governments. 5.2 Extrabudgetary local government units: Municipal Enterprise Vilniaus Miesto Bustas (Vilnius City Housing) and public health care institutions established by municipalities.
Compilation Practices	
Breaks in Series	Starting in 2010 due to changed methodology in 2014, 4 additional State Enterprises have been included into the subsector of Extrabudgetary Funds: Deposit and Investment Insurance, Lithuanian Oil Products Agency, National Centre of Remote Sensing and Geoinformatics „GIS-Centras", Agriculture Information and Rural Business Centre. Starting in 2011, the State Enterprise Ignalina Nuclear Power Plant is included in the Central Government subsector. Starting in 2009, the following revisions were introduced: interest expenditure of local governments is on an accrual basis, as well as other current expesne. From 2006, the data on the central government includes joint-stock company "Turto Bankas" and the "Public Enterprise State Property Fund". From October 2014 Public Enterprise State Property Fund was reorganised and merged with Public Enterprise Turto Bankas. In 2007 the data on central government for 2001-2005 was revised to include the recording of guarantees, on-lent loans, and some capital transfers to households (restitution of confiscated property through financial compensation, and compensation for lost savings). From 2001, the data on central government was revised to include revenue includes grants received from the European Union; accruals of value-added taxes and excises are derived from time-adjusted cash data; accruals of interest are calculated for budgetary central government; consumption of fixed capital is introduced (the data are provided by Statistics Lithuania); and privatization outlays and receipts of local governments are included. From 2000, data for social security funds are reported on an accrual basis.
Compilation Notes	Data cover the operations of subsectors 1, 2, 3, and 5. Data for all subsectors are reported on a noncash basis, in accordance with the European System of Accounts, 2010. Assets and liabilities are valued at market value. Foreign currency-denominated liabilities are converted into domestic currency at the official exchange rate at the end of each accounting period. Gross debt at face value is also reported, whereas the accrued interest is not added to the principal of the underlying instrument but is classified under accounts payable or receivable. Government Finance Statistics are compiled by the Ministry of Finance.
Implementation of GFSM 2001/2014	Latvia participates in the Eurostat GFS convergence project with the IMF since 2012.

Luxembourg (137)

Information Last Updated	2017
Units of General Government	
1. Budgetary Central Government	Covered. 1.1 judiciary and legislative power, the Ministries and the Monarchy; 1.2 33 special funds and 60 "Services de l'Etat à Gestion Séparé".
2. Extrabudgetary Central Government	Covered. 2.1 various non-market public establishments with financial autonomy, e.g., the National Solidarity Fund and the Regional Development Fund for the Kirchberg Plateau 2.2 various non-market public corporations, e.g., the Luxembourgian National Railway Company (SNCFL).
3. Social Security Funds	Covered. 19 Social Protection Organisms.
4. State Government	Not applicable.
5. Local Government	Covered. 5.1 123 municipalities, of which 105 exist as per 01.01.2016 as the number of municipalities is steadily being reduced by the merger of municipalities; 5.2 30 social offices and 73 inter-communal associations of which 56 conduct activities, 15 ceased business operations and 3 were inactive (newly established or temporarily cessation of business) as per 01.01.2016.
Compilation Practices	
Breaks in Series	Coverage: Data in central government tables cover operations of subsectors 1–2. Data in Social Security Funds tables cover operations of subsector 3. Data in local government tables cover operations of subsector 5 and are based on information from all local governments. Valuation: Financial assets at market prices; loans and bonds at market value.
Compilation Notes	Liquidation or complementary period: The complementary period taken into account comprising January to March of the following year.
Implementation of GFSM 2001/2014	Data are consistent with public sector accounts and are on an accrual basis in accordance with ESA2010. This institutional table is based on information reported in 2015.

Macedonia, FYR (962)

Information Last Updated	2015
Units of General Government	
1. Budgetary Central Government	1.1 Legislative, Judiciary, and Executive bodies including ministries/departments. 1.2 Other agencies or funds: No information available.
2. Extrabudgetary Central Government	Special Revenue Accounts and Road Fund.
3. Social Security Funds	Health Insurance Fund, Employment Fund, and Pension and Disability Insurance Fund.
4. State Government	Not applicable.
5. Local Government	5.1 Budgetary local government units/entities: 85 Municipalities including the city of Skopje 5.2 Extrabudgetary local government units: No information available.
Compilation Practices	
Breaks in Series	None reported.
Compilation Notes	Data cover activities of subsectors 1-3. Government Finance Statistics are compiled by the Ministry of Finance.
Implementation of GFSM 2001/2014	No information available.

Madagascar (674)

Information Last Updated	2017
Units of General Government	
1. Budgetary Central Government	Covered. Legislative, executive and jurisdictional institutions.
2. Extrabudgetary Central Government	Partially covered. Government agencies (approximately 139 including 12 chambers of commerce, national printer and post office)
3. Social Security Funds	Covered. Caisse Nationale de la Prévoyance Sociale
4. State Government	Not applicable.
5. Local Government	Not covered. 22 regions, 119 districts, and 1693 communities.
Compilation Practices	
Breaks in Series	Madagascar changed its currency in 2005 from the Malagasy Franc to the Ariary Malagasy. There are no breaks in data series.
Compilation Notes	
Implementation of GFSM 2001/2014	Plans include moving concepts and valuation and to an "accrual basis".

Malawi (676)

Information Last Updated	2015
Units of General Government	
1. Budgetary Central Government	1.1 Legislative, Judiciary, and Executive bodies including ministries/departments. 1.2 Other agencies or funds: Malawi Human Rights Commission, Roads Fund.
2. Extrabudgetary Central Government	Competitions and Fair Trading Commission (CFCT), Health Service Regulatory Authority, Lilongwe University of Agriculture and Natural Resources (LUANAR), Malawi Broadcasting Corporation (MBC), Malawi College of Health Sciences (MCHS), Malawi Communications Regulatory Authority, Malawi Council for the Handicapped (MACOHA), Malawi Energy Regulatory Authority, Malawi Gaming Board (MGB), Malawi Institute of Education (MIE), Malawi Investment and Trade Centre (MITC), Malawi National Commission for UNESCO (MNC-UNESCO), Malawi National Council of Sports (MNCS), Malawi National Examination Board (MANEB), Malawi Revenue Authority, Malawi University of Science and Technology (MUST), Medical Council of Malawi (MCM) Mzuzu University, National Council for Higher Education (NCHE), National Herbarium and Botanic Gardens of Malawi (NHBG), National Commission of Science and Technology (NCST), National Construction Industry Council (NCIC), National Food Reserve Agency, National Library Services, National Oil Company of Malawi (NOCMA), National Water Resources Board (NWRB), National Youth Council of Malawi (NYCM), Nurses and Midwives Council of Malawi (NMCM), Pharmacy, Medicines and Poisons Board (PMPB), Public Private Partnership Commission, Small Medium Entrepreneurs Development Institute (SMEDI), Roads Authority (RA), Road Fund Administration, Technical, Entrepreneurial, Vocational Education and Training Authority (TEVETA), Tobacco Control Commission, University of Malawi.
3. Social Security Funds	Not applicable.
4. State Government	Not applicable.
5. Local Government	5.1 Budgetary local government units/entities: 4 city councils, 2 municipal councils, 1 town council, 28 district councils. 5.2 Extrabudgetary local government units: Not applicable.
Compilation Practices	
Breaks in Series	Data in central government tables cover operations of subsector 1.
Compilation Notes	Liabilities are recorded at issue price.
Implementation of GFSM 2001/2014	Over the next two years the authorities plan to implement a formal process to collect GFSM 2001/2014 data from extrabudgetary units, which will likely be on a noncash basis, with a view to widening coverage to general government. A working group is being established to consider options for moving to a modified cash basis of reporting of expenditure.

Malaysia (548)

Information Last Updated	2016
Units of General Government	
1. Budgetary Central Government	Covered. Legislative, Judiciary, and Executive bodies including ministries/departments.
2. Extrabudgetary Central Government	Not covered. 79 statutory bodies.
3. Social Security Funds	Covered. Social Security Organization (SOCSO) is included under the statutory bodies.
4. State Government	Not covered. 13 state governments.
5. Local Government	Not covered. 12 city councils, 38 municipal councils, 97 district councils, and 2 agencies with the functions of a local government (based on a list of entities used for the survey of the MOF's Economic Report.
Compilation Practices	
Breaks in Series	None reported.
Compilation Notes	Data cover the operations of subsector 1. In the Economic Report (ER) published by the Ministry of Finance of Malaysia (MOF), loans for development purposes (and the respective repayments) are considered part of expenditure. For the Government Finance Statistics Yearbook (GFSY), however, those items were reclassified into net acquisition of financial assets, according to the GFSM 2001 framework. Because of this, some aggregates and balancing items of the two publications are not directly comparable. The Federal Government debt data in the ER and the reclassified debt data under GFSM 2001 format are not directly comparable. The Federal Government debt data published by the MOF classifies debt based on currency of issue. Under the GFSM 2001 format, foreign holding of Federal Government domestic debt and financing are treated as foreign liabilities.
Implementation of GFSM 2001/2014	No information available.

Maldives (556)

Information Last Updated	2015
Units of General Government	
1. Budgetary Central Government	1.1 Legislative, Judiciary, and Executive bodies including ministries/departments. 1.2 Other agencies or funds: Independent Commissions, Schools and Hospitals, and other offices.
2. Extrabudgetary Central Government	Not applicable.
3. Social Security Funds	Not applicable.
4. State Government	Not applicable.
5. Local Government	Not applicable.
Compilation Practices	
Breaks in Series	None reported.
Compilation Notes	Data cover activities of subsector 1. Government Finance Statistics are compiled by the Ministry of Finance and Treasury.
Implementation of GFSM 2001/2014	The general government's cash flow statement is compiled according to the GFSM 2001 framework.

Mali (678)

Information Last Updated 2015

Units of General Government

1. Budgetary Central Government

1.1 Legislative, Judiciary, and Executive bodies including ministries/departments:
1.2 Other agencies or funds:
Cultural council, economic council, high council for local governments and territories, social council. These units are generally subdivided into one or more of the following services: administrative superstructures, centralized departments; headquarters staff; and connected and/or otherwise dependent units, funds, and commissions.

2. Extrabudgetary Central Government

Publicly owned administrative units (78).

3. Social Security Funds

National Institute of Social Providence.

4. State Government

Not applicable.

5. Local Government

5.1 Budgetary local government units/entities:
District (1), Regions (8), Cercles (49), and Communes (703).
5.2 Extrabudgetary local government units:
No information available.

Compilation Practices

Breaks in Series

None reported.

Compilation Notes

Data cover activities of subsector 1.
Government Finance Statistics are compiled by the Central Bank of West African States (BCEAO).

Implementation of GFSM 2001/2014

Mali is a member country of the West Africa Economic and Monetary Union (WAEMU).
In June 2009, the WAEMU Council of Ministers adopted a new public finance harmonized framework which includes six directives of which the common reporting format on Government Financial Operations (Tableau des Opérations Financières de l'Etat - TOFE) which is compatible with the international statistical methodology adopted by the Government Finance Statistics Manual 2001 (GFSM 2001). The member countries have until 2017 for full implementation of the framework after having incorporated the guidelines in their own legislation by late 2011.

Malta (181)

Information Last Updated 2015

Units of General Government

1. Budgetary Central Government

Covered.
1.1 Legislative, Judiciary, and Executive bodies including ministries/departments.
1.2 Other agencies or funds:
Not applicable.

2. Extrabudgetary Central Government

Covered.
Appoġġ, Bord Tal-Koperattivi, Broadcasting Authority, Employment and Training Corporation, Environment Protection Fund, Foundation for Educational Services, Foundation for Medical Services, Foundation for Tomorrow's Schools, Gozo Ferries Co Ltd, Grand Harbour Regeneration Corporation, Heritage Malta, Housing Authority, Identity Malta, Industrial Projects and Services Ltd, International Institute on Ageing, Karin Grech Rehabilitation Centre, Kunsill Malti għall-Isport, Malta College of Arts, Science and Technology, Malta Communications Authority , Malta Competition and Consumer Affairs Authority, Malta Council for Culture and the Arts, Malta Council for Economic and Social Development, Malta Council for Science and Technology, Malta Enterprise Corporation, Malta Gaming Authority, Malta Government Investments Ltd, Malta Government Technology Investments Ltd, Malta Information Technology Agency, Malta Philharmonic Orchestra, Malta Resources Authority, Malta Statistics Authority, Malta Tourism Authority, Manoel Theatre Management Committee, Medicines Authority, MEPA, MIMCOL, Mount Carmel Hospital, National Audit Office, National Commission Persons with Disability, Occupational Health and Safety Authority, Office of the Ombudsman, Property Management Services, Sapport, Sedqa - Agency against Drug and Alcohol Abuse, St James Cavalier Creativity Centre, Superintendence of Cultural Heritage, University of Malta, Valletta 2018 Foundation, WasteServ Malta Ltd.

3. Social Security Funds

Not applicable.

4. State Government

Not applicable.

5. Local Government

Covered.
5.1 Budgetary local government units/entities:
68 Local councils
5.2 Extrabudgetary local government units:
Not applicable.

Compilation Practices

Breaks in Series

Prior to 2007, the unit of currency is Liri. From 2008, the unit of currency is Euro.
From 2003, all data are on an accrual basis.
Prior to 1996, data are not strictly comparable with those from 1996 onwards. From 1996 through 2002, data reflect reclassifications in line with the GFSM 1986 methodology.

Compilation Notes

Data cover activities of subsectors 1, 2, and 5.

Implementation of GFSM 2001/2014

No information available.

Marshall Islands, Republic of (867)

Information Last Updated	2017
Units of General Government	
1. Budgetary Central Government	1.1 Legislative, Judiciary, and Executive bodies including ministries/departments. 1.2 Other agencies or funds: No information available.
2. Extrabudgetary Central Government	College of the Marshall Islands-CMI, Environmental Protection Authority-EPA, Land Registration Authority-LPA, Marshall Islands Marine Resources Authority-MIMRA, Marshall Islands scholarship grant and Loan Board, Marshall Islands Visitors Authority-MIVA, Marshall Islands Nuclear Claims Tribunal, The Health Care Revenue Fund.
3. Social Security Funds	Marshall Islands Social Security Administration, The Marshall Islands Health Fund.
4. State Government	Not applicable.
5. Local Government	5.1 Budgetary local government units/entities: Ailinglaplap Atoll, Ailuk Atoll, Arno Atoll, Aur Atoll, Bikini Atoll, Ebon Atoll, Enewetek-Ujelang Atoll, Erikub Atoll, Jabat Atoll, Jaluit Atoll, Kili Atoll, Kwajalein Ebeye Atoll, Lae Atoll, Lib Atoll, Likiep Atoll, Majuro Atoll, Maloelap Atoll, Mejit Atoll, Mili Atoll, Namdrik Atoll, Namu Atoll, Rongelap Atoll, Ujae Atoll, Utrik Atoll, Wotje Atoll. 5.2 Extrabudgetary local government units: Not applicable.
Compilation Practices	
Breaks in Series	None reported.
Compilation Notes	Data cover activities of subsectors 1, 2, and 5. No breakdown into subsector 5 is available. Expenditure by functions of government (Table 7) shows the composition of Expense, not including Net investment in nonfinancial assets. Government Finance Statistics are compiled by the Ministry of Finance.
Implementation of GFSM 2001/2014	No information available.

Mauritius (684)

Information Last Updated	2016
Units of General Government	
1. Budgetary Central Government	Covered. Legislative, Judiciary, and Executive bodies including ministries/departments.
2. Extrabudgetary Central Government	Covered. 116 Extra-Budgetary Units (including 7 Special Funds).
3. Social Security Funds	Covered. Social Security Fund.
4. State Government	Covered. Rodrigues Regional Assembly.
5. Local Government	Covered. 12 Local Government units comprising 5 Municipalities and 7 District Councils.
Compilation Practices	
Breaks in Series	Starting in 2010, all data are reported on a calendar year basis. Data prior to 2010 are on a financial year basis ending June 30. The intermediate six month (July to Dec 2009) period is not reflected in the database but is available on request. Starting in 2009, the Civil Service Protection Scheme became an integral part of the Budgetary Central Government. From 2002, data for the subsectors of central government are presented on a gross basis, and reciprocal transactions among them are eliminated separately. Starting in 2009, interest for the Budgetary Central Government is reported on a noncash basis (Cash data adjusted for accrued interest).
Compilation Notes	Data cover activities of the Consolidated General Government Sector comprising the units listed at 2.
Implementation of GFSM 2001/2014	Implementation of GFSM 2014 has started in 2015 and will continue in 2016. Social Security Funds has now been reclassified outside Central Government but within General Government. Compilation of the first Balance Sheet for Budgetary Central Government for period 2013 is still under process and will be submitted in 2016.

Micronesia, Federated States of (868)

Information Last Updated	2017
Units of General Government	
1. Budgetary Central Government	1.1 Legislative, Judiciary, and Executive bodies including ministries/departments. 1.2 Other agencies or funds: FSM National Postal Service, FSM Banking Board, FSM Insurance Board.
2. Extrabudgetary Central Government	Coconut Development Authority, College of Micronesia, National Oceanic Resource Management Authority(NORMA), Chuuk State Housing Authority, Kosrae Port Authority, Pohnpei Port Authority, Pohnpei State Housing Authority, Yap Fishing Authority, Yap Visitor's Bureau.
3. Social Security Funds	FSM Social Security Administration , Micare Plan Incorporated, Chuuk State Health Care Plan.
4. State Government	4.1 Budgetary state government units/entities: Chuuk State, Kosrae State, Pohnpei State, Yap State 4.2 Extrabudgetary state government units: Not applicable.
5. Local Government	5.1 Budgetary local government units/entities: 75 local governments. 5.2 Extrabudgetary local government units: Not applicable.
Compilation Practices	
Breaks in Series	None reported.
Compilation Notes	Data cover activities of subsector 1. Expenditure by functions of government (Table 7) shows the composition of Expense, not including Net investment in nonfinancial assets. Government Finance Statistics are compiled by the Ministry of Finance.
Implementation of GFSM 2001/2014	The general government's cash flow statement is compiled according to the GFSM 2001 framework.

Moldova (921)

Information Last Updated	2017
Units of General Government	
1. Budgetary Central Government	Covered. 1.1 Legislative, Judiciary, and Executive bodies including ministries/departments. 1.2 Other agencies or funds: Other central administrative authorities (8), other institutions and agencies (21).
2. Extrabudgetary Central Government	Not applicable.
3. Social Security Funds	Covered. Compulsory Medical Insurance Fund and State Social Insurance Budget.
4. State Government	Not applicable.
5. Local Government	Covered. 5.1 Budgetary local government units/entities: Two levels of local governments: the first level includes 898 city halls of municipalities, towns and villages, and the second level includes 32 rayons, 2 municipalities, 1 autonomous territorial unit. 5.2 Extrabudgetary local government units: Not applicable.
Compilation Practices	
Breaks in Series	Since 2004, data on shares and other equity are included. Since 2002, central government data includes operations of subsector 3 (Social Security Funds).
Compilation Notes	Data cover activities of subsectors 1, 3, and 5. Government Finance Statistics are compiled by the Ministry of Finance.
Implementation of GFSM 2001/2014	The Strategy on Development of Public Finance Management for 2013-2020 was approved. This strategy provides using of a new chart of accounts for all budget institutions, aligned to the requirements of GFSM 2001. The new budget classification that is integrated with the unique chart of accounts was developed. The new Law of public finance and fiscal budgetary responsibility was approved. A new informational system was developed. Implementation of the new budget classification, the new Chart of Accounts and the reporting system started on January 1, 2016.

Mongolia (948)

Information Last Updated	2015
Units of General Government	
1. Budgetary Central Government	1.1 Legislative, Judiciary, and Executive bodies including ministries/departments. 1.2 Other agencies or funds: Culture and Art Fund, Employment and Promotion Fund, Environment Fund, Government agencies (except self-financed), Road Department, and State Property Committee (before 2002 and from 2004 onward).
2. Extrabudgetary Central Government	Assistance of Disabled Citizens Fund, Construction Department, Foreign Citizens and Citizenship Issues Department, Fuel and Energy Authority, Intellectual Rights Department, Departments Development Fund, Environment Protection Fund, Grains Fund, Herd Protection Fund, KR-1 Fund, KR-2 Fund, Oil and Gas agency, Travel Fund, Service of Diplomatic Missions Department, State Center of Standardization and Metrology, State Citizens' Registration and Information Center, State Property Committee (2002 and 2003), Telecommunications Department, Ukraine Fund, USA1 Fund, USA2 Fund, Road Fund, and Wild Goats Fund.
3. Social Security Funds	Health Insurance Fund, Industrial Accidents and Occupational Disease Insurance Fund, Pension Insurance Fund, Social Benefits Insurance Fund, and Unemployment Insurance Fund.
4. State Government	Not applicable.
5. Local Government	5.1 Budgetary local government units/entities: 9 districts (Ulaanbaatar), 21 provinces (aimags), and 331 districts (soums). 5.2 Extrabudgetary local government units: No information available.
Compilation Practices	
Breaks in Series	Prior to 2002, data for central government subsectors was consolidated. From 1997, the data for xx cover the expenditures of the Reserve Funds. Before 1993, in table 7, the data on general government subsectors for public order and safety were classified in the line with the national budget allocations for general public services. From 2007, data for central government includes social security funds.
Compilation Notes	Data cover activities of subsectors 1-3 and 5. Government Finance Statistics are compiled by the Ministry of Finance and Economy.
Implementation of GFSM 2001/2014	No information available.

Montserrat (351)

Information Last Updated	2015
Units of General Government	
1. Budgetary Central Government	1.1 Legislative, Judiciary, and Executive bodies including ministries/departments: 1.2 Other agencies or funds: Office of the Premier, and Royal Montserrat Police Service.
2. Extrabudgetary Central Government	Montserrat Info-Communication Authority, Montserrat Volcano Observatory, Montserrat Tourist Board, Land and Development Authority, Disaster Management Coordination Agency, Montserrat Development Corporation, Spirit of Montserrat.
3. Social Security Funds	Montserrat Social Security Fund.
4. State Government	Not applicable.
5. Local Government	Not applicable.
Compilation Practices	
Breaks in Series	None reported.
Compilation Notes	Data cover activities of subsector 1. Government Finance Statistics are compiled by the Ministry of Finance.
Implementation of GFSM 2001/2014	No information available.

Morocco (686)

Information Last Updated	2015
Units of General Government	
1. Budgetary Central Government	1.1 Legislative, Judiciary, and Executive bodies including ministries/departments. 1.2 Other agencies or funds: General government budget, Special treasury accounts.
2. Extrabudgetary Central Government	Government administrative agencies.
3. Social Security Funds	Moroccan Retirement Fund(caisse Marocaine de Retraite), Mutual associations, National Social Security Fund (caisse Nationale de Securite sociale), Pension Fund (Regime collectif d'Allocation de Retraites), Special systems.
4. State Government	Not applicable.
5. Local Government	5.1 Budgetary local government units/entities: Arrondissements(41), Prefectures and provinces(61), Regions (16),Rural communes(1298), Trade unions (132), Urban communes (200). 5.2 Extrabudgetary local government units: Not applicable.
Compilation Practices	
Breaks in Series	None reported.
Compilation Notes	Data cover activities of subsectors 1, 2, 3, and 5. Through 2001, data in central government tables only cover subsector 1. Government Finance Statistics are compiled by the Ministry of Finance.
Implementation of GFSM 2001/2014	No information available.

Mozambique (688)

Information Last Updated	2015
Units of General Government	
1. Budgetary Central Government	1.1 Legislative, Judiciary, and Executive bodies including ministries/departments: 1.2 Other agencies or funds:
2. Extrabudgetary Central Government	Mining Development Fund, Water Supply Equipment and Investment Fund, Environment Fund, Economic Rehabilitation Support Fund, Cultural and Artistic development fund, Commerce Fund, Sports Promotion Fund, Tourism National Fund, Agriculture Development Fund, Road Fund, Energy Fund, Housing Development Fund, Research National Fund, Dredging National Fund, Universal Access Service Fund, Navy National Institute, Oil National Institute, Mozambique Communication National Institute, Civil Servants High Studies Institute, Legal Support Institute , Polytechnic Institutes of Gaza, Manica, and Tete, Health Sciences University, Accounting and Auditing University, Audiovisual and Cinema National Institute , Literature and Music National Institute, Adult Training National Institute, Education Development National Institute, Long Distance Education National Institute, Studentship Institute, Language Institute, Road National Institute, Meterology National Institute, Navigation and Hydrograpic National Instiute, Meterology National Institute and Hydrograpic National Institute, Small Scale Fishing Development National Institute, Fishing Inspection National Institute, Mozambican Communities Abroad Support National Institute, Demining National Institute, State Holdings Management Institute.
3. Social Security Funds	National Social Security Institute (INSS).
4. State Government	Not applicable.
5. Local Government	5.1 Budgetary local government units/entities: 43 municipalities. 5.2 Extrabudgetary local government units: Not applicable.
Compilation Practices	
Breaks in Series	None reported.
Compilation Notes	Data cover activities of subsectors 1. Government Finance Statistics are compiled by the Ministry of Finance.
Implementation of GFSM 2001/2014	No information available.

Information Last Updated	2016
Units of General Government	
1. Budgetary Central Government	Covered. 2.1 Legislative, Judiciary, Executive bodies as well as Offices, ministries and Agencies (OMA)
2. Extrabudgetary Central Government	Partially covered. 2.2 Meat Board of Namibia*, Namibia Agronomic Board*, Development Fund of Namibia*, Road Fund Administration*, Road Authority*, Air Namibia*, Namibia Tourism Board, Diamond Board of Namibia, Guardian's Funds, Karakul Board of Namibia, Labour Promotion Funds, Motor Vehicles Accident Fund, Namibia Broadcasting Corporation, Namibia Central Intelligence Services, Namibia Press Agency (NAMPA), National Monuments Council, New Era Production, Polytechnic of Namibia, Sea Fisheries Fund, Vocational Training, Sport Development Fund, University of Namibia.
3. Social Security Funds	Partially covered. 2.3 Social Security Commission, Employees' Compensation Fund, Maternity Leave, Sick and Death Benefit Fund
4. State Government	Partially covered. 13 Regional councils: Khomas regional council, Erongo regional council, Karas regional council, Oshana regional council, Ohangwena regional council, Oshikoto regional council, Omaheke regional council, Zambezi regional council, Kavongo regional council, Omusati regional council, Otjozondjupa regional council, Kunene regional council and Hardap regional council.
5. Local Government	Partially covered. 2.5 Budgetary Local Government units: 13 Regional Councils, 1 Covered, 16 Municipalities (8 covered), 16 Town Councils (2 covered), 19 Villages (not yet covered).
Compilation Practices	
Breaks in Series	Fiscal statistics data reporting is in conformity with the GFSM 2014, in terms of methodology, classification and valuation.
Compilation Notes	Coverage: General government coverage is expected to start next reporting data 2016.
Implementation of GFSM 2001/2014	GFSM 2001/2014 Implementation plan: Review and enhance the Integrated Financial Management System (IFMS) functionalities, i.e. implement new Chart of Acount and further develop the budget module, aligning these to GFSM 2014 by end-2017. By 2018/2019 financial year, adopt accrual recording, as relevant.

Nepal (558)

Information Last Updated	2016
Units of General Government	
1. Budgetary Central Government	Partially covered. Office of the President, Constituent Assembly, Parliament, Supreme Court, Office of the Auditor General, Office of the Prime minister and Council of Ministers, Ministries, Departments.
2. Extrabudgetary Central Government	Partially covered. Local Development Fees Fund, National Level Welfare Fund, Pashupati Area Development Trust, Peace Fund, Roads Board, Rural Water and Sanitation Fund Development Board, Social Welfare Council, universities, and others.
3. Social Security Funds	Not applicable.
4. State Government	Not applicable.
5. Local Government	Covered. 75 District Development Committees, 58 Municipalities, and 3,915 Village Development Committees.
Compilation Practices	
Breaks in Series	Data on the central government cover Subsector 1. Data include transactions in kind. Data for foreign grants and borrowing have been adjusted to eliminate receivable items. From 1991 onward, data on public order and safety are included in the line on general public services in Table 7.
Compilation Notes	Data for budgetary central government are reported on a non-cash basis (including transactions in kind). Liquidation or complementary period: One month. Valuation of assets and liabilities: 14 Financial assets in the form of loans, most part of the outstanding liabilities is valued at the fixed (face) value. The data on accounts receivable/payable are not compiled. The outstanding liabilities in foreign currency are converted in the national currency at the rate prevailing at the year-end.
Implementation of GFSM 2001/2014	In March 2014, the inter-agency GFS Steering Committee and Task Force were created to support the GFS developments in Nepal. Nepal is participating in the Japan Administered Account for Selected IMF Activities GFS Capacity Building Project for Asian Countries. The Implementation Plan includes reporting quarterly GFS for budgetary central government, integrating classification of flows and stocks, developing a financial balance sheet for budgetary central government, progressively extending GFS coverage to general government. This institutional table is based on information submitted in 2014.

Netherlands (138)

Information Last Updated	2015
Units of General Government	
1. Budgetary Central Government	Partially covered. 1.1 Legislative, Judiciary, and Executive bodies including ministries/departments. 1.2 Other agencies or funds: Animal Health Fund, Economic Structure Support Fund, Infrastructure Fund, Municipalities Fund, Provinces Fund, Saving Fund for Old Age Pensions, VAT Compensation Fund, and 40 government agencies.
2. Extrabudgetary Central Government	Partially covered. 14 universities, 18 public corporate organizations and various non-profit institutions financed and controlled by government.
3. Social Security Funds	Covered. 7 executive bodies, including 9 social security funds.
4. State Government	Not applicable.
5. Local Government	Covered. 5.1 Budgetary local government units/entities: 316 communal arrangements, 418 municipalities, 12 provinces, and 26 public water boards. 5.2 Extrabudgetary local government units: Schools (not part of municipalities and financed by government) and various non-profit institutions financed and controlled by government (among others: Central Refugee Centre Organization (COA), Chambers of Commerce, Legal aid organizations, Police districts (25), Public museums, Public libraries, Sheltered workshops, Youth welfare work organizations).
Compilation Practices	
Breaks in Series	None reported.
Compilation Notes	Data cover activities of subsectors 1-3 and 5. Data are reported after FISIM allocation. Data for all subsectors are reported on a noncash basis, consistent with the European System of Accounts, 2010 (ESA2010). Financial assets and liabilities are reported at face value for non-negotiable instruments and at market value for negotiable instruments. Government Finance Statistics are compiled by the Statistics Netherlands.
Implementation of GFSM 2001/2014	Netherlands participates in the Eurostat GFS convergence project with the IMF.

Information Last Updated 2015

Units of General Government

1. Budgetary Central Government

Covered.
1.1 Legislative, Judiciary, and Executive bodies including ministries/departments.
1.2 Other agencies or funds:
New Zealand Superannuation Fund.

2. Extrabudgetary Central Government

Covered.
9 Crown research institutes, 12 Fish and Game councils, 21 District health boards, 24 Reserve boards, 33 Tertiary education institutions, 2463 School boards of trustees, Accounting Standards Review Board, Agricultural and Marketing Research and Development Trust, Alcohol Advisory Council of New Zealand, Arts Council of New Zealand Toi Aotearoa (Creative NZ), Asia 2000 Foundation of New Zealand, Broadcasting Commission, Broadcasting Standards Authority, Career Services, Children's Commissioner, Civil Aviation Authority of New Zealand, Commerce Commission, Crown Health Financing Agency, Earthquake Commission, Electoral Commission, Electricity Commission, Energy Efficiency and Conservation Authority, Environmental Risk Management Authority (ERMA), Families Commission, Foundation for Research, Government Superannuation Fund Authority, Guardians of New Zealand Superannuation, Health and Disability Services Commissioner, Health Research Council of New Zealand, Health Sponsorship Council, Housing New Zealand Corporation, Human Rights Commission, Land Transport New Zealand, Law Commission, Leadership Development Centre Trust, Legal Services Agency, Maritime Safety Authority of New Zealand, Mental Health Commission, Museum of New Zealand Te Papa Tongarewa, New Zealand Antarctic Institute (Antarctic New Zealand), New Zealand Artificial Limb Board, New Zealand Blood Service, New Zealand Film Commission, New Zealand Fire Service Commission, New Zealand Fish and Game Council, New Zealand Game Bird Habitat Trust Board, New Zealand Government Property Corporation, New Zealand Historic Places Trust (Pouhere Toanga), New Zealand Lotteries Commission, New Zealand Lottery Grants Board, New Zealand Qualifications Authority, New Zealand Sports Drug Agency, New Zealand Symphony Orchestra, New Zealand Teachers Council, New Zealand Tourism Board, New Zealand Trade and Enterprise, New Zealand Venture Investment Fund, Ngai Tahu Ancillary Claims Trust.

3. Social Security Funds

Covered.
Accident Compensation Corporation.

4. State Government

Not applicable.

5. Local Government

Covered.
5.1 Budgetary local government units/entities:
89 Local government units
5.2 Extrabudgetary local government units:
10 Museums

Compilation Practices

Breaks in Series

Starting 2009, the GFS presented are based on data produced from two different data sources: The local government GFS data come from Statistics NZ, and higher level central government GFS data were produced by the New Zealand Treasury as part of its budget forecast information while more detailed transaction data have been produced by the IMF base on the Financial Statements of the Government of New Zealand.
From 2006, in the Statement of Sources and Uses of Cash for the central and general government, compensation of employees also includes purchases of goods and services, and social benefits includes subsidies, grants, and other payments.
Prior to 2001, data in all tables are compiled in accordance with the methodology of the GFSM 1986.
Prior to 1991, data on public order and safety were included in the line on general public services.
From 1990, Fiscal Year ending changed.

Compilation Notes

Data cover activities of the central and local government subsectors.
Government Finance Statistics are compiled by Statistics NZ.
Significant balance sheet revisions were made in the central government GFS year ended June 2014 release.

Implementation of GFSM 2001/2014

Over the medium term, the next steps will include advancing the public financial accounting system in line with international standards and developing a single data collection, processing and output system to produce GFS according to the GFSM 2001/2014 (across all levels of government).
In the short term we aim to implement the GFSM 2014 standards and produce a general government GFS reconciliation from our central and local government subsectors.

Nicaragua (278)

Information Last Updated	2015
Units of General Government	
1. Budgetary Central Government	1.1 Legislative, Judiciary, and Executive bodies including ministries/departments.
2. Extrabudgetary Central Government	Attorney's Office for Human Rights, 8 public universities, and 49 various nonprofit government institutions.
3. Social Security Funds	Nicaraguan Social Security Institute (INSS), Social Security and Human Development Institute (ISDHU), and Social Security Institute for Military Personnel (MIDEF).
4. State Government	4.1 Budgetary state government units/entities: North Atlantic Regional Government and South Atlantic Regional Government. 4.2 Extrabudgetary state government units: Not applicable.
5. Local Government	5.1 Budgetary local government units/entities: 152 Municipalities. 5.2 Extrabudgetary local government units: Not applicable.
Compilation Practices	
Breaks in Series	None reported.
Compilation Notes	Data in central government sector cover activities of subsectors 1-3. Data in central government cover tables 1, 2, and partially 3. Data time series cover 1990 to 2011. Data are recorded on cash basis for subsectors 1-3. Government Finance Statistics are compiled by the Ministry of Finance (http://dsbb.imf.org/).
Implementation of GFSM 2001/2014	No information available.

Nigeria (694)

Information Last Updated	2015
Units of General Government	
1. Budgetary Central Government	1.1 Legislative, Judiciary, and Executive bodies including ministries/departments: 1.2 Other agencies or funds: Central government offices and commissions.
2. Extrabudgetary Central Government	Federation accounts, Special Funds and other central government units with individual budgets.
3. Social Security Funds	Not applicable.
4. State Government	4.1 Budgetary state government units/entities: Abuja (Federal Capital Territory) and 36 state governments. 4.2 Extrabudgetary state government units: No information available.
5. Local Government	5.1 Budgetary local government units/entities: 774 local governments 5.2 Extrabudgetary local government units: No information available.
Compilation Practices	
Breaks in Series	None reported.
Compilation Notes	Data cover activities of subsector 1. Government Finance Statistics are compiled by the Federal Ministry of Finance.
Implementation of GFSM 2001/2014	No information available.

Norway (142)

Information Last Updated	2015
Units of General Government	
1. Budgetary Central Government	Covered. 1.1 Legislative, Judiciary, and Executive bodies including ministries/departments. 1.2 Other agencies or funds: National insurance scheme.
2. Extrabudgetary Central Government	Covered. Extrabudgetary funds (includes advance and deposit accounts, other guarantee funds, and special accounts of the central government), Government Pension Fund - Global, Government Pension Fund - Norway, Government Petroleum Insurance Fund, Miscellaneous other government funds (including Innovation Norway, environmental funds, culture funds, etc.), Norwegian Research Council and Norwegian Trade Council, Price regulation funds, Public colleges and universities, Public hospitals, Public Service Pension Fund, Seamen's Pension Insurance Fund, and War Pension Scheme for the Military.
3. Social Security Funds	Not applicable. Integrated in subsector 1 and subsector 2.
4. State Government	Not applicable.
5. Local Government	Covered. 5.1 Budgetary local government units/entities: 18 counties and 428 municipalities 5.2 Extrabudgetary local government units: 300 nonmarket corporations classified within Local Government and 428 joint parish councils.
Compilation Practices	
Breaks in Series	None reported.
Compilation Notes	Data cover activities of subsectors 1-3 and 5. Government Finance Statistics are compiled by Statistics Norway.
Implementation of GFSM 2001/2014	The GFSM 2014 format was implemented in national publications in late 2014. The most important changes are that research and development services (R&D) and major military procurements will now be recognized as investments and not as ongoing operating expenses. In addition, the general government sector has been expanded by approximately 100 units. Most of these are cultural institutions such as museums and theatres. The previous questionnaire followed the GFSM 2001 format. As of 2015, the questionnaires will follow the GFSM 2014 format. More details regarding new units will also be provided with the 2015 questionnaire.

Oman (449)

Information Last Updated	2015
Units of General Government	
1. Budgetary Central Government	1.1 Legislative, Judiciary, and Executive bodies including ministries/departments. 1.2 Other agencies or funds: Secretariat of the Supreme Committee for Town Planning, Sultan Qaboos University, 42 municipalities.
2. Extrabudgetary Central Government	State General Reserve Fund and Several fully owned Government Agencies.
3. Social Security Funds	Employee pension fund, Public Authority for Social Insurance (PASI).
4. State Government	Not applicable.
5. Local Government	Not applicable.
Compilation Practices	
Breaks in Series	None reported.
Compilation Notes	Data cover activities of subsector 1. Government Finance Statistics are compiled by the Central Bank of Oman The (42) municipalities, which are legally local government, are considered dependent agencies of central government when compiling government finance statistics because they do not have sufficient financial independence to be considered as a separate level of general government.
Implementation of GFSM 2001/2014	No information available.

Pakistan (564)

Information Last Updated 2015

Units of General Government

1. Budgetary Central Government
1.1 Legislative, Judiciary, and Executive bodies including ministries/departments:
1.2 Other agencies or funds:
No information available.

2. Extrabudgetary Central Government
Several universities, and other nonprofit public institutions serving households.

3. Social Security Funds
Not applicable.

4. State Government
4.1 Budgetary state government units/entities:
4 provinces.
4.2 Extrabudgetary state government units:
Not applicable.

5. Local Government
5.1 Budgetary local government units/entities:
District councils, local councils, and municipalities.
5.2 Extrabudgetary local government units:
Not applicable.

Compilation Practices

Breaks in Series
None reported.

Compilation Notes
Data cover activities of subsector 1.
Government Finance Statistics are compiled by the Ministry of Finance.

Implementation of GFSM 2001/2014
The budgetary central government cash flow statement is compiled according to the GFSM 2001 framework.

Palau (565)

Information Last Updated 2017

Units of General Government

1. Budgetary Central Government
1.1 Legislative, Judiciary, and Executive bodies including ministries/departments.
1.2 Other agencies or funds:
Palau Environmental Quality Protection Board, National Postal Service, National Aviation Administration, Foreign Investment Board, Palau Election Commission, Palau Code Commission, Palau Public Lands Authority, Parole Board, Ethics Commission, Financial Institutions Commission, Language Commission.

2. Extrabudgetary Central Government
Palau Community College, Palau Community Action Agency, Palau International Coral Reef Center, Palau Visitors Authority, Palau District Housing Authority, Palau National Museum, Ngarmau Free Trade Zone Authority, Micro Legal Service, Palau Workforce Investment Act (WIA), 4 universities, Government institutions.

3. Social Security Funds
Palau Social Security Retirement Fund, Palau Civil Service Pension Trust Fund, National Health Care Fund.

4. State Government
4.1 Budgetary state government units/entities:
Aimeliik State, Angaur State, Airai State,Hatohoboi State, Kayangel State, Koror State, Melekeok State, Ngarchelong State, Ngaraad State, Ngardmau State, Ngaremlengui State, Ngatpang State, Ngiwal State, Peleliu State, Sonsorol State.
4.2 Extrabudgetary state government units:
Not applicable.

5. Local Government
Not applicable.

Compilation Practices

Breaks in Series
None reported.

Compilation Notes
Data cover activities of subsectors 1-3.
Expenditure by functions of government (Table 7) shows the composition of Expense, not including Net investment in nonfinancial assets.
Government Finance Statistics are compiled by the Ministry of Finance and Office of the Controller General of the Republic.

Implementation of GFSM 2001/2014
Over the medium term, the next steps will include improving the migration plan towards the GFSM 2001 framework.

Paraguay (288)

Information Last Updated	2015
Units of General Government	
1. Budgetary Central Government	1.1 Legislative, Judiciary, and Executive bodies including ministries/departments. 1.2 Other agencies or funds: Retirement and Pension Fund of Government Employees.
2. Extrabudgetary Central Government	National Animal Health Service, National Commission of Communications, National Commission of Stock Market, National Council of Housing, National Directorate of Customs, National Directorate of Public Procurement, National Directorate of Transportation, National Directorate of Welfare, National Forestry Institute, National Fund of Culture and Arts, National Institute for Cooperatives, National Institute for Indigenous People, National Institute of Rural and Land Development, National Institute of Technology and Normalization, National Plant and Seed Health and Quality Service, National University of Asunción, National University of Caaguazu, National University of Concepción, National University of East, National University of Itapúa, National University of Pilar, National University of Villarica del Espiritu Santo, National Vegetable and Seed Quality Service , Paraguayan Institute of Handicrafts, Regulation Entity for Sanitary Services, Secretariat of Transportation for the Metropolitan Area of Asunción.
3. Social Security Funds	Social Security Institution.
4. State Government	4.1 Budgetary state government units/entities: 17 departments. 4.2 Extrabudgetary state government units: No information available.
5. Local Government	5.1 Budgetary local government units/entities: Capital and 239 municipalities. 5.2 Extrabudgetary local government units: No information available.
Compilation Practices	
Breaks in Series	From 1990-1993, data in local government tables cover operations of Asunción (capital) only.
Compilation Notes	Data cover activities of subsectors 1-4 and partially 5. Government Finance Statistics are compiled by the Ministry of Finance.
Implementation of GFSM 2001/2014	No information available.

Peru (293)

Information Last Updated	2015
Units of General Government	
1. Budgetary Central Government	1.1 Legislative, Judiciary, and Executive bodies including ministries/departments. 1.2 Other agencies or funds: 7 other decentralized agencies, 9 entities of enterprise treatment, 31 universities, 58 public institutions, and 101 public welfare agencies.
2. Extrabudgetary Central Government	Mortgage Fund for Housing Promotion and National Fund for Housing (in liquidation).
3. Social Security Funds	Consolidated Pensions Reserves Fund (Fondo Consolidado de Reservas Previsionales), Public Pension Fund (Oficina de Normalización Previsional), and Social Security of Health.
4. State Government	4.1 Budgetary state government units/entities: 25 regions. 4.2 Extrabudgetary state government units: No information available.
5. Local Government	5.1 Budgetary local government units/entities: 7 decentralized agencies, 194 provincial councils, 1,836 district councils. 5.2 Extrabudgetary local government units: No information available.
Compilation Practices	
Breaks in Series	From 1995, data for subsectors of central government are aggregated (i.e., before consolidation).
Compilation Notes	Data cover activities of subsectors 1-5. Government Finance Statistics are compiled by the Central Reserve Bank of Peru (BCRP).
Implementation of GFSM 2001/2014	No information available.

Philippines (566)

Information Last Updated	2015
Units of General Government	
1. Budgetary Central Government	1.1 Legislative, Judiciary, and Executive bodies including ministries/departments. 1.2 Other agencies or funds: 2 autonomous regions, 3 constitutional offices, Commission on Human Rights, Joint Legislative Executive Debt Council, and ombudsman's office.
2. Extrabudgetary Central Government	Central Bank Board of Liquidators, Government Owned and Controlled Corporations involved in non-market activities, Government service insurance system, Lung Center of the Philippines, Medical care plan, National Kidney Institute, National Post-harvest Institute for Research and Extension, Philippine Children's Medical Center, Philippine Heart Center Philippine High School for the Arts, Philippine Rice Research Institute, and Philippine Tourism Authority.
3. Social Security Funds	Social security system.
4. State Government	Not applicable.
5. Local Government	5.1 Budgetary local government units/entities: 13 regions, 64 cities, 76 provinces, 1,541 municipalities, and 41,924 barangays (municipal subunits). 5.2 Extrabudgetary local government units: No information available.
Compilation Practices	
Breaks in Series	Prior to 2001, the net operations of "nonbudget accounts" were incorrectly classified as domestic financing. From 2002, the "nonbudget accounts" transactions are appropriately classified to revenues, expenses, and financing. From 1998, the budgetary central government stock of liabilities (outstanding debt data) is consolidated with the Bond Sinking Fund, and other subsectors of general government's debt are appropriately consolidated. From 1994, data exclude interest paid for restructuring of the Central Bank of the Philippines. From 1992, data for local government covered operations of subsector 5 and were based on information from all local governments.
Compilation Notes	Data cover activities of subsector 1. Government Finance Statistics are compiled by the Department of Finance.
Implementation of GFSM 2001/2014	A migration plan to the GFSM 2001/2014 is under consideration.

Poland (964)

Information Last Updated	2015
Units of General Government	
1. Budgetary Central Government	1.1 Legislative, Judiciary, and Executive bodies including ministries/departments. 1.2 Other agencies or funds: Energy Regulatory Authority, Financial Supervision Authority, Office for Competition and Consumer Protection, Office of Public Procurement, Polish Committee for Standardization, Polish Patent Office, State Mining Authority, and various other agencies.
2. Extrabudgetary Central Government	Agency of Material Stocks, Municipal Investments Development Fund, National Capital Fund, National Road Fund, and Railway Fund, Polish Academy of Science, Polish Agency for Enterprise Development, Polish Centre for Accreditation, Polish Science and Technology Fund, Pupils' Sport and Recreation Classes Fund, Student Loan and Credit Fund, Technology Credit Fund, and universities, Thermo-modernization Fund, Agency of Medical Technology Assessment, Alimony Fund, Employee Guaranteed Benefits Fund, Health care institutions, Physical Education Development Fund, and State Fund for Rehabilitation of the Disabled, Central Fund for Management of Geodetic and Cartographic Resources, Agency of Military Property, Agency of Restructuring and Modernization of Agriculture, Agricultural Land Protection Fund, Agricultural Market Agency, Agricultural Property Agency and Agricultural Property Resource of the State Treasury, Armed Forces Modernization Fund, Auxiliary units, budget establishments, and special units, Border Guard Support Fund, Central Record of Drivers and Vehicles Fund, Compensation Fund, Cultural Promotion Fund, Insurance Ombudsman Office, Military Agency for Housing, Motivation fund, National Research and Development Centre, Office of Technical Supervision, Police Support Fund, Polish Institute of International Affairs, Polish Organization of Tourism, Post-penitentiary Aid Fund, Prison Enterprises Development Fund, Public Security Modernization Fund, Reprivatization Fund, State Treasury Fund, Zone Fund, and Transport Technical Supervision, Inland Waterways Fund, National Fund for Environmental Protection and Water Management, Agricultural Advisory Centre, Arts Promotion Fund, Cultural institutions, Entrepreneurs Restructuring Fund, Agricultural Land Protection Fund, Gambling Problem Solving Fund, Insurance Ombudsman Office, Logistic Services Centre, motivation funds, own revenue funds, Polish Film Institute, and Polish National School of Judiciary and Public Prosecution.
3. Social Security Funds	Administrative Fund, Contributions' Fund, Demographic Reserve Fund, Motivation Fund, Social Insurance Fund, Social Insurance Institution, Labor Fund, National Health Fund, Prevention and Rehabilitation Fund, Pension and Disability Fund (for farmers), and Bridge
4. State Government	Not applicable.
5. Local Government	5.1 Budgetary local government units/entities: 16 districts, 314 Counties, and 2479 communes. 5.2 Extrabudgetary local government units: Auxiliary units, budget establishments, own revenue funds, and special-purpose funds.
Compilation Practices	
Breaks in Series	From 2002, some data are compiled on an accrual basis and are classified in accordance with the GFSM 2001.
Compilation Notes	Data cover activities of subsectors 1-3 and 5. Government Finance Statistics are compiled by the Ministry of Finance.
Implementation of GFSM 2001/2014	An inter-institutional working group has been established with the main objective to discuss and resolve technical and methodological issues regarding the implementation of the European System of Accounts, 2010 (ESA 2010). Data compiled for GFS are routinely compared with data compiled in accordance with EU requirements.

Portugal (182)

Information Last Updated	2015
Units of General Government	
1. Budgetary Central Government	1.1 Legislative, Judiciary, and Executive bodies including ministries/departments. 1.2 Other agencies or funds: Health Service for Government Employees (Assistência na Doença aos Servidores do Estado) and Pension Scheme for Government Employees (Caixa Geral de Aposentações).
2. Extrabudgetary Central Government	4 agencies in education, 33 agencies in health, 1 agency in defense, 4 in internal affairs, 2 in justice, 6 in presidency of the council of ministers, 2 agencies in agriculture, rural development and fisheries, 6 in cultural activities, 6 in economy innovation and development, 15 in environment and spatial planning, 5 in public works, transport and communications and 2 in foreign affairs, 7 agencies in finance and public administration, 30 in labour and social solidarity, 8 in miscellaneous activities, 22 public corporations and 33 nonprofit institutions classified in the central government subsector, such as, Rádio e Televisão de Portugal, S.A.; Estradas de Portugal, S.A.; Santa Casa da Misericórdia de Lisboa; Parque Escolar E.P.E., 98 agencies in science, technology, and higher education (including universities).
3. Social Security Funds	Security Financial Management Institute (Instituto de Gestão Financeira da Segurança Social).
4. State Government	Not applicable.
5. Local Government	5.1 Budgetary local government units/entities: Regional governments of the Azores and Madeira, 18 districts, and 308 municipalities, Parishes (4,260). 5.2 Extrabudgetary local government units: 265 agencies of local government and municipal corporations reclassified into the government sector, 84 non-profit institutions of local governments, and 131 agencies of regional government and regional corporations reclassified into the government sector.
Compilation Practices	
Breaks in Series	From 1995, the budgetary central government which was previously recorded under the social security funds includes Caixa Geral de Aposentações. The 2010 data submission revises the data series from 1995-2008, except for Table 7 which only incorporates revisions from 2006 onward. For this reason, the functional classification of expense prior to 2006 may not be directly comparable with that of most recent years.
Compilation Notes	Data cover activities of subsectors 1-3 and 5. Government Finance Statistics are compiled by the Ministério das Finanças.
Implementation of GFSM 2001/2014	Portugal participates in the Eurostat GFS convergence project with the IMF.

Romania (968)

Information Last Updated	2015
Units of General Government	
1. Budgetary Central Government	1.1 Legislative, Judiciary, and Executive bodies including ministries/departments. 1.2 Other agencies or funds: External and internal credits, Central Treasury Budget, Risk Fund, EU Transfers.
2. Extrabudgetary Central Government	Public institutions partially or totally financed from own revenues subordinated to ministries and subsidized from state budget, External aid managed by Ministry of Public Finance, 82 other extrabudgetary funds, including public corporations operating on a nonmarket basis.
3. Social Security Funds	State Social Security, Unemployment Fund, Health Social Insurance Fund, Public institutions financed partially or totally from own revenue (from unemployment fund), External credits granted to unemployment and state social security budgets.
4. State Government	Not applicable.
5. Local Government	5.1 Budgetary local government units/entities: Bucharest, 2,850 communes, 41 counties, 103 municipalities, and 211 towns 5.2 Extrabudgetary local government units: External and internal credits granted to local authorities, Self-financing institutions subordinated to local authorities, Revenue and expenditure outside the local budgets, Airports, District Heating Units, Other local units.
Compilation Practices	
Breaks in Series	None reported.
Compilation Notes	Data in central government tables cover operations of subsectors 1–3; Data in local government tables cover operations of subsector 5. Data are reported on an accrual basis. Accrual data are derived from cash data using various methods: tax revenue data are adjusted using time-adjusted cash method; expense data are adjusted using due-for-payments data; and interest payments are calculated on an accrual basis.
Implementation of GFSM 2001/2014	No information available.

Russian Federation (922)

Information Last Updated	2017
Units of General Government	
1. Budgetary Central Government	Covered. Legislative, Judiciary, and Executive bodies including ministries/departments, Other Federal institutions of the government of the Russian Federation.
2. Extrabudgetary Central Government	Covered. Federal budgetary and autonomic organizations (Extra budgetary units of central government), The Government corporation of the Russian Federation "Fund of assistance to housing and communal services reforming", open joint-stock company "RUSNANO", government company "Russian highways" (Extra budgetary units).
3. Social Security Funds	Covered. Mandatory medical insurance funds – federal and territorial, Pension fund of the Russian Federation, Russian Federation social insurance fund.
4. State Government	Covered. 4.1 Budgetary state government units/entities: Regional institutions ("subjects") of the government of the Russian Federation. Extrabudgetary state government units: Regional budgetary and autonomic organizations (Extra budgetary units of regional government).
5. Local Government	Covered. Budgetary local government units/entities: Local government(approximately 23,100). Extrabudgetary local government units: Local budgetary and autonomic organizations.
Compilation Practices	
Breaks in Series	Starting in 2007, data reported in the Table 1, Table 2, Table 3, Table 7, and Table 8 are on an accrual basis. Starting in 2005, data reported in the Statement of Government Operations, Table 4, Table 5, Table 6, and Table 9 are on an accrual basis. Starting in 2002, data are on a noncash basis. In 2002, federal budget data include the operations of the Ministry of Atomic Energy Fund, and the local government budgets data include the operations of the Territorial Road Funds and the Territorial Ecological Funds. In 2002, the opening balances of budgetary, central government, local governments, and general government liabilities were different from the 2001 closing balances. The 2001 closing balances were replaced by 2002 opening balances for publication purposes. For 2001, central and local government extrabudgetary data include a wider coverage of off-budget transactions of budget institutions. Before 2000, local government debt guaranteed by the central government is included under central government debt. From 1999 onward, the budgetary data include transactions of budgetary institutions related to own revenue and its expenditure. For 1998, debt data exclude certain operations on the rescheduling of government debt in the form of securities, which should have been included under internal debt. From 1998 onward, the operations of three additional extrabudgetary funds—the Atomic Energy Ministry Fund, Earmarked Budgetary Fund to Assist Military Reform, and Federal Fund for Replenishment of Mineral and Raw Material Base—are included with budgetary data. From 1995 onward, the operations of six former extrabudgetary funds—the Federal Ecological Fund, Federal Roads Fund, Fund for Development of the Customs System, State Fund for Combating Criminal Activities, Tax Police Fund, and Tax Service Fund—are included with budgetary data. From 2011 onward, the operations of extrabudgetary central, state and local government units include budgetary and autonomous institutions established by government authorities to perform activities on behalf of the government.
Compilation Notes	Data cover activities of subsectors 1-5. Data are presented on an accrual basis. Statement of sources and uses of cash - Cash basis. Government Finance Statistics are compiled by the Federal Treasury. Data on operations of the general government are compiled in billions of rubles.
Implementation of GFSM 2001/2014	Over the medium term, the next step is to produce sub-annual financial balance sheets consisting of all Units of General Government.

Rwanda (714)

Information Last Updated	2015
Units of General Government	
1. Budgetary Central Government	1.1 Legislative, Judiciary, and Executive bodies including ministries/departments: 1.2 Other agencies or funds: 63 other government bodies.
2. Extrabudgetary Central Government	Experimental farms, funds, government bureaus, institutes, offices, national museum, national university, Road Fund, schools.
3. Social Security Funds	Rwanda Social Security Board.
4. State Government	Not applicable.
5. Local Government	5.1 Budgetary local government units/entities: 30 districts and Kigali City Council. 5.2 Extrabudgetary local government units: No information available.
Compilation Practices	
Breaks in Series	None reported.
Compilation Notes	Data cover activities of subsectors 1-3. Government Finance Statistics are compiled by the Ministry of Finance and Economic Planning.
Implementation of GFSM 2001/2014	No information available.

Samoa (862)

Information Last Updated	2015
Units of General Government	
1. Budgetary Central Government	1.1 Legislative, Judiciary, and Executive bodies including ministries/departments. 1.2 Other agencies or funds: 14 Ministries, Office of the Electoral Commissioner, Public Service Commission, Samoa Bureau of Statistics, Attorney General's Office, Audit Office, Legislative Department, Ombudsmen's Office, Telecom Regulatory Office.
2. Extrabudgetary Central Government	Scientific Research Organization of Samoa, Unit Trust of Samoa, National University of Samoa, Samoa Qualifications Authority, Samoa Sports Facilities Authority, Samoa Tourism Authority, Samoa Water Authority, Samoa Airports Authority, Samoa Fire and Emergency Services Authority, Samoa Post Limited, National Kidney Foundation of Samoa, Samoa Public Trust, Samoa Trust Estates Corporation, Samoa Ports Authority, National Health Service of Samoa, Land Transport Authority.
3. Social Security Funds	Accident Compensation Corporation.
4. State Government	Not applicable.
5. Local Government	Not applicable.
Compilation Practices	
Breaks in Series	None reported.
Compilation Notes	Data cover activities of subsector 1. Government Finance Statistics are compiled by the Ministry of Finance.
Implementation of GFSM 2001/2014	It is planned to collect data on an accrual basis for selected items and compile financial balance sheet in 2015. Also in 2015, it is planned to start collecting data on nonfinancial assets at historic cost, as a pilot exercise.

San Marino (135)

Information Last Updated	2017
Units of General Government	
1. Budgetary Central Government	Covered. 1.1 Legislative, Judiciary, and Executive bodies including ministries/departments. 1.2 Other agencies or funds: No information available.
2. Extrabudgetary Central Government	Covered. Civil Aviation Authority, Public Services Company, Public Works Company, State Dairy, University of San Marino, Game Company, National Mailing Office, CONS(National Olympic Committee of San Marino).
3. Social Security Funds	Covered. Social Security Institute.
4. State Government	Not applicable.
5. Local Government	Not applicable.
Compilation Practices	
Breaks in Series	Starting in 2005, data include the financial assets held by general government units as holders of non-life insurance policies. Starting in 2014, the Coin Minting and Stamp Printing Company is no longer part of the extrabudgetary central government and the National Post Office has been reclassified from budgetary to extrabudgetary.
Compilation Notes	Data cover activities of subsectors 1-3. Data for all subsectors are reported on a noncash basis, consistent with the European System of Accounts, 2010 (ESA 2010). Government Finance Statistics are compiled by the National Statistic Office.
Implementation of GFSM 2001/2014	Data for all subsectors are reported on a noncash basis, consistent with the European System of Accounts, 2010 (ESA 2010).

São Tomé and Príncipe (716)

Information Last Updated	2015
Units of General Government	
1. Budgetary Central Government	1.1 Legislative, Judiciary, and Executive bodies including ministries/departments. 1.2 Other agencies or funds: Commissions.
2. Extrabudgetary Central Government	Central government autonomous funds and administrative agencies.
3. Social Security Funds	Social Security Fund.
4. State Government	Not applicable.
5. Local Government	5.1 Budgetary local government units/entities: Autonomous Region of Principe and Local Governments. 5.2 Extrabudgetary local government units: Not applicable.
Compilation Practices	
Breaks in Series	None reported.
Compilation Notes	Data cover activities of subsector 1. Government Finance Statistics are compiled by the Ministry of Finance.
Implementation of GFSM 2001/2014	Over the medium term, the next steps include improving the classification of cash data in GFSM 2001 format, collecting additional noncash flow data, and compiling financial balance sheets.

Senegal (722)

Information Last Updated	2015
Units of General Government	
1. Budgetary Central Government	1.1 Legislative, Judiciary, and Executive bodies including ministries/departments: 1.2 Other agencies or funds: Constitutional court, Economic and Social Council, High Authority for Audiovisual Affairs and Communication.
2. Extrabudgetary Central Government	40 units reported.
3. Social Security Funds	Social security fund.
4. State Government	Not applicable.
5. Local Government	5.1 Budgetary local government units/entities: Communes (171), Conseil Régional (14), Communautés rurales (385). Communes (municipalities) and rural districts 5.2 Extrabudgetary local government units: No information available.
Compilation Practices	
Breaks in Series	None reported.
Compilation Notes	Data cover activities of subsector 1. Government Finance Statistics are compiled by the National Statistics and Demographic Agency (ANSD) Ministry of Economy and Finance (MOF).
Implementation of GFSM 2001/2014	Senegal participates in the West African Economic and Monetary Union Project on harmonizing the public finances by 2017.

Serbia, Republic of (942)

Information Last Updated	2015
Units of General Government	
1. Budgetary Central Government	1.1 Legislative, Judiciary, and Executive bodies including ministries/departments. 1.2 Other agencies or funds: Army, cultural institutions, public education institutions, and social protection centers.
2. Extrabudgetary Central Government	Road Fund.
3. Social Security Funds	Health Fund, National Employment Agency, and Pension Fund.
4. State Government	Not applicable.
5. Local Government	5.1 Budgetary local government units/entities: Autonomous Province Vojvodina, cities, and municipalities. 5.2 Extrabudgetary local government units: No information available.
Compilation Practices	
Breaks in Series	None reported.
Compilation Notes	Data cover activities of subsectors 1-3 and 5. Government Finance Statistics are compiled by the Ministry of Finance.
Implementation of GFSM 2001/2014	Over the medium term, the next steps will include improving the classification of flows and stocks.

Seychelles (718)

Information Last Updated	2015
Units of General Government	
1. Budgetary Central Government	1.1 Legislative, Judiciary, and Executive bodies including ministries/departments. 1.2 Other agencies or funds: 28 regulatory bodies and agencies (Constitutional Appointments Authority; Electoral Commissioner's Office; Financial Intelligence Unit; Mayor of Victoria; National Arts Council; National Assembly Secretariat; National Drug Enforcement Agency; National Human Resources Development Council; National Sports Council; National Statistics Bureau; Office of the Auditor General; Office of Fair Trading; Office of the Ombudsman; Office of the Public Service Appeals Board; Public Officers' Ethics Commission; Seychelles Bureau of Standards; Seychelles Civil Aviation Authority; Seychelles Centre for Marine Research & Technology; Seychelles Fishing Authority; Seychelles Heritage Foundation; Seychelles Institute of Management; Seychelles Investment Bureau; Seychelles Licensing Authority; Seychelles Planning Authority; Seychelles Qualifications Authority; Seychelles Revenue Commission; Seychelles Tourism Board; and Social Welfare Agency.
2. Extrabudgetary Central Government	Not applicable.
3. Social Security Funds	Not applicable.
4. State Government	Not applicable.
5. Local Government	Not applicable.
Compilation Practices	
Breaks in Series	In 2011, the Social Security Fund (SSF) was eliminated as an entity. The assets (funds on hand) were either transferred to government or given to the Seychelles Pension Fund. SSF functions are now managed in part directly as social benefits paid by government (BA) or handled by the Seychelles Provident Fund (SPF). The SPF was reclassified as a Financial Public Corporation in 2011 as well.
Compilation Notes	Data cover activities of subsectors 1 and 3. Government Finance Statistics are compiled by the Ministry of Finance.
Implementation of GFSM 2001/2014	No information available.

Sierra Leone (724)

Information Last Updated	2015
Units of General Government	
1. Budgetary Central Government	1.1 Legislative, Judiciary, and Executive bodies including ministries/departments: 1.2 Other agencies or funds: Not applicable.
2. Extrabudgetary Central Government	Anti-Corruption Commission, Office of the Ombudsman, Independent Media Commission, Registration of Political Parties Commission, Law Reform Commission, Sierra Leone Insurance Commission, National Assets Commission, Local Government Services Commission, Audit Services, National Authorising Office, Electoral Commission of Sierra Leone, National Commission for Democracy, Statistics- Sierra Leone, National Commission for Privatisation, Mass Media Services, National Public Procurement Authority, Justice and Legal Services Commission, National Commission for Human Rights, University of Sierra Leone, Teacher Training Colleges, Other Tertiary Educational Institutions, Pharmacy Board Services, National Tourist Board, SALWACO (Sierra Leone Water Company), Sierra Leone Investment and Export Promotion Agency, National Telecommunications Commission, Sierra Leone Maritime Administration, Civil Aviation Authority, Sierra Leone Agricultural Research Institute, Sierra Leone Environment Protection Agency.
3. Social Security Funds	NASSIT (National Social Security and Insurance Trust).
4. State Government	Not applicable.
5. Local Government	5.1 Budgetary local government units/entities: 149 chiefdoms, Freetown City Council, 1 rural area council (Western Rural), 4 rural district councils (Koya, Mountain, Waterloo, and York) , 5 town councils (Bo, Kenema, Koidu, Makeni, and Sherbro Urban District), and 12 district councils. 5.2 Extrabudgetary local government units: No information available.
Compilation Practices	
Breaks in Series	Prior to 1998, fiscal year ends June 30. From 1991, revenue data include loan repayments, and expense data include lending operations. These data cannot be disaggregated from existing source data.
Compilation Notes	Data cover activities of subsector 1. Government Finance Statistics are compiled by the Ministry of Finance.
Implementation of GFSM 2001/2014	No information available.

Singapore (576)

Information Last Updated	2015
Units of General Government	
1. Budgetary Central Government	1.1 Legislative, Judiciary, and Executive bodies including ministries/departments. 1.2 Other agencies or funds: Not applicable.
2. Extrabudgetary Central Government	8 community development authorities, boards and councils, 12 economic affairs and service agencies, boards and councils, 7 education agencies (including universities and polytechnics).
3. Social Security Funds	Not applicable.
4. State Government	Not applicable.
5. Local Government	Not applicable.
Compilation Practices	
Breaks in Series	In Table 7, data for pre-primary and primary education outlays (7091) are included in secondary education outlays (7092). Full consolidation for the subsectors of central government could not be effected prior to 1994. Starting in 2005, revenue and expense data for the subsectors budgetary and extrabudgetary central government are presented on a gross basis, consistent with the GFSM 2001 methodology. Data through 2004 are presented net of grants among these central government units.
Compilation Notes	Data in central government on tables cover operations of subsectors 1 and partially subsector 2. Liabilities are reported at face value.
Implementation of GFSM 2001/2014	No information available.

Slovak Republic (936)

Information Last Updated	2015
Units of General Government	
1. Budgetary Central Government	1.1 Legislative, Judiciary, and Executive bodies including ministries/departments. 1.2 Other agencies or funds: Office of the national council, office of the ombudsman, and various agencies.
2. Extrabudgetary Central Government	National Property Fund, and State Fund for Dwelling Development, 20 Public Universities, Healthcare Oversight Office, Slovak National Centre for the Human Rights, Radio and Television of Slovakia, Danubiana, Slovak Press Agency, Audiovisual Fund, Central semi-budgetary organizations, National Nuclear Fund, Slovak Consolidation Agency, Slovak Land Fund, Slovak National Centre for the Human Rights, RTVS, Audit Oversight Office, Environmental Fund, and Nation's Memory Institute.
3. Social Security Funds	General Health Insurance Company, Spolocna Health Insurance, Social Insurance Company, Dovera Health Insurance Company, Union Health Insurance Company.
4. State Government	Not applicable.
5. Local Government	5.1 Budgetary local government units/entities: 8 regions, and 2,900 municipalities and other units. 5.2 Extrabudgetary local government units: No information available.
Compilation Practices	
Breaks in Series	From 2009, data are compiled in Euros. From 2008, liabilities are recorded at face value plus accrued interest. From 2003, some data components are on an accrual basis.
Compilation Notes	Data cover activities of subsectors 1-3 and 5. Government Finance Statistics are compiled by the Ministry of Finance of Slovak Republic. Data for all subsectors are reported on a noncash basis, consistent with the European System of Accounts, 2010 (ESA2010).
Implementation of GFSM 2001/2014	No information available.

Slovenia (961)

Information Last Updated	2015
Units of General Government	
1. Budgetary Central Government	1.1 Legislative, Judiciary, and Executive bodies including ministries/departments. 1.2 Other agencies or funds: No information available.
2. Extrabudgetary Central Government	Agency for Public Legal Records and Related Services, Agency for Energy, Agency for Radioactive Waste, Agency for Railways, Agency of the Republic of Slovenia for Entrepreneurship and Foreign Investment, Post and Electronic Communications Agency of the Republic of Slovenia, Slovenian Technology Agency, Slovenian research Agency, Agency for Public Oversight of Auditing, Film Fund, Employment Service of Slovenia, Fund for Employment of the Disabled, Guarantee and Alimony Fund, Krško Nuclear Plant Decommissioning Fund, Nonprofessional Cultural Activities Fund, Restitution Fund, Slovene Enterprise Fund, Succession Fund, Human Resources Development and scholarship fund, Regional Development Fund, Ecological Development Fund, Housing Fund of the Republic of Slovenia, Various other central government institutions (330 units), Public companies (23 units).
3. Social Security Funds	Pension Management Fund, Health Insurance Fund, Pension and Disability Insurance Fund.
4. State Government	Not applicable.
5. Local Government	5.1 Budgetary local government units/entities: 211 municipalities. 5.2 Extrabudgetary local government units: Other local government institutions (1007 units).
Compilation Practices	
Breaks in Series	Data prior to Slovenia joining the European Economic and Monetary Union in 2007 are in billions of Tolars. Starting with 2007 data are in millions of Euros.
Compilation Notes	Data in central government tables cover operations of subsectors 1–3. Data in local government tables cover operations of subsector 5 and are based on information from all local governments. Data for all subsectors are reported on a cash basis except for some units in extrabudgetary and social security funds subsectors. There are 23 units in extrabudgetary subsector which are public companies and therefore report on an accrual basis. These units were added to align with ESA95 classification of institutional sectors. Pension Management Fund (KAD) in social security funds subsector also reports on an accrual basis. For all of these units data from ESA95 EDP report are used.
Implementation of GFSM 2001/2014	No information available.

Information Last Updated	2017
Units of General Government	
1. Budgetary Central Government	Covered. Ministry of Agriculture and Livestock Development, Office of the Auditor General, Ministry of Education and Human Resources Development, Ministry of Finance and Treasury, Ministry of Foreign Affairs and External Trade, Office of the Governor General, Ministry of Health and Medical Services, Ministry of Infrastructure Development, National Debt Servicing, National Parliament. Ministry of Forestry and Research Office of the Prime Minister, and Cabinet Pensions and Gratuities Ministry of Police, National Security and Correctional Services Ministry of Provincial Government and Institutional Strengthening Ministry of Lands, Housing and Survey Ministry of Development Planning and Aid Co-ordination Ministry of Culture and Tourism Ministry of Commerce, Industries, Labour and Immigration Ministry of Communication and Aviation Ministry of Fisheries and Marine Resources Ministry of Public Service Ministry of Justice and Legal Affairs Ministry of Home Affairs Ministry of National Unity, Reconciliation and Peace Ministry of Mines and Energy National Judiciary Ministry of Women, Youth and Children's Affairs Ministry of Rural Development Ministry of Environment, Climate Change, Disaster Management and Meteorology
2. Extrabudgetary Central Government	Covered. Solomon Islands National University(SINU), Solomon Islands Visitors Bureau (SIVB).
3. Social Security Funds	Not applicable.
4. State Government	Covered. Guadalcanal Province, Central Province, Western Province, Isabel Province, Malaita Province, Makira Province, Temotu Province, Choisel Province, Rennell & Bellena Province.
5. Local Government	Covered. Honiara City Council
Compilation Practices	
Breaks in Series	There is a break in series for grants and corresponding expenditure items (use of goods and services; gross investment in nonfinancial assets) as data for grants for 2013-2015 are taken from the balance of payments survey and reflected in the expenditure side. Prior to 2013, non-appropriated expenditure funded with grants directly received by ministries and implementing agencies are not covered as these grants and expenditures are not administered by the Ministry of Finance and Treasury.
Compilation Notes	The budgetary central government data are sourced from administrative data from the financial system of the Ministry of Finance and Treasury. Financial transactions and balance sheet data are sourced from the monetary survey data of the Central Bank of Solomon Islands. Data for 2013-2015 are based on the new chart of accounts, implemented in 2013. Data for 2011-2012 are based on an old chart of accounts with mapping to GFSM 2014 classifications. Grants data for 2013-2015 are taken from the balance of payments survey. The budgetary central government data do not cover non-appropriated expenditures with grants directly received by ministries and implementing agencies as these revenues and expenditures are not administered by the Ministry of Finance and Treasury.
Implementation of GFSM 2001/2014	GFSM 2014 was implemented in the second quarter of 2015. Noncash data such as other accounts receivable and payable are being collected. The Solomon Islands government is in the process of expanding the coverage to general government which includes budgetary central government, provincial governments, extra-budgetary units and local governments. According to the current plan, a consolidated general government sector will be produced in 2016, the public corporations sector in 2017, and a consolidated public sector in 2018.

Information Last Updated	2017
Units of General Government	
1. Budgetary Central Government	1.1 Legislative, Judiciary, and Executive bodies including ministries/departments. 1.2 Other agencies or funds: Not applicable.
2. Extrabudgetary Central Government	171 major councils, funds, museums, sector education and training authorities (22 with effect from 2000); Technikon (college providing advanced technical education); 6 universities of technology, 17 other universities, and various other agencies for the development of specific activities.
3. Social Security Funds	Compensation Fund, Mines and Workmen Compensation Fund, Road Accident Fund (since 1996), South African Social Security Agency (SASSA) (since 2006), and Unemployment Insurance Fund.
4. State Government	4.1 Budgetary state government units/entities: 9 provinces (Eastern Cape, Free State, Gauteng, KwaZulu Natal, Limpopo, Mpumalanga, North West, Northern Cape, and Western Cape). 4.2 Extrabudgetary state government units: No information available.
5. Local Government	5.1 Budgetary local government units/entities: 278 local government units. 5.2 Extrabudgetary local government units: No information available.

Compilation Practices

Breaks in Series

In May 2011, local government elections for newly demarcated local governments were held. The demarcation process reduced the number of local governments to 278 units. Financial reporting on the new structures took effect from July 2001.

As from fiscal 2007/08, survey conducted by Stats SA was based on the newly local government financial census (Quarterly Financial Statistics and Municipal Financial Census) introduced in 2008. Thus the data is not comparable with prior years. Accrual data includes all non-cash items such as, depreciation, doubtful debt and loss/gains on disposal of Property Plant and Equipment (PPE). Some local authorities are reporting on Institute for Municipal Finance Officers (IMFO) while others use the GRAP/GAMAP reporting standards, according to the Municipal Finance Management Act (MFMA).

From 2006 onward, South African Social Security Agency (SASSA) is included under extrabudgetary units.

From 1997 onward, domestic debt data include part of Namibia's debt, guaranteed by South Africa before Namibia's independence and subsequently assumed by South Africa.

From 1996 onward, data for the social security funds include the Road Accident Fund. The Multilateral Motor Vehicle Accident Fund, which was a public insurer, was transformed into a social security fund.
From 1996 onward, data are classified according to the GFSM 2001 classifications, and the subsectors of central government's data are presented on a gross basis (i.e., before consolidation). Prior to 1996, the subsectors of central government's data are presented on a net basis (i.e., after consolidation). As a result, the subsectors of central government, but not central government's, data are not comparable.

Data for 1995 reflect further changes, which also were implemented according to the 1993 constitution, in the composition of government. Receipts from certain taxes formerly constituted a portion of the revenue of self-governing territories and independent states (and, in 1994, of the provincial administrations). In 1995, receipts from these taxes became part of budgetary central government revenue. Transfers from budgetary central government to the provincial governments were increased correspondingly to compensate for lost revenue and the devolution of further functions to provinces associated with implementation of the 1993 constitution.

From 1994 onward, data reflect changes that were implemented, according to the 1993 constitution, in the composition of government. Through 1993, the former Transkei, Bophuthatswana, Venda, Ciskei (TBVC-countries), and self-governing territories were treated as extrabudgetary institutions of the central government. In 1994, these self-governing territories and independent states were phased out; the number of provinces increased from four to nine; and operations of the self-governing territories and independent states were transferred either to national government or new provincial governments or were abolished. Domestic debt data include debt of the former independent states; this debt was assumed, on the basis of section 239 of the 1993 constitution, by the central government.

Compilation Notes

Data cover activities of subsectors 1-5.

Financial reporting on the new structures took effect from July 2001. The financial statements of the 37 and 38 national departments for fiscal 2010/11 and 2011/12 respectively, as well as documentation received from South African Revenue Service (SARS) were used as the source for adjusted accrual data for national government. However, for fiscal 2012/13, the Statement of the National Revenue, Expenditure and Borrowing from 38 national departments was used as a source for cash and proxy for accrual by adding consumption of fixed capital estimated by the National Accounts Division.

Government Finance Statistics are compiled by the South African Reserve Bank (SARB).

Implementation of GFSM 2001/2014

The South African Reserve Bank converted cash GFS data into the GFSM 2001 format in 2003. Starting in 2005, additional non-cash data, as contained in audited financial statements, are included. The release of the Public Finance Management Act, Act 1 of 1999 (as amended), lays the foundation for a number of reforms; the Minister of Finance established the Accounting Standards Board as a juristic person to establish generally recognized accounting practices. The Minister of Finance will, in due course, determine a date of implementation of Statements of Generally Recognized Accounting Practices. Full implementation is regarded as a medium- to long-term project.

Spain (184)

Information Last Updated	2015
Units of General Government	
1. Budgetary Central Government	1.1 Legislative, Judiciary, and Executive bodies including ministries/departments: 1.2 Other agencies or funds: Monarchy.
2. Extrabudgetary Central Government	Extrabudgetary funds, agencies, and other units.
3. Social Security Funds	National Mutual Pension Fund for local governments, Social security funds.
4. State Government	4.1 Budgetary state government units/entities: Autonomous communities 4.2 Extrabudgetary state government units: Several government agencies that belong to these autonomous communities.
5. Local Government	5.1 Budgetary local government units/entities: 9,000 (approximately) municipalities and other local authorities 5.2 Extrabudgetary local government units: No information available.
Compilation Practices	
Breaks in Series	None reported.
Compilation Notes	Data cover activities of subsectors 1-5. Government Finance Statistics are compiled by the Ministerio de Economía y Hacienda.
Implementation of GFSM 2001/2014	Spain participates in the Eurostat GFS convergence project with the IMF.

Sri Lanka (524)

Information Last Updated	2017
Units of General Government	
1. Budgetary Central Government	Covered. 1.1 Legislative, Judiciary, and Executive bodies including ministries/departments. 1.2 Other agencies or funds: Not applicable.
2. Extrabudgetary Central Government	Not covered.
3. Social Security Funds	Not covered.
4. State Government	Not covered. 4.1 Budgetary state government units/entities: 8 provincial councils. 4.2 Extrabudgetary state government units: No information available.
5. Local Government	Not covered. 5.1 Budgetary local government units/entities: 18 municipal councils, 37 urban councils, and 256 village councils (pradesheeya sabhas). 5.2 Extrabudgetary local government units: No information available.
Compilation Practices	
Breaks in Series	None reported.
Compilation Notes	Data cover activities of subsector 1. Government Finance Statistics are compiled by the Central Bank of Sri Lanka.
Implementation of GFSM 2001/2014	A migration plan to GFSM 2001/2014 was adopted. The Ministry of Finance (State Accounts Department)and the Central Bank of Sri Lanka are in the process of formulating a strategy to implement this over the medium term.

St. Kitts and Nevis (361)

Information Last Updated	2015
Units of General Government	
1. Budgetary Central Government	1.1 Legislative, Judiciary, and Executive bodies including ministries/departments. 1.2 Other agencies or funds: Not applicable.
2. Extrabudgetary Central Government	National Handicraft and Cottage Industries Development Board, Tourism Authority, Trust funds.
3. Social Security Funds	Social security fund.
4. State Government	Not applicable.
5. Local Government	Not applicable.
Compilation Practices	
Breaks in Series	None reported.
Compilation Notes	Data cover activities of subsectors 1. Government Finance Statistics are compiled by the Ministry of Finance.
Implementation of GFSM 2001/2014	No information available.

St. Lucia (362)

Information Last Updated	2015
Units of General Government	
1. Budgetary Central Government	1.1 Legislative, Judiciary, and Executive bodies including ministries/departments. 1.2 Other agencies or funds: Not applicable.
2. Extrabudgetary Central Government	Not applicable.
3. Social Security Funds	Not applicable.
4. State Government	Not applicable.
5. Local Government	5.1 Budgetary local government units/entities: 11 parishes, Castries City Council. 5.2 Extrabudgetary local government units: Not applicable.
Compilation Practices	
Breaks in Series	None reported.
Compilation Notes	Data cover activities of subsectors 1. Government Finance Statistics are compiled by the Ministry of Finance.
Implementation of GFSM 2001/2014	No information available.

St. Vincent and the Grenadines (364)

Information Last Updated	2015
Units of General Government	
1. Budgetary Central Government	1.1 Legislative, Judiciary, and Executive bodies including ministries/departments. 1.2 Other agencies or funds: No information available.
2. Extrabudgetary Central Government	Not applicable.
3. Social Security Funds	National Insurance Fund.
4. State Government	Not applicable.
5. Local Government	5.1 Budgetary local government units/entities: 6 parishes. 5.2 Extrabudgetary local government units: Not applicable.
Compilation Practices	
Breaks in Series	None reported.
Compilation Notes	Data cover activities of subsector 1. Government Finance Statistics are compiled by the Eastern Caribbean Central Bank.
Implementation of GFSM 2001/2014	No information available.

Suriname (366)

Information Last Updated	2015
Units of General Government	
1. Budgetary Central Government	1.1 Legislative, Judiciary, and Executive bodies including ministries/departments. 1.2 Other agencies or funds: No information available.
2. Extrabudgetary Central Government	No information available.
3. Social Security Funds	Public Pension, a universal PAYG system, Pension Fund Suriname (PFS), covering approximately 40,000 public sector employees.
4. State Government	Not applicable. =
5. Local Government	5.1 Budgetary local government units/entities: 11 local governments 5.2 Extrabudgetary local government units: Not applicable.
Compilation Practices	
Breaks in Series	None reported.
Compilation Notes	Data cover activities of subsectors 1. Government Finance Statistics are compiled by the Ministry of Finance.
Implementation of GFSM 2001/2014	No information available.

Swaziland (734)

Information Last Updated	2015
Units of General Government	
1. Budgetary Central Government	1.1 Legislative, Judiciary, and Executive bodies including ministries/departments: 1.2 Other agencies or funds: Office of the king and various other agencies.
2. Extrabudgetary Central Government	Central Transport Administration, Community Development Fund, Disabled Soldiers and Dependent Fund, Fairview Township, Guardian Fund, Japanese Aid Fund, King Sobhuza II Memorial Park, Prison Officers' Reward Fund, Matsapha Dry Expansion, Regional Development Fund, Ngwane Park Township, Police Reward Fund, Resettlement Fund, Sibhimbi Fund, Special Care Medical Aid Fund, Commission for Mediation, Arbitration and Conciliation, Motor Vehicle Accident Fund, National Agricultural Marketing Board, National Emergency Response Commission on HIV/AIDS, Sebenta National Institution, Small Enterprises Development Company, Strategic Oil Reserve Fund, Swaziland Cotton Board, Swaziland Investment Promotion Authority, Swaziland National Trust Commission, Swaziland Tourism Authority, Swaziland Television Authority, Swaziland Water and Agricultural Development Enterprise, University of Swaziland, and Water Relief Fund.
3. Social Security Funds	Not applicable.
4. State Government	Not applicable.
5. Local Government	5.1 Budgetary local government units/entities: 2 city councils, 3 town councils, and various smaller town boards. 5.2 Extrabudgetary local government units: No information available.
Compilation Practices	
Breaks in Series	None reported.
Compilation Notes	Data cover activities of subsector 1. Government Finance Statistics are compiled by the Central Bank of Swaziland.
Implementation of GFSM 2001/2014	No information available.

Sweden (144)

Information Last Updated	2015
Units of General Government	
1. Budgetary Central Government	Covered. 1.1 Legislative, Judiciary, and Executive bodies including ministries/departments: Agencies, Monarchy, National Debt Office (approximately 230 units). 1.2 Other central government bodies or funds: Central government controlled funds and central government owned and controlled non-market corporations (15 units).
2. Extrabudgetary Central Government	Not applicable.
3. Social Security Funds	Covered. General Pension Funds, Swedish Pensions Agency.
4. State Government	Not applicable.
5. Local Government	Covered. 5.1 Budgetary local government units/entities: 290 municipalities, 200 municipal associations, 20 county councils, 20 other local government bodies (local government owned and controlled non-market corporations). Extrabudgetary local government units: No information available.
Compilation Practices	
Breaks in Series	From 2010, The Swedish Pension Agency was established (classified within social security funds subsector). From 2000, the church is separated from local government. From 1998, voluntary pension schemes were included in the balance sheet of both central and local government which affect imputed social contributions and corresponding items. From 1998, the Unemployment Fund is included in the budgetary central government. Previously, this fund formed part of social security funds. From 1995, the fiscal year end changed.
Compilation Notes	Data cover activities of subsectors 1, 3 and 5. Government Finance Statistics are compiled by Statistics Sweden.
Implementation of GFSM 2001/2014	Sweden participates in the Eurostat GFS convergence project with the IMF. Data are based on information in the European ESA Transmission Program (ESA 2010) but then adjusted according to the requirements in the IMF GFS Yearbook.

Information Last Updated	2017
Units of General Government	
1. Budgetary Central Government	Covered. Central federal administration: Legislative, Judiciary, and Executive bodies including ministries/departments
2. Extrabudgetary Central Government	Covered. 12 units reported, separate accounts to be approved by parliament: Fund for major railway projects, Infrastructure Fund, Area of Swiss federal Institutes of Technology, Swiss Alcohol Board, Swiss Federal Institute for Vocational Education and Training, Swiss Federal Institute of Metrology, Swiss National Museum, Pro Helvetia (Swiss Arts Council), Swiss National Science Foundation, Switzerland Tourism, Swiss Grid Supplement Fund, Foundation for Buildings for International Organisations (FIPOI).
3. Social Security Funds	Covered. 6 units reported: Old-age and survivors' insurance (AHV), Disability insurance (IV), Compensation fund for loss of earnings (EO), Agriculture family allowances (FL), Unemployment insurance (ALV), Geneva maternity insurance.
4. State Government	Covered. 26 units reported: Cantons (26/26), Aggregation of Cantonal Concordats.
5. Local Government	Covered. 2396 units reported out of a sample of 900: Municipalities (2396/2396), Including nonfinancial special purpose entities at the level of local governments.
Compilation Practices	
Breaks in Series	In principle, the GFS Model posts all transactions and indicators on an accrual basis. The source data are collected on an accrual basis except for the Central Government whose data were collected on a cash basis before 2008. The national accounting models are aligned to follow the International Public Sector Accounting Standards (IPSAS). Where the GFSM 2014 deviates from European System of Accounts (ESA 2010), is that the latter is adopted for the treatment of accounting transactions. During the reconciliation with the system of national accounts, it was found that efficient processing of the data for the Confederation and social security funds could be guaranteed under the new conditions only by implementing an IT application on a time series basis. As a result, the Confederation and social security funds sub-sectors have been completely rerecorded from fiscal 2008 onward. Furthermore, the Confederation sub-sector has been extended to include the Building Foundation for International Organisations (FIPOI) and feed-in remuneration at cost (CRF fund). Switching the national financial statistics model to the HAM2 resulted in a series break in the cantons and municipalities' sub-sectors because from fiscal 2008 on, hospitals and retirement and nursing homes are no longer included in accordance with the ESA 2010 sectoring guidelines. If they are contained in a government unit's accounts, they are eliminated. According to the ESA 2010 delimitation criteria, these entities are not part of the general government sector. With the implementation of the GFSM 2014, this series break in the basic data was removed by eliminating the hospitals and retirement and nursing homes of the cantons and municipalities contained in the FS Model up to fiscal 2007 without affecting the balance from 1990 to 2007. Another series break in the basic statistics was eliminated in the GFS Model relates to contributions and compensation from and to public authorities. Prior to 2008, these two items were not recorded separately, but rather as contributions. In the GFS Model, these items were divided up into compensation and contributions for the 1990–2007 period using the average share for each task area during the 2008–2012 period. This subdivision is important from an economic perspective, as compensation payments are considered as intermediate consumption and received compensation as production. In contrast, contributions are grants, as they are not paid in return for something. A further correction concerns the recording of the Confederation's receipts from the auction of mobile radio licenses in 2001, 2002 and 2012. For the sake of consistency with the ESA 2010 guidelines, these receipts are recorded as receipts from the disposal of nonproduced assets under transactions in non-financial assets. They thus have a positive effect on net lending/borrowing for the years in question.
Compilation Notes	Data cover activities of all subsectors included in the definition of general government (see above). Data disseminated for general government sector covers tables 1-3, 6 and 7. Time series for revenue, expense and net acquisitions of non-financial assets for general government sector covers the time span 1990 to 2014. Balance Sheet data for the same time span are available for all general government subsectors except local government. Local Balance Sheet data and therefore general government Balance Sheet are available from 2008 to 2014. Data are recorded on accrual basis for all subsectors since 1990, except Central Government data, which are recorded on a time corrected cash basis (accrual) until 2006. Since 2007 Central Government applies the International Public Sector Accounting Standards (IPSAS), so that beginning with 2007 all general government data are all recorded on a fully accrual basis. Tradable assets and liabilities are valued at market price. Contrary to ESA 2010, GFSM 2014 data are also fully consolidated. All subsectors are based on a complete census, except for the local government. Local government data are based on an annual survey of about 900 municipalities and on sample based estimates for the remainder. Latest methodological information can be fund on the following website: https://www.efv.admin.ch/efv/en/home/themen/finanzstatistik/berichterstattung.html See Annual report --> See Basic documentation
Implementation of GFSM 2001/2014	The Financial Statistics Section of the Federal Finance Administration (FFA) published data and indicators in accordance with the new financial statistics guidelines (GFSM 2014) of the International Monetary Fund (IMF) for the first time on September 2015. As part of the changeover to the GFSM 2014, a methodological reconciliation is being performed with the system of national accounts of the Federal Statistical Office (FSO). Where necessary, the results of the GFS Model have been reconciled with those of the system of national accounts and its data has been included. The harmonization between the Swiss system of national accounts and the international GFS Model of financial statistics has also led to adjustments to the basic statistics. The data published in the GFS Model is of a provisional nature for the time being, as the reconciliation with the Swiss system of national accounts has not yet been completed. The items regarding the recording, coverage and valuation of contributions for the restructuring and funding of public-sector pension funds, as well as the amount of the resultant employee retirement benefits that were still outstanding within the scope of the 2015 reconciliation have been clarified in the meantime, but they have not yet been implemented. It is planned to publish the data adjustments associated with the finalization of the reconciliation and thus the definitive figures for the GFS Model in the summer of 2017.

Information Last Updated 2017

Units of General Government

1. Budgetary Central Government

Covered.
National Irrigation Commission, President's Delivery Bureau, Treasury Registrar, Secretariat of The Public Remuneration, Joint Finance Commission, Judiciary Service Commission, Financial Intelligence Unit, Fire and Rescue Force, Commission for Mediation and Arbitration, Attorney General's Office, State House, The Treasury, Public Debt and General Services, Accountant General's Department, Ministry of Co-operatives and Marketing, Prime Minister, Vice President, Registrar of Political Parties, Ministry of Home Affairs - Police Force, Ministry of Home Affairs - Prison Services, President`s Office and Cabinet Secretariat, Vice President's Office, President's Office - Public Service Management, Ethics Secretariat, Ministry of Foreign Affairs and International Co-operation, Public Prosecutions Division, Regional Administrative Secretariat Katavi, Prime Minister's Office, Defense, National Service, Judiciary, Ministry of Constitutional, Affairs and Justice, The National Assembly Fund, Ministry of Agriculture, Food Security and Cooperatives, Ministry of Industry, Trade and Marketing, Ministry of Education and Vocational Training, Regional Administrative Secretariat Simiyu, Ministry of Lands and Human Settlements Development, Ministry of Water and Irrigation, Ministry of Finance, Ministry of Home Affairs, Ministry of Health and Social Welfare, Ministry of Community Development, Gender and Children, Regional Administrative Secretariat Njombe, Commission for Human Rights and Good Governance, Prime Minister's Office - Regional Administration and Local Government, Ministry of Defense & National Service, Ministry of Energy and Minerals, Law Reform Commission, Electoral Commission, Ministry of Transport, Ministry of Labor, Employment and Youth Development, President's Office - Planning Commission, Public Service Recruitment Secretariat, Ministry of Communication, Science and Technology, Ministry of Natural Resources and Tourism, Regional Administrative Secretariat Arusha, Regional Administrative Secretariat Coast, Regional Administrative Secretariat Dodoma, Regional Administrative Secretariat Iringa, Regional Administrative Secretariat Kigoma, Regional Administrative Secretariat Kilimanjaro, Regional Administrative Secretariat Lindi, Regional Administrative Secretariat Mara, Regional Administrative Secretariat Mbeya, Regional Administrative Secretariat Morogoro, Regional Administrative Secretariat Mtwara, Regional Administrative Secretariat Mwanza, Regional Administrative Secretariat Ruvuma, Regional Administrative Secretariat Shinyanga, Regional Administrative Secretariat Singida, Regional Administrative Secretariat Tabora, Regional Administrative Secretariat Tanga, Regional Administrative Secretariat Kagera, Regional Administrative Secretariat Dar es Salaam, Regional Administrative Secretariat Rukwa, Anti Drug Commission, TACAIDS (Tanzania Commission for AIDS), Immigration Department, Public Service Commission, Regional Administrative Secretariat Manyara, Ministry for East African Cooperation, Ministry of Works, Ministry of Livestock Development and Fisheries.

2. Extrabudgetary Central Government

Covered.
Agency for Development Education Management, Agriculture Seed Agency, Architects and Quantity Surveyors Registration Board (AQRB), Ardhi University, Arusha Technical College, Board of External Trade (Tan Trade), CAMARTEC, Capital Development Authority (CDA), Cashewnut Board of Tanzania, Cereals & Other Produce Board, College of African Wildlife Management (MWEKA), College of Business Education (CBE), Co-operative Audit & Supervision Corporation (COASCO), Copyright Society of Tanzania, Dar es Salaam College of Education (DUCE), Dar es Salaam Institute of Technology (DIT), Dar es Salaam Maritime Institute (DMI), Dar Rapid Transport, Diary Board of Tanzania, East Africa Statistical Centre, Engineers Registration Board, Export Processing Zones Authority, Fair Competition Commission (FCC), Fair Competition Tribunal (FCT), Government Chemist Laboratory Agency, Government Procurement Services Agency (GPSA), Higher Education Students Loans Board, Institute of Accountancy Arusha, Institute of Finance Management (IFM), Institute of Judicial Administration (IJA), Institute of Rural Development Planning, Institute of Social Works, Kibaha Education Centre, Kivukoni College (MwalimuNyerere Memorial Academy), Law School of Tanzania, Local Government Training Institute (Hombolo), Mbeya Institute of Technology, Mkwawa University College of Education, Moshi University College of Coperative and Business, Mozambique - Tanzania Centre for Foreign Relation, Muhimbili National Hospital (MNH), MuhimbiliOrthopaedic Institute (MOI), Muhimbili University of Health & Allied Sciences (MUHAS), Mzinga Corporation, National Arts Council, National Board of Accountants and Auditors (NBAA), National Bureau of Statistics, National College of Tourism, National Construction Council, National Council fro Technical Education (NACTE), National Economic Empowerment Council (NEEC), National Environment Management Council (NEMC), National Examination Council of Tanzania, National Food Reserve Agency, National Housing & Building Research Agency, National Identification Authority, National Institute for Medical Research (NIMRI), National Institute of Transport, National Kiswahili Council of Tanzania, National Land Use Planning Commission, National Museum of Tanzania, National Sports Council, National Sugar Institute, Nelson Mandela African Institute of Science and Technoligy (NM-AIST), Occupational Safety and Health Authority (OSHA), Ocean Road Cancer Institute, Open University of Tanzania (OUT), Procurement & Supplies Professionals and Technicians Board, Public Procurement Appeal Authority, Public Procurement Regulatory Authority (PPRA) Registration, Insolvency & Trusteeship Agency (RITA), Rufiji Basin Development Authority (RUBADA), Rural Energy Fund, Small Industries Development Organization (SIDO), Social Security Regulatory Authority, Sokoine University of Agriculture (SUA), State Mining Corporation (STAMICO), Tanzania Sanaa naUtamaduniBagamoyo, Tanzania Airport Authority, Tanzania Atomic Energy Commission, Tanzania Automotive Technology Centre (NYUMBU), Tanzania Building Authority, Tanzania Bureau of Standards (TBS), Tanzania Coffee Board, Tanzania Commission for Science and Technology, Tanzania Commission for Universities (TCU), Tanzania Cotton Board, Tanzania Education Authority, Tanzania Employment Services Agency, Tanzania Engineering & Manufacturing Design Organization, Tanzania Fisheries Research Institute, Tanzania Food and Drugs Authority, Tanzania Food and Nutrition Centre (TFNC), Tanzania Forestry Research Institute, Tanzania Industrial Research & Development Organization (TIRDO), Tanzania Institute of Accountancy, Tanzania Institute of Adult Education, Tanzania Institute of Education, Tanzania Investment Centre (TIC), Tanzania Library Services Board, Tanzania Marine Parks (Marine Parks and Reserve Unit), Tanzania Meteological Agency, Tanzania Minerals Audit Agency (TMAA), Tanzania National Business Council, Tanzania National Roads Agency, Tanzania Officia l Seed Certification Agency, Tanzania Public Service College, Tanzania Pyrethrum Board, Tanzania Revenue Authority, Tanzania Sisal Board, Tanzania Smallholders Tea Development Agency, Tanzania Tobacco Board, Tanzania Tourist Board, Tanzania Tree Seed Agency, Tanzania Warehouse Licensing Board, Tanzania Wildlife Research Institute (TAWIRI), Tea Board of Tanzania, Tropical Pesticides Research Institute, UNESCO National Commission, University of Dar es Salaam, University of Dodoma, University of Mzumbe, Business Registrations & Licensing Agency (BRELA), Contractors Registration Board, Drilling and Dam Construction Agency, Energy & Water Utilities Regulatory Authority (EWURA), Medical Store Department (MSD), National Development Corporation, National Institute for Productivity, National Ranching Company Limited (NARCO), Sugar Board of Tanzania, Surface and Marine Transport Authority SUMATRA, Tanzania Civil Aviation Authority, Tanzania Communication Regulatory Authority, Tanzania Government Flights Agency, TEMESA, VETA, Weights and Measures Agency, Gaming Board of Tanzania, Pangani Water Basin, Wami Ruvu Water Basin, Ziwa Tanganyika Water Basin, Mt Ruvuma Water Basin, Rufiji Water Basin, Lake Nyasa Water Basin, Lake Rukwa Water Basin, Kati Water Basin, Lake Victoria Water Basin, Mt Songwe Water Basin, Lake Victoria Environment Management Project (LVEMP), Fisheries Education Training Agency (FETA), Geological Survey of Tanzania (GST), Tanzania Forest Services Agency (TFSA), Tanzania Veterinary Laboratory Agency (TVLA), Tanzania Meat Board (TMB), Tanzania Revenue Appeals Board (TRAB), Tax Revenue Appeal Tribunal (TRAT), Corporation Sole Works Superintendent (CSWS), Tanzania Fertilizer Regulatory Authority (TFRA), Pharmacy Council of Tanzania (PCTz), Tanzania Nurses and Midwifery Council (TNMC), Agriculture Input Trust Fund (AGITF), Road Fund Board (RFB), Appropriate Technology Transfer Institute (ATTI) – Mbeya, Livestock Training Agency (LITA), Morogoro Works Trainnig Institute (MWTI), Tengeru Community Development Training(TCDTI), Tanzania Coffee Research Institute (TACRI), Tea Research Insitute of Tanzania (TRIT), Tobacco Research Institute of Tanzania (TORITA).

3. Social Security Funds

Covered.
National Health Insurance Fund (NHIF), National Social Security Fund (NSSF), GEPF Retirement Benefit Fund, Local Authorities Pension Fund, Parastatal Pension Fund (PPF), Public Service Pension Fund (PSPF).

4. State Government

Not applicable.

5. Local Government

Covered.
Arusha City Council, Arusha District Council, Babati District Council, Babati Town Council, Bagamoyo District Council, Bahi District Council, Bariadi District Council, Bariadi Town Council, Biharamulo District Council, Buhigwe District Council, Bukoba District Council, Bukoba Municipal Council, Bukombe District Council, Bumbuli District Council, Bunda District Council, Busega District Council, Busokelo District Council, Butiama District Council, Chamwino District Council, Chato District Council, Chemba District Council, Chunya District Council, Dar es Salaam City Council, Dodoma Municipal Council, Gairo District Council, Geita District Council, Geita Town Council, Hai District Council, Hanang District Council, Handeni District Council, Handeni Town Council, Igunga District Council, Ikungi District Council, Ilala Municipal Council, Ileje District Council, Ilemela Municipal Council, Iramba District Council, Iringa Municipal Council, Iringa District Council, Itilima District Council, Kahama District Council, Kahama Town Council, Kakonko District Council, Kalambo District Council, Kaliua District Council, Karagwe District Council, Karatu District Council, Kasulu District Council, Kasulu Town Council, Kibaha District Council, Kibaha Town Council, Kibondo District Council, Kigoma District Council, Kigoma/Ujiji Municipal Council, Kilindi District Council, Kilolo District Council, Kilombero District Council, Kilosa District Council, Kilwa District Council, Kinondoni Municipal Council, Kisarawe District Council, Kishapu District Council, Kiteto District Council, Kondoa District Council, Kongwa District Council, Korogwe Town Council, Korogwe District Council, Kwimba District Council, Kyela District Council, Kyerwa District Council, Lindi Municipal Council, Lindi District Council, Liwale District Council, Longido District Council, Ludewa District Council, Lushoto District Council, Mafia District Council, Magu District Council, Makambako Town Council, Makete District Council, Manyoni District Council, Masasi Town Council, Masasi District Council, Maswa District Council, Mbarali District Council, Mbeya CC City Council, Mbeya District Council, Mbinga District Council, Mbogwe District Council, Mbozi District Council, Mbulu District Council, Meatu District Council, Meru District Council, Misenyi District Council, Misungwi District Council, Mkalama District Council, Mkinga District Council, Mkuranga District Council, Mlele District Council, Momba District Council, Monduli District Council, Morogoro District Council, Morogoro MC Municipal Council, Moshi Municipal Council, 5Moshi District Council, Mpanda District Council, Mpanda Town Council, Mpwapwa District Council, Msalala District Council, Mtwara Municipal Council, Mtwara District Council, Mufindi District Council, Muheza District Council, Muleba District Council, Musoma Municipal Council, Musoma District Council, Mvomero District Council, Mwanga District Council, Mwanza/Nyamagana City Council, Nachingwea District Council, Namtumbo District, Council, Nanyumbu District Council, Newala District Council, Ngara District Council, Ngorongoro District Council, Njombe District Council, Njombe Town Council, Nkasi District Council, Nsimbo District Council, Nyang'hwale District Council, Nyasa District Council, Nzega District Council, Nzega Town Council, Pangani District Council, Rombo District Council, Rorya District Council, Ruangwa District Council, Rufiji District Council, Rungwe District Council, Same District Council, Sengerema District Council, Serengeti District Council, Shinyanga Municipal Council, Shinyanga District Council, Siha District Council, Sikonge District Council, Simanjiro District Council, Singida Municipal Council, Singida District Council, Songea Municipal Council, Songea District Council, Sumbawanga Municipal Council, Sumbawanga District Council, Tabora Municipal Council, Tabora/Uyui District Council, Tandahimba District Council, Tanga City Council, Tarime District Council, Tarime Town Council, Temeke Municipal Council, Tunduru District Council, Tunduma Town Council, Ukerewe District Council, Ulanga District Council, Urambo District Council, Ushetu District Council, Uvinza District Council, Wanging'ombe District Council.

Compilation Practices

Breaks in Series

None reported.

Compilation Notes

Data cover activities of subsectors 1 and 5. Government Finance Statistics are compiled by the Ministry of Finance.

Implementation of GFSM 2001/2014

Improve the classification of cash data in GFSM 2001 format, decide sector classification of other government entities, expand coverage of data to include all general government units, collect additional noncash flow data, and compile financial balance sheets.

Thailand (578)

Information Last Updated

2017

Units of General Government

1. Budgetary Central Government

Covered.
194 units reported. 20 ministries, The Office of His Majesty's Principal Private Secretary, Bureau of the Royal Household, Office of National Buddhism, Office of the Royal Development Project Board, The National Research Council of Thailand, The Royal Institute, The National Police Office, Office of Prevention and Suppression of Money, Southern Boarder Provinces Administrative Center, The Secretariat of Thailand Senate, The Secretariat of the House of Representatives, Office of the Constitution Court, The Office of the Administrative Courts, The office of the Court of Justice, Office of the Attorney General, National Economic And Social Advisory Council, Office of the Election Board, The State Audit Office, Office of the Ombudsman, Office of the National Counter Corruption Commission, Office of the National Human Rights Commission, Law Reform Commission of Thailand, Boat Building Training Center, Committee for the Coordination of the Investigation of the Lower Mekong Basin, Council of Social Welfare in Thailand, Fisheries Development Center, Hoop Krapong Community Development Center, Plant Protection Service Center, Red Cross Society, Thailand Management and Productivity Development Center, Vegetable Seed Research Center, War Veteran's Organization, Public Hospitals, Public Schools, 24 Universities , 19 Public Organizations, and 94 Provinces and cluster of Provinces.

2. Extrabudgetary Central Government

Covered.
116 units reported. Education Loan Fund, Oil Fund, Fund for Promoting Conservation of Energy, Research Fund, Sugar Canes and Sugar Fund, Fund for Promotion of Small and Medium Enterprises, National Village and Urban Community Fund, Thai Health Promotion Foundation, National Science and Technology Development Agency, National Health Security Office, Revolving Fund for producing Royal Thai, Bypass fee fund, other 97 Extrabudgetary Funds, and 8 autonomous government agencies.

3. Social Security Funds

Covered.
2 units reported: Social Security Fund and Workmen's Compensation Fund.

4. State Government

Not applicable.

5. Local Government

Covered.
Budgetary local government units/entities: 7,853 units reported. 76 Provincial Administration, 2,440 Municipalities, 5,335 Subdistrict Administration Organizations, Bangkok, and Pattaya City. Extrabudgetary local government units: No extrabudgetary information was provided.

Compilation Practices

Breaks in Series

From 2005, budgetary central government and consolidated central government data include consumption of fixed capital. From 2003, extrabudgetary central government and social security funds data are on an accrual basis.

Compilation Notes

Data cover activities of subsectors 1-3 and 5.
Data disseminated for general government sector cover table 1, 2, 3, partially 6, partially 7 and 8. Time series for revenue and expense for general government sector cover 1995 to 2015. Data are recorded on cash basis for subsectors 5. Data are recorded on mixed cash, commitment, and/or accrual basis for subsectors 1, 2, and 3. The following flows are consolidated: Grants

Implementation of GFSM 2001/2014

Government Finance Statistics are compiled by the Ministry of Finance. Thailand will disseminate monthly General Government data on the Ministry of Finance's website starting in fiscal year 2016.

Timor-Leste, Dem. Rep. of (537)

Information Last Updated	2017
Units of General Government	
1. Budgetary Central Government	Covered. 1.1 Legislative, Judiciary, and Executive bodies including ministries/departments. 1.2 Other agencies or funds: Combined Fund of Timor Leste (CFTL), Human Capital Development Fund (HCDF), 13 districts, 65 subdistricts, 21 autonomous agencies, Infrastructure fund (until 2016).
2. Extrabudgetary Central Government	Not applicable. Television and Radio Corporation of Timor-Leste (RTTL), Timor-Gap, Petroleum Fund, Donor Fund
3. Social Security Funds	Not applicable.
4. State Government	Not applicable.
5. Local Government	Not applicable.
Compilation Practices	
Breaks in Series	None reported.
Compilation Notes	From August 2005, the Petroleum Fund collects all revenue receipts from energy sector activities. Beginning in 2014, Local governments will replace the current district system noted above. Since 2014, the Western district of Oecusse is an autonomous agency. From 2017 onwards, the infrastructure fund ceases to exist.
Implementation of GFSM 2001/2014	From 2010 onward, cash based data in accordance with GFSM 2001 framework were reported for publication in the GFS Yearbook. The action plan is being implemented to introduce some aspects of the GFSM 2001 framework.

Togo (742)

Information Last Updated	2015
Units of General Government	
1. Budgetary Central Government	1.1 Legislative, Judiciary, and Executive bodies including ministries/departments. 1.2 Other agencies or funds: No information available.
2. Extrabudgetary Central Government	30 extrabudgetary central government units/entities : Togo Copyright Office, Construction and Housing Center, National Center for Blood Transfusion, 10 Regional Hospital Centers, 3 University Hospital Centers (Tokoin, Campus, and Kara), Togo National Publishing Company, National School of Administration, Independent Company for the Financing of Road Maintenance, National Apprenticeship, Vocational Training and Development Fund, Fund for the Promotion and Development of Tourism, Special Fund for Housing Development, National Institute for Agricultural Training in Tové, National Institute of Hygiene, Togolese Agricultural Research Institute, Institute for Technical Support and Advice, Togo Free Zone Authority, University of Kara, University of Lomé, National Center for Professional Development, National Agency for Food Security in Togo, Support Fund for Youth Economic Initiatives, Youth Integration Fund, Young Farmer Support and Guarantee Fund, Support Fund for Local Economic and Social Development Initiatives, Nation Fund for Inclusive Financing, National Employment Promotion Agency, National Health Insurance Institute, National Environmental Management Agency, National Agency for the Promotion and Financing Guarantee of SMEs/SMIs.
3. Social Security Funds	National Social Security Fund, Pension Fund.
4. State Government	Not applicable.
5. Local Government	5.1 Budgetary local government units/entities: 30 municipalities, 35 prefectures, Public enterprise for the administration of markets, 1 subprefecture. 5.2 Extrabudgetary local government units: No information available.
Compilation Practices	
Breaks in Series	None reported.
Compilation Notes	Data cover the operations of subsector 1. Receipts are recorded on a cash basis and expenditures are based on commitments with some adjustments for arrears.
Implementation of GFSM 2001/2014	Togo is a member country of the West Africa Economic and Monetary Union (WAEMU). In June 2009, the WAEMU Council of Ministers adopted a new public finance harmonized framework which includes six directives of which the common reporting format on Government Financial Operations (Tableau des Opérations Financières de l'Etat – TOFE) which is compatible with the international statistical methodology adopted by the GFSM 2001.

Trinidad and Tobago (369)

Information Last Updated	2015
Units of General Government	
1. Budgetary Central Government	1.1 Legislative, Judiciary, and Executive bodies including ministries/departments. 1.2 Other agencies or funds: Public Service Appeal Board, Registration, Recognition, and Certification Board, Service Commissions Department, Statutory Authorities Service Commission, Trinidad and Tobago Police Service, Tax Appeal Board.
2. Extrabudgetary Central Government	Agricultural Society of Trinidad and Tobago, Airports Authority of Trinidad and Tobago, Board of Industrial Training, Cipriani Labor College, Chaguaramas Development Authority, Cocoa and Coffee Board, College of Science, technology and Applied Arts, Institute of Marine Affairs, National Institute of Higher Education (Research, Science and Technology), Land Settlement Agency, National Agricultural Marketing and Development Company(NAMDEVCO), Naparima Bowl, National Carnival Commission, National Library and Information System (NALIS), Port Authority of Trinidad and Tobago, Public Transport Service Corporation, Princess Elizabeth Home, Queens Hall, Regulated Industries Commission, Sugar Industry Labor Welfare Fund, Trinidad and Tobago Association for the Hearing Impaired, Trinidad and Tobago Blind Welfare Association, Trinidad and Tobago Association for Retarded Children, Trinidad and Tobago Bureau of Standards, Trinidad and Tobago Civil Aviation Authority, Trinidad and Tobago National Commission for United Nations Educational, Scientific, and Cultural Organization, Zoological Society of Trinidad and Tobago, Water and Sewerage Authority.
3. Social Security Funds	National Insurance Board.
4. State Government	Not applicable.
5. Local Government	5.1 Budgetary local government units/entities: Port of Spain City Corporation, San Fernando City Corporation, Arima Borough Corporation, Point Fortin Borough Corporation, Chaguanas Borough Corporation, Diego Martin Regional Corporation, San Juan/ Laventille Regional Corporation, Tunapuna/Piarco Regional Corporation, Sangre Grande Regional Corporation, Couva/Tabaquite Regional Corporation, Mayaro/Rio Claro Regional Corporation, Siparia Regional Corporation, Penal/Debe Regional Corporation, Princess Town Regional Corporation, Tobago House of Assembly. 5.2 Extrabudgetary local government units: Not applicable.
Compilation Practices	
Breaks in Series	None reported.
Compilation Notes	Data in central government tables cover operations of subsectors 1–3 and subsector 5.
Implementation of GFSM 2001/2014	No information available.

Tunisia (744)

Information Last Updated	2015
Units of General Government	
1. Budgetary Central Government	1.1 Legislative, Judiciary, and Executive bodies including ministries/departments. 1.2 Other agencies or funds: No information available.
2. Extrabudgetary Central Government	Administrative government agencies.
3. Social Security Funds	National Pension and Social Welfare Fund, National Social Security Fund, National Health Insurance Fund.
4. State Government	Not applicable.
5. Local Government	5.1 Budgetary local government units/entities: 24 government councils and 264 municipalities 5.2 Extrabudgetary local government units: Not applicable.
Compilation Practices	
Breaks in Series	From 1994 onward, data for the Old Age, Disability, and Survivor Insurance Fund are included in the accounts of the National Social Security Fund. Until 1998, outstanding external debt as of December 31 is valued at average annual exchange rates. Thereafter, end-of-year exchange rates are used.
Compilation Notes	Data in consolidated central government tables cover operations of subsectors 1 and 3. The domestic budget excludes foreign-financed spending and lending for policy purposes. Data for budgetary central government include those transactions. In Table 7, data for expenditures on fuel and energy are included in other economic affairs and services categories.
Implementation of GFSM 2001/2014	No information available.

Turkey (186)

Information Last Updated	2017
Units of General Government	
1. Budgetary Central Government	Covered. 1.1 Constitutional court, Grand National Assembly of Turkey, judiciary, ministries, presidency, prime ministry, supreme court, undersecretariats 1.2 Special budgeted institutions – mainly universities, high technology institutes 1.3 Regulatory and supervisory institutions, except BRSA and capital markets 1.4 Risk Account 1.5 Supporting and Price Stability Fund
2. Extrabudgetary Central Government	Covered. 2.1 Extrabudgetary funds (Defense Industry Support Fund, Privatization Fund, Prime Ministry Promotion Fund) 2.2 Revolving funds 2.3 Social facilities 2.4 Other extrabudgetary units (such as Turkey Radio and Television Institution, and Turkey Accounting Standards Board)
3. Social Security Funds	Covered. 3.1 Social security institution 3.2 General Directorate of Turkish Labor Administration 3.3 Unemployment Insurance Fund
4. State Government	Not applicable.
5. Local Government	Covered. 5.1 Municipalities (1,391) 5.2 Provincial special administrations (53) 5.3 Local government unions (988) 5.4 Development agencies (26) 5.5 Youth and sports provincial administrations (81)
Compilation Practices	
Breaks in Series	Data Coverage: Data of central government tables cover operations of subsector 1-3. Data in local governments tables cover operations of subsector 5.
Compilation Notes	Accounting Practices: 1. Bases of recording: Data for all subsectors are reported on a noncash basis. (Except in the budgetary subsector, tax revenues are time adjusted cash revenues and in the social security subsector, social contributions are cash revenues.) 2. Liquidation or complementary period: Not reported. 3. Valuation of assets and liabilities: Domestic and external government bonds are recorded at market value
Implementation of GFSM 2001/2014	The institutional units within the general government sector have been implementing the new Public Financial Management and Control Law since 2006. This law requires the institutional units to apply a new accounting system based on accrual principles. The authority to compile government finance statistics was given at that time to the Ministry of Finance (MOF). Beginning in 2009, data are available for general government and its sub-sector. General government sector scope has been changed in 2012 February; institutions affiliated with municipalities are removed from the scope; and 2008, 2009, 2010 years GFS tables have been revised on this scope.

Uganda (746)

Information Last Updated	2015
Units of General Government	
1. Budgetary Central Government	1.1 Legislative, Judiciary, and Executive bodies including ministries/departments. 1.2 Other agencies or funds: Includes referral hospitals, agencies, commissions, and state house.
2. Extrabudgetary Central Government	9 universities, 13 district referral hospitals, 39 missions abroad, the Uganda Revenue Authority, and Other semi-autonomous agencies.
3. Social Security Funds	National Social Security Fund.
4. State Government	Not applicable.
5. Local Government	5.1 Budgetary local government units/entities: 1 city council, 111 districts, 22 municipalities, and 179 town councils. 5.2 Extrabudgetary local government units: Not applicable.
Compilation Practices	
Breaks in Series	None reported.
Compilation Notes	Data cover activities of subsectors 1 and 2. Government Finance Statistics are compiled by the Ministry of Finance.
Implementation of GFSM 2001/2014	No information available.

Ukraine (926)

Information Last Updated	2017
Units of General Government	
1. Budgetary Central Government	Covered. Parliament (Verkhovna Rada); President's office; Cabinet of Ministers, ministries, state services, state agencies and inspections, state executive bodies with special status, national commissions; Constitutional Court, general jurisdiction courts, other bodies and budgetary units financed from the central budget.
2. Extrabudgetary Central Government	Not applicable.
3. Social Security Funds	Covered. 4 units reported. Pension Fund, Social Insurance Fund against Occupation Accident and Diseases of Ukraine, Social Insurance Fund against Temporary Loss of Working Capacity, and Unemployment Social Insurance Fund.
4. State Government	Not applicable.
5. Local Government	Covered. Budgetary local government units/entities: Local government units (11501/11761 budgets) of which: oblasts(24/24), republic Crimea(0/1), cities with special status: Kyiv and Sevastopol(1/2), municipalities(147/170), districts(464/474). Extra budgetary local government units: Not applicable.
Compilation Practices	
Breaks in Series	Starting April, 2014 and onwards budgetary and financial reporting do not cover the data on temporarily occupied territory of the Autonomous Republic of Crimea and Sevastopol city, as well as the part of the anti-terrorist operation zone. Starting 2001, operations of the social security funds do not include to the budgetary central government data. 2000-2001, budgetary central government data included operations of the Social Insurance Fund. In 2001 the Social Insurance Fund was liquidated. 1996-2000, budgetary central government data included operations of the Unemployment Social Insurance Fund. 1994-1996, budgetary central government data included operations of the Pension Fund.
Compilation Notes	Data cover activities of subsectors 1, 3, 5. Government Finance Statistics is complied by the Ministry of Finance of Ukraine. There is no single standard in accounting and reporting in the General Government Sector.
Implementation of GFSM 2001/2014	Implementation of the Common Chart of Accounts in Public Sector is provided in 2017, and further improvement the government finance statistics compiling according to the Government Finance Statistics Manual 2014. This institutional information was reported in 2016 in the Government Finance Statistics Yearbook (GFSY).

United Arab Emirates (466)

Information Last Updated	2015
Units of General Government	
1. Budgetary Central Government	1.1 Legislative, Judiciary, and Executive bodies including ministries/departments. 1.2 Other agencies or funds: Not applicable.
2. Extrabudgetary Central Government	Securities and Commodities Authority, United Arab Emirates University, Sheikh Zayed Housing Program, Zakat Fund, National Bureau of Statistics, Foreign Aid Coordination Office, Federal Customs Authority, Higher Colleges of Technology, General Authority for Islamic Affairs and Endowment, Emirates Authority for Standardization & Metrology, Minister of state office, National Transport Authority, General Authority of Youth and Sports Welfare, Marriage Fund, National Conference Committee, Institute of Training & Judicial Studies, Zayed University, National Human Resource Development & Employment Authority, Insurance Authority, National Council of Tourism and Antiquities, Emirates Identity Authority, Federal Water & Electricity Authority, Red Crescent, National Media Council, Emirates General Petroleum corporation, Federal Authority for Government Human Resources, Emirates Real Estate Corporation, General Civil Aviation Authority, Higher Committee for UAE Civil Seaports & Airports Security, Federal Demographic Council, Telecommunications Regulatory Authority, Federal Authority for Nuclear Regulation, National Qualifications Authority (NQA).
3. Social Security Funds	The General Pension & Social Security Authority.
4. State Government	Emirate of Abu Dhabi, Emirate of Ajman, Emirate of Dubai, Emirate of Al Fujairah, Emirate of Ras Al Khaimah, Emirate of Sharjah, Emirate of Um Al Quwain.
5. Local Government	Not applicable.
Compilation Practices	
Breaks in Series	None reported.
Compilation Notes	Data in central government tables cover operations of subsectors 1, 2, and 3. Data in state government tables cover operations of subsector 4. For Emirates of Um Al Quwain and Ajman some important government units are excluded from the coverage. The extra-budgetary funds were excluded from all of the Emirates except Emirates of Ras Al khaimah and Al Fujairah. This is the reason for some discrepancies between revenue and expense in current grants recorded by central and state government. Data for all subsectors are reported on a noncash basis. The Emirates of Dubai and Ajman as well as some extrabudgetary central government units use accrual-based accounting. Nonfinancial assets are valued at historical cost. Financial assets and liabilities are valued at fair market value.
Implementation of GFSM 2001/2014	In 2010 the cabinet issued Ministerial decree number (67/5w/1) to support Ministry of Finance efforts in gathering and compiling UAE Federal and Emirate government's financial data and present UAE combined financials following the GFSM 2001 standards and guidelines.

United Kingdom (112)

Information Last Updated	2015
Units of General Government	
1. Budgetary Central Government	Partially covered. 1.1 Legislative, Judiciary, and Executive bodies including ministries/departments. 1.2 Other agencies or funds: Monarchy, national insurance funds, non-departmental public bodies such as national museums, devolved administrations in Scotland, Wales and Northern Ireland, and parliament, Also included are National Health Service Institutions including hospitals and Academics (Central Government Controlled and funded schools).
2. Extrabudgetary Central Government	Not applicable.
3. Social Security Funds	Not applicable.
4. State Government	Not applicable.
5. Local Government	Partially covered. 5.1 Budgetary local government units/entities: 540 (approximately) local councils and local government units 5.2 Extrabudgetary local government units: Not applicable.
Compilation Practices	
Breaks in Series	From 2010, Northern Rock Asset Management and Brasford and Bingley, formerly classified as financial corporations are included within Central Government. From 2010, there has been an increase in the number of Academics, and a reduction in schools classified within the local government sector. Government revenue in 2012 is affected by the substantial one off receipt of £28bn from the transfer of assets from the Royal Mail Pension Plan. The introduction of ESA10 lead to the reclassification from 2004Q2 of Network Rail into Central Government.
Compilation Notes	Data in general government sector covers operations of subsectors 1, 2, and 5. Government Finance Statistics are compiled by the Office for National Statistics.
Implementation of GFSM 2001/2014	The United Kingdom participates in the Eurostat GFS convergence project with the IMF.

United States (111)

Information Last Updated	2017
Units of General Government	
1. Budgetary Central Government	Covered. Congress, Federal Judiciary, and departments and agencies of the Executive Branch of the Federal Government.
2. Extrabudgetary Central Government	Not applicable.
3. Social Security Funds	Covered. Old-Age and Survivors Insurance, Disability Insurance, Hospital Insurance, Supplementary Medical Insurance, Railroad Retirement, Unemployment Insurance, Pension Benefit Guaranty, Veterans' Life Insurance, Workers' Compensation, Military Medical Insurance.
4. State Government	Covered. 50 state governments. Five state temporary disability insurance systems. 50 state workers' compensation systems.
5. Local Government	Covered. 90056 units reported. 38910 general purpose governments, 38266 special district governments, 12880 public school systems.
Compilation Practices	
Breaks in Series	Starting in 2001, the breakdown between subsectors 4 and 5 is not available; local government data are combined with state government data. Starting in 2001, data are based on the summation of calendar year quarters.
Compilation Notes	Data cover activities of subsectors 1-5. Data in general government sector cover Tables 1-3 and 6. Data are recorded largely on an accrual basis (some data are on a cash or mixed cash/accrual basis). The following flows are consolidated: Grants from/to other general government units. The following stocks are consolidated: Debt securities.
Implementation of GFSM 2001/2014	Government Finance Statistics are compiled by the U. S. Bureau of Economic Analysis largely on a GFSM 2014 basis. The number of market value or partial market value estimates in the balance sheet (Table 6) is likely to be expanded. This institutional information was reported in 2015.

Uruguay (298)

Information Last Updated	2015
Units of General Government	
1. Budgetary Central Government	1.1 Legislative, Judiciary, and Executive bodies including ministries/departments. 1.2 Other agencies or funds: National Administration for Public Education and University of the Republic.
2. Extrabudgetary Central Government	Various extrabudgetary funds (Fondos de Libre Disponibilidad).
3. Social Security Funds	Social Insurance Fund.
4. State Government	Not applicable.
5. Local Government	5.1 Budgetary local government units/entities: 19 Departmental governments 5.2 Extrabudgetary local government units: Not applicable.
Compilation Practices	
Breaks in Series	In 2009, the data for revenue and expenditure were compiled from different data sources, and some variables are not directly comparable with previous years' data. From 2009, data for budgetary central government also cover extrabudgetary central government units. From 2003 until 2006, detailed data for budgetary central government included in Table 7 are reported on an accrual basis, while Total Outlays (code 7) remained on a cash basis to ensure internal consistency of the dataset. The discrepancy between accrual and cash data for total outlays is reported in the statistical discrepancy line of Table 7. In 1999, new budget classifications were introduced.
Compilation Notes	Data cover activities of subsectors 1-3 and 5. The revenue total refunds are registered in item 116 Other Taxes with a negative sign. Government Finance Statistics are compiled by the Ministry of Economy and Finance.
Implementation of GFSM 2001/2014	No information available.

Uzbekistan (927)

Information Last Updated	2015
Units of General Government	
1. Budgetary Central Government	1.1 Legislative, Judiciary, and Executive bodies including ministries/departments: 1.2 Other agencies or funds: State committees, agencies and other government establishments.
2. Extrabudgetary Central Government	Fund for the Reconstruction and Development of Uzbekistan (FRD), Fund for the Reconstruction , Repair, and Equipping of Educational and Medical Establishments, Fund for the Reclamation of Irrigated Land, Republican Road Fund, Special Account of the State Committee for Competition, Fund for Children's Sports, Book Fund.
3. Social Security Funds	Pension Fund of Uzbekistan, Employment Promotion Fund.
4. State Government	Autonomous Republic of Karakalpakstan, 12 provinces and Tashkent City.
5. Local Government	5.1 Budgetary local government units/entities: 194 districts and towns which are considered dependent agencies of the central or regional governments when compiling government finance statistics because they do not have sufficient financial independence to be considered as a separate level of the general government sector. 5.2 Extrabudgetary local government units: Not applicable.
Compilation Practices	
Breaks in Series	None reported.
Compilation Notes	Data cover activities of subsectors 1-3 and 5. Government Finance Statistics are compiled by the Ministry of Finance.
Implementation of GFSM 2001/2014	From January 1, 2014, the Republic of Uzbekistan adopted a new Budget Code, a new Chart of Accounts and a reporting system aligned with the GFSM 2001 classifications.

Vanuatu (846)

Information Last Updated	2015
Units of General Government	
1. Budgetary Central Government	1.1 Legislative, Judiciary, and Executive bodies including ministries/departments. 1.2 Other agencies or funds: Not applicable.
2. Extrabudgetary Central Government	Government agencies (approximately 30).
3. Social Security Funds	Not applicable.
4. State Government	Not applicable.
5. Local Government	5.1 Budgetary local government units/entities: Municipalities of Luganville and Port Villa, 6 provinces. 5.2 Extrabudgetary local government units: Not applicable.
Compilation Practices	
Breaks in Series	None reported.
Compilation Notes	Data in the central government tables cover operations of subsector 1.
Implementation of GFSM 2001/2014	No information available.

Vietnam (582)

Information Last Updated	2015
Units of General Government	
1. Budgetary Central Government	1.1 Legislative, Judiciary, and Executive bodies including ministries/departments: 1.2 Other agencies or funds: Partial information was provided. Agencies, institutes.
2. Extrabudgetary Central Government	16 units reported. Health Insurance Fund, Unemployment Insurance Fund, State Owned Enterprises Restructuring and Equitization Fund, Science and Technology Development Fund, Environmental Protection Fund, National Fund for Job Creation, Public Telecommunication Services Fund, Vietnam Child Safety Net Fund (Child Protection Fund), Legal Assistance Fund, Fund in Support of Orange Agent Victims, Drug Abuse Prevention and Control Fund, Vietnamese Overseas Assistance and Mobilization Fund, Training Credit Fund, Fund in Support of HIV Carriers, Farmer Assistance Fund under the Vietnam Farmers' Union, Cooperative Development Assistance Fund.
3. Social Security Funds	Partial information was provided. Social Security Insurance Fund, and Health Fund.
4. State Government	Not applicable.
5. Local Government	5.1 Budgetary local government units/entities: Partial information was provided. Commune governments for 11,000 communes, district towns, and wards, District government for 700 districts, Provincial governments for 63 provinces, and Various funds at the local government level. 5.2 Extrabudgetary local government units: 8 units reported. Gratitude Fund for National Services and Merits, Health Care Fund for the Poor, Local Housing Development Fund, Flood and Storm Prevention and Control Fund, Security and Social Order Fund, Local Development Investment Fund, SME Guarantee Fund, Local Farmer Assistance Fund.
Compilation Practices	
Breaks in Series	
Compilation Notes	Data cover activities of subsector 1. Data disseminated for general government sector cover table 1 and partially 7. Time series for revenue and expense for general government sector cover 1994 to 2004. Data are recorded on cash basis for subsector 1. No information was provided.
Implementation of GFSM 2001/2014	Government Finance Statistics are compiled by the Ministry of Finance. Over the medium term, the next steps were not yet provided. This institutional information was reported in 2012 in the Government Finance Statistics Yearbook (GFSY).

West Bank and Gaza (487)

Information Last Updated 2015

Units of General Government

1. Budgetary Central Government
1.1 Legislative, Judiciary, and Executive bodies including ministries/departments:
1.2 Other agencies or funds:
Palestinian Central Bureau of Statistics, Palestinian Energy Authority Palestinian Water Authority, and Pension Fund Committee.

2. Extrabudgetary Central Government
Not applicable.

3. Social Security Funds
Social security fund.

4. State Government
Not applicable.

5. Local Government
5.1 Budgetary local government units/entities:
428 localities/municipalities, and 16 main governorates.
5.2 Extrabudgetary local government units:
Not applicable.

Compilation Practices

Breaks in Series
Prior to 2006, data were compiled on a cash basis.

Compilation Notes
Data cover activities of subsectors 1, 3, and partially 5.
Government Finance Statistics are compiled by the Ministry of Finance.

Implementation of GFSM 2001/2014
No information available.

Yemen, Republic of (474)

Information Last Updated 2015

Units of General Government

1. Budgetary Central Government
1.1 Legislative, Judiciary, and Executive bodies including ministries/departments.
1.2 Other agencies or funds:
Universities.

2. Extrabudgetary Central Government
General Board for Agricultural Development, General Board for Agricultural Research, General Board for Al-Thawra Hospital, General Board for Development of Eastern Region, General Board for Development of Tihama, Martyrs' Bureau, Ministry of Interior Employee Fund, Promotion of Agricultural and Fisheries Production Fund, Roads and Bridges Maintenance Fund, Social Development Fund, Social Welfare Fund, Waqf Fund (religious endowments authority), and Youths and Sports Care Fund.

3. Social Security Funds
Defense Employees' Pension Fund, and General Authority for Social Security (Government and Public Enterprise Employees' Pension Fund).

4. State Government
Not applicable.

5. Local Government
5.1 Budgetary local government units/entities:
21 governorates.
5.2 Extrabudgetary local government units:
No information available.

Compilation Practices

Breaks in Series
None reported.

Compilation Notes
Data cover activities of subsectors 1-3 and 5.
Government Finance Statistics are compiled by the Ministry of Finance.

Implementation of GFSM 2001/2014
No information available.

Zambia (754)

Information Last Updated 2015

Units of General Government

1. Budgetary Central Government

1.1 Legislative, Judiciary, and Executive bodies including ministries/departments.
1.2 Other agencies or funds:
Not applicable.

2. Extrabudgetary Central Government

Bangwelu Water Transport, Copperbelt University, Counterpart funds of budgetary organizations, Government Communication Flight, Government Stores Department, Hostel Board of Management, Industrial Plantations Division, Land Development Services Account, Miscellaneous funds, Mweru Water Transport, Prices and Income Commission, Special (revolving) funds, State-supported schools, University of Zambia, Water and waste management, and Zambia National Tourist Bureau.

3. Social Security Funds

Workmen's Compensation Fund.

4. State Government

Not applicable.

5. Local Government

5.1 Budgetary local government units/entities:
55 district councils.
5.2 Extrabudgetary local government units:
No information available.

Compilation Practices

Breaks in Series

None reported.

Compilation Notes

Data cover activities of subsector 1.
Government Finance Statistics are compiled by the Ministry of Finance and National Planning.

Implementation of GFSM 2001/2014

No information available.

Zimbabwe (698)

Information Last Updated 2015

Units of General Government

1. Budgetary Central Government

1.1 Legislative, Judiciary, and Executive bodies including ministries/departments.
1.2 Other agencies or funds:
72 units, which include revenue retention agencies, statutory funds, and the National Development Fund.

2. Extrabudgetary Central Government

101 extrabudgetary units, which include Agriculture Rural Development, District Development Fund, Grain Marketing Board, National AIDS Council, Parirenyatwa Group of hospitals, University of Zimbabwe, Zimbabwe National Roads Authority, and Zimbabwe Revenue Authority.

3. Social Security Funds

National Social Security Authority.

4. State Government

Not applicable.

5. Local Government

5.1 Budgetary local government units/entities:
32 urban councils and 60 rural district councils. The urban councils include Bulawayo, Chiredzi, Chitungwiza, Kwekwe, and Harare. The rural councils include Beitbridge, Guruwe, Matobo, and Ruwa.
5.2 Extrabudgetary local government units:
No information available.

Compilation Practices

Breaks in Series

None reported.

Compilation Notes

Data cover activities of subsector 1.
Government Finance Statistics are compiled by the Ministry of Finance.

Implementation of GFSM 2001/2014

Over the medium term, the next steps include implementing the migration plan towards the GFSM 2001 framework, depth of data in the cash flow statement, transactions in assets and liabilities, gross debt, financial balance sheet, and broadening the statistical coverage to central government.